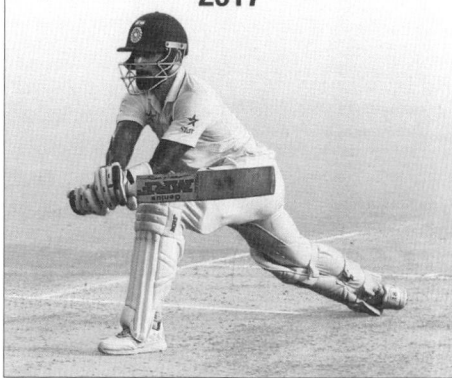

WISDEN

CRICKETERS' ALMANACK

2017

EDITED BY LAWRENCE BOOTH

WISDEN

CRICKETERS' ALMANACK

2017

154th EDITION

John Wisden & Co

An imprint of Bloomsbury Publishing Plc

John Wisden & Co Ltd
An imprint of Bloomsbury Publishing Plc

50 Bedford Square
London
WC1B 3DP
UK

1385 Broadway
New York
NY 10018
USA

www.bloomsbury.com

WISDEN CRICKETERS' ALMANACK
Editor **Lawrence Booth**
Co-editor **Hugh Chevallier**
Deputy editors **Steven Lynch** and **Harriet Monkhouse**
Assistant editor **James Gingell**
Contributing editor **Richard Whitehead**
Production co-ordinator **Peter Bather**
Chief statistician **Philip Bailey**
Proofreader **Charles Barr**
Database and typesetting **Stephen Cubitt**
Publisher **Charlotte Atyeo**
Consultant publisher **Christopher Lane**

Reader feedback: almanack@wisden.com
www.wisden.com
www.wisdenrecords.com
Follow Wisden on Twitter @WisdenAlmanack
and on Facebook at Wisden Sports

British Library Cataloguing-in-Publication Data
A catalogue record for this book is available from the British Library.

Hardback 978-1-4729-3519-9 £50
Soft cover 978-1-4729-3518-2 £50
Large format 978-1-4729-3517-5 £65
Leatherbound 978-1-4729-3520-5 £285
The Shorter Wisden (eBook) 978-1-4729-3523-6 £8.99

2 4 6 8 10 9 7 5 3 1

Typeset in Times New Roman and Univers by David Lewis XML Associates, Bungay NR35 1EF
Printed and bound in Italy by Grafica Veneta S.p.A., Trebaseleghe (PD)

To find out more about our authors and books visit www.wisden.com. Here you can also sign up for our e-newsletter for year-round news and views from *Wisden*.

A Taste of Wisden 2017

The Cook who gave honours-board engravers repetitive strain injury shed the cocoon of accumulation that once habitually formed around his innings.

Curiouser and Curiouser, page 27

* * *

The Roundhead county of boots and the Battle of Naseby has nurtured an innovative, risk-taking Cavalier.

Five Cricketers of the Year, page 87

* * *

"I strongly believe this book is not my story, it is the story of what God has planned and realised through me." Heavenly choirs sing out from every page.

Cricket Books in 2016, page 132

* * *

A group of Donald Trumps were booed as they took their seats, the loudest abuse coming from a group of Mexican sombreros.

England v Sri Lanka in 2016, First Test, page 269

* * *

One delicious over, costing 16, explained why: defended, reverse-swept, swept; defended, reverse-swept, swept. The immaculate execution showed Misbah as contemptuous of spin as Henry VIII of wives.

England v Pakistan in 2016, First Test, page 300

* * *

The closest thing to a security breach came when three old ladies on a tuk-tuk slipped their way into the convoy en route to the one-day warm-up at Fatullah. By the end of the tour, Reg Dickason had proved an unlikely Bangladeshi hero.

Bangladesh v England in 2016-17, page 326

* * *

The fourth six felt sadistically emphatic – like shooting a corpse between the eyeballs.

The World Twenty20 final in 2015-16, page 825

* * *

He returned like an old Soviet soldier in Eastern Europe; he shouldn't have been there, but his occupation was undeniable.

New Zealand v Australia in 2015-16, page 956

LIST OF CONTRIBUTORS

Kamran Abbasi
Timothy Abraham
Andrew Alderson
Tanya Aldred
Chris Aspin
Philip August
Vaneisa Baksh
Philip Barker
Marcus Berkmann
Benedict Bermange
Scyld Berry
Edward Bevan
Paul Bird
Paul Bolton
Stephen Brenkley
Daniel Brettig
Liam Brickhill
Gideon Brooks
Colin Bryden
Ian Callender
Brian Carpenter
Adam Collins
Clare Connor
James Coyne
Jon Culley
John Curtis
Martin Davies
Geoffrey Dean
Peter della Penna
William Dick
George Dobell
Paul Edwards
Vithushan Ehantharajah
Mark Eklid
Matthew Engel
Peter English
John Etheridge
Melinda Farrell
Fidel Fernando
Chris Foy
Alan Gardner
Mark Geenty
Richard Gibson
Haydn Gill
Julian Guyer
Gideon Haigh
Kevin Hand
David Hardy
Shahid Hashmi
Douglas Henderson
Andrew Hignell
Paul Hiscock
Tristan Holme
Jon Hotten
Nick Hoult
Steve James
Paul Jones
Nishant Joshi
R. Kaushik
Abid Ali Kazi
Karthik Lakshmanan
Richard Latham
Geoff Lemon
Jonathan Liew
Will Macpherson
Neil Manthorp
Vic Marks
Ali Martin
Alex Massie
Kalika Mehta
Andrew Miller
Mohammad Isam
R. Mohan
Sidharth Monga
Firdose Moonda
Benj Moorehead
Kritika Naidu
Raf Nicholson
Vladimir Ninković
Andrew Nixon
Sidhanta Patnaik
Mark Pennell
John Pitt
Dileep Premachandran
Derek Pringle
Andrew Radd
Paul Radley
Barney Ronay
Nick Sadleir
Alvin Sallay
Osman Samiuddin
Neville Scott
Utpal Shuvro
Rob Smyth
Richard Spiller
John Stern
Fraser Stewart
Andy Stockhausen
Chris Stocks
Bharat Sundaresan
Pat Symes
Bruce Talbot
Sa'adi Thawfeeq
Anand Vasu
Telford Vice
Phil Walker
John Ward
David Warner
Tim Wellock
Tim Wigmore
Simon Wilde
Marcus Williams
Dean Wilson
Andy Zaltzman

Photographers are credited as appropriate. Special thanks to Graham Morris and Philip Brown. **Cartoons** by Nick Newman. Contributors to the **Round the World** section are listed after their articles.

The editor also acknowledges with gratitude assistance from the following: Robin Abrahams, Dave Allen, Derek Barnard, Mike Bechley, Josh Burrows, Norman Bygrave, Derek Carlaw, Howard Clayton, Brian Croudy, Alan Curr, Prakash Dahatonde, Nigel Davies, Charles Davis, Ted Dexter, Gulu Ezekiel, M. L. Fernando, Ric Finlay, Alan Fordham, David Frith, Nagraj Gollapudi, Victoria Groves, Richard Heller, Clive Hitchcock, Robin Hobbs, Julia and John Hunt, Doug Insole, David Kendix, Rajesh Kumar, Edward Liddle, Daniel Lightman, Roger Long, Nirav Malavi, Mahendra Mapagunaratne, Colin Maynard, Pat Murphy, Clayton Murzello, Michael Owen-Smith, Francis Payne, Mick Pope, Roger Prideaux, Qamar Ahmed, Abdul A. Ravat, Andrew Samson, Clare Skinner, Steven Stern, Jeremy Tagg, Tushar Trivedi, Derek Ufton, Chris Walmsley, Charlie Wat, Jean and Chris Whipps, Alan Williams, Oliver Wise, John Woodcock.

The production of *Wisden* would not be possible without the support and co-operation of many other cricket officials, county scorers, writers and lovers of the game. To them all, many thanks.

PREFACE

There were moments in 2016, with experts routinely derided and facts apparently consigned to history, when *Wisden* might have wondered about its place in the world. But there's more than one way of keeping up with the times. This year's cover depicts the game's best batsman, Virat Kohli, playing a reverse sweep – a stroke once regarded as infra dig, but now part of the furniture. It felt like a celebration, of a special talent and of cricket's evolution.

I like to think Tony Cozier would have approved. Tony, who died last year, contributed to every Almanack from 1977 to 2016, and spent his career trying to keep the game's authorities honest, with a diligence not always found in the commentary box. He was cricket journalism's great all-rounder. In recent times, broadcasting has lost Tony Greig, Christopher Martin-Jenkins, Richie Benaud and now Cozier. The sport was lucky to have had so many at once.

As ever, the winning entry in our photograph competition – this year taken by Saqib Majeed, amid the stunning colours of a Kashmiri autumn – is published in the first colour section, along with the two runners-up; thanks go to MCC, especially Clare Skinner, and our panel of independent judges. Meanwhile, all the pages from previous schools sections can be found at schoolscricketonline.co.uk. We encourage new schools to submit their results, especially from the state sector, which – as Phil Walker explains on page 55 – may not quite be the lost cause many fear.

One tiny scorecard tweak: bowling figures in Twenty20 games have a new second column – dot balls, which are like gold dust in 20-over cricket, instead of maidens, which are more like the holy grail. Last year, the dot balls lived in brackets after each analysis; we think we've settled on an answer.

The work ethic of the Almanack's editorial team was unrelenting once more. Co-editor Hugh Chevallier never allowed standards to slip, though deputy editors Harriet Monkhouse and Steven Lynch would not have countenanced the possibility anyway. Our new recruit, assistant editor James Gingell, has fitted in like a dream. Christopher Lane, our consultant publisher, was as indispensable as always; many thanks, too, to Peter Bather, our production co-ordinator, and Richard Whitehead, our contributing editor.

It's futile trying to list all the people who make Wisden what it is, but a few others deserve special gratitude. At Bloomsbury, Charlotte Atyeo was again the best boss an editor can hope for, and Richard Charkin nothing but supportive. Thanks to Stephen Cubitt for his typesetting and technical wizardry, Charles Barr for his sharp-eyed proofreading, and Philip Bailey for his inexhaustible statistics. At the *Daily Mail*, sports editor Lee Clayton generously gave me the breathing space I always need.

My wife, Anjali Doshi, knows better than most what this job entails. That she doesn't merely put up with the strange working hours, but cajoles and advises me, is its own annual miracle. To her, my love.

LAWRENCE BOOTH
Barnes, February 2017

CONTENTS

Part One – Comment

Wisden Honours 14
Notes by the Editor 15
Alastair Cook passes 10,000 Test runs *by Andy Zaltzman* 25
Cricket and politics *by Alex Massie* 31
The story of the six *by Gideon Haigh* 37
Joe Root scores 254 against Pakistan *by Jon Hotten* 43
Sixty years of *Test Match Special by Matthew Engel* 49
Cricket's battle for the working classes *by Phil Walker* 55
Tony Cozier 1940–2016 *by Vic Marks* 62
Cricket and climate change *by Tanya Aldred* 65
What makes a good coach? *by Benj Moorehead* 71
The secrets of ball-tampering *by Derek Pringle* 77
▷Bites, boots and bottle tops *by Steven Lynch* 81
The return of the cable knit *by Philip Barker* 84
Five Cricketers of the Year
Ben Duckett *by Andrew Radd* 87
Misbah-ul-Haq *by Osman Samiuddin* 89
Toby Roland-Jones *by John Stern* 91
Chris Woakes *by George Dobell* 93
Younis Khan *by Kamran Abbasi* 95
Twenty-five years of Durham *by Stephen Brenkley* 97
Rachael Heyhoe Flint 1939–2017 *by Clare Connor* 102
The other side of the IPL *by Anand Vasu* 104
The Leading Cricketer in the World
Virat Kohli *by Bharat Sundaresan* 110
Wisden's writing competition
One over – memories for life *by John Pitt* 112
Peculiar cricketing educations *by Rob Smyth* 114

Part Two – The Wisden Review

Books *by Marcus Berkmann* 123
Media *by Barney Ronay* 141
▷Rugby's cricket-loving coach *by Chris Foy* 145
Blogs *by Brian Carpenter* 150
▷Twitter *by Nishant Joshi* 152
Retirements *by Steve James* 154
Cricketana *by Marcus Williams* 159
Weather *by Andrew Hignell* 165
People *by James Gingell* 166
Courts 169
Laws *by Fraser Stewart* 170
Theatre *by Hugh Chevallier* 172
Obituaries 174
▷Obscured by clouds 219

Part Three – English International Cricket

The England team *by Nick Hoult* 242
England players *by Lawrence Booth* 248
England international averages in 2016 256
England v Sri Lanka 259
England v Pakistan 289
▷Stat attack 318
Bangladesh v England 323
India v England 342

Part Four – English Domestic Cricket

STATISTICS

First-class averages 380
Scores of 100 and over 387
Ten wickets in a match 391

SPECSAVERS COUNTY CHAMPIONSHIP

Review and statistics 392
Derbyshire 404
Durham 417
Essex 431
Glamorgan 445
Gloucestershire 459
Hampshire 473
Kent 488
Lancashire 502
Leicestershire 516
Middlesex 529
Northamptonshire 542
Nottinghamshire 556
Somerset 570
Surrey 584
Sussex 599
Warwickshire 613
Worcestershire 627
Yorkshire 640

ONE-DAY COUNTY COMPETITIONS

NatWest T20 Blast 655
Royal London One-Day Cup 683

OTHER ENGLISH CRICKET

Pakistan A and Sri Lanka A in England 702
England Lions v Pakistan A v Sri Lanka A 707
The Universities 710
MCC 718
MCC v Yorkshire 718
The Minor Counties 720
Second Eleven Championship 724
League Cricket 726
The ECB City Cup 734
Royal London Club Championship and NatWest Club T20 735
Davidstow Village Cup 737
Disability Cricket 739
England Under-19 v Sri Lanka Under-19 741
Youth Cricket 745
▷Bunbury Festival 746
Schools Cricket 747
▷Archive of schools cricket 783

EUROPEAN CRICKET

Ireland 784
Ireland v Sri Lanka 785
Ireland v Afghanistan 786
Ireland v Pakistan 787
Ireland v Hong Kong 787
Scotland 788
Scotland v Afghanistan 789
Scotland v Hong Kong 789
The Netherlands 790

Part Five – Overseas Cricket

THE WORLD TWENTY20

Review *by Dileep Premachandran* 793

Statistics 799 | Reports 802

ICC UNDER-19 WORLD CUP

Review *by Sidhanta Patnaik* 827 | Reports 828

CRICKET IN AUSTRALIA

The rollercoaster ride *by Daniel Brettig* 836
▷Phillip Hughes's death: "no one to blame" 839
Australia v India 840
Australia v South Africa 850
Australia v New Zealand 860
Australia v Pakistan 864
KFC T20 Big Bash League 878
Domestic Cricket in Australia 881

CRICKET IN BANGLADESH

Tigers' balm *by Utpal Shuvro* 889
Bangladesh v Zimbabwe 891
Asia Cup 893
Bangladesh v Afghanistan 900
Domestic Cricket in Bangladesh 902

CRICKET IN INDIA

Top of the world, but shrouded in mist *by Dileep Premachandran* 908
India v Sri Lanka 912
India v New Zealand 915
The Indian Premier League 928
Domestic Cricket in India 931

CRICKET IN NEW ZEALAND

Life after McCullum *by Andrew Alderson* 943
New Zealand v Pakistan 946
New Zealand v Australia 951
New Zealand v Pakistan 961
New Zealand v Bangladesh 966
Domestic Cricket in New Zealand 973

CRICKET IN PAKISTAN

On top – but not for long *by Osman Samiuddin* 980
Pakistan v West Indies 983
Domestic Cricket in Pakistan 998

CRICKET IN SOUTH AFRICA

Heading for the shires? *by Colin Bryden* 1007
South Africa v Australia 1010
South Africa v New Zealand 1013
South Africa v Ireland 1017
South Africa v Australia 1018
South Africa v Sri Lanka 1024
Domestic Cricket in South Africa 1040

CRICKET IN SRI LANKA

Old faces, young guns *by Sa'adi Thawfeeq* 1052
Sri Lanka v Australia 1055
Domestic Cricket in Sri Lanka 1070

CRICKET IN THE WEST INDIES

Parties and politics *by Vaneisa Baksh* 1078
Triangular ODI series (WI/A/SA) 1081
West Indies v India 1090
Domestic Cricket in West Indies 1101

CRICKET IN ZIMBABWE

Time for a hot Streak *by Liam Brickhill* 1107
Zimbabwe v India 1109
Zimbabwe v New Zealand 1112
Zimbabwe v Sri Lanka 1117
Triangular ODI series (Z/SL/WI) 1122
Domestic Cricket in Zimbabwe 1125

WORLD TABLES, RANKINGS AND AVERAGES

International results 1129
ICC team rankings 1130
ICC player rankings 1131
Test, ODI, T20I averages 1132

OTHER OVERSEAS INTERNATIONAL CRICKET

Other first-class tours 1137
ICC Intercontinental Cup 1141
Cricket in Afghanistan 1145
Cricket in Hong Kong 1146
Cricket in Oman 1148
Cricket in Papua New Guinea 1149
Cricket in the United Arab Emirates 1150
England Lions in the UAE 1152
Cricket Round the World 1154
▷European native cricket sixes *by Vladimir Ninković* 1161

Part Six – Women's Cricket

International cricket *by Melinda Farrell* 1166
▷Charlotte Edwards steps down *by Vithushan Ehantharajah* 1167
THE LEADING CRICKETER IN THE WORLD
Ellyse Perry *by Raf Nicholson* 1169
ICC WOMEN'S WORLD TWENTY20 1170
INTERNATIONAL SERIES 1178
South Africa v England 1179
England v Pakistan 1183
West Indies v England 1189
Sri Lanka v England 1192
ICC rankings 1196
ODI averages 1197
Women's Big Bash League 1198
Kia Super League 1200
English domestic cricket 1202

Part Seven – Records and Registers

Features of 2016 1206

RECORDS

Contents 1217
Notes on Records *by Rob Smyth* 1223
Roll of dishonour 1223
First-class 1225
List A one-day 1253
List A Twenty20 1256
Test (overall) 1258
Test (series by series) 1290
One-day international 1331
Twenty20 international 1341
Miscellaneous 1346
Women's Test, ODI and T20I 1351

BIRTHS AND DEATHS

Test cricketers 1356
Other notables 1445

REGISTER

Cricketers of the Year, 1889–2017 1451

Part Eight – The Almanack

Official bodies 1456
Crime and punishment 1461
International umpires 1463
ICC referees 1463
ECB umpires 1464
The Duckworth/Lewis/Stern method 1464
Powerplays 1465
Meetings and decisions 1466
Dates in cricket history 1476
Anniversaries 1481
One hundred and fifty years ago 1483
One hundred years ago 1483
Fifty years ago 1485
Honours and Awards 1490
2017 Fixtures 1496
Errata 1506
Charities 1509
Cricket trade directory 1512
Chronicle of 2016 1516
Index of advertisements 1533
Index of Test matches 1534
Index of unusual occurrences 1536

SYMBOLS AND ABBREVIATIONS

*	In full scorecards and lists of tour parties signifies the captain. In short scorecards, averages and records signifies not out.
†	In full scorecards signifies the designated wicketkeeper. In averages signifies a left-handed batsman.
‡	In short scorecards signifies the team who won the toss.
MoM/PoM	In short scorecards signifies the Man/Player of the Match.
MoS/PoS	In short scorecards signifies the Man/Player of the Series.
DLS	Signifies where the result of a curtailed match has been determined under the Duckworth/Lewis/Stern method.

Other uses of symbols are explained in notes where they appear.

FIRST-CLASS MATCHES

Men's matches of three or more days' duration are first-class unless otherwise stated. All other matches are not first-class, including one-day and Twenty20 internationals.

SCORECARDS

Where full scorecards are not provided in this book, they can be found at Cricket Archive (www.cricketarchive.co.uk) or ESPNcricinfo (www.cricinfo.com). Full scorecards from matches played overseas can also be found in the relevant *ACS Overseas First-Class Annuals*.

In Twenty20 scorecards, the second figure in a bowling analysis refers to dot balls, and not maidens (as in first-class and List A games).

RECORDS

The entire Records section (pages 1225–1355) can now be found at www.wisdenrecords.com. The online Records database is regularly updated and, in many instances, more detailed than in *Wisden 2017*. Further information on past winners of tournaments covered in this book can be found at www.wisden.com/almanacklinks.

PART ONE

Comment

Wisden Honours

THE LEADING CRICKETERS IN THE WORLD

Virat Kohli (page 110)
Ellyse Perry (page 1169)

The Leading Cricketers in the World are chosen by the editor of *Wisden* in consultation with some of the world's most experienced writers and commentators. Selection is based on a player's class and form shown in all cricket during the calendar year, and is merely guided by statistics rather than governed by them. There is no limit to how many times a player may be chosen. A list of past winners can be found on page 111. A list of notional past winners, backdated to 1900, appeared on page 35 of *Wisden 2007*.

FIVE CRICKETERS OF THE YEAR

Ben Duckett (page 87)
Misbah-ul-Haq (page 89)
Toby Roland-Jones (page 91)
Chris Woakes (page 93)
Younis Khan (page 95)

The Five Cricketers of the Year are chosen by the editor of *Wisden*, and represent a tradition that dates back to 1889, making this the oldest individual award in cricket. Excellence in and/or influence on the previous English summer are the major criteria for inclusion. No one can be chosen more than once. A list of past winners can be found on page 1451.

WISDEN SCHOOLS CRICKETER OF THE YEAR

A. J. Woodland (page 748)

The Schools Cricketer of the Year, based on first-team performances during the previous English summer, is chosen by *Wisden's* schools correspondent in consultation with the editor and other experienced observers. The winner's school must be in the UK, play cricket to a standard approved by *Wisden* and provide reports to this Almanack. A list of past winners can be found on page 749.

WISDEN BOOK OF THE YEAR

Following On by Emma John (page 135)

The Book of the Year is selected by *Wisden's* guest reviewer; all cricket books published in the previous calendar year and submitted to *Wisden* for possible review are eligible. A list of past winners can be found on page 136.

WISDEN–MCC CRICKET PHOTOGRAPH OF THE YEAR

was won by Saqib Majeed (whose entry appears opposite page 64)

The Wisden–MCC Cricket Photograph of the Year is chosen by a panel of independent experts; all images on a cricket theme photographed in the previous calendar year are eligible.

WISDEN'S WRITING COMPETITION

was won by John Pitt (page 112)

Wisden's Writing Competition is open to anyone (other than previous winners) who has not been commissioned to write for, or has a working relationship with, the Almanack. Full details appear on page 113.

Full details of past winners of all these honours can be found at www.wisden.com

NOTES BY THE EDITOR

The England team in 2016 brought to mind a conversation, maybe apocryphal, between John Major and Boris Yeltsin, in the days when Britain and Russia could just about share a joke. Major asked Yeltsin to sum up his country's economy in a word. "Good," said Yeltsin. And in two words? "Not good." History doesn't record whether Major took the chance to point out the tendency of both Russia's finances and England's cricketers to collapse at the slightest provocation. But there was another political parallel: England promised plenty – and, at Test level, delivered rather less. By the end of their 4–0 defeat in India in December, they were fifth in the Test rankings, precisely where they had been after winning in South Africa in January. From there, a gruelling schedule of 14 games in seven months had simply taken them back to the beginning. For one of the best-resourced sides in the world, it felt like money poorly spent.

As the year progressed, England's ability to hint at one course of action before settling on its opposite assumed a faintly pathological air. At Mirpur, they were 100 without loss, before losing all ten wickets in a session. At Mohali, they reduced India to 156 for five, but allowed them to score 417. At Mumbai, they made 400, and lost by an innings; and they also lost by an innings at Chennai, after racking up 477, then conceding the highest total in their 983-Test history. A trip to India is a tough gig, especially when Virat Kohli has a glint in his eye and a score to settle. But 759-for-seven tough? Not even President Trump's most outrageous alternative fact could salvage that.

Above all, England failed to build on the gains of 2015, when their fearlessness made them the most watchable team in the world. It was no coincidence that their best cricket had come against New Zealand, Australia and South Africa, three sides cut from the same cultural cloth, full of bouncers, machismo and token spinners. But in 2016 England faced the subtler flavours of the east, of Sri Lanka and Pakistan, then Bangladesh and India. This kind of menu used to be regarded as a trial, as if England's players were obliged to grin and bear another prawn dhansak before returning to the comforts of meat and two veg. Yet weren't countless expensive training camps in Asia for age-group teams and Lions squads supposed to have attuned the tastebuds?

Of those four series, England won only one – Sri Lanka at home, among the easiest assignments in the world game now their batting stars have retired. They drew with Pakistan – a result put into perspective when the Pakistanis were whitewashed in New Zealand and Australia. England became the first major side to lose a Test to Bangladesh; and, for the first time, they lost four in a series to India. Too often, they played as if they had failed to absorb the change in opponent, conditions or tempo.

Yet they clearly had it in them. At Old Trafford, Edgbaston, Rajkot and Chennai, Pakistan's Yasir Shah and India's Ravichandran Ashwin – two of the game's best spinners – returned collective figures of eight for 939. In five other Tests apparently taking place in a parallel universe, Yasir and Ashwin managed 39 for 682. England were nothing if not maddeningly inconsistent, except when they were maddeningly consistent: collapses of six for 15 at

Mumbai and Chennai suggested a side unable to learn from their mistakes. Last year, no serious Test nation won a lower percentage of their games than England's 35.

In 2013, these pages were not alone in warning that England would struggle to win again in India if they failed to address their spin-bowling crisis, camouflaged for a while by Graeme Swann and Monty Panesar. But the attack they took to South Asia was a reminder of the priorities of a county game that has taken far too long to accept the folly of preparing greentops for medium-pacers. The forward-thinking experiment to allow visiting captains the chance to bowl first in the Championship has already helped flatten pitches and encourage spinners. But the benefits will not be immediate. In India, while Adil Rashid exceeded expectations with 23 wickets, four other frontline slow bowlers managed 15 between them at 67, and leaked almost 3.5 an over. The contrast with Ashwin and Ravindra Jadeja, who took 54 at 28 with an economy-rate of around 2.5, was painful.

Confusion over England's best spin-bowling line-up spread. Hell-bent on getting the most out of their quicker bowlers, they rested and rotated them into virtual irrelevance. Injuries didn't help, but it was absurd that Ben Stokes's 106 overs in five Tests were the most by a seamer. He and his colleagues were just as likely to succumb to tedium as tendonitis.

England's brightest light came in the batting. At Rajkot, Haseeb Hameed brought to mind the debuts made by England's three batting giants of the last ten years: Kevin Pietersen, Alastair Cook and Joe Root. He could end up with more Test runs than any of them. And he deserved better than to begin his career with England's most hopeless performance since the 2013-14 Ashes. With one or two exceptions, the time for this team to be talking about potential is over.

Steady as he goes

On a cold, sunny February morning, Cook walked into a cramped hospitality box at Lord's and cheerfully apologised for disturbing journalists on what he imagined was a day off. He didn't look like a man relieved to have shed the burdens of office – not quite. Then again, he didn't look especially devastated either. But of one thing he was certain: after 59 Tests in charge, more than any England captain, his time was up.

The Cook years will go down as a period of stunning feats (two home Ashes wins, plus victories in India and South Africa) and navel-gazing misery (nine of his England-record 22 defeats came in two series, including an Ashes whitewash). In that respect, the team felt out of kilter with the captain: Cook was not naturally inclined to the end of any spectrum. Indeed, at the time of his resignation, he averaged fractionally more as captain (46.57) than he did in the ranks (46.36). He was reluctant to satisfy those in search of an easy headline, and stayed off Twitter, which was probably for the best, though some of the nastier stuff filtered through. During the winter in Asia, he displayed the sort of perspective that often suggests a captain has glimpsed life beyond coin tosses and bowling changes. Even his stubbornness had an endearingly human quality, though his delayed departure from the one-day job contributed to another World Cup fiasco, in 2015. Mainly, he emitted calm.

But he chose the right time to go. By his own admission, England's Test cricket had stagnated. This was partly a result of being lumbered with seven matches in less than nine weeks in Bangladesh and India, a touring schedule that must never be repeated. But the two meltdowns during his reign – Australia 2013-14 and India 2016-17 – reflected an abiding weakness. Lacking the tactical acumen to influence a game on its own, Cook was half the leader when he wasn't scoring runs. That his team lost only four of his 17 Test series in charge was testament to a very English grit: understated, occasionally self-conscious, always bloody-minded. It proved an exhausting combination.

Cook can now focus on the business of breaking more records with the bat, and offering advice from the slips to Joe Root. And he is well placed to suggest Root ignore the native pessimism about saddling the star batsman with the cares of captaincy. After all, Root's three main rivals among Test batting's twentysomething starlets have all flourished as leaders: when Cook stepped down, New Zealand's Kane Williamson had averaged 55 as captain (compared with 49 beforehand), Australia's Steve Smith 73 (compared with 51), and Kohli 63 (41). All three took over after fewer Tests than Root. If he's not ready now, he never will be.

Changing planes

Since England captains rarely learn on the job at county level any more, Root will have to absorb plenty, quickly – not least the quaint and enduring belief that he should operate on a higher moral plane than the rest of us. In September, the white-ball captain Eoin Morgan (along with Alex Hales) pulled out of the tour to Bangladesh because of security concerns. It was manna for the amateur psychologists. Some sympathised with the decision, while others regarded it as expediency disguised as principle: would Morgan and Hales, they wondered, have pulled out of a trip to India?

It's true that Morgan partly explained his nervousness by citing two explosions outside the Chinnaswamy Stadium in 2010, when he was in Bangalore's IPL squad, though he had returned to India in the meantime. But his point was that no team had toured Bangladesh since a terrorist attack in Dhaka on July 1. Despite the fact that the Foreign Office were offering similarly careful advice about Bangladesh and India, common sense told you one was riskier than the other. Any charge of hypocrisy had to look beyond the mandarins' caution.

In the event, the Bangladeshis put on a faultless security display, though that only strengthened the view of those who felt Morgan and Hales should have gone. And yet isn't the idea of safety deeply personal? Everyone has their own threshold; some may regard the assurances of security experts as too theoretical for comfort. Morgan said he couldn't be sure he would have been able to concentrate on the cricket, which ought to have silenced those who wondered about his commitment (and since when has not singing the national anthem been proof of anything?). Morgan's world-class hundred in Cuttack in January, in his second game back in charge, suggested his focus was better than ever. And England now knew that Jos Buttler could do the job too, having given a good account of himself in Bangladesh.

Morgan's next job is to translate England's white-ball potential into something tangible – and silver. As in Test cricket, they finished the year placed fifth in both the one-day and Twenty20 rankings, but those mid-table positions felt misleading rather than mediocre. Between the start of 2016 and the end of their 50-over runfest in India in January 2017, they had passed 300 ten times (more than any side in the world over the same period) and scored at 6.32 an over (no one else managed a run a ball). In April at Kolkata, they should have won the World Twenty20; in August at Trent Bridge, they made 444 for three against Pakistan, a 50-over world record; in January, they might have won a Twenty20 series in India if the umpiring had been more alert. They were rarely less than thrilling. This summer's Champions Trophy and the 2019 World Cup, both at home, will be ideal stages to remind critics that the English game is lucky to have Morgan.

With friends like that

In February in Dubai – four words that now loom annually over cricket – something remarkable happened: the world ganged up on India. At stake was the redistribution of ICC finances following the Big Three carve-up in early 2014, as craven an example of maladministration as cricket has seen. At the heart of the latest new world order was payback, quite literally.

Shashank Manohar, the ICC chairman and that rarest of beasts – an Indian administrator with a conscience – had promised to spread the funds more fairly, or less unfairly, which is the best cricket can generally hope for. Yet when the majority of Full Members came down in favour of a proposal to cut India's net share of the profits from the 2015–2023 broadcasting-rights cycle from \$450m to \$260m, the BCCI's complaints would have rung a bell with anyone who recoiled at their heist three years earlier: India felt blindsided and bullied, and grumbled that two wrongs didn't make a right. It just wasn't… fair!

Not only did this suggest the Indians were finally ackowledging the iniquities of that heist, but it sounded suspiciously like the objection many had raised against the BCCI's behaviour under N. Srinivasan. During his reign, Indian officials would happily let it be known that they were simply doing to cricket what England and Australia had done for decades – treating it like a fiefdom. For many, the boardroom bargaining of February 2017 was a delightful irony.

Yet *Schadenfreude* isn't all it's cracked up to be. The provisional vote in Dubai took place at a time when the BCCI were struggling to rebuild after being hobbled by India's Supreme Court, and thus at their most vulnerable. Machiavelli would have approved of the ruthlessness, but it didn't say much for cricket's democratic processes. And among those happy to undo the bad work of 2014 were – you guessed it – England and Australia, the junior partners of Big Three Inc, who seemed determined to prove that opportunism takes many shapes and sizes.

If the proposals are officially approved later this year (though even an enfeebled BCCI can suck others into their orbit), then cricket could find itself on a new kind of *terra infirma*. The sport may be closer to financial equality than it was three years ago. But it will have got there using the same machinations that caused it such grief in the first place.

Contextual healing

India's hosting of 13 successive Tests between September 2016 and March 2017 was a kitchen-sink attempt to reintroduce the red ball to a nation that had fallen for the white (and, as luck would have it, a guarantee that India would go top of the rankings). Before last winter, their TV audiences for Test matches had halved since 2012, although the victory over England in Mumbai, where Kohli's 235 was more an apotheosis than an innings, was India's most-watched Test since the retirement of Sachin Tendulkar.

But the spike could not hide the trend: broadcasting rights for Tests around the world have plummeted in value. These days, the most lucrative games *not* involving Kohli take place in ICC global events and between Twenty20 franchises. Bilateral series struggling for TV money are beginning to feel like Warren Buffett's appraisal of the 2008 economic crash: you can't see who's swimming naked until the tide goes out. The Ashes are always well protected, though that is of little consolation to everyone else.

If the game really is serious about saving Test cricket – and too often Test cricket has had to take the administrators at their word – it must go further than skew the schedule. It must build a window in the international calendar for the IPL, the Big Bash and possibly one other domestic Twenty20 shindig. And – to beat an old drum – it must supplement the international game with the kind of context that makes those Twenty20 shindigs so easy to grasp for the casual sports fan, the key to cricket's survival in the years to come.

A proposal in February suggested a solution of sorts, a nine-team Test league spread over two years, culminating in a one-off final; three other sides – Zimbabwe plus, in all likelihood, Ireland and Afghanistan – would be assured of regular matches. It is a step in the right direction. But they need to go further.

Several months earlier, an eminently sensible proposal to split Test cricket into two divisions had met with predictable resistance. Objecting to a 12-team structure – seven in the first division, five in the second, with promotion, relegation, context, talking points, and a structure to grab that casual fan – Thilanga Sumathipala, president of Sri Lanka Cricket, complained: "We feel that, to make it a top seven, you are virtually relegating the bottom three [Full Members] to a different level." Surely not! Yet his objection, backed by India, won the day. And what emerged smacked of compromise: a nine–three split means the three are not so much a division as their own obscure genus.

By precluding, for the time being, the possibility of relegation, cricket has passed up the chance to borrow the seat-of-the-pants six-pointer from football, a refreshingly scrappy antidote to the glorious chase for the title. For a while now, the only headlines made by the rankings have revolved around who is top. This has provided some strong narratives, not least when Pakistan briefly became No. 1 in August, despite not having played a home Test for seven years. But a proper league structure needs every game to count. And nothing would focus the minds of complacent executives quite like the threat of relegation.

Perfect guests

Like the 2015 New Zealanders, the 2016 Pakistanis left England with everyone craving a decider; unlike them, Pakistan had arrived expecting headlines that went beyond the cricket. But, once Mohammad Amir had refused to overstep at Lord's, the cricket is precisely what made the headlines. This had plenty to do with the leadership of Misbah-ul-Haq, who showed it was possible to combine dignity and success. He also provided a poignant reminder of the human cost of Pakistan's exile, when – after his side's victory at The Oval – he quietly pointed out that he saw his sister and mother only once a year. And, flourishing as an international sportsman in his early forties, he gave hope to more of us than he probably realised.

Misbah was once mocked by sceptical fans for his "tuk tuk" approach, as another ball thudded off the face of a dead bat. But it was a simplification. Captaining Pakistan has always required skills more suited to defusing a brawl. To do so in the years since the 2009 terrorist attack in Lahore has also required a more nuanced ability – to persuade players they are doing something worthwhile. Pakistan's time as Test cricket's No. 1 side was fleeting, but it was a miracle they got there at all. And throughout, Misbah seemed to be enacting Hemingway's definition of courage as "grace under pressure".

A funny kind of home

A visit to Mumbai provides confirmation that cricket is, more than it has ever been, an Indian sport. Its greatest metropolis has three Test grounds past and present within 20 minutes' walk, as well as countless future stars on the maidans and in the backstreets. Mumbai has cricket in every pore and artery. There are days when nothing else matters.

This makes what happened at the Wankhede Stadium during the Fourth Test against England all the sadder. While Indian cricket administrators were busy trying to save their careers during a stand-off with the Supreme Court, Indian cricket lovers suffered a string of indignities as they sought a pleasant time at the Test.

Queues outside the ground suggested little room for manoeuvre within, though the opposite was the case. If they hadn't lost the will to live by the time they reached the gates, Indian fans had to dump their rucksacks in an unguarded pile outside the stadium, while their English counterparts were allowed to take theirs in – because, according to one policeman, they couldn't be parted from their passports. One local was told that bottled water inside the ground was on sale to tourists only, an oversight that wasn't corrected until he took his grievance to Twitter. Many seats were soiled by bird poo, but then many seats were useless anyway, exposed to the sun until around 4pm, half an hour before the scheduled close; and, of course, bottles of sunscreen were also banned. Those seats that *were* shaded often sparked squabbles, regardless of who had booked what. The toilets were filthy. An Indian friend swore never to go again.

Yet Mumbai was hardly alone in turning what should have been a pleasure into an ordeal. The stadiums at Rajkot and Visakhapatnam, both making their Test debuts during the England series, are unhelpfully situated out of town; at Chennai, three vast stands stood empty because of an ongoing political dispute, which mocked the hordes of supporters stranded outside. Those who did gain entry should have been able to read all about it, except that staff were confiscating newspapers, without explanation.

Such is the lot of cricket lovers in India, who are fast becoming television's useful idiots – reassuring proof to those who invest in the game that it really is a sport for the masses.

Just when you thought you were safe…

As if the Plague, the Great Chinese famine and the Holocaust had never happened, some wondered whether 2016 was the worst year in history. The climax of the County Championship clearly passed them by. In St John's Wood in late September, two of domestic cricket's most celebrated sides took the title to the wire. It needed a hat-trick from Toby Roland-Jones for Middlesex to pip Yorkshire – and Somerset, watching helplessly in the West Country. Even the tabloids took an interest.

But what Lord's giveth, it taketh away. Ten days after this good-news finale, it was announced that Durham – who had finished fourth – had been bailed out of financial strife by the ECB, but punished with relegation, a points deduction, and various other sanctions, not all suggesting even-handedness. Up in the North-East, they may have wondered whether the historians had a point. Expecting flak, the ECB depicted their ruling as the saviour of cricket in the region, and as a warning to others. Accusations flew back and forth on social media; simplified positions grew entrenched. The truth was somewhere in the middle: Durham had been reckless, the board draconian.

Yet serious questions demanded answers. When, for instance, had Durham's relegation been decided? A leak from a meeting suggested the board knew in May, though they deny this. But the *possibility* of relegation – and all involved must have known it was a possibility – was not conveyed to Durham's players. They deserved to know.

In September, believing they were fighting for their first-division lives, Durham fielded fast bowler Mark Wood against Surrey; Wood aggravated an ankle injury, and was ruled out of England's winter tours, when his skiddy pace might have come in handy. Not only that, but other teams threw everything into avoiding a relegation which was 50% less likely than they realised. It would have been better to come clean about Durham's fate at the time. Instead, with games taking place which some officials appeared to know would be meaningless, the County Championship was brought into disrepute.

A few months after Durham's relegation, it emerged that their Academy had produced a higher percentage of first-team cricketers than any other. So the ECB must have squirmed when Hampshire, who would have been relegated in any normal year, bolstered their ranks at the start of 2017 with two South African Kolpaks, Rilee Rossouw and Kyle Abbott. Hampshire have not won the Championship since 1973; Durham, who didn't become a first-class county until 1992, have won three of the last nine.

Part of their problem since building an international venue – to satisfy the ECB's requirements for first-class status – was that they were always in the wrong place (in isolated Chester-le-Street, near a motorway junction, rather than in Newcastle or Durham itself), and usually at the wrong time (five of their six Tests were over by mid-June, before the arrival of the summer's sexier tourists). They have also lacked a powerful and reliable advocate. Other counties have had the help of rich personal backers (Graves and his family at Yorkshire, Rod Bransgrove at Hampshire), or generous county councils (Warwickshire), or even national assemblies (Glamorgan). Durham have had less luck. To punish them doubly, triply and more, felt like cricket's version of the postcode lottery. If they go straight back up in 2017 – and, despite a 48-point penalty, just you try stopping them – few promotions will have been cheered more loudly.

Free hit

Channel 5's bold decision to give Saturday-morning airtime to Australia's 2016-17 Big Bash League made some resounding points, none of them a pat on the back for the English game. They ensured the presence of live cricket on one of the UK's major free-to-air channels for the first time since the 2005 Ashes, when older readers may recall the sport felt like a national event. British fans who couldn't afford a satellite subscription thus had to rely on overseas matches for their fix. And, in the razzle-dazzle stakes, the Big Bash has left its English counterpart for dead. We knew this already, but live TV has a way of nailing the point.

While Colin Graves's eve-of-tournament description in May of the NatWest T20 Blast as "mediocre" had hints of Gerald Ratner and his crap jewellery, he was also on to something. Would an Australian broadcaster have done a Channel 5 in reverse and pay for the privilege of televising it? The answer is an unambiguous no.

An English city-based 20-over tournament will probably be with us in 2020, but it would have been sooner had the counties not argued over the details. It is a delay our game can barely afford, not least because part of the new competition's allure will be free-to-air coverage. Advocates of satellite paywalls insist the world has changed: youngsters, they say, barely watch television any more; the digital dissemination of cricket, they argue, is about creating noise in bitesized chunks on social media. Since recent research by the ECB suggested that more British children aged 7–15 recognised American wrestler John Cena than Alastair Cook, they could do with cranking up the volume.

There may be some truth in the advocates' argument. But it doesn't sit easily with Channel 5's claim that a total of 3.3 million viewers tuned into their six BBL shows. The debate over free-to-air cricket has disappeared so far up its own fundament that a basic truth has been lost: the sport needs viewers as much as it needs cash and coaches. Why else are the ECB pushing for terrestrial coverage in 2020? It's a nice idea. Here's hoping it's not too late.

Cricket's first lady

The coincidence was strange. The day someone suggested MCC were thinking of making their Laws gender-inclusive – adding "or she" after every mention of "he" – news came through that Rachael Heyhoe Flint had died, at the age of 77. Death was the one thing she seemed incapable of; as Clare Connor explains later in these pages, she was a force of nature.

Heyhoe Flint would probably have chuckled at the extra pronoun, and no doubt regarded it as a sign of cricket's slow, awkward, but necessary embrace of the women's game. Truth be told, *Wisden* is not speaking from the moral high ground: she should have been a Cricketer of the Year – probably in 1974, the summer after she had beaten the men to it, and driven through the first women's World Cup.

That last sentence sums up part of the problem, for coverage of women's cricket has long fallen prey to unhelpful references to what the men have or haven't done. But, in the case of one of Heyhoe Flint's astute observations, we can probably make an exception. "Professional coaching," she reckoned, "is a man trying to get you to keep your legs together, when other men have spent a lifetime trying to get them apart." For her humour, as well as her revolutionary zeal, she will be missed.

Heavyweight champions

As Northamptonshire biffed their way to more Twenty20 success, it felt as if we finally had the answer to one of sport's oldest riddles: who ate all the pies? *Wisden* often looks for polite ways of describing the larger cricketer – portly, generously built, well upholstered. But Northamptonshire are used to the jibes, and didn't play as if they cared about euphemism. As much as anything, their two finals-day wins at Edgbaston against teams who clearly counted their calories were a reminder that, for all cricket's obsession with professionalism, there's still room for indulgence.

Leaders of the Weston world

Cricket was way ahead of the pollsters. As *The Cricketer's* February 2017 edition suggested, the result of last year's seismic election across the Atlantic was foretold by the scorecard of a humble county match at Weston-super-Mare, some three decades earlier. Surrey chose to bat against Somerset, quickly giving rise to the prophetic moment: Clinton c and b Trump 16. Never let anyone tell you sport and politics don't mix.

ALASTAIR COOK PASSES 10,000 TEST RUNS

Curiouser and curiouser

ANDY ZALTZMAN

At some point in the future, historians – should they remain legal in the post-factual galaxy – will sit down to write *The Definitive History of Planet Earth: 2006 to 2016*. They will pick over a world of bewildering social change, breakneck technological evolution and frenetic, furious politics. When they scrutinise cricket, they will see a sport buffeted and renewed by these riptides of revolution. Yet amid it all has been an immutable bulwark, apparently standing outside time: in a world devoted to the instantaneous, Alastair Cook's Test career has been an epic of throwback pragmatism.

Cook has played 140 Test matches in 11 years, scoring over 11,000 runs, with 83 innings of 50 or more. He has batted for 551 hours in Tests, of which a record 522 as an opener is three days more than the next man, Geoffrey Boycott. Ever present since illness ruled him out of the third Test of his debut series, in India, he has been nothing if not stoic. And, during the course of a golden-goose-squeezing 31 Tests between April 2015 and December 2016, Cook overtook Graham Gooch's England record of 8,900, crossed the 10,000 mark, and finished the tour of India with 11,057 and 30 hundreds, another England record.

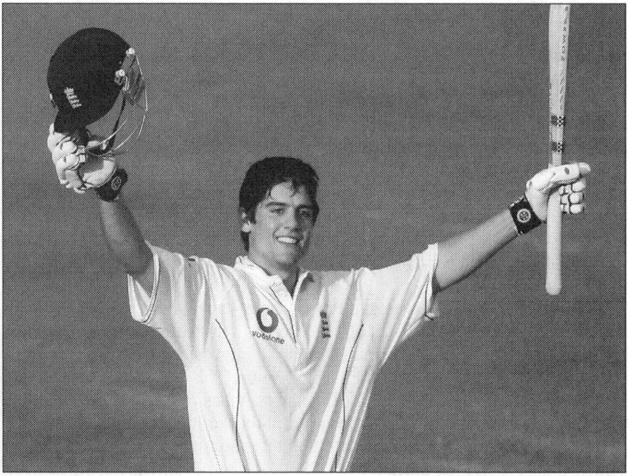

The start of something big: Alastair Cook reaches a century on debut, Nagpur, March 2006.

Beneath the surface, however, lies a career of curious inconsistencies, of mountainous achievements and prolonged plateaus; certainties have been transformed, as if elements of his batting have had their polarity reversed.

Cook's Test career can be broadly broken into four phases. The first consists of his stellar initial burst, starting with his debut at Nagpur when, aged 21, he made 60 and 104 not out against Anil Kumble and Harbhajan Singh following a three-day journey from the West Indies to the heart of India. He added two more centuries, as well as 89 and 83, in the summer of 2006, becoming the first Englishman to score three Test hundreds before his 22nd birthday. It is the kind of stat that has followed him around ever since.

Phase Two stretched from the 2006-07 Ashes to the end of the 2010 season, during which his returns against the best opposition were unspectacular. In England's 5–0 whitewash in Australia, Cook made a hundred at Perth but otherwise did not reach 50, as the naggery of Glenn McGrath and Stuart Clark produced his first prolonged struggle. His overall numbers were buttressed by

THE FOUR PHASES OF COOK

	T	*I*	*NO*	*Runs*	*HS*	*100*	*50*	*Avge*
March 2006 to August 2006	9	16	2	761	127	3	3	54.35
November 2006 to August 2010	51	92	4	3,603	173	10	19	40.94
November 2010 to December 2012	27	46	4	2,753	294	10	7	65.54
March 2013 to December 2016	53	99	5	3,940	263	7	24	41.91

runs against West Indies and Bangladesh, but against top-seven teams Cook averaged 33 in 36 Tests, with just four hundreds in 66 innings. The period included another low-key Ashes (he averaged 24 in 2009), excellent hundreds in Sri Lanka and South Africa, and a horror run against Pakistan in 2010, when a century at The Oval dispersed the first and only selectorial vultures to hover over his Test place.

The sheer size of Cook's numbers stems not only from his enduring quality and remarkable fitness record, but also from the era in which he has played. Since 2000, England have had an average of 13 Tests a year, the most intensive schedule in history. He has benefited from belonging to the age of central contracts: the trapdoor-trigger selectors of yore might not have tolerated his second-phase lull. This stability is highlighted by the fact that Cook has had 63 England team-mates in his 140 Tests; Michael Atherton acquired 64 in his first 57 Tests alone.

From the ruins of 2010 emerged Phase Three – a number-crunching peak in which he averaged 65 in 27 Tests and scored ten centuries, five over 175, including a career-best 294 against India at Edgbaston, the second-highest score by an England player in the past 52 years. This period was bookended by Cook's two greatest series: his Himalayan Ashes of 2010-11, and – in his first series as full-time captain – a triumphant tour of India two winters later.

His overall Ashes performance highlights the statistical oddness of his career. Of the six he has taken part in, 2010-11 was his only major success – a methodical, 766-run disembowelment of Australia, second only to Wally

Happier times: the productive partnership of Alastair Cook and Kevin Pietersen.

Hammond's 905 in 1928-29 among English Ashes aggregates; Cook's average that winter of 127 is second to Don Bradman's 139 in 1930 among those who have played a complete Ashes series. But he averaged below 30 in 2006-07, 2009, 2013 and 2013-14, and a modest 36 in 2015. In England, he is without an Ashes hundred in 28 innings over three winning series, and has passed 51 only once in eight home Test wins against Australia.

Phase Four comprises everything since the start of 2013, when he has remained a consistent run-maker and milestone-passer, averaged just under 42 in 53 Tests, but made relatively few centuries (seven), and defined and dominated few matches.

Alongside, and sometimes overlapping, these phases have been peaks, troughs and assorted crinkles in Cook's underlying statistical substrata. Take his conversion stats. By the end of June 2007, he had turned six of his first 11 half-centuries into hundreds. Between then and the end of the Third Test in the Caribbean in February 2009, it was only one out of 14. But between the Fourth, in Barbados, where he scored 94 and 139 not out on a futile featherbed, and the start of the 2013 Ashes, he converted 18 out of 29 (along with five dismissals in the nineties) – the second-best out of the 46 batsmen with at least ten half-centuries in that period, behind only Jacques Kallis.

Between July 2013 and December 2016, by contrast, Cook converted only five of his 29 fifties into hundreds – the second-*worst* conversion rate among the 38 players with ten or more, ahead only of West Indies' Jermaine Blackwood. In other words, while he reached 50 with almost precisely the same regularity over both periods (once every three-and-a-bit innings), the Cook who gave honours-board engravers repetitive strain injury shed the cocoon of accumulation that once habitually formed around his innings. This may be attributable to the burden of captaincy, which he relinquished in

February 2017. After all, he scored six hundreds in his first seven Tests in charge – including two as stand-in captain for Andrew Strauss in Bangladesh in early 2010 – but only six more in 52 games since. The regularity of his half-centuries suggests his form has remained largely intact; his downward-spiralling conversion rate suggests his intensity has not.

Other aspects of Cook's batting have undergone similarly enigmatic mutations. For much of his career, he was virtually unbowlable. His weakness lay in the poke outside off, which – allied to his strength off his legs – led bowlers to steer clear of the stumps. They were disturbed only 12 times in his first 98 Tests – once every 1,400 deliveries (for other Test openers across the same period the average figure was 449). Cook played on nine times, and was bowled off his pads once. So he had been clean-bowled twice in more than 17,000 balls, by two Pakistani Mohammads – Sami at Lord's in 2006, and Amir at Edgbaston in 2010.

MASTERCHEF

The leading Test run-scorers since Cook made his debut on March 1, 2006:

Runs		*T*	*I*	*NO*	*HS*	*100*	*Avge*
11,057	**A. N. Cook (E)**	**140**	**253**	**15**	**294**	**30**	**46.45**
8,463	K. C. Sangakkara (SL)	80	144	12	319	30	64.11
7,737	H. M. Amla (SA)	97	163	13	311*	26	51.58
7,571	M. J. Clarke (A)	95	167	20	329*	26	51.50
7,507	K. P. Pietersen (E)	96	165	7	227	21	47.51
6,955	A. B. de Villiers (SA)	92	151	15	278*	18	51.13
6,946	I. R. Bell (E)	107	186	22	235	20	42.35
6,538	Younis Khan (P)	73	133	16	313	23	55.88
6,455	D. P. M. D. Jayawardene (SL)	74	130	5	374	21	51.64
6,015	L. R. P. L. Taylor (NZ)	80	145	17	290	16	46.99

As at February 8, 2017.

But in his 99th Test, at Adelaide in 2013-14, Mitchell Johnson bowled him one of Test cricket's least defendable deliveries, a 93mph outswinging masterpiece that, even with a month's advance notice in writing, would still have smashed into off stump. Then, in his 100th, Ryan Harris produced an even better delivery, and Cook was cleanly castled again. His stumps have never regained their sense of undisturbability: perhaps because he has become more adept at avoiding edges, bowlers have aimed a fraction straighter, and so in his last 42 Tests Cook has been bowled 16 times, once every 421 deliveries. His timbers were even shivered twice by spinners over the winter – he played on attempting to sweep Shakib Al Hasan in Chittagong, and was clean bowled by Ravichandran Ashwin in Mohali, the third and fourth time he had been bowled by spinners in 8,472 deliveries.

For most of his career, Cook was one of the world's most secure players of slow bowling. Until the start of the 2015 summer, he averaged 67 against spin, falling once every 150 balls; against pace, he averaged 40, falling once every 84. Over the span of Cook's career, only Kumar Sangakkara and Joe Root had proved harder for spinners to dismiss. Then came another reversal: from the

To boldly go: Alastair Cook loses sight of a ball from Sohail Khan, The Oval, August 2016.

2015 summer onwards, he has averaged 34 against spin and 59 against seam. Until then, his spin-average was comfortably the best among the 15 batsmen who had opened in at least 50 innings during that period of Cook's career; against pace, he was ninth best. Since then, his pace-average is the best of the 15 most regular openers, but his spin-average the tenth.

Loitering within this metamorphosis lies a further anomaly. Against the six all-time leading wicket-takers among Test spinners – Muttiah Muralitharan, Shane Warne, Kumble, Harbhajan, Daniel Vettori and Rangana Herath – Cook has an aggregate of 598 for nine. Against part-timers Mohammad Hafeez, Ryan Hinds, Mahmudullah and Kane Williamson, it is 169 for ten. Bangladesh's teenage debutant off-spinner Mehedi Hasan dismissed him three times in 82 balls in October; in six Tests, Murali got him twice in 450. And before the 2016-17 series in India, Cook averaged 101 against left-arm spin. Then Ravindra Jadeja dismissed him six times, for 75 runs. In a universe that has delivered Donald Trump as president of the United States, perhaps quirks such as these should no longer surprise us.

Cook has been an opener for the ages, yet has never found an ideal partner. He has opened England's batting in 240 Test innings, 117 times with Andrew Strauss, and 123 times with 13 others. His partnership with Strauss produced an average of 40 per stand, a reasonable figure, but lower than you might expect from two successful Test openers. Strauss was far more productive with the more aggressive Marcus Trescothick and, in a delight for irony aficionados,

Cook's most fruitful regular partner in Tests for any wicket has been Kevin Pietersen – and Pietersen's, Cook.

In 58 Test partnerships, before one of sport's less amicable partings of the ways, they added 50 or more 28 times, including 13 century stands (of which eight contributed to victories), and averaged a superb 64. There is more: of the 61 England pairings to have shared at least 25 partnerships, Cook and Pietersen are fourth, behind Hobbs and Sutcliffe (average 87), Barrington and Dexter (66), and Barrington and Cowdrey (64). Cook and Strauss are 40th, and Strauss and Pietersen 59th, with a monosyllable-overheard-on-a-microphone-foreboding average of just 28.

Curiosities naturally dwell within the statistics of almost every player, particularly those who have played as much as Cook. Yet some of his curiosities are especially curious. Before May 2010, for example, he averaged more in the first and fourth innings of Tests (50 and 46) than in the second and

THE ROAD TO 10,000 – AND BEYOND

How Alastair Cook made it to five figures:

Runs	*T*	*I*	*Score*	*Opposition*	*100*	*Avge*
1,000	13	24	7* (20)	v Australia at Melbourne, 2006-07	4	46.04
2,000	26	48	13* (44)	v New Zealand at Wellington, 2007-08	7	44.15
3,000	40	73	97* (139*)	v West Indies at Bridgetown, 2008-09	8	44.08
4,000	53	96	31* (39)	v Bangladesh at Chittagong, 2009-10	11	44.04
5,000	65	115	59* (189)	v Australia at Sydney, 2010-11	16	47.50
6,000	75	131	22* (49)	v Pakistan at Dubai, 2011-12	19	48.60
7,000	86	151	88* (190)	v India at Kolkata, 2012-13	23	50.36
8,000	101	181	18* (51)	v Australia at Melbourne, 2013-14	25	46.97
9,000	114	204	56* (56)	v New Zealand at Leeds, 2015	27	46.87
10,000	**128**	**229**	**5* (47*)**	**v Sri Lanka at Chester-le-Street, 2016**	**28**	**46.49**
11,000	**140**	**252**	**2* (10)**	**v India at Chennai, 2016-17**	**30**	**46.44**

Figures for hundreds and averages are to the end of the innings in which he achieved the milestone.

third (37 and 42). Since then, he has averaged almost twice as many in the second and third (60 apiece) as in the first and fourth (32 and 33). Scientists may well unravel the mysteries of life itself before they concoct a satisfactory explanation.

Cook has been an accumulator in the Age of Biff, a totem of anti-flamboyance in an era of compulsory entertainment, England's immovable island of certainty during years of cricketing flux. Yet beneath his changeless facade of hawk-eyed focus and impassive resolve – and camouflaged by the jerky unorthodoxies that sporadically bloom into a majestic pull, a surgical cut or a weighty clip – lurks a narrative of sweeping and sometimes inexplicable undulations, a patchwork of triumphs and failures, mastery and struggle, that has shaped English Test cricket for more than a decade.

Andy Zaltzman is a stand-up comedian, podcaster, ESPNcricinfo contributor and Test Match Special *scorer. He was formerly a grindingly tedious village-level opening batsman.*

CRICKET AND POLITICS

By the right, quick march

ALEX MASSIE

Beefy, of course, was for Brexit. How could it have been otherwise? How could English cricket's greatest living champion be expected to truckle or bend the knee to Brussels or Strasbourg? Announcing his enthusiasm for leaving the European Union, Ian Botham declared: "Cricket is a game where you achieve the greatest success when you are confident in your own ability to go out and stand proud. Britain has that spirit." You may not agree with the analogy, but when Botham complained "we have lost the right to govern ourselves", he was – as the referendum confirmed – speaking for many. Similarly, his bullish declaration that "England should be England" revealed the essence of the Brexit debate: this was a very English revolution; Scotland, Wales and Northern Ireland had walk-on parts.

It transpired that Botham – parroting lines from the standard Brexit texts – was resolutely on-message (more so, certainly, than when he suggested republicans should be hanged). "In my cricketing career," he said, "I played alongside team-mates and opposition from all over the world – from India,

Cheers, and cheerio: Brexiteers Boris Johnson and Ian Botham at Chester-le-Street CC.

Australia, the Caribbean. Countries like these are our natural friends." There was no need to add that countries like France and Italy and Germany are not, and we know this because, mystifyingly, they cannot appreciate the genius of cricket. If that means ditching the Dutch, so be it…

In fact, Botham was closer to an older spirit of cricket than he knew. As long ago as 1877, one writer – Charles Box – observed: "The effete inhabitants of cloudless Italy, Spain and Portugal would sooner face a solid square of British infantry than an approaching ball from the sinewy arms of a first-class bowler." A joke, yes, but not entirely – and a reminder that, for a certain kind of Englishman, foreigners are always odd. It is a conceit not always discouraged by cricket.

Even in a country obsessed with football, this tendency to seek greater truths in cricket lives on. Writing about the then prime minister David Cameron, journalist Peter Oborne once noted that, though expansive, he was too heavily geared towards the leg side. "This tendency to strike across the line," wrote Oborne, "allied perhaps to a lack of basic concentration, too often brought about a premature return to the pavilion." As in cricket, you may think, so in politics.

Corbyn enjoys cricket, perhaps explaining why his politics is soaked in nostalgia

Be that as it may, Brexit was also – according to Michael Gove, one of its leading advocates – a protest against the experts and a revolt against the liberal elite: a triumph for provincial England over metropolitan Britain and, given the balance of informed opinion, of the amateur over the professional. Pre-1963 county cricket, before the abolition of the Gentleman–Player divide, would have been proud.

Cricket, or at least the counties, had an explicit reason to be interested in Brexit too, since leaving the European Union – whenever and however it occurs – may have an impact on their ability to sign Kolpak players. But the divides revealed by the vote also map neatly on to some of the divides long apparent in English cricket. Alastair Cook, for instance, happiest on his Bedfordshire farm, is believed to have backed the Leave campaign; one or two of his more metropolitan team-mates did not.

Just as Brexit relied on some left-wingers supporting an argument largely led by the right, so cricket's popularity crosses the class divide, even if it is largely defined by a particular, conservative, tradition. Or, as historian Derek Birley put it: "Cricket mythology requires us to believe in progression from rustic innocence to a golden age, followed by a decline." What could be more conservative – or more English and Brexitish – than that? Paradoxically, this sentiment is not confined to the right. The Labour leader Jeremy Corbyn enjoys cricket, which could explain why his politics is soaked in nostalgia for a left that never quite was, but may be once again.

If this is unfair, then doubtless it is also unfair to note that Theresa May, daughter of a cricket-loving vicar – and wife of cricket-loving Philip – said in 2012 she had been a "Geoff Boycott fan all my life", admiring the manner in which "he solidly got on with what he was doing". It is hard to avoid the

The way we weren't? The opening ceremony of London's 2012 Olympics created a picture-perfect game on an impossibly bijou pitch.

thought that this is how the prime minister sees herself. An entire generation of Yorkshiremen must feel reassured.

In reality there is no famous cricketing counterpart to a much-quoted line from Bill Shankly: "The socialism I believe in is everyone working for each other, everyone having a share of the rewards. It's the way I see football, the way I see life." On the contrary, a large part of cricket's tension lies in the interplay between the individual and the collective; if the game does not encourage selfishness, it can still reward it. Indeed the newspaperman and Labour MP Woodrow Wyatt, a cousin of former England captain Bob Wyatt, once cheerfully observed: "No country which has cricket as one of its national games has yet gone communist." (Causation, of course, does not imply correlation.)

Mind you, it is always wise to be on your guard. In *The Cricketer* in 1922, Lord Harris harrumphed: "Bolshevism is rampant and seeks to abolish all laws and rules, and this year cricket has not escaped its attack." The attack? Nothing less than the lax application of county cricket's residential qualifications.

No wonder cricket, at least in England, is reckoned a profoundly conservative expression of the national psyche. It seems notable that the sport's soul – if it possesses such a thing – is southern and pastoral, not northern and industrial. It speaks to the soft romance of the village green, and an England that is eternal, even as it disappears year by year. The reaction against a city-based Twenty20 competition owes something to this sense of rustic tradition too.

The histories of the Yorkshire and Lancashire leagues tell different stories, of course. So too does the emergence of a generation of city-spawned English-

Asian cricketers. Ahead of his time, Basil D'Oliveira ended his autobiography thus: "I shall always offer Britain as my model example of the decent, multiracial society any country should be proud to copy." Given the manner in which he was treated by the game's authorities, this was a generous appraisal.

Times change, and so do attitudes. Norman Tebbit's cricket test seems a less burning question now that identity is more readily acknowledged as multi-layered. When Moeen Ali is booed at Edgbaston by other English-Asians, the dominant reactions are sadness and even pity, not anger. We are a little more relaxed these days. In that respect, the game is a mirror for an evolving society. A cricketer in England fending off accusations of dual loyalty is as likely to be white and from Durban as brown and from Birmingham. Yet, except when playing Australia, English cricket can be so lacking in nationalist fervour it might be thought of as post-national. There is a pleasure in seeing England play well, though also a peculiar enjoyment in seeing them play dreadfully. In general, the game's the thing: caps are doffed to Bangladesh in 2016, just as they were to Pakistan in 1954.

> There is a pleasure in seeing England play well, and in seeing them play dreadfully

What of the cricketers themselves? John Arlott's observation that there were never more than half a dozen left-wingers on the county circuit may have been exaggerated, but only to a degree. After all, Mike Edwards, the former Surrey batsman, suggested cricketers were "the only group of employees more right-wing than their employers". And Simon Hughes recalled that Jack Russell was an oddity in more ways than one: he voted Labour at a time when "you could probably count the socialist cricketers on the fingers of one hand. After a couple had been amputated."

So no one was surprised when Ted Dexter stood as a Conservative candidate in the 1964 election in Cardiff South-East, where he helped Jim Callaghan increase Labour's majority from 868 to 8,000. Nor that, when Andrew Strauss was linked with a political career following his retirement in 2012, it was the Conservatives who were said to be thinking of adopting him. Nor that the prime ministers most associated with cricket – Alec Douglas-Home and John Major – were both Tories. Nor again that, if you select a team of Victorian MPs with first-class experience, Tories outnumber Liberals five to one.

Two nations, as Disraeli put it, but only one of them got to own, or define, the game. And cricket's attitude towards class was often not so much conservative as grimly, extravagantly, blimpishly reactionary. As late as the 1950s, the cricket writer G. D. Martineau could claim: "Professionals are as much the backbone of English first-class cricket as non-commissioned officers are the backbone of the British army." They were necessary, in other words, but not quite the thing. And it was a reminder, for some, that Orwell's appraisal of England as "a family with the wrong members in control" has applied to its cricket too.

John Major's panegyric to an eternal idea of a "country of long shadows on county grounds, warm beer, invincible green suburbs, dog lovers and pools fillers" was nostalgic tosh even 25 years ago. But his plea for a "classless

Cut and thrust: political adversaries Ian Paisley and Martin McGuinness cross bats at Stormont in 2007. Joining them are Ireland cricketers Kyle McCallan and Trent Johnston.

society" and "a country at ease with itself" indicated that these virtues had not always been apparent. Cricket could have told him this. It seems equally telling that Tony Blair's New Labour government, the most thrusting and self-consciously modern administration in recent memory, also had the least evident enthusiasm for the sport. Cool Britannia had more time for football.

Cricket and the European question have some history, too. When Geoffrey Howe resigned from Margaret Thatcher's cabinet in 1990, precipitating the crisis that led to her defenestration, she chose her metaphor carefully. "I am still at the crease," she said, "though the bowling has been pretty hostile of late." There would be "no ducking the bouncers, no stonewalling, no playing for time". On the contrary, "the bowling's going to get hit all round the ground. That is my style." The bowlers disagreed, as did some of her own team. As Howe told the Commons next day, Thatcher's relationship with her senior ministers had broken down. Her approach, he suggested, was "rather like sending your opening batsmen to the crease, only for them to find, the moment the first balls are bowled, that their bats have been broken before the game by the team captain".

The day after Brexit was confirmed, and Cameron had returned to the pavilion for the final time, all eyes turned to an improbable man of the moment: Alexander Boris de Pfeffel Johnson. Would he be Britain's next PM? What, now that he and his buccaneering band of Brexiteers had won the day, was the plan? Trapped by reporters outside his London home, Boris mumbled that this was not the moment for such trivia. "Christ," he said, "I've got to go and play cricket." And off he tootled to a charity match at Althorp House, home of Earl Spencer. According to his critics, this was a suitably ludicrous coda to a fantastical series of events. But there was also something reassuring about it: even in the midst of political crisis, there must be space for cricket.

It was surprising Johnson missed the opportunity to quote Henry Newbolt's "Vitaï Lampada": "And it's not for the sake of a ribboned coat/Or the selfish hope of a season's fame/But his captain's hand on his shoulder smote/'Play up! Play up! And play the game!'" The poem represents the acme of cricket's embodiment of a particular Englishness; it also matches the spirit of Brexit, as imagined by Johnson and Botham. In politics, as in cricket, we bat on.

Alex Massie writes about politics for The Times *and* The Spectator. *He also plays for Selkirk in division three of the East of Scotland league.*

THE STORY OF THE SIX

The currency of cricket's economy

GIDEON HAIGH

In *Death of a Gentleman*, the rise of the Indian Premier League is symbolised by shots of seething crowds, comely cheerleaders and the flailing bat of Chris Gayle, while his voice sing-songs through the ecstatic din. "Because it's a different feeling, I'm telling you, when you see so many flags going, right around the ground, and they are shouting your name, and saying 'We want a six!'" As various of his strokes are seen soaring into stands, Gayle slips into a seeming trance. "It's like, damn, OK, I'll give them a six… It's a great feeling… Going, going, going, gone… Beautiful."

Had there been a soundtrack, only Barry White would have been suitable: "Keep on doin' it, right on/Right on doin' it." And, as ever with zeitgeisty Gayle, it was on point. The game has had rhapsodic romances with certain shots, from the cover-drive and the leg glance to the reverse sweep and the ramp. Today it is smitten with a quantity, a unit: the six has become the currency of cricket's economy. How many in a Test career, a record seized last year by Brendon McCullum from Adam Gilchrist, has become a kind of blue riband. How many in any given T20 game, as tournament six-counters spin like fruit machines, is a favourite gee-whizz stat, an excitement index. Sponsors, from DLF to Yes Bank, have competed for naming rights to IPL maximums. By calling his autobiography *Six Machine*, Gayle himself incorporated the big hit into his personal brand.

Contemplating the way the six collapsed distance between player and crowd, John Arlott once called it "the most companionable of cricket acts". Today it is in some ways a marketing device, an act of consumer outreach. As the camera hovers over the expectant terraces, we're invited to share in the rapture. Look at the fans! Look at them having fun! And – all of a piece with fans having fun – look at the product we're pitching you!

Oddly enough, the most pronounced growth in the six supply has been experienced in neither Twenty20 nor Test cricket, but in one-day internationals – indicative of the overall tide of aggression and enhancements in technology, but perhaps also of the contrivances adopted to revive the format. Many of the 38 sixes that descended on fans at Bangalore's Chinnaswamy Stadium during a one-day international between India and Australia in November 2013 seemed almost perfunctory, so far away were fielders kept by restrictions.

Expectations have changed irrevocably. When Robin Smith (167 not out) set England's one-day benchmark in 1993, they hit their four sixes in the full 55 overs. When Alex Hales (171) moved that benchmark last year, they hit 16 in 50. The four consecutive sixes with which West Indies' Carlos Brathwaite lowered the boom on England in the World Twenty20 final a few months earlier still qualified as extraordinary, although not, perhaps, miraculous.

All-out attack: umpire Martin Saggers signals another six.

No one had counted West Indies out, even though they needed 19 in the final over. That was the way they had approached the tournament: 43 sixes, to go with the 43% of deliveries from which they did not score.

How and why has this changed? In the game's earliest days, the scarcity of sixes was as notable as their abundance now. That was partly because six was awarded only if the ball left the ground itself, rather than simply the playing area. Australians awarded five runs for hits into the crowd, although this required the batsman to change ends – a penalty of sorts. Everywhere else, the hit beyond the ropes that remained within the ground was worth only four.

If the six has an ideological forefather, it was the broad-shouldered, horseshoe-moustached South Australian Joe Darling, who was irked on his first tour of England in 1896 to hit two balls over the pavilion at Crystal Palace and earn only four for them, as the venue's defined precinct extended another 100 yards. "Those two hits of mine would have gone right out of the Melbourne Cricket Ground," he griped.

Eighteen months later, at Adelaide Oval, Darling got a little of his own back by transiting from 98 to 104 in one hit, off England's Johnny Briggs – the first blow of its kind in an international match, causing nearly a delirium. "Most batsmen display extreme caution when they approach the coveted century," reported the *Register*. "Not so Darling, who, getting from Briggs a ball to leg which was just the right height to have a pop at, put all his strength into a hit to square leg and sent the ball sailing out of the Oval. Then the hats left the heads of excited spectators and the cheering continued until the ball was found in the Park Lands, and Darling was ready to take strike again."

Darling must have enjoyed the sensation, because he wanted to share it, taking on the six as a personal mission. When Surrey hosted a dinner for the Australians in 1899, and discussion turned to the timidity of modern batting, Darling enjoined English administrators to "alter the rules to enable a batsman to take risks by giving six for every hit over the boundary". He was unsuccessful in the first instance: when Middlesex's Albert Trott accomplished his unique blow at Lord's shortly afterwards, wellying his fellow Australian Monty Noble over the Pavilion and into the squash courts, it was worth only four. But when Darling led the touring Australians in 1905, their sixes for the first time had only to clear the fence, which quickly became the Australian first-class norm, and five years later the English norm too.

To hit in these times was to indulge in an almost guilty pleasure. The notion – so common today it verges on cliché – that players were entertainers, had little traction. Even Gilbert Jessop, the definitive hitter of his day, felt no such duty: "Playing to the gallery in all sports is one of the most offensive forms of diseased vanity, and to hit simply in order to extort applause would indeed be a lamentable method of seeking cheap popularity." Yet he could not deny that it was fun, that there was "some satisfaction in feeling that you are giving pleasure to the vast throng surrounding the field of play, that they are glad to see you appear".

Even the most bloody-minded batsmen admitted the big hit's particular frisson, while remaining reticent about such exhibitionism. In 1919, the first season of their famously stubborn and prolific partnership, Yorkshire's Percy Holmes and Herbert Sutcliffe were enjoying themselves at Northampton, vying with each other to be first to three figures. In his 1935 autobiography, *For England and Yorkshire*, Sutcliffe recalled the illicit pleasure of straight-driving 40 yards beyond the boundary into the tennis courts, a shot that took him from 94 to his maiden first-class century. In the next breath, though, he was excusing such self-indulgence: "The thrill stayed with me for a long time – there is a touch of it now when I think of the shot – but the hit was one I should not have attempted had there not been a race with Percy for the pleasure of scoring the first hundred for the county."

The six was transgressive not only because cricket was conservative. It was also risky. Bats were slim and light. Boundaries hugged fences. At lower levels there was even the inhibition of six and out, lest a precious ball be lost. So for a long time batting's most rewarding stroke was not identified with its foremost exponents. There was attacking batsmanship, of course. But six-hitting tended to be a facility of specialist practitioners, usually down the order: West Indies' Learie Constantine, South Africa's Jimmy Sinclair, Somerset's Arthur Wellard, Middlesex's Jim Smith.

The pre-war batsman of stature most notable for hitting was an outsider. C. K. Nayudu was a straight hitter of withering force. A six out of Chepauk in

Popperfoto/Getty Images

Popperfoto/Getty Images

Striking early: Joe Darling, in a pastel drawing by Albert Chevallier Tayler, and Albert Trott, photographed by George Beldam.

December 1920 ended up near a coconut tree 50 yards beyond the ground. Six years later, 11 sixes in a two-hour 153 against MCC at Bombay Gymkhana advanced India's case for Test recognition. And one of Nayudu's 32 sixes on India's 1932 tour of England, at Edgbaston, was said to have cleared the county, crossing the River Rea, which then formed the boundary between Warwickshire and Worcestershire. Including Nayudu among the Five Cricketers of the Year, *Wisden* reported: "Possessed of supple and powerful wrists and a very good eye, he hit the ball tremendously hard but, unlike the modern Australian batsmen, he lifted it a fair amount." Most did not: Hobbs hit eight sixes in 61 Tests, Bradman six in 52, Walter Hammond 27 in 85, with the boost of ten in one innings against New Zealand. Nayudu was even an outlier among his countrymen: Vijay Merchant's best first-class score, an unbeaten 359, was unaided by a single six; B. B. Nimbalkar's record-breaking unbeaten 443 included just one.

If sixes grew more regular after the Second World War, one thing did not change: the conviction that they should be spontaneous. "It is unwise for a batsman specifically to make up his mind before the ball is bowled where he will hit it," counselled Bradman. "The really fast scorer over a period is not the wild slogger." Even the free-swinging Australian Alan Davidson, who hit two sixes in a famous over during the tight 1961 Old Trafford Test, insisted it must "be an instinctive thing", that "the best shots are rarely premeditated". When Garfield Sobers hit his fabled six sixes at Swansea in 1968, he formed the ambition only after four deliveries: "I thought I should give it a go; there was nothing to lose."

The taboo was loosened at last by Sobers's West Indian heirs, licensed by limited-over incentives, empowered by ever-heavier bats. In the course of an 85-ball 102 in the 1975 World Cup final at Lord's, Clive Lloyd deployed a 3lb Duncan Fearnley to hit Dennis Lillee into the top tier of the Tavern Stand and flail Max Walker into the Grand Stand. In the final against England four years later, Viv Richards used a hump-backed Stuart Surridge Jumbo to hit the last ball of his undefeated 138, a near-yorker from Mike Hendrick, into the Mound Stand. Seeing mid-off and mid-on back, he anticipated a full delivery, stepped to off and aimed to leg. "I left the field thinking: 'That shot is my invention'," he wrote in *Sir Vivian*. "I was very proud of the option I had taken. It wasn't arrogance. It was pure one-day cricket." It was also pure Richards, who bestowed his gifts, and sixes, liberally: six of them in his record-breaking 56-ball Test hundred in Antigua in April 1986, including one, off John Emburey, with one hand.

In the same week, fastidious premeditation informed perhaps the most reverberating six of all. Footage of Javed Miandad awaiting the last ball of the Austral-Asia Cup final in Sharjah shows him standing a full minute, scanning the field, weighing his options and calling on his deity, with four needed to win. Like Richards at Lord's, he anticipated the pitched-up delivery, and stepped forward, nailing a full toss from India's luckless Chetan Sharma into the stands. It remains the maximum of maximums: the luxury Mercedes Miandad was given, and the umrah he was enabled to perform at the Holy Kaaba in Mecca, are a unique temporal and spiritual double.

Thus, perhaps, the beginnings of cricket's genuflection to the six: Miandad scored an unbeaten 116 that day, though few remember any detail of the first 110. Certainly the six suited the priorities of a game increasingly preoccupied with television. The slow-motion replay broke it down for delectation; the umpire's ceremonial raise of the arms provided an interlude of celebration; the commentator revelled in descriptive possibilities. Ian Botham's straight-drive beyond the Headingley boundary during his 1981 command performance will for ever be associated with Richie Benaud's call: "Don't bother looking for that, let alone chasing it – that's gone straight into the confectionery stall and out again."

A first generation of sponsors embraced the big blow: National Power in England with its Six Award for the first-class season, Mercantile Mutual in Australia with its Six Targets in domestic one-day cricket – for hitting one of them, at the River End of the WACA in October 1995, Steve Waugh won $A140,000. And when Waugh slog-swept Steve Elworthy into the Headingley bleachers during the 1999 World Cup, he foretold how batting's frontiers would move in the search for extra heft and leverage.

Slog-sweeps and reverse sweeps appear in Bob Woolmer's magnum opus, *Art and Science of Cricket* (2008) – perhaps the first instructional book to give them their due. Yet so profuse have been batting's Twenty20-inspired innovations since then that much else about the book's stroke catalogue, demonstrated by a sombre Jacques Kallis, now appears rather staid. Certainly there are no elucidations of how best to set oneself to hit a six when it is needed – a skill that since the advent of the IPL has been worth ever more, and proved

"The most companionable of cricket acts": sixes can give the crowd a piece of the action.

transferable. The sixes that crowned Virender Sehwag's first Test triple-century and M. S. Dhoni's match-winning World Cup innings were batting's new age incarnate.

Some have raised alarms about the spirit of this age, and in December 2016 MCC's world cricket committee recommended a limit on the dimensions of the modern bat, a miracle of balance, mass and rebound. In the Australian summer of 2015-16, a photograph circulated of that *beau idéal* of 1970s batting, Barry Richards, holding up one of his own bats alongside one of David Warner's, wand versus claymore. Into the Big Bash League, Gayle then flourished a gleaming gold bat, almost the perfect fetish object and symbol of cricket's six-propelled bling economy.

Yet the rise and rise of the six is not just about power. It is also about time, urgency, gratification. Who can wait for centuries? Who can wait for fame? It took Darren Lehmann 30 first-class hundreds over a decade to secure a Test cap. It took his son Jake one ball – sliced inside-out for six to win a BBL game for Adelaide Strikers in January 2016 – to become an instant celebrity.

Curiously, the junior Lehmann didn't even seem to hit it that well: the ball fell just the right side of an alluring rope. But perhaps that is another dimension of the phenomenon. The hit for six has been less the characteristic shot of the last decade than the mis-hit. Certainly the days when six implied perfect connection, complete mastery, are past. So excellent are bats, so conducive are conditions and so lush are incentives that it hardly matters how – it is how much. Size matters. As Gayle is also bound to have said at some point.

Gideon Haigh's latest book is Stroke of Genius: Victor Trumper and the Shot That Changed Cricket.

JOE ROOT SCORES 254 AGAINST PAKISTAN

The right kind of hunger

JON HOTTEN

It is July 22, 2016. Joe Root wakes up in his room at Manchester's Lowry Hotel with a plan. His Test summer has been OK, not great. He is being talked about as one of the best batsmen in the world across all formats – with Steve Smith, Virat Kohli, Kane Williamson and A. B. de Villiers. He was one of the stars of England's Ashes win in 2015, then played superbly in the disparate conditions of the UAE and South Africa.

He's dipped a little in the cold early summer against Sri Lanka, though, making nought, 80, three and four. And, in the First Test against Pakistan at Lord's, he fell to two poorly executed shots, mis-hitting a slog-sweep off Yasir Shah on 48, then fluffing a pull off Rahat Ali on nine. Days later, he's still upset by the first innings, because he and Alastair Cook had put on over a hundred and made the wicket look flat. When he got out, England stumbled. He is frustrated, too, because he knows he was in form but not scoring, which to him is a greater sin than not being in form in the first place.

After Lord's, England's batting coach, Mark Ramprakash, asks if he's happy with how he's playing. Root says yes, he feels generally fine. Ramprakash says he might still be in one-day mode. He disagrees. One of the things he prides himself on is the ability to adjust between formats. Over the next couple of days, Ramprakash's words nag at him, one thought recurring in particular: he

Jan Kruger, Getty Images

Calculated risk: Joe Root slog-sweeps Yasir Shah on the first day at Old Trafford.

had swept the ball before he fell to Yasir for four. The next was tossed up outside off, and he thought: "There's fifty." It was the wrong kind of hunger.

For a professional batsman, getting out is an endless reality. But the dismissals that hurt Root most are the ones such as the first innings at Lord's, mini-nightmares that lead to damage. Afterwards, the team spend a long time talking about Yasir. He bowled well for his ten wickets, sure, but England had played him badly, let him settle, thrown their wickets away with cross-bat shots.

"Sometimes you need to get it wrong to get it right," says Root. "I remember I had real clarity in the lead-up to that week at Old Trafford. Ramps had got this dog-stick and I faced a lot of that, getting my angles right for their left-armers; over the wicket, round, reverse swing, new ball… It was about being a little bit more greedy, and a little bit more stubborn."

> You're almost taking lbw out of the game

In the Old Trafford nets he works on alignment, in readiness for Pakistan's three left-arm seamers: Mohammad Amir, quick and skiddy, with late swing and a nasty low bouncer; Wahab Riaz, the enforcer, full or short, with brute pace and reverse swing; Rahat Ali, somewhere in between. He works and works with Ramps and his dog-stick, works on getting greedy, getting stubborn…

"In the UAE against them I got caught behind three times. There was a big thing made of my mode of dismissals against left-arm seamers, so I knew how they'd try to get me out. I practised leaving the ball, and moved further across my stumps to make sure I knew exactly where off stump was. If the ball was outside my right eye, I felt comfortable leaving it. If it was going to swing in, I was aligned to hit back down the ground. You're almost taking lbw out of the game. I had a strange feeling, you don't get it very often. My movement was right, feet in sync. I had confidence. My weight felt well balanced."

He's never been a great sleeper, and sometimes he'll lie in bed before a game playing the bowling in his head. But when he wakes at the Lowry he feels the rush. He knows what it is: he can't wait for this game. Cook wins a toss – about time, after losing four in a row to Misbah-ul-Haq. Root gets his gear ready, finds a seat, has a cup of tea. His supplier had given him a couple of nice new bats for Lord's, and he later realised he hadn't taped the handles up as he usually does – another sign he hadn't prepared as well as he thought.

"I like a bat that has consistency through the whole blade, not just the sweet spot. I'm not good enough to hit the sweet spot every time…"

Cook and Alex Hales walk out. Amir opens from the Pavilion End, Rahat from the Brian Statham End. Root watches from the balcony, but not too hard: if you watch like you're already out in the middle, it can drain you, amplify your doubts and make the bowlers look better than they are. After 30 minutes, Hales is bowled by Amir. From the balcony it looks unplayable, a rapid, full inswinger that comes back wickedly late to hit off stump. But as Root gathers his kit to make his way down, he sees the replay – good though the delivery was, Hales has played the wrong line. It settles him a little.

"When you're watching telly it looks like it's moving more than it is. You mustn't talk yourself out of scoring runs, or feel like it's difficult, or think about all this stuff when you're going out there. The best way I can describe it is that it's like learning to drive a car. The first time it seems everything's happening at once, but the more you do it, the more naturally it comes. You don't think. The ideal place when you walk out is just: right, watch the ball."

He takes a middle-and-off guard. Rahat is bowling. The first delivery is a little short, and he goes back and defends. The second is wide, and he watches it go past, a positive leave. The third is full. He sees it early and moves silkily towards it, making contact just outside off stump. It's back past Rahat before he's finished his follow-through. A couple of overs later he pumps Amir down the ground too: another great contact. The short one comes – Amir's arm suddenly twice as quick – and he can't duck or sway, so he takes it on the shoulder. It hurts, but the memory of being hit in the same place by Mitchell Johnson flashes through his head. No comparison: that one had felt like being knifed. He had tried to smile, but the pain was too much; all he could manage was an unconvincing grimace. This one sharpens him up, brings him clarity.

Graham Morris

Raising his profile: Joe Root celebrates 200.

"Five runs at a time, try to get a partnership going. That's all I practise, regardless of the situation. Make it feel like it's the two of you playing the delivery, not just the guy on strike. Cooky likes to get on with his own thing, and it helped to see the way he was playing and leaving."

Yasir comes on for the over before drinks. Watch the ball. Right forward or right back. Play straight. Aim to beat mid-off and mid-on with the drive, and punch the shorter ones either side of cover or midwicket. The second ball of his second over is short, and Root gets back and cuts it in front of square, smooth and controlled.

"Yasir bowls a lot out the front of his hand. It feels as if drift is his biggest asset in the first innings, trying to keep the stumps and lbw in play. He's just got ten wickets. You want to nullify that. Make him get you out with a ball that does turn big."

They bat comfortably until lunch. Just before the interval, Yasir bowls two bad balls – one short, one a full toss – and Root hits both for four. Hungry yet patient, patient and stubborn.

"I struggle to eat at lunch when I'm batting. I usually try to get a protein shake or some sort of liquid down. Get something on board, a banana, protein bar, try and calm down…"

The afternoon session is about the labour of batting. Playing Misbah's Pakistan has a rhythm unique in international cricket. They tend to sit in during quiet periods, set sweepers on both sides, and wait for something to happen. He tells himself not to fall for it, because when a wicket goes they're all over you in an instant. He passes 50, but feels the weight of his lull. In the time he goes from 53 to 66, Cook goes from 55 to 97. Cooky never outscores him. Root nails the slog-sweep off Shah – his first since Lord's – to move to 70. Cook gives him a look that says: "Rein it in a bit."

"Prior to that game, if Yasir went outside off stump, I tried to hit it over wide mid-on. So I spent a lot of time on a hard sweep in front of square along the floor – try and take the top edge out of it. Anything on leg stump or just outside I'd lap – try to beat the man at 45 on either side."

Cook's hundred comes with a clip for two off Amir. It's his 29th in Tests, level with Bradman. Not bad, that, thinks Root. He edges into the eighties, feels the tension gather inside him. He wills himself to let the runs come, just five more, then another five… They inch towards tea until, with three deliveries left, Cook gets a fast, full ball from Amir that keeps low and scuttles through him. After the interval, Pakistan sense an opening. Root moves to 97, then Rahat gets James Vince.

> When you get to a hundred, the overriding feeling is relief

"I felt Yasir had bowled a lot of overs and I wanted to face him as I got towards a hundred because I might get a tired delivery, even though he's got that ball that can make you feel unsettled. I managed to get one between midwicket and mid-on. It's a strange feeling when you get to a hundred, because there's that excitement, but the overriding feeling is relief. When I got them as a kid, it was all excitement, all happy, but it changes slightly. It's different now."

The hard part is staying patient, staying hungry. A hundred's not enough to win this match; a hundred's never enough for the big players. He feels the air go out of Pakistan again. They're waiting for the second new ball. Yasir gets a warning for running on the pitch. He's bowled 30 overs for 110, no wickets and only five maidens. Gary Ballance falls just before the close, but by stumps Root has scored 141, batted for six hours and a minute, faced 246 deliveries and, he thinks, played and missed just twice.

"I found it very draining. They spent a lot of time with men back, so we got a lot of singles. It was slow. You have to grit your teeth and be more stubborn than they are, but it was quite exhausting. There was a real element of satisfaction, though. When you wake up in the morning, there's nothing better than that enjoyable sort of tiredness and stiffness."

A new day, and Chris Woakes starts batting like a god, smashing it everywhere, so Root gives him the strike, props on his bat and enjoys the show. By the time he's eased his way to 150, Woakes has raced from two to 33. Then Yasir bowls Root a big, drifting leg-break from wide on the crease,

Board of control: Lancashire welcome an all-conquering Yorkshireman.

and draws a stunted little poke that takes the edge and brushes Younis Khan's fingertips at slip.

"That was the first real error I'd made – the first one off Yasir I thought I got wrong. It was a nice way of getting grounded again. I told myself to make it count, drive the point home, bring the declaration into it. Up to lunch, I may have got 20 or 30. After that, Stokes came in, and it's inevitable that something's going to happen one way or the other."

Yasir goes round the wicket and bowls a defensive line, trying to bore Root into a mistake. He and Stokes drag the field around with singles, getting into Misbah's head. Eventually, Misbah has to stop them playing drop-and-run; he takes a man out of backward point to plug square leg. The gap appears. Root is on 197.

"The safest shot for me, bizarrely, was the reverse sweep. It just happened. I remember one of the analysts had said that, from my last ten or so reverse sweeps, I'd scored 25 runs and been out six times…"

Yasir floats another towards his pads, and instinct takes over: the bat handle flips in his hands, he drops his knee and swings like a lefty. For the briefest of seconds Root – and only Root – knows how perfectly he's hit it, the contact an instant longer on the bat face, the ball fizzing through Misbah's gap to the rope. Then the world knows it too. He hears one thing: "Roooooot!"

"I felt I'd had a really solid plan for everything they threw at me – I had a couple of boundary options and a solid defence. Stokes got out right after, and then me and Jonny Bairstow scored rapidly. I wanted to get through to the declaration, really do my job."

England have a mountain of runs. His previous Test best – 200 not out against Sri Lanka at Lord's in 2014 – is a speck in the rear-view mirror. Wahab begins the 151st over of an innings that, for Pakistan, has become a nightmare.

Bairstow takes a single. The next ball is in the slot, but Root gets under it like a Sunday hacker, and watches Mohammad Hafeez gallop in and hold on. It's over at last. He bangs his bat into the ground.

"I'd started to think that 300 wasn't miles away. We were scoring quickly and we were only halfway through the second day. The ball was there. I just mis-hit the shot. After, it was a blur really. All of the lads were saying well played, but you're still in the middle of a Test match. I don't think it even hits you once the game's won – maybe it's a long time later, when you're driving along and you think, yeah, you know, that was a special day."

Jon Hotten is the author of The Meaning of Cricket.

SIXTY YEARS OF TEST MATCH SPECIAL

From Alston to Zaltzman

MATTHEW ENGEL

Hours before the start of the 1968 Ashes, news came through from Los Angeles that Senator Robert Kennedy had died, the day after he was shot in his moment of triumph at the California presidential primary. John Arlott welcomed listeners to *Test Match Special* from Old Trafford "on this sombre morning of world news". Maybe that was not the precise phrase, but I remember with ringing clarity the Arlottian word "sombre". It contained a multitude of meanings: that we knew what had happened; that it mattered to us as human beings; and that, in due course – probably over much claret, in Arlott's case – we would discuss its meaning. But for now the cricket would go on, and that was the business in hand.

Would such an event penetrate a modern cricket TV commentary box? Would the blazered Mammonites even mention it?

There is a fundamental difference between the broadcasting of cricket on radio and on television, and it has grown wider with the years. On TV, the orthodoxy is that This Is Thrilling And It Really Matters, no matter what. On radio, there is a tacit pact with the listener, who will be registering the cricket as an agreeable extra in their own day-to-day routine. The context is whatever else is worrying us, from sick kids to distant assassinations.

When *TMS* began, 60 years ago, this hardly needed saying. Everyone involved with the game had lived through the war; some who fought were still playing (Keith Miller, who famously described pressure as "a Messerschmitt

Clare Skinner

An A–Z of *TMS*: Rex Alston and Andy Zaltzman.

up your arse", had just retired); almost all the players had done national service; no one was paid much. Yet cricket remained supreme as the summer game.

Now, many professionals have done little in their lives except play cricket, and get paid well, even if no one has heard of them. TV commentators, who are paid exceedingly well, act as though nothing on the planet is as significant as the umpteenth iteration of a computer's opinion of an lbw. In the meantime, cricket is disappearing from Britain's parks, greens and consciousness to its new home, up its own backside.

Against this background, *TMS* is a miraculous survivor. It is the game's prime ambassador to the outside world, as it has been since it began, on May 30, 1957. It has changed since then, of course it has. But, unlike the game it serves, it has changed organically, in keeping with its own traditions. Survival rests on a number of happy accidents. One is stability. There have only ever been three producers: Michael Tuke-Hastings for 16 years, Peter Baxter for 34, Adam Mountford for the past decade.

The basis of *TMS* is that of all great art: a disciplined line and a wild imagination

Neil Durden-Smith, now the senior surviving *TMS* commentator (sounding in his eighties exactly as he did in his thirties), did a handful of Tests in the early 1970s, before concentrating on PR. He remembers how straightforward it all was: "You came into the box in the morning, and there would be a note pinned up with your times, and that's what you did. You just sat down and got on with it. If you were last on, you had to hand over to Jim Swanton to do the summary. It was very relaxed, very informal."

Indeed. Tuke-Hastings had a good many other BBC responsibilities, such as producing quizzes. He oversaw the non-London Tests from a distance, as did Baxter in the early days, leaving the on-the-spot role to regional men, including Dick Maddock in the Midlands and an interesting cove in the North called Don Mosey. But the informality had a firm foundation. The basis of *TMS* is that of all great art: a disciplined line combined with a wild imagination. Shane Warne's bowling worked the same way. For the commentators, that means describing every ball accurately, giving the score regularly and judging the mood astutely: when to concentrate on the game, and when to discuss last night's dinner, Blowers's trousers, or the latest email from Mongolia.

Deviation from those rules can be fatal. Alan Gibson rivalled Arlott in his gifts as a commentator: he had a voice like honey and a marvellous way with words. Like Arlott, he enjoyed a drink; unlike Arlott, he could not judge his intake. He was despatched after a slurred performance at Headingley in 1975.

It was Arlott who created the tone. More than anyone else, he reached out beyond the core audience. People would say – especially women, who were considered tangential to the sport in those distant days – that they liked him "because he didn't talk about the cricket". He did, but he made it accessible, using his broad sensibilities, wit and command of metaphor. From 1946, long before *TMS* brought in ball-by-ball coverage, Arlott set the standard. It did not at first include much hilarity. That didn't come until Brian Johnston was added to the team in 1966; he joined it full-time when he was booted off TV four years later. Producers said he did not have the discipline to match his words to the pictures. Johnston said: "The emphasis was to be on an analysis of technique and tactics… So be it. But it was not my cup of tea."

Radio and TV coverage now went in different directions. Johnston's 24 years on *TMS* helped encourage the habit (more difficult now that satellites are involved) of turning the radio on and the TV sound down. And when the BBC's TV coverage finally expired in 1999, it did so – for all Richie Benaud's brilliance – mainly of boredom.

Yet the idyllic image of choccy cake and old chestnuts in the radio box was not quite accurate. The two stars of the 1970s – Arlott and Johnston – were far from close friends. Arlott and Tuke-Hastings both retired to the island of Alderney (population: 2,000 or so) but did not speak. Mosey, who joined the commentary team in 1974, could start a fight in an empty room. No one who scored as meticulously as Bill Frindall was likely to be happy-go-lucky.

But the upshot was a remarkable creative tension. *TMS* was a trailblazer both in cricket – its influence yanked Australian commentary away from its old solemnity – and beyond. Brough Scott, host of Channel 4's once-stylish (and now sadly lost) horse racing, described his programme's formula as "a mix of *Test Match Special* and drive time". Cricket was also a flagship for the dear old wireless itself. Once it was assumed that radio would slowly wither. *TMS* is one of the reasons it has done no such thing.

And the programme has had a knack of chance discoveries. On the Saturday of the 1976 Lord's Test – a rare damp day in that blazing summer – the panel were allowed to keep chatting, instead of handing back to the studio. The BBC found people enjoyed it as much as, or more than, the actual cricket. Jonathan Agnew, an intermittently excellent fast bowler, turned out to be a consistently excellent broadcaster, whose skills and growing stature helped lead the programme almost seamlessly through the deaths of Frindall, Christopher Martin-Jenkins and now Tony Cozier, all well before their powers might have waned.

There was a rocky patch in the mid-to-late 2000s. Clouds appeared during the last years of Baxter's long, sunny reign in the shape of men in suits who wanted the measured tones of *TMS* to match the zippier style of Radio 5. The rota had indeed become too much of a closed shop. But Baxter was pushed into giving young men

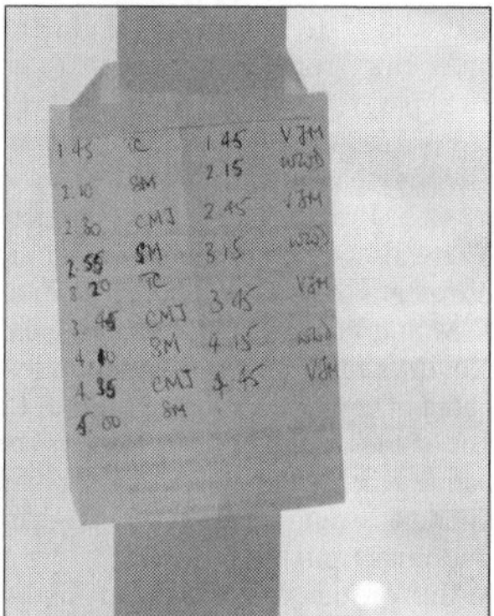

Patrick Eagar, Popperfoto/Getty Images

All in the timing: the afternoon session of a West Indies match in the 2006-07 World Cup, featuring Tony Cozier, Simon Mann, Vic Marks, Christopher Martin-Jenkins, and a rare appearance by Wayne Daniel. The hand is Peter Baxter's.

from the sports room their commentary debuts, whether he was convinced by them or not.

Among those was Arlo White, a highly competent broadcaster who was chosen for the post-2005 Ashes tour of Pakistan, and then for a couple of home Tests. White had played for Leicestershire Under-11s, but when he commentated in his head it was on football, and he readily admits he was not exactly Swantonian in his grasp of cricketing lore and history. He was monstered in the press, mainly by the serial controversialist Michael Henderson, whose other *TMS* victims have included Vic Marks, Ed Smith, Alison Mitchell – and Swanton. "The criticism stung and hurt," says White. "But I got to see some great places and worked with some of the world's most talented broadcasters, and I wouldn't take a second of it back. Anything I do now is based on what I learned on *TMS*." He's fine: chief English soccer commentator for NBC, purveyors of the Premier League to the eager Americans.

Tufnell's sharp cricket brain and sharper wit have been a huge plus

Mountford himself seemed to make a shaky start. The commentary team settled down, but the summarisers went a bit haywire. For most of *TMS's* life, this role had comprised serial duopolies: Freddie Brown and Norman Yardley; Trevor Bailey and Fred Trueman; Marks and Mike Selvey. Now there was a cacophony of voices, many brought over from Mountford's previous berth on Radio 5, and not all the voices were any good.

But it fell into place quite rapidly. Mountford had unearthed one diamond: Phil Tufnell, a find he credited to CMJ, who had worked with him in Sri Lanka, and said, "He's brilliant." Tufnell, like White, might not be up to speed on Victor Trumper. But his sharp cricket brain and sharper wit have been a huge plus.

For me, there are lingering issues. There is the Geoff Boycott problem. Geoffrey has now discovered that cricket is indeed a team game, and judges it as such; I'm not sure he has cottoned on that the same applies to commentary. There also seems to me too much movement in and out of the box, too many different voices in too short a time, the key changes stifling the melody.

Mountford insists this is unavoidable. "For years Peter just had to do a list. Now it's more like a jigsaw puzzle. I've got so many other outlets to worry about. They're dodging to 5 Live, Radio 1, Radio 2. They might have to nip out of the ground to do TV news, because we don't have the rights, and the cameras are not allowed in. The big change is social media. I might have to get Graeme Swann or Michael Vaughan to do half an hour on Facebook, taking questions from the audience."

But on the whole *TMS* is in rude health. Mountford hears nothing but support from the BBC hierarchy. It is said British emigrés to France settled in the Dordogne because that was the most southerly place with reliable reception of Radio 4 Long Wave. Now the internet takes it across the planet.

Though Frindall was the master statistician of his generation, he had no love of computers and no patience with weird stats. Andrew Samson and his extraordinary database give radio the lead in off-the-wall facts: "Player most

Mirror image: *TMS* has long reflected its time – here in the guise of Phil Tufnell and Henry Blofeld.

often out for two in a one-day international? Just wait a moment." Women, led by Alison Mitchell, are in the box on their merits and on equal terms.

The most interesting commentator of the new generation is Daniel Norcross, who made his Test debut at Edgbaston last summer. The route to commentary now is usually a slow progress through the BBC ranks (Simon Mann and Mitchell), or playing (Smith), or both (Charlie Dagnall). Norcross made a living for a while playing pub quiz machines, had a spell in the City, and drifted in and out of dot-com jobs before setting up *Test Match Sofa*, an anarchic internet-based non-rival to the real *TMS*: a group of blokes watching TV and chatting, with the ECB going berserk and accusing them of destroying the world of sporting media rights. "It was the most fun, the most silly enterprise I have ever been involved with," he says. "I was doing the one thing I had always wanted to do, even though I had none of the qualifications to do it."

He finally wrote a hopeless gissa-job letter to Mountford, who had a hunch Norcross *could* do it. I think so too: he has knowledge, enthusiasm and a smile in his voice. And, like the policeman/poet Arlott, an unusual perspective. Even more improbable is the one-day scorer Andy Zaltzman. It is not unusual for *TMS* to be a route into comedy gigs; Zaltzman has done it the other way round. But he is a serious scorer nonetheless.

In his last years, I got to know Rex Alston, the straight-man commentator of the early *TMS*. He was a classic public-school master of his generation: benign and humorous, but deeply conservative. He would have been startled out of his wits by the clown-haired Zaltzman. But they are both legitimate members of a great tradition.

I was standing by the school dining hall when I heard Arlott say "sombre". While I was listening to Norcross make his debut 48 years later, I was chopping thistles. I heard England beat West Indies at Lord's in 2000 from the car park at a niece's wedding. Funny how these associations remain in the mind more readily than the Tests one actually saw.

For others, it can be even more important. "Thank you, *TMS*," a listener in Ankara wrote last year. "You've meant more than cricket for us." It has never been more vital to our game, and our lives.

Matthew Engel attended every England Test as cricket correspondent of The Guardian *from 1982-83 to 1987. Otherwise,* TMS *has been part of the musical accompaniment of his life.*

CRICKET'S BATTLE FOR THE WORKING CLASSES

Breaking the grass ceiling

PHIL WALKER

Moeen Ali grew up in Sparkhill, Birmingham, played in the parks and went to a large comprehensive, where two-fifths of pupils receive free school meals. Ben Stokes, son of a nine-fingered rugby league coach from New Zealand, landed up in Cockermouth, Cumbria, and learned his cricket at the local club. Today they bowl right-handed, bat cack-handed, chase wide ones and go after short ones. They're an unlikely double act in England's middle order – Stokes's inky sleeve to Ali's "Save Gaza" bangle – yet dazzling to watch. But of England's top seven for the First Test against India at Rajkot, where both hit centuries, they were the only two who completed their education at a state secondary school.

These days we may not be too keen on all that hidebound stuff about class. But the problem with the idea of meritocracy, noted the British sociologist Richard Hoggart in 1989, is that "class distinctions do not die; they merely learn new ways of expressing themselves. Each decade we shiftily declare we have buried class; each decade the coffin stays empty."

In 2013, *All Out Cricket* magazine carried out some research for Chance to Shine, the charity focused on reversing the decline of the game in state schools. Of 413 county players, they found that 207 were educated by the state, and 119 privately (the other 87 abroad). In other words, 36% of county cricketers educated in the UK had attended private school, against just 7% of the overall population. That year, *The Economist* published its own research into the changing social make-up of England Test teams, using schooling as a "broad measure of class" to reveal a growing trend towards privately educated players: while state-school kids had comprised at least 60% of every England team between 1960 and 1990, that figure had dropped to a third in 2013.

Wasim Khan, Chance to Shine's chief executive at the time – and another to have emerged from a working-class area of Birmingham to play professionally – stressed that the charity were "striving to bring the standard of cricket in state schools up, not independent schools down". But the reality was stark: fewer working-class people were reaching the top of the English game than at any other time in its history.

Some argue that the specialist cricket scholarships offered by certain private schools to handfuls of kids from modest backgrounds skew the stats. Joe Root attended King Ecgbert secondary school in Sheffield before receiving a scholarship from fee-paying Worksop College; Haseeb Hameed, a working-class lad from a Bolton estate, earned one from Bolton School. There is truth in the argument. But while these gifted cricketers get access to top facilities and professional coaching, what of the mates they leave behind? All they have

Counter point: Harold Larwood at his sweet and tobacco shop in Blackpool, 1949.

gained is a lost inspiration, and another reason to kick a football around. A few success stories speak of little but the largesse of private money.

Cricket may be among England's "most cherished institutions", as Derek Birley wrote in *A Social History of English Cricket*, yet it is "freighted with extraneous moral overtones" embedded through centuries of deference. Indeed, it wasn't until 1952 that a professional, Len Hutton, was considered capable of captaining England. Writing in *The Times*, Geoffrey Green (Shrewsbury School) seemed to sound a warning: "In an age of so-called equal opportunity for all, the professional player has at last attained his fullest stature, and it is now up to Hutton to prove not only himself but also his colleagues worthy of the new principle which has been established." The *Financial Times* saw Hutton's elevation "as quietly cocking a snook at the cricketing Establishment", concluding with a sentence that's barely gathered moss since: "Cricketers in England had, for as long as anyone could remember, been divided by social hierarchy."

In truth, it wasn't quite Hutton's style to cock snooks; he preferred to suppress his Yorkshire accent for the job in hand. Others have stayed truer to their roots. Botham, Flintoff and Stokes have presented earthiness as a roguish virtue – and been cheered from the rafters for doing so. Botham was a state-school boy with an unignorable talent at a county, Somerset, keen on recruiting from private schools. But where his strident anti-authoritarianism did rather more to advance his everyman credentials than his country pile or grouse shoots, his latest heir takes a more straightforward approach. "I started off saying what I thought people wanted to hear," says Stokes. "But now I just say what I want." Perhaps despite itself, English cricket has always had fun with its working-class heroes. They refresh the parts other cricketers can't reach.

Stokes and Ali, then, should be perfect for their time and place. Ali's appeal is widespread, most obviously among British-Asians – now around 40% of the known recreational playing force – but also in the hearts of romantics, who weep for leg-side flicks, and of progressives, who salute a Muslim in an England cap. Stokes is less complicated: there is no more watchable sportsman in Britain. And yet not enough *have* been watching – or listening, reading, thinking or playing.

When, in 2014, the ECB carried out their own research, they uncovered some chilling trends. Among children aged 7–15, only 2% ranked cricket as their favourite sport; asked to name ten sports, three in five made no mention of it. Those figures, combined with the number of recognised club players dropping from 908,000 to 844,000 in a year, caused shock waves at the ECB. The voices which, a decade earlier, had cracked with despair when live TV coverage of England's home matches was sold to Sky, could be heard once more. After years of complacency from a central governing body – with their faith in a top-down approach relying on the marketing power of a paywalled England team – came an equation of devastating simplicity: extrapolate those numbers across a generation, and the game becomes irrelevant.

This is the message rammed home by Matt Dwyer, urgently appointed in 2015 as the ECB's director of participation and growth. Dwyer, an Australian, had initially been employed by Cricket Australia in 2011 to adapt his sales and marketing expertise to a model for cricket that could, in CA's words, "win the battle of the schoolyard and inspire the next generation". The programme – founded at the inception of the Big Bash, and what Dwyer calls an "unashamed focus on kids and mums" – has helped reinvigorate interest in Australian cricket, and persuaded the English game to get him on board.

"There are some very good people at the ECB," says Simon Prodger, managing director of the National Cricket Conference, which represents 1,100 clubs across the country. "But I think they've taken a long time to admit the truth about certain things. They used to be very instructional: 'This is what you will do!' Because they thought they were the owners of the game, they thought they could just dictate to you, without understanding the collateral effect."

The ECB have bolstered their ranks by the addition of Lord Patel of Bradford – Kamlesh, to those he meets – as an independent director. Until recently chairman of the Mental Health Act Commission, he hopes his experience will feed into his other passion. "The new [ECB] leadership have a tough job, but they're doing it for cricket, not for personal gain. I don't mean they weren't before... but it *felt* like it."

Patel comes up with an analogy. "If you look at the NHS over the last ten years, we've disinvested, so now we find ourselves in a catastrophic state. We don't have enough nurses, people are living longer, demand is outstripping supply: we're in big trouble. Cricket has done it gradually. And it's not just been cricket – councils and schools have not had the money. It's much cheaper to cut cricket than football. It's expensive for councils to look after pitches and keep the groundsmen going. We're fortunate there's a group of people, largely from South Asia, who are used to playing in the backstreets."

There is another group of cricketers, even more hidden. From the Bangladeshi restaurateurs playing at sunrise, to the taxi-drivers grabbing a couple of hours in a floodlit east London car park, self-made worlds of taped-up tennis balls, rudimentary kit and boundless invention throb in the nooks and crannies of urban life. And it's not limited to particular communities. The Last Man Stands leagues – post-work, eight-a-side, 20 five-ball overs, get changed under a tree – have gained traction too. "I love these leagues," says Prodger. "Cricket can be played in so many different forms – that's the beauty of it." Belatedly, the ECB have recognised these vast untapped markets, offering funding support to bring them into the fold – not least because an increase in registered players means more favourable funding from Sport England.

"I think the ECB are the only sporting organisation in the country that can tap into that massive [South Asian] population," says Patel. "Take Bradford, where 30% of under-10s are overweight or obese. In 15 years, they'll all have diabetes or heart disease, and yet we don't do anything. Cricket has the potential to change that. The door is open." And the delicate question of community friction, particularly in working-class areas? "There are stories, yeah. I work in the inner city, and cultural tensions spill over on to the pitch. You'll get the odd gripe afterwards – 'They'll bugger off without having a pint,' and so on. But that's society, not cricket. Cricket is just one small vehicle that potentially can help with health, mental health and community cohesion."

One evening about a decade ago, Scyld Berry, then *Wisden* editor, asked Angus Fraser where all the inner-city non-white cricketers had gone. "Owais Shah was basically the only non-middle-class person on the Middlesex staff," says Berry. Thus the Wisden City Cup was born, for 16–22-year-olds. "It's designed to create a perception, so people feel there's a pathway to the top, to get on to the county staff by some other way. In the first year the team were so good they beat the Middlesex Academy." Berry contends that the City Cup, running since 2009, is now an established part of a growing number of schemes designed to revive cricket in the inner cities. "Between Matt Dwyer and Kamlesh Patel, they're constructing a pyramid, a pathway, connecting all the various projects. Those two have the vision, particularly for Asian cricket, to blend it into the mainstream. Until recently, official cricket was happy to ignore them, but now the numbers are so great they cannot be ignored any longer."

The most celebrated project is Chance to Shine. Conceived in 2003 by Mark Nicholas, Duncan Fearnley and Mervyn King, appointed governor of the Bank of England that year, to address the mess of state-school cricket, the charity have so far provided sessions for over three million children, and are closely aligned with the ECB, who now contribute £2.5m a year. The ECB's new strategy Cricket Unleashed will be rolled out in 2017, with a key aspect the entry-level All Stars Cricket programme, produced in conjunction with Chance to Shine. A series of eight-week sessions directed at under-9s to be staged at clubs across the country, All Stars has already received a huge take-up from clubs who know a thriving colts section is their best hope of future security.

Leap forward: Tom Walsh, a graduate of the Taunton hub, bowls for Somerset during the 2016 Bunbury Festival.

"When we first started, the ECB supported us with half a million a year," says Chance to Shine's Fabian Devlin. "It was a leap in the dark for them, but the fact was they weren't doing anything in schools. It was almost a case of them giving us some money and letting us get on with it. Now there is a much tighter partnership." In 2016, Chance to Shine delivered sessions for 434,094 state-school children, of whom 46% were girls. Tellingly, the ECB's own research has found that, of pupils who play cricket in school, 58% like the sport; in schools where there is no cricket, it is 1%. But the charity is no panacea: only 3–4% of these children end up in a local club. "What we're still missing is white working-class boys and girls from white sink estates," says Patel. "I still don't think we're there. I know Chance to Shine are doing things, but I've worked in lots of white working-class areas, and it's a tough life. We're constantly focused on black or South Asian kids, and rightly so, but there's a group of kids we've left behind, say from mining villages. We need to realise the potential there."

Pockets of hope can still be found among the white working class. Five years ago, Ciaran O'Sullivan and his mates were discovered by a Chance to Shine coach playing cricket in a park in west London, and persuaded to join the charity's White City Estate street project. Cricket hadn't really been a thing at O'Sullivan's school ("We'd just play during lunch to pass the time"), but the project fired a passion that propelled the boys to Shepherd's Bush CC and, in O'Sullivan's case, a Level 2 coaching badge and a place in the first team. "Cricket, for me? It's done a lot!" he says. "I used to be really quiet. I wouldn't talk. I'm more confident now. When I joined Shepherd's Bush, I didn't know about cricket – it was just something to do to get me out the house. But then I got integrated into the club." And what do his non-cricket mates from White City make of it? "Nah. They just think it's a waste of time standing around in a field all day…"

Getting talented kids from secondary schools into clubs, and keeping them there, remains vital. To that end, Susan Brealey is a woman on a mission. "That so many come from 7% of schools seemed to me completely ludicrous, especially when 40 years ago the reverse was true," she says. In 2011, Brealey launched the first MCC Foundation cricket hubs, with a view to providing high-class coaching sessions, free of charge, to promising state-school-educated cricketers aged 11–15. Local comprehensives nominate their best athletes for a trial, with sessions at nearby independent schools. Six pilot hubs were set up in the first year, and there are scheduled to be at least 40 in 2017. "It's only 1,500 children a year at the moment," says Brealey. "But if you start multiplying that out, you develop something significant." She wants 200 hubs in place within five years.

What's more, it's a competitive environment: hub cricketers get to represent their region in organised matches, and need to perform to be retained. The most notable result so far came when the Langley hub from Slough beat Eton's B-team. Tom Walsh, meanwhile, a promising fast bowler, recently graduated from the Taunton hub on to Somerset's emerging player programme. "I don't think I'd have got anywhere near as far as I have [without the hub]," he says. "It's given me that time with great coaches that I wouldn't have had otherwise. And we've been able to use these amazing facilities at King's College, which are completely different to what anybody has seen before." And the unity it fosters? "Massive. Totally. Everyone had the same background. No one was coming in with a brand-new bat every five minutes. We were all equal, you know? So when we go and play King's, or Taunton School, my mates are like: 'We're not being beaten by this lot.' We have just as much raw talent as them."

Brealey says she would love to find an England cricketer one day. "But what I really want to do is to help clubs. If you can get to children at state schools, then you can connect them with clubs."

With fewer good cricketers coming through the leagues, such initiatives are crucial. "Clubs are beginning to lose second teams," says Andy Compton, master in charge of cricket at Bolton School, Hameed's alma mater, as well as the key co-ordinator of the Bolton hub and a stalwart Lancashire League player. "The standard is not as good, and so there's scrabbling around to pay players to come and play. You just aren't getting the same number of cricketers, so they will migrate to the better clubs, or the ones that are throwing money at them."

This concentration of talent in the richest clubs echoes societal patterns, and risks more have-nots going to the wall. "Not enough central money is given to the amateur game," says Prodger. "The big beef I've had with the ECB is that 99.98% of participation in this country plays recreational, not elite, cricket, yet

95% of all money goes to the elite game. To me, the recreational game needs to be celebrated in its own right, not with a pretence that it's a pathway to becoming a professional cricketer. That's bullshit: it doesn't happen any more, and it hasn't for a while." Prodger and others have been sparring with the ECB for years; at least now, he says, "there's more of a listening ear". And Patel sounds optimistic: when he says "a significant sum of any lucrative media deal we get in the coming years will go into working-class grassroots cricket", there is a sense that he speaks for all.

As the club game drags itself into the 21st century – an age of funding crises, council cuts, volunteering crunches, time-poor families, weekend work, crumbling bar revenues, red cards for player behaviour, and an umpiring exodus from a game that goes on too long in an individualistic culture at odds with even the *idea* of team – it's tempting to pause and wonder how much further it can go. And then, in the next breath, to stand in wonder at how far it's come.

Phil Walker is editor of All Out Cricket *and a long-standing club cricketer in the Essex part of north-east London.*

TONY COZIER 1940–2016

Master of all trades

VIC MARKS

There has never been a better place to follow a Test match than from the seat next to Tony Cozier. From a BBC commentary box, with West Indies either demolishing the opposition or being demolished – there has not been much middle ground over the last four decades – you were informed, educated and entertained, just as Lord Reith once demanded. Whatever was happening at the Kennington Oval, or the Kensington Oval, the listener would be soothed and transported by the soft, lilting Bajan tones of a master broadcaster.

Tony would first inform by effortlessly describing the action. He always obeyed the old *Test Match Special* rules because he never missed a ball; he rarely made a mistake but, when he did, he would interject quickly with a "Correction: that was Richards's 11th boundary – there was also an all-run four." Accurate reporting was his first, essential, port of call. Then, if there was time and space – but only if that was the case because of a lull in the cricket – he would both educate and entertain by disappearing down some byway, which might unwittingly reveal his encyclopaedic knowledge of the game.

The meander might relate to Everton Weekes's six-hitting in Test cricket. Why were there so few? Tony might explain how Weekes, a majestic third of Barbados's Three Ws, was a pragmatic powerhouse who considered aerial shots too great a risk. Tony would know that at first hand from watching

The heart and soul of Caribbean cricket: Tony Cozier interviews Mike Atherton in 1998.

Weekes as a boy, and because he was a friend for over six decades – just as he remained a friend of just about every West Indian cricketer thereafter, from Holder (Vanburn) to Holder (Jason).

So Weekes, by now 91, was far from the only prominent cricketer at Cozier's funeral in Bridgetown in May 2016. Garry Sobers and Clive Lloyd were there; Wes Hall conducted the service. Phil Simmons, the West Indies coach at the time, attended too, his presence a reminder of Tony's fearlessness as a journalist. Indirectly, Simmons once caused Tony to be abused in Trinidad because he had dared to suggest in a column that Simmons, a local, should be dropped from the Test team. This was never going to go down well in Port-of-Spain, but it did not stop Tony expressing his view.

Michael Holding was committed to work at the Headingley Test against Sri Lanka at the time of the funeral, but his love of Tony was obvious in a moving, tearful recollection of his great friend during a tribute on *TMS*. Holding explained that, if Cozier had something to say, true lovers of Caribbean cricket always listened. And so did the players.

It would be commonplace to see Cozier, Holding and Viv Richards meet up after another disappointing day of Test cricket for West Indies (we are now in the 21st century). They would share their frustrations, which accelerated from their tongues – one Bajan, one Jamaican, one Antiguan – at alarming speed. Soon it became impossible to decipher what they were saying. But the general impression was clear: they cared deeply about the game in the Caribbean.

Cozier was the most objective of broadcasters in the best traditions of *TMS*, but away from the microphone he was no neutral. The decline of West Indies cricket, especially in the Test arena, pained him, and he wrote about it passionately and clear-sightedly, latterly on ESPNcricinfo – to the extent that the West Indies board no longer welcomed him as a TV broadcaster. For a doyen of cricket journalism, this was a travesty and an insult. Needless to say, it did not prevent Tony from speaking his mind.

To watch him at work at a Test match was an education. He would move from the TV commentary box to the press room to the radio box, never hurried, yet never stopping. He mastered all three disciplines long before most of those around him had entered a media centre. On TV, he recognised it was not necessary to talk all the time, a lost art; he concentrated on the game, rather than the cringeworthy in-jokes of a previous generation of cricketers. And he might write three newspaper pieces a day, in crystal-clear prose.

Yet he will be remembered most for his work on radio. He had all the tools of the great broadcaster, among them that soothing voice and a fount of knowledge unsurpassed by any other commentator or summariser of my experience. He may not have been a first-class cricketer, but in his youth he opened at club level against Hall and Griffith: he knew the problems of playing. Add humour and a sense of timing, plus a deep love of the game, and you have an all-rounder of Sobers proportions.

He was always a generous broadcaster, never seeking to dominate. Yet he could be ruthless. Just occasionally, if he decided, say, that the great Geoffrey Boycott was proffering a particular point of view a little too frequently, he would talk on and on himself, never to the detriment of the coverage.

... but someone's got to do it. The guests at a 1986 Cozier beach party include two future *Wisden* editors, while the photographer has just stepped down from the post. Matthew Engel is behind the outstretched arm, Scyld Berry wears a Cockspur Rum T-shirt, and behind the camera is John Woodcock. The host (second left) is in a white cap; Christopher Martin-Jenkins is in front of Engel.

Beyond the confines of the media centre he possessed a wonderful zest for life. Tony liked to party. And, with the help of his wife, Jillian, whose wedding anniversary he never forgot (the crafty Cozier contrived to get married on his birthday), and his children, Natalie and Craig, he threw wonderful bashes. In tributes to Tony, just about every cricket journalist on the planet mentioned getting lost on the way to his beach hut somewhere on the east coast of Barbados. Everybody was invited; everybody accepted; most got there in the end.

The last time I saw him was in 2013 in Cardiff. His body was frail, though not his voice, nor his mind. Towards the end of a meal in the basement of an Italian restaurant there came the strains of Elvis Presley. Tony's antennae were alerted: he started to sing. The diners on the next table were South Africans following the cricket – and, it turned out, just as keen on Elvis. And there was Tony, delicately dancing around the tables with one of the wives, a smile on his face, and a sparkle in his eye.

Vic Marks played for Somerset and England, and is the cricket correspondent of The Observer, *as well as a regular summariser on* Test Match Special. *He and Cozier first worked together in 1990.*

Saqib Majeed

THE WISDEN–MCC CRICKET PHOTOGRAPH OF 2016 Saqib Majeed wins the award for his image of autumnal cricket in Srinigar, Kashmir.

Asanka Brendon Ratnayake

THE WISDEN–MCC CRICKET PHOTOGRAPH OF 2016 Asanka Brendon Ratnayake is one of two runners-up, for his photograph of Virat Kohli warming his hands during the Twenty20 international between Australia and India at Melbourne, January 29. (Kohli is also Wisden's Leading Cricketer in the World.)

The seventh Wisden–MCC Cricket Photograph of the Year competition attracted over 350 entries. First prize was £2,000; the two runners-up received £1,000, and eight other shortlisted entries £250 each. Any image with a cricket theme taken during 2016 was eligible. The independent judging panel, chaired by former *Sunday Times* chief photographer Chris Smith, comprised award-winning photographers Patrick Eagar, Adrian Murrell and Kevin Cummins, broadcaster Ali Mitchell and Nigel Davies, the former art director of *The Cricketer*. For more details, go to www.lords.org/photooftheyear

Philip Brown

THE WISDEN–MCC CRICKET PHOTOGRAPH OF 2016 The other runner-up is Philip Brown – whose image of Bangladesh's Shakib Al Hasan batting against England in October – captures a golden moment.

THE SWEET TASTE OF SUCCESS Pakistan, with Younis Khan to the fore, mark victory in the First Test at Lord's with a nod to their army training camp. Meanwhile, the Southern Vipers celebrate a healthy prize for winning the inaugural Kia Super League, in Chelmsford.

OFF-BREAKS? In the Second Test at Visakhapatnam, Alastair Cook is undone by a cracking ball from Mohammed Shami. And at Lord's, during the most compelling climax to a Championship season for years, Middlesex's Toby Roland-Jones dismisses Yorkshire's Andrew Hodd.

ENGLAND 444 for 3
Roy 15 (19)
Hales lbw b Hasan Ali 171 (122)
85 (86)
Buttler† not out 90 (51)
Morgan* not out 57 (27)
Stokes
Ali
Woakes
Rashid
Plunkett
Wood
Extras (b6, lb8, w3, nb9, pen0) 26
Total (3 wickets, 50 overs) 444
ENGLAND won the toss and elected to bat
IPA TIME WELL SPENT IPA

LEAP FOR THE STARS At Trent Bridge in August, England smack a one-day international record 444 against Pakistan, while at Lord's in July, Middlesex's Steven Finn seizes the moment, bringing Kent's Sam Northeast down to earth.

SCILLY GAME The Scillonian island of St Agnes has one of cricket's wilder outposts. In Derby last April, play continues, despite snow: Neil Broom bats; Glamorgan's Chris Cooke shivers.

THE LEADING WOMAN CRICKETER IN THE WORLD   Ellyse Perry

CRICKET AND CLIMATE CHANGE

How green is your sward?

TANYA ALDRED

Cricket's global administrators do love a board meeting, all mahogany chairs, glass tables and endless supplies of upmarket coffee. There is much to discuss, after all. Dollars. Participation. TV deals. Future tours. Behaviour. Match-fixing. Governance.

But something is missing, something that more than 97% of climate scientists agree on – from NASA to the Geological Society of London, and the nearly 200 countries who signed the Paris Agreement in December 2015. Climate change is real, and it is extremely likely to be man-made. In July 2016, NASA reported that January to June had been the hottest on record for each respective month, part of a trend in which almost every year since 2000 has been hotter than the last. In November, Danish and US researchers found that air temperatures above the Arctic were an astonishing 20°C warmer than expected. The Arctic Resilience Report warned that the melting of the ice cap risks triggering "19 tipping points", which could cause uncontrollable change worldwide. The bad news just kept on rolling.

Cricket, like everything else, will be fundamentally affected. And yet, despite all the warnings, the ICC have done almost nothing. By the end of 2016 they had not commented publicly on climate change or the challenges it presents to the game, nor outlined a grand plan. They are keen to stress that action is on the agenda, but have done little in terms of mitigation (reducing emissions) or adaptation to a changing world. They set no environmental targets for their members. They do not currently employ a sustainability officer. And while their laudable social responsibility work with UNICEF is detailed on their website, there is no reference to the environment.

Tours are arranged on a distinctly ungreen basis, with no pressure on members to plan a lower-impact itinerary. England's winter series in India, for instance, included a mishmash of cross-country flights, when the whole thing could have been done in a more sustainable circle. The ICC offices are in Dubai, which relies on energy-intensive air-conditioning and desalinated water. Those offices are, to give the ICC their due, undergoing an environmental audit, with the aim of becoming carbon neutral. But, in the words of communications officer Claire Furlong, progress has "historically been a little ad hoc".

The men (and it is still predominantly men) who run the game are not scientists or activists: they're often ex-players, sometimes businessmen. They are juggling huge budgets, balancing television deals with the need to proselytise. No one pretends it is easy. As Gideon Haigh has written, the role of administrators has traditionally been to "inure cricket against change rather than to enact it". Perhaps they are not worried about the climate, or don't

Sam Panthaky AFP/Getty Images

Bowling dry: children at Sarkhej Roza, near Ahmedabad in India. The 15th-century buildings once gave on to a lake, but the rains have dwindled – better news for cricketers than farmers.

see the urgency, or are too busy. But prudent businessmen always look to the future.

Shortly after the election of Donald Trump as president of the United States last November, 300 American businesses wrote an open letter, urging him not to pull out of the Paris deal. These were not lentil-weaving anti-capitalists: 72 of the companies had an annual revenue of over $100m. But climate change is beginning to bite. "We want the US economy to be energy-efficient and powered by low-carbon energy," they wrote. "Failure to build a low-carbon economy puts American prosperity at risk." As Barack Obama put it: "We are the first generation to feel the effect of climate change, and the last generation who can do something about it."

Many sporting organisations are lagging behind business in recognising the threat, despite the fact they will be significantly affected. Cricket has plenty to lose. It also has a moral responsibility to act.

If you put to one side winter and water activities, there are few sports more intrinsically connected with their environment than cricket. Of all the major pitch games, it will be hardest hit by climate change. From barren refugee camps to the ice of St Moritz, from the ochre Australian outback to the windswept Scottish coast, cricket is defined almost entirely by the conditions. If they change, so does the essence of the game.

That is truest of all in Britain, land of Blake's pleasant pastures, the menacing cloud from across the moors, the Hove sea fret, the misty morning in the Quantocks. Here, there has been a tendency among writers and players of all abilities to romanticise the greensward, to link cricket with the pastoral and the pre-industrial. Yet there is a looming danger: traditional English

Probal Rashid, LightRocket/Getty Images

Damp outfield: little room for play at Shyamnagar, southern Bangladesh. Climatologists fear such landscapes will vanish below rising seas – bad news for cricketers and the millions who live here.

conditions could be gone in 20 years. MCC's Russell Seymour is the UK's only cricket sustainability manager, having been in the job since 2009, and he is more than worried.

"A match can be changed fundamentally with a simple change in the weather," he says. "In the morning, sunny conditions make batting easier, because the bowlers can't get any movement in the warm, dry air. Cloud cover after lunch increases humidity, and the ball starts to move. After a shower, conditions change again. Now imagine what happens with climate change. There will be alterations to soil-moisture levels, and higher temperatures will bring drier air, then drier pitches. This will bring a change to grass germination and growth, which in turn affects the pitch and outfield."

In other words, the assumptions we make about English cricket, its landscapes and rhythms, will no longer apply. The ball may not move in 2025 the way it did in 1985, or even during that holy summer of 2005. The old-fashioned English seamer could be on his last legs.

Then there's rain. According to data from the Met Office there is more of it, and the increase is continuing. Because of the complexity of the weather system, it is unclear how things will pan out. Indeed, the UK Climate Projections (2009) show an increased likelihood of *drier* summers. Experts do agree that more extreme weather events are likely, along with wetter, warmer winters and more intense summer downpours. The ECB won't release precise data on how much cricket has been lost to rain over the last ten years. But, according to Dan Musson, their national participation manager, it is considerable.

"There is clear evidence that climate change has had a huge impact on the game in the form of general wet weather and extreme weather events," he says.

"I've been at the ECB since 2006 and we have had to implement flood relief efforts on half a dozen occasions, both in season – particularly in 2007, with flooding in the Midlands and the Thames Valley – and out of season, when winter storms Desmond and Eva ran through the north of England in December 2015. Wet weather has caused a significant loss of fixtures every year in the last five at recreational level, and posed challenges to the professional game."

The recreational game is most at risk: clubs have fewer resources to protect against the threat, and more difficulty with insurance. And because the land on floodplains is usually cheap and fertile, that's where many municipal grounds can be found. Games are repeatedly called off; people eventually give up and do something else. At grassroots level, the ECB have made good progress. They have commissioned research from Cranfield University to identify flood risk, and produced guidance for clubs; and they run a small-grants scheme to fund wet-weather management and preventative measures. In 2016, more than £1m was doled out to flooded clubs, which are also encouraged to install solar panels, recycle rainwater and look after their equipment: to think green in order to reduce costs, and survive. A further £1.6m has been set aside for 2017.

No one can name the greenest county as there is no central data

But for the first-class counties there is not yet an overarching strategy, nor much guidance. Individual clubs are taking action, but no one can name the greenest county, as there is no central data. Clubs that should be audited for climate risk, and making sustainable development part of every decision, are doing neither.

And yet, given money and encouragement, there are so many possibilities. Could counties reduce the travel footprint of players and spectators? Could there be rebates for fans who use public transport? Could clubs integrate sustainability into procurement and purchasing policy? Can they avoid single-use plastics? How do they use water? What food are they providing? Can they buy from ethical suppliers? If they are rebuilding, are they using sustainable materials? Can they generate renewable electricity? Offset carbon? Educate fans? Leave a positive legacy? One Planet Living, the blueprint for London 2012's environmental approach, gives practical guidance.

Nudging organisations to change their behaviour requires carrot as well as stick. Positive action could be rewarded by the ECB, whether financially or in terms of match allocation. The benefits of thinking long-term also need to be spelled out: central investment in drainage, for example, has meant counties can get back on the pitch after bad weather far sooner than previously.

On paper, the ECB have committed to action. Their 2016 strategy document, Cricket Unleashed, says: "We will work to promote environmental sustainability throughout the game. We recognise our role in society and the natural landscape, and will work on reducing our impact on the environment."

It's vague, but it's there. The ECB are already a member of BASIS (the British Association for Sustainable Sport, founded by Russell Seymour), and there are those at Lord's who are impatient to change: a steering group have been formed to engage with the professional game, and make good the

Michael Webster

In thrall to the elements: much of the pitch at Threlkeld, in Cumbria, was swept away in June 2012. The next match was played here three years later.

promises in the document. Whereas efforts from interested ECB employees have foundered further up the ladder, there is now more optimism. It is a golden opportunity for those at the top to be bold.

There are three international tournaments coming up in England – the Champions Trophy and the women's World Cup in 2017, and the men's World Cup in 2019. The ECB's steering group hope to use the first two as pilot schemes, then gain ISO 20121 certification for the 2019 World Cup. It is the minimum they should be doing. ISO 20121 is an international standard for sustainability in event management inspired by the London Olympics and Paralympics, and since certified for the French Open tennis at Roland Garros, football's 2016 European Championships, and the Rio Olympics.

Other sports have started to change their behaviour. The north American National Hockey League, uniquely among sporting leagues, produce a sustainability report, and all the commissioners of the major US sports have made statements on the environment and climate change. Unlike in the UK, the French government are encouraging sustainability through sport. Golf, cricket's fuddy-duddy cousin, is being pushed by the R&A and the Golf Environment organisation. FIFA, despite major governance issues, have embraced sustainability around the World Cup. Sailing is well ahead of cricket, too.

Could English cricket step forward to take the international lead? Be progressive! Innovative! Principled! The ECB need only look over their shoulder: in February 2017, MCC announced they would buy electricity generated solely from renewable sources. To millennials and post-millennials, climate change is no global conspiracy, but a living, breathing, terrifying threat. They are looking for action – and organisations who put their head in the sand will be scorned. Sport communicates passionately, and reaches the parts governments or NGOs cannot. Cricket can positively influence fan behaviour by example, and win back the trust of those disillusioned by the raging giant of unbridled commercialism.

On their rocky outpost in the north Atlantic, the British are protected to some extent by wealth and geography. But other cricket nations are in the front line. In 2016, the IPL was forced to relocate matches from Maharashtra because of a water shortage. Bangladesh is what the World Bank calls a "potential impact hotspot," threatened by "extreme river floods, more intense tropical cyclones, rising sea levels and very high temperatures". Sri Lanka and West Indies are also vulnerable to rising sea levels. Rainfall patterns in Zimbabwe are ever more uncertain. The southern part of Australia is projected to have more extreme droughts.

Yes, there are ways to manage the environment. Qatar is even working on technology that cools open-air arenas, and cricket has experimented with enclosed stadiums. But is that really the future it wants? We must either accept fundamental changes to the game, or alter how we behave if we are to maintain, as far as possible, what we have.

No one is pretending cricket can change the world. But it can set a moral tone and show a concern for the environment that has nurtured and shaped it over hundreds of years. Do nothing, and it has everything to lose.

Tanya Aldred is co-editor of The Nightwatchman.

WHAT MAKES A GOOD COACH?

"No one particularly cares in China"

BENJ MOOREHEAD

Micky Stewart

Towards the end of my ten years as Surrey captain I could see cricket was changing. The commercial side of the game was getting bigger, and winning trophies was the priority. County captains had always run the show, on and off the field, but I could see that the increased demand for success was going to require someone akin to a football manager to help bear the load.

I was aware of the opposition within the game, particularly as it conjured up the structure of a professional football club. Even so, Surrey invited me to be their first cricket manager in 1979, and seven years later I was asked to do the job for England – mind you, I didn't accept it until the TCCB agreed to the title of team manager. Their preference was for assistant manager, again because it had less of a football connotation.

I was lucky that the England side contained talented cricketers, but as a unit they were sadly lacking. In 1986, they lost at home to India and, for the first time, New Zealand. A team including Gower, Botham, Lamb, Edmonds, Emburey and Dilley should not have. Mike Gatting – the captain – and I emphasised this to the players prior to the 1986-87 tour to Australia, and they responded magnificently.

All that was 30 years ago, and it gives me great satisfaction to know that the position I started has been retained – though things have changed a bit, too. When I took over, my non-playing staff numbered two: Lawrie Brown, our experienced physiotherapist, and Peter Lush, the tour manager. Today, it's around 15!

Micky Stewart was England manager between 1986 and 1992.

Gary Kirsten

I don't think the cricketing fraternity takes professional coaching seriously enough. We continue to say the captain is more important than the coach, but that's short-sighted. It requires a highly skilled individual to run a modern international team across three formats.

Effectively, you are the CEO of a business. You're looking after contracting, recruitment, the entire coaching structure, man-management, creating the right environment, scheduling, rotating players across formats, checking facilities, looking after relationships with all stakeholders of the team... the list goes on! There might be a player who calls you in the middle of the night to say: "I need to get home. My wife hasn't seen me for three months."

When I was with India, we did a lot of research into how Indians respond to types of leadership. Generally speaking, they are a flair-orientated people who like to do things in a more spontaneous manner. So, for instance, we brought in optional practice sessions and removed fines for being late: we knew, if the culture was right, the players would feel responsible to their team-mates. That said, my South African instinct for structure and organisation could also blend nicely with India's free-spirited nature.

As South Africa coach, I considered going the other way, encouraging flair and instinct, and giving the players more chance to make their own decisions. We tried to introduce more flexibility. It wasn't always popular, because South Africans like a little more structure.

I like the idea of a foreign coach, because they bring a fresh perspective, and I warmed to the role in India. There is a lot of hype around Indian cricket but, when it came to the nuts and bolts of coaching, I was left to get on with it. I wasn't part of the greater political agenda, and rarely had to speak to the media: I did only two press conferences during the 2011 World Cup. Throughout, we never spoke about winning – there was enough of that around us as it was. Instead we highlighted an image from a Nike advert, which showed the people walking hand in hand with the players, and crossing a line, like the end of a marathon. It showed this was not about the burden of millions of fans on our shoulders: it was a journey *with* them.

Gary Kirsten coached India from December 2007 until after the World Cup win in April 2011. He coached South Africa for two years from June 2011.

Phil Simmons

As the Zimbabwe coach on my first visit to the National Academy in Harare in 2004, I didn't allow anyone to practise with their shirt untucked. I've since realised those things are not important. Now I'm trying to discern what Player A needs to do differently from Player B for the team to be successful. It's about how you practise, not how you dress.

When I joined Ireland in 2007 they had just started playing regular international cricket. I had to create a culture of professional practice – and be quite strict. Once the players became wise to the demands, I could back off and become more of a facilitator, because these things were done instinctively.

I remember Bob Woolmer talking to me about going on tour: "You have to get a feel for the culture. You can't sit in a hotel room and then go out and play." That was the attitude I took to being a foreign coach in Ireland. I was out and about, watching club cricket and talking to their members. Because I made myself seen, people would come up to me without hesitation. That's how I established a connection with Irish grassroots.

In the West Indies, it's a challenge to teach the skills required for Test cricket. From a young Caribbean player's perspective, you can play in two or three global Twenty20 leagues and be financially secure. But we can't make excuses for our Test performance by saying Twenty20 is our natural game.

Shiny coachwork: Phil Simmons gets his point across at the World Twenty20, March 2016. West Indies went on to lift the trophy.

Look at Australia's David Warner: he was a Twenty20 player who has become one of Test cricket's best batsmen. The transition is possible.

Phil Simmons has coached Zimbabwe, Ireland (from 2007 until 2015) and West Indies, who sacked him in September 2016.

John Buchanan

When I met the Australian team in 1999, I told them that I wanted to go against convention, that I wanted to coach them as people rather than just cricketers, that I saw us as a family unit. And that it was all about improvement, regardless of results. I put it in terms of a journey to Everest.

I wanted to link the present with the past, so I talked about Australia's 1948 Invincibles. Both Steve Waugh and I were adamant about the symbolic importance of the Baggy Green. The Invincibles had been remembered for something special they had achieved for Australian cricket; I told the team that, by the time we disbanded, we should have left our own imprint.

Players and coaches can become too caught up in the game, insulated from the real world. A young coach who has been in a cricket environment for 15 or 20 years needs to spend time out of it to develop life skills that will help with coaching a set of individuals. I introduced education sessions in which the Australian players were required to talk about something they were passionate about other than cricket. There was everything from fly-fishing to wrestling to poetry. I took the players on a trip to an albatross rookery in Dunedin. It was all aimed at showing there was life outside the dressing-room.

I started using data analysis with Queensland in 1994, and eventually introduced it to the Australian team. Importantly, Waugh had seen me using it with Queensland when we played against his New South Wales side, setting up a game plan in a way no other team were doing.

It was harder to convince other seniors. Shane Warne thought all the data and team meetings made the game complicated. What Shane didn't understand was how skilled he was. That was probably true of Glenn McGrath as well. Both had the capacity to retain so much knowledge and experience in their own mental filing systems, and to use it to their advantage during a match. So they couldn't see the point of all this information. But few players I coached and met possessed their powers of recall. That's one of the things that made Warne and McGrath great players.

The big challenge for coaches today is balancing three formats. It used to be that you learned the long game and adapted those skills to the short format. These days, coaches and players are learning their trade in Twenty20, which means the 50-over game has become the transitional format to Test cricket. That's a dynamic with which coaches are constantly grappling.

John Buchanan was coach of Australia from 1999 until 2007; they won his first 15 Tests in charge, and two World Cups. He has also coached Queensland and Middlesex.

John Wright

In some ways I'm in Ian Chappell's camp: coaches should be responsible for getting players to the ground. The more in the background you are, the better. You lead from behind.

For a genius like Virender Sehwag, the key was to give him absolute freedom. The only technical aspect was making sure he kept his head still. On the morning of a match there were just two things I asked Viru: how was his mum's back (she had a chronic condition), and how was he going to play today. He'd reply: "Play straight and watch the ball." The biggest harm I could do was to get in his way – so long as he was playing within the confines of the team's objective.

Perhaps I'm old-fashioned, but I still think a player's best coaching tool is his peer group. As a young Derbyshire opener, I learned more speaking to Sunil Gavaskar at Somerset or Geoff Boycott at Yorkshire than I did from any coach. Similarly, I wanted the young Indian players to ask Sachin Tendulkar or Rahul Dravid about batting. It was much more powerful coming from them. I hardly did any batting coaching with India.

When I started with them, young players would ask: "Do you think I should have a net, sir?" We tried to break down every piece of seniority: everyone was encouraged to have their opinion. Sourav Ganguly, the captain, would invite young players to drink tea in his room. That way we felt more like a family.

A coach can't make excuses for bad results: talking about a five-year plan is like a batsman moaning about the wicket. I hardly looked beyond the present. I recall exchanging a look with Javed Miandad, my opposite number, before a Test series in Pakistan, as if to say: "Whoever loses will get the sack." Sure enough, Javed lost his job. That's just the way it is – in fact, it's part of the thrill. Besides, it's just a game. "There may be a bit of a pressure on us," I used to tell the boys, "but no one particularly cares in China."

John Wright coached India between 2000 and 2005, and New Zealand from 2010 for nearly two years. He is Derbyshire's specialist Twenty20 coach.

Graham Ford

To have been an international cricketer has to be an advantage for a coach, but I was lucky to work with great players in my early days. At Natal, I had senior guys with brilliant cricketing brains, such as Malcolm Marshall and Clive Rice. Malcolm once told me: "Any fool can castigate a player for a poor performance. What it's really about is finding a way to improve him quietly and in small steps." After Natal I was assistant, then head coach, of South Africa when still in my thirties. An advantage of *not* having played at international level is that I am hungry to learn, and happy to be involved.

A lot of coaching is about questioning the players and getting their feedback, and one of the huge challenges for a foreign coach in Sri Lanka is the language barrier with younger members of the team. Your seniors are particularly important: they can be your ear on the training ground and help pass on messages. Previously my go-to guys were Mahela Jayawardene and Kumar Sangakkara, which made it easy. Angelo Mathews has been outstanding in taking on that role.

There can be too much coaching, too many messages. You have to allow for individual flair. In Sri Lanka there is a tradition of coaches who don't have a lot of official badges, but encourage emerging talents to play in their own unique way. Combined with a diet of soft-ball cricket, this has produced some wonderful, freak players. At the same time, a coach should never forget the basics for a batsman or a bowler: get your head and eyes into the right position at the crucial moment.

Graham Ford has had two stints with Sri Lanka, one with South Africa, and also coached Kent and Surrey.

Philip Brown, SilverHub Media

Ford focus: Sri Lanka coach Graham Ford and the tools of his trade.

John Bracewell

A rugby or football player has the game of his life, but his team loses and he feels rubbish. A cricketer scores a hundred, but the team loses and, generally, he feels OK. That's because cricket is an individualistic team sport. Being a cricket coach is a social experiment: you are managing private individuals, team players, givers, takers. Rugby doesn't tolerate that. As the All Blacks' motto goes: "No dickheads". You're with us or you're out. Cricket tolerates difference – it has to. That's why I love it so much.

Bob Woolmer and John Buchanan were two passionate – but polar-opposite – coaches who influenced me. Bob was focused on the improvement of technique through practice, and was extraordinarily innovative. I once went to his old club in Cape Town and found nets with gutters down the side. "Oh, I invented that," he said. "That way I can gather the balls from one spot." It made things easier, but it was slightly nuts!

John was focused on the improvement of a team through man-management. He came to talk to us in New Zealand once, and told us about the first day he handed out analysis sheets to his Queensland players: Matthew Hayden loved it, Andrew Symonds was a little confused, Allan Border threw his in the bin. John knew his players would react differently, but it didn't faze him.

I've never been averse to trying something new that seems a bit crazy. When I was New Zealand coach, one of my big concerns was that, with so many staff and so much data, players had stopped thinking for themselves and communicating with one another. So we looked at a system of peer appraisals used in Australian Rules, where the players would fill in an assessment of the team's performance at the end of a day's play. We made some mistakes along the way – it took too long and it wasn't suited to Test cricket – but I make no apologies for that. Somebody has to get the ball rolling. As a coach you've got to be self-assured and unafraid of failure.

The Ireland job has been very enjoyable because it's a case of back to the future. It's a bit like New Zealand in the 1980s. A lack of facilities means the players practise at their clubs, and the coach goes with them, so I'll book a net with Kevin O'Brien at Railway Union CC. Ireland players have a massive affiliation with their local club. It's earthy, based around families and communities, and makes for self-sufficient cricketers.

In terms of teaching the skills of cricket, I have one overriding philosophy: coach the player using *his* technique, not *a* technique.

John Bracewell coached New Zealand for five years from November 2003, and in April 2015 took over the Ireland job. He has had two spells at Gloucestershire.

Benj Moorehead is a freelance cricket writer and editor.

THE SECRETS OF BALL-TAMPERING

Hell for leather

DEREK PRINGLE

When Faf du Plessis appealed against his punishment for ball-tampering during South Africa's Test series in Australia in November, his reasons were understandable. He didn't want to be penalised for a practice that – in one form or another – has gone on since before W. G. Grace. And he did not believe he deserved to be labelled a cheat for a deed most cricketers consider little more than mischief. His offence had been to coat the ball in sugary saliva – he was sucking a mint to improve aerodynamics rather than halitosis – and it was the second time he had fallen foul of Law 42.3. With the ICC determined to clamp down on such methods, his appeal failed.

But the episode was a reminder that nothing stirs cricket's moral ire like claims of ball-tampering. From John Lever's Vaseline strips in India, via Michael Atherton's dirt in the pocket at Lord's, to Pakistan's forfeiture at The Oval, judgment is usually severe – especially by the media.

This righteousness is not shared by most cricketers. When it comes to altering the condition of the ball, they see any creativity, within limits, as acceptable, which explains why they feel hard done by when they are caught. Hence the double standard – of ball-tampering as a crime many are happy to commit, but few are prepared to admit. I should know.

My moment of denial came after a day's play at Chelmsford in 1985, during Australia's tour match against Essex. Faced with a docile pitch, I had lifted up the quarter-seam to create a flap on the non-shiny side of the ball. To my slight surprise (these things didn't always succeed) the response was instant: reverse swing into the right-handers, which interested the umpires. When they saw the ball's state, they changed it and demanded to see Graham Gooch, Essex's acting-captain, at the close. Gooch knew what I'd been up to but, when he formally asked us who had done the tampering, I could not bring myself to own up in front of team-mates.

I don't know why I demurred. With a side's interests best served when their bowlers are potent, few players have ever complained about tampering, at least not outside the dressing-room. Only when one team's bowlers cannot achieve the same influence as their opponents' do the batsmen tend to carp, a hypocrisy that occurred when Pakistan won in England in 1992. Reverse swing can be achieved legally, though usually after 30 overs or so. During that summer, Wasim Akram and Waqar Younis often achieved it much sooner, prompting several England batsmen to cry foul.

Bowlers are cricket's innovators and, after Wasim had uprooted my stumps with a late outswinger in the final Test at The Oval, I asked umpires Dickie Bird and David Shepherd if I might see the ball. This was not done out of protest, but as a matter of research: Wasim was as close to genius as was possible on a cricket field. What I saw was revelatory, at least for a ball 78 overs old. Most striking was the distinctly two-toned appearance: one side dark but smooth, with the cool clamminess of a marble floor; the other dry and dusty, much lighter in colour, but pitted all over, like the dimples on a golf ball.

It was a work of art, however the alchemy was achieved – and it could have occurred naturally, as Pakistan were scrupulous about keeping one side dry, while applying sweat, but never spit, to the other. In its sudden and late swing, that ball moved like no other I have experienced: England slumped from 182 for three to 207 all out, with Wasim taking five for 18 in seven overs, as the ball homed in on stumps – and toes – like a guided missile. Only wrist-spinner Mushtaq Ahmed did not benefit: with one side light and the other dark, batsmen were able to pick his googly a mile off.

Nine Network Australia

A good licking: Faf du Plessis is caught on TV.

The animosity between the teams came to a head soon after, when the umpires changed the ball during England's innings in the one-day international at Lord's. Some claimed it had been deliberately disfigured, and the ball was spirited away by officials. It has yet to resurface, and accusations of cheating can still pique the protagonists even a quarter of a century later.

That stigma has led to some bruising encounters off the pitch. Court battles between Imran Khan on one side, and Ian Botham and Allan Lamb on the other, and between Lamb and his old Northamptonshire team-mate Sarfraz Nawaz, arose from accusations of tampering. I was subpoenaed by Imran's legal team to give evidence following a piece I had written for *The Independent on Sunday* about my own tampering exploits. I wrote that any English bowler worth his salt would have picked the seam at some stage during his career, something Botham denied in court. The jury, though bewildered by the arcane details, found in Imran's favour.

As a bowler never quick enough to intimidate, I always sought ways of getting the ball to move laterally, either off the seam or through the air. Most were legal, such as applying sweat or spit, and rubbing it on my trousers or shirt to get a shine. Players are also allowed to remove bits of grass or mud from the seam. All other means, and there are plenty, are probably illicit.

When Marcus Trescothick admitted sucking Murray Mints during the 2005 Ashes to give the ball a sheen, the use of sugary saliva was a new one on me. England's bowlers deployed reverse swing superbly during their 2–1 win, and Australia knew what they were up to, even if the press and public did not. John

Buchanan, Australia's coach, told me over a beer in Manchester how he believed England's sweet tooth was aiding Andrew Flintoff and Simon Jones, their best exponents of reverse swing. Buchanan did not want to appear a whinger, so forbade the story being published. I remained sceptical, though it did explain why England's twelfth men were occasionally seen flinging sweets on to the outfield for Trescothick and others to stuff in their pockets, ready to be sucked into service.

Yet it seems the use of sweets comfortably pre-dates 2005. One prominent county batsman, who prefers not to be named, told me he believed the practice began at Warwickshire in the mid-1990s. And Atherton has written about the time he sent England's twelfth man to buy chewing-gum, only for him to return with a sugar-free version, "ensuring his twelfth-man career was brief". Quite why sugary saliva is supposed to work better is a mystery yet to be explained.

Essex were not alone in buying Lipice in bulk

At Essex in the 1970s and '80s, in an era before the cameras got up close and personal, we used Lipice (a brand of lip screen) to shine the ball. Our captain Keith Fletcher had drummed into every player the fact that the team got only one ball per innings, and needed to look after it. Besides, John Lever was the best swing bowler in county cricket, so keeping it shiny for as long as possible was simply good sense. According to Fletcher, Lipice became prominent after Australia's Bob Massie had swung England to defeat at Lord's in 1972, with 16 wickets in his debut Test. Accusations that he used Lipice arose on the back of that incredible performance, though they were never proved.

"Massie just bowled better than everybody else," said Fletcher. "The ball swung, but you still needed skill to control it. Anyway, England didn't have any swingers except Basil D'Oliveira, so couldn't really take advantage of the conditions, as Massie did." Yet, whether or not Massie used Lipice, swing bowlers everywhere took note; Essex were not alone in buying it in bulk.

Prior to that, hair gels such as Brylcreem seem to have been the illegal substance of choice – Denis Compton and Fred Trueman even advertised the stuff. But uncovered pitches meant bowlers in those days were less reliant on movement through the air: if pitches were gripping after rain, the ball's seam was often enough. It could be cleaned, but it was not meant to be raised, at least not deliberately, though many bowlers could not resist, turning plaited twine into a bristling edge with a swift twist of their thumbnail. Not that picking the seam suited everyone. At Essex, Lever felt it made the seam go soft, so the practice was discouraged, although the slow left-armer Ray East would lift half an inch to give his spinning finger some purchase.

Umpires, who back then were all ex-pros, might have tut-tutted, but generally turned a blind eye. Only when the TV camera was able to zoom in and expose the chicanery for all to see did they have to become policemen as well. Umpire Judah Reuben famously queried Lever's use of Vaseline during England's 1976-77 tour of India. Lever had swung them to victory with ten for 70 on debut in the First Test at Delhi. After a second win followed in Calcutta, India were under severe pressure when the series reached Madras.

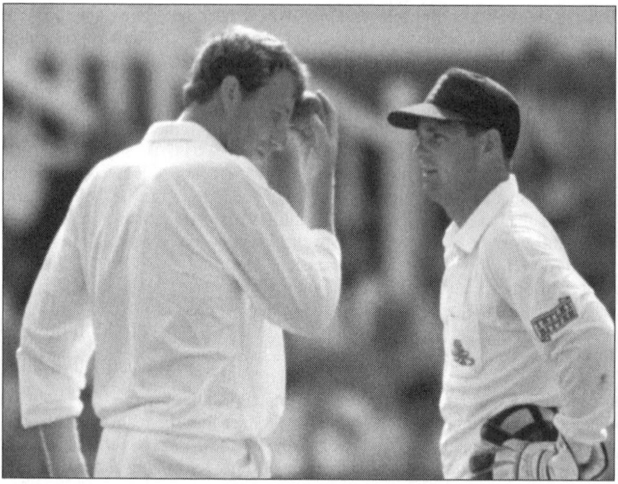

By the sweat of his brow: in the dirt-in-the-pocket Test of July 1994, England captain Mike Atherton – here with Steve Rhodes – tries to get his head round the problem of swing.

"Most of us had long hair in those days, so the extra sweat I was pumping out in Madras, which was hot and humid, was getting into my eyes and making them sting," says Lever. "I used to play football in the off season, and sometimes put Vaseline across my forehead and eyebrows to channel the sweat away from the eyes. So I asked Bernard Thomas, the England physio, whether he could do the same. With no Vaseline, the best he could come up with at short notice was Vaseline-impregnated gauze.

"I wore the gauze after lunch on the third day, when we had them seven down, but discarded it quite quickly as it didn't really work. I put it behind the stumps, but the umpire picked it up and claimed it had come adrift while I was bowling. He obviously felt there was something underhand going on, and he reported it to Bishan Bedi, India's captain, and then to the Indian board, who leaked it to the press."

Lever, who admits some of the Vaseline got on to his hands and therefore the ball, reckons a technical breach of the Laws probably did occur, but not a deliberate one. "If I'd wanted to get Vaseline on the ball I would not have advertised the fact in such an obvious way," he says. The subsequent furore proved stressful for him and his family back in England. "Dad suffered a heart attack soon after, which I'm convinced was brought on by the press intrusion," says Lever. "I found it very hard to forgive Bedi for stirring it up the way he did in order to divert the pressure of a series defeat. It wasn't until 30 years later that I was able to finally shake his hand and let bygones be bygones."

A BRIEF HISTORY

Bites, boots and bottle tops

STEVEN LYNCH

1899 C. B. Fry's *Book of Cricket* includes a photograph of Sussex seamer Fred Tate rubbing the ball on the ground to take the shine off.

1925 Middlesex fast bowler Nigel Haig accused of lifting the seam during a county match against Worcestershire.

1951-52 West Indies captain John Goddard vigorously rubs a new ball on the ground during a Test in Australia, to remove the shine for his spinners, Sonny Ramadhin and Alf Valentine. This practice was frowned on, but not officially banned until 1980.

1981 Imran Khan admits (in a 1994 biography) that, with "the ball not deviating at all" during a county match for Sussex, "I got the twelfth man to bring on a bottle top, and it started to move around a lot. I occasionally scratched the side and lifted the seam."

1990-91 New Zealand seamer Chris Pringle uses a bottle top to scratch the ball during a Test against Pakistan at Faisalabad, and takes 11 wickets (his other 13 Tests brought him 19 victims). He later writes that the umpires knew what he was doing but "didn't want to get involved in anything controversial".

1992 England's Allan Lamb is fined around £7,000 by the ECB after claiming in a newspaper article that Pakistan's bowlers were tampering with the ball. Shortly afterwards, the ball is changed while Pakistan are bowling during a one-day international at Lord's.

2000 Waqar Younis is the first player to be suspended for ball-tampering, benched for one match by referee John Reid during a triangular ODI tournament in Sri Lanka in July.

2001-02 Indians are outraged after Sachin Tendulkar is penalised for ball-tampering by referee Mike Denness during a Test in South Africa. In the subsequent arguments the tour is jeopardised, and the Third Test replaced by an unofficial game after ICC refused to sanction it. The offence was later downgraded..

2006 Pakistan refuse to play on in the final Test at The Oval after incurring a five-run penalty for ball-tampering imposed by Australian umpire Darrell Hair, and forfeit the match.

2009-10 Pakistan's Shahid Afridi is caught biting the ball during an ODI in Australia, and banned from the next two Twenty20 internationals. "There is no team in the world that doesn't tamper with the ball," he said, but admitted: "My methods were wrong. I am embarrassed, I shouldn't have done it."

2009-10 South Africa query England's methods in a Cape Town Test in which Jimmy Anderson is filmed working hard on the ball, and Stuart Broad seen stepping on it. "Over the years we have seen a lot of tall fast bowlers stop the ball with their boot," said England's then coach, Andy Flower.

2013-14 Pakistan awarded five penalty runs in a Test in Dubai after South Africa's Faf du Plessis scratches the ball on a zip in his trousers. He is fined, and zips are later outlawed.

2015-16 Victoria's assistant coach Mick Lewis scratches the ball in a concrete gutter near the boundary during the Sheffield Shield final in Adelaide. South Australia are awarded five penalty runs, and Lewis fined $A2,266.

2016-17 Du Plessis, by now South Africa's captain, fined 100% of match fee following a Test in Australia, after being filmed applying saliva to the ball with a sweet in his mouth.

If lotions, potions and seam picking represent the traditional, almost acceptable, face of ball-tampering, the relatively recent phenomenon of reverse swing has produced even more bizarre ways of contravening the Laws. Its aerodynamics, with most of the technique going into preparing the ball, are still not completely understood, but it is different from conventional swing, where the skill and technique go into *bowling* the ball, with finger and wrist actions crucial.

Reverse swing requires a ball of opposites, a yin and yang, with one side smooth and shiny, the other rough, dry and pockmarked. Most abuses occur when trying to achieve the latter, though roughening a new ball, so spinners might open the bowling, used to be commonplace in county cricket before the 1980s. They still talk about Wilf Wooller, Glamorgan's post-war captain, walking down the 70 or so steps at Swansea and scraping the ball on each, because he wanted to open with Len Muncer's off-breaks.

THE FINAL
TOUCH . . .
BRYLCREEM
your hair
Getty Images

Innocent times? Denis Compton and a versatile hair product.

The leather on cricket balls is tough, so abrading one side is not easily done with fingernails. That is why Atherton, at least to my mind, was not tampering when he was caught applying dirt to the ball against South Africa in 1994. The incident, which almost cost him the captaincy, occurred when his team were trying to harness reverse swing with only a rudimentary knowledge of how to do so. With dirt scooped from old pitch ends in his pocket, he was trying to make one side of the ball drier than the other – crucial for reverse swing to be achieved on a humid day – by lightly rubbing it with soil. The Laws allow players to maintain the ball's condition, but not increase its rate of deterioration. In Atherton's case, it was possible to argue both viewpoints.

More brutish means have been used. In the early days of reverse swing, Imran Khan admitted using a bottle top, as did New Zealand seamer Chris Pringle. Fed up with his team being bowled out in Pakistan in 1990-91, Pringle scratched up one side of the ball and skittled the home side for 102 in Faisalabad with seven for 52. But Waqar took 12, and New Zealand still lost.

According to some, scalpels and razor blades have been employed to cut the leather in search of swing. Mike Smith, who played one Test for England against Australia in 1997 and is now a lawyer, reckons one player had an emery board taped to his finger. I've heard of another who sewed a sheet of sandpaper, coloured white, into his trousers, allowing him to polish the ball on the outside, and scrape it on the inside.

One simple way to stop the worst abuses is to allow bowlers to do what they like to the ball, using only what is available in the course of a day's play. Fingernails, sun lotions and lip screens (from their skin only, not shirts or trousers impregnated with the stuff), sugary saliva (if they want large dentist bills, so be it) and hair gels, along with spit and sweat, would all be allowed. Outside agents, such as knives or bottle tops, would not, their use incurring both financial and run penalties.

The late Bob Woolmer advocated something similar after his Pakistan side forfeited the 2006 Oval Test following umpire Darrell Hair's insistence that they had been guilty of tampering. Like many who have played and watched a lot of cricket, Woolmer was adamant a balance was needed between bat and ball if the game was to have meaning, and that a moving ball, in all its guises, helps provide that.

Tampering, in one form or another, has gone on for over 100 years. It is as much a part of the fabric of the game as bats, pads and gloves, and it is time MCC acknowledged as much. Loosening the Laws would also remove morality – and hypocrisy – from the equation. As the American man of letters H. L. Mencken once said: "The truth that survives is simply the lie that is pleasantest to believe."

Derek Pringle played for Essex and England before becoming cricket correspondent for various national newspapers. He continues to write today.

THE RETURN OF THE CABLE KNIT

Lions in sheep's clothing

PHILIP BARKER

The American satirist Ambrose Bierce called the sweater a "garment worn by a child when its mother is feeling chilly". This may explain the almost parental coo that echoed around Twitter when it emerged in November that England's Test team were planning to revert to the traditional cream-coloured cable-knit sweater for the 2017 summer. It felt like more than the return of pure new wool, which they had last worn in 2008: it felt like the return of an entire way of life.

It also called into question the judgment of Michael Vaughan, then the England captain, who had thrilled at the demise of the cable knit, calling it "my bugbear for many a year", and claiming that the new, brilliant-white Climawarm top would give his players a "lighter feel". It made little difference to England's fortunes: four months later, after leading his side to defeat by South Africa, Vaughan was out of a job. Lancashire started the trend in 2000 and, by the time England began wearing the Climawarm, most counties had already switched to a fleece. This was not just a fleece, but – in the words of Adidas, its creator – "an integrated system of technologies which work together to regulate the temperature of the athlete".

PA Photos

Non-Test sweater: Alan Jones at Lord's, 1970.

Before England's volte-face – the result of a change of supplier, with American firm New Balance keen to show they are in touch with cricket's traditions – only Australia and New Zealand had championed the cable knit. Yet a trusty woollen top had once been synonymous with the game. Two summers ago, there was a false dawn, with the introduction of a hybrid – part fleece, part knitted – with red trim at the base. Now the real thing is back.

England's away sweater actually came first. Between the wars, the touring model – yellow, red and blue trim – became a familiar sight. Supplied by Jaeger of London, it was topped off with a dark blue cap bearing St George and the dragon. This design had first been seen in 1903, when MCC began organising

England's tours, and captain Pelham Warner was despatched to the outfitters Beale and Inman to obtain a sample. MCC records indicate that home England sweaters, with their crown and three lions, did not appear until 1948. Before that, players wore MCC or county colours in home Tests. Post-war rationing may explain why those worn by Len Hutton and Cyril Washbrook look distinctly modest compared with Ian Botham's chunkier version for his 1981 Ashes heroics, or the MCC touring knit he sported in his Shredded Wheat adverts.

The England badge was introduced during the reign of Edward VII, in 1908. Former Test captain R. E. "Tip" Foster suggested silver lions on "a cap for all England". Sir Alfred Scott-Gatty of the College of Arms wrote to Lord Harris at Lord's, with a self-satisfied chuckle about "Mr Foster's Tip": "These beasts are always gold – silver lions remind one of Aesop's fables. Sport and Heraldry do not mix!" Undeterred, MCC introduced their (home) cap a few months later, "with the gracious approval of His Majesty the King". In away series, England's caps retained George and the dragon until 1996-97.

In 1953, Anthony Asquith's film of Terence Rattigan's play *The Final Test* was released, the cast including Hutton and Denis Compton. The star was Jack Warner, later Dixon of Dock Green, and the costume the official England cable sweater, then made by Paine of Godalming. By now, MCC had sought "covering authority for the badge being used for all purposes connected with the Test team". The Home Office gave permission grudgingly, with a stern warning: "The incorporation of the crown is a special privilege and not one to be abused." It was, they added, to be worn only "on cricket occasions". This complicated matters when the BBC commissioned another adaptation of Rattigan's play in 1961. "We have to dress certain artistes as cricketers," wrote theatrical agents Bermans, requesting six England sweaters from MCC. The club's assistant secretary Billy Griffith replied: "I regret we cannot give permission because the badge has on it a Tudor crown."

The allocation of one long-sleeved and one sleeveless sweater, both meant to last five years, seems parsimonious today. There were no on-field presentations back then, but the sweaters were treasured just as much. In 1966, Warwickshire's Dennis Amiss was said to have kept his under his pillow. The sweater belonging to Glamorgan's Alan Jones, meanwhile, assumed an elegiac air. After the cancellation of South Africa's tour in 1970, he was called up to face the Rest of the World at Lord's, twice falling cheaply to Mike Procter. But the game later lost its Test status, and Jones never did appear in an official Test.

The Tudor crown had its last outing against Pakistan in August 1996. At the start of the following year, the ECB came into being, with the first series under the new order taking place in New Zealand. England wore old-style tour sweaters over mix-and-match logos on their shirts – a nightmare for the marketing men. From then on, the official ECB cap and sweater were to be used home and away, and issued to substitute fielders too. The Kent and Curwen woollens were still cable knit, but the crown was replaced by a stylised coronet.

Freed from crown copyright, a range of replica gear appeared, all with the newly registered badge. For England A the logo was rendered in red, for the

Under-19s in gold. Women's cricket came under the ECB's umbrella in 1998, and used the same kit. Before that, their jumpers were plain white, or trimmed with blue and red – as when they lifted the 1993 World Cup.

Wolf in sheep's clothing: Australia's Ross Edwards models the proposed England kit for the 1979-80 technicolour tour.

A different sweater had been introduced for home one-day internationals from 1972 to 1976, with an embroidered single lion in lighter blue. It was worn by, among others, David Gower, Derek Randall and David Lloyd to make their international debuts – in whites, of course. England did not play in coloured clothing at home until the late 1990s.

Their first day/night matches were part of a 1979-80 tri-series on what Scyld Berry dubbed the technicolour tour. Australia and West Indies also took part, and Australian sporting goods firm Whitmont supplied the kit. The teams were offered a predominantly white top with coloured flashes, and the media launch featured England's jumper being modelled by an Australian, Ross Edwards. Mike Brearley and his team were unimpressed with the design: they would have been happy with full colour outfits, but felt stripes alone did not provide a sufficiently clear background to pick up the white ball.

As the floodlights blazed, England cut a strange sight in traditional whites and MCC sweaters, and dark blue pads – while Australia stuck with the Whitmont kit.

England finally embraced technicolour in 1983 (Hampshire's Trevor Jesty spent his entire ten-match international career in light-blue pyjamas). By the 1992 World Cup, all nine participating teams wore similar jerseys: a multicoloured yoke across the top, with the remainder in national colours (light blue for England). A decade later, Twenty20 presented a further marketing opportunity: England wear dark-blue tops in one-day internationals; red in Twenty20.

Since 2001, their shirts have included the player's place in the grand scheme, just under the badge: in December, Liam Dawson became their 676th Test player. The first English batsman to achieve that feat played his entire career long before such official recognition: the closest W. G. Grace came was the purple, red and gold cap – still on display at Lord's – from Lord Sheffield's 1891-92 tour of Australia.

Philip Barker is a writer, broadcaster and specialist in sporting history.

FIVE CRICKETERS OF THE YEAR

The Five Cricketers of the Year represent a tradition that dates back in Wisden *to 1889, making this the oldest individual award in cricket. The Five are picked by the editor, and the selection is based, primarily but not exclusively, on a player's influence on the previous English season. No one can be chosen more than once. A list of past Cricketers of the Year appears on page 1451.*

Ben Duckett

ANDREW RADD

The late Brian Reynolds would have turfed him out of the Wantage Road nets before you could say "improvisation". Northamptonshire's long-serving coach, a heart-and-soul, one-county man from the national service generation, was no fan of the reverse sweep, considering it on a par with grubby pads and facial hair. Any young cricketer attempting it could expect to be pointed to the dressing-room and replaced by someone prepared to play properly. And yet the emergence of Ben Duckett as a standard-bearer for 360-degree English batsmanship is arguably the best news in years for the club Reynolds loved so dearly. The Roundhead county of boots and the Battle of Naseby has nurtured an innovating, risk-taking Cavalier.

For all but the boldest, savviest or most parochial of springtime punters, Duckett would not have figured among the contenders to finish the summer as the leading run-getter in all cricket. In the event, his tally of 2,706 was the highest since Marcus Trescothick's 2,934 in 2009. It included innings of 163 and 220, both unbeaten, in a one-day series for England Lions, and four first-class hundreds, the smallest of them 185. He batted with panache, impish ingenuity, confidence and courage – all before turning 22. In September, he reaped the rewards with a cupboardful of prizes, and selection for the tours to Bangladesh and India, becoming only the 24th cricketer to represent England at Test level while on Northamptonshire's books, and the first since Monty Panesar seven years earlier.

"Technically I don't think I changed very much," he says. "But I was given a different role at the top of the order, with the chance to go out and play with freedom. At one stage I was trying to be a player I wasn't. I thought: 'I've got to bat like an opener and leave the ball.'" So when David Ripley, his county coach, told him to play his natural game, Duckett took him at his word.

If the headlines were made last summer, the seeds had been sown midway through the 2015 season, when Ripley made him a Championship opener. In his second match in the role, against Lancashire at Old Trafford, Duckett scored 134 (from 151 balls) and 88, then followed up with centuries against Derbyshire, Kent and Surrey. Talent was never an issue, but doubts persisted about his stickability at the crease. "I'm not the most focused person, and can lose concentration in quite a lot of things," he says. "But, right now, scoring runs is the most important thing in life." Batting eight and a half hours for 282 not out in the opening fixture of 2016 against Sussex at Northampton – where he was denied all manner of records by rain and a sodden outfield – indicated a tougher mental approach. "I've had patches of not scoring runs, and that's going to happen with the way I play. That's why I'm determined to cash in and get those big scores when the opportunity is there."

BEN MATTHEW DUCKETT, born in Farnborough, Kent, on October 17, 1994, made his mark in Northamptonshire's youth set-up by averaging 106 at the age of 11. He also showed promise as a wicketkeeper, and carried that into his senior career. Competitive sport was in the blood: his father Graham turned out for Surrey Second XI in the 1970s, while his mother Jayne has played and coached lacrosse, not a game for the faint-hearted. At Stowe School, opposing bowlers were already having to contend with his future trademark – Reynolds's bête noire, the reverse sweep. Phil Rowe, now assistant coach and Academy director at Wantage Road, has worked with Duckett for many years, and attributes his success with the shot to a handful of factors: his diminutive stature, the fact that – though a left-handed batsman – he is naturally right-handed, and his proficiency at hockey. Rowe believes Duckett's "funky" strokes are no more difficult for him than the leg glance or late cut for a more orthodox player.

Having those weapons is one thing; knowing when and how to employ them quite another. In his short career he has made a habit of rising to the big occasion – from an eye-catching century against Australia in the Under-19 World Cup in Dubai in 2014, to last summer's T20 Blast semi-final against Nottinghamshire at Edgbaston, where his spectacular 84 from 47 balls paved the way for Northamptonshire's second title in four years. Duckett had discussed his plan of attack in the dressing-room, and executed it with clinical assurance. Then, after a pair of sixties in England's one-day series win in Bangladesh, came the Second Test at Mirpur. He had made only 36 runs in his first three Test innings, so circumspection would have been understandable as he and Alastair Cook launched a pursuit of 273. Instead, Duckett backed himself to wrest the initiative from the Bangladesh spinners. Though England lost, his sparkling 56 encapsulated everything that is refreshing and exciting about his cricket. A sobering time in India at the hands of Ravichandran Ashwin brought him back to earth, but he will be wiser for the experience.

That was a reminder that it hasn't all been plain sailing. In March 2015, Duckett was dropped from a pre-season tour of the Caribbean after returning in less-than-perfect shape from grade cricket in Sydney. But Northamptonshire continued to back him, and he soon became their hottest property – to the extent that, as the club's members contemplated the momentous switch last year to a limited company, it was common to hear: "Will it mean we keep Duckett?" He agreed a contract extension to the end of 2018. "They're a small club that's done big things over the last few seasons," he says. "Growing up at Northants has been great for me." They are sentiments Reynolds would have applauded – wherever the ball ended up, and however it got there.

Misbah-ul-Haq

OSMAN SAMIUDDIN

In January 2017 at the SCG, after Misbah-ul-Haq had finished his last press conference on the tour of Australia, he was pursued by a gaggle of Pakistani journalists. One of them wanted to ask a question that had escaped his mind earlier. Misbah, who had just presided over a 3–0 Test defeat, turned around and asked him to fire away. "How," the journalist wondered, "did Pakistan fall so far, from No. 1 to 5, in just three months?" Without breaking step, or pausing for breath, Misbah replied in Punjabi and a pop-philosophical vein: "If a man who has lived for 70 years can suddenly die one day, what's a team falling from the ranking in three months?"

Sydney was Pakistan's sixth Test defeat in a row, five of them under Misbah. Yet only during the course of that Australia series had the fog cleared: it had been a series too far for Misbah – and for Misbah's Pakistan. Maybe three too far. With hindsight, the golden haze of an August afternoon at The Oval – where he joked with Alastair Cook about wanting a Fifth Test – was their zenith.

Pakistan's ten-wicket win over England to secure a 2–2 draw came in front of an adoring crowd, at the scene of one of Pakistan's greatest early triumphs. It was August 14, the anniversary of the country's founding. As the Test played out, it became a tribute to the passing, in July, of one of Pakistan's greatest men, the humanitarian Abdul Sattar Edhi, and one of its greatest openers, Hanif Mohammad, who had died on the first day. A week later, Pakistan would become the top-ranked Test side – only six years after losing the spot-fixing Test at Lord's, when they were sixth in the rankings and much further down in the rankings of goodwill.

In fact, it was the England trip that had promised to be a tour too far. Misbah had not appeared for Pakistan since they defeated England in Sharjah in November 2015, and had played no first-class match in the six months before they arrived. In May, he had turned 42. For a few months he contemplated retirement.

He had failed to secure a short-term county deal, but instead got the best preparation for a tour a modern Pakistan team have ever had. It began with an old-school boot camp at the army academy in Kakul, Abbottabad – Misbah emerged as one of the fittest of the intake – and was followed by a short skills-based camp in Lahore, then acclimatisation in Hampshire. As it was Ramadan, most players were fasting, but there was no let-up on training. "Fitness was at such a high," says Misbah. "That really helped us. As a challenge of fitness, Test matches were pretty easy."

MISBAH-UL-HAQ KHAN NIAZI was born in Mianwali, on May 28, 1974. On the cusp of Punjab and Khyber Pakhtunkhwa (once part of the latter, it now comes officially under the former), Mianwali is the ancestral home of another Niazi, Imran Khan. The two share little but a vast tribe. Nothing in his early years presaged the extraordinariness of Misbah's career.

He grew up in conventional circumstances, the youngest child and only son of two teachers. He took to many sports, especially hockey, football and snooker – interests frowned upon by his father. In the end, Misbah acceded to, and disobeyed, his strictures: he settled on cricket, but only after completing a university education. Until then, he had roamed the streets as a champion tape-ball batsman. Once he began in earnest, he rose swiftly, but not always smoothly: for 11 years after his first-class debut, he would remain more out than in at international level.

With Pakistan scrambling around in 2010 for a fifth Test captain that year, the PCB chairman Ijaz Butt met Misbah – recently discarded as a batsman – in great secrecy, in a clerk's room at board HQ in Lahore. Misbah received an offer, while being reminded there were no other candidates around; for a while, he didn't tell even his wife. Few are the great sporting careers that begin properly at 36.

In six years he turned Pakistan into an image of himself: head-down focus, unquestioning commitment, deep discipline. But he knew how to let his hair down, equalling Viv Richards's then Test record 56-ball hundred, against Australia at Abu Dhabi in 2014 – the second of three successive centuries.

Last summer was the high-water mark, even if he prefers the 2011-12 clean sweep of England in the UAE: "They were No. 1 at the time, and 2010 was still fresh in everyone's minds." In his first Test innings on English soil, at Lord's in July, Misbah set the tone: Pakistan were here to win matches and influence people. He came in at 77 for three, and might have been dismissed three times before reaching 20. But he ended up playing as well as he can recall, going on to a five-hour century: "If you take in the whole scenario – the history of the ground, the fact that I'd almost retired, 2010 – it was probably the top innings of my Test career." To celebrate, he provided the image of the summer, possibly the year – an impromptu set of ten push-ups, in gratitude to the soldiers who had helped with training. "It was a really emotional game for us," says a man defined by his own lack of public emotion.

After that, his leadership took over. Pakistan's defeat at Old Trafford was comprehensive, and their late demise at Edgbaston spirit-sucking, though Misbah did his best with a fighting half-century in both. But such was the character of the side that his faith in his players and their preparation never wavered. There was, he says, a rare "energy" in the squad – an energy he helped generate. Victory at The Oval confirmed as much.

He had also instigated an off-field PR coup by on-field deed. This was Pakistan's first non-rancorous tour to England in 20 years. The attention, he knew, would be fierce, but it couldn't be as fierce as the 2011-12 series, when he underwent some of the toughest media interactions of his career. "We knew we had controlled these things this time," he says. "After six years of this side, we had no issues off the field, so I was confident nothing would happen." Nothing, that is, other than magic.

Toby Roland-Jones

JOHN STERN

Toby Roland-Jones, the scourge of Yorkshire, breakfasts on champions. Three times in the space of 13 months he cut down the White Rose with zeal, culminating in a hat-trick at Lord's to finish off an epic title decider, and deliver Middlesex their first County Championship since 1993.

In September 2015, Roland-Jones had transformed the Lord's match against Yorkshire with a maiden first-class century, followed by a five-wicket haul. Then, last July, he launched Middlesex's title tilt with another blistering batting display, this time at Scarborough. Two months on, in the late September sun, he charged in from the Pavilion End to take five wickets in 16 balls, the hat-trick the *coup de grâce*. He finished with ten in the match and 54 for the season, including 29 at 27 apiece on Lord's pitches which drove less skilled bowlers to distraction. It took his averages against Yorkshire to 37 with the bat and 18 with the ball. Amid it all, it was easy to forget he had been called up to the Test squad against Pakistan at Lord's. After a season to cherish, he briefly captained England Lions in the UAE.

Reaching the crease from a long run-up (exactly 20.1m, he says), Roland-Jones seams the ball from an awkward length. With Tim Murtagh, he has formed a daunting new-ball partnership which has taken two-fifths of Middlesex's Championship wickets over the past five seasons. The pair embody the unflinching pride in the club advocated by Angus Fraser, their managing director of cricket. The Lord's flourish would not have been possible without the years of hard work that preceded it.

TOBIAS SKELTON ROLAND-JONES, born in Ashford, west London, on January 29, 1988, grew up in nearby Sunbury-on-Thames, a town once in Middlesex, now in Surrey. This geographical ambiguity still prevails in his life: he and his girlfriend, Harriet, live in Surrey – "behind enemy lines", as he puts it. He first experienced cricket aged four at the Sunbury club – where his father, Russell, coached junior sides – and attended the sporty Hampton School, which was also the alma mater of Surrey's Zafar Ansari and where England's assistant coach, Paul Farbrace, once taught. Roland-Jones began as a batsman, but a growth spurt in his late teens meant fast bowling became the priority. Even so, it was not until his final year studying accounting and management at Leeds University that a professional career dawned on him.

Positive feedback from umpires helped earn trials in 2009 with Surrey and Middlesex, who offered him a one-year contract. In a grim 2010, when they finished eighth in Division Two, he topped the averages with 36 wickets at 19. Injuries restricted him to a supporting role in their promotion year of 2011, but he bounced back spectacularly. The following summer he took 61 Championship wickets to help Middlesex finish third in the first division, was named their Player of the Year, and earned selection for the England Performance Programme. He believes he has never bowled better.

A hat-trick in 2013 against Derbyshire, who were dismissed for 60 at Lord's, suggested an instinct for game-changing moments. And in 2014 he blitzed Northamptonshire with 12 wickets and a 30-ball 60. Freer from injuries, Roland-Jones was performing more reliably, but without losing his show-stopping capability – nor his competitive instinct. Watching Yorkshire retain the Championship on the first day of the 2015 game at Lord's "did smart a bit. It's tough to concede a title to a team on your home ground, even if they were worthy winners."

But that game wasn't over, and the response from Middlesex, though in vain, was ferocious. They had been dismissed for 106, and trailed on first innings by 193, but by the end of the third day had 573 for eight, with Roland-Jones 103. Misinterpreting a signal from the dressing-room, he had thought a declaration imminent. "So I started going bananas with two overs to go and luckily managed to avoid a few fielders – everything came off." Five for 27 on the final day secured the match.

Last July he effected a more meaningful result. This time it was at Scarborough, where Yorkshire had never previously lost a Championship match by an innings. Middlesex resumed on the final day on 470 for eight, ahead by 64; after Roland-Jones's unbeaten 79, from 51 balls with six sixes, the lead had grown to 171. He then took three wickets as Yorkshire were bowled out for 167.

After drawing their first six Championship matches, Middlesex were up and running. "We needed to find a way to win key battles and key matches. We felt we'd started to turn up against the big teams." There are none bigger than Yorkshire, their opponents in the excruciatingly tense finale. "It was the toughest experience I've had," he says. "The pressure, the crowd, the TV – it was all on the line. I was fielding in front of the Middlesex hospitality box and never looked up once – I just took deep breaths and kept looking at the ground. I wanted to try and find a way."

And find a way he did. At 174 for six, with 66 needed from six overs, Yorkshire's title hopes had disintegrated; a draw would leave Somerset champions. But Roland-Jones had Azeem Rafiq caught behind off the last ball of his 12th over, then – after Steven Finn knocked over Steve Patterson – bowled Andrew Hodd with the first of his 13th.

As Roland-Jones reached the start of his run-up, he glanced towards Murtagh, at mid-on. Both men puffed their cheeks, and exhaled: "I was just trying to remember how to bowl." The next delivery, to the left-handed Ryan Sidebottom, was straight. Sidebottom moved too far to the off side – and lost his leg stump. Roland-Jones did not even realise he had taken a hat-trick. No matter: Middlesex had their first title for 23 years and, for the first time since 1947, the summer of Compton and Edrich, had secured the Championship at Lord's.

A batsman who became a bang-it-in, seam-bowling all-rounder, and appears to thrive under pressure… there is a touch of Stuart Broad about Roland-Jones. "I want to be the guy who's there when it counts, the guy the captain knows he can turn to," he says. "If I'm judged at the end of my career as someone who pitched up when it mattered, I'll be a very proud man."

Chris Woakes

GEORGE DOBELL

By the time the summer started, Chris Woakes feared his Test career was over. He had just returned from a frustrating tour of South Africa and, aged 27, suspected the selectors might look elsewhere. That trip could have turned out differently. Playing in the First Test at Durban because of an injury to James Anderson, Woakes found the edge of Hashim Amla's bat in his first spell, only for Jonny Bairstow to drop the chance. He bowled tidily for the rest of the match but, when Anderson returned for the next game, Woakes made way.

It was an episode that seemed to sum up his career. Nobody doubted his character. But it appeared he might be one of Test cricket's nearly men, not quite able to bridge the gap from the county game. Recalled for the final Test, at Centurion, but lacking rhythm after three weeks without a match and aware his future was on the line, he produced a nervy performance, taking one for 144 as England succumbed to defeat. For the first time in his Test career, he felt he had let himself down. In six matches his bowling average was 63.

"I was still confident I could succeed at that level," he says. "But I wasn't sure I would have another chance to prove it. When you've had that many opportunities, you can't complain." Had it not been for a knee injury to Ben Stokes, that chance might never have arrived. But on the day Woakes was recalled to the Test squad in May, he claimed career-best figures of nine for 36 for Warwickshire against Durham. "It was like facing 90mph leg-breaks," said their captain Paul Collingwood.

Even then, Woakes was far from certain to play in the Second Test against Sri Lanka at Chester-le-Street. Both Trevor Bayliss and Paul Farbrace, coach and assistant coach, favoured Nottinghamshire's Jake Ball, but Alastair Cook valued Woakes's extra ability as a batsman. Cook prevailed.

This time Woakes seized his chance. He produced career-bests with bat and ball, then hit a maiden half-century in the next Test, at Lord's, and followed it with a superb rearguard to help England tie the first one-dayer at Trent Bridge. They had been 82 for six in pursuit of Sri Lanka's 287, when Woakes and Jos Buttler put on 138. Woakes finished unbeaten with 95 from 92 balls – the highest score by anyone at No. 8 or below in one-day internationals. A last-ball six from Liam Plunkett completed the escape.

Better was to come. At Lord's against Pakistan, Woakes claimed 11 for 102, becoming the first England bowler since Ian Botham in 1978 to take a five-for in each innings of a Test there. He picked up seven wickets at Manchester (and hit a composed half-century as nightwatchman), then five more on his home ground in Birmingham. His 26 wickets at 16 apiece – a series record for England against Pakistan – were testament to his pace, control and movement. He had proved, to himself as much as anyone, that he could thrive in Test cricket.

It was a surprise it had taken him so long. CHRISTOPHER ROGER WOAKES was born into a sport-loving family in Birmingham on March 2,

1989. Strongly influenced by his father and two older brothers, he showed ability in all sports and, by the age of 11, was in the youth systems of both Walsall FC and Warwickshire CCC. Spotted by Steve Perryman, a former Warwickshire medium-pacer, Woakes was taught the art of swing bowling – partially by use of a yo-yo to drill the correct wrist position – and by the age of 14 was moving the ball both ways.

He made his first-class debut as a 17-year-old in 2006, and two years later became the youngest man to finish a season as Warwickshire's highest Championship wicket-taker. He also developed so much as a batsman that, by the time he made his Test debut at the end of the 2013 Ashes, he went in at No. 6.

"It was his attitude that impressed me," says Ashley Giles, his Warwickshire coach. "He was a bit of a weedy boy physically, but he wasn't intimidated by any challenge. I've worked with a few more talented cricketers – though not many – but never with one who offered more in terms of attitude, commitment and professionalism. If I could clone anyone I've worked with, it would be Chris Woakes."

He had actually made his international debut in a Twenty20 game at Adelaide in January 2011. In those days, England still used white-ball cricket to gauge a player's readiness for Tests. And, while he claimed six for 45 in a 50-over match against Australia later that month – indeed, he has two of England's three one-day six-fors – his skills seemed better suited to the longer form of the game. But he lacked the pace to trouble good batsmen on the flat surfaces prevalent in international cricket. So he worked, largely with Graeme Welch, then Warwickshire's bowling coach, on running in faster and making greater use of his front arm. He developed from a medium-pace swing bowler into one capable of hitting 90mph – and batsmen.

"Those early experiences of international cricket were vital," says Woakes. "They taught me how much I had to improve, and how big the gap was between county and international cricket." There had been moments he seemed on the brink of establishing himself. In 2014 he played three successive Tests against India and, while the wickets didn't flow (he claimed five at 43), his temperament left an impression. "It felt like a breakthrough," he says.

Then injuries intervened. He suffered a stress fracture of the foot, allowing Chris Jordan to take his spot in the Caribbean in 2015. A knee problem let Stokes cement his place as England's first-choice all-rounder. And a quad strain ruled him out of the tour to the UAE later that year. A disappointing World Cup had not helped.

The 2016 summer started badly too: he describes learning of his friend James Taylor's illness as "my worst moment in the game". But it ended with the pair planning to be ushers at each other's weddings, and Woakes established as a first-choice player in the Test side. And, at a time when the modern face of sport often wears a snarl, he provided a reminder that nice guys can reach the top. "My dream was always to play for Warwickshire," he says. "But it has gone better than I could have imagined."

Younis Khan

KAMRAN ABBASI

At The Oval, in the final Test of a demanding tour that examined both form and longevity, Younis Khan scored a faultless double-hundred. It was an innings of class and unshakeable determination – and it brought immense relief. Until then, his performances had not been those of Pakistan's premier batsman. But the problem went deeper than a series average of 20; even great players suffer fallow periods.

Younis wasn't just playing badly: he looked a shambles, hopping about the crease on one leg, executing shots in mid-air, living his trauma before the world's eyes. His supporters excused it all as a caricature of his usual style. Whatever the reason, it was a quirk rarely seen in a batsman of his stature, and unlikely to produce results against England's threatening swing and seam.

After a stunning win at Lord's celebrated with press-ups and – led by Younis – a mass salute in front of the Pavilion, Pakistan were well beaten at Old Trafford and Edgbaston. They were desperate to draw level – not only to square the series, but to give themselves a crack at the No. 1 ranking. Yet Younis's form cast a shadow over their chances: his six innings going into The Oval had been 33, 25, 1, 28, 31 and 4.

On the second day, with Pakistan 127 for three in reply to England's 328, he joined Asad Shafiq. Younis had built his reputation on scoring decisive hundreds in adversity. Here was another such hour – but where was the man? Pakistan supporters needn't have worried. The Younis who emerged was the lithe, silky champion of repute. It was a serene innings, utterly calm and – coupled with his customary brilliance against spin – in full command of England's pace attack.

A stand of 150 with Shafiq was only part of the story, as Younis's masterclass coaxed contributions from a suspect lower order. When he was finally leg-before to James Anderson for 218, made in seven and a half hours, Pakistan led by over 200; the game was theirs. Younis had played one of the great innings by a Pakistani in England: only Zaheer Abbas (twice) and Javed Miandad had gone higher. He had delivered, as he often does, when it mattered.

Afterwards, he made little of his battle with form, but revealed a conversation with – of all people – an Indian Test captain. "I received a call before the game from India, from Mohammad Azharuddin, and he talked about my batting, and told me to stay in the crease. I was very calm before the innings at The Oval. I waited and gathered myself for my form to turn around. I was relieved and happy when it happened. Squaring the Test series in England was a high point of the year for me."

Soon after, Azharuddin told Wisden India: "Younis is a good friend. It pained me to watch him bat in the first three Tests. I felt he was too good to be batting in that fashion, so I decided to speak to him. It was nice of him to hear me out, and adapt in such a short period of time. The result speaks for itself."

On his return to Pakistan, Younis was hospitalised with dengue fever, and missed the opening encounter against West Indies in the UAE, Pakistan's first day/night Test. But he returned for the second match, and scored another influential hundred. He has rarely had his fill.

MOHAMMAD YOUNIS KHAN was born on November 29, 1977, in Mardan, in the North-West Frontier Province (Khyber Pakhtunkhwa). One of seven brothers – he also had three sisters – he moved to Karachi in the early 1980s, where he played for Steel Town Gymkhana and Malir Gymkhana. His first coaches included Shamshad Khan, one of his brothers, and Anwarul Haq, a former first-class cricketer; Younis learned about courage by watching Ayub, another brother, sweep the fast bowlers, despite his father's warning that he would lose his teeth. Domestic runs meant Younis was fast-tracked into the Test team, making his debut against Sri Lanka at Rawalpindi in February 2000. Pakistan lost by two wickets, but he left his mark with a second-innings century from No. 7.

He established himself in all formats, but disagreements with the board, a lack of interest in Twenty20 – which he likened to WWE wrestling after leading Pakistan to the World T20 title in England in 2009 – and flaky form meant he focused on Tests. The strategy paid off. He is now Pakistan's leading Test run-scorer (9,977) and centurion, making his 34th against Australia at Sydney earlier this year.

In February 2009, he compiled 313 against Sri Lanka in Karachi – his last international innings on home soil before the terrorist attack in Lahore six days later – and The Oval was his sixth double (only five men have more in Tests). He averages 53 in the fourth innings of Tests, the same as in the first. His conversion rate (he has more hundreds than fifties) is remarkable.

Younis's career is tinged with tragedy: several close family members have died prematurely, as did his coach and mentor Bob Woolmer during the 2007 World Cup. But his drive has never waned: a proud man with a fiercely independent streak, he is still one of Pakistan's fittest players, and practises relentlessly with his own drills and warm-up routines. And, despite a record that places him above Miandad, Inzamam-ul-Haq, Mohammad Yousuf and Zaheer, Younis remains humble.

"They are legendary cricketers," he says, "and I'd never compare myself with them. I have learned from my hard times, and my hunger for learning and hard work is my greatest attribute. I want to keep going and contribute as much as I can." While the achievements of Pakistan's other leading batsmen have a powerful emotional pull, Younis has a strong argument to be a notch above them all.

FIVE CRICKETERS OF THE YEAR   Ben Duckett

FIVE CRICKETERS OF THE YEAR Misbah-ul-Haq

FIVE CRICKETERS OF THE YEAR Toby Roland-Jones

FIVE CRICKETERS OF THE YEAR   Chris Woakes

FIVE CRICKETERS OF THE YEAR   Younis Khan

WATER SPORT A construction site in Mumbai, or a dais beside the Ganges in Varanasi – always time for an impromptu game.

DUST TO DUSK Children in Bangladesh play cricket beside a rice mill; their parents work in the background. In Mumbai there is another good reason for keeping the ball on the ground.

FANFARE Spectators at Scarborough stroll on the outfield, and in Bangladesh they throng around giant screens showing the final of the Asia Cup.

TWENTY-FIVE YEARS OF DURHAM

Tales from the Riverside

STEPHEN BRENKLEY

The birth of modern Durham was almost an afterthought. On December 5, 1988, while they were still a Minor County, a meeting of the club committee reached Any Other Business. The minutes record: "The chairman outlined the discussions which had been held on an informal basis with a group which was interested in the idea of Durham forming a first-class side." The statement's blandness did not anticipate the drama that would unfold. In 1992, after protracted negotiations, the idea became reality, and Durham were installed as the 18th first-class county. Their 25th anniversary should be a time to celebrate glorious deeds.

But it will also be marked by gloom and a sense of injustice, accompanied by the suspicion that a legacy has been either squandered or crushed, depending on your perspective. At least there is a future of sorts. Throughout the first nine months of 2016 – and, in truth, for years before – Durham were close to financial collapse.

Shortly after the end of the season, when they finished fourth in the Championship and runners-up in the NatWest T20 Blast, the ECB announced Durham would be relegated, and docked points in all competitions in 2017 – 48 in the Championship, four in the Blast, two in the Royal London Cup. This was the cost of the ECB all but wiping out their unmanageable debts, in a package worth £3.8m.

No one can doubt Durham have made a substantial contribution to the game, justifying the view that English cricket needs a northern outpost. They have been county champions three times, and have won the 50-over competition twice. Their purpose-built stadium, integral to their original application, has hosted six Tests, 15 one-day and two Twenty20 internationals. They have provided nine England players from their admirable Academy, five of them Ashes winners. There has evolved almost a production line of fast bowlers. And, in Shotley Bridge's Paul Collingwood, their most capped home-grown player, they can claim England's only World Cup-winning captain: he lifted the World Twenty20 in 2010.

To guide them through a convulsive fallout, Durham turned to Ian Botham as their chairman, an appointment promoted by the ECB. In his last great adventure as a player, he scored the club's first Championship hundred. Now he is back, ready to use his charisma to salvage something from the mess.

The board insisted they had no choice but to impose stringent penalties: Durham needed the money, but there needed to be a deterrent to preserve cricket's integrity. Opinion in the county – and elsewhere – was that, in being made an example of, they had been discriminated against. In the House of Commons, Kevan Jones, MP for North Durham, called the ECB's behaviour

One of a kind: Paul Collingwood leads England to the World T20 in Barbados, May 2010.

"disgraceful and shameless". Durham already had experience of losing points – though in 2013, it was only 2.5 for breaching the ECB salary cap the previous summer. That did not prevent them securing their third Championship in six years. And though the transgression – which they reported – was only £14,000 above the £2m limit, it was evidence of inattentive book-keeping.

In November 2015, they wrote to the ECB outlining their plight. By May, the board – sensing the game could not allow the collapse of its northern frontier – agreed to help. Throughout the negotiations, it was an open secret at the ECB that one of the prices of rescue would be playing penalties. The trouble was that Durham were not made aware of this until late September, when they were given 48 hours to accept or fold. It still rankles with David Harker, their chief executive. "Relegation had not been discussed since we started talking in May," he said. "I think there are people in the cricket world who had made their minds up that this might very well be the penalty, and might well have spoken to other people in the cricket world."

Gordon Hollins, the ECB's chief operating officer (who once worked at Durham), sees things differently. "You can't say they didn't do anything wrong," he said. "Nobody else on the planet looks at it that way. You can say the sanctions were too harsh. I understand that, because it's emotional and there are different degrees of opinion. But this was the decision."

It was a crisis years in the making – and everyone could see what was happening. As Harker put it: "By about 1995 it was becoming apparent that the club's business model wasn't stacking up." In essence, the Riverside ground created most of the subsequent problems. Yet if it had not been built, there would have been no first-class status, no Championships, and many fewer Durham Test cricketers. The old Test and County Cricket Board made it a condition that Durham build a stadium of international standard – perhaps partly, Harker muses, to deter them from pursuing their application. But Durham entered into the arrangement enthusiastically. Their bid brochure spoke of a scheme at the newly named Riverside Park which demonstrated "the concept of improving leisure amenities in the area, while at the same time, through developing houses and offices on a small part of the site, providing funds towards the cost of a cricket ground".

DURHAM'S ENGLAND PLAYERS

	Tests	*ODIs*	*T20Is*	*Debut*
I. T. Botham	2	5	–	1992
S. J. E. Brown†	1	–	–	1996
P. D. Collingwood†	68	197	35	2001
S. J. Harmison‡	63	58	2	2002
L. E. Plunkett‡	9	29	1	2005-06
P. Mustard†	–	10	2	2007-08
G. Onions†	9	4	–	2009
B. A. Stokes‡	32	50	21	2011
S. G. Borthwick†	1	2	1	2011
M. A. Wood‡	8	11	1	2015
K. K. Jennings‡	2	–	–	2016-17

As at 1.2.2017. † *Born in Durham.* ‡ *Born outside Durham, but a product of the Academy.*

The following, born in Co. Durham, represented England before 1992: J. E. McConnon, C. Milburn, C. H. Parkin, R. T. Spooner, A. E. Stoddart, D. C. H. Townsend, P. Willey and R. G. D. Willis. R. C. Blunt (New Zealand) and J. Middleton (South Africa) were also born in the county.

They also made a virtue of its "ideal" location near a junction of the A1 motorway, but away from the conurbations of Newcastle, Darlington, Hartlepool and Durham. As Harker concedes, it has – when hosting international cricket over the past decade – proved short of ideal. The only viable route is by road and, though the motorway junction is barely a mile away, the ground has never dispelled the feeling it is off the beaten track. Harker believes Durham could have acted little differently. He also emphasises that they had been trying for nigh on ten years to persuade the ECB to discuss the issue of how county cricket was financed.

"It's not fair to sit at Lord's and say this problem is entirely of our own making," he said. "It isn't. I look back over the years – the bidding for international cricket, the salary-cap breach – and what could we have done? Where have we let ourselves down? I am happy to sit with anyone who can point to me and say that's what you should have done instead."

What about that salary-cap breach? Harker says the club were a victim of their own success in producing England players. "What tipped us over the edge was Graham Onions coming back to us after losing a central contract. When the cap was introduced I remember saying that, unless some sort of transitioning was in place, we would breach it in a couple of years because we already had contracts in place for people who were international players."

Durham's results were initially pretty hopeless. They finished in the bottom three of the Championship in each of their first six seasons. It became clear,

Cap in hand: Clive Leach and David Harker present Gordon Muchall and Mark Davies with their Durham caps, July 2005.

both to them and the ECB, that the international-class stadium to which they had moved in 1995 – after spending three summers playing at six different club grounds in the North-East – needed international matches.

But the status and timing of those matches – low-key opposition in early June when the northern spring has hardly sprung – were misguided. Zimbabwe came in 2003, Bangladesh in 2005, West Indies in 2007 and again in (May) 2009, when Chris Gayle did not help matters by saying, a few days before the game, that he would not mind if Test cricket died.

Crowds were sparse, it was usually cold, the games were barely contests. Not until 2013, when Australia arrived in August, did the ground host an alluring Test. Even then, despite England retaining the Ashes, it was not a sell-out. The visit of Sri Lanka last May was another costly disappointment. There is now a rueful acknowledgment at the ECB that Durham should never have staged Tests – though England have won all six – and that one-day and Twenty20 internationals are the future.

Harker begged to differ: "I don't think there was an alternative to trying to get involved. It wasn't necessarily that we were losing money on these games: we just weren't earning enough. So, if you weren't involved you would be earning even less. This is still a challenge for cricket. It doesn't matter how much you promote the game or how much you charge for a ticket. If people don't want to be there, they're not going to come."

Durham targeted team improvement when Clive Leach, a former Warwickshire batsman and retired chairman of Yorkshire–Tyne Tees Television, became chairman in 2004. He was motivated by their bottom-place finish in Division Two of the Championship that summer, and the belief that a winning team might bring in cash to invest in the ground, and arrest the financial decline.

Gradually, Durham became harder to beat. With the sage counselling of Geoff Cook, their director of cricket who had been there from the start, they made astute signings, Dale Benkenstein and Michael Di Venuto among them. The Academy began to bear fruit. But they also drastically reassessed their financial strategy. Leach, born in India, turned to two businessmen he knew there: the Radia brothers – Gautam, who runs several radio stations, and Hiren.

Without fanfare, Durham, who had started their first-class life as a company limited by guarantee, became a private company, in return for nearly £2.5m from the Radias. The ECB were not in a position to veto the move but, having exclusively overseen members' clubs, they were averse to the dangers this threw up, and reluctant to put cricket's money into such a set-up, ailing or not. The Radia brothers were hardly asset strippers, but nor – it turned out – did they have the funds to prevent Durham sliding further. The global financial crisis of 2008, the year they landed their first Championship, virtually ended the brothers' involvement with a county they nominally owned. The club looked to Durham County Council for help, and negotiated two separate loans, in 2009 and 2013, totalling £4.3m. The council's agreement, at the ECB's behest last autumn, to convert most of these loans into preferential shares was instrumental in Durham staying afloat. They are now becoming a community interest company.

Harker and Leach robustly defend their decision to invest in the team. "We always took the view that we had to be successful at our core activity in order to promote the sport, the brand and the business," said Harker. "That wasn't a reckless decision, a case of chasing cricketing glory for the sake of it."

Various attempts have been made (as per the original bid brochure) to develop the area around the Riverside. The latest, probably last, to founder was for a five-star hotel. Several backers were courted, but all declined, suggesting development may not have been commercially feasible.

Durham now find themselves in a more favourable financial position than at any time since the early days. But they may have to accept a lesser status, which will mean, for instance, nurturing players, only to see them leave. Two senior men, Mark Stoneman and Scott Borthwick, have gone to Surrey, and they had to fight to keep Keaton Jennings, the most recent Academy product to play for England. Harker foresees Durham possibly breaking even each year, but refuses to settle for second best on the field, or be prepared to lose the players they will still be expected to develop.

This is not necessarily the ECB's view. "The definition of success used to be winning competitions," said Hollins. "But my argument is that the role of the first-class county is a lot broader than that – it's about participating and inspiring people to engage. This could become a genuine community club." Which, of course, may be a brutally polite way of saying you should never expect to win anything ever again.

Stephen Brenkley, who lives in Barnard Castle, Co. Durham, is the former cricket correspondent of The Independent.

RACHAEL HEYHOE FLINT 1939–2017

A peer without peer

CLARE CONNOR

She never knew it, but Rachael Heyhoe Flint once made me cry. It was 2015, and I was presenting plans for the Kia Super League to the ECB board, of which she was a member. It was a fairly radical idea at the time – particularly as we were moving away from the traditional county structure – and I had wanted, as usual, to discuss it with Rachael beforehand. She was always my go-to person for things like this; she would ask me questions, and provide suggestions that left me better prepared. This time, though, there hadn't been an opportunity to brief her fully.

When it came to the meeting, she didn't just say: "Oh yes, Clare, that's a good idea." She challenged me really hard. It put me on the back foot and made me realise we still had a lot to think about. It was a harsh lesson, but also a true mark of her character. While both of us wanted to promote the women's game, she wasn't going to give me an easy ride just because of our shared passion; she was robust, independent and professional.

I had got to know Rachael well after starting my job as the director of England Women's cricket in 2008. We worked closely together through the Lady Taverners – where her energy helped get thousands of girls playing cricket – and even more so after 2010, when she joined the ECB board. I came to appreciate her personality, humour and strength. She also had traits I think are common to all game-changers: rebelliousness, a taste for mischief, and a challenging streak.

Of course, I knew *of* Rachael long before I met her. I'd read about her and heard all the stories. She had been a supremely successful captain of the England team, their best batsman, their manager and their press officer. But her commitment and desire to advance the sport went beyond just being brilliant at it. She devised the first World Cup in 1973 – two years before the men's – she drummed up sponsorship, and she sold the tickets. She wrote the reports and the publicity releases. And in 1999, she was one of the first female members of MCC. In an era when women's cricket had little or no profile, she made herself a household name; she understood the power of celebrity in promoting a cause. And she did it all without a trace of selfishness or ego.

Rachael might have said she wasn't a feminist but, in my eyes, she was. She talked convincingly about equality, about women's cricket being accepted and included and valued. It was just that she didn't identify as a militant; she got her way with charm, persistence and intellect. She once said she would never chain herself to the Grace Gates or go on hunger strike to get what she wanted. She didn't need to.

She was an extremely busy woman, always charging up and down the motorway between the Midlands, where she looked after her husband, Derrick,

Pioneer: Rachael Heyhoe Flint (far right) leads the first women's team to play at Lord's, in 1976.

Dennis Oulds, Getty Images

and London, to work at Lord's – and the Lords. She also had countless charity appointments. But she always had time for you. When you see people with power or vast amounts of responsibility, they don't always talk to others as politely or as gently or with as much patience as they should. Rachael was different: she made everybody feel special.

She was ennobled by David Cameron in 2010, and once took me on a tour of the House of Lords, joking with everyone we met: the police, the cafe assistants, and the cloakroom attendant. Later in the day she introduced me to some senior politicians, and she was the same with all of them. I've seen her mix with children aged eight or nine from deprived backgrounds, and with Tony Blair or Gordon Brown in the gardens of Downing Street. By most people's standards she was posh, but she had that rare common touch.

She was deeply proud of where the women's game is now, and it gave her immense joy to watch the current England team play as fully fledged professional cricketers. I know for certain I wouldn't be where I am today without her hard work. And the players know they owe her a debt of gratitude, too. They will play in a World Cup this summer, 44 years after Rachael pulled the first one together. It would be wonderful to win it – of course it would. But, without her, they wouldn't even be taking part.

Clare Connor, who captained England in 79 of her 111 internationals, was speaking to James Gingell. A full obituary of Rachael Heyhoe Flint will appear in Wisden 2018.

THE OTHER SIDE OF THE IPL

Chewed up and spat out

ANAND VASU

In the dusty village of Nadwa Sarai in Uttar Pradesh, where the population was 5,000 last time anyone bothered to count, a 25-year-old in a Pune Warriors jersey is working the wheat fields. Depending on the season, he sows or reaps; either way, it's tough, and times are hard. He is used to bending his back – he's no shirker – but this son of a woodcutter seemed destined for glory in a different field.

A few years earlier, in 2009, the Indian Premier League moved to South Africa because of a general election back home: police could not be spared to provide security at the cricket. At picturesque Newlands, far removed from the fields of Nadwa Sarai, Rajasthan Royals captain Shane Warne threw the ball to Kamran Khan, an unknown, freakish left-arm seamer, just turned 18. Kolkata Knight Riders needed seven off the last over, and Sourav Ganguly was at the crease. The move was brave – but it paid off. Kamran kept Kolkata down to six, forcing a super over, which he himself bowled. Rajasthan won; a star was born. Kamran said Warne spoke English so fast he was unable to understand his instructions, but was effusive anyway. "I had not played any serious cricket before this, and if I am playing at this level all credit goes to

Part of the family? Kamran Khan and Rajasthan Royals team-mates during the 2010 IPL.

Warne," he said at the time. "His faith in me is the biggest factor in my success."

The rise and fall of Kamran is hardly a unique sporting tale, but this does not make it any less poignant. After his father died of a lung ailment, his mother – desperate to make ends meet – took to rolling *beedis*, the cheap cigarettes made from unprocessed tobacco, and smoked in rural India. Two years later, she died too. Then, at his lowest ebb, cricket handed him a lifeline. In March 2009, Darren Berry, the former Victoria wicketkeeper who was working with the Royals, spotted him playing for a police team in a local Twenty20 tournament, and signed him for $24,000, more than the boy had ever heard of. Several weeks later, he was in Cape Town.

But before he could enjoy his new-found wealth, life changed again. Kamran's action – a loping approach followed by a full-bodied explosion – was declared suspect, and he was banned from bowling. A spell of rehabilitation helped, but in 2011 Kamran – now with Pune Warriors – played just one IPL match, against Royal Challengers Bangalore. He fell in a heap trying to deliver his first ball, and was smashed by Chris Gayle: his first two overs cost 37, and he was not picked again. He was reduced to serving as a net bowler for Mumbai Indians.

"When I was called to Wankhede Stadium to bowl in the nets, I felt ashamed," he says. "It was not a good feeling. I did my best to hide, hoping nobody would notice me or recognise me." But Allan Donald, who had coached him at Pune, did notice – and was shocked to hear he had not played a serious game of cricket in years. "Of course it was the highlight of my life to play in the IPL," Kamran says. "I only wish it had happened a little earlier. Then I could've used the money for the medical treatment of my parents." He has all but given up on a game that gave up on him.

The IPL is excellent at blowing its own trumpet, so you might have heard how West Indian all-rounder Kieron Pollard used his earnings to build a huge house for his mother, who had raised him in a Port-of-Spain slum. But have you heard the story of Harmeet Singh?

A wiry left-arm spinner, he came to attention in New Zealand in January 2010, when he was playing the second of two Under-19 World Cups. Tossing the ball up fearlessly with a repeatable, easy action that had purists purring and batsmen guessing, Harmeet was the darling of the commentators. Writing on ESPNcricinfo, Ian Chappell likened him to Bishan Bedi, "with that same natural flight and guile that would right now place him as the best spin bowler in any Test side bar England".

The fanfare travelled swiftly from Christchurch to Mumbai, where Harmeet, the son of a property dealer, had barely begun making a name for himself. Ahead of that World Cup, he had played two Ranji Trophy matches, picking up 12 wickets against Himachal Pradesh and Railways, both relatively weak. But when he came back from New Zealand, the praise went to his head: he started to believe he really was good enough to walk into most Test teams. Seasoned Ranji Trophy campaigners begged to differ. Rumours of Harmeet's fondness for a drink, coupled with tales of indiscipline, did not help, and batsmen set out to teach the young tyke a lesson. Harmeet played only one

Ian Hitchcock, ICC/Getty Images

Left spinning: Harmeet Singh at the 2012 Under-19 World Cup. His career has since stalled.

match for Mumbai in 2010-11, and would not play first-class cricket again for two seasons. Picked by Rajasthan Royals for the 2013 IPL, he seemed ready to mix with the big boys once more. But he managed a single game before getting caught in the match-fixing controversy that would result in the suspension of Sreesanth, the former Test seamer, and Ajit Chandila. Harmeet had reportedly been introduced by Chandila to bookies, though he says he thought he was meeting Chandila's cousins – a plausible explanation given the two had been team-mates for several years. Yet Harmeet never reported the approach, which he claims he turned down. Released by Mumbai, and unable to play for Vidarbha – who wanted his services – until he was cleared by the disciplinary committee, Chappell's next Bedi couldn't get a game anywhere. Since then, no IPL team have touched him.

"I was given a clean chit by the BCCI, and the Delhi Police also said I never had anything to do with spot-fixing," he says. "I don't think that is the reason I have not been picked in the IPL. I was keen to play, but sometimes this happens in auctions. Maybe teams had already formed their squads by the time I came up for bidding. Sometimes it's about having the right luck also."

A player who was an integral part of India's victory at the Under-19 World Cup not getting an IPL offer? No matter how hard Harmeet tries to convince himself, that's down to more than luck. By the end of 2016, still only 24, he had played only 14 first-class matches, most recently for unfancied Jammu & Kashmir. His left-arm spin, which once floated like the prettiest butterfly, was stung by the IPL. He now waits in limbo.

While cricket may still be regarded in some quarters as the gentleman's game, the IPL has never thought it crass to splash the cash. And you might have heard how Chris Morris, the South African all-rounder, went from being a franchise player with a modest salary to a Rand millionaire in the space of ten minutes at an auction. But the IPL would rather you did not ask about Paul Valthaty, once toasted as all that was good about cricket's glitziest spectacle.

In 2011, aged 27, Valthaty was bold enough to say that wearing the India cap was every cricketer's dream, and he had "taken a small step in that direction". He was referring to his own blistering 120 not out from 63 balls for Kings XI Punjab against a Chennai Super Kings attack including Ravichandran Ashwin, Tim Southee and Morne Morkel. He had not even come close to playing first-class cricket, yet this innings – in which he comfortably outscored his opening partner Adam Gilchrist – had emboldened him to speak about playing for India.

Valthaty brimmed with promise as a youngster, put in the work, and made it to the Under-19 World Cup team in 2002. But a blow to his right eye when he was batting against Bangladesh cost him a year in the game, and he never quite graduated to the next level. Playing club cricket in Mumbai, he stuck with the dream, eventually building a reputation as a Twenty20 specialist. Then the IPL came calling. Abhishek Nayar, a Mumbai regular and India occasional, persuaded Kings XI Punjab to give Valthaty a go, and that century against CSK looked like his breakthrough. It would prove the falsest of dawns.

Himachal Pradesh picked Valthaty in the Ranji Trophy in 2011, but he averaged only 20 in five matches, and has not played first-class cricket since. He was given six games by Kings XI in the 2012 IPL, but averaged five. In 2013, he played once, scoring six. Since then all doors, IPL or otherwise, have stayed shut. The son of an engineer and a doctor, he was a rarity among Indian middle-class children, encouraged to pursue sport over academia. "My father used to push me a lot to play cricket," he says. "He is a great enthusiast of the sport. My mother, too, supported me. My family and friends have been behind me through thick and thin, which has motivated me to do well." Now aged 33, Valthaty is all but forgotten.

Shreyas Iyer, the latest wunderkind from the Mumbai school of batsmanship, had to be dragged to the Wankhede by his friends to watch the home team in action: he preferred playing to spectating. Barely a year later, he entered an IPL auction at Rs10 lakh (about £1,200), and was bought by Delhi Daredevils for Rs2.6 crore (about £310,000). He wasn't quite as reluctant to attend IPL matches after that.

Not everyone is so fortunate. "Don't feel bad if someone *rejects or ignores* you," began a pointedly asterisked tweet from Manpreet Gony in July 2016. "People usually reject and ignore *precious things*, because they cannot *afford* them." For two years Punjab, his state team, had all but ignored him, and for three the IPL had rejected him. Kings XI Punjab were the last to take a punt on this tall, strapping seamer.

Gony owes his two-ODI career entirely to the IPL. In 2008, its inaugural season, he had a fine run with Chennai Super Kings, whose captain M. S. Dhoni was sufficiently impressed to alert the national selectors. In an international career that lasted four days, Gony took none for 11 against Hong Kong and two for 65 from eight overs against Bangladesh. He has never been seriously considered for India since.

Gony had already seen a bit of life before the IPL turned everything upside down. When he married Manpreet (they do indeed share a first name), Gony was ostracised by his family, who disapproved of his choice. The couple took

Rise and fall: Paul Valthaty beams at Punjab colleague Adam Gilchrist during the 2011 IPL.

refuge in each other's arms, but personal tragedy struck when their child died after only 15 days. The IPL lifted him for a time, but when it dropped him, the fall was precipitous. Embroiled in a property dispute with his mother, who claimed Gony had sent her death threats, separated from his wife, and abandoned by cricket, he put on a brave face, posting photos of rides on his beloved Harley-Davidson, growing a luxuriant beard, and posing as the successful cricketer he was not.

Desperate for money, he went to America and bowled in leagues that were beneath him. "I was not thinking clearly because my personal life was a mess and there was a lot of pressure on me," he says. "In India, it's difficult to make a living from cricket if you're not playing at a certain level. I couldn't concentrate on cricket, so I left India. At least I could pay my bills, but now I know I wasted two years of my career." In 2016, Gony – at the age of 32 – was trying to rebuild his life and career in the Ranji Trophy, but he knew, in his heart of hearts, that his best days were behind him.

At 37, Australian left-arm wrist-spinner Brad Hogg had hit rock bottom. In an effort to save his marriage, he retired from international cricket, though he was desperate to play more. Life behind a desk was not easy; soon he had lost both family and vocation, and seriously contemplated suicide. Four years later, the IPL resurrected him. But life does not begin at 40 for all cricketers.

Bharat Chipli, a promising batsman who once racked up the runs for Karnataka in the Ranji Trophy, now plays in the Karnataka Premier League, a tournament that includes a team of film stars who have not won a game in five seasons. Chipli was obsessed with cricket from a young age, but admits he never thought he would play at a serious level.

Not a natural thumper of the ball, he added muscle to his batting, and in 2011 Deccan Chargers came calling. A 35-ball 61 against Royal Challengers Bangalore brought Chipli front and centre, even in a team containing some of the biggest names in the business. "Kumar Sangakkara would give me a bat whenever I wanted," he says. "Dale Steyn never showed any attitude, and Darren Lehmann, our coach, would take me out for a cold beer whether I had performed or not." But he hasn't added to his 20 first-class appearances since 2012: form deserted him, and other young batsmen – K. L. Rahul, Mayank Agarwal and Karun Nair – jumped the queue.

Kamran bends his back only in the fields these days. Harmeet can't toss it up or make it dip, no matter how hard he tries. Valthaty would love to clear the ropes, but he can't find a team. Gony is starting again, but is not sure where it will lead. Chipli aimed to be a serious cricketer, and had to settle for a lot less.

The IPL has its success stories – of course it does. But the seduction of dollars, the flirtation with the spotlight, the embrace of fame – these can all be followed by a kiss of death. They loved the IPL, these young men, but the feeling was only fleetingly mutual.

Anand Vasu has written on cricket for nearly two decades.

THE LEADING CRICKETER IN THE WORLD IN 2016

Virat Kohli

BHARAT SUNDARESAN

Back in July 2011, Virat Kohli spoke of his desire to become the batsman India's opposition "need to get out". It sounded an ambitious claim: he had just flopped in his maiden Test series, in the Caribbean, where he had been worked over by Fidel Edwards, and was left out of the squad for the subsequent tour of England.

Fast-forward to 2016, and Kohli was very much the man the opposition needed to get out. They just couldn't fathom how. No matter where they bowled, he seemed to have an answer. In a year when the Indian economy experienced more bumps than an autorickshaw ride, his stock rose steadily, with the odd dramatic spike. And his eventual figures were eye-popping.

In all three genres, Kolhi averaged more than anyone: 75 in Tests, 92 in one-dayers and a phenomenal 106 in Twenty20 internationals. His 51-ball unbeaten 82 at Mohali to send Australia home from the World T20 in March was one of the limited-overs performances of the year, typifying his mastery of the chase. In 13 Twenty20 innings for India, he was undefeated seven times, and scored seven half-centuries. And by the end of 2016, his career average in all three formats was over 50. It needed something special to outshine team-mate and off-spinner Ravichandran Ashwin, who was taking wickets by the bucketload and scoring useful runs too – but Kohli managed it.

When a young Sachin Tendulkar had reached the summit a couple of decades earlier, it had been no surprise. But Kohli was no wonder kid, and you might argue – though not too loudly in his home city of Delhi – that he isn't as naturally gifted as some of his peers. That he is now the complete package is testament to his will. Like a man possessed, he has simply forced his way to the top. And he is still only 28.

Take the 2014-15 Test series in Australia, which he began with a question mark hanging over his ability against seam bowling after struggling in England. Instead, he mastered the likes of Mitchell Johnson and Ryan Harris by daring to bat outside his crease, and finished with four hundreds. Then there was the 2016 IPL, which he started in the shadow of Bangalore team-mates Chris Gayle and A. B. de Villiers. Yet Kohli totalled 973 runs – 125 more than the next best, David Warner – and averaged 81, hitting four of the tournament's seven hundreds. And he did it all without obviously changing his game.

Where once his puppy fat was conspicuous, today he is the author and epitome of the body-over-mind revolution that has changed the way Indian cricketers prepare. His training videos are all the rage. He attributes his transformation in Test cricket to his approach to fitness, embracing boredom off the field to ensure entertainment on it. It was no coincidence that, in 2016, he turned three of his four Test hundreds into doubles.

Whatever the scenario, Kohli knew what he had to do. Against West Indies in Antigua, he took the game by its scruff and scored 200. Against New Zealand at Indore, he curbed his natural instincts and compiled a patient 211. Against England at Mumbai, he hit a breathtaking 235, and finished a series he had bent to his will with an average of 109. That innings marked him out as Tendulkar's heir, but he was not finished: in February 2017, against Bangladesh at Hyderabad, he became the first to score a double-century in four successive Test series, beating Don Bradman and Rahul Dravid, who managed three.

Being India's captain – and Kohli is now in total charge, after M. S. Dhoni stepped down as skipper of the white-ball teams in January 2017 – is akin to being a reality star. He lives his life in the public eye, the cameras always turned towards him, the scrutiny never-ending. Yet Kohli has thrived. By the time England left India nursing a 4–0 defeat, he averaged almost 64 as captain, the best for an Indian, with Tendulkar's 51 a far-off second. And he capped his gargantuan year with the bat by warding off rumours on social media about his engagement to a Bollywood star, treating the gossip as he had every overpitched delivery during the preceding 12 months: with disdain.

A lack of runs in England remains the only blip on his CV, as Jimmy Anderson had the temerity to suggest during the Mumbai Test. The reaction next morning of Ashwin, who questioned Anderson's sanity as he walked out to bat in the game's dying moments, said something about Kohli's standing among his team-mates. And it would take an equally brave man to bet against him setting the record straight when India return to England in 2018.

THE LEADING CRICKETER IN THE WORLD

2003	Ricky Ponting (Australia)	2010	Sachin Tendulkar (India)
2004	Shane Warne (Australia)	2011	Kumar Sangakkara (Sri Lanka)
2005	Andrew Flintoff (England)	2012	Michael Clarke (Australia)
2006	Muttiah Muralitharan (Sri Lanka)	2013	Dale Steyn (South Africa)
2007	Jacques Kallis (South Africa)	2014	Kumar Sangakkara (Sri Lanka)
2008	Virender Sehwag (India)	2015	Kane Williamson (New Zealand)
2009	Virender Sehwag (India)	**2016**	**Virat Kohli (India)**

A list of notional past winners from 1900 appeared in Wisden 2007, *page 32.*

WISDEN WRITING COMPETITION WINNER IN 2016

One over – memories for life

JOHN PITT

It's pretty dark now, and I'm sprinting through a slightly run-down station to catch a train; my father hurries ahead. It's nine o'clock and, since I'm only eight, well past my bedtime. We still have to get back from Manchester to Liverpool. But I don't care, because something extraordinary has happened. Minutes earlier, I finished watching my first live game of cricket, and I know, as the darkness draws in around Warwick Road station outside Old Trafford, that my life has changed for ever.

It is July 28, 1971, and no Lancashire fan will need telling it was the Gillette Cup semi-final in which David Hughes hit 24 in an over from Gloucestershire's John Mortimore. Look at the clips on YouTube, and you see a different era. The crowd, all sideburns and long hair, are packed in, sitting on the grass and, extraordinarily, running on to collect the ball before it reaches the boundary. It was during Lancashire's early one-day success and, at ten that morning, I had waited anxiously – having entered through a children-only turnstile – for my father to get in, amid rumours they were about to close the gates.

The rest of the day remains cinematically clear: a spectacular run-out by Clive Lloyd, lithe and athletic in his mid-twenties; a powerful 60-odd from Mike Procter; a steady start from David Lloyd and Barry Wood, with tension building; a mid-innings collapse, with Farokh Engineer slipping on to his stumps; Jacks Bond and Simmons edging us closer as evening fell. And then, of course, Hughes's unforgettable assault, launching the ball into the murk. That Lancashire side have a kind of luminous brilliance even now, the list of their names like a form of prayer: Lloyd (D.), Wood, Pilling, Lloyd (C. H.), Sullivan, Engineer, Bond, Simmons, Hughes, Lever, Shuttleworth. They are heroic figures from a glamorous, bygone age.

My father, who had woken me early that morning to suggest the trip, died in 2015, aged 93. He had grown up in Birmingham, a Warwickshire fan, and when I cleared his house I came across his old autograph book, dated 1934, and filled with names largely meaningless to me, but no doubt resonant to him: Peter Cranmer, H. E. Dollery, J. S. Ord. Then I think of my own two sons, both adults now, and their first games: for Joe, Murali's 16 wickets at The Oval; for Tom – a Gloucestershire fan – a tense 40-over affair at Cheltenham.

What strikes me is that such memories link us not, as Philip Larkin believed, to our losses, but to our excited younger selves. So that now, in my mid-fifties, nearing retirement, I'm still in part that young boy running through a poorly lit station on a summer night, intoxicated by the sight of a man hitting sixes into the gloom as the crowd exploded in joy, exhilarated beyond words.

John Pitt, a lifelong Lancashire fan, teaches English in Gloucestershire.

THE COMPETITION

Wisden received 85 entries for its fifth writing competition. They arrived from all corners of the globe, all ages, and both genders. Some entries arrived months before the deadline; others with seconds to spare. In all five years of the competition, the standard has been high, and the business of judging remains exacting. The prize is unchanged: publication, adulation, and an invitation to the launch dinner, held at Lord's in April.

The rules are also unchanged. Anyone who has never been commissioned by Wisden can take part. Entries, which should not have been submitted before (and are restricted to a maximum of two per person), must be:

1. the entrant's own work
2. unpublished in any medium
3. received by the end of 30 November, 2017
4. between 480 and 520 words (excluding the title)
5. neither libellous nor offensive
6. related to cricket, but not a match report.

Articles should be emailed to almanack@wisden.com, with "Writing Competition 2017" as the subject line. (Those without access to email may post their entry to Writing Competition 2017, John Wisden & Co, 13 Old Aylesfield, Golden Pot, Alton, Hampshire GU34 4BY, though email is preferred.) Please provide your name, address and telephone number. All entries will be acknowledged by the end of 2017, and the winner informed by the end of January 2018. Bloomsbury staff and those who in the editor's opinion have a working relationship with Wisden are ineligible. The editor's decision is final. Once again, we look forward to receiving your contributions. Your hard work and imagination are much appreciated.

THE 2016 ENTRANTS

Alex Abel, Nick Alford, Anubhav Anand, Mike Battrum, Archie Berens, David Brown, Michael Brown, Nick Brown, Samuel Bruning, Andrew Burrill, Simon Burrowes, Andrew Carr, Michael Cartwright, Paul Caswell, Paul Clifford, Oliver Colling, Steve Crudge, David Cuffley, Glynis Cuffley, Philip Fisher, David Fraser, Mark Gannaway, Allan Garley, Nick Gormack, Ian Gray, Steve Green, Rowena Haigh, Steven Haigh, Philip Hardman, Mike Harfield, Anthony Hodges, Edward Hodgson, Michael Jones, Ullas Krishnan, Gareth Langley, Anthony McKenna, Duncan McLeish, Paul McLeod, Jim MacPherson, Ian Marshall, Samuel Martin, Lawson Mayor, Mark Milbank, James Mitchell, Louis Moen, Adrian Morris, Anthony Morrissey, Geoffrey Myton, Colin Norton, Neil Okninski, Hugh Oxlade, Patrick Paul, M. Pawan, Greg Philp, Stephen Pickles, John Pitt, David Potter, Ramanan Raghavendran, Harry Reardon, Richard Reardon, Chris Rigby, Wayne Rimmer, Steve Robinson, Mark Sanderson, Abhijato Sensarma, Christopher Sharp, John Sleigh, Chris Smith, Matthew Stevenson, Peter Stone, Richard Stone, Richard Unwin, David Walsh, Rick Walton, Stephen Ward, Jakub Widlarz, Benedict Wiles.

WINNERS

Brian Carpenter 2012
Liam Cromar 2013
Peter Casterton 2014
Will Beaudouin 2015
John Pitt 2016

PECULIAR CRICKETING EDUCATIONS

Freaks of nurture

ROB SMYTH

Shortly before Christmas in Chennai, Joe Root put an old spin on a new theme. Cyclone Vardah had made net practice impossible before the Fifth Test against India, so Root – keen to hone his footwork against the seamers – opted for a concrete road near the M. A. Chidambaram Stadium. Using a pair of batting gloves for a wicket, he briefly revisited simpler times. "Something just clicked into place," he said. "To go back to being a kid again, and to remember what it's like to play on a street with your mates, why you love playing and why you first got into cricket – to park all the pressure and think about the game… that was nice." Two days later, on a different kind of road, he stroked a breezy 88.

As a child, Root developed his classical style in the back garden, where his father and brother threw balls at him. His physical limitations – he could barely get it off the square in his early teens – obliged him to concentrate on a solid technique: he knew he would have to bat a long time to make significant runs. "Whenever I went to practise," he said, "it was always about trying to be as technically correct as possible." *Plus ça change…*

Every player has a story about the influence of their upbringing on their cricket. Despite Andy Caddick's homage to the bowling action of Richard Hadlee, no two techniques are identical, and a cricketer's game is a window on his childhood. For all its status, the word of the MCC coaching manual has never been gospel – not least because many players developed everlasting idiosyncrasies long before they first received formal tuition. And if hitting a golf ball against a water tank with a stump was good enough for Don Bradman, the rest of us shouldn't be too sniffy.

The Telegraph
HOME | NEWS
Sport | Cricket
Cricket | Fixtures | Results | Tables | Kia Super League | Counties | International | The Ashes

'No nets? No problem': England practice in road as Cyclone Vardah disrupts preparation for fifth Test against India

Streetwise: Joe Root leaves the Chennai stadium after the nets became unplayable, December 2016.

A young Kevin Pietersen worked on his own urban coaching manual round the back of his home in Pietermaritzburg, particularly on an early version of his flamingo shot – back foot in the air as the ball disappears through midwicket. The confined space and bespoke rules (one-hand-one-bounce, out if you hit the wall on the full) meant Pietersen had to develop the wristy placement that became a trademark. Not long after Kevin's first Test, in 2005, Pietersen's father, Jannie, expressed disbelief that he had taken his backyard game into the Test arena. Yet the backyard, it turns out, is where many cricketers made their international debut.

Viv Richards would play out West Indies v England with his brother, Mervyn. Moeen Ali and his two brothers, Kadeer and Omar, enacted entire Tests in the garden. And Stuart Broad would pretend he was Glenn McGrath, Shane Warne or Matthew Hayden. "They were so successful," he said, demonstrating an affinity for Australians that has since waned. "They were winners." It was a telling insight into Broad's character, and his backyard tribute later became back-handed: his Australian toughness helped him become the only Englishman to be named Man of the Match in three Ashes-clinching victories.

> When Ben Stokes mastered the straight-drive, he was still in nappies

Steve Cannane's book *First Tests* details the unique circumstances in which many of Australia's greatest cricketers learned the game. It includes the story of how Greg Chappell developed his trademark flick off the hip. The leg side of his backyard pitch was full of fruit trees, protected by wire cages and doubling up as fielders. Chappell could hit the ball safely only between the citrus and the almonds; or, if you prefer, forward square leg and backward square leg.

The manipulation of space, both at the crease and between fielders, is so fundamental to batsmanship that it's no surprise many greats bore the stamp of their childhood. Gordon Greenidge, Sunil Gavaskar, Geoff Boycott and Ben Stokes all learned to play straight because of the narrowness of their improvised pitch. Greenidge practised on a 12ft-wide concrete strip between two houses, and Gavaskar in a similar area next to his family's apartment in Chikhalwadi, Maharashtra; such was his mastery of the shot, he even called one of his books *Straight Drive*. Boycott played in a T-junction in Fitzwilliam, with back gardens all around. "Anybody who hit the ball into a garden was out, no argument allowed, so we were pretty selective in our strokemaking," he said in his autobiography. "Psychologists can make of that what they will."

When he mastered the straight-drive, Stokes was wearing whites of a different kind: he was still in nappies. He wasn't even two when, in the tight hallway of his New Zealand home, armed with a plastic bat, he started rifling his dad Ged's underarm deliveries whence they came. "He was able to straight-drive the ball down the hallway without a problem, and was pulling the nappies up as he ran," said Ged. "He just seemed a natural." Stokes was not told to avoid the wall, but instinctively did so: "I couldn't talk, other than a bit of jibber-jabber, but I could hit a perfect straight-drive." Sure enough, the stroke was a startling feature of his maiden Test century, at Perth in 2013-14.

For a young Ricky Ponting, hitting the ball into one particular garden meant a fate worse than dismissal. "Like all kids we built the rules of cricket around the circumstances of our backyard," he wrote in *At the Close of Play*. "Over the fence was out, and God help you if the old man caught you wading into his prized vegetable patch to fetch a ball. He loved that garden and it lay in wait

Paving the way: on this Chennai strip, right-handers tend to eschew the steer to third man.

from point to long-on, ready to swallow a ball. Drew [Ponting's brother] reckons I mastered the art of hitting the ball over the garden and into the fence." Viv Richards had a different motivation for hitting the fence at the end of the garden – it counted as six. That fence created a world of misery for bowlers.

Others were less inclined to hit the ball in the air. Haseeb Hameed, who made his Test debut over the winter, aged 19, started learning the value of keeping the ball on the ground when he was just four. "Even now I can picture myself in the living-room, with the TV to my left and my dad sitting on the sofa right in front of me and throwing balls at me," he said in *The Daily Telegraph*. "I don't remember being told to keep the ball down, but it's a pretty natural thing to do if you've got things on the wall. I also remember I'd have a bat in one hand and throw the ball at the wall and do drills like giving myself room to drive over extra cover."

If the so-called Baby Boycott was born in the living-room, so was the Little Master. Sachin Tendulkar cut one side of a golf ball so that it was almost oval-shaped and got his aunt to throw it at him in the lounge. The ball would deviate sharply, and Tendulkar said his fear of breaking anything valuable helped him develop the Andrex-soft hands that were among his greatest qualities.

The need to manipulate space seems less obvious in bowling, yet many run-ups have evolved in unusual ways. South African fast bowler Morne Morkel's anti-clockwise twirl at the top of his mark came about because there was no additional room in the nets, while compatriot Makhaya Ntini went wide on the crease because his spikes clashed with the slabs of concrete at each end of the pitch in his home village of King William's Town. Lasith Malinga developed a round-arm action to make the ball skid on the beaches of Galle. Generations of Pakistan fast bowlers have learned the magic of reverse swing by playing tape-ball cricket. And Indian death-bowling specialist Jasprit Bumrah worked on the yorker to allow his mother her afternoon nap: if he hit the skirting board where the floor met the wall, it made scarcely a noise.

Bumrah improvised to create a blockhole; others have used their imagination to produce their own equipment. "Poverty is good for nothing," said the World Cup-winning Argentinian Jorge Valdano, "except perhaps for football." And cricket. Never mind jaffas: Trinidad's Sonny Ramadhin pioneered mystery spin by practising with limes and oranges; Yorkshire's Hedley Verity bowled with lumps of coal. Batsmen have used everything from a broomstick (W. G. Grace) to a coconut branch (Brian Lara). When Boycott says he could play a bowler with a stick of rhubarb, he may even be talking from experience.

Fred Spofforth would catch sparrows as they flew out of the hedge

As with all forms of education, not everything endures. Paul Collingwood became a bottom-handed player in spite of, not because of, his early experiences. "My first coach was Dad in the kitchen – the smallest kitchen-cum-dining-room you could imagine, about six yards across," he said. "He bowled at me with a sponge ball and I had to keep my left elbow up – though you'd never know it now – and hit through the V." Ian Botham was at school when he first made money from cricket. Mr Hibbert, the sports master, put a coin on a good length and said anyone who hit it could keep it. "I cleaned up," said Botham. But when he later became a golden-armed swing bowler, his boredom threshold was not so conducive to line and length.

In general, though, old habits die hard. Botham's old mate Richards ascribed his superb outfielding to throwing stones at lizards as a child, a pastime that would decide the first World Cup final, in 1975. Fred Spofforth, a superb short slip, had also made use of nature. As a youngster, he would get somebody to throw stones into a hedge, so he could catch the sparrows as they flew out.

Often the circumstances that influence a young player are beyond their control. Like Root, Alastair Cook developed a strong defensive technique because he did not have the power to hit boundaries. And the classical approach of Keith Miller, who was also small as a child, was not compromised even when he grew into a virile, unfettered six-hitter.

In the modern game, Generation Six deal in the brazenly unorthodox. Sam Billings, one of the foremost exponents of 360-degree batting in the English game, believes his multi-sport upbringing was a major factor in his development. "You look around the world and most of the top performers in all sports have played several different sports as a kid," he said. "There are so many things that culminate in you being good at one skill."

A. B. de Villiers is the most famous example, a jock of all trades and master of each and every one, while a young Jos Buttler started to work on his ramp shot after playing hockey: the ball ricocheted off another player's stick and on to the crossbar, making Buttler realise the potential for helping the ball on its way with the merest touch. Even sports with little in common can help each

Rough cut? Children in Melbourne make do with a tricky surface.

other. Billings has taken plenty from rugby: "Spacial awareness, foot movement, balance. Things you don't even think about, like throwing from the outfield when you're running full pelt and off balance. It's very similar to when you take a ball on the back foot in rugby and have to offload it."

His hand speed comes from a more obvious place – squash, tennis, and particularly rackets, a forerunner of squash that is played in a deeper court, with a harder ball, at almost demented speed. He was encouraged to play at Haileybury by his teacher Mike Cawdron, the former Gloucestershire and Northamptonshire all-rounder. "He was a massive influence on me. Historically, cricketers are very good at rackets because of the speed of the ball and the hand–eye co-ordination, so he tried to get as many of the cricketers playing it as possible."

School influences and mentors sit in the background, smiling proudly, throughout cricket history. Dennis Lillee attributes his never-ever-say-die attitude to a teacher called Ken Waters. In November 2016, Lillee put out a radio appeal to find him; the pair were reunited over the phone a few hours later. "The fierce determination in him rubbed off on me," said Lillee. "It wasn't just about playing the game, it was about winning. I hated losing tiddlywinks, I hated losing marbles. I ended up with thousands of marbles because I won most of my games. He was fantastic, and I owe him a lot."

The development of character through childhood cricket can be even more influential than technique. And nobody does mental disintegration like a sibling. De Villiers's brothers were six and nine years older, and believed in the toughest of brotherly love. If they couldn't get him out, they would happily bowl beamers. "My brothers were merciless," said AB. "They were monsters. There were always a lot of tears – usually mine."

Greg Chappell tells similar stories of being intimidated by Ian, a dynamic that worked out reasonably well for Australia. And the Waugh twins benefited from geology as well as biology: the unusual slope in their front garden helped both become ruthless off their pads, and might even have played some part in their Test records at Lord's, where Steve averaged 115 and Mark 80.

Steve Smith's ability against spin came from playing on uneven paving. His father would flick a softball in the back garden that would deviate sharply; the flower beds on either side represented fielders, and any ball entering them was out. Lara's status as one of the great players of slow bowling stemmed from batting against a rolled-up ball of foil; every time it hit his bare legs, he winced with pain.

There is a romance surrounding the idea of the street footballer. Few talk about street or garden cricketers, yet they are probably even more prevalent, such is the scope for quirks in batting and bowling. In cricket, technique is nurture's version of DNA. The details are unique to each player, yet each player can recognise another's experience. They are all freaks of nurture.

Rob Smyth is the author of Gentlemen and Sledgers: A History of the Ashes in 100 Quotations and Confrontations.

THE
Nightwatchman
THE WISDEN CRICKET QUARTERLY
WISDEN
MORE BRILLIANT CRICKET
WRITING FROM WISDEN
FOUR TIMES A YEAR
17
SPRING 2017
THE
Nightwatchman
WISDEN
www.thenightwatchman.net

PART TWO

The Wisden Review

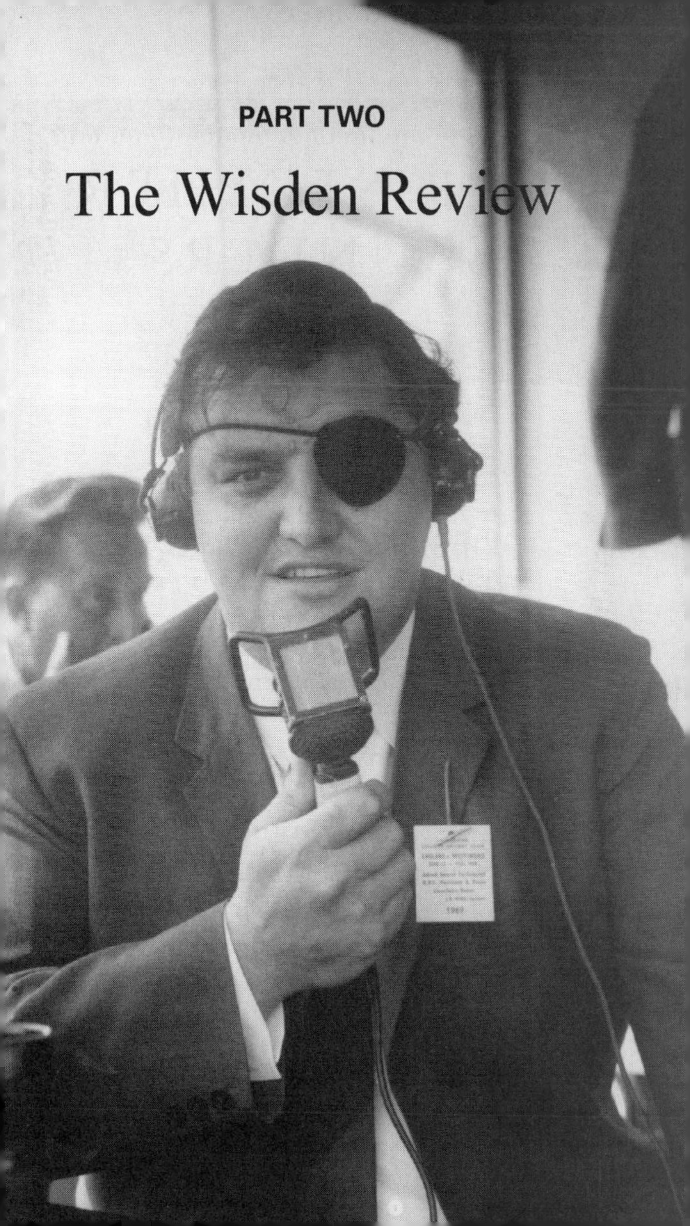

CRICKET BOOKS IN 2016

Friends, poems, countrymen

MARCUS BERKMANN

The boxes arrive and, within them, huge, unimaginable numbers of cricket books. Who said cricket publishing was dying? Clearly, no one told the writers or the publishers. The curious thing is that, while the 2016 season was still up and running, I found it very difficult to get through them. I think I managed two in about three months. And then the season came to an end, and I looked around for something to do, and there were all these wonderful books to read...

We begin with something suitably stately. A couple of years ago, Peter Oborne's history of Pakistani cricket, *Wounded Tiger*, was crowned *Wisden's* Book of the Year. Following this, after a fashion, is **White On Green**, credited to Richard Heller and Oborne, a collection of 40 unlinked essays on aspects of the Pakistan game not covered by the first book. Heller had helped Oborne with his research on *Wounded Tiger*, and his slightly fussier style is more in evidence this time round. But it isn't without interest: Heller and Oborne have interviewed many stalwarts of cricket in Pakistan, including Tauseef Ahmed, neither the first nor the last net bowler to find himself promoted to the national team on the whim of a captain.

Best of all is the famous match in December 1964 between Pakistan Railways, full to bursting with international talent, and Dera Ismail Khan, a sleepy town on the North-West Frontier famous for its dates and mangoes. Railways made 419 for two on the first day. On the second, they reached 825 for six. They declared early on the last, at 910 for six. Had they left it too late?

Possibly not. Dera Ismail Khan were all out for 32, followed on, and were all out for 27. They returned home, "thinking themselves fortunate that they had brought no travelling supporters and that the few scanty match reports had not mentioned their names". Fifty-two years later, one or two of the psychological wounds incurred that day may have started to heal.

Jon Hotten is another winner of the Book of the Year award, having lifted the title in 2016 for his collaboration with Simon Jones, *The Test*. He returns, alone, with **The Meaning Of Cricket**, his go at the why-do-we-love-this-crazy-game-so-much book. It's based on his blog, *The Old Batsman*, and thus has the slightly random, thrown-together feel of a load of articles without a strong theme. Hotten, though, is a lovely writer, who can say many of the same old things but somehow make them seem new. Here he is meditating on the time, long ago, when a team-mate, Simon Locke, took all ten wickets: "It's a melancholic feeling recalling that day, and the memory has a dreamlike quality. I wonder what happened to Simon Locke, and to everyone who played. Have they had good lives since then? I hope so. Nothing ties us except that game, but I doubt that anyone who played has forgotten it. And out there are thousands of people I have played cricket with and against in hundreds

of matches. Maybe we sometimes pass each other in the street without knowing."

Hotten is very good on Chris Gayle, whom he calls "the Bradman of T20". One in every nine deliveries Gayle has faced in T20 has been hit for six. One in nine! His book, the teasingly titled **Six Machine**, is nearly as much fun. Gayle is unencumbered by modesty, real or false. "Who wouldn't want to be me?" he asks on page 6. "Don't get me wrong. It's good fun being me," he adds two pages later. This could get tiresome, but there's an immense charm to the book, and time and again you find yourself laughing out loud at his sheer chutzpah. Gayle wanted to be a fast bowler, but "ended up doing spin because I couldn't be bothered running that far". Why is that no surprise? "The pitches you play on are different. When you're chatting up a girl on Jamaican soil, it's very different to chatting up an English girl." You never read that in Brian Statham's autobiography.

Perhaps paradoxically, Gayle emphasises how hard he has had to work to reach his current state of grace. It takes a lot of effort to look that effortless. Mark Nicholas, one gets the impression, has had an easier climb up the greasy pole. Captain of Hampshire in his mid-twenties – Trevor Jesty complained he had been passed over because he had only two initials to MCJ's three – he then progressed seamlessly into a TV and journalistic career that remains the envy of us all. Still unfeasibly young-looking at 59, and with all his own hair, he is the extrovert's extrovert, and it comes as a shock to learn he hasn't written a book before. But here it is. **A Beautiful Game: My Love Affair With Cricket** is a whopping great 400-pager, unghosted, and full of the stuff of Nicholas.

And what a curious book it is. Nicholas has got to the top by being authentically himself: a posh boy with a streak of vulgarity a mile wide. But he is also bright, and he has met everyone, and he has listened to what they said. His book comes in three sections: Playing the Game; Thinking about the Game; and Talking and Writing about the Game. The first and the third are a little dull. Like many broadcasters, Nicholas is prone to blandness as a writer. His signature phrase is "we got along famously". But the middle section is the goods. Years of playing and watching – and most importantly chatting with friends over a drink or two afterwards – have given him a wealth of insights into this impossible sport. He is particularly sound on the genius of his two most illustrious team-mates at Hampshire, Barry Richards and Malcolm Marshall. And he has many glorious stories to tell, a few of which he tells only once. Some ruthless blue pencil might have transformed an interesting book into a considerable one.

Team Mates is delightful. Edited by John Barclay and Stephen Chalke, in aid of the Arundel Castle Cricket Foundation, it's a collection of 27 pieces donated by cricket's great and good, each discussing a particular colleague. Mike Atherton nominates Angus Fraser ("his personal example was outstanding"), Chris Cowdrey ruminates on Alan Knott ("I am proud to be able to say he is my friend"), and so forth. As every essay commissioned had to be included, there are necessarily one or two duds. Indeed, the profusion of exclamation marks suggests the book has been lightly edited, if at all.

But for all its rough edges, this is an inspiring and deeply pleasurable piece of work. Mike Selvey, in one of the most engaging contributions, discusses Middlesex's pace attack of 1980: Wayne Daniel and Vintcent van der Bijl. The latter "reminded me, bizarrely, of what might happen if an upright piano was being shifted, got loose and started to run down a slope". As ever, most of the funniest pieces are by amateur cricketers. Actor Michael Simkins writes joyously about Stephen Isted: "Underneath this mild-mannered, portly, Clark Kent demeanour, there beat the heart and physique of Superman." And Charles Collingwood, better known as Brian Aldridge from *The Archers*, tells of the occasion when, trying to get a team together for The Stage, he reached the last name on his list: H. Pinter. Nervously he dialled the number at 8.30 on the morning of the match. After what seemed like an eternity, the receiver was lifted.

"Hello," a deep, husky voice said.

"Is that Harold Pinter?" ventured Collingwood.

"Yes."

With an audible tremor, Collingwood asked whether he would be free to play for The Stage against Richmond that afternoon.

"Fuck off," said Pinter, and hung up.

John Stern's **The Periodic Table of Cricket** is an odd one, if only because, unlike most of these books, it appears to be aimed at the casual fan rather than the dedicated loon. But are there any casual cricket fans these days? I haven't met one for years. Stern, a former editor of *The Wisden Cricketer*, takes the basic structure of the periodic table of elements, throws away the content and fills the gaping holes with his 114 favourite cricketers. He has divided them into five categories: Defenders & Pragmatists, Stylists & Entertainers, Mavericks & Rebels, Aggressors & Enforcers, Innovators & Pioneers.

It is, then, a long, drunken pub conversation turned into a nifty little hardback. H, for Hobbs rather than hydrogen, is No. 1 in his table, but No. 2 is

Hu (Hutton) rather than He (helium). This is a more entertaining book than it looks, because Stern brings a sharp intelligence and a perceptive eye to these pen portraits. Jacques Kallis had "the physique of a rugby No. 8 and the equable temperament of a surgeon". Inzamam-ul-Haq is "an advertisement for the larger gentleman". But I'm still not sure who is going to buy it, especially as the series style – other titles include wine, cocktails and hip hop – dictates that Stern's name, shamefully to my mind, is not found anywhere on the cover.

Andrew Murtagh's **Test of Character** is a biography of John Holder, one-time Hampshire fast bowler and, more famously, Test umpire, written very much with its subject's approval. Holder always seemed to me the calmest and most judicious of umpires, so it's strange to learn he stood in only 11 Tests. But this amiable, baggy book does him justice. Murtagh, uncle of Middlesex's Tim, clearly has a great fondness for his old friend – they played together for Hampshire Seconds in the late 1960s – and is still infuriated that Holder, genuinely quick in his day, had his action changed by the county's coaches, then hurt his back and had to retire. Holder himself doesn't seem to mind half as much. "The only constant in his topsy-turvy career was his smile," writes Murtagh. At one point he asks Holder how he got on with Ian Botham. "Absolutely fine," says John. "He was as good as gold. I used to greet him, 'Morning, Both. Why are you so ugly?' And he would reply, 'Morning, John. Why are you so black?'" And they would piss themselves laughing. You probably had to be there.

Holder and Murtagh are lovely about everybody. Even Roy Gilchrist, the beamer-bowling, wife-beating madman of a fast bowler who terrorised sides in the early 1960s, is gently described as "a loose cannon, liable to detonate at any moment". Jarrod Kimber, in **Test Cricket: The Unauthorised Biography**, is more straightforward – Gilchrist was "a shocking human being". Kimber is an Australian cricket tragic of the old school: this is his fourth book, and his fourth about cricket. It's a history of the game, in 63 shortish chapters, written in the terse, tabloidy style for which Kimber is renowned. Many sentences are short. Some are shorter. A few. Are. Very. Short. Indeed. I have to admit, this tends to grate after a while, but the judgments are sound, and the observations rarely less than original. "Murali would look at the pitch, find his line, and then just keep going until all the batsmen were gone." Kimber is alert to class differentials, racism and sexism in cricket; he's not a cosy writer. "There is a strong line of hard-as-nails Australian captains. Allan Border was made of the collective spittle of Australian disappointment." That's our quiz team-name for this week sorted: The Collective Spittle of Australian Disappointment.

That's our quiz team-name: The Collective Spittle of Australian Disappointment

Anyone who has ever doubted that Australians are fundamentally different from the rest of us should read their cricket books. **The Grade Cricketer**, by Dave Edwards, Sam Perry and Ian Higgins, is the faux memoir of a low-level Australian cricketer who used to be quite good as a 12-year-old, before puberty intervened. Having written a couple of books about village cricket myself, I have often felt uncomfortable reviewing the works of others on similar subjects.

If they're not as good as my books, who's going to believe me when I say so? And if they're as good or better, that's just annoying. But *The Grade Cricketer* is so strange and, I suspect, brilliant, that for once I must make an exception.

The unnamed narrator has spent ten years playing grade cricket with team-mates he alternately idolises and despises. While his brother, who was good at school, has just bought a new harbourside apartment, our friend is paying his Grade cricket registration fees in nine instalments. He has long since grown used to the idea that scoring runs and taking wickets matter less than the possession of a good "rig" (torso) and a decent grasp of *Anchorman* quotes. Thomas Keneally called it "the best cricket book in yonks" and, although you probably need to have lived in the southern hemisphere for an extended period to get all the jokes, its terrible bleakness lifts it right out of the general swim of things. "Most Grade cricketers have contemplated switching clubs at one stage or another. As humans, we have an inherent tendency to think the grass is greener on the other side. But all grass looks the same when you're standing on it for six fucking hours every Saturday, wondering what you're doing with your life."

Gideon Haigh named his cat after Victor Trumper. His 31st book, **Stroke Of Genius**, takes the famous photograph of Trumper about to play a booming straight-drive, and somehow builds a book around it. Haigh's problem, in his own words, is that Trumper is "an elusive historical figure". He left no memoirs or papers, gave almost no interviews, and died young. We don't really know what he was like, either as a person or as a cricketer, but we do know that for a few years at the beginning of the 20th century he was the best batsman in the world. And his sole legacy seems to be that photo, taken by George Beldam, the Middlesex cricketer, who pioneered action photography, and even invented the term. It's a characteristically bold venture, adorned by Haigh's elegant prose, but it feels like a slightly thin idea stretched further than it will naturally go. (As I know to my cost, you sometimes have to write the whole book before you realise it's not that good.) If we don't get to the heart of Trumper's gnomic personality, though, we at least get a couple of poems about him. This one was by Victor Daley, and was written in 1904:

Ho Statesmen, Patriots, Bards make way!
Your fame has sunk to zero:
For Victor Trumper is today
Our one Australian Hero.

It goes on for rather longer, but I think that'll do for now.

Ken Piesse's **A Pictorial History of Australian Test Cricket** is a coffee-table book, pure and simple, less for reading than for idly flicking through on a cold winter's afternoon. But it's nicely done, with an excellent selection of photos, postcards and magazine covers – few of which I had seen before – and Piesse's pithy prose linking it all up. This is his 51st cricket book, and I'm guessing not his first that doesn't like Bradman very much. The emphasis is primarily on Australia at home, and on Australia winning, which means we jump straight from England touring in 2002-03 to England touring in 2006-07, and losing badly both times. He does mention the intervening series a bit later, but only in passing, as though not wanting to linger on bad news. Seeing these unfamiliar photographs, you realise with a jolt that once, long ago, Dennis Lillee was very young indeed. Gideon Haigh's pic of Trumper turns up on page 55.

Back to Blighty for **The War of the White Roses**, Stuart Rayner's compelling account of Yorkshire cricket's civil war between 1968 and 1986. After winning the Championship for the 29th time, they embarked on nearly 20 years of madness, sacking their best players, making Geoffrey Boycott captain for eight seasons, and continuing to deny selection for anyone except native Tykes. Rayner was born halfway through this tale of woe, but writes with lip-smacking relish. Boycott's man-management skills are a frequent theme. Players would turn up to practise before a home match and the putative twelfth man would say to him, "Do I put on my bowling boots or my fielding boots?" (Meaning, am I twelfth man or not?) And Boycott would say "What's it to you?" and walk away without another word.

It's absolutely true: he doesn't give a monkey's

Graeme Fowler's *Fox On The Run*, published in 1988, has long been one of my favourite cricket books, an honest and intelligent account of a disastrous loss of form. Fowler was considering giving up the game in the mid-1980s, until he discovered he had been playing with a broken neck for seven years. **Absolutely Foxed** is a belated follow-up, and every bit as enjoyable. Reviewers sometimes look for the defining sentence, the one that makes sense of the whole book, and this one comes on page 232: "I've never bothered what people thought about me." It's absolutely true: he doesn't give a monkey's. Fowler is a complete one-off. He loved Derek Randall, my all-time favourite cricketer, whom he considered ill-used by the selectors, which he was, brutally. He writes superbly on two of his great friends in cricket, David Lloyd and Ian Botham. The thing about Bumble, he says, is that "whatever he's focused on at the time is the most important thing. If it was fly-fishing, everything in life would revolve around fly-fishing. If it was golf, everything would revolve around golf." When Lloyd left Lancashire, he worked for a double-glazing firm. When Fowler saw him, he was full of enthusiasm for his new job.

"It's brilliant. Windows? Everybody needs windows. Look around you, there's windows everywhere."

When Fowler saw him again a couple of months later, Bumble told him he'd jacked it in.

"What? You said everybody needs windows."

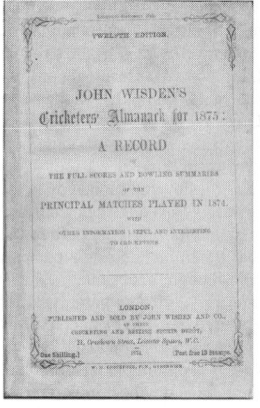

"They've all got 'em. Have a look round. Have you seen a space where there isn't a window?"

That seems wholly authentic to me.

Botham, as Sky viewers know, has become a bit of an old bore on screen, but Fowler writes about his boundless generosity, his love of life, his absolute sincerity and his unexpected sensitivity. In return, Sir Beef supplies a good and thoughtful foreword. "As a player, Foxy was one of the gutsiest I ever encountered… He made a dressing-room tick. His humour and wit were legendary." As this book testifies, they still are.

In recent years Fowler has suffered badly from depression. There's a seam of cricket publishing which one might call the Depression Memoir, in which an apparently cheerful player reveals he has spent the past nine months sitting in a chair staring at the wall. Fowler's book, happily, is much better and broader than that, and so too is Jonathan Trott's **Unguarded**. Having scored runs at will for four years, Trott came a cropper in the 2013-14 Ashes and flew home early, suffering from a "stress-related illness". Michael Vaughan put out a spectacularly nasty tweet suggesting everyone had been "conned" by Trott's breakdown, and there's clearly no love lost between them. "It's funny. Michael Vaughan and I both batted at No. 3 for England with reasonable success, but it is almost the only thing we have in common. I have a bald head and chipped teeth; he has new hair and suddenly has brilliant white teeth. I think that's a pretty reasonable reflection of our differing characters." I like that.

Actually, I like the whole book, not least because of Trott's wry humour. Shane Watson, you will be delighted to learn, is a bit thick. Trott doesn't think much of David Warner, either. "Maybe he's a great guy if you get to know him. Suffice to say, I haven't got to know him. I momentarily wonder if he was brought up in captivity and if it might be kinder to release him back into the wild."

Trott was among the more intense and driven of England batsmen, and his book, admirably ghosted by George Dobell, suggests he was lucky to last as long as he did. In South Africa his parents drove him relentlessly and, although he absolves them of blame, "between us, we created something of a monster". Like many cricket tragics, he has a bit of a thing about kit, and spent hours knocking in other people's bats as a child at his parents' sports shop. "It was instilled in me early on that, if you wanted something, you had to work for it." He was the only guy in the England dressing-room who could put a grip on a bat so it was an absolute fit. Alastair Cook always got him to do his. Trott asks: "Do you know how difficult it is to reach the top in international sport? And how difficult it is to stay there? … You have to be a bit of a mess to want it as badly as you need to if you're going to make it. There are some exceptions, but they are few and far between."

Ben Stokes may or may not be one of those exceptions. There's a freedom to the way he plays that can make you glad to be alive. Unfortunately his first memoir, **Firestarter**, is a waste of ink and paper. He is only 25, for goodness' sake; I have tins in the cupboard older than him. No cricketer under the age of 30 should be allowed to write – or even "write" – an autobiography. They have nothing to say, and far too many pages in which to say it.

AB: The Autobiography is longer and more serious, but it's just as boring. Whereas Stokes is hamstrung by youth, A. B. de Villiers has the more typically South African burden of extreme humility filtered through intense religious faith. "I am a Christian, a child of God. I strongly believe this book is not my story, it is the story of what God has planned and realised through me." Heavenly choirs sing out across every page. Everything is wonderful, and everyone is wonderful too. Jacques Kallis is the best all-rounder of all time; Graeme Smith led from the front; even Hansie Cronje only "erred in communicating with betting syndicates". And AB's hard work pays off, with century after century after century. It's all crucifyingly dull, although there is the welcome news that AB's oldest brother, Jan, is the owner of an "outstanding boutique guesthouse" called The Purple Trumpet. Hmm, wonder what type of person goes there.

Things could always be worse. Had I been in this chair a year ago, I should have had to deal with the tsunami of Richie Benaud memorial volumes, which, for a while at least, seemed the only books about cricket published anywhere in the world. This year there's just one, **Richie: The Man Behind The Legend**, a collection of 88 articles by friends and acquaintances telling us how marvellous he was. This may feel like about 80 more than we truly need, but there's a good spread here, from one or two nonagenarians who knew him when he was but a nipper, through cricketing colleagues from far and wide, to fellow journalists and commentators from the latter part of his long career. "A fierce competitor, but a charming and intelligent man," says Sir Garfield Sobers. "Richie led a full and creative life in which fear may have played a very minuscule, inconsequential part," says Greg Chappell. There are many good lines. On one occasion Glenn McGrath was out for two, and Richie noted that he was "just 98 runs short of his century". David Norrie recounts a conversation Richie had with Raman Subba Row, then chairman of the TCCB. Subba Row was worried there was too much Test cricket and wanted to know what could be done about it. Richie's suggestion: "Play less."

Bill Lawry, meanwhile, is outed as the man who nailed Richie's shoes to the floor of the SCG dressing-room in the early 1960s. And the many splendid photographs reveal something I hadn't spotted before: while on television he looked like a smallish man with a very large head, he was in fact a rather tall man with a surprisingly small head. The camera never lies.

A few years ago Patrick Ferriday and Dave Wilson gave us *Masterly Batting*, in which they put the 100 greatest Test innings in strict numerical order according to some complicated algorithm of their own making. They described it as "a fun exercise with a rigorously researched backbone", and the same might apply to the follow-up, **Supreme Bowling: 100 Great Test Performances**. How can you compare the incomparable? Actually, they explain how at some length, but the upshot is that Jim Laker's nine for 37 in the first innings at Manchester in 1956 is the 21st-best bowling performance ever, and his ten for 53 in the second innings is the 50th. The top five are as follows. Fifth: Devon Malcolm's nine for 57 at The Oval against South Africa in 1994 ("You guys are history!"). Fourth: Bob Willis's eight for 43 at Headingley against Australia in 1981. Third: Stuart Broad's eight for 15 at Trent Bridge against Australia in 2015. (Third best? Really?) Second: Harbhajan Singh's eight for 48 at Chennai against Australia in 2000-01. And first is Hugh Tayfield's nine for 113 at Johannesburg against England in 1956-57. Each performance from 100–51 gets a page, from 50–26 two pages, and for 25–1 you basically sit there and read about every ball individually. Very sensibly, Ferriday and Wilson – whose strengths may be more statistical than literary – have hired good writers to describe the top 25: Stephen Chalke is here, as is David Frith. The result is a monumental labour of love, which will make them no money at all: it's both completely pointless and oddly sublime. Only cricket could generate a book like this.

The result is a monumental labour of love, which will make them no money

As could surely be said of Brian Levison's **Remarkable Cricket Grounds**, which, in the grand Ronseal tradition, is a collection of photographs of remarkable cricket grounds. Lord's and the MCG are in there, of course, but so are Hambledon and the Parks. And Raby Castle in Staindrop, County Durham, whose pictures transport me to a place of immense inner calm and well-being. Levison admits he has watched cricket at only six of these venues; I will admit to having *played* at three: Blenheim Palace, the Hong Kong Cricket Club and Sir Paul Getty's ground at Wormsley (nought, nought not out and nought, should you be wondering.) The photos are spectacular; Levison's words are judicious; the whole is magnificent, and one of very few of these books I have actually kept.

I should explain. I live in a small flat that is full of teenagers and books. My cricket shelves groan and occasionally creak, so when I started this project I was determined to keep only the very best. The ones that make the cut are the

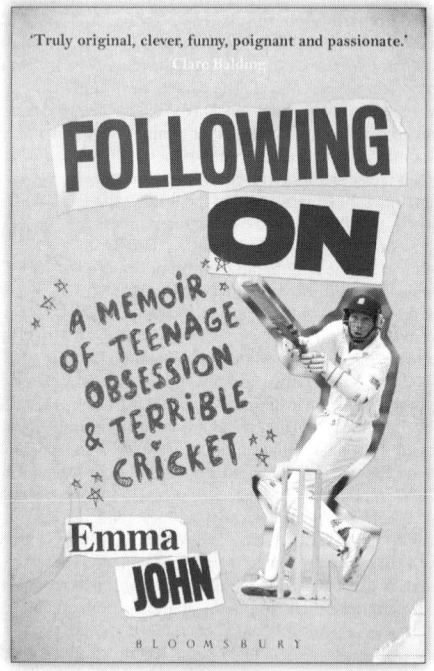

Levison, the Trott, the Fowler, the Nicholas (to my slight surprise), Barclay and Chalke's *Team Mates*, Hotten's *The Meaning Of Cricket*, and *The Grade Cricketer*. And one other, which was curiously the first of these books I read. I had been sent an advance copy of Emma John's **Following On** in the hope I would provide a nifty quote for the hardback. "Elegantly turned and strikingly perceptive," I said, and I think I was right. *Following On* is a cricketing memoir of the 1990s, when the teenage Emma followed the famously dismal England team with extraordinary passion. Twenty years on, she looks back on this lunacy with great warmth and wit, and interviews her favourite 11 cricketers from the era to find out what they made of it, too. When I read it in the spring, I was bowled over by its excellence. When I reread it in the autumn, I was thrilled to discover it was every bit as good as I had thought.

Following On was not widely reviewed. At the time of publication, Emma John was the deputy editor of the *Observer* magazine, and newspapers are often disinclined to review books by staff members of rivals. Their loss. Graeme Hick is "the kind of man who would get led into trouble by a wily village girl in a George Eliot novel". Angus Fraser bowled "with an air of modesty and exhaustion". Alec Stewart "held himself with the open-chested deportment of an off-duty soldier, and at 14 years old I instinctively understood, without even knowing the phrase, that this was a man's man". She's spot on so often, you simply have to marvel. "I am thrilled. My first encounter with Phil Tufnell, and he has a genuine hangover. He squints at the menu quietly for a long while, then asks for a sausage sandwich." Very occasionally, there might be a little too much about her adolescent angst, and the mind might begin to wander. But the quality of the writing is exceptional throughout, and her interviews with the cricketers are consistently insightful and unexpected. It wasn't a hard decision in the end. Emma John's *Following On* is *Wisden's* Book of the Year.

Marcus Berkmann is the author of several cricket books, including Rain Men, Zimmer Men *and* Ashes To Ashes. *He was one of three players in his team to end the 2016 season with a batting average of exactly nought.*

"Bowlers would have been forgiven phantom ailments on the way to Trent Bridge: seven of the ten worst figures in this year's competition were recorded at Cardus's lotus land for batting."

The Royal London One-Day Cup in 2016, page 683

WISDEN BOOK OF THE YEAR

Since 2003, *Wisden's* reviewer has selected a Book of the Year. The winners have been:

2003 *Bodyline Autopsy* by David Frith
2004 *No Coward Soul* by Stephen Chalke and Derek Hodgson
2005 *On and Off the Field* by Ed Smith
2006 *Ashes 2005* by Gideon Haigh
2007 *Brim Full of Passion* by Wasim Khan
2008 *Tom Cartwright: The Flame Still Burns* by Stephen Chalke
2009 *Sweet Summers: The Classic Cricket Writing of JM Kilburn* edited by Duncan Hamilton
2010 *Harold Larwood: The authorized biography of the world's fastest bowler* by Duncan Hamilton
2011 *The Cricketer's Progress: Meadowland to Mumbai* by Eric Midwinter
2012 *Fred Trueman: The Authorised Biography* by Chris Waters
2013 *Bookie Gambler Fixer Spy: A Journey to the Heart of Cricket's Underworld* by Ed Hawkins
2014 *Driving Ambition* by Andrew Strauss
2015 *Wounded Tiger: A History of Cricket in Pakistan* by Peter Oborne
2016 *The Test: My Life, and the Inside Story of the Greatest Ashes Series* by Simon Jones and Jon Hotten
2017 ***Following On: A memoir of teenage obsession and terrible cricket*** **by Emma John**

OTHER AWARDS

The Cricket Society Literary Award has been presented since 1970 to the author of the cricket book judged best of the year. The 2016 award, made by the Cricket Society in association with MCC, was won in April by Simon Lister for **Fire in Babylon: How the West Indies cricket team brought a people to its feet** (Yellow Jersey); he received £3,000. In June, Tim Lane and Elliot Cartledge won the cricket category at the British Sports Book Awards with **Chasing Shadows: The Life & Death of Peter Roebuck** (Hardie Grant).

BOOKS RECEIVED IN 2016

GENERAL

Allen, Dave **Forever Changes** Living with English County Cricket (Moyhill, paperback, £9.95)
Battersby, David **In the Shadow of Packer** England's Winter Tour of Pakistan and New Zealand 1977/78 Foreword by Bob Willis (Pitch, paperback, £12.99)
Bird, Jeffrey, and Woolley, Malcolm **1840 and all that** History and Reflections of Cowbridge Cricket Club (cowbridgecricket.co.uk)
Brooks, Tim **Cricket on the Continent** (Pitch, paperback, £12.99)
Cawkwell, Tim **Cricket's Pure Pleasure** The story of an extraordinary match: Middlesex v Yorkshire, September 2015 (Sforzinda Books, paperback, £8.90, ebook £3.50)
Dolman, Steve **In Their Own Words** Derbyshire Cricketers in Conversation Foreword by Wayne Madsen (Pitch, £16.99)
Drew, John **When Cricket First Came to India** (Cricket Wicket Press, paperback)
Ferriday, Patrick and Wilson, Dave, ed. **Supreme Bowling** 100 Great Test Performances (von Krumm, £15)
Fuller, John **All Wickets Great and Small** In search of Yorkshire's Grassroots Cricket (Pitch, paperback, £9.99)
Haigh, Gideon **Stroke Of Genius** Victor Trumper and the shot that changed cricket (Simon & Schuster, £18.99)
Hauser, Liam **A History of Test Cricket** The Story and Statistics of Every Test Playing Nation (New Holland, paperback, £16.99)
Heller, Richard and Oborne, Peter **White on Green** Celebrating the Drama of Pakistan Cricket (Simon & Schuster, £20)
Hill, Stephen, with Phillips, Barry **Somerset Cricketers 1882–1914** Foreword by Vic Marks (Halsgrove, £16.99)

Hotten, Jon **The Meaning of Cricket** Or, How to Waste Your Life on an Inconsequential Sport (Yellow Jersey, £12.99)
Kimber, Jarrod **Test Cricket** The Unauthorised Biography (Hardie Grant, paperback, £14.99)
Laughton, Tony **Bibliography of the works of Albert Craig, Cricket & Football Rhymester** (Boundary Books, limited edition of 75, paperback, £25)
Morgan, Roy **Real International Cricket** A History in One Hundred Scorecards (Pitch, paperback, £12.99)
Nicholls, Barry **The Test of the Century** The Story Behind 1977's Centenary Test Foreword by Rick McCosker (New Holland, paperback, £14.99)
Rayner, Stuart **The War of the White Roses** Yorkshire Cricket's Civil War 1968–1986 (Pitch, £17.99)
Rowe, Mark **The Summer Field** A History of English Cricket Since 1840 (ACS, paperback, £18)
Samson, Andrew **The Moon is Toast** A Year in The Life Of A Cricket Statistician (TSL Publications, £13.56)
Smith, Tom, with Grime, Ken **Boulder Rolling** The inside story of an extraordinary 2015 season (Max Books, paperback, £9)
Stern, John **The Periodic Table of Cricket** (Ebury Press, £9.99)
Suthar, Nihar **The Corridor of Uncertainty** How Cricket Mended a Torn Nation (Pitch, paperback, £9.99)
Tossell, David **The Girls of Summer** An Ashes Year with the England Women's Cricket Team Foreword by Charlotte Edwards (Pitch, paperback, £12.99)
Waterhouse, Ann **Cricket Made Simple** An Entertaining Introduction to the Game for Mums & Dads (Meyer & Meyer Sport, paperback, £6.95)

BIOGRAPHY

Booth, Keith and Booth, Jennifer **Rebel With A Cause** The Life and Times of Jack Crawford (Chequered Flag, paperback, £11.99)
Hudd, Gerald **John Jackson** The Nottinghamshire Foghorn (ACS, paperback, £14)
Murtagh, Andrew **Test of Character** The Story of John Holder, Fast Bowler and Test Match Umpire (Pitch, £18.99)
Musk, Stephen **George Pilch** His Day in the Sun (Red Rose Books, £7.95)
Potter, David **'Sivvy'** R. W. Sievwright – Arbroath, Forfarshire and Scotland – Scotland's Greatest Cricketer? Foreword by George Salmond (paperback, £7.99, more from david.potter@blueyonder.co.uk)
Senior, Darren **Lionel Palairet** Stylist 'Par Excellence' (ACS, paperback, £14)
Walmsley, Keith **Brief Candles 2** More One-Match Wonders (ACS, paperback, £14)

AUTOBIOGRAPHY

Best, Tino, with Wilson, Jack **Mind the Windows** My Story Foreword by Andrew Flintoff (John Blake, £18.99)
Butcher, Alan **The Good Murungu** A Cricket Tale of the Unexpected (Pitch, paperback, £12.99)
de Villiers, A. B. **AB** The Autobiography Foreword by Jonty Rhodes (Pan Macmillan, £18.99)
Fowler, Graeme, with Woodhouse, John **Absolutely Foxed** Foreword by Sir Ian Botham (Simon & Schuster, £18.99)
Gayle, Chris, with Fordyce, Tom **Six Machine** I Don't Like Cricket… I Love It (Viking, £16.99)
John, Emma **Following On** A memoir of teenage obsession and terrible cricket (Bloomsbury, £16.99)
Nicholas, Mark **A Beautiful Game** My Love Affair With Cricket (Allen & Unwin, £20)
Stokes, Ben with Gibson, Richard **Firestarter** Me, Cricket and the Heat of the Moment (Headline, £20)
Trott, Jonathan with Dobell, George **Unguarded** My Autobiography (Sphere, £20)
Yardy, Mike, with Talbot, Bruce **The Hard Yards** Highs and Lows of a Life in Cricket (Pitch, £18.99)
Younis Ahmed, with Booth, Keith **Lahore To London** (Chequered Flag, £20)

ANTHOLOGY

Barclay, John and Chalke, Stephen **Team Mates** (Fairfield Books, £15)
Tasker, Norman and Heads, Ian, ed. **Richie** The Man Behind the Legend Foreword by John Benaud (Pitch, £18.99)
Walker, Julian, ed. **The Roar of the Crowd** A Sporting Anthology (British Library, paperback, £12.99)

ILLUSTRATED

Bolloten, John **Shabash** A Season of Cricket in Inner-City Bradford (paperback, £7 plus p&p, more from johnbolloten.co.uk)
Levison, Brian **Remarkable Cricket Grounds** (Pavilion, £25)
Piesse, Ken **A Pictorial History of Australian Test Cricket** Foreword by Chris Rogers (Echo, $A50 plus p&p)

FICTION

Edwards, Dave, Perry, Sam and Higgins, Ian **The Grade Cricketer** (Melbourne Books, paperback, £23.50)
Haselhurst, Alan **Politically Cricket** (P&H, £20)
Pearson, Orlando **The Redacted Sherlock Holmes** Volume III (MX Publishing, paperback, £8.99)
Sengupta, Arunabha **Sherlock Holmes and the Birth of the Ashes** (Max Books, paperback, £6)

POETRY

Parker, R. T. A., ed. **Leg Avant** The New Poetry of Cricket (Crater Press, paperback, £8 plus p&p, more from richie_fire@hotmail.com)

STATISTICAL

Bailey, Philip, comp. **First-Class Cricket Matches 1951** (ACS, acscricket.com, paperback, £30)
Bryant, John, ed. **First-Class Matches Australia 2005/06 and 2006/07, South African Airways Provincial Challenge 2006/07** (ACS, paperback, £20)
Hawkes, Chris **World Cricket Records** (Carlton, £19.99)
Lawton Smith, Julian, ed. **The Minor Counties Championship 1910** and **1911** (ACS, paperback, £16 each)

HANDBOOKS AND ANNUALS

Bailey, Philip, ed. **ACS International Cricket Year Book 2016** (ACS, paperback, £30)
Brigham, Daniel, ed. **The Cricketers' Who's Who 2016** Foreword by Joe Root (Jellyfish Publishing, £19.99)
Bryant, John, ed. **ACS Overseas First-Class Annual 2016** (ACS, paperback, £65)
Full scorecards for first-class matches outside England in 2015-16.
Bryden, Colin, ed. **South African Cricket Annual 2016** (CSA, www.sacricketshop.co.za, R199.90 plus p&p)
Clayton, Howard, ed. **First-Class Counties Second Eleven Annual 2016** (ACS, paperback, £12)
Colliver, Lawrie, ed. **Australian Cricket Digest 2016-17** (paperback, $A30 plus p&p; more from lawrie.colliver@gmail.com)
Marshall, Ian, ed. **Playfair Cricket Annual 2016** (Headline, paperback, £8.99)
Payne, Francis and Smith, Ian, ed. **2016 New Zealand Cricket Almanack** (Upstart Press, $NZ55)
Piesse, Ken, ed. **Pavilion** The annual magazine of the Australian Cricket Society ($A10 plus p&p)

REPRINTS AND UPDATES

Benaud, Richie & friends **Remembering Richie** Foreword by Michael Parkinson (Hodder, paperback, £9.99)
Berry, Scyld **Cricket: The Game of Life** Every reason to celebrate (Hodder, paperback, £10.99)
Flintoff, Andrew, with Smith, Ed **Second Innings** My Sporting Life (Hodder, paperback, £10.99)
Jones, Simon, and Hotten, Jon **The Test** My Life, and the Inside Story of the Greatest Ashes Series (Yellow Jersey, £9.99)
Ward, Andrew **Cricket's Strangest Matches** (Portico, paperback, £7.99).

PERIODICALS

All Out Cricket (monthly) ed. Phil Walker (PCA Management/TriNorth, £4.25 (£2.99 digital); £44.99 for 12 print issues, £29.99 digital. Subscriptions: alloutcricket.com)
The Cricketer (monthly) ed. Simon Hughes (The Cricketer Publishing, £4.95; £44.99 for 12 print issues, £44.99 digital, £49.99 print & digital. Subscriptions: www.thecricketer.com or ring 0844 815 0864)
The Cricket Paper (weekly) ed. David Emery (Greenways Publishing, £1.50; £20 for ten issues inc p&p, from www.thecricketpaper.com)
The Cricket Statistician (quarterly) ed. Simon Sweetman (ACS, £3 to non-members)
The Journal of the Cricket Society (twice yearly) (from D. Seymour, 13 Ewhurst Road, Crofton Park, London, SE4 1AG, £5 to non-members)

CRICKET IN THE MEDIA IN 2016

Goodbye to all that

BARNEY RONAY

This was the year the big newspaper beasts began, finally, to shuffle off the reservation – though not without the odd snort and grizzle, a last bare of the teeth. The role of all-seeing cricket correspondent dates back to the bloom of the popular press in the early 20th century, from the writerly stylings of Neville Cardus to the recent vogue for muscular scribes, often ex-pros, embedded year-round with the itinerant juggernaut of the England team.

Like all alpha species, the correspondent remains vulnerable to changes in his environment, not least the dying back of column inches, indeed of newspapers themselves. In 2016 came the departure of Mike Selvey after three decades as cricket correspondent of *The Guardian*. Stephen Brenkley, who had been at *The Independent* and its Sunday title for 18 years, was another victim. Steve James of Glamorgan and England, a fine writer on cricket and rugby, was squeezed out of *The Daily Telegraph* in a shake-up that saw ex-footballer Ryan Giggs hired to speak his brains in a weekly ghosted column. In January 2017, James made his way back into the fold

Bowing out: Mike Selvey wins the ECB Special Award at the PCA dinner, in September 2016.

when he was appointed deputy cricket correspondent of *The Times*, to replace Richard Hobson, who quit after 19 years. And back in November, Gideon Brooks, cricket correspondent of the *Daily Express*, had been temporarily reassigned to cover Premier League football instead of England's Test tour of India.

Selvey's 31 years at *The Guardian* are unlikely to be matched, and few have written with such journalist–practitioner clarity, or such beauty, about the art of seam and swing bowling. As Vic Marks put it in *The Observer*, Selvey was "always an independent soul, reluctant to follow the pack, especially if they were heading for a press conference". Fittingly, his final pieces came from his old team Middlesex's Championship triumph at Lord's – from Nick Gubbins's first-day knock ("grittier than an egg sandwich on a windblown beach") to an improbable hat-trick for Toby Roland-Jones.

A brilliantly lyrical long-form Brathwaite riff

All told Brenkley spent 41 years as a newspaper cricket writer. He was once hung on a coat-hook by an enraged Ian Botham. Later he was throttled across a dinner table by an enraged ECB chairman Giles Clarke. Both incidents suggest a journalist asking the right questions. Brenkley's final report – a characteristically zesty account of West Indies' World Twenty20 triumph – ended with what might have been a cryptic farewell: "This could be the start of something. The moment must be seized."

It is a fair assessment on many fronts. "Lack of newspaper content reflects an uncomfortable reality about the growing unpopularity of a game I have loved all my life," wrote media sage Roy Greenslade in *The Guardian* during a gloomy June. Greenslade was responding to a stirring piece on ESPNcricinfo by David Hopps, who cited the cutbacks at regional newspapers and the move into largely unmonetised digital coverage. For all the valedictory notes, both Hopps and Greenslade pointed to the vibrancy of cricket writing among a younger, more footloose brand of freelancer, the pop-up correspondent who still scrutinises the details and picks out notes of beauty for websites, papers and magazines.

The World T20 in India was both the biggest event of the year, and an exception to Greenslade's rule. Mid-football season, it made the back pages of *The Sun*, *Daily Mirror* and *Daily Star*, as England were beaten in sensational fashion by West Indies. "Ben has a Waite problem," was the *Sun* headline, hailing "one of the most dramatic finishes ever to a cricket match" after Carlos Brathwaite spanked Ben Stokes for four sixes. On ESPNcricinfo, Jarrod Kimber produced a brilliantly lyrical long-form Brathwaite riff, strolling in cinematic, flashback-heavy detail through an extraordinary feat of hitting – blows that "couldn't have had more effect on England if he'd gone from player to player smashing them with his bat".

In *The Daily Telegraph* Jonathan Liew, one of the younger breed of highly skilled generalists, noted the binding effect of trauma and slur on West Indies' T20 travellers. "This is a team who have had enough of insults," he wrote, citing not just the inanity of their own board, but Mark Nicholas's suggestion in a pre-tournament column that they were "short on brains".

His own man: The *Independent's* cricket correspondent Stephen Brenkley in 2005.

Beyond the glory of the spectacle, it was notable how quickly Twenty20 reverted to being a source of anxiety. Simon Heffer cautioned in the *Telegraph* that "Test cricket must not be callously swept aside for the faddish appeal of Twenty20". Identifying himself as a "purist", and speaking out against the idea of a block of county T20 matches, Heffer pleaded: "Isn't it time someone took the lead in making cricket formally into two codes and setting about saving the first-class game in all its forms?"

The excellent Mike Atherton – destined, perhaps, to be the last of the big beasts – was more sanguine in *The Times*, calling for temperance over T20's moreish appeal: "Without careful strategic thought, there is a chance it could cannibalise everything else." On ESPNcricinfo, Ian Chappell went further, demanding the outright stigmatising of excessive six-hitting. "I liken six-craving fans to guys who frequent an establishment because the waitresses are topless," he counselled. "When another bar opens down the road... with waitresses who are even more skimpily attired, they quickly shift their patronage."

During England's traditional early-summer dismantling of some poor frozen unfortunates, James Anderson took ten for 45 against Sri Lanka at Leeds – a Lancastrian achievement welcomed with magnanimity by the *Yorkshire Post*, who still found something to grumble about. "It is difficult enough for Yorkshire to sell tickets for a Test match at Headingley in May," the paper tutted. "It is even more difficult when the opponents are as feeble as Sri Lanka."

The arrival of Pakistan and Mohammad Amir was a media event of a different kind. His failings had been exposed by a newspaper sting six years earlier, and he returned as both a victim and, more resoundingly, an unreconstructed villain. Above all, he presented a challenge of language. *The Guardian* noted the warm applause that greeted his first bowl of the tour. To the *Daily Mail* and the *Mirror* he remained "disgraced bowler Mohammad Amir".

It was a recurrent divergence of opinion. "Cricket cheat Mohammad Amir's return to Lord's sickens me – this match-fixer should have been banned for life," was both the headline and the gist of Graeme Swann's *Sun* column. Kevin Pietersen agreed in the *Telegraph*, where Liew pointed out that such "zero tolerance leaves nowhere else to go", and listed Amir's very real deprivations as a prisoner of the English justice system.

Alastair Cook continued to ease his way through the mature peaks of a thrillingly distinguished Test career, his 10,000th run at Chester-le-Street against Sri Lanka applauded in *The Sun* as a triumph for "England's quiet hero". "Opponents do not fear Cook," wrote John Etheridge, placing him in

RUGBY'S CRICKET-LOVING COACH

"We've got to play Bodyline"

CHRIS FOY

England's rugby revolution has had a strong cricket flavour. Their Australian coach Eddie Jones transformed the national team following the 2015 World Cup debacle (rugby and cricket have more in common than you might imagine), and admitted he was regularly inspired by his other sporting passion.

It was clear from his first press conference. When, in November 2015, Jones arrived at Twickenham as the new head coach, he was asked if he would continue beyond rugby's next World Cup, in 2019. "I will be 59 then, mate, and watching cricket in Barbados," he replied. "That is one of my dreams." The choice of location may reflect a relish for sun and sand, but there was also a sense that Jones's views of international cricket had been shaped decades ago. In his mind, West Indies' pace bowlers will for ever be cricket's dangermen.

A year later, he opted not to select Bath wing Semesa Rokoduguni to take on South Africa at Twickenham, saving him for a less daunting assignment against Fiji the following week. Jones explained: "Do you make your debut as a Test match batsman at the WACA against the Windies and four quicks, or on the flat track in Melbourne against spinners? You want to pick the right time to bring a player in."

From a young age, Jones played rugby and cricket with equal gusto – often on the same day. He was a handy batsman with grand ambitions. "I loved cricket and I wanted to play for Australia, but I just wasn't good enough," he told *Test Match Special* last summer. Growing up, he idolised the anti-establishment Ian Chappell.

Since taking charge of England, he has initiated inter-management cricket matches at the squad's Surrey HQ, and in July showed a sound technique when scoring 30 for an RFU XI against the rugby writers in Richmond. He has also enlisted the psychologist services of former England all-rounder Jeremy Snape. There have been tales of Jones wielding a bat and ball during training camps – aiming the ball at those he suspects of not paying attention, and lambasting them if they drop it. If that conveys a certain menace, cricket has also provided a template for his team's ferocity.

Before England faced Wales in the Six Nations last year, Jones said: "You go back to the great Ashes series. When have England won Test matches? When they've had two fast bowlers who want to rip every Aussie batsman's head off. To me, that's English sport. We need to be aggressive."

That mindset was given added substance when England travelled to Jones's home country for three internationals in June. He made it plain he wanted his players to smash the Wallabies with a Bodyline approach, showing them footage of the dismantling of Don Bradman and Co to ram home the message.

"Larwood and Jardine did something different," he said. "They neutralised Australia's greatest weapon. In terms of how we have to play, it will be exactly the same. We've got to play Bodyline. We've got to have a completely physical, aggressive team approach." It worked: England stormed to a historic 3–0 triumph. After the opening victory in Brisbane, Jones quipped: "It is very hard to play Bodyline with rugby. You can't put seven on the leg side and you can't bowl short – there wasn't enough grass on the wicket!"

The joker in him surfaces often. But he is deadly serious about his work – and that won't change, until the Barbados retirement plan takes effect.

Chris Foy is the rugby correspondent of the Daily Mail.

BT Sport

Sofa, so good: Greg James, Michael Vaughan, Ricky Ponting and Graeme Swann in the studio.

the second rank of top players. A few inches away, Swann disagreed. "I would class Alastair Cook as an all-time great," he wrote. "Those that don't appreciate how good he is just don't get the game."

Before they were duffed up in India, England's low point of the year had come in an alarmingly brittle collapse against Bangladesh in Mirpur. The *Mirror* called it an "extraordinary defeat… the worst collapse in Test history". The *Star* saw "a humiliating implosion" that would leave England "scarred". The *Sun* settled for "shocking and embarrassing". Amid a cacophony of doom, Alan Tyers in the *Telegraph* enjoyed Bob Willis's fury on Sky Sports. "In terms of cricketing disasters this is right at the top of the tree," Willis told viewers, raising the prospect of The Bob Willis Cricket Disaster Tree being an actual thing he keeps at home and gets down from the attic now and then.

One of the more intriguing turns on the airwaves was the appearance of Daniel Norcross on *Test Match Special*. Norcross was previously chief buccaneer of piratical internet interlopers *Test Match Sofa,* a slightly woozy backwater of cricket broadcasting that so angered the BBC's correspondent Jonathan Agnew in 2011 he was moved to froth on social media about commercial "predators". Fascinating, then, to hear Agnew and the genial Norcross broadcasting expertly in rotation. Agnew had an interesting summer, flying to Rio in August to commentate on horse dancing from a decommissioned military base in the dreaded Deodora Olympic Park. He simultaneously engaged in an unlikely blog-based feud with the heavyweight journalistPeter Oborne, who had objected to Agnew's absence from the national summer sport on the national broadcaster.

James Taylor also made his commentating bow, if in sad circumstances, after his retirement on health grounds. The *Independent on Sunday* noted that

Taylor made "an assured and thoughtful debut" in early July. As the summer wore on, the familiar challenge was to prevent a fascinating proximity to the current players becoming a corseting proximity to the current players.

TalkSport2 also arrived on the scene, and stepped in to take the vacant radio rights for England's one-day tour of Bangladesh after the BBC turned them down. Broadcasting live from a studio in Southwark, they had promised to "change the way cricket fans listen to the sport". Happily they did nothing of the kind, sounding reassuringly similar to the way cricket fans have always listened to the sport, though with more adverts for van hire and special offers on sacks of gravel.

On television, Sky Sports began, for the first time in a while, to feel the pinch, caused by the mind-boggling expenditure on football rights. Another popular voice disappeared, when the network's cricket news reporter Tim Abraham was recalled from India midway through England's tour, and made redundant.

BT Sport continued to intrude on the digital monopoly. Their first cricket broadcast was a gripping Test series win for South Africa in Australia. The BT studio saw Swann, Ricky Ponting and the ever-banterous Michael Vaughan lounging around on comfy sofas, helmed by the agreeably perky music and radio presenter Greg James. "Overnight highlight of the @btsportcricket coverage," James tweeted after the Second Test. "Aussie captain Steve Smith being hit in the goolies." Which is frankly a bit of a change from Peter West in a cardigan saying "Hello and welcome to Lord's."

Coverage of women's cricket continued to grow stealthily. Supriya Nair in the *Financial Times* noted the enthusiasm of the crowds at the Women's World T20, in a region where "barriers to entering the sporting system are dauntingly high for almost every woman". Selvey, meanwhile, took pleasure in the no-nonsense approach of the new England women's coach, Mark Robinson. He had given his charges "a harsh insight into the world of the professional cricketer", describing their performance during the semi-final defeat by Australia – while captain Charlotte Edwards sat next to him – as "dismal". "Some believe it was bizarre," wrote Selvey. "But it was, to be honest, rather refreshing." Edwards was soon forced to retire.

The concluding round of Championship matches, meanwhile, brought a bravura end to the season, with a rush to cover a finely poised set of games. "Alive and kicking," *The Sunday Times* concluded, seeing a "stunning climax" that proved the county game was "in rude health". In *The Observer*, Vic Marks wrote "suddenly county cricket is sexy", and talked hopefully of attracting a fresh audience. The final day of Middlesex's triumph at Lord's drew 555 words in the *Mirror* and 300 in *The Sun*, under the crunchy strap-line "Toby Treble Takes Title".

Returning to the yearly theme of departures and last things, cricket showed it does the newspaper obituary like nothing else. The death of Tony Cozier inspired a wonderfully warm farewell in *The Guardian*, remembering "the inimitable lilting tones of his commentary". Australian seamer Max Walker's obituary in the *Telegraph* had some knockabout moments, among them the revelation that he liked to use a "sticky brown fluid" to protect his hands while playing Tests. "I remember shaking hands with the Queen at Lord's," Walker recalled. "She had these white silk gloves on and I almost dragged the glove off her hand when I let go." Another major geopolitical incident narrowly avoided.

Barney Ronay is senior sportswriter for The Guardian.

CRICKET AND BLOGS IN 2016

The lie of the emotional landscape

BRIAN CARPENTER

People play and watch cricket; they read and write about it. But their relationship with the game often goes further. Simply doing these things is not enough; cricket compels its followers to live it, feel it and think about it in ways most games don't. No other sport provokes the same range of emotion. In 2016, blogs reflected the responses to cricket of people with backgrounds and experiences of the game as diverse as those blogs' design and content.

From Pembrokeshire, on the wild western fringes of the British game, Rick Walton's blog **cricketmanwales.com** reflects, in an urgent and compelling style that is one part Christian Ryan to three parts Simon Barnes, on his experiences as a coach for Cricket Wales and the game's role as a catalyst for personal development. Walton began 2016 captivated by England's performance at Newlands, and what it said about the value of Test cricket. As the year wore on, he deconstructed the essence of the retiring Brendon McCullum, revelled in the World Twenty20 and the denouement of the County Championship, and outlined the transformative power of cricket on the life of a west Walian boy called Dylan. It is clear that everyday life presents challenges that cricket has helped him confront and surmount. Of his performances on one tour, Walton wrote: "He scored 37 not out in our final game and smashed more boundaries than anyone else in our posse. He entertained us, with his beefy bludgeoning and his centrifugal anything-might-happenness. People cheered him on."

Of McCullum, meanwhile, Walton had this to say: "When Brendon connects, things fly. Our spirits have, the ball has. Though he has not gone, we should hoist him shoulder high; he's special, we needed him, he enriched us all. Whenever games get dull, or challenges remain unmet, or situations bleak, let's remember him, eh?"

Patrick Medhurst-Feeney's **thecrippledcricketer.wordpress.com** testifies to the sport's redemptive power. He plays most of his cricket for a Devon village club called Yelverton Bohemians, but his time away from the game is spent confronting the demons that are the legacy of active service in Afghanistan. The long posts reflect the difficulties faced by many ex-service personnel. In his case, though, exposure to the game is easing the pain. This is cricket as salvation.

As Walton and Medhurst-Feeney illustrate, cricket can be fun, inspiring and enriching. It can also change lives. Those of us who have followed it since childhood know this. But for others there is joy to be drawn from rediscovering its pleasures. Nick Brown, at **notesfromacricketnovice.wordpress.com**, spent last summer doing just that, although he had never watched the sport live, only in the distant days when it was on BBC television. The result was an observant

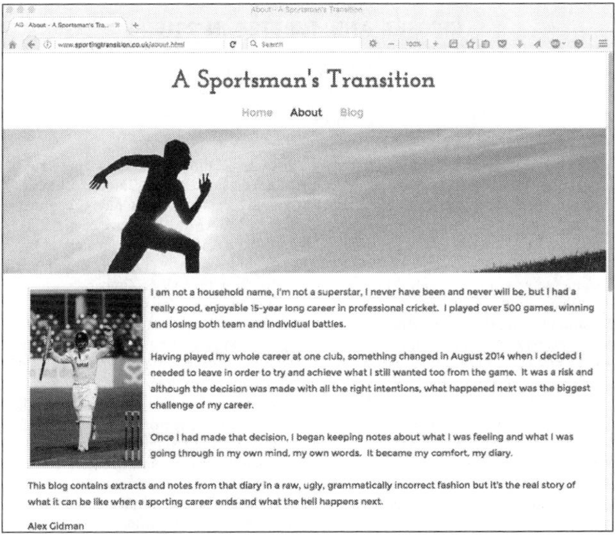

travelogue through the county game – mostly the sights and sounds of Old Trafford as Lancashire strove to stay in Division One, but also sleet at Edgbaston, rain at Lord's and blazing sun at Colwyn Bay, with side orders of football and punk rock. Before the year was out, Brown was at the WACA as Australia succumbed to South Africa – a reminder of how, when cricket gets you, it really gets you.

Further evidence came from Nick Slough (**newcrimsonrambler.wordpress.com**), who filled his boots with East Midlands cricket, and provided a ripe seam of ironic comment. From early-season visits to Trent Bridge ("cricket crowds are hardy organisms who, like lichen, can thrive in apparently inhospitable terrain") to a late-season visit to Grace Road by an ECB delegation, via the rise of Ben Duckett and the glorious autumn of Marcus Trescothick's career, to read Slough is to experience the perpetually threatened world of county cricket in all its understated glory.

Subash Jayaraman declared the innings of his innovative Couch Talk podcast closed, but his chief contribution to the blogosphere lay in exposing that an ESPNcricinfo column by former England batsman Ed Smith bore a strong resemblance to one previously published in *The Economist.* This illustrated how amateur observers, with sufficient confidence and determination, could boldly go where the mainstream – for reasons of loyalty, friendship or employment – may fear to tread. Jayaraman demonstrated that the strength of blogs remains the opportunity they give to anyone to write whatever they want,

CRICKET AND TWITTER IN 2016

Plenty to add

NISHANT JOSHI

Another year, another Twitter outburst by a cricketer. Calling your boss a "big idiot" is a ballsy move in any profession, and West Indies batsman Darren Bravo succumbed to a moment of madness after it emerged he would receive a lowly Grade C contract from his board. His target was board president Dave Cameron. "You have been failing 4 d last 4yrs," tweeted Bravo, showing none of the discipline that characterises his batting. "Y don't u resign and FYI I've neva been given an A contract. Big idiot." Cameron was unimpressed – and Bravo sent home from the tour of Zimbabwe.

When Bollywood mixes with cricket, the Twittersphere is assured of fireworks. During the World Twenty20, movie megastar Amitabh Bachchan provoked a strong response by tweeting: "With all due respects, it would be really worthy of an Indian commentator to speak more about our players than others all the time." An odd sentiment, you might think, while India were hosting a global tournament.

The follow-up, from M. S. Dhoni, came as a thunderbolt: "Nothing to add." It sounded innocuous, in keeping with the stoic, pursed-lipped approach to controversial topics and the magnolia dullness of his Twitter account, where he usually posts pictures of his many motorcycles. But when he lends his voice to any debate, it comes with the heft of five million followers. Through further cryptic tweets, it was clear Bachchan was talking about Harsha Bhogle, the well-respected commentator. Within weeks, Bhogle had been dropped from the IPL roster, apparently without explanation. Is it possible that two tweets turned the opinions of both the public and the broadcaster? The mystery has yet to be solved.

Meanwhile, Virat Kohli's on–off girlfriend Anushka Sharma, another Bollywood fixture, was subjected to vitriolic online abuse, seemingly triggered by Kohli's every dismissal and India's every loss. Was she a distraction? Did he lose concentration when she was at the game? According to many, it was all her fault. In March, Kohli took a stand, with a post shared over 40,000 times: "Shame on people for trolling @AnushkaSharma non-stop. Have some compassion. She has always only given me positivity." It was a welcome antidote to much of the bile.

The most optimistic tweet of the year went to Surrey Cricket, who were offering unpaid work on a drizzly day in May: "ICYMI [in case you missed it]: To win the chance to go out with the groundsmen and help work the pitch at tea time, simply tell us why it should be you." The worst prediction of the year came from Tim Bresnan, when West Indies needed 19 off the last over to beat England in the World Twenty20 final: "No chance for WI now. Stokes has been getting them in the hole. All tournament."

Others were concerned with weightier matters. After Donald Trump won the US election, Kevin Pietersen shouted: "NAIL ON HEAD! People are sick & tired of the generic, pompous, elitist bulls**t! Good luck to him!" And, as always, a special mention for Ravi Bopara, whose prediction about Leicester City winning football's Premier League came the day after they were crowned champions: "Have to say a big congrats to my 2nd best team for winning the PL. Leicester City. Knew we would do it."

Nishant Joshi tweets @AltCricket.

without the need to bow to an editor, a newspaper proprietor, or the commercial demands of a changing media environment.

The majority, though, are not written by people who earn their living through the game, or feel it slipping through their fingers. The nature of blogging – time-consuming and unpaid – means bloggers regularly fall by the wayside. But, as the 2017 English season begins, most of the writers featured here will be doing what they have always done because they choose to, and nobody has the power to stop them.

For players, things are different. In 2016, Alex Gidman, a long and distinguished career with Gloucestershire behind him, posted a series of raw and searingly honest extracts from a diary of the 2015 season, at **sportingtransition.co.uk**. Having joined Worcestershire, he found his career unravelling amid injuries and declining form. By the end of the season, at 34, his time was up. While Gidman knew what it was to leave first-class fields with applause ringing in his ears, a ghosted autobiography was never likely. But blogging gave him the chance to tell his story, which showed a recognition of the bleak place his career had come to, and an awareness of what he had lost.

As he said at the start of his diary, "being a sportsman of any type is every boy's dream, to do it and to have been successful is as good as it gets". But by season's end, things were very different: "It would seem that I'm just not good enough in the management's eyes to be in this team. I've had all my belief and confidence ripped away from me and, although I have developed very thick skin over the years and can take all sorts of criticism and disappointment, I had no idea what this feels like."

There is often regret in cricket's emotional landscape. In 2016, among the saddest stories was the premature retirement of James Taylor, because of a heart condition. At **chrispscricket.wordpress.com**, Chris Smith wrote that Taylor "would now be deprived of the heightened experience of cricket played at its most intense: duelling with fast bowlers, challenging fielders with aggressive running and steeling himself not to flinch when crouched close at short leg". The way in which Taylor coped with this was as moving as it was inspirational.

As the work of the greats shows, from Cardus and Ross to Haigh and beyond, a deep relationship with cricket has given rise to memorable writing. The web – sometimes for good, often for ill – has democratised the dissemination of opinion, opening up space in cricket's global chatroom for writing that touches on wider themes, of atmosphere, technique, the politics of selection, discovery and loss. Writing about cricket is a way of making sense of a complex and infatuating game; the world's bloggers continue to do this very well.

Brian Carpenter blogs at differentshadesofgreen.blogspot.com. In 2013, he was the inaugural winner of Wisden's *writing competition.*

RETIREMENTS IN 2016

Happy to be alive

STEVE JAMES

A career cut short always provokes sadness, but the retirement of **James Taylor** generated outright shock. In April, he turned up at Fenner's for the second day of Nottinghamshire against Cambridge MCCU. He experienced tightness in his chest during the warm-up, and his heart started to race. "I thought I was going to die," he said. By 5pm he was in hospital, where he remained for 16 days.

Taylor was diagnosed with a rare congenital heart condition (arrhythmogenic right ventricular cardiomyopathy) that can be managed but not cured. He underwent surgery to have an internal defibrillator fitted, but – at the age of 26 – his playing career was over. In truth, Taylor was fortunate: the condition is usually discovered post-mortem. "The outpouring of emotion was like I had died," he said. "But I was lucky enough to read the messages people sent to me."

The sadness was compounded by the timing. After something of a struggle – because of his stature (5ft 6in) and a bottom-handed technique that inevitably favoured the leg side – he finally appeared to be cracking international cricket. In 2015-16, he had played his part in England's Test victory in South Africa, where he had taken some stunning catches at short leg. He was such a

Julian Finney, Getty Images

Pulling up: James Taylor shone in South Africa before his early retirement.

determined cricketer, fleet-footed and apparently so fit, whether dancing down the pitch to spinners or scampering between the wickets. And he was a fine batsman: he averaged 46 in first-class cricket (with 20 centuries), and a remarkable 53 in one-day matches.

The retirement of **Andrew Gale** was sudden, too: in November, he replaced the departed Jason Gillespie as Yorkshire's coach. Gale made his Yorkshire debut in 2004, became captain from 2010, and led them to the Championship in 2014 and 2015, though the first triumph was marred by his absence at the denouement: he had been banned after an altercation with Lancashire's Ashwell Prince. He was a gritty left-hander, whose aggressive leadership was once admired by the England hierarchy.

By contrast, the departure of Australian left-hander **Chris Rogers** was entirely expected. He left Test cricket in 2015, and in 2016 very nearly captained Somerset, his fifth county, to their first Championship. He was an old-fashioned batsman – nuggety, watchful, always playing the ball late – and found a way to prosper in the muscular modern world. He finished with 25,470 first-class runs, including 76 centuries. Rogers played his first Test against India in 2008, and for many years it appeared that would be his last. But he returned for the 2013 Ashes and, in the fourth match, at Chester-le-Street, scored a maiden Test hundred. He spent 19 deliveries on 96 before getting there, demonstrating that nerves can affect anyone at any age (it was three weeks before his 36th birthday). Four of his five Test centuries came against England.

> He became Kent's rock, and led them to the Twenty20 Cup in 2007

Rob Key had been preparing to appear, as usual, for Kent, when he accepted an offer to work on Sky Sports' coverage of the World Twenty20 in India in March and April. It was clear he had found his next career: he is superb on television, combining technical expertise, wit and self-deprecation. Ruddy-cheeked and prone to carrying an extra pound or two, he was always among the most popular of cricketers. He became Kent's rock, playing for 18 seasons, captaining them for nine – in two spells – and leading them to the Twenty20 Cup in 2007. And he was not a bad batsman either. In first-class cricket he scored 19,419 runs, with 54 centuries and an average just over 40. He passed 1,000 first-class runs in a season seven times, his highest being 1,896 in 2004, when he also scored 221 against West Indies at Lord's. He played 15 Tests in all, but lost his place after the winter of 2004-05. You wonder how he might have fared later in his career, when he seemed more content and confident.

Graham Napier did not play international cricket, though he was part of the 2009 World T20 squad, and one of the first English players at the IPL. He also produced some stunning moments in 19 seasons at Essex – none more so than a 58-ball 152 not out against Sussex at Chelmsford in 2009, when he hit 16 sixes (then a record for T20 matches, since surpassed by Chris Gayle). He also equalled Andrew Symonds's 16 sixes in a first-class innings (another world record at the time) during an innings of 196 against Surrey in 2011 at Whitgift School. He was a slingy bowler and quicker than you expected – his yorker once surprised me – and he took four wickets in four balls in a 40-over match, again against Surrey, in 2013. He was an excellent county all-rounder, and finished on a high: his 63 Championship wickets helped Essex to promotion.

His colleague, the seamer **David Masters**, was another high-quality cricketer. He played 17 seasons at Kent, Leicestershire and finally Essex, taking 672 first-class wickets at 25. In 2011, aged 33, he claimed 93 at 18, including eight for ten to dismiss Leicestershire for 34 at Southend. He was the archetypal nagging medium-pacer, and his success was often held up as evidence of over-fruity pitches. This was unfair: there is considerable skill in hitting the right line and length time and again.

Hampshire's left-armer **James Tomlinson** did not have the statistics to match Masters – he took 382 first-class wickets at just under 32 – but deserves mention for his superb valedictory statement: "I would most like to thank the opposition batters, who for over a decade missed the straight ones and nicked the half-volleys… to you all I will be forever grateful!"

An old colleague of mine, **Dean Cosker**, the last active player from Glamorgan's 1997 Championship-winning side, also retired. He took 29 wickets that year, his second in senior cricket, and forged a long career from accurate left-arm spin and electric fielding at backward point.

Lewis Hatchett, a left-arm swing bowler for Sussex, retired on medical advice after six years and 72 first-class wickets. That he had enjoyed a professional career at all was remarkable: he lived with Poland Syndrome, which means he has neither a right pectoral muscle nor the two ribs that would normally sit behind it. Derbyshire wicketkeeper **Tom Poynton** also battled bravely: a car crash in 2014 killed his father and left him needing ankle surgery. In July, he decided the ankle could not stand up to the strain.

Alex Gidman retired in February 2016 after finding himself unable to flex his left index finger. He scored 11,622 first-class runs at 36, mainly for Gloucestershire, but with one final season with Worcestershire. He was especially strong on the leg side and was once considered for England's one-day team. Durham's **Gordon Muchall** was talented enough to be part of the ECB Academy side that went to Australia in 2002-03. But he never kicked on, and ended his career with an average of just under 30.

CAREER FIGURES

Players not expected to appear in county cricket in 2017

(minimum 40 first-class appearances)

BATTING

	M	I	NO	R	HS	100	Avge	1000r/season
Azhar Mahmood	176	274	32	7,703	204*	9	31.83	–
A. W. R. Barrow	40	67	5	1,201	88	0	19.37	–
G. Chapple	315	436	75	8,725	155	6	24.16	–
D. A. Cosker	248	329	96	3,444	69	0	14.78	–
W. J. Durston	109	188	28	5,346	151	6	33.41	1
A. W. Gale	156	245	17	8,211	272	20	36.01	2
A. P. R. Gidman	204	348	28	11,622	264	24	36.31	6
R. W. T. Key	299	517	37	19,419	270*	54	40.45	7
D. D. Masters	202	246	40	2,829	119	1	13.73	–
J. C. Mickleburgh	101	175	3	4,978	243	10	28.94	–
G. J. Muchall	163	282	17	7,947	219	14	29.98	2
J. K. H. Naik	77	118	29	1,888	109*	1	21.21	–
G. R. Napier	179	239	43	5,739	196	7	29.28	–
M. S. Panesar	219	270	87	1,536	46*	0	8.39	–
A. N. Petersen	226	388	19	14,765	286	42	40.01	2+2
T. Poynton	47	70	8	1,155	106	1	18.62	–
C. J. L. Rogers	313	554	40	25,470	319	76	49.55	9+2
T. C. Smith	107	160	25	3,972	128	3	29.42	–
J. W. A. Taylor	139	231	29	9,306	291	20	46.06	5
R. M. L. Taylor	44	75	11	1,461	101*	1	22.82	–
J. A. Tomlinson	129	162	73	945	51	0	10.61	–
D. J. Wainwright	81	114	28	2,270	109	3	26.39	–
M. A. Wallace	264	422	36	11,159	139	15	28.90	1

1+1 indicates one season in England and one overseas.

BOWLING

	R	W	BB	Avge	5I	10M	Ct/St
Azhar Mahmood	15,337	611	8-61	25.10	27	3	142
A. W. R. Barrow	36	1	1-4	36.00	–	–	71
G. Chapple	26,314	985	7-53	26.71	39	3	104
D. A. Cosker	21,683	597	6-91	36.31	12	1	150
W. J. Durston	4,751	119	6-109	39.92	4	–	113
A. W. Gale	238	1	1-33	238.00	–	–	49
A. P. R. Gidman	4,538	103	4-47	44.05	–	–	141
R. W. T. Key	331	3	2-31	110.33	–	–	154
D. D. Masters	16,905	672	8-10	25.15	31	–	60
J. C. Mickleburgh	50	0	0-4	–	–	–	71
G. J. Muchall	657	15	3-26	43.80	–	–	117
J. K. H. Naik	6,657	170	8-179	39.15	6	–	42
G. R. Napier	14,760	490	7-21	30.12	17	–	63
M. S. Panesar	22,135	709	7-60	31.22	39	6	44
A. N. Petersen	876	17	3-58	51.52	–	–	175
T. Poynton	96	2	2-96	48.00	–	–	107/10
C. J. L. Rogers	137	1	1-16	137.00	–	–	244
T. C. Smith	6,882	241	6-46	28.55	7	–	112
J. W. A. Taylor	176	0	0-2	–	–	–	91
R. M. L. Taylor	3,691	90	5-55	41.01	3	–	22
J. A. Tomlinson	12,196	382	8-46	31.92	12	1	27
D. J. Wainwright	6,991	181	6-33	38.62	6	–	28
M. A. Wallace	3	0	0-3	–	–	–	707/56

CRICKETANA IN 2016

To cap it all

MARCUS WILLIAMS

Vic Richardson, Herbert Sutcliffe, Victor Trumper, K. S. Ranjitsinhji, Archie Jackson, W. G. Grace, Gubby Allen, Fred Trueman, Dennis Lillee, Johnny Briggs, Colin Blythe.

That's a pretty handy Ashes XI, strong in batting and bowling, even if the spin department lacks a little variety: Briggs and Blythe were both left-armers. It's true there is no specialist wicketkeeper, but either Richardson or Grace could do a decent job behind the stumps. Of course, this side – whose careers spanned more than a century from 1864 to 1988 – never took the field. Yet the players are linked: various items of their memorabilia were offered in English salerooms during 2016.

Top scorer, in terms of price, was Richardson, whose Baggy Green from the 1932-33 Bodyline series made a remarkable £25,788 (this includes buyer's premium, as do all sums in these pages) at a Knights sale in Leicester. An Australian Test cap is always sought after by collectors, but its good condition, the presence of Richardson's handwritten name on the label inside, and the inexhaustible cachet of Bodyline all pushed bidding to new levels. Caps from this series have been sold before – those belonging to Clarrie Grimmett, Bert Oldfield and Bill Woodfull have gone under the hammer in Australia – but the record, set by Oldfield's back in 2000, had been just £15,000.

The premium that Bodyline commands was confirmed when a Baggy Green from a different era came up, but still belonging to one of the most celebrated figures of modern times. Dennis Lillee had given his cap, still in fine condition, to an English opponent of the 1970s, though in November at Graham Budd Auctions in London it changed hands for £8,470.

Back in May, several items once belonging to Herbert Sutcliffe were sold by Mullock's in Shropshire. They included a silver-cased travelling clock, also dating from Bodyline. It is inscribed "From Fergy" – Bill Ferguson, the Australian who was official scorer and baggage-master to this and many other touring teams for more than half a century. The clock, in full working order, sold for £491.

On the 1924-25 tour of Australia, Sutcliffe had amassed 734 runs in five Tests at an average of 81, reaching several landmarks on the way: the first to score a hundred in each innings of a Test against Australia, the first to make four hundreds in a series, and the first Englishman to hit three successive Test hundreds. His achievements were recognised by "A Few Yorkshire Admirers" with a silver-plated drinks tray, which went for £295. A larger item, an oak side-table canteen complete with set of silver cutlery, presented to Sutcliffe by Yorkshire in 1938 to commemorate his 100th century for them, realised £1,473.

Elsewhere, there came up for sale a signed photograph of Trumper at the wicket (Knights, £1,719) and, at Christie's in London, Ranji's palm-wood walking stick with gold band, previously owned by Henry Blofeld, plus six framed photos; the combined lot made £4,550. Archie Jackson, meanwhile, featured in a rare complete set of postcard-size photos of the 1930 Australian tour party, signed by each player; they fetched £4,175 at Knights. And one of Grace's bats – believed to have been used when he played for Gloucestershire against Surrey in 1872 – was sold by Anderson & Garland in Newcastle. Despite a fair bit of woodworm, it fetched £4,340, more than ten times the estimate. The bat had been given to George Strachan, one of Grace's team-mates against Surrey. In his obituary – Strachan died while in command of a Boer War concentration camp – *Wisden 1903* described him as "one of the finest all-round players in the world", particularly noted for his fielding. That 1872 summer, he had also turned out *for* Surrey, said to be the catalyst for the adoption the next year of an official system of county qualification.

Gubby Allen's Doulton Lambeth lemonade jug and two beakers, all decorated with vignettes of cricketers, made £1,167 at Knights, while a silver ashtray presented to Fred Trueman by Claude R. Harper – a racehorse owner and cricket lover who gave a dinner in honour of the 1953 Ashes-winning team – fetched £508 (Graham Budd). And a medal, complete with ribbon, awarded to Johnny Briggs for his feats in 1890, when he topped Lancashire's bowling averages (and was second in the batting), soared far in excess of its valuation to £3,316.

Mullock's

A great healer: the wounds caused by Bodyline mended eventually. This travelling clock belonged to Herbert Sutcliffe.

Last man in this eclectic team is Colin Blythe of Kent and England, whose navy blue cap from the 1901-02 tour of Australia realised £11,666, more than three times the estimate, again at Knights. It sported a small peak typical of the time, as well as the royal coat of arms, adopted by the captain, Archie MacLaren, as his team's colours. Blythe's cap is a rare memento of the last privately organised English tour of Australia. Two years later, MCC took charge and introduced the more familiar badge of St George and Dragon.

Bidding online – or at the end of a telephone – has long been an alternative to turning up in person, while websites such as eBay are an established part of the modern retail landscape. Christie's, however, had never run an online-only book sale before. One advantage over traditional printed catalogues is the option to run as much text and as many photographs as desired. After a disappointing sale earlier in the year – it coincided with a fall in financial confidence after the Brexit vote – Christie's felt an online auction devoted solely to cricket books, and not overshadowed by more expensive items, might attract more attention.

Their experienced cricket specialist, Rupert Neelands, was pleased with December's online sale, whose 65 lots included two runs of *Wisden*, as well as several more general titles. "We sold 80% of the lots, which is high in present times, for a total of £99,000 on the hammer price," he said. "We also got many new buyers. As a bidder, you have a greater sense of control than in the saleroom, where the auctioneer conducts everything. However, the disadvantage is that there is no historical record, and you don't get to meet your friends" – or, indeed, the chance to judge the competitiveness of your rivals!

While *Wisden* remains probably the most collected item in cricketana, it is currently a buyer's market. One indication of this was that a bound volume containing the 1872–1875 Almanacks, formerly part of the MCC collection, sold for £22,500, around 60% of what it had made in 2010. There are many editions available from specialist booksellers or on dedicated websites, such as Chris Ridler's wisdenauction.com, which last year received its three millionth hit since starting in 2008. In the last three years, Christie's have sold six sets of *Wisden*, even though their cricket sales are no longer routine.

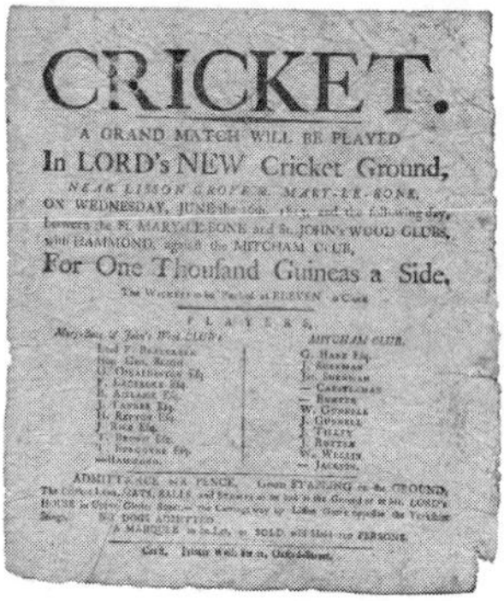

Knights

Quite a scrap: the buyer of this modest handbill paid almost £3,000.

The disappointing price paid for those 1870s editions does not necessarily mean that, when a rare or unusual *Wisden* is for sale, it is not snapped up. Last year a softback copy of the rare 1941 edition came on to the market. It was slightly battered – hardly surprising since it had been in the library of Oflag VII-B, an Allied prisoner of war camp in Bavaria. The book had belonged to Keith Jackson, who spent five years as a POW; at the time of his liberation, he made sure he liberated his *Wisden* too. Jackson, who died in 1997, played for Durham after the War, and took five Invincibles wickets at Sunderland in 1948. A bid of £540 gave his Almanack a new home in Taunton.

Since 1995, *Wisden* has been available in a numbered, leatherbound limited edition. Nos 1–5 are presented to the Five Cricketers of the Year, but in 2011 the editor, Scyld Berry, chose to name only four, on the grounds that the choice of the fifth was inappropriate because of the previous summer's spot-fixing scandal. In November, the unpresented No. 5 appeared on wisdenauction.com (where the 1941 softback had also been sold). There was interest from around the world, and the 49th and winning bid was for £3,100. The purchaser was from Dubai, and his prize reached him on Christmas Day.

The same website also oversaw the disposal of a complete run of 22 leatherbound *Wisdens*, stamped No. 7 – the second-lowest publicly available number – for £5,580. And the 1995 volume bearing No. 51 sold within 30 minutes for £2,200. (Since 1996, the limited edition has been capped at 150 copies, but in the first year the number was 100, making it more collectable.)

Scarcity has always been the major determinant of value and, in May, copies of *Wisden's* first two hardback editions, from 1896 and 1897, were up for sale at Chiswick Auctions in London. The books showed minor wear, but still went for £29,072.

The notion of a game of cricket for a vast prize is nothing new. In June 1813, the short-lived second Lord's Ground hosted a match between a Marylebone and St John's Wood XI, and a Mitcham XI. The purse was a scarcely believable 1,000 guineas (won by Mitcham). The first lot in Knights' February sale was a handbill for this game, which advertised "good stabling on the ground", and forbade dogs. It fetched £2,947. Almost 200 years later, in 2008, teams from England and the West Indies met in Antigua for the Allen Stanford Twenty20 for $20m match. A large batch of memorabilia from the occasion – including a T-shirt autographed by England coach Peter Moores and his 15-man squad, as well as caps signed by Andrew Flintoff and Kevin Pietersen – went under the hammer at Graham Budd Auctions. The lot made £218.

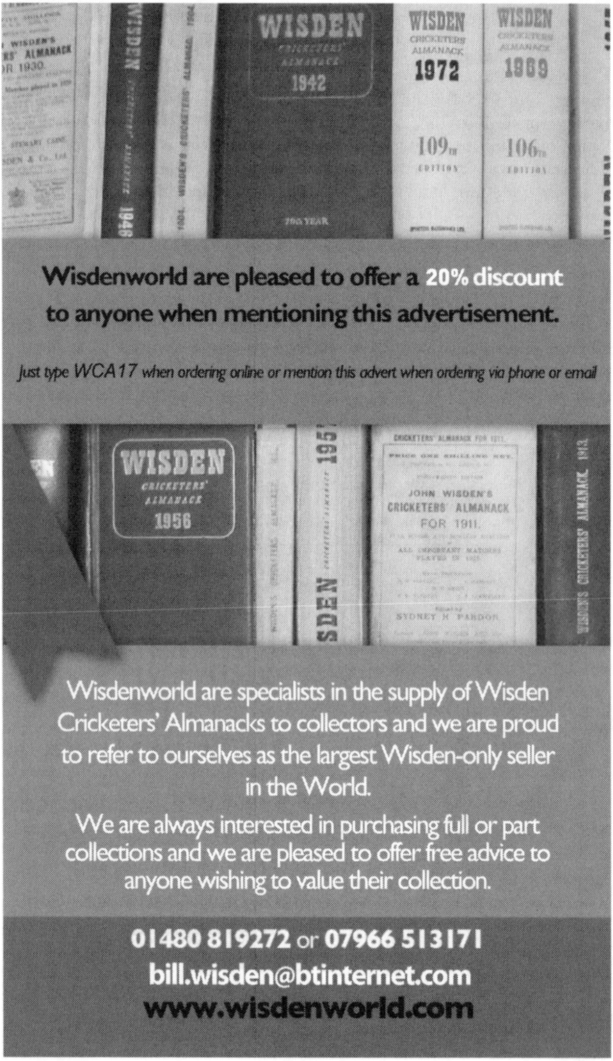
Wisdenworld are pleased to offer a 20% discount
to anyone when mentioning this advertisement.
Just type WCA17 when ordering online or mention this advert when ordering via phone or email
Wisdenworld are specialists in the supply of Wisden Cricketers' Almanacks to collectors and we are proud to refer to ourselves as the largest Wisden-only seller in the World.
We are always interested in purchasing full or part collections and we are pleased to offer free advice to anyone wishing to value their collection.
01480 819272 or 07966 513171
bill.wisden@btinternet.com
www.wisdenworld.com

CRICKET AND THE WEATHER IN 2016

The north wind doth blow

ANDREW HIGNELL

It was an El Niño year. An abnormal pattern of ocean currents develops off the coast of Peru, triggering major changes to rainfall in South America, and freak weather elsewhere. The jet streams – strong winds several miles above the earth – are disrupted, and in April 2016 these disturbances caused fronts to sweep in from the Atlantic. Then came an unseasonal blast of Arctic air. The essence of El Niño is that the unexpected becomes more likely, and on April 26 snow stopped play at Chester-le-Street, Edgbaston, Leicester, Derby and The Oval.

Last year also saw periods of intense rainfall. The matches between Worcestershire and Kent (at New Road in April), and Derbyshire and Northamptonshire (at Chesterfield in July), were both washed out, though drainage was also a factor. May 10 was especially wet: five Championship matches had no play. The Chesterfield washout partly explains why Northamptonshire and Derbyshire were two of the counties most badly affected in 2016. There is the possibility in 2017, when Championship fixtures dwindle from 16 to 14, that the weather could wreak even more damage to the fixture list – or the rain could whistle through on practice days... Overall, the playing time lost in the 2016 Championship increased by 94 hours, though some counties experienced less disruption than usual: Gloucestershire, Somerset and Lancashire were all relatively dry – thanks to that unpredictable little boy, El Niño.

HOURS LOST TO THE WEATHER IN THE 2016 CHAMPIONSHIP

	Home	*Away*	*2016*	*2015*	*Difference*
Derbyshire	**58.75**	19.50	78.25	46.75	**31.50**
Durham	41.75	**12.00**	53.75	**25.00**	28.75
Essex	21.00	19.75	40.75	58.00	–17.25
Glamorgan	32.50	12.25	44.75	61.75	–17.00
Gloucestershire	16.00	26.25	42.25	63.50	**–21.25**
Hampshire	32.00	31.50	63.50	34.25	29.25
Kent	26.50	53.75	80.25	59.00	21.25
Lancashire	17.50	13.50	**31.00**	52.25	**–21.25**
Leicestershire	35.25	25.75	61.00	49.75	11.25
Middlesex	30.75	33.50	64.25	43.75	20.50
Northamptonshire	36.50	**63.25**	**99.75**	**72.00**	27.75
Nottinghamshire	13.75	43.50	57.25	41.75	15.50
Somerset	**9.75**	47.50	57.25	42.25	15.00
Surrey	31.50	14.75	46.25	52.50	–6.25
Sussex	15.75	34.00	49.75	37.00	12.75
Warwickshire	49.25	16.50	65.75	54.00	11.75
Worcestershire	41.25	23.00	64.25	41.00	23.25
Yorkshire	18.00	37.50	55.50	33.00	22.50
Total	527.75	527.75	1055.50	867.50	188.00

CRICKET PEOPLE

Olympic spirit

JAMES GINGELL

In January 2011, the pavilion at Hightown Cricket Club burned down because of an electrical fault. They got by with Portakabins for two seasons, but it was a strain. A couple of years later, after they were relegated from the Liverpool & District Competition, a raft of senior players left.

In 2016, **Tatenda Taibu**, the former captain of Zimbabwe, came to Liverpool to write his autobiography away from the chaos of his home nation. But nearly four years after retiring from professional cricket he was itching for a game. Taibu searched online for a club, found Hightown St Mary's (they had changed their name after merging with nearby Crosby St Mary's), and asked if he could join. Initially, they thought it was a hoax, but asked for a reference, just to be sure. "I can get one of my former coaches," Taibu replied. "Like John Buchanan." That was enough to convince the club, and when they told Taibu of their recent difficulties, he identified with their fortitude. He felt nerves before his first game – he had not picked up a bat since July 2012 – but scored an unbeaten 61 out of 107, and finished the season averaging 50.

During the summer he was drawn to an even more challenging project: after repeated overtures, he became convenor of selectors for Zimbabwe Cricket. Tavengwa Mukuhlani, the chairman, told him he was the only candidate. "They had to look for a person trusted by the blacks, the whites and the Asians," says Taibu. "With me, it's easy. What you see is what you get." Taibu, now 33, splits his schedule between the UK and Zimbabwe, and admits it can be a stretch. But if his time is limited, his passion is not. He remembers, as a boy, driving through a provincial town with his mum and spotting Dave Houghton's Zimbabwe team washing cars to raise money for a tour. "I've always had that picture in my head when I think about where Zimbabwe cricket has come from." He's determined not to let their hard work go to waste.

"I had a very fast arm: they never took a single to me," says **Sunette Viljoen** of her time as a young cricketer in South Africa's North West province. Her arm was so potent, in fact, that it won her a silver medal for the javelin at the 2016 Olympics. Having come fourth in London four years previously, she felt catharsis. "When I stood on the Rio podium, I had tears in my eyes… just to be an Olympic medallist is so overwhelming."

Cricket had come earlier, though. She was the first girl from her school to play with the boys, earning their respect, before gaining the attention of the national selectors: at 17, she was picked for the 2000 World Cup in New Zealand. Viljoen contributed with bat and ball, including an unbeaten 54 that helped beat England in the group stages; South Africa made it to the semi-finals, where they lost to eventual winners Australia.

In 2002 she was offered a university athletics scholarship. But there was a dilemma. Over Skype, she demonstrates the difference between the javelin throw and the bowling action: where javelin throwers must remain tall as the arm comes over, bowlers have to force their weight down, with their knuckles plunging towards the grass. Her coach was unequivocal: the two were not compatible, and the cricket had to stop. "It was heartbreaking. But at that stage I wasn't sure you could make a living playing cricket."

With her silver medal safely pouched, Viljoen is keen to come back to her first love. Now 33, and playing club cricket again – for Randburg, just outside Johannesburg – she has half an eye on the World Cup in England in 2017 (a month before the World Championships in Athletics in London). "I have the ability; I have the belief. I will start at the lowest point and work up." Sometimes, she says, you just have to do the things you're passionate about. "My son loves it as well. He just wants his mum to play cricket again."

In 2006, **Scott Brooker** was working for Statistics New Zealand when the University of Canterbury alerted him to the opportunity of a PhD project in sport analytics, helping Dr Seamus Hogan build a computer program that could model a batsman's strategic nous in limited-overs games. Brooker signed up instantly. "He was crazy with his cricket history!" he says. "The amount he knew about stuff that happened before he was born was incredible."

One of the outcomes of their project was a tool called WASP (winning and score predictor), picked up by Sky Sports in 2012. During televised games, it forecasts first-innings totals, then quantifies the probability of the chasing team reaching their target: similar in purpose, then, to Duckworth/Lewis/Stern. The key difference is conceptual, which Brooker illustrates with an extreme case. "From time to time, a team will be doing well in their chase when the game gets interrupted," he says. "Under DLS, a new target score is set, but occasionally the chasing team are doing so well, they've already exceeded their target score." A stark example came in 2007-08, when New Zealand were 213 for six after 37 overs chasing 243 against England at Christchurch. After a rain delay, there were four overs left, but New Zealand had already overhauled their revised target of 180.

That scenario would be impossible under WASP, which Brooker believes makes it a fairer arbiter. "If a team had a 99% probability of winning before the break, WASP would set them a target that gave them a 99% chance of winning. Even if that was a ridiculously simple task, like ten off ten overs, WASP would still set them some task to give the fielding team a chance."

So could WASP replace DLS? "I'd love that to be the case," he says. "But this isn't something where the ICC will come knocking on my door and say: 'Hey, we want a new system.'" The program needs constant refinement and updates with the latest match data and rule changes. And, since Hogan died suddenly after a brain aneurysm in 2015, that has been solely Brooker's responsibility. "The biggest challenge is finding the time," he says. And that's far from easy: he is now head of business intelligence at Yellow New Zealand and has two young children. Even cricket must bow to that.

CRICKET IN THE COURTS IN 2016

The many arms of the law

FAN JAILED FOR FLYING WRONG FLAG

A Pakistani fan of Indian star Virat Kohli spent a month in jail – and was threatened with ten years – after hoisting the Indian flag from his house in honour of his hero. Umar Daraz, 22, was celebrating Kohli's match-winning innings in a one-day international against Australia on January 26. After his arrest, regional police officer Faisal Rana said Daraz had been charged with acting against Pakistan's sovereignty. "Daraz initially told us that he is a true Pakistani, but likes Kohli and never knew that was a crime," Rana said. However, he added that the action had been against Pakistan's ideology. Daraz was finally bailed on February 27.

DHONI AS GOD: NO CRIME, SAYS COURT

After more than three years, the Indian Supreme Court finally quashed an action to bring criminal proceedings against then Indian captain M. S. Dhoni, after he was portrayed on a magazine cover as the god Vishnu. In his eight hands were various products he endorsed, including a phone, a shoe and a packet of crisps. The artwork appeared on *Business Today* in April 2013. In 2015, the Karnataka High Court supported a petition filed by activist Jayakumar Hiremath, saying: "A celebrity and a cricketer like Dhoni should know the consequences of hurting religious sentiments… These celebrities only sign ads without any responsibility. Their aim is to earn easy money without considering the problems it may create." A year later, on September 5, the Supreme Court said the ruling was a breach of due process.

CLUB TREASURER STOLE FUNDS

Matthew Essex, the treasurer of Lascelles Hall CC in Huddersfield, pleaded guilty to stealing £20,000 from club funds. He was given a suspended prison sentence by Leeds Crown Court on June 28, and ordered to do 160 hours' community service.

CRICKET AND THE LAWS IN 2016

Through thick and thin

FRASER STEWART

MCC spent much of the year redrafting a new Code of the Laws, which will come into force on October 1, 2017. Unlike recent tweaks, which had occurred every few years since the launch of the 2000 Code, the latest version is a result of a thorough review of all 42 Laws, following a global consultation process with governing bodies and umpires. The proposed changes include limiting the edges and the depths of bats, combining obstructing the field and handled the ball into one dismissal, giving the umpires more powers to deal with player behaviour, and allowing catches and stumpings after the ball has struck a helmet worn by any fielder. And, for the first time, the Laws will be gender-neutral; previously, all wording had been male only, prefaced by a disclaimer saying it applied to females too. With participation and interest in women's cricket on the rise, this was felt to be an important shift.

The expanding size of the edges of bats prompted MCC to bring in limits. The world cricket committee publicly suggested the edge should be no thicker than 40mm, with the bat's overall depth set at 67mm. Others had suggested slightly less generous measurements, with edges of around 35mm, but the MCC committee will determine the final dimensions. There is scientific and statistical evidence to suggest that bats have become more powerful, although there are other factors – such as the style of play, better pitches and shorter boundaries. A full report on these issues is available on MCC's website.

The decision to merge obstructing the field and handled the ball followed plenty of discussion about whether handled the ball was little more than a form of obstruction. In 2013, MCC tried to draw a distinction between the two, limiting the timeframe within which a batsman could be given out handled the ball – while receiving the delivery, or in its immediate aftermath. The two will now come under the broad heading of obstructing the field, leaving cricket – pub-quiz setters, please note – with nine forms of dismissal.

Previously, a batsman could be not out if the ball touched the helmet of a fielder. But with helmets now being worn more widely at many levels of the game, MCC decided to treat them as a part of the fielder; equally, MCC did not want to put fielders off wearing them.

Cricket has changed greatly since the 2000 Code, and so has society, with leagues and governing bodies facing more disciplinary issues. MCC's global consultation in 2015 had seen a strong request from umpires for more powers, as the Laws currently allow punishments only *after* a match. Almost all other sports have procedures to remove players from the field. Many cricket leagues around the world have already introduced their own on-field disciplinary systems aimed at punishing and preventing poor behaviour. In 2016, MCC trialled their own system in three Premier Leagues and in matches between the

MCC Universities. The feedback from players and umpires was encouraging, and MCC are debating whether and how such a system could be enshrined within the Laws. In December 2016, MCC's world cricket committee called for sending-offs to be included in the Laws.

During the Test in Mirpur between Bangladesh and England in October, Chris Woakes was reprieved after being caught off a loopy leg-break from Sabbir Rahman. MCC's Laws currently draw a distinction between slow and non-slow full tosses. A slow ball will be legal if it passes, or would have passed, below the batsman's shoulders, judged on his standing upright at the crease; a non-slow ball must be below the waist. In Mirpur, the third umpire ruled that the ball was just above waist height, the point at which – under the ICC's playing conditions – a delivery of *any* speed is a no-ball. Because those playing conditions override the Laws, Woakes was given not out. MCC are amending this Law, with all non-pitching deliveries over waist height deemed unfair, regardless of pace.

Another controversy followed at Rajkot, where Joe Root was caught and bowled by India's Umesh Yadav. But Yadav quickly lost control of the ball as he attempted to throw it up in celebration, reminiscent of Herschelle Gibbs dropping Steve Waugh during the 1999 World Cup. Yadav made an attempt to catch the ball again, but failed. The relevant part of Law 19.4 states: "The act of making the catch… shall end when a fielder obtains complete control both over the ball and over his own movement." In slow motion, it looked as if Yadav had control for long enough to complete the catch, but in real time it was less clear.

The on-field umpires, Kumar Dharmasena and Chris Gaffaney, referred the decision to the third umpire, Rod Tucker, but gave a soft signal of out. The soft signal is used by the ICC for borderline dismissals, where officials indicate what their decision would have been if the game were not televised. Unless the third umpire has evidence to overturn their opinion, he will follow their guidance. At Rajkot, the on-field umpires' soft signal was key: had it been not out, Root would probably have survived. Instead, Dharmasena and Gaffaney must have been happy with their gut reaction, and so Tucker followed suit.

In November, South Africa captain Faf du Plessis was fined for unlawfully altering the condition of the ball during a Test against Australia in Hobart, after footage appeared to show him rubbing his finger directly on a sweet in his mouth, then rubbing the finger on the ball. Law 42.3 allows fielders to polish it, provided no artificial substance is used. Saliva is not artificial, but the residue from a sweet does breach this Law.

In 2016, MCC launched a Laws of Cricket app, which is free to download on most platforms. The app contains all the Laws, as well 15 animations explaining some of the more complicated ones, and a quiz to test the user's knowledge.

Fraser Stewart is Laws Manager at MCC. The Laws appear on MCC's website (www.lords.org/laws).

CRICKET AND THE THEATRE

When The Eye Has Gone

HUGH CHEVALLIER

> "By the way, this here's me namesake. Tell the nice people your name... He says he's shy... You don't have to be shy, Milburn. That's his name, see: 'Milburn'. From the early '60s in Northampton at the Abington, Ken Ball was the landlord – he was the one who named him."

"Milburn" is in fact a large – very large – gin and Coke, and he's the drink of choice of Colin Milburn, a large – very large – cricketer, whose life is the subject of a new play by Dougie Blaxland. These opening moments of *When The Eye Has Gone* set the scene: Milburn sits in the North Briton pub in Newton Aycliffe, County Durham, and the date is February 28, 1990, the day of his death. Over the next 75 minutes, the solitary drinker, with only his namesake for company, introduces the audience to an array of figures from his 48 years. His mum, dad, school friends, team-mates, fans, detractors, selectors and many more all make brief appearances. They have their influence, their part to play, but everything turns on one moment.

That moment is May 23, 1969, and Northamptonshire have just beaten the touring West Indians. Milburn hadn't done that much in the victory, but he was peering through the mist towards the peaks of greatness. A couple of months earlier, he had been parachuted into England's most recent Test, at Karachi, and made a century of real beauty. From nine Tests, his average was 46, and heading upwards: no one doubted he would open in the West Indies series. Time and again, he lit up the game with exhilarating, seemingly effortless, batting. As Viv Richards would in decades to come, he emptied bars with the unfettered joy of his strokeplay.

Trouble was, he could empty bars of drink, as well as drinkers. That May evening, he lost control of his car, and suffered life-changing injuries. The gods, who had given him the quickest of touches, in a split second ripped all the sight from his left eye and some from his right. There never had been a proper Plan B, and the tragedy – the word is overused, but it fits here like a pint pot in a thirsty hand – of the play is to see a gifted man drown in a sea of indecision. He barely fights against a tide that takes him towards self-annihilation, a journey punctuated by failed comebacks and measured by how many times he could deflect the question: "What are you going to do instead of cricket?" The grim answer was watch telly in an ever-darkening winter of the soul.

So it does not always make for easy watching, though the humour – and there's plenty of it – stays firmly on the right side of the mordant–mawkish divide. Nor can it have been an easy play to work on, since a one-man show always places a huge workload on a single pair of shoulders. Small budgets might have been a factor, though it is wholly justified on an artistic level. The

Sport & General, PA Photos

Lisa Hounsome Photography

Boycott and Milburn… Milburn and Milburn. England's openers walk out against West Indies at Lord's in 1966. Fifty years on, Dan Gaisford gives a poignant performance in *When The Eye Has Gone*.

action, for all its exhausting physicality, takes place essentially in Milburn's head, and it makes sense for the myriad characters, from E. W. Swanton to the consultant ophthalmologist, to be filtered through his imperfect lens. If there is an occasional blurring of characters, that isn't necessarily a fault in a play where the imagery of sight is never far beneath the surface.

The demands on Dan Gaisford are immense. Yet his restive energy, Blaxland's lively, conversational script, and taut direction from Shane Morgan all make light of his burden. Gaisford, it has to be said, looks nothing like the 19-stone Milburn; given how much movement is asked of him, that is no bad thing. A fat suit was considered, then ditched in favour of some discreet padding. It is the right choice: the audience connect with the poignancy of the drama partly because Milburn is an Everyman figure.

Blaxland is in fact James Graham-Brown, a former professional with Kent and Derbyshire, and a prolific writer, though this is his first play about cricket. His primary motivation was to help the Professional Cricketers' Association raise awareness – and funds – for their mental well-being initiative, though he has another connection with Milburn: he recently lost the sight of his right eye.

In November 2016, *When The Eye Has Gone* toured all 18 county grounds, plus a few other small venues. Many performances were sold out, and the reception for an inspired and courageous production was rightly enthusiastic, with countless standing ovations for an exhausted Gaisford.

Colin Milburn played nine Tests for England, hitting 654 runs – including two hundreds – at an average of 46. In May 1973, four years to the day after his accident, he returned to first-class cricket. In 28 more games for Northamptonshire, he reached 50 just once, and averaged 17. His last match, a ten-wicket defeat by Hampshire, was in July 1974; Milburn made two and eight.

OBITUARIES

AARON, SANDY, who died on April 26, aged 86, was a brisk inswing bowler and useful batsman who took five for 77 – and scored 69 runs for once out – on his Ranji Trophy debut for Kerala, against Andhra in January 1957. The following season he bowled respectably in three more matches – taking all the wickets, including future Test batsman M. L. Jaisimha, as Hyderabad slipped to 46 for three – but faded away. His brother, Leslie, played once for Kerala, in 1958-59.

ABDUL SATTAR EDHI, who died on July 8, aged 88, was a Pakistani humanitarian who set up several charitable organisations, including the world's largest free ambulance service. The BBC said he was "Pakistan's most respected figure, seen by some as almost a saint". Despite raising millions, Edhi continued to live in a small apartment adjoining his Foundation's offices in Karachi, and reportedly owned only two sets of clothes. The Pakistan team in England, which sported the Foundation's logo on their kit, observed a minute's silence before the tour match against Sussex, while former PCB chairman Najam Sethi suggested Lahore's Gaddafi Stadium be renamed after him.

ADISESH, LINGHANATHA THAMMAIAM, who died on November 19, aged 89, was a handy all-rounder who came close to Test selection for India in the early 1950s. After making 70 and 183 (entering at nought for two) for Mysore against Hyderabad at Bangalore in December 1951, he was called up for South Zone's match against the England tourists, and top-scored with 69 before being bowled by Derek Shackleton. The following season he made 87 against the Pakistanis, and was one of four South Zone players chosen for the tour of the West Indies – but all four pulled out, apparently bothered by the preponderance of West Zone names in the squad. He was not considered by India again. Adisesh moved to England to complete his medical studies, and played in the northern leagues, latterly for Liverpool.

AITKEN, ROBERT, died on May 16, aged 76. Usually known as "RA", Bobby Aitken was an unmistakable figure in Sydney club cricket for nearly three decades, mostly with Richie Benaud's old team Central Cumberland. He bowled off-spin with the aggression and glower of a fast bowler, and took 816 first-grade wickets, the sixth highest haul; he was also a useful batsman. However, he frequently ended up before the disciplinary committee; he should have played for New South Wales, but his temperament was seen as too combustible.

ALI, HAMZA SHABBIR, died on June 9 after an incident in the River Avon at Saltford, between Bristol and Bath. He was 20. An inquest – which returned a verdict of accidental death – was told that Ali, a non-swimmer, had been goaded into the water by two other youths, who stayed on the bank as he got into difficulties. Passers-by eventually managed to get him out, but he died the following morning. A seamer who had played limited-overs matches for Rawalpindi in Pakistan, Ali made his first-class debut for Hampshire against Cardiff MCCU two months before his death, taking two wickets; he had just joined the MCC cricket staff at Lord's. "He was an extremely talented young man and a beauty of a guy," said Hampshire team-mate Gareth Andrew.

ALLIN, THOMAS WILLIAM, died on January 4, aged 28, after jumping from the Torridge Bridge in Bideford, Devon. Tom Allin was a seamer who played one first-class match for Warwickshire. His mother told an inquest he had been through "a tough few months": several weeks earlier, he had been cut from his car after a head-on crash and, though his physical recovery was progressing well, he told a nurse his mood was "up and down". He was also concerned about his brother, who had been seriously ill. The inquest recorded a verdict of suicide. The son of Tony Allin, who took 44 wickets for Glamorgan in one summer of first-class cricket in 1976, Tom progressed through Devon's age-group teams, and made his Minor Counties debut against Wiltshire in 2007. By the following summer he was playing for Warwickshire's Second XI. He spent six years at Edgbaston, and made his first-team debut against Surrey in a 40-over game in August 2011. His single Championship appearance came against Middlesex in May 2013. He finished wicketless in both. Allin was released by Warwickshire in 2013, and returned to Devon, making one Minor Counties appearance in 2015. He played for North Devon in the Devon League, was involved in primary-school sports coaching in Barnstaple and Bideford, and was head of cricket at Shebbear College. "Such sad news to hear of Tom's passing," tweeted the England all-rounder Chris Woakes, a former team-mate at Edgbaston. "A great lad who always had a smile on his face."

ANWAR ELAHI, who died on October 19, aged 79, was a leg-spinner who played in the first Quaid-e-Azam Trophy match in Pakistan, for Sind against Bahawalpur (for whom Hanif Mohammad carried his bat) at Dacca in 1953-54. He played on for various teams until 1969-70, but never bettered his four for 64 on debut. His brother, Ikram Elahi, toured England in 1954 and West Indies in 1957-58 without winning a Test cap.

APPLEBY, EDGAR, who died on May 8, 2015, aged 84, was a bookseller in Keswick, in the Lake District, and president of the local cricket club. The shop's profits were not significantly harmed by his habit of discounting books – especially on cricket, where he specialised in overseas annuals – if the potential buyer could answer questions about the contents. Appleby was a sought-after speaker on a diverse range of subjects, including cricket, the sinking of the *Bismarck* and the *Titanic*, and the assassination of Archduke Franz Ferdinand. He recited his speeches without notes, having fine-tuned them on long walks with his otterhound, Hotspur.

ARMISHAW, CHRISTOPHER JOHN, died on March 12, aged 63. Seamer Chris Armishaw played five one-day games for Derbyshire in 1973, taking the wicket of Clive Radley with his first ball on the way to four for 31 on debut, against Middlesex at Chesterfield. But the other matches produced only one wicket, and he faded from the scene, remaining a feared opponent at Tutbury CC.

ARUNACHALAM, K. V., who died on September 13, aged 78, was an Indian umpire who stood in 15 Ranji Trophy matches between 1979-80 and 1991-92. Soon after, he called a one-ball over in a limited-overs game in Chennai, a mistake which probably affected the result of a close match; he quit umpiring immediately.

BAILEY, JAMES HENRY, died on April 10, aged 66. For many years Henry Bailey was the groundsman at Boland Park in Paarl, before handing over to his son, Rupert. He had been a keen player with the local Young People's club, and later their chairman. Former South African Test spinner Omar Henry remembered "a friend, club team-mate, colleague and phenomenal human being".

BAINDOOR, RANJAN, who died on April 4, aged 66, played 16 matches for Bombay from 1974-75, and was part of the team, captained by Sunil Gavaskar, which won the Ranji Trophy in 1983-84. That season he made 96 and 86 – his only two first-class fifties – in the semi-final against Haryana at the Wankhede Stadium. His off-breaks were also occasionally effective, and he took four for 32 against the Rest of India in the Irani Trophy at Delhi in October 1976. He became an administrator, and chairman of selectors for Mumbai Under-19s.

BANERJEE, SUBRATA, who died on August 19, aged 71, was a long-serving umpire from Kolkata who stood in 13 one-day internationals and 64 first-class matches in a career that stretched from 1967-68 (when he was only 22) to 2002-03. His father, Sunil, was also a first-class umpire, and officiated in a Test against England in 1963-64.

BANNISTER, JOHN DAVID, died on January 23, aged 85. Long after he had retired from playing, Jack Bannister was sometimes described as the most powerful man in English cricket. He was the mainstay of the players' trade union – now the Professional

Cricketers' Association – and later an influential journalist and broadcaster as well. And he performed important behind-the-scenes roles in the game's two great schisms in the 1970s and '80s – the Kerry Packer breakaway and the South African rebel tours. "Don't talk to that man," one old-fashioned county captain advised his players. "He's a communist." Given the third strand of his life, that seems highly improbable: Bannister built up a chain of betting shops before selling them, and was always a committed and clever punter. The word "shrewd" clung to him in just about everything he did: bowling, betting, broadcasting and being bolshie (if not exactly Bolshevik). He was a great talker off-air as well: "Argumentative, belligerent and stubborn," summed up his daughter Elaine, "but that was all part of his charm."

His cricket career contained one sensational performance, still enshrined in *Wisden*: he took all ten for 41 in a Warwickshire friendly against a far-from-hopeless Combined Services team in 1959. (He was immediately dropped.) Bannister's other 1,188 wickets – all but for 17 for Warwickshire – were harder won, and often came upwind. "Jack was sharp," recalled team-mate David Brown, "and he was a proper seam bowler. Line and length were paramount to him, and he hated to see anyone do anything else. When he bowled together with Tom Cartwright, you could see the two patches where they had both landed the thing." His boots were a particular source of wonder: "They were massive things. It wasn't that his feet were particularly large, it was just the boots. The soles would have been half an inch thick, and he'd knock metal spikes into them. The whiting got thicker and thicker. The laces went right up the shin. He had quite a high knee action, but how he lifted his feet no one knew." Bannister still had enough energy to nip off most evenings to the nearest greyhound track (most easily done in Taunton, where the dogs raced round the boundary).

Bob Thomas/Getty Images

Seam attack: Jack Bannister bowls for Warwickshire at Gloucester, July 1965.

He was a grammar-school boy with a mind that in another era might have taken him to a job in the City. Instead, towards the end of his career, he found part of his destiny in 1967 when his Warwickshire team-mates sent him to the first meeting of a putative body initially called the County Cricketers' Association. He was immediately elected treasurer, and became chairman a year later; after giving up cricket, he spent 19 years as secretary, and the strong-minded and well-funded PCA that exist 50 years on could never have happened without the persistence Bannister brought to the fledgling organisation.

"Jack was absolutely tireless," said his successor David Graveney. "The subscriptions were token, really, and there was no level of funding. But the game was Victorian in many of its attitudes. And Jack was willing to lobby whoever, however, whenever, to make people realise they had to join the modern world. Others later picked up the bat and ran with it. But he created the bat."

He also had great skills as a conciliator. When World Series Cricket split the game in 1977, both Bannister and the Association saw it as a grave threat to the members' interests. Dennis Amiss's decision to sign up was so contentious he was almost forced out of

Warwickshire; Bannister helped patch up the wounds. When other players joined rebel tours in South Africa in the 1980s, his position was more equivocal: he had always enjoyed being there himself; he was a friend of the tours' organiser Ali Bacher, and strongly opposed to the boycott in that period when South African cricket had reformed, but the country had not. Those closest to the PCA say he steered a careful course.

By now, he had also become a high-profile commentator. Mike Blair, sports editor of the small but well-regarded *Birmingham Post*, had talked him into becoming its cricket reporter, and he took over as *Wisden's* Warwickshire correspondent, from 1983 to 2001. Though Bannister was more fluent as a talker than a writer, his knowledge and contacts served the paper and the Almanack well, and the job gave him a springboard into broadcasting. He broke through the glass ceiling that normally stops non-Test players becoming *Test Match Special* summarisers, then did the same in the TV commentary box, where his Brummie tones, analytical gifts and light touch made him a favourite. His judgment was also respected in the press box. As one journalist explained: "If ever I had an off-the-wall thought, say that 200 all out on the first day was not as bad as it looked, I'd run the idea past Jack. If he didn't rubbish it instantly, I'd know I was on to something."

He was also a lively, if erratic, raconteur. His anecdotes about his contemporaries were often brilliant and adorned *Wisden* obituaries for many years. He could sometimes go on a bit, especially when misjudging the interest level in his latest round of golf: "Watch out!" one pressman would whisper. "He's in his when-I-got-to-the-fifth mood."

Bannister loved betting every bit as much as golf and cricket, but he was not infallible: he said himself he usually lost his 30-year sequence of tipping contests with Richie Benaud (see *Wisden 2016*, page 194) and at the halfway stage of the 1983 World Cup final rashly offered 100/1 against an Indian victory. He also loved the companionship of cricket, but the game overrode all that: in notional retirement, he would sit at home in Brecon and do score flashes on big matches for Talksport radio. Neither he nor the station ever said he was at the game – but then again they never said he wasn't. Listeners might just have picked up a hint the day he cried out: "Bessie! Get off the sofa!"

BARBOUR, BRIAN DOUGLAS, who died on December 5, 2014, aged 61, was an aggressive left-hander for Rhodesia (later Zimbabwe). He hit 97 on debut, against Transvaal in 1971-72 aged 18, and later made three centuries, the highest 106 against Natal at Bulawayo in March 1972. Probably his best-remembered innings came six years later at the Wanderers, where he joined Mike Procter at 81 for five against Eastern Province in the final of the Datsun Shield, South Africa's limited-overs competition. They put on an unbroken 135 – Procter made 102 and Barbour 57 – to secure Rhodesia's first title.

BENTLEY, WILLIAM LESLIE, died on May 26, aged 87. Les Bentley was Northamptonshire's head groundsman from 1979 to 1982, when his dismissal prompted a very public row. He had been recruited from Harrogate to replace Albert Lightfoot at Wantage Road, where the ground conditions "left a lot to be desired", according to the committee minutes in 1978. But club officials – notably secretary Ken Turner – did not see the improvements they were hoping for, issued an ultimatum to Bentley ahead of the 1982 season, and sacked him after an Under-19 Test against West Indies was played on a used pitch and finished before lunch on the third of four days. Northamptonshire were taken to an industrial tribunal, but Bentley lost, despite strong backing from Wayne Larkins, Peter Willey and former captain Jim Watts, who resigned from the committee over the affair. More recently, Bentley had been a popular groundsman at Northampton Saints CC, where he dispensed dry wit and cricketing wisdom from his corner near the scoreboard.

BHARGAV, KARAN, who died of dengue fever on April 18, aged 20, was a promising slow left-armer who had played for Punjab's junior teams. He took 33 wickets as the Under-19s reached the final of the Cooch Behar Trophy in 2014-15.

BHAT, NAYEEM QADIR, was one of five people shot dead by police on April 12 during an outbreak of violence in Handwara, 50 miles north of Srinagar in India, following demonstrations about the alleged molestation of a local schoolgirl. He was 22, and a dedicated cricketer who had been the first from his district, Kupwara, to attend a national Under-19 training camp. "Bring my Gavaskar back," beseeched his grieving mother.

BHATTACHARJEE, ALOKE, who died on December 24, aged 63, was an unorthodox spinner who took 134 wickets, mainly for Bengal, at an average of 22. After a sobering debut in 1970-71 – one for 150 in a Ranji Trophy semi-final against Bombay – he had to wait four seasons for his second game, but produced match figures of 12.2–6–11–10 as Assam were dismembered for 33 and 35. Dilip Doshi took six for six in the first innings, and Bhattacharjee seven for seven in the second – all bowled or lbw – which remained the best figures of a career stretching to 1986-87. "His stock delivery was a fastish leg-spinner which did not always turn, so was most deceptive," said his former team-mate Raju Mukherji. "Occasionally he would bowl off-spin with a similar wrist action but at a slightly slower pace, which could turn yards on Indian pitches. He was also by far the best Indian outfielder in the 1970s – he got a very raw deal from the selectors." Bhattacharjee could bat, too: he top-scored with 55 for East Zone against the 1979-80 Australian tourists. He became an umpire, standing in three men's one-day internationals, and the women's World Cup final in Kolkata in December 1997, and was later a Bengal selector.

BIRCH, BETTY DOROTHY, who died on September 20, aged 93, was a batsman – and fine fielder with a good throw from the deep – who played eight Tests for England in the 1950s, scoring 83 not out against New Zealand at Worcester in 1954, and 72 (also undefeated) in what turned out to be her last match, against Australia at Perth in 1957-58. She later taught PE at her old school, Lady Margaret in Parsons Green, west London.

BIRTWISTLE, IAN HOWARD, who died on March 19, aged 70, took more than 1,000 wickets over 30 years for Accrington from 1965 with his gentle swingers, 811 of them at 16 apiece in the Lancashire League. "Birty and I and a few others would net all day during the school holidays," remembered future England coach David Lloyd, a club team-mate. "Those swingers were slow – a touch of the Chris Harris or Jeremy Coney." Birtwistle's best two performances both came in 1988, when he trumped eight for 63 at Haslingden with eight for 49 against Ramsbottom.

CAMERON, DONALD JOHN, died on September 7, aged 83. Over four decades on *The New Zealand Herald*, Don Cameron became one of his country's most familiar sports journalists. DJ – as he was usually bylined – wrote about rugby and yachting, but was best known as the paper's cricket correspondent. He covered New Zealand cricket through its highs and more frequent lows, developing close friendships with many players, and was *Wisden's* New Zealand correspondent from 2000 to 2012. For ESPNcricinfo, he named John Wright as his favourite cricketer and wrote a fine appreciation of Richard Hadlee, who lacked, said Cameron, "the homespun warmth that New Zealanders seek in their sporting heroes". His books were mostly on rugby, but included *Caribbean Crusade*, an account of New Zealand's tour of the West Indies in 1971-72. He was a genial press-box companion, and unfailingly kind to young journalists who might be touring the country for the first time. And he loved Test cricket. In his report for *Wisden 2009*, on New Zealand v England at Hamilton, he wrote that "this game in the modest surroundings of Seddon Park may have seemed a minor, even nondescript affair. To the 23,500 spectators (perhaps half imported from England) it was a sheer joy – Test cricket restored to its legendary grace and traditional style, a match played under the sun, with old-fashioned gentlemanliness and never a hint of the churlish behaviour, the inquests and inquiries and bitterness, that have besmirched recent international cricket."

CANNINGS, VICTOR HENRY DOUGLAS, died on October 27, aged 97. Vic Cannings was a prolific new-ball partner for Derek Shackleton at Hampshire in the 1950s. They operated in tandem for ten summers, Cannings bowling slightly faster outswingers than

Catch-as-catch-can: Desmond Eagar and Vic Cannings teach slip fielding to Hampshire boys.

Shackleton's canny inswingers, and their accuracy drove opposing batsmen to distraction. "Derek and I were a great partnership in all sorts of ways," Cannings recalled. "Shack would be allowed one half-volley a season, and I would be allowed two."

He was a late starter, and took a circuitous route to play for his home county. His family moved from the village of Bighton to Farnham when he was in his teens, and he was recommended to Surrey, appearing for one of their junior teams alongside the Bedser twins. Playing for Farnham against a Surrey Club & Ground team, he bowled to Jack Hobbs. "Our umpire, a hairdresser in Farnham, reckoned I had him lbw and didn't appeal. But I don't think I did."

Cannings ruled himself out of county cricket, however, joining the Palestine Police in 1938 and serving with them throughout the war. There was no shortage of cricket: he played with or against Jim Laker, Lindsay Hassett, Norman Yardley and Bob Appleyard. When he came home he had trials with Hampshire, Middlesex and Glamorgan, but Hampshire couldn't afford a contract. Instead, recommended by a major who had been serving in Nazareth, he joined Warwickshire, completing the £5-a-week deal on Paddington station. He made an excellent start with 61 wickets in 1947, but competition for places at Edgbaston was stiff, and at the end of 1949 he did finally join Hampshire. He teamed up with Shackleton for the first time against Middlesex at Lord's and, after two days of rain, they shared six wickets in a total of 103. One of his victims was Denis Compton (bowled for four). "He was known as my rabbit," said Cannings. "I simply watched his feet when I ran up to bowl."

Cannings was a cheery, amiable man, but he took his cricket seriously: Hampshire wicketkeeper Leo Harrison considered him a more thoughtful bowler than Shackleton. For four successive summers from 1951 he passed 100 wickets, and in 1955, when Hampshire finished second in the Championship – then their highest position – he took 94 at 17. He always felt the team were held back by an inferiority complex.

He was 40 by the time he retired in 1959, after taking 834 wickets for Hampshire, eighth on their all-time list. Cannings was already an experienced coach from winter spells in

South Africa, Pakistan, Argentina and Trinidad, and was in the Caribbean when he received two letters in a week offering coaching roles at Eton and Tonbridge. He chose Eton, and stayed for 25 years as a kindly, sometimes eccentric, mentor to the likes of John Barclay and Matthew Fleming. He supervised Barclay's switch from seam to spin, although Barclay does not recall much technical advice. "You just bowl," he would say, "and they'll get out."

CARNILL, DENYS JOHN, who died on March 30, aged 90, captained the British hockey team at three Olympic Games, winning a bronze medal at the first, in Helsinki in 1952. Also a left-hand batsman and leg-spinner, he played Minor Counties cricket for Hertfordshire; entering at 73 for five against Norfolk at Lakenham in 1953, he hit 167 in an unbroken stand of 333 with Les Bateman. Carnill appeared in one first-class match while at Oxford University, against Free Foresters in 1950. He taught history and hockey at Dean Close School in Cheltenham.

CARR, DONALD BRYCE, OBE, who died on June 12, aged 89, spent 40 years at the heart of English cricket, acquiring a CV that may never be matched. He was captain of Oxford University, Derbyshire and, on one occasion, England. He was assistant secretary of MCC, secretary of the Test and County Cricket Board and the Cricket Council, and manager of two England tours. He attended the infamous selection meeting in 1968 that sparked the D'Oliveira Affair, and faced Kerry Packer across the High Court in 1977. Few in cricket have been so close to so much for so long.

It wasn't all plain sailing. In 1955-56, as captain of an MCC team in Pakistan, Carr was involved in a prank in which umpire Idris Baig was kidnapped and doused with buckets of water. A row ensued, and the tour was almost called off. Back home, Carr took the flak, though he emerged largely unscathed. "His reputation as a captain is such that he is better fitted than most to bear the blame," wrote Michael Melford in *The Daily Telegraph*.

His long years as an administrator tended to overshadow his career as a fluent, attractive batsman, and a bold, popular leader. Strong on the cut and pull, he relished fast bowling; short and nimble, he was swift between the wickets, and a brilliant close catcher. For Derbyshire, he formed a predatory leg trap with Alan Revill and Derek Morgan for the inswingers of Cliff Gladwin. He batted right-handed but bowled slow left-arm, orthodox at first, then a mixture of wrist-spin and chinamen.

Carr was born in Germany, where his father was serving in the army, and spent four years in India before returning to England with his mother and two brothers. His early passion for cricket was fuelled by trips to watch Hampshire at Bournemouth. It was there, aged six, that the Essex fast bowler Ken Farnes took pity on him after he was manhandled to the back of a queue for autographs. Farnes led him to the visitors' dressing-room, where Carr collected signatures and was given chocolates and orange squash.

His father left the army to become bursar at Repton School, establishing the family connection with Derbyshire. Donald captained Repton in 1944, and was selected to lead the Public Schools against a Lord's XI in a match interrupted when a German V1 flying bomb exploded just outside the ground. The players and umpires lay prone, but the game soon resumed. After Repton, Carr joined the army and was on camp in Kent one July morning in 1945 when he was called into the adjutant's office and told he was needed at Lord's to play for England in the Third Victory Test against the Australian Services. Carr joined two other teenagers making their first-class debuts, John Dewes and Luke White, in a team captained by 42-year-old Walter Hammond. "When I arrived in the dressing-room he looked straight through me," Carr told Stephen Chalke in 2006. "I think he thought I was carrying someone else's bag."

Carr walked out to bat in gloomy light after Keith Miller had bowled Len Hutton for 104. "Good luck, kid," said Miller, and bowled him third ball. That night the team went to a greyhound meeting at White City, with the three tyros placing Hammond's bets. "I had to collect his winnings," Carr recalled. "I think he got a couple of quid and gave me sixpence."

Donald Carr at The Oval in 1956. The Surrey keeper is Roy Swetman, and the slip Peter May.

He played for Derbyshire and Combined Services in 1946 but, after missing the following season because of an overseas posting, he left the army and went to Oxford in 1948. In the last of his three Varsity Matches, in 1951, he made 34 and 50 in a victory over a strong Cambridge side. He also won Blues for hockey and football, and was part of the Pegasus team that won two FA Amateur Cup finals at Wembley.

Carr had not realised his full potential until 1949, when he passed 1,000 first-class runs. After repeating the feat in 1950, and getting close in 1951, he was chosen as vice-captain to another amateur, Nigel Howard, in an understrength England team to play five Tests in India. While Howard fretted constantly about his health, Carr relished returning to the country of his youth. "I loved India," he said. "The people were so delighted to see you. The history was fascinating. I even liked the smells and all the beastliness."

He made his debut in the First Test in Delhi, contributing 76 to a five-hour match-saving partnership of 158 with Allan Watkins, but was dropped for the next three games as Howard, though clearly out of his depth, resisted suggestions he should stand down. With England 1–0 up, Howard succumbed to a temperature before the final Test, at Madras, and Carr took over. It was a notable occasion: the death of King George VI was announced at tea on the first day, and India achieved their first Test victory, at the 25th attempt. There was little triumphalism. "They were all very polite to us," said Carr. "They said the reason we had lost was because we were so upset that the King had died."

Carr's leadership qualities were not forgotten, and in 1955-56 he was asked to captain a youthful MCC A team on a hastily arranged tour of Pakistan. There were portents of what lay ahead at an early function, when Carr made a speech that included an anecdote about his former Oxford team-mate Abdul Hafeez Kardar, by now the Pakistan captain. Carr recalled how Kardar's Oxford nickname, "the mystic of the East", had been mistranslated as "the mistake of the East". Kardar was unamused.

Matters came to a head in Peshawar during the third representative match. Baig's umpiring had rankled with the MCC players throughout the tour, and they were incensed by four leg-before decisions in their first innings. On the evening before the rest day, Carr was one of a posse of players who took a pony and trap to the umpire's hotel, brought him back to their own, and soaked him with buckets of water in Billy Sutcliffe's room. Several eye-witnesses claimed Baig took it in good part – until two passing Pakistan players started laughing at him. Back at his hotel, and roused to outrage by Kardar, Baig's view changed. Next morning he had his arm in a sling, claiming that it had been twisted behind his back and that he had been gagged. Carr was playing squash when tour manager Geoffrey Howard approached him: "I think we've got a problem."

There were student demonstrations, troops despatched to protect the MCC tourists, and an exchange of telegrams between Karachi and St John's Wood. Journalists Crawford White (*News Chronicle*) and Brian Chapman (*Daily Mirror*) made sure the story was kept to the fore at home; it achieved enough exposure for the comedian Tommy Trinder to joke about it on television. Carr called MCC secretary Ronny Aird to accept responsibility, but saw it as little more than youthful exuberance. "Quite honestly, when I look back on the Peshawar incident I think it was about the funniest thing I have ever seen in my life," he told the MCC committee.

There was a happy postscript: in 1970 Carr managed an international team which flew to Karachi to raise funds for victims of cyclones in East Pakistan. Baig was put in charge of the match and greeted Carr warmly. As they chatted, the Warwickshire seamer David Brown appeared behind his manager with a bucket of water, and asked: "Would this help?"

Carr had become Derbyshire captain in 1955, and moulded them into an enterprising side. Sometimes his keenness to make a game of it went too far for his team-mates – they once locked him in the dressing-room to prevent an early declaration against Worcestershire. But he was popular. "He was equally at home having tea with the Duke and Duchess of Devonshire at Chatsworth House or drinking a pint in the miners' welfare," said one of his players. He was no soft touch, though. "He could be severe on people who were sloppy," recalled Bob Taylor. "I remember being told off in no uncertain terms when my lobs back to the bowler fell short." Carr led Derbyshire for eight seasons, and his best summer came in 1959, when he became their first player to score more than 2,000 runs in a season. He was named a *Wisden* Cricketer of the Year.

He became secretary of Derbyshire in 1960 and, after retiring as a player in 1962, assistant secretary of MCC. In August 1968, he was one of ten people at the meeting that resulted in Basil D'Oliveira's omission from the England team to tour South Africa. Carr admitted he "probably" wrote the minutes, which have long been absent from MCC's archives. Speaking to Rob Steen for *The Wisden Cricketer* in 2008, Carr recalled: "I would say the original decision was made on the basis of cricketing ability, but it all looked so awful. I think I believed, or was talked into believing, that it was all on cricketing grounds." The tour was later cancelled after the South African government objected when D'Oliveira was called up as a replacement for Tom Cartwright. "I felt it had not been very well handled," Carr admitted.

In 1974 he moved from MCC to the new TCCB, where he formed a close alliance with chairman Doug Insole. Carr's strengths as an administrator were those that had served him well as a captain. "He was extremely good with people," Insole said. "As a former player he had a good sense of what the game wanted. He was very popular around the world." The pair were thrust into the spotlight in the summer of 1977, when Packer's World Series Cricket divided the sport. Carr had to call Tony Greig and tell him he was being sacked as England captain.

In Trinidad on the 1973-74 tour of the West Indies, Greig had provided one of Carr's most testing moments as a tour manager, almost provoking a riot by running out Alvin

Bob Thomas, Popperfoto/Getty Images

... they do things differently there: the MCC team of 1951-52 with the Nizam of Hyderabad and his wife. Donald Carr is seated on the right. Tour manager Geoffrey Howard is seated on the left.

Kallicharran in the First Test when he left his crease before time had been called at the end of the day. After three hours of talks, it was agreed England would withdraw the appeal. Carr retired in 1986 and briefly served as an ICC match referee. His son John – who was born in a house adjoining Lord's while his father worked for MCC – flourished as a prolific batsman for Middlesex, before following Donald's example by becoming a prominent administrator.

One of the senior Carr's jobs at the TCCB was to police the written output of England players. His experience of dealing with Pakistani umpires proved useful in a conversation with Angela Patmore, ghostwriter of Mike Gatting's autobiography. After reading the section dealing with Gatting's row with Shakoor Rana, he told her: "We want Mike to play for England again, don't we? What we would like is for you to write 2,000 words that are very bland." He also earned a rebuke in a *Sun* leading article in 1983 after he tried to block Ian Botham's column: "We hope that Donald Duck has learnt his lesson," the paper fumed. "This is a free country."

COCKBAIN, RONALD GEORGE, died on October 23, aged 83. Ronnie Cockbain was a stalwart of the Bootle club in the Liverpool Competition, scoring 9,197 runs and taking 453 wickets at 16 between 1949 and 1983. He also appeared in seven matches for Cheshire. His son and grandson, both called Ian, played first-class cricket.

COLLINGE, OLIVER, who died of cancer on July 4, aged 28, had been a keen cricketer for Booth CC in Halifax since the age of nine, and featured in the Schools section of *Wisden 2006* after heading the bowling averages for Bradford Grammar. "Ollie's Bell" has been installed outside the umpires' room at Booth's ground in his memory, and will be rung to start matches.

COLLIS, JOHN MORLEY, who died on December 3, aged 72, was music editor of *Time Out* in the 1970s and '80s, and one of the founders of the influential magazine *Let it Rock*. He wrote biographies of Van Morrison and John Denver, plus an essential reference guide to the music industry, and was especially proud of his history of Chess Records, published after six years of research. At *Time Out*, he played cricket for SW Litho, formed by staff of the *Socialist Worker*, and helped expand their fixture list. Eventually the team became Millfields, named after the Hackney park ground where they played. Collis assumed the captaincy and appointed himself "chairman for life: Mugabe style". His wily outswingers once produced figures of nine for 14, still a club record. The team are now run by his son Tom. He collected *Wisdens*, and was given a chance to share his love of the game with *Guardian* readers when he joined their list of county writers in 2001. He wrote engagingly. Of the combustible fast bowler Steve Kirby, he said: "He is red-haired, but when he feels cruelly cheated of a wicket his whole head appears to catch fire." But he did not necessarily believe that attending a press conference was more important than getting to the pub.

CORBETT, RONALD BALFOUR, CBE, died on March 31, aged 85. Best known as the (much) smaller half of the Two Ronnies, the comedian Ronnie Corbett had a long and varied show-business career, one of his earliest roles coming in the children's TV programme *Crackerjack*. Interested in most sports, he was twice president of the Lord's Taverners, in 1982 and 1987. A photograph from England's 1979-80 tour of Australia showed Peter Willey batting, with Corbett – barely higher than the stumps – keeping wicket behind him.

CORDNER, JOHN PRUEN, who died on December 10, aged 87, was a member of a famous Melbourne football and medical family. A left-arm seamer, he played three times for Victoria in 1951-52, then once for Warwickshire the following August – going wicketless against the Indian tourists – while he was in England studying nuclear science.

CORRIGAN, ALFRED BRIAN, AM, died on December 9, aged 87. Brian Corrigan was a distinguished doctor, and a pioneer of sports medicine in Australia. In 1961, he treated Richie Benaud, who had badly injured his shoulder in the first match of the Ashes tour, and watched with satisfaction as, a few weeks later, Benaud's leg-breaks turned the Old Trafford Test. Not long before, "Doc" Corrigan had patiently nursed fast bowler Gordon Rorke back to health after a severe bout of hepatitis in India. "He was a doctor with a glint in his eye," said Ian Chappell. "A wonderful character."

COX, HELEN JOANNE, MP, was killed on June 16, aged 41, a week before the EU referendum. A supporter of the Remain campaign, Jo Cox was in her West Yorkshire seat of Batley & Spen to hold a constituency surgery when she was shot and stabbed by a far-right fanatic. Elected in May 2015, she was already a rising star in the Labour Party. Cox was proud to represent her home town, and a keen supporter of Mount CC, a Muslim club in Batley, which in April 2016 won the Duke of York's community initiative award: ECB chairman Colin Graves called Mount "a shining example of what a community club should be". Cox had visited it just a few weeks before her murder, and sent a video message from Westminster. "She mingled with the children and played with a bat and ball," said club official Abdul Ravat. "She was full of energy and she loved people." There was a minute's silence before all matches in the Bradford League on the weekend after she died, and Yorkshire's players wore black armbands during their T20 Blast match against Derbyshire at Headingley on June 19. The Mount club tweeted: "We won't forget your efforts and hard work. Let us build unity not hate."

COZIER, WINSTON ANTHONY LLOYD, died on May 11, aged 75. As Tony Cozier approached his half-century as an international cricket commentator, he was probably the most respected and best-loved of all the game's broadcasters. Though not a great player, he upended modern convention, and was called on regularly to work on television across the world, whether his native West Indies were playing or not. Colleagues were in awe of his ability to switch seamlessly from radio, which requires words above all, to TV, which values a certain amount of silence. Listeners just loved his voice: "A melodic lilt that brought to mind waves gently lapping on a Caribbean beach," as Mike Dickson wrote in the *Daily Mail*. If he was dishonoured anywhere, it was at home, where – to his great

Abdul A. Ravat/Mount CC

Mingling with the children: Jo Cox MP at Mount Cricket Club, Batley.

distress – his last years were clouded by disputes with West Indian administrators. There can be no question which side of the argument commanded more respect within the game.

To British listeners, Cozier sprang from nowhere when he became the visiting commentator on *Test Match Special*, aged just 25, in 1966. In fact, he was already a journalistic veteran. He had commentated on the 1964-65 home series against Australia; he had freelanced his way round England, sleeping in YMCAs and on friends' sofas, to cover the epic 1963 tour; long before, he had written his first professional Test report, aged 14, on the Bridgetown Test of 1954-55 for the *St Lucia Voice*. He did have one advantage: his father was the editor. There had been Coziers in Barbados since the late 18th century, and Jimmy Cozier made his own name as a journalist in the late imperial phase, working in several different colonies before starting his own paper in Barbados, the short-lived *Daily News*, then becoming an influential columnist on the *Advocate*. He wrote mainly on non-sporting matters, but covered West Indies' 1950 tour of England. In Jimmy's wandering phase, Tony went to boarding school in Barbados, where he thrived, and then to study journalism at university in Ottawa, where he did not. He lasted just one long Canadian winter before coming home to play hockey (at which he represented Barbados) and club cricket (facing top fast bowlers, but not normally for long), and make his way in the world.

Various elements defined Cozier's career. There was the length and breadth of it: perhaps only Richie Benaud can have covered more international matches. Then there was his professionalism. "He was just never stumped," recalled Peter Baxter, the former producer of *TMS*. "He seemed to have seen and heard every game, even obscure county matches when he was on a different continent. It was as though he had been watching two games at once." There was also his commitment to Caribbean cricket: he believed passionately in its importance as a unifying factor in a splintered region and, by his popularity, became a de facto PR man for the West Indian game. For his first three decades in the business, the team were usually outstanding. As a white man from Barbados – a country with a firm racial divide before independence – he was in an unusual position; but he had established his credentials early, resigning from Bridgetown's Carlton CC after they rejected a potential black member, and joining Wanderers. He was trusted by generations of West Indies players, but his good nature and geniality also embodied all the most beguiling aspects of the Caribbean game to the outside world.

In 1966, there were reputedly letters to the BBC complaining about the employment of a "black bastard" and, in the days before his face became more widely known, he was accustomed to jaws dropping when people met him for the first time and discovered he was not black. Indeed, when in animated discussion with the players – fellow Bajans especially – that melodic lilt could mutate into a rapid-fire and, to outsiders, incomprehensible patois. His reputation as a players' man was bolstered when, reputedly at the request of the boss, he went to join Kerry Packer's commentary team during World Series Cricket. It was a good career move too, giving him a chance to break into TV.

Graham Morris

Good-natured and genial: Tony Cozier at the microphone.

Cozier had an extraordinary work ethic. He edited all 22 editions of the *West Indies Cricket Annual* between its birth in 1970 and its demise in 1991; for the next 11 years he produced the *Caribbean Cricket Quarterly*; he wrote a history of West Indian Test cricket, ghosted books for Garry Sobers, Clive Lloyd and Michael Holding, wrote columns for papers round the world, and contributed to *Wisden* regularly from 1977 to 2016. Eventually, his son Craig, now a freelance cricket producer and statistician, joined the cottage industry. Everything was done to impeccable standards. Yet there was always fun and laughter: the beach party given by Tony and his wife Jillian was a highlight of any Barbados Test.

He had to tread a difficult line amid the complex politics of Caribbean cricket. Once, he had to keep a low profile in Trinidad, having dissed the local favourite Phil Simmons. As the players became less heroic, the administrative ineptitude more blatant, and Cozier's criticisms more forceful, that task grew harder. On the 2014-15 England tour of the Caribbean, the West Indian board prevented him from doing TV commentary; their president, Dave Cameron, claimed Cozier's eyesight was failing (a slander action was still pending when he died). More objective observers thought lack of vision was indeed the problem, but not on Tony's side: he did his normal professional job for the BBC. On his death, even the board could not continue the grudge. "He represented West Indies wherever he went," they said in a statement. "He educated people around the world about our cricket, our people, our culture and who we are."

CROCKWELL, FIQRE SALASSIE, was shot dead early on June 20, shortly after leaving a Bermuda Heroes Weekend celebration. Another partygoer was stabbed nearby; two men were later arrested. Crockwell was 30, and still part of the national squad, despite a conviction for possession of heroin the previous year. An opening batsman who often kept wicket, he played two one-day internationals for Bermuda during the World Cup qualifying tournament in South Africa in 2009, and scored 45 against Kenya on debut, in a first-wicket stand of 107 with David Hemp. He made several appearances for St George's in Bermuda's prestigious annual Cup Match, and was also a talented footballer.

CROWE, MARTIN DAVID, MBE, died of cancer on March 3, aged 53. In the second half of the 1980s, Martin Crowe had a claim to be the best batsman in the world. With his upright elegance and classical technique, he was certainly the purists' favourite. But he was no mere aesthete: many of his 17 Test hundreds for New Zealand were made in hostile environments.

Crowe's immaculate appearance and unflappable demeanour made it appear as if the life of an international sportsman came easily, but – in his playing days at least – he could be intense and moody. "Martin was a sensitive man," said his former team-mate Jeremy Coney. "He felt things keenly, was strongly opinionated and quick to take offence, so he polarised people." Later Crowe gained perspective on his complexities and, in a sometimes self-lacerating second autobiography, *Raw*, traced many of his problems back to being thrust into top-level sport in his teens. By his own admission, he was "the record holder for grievances".

An original thinker, Crowe was always ready to challenge orthodoxy. His captaincy brought innovation to the 1992 World Cup, where New Zealand opened the bowling with a spinner, Dipak Patel, and the batting with a pinch hitter, Mark Greatbatch. They might have won the trophy, but Crowe was injured while making 91 during the semi-final against Pakistan, and off the field as his team lost their way against Inzamam-ul-Haq.

After retiring, he made the transition to writing. His columns on ESPNcricinfo were frequently trenchant, always thoughtful and never routine. He wrote with empathy about Jonathan Trott's withdrawal from the 2013-14 Ashes, and in *Wisden 2014* he vigorously attacked the sledging that had scarred that series: "The truth is, we have all been guilty of taking cricket too seriously." He responded to the death of Phillip Hughes later that year with a heartfelt appeal for a more compassionate game.

Crowe was born in Auckland, with cricket in his blood. His father Dave had appeared for Wellington and Canterbury, and his mother Audrey excelled at many sports; the family bookshelves were lined with *Wisdens*. His brother Jeff was four years older, but the two quickly became ferocious competitors at whichever sport they tackled. At Auckland Grammar, Martin was in the rugby XV alongside future All Black Grant Fox, and played tennis and golf to a high standard. But cricket was his strongest suit, and he was fast-tracked through New Zealand age-group teams.

At 17, he made a fifty on his first-class debut for Auckland, earning a scholarship to Lord's with the MCC Young Cricketers. He came under the shrewd guidance of Don Wilson, who tightened up his technique and added to his education, telling Crowe: "No one remembers 60, lad, only big hundreds." Early in his stay – in bitter May weather – he made a brilliant century to take the Young Cricketers to victory against a strong MCC team, finishing the match with a six into the Tavern Stand. "When he arrived he had an outsize determination to be No. 1," wrote Wilson, "and nothing was going to stop him."

In January 1982, Crowe scored his first century for Auckland; less than a month later he was making his Test debut, against Australia at Wellington. It was an unhappy baptism: in a rain-ruined match he did not get on the field until the fifth day, was promptly hit on the head twice by Jeff Thomson, and run out for nine. He made just 20 in four innings in the series, and was given a chilly reception from colleagues who resented his promotion. "Greg Chappell and Rod Marsh were nicer to me than my own team-mates," he said. His figures improved in England in 1983, and he hit his first Test hundred, against England at Wellington, the following winter. By now, his brother Jeff was also a member of the New Zealand team, to the undisguised delight of their father, who told one of his former coaches: "You said I'd never make a Test player – well, I made two." The brothers played 36 Tests together.

A watershed in Crowe's development came in 1984, when he stood in for Viv Richards as one of Somerset's overseas players. He moved in with Ian Botham, but got off to a shaky start, including five consecutive single-figure scores. Things improved in June, when he made over 700 runs, and by the end of the season he had 1,769 at 53 in the Championship, and 2,620 in all formats. One turning point was an unbeaten 70 out of 192 against Leicestershire, and Andy Roberts in full cry; another was finding his own

Adrian Murrell, Allsport/Getty Images

"Part dancer, part fencer, part keen-eyed executioner": Martin Crowe at The Oval in 1983.

accommodation. According to Vic Marks, the Somerset all-rounder: "We met him in New Zealand the previous winter, and Both said, 'You must come and live with me,' which was a hard invitation to turn down. After about three or four weeks when he had hardly scored a run, he plucked up the courage to say: 'I don't think this is going to work.' I really admired him for doing that, and when I asked him about it, he said he told Both when he was in the bath. He reckoned there wasn't much he could do about it from there.

"He was very serious about his game and very analytical. Sometimes you worried he was too keen to be the perfect batsman. He threw himself with great energy into the role of being a guide and mentor to the younger players." Crowe was named a *Wisden* Cricketer of the Year, and admitted: "I probably learned more in six months than in six years before."

The experience benefited a Test career that until now had been no more than promising. His breakthrough innings came in Georgetown in April 1985, when he made 188 against a West Indies attack including Malcolm Marshall, Joel Garner and Michael Holding. Seven months later, he made another 188, at Brisbane, with New Zealand going on to win a series against Australia for the first time. And in March 1986, he made a brilliant 137 against the Australians at Christchurch, returning to the crease after a blow on the head from Bruce Reid. "He simply eviscerated the bowlers to every sector of Lancaster Park," Coney recalled. "He looked angry with himself. He saw the injury as his error – and he wanted to show the Australians that."

Under Coney's sparky captaincy, and with Richard Hadlee at the height of his powers, New Zealand earned their first series victory in England, in 1986, with Crowe making a masterly 106 at Lord's. He was a joy to watch – "part dancer, part fencer, part keen-eyed executioner: Martin didn't do ugly," according to Coney. Back home, he proved the point with 328 runs at 65, as New Zealand came from behind to draw a three-match series against West Indies, then enjoyed another productive time in Australia.

He returned to Taunton in 1987 to be greeted by a sulphurous atmosphere following the departures of Botham, Richards and Garner. But his commitment won admirers. "He was still brilliant, but a bit more self-contained," said Marks. "He had been playing Test cricket for five years by then, and there was not the same energy." Crowe provided stability in a difficult summer for Somerset, with 1,627 Championship runs at 67.

Crowes' nest: Martin Crowe (front left), brother Jeff (with bottle), Jeremy Coney (holding Cornhill trophy) and the 1986 New Zealand team celebrate their 1–0 victory, at The Oval.

He took over the New Zealand captaincy from John Wright in 1990-91, but the retirement of Hadlee deprived him of his main weapon, and his first series was lost 3–0 in Pakistan, setting a template for his time in charge. Just two matches of 16 were won, amid suggestions Crowe was unable to inspire his players. "Martin cultivates that class thing, with all his talk about wine and fine restaurants," grumbled off-spinner John Bracewell. "That irritates the hell out of everybody outside Auckland."

Nevertheless, Crowe averaged 54 as captain, and against Sri Lanka at Wellington in 1990-91 mounted a remarkable feat of escapology in a third-wicket stand of 467 with Andrew Jones, then a Test record for any wicket. On 299, Crowe's concentration was scrambled by the thought of becoming the first New Zealander to make a triple-century, and he was caught behind in the game's final over. He smashed his bat against the boundary fence and hurled it across the dressing-room. He later concluded that the "toxic suppression" caused by his near miss contributed to his cancer. "Not a week would go by when I wouldn't be reminded of the one run I craved so much," he wrote. "It tore at me like a vulture pecking dead flesh. I did not know how to let it go." He was delighted when Brendon McCullum finally passed the landmark in 2014.

His captaincy ended at the WACA in 1993-94 when, while helping save the First Test, he aggravated a knee injury and missed the rest of the tour. By the time he returned, in England in 1994, Ken Rutherford was in charge, although Crowe reminded the world of his enduring class with another beautiful Lord's century. He made a hundred in the next match, too, at Old Trafford, but after seven more Tests the chronic knee condition forced his retirement, in 1996. In all, he played in 77, scoring 5,444 runs at 45.

He was never likely to go quietly. Grasping the need for a new shorter form of the game, he devised Cricket Max, launching it in New Zealand in 1996. Teams of 13 players batted in two innings of ten eight-ball overs each, with 12 runs for a straight hit over the boundary in a marked zone between long-on and long-off. It did not catch on, but the arrival of Twenty20 showed how far-sighted his vision had been. As a member of MCC's world cricket committee, he badgered the ICC to commit to a Test championship, and came to believe that their failure to do so had dealt the format a mortal blow. He became a mentor to New Zealand batsmen Martin Guptill and Ross Taylor, whose removal as Test captain in 2012 outraged him. Taylor described Crowe as a "passionate, emotional genius", adding: "He was a pretty hard taskmaster, but he knew when to cuddle you as well."

Crowe was inducted into the ICC Hall of Fame during the 2015 World Cup group match between New Zealand and Australia at Auckland. As his health worsened, it seemed as if he might die while New Zealand were in England later that year. Taylor said: "He sent a message through before the Test at Leeds saying, 'If I pass away, please do not come home for the funeral'." He lived another nine months. One of the pallbearers was his cousin Russell, the Hollywood actor, and there were eulogies from his brother, and former New Zealand team-mate Ian Smith.

A memorable accolade came from Wasim Akram, who rated him the best batsman he had bowled to. "Only Martin Crowe knew how to play reverse swing," he said. "He was always playing on the front foot, always playing for inswing. He was very calm, and his concentration was 100% every delivery – he never gave you a chance."

DALE, JOHN ROBERT, who died on November 19, aged 86, was a slow left-armer who played just once for Kent – Ted Dexter was his only wicket, in 1958 – but had a long career for his native Lincolnshire. He started for them in 1949, then had spells on the staff at Northampton and Canterbury, before returning to teaching and Minor Counties cricket. In 1974, aged 43, he took three for 33 against Glamorgan at Swansea, as Lincolnshire became only the second Minor County to defeat first-class opposition in the Gillette Cup. The same season he took eight for 54 against Yorkshire Second XI, and finished with 151 wickets for Lincolnshire at a shade over 20.

DALTON, JOYCE, who died on December 16, aged 83, played three Tests for Australia in 1957-58, making 59 not out in her final innings, at Perth. Though born in Queensland, she started with New South Wales in 1952-53, skippering them for two seasons, then spent most of the 1960s as vice-captain after returning from a teaching stint in New Zealand. Team-mate Muriel Picton remembered "a classic style of player, whose delicacy and timing were particularly evident in the effortless ease of her driving", and a lithe and fleet-footed fielder. In New Zealand, Dalton made 141 for Wellington against Canterbury in January 1960. A year later, now with Canterbury, she made 93 against her old colleagues in the Australian touring team. Back home, Dalton helped keep women's cricket in 1960s Australia alive, in the face of declining public interest and apathy from the male Establishment. She also represented NSW at hockey and squash.

DATTA, PUNYA BRATA, died on November 12, aged 92. "Badal" Datta was an elegant left-hand batsman from Bengal (he was born in Sylhet in modern-day Bangladesh), although he was used more as a bowler in 1947, when he featured in a strong Cambridge University side. "He was delightful," wrote Trevor Bailey. "He bowled accurately but hardly spun the ball." Bailey also recalled that he and Datta looked similar from a distance, which led one elderly Somerset supporter to marvel at the versatility of a chap who could take the new ball with right-arm medium-pace, then switch to left-arm spin. Datta's best score that year was a modest 47; he did claim five for 52 from 31.3 overs against Essex at Fenner's, but failed to strike in the drawn Varsity Match. Back home, and now opening, he hit 62 and 143 for Bengal against Bihar in 1952-53, then 141 against a Holkar side captained by the veteran C. K. Nayudu. But India had no Tests that season, and Datta's moment had passed. He soon faded out of the first-class game, although he remained active in club cricket into his fifties, and did administrative work for the Cricket Association of Bengal.

DAVIES, TREFFOR ELLIOTT, who died on December 21, 2013, aged 75, joined the Worcestershire staff at 16 in 1954, and made his debut the following year. But national service intervened, and he eventually played only 20 matches, more than half in 1961 – his final season – which brought his highest score of 76, against Glamorgan at Cardiff Arms Park. He had met his future wife while stationed in the Bahamas, and they later

Patrick Eagar, Popperfoto/Getty Images

"Ladies and gentlemen, boys and girls..." Johnny Dennis in his Lord's eyrie, 2003.

moved back there; he taught English and coached cricket, as well as leading the Cosmopolitans club to the national title in 1962.

DENNIS, JOHN WILLIAM, died on December 3, aged 76. Johnny Dennis was the PA announcer for most major matches in England for around 20 years to 2014, his warm, mellifluous voice a reassuring companion to the day's play. In all, he manned the microphone at 136 Test matches. An actor by profession, he had an amusing turn of phrase, once asking for the aisles at a cup semi-final to be kept free of "picnic impedimenta". A regular performer at the Players' Theatre near Charing Cross, Dennis was held up by a late finish at Lord's one evening, and left the ground with just 20 minutes to spare before curtain-up in the West End.

DESAI, KANTILAL RANCHHODJI, died on July 23, aged 84. Kanti Desai played 19 Ranji Trophy matches for Gujarat in the 1960s. His highest score was 117, against Maharashtra in December 1960, although his unbeaten 95 against serial Ranji Trophy champions Bombay the following November was probably a better innings. Desai later helped popularise cricket in his home city of Valsad, where he was instrumental in the building of a new first-class ground; he became a vice-president of the Gujarat Cricket Association.

DEVEREUX, ALAN, died on May 29, aged 75. For almost 50 years the actor Alan Devereux was known to devotees of *The Archers* as Sid Perks, landlord of The Bull, the pub at the heart of social life in Ambridge. Sid's distinctive Brummie tones were first heard in 1963, when he arrived in Borsetshire as a teenage tearaway. Devereux was born in Sutton Coldfield, where his father was a keen cricketer. Apart from charity matches with fellow cast members, he did not play the game, but watched it keenly on television. Sid, however, was a stalwart of the Ambridge XI, re-forming the club in 1970, taking over as captain in 1990, and plotting many triumphs in the annual grudge match against Penny Hassett. In 1998, he became team manager, but his tenure ended in disgrace: Sid did not like the fact that Adam Macy, Ambridge's star batsman, was gay, and they fought – which ultimately led to his being forced to resign as captain. In 2007, Sid and Jolene, his wife,

Central Press/Getty Images

The hard yards? Audrey Disbury (right) fields as Rachael Heyhoe Flint bats on a Perth beach in 1968; Edna Barker waits for an edge.

took part in a special episode recorded live at Lord's during the Village Cup final. It featured a guest appearance by Mike Gatting, who offered Sid the hospitality of an MCC box, leading his wife – watching from a distance – to conclude he was being kidnapped by a bearded stranger.

DEVEREUX, LOUIS NORMAN, who died on November 12, aged 85, was a handy county all-rounder throughout the 1950s with Worcestershire and Glamorgan. He had been on the Lord's groundstaff in 1948 – alongside his future county colleague Don Shepherd – and the following year, still only 17, played for Middlesex against both Universities. He also found time to represent England at table tennis. After being restricted by national service, he found a regular place at New Road, scoring 732 runs and taking 55 wickets in 1953. Diminishing returns saw him released two years later, but Devereux prospered after a move to Glamorgan: he was capped during his debut season of 1956, which produced 833 runs, plus a career-best six for 29 with his off-breaks against Yorkshire at Middlesbrough; a fortnight later he took five for 11 as Gloucestershire collapsed from 61 without loss to 81 all out at Newport. Devereux made his only century in 1957, an unbeaten 108 against Lancashire at Old Trafford, but was let go after a handful of games in 1960; he read of his sacking in the *Western Mail*. After a spell in Scottish league cricket, he moved back to Wales, and ran the Central Hotel in Aberystwyth for 30 years from 1965.

DISBURY, AUDREY DELPH, who died on June 17, aged 82, played ten Tests for England, most notably in the team that retained the Ashes (and also defeated New Zealand 2–0) in 1968-69. On that tour, Disbury helped nurture the talent of fellow opener Enid Bakewell, and their partnership prospered: they put on 48 and 59 in the First Test at the Barton Oval, Adelaide, then 84 to set up victory at Christchurch, and 95 during the series-clinching win at Auckland. "Dis", as she was known, was an engaging tourist, valued as much for her humour as her ultra-competitiveness. For Bakewell, hitherto a slow scorer, she provided a template for a new aggressive approach: "She inspired me to score quickly and always look for runs. Until then I didn't have the confidence she had."

For the first time, the team had flown to Australia, a contrast to the leisurely sea trip of Disbury's first tour, in 1957-58. Back then, despite being given paid leave by the Women's Royal Naval Service, she had to raise more than £300 for the voyage, washing cars, working as a waitress and a cinema usherette, and selling raffle tickets. Once aboard ship, the main problem was maintaining her pristine white blazer. She played in three Tests on that tour without conspicuous success, but made 44 against New Zealand at The Oval in 1966, her only home Test.

Disbury was born in Bedford and honed her game in the garden with her brother Brian, later of Kent (see below): he bowled a golf ball, she batted with a cricket stump. She joined the Wrens after training as a nurse, and served as a vehicle mechanic and later as a welfare officer. She played cricket for Kent and was captain of the International XI at the first women's World Cup in 1973, helping weld a disparate bunch into what *Wisden* called a "capable fighting unit". The team finished third.

After leaving the Wrens, she ran a B&B in Ashford that became renowned for its cooked breakfasts. For many years she drove a clapped-out Fiat that sometimes required the passenger to change gear with a pair of pliers on Disbury's command of "Now!" She was a familiar figure in Kent golf circles, and county captain in 1996 and 1997. She played every game hard, but with a smile never far away. "She was a card," said Bakewell, "but she was *so* competitive."

DISBURY, BRIAN ELVIN, who died in April, aged 86, was the older brother of Audrey Disbury. Brian was a tidy batsman who did well for Bedford School, then for Bedfordshire: inside a week in August 1951, he hit 119 against Cambridgeshire, and 151 against Buckinghamshire, sharing opening stands of 235 and 246 with George August. Disbury joined Kent, but struggled at first-class level. In 14 county matches he passed 26 only once, knuckling down for three hours to reach 74 not out against Leicestershire at Tunbridge Wells in 1956. An accountant, he later emigrated to America, where he died.

EARLS-DAVIS, MICHAEL RICHARD GRATWICKE, who died on April 5, aged 95, was one of several amateurs mooted as a possible Somerset captain in 1950. In the event, he played for them only once, failing to take a wicket at Worcester. A seamer, he had appeared in five matches in 1947 while at Cambridge, taking five wickets in the first, against Worcestershire, and four for 87 in the first innings of the next, against Gloucestershire. But he managed only three more wickets, and was not selected for the Varsity Match. His grandfather W. G. Heasman played for Sussex in the 19th century, and Earls-Davis turned out for them in wartime games before being injured in action with the Irish Guards in 1944. He became a teacher at Sherborne, his old school.

EASTER, JOHN NICHOLAS CAVE, who died on January 11, aged 70, was one of the world's foremost squash players in the 1970s, second only to Jonah Barrington in the British ranks. Tall and good-looking – he worked for a time as a model – Easter was also a useful opening bowler, an Oxford Blue in 1967 and 1968. In the first of those years he claimed a career-best five for 62 in The Parks, bowling Northamptonshire's captain Roger Prideaux for 99 as the first part of a hat-trick. His son Nick won more than 50 rugby caps for England.

EVANS, ANTHONY RHYS, who died on August 19, aged 73, played 15 first-class matches for Orange Free State, scoring 126 against Border at Bloemfontein in 1969-70, when he was dismissed by Tony Greig for a duck in the second innings. The same season he made 49 in OFS's first official List A match, against Eastern Province. He ran the family farming business from 1972 until his death.

EVANS, GEOFFREY ROSSALL, died on September 13, aged 77. Geoff Evans had been involved with cricket in his native Devon for more than 60 years, first as a player, then an administrator. For most of the 1970s he kept wicket, and was in the Devon side that won the Minor Counties Championship for the first time, in 1978. He was their secretary from 1986 to 2009, then chairman. In 2001, Evans took over as secretary of the Minor Counties Cricket Association, and was still in office at his death; he was given honorary life membership of MCC in 2012. "Geoff's contribution to Devon cricket was second to none," said their president, Roger Moylan-Jones. Evans's coffin was draped with the county club's flag, with his Devon cap on top; the pall-bearers were all former Devon players.

FARLEY, CECIL FREDERICK, died on April 18, aged 97. Gus Farley worked at Lord's for 45 years, latterly as ground superintendent, organising the gatemen and stewards, among myriad other tasks. He was well suited to it, as he had done almost every conceivable job on the ground; even after his official retirement, he was MCC's head steward for a while, then ran the staff canteen, reprising the skills he had learned in the army catering corps. He had an endless fund of stories about Lord's and the war, usually dispensed with a smile and a suitable swear word.

FINLAY, AUBREY JAMES, who died on April 4, aged 78, was a batsman most associated with Ulster's Sion Mills club, who played 18 matches for Ireland, nine of them first-class. His highest score was 49 against the Free Foresters in 1957, aged 19.

FLEMING, ANTHONY WILLIAM PATRICK, died on January 5, aged 84. Tony Fleming was the first manager of MCC's indoor school in 1977, and later moved over to the Pavilion as ground administrator, where he proved popular with members and staff alike. He had arrived fresh from the RAF, but decided not to use his rank of flight lieutenant when he spotted that MCC's other senior staff included a group captain and a wing commander (soon to be joined by a couple of colonels). Fleming was a fine wicketkeeper, despite coming late to cricket: he was 24 when posted to Headley Court, a military hospital, whose team had only ten players and no keeper. He learned how to keep in the nets and, having started that way, almost invariably stood up to the stumps, surprising many a batsman with lightning reflexes. He was the right size, despite having played international basketball. "I was a lot taller then," he would explain with a smile from behind an ever-present Camel cigarette. Colin Maynard, MCC's deputy secretary, remembered how, "especially on a winter's day, Tony's office could have been mistaken for a scene from *The Hound of the Baskervilles*. He was in there somewhere, in the centre of a thick fog." Aged 50, Fleming was recruited to captain Uxbridge, and led them to the Thames Valley League title in 1982. "He was bloody old," recalled team-mate Colin Sargent, "but bloody fit."

FOREMAN, DENIS JOSEPH, who died on July 23, aged 83, was the first non-white South African to play county cricket after the Second World War, a trailblazer for the likes of Basil D'Oliveira. Foreman had actually appeared in a few first-class matches for Western Province as an "honorary white" before apartheid was so rigidly enforced. He did little in his three Currie Cup games in 1951-52, under the South African Test captain Jack Cheetham. "Nobody made a fuss," WP's off-spinner Ronnie Delport – who played in those matches – told the former *Wisden* editor Scyld Berry in 2012, "though there were the crude comments from those days that he had 'a touch of the tar-brush'."

Foreman was probably a better footballer than cricketer, and signed to play in the Football League after talent scouts visited South Africa. But he remembered to pack his bat when he set sail to play for Brighton & Hove Albion, for whom he made 219 appearances and scored 69 goals as a nippy inside-left. On his second day in England, in

1952, he was taken to a cricket dinner at Hove Montefiore CC, where a long association began with his wonderment that he was allowed to sit and eat alongside white people.

He joined the Sussex staff after the football season, and played on and off for 15 years. He started with 54 and five wickets against an Oxford University side including Colin Cowdrey, but his subsequent figures were modest. There were only four more wickets in 126 further matches, and he finished with a batting average of 18, and just one century, 104 against Nottinghamshire at Hove in 1967, his final season. But he was a fine fielder, and universally popular.

FOX, JOHN GEORGE, died on August 2, aged 87. Jackie Fox was a tidy wicketkeeper who joined Warwickshire after several seasons of Minor Counties cricket with his native Durham. He made his first-class debut in 1959, when nearly 30, and replaced Dick Spooner as the regular keeper for most of the following season, in which he made 51 dismissals. His batting made strides too: he scored 52 against the 1959 Indian tourists at Edgbaston. But Warwickshire also had the Oxford University wicketkeeper Alan Smith, a far better batsman; when Smith was available full-time in 1961, Fox made only three Championship appearances, and never represented the first team again. He later played a few games for Devon.

FRANS, VERNON, who died on December 12, aged 56, was one of four brothers who represented Eastern Province's non-white team. "The Frans family were legends," said Cricket South Africa's chief executive Haroon Lorgat, a former team-mate. A fast bowler, Vernon took 44 wickets in 13 matches now considered first-class, including six for 90 against Transvaal in 1986-87. He also played representative football, baseball and hockey.

GANTEAUME, ANDREW GORDON, who died on February 17, aged 95, became a celebrated victim of the politics that afflicted West Indies cricket in the years before Frank Worrell became the team's first permanent black captain. Ganteaume made one Test appearance, against Gubby Allen's England at Port-of-Spain in 1947-48, and scored a century, but he was promptly dropped – allegedly for slow scoring – and never chosen again. It gave him a Test average of 112, the highest in history. But if the stat delighted cricket geeks, Ganteaume was less impressed. He kept his counsel for 59 years, until his autobiography blamed the white Establishment for his exile.

A slim, diminutive opener of mixed African and Indian descent, Ganteaume had appeared for Trinidad as a wicketkeeper-batsman since 1941, and staked a claim to play in West Indies' first post-war series with scores of 101, 47 not out and 90 in two warm-up matches against MCC. "I was not a privileged boy," he said. "I had to make a hundred even to get into the argument." But he was called up only because of an injury to his compatriot, the white Jeffrey Stollmeyer. Gerry Gomez, another white Trinidadian, stood in for Stollmeyer as captain. Ganteaume was told of his selection by administrator Edgar Marsden, and wrote: "He could not disguise his resentment at having to announce something that he did not want to happen."

Replying to England's 362, Ganteaume and George Carew, batting in a brown felt hat, put on 173 for the first wicket. After Carew was dismissed by Jim Laker for 107, Ganteaume batted on and, after taking a drinks break on 99, completed his hundred. Gomez sent out a note – which Ganteaume kept, and reproduced in his book – asking the batsmen to step up the rate. Soon after, Ganteaume holed out on the boundary, having batted for nearly five hours was greeted by a stony-faced captain. "That's not what I meant," said Gomez. His local supporters were more pleased: a public subscription raised enough money for an engraved silver jug and a bicycle.

Rain frustrated West Indies' bid for victory, prompting more discussion about Ganteaume's scoring-rate. The next Test was in British Guiana, but John Goddard, also white, came in as captain, West Indies' custom then being to choose a different one for each Test. Goddard also opened the batting with Carew, despite having no experience in the position. Ganteaume was not selected for the tour of India later that year. He had no doubt that the white power brokers – in particular Stollmeyer and Gomez – were to blame. As Everton Weekes put it: "Myself and Frank [Worrell] simply couldn't follow what was happening, although we had a pretty fair opinion of what was behind it."

There was an odd postscript when, out of the blue, Ganteaume was chosen for the tour of England in 1957. Now aged 36, he scored 800 runs at 27, but did not get near the Test team. He played until 1957-58, and retired after a one-match comeback in 1962-63; in 50 matches, he had scored 2,785 runs at almost 35.

He stayed closely involved with cricket: he was a long-serving Trinidad and West Indies selector, and managed the team in home series against England and Australia in the 1970s. He wrote about cricket and commentated on radio in Trinidad. Most assumed he had long forgiven those responsible for his brief Test career, until his book, *My Story: the Other Side of the Coin*, was published in 2007. As Weekes put it: "It says a lot about Andy's character that he kept his emotions to himself for all that time before choosing his moment to state his case."

GARUDACHAR, B. K., who died on February 26, aged 99, was a leg-spinning all-rounder who played for a variety of Indian teams either side of the war. His highest score, 164, came for Mysore in the Ranji Trophy semi-final against Holkar at Indore in March 1946. This followed a marathon effort with the ball: four for 301 from 69 overs as Holkar piled up 912 for eight, with six centuries. "Holkar batted for two and a half days," he said. "I felt if we had run all the way to Bangalore, we would have reached it earlier than the time we took running around fetching the ball from the boundary." Five years earlier, against Madras, he followed six for 56 with eight for 99, to spirit Mysore to a 22-run victory. They reached the Ranji final for the first time that year, but lost by an innings to ever-powerful Bombay, despite the persistent Garudachar's three for 161. An engineer, he remained involved in cricket in various administrative posts. He had been India's oldest first-class cricketer, a mantle that passed to the former Baroda and Bombay player (and cricket historian) Vasant Raiji.

GATHORNE, ROY, who died on March 17, aged 95, played six Currie Cup matches for Eastern Province, all in 1952-53, scoring 64 against Western Province at Newlands. He eventually returned to Michaelhouse, his old school, to head up the English department, and ran the cricket there for many years; the ground is named after him.

GAUSTAD, JOHN NEVILLE, who died on June 3, aged 68, was a New Zealander who revolutionised the selling of sports books in Britain in 1985 when he opened Sportspages, a small shop off the Charing Cross Road. In the early days, cricket was very much its No. 1 sport, but it was the post-1990 football boom that helped the business expand, first next door – mainly to accommodate the fad for fanzines – and then to Manchester. For various reasons, the wind changed against him even before the internet took off, and Sportspages closed in 2005. It is remembered with great affection, like Gaustad himself, and his legacy lives on through the William Hill Sports Book award, which he co-founded in 1989; he chaired the judging panel until he retired in 2015.

GHULAM MUSTAFA KHAN, who died on January 3, aged 83, was an administrator and cricket statistician who was *Wisden's* Pakistan correspondent from 1959 to 1983, and a contributor to each subsequent edition until 2015. He also wrote extensively for *The Cricketer*, edited the PCB's annual, and produced other statistical works. He had joined the board as a clerk in 1956, and rose to become secretary for two years before his retirement in 1997. For much of the time he was the sole employee, holed up in a small office at Karachi's National Stadium.

GILL, WALTER, who died on July 28, aged 86, was a fine all-round sportsman who had spells as a professional with the northern cricket clubs Bradshaw, Little Lever and Egerton. He also played semi-pro football for Chorley. A teacher in Cheshire, Gill underwent a heart transplant in 1991. He was told it might give him another ten years, but it lasted 25, during which time he umpired in the Bolton League, and took part in athletics (shot put), bowls and golf at the British Transplant Games.

GLEESON, JOHN WILLIAM, died on October 8, aged 78. During the 1950-51 Ashes, a 12-year-old boy became fascinated by Jack Iverson's experiments with a table-tennis ball. These had helped him become the feared mystery spinner who confounded England. He flicked the ball out from a folded middle finger, and it turned to leg or off – and often rose sharply – with no discernible change in action. Iverson soon faded from view, undone by a lack of confidence, but young Johnny Gleeson tried to master the trick, while assisting his parents in their general store in Wiangaree, near the foothills of the McPherson Range on the New South Wales–Queensland border.

Gleeson left school at 15, and joined the old Postmaster General's Department as a telephone technician: he spent his working life helping Australians communicate with one another, though his cricket was founded on deception. He started as a wicketkeeper who made a few runs in the lower grades for the Sydney club Western Suburbs, all the while honing those Iverson impersonations in the nets. Quite when Gleeson first delivered a mystery ball in earnest is unclear, but there is no dispute about when they were first widely noticed. Jack Chegwyn, a former NSW batsman, used to take strong sides around the state to give the locals a taste of big cricket. Late in 1965, at Gunnedah – 50 miles west of his home town of Tamworth – Gleeson flummoxed Richie Benaud with an off-break disguised as a leg-break. Benaud immediately organised a place at Sydney's Balmain club, where Gleeson prospered so quickly that he played for NSW in 1966-67. When they visited Adelaide, he met Don Bradman, who – after facing him in the nets without pads or bat – said: "By the end of the season, I think you'll be playing for Australia."

Later that season, Gleeson was picked for what would now be called an A team, in New Zealand, and in December 1967, after only 15 first-class matches, he won the first of his 29 Test caps, against India at Adelaide. Four wickets from 29 eight-ball overs set the tone for his career: at the highest level, Gleeson became a stock bowler whose accuracy allowed batsmen few liberties, while his folded middle finger, from which he flicked out his variations, kept them wary. A Test strike-rate of 95 may sound innocuous, but it should be balanced against an economy-rate of 2.28.

In 1968, he made the first of two trips to England. Memories of Iverson meant batsmen were apprehensive and, although Gleeson never ran through them, he took 12 wickets and kept the runs down. On tour, his polite withdrawals from boisterous night-time activities cemented his nickname of "Cho" – Cricket Hours Only – which had started when he would return to Tamworth after grade games in Sydney. Back home, Gleeson enjoyed his best season in 1968-69. He finished with 50 first-class wickets – only Graham McKenzie and Tony Lock took more – including 26 in five Tests against West Indies, and five for 61, which remained his best figures, to bowl Australia to victory at Melbourne. He also made a Test-best 45 in the final match at Sydney, showing the adhesive technique which had served him well in his early days.

Ashley Mallett – a friend and fellow Test spinner – captured his essence. "In my mind's eye, I can see Cho now," he said. "He moves in with a funny gait, a bit like a comical mix of Groucho Marx and Ronnie Corbett. He's not a short man, but stays low. The delivery doesn't make a fizzing sound, like Prasanna's or Shane Warne's. It glides out of that folded-finger grip, always on target, but devoid of loop or shape."

Gleeson was a man of principle, and never resorted to sledging. In 1969-70, he was one of those who, led by skipper Bill Lawry, spoke up against the Australian administrators' desire to milk another Test out of a team frazzled by the stresses and strains of a 4–0 shellacking in South Africa, straight after five games in India. On the field, Gleeson's bowling kept the South Africans quiet: he teased out 19 wickets, and even Barry Richards had to watch him like a cat. He continued to toil during the dull 1970-71 Ashes, played out on lifeless pitches. He sent down 221 parsimonious eight-ball overs in the first five Tests, before becoming collateral damage when Lawry was axed for the last. Gleeson took a career-best seven for 52 for NSW against Queensland at the SCG in 1971-72, but the

James Jackson, *Evening Standard*/Getty Images

Sleight of hand: John Gleeson glides down another at Lord's, 1972, watched by David Constant.

following summer in England it became apparent he was an anachronism in the all-action Ian Chappell era, with its emphasis on pace and facial hair. He became a back number behind Mallett, who replaced him in the last two Tests. He finished with 93 Test wickets.

The next season was Gleeson's last at home, although he did tour South Africa again in 1973-74 with the multiracial team organised by Derrick Robins. And he played the following season there for Eastern Province, when his 24 wickets included seven for 73 against Western Province at Newlands. He lived out his retirement in Tamworth, assuring Chappell in his last days: "Don't fret mate, I'm in good shape."

GODDARD, TREVOR LESLIE, who died on November 25, aged 85, provided the glue that bound South Africa together between the emerging mid-1950s team of Neil Adcock and Peter Heine, and the box-office pre-isolation line-up of Richards and Procter. He was a serious Test cricketer – a measured opening batsman, an accurate left-arm seamer, and a superb close fielder. After Aubrey Faulkner in the first quarter of the 20th century, Goddard was his country's next great all-rounder, followed by Procter and Jacques Kallis. He was the first South African to make 2,000 runs and take 100 wickets in Tests, though perhaps his most enduring statistic is the best economy-rate – 1.64 – by any bowler with more than 75 Test wickets. He was captain in 13 Tests in the mid-1960s, ushering in a new generation that included the Pollock brothers, Colin Bland and Eddie Barlow.

Goddard was a thinker, adept at analysing opponents' strengths and weaknesses. Lean and tall, he had batting and bowling techniques that were flawlessly classical – "A walking coaching manual," wrote the journalist Neil Manthorp. He was also one of cricket's most popular figures: Don Bradman praised his "qualities of sincerity and integrity", and he later became an evangelical preacher. Just before making his only Test hundred – against England at Johannesburg in 1964-65 – he was almost run out by Tom Cartwright. "It missed by a whisker," said Cartwright. "I nearly ran him out for 99 – and forever I've been glad that I didn't. He was such a nice man."

Born in Durban, Goddard played more football than cricket until he was selected for South African Schools in 1949. He made his debut for Natal in 1952-53, but was on the point of giving up, when he was promoted to open. In the second match in his new role, he made 174 against Western Province at Newlands. It was the impetus he needed. He was selected to tour England under Jack Cheetham in 1955, and made his debut in the First Test at Trent Bridge, opening the bowling and the batting. South Africa went 2–0 down, but fought back to level the series at Headingley. Goddard made 74 in the second innings, and – with Adcock nursing a foot injury – bowled unchanged on the fifth day from 11.30 until the match was won at 4.12, taking five for 69 in 62 overs, 37 of them maidens. He later confessed it was only the whispered encouragement of umpire Frank Chester that kept him going. Although they lost the decider at The Oval, it was the first time South Africa had won two Tests in England. *Wisden* called Goddard "a cricketer of great possibilities".

William Vanderson, Picture Post/Getty Images

All-round nice guy: Trevor Goddard's classical action graces Trent Bridge in 1955.

When England visited in 1956-57, South Africa again recovered from 2–0 down, this time securing a draw. Goddard struggled to make an impact with the ball but, settling on a disciplined leg-stump line, conceded just 1.28 an over in the five matches. In the final Test, at Port Elizabeth, with South Africa needing a win to square the series, he top-scored in their second innings with 30 in 193 minutes on a dreadful pitch to help set England 189; they managed only 130, with Goddard claiming the prize wicket of Peter May.

But a heavy home defeat by Australia in 1957-58 was followed by an unhappy tour of England in 1960. With Geoff Griffin no-balled for throwing at Lord's, Goddard bowled more than 200 overs in the Tests. At The Oval he was on 99 when he edged Brian Statham to slip, where Colin Cowdrey completed a tumbling low catch, with the ball obscured from view. Umpire Eddie Phillipson consulted his colleague Charlie Elliott, before giving Goddard out, but he remained convinced Cowdrey knew the catch had not been taken cleanly.

After that tour, he retired from first-class cricket and moved his family to England, partly so his son's bronchial condition could be treated in London. He worked as a draughtsman, and played for Great Chell in the Staffordshire League, breaking Frank Worrell's record run aggregate, and discovering a more aggressive style.

But Goddard returned to South Africa and, after three years out of Test cricket, was asked to lead the team in Australia in 1963-64. It was hardly a ringing endorsement: Roy McLean, the expected choice, was unavailable, and Peter van der Merwe did not want to make his Test debut as captain. "The Australians wanted to call the tour off because they thought it would be a financial disaster," Peter Pollock recalled. "No one had heard of any of us." One scribe called them "Goddard's Cinderellas".

On the field, Goddard proved a cautious leader, but he was a quietly inspirational mentor to a group of young players. South Africa had six debutants in the drawn First Test at Brisbane but, after a heavy defeat in the Second, at Melbourne, Goddard made 80 and 84 at Sydney, batting over seven hours in all to secure a draw. At Adelaide, he took five for 60 in Australia's first innings to set up victory. With a little more enterprise, South Africa might even have won the series. "Time and time again," said Australia's wicketkeeper Wally Grout, "when a little boldness would have carried them through, they chose caution." On the subsequent three-Test tour of New Zealand, Goddard was at his most miserly, bowling 140 overs (including 81 maidens) for 142 runs. "I have never seen anyone like him for the ability to block up an end," said Pollock. "It's an art that has disappeared."

Goddard continued as leader for the visit of England in 1964-65, but came under criticism when the First Test at Durban was lost heavily. After the third match, the selectors asked him to stand down, offering to tell the public he was feeling the pressure, but he told them they should have the courage to fire him. "They thought he was too nice," said Pollock. A compromise was reached: at the end of the series, won 1–0 by England, Goddard resigned. His sportsmanship was demonstrated in the fourth match, at Johannesburg, where England captain Mike Smith was run out by van der Merwe after wandering out of his crease to pat down the pitch. Smith was given out, but Goddard withdrew the appeal.

He retired from Test cricket again, and missed the subsequent tour of England, but was in magnificent form at the start of 1966-67, and was persuaded back for the visit of Australia. In the First Test at the Wanderers, he bowled a more attacking line than usual, with swing and subtle variations of pace. He took six for 53 in the second innings – his best Test figures – as South Africa beat Australia at home for the first time in 22 attempts. Goddard was carried off on his team-mates' shoulders. The series was won 3–1.

South Africa did not play another Test for three years, but Goddard, now 38, was still in the team when Australia returned in 1969-70. He had already announced he would not be available for the planned tour of England and, when he performed modestly, the selectors decided to look to the future. Goddard wrapped up a thumping win at Johannesburg – the third part of a 4–0 whitewash – with the wicket of Alan Connolly, but it was his final ball in Test cricket: when he walked off, he was told he had been dropped. "I wouldn't be human if I did not say I was disappointed, but that's life," he said. In 41 Tests Goddard made 2,516 runs at 34, and took 123 wickets at 26. In his final first-class match a month later, he took a hat-trick for Natal against Rhodesia. He had a simple philosophy: "Play it hard and straight, and give your best."

He had always been religious and, soon after leaving cricket, attended a mission in Durban with his wife Jean. It inspired him to become an evangelical Christian minister. He worked with aspiring South African sportsmen and in the townships, unpaid roles supported by individual donations. In 1985, he was seriously injured in a car accident after he fell asleep at the wheel. Goddard's death illustrated South Africa's continuing issues with the legacy of apartheid-era cricketers. The national side were playing a Test at Adelaide, but the black armbands they wore on the fourth day were to mark the second anniversary of the death of Phillip Hughes.

GOHEL, BHARAT, who died on May 9, aged 60, was a slow left-armer who played for Hong Kong in the ICC Trophy in the English Midlands in 1986, taking six for 11 in his first match, against Fiji.

GOODWIN, FREDERICK, died on February 19, aged 82. Freddie Goodwin took the new ball in 11 first-class matches for Lancashire in 1955 and 1956, making a considerable impact in his debut season, before drifting out of cricket to concentrate on his main suit as a wing-half for Manchester United. Goodwin's seamers had been spotted while he was playing for Radcliffe in the Central Lancashire League, and he took five wickets on debut, against Kent at Old Trafford. Later that summer he managed a career-best five for 35 against Middlesex at Lord's, including the wickets of Jack Robertson and Bill Edrich. He finished the season with 26 at 18, but took just one wicket in three appearances in 1956. At the other Old Trafford, Goodwin was understudy to Duncan Edwards and Eddie Colman, but their deaths in the 1958 Munich air crash thrust him into the first team. He was a member of the patchwork side that reached that season's FA Cup final, and ever-present as United were First Division runners-up in 1958-59. He was sold to Leeds United in 1960, and later became player-manager of Scunthorpe United, then a well-known and innovative manager with Birmingham City in the 1970s, nurturing the talents of Trevor Francis, Britain's first £1m footballer.

GOODYEAR, WALTER, who died on December 20, aged 99, was Derbyshire's groundsman for more than half a century. He started at Queen's Park in Chesterfield in 1931, aged 14, becoming head groundsman two years later; in 1938 he moved to Derby. Goodyear's pitches were usually well grassed, which suited Derbyshire's production line of seamers. "For a long time I prepared them for Les Jackson," he admitted. "People used to turn up and ask me how it would play. My answer was usually: 'If we win the toss we'll put the buggers in, and Les will have three or four wickets before lunch.' He usually did, you know. If he didn't, I was for it!" Tommy Mitchell, the Derbyshire leg-spinner who won five England caps in the 1930s, was less impressed. "Tommy wanted turning wickets," Goodyear would chuckle. "He never got them, though." Derbyshire won the Championship for the only time in 1936, early in Goodyear's career, and marked his final season by winning the NatWest Trophy in 1981.

GRAY, JAMES ROY, died on October 31, aged 90. Jimmy Gray was the most prolific Hampshire batsman born within the county's borders but, as much as his runs, it was his calm authority and bearing on the field that left an impression. His sleeves rolled with military precision, his boots and pads whitened, Gray was never less than immaculate. At the crease he stood straight-backed, with a grooved defensive technique – the ideal foil for the Caribbean pyrotechnics of his long-time opening partner Roy Marshall.

Over 18 summers, Gray made 22,450 runs for Hampshire, putting him fourth on their all-time list. He assessed bowlers and conditions with caution, content to let Marshall blaze away. "He would have fitted well into the modern game with the way he prepared and his professionalism," said team-mate Brian Timms. Few risks were taken. As John Arlott wrote: "It would violate the laws of cricketing nature if Jimmy Gray were out to a careless or untidy stroke." He was also a handy medium-pacer, taking 451 wickets.

But county cricket would have seen little of Gray had he succeeded in his first ambition of becoming a footballer. Although he was born in the Portswood area of Southampton, his potential was missed by the local clubs, and he signed for Arsenal as a right-back at the start of the 1946-47 season, turning professional a year later. The Compton brothers were already on the staff at Highbury, and he struck up a lasting friendship with another Arsenal footballer-cum-cricketer, Arthur Milton. Gray progressed no further than the reserves, but learned an important lesson. "The will to win, the desire and the need to fight for your team-mates was instilled into me there," he told the journalist Pat Symes. "I carried those things into cricket."

Gray made his debut for Hampshire against Combined Services in Aldershot cricket week in 1948. Another new recruit was Derek Shackleton, who had made his own debut in the previous match. Field Marshal Montgomery was a visitor and, after a dressing-room inspection, gave a shrewd analysis of the Hampshire team. "You've too many old'uns," he said. "I sacked all my older generals, replaced them with younger ones. I suggest you do the same." Gray appreciated the point. "Shack and I were lucky because we came on the scene when there were opportunities," he said. "Hampshire were desperate for young players at the time. His breakthrough came in 1951, when he made his first century and passed 1,000 runs for the first time. In those difficult early seasons he had roomed with the veteran Neil McCorkell, who offered priceless advice – "absolute gold dust", said Gray. He first opened the batting in 1952, and in 1955 began his formidable partnership with

Marshall. Between them they made almost 3,000 runs in the Championship, as Hampshire came third, then their highest finish. Gray saw batting with Marshall in simple terms: "My job is to admire, and let him have as much of the bowling as possible."

Hampshire had attracted criticism for playing cautiously, but the arrival of Colin Ingleby-Mackenzie as captain in 1958 removed the handbrake. In 1961, they were champions for the first time, and Gray contributed more than 2,000 runs. His consistency was remarkable: he scored 1,000 in 12 consecutive seasons. When that sequence ended in 1964, mainly because he played fewer matches in order to concentrate on his new career as a schoolteacher, he still passed 900. He played intermittently in 1965 and 1966 before retiring. Gray became deputy head of Stroud School in Romsey, and later ran a sports shop in Southampton with his former team-mate Peter Sainsbury. He was chairman of the Hampshire cricket committee in the 1990s.

GRAY, ROBERT JOHN, died on May 22, aged 78. Bob Gray was a long-serving Australian journalist who wrote entertainingly for a time on cricket, covering the acrimonious tour of West Indies in 1964-65, but cut down on travelling after his marriage in 1968. He remained on the sports beat, and enjoyed a lifelong friendship with Richie Benaud. It had flowered one night in 1962-63, when they decided to eat before writing their articles: Benaud duly filed his, then – noting his colleague was fast asleep – ad-libbed a story about Graham McKenzie through to Gray's Sydney *Mirror*. Gray found it highly amusing when, early next morning, Benaud was roused by an irate sports editor, complaining he had been scooped. He remained one of the few capable of cracking Benaud's sangfroid, to provoke a rich belly laugh about the details of his latest exploits.

GREEN, DAVID MICHAEL, who died on March 19, aged 76, was one of the most talented and enigmatic of English county batsmen in the 1960s. He again became a regular on county grounds for nearly three decades from 1982, when his presence was normally advertised by the sound of laughter emanating from the press box. His journalistic career, however, was also somewhat enigmatic.

David Green was a golden boy: Manchester Grammar (when it was still a state school) and Oxford; he was blond, stocky and good-looking. He was a cricket Blue in each of his three years, and might have got a rugby Blue as well. But there were two issues: national service was fading away, so teenagers had to compete against men who had served in the forces; and the Oxford rugby Establishment took a surprisingly dim view of Green's penchant for a few pints. With a leisurely third-class degree, he drifted into county cricket with Lancashire, fortuitously at the very moment the old distinctions were abolished, and Oxford men were no longer expected to play as amateurs. He made his mark with a century against the Australians in 1964, to the delight of Tony Pawson in *The Observer*.

MOST FIRST-CLASS RUNS IN A SEASON WITHOUT A CENTURY

Runs		*Season*	*I*	*NO*	*HS*	*50*	*Avge*
2,037	**D. M. Green (Lancs)**	**1965**	**63**	**1**	**85**	**14**	**32.85**
1,709	C. B. Harris (Notts)	1935	49	3	92	12	37.15
1,678	D. E. Davies (Glam)	1952	52	1	97	13	32.90
1,665	C. Washbrook (Lancs)	1939	51	8	91	8	31.72
1,660	D. W. Richardson (Worcs)	1960	61	2	88	12	28.13
1,655	P. E. Richardson (Kent)	1960	53	6	96	11	35.21
1,653	H. T. Bartlett (Sussex)	1947	52	3	95	14	33.73
1,606	M. H. Denness (Kent)	1966	55	4	97	10	31.49
1,570	T. H. Clark (Surrey)	1957	52	4	99	12	32.70
1,562	J. Briggs (Yorks)	1883	50	1	84	12	31.87

D. W. and P. E. Richardson were brothers. There have been six instances of batsmen scoring 1,000 runs in a season without a century since 2000, most recently by M. J. Richardson (Durham) in 2015.

Graham Morris

County blazer: David Green in 2013.

Green, he said, "has always been carefree and too often merely careless. But he was supremely confident in his stance… The same powerful assurance was reflected in his shots." He also showed a flair that season in the new Gillette Cup.

The following year, damp and difficult for batting, Green passed 2,000 runs, mostly opening with Geoff Pullar. But, uniquely, he did so without a single century: 14 fifties, highest score 85. In later years he was ambivalent about this, and called it "part of my wider failure to hit loftier heights as a first-class batsman". It may also have been a sign that, beneath his surface self-assurance, sense of fun and not infrequent truculence, there was a good deal of insecurity. And when his form fell away, the truculence played a part: he called the Lancashire chairman "a prat"; after this led to its predictable conclusion in 1967, he burned his county blazer.

Green found a happy new home at Gloucestershire, where the committee were less censorious, and immediately had another 2,000-run season, this time complete with centuries, including 233 after an epic opening stand of 315 with Arthur Milton at Hove. Green was named one of *Wisden's* Five Cricketers of the Year. His team-mate Tony Brown gives much credit to Milton for teaching him how to play spin better: "Arthur and Greeny struck up a really good partnership, both in the pub and the field, and he would remind him he couldn't hit every ball for four."

But this phase did not last either and, after two more seasons – when still only 31, but with a young family – Green accepted an offer from Ken Graveney, Tom's brother, to help run his catering business. He carried on for a while in one-day cricket, and was in the Gloucestershire team that lost the epic day/night-but-no-floodlights semi-final at Old Trafford in 1971; he was also able to continue with his club rugby, which had started in the Sale back row and went on to include several West Country sides. But he seemed to have reached a judgment on himself: "My spells of good form were neither long enough nor frequent enough. A worrier by nature, I could at times work myself into a state of virtual paralysis," he reflected in his self-published 2013 memoir, *A Handful of Confetti*.

He grew bored with business ("proper work," he wrote, "and I was never all that keen on that"), and in 1982, when Tony Lewis suggested he might write regularly for the *Telegraph*, he jumped at it. And so, for the next 27 years, Green enjoyed life on the cricket and rugby circuits for the daily, and later its Sunday sister. His colleagues much enjoyed having him there, since a day with Greeny meant a stream of high-class anecdotes, insights and playful insults, with a night to follow for those strong enough to keep pace. But little of the joy found its way into the paper: his reports were technically strong, but weak on flavour. "He was a Cavalier at the crease but a Roundhead in print," mused his friend Mark Baldwin, chairman of the Cricket Writers' Club. Friends would urge him to change his style, this time to play *more* shots; but it seems the self-doubt never left him. He did make peace with Lancashire, and they gave him a new blazer.

GUDGE, SUNIL CHANDRAKANT, who died of a heart attack on May 3, aged 56, was a leg-spinner who took more than 100 wickets for Rajasthan, with a best of five for 46 against Gujarat in only his fourth match, in 1979-80. He came close to representative honours, playing two Under-19 Tests against Pakistan, while for India Under-22s against the 1981-82 England tourists in his native Pune, he went wicketless as Geoff Boycott compiled a century. In December 1986, Gudge took all four wickets (for 171) as the visiting Sri Lankans romped to 501 for four against the Board President's XI at Gwalior. He also became a useful batsman, and made 125, his only century, against Gujarat at Pune in 1994-95. He was also a BCCI match referee.

HANIF MOHAMMAD, who died on August 11, aged 81, was only 16 when he walked out to bat in the first unofficial Test between Pakistan and MCC at Lahore in November 1951. It was his first-class debut, and a match of overwhelming significance for his country. He stood 5ft 3in and weighed barely nine stone. "He looked about 12," said Brian Statham. But, as the day progressed, sympathy evaporated: Hanif made 26 in 165 minutes. "We never looked like shifting him."

The MCC attack were the first to experience what bowlers around the world would discover over the next two decades: bowling to Hanif was the most thankless job in cricket. In the next game, he batted more than four hours for 64, as Pakistan chased down 288. It was an innings of incalculable value: eight months later, they were granted Test status.

Having dug Pakistani cricket's foundations, Hanif set about erecting its walls. With Abdul Hafeez Kardar as captain and Fazal Mahmood as strike bowler, he was part of a formidable triumvirate who carried the emerging nation's hopes. Despite his stature, Hanif shouldered the responsibility – time after time constructing monumental innings of concentration, courage and exemplary defence. "He lacked a sense of cricket as a sport, let alone entertainment," wrote Peter Oborne in *Wounded Tiger*, a history of Pakistan cricket. "For Hanif it was a solemn duty, indeed a vocation, whose fundamental purpose was to ensure that his country was not defeated."

There was no better example than his match-saving 337 in 16 hours ten minutes – Hanif remained convinced it was 16 hours 39 (or 999 minutes) – against West Indies in Barbados in 1957-58. Pakistan seemed destined for a crushing defeat when they followed on 473 adrift, with more than three days of the six remaining. Hanif reached stumps on 61, having survived a barrage of bouncers from Roy Gilchrist by opting not to hook, after a word of advice from Clyde Walcott. On the fourth day, he added exactly 100 – Pakistan lost only one wicket – and began to entertain the possibility of a draw. Back in his hotel room, Hanif found motivational messages from Kardar: "You are the only hope to save Pakistan." On the fifth, he defied pain from thighs bruised by Gilchrist, and sunburn that caused the skin under his eyes to peel away. During intervals he would sit in a corner of the dressing-room and eat a piece of chicken. By stumps he had 270, and Pakistan a small lead. That night he allowed himself to fantasise about Len Hutton's Test-record 364 and, after tuning in to Radio Pakistan, realised the impact he was having at home. On a deteriorating final-day pitch, he was within 28 of passing Hutton when he edged Denis Atkinson to wicketkeeper Gerry Alexander. It was then the longest first-class innings, and remains the longest in Tests. He slept all night in his kit.

Hanif was the most celebrated member of perhaps the most remarkable family in cricket history. He was the third of five brothers, three of whom – Wazir, Mushtaq and Sadiq – also became Test players, while the other, Raees, was once Pakistan's twelfth man. Hanif, Mushtaq and Sadiq all played against New Zealand at Karachi in 1969-70 – Hanif's final Test – thus emulating W. G., E. M. and G. F. Grace, for England against Australia in 1880. At least one of the brothers played in Pakistan's first 89 Tests, and Hanif's son Shoaib later played in 45.

Hanif was born in Junagadh in the Indian state of Gujarat, where the family enjoyed an affluent lifestyle, with space for matches that frequently involved him batting all day. They played with a tennis ball shaved on one side for prodigious swing, or a cork ball that flew off a concrete terrace. Techniques were honed, reflexes sharpened. Batsmen were given out for shots that rebounded off trees, and he quickly learned to keep the ball on the ground. Following Partition in 1947, his extended family left their possessions and travelled to Karachi, where high rents forced them to live in an abandoned Hindu temple. "We lost everything," Hanif said. His father, a good club cricketer, soon died, but the boys were urged to excel at sport by their mother, Ameerbi, a successful badminton and carrom player. Hanif's potential was quickly identified, and he moved schools to work with Abdul Aziz Durani, who advised him to concentrate on cricket and spent hours in one-to-one sessions. Durani threw golf balls to teach him to pull and cut, and umpired matches so he could bat for as long as possible. A triple-century in an important schools' final earned his first extensive newspaper coverage. And, playing for Sind and Karachi Muslims against an experienced Northern Muslims side, including Fazal, on a matting wicket at the Karachi Gymkhana, he made 158 in almost eight hours, admitting: "I surprised myself." His reward was a bicycle from an admiring businessman.

Allsport/Getty Images

Vocation: Hanif Mohammad on his way to an unbeaten 102 at Osterley, April 1962.

In 1952, Hanif toured England for the first time with the Pakistan Eaglets, an initiative aimed at exposing the country's emerging talents to English conditions. At his indoor school in south London, Alf Gover instantly compared Hanif to Don Bradman: "Everything is already perfect." Against Devon at Torquay, Hanif was bowled in the first over by a ball that swung in the sea breeze. When his room-mate Sultan Mahmud returned after midnight from a party, he found Hanif, still kitted up, repeating the stroke he should have played in front of a mirror.

During Pakistan's first Test tour, in India in 1952-53, Hanif began with a hundred in each innings against North Zone. In the Tests – where he also kept wicket in the first three games – he made 287 runs at nearly 36, including a six-hour 96 in the Third, at Bombay. He was dubbed the Little Master, which stuck. In 1954, Pakistan sailed to England, then the world's most powerful team. It was a dismal summer and, in a rain-ruined opener at Lord's, Hanif – free of wicketkeeping duties – batted 340 minutes in total for 59 runs. Pakistan lost the Second Test by an innings and, when they were bowled out cheaply again in the drawn Third at Old Trafford, some influential voices suggested their elevation to Test status had been hasty. Kardar's team responded by squaring the series at The Oval with a nerve-shredding 24-run victory, sealed by Hanif's direct hit to run out Jim McConnon.

Wazir led the tour averages, but 19-year-old Hanif – who by now had grown three inches – top-scored, with 1,623 at 36. His mannerisms were becoming familiar: between balls he would twiddle his bat, adjust his sweater, and tug his cap. He did not move forward or back, relying on his eye to assess length. "At first purely defensive," said *Wisden*, "he later blossomed into a most attractive opening batsman, bringing off delightful all-round strokes with a power his slight build belied." Against India the following winter, in Pakistan's first home series, he scored his first Test hundred – 142 in eight and a half hours at Bahawalpur.

His feats brought him celebrity, and its trappings. "He was recognised everywhere – every street, every building, every hotel," said his brother Sadiq. To avoid the distraction of making a living, he was awarded public-sector jobs that meant he could concentrate on cricket, and given land to build a bungalow after his heroics in the Caribbean. Perhaps in response to the pressure, he became a solitary, self-contained figure, retreating to his room on tour to listen to sitar music.

In January 1959, he cemented his status with the highest score in first-class cricket. His 499 for Karachi against Bahawalpur in the Quaid-e-Azam Trophy semi-final surpassed Bradman's 452 for New South Wales 29 years earlier. It took less than 11 hours, with Hanif scoring 230 runs on one day, and 244 the next – numbers he would often quote to prove he was no blocker. He recalled just one chance, given on one of only two occasions he hit the ball in the air, and was run out going for a second from the penultimate ball of the day. He thought he had made 497, only to learn that the boys manning the scoreboard had short-changed him by two. "I was really furious," he said. "Had I known that, I would have waited for the last delivery to get the required runs." He remained at the summit until 1994, when Brian Lara made his unbeaten 501 for Warwickshire against Durham.

Patrick Eagar, Popperfoto/Getty Images

Captain rock: Hanif Mohammad on the 1967 tour of England.

For Pakistan, Hanif remained rock-like, often showing bravery as well as skill. Against West Indies at Karachi in 1958-59, he suffered a broken finger late on the fourth day as Pakistan chased 88. He batted on to spare a team-mate an awkward few minutes, retiring hurt next morning and missing the rest of the series. And in India in 1960-61, he appeared in all five Tests, despite having had his toenails removed because of a foot infection: his mother had convinced him national pride was at stake. In the First Test at Bombay, he ignored medical advice, playing in a pair of specially adapted shoes. "It was like batting with nails piercing your feet – a cricketing crucifixion," he said. He rated his first-innings 160 as his greatest performance.

And Hanif was also at the crease on the fourth day against Australia at Karachi in 1959-60, when Dwight D. Eisenhower arrived with Pakistan's recently installed military leader, General Ayub Khan, who was keen for his visitor to see the country's most famous sportsman. Hanif batted most of the day for 40 not out, but Eisenhower left early as Pakistan dawdled to 104 by stumps – the second slowest complete day in Test history. No American president has watched Test cricket since.

The 1960s were a struggle for Pakistan and, as the pioneers slipped into retirement, the captaincy passed to Hanif. His first assignment, a solitary Test against Australia in Karachi in 1964-65, saw six players make their debuts, including Asif Iqbal and Majid Khan, and there were three more new faces for the return at the MCG a month later. It was the first time Hanif had batted in Australia but – just as he had in England in 1954 and the West Indies in 1957-58 – he adapted instantly, making 104 and 93. "That second innings was the best I saw him play," said Asif. "It was grey overhead and the pitch was difficult, but his technique was equal to it." Hanif met Bradman, who had expected a tall, powerful figure, and was delighted to discover otherwise.

In 1967, he brought a team of tyros to England. At Lord's he shared an eighth-wicket partnership of 130 with Asif, who was caught in the deep for 76: "Afterwards in the Pavilion he said, 'I'm proud of you, but very disappointed with how you got out. As a batsman you have to go on and get hundreds – your concentration needs to be much better.'" Hanif underlined his point by batting more than nine hours across three days in a match-saving undefeated 187. *Wisden* made him a Cricketer of the Year.

Despite that, Pakistan lost 2–0, and Hanif was stripped of the captaincy. He played just four more Tests, and became embroiled in a bitter disagreement with Kardar, now the chairman of selectors. Hanif thought he could still contribute, but Kardar wanted him to retire immediately, and suggested it might be better for the careers of his brothers if he did. Feeling he was being blackmailed, Hanif stepped down, having played 55 Tests and scored 3,915 first-class runs at 44, with 12 hundreds. He carried on in domestic cricket until the mid-1970s, ending with 17,059 first-class runs at 52.

He worked for Pakistan International Airlines, managing their team to three successive Wills Cup wins in the 1980s, ran the PIA colts scheme with his trademark zeal, and oversaw the early development of several future Test players. He was also a selector. His death marked the end of an era, and sparked an inevitable discussion about whether he ranked above Javed Miandad, Inzamam-ul-Haq and Younis Khan as Pakistan's greatest batsman. "I have no doubt he was," said Asif. "He played in an era when Pakistan were one of the weakest sides, and had a huge responsibility. If you look at all the people who have scored Test triple-centuries, very few did so in conditions alien to them, against strong bowling attacks and without the benefit of protective clothing." Sadiq put it more succinctly: "Whenever he went in to bat, the country was glad he was there."

HARRAGAN, ROBERT, died on January 26, aged 61. Bob Harragan was a cricket obsessive who wrote one of the cheeriest columns in local journalism: Bits and Bobs in the *South Wales Guardian*. It was supposedly a column about everything, but as the paper's editor Steve Adams recalled: "If Bob was writing about the county council's policy on street lights, he would somehow find an analogy about Glamorgan openers of the 1980s." Previously, he had covered local cricket for the *South Wales Evening Post*, and championed players such as Robert Croft and Simon Jones. He was also a much-valued contributor to *Wisden's* Chronicle, which was regularly enlivened by his reports of strange events in the Welsh leagues.

HARRISON, LEO, who died on October 12, aged 94, began his first-class career for Hampshire nine days before Hitler invaded Poland, and ended it in the middle of the Swinging Sixties. He made 396 appearances in all, most of them as a neat, jaunty, bespectacled wicketkeeper, one of the most reliable on the circuit. His send-off to batsmen was invariably "It ain't half a bloody game, mate," a catchphrase turned into the title of a short story by Harrison's close friend John Arlott. It was Arlott's only attempt at fiction, and he was fuming when his prudish publisher changed bloody to bloomin'.

Harrison was initially seen as a batsman of great promise, but took several seasons to contribute regular runs, and even longer to establish himself behind the stumps. Once he got an extended go, however, he proved hard to dislodge. "He was always very relaxed, almost to the point of being casual," said his protégé and successor Brian Timms. "Everything he did was stylish." Harrison made 681 dismissals, 103 of them stumpings, many standing up to Derek Shackleton, whose unfailing accuracy left him in awe: "I've picked up the ball and seen six green marks on the seam and none on the shiny part." They became clinical in analysing opponents' weaknesses. "When we saw a batsman go on to the back foot, we just knew it wouldn't be long before he would be in serious trouble."

The son of a builder from the fishing village of Mudeford near Christchurch (now in Dorset, but then part of Hampshire), Harrison joined the county staff in 1938, making his debut against Worcestershire the following summer, a few miles from home at Dean Park, Bournemouth. In the second game of the week, he played against a Yorkshire side including Herbert Sutcliffe in his final Championship match, and Hedley Verity in his last but one.

Harrison served in the RAF during the war, although poor eyesight quickly ended ambitions of becoming a pilot. Instead he made instruments for Bomber Command, stationed at bases on the east coast, and never forgot the high spirits of the crews who knew the odds were stacked against their survival. He remained in the RAF, and in 1946 played first-class matches for them and the Combined Services, as well as for Hampshire. There, a queue of keepers was waiting to replace Neil McCorkell, and Harrison was one of several given a chance. With the bat he struggled to live up to pre-war expectations, and needed his excellent fielding to stay in the team. But in 1951 he passed 1,000 runs for the first time, a feat he repeated the following year. By now Harrison's problems with his vision had forced him to play in glasses, but in 1955 he became Hampshire's regular keeper, and was selected for the Players against the Gentlemen at Lord's. Three years later, Colin Ingleby-Mackenzie took on the Hampshire captaincy. The Old Etonian and the builder's son were an unlikely alliance, but they became firm friends and regular partners at the races and at parties, often creeping back to the team hotel as the morning milk arrived. Thanks to Ingleby-Mackenzie, Harrison was able to show off his poker skills at some of England's finest country houses. Hampshire's unexpected title triumph in 1961 was the crowning of Harrison's career, and he made a telling contribution with 656 runs and 62 dismissals. But he was 39 by then and, after one more productive year, Timms took over, although Harrison returned for a farewell appearance against Surrey in 1966.

His friendship with Arlott had begun when Arlott was a young Southampton policeman who would ensure his beat took in the nets at the county ground. Harrison often dined at his house in Alresford, and was guest of honour at the unveiling of a plaque there in 2009. He was a regular visitor when Arlott retired to Alderney. "Honest as the day," Arlott wrote of his friend. "And a trier to the last gasp." His death left John Manners, also of Hampshire, as the last survivor of pre-war county cricket (see *Wisden 2016*, page 65).

In their pomp, Shackleton and Harrison exerted such a stranglehold over the Glamorgan batsman Bernard Hedges that his dismissal gathered an air of inevitability. On one occasion, he edged Shackleton's third ball into Harrison's gloves, and turned round in exasperation: "You two bastards must burst out laughing every time you see me come in." Harrison paused. "No, we don't laugh, Bernard – we're very happy to see you."

HARRISON, ROLAND, who died on August 2, aged 73, was a tough opening batsman who scored more than 10,000 runs in the Lancashire League for Burnley. He captained them to three titles in the 1970s. Playing against Rishton in 1981, he batted on after Michael Holding broke his jaw.

HARVEY, CLARENCE EDGAR, died on October 5, aged 95. Born on St Patrick's Day in 1921, "Mick" Harvey was the second of six brothers, all of whom turned out for Melbourne's Fitzroy club. Four played for Victoria, and two – Neil and Merv – for Australia. Mick, who had been an infantryman on the infamous Kokoda Trail in New Guinea during the war, had three matches for Victoria in 1948-49, before accepting a job as a printer in Queensland. He had spotted that batting opportunities were more plentiful up there, especially as the stalwart Bill Brown was about to retire. By the end of 1949-50, Harvey had made his debut for Queensland, and the following summer hit the first of three hundreds for them, against New South Wales. Neil Harvey, the most famous of the brethren, wrote that Mick "was a much more solid batsman than the rest of the family, having a good defence, but he was not really a good player of spin bowling". He became an umpire, and stood in two Tests, both in 1979, and six one-day internationals.

HEALD, TIMOTHY VILLIERS, who died on November 20, aged 72, was a writer able to turn his hand to almost any subject. Among his many books were two series of crime novels, an account of Hong Kong in its final days as a British colony, and a study of the old boys' network; the aristocratic subjects of his biographies included the Queen, the Duke of Edinburgh, Prince Charles, and John Steed of *The Avengers*. At Sherborne School, Heald was commissioned by the head boy, Stanley Johnson – father of Boris – to write a polemic attacking the fagging system. It was abolished soon after. Johnson's daughter Rachel appointed him royal correspondent of *The Lady*, and he also worked for a variety of newspapers. His output included several cricket books, notably biographies of Brian Johnston and Denis Compton. Heald recalled encountering Compton at the wake following Johnston's funeral in 1994. Unusually, he was without a drink, and Heald asked if he could fetch one. "No thanks, old boy," replied Compton. "The prime minister's getting me one." Seconds later, John Major appeared with a full glass.

HEWES, LEONARD BRIAN, died on April 11, aged 80, after collapsing in the Trent Bridge Inn. Brian Hewes was Nottinghamshire's scorer from 2007 to 2011, after several seasons in charge of the Second XI book. The pavilion flag flew at half mast in his memory during the Championship match against Surrey on April 12.

HEYS, WILLIAM, died on May 21, aged 85. Bill Heys was one of three wicketkeepers tried by Lancashire in 1957. He played five first-class matches that year, two of them against the West Indian tourists, making a career-best 46 in the first. He did well enough with the gloves, pulling off three stumpings in his first two games, but better batsmen were preferred, and he never appeared again. Heys played for Church in the Lancashire League for 22 seasons from 1949, and was part of the club for almost 70 years.

HEYWOOD, MALCOLM, who died on January 22, aged 81, was a well-known figure in the Lancashire League, and president from 2001 to 2004. A consistent opening batsman, he played for Todmorden for 20 years, captaining for five in the mid-1960s, when his team once included a handy substitute professional in Garry Sobers. Heywood outscored him – 52 to 12 – and came up against many other big names, once making 83 not out against Sobers's fearsome West Indies team-mate Charlie Griffith. A teacher, he later produced several books on local themes, including a lavish history of Todmorden cricket, *Cloth Caps & Cricket Crazy*, co-written with his wife Freda and son Brian, who also played for the club.

HIGGS, KENNETH, died on September 7, aged 79. A letter to Old Trafford in 1957 from Staffordshire captain Denis Haynes changed Ken Higgs's life. Higgs was 20, and intent on becoming a footballer, until Haynes suggested Lancashire take a look at the strapping seamer who was jarring bat handles in Minor Counties cricket. The Lancashire coach Stan Worthington returned to Manchester with a firm recommendation: Higgs could be "the next Alec Bedser".

He quickly lived up to expectations. Against Hampshire on his Championship debut in 1958, he took a wicket in his first over, and in the second innings claimed seven for 36. By the end of the season, he had 67 at 22. When Brian Statham was away on Test duty, Higgs became the indefatigable leader of the attack. From 1959, he topped 100 wickets in three successive summers. "He did not have days when he sprayed it around, and he did not bowl long hops. He was just so consistent," said Lancashire captain Bob Barber.

Off a gently curving run-up of no more than 15 strides, Higgs generated cut and swing with a snap of the wrist and an action that harnessed all his strength. He was an imposing figure – the writer Paul Edwards described him as having "an arse that crossed two postcodes" – and operated at around 80mph, slower than Statham but with a similar premium on accuracy. Later, at Leicestershire, he became a more voluble figure, prone to

Central Press/Getty Images

One for the camera: John Snow and Ken Higgs swap pint pot for cup and saucer at The Oval, 1966.

volcanic eruptions and seldom short of a word for batsmen. "He was like a raging bull on the field, but the kindest, gentlest man off it," said his Leicestershire team-mate Jonathan Agnew. "He had a chihuahua, which summed him up really – this massive man with a tiny dog."

His Test statistics suggest he was unlucky not to win more caps. In 15 matches he took 71 wickets at 20, with an economy-rate of 2.14. On debut against South Africa at The Oval in 1965, he took the new ball in the second innings with Statham, in his final Test. Higgs claimed eight in the match, and was selected for the winter's Ashes tour. He played in the First Test at Brisbane, but succumbed to injury and illness, and did not get back into the team until the New Zealand leg of the trip, when he took 17 wickets in the three Tests, including figures of 9–7–5–4 in the second innings at Christchurch. He retained his place at home against West Indies, and was the only England player to appear in all five Tests, taking 24 wickets at 25, including six for 91 at Lord's – "a triumph for industry and wholeheartedness" said *The Times*. Many of his victims were top-order batsmen: Conrad Hunte and Rohan Kanhai were bagged four times each. At The Oval, Higgs and last man John Snow put on 128. Higgs finally gave a return catch to David Holford when 63, with the pair unaware they were two short of the Test record for the tenth wicket. As they celebrated with pints in the dressing-room, they were asked to pose for photographs on the pavilion balcony. But they were told frothing glasses might give the wrong message, and ordered to replace them with teacups.

As a schoolboy, Higgs had shown greater potential as a footballer, and was signed up by Port Vale as a centre-half. He was selected for an FA youth tour of West Germany, but national service intervened, and in the army he began to play more cricket. His enthusiasm grew and, when his brother's Staffordshire League team were a man short, he was pressed into playing. He soon became a regular. Higgs's performances for Lancashire dipped in the early 1960s. He began straying down the leg side, but his problems had more to do with anxiety about the annual round of contract negotiations and lack of financial security. He did not drive, and commuted each day from Staffordshire by train and bus. When Lancashire were playing Northamptonshire he was accompanied by fellow Potteries resident David Steele – until Steele failed to walk for an edge, and Higgs pointedly caught a different train home.

It was hard to avoid Old Trafford's complex internal politics. Before playing Nottinghamshire at Worksop in 1961, the team were about to leave their hotel when Barber took a call from Worthington at Old Trafford telling him the committee thought Higgs was tired, and demanding he be sent home. Barber refused, and asked why: "Stan said because he had taken fewer wickets than at the same point in the previous season." Barber agreed to ask Higgs how he felt. "He said he wasn't tired and wondered why I was asking. I said, 'Because the committee think you haven't taken enough wickets this season.' Ken just said, 'Aye, it's because I haven't bowled enough.'"

He put his slump behind him in 1965 to pass 100 wickets for the fourth time and earn his Test call-up. He was a *Wisden* Cricketer of the Year in 1968, and chosen for the tour of the Caribbean in 1967-68, but was furious when he was ignored for the Tests, as the selectors opted for the greater pace of Snow, David Brown and Jeff Jones. He played only once more for England.

But, when nerveless accuracy was called for, he was still one of the best on the circuit. In 1969, he bowled at the death in two remarkable Championship finishes. Warwickshire needed five runs from the final over with five wickets in hand, but Higgs took two wickets, and kept them to three. And, at Bramall Lane, with Yorkshire requiring one to win off the last over, he bowled a triple-wicket maiden. He left Lancashire at the end of the season, feeling that the newly arrived overseas players were being disproportionately rewarded, and sought more lucrative employment with Rishton in the Lancashire League. Two years later, he was enticed to Leicestershire, where he was a regular for eight summers. Under Ray Illingworth's canny captaincy he played a leading role in their 1970s successes. When Leicestershire were champions in 1975, he bowled 560 overs and took 50 wickets at 29.

He was never less than combative. "He had battles with Javed Miandad," recalled Agnew. "In one game, Javed played him back down the pitch defensively, and Ken stared at him, determined not to be the one to break eye contact. The trouble was, he was still staring at him when he bent down to pick up the ball, and couldn't find it. After it rolled past him, Javed ran a quick single."

Higgs was captain in 1979 but played less often, and became the county coach, dispensing kindly wisdom to emerging seamers such as Agnew, Les Taylor, Gordon Parsons and Phil DeFreitas. In 1986, aged 49, he was summoned for two final Championship matches. Against Yorkshire at Grace Road, bowling off three paces but observing the time-honoured principles of line and length, he took five for 22 off 11 overs. "I don't know what the fuss is about," he told reporters afterwards. "I'm still getting 2,000 wickets a week in the nets."

HINTZ, ANDREW JOHN, who died of cancer on February 7, aged 52, was a seamer who played six first-class and ten List A games for Canterbury in the late 1980s, before suffering stress fractures in the back. He took four for 23 in a Shell Cup one-day game at Auckland on New Year's Eve in 1986, and five more the following season – opening the bowling with Michael Holding – as Canterbury beat Auckland in a first-class match.

HOBDEN, MATTHEW EDWARD, who died on January 2, aged 22, was a fast bowler of enormous potential whose muscular presence and 6ft 4in frame earned him the nickname "The Beast" in the Sussex dressing-room. He was a big personality, too: rebellious, roguish, greatly popular. "He was always in some sort of scrape, but he was a good kid," said the former Sussex coach Mark Robinson. "You could not help but like him." His promise was noted beyond Hove, and Kevin Shine – the ECB's lead fast-bowling coach – called him "the strongest, most powerful cricketer I've ever seen on the England Performance Programme". Shine was certain he would have gone on to play international cricket.

Hobden was born in Eastbourne, but owed his opportunity at Sussex to eye-catching performances for Cardiff MCCU, including five for 62 against Warwickshire in his second first-class match. In June 2013 he was thrust into the Sussex team for a televised 40-over

Bob Thomas/Getty Images

Hitting the heights: Bishan Bedi, Mushtaq Mohammad, Alan Hodgson, Peter Willey, Jim Yardley, Wayne Larkins and George Sharp celebrate Northamptonshire's first trophy, the 1976 Gillette Cup.

game against Nottinghamshire at Trent Bridge, and did not look out of his depth. A year later he made his Championship debut against the same opponents at Hove, where his first-innings wickets were the Test trio of Phil Jaques, James Taylor and Samit Patel. "He was a muscle bowler who hit the pitch hard and made the ball go away," said Robinson. "People did not want to face him in the nets." He was also blessed with a magnificent arm, and against Durham at Chester-le-Street in April 2015 showed his capabilities as a batsman, with a pugnacious unbeaten 65 in a last-wicket stand of 164 with Ollie Robinson.

Hobden had been celebrating New Year in Scotland with friends, when he died after falling from a roof. The county retired his No. 19 shirt, and planted a tree at Hove in his memory; the players gathered around it to celebrate a late-season victory over Gloucestershire. But his death cast a pall over Sussex's summer. "When we came back in pre-season and the full squad were together, his absence was really obvious," said wicketkeeper Ben Brown. "There have been moments where we've thought, 'Matt would have been good here' – and the memories of when he played come back. He gave us so many funny moments."

HODGSON, ALAN, who died on October 6, aged 64, was one of many cricketers from the North-East to head Northamptonshire's way during the 1960s and '70s. A tall, strongly built fast bowler from Consett, he caught the eye as a 16-year-old triallist in 1968, and two years later made the first of 99 first-class appearances. His best season was 1976, when he, Sarfraz Nawaz and John Dye formed what *Wisden* called "a match-winning combination", as Northamptonshire finished runners-up in the Championship and won the Gillette Cup, their first major trophy. He took 41 first-class wickets that year, including a career-best five for 30 against Oxford University. In 1977, he grabbed six for 22 in a Sunday League game against Derbyshire. "His height was his main asset," said former captain Jim Watts, "but he always did enough with the ball to trouble batsmen, and often took two or three wickets in the middle of the innings, when they were not always noticed."

A few weeks before his death, Hodgson posed for a photograph on the outfield at Northampton with five other members of Mushtaq Mohammad's 1976 side at the annual former players' day, an event he helped organise for many years. Back trouble had ended his county career in 1979, but he enjoyed success in local club cricket, returned to Wantage Road as a coach and manager of the indoor school, and also served as vice-chairman of the Northamptonshire Cricket League. A convivial man, he shared a flat with Colin Milburn for a time, and was an important source of insight and anecdote when James Graham-Brown set about writing his acclaimed play *When The Eye Has Gone*, about Milburn's tragic decline (see page 172). Sadly, Hodgson did not live to see it performed.

HOLDSWORTH, WILLIAM EDGAR NEWMAN, died on July 31, aged 87. Bill Holdsworth was a seamer who played 27 matches for Yorkshire, the first in 1952. He began the following season by taking five for 21 against Essex, and claimed a career-best six for 58 against Derbyshire at Scarborough. After that he was a professional for various league teams. He later became president of Otley Golf Club.

HURD, ALAN, who died on April 11, aged 78, was an off-spinner who made a spectacular debut for Essex, taking a wicket with his first ball on the way to six for 15 – and ten for 77 in the match – to set up victory over Kent on a helpful track at Clacton in 1958. Not long before that he had helped Cambridge win the Varsity Match "Well, 'Hurdy-Gurdy' was my secret weapon," remembered his captain Ted Dexter, "because he bowled his off-spin really slow and loopy, which was very useful against the tail. He was the bowler I turned to in the closing overs, and we beat Oxford in the last few minutes." Hurd took 34 wickets in six matches for Essex that year, but he was no batsman, and Trevor Bailey, his county captain, once pronounced him "the worst fielder ever to have played first-class cricket", although Bailey did smile about an incident when Hurd was barracked loudly from the cheap seats at Leyton after letting a boundary through his legs. A member responded with: "But he's terribly kind to his mother!" Hurd's three seasons of first-class cricket were split between university and county: he took 73 wickets in 1958, then 82 in 1959, and 94 in 1960. After that he turned full-time to teaching – Chris Tavaré and Paul Downton came under his wing at Sevenoaks School – and played for Sevenoaks Vine.

IMTIAZ AHMED, who died on December 31, five days before his 89th birthday, was a mainstay of Pakistan's early Test teams: he played in their first 39 matches, from 1952-53, until missing one in England in 1962. He was an attacking batsman – a good driver and hooker – and a dependable wicketkeeper who took seven catches off Fazal Mahmood in one of Pakistan's greatest triumphs, the victory at The Oval to square their first series in England, in 1954. Imtiaz finished that trip with 87 first-class victims, a record for a touring keeper that is unlikely to be beaten.

He was born in 1928 in Lahore. Early coaching came from his father, also a wicketkeeper, who drummed in the importance of the stance, ideally moving only one of the feet to collect the ball. Imtiaz preferred standing back to the seamers, and recalled dropping just one chance off Fazal (Denis Compton on 13), when he stood up to him at Trent Bridge in 1954, as Fazal's pace was down because of an injury. Compton went on to 278.

Imtiaz played four Ranji Trophy matches for Northern India before Partition, and hit an unbeaten 138 against Lindsay Hassett's Australian Services team in October 1945, when he shared a seventh-wicket stand of 268 with his future Test captain, Abdul

L. Blandford, Topical Press Agency/Getty Images

Permanent fixture: Imtiaz Ahmed in 1954.

Hafeez Kardar. After the creation of Pakistan in 1947, Imtiaz stayed in Lahore, and in 1948-49 made 76 and 131 while opening in the first official match played by the new national team, against the West Indian tourists. Three years later, in Karachi, he top-scored with 43 in the first innings against MCC, in a game Pakistan eventually won by four wickets, helping their bid for Test status.

The previous season, Imtiaz had made what remained his highest score, in unusual circumstances. He was one of three Pakistanis invited to play for the Indian Prime Minister's XI against the Commonwealth XI touring team in Bombay, and things were not looking good when his side were forced to follow on. But Imtiaz went on the counter-attack, and had reached 263 when he was hit in the face by a ball from the Kent off-spinner Ray Dovey. He retired hurt, but returned later to take his score to 300 not out.

Pakistan attained Test status in 1952-53, and Imtiaz was among the first on the teamsheet for the inaugural tour of India. To start with, their wicketkeeper was 17-year-old Hanif Mohammad, but Kardar realised Hanif was going to be his leading batsman, and Imtiaz was given the gloves from the Fourth Test. He kept them for the rest of the 1950s, and beyond. It led to his being shuffled up and down the batting order – his only Test double-century, 209 against New Zealand at Lahore in 1955-56, came from No. 8 – but Imtiaz was not one for complaining. In the West Indies in 1957-58, he was asked to open at Kingston, and kicked off the Third Test with a superb 122 against an attack led by the ferocious Roy Gilchrist, although his efforts were rather forgotten when Garry Sobers scorched to 365 not out. The following season, back in Pakistan, the 12-year-old Majid Khan was inspired by the sight of Imtiaz hooking another speedy West Indian, Wes Hall.

After Kardar retired, Imtiaz captained Pakistan against England in 1961-62, before being shoved aside in favour of the Oxford Blue Javed Burki for the subsequent tour of England. Burki, only 23 when that trip started, was taken aback: "Imtiaz was head and shoulders above everyone in terms of character, respect of fellow players, standing in the game and general reputation. I thought he was the best captain I had ever played under." Injury meant Imtiaz finally missed a Test – the Third at Leeds – in a forgettable tour for Pakistan. They had no more fixtures for 26 months, by which time his long career was finally over.

Imtiaz served for many years in the Pakistan Air Force, rising to the rank of wing commander, and filled several coaching and administrative roles: he was chairman of the Test selectors from 1976 to 1978, the year he managed the team which toured England under Wasim Bari. Imtiaz was eventually given a lifetime achievement award by the Pakistan board. He had become Pakistan's oldest surviving Test cricketer when Israr Ali died at the start of 2016, a distinction passed to Wazir Mohammad, the oldest of the famous brotherhood.

ISRAR ALI, who died on February 1, aged 88, was a slender left-arm seamer who played in Pakistan's inaugural Test, in Delhi in 1952-53. His captain Abdul Hafeez Kardar apparently thought he was a batsman, so put him at No. 3: Israr made one and nine, didn't bowl, and was dropped. He was back for the Third Test, but did not take a wicket, and – one of several to fall foul of the autocratic Kardar – had to wait seven years for another chance, returning for two matches against Australia in 1959-60. At last he made his mark, bowling Australia's opener Les Favell for a duck at Dacca with a ball that broke a stump. He removed Favell again in the second innings, and twice more in the Second Test at Lahore; his only other victim was Alan Davidson (twice). Outside his Test appearances, Israr took more than 100 first-class wickets, including nine for 58 – the first nine, before Zulfiqar Ahmed took the tenth – for Bahawalpur against Punjab in 1957-58. Later that season he had the remarkable figures of 11–10–1–6 (five bowled and one lbw) as Dacca University were skittled for 39 in the Quaid-e-Azam Trophy semi-final; he had earlier scored 79 as opener. Bahawalpur won the trophy that year, Israr taking four for 18 in the fourth innings as Karachi C were despatched for 82. He had two successful seasons in the Lancashire leagues with Bacup in 1959 and Ashton in 1960, but soon afterwards was badly injured in a road accident, which ended his cricket career. A farmer and land-owner, he was a national selector in 1983-84.

JACOBS, JENNIFER MARY, died on July 20, aged 60. Jen Jacobs played seven Tests and 13 one-day internationals for Australia. Equally steady as batsman or off-spinner, she followed 48 at Ahmedabad in 1983-84 with four for 72 at Bombay. Originally from Adelaide, she moved to Melbourne in 1983, and played for Victoria for several seasons.

JAVED AKHTAR, who died on July 8, aged 75, played one Test for Pakistan, but was better known as an umpire, standing in 18 Tests and 40 one-day internationals between 1976-77 and the 1999 World Cup. His later matches were mired in controversy, particularly in England in 1998; South African administrator Ali Bacher accused him of being on a bookmaker's payroll after some peculiar decisions, especially during the Headingley Test which England won narrowly to take the series. Akhtar sued, and was cleared of any wrongdoing after Bacher failed to turn up for the court hearing in Pakistan. An off-spinner, he had taken seven for 56 – which remained a career-best – in only his fifth first-class match, for the President's XI against Ted Dexter's MCC tourists in his home town of Rawalpindi in 1961-62. Despite that, Akhtar originally missed out on selection for the England tour that followed, only to be called up late as a replacement for Haseeb Ahsan. He went straight into the Third Test at Headingley, where he failed to take a wicket in England's only innings. Six county games produced ten victims, but he never had another Test. Akhtar played on for Rawalpindi – finishing with 187 wickets at 18 – until 1975-76, by which time he had already started umpiring.

JENKINSON, NEIL, who died on July 20, aged 77, was a diligent researcher and historian whose books included biographies of Philip Mead, Richard Daft and Charles Llewellyn, a history of Hambledon CC, and *Cricket's Greatest Comeback,* the story of how Hampshire defeated Warwickshire in 1922 after being dismissed for 15. He was Hampshire's honorary curator, and as a solicitor in Winchester numbered John Arlott among his clients.

JONES, WILLIAM GEORGE, died on October 18, aged 65. Bill Jones was a well-built left-arm seamer who was on the MCC cricket staff in the early 1970s alongside Ian Botham, who remained a firm friend: Jones made an appearance when Botham was featured on *This Is Your Life*. He played for several county Second XIs, and eventually turned to coaching, invariably referring to the children in his charge as "anklebiters". A regular in the Lord's indoor nets, Jones coached at University College School in Hampstead for 42 years from 1973, before retiring because of ill health. Botham was one of several celebrities who attended a fundraising dinner for him early in 2016.

JUNAID JAMSHED, one of 47 casualties when a PIA plane crashed in mountains in northern Pakistan on December 7, had been a prominent pop star and fashion designer before becoming a Muslim cleric. He was 52. His song "Dil Dil Pakistan" had been adopted as an unofficial anthem for the national team, and was sung at most of their matches.

KHALID QURESHI, who died on February 10, two days before his 88th birthday, was a member of the team which visited India for Pakistan's first official Test series, in 1952-53. A slow left-armer, he played in six tour games, but none of the Tests. After that, Qureshi trained as an electrical engineer in England, where he had some success for Lowerhouse in the Lancashire League, and back home in 1956-57 he claimed 12 for 77 as Punjab beat Bahawalpur by an innings. His best figures, nine for 28, came four years later in an Ayub Trophy quarter-final for Lahore, and he ended up with 143 wickets at 19. For Lahore Gymkhana in 1962, Qureshi took nine for none as the Punjab Club were skittled for three. His father and two brothers also played first-class cricket.

LAMBERT, DENNIS ALFRED, who died on November 13, aged 82, was one of the founders of the Association of Cricket Statisticians; in 1972, he and Robert Brooke placed an advertisement in *The Cricketer*, seeking like-minded recruits. Lambert was the ACS's first secretary, and chairman from 1979 to 1981. An accountant, he was also Leicestershire's official statistician, and wrote their book in the Christopher Helm county history series.

LEE, DONALD, died on August 10, aged 83. Don Lee played 31 first-class matches in South Africa over 15 years from 1952-53, mainly for Griqualand West. An off-spinning all-rounder, he never bettered his debut match haul of seven wickets, in a victory over North Eastern Transvaal in Pretoria. His only century, 111 against Orange Free State, came four seasons later. Lee became a first-class umpire; his brother, Lennard, also played for Griqualand West.

LLOYD, BARRY JOHN, who died on December 1, aged 63, was an accurate off-spinner who played for Glamorgan from 1972 to 1983, sharing the captaincy with Javed Miandad in 1982. Lloyd took 55 wickets that season, his best return, although his best figures – eight for 70 – had come the year before, against Lancashire at Cardiff. He was also an effective one-day container, going for less than four an over. "A terrific servant to cricket in Wales, and a bloody good bloke," said Glamorgan's coach Robert Croft. Lloyd later played for Wales Minor Counties, and turned out for his club, Pontarddulais, until 2010. His daughter Hannah played five one-day internationals for England.

McCAY, DAVID LAWRENCE CORNELIUS, who died on September 20, aged 72, was a bespectacled all-rounder who top-scored with 82 – starting with a six – on his debut for Western Province, against the touring Australians at Cape Town in November 1966. After that he was more of a hit with the ball, two months later taking eight for 76 – and 14 for 154 in the match – against Natal B at Newlands. "He was a big bloke, and could swing it both ways," said former WP selector Fritz Bing. "You could compare his bowling speed to Eddie Barlow." McCay toured England in 1967 with a strong South African Universities side, but never quite recaptured the form of his early matches, and embarked on a successful business career. He was the owner of the winery and restaurant at Constantia Uitsig, where he established a well-appointed cricket ground which has been used for tour and academy games.

MADDOCKS, LEONARD VICTOR, died on August 27, aged 90. Len Maddocks features in one of the most famous pieces of archive cricket film: rapped on the pads at Old Trafford in 1956, he is given out lbw as Jim Laker takes his 19th wicket. Maddocks batted four times against Laker and Tony Lock in his two Tests on that tour, and lasted 27 minutes in total. Luckily, he wasn't in that side for his batting: Maddocks was a slender, unflashy wicketkeeper, although it was his misfortune to be an almost permanent understudy. He was first chosen for Victoria as a 20-year-old in 1946-47, but had to serve a long apprenticeship under Bill Baker and Ian McDonald, the older brother of Maddocks's future Test team-mate Colin. Not until 1953-54 did Maddocks nail down a spot, but his anticipation and sound glovework – which contrasted with the flair of Don Tallon and the rustic effectiveness of Gil Langley – marked him out as one to watch. Maddocks also averaged 40 in his first full season, presenting a straight bat.

When Len Hutton's side arrived for the 1954-55 Ashes, the selectors chose Maddocks for an Australian XI early in the tour. Then, after Langley suffered an eye injury while keeping in a Sheffield Shield game, Maddocks was drafted in for the last three Tests. He kept quiet about a broken finger on his right hand, which his crossed-gloves stance exposed to further damage, but his batting remained solid: on debut at Melbourne, he top-scored with 47 from No. 8 as the last four wickets doubled the score to 231 to give Australia a narrow lead. In the second innings, however, he was castled first ball – one of Frank Tyson's seven for 27 – as they were blown away for 111. In the next match, at Adelaide, Maddocks again batted grittily, again top-scored (this time with 69), and again pushed

Australia to a respectable first-innings total, topped off by a 92-run stand for the ninth wicket with his skipper, Ian Johnson. But Australia crumbled once more, and England clinched the match, and the Ashes.

In England in 1956, Langley was first choice behind the stumps, until he broke a finger against Somerset. Back came Maddocks, although he was unfortunate to play on spin-friendly surfaces in the Third and Fourth Tests which rankled for ever with the tourists. He kept well, but his batting failed completely.

Maddocks played one more Test, in India on the way home, but pressure of work – he was an accountant with Australian Paper Manufacturers – forced him to withdraw from the 1957-58 tour of South Africa, where Wally Grout became the permanent replacement for the retired Langley. Maddocks continued to captain Victoria, scoring a century in an unofficial Test in New Zealand in 1959-60. Work took him to Tasmania in the 1960s, and he played for them in pre-Shield days.

Sport & General/PA Photos

And that's 19! Len Maddocks follows the herd and falls victim to Jim Laker. Godfrey Evans is the keeper; Frank Lee the umpire.

He devoted his later life to cricket administration, spending a decade from 1973 as a Victorian delegate to the Australian board. During that period he received the poisoned chalice of managing the 1977 tour of England, which was derailed by most of the side having signed secret contracts to play in Kerry Packer's World Series Cricket. His younger brother Dick also played for Victoria, as did his son Ian, another wicketkeeper. Len Maddocks had been Australia's oldest living Test cricketer, a distinction which passed to Ken Archer.

MAINWARING, EDWARD STEWART, died on January 9, aged 74. Ed "Stewpot" Stewart was a familiar face on TV – and an even more familiar voice on radio, whether presenting music programmes or the BBC's *Sunday Sport*. He regularly turned out in charity football and cricket games, and dismissed Brian Clough in a Taverners match at Lord's in 1975.

MASINGATHA, LAZOLA, died on April 29, aged 32, a few days after being injured in a road accident in Breidbach, South Africa. He was one of five municipal employees who died when their light truck crashed. At the memorial service, the local mayor was forced to flee through a hole hurriedly cut in the back of a marquee as other workers, who felt they were owed back pay, started chanting menacingly. Masingatha, a handy batsman, had played several matches for Border, scoring 75 against South Western Districts at East London in October 2007.

MAY, NORMAN ALFRED, AM, who died on September 10, aged 88, became one of Australia's best-known sporting commentators during his 26 years with the ABC, an association that started with a casual invitation to cover a Sydney surf carnival in 1958. "Nugget", as he was universally known because of his solid build, went on to span all sports, and gained a kind of national immortality after a spirited account of the climax of the men's medley relay swim at the 1980 Olympics in Moscow: "Five metres now, four, three, two, one... Gold! Gold to Australia! Gold!" He had a long association with cricket, both on radio and television, his work marked by broad knowledge, thorough preparation and an innate feel for the game. Occasional criticisms of bias might be answered by May removing his glass eye – the legacy of a childhood accident with a bow and arrow – and agreeing with his accuser that he was indeed one-eyed.

MELVILLE, JAMES EDWARD, who died on June 2, aged 80, was a lively seamer with a well-disguised slower ball who took nine for 94 in his second match for Kent's second team, against Sussex at Hove in 1960. The following season, he ambushed the Australians in a one-day game on his home pitch at Blackheath, taking six for 46 as the Club Cricket Conference inflicted the only defeat on Richie Benaud's tourists outside the Tests. Melville made his first-class debut in 1962. Against eventual champions Yorkshire at Middlesbrough, he took three for 28 in the first innings and four for 78 in the second, bowling Geoff Boycott – in one of his earliest Championship appearances – for a duck. But three further games that summer brought only three wickets, and a dressing-down from Kent's manager Les Ames for arriving late one morning after spending the previous night driving a minicab. He made one more appearance in 1963, before returning to club cricket with Blackheath.

MICHELMORE, ARTHUR CLIFFORD, CBE, died on March 19, aged 96. Cliff Michelmore was the dependable TV anchorman for many big occasions, including the moon landings and the Investiture of the Prince of Wales in 1969. A long-time host of the BBC's *Tonight* magazine show, he had started with the British Forces Network in Germany, where his work included cricket commentary. Once he joined the BBC, he interviewed Denis Compton and Godfrey Evans, among other famous sportsmen.

MILLER, MARTIN ELLIS, who died on October 28, aged 75, was an off-spinner who took 33 wickets in a dozen matches in 1963 for Cambridge University, under the captaincy of Mike Brearley. He booked a place in the Varsity Match with six for 89 – the top six in the order – against Middlesex at Fenner's, and also claimed five for 53 to give Worcestershire a scare at New Road (chasing 192, they won by two wickets). *Wisden* wrote that Miller "varied the flight and pace of his off-breaks artfully, and could bowl for unlimited periods", but that was his only year in the side. He turned down approaches from Worcestershire over concerns about his eyesight, which eventually failed completely and led to early retirement from the civil service.

MINNEY, JOHN HARRY, who died on April 1, aged 76, was a gifted amateur who played 14 matches for Cambridge between 1957 and 1959, without managing a Blue, then five more in a peculiar career for Northamptonshire. He played three county games in 1961, then waited six years for a recall. After battling to 42 in his first comeback match on what *Wisden* called "a dubious pitch" at Worksop, he made a "rousing" 58 – his only half-century – in a victory over Middlesex at Wantage Road. After that, Minney returned to club cricket and the family footwear firm, once causing traffic chaos in Finedon when he invited the pop group Showaddywaddy – at the height of their 1970s fame – to visit the factory after spotting them on TV wearing his company's shoes.

MOORE, FREDERICK, died on March 17, aged 85. Freddie Moore was a seamer from Rochdale who played 24 times for Lancashire in the 1950s without becoming a regular. But he did have one memorable match: taking advantage of the absence of Brian Statham on England duty, Moore claimed five for 36 – including a hat-trick – against Essex at Chelmsford in 1956, and followed that with a career-best six for 45 in the second innings. He played for the Second XI for ten years, and had spells as a league professional with East Lancashire and Lowerhouse.

MOULE, HARRY GEORGE, who died on June 15, aged 94, was a prolific club batsman from Kidderminster who made one first-class appearance, opening for an understrength Worcestershire against Cambridge University at New Road in 1952, and scoring 45 and 57. Despite his efforts, the students successfully chased a target of 373, David Sheppard

GREAT WAR OBITUARY – 100 YEARS ON

Obscured by clouds

MOON, 2ND LT LEONARD JAMES, died of self-inflicted wounds on November 23, 1916, aged 38. Leonard Moon, who made four Test appearances for England under the captaincy of Plum Warner in South Africa in 1905-06, was serving with the Devon Regiment near Salonika, Greece, when he committed suicide with a pistol shot to the head. Three months earlier, some of his men had reported that he was behaving in an odd manner, and suspected him of cowardice. An inquiry found he was suffering from depression, although a day before his death he was said to be in high spirits in the mess.

A fine sportsman, Moon was in the first XI at Westminster for three years from 1894, opening the batting and keeping wicket. He made 53 in a low-scoring game against Charterhouse in 1896. He confirmed his potential at Cambridge, where he won a Blue in 1899 and 1900, making 58 and 60 in his second Varsity Match, a high-scoring draw dominated by the batting of Oxford's Tip Foster. But his most eye-catching performance came in 1899, when he scored 138 in two hours 20 minutes against Joe Darling's Australians at Fenner's. On a day shortened to four and a half hours because it coincided with the Cambridge Bumps, Moon hit a six and 21 fours in what *The Times* called "a very remarkable performance".

George Beldam, Popperfoto/Getty Images

Leonard Moon, 1905.

He made 808 runs at 24 that summer, and played for Middlesex for the first time. He went on to share two notable partnerships with Warner at Lord's. In 1903, they put on 248 for the first wicket against Gloucestershire, although their efforts were overshadowed by pyrotechnics from Albert Trott later in the day. And in 1908, they managed 212 against Sussex, Moon showing the power of his trademark cut shot, and using his feet impressively to the leg-spinner Joe Vine. The innings came in the midst of Moon's most prolific season: 918 runs at 38. In 96 first-class matches, he scored 4,166 runs at almost 27.

He had made his Test debut at the Old Wanderers in the second match of the 1905-06 series. He got several starts, but his highest score was 36 in the Third Test, again in Johannesburg, when he also kept wicket. In all matches on the tour, he made 373 runs at almost 25.

Moon was also a fine footballer who earned a Blue at Cambridge, and played for Corinthians. His brother Billy, who made two first-class appearances for Middlesex, was England's first teenage goalkeeper, winning seven caps between 1888 and 1891.

Wisden *first published an obituary for Moon in 1917. For the next two years, an updated appreciation of a player who died in the Great War will appear 100 years after the original notice.*

Sport & General/PA Photos

The greatest? Garry Sobers meets Muhammad Ali at Lord's, 1966.

making 239 not out. Moule, who was never asked to play again, had been Worcestershire's oldest surviving cricketer, a distinction that passed to John Ashman, one of five former players who celebrated their 90th birthdays in 2016.

MUBEEN MUGHAL, MOHAMMAD, who died of hepatitis on February 2, aged 23, kept wicket in six first-class matches for Sialkot in Pakistan. On debut, against Habib Bank in October 2011, he scored 47 and took five catches, all Test players. The local cricket association have set up a club tournament in his memory.

MUHAMMAD ALI died on June 3, aged 74. During his boxing heyday and beyond, the three-time world heavyweight champion Muhammad Ali was the most famous sportsman – and arguably the most recognisable human being – on the planet. In May 1966, five days before a title defence against Henry Cooper, he was taken to Lord's to see the West Indians play Middlesex, and met Garry Sobers. Fifty years later, on the day of Ali's funeral in his home town of Louisville, Kentucky, Sobers was at Lord's again – and rang the five-minute bell after a special tribute during lunch on the second day of England's Test against Sri Lanka.

MUKHERJEE, PRABIR, who died on May 31, aged 86, was the head groundsman at Eden Gardens in Kolkata for around 30 years, although his reign ended in acrimony after the Cricket Association of Bengal blamed him for a waterlogged outfield that led to the abandonment of a Twenty20 international against South Africa in October 2015. Three years previously, the strong-willed Mukherjee had defied India's captain M. S. Dhoni,

Graham Morris

The gardener of Eden: Prabir Mukherjee in 2012.

who wanted a spin-friendly track for the Third Test against England. After grumbling to the media and then claiming sickness, Mukherjee returned to his post, and prepared what he felt was a normal pitch: England won to take a 2–1 lead, before clinching the series in Nagpur. Mukherjee had been a fast bowler and a goalkeeper in his youth, and started working for the CAB in 1979, eventually moving into groundsmanship. In 1987, he prepared the pitch for the World Cup final between Australia and England.

MUKHTAR BHATTI, who died on February 7, aged 84, was a much-travelled Pakistani journalist who covered many sports as an agency reporter. He was a diligent historian, producing several sporting record books, including one marking Pakistan's 50 years as a Test nation. He died in harness, working on a book on Pakistan hockey.

MULVANEY, DEREK JOHN, AO, died on September 21, aged 90. Professor John Mulvaney was the first university-trained archaeologist to work in Australia; his work demonstrated that the Aboriginal presence stretched back at least to the Ice Age. His understanding of native culture was reflected in his 1967 work *The Australian Aboriginal Cricketers on Tour 1867-68*, which examined the players as real people with real histories. Mulvaney was made an Officer of the Order of Australia in 1991, partly for his study of Aboriginal cultural heritage.

MUNDEN, VICTOR STANISLAUS, died on September 22, aged 88. A left-arm spinner and handy batsman, Vic Munden had a 12-year career with Leicestershire, being a regular for six. He mostly had to play second fiddle to the unorthodox Australian slow left-armer Jack Walsh. But when Walsh was restricted by injury in 1951, Munden took his chance. He claimed 51 wickets at 22 – including five for 33 to consign Surrey to a two-day defeat at Ashby-de-la-Zouch – received his cap, and was rarely left out after that. In 1955, he took 87, his season's best. His best figures – six for 33, and ten for 42 in the match – had come against Somerset at Bath two years earlier; a hat-trick against Derbyshire helped set up another win at Ashby. With the bat, his most productive season was 1952, when 1,259 runs included his only two centuries – 103 against Kent at Folkestone in July, and 100 a week later against Lancashire at Liverpool. Trevor Bailey recalled that Munden's batting taught him a lesson: "He was scoring runs off my bowling rather too easily for comfort, so I slipped him my beamer, which not only hit him but fractured his cheekbone. I saw Vic in hospital, and never bowled another in my life." Brothers Donald and Paul also played for Leicestershire, while his son, David, toured with England Under-19s and later became a noted cricket photographer, before being forced to retire by Parkinson's disease.

MUNRO, ANTHONY JOHN, died on April 23, aged 52, following a stroke. Tony Munro was an industrious writer with a zeal for publicising cricket in such unusual outposts as Malta or the Maldives; his brother drew parallels between Munro's dwarfism and his passion for the smaller nations. He collated *Wisden's* Cricket Round the World section between 2003 and 2011, and did similar work for ESPNCricinfo. The Almanack's co-editor Hugh Chevallier said: "He never thought twice about calling from Australia, no matter what time of day it was, to check whether we might be interested in a particular angle."

MUZUNGUZIKA, ROBINA, died on May 17, aged 28, after complications in childbirth; her baby died too. A good enough player to have been in Mashonaland Eagles' squad, Muzunguzika also became one of three scorers contracted to Zimbabwe Cricket.

NANAN, RANGY, who died on March 23, aged 62, had the misfortune of being probably the best slow bowler in the Caribbean when the all-conquering West Indians relied predominantly on pace. He played just one Test – in Pakistan in December 1980 – taking four wickets in a series-clinching victory. "Nobody got a long run," he told ESPNCricinfo in 2008, adding that "captains of West Indies teams didn't really know how to set fields for spinners. Cricket is a game of angles, and you had to think differently for spinners. If Shane Warne was living in the West Indies, nobody would have heard of him." Still, Nanan played on for Trinidad & Tobago until 1991, finishing with 272 wickets for them – a record, until surpassed by leg-spinner Imran Khan in November 2016. "It always felt as if I was at school when facing his prodigiously turning off-breaks," said his fellow countryman Brian Lara. "I learned a lot about the art of playing spin from him." Nanan took seven for 109 against the Leeward Islands in Antigua in 1981-82 – Viv Richards, with 167, rather spoiled his figures – and topped the domestic wicket-takers that season with 32. The following year he made his only century, 125 against the Leewards at Pointe-à-Pierre. A policeman, Nanan later acted as a liaison officer for West Indian teams, and during the 2007 World Cup in the Caribbean.

O'LINN, SIDNEY, died on December 11, aged 89. Sid O'Linn (a contraction of the original "Olinsky": his father was a kosher butcher) was a South African double international, following a solitary football cap with seven Test appearances. He first came to England in 1947, and played 194 times for Charlton Athletic over the next decade as a no-nonsense midfielder with a powerful shot, which brought most of his 33 goals. In summer he turned out for Kent, originally as a wicketkeeping understudy when Godfrey Evans was with England. A dogged left-hander, O'Linn had almost a full season in 1952, scoring 1,080 runs, including an unbeaten 111 against Surrey at The Oval, his only county century. But he had just one more match for Kent; some felt this was because he was disinclined to call the amateur captains "Mister".

After returning home in 1957, he resumed his domestic first-class career ten years after a couple of games for Western Province, and did so well in 1959-60 for Transvaal – 619 runs at 68, including 120 not out against Griqualand West – that he was a surprise inclusion for the tour of England. Having learned of a board directive that wives and girlfriends were not allowed, and desperate to go, a frantic O'Linn rushed through a divorce from his first wife. She was living in England, and he was paranoid about bumping into her.

Jackie McGlew's weakish side were further depleted when the bent-armed seamer Geoff Griffin was prevented from bowling, and they lost 3–0. But O'Linn played in all five Tests. The highlight came in the Third at Trent Bridge where, having kept wicket for most

PA Photos

Faces in the Worcester mist. Three of the 1960 South African tourists died in 2016: Jim Pothecary (extreme left), Sid O'Linn (second right) and Trevor Goddard (seated, second right).

of England's first innings after John Waite injured a finger, O'Linn prolonged the match by batting nearly six hours for 98 as South Africa followed on. He missed his century when Colin Cowdrey – a former Kent team-mate – stuck out a hand and intercepted an edge that seemed destined for the boundary. O'Linn ended the series with 261 runs, more than either of the highly rated openers, McGlew and Trevor Goddard, and against Warwickshire in August equalled his career-best 120 not out.

He was no stylist. "His footwork is at times almost grotesque," wrote John Arlott, "and often it seems as if he is quite incapable of playing forward at all." However, Arlott concluded, "he has immense guts, unending patience and an almost scientific understanding of his own limitations". O'Linn played two further Tests, at home against New Zealand in 1961-62 but, pushing 35 years of age, failed to reach 20 and was sidelined. He later ran a sports shop in Johannesburg, in partnership with his old team-mate Waite.

PARKER, WILLIAM BRADLEY, died on February 17, aged 68. Bill Parker was an excellent all-round sportsman who played good-class cricket and rugby in and around Tyneside. He was a heavy scorer for South Shields, and played six Minor Counties Championship matches for Durham in the early 1980s. He also taught and coached, and his rugby charges included England internationals Kyran Bracken, Austin Healey and Tony Underwood.

PAUL, T. VIJAY, who died on December 16, aged 66, was a batsman who made two centuries in a long career for Hyderabad, both against Tamil Nadu, the higher 156 not out at Secunderabad in 1982-83. Soon after, he stood down to make room for the young Mohammad Azharuddin. Paul became a noted coach, bringing on V. V. S. Laxman – who called him "the most passionate and knowledgable coach I have seen" – and Test left-arm spinner Pragyan Ojha.

PAYNE, ANDREW DAVID, died of leukaemia on July 22, aged 55. Andy Payne was a keen cricketer – and later coach – for the Kings Heath club in Birmingham. Warwickshire's players wore red armbands in his memory over their dark one-day kit for the Royal London Cup game against Worcestershire at Edgbaston.

PEEL, NIGEL DAVID, who died of a brain tumour on January 28, aged 48, was a seamer who took 159 wickets for Cheshire in the Minor Counties Championship, including eight for 62 against Dorset at Weymouth in 1990. "If ever there was a cricketer who was too

Essex boys: Paddy Phelan and Les Savill, 1961.

nice to be a fast bowler, it was Peely," said Ian Milligan, a former team-mate and now chairman of their old club, Bramhall.

PHELAN, PATRICK JOHN, died on July 7, aged 78. Paddy Phelan was a flighty off-spinner who turned the ball a lot, and took 300 wickets for Essex. He started in 1958, under a demanding captain: "When Paddy came into the side, Trevor Bailey just couldn't accept that he couldn't put six balls an over on the spot," said Robin Hobbs. Despite this, Phelan took 50 wickets at 26 in his first summer, with five for 22 in victory over Northamptonshire at Leyton – and was, Hobbs remembered, unamused to be dropped for the last few games of the season when the Cambridge Blue Alan Hurd (see above) was persuaded to play instead. After two years of national service, Phelan was a regular until 1965, when he was released in a bout of cost-cutting that left Essex with just 12 contracted players. It also left them without a regular driver for their kit van, Phelan's usual task.

His best season was 1964, when his 64 wickets included a career-best eight for 109 against Kent at Blackheath, and ten in a historic victory over the touring Australians at Southend – Essex's first since 1905. He took five for 94 to make the tourists follow on after a century from 20-year-old Keith Fletcher had lifted Essex to 425, still their highest total against the Australians; Phelan added five for 154 in the second innings. Not a great batsman, he did make 63 against Gloucestershire at Leyton in 1963. He returned to club cricket after being released by Essex and, 21 years later, played a couple of Minor County matches for Cambridgeshire.

PIERIS, PERCIVAL IAN, died on January 1, aged 82. A bespectacled purveyor of what his captain Ted Dexter called "old-fashioned swing and cutters", Ian Pieris formed a useful new-ball partnership with Ossie Wheatley for Cambridge University between 1956 and 1958. A Blue in each of his three years, Pieris took 77 wickets in 36 university matches, with a best of five for 44 against Douglas Jardine's XI at Eastbourne in 1958. He also made 55 not out against Kent at Fenner's in 1957. Pieris improved his best figures in 1966-67, with six for 30 – four of them Test batsmen – for the Ceylon Prime Minister's XI against the State Bank of India in his native Colombo. With no domestic first-class structure in the country at the time, he had few other chances to shine, though he did make a mark in an unofficial Test against West Indies in March 1967, during a last-wicket stand of 110 in 53 minutes with Neil Chanmugam. "I was angry with the captain, the selectors and with everybody because I was sent to bat at No. 11," he recalled. "I thought 'I am going to show these chaps that I can bat.' I scored 46 not out, fuelled in cold fury." A product of St Thomas' College, Pieris played four times in the annual match against Royal College in Colombo, scoring 123 as captain in the last, in March 1953. Later that month he played for Ceylon against the Australian team en route to England, bowling Arthur Morris. He was president of Sri Lanka Cricket in 1989 and 1990.

PINKERTON, ANTHONY DAVID, died on November 9, aged 86. Calcutta-born Tony Pinkerton played 13 matches for Transvaal in the early 1950s, scoring 76 not out against Natal and 82 against Griqualand West in successive games in 1952-53, Transvaal's only season in the B section of the Currie Cup.

PLEASS, JAMES EDWARD, died on February 16, aged 92. Jim Pleass was the last survivor of the first Glamorgan team to win the County Championship, in 1948. His contribution to that famous triumph was modest: appearing in around half the matches, he averaged 16 and made just one half-century. But that unbeaten 77 helped beat Hampshire at Cardiff Arms Park, one of Glamorgan's 13 wins as they finished four points clear of Surrey. The title was secured with an innings victory in the return game at Bournemouth, the final decision given by Dai Davies, a former Glamorgan stalwart. "Dai was proudly wearing a red tie with a dragon motif," recalled Pleass. "Their last batsman Charlie Knott missed his intended stroke against Johnnie Clay… before he had finished the appeal, Dai had already said: 'That's out and we've won!'" It was a momentous conclusion to Pleass's first full season, after an eventful war during which he survived the Normandy landings when another boat cut in front of his, but hit a German mine, killing all hands.

He remained an unsung member of the Glamorgan line-up, making occasional runs and fielding expertly in the covers. In 1951 he was part of the side that upset the South Africans at Swansea: "Without question, the most exciting game I ever played in," said Pleass of a match in which the tourists – who reached 54 for none chasing 148 – were bowled out for 83. Four years later, he made his only county century, an unbeaten 102 at Harrogate which spirited Glamorgan past a target of 344 to complete their first victory in Yorkshire. But the following year he retired, fed up with in-and-out form and a batting average that stubbornly refused to exceed 20. He began a successful business career, initially working for an insurance firm run by Wilf Wooller, his long-time county captain. For some time he was on the Glamorgan committee, and also ran the former players' association.

PORTER, CLIVE WILLOUGHBY, who died on June 8, aged 71, was devoted to the study of cricket in Kent. He produced three books: a history of the county's matches against the Australians, a study of the Test career of Jack Hobbs, and *Kent Cricket Champions, 1906* – which was, according to another Kent historian, Derek Carlaw, "the very model of what such a book should be, meticulously researched, making much use of contemporary newspapers and exhibiting a deep knowledge of the period". Porter was the editor of the *Cricket Society Journal* from 1984 to 2005, a contributor to other cricket magazines and journals, and occasionally a scorer for BBC radio and television. He spent a lifetime working in education.

POTHECARY, JAMES EDWARD, died on May 11, aged 82. Western Province seamer Jim Pothecary had endured five unspectacular seasons, before taking 25 wickets at 14 in 1959-60 – including a career-best five for 29 against Rhodesia – which won him a spot in the team that toured England in 1960. Pothecary possessed a handy late outswinger, but lacked the pace to do serious damage. He missed the first two Tests, but was then given the chance to share the new ball with Neil Adcock, after Geoff Griffin was called for throwing at Lord's. He went wicketless as England took a 3–0 lead at Trent Bridge, but did better in the last two matches, both drawn: Pothecary took five at Old Trafford and four at The Oval, all batsmen in the top seven. He finished the tour with 53 wickets at 29 in first-class matches, and was perhaps unfortunate to be singled out by *Wisden* as "probably the biggest disappointment" of an underwhelming trip. He played only nine more games over the next five home seasons – improving his career-best with the bat to 81 not out against Eastern Province in 1963-64 – and did not challenge for another cap.

PREMASIRI, HALAMBAGE, was shot dead near his home in Ambalangoda, Sri Lanka, on August 12. He was 52, and had recently been elected president of the Galle Cricket Association in a controversial campaign, after which the Sri Lankan board refused to accept the results. The killing, though, was not thought to be cricket-related: Premasiri's brother had been murdered in similar circumstances in 2011, amid rumours of underworld involvement. Two men were later arrested. In his playing days, Premasiri had come close to national selection: he played for Sri Lanka A against England A in 1990-91, his first season, scoring 56 in the first representative match. He continued with the Singha club in Colombo, making three hundreds for them – the highest 147 at Moratuwa in 1994-95 – and three more for Southern Province in the President's Trophy. In all, he played 70 first-class matches before concentrating on his business career.

PRESSDEE, JAMES STUART, died on July 20, aged 83. Jim Pressdee was one of Glamorgan's best home-grown all-rounders, and enjoyed his finest hour at Swansea, just a few miles from The Mumbles, where he grew up. Over three days in August 1964, in front of large crowds and amid a feverish atmosphere, he contributed ten wickets to Glamorgan's first win over the Australians, prompting a ground invasion and renditions of "Land of my Fathers". "There were ships in the bay, thousands of people in the ground, and not a cloud in the sky," reported *The Times*.

Pressdee was a gritty, stubborn batsman, an orthodox slow left-armer, and good enough to do the double twice. In the mid-1950s, there was talk he might follow his Glamorgan team-mate Jim McConnon into the England team. But for several summers he hardly bowled – after constant disagreements with captain Wilf Wooller about how he should do so, and who should set his fields.

A fighter: Jim Pressdee at Dartford in 1959.

He was also a talented footballer, playing for Wales Schoolboys and making eight league appearances for Swansea Town. When he made his Glamorgan debut, against Nottinghamshire at Cardiff Arms Park in August 1949, he was 16 years 59 days old, the county's youngest post-war player. National service hindered his progress, but the departures of Len Muncer and Norman Hever in 1954 meant more opportunities, and next summer Pressdee took 65 Championship wickets and made 773 runs. He showed a particular relish for touring teams, scoring his first century against the Indians in 1959; two years later, he became the first Glamorgan batsman to score a hundred against the Australians.

His bowling form returned with the encouragement of new captain Ossie Wheatley, who wisely allowed him to set his own fields. Wheatley's commitment to attacking cricket also suited Pressdee, and in 1963 he took 106 wickets at 21, scored 1,467 runs at 33, and held 41 catches as the club finished second in the Championship. He did the double again in 1964 – no Glamorgan player has managed it since – and passed 1,000 runs in 1965, when they challenged for the Championship once more, Pressdee claiming a career-best nine for 43 against Yorkshire at Swansea.

He had already decided to move to South Africa, where he had been coaching, when his relationship with Wooller, by now Glamorgan's secretary, came to a head after the final match of the 1965 season, against Essex at Llanelli. Pressdee attempted to leave the pavilion by a back room used as an office by the county staff. Wooller had declared it out of bounds because of the cash and valuables kept there, but Pressdee insisted on going through. A shouting match ensued. When Pressdee eventually left, he made straight for the press tent to inform journalists that Wooller's behaviour was one of the main reasons he was leaving the country. He captained North Eastern Transvaal for four seasons, including successive Currie Cup section B titles. In the 1980s, he returned briefly to Wales, and led Glamorgan Colts, helping develop players such as Steve James and Tony Cottey.

After a memorial service in Swansea, his ashes were taken to Mumbles CC, where a tree will be planted in his memory. "He was a fighter, and a man you wanted on your side," said team-mate Don Shepherd.

PRICE, JAMES MURRAY GRANT, died on June 6, aged 81. Murray Price kept wicket in 28 matches for Border in South Africa over a decade from 1955-56. He marked his debut, against Orange Free State, with two stumpings off the former Test opening bowler Ossie Dawson, and finished the season with seven – and six catches. Price had few pretensions to batting, making a highest score of 40 not out against Natal in 1957-58. For many years he ran the family stud farm.

PRIDEAUX, RUTH EMILY (née Westbrook), who died on April 7, aged 85, became the first full-time coach of the England women's team in 1988, and guided them to World Cup victory at Lord's five years later, having modernised the backroom staff, bringing in physiotherapists, sports scientists and nutritionists. "She was the best coach I ever had," said Barbara Daniels, one of that victorious 1993 side. "Inspiring, innovative, empathetic, and a bit scary." Prideaux had played 11 Tests as a wicketkeeper-batsman, scoring 87 against South Africa at Cape Town in January 1961, not long before becoming (with team-mate Mary Duggan) one of the first two women to earn the MCC's advanced coaching badge. She had started young. "My father was not pleased," she told cricket writer Raf Nicholson. "I had three brothers, and he thought they should be playing cricket, not me. And I was the only one that really wanted to!" In 1963 she married the Northamptonshire captain Roger Prideaux, who would play three Tests; part of the honeymoon was spent at the Scarborough Festival. They had four children, but separated in 1972. They were the only husband and wife to play Test cricket until 1998, when Rasanjali Chandima Silva joined Guy de Alwis in winning a Sri Lankan cap.

PUGH, CHARLES THOMAS MICHAEL, died on February 1, aged 78. Tom Pugh was almost certainly the only county captain who claimed to have been a candidate to play James Bond. His acting experience was limited to a TV advert for cigarettes, but he was suave, good-looking, and blessed with an Etonian's poise. And he loved to tell the story of how, aged 24, he made it to the last five or six on the shortlist, compiled by the producer Cubby Broccoli and author Ian Fleming, for *Dr No*, the first Bond film. The gig went to Sean Connery.

Had he got the part, Pugh would have had to choose between Hollywood and Nevil Road. Connery ensured it was cricket, only for Gloucestershire to sack him at the end of the 1962 season, matching the suddenness of his appointment as captain two years earlier. Pugh, then a Lloyds insurance broker, owed his move to Bristol to Percy Fender, who had been asked by Sir Percy Lister, the county's vice-chairman, to identify a promising amateur batsman who might later assume the captaincy. Fender recalled seeing Pugh make 76 against Harrow in 1954, and suggested they could be recruiting the next Ted Dexter.

Man of action: Tom Pugh (right), Conservative MP John Biggs-Davison and Ross McWhirter (centre) in Downing Street to protest at the cancellation of the 1970 South Africa tour.

The deal was sealed over lunch at The Savoy, where Pugh ordered the lobster soup, fell ill, and earned a rebuke from his father for drinking red wine with seafood.

He made just six appearances in 1959 but, amid an injury crisis, played in 23 Championship matches in 1960, scoring 844 runs at 22. At Chesterfield in early June, he and Tom Graveney put on 256, still a Gloucestershire second-wicket record, against Derbyshire. Pugh made 137, his only first-class hundred. "There was Tom Graveney at one end with his eloquent batting, and Tom Pugh at the other, hitting it here, there and everywhere," recalled the all-rounder Tony Brown. Pugh was a champion rackets player, and batted accordingly. "He was used to a high bouncing ball, so when they pitched short, like that day at Chesterfield, it played to his strength," said Brown. "Instead of three slips, they should have had three third men."

Pugh's runs that summer convinced the county to make him captain in place of Graveney, who resigned in protest; *The Daily Telegraph* opined that Pugh's cricket would "hardly surpass Old Etonian standard". He was robbed of the chance to prove the critics wrong when, early in the 1961 season, Northamptonshire's David Larter broke his jaw after he ducked into a low full toss; he was given out lbw. Pugh returned a few weeks later, and in 1962 led Gloucestershire to fourth place, with six wins in their final eight games – including victory over Glamorgan, at the steelworks ground at Margam, Port Talbot; no innings reached three figures. Pugh expressed frustration to Sam Cook that his batsmen were failing to get on top of Glamorgan's bowlers, and promised to do something about it. When Pugh returned, having thrashed around for three (bowled by Don Shepherd), Cook remarked: "They don't seem to be having any trouble with that swarm of bees now, skipper." "What swarm of bees?" demanded Pugh. "The one you were trying to swat out there just now." Despite fourth place and his bold captaincy, Pugh contributed just 832 runs at 16, and was replaced by Tom's brother, Ken Graveney, who had been out of first-class cricket for 11 years, but fulfilled the committee's wish for another amateur. Pugh was devastated.

He had another brush with Bond later in the 1960s when he married Kitty Green, a model who had featured in *Thunderball*. He would have fitted the criteria for the role in one important respect: he drove a two-seater sports car, often at high speed. Eventually, Brown was the only Gloucestershire player prepared to keep him company: "You just had to remind him from time to time that the roads are governed by certain regulations." He often lived life on the edge: he was once arrested on suspicion of running a brothel on the King's Road, but later acquitted.

RAMPRASAD, BAJINA, who died on March 30, aged 75, had a long career with Andhra, starting as their wicketkeeper in 1959-60 and spanning 17 seasons. Stylish and determined, he often opened, and hit 132 against Kerala in January 1965. His best innings, though, came almost nine years later: by now Andhra's captain, Ramprasad made 122 against a Karnataka attack including Test spinners Bhagwat Chandrasekhar and Erapalli Prasanna.

REYNOLDS, STANLEY AMBROSE HARRINGTON, who died on November 28, aged 82, was an American journalist who settled in England and fell in love with cricket. His love, however, was not too blind to prevent him observing it with wry bewilderment expressed in witty columns, particularly for *The Guardian* and *Punch* in the 1970s. Nor did it stop Reynolds rapidly becoming as fogeyish as any Englishman in defence of its sacred values. "He loved the otherness of cricket, the white clothes and all the rituals," said his former wife Gillian, the *Telegraph's* radio critic for more than 40 years. He became interested because he lived opposite the Aigburth ground in Liverpool, and struck up a friendship with the groundsman, Cedric. But his writing was sharp rather than sentimental. In 1972 he noted how the queue for tickets at Lord's had to cross the entrance to the members' car park: "Cravated old colonels seated behind long, gleaming bonnets regularly parted our queue as deftly as Charlton Heston handled the Red Sea... If we ever have a revolution in England it will not start, as so many say, on the Liverpool docks, but in a queue outside Lord's when Lancashire is playing in the Gillette Cup final."

RIDLEY, MALCOLM JAMES, who died on August 21, aged 75, was a director of John Wisden & Co from 1996 to 2003, and a member of its management committee for ten years. An accountant, Ridley was a professional advisor to Paul Getty, overseeing the purchase of John Wisden & Co in 1993 and, ten years later, the acquisition of Cricinfo and *The Cricketer*. As a lifelong Surrey supporter, he took great pleasure in meeting many of his childhood heroes at Getty's private matches at Wormsley. "He was a true gentleman," said Christopher Lane, Wisden's managing director while Ridley was on the board. "He had great integrity and kindness, and his wise counsel contributed much to Wisden."

RIX, LORD (Brian Norman Roger), CBE, DL, who died on August 20, aged 92, was one of Britain's most successful post-war comic actors, and became synonymous with Whitehall farces: few men were caught more often in public with their trousers down. Rix enjoyed enormous success in theatre management, and was said to be one of the highest-paid performers on television. In the late 1970s he changed tack, and became a vigorous campaigner on behalf of mental illness.

Yet all he had ever wanted to do was play for Yorkshire. Rix was the son of a cricket-loving ship owner from Hull, who was desperate for his son to go to Oxford to develop his game. He had to be content with representing Hull and later the Lord's Taverners, though he credited some of his success on stage to his years spent playing as a boy: "As with batting, timing is everything." He relished appearing at Lord's in 1973, alongside Elton John, David Frost, Peter Cook and Michael Parkinson, to play Middlesex for Fred Titmus's benefit. Rix took two for 30, made 23 not out and held a fine one-handed catch at backward point to dismiss Norman Featherstone off the bowling of Ed Stewart.

He was one of 42 people to have made two appearances on *This is Your Life*. In 1961, one of his guests was Colin Cowdrey, who said Rix possessed the talent to have played county cricket. When he returned in 1977, his final guest was Wes Hall, a friend since West Indies' tour 14 years earlier.

ROBINSON, IAN DAVID, who died on April 3, aged 69, was the first Zimbabwean umpire on the ICC's international panel. He stood in Zimbabwe's inaugural Test, in October 1992, not long after being their representative at that year's World Cup, and in all oversaw 28 Tests and 90 one-day internationals, in addition to various administrative roles in Zimbabwean cricket. The English-born Robinson was popular, with a dry sense of humour. "I shared some fun cross-Zim road trips with him," said the former England batsman Alan Butcher, who had a spell as the national coach in Harare. Perhaps the most famous passage of play involving Robinson came at the end of England's first Test in Zimbabwe, at Bulawayo in 1996-97. With England pushing for victory, he turned a blind eye to several wide deliveries from the home seamer Heath Streak, particularly in the last over of a match in which the scores finished level. He hung up his white coat in 2008, and became the ICC's umpires' performance manager for Africa.

ROBSON, JAMES DONALD, CBE, DL, died on March 10, aged 82. Don Robson's passion, energy and vision drove Durham's elevation to first-class cricket in 1992. He became chairman when they were still a Minor County, but his ambition was always to make them the first new first-class side since Glamorgan in 1921. Part of his masterplan was to establish a new ground capable of staging international cricket in the region and, when he was offered the lease on farmland at Chester-le-Street, in the shadow of Lumley Castle, he immediately saw the possibilities. The Riverside ground opened in 1995, staged matches in the 1999 World Cup, its first Test in 2003 and – to Robson's immense pride – an Ashes Test in 2013. The pavilion, opened by the Queen in 1996, is named in his honour. But his impact went beyond bricks and mortar. He wanted to ensure that talented players from the North-East no longer had to leave to fulfil their ambitions. The success of the club's Academy, and the players who went on to represent England, gave him as much satisfaction as anything.

Robson had been involved in local politics since the mid-1960s, and was a long-serving Labour leader of Durham County Council. He launched a number of initiatives to regenerate the local economy, and saw Durham's promotion to first-class status as part of the strategy. He stood down as chairman before the club won their first Championship in 2008.

It had taken two years of lobbying by Robson to convince the TCCB that Durham had the finance and infrastructure to make the step up, and he raised £1m in the process. Once their elevation was confirmed, a team were assembled consisting of established international stars – Ian Botham and Dean Jones – plus discards from other counties and callow local youngsters. "He was conspicuous around the place when we arrived, and made everyone feel very welcome," said Simon Hughes, who had arrived from Middlesex. "He was always genial, friendly and asking if everyone was OK."

Those years in local government had given Robson an extensive contacts book, and he was known as a formidable organiser. Durham's first match, a Sunday League game against Lancashire at the Racecourse ground, was televised, but a late change of pitch meant the cameras were in the wrong position, looking over mid-off. Robson was furious that Durham had been made to look amateurish on their big day. "Within an hour, two trucks with elevated platforms had arrived," said Hughes. "The cameras were loaded on to them, and moved to the right places by the time the second innings started. That summed him up."

ST JOHN, ADRIAN, was shot dead on April 12, after being caught up in an attempted robbery while on holiday in Trinidad. A man was later charged with murder. St John, who was 22, grew up near The Oval, and was a promising batsman who had captained Chris

Gayle's academy team in London. The players called him "a lovely man, a fine cricketer, a leader of men". He worked as a recruitment consultant, but had been thinking of trying his luck in professional cricket in the West Indies.

SETH, KAPIL, who died of hepatitis on July 2, aged 36, had just one first-class match for Madhya Pradesh, against Vidarbha in November 2000 – and made a century from No. 10. Coming in at 276 for eight, Seth joined his fellow 20-year-old, wicketkeeper Amkit Srivastava. They doubled the score to 552, before Srivastava retired hurt on reaching his double-century; Seth finished with 125 not out. But he was less successful in his primary role, sending down four expensive overs of medium-pace. Apart from a single List A game shortly afterwards, he never played for the state again.

CENTURY IN ONLY FIRST-CLASS INNINGS

N. F. Callaway (207)	New South Wales v Queensland at Sydney	1914-15
S. E. Wootton (105)	Victoria v Tasmania at Hobart	1923-24
H. H. E. Grangel (108)	Victoria v Tasmania at Melbourne	1935-36
M. N. Harbottle (156)	Army v Oxford University at Camberley	1938
S. Harding (100*)	Sinhalese SC v Burgher RC at Colombo	1988-89
K. Seth (125*)	**Madhya Pradesh v Vidarbha at Indore**	**2000-01**
J. S. D. Moffat (169)	Cambridge University v Oxford University at Oxford	2002
A. S. Sharma (185*)	Oxford University v Cambridge University at Oxford	2010
Shahbaz Bashir (102)	Netherlands v United Arab Emirates at Deventer	2012

SHAH, BHARATKUMAR KANTILAL, died on January 18, aged 70. Bharat Shah played one match for Saurashtra in 1965-66, making nought and five against Bombay at the Brabourne Stadium. He was later president of the Saurashtra Cricket Association for more than 17 years, before stepping down in 2013.

SHARPE, CARL, OAM, died on March 1, aged 78. Throughout the vast western region of New South Wales, Sharpe's name was synonymous with cricket administration, and he organised coaching, tours, and visits by leading players. He nurtured the grassroots over 50 years, and around 1,500 attended his funeral in the city of Orange.

SHODHAN, ROSHAN HARSHADLAL, died on May 16, aged 87. A tall, stylish left-hander, "Deepak" Shodhan was the first Indian to score a century in his maiden Test innings – but played only two more matches, finishing with an average of 60. He fell foul of the politics that bedevilled Indian cricket in the 1950s: "When I got into the team, Vinoo Mankad asked me whether I chose to support him or Vijay Hazare. I told him I support India and the team. That ticked him off." Shodhan had been drafted into the side in Calcutta for the final match of the 1952-53 series against Pakistan after Hazare pulled out injured. He came in at No. 8 and started well, although Shodhan remained convinced that two batsmen hit out recklessly in an attempt to deny him a century. He finished with 110 as the last four wickets added 218. He went on the West Indian tour that followed, and played only twice because of illness, but still managed to save the final Test at Kingston. "He was down with flu and was admitted to the hospital," said team-mate Madhav Apte. "In the second innings we needed someone to delay West Indies. Deepak consumed enough time to help India draw that match." And that was it: afterwards, Shodhan was confined to domestic cricket, first with his native Gujarat and then Baroda, for whom he hit 261 against Maharashtra in 1957-58. In his early days he was also a handy left-arm seamer, and took five for 49 against the Commonwealth XI in 1950-51, his victims including Les Ames. His brother, Jyotindra ("a much better cricketer than me"), also captained Gujarat. Shodhan had been India's oldest Test cricketer, a distinction that passed to his friend Dattajirao Gaekwad.

SMITH, GEOFFREY, died on November 8, aged 90. Geoff Smith was an energetic fast bowler who took time off from his day job as a heating engineer to play a few matches for

Kent every season between 1951 and 1958. He was capped in 1953 after taking 31 wickets in six matches, and four years later topped the county's averages with 57 at 16; inside a week in June 1957 he twice improved his career-best, taking six for 60 against Warwickshire at Dartford, then eight for 110 against Sussex at Tunbridge Wells. But, bothered by an irregular heartbeat, he played only one more match. Away from cricket, he worked on prestigious building projects, including the Sydney Opera House and the Shell Centre on London's South Bank.

SMITH, KEITH FREDERICK HENRY, who died on June 6, aged 87, scored an unbeaten 141 on first-class debut, for Wellington against Central Districts at the Basin Reserve in December 1953. He never bettered that, although he did make another century six years later, playing *for* CD against Wellington. In the next match, against Canterbury, he took three for none – all Test players – with his slow left-armers. He had a long career as a teacher, including a spell at a school in Western Samoa, and was a Wellington selector.

SPANSWICK, JOHN GEORGE, who died on October 15, aged 83, was a lively seamer from Folkestone who deputised for the ailing Fred Ridgway for Kent in 1955, taking 31 wickets in 15 matches. His three for 23 helped skittle Northamptonshire for 60 at Tunbridge Wells, and he later took four for 64 against Lancashire at Maidstone. But with Ridgway fit again, Spanswick appeared only once in 1956, taking five wickets against Cambridge University, and faded from the scene.

SUBRAMANIAM, UDIRAMALA, who died on November 28, aged 69, played only six first-class games, but had one great day in January 1972, when his five wickets in Kerala's Ranji Trophy match against Hyderabad were all Test players – Mansur Ali Khan Pataudi, Syed Abid Ali, Abbas Ali Baig, Kenia Jayantilal and Pochiah Krishnamurthy. To round things off, Subramaniam caught another Test man, Bobjee Narasimha Rao. His other five matches brought eight wickets.

TAILANG, SUDHIR, who died of a brain tumour on February 6, aged 55, was a prominent cartoonist who worked for several of India's leading newspapers. His usual targets were politicians, but he had a soft spot for cricket, and in 2003 produced a book featuring his work called *Cricket Here and Now*.

TSIKI, LUKHANYA, died of a heart attack on April 18, aged 22, while training at the cricket academy in South Africa's Eastern Cape. A left-hand batsman and right-arm seamer, he had played for Border's age-group teams. "We wanted to check where the guys were with fitness," said Mfuneko Ngam, the former Test fast bowler who runs the academy. "He was fine, he didn't have any problems… after he was finished, he sat with his mates, coughed, and collapsed. We took him to the hospital but it was too late."

TUCKETT, LINDSAY THOMAS DELVILLE, who died on September 5, aged 97, followed his father – also Lindsay, but usually known as Len – as a seamer for Orange Free State and South Africa. Lindsay made his first-class debut in 1934-35, shortly after his 16th birthday, only five years after his father's last game. Len had gone wicketless in his only Test, against England in 1913-14, but Lindsay made a better start, taking five for 68 on debut at Trent Bridge in 1947, and five for 115 in the Second Test at Lord's. His selection for that tour owed much to a fine performance for OFS against North Eastern Transvaal in the previous home season, when he followed eight for 64 – seven bowled and one lbw – with five for 41 at Bloemfontein.

A strapping figure, with a good action and decent pace, Tuckett seemed ideal for English conditions. Early on, he collected seven for 63 against Surrey, and the following week six for 64 against MCC at Lord's. But during a long spell in the First Test he picked up a groin strain. He did play in all five but, bothered by the injury – and even more by Denis Compton and Bill Edrich, in their golden summer – claimed only five more wickets. Tuckett impressed John Arlott. "He had all the apparent qualifications for a fast-medium bowler," he wrote. "His run was little more than a dozen yards long, and he

Eye on the bat: Lindsay Tuckett (second right) with fellow South African Test players Ken Viljoen, Athol Rowan and (cigarette in mouth) Jack Plimsoll.

covered those with a loping, almost lolling, lazy stride, his eyes half-shut... His danger to the batsmen lay not in his swing, but in his pace off the wicket." But Arlott spotted a flaw: "When Norman Yardley came in to bat in the Second Test, his first ball from Tuckett pitched on a good length and rose to strike the batsman in the jaw. For the remainder of the over Tuckett bowled half-volleys... That was his great failing – an apparent inability to bowl just short of a length with the new ball. He gave runs away by overpitching."

England toured South Africa in 1948-49, and Tuckett sent down the final over of the First Test at Durban, which England's ninth-wicket pair won by scrambling a leg-bye off the last ball. Tuckett played in four of the Tests, but managed only four wickets, and finished his international career with 19 at the unflattering average of 51.

He continued with OFS until the mid-1950s, taking a career-best eight for 32 – and 13 for 66 in the match – against Griqualand West at Kimberley in 1951-52. He made one first-class century – 101 against North Eastern Transvaal at Pretoria in 1939-40, just before turning 21. Tuckett was the oldest surviving Test cricketer when he died, a distinction that passed to another South African, John Watkins.

UNDERWOOD, ARTHUR JOSEPH, who died on June 29, aged 88, was a left-arm seamer who did well for Nottinghamshire's Second XI – he took seven for 31 at Northampton in 1953 – but struggled in the first team: he scraped together only eight wickets in 14 matches between 1949 and 1954 at an average nudging 100, before returning to club cricket with Steetley in the Bassetlaw League.

WALKER, MAXWELL HENRY NORMAN, OAM, died on September 28, aged 68. Every big draw needs a good support act. In the 1970s, the Australian Test side boasted the precision and purpose of Dennis Lillee, the anarchic destructiveness of Jeff Thomson – and the apparent artlessness of Max Walker. The action he described as "right arm over

Patrick Eagar, Popperfoto/Getty Images

"Tangles": Max Walker bowling at Lord's in 1975; Bill Alley is the umpire.

left ear'ole", and the seemingly crossed legs at the point of delivery, produced an almost comic effect, masking the skill which brought him 138 wickets in 34 Tests with incisive inswing. Walker's nickname of "Tangles" had an amiable ring, but there were plenty of Test batsmen who found him as searching and relentless as his more vaunted team-mates. After his cricket finished, he remained in the national consciousness, with media work, prolific writing, and skilfully honed performances on the public-speaking circuit.

Walker was born in Hobart, but decamped in 1967 to study architecture at the Royal Melbourne Institute of Technology – and play Australian Rules football for Melbourne, where he had 85 games as a ruckman over six seasons. He became a fixture in Victoria's cricket team from 1971-72, and a Test player the following season. He was a surprise selection, but not for long: an inspired spell of six for 15 from 16 overs won the Sydney Test after Pakistan had started the last day needing only 111 with eight wickets in hand. In the West Indies immediately afterwards, Walker heroically picked up the baton when Lillee went down with back trouble, and Bob Massie lost form. Walker averaged more than 50 overs per Test, and took 26 wickets as Australia won 2–0. Radio commentator Alan McGilvray told of his bravery in bowling with badly bruised legs and ankles during the Georgetown Test, but Walker's own approach was simple: "Dennis and Bob can't, so I must."

During the 1974-75 Ashes, Lillee and Thomson prised open England's batting, yet Walker gave them no respite, bowling long spells without slackening the pressure. In the final match, which England won by by an innings, Walker found himself leading the attack again: Thomson had injured his shoulder playing tennis, while Lillee went off with a bruised foot after six overs. Walker responded with his best Test return – eight for 143, the last five for 17. "His figures made amazing reading," wrote Frank Tyson, "when one considered that the English total was in excess of 500."

Walker had two tours of England, playing in the inaugural World Cup final at Lord's in 1975, and taking 53 wickets at 22 in 1977, including seven for 19 as Gloucestershire were skittled for 63. He also made a career-best 78 – and shared a ninth-wicket partnership of 100 with Mick Malone – in what turned out to be his final Test, at The Oval. He had played his part in the helter-skelter of the first two days of the Centenary Test in March 1977, bowling almost unchanged through the first England innings of 95. The most memorable of his four wickets was Tony Greig, whose stumps went cartwheeling, to the delight of Walker's home MCG crowd. He eagerly signed for Kerry Packer, and had no compunction about being part of the new order. He and Lillee were the only two bowlers to capture seven wickets in an innings during the World Series Cricket Super Tests. Walker was 31 when peace was brokered and, although a Test return proved beyond him, he had three more successful seasons with Victoria, taking 88 wickets in 24 matches.

He spent the rest of his life, as sportswriter Greg Baum put it, being "his own industry". He did radio and television commentary, anchored shows for Channel Nine, starred in a long-running advert for fly spray, and produced 14 largely humorous books, with titles such as *How to Kiss a Crocodile* and *How to Hypnotise Chooks*. He didn't pretend they were profound or literary, but they were read avidly by an otherwise non-bookish public. There was charity work, too, marked by an honesty of spirit; he earned perhaps Australia's highest accolade, of being "a good bloke".

Walker's old team-mate Keith Stackpole said he was "lovable, uncomplicated and astute". And, although he hardly needed it, he was kept in the public eye by the spoof "12th Man" tapes of impressionist Billy Birmingham, who invented a long-running saga featuring Walker trying to reclaim his berth in the Channel Nine commentary box by buttering up Richie Benaud. One attempt has Max ringing up to see if Benaud had a copy of his latest book: "Of course I haven't," replies the faux Richie.

WAQAR AHMED, who died on February 23, aged 68, toured England with Hanif Mohammad's Pakistan team as a 19-year-old in 1967, but did not crack the Test side, and returned home early after the death of his father, the former Indian wicketkeeper Dilawar Hussain. Waqar was an attractive batsman for various domestic teams, and scored three centuries – the highest 199 against Sargodha in November 1968, when he and Shafqat Rana put on 330 for Lahore's fourth wicket. He had made his first-class debut for Punjab University in 1964-65, just before his 17th birthday, and hit 195 against Lahore Reds in his third match. "He was a man of many parts," recalled the former Test opener Aftab Gul. "A wit, a raconteur, a man of learning and a joy to be with." He was secretary of the Pakistan Cricket Board from 1997 to 1999.

WARR, JOHN JAMES, who died on May 9, aged 88, spent a lifetime cheerfully mocking his own efforts for England on the 1950-51 Ashes tour. In two Tests, Warr bowled 73 eight-ball overs, conceded 281 runs and took one wicket – when Ian Johnson walked after edging to Godfrey Evans at Adelaide. Warr's Test average remained the worst in history, until surpassed by Sri Lanka's Roger Wijesuriya in the 1980s, and his brief international career provided a fund of material when he later became an outstanding after-dinner speaker. His habitual good humour, bonhomie and talent for the one-liner tended to obscure the fact that, for more than a decade, he was a fine county bowler and, late in his career, a shrewd captain of Middlesex. When Warr – always "JJ" – retired in 1960 to spend more time at his desk in the City, he had taken 956 first-class wickets at 22.

Warr had been a surprise pick to tour Australia under Freddie Brown's captaincy while still at Cambridge, though his figures in the summer of 1950 were good: 84 wickets at 24. That was slightly worse than rivals left at home – Derek Shackleton took 111 at 22, and Les Jackson 92 at 20 – but after the squad was announced E. W. Swanton wrote in *The Daily Telegraph*: "If Warr is lucky to be chosen, he is no more so than several whose names were announced earlier. Ideally, of course, he is not sufficiently fast, but that applied to all the candidates. His virtues are that he is lean, wiry and strong, and that he is a dauntless fellow who will really look to be hoping for a bowl at five o'clock on the hottest day."

Unable to find his customary swing, he struggled in the early state games – and dropped a sitter against Queensland – but six wickets in the match against New South Wales at Sydney convinced the selectors he was ready for the Third Test. Warr finished wicketless, and England lost by an innings to go 3–0 down with two to play. He kept his place for the Fourth at Adelaide, again toiling in vain in the first innings, but in the second was finally

"Lean, wiry and strong": J. J. Warr bustles in for Middlesex against Northamptonshire in 1957.

rewarded. "I got the faintest of faint touches, and Evans went up, half-heartedly," Johnson recalled. "John followed him, but the umpire said not out. Well, I saw John's shoulders sag, and he looked so crestfallen that on the spur of the moment I nodded to the umpire and walked. It's the only time I ever did it, I can tell you, but it seemed in keeping with the spirit of the game." Friends in England sent Warr a telegram, saying simply "*Hymns Ancient and Modern*, 281", a reference to his average. He found that hymn No. 281 was *Lead Us, Heavenly Father, Lead Us*, containing the apt lines: "Lone and dreary, faint and weary/Through the desert thou didst go."

He had made his first-class debut for Cambridge against Yorkshire in 1949 in a match that also launched the careers of Fred Trueman, Brian Close and Frank Lowson (in the match report, *Wisden* described Trueman as "a spin bowler"). Warr's Middlesex debut was also against Yorkshire, at Bramall Lane later that summer. In eight Championship games he took 30 wickets and, in the last, against Derbyshire at Lord's, his five for 36 helped Middlesex to a share of the title with Yorkshire. He had an ugly action, but swung the ball at a useful pace.

Warr played in four Varsity Matches, and made a decisive impact in Cambridge's victory in 1949, demanding the ball when Oxford's tenth-wicket pair were digging in, and instantly removing the last man. He was captain in 1951, leading a side that included David Sheppard, Peter May and Raman Subba Row.

Warr worked as a broker in the City, and his employers granted him generous time off. His best year was 1956, when he took 116 wickets at 18, including a career-best nine for 65 against Kent at Lord's. He took over the captaincy from Bill Edrich two years later, and proved a popular leader of a young side. "On the field he was as good as any captain I played under," said John Murray, their wicketkeeper. "He was a very intelligent man. He made it fun, but he played the game seriously." He formed a fine new-ball partnership with Alan Moss, and in 1960 led Middlesex to third place. "He knew the talent he had at his disposal and how to use it," said Murray. But, at 33, Warr felt it was the right moment to devote himself to his career.

He was recognised as the best speaker on the circuit and, although constantly in demand, gave his services for free. He also wrote a cricket column for *The Sunday Telegraph*, was a keenly competitive golfer and, as a racing enthusiast, a steward at Goodwood and Windsor, and a member of the Jockey Club. In 1970 he won the Binney Memorial Medal for bravery after pursuing two men who had stolen cash boxes containing £2,000 from an office. A third man fired a shot which passed through the fabric of Warr's trousers.

He was perplexed in 1974 to be asked to represent the Australian Cricket Board at ICC meetings in England, having not visited the country since his ill-starred tour. "The only quality I had on that tour which they might have admired was that I never caught any of them out," he said. He was president of MCC (and thus chairman of the ICC) in 1987-88, taking over towards the end of the club's stormy bicentenary year.

His legacy, however, was his store of jokes and quips. He described his great friend Denis Compton's call for a single as merely "the basis for negotiation"; he told Trueman they "shared 308 Test wickets"; and he described Swanton's prose style as "a mixture of Enid Blyton and the Ten Commandments". One of his best lines was saved for Edrich's fourth wedding. "Bride or groom?" asked the usher. "Season ticket," said Warr.

WATT, ARTHUR DAVID WILLIAMSON, died on September 25, aged 98. Dave Watt played for Western Australia either side of the war, at a time when the state was treated almost as a foreign country by the cricket panjandrums in the east. In 1946-47 he followed 85 for WA against the MCC tourists with a four-hour 157 for a Combined XI, also at Perth, marked by good footwork and punishing strokeplay. "Watt mastered the bowling," reported *Wisden.* Making their debut in the competition, and allowed only a reduced programme, WA jolted the Establishment by winning the Sheffield Shield the following summer, Watt making 129 in the victory over Queensland at Brisbane. He dropped out of first-class cricket after one more season, to concentrate on accountancy.

WIGHT, NORMAN DELISLE, who died on January 23, aged 87, was one of four brothers who all played for British Guiana. Leslie won one Test for West Indies in 1952-53, Peter (who died in December 2015) was a prolific scorer for Somerset, before becoming a first-class umpire, and Arnold opened the batting. Norman, a big-turning off-spinner, had the longest domestic career, playing 23 matches over 13 years from 1946-47, with a best of six for 51 in Trinidad in March 1947. He came close to a Test cap when the touring Australians reached Georgetown in 1954-55, but the Barbadian Norman Marshall, a better batsman, was preferred as a replacement for the out-of-form Collie Smith. Wight also played football, hockey and rugby for British Guiana.

WILSON, ALAN, who died on April 6, 2015, aged 94, was Lancashire's wicketkeeper for most of the 1950s, although his negligible batting meant his place was never entirely secure. After he was capped in 1951, his highest score in 24 matches the following season was six, and overall in 171 games he reached 30 only once – although that unbeaten 37, against Leicestershire at Old Trafford in 1958, did form part of an unlikely last-wicket stand of 105 with Roy Tattersall. "In the nets he didn't look a bad batsman," remembered Brian Statham, "and in the middle he shaped pretty well, too – until he tried to make a shot. And then he got out." The upshot was that Wilson – whose swarthy complexion earned him the nickname "Ranji" – often lost his place to better batsmen. But he was a tidy keeper, who took a high proportion of stumpings; and according to Statham "no pleasanter fellow has worn the Lancashire cap". He seemed to have lost his place for good after 1959, but remained on the staff and returned to the first team in 1962 for his benefit match, against Hampshire, which raised £4,023.

WOGAN, SIR MICHAEL TERENCE, KBE, DL, died on January 31, aged 77. Terry Wogan was one of Britain's best-loved broadcasters, famous for his long-running radio programme, TV chat show and caustic commentary on the Eurovision Song Contest. As a youngster he enjoyed most sports, having "a passing interest in everything that involved a ball", but

Lovely man, awful batsman: Alan Wilson was happier wearing wicketkeeping gloves.

came late to cricket, which was played little in his (Catholic) part of Ireland. He was president of the Lord's Taverners in 1983-84, and fielded his own side in charity matches, with several famous names – including, occasionally, Denis Compton. "The legendary Compo," wrote Wogan, "slower, more rotund, more florid than in his glory days, but still with the eye of a hawk, the reactions of a snake."

WRIGHT, GERALD LESLIE, died on March 30, 2015, aged 84. Gerry Wright was an artist who specialised in bright, colourful paintings. He had a special interest in cricket, and brought several of the stars of the Golden Age – usually seen only in black-and-white photographs – to life in imagined outdoor settings. Cricket historian David Frith collaborated on a book featuring Wright's works in 1985, and wrote: "Heroes like Gilbert Jessop, C. B. Fry, Prince Ranjitsinhji and the Old Man, WG himself, gaze back at us from their Arcadian garden as if confident their epic deeds have never been surpassed." The paintings proved popular with collectors ranging from Sir Paul Getty to Charlie Watts of the Rolling Stones, and featured in an exhibition at Lord's in 2016. An enthusiastic fast bowler in his youth, Wright was vice-president of Linton Park, the Kent club that won the National Village Championship in 1978.

ZAFAR KHAN, who died on September 5, aged 80, was a tall, portly and bespectacled batsman who played 23 matches for various teams in Pakistan over 13 seasons from 1955-56. His highest score of 84 came in 1960-61, when captaining Hyderabad & Khairpur against a Karachi Schools side including the future Test opener Sadiq Mohammad.

The obituaries section includes those who died, or whose deaths were notified, in 2016. Wisden *always welcomes information about those who might be included: please send details to almanack@wisden.com, or to John Wisden & Co, 13 Old Aylesfield, Golden Pot, Alton, Hampshire GU34 4BY.*

BRIEFLY NOTED

The following, whose deaths came to *Wisden's* attention during 2016, played or umpired in a small number of first-class (fc) matches. Those marked by a dagger died longer ago, and will be given more extended treatment when *Wisden* next produces a set of supplementary obituaries (see *Wisden 1994* and *Wisden 2015*).

	Died	*Age*	*Main team(s)*
ABBOTT, David William	5.3.2016	81	Umpire

Stood in one fc match in New Zealand, and a women's World Cup game in 1981-82.

ABHYANKAR, A. N.	15.3.2016	*c*79	Vidarbha

Played five fc matches over three seasons from 1958-59; scored 51 against Rajasthan.

BAWDEN, David Barry Ellis	13.4.2016	72	Rhodesia

Opener who played 11 fc matches, scoring 64 v Eastern Province B in 1980-81. School headmaster.

BEZANT, Colin John ("Buzz")	14.3.2016	72	Umpire

Stood in four fc matches at Perth in Western Australia during the 1980s.

BROOM, Roland Francis	24.12.2016	91	Wellington

Left-arm seamer who played three fc matches in 1954-55; 3-18 on debut v Canterbury.

CARTRIDGE, Donald Colin	24.9.2015	81	Hampshire

Stylish club batsman who managed only six runs in six fc innings in 1953. Later a teacher and coach.

DARVELL, Bruce Stanley	21.12.2005	74	Kent

Off-spinner who played one fc match in 1952, v Oxford University. Also played for Hertfordshire.

HANNIE, Ralph Edwin	12.8.2016	50	Griqualand West

Left-handed all-rounder who played six fc matches in the early 1990s.

KOLBE, Clive	20.9.2016	72	Western Province

Leg-spinning all-rounder who played four fc matches for WP's non-white team in the early 1970s.

†**MORRIS,** William Bancroft	2.3.2004	86	Essex

Jamaican-born leg-spinning all-rounder: 48 fc matches 1946-50; 65 and 68 v Camb U, 1949.

†**PASSAILAIGUE**, Charles Clarence	7.1.1972	70	Jamaica/W Indies

Scored 261 against Lord Tennyson's XI in 1931-32, sharing a world-record sixth-wicket stand of 487* with George Headley. One Test against England, the nine-day game at Kingston in 1929-30.*

PURSHOTTAM, K.	17.10.2016	58	Karnataka

Brisk swing bowler who played four fc matches in 1980-81, taking ten wickets at 21.

RAGHUNATH, Ponnambath Mambally Krishnan	14.1.2016	65	Kerala

Seamer who took 11 wickets in nine fc matches in the 1970s; 3-66 v Tamil Nadu in 1973-74.

SHILLINGLAW, Harold Arthur Edward	15.4.2016	88	Victoria

Fitzroy stalwart who played three fc matches, all against Tasmania; 48 and 3-33 in 1953-54.

TALWALKAR, Hemant Sharad	20.11.2016	62	Maharashtra

Left-handed all-rounder who played ten fc matches; 87 v Baroda in 1980-81.

TENNANT, Peter Norie	23.6.2016	74	Warwickshire

Wicketkeeper from Solihull who played one fc match, against Scotland in 1964.

A LIFE IN NUMBERS

	Runs	*Avge*	*Wkts*	*Avge*
Aaron, S.	124	17.71	13	22.23
Adisesh, L. T.	990	38.07	23	29.78
Allin, T. W..	0	0.00	0	–
Anwar Elahi	214	12.64	28	21.64
Baindoor, R.	316	19.75	20	37.20
Bannister, J. D.	3,142	9.43	1,198	21.91
Barbour, B. D.	1,758	24.76	0	–
Bhattacharjee, A.	575	15.54	134	22.67
Cannings, V. H. D.	2,670	10.89	927	22.73
Carnill, D. J.	8	8.00	1	33.00
Carr, D. B.	19,257	28.61	328	34.74
Cordner, J. P..	13	6.50	3	78.66
Crowe, M. D.	19,608	56.02	119	33.69
Dale, J. R.	0	0.00	1	31.00
Datta, P. B.	1,459	29.77	41	37.09
Davies, T. E.	481	19.24	6	28.16
Desai, K. R.	795	28.39	8	29.62
Devereux, L. N.	5,560	19.85	178	35.31
Disbury, B. E.	288	16.00	5	40.80
Earls-Davis, M. R. G.	14	2.33	12	30.08
Easter, J. N. C..	90	3.91	58	33.44
Evans, A. R.	640	21.33	0	–

	Runs	Avge	Wkts	Avge
Finlay, A. J.	170	11.33	–	–
Foreman, D. J.	3,277	18.20	9	30.33
Fox, J. G.	515	10.72	0	–
Frans, V.	119	7.43	44	19.43
Ganteaume, A. G.	2,785	34.81	0	–
Garudachar, B. K.	1,126	29.63	100	26.20
Gathorne, R.	210	19.09	5	23.40
Gleeson, J. W.	1,095	11.06	430	24.95
Goddard, T. L.	11,289	40.60	533	21.69
Goodwin, F.	47	7.83	27	26.48
Gray, J. R.	22,650	30.73	457	30.01
Green, D. M.	13,381	28.83	116	38.44
Gudge, S. C.	1,033	24.02	110	46.66
Hamza Ali	–	–	2	29.50
Hanif Mohammad	17,059	52.32	52	28.49
Harrison, L.	8,854	17.49	0	–
Harvey, C. E.	1,716	27.23	0	–
Heys, W.	74	10.57	–	–
Higgs, K.	3,648	11.29	1,536	23.61
Hintz, A. J.	108	13.50	11	33.18
Hobden, M. E.	121	9.30	48	39.35
Hodgson, A.	909	9.67	206	28.95
Holdsworth, W. E. N.	111	7.92	53	30.15
Hurd, A.	376	5.37	249	30.80
Imtiaz Ahmed	**10,393**	**37.38**	**4**	**41.50**
Israr Ali	1,130	20.54	114	22.63
Javed Akhtar	835	15.75	187	18.21
Khalid Qureshi	370	10.57	143	19.60
Lee, D.	846	19.22	58	30.24
Lloyd, B. J.	1,631	11.90	247	41.02
McCay, D. L. C.	345	15.68	49	21.85
Maddocks, L. V.	4,106	32.84	1	4.00
Masingatha, L.	478	21.72	–	–
Miller, M. E.	48	4.80	33	23.33
Minney, J. H.	572	19.06	0	–
Moore, F.	151	7.94	54	28.07
Morris, W. B.	1,219	17.92	43	45.93
Moule, H. G.	102	51.00	–	–
Mubeen Mughal	106	10.60	–	–
Munden, V. S.	5,786	17.87	371	28.57
Nanan, R.	2,607	20.85	366	23.10
O'Linn, S.	4,525	35.62	2	59.50
Passailaigue, C. C.	788	52.53	1	56.00
Paul, T. V.	1,583	35.97	–	–
Phelan, P. J.	1,693	13.22	314	28.68
Pieris, P. I.	917	17.30	101	34.95
Pinkerton, A. D.	508	28.22	6	61.66
Pleass, J. E.	4,293	19.33	0	–
Pothecary, J. E.	1,039	15.74	143	28.34
Premasiri, H.	3,366	28.28	1	45.00
Pressdee, J. S.	14,267	28.82	481	22.17
Price, J. M. G.	442	10.27	–	–
Pugh, C. T. M.	2,469	18.56	1	30.00
Ramprasad, B.	2,240	20.18	0	–
Seth, K.	125	–	0	–
Shah, B. K.	5	2.50	–	–
Shodhan, R. H.	1,802	31.61	73	34.05
Smith, G.	728	12.33	165	22.82
Smith, K. F. H.	1,719	25.65	35	22.37
Spanswick, J. G.	135	6.42	36	32.63
Subramaniam, U.	26	5.20	13	26.53
Tuckett, L. T. D.	1,496	17.60	225	23.07
Underwood, A. J.	109	9.90	10	90.70
Walker, M. H. N.	2,014	15.49	499	26.47
Waqar Ahmed	1,705	27.88	1	67.00
Warr, J. J.	3,838	11.45	956	22.79
Watt, A. D. M.	1,079	38.53	7	23.42
Wight, N. D.	527	23.95	60	37.93
Wilson, A.	760	5.98	–	–
Zafar Khan	523	14.94	6	31.50

Test players are in bold; their career figures can be found on page 1356.

Fox made 91 catches and 14 stumpings; Ganteaume 34 and three; Hanif Mohammad 178 and 12; Harrison 578 and 103; Heys five and three; Imtiaz Ahmed 322 and 82; Maddocks 210 and 67; Mubeen Mughal 21 and none; O'Linn 97 and six; Price 57 and 17; Wilson 287 and 59.

PART THREE

English International Cricket

THE ENGLAND TEAM IN 2016

The Cook conundrum

NICK HOULT

Alastair Cook knew what to expect as he walked into the fiercely air-conditioned press room of Chennai's Chepauk in December, following another collapse and another innings defeat by India. England had just finished the last of their 17 Tests in 2016, their most in a calendar year and the most by any country since India in 1983. They had conceded the highest total in their history. They had lost 4–0. It was not long before Cook was asked the big one: after four years and 59 Tests as captain, was it time to step down?

Rewind 11 months and, in a similarly cramped room at Johannesburg's Wanderers, he had faced a very different question. His team had clinched a series win at South Africa's fortress, and Cook was asked if this was the finest

ENGLAND IN 2016

	Played	*Won*	*Lost*	*Drawn/No result*
Tests	17	6	8	3
One-day internationals	18	11	5	2
Twenty20 internationals	10	5	5	–

DECEMBER / JANUARY / FEBRUARY	4 Tests, 5 ODIs and 2 T20Is (a) v South Africa	(see *Wisden 2016*, page 403)
MARCH / APRIL	ICC World Twenty20 (in India)	(page 793)
MAY / JUNE / JULY	3 Tests, 5 ODIs and 1 T20I (h) v Sri Lanka	(page 259)
AUGUST / SEPTEMBER	4 Tests, 5 ODIs and 1 T20I (h) v Pakistan	(page 288)
OCTOBER	2 Tests and 3 ODIs (a) v Bangladesh	(page 323)
NOVEMBER / DECEMBER / JANUARY / FEBRUARY	5 Tests, 3 ODIs and 3 T20Is (a) v India	(page 342)

MOST TEST RUNS BY A WICKETKEEPER IN A CALENDAR YEAR

		T	I	NO	HS	100	Avge	Year
1,470	**J. M. Bairstow (England)**	**17**	**29**	**4**	**167***	**3**	**58.80**	**2016**
1,045	A. Flower (Zimbabwe)	9	16	3	232*	3	80.38	2000
933	A. B. de Villiers (South Africa)	9	13	1	164	4	77.75	2013
899	A. Flower (Zimbabwe)	9	14	4	199*	3	89.90	2001
891	K. C. Sangakkara (Sri Lanka)	12	17	1	140	3	55.68	2001
870	A. C. Gilchrist (Australia)	14	19	2	152	3	51.17	2001
837	A. C. Gilchrist (Australia)	14	25	3	144	3	38.01	2004
836	A. C. Gilchrist (Australia)	15	22	2	162	3	41.80	2005
792	A. C. Gilchrist (Australia)	11	16	5	204*	2	72.00	2002
777	M. J. Prior (England)	15	22	2	91	0	38.85	2012

moment of his captaincy. His answers on both occasions were non-committal – and it was an equivocation which reflected England's Test year.

The victory in South Africa, No. 1 at the time, had taken them fifth in the rankings. They moved second in the summer during a thrilling 2–2 draw with Pakistan, though it ended with a listless performance at The Oval. And they slipped back to fifth after the hammering in India. In all, England were beaten eight times in 2016, their joint-worst tally (also in 1984, 1986 and 1993), including their first defeat by Bangladesh. After Chennai, an exhausted Cook agreed the Test side had stagnated. Inevitably, his captaincy again came under scrutiny. His conservatism allowed opponents off the hook, and England often stopped attacking with the new ball, which cost them in India, where the spinners lacked menace. In February, he confirmed what he had suspected as he boarded the flight home, and stepped down. The job soon passed to Joe Root.

The limited-overs teams, by contrast, continued to bloom, their aggressive batting making them hard to beat and wonderful to watch. A world-record 444 for three at Trent Bridge against Pakistan, including an England-best 171 from Alex Hales, was the highlight; not far behind was a ten-wicket win over Sri Lanka at Edgbaston, in which both Hales and Jason Roy hit hundreds. Three months earlier, Eoin Morgan's side had surprised many by reaching the final of the World Twenty20 in India. It ultimately proved a galling experience after Ben Stokes, tasked with defending 19 from the final over, was belted for four successive sixes by West Indies' Carlos Brathwaite. But the near miss confirmed England's stature in the white-ball formats.

In Test cricket, however, it was a familiar tale. England were dangerous when conditions favoured their seam and swing bowlers – and thus their batsmen, who enjoyed pace and bounce – but vulnerable on slower surfaces. Too often Nos 6–8 had to bail them out. Sri Lanka were easily beaten 2–0 in early summer, but Pakistan won both London Tests, where the pitches were flat and the ball turned just enough. A 1–1 draw in Bangladesh could have been a 2–0 defeat, with England's batsmen exposed by the off-breaks of teenager Mehedi Hasan. Stokes saved them in Chittagong, but they lost ten wickets in a session in Mirpur, a sign of things to come in India.

There, they were only ever surefooted on a flat track in Rajkot. But, as India's spinners gained rhythm, England floundered. They had no excuses:

Michael Steele, Getty Images

White ball, red hot: Ben Stokes and Jonny Bairstow, armed for the fray.

Cook won four tosses, and the pitches were fair – certainly not the outrageous turners that greeted South Africa a year earlier. In desperation, England picked five spinners in seven Tests, including the 39-year-old Gareth Batty and Hampshire's Liam Dawson, who had taken only 20 (expensive) Championship wickets in the summer.

Like so much of England's year, their slow bowling was a mixture of the good, the bad and the downright awful. Adil Rashid collected 23 wickets against India, who at first struggled with his variations. But they became more confident at picking his googly, and he was hammered in the last two Tests, when his five wickets cost 69 apiece. Moeen Ali could neither attack nor contain, and paid 53 for each of his 37 Test wickets in 2016, a worrying figure for a first-choice spinner. Batty and Zafar Ansari, meanwhile, were not up to the challenge, and – with Somerset's Jack Leach correcting an illegal action – Dawson was no more than a stopgap. Cook admitted he wished he could have called on Ravichandran Ashwin and Ravindra Jadeja.

The retirement in April of James Taylor with a life-threatening heart condition was a cruel blow. Less importantly, it disrupted England's plans, but coach Trevor Bayliss's habit of giving players one Test too many, rather than one too few, led to some strange selections. An out-of-form Nick Compton was retained against Sri Lanka, and averaged 12. Gary Ballance was recalled against Pakistan, despite inconsistent form for Yorkshire, and lasted only six Tests, while James Vince occasionally looked wonderful, but didn't pass 42. The squad for India was chosen before the final Test in Bangladesh, which saddled England with an unselectable Ballance, and an out-of-form Steven Finn. After a promising start to his one-day international career, in Bangladesh, Ben Duckett had his technique exposed by Ashwin in India.

PERFECT PARTNERS

Most runs added by a particular wicket in Tests in a calendar year:

Runs	*Wkt*	*Tests*		
2,341	3rd	12	Pakistan	2006
1,921	**6th**	**17**	**England**	**2016**
1,800	2nd	15	South Africa	2008
1,790	2nd	15	Australia	2005
1,731	4th	11	Australia	2012
1,704	4th	14	England	2015
1,687	2nd	12	Australia	2003
1,662	1st	15	South Africa	2008
1,645	1st	15	India	2008
1,642	3rd	10	South Africa	2012

The previous best for the sixth wicket was 1,223 runs by West Indies in 15 Tests in 1984.

Despite the confusion, the year also ended with reasons to be cheerful: after waiting four years to find a convincing opening partner for Cook, England seemed to unearth two at once, in Haseeb Hameed and Keaton Jennings. Hameed took to Test cricket like a natural, sound of technique, unflappable of temperament. And his "Baby Boycott" nickname, though misleading, earned what felt like the royal seal of approval, when Geoffrey himself started using it on the radio. A broken finger cut short Hameed's highly promising debut series after three Tests in India, but he returned after surgery to watch the last two, and in Mumbai saw Jennings become the first England player since Billy Griffith in 1947-48 to score a hundred on his first day of Test cricket.

Chris Woakes developed into a genuine international all-rounder, taking 11 wickets against Pakistan at Lord's and regularly chipping in with lower-order runs, but he faded in India, where he managed three wickets at 81. Ali's four Test centuries confirmed his class, but his yo-yoing around the order continued, and England finished the winter *still* unsure about his best position.

For the three longest-serving members of the side, there were similar ups and downs. At Chester-le-Street in May, Cook passed 10,000 Test runs, and in July he scored a century against Pakistan at Old Trafford. But Jadeja dismissed him six times in India (where he passed 11,000), and an average of 42 confirmed a middling year. James Anderson reached a landmark of his own – 450 Test wickets – and twice topped the rankings during the summer, but a shoulder injury forced him out of five games. Stuart Broad had been No. 1, too, after his decisive spell at Johannesburg, but also struggled with fitness in Asia. England's main seam-bowling quartet of Anderson, Broad, Woakes and Stokes all averaged in the mid-twenties during the year, though that didn't quite tell the whole story.

Quietly, a new leadership group emerged, of Root, Stokes and Jonny Bairstow. Root fell only four runs short of Michael Vaughan's England record tally for a Test year (1,481 in 2002), but was more frustrated by his conversion rate, departing six times between 62 and 88. Despite that, he still played one of the innings of 2016: a faultless 254 against Pakistan at Old Trafford, having just been promoted to No. 3.

Bairstow was England's player of the year, scoring more runs (1,470) and making more dismissals (70) in a calendar year than any wicketkeeper in history. He also defied expectations with vital contributions in both Bangladesh and India, and was the saviour of many a lost cause: thanks in large part to his contributions, England's sixth-wicket partnership yielded an astonishing 1,921 runs. Bairstow's pursuit of perfection included training with the goalkeepers at Newcastle United, and his glovework improved hugely.

The year had started with him and Stokes putting on 399 in Cape Town, Test cricket's highest sixth-wicket stand. Bairstow reached his maiden century, and looked to the heavens in memory of his father, David. At the other end Stokes produced an exhilarating exhibition of six-hitting, striking 11 in his 258 from 198 balls – the highest Test score by a No. 6. Fans were left hoping his description of the innings as "once in a lifetime" was false modesty.

MOST WICKETKEEPING DISMISSALS IN A CALENDAR YEAR

Dis		*T*	*Ct*	*St*	
70	**J. M. Bairstow (England)**	**17**	**66**	**4**	**2016**
67	M. V. Boucher (South Africa)	13	65	2	1998
67	I. A. Healy (Australia)	16	58	9	1993
66	A. C. Gilchrist (Australia)	14	58	8	2004
59	I. A. Healy (Australia)	15	55	4	1997
58	M. V. Boucher (South Africa)	15	56	2	2008
57	R. D. Jacobs (West Indies)	14	55	2	2000
57	A. C. Gilchrist (Australia)	14	52	5	2001
56	M. J. Prior (England)	14	54	2	2010
55	P. J. L. Dujon (West Indies)	15	54	1	1984
55	A. C. Gilchrist (Australia)	15	50	5	2005

Whether with bat or ball, or diving for every lost cause in the field, Stokes was the leader others followed. It was no coincidence that England won both Tests he played during the summer, but only two out of five when he was absent through injury. He seized the moment at Chittagong, first propping up the batting, then taking the final two wickets on a tense last morning to steal a 22-run win. A one-day hundred in Mirpur and a Test century at Rajkot underlined the work he had put in against spin. And, while his spats with Virat Kohli earned him an ICC reprimand, his competitiveness rallied the team when they were low.

The Test series against Pakistan had been among the most entertaining in England for years. The tourists had arrived under the cloud of the 2010 spot-fixing scandal, but the ghosts of that trip were exorcised by a wonderful series, in which both teams came from behind, before settling for Test cricket's first 2–2 draw since South Africa visited England in 2003. Yasir Shah provided an early reminder of England's old failings against spin with ten wickets at Lord's (and later added five in the second innings at The Oval) while Wahab Riaz reversed the ball more than the home seamers. England bounced back at Old Trafford, where Yasir was tamed by batsmen content to play the long innings, and nosed ahead at Edgbaston, where Ali and the seamers produced the best all-round bowling performance of the summer.

But discipline evaporated at The Oval: Hales, struggling to cement his place as a Test opener, stormed into the third umpire's room to complain about his dismissal, catches were dropped as standards slipped in the absence of Stokes, and there was a lack of urgency with the ball as Younis Khan made a double-hundred.

Throughout that game, the Bangladesh tour loomed over England, with security fears putting it in doubt following a terrorist attack in Dhaka in early July. A long meeting on the eve of the one-day series against the Pakistanis ended in the decision to tour, but the players were given the option to pull out: Morgan and Hales took it. Hales largely escaped criticism, but Morgan, as white-ball captain, was expected by some to set an example, though he appeared to anger those outside the dressing-room more than those in it. In his absence, under the impressive leadership of Jos Buttler, England became the first side to win a one-day series in Bangladesh for over two years.

The result confirmed England's white-ball cricket as a new source of pride. They lost only one 50-over match at home all summer – a dead game against Pakistan at Cardiff – and earlier in the year should have won in South Africa, where a dropped catch by Rashid gave Chris Morris the chance to play a match-winning innings in Johannesburg. Having been 2–0 up, England went down 3–2.

Character, though, courses through the team. After suffering a heavy defeat by West Indies in their opening World Twenty20 match, they faced elimination after conceding 229 against South Africa. But Root played a sublime innings to lead England to the highest successful run-chase in Twenty20 internationals. From then, they got their game together – until they met Brathwaite in Kolkata.

ENGLAND PLAYERS IN 2016

LAWRENCE BOOTH

The following 32 players (there were 33 in both 2015 and 2014) appeared in 2016, when England played 17 Tests, 18 one-day internationals and ten Twenty20 internationals. Statistics refer to the full year, not the 2016 season.

MOEEN ALI — Worcestershire

Ali's role evolved yet again, this time into a middle-order Test batsman: his four hundreds in 2016 were equalled by only Virat Kohli and Steve Smith. He could still be frustrating – sometimes flapping at the short ball, sometimes flopping against spin – but it was hard to stay angry for long: every waft and miss was followed by something dreamy through the covers. After a slow start, he touched the heights against Pakistan, and two centuries in India were extended sighs of delight. His off-breaks were expensive – at times, not even he believed in them – and his limited-overs returns underwhelming. His advocates pointed out that only Ian Botham and Jacques Kallis had scored 1,000 runs and taken 30 wickets in a Test year. Above all, team-mates cherished his flexibility: across the formats, he filled seven different positions.

17 Tests: 1,078 runs @ 46.86; 37 wickets @ 53.02.
15 ODI: 145 runs @ 16.11, SR 81.46; 10 wickets @ 70.50, ER 5.30.
9 T20I: 70 runs @ 17.50, SR 106.06; 7 wickets @ 28.85, ER 8.78.

JAMES ANDERSON — Lancashire

It was the story of his career: unplayable at home, unpredictable away. Six Tests in South Africa and India yielded 11 wickets at 46; six at home to Sri Lanka and Pakistan brought 30 at 15. Against the Sri Lankans, he was at his best, taking ten for 45 at Headingley. And he finished the year with 467 Test victims, overhauling Kapil Dev and Richard Hadlee to go sixth on the all-time list. But, at 34, wear and tear played their part too, and – from the start of the Pakistan series – Anderson missed five Tests because of a troublesome right shoulder. For the first time in years, his future looked uncertain.

12 Tests: 66 runs @ 8.25; 41 wickets @ 23.73.

Steve Paston, PA Photos

ZAFAR ANSARI — Surrey

Ansari's winter was a reminder of Test cricket's inherent cruelty. He deserved more than two wickets with his left-arm spin on debut at Mirpur, and hung around for almost two hours in the First Test against India at Rajkot. But otherwise he looked overawed; sickness and back spasms at Visakhapatnam made for a miserable conclusion. He flew home early, chastened, perhaps wiser.

3 Tests: 49 runs @ 9.80; 5 wickets @ 55.00.

JONNY BAIRSTOW **Yorkshire**

Question marks gave way to exclamation marks. While Bairstow's middle-order solidity became a regular talking point, his keeping was no longer a subject of whispers. His 70 Test dismissals were a world record for a calendar year, and twice as many as his nearest rival, Pakistan's Sarfraz Ahmed. And, beginning with his heady 150 not out in Cape Town, he came within 12 of breaking Michael Vaughan's England record for most runs in a year (having already scored the most for a wicketkeeper of any nationality). Two big hundreds followed at home to Sri Lanka, and the only grumble was that he passed 40 in 12 subsequent innings without another century. His batting against – and keeping to – spin improved beyond measure, the result of a fierce work ethic and an ingrained desire to prove critics wrong.

17 Tests: 1,470 runs @ 58.80; 66 catches, 4 stumpings.
10 ODI: 198 runs @ 28.28, SR 77.95; 1 catch and 1 stumping in 2 games as wicketkeeper.
1 T20I: did not bat.

JAKE BALL **Nottinghamshire**

His Test returns didn't convey the promise of a natural, bounding action and a sharp bouncer. But he now had a place in the pecking order, and a five-wicket haul in Mirpur – the first by an England one-day debutant – boded well.

3 Tests: 52 runs @ 8.66; 2 wickets @ 114.00.
3 ODI: 28 runs @ 28.00, SR 127.27; 7 wickets @ 19.85, ER 5.38.

GARY BALLANCE **Yorkshire**

The raised eyebrows that greeted Ballance's recall against Pakistan, a year after he had been dropped against Australia, never quite lowered. A nuggety 70 at Edgbaston was as good as it got and, if Ballance didn't stay *quite* as deep in his crease as he had previously, he kept getting out to spin down the leg side. After 24 runs in four innings in Bangladesh, his winter was done, though not before – as if obliged to repent – he was dragged round India.

6 Tests: 219 runs @ 19.90.

STUART BROAD **Nottinghamshire**

Broad got on one of his rolls only once, taking six for 17 at the start of the year in Johannesburg. But he still finished the year with more Test wickets than any team-mate (and any seamer bar Australia's Mitchell Starc), and England missed his knack for disturbing a game's balance during the three Tests he sat out in Asia. His second-innings four for 33 at Visakhapatnam – full of fast leg-cutters, despite a damaged right foot – was among England's most skilled bowling displays of the year. His batting stats were the stuff of a No. 11, even while some of his strokeplay was not. And if Broad barely played any white-ball cricket, his desire to take part in the 2019 World Cup was backed up by a stint in the Big Bash.

14 Tests: 145 runs @ 8.52; 48 wickets @ 26.56.
2 ODI: 19 runs @ 9.50, SR 67.85; 1 wicket @ 89.00, ER 5.56.

JOS BUTTLER **Lancashire**

Buttler's arrival at the crease in white-ball games came with guaranteed frisson. His 41 sixes in limited-overs internationals were 19 more than any other England player, and his 50-over strike-rate of almost 130 was the highest of anyone, anywhere, to pass 400 runs. Appropriately, it was he who spanked the cover-drive that sealed England's world-record 444 for three against Pakistan at Trent Bridge. And when Morgan declined to tour Bangladesh, Buttler assumed the captaincy, presiding over a 2–1 win and revealing a steel few had imagined. England finally found a place for him in the Test team, too – as a specialist batsman – and an intelligent 76 in Mumbai made a mockery of the concerns over his lack of red-ball cricket. He was too gifted for that to matter.

3 Tests: 154 runs @ 38.50.
16 ODI: 573 runs @ 57.30, SR 129.93; 17 catches, 4 stumpings.
10 T20I: 366 runs @ 61.00, SR 151.23; 3 catches.

NICK COMPTON **Middlesex**

Compton's second crack at Test cricket dribbled away. An innings of 45 at Cape Town in January 2016 was followed by nothing higher than 26 in ten attempts, including five single-figure dismissals. By the end, against Sri Lanka at Lord's, he was edging balls he should have sent whistling through cover. He looked exhausted, and opted to take a short break from the game, leaving the No. 3 spot free for Root. It was hard to see a way back.

6 Tests: 162 runs @ 16.20.

ALASTAIR COOK **Essex**

Cook's entry into Test batting's five-figure club couldn't mask the disappointment of a year which ended with four defeats in India. His batting remained solid, though statistically unspectacular, thanks mainly to Ravindra Jadeja, who removed him six times. Only during the home summer, when Cook averaged 63 against Sri Lanka and Pakistan, and scored at 60 per 100 balls – quicker than ever – did he lord it; even then, it felt as if he had not fully exploited his fluency. Despite becoming the first Englishman to pass 10,000 Test runs, followed 12 games later by 11,000, Cook spent the India trip fending off questions about his future. In February, he announced he would relinquish the captaincy.

17 Tests: 1,270 runs @ 42.33.

BEN DUCKETT **Northamptonshire**

Few quibbled with Duckett's selection for his first senior tour after a prolific summer for his county and England Lions, and a sixty in each of the one-day wins in Bangladesh confirmed his quirky promise. But Test cricket's nut proved tougher to crack. A flaw against off-spin – he planted his front foot outside leg stump to the ball pitched on middle and leg – was exposed first by Mehedi Hasan, then Ravichandran Ashwin. By the Third Test in Mohali, Duckett was gone, with only the memory of a scintillating 56 before the collapse in Mirpur to sustain him.

4 Tests: 110 runs @ 15.71.
3 ODI: 123 runs @ 41.00, SR 80.92.

STEVEN FINN **Middlesex**

Finn played more Tests than in any year since his first, in 2010, but highlights were worryingly few. An exacting spell of reverse swing in tandem with Woakes on the last afternoon against Pakistan at Edgbaston stood out, which merely reinforced the idea of a talent struggling to find expression. In Mirpur came a sadly apt coda: 11 wicketless overs, a pair with the bat. The rhythm that seemed more important to him than to any other England seamer was as elusive as ever.

9 Tests: 89 runs @ 9.88; 17 wickets @ 46.64.

ALEX HALES **Nottinghamshire**

A tiring year came to an abrupt halt in September, when Hales opted out of the trip to Bangladesh, though he would have been dropped from the Test squad in any case. Murderous in 50-over cricket, he had been muddled in Tests, carefully reaching 80 three times against Sri Lanka, but either side averaging 17 against South Africa and Pakistan, whose best bowlers homed in on a weakness outside off; a meltdown at The Oval while disputing a catch didn't help. Hales's real value came in the one-day game, in which he peaked with an England-record 171 against Pakistan at Trent Bridge. On such days, he appeared capable of anything. But they also revealed the gap between the two batsmen he was trying to be. For the time being, two into one did not go.

10 Tests: 537 runs @ 28.26; no wicket for 2 runs.
14 ODI: 743 runs @ 61.91, SR 101.36.
8 T20I: 146 runs @ 18.25, SR 119.67.

HASEEB HAMEED **Lancashire**

Like Alastair Cook, Kevin Pietersen and Joe Root – England's three batting giants of the last decade – Haseeb Hameed took to Test cricket as if he'd been doing it all his life. Unlike them, he was a teenager when he made his debut, scoring 31 and 82 in Rajkot, then defending expertly in vain pursuit of a draw in Visakhapatnam. His first Test tour ended early because of a broken finger, but not before he had ridden the pain to make an impish 59 not out from No. 8 in Mohali. Hameed was far more than the "Bolton Blocker", though his judgment outside off was precocious. He leapt out to drive the spinners, slog-swept with precision, and left English cricket wanting much, much more.

3 Tests: 219 runs @ 43.80.

CHRIS JORDAN **Sussex**

Jordan's share price rose during the World Twenty20, when his yorkers at the death – he took four for 28 in the vital group game against Sri Lanka in Delhi – helped England to the final, and earned him an IPL gig with Royal Challengers Bangalore. But he was hittable with the new ball, and unwanted by the Test side, encouraging an uneasy sense that his international career remained in limbo.

7 ODI: 32 runs @ 16.00, SR 96.96; 4 wickets @ 81.50, ER 6.41.
10 T20I: 48 runs @ 12.00, SR 94.11; 12 wickets @ 25.33, ER 8.76.

EOIN MORGAN **Middlesex**

Morgan's decision not to tour Bangladesh because of security worries cast a pall over a year in which his own white-ball batting failed to keep pace with his team-mates'. Only Carlos Brathwaite prevented him from becoming the second England captain to lift the World Twenty20, and he had to settle for leading his side to a 50-over world record, against Pakistan. That only partly obscured a personal tally of two half-centuries in 23 innings, though an 81-ball 102 at Cuttack in January 2017 contained much of the old magic.

15 ODI: 328 runs @ 29.81, SR 87.00.
10 T20I: 175 runs @ 21.87, SR 117.44.

LIAM PLUNKETT **Yorkshire**

A bowler possessing the physique of a rugby centre worked best as an impact player. His introduction during the World Twenty20 for the matches in Delhi gave the attack an edge, and his last-ball six to tie the Trent Bridge one-dayer against Sri Lanka was an easily forgotten champagne moment.

10 ODI: 31 runs @ 31.00, SR 206.66; 15 wickets @ 34.33, ER 5.72.
6 T20I: 4 runs @ 4.00, SR 100.00; 4 wickets @ 38.25, ER 7.00.

ADIL RASHID **Yorkshire**

In India, Rashid equalled the record for most wickets (23) in a Test series by an England leg-spinner, but the feeling persisted that he had not won his captain's trust. He had improved since his debut a year earlier in the UAE, and five four-wicket hauls in seven subcontinental Tests made him incontestably England's leading slow bowler. But, to Cook's occasional exasperation, an ability to shape matches eluded him. In 50-over cricket, Rashid was England's most penetrative bowler, taking 12 more wickets than the next man (Woakes, with 17). And, all told, only four bowlers claimed more international victims in 2016 than his 67. Rashid's Test batting stats, like his fallible catching, were beneath him: a hard-working 60 in Chennai exposed his other efforts, including nine – often feckless – single-figure dismissals in 13 innings.

7 Tests: 192 runs @ 17.45; 30 wickets @ 35.66.
17 ODI: 96 runs @ 32.00, SR 107.86; 29 wickets @ 28.34, ER 5.19.
10 T20I: 8 runs @ 4.00, SR 61.53; 8 wickets @ 33.50, ER 7.65.

JOE ROOT **Yorkshire**

Such were his standards that even a year in which only Virat Kohli outdid his all-format tally of 2,570 felt a notch below what was possible. Root was rarely less than awe-inspiring, his palette ranging from a wondrous 254 against Pakistan at Old Trafford in his new guise as No. 3, to a raucous Twenty20 takedown of South Africa in Mumbai. But, as in 2015, he turned only three of his 13 Test fifties into hundreds, and finished too many innings with a rueful shake of the head. A faulty conversion rate was all that stood between him, his back-foot cover-drive, and greatness – though, following Cook's resignation, he now had the Test captaincy to deal with too.

17 Tests: 1,477 runs @ 49.23; 3 wickets @ 58.00.
15 ODI: 796 runs @ 61.23, SR 91.81; 1 wicket @ 41.00, ER 5.85.
9 T20I: 297 runs @ 37.12, SR 142.78; 2 wickets @ 16.00, ER 10.66.

JASON ROY **Surrey**

Philip Brown, SilverHub

Every so often, Roy revealed his special gift. A 16-ball 43 set up the World Twenty20 chase against South Africa, and a 44-ball 78 swung the semi-final against New Zealand. The summer produced 50-over gems, including two centuries in three innings against Sri Lanka – enough to relegate concerns about his struggles earlier in the year in South Africa. Even in a batting line-up that seemed to boast every shot in the book, Roy looked innovative. His next challenge was a Test place.

17 ODI: 647 runs @ 43.13, SR 108.01.
10 T20I: 228 runs @ 22.80, SR 133.33.

BEN STOKES **Durham**

You name it, Stokes was at the heart of it, confirming his status as the most talked-about England cricketer since Kevin Pietersen. Usually, the headlines hummed with praise: a 198-ball 258 at Cape Town, a one-man show to clinch the nail-biter in Chittagong, and a set of figures – including 21 sixes, more than anyone in the world – that would decorate the CV of the best Test all-rounders. His batting on the subcontinent, though fading in India, revealed the cricket brain inside the fiery redhead, as did his one-day contributions from No. 5. His combative nature could also bring out the best in opponents: Carlos Brathwaite's four successive sixes off him to win the World T20 for West Indies in Kolkata was among the vignettes of the year, and Stokes became involved in several squabbles in Bangladesh, then with Virat Kohli in India. Deep down, they were all compliments disguised as insults.

12 Tests: 904 runs @ 45.20; 33 wickets @ 25.81.
13 ODI: 490 runs @ 49.00, SR 105.60; 7 wickets @ 53.85, ER 5.43.
9 T20I: 72 runs @ 10.28, SR 144.00; 5 wickets @ 50.00, ER 9.03.

JAMES TAYLOR **Nottinghamshire**

Taylor stunned the sport in April when he announced his immediate retirement because of an incurable heart condition. Having felt unwell during Nottinghamshire's trip to Cambridge, he underwent hospital tests which diagnosed a potentially fatal heart condition. Though his form during the Test series in South Africa had ebbed away, Taylor had been part of England's middle-order plans, not least because he was adept against spin; and his short-leg fielding was becoming a thing of wonder. A popular figure, he found an instant home on Sky and BBC radio, and as a columnist for the *Evening Standard*.

3 Tests: 74 runs @ 14.80.

REECE TOPLEY **Hampshire**

It turned into a year to forget. Topley had his moments during the 3–2 one-day defeat in South Africa, claiming four wickets in the win at Port Elizabeth, then reducing the hosts to 22 for three in the decider at Cape Town. But he fluffed a run-out chance that would have forced a super over in the Twenty20 match, also at Cape Town, and was dropped during the World T20 after 4.1 overs in Mumbai cost 55. There would be no stirring comeback: he broke his right hand on Hampshire debut in April, and in May was ruled out for the season with a stress fracture of the back.

5 ODI: 1 run without being dismissed, SR 11.11; 10 wickets @ 21.90, ER 6.08.
4 T20I: 1 run without being dismissed, SR 50.00; 1 wicket @ 114.00, ER 12.43.

JAMES VINCE — Hampshire

Vince had an important advocate in Trevor Bayliss, but his cover-drive proved a flourish that became a flaw. Time and again, unable to resist the bait, he was caught on the off side, leaving him with no fifty in seven Tests, and four tantalising scores between 35 and 42. A string of missed half-chances in the slips did not help. England decided their No. 4 could not be averaging 19, though they gave him a chance at the top of the one-day order in Bangladesh, where he didn't pass 32.

7 Tests: 212 runs @ 19.27; no wicket for 13 runs.
4 ODI: 104 runs @ 26.00, SR 84.55.
2 T20I: 38 runs @ 19.00, SR 118.75.

DAVID WILLEY — Yorkshire

His thoughtful left-arm swing was one of the highlights of the World Twenty20 (and his batting helped avert embarrassment against Afghanistan). But his 50-over returns declined after a four-for against Sri Lanka at Cardiff. There were six wicketless games out of 12 and, without movement through the air, he looked vulnerable. Even so, he was part of England's white-ball furniture.

12 ODI: 44 runs @ 14.66, SR 55.69; 11 wickets @ 47.72, ER 5.54.
8 T20I: 60 runs @ 20.00, SR 122.44; 10 wickets @ 19.00, ER 7.60.

CHRIS WOAKES — Warwickshire

Philip Brown, SilverHub

There are breakthroughs – and there is the summer Woakes enjoyed in 2016. Backed by Cook to replace the injured Stokes for the Second Test against Sri Lanka at Chester-le-Street (the coaches wanted Ball), he responded with pace, accuracy and hostility, instantly looking like a banker. Riches followed against Pakistan – 26 wickets at 16 – and his batting was on the up too. By the end of the year, he had reached 25 on 12 occasions in Tests, all but two from No. 8 or below. He had begun 2016 by struggling for rhythm in South Africa, and finished it in search of seam movement in India. But few held that against him.

12 Tests: 493 runs @ 30.81; 41 wickets @ 25.41.
14 ODI: 212 runs @ 42.40, SR 104.43; 17 wickets @ 36.35, ER 5.35.

MARK WOOD **Durham**

English cricket grimaced when Wood was ruled out of the winter tours after breaking a bone giving his all for Durham. His frail left ankle had already limited him to four 50-over internationals in late summer, though they provided a wistful reminder of his pace, zest and joy – especially when he helped reduce Pakistan to two for three at Lord's. But his latest injury setback did little to silence comparisons to the equally explosive, equally fragile Simon Jones.

4 ODI: 8 runs without being dismissed, SR 160.00; 7 wickets @ 33.42, ER 5.85.

AND THE REST...

Gareth Batty (Surrey; 2 Tests) collected four wickets at Chittagong, in his first Test for over 11 years, then was all but ignored in Mohali, and thanked for his time. **Keaton Jennings** (Durham; 2 Tests) sparkled on Test debut with a hundred in Mumbai, and – with a half-century in Chennai – showed his taming of India's spinners was no fluke. **Sam Billings** (Kent; 1 ODI, 2 T20Is) was unlucky to make only three appearances, but his innovative 62 as opener in the one-day decider in Chittagong underlined his rare talent. **Liam Dawson** (Hampshire; 1 Test, 1 ODI, 1 T20I) prospered on Twenty20 debut, against Sri Lanka in Southampton, but found Pakistan's middle order less supine in his first 50-over game, at Cardiff. A Test debut in Chennai brought an unbeaten 66, but little for his left-arm spin. **Tymal Mills** (Sussex; 1 T20I) was selected for the Twenty20 game against Sri Lanka because of his pace, though he made more impact with his crafty slower balls.

ENGLAND TEST AVERAGES IN CALENDAR YEAR 2016

BATTING AND FIELDING

	T	I	NO	R	HS	100	50	Avge	SR	Ct/St
L. A. Dawson	1	2	1	66	66*	0	1	66.00	42.58	0
J. M. Bairstow	17	29	4	1,470	167*	3	8	58.80	58.21	66/4
J. E. Root	17	32	2	1,477	254	3	10	49.23	60.70	26
†M. M. Ali	17	29	6	1,078	155*	4	5	46.86	53.79	7
†B. A. Stokes	12	21	1	904	258	2	3	45.20	66.76	9
H. Hameed	3	6	1	219	82	0	2	43.80	34.21	4
†A. N. Cook	17	33	3	1,270	130	2	7	42.33	51.90	17
†K. K. Jennings	2	4	0	167	112	1	1	41.75	46.64	2
J. C. Buttler	3	6	2	154	76	0	1	38.50	48.27	5
C. R. Woakes	12	21	5	493	66	0	2	30.81	44.49	6
A. D. Hales	10	19	0	537	94	0	5	28.26	44.71	8
†G. S. Ballance	6	11	0	219	70	0	1	19.90	43.19	6
J. M. Vince	7	11	0	212	42	0	0	19.27	52.21	3
A. U. Rashid	7	13	2	192	60	0	1	17.45	38.24	3
N. R. D. Compton	6	11	1	162	45	0	0	16.20	38.84	3
†B. M. Duckett	4	7	0	110	56	0	1	15.71	57.89	1
J. W. A. Taylor	3	6	1	74	27	0	0	14.80	37.56	3
S. T. Finn	9	12	3	89	17	0	0	9.88	35.31	2
†Z. S. Ansari	3	5	0	49	32	0	0	9.80	36.02	1
J. T. Ball	3	6	0	52	31	0	0	8.66	47.70	1
†S. C. J. Broad	14	18	1	145	19	0	0	8.52	42.52	7
†J. M. Anderson	12	15	7	66	17	0	0	8.25	66.66	6
G. J. Batty	2	4	1	5	3	0	0	1.66	10.63	0

BOWLING

	Style	O	M	R	W	BB	5I	Avge	SR
J. M. Anderson	RFM	394.1	103	973	41	5-16	3	23.73	57.68
C. R. Woakes	RFM	339.2	78	1,042	41	6-70	2	25.41	49.65
B. A. Stokes	RFM	279.2	46	852	33	5-73	1	25.81	50.78
S. C. J. Broad	RFM	463.4	117	1,275	48	6-17	1	26.56	57.95
A. U. Rashid	LBG	287.1	23	1,070	30	4-52	0	35.66	57.43
G. J. Batty	OB	53.2	4	181	4	3-65	0	45.25	80.00
S. T. Finn	RFM	235.1	33	793	17	3-26	0	46.64	83.00
M. M. Ali	OB	532	83	1,962	37	5-57	1	53.02	86.27
Z. S. Ansari	SLA	68	3	275	5	2-76	0	55.00	81.60
J. E. Root	OB	55.2	9	174	3	2-31	0	58.00	110.66
L. A. Dawson	SLA	43	4	129	2	2-129	0	64.50	129.00
J. T. Ball	RFM	76	19	228	2	1-47	0	114.00	228.00
A. D. Hales	RM	3	1	2	0	0-2	0	–	–
J. M. Vince	RM	4	1	13	0	0-0	0	–	–
K. K. Jennings	RM	5	1	20	0	0-20	0	–	–

ENGLAND ONE-DAY INTERNATIONAL AVERAGES IN CALENDAR YEAR 2016

BATTING AND FIELDING

	M	*I*	*NO*	*R*	*HS*	*100*	*50*	*Avge*	*SR*	*Ct/St*
S. W. Billings	1	1	0	62	62	0	1	62.00	89.85	0
A. D. Hales	14	13	1	743	171	3	4	61.91	101.36	6
J. E. Root	15	14	1	796	125	2	6	61.23	91.81	5
J. C. Buttler	16	13	3	573	105	1	5	57.30	129.93	17/4
†B. A. Stokes	13	12	2	490	101	1	4	49.00	105.60	5
J. J. Roy	17	17	2	647	162	2	2	43.13	108.01	3
C. R. Woakes	14	9	4	212	95*	0	1	42.40	104.43	5
†B. M. Duckett	3	3	0	123	63	0	2	41.00	80.92	0
A. U. Rashid	17	5	2	96	39	0	0	32.00	107.86	2
L. E. Plunkett	10	2	1	31	22*	0	0	31.00	206.66	5
†E. J. G. Morgan	15	13	2	328	68	0	2	29.81	87.00	5
J. M. Bairstow	10	8	1	198	61	0	1	28.28	77.95	5/1
J. T. Ball	3	1	0	28	28	0	0	28.00	127.27	0
J. M. Vince	4	4	0	104	51	0	1	26.00	84.55	3
†M. M. Ali	15	12	3	145	45*	0	0	16.11	81.46	6
C. J. Jordan	7	3	1	32	15*	0	0	16.00	96.96	3
†D. J. Willey	12	7	4	44	13*	0	0	14.66	55.69	7
L. A. Dawson	1	1	0	10	10	0	0	10.00	76.92	0
†S. C. J. Broad	2	2	0	19	13	0	0	9.50	67.85	0
M. A. Wood	4	1	1	8	8*	0	0	–	160.00	2
R. J. W. Topley	5	3	3	1	1*	0	0	–	11.11	2

BOWLING

	Style	*O*	*M*	*R*	*W*	*BB*	*4I*	*Avge*	*SR*	*ER*
J. T. Ball	RFM	25.5	0	139	7	5-51	1	19.85	22.14	5.38
R. J. W. Topley	LFM	36	3	219	10	4-50	1	21.90	21.60	6.08
A. U. Rashid	LBG	158.2	0	822	29	4-43	2	28.34	32.75	5.19
M. A. Wood	RFM	40	1	234	7	3-46	0	33.42	34.28	5.85
L. E. Plunkett	RFM	90	0	515	15	3-44	0	34.33	36.00	5.72
L. A. Dawson	SLA	8	0	70	2	2-70	0	35.00	24.00	8.75
C. R. Woakes	RFM	115.3	8	618	17	4-41	1	36.35	40.76	5.35
J. E. Root	OB	7	0	41	1	1-26	0	41.00	42.00	5.85
D. J. Willey	LFM	94.4	8	525	11	4-34	1	47.72	51.63	5.54
B. A. Stokes	RFM	69.2	1	377	7	2-45	0	53.85	59.42	5.43
M. M. Ali	OB	133	2	705	10	3-43	0	70.50	79.80	5.30
C. J. Jordan	RFM	50.5	1	326	4	2-42	0	81.50	76.25	6.41
S. C. J. Broad	RFM	16	1	89	1	1-55	0	89.00	96.00	5.56

"The fourth six felt sadistically emphatic – like shooting a corpse between the eyeballs."

The World Twenty20 in 2015-16, page 825

ENGLAND TWENTY20 INTERNATIONAL AVERAGES IN CALENDAR YEAR 2016

BATTING AND FIELDING

	M	*I*	*NO*	*R*	*HS*	*50*	*Avge*	*SR*	*4*	*6*	*Ct*
J. C. Buttler	10	10	4	366	73*	3	61.00	**151.23**	24	20	3
†B. A. Stokes	9	8	1	72	15	0	10.28	**144.00**	6	4	6
J. E. Root	9	9	1	297	83	2	37.12	**142.78**	29	9	7
J. J. Roy	10	10	0	228	78	1	22.80	**133.33**	25	9	1
†D. J. Willey	8	5	2	60	21	0	20.00	**122.44**	2	4	4
A. D. Hales	8	8	0	146	37	0	18.25	**119.67**	19	2	5
J. M. Vince	2	2	0	38	22	0	19.00	**118.75**	6	0	0
†E. J. G. Morgan	10	10	2	175	47*	0	21.87	**117.44**	5	9	5
†M. M. Ali	9	7	3	70	41*	0	17.50	**106.06**	5	2	4
L. E. Plunkett	6	2	1	4	4	0	4.00	**100.00**	0	0	0
C. J. Jordan	10	5	1	48	15	0	12.00	**94.11**	6	0	4
S. W. Billings	2	1	0	5	5	0	5.00	**83.33**	1	0	0
A. U. Rashid	10	4	2	8	4*	0	4.00	**61.53**	0	0	3
R. J. W. Topley	4	1	1	1	1*	0	–	**50.00**	0	0	0
J. M. Bairstow	1	–	–	–	–	–	–	–	0	0	0
L. A. Dawson	1	–	–	–	–	–	–	–	0	0	1
T. S. Mills	1	–	–	–	–	–	–	–	0	0	1

BOWLING

	Style	*O*	*Dots*	*R*	*W*	*BB*	*4I*	*Avge*	*SR*	*ER*
T. S. Mills	LF	4	11	22	0	0-22	0	–	–	**5.50**
L. A. Dawson	SLA	4	4	27	3	3-27	0	9.00	8.00	**6.75**
L. E. Plunkett	RFM	21.5	58	153	4	2-27	0	38.25	32.75	**7.00**
D. J. Willey	LFM	25	71	190	10	3-20	0	19.00	15.00	**7.60**
A. U. Rashid	LBG	35	73	268	8	2-18	0	33.50	26.25	**7.65**
C. J. Jordan	RFM	34.4	76	304	12	4-28	1	25.33	17.33	**8.76**
M. M. Ali	OB	23	40	202	7	2-22	0	28.85	19.71	**8.78**
B. A. Stokes	RFM	27.4	63	250	5	3-26	0	50.00	33.20	**9.03**
J. E. Root	OB	3	5	32	2	2-9	0	16.00	9.00	**10.66**
R. J. W. Topley	LFM	9.1	19	114	1	1-22	0	114.00	55.00	**12.43**

ENGLAND v SRI LANKA IN 2016

REVIEW BY GEORGE DOBELL

Test matches (3): England 2, Sri Lanka 0
One-day internationals (5): England 3, Sri Lanka 0
Twenty20 international (1): England 1, Sri Lanka 0
Super Series: England 20pts, Sri Lanka 4pts

Perhaps it was the weight of recent history, perhaps it was the schedule, perhaps it was simply the gulf in class – but Sri Lanka's attempt to replicate the success of their 2014 tour was thwarted by a resurgent England, who prevailed in all three formats.

Comparisons with the team of two years earlier, who had themselves won in all three formats, did the Sri Lankans no favours. As if it wasn't tough enough trying to repeat that success so soon, their chief selector, Sanath Jayasuriya, hardly tempered expectations ahead of the series by laying claim to "the best bowling side in the world". The truth was rather less palatable, and their batting wasn't up to much either.

There was no Kumar Sangakkara, who was playing for Surrey, and no Mahela Jayawardene, who was commentating for Sky – and had recently been helping England as a consultant. As injury ravaged the bowling attack, there would soon be no Dammika Prasad and no Dushmantha Chameera; Shaminda Eranga was banned for an illegal action after the Tests. Trevor Bayliss and Paul Farbrace, the Sri Lanka coaching duo a few years earlier, were working

Stu Forster, Getty Images

The dream: Jonny Bairstow hit 387 runs in four innings, including a century at Headingley.

for England, too. Angelo Mathews remained, but was troubled by a hamstring problem and by the burden of carrying an inexperienced batting line-up, in which Dinesh Chandimal topped the Test averages with a modest 34. Mathews himself, so significant in 2014, averaged just 25.

It was also a significantly different itinerary. In 2014, the limited-overs games had been played first, with the Test series not starting until June 12, on a benign surface at Lord's. This time, the Tests came first – and in the damp North, on May 19. While some in Sri Lanka sensed a conspiracy, the reality was more prosaic: Lord's was in the middle of its latest round of renovations, and would not be ready until June. But Leeds and Chester-le-Street presented the sort of conditions of which English seamers (if not English spectators, who stayed away in their droves) dream. And, in James Anderson, England had the man to exploit them. Sri Lanka's first three Test innings lasted barely 115 overs in total, and included a lone half-century – Kusal Mendis made a punchy 53 in the second innings at Leeds – and 22 single-figure scores. Mathews described their performance in the First Test, which would have ended inside two days but for rain, as "embarrassing". Had the weather not intervened on the last day at Lord's, they might easily have lost 3–0.

If Sri Lanka didn't present the stiffest opposition, then the challenge of facing Anderson & Co in such circumstances is one of cricket's toughest, as

FIVE STATS YOU MAY HAVE MISSED

BENEDICT BERMANGE

- At Leeds, England enforced the follow-on after making 298. Only once since 1967, when the required lead was raised worldwide from 150 to 200, has a lower total led to a follow-on: at Chandigarh in 1990-91, India asked Sri Lanka to bat again after scoring 288.

- On the first afternoon at Headingley, England were 83 for five. Only two teams, batting first, have had a lower score at the fall of the fifth wicket, yet gone on to win by an innings:

47-5	England (446) beat Pakistan (74 & 147) by an innings and 225 runs at Lord's	2010
51-5	Australia (284) beat England (65 & 72) by an innings and 147 runs at Sydney	1894-95
83-5	**England (298) beat Sri Lanka (91 & 119) by an innings and 88 runs at Leeds**	**2016**

- Also in the First Test, Dasun Shanaka became the third bowler to take two Test wickets before conceding any runs:

T. P. Horan	Australia v England at Sydney	1882-83
R. L. Johnson	England v Zimbabwe at Chester-le-Street	2003
M. D. Shanaka	**Sri Lanka v England at Leeds**	**2016**

- England have never lost a home Test that started earlier than May 28. Their record for all home Tests beginning in May is: P33 W24 L3 D6. Those three defeats came against Australia (in a match starting on May 28, 1921), New Zealand (May 29, 2015) and Pakistan (May 31, 2001).

- England have won all six Tests at Chester-le-Street. Second on the list of grounds with most consecutive home wins since its inaugural Test is Bloemfontein, in South Africa, with four.

Benedict Bermange is the cricket statistician for Sky Sports.

Australia had discovered the previous summer. By the time they found themselves in easier conditions – from the second innings in Durham – the series was all but gone.

It was a different England, too. Whereas their 2014 side had just lost 5–0 in Australia, this team had been emboldened by an Ashes success, victory in South Africa, and a new, carefree approach in limited-overs cricket. In Joe Root and Ben Stokes, they possessed two of the game's most exciting talents; in Anderson and Alastair Cook, the experience to guide them through the tough times. They were hungry, united, and very much at home. Most of all, they had depth. Even after Stokes was forced to pull out midway through the First Test with a knee injury, England had a batting order that extended beyond the horizon.

This was just as well. Their top order remained fragile, with Root failing three times out of four, James Vince making an uncertain start to his Test career, and Nick Compton's spluttering to a halt. But the middle order were able to compensate: their Nos 6 and 7 contributed 603 runs at an average of 120. Central to this was Jonny Bairstow. Coming to the crease at 83 for five at Headingley, he made an imperious century, his first in Tests on his home ground; at Lord's, he responded to the threat of 84 for four with an unbeaten 167. He averaged 129 and was named England's Man of the Series. Bairstow also finished with 19 catches. But along the way he missed several relatively easy chances, leaving Bayliss to reflect that the selectors would have to think carefully about the choice of keeper.

Moeen Ali, who hit a sparkling unbeaten 155 from No. 7 at Chester-le-Street, added to Sri Lanka's frustrations; Chris Woakes, a batsman good enough to have made his Test debut at No. 6 in 2013, now came in at No. 8, and averaged over 50, as well as bowling with pace, skill and control.

There were some signs of improvement from the top order as well. Alex Hales, who had opted for an extra couple of weeks' rest at the end of a long winter before returning to county cricket, passed 80 in each Test, though without reaching a maiden century. Demonstrating greater certainty around off stump, he seemed – for a while at least – to be providing one of the ingredients England had been searching for since the retirement of Andrew Strauss: a reliable partner for Cook.

It was a role Compton had once fulfilled. But here, perhaps still bearing the mental scars from being dropped

Gareth Copley, Getty Images

The scream: Nick Compton rails at another failure.

before the 2013 Ashes, he looked stiff with anxiety. Unwilling to settle for the unfashionable role of anchor, and possibly unsettled by Bayliss's desire – made explicit during the tour of South Africa – for "attacking-style batters", he was drawn into some out-of-character strokes, and didn't pass 22. He later announced he would be taking a break from the game.

Anderson, with 21 wickets – nine more than anyone else – at an average of under 11, enjoyed an outstanding series. After claiming ten for 45 in ideal conditions at Leeds, he picked up five for 58 in the second innings at Durham in conditions offering him almost nothing. He passed 450 Test wickets in the process, and his haul here was the biggest in a three-match series for England since Ryan Sidebottom took 24 in New Zealand in 2007-08. Anderson finished as the sixth-highest wicket-taker in Test history, and third among seamers.

BEST TEST SERIES AVERAGE FOR ENGLAND

Avge		*T*	*Balls*	*Runs*	*W*		
4.80	J. Briggs	2	391	101	21	v South Africa	1888-89
5.80	G. A. Lohmann	3	520	203	35	v South Africa	1895-96
7.47	G. A. R. Lock	5	1,056	254	34	v New Zealand	1958
7.54	R. Peel	3	442	181	24	v Australia	1888
8.29	S. F. Barnes*	3	768	282	34	v South Africa	1912
8.80	J. H. Wardle	4	857	176	20	v Pakistan	1954
9.16	D. L. Underwood	3	900	220	24	v New Zealand	1969
9.60	J. C. Laker	5	1,703	442	46	v Australia	1956
10.38	C. Blythe	3	603	270	26	v South Africa	1907
10.80	**J. M. Anderson**	**3**	**580**	**227**	**21**	**v Sri Lanka**	**2016**

Minimum 20 wickets.

* *Barnes took 39 wickets at 10.35 in the triangular series of 1912, including five v Australia.*

Cook reached a significant milestone in Durham, too. He not only became the youngest to make 10,000 Test runs, but the quickest to do so (ten years 90 days from his debut). How Sri Lanka could have used such experience.

It looked, at least for a couple of hours, as if the limited-overs series might provide the tourists with some respite. After thrashing Ireland in two one-day games in Dublin, they appeared to have England on the floor during the series opener at Nottingham. Having made a competitive 286, they reduced England to 82 for six. But Woakes added 138 with Jos Buttler, then an unbroken 51 with Liam Plunkett, who thumped the last ball for six to secure a tie. England celebrated as if they had won; Sri Lanka looked as if their spirit was broken. Eoin Morgan's team went on to win the five-match series 3–0 (it rained in Bristol), before Buttler propelled them to another comfortable victory in the one-off Twenty20 international at Southampton.

Perhaps the nadir of Sri Lanka's tour came at Edgbaston, where Hales and Jason Roy made centuries as England, set 255, won by ten wickets. Five days later at The Oval, Roy creamed 162 to help them chase down 308 in 42 overs. For a side on the wrong end of many thrashings from Sri Lanka over the years, this was confirmation of their improvement. For Sri Lanka, it was just chastening.

"For the past two months, we've been having the same problems," admitted a weary Mathews at the end of the tour. "Either our batting, bowling or fielding has let us down in every game. This is a tough time for me as captain. But you can't run away from it. You have to deal with the issues."

It all meant that the Super Series – a concept adopted from women's cricket by Andrew Strauss, with each game offering points (four for a Test win, and two in limited-overs matches) in an attempt to add interest and relevance to the overall contest – never gained traction.

In truth, things had started to go wrong for Sri Lanka long before they arrived. The previous December, wicketkeeper-batsman Kusal Perera had been accused of a doping offence and suspended from all cricket. However, on May 11, between the Sri Lankans' two county fixtures, the charges were dropped when an ICC-appointed independent expert cast doubt on the findings of the laboratory, based in Qatar, that claimed to have detected small quantities of a performance-enhancing steroid. Perera, who had maintained his innocence, flew to the UK, and played in the Third Test, as well as the limited-overs internationals.

In April, opening batsman Kaushal Silva had been hospitalised after taking a blow to the head while fielding in a practice match in Pallekele, though he was fit for the tour. And Prasad, who in 2014 had claimed a match-winning five-for at Leeds, was ruled out after sustaining a shoulder injury during the warm-up game against Essex, in which the county seemed the stronger team. Chameera, who looked sharp at Leeds, was diagnosed with a stress fracture before the Second Test, while Eranga, having had his bowling action deemed illegal after the Third, was admitted to a Dublin hospital suffering from an elevated heart rate ahead of the one-dayers.

Gareth Copley, Getty Images

Island express: Nuwan Pradeep Fernando, most hostile of the Sri Lankan pace attack.

There were a couple of consolations. The figures might not have reflected it, but Rangana Herath defied unhelpful conditions, and his age, to contribute with bat, ball and in the field, reaching 300 Test wickets in Durham. Nuwan Pradeep Fernando, meanwhile, was Sri Lanka's top wicket-taker in the Tests and – jointly with Suranga Lakmal – the one-day series, bowling with skill and stamina. Had he enjoyed a bit more luck from umpires and fielders, those figures would have been far better. Silva, recovered from his accident, twice passed 50 and was named their Man of the Series, Chandimal hit a brilliant century in the second innings in Durham – Sri

Graham Morris

Just for openers: Jason Roy and Alex Hales celebrate England's ten-wicket win at Edgbaston.

Lanka's only hundred against England all tour – and Mathews suggested that Mendis had earned the right to a prolonged run at No. 3.

Misfields and dropped catches were another theme of the tour. All three of England's Test centuries followed let-offs, and each time Pradeep Fernando was the unfortunate bowler. If he could blame only himself for missing a caught-and-bowled chance offered by Bairstow on 70 at Leeds, he was blameless when Ali was missed in the gully on 36 in Durham, and Bairstow on 11 at midwicket at Lord's.

While there was sympathy for Sri Lanka when umpire Rod Tucker denied Pradeep Fernando a wicket at Lord's (incorrectly calling a no-ball to reprieve Hales, who had been bowled), there were also raised eyebrows when they reacted by hanging their flag from their dressing-room balcony. It was claimed as an act of "solidarity" with the team, but it was hard to avoid the suspicion that Sri Lanka were also implying they had been on the rough end of decisions – and the schedule – throughout their trip. The fact that Hales had already been dropped twice in that innings was a more accurate reflection of a tour that never got going.

SRI LANKAN TOURING PARTY

*A. D. Mathews (T/50/20), K. M. C. Bandara (T/50/20), P. V. D. Chameera (T), L. D. Chandimal (T/50/20), D. M. de Silva (T/50/20), D. P. D. N. Dickwella (T/50/20), R. M. S. Eranga (T/50), A. N. P. R. Fernando (T/50/20), M. D. Gunathilleke (50/20), H. M. R. K. B. Herath (T), F. D. M. Karunaratne (T), R. A. S. Lakmal (T/50/20), M. F. Maharoof (50/20), B. K. G. Mendis (T/50/20), M. D. K. Perera (T), M. D. K. J. Perera (T/50/20), K. T. G. D. Prasad (T), S. Prasanna (50/20),

R. L. B. Rambukwella (20), S. Randiv (50/20), M. D. Shanaka (T/50/20), J. K. Silva (T), T. A. M. Siriwardene (T), W. U. Tharanga (50), H. D. R. L. Thirimanne (T).

Prasad, a seam bowler, injured his shoulder in the first warm-up and returned to Sri Lanka; his replacement was batsman M. D. K. J. Perera. After the First Test, Chameera was diagnosed with a stress fracture of the lower back, and replaced by Bandara. Thirimanne was originally selected for both limited-overs squads, but withdrew with back trouble, and was replaced by Dickwella. Eranga was suspended after the Irish leg of the tour.

Coach: G. X. Ford. *Manager:* C. P. Senanayake. *Bowling coach:* C. P. H. Ramanayake. *Fielding coach:* N. Seneviratne. *Trainer:* M. Maine. *Analyst:* D. Samarasinghe. *Physiotherapist:* S. Mount. *Masseur:* L. Thamel. *Communications manager:* C. Perera.

TEST MATCH AVERAGES

ENGLAND – BATTING AND FIELDING

	T	*I*	*NO*	*R*	*HS*	*100*	*50*	*Avge*	*Ct*
J. M. Bairstow	3	4	1	387	167*	2	0	129.00	19
†A. N. Cook	3	5	2	212	85	0	1	70.66	1
†M. M. Ali	3	4	1	189	155*	1	0	63.00	0
A. D. Hales	3	5	0	292	94	0	3	58.40	1
C. R. Woakes	2	3	1	105	66	0	1	52.50	0
J. E. Root	3	4	0	87	80	0	1	21.75	6
J. M. Vince	3	4	0	54	35	0	0	13.50	2
†J. M. Anderson	3	3	2	13	8*	0	0	13.00	2
N. R. D. Compton	3	5	1	51	22*	0	0	12.75	2
S. T. Finn	3	4	0	41	17	0	0	10.25	2
†S. C. J. Broad	3	3	0	23	14	0	0	7.66	2

Played in one Test: †B. A. Stokes 12 (1 ct).

BOWLING

	Style	*O*	*M*	*R*	*W*	*BB*	*5I*	*Avge*
J. M. Anderson	RFM	96.4	30	227	21	5-16	3	10.80
C. R. Woakes	RFM	53.3	18	150	8	3-9	0	18.75
S. C. J. Broad	RFM	94	20	295	12	4-21	0	24.58
S. T. Finn	RFM	59	4	197	7	3-26	0	28.14

Also bowled: M. M. Ali (OB) 49–12–180–2; J. E. Root (OB) 2.2–0–19–0; B. A. Stokes (RFM) 7–2–25–1; J. M. Vince (RM) 2–1–10–0.

SRI LANKA – BATTING AND FIELDING

	T	*I*	*NO*	*R*	*HS*	*100*	*50*	*Avge*	*Ct/St*
L. D. Chandimal	3	5	0	172	126	1	0	34.40	5/1
J. K. Silva	3	6	0	193	79	0	2	32.16	1
B. K. G. Mendis	3	6	1	156	53	0	1	31.20	6
†F. D. M. Karunaratne	3	6	1	129	50	0	1	25.80	1
A. D. Mathews	3	5	0	125	80	0	1	25.00	4
†H. M. R. K. B. Herath	3	5	0	109	61	0	1	21.80	3
†H. D. R. L. Thirimanne	3	5	0	87	22	0	0	17.40	2
A. N. P. R. Fernando	3	5	4	15	13*	0	0	15.00	1
R. A. S. Lakmal	2	3	0	11	11	0	0	3.66	2
R. M. S. Eranga	3	5	1	7	2*	0	0	1.75	0

Played in one Test: P. V. D. Chameera 2, 0 (1 ct); †M. D. K. J. Perera 42; M. D. Shanaka 0, 4; †T. A. M. Siriwardene 0, 35.

BOWLING

	Style	O	M	R	W	BB	5I	Avge
M. D. Shanaka	RM	13	3	46	3	3-46	0	15.33
P. V. D. Chameera	RF	17	0	64	3	3-64	0	21.33
T. A. M. Siriwardene	SLA	15.2	0	72	3	2-35	0	24.00
A. N. P. R. Fernando	RFM	96	21	316	10	4-107	0	31.60
H. M. R. K. B. Herath	SLA	106.3	15	303	7	4-81	0	43.28
R. A. S. Lakmal	RFM	72	8	259	5	3-90	0	51.80
R. M. S. Eranga	RFM	86.4	10	324	5	3-58	0	64.80

Also bowled: A. D. Mathews (RFM) 39–12–98–1.

ESSEX v SRI LANKANS

At Chelmsford, May 8–10. Drawn. Toss: Sri Lankans. First-class debut: A. P. Beard. County debut: M. H. Cross.

Aaron Beard, an 18-year-old member of the Essex Academy, made an immediate impact, removing the Sri Lankan openers with the game's fourth and 15th deliveries after Mathews had chosen to bat. He found swing at a bristling pace and, although Mendis looked more comfortable than his team-mates, he too fell to Beard, for 66. Three late wickets for Moore ended the innings at 254. After twin hundreds against Cambridge MCCU, Mickleburgh made a workmanlike century. Next came Westley, showcasing his blossoming talent with the fourth of a productive season. Against an anaemic Sri Lankan attack – Prasad was best, but he picked up a shoulder injury that ruled him out of the tour – Westley helped himself, especially to leg. And finally the classy Bopara picked off runs at will. He would doubtless have been the third home centurion had the ECB not ruled that the first innings should be limited to 100 overs. Trailing by 158, Sri Lanka lost two wickets before stumps. Outplayed for two days, they were spared further embarrassment on the last, which was washed out.

Close of play: first day, Essex 81-2 (Mickleburgh 42); second day, Sri Lankans 42-2 (Karunaratne 16).

Sri Lankans

F. D. M. Karunaratne lbw b Beard	8	– not out	16
J. K. Silva c Cross b Beard	0	– lbw b Beard	7
B. K. G. Mendis c Cross b Beard	66	– c Westley b Dixon	16
†L. D. Chandimal c Westley b Ryder	27		
*A. D. Mathews c Moore b Bopara	30		
T. A. M. Siriwardene b Beard	5		
D. M. de Silva lbw b Ryder	5		
D. P. D. N. Dickwella c Cross b Moore	53		
K. T. G. D. Prasad c Bopara b Moore	13		
R. M. S. Eranga not out	1		
A. N. P. R. Fernando b Moore	11		
B 20, lb 5, w 4, nb 6	35	W 2, nb 1	3
1/1 (2) 2/16 (1) 3/104 (4) 4/127 (3) 5/142 (6) 6/155 (7) 7/207 (5) 8/231 (9) 9/242 (8) 10/254 (11) (63 overs)	254	1/9 (2) 2/42 (3) (2 wkts, 13 overs)	42

Beard 16–3–62–4; Dixon 12–1–44–0; Moore 13–1–48–3; Ryder 10–0–48–2; ten Doeschate 6–1–16–0; Westley 1–0–3–0; Bopara 5–2–8–1. *Second innings*—Beard 6–1–19–1; Dixon 4–0–17–1; Moore 3–0–6–0.

Essex

N. L. J. Browne lbw b Prasad	28
J. C. Mickleburgh lbw b Prasad	109
T. C. Moore b Eranga	3
T. Westley c de Silva b Fernando	108
R. S. Bopara not out	87
D. W. Lawrence not out	57
B 1, lb 13, w 1, nb 5	20
1/78 (1) 2/81 (3) 3/213 (2) 4/299 (4) (4 wkts dec, 100 overs)	412

J. D. Ryder, *R. N. ten Doeschate, †M. H. Cross, A. P. Beard and M. W. Dixon did not bat.

Prasad 17.3–3–78–2; Fernando 18–1–62–1; Eranga 19–7–55–1; Mathews 10–5–19–0; Siriwardene 19–0–118–0; Karunaratne 9.3–1–37–0; de Silva 7–0–29–0.

Umpires: S. C. Gale and S. J. O'Shaughnessy.

LEICESTERSHIRE v SRI LANKANS

At Leicester, May 13–15. Drawn. Toss: Sri Lankans.

The Sri Lankans' shaky build-up to the Test series continued against an inexperienced Leicestershire, who made nine changes from their previous game. After choosing to bat, the tourists careered to 192 for eight, before Shanaka – who struck four sixes in a 132-ball 112 – and Herath added 174. But respite was temporary, as several Leicestershire batsmen seized their chance. Burgess and Wells both hit career-bests, with Wells missing out on a maiden hundred when he failed to accelerate on the final morning. Stranded on 87 – like Ravi Bopara in the previous warm-up match – he was apparently unaware that after 100 overs the curtain would fall on the innings. Sri Lanka were better in their second, with Karunaratne retiring after reaching a hundred, but plenty of questions remained ahead of the First Test at Headingley.

Close of play: first day, Sri Lankans 318-8 (Shanaka 91, Herath 28); second day, Leicestershire 304-5 (Wells 53, Taylor 1).

Sri Lankans

F. D. M. Karunaratne b Sheikh	0	– retired out	100
J. K. Silva c Sykes b Sayer	38	– b Taylor	43
B. K. G. Mendis c Eckersley b Sayer	65		
*L. D. Chandimal b Sykes	30		
H. D. R. L. Thirimanne c Wells b Taylor	6	– (3) not out	40
T. A. M. Siriwardene c Ali b Wells	8	– (5) b Sayer	0
†D. P. D. N. Dickwella lbw b Naik	19	– (4) c Taylor b Wells	0
M. D. Shanaka c Hill b Wells	112		
P. V. D. Chameera c Eckersley b Naik	2		
H. M. R. K. B. Herath c Hill b Taylor	55		
R. A. S. Lakmal not out	0		
B 28, w 3, nb 1	32	B 12, lb 3, w 2	17
1/0 (1) 2/101 (2) 3/124 (3) (97.1 overs)	367	1/100 (2) (4 wkts dec, 50.2 overs)	200
4/131 (5) 5/153 (6) 6/173 (4)		2/179 (1) 3/191 (4)	
7/185 (7) 8/192 (9) 9/366 (10) 10/367 (8)		4/200 (5)	

Sheikh 21–4–86–1; Taylor 16–3–55–2; Naik 15–2–61–2; Wells 18.1–2–72–2; Sykes 15–5–24–1; Sayer 12–1–41–2. *Second innings*—Sheikh 3–0–17–0; Taylor 11–3–29–1; Wells 9–2–45–1; Sykes 8–2–28–0; Naik 8–3–19–0; Sayer 11.2–0–47–1.

Leicestershire

*A. J. Robson lbw b Herath	39
L. J. Hill b Herath	30
A. M. Ali lbw b Lakmal	46
†E. J. H. Eckersley st Dickwella b Siriwardene	21
M. G. K. Burgess c and b Siriwardene	98
T. J. Wells not out	87
R. M. L. Taylor not out	37
B 10, lb 2, nb 5	17
1/71 (1) (5 wkts dec, 100 overs)	375
2/82 (2) 3/128 (4)	
4/175 (3) 5/303 (5)	

R. J. Sayer, J. S. Sykes, J. K. H. Naik and A. Sheikh did not bat.

Lakmal 19–3–65–1; Chameera 17–3–104–0; Shanaka 16–0–68–0; Karunaratne 6–0–30–0; Herath 24–8–39–2; Siriwardene 18–3–57–2.

Umpires: N. G. B. Cook and A. G. Wharf.

ENGLAND v SRI LANKA

First Investec Test Match

JONATHAN LIEW

At Leeds, May 19–21. England won by an innings and 88 runs. England 4pts. Toss: Sri Lanka. Test debuts: J. M. Vince; M. D. Shanaka.

You can generally rely on a Leeds crowd to provide their own entertainment, especially on Test-match Saturday. A bunch of guys in butchers' overalls chased a cow. A troop of huntsmen in traditional pink spotted a fox, and pursued him mercilessly across the West Stand. A group of Donald Trumps were booed as they took their seats, most loudly by a group of Mexican sombreros. All good clean fun, then – but, as a hapless Sri Lanka were blown away inside three days (and the equivalent of less than two), it was as though the action in the stands was becoming more competitive than the action on the field.

Sri Lanka were well beaten, though not entirely to blame. Their subsidence had been widely predicted, which only underlined the folly of inviting them to the North in rainy May. They were greeted with a surface even more helpful to bowlers than those served up for Yorkshire in the County Championship. Swing and seam were abundant, and the odd ball reared off a length. And, while their pace attack bowled well enough in the conditions, their batsmen came and went in a fiesta of prods and edges: Sri Lanka were bowled out twice in six hours' play. When Anderson castled Pradeep Fernando to end proceedings, it felt merciful rather than clinical, and that is surely not the hallmark of great Test cricket.

For England, well, you can only beat what the Future Tours Programme puts in front of you. Yet, in this first outing of the Test summer, a crushing victory was tempered both by the weakness of the opposition, and by the patchiness of England's own performance. It was a win built almost entirely on four players: Hales and Bairstow with the bat, Anderson and Broad with the ball. They contributed 75% of their team's runs and wickets, and close to 100% of the resolve.

How different things had looked on the first afternoon, when England were 83 for five, and the ghosts of 2014 – and their penultimate-ball defeat by the same opposition at the same venue – were beginning to stir. Bowling first under chrome skies had been an easy decision for Mathews, despite the absence of the injured Dammika Prasad. And there was an unlikely star on an opening day limited to 53 overs by rain, as debutant Dasun Shanaka – selected largely on the strength of a rapid century at Leicester – began his Test career with wickets from his seventh, tenth and 14th balls, at which point his figures read 2.2–2–1–3.

As if he had been doing it all his life, Shanaka located the perfect Headingley length: a little fuller than usual, tempting the drive, but not allowing the batsman to cover any movement. Cook, needing 36 runs for 10,000 in Tests, was lured by a wide one. Compton, fighting for his England career, was neither forward nor back, and edged to slip for an unhappy duck. Root's dismissal was probably the cleverest of all, Shanaka banging in a

---

TEST CENTURIES BY YORKSHIRE PLAYERS AT HEADINGLEY

246*	G. Boycott	v I	1967
191	G. Boycott	v A	1977
144*	F. S. Jackson	v A	1905
140	**J. M. Bairstow**	**v SL**	**2016**
115	G. Boycott	v NZ	1973
112	G. Boycott	v P	1971
107	A. Lyth	v NZ	2015
104	J. E. Root	v NZ	2013
103	M. P. Vaughan	v WI	2007
101	L. Hutton	v NZ	1949
100	L. Hutton	v SA	1947
100	L. Hutton	v SA	1951

S. R. Tendulkar scored one Test hundred for India after playing for Yorkshire; M. T. G. Elliott and D. R. Martyn each scored one for Australia and Younis Khan one for Pakistan before playing for Yorkshire.

Nigel French, PA Photos

There's another: Jimmy Anderson bowls Kusal Mendis for a fighting fifty, and Sri Lanka hurtle towards an innings defeat.

couple just short of a length, before offering him a wider, fuller delivery in his next over that Root could only steer to third slip. That brought in James Vince on debut: after taking 19 balls to get off the mark, then unfurling a couple of attractive strokes, he too was caught on the drive. Stokes pummelled three successive fours off Eranga, then chipped tamely to mid-on.

Meanwhile Hales, so indulgent in short-form cricket, was attaining monastic levels of self-deprivation. He made just three scoring shots in the first hour and, despite never quite finding his flow, carved out what was then his highest Test score, with a combination of judicious leaves and – his pressure-release shot – back-foot drives. It was a vital innings, not just personally but in the context of the game: after his 141-run partnership with Bairstow, which ended on the second morning when Hales tried to launch Herath down the ground, Sri Lanka never regained the upper hand.

On his home ground, Bairstow alone made scoring look remotely easy. He successfully reviewed an lbw decision after Mathews seemed to have trapped him on 40, and should have been caught and bowled by Pradeep Fernando on 70. But mostly he looked a class apart. Anything straight was shovelled through midwicket; anything wide slapped through point. His voracious running shifted the pressure to the fielders, and he overtook Hales on the second morning, having given him a 32-over head start. As he reached his second Test century, his eyes shot to the heavens. This was the ground where his late father, David, was once cock of the walk, and where his mother, Janet, still works as an administrator. " I knew exactly where she was," said Bairstow. "Just up on the third floor. I'm sure mum will have had a glass of wine this afternoon to celebrate."

Finn helped him add 56 for the ninth wicket, but Bairstow's majestic assurance was the exception, not the rule – as Sri Lanka soon proved. Only Mathews provided much resistance, and he was partially culpable for his downfall, declining to review an lbw to Anderson on the advice of his batting partner, Thirimanne. Hawk-Eye had it missing leg.

Anderson then bowled one of his insouciantly brilliant spells, the sort that renders the middle of the bat superfluous; figures of five for 16, his cheapest five-for in Tests, moved him past Kapil Dev's 434 wickets on the all-time list. Broad, charging down the hill from

CHEAPEST TEN-FORS IN TEST CRICKET

11-24	H. Ironmonger	Australia v South Africa at Melbourne	1931-32
10-27	G. D. McGrath	Australia v West Indies at Brisbane	2000-01
15-28	J. Briggs	England v South Africa at Cape Town	1888-89
11-31	E. R. H. Toshack	Australia v India at Brisbane	1947-48
15-45	G. A. Lohmann	England v South Africa at Port Elizabeth	1895-96
10-45	**J. M. Anderson**	**England v Sri Lanka at Leeds**	**2016**
11-48	G. A. R. Lock	England v West Indies at The Oval	1957
10-49	F. E. Woolley	England v Australia at The Oval	1912
13-55	C. A. Walsh	West Indies v New Zealand at Wellington	1994-95
13-57	S. F. Barnes	England v South Africa at The Oval	1912
10-57	W. Voce	England v Australia at Brisbane	1936-37

the Kirkstall Lane End, chipped in with four, prompting Anderson – whose 19 Test wickets at Headingley before this game had cost 41 apiece – to reveal a fundamental change of tactics. "It's taken us nine years to realise we've been bowling at the wrong ends," he deadpanned.

With Sri Lanka's last six wickets falling for 14 inside ten overs, Cook pugnaciously imposed the follow-on late on the second day. Despite three hours of rain that briefly threatened to take the match into a fourth, the clouds parted for long enough on the Saturday for Sri Lanka to fold a second time. A knee injury to Stokes, suffered while bowling on the second evening, left England's attack a man short, but it scarcely mattered.

Anderson ripped out the top order, finishing with match figures of ten for 45, England's best against Sri Lanka (beating Graeme Swann's ten for 181 at Colombo's P. Sara Oval in 2011-12), and the first ten-wicket haul by an England seamer at Headingley since Fred Trueman against Australia in 1961. Finn, preferred to the uncapped Jake Ball of Nottinghamshire, looked out of sorts, but massaged his figures with three wickets in five balls. Mendis scrapped his way to a maiden Test fifty, having been dropped by Bairstow and Vince, though Bairstow finished with nine catches in his first home Test as a wicketkeeper. Sri Lanka's aggregate of 210 runs, meanwhile, was their lowest in a Test in which they had lost all 20 wickets.

In years to come, we may look back on May Test matches in England as a passing phase, a fleeting eccentricity, like the two-day County Championship or aluminium bats. There was little public appetite for this game, with spectators dissuaded by poor forecasts and steep ticket prices. The new Super Series format, under which England claimed the first four points, was on nobody's lips. And so, as the fox and the cow, the butchers and the hunters, Donald Trump and the Mexicans, filed out of Headingley, it was tempting to wonder what it had all been for.

Man of the Match: J. M. Bairstow. *Attendance:* 37,863.

Close of play: first day, England 171-5 (Hales 71, Bairstow 54); second day, Sri Lanka 1-0 (Karunaratne 0, Silva 0).

BEST MATCH FIGURES IN A HEADINGLEY TEST

38.3–10–99–15	C. Blythe	England v South Africa	1907
53.3–33–65–11	G. A. R. Lock	England v New Zealand	1958
42.2–11–85–11	C. G. Macartney	Australia v England	1909
37.5–10–88–11	F. S. Trueman	England v Australia	1961
70.3–31–113–11	J. C. Laker	England v Australia	1956
25.1–11–45–10	**J. M. Anderson**	**England v Sri Lanka**	**2016**
38.1–8–77–10	Imran Khan	Pakistan v England	1987
52–22–82–10	D. L. Underwood	England v Australia	1972
43.2–12–115–10	S. F. Barnes	England v South Africa	1912
56–25–122–10	W. J. O'Reilly	Australia v England	1938

England

*A. N. Cook c Chandimal b Shanaka	16
A. D. Hales c Chameera b Herath	86
N. R. D. Compton c Thirimanne b Shanaka	0
J. E. Root c Mendis b Shanaka	0
J. M. Vince c Mendis b Eranga	9
B. A. Stokes c Mathews b Fernando	12
†J. M. Bairstow c Fernando b Chameera	140
M. M. Ali c Mendis b Chameera	0
S. C. J. Broad b Chameera	2
S. T. Finn st Chandimal b Herath	17
J. M. Anderson not out	1
Lb 8, w 4, nb 3	15
(90.3 overs)	298

1/49 (1) 2/49 (3) 3/51 (4) 4/70 (5) 5/83 (6) 6/224 (2) 7/231 (8) 8/233 (9) 9/289 (7) 10/298 (10)

Eranga 19–4–68–1; Fernando 19–7–56–1; Mathews 11–2–31–0; Chameera 17–0–64–3; Shanaka 13–3–46–3; Herath 11.3–1–25–2.

Sri Lanka

F. D. M. Karunaratne c Bairstow b Broad	0	c Bairstow b Anderson	7
J. K. Silva c Bairstow b Anderson	11	c Bairstow b Anderson	14
B. K. G. Mendis c Bairstow b Broad	0	b Anderson	53
†L. D. Chandimal c Vince b Stokes	15	b Ali	8
*A. D. Mathews lbw b Anderson	34	c Bairstow b Broad	5
H. D. R. L. Thirimanne c Finn b Broad	22	c Root b Finn	16
M. D. Shanaka c Bairstow b Anderson	0	c Bairstow b Anderson	4
H. M. R. K. B. Herath c Stokes b Anderson	1	c Broad b Finn	4
P. V. D. Chameera c Finn b Broad	2	c Compton b Finn	0
R. M. S. Eranga c Bairstow b Anderson	1	not out	2
A. N. P. R. Fernando not out	0	b Anderson	0
Nb 5	5	Lb 5, nb 1	6
(36.4 overs)	91	(35.3 overs)	119

1/10 (1) 2/12 (2) 3/12 (3) 4/43 (4) 5/77 (5) 6/81 (7) 7/83 (8) 8/90 (9) 9/91 (6) 10/91 (10)

1/10 (1) 2/35 (2) 3/79 (4) 4/93 (5) 5/93 (3) 6/101 (7) 7/111 (8) 8/117 (9) 9/118 (6) 10/119 (11)

Anderson 11.4–6–16–5; Broad 10–1–21–4; Stokes 7–2–25–1; Vince 1–0–10–0; Finn 7–0–19–0. *Second innings*—Anderson 13.3–5–29–5; Broad 13–0–57–1; Finn 8–0–26–3; Ali 1–0–2–1.

Umpires: Aleem Dar and R. J. Tucker. Third umpire: S. Ravi.
Referee: A. J. Pycroft.

ENGLAND v SRI LANKA

Second Investec Test Match

FIDEL FERNANDO

At Chester-le-Street, May 27–30. England won by nine wickets. England 4pts. Toss: England.

After taking four outstanding catches on day one, Sri Lanka returned next morning full of pep. Then, like an untied balloon, they deflated at an alarming rate and flew around haphazardly, making rude noises. The pitch was fair, but the Sri Lankans could take the match only as far as the fourth day, when Cook finally moved past 10,000 Test runs and England moved 2–0 up with one to play. On three of those days, Sri Lanka had competed; on the second, their cricket was abysmal enough to define their series.

It was in the rotation of Moeen Ali's velvet wrists that the match turned for England, his second-morning reprieve signalling the moment Sri Lanka let the Test slip. He had 36 when Pradeep Fernando drew a thick edge in the third over – but the ball burst through Karunaratne's fingers at a wide second slip. Next over, wicketkeeper Chandimal missed a straightforward chance – Woakes, on eight, edging Eranga. Sri Lanka had entered freefall.

Like those for whom a near-death experience spurs a fearless attitude, England's overnight batsmen did not merely progress from 310 for six – they surged. And the threat

Gareth Copley, Getty Images

Here's one we made earlier: officials mark Alastair Cook's 10,000th run with a giant banner; Cook was rather more self-effacing.

Sri Lanka posed in the early overs didn't simply go flat – it flatlined. Even when boundaries were not forthcoming, the outfield became a wellspring of runs, the bowlers tiring, Mathews's captaincy worsening. Such mis-hits as there were fell into gaps where catchers had stood in the early morning.

As Ali flitted about the crease, skipping forward, slinking back, even the poise of Herath, their most experienced bowler, was upset. His second ball of the day was thunked over mid-off by Ali, who passed 50; in Herath's next over, Ali swatted him in front of point, then scorched him through the covers. Sri Lanka did manage the wickets of Woakes – to end a seventh-wicket stand worth 92 – and Broad in quick succession before lunch. But, for England, these proved minor hiccups. After the break, Ali manoeuvred Sri Lanka into submission.

Mathews's tactics betrayed a startling lack of intent. There were catchers for Finn, but vast spaces for Ali. The ground-fielding nosedived: balls were fumbled, missed completely and, in some cases, escorted gallantly to the boundary. Ali began the afternoon session on 85, and needed only 17 deliveries to move to his second Test hundred, both against Sri Lanka. On 105, he was dropped again, this time by Siriwardene at deep midwicket off Eranga (whose tour was about to get worse: the day after the game, he was reported for a suspect action). Ali crashed the next two balls either side of square in an over costing 13. Mathews cut a beleaguered figure, regularly declining to bring the field in for the last two balls of the over, which allowed Ali to retain the strike with minimal difficulty.

Towards the end of the innings, with Sri Lanka firing it down the leg side to delay the declaration, Herath wangled a top-edge out of an ambitious Finn, and took the catch himself. It was his 300th Test wicket. Only two other Sri Lankans – Muttiah Muralitharan and Chaminda Vaas – had beaten him to it.

The declaration eventually came at 498 for nine, with Ali unbeaten on 155, yet Sri Lanka's day soon deteriorated further. At Headingley, they had played as if given only rough coordinates for the off stump. The Chester-le-Street pitch was friendlier, but once more they found themselves poking, wafting and prodding against Anderson, Broad and Woakes, in for the injured Ben Stokes. Balls continued to seek out edges, then fielders: in the 40 overs before stumps, seven catches went to keeper or cordon.

Amid the wreckage came Mathews's tour nadir: having been ruled caught behind on three off the energetic Woakes, he asked for a review, only for Hot Spot and Snicko to

HIGHEST TEST SCORE BY AN ENGLAND NO. 7

175	K. S. Ranjitsinhji	v Australia at Sydney	1897-98
169*	J. Hardstaff, jnr.	v Australia at The Oval	1938
164	D. W. Randall	v New Zealand at Wellington	1983-84
155*	**M. M. Ali**	**v Sri Lanka at Chester-le-Street**	**2016**
150*	J. M. Bairstow	v South Africa at Cape Town	2015-16
149*	I. T. Botham	v Australia at Leeds	1981
142	A. Flintoff	v South Africa at Lord's	2003
140	**J. M. Bairstow**	**v Sri Lanka at Leeds**	**2016**

confirm his downfall. Of the frontline quicks, only an off-rhythm Finn went wicketless. Sri Lanka had begun the day with realistic hopes of keeping England's first innings to 350. They ended it at 91 for eight – 407 adrift. Only ten more runs were added next morning, as Broad finished with four for 40. In three successive innings, Sri Lanka had totalled 311.

That second day was more calamitous for having followed three sessions of competent English batting. While Hales shelved aggression in his bid to crack Test cricket, Cook had been well caught for 15 by a tumbling second slip off Lakmal, leaving him on 9,995 Test runs; only Brian Lara (out twice on 9,993 against England in 2004), and Mahela Jayawardene (run out on 9,999 at Centurion in 2011-12) had previously succumbed in the nervous 9,990s. Shortly before lunch, Compton hooked Pradeep Fernando towards long leg, where Lakmal appeared to dart in several directions at once, then threw his hands up as if in supplication, found the ball lodged within them, and – sliding backwards – came to a halt inches from the boundary.

Root brought dynamism, apparently picking Sri Lanka's pockets rather than scoring runs. While Hales lumbered along, Root filled his sack with ones and twos to unconventional parts of the ground. Every time Mathews attempted to tighten the net around him, Root slipped through. He ventured boundaries only occasionally, hitting five in his 119-ball 80.

It took two more outstanding catches for Sri Lanka to regain their footing on the first day. Hales fell in the eighties to a left-arm spinner for the second time in the series, when his cut off Siriwardene was snaffled by a diving Mathews at slip. Later, Thirimanne climbed to his right at short cover to cling on to Vince's uppish drive. This alertness would desert them on day two, but return on days three and four.

Also relocated while following on – the first time Sri Lanka had done so in successive Tests since their tour of India in 1993-94 – was the elusive off stump. As England's quicks came at him again on the third morning, Silva left the ball decisively, defended resolutely, and leaned confidently into sumptuous drives. He scored 60, while others got starts. When the pitch eased further, Mathews made bruising advances against spin: in a combative 80, he hit six fours and a six off Ali, in all taking 46 runs from the 46 balls he faced against him. But it was Chandimal who played Sri Lanka's most consequential innings, and spurred the tail to defiance for the first time in the series.

He hunkered down against the seamers early in his innings, before unfurling his off-kilter attacking strokes, mainly against Ali. The bowlers, who had delivered more than 95 consecutive overs when Chandimal arrived, were soon visibly tiring. He moved past 50 from his 95th delivery, had an inside edge badly dropped by Bairstow off Anderson on 69, and completed his sixth Test hundred, and first outside Asia, from his 172nd; it was also his fourth in nine innings from No. 6.

En route, he added 92 for the sixth wicket with Siriwardene, then a heartening 116 for the seventh with Herath, whose 61 bristled with characteristic short-arm pulls and booming sweeps. By the time he provided Anderson with his 450th Test wicket, Sri Lanka had crept into a 33-run lead. But thoughts of a miracle were disrupted by Anderson, who completed his 21st five-wicket haul: he conceded only 58 runs from 27 overs, and looked a class above his colleagues.

Ian Horrocks, Getty Images

Handicraft: Rangana Herath is hugged after reaching a landmark of his own – 300 Test wickets.

England needed 79 for victory, and – the loss of Hales aside – there were no jitters. The only question was whether Cook could become the first England batsman to tick off 10,000. Typically, the milestone arrived not from anything imperious, but from a run-of-the-mill whip off the pads, which trickled over the rope at midwicket. Of the 12 batsmen to reach five figures, Cook – at 31 years 157 days – was the youngest, beating Sachin Tendulkar by 169 days. And, in the course of his unbeaten 47, he overtook Mike Atherton (3,815) as the leading Test run-scorer among England captains. A banner was unfurled for him in the stands, which were disappointingly empty.

Two years after the trauma of losing to Sri Lanka at Headingley, England had sailed to a series victory with time to spare.

Man of the Match: J. M. Anderson. *Attendance:* 29,310.

Close of play: first day, England 310-6 (Ali 28, Woakes 8); second day, Sri Lanka 91-8 (Thirimanne 12, Lakmal 0); third day, Sri Lanka 309-5 (Chandimal 54, Siriwardene 35).

England

*A. N. Cook c Karunaratne b Lakmal	15	– not out	47
A. D. Hales c Mathews b Siriwardene	83	– b Siriwardene	11
N. R. D. Compton c Lakmal b Fernando	9	– not out	22
J. E. Root c Silva b Fernando	80		
J. M. Vince c Thirimanne b Siriwardene	35		
†J. M. Bairstow c Chandimal b Fernando	48		
M. M. Ali not out	155		
C. R. Woakes c Mendis b Lakmal	39		
S. C. J. Broad c Mendis b Fernando	7		
S. T. Finn c and b Herath	10		
J. M. Anderson not out	8		
B 1, lb 8	9		
1/39 (1) 2/64 (3) (9 wkts dec, 132 overs)	498	1/35 (2) (1 wkt, 23.2 overs)	80

3/160 (2) 4/219 (4) 5/227 (5)
6/297 (6) 7/389 (8) 8/400 (9) 9/472 (10)

LORD'S
THE HOME OF CRICKET
LORD'S TOURS & MUSEUM
Visit lords.org/tours

Eranga 27–3–100–0; Lakmal 29–4–115–2; Fernando 33–5–107–4; Herath 29–1–116–1; Mathews 6–2–16–0; Siriwardene 8–0–35–2. *Second innings*—Herath 10–3–18–0; Fernando 2–0–12–0; Siriwardene 7.2–0–37–1; Lakmal 3–0–9–0; Eranga 1–0–4–0.

Sri Lanka

F. D. M. Karunaratne b Anderson	9	– c Root b Woakes	26
J. K. Silva c Bairstow b Broad	13	– c Bairstow b Finn	60
B. K. G. Mendis c Anderson b Woakes	35	– c Bairstow b Anderson	26
†L. D. Chandimal c Cook b Anderson	4	– (6) b Broad	126
*A. D. Mathews c Bairstow b Woakes	3	– c Bairstow b Anderson	80
H. D. R. L. Thirimanne c Compton b Anderson	19	– (4) b Ali	13
T. A. M. Siriwardene c Bairstow b Woakes	0	– c Hales b Anderson	35
H. M. R. K. B. Herath c Anderson b Broad	12	– lbw b Anderson	61
R. M. S. Eranga c Root b Broad	2	– b Anderson	1
R. A. S. Lakmal c Bairstow b Broad	0	– c Broad b Woakes	11
A. N. P. R. Fernando not out	2	– not out	13
Lb 1, nb 1	2	B 5, lb 11, w 1, nb 6	23
1/10 (1) 2/44 (2) 3/53 (4) 4/58 (5) 5/67 (3) 6/67 (7) 7/88 (8) 8/90 (9) 9/93 (10) 10/101 (6) (43.3 overs)	101	1/38 (1) 2/79 (3) 3/100 (4) 4/182 (2) 5/222 (5) 6/314 (7) 7/430 (8) 8/442 (9) 9/453 (6) 10/475 (10) (128.2 overs)	475

Anderson 12.3–2–36–3; Broad 13–2–40–4; Woakes 7–4–9–3; Finn 7–3–15–0; Ali 4–4–0–0. *Second innings*—Anderson 27–9–58–5; Broad 24–6–71–1; Woakes 27.2–8–103–2; Finn 19–0–78–1; Ali 28–5–136–1; Vince 1–1–0–0; Root 2–0–13–0.

Umpires: Aleem Dar and S. Ravi. Third umpire: R. J. Tucker.
Tucker replaced Aleem Dar (ill) on the fourth day; D. J. Millns replaced Tucker as third umpire.
Referee: A. J. Pycroft.

ENGLAND v SRI LANKA

Third Investec Test Match

STEVEN LYNCH

At Lord's, June 9–13. Drawn. England 2pts, Sri Lanka 2pts. Toss: England.

The shoulders said it all – and two pairs of them defined the match. Jonny Bairstow's threatened to burst out of his shirt, which looked as if he'd left the coat-hanger in, as he reeled off another fine century. But Nick Compton's were hunched, as he sloped off after a double failure almost certainly ended his Test career.

Hopes of an England clean sweep, however, were washed away by the rain. Only 45 overs were possible on the fourth day, and 12.2 – in two soggy spells – on the fifth. This, plus patches of decent batting on a placid pitch, allowed Sri Lanka to escape with a draw – their first in 17 Tests, of which ten had been lost, since July 2014, but their fifth in a row at Lord's. It was also the first draw in 14 in England, since the opening Test against India at Nottingham that same month.

Before play, Cook was presented with a silver bat to mark 10,000 Test runs (two days later he was awarded a CBE), and he would have been delighted to win the toss: England had not lost here after batting first since South Africa upset them in 2003. The start was promising, too. Hales square-drove Lakmal for a juicy four, and soon Cook was posting England's first half-century opening partnership for 14 innings at home.

And then, in line with recent form, England hit trouble. Tied down by Herath, Hales thick-edged an ugly mow to slip; then the enthusiastic Lakmal had Compton nicking behind and, four balls later, Root lbw on review. It was the 21st time in 37 Test innings that England had lost their third wicket before reaching 75. Soon after lunch Vince was

Sarah Ansell Getty Images

Silva lining: Kaushal Silva flexes his elbows in a century opening stand with Dimuth Karunaratne.

beaten by one which seamed up the hill from Pradeep Fernando, the liveliest of the bowlers. And, if Eranga at midwicket had held on waist-high to a firm clip from Bairstow – 11 at the time – they would have been 102 for five. It was a surprise that Eranga was playing at all, after his action was reported at Chester-le-Street (he was tested at Loughborough before this game, and suspended soon afterwards). Sri Lanka's only alteration was to recall Kusal Perera – a recent arrival after doping charges had been dropped – for Milinda Siriwardene. England were unchanged.

Bairstow made the most of his reprieve, leading the rescue act that eventually lifted England past 400. Standing still at the crease and playing late, he showed intent from the first ball, which he bottom-handed towards point, a shot more croquet than cricket.

A quiet session followed, as the fifth-wicket pair rebuilt against some disciplined bowling, only for Cook to play across Pradeep Fernando and fall leg-before for 85, having passed Sunil Gavaskar's 10,122 Test runs. Ali uncorked a lip-smacking cover-drive, and helped add 63 before edging to slip; but Bairstow drove well against the new ball, and Woakes joined in with a couple of crisp drives of his own.

Just before the first-day close, Bairstow nurdled a leg-side single to bring up his third Test hundred, becoming only the second England wicketkeeper – after Les Ames in the West Indies in 1929-30 – to make two in the same series. He and Woakes stretched their stand to 144 next day, England's seventh-wicket best against Sri Lanka, beating 109 by Ian Bell and Matt Prior at Kandy in 2007-08.

The persistent Herath juggled a return catch to dismiss Woakes for a career-best 66, but Bairstow was not done, purring past 150 (and his own highest Test score) in the following over. The tail did little, and Bairstow was stranded on 167, one short of Clyde Walcott's record for a wicketkeeper in a Test in England, and six behind Alec Stewart's overall England mark, set at Auckland in 1996-97.

Sri Lanka's reply had a frenetic start: Karunaratne lashed Anderson over the covers and leaned back to carve Broad for four and three, then Silva joined in, cover-driving Anderson: the first three overs cost 23. But the bowlers – and the batsmen – settled down. By tea the stand was worth 62, helped when Bairstow shelled a regulation nick from Woakes's first ball, with Karunaratne 28. Coming so soon after his superb innings, it fuelled the debate over whether he should hand the gloves to Jos Buttler, still in Test exile, and concentrate on batting. Bairstow was in little doubt, and finished with 19 dismissals, an England record for a three-match series, beating Geraint Jones's 17 – also against Sri Lanka – in 2006. Only Sri Lanka's Amal Silva, with 22 against India in 1985-86, had taken more.

That evening the openers took the score to 108. Karunaratne escaped a marginal lbw shout from Woakes, on 31, but possibly lost concentration after reaching 50 when, with drinks imminent, he flicked Finn down leg and was caught behind. In came the dapper Mendis, who kept the boundaries flowing, edging Broad not far from the leaping Root at third slip, then flaying Woakes through point. In between, Silva brought up the 150 with a cover-driven four off Broad.

Sri Lanka were sitting pretty at 162 for one by the close, but the game took a twist on the third morning, both batsmen falling without adding to their scores. Mendis was trapped by the first ball of the second over, while Silva provided Bairstow with another victim. Mathews – a centurion at Lord's in 2014 – soon edged to Root, and Sri Lanka were up against it once more.

HIGHEST TEST SCORES IN ENGLAND BY WICKETKEEPERS

168*	C. L. Walcott	West Indies v England at Lord's	1950
167*	**J. M. Bairstow**	**England v Sri Lanka at Lord's**	**2016**
164	A. J. Stewart	England v South Africa at Manchester	1998
152	A. C. Gilchrist	Australia v England at Birmingham	2001
148*	L. E. G. Ames	England v South Africa at The Oval	1935
140	**J. M. Bairstow**	**England v Sri Lanka at Leeds**	**2016**
137	L. E. G. Ames	England v New Zealand at Lord's	1931
135	A. P. E. Knott	England v Australia at Nottingham	1977
128*	R. C. Russell	England v Australia at Manchester	1989
126*	M. J. Prior	England v West Indies at Lord's	2007
126	M. J. Prior	England v Sri Lanka at Lord's	2011
126	**L. D. Chandimal**	**Sri Lanka v England at Chester-le-Street**	**2016**

The highest score by a wicketkeeper in any Test is A. Flower's 232 for Zimbabwe v India at Nagpur in 2000-01; there have been seven other double-centuries.*

Cook displayed some innovative captaincy, preferring Woakes – the slipperiest bowler on show – to Anderson. Then he tried a 7–2 field and, although that produced no breakthroughs, turning to Finn did: Chandimal was lbw on review, and in his next over Thirimanne's loose drive flew to second slip. Perera paid Finn back with cuts and drives for four in the last over before lunch, but England still bossed the session with five for 56. Perera and Herath stemmed the collapse, putting on 71. But, after Herath chopped on, Anderson removed the swishing Perera – his first Test wicket at Lord's for 68.2 overs – and the immobile Lakmal, before Woakes returned to grab another wicket with his first delivery, which Eranga steered to third slip.

It was tea on the third day. England led by 128, but the forecast was dire and Cook, who had an X-ray after his knee collected a meaty Perera drive at silly point, was injured. In his absence, England's innings was opened by two right-handers for the first time since 2002 (Robert Key and Michael Vaughan against India). But Compton and Root failed again, and Vince misjudged the slope for a second time, leaving Pradeep Fernando on a hat-trick. The combined total of eight runs by England's Nos 3 and 4 was their lowest in any Test in which they batted four times; soon after, Compton announced he would be taking a break from cricket.

When nightwatchman Finn departed early on the fourth morning, Cook emerged and, freed from the hazards of the new ball, cut Pradeep Fernando for a couple of felicitous fours. His normal opening partner, Hales, should have departed when 58, his stumps demolished by a Pradeep Fernando shooter – but Rod Tucker had called no-ball, erroneously, as replays showed. Feelings ran high: the Sri Lankan flag was draped over their dressing-room balcony in protest, until MCC asked for it to be removed. Unabashed, Hales clattered Herath straight for six, then swept him for four. He was soon in the eighties for the third time in the series, but a maiden hundred remained elusive: at 94, with the light fading, Mathews won a reviewed lbw.

After tea, Cook continued to show every sign of enjoying the No. 7 spot, trying a ramp and a reverse sweep – and then, just before declaring 361 ahead, clonking Eranga over midwicket for his first six in 43 Tests since December 2012. He walked off one short of another half-century, having taken his record against Sri Lanka at Lord's to 470 runs at 78.

Theoretically, Sri Lanka had 110 overs to survive but, after they negotiated a tricky spell at the end of the fourth day, the weather played spoilsport on the fifth. England took the series 2–0, an emphatic turnaround from their narrow defeat by Sri Lanka two years previously.

Man of the Match: J. M. Bairstow. *Attendance:* 103,691.

Men of the Series: England – J. M. Bairstow; Sri Lanka – J. K. Silva.

Close of play: first day, England 279-6 (Bairstow 107, Woakes 23); second day, Sri Lanka 162-1 (Silva 79, Mendis 25); third day, England 109-4 (Hales 41, Finn 6); fourth day, Sri Lanka 32-0 (Karunaratne 19, Silva 12).

England

*A. N. Cook lbw b Fernando	85	– (7) not out	49
A. D. Hales c Mathews b Herath	18	– lbw b Mathews	94
N. R. D. Compton c Chandimal b Lakmal	1	– (1) c Chandimal b Eranga	19
J. E. Root lbw b Lakmal	3	– (3) b Fernando	4
J. M. Vince b Fernando	10	– (4) b Fernando	0
†J. M. Bairstow not out	167	– (5) b Fernando	32
M. M. Ali c Mathews b Herath	25	– (8) c Herath b Eranga	9
C. R. Woakes c and b Herath	66	– (9) not out	0
S. C. J. Broad c Mendis b Lakmal	14		
S. T. Finn c Lakmal b Herath	7	– (6) lbw b Eranga	7
J. M. Anderson c Chandimal b Eranga	4		
Lb 16	16	B 6, lb 4, w 1, nb 8	19
1/56 (2) 2/67 (3) 3/71 (4) 4/84 (5) 5/164 (1) 6/227 (7) 7/371 (8) 8/396 (9) 9/411 (10) 10/416 (11) (128.4 overs)	416	1/45 (1) 2/50 (3) 3/50 (4) 4/101 (5) 5/120 (6) 6/202 (2) 7/224 (8) (7 wkts dec, 71 overs)	233

Eranga 25.4–2–94–1; Lakmal 27–2–90–3; Fernando 27–4–104–2; Mathews 13–5–31–0; Herath 36–8–81–4. *Second innings*—Lakmal 13–2–45–0; Eranga 14–1–58–3; Fernando 15–5–37–3; Herath 20–2–63–0; Mathews 9–3–20–1.

Sri Lanka

F. D. M. Karunaratne c Bairstow b Finn	50	– not out	37
J. K. Silva c Bairstow b Broad	79	– lbw b Anderson	16
B. K. G. Mendis lbw b Woakes	25	– not out	17
H. D. R. L. Thirimanne c Root b Finn	17		
*A. D. Mathews c Root b Woakes	3		
†L. D. Chandimal lbw b Finn	19		
M. D. K. J. Perera c Bairstow b Anderson	42		
H. M. R. K. B. Herath b Broad	31		
R. M. S. Eranga c Vince b Woakes	1		
R. A. S. Lakmal c Root b Anderson	0		
A. N. P. R. Fernando not out	0		
B 4, lb 16, w 1	21	B 1, lb 6, nb 1	8
1/108 (1) 2/162 (3) 3/166 (2) 4/169 (5) 5/202 (6) 6/205 (4) 7/276 (8) 8/288 (7) 9/288 (10) 10/288 (9) (95.1 overs)	288	1/45 (2) (1 wkt, 24.2 overs)	78

Anderson 23–6–61–2; Broad 23–7–79–2; Finn 18–1–59–3; Woakes 17.1–5–31–3; Ali 14–2–38–0. *Second innings*—Broad 11–4–27–0; Anderson 9–2–27–1; Woakes 2–1–7–0; Ali 2–1–4–0; Root 0.2–0–6–0.

Umpires: S. Ravi and R. J. Tucker. Third umpire: Aleem Dar.
Referee: A. J. Pycroft.

At Malahide, June 16. SRI LANKA beat IRELAND by 76 runs (DLS) (see Cricket in Ireland, page 785).

At Malahide, June 18. SRI LANKA beat IRELAND by 136 runs (see Cricket in Ireland, page 785).

Limited-Overs International Reports by Dean Wilson

ENGLAND v SRI LANKA

First Royal London One-Day International

At Nottingham, June 21 (day/night). Tied. England 1pt, Sri Lanka 1pt. Toss: England.

England recovered from a seemingly hopeless position to conjure a tie, sealed by Plunkett's last-gasp six. Sri Lanka's total had owed much to Mathews, who faced 109 deliveries for his 73, and a turbocharged 59 off 28 from Prasanna. He smacked four sixes, and only three of his runs did not come in boundaries. Shanaka and Maharoof, who had been recalled for this tour after four years out of favour, helped boost the total to 286, before Mathews took two quick wickets as England lurched to 30 for four. Despite 43 from captain Morgan, it was soon 82 for six – but Mathews had left the field with a hamstring twinge, and Sri Lanka fell apart as Buttler got going. He and Woakes put on 138, the second-best for the seventh wicket in all one-day internationals, behind Buttler's own 177 with Rashid against New Zealand at Edgbaston a year earlier. Buttler finally fell in the 43rd over, well caught by Shanaka perilously close to the long-on boundary, but Woakes carried on, more than doubling his previous-highest ODI score of 42. He and Plunkett – one of five Yorkshire players for England, a record for any county in a one-day international – required 30 from two overs, then 14 from the last, bowled by Pradeep Fernando. When the penultimate ball failed to reach the boundary, the Sri Lankans started celebrating – too early, as the batsmen scrambled three. Plunkett made room, and hammered the last delivery high over mid-off to force the first tie between the countries. Woakes, meanwhile, finished unbeaten on 95, the highest ODI score from No. 8 or below, beating Andre Russell's 92 not out (from No. 9) for West Indies against India in Antigua in 2011.

Man of the Match: C. R. Woakes. *Attendance:* 17,007.

ENGLAND'S TIED ONE-DAY INTERNATIONALS

England (226-5) v Australia (226-8) at Nottingham	1989
New Zealand (237) v England (237-8) at Napier	1996-97
England (270-5) v South Africa (270-8) at Bloemfontein	2004-05
Australia (196) v England (196-9) at Lord's	2005
England (340-6) v New Zealand (340-7) at Napier	2007-08
India (338) v England (338-8) at Bangalore†	2010-11
India (280-5) v England (270-8) at Lord's‡	2011
Sri Lanka (286-9) v England (286-8) at Nottingham	**2016**

† *World Cup* ‡ *D/L method.*

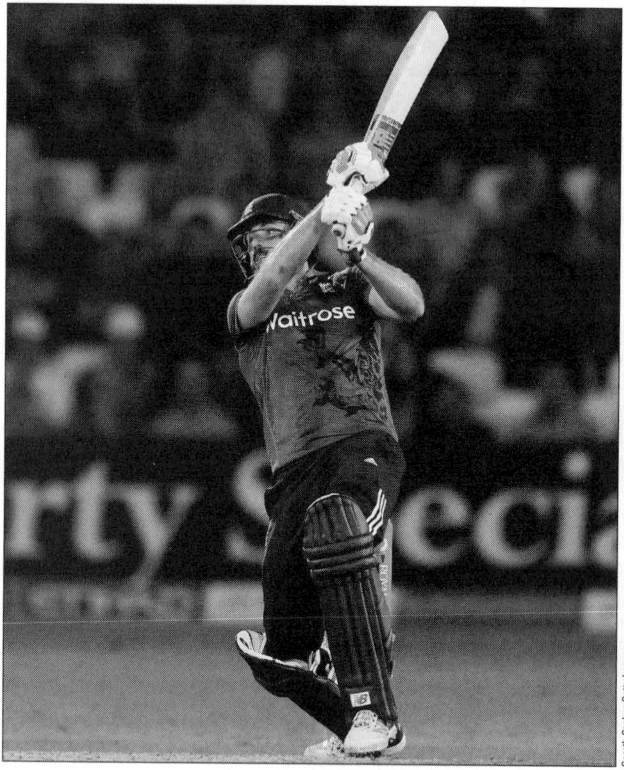

Gareth Copley, Getty Images

Equal to the task: Liam Plunkett smites a last-ball six to level the scores at Trent Bridge.

Sri Lanka

M. D. K. J. Perera c Roy b Willey	24
M. D. Gunathilleke c Bairstow b Willey	9
B. K. G. Mendis c Buttler b Woakes	17
†L. D. Chandimal c Woakes b Ali	37
*A. D. Mathews c Woakes b Plunkett	73
S. Prasanna c and b Woakes	59
W. U. Tharanga c Buttler b Plunkett	3
M. D. Shanaka run out	20
M. F. Maharoof not out	31
R. A. S. Lakmal run out	7
Lb 2, w 3, nb 1	6
1/27 (2) 2/50 (1) (9 wkts, 50 overs)	286

3/56 (3) 4/120 (4)
5/188 (6) 6/197 (7) 7/225 (8)
8/266 (5) 9/286 (10) 10 overs: 59-3

A. N. P. R. Fernando did not bat.

Woakes 10–0–56–2; Willey 10–0–56–2; Rashid 10–0–36–0; Plunkett 10–0–67–2; Ali 10–0–69–1.

England

J. J. Roy lbw b Mathews	3	D. J. Willey c Mendis b Maharoof	7
A. D. Hales c Perera b Lakmal	4	L. E. Plunkett not out	22
J. E. Root b Mathews	2		
*E. J. G. Morgan c Chandimal b Fernando	43	Lb 2, w 5	7
J. M. Bairstow c Gunathilleke b Lakmal	3		
†J. C. Buttler c Shanaka b Prasanna	93	1/3 (1) 2/7 (2) (8 wkts, 50 overs)	286
M. M. Ali b Fernando	7	3/17 (3) 4/30 (5) 5/72 (4)	
C. R. Woakes not out	95	6/82 (7) 7/220 (6) 8/235 (9) 10 overs: 39-4	

A. U. Rashid did not bat.

Lakmal 10–0–65–2; Mathews 6–0–22–2; Shanaka 3–0–21–0; Fernando 10–0–64–2; Maharoof 10–0–59–1; Prasanna 10–0–43–1; Gunathilleke 1–0–10–0.

Umpires: R. J. Bailey and P. R. Reiffel. Third umpire: B. N. J. Oxenford.
Referee: D. C. Boon.

ENGLAND v SRI LANKA

Second Royal London One-Day International

At Birmingham, June 24 (day/night). England won by ten wickets. England 2pts. Toss: Sri Lanka.

England surged to only their sixth ten-wicket victory in one-day internationals, clinching – virtually unnoticed – the Super Series with four matches to play. Sri Lanka had been restricted to 254 for seven, with Rashid producing an especially probing spell; the highlight was a sprightly unbeaten 53 from Tharanga, formerly an opener but now down at No. 7. England's openers soon made the target look insignificant, sprinting to centuries – Hales from 91 balls, Roy from 92. Hales hit six sixes to Roy's four, and both finished with format-bests; Hales's 133 not out, which included

ENGLAND'S TEN-WICKET WINS IN ONE-DAY INTERNATIONALS

171-0	v West Indies (169-8) at Chester-le-Street	2000
192-0	v Bangladesh (190) at The Oval	2005
85-0	v South Africa (83) at Nottingham	2008
171-0	v Sri Lanka (174) at Nottingham†	2011
73-0	v Sri Lanka (67) at Manchester	2014
256-0	**v Sri Lanka (254-7) at Birmingham**	**2016**

† *D/L method.*

26 from an over of Prasanna's leg-spin costing 27, was for five days an England record against Sri Lanka, surpassing David Gower's 130 at Taunton during the 1983 World Cup. Their eventual stand of 256 was also the highest for any England wicket, beating 250 for the second between Andrew Strauss and Jonathan Trott against Bangladesh here six years earlier, and the highest total to win without loss in ODIs, beating 236 by New Zealand to defeat Zimbabwe at Harare in August 2015. After victory was completed with more than 15 overs to spare, Hales and Roy strode off to raucous singing from the Edgbaston crowd. Umpire Oxenford sported a lollipop-shaped perspex shield for the first time in England; despite the openers' onslaught, he did not need to employ its circular screen to protect himself.

Man of the Match: J. J. Roy. *Attendance:* 23,579.

Sri Lanka

M. D. K. J. Perera run out	37
M. D. Gunathilleke c Buttler b Plunkett	22
B. K. G. Mendis lbw b Plunkett	0
†L. D. Chandimal run out	52
*A. D. Mathews c Plunkett b Rashid	44
S. Prasanna c Willey b Rashid	2
W. U. Tharanga not out	53
M. F. Maharoof b Willey	2
S. Randiv not out	26
B 1, lb 13, w 2	16
1/39 (2) 2/47 (3) 3/77 (1) 4/159 (5) 5/163 (6) 6/188 (4) 7/191 (8) (7 wkts, 50 overs)	254
10 overs: 51-2	

R. A. S. Lakmal and A. N. P. R. Fernando did not bat.

Willey 10–0–65–1; Woakes 8–0–36–0; Plunkett 10–0–49–2; Ali 9–0–41–0; Rashid 10–0–34–2; Root 3–0–15–0.

England

J. J. Roy not out	112
A. D. Hales not out	133
Lb 3, w 8	11
(no wkt, 34.1 overs)	256
10 overs: 57-0	

J. E. Root, *E. J. G. Morgan, J. M. Bairstow, †J. C. Buttler, M. M. Ali, C. R. Woakes, D. J. Willey, L. E. Plunkett and A. U. Rashid did not bat.

Maharoof 7–1–47–0; Lakmal 5–0–21–0; Randiv 8–0–62–0; Fernando 4–0–31–0; Prasanna 8.1–0–78–0; Gunathilleke 2–0–14–0.

Umpires: M. A. Gough and B. N. J. Oxenford. Third umpire: P. R. Reiffel.
Referee: D. C. Boon.

ENGLAND v SRI LANKA

Third Royal London One-Day International

At Bristol, June 26. No result. England 1pt, Sri Lanka 1pt. Toss: England.

For the second time in three years, following a washout against India, Bristol's big day fell foul of the weather. This one was little more than half over when the rain came, frustrating not only the locals – Gloucestershire had spent huge sums on ground improvements – but also England, whose bowlers had again done well. Mendis made a neat 53, then Chandimal and Mathews put on 80. But Tharanga was the only other player to reach double figures, as the tidy Woakes and Plunkett shared six wickets. After the first rain break, Hales was caught behind first ball; soon the weather closed in for good.

Attendance: 13,676.

Sri Lanka

M. D. K. J. Perera c Buttler b Plunkett	9
M. D. Gunathilleke b Willey	1
B. K. G. Mendis c Hales b Plunkett	53
†L. D. Chandimal c Jordan b Woakes	62
*A. D. Mathews c Buttler b Jordan	56
S. Prasanna c Bairstow b Plunkett	2
W. U. Tharanga b Woakes	40
M. D. Shanaka run out	2
M. F. Maharoof c Bairstow b Woakes	9
R. A. S. Lakmal not out	3
A. N. P. R. Fernando not out	2
Lb 4, w 5	9
1/3 (2) 2/32 (1) 3/88 (3) 4/168 (4) 5/171 (6) 6/209 (5) 7/215 (8) 8/242 (9) 9/242 (7) (9 wkts, 50 overs)	248
10 overs: 34-2	

Willey 10–0–55–1; Woakes 10–1–34–3; Plunkett 10–0–46–3; Jordan 10–0–49–1; Rashid 10–0–60–0.

England

J. J. Roy not out		5
A. D. Hales c Chandimal b Lakmal		0
J. E. Root not out		11
1/1 (2)	(1 wkt, 4 overs)	16

*E. J. G. Morgan, J. M. Bairstow, †J. C. Buttler, C. R. Woakes, C. J. Jordan, D. J. Willey, L. E. Plunkett and A. U. Rashid did not bat.

Lakmal 2–0–8–1; Mathews 2–0–8–0.

Umpires: P. R. Reiffel and R. T. Robinson. Third umpire: B. N. J. Oxenford.
Referee: D. C. Boon.

ENGLAND v SRI LANKA

Fourth Royal London One-Day International

At The Oval, June 29 (day/night). England won by six wickets (DLS). England 2pts. Toss: England.

On his home ground, Jason Roy came within a hit of overhauling England's long-standing individual record score. But, having pillaged a spectacular 162, he aimed a tired hoick at Pradeep Fernando, and was bowled. It meant the record remained Robin Smith's unbeaten 167, made against Australia at Birmingham in 1993, though it would fall before the summer was out. Roy faced 118 balls, and hit 13 fours and three sixes. Just as impressive was his work-rate: he scampered 16 twos and 54 singles. By the time he fell in the 38th over of a game restricted to 42 a side by the weather, England were in sight of a series-clinching victory. After Ali (promoted to open because Alex Hales had jarred his back) went cheaply, Root helped pile on 149 in 18 overs, an England record for the second wicket against Sri Lanka. Then Morgan and Bairstow sat back and let Roy run riot; the pick of his innings was a massive straight strike off Prasanna that sailed into the pavilion. Earlier, Sri Lanka had produced their best batting performance of the series on a flat Oval track, easing past 300 following an interruption for rain in the 19th over. England's target was swelled slightly to 308 – but it was nowhere near enough, and they sailed to their second-highest successful run-chase with 11 balls to spare.

Man of the Match: J. J. Roy. *Attendance:* 24,443.

Sri Lanka

M. D. K. J. Perera run out	1
M. D. Gunathilleke c Ali b Rashid	62
B. K. G. Mendis c Plunkett b Rashid	77
†L. D. Chandimal b Willey	63
*A. D. Mathews not out	67
S. Prasanna b Willey	9
M. D. Shanaka not out	19
Lb 2, w 5	7
1/8 (1) 2/136 (3) 3/158 (2) 4/245 (4) 5/259 (6) (5 wkts, 42 overs)	305
10 overs: 64-1	

W. U. Tharanga, M. F. Maharoof, R. A. S. Lakmal and A. N. P. R. Fernando did not bat.

Willey 8–0–58–2; Woakes 9–0–65–0; Plunkett 8–0–65–0; Rashid 9–0–57–2; Ali 8–0–58–0.

England

J. J. Roy b Fernando	162
M. M. Ali c Chandimal b Fernando	2
J. E. Root c Fernando b Gunathilleke	65
*E. J. G. Morgan c Gunathilleke b Lakmal	22
J. M. Bairstow not out	29
†J. C. Buttler not out	17
Lb 5, w 7	12
1/18 (2) 2/167 (3) 3/221 (4) 4/281 (1) (4 wkts, 40.1 overs)	309
9 overs: 52-1	

A. D. Hales, C. R. Woakes, D. J. Willey, L. E. Plunkett and A. U. Rashid did not bat.

Lakmal 7–0–48–1; Fernando 9–0–78–2; Mathews 3–0–17–0; Maharoof 8–0–58–0; Shanaka 1–0–12–0; Prasanna 7.1–0–61–0; Gunathilleke 5–0–30–1.

Umpires: R. J. Bailey and B. N. J. Oxenford. Third umpire: P. R. Reiffel.
Referee: D. C. Boon.

ENGLAND v SRI LANKA

Fifth Royal London One-Day International

At Cardiff, July 2. England won by 122 runs. England 2pts. Toss: Sri Lanka. One-day international debut: K. M. C. Bandara.

England eased to their third large victory of the series after running up a total that always looked beyond Sri Lanka. With Hales still injured, Vince came in for Moeen Ali and made his first international half-century, before Root struck out sweetly for 93. Then came Buttler, spraying the ball everywhere in a 45-ball 70. Newcomer Chaminda Bandara, a 29-year-old left-arm seamer, went for 83 in his ten overs, although he did have the late consolation of Buttler's wicket. Despite Chandimal's fourth fifty of the series, Sri Lanka were never in the hunt, and they lost Mathews and Tharanga in the space of three balls. With Willey taking four in an international innings for the first time, all the wickets fell to Yorkshire bowlers; even the run-out of Mendis came from a throw from Bradford's Bairstow at deep midwicket. It was only the second time, after losing 5–0 in India in 2014-15, that Sri Lanka had failed to win a game in a bilateral five-match one-day series.

Man of the Match: J. C. Buttler. *Attendance:* 13,354.
Man of the Series: J. J. Roy.

England

J. J. Roy c Perera b Lakmal	34	L. E. Plunkett run out	9
J. M. Vince st Chandimal b Gunathilleke	51		
J. E. Root b Fernando	93	Lb 4, w 4	8
*E. J. G. Morgan c Mendis b Gunathilleke	20		
J. M. Bairstow c Shanaka b Gunathilleke	22	1/67 (1) 2/108 (2) (7 wkts, 50 overs)	324
†J. C. Buttler b Bandara	70	3/137 (4) 4/182 (5)	
C. R. Woakes not out	17	5/291 (6) 6/314 (3) 7/324 (8)	10 overs: 60-0

C. J. Jordan, D. J. Willey and A. U. Rashid did not bat.

Lakmal 10–0–65–1; Bandara 10–0–83–1; Fernando 8–0–59–1; Gunathilleke 10–0–48–3; Prasanna 10–0–52–0; Mendis 2–0–13–0.

Sri Lanka

M. D. K. J. Perera lbw b Willey	6	A. N. P. R. Fernando c Woakes b Willey	7
M. D. Gunathilleke lbw b Plunkett	48	K. M. C. Bandara not out	1
B. K. G. Mendis run out	22		
†L. D. Chandimal b Willey	53	Lb 7, w 8	15
*A. D. Mathews b Plunkett	13		
W. U. Tharanga b Rashid	0	1/9 (1) 2/66 (3) 3/83 (2) (42.4 overs)	202
M. D. Shanaka st Buttler b Rashid	22	4/105 (5) 5/106 (6) 6/140 (7)	
S. Prasanna c Willey b Plunkett	5	7/170 (8) 8/194 (9) 9/195 (4)	
R. A. S. Lakmal c Morgan b Willey	10	10/202 (10)	10 overs: 41-1

Woakes 9–0–36–0; Willey 8.4–0–34–4; Jordan 7–0–40–0; Plunkett 8–0–44–3; Rashid 10–0–41–2.

Umpires: M. A. Gough and P. R. Reiffel. Third umpire: B. N. J. Oxenford.
Referee: D. C. Boon.

ENGLAND v SRI LANKA

Royal London Twenty20 International

At Southampton, July 5 (floodlit). England won by eight wickets. England 2pts. Toss: Sri Lanka. Twenty20 international debuts: L. A. Dawson, T. S. Mills; K. M. C. Bandara, A. N. P. R. Fernando, B. K. G. Mendis.

In years gone by, England players had their jobs and stuck to them, whether the target was 150 or 350. But times have changed: after beefing up the middle in the 50-over games, Buttler stepped into the role of opener. And, unfazed by the first-over departure of Roy, he monstered an unbeaten 73, his best score in all Twenty20 cricket, to take his side home with 15 balls to spare after an unbroken stand of 114 with Morgan. For Sri Lanka, Gunathilleke top-scored in a middling total, in which Jordan and Liam Dawson – making his international debut, on his home ground – took three wickets apiece. England's other newcomer, left-armer Tymal Mills, went wicketless, but showed off some clever slower balls in between his customary pace. Sri Lanka returned home without a win in any format.

Man of the Match: J. C. Buttler. *Attendance:* 12,796.

Sri Lanka

		B	*4/6*
1 M. D. K. J. Perera *c 11 b 9*	13	15	1
2 M. D. Gunathilleke *c 8 b 7*	26	16	4
3 B. K. G. Mendis *c and b 7*	21	16	0/1
4 *A. D. Mathews *b 7*	11	10	1
5 †L. D. Chandimal *c 4 b 8*	23	22	1/1
6 M. D. Shanaka *run out*	1	1	0
7 R. L. B. Rambukwella *run out*	19	16	1/1
8 S. Prasanna *c 2 b 9*	1	3	0
9 M. F. Maharoof *c 12 b 8*	10	16	0
10 K. M. C. Bandara *not out*	2	4	0
11 A. N. P. R. Fernando *b 8*	0	1	0
B 1, lb 9, w 3	13		
6 overs: 51-1 (20 overs)	140		

1/17 2/58 3/74 4/81 5/82 6/106 7/122 8/129 9/140

Jordan 4–11–29–3; Mills 4–11–22–0; Plunkett 4–11–27–2; Dawson 4–4–27–3; Rashid 4–11–25–0.

England

		B	*4/6*
1 J. J. Roy *b 4*	0	3	0
2 †J. C. Buttler *not out*	73	49	3/4
3 J. M. Vince *st 5 b 4*	16	14	2
4 *E. J. G. Morgan *not out*	47	39	1/2
B 1, w 7	8		
6 overs: 41-2 (17.3 overs)	144-2		

1/0 2/30

5 J. M. Bairstow, 6 S. W. Billings, 7 L. A. Dawson, 8 C. J. Jordan, 9 L. E. Plunkett, 10 A. U. Rashid and 11 T. S. Mills did not bat.

12th man D. J. Willey

Mathews 4–11–27–2; Rambukwella 2.3–3–27–0; Maharoof 3–7–26–0; Prasanna 4–4–31–0; Gunathilleke 1–2–9–0; Fernando 2–3–12–0; Bandara 1–1–11–0.

Umpires: R. J. Bailey and M. A. Gough. Third umpire: R. T. Robinson.
Referee: D. C. Boon.

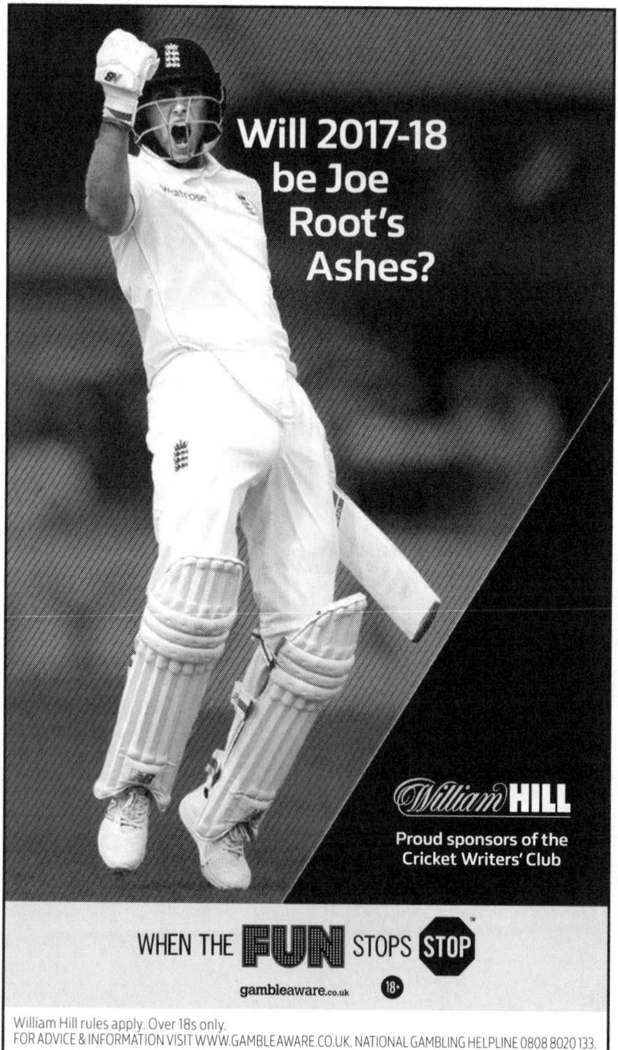
Will 2017-18
be Joe
Root's
Ashes?
William HILL
Proud sponsors of the
Cricket Writers' Club
WHEN THE FUN STOPS STOP
gambleaware.co.uk
18+
William Hill rules apply. Over 18s only.
FOR ADVICE & INFORMATION VISIT WWW.GAMBLEAWARE.CO.UK. NATIONAL GAMBLING HELPLINE 0808 8020 133.

ENGLAND v PAKISTAN IN 2016

REVIEW BY GIDEON BROOKS

Test matches (4): England 2, Pakistan 2
One-day internationals (5): England 4, Pakistan 1
Twenty20 international (1): England 0, Pakistan 1
Super Series: England 16pts, Pakistan 12pts

At the end of an enthralling Test series, Misbah-ul-Haq sat in the cavernous Ken Barrington Cricket Centre, deep in the bowels of The Oval, and reflected on his six years in charge of Pakistan. He spoke movingly – as much as his flat monotone allowed – of life on the road, of endless hotel rooms, of families and friends waiting indefinitely at home.

Yet when he looks back, both at this tour and a reign which began after the Lord's spot-fixing scandal of 2010, he will do so with pride. A drawn Test series – which could have been even better had Pakistan exploited a commanding position in the Third match at Edgbaston – was enough to keep them at No. 3 in the rankings. Three days later, following Australia's 3–0 defeat in Sri Lanka, they went second. The final step would come five days after that, when Trinidadian rain deprived India, briefly top themselves, of the chance to stay there. India did regain the No. 1 ranking in early October, but the temporary ascent of Pakistan, shorn of home comforts since the Lahore terrorist attack in March 2009, was a story for the ages.

Free from the conflict that had marred previous England–Pakistan encounters, this one developed a compelling narrative nevertheless. And, following the lukewarm Sri Lanka series, it lit up the summer. Not since the visit of South Africa in 2003 had any Test series ended 2–2. Fans craved a decider.

TEST SERIES THAT ENDED 2–2

1882-83	Australia v England (4 Tests)	1972	England v Australia (5)
1927-28	South Africa v England (5)	1991	England v West Indies (5)
1952-53	Australia v South Africa (5)	1995	England v West Indies (6)
1953-54	West Indies v England (5)	1998-99	West Indies v Australia (4)
1956-57	South Africa v England (5)	2003	England v South Africa (5)
1961-62	South Africa v New Zealand (5)	**2016**	**England v Pakistan (4)**

Pakistan, who had not played a Test since hosting England in the UAE in late 2015, arrived fitter than usual, after a two-week military boot camp in Abbottabad in May. It sparked a series of tributes to the country's soldiers: as so often, 42-year-old Misbah led by example, with ten press-ups at Lord's to celebrate his century on the opening evening of the series. Once a memorable victory had been secured three days later, the whole squad followed suit. This irritated Alastair Cook, who said it was hard to watch the tourists' massed ranks hitting the turf, then jumping up to salute, and muttered grumpily about

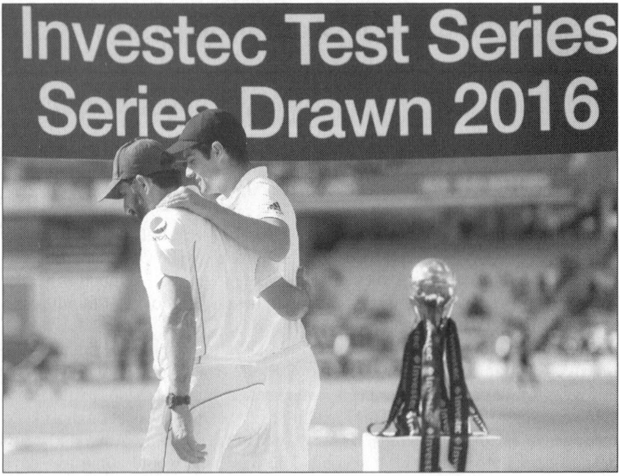

Drawing comfort: Misbah-ul-Haq and Alastair Cook reflect the spirit of the series.

the "cricketing gods". No matter: the press-ups went viral. The Pakistanis were making friends.

From Abbottabad, they had headed for a week-long skills camp in Lahore, and teamed up with their new coach, the South African Mickey Arthur, back in international cricket for the first time since his axing by Australia before the 2013 Ashes. Next came acclimatisation in Southampton. If anything, Pakistan seemed better prepared for the First Test than an England side without Ben Stokes or Jimmy Anderson, who was wrapped in cotton wool by the selectors, despite his insistence he was fit to play after recovering from a shoulder injury. It was another decision which annoyed Cook, as well as coach Trevor Bayliss; England's denials of a rift down the middle of the selectorial table were unconvincing.

The return of Mohammad Amir occupied thoughts on both sides, as well as column inches. Cook stated repeatedly that, though Amir had served his punishment for bowling deliberate no-balls at Lord's in 2010, anyone now found guilty of corruption should be banned for life. But it was impossible to ignore the symbolism of a Test return at the venue where Amir's career and reputation had come crashing down six years earlier.

Expecting a media maelstrom, Pakistan employed a (British) PR consultant, Jonathan Collett. Yet, while Amir's reception at Lord's did produce stray shouts of "No-ball!" to balance out a smattering of sympathetic applause, the public reaction was, on the whole, forgiving. His reception at Old Trafford and Edgbaston was livelier, but most seemed to think he had done his time. His bowling added to the compassion: not helped by several dropped catches, Amir managed only 12 Test wickets at 42. One or two opening spells aside, he lacked the diamond edge that memory had bestowed.

The incision was provided initially by the leg-spin of Yasir Shah, who claimed ten for 141 at Lord's, in his first Test outside Asia. But England worked out he did not turn it as much as they thought, and resolved to play him straighter. In Manchester, where they drew level, in Birmingham, where they secured a brilliant come-from-behind victory, and in the first innings at The Oval, Yasir racked up figures of four for 562. It was to his credit that he took five for 71 in the second innings, as Pakistan put their two defeats behind them with a series-levelling win.

MOST WICKETS IN AN ENGLAND–PAKISTAN SERIES

W		*T*	*O*	*R*	*BB*	*Avge*	
30	Abdul Qadir (P)	3	234.4	437	9-56	14.56	1987-88
26	**C. R. Woakes (E)**	**4**	**148.3**	**435**	**6-70**	**16.73**	**2016**
24	Saeed Ajmal (P)	3	147	353	7-55	14.70	2011-12
23	J. M. Anderson (E)	4	140.3	316	6-17	13.73	2010
22	G. P. Swann (E)	4	106.5	269	6-65	12.22	2010
22	F. S. Trueman (E)	4	164.5	439	6-31	19.95	1962
22	Waqar Younis (P)	5	166	557	5-52	25.31	1992
21	Imran Khan (P)	3	178.1	390	7-52	18.57	1982
21	Imran Khan (P)	5	168.2	455	7-40	21.66	1987
21	Wasim Akram (P)	4	168.5	462	6-67	22.00	1992
20	J. H. Wardle (E)	4	142.5	176	7-56	8.80	1954
20	Fazal Mahmood (P)	4	165	408	6-46	20.40	1954
20	S. J. Harmison (E)	4	151.3	542	6-19	27.10	2006

If Yasir earned plaudits for his three-dimensional cricket – 19 wickets, 92 gritty runs and five catches (no fielder outside the slip cordon took more on either side) – he met his match in Chris Woakes. After taking two wickets for 197 in South Africa over the winter, Woakes laid a claim to regular inclusion in England's Test team with 26 at 16, including 11 at Lord's. No England bowler had claimed so many in a series against Pakistan. He also weighed in with 177 runs at 35, mainly from No. 8. Something had clicked. Likeable and modest, he attributed the improvement to consistency of selection, extra pace brought about by a more aggressive run-up and more dynamic use of his front arm, and even the use of a yo-yo to hone his wrist action. It seemed an appropriate toy given the ups and downs of his career, though this series felt like the end of the metaphor.

England had three centurions in Cook, Joe Root and Moeen Ali, with Root producing the finest innings of his career: 254 at Old Trafford, full of glorious strokemaking and unbending discipline after two airy dismissals at Lord's. He and Cook, who also reached three figures in Manchester, shone so brightly that both Misbah and Arthur suggested England were perilously close to becoming a two-man batting line-up.

That seemed a little harsh on Moeen, who made two delightful fifties as England fought back in Birmingham, and Jonny Bairstow, whose keeping

Philip Brown, SilverHub

Mitchell Gunn, Getty Images

In the swing: Joe Root hit more runs than anyone else, while Chris Woakes – here dismissing Wahab Riaz at Lord's – was comfortably the leading wicket-taker.

improved markedly, made four half-centuries. But the rest had forgettable series. James Vince, repeatedly undone by his love of the cover-drive, and Alex Hales managed one fifty between them. Hales also suffered a meltdown at The Oval after being given out caught at square leg by a tumbling Yasir, then storming into the third umpire's office to remonstrate about the legality of the catch. It cost him £1,500 (Stuart Broad, perhaps disproportionately, was fined £2,000 for tweeting about the dismissal).

But a series haul of 145 runs at an average of just 18 was not enough for Hales to retain his Test spot for the winter, though he pulled out of the trip to Bangladesh for security reasons in any case. Cook's eighth opening partner in the four years since the retirement of Andrew Strauss had lasted longer than the other seven, but ultimately met the same fate. Gary Ballance, who admitted his surprise at his recall a year after being dropped during the Ashes, appeared at least to have a plan, even if he was able to execute it to good effect only twice.

Both Anderson and Broad, who took 13 wickets without ever hitting one of his hot streaks, operated in Woakes's shadow. Anderson had returned at Old Trafford after recovering from a stress fracture to his right shoulder. A yard or two down on pace, he likened himself to an old defender in football – lacking the nip of a striker but staying "two steps ahead of him upstairs". About to turn 34, he said he hoped to make it to 37. Yet he had missed at least one Test in three of England's last five series and, with more than 50,000 competitive deliveries behind him, it was becoming necessary to manage his workload. The news that he would miss the tour of Bangladesh to allow him more time to recover came as no great shock – and seemed to vindicate the selectors' earlier caution.

FIVE STATS YOU MAY HAVE MISSED

BENEDICT BERMANGE

- At Old Trafford, Joe Root became only the third man to score a double-century and take four catches in an innings in the same Test:

R. B. Simpson	Australia v West Indies at Bridgetown	1964-65
J. H. Kallis	South Africa v Sri Lanka at Cape Town	2011-12
J. E. Root	**England v Pakistan at Manchester**	**2016**

- Only three bowlers have missed more Tests than Sohail Khan, then taken a five-for in their first match on return:

Missed			
46	T. W. J. Goddard (6-29)	England v New Zealand at Manchester	1947
45	C. D. Collymore (5-66)	West Indies v Sri Lanka at Gros Islet	2003
41	C. T. Tremlett (5-87)	England v Australia at Perth	2010-11
38	**Sohail Khan (5-96)**	**Pakistan v England at Birmingham**	**2016**
37	W. E. Hollies (5-123)	England v South Africa at Nottingham	1947
37	R. J. Peterson (5-33)	South Africa v Bangladesh at Chittagong	2007-08

- At Edgbaston, England totalled 742 without a century, the third-highest aggregate:

Runs	*HS*		
763	76	Australia v England at Nottingham	1997
753	85	England v Australia at Adelaide	1932-33
742	**86***	**England v Pakistan at Birmingham**	**2016**
732	92	South Africa v Australia at Melbourne	1952-53
732	99	Australia v New Zealand at Perth	2001-02

- Younis Khan's double-century at The Oval was his sixth against different opposition, to equal the Test record:

Countries		*Against*
6	K. C. Sangakkara (SL)	Bang 3, Pak 3, SA 2, India 1, NZ 1, Zim 1
6	**Younis Khan (Pak)**	**Aus 1, Bang 1, Eng 1, India 1, SL 1, Zim 1**
5	B. C. Lara (WI)	Aus 3, Eng 2, SL 2, Pak 1, SA 1
5	D. P. M. D. Jayawardene (SL)	India 2, SA 2, Bang 1, Eng 1, Pak 1
5	Javed Miandad (Pak)	NZ 2, Aus 1, Eng 1, India 1, SL 1
5	S. R. Tendulkar (India)	Aus 2, Bang 1, NZ 1, SL 1, Zim 1
5	R. Dravid (India)	Aus 1, Eng 1, NZ 1, Pak 1, Zim 1

- Yasir Shah's series bowling average was the fourth-worst to include a ten-wicket haul:

Avge	*T*	*Wkts*			
42.13	5	22	S. P. Gupte	India v West Indies	1958-59
41.61	3	13	M. D. Craig	New Zealand v Pakistan	2014-15
40.90	4	11	Abdul Qadir	Pakistan v England	1987
40.73	**4**	**19**	**Yasir Shah**	**Pakistan v England**	**2016**
37.88	3	17	A. Kumble	India v Pakistan	2004-05

Moeen's off-spin proved expensive, as Pakistan despatched him at 4.65 an over – the worst economy-rate of any of his nine series – yet he continued to take key wickets, snaring Misbah, Azhar Ali and Younis Khan twice each. If he was costly, he was by no means a luxury. And, after fatally charging Yasir at Lord's, he batted beautifully, passing 50 in three consecutive innings.

Pakistan shared their batting successes around. Misbah, Azhar and Asad Shafiq all scored centuries and, after three difficult Tests which led to questions about his future, Younis made a brilliant 218 at The Oval. It rivalled Root for the innings of the summer, and underlined his status as one of the game's all-time greats.

The tourists belatedly discovered a tidy opener in Sami Aslam, who replaced Shan Masood after two Tests; at Manchester, Masood was dismissed twice by Anderson, which meant he had fallen to him in six innings out of six. In Sarfraz Ahmed, the Pakistanis could boast one of the best wicketkeeper-batsmen in world cricket. Among their bowlers, the surprise success story was Sohail Khan, the lone right-armer of the main pace quartet, who returned for his first Test in almost five years and responded with five-fors at Edgbaston and The Oval.

MOST RUNS IN AN ENGLAND–PAKISTAN SERIES

Runs		*T*	*I*	*NO*	*HS*	*100*	*50*	*Avge*	
631	Mohammad Yousuf (P)	4	7	0	202	3	0	90.14	2006
512	**J. E. Root (E)**	**4**	**8**	**1**	**254**	**1**	**2**	**73.14**	**2016**
488	Salim Malik (P)	5	8	2	165	1	3	81.33	1992
453	D. C. S. Compton (E)	4	5	0	278	1	2	90.60	1954
450	A. N. Cook (E)	3	5	0	263	1	2	90.00	2015-16
449	D. I. Gower (E)	3	5	1	173*	2	2	112.25	1983-84
446	E. R. Dexter (E)	5	6	1	172	1	3	89.20	1962
445	M. W. Gatting (E)	5	8	1	150*	2	1	63.57	1987
444	A. J. Strauss (E)	4	7	0	128	2	1	63.42	2006
431	Inzamam-ul-Haq (P)	3	5	1	109	2	3	107.75	2005-06
426	K. F. Barrington (E)	3	5	2	148	3	0	142.00	1967
423	**A. N. Cook (E)**	**4**	**8**	**1**	**105**	**1**	**3**	**60.42**	**2016**

But it was a different story in the 50-over matches, claimed 4–1 by a vibrant England. This was entirely expected: Pakistan were ranked ninth, and had not won a one-day series in England since their first, in 1974. Even so, they were well and truly thrashed, their pain eased only by a consolation win in Cardiff, then victory in the solitary Twenty20 international at Old Trafford, where Pakistan's fans turned out in numbers not seen all tour.

England's white-ball dominance had peaked at Trent Bridge, where they bludgeoned a world record 444 for three. Hales, clearly more comfortable in blue, broke Robin Smith's 23-year-old national record with a magnificent 171, as England won by 169 runs. It was men against boys. Woakes once again showed his versatility, finishing as the leading wicket-taker, with nine at 19. He truly had the summer of his life.

But so too did Misbah, who had celebrated victory at The Oval on Pakistan's Independence Day. "Sometimes people think it's easy, that the UAE suits us and we win," he said in those indoor nets. "But just living every day away from our country, without family and friends – it's really difficult. I see my mother and sister only once a year, and some friends not for three or four years." Like New Zealand the previous year, the Pakistanis left England supporters pining for their return. The contrast with 2010 could not have been

Philip Brown, SilverHub

Louder than words… Mohammad Amir bowls his first ball in Test cricket since the end of his ban for corruption. Few voiced dissatisfaction over his selection.

greater. "Cricket matches are won and lost," said Misbah. "But to win an audience, people and supporters – that's important."

PAKISTAN TOURING PARTY

*Misbah-ul-Haq (T), Amad Butt (20), Asad Shafiq (T), Azhar Ali (T/50), Babar Azam (50/20), Hasan Ali (50/20), Iftikhar Ahmed (T), Imad Wasim (50/20), Imran Khan snr (T), Khalid Latif (20), Mohammad Amir (T/50/20), Mohammad Hafeez (T/50), Mohammad Irfan (50), Mohammad Nawaz (50/20), Mohammad Rizwan (T/50/20), Rahat Ali (T), Sami Aslam (T/50), Sarfraz Ahmed (T/50/20), Shan Masood (T), Sharjeel Khan (50/20), Shoaib Malik (50/20), Sohail Khan (T), Sohail Tanvir (20), Umar Gul (50), Wahab Riaz (T/50/20), Yasir Shah (T/50), Younis Khan (T), Zulfiqar Babar (T).

Azhar Ali captained in the 50-over matches, and Sarfraz Ahmed in the Twenty20 international. Mohammad Hafeez injured his calf before the second one-day international, and was replaced by Mohammad Irfan. Irfan was originally named in the Twenty20 squad, but returned home after suffering cramp during the fourth ODI, and was replaced by Hasan Ali.

Coach: J. M. Arthur. *Batting coach:* G. W. Flower. *Bowling coach:* Azhar Mahmood. *Spin-bowling coach:* Mushtaq Ahmed. *Fielding coach:* S. J. Rixon. *Manager:* Intikhab Alam. *Assistant manager:* Shahid Aslam. *Trainer:* G. Luden. *Physiotherapist:* S. Hayes. *Masseur:* Malang Ali. *Security manager:* Azhar Arif. *Analyst:* Muhammad Talah Ejaz (T), Talah Butt (50/20). *Media manager:* Agha Akbar (to First Test), Amjad Husain Bhatti (Second to Fourth Tests), Raza Rashid (50/20). *Social media manager:* Aun Zaidi.

"Like the old submarine on Visakhapatnam's Ramakrishna Mission Beach, England's chances had long been decommissioned."

India v England in 2016-17, Second Test, page 356

TEST MATCH AVERAGES

ENGLAND – BATTING AND FIELDING

	T	I	NO	R	HS	100	50	Avge	Ct/St
J. E. Root	4	8	1	512	254	1	2	73.14	9
†M. M. Ali	4	7	2	316	108	1	2	63.20	3
†A. N. Cook	4	8	1	423	105	1	3	60.42	6
J. M. Bairstow	4	7	0	366	83	0	4	52.28	14/1
C. R. Woakes	4	7	2	177	58	0	1	35.40	3
†G. S. Ballance	4	7	0	195	70	0	1	27.85	3
S. T. Finn	3	5	3	48	16*	0	0	24.00	0
J. M. Vince	4	7	0	158	42	0	0	22.57	1
A. D. Hales	4	8	0	145	54	0	1	18.12	6
†J. M. Anderson	3	3	1	28	17	0	0	14.00	0
†S. C. J. Broad	4	5	0	36	17	0	0	7.20	3

Played in one Test: J. T. Ball 4, 3; †B. A. Stokes 34.

BOWLING

	Style	O	M	R	W	BB	5I	Avge
C. R. Woakes	RFM	148.3	33	435	26	6-70	2	16.73
J. M. Anderson	RFM	100.1	27	231	9	3-41	0	25.66
S. C. J. Broad	RFM	146.3	40	372	13	3-38	0	28.61
M. M. Ali	OB	110	11	512	11	3-88	0	46.54
S. T. Finn	RFM	105.1	19	352	5	3-110	0	70.40

Also bowled: J. T. Ball (RFM) 35–12–88–1; J. E. Root (OB) 11–3–27–1; B. A. Stokes (RFM) 20.2–1–60–2; J. M. Vince (RM) 2–0–3–0.

PAKISTAN – BATTING AND FIELDING

	T	I	NO	R	HS	100	50	Avge	Ct
†Sami Aslam	2	4	1	167	82	0	2	55.66	0
Younis Khan	4	7	0	340	218	1	0	48.57	6
Azhar Ali	4	8	1	295	139	1	0	42.14	4
Misbah-ul-Haq	4	7	0	282	114	1	2	40.28	2
Asad Shafiq	4	7	0	274	109	1	1	39.14	1
Sarfraz Ahmed	4	7	1	193	46*	0	0	32.16	15
†Mohammad Amir	4	7	2	107	39*	0	0	21.40	0
†Shan Masood	2	4	0	71	39	0	0	17.75	0
Mohammad Hafeez	3	6	0	102	42	0	0	17.00	5
Yasir Shah	4	7	1	92	30	0	0	15.33	5
Sohail Khan	2	3	0	45	36	0	0	15.00	0
Wahab Riaz	3	5	0	62	39	0	0	12.40	0
Rahat Ali	3	6	3	31	15*	0	0	10.33	0

Played in one Test: Iftikhar Ahmed 4 (1 ct).

BOWLING

	Style	O	M	R	W	BB	5I	Avge
Sohail Khan	RFM	87.4	9	325	13	5-68	2	25.00
Wahab Riaz	LF	88.5	3	360	10	3-93	0	36.00
Yasir Shah	LBG	238	34	774	19	6-72	2	40.73
Mohammad Amir	LFM	162.3	33	509	12	2-39	0	42.41
Rahat Ali	LFM	106	17	407	8	3-47	0	50.87

Also bowled: Azhar Ali (LBG) 18–0–95–0; Iftikhar Ahmed (OB) 4.2–1–13–1; Shan Masood (RM) 3–0–19–0.

SOMERSET v PAKISTANIS

At Taunton, July 3–5. Drawn. Toss: Pakistanis. First-class debuts: D. M. Bess, A. J. Hose. County debuts: T. D. Rouse, P. A. van Meekeren.

Trescothick, who had first played the touring Pakistanis exactly 20 years earlier, helped save the match for Somerset with a 105-ball century – his third of the season and 61st in first-class cricket. But, apart from the result, the Pakistanis were satisfied with their tour opener. There were centuries for Younis Khan – who put on 179 with the tidy Asad Shafiq after Misbah-ul-Haq fell second ball – and, in the second innings, Azhar Ali. In between, the seamers shared eight wickets as Somerset were dismantled for 128, in which Hildreth was the lone batting success. More runs from Shafiq left Somerset 73 overs to survive. They held on, despite a Yasir Shah-inspired wobble after Trescothick was finally caught behind off Rahat Ali. Dom Bess, an 18-year-old off-spinner, made up for going wicketless on debut by resisting for almost an hour, before the ninth-wicket pair negotiated 16 balls.

Close of play: first day, Pakistanis 324-5 (Younis Khan 99, Sarfraz Ahmed 6); second day, Pakistanis 140-4 (Azhar Ali 50, Asad Shafiq 26).

Pakistanis

Mohammad Hafeez b van Meekeren	20	– c Barrow b Davey	10
Shan Masood lbw b Groenewald	62	– c Leach b Groenewald	29
Azhar Ali c Barrow b van Meekeren	26	– not out	101
Younis Khan c Rouse b Davey	104		
*Misbah-ul-Haq c Rouse b Groenewald	0	– (4) c Trescothick b Leach	19
Asad Shafiq c Bess b Leach	80	– not out	69
†Sarfraz Ahmed not out	17	– (5) lbw b Leach	0
Mohammad Amir c Barrow b Davey	0		
Sohail Khan c Barrow b van Meekeren	5		
Yasir Shah not out	11		
B 5, lb 19, w 2, nb 8	34	B 1, lb 2, w 1, nb 4	8
1/44 (1) 2/100 (3) 3/132 (2) 4/132 (5) 5/311 (6) 6/335 (4) 7/336 (8) 8/341 (9) (8 wkts dec, 100 overs)	359	1/11 (1) 2/63 (2) 3/98 (4) 4/98 (5) (4 wkts dec, 59.4 overs)	236

Rahat Ali did not bat.

Davey 22–7–71–2; van Meekeren 26–8–78–3; Groenewald 12–5–24–2; Trego 6–0–37–0; Bess 17–3–72–0; Leach 17–1–53–1. *Second innings*—Davey 4–1–20–1; van Meekeren 11–2–49–0; Groenewald 9.4–1–42–1; Trego 4–1–5–0; Leach 18–5–61–2; Bess 13–2–56–0.

Somerset

M. E. Trescothick c Sarfraz Ahmed b Mohammad Amir	8	– c Sarfraz Ahmed b Rahat Ali	106
A. J. Hose b Mohammad Amir	10	– lbw b Yasir Shah	8
T. D. Rouse c Sarfraz Ahmed b Sohail Khan	1	– lbw b Yasir Shah	41
J. C. Hildreth not out	47	– c Sarfraz Ahmed b Mohammad Amir	48
*P. D. Trego b Mohammad Amir	23	– b Rahat Ali	0
†A. W. R. Barrow b Rahat Ali	6	– lbw b Sohail Khan	7
J. H. Davey c Younis Khan b Rahat Ali	10	– b Yasir Shah	9
D. M. Bess b Yasir Shah	4	– lbw b Yasir Shah	21
M. J. Leach c Younis Khan b Sohail Khan	1	– not out	6
T. D. Groenewald lbw b Sohail Khan	0	– not out	4
P. A. van Meekeren lbw b Yasir Shah	0		
B 7, lb 11	18	Lb 8	8
1/12 (1) 2/23 (2) 3/23 (3) 4/62 (5) 5/79 (6) 6/103 (7) 7/116 (8) 8/123 (9) 9/123 (10) 10/128 (11) (34.1 overs)	128	1/47 (2) 2/145 (3) 3/183 (1) 4/191 (5) 5/203 (6) 6/226 (4) 7/234 (7) 8/251 (8) (8 wkts, 73 overs)	258

Mohammad Amir 11–2–36–3; Sohail Khan 10–2–26–3; Rahat Ali 9–1–38–2; Yasir Shah 4.1–0–10–2. *Second innings*—Mohammad Amir 15–6–42–1; Sohail Khan 13–1–66–1; Yasir Shah 32–9–107–4; Rahat Ali 12–2–30–2; Azhar Ali 1–0–5–0.

Umpires: T. Lungley and B. V. Taylor.

SUSSEX v PAKISTANIS

At Hove, July 8–10. Drawn. Toss: Sussex. First-class debuts: J. C. Archer, P. D. Salt. County debut: A. Sakande.

The loss of the last day to persistent drizzle prevented a result, although a good batting pitch might have precluded one anyway. Azhar Ali batted carefully for a second successive century, and his stands of 125 and 146 with Younis Khan and Misbah-ul-Haq propelled the Pakistanis to 363 on the first day. Fast bowler Jofra Archer – born in Barbados and a former West Indies Under-19 representative – took four of the five wickets to fall (the other first-class debutant, 19-year-old Welshman Philip Salt, later made a tidy unbeaten 37). Sussex replied in kind, the openers putting on 212: Wells fell just short of a century, but Finch completed his second in first-class cricket. Brown declared 72 behind, then Pakistan's top three all but doubled that by the end of the second day.

Close of play: first day, Pakistanis 363-5 (Asad Shafiq 13, Sarfraz Ahmed 21); second day, Pakistanis 71-1 (Shan Masood 38, Azhar Ali 9).

Pakistanis

Mohammad Hafeez lbw b Archer	17	– c Cachopa b Archer	23
Shan Masood c Brown b Archer	4	– not out	38
Azhar Ali c Brown b Archer	145	– not out	9
Younis Khan c Shahzad b Briggs	59		
*Misbah-ul-Haq lbw b Archer	68		
Asad Shafiq not out	13		
†Sarfraz Ahmed not out	21		
B 19, lb 12, w 4, nb 1	36	Lb 1	1
1/16 (2) 2/49 (1) 3/174 (4) 4/320 (5) 5/335 (3) (5 wkts dec, 99 overs)	363	1/48 (1) (1 wkt, 24 overs)	71

Wahab Riaz, Sohail Khan, Zulfiqar Babar and Imran Khan snr did not bat.

Shahzad 21–3–74–0; Archer 22–7–49–4; Sakande 20–3–52–0; Finch 8–0–39–0; Briggs 19–4–70–1; Beer 7–0–36–0; Wells 2–0–12–0. *Second innings*—Shahzad 7–3–18–0; Archer 9–2–24–1; Sakande 6–0–24–0; Briggs 2–1–4–0.

Sussex

L. W. P. Wells c Sarfraz Ahmed b Wahab Riaz	93
H. Z. Finch c Mohammad Hafeez b Wahab Riaz	103
M. W. Machan lbw b Imran Khan	13
C. Cachopa lbw b Zulfiqar Babar	19
*†B. C. Brown c Sarfraz Ahmed b Imran Khan	0
P. D. Salt not out	37
Lb 9, nb 17	26
1/212 (1) 2/228 (2) 3/233 (3) 4/233 (5) 5/291 (4) (5 wkts dec, 63.5 overs)	291

W. A. T. Beer, A. Shahzad, D. R. Briggs, J. C. Archer and A. Sakande did not bat.

Imran Khan 13–2–60–2; Sohail Khan 16–2–79–0; Wahab Riaz 11–0–62–2; Zulfiqar Babar 17.5–3–66–1; Asad Shafiq 1–0–1–0; Azhar Ali 5–0–14–0.

Umpires: J. H. Evans and R. J. Warren.

ENGLAND v PAKISTAN

First Investec Test Match

HUGH CHEVALLIER

At Lord's, July 14–17. Pakistan won by 75 runs. Pakistan 4pts. Toss: Pakistan. Test debut: J. T. Ball.

The Lord's hum is a civilised affair, the distilled hubbub of 30,000 contented souls accepting the offer of another glass of white, rustling a copy of *The Daily Telegraph*, apologising to a neighbour who knocks their cheese straw to the ground – maybe even chatting about the cricket. But at intervals on the Friday and Sunday of a cracking Test, the hum was pierced by something discordant: an elemental howl, as though a domestic animal was being slaughtered. But the slaughter was of home batsmen, and the cry the unique celebration of Yasir Shah, the latest in a long line of wrist-spinners to get inside English heads (and in this instance eardrums).

If the Yasir yell – perhaps the Shah shriek – proved the soundtrack to a deserved Pakistan victory, its rasp was almost the only dissonant note of a fizzing encounter. With rain dampening the early summer, and controversy so often dogging England–Pakistan Tests, it was a relief that the atmosphere, meteorological and metaphorical, was benign. The standard of cricket was reassuringly high, and the crowd lapped up the first genuinely competitive home Test for well over a year. No wonder Lord's was abuzz.

NOTTINGHAMSHIRE PAIR OPENING THE BOWLING FOR ENGLAND

H. Larwood and W. Voce	v Australia (3 Tests)	1932-33
S. C. J. Broad and D. J. Pattinson	v South Africa at Leeds	2008
S. C. J. Broad and G. P. Swann	v West Indies at Lord's	2009
S. C. J. Broad and J. T. Ball	**v Pakistan at Lord's**	**2016**
S. C. J. Broad and J. T. Ball	**v India at Chennai**	**2016-17**

At Colombo (SSC) in 2007-08 – after Broad had left Leicestershire but before he had played for Nottinghamshire – he and R. J. Sidebottom opened the bowling against Sri Lanka.

England made two changes from the side who had enjoyed the better of a rainy draw five weeks earlier (Lord's was hosting successive Tests for the first time in 104 years after the Sri Lankan series had been rejigged to give more time for the redevelopment of the Warner Stand). Nick Compton had jumped before he was pushed, while neither Ben Stokes, who had undergone knee surgery in May, nor Jimmy Anderson, who had hurt his shoulder, was deemed fit. Anderson did not agree, and made clear his disgruntlement at being left out. In came Ballance, more on reputation as a scrapper than on county form, and – in a happy moment for the school of nominative determinism – Nottinghamshire's young seamer Jake Ball, nephew of former England wicketkeeper Bruce French, who presented him with his cap.

As the Test began, new prime minister Theresa May was finalising her Brexit cabinet, determining how best to deploy figures who had contributed to the downfall of her predecessor, David Cameron. There were parallels at Lord's, where Pakistan captain Misbah-ul-Haq had to handle the return of Mohammad Amir, who had played a central role in one of cricket's darkest episodes.

After delivering a couple of cricket's most notorious no-balls, Amir had done time behind bars, as well as most of a five-year ban, and some colleagues had opposed his rehabilitation, while Cook said anyone now convicted of corruption should never play again. As it turned out, Amir's first Test, six years after his downfall, was at the scene of the crime.

PLAYERS BORN ON THE SAME DAY IN THE SAME TEST TEAM

	Date of birth	*Span*	*Tests*
E. J. Gregory and N. F. D. Thomson (Australia)	29.5.1839	1876-77	1
E. H. Hendren and E. Tyldesley (England)	5.2.1889	1921–1928-29	5
J. F. Crapp and J. A. Young (England)	14.10.1912	1948–1948-49	4
M. V. Narasimha Rao and Yashpal Sharma (India).	11.8.1954	1979-80	2
A. O. Malhotra and N. S. Yadav (India)	26.1.1957	1983-84	3
D. C. Boon and D. R. Gilbert (Australia).	29.12.1960	1985-86–1986-87	8
M. E. Waugh and S. R. Waugh (Australia)	2.6.1965	1990-91–2002-03	108
Naved-ul-Hasan and Yasir Hameed (Pakistan)	28.2.1978	2004-05–2006-07	5
H. J. H. Marshall and J. A. H. Marshall (New Zealand) .	15.2.1979	2004-05–2005-06	5
Al-Amin Hossain and Rubel Hossain (Bangladesh)	1.1.1990	2013-14–2014-15	3
J. T. Ball and J. M. Vince (England)	**14.3.1991**	**2016**	**1**

The only pair to make their debut in the same match on the same side were Gregory and Thomson, in the very first Test, at Melbourne in 1876-77.

His entrance would have to wait, however: Misbah won his seventh toss in a row, and chose to bat. There was little in the strip for England's opening bowlers who, despite their county connection, failed to tie Pakistan up in Notts. But Woakes did find swing – initially away from the right-handers, then in as well – to claim two wickets. Every now and again Ball beat bat and hit pad, and eventually his yorker did for Azhar Ali, the first of many victims for the inbuilt bias of the DRS: in favour of the on-field umpire, whenever the decision was borderline. The victim of ultra-marginal calls in both innings, Azhar was especially unlucky.

His downfall left Pakistan teetering at 77 for three, their grand old men together. Despite a combined 80 years or more, Younis Khan and Misbah had only one Lord's Test between them – by Younis back in 2001. Their techniques were different: Younis's shots were accompanied by an eccentric flourish of the back leg, while Misbah's cushiony hands mitigated any lateral movement, especially from Woakes. Yet it was an edge off Finn that had Misbah's heart in his mouth, Root fluffing a tough but catchable chance at second slip. Younis perished when a flick off his toes fetched up at midwicket and, at 134 for four, Pakistan could easily have flumped for under 200. As so often, much rested on Misbah's shoulders.

With a deftness and athleticism belying his years, he set about resurrecting the innings in the company of the resolute Asad Shafiq, a favourite ally: the 148 they added made them the first fifth-wicket pair to compile seven century stands in Tests. Cook, still scarred by Misbah's dismantling of English slow bowling in late 2015, used Moeen Ali sparingly. One delicious over, costing 16, explained why: defended, reverse-swept, swept; defended, reverse-swept, swept. The immaculate execution showed Misbah as contemptuous of spin as Henry VIII of wives.

Soon afterwards, he became the oldest to score a Test century for 82 years – and the oldest Test captain ever to do so. And he celebrated, not with a roar, but a salute and ten press-ups, a nod to the hard work put in with the Pakistan army (as well as the remarkable fitness of a 42-year-old). Grizzled hacks in the media centre burst into laughter. Shafiq departed to the new ball, caught in two minds by a Woakes outswinger, and then, from the last delivery of the day, nightwatchman Rahat Ali provoked more hilarity when an almighty off-side heave cannoned into the stumps.

Next morning brought an exquisite one–two from Woakes, who followed a sizzling awayswinger with one that came back in to Wahab Riaz. Enter Amir. His reception was hard to gauge, since the crowd were still cheering Woakes's six-for. There was no doubt, though, that from 282 for four on a blameless pitch, a total of 339 was disappointing.

If there was no wag from the Pakistan tail, there were a couple in the crowd who amused themselves (and few others) with cries of "No-ball!" when Amir ran in from the Pavilion End, an attempt at humour as feeble as it was foreseeable. Hales fell quickly to Rahat,

Resounding success: Yasir Shah shares his delight at the dismissal of Chris Woakes.

least celebrated of Pakistan's left-arm troika, while Cook was twice dropped off Amir: on 22 by Mohammad Hafeez at slip, then a simpler chance behind the wicket on 55. Root, who had looked more comfortable than an old shoe, decided to give Yasir the boot. A miscued slog-sweep later, England were 118 for two, Yasir poised to run riot in the middle order. Vince vanished like an English summer – three fine shots and a dismissal – Ballance botched a forward defensive, Bairstow blithely went back to cut a ball that was too full, and Moeen missed a sweep. Sandwiched in the middle of Yasir's full-throated five was one for Amir, who eventually removed Cook for 81, an innings uncharacteristic both in speed (a 60-ball half-century was his second-quickest in Tests) and conclusion (bowled for the first time in 20 innings). England closed on 253 for seven. Yasir grabbed a sixth on the third morning: different tail, same limp ending.

OLDEST TEST CENTURIONS

Years	*Days*			
46	82	J. B. Hobbs (142)	England v Australia at Melbourne	1928-29
45	151	E. H. Hendren (132)	England v Australia at Manchester	1934
43	202	W. Bardsley (193*)	Australia v England at Lord's	1926
42	295	A. W. Nourse (111)	South Africa v Australia at Johannesburg	1921-22
42	61	F. E. Woolley (154)	England v South Africa at Manchester	1929
42	**47**	**Misbah-ul-Haq (114)**	**Pakistan v England at Lord's**	**2016**
42	6	E. A. B. Rowan (236)	South Africa v England at Leeds	1951
41	360	R. B. Simpson (100)	Australia v India at Adelaide	1977-78
41	268	W. W. Armstrong (123*)	Australia v England at Melbourne	1920-21
41	264	T. W. Graveney (105)	England v Pakistan at Karachi	1968-69

Only the last century is shown for each player (Hobbs would otherwise have seven entries). Nourse's hundred was his only one in Tests, 19 years after his debut.

Trailing by 67, England had to unpick the Pakistan batting, and pronto. Broad did his bit, inveigling Hafeez into the cordon, and five balls after lunch Woakes removed Shan Masood to usher in a session of intense cricket: cat and mouse one moment, dog eat dog the next. Woakes did for Azhar, while Finn, anodyne on the opening day, summoned some mojo. He should have had a couple, but he went wicketless for the first time in his 33 Tests. Then Misbah faced his first ball from Moeen. He timed his slog; Hales timed his run on the midwicket boundary; the scorecard timed Misbah's innings as an 11-minute duck.

Sensing this was England's last route back into the game, the crowd, in very un-Lord's (or ladylike) mood, bayed for more blood. Though the teams traded punches, neither could floor the other. Woakes's consistent hostility brought a maiden Test ten-wicket haul – then

BEST BOWLING FOR ENGLAND IN A TEST DEFEAT

13-163	S. F. Barnes	v Australia at Melbourne	1901-02
13-244	T. Richardson	v Australia at Manchester	1896
11-76	W. H. Lockwood	v Australia at Manchester	1902
11-83	N. G. B. Cook	v Pakistan at Karachi	1983-84
11-102	**C. R. Woakes**	**v Pakistan at Lord's**	**2016**
11-110	A. R. C. Fraser	v West Indies at Port-of-Spain	1997-98
11-176	I. T. Botham	v Australia at Perth	1979-80
11-215	D. L. Underwood	v Australia at Adelaide	1974-75
11-228	M. W. Tate	v Australia at Sydney	1924-25

made him the first England bowler to claim two five-fors in a Lord's Test since Ian Botham against New Zealand in 1978 – though by the close some useful biffs had swollen Pakistan's lead. Next day, the overnight innings again tapered off, but the target was 283; only once in 132 Lord's Tests had a team made as many in the fourth innings to win.

As if preoccupied by the looming menace of Yasir, the batsmen underestimated the seamers. An honest, if unexceptional, ball pecked the varnish of Cook's bat, while Hales cut a lifter to slip. And when Root swivel-pulled half-heartedly to deepish midwicket to make it 47 for three, all to Rahat, Pakistani nostrils scented success. In his short Test career, Vince had rarely radiated permanence. Now he collected five boundaries in six balls, though two could have gone anywhere. Before long, his detractors were wearing I-told-you-so expressions when another ambitious drive – from his third ball after lunch – warmed second slip's hands. The target was still 187 away.

Could England repair the damage? Such gaping holes called for quarry-loads of Yorkshire grit. Ballance and Bairstow dug deep – until Lord's resounded again to the Yasir yell. Ballance had stepped outside off when a delivery spat out of the rough, turned sharply and clobbered leg stump. Moeen had signalled he would attack Yasir, and was as good as his word: fourth ball, he lost his wits – dancing down the pitch in a gamble too far – and his middle stump.

For England supporters, the head was clear: 139 for six meant only one winner. Yet with Bairstow and Woakes clinging on, the heart harboured absurd notions of victory. Misbah brought back Wahab, and battle royal ensued. One spell to Woakes was the very manifestation of menace: time and again Wahab beat the bat with 90mph reverse swing. But the wicket would not come, each single prompted wild applause, the score crept up, and those notions didn't seem quite so absurd. The target less than 100 away; the fifty stand in 28 overs.

And then the dam broke. Bairstow went back to pull Yasir, as he had so often, and missed. The seventh in the match to fall within ten of a fifty – three of them to Yasir, giving a new slant on the roaring forties – Bairstow bent over his bat, distraught. Victory came in a rush, with Yasir taking ten for 141, the best match figures of his career, the best for Pakistan at Lord's (beating Waqar Younis's eight for 154 in 1996), and the best by a spinner here since Derek Underwood claimed 13 for 71 against Pakistan in 1974. And in a gesture oozing mischief as much as *joie de vivre*, Younis Khan orchestrated celebrations in front of the Pavilion: press-ups for all, followed by a team salute.

Man of the Match: Yasir Shah. *Attendance:* 113,637.

Close of play: first day, Pakistan 282-6 (Misbah-ul-Haq 110); second day, England 253-7 (Woakes 31, Broad 11); third day, Pakistan 214-8 (Yasir Shah 30, Mohammad Amir 0).

Pakistan

Mohammad Hafeez c Bairstow b Woakes	40	– c Root b Broad	0
Shan Masood c Bairstow b Woakes	7	– c Cook b Woakes	24
Azhar Ali lbw b Ball	7	– lbw b Woakes	23
Younis Khan c Ali b Broad	33	– b Ali	25
*Misbah-ul-Haq b Broad	114	– c Hales b Ali	0
Asad Shafiq c Bairstow b Woakes	73	– b Woakes	49
Rahat Ali b Woakes	0	– (11) not out	0
†Sarfraz Ahmed c Vince b Woakes	25	– (7) c Bairstow b Woakes	45
Wahab Riaz b Woakes	0	– c Bairstow b Woakes	0
Mohammad Amir c Root b Broad	12	– c Bairstow b Broad	1
Yasir Shah not out	11	– (8) c Bairstow b Broad	30
B 4, lb 10, w 2, nb 1	17	B 6, lb 11, nb 1	18
1/38 (2) 2/51 (1) 3/77 (3) (99.2 overs)	339	1/2 (1) 2/44 (2) (79.1 overs)	215
4/134 (4) 5/282 (6) 6/282 (7)		3/59 (3) 4/60 (5)	
7/310 (8) 8/310 (9) 9/316 (5) 10/339 (10)		5/129 (4) 6/168 (6) 7/208 (7)	
		8/214 (9) 9/214 (8) 10/215 (10)	

Broad 27.2–9–71–3; Ball 19–5–51–1; Woakes 24–7–70–6; Finn 21–2–86–0; Ali 7–0–46–0; Vince 1–0–1–0. *Second innings*—Broad 19.1–7–38–3; Ball 16–7–37–0; Finn 13–4–42–0; Woakes 18–6–32–5; Ali 13–3–49–2.

England

*A. N. Cook b Mohammad Amir	81	– c Sarfraz Ahmed b Rahat Ali	8
A. D. Hales c Azhar Ali b Rahat Ali	6	– c Mohammad Hafeez b Rahat Ali	16
J. E. Root c Mohammad Hafeez b Yasir Shah	48	– c Yasir Shah b Rahat Ali	9
J. M. Vince lbw b Yasir Shah	16	– c Younis Khan b Wahab Riaz	42
G. S. Ballance lbw b Yasir Shah	6	– b Yasir Shah	43
†J. M. Bairstow b Yasir Shah	29	– b Yasir Shah	48
M. M. Ali lbw b Yasir Shah	23	– b Yasir Shah	2
C. R. Woakes not out	35	– c Younis Khan b Yasir Shah	23
S. C. J. Broad b Wahab Riaz	17	– b Mohammad Amir	1
S. T. Finn lbw b Yasir Shah	5	– not out	4
J. T. Ball run out	4	– b Mohammad Amir	3
Nb 2	2	B 1, lb 5, w 1, nb 1	8
1/8 (2) 2/118 (3) 3/139 (4) (79.1 overs)	272	1/19 (1) 2/32 (2) (75.5 overs)	207
4/147 (5) 5/173 (1) 6/193 (6)		3/47 (3) 4/96 (4)	
7/232 (7) 8/260 (9) 9/267 (10) 10/272 (11)		5/135 (5) 6/139 (7) 7/195 (6)	
		8/196 (9) 9/204 (8) 10/207 (11)	

Mohammad Amir 18–2–65–1; Rahat Ali 14–1–68–1; Wahab Riaz 18.1–0–67–1; Yasir Shah 29–6–72–6. *Second innings*—Mohammad Amir 17.5–4–39–2; Rahat Ali 14–0–47–3; Yasir Shah 31–9–69–4; Wahab Riaz 13–1–46–1.

Umpires: H. D. P. K. Dharmasena and J. S. Wilson. Third umpire: R. J. Tucker.
Referee: R. B. Richardson.

ENGLAND v PAKISTAN

Second Investec Test Match

TANYA ALDRED

At Manchester, July 22–25. England won by 330 runs. England 4pts. Toss: England.

After the Lord's misadventure, the northern triumph. Old Trafford, plain but faithful old girl that she is, was the backdrop to a four-day England win that whipped the rug from under the Pakistanis. The match provided a cautionary tale: the exchange of fortunes between two sides and their talismanic princelings.

First, the seemingly unstoppable Yasir Shah proved mortal – returning clodden-shod match figures. Then there was Root, uncharacteristically careless the week before, classically magnificent here. He fashioned an innings of iron restraint, combined with a near-perfect touch, easing onwards and upwards to his highest score and beyond. So perfect was his batting, so timeless, that a mouthy Manchester crowd were turned tummy-side up to purr at this batsman from over the Pennines. Cook provided the ballast, while Woakes – with seven wickets and a cameo 58 – hinted at a golden future.

The only PR hiccup for England came on the third afternoon, when Cook cautiously chose not to enforce the follow-on, with Pakistan 391 behind and suitably demoralised. A scathing editorial in the Pakistan daily *Dawn* thundered that this was "one of the most glaring incidences of cowardice in cricket history". Never before in a time-restricted Test had England led by so many without asking the opposition to bat again.

Former captains, and sections of the crowd, were also bemused. No matter, for Cook had his reasons: rest for bowlers, the desire to bat in the best of the conditions, a chance to put more overs in the legs of the Pakistan bowlers. In any event, the threatened rain didn't stick around for long enough to make a difference.

HIGHEST TEST SCORES AT OLD TRAFFORD

311	R. B. Simpson	Australia v England	1964
256	K. F. Barrington	England v Australia	1964
254	**J. E. Root**	**England v Pakistan**	**2016**
223	C. G. Greenidge	West Indies v England	1984
210	G. Kirsten	South Africa v England	1998
205	Aamir Sohail	Pakistan v England	1992
191	W. J. Edrich	England v South Africa	1947
187	M. J. Clarke	Australia v England	2013
182	C. C. Hunte	West Indies v England	1963
179	M. Azharuddin	India v England	1990

It had been on a sunny Friday morning and a perfect-looking pitch that Misbah-ul-Haq finally lost a toss. Cook was tightening the last buckle on his pad as the coin hit the ground: of 38 previous Manchester Tests in which England had batted first, they had lost only three, most recently in 1989. Pakistan retained their team from Lord's, but England brought back Anderson (now officially fit) for Jake Ball, and Stokes for Steven Finn.

A throaty turnout of over 17,000 filled Old Trafford – a mix of football shirt and the occasional salwar kameez, with a side order of Mr Whippy – and it was difficult to know whether it was mean-spiritedness or ale or both which led a section of them to no-ball Mohammad Amir throughout his first over, and on his return for later spells. Not that it seemed to faze him: he buzzed with intent as spiky as his haircut, and in his first over drew Cook into an edge through a non-existent fourth slip. But it was Hales, back on trial once more despite a successful series against Sri Lanka, who went early. After being dropped at

Corbis/Getty Images

Every knee shall bow: Joe Root cracks on towards a career-best 254; Sarfraz Ahmed is the keeper.

gully by Asad Shafiq off Amir in the seventh over, he lost his off stump to an Amir inswinger three balls later.

Just after midday, Yasir was on at the Statham End, but Cook and Root had done their homework. Gone were the cross-bat shots that had derailed England at Lord's, parked in batting purgatory next to wafting drives at the left-arm seamers. At lunch, they were 95 for one, and progress continued serenely in the afternoon, as both men reached centuries. It was Cook's 29th in Tests (and first in 20 innings), leaving him level with Bradman and slightly abashed: "He did it in less than half the games I did." And it was Root's tenth, his first since being repositioned to No. 3.

Cook fell on the stroke of tea, bowled for 105 by a skidder from Amir that exposed the middle order to their familiar struggles. Vince hit a handful of pretty fours, before driving at Rahat Ali, having been dropped on six by Younis Khan at second slip off Amir playing precisely the same stroke. Ballance also misjudged Rahat, dragging on a cut at a ball that was too close. But Root batted on, beautiful back-foot drive after beautiful back-foot drive. He had 141 by the close, when he was applauded off by the crowd and the Pakistanis, who queued up to shake his hand.

On the second morning, the outfield ran even more quickly, and Woakes (a nightwatchman in name only) reeled off a selection of deft drives before unleashing a sublime upper-cut for six – his first in Tests – off Amir, casually leaning back as if to knock an apple off a tree. Root was content to watch and admire as he eased past 150, only to be given a lifeline a few balls later when Younis put down a tough low chance at slip off Yasir.

And so it went on: Woakes and Stokes provided the big hitting, while Root inched to 197 with 17 successive singles, before moving past 200, and his highest Test score, with a reverse-sweep for four off Yasir. When Stokes fell, via DRS, for 34, Bairstow replaced him as England's attack dog, crashing a full toss from Yasir for four, before being dropped by wicketkeeper Sarfraz Ahmed two balls later, on nine. Yasir, whose smiling countenance never slipped, merrily tugged at his thick white wristbands and the elastic of his stout-bottomed trousers, all the while totting up the most runs conceded by a Pakistani against England. He would finish with one for 213 in the innings (beating Fazal Mahmood's two for 192 at The Oval in 1962), and one for 266 in the match (beating Danish Kaneria's four for 237 at Leeds in 2006).

Finally, after ten hours and 14 minutes, 406 balls and 27 fours, Root – to his obvious frustration – misread Wahab Riaz's slower ball and was caught by Mohammad Hafeez for 254. It was the 15th-highest score in England's history, and the third-highest by an England No. 3, behind Wally Hammond (336 not out at Auckland in 1932-33) and Tom Graveney (258 against West Indies at Trent Bridge in 1957). Two overs later, when Bairstow was caught at long-off for a cracking fifty, England declared at 589 for eight.

Pakistan trooped off, but the best of the conditions had gone. A wind had been whistled, the clouds were thickening and the beer snake in the party stand stretched from top to bottom. Underneath people staggered around with traffic cones on their heads trying to open the doors to the stinking Portaloos.

MOST RUNS IN A TEST IN ENGLAND

456	G. A. Gooch (333 and 123)	England v India at Lord's	1990
364	L. Hutton (364)	England v Australia at The Oval	1938
362	G. C. Smith (277 and 85)	South Africa v England at Birmingham	2003
334	D. G. Bradman (334)	Australia v England at Leeds	1930
325	**J. E. Root (254 and 71*)**	**England v Pakistan at Manchester**	**2016**
321	D. G. Bradman (244 and 77)	Australia v England at The Oval	1934
315	P. B. H. May (30 and 285*)	England v West Indies at Birmingham	1957
315	R. B. Simpson (311 and 4*)	Australia v England at Manchester	1964
311	H. M. Amla (311*)	South Africa v England at The Oval	2012
310	J. H. Edrich (310*)	England v New Zealand at Leeds	1965
309	B. Mitchell (120 and 189*)	South Africa v England at The Oval	1947
304	D. G. Bradman (304)	Australia v England at Leeds	1934

In less than two hours before the close, Pakistan were reduced to 57 for four, with Woakes, full of bounce and verve, picking up three. Hafeez was held by Root at second slip (his first of four catches in the innings), Azhar Ali caught and bowled, and nightwatchman Rahat snaffled at short leg. In between, a crabbed Younis, who had never looked at ease, was caught behind off Stokes. The tourists headed for the pavilion, 532 in arrears.

On the more prosaic third day, Pakistan lurched to lunch, either side of an hour's break for rain, on 119 for eight. Anderson got Shan Masood for the fifth consecutive innings, and only a ninth-wicket stand of 60 between Misbah and Wahab slowed England down. The sight of Hales, having ended the fun by catching Wahab at deep midwicket, immediately running for the dressing-room signalled Cook's decision to bat again. With the floodlights on, and rain in the air, it felt like a vote for methodical victory over ruthlessness.

England's reply was interrupted by spreadeagled groundsheets before tea, but they lost only Hales in 21 lively overs by stumps. On the fourth morning, Cook moved to his fastest half-century in Tests, from 55 balls, as he and Root rattled through a stand of 105 in 85 deliveries. By the time Cook declared for a second time, the pair had scored 506 of England's 733 runs off the bat. Pakistan needed to make 565 to win, or to survive 11 hours to draw. Both were fanciful. Anderson ensured a dismal start when he removed Masood again, for one. And, with the dismissal of Azhar, he overtook Glenn McGrath as the leading fast bowler in home Tests, with 290 wickets.

Pakistan resisted in parts, but Woakes and Moeen Ali collected three apiece, and a series-levelling 330-run victory, England's first over Pakistan in eight Tests, left Cook delighted. Man of the Match Root pondered a little, and said: "I think I can get better."

The one shadow was an injury to Stokes, who had hobbled from the pitch two deliveries into his sixth over. Scans showed a torn muscle in his right calf, ruling him out of the rest of the series. For Pakistan, it was back to the drawing board.

Man of the Match: J. E. Root. *Attendance:* 53,257.

Close of play: first day, England 314-4 (Root 141, Woakes 2); second day, Pakistan 57-4 (Shan Masood 30, Misbah-ul-Haq 1); third day, England 98-1 (Cook 49, Root 23).

England

*A. N. Cook b Mohammad Amir	105	– not out	76
A. D. Hales b Mohammad Amir	10	– c Sarfraz Ahmed b Mohammad Amir	24
J. E. Root c Mohammad Hafeez b Wahab Riaz	254	– not out	71
J. M. Vince c Sarfraz Ahmed b Rahat Ali	18		
G. S. Ballance b Rahat Ali	23		
C. R. Woakes c and b Yasir Shah	58		
B. A. Stokes c Sarfraz Ahmed b Wahab Riaz	34		
†J. M. Bairstow c Misbah-ul-Haq b Wahab Riaz	58		
M. M. Ali not out	2		
Lb 9, w 8, nb 10	27	Lb 2	2
1/25 (2) 2/210 (1) (8 wkts dec, 152.2 overs)	589	1/68 (2) (1 wkt dec, 30 overs)	173
3/238 (4) 4/311 (5)			
5/414 (6) 6/471 (7) 7/577 (3) 8/589 (8)			

S. C. J. Broad and J. M. Anderson did not bat.

Mohammad Amir 29–6–89–2; Rahat Ali 29–4–101–2; Wahab Riaz 26.2–1–106–3; Yasir Shah 54–6–213–1; Azhar Ali 11–0–52–0; Shan Masood 3–0–19–0. *Second innings*—Mohammad Amir 11–2–43–1; Rahat Ali 8–0–54–0; Yasir Shah 9–0–53–0; Azhar Ali 2–0–21–0.

Pakistan

Mohammad Hafeez c Root b Woakes	18	– c Ballance b Ali	42
Shan Masood c Root b Anderson	39	– c Cook b Anderson	1
Azhar Ali c and b Woakes	1	– lbw b Anderson	8
Younis Khan c Bairstow b Stokes	1	– c Hales b Ali	28
Rahat Ali c Ballance b Woakes	4	– (11) not out	8
*Misbah-ul-Haq c Cook b Ali	52	– (5) b Woakes	35
Asad Shafiq c Hales b Broad	4	– (6) lbw b Anderson	39
†Sarfraz Ahmed c Root b Stokes	26	– (7) c Bairstow b Woakes	7
Yasir Shah c Root b Woakes	1	– (8) lbw b Ali	10
Wahab Riaz c Hales b Ali	39	– (9) c Cook b Root	19
Mohammad Amir not out	9	– (10) c Broad b Woakes	29
Lb 2, nb 2	4	B 2, lb 4, w 1, nb 1	8
1/27 (1) 2/43 (3) 3/48 (4) (63.4 overs)	198	1/7 (2) 2/25 (3) (70.3 overs)	234
4/53 (5) 5/71 (2) 6/76 (7)		3/83 (1) 4/102 (4)	
7/112 (8) 8/119 (9) 9/179 (6) 10/198 (10)		5/145 (5) 6/163 (7) 7/167 (6)	
		8/190 (8) 9/208 (9) 10/234 (10)	

Anderson 13–5–27–1; Broad 12–5–20–1; Ali 7.4–0–43–2; Woakes 16–1–67–4; Stokes 15–1–39–2. *Second innings*—Anderson 16–2–41–3; Broad 14–3–37–0; Stokes 5.2–0–21–0; Ali 18.4–1–88–3; Woakes 15.3–2–41–3; Root 1–1–0–1.

Umpires: H. D. P. K. Dharmasena and R. J. Tucker. Third umpire: J. S. Wilson.
Referee: R. B. Richardson.

At Worcester, July 29–30 (not first-class). **Drawn. Pakistanis 261-3 dec** (80 overs) (Shan Masood 67, Azhar Ali 81); ‡**Worcestershire 260-6** (76 overs) (J. M. Clarke 58, T. Köhler-Cadmore 73). *Shan Masood batted more than three hours for his 67 – but lost his Test place to his opening partner, Sami Aslam, who was out for 17. After Azhar Ali departed at 181-3, Iftikhar Ahmed (41*) and Mohammad Rizwan (49*) put on 80 before a late declaration. Worcestershire survived 11 overs on the first evening, and had few problems on the second day, mostly against a second-string attack.*

ENGLAND v PAKISTAN

Third Investec Test Match

LAWRENCE BOOTH

At Birmingham, August 3–7. England won by 141 runs. England 4pts. Toss: Pakistan.

As Chris Woakes ran in to deliver the last ball of the second day, Pakistan were ready to make England regret their laxity. Azhar Ali was on strike, 139 to the good, and the scoreboard read 257 for two in reply to 297. The game was at their mercy, maybe even the series. But Azhar's concentration wavered, and a loose drive flew to Cook at first slip. For England, the door creaked ajar. Over the next three days – cautiously at first, then with a flourish – they prised it open. At 5.24 on a final afternoon full of drama, Sohail Khan drove a return catch into the midriff of Moeen Ali, and England were celebrating one of their best wins under Cook. It was a fitting way to mark their 500th home Test.

Lovers of karmic twists noted that the last-day damage was done by reverse swing, the weapon deployed by Wasim Akram and Waqar Younis when Pakistan won in England 24 years earlier. With a grim chuckle, Misbah-ul-Haq said his batsmen had been clueless, especially while Woakes and Finn – restored for the injured Ben Stokes – were claiming four for one in 23 balls before tea. By next morning, as a Pakistan TV channel insinuated ball-tampering, the irony had come full circle. No one could accuse anyone of conforming to stereotype.

The shape of this Test, though, was very much an England–Pakistan classic: slow burner followed by raging inferno. Misbah had invited comparisons with Ricky Ponting by putting England in, but no side batting first had won at Edgbaston since that fabled match in 2005, and Misbah had lost none of the previous nine Tests in which he had chosen to field. As if instinctively grasping all this, his bowlers set about vindicating his decision.

Philip Brown, SilverHub

If you're happy and you know it. . . A muscular Sohail Khan adds a clap to his celebratory press-ups after a maiden Test five-for.

Front and centre was Sohail Khan, a replacement for Wahab Riaz, and Pakistan's first right-arm quick of the summer. His Test record did not demand attention: one for 245 in two games, most recently in 2011. Now, as England slapdashed their way to 158 for five, he picked up four. Hales got a good one that left him, but Root, Vince and Bairstow all committed indiscretions outside off; in between, Rahat Ali removed Cook for 45. Sohail had spent his youth building muscle by hurling rocks down mountains in the old North-West Frontier Province. At the close – which he hastened by trapping Anderson – he put his biceps to work once more, punctuating each press-up with a clap of the hands, and taking care of the following morning's back pages.

England were in less playful mood. Only during a sixth-wicket stand of 66 between Ballance and Moeen had their innings settled, and even that was relative. On 70, Ballance tickled Yasir Shah down the leg side, and it needed a sensible approach from Moeen – imagining himself, he said, as Worcestershire's No. 3 – to lift the score towards 300. That evening, Ballance claimed it was a decent total in nibbly conditions. No one was quite buying that, least of all the Pakistanis.

THE ROAD TO 500

Edgbaston 2016 was England's 500th home Test:

	P	*W*	*L*	*D*	*% W*	*% L*	*% D*	*First*
v Australia	166	51	49	66	30.72	29.51	39.75	1880
v South Africa	64	27	13	24	42.18	20.31	37.50	1907
v West Indies	83	32	29	22	38.55	34.93	26.50	1928
v New Zealand	54	30	5	19	55.55	9.25	35.18	1931
v India	57	30	6	21	52.63	10.52	36.84	1932
v Pakistan	50	22	10	18	44.00	20.00	36.00	1954
v Sri Lanka	18	8	3	7	44.44	16.66	38.88	1984
v Zimbabwe	4	3	0	1	75.00	–	25.00	2000
v Bangladesh	4	4	0	0	100.00	–	–	2005
	500	**207**	**115**	**178**	**41.40**	**23.00**	**35.60**	

Anderson, it's true, struck with the fourth delivery of the second day, as Mohammad Hafeez slapped a long hop to point, giving him 50 Test wickets against everyone bar Bangladesh and Zimbabwe (only Muttiah Muralitharan could boast all nine). But, between that and Woakes's last-ball heist, England's only succour was the run-out of Sami Aslam, a neat left-handed opener and a happy improvement on Shan Masood. England's struggles could be partly ascribed to the heavy roller and to a slow surface more like Lord's than Manchester – but only partly. Where their batsmen snatched and grasped, Pakistan's played harder to get.

Other than a chance to Root at second slip in the first over after lunch when Azhar had 38, he and Aslam were untroubled. England offered too much width; Pakistan disdained it. This was not a sequence designed to bolster Colin Graves's plans for four-day Tests, but the impasse was absorbing, and England were getting tetchy. Anderson lost his cool after twice being warned for running on the pitch in the 68th over by Bruce Oxenford – a display of petulance for which he later apologised, cannily sidestepping a fine – and Cook barely used Moeen's off-breaks before the 48th over. The game was drifting away.

A direct hit from Vince after a dreadful call for a single from Azhar sent Aslam on his way for 82 – an inglorious end to a stand of 181. But that was merely the prelude to further Pakistani circumspection. Azhar, who had made a 32-ball duck here six years earlier, reached his tenth Test century – and first outside Asia – when he tucked Broad off his hip for four. Under the grumpy gaze of Anderson, he did his press-ups and carried on – only to edge Woakes as stumps beckoned.

On a bright Friday morning, England looked bushy-tailed. Younis Khan's travails continued when Woakes, in his first Test on his county ground, strangled him down the

Rui Vieira, PA Photos

Rarely missing a beat: Jonny Bairstow and Moeen Ali, the heart of England's middle order.

leg side, and Pakistan still trailed by one run when Broad bowled the strokeless Asad Shafiq. As he had done against England in the UAE, however, Misbah blocked the seamers and pursued Moeen; Sarfraz Ahmed followed suit. At 358 for five, Pakistan were pulling clear again. But Anderson bowled Misbah via front boot and back leg, and the last five tumbled for 42 – though not before Anderson was finally removed from the attack by Oxenford. The lead was 103. It ought to have been enough.

Yet, by stumps on day three, England were in credit, their openers intact. Cook became their leading scorer in all formats, passing Kevin Pietersen's 13,779, while Hales reached his only fifty of the series; it was their first century stand for the first wicket, at the 18th attempt. With runs in the bank, Hales felt emboldened to refund a spectator who had tweeted his outrage at England's glacial over-rate: on a day of 81 overs, they managed just 20 between lunch and tea. The 10% shortfall equated to compensation worth £4.10, which the spectator passed on to the Lord's Taverners. Meanwhile, to no one's surprise, the officials found a way of justifying all but one of the nine missing overs.

England resumed next morning 17 in front, but within 20 minutes both openers were gone – Cook driving to point, Hales poking to second slip. Misbah could have attacked, but preferred to grind. Rahat sent down five successive maidens, and had Root dropped at first slip on 25 by Hafeez. Vince resisted temptation. One leave followed another, and a tense session yielded 63 runs. The monasticism ended when Root, on 62, top-edged a sweep off Yasir to short fine leg. Vince, forgetting himself, dangled his bat at Mohammad Amir and the second new ball, and when Ballance moved fatally across his stumps against Yasir for the third time in the series – this time glancing to leg slip – England were five down and 179 ahead.

IF AT FIRST YOU DON'T SUCCEED

Tests in which England batted first, conceded a lead of 100 or more – and went on to win:

Deficit		
171	England (133 and 353) beat South Africa (304 and 111) at Lord's	1955
142	England (152 and 346) beat Australia (294 and 111) at Sydney	1978-79
134	England (389 and 478) beat New Zealand (523 and 220) at Lord's	2015
117	England (133 and 428) beat South Africa (250 and 224) at Cape Town	1927-28
106	England (145 and 237) beat South Africa (251 and 99) at Johannesburg	1898-99
103	**England (297 and 445-6 dec) beat Pakistan (400 and 201) at Birmingham**	**2016**

This excludes the 2006 Oval Test, when England (173 and 298-4) conceded a first-innings lead of 331, but were awarded the match after Pakistan (504) refused to play on.

They had chiselled out 142 runs in two sessions, but Bairstow, scampering furiously, and Moeen now made the Test's first decisive break. An effervescent final session yielded 152: Pakistan's chance had gone. Moeen smashed 19 of the 20 conceded by Yasir in the first over next morning, leaving him with four for 502 since his Lord's ten-for. And, shortly after Bairstow went for 83 – having breezed past Matt Prior's record for an England wicketkeeper of 777 Test runs in a calendar year, with eight games still to go – Cook declared on 445 for six, their highest third-innings total against Pakistan.

The tourists needed 343 in 84 overs, but Hafeez again went carelessly, scooping Broad to long leg, before Aslam and Azhar dug in. At lunch in sunny Birmingham, thoughts turned to a draw. But not England's. A helpful breeze in the direction of the Hollies Stand provided Moeen with the drift to induce an edge to gully by Azhar. And when Anderson replaced the thrifty Broad, the ball began to reverse. Younis edged Anderson to make it 92 for three, but it wasn't until Finn and Woakes joined forces that the innings went into free fall.

Finn picked up his first Test wicket in 430 deliveries when Misbah fiddled at one that straightened, and Shafiq completed a pair when – for the sixth time in the series – Woakes struck in the first over of a new spell. He then winkled out Sarfraz, edging low to second slip, before Aslam shouldered arms to Finn and had his off stump grazed. To Edgbaston's delight, Pakistan were 125 for seven.

Yasir and Amir went quickly after tea, extending the collapse to eight for 72, and only some last-wicket frolics took the Test into its final hour. Moeen's caught-and-bowled completed a team effort in which five England bowlers claimed two wickets in an innings for the first time since Delhi in 1981-82. And, having been 1–0 down, Cook's men now led 2–1. They headed for the capital, ready to apply the icing.

Man of the Match: M. M. Ali. *Attendance:* 81,823.

Close of play: first day, England 297; second day, Pakistan 257-3 (Younis Khan 21); third day, England 120-0 (Cook 64, Hales 50); fourth day, England 414-5 (Bairstow 82, Ali 60).

England

*A. N. Cook lbw b Rahat Ali	45	– c Yasir Shah b Sohail Khan	66
A. D. Hales c Sarfraz Ahmed b Sohail Khan	17	– c Younis Khan b Mohammad Amir	54
J. E. Root c Mohammad Hafeez b Sohail Khan	3	– c Mohammad Hafeez b Yasir Shah	62
J. M. Vince c Younis Khan b Sohail Khan	39	– c Younis Khan b Mohammad Amir	42
G. S. Ballance c Sarfraz Ahmed b Yasir Shah	70	– c Asad Shafiq b Yasir Shah	28
†J. M. Bairstow c Sarfraz Ahmed b Sohail Khan	12	– lbw b Sohail Khan	83
M. M. Ali c Sarfraz Ahmed b Mohammad Amir	63	– not out	86
C. R. Woakes c Sarfraz Ahmed b Rahat Ali	9	– not out	3
S. C. J. Broad c Azhar Ali b Mohammad Amir	13		
S. T. Finn not out	15		
J. M. Anderson lbw b Sohail Khan	5		
Lb 1, w 1, nb 4	6	B 4, lb 7, w 2, nb 8	21
1/36 (2) 2/48 (3) 3/75 (1) (86 overs)	297	1/126 (1) (6 wkts dec, 129 overs)	445
4/144 (4) 5/158 (6) 6/224 (5)		2/126 (2) 3/221 (3)	
7/244 (8) 8/276 (9) 9/278 (7) 10/297 (11)		4/257 (4) 5/282 (5) 6/434 (6)	

Mohammad Amir 16–3–53–2; Sohail Khan 23–3–96–5; Rahat Ali 20–4–83–2; Yasir Shah 27–3–64–1. *Second innings*—Mohammad Amir 31–8–75–2; Sohail Khan 29–3–111–2; Rahat Ali 21–8–54–0; Yasir Shah 43–4–172–2; Azhar Ali 5–0–22–0.

Pakistan

Mohammad Hafeez c Ballance b Anderson	0	– c Woakes b Broad	2
Sami Aslam run out	82	– b Finn	70
Azhar Ali c Cook b Woakes	139	– c Cook b Ali	38
Younis Khan c Bairstow b Woakes	31	– c Bairstow b Anderson	4
*Misbah-ul-Haq b Anderson	56	– c Bairstow b Finn	10
Asad Shafiq b Broad	0	– lbw b Woakes	0
†Sarfraz Ahmed not out	46	– c Root b Woakes	0
Yasir Shah run out	7	– c Hales b Anderson	7
Mohammad Amir lbw b Woakes	1	– c Woakes b Broad	16
Sohail Khan lbw b Broad	7	– c and b Ali	36
Rahat Ali c Root b Broad	4	– not out	15
B 5, lb 21, nb 1	27	Lb 2, nb 1	3
1/0 (1) 2/181 (2) 3/257 (3) 4/274 (4) 5/296 (6) 6/358 (5) 7/367 (8) 8/368 (9) 9/386 (10) 10/400 (11) (136 overs)	400	1/6 (1) 2/79 (3) 3/92 (4) 4/124 (5) 5/125 (6) 6/125 (7) 7/125 (2) 8/149 (8) 9/151 (9) 10/201 (10) (70.5 overs)	201

Anderson 29.1–7–54–2; Broad 30–4–83–3; Finn 27.5–7–76–0; Woakes 30–7–79–3; Ali 17–2–79–0; Vince 1–0–2–0; Root 1–0–1–0. *Second innings*—Anderson 13–3–31–2; Broad 15–7–24–2; Woakes 11–2–53–2; Finn 13–5–38–2; Ali 17.5–4–49–2; Root 1–0–4–0.

Umpires: B. N. J. Oxenford and J. S. Wilson. Third umpire: H. D. P. K. Dharmasena. Referee: R. B. Richardson.

ENGLAND v PAKISTAN

Fourth Investec Test Match

OSMAN SAMIUDDIN

At The Oval, August 11–14. Pakistan won by ten wickets. Pakistan 4pts. Toss: England. Test debut: Iftikhar Ahmed.

All series long he had hopped, skipped and fidgeted. He had crouched much lower than during his last series in England, a decade earlier – a result of playing almost exclusively since then on low, slow surfaces. To greet each ball he would not so much rise up as jump at it, as if from behind a sofa, then move across to cover for that ancient Pakistani failing in England: the edge to slip. As a result, the back leg seemed to develop a mind of its own, sometimes flamingoing up, more often slipping away. There was no balance. It wasn't pretty, but neither was it entirely ugly.

Younis Khan has always been a twitchy presence, his odd movements dictated by an unusually long reach and torso. But, officially aged 38 (unofficially, he was probably over 40), he had raised questions by failing in the first three Tests. In truth, his failures were relative, with four scores between 25 and 33. And he was getting out carelessly: twice caught down leg, once to midwicket, once on the slog.

The glitches were mental as much as technical. And, like the finest, he knew his time would come – that day when body, feet, hands and mind would achieve harmony. Here, with Pakistan needing a win to square a series they had led less than a month earlier, Younis stood a little taller and recalibrated his point of impact with the ball, letting it come to him further back in the crease. There had been input from Mickey Arthur and Grant Flower, coach and batting coach as well as a surprise phone call from former Indian captain Mohammad Azharuddin, but Younis has always been an autodidactic kind of guy.

The result, an incandescent 218 by the third afternoon, was nothing less than his fierce will emerging from a personal swamp. It contained all the qualities for which he is renowned – punches and drives in the arc between the umpire and point, dominance of the spinner – but there were lesser-seen gems too, including some flashing cuts.

Younis also batted wonderfully with the tail. He had 128 when Sarfraz Ahmed fell (for another important forty), at which point Pakistan were 397 for seven in reply to England's 328. Yet with care, authority and trust, he helped add 145 to the team total, and 90 to his own. He was intelligent, too: on the third afternoon, facing a deep-set field, he dinked Moeen Ali to midwicket with exactly the right force to fetch him two. The next ball went into the stands beyond wide long-on to bring up his sixth double-century, equalling Javed Miandad's Pakistan record. And with it came a reminder of Younis's capacity to go big: this was his 32nd Test hundred to set against 30 fifties (and only one dismissal in the nineties). It was among the very best conversion rates of any era.

The key partnership, however, had come on the second day with Asad Shafiq, who should, in time, take over as Pakistan's best batsman. He had looked impressive without setting the series alight, and a pair at Edgbaston had been dispiriting. But Pakistan not merely kept faith: they moved him up the order, having brought in Iftikhar Ahmed for opener Mohammad Hafeez. So often it had been Younis guiding a younger player through a partnership. But here the roles were neatly reversed: it was Shafiq's presence that seemed to calm Younis at the start of a 150-run stand.

Thus began a demonstration of a liquid exquisiteness

England had unsettled Shafiq with inswing, but he put himself right. It was not flawless, and Anderson missed a tough catch at third slip off Woakes when he had only seven. But it was everything a Shafiq innings should be: aesthetically pleasing, nimble-footed, runs everywhere, all wrapped up in a charming discretion.

Tough as the Anderson miss was, it summed up England's catching throughout the series, and their sloppiness in this Test. Having won the toss, and armed with a 2–1 lead, their dismissal inside 77 overs was a waste – not that it necessarily felt that way at the time. Rather, the sense was that Pakistan had let England off the hook, after a mixture of poor shots and energetic bowling from Wahab Riaz – back in the side at the expense of Rahat Ali – had them 74 for four before lunch.

Briefly, and for perhaps the only time all summer, the mood had threatened to turn sour. In the seventh over, Hales clipped Mohammad Amir to square leg, where Yasir Shah dived forward and claimed a low catch. Replays were blurry, but the soft signal had been out, and – with no contrary evidence available – Hales had to go. Lip-readers deciphered obscenities, but worse was to come: Hales took his grievance to TV official Joel Wilson's room, earning himself a £1,500 fine and the derision of social media.

Out in the middle, his team-mates could have been in even deeper strife. Bairstow, on 13, was caught at point shortly after lunch off a Wahab no-ball. And, after Azhar Ali held Ballance at third slip off Wahab to make it 110 for five, he dropped Moeen Ali, on nine, off the unfortunate Amir. Much in the manner of their second-innings partnership at Edgbaston, the pair cashed in, adding a bristling 93. Bristling is what Bairstow does best anyway, in attack or defence, and he had done it all summer. But Moeen's was the innings that made England's day.

He had begun inauspiciously, in the middle of a brutal Wahab spell, his helmet pinged so hard that the first ball he faced rebounded to backward point. Three deliveries later he flicked Wahab through square leg almost as cleanly as he had been hit. Thus began not an innings but a demonstration, of a liquid exquisiteness of sporting movement more commonly associated with tennis star Roger Federer – whips here, lashes there, the entire operation orchestrated by soft and powerful wrists. It was the best of his three Test hundreds. After adding 79 with Woakes, Moeen was last out, hooking to deep square leg to give Sohail Khan a second five-for in two Tests, a pleasant surprise given how exhausted he had looked at Edgbaston.

Out of the middle, not the manual: Younis Khan's distinct style brings more runs at The Oval.

Once Pakistan had opened up a lead of 214, the only question was how they would exploit it. At Edgbaston, where their first-innings advantage had been 103, they bowled as if they were the team in arrears, while their opening spells through the series had mixed class with dross. Finally, they got it right. Amir began with a maiden for the first time all summer, Sohail produced another, and the mood was set. After nine overs, England had only nine runs; in the tenth, Wahab's first, Cook was caught at slip.

It was left to Yasir to work a way to victory. After Lord's, he had been muted. But at The Oval he had a surface to work with, one with grip and life. Sure enough, he emerged a different beast, taking care of England's top order with balls that did not spin much, but zipped off the pitch.

There was resistance, marshalled inevitably by Bairstow, but for such moments exist bowlers like Wahab. England were close to level, with four wickets in hand, when – troubled by no-balls and warnings for running on the pitch – he breezed in for a new spell. Almost immediately he ran out Woakes with a superb piece of fielding off his own bowling, then dismissed Bairstow next ball. A few overs later he was out of the attack for transgressing again. It didn't matter: he had done his job.

Pakistan needed only 40, and not long after tea Azhar launched Moeen over long-on, with one stroke winning the Test, levelling the series, and taking his team to the brink of the No. 1 ranking. It was a euphoric moment, arriving on the 69th anniversary of the founding of the country, and lifting spirits back home after a terrorist attack in Quetta. The result also came as a tribute to Hanif Mohammad, who had played a part in their grandest triumph, at The Oval in 1954, and who died during this Test. For Pakistanis everywhere, this game took its place in the pantheon.

Man of the Match: Younis Khan. *Attendance:* 81,592.

Men of the Series: England – C. R. Woakes; Pakistan – Misbah-ul-Haq.

Close of play: first day, Pakistan 3-1 (Azhar Ali 0, Yasir Shah 0); second day, Pakistan 340-6 (Younis Khan 101, Sarfraz Ahmed 17); third day, England 88-4 (Ballance 4, Bairstow 14).

England

*A. N. Cook b Sohail Khan	35	– c Iftikhar Ahmed b Wahab Riaz	7
A. D. Hales c Yasir Shah b Mohammad Amir	6	– lbw b Yasir Shah	12
J. E. Root c Sarfraz Ahmed b Wahab Riaz	26	– lbw b Yasir Shah	39
J. M. Vince c Sarfraz Ahmed b Wahab Riaz	1	– c Misbah-ul-Haq b Yasir Shah	0
G. S. Ballance c Azhar Ali b Wahab Riaz	8	– c Sarfraz Ahmed b Sohail Khan	17
†J. M. Bairstow c Sarfraz Ahmed b Mohammad Amir	55	– c Azhar Ali b Wahab Riaz	81
M. M. Ali c Yasir Shah b Sohail Khan	108	– c Sarfraz Ahmed b Yasir Shah	32
C. R. Woakes c Sarfraz Ahmed b Sohail Khan	45	– run out	4
S. C. J. Broad lbw b Sohail Khan	0	– c Younis Khan b Yasir Shah	5
S. T. Finn b Sohail Khan	8	– not out	16
J. M. Anderson not out	6	– lbw b Iftikhar Ahmed	17
B 8, lb 7, w 7, nb 8	30	B 8, lb 10, nb 5	23
1/23 (2) 2/69 (1) 3/73 (3) 4/74 (4) 5/110 (5) 6/203 (6) 7/282 (8) 8/282 (9) 9/296 (10) 10/328 (7) (76.4 overs)	328	1/14 (1) 2/49 (2) 3/55 (4) 4/74 (3) 5/128 (5) 6/193 (7) 7/209 (8) 8/209 (6) 9/221 (9) 10/253 (11) (79.2 overs)	253

Mohammad Amir 18–1–80–2; Sohail Khan 20.4–1–68–5; Wahab Riaz 20–0–93–3; Yasir Shah 16–2–60–0; Iftikhar Ahmed 2–0–12–0. *Second innings*—Mohammad Amir 21.4–7–65–0; Sohail Khan 15–2–50–1; Wahab Riaz 11.2–1–48–2; Yasir Shah 29–4–71–5; Iftikhar Ahmed 2.2–1–1–1.

Pakistan

Sami Aslam lbw b Broad	3	– not out	12
Azhar Ali c Bairstow b Ali	49	– not out	30
Yasir Shah c Root b Finn	26		
Asad Shafiq c Broad b Finn	109		
Younis Khan lbw b Anderson	218		
*Misbah-ul-Haq c Hales b Woakes	15		
Iftikhar Ahmed c Ali b Woakes	4		
†Sarfraz Ahmed c Bairstow b Woakes	44		
Wahab Riaz st Bairstow b Ali	4		
Mohammad Amir not out	39		
Sohail Khan c Broad b Finn	2		
B 18, lb 6, w 3, nb 2	29		
1/3 (1) 2/52 (3) 3/127 (2) 4/277 (4) 5/316 (6) 6/320 (7) 7/397 (8) 8/434 (9) 9/531 (5) 10/542 (11) (146 overs)	542	(no wkt, 13.1 overs)	42

Anderson 29–10–78–1; Broad 29–5–99–1; Finn 30–1–110–3; Woakes 30–8–82–3; Ali 23–1–128–2; Root 5–0–21–0. *Second innings*—Woakes 4–0–11–0; Finn 0.2–0–0–0; Ali 5.5–0–30–0; Root 3–2–1–0.

Umpires: M. Erasmus and B. N. J. Oxenford. Third umpire: J. S. Wilson.
Referee: R. B. Richardson.

At Malahide, August 18. PAKISTAN beat IRELAND by 255 runs (see Cricket in Ireland, page 787).
Sharjeel Khan hits 152 from 86 balls, with nine sixes.

At Malahide, August 20. IRELAND v PAKISTAN. Abandoned (see Cricket in Ireland, page 787).

LIMITED-OVERS INTERNATIONAL REPORTS BY JULIAN GUYER

ENGLAND v PAKISTAN

First Royal London One-Day International

At Southampton, August 24 (day/night). England won by 44 runs (DLS). England 2pts. Toss: Pakistan.

Following a closely fought Test series, England comfortably ended a run of five straight one-day defeats at the Rose Bowl, thanks to sixties from Roy and Root. Roy got the chase going with three fours in four balls from Umar Gul, the first an astonishing straight-batted punch through midwicket. In the next over, the fourth, he suffered a disconcerting dizzy spell that held up play; in the sixth – having launched a pull shot straight up in the air – he was dropped by Sarfraz Ahmed off Mohammad Amir on 24. Undeterred, he carried on to a delightful 65 off 56 balls, while Root proved it was possible to score briskly without resorting to extravagance. Their target of 261 never looked a problem. So it was a surprise when Roy was dismissed, his slog off Mohammad Nawaz well held by Babar Azam at long-off, and Root was cursing himself after being run out by Azhar Ali. But Morgan and Stokes settled in, before a rain break left England needing only 59 more from 14 overs; three balls after the resumption, the rain returned, this time for good. Earlier, Wood – back from an ankle injury for his first international since October 2015 – repeatedly topped 90mph, and had the dangerous Sharjeel Khan caught behind in his third over. Pakistan's innings only briefly threatened to get out of second gear against some accurate bowling. Azhar's 110-ball 82 typified their struggle, and they managed only four fours in the last ten overs.

Man of the Match: J. J. Roy. *Attendance:* 17,117.

Pakistan

*Azhar Ali c Ali b Rashid	82	Imad Wasim not out	17
Sharjeel Khan c Buttler b Wood	16		
Mohammad Hafeez c Hales b Root	11	Lb 1, w 4	5
Babar Azam lbw b Rashid	40		—
†Sarfraz Ahmed c Wood b Woakes	55	1/25 (2) 2/52 (3) (6 wkts, 50 overs)	260
Shoaib Malik c Rashid b Plunkett	17	3/113 (4) 4/178 (1)	
Mohammad Nawaz not out	17	5/224 (6) 6/226 (5)	10 overs: 45-1

Wahab Riaz, Mohammad Amir and Umar Gul did not bat.

Woakes 10–2–43–1; Wood 10–0–57–1; Plunkett 10–0–52–1; Root 4–0–26–1; Ali 7–0–30–0; Rashid 9–0–51–2.

England

J. J. Roy c Babar Azam b Mohammad Nawaz	65	B. A. Stokes not out	15
A. D. Hales c Mohammad Hafeez b Umar Gul	7	Lb 6, w 7	13
			—
J. E. Root run out	61	1/27 (2) 2/116 (1) (3 wkts, 34.3 overs)	194
*E. J. G. Morgan not out	33	3/158 (3)	10 overs: 66-1

†J. C. Buttler, M. M. Ali, C. R. Woakes, A. U. Rashid, L. E. Plunkett and M. A. Wood did not bat.

Imad Wasim 5–0–23–0; Mohammad Amir 6–0–33–0; Umar Gul 6–0–46–1; Wahab Riaz 6–0–30–0; Mohammad Nawaz 6.3–0–31–1; Shoaib Malik 5–0–25–0.

Umpires: R. J. Bailey and S. D. Fry. Third umpire: M. Erasmus.
Referee: J. J. Crowe.

ENGLAND v PAKISTAN

Second Royal London One-Day International

At Lord's, August 27. England won by four wickets. England 2pts. Toss: Pakistan.

Sarfraz Ahmed became the first Pakistani to score a one-day international hundred at Lord's, but a lack of runs again proved his side's undoing. Sarfraz's century was chiselled from the adversity of two for three, after Azhar Ali had chosen to bat on a cloudy morning. Woakes and Buttler combined to remove both Sami Aslam, caught down the leg side on review despite questionable evidence, and Azhar himself; Sharjeel Khan was bowled by an excellent delivery from Wood that cut in sharply. But Sarfraz, whose only previous hundred in the format had come against Ireland during the 2015 World Cup, defied the bowlers with largely conventional strokeplay, if unconventional footwork that aggressively challenged their lengths. He completed a 124-ball century when he glanced Plunkett for his sixth four, and no one could begrudge him his roar of delight. Imad Wasim made a combative, career-best unbeaten 63, but received little support from the tail. Mohammad Amir bowled Roy with the second ball of the reply, and Hales followed cheaply. But a third-wicket partnership of 112 between Root, who had shaken off a collision in the field with Rashid while catching Hasan Ali, and Morgan – ending a run of 23 international innings without a fifty – reasserted England's control. Stokes's brutal 30-ball 42 put the result beyond doubt. In the 36th over, Hasan became the first bowler to be no-balled by the third official under an ICC trial system, when, with a vibrating pager, Simon Fry alerted Marais Erasmus.

Man of the Match: J. E. Root. *Attendance:* 27,481.

Pakistan

Sami Aslam c Buttler b Woakes	1
Sharjeel Khan b Wood	0
*Azhar Ali c Buttler b Woakes	0
Babar Azam b Plunkett	30
†Sarfraz Ahmed c Hales b Rashid	105
Shoaib Malik c Buttler b Wood	28
Imad Wasim not out	63
Hasan Ali c Root b Plunkett	0
Wahab Riaz c Plunkett b Woakes	6
Yasir Shah c Roy b Wood	0
Mohammad Amir run out	6
B 4, lb 4, w 4	12
1/2 (1) 2/2 (2) 3/2 (3) 4/66 (4) 5/125 (6) 6/202 (5) 7/223 (8) 8/236 (9) 9/238 (10) 10/251 (11) (49.5 overs)	251
10 overs: 46-3	

Wood 10–1–46–3; Woakes 9.5–2–42–3; Rashid 10–0–51–1; Plunkett 10–0–50–2; Ali 10–0–54–0.

England

J. J. Roy b Mohammad Amir	0
A. D. Hales b Imad Wasim	14
J. E. Root c Shoaib Malik b Wahab Riaz	89
*E. J. G. Morgan b Imad Wasim	68
B. A. Stokes b Hasan Ali	42
†J. C. Buttler run out	4
M. M. Ali not out	21
C. R. Woakes not out	7
Lb 8, nb 2	10
1/0 (1) 2/35 (2) 3/147 (4) 4/203 (5) 5/219 (6) 6/240 (3) (6 wkts, 47.3 overs)	255
10 overs: 39-2	

A. U. Rashid, L. E. Plunkett and M. A. Wood did not bat.

Mohammad Amir 10–2–39–1; Hasan Ali 9–0–52–1; Imad Wasim 7–0–38–2; Wahab Riaz 10–0–46–1; Yasir Shah 9.3–0–62–0; Shoaib Malik 2–0–10–0.

Umpires: M. Erasmus and R. T. Robinson. Third umpire: S. D. Fry.
Referee: J. J. Crowe.

ENGLAND v PAKISTAN

Third Royal London One-Day International

At Nottingham, August 30 (day/night). England won by 169 runs. England 2pts. Toss: England.

During the 2015 World Cup, the only one-day records it was possible to imagine England setting were of the runs-conceded variety. Not even 18 months on, they managed a world-record 444 for three, with Hales – putting a run of low scores behind him – making an England-best 171 on his home ground. Almost incidentally, they claimed the series. It was carnage from start to finish, aided by shoddy Pakistan fielding and badly timed no-balls from Wahab Riaz, who would otherwise have removed Hales on 72 and Buttler on 75; he ended up conceding 110. Hales also gave a chance, on 114, when he flayed Yasir Shah to short extra cover, but Azhar Ali was unable to hold on. Next ball, he hoisted Yasir for six, and eight overs later broke Robin Smith's 23-year-old England record of 167 not out when he pummelled a short delivery from Hasan for four. With the innings not yet

STAT ATTACK

The records that tumbled at Trent Bridge:

444 England's total was the highest in one-day internationals, beating Sri Lanka's 443-9 against the Netherlands at Amstelveen in 2006. It was the first time England had held the overall record in ODIs since March 1996, when their 363-7 against Pakistan at Nottingham in 1992 was overtaken by Sri Lanka's 398-5 against Kenya at Kandy during the World Cup.

408 England's previous highest one-day total, against New Zealand at Birmingham in June 2015. By the end of the 2015 World Cup, England had reached 350 only twice in ODIs; this was their sixth instance since.

392 The previous largest score conceded by Pakistan in ODIs, against South Africa at Centurion in 2006-07. Shoaib Malik played in both.

248 The partnership between Alex Hales and Joe Root was the highest against Pakistan in ODIs, beating 238 by Hashim Amla and A. B. de Villiers for South Africa's third wicket at Johannesburg in 2012-13. The only higher second-wicket stand for England was 250, by Andrew Strauss and Jonathan Trott against Bangladesh at Birmingham in 2010.

171 Alex Hales made the highest individual score for England in ODIs, beating Robin Smith's 167* against Australia at Birmingham in May 1993. It was England's seventh innings of 150 or more, three of them by Strauss. Hales was also the only England batsman to have scored a T20I hundred.

110 Wahab Riaz surpassed his own mark for the most runs conceded by a Pakistan bowler in an ODI. Against South Africa at Johannesburg in 2012-13, his figures were 10–0–93–2 (Bilawal Bhatti also conceded 93, v New Zealand at Napier in 2014-15). Only Australia's Mick Lewis, with 10–0–113–0 against South Africa at Johannesburg in 2005-06, had conceded more.

59 Between them, England's batsmen hit 59 boundaries – 43 fours and 16 sixes – equalling the overall record for any ODI innings, set by Sri Lanka (56 fours and three sixes) in their 443-9 in 2006. England's total of 268 from boundaries had been surpassed only once in ODIs, by South Africa, with 272 (38 fours and 20 sixes) against India in Mumbai in 2015-16.

58 Mohammad Amir made the first half-century by a No. 11 in 3,773 ODIs. The previous best was also for Pakistan against England: Shoaib Akhtar hit 43 at Cape Town during the 2003 World Cup.

22 Jos Buttler reached his half-century from 22 balls, beating the England record of 24, set by Paul Collingwood against New Zealand at Napier in 2007-08. Eoin Morgan made 50 from 24 balls in this match.

16 England's batsmen hit 16 sixes, edging their old record of 15, set seven months earlier against South Africa at Bloemfontein.

Graham Morris

On the up: Alex Hales takes England's one-day form to new heights.

37 overs old, a possible double-century was on the cards. Instead, Hales was plumb lbw next ball. In all, he had faced 122 deliveries, and hit 22 fours and four sixes. Root fell in the next over, having made a virtually unnoticed 86-ball 85. But the fun was not over, as Buttler (90 off 51) and Morgan (57 off 27) smote a dozen sixes in an unbroken stand of 161 off 12 overs. The world record came from the very last ball, after Buttler had played and missed at the fourth and fifth deliveries of Hasan's final over. To the delight of a capacity crowd, the sixth disappeared over extra cover for four. Pakistan steadily lost wickets in reply, only for Mohammad Amir to delay the inevitable with a 22-ball half-century from No. 11, before becoming a fourth victim for Woakes.

Man of the Match: A. D. Hales. *Attendance:* 17,061.

England

J. J. Roy c Sarfraz Ahmed b Hasan Ali	15
A. D. Hales lbw b Hasan Ali	171
J. E. Root c Sarfraz Ahmed b Mohammad Nawaz	85
†J. C. Buttler not out	90
*E. J. G. Morgan not out	57
B 6, lb 8, w 3, nb 9	26
1/33 (1) 2/281 (2) 3/283 (3) (3 wkts, 50 overs)	444
10 overs: 64-1	

B. A. Stokes, M. M. Ali, C. R. Woakes, A. U. Rashid, L. E. Plunkett and M. A. Wood did not bat.

Mohammad Amir 10–0–72–0; Hasan Ali 10–0–74–2; Wahab Riaz 10–0–110–0; Mohammad Nawaz 10–0–62–1; Yasir Shah 6–0–48–0; Azhar Ali 1–0–20–0; Shoaib Malik 3–0–44–0.

Pakistan

Sami Aslam c Ali b Woakes	8
Sharjeel Khan c Stokes b Woakes	58
*Azhar Ali c Rashid b Woakes	13
Babar Azam c Morgan b Stokes	9
†Sarfraz Ahmed c Root b Rashid	38
Shoaib Malik c Buttler b Plunkett	1
Mohammad Nawaz c Morgan b Rashid	34
Hasan Ali b Ali	4
Wahab Riaz lbw b Wood	14
Yasir Shah not out	26
Mohammad Amir c and b Woakes	58
B 4, lb 2, w 5, nb 1	12
1/21 (1) 2/50 (3) 3/83 (2) 4/106 (4) 5/108 (6) 6/155 (5) 7/164 (8) 8/180 (7) 9/199 (9) 10/275 (11) (42.4 overs)	275
10 overs: 83-3	

Wood 10–0–75–1; Woakes 5.4–1–41–4; Plunkett 6–0–30–1; Stokes 4–0–14–1; Ali 7–0–36–1; Rashid 10–0–73–2.

Umpires: S. D. Fry and R. A. Kettleborough. Third umpire: M. Erasmus.
Referee: J. J. Crowe.

ENGLAND v PAKISTAN

Fourth Royal London One-Day International

At Leeds, September 1 (day/night). England won by four wickets. England 2pts. Toss: Pakistan.

Pakistan's lack of runs again led to defeat, despite a spirited display in the field that reduced England to 72 for four. The hosts were indebted to a pugnacious fifth-wicket stand of 103 between Stokes and Bairstow, playing on his home ground only because Jos Buttler had tweaked a hamstring during the warm-up. The outcome, though, might have been different had the giant left-armer Mohammad Irfan, a late call-up to the squad, been able to bowl his ten overs. He had Roy well caught in the slips by Mohammad Rizwan; then, going around the wicket after twice being warned for running on the pitch, he removed Hales – fresh from his Trent Bridge heroics – caught behind off an excellent full-length ball. But, with figures of two for 25 in five overs, Irfan twice left the field, and bowled only one more delivery (a wide), before walking off with cramp, to the obvious consternation of Pakistan's coach Mickey Arthur. In a mirror image of the conclusion to the Oval Test, Moeen Ali – who added 50 with Bairstow – won the match by hitting Azhar Ali for six. Azhar and the elegantly aggressive Imad Wasim, who faced only 41 balls for his undefeated 57, once more provided the bulk of Pakistan's runs. With England now 4–0 up, ensuring they could not be caught in the Super Series, Arthur described the state of his team's 50-over cricket as "eye-opening".

Man of the Match: J. M. Bairstow. *Attendance:* 15,823.

Pakistan

Sami Aslam c Stokes b Plunkett	24
Sharjeel Khan c Stokes b Jordan	16
*Azhar Ali c Willey b Rashid	80
Babar Azam c Plunkett b Ali	12
†Sarfraz Ahmed c Plunkett b Rashid	12
Mohammad Rizwan lbw b Rashid	6
Mohammad Nawaz st Bairstow b Ali	13
Imad Wasim not out	57
Hasan Ali c Root b Jordan	9
Umar Gul not out	6
Lb 3, w 6, nb 3	12
1/24 (2) 2/61 (1) 3/110 (4) 4/136 (5) 5/152 (6) 6/169 (3) 7/180 (7) 8/236 (9) (8 wkts, 50 overs)	247
10 overs: 40-1	

Mohammad Irfan did not bat.

Willey 8–2–40–0; Jordan 9–1–42–2; Stokes 4–0–15–0; Plunkett 9–0–61–1; Rashid 10–0–47–3; Ali 10–0–39–2.

England

J. J. Roy c Mohammad Rizwan b Mohammad Irfan	14
A. D. Hales c Sarfraz Ahmed b Mohammad Irfan	8
J. E. Root c Mohammad Irfan b Hasan Ali	30
*E. J. G. Morgan c Sharjeel Khan b Umar Gul	11
B. A. Stokes c Babar Azam b Imad Wasim	69
†J. M. Bairstow run out	61
M. M. Ali not out	45
D. J. Willey not out	4
Lb 3, w 7	10
1/15 (1) 2/36 (2) 3/59 (3) 4/72 (4) 5/175 (5) 6/225 (6) (6 wkts, 48 overs)	252
10 overs: 52-2	

A. U. Rashid, L. E. Plunkett and C. J. Jordan did not bat.

Mohammad Irfan 5–1–26–2; Umar Gul 10–1–39–1; Hasan Ali 10–0–53–1; Imad Wasim 10–0–50–1; Mohammad Nawaz 10–0–54–0; Azhar Ali 3–0–27–0.

Umpires: M. Erasmus and R. T. Robinson. Third umpire: S. D. Fry.
Referee: J. J. Crowe.

ENGLAND v PAKISTAN

Fifth Royal London One-Day International

At Cardiff, September 4. Pakistan won by four wickets. Pakistan 2pts. Toss: Pakistan. One-day international debut: L. A. Dawson.

At 77 for three chasing 303, Pakistan looked set to become the first team to lose a one-day series 5–0 in England. But Sarfraz Ahmed produced a splendid 90 from 73 balls, and put on 163 with Shoaib Malik, a fourth-wicket record for Pakistan in this fixture. The pair came together after Wood had taken two wickets in three balls, bowling Babar Azam and having Azhar Ali caught behind on review. Shoaib, who in 34 previous international innings in the UK had not gone beyond 38, twice lofted Hampshire's debutant left-arm spinner Liam Dawson for six; Sarfraz whacked Woakes over midwicket, where he was caught one-handed by a spectator leaning over the boundary boards – earning him a trip to Australia. Dawson eventually removed both, though his two for 70 in eight overs was the most expensive analysis by an England one-day debutant. And when Bairstow ran out Mohammad Nawaz, Pakistan still needed 37. But Mohammad Rizwan and Imad Wasim, born in nearby Swansea where his father was working as an engineer, kept their cool to take Pakistan to their highest successful chase outside Asia, and only their second ODI win over England in 14 matches. Imad finished with 153 runs in the series without being dismissed. Earlier, Roy had again been in excellent touch before top-edging a pull off Mohammad Amir's clever slower-ball bouncer, while Stokes's format-best 75 ended when he scooped to short fine leg. That was one of four wickets for Hasan Ali, who ensured that England's threatening 258 for five in the 42nd over did not translate into a match-winning total. In overcast conditions favouring seam, Imad took a miserly one for 33 in ten overs with his left-arm darts; by the end of the game, Glamorgan fans were struggling to remember a better all-round performance by a Welsh-born cricketer all summer.

Man of the Match: Sarfraz Ahmed. *Attendance:* 14,197.
Man of the Series: J. E. Root.

England

J. J. Roy c Hasan Ali b Mohammad Amir	87
A. D. Hales c Shoaib Malik b Mohammad Amir	23
J. E. Root b Hasan Ali	9
*E. J. G. Morgan c and b Imad Wasim	10
B. A. Stokes c Umar Gul b Hasan Ali	75
†J. M. Bairstow c Mohammad Rizwan b Umar Gul	33
L. A. Dawson c Umar Gul b Mohammad Amir	10
C. R. Woakes b Hasan Ali	10
D. J. Willey c Mohammad Nawaz b Hasan Ali	6
C. J. Jordan not out	15
M. A. Wood not out	8
B 4, lb 6, w 5, nb 1	16
1/37 (2) 2/64 (3) 3/92 (4) 4/164 (1) 5/219 (6) 6/258 (5) 7/270 (8) 8/274 (7) 9/283 (9) (9 wkts, 50 overs)	302
10 overs: 69-2	

Mohammad Amir 10–0–50–3; Umar Gul 10–0–77–1; Hasan Ali 10–0–60–4; Shoaib Malik 6–0–40–0; Imad Wasim 10–0–33–1; Mohammad Nawaz 4–0–32–0.

Pakistan

*Azhar Ali c Bairstow b Wood	33
Sharjeel Khan c Wood b Woakes	10
Babar Azam b Wood	31
Shoaib Malik c Roy b Dawson	77
†Sarfraz Ahmed c Hales b Dawson	90
Mohammad Rizwan not out	34
Mohammad Nawaz run out	2
Imad Wasim not out	16
W 10, nb 1	11
1/22 (2) 2/76 (3) 3/77 (1) 4/240 (5) 5/256 (4) 6/266 (7) (6 wkts, 48.2 overs)	304
10 overs: 64-1	

Hasan Ali, Mohammad Amir and Umar Gul did not bat.

Woakes 7–0–47–1; Willey 8–2–32–0; Wood 10–0–56–2; Stokes 8–0–47–0; Jordan 7.2–0–52–0; Dawson 8–0–70–2.

Umpires: R. J. Bailey and S. D. Fry. Third umpire: M. Erasmus.
Referee: J. J. Crowe.

ENGLAND v PAKISTAN

NatWest Twenty20 International

At Manchester, September 7 (floodlit). Pakistan won by nine wickets. Pakistan 2pts. Toss: England. Twenty20 international debuts: Babar Azam, Hasan Ali.

With Old Trafford transformed into a sea of green and white, Pakistan rounded off their tour in style, winning with 31 balls to spare in Sarfraz Ahmed's first match as Twenty20 captain. England, fielding the XI that had lost the World Twenty20 final in April, were restricted to 135 for seven after racing to 56 without loss in the seventh over. Imad Wasim removed both openers, and Pakistan's quicks – led by Wahab Riaz – adjusted their line to get England hitting towards Old Trafford's longer, square boundaries: they managed just one four in the final ten overs, which yielded only 58 runs. Morgan later suggested the arrival of dew in the brief innings break had improved batting conditions, but England's bowling was poor. Sharjeel Khan and Khalid Latif, who put on 107 for the first wicket, shared 20 boundaries, each greeted by a joyous wall of sound in the closest thing to a home crowd many present-day Pakistan players had experienced. The mood changed slightly when a Pakistan fan evaded the stewards and ran on to the field in an attempt to get a selfie with Morgan. The match finished with England security manager Reg Dickason – whose decision to give the upcoming Bangladesh tour the go-ahead on safety grounds would not persuade Morgan or Hales to make the trip – shepherding the players off the field.

Man of the Match: Wahab Riaz. *Attendance:* 20,018.

England

		B	*4/6*
1 J. J. Roy *lbw b 7*	21	20	2/1
2 A. D. Hales *b 7*	37	26	5
3 J. E. Root *c 6 b 9*	6	9	0
4 †J. C. Buttler *c 2 b 10*	16	15	2
5 *E. J. G. Morgan *c 4 b 10*	14	16	0
6 B. A. Stokes *c 3 b 9*	4	7	0
7 M. M. Ali *not out*	13	15	0
8 D. J. Willey *c 6 b 10*	12	12	1
9 L. E. Plunkett *not out*	0	0	0
Lb 8, w 4	12		
6 overs: 53-0 (20 overs)	135-7		

1/56 2/67 3/67 4/93 5/104 6/110 7/132

10 A. U. Rashid and 11 C. J. Jordan did not bat.

Imad Wasim 4–9–17–2; Sohail Tanvir 4–9–35–0; Mohammad Amir 4–6–33–0; Hasan Ali 4–8–24–2; Wahab Riaz 4–12–18–3.

Pakistan

		B	*4/6*
1 Sharjeel Khan *c 7 b 10*	59	36	7/3
2 Khalid Latif *not out*	59	42	8/2
3 Babar Azam *not out*	15	11	2
W 6	6		
6 overs: 73-0 (14.5 overs)	139-1		

1/107

4 *†Sarfraz Ahmed, 5 Mohammad Rizwan, 6 Shoaib Malik, 7 Imad Wasim, 8 Sohail Tanvir, 9 Hasan Ali, 10 Wahab Riaz and 11 Mohammad Amir did not bat.

Willey 2–8–16–0; Jordan 1–2–16–0; Plunkett 1.5–2–24–0; Stokes 2–4–20–0; Root 1–2–10–0; Rashid 4–9–29–1; Ali 3–8–24–0.

Umpires: M. A. Gough and R. T. Robinson. Third umpire: R. J. Bailey.
Referee: J. J. Crowe.

BANGLADESH v ENGLAND IN 2016-17

REVIEW BY WILL MACPHERSON

One-day internationals (3): Bangladesh 1, England 2
Test matches (2): Bangladesh 1, England 1

Throughout England's 34-day stay, Bangladesh sent two emphatic messages to the world. First, that the country was open for business, three months after an attack on an upmarket Dhaka cafe in which 29 died, including 20 hostages – many of them Westerners. Eoin Morgan and Alex Hales subsequently pulled out of the trip, citing safety worries, but the Bangladeshi government and cricket board, as well as the ECB's security adviser – the hard-nosed former Melbourne cop Reg Dickason – arranged protection normally reserved for visiting heads of state. Happily, the tour passed without a snag.

The other message, eloquently expressed on the pitch, was that Bangladesh had genuinely arrived as an international force. When debutant off-spinner Mehedi Hasan, who turned 19 between the two Tests, trapped Steven Finn in Mirpur to complete an England collapse of ten for 64, the Shere-Bangla Stadium erupted. Bangladesh's players ran wild, the stands – rowdy, rather

Philip Brown, Getty Images

Miss and hit: Eoin Morgan, the one-day captain, stayed away, but England endeared themselves to Bangladeshi spectators simply by being there.

than rammed – went berserk, local residents strained for a view from rooftops, and armed guards downed their weapons to dance.

After 16 years and 95 Tests, Bangladesh had claimed their greatest win – their eighth in all, but their first over opposition other than Zimbabwe or Floyd Reifer's weakened West Indians of 2009. They had played to their strengths, which were growing by the day – and dovetailed perfectly with England's glaring flaws. Given the narrowness of the Bangladeshis' defeat in the First Test at Chittagong, it could easily have been 2–0.

The contrast with England's previous tour, in early 2010, could not have been starker. Then, Andrew Strauss had rested up for sterner challenges, handing Alastair Cook his first crack at the captaincy, while the two Tests were played on the flattest of tracks. England won both. Bangladesh went into this series without a Test for 15 months but, unlike six years earlier, their ambition was brazen, their plan clear. As the captain, Mushfiqur Rahim, said after the Second Test: "We planned to make wickets that last three to four days. They would help our spinners and trouble the English batsmen." Cook was magnanimous: "They decided they wanted to be brave and try to win – and why wouldn't you?"

Both pitches turned extravagantly, but were not identical. In Chittagong, on a surface drier than the England players had ever seen, the hosts picked two seamers and a smorgasbord of spinners, and it turned from the word go. Thanks to a remarkable all-round effort from Ben Stokes, England left with a stomach-tightening 22-run win. In Mirpur, the pitch was darker and damper, but again produced English jitters. Bangladesh left out a medium-pacer and squeezed in another spinner; their one seamer, Kamrul Islam, sent down 18 balls and scored seven runs. In effect, Bangladesh levelled the series with ten men.

They looked a less brittle side than those England had faced before. At the 2015 World Cup (before they knocked England out in Adelaide), Chandika Hathurusinghe, their tough Sri Lankan coach, had been shocked to see his team celebrating victory over Afghanistan as if they had won the tournament, and handed out a rollicking. In 20 months, he had guided them to a bigger cause for celebration. If, like England, they suffered maddening collapses – nine for 49 and six for 58 in the Second Test alone – they dusted off the disappointment of Chittagong, and created history.

Bangladesh's lack of Test cricket created some startling discrepancies. Before the First Test, where Cook became England's most capped player, Mushfiqur observed: "He debuted after me and he's playing his 134th Test. I've got 48!" Cook had even led England in more Tests than Mushfiqur had played, yet Mushfiqur was the most capped player in his squad. Still, this represented perhaps the most promising side in the captain's 11-year career. Mehedi was one of three debutants, while another, Sabbir Rahman, looked to the manner born, relishing his duel with Stokes in Mirpur.

The emergence of Mehedi, who bowled with no great frills or variation in taking 19 wickets, the most by a Bangladeshi in a Test series, was thrilling, while Tamim Iqbal, the senior pro, challenged him for the series award. The Mirpur win was underpinned by his third century against England (and the

Gareth Copley, Getty Images

Horses for courses: Gareth Batty, Moeen Ali and Adil Rashid – England's spinners for the First Test.

only one of the series), while he took over in the field during the series-ending capitulation, even with Mushfiqur still out there. The other key players were Mehedi's fellow twirlers: left-arm spinners Shakib Al Hasan, though hare-brained with the bat, and Taijul Islam.

Bangladesh's victory was cheered with added vigour, given that the tour might not have happened at all. Following the cafe attack on July 1, Bangladesh looked set to follow Pakistan into nomadism. Australia had already withdrawn from a scheduled visit in 2015, and refused to send a side to the Under-19 World Cup four months later. But Dickason and David Leatherdale, the PCA chief executive, travelled to Bangladesh in August, and declared it safe to tour.

Despite that, Morgan, the white-ball captain, and opener Hales – who would have been dropped from the Test side anyway – could not be persuaded, which cast a shadow over the build-up. Some journalists and supporters seemed to equate their withdrawal with treason; as a leader (or perhaps as an Irishman) Morgan attracted particular vitriol. England's management made it clear they respected personal choice, while expressing their disappointment, but the players backed their comrades. The Barmy Army, less certain about safety, also stayed at home, though a hardy band of around 30 fans watched the Tests.

The threat of terror in Bangladesh was real enough for expats to leave home only for work. Dickason's approach was to "take a driver on a par three"– he was taking no chances. In Dhaka, 2,000 security personnel were involved in the convoy transporting the touring party from hotel to ground, while a 1km blockade was enforced around the stadium, covered for the first time by CCTV.

Players, officials and media were treated like royalty, but the constant presence of police, soldiers, rifles and even an armoured tank created a unique environment. "Even for those of us who have been around for a while, it's been quite a daunting trip," said England's assistant coach Paul Farbrace, who like coach Trevor Bayliss had been in the Sri Lankan team bus attacked by terrorists in Lahore in 2009. Still, the closest thing to a security breach came when three old ladies on a tuk-tuk slipped into the convoy en route to the one-day warm-up at Fatullah. By the end of the tour, Dickason had become an unlikely Bangladeshi hero.

Both Tests gave England plenty to ponder as they left for India. They struggled to bat against spin, and struggled to bowl it. Cook was left to admit – bluntly but not unfairly – that he had no world-class slow bowler at his disposal. The closest was the ever-evolving Moeen Ali, who bowled with pace,

MOST WICKETS AFTER TWO TESTS

24	N. D. Hirwani	India v West Indies and New Zealand	1987-88 and 1988-89
22	A. V. Bedser	England v India	1946
21	R. A. L. Massie	Australia v England	1972
19	S. F. Barnes	England v Australia	1901-02
19	**Mehedi Hasan**	**Bangladesh v England**	**2016-17**
18	J. J. Ferris	Australia v England	1886-87
18	C. V. Grimmett	Australia v England	1924-25 and 1925-26
18	A. L. Valentine	West Indies v England	1950
18	B. A. W. Mendis	Sri Lanka v India	2008

turn and drift, especially from around the wicket to Bangladesh's left-handers. Yet there were still too many poor deliveries, and Ali's modesty summed up England's travails. After picking up only his second Test five-for, in Mirpur, he ascribed his wickets to luck. "I'm nowhere near where I want to be as a spinner," he said. "I don't really have much success."

The Surrey pair of Gareth Batty and Zafar Ansari played a Test each. Batty's, in Chittagong, was his first in 11 years and, while he bowled with trademark fervour, he looked unlikely to run through Bangladesh. For Mirpur, Ansari came in, so he would not be uncapped if required in India; he struggled on the first morning, then improved. Meanwhile, the summer's two most successful English spinners, Jack Leach of Somerset and Middlesex's Ollie Rayner, wintered with the Lions.

However, Cook's quest to make a silk purse out of a sow's ear was hampered by some peculiarly defensive fields. The captain betrayed his mistrust of Adil Rashid by ignoring his leg-spin for much of the vital third morning in Mirpur; when he eventually bowled, he burgled four wickets, though he never offered control. The reverse swing of Stokes, the man of the tour, and Broad masked the spinners' shortcomings in Chittagong, but an absurd schedule of seven Tests in 62 days meant Broad was rested for Mirpur, with 99 caps to his name. In a topsy-turvy series in which the slow bowlers opened the attack to take the shine off the new ball, allowing the quicker ones to exploit reverse swing, it was to seam, not spin, that Cook turned.

FIVE STATS YOU MAY HAVE MISSED

BENEDICT BERMANGE

- The First Test at Chittagong was the first since Edgbaston 1992 – and the 23rd in all – that England had fielded a team of 11 first-class centurions.

- Mehedi Hasan became the fourth-youngest bowler to take at least five wickets in an innings on Test debut:

Yrs	*Days*			
18	196	P. J. Cummins (6-79)	Australia v South Africa at Johannesburg	2011-12
18	236	Shahid Afridi (5-52)	Pakistan v Australia at Karachi	1998-99
18	319	Shahid Nazir (5-53)	Pakistan v Zimbabwe at Sheikhupura	1996-97
18	**361**	**Mehedi Hasan (6-80)**	**Bangladesh v England at Chittagong**	**2016-17**
19	88	N. D. Hirwani (8-61, 8-75)	India v West Indies at Madras	1987-88

- At Chittagong, Gareth Batty took his first Test wicket for more than 11 years, the sixth-longest such gap for England:

Yrs	*Days*		*From*	*To*
15	194	L. Hutton	1939	1954-55
12	84	W. E. Hollies	1934-35	1947
11	364	F. R. Brown	1937	1949
11	345	H. L. Jackson	1949	1961
11	230	D. Shackleton	1951-52	1963
11	**139**	**G. J. Batty**	**2005**	**2016-17**
11	35	K. W. R. Fletcher	1970-71	1981-82
11	15	G. O. B. Allen	1936-37	1947-48
10	14	M. P. Bicknell	1993	2003

- The Mirpur Test provided only the second instance of a team gaining a first-innings lead after losing their eighth wicket at a lower total than the team batting first had lost their second. At Bombay in 1960-61, Pakistan went from 301 for one to 350 all out, before India recovered from 300 for eight to reach 449 for nine declared.

- England's ten-wicket collapse at Mirpur was their worst. Only one lower Test total had been recorded by a side reaching 100 before losing a wicket.

Runs	*From*	*To*		
46	124-0	170	India v England at Manchester	1946
51	107-0	158	New Zealand v Australia at Auckland	1973-74
64	**100-0**	**164**	**England v Bangladesh at Mirpur**	**2016-17**
73	135-0	208	Pakistan v New Zealand at Christchurch	1995-96
75	106-0	181	New Zealand v India at Hyderabad	1969-70
83	153-0	236	Zimbabwe v Sri Lanka at Galle	2001-02
85	121-0	206	India v Australia at Delhi	1959-60
86	**158-0**	**244**	**Australia v South Africa at Perth**	**2016-17**
88	101-0	189	England v Sri Lanka at Galle	2000-01
89	276-0	365	West Indies v New Zealand at Hamilton	1999-2000

The batting was just as shaky. Conditions were unrelenting, and especially alien for those at the top of the order: Cook admitted they were the toughest he had known. Having dashed back to Chittagong following the birth of his second daughter, he was partnered by Ben Duckett, rather than another greenhorn, Haseeb Hameed; Duckett looked out of his depth before throwing off the shackles in his final innings. Gary Ballance suffered most, managing just 24 runs, and was dropped in India. England had no tail, but five left-handers in their top six, and their dependence on a middle-order raft of all-rounders was exposed in Mirpur, where Ali, Stokes and Jonny Bairstow all failed. Only Chris Woakes averaged more than 32, and no one passed 50 more than once.

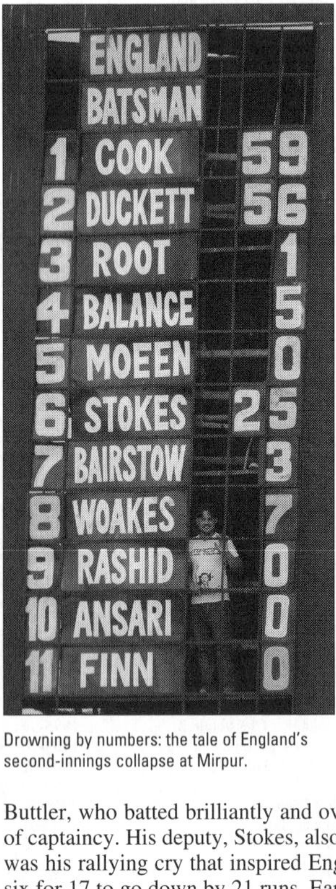

ENGLAND
BATSMAN
1 COOK 59
2 DUCKETT 56
3 ROOT 1
4 BALANCE 5
5 MOEEN 0
6 STOKES 25
7 BAIRSTOW 3
8 WOAKES 7
9 RASHID 0
10 ANSARI 0
11 FINN 0

Philip Brown, Getty Images

Drowning by numbers: the tale of England's second-innings collapse at Mirpur.

Also a mess was the umpiring. The surfaces, inept batting, and new DRS regulations – that required the ball to hit less of the stumps to be given out on review – combined to produce a record 26 reviews in the First Test alone. Kumar Dharmasena had a particularly difficult series: 27 of his decisions during the Tests were challenged, and 13 overturned.

The Tests followed three magnificent one-day games. Bangladesh had won their previous six 50-over series at home, but threw away a strong position in the opening match – before England did the same in the second, when tempers flared. Jos Buttler, their captain in Morgan's stead, was furious to receive a send-off, before Stokes clashed with Tamim, who had barged Bairstow and ranted at Jason Roy. The sanctions – fines for Bangladesh captain Mashrafe bin Mortaza and his team-mate Sabbir, but only a reprimand for Buttler – and Tamim's end-of-series apology to Roy were instructive. By the time the teams shared a charter flight to Chittagong, where England won the decider, the ruckus had calmed.

"What we have achieved here should not be underestimated," said Buttler, who batted brilliantly and overcame his struggles with the extra duty of captaincy. His deputy, Stokes, also revelled in his new responsibility, and it was his rallying cry that inspired England's opening victory: Bangladesh lost six for 17 to go down by 21 runs. Earlier in the day, he had scored his maiden one-day international century, proof of his improvement against spin.

Buttler was right. With Roy injured, Root rested, and Hales and Morgan absent, England won the third game without any of their first-choice top four. While Farbrace said the absentees would return in India, he suggested it was "probably even a good thing that some didn't come". England learned plenty: Buttler and Stokes were long-term leaders, while Duckett and Sam Billings thrived with the bat. Jake Ball became the first Englishman to take a five-for on ODI debut, and Rashid's ten wickets were the joint-most by a spinner in a three-match one-day series.

As Buttler collected the trophy, a crowd of Bangladesh fans – so partisan during the game – stayed back to chant "England, thank you". That was the motif of a remarkable tour, during which the depth of gratitude was as heart-warming as the cricket.

ENGLAND TOURING PARTY

*A. N. Cook (Essex; T), M. M. Ali (Worcestershire; T/50), Z. S. Ansari (Surrey; T), J. M. Bairstow (Yorkshire; T/50), J. T. Ball (Nottinghamshire; T/50), G. S. Ballance (Yorkshire; T), G. J. Batty (Surrey; T), S. W. Billings (Kent; 50), S. C. J. Broad (Nottinghamshire; T), J. C. Buttler (Lancashire; T/50), L. A. Dawson (Hampshire; 50), B. M. Duckett (Northamptonshire; T/50), S. T. Finn (Middlesex; T/50), H. Hameed (Lancashire; T), L. E. Plunkett (Yorkshire; 50), A. U. Rashid (Yorkshire; T/50), J. E. Root (Yorkshire; T), J. J. Roy (Surrey; 50), B. A. Stokes (Durham; T/50), J. M. Vince (Hampshire; 50), D. J. Willey (Yorkshire; 50), C. R. Woakes (Warwickshire; T/50).

Buttler captained in the one-day internationals. M. A. Wood (Durham) was originally named in both squads, and J. M. Anderson (Lancashire) for the Tests, but both withdrew unfit; Finn was added to the one-day squad and Ball the Test squad.

Coach: T. H. Bayliss (T/50). *Assistant coach:* P. Farbrace (50), O. D. Gibson (T). *Batting coach:* P. D. Collingwood (50), M. R. Ramprakash (T). *Specialist coach:* A. Hurry (50), S. J. Rhodes (T). *Strength and conditioning coach:* P. C. F. Scott (T/50). *Operations manager:* P. A. Neale (T/50). *Doctor:* G. Bhogal (T/50). *Physiotherapist:* C. A. de Weymarn (T/50). *Masseur:* M. E. S. Saxby (T/50). *Security manager:* R. C. Dickason (T/50). *Assistant security manager:* T. Minish (T/50). *Analyst:* G. Lindsay (T/50). *Head of team communications:* D. Reuben (T/50).

At Fatullah, October 4, 2016. **England XI won by four wickets.** ‡**Bangladesh Cricket Board Select XI 309-9** (50 overs) (Imrul Kayes 121, Mushfiqur Rahim 51; C. R. Woakes 3-52); **England XI 313-6** (46.1 overs) (J. C. Buttler 80*, M. M. Ali 70). *England looked in a spot of bother when Ben Stokes fell in the 29th over of the chase, making it 170-5. But skipper Jos Buttler, who hit four sixes (but only three fours), put on 139 with Moeen Ali in 17 overs to ensure victory. Earlier, Imrul Kayes's rapid 121 – he hit six sixes from 91 balls – propelled the BCB XI towards 300. Test captain Mushfiqur Rahim chipped in with 51, and Nasir Hossain a sprightly 46. Jason Roy (28 from 22 balls) and James Vince (48 from 39) gave England's reply a lively start with an opening stand of 72 in 8.4 overs.*

ONE-DAY INTERNATIONAL REPORTS BY WILL MACPHERSON

BANGLADESH v ENGLAND

First One-Day International

At Mirpur, October 7, 2016 (day/night). England won by 21 runs. Toss: England. One-day international debuts: J. T. Ball, B. M. Duckett.

The cricket had been a long time coming, but it was worth the wait. Poised for their third straight one-day win over England, spread across more than five years, Bangladesh contrived to lose their last six for 17 – three to Jake Ball, who returned the best figures on one-day international debut for England. Victory was built on the belligerence of Stokes, who – five years after his first appearance in the format – scored a dazzling maiden century, and Duckett, another debutant, who made a patient but innovative 60. After their fourth-wicket stand of 153, Buttler kicked on in his first ODI as captain, pilfering 63 from 38 balls; like Stokes, he hit four sixes. England's 309 for eight was their highest

BEST FIGURES ON ONE-DAY DEBUT FOR ENGLAND

5-51	**J. T. Ball**	**v Bangladesh at Mirpur**	**2016-17**
4-23	A. J. Hollioake	v Pakistan at Birmingham	1996
4-32	C. T. Tremlett	v Bangladesh at Nottingham	2005
4-33	G. B. Stevenson	v Australia at Sydney	1979-80
4-44	P. J. Martin	v West Indies at The Oval	1995
4-45	M. V. Fleming	v India at Sharjah	1997-98
4-46	†W. B. Rankin	v Ireland at Malahide	2013
4-67	D. V. Lawrence	v West Indies at Lord's	1991

† *Rankin had already played 37 one-day internationals for Ireland.*

score in Bangladesh, who needed to pull off their biggest second innings on this ground to win. For 41 overs, they were cruising. Imrul Kayes made his second century against the tourists in four days, while Shakib Al Hasan was in scintillating touch. At 271 for four, Bangladesh needed 39 from 52 balls. But Stokes, vice-captain and talisman, gathered England together for a pep talk. Ball immediately dismissed Shakib, caught at midwicket for 79 from 55 deliveries, and Mosaddek Hossain, who chopped on for a golden duck. Rashid ripped a leg-break at Mashrafe bin Mortaza, who edged behind, then saw the elegant Kayes coming, and sent it wide of off stump. Buttler pulled off a sharp stumping, and Rashid finished with a career-best four for 49. Appropriately, it was Rashid – with a direct hit from mid-off to account for Shafiul Islam – and Ball who together completed the heist. A crowd of 25,000, so loud for so long, had been silenced.

Man of the Match: J. T. Ball.

England

J. J. Roy c Sabbir Rahman b Shakib Al Hasan	41
J. M. Vince c Mashrafe bin Mortaza b Shafiul Islam	16
B. M. Duckett b Shafiul Islam	60
J. M. Bairstow run out	0
B. A. Stokes c Sabbir Rahman b Mashrafe bin Mortaza	101
*†J. C. Buttler c Mosaddek Hossain b Shakib Al Hasan	63
M. M. Ali c Tamim Iqbal b Mashrafe bin Mortaza	6
C. R. Woakes run out	16
D. J. Willey not out	0
B 1, lb 3, w 2	6
1/41 (2) 2/61 (1) 3/63 (4) 4/216 (3) 5/230 (5) 6/245 (7) 7/308 (6) 8/309 (8) (8 wkts, 50 overs)	309
10 overs: 53-1	

A. U. Rashid and J. T. Ball did not bat.

Mashrafe bin Mortaza 10–0–52–2; Shafiul Islam 9–0–59–2; Shakib Al Hasan 10–0–59–2; Mosaddek Hossain 9–0–50–0; Mahmudullah 3–0–24–0; Mosharraf Hossain 3–0–23–0; Taskin Ahmed 6–0–38–0.

Bangladesh

Tamim Iqbal c Vince b Ball	17
Imrul Kayes st Buttler b Rashid	112
Sabbir Rahman c Willey b Ball	18
Mahmudullah c sub (S. W. Billings) b Rashid	25
†Mushfiqur Rahim c sub (S. W. Billings) b Rashid	12
Shakib Al Hasan c Willey b Ball	79
Mosaddek Hossain b Ball	0
*Mashrafe bin Mortaza c Buttler b Rashid	1
Mosharraf Hossain not out	7
Shafiul Islam run out	0
Taskin Ahmed c Buttler b Ball	1
B 1, lb 4, w 10, nb 1	16
1/46 (1) 2/82 (3) 3/132 (4) 4/153 (5) 5/271 (6) 6/271 (7) 7/274 (8) 8/280 (2) 9/280 (10) 10/288 (11) (47.5 overs)	288
10 overs: 50-1	

Woakes 7–1–38–0; Willey 7–1–46–0; Ball 9.5–0–51–5; Stokes 5–0–37–0; Rashid 9–0–49–4; Ali 10–0–62–0.

Umpires: M. Erasmus and Sharfuddoula. Third umpire: Aleem Dar.
Referee: J. Srinath.

BANGLADESH v ENGLAND

Second One-Day International

At Mirpur, October 9, 2016 (day/night). Bangladesh won by 34 runs. Toss: England.

The teams served up another thrilling game – but with extra spice. Having this time chosen to bowl, and with England chasing 239, Buttler found himself sifting through the rubble of 26 for four, following an inspired burst from Mashrafe bin Mortaza. He played a superb hand, pulling with control, until Taskin Ahmed – who had already disposed of Bairstow – rapped him on the pads. The umpire said no, but the review proved successful. Mortaza and Sabbir Rahman irked Buttler by giving him a mighty mouthful, for which they lost 20% of their match fees; Buttler himself was reprimanded for turning round to confront the fielders. "There is no need to run in someone's face and celebrate," he said. England's tail wagged, before Mortaza had Ball caught on the slog to finish with four for 29. Earlier, the efforts of England's bowlers ought to have been enough to clinch the series. After Woakes bounced out the openers, Mahmudullah held things together, before Mortaza produced the first of his match-turning contributions, adding 69 for the eighth wicket in 49 balls with Nasir Hossain, and later admitting: "I just slogged, man!" There was another flare-up after Bangladesh had sealed victory – their fourth in six one-day internationals against England, after losing the first 12. Stokes was furious with Tamim Iqbal over a verbal volley at Roy, and what he perceived to be a cursory handshake with Bairstow. The tour headed for Chittagong, bitter but beautifully balanced.

Man of the Match: Mashrafe bin Mortaza.

Bangladesh

Tamim Iqbal c Ali b Woakes	14
Imrul Kayes c Willey b Woakes	11
Sabbir Rahman b Ball	3
Mahmudullah lbw b Rashid	75
†Mushfiqur Rahim c Ali b Ball	21
Shakib Al Hasan c Buttler b Stokes	3
Mosaddek Hossain c Ali b Rashid	29
Nasir Hossain not out	27
*Mashrafe bin Mortaza run out	44
Shafiul Islam not out	0
Lb 4, w 6, nb 1	11
1/25 (2) 2/26 (1) 3/39 (3) 4/89 (5) 5/113 (6) 6/161 (4) 7/169 (7) 8/238 (9) (8 wkts, 50 overs)	238
10 overs: 30-2	

Taskin Ahmed did not bat.

Woakes 9–0–40–2; Willey 8–1–36–0; Rashid 10–0–53–2; Ball 8–0–44–2; Stokes 6–1–22–1; Ali 9–0–39–0.

England

J. J. Roy lbw b Mashrafe bin Mortaza	13
J. M. Vince c Mosaddek Hossain b Mashrafe bin Mortaza	5
B. M. Duckett b Shakib Al Hasan	0
J. M. Bairstow c Mushfiqur Rahim b Taskin Ahmed	35
B. A. Stokes b Mashrafe bin Mortaza	0
*†J. C. Buttler lbw b Taskin Ahmed	57
M. M. Ali c Shakib Al Hasan b Nasir Hossain	4
C. R. Woakes c Mushfiqur Rahim b Taskin Ahmed	7
A. U. Rashid not out	33
D. J. Willey lbw b Mosaddek Hossain	9
J. T. Ball c Nasir Hossain b Mashrafe bin Mortaza	28
Lb 7, w 6	13
1/12 (2) 2/14 (3) 3/24 (1) 4/26 (5) 5/105 (4) 6/120 (7) 7/123 (6) 8/132 (8) 9/159 (10) 10/204 (11) (44.4 overs)	204
10 overs: 31-4	

Shakib Al Hasan 9–0–50–1; Mashrafe bin Mortaza 8.4–0–29–4; Shafiul Islam 8–0–37–0; Taskin Ahmed 8–0–47–3; Nasir Hossain 10–1–29–1; Mosaddek Hossain 1–0–5–1.

Umpires: Aleem Dar and Sharfuddoula. Third umpire: M. Erasmus.
Referee: J. Srinath.

BANGLADESH v ENGLAND

Third One-Day International

At Chittagong, October 12, 2016 (day/night). England won by four wickets. Toss: England.

Heavy rain during the build-up threatened to deny an engrossing series its fitting finale, but the clouds – and the stormy relationship between the sides – passed as England clinched a 2–1 win. No side had successfully chased more than 226 on this ground, but they were home with 13 balls to spare. Already without Alex Hales, Eoin Morgan and the rested Joe Root, England had lost Jason Roy to a quad complaint on the morning of the game. Billings seized his chance at the top of the order, putting on 63 with Vince – whom he would have replaced had Roy been fit – then 64 with Duckett, who made his second sixty of the series. Having already swept Mashrafe bin Mortaza into the stands, Billings attempted a repeat, but top-edged to deep square leg. Bairstow and Duckett fell in quick succession to Shafiul Islam, then Ali followed Buttler to leave England 236 for six. But Stokes was playing maturely, and added a rapid unbroken 42 with Woakes, who was dropped at slip by Imrul Kayes with 21 still needed, but completed the job with a straight six. Earlier, Bangladesh had raided 85 from their final 71 balls having teetered at 192 for six. Rashid took another career-best four-for (two with long hops, one with a full toss) and lifted his series haul to ten. The seamers, with the fit-again Plunkett replacing David Willey, had been largely impotent, until the introduction of Stokes, who persuaded Kayes to clip to midwicket. Buttler fortuitously stumped Shakib Al Hasan off Ali as the ball ricocheted off his gloves. And, for all the intelligence and dynamism of Mushfiqur Rahim and Mosaddek Hossain, Bangladesh did not have quite enough to extend their string of home one-day series wins to seven.

Man of the Match: A. U. Rashid. *Man of the Series:* B. A. Stokes.

Bangladesh

Tamim Iqbal c Vince b Rashid	45
Imrul Kayes c sub (L. A. Dawson) b Stokes	46
Sabbir Rahman c Buttler b Rashid	49
Mahmudullah c Bairstow b Rashid	6
†Mushfiqur Rahim not out	67
Shakib Al Hasan st Buttler b Ali	4
Nasir Hossain c Vince b Rashid	4
Mosaddek Hossain not out	38
B 4, lb 3, w 11	18
1/80 (2) 2/106 (1) 3/122 (4) 4/176 (3) 5/184 (6) 6/192 (7) (6 wkts, 50 overs)	277
10 overs: 42-0	

*Mashrafe bin Mortaza, Shafiul Islam and Taskin Ahmed did not bat.

Woakes 8–0–66–0; Ball 8–0–44–0; Plunkett 9–0–51–0; Ali 10–0–42–1; Stokes 5–0–24–1; Rashid 10–0–43–4.

England

J. M. Vince lbw b Nasir Hossain	32
S. W. Billings c Imrul Kayes b Mosaddek Hossain	62
B. M. Duckett c Mushfiqur Rahim b Shafiul Islam	63
J. M. Bairstow b Shafiul Islam	15
B. A. Stokes not out	47
*†J. C. Buttler b Mashrafe bin Mortaza	25
M. M. Ali c Mahmudullah b Mashrafe bin Mortaza	1
C. R. Woakes not out	27
W 6	6
1/63 (1) 2/127 (2) 3/172 (4) 4/179 (3) 5/227 (6) 6/236 (7) (6 wkts, 47.5 overs)	278
10 overs: 49-0	

L. E. Plunkett, A. U. Rashid and J. T. Ball did not bat.

Mashrafe bin Mortaza 10–1–51–2; Shafiul Islam 9.5–0–61–2; Shakib Al Hasan 8–0–45–0; Taskin Ahmed 9–0–46–0; Nasir Hossain 7–0–53–1; Mosaddek Hossain 4–0–22–1.

Umpires: Anisur Rahman and M. Erasmus. Third umpire: Aleem Dar.
Referee: J. Srinath.

At Chittagong (M. A. Aziz), October 14–15, 2016. **Drawn.** ‡**England XI 137-4 dec** (45 overs) (B. M. Duckett 59; Sabbir Rahman 3-27); **Bangladesh Cricket Board XI 136-4** (44 overs) (Shahriar Nafees 51). *England's Test preparations were hamstrung by the loss of the first day to rain. There was time on the second for Ben Duckett to stake a claim for a place with 59 in 63 balls before retiring out; his opening partner, Haseeb Hameed, made 16 from 56. The teams chose from 12 players.*

At Chittagong (M. A. Aziz), October 16–17, 2016. **Drawn.** ‡**Bangladesh Cricket Board XI 294** (74.4 overs) (Abdul Mazid 106, Nazmul Hossain 72; Z. S. Ansari 4-68); **England XI 256** (78.2 overs) (H. Hameed 57, B. M. Duckett 60; Tanveer Haider 4-53). *Both teams chose from 14 players. The BCB XI's opener Abdul Mazid made 92* before lunch on the first day before retiring hurt; he resumed later and completed a 90-ball century. Nazmul Hossain was more cautious, as the middle order struggled against Surrey's spin twins: although Zafar Ansari took four wickets to Gareth Batty's two, it was Batty who lined up in the First Test. England started brightly with an opening stand of 90 in 27 overs, before Duckett retired out; Hameed ploughed on, batting for 262 minutes before also retiring.*

BANGLADESH v ENGLAND

First Test Match

SIMON WILDE

At Chittagong, October 20–24, 2016. England won by 22 runs. Toss: England. Test debuts: Kamrul Islam, Mehedi Hasan, Sabbir Rahman; B. M. Duckett.

This taut contest was unrecognisable from the eight previous Tests between the sides, all comprehensive England wins. At 21 for three on the first morning, they knew they were in a tussle, and during the course of four days and 21 balls there remained little to separate the teams. The final margin was England's closest win by runs outside the Ashes, and Bangladesh's narrowest defeat – and the difference was made by England's all-rounders.

Stokes was sound in defence, measured in his aggression, and tireless and skilful with the old ball. This was his best Test to date, with 103 runs and six wickets on a pitch whose sharp turn meant ten different spinners had a bowl. It was he who landed the two knockout blows on the final morning. Moeen Ali, surviving a record five lbw reviews – including

Philip Brown, Getty Images

Hands up! Ben Stokes's aggression helped England edge home.

three in six balls against Shakib Al Hasan either side of lunch on the first day – hit his best score in overseas Tests, and spun the ball at pace to take five wickets. And Bairstow made runs in both innings, becoming the first to pass 1,000 in Tests in 2016, and overtaking Andy Flower's record for most in a calendar year by a wicketkeeper; in demanding conditions, he made only one clear mistake behind the stumps.

English escapology was a constant theme. Bairstow's stands of 88 with Ali in the first innings (from 106 for five), and 127 with Stokes in the second (from 62 for five), were England's best of the match. By extending to seven the number of successive fifty partnerships for their sixth wicket, England set a Test record. Showing genuine belief, Bangladesh faltered only after tea on the fourth day, when they were 179 for five, needing another 107. Cook belatedly turned to his seamers to dry up the runs and test the patience of opponents unused to victory.

Two debutants had given them unexpected edge. Mehedi Hasan, unfazed by being his captain's go-to bowler in the week before his 19th birthday, proved an off-spinner of accuracy and nerve, while Sabbir Rahman kept alive hopes of a famous upset with a courageous and composed 64 not out; if Sabbir erred, it was in agreeing to a single off the last ball of the third over on the final morning, leaving No. 10 Taijul Islam to face Stokes. Within three deliveries, he removed both Taijul and Shafiul Islam leg-before. Both went to review: England challenged the not-out verdict against Taijul on the basis that he had gone across his stumps; replays showed the ball hitting leg. It transpired that Taijul would have been not out under DRS as it was before September 22, when the required target area on the stumps was smaller. The second struck Shafiul outside the line, but his bat was behind his leg and he was not obviously playing a shot. Bangladesh challenged in vain.

It was fitting that the denouement involved DRS and umpire Dharmasena. The game had spawned a record 26 reviews, 16 at Dharmasena's end, of which eight – another record – were overturned. And the ten reviews in England's first innings broke the old mark of eight. Chris Gaffaney had ten decisions challenged and three overturned. Both umpires deserved sympathy. With the pitch providing unpredictable degrees of turn, and spinners operating with new ball and old, they found their judgment as sorely tested as the batsmen.

England played three spinners, one of them the 39-year-old Gareth Batty, recalled after a world record absence of 142 Tests – passing the 114 of Martin Bicknell, another Surrey man. He found himself opening the bowling in both innings, the first England slow bowler to do so since Sam Staples in 1927-28 on the Durban matting. Here, the trio ended with 12 wickets, but gave their captain headaches setting fields to bowling of variable length, as an economy-rate of 3.5 betrayed. They compared unfavourably with Bangladesh's three frontline spinners, who claimed 18 wickets and went for 2.3.

In opting to go with Ben Duckett as Cook's latest opening partner, England resisted the temptation to make Haseeb Hameed their sixth teenage Test cricketer in 139 years, highlighting a cultural difference with Bangladesh, for whom Mehedi was their 26th in 16 years as a Test nation. Cook, meanwhile, was playing his 134th Test, putting him clear of Alec Stewart as England's most capped cricketer, and started by winning the toss.

The first day introduced England to the particular nature of this Test tour, as a game of unusually fine margins unfolded, even if the loss of early wickets followed by a recovery

---

SLEEPLESS NIGHTS...

Tests in which the last day started with the batting side needing fewer than 40 runs and the bowling side fewer than three wickets:

England 348-8 (needing 375) lost to Australia by 11 runs at Adelaide	1924-25
Australia 255-9 (needing 292) lost to England by three runs at Melbourne.	1982-83
South Africa 185-8 (needing 219) lost to England by 23 runs at Leeds.	1998
Bangladesh 253-8 (needing 286) lost to England by 22 runs at Chittagong	**2016-17**

Philip Brown, Getty Images

Comfort zone: Joe Root consoles Sabbir Rahman after Bangladesh lose by 22 runs.

conformed to a familiar pattern. Duckett showed glimpses of positivity before he was bowled trying to stay leg side of the ball; Cook was also bowled, tangled up in a sweep; and Ballance fell lbw when Mehedi called for a review, detecting that ball had struck pad fractionally before bat.

Ali, focusing on covering off stump and sweeping prodigiously, tightrope-walked his way through three and a half hours for 68, though only Root's persuasions convinced him to ask for two reviews in the first over after lunch. But there was no saving Root himself moments later, when he edged to slip via the keeper's leg. Although Shakib breached Stokes's defence, and Ali was eventually caught behind by one that left him, life was obviously easier once the ball grew soft, and it took the arrival of the second new ball for Bairstow to be undone by a skidding delivery. That wicket made the hard-worked Mehedi the first spinner to claim five on his first day of Test cricket since slow left-armer Alf Valentine took eight for West Indies at Manchester in 1950.

England's last three fell cheaply on the second morning, but a total of 293 looked useful. However, Bangladesh responded strongly thanks to Tamim Iqbal, who held firm for 78, despite losing two fellow left-handers to Ali shortly before lunch. Rashid accounted for Mahmudullah, and Batty for Tamim, but England's spinners failed to repay Cook's faith. Not until the 67th and 68th overs did he use seam from both ends, and Stokes's leg-cutters soon had an impact: he removed Mushfiqur Rahim for an impish 48, a strike that seemed all the more telling next morning when Bangladesh's last five tumbled for 27, starting with Shakib's rash charge at Ali's second delivery. Stokes clattered Sabbir on the helmet – sending him to hospital for observation – and produced an impressive spell of 10–5–10–4, spread over two days.

It did not take long for England to surrender momentum, or for Shakib to make amends, as Cook, Root and Duckett departed in the space of 20 balls, Root wasting a review as he did so. It was only after the loss of both Ballance, who fell at leg slip, to a smart catch by Imrul Kayes, and Ali that England found two batsmen – Stokes and Bairstow – able to pick off the bad balls. Both were gone by stumps, along with Rashid,

ALL FOUR INNINGS ALL OUT FOR 200–299 IN A TEST

Australia (280 and 277) beat South Africa (221 and 240) by 96 runs at Brisbane	1952-53
South Africa (269 and 289) beat England (240 and 224) by 94 runs at Nottingham	1965
England (284 and 294) beat Australia (287 and 288) by three runs at Melbourne	1982-83
Pakistan (259 and 226) beat South Africa (231 and 225) by 29 runs at Durban	1997-98
Pakistan (238 and 286) beat India (254 and 258) by 12 runs at Chennai	1998-99
New Zealand (275 and 272) beat West Indies (257 and 263) by 27 runs at Auckland	2005-06
England (293 and 240) beat Bangladesh (248 and 263) by 22 runs at Chittagong	**2016-17**

but their three-figure stand, on a day on which 13 wickets fell for 255 (five to Shakib) felt match-shaping.

If Bangladesh were discouraged, they did not let on. England could add only 12 for their last two wickets on the fourth morning, as the hosts claimed all 20 for the first time against a side other than Zimbabwe or West Indies. It left them needing 286, and Kayes seemed in an impudent hurry to knock them off. As Bangladesh rattled along, Cook's faith in spin again appeared misplaced, but by tea Ali, Rashid and Batty had five wickets between them. There followed a tense passage as England switched to seam, hoping Bangladeshi nerves would crack. But when Broad created an opportunity against Sabbir, Bairstow spilled a leg-side offering. Finally, Batty produced a snorter to have the redoubtable Mushfiqur caught at short leg, ending a stand of 87. Through the breach piled Broad, picking up two wickets towards the end of a harrying nine-over spell full of reverse swing.

England might have won that evening, but Sabbir remained immovable, and Taijul swung with abandon in fading light. Cook was content to come back next morning, refreshed and with a new ball – if needed – available after two overs, and Bangladesh having had a night contemplating history. A couple of streaky shots set English minds on edge, but Stokes got the job done.

Man of the Match: B. A. Stokes.

Close of play: first day, England 258-7 (Woakes 36, Rashid 5); second day, Bangladesh 221-5 (Shakib Al Hasan 31, Shafiul Islam 0); third day, England 228-8 (Woakes 11, Broad 10); fourth day, Bangladesh 253-8 (Sabbir Rahman 59, Taijul Islam 11).

England

*A. N. Cook b Shakib Al Hasan	4	– c Mahmudullah b Mehedi Hasan	12
B. M. Duckett b Mehedi Hasan	14	– c Mominul Haque b Shakib Al Hasan	15
J. E. Root c Sabbir Rahman b Mehedi Hasan	40	– lbw b Shakib Al Hasan	1
G. S. Ballance lbw b Mehedi Hasan	1	– c Imrul Kayes b Taijul Islam	9
M. M. Ali c Mushfiqur Rahim b Mehedi Hasan	68	– c Mushfiqur Rahim b Shakib Al Hasan	14
B. A. Stokes b Shakib Al Hasan	18	– lbw b Shakib Al Hasan	85
†J. M. Bairstow b Mehedi Hasan	52	– b Kamrul Islam	47
C. R. Woakes c Mominul Haque b Taijul Islam	36	– not out	19
A. U. Rashid c Sabbir Rahman b Taijul Islam	26	– lbw b Shakib Al Hasan	9
S. C. J. Broad c Mushfiqur Rahim b Mehedi Hasan	13	– run out	10
G. J. Batty not out	1	– lbw b Taijul Islam	3
B 14, lb 4, w 2	20	B 3, lb 8, p 5	16
1/18 (2) 2/18 (1) 3/21 (4) 4/83 (3) 5/106 (6) 6/194 (5) 7/237 (7) 8/258 (8) 9/289 (9) 10/293 (10) (105.5 overs)	293	1/26 (1) 2/27 (3) 3/28 (2) 4/46 (4) 5/62 (5) 6/189 (7) 7/197 (6) 8/213 (9) 9/233 (10) 10/240 (11) (80.2 overs)	240

Shafiul Islam 9–1–33–0; Mehedi Hasan 39.5–7–80–6; Kamrul Islam 8–0–41–0; Shakib Al Hasan 19–6–46–2; Taijul Islam 24–11–47–2; Sabbir Rahman 3–0–11–0; Mahmudullah 2–0–17–0; Mominul Haque 1–1–0–0. *Second innings*—Mehedi Hasan 20–1–58–1; Shakib Al Hasan 33–7–85–5; Taijul Islam 15.2–2–41–2; Kamrul Islam 8–0–24–1; Mahmudullah 1–0–6–0; Shafiul Islam 3–0–10–0.

Bangladesh

Tamim Iqbal c Bairstow b Batty	78	– c Ballance b Ali	9
Imrul Kayes b Ali	21	– c Root b Rashid	43
Mominul Haque c Stokes b Ali	0	– lbw b Batty	27
Mahmudullah c Root b Rashid	38	– lbw b Batty	17
*†Mushfiqur Rahim c Bairstow b Stokes	48	– (6) c Ballance b Batty	39
Shakib Al Hasan st Bairstow b Ali	31	– (5) c Bairstow b Ali	24
Shafiul Islam c Broad b Rashid	2	– (11) lbw b Stokes	0
Sabbir Rahman c Cook b Stokes	19	– (7) not out	64
Mehedi Hasan lbw b Stokes	1	– (8) lbw b Broad	1
Taijul Islam not out	3	– lbw b Stokes	16
Kamrul Islam b Stokes	0	– (9) c Ballance b Broad	0
B 2, lb 4, w 1	7	B 9, lb 13, w 1	23
1/29 (2) 2/29 (3) 3/119 (4) 4/163 (1) 5/221 (5) 6/221 (6) 7/238 (7) 8/239 (9) 9/248 (8) 10/248 (11) (86 overs)	248	1/35 (1) 2/81 (2) 3/103 (3) 4/108 (4) 5/140 (5) 6/227 (6) 7/234 (8) 8/238 (9) 9/263 (10) 10/263 (11) (81.3 overs)	263

Broad 8–2–12–0; Batty 17–1–51–1; Woakes 7–2–15–0; Rashid 16–1–58–2; Ali 22–4–75–3; Stokes 14–5–26–4; Root 2–0–5–0. *Second innings*—Batty 17–3–65–3; Ali 14–2–60–2; Woakes 7–3–10–0; Rashid 17–2–55–1; Broad 15–4–31–2; Stokes 11.3–2–20–2.

Umpires: H. D. P. K. Dharmasena and C. B. Gaffaney. Third umpire: S. Ravi.
Referee: R. S. Madugalle.

BANGLADESH v ENGLAND

Second Test Match

VIC MARKS

At Mirpur, October 28–30, 2016. Bangladesh won by 108 runs. Toss: Bangladesh. Test debut: Z. S. Ansari.

Bangladesh's first Test victory over England was a triumph of planning, skill and derring-do. It was fashioned by two cricketers – one well known to the tourists at the start of their trip, the other cunningly kept out of view.

Tamim Iqbal, a frequent tormentor of England, scored 144 runs on a pitch that would have had any self-respecting spinner salivating. Somehow, he made it look like a road; when the rest were batting, it resembled a sandpit. Less familiar, at least until the First Test, was Mehedi Hasan, just turned 19, who had been omitted from Bangladesh's one-day side against Afghanistan a few days before England's arrival so that they remained unaware of his talents. After seven wickets at Chittagong, Mehedi finished with 12 for 159 here, Bangladesh's best match figures, beating Enamul Haque's 12 for 200 against Zimbabwe across Dhaka at the Bangabandhu National Stadium in January 2005. Mehedi mesmerised the English batsmen with pure orthodoxy. Allied to a fervour for the game that had him lapping up his coaches' every word, this suggested he would be integral to Bangladesh cricket for the next decade or more.

Here was another Test whose outcome was pleasingly hard to predict almost until the end. After Tamim's brilliant first-day century, the match was often a trial for batsmen as

OVERCOMING THE OLD COUNTRY

How long it took each team to defeat England in a Test:

Tests		*1st Test*	*1st win*	*Tests*		*1st Test*	*1st win*
1	Australia	1876-77	1876-77	9	South Africa	1888-89	1905-06
4	Pakistan	1954	1954	**10**	**Bangladesh**.....	**2003-04**	**2016-17**
5	Sri Lanka	1981-82	1992-93	15	India	1932	1951-52
6	West Indies	1928	1929-30	48	New Zealand	1929-30	1977-78

Zimbabwe have played six Tests against England (between 1996-97 and 2003), without a win.

the ball spun or skidded. Not long after lunch on the third day, England were set an unlikely 273 for victory. By tea they were 100 for none. An hour and fifty minutes later they were all out for 164, and the Bangladesh side – along with a host of supporters who had suddenly swelled the crowd – were rejoicing in a historic victory. It was the first time England had lost all ten in a session since Headingley 1938 against Australia. Mehedi caused most of the havoc, with the canny Shakib Al Hasan backing him up.

The result was an expression of Bangladesh's burgeoning self-confidence. By preparing spin-friendly tracks, they demonstrated their willingness to lose in pursuit of a win. The draw was of little interest. In the past, they might have preferred docile surfaces, aimed at runs and – in theory, at least – respectability. Now they sought to exploit England's Achilles heel. Bangladesh's slow bowlers – now numbering four specialists, after Shuvagata Hom replaced seamer Shafiul Islam – proved more accurate and accomplished than England's, and several of their batsmen were more adept at counteracting the spinning ball, usually with aggressive intent.

Their positive thinking might have emanated from head coach Chandika Hathurusinghe, and it streamed through the entire squad. The result gave him a unique double: in March 1993, he had been part of the first Sri Lankan side to achieve a Test victory over England, in Colombo. Here, he delivered some well-chosen words at tea on the third day, just when Bangladesh seemed to be squandering a golden opportunity. Hathurusinghe had overseen

Philip Brown, Getty Images

Smoking gun: Tamim Iqbal attacks on the second day.

a fine campaign with panache, sanctioning the idea of tossing the second over of the series to Mehedi.

Bangladesh had the benefit of batting first and, after the early loss of Imrul Kayes, who cut a short ball from Woakes straight to point, Tamim batted sublimely, with lively support from Mominul Haque. The seamers – including Finn, playing for the rested Stuart Broad – were pulled or caressed off the front foot; the spinners were often treated with disdain, as Tamim drifted down the pitch for another extravagant drive. Test debutant Zafar Ansari, who had replaced his county captain Gareth Batty, yielded 13 runs from his first over of left-arm spin. And it really wasn't a bad one.

Together this pair added 170, easily the highest partnership of the series, whereupon Tamim was out tamely, shortly after reaching his eighth Test century with successive lofted extra-cover drives off Ali. Having put every English bowler to the sword, with the exception of the miserly Stokes, he opted to pad up to Ali, and was lbw. Ali was, by a disturbing margin, England's best spinner, and soon a rare straight delivery defeated Mominul, part of a collapse in which Bangladesh lost their last nine for 49. Cook had finally found a potent combination of spin and pace: Ali – who finished with his second Test five-for, more than two years after his first – and Stokes. It meant the stand between Tamim and Mominul accounted for 77.27% of the Bangladesh total – the second-highest for a completed Test innings, behind the 77.78% of Kumar Sangakkara and Mahela Jayawardene (168 out of 216) at Durban in 2000-01. It would prove decisive.

England could have ended the day on a high, but stuttered to 50 for three. Duckett hit his third ball, from Shakib, over long-on, then fell to his fifth, while Mehedi defeated Cook and Ballance. On the second morning, the only resistance came from Root, who survived a drop at slip on 19 by Mahmudullah to hit a dutiful half-century, and Bairstow. When Root was out, they were 144 for eight, only for Woakes and Rashid – happy to glean singles from a strangely deep-set field – to put on 99, England's highest ninth-wicket stand in Asia.

Woakes had an extraordinary escape on 38 against the occasional wrist-spin of Sabbir Rahman. He received a high full toss, which would have been deemed ugly on the village green. Unsure whether to smash it for four or six, he hit it straight to short midwicket, and set off towards the pavilion, crestfallen and angry. But the TV umpire, Chris Gaffaney, decreed it would have passed him above hip height, and was therefore a no-ball. This seemed an affront to natural justice, since the regulation had been introduced only because of the proliferation of high full tosses from seamers towards the end of limited-overs games. Had Gaffaney used the ball-tracking data, he might have deemed the delivery legal.

Against the odds, England acquired a first-innings lead of 24, but were no more successful at containing Bangladesh than in the first innings. Despite the vagaries of the surface, the runs ticked along at five an over. Tamim was again irrepressible, Kayes unfurled a variety of sweeps, and Mahmudullah was majestic – until the last ball of the day, when he had a horrible heave at Ansari and was bowled. This was Ansari's second Test wicket, his first (Tamim) having come courtesy of a sharp catch at leg slip by an increasingly desperate England captain.

Bangladesh led by 128 at the close, and continued to attack next day. Eventually Cook turned to Rashid, apparently as a last resort. The runs kept flowing, but wickets fell at

---

THAT ENGLAND COLLAPSE IN FULL

After reaching tea on the third day at 100 without loss, England lost ten for 64 runs in 22.3 overs:

W (*Duckett*) 14••• // W (*Root*) 1•11• // 1••••1 // •••••• // •••••• // •1•1•1 // ••1121 // •24••• // •W (*Ballance*) •••W (*Ali*) // 2••••• // •1••W (*Cook*) • // 2••••1 // 1•••14 // 1••••• // 11W (*Bairstow*) 31• // 11•1•1 // •1•••1 // •••1•• // •6••1• // •4W (*Stokes*) W (*Rashid*) •W (*Ansari*) // •1•••• // ••1••• // •1W (*Finn*)

Teenage dream: 19-year-old Mehedi Hasan spins Bangladesh to a historic Test win.

regular intervals, despite four dropped catches, which ranged from the practically impossible (Finn, back-pedalling at mid-off, when Mushfiqur Rahim had six) to the utterly routine (Duckett at deep midwicket, when Shakib had 23). England also made a hash of DRS, twice failing to review lbw shouts from Ali which would have brought a wicket. As tempers frayed, Stokes overheated in a duel with Sabbir, which cost him 15% of his match fee.

England were left needing 64 more than they had successfully chased in the fourth innings of a Test in Asia, yet by tea they had taken 100 from just 23 overs. Duckett played a brave, barnstorming innings. Twice in an over he reverse-swept Shakib to the boundary, and meted out similar treatment to Mehedi. Cook cruised along in his wake. The pitch seemed to be having a siesta.

Everything changed after the interval. Duckett was bowled by the first ball of the session, a skidder from Mehedi, and England became paralysed. Apart from the openers, Stokes alone reached double figures. Ballance failed again, jeopardising his position in a team that now looked ill-equipped to take on India. Shakib hastened the conclusion with three wickets in four balls, saluting the crowd after bowling Stokes, invoking Marlon Samuels in Grenada the previous year.

But, appropriately, it was Mehedi who claimed the last wicket. When umpire Dharmasena's finger was raised – which in this series was never a sure sign of a batsman's dismissal – the Bangladesh side celebrated wildly, while Finn sought a review without realising England had none left. It was a sad little vignette, highlighting their haplessness. Mehedi became just the third bowler to take a six-wicket haul in each of his first two Tests, after Alec Bedser and Narendra Hirwani.

Mushfiqur hoped this would be a landmark victory, pleading with the ICC to "send us series against the big boys". Cook managed a sense of perspective. "People need to come here and play cricket," he said. "You can see their development. It's not easy for me to say, but it's a good win for Bangladesh cricket. Maybe some things are bigger than one game."

Man of the Match: Mehedi Hasan. *Man of the Series:* Mehedi Hasan.

Close of play: first day, England 50-3 (Root 15, Ali 2); second day, Bangladesh 152-3 (Imrul Kayes 59).

Bangladesh

Tamim Iqbal lbw b Ali	104	– c Cook b Ansari	40
Imrul Kayes c Duckett b Woakes	1	– lbw b Ali	78
Mominul Haque b Ali	66	– c Cook b Stokes	1
Mahmudullah c Cook b Stokes	13	– b Ansari	47
Shakib Al Hasan c Bairstow b Woakes	10	– b Rashid	41
*†Mushfiqur Rahim c Cook b Ali	4	– c Cook b Stokes	9
Sabbir Rahman c Bairstow b Stokes	0	– lbw b Rashid	15
Shuvagata Hom c Bairstow b Woakes	6	– not out	25
Mehedi Hasan lbw b Ali	1	– (10) c Root b Rashid	2
Taijul Islam not out	5	– (9) c Bairstow b Stokes	5
Kamrul Islam c Root b Ali	0	– c and b Rashid	7
B 1, lb 9	10	B 17, lb 7, w 1, nb 1	26
1/1 (2) 2/171 (1) 3/190 (3) 4/196 (4) 5/201 (6) 6/202 (7) 7/212 (8) 8/213 (9) 9/215 (5) 10/220 (11) (63.5 overs)	220	1/65 (1) 2/66 (3) 3/152 (4) 4/200 (2) 5/238 (5) 6/238 (6) 7/268 (7) 8/273 (9) 9/276 (10) 10/296 (11) (66.5 overs)	296

Woakes 9–3–30–3; Finn 8–1–30–0; Ali 19.5–5–57–5; Ansari 6–0–36–0; Stokes 11–5–13–2; Rashid 10–0–44–0. *Second innings*—Finn 3–0–18–0; Ali 19–2–60–1; Ansari 19–0–76–2; Stokes 12–2–52–3; Rashid 11.5–1–52–4; Woakes 2–0–14–0.

England

*A. N. Cook lbw b Mehedi Hasan	14	– c Mominul Haque b Mehedi Hasan	59
B. M. Duckett c Mushfiqur Rahim b Shakib Al Hasan	7	– b Mehedi Hasan	56
J. E. Root lbw b Taijul Islam	56	– lbw b Shakib Al Hasan	1
G. S. Ballance c Mushfiqur Rahim b Mehedi Hasan	9	– c Tamim Iqbal b Mehedi Hasan	5
M. M. Ali b Mehedi Hasan	10	– lbw b Mehedi Hasan	0
B. A. Stokes c Mominul Haque b Taijul Islam	0	– b Shakib Al Hasan	25
†J. M. Bairstow lbw b Mehedi Hasan	24	– c Shuvagata Hom b Mehedi Hasan	3
Z. S. Ansari c Shuvagata Hom b Mehedi Hasan	13	– (10) c Imrul Kayes b Shakib Al Hasan	0
C. R. Woakes c Shuvagata Hom b Mehedi Hasan	46	– (8) not out	9
A. U. Rashid not out	44	– (9) lbw b Shakib Al Hasan	0
S. T. Finn c Mushfiqur Rahim b Taijul Islam	0	– lbw b Mehedi Hasan	0
B 13, lb 7, nb 1	21	B 4, lb 2	6
1/10 (2) 2/24 (1) 3/42 (4) 4/64 (5) 5/69 (6) 6/114 (7) 7/140 (8) 8/144 (3) 9/243 (9) 10/244 (11) (81.3 overs)	244	1/100 (2) 2/105 (3) 3/124 (4) 4/124 (5) 5/127 (1) 6/139 (7) 7/161 (6) 8/161 (9) 9/161 (10) 10/164 (11) (45.3 overs)	164

Mehedi Hasan 28–2–82–6; Shakib Al Hasan 16–5–41–1; Taijul Islam 25.3–3–65–3; Kamrul Islam 3–0–16–0; Shuvagata Hom 4–0–8–0; Sabbir Rahman 5–0–12–0. *Second innings*—Mehedi Hasan 21.3–2–77–6; Shakib Al Hasan 13–1–49–4; Shuvagata Hom 6–0–25–0; Taijul Islam 5–2–7–0.

Umpires: H. D. P. K. Dharmasena and S. Ravi. Third umpire: C. B. Gaffaney.
Referee: R. S. Madugalle.

INDIA v ENGLAND IN 2016-17

REVIEW BY JOHN ETHERIDGE

Test matches (5): India 4, England 0
One-day internationals (3): India 2, England 1
Twenty20 internationals (3): India 2, England 1

Any optimism England might have had about repeating their win in India four years earlier lasted roughly a week. After a strong performance in the First Test, Alastair Cook's team were systematically duffed up by a side led with passion, animation and ruthlessness by Virat Kohli. A vastly superior India won 4–0, extending their sequence at home to 16 victories in 18 Tests, and their unbeaten run – home and abroad – to 18, a national record. By the end, England's batsmen were regularly tossing away their wickets, unsure how to balance aggression with adhesion on slow turners, not the fizzing, spitting surfaces many had expected. Their spin bowling was alarmingly ineffective, and the glory days of James Anderson's new-ball partnership with Stuart Broad seemed to be drawing to a close.

Above all, Cook's future as captain was clouded in doubt. His cautious tactics, handling of England's bowlers, and submissive body language all came under the microscope. And while the noises from the dressing-room were supportive, Cook himself had much to contemplate: a welcoming atmosphere and good work behind the scenes can prop up a captain for only so long. When he met director of England cricket Andrew Strauss in January for a tour debrief, his leadership was top of the agenda. In February, he announced he was stepping down.

Yet Cook had been partly responsible for the uncertainty. On the eve of the tour, he had admitted in an interview with *The Cricketer* magazine that he did not know how much longer he would continue as captain, and said he fancied playing for a couple of years as batsman and senior pro. There was nothing unusual about these observations – he had expressed similar sentiments before – but the timing encouraged speculation.

While England's captain often looked tired and careworn, and naturally missed the baby daughter he had left to come on tour when she was only 18

MOST RUNS IN AN INDIA–ENGLAND TEST SERIES

Runs		*T*	*Avge*	
752	G. A. Gooch (England)	3	125.33	1990
655	**V. Kohli (India)**	**5**	**109.16**	**2016-17**
615	M. P. Vaughan (England)	4	102.50	2002
602	R. Dravid (India)	4	100.33	2002
594	K. F. Barrington (England)	5	99.00	1961-62
586	V. L. Manjrekar (India)	5	83.71	1961-62
575	M. W. Gatting (England)	5	95.83	1984-85
562	A. N. Cook (England)	4	80.28	2012-13
542	S. M. Gavaskar (India)	4	77.42	1979
533	K. P. Pietersen (England)	4	106.60	2011

Danish Siddiqui, Reuters

Running smoothly: between them, Cheteshwar Pujara and Virat Kohli made more than 1,000 runs.

hours old, Kohli was the dominant figure on either side. India had lost their three previous series against England, and he had played in two of them, averaging 20. This was a mission driven partly by revenge, and wholly by ambition. He was everywhere. Whether it was making runs (he averaged 109), urging groundsmen to prepare pitches with less grass, trying to manipulate umpires, niggling the opposition at media conferences or in the middle, or setting sky-high standards of fitness, preparation and fielding, he could rarely be ignored.

Such was his ubiquity that England believed he was something of a protected species. When Kohli gave Ben Stokes an abusive send-off during the Third Test at Mohali, and Stokes responded in kind, it was Stokes who got into trouble with the ICC. Kohli was also sucked into the mint-in-the-mouth ball-shining debate after pictures emerged of a Tic Tac rattling around his teeth during the First Test at Rajkot; only newspaper journalists asked him for an explanation. England's sense of injustice reached its peak in Mumbai, where – with India about to seal the series – Ravichandran Ashwin walked alongside Anderson to dispense abuse for a perceived slight on Kohli at the previous evening's press conference, but escaped censure.

Ashwin was hardly less influential than his captain. He and left-armer Ravindra Jadeja shared 54 wickets, and finished the series first and second in the Test rankings – the first Indians to do so since fellow spinners Bishan Bedi and Bhagwat Chandrasekhar in 1974. Ashwin also scored 306 runs, and Jadeja 224; completing a formidable trio was the debutant off-spinner Jayant Yadav, who took nine wickets in three Tests and hit a century in Mumbai. Ashwin's nous and variations of flight and angle made him a huge threat in

Danish Siddiqui, Reuters

A shoulder to lean on: Saqlain Mushtaq (right) with Adil Rashid (centre) and Moeen Ali.

the middle three Tests, though his aggregate from the First and Fifth was four for 437. Perhaps most crucially, Jadeja dismissed Cook six times – frequently aiming across the line to deliveries that tended to skid on – and finished with seven for 48 in Chennai. His economy-rate of 2.31 confirmed he was almost unhittable.

The spinners were made even more threatening by India's first home use of the DRS, and their first in any bilateral series since touring Sri Lanka in 2008. Anil Kumble, their coach, had been suspicious of ball-tracking technology as a player, but his opinion changed on a visit to the Massachusetts Institute of Technology in his role on the ICC cricket committee. A pre-series presentation by the ICC's Geoff Allardice clinched India's acceptance. Despite their lack of DRS experience, they made marginally better use of it than their opponents, succeeding in 11 of their 37 reviews, to England's eight from 32.

A captain is normally only as good as his bowlers and, while Cook had been able to call on Graeme Swann and Monty Panesar during the 2–1 triumph in 2012-13, this time he had to make do with Moeen Ali, Adil Rashid and assorted others. Ali managed just ten wickets at 64. Rashid took 23, but averaged 37, and got worse as the series wore on. He had started by reducing his ratio of long hops and full tosses, prompting optimism about his progress. But he reverted to his old faults, and ended a near liability. In the Fifth Test at Chennai, where India racked up 759 for seven – their highest score, and the highest against England – Ali and Rashid had combined figures of two for 343, with just two maidens. When wicketkeeper Parthiv Patel criticised England's spinners in Mumbai, he was both mischievous and spot on. Maybe it was no coincidence that the fortunes of Rashid in particular dipped when the former

Pakistan off-spinner Saqlain Mushtaq left his position as part-time coach after the Third Test. Saqlain had been both technical adviser and emotional crutch, and he made it clear he would relish a permanent role.

England's slow-bowling department had other problems. When Zafar Ansari was ruled out after the third game because of a back injury, Hampshire's Liam Dawson – to much bemusement – was summoned as his replacement. Somerset's Jack Leach had been the leading English spinner during the 2016 summer, with 68 first-class wickets at 22, while Dawson had managed 66 in the previous three seasons put together. But, during the Chennai Test, it emerged that Leach had exceeded the permitted 15 degrees of flexion in routine testing at the National Performance Centre in Loughborough, and undergone remedial work with the Lions. At 39, Gareth Batty failed to provide the control, threat or mentoring role England had hoped for. Ansari, his Surrey team-mate, looked out of his depth and may also struggle to play Test cricket again.

There was little or no reverse swing for England's quicker bowlers, who were outperformed by India's. Mohammed Shami and Umesh Yadav were faster and more threatening, and Shami's screamer in Visakhapatnam to bowl Cook – snapping his off stump in two – was the most spectacular ball of the series. England's seamers were rotated and rested: apart from all-rounder Stokes, none played more than three Tests – and none took more than eight wickets. Anderson had worked hard at home to recover from the shoulder injury that interrupted his summer, and arrived in time for the Second Test. But he was wicketless in two of his three games, and strategically rested at Chennai amid vague talk of "body soreness". Stokes took England's only five-for, in Mohali, and for a while his career batting average exceeded his bowling – the definition of an all-rounder. But, as he tired, his impact faded in both disciplines. England's combined bowling average of 49 was their worst in a series of five or more Tests against anyone other than Australia.

They did not help themselves by misreading the conditions, choosing three spinners in Mohali and four seamers in Mumbai, when it should have been the other way round. It meant they often fielded a near-redundant player. As if trying to win in India with ten men wasn't hard enough, the Indians often appeared to have 12, especially once Jayant – a middle-order batsman for his state side – bolstered the tail. Including the two Tests in Bangladesh which preceded this series, Cook had four opening partners (Ben Duckett, Haseeb Hameed, Joe Root and Keaton Jennings), while five men walked out at No. 4 (Gary Ballance, Duckett, Stokes, Ali and Jonny Bairstow). For the last three Tests, Jos Buttler played as a specialist batsman, with some success.

One undoubted highlight was Hameed, who scored 219 runs at 43 before his tour was ended by a broken little finger. Aged just 19, he allied a remarkable unflappability to a technique that could have been cut-and-pasted from a 1950s coaching manual. He stands side-on, feet shoulder-width apart, head still; his balance is perfect, his footwork precise, his demeanour unhurried. The "Baby Boycott" tag had a ring to it, but was palpable nonsense, as a six down the ground off Jadeja at Rajkot proved. He showed bravery, too, shrugging off the fracture to make a half-century from No. 8 at Mohali. As he worked the strike during a last-wicket stand with Anderson, Hameed displayed acumen in a team

Amit Dave, Reuters

Stronger suit: Moeen Ali fared better as a batsman than a bowler.

that were often soft and unthinking. Right on cue, Anderson allowed himself to be dozily run out. Hameed went home for surgery, but returned for the final two games to be with his family, who had booked in for all seven Asian Tests and had no intention of leaving. They watched Jennings, his replacement, make a century and a golden duck on Test debut at Mumbai.

It was a reminder that maybe their batting wasn't the problem: with Cook winning four tosses out of five, their first-innings totals included 537, 400 and 477, yet they still lost those final two Tests by an innings. Nine batsmen averaged 36 or above but, while they recorded just two centuries in the final four Tests (after four in the First), India had Kohli's series-defining 235 at Mumbai, plus K. L. Rahul's 199 and newcomer Karun Nair's unbeaten 303, both at Chennai. The home team went big, scoring 400 in each game, and 1,390 in their final two innings alone.

England never quite matched them. Root made a hundred on the first day of the series, and passed 50 in each Test, but by the end of the series he had converted only three of his last 17 half-centuries. Ali scored two centuries and a fifty, but his modes of dismissal often caused exasperation. Bairstow was consistency personified on both sides of the stumps, but without reaching 90.

There also appeared to be a difference in philosophy between Cook and head coach Trevor Bayliss. After England tried to block their way to a draw in the Second Test – Cook and Hameed took 50 overs to put on 75, before all ten wickets tumbled for 83 – Cook insisted "everybody bought into" the tactic. Bayliss seemed to contradict this and, before the Fourth Test, said he would make his views clear to the team: "It will be up to me to play a role in this. It's time I stepped up to the mark. I'll remind the players how we've played well,

FIVE STATS YOU MAY HAVE MISSED

BENEDICT BERMANGE

- In the First Test at Rajkot, Alastair Cook scored his 12th century as captain, the most for England:

100s	*Capt*		*100s*	*Capt*	
12	**59**	**A. N. Cook**	9	50	A. J. Strauss
11	34	G. A. Gooch	9	51	M. P. Vaughan
10	41	P. B. H. May	8	54	M. A. Atherton

- On his return to India's side for the Third Test at Mohali, Parthiv Patel became only the fourth player to have missed 40 or more successive matches *twice* during his Test career:

	Tests missed
D. B. Close (Eng)	44 between 1950-51 and 1955; 75 between 1967 and 1976
F. J. Titmus (Eng)	59 between 1955 and 1962; 62 between 1967-68 and 1974-75
G. B. Hogg (Aus)	78 between 1996-97 and 2002-03; 45 between 2003-04 and 2007-08
P. A. Patel (India) . . .	**43 between 2004-05 and 2008; 83 between 2008 and 2016-17**

- Before India made 631 at Mumbai and 759 for seven at Chennai, England had only once conceded totals of 600-plus in successive Tests: Australia scored 645 at Brisbane and 659 for eight at Sydney in 1946-47.

- In the Fifth Test at Chennai, Joe Root reached 50 in an innings for the 11th successive Test against India, extending his own record for the most matches against one opponent with at least a half-century:

T			*Span*
11	**J. E. Root (England)**	**v India**	**2012-13 to 2016-17**
9	R. N. Harvey (Australia).	v South Africa	1949-50 to 1952-53
9	J. H. Edrich (England)	v Australia	1968 to 1970-71
9	K. D. Walters (Australia)	v West Indies	1968-69 to 1972-73
9	D. P. M. D. Jayawardene (Sri Lanka).	v India	2001 to 2009-10
9	K. C. Sangakkara (Sri Lanka).	v Pakistan.	2009 to 2013-14

- At Chennai, India became only the fourth team to make a total of 400 or more in every match of a series of five or more Tests:

T			*T*		
6	Australia v England	1989	5	Australia v Pakistan	1983-84
5	India v New Zealand.	1955-56	**5**	**India v England**.	**2016-17**

which is with a nice positive approach." Cook later said he endorsed Bayliss's comments, but the suspicion remained that the coach's doctrine was more aggressive than his captain's.

Some of England's problems were in place even before they arrived. A schedule of seven almost back-to-back Tests left no chance for out-of-form or fringe players to discover touch and confidence. The ECB claimed the itinerary had been agreed by a previous regime, though Strauss, chief executive Tom Harrison and chairman Colin Graves had been in place for 18 months. The likes of Ballance and Steven Finn ran drinks for several weeks with little hope of a game. A mini-holiday was built into the schedule, and most players decamped to Dubai for a few days' R&R before the Mumbai Test. They might have felt refreshed, but the two heaviest defeats of the tour followed.

Ansari, Ballance, Batty and Finn were poor selections – either out of nick, too old, or probably not good enough – while Duckett was brutally exposed by Ashwin. The arrival of Jennings and, to a lesser extent, Dawson, who began with an unbeaten 66, showed that players could be flown in and enjoy success – and suggested some of the passengers should have gone home. In the end, India were so good it would probably have made little difference.

John Stern writes: Home advantage, greater experience and star quality gave India the edge in two compelling white-ball series played in front of packed houses. The recall of Yuvraj Singh to their one-day squad after an absence of three years gave Kohli, the new limited-overs captain, a brains trust that, along with M. S. Dhoni, had more than 900 limited-overs internationals between the three of them. All hit hundreds, and took part in double-century stands that sealed the run-splattered 50-over series with a game to spare. In all, 2,090 were scored, making it the highest-scoring three-match series in ODI history.

England's victories in the final one-dayer, at Kolkata, and the first Twenty20 game, at Kanpur, came on pitches with pace and bounce. On slower surfaces elsewhere, their attack were mainly one-dimensional. Death bowling remained a mostly unmastered skill, with the exception of Chris Woakes, who demonstrated bottle at Eden Gardens. The introduction for the Twenty20 games of Tymal Mills and Chris Jordan, who both showed off their variations, sharpened England up.

That series was marred by an old-fashioned umpiring row. The performance of Chettithody Shamshuddin in the second match prompted England to make an official complaint to match referee Andy Pycroft. Shamshuddin, who had been a late appointment, and was flown in from Australia less than 24 hours before, then asked to stand down from his on-field duties only hours before the final T20. Both the captain, Eoin Morgan, and Root called for DRS to be introduced for 20-over internationals. Six days later, the ICC proposed exactly that.

Having chosen to miss the one-day tour of Bangladesh in October, Morgan was under pressure, but his brilliant century in the second ODI at Cuttack, even in a losing cause, had the stamp of class. He finished with his reputation as leader and batsman intact, despite England's tired collapse of eight wickets for eight runs in the final T20 at Bangalore.

ENGLAND TOURING PARTY

*A. N. Cook (Essex; T), M. M. Ali (Worcestershire; T/50/20), J. M. Anderson (Lancashire; T); Z. S. Ansari (Surrey; T), J. M. Bairstow (Yorkshire; T/50), J. T. Ball (Nottinghamshire; T/50/20), G. S. Ballance (Yorkshire; T), G. J. Batty (Surrey; T), S. W. Billings (Kent; 50/20), S. C. J. Broad (Nottinghamshire; T), J. C. Buttler (Lancashire; T/50/20), L. A. Dawson (Hampshire; T/50/20), B. M. Duckett (Northamptonshire; T), S. T. Finn (Middlesex; T), A. D. Hales (Nottinghamshire; 50/20), H. Hameed (Lancashire; T), K. K. Jennings (Durham; T), C. J. Jordan (Sussex; 20), T. S. Mills (Sussex; 20), E. J. G. Morgan (Middlesex; 50/20), L. E. Plunkett (Yorkshire; 50/20), A. U. Rashid (Yorkshire; T/50/20), J. E. Root (Yorkshire; T/50/20), J. J. Roy (Surrey; 50/20), B. A. Stokes (Durham; T/50/20), D. J. Willey (Yorkshire; 50/20), C. R. Woakes (Warwickshire; T/50).

Hameed (broken finger) and Ansari (back trouble) returned home during the Test series, and were replaced by Jennings and Dawson. Anderson joined the squad late after a shoulder problem. Morgan captained in the limited-overs matches.

Coach: T. H. Bayliss (T/50/20). *Assistant coach:* P. Farbrace (T/50/20). *Batting coach:* M. R. Ramprakash (T), G. P. Thorpe (50/20). *Fast-bowling coach:* O. D. Gibson (T/50/20). *Spin-bowling coach:* Saqlain Mushtaq. *Wicketkeeping coach:* B. N. French (to end of First Test). *Strength and conditioning coach:* P. C. F. Scott (T/50/20). *Operations manager:* P. A. Neale (T/50/20). *Doctor:* R. Young (T), M. G. Wotherspoon (50/20). *Physiotherapist:* C. A. de Weymarn (T/50/20). *Masseur:* M. E. S. Saxby (T), K. S. Bansil (50/20). *Analyst:* R. Lewis (T), N. A. Leamon (50/20). *Security manager:* R. C. Dickason (T/20). *Assistant security manager:* T. S. Minish (T/50), J. A. Shaw (20). *Head of team communications:* D. Reuben (T/50/20).

TEST MATCH AVERAGES

INDIA – BATTING AND FIELDING

	T	*I*	*NO*	*R*	*HS*	*100*	*50*	*Avge*	*Ct/St*
K. K. Nair	3	3	1	320	303*	1	0	160.00	3
V. Kohli	5	8	2	655	235	2	2	109.16	5
J. Yadav	3	4	1	221	104	1	1	73.66	1
†P. A. Patel	3	4	1	195	71	0	2	65.00	11/2
K. L. Rahul	3	4	0	233	199	1	0	58.25	3
C. A. Pujara	5	8	0	401	124	2	1	50.12	2
M. Vijay	5	8	0	357	136	2	0	44.62	3
R. Ashwin	5	7	0	306	72	0	4	43.71	1
†R. A. Jadeja	5	7	1	224	90	0	2	37.33	6
Mohammed Shami	3	4	3	35	19	0	0	35.00	0
A. M. Rahane	3	5	0	63	26	0	0	12.60	3
W. P. Saha	2	4	0	49	35	0	0	12.25	6
U. T. Yadav	5	6	2	38	13	0	0	9.50	6

Played in two Tests: A. Mishra 0 (1 ct). Played in one Test: Bhuvneshwar Kumar 9; †G. Gambhir 29, 0; I. Sharma did not bat.

BOWLING

	Style	*O*	*M*	*R*	*W*	*BB*	*5I*	*Avge*
I. Sharma	RFM	31	8	59	3	2-42	0	19.66
Mohammed Shami	RFM	103	22	252	10	3-63	0	25.20
R. A. Jadeja	SLA	290.1	67	672	26	7-48	1	25.84
J. Yadav	OB	81.3	17	266	9	3-30	0	29.55
R. Ashwin	OB	307.1	45	847	28	6-55	3	30.25
A. Mishra	LBG	75.5	12	275	5	2-60	0	55.00
U. T. Yadav	RF	143.5	23	464	8	2-58	0	58.00

Also bowled: Bhuvneshwar Kumar (RFM) 17–1–60–1; K. K. Nair (OB) 1–0–4–0.

ENGLAND – BATTING AND FIELDING

	T	*I*	*NO*	*R*	*HS*	*100*	*50*	*Avge*	*Ct/St*
J. E. Root	5	10	0	491	124	1	4	49.10	5
J. M. Bairstow	5	9	1	352	89	0	3	44.00	11/2
H. Hameed	3	6	1	219	82	0	2	43.80	4
†M. M. Ali	5	9	0	381	146	2	1	42.33	3
†K. K. Jennings	2	4	0	167	112	1	1	41.75	2
J. C. Buttler	3	6	2	154	76	0	1	38.50	5
†B. A. Stokes	5	10	1	345	128	1	1	38.33	5
†A. N. Cook	5	10	0	369	130	1	1	36.90	3
A. U. Rashid	5	9	1	113	60	0	1	14.12	2
C. R. Woakes	3	5	0	70	30	0	0	14.00	3
†Z. S. Ansari	2	3	0	36	32	0	0	12.00	1
J. T. Ball	2	4	0	45	31	0	0	11.25	1
†S. C. J. Broad	3	5	1	44	19	0	0	11.00	0
†B. M. Duckett	2	3	0	18	13	0	0	6.00	0
†J. M. Anderson	3	6	2	20	13*	0	0	5.00	2

Played in one Test: G. J. Batty 1, 0; L. A. Dawson 66*, 0.

BOWLING

	Style	O	M	R	W	BB	5I	Avge
S. C. J. Broad	RFM	89	24	248	8	4-33	0	31.00
A. U. Rashid	LBG	232.2	19	861	23	4-82	0	37.43
B. A. Stokes	RFM	106.2	16	357	8	5-73	1	44.62
J. M. Anderson	RFM	79	17	214	4	3-62	0	53.50
Z. S. Ansari	SLA	43	3	163	3	2-77	0	54.33
M. M. Ali	OB	188.1	21	649	10	3-98	0	64.90
C. R. Woakes	RFM	77	16	244	3	1-6	0	81.33

Also bowled: J. T. Ball (RFM) 41–7–140–1; G. J. Batty (OB) 19.2–0–65–0; L. A. Dawson (SLA) 43–4–129–2; K. K. Jennings (RM) 5–1–20–0; J. E. Root (OB) 16–2–57–2.

INDIA v ENGLAND

First Test Match

SCYLD BERRY

At Rajkot, November 9–13, 2016. Drawn. Toss: England. Test debut: H. Hameed.

It was a far more satisfactory draw for the tourists than the hosts, to the extent that Trevor Bayliss said it was for sheer effort, the best of his tenure. Having noted England's debacle at Mirpur, India made the mistake of underestimating them: they had steamrollered the opposition in 12 of their previous 13 home Tests (the other was rain-affected) rising to No. 1 in the rankings on the back of Ashwin's own rise to the top of the bowling table. But England, at ease with being underdogs, responded in their inconsistent way: having been Bangladesh's first pukka Test victims, they controlled this match from the time Root took charge on the first afternoon. By the end, with Kohli holding on, India were simply grateful to survive.

England's three spinners, having been outbowled by Bangladesh, grew in stature to take 13 of India's 16 wickets, a feather in the cap of their consultant Saqlain Mushtaq (whose contract was extended until the end of the Third Test). Rashid was the most improved in accuracy, and outdid Ashwin – who conceded 230 runs in all – by seven wickets to three. He concentrated on his stock ball, and did not immediately fall back on variations when his leg-break was hit. Rashid said Saqlain had told him to focus on bowling at the pace at which his leg-break turned most; gone were the long hops of Chittagong and Mirpur.

But the most outstanding performance among the four British Asians – the first time so many had represented England in the Test team, reflecting almost exactly the proportion in all cricket in England and Wales – came not from Rashid, nor even Ali, who was Man of the Match. It came from Haseeb Hameed, who made one of the most dazzling debuts ever for England – perhaps since 1896 and K. S. Ranjitsinhji, also from Gujarat, like Hameed's parents, and who had attended school in Rajkot.

The pitch, of black cotton soil, did not deteriorate nearly as quickly as expected, given the initial cracks. It had some live grass in the middle, which upset Kohli, who pronounced after the game: "That should not have been the case." And it enabled Woakes to bounce India's batsmen and score five direct hits – three in successive overs on Pujara. What

Amit Dave, Reuters

Little acorn, great oak: Haseeb Hameed in his first Test, and Alastair Cook in his 136th.

stopped England pressing home their advantage was the lushness of the square and outfield – being a new stadium, it had an inbuilt sprinkler system – so the ball barely reversed, and a draw was always the likeliest result. India's 23rd Test venue was well appointed, eco-friendly and solar-powered – except for the floodlights – with splendid net facilities. But it was out of town, so the crowd never numbered more than a few thousand, even when schoolchildren were bussed in.

After Cook had won the toss – and Kohli had lost his first in eight at home – three England batsmen scored a century in a Test innings in India for only the second time, after Geoff Pullar, Ken Barrington and Ted Dexter at Kanpur in 1961-62. If Ali's was the most gorgeous, and Stokes's the most physical, Root's was the most valuable. In spite of the pitch's easiness, England – 102 for three at lunch – had been wobbling, and vulnerable to Ashwin, before Root was partnered by Ali in a stand of 179. Root played with a straight bat, driving felicitously, and did not sweep until he had reached 28, or reverse-sweep until he had made his 11th Test hundred – his first in Asia, and the first in India by a tourist since Australian captain Michael Clarke in February 2013. The fourth-wicket pair showed up India's fielding, which was often shoddy – five chances were dropped – with the great exception of Kohli, whose annoyance was clear. Root's dismissal was mildly controversial: some argued that Yadav, in his follow-through, did not have full control of the ball before throwing it up, then trying – and failing – to catch it again, but all three umpires were satisfied. Ali ended day one on 99, and next morning hit three fours in four balls off Yadav, before shouldering arms to Mohammed Shami.

A year before in the UAE, Stokes had been all at sea against spin. Now his defence was calm as he played himself in and hit the ball into the ground, before running India ragged with Bairstow in a stand of 99. Saha, moving wide to his left, dropped Stokes on 60 and

61 as Yadav built up full steam. Having scored a hundred in his second Test in Australia, Stokes now made one in his third in the subcontinent; all three of his previous Test innings against India, in England in 2014, had been ducks. England's eventual 537 was the highest total India had conceded at home since West Indies made 590 at Mumbai in November 2011, but India's opening pair saw out the second day.

Broad celebrated his 100th Test by pinning Gambhir early next morning as he fell across the crease, but then Vijay and Pujara put on 209 in 67 overs, both making hundreds. Vijay was more composed against Woakes's bouncers, swaying and keeping an eye on them, whereas Pujara turned his back. Vijay straight-drove England's spinners for four sixes, whereas Pujara, watched on his home ground by his family – including, for the first time at a game, his father and coach, Arvind – kept the ball on the ground. But England persevered in the dry, cloudless heat to take four wickets on the third day, two of them in the last four deliveries. At the close, India were still 218 behind.

ENGLAND'S TEENAGE TEST CRICKETERS

Yrs	*Days*			
18	149	D. B. Close	v New Zealand at Manchester	1949
19	32	J. N. Crawford	v South Africa at Johannesburg	1905-06
19	83	D. C. S. Compton	v New Zealand at The Oval	1937
19	269	B. C. Hollioake	v Australia at Nottingham	1997
19	**297**	**H. Hameed**	**v India at Rajkot**	**2016-17**
19	338	I. A. R. Peebles	v South Africa at Johannesburg	1927-28

Hameed was the youngest to open the batting in his first Test; Crawford (who played five Tests as a teenager, an England record) did so in his second, when younger than Hameed.

After Kohli trod on his leg stump working Rashid to midwicket, India lacked a third century-maker, but Ashwin guided the tail until they came close to parity. England's lead would have been 77 if Cook, at wide slip, had caught as simple a chance as there could be off Broad, offered by Shami. The 28 runs which India's last pair then added ate up at least half an hour, which England might have used profitably in the final session.

Before that, however, came Hameed. He had tackled India's pace with maturity in his first innings, leaving the ball especially well: to his first delivery in Test cricket, short but barely outside off stump, he simply dropped his hands, instead of a nervous twitch to feel bat on ball. To his second, he played a they-shall-not-pass forward defensive, his back leg swivelling round so that everything was behind the ball. With Cook at his scratchiest at the start of his 55th Test as captain, breaking Mike Atherton's England record, he looked the debutant while Hameed looked the veteran. But Hameed's handling of pace was surpassed in his second innings by his handling of spin.

After Mirpur, England could have collapsed against Ashwin and Jadeja if their second innings had begun hesitantly. Hameed, with the game sense of a master, was having none of it. Jadeja took the new ball as the quickest, and therefore most dangerous, of India's spinners on a pitch that was basically slow, though with the odd delivery spitting. Hameed calmly took a step out and drove him for six over long-off. Vijay had straight-driven four sixes, so Hameed asked: why not? He followed up by cutting and cover-driving fours in an Ashwin over. "We knew he could play," said Cook of his tenth opening partner post-Andrew Strauss. "He's an unbelievable player."

Hameed's counter-attack made the threat of India's three spinners evaporate. He throttled back to reach 62 by stumps on day four, and Cook grew in confidence. On the fifth morning, Hameed had a chance of beating Denis Compton as the youngest England batsman to make a Test century. But he may have been tired in his first five-day game, after hours at short leg in a hot helmet. In any event he did not play for three figures but for a declaration, lashing a return catch to Mishra on 82 – and settling for the highest Test score by an England teenager, beating Jack Crawford's 74 at Cape Town 111 years earlier. Hameed's stand with Cook was worth 180, another record: England's best for the first wicket in India, surpassing 178 by Tim Robinson and Graeme Fowler at Madras in 1984-85. The effect of his innings was to give his side the psychological ascendancy: never, surely, had any England debutant opener so dominated quality spin.

Had Cook not been batting – becoming the first England player to score 1,000 Test runs in India, and completing his 30th century – he might have declared shortly before the lead passed 300. As it was, England had a minimum of 49 overs to scare, or conceivably dismiss, India – which they turned into 53 by whisking through them and posting their subs round the boundary to throw the ball back in the last hour.

MOST TEST HUNDREDS IN ASIA BY VISITING BATSMEN

100	*T*		*100*	*T*	
9	**28**	**A. N. Cook (England)**	5	14	B. C. Lara (West Indies)
8	25	J. H. Kallis (South Africa)	5	17	D. M. Bravo (West Indies)
7	23	H. M. Amla (South Africa)	5	21	A. Flower (Zimbabwe)
6	22	A. R. Border (Australia)	5	28	R. T. Ponting (Australia)

After Woakes had bounced out Gambhir, India regained their composure, until Rashid trapped Pujara just before tea – though the ball pitched outside leg. Rashid, having taken four wickets first time round, was England's likeliest match-winner, but he was underused. Even though his leg-break was turning ever more sharply – and one ball from Ansari bounced head high – Rashid had only one close catcher on the off side. Ali, meanwhile, thwarted by the fact that India had six right-handers in their top seven, did not bowl round the wicket enough.

Spinning out the opposition on the last afternoon had been the speciality of Ray Illingworth a generation or two before, and – once Saha was sixth out with what proved to be ten overs left – he might have finished the job. But spin has assumed such a low profile in county cricket that England did not know how to win.

Man of the Match: M. M. Ali.

Close of play: first day, England 311-4 (Ali 99, Stokes 19); second day, India 63-0 (Vijay 25, Gambhir 28); third day, India 319-4 (Kohli 26); fourth day, England 114-0 (Cook 46, Hameed 62).

England

*A. N. Cook lbw b Jadeja	21	– c Jadeja b Ashwin	130
H. Hameed lbw b Ashwin	31	– c and b Mishra	82
J. E. Root c and b Yadav	124	– c Saha b Mishra	4
B. M. Duckett c Rahane b Ashwin	13		
M. M. Ali b Mohammed Shami	117		
B. A. Stokes c Saha b Yadav	128	– (4) not out	29
†J. M. Bairstow c Saha b Mohammed Shami	46		
C. R. Woakes c Saha b Jadeja	4		
A. U. Rashid c Yadav b Jadeja	5		
Z. S. Ansari lbw b Mishra	32		
S. C. J. Broad not out	6		
B 5, lb 4, nb 1	10	B 11, lb 3, nb 1	15
1/47 (1) 2/76 (2) 3/102 (4) 4/281 (3) 5/343 (5) 6/442 (7) 7/451 (8) 8/465 (9) 9/517 (6) 10/537 (10) (159.3 overs)	537	1/180 (2) 2/192 (3) 3/260 (1) (3 wkts dec, 75.3 overs)	260

Mohammed Shami 28.1–5–65–2; Yadav 31.5–3–112–2; Ashwin 46–3–167–2; Jadeja 30–4–86–3; Mishra 23.3–3–98–1. *Second innings*—Mohammed Shami 11–1–29–0; Jadeja 15–1–47–0; Ashwin 23.3–4–63–1; Yadav 13–2–47–0; Mishra 13–0–60–2.

India

M. Vijay c Hameed b Rashid	126	– c Hameed b Rashid	31
G. Gambhir lbw b Broad	29	– c Root b Woakes	0
C. A. Pujara c Cook b Stokes	124	– lbw b Rashid	18
*V. Kohli hit wkt b Rashid	40	– not out	49
A. Mishra c Hameed b Ansari	0		
A. M. Rahane b Ansari	13	– (5) b Ali	1
R. Ashwin c Ansari b Ali	70	– (6) c Root b Ansari	32
†W. P. Saha c Bairstow b Ali	35	– (7) c and b Rashid	9
R. A. Jadeja c Hameed b Rashid	12	– (8) not out	32
U. T. Yadav c Stokes b Rashid	5		
Mohammed Shami not out	8		
B 23, lb 2, w 1	26		
1/68 (2) 2/277 (3) 3/318 (1) 4/319 (5) 5/349 (6) 6/361 (4) 7/425 (8) 8/449 (9) 9/459 (10) 10/488 (7) (162 overs)	488	1/0 (2) 2/47 (3) 3/68 (1) 4/71 (5) 5/118 (6) 6/132 (7) (6 wkts, 52.3 overs)	172

Broad 29–9–78–1; Woakes 31–6–57–0; Ali 31–7–85–2; Ansari 23–1–77–2; Rashid 31–1–114–4; Stokes 17–2–52–1. *Second innings*—Broad 3–2–8–0; Woakes 4–1–6–1; Ansari 8–1–41–1; Ali 19–5–47–1; Rashid 14.3–1–64–3; Stokes 2–1–1–0; Root 2–0–5–0.

Umpires: H. D. P. K. Dharmasena and C. B. Gaffaney. Third umpire: R. J. Tucker.
Referee: R. S. Madugalle.

INDIA v ENGLAND

Second Test Match

ALI MARTIN

At Visakhapatnam, November 17–21, 2016. India won by 246 runs. Toss: India. Test debut: J. Yadav.

Test cricket was played among the verdant hills of coastal Visakhapatnam for the first time, but for India there was a distinct sense of familiarity. This game fitted a template established over four years of home dominance: win the toss, compile a formidable first-innings total, then weave a spinners' web on a pitch of ever-diminishing returns. England were powerless to escape.

Kohli loomed large throughout his 50th Test, starting with some none-too-subtle instructions to groundsman Kasturi Sriram following the stalemate in Rajkot, where grass on the pitch had displeased him. Here, the only grass – imported from St Lucia – was on the outfield, and it was too lush to aid England's quest for significant reverse swing. Kohli made his 14th Test century, captained with aggression, if frenetically at times, and finished the game with 248 runs, two more than India's margin of victory. It all meant that, while Ashwin picked up eight wickets, including his 22nd Test five-for, the oversized cheque at the presentation ceremony was Kohli's. It was his first match award in 19 Tests in charge.

The scoreline said little about England's fight over four and a half days, but plenty about their batting either side of tea on the second, when they subsided to 80 for five in reply to India's 455 (though keeping them below 500 had – from 351 for four – been a minor triumph for the tourists). The procession began when Cook's off stump was snapped like a breadstick by Mohammed Shami, before Hameed played fall guy in a farcical run-out.

Danish Siddiqui, Reuters

Look back in horror: Ben Duckett is put out of his misery by Ravichandran Ashwin.

Duckett endured the first of two torture-chamber innings against Ashwin, and Root – having batted with authority for 53 – holed out to mid-off. Ali became a first Test victim for the debutant off-spinner Jayant Yadav. With the next rain forecast for January, a 1–0 lead for India was inevitable.

The *coup de grâce* came when Anderson was trapped by Jayant on review 20 minutes after lunch on the fifth day – the first to register a king pair for England since Ernie Hayes in Cape Town in 1905-06, and the first to 21 Test ducks for them (Anderson had gone 54 innings, and more than six years from his debut in 2003, without one). It was also his side's tenth lbw in the match, another England record. More importantly, they had been bowled out for 158 in the 98th over of the fourth innings, chasing – or, more accurately, scorning – a target of 405. Thus the tongue-twisting Dr Y. S. Rajasekhara Reddy ACA-VDCA Cricket Stadium began life as India's 25th Test venue (and the third new one in three matches) with a textbook home triumph. As holidaymakers remained mostly on the promenade, it was a pity the ground came close to threatening its 25,000 capacity only on the fourth day.

Anderson's return for the rested Chris Woakes, after 13 weeks out because of the shoulder injury that dogged his summer, was a boon for England, as first-innings figures of three for 62 confirmed. But from the moment Cook lost the toss, there was a sense of foreboding; even he said his side now had "nothing to lose" on a surface tipped by the groundsman to turn from tea on the second day. As it transpired, variable bounce proved the greatest challenge.

As well as awarding Jayant his first cap, in place of leg-spinner Amit Mishra, India restored Rahul as opener after a hamstring injury, with Gautam Gambhir dropping out. Rahul's return lasted just five balls: in the second over, Broad had him fencing to slip. Anderson then bounced out Vijay in the fifth to make it 22 for two, but Broad was soon off the field after reopening a wound on his right wrist, and would later hobble off with a strained tendon in his right foot. His early absence meant Cook turned to spin by the 11th over, but Ansari's introduction at the Dr Vizzy End brought a palpable release of pressure, allowing Pujara and Kohli to set about a stand of 226, more than double the game's next best. And, like Broad, Ansari was not in good shape, suffering illness and back spasms, and bowled only 12 overs in the match.

The Indian pair were immense. While Pujara's 119 was a controlled innings of dancing feet to the spinners, 12 crisply timed fours and two murderous sixes – the second of which, as Rashid dropped short after tea, brought up his third century in successive Tests, and tenth overall – Kohli's 167 oozed purpose from the outset. He celebrated each milestone in the subdued fashion of a batsman with an eye on the bigger picture. Even attempts to bore him into submission with packed off-side fields did not work: he simply found a way through with laser precision.

Aside from a stray dog entering the fray to fertilise the outfield and bring about an early tea, with both men in the nineties, Kohli's one lapse in concentration came when he had 56. A short-ball barrage from Stokes produced a mistimed pull towards long leg, where Rashid dived forward but couldn't hold on. It was a mistake England would rue for the rest of the Test. Did Cook not want a safer pair of hands in place for the plan? Like the absent gully that gave Ashwin, yet to score, a let-off during Anderson's burst with the second new ball late in the day, it felt a big oversight.

Some redemption for Rashid would come on the second day, when he and Ali shared five wickets – including Kohli, caught at slip by Stokes the ball after he had dropped Ashwin on 17. But a total of 455 still required England's batsmen to respond in kind. Instead, Cook received that jaffa from Shami, and the run-out of Hameed, courtesy of Root's late refusal of a second, and Jayant's smart work at square leg, caused panic.

Stokes and Bairstow demonstrated what was possible, first resisting until stumps, then stretching their stand to 110 in 44 overs on the third morning, by which time England's sixth wicket had broken their all-wicket record for most runs in a calendar year (overtaking the 1,704 added by the fourth in 2015). But the damage had been done; when Umesh Yadav yorked Bairstow shortly before lunch, they were back in the mire at 190 for six. Ashwin then won three lbw shouts and, for the first time against England, raised the ball in celebration of a five-for. He would finish the game top of the Test wicket-taking list for the year, passing Rangana Herath's 54 for Sri Lanka.

India led by 200, but Kohli gave no thought to the follow-on. Instead, he transcended the conditions with a majestic 81 out of 204, though even that total required a last-wicket stand of 42. Despite his injured foot, Broad's leg-cutters exploited an increasingly capricious pitch to claim four for 33 – easily his best figures in India, which wasn't saying much – while Rashid collected four more himself. But England's spirited response made a draw less likely: they now needed to survive at least 150 overs.

For more than 50, spread across three hours, the openers resisted, to the growing frustration of Kohli, who burned two reviews in quick succession. Hameed, struck on the glove first ball by Shami, gave a demonstration of his adhesive qualities over 144 balls, before falling to a grubber from Ashwin. But the hammer blow to England's hopes came in the final over of the day, when Cook – who had compiled his slowest Test fifty, from 171 balls – was hit in front by Jadeja, and reviewed in vain. It meant Duckett striding out with Root on the last morning, but with little sense of optimism following his first-innings working-over by Ashwin. This time, he needed just six balls to get him, for the third time in a row, a half-hearted sweep popping up via glove to Saha.

From there – and with the exception of the insatiable Bairstow – the innings disintegrated, as the trickery of Ashwin, the skiddy left-arm of Jadeja, and the bounding Jayant picked away the stitches, and the guts came tumbling out. Cook later revealed the plan had been to recreate South Africa's block fest in Delhi the previous year, when they made 143 at one an over (and still lost). Emboldened by victory, Kohli damned his opponents for a lack of intent that allowed his spinners to swarm. It all felt immaterial. Like the old submarine on Visakhapatnam's Ramakrishna Mission Beach, England's chances had long since been decommissioned.

Man of the Match: V. Kohli.

Close of play: first day, India 317-4 (Kohli 151, Ashwin 1); second day, England 103-5 (Stokes 12, Bairstow 12); third day, India 98-3 (Kohli 56, Rahane 22); fourth day, England 87-2 (Root 5).

India

M. Vijay c Stokes b Anderson	20	– c Root b Broad	3
K. L. Rahul c Stokes b Broad	0	– c Bairstow b Broad	10
C. A. Pujara c Bairstow b Anderson	119	– b Anderson	1
*V. Kohli c Stokes b Ali	167	– c Stokes b Rashid	81
A. M. Rahane c Bairstow b Anderson	23	– c Cook b Broad	26
R. Ashwin c Bairstow b Stokes	58	– c Bairstow b Broad	7
†W. P. Saha lbw b Ali	3	– lbw b Rashid	2
R. A. Jadeja lbw b Ali	0	– c Ali b Rashid	14
J. Yadav c Anderson b Rashid	35	– not out	27
U. T. Yadav c Ali b Rashid	13	– c Bairstow b Rashid	0
Mohammed Shami not out	7	– st Bairstow b Ali	19
B 4, lb 5, w 1	10	B 5, lb 8, w 1	14
1/6 (2) 2/22 (1) 3/248 (3) 4/316 (5) 5/351 (4) 6/363 (7) 7/363 (8) 8/427 (6) 9/440 (9) 10/455 (10) (129.4 overs)	455	1/16 (1) 2/17 (2) 3/40 (3) 4/117 (5) 5/127 (6) 6/130 (7) 7/151 (4) 8/162 (8) 9/162 (10) 10/204 (11) (63.1 overs)	204

Anderson 20–3–62–3; Broad 16–2–49–1; Stokes 20–4–73–1; Ansari 12–1–45–0; Rashid 34.4–2–110–2; Ali 25–1–98–3; Root 2–0–9–0. *Second innings*—Anderson 15–3–33–1; Broad 14–5–33–4; Rashid 24–3–82–4; Stokes 7–0–34–0; Ali 3.1–1–9–1.

England

*A. N. Cook b Mohammed Shami	2	– lbw b Jadeja	54
H. Hameed run out	13	– lbw b Ashwin	25
J. E. Root c U. T. Yadav b Ashwin	53	– lbw b Mohammed Shami	25
B. M. Duckett b Ashwin	5	– c Saha b Ashwin	0
M. M. Ali lbw b J. Yadav	1	– c Kohli b Jadeja	2
B. A. Stokes lbw b Ashwin	70	– b J. Yadav	6
†J. M. Bairstow b U. T. Yadav	53	– not out	34
A. U. Rashid not out	32	– c Saha b Mohammed Shami	4
Z. S. Ansari lbw b Jadeja	4	– b Ashwin	0
S. C. J. Broad lbw b Ashwin	13	– lbw b J. Yadav	5
J. M. Anderson lbw b Ashwin	0	– lbw b J. Yadav	0
B 6, lb 3	9	Lb 3	3
1/4 (1) 2/51 (2) 3/72 (4) 4/79 (3) 5/80 (5) 6/190 (7) 7/225 (6) 8/234 (9) 9/255 (10) 10/255 (11) (102.5 overs)	255	1/75 (2) 2/87 (1) 3/92 (4) 4/101 (5) 5/115 (6) 6/115 (3) 7/129 (8) 8/143 (9) 9/158 (10) 10/158 (11) (97.3 overs)	158

Mohammed Shami 14–5–28–1; U. T. Yadav 18–2–56–1; Jadeja 29–10–57–1; Ashwin 29.5–6–67–5; J. Yadav 12–3–38–1. *Second innings*—Mohammed Shami 14–3–30–2; U. T. Yadav 8–3–8–0; Ashwin 30–11–52–3; Jadeja 34–14–35–2; J. Yadav 11.3–4–30–3.

Umpires: H. D. P. K. Dharmasena and R. J. Tucker. Third umpire: C. B. Gaffaney.
Referee: R. S. Madugalle.

INDIA v ENGLAND

Third Test Match

LAWRENCE BOOTH

At Mohali, November 26–29, 2016. India won by eight wickets. Toss: England. Test debut: K. K. Nair.

Visitors to neighbouring Chandigarh have often gone the extra mile to leave their mark. In the 1950s, the Swiss-French architect Le Corbusier rebuilt the city along its distinctive grid system, while the West Indians settled for winning the inaugural Test here in 1994-95.

Cleaning up: Chris Woakes transforms a poor ball from Adil Rashid into the valuable wicket of Cheteshwar Pujara.

Otherwise, tourists have drawn a blank. There was a brief period on the second afternoon, as India lost three for eight, when England stirred, but the rebellion was quickly crushed. In this most orderly of Indian cities, Kohli's men ended up taking a bloodless route to a four-day victory – and a 2–0 lead.

England's defeat at Visakhapatnam had been hastened by the toss, but they had no such excuse here, and the result gave Kohli ammunition against those who claimed India were less potent when they batted second. England, on the other hand, were careless with the bat, and mainly toothless with the ball. Cook looked disorientated in the post-match press conference, admitting he had gone in with the wrong team – Batty spent much of the game impersonating a statue at deep cover – and drawing the only credible conclusion: his side had been outmanoeuvred at every turn.

To compound English fears that the tour was beginning to unravel, Hameed broke his left little finger. It had been hit by Mohammed Shami during the previous Test, and now Umesh Yadav repeated the dose with a snorter that flew to gully on the first morning. Scans revealed a fracture but, coming in at No. 8 on the fourth day, Hameed played an innings so full of courage and class that England were unsure whether to laugh or cry: a prince had arrived, all too briefly. Despite his protestations, he would play no further part in the series.

His determination further exposed what had come before. During that first morning – amid a gentle haze, on a pitch at its best, with a series to be squared – England had limped to lunch on 92 for four. Hameed was blameless, but Root fell to the first ball after drinks, misjudging a pull off Jayant Yadav, and Cook contrived to edge Ashwin's opener, a wide loosener he would normally hit for four. As if trying to outdo both, Ali hooked Shami to fine leg ten minutes before the break – reminiscent of the shot that all but cost David Gower his Test career at Adelaide in 1990-91. It was as mindless a session as England had endured all tour.

In the afternoon, Stokes ran past a straight one from Jadeja to make it 144 for five, pausing to return an expletive to Kohli in India's celebratory huddle, and earning a demerit point from the ICC (Kohli escaped scot-free). Bairstow and Buttler, picked as a specialist batsman for his first Test in over a year after replacing Ben Duckett, added 69. But on 43 Buttler chipped to Kohli, making swift ground from short cover to intercept a lofted drive at mid-off; and on 89 Bairstow fell lbw on review to Jayant, having been dropped behind the previous ball. Woakes, back for Stuart Broad, who was nursing his right foot, hustled to 25, but England's close-of-play 268 for eight was an opportunity wasted. Next morning, they were all out for 283.

The only surprise before lunch on the second day came when Vijay walked for a catch behind off Stokes after umpire Gaffaney had declined the appeal. But when India reached 148 for two at tea, their reply was taking as predictable a course as one of Le Corbusier's streets. Instead, Pujara swung a Rashid long hop towards deep midwicket, where Woakes held a superb tumbling catch, and Rahane's poor form was prolonged by Rashid's googly.

BATTING IN TESTS AT EVERY POSITION FROM No. 1 TO No. 9

M. M. Ali (England)
T. J. E. Andrews (Australia)
*W. W. Armstrong (Australia)
T. E. Bailey (England)
†F. M. Engineer (India)
J. M. Gregory (Australia)
‡S. E. Gregory (Australia)
†S. P. Jones (Australia)
C. Kelleway (Australia)
B. B. McCullum (New Zealand)
‡V. Mankad (India)
M. A. Noble (Australia)
‡W. Rhodes (England)
A. J. Richardson (Australia)
†R. J. Shastri (India)
G. J. Whittall (Zimbabwe)

* *Also No. 11.* † *Also No. 10.* ‡ *Also Nos 10 and 11.*

Six other England players have batted in nine different positions (but not Nos 1–9): J. M. Anderson, W. Barnes, M. J. Hoggard, A. E. Relf, F. J. Titmus and D. L. Underwood.

When the debutant Karun Nair was sent back by Kohli, only to be beaten by an alert throw from point by Buttler, India were 156 for five. The English contingent in a modest crowd began clearing their throats.

The equation seemed straightforward: get Kohli quickly, and England would have a potentially decisive first-innings lead. The first part went well. Stokes returned to find his edge, and celebrated with a self-mocking hand over mouth. Only the bowlers stood in England's way, yet – like exhibits in the nearby Rock Garden – they refused to budge. By the close, Ashwin and Jadeja had taken India within 12 of England, and next morning extended their stand to 97, before Ashwin drove Stokes to backward point. But Jadeja kept going, past his previous Test best (68 at Lord's in 2014), and Jayant got stuck in. By the time England removed Jadeja for 90, caught at long-on off Rashid, India had regained control. For the first time, their Nos 7–9 all made fifties in the same Test innings. It was the game's most telling passage. Their eventual 417 would have been par for the team batting first; as it was, they led by 134.

England's only consolations were statistical: Stokes completed his third Test five-for (and first outside the Ashes), while Umesh was Bairstow's 68th dismissal in 2016, the most by a Test wicketkeeper in a calendar year. Other numbers simply confirmed their misreading of the pitch: while Rashid got through 38 overs of probing leg-breaks, their two off-spinners, Ali and Batty – recalled for Zafar Ansari, who had a bad back but would have been dropped anyway – combined for only 29. Once more, England seemed a player short.

With Hameed beavering away in the nets like a scientist in a garden shed, trying to discover a grip that eased the pressure on his finger, Root walked out to open with Cook – an unexpected reprise of the 2013 Ashes. But the returnee looked more at home than the

Stoking the flames: Virat Kohli marks the departure of Ben Stokes.

incumbent: Cook played the spinners as if in a darkened room, narrowly surviving a Jadeja review for leg-before, then overturning a successful lbw appeal from Ashwin next ball he faced. On 12, he was put out of his misery, playing outside the line of an Ashwin delivery that was more arm-ball than off-break. It barely registered that Cook had passed Steve Waugh to move into the top ten of Test cricket's highest scorers.

Ali had batted at No. 4 in the first innings for the first time in Tests, and now came in at No. 3 for the first time too, though it was his position at Worcestershire. Like Wilfred Rhodes and Trevor Bailey, he had thus filled every Test slot in the top nine, and immediately auditioned for the role of No. 10 with a lame chip to mid-on off Ashwin, who had foxed him in the flight. Bairstow edged Jayant, and England closed the third day on 78 for four after Stokes was hit on the back leg by Ashwin, who sensibly asked for a review. Kohli ostentatiously put his finger to his lips – stirring things up even while apparently calming them down. He needn't have bothered: England were speechless in any case.

A hasty defeat beckoned when nightwatchman Batty fell in the second over of the fourth day, and Buttler swung Jayant to deep midwicket to make it 107 for six. But Root was in the mood for a scrap, completing his slowest Test half-century since his debut, from 147 balls, and Hameed knuckled down too. Had Rahane not pulled off a reflex one-handed slip catch shortly before lunch to snaffle Root for 78, India might have got twitchy. As it was, they were merely made to sweat. Having defended his way to 17 from 110 balls, Hameed nailed a slog-sweep for four off Ashwin. And, after losing Woakes and Rashid in the same over to short balls from Shami, he set about the stroke with abandon, moving to a valiant fifty – also from 147 balls – by hammering Ashwin for six. By the time Anderson was run out attempting a second, Hameed had 59, earning a handshake from Kohli. India needed 103.

Woakes removed Vijay for a duck, edging to a widish second slip, but wicketkeeper Parthiv Patel – in for the injured Wriddhaman Saha – was enjoying his chance to open in his first Test for eight years (his 83-game absence was an Indian record), and crashed a 39-ball fifty. Rashid winkled out Pujara but, with more than an hour to go before stumps, Patel supplied the finishing touch. India had avoided a series defeat against England for the first time since 2008-09. England, meanwhile, found themselves propelled to No. 2 in the Test rankings following Australia's defeat at home by South Africa – which didn't say much for the rankings.

Explaining his decision to commission Le Corbusier, the former Indian prime minister Jawaharlal Nehru once said: "The one thing which India requires in many fields is being hit on the head so that it may think." But only one side left Chandigarh with a headache.

Man of the Match: R. A. Jadeja.

Close of play: first day, England 268-8 (Rashid 4, Batty 0); second day, India 271-6 (Ashwin 57, Jadeja 31); third day, England 78-4 (Root 36, Batty 0).

England

*A. N. Cook c Patel b Ashwin	27	– b Ashwin	12
H. Hameed c Rahane b U. T. Yadav	9	– (8) not out	59
J. E. Root lbw b J. Yadav	15	– (2) c Rahane b Jadeja	78
M. M. Ali c Vijay b Mohammed Shami	16	– (3) c J. Yadav b Ashwin	5
†J. M. Bairstow lbw b J. Yadav	89	– (4) c Patel b J. Yadav	15
B. A. Stokes st Patel b Jadeja	29	– (5) lbw b Ashwin	5
J. C. Buttler c Kohli b Jadeja	43	– c Jadeja b J. Yadav	18
C. R. Woakes b U. T. Yadav	25	– (9) c Patel b Mohammed Shami	30
A. U. Rashid c Patel b Mohammed Shami	4	– (10) c U. T. Yadav b Mohammed Shami	0
G. J. Batty lbw b Mohammed Shami	1	– (6) lbw b Jadeja	0
J. M. Anderson not out	13	– run out	5
B 8, lb 3, nb 1	12	B 8, lb 1	9
1/32 (2) 2/51 (3) 3/51 (1) 4/87 (4) 5/144 (6) 6/213 (7) 7/258 (5) 8/266 (8) 9/268 (9) 10/283 (10) (93.5 overs)	283	1/27 (1) 2/39 (3) 3/70 (4) 4/78 (5) 5/78 (6) 6/107 (7) 7/152 (2) 8/195 (9) 9/195 (10) 10/236 (11) (90.2 overs)	236

Mohammed Shami 21.5–5–63–3; U. T. Yadav 16–4–58–2; J. Yadav 15–5–49–2; Ashwin 18–1–43–1; Jadeja 23–4–59–2. *Second innings*—Mohammed Shami 14–3–37–2; U. T. Yadav 8–3–26–0; Ashwin 26.2–4–81–3; Jadeja 30–12–62–2; J. Yadav 12–2–21–2.

India

M. Vijay c Bairstow b Stokes	12	– c Root b Woakes	0
†P. A. Patel lbw b Rashid	42	– not out	67
C. A. Pujara c Woakes b Rashid	51	– c Root b Rashid	25
*V. Kohli c Bairstow b Stokes	62	– not out	6
A. M. Rahane lbw b Rashid	0		
K. K. Nair run out	4		
R. Ashwin c Buttler b Stokes	72		
R. A. Jadeja c Woakes b Rashid	90		
J. Yadav c Ali b Stokes	55		
U. T. Yadav c Bairstow b Stokes	12		
Mohammed Shami not out	1		
B 8, lb 4, w 3, nb 1	16	B 4, lb 1, nb 1	6
1/39 (1) 2/73 (2) 3/148 (3) 4/152 (5) 5/156 (6) 6/204 (4) 7/301 (7) 8/381 (8) 9/414 (9) 10/417 (10) (138.2 overs)	417	1/7 (1) 2/88 (3) (2 wkts, 20.2 overs)	104

Anderson 21–4–48–0; Woakes 24–7–86–0; Ali 13–1–33–0; Rashid 38–6–118–4; Stokes 26.2–5–73–5; Batty 16–0–47–0. *Second innings*—Anderson 3–2–8–0; Woakes 2–0–16–1; Rashid 5–0–28–1; Stokes 4–0–16–0; Ali 3–0–13–0; Batty 3.2–0–18–0.

Umpires: M. Erasmus and C. B. Gaffaney. Third umpire: H. D. P. K. Dharmasena.
Referee: R. S. Madugalle.

INDIA v ENGLAND

Fourth Test Match

TIM WIGMORE

At Mumbai, December 8–12, 2016. India won by an innings and 36 runs. Toss: England. Test debut: K. K. Jennings.

November 1988 was a time before the assassination of Rajiv Gandhi, the fall of the Berlin Wall, and the creation of the Spice Girls. It was also the last time India had played a Test at Mumbai without Sachin Tendulkar. To judge by the intermittent chants of his name, and the T-shirts worn in the crowd, the reverence in his home town had not dimmed. But the spectators had room in their hearts for a new champion. As Virat Kohli turned to salute them on the fourth afternoon, after an imperious 235, he had produced a performance fit to rank with Tendulkar himself. This was Kohli's 41st international century. And if Tendulkar's round 100 remained a world away, Kohli – born three weeks before that 1988 Mumbai Test – has the desire and skill to get close.

George Foreman once fought five bouts on one night. Here, Kohli confronted six frontline bowlers over two days, dismantling them all in compiling his fourth Test century of the year, and third double. He wowed in glorious technicolour, with serene straight-drives, dextrous sweeps and meticulous placement; in stifling heat, he also scampered twos throughout his 515 minutes at the crease. It was the measure of a cricketer who gauges his fitness not against team-mates or opponents, but the world's best athletes.

INDIA'S BEST MATCH FIGURES AGAINST ENGLAND

12-108	V. Mankad	at Chennai	1951-52
12-167	**R. Ashwin**	**at Mumbai**	**2016-17**
12-181	L. Sivaramakrishnan	at Mumbai	1984-85
10-154	**R. A. Jadeja**	**at Chennai**	**2016-17**
10-177	S. A. Durani	at Chennai	1961-62
10-188	C. Sharma	at Birmingham	1986
10-233	A. Kumble	at Ahmedabad	2001-02

Earlier in the year, he discovered that his body-fat percentage was nine, among the lowest for any cricketer, and set his sights on tennis star Novak Djokovic's 7.5. England's attempts to unsettle him – three of Kohli's first eight deliveries were bouncers from Ball – proved futile. This was, he reckoned, his second-best Test innings, behind his audacious 141 at Adelaide in December 2014. A Sunday morning stroll to the Oval Maidan, with Kohli 147 not out overnight, confirmed his silky late cuts were inspiring a new generation.

And yet he was only one of two Indian giants on show. With 12 wickets, a product of subtle variations, a shrewd cricketing brain and remorseless accuracy, Ashwin took his series haul to 27. England had not merely encountered the world's pre-eminent batsman and bowler in these conditions: after dominating a draw in Rajkot, they had been treated more brutally with every Test. It didn't help that their selection was again awry, as Cook admitted. Having picked a spinner too many in Mohali, they overcorrected, picking a spinner too few *and* a bowler too many. Ali and Rashid were in tandem from the eighth over and, when England fielded for the duration of the third day, Woakes bowled only three overs, even as Rashid bowled 28 straight.

England could rue sliding-doors moments, too. In the first innings, they looked refreshed – most of the players had gone to Dubai between Tests – and made good on

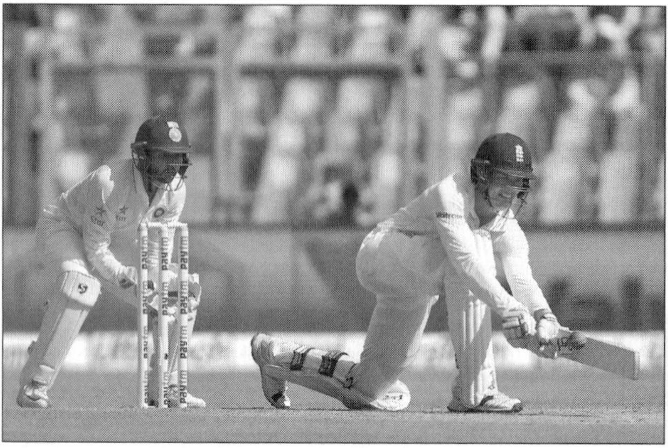

Sweeping statement: Keaton Jennings announces himself in Test cricket with a first-day hundred.

their promise to greet India's slow bowlers with renewed intent. After becoming the first England batsman to score 2,000 Test runs against India, Cook was even stumped, charging Jadeja's third ball, having played positively for 46. And debutant Keaton Jennings made almost as powerful an impression as the man he had replaced, Haseeb Hameed, now watching in the stands where he was nursing his newly operated little finger. Jennings made a jittery start – he was dropped by Nair in the gully before he had scored – but he was compact and unruffled, and proficient on the cut, pull and drive. Despite concerns about how another left-hander would cope with Ashwin, he repeatedly unfurled his reverse sweep, using it to bring up his century – the first by an England opener on debut since Cook, at Nagpur, a decade earlier, and only the fourth by an England batsman on his first day of Test cricket, after W. G. Grace (1880), George Gunn (1907-08) and Billy Griffith (1947-48).

The only shame was that the moment escaped his parents: Alison and Ray – the former South Africa coach – were holidaying in Mauritius, where their hotel lost power for an hour when he was on 96. Umpire Paul Reiffel was also absent, having been hit on the back of the head at square leg by a gentle return throw from Bhuvneshwar Kumar halfway through the day. He was taken to hospital with concussion, and third official Marais Erasmus stepped in for the rest of the match.

During a 94-run partnership with Ali, Jennings lifted England to 230 for two – from which they should have made 450. But, two balls after reaching an enterprising half-century, Ali fell slog-sweeping Ashwin; when Jennings prodded to gully two balls later, India had a route back into the match. Like Cook and Ali, Bairstow was complicit in his own downfall, top-edging a sweep to deep backward square. And, after England had slipped to 334 for eight, it required Buttler's most mature Test innings – a mix of nimble footwork, reverse sweeps and judicious defence – and freewheeling from Ball to lift them to 400. It felt a touch over par: no side had lost at the Wankhede after making more than England's 347 in 1992-93. But Kohli did not care.

Incongruously, given what transpired, England threatened a first-innings lead. On the third afternoon, after Root – briefly in charge while Cook was off the field – had burgled two wickets, India were 307 for six. Eight runs later, Rashid enticed Kohli, on 68, into a drive; he mistimed it back to the bowler's left hand, but survived. It was

Jayant stride: Yadav hits India's first Test hundred from No. 9.

not England's only error. Bairstow had missed a stumping off a Rashid googly when Vijay had 45; later, from the fourth delivery of the second new ball, delayed until the 130th over, Root spilled Jayant off Anderson at second slip on eight. The three chances cost a combined 354.

In Australia three years earlier, England had been mocked for their copious support staff; *The Sun* harangued the 61 "guilty men", including 29 non-players, involved in that disastrous tour. Now, they could be accused of a shortfall. They lacked a specialist fielding, wicketkeeping and spin-bowling coach; consultant keeping and spin coaches had been used earlier in the tour, but both left before this Test.

Desperate for a breakthrough, Cook frittered away his reviews. And when Jayant, on 28, edged Ali to Bairstow down the leg side, umpire Oxenford failed to spot it. Kohli, who was having a better game than the officials, gleefully performed a mock review signal. England's humiliation was far from over. Kohli accelerated effortlessly: his first 50 took 111 balls, his second 76, his third 59, his fourth 56, and his final 35 another 38. He finished with India's highest score against England (for eight days at least), beating Vinod Kambli's 224 at the Wankhede in 1992-93, as well as the highest score by an Indian captain, and – for the first time – a Test average above 50. Jayant, meanwhile, compiled a maiden Test century, the first by an Indian No. 9. They added 241 for the eighth wicket, another Indian record, and two short of the overall record against England, set at Adelaide in 1907-08 by Roger Hartigan and Clem Hill. Having expected their own lower order to be an advantage, England were again left ruing the depth of India's batting.

As the stadium revelled in India's omnipotence, Jennings's golden duck – a victim of Bhuvneshwar's late swing – was suitably chastening. Given the quality of the bowling, Root and Bairstow later showed chutzpah as they swept with power and intent to force Kohli on the defensive. Yet, beyond their stand of 92, England's innings betrayed the effects of India's relentlessness. It was absurd that Ali, fresh – or not – from bowling 53 overs, was batting by the 12th over at No. 4, with Buttler down at No. 8 because Ball was used as a nightwatchman. After a sparkling 77, Root misread Jayant's length, before

Stokes was caught at slip when a reverse sweep rebounded off his boot. The fourth day ended when Ball edged Ashwin behind, leaving England 182 for six.

Most had expected a quick kill on the final morning, yet few envisaged quite how quick. A blur of raucous appeals and beguiling bowling from Ashwin – especially a wondrous carrom ball to snare Bairstow – secured India the series with a spell of six for seven in 37 balls either side of stumps. Ashwin even had the pleasure of riling Anderson, forlornly walking out at No. 11; at a press conference the previous evening, Anderson had the temerity to suggest that home conditions disguised the technical flaws England had exposed in Kohli in 2014. In this game, criticising him was not the done thing.

HUNDRED AND DUCK ON TEST DEBUT

0 and 137	G. R. Viswanath	India v Australia at Kanpur	1969-70
163 and 0	A. C. Hudson	South Africa v West Indies at Bridgetown	1991-92
0 and 109*	Mohammad Wasim	Pakistan v New Zealand at Lahore	1996-97
112 and 0	**K. K. Jennings**	**England v India at Mumbai**	**2016-17**

Jennings alone made a first-ball duck; Hudson faced two balls, Wasim four and Viswanath 17. B. R. Taylor scored 105 and 0 on debut for New Zealand v India at Calcutta in 1964-65.*

As Ashwin and Kohli led India's victory lap, the spectators unperturbed that the final day had lasted barely half an hour, there seemed a wider significance. Crowds were excellent throughout, even though the absence of Ajinkya Rahane – who broke a finger facing pre-match throwdowns – meant a Mumbai Test lacked a local player for the first time. TV executives talked giddily of the "Virat effect", with audiences up a quarter on the series with South Africa a year earlier. Suddenly Test cricket in India seemed altogether more vibrant. If the format's *raison d'être* is as a bastion of excellence, undiluted by the constraints of time, the ideal was embodied, once again, by India's two totems, leaving boisterous supporters little reason to feel nostalgic for the age of Tendulkar.

Man of the Match: V. Kohli.

Close of play: first day, England 288-5 (Stokes 25, Buttler 18); second day, India 146-1 (Vijay 70, Pujara 47); third day, India 451-7 (Kohli 147, J. Yadav 30); fourth day, England 182-6 (Bairstow 50).

England

*A. N. Cook st Patel b Jadeja	46	– lbw b Jadeja	18
K. K. Jennings c Pujara b Ashwin	112	– lbw b Bhuvneshwar Kumar	0
J. E. Root c Kohli b Ashwin	21	– lbw b J. Yadav	77
M. M. Ali c Nair b Ashwin	50	– c Vijay b Jadeja	0
†J. M. Bairstow c U. T. Yadav b Ashwin	14	– lbw b Ashwin	51
B. A. Stokes c Kohli b Ashwin	31	– c Vijay b Ashwin	18
J. C. Buttler b Jadeja	76	– (8) not out	6
C. R. Woakes c Patel b Jadeja	11	– (9) b Ashwin	0
A. U. Rashid b Jadeja	4	– (10) c Rahul b Ashwin	2
J. T. Ball c Patel b Ashwin	31	– (7) c Patel b Ashwin	2
J. M. Anderson not out	0	– c U. T. Yadav b Ashwin	2
B 1, lb 2, nb 1	4	B 15, lb 2, nb 2	19
1/99 (1) 2/136 (3) 3/230 (4) 4/230 (2) 5/249 (5) 6/297 (6) 7/320 (8) 8/334 (9) 9/388 (10) 10/400 (7) (130.1 overs)	400	1/1 (2) 2/43 (1) 3/49 (4) 4/141 (3) 5/180 (6) 6/182 (7) 7/185 (5) 8/189 (9) 9/193 (10) 10/195 (11) (55.3 overs)	195

Bhuvneshwar Kumar 13–0–49–0; U. T. Yadav 11–2–38–0; Ashwin 44–4–112–6; J. Yadav 25–3–89–0; Jadeja 37.1–5–109–4. *Second innings*—Bhuvneshwar Kumar 4–1–11–1; U. T. Yadav 3–0–10–0; Jadeja 22–3–63–2; Ashwin 20.3–3–55–6; J. Yadav 6–0–39–1.

India

K. L. Rahul b Ali	24
M. Vijay c and b Rashid	136
C. A. Pujara b Ball	47
*V. Kohli c Anderson b Woakes	235
K. K. Nair lbw b Ali	13
†P. A. Patel c Bairstow b Root	15
R. Ashwin c Jennings b Root	0
R. A. Jadeja c Buttler b Rashid	25
J. Yadav st Bairstow b Rashid	104
Bhuvneshwar Kumar c Woakes b Rashid	9
U. T. Yadav not out	7
B 5, lb 8, w 3	16
1/39 (1) 2/146 (3) 3/262 (2) 4/279 (5) 5/305 (6) 6/307 (7) 7/364 (8) 8/605 (9) 9/615 (4) 10/631 (10) (182.3 overs)	631

Anderson 20–5–63–0; Woakes 16–2–79–1; Ali 53–5–174–2; Rashid 55.3–5–192–4; Ball 18–5–47–1; Stokes 10–2–32–0; Root 10–2–31–2.

Umpires: B. N. J. Oxenford and P. R. Reiffel. Third umpire: M. Erasmus.
Erasmus replaced Reiffel when he was injured on the first day, and C. Shamshuddin took over as third umpire.
Referee: J. J. Crowe.

INDIA v ENGLAND

Fifth Test Match

DILEEP PREMACHANDRAN

At Chennai, December 16–20, 2016. India won by an innings and 75 runs. Toss: England. Test debut: L. A. Dawson.

England's previous Test at Chennai, in December 2008, had taken place in the shadow of the Mumbai terror attacks. Eight years on, they were greeted by a natural calamity: Cyclone Vardah had swept through the city four days before the start. Thousands of trees were uprooted, and normal life had ground to a halt, but intrepid groundstaff repaired a fallen sightscreen, and used trays of hot coals to dry the pitch. The cricket had to go on.

India were thankful it did. Years from now, England will still be scratching their heads and wondering how they lost. They kept Ashwin to match figures of one for 207 on his home ground, and dismissed Pujara and Kohli for a combined 31. Yet they ended up breaking some grim records: no team had lost a Test by an innings after scoring more than their 477 first time round, nor conceded more in an innings against India.

As they had throughout the series, the Indians found heroes for every decisive passage of play. Ishant Sharma, in his first Test of the home season, was a constant threat, while

---

HIGHEST MAIDEN TEST HUNDREDS

365*	G. S. Sobers	West Indies v Pakistan at Kingston	1957-58
311	R. B. Simpson	Australia v England at Manchester	1964
303*	**K. K. Nair**	**India v England at Chennai**	**2016-17**
287	R. E. Foster†	England v Australia at Sydney	1903-04
277	B. C. Lara	West Indies v Australia at Sydney	1992-93
274	Zaheer Abbas	Pakistan v England at Birmingham	1971
256	R. B. Kanhai	West Indies v India at Calcutta	1958-59
255*	D. J. McGlew	South Africa v New Zealand at Wellington	1952-53
251	W. R. Hammond	England v Australia at Sydney	1928-29
250	S. F. A. F. Bacchus	West Indies v India at Kanpur	1978-79

† *On debut.*

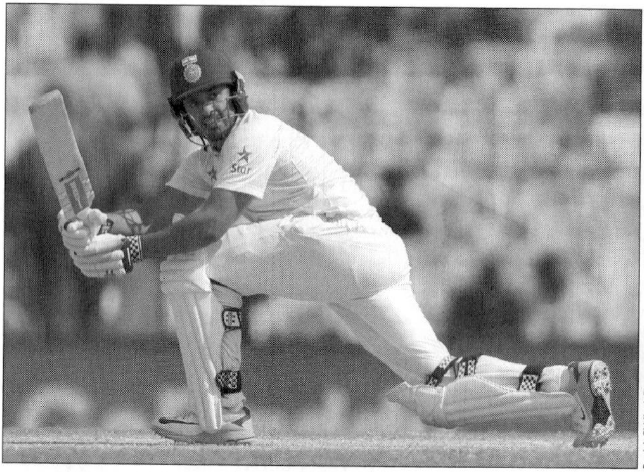

Triple jump: Karun Nair leapt to third on the list of highest innings for India with an unbeaten 303.

Jadeja kept England from disappearing over the horizon on the first day. With the bat, Rahul and Patel stitched together India's first three-figure opening partnership in 18 months. That was built on by a colossal triple-century from Karun Nair, in only his third Test. With England left to negotiate the final day, it was Jadeja – his pace and trajectory perfect for a placid surface – who landed the telling blows to give India four Test wins in a series against England for the first time.

That had seemed implausible at tea on the second day, with England having ridden on Ali's 146 and the lower-order pluck of Rashid and debutant Liam Dawson to secure a handy total. Following the early demise of Jennings and Cook – who had reached 11,000 Test runs from the first ball of the match, pushing Umesh Yadav into the covers for two – Ali had been fortunate to get off the mark, an uppish flick off Jadeja bursting through Rahul's hands at midwicket. But once he settled, he played some delightful strokes, wresting the initiative away from India with the help of Root. Ali was initially flummoxed by Ashwin's variations, but Root's more decisive footwork helped upset the spinners' rhythm. He played a succession of superb sweeps, while Ali was unafraid to hit Mishra's leg-breaks against the turn and on the up, even if Mishra – recalled in place of the hamstrung Jayant Yadav – was serving up some freebies.

The partnership was worth 146 by the time Jadeja had Root caught behind sweeping for a very Rootish 88 shortly before tea: Kohli asked for a review, and UltraEdge showed the thinnest of bottom edges. But there was no let-up in England's intensity. Bairstow smashed Jadeja for a straight six and, after the break, heaved him and Ashwin over midwicket. With Ali making languid progress, India were in danger of wilting in the late-afternoon heat. Once more, a false shot opened the door – Bairstow, too early on the drive, lofting Jadeja to short cover to depart for 49. A lovely inside-out drive off Mishra took Ali to 99, then a tap and run to his second hundred of the series, and fourth of the year. At stumps, England were a commanding 284 for four.

India needed a little over an hour to redress the balance next morning. Stokes feathered the fifth ball, from Sharma, who then persuaded Buttler to play round a straight one. Ali lofted Ashwin for six, then clipped him through midwicket, but grew jittery against the short stuff, used sparingly the previous day. Sharma greeted Dawson with a bouncer that thudded into his helmet, though it was Ali who fell next, top-edging Umesh's fourth delivery after drinks to Jadeja in the deep.

At 321 for seven, another sub-par total loomed for England, but Dawson and Rashid were in defiant mood. They built slowly at first, but played some attractive shots as confidence soared with the mercury. Kohli tried several combinations, but nothing worked, and Mishra came in for heavy punishment. The partnership was worth 108, England's highest in India for the eighth wicket, by the time Rashid flailed at Umesh. But Broad clattered 19, his highest Test score of the year, and both Dawson and Ball struck sixes in an Ashwin over that cost 17. A Mishra googly ended India's misery, leaving Dawson unconquered on 66 – the highest score by an England No. 8 on debut, surpassing David Bairstow's 59 against India at The Oval in 1979.

NO SAFETY IN NUMBERS

Teams who batted first and scored 400 – but lost by an innings:

England (405 and 251) lost to Australia (695) at The Oval	1930
Sri Lanka (400 and 82) lost to England (496-5 dec) at Cardiff	2011
England (400 and 195) lost to India (631) at Mumbai	**2016-17**
England (477 and 207) lost to India (759-7 dec) at Chennai	**2016-17**
Pakistan (443-9 dec and 163) lost to Australia (624-8 dec) at Melbourne	**2016-17**

India needed to start well, and Rahul and Patel – opening because Vijay had injured his shoulder – married circumspection with some pleasing shots before stumps. Their intent was clear the following morning: Rahul twice struck Dawson down the ground, while Patel was typically busy. Runs came at a clip, before Patel finally fell for a Test-best 71, to a leading edge off Ali. England got the ball changed three deliveries into the second session, and Stokes snared Pujara with the replacement, driving loosely at one that shaped away. Kohli strode out to loud cheers, but failed for the first time in the series, picking out Jennings at short cover as Broad came round the wicket.

With India 211 for three, England had a glimmer – but Rahul, having eased to a century thanks to an overthrow, consolidated with the help of a man he first met when they were 11. Nair had seemed ill at ease in his first two appearances, but a sumptuous straight-drive off Broad got him going. England dried up the runs after Ball struck Rahul in the ribs. But when Nair edged Ball on 34, the chance brushed Cook's fingertips at slip on the way to the boundary, and when he survived a review off Ali on 69, England sensed it wouldn't be their day. They had to settle for spoiling Rahul's. On 199, he latched on to a poor delivery from Rashid – and sliced it to Buttler at point, sinking to his haunches in despair. Among Indian batsmen, only Mohammad Azharuddin – 30 years earlier, against Sri Lanka at Kanpur – had been dismissed one short of a Test double.

Vijay fell next morning for 29, giving Dawson his first Test wicket. And India were kept to 72 in the session, thanks to the thrift of both Dawson and Stokes, who took a chunk out of Nair's bat, but not before he had reached his maiden Test hundred. What followed was carnage. If the ball was full, he drove or swept, orthodox and reverse; if it was short, he pulled and cut. When Nair had 154, Bairstow caught a reverse sweep off Rashid but, with few supporting his appeal, the umpire wasn't interested. Ashwin was the perfect foil, as Nair went from 100 to 200 in 121 balls. By the time Buttler took a brilliant catch to send back Ashwin, they had added 181.

The punishment wasn't over. Root dropped Nair at slip off Ball on 217, and Bairstow fluffed a stumping off Ali on 246. Nair's bat then produced tom-tom drumbeats against the tired Rashid and Ali. With Jadeja racing to a half-century in 52 deliveries, the two

More questions than answers: Ravindra Jadeja dismisses Joe Root to send England hurtling towards an innings defeat.

added 138 in 115. Nair's third hundred needed just 75, making him only the second Test player – after Wally Hammond at Auckland in 1932-33 – to pass 200 and 300 in the same session. In all, he struck 32 fours and four sixes; only Virender Sehwag (twice) had scored more for India. They declared on 759 for seven, beating their 726 for nine against Sri Lanka at Mumbai's Brabourne Stadium in 2009-10. It was also the most England had conceded, surpassing 751 for five by West Indies in Antigua in 2003-04, when Brian Lara made his 400 not out.

Trailing by 282, England negotiated the fifth morning to raise hopes of a draw. And, although Kohli didn't bring Jadeja on until the 20th over of the day, it was the catalyst for a stunning collapse. After an opening stand of 103, Cook fell to him for the sixth time in the series, flicking to leg slip; Jennings was caught and bowled, deceived in the flight, and Root given out lbw on review after missing a sweep. Bairstow then checked a flick off Sharma, only for Jadeja to hare towards deep midwicket and take a stunning catch over his shoulder. Like Root, Bairstow had fallen just short of overhauling Michael Vaughan's England record of 1,481 Test runs in a calendar year.

England were four down at tea, but the meltdown – when it came – was spectacular. Ali was taken athletically by Ashwin at mid-on, and Stokes chipped to Nair at short midwicket. Dawson fell to a Mishra googly, Rashid to the new ball, and Broad to backward short leg. When Ball edged – fittingly, to Nair – Jadeja had taken seven for 48 and, for the first time, ten in the match; as at Mumbai, England had lost their last six wickets for 15. It was a day that summed up their cataclysmic tour, with isolated pockets of defiance not nearly enough against a rampaging India.

Man of the Match: K. K. Nair. *Man of the Series:* V. Kohli.

Close of play: first day, England 284-4 (Ali 120, Stokes 5); second day, India 60-0 (Rahul 30, Patel 28); third day, India 391-4 (Nair 71, Vijay 17); fourth day, England 12-0 (Cook 3, Jennings 9).

England

*A. N. Cook c Kohli b Jadeja	10	– c Rahul b Jadeja	49
K. K. Jennings c Patel b Sharma	1	– c and b Jadeja	54
J. E. Root c Patel b Jadeja	88	– lbw b Jadeja	6
M. M. Ali c Jadeja b Yadav	146	– c Ashwin b Jadeja	44
†J. M. Bairstow c Rahul b Jadeja	49	– c Jadeja b Sharma	1
B. A. Stokes c Patel b Ashwin	6	– c Nair b Jadeja	23
J. C. Buttler lbw b Sharma	5	– not out	6
L. A. Dawson not out	66	– b Mishra	0
A. U. Rashid c Patel b Yadav	60	– c Jadeja b Yadav	2
S. C. J. Broad run out	19	– c Pujara b Jadeja	1
J. T. Ball b Mishra	12	– c Nair b Jadeja	0
B 4, lb 5, w 1, p 5	15	B 12, lb 8, w 1	21
1/7 (2) 2/21 (1) 3/167 (3) 4/253 (5) 5/287 (6) 6/300 (7) 7/321 (4) 8/429 (9) 9/455 (10) 10/477 (11) (157.2 overs)	477	1/103 (1) 2/110 (2) 3/126 (3) 4/129 (5) 5/192 (4) 6/193 (6) 7/196 (8) 8/200 (9) 9/207 (10) 10/207 (11) (88 overs)	207

Yadav 21–3–73–2; Sharma 21–6–42–2; Jadeja 45–9–106–3; Ashwin 44–3–151–1; Mishra 25.2–5–87–1; Nair 1–0–4–0. *Second innings*—Sharma 10–2–17–1; Ashwin 25–6–56–0; Jadeja 25–5–48–7; Yadav 14–1–36–1; Mishra 14–4–30–1.

India

K. L. Rahul c Buttler b Rashid	199	R. A. Jadeja c Ball b Dawson	51
†P. A. Patel c Buttler b Ali	71	U. T. Yadav not out	1
C. A. Pujara c Cook b Stokes	16	B 2, lb 4, w 1	7
*V. Kohli c Jennings b Broad	15		
K. K. Nair not out	303	1/152 (2) (7 wkts dec, 190.4 overs)	759
M. Vijay lbw b Dawson	29	2/181 (3) 3/211 (4)	
R. Ashwin c Buttler b Broad	67	4/372 (1) 5/435 (6) 6/616 (7) 7/754 (8)	

A. Mishra and I. Sharma did not bat.

Broad 27–6–80–2; Ball 23–2–93–0; Ali 41–1–190–1; Stokes 20–2–76–1; Rashid 29.4–1–153–1; Dawson 43–4–129–2; Root 2–0–12–0; Jennings 5–1–20–0.

Umpires: M. Erasmus and S. D. Fry. Third umpire: B. N. J. Oxenford.
Referee: J. J. Crowe.

At Mumbai (Brabourne), January 10, 2017 (day/night). **England XI won by three wickets. India A 304-5** (50 overs) (S. Dhawan 63, A. T. Rayudu 100, Yuvraj Singh 56, M. S. Dhoni 68*); ‡**England XI 307-7** (48.5 overs) (J. J. Roy 62, S. W. Billings 93; Kuldeep Yadav 5-60). *Chris Woakes (0-71) and Jake Ball (2-61) proved expensive as a strong India A line-up passed 300, thanks to a round 100 from Ambati Rayudu (who retired out) and rapid half-centuries from the veterans Yuvraj Singh and skipper M. S. Dhoni, whose 68* took just 40 balls. But after openers Jason Roy and Alex Hales put on 95 in 14.3 overs, Sam Billings shared stands of 79 with Jos Buttler and 99 with Liam Dawson, as England overcame the threat posed by the unorthodox slow left-armer Kuldeep Yadav, who finished with his best List A figures.*

At Mumbai (Brabourne), January 12, 2017. **India A won by six wickets.** ‡**England XI 282** (48.5 overs) (A. D. Hales 51, J. M. Bairstow 64; Parvez Rasool 3-38); **India A 283-4** (39.4 overs) (A. M. Rahane 91, S. P. Jackson 59, R. R. Pant 59). *An entirely different India A side looked weaker on paper than two days previously – but raced to victory. It would have been even more of a stroll, but for a tenth-wicket stand of 71 between Adil Rashid and David Willey. England's white-ball captain Eoin Morgan, out for three in the previous game, went first ball this time, as did Buttler. India A's openers Ajinkya Rahane and Sheldon Jackson started with 119 in 18.5 overs, then the prolific Rishabh Pant spanked 59 from 36 deliveries. Both sides chose from 12 players.*

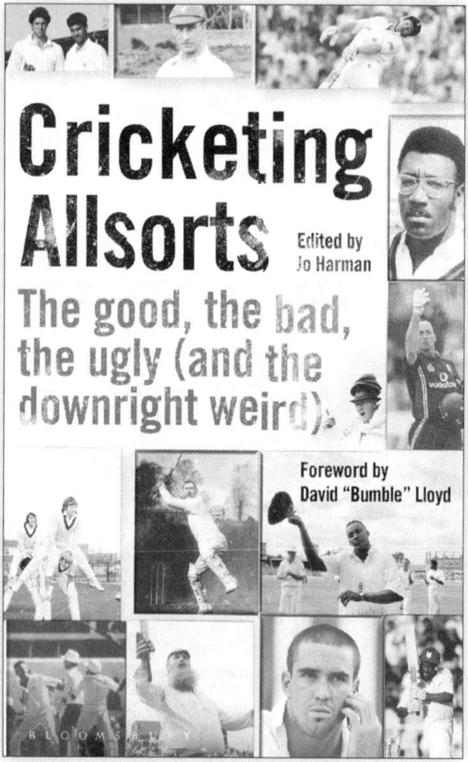
Cricketing
Allsorts
Edited by
Jo Harman
The good, the bad, the ugly (and the downright weird)
Foreword by
David "Bumble" Lloyd
BLOOMSBURY

LIMITED-OVERS INTERNATIONAL REPORTS BY JOHN STERN

INDIA v ENGLAND

First One-Day International

At Gahunje, January 15, 2017 (day/night). India won by three wickets. Toss: India.

England's highest one-day total against India – for four days – was still no match for the class of Kohli. His 27th ODI century was a gem, even by his standards, and his 15th in a successful chase, surpassing Sachin Tendulkar's record of 14. It included an array of audacious shots, none better than an outrageous clip-cum-pull to despatch a Woakes slower ball for six over wide long-on. Kohli's improbable alliance for the fifth wicket with Kedar Jadhav, playing on his home ground, yielded a scarcely believable 200 in 147 balls, and rescued India from 63 for four as they pursued a daunting 351. England's plan, according to Morgan, was to keep Kohli off strike, but they had reckoned without Jadhav's uncomplicated hitting. His 65-ball hundred was the sixth fastest by an Indian, yet it was barely noticed by a Kohli-obsessed full house. That England scored as many as they did was down largely to Stokes's late barrage. He made 62 off 40 balls, with five sixes on this small ground, as England plundered 105 from the final eight overs. They had, however, scored only 30 between the 35th and 40th, and Morgan's post-match assessment was that the flourish disguised other flaws. Roy was out-thought by Jadeja, and stumped, having cracked 73 from 61 balls. As so often, Root, who had joined the limited-overs leg of the tour late because of the birth of his first child, anchored the innings, though his 78 took 95. Willey struck twice with the new ball, before Yuvraj Singh (in his first ODI for more than three years) and Dhoni (back in the ranks after ceding the captaincy to Kohli) fell cheaply. For England, though, that was as good as it got.

Man of the Match: K. M. Jadhav.

England

J. J. Roy st Dhoni b Jadeja	73
A. D. Hales run out	9
J. E. Root c Pandya b Bumrah	78
*E. J. G. Morgan c Dhoni b Pandya	28
†J. C. Buttler c Dhawan b Pandya	31
B. A. Stokes c Yadav b Bumrah	62
M. M. Ali b Yadav	28
C. R. Woakes not out	9
D. J. Willey not out	10
B 1, lb 11, w 6, nb 4	22
1/39 (2) 2/108 (1) 3/157 (4) 4/220 (5) 5/244 (3) 6/317 (6) 7/336 (7) (7 wkts, 50 overs)	350
10 overs: 67-1	

A. U. Rashid and J. T. Ball did not bat.

Yadav 7–0–63–1; Pandya 9–0–46–2; Bumrah 10–0–79–2; Jadeja 10–0–50–1; Ashwin 8–0–63–0; Jadhav 4–0–23–0; Yuvraj Singh 2–0–14–0.

India

K. L. Rahul b Willey	8
S. Dhawan c Ali b Willey	1
*V. Kohli c Willey b Stokes	122
Yuvraj Singh c Buttler b Stokes	15
†M. S. Dhoni c Willey b Ball	6
K. M. Jadhav c Stokes b Ball	120
H. H. Pandya not out	40
R. A. Jadeja c Rashid b Ball	13
R. Ashwin not out	15
B 1, lb 4, w 11	16
1/13 (2) 2/24 (1) 3/56 (4) 4/63 (5) 5/263 (3) 6/291 (6) 7/318 (8) (7 wkts, 48.1 overs)	356
10 overs: 51-2	

U. T. Yadav and J. J. Bumrah did not bat.

Woakes 8–0–44–0; Willey 6–0–47–2; Ball 10–0–67–3; Stokes 10–0–73–2; Rashid 5–0–50–0; Ali 6.1–0–48–0; Root 3–0–22–0.

Umpires: H. D. P. K. Dharmasena and C. K. Nandan. Third umpire: R. S. A. Palliyaguruge.
Referee: A. J. Pycroft.

INDIA v ENGLAND

Second One-Day International

At Cuttack, January 19, 2017 (day/night). India won by 15 runs. Toss: England.

India clinched the series after producing another middle-order double-century partnership. And again, England could not capitalise on a strong position. Kohli failed for once, dismissed for eight in a superb opening spell by Woakes which left India 25 for three. But, after three successive maidens, he was taken out of the attack – and the pressure released. Yuvraj Singh and Dhoni, both 35, and with 580 one-day internationals between them, hit the short-pitched strategy of England's wayward pace attack – including Plunkett, in for Adil Rashid – to all parts of the heavily fenced Barabati Stadium. They ended up adding 256, the second-highest stand for the fourth wicket in one-day internationals, behind compatriots Mohammad Azharuddin and Ajay Jadeja, against Zimbabwe here in April 1998. Yuvraj made his first 50-over century since the 2011 World Cup, and in the meantime had survived cancer. Now he broke his own record for the highest score for India against England (previously 138 not out at Rajkot in 2008-09), facing 127 balls in all; Dhoni faced 122, and hit six sixes. Roy made a bright 82 off 73, though England were never truly in the hunt until Morgan, making his first ODI hundred since June 2015, and Plunkett hit 50 off 25 balls for the eighth wicket. But Morgan's run-out after backing up too far extinguished all hope. Earlier, Root had made his seventh fifty in nine one-day internationals, without converting any into centuries. Hales was later ruled out for the rest of the trip after breaking his right hand attempting a catch.

Man of the Match: Yuvraj Singh.

India

K. L. Rahul c Stokes b Woakes	5	R. A. Jadeja not out	16
S. Dhawan b Woakes	11		
*V. Kohli c Stokes b Woakes	8	B 4, lb 2, w 9, nb 1	16
Yuvraj Singh c Buttler b Woakes	150		
†M. S. Dhoni c Willey b Plunkett	134	1/14 (1) 2/22 (3) (6 wkts, 50 overs)	381
K. M. Jadhav c Ball b Plunkett	22	3/25 (2) 4/281 (4)	
H. H. Pandya not out	19	5/323 (6) 6/358 (5) 10 overs: 43-3	

R. Ashwin, Bhuvneshwar Kumar and J. J. Bumrah did not bat.

Woakes 10–3–60–4; Willey 5–0–32–0; Ball 10–0–80–0; Plunkett 10–1–91–2; Stokes 9–0–79–0; Ali 6–0–33–0.

England

J. J. Roy b Jadeja	82	L. E. Plunkett not out	26
A. D. Hales c Dhoni b Bumrah	14	D. J. Willey not out	5
J. E. Root c Kohli b Ashwin	54	Lb 7, w 4, nb 1	12
*E. J. G. Morgan run out	102		
B. A. Stokes b Ashwin	1	1/28 (2) 2/128 (3) (8 wkts, 50 overs)	366
†J. C. Buttler st Dhoni b Ashwin	10	3/170 (1) 4/173 (5)	
M. M. Ali b Bhuvneshwar Kumar	55	5/206 (6) 6/299 (7)	
C. R. Woakes b Bumrah	5	7/304 (8) 8/354 (4) 10 overs: 66-1	

J. T. Ball did not bat.

Bhuvneshwar Kumar 10–1–63–1; Bumrah 9–0–81–2; Jadeja 10–0–45–1; Pandya 6–0–60–0; Ashwin 10–0–65–3; Jadhav 5–0–45–0.

Umpires: A. K. Chaudhary and R. S. A. Palliyaguruge. Third umpire: H. D. P. K. Dharmasena. Referee: A. J. Pycroft.

INDIA v ENGLAND

Third One-Day International

At Kolkata, January 22, 2017 (day/night). England won by five runs. Toss: India.

England won their first match of the winter against India as the one-day series enjoyed a noisy conclusion in front of 56,770 at Eden Gardens. When Jadhav scooped the first two balls of the final over, from Woakes, over extra cover for six and four, India needed only six to complete a whitewash. Instead, for the first time in the series, England's death bowling matched India's ferocious hitting: Woakes produced two dot balls, before Jadhav smeared him to Billings at deep cover to depart for 90 from 75. Bhuvneshwar Kumar was unable to score off the final delivery. After India had inserted England on a pitch of unexpected pace and bounce, Roy and Billings played and missed 15 times in the first eight overs. Roy passed 50 for the third time in the series, before once again falling to Jadeja. Bairstow, replacing the injured Joe Root, was caught at third man off a Bumrah no-ball on 28, and overturned a caught-behind decision off Pandya on 46, but did not exploit his fortune, tamely cutting Pandya to point ten runs later. It was left to Stokes to refuel the innings on the ground where, nine months earlier, Carlos Brathwaite had ruined his and England's hopes of the World Twenty20 title. Stokes's unbeaten 57 from 39 balls was his fifth score above 50 in his last eight one-day internationals, and he added a crucial 73 in 6.4 overs with Woakes after England had threatened to stagnate at 246 for six. Three wickets – including Kohli for 55 and Pandya, whose maiden ODI fifty in a sixth-wicket stand of 104 from 83 balls with Jadhav had taken India so close – three wickets for Stokes confirmed he would pick up the match award. It was Kohli's first home defeat as captain in 20 matches in all formats.

Man of the Match: B. A. Stokes. *Man of the Series:* K. M. Jadhav.

England

J. J. Roy b Jadeja	65
S. W. Billings c Bumrah b Jadeja	35
J. M. Bairstow c Jadeja b Pandya	56
*E. J. G. Morgan c Bumrah b Pandya	43
†J. C. Buttler c Rahul b Pandya	11
B. A. Stokes not out	57
M. M. Ali c Jadeja b Bumrah	2
C. R. Woakes run out	34
L. E. Plunkett run out	1
B 1, lb 8, w 7, nb 1	17
1/98 (2) 2/110 (1) 3/194 (4) 4/212 (5) 5/237 (3) 6/246 (7) 7/319 (8) 8/321 (9) (8 wkts, 50 overs)	321
10 overs: 43-0	

D. J. Willey and J. T. Ball did not bat.

Bhuvneshwar Kumar 8–0–56–0; Pandya 10–1–49–3; Bumrah 10–1–68–1; Yuvraj Singh 3–0–17–0; Jadeja 10–0–62–2; Ashwin 9–0–60–0.

India

A. M. Rahane b Willey	1
K. L. Rahul c Buttler b Ball	11
*V. Kohli c Buttler b Stokes	55
Yuvraj Singh c Billings b Plunkett	45
†M. S. Dhoni c Buttler b Ball	25
K. M. Jadhav c Billings b Woakes	90
H. H. Pandya b Stokes	56
R. A. Jadeja c Bairstow b Woakes	10
R. Ashwin c Woakes b Stokes	1
Bhuvneshwar Kumar not out	0
J. J. Bumrah not out	0
Lb 8, w 13, nb 1	22
1/13 (1) 2/37 (2) 3/102 (3) 4/133 (4) 5/173 (5) 6/277 (7) 7/291 (8) 8/297 (9) 9/316 (6) (9 wkts, 50 overs)	316
10 overs: 52-2	

Woakes 10–0–75–2; Willey 2–0–8–1; Ball 10–0–56–2; Plunkett 10–0–65–1; Stokes 10–0–63–3; Ali 8–0–41–0.

Umpires: A. K. Chaudhary and H. D. P. K. Dharmasena. Third umpire: R. S. A. Palliyaguruge.
Referee: A. J. Pycroft.

INDIA v ENGLAND

First Twenty20 International

At Kanpur, January 26, 2017 (floodlit). England won by seven wickets. Toss: England. Twenty20 international debut: Parvez Rasool.

As at Eden Gardens, England found conditions to their liking at Green Park, where pace and uneven bounce helped their muscular seam attack keep India's batsmen on a tight leash. Their batsmen then strolled home with 11 balls to spare. It was, according to Morgan, "as complete a performance as we've produced on this trip". Tymal Mills won his second cap, took his first international wicket and pushed 93mph – but it was his back-of-the-hand slower ball that drew praise from Kohli. With Dhoni looking to hit out at the death, Mills's variations limited him to eight runs from the seven deliveries he sent down to him. England's most miserly bowling, though, came from Ali, who removed Kohli for 29 via a sharp catch from Morgan at midwicket. The chase began brazenly, with 42 coming from the first 19 balls, and stalled only briefly, when Roy and Billings were both bowled in the same over by leg-spinner Yuzvendra Chahal. Raina had hit India's solitary six, but England managed seven, including four from Morgan in a powerful fifty. He added 83 in 11.3 overs for the third wicket with Root, whose unbeaten 46 meant this was the first match of the Indian tour in which he failed to score a half-century.

Man of the Match: M. M. Ali.

India

		B	4/6
1 *V. Kohli *c 4 b 7*	29	26	4
2 K. L. Rahul *c 10 b 9*	8	9	1
3 S. K. Raina *b 5*	34	23	4/1
4 Yuvraj Singh *c 10 b 8*	12	13	1
5 †M. S. Dhoni *not out*	36	27	3
6 M. K. Pandey *lbw b 7*	3	5	0
7 H. H. Pandya *c 2 b 11*	9	12	0
8 Parvez Rasool *run out*	5	6	0
9 J. J. Bumrah *not out*	0	0	0
Lb 3, w 7, nb 1	11		
6 overs: 47-1 (20 overs)	147-7		

1/34 2/55 3/75 4/95 5/98 6/118 7/145

10 Y. S. Chahal and 11 A. Nehra did not bat.

Mills 4–6–27–1; Jordan 4–11–27–1; Plunkett 4–8–32–1; Stokes 4–7–37–1; Ali 4–9–21–2.

England

		B	4/6
1 J. J. Roy *b 10*	19	11	0/2
2 S. W. Billings *b 10*	22	10	3/1
3 J. E. Root *not out*	46	46	4
4 *E. J. G. Morgan *c 3 b 8*	51	38	1/4
5 B. A. Stokes *not out*	2	5	0
B 1, lb 2, w 4, nb 1	8		
6 overs: 48-2 (18.1 overs)	148-3		

1/42 2/43 3/126

6 †J. C. Buttler, 7 M. M. Ali, 8 L. E. Plunkett, 9 C. J. Jordan, 10 A. U. Rashid and 11 T. S. Mills did not bat.

Nehra 3–5–31–0; Bumrah 3.1–9–26–0; Chahal 4–11–27–2; Parvez Rasool 4–6–32–1; Raina 2–1–17–0; Pandya 2–4–12–0.

Umpires: A. K. Chaudhary and N. N. Menon. Third umpire: C. K. Nandan.
Referee: A. J. Pycroft.

INDIA v ENGLAND

Second Twenty20 International

At Nagpur, January 29, 2017 (floodlit). India won by five runs. Toss: England.

Once Buttler had helped take 16 from the penultimate over, bowled by Nehra, England needed eight off the last. But a combination of precise death bowling by Bumrah, and – to the tourists' exasperation – a third poor decision of the night from umpire Shamshuddin, meant they managed just two. Root was given out lbw for 38 from the first ball, despite a thick bottom edge, and Buttler bowled by the fourth, sending a sell-out crowd of 45,000 into raptures. Earlier, both Kohli and Yuvraj Singh had been given not out by Shamshuddin; replays suggested the leg-before shouts should have been upheld. A slow pitch placed a premium on patience for batsmen, and precision for bowlers. Jordan, with his most economical four-over spell in Twenty20 internationals, and Ali bowled expertly for England, while Rahul was a beacon of fluidity among some staccato Indian innings. His 71 from 47 balls was the only half-century of the match, and the highest T20 score for

India against England, beating Virender Sehwag's 68 a decade earlier. Late in England's faltering innings, Stokes grasped the initiative with 38 from 27 balls, but his departure in the 17th over, lbw to Nehra, slowed the chase once again. With Bumrah conceding only four off the bat in his last two overs, India had somehow set up a series decider.

Man of the Match: J. J. Bumrah.

India

		B	4/6
1 *V. Kohli *c 9 b 8*	21	15	2/1
2 K. L. Rahul *c 5 b 8*	71	47	6/2
3 S. K. Raina *c 8 b 10*	7	10	0
4 Yuvraj Singh *lbw b 7*	4	12	0
5 M. K. Pandey *b 11*	30	26	0/1
6 †M. S. Dhoni *b 8*	5	7	0
7 H. H. Pandya *run out*	2	3	0
8 A. Mishra *run out*	0	0	0
9 J. J. Bumrah *not out*	0	0	0
Lb 1, w 3	4		
6 overs: 46-1 (20 overs)	144-8		

1/30 2/56 3/69 4/125 5/139 6/143 7/144 8/144

10 Y. S. Chahal and 11 A. Nehra did not bat.

Dawson 2–2–20–0; Mills 4–7–36–1; Jordan 4–9–22–3; Stokes 3–5–21–0; Ali 4–8–20–1; Rashid 3–5–24–1.

England

		B	4/6
1 J. J. Roy *c 3 b 11*	10	11	0/1
2 S. W. Billings *c 9 b 11*	12	9	0/1
3 J. E. Root *lbw b 9*	38	38	2
4 *E. J. G. Morgan *c 7 b 8*	17	23	1
5 B. A. Stokes *lbw b 11*	38	27	2/2
6 †J. C. Buttler *b 9*	15	10	1/1
7 M. M. Ali *not out*	1	2	0
8 C. J. Jordan *not out*	0	1	0
B 1, lb 2, w 4, nb 1	8		
6 overs: 36-2 (20 overs)	139-6		

1/22 2/22 3/65 4/117 5/137 6/138

9 L. A. Dawson, 10 A. U. Rashid and 11 T. S. Mills did not bat.

Chahal 4–7–33–0; Nehra 4–6–28–3; Bumrah 4–14–20–2; Mishra 4–8–25–1; Raina 4–6–30–0.

Umpires: A. K. Chaudhary and C. Shamshuddin. Third umpire: N. N. Menon.
Referee: A. J. Pycroft.

INDIA v ENGLAND

Third Twenty20 International

At Bangalore, February 1, 2017 (floodlit). India won by 75 runs. Toss: England. Twenty20 international debut: R. R. Pant.

A closely fought series ended with a rout, as England lost eight for eight in 19 balls – the second-worst eight-wicket collapse in international history. On a notoriously high-scoring ground, they had rated their chances of chasing down 203, and a third-wicket stand of 64 in 7.1 overs between Root and Morgan, who hit three sixes in three legitimate balls from Raina, suggested their faith was not misplaced. But Mishra's leg-breaks gave away only three in the 13th over, before Morgan and Root – who laboured slightly – fell in successive balls in the next, from leg-spinner Chahal. The rest of England's order went down swinging blindly, displaying a lack of discipline unworthy of their

---

EIGHTSOME REELS

The worst eight-wicket collapses in international cricket:

Runs	*From*	*To*		
5	37-2	42	New Zealand v Australia (Test) at Wellington	1945-46
8	**119-2**	**127**	**England v India (T20) at Bangalore**	**2016-17**
10	45-2	55	Sri Lanka v West Indies (ODI) at Sharjah	1986-87
10	121-2	131	New Zealand v Pakistan (Test) at Auckland	2000-01
10	11-1	21-9	Australia v South Africa (Test) at Cape Town	2011-12
11	183-2	194	England v West Indies (ODI) at Lord's *(World Cup final)*	1979
14	21-2	35	South Africa v England (Test) at Cape Town	1898-99
14	85-2	99	South Africa v Australia (Test) at Durban	1949-50
14	44-2	58	Bangladesh v India (ODI) at Mirpur	2014

In 1898-99 South Africa were 18-0, and 21-1.

abilities; in all, six batsmen failed to score. Chahal's final figures were six for 25, the third-best in Twenty20 internationals. Earlier, Raina had responded to the second-over run-out of Kohli with a punishing 45-ball 63 – his first Twenty20 international half-century since June 2010 – before India were restricted in the middle overs. But they managed 70 from the final five, with Yuvraj Singh carting Jordan for 22 in four balls, and Dhoni scoring what was, remarkably, his first fifty in his 76th T20 international. Umpire Shamshuddin asked to step down from on-field duty after his mistakes at Nagpur.

Man of the Match: Y. S. Chahal. *Man of the Series:* Y. S. Chahal.

India

		B	*4/6*
1 *V. Kohli *run out*	2	4	0
2 K. L. Rahul *b 6*	22	18	2/1
3 S. K. Raina *c 4 b 8*	63	45	2/5
4 †M. S. Dhoni *c 10 b 9*	56	36	5/2
5 Yuvraj Singh *c 5 b 11*	27	10	1/3
6 R. R. Pant *not out*	5	3	1
7 H. H. Pandya *run out*	11	4	0/1
B 4, lb 4, w 8	16		
6 overs: 53-1 (20 overs)	202-6		

1/4 2/65 3/120 4/177 5/191 6/202

8 A. Mishra, 9 J. J. Bumrah, 10 Y. S. Chahal and 11 A. Nehra did not bat.

Mills 4–8–31–1; Jordan 4–8–56–1; Plunkett 2–3–22–1; Stokes 4–8–32–1; Ali 4–6–30–0; Rashid 2–3–23–0.

England

		B	*4/6*
1 J. J. Roy *c 4 b 8*	32	23	4/1
2 S. W. Billings *c 3 b 10*	0	1	0
3 J. E. Root *lbw b 10*	42	37	4/2
4 *E. J. G. Morgan *c 6 b 10*	40	21	2/3
5 †J. C. Buttler *c 1 b 9*	0	2	0
6 B. A. Stokes *c 3 b 10*	6	7	1
7 M. M. Ali *c 1 b 10*	2	3	0
8 L. E. Plunkett *b 9*	0	1	0
9 C. J. Jordan *st 4 b 10*	0	2	0
10 A. U. Rashid *not out*	0	0	0
11 T. S. Mills *c 1 b 9*	0	2	0
Lb 2, w 3	5		
6 overs: 55-1 (16.3 overs)	127		

1/8 2/55 3/119 4/119 5/119 6/123 7/127 8/127 9/127

Nehra 3–10–24–0; Chahal 4–13–25–6; Bumrah 2.3–7–14–3; Mishra 4–10–23–1; Pandya 2–5–17–0; Raina 1–0–22–0.

Umpires: A. K. Chaudhary and N. N. Menon. Third umpire: C. Shamshuddin.
Referee: A. J. Pycroft.

PART FOUR
English Domestic Cricket

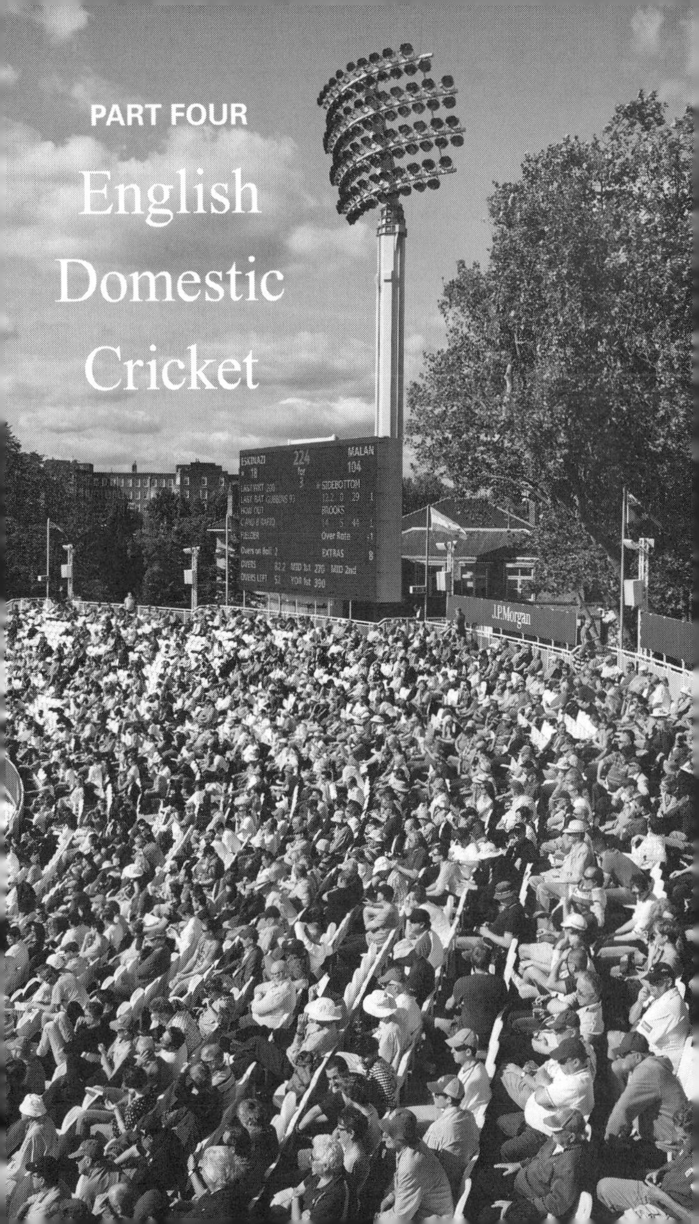

FIRST-CLASS AVERAGES IN 2016

These include MCC v Yorkshire at Abu Dhabi.

BATTING AND FIELDING (10 innings)

		M	I	NO	R	HS	100	50	Avge	Ct/St
1	S. A. Northeast (*Kent*)	16	23	6	1,402	191	5	4	82.47	5
2	J. M. Bairstow (*Yorks & England*)	11	17	1	1,286	246	4	4	80.37	38/2
3	†A. N. Cook (*Essex & England*)	14	24	7	1,278	142	4	6	75.17	15
4	M. Klinger (*Glos*)	7	12	4	589	140	3	2	73.62	8
5	†M. M. Ali (*Worcs & England*)	10	15	4	778	155*	3	4	70.72	3
6	R. N. ten Doeschate (*Essex*)	17	23	5	1,226	145	4	6	68.11	13
7	D. J. Bell-Drummond (*Kent*)	13	20	6	953	206*	2	6	68.07	1
8	S. J. Thakor (*Derbys*)	9	13	4	606	130	2	2	67.33	0
9	†K. K. Jennings (*Durham*)	17	29	4	1,602	221*	7	3	64.08	18
10	Azhar Ali (*Pakistanis*)	6	12	3	576	145	3	0	64.00	4
11	†E. C. Joyce (*Sussex*)	13	18	1	1,059	250	3	6	62.29	4
12	†N. R. T. Gubbins (*Middx*)	16	24	1	1,409	201*	4	9	61.26	6
13	J. E. Root (*Yorks & England*)	9	15	1	839	254	2	3	59.92	20
14	W. L. Madsen (*Derbys*)	15	26	4	1,292	163	6	3	58.72	11
15	†B. M. Duckett (*Northants*)	15	25	2	1,338	282*	4	5	58.17	9/1
16	†S. M. Ervine (*Hants*)	13	23	4	1,090	158*	4	5	57.36	10
17	T. Westley (*MCC & Essex*)	19	27	0	1,515	254	5	8	56.11	19
18	C. D. Nash (*Sussex*)	15	24	1	1,256	144	3	9	54.60	20
19	Asad Shafiq (*Pakistanis*)	6	10	2	436	109	1	3	54.50	1
20	B. C. Brown (*Sussex*)	18	24	6	980	159*	4	4	54.44	43
21	†P. Mustard (*Durham & Glos*)	7	11	2	485	107*	1	3	53.88	23
22	†C. F. Hughes (*Derbys*)	11	19	4	806	137*	3	4	53.73	8
23	†M. E. Trescothick (*Somerset*)	17	29	3	1,353	218	5	4	52.03	34
24	H. Z. Finch (*Sussex*)	9	11	3	413	135*	2	2	51.62	5
25	†R. McLaren (*Hants*)	16	26	9	869	100	1	6	51.11	7
26	J. M. Clarke (*Worcs*)	16	27	1	1,325	194	6	4	50.96	7
27	L. S. Livingstone (*Lancs*)	15	23	7	815	108*	2	6	50.93	26
28	J. C. Hildreth (*Somerset*)	17	25	3	1,107	166	4	2	50.31	9
29	H. Hameed (*Lancs*)	16	27	3	1,198	122	4	7	49.91	6
30	†K. C. Sangakkara (*Surrey*)	12	22	1	1,039	171	1	7	49.47	10
31	A. N. Petersen (*Lancs*)	15	24	1	1,134	191	3	6	49.30	8
32	†M. J. Cosgrove (*Leics*)	16	27	1	1,279	146	5	5	49.19	10
33	R. I. Newton (*Northants*)	11	20	3	827	202*	3	2	48.64	5
34	D. W. Lawrence (*Essex*)	17	24	2	1,070	154	3	6	48.63	13
35	B. T. Foakes (*MCC & Surrey*)	17	28	8	959	141*	1	5	47.95	49/4
36	L. R. P. L. Taylor (*Sussex*)	8	11	1	478	142*	1	4	47.80	6
37	†C. D. J. Dent (*Glos*)	17	31	3	1,336	180	3	8	47.71	19
38	†N. L. J. Browne (*MCC & Essex*)	19	30	3	1,277	255	3	6	47.29	14
39	†M. D. Stoneman (*Durham*)	17	29	1	1,317	141*	2	6	47.03	8
40	A. M. Rossington (*Northants*)	13	18	5	606	138*	1	4	46.61	15/3
41	D. I. Stevens (*Kent*)	15	17	0	782	140	2	5	46.00	8
42	G. L. van Buuren (*Glos*)	7	12	2	459	172*	2	0	45.90	4
43	I. J. L. Trott (*Warwicks*)	17	26	3	1,051	219*	2	6	45.69	4
44	A. J. A. Wheater (*Hants & Essex*)	15	25	4	948	204*	2	4	45.14	23/1
45	S. D. Robson (*Middx*)	14	21	1	899	231	3	4	44.95	16
46	L. E. Plunkett (*Yorks*)	8	13	3	449	126	1	3	44.90	3
47	P. D. Trego (*Somerset*)	17	26	2	1,070	154*	2	6	44.58	5
48	†S. M. Davies (*Surrey*)	16	28	2	1,147	117	3	5	44.11	10
49	†C. J. L. Rogers (*Somerset*)	16	25	2	1,010	132	3	6	43.91	8
50	C. R. Woakes (*Warwicks & England*)	12	19	6	567	121	1	3	43.61	5
51	S. S. Eskinazi (*Middx*)	9	15	1	609	157	2	2	43.50	4
52	†L. W. P. Wells (*Sussex*)	17	23	1	955	181	4	2	43.40	6

		M	I	NO	R	HS	100	50	Avge	Ct/St
53	J. C. Mickleburgh (*Essex*)	10	15	0	650	125	4	1	43.33	9
54	†J. A. Simpson (*Middx*)	16	23	5	779	100*	1	7	43.27	45/1
55	†D. J. Malan (*Middx*)	15	23	1	951	147	3	5	43.22	6
56	T. T. Bresnan (*Yorks*)	12	21	4	731	142*	1	5	43.00	12
57	†J. E. C. Franklin (*Middx*)	14	19	4	641	99	0	4	42.73	10
58	†R. J. Burns (*MCC & Surrey*)	18	34	2	1,326	122	2	9	41.43	16
59	T. R. Ambrose (*Warwicks*)	15	20	4	653	104	1	7	40.81	55/4
60	S. P. Crook (*Northants*)	10	15	3	484	145	2	1	40.33	1
61	†A. Z. Lees (*Yorks*)	18	34	2	1,285	132	3	8	40.15	15
62	†S. G. Borthwick (*Durham*)	17	29	2	1,084	188*	3	5	40.14	26
63	A. G. Wakely (*Northants*)	13	20	3	678	104	1	4	39.88	11
64	J. S. Foster (*Essex*)	16	20	3	677	113	1	3	39.82	48/1
65	D. K. H. Mitchell (*Worcs*)	16	29	2	1,069	155	3	5	39.59	15
66	S. J. Mullaney (*Notts*)	17	31	2	1,148	165	4	3	39.58	20
67	R. S. Bopara (*Essex*)	17	24	2	870	99	0	7	39.54	7
68	†N. J. O'Brien (*Leics*)	9	14	3	432	93	0	2	39.27	30
69	J. J. Roy (*Surrey*)	11	19	0	745	120	2	3	39.21	9
70	S. R. Dickson (*Kent*)	15	21	3	701	207*	1	4	38.94	8
71	†B. A. Godleman (*Derbys*)	13	24	0	934	204	3	2	38.91	6
72	O. E. Robinson (*Sussex*)	12	14	4	389	81	0	3	38.90	4
73	C. B. Cooke (*Glam*)	8	14	2	465	63	0	3	38.75	6
74	H. J. H. Marshall (*Glos*)	17	27	0	1,046	135	4	5	38.74	15
75	J. L. Denly (*Kent*)	15	21	2	733	206*	1	4	38.57	7
76	†A. Lyth (*Yorks*)	17	32	2	1,153	202	4	3	38.43	25
77	E. J. H. Eckersley (*Leics*)	12	19	2	645	117	3	1	37.94	31
78	L. D. McManus (*Hants*)	11	14	1	493	132*	1	3	37.92	21/6
79	†A. Harinath (*Surrey*)	12	22	1	777	137	1	5	37.00	5
80	Misbah-ul-Haq (*Pakistanis*)	6	10	0	369	114	1	3	36.90	2
81	V. Chopra (*Warwicks & Essex*)	17	26	2	885	107	1	7	36.87	23
82	N. J. Dexter (*Leics*)	16	27	1	958	136	3	4	36.84	4
83	G. G. Wagg (*Glam*)	14	23	3	736	106	1	5	36.80	5
84	J. Leach (*Worcs*)	16	22	5	620	107*	1	4	36.47	4
85	†W. D. Bragg (*Glam*)	17	32	1	1,126	161*	2	8	36.32	10
86	A. H. T. Donald (*Glam*)	17	31	1	1,088	234	2	5	36.26	12
87	A. D. Hales (*Notts & England*)	9	16	0	580	94	0	5	36.25	7
88	†J. H. K. Adams (*Hants*)	14	25	0	897	99	0	8	35.88	13
89	J. M. R. Taylor (*Glos*)	16	26	2	860	107*	2	4	35.83	10
90	†S. M. Curran (*Surrey*)	10	16	2	499	96	0	5	35.64	4
91	†A. J. Blake (*Kent*)	8	11	3	285	89*	0	2	35.62	5
92	I. R. Bell (*MCC & Warwicks*)	17	25	2	813	174	1	4	35.34	7
93	T. C. Fell (*Worcs*)	8	16	1	530	85	0	4	35.33	4
94	†T. P. Alsop (*Hants*)	13	21	0	737	117	1	6	35.09	12
95	P. J. Horton (*Leics*)	16	28	2	908	117*	2	6	34.92	8
96	O. B. Cox (*Worcs*)	16	24	2	761	75	0	6	34.59	38/2
97	D. P. Sibley (*Surrey*)	7	13	2	377	99	0	3	34.27	6
98	†L. A. Procter (*Lancs*)	16	25	1	822	137	2	3	34.25	5
99	B. L. D'Oliveira (*Worcs*)	15	27	1	888	202*	3	2	34.15	9
100	J. D. Libby (*Northants & Notts*)	16	28	1	920	144	2	4	34.07	4
101	†G. S. Ballance (*Yorks & England*)	18	34	2	1,089	132	3	5	34.03	12
102	G. H. Roderick (*Glos*)	15	26	3	781	102	1	7	33.95	29/2
103	S. R. Patel (*MCC & Notts*)	18	32	0	1,085	124	2	7	33.90	14
104	L. A. Dawson (*Hants*)	12	20	1	644	116	1	5	33.89	2
105	†M. T. Coles (*Kent*)	11	10	0	333	70	0	3	33.30	5
106	P. D. Collingwood (*Durham*)	14	24	6	595	106*	1	3	33.05	12
107	Sarfraz Ahmed (*Pakistanis*)	6	10	3	231	46*	0	0	33.00	21
108	†T. C. Smith (*Lancs*)	8	13	0	417	87	0	4	32.07	9
109	†K. H. D. Barker (*Warwicks*)	17	22	3	608	113	1	4	32.00	7
110	C. M. W. Read (*Notts*)	13	22	4	572	101	1	4	31.77	38/2
111	B. R. M. Taylor (*Notts*)	14	26	2	762	114	2	3	31.75	11
112	†F. D. M. Karunaratne (*Sri Lankans*)	5	10	2	253	100	1	1	31.62	1

		M	I	NO	R	HS	100	50	Avge	Ct/St
113	M. H. Wessels (*Notts*)	13	22	2	632	159*	2	3	31.60	22/2
114	T. Köhler-Cadmore (*Worcs*)	14	23	2	648	169	2	2	30.85	20
115	R. I. Keogh (*Northants*)	11	17	0	519	154	1	2	30.52	3/1
116	R. E. Levi (*Northants*)	10	14	0	427	104	1	1	30.50	11
117	G. H. Rhodes (*Worcs*)	6	11	2	274	59	0	2	30.44	2
118	†M. A. Wallace (*Glam*)	15	27	5	669	78	0	6	30.40	53/1
119	D. L. Lloyd (*Glam*)	16	28	1	817	107	3	2	30.25	5
120	R. K. Kleinveldt (*Northants*)	11	15	2	391	97	0	3	30.07	11
121	S. J. Croft (*Lancs*)	16	25	1	713	100	1	4	29.70	30
122	J. A. R. Harris (*MCC & Middx*)	8	11	4	207	78	0	2	29.57	3
123	J. T. A. Burnham (*Durham*)	15	25	2	680	135	1	4	29.56	6
124	W. R. Smith (*Hants*)	16	28	0	827	210	1	3	29.53	11
125	†M. A. Carberry (*Hants*)	8	15	1	411	107	1	1	29.35	4
126	†J. C. Tredwell (*MCC & Kent*)	13	13	3	293	124	1	0	29.30	14
127	E. G. Barnard (*Worcs*)	15	21	5	468	73	0	2	29.25	5
128	A. O. Morgan (*Glam*)	9	17	3	406	103*	1	1	29.00	3
	T. S. Roland-Jones (*Middx*)	15	14	3	319	79*	0	2	29.00	4
130	M. L. Pettini (*Leics*)	16	26	2	694	142*	2	1	28.91	3
131	G. K. Berg (*Hants*)	10	13	3	288	56	0	1	28.80	3
132	M. J. Richardson (*Durham*)	16	25	3	625	115*	1	3	28.40	34/1
133	T. D. Groenewald (*Somerset*)	13	18	13	142	26*	0	0	28.40	1
134	†J. D. Shantry (*Worcs*)	12	13	4	255	106	1	0	28.33	4
135	J. K. Silva (*Sri Lankans*)	5	10	0	281	79	0	2	28.10	1
136	†B. T. Slater (*Derbys*)	9	15	1	393	110	1	1	28.07	3
	A. U. Rashid (*Yorks*)	10	16	2	393	88	0	3	28.07	7
138	D. A. Payne (*Glos*)	15	18	4	389	67*	0	3	27.78	9
139	†R. A. Whiteley (*Worcs*)	14	24	3	581	71	0	4	27.66	13
140	N. J. Selman (*Glam*)	10	19	2	470	122*	2	2	27.64	7
141	†M. W. Machan (*Sussex*)	9	11	0	304	66	0	1	27.63	6
142	†I. J. Westwood (*Warwicks*)	11	17	1	442	127	1	2	27.62	3
143	†H. D. Rutherford (*Derbys*)	10	17	1	441	78	0	3	27.56	8
144	A. J. Robson (*Leics*)	17	29	1	771	84	0	9	27.53	14
145	†Z. S. Ansari (*Surrey*)	10	17	1	439	53	0	2	27.43	5
146	L. Gregory (*Somerset*)	12	16	4	329	73*	0	2	27.41	3
147	J. M. Vince (*Hants & England*)	15	25	0	685	119	1	2	27.40	8
148	D. Murphy (*Northants*)	12	17	4	355	60*	0	1	27.30	33/2
149	C. A. J. Meschede (*Glam*)	14	23	5	491	78	0	4	27.27	3
150	†B. A. Stokes (*Durham & England*)	8	11	1	272	51	0	2	27.20	2
151	†M. J. Lumb (*Notts*)	17	31	0	842	108	1	3	27.16	6
152	R. Clarke (*MCC & Warwicks*)	17	23	4	499	74	0	5	26.26	32
153	J. Allenby (*Somerset*)	12	17	0	446	63	0	5	26.23	20
154	A. J. Hodd (*Yorks*)	13	20	3	444	96*	0	2	26.11	37/6
155	†J. D. Ryder (*Essex*)	8	10	1	234	51	0	2	26.00	4
156	C. N. Miles (*Glos*)	14	21	5	413	60*	0	3	25.81	4
157	T. B. Abell (*Somerset*)	13	22	1	538	135	2	1	25.61	10
158	C. Overton (*Somerset*)	13	19	2	435	138	1	0	25.58	11
159	N. T. Broom (*Derbys*)	14	22	1	530	96	0	2	25.23	7
160	J. A. Brooks (*Yorks*)	15	22	11	275	48	0	0	25.00	4
	J. Clark (*Lancs*)	7	10	1	225	84*	0	2	25.00	1
162	†J. A. Rudolph (*Glam*)	16	30	2	688	87	0	3	24.57	10
163	G. T. Hankins (*Glos*)	10	17	0	416	116	1	1	24.47	6
164	N. R. D. Compton (*Middx & England*)	13	22	2	487	131	1	2	24.35	11
165	G. J. Batty (*Surrey*)	17	26	5	505	110*	1	0	24.04	4
166	M. J. J. Critchley (*Derbys*)	7	12	1	263	70*	0	1	23.90	3
167	†K. Noema-Barnett (*Glos*)	9	13	0	300	84	0	3	23.07	7
168	B. A. Hutton (*Notts*)	13	21	3	411	74	0	2	22.83	4
169	†W. M. H. Rhodes (*Yorks & Essex*)	8	10	0	224	95	0	1	22.40	4
170	R. D. Pringle (*Durham*)	12	13	2	243	57*	0	1	22.09	9
171	B. J. McCarthy (*Durham*)	7	10	2	176	51*	0	1	22.00	2
172	G. Onions (*MCC & Durham*)	18	20	7	285	65	0	1	21.92	2

		M	*I*	*NO*	*R*	*HS*	*100*	*50*	*Avge*	*Ct/St*
173	G. R. Napier (*Essex*)	15	16	2	304	124	1	0	21.71	3
174	G. P. Smith (*Notts*)	7	12	0	257	54	0	1	21.41	3
175	A. G. Salter (*Glam*)	7	11	3	171	45*	0	0	21.37	5
176	†A. W. Gale (*Yorks*)	16	28	1	571	83	0	2	21.14	2
177	R. C. Davies (*Somerset*)	15	19	1	380	86	0	3	21.11	27/6
178	†T. J. Murtagh (*Middx*)	14	12	4	168	47	0	0	21.00	4
	D. D. Masters (*Essex*)	9	10	5	105	47*	0	0	21.00	0
180	S. R. Hain (*Warwicks*)	16	23	1	457	135	1	1	20.77	19
181	S. C. Kerrigan (*Lancs*)	13	18	7	225	48	0	0	20.45	6
182	P. Coughlin (*Durham*)	7	11	1	202	39	0	0	20.20	4
183	†T. J. Moores (*Lancs & Notts*)	6	10	0	201	41	0	0	20.10	7
184	R. E. van der Merwe (*Somerset*)	7	10	1	180	102*	1	0	20.00	3
185	K. R. Brown (*Lancs*)	10	17	0	337	61	0	2	19.82	6
186	D. R. Briggs (*Sussex*)	13	13	3	197	49	0	0	19.70	6
187	L. C. Norwell (*Glos*)	12	15	3	224	102	1	0	18.66	1
188	J. S. Patel (*Warwicks*)	16	21	5	298	31	0	0	18.62	8
189	T. Poynton (*Derbys*)	9	11	2	167	53	0	1	18.55	15/1
190	A. R. I. Umeed (*Warwicks*)	6	10	1	165	101	1	0	18.33	4
191	A. P. Palladino (*Derbys*)	14	20	5	268	49	0	0	17.86	2
192	†S. C. J. Broad (*Notts & England*)	11	14	0	250	55	0	1	17.85	8
193	†B. A. Raine (*Leics*)	14	19	1	321	64	0	1	17.83	2
194	J. A. Leaning (*Yorks*)	11	18	2	285	51	0	1	17.81	9
195	K. M. Jarvis (*Lancs*)	16	23	4	338	57	0	1	17.78	3
196	Mohammad Hafeez (*Pakistanis*)	5	10	0	172	42	0	0	17.20	6
197	T. K. Curran (*Surrey*)	16	27	1	435	54	0	3	16.73	6
198	C. J. C. Wright (*Warwicks*)	10	15	2	207	45	0	0	15.92	2
199	Imran Tahir (*Notts*)	7	12	4	127	25	0	0	15.87	3
200	C. J. McKay (*Leics*)	15	20	1	300	65	0	2	15.78	0
201	†M. E. Claydon (*Kent*)	15	15	3	187	55	0	1	15.58	1
202	S. A. Patterson (*Yorks*)	16	22	1	305	63*	0	2	14.52	1
203	S. C. Meaker (*Surrey*)	11	15	6	126	41	0	0	14.00	5
204	J. Shaw (*Glos & Yorks*)	15	19	6	168	29	0	0	12.92	5
205	B. D. Cotton (*Derbys*)	8	11	3	102	26	0	0	12.75	1
206	M. G. Hogan (*Glam*)	16	22	6	191	30	0	0	11.93	8
207	S. T. Finn (*Middx & England*)	14	16	4	139	22*	0	0	11.58	3
208	W. A. Tavaré (*Glos*)	6	10	0	112	36	0	0	11.20	6
209	C. Rushworth (*Durham*)	14	16	5	114	31*	0	0	10.36	3
210	L. J. Fletcher (*Derbys & Notts*)	10	14	2	122	32	0	0	10.16	4
	†S. J. Magoffin (*Sussex*)	16	16	4	122	23*	0	0	10.16	4
212	O. P. Rayner (*Middx*)	13	13	3	100	26	0	0	10.00	18
	J. A. Porter (*Essex*)	15	13	7	60	20*	0	0	10.00	7
214	T. van der Gugten (*Glam*)	14	20	4	159	36	0	0	9.93	3
215	†M. J. Leach (*Somerset*)	16	18	5	128	27*	0	0	9.84	6
216	M. S. Crane (*Hants*)	13	19	6	126	24*	0	0	9.69	4
217	J. T. Ball (*MCC, Notts & England*)	14	21	2	179	33	0	0	9.42	3
218	†R. J. Sidebottom (*Yorks*)	9	11	3	75	23	0	0	9.37	1
219	†N. Wagner (*Lancs*)	9	12	0	111	37	0	0	9.25	2
220	†J. M. Anderson (*Lancs & England*)	10	10	4	55	17	0	0	9.16	3
221	H. F. Gurney (*Notts*)	14	22	10	83	27*	0	0	6.91	2
222	C. E. Shreck (*Leics*)	16	20	12	51	20	0	0	6.37	6
223	M. H. A. Footitt (*Surrey*)	9	11	3	49	16	0	0	6.12	3
224	Azharullah (*Northants*)	13	15	3	72	14*	0	0	6.00	1
225	B. W. Sanderson (*Northants*)	15	15	3	58	19	0	0	4.83	1

"It was death bowling by asphyxiation."

The World Twenty20 in 2015-16, page 5.01/34?

BOWLING (10 wickets in 5 innings)

		Style	*O*	*M*	*R*	*W*	*BB*	*5I*	*Avge*
1	J. M. Anderson (*Lancs & England*)	RFM	334.4	103	765	45	5-16	3	17.00
2	C. R. Woakes (*Warwicks & England*)	RFM	351.1	85	1,052	59	9-36	3	17.83
3	G. C. Viljoen (*Kent*)	RFM	103.5	12	385	20	5-55	1	19.25
4	S. J. Magoffin (*Sussex*)	RFM	523.1	144	1,249	62	5-32	5	20.14
5	D. M. Bess (*Somerset*)	OB	89.5	25	264	13	6-28	2	20.30
6	W. J. Weighell (*Durham*)	RM	112.5	22	329	16	5-33	1	20.56
7	D. D. Masters (*Essex*)	RFM	325.1	92	824	40	7-52	1	20.60
8	Hasan Ali (*Pakistan A*)	RFM	83.4	18	290	14	4-63	0	20.71
9	M. V. T. Fernando (*Sri Lanka A*)	LFM	74.1	11	253	12	5-37	1	21.08
10	G. G. White (*Northants*)	SLA	122	27	317	15	6-44	1	21.13
11	R. J. Sidebottom (*Yorks*)	LFM	245	63	657	31	5-51	1	21.19
12	M. R. Quinn (*Essex*)	RFM	142	24	473	22	7-76	1	21.50
13	J. E. Poysden (*Warwicks*)	LBG	80.4	7	323	15	5-53	1	21.53
14	B. W. Sanderson (*Northants*)	RFM	420.5	98	1,204	55	8-73	4	21.89
15	G. R. Napier (*Essex*)	RFM	470.3	100	1,539	69	5-29	5	22.30
16	J. Overton (*Somerset*)	RFM	133.3	27	382	17	5-42	1	22.47
17	C. J. McKay (*Leics*)	RFM	411.1	78	1,260	56	6-73	1	22.50
17	W. A. White (*Leics*)	RFM	64.1	13	225	10	4-24	0	22.50
19	M. J. Leach (*Somerset*)	SLA	561.3	123	1,536	68	6-42	5	22.58
20	K. H. D. Barker (*Warwicks*)	LFM	540.4	156	1,426	62	5-53	1	23.00
21	J. T. Ball (*MCC, Notts & England*)	RFM	415	84	1,342	57	6-57	3	23.54
22	O. P. Rayner (*Middx*)	OB	444.5	108	1,202	51	6-79	3	23.56
23	D. Wiese (*Sussex*)	RFM	152.2	34	456	19	4-18	0	24.00
24	J. S. Patel (*Warwicks*)	OB	616.4	168	1,658	69	5-32	4	24.02
25	R. Rampaul (*Surrey*)	RFM	128.5	13	510	21	5-85	2	24.28
26	T. C. Smith (*Lancs*)	RFM	133	31	374	15	5-25	1	24.93
27	M. A. Wood (*Durham*)	RFM	78	7	275	11	3-24	0	25.00
28	M. L. Cummins (*Worcs*)	RF	96.2	12	377	15	7-84	2	25.13
29	L. J. Carey (*Glam*)	RFM	84.4	13	330	13	4-92	0	25.38
30	Mir Hamza (*Pakistan A*)	LFM	104.4	23	286	11	4-53	0	26.00
31	R. S. Bopara (*Essex*)	RM	355.2	69	1,171	45	5-49	2	26.02
32	M. H. A. Footitt (*Surrey*)	LFM	269.3	50	991	38	7-62	3	26.07
33	J. A. Brooks (*Yorks*)	RFM	459.2	112	1,583	60	6-65	3	26.38
34	T. van der Gugten (*Glam*)	RFM	461	74	1,485	56	5-52	5	26.51
35	M. J. Henry (*Worcs*)	RFM	234	48	716	27	5-36	1	26.51
36	R. I. Keogh (*Northants*)	OB	242.2	42	828	31	9-52	1	26.70
37	T. D. Groenewald (*Somerset*)	RFM	369	91	1,071	40	5-90	2	26.77
38	T. E. Bailey (*Lancs*)	RFM	215.4	51	592	22	5-110	2	26.90
39	M. G. Hogan (*Glam*)	RFM	512.4	140	1,322	49	5-36	2	26.97
40	H. W. Podmore (*Glam & Middx*)	RM	144.3	26	465	17	4-54	0	27.35
41	J. Leach (*Worcs*)	RFM	519.4	81	1,842	67	5-60	5	27.49
42	C. J. C. Wright (*Warwicks*)	RFM	280.2	54	833	30	4-41	0	27.76
43	J. C. Archer (*Sussex*)	RFM	243.1	54	778	28	4-31	0	27.78
44	W. B. Rankin (*Warwicks*)	RFM	181.2	23	556	20	3-33	0	27.80
45	R. E. van der Merwe (*Somerset*)	SLA	203.4	40	614	22	4-45	0	27.90
46	S. C. J. Broad (*Notts & England*)	RFM	356.3	95	979	35	4-21	0	27.97
47	T. S. Roland-Jones (*Middx*)	RFM	482.2	95	1,524	54	6-54	2	28.22
48	M. T. Coles (*Kent*)	RFM	309.5	57	1,134	40	5-116	1	28.35
49	N. J. Dexter (*Leics*)	RM	261.5	50	824	29	5-52	1	28.41
50	J. Allenby (*Somerset*)	RM	243.2	57	598	21	4-67	0	28.47
51	T. T. Bresnan (*Yorks*)	RFM	318.1	76	997	35	5-36	1	28.48
52	J. A. Porter (*Essex*)	RFM	478.2	80	1,683	59	5-46	2	28.52
53	T. J. Murtagh (*Middx*)	RFM	457.2	116	1,227	43	5-53	1	28.53
54	C. N. Miles (*Glos*)	RFM	404.2	62	1,641	57	5-54	2	28.78
55	L. C. Norwell (*Glos*)	RFM	413.5	94	1,271	44	4-65	0	28.88
56	S. M. Curran (*Surrey*)	LFM	226	50	784	27	7-58	2	29.03
57	Sohail Khan (*Pakistanis*)	RFM	126.4	14	496	17	5-68	2	29.17
58	R. Clarke (*MCC & Warwicks*)	RFM	452.5	107	1,285	44	4-20	0	29.20

		Style	O	M	R	W	BB	5I	Avge
59	N. Wagner (*Lancs*)	LFM	286.4	52	937	32	6-66	2	29.28
60	S. A. Patterson (*Yorks*)	RFM	465.5	145	1,205	41	6-56	1	29.39
61	H. F. Gurney (*Notts*)	LFM	426.5	79	1,326	45	6-61	2	29.46
62	D. I. Stevens (*Kent*)	RM	415.1	106	1,172	39	4-74	0	30.05
63	G. Onions (*MCC & Durham*)	RFM	587	105	1,807	59	5-90	1	30.62
64	B. A. Stokes (*Durham & England*)	RFM	210.5	39	645	21	4-54	0	30.71
65	A. P. Palladino (*Derbys*)	RFM	453.5	110	1,201	39	5-74	2	30.79
66	L. Gregory (*Somerset*)	RFM	276.5	61	894	29	4-58	0	30.82
67	S. C. Meaker (*Surrey*)	RF	298.5	42	1,145	37	4-40	0	30.94
68	S. J. Thakor (*Derbys*)	RM	188	24	687	22	5-63	1	31.22
69	Z. S. Ansari (*Surrey*)	SLA	236.4	39	691	22	6-36	1	31.40
70	C. Rushworth (*Durham*)	RFM	355.2	74	1,071	34	5-93	1	31.50
71	B. J. McCarthy (*Durham*)	RFM	177.1	25	632	20	5-70	1	31.60
72	B. A. Raine (*Leics*)	RFM	338	77	1,108	35	5-66	1	31.65
73	M. E. Claydon (*Kent*)	RFM	416.4	76	1,600	50	5-42	2	32.00
73	S. G. Whittingham (*Sussex*)	RFM	153.4	18	576	18	4-58	0	32.00
75	G. J. Batty (*Surrey*)	OB	444.1	93	1,325	41	7-32	2	32.31
76	J. K. Fuller (*Middx*)	RFM	100	17	393	12	5-70	1	32.75
77	K. M. Jarvis (*Lancs*)	RFM	545.2	130	1,673	51	6-70	2	32.80
78	D. A. Payne (*Glos*)	LFM	461	84	1,412	43	5-36	1	32.83
79	C. E. Shreck (*Leics*)	RFM	442.3	85	1,455	44	4-33	0	33.06
80	M. W. Dixon (*Essex*)	RF	123.1	22	498	15	5-124	1	33.20
81	B. A. Hutton (*Notts*)	RM	276.3	50	1,048	31	4-6	0	33.80
82	A. U. Rashid (*Yorks*)	LBG	293.2	36	1,083	32	4-17	0	33.84
83	O. P. Stone (*Northants*)	RFM	106.4	11	339	10	4-56	0	33.90
84	T. P. Milnes (*Derbys*)	RFM	172	37	509	15	6-93	1	33.93
85	S. T. Finn (*Middx & England*)	RFM	423.1	64	1,461	43	4-54	0	33.97
86	B. T. J. Wheal (*Hants*)	RFM	229	41	749	22	6-51	1	34.04
87	C. Overton (*Somerset*)	RFM	380.5	83	1,168	34	4-54	0	34.35
88	A. N. P. R. Fernando (*Sri Lankans*)	RFM	114	22	378	11	4-107	0	34.36
89	J. A. Tomlinson (*Hants*)	LFM	151.3	40	483	14	4-74	0	34.50
90	S. R. Patel (*MCC & Notts*)	SLA	387.5	70	1,243	36	4-71	0	34.52
91	W. S. Davis (*Derbys*)	RFM	170.2	20	733	21	7-146	1	34.90
92	L. Wood (*Notts*)	LM	98.5	17	350	10	5-40	1	35.00
93	Wahab Riaz (*Pakistanis*)	LF	99.5	3	422	12	3-93	0	35.16
94	C. J. Haggett (*Kent*)	RFM	158.4	30	529	15	4-15	0	35.26
95	P. Coughlin (*Durham*)	RFM	159.5	31	460	13	3-65	0	35.38
96	Yasir Shah (*Pakistanis*)	LBG	274.1	43	891	25	6-72	2	35.64
97	B. A. Carse (*Durham*)	RF	158.2	24	607	17	3-38	0	35.70
98	R. K. Kleinveldt (*Northants*)	RFM	302.1	60	930	26	5-53	1	35.76
99	M. W. Parkinson (*Lancs*)	LBG	114.1	23	363	10	5-49	1	36.30
100	R. N. ten Doeschate (*Essex*)	RM	132	17	473	13	4-31	0	36.38
101	G. K. Berg (*Hants*)	RFM	251.2	73	694	19	6-56	1	36.52
102	Mohammad Amir (*Pakistanis*)	LFM	188.3	41	587	16	3-36	0	36.68
103	Imran Tahir (*Notts*)	LBG	288.4	51	930	25	7-112	1	37.20
103	J. M. Bird (*Notts*)	RFM	157.3	27	558	15	4-56	0	37.20
105	J. Shaw (*Glos & Yorks*)	RFM	405.3	73	1,537	41	5-79	1	37.48
106	J. C. Tredwell (*MCC & Kent*)	OB	365	83	1,053	28	4-45	0	37.60
107	S. C. Kerrigan (*Lancs*)	SLA	498.4	106	1,326	35	6-86	2	37.88
108	C. F. Parkinson (*Derbys*)	SLA	170.4	28	531	14	4-90	0	37.92
109	G. H. S. Garton (*Sussex*)	LFM	106.1	10	420	11	3-93	0	38.18
110	G. G. Wagg (*Glam*)	SLA/LM	434	73	1,426	37	5-90	1	38.54
111	R. McLaren (*Hants*)	RFM	387	83	1,249	32	5-104	1	39.03
112	L. J. Fletcher (*Derbys & Notts*)	RFM	282.1	73	745	19	4-25	0	39.21
113	T. L. Best (*Hants*)	RFM	136.5	20	554	14	5-90	1	39.57
114	Rahat Ali (*Pakistanis*)	LFM	127	20	475	12	3-47	0	39.58
115	W. M. H. Rhodes (*Yorks & Essex*)	RFM	161	34	518	13	2-34	0	39.84
116	C. J. Jordan (*Sussex*)	RFM	201	38	678	17	4-36	0	39.88
117	E. G. Barnard (*Worcs*)	RFM	382.2	76	1,423	35	4-62	0	40.65
118	B. L. D'Oliveira (*Worcs*)	LBG	271.1	33	786	19	4-80	0	41.36

		Style	O	M	R	W	BB	5I	Avge
119	R. J. Gleeson (*Northants*)	RFM	166	32	538	13	4-105	0	41.38
120	J. Clark (*Lancs*)	RM	132	23	456	11	3-20	0	41.45
121	M. D. Taylor (*Glos*)	LM	143	15	543	13	4-56	0	41.76
122	Azharullah (*Northants*)	RFM	291.2	47	1,048	25	6-68	1	41.92
123	T. K. Curran (*Surrey*)	RFM	469.2	93	1,565	37	4-58	0	42.29
124	M. S. Crane (*Hants*)	LBG	399	55	1,498	35	3-19	0	42.80
125	K. Noema-Barnett (*Glos*)	RM	225.2	54	604	14	3-56	0	43.14
126	L. A. Dawson (*Hants*)	SLA	306.5	56	877	20	4-100	0	43.85
127	R. D. Pringle (*Durham*)	OB	242.2	32	924	21	7-107	1	44.00
128	C. A. J. Meschede (*Glam*)	RM	360.5	67	1,199	27	5-84	1	44.40
129	D. R. Briggs (*Sussex*)	SLA	381.5	71	1,176	26	5-93	2	45.23
130	J. M. R. Taylor (*Glos*)	OB	293.5	52	998	22	4-16	0	45.36
131	S. J. Mullaney (*Notts*)	RM	148.5	37	454	10	3-54	0	45.40
132	A. Carter (*Derbys & Hants*)	RFM	143	20	566	12	4-52	0	47.16
133	B. D. Cotton (*Derbys*)	RFM	202.3	50	661	14	4-28	0	47.21
134	J. D. Shantry (*Worcs*)	LFM	384.3	98	1,114	23	5-46	1	48.43
135	O. E. Robinson (*Sussex*)	RFM/OB	282.3	48	951	19	4-110	0	50.05
136	L. A. Procter (*Lancs*)	RFM	152.5	28	505	10	3-14	0	50.50
137	A. Shahzad (*Sussex*)	RFM	225.5	32	817	16	3-34	0	51.06
138	C. A. J. Morris (*Worcs*)	RFM	144.1	26	563	11	2-35	0	51.18
139	S. G. Borthwick (*Durham*)	LBG	313.3	34	1,200	23	5-79	1	52.17
140	J. A. R. Harris (*MCC & Middx*)	RFM	254.2	36	898	17	3-67	0	52.82
141	D. L. Lloyd (*Glam*)	RM	161.1	20	623	11	3-36	0	56.63
142	A. O. Morgan (*Glam*)	SLA	232	34	740	13	2-37	0	56.92
143	S. P. Crook (*Northants*)	RFM	139.2	18	578	10	2-7	0	57.80
144	J. E. C. Franklin (*Middx*)	LFM	205	39	646	11	3-26	0	58.72
145	L. E. Plunkett (*Yorks*)	RFM	172.1	23	602	10	2-46	0	60.20
146	M. M. Ali (*Worcs & England*)	OB	201	28	853	14	3-88	0	60.92

BOWLING STYLES

LBG Leg-breaks and googlies (8)
LF Left-arm fast (1)
LFM Left-arm fast medium (15)
LM Left-arm medium (3)
OB Off-breaks (10)
RF Right-arm fast (4)
RFM Right-arm fast medium (82)
RM Right-arm medium (14)
SLA Slow left-arm (11)

The total comes to 148 because O. E. Robinson and G. G. Wagg have two styles of bowling.

INDIVIDUAL SCORES OF 100 AND OVER

There were **299** three-figure innings in 171 first-class matches in 2016, 55 more than in 2015, when 170 first-class matches were played. Of these, 26 were double-hundreds, compared with 17 in 2015. The list includes 254 hundreds in the County Championship, compared with 208 in 2015.

K. K. Jennings (7)
116 } 105* } Durham v Somerset, Chester-le-Street
113 Durham v Warwicks, Birmingham
221* Durham v Yorks, Chester-le-Street
129 Durham v Hants, Chester-le-Street
171* Durham v Notts, Chester-le-Street
201* Durham v Surrey, Chester-le-Street

J. M. Clarke (6)
119 Worcs v Oxford MCCU, Oxford
135 Worcs v Glos, Bristol
133 Worcs v Glam, Cardiff
123 Worcs v Leics, Worcester
125 Worcs v Northants, Worcester
194 Worcs v Derbys, Worcester

W. L. Madsen (6)
150 Derbys v Glos, Bristol
103 Derbys v Kent, Derby
109 Derbys v Worcs, Derby
163 Derbys v Kent, Canterbury
134* Derbys v Leics, Derby
100 Derbys v Worcs, Worcester

M. J. Cosgrove (5)
122 Leics v Kent, Leicester
119 Leics v Kent, Canterbury
146 Leics v Worcs, Worcester
111 Leics v Northants, Northampton
110 Leics v Derbys, Derby

S. A. Northeast (5)
189 Kent v Glos, Canterbury
191 Kent v Derbys, Canterbury
166* Kent v Essex, Chelmsford
190 Kent v Sussex, Tunbridge Wells
178* Kent v Essex, Canterbury

M. E. Trescothick (5)
127 Somerset v Surrey, The Oval
129* Somerset v Lancs, Taunton
106 Somerset v Pakistanis, Taunton
124 Somerset v Middx, Taunton
218 Somerset v Notts, Nottingham

T. Westley (5)
110 Essex v Cambridge MCCU, Cambridge
121 Essex v Glos, Chelmsford
125 Essex v Worcs, Worcester
108 Essex v Sri Lankans, Chelmsford
254 Essex v Worcs, Chelmsford

J. M. Bairstow (4)
246 Yorks v Hants, Leeds
198 Yorks v Surrey, Leeds
140 England v Sri Lanka, Leeds
167* England v Sri Lanka, Lord's

B. C. Brown (4)
126* Sussex v Leeds/Brad MCCU, Hove
159* Sussex v Glam, Hove
113 Sussex v Glos, Hove
118* Sussex v Glos, Bristol

A. N. Cook (4)
105 Essex v Glos, Chelmsford
127* Essex v Sussex, Hove
142 Essex v Worcs, Worcester
105 England v Pakistan, Manchester

B. M. Duckett (4)
282* Northants v Sussex, Northampton
189 Northants v Essex, Northampton
185 Northants v Glam, Northampton
208 Northants v Kent, Beckenham

S. M. Ervine (4)
123 Hants v Yorks, Leeds
103 } 106 } Hants v Somerset, Taunton
158* Hants v Surrey, The Oval

N. R. T. Gubbins (4)
109 Middx v Somerset, Lord's
201* Middx v Lancs, Lord's
145 Middx v Durham, Lord's
125 Middx v Yorks, Lord's

H. Hameed (4)
103 Lancs v Warwicks, Manchester
122 Lancs v Notts, Nottingham
114 } 100* } Lancs v Yorks, Manchester

J. C. Hildreth (4)
130 Somerset v Lancs, Taunton
166 Somerset v Yorks, Taunton
152 Somerset v Hants, Southampton
135 Somerset v Notts, Taunton

A. Lyth (4)
111 Yorks v Hants, Leeds
106 Yorks v Somerset, Taunton
202 Yorks v Surrey, The Oval
114* Yorks v Durham, Leeds

H. J. H. Marshall (4)
135 Glos v Worcs, Bristol
112 Glos v Kent, Canterbury
118 Glos v Kent, Bristol
101 Glos v Glam, Cardiff

J. C. Mickleburgh (4)
125 }
102 } Essex v Cambridge MCCU, Cambridge
109 Essex v Sri Lankans, Chelmsford
103 Essex v Northants, Northampton

S. J. Mullaney (4)
139 Notts v Cambridge MCCU, Cambridge
113 Notts v Surrey, Nottingham
165 Notts v Somerset, Nottingham
137 Notts v Hants, Nottingham

R. N. ten Doeschate (4)
145 Essex v Northants, Northampton
109 Essex v Sussex, Colchester
109* Essex v Worcs, Chelmsford
117 Essex v Glam, Chelmsford

L. W. P. Wells (4)
116 Sussex v Derbys, Derby
104 Sussex v Derbys, Hove
181 Sussex v Glam, Hove
120 Sussex v Glos, Hove

M. M. Ali (3)
136* Worcs v Glos, Bristol
155* England v Sri Lanka, Chester-le-Street
108 England v Pakistan, The Oval

Azhar Ali (3)
101* Pakistanis v Somerset, Taunton
145 Pakistanis v Sussex, Hove
139 Pakistan v England, Birmingham

G. S. Ballance (3)
105 Yorks v MCC, Abu Dhabi
132 Yorks v Middx, Scarborough
101* Yorks v Notts, Scarborough

S. G. Borthwick (3)
134 }
103* } Durham v Lancs, Chester-le-Street
188* Durham v Notts, Nottingham

N. L. J. Browne (3)
101 Essex v Cambridge MCCU, Cambridge
255 Essex v Derbys, Chelmsford
229* Essex v Derbys, Derby

S. M. Davies (3)
115 }
109 } Surrey v Lough MCCU, The Oval
117 Surrey v Yorks, Leeds

C. D. J. Dent (3)
180 Glos v Derbys, Bristol
138* Glos v Worcs, Bristol
165 Glos v Leics, Leicester

N. J. Dexter (3)
131 Leics v Kent, Leicester
136 Leics v Glos, Leicester
109 Leics v Worcs, Worcester

B. L. D'Oliveira (3)
122 Worcs v Oxford MCCU, Oxford
128 Worcs v Essex, Worcester
202* Worcs v Glam, Cardiff

E. J. H. Eckersley (3)
117 }
104 } Leics v Derbys, Leicester
107 Leics v Northants, Northampton

B. A. Godleman (3)
204 Derbys v Worcs, Derby
106 Derbys v Glam, Colwyn Bay
100 Derbys v Essex, Derby

C. F. Hughes (3)
137* Derbys v Glos, Bristol
109* Derbys v Northants, Northampton
122 Derbys v Glam, Colwyn Bay

E. C. Joyce (3)
250 Sussex v Derbys, Derby
106 Sussex v Derbys, Hove
106 Sussex v Glam, Hove

M. Klinger (3)
140 Glos v Northants, Bristol
102* Glos v Worcs, Worcester
129* Glos v Sussex, Hove

D. W. Lawrence (3)
116 Essex v Derbys, Chelmsford
127 Essex v Glos, Cheltenham
154 Essex v Leics, Leicester

A. Z. Lees (3)
107 Yorks v Notts, Nottingham
114* Yorks v Lancs, Manchester
132 Yorks v Durham, Leeds

D. L. Lloyd (3)
105 Glam v Cardiff MCCU, Cardiff
107 Glam v Kent, Canterbury
102* Glam v Sussex, Hove

D. J. Malan (3)
121 Middx v Hants, Southampton
147 Middx v Hants, Northwood
116 Middx v Yorks, Lord's

D. K. H. Mitchell (3)
155 Worcs v Oxford MCCU, Oxford
107* } Worcs v Northants, Worcester
103 }

C. D. Nash (3)
119 Sussex v Essex, Hove
144 Sussex v Leics, Hove
132 Sussex v Glam, Cardiff

R. I. Newton (3)
108 Northants v Glos, Bristol
202* Northants v Leics, Northampton
130 Northants v Glos, Northampton

A. N. Petersen (3)
105 Lancs v Surrey, Manchester
191 Lancs v Middx, Lord's
155 Lancs v Somerset, Manchester

S. D. Robson (3)
231 } Middx v Warwicks, Lord's
106 }
114* Middx v Notts, Lord's

C. J. L. Rogers (3)
109 Somerset v Middx, Lord's
132 } Somerset v Notts, Taunton
100* }

T. B. Abell (2)
104 Somerset v Warwicks, Birmingham
135 Somerset v Lancs, Manchester

B. M. R. Akram (2)
160 Lough MCCU v Surrey, The Oval
100* Lough MCCU v Kent, Canterbury

D. J. Bell-Drummond (2)
206* Kent v Lough MCCU, Canterbury
124 Kent v Leics, Leicester

W. D. Bragg (2)
129 Glam v Derbys, Derby
161* Glam v Essex, Cardiff

R. J. Burns (2)
122 Surrey v Hants, Southampton
101 Surrey v Hants, The Oval

S. P. Crook (2)
103* Northants v Glos, Bristol
145 Northants v Worcs, Worcester

A. H. T. Donald (2)
105 Glam v Cardiff MCCU, Cardiff
234 Glam v Derbys, Colwyn Bay

S. S. Eskinazi (2)
106 Middx v Lancs, Lord's
157 Middx v Yorks, Scarborough

H. Z. Finch (2)
135* Sussex v Leeds/Brad MCCU, Hove
103 Sussex v Pakistanis, Hove

P. J. Horton (2)
100 Leics v Sussex, Hove
117* Leics v Worcs, Worcester

T. Köhler-Cadmore (2)
119* Worcs v Essex, Worcester
169 Worcs v Glos, Worcester

J. D. Libby (2)
102 Northants v Derbys, Northampton
144 Notts v Durham, Chester-le-Street

L. S. Livingstone (2)
108* Lancs v Somerset, Taunton
106* Lancs v Warwicks, Manchester

S. R. Patel (2)
124 Notts v Warwicks, Nottingham
100 Notts v Middx, Nottingham

M. L. Pettini (2)
142* Leics v Sussex, Hove
117 Leics v Northants, Northampton

L. A. Procter (2)
137 Lancs v Hants, Manchester
122 Lancs v Durham, Southport

J. E. Root (2)
213 Yorks v Surrey, Leeds
254 England v Pakistan, Manchester

J. J. Roy (2)
110 Surrey v Middx, Lord's
120 Surrey v Durham, Chester-le-Street

N. J. Selman (2)
122* Glam v Northants, Swansea
101 Glam v Glos, Cardiff

D. I. Stevens (2)
140 Kent v Glos, Bristol
136 Kent v Essex, Canterbury

M. D. Stoneman (2)
141* Durham v Middx, Chester-le-Street
137 Durham v Hants, Southampton

B. R. M. Taylor (2)
114 }
105* } Notts v Durham, Nottingham

J. M. R. Taylor (2)
105 Glos v Worcs, Bristol
107* Glos v Worcs, Worcester

S. J. Thakor (2)
130 Derbys v Kent, Derby
123 Derbys v Kent, Canterbury

P. D. Trego (2)
138 Somerset v Middx, Taunton
154* Somerset v Lancs, Manchester

I. J. L. Trott (2)
219* Warwicks v Middx, Lord's
123 Warwicks v Surrey, Guildford

G. L. van Buuren (2)
172* Glos v Worcs, Worcester
121* Glos v Leics, Leicester

M. H. Wessels (2)
143 Notts v Cambridge MCCU, Cambridge
159* Notts v Durham, Nottingham

A. J. A. Wheater (2)
204* Hants v Warwicks, Birmingham
102 Hants v Notts, Nottingham

Younis Khan (2)
104 Pakistanis v Somerset, Taunton
218 Pakistan v England, The Oval

The following each played one three-figure innings:

T. P. Alsop, 117, Hants v Surrey, The Oval; T. R. Ambrose, 104, Warwicks v Hants, Birmingham; Asad Shafiq, 109, Pakistan v England, The Oval.

G. J. Bailey, 110*, Middx v Surrey, Lord's; K. H. D. Barker, 113, Warwicks v Notts, Nottingham; C. A. Barrett, 114*, Northants v Worcs, Worcester; G. J. Batty, 110*, Surrey v Hants, Southampton; I. R. Bell, 174, Warwicks v Hants, Southampton; S. W. Billings, 171, Kent v Glos, Bristol; T. T. Bresnan, 142*, Yorks v Middx, Lord's; J. T. A. Burnham, 135, Durham v Surrey, The Oval.

M. A. Carberry, 107, Hants v Middx, Southampton; K. S. Carlson, 119, Glam v Essex, Chelmsford; L. D. Chandimal, 126, Sri Lanka v England, Chester-le-Street; V. Chopra, 107, Warwicks v Yorks, Birmingham; I. A. Cockbain, 129*, Glos v Durham MCCU, Bristol; P. D. Collingwood, 106*, Durham v Surrey, The Oval; N. R. D. Compton, 131, Middx v Durham, Lord's; S. J. Croft, 100, Lancs v Warwicks, Manchester.

L. A. Dawson, 116, Hants v Warwicks, Birmingham; J. L. Denly, 206*, Kent v Northants, Northampton; S. R. Dickson, 207*, Kent v Derbys, Derby.

D. A. Escott, 125, Oxford Univ v Cambridge Univ, Oxford.

A. J. Finch, 110, Surrey v Warwicks, Guildford; B. T. Foakes, 141*, Surrey v Hants, Southampton; J. S. Foster, 113, Essex v Northants, Northampton.

S. R. Hain, 135, Warwicks v Hants, Birmingham; G. T. Hankins, 116, Glos v Northants, Northampton; A. Harinath, 137, Surrey v Notts, Nottingham; H. R. Hosein, 108, Derbys v Worcs, Worcester; A. L. Hughes, 140, Derbys v Glos, Derby; M. S. T. Hughes, 116, Oxford Univ v Cambridge Univ, Oxford.

R. P. Jones, 106*, Lancs v Middx, Manchester; C. J. Jordan, 131, Sussex v Essex, Colchester.

F. D. M. Karunaratne, 100, Sri Lankans v Leics, Leicester; R. I. Keogh, 154, Northants v Worcs, Worcester.

J. Leach, 107*, Worcs v Derbys, Worcester; J. S. Lehmann, 116, Yorks v Somerset, Leeds; R. E. Levi, 104, Northants v Derbys, Northampton; M. J. Lumb, 108, Notts v Warwicks, Nottingham.

R. McLaren, 100, Hants v Surrey, The Oval; L. D. McManus, 132*, Hants v Surrey, Southampton; Misbah-ul-Haq , 114, Pakistan v England, Lord's; A. O. Morgan, 103*, Glam v Worcs, Worcester; P. Mustard, 107*, Glos v Derbys, Derby; J. G. Myburgh, 110, Somerset v Hants, Southampton.

G. R. Napier, 124, Essex v Sussex, Colchester; L. C. Norwell, 102, Glos v Derbys, Bristol.

C. Overton, 138, Somerset v Hants, Taunton.

L. E. Plunkett, 126, Yorks v Hants, Leeds.

C. M. W. Read, 101, Notts v Yorks, Nottingham; M. J. Richardson, 115*, Durham v Durham MCCU, Chester-le-Street; G. H. Roderick, 102, Glos v Essex, Cheltenham; W. T. Root, 133, Leeds/Brad MCCU v Sussex, Hove; A. M. Rossington, 138*, Northants v Sussex, Arundel.

K. C. Sangakkara, 171, Surrey v Somerset, The Oval; M. D. Shanaka, 112, Sri Lankans v Leics, Leicester; J. D. Shantry, 106, Worcs v Glos, Worcester; A. R. S. Silva, 109, Sri Lanka A v Durham, Chester-le-Street; J. A. Simpson, 100*, Middx v Hants, Northwood; B. T. Slater, 110, Derbys v Glos, Derby; W. R. Smith, 210, Hants v Lancs, Southampton.

L. R. P. L. Taylor, 142*, Sussex v Kent, Tunbridge Wells; J. C. Tredwell, 124, Kent v Essex, Chelmsford.

A. R. I. Umeed, 101, Warwicks v Durham, Birmingham.

R. E. van der Merwe, 102*, Somerset v Hants, Taunton; J. M. Vince, 119, Hants v Yorks, Leeds; A. C. Voges, 160*, Middx v Hants, Northwood.

G. G. Wagg, 106, Glam v Kent, Canterbury; A. G. Wakely, 104, Northants v Glos, Northampton; I. J. Westwood, 127, Warwicks v Durham, Chester-le-Street; C. R. Woakes, 121, Warwicks v Notts, Nottingham.

FASTEST HUNDREDS BY BALLS...

Balls	*Mins*		
68	98	S. R. Patel	Notts v Warwicks, Nottingham.
71	88	J. M. R. Taylor	Glos v Worcs, Worcester.
79	97	B. R. M. Taylor	Notts v Durham, Nottingham.
80	116	A. H. T. Donald	Glam v Derbys, Colwyn Bay.
81	100	B. M. Duckett	Northants v Glam, Northampton.
82	74	L. E. Plunkett	Yorks v Hants, Leeds.
85	107	J. S. Foster	Essex v Northants, Northampton.
90	147	A. J. Finch	Surrey v Warwicks, Guildford.
93	109	J. D. Shantry	Worcs v Glos, Worcester.
94	121	K. C. Sangakkara	Surrey v Somerset, The Oval.
96	124	J. M. Bairstow	Yorks v Surrey, Leeds.
96	137	J. M. R. Taylor	Glos v Worcs, Bristol.
98	141	N. L. J. Browne	Essex v Cambridge MCCU, Cambridge.

...AND THE SLOWEST

Balls	*Mins*		
291	338	H. Hameed	Lancs v Warwicks, Manchester.
285	381	W. R. Smith	Hants v Lancs, Southampton.
276	386	R. P. Jones	Lancs v Middx, Manchester.
276	377	W. L. Madsen	Derbys v Glos, Bristol.
266	346	N. L. J. Browne	Essex v Derbys, Derby.
257	335	C. D. Nash	Sussex v Leics, Hove.
253	295	L. A. Procter	Lancs v Hants, Manchester.
243	322	S. R. Dickson	Kent v Derbys, Derby.
242	337	A. O. Morgan	Glam v Worcs, Worcester.
240	290	H. R. Hosein	Derbys v Worcs, Worcester.

TEN WICKETS IN A MATCH

There were **15** instances of bowlers taking ten or more wickets in a first-class match in 2016, one more than in 2015. Twelve were in the County Championship.

The following each took ten wickets in a match on one occasion:

J. M. Anderson, 10-45, England v Sri Lanka, Leeds.

G. J. Batty, 10-115, Surrey v Somerset, Taunton.

M. L. Cummins, 12-166, Worcs v Sussex, Hove.

K. M. Jarvis, 11-119, Lancs v Surrey, Manchester.

R. I. Keogh, 13-125, Northants v Glam, Northampton; S. C. Kerrigan, 10-166, Lancs v Middx, Manchester.

S. J. Magoffin, 10-70, Sussex v Worcs, Hove.

J. S. Patel, 10-123, Warwicks v Surrey, Guildford; R. D. Pringle, 10-260, Durham v Hants, Southampton.

M. R. Quinn, 11-163, Essex v Glos, Cheltenham.

T. S. Roland-Jones, 10-127, Middx v Yorks, Lord's.

B. W. Sanderson, 10-89, Northants v Glam, Swansea.

N. Wagner, 11-111, Lancs v Notts, Manchester; C. R. Woakes, 11-102, England v Pakistan, Lord's.

Yasir Shah, 10-141, Pakistan v England, Lord's.

SPECSAVERS COUNTY CHAMPIONSHIP IN 2016

ALAN GARDNER

***Division One** 1 Middlesex 2 Somerset*
***Division Two** 1 Essex*

The final 16-game Championship season – at least for now – was always likely to leave its mark on posterity. Changes voted through shortly before it began decreed that, from 2017, Division One would consist of eight teams and Division Two ten; accordingly, in 2016 two teams would be relegated and only one promoted. At the same time, the centuries-old tradition of the toss was tweaked to give the visiting side the right to bowl first, an attempt to recalibrate the balance between seam and spin; the toss was used only if the visitors wanted to bat. Once again, county cricket felt like a Petri dish.

But if it began as a science experiment, the finish was pure theatre. Going into the last half-hour of the final round, the fates of three teams were intertwined. Somerset watched on from afar, helplessly hoping to be delivered of a first Championship pennant; Middlesex and Yorkshire battled in front of

COUNTY CHAMPIONSHIP TABLE

						Bonus points			
	Division One	*Matches*	*Won*	*Lost*	*Drawn*	*Batting*	*Bowling*	*Penalty*	*Points*
1	Middlesex (**2**)	16	6	0	10	48	40	4	230
2	Somerset (**6**)	16	6	1	9	44	41	0	226
3	Yorkshire (**1**)	16	5	3	8	49	42	0	211
4	Durham† (**4**)	16	5	3	8	39	41	0	200
5	Surrey (*1*)	16	4	6	6	46	42	0	182
6	Warwickshire (**5**)	16	3	4	9	39	44	0	176
7	Lancashire (*2*)	16	3	5	8	39	38	0	165
8	Hampshire (**7**)	16	2	4	10	41	35	3	155
9	Nottinghamshire (**3**)	16	1	9	6	34	44	0	124

						Bonus points			
	Division Two	*Matches*	*Won*	*Lost*	*Drawn*	*Batting*	*Bowling*	*Penalty*	*Points*
1	Essex (*3*)	16	6	3	7	58	46	0	235
2	Kent (*7*)	16	5	2	8*	49	38	0	212
3	Worcestershire (*9*)	16	6	4	5*	42	35	0	203
4	Sussex (**8**)	16	4	2	10	40	38	0	192
5	Northamptonshire (*5*)	16	4	3	8*	42	33	0	184
6	Gloucestershire (*6*)	16	4	5	7	44	40	0	183
7	Leicestershire (*9*)	16	4	4	8	39	40	1	182
8	Glamorgan (*4*)	16	3	8	5	34	42	1	148
9	Derbyshire (*8*)	16	0	5	10*	32	32	0	119

2015 positions are shown in brackets: Division One in bold, Division Two in italic.

† *Ten days after the completion of the Championship, Durham were relegated from Division One for financial reasons, while Hampshire were reprieved.*

* *Plus one match abandoned.*

Win = 16pts; draw = 5pts. *Penalties deducted for slow over-rates.*

7,400 spectators at Lord's, and many more following via television, radio and online. As if all this wasn't enough, Middlesex's first title in 23 years was sealed – uniquely – by a hat-trick. It might not have been as preposterous as Leicester City winning the Premier League, but it was majestic in its own way. The 2016 Championship refused to go gentle into that good night.

Another first, less edifying, swiftly followed. Despite finishing fourth, Durham were summarily demoted to Division Two – where they would start life in 2017 with a 48-point penalty – as punishment for requiring a financial rescue package from the ECB. No matter that Durham, champions three times between 2008 and 2013, had been one of the most reliable producers of England players, or that their debts sprang in part from the expensive process of bidding for international matches, encouraged by the ECB. They had to take their medicine, while others returned to questioning the health of the game.

It was preferable to dwell on that sun-dappled afternoon at Lord's, and the most thrilling climax to the Championship since Nottinghamshire's bonus-points trolley dash in 2010. The match between Yorkshire, aiming for a third title in three years, and Middlesex had been signposted as a potential decider many weeks earlier, but few had foreseen Somerset emerging to throw a maroon cap into the ring. In fact, the three title bids were closely linked, and the eventual destination of the trophy was a study in chaos theory. As with the triptych of plotlines in the film *Run Lola Run*, it was possible to imagine resetting the race, each time watching it veer off towards an alternative ending.

Middlesex were perfectly content with the result they got. Having started with six consecutive draws – the early combination of flat pitches and inclement weather was nowhere more apparent than at Lord's – they signalled a more ruthless intent by sacking Scarborough in July. Meandering towards another stalemate, the match was upturned by Middlesex's ninth-wicket pair, Toby Roland-Jones and Tim Murtagh, who thrashed 107 in 58 balls on the final morning, then took six wickets to inflict Yorkshire's first defeat. In their two title-winning campaigns, Yorkshire had suffered isolated losses against Middlesex, both at Lord's, but this hit uncomfortably closer to home. It also took Middlesex top of the table, a position they would never relinquish, despite being harried all the way.

That **Yorkshire** matched them almost stride for stride indicated the character of Jason Gillespie's side. With two games to go, only a point separated the teams but, by the third afternoon at Lord's, Yorkshire were nine down, and their hopes dependent on a fourth batting point, a necessity if they were to stay in contention; they got there when last man Ryan Sidebottom struck a four just after a rain break. It meant there would have to be contrivance if the trophy was not to make a sharp detour to Taunton, where Somerset had already won, and the sight of Yorkshire's declaration bowling harked back to another era. But the alternative – both teams quietly playing out a draw – would have been worse. As the overs threatened to run out, Roland-Jones, by now something of a Yorkshire nemesis, settled the argument with that hat-trick.

In the West Country, **Somerset's** disappointment at finishing runners-up for the third time in seven years was balanced by an acceptance that it was preferable to another relegation fight. They too had drawn their first six, before

Dan Mullan, Getty Images

Tiers of joy: Middlesex soak in the atmosphere in front of the Lord's Pavilion.

stealing a nerve-jangling one-wicket win against Surrey, when defeat would have pushed them into eighth. Captain Chris Rogers called it a turning point. There was another six weeks later, when Middlesex emerged victorious from their own Taunton thriller, following a Rogers declaration. Boethius was writing about the Wheel of Fortune as long ago as the sixth century, though few sportsmen take much consolation in philosophy.

But the wheel turned again, as did Somerset's pitches from August. Left-arm spinner Jack Leach emerged as a match-winner, and they prevailed in five of their last seven games, including tense low-scorers against Durham and Warwickshire. An emphatic victory at Headingley in the penultimate round suddenly made it a three-horse race. Somerset's sole defeat remained that one against the eventual champions; they were also the only team apart from Middlesex to beat Yorkshire.

The new toss regulations had introduced an element of unpredictability, while more draws kept the teams bunched together, but it was a surprise to see Lancashire, newly promoted, leading at the halfway stage. Yorkshire were briefly level with them, before Durham, then Middlesex, took over. **Durham** could not sustain such a lofty position, despite the run-making feats of Keaton Jennings. But their pain at being relegated after the event was heightened after their rejoicing at apparently preserving Division One status, with a game to go, for what would have been a 12th consecutive season (no team had remained in the top flight longer). That they went on to win at the Rose Bowl, snuffing out **Hampshire's** hopes of another great escape, added to the narrative complexity. Hampshire, having finished next to bottom, were the club handed a reprieve by the ECB.

Nottinghamshire found themselves adrift well before the end, despite picking up maximum points from their opening game; they never won again. **Surrey**, beaten in that match at Trent Bridge, had to wait until late June for their first victory – over Nottinghamshire – but came through strongly, led by the indefatigable Gareth Batty, to finish fifth. **Warwickshire**, with Ian Bell and Jonathan Trott back in the ranks, and Jeetan Patel as effective as ever, had been expected to mount a challenge, but were uncertain of staying up until the final round; Dougie Brown, the coach, paid the price with his job, despite lifting the Royal London One-Day Cup. Ultimately they overleapt **Lancashire**, who won three of their first five but none thereafter, and were left waiting nervously on news from Southampton.

While the change to the toss had seemingly done its job in the top tier, Division Two provided a stiffer test for the ECB's experiment. With only one promotion spot to play for, expedience took precedence. **Essex** finally put together a campaign sturdy enough to return them to Division One, after six years away, but they did so on barely 150 overs of (part-time) spin. If there was some irony in Essex coming up with a successful strategy after the clampdown on green seamers – Chelmsford was viewed as a chief culprit – then it was lost on Chris Silverwood, who simply urged his batsmen to be greedy on better surfaces. The seam attack, led for the last time by the canny Graham Napier and David Masters, redoubled their efforts, to capitalise on scoreboard pressure.

Essex's six wins all came by an innings or ten wickets, and no team in either division collected more batting or bowling points. They led more or less throughout, and few would argue they were not worthy winners, though **Kent** had just cause for disgruntlement after coming second – enough for promotion in any other year. The abandonment of their opening match, at New Road, undermined their chances, and they continued to suffer with the weather: by June, their matches had lost almost 1,000 overs. The ECB's decision to grant Hampshire another life, rather than send Kent up, sharpened the sense of frustration at Canterbury and led to the threat of legal action.

The teams below scrapped gamely to the finish. **Worcestershire** could not quite summon the momentum to yo-yo their way to a sixth promotion, although in Joe Leach they had the division's leading bowler. They were crushed at Chelmsford in early September but won their last two games to climb above **Sussex**, who were hamstrung by injuries – their captain, Luke Wright, played only six games – and bogged down by ten draws.

Northamptonshire, a cricketing version of Wimbledon's "Crazy Gang", remained unfashionable and impecunious, but revelled in their success: a second Twenty20 title was followed by a surge to fifth, and the emergence of Ben Duckett gave them one of the jewels of the game. **Gloucestershire** pushed themselves into contention before falling back, as did **Leicestershire**, whose seventh-place finish was nevertheless a stirring achievement after three consecutive wooden spoons. Two points separated those three, with **Glamorgan** lagging some way behind, although there were signs of Welsh talent emerging under new head coach Robert Croft, including Kiran Carlson, their youngest first-class centurion, and Aneurin Donald. **Derbyshire** lost their coach, Graeme Welch, midway through the season and ended up winless; the call to Kim Barnett to take charge went out soon after.

Giving the away team the option to insert – four captains out of five did so on the opening day of the season – was a practical solution to a perennial problem, and it proved a qualified success. Draws proliferated early on, with just 11 results from 43 matches in the first six rounds, and batsmen had it unusually easy: for the first time, four double-hundreds were scored before the end of April. Groundsmen were not helped by the changeable weather, either. Four games were interrupted by snow and sleet on April 26, while the penultimate round saw crowds basking on the hottest September day in over 100 years.

As the season developed, a better balance was struck. There were 71 results overall, a noticeable drop but still more than in the bedraggled summer of 2012; of those, 30 were concluded in the equivalent (by overs) of three days or less. But bowlers generally had to work harder for their wickets, with strike-rates in both divisions rising to around 61.

In Division One, the rejuvenating effect on spinners was pronounced: Patel and Jack Leach were the leading wicket-takers, while Middlesex's title win was in no small part down to the development of Ollie Rayner. Not since 2010 had three slow bowlers taken more than 50 – and that was across both divisions. The returns were less encouraging in Division Two, where experienced practitioners were in short supply. Northamptonshire's Rob Keogh had most success, claiming 31 wickets with his occasional off-spin, and sharing all 20 with slow left-armer Graeme White on an old-fashioned Wantage Road bunsen against Glamorgan. Altogether, spin accounted for nearly a quarter of the overs and a fifth of the wickets, a promising upswing after the previous year's low, and enough to suggest the trial merited persistence.

Further change was anticipated, with a round of floodlit games announced for 2017, and the prospect of city-based Twenty20 continuing to cast its shadow. Like much of British life in the summer of 2016, the future was uncertain. The appearance of cricket on newspaper front pages in June, when Boris Johnson was photographed playing a country-house match the weekend after the EU referendum, did not necessarily augur well. Thankfully, it captured the back pages again after Middlesex's memorable triumph.

Pre-season betting (best available prices): *Division One* – 13-8 Yorkshire; 6-1 Warwickshire; 13-2 Nottinghamshire; 15-2 MIDDLESEX; 8-1 Surrey; 12-1 Durham; 16-1 Lancashire; 20-1 Somerset and Hampshire. *Division Two* – 2-1 Sussex; 4-1 Worcestershire; 5-1 ESSEX; 9-1 Kent; 14-1 Glamorgan and Gloucestershire; 16-1 Derbyshire and Northamptonshire; 25-1 Leicestershire.

"The Cook who gave honours-board engravers repetitive strain injury has shed the cocoon of accumulation that once habitually formed around his innings."

Curiouser and Curiouser, page 27

Prize money

Division One
£532,100 for winners: MIDDLESEX.
£221,020 for runners-up: SOMERSET
£103,022 for third: YORKSHIRE.
£27,000 for fourth: DURHAM†.
£24,000 for fifth: SURREY.

Division Two
£111,050 for winners: ESSEX.
£51,052 for runners-up: KENT.

† *Durham were paid £27,000 players' prize money but not the £5,121 county performance payment usually included in the total.*

Leaders: *Division One* – from April 13 Nottinghamshire; April 27 Warwickshire; May 4 Nottinghamshire; May 11 Yorkshire; May 18 Warwickshire; May 24 Lancashire; June 1 Lancashire and Yorkshire; June 29 Lancashire; July 6 Middlesex. Middlesex became champions on September 23.
Division Two – from April 13 Essex; June 29 Kent; July 6 Essex. Essex became champions on September 13.

Bottom place: *Division One* – from April 20 Surrey; May 11 Hampshire; May 25 Surrey; June 1 Hampshire and Surrey; June 22 Hampshire; August 16 Nottinghamshire.
Division Two – from April 20 Glamorgan, Kent and Worcestershire; April 27 Northamptonshire; May 4 Glamorgan; July 20 Northamptonshire; August 6 Glamorgan; August 16 Derbyshire.

Scoring of Points

(*a*) For a win, 16 points plus any points scored in the first innings.
(*b*) In a tie, each side score eight points, plus any points scored in the first innings.
(*c*) In a drawn match, each side score five points, plus any points scored in the first innings.
(*d*) If the scores are equal in a drawn match, the side batting in the fourth innings score eight points, plus any points scored in the first innings, and the opposing side score five points, plus any points scored in the first innings.
(*e*) First-innings points (awarded only for performances in the first 110 overs of each first innings and retained whatever the result of the match):

(i) A maximum of five batting points to be available: 200 to 249 runs – 1 point; 250 to 299 runs – 2 points; 300 to 349 runs – 3 points; 350 to 399 runs – 4 points; 400 runs or over – 5 points. Penalty runs awarded within the first 110 overs of each first innings count towards the award of bonus points.

(ii) A maximum of three bowling points to be available: 3 to 5 wickets taken – 1 point; 6 to 8 wickets taken – 2 points; 9 to 10 wickets taken – 3 points.

(*f*) If a match is abandoned without a ball being bowled, each side score five points.
(*g*) The side who have the highest aggregate of points shall be the champion county of their respective division. Should any sides in the Championship table be equal on points, the following tie-breakers will be applied in the order stated: most wins, fewest losses, team achieving most points in head-to-head contests, most wickets taken, most runs scored.
(*h*) The minimum over-rate to be achieved by counties will be 16 overs per hour. Overs will be calculated at the end of the match, and penalties applied on a match-by-match basis. For each over (ignoring fractions) that a side have bowled short of the target number, one point will be deducted from their Championship total.
(*i*) Penalties for poor and unfit pitches are at the discretion of the Cricket Discipline Commission.

Under ECB playing conditions, two extras were scored for every no-ball bowled, whether scored off or not, and one for every wide. Any runs scored off the bat were credited to the batsman, while byes and leg-byes were counted as no-balls or wides, as appropriate, in accordance with Law 24.13, in addition to the initial penalty.

CONSTITUTION OF COUNTY CHAMPIONSHIP

At least four possible dates have been given for the start of county cricket in England. The first, patchy, references began in 1825. The earliest mention in any cricket publication is in 1864, and eight counties have come to be regarded as first-class from that date, including Cambridgeshire, who dropped out after 1871. For many years, the County Championship was considered to have started in 1873, when regulations governing qualification first applied; indeed, a special commemorative stamp was issued by the Post Office in 1973. However, the Championship was not formally organised until 1890, and before then champions were proclaimed by the press; sometimes publications differed in their views, and no definitive list of champions can start before that date. Eight teams contested the 1890 competition – Gloucestershire, Kent, Lancashire, Middlesex, Nottinghamshire, Surrey, Sussex and Yorkshire. Somerset joined the following year, and in 1895 the Championship began to acquire something of its modern shape, when Derbyshire, Essex, Hampshire, Leicestershire and Warwickshire were added. At that point MCC officially recognised the competition's existence. Worcestershire, Northamptonshire and Glamorgan were admitted in 1899, 1905 and 1921 respectively, and are regarded as first-class from these dates. An invitation in 1921 to Buckinghamshire to enter the Championship was declined, owing to the lack of necessary playing facilities, and an application by Devon in 1948 was unsuccessful. Durham were admitted in 1992 and were granted first-class status prior to their pre-season tour of Zimbabwe.

In 2000, the Championship was split for the first time into two divisions, on the basis of counties' standings in the 1999 competition. From 2000 onwards, the bottom three teams in Division One were relegated at the end of the season, and the top three teams in Division Two promoted. From 2006, this was changed to two teams relegated and two promoted. In 2016, two were relegated and one promoted, to create divisions of eight and ten teams.

COUNTY CHAMPIONS

The title of champion county is unreliable before 1890. In 1963, *Wisden* formally accepted the list of champions "most generally selected" by contemporaries, as researched by the late Rowland Bowen (see *Wisden 1959*, pp 91). This appears to be the most accurate available list but has no official status. The county champions from 1864 to 1889 were, according to Bowen: 1864 Surrey; 1865 Nottinghamshire; 1866 Middlesex; 1867 Yorkshire; 1868 Nottinghamshire; 1869 Nottinghamshire and Yorkshire; 1870 Yorkshire; 1871 Nottinghamshire; 1872 Nottinghamshire; 1873 Gloucestershire and Nottinghamshire; 1874 Gloucestershire; 1875 Nottinghamshire; 1876 Gloucestershire; 1877 Gloucestershire; 1878 undecided; 1879 Lancashire and Nottinghamshire; 1880 Nottinghamshire; 1881 Lancashire; 1882 Lancashire and Nottinghamshire; 1883 Nottinghamshire; 1884 Nottinghamshire; 1885 Nottinghamshire; 1886 Nottinghamshire; 1887 Surrey; 1888 Surrey; 1889 Lancashire, Nottinghamshire and Surrey.

1890	Surrey
1891	Surrey
1892	Surrey
1893	Yorkshire
1894	Surrey
1895	Surrey
1896	Yorkshire
1897	Lancashire
1898	Yorkshire
1899	Surrey
1900	Yorkshire
1901	Yorkshire
1902	Yorkshire
1903	Middlesex
1904	Lancashire
1905	Yorkshire
1906	Kent
1907	Nottinghamshire
1908	Yorkshire
1909	Kent
1910	Kent
1911	Warwickshire
1912	Yorkshire
1913	Kent
1914	Surrey
1919	Yorkshire
1920	Middlesex
1921	Middlesex
1922	Yorkshire
1923	Yorkshire
1924	Yorkshire
1925	Yorkshire
1926	Lancashire
1927	Lancashire
1928	Lancashire
1929	Nottinghamshire
1930	Lancashire
1931	Yorkshire
1932	Yorkshire
1933	Yorkshire
1934	Lancashire
1935	Yorkshire
1936	Derbyshire
1937	Yorkshire
1938	Yorkshire
1939	Yorkshire
1946	Yorkshire
1947	Middlesex
1948	Glamorgan
1949	Middlesex Yorkshire
1950	Lancashire Surrey
1951	Warwickshire
1952	Surrey
1953	Surrey
1954	Surrey
1955	Surrey
1956	Surrey
1957	Surrey
1958	Surrey
1959	Yorkshire
1960	Yorkshire
1961	Hampshire
1962	Yorkshire
1963	Yorkshire
1964	Worcestershire
1965	Worcestershire
1966	Yorkshire
1967	Yorkshire
1968	Yorkshire
1969	Glamorgan
1970	Kent
1971	Surrey
1972	Warwickshire
1973	Hampshire
1974	Worcestershire
1975	Leicestershire
1976	Middlesex
1977	Middlesex Kent
1978	Kent
1979	Essex
1980	Middlesex
1981	Nottinghamshire
1982	Middlesex
1983	Essex

1984	Essex	1995	Warwickshire	2006	Sussex
1985	Middlesex	1996	Leicestershire	2007	Sussex
1986	Essex	1997	Glamorgan	2008	Durham
1987	Nottinghamshire	1998	Leicestershire	2009	Durham
1988	Worcestershire	1999	Surrey	2010	Nottinghamshire
1989	Worcestershire	2000	Surrey	2011	Lancashire
1990	Middlesex	2001	Yorkshire	2012	Warwickshire
1991	Essex	2002	Surrey	2013	Durham
1992	Essex	2003	Sussex	2014	Yorkshire
1993	Middlesex	2004	Warwickshire	2015	Yorkshire
1994	Warwickshire	2005	Nottinghamshire	2016	Middlesex

Notes: Since the Championship was constituted in 1890 it has been won outright as follows: Yorkshire 32 times, Surrey 18, Middlesex 11, Lancashire 8, Warwickshire 7, Essex, Kent and Nottinghamshire 6, Worcestershire 5, Durham, Glamorgan, Leicestershire and Sussex 3, Hampshire 2, Derbyshire 1. Gloucestershire, Northamptonshire and Somerset have never won.

The title has been shared three times since 1890, involving Middlesex twice, Kent, Lancashire, Surrey and Yorkshire.

Wooden spoons: Since the major expansion of the Championship from nine teams to 14 in 1895, the counties have finished outright bottom as follows: Derbyshire 16; Leicestershire and Somerset 12; Northamptonshire 11; Glamorgan 10; Gloucestershire 9; Nottinghamshire and Sussex 8; Worcestershire 6; Durham and Hampshire 5; Warwickshire 3; Essex and Kent 2; Yorkshire 1. Lancashire, Middlesex and Surrey have never finished bottom. Leicestershire have also shared bottom place twice, once with Hampshire and once with Somerset.

From 1977 to 1983 the Championship was sponsored by Schweppes, from 1984 to 1998 by Britannic Assurance, from 1999 to 2000 by PPP healthcare, in 2001 by Cricinfo, from 2002 to 2005 by Frizzell, from 2006 to 2015 by Liverpool Victoria (LV), and from 2016 by Specsavers.

COUNTY CHAMPIONSHIP – FINAL POSITIONS, 1890–2016

	Derbyshire	Durham	Essex	Glamorgan	Gloucestershire	Hampshire	Kent	Lancashire	Leicestershire	Middlesex	Northamptonshire	Nottinghamshire	Somerset	Surrey	Sussex	Warwickshire	Worcestershire	Yorkshire
1890	–	–	–	–	6	–	3	2	–	7	–	5	–	1	8	–	–	3
1891	–	–	–	–	9	–	5	2	–	3	–	4	5	1	7	–	–	8
1892	–	–	–	–	7	–	7	4	–	5	–	2	3	1	9	–	–	6
1893	–	–	–	–	9	–	4	2	–	3	–	6	8	5	7	–	–	1
1894	–	–	–	–	9	–	4	4	–	3	–	7	6	1	8	–	–	2
1895	5	–	9	–	4	10	14	2	12	6	–	12	8	1	11	6	–	3
1896	7	–	5	–	10	8	9	2	13	3	–	6	11	4	14	12	–	1
1897	14	–	3	–	5	9	12	1	13	8	–	10	11	2	6	7	–	4
1898	9	–	5	–	3	12	7	6	13	2	–	8	13	4	9	9	–	1
1899	15	–	6	–	9	10	8	4	13	2	–	10	13	1	5	7	12	3
1900	13	–	10	–	7	15	3	2	14	7	–	5	11	7	3	6	12	1
1901	15	–	10	–	14	7	7	3	12	2	–	9	12	6	4	5	11	1
1902	10	–	13	–	14	15	7	5	11	12	–	3	7	4	2	6	9	1
1903	12	–	8	–	13	14	8	4	14	1	–	5	10	11	2	7	6	3
1904	10	–	14	–	9	15	3	1	7	4	–	5	12	11	6	7	13	2
1905	14	–	12	–	8	16	6	2	5	11	13	10	15	4	3	7	8	1
1906	16	–	7	–	9	8	1	4	15	11	11	5	11	3	10	6	14	2
1907	16	–	7	–	10	12	8	6	11	5	15	1	14	4	13	9	2	2
1908	14	–	11	–	10	9	2	7	13	4	15	8	16	3	5	12	6	1
1909	15	–	14	–	16	8	1	2	13	6	7	10	11	5	4	12	8	3
1910	15	–	11	–	12	6	1	4	10	3	9	5	16	2	7	14	13	8
1911	14	–	6	–	12	11	2	4	15	3	10	8	16	5	13	1	9	7
1912	12	–	15	–	11	6	3	4	13	5	2	8	14	7	10	9	16	1

	Derbyshire	Durham	Essex	Glamorgan	Gloucestershire	Hampshire	Kent	Lancashire	Leicestershire	Middlesex	Northamptonshire	Nottinghamshire	Somerset	Surrey	Sussex	Warwickshire	Worcestershire	Yorkshire
1913	13	–	15	–	9	10	1	8	14	6	4	5	16	3	7	11	12	2
1914	12	–	8	–	16	5	3	11	13	2	9	10	15	1	6	7	14	4
1919	9	–	14	–	8	7	2	5	9	13	12	3	5	4	11	15	–	1
1920	16	–	9	–	8	11	5	2	13	1	14	7	10	3	6	12	15	4
1921	12	–	15	17	7	6	4	5	11	1	13	8	10	2	9	16	14	3
1922	11	–	8	16	13	6	4	5	14	7	15	2	10	3	9	12	17	1
1923	10	–	13	16	11	7	5	3	14	8	17	2	9	4	6	12	15	1
1924	17	–	15	13	6	12	5	4	11	2	16	6	8	3	10	9	14	1
1925	14	–	7	17	10	9	5	3	12	6	11	4	15	2	13	8	16	1
1926	11	–	9	8	15	7	3	1	13	6	16	4	14	5	10	12	17	2
1927	5	–	8	15	12	13	4	1	7	9	16	2	14	6	10	11	17	3
1928	10	–	16	15	5	12	2	1	9	8	13	3	14	6	7	11	17	4
1929	7	–	12	17	4	11	8	2	9	6	13	1	15	10	4	14	16	2
1930	9	–	6	11	2	13	5	1	12	16	17	4	13	8	7	15	10	3
1931	7	–	10	15	2	12	3	6	16	11	17	5	13	8	4	9	14	1
1932	10	–	14	15	13	8	3	6	12	10	16	4	7	5	2	9	17	1
1933	6	–	4	16	10	14	3	5	17	12	13	8	11	9	2	7	15	1
1934	3	–	8	13	7	14	5	1	12	10	17	9	15	11	2	4	16	5
1935	2	–	9	13	15	16	10	4	6	3	17	5	14	11	7	8	12	1
1936	1	–	9	16	4	10	8	11	15	2	17	5	7	6	14	13	12	3
1937	3	–	6	7	4	14	12	9	16	2	17	10	13	8	5	11	15	1
1938	5	–	6	16	10	14	9	4	15	2	17	12	7	3	8	13	11	1
1939	9	–	4	13	3	15	5	6	17	2	16	12	14	8	10	11	7	1
1946	15	–	8	6	5	10	6	3	11	2	16	13	4	11	17	14	8	1
1947	5	–	11	9	2	16	4	3	14	1	17	11	11	6	9	15	7	7
1948	6	–	13	1	8	9	15	5	11	3	17	14	12	2	16	7	10	4
1949	15	–	9	8	7	16	13	11	17	1	6	11	9	5	13	4	3	1
1950	5	–	17	11	7	12	9	1	16	14	10	15	7	1	13	4	6	3
1951	11	–	8	5	12	9	16	3	15	7	13	17	14	6	10	1	4	2
1952	4	–	10	7	9	12	15	3	6	5	8	16	17	1	13	10	14	2
1953	6	–	12	10	6	14	16	3	3	5	11	8	17	1	2	9	15	12
1954	3	–	15	4	13	14	11	10	16	7	7	5	17	1	9	6	11	2
1955	8	–	14	16	12	3	13	9	6	5	7	11	17	1	4	9	15	2
1956	12	–	11	13	3	6	16	2	17	5	4	8	15	1	9	14	9	7
1957	4	–	5	9	12	13	14	6	17	7	2	15	8	1	9	11	16	3
1958	5	–	6	15	14	2	8	7	12	10	4	17	3	1	13	16	9	11
1959	7	–	9	6	2	8	13	5	16	10	11	17	12	3	15	4	14	1
1960	5	–	6	11	8	12	10	2	17	3	9	16	14	7	4	15	13	1
1961	7	–	6	14	5	1	11	13	9	3	16	17	10	15	8	12	4	2
1962	7	–	9	14	4	10	11	16	17	13	8	15	6	5	12	3	2	1
1963	17	–	12	2	8	10	13	15	16	6	7	9	3	11	4	4	14	1
1964	12	–	10	11	17	12	7	14	16	6	3	15	8	4	9	2	1	5
1965	9	–	15	3	10	12	5	13	14	6	2	17	7	8	16	11	1	4
1966	9	–	16	14	15	11	4	12	8	12	5	17	3	7	10	6	2	1
1967	6	–	15	14	17	12	2	11	2	7	9	15	8	4	13	10	5	1
1968	8	–	14	3	16	5	2	6	9	10	13	4	12	15	17	11	7	1
1969	16	–	6	1	2	5	10	15	14	11	9	8	17	3	7	4	12	13
1970	7	–	12	2	17	10	1	3	15	16	14	11	13	5	9	7	6	4
1971	17	–	10	16	8	9	4	3	5	6	14	12	7	1	11	2	15	13
1972	17	–	5	13	3	9	2	15	6	8	4	14	11	12	16	1	7	10
1973	16	–	8	11	5	1	4	12	9	13	3	17	10	2	15	7	6	14
1974	17	–	12	16	14	2	10	8	4	6	3	15	5	7	13	9	1	11
1975	15	–	7	9	16	3	5	4	1	11	8	13	12	6	17	14	10	2
1976	15	–	6	17	3	12	14	16	4	1	2	13	7	9	10	5	11	8

	Derbyshire	Durham	Essex	Glamorgan	Gloucestershire	Hampshire	Kent	Lancashire	Leicestershire	Middlesex	Northamptonshire	Nottinghamshire	Somerset	Surrey	Sussex	Warwickshire	Worcestershire	Yorkshire
1977	7	–	6	14	3	11	1	16	5	1	9	17	4	14	8	10	13	12
1978	14	–	2	13	10	8	1	12	6	3	17	7	5	16	9	11	15	4
1979	16	–	1	17	10	12	5	13	6	14	11	9	8	3	4	15	2	7
1980	9	–	8	13	7	17	16	15	10	1	12	3	5	2	4	14	11	6
1981	12	–	5	14	13	7	9	16	8	4	15	1	3	6	2	17	11	10
1982	11	–	7	16	15	3	13	12	2	1	9	4	6	5	8	17	14	10
1983	9	–	1	15	12	3	7	12	4	2	6	14	10	8	11	5	16	17
1984	12	–	1	13	17	15	5	16	4	3	11	2	7	8	6	9	10	14
1985	13	–	4	12	3	2	9	14	16	1	10	8	17	6	7	15	5	11
1986	11	–	1	17	2	6	8	15	7	12	9	4	16	3	14	12	5	10
1987	6	–	12	13	10	5	14	2	3	16	7	1	11	4	17	15	9	8
1988	14	–	3	17	10	15	2	9	8	7	12	5	11	4	16	6	1	13
1989	6	–	2	17	9	6	15	4	13	3	5	11	14	12	10	8	1	16
1990	12	–	2	8	13	3	16	6	7	1	11	13	15	9	17	5	4	10
1991	3	–	1	12	13	9	6	8	16	15	10	4	17	5	11	2	6	14
1992	5	18	1	14	10	15	2	12	8	11	3	4	9	13	7	6	17	16
1993	15	18	11	3	17	13	8	13	9	1	4	7	5	6	10	16	2	12
1994	17	16	6	18	12	13	9	10	2	4	5	3	11	7	8	1	15	13
1995	14	17	5	16	6	13	18	4	7	2	3	11	9	12	15	1	10	8
1996	2	18	5	10	13	14	4	15	1	9	16	17	11	3	12	8	7	6
1997	16	17	8	1	7	14	2	11	10	4	15	13	12	8	18	4	3	6
1998	10	14	18	12	4	6	11	2	1	17	15	16	9	5	7	8	13	3
1999	9	8	12	14	18	7	5	2	3	16	13	17	4	1	11	10	15	6
2000	**9**	**8**	*2*	*3*	*4*	**7**	**6**	**2**	**4**	*8*	*1*	*7*	**5**	**1**	*9*	*6*	*5*	**3**
2001	*9*	*8*	**9**	**8**	*4*	*2*	**3**	**6**	**5**	*5*	**7**	*7*	**2**	**4**	*1*	*3*	*6*	**1**
2002	*6*	*9*	*1*	*5*	*8*	**7**	**3**	**4**	**5**	*2*	*7*	*3*	**8**	**1**	**6**	**2**	*4*	**9**
2003	*9*	*6*	**7**	*5*	*3*	*8*	**4**	**2**	**9**	**6**	*2*	**8**	*7*	**3**	**1**	**5**	*1*	*4*
2004	*8*	*9*	*5*	*3*	**6**	*2*	**2**	**8**	*6*	**4**	**9**	*1*	*4*	**3**	**5**	**1**	**7**	*7*
2005	*9*	*2*	*5*	**9**	**8**	**2**	**5**	*1*	*7*	**6**	*4*	**1**	*8*	**7**	**3**	**4**	*6*	*3*
2006	*5*	**7**	*3*	*8*	*7*	**3**	**5**	**2**	*4*	**9**	*6*	**8**	*9*	*1*	**1**	**4**	*2*	**6**
2007	*6*	**2**	*4*	*9*	*7*	**5**	**7**	**3**	*8*	*3*	*5*	*2*	*1*	**4**	**1**	**8**	**9**	**6**
2008	*6*	**1**	*5*	*8*	*9*	**3**	**8**	**5**	*7*	*3*	*4*	**2**	**4**	**9**	**6**	*1*	*2*	**7**
2009	*6*	**1**	*2*	*5*	*4*	**6**	*1*	**4**	*9*	*8*	*3*	**2**	**3**	*7*	**8**	**5**	**9**	**7**
2010	*9*	**5**	**9**	*3*	*5*	**7**	**8**	**4**	*4*	*8*	*6*	**1**	**2**	*7*	*1*	**6**	*2*	**3**
2011	*5*	**3**	*7*	*6*	*4*	**9**	*8*	**1**	*9*	*1*	*3*	**6**	**4**	*2*	**5**	**2**	**7**	**8**
2012	*1*	**6**	*5*	*6*	*9*	*4*	*3*	**8**	*7*	**3**	*8*	**5**	**2**	**7**	**4**	**1**	**9**	*2*
2013	**8**	**1**	*3*	*8*	*6*	*4*	*7*	*1*	*9*	**5**	*2*	**7**	**6**	**9**	**3**	**4**	*5*	**2**
2014	*4*	**5**	*3*	*8*	*7*	*1*	*6*	**8**	*9*	**7**	**9**	**4**	**6**	*5*	**3**	**2**	*2*	**1**
2015	*8*	**4**	*3*	*4*	*6*	**7**	*7*	*2*	*9*	**2**	*5*	**3**	**6**	*1*	**8**	**5**	**9**	**1**
2016	*9*	**4**	*1*	*8*	*6*	**8**	*2*	**7**	*7*	**1**	*5*	**9**	**2**	**5**	*4*	**6**	*3*	**3**

For the 2000–2016 Championships, Division One placings are in bold, Division Two in italic.

MATCH RESULTS, 1864–2016

County	*Years of Play*	*Played*	*Won*	*Lost*	*Drawn*	*Tied*	*% Won*
Derbyshire	1871–87; 1895–2016	2,546	622	937	986	1	24.43
Durham	1992–2016	410	112	169	129	0	27.31
Essex	1895–2016	2,509	731	727	1,045	6	29.13
Glamorgan	1921–2016	2,040	452	701	887	0	22.15
Gloucestershire	1870–2016	2,782	811	1,024	945	2	29.15
Hampshire	1864–85; 1895–2016	2,618	689	878	1,047	4	26.31
Kent	1864–2016	2,905	1,034	869	997	5	35.59
Lancashire	1865–2016	2,980	1,098	618	1,261	3	36.84

County	*Years of Play*	*Played*	*Won*	*Lost*	*Drawn*	*Tied*	*% Won*
Leicestershire	1895–2016	2,475	553	901	1,020	1	22.34
Middlesex	1864–2016	2,685	977	682	1,021	5	36.38
Northamptonshire	1905–2016	2,243	558	765	917	3	24.87
Nottinghamshire	1864–2016	2,815	851	768	1,195	1	30.23
Somerset	1882–85; 1891–2016	2,517	608	969	937	3	24.15
Surrey	1864–2016	3,060	1,193	683	1,180	4	38.98
Sussex	1864–2016	2,954	841	1,001	1,106	6	28.46
Warwickshire	1895–2016	2,489	696	705	1,086	2	27.96
Worcestershire	1899–2016	2,427	624	845	956	2	25.71
Yorkshire	1864–2016	3,084	1,335	543	1,204	2	43.28
Cambridgeshire	1864–69; 1871	19	8	8	3	0	42.10
		22,779	13,793	13,793	8,961	25	

Matches abandoned without a ball bowled are wholly excluded.

Counties participated in the years shown, except that there were no matches in 1915–1918 and 1940–1945; Hampshire did not play inter-county matches in 1868–1869, 1871–1874 and 1879; Worcestershire did not take part in the Championship in 1919.

COUNTY CHAMPIONSHIP STATISTICS FOR 2016

	For			*Runs scored*	*Against*		
County	*Runs*	*Wickets*	*Avge*	*per 100 balls*	*Runs*	*Wickets*	*Avge*
Derbyshire (*9*)	7,866	225	34.96	55.96	7,953	173	45.97
Durham (**4**)	8,128	235	34.58	56.91	8,418	238	35.36
Essex (*1*)	8,411	199	42.26	58.15	8,195	276	29.69
Glamorgan (*8*)	7,875	275	28.63	58.83	8,275	230	35.97
Gloucestershire (*6*)	8,335	243	34.30	56.39	8,476	231	36.69
Hampshire (**8**)	8,261	235	35.15	51.94	8,195	183	44.78
Kent (*2*)	7,425	170	43.67	60.04	7,420	217	34.19
Lancashire (**7**)	7,667	232	33.04	50.08	7,935	219	36.23
Leicestershire (*7*)	7,508	239	31.41	54.58	6,671	213	31.31
Middlesex (**1**)	8,022	187	42.89	55.37	7,607	237	32.09
Northamptonshire (*5*)	7,230	201	35.97	61.44	6,972	203	34.34
Nottinghamshire (**9**)	7,323	273	26.82	54.26	8,374	234	35.78
Somerset (**2**)	7,827	217	36.06	61.31	7,058	252	28.00
Surrey (**5**)	8,608	256	33.62	54.80	8,006	228	35.11
Sussex (*4*)	7,366	198	37.20	57.80	8,150	227	35.90
Warwickshire (**6**)	6,305	216	29.18	53.80	7,367	269	27.38
Worcestershire (*3*)	7,877	221	35.64	60.65	7,781	201	38.71
Yorkshire (**3**)	8,572	246	34.84	56.28	7,753	237	32.71
	140,606	4,068	34.56	56.42	140,606	4,068	34.56

2015 Championship positions are shown in brackets; Division One in bold, Division Two in italic.

ECB PITCHES TABLE OF MERIT IN 2016

	First-class	*One-day*		*First-class*	*One-day*
Derbyshire	4.63	5.32	Surrey	5.00	5.50
Durham	4.68	5.55	Sussex	5.10	5.09
Essex	5.11	5.54	Warwickshire	5.00	5.27
Glamorgan	4.89	5.13	Worcestershire	4.50	5.36
Gloucestershire	4.56	5.33	Yorkshire	5.50	5.17
Hampshire	4.78	5.50			
Kent	4.56	5.20			
Lancashire	5.22	4.82	Cambridge MCCU	5.00	
Leicestershire	4.30	5.10	Cardiff MCCU	5.00	
Middlesex	4.00	4.96	Durham MCCU	5.00	
Northamptonshire	4.44	5.47	Leeds/Bradford MCCU	5.50	
Nottinghamshire	4.75	5.83	Loughborough MCCU	4.75	
Somerset	4.25	5.42	Oxford MCCU	4.33	

Each umpire in a match marks the pitch on the following scale: 6 – Very good; 5 – Good; 4 – Above average; 3 – Below average; 2 – Poor; 1 – Unfit.

The tables, provided by the ECB, cover major matches, including Tests, Under-19 internationals, women's internationals and MCCU games, played on grounds under the county's or MCCU's jurisdiction. Middlesex pitches at Lord's are the responsibility of MCC. The "First-class" column includes Under-19 and women's Tests, and inter-MCCU games.

Yorkshire had the highest marks for first-class cricket, and Nottinghamshire for one-day cricket, though the ECB point out that the tables of merit are not a direct assessment of the groundsmen's ability. Marks may be affected by many factors, including weather, soil conditions and the resources available.

COUNTY CAPS AWARDED IN 2016

Glamorgan*	C. B. Cooke.
Gloucestershire*	C. T. Bancroft, J. R. Bracey, G. T. Hankins, P. Mustard, J. Shaw, G. L. van Buuren.
Hampshire	G. K. Berg, A. J. A. Wheater.
Kent	M. E. Claydon.
Lancashire	H. Hameed, A. N. Petersen.
Middlesex	N. R. T. Gubbins, P. R. Stirling, A. C. Voges.
Northamptonshire	B. M. Duckett, R. K. Kleinveldt.
Nottinghamshire	J. T. Ball, J. M. Bird, D. T. Christian.
Somerset	T. D. Groenewald, C. Overton.
Surrey	T. K. Curran, B. T. Foakes, A. Harinath.
Sussex	L. W. P. Wells.
Worcestershire*	K. J. Abbott, M. L. Cummins, M. J. Henry, G. H. Rhodes, M. J. Santner.
Yorkshire	Azeem Rafiq, A. J. Hodd, J. A. Leaning, D. J. Willey.

** Glamorgan's capping system is now based on a player's number of appearances; Gloucestershire now award caps to all first-class players; Worcestershire have replaced caps with colours awarded to all Championship players. Durham abolished their capping system after 2005.*

No caps were awarded by Derbyshire, Essex, Leicestershire or Warwickshire.

COUNTY BENEFITS AWARDED FOR 2017

Derbyshire	W. L. Madsen.
Durham	P. D. Collingwood.
Kent	J. C. Tredwell.
Nottinghamshire	S. R. Patel.
Somerset	J. C. Hildreth.
Surrey	G. J. Batty.
Sussex	C. D. Nash.
Yorkshire	S. A. Patterson and R. J. Sidebottom.

None of the other ten counties awarded a benefit for 2017.

DERBYSHIRE

Demolition Derby

MARK EKLID

The best news from the County Ground came from outside the boundary. The opening of a new £1.75m business and media centre completed a two-year redevelopment, following a remodelled pavilion and vastly improved player facilities. A venue whose amenities have rarely been viewed fondly has been transformed.

The rebuilding of Derbyshire's team was less successful. The elite performance system, drawn up three seasons earlier to establish a "player development pathway", was undermined by the mid-season resignation of the man who had been chosen to implement it, Graeme Welch. It was then discredited in an internal review, and largely dismantled at the end of the summer.

That final act of demolition was the result of a season that seemed like a relic from the past. Derbyshire finished bottom of the Championship, extending their record to a 16th wooden spoon. And, for the first time since 1924 – but the fifth in all, another record – they failed to win a match. Their batsmen collected the fewest bonus points in either division; so did their bowlers, who could not take 20 wickets in a Championship match even once. There was no solace in the white-ball formats: Derbyshire narrowly missed out on the knockout stage of both competitions.

New signings in key positions failed, long-term injuries struck, and then there was the sudden departure of Welch, appointed elite performance director in early 2014. It came on the morning of the first home match in the NatWest T20 Blast, in June, only ten weeks after his contract had been extended to the end of 2018. After a poor start, however, and the deterioration of his relationship with senior players, Welch decided it was time to go. Ant Botha, his chief ally on the coaching staff, soon followed.

Batting coach John Sadler was named head coach until the end of the season and, in the first weeks of readjustment, results were encouraging. But two defeats in three days at the end of July – at Chester-le-Street in the final Twenty20 match, and Northampton in the penultimate Royal London One-Day Cup game – proved pivotal. In both tournaments, victory would have seen Derbyshire qualify for the quarter-finals ahead of their opponents. The remaining eight weeks of the season could have had an entirely different sheen, but that weekend their purpose evaporated. Sadler left at the end of October.

The players brought in to increase the squad's experience did not provide the solution. Neil Broom, a 32-year-old New Zealand batsman who arrived on a two-year deal with a British passport, struggled to adapt and later asked to be released from his contract so he could resume his international career. He and his countryman Hamish Rutherford, who had prospered in a shorter spell the previous season, failed to muster a first-class century between them; Rutherford was not selected for the last five Championship games. Andy Carter, recruited from Nottinghamshire to lead an attack trying to absorb the loss of Mark Footitt to Surrey, made little impact and left abruptly in July.

Tony Marshall, Getty Images

Tony Palladino

Bowling options were further restricted by the loss of Tom Taylor in June, to a stress fracture in his back. Shiv Thakor suffered a similar injury in August, cutting short a season in which he had moved closer to fulfilling his outstanding potential as an all-rounder. An additional blow came when wicketkeeper Tom Poynton was forced to retire, aged 26, because of a flare-up of the injury to his right ankle sustained in the car accident that killed his father, Keith, two years earlier.

By October, Wes Durston – Derbyshire's one-day captain for the past two seasons – and Chesney Hughes had been released at the end of their contracts. Hughes, aged 25, scored three Championship centuries, taking him to ten in his seven seasons with the county; though he was yet to live up to the promise of his teens, his departure was a sad one.

With Durston, Hughes and Poynton gone, only two of the 17 players who helped Derbyshire win Division Two in 2012 remained – Tony Palladino and Wayne Madsen. Palladino, who is to combine playing with a coaching role in 2017, was Derbyshire's leading Championship wicket-taker with 39, while Madsen fully justified his decision in March to hand over the captaincy to Billy Godleman, and concentrate on his batting. Godleman also took charge of the 50-over team. Madsen scored a career-best aggregate of 1,292 at 58, his fourth 1,000-run season in a row, with six centuries.

At the end of September, Kim Barnett – Derbyshire's long-time former captain and leading run-scorer – stepped down as club president to become director of cricket. Earlier, he had been commissioned by the board to assess the elite performance system; his report recommended reducing the number of coaching positions, but advocated a Twenty20 specialist. The job went to former New Zealand batsman John Wright, a Derbyshire player for 12 seasons, and more recently coach of India and his own country. The playing squad was strengthened by signing South Africa's leg-spinner Imran Tahir – who will represent his sixth county, equalling the record held by Marcus North and Yasir Arafat – and Sri Lankan all-rounder Jeewan Mendis to share overseas duties, plus Ireland wicketkeeper Gary Wilson and former Lancashire opener Luis Reece. South African fast-bowler Hardus Viljoen, who had briefly appeared for Kent in 2016, joined as a Kolpak. The rebuilding of Derbyshire had begun, again.

Championship attendance: 8,583.

DERBYSHIRE RESULTS

All first-class matches – Played 15: Lost 5, Drawn 10. Abandoned 1.
County Championship matches – Played 15: Lost 5, Drawn 10. Abandoned 1.

Specsavers County Championship, 9th in Division 2;
NatWest T20 Blast, 7th in North Group; Royal London One-Day Cup, 7th in North Group.

COUNTY CHAMPIONSHIP AVERAGES, BATTING AND FIELDING

Cap		*Birthplace*	*M*	*I*	*NO*	*R*	*HS*	*100*	*Avge*	*Ct/St*
	H. R. Hosein	*Chesterfield‡*	4	8	4	423	108	1	105.75	9
	S. J. Thakor	*Leicester*	9	13	4	606	130	2	67.33	0
2011	W. L. Madsen	*Durban, SA*	15	26	4	1,292	163	6	58.72	11
	†C. F. Hughes	*Anguilla*	11	19	4	806	137*	3	53.73	8
2015	†B. A. Godleman	*Islington*	13	24	0	934	204	3	38.91	6
	A. L. Hughes	*Wordsley*	5	9	0	299	140	1	33.22	7
	†B. T. Slater	*Chesterfield‡*	9	15	1	393	110	1	28.07	3
	†H. D. Rutherford¶	*Dunedin, NZ*	10	17	1	441	78	0	27.56	8
	N. T. Broom††	*Christchurch, NZ*	14	22	1	530	96	0	25.23	7
	T. A. I. Taylor	*Stoke-on-Trent*	3	6	0	147	80	0	24.50	0
	M. J. J. Critchley	*Preston*	7	12	1	263	70*	0	23.90	3
	A. Carter	*Lincoln*	4	4	1	68	39	0	22.66	2
	T. P. Milnes	*Stourbridge*	5	9	0	188	56	0	20.88	1
	T. Poynton	*Burton-on-Trent*	9	11	2	167	53	0	18.55	15/1
2012	A. P. Palladino	*Tower Hamlets*	14	20	5	268	49	0	17.86	2
	C. F. Parkinson	*Bolton*	4	7	2	80	48*	0	16.00	0
2012	W. J. Durston	*Taunton*	4	4	0	63	43	0	15.75	3
	B. D. Cotton	*Stoke-on-Trent*	8	11	3	102	26	0	12.75	1
	L. J. Fletcher	*Nottingham*	4	4	0	34	14	0	8.50	1
	T. A. Wood	*Derby‡*	2	4	0	32	14	0	8.00	1
	W. S. Davis	*Stafford*	6	8	1	34	15	0	4.85	0

Also batted: G. T. G. Cork (*Derby‡*) (1 match) 49, 4; R. P. Hemmings (*Newcastle-under-Lyme*) (1 match) did not bat (1 ct); C. M. Macdonell (*Basingstoke*) (1 match) 21, 35*; †A. J. Mellor (*Stoke-on-Trent*) (2 matches) 27, 44, 0 (7 ct).

‡ *Born in Derbyshire.* ¶ *Official overseas player.* †† *Other non-England-qualified.*

BOWLING

	Style	*O*	*M*	*R*	*W*	*BB*	*5I*	*Avge*
A. P. Palladino	RFM	453.5	110	1,201	39	5-74	2	30.79
S. J. Thakor	RM	188	24	687	22	5-63	1	31.22
T. P. Milnes	RFM	172	37	509	15	6-93	1	33.93
W. S. Davis	RFM	170.2	20	733	21	7-146	1	34.90
C. F. Parkinson	SLA	170.4	28	531	14	4-90	0	37.92
B. D. Cotton	RFM	202.3	50	661	14	4-28	0	47.21

Also bowled: N. T. Broom (OB) 17–2–64–3; A. Carter (RFM) 101–12–440–6; G. T. G. Cork (LFM) 17–2–70–0; M. J. J. Critchley (LBG) 122.2–3–639–4; W. J. Durston (OB) 101.4–14–397–9; L. J. Fletcher (RFM) 99–25–276–4; R. P. Hemmings (RM) 19–5–58–0; A. L. Hughes (RM) 53–10–169–1; C. F. Hughes (SLA) 106.3–11–430–9; W. L. Madsen (OB) 165.1–21–527–7; H. D. Rutherford (SLA) 2–0–8–0; B. T. Slater (LBG) 13–0–71–0; T. A. I. Taylor (RFM) 63–13–250–4.

LEADING ROYAL LONDON CUP AVERAGES (100 runs/4 wickets)

Batting	*Runs*	*HS*	*Avge*	*SR*	*Ct*
B. T. Slater	328	148*	82.00	84.97	0
B. A. Godleman	298	91	59.60	82.32	0
N. T. Broom	177	90	59.00	97.25	3
H. D. Rutherford	195	104	48.75	101.56	1
W. L. Madsen	168	69*	42.00	80.00	7

Bowling	*W*	*BB*	*Avge*	*ER*
A. Carter	5	3-59	19.40	5.06
B. D. Cotton	10	4-43	25.80	5.45
S. J. Thakor	10	3-36	26.80	6.53
M. J. J. Critchley	6	2-53	58.33	7.29

LEADING NATWEST T20 BLAST AVERAGES (150 runs/15 overs)

Batting	*Runs*	*HS*	*Avge*	*SR*	*Ct*
W. J. Durston	223	51	27.87	**162.77**	3
H. D. Rutherford	343	71*	31.18	**142.91**	0
J. D. S. Neesham	199	45	24.87	**135.37**	4
W. L. Madsen	257	59*	32.12	**134.55**	5
C. F. Hughes	244	46	24.40	**127.74**	8
N. T. Broom	232	68	21.09	**118.36**	3

Bowling	*W*	*BB*	*Avge*	*ER*
M. J. J. Critchley	11	3-36	23.54	**6.84**
A. L. Hughes	6	3-23	47.83	**7.55**
S. J. Thakor	11	3-17	24.36	**7.92**
W. J. Durston	5	2-17	24.60	**8.20**
A. Carter	9	3-34	29.55	**8.96**
J. D. S. Neesham	15	4-35	25.40	**9.40**

FIRST-CLASS COUNTY RECORDS

Highest score for	274	G. A. Davidson v Lancashire at Manchester	1896
Highest score against	343*	P. A. Perrin (Essex) at Chesterfield	1904
Leading run-scorer	23,854	K. J. Barnett (avge 41.12)	1979–98
Best bowling for	10-40	W. Bestwick v Glamorgan at Cardiff	1921
Best bowling against	10-45	R. L. Johnson (Middlesex) at Derby	1994
Leading wicket-taker	1,670	H. L. Jackson (avge 17.11)	1947–63
Highest total for	801-8 dec	v Somerset at Taunton	2007
Highest total against	677-7 dec	by Yorkshire at Leeds	2013
Lowest total for	16	v Nottinghamshire at Nottingham	1879
Lowest total against	23	by Hampshire at Burton-upon-Trent	1958

LIST A COUNTY RECORDS

Highest score for	173*	M. J. Di Venuto v Derbys County Board at Derby	2000
Highest score against	158	R. K. Rao (Sussex) at Derby	1997
Leading run-scorer	12,358	K. J. Barnett (avge 36.67)	1979–98
Best bowling for	8-21	M. A. Holding v Sussex at Hove	1988
Best bowling against	8-66	S. R. G. Francis (Somerset) at Derby	2004
Leading wicket-taker	246	A. E. Warner (avge 27.13)	1985–95
Highest total for	366-4	v Combined Universities at Oxford	1991
Highest total against	369-6	by New Zealanders at Derby	1999
Lowest total for	60	v Kent at Canterbury	2008
Lowest total against	42	by Glamorgan at Swansea	1979

TWENTY20 COUNTY RECORDS

Highest score for	111	W. J. Durston v Nottinghamshire at Nottingham	2010
Highest score against	158*	B. B. McCullum (Warwickshire) at Birmingham	2015
Leading run-scorer	**2,114**	**W. J. Durston (avge 28.95)**	**2010–16**
Best bowling for	5-27	T. Lungley v Leicestershire at Leicester	2009
Best bowling against	5-14	P. D. Collingwood (Durham) at Chester-le-Street	2008
Leading wicket-taker	51	T. D. Groenewald (avge 27.52)	2009–14
Highest total for	222-5	v Yorkshire at Leeds	2010
Highest total against	242-2	by Warwickshire at Birmingham	2015
Lowest total for	72	v Leicestershire at Derby	2013
Lowest total against	84	by West Indians at Derby	2007

ADDRESS

The 3aa Ground, Nottingham Road, Derby DE21 6DA; 0871 350 1870; info@derbyshireccc.com; www.derbyshireccc.com.

OFFICIALS

Captain B. A. Godleman
(limited-overs) **2016** W. J. Durston
Elite performance director 2016 G. Welch
Head coach 2016 J. L. Sadler
Director of cricket 2017 K. J. Barnett
Twenty20 coach J. G. Wright
Academy director 2016 A. J. Harris
Development coach 2017 M. B. Loye
President 2016 K. J. Barnett
Chairman C. I. Grant
Chief executive S. Storey
Head groundsman N. Godrich
Scorer J. M. Brown

At Derby, April 11–13 (not first-class). **Drawn. Derbyshire 396-6 dec** (82.3 overs) (B. T. Slater 67, W. L. Madsen 100, W. J. Durston 100, S. J. Thakor 50) **and 16-0 dec** (3.3 overs); **‡Durham MCCU 287** (106.3 overs) (C. M. Macdonell 109; A. P. Palladino 3-40). *County debut:* N. T. Broom. *Charlie Macdonell, a product of the Northamptonshire junior system, scored 109 – not a maiden first-class century, because Durham MCCU had already played their two first-class matches for the season. On the opening day of a rain-shortened contest, Wayne Madsen and Wes Durston both retired out after reaching three figures.*

At Bristol, April 17–20. DERBYSHIRE drew with GLOUCESTERSHIRE.

DERBYSHIRE v GLAMORGAN

At Derby, April 24–27. Drawn. Derbyshire 11pts, Glamorgan 12pts. Toss: Glamorgan.

An almighty snow and hailstorm ended a game played in miserably cold weather – though the two No. 11s, van der Gugten and Carter, raised the temperature with two sixes each. Dutch international van der Gugten helped Glamorgan add a fourth batting point in a last-wicket stand of 63 with Salter; Carter, making his home debut after joining from Nottinghamshire, hit a career-best 39 while putting on 56 with Poynton to keep Glamorgan's lead down to 32. The two tailenders were the only players to clear the ropes, though their adventurous batting actually made a positive outcome less likely, delaying the progress of a match which lost 138 overs in all. On the opening day, which lost only two, Bragg scored a solid career-best 129. Palladino went on to take five wickets for the first time in nearly two years, before Madsen fell three short of completing hundreds in Derbyshire's first three games of the season.

Close of play: first day, Glamorgan 308-6 (Wagg 14, Meschede 3); second day, Derbyshire 98-2 (Slater 41, Madsen 23); third day, Derbyshire 331-9 (Poynton 30, Carter 31).

Glamorgan

J. M. Kettleborough b Palladino	22	– b Fletcher	20
*J. A. Rudolph c Poynton b Palladino	35	– not out	31
W. D. Bragg lbw b Durston	129	– lbw b Durston	10
†C. B. Cooke b Palladino	40	– not out	22
A. H. T. Donald c Poynton b Carter	45		
D. L. Lloyd lbw b Carter	0		
G. G. Wagg c Hughes b Palladino	14		
C. A. J. Meschede b Fletcher	3		
A. G. Salter not out	25		
M. G. Hogan c Rutherford b Palladino	5		
T. van der Gugten c Madsen b Durston	36		
B 4, lb 11, nb 8	23	Nb 4	4
1/58 (1) 2/72 (2) 3/185 (4) 4/260 (5) 5/260 (6) 6/299 (3) 7/308 (8) 8/308 (7) 9/314 (10) 10/377 (11) (114.4 overs)	377	1/26 (1) 2/43 (3) (2 wkts, 32 overs)	87
110 overs: 356-9			

Fletcher 27–10–53–1; Palladino 27–8–83–5; Carter 27–7–94–2; Durston 10.4–2–34–2; Critchley 14–0–73–0; Hughes 7–1–21–0; Madsen 2–0–4–0. *Second innings*—Fletcher 10–2–18–1; Palladino 4–1–20–0; Carter 8–1–33–0; Durston 9–4–9–1; Critchley 1–0–7–0.

Derbyshire

B. T. Slater lbw b Salter	62
C. F. Hughes b Hogan	19
*H. D. Rutherford c Salter b Hogan	10
W. L. Madsen b Salter	97
N. T. Broom b van der Gugten	4
W. J. Durston c Cooke b Lloyd	43
M. J. J. Critchley c Rudolph b Salter	5
†T. Poynton not out	36
A. P. Palladino c Cooke b Hogan	0
L. J. Fletcher c Hogan b Meschede	6
A. Carter c Wagg b Hogan	39
Lb 9, w 5, nb 10	24
1/36 (2) 2/58 (3) 3/161 (1) 4/182 (5) 5/241 (6) 6/252 (7) 7/267 (4) 8/274 (9) 9/289 (10) 10/345 (11) (94.5 overs)	345

Hogan 25.5–6–74–4; Wagg 19–4–67–0; Meschede 15–1–68–1; van der Gugten 12–3–43–1; Lloyd 9–2–28–1; Salter 14–2–56–3.

Umpires: N. L. Bainton and N. J. Llong.

At Northampton, May 1–4. DERBYSHIRE drew with NORTHAMPTONSHIRE.

DERBYSHIRE v SUSSEX

At Derby, May 8–11. Drawn. Derbyshire 6pts, Sussex 13pts. Toss: uncontested. County debut: S. G. Whittingham.

Joyce and Wells piled up records as they dismantled an ineffective Derbyshire attack on an increasingly placid pitch, but they were ultimately frustrated by rain. Their partnership of 310, unsurpassed in this fixture, led to Sussex's biggest total at Derby, beating their 429 in 2010. Joyce started cautiously, taking 57 overs to reach 67, then unleashed the full array of his attacking strokes. He reached his double-century with a six while hitting 24 off an over from Carter, swiftly overhauled his previous first-class best of 231, and finished with 34 fours and two sixes. Wells, initially more dominant, was happy to ease off, but steadily compiled a tenth first-class hundred. Sussex took a lead of 277, having bowled out Derbyshire for a feeble 191 on the first day, when Hatchett took five wickets, and Stu Whittingham – born in Derby but brought up in Sussex – marked his debut for the senior team with two. The home side were saved from probable defeat when rain allowed only 26.3 overs across the last two days.

Close of play: first day, Sussex 83-1 (Joyce 41, Wells 3); second day, Sussex 468-5 (Finch 16, Brown 22); third day, no play.

Derbyshire

C. F. Hughes c Brown b Hatchett	8	– (2) not out	58
*B. A. Godleman b Magoffin	28	– (1) c Robinson b Wells	16
H. D. Rutherford c Wells b Whittingham	32	– c Finch b Whittingham	0
W. L. Madsen lbw b Hatchett	9	– not out	8
N. T. Broom b Whittingham	10		
W. J. Durston c Finch b Hatchett	8		
S. J. Thakor not out	36		
†T. Poynton c Brown b Magoffin	6		
A. P. Palladino c Nash b Hatchett	13		
L. J. Fletcher c and b Hatchett	14		
A. Carter b Robinson	5		
Lb 5, w 1, nb 16	22	B 6, lb 2, nb 2	10
1/30 (1) 2/78 (3) 3/78 (2) 4/103 (5) 5/105 (4) 6/118 (6) 7/148 (8) 8/164 (9) 9/184 (10) 10/191 (11) (68 overs)	191	1/79 (1) 2/81 (3) (2 wkts, 26.3 overs)	92

Magoffin 19–6–35–2; Robinson 17–5–41–1; Whittingham 11–1–38–2; Hatchett 14–3–58–5; Wells 6–1–9–0; Finch 1–0–5–0. *Second innings*—Magoffin 6–2–12–0; Robinson 5–0–15–0; Whittingham 5.3–0–12–1; Hatchett 5–2–21–0; Wells 5–0–24–1.

Sussex

C. D. Nash lbw b Thakor	37
E. C. Joyce lbw b Durston	250
L. W. P. Wells c Madsen b Durston	116
L. R. P. L. Taylor c Hughes b Thakor	6
M. W. Machan c Poynton b Thakor	12
H. Z. Finch not out	16
*†B. C. Brown not out	22
Lb 1, nb 8	9
1/71 (1) 2/381 (3) 3/408 (4) 4/430 (2) 5/430 (5) (5 wkts dec, 122 overs)	468
110 overs: 418-3	

O. E. Robinson, L. J. Hatchett, S. J. Magoffin and S. G. Whittingham did not bat.

Fletcher 21–2–102–0; Palladino 22–6–61–0; Carter 19–0–115–0; Thakor 23–6–59–3; Durston 27–3–106–2; Madsen 9–0–21–0; Hughes 1–0–3–0.

Umpires: M. Burns and R. T. Robinson.

At Chelmsford, May 15–18. DERBYSHIRE drew with ESSEX.

DERBYSHIRE v KENT

At Derby, May 22–25. Kent won by seven wickets. Kent 21pts, Derbyshire 7pts. Toss: Derbyshire.

Kent achieved an unlikely win with a flourish, despite conceding 492 and finding themselves a batsman short. After two days, Denly had dashed home for the birth of his first child (which he missed by ten minutes), but Dickson carried his bat for a maiden Championship century, which became a flawless unbeaten 207 and restricted Kent's first-innings deficit to 80. Dickson's double-hundred was the third against Derbyshire in successive matches. The advantage was still marginally with the home side on a wearing pitch – until they slumped to 94, with four apiece for Tredwell (including his 400th) and Haggett (in a career-best). Kent needed 175, and Bell-Drummond paved the way; Blake clubbed the only three balls he faced for six to complete victory before tea on the final day. Only once before in first-class cricket is a batsman known to have hit 18 not out from three balls: Don Wilson for Yorkshire against MCC at Scarborough in 1965. And only once had Derbyshire scored more than 492 and lost, though it would happen again in July; 398 was their biggest difference between totals in the same match. It was harsh on Thakor, their 11th player to combine a century with five wickets in an innings. He had put on 150, a county eighth-wicket record against Kent, with Taylor (who made a maiden fifty), after Madsen scored his 20th century for Derbyshire.

DOUBLE TROUBLE

Double-hundreds conceded in three successive Championship matches:

Somerset	J. H. Board (Glos), A. E. Stoddart (Middx), K. S. Ranjitsinhji (Sussex)	1900
Worcs	F. A. Tarrant (Middx), F. R. Foster (Warwicks), V. W. C. Jupp (Sussex)	1914
Northants*	A. Sandham (Surrey), J. R. Freeman (Essex), A. C. Russell (Essex)	1921
Derbys	**E. C. Joyce (Sussex), N. L. J. Browne (Essex), S. R. Dickson (Kent)**	**2016**

* *Northamptonshire's sequence was interrupted by a match against the touring Australians, for whom C. G. Macartney made 193.*

Close of play: first day, Derbyshire 381-7 (Thakor 86, Taylor 39); second day, Kent 79-1 (Dickson 31, Denly 34); third day, Derbyshire 9-3 (Madsen 5, Broom 3).

Derbyshire

C. F. Hughes lbw b Coles	0	– b Tredwell	1
*B. A. Godleman c Denly b Coles	3	– lbw b Tredwell	3
H. D. Rutherford b Coles	5	– (4) c Rouse b Coles	0
W. L. Madsen c Ball b Tredwell	103	– (5) lbw b Haggett	37
N. T. Broom lbw b Ball	96	– (6) c Ball b Tredwell	18
S. J. Thakor st Rouse b Tredwell	130	– (7) b Tredwell	10
†T. Poynton c Rouse b Claydon	10	– (8) lbw b Haggett	3
M. J. J. Critchley lbw b Coles	3	– (9) lbw b Haggett	18
T. A. I. Taylor c Coles b Ball	80	– (3) lbw b Coles	0
A. P. Palladino b Coles	15	– not out	1
B. D. Cotton not out	7	– lbw b Haggett	1
B 12, lb 4, w 3, nb 21	40	Nb 2	2
1/4 (1) 2/12 (3) 3/35 (2) 4/196 (4) 5/281 (5) 6/309 (7) 7/312 (8) 8/462 (9) 9/474 (6) 10/492 (10) (125.5 overs) 110 overs: 444-7	492	1/1 (1) 2/1 (3) 3/4 (4) 4/49 (6) 5/61 (5) 6/61 (2) 7/64 (8) 8/82 (7) 9/92 (9) 10/94 (11) (28.4 overs)	94

In the second innings Godleman, when 0, retired hurt at 1-0 and resumed at 49-4.

Coles 34.5–7–116–5; Claydon 24–3–121–1; Haggett 25–1–103–0; Tredwell 28–1–89–2; Ball 13–0–46–2; Denly 1–0–1–0. *Second innings*—Coles 8–0–34–2; Tredwell 14–1–45–4; Haggett 6.4–0–15–4.

Kent

D. J. Bell-Drummond c Poynton b Cotton	4	– not out	80
S. R. Dickson not out	207	– b Taylor	16
J. L. Denly retired not out	34		
*S. A. Northeast c Poynton b Thakor	12	– c Godleman b Hughes	30
A. J. Blake c Hughes b Thakor	6	– not out	18
A. J. Ball c Poynton b Cotton	40	– (3) lbw b Palladino	23
†A. P. Rouse b Cotton	25		
C. J. Haggett lbw b Thakor	15		
J. C. Tredwell lbw b Thakor	0		
M. T. Coles b Taylor	41		
M. E. Claydon b Thakor	0		
B 14, lb 7, nb 2, p 5	28	Lb 7, nb 2	9
1/9 (1) 2/99 (4) 3/113 (5) (126 overs)	412	1/46 (2) (3 wkts, 32.3 overs)	176
4/188 (6) 5/227 (7) 6/285 (8)		2/100 (3) 3/152 (4)	
7/285 (9) 8/382 (10) 9/412 (11) 110 overs: 335-7			

In the first innings Denly retired not out at 79-1.

Palladino 29–9–52–0; Cotton 26–5–66–3; Taylor 17–5–58–1; Thakor 19–3–63–5; Critchley 16–0–60–0; Hughes 10–1–45–0; Madsen 9–0–42–0. *Second innings*—Palladino 8–2–31–1; Cotton 9–2–32–0; Madsen 4–0–14–0; Taylor 3–0–22–1; Thakor 3–0–15–0; Critchley 4.3–0–44–0; Hughes 1–0–11–1.

Umpires: N. A. Mallender and D. J. Millns.

At Hove, May 28–31. DERBYSHIRE lost to SUSSEX by ten wickets.

DERBYSHIRE v WORCESTERSHIRE

At Derby, June 20–23. Drawn. Derbyshire 12pts, Worcestershire 6pts. Toss: uncontested. First-class debut: R. P. Hemmings. Championship debut: W. S. Davis.

Worcestershire enjoyed a brief moment of dominance in the fourth over of this match – a double-wicket maiden from Leach. But the next two days belonged to Derbyshire. After an opening-day washout, Godleman's first double-century was their highest score against Worcestershire, overhauling Stan Worthington's unbeaten 200 at Chesterfield in 1933. He put on 251, the highest third-wicket stand between these counties, with Madsen, who scored his third Championship century of the season. It was Shantry who finally dismissed Godleman, his 250th first-class victim, but – after Derbyshire declared at lunch on day three – Cotton and Palladino made Worcestershire follow on that evening. At 24 for two in the first over of the final day, they still trailed by 279, and Derbyshire's first victory of 2016 seemed possible. Only four more wickets fell, however – two to Championship newcomer Will Davis – as nightwatchman Barnard batted three and a half hours for a dogged career-best 73.

Close of play: first day, no play; second day, Derbyshire 319-3 (Godleman 157, Broom 28); third day, Worcestershire 24-1 (D'Oliveira 14, Barnard 4).

Derbyshire

H. D. Rutherford b Leach	5
*B. A. Godleman c Köhler-Cadmore b Shantry	204
C. F. Hughes lbw b Leach	0
W. L. Madsen c Cox b Shantry	109
N. T. Broom c Shantry b D'Oliveira	93
B. T. Slater not out	28
†T. Poynton not out	3
B 8, lb 7, nb 10	25
1/13 (1) 2/13 (3) 3/264 (4) 4/419 (2) 5/458 (5) (5 wkts dec, 127 overs)	467

110 overs: 385-3

R. P. Hemmings, A. P. Palladino, B. D. Cotton and W. S. Davis did not bat.

Henry 26–4–79–0; Leach 25–3–90–2; Shantry 33–7–102–2; Barnard 20–4–103–0; D'Oliveira 15–1–57–1; Kervezee 7–2–20–0; Mitchell 1–0–1–0.

Worcestershire

*D. K. H. Mitchell b Cotton	2	– c Madsen b Cotton 6
B. L. D'Oliveira c Slater b Cotton	4	– lbw b Palladino 14
J. M. Clarke c Hemmings b Cotton	0	– (4) c Broom b Davis 63
A. N. Kervezee b Palladino	0	– (5) c Poynton b Cotton 41
T. Köhler-Cadmore b Palladino	29	– (6) c Cotton b Hughes 48
R. A. Whiteley c Hughes b Palladino	2	– (7) not out 9
†O. B. Cox lbw b Palladino	40	– (8) not out 15
J. Leach b Davis	5	
E. G. Barnard c Broom b Hughes	28	– (3) c Rutherford b Davis 73
M. J. Henry c Poynton b Cotton	31	
J. D. Shantry not out	12	
B 4, lb 1, nb 6	11	B 14, lb 3, nb 8 25
1/5 (2) 2/5 (3) 3/6 (1) 4/16 (4) 5/18 (6) 6/84 (7) 7/91 (8) 8/91 (5) 9/144 (10) 10/164 (9) (53.1 overs)	164	1/12 (1) 2/24 (2) 3/170 (4) 4/179 (3) 5/243 (5) 6/275 (6) (6 wkts, 104.3 overs) 294

Cotton 14–8–28–4; Palladino 15–7–32–4; Hemmings 11–2–32–0; Davis 10–2–52–1; Madsen 2–0–8–0; Hughes 1.1–0–7–1. *Second innings*—Cotton 18–7–34–2; Palladino 16–6–32–1; Hemmings 8–3–26–0; Davis 20.3–3–87–2; Hughes 28–9–61–1; Madsen 10–2–21–0; Slater 4–0–16–0.

Umpires: P. K. Baldwin and N. G. C. Cowley.

At Canterbury, June 26–29. DERBYSHIRE drew with KENT.

DERBYSHIRE v NORTHAMPTONSHIRE

At Chesterfield, July 4–7. Abandoned. Derbyshire 5pts, Northamptonshire 5pts.

A Queen's Park outfield left waterlogged by heavy rain allowed no play, despite glorious sunshine. The match was called off on the third afternoon – the first total washout of a Championship game involving Derbyshire since May 1981, and their 26th in all first-class cricket.

At Derby, July 15. DERBYSHIRE lost to SRI LANKA A by seven wickets (see Sri Lanka A tour section).

At Colwyn Bay, July 17–20. DERBYSHIRE lost to GLAMORGAN by four wickets. *Derbyshire lose despite scoring 536 in the follow-on.*

At Leicester, August 4–7. DERBYSHIRE drew with LEICESTERSHIRE.

DERBYSHIRE v ESSEX

At Derby, August 13–16. Essex won by an innings and 62 runs. Essex 23pts, Derbyshire 1pt. Toss: Essex. First-class debut: P. I. Walter. County debut: W. M. H. Rhodes. Championship debut: C. M. Macdonell.

Essex opener Browne followed his 255 at Chelmsford in May with an unbeaten 229, the fourth century in his six innings against Derbyshire, taking his aggregate to 794 at 264. Derbyshire contained the batting reasonably well on the first day, when Browne was dropped on 60 off Milnes; next day, Milnes completed Championship-best figures of six for 93, but Essex took control, stepping up the scoring-rate to nearly five an over. Then Paul Walter, a 22-year-old seamer from Basildon, reduced Derbyshire to 79 for six, striking three times in his first seven overs in first-class cricket. Trailing by 365, Derbyshire followed on, and Godleman's third century of the season could not prevent an innings defeat on the final morning. Napier finished with four wickets in each innings, and Essex increased their lead at the top of the second division to 23 points.

DOUBLE DOUBLE

Home and away double-hundreds against the same county in one Championship season:

W. G. Grace	243* at Hove and 301 at Bristol	Glos v Sussex	1896
C. B. Fry	201* at Hove and 233 at Nottingham	Sussex v Notts	1905
P. Holmes	209 at Birmingham and 220* at Huddersfield	Yorks v Warwicks	1922
N. L. J. Browne	**255 at Chelmsford and 229* at Derby**	**Essex v Derbys**	**2016**

A. E. Fagg scored 244 and 202 in the same match, for Kent v Essex at Colchester in 1938.*

Close of play: first day, Essex 291-4 (Browne 116, ten Doeschate 15); second day, Derbyshire 116-6 (Mellor 20, Critchley 17); third day, Derbyshire 213-5 (Parkinson 0, Macdonell 3).

Essex

N. L. J. Browne not out	229
J. C. Mickleburgh c Hughes b Milnes	7
T. Westley c Mellor b Critchley	72
R. S. Bopara c Mellor b Parkinson	44
K. S. Velani lbw b Milnes	19
*R. N. ten Doeschate b Milnes	60
†J. S. Foster c Palladino b Milnes	13
W. M. H. Rhodes c Broom b Milnes	1
G. R. Napier c Mellor b Milnes	4
P. I. Walter b Palladino	47
B 14, lb 6, nb 14	34
(9 wkts dec, 144.5 overs)	530

1/14 (2) 2/142 (3) 3/217 (4) 4/252 (5) 5/392 (6) 6/436 (7) 7/441 (8) 8/447 (9) 9/530 (10) 110 overs: 360-4

J. A. Porter did not bat.

Palladino 26.5–5–73–1; Milnes 32–4–93–6; Parkinson 38–4–149–1; Hughes 12–2–25–0; Madsen 5–0–21–0; Critchley 27–1–128–1; Broom 4–0–21–0.

Derbyshire

B. T. Slater lbw b Porter	0	– c Westley b Napier	29
*B. A. Godleman b Walter	10	– lbw b Napier	100
A. L. Hughes c Foster b Napier	13	– c Foster b Walter	23
W. L. Madsen lbw b Walter	0	– c Mickleburgh b Rhodes	37
N. T. Broom c Browne b Napier	31	– b Bopara	13
C. M. Macdonell c Foster b Walter	21	– (7) not out	35
†A. J. Mellor c Foster b Napier	44	– (8) c Browne b Bopara	0
M. J. J. Critchley c Mickleburgh b Bopara	36	– (9) c Napier b Porter	43
T. P. Milnes b Napier	0	– (10) c Browne b Napier	8
A. P. Palladino not out	3	– (11) lbw b Napier	0
C. F. Parkinson b Bopara	2	– (6) c ten Doeschate b Bopara	0
Lb 5	5	B 6, lb 3, nb 6	15
(65.3 overs)	165	(95.2 overs)	303

1/0 (1) 2/16 (2) 3/16 (4) 4/34 (3) 5/74 (5) 6/79 (6) 7/149 (7) 8/149 (9) 9/161 (8) 10/165 (11)

1/75 (1) 2/151 (3) 3/167 (2) 4/210 (4) 5/210 (5) 6/213 (6) 7/213 (8) 8/285 (9) 9/297 (10) 10/303 (11)

Porter 16–4–44–1; Walter 14–5–44–3; Napier 15–5–28–4; Rhodes 7–2–18–0; Bopara 10.3–6–15–2; Westley 2–1–6–0; Velani 1–0–5–0. *Second innings*—Porter 18–0–74–1; Walter 17–0–68–1; Napier 18.2–6–50–4; Rhodes 16–7–33–1; Bopara 15–1–39–3; ten Doeschate 5–0–15–0; Westley 6–1–15–0.

Umpires: S. C. Gale and J. W. Lloyds.

DERBYSHIRE v GLOUCESTERSHIRE

At Derby, August 31–September 3. Drawn. Derbyshire 9pts, Gloucestershire 11pts. Toss: Derbyshire.

Rain washed out day four, when the match was finely balanced, with Gloucestershire ten for no wicket in pursuit of 272. On the opening day, Slater had hit his first first-class century of the summer, but Derbyshire fell away disappointingly, losing seven for 67. Mustard, on loan from Durham, completed his first Championship hundred for five years to help Gloucestershire take a first-innings lead of 89, despite Palladino taking five wickets (including his 350th). By the third morning, Derbyshire faced trouble – four down in their second innings and still 28 in arrears – but Alex Hughes showed tremendous resilience to get them back in contention with his second hundred, a career-best, supported by valuable lower-order fifties from Hosein and Milnes. Miles finished with eight wickets in the match, but both sides felt rain denied them the opportunity to win.

Close of play: first day, Gloucestershire 27-1 (Dent 10, Tavaré 11); second day, Derbyshire 16-2 (Parkinson 5, Hughes 0); third day, Gloucestershire 10-0 (Roderick 6, Dent 4).

Derbyshire

B. T. Slater c Mustard b Miles	110	– lbw b Payne	6
*B. A. Godleman c Taylor b Miles	31	– c Mustard b Norwell	5
A. L. Hughes c Mustard b Norwell	1	– (4) lbw b Dent	140
W. L. Madsen c Hankins b Miles	0	– (5) c Marshall b Miles	0
N. T. Broom c Tavaré b Miles	36	– (6) b Miles	42
M. J. J. Critchley c and b Taylor	3	– (7) c Mustard b Taylor	32
†H. R. Hosein not out	10	– (8) not out	52
T. P. Milnes run out	9	– (9) c Dent b Payne	56
A. P. Palladino b Shaw	18	– (10) c Payne b Shaw	2
C. F. Parkinson lbw b Payne	2	– (3) c Mustard b Miles	12
W. S. Davis c Tavaré b Shaw	13	– c Mustard b Miles	0
B 2, lb 6, w 1	9	B 5, lb 6, nb 2	13
1/91 (2) 2/94 (3) 3/97 (4) 4/175 (5) 5/182 (6) 6/190 (1) 7/199 (8) 8/218 (9) 9/229 (10) 10/242 (11) (81.5 overs)	242	1/6 (1) 2/16 (2) 3/61 (3) 4/61 (5) 5/161 (6) 6/219 (7) 7/261 (4) 8/343 (9) 9/359 (10) 10/360 (11) (95.2 overs)	360

Payne 11–0–38–1; Norwell 16–7–38–1; Taylor 24–6–61–1; Shaw 12.5–2–65–2; Miles 17–3–30–4; Dent 1–0–2–0. *Second innings*—Payne 23–9–66–2; Norwell 20–5–62–1; Shaw 11–1–47–1; Miles 16.2–1–82–4; Taylor 18–2–73–1; Dent 7–2–19–1.

Gloucestershire

*G. H. Roderick c Madsen b Milnes	4	– not out 6
C. D. J. Dent c Godleman b Parkinson	94	– not out 4
W. A. Tavaré c Hosein b Milnes	11	
G. T. Hankins b Parkinson	34	
H. J. H. Marshall lbw b Palladino	11	
†P. Mustard not out	107	
J. M. R. Taylor c Critchley b Palladino	36	
C. N. Miles b Palladino	5	
D. A. Payne b Palladino	1	
L. C. Norwell c Hosein b Davis	0	
J. Shaw c Milnes b Palladino	16	
B 6, lb 1, w 1, nb 4	12	
1/5 (1) 2/27 (3) 3/84 (4) 4/108 (5) 5/193 (2) 6/267 (7) 7/281 (8) 8/293 (9) 9/300 (10) 10/331 (11) (98.5 overs)	331	(no wkt, 5 overs) 10

Palladino 25.5–7–74–5; Milnes 22–5–57–2; Davis 21–4–89–1; Parkinson 15–3–56–2; Critchley 4–0–21–0; Madsen 7–0–20–0; Hughes 4–2–7–0. *Second innings*—Palladino 3–1–6–0; Milnes 2–1–4–0.

Umpires: J. H. Evans and R. J. Evans.

DERBYSHIRE v LEICESTERSHIRE

At Derby, September 12–15. Drawn. Derbyshire 11pts, Leicestershire 9pts. Toss: uncontested. First-class debuts: T. A. Wood; H. E. Dearden.

Leicestershire's ninth-wicket pair, Sayer and Jones – who needed a runner after damaging his hand while bowling – saw out the last 23.5 overs. Their stubbornness condemned Derbyshire to the Championship's wooden spoon after a second successive season without a home win. In truth, neither side deserved to lose. Hosein's career-best 83 had steered Derbyshire past 300 on the second morning, and Leicestershire were 60 behind after the first innings; Cosgrove, forced to retire for a while by his own hand injury, was stranded on 95. Derbyshire were thankful for that edge when they stumbled to 57 for five; McKay removed both openers to complete his 50 for the season. But Madsen, with an unbeaten 134, and Hosein steadied them in a stand of 143, and they declared at the start of day four, setting 347. At 200 for three, Leicestershire were well placed, with Cosgrove approaching a century again. He got there this time – like Madsen, his fifth of the season – but was one of five wickets lost for 42, tipping the balance back towards Derbyshire. They were unable to complete the job.

Close of play: first day, Derbyshire 282-8 (Hosein 79, Parkinson 6); second day, Leicestershire 228-8 (Cosgrove 81, Jones 2); third day, Derbyshire 286-8 (Madsen 134, Parkinson 8).

Derbyshire

B. T. Slater c Pettini b Shreck	27	– c Pettini b McKay	0
*B. A. Godleman lbw b McKay	9	– b McKay	13
A. L. Hughes c Eckersley b Shreck	55	– run out	3
W. L. Madsen c Eckersley b Jones	38	– not out	134
N. T. Broom c Robson b Shreck	15	– lbw b Dexter	3
T. A. Wood b Dexter	8	– lbw b Shreck	14
†H. R. Hosein not out	83	– c Eckersley b Shreck	58
T. P. Milnes c Eckersley b Sayer	19	– c Eckersley b Dexter	20
A. P. Palladino c Eckersley b Dexter	12	– c sub (L. J. Hill) b Sayer	15
C. F. Parkinson c Eckersley b McKay	8	– not out	8
W. S. Davis c Dearden b Shreck	15		
B 9, lb 2, w 5, nb 2	18	B 4, lb 1, w 1, nb 12	18
1/21 (2) 2/40 (1) 3/124 (4) 4/140 (3) 5/151 (5) 6/177 (6) 7/212 (8) 8/250 (9) 9/288 (10) 10/307 (11) (91.2 overs)	307	1/0 (1) 2/17 (2) 3/25 (3) 4/32 (5) 5/57 (6) 6/200 (7) 7/245 (8) 8/266 (9) (8 wkts dec, 80 overs)	286

McKay 18–4–50–2; Jones 15–2–45–1; Sayer 13–1–49–1; Dexter 19–3–60–2; Shreck 22.2–3–78–4; Cosgrove 4–1–14–0. *Second innings*—McKay 17–3–61–2; Jones 2–0–6–0; Dexter 25–7–68–2; Shreck 19–3–61–2; Cosgrove 4–1–14–0; Sayer 12–1–63–1; Horton 1–0–8–0.

Leicestershire

P. J. Horton c Hosein b Davis	19	– lbw b Palladino	61
A. J. Robson lbw b Palladino	0	– c Hosein b Palladino	0
N. J. Dexter c Madsen b Parkinson	14	– (5) lbw b Palladino	26
*M. J. Cosgrove not out	95	– c Godleman b Parkinson	110
†E. J. H. Eckersley lbw b Palladino	27	– (6) c Hosein b Davis	20
M. L. Pettini c Hughes b Davis	44	– (7) c Slater b Parkinson	1
H. E. Dearden c Hosein b Parkinson	13	– (3) c Madsen b Palladino	2
C. J. McKay c Hughes b Davis	21	– c Hughes b Davis	0
R. J. Sayer c Broom b Davis	0	– not out	32
R. A. Jones c Hosein b Milnes	7	– not out	19
C. E. Shreck c Hughes b Palladino	0		
Lb 5, nb 2	7	B 4, lb 13, w 1, nb 12	30
1/15 (2) 2/28 (1) 3/44 (3) 4/137 (5) 5/181 (7) 6/220 (8) 7/220 (6) 8/221 (9) 9/236 (10) 10/247 (11) (90.1 overs)	247	1/5 (2) 2/7 (3) 3/122 (1) 4/200 (5) 5/232 (4) 6/238 (7) 7/241 (8) 8/242 (6) (8 wkts, 96 overs)	301

In the first innings Cosgrove, when 77, retired hurt at 142-4 and resumed at 220-6.

Palladino 16.1–7–27–3; Milnes 23–4–67–1; Hughes 3–0–8–0; Davis 23–2–68–4; Parkinson 25–5–72–2. *Second innings*—Palladino 25–3–64–4; Milnes 17–8–39–0; Hughes 7–1–28–0; Davis 17–4–45–2; Parkinson 22–5–76–2; Madsen 6–1–26–0; Broom 2–0–6–0.

Umpires: J. H. Evans and G. D. Lloyd.

At Worcester, September 20–23. DERBYSHIRE lost to WORCESTERSHIRE by nine wickets. *Derbyshire go through the season without a Championship victory.*

DURHAM

Ambition's debt is paid

TIM WELLOCK

Inspired by a remarkable sequence from Keaton Jennings, Durham defied prophets of doom by retaining fourth place in the Championship and reaching the Twenty20 final. Then came the bombshell.

Ten days after Durham won their last game, at Southampton, the ECB announced they would be relegated, thus reprieving Hampshire (45 points below them). The punishment was the price of a £3.8m bailout, and ended a record 11 consecutive seasons in Division One. There was also a 48-point deduction for the 2017 Championship, plus four points in the Twenty20 Blast and two in the 50-over competition. Only the players' share of the prize money was paid, and Durham lost the right to stage Test cricket.

Captain Paul Collingwood described it as "a kick in the nuts", and it was a sad legacy for Clive Leach, who bowed out after 12 years as chairman. Durham were bottom of Division Two when he arrived, but captured five trophies in eight seasons before interest on loans totalling almost £7.5m began to bite. There was also a shortfall of income, particularly from the Sri Lanka Test in May 2016 – part of a package that came with the 2013 Ashes Test.

The accounts up to September 2015 showed an operating profit of £650,000, compared with a loss of over £1m the previous year. But loans for ground development and floodlights meant the overall debt soared by £700,000 to almost £7.5m. The ECB statement forecast that insufficient funds would be generated over the next year to meet liabilities, and expressed doubt that the company could continue as a going concern. The cash injection lifted that fear, and an EGM in September had already approved the club becoming a community interest company to access more sources of finance. In November it was announced that Ian Botham, who played for Durham in their first two first-class seasons, would succeed Leach as chairman.

On the field, it was a similar story to 2015: Durham were Championship contenders in mid-season, before problems with spin – bowling it or batting against it – caused a stutter. The title challenge ended in a pivotal 17 minutes on a turning pitch at Taunton, where they surrendered their last five wickets for six runs to lose by 39. The next match, at Lord's, was an innings defeat; across the two games, 27 Durham wickets fell to slow bowling, while Scott Borthwick's leg-breaks claimed just one. He sometimes bowled effectively in Twenty20, but his only notable four-day spell came at Trent Bridge in May, when he became the fourth Durham player to combine a century and a five-for in the same match. Borthwick and limited-overs captain Mark Stoneman passed 1,000 Championship runs for the fourth successive season. But, as rumours of financial hardship spread, both joined Surrey.

Collingwood, now 40, signed for a third season beyond his intended retirement, the same day Stoneman announced his move – prompting

Keaton Jennings

Collingwood to take back the one-day captaincy. Australian all-rounder John Hastings had not returned because of injuries, and finances dictated that Durham did without an overseas player, although Stephen Cook and Tom Latham were signed up for 2017. Phil Mustard was told he would be released, spent two months on loan to Gloucestershire, and joined them for 2017; Gordon Muchall retired. Others released were Calum MacLeod and Jamie Harrison, plus development players Gurman Randhawa and Gavin Main.

The Johannesburg-born Jennings was coveted by other counties, but signed a four-year contract. He scored 1,548 Championship runs – more than anyone in the country – and was the first to hit seven centuries in a season for Durham, two of them doubles. He also contributed heavily in one-day cricket, and his 88 was the highest score in an English Twenty20 final. Initially picked only for the Lions' winter tour, he was promoted to the senior squad and scored a century on Test debut at Mumbai.

Another South African with England ambitions, the pacy Brydon Carse, stayed on, as did Paul Coughlin, acknowledging he had been nurtured by the county. Although primarily a seamer, he made a match-winning 231 in the Second XI Championship final against Middlesex. He also led Durham against Sri Lanka A, when the team included his brother Josh. Teessider James Weighell signed a two-year deal, so too Irish internationals Barry McCarthy and wicketkeeper Stuart Poynter. If there was any consolation in relegation and the departures, it was that they might help young batsmen develop. Those were in short supply, although Jack Burnham looked to have a bright future, and Adam Hickey showed all-round promise.

The seam department remained strong, despite Graham Onions, now 34, nearing the end of his career. He took 50 first-class wickets for the seventh time, and needed 24 more to break Simon Brown's county record of 518. After passing 50 in each of the previous three seasons, Chris Rushworth had to settle for 34.

Mark Wood had needed two operations on his ankle the previous winter, and played only three Championship games – culminating in a thrilling win at home to Surrey, which appeared to have secured survival. Wood bowled 35 overs in the match, and was later found to have fractured a bone in the suspect ankle. "I was 60% fit and probably shouldn't have played," he said. "But I was desperate to help us avoid relegation." It was a relief to Durham when Wood's central contract for Test cricket was renewed, but an embarrassment for the ECB that allowing him to play against Surrey had ruled him out of the winter tours.

The season was the last scored by the dedicated Brian Hunt, a fixture at the club for 41 years. Unusually for a scorer, he received a benefit, in 2009.

Championship attendance: 28,944.

DURHAM RESULTS

All first-class matches – Played 18: Won 5, Lost 3, Drawn 10.
County Championship matches – Played 16: Won 5, Lost 3, Drawn 8.

Specsavers County Championship, 4th in Division 1 (but relegated);
NatWest T20 Blast, finalists; Royal London One-Day Cup, 5th in North Group.

COUNTY CHAMPIONSHIP AVERAGES, BATTING AND FIELDING

Cap		*Birthplace*	*M*	*I*	*NO*	*R*	*HS*	*100*	*Avge*	*Ct/St*
	†K. K. Jennings	*Johannesburg, SA*	16	28	4	1,548	221*	7	64.50	18
	†M. D. Stoneman	*Newcastle-u-Tyne*	16	28	1	1,234	141*	2	45.70	8
	†S. G. Borthwick	*Sunderland‡*	16	28	2	1,060	188*	3	40.76	25
1998	P. D. Collingwood	*Shotley Bridge‡*	14	24	6	595	106*	1	33.05	12
	B. A. Carse††	*Port Elizabeth, SA*	8	8	2	176	47	0	29.33	2
	G. Clark	*Whitehaven*	3	6	0	170	58	0	28.33	0
	†B. A. Stokes§	*Christchurch, NZ*	6	9	1	226	51	0	28.25	1
	J. T. A. Burnham	*Durham‡*	14	24	1	630	135	1	27.39	6
	R. D. Pringle	*Sunderland‡*	10	12	2	243	57*	0	24.30	9
	G. Onions	*Gateshead‡*	16	19	7	282	65	0	23.50	2
	M. J. Richardson	*Port Elizabeth, SA*	15	24	2	510	99*	0	23.18	33/1
	B. J. McCarthy	*Dublin*	7	10	2	176	51*	0	22.00	2
	M. A. Wood§	*Ashington*	3	6	0	130	36	0	21.66	0
	†A. J. Hickey	*Darlington‡*	3	6	3	64	36*	0	21.33	1
	P. Coughlin	*Sunderland‡*	6	10	0	198	39	0	19.80	3
	W. J. Weighell	*Middlesbrough*	3	4	1	53	22	0	17.66	1
	S. W. Poynter	*Hammersmith*	4	7	0	119	42	0	17.00	12
	C. Rushworth	*Sunderland‡*	13	16	5	114	31*	0	10.36	3

Also batted: U. Arshad (*Bradford*) (2 matches) 32, 3, 84; G. J. Muchall (*Newcastle-upon-Tyne*) (cap 2005) (1 match) 13, 17 (1 ct).

‡ *Born in Durham.* § *ECB contract.* †† *Other non-England-qualified.*

BOWLING

	Style	*O*	*M*	*R*	*W*	*BB*	*5I*	*Avge*
W. J. Weighell	RM	112.5	22	329	16	5-33	1	20.56
M. A. Wood	RFM	78	7	275	11	3-24	0	25.00
B. A. Stokes	RFM	183.3	36	560	18	4-54	0	31.11
G. Onions	RFM	544	95	1,688	54	5-90	1	31.25
B. J. McCarthy	RFM	177.1	25	632	20	5-70	1	31.60
C. Rushworth	RFM	343.2	68	1,049	32	5-93	1	32.78
B. A. Carse	RF	148.2	21	569	17	3-38	0	33.47
P. Coughlin	RFM	137.3	26	395	10	2-31	0	39.50
R. D. Pringle	OB	201.2	24	804	19	7-107	1	42.31
S. G. Borthwick	LBG	310.3	33	1,194	23	5-79	1	51.91

Also bowled: U. Arshad (RFM) 30–4–103–0; P. D. Collingwood (RM/OB) 39.1–6–127–1; A. J. Hickey (OB) 47.5–6–143–6; K. K. Jennings (RM) 55–14–159–6; M. D. Stoneman (OB) 5–1–28–0.

LEADING ROYAL LONDON CUP AVERAGES (150 runs/4 wickets)

Batting	*Runs*	*HS*	*Avge*	*SR*	*Ct*
M. J. Richardson	156	64	52.00	96.29	2
M. D. Stoneman	247	93	35.28	85.17	2
S. G. Borthwick	238	84	34.00	88.14	5
P. Mustard	161	88	32.20	99.38	2
R. D. Pringle	209	125	29.85	119.42	3
P. D. Collingwood	168	69	28.00	105.66	1

Bowling	*W*	*BB*	*Avge*	*ER*
J. Harrison	6	4-40	24.16	5.57
C. Rushworth	12	3-19	32.41	6.27
U. Arshad	5	3-50	45.20	5.62
R. D. Pringle	4	2-39	53.00	5.57
S. G. Borthwick	4	1-48	101.00	6.41

LEADING NATWEST T20 BLAST AVERAGES (125 runs/18 overs)

Batting	Runs	HS	Avge	SR	Ct/St
C. S. MacLeod	165	83	33.00	**142.24**	3
M. D. Stoneman	356	82*	25.42	**137.45**	7
P. D. Collingwood	139	44*	69.50	**134.95**	5
P. Mustard	290	75*	29.00	**131.81**	11/1
R. D. Pringle	139	33	11.58	**129.90**	6
K. K. Jennings	348	88	43.50	**126.54**	3
M. J. Richardson	188	37	18.80	**109.94**	12

Bowling	W	BB	Avge	ER
M. A. Wood	9	4-25	13.55	**6.10**
C. Rushworth	19	3-14	15.63	**6.45**
S. G. Borthwick	18	4-18	20.72	**7.36**
K. K. Jennings	9	2-18	40.88	**7.36**
P. Coughlin	17	5-42	19.29	**8.66**
B. J. McCarthy	7	3-23	23.71	**8.97**
U. Arshad	12	3-30	39.66	**9.74**

FIRST-CLASS COUNTY RECORDS

Highest score for	273	M. L. Love v Hampshire at Chester-le-Street	2003
Highest score against	501*	B. C. Lara (Warwickshire) at Birmingham	1994
Leading run-scorer	**10,644**	**P. D. Collingwood (avge 34.11)**	**1996–2016**
Best bowling for	10-47	O. D. Gibson v Hampshire at Chester-le-Street	2007
Best bowling against	9-34	J. A. R. Harris (Middlesex) at Lord's	2015
Leading wicket-taker	518	S. J. E. Brown (avge 28.30)	1992–2002
Highest total for	648-5 dec	v Nottinghamshire at Chester-le-Street	2009
Highest total against	810-4 dec	by Warwickshire at Birmingham	1994
Lowest total for	67	v Middlesex at Lord's	1996
Lowest total against	18	by Durham MCCU at Chester-le-Street	2012

LIST A COUNTY RECORDS

Highest score for	164	B. A. Stokes v Nottinghamshire at Chester-le-St	2014
Highest score against	151*	M. P. Maynard (Glamorgan) at Darlington	1991
Leading run-scorer	**5,764**	**P. D. Collingwood (avge 32.75)**	**1995–2016**
Best bowling for	7-32	S. P. Davis v Lancashire at Chester-le-Street	1983
Best bowling against	6-22	A. Dale (Glamorgan) at Colwyn Bay	1993
Leading wicket-taker	298	N. Killeen (avge 23.96)	1995–2010
Highest total for	353-8	v Nottinghamshire at Chester-le-Street	2014
Highest total against	361-7	by Essex at Chelmsford	1996
Lowest total for	72	v Warwickshire at Birmingham	2002
Lowest total against	63	by Hertfordshire at Darlington	1964

TWENTY20 COUNTY RECORDS

Highest score for	91*	G. Clark v Yorkshire at Leeds	2015
Highest score against	**127**	**T. Köhler-Cadmore (Worcs) at Worcester**	**2016**
Leading run-scorer	**3,207**	**P. Mustard (avge 25.05)**	**2003–16**
Best bowling for	5-6	P. D. Collingwood v Northants at Chester-le-St	2011
Best bowling against	5-16	R. M. Pyrah (Yorkshire) at Scarborough	2011
Leading wicket-taker	93	G. R. Breese (avge 21.56)	2004–14
Highest total for	225-2	v Leicestershire at Chester-le-Street	2010
Highest total against	**225-6**	**by Worcestershire at Worcester**	**2016**
Lowest total for	93	v Kent at Canterbury	2009
Lowest total against	47	by Northamptonshire at Chester-le-Street	2011

ADDRESS

Emirates Durham International Cricket Ground, Riverside, Chester-le-Street, County Durham DH3 3QR; 0191 387 1717; reception@durhamccc.co.uk; www.durhamccc.co.uk.

OFFICIALS

Captain P. D. Collingwood
(50-overs) K. K. Jennings
Director of cricket G. Cook
First-team coach J. J. B. Lewis
Academy coach J. B. Windows
Chairman 2016 C. W. Leach
2017 Sir Ian Botham

Chief operating officer R. Dowson
Chief executive D. Harker
Head groundsman V. Demain
Scorer 2016 B. Hunt
2017 W. R. Dobson

DURHAM v DURHAM MCCU

At Chester-le-Street, April 5–7. Drawn. Toss: Durham MCCU. First-class debut: B. A. Carse.

There was no play on the first day, and only 55 overs on the third. Between showers the ball swung, but in the cold there was little encouragement for seamers in a placid pitch, though Brydon Carse, a 20-year-old South African with England ambitions, generated impressive pace on the last day. Stoneman made a patient 83, which laid the platform for an untroubled century from Richardson. After the county declared, Cameron Steel and Charlie Macdonell put on 130 for the students' third wicket, the biggest stand of the match.

Close of play: first day, no play; second day, Durham MCCU 32-0 (Kurtz 17, Clark 15).

Durham

*M. D. Stoneman c and b Phillips	83
K. K. Jennings c Clark b Phillips	54
S. G. Borthwick st Dunford b Dewes	24
†M. J. Richardson not out	115
J. T. A. Burnham not out	50
B 4, lb 5, w 5, nb 10	24
1/92 (2) (3 wkts dec, 78 overs)	350
2/137 (3) 3/236 (1)	

G. J. Muchall, R. D. Pringle, U. Arshad, B. A. Carse, C. Rushworth and G. Onions did not bat.

Wood 12–3–47–0; Alexander 10–0–52–0; Phillips 14–1–68–2; Dewes 21–1–89–1; Macdonell 21–1–85–0.

Durham MCCU

E. E. Kurtz c Arshad b Rushworth	17
*J. Clark c Borthwick b Rushworth	17
C. T. Steel c Muchall b Onions	56
C. M. Macdonell not out	81
E. J. Pollock c Richardson b Jennings	11
R. A. M. Gibson not out	3
B 1, lb 1, nb 4	6
1/32 (1) 2/35 (2) (4 wkts, 67 overs)	191
3/165 (3) 4/188 (5)	

W. D. B. Phillips, †J. E. Dunford, J. M. Wood, T. D. Alexander and J. J. N. Dewes did not bat.

Rushworth 12–6–22–2; Onions 17–4–48–1; Carse 10–3–38–0; Pringle 8–2–30–0; Arshad 11–5–28–0; Jennings 6–0–17–1; Borthwick 3–1–6–0.

Umpires: M. A. Gough and S. J. O'Shaughnessy.

DURHAM v SOMERSET

At Chester-le-Street, April 10–13. Drawn. Durham 10pts, Somerset 8pts. Toss: uncontested. County debuts: R. C. Davies, C. J. L. Rogers. Championship debuts: B. A. Carse; R. E. van der Merwe.

Keaton Jennings joined Dean Jones (against the Pakistanis in 1992) and Paul Collingwood (also against Somerset, in 2005) as only the third batsman to score two centuries in a match for Durham – though there was to be a fourth in May. With the Riverside floodlights shining on Championship cricket for the first time, Jennings followed a diligent 116 with a fluent unbeaten 105. On the first day, he had grafted to 50 in 130 balls; on the second, his half-century needed only 63, helped by dreadful bowling – the innings' first three overs yielded 32, of which 24 came off Gregory. Four players were making Championship debuts for Somerset: Australian batsman and new captain Chris Rogers, wicketkeeper Ryan Davies, South African all-rounder Roelof van der Merwe and Scottish seamer Josh Davey. Rogers held firm against far better bowling by Onions, who claimed three wickets in ten deliveries on the second morning – only to be run out when Trego tried to steal a first-ball single to mid-off. There were also two wickets for Carse, who looked the quickest bowler. But rain washed out the last two days.

Close of play: first day, Somerset 30-3 (Rogers 3, Hildreth 4); second day, Durham 223-4 (Jennings 105, Collingwood 39); third day, no play.

Durham

M. D. Stoneman c Abell b Groenewald	14	– c Trescothick b van der Merwe	41
K. K. Jennings c Trescothick b Davey	116	– not out	105
S. G. Borthwick lbw b Gregory	14	– c Trescothick b Groenewald	25
J. T. A. Burnham b Davey	33	– c van der Merwe b Gregory	5
†M. J. Richardson lbw b Gregory	9	– lbw b Gregory	0
*P. D. Collingwood b Gregory	0	– not out	39
R. D. Pringle c Davey b Groenewald	10		
U. Arshad lbw b Groenewald	32		
B. A. Carse lbw b van der Merwe	0		
C. Rushworth c Allenby b Gregory	4		
G. Onions not out	0		
Lb 11, w 1, nb 12	24	Nb 8	8
1/30 (1) 2/55 (3) 3/134 (4) (81.4 overs)	256	1/74 (1) (4 wkts, 57 overs)	223
4/159 (5) 5/159 (6) 6/172 (7)		2/135 (3) 3/149 (4)	
7/244 (2) 8/244 (9) 9/252 (8) 10/256 (10)		4/151 (5)	

Gregory 17.4–2–58–4; Groenewald 15–2–54–3; Allenby 12–4–37–0; Trego 14–6–25–0; Davey 13–2–39–2; van der Merwe 10–2–32–1. *Second innings*—Gregory 12–4–54–2; Groenewald 13–3–44–1; Trego 5–1–24–0; Davey 7–1–40–0; van der Merwe 8–1–36–1; Allenby 12–3–25–0.

Somerset

M. E. Trescothick b Onions	3
T. B. Abell lbw b Rushworth	10
J. H. Davey lbw b Rushworth	10
*C. J. L. Rogers run out	23
J. C. Hildreth c Pringle b Onions	27
J. Allenby lbw b Onions	0
R. E. van der Merwe c Richardson b Onions	3
P. D. Trego c Rushworth b Carse	45
†R. C. Davies c and b Carse	14
L. Gregory lbw b Rushworth	27
T. D. Groenewald not out	5
B 2, lb 6, nb 4	12
1/11 (2) 2/21 (3) 3/23 (1) (48.1 overs)	179
4/73 (5) 5/73 (6) 6/85 (7)	
7/85 (4) 8/102 (9) 9/168 (10) 10/179 (8)	

Rushworth 18–1–70–3; Onions 19–2–62–4; Carse 6.1–2–13–2; Arshad 5–0–26–0.

Umpires: R. J. Bailey and N. G. C. Cowley.

DURHAM v MIDDLESEX

At Chester-le-Street, April 24–27. Drawn. Durham 11pts, Middlesex 10pts. Toss: Middlesex.

Middlesex captain Voges said he had never seen snow before, but he got a crash course here. It ended the second day, when a biting north wind had caused the umpires to send for heavier bails, while the third day fell victim to showers of sleet, and only 14 deliveries were bowled on the fourth. The previous week had been warm and sunny, and groundsman Vic Demain had prepared a run-laden pitch. Voges decided to bat, and Middlesex's top seven all passed 25, but there were a few careless dismissals and the top score was Malan's 74. In his first appearance since being hit for four successive sixes in the World Twenty20 final, Stokes began his opening spell with 11 dot balls and finished with four wickets. Next day, Stoneman was dropped by Harris at long leg on 19, but was otherwise flawless on his way to an unbeaten century. He scored heavily through backward point and put on 131 with the 19-year-old Burnham, who drove confidently in a career-best 61. Finn conceded 30 in his first four overs, but settled down to take three wickets.

Close of play: first day, Middlesex 358-7 (Stirling 41); second day, Durham 295-4 (Stoneman 139, Richardson 31); third day, no play.

Middlesex

S. D. Robson b Carse	26	T. J. Murtagh c Richardson b Onions	5
N. R. T. Gubbins lbw b Onions	60	S. T. Finn b Stokes	5
N. R. D. Compton b Pringle	38		
D. J. Malan c Richardson b Rushworth	74	B 5, lb 11, nb 12	28
*A. C. Voges c Borthwick b Stokes	50		—
†J. A. Simpson lbw b Onions	38	1/58 (1) 2/101 (2) (103.1 overs)	389
P. R. Stirling c Richardson b Stokes	44	3/177 (3) 4/267 (4)	
J. A. R. Harris lbw b Stokes	8	5/267 (5) 6/338 (6) 7/358 (8)	
T. S. Roland-Jones not out	13	8/361 (7) 9/368 (10) 10/389 (11)	

Rushworth 18–7–49–1; Onions 21–1–71–3; Stokes 25.1–5–80–4; Carse 11–1–75–1; Pringle 22–3–73–1; Borthwick 6–0–25–0.

Durham

M. D. Stoneman not out	141	†M. J. Richardson not out	39
K. K. Jennings c Simpson b Finn	34	B 2, lb 6, nb 8	16
S. G. Borthwick c Simpson b Harris	5		—
J. T. A. Burnham lbw b Finn	61	1/71 (2) 2/82 (3) (4 wkts, 86.3 overs)	305
B. A. Stokes c Stirling b Finn	9	3/213 (4) 4/231 (5)	

*P. D. Çollingwood, R. D. Pringle, B. A. Carse, C. Rushworth and G. Onions did not bat.

Murtagh 15–1–60–0; Finn 18–2–64–3; Harris 17–2–57–1; Roland-Jones 17.3–0–71–0; Stirling 19–2–45–0.

Umpires: I. J. Gould and G. D. Lloyd.

At The Oval, May 1–4. DURHAM drew with SURREY.

DURHAM v LANCASHIRE

At Chester-le-Street, May 15–18. Durham won by 73 runs. Durham 23pts, Lancashire 6pts. Toss: Durham.

Borthwick was the second Durham batsman in four games to score twin hundreds, after only two in their previous 24 seasons as a first-class county. By emulating Jennings's feat against Somerset, he set up their first win of 2016 – and Lancashire's first defeat. Immaculate timing was the essence of Borthwick's classy batting, and he maintained an even tempo throughout his 134 off 221 balls. Collingwood just missed a second successive hundred as he steered his side towards 400. The improved pitches would ultimately provide for that Riverside rarity, an uninterrupted match reaching the final session, but there were also rewards for bowlers hitting the right length: Bailey and McCarthy both collected five-wicket hauls in their first games of the season. With Hameed providing a solid anchor, then Kerrigan making 48 as nightwatchman, Lancashire were content to score under three an over in accumulating 220 for four before McCarthy's persistence paid off. Borthwick completed his second century just before the third-day close, and Collingwood declared 324 ahead. Victory arrived six overs after tea, with Weighell (playing because of Chris Rushworth's torn buttock muscle) and Carse claiming three wickets each.

Close of play: first day, Durham 341-6 (Collingwood 85, Weighell 14); second day, Lancashire 205-4 (Croft 31, Kerrigan 2); third day, Durham 239-4 (Borthwick 103, Collingwood 9).

Durham

M. D. Stoneman c Brown b Bailey	31	– c Davies b Bailey	62
K. K. Jennings c Davies b Bailey	1	– c Livingstone b Jarvis	20
S. G. Borthwick c Petersen b Kerrigan	134	– not out	103
J. T. A. Burnham c Livingstone b Bailey	44	– run out	1
†M. J. Richardson c Livingstone b Jarvis	1	– c Livingstone b Kerrigan	35
*P. D. Collingwood c Brown b Jarvis	97	– not out	9
R. D. Pringle c Livingstone b Bailey	25		
W. J. Weighell c Petersen b Bailey	14		
B. A. Carse c Livingstone b Jarvis	1		
B. J. McCarthy c Petersen b Kerrigan	37		
G. Onions not out	14		
Lb 8, nb 4	12	Lb 9	9
1/25 (2) 2/46 (1) 3/134 (4) (117 overs)	411	1/55 (2) (4 wkts dec, 60 overs)	239
4/151 (5) 5/274 (3) 6/317 (7) 7/341 (8)		2/146 (1) 3/150 (4)	
8/342 (9) 9/375 (6) 10/411 (10) 110 overs: 376-9		4/216 (5)	

Bailey 31–6–110–5; Jarvis 32–5–86–3; Procter 11–1–50–0; Wagner 24–6–89–0; Kerrigan 17–4–58–2; Croft 2–0–10–0. *Second innings*—Bailey 16–2–57–1; Jarvis 14–0–47–1; Wagner 8–1–28–0; Procter 4–0–29–0; Kerrigan 18–3–69–1.

Lancashire

K. R. Brown c Pringle b Weighell	9	– lbw b Onions	41
H. Hameed b Borthwick	74	– lbw b Weighell	4
L. A. Procter c Pringle b Weighell	1	– c Borthwick b Carse	21
A. N. Petersen lbw b Onions	61	– c Jennings b Carse	22
*S. J. Croft lbw b McCarthy	35	– c Richardson b McCarthy	1
S. C. Kerrigan lbw b McCarthy	48	– (11) b Onions	2
†A. L. Davies b McCarthy	31	– (6) c Richardson b Weighell	39
L. S. Livingstone c Richardson b McCarthy	4	– (7) not out	60
T. E. Bailey c Pringle b McCarthy	2	– (8) c Richardson b Carse	15
N. Wagner run out	10	– (9) c Jennings b Borthwick	4
K. M. Jarvis not out	14	– (10) c Jennings b Weighell	28
B 15, lb 13, w 1, nb 8	37	B 8, lb 6	14
1/19 (1) 2/21 (3) 3/125 (4) (106.4 overs)	326	1/12 (2) 2/50 (1) (67 overs)	251
4/202 (2) 5/220 (5) 6/282 (7)		3/94 (4) 4/97 (3)	
7/286 (8) 8/298 (9) 9/309 (6) 10/326 (10)		5/97 (5) 6/164 (6) 7/181 (8)	
		8/188 (9) 9/244 (10) 10/251 (11)	

Onions 24.4–7–53–1; Weighell 23–3–53–2; Carse 17–3–66–0; McCarthy 22–5–70–5; Borthwick 13–1–37–1; Pringle 2–0–6–0; Jennings 5–2–13–0. *Second innings*—Onions 15–3–65–2; Weighell 15–4–45–3; McCarthy 13–1–51–1; Carse 15–3–38–3; Borthwick 8–0–24–1; Pringle 1–0–14–0.

Umpires: S. C. Gale and R. A. Kettleborough.

At Birmingham, May 22–25. DURHAM beat WARWICKSHIRE by four wickets.

At Nottingham, May 28–31. DURHAM drew with NOTTINGHAMSHIRE.

DURHAM v YORKSHIRE

At Chester-le-Street, June 20–23. Drawn. Durham 8pts, Yorkshire 11pts. Toss: uncontested. First-class debut: B. O. Coad.

When Durham were 105 for four second time round, still 46 behind, Yorkshire were eyeing a three-day win. But Jennings batted 578 minutes for an unbeaten 221, which eventually allowed Durham to set a target of 357. Collingwood had defied a fractured thumb to make 61, and Arshad contributed a career-best 84 to a total of 507 for eight. Both that and the double-century were county records for the second innings. Jennings, born in South Africa, made Durham's fifth-highest score, exceeded only by Australians – Martin Love (twice), Michael Di Venuto and Mike Hussey. With six bowlers unfit or with England, Yorkshire introduced Ben Coad and recalled Josh Shaw from a loan spell with Gloucestershire. But with moisture around they chose to bowl, and Patterson's accuracy earned a career-best six for 56 – before Rushworth grabbed four to make it 14 wickets on the first day. Things calmed down as the pitch grew docile, until only five fell on the last. Yorkshire settled for a draw after an opening stand of 112 ended when Lyth was caught at slip by Stokes – substituting for Collingwood, with ECB approval, as he recovered from knee surgery. In an excellent spell, McCarthy trapped Williamson next ball. But sixth-wicket pair Leaning and Bresnan survived the last 25 overs.

Close of play: first day, Yorkshire 129-4 (Ballance 35, Gale 1); second day, Durham 98-3 (Jennings 46, Richardson 6); third day, Durham 452-8 (Jennings 185, Rushworth 16).

Durham

M. D. Stoneman lbw b Patterson	45	– c and b Bresnan	28
K. K. Jennings b Shaw	20	– not out	221
S. G. Borthwick run out	2	– b Lyth	4
J. T. A. Burnham c Williamson b Patterson	49	– lbw b Patterson	8
†M. J. Richardson c Hodd b Patterson	18	– run out	13
*P. D. Collingwood c Ballance b Patterson	4	– lbw b Williamson	61
R. D. Pringle b Patterson	3	– b Bresnan	20
U. Arshad c Hodd b Bresnan	3	– c Hodd b Coad	84
B. J. McCarthy c and b Shaw	9	– c Hodd b Patterson	11
C. Rushworth c Leaning b Patterson	13	– not out	31
G. Onions not out	0		
B 1, lb 5	6	B 11, lb 9, w 2, nb 4	26
1/49 (2) 2/56 (3) 3/74 (1) 4/98 (5) 5/106 (6) 6/110 (7) 7/122 (8) 8/148 (9) 9/172 (10) 10/172 (4) (61.1 overs)	172	1/46 (1) 2/65 (3) 3/83 (4) 4/105 (5) 5/222 (6) 6/252 (7) 7/408 (8) 8/425 (9) (8 wkts dec, 145 overs)	507

Bresnan 14–3–34–1; Coad 17–5–38–0; Patterson 20.1–4–56–6; Shaw 10–1–38–2. *Second innings*—Bresnan 35–5–145–2; Coad 18–5–70–1; Patterson 38–17–77–2; Shaw 19–2–81–0; Lyth 15–3–54–1; Williamson 14–2–40–1; Leaning 6–1–20–0.

Yorkshire

A. Lyth c Richardson b Rushworth	12	– c sub (B. A. Stokes) b McCarthy	50
A. Z. Lees b Rushworth	71	– b Pringle	74
K. S. Williamson c Jennings b Rushworth	10	– lbw b McCarthy	0
G. S. Ballance c Borthwick b Onions	78	– c Richardson b Onions	32
S. A. Patterson b Rushworth	0		
*A. W. Gale c Stoneman b Pringle	28	– (5) c Richardson b Pringle	17
J. A. Leaning b Onions	9	– (6) not out	22
T. T. Bresnan c Burnham b McCarthy	63	– (7) not out	27
†A. J. Hodd lbw b Rushworth	3		
J. Shaw b Borthwick	24		
B. O. Coad not out	17		
Lb 8	8	B 12, lb 4	16
1/30 (1) 2/54 (3) 3/125 (2) 4/125 (5) 5/193 (6) 6/210 (7) 7/229 (4) 8/236 (9) 9/279 (10) 10/323 (8) (90.1 overs)	323	1/112 (1) 2/112 (3) 3/149 (4) 4/176 (5) 5/179 (2) (5 wkts, 82 overs)	238

Rushworth 25–3–93–5; Onions 24–3–90–2; McCarthy 17.1–0–67–1; Arshad 16–3–46–0; Borthwick 6–2–9–1; Pringle 2–0–10–1. *Second innings*—Rushworth 10–1–25–0; Onions 15–5–29–1; Borthwick 20–7–70–0; Pringle 16–3–35–2; Arshad 9–1–31–0; McCarthy 11–2–27–2; Stoneman 1–0–5–0.

Umpires: S. A. Garratt and J. W. Lloyds.

At Chester-le-Street, June 26–29. DURHAM drew with SRI LANKA A (see Sri Lanka A tour section).

DURHAM v HAMPSHIRE

At Chester-le-Street, July 3–6. Drawn. Durham 12pts, Hampshire 12pts. Toss: Durham.

Hampshire wanted to bat and Durham obliged them, only to concede an opening stand of 160, which developed into 472 for nine. The top six plus Berg all reached 40. Searching for a breakthrough, Durham kept Rushworth going for 16 of the first 40 overs; he conceded only 30, but departed with a hamstring strain (as did Hampshire's McLaren two days later). Jennings dashed to 20 in 16 balls, then steadied himself to complete a century in 201, his fifth of the season. By the time he fell, he had survived 15 hours 22 minutes over two innings against Yorkshire and Hampshire. Stokes, though still unable to bowl post-operation, had replaced the injured Collingwood and scored 51; there was also a maiden half-century from McCarthy, who was joined by last man Onions with 51 needed from ten overs for maximum batting points. They did it with ten balls to spare. Most of the second evening was washed out, and Durham declared behind to put Hampshire in for six overs on the third. They reached the close unscathed and opted for safety on the final day; Adams spent 60 overs scoring 49, and rain ended play after tea.

Close of play: first day, Hampshire 319-6 (Ervine 14, McManus 5); second day, Durham 79-2 (Jennings 36, Burnham 19); third day, Hampshire 9-0 (Adams 4, Smith 4).

Hampshire

*W. R. Smith c Richardson b Jennings	67	– (2) c Richardson b Onions	10
J. H. K. Adams c Jennings b McCarthy	86	– (1) c Jennings b Coughlin	49
T. P. Alsop lbw b Pringle	40	– b Borthwick	34
M. A. Carberry b Onions	48	– b McCarthy	59
A. J. A. Wheater lbw b McCarthy	44	– not out	10
S. M. Ervine b Coughlin	93	– not out	0
R. McLaren c Jennings b Coughlin	4		
†L. D. McManus c sub (A. W. O. Appleby) b Onions	5		
G. K. Berg c Burnham b Jennings	56		
G. M. Andrew not out	15		
B 6, lb 5, w 1, nb 2	14	B 3, lb 8, w 1	12
1/160 (1) 2/178 (2) (9 wkts dec, 138.1 overs)	472	1/18 (2) (4 wkts, 67 overs)	174
3/215 (3) 4/289 (4)		2/70 (3) 3/149 (1)	
5/301 (5) 6/310 (7)		4/173 (4)	
7/320 (8) 8/415 (9) 9/472 (6) 110 overs: 361-7			

T. L. Best did not bat.

Rushworth 16–6–30–0; Onions 29–3–95–2; McCarthy 29–7–88–2; Coughlin 22.1–5–55–2; Pringle 17–1–90–1; Jennings 13–1–34–2; Borthwick 12–0–69–0. *Second innings*—Onions 11–2–20–1; Coughlin 16–7–32–1; McCarthy 8–3–20–1; Pringle 16–0–37–0; Jennings 2–0–10–0; Borthwick 14–3–44–1.

Durham

*M. D. Stoneman b McLaren	17
K. K. Jennings c Adams b Berg	129
S. G. Borthwick b McLaren	5
J. T. A. Burnham c Alsop b McLaren	74
B. A. Stokes b Smith	51
†M. J. Richardson c Smith b Andrew	5
R. D. Pringle c sub (M. S. Crane) b Berg	18
P. Coughlin c McManus b Andrew	23
B. J. McCarthy not out	51
C. Rushworth c sub (M. S. Crane) b Andrew	0
G. Onions not out	23
B 5, lb 11, w 1, nb 8	25
1/37 (1) 2/47 (3) (9 wkts dec, 112 overs)	421
3/205 (4) 4/295 (5)	
5/304 (2) 6/310 (6) 7/342 (8)	
8/348 (7) 9/349 (10) 110 overs: 409-9	

Best 19–2–104–0; McLaren 20–1–78–3; Berg 30–13–70–2; Andrew 30–9–104–3; Ervine 6–0–32–0; Smith 7–1–17–1.

Umpires: R. J. Evans and S. J. O'Shaughnessy.

At Southport, July 16–19. DURHAM beat LANCASHIRE by two wickets.

At Taunton, August 4–6. DURHAM lost to SOMERSET by 39 runs.

At Lord's, August 13–15. DURHAM lost to MIDDLESEX by an innings and 80 runs.

DURHAM v WARWICKSHIRE

At Chester-le-Street, August 23–26. Drawn. Durham 8pts, Warwickshire 11pts. Toss: uncontested.

Barker has often been Durham's nemesis – when he bowled Stoneman, it was his 50th wicket in 11 Championship encounters – and, in the first day's seam-friendly conditions, the home batsmen had to battle hard. But it was Patel's off-spin that mopped up their last five wickets, starting with Collingwood, who had faced 108 balls for 23. There was still plenty of movement on the second day, but Westwood survived two chances to the slips and other close shaves during a six-hour 127; his previous Championship-best in 2016 was just 45. Rain and bad light meant only eight overs were bowled on the third day, though Warwickshire still fancied their chances, as they led by 137 with three wickets standing. They added 37 on the final morning before giving themselves 84 overs to bowl out Durham. In the best conditions of the match, a stand of 151 between Stoneman and Borthwick ensured stalemate.

Close of play: first day, Warwickshire 25-1 (Westwood 13, Wright 2); second day, Warwickshire 315-7 (Ambrose 27, Barker 13); third day, Warwickshire 344-7 (Ambrose 38, Barker 26).

Durham

M. D. Stoneman b Barker	3	– b Patel	80
K. K. Jennings c Chopra b Barker	21	– c Ambrose b Barker	0
S. G. Borthwick c Ambrose b Clarke	19	– b Clarke	92
J. T. A. Burnham c Clarke b Wright	30	– not out	10
*P. D. Collingwood c Chopra b Patel	23	– not out	4
M. J. Richardson c Clarke b Barker	55		
†S. W. Poynter b Patel	17		
P. Coughlin c Hain b Patel	14		
B. J. McCarthy b Patel	4		
G. Onions c Ambrose b Patel	15		
C. Rushworth not out	0		
B 4, lb 2	6	B 2, w 5, nb 2	9
1/16 (1) 2/29 (2) 3/59 (3) (81.3 overs)	207	1/13 (2) (3 wkts dec, 62 overs)	195
4/81 (4) 5/151 (6) 6/173 (5)		2/164 (1) 3/191 (3)	
7/174 (7) 8/178 (9) 9/203 (8) 10/207 (10)			

Barker 17–8–29–3; Wright 15–1–52–1; Clarke 24–9–48–1; Hannon-Dalby 9–1–37–0; Patel 15.3–5–32–5; Trott 1–0–3–0. *Second innings*—Barker 12–4–32–1; Wright 7–1–37–0; Clarke 12–2–44–1; Patel 20–7–43–1; Hannon-Dalby 10–3–35–0; Westwood 1–0–2–0.

Warwickshire

V. Chopra c Poynter b Rushworth	10
I. J. Westwood c Collingwood b Rushworth	127
C. J. C. Wright lbw b Onions	15
I. J. L. Trott c Coughlin b McCarthy	48
*I. R. Bell c Poynter b Rushworth	45
S. R. Hain c Poynter b Coughlin	6
†T. R. Ambrose c Coughlin b McCarthy	50
R. Clarke b McCarthy	2
K. H. D. Barker not out	43
J. S. Patel not out	1
B 11, lb 15, w 6, nb 2	34
1/20 (1) (8 wkts dec, 126 overs)	381
2/51 (3) 3/157 (4)	
4/265 (5) 5/266 (2) 6/272 (6)	
7/292 (8) 8/378 (7) 110 overs: 316-7	

O. J. Hannon-Dalby did not bat.

Rushworth 36–6–94–3; Onions 34–9–94–1; Borthwick 9–1–38–0; McCarthy 18–5–56–3; Coughlin 22–3–64–1; Jennings 7–4–9–0.

Umpires: N. L. Bainton and P. J. Hartley.

DURHAM v NOTTINGHAMSHIRE

At Chester-le-Street, August 31–September 3. Drawn. Durham 9pts, Nottinghamshire 11pts. Toss: Durham.

The final day's washout ruined the prospect of an interesting finish to a fluctuating game. Durham had sped to 77 without loss in 14 overs, but later lost nine wickets between lunch and tea, with Gurney taking six for the first time. He also struck Collingwood in the box, causing him to retire for a while. Nottinghamshire opener Libby looked composed, batting three sessions for a career-best 144 full of leg-side runs, before he was last out, though he had been badly missed on 87 by Richardson at leg gully. Trailing by 69, Durham lost three wickets late on the second day, but nightwatchman Onions batted through the next morning and contributed a maiden fifty to a stand of 162 with Jennings, whose sixth century of the season equalled the county record set by Collingwood in 2005 and matched by Michael Di Venuto in 2009. Durham declared during a break for bad light, when they led by 316. Onions had time to dismiss Libby, but there would be no more play.

Close of play: first day, Nottinghamshire 129-2 (Libby 51, Lumb 68); second day, Durham 83-3 (Jennings 34, Onions 1); third day, Nottinghamshire 17-1 (Mullaney 7).

Durham

M. D. Stoneman c Read b Mullaney	49	– c Taylor b Mullaney	39
K. K. Jennings lbw b Gurney	33	– not out	171
S. G. Borthwick c Read b Gurney	20	– lbw b Gurney	0
J. T. A. Burnham c Read b Gurney	0	– b Imran Tahir	3
*P. D. Collingwood not out	33	– (6) c Lumb b Fletcher	9
M. J. Richardson lbw b Gurney	0	– (7) lbw b Fletcher	9
†S. W. Poynter b Patel	42	– (8) b Imran Tahir	22
P. Coughlin lbw b Imran Tahir	19	– (9) c Mullaney b Gurney	5
B. J. McCarthy b Patel	9	– (10) not out	28
G. Onions b Gurney	19	– (5) lbw b Patel	65
C. Rushworth c Mullaney b Gurney	0		
B 3, lb 7, nb 10	20	B 5, lb 14, w 1, nb 14	34
1/77 (2) 2/115 (3) 3/115 (1) 4/121 (4) 5/121 (6) 6/157 (8) 7/187 (7) 8/196 (9) 9/232 (10) 10/244 (11) (64.4 overs)	244	1/67 (1) 2/68 (3) 3/78 (4) 4/240 (5) 5/261 (6) 6/273 (7) 7/317 (8) 8/334 (9) (8 wkts dec, 117 overs)	385

In the first innings Collingwood, when 7, retired hurt at 122-5 and resumed at 187-7.

Wood 8–1–41–0; Fletcher 8–1–25–0; Gurney 16.4–4–61–6; Imran Tahir 19–5–62–1; Mullaney 6–2–14–1; Patel 7–2–31–2. *Second innings*—Fletcher 22–7–54–2; Wood 17–4–45–0; Gurney 29–1–93–2; Mullaney 11–2–42–1; Imran Tahir 24–5–78–2; Patel 13–1–51–1; Libby 1–0–3–0.

Nottinghamshire

S. J. Mullaney c Poynter b Onions	7	– not out	7
J. D. Libby lbw b Coughlin	144	– b Onions	5
T. J. Moores c Borthwick b Rushworth	1		
M. J. Lumb c Borthwick b Onions	82		
B. R. M. Taylor c Coughlin b McCarthy	5		
S. R. Patel b Jennings	37		
*†C. M. W. Read b Rushworth	2		
L. Wood c Richardson b Onions	5		
L. J. Fletcher c Collingwood b Rushworth	1		
Imran Tahir c Burnham b Borthwick	13		
H. F. Gurney not out	0		
B 8, nb 8	16	Lb 4, w 1	5
1/13 (1) 2/16 (3) 3/157 (4) 4/186 (5) 5/268 (6) 6/272 (7) 7/281 (8) 8/286 (9) 9/313 (10) 10/313 (2) (94.2 overs)	313	1/17 (2) (1 wkt, 7.2 overs)	17

Rushworth 22–4–75–3; Onions 26–2–84–3; Coughlin 16.2–1–45–1; McCarthy 14–1–65–1; Borthwick 13–2–28–1; Stoneman 1–0–5–0; Jennings 2–0–3–1. *Second innings*—Rushworth 4–0–10–0; Onions 3.2–2–3–1.

Umpires: G. D. Lloyd and J. W. Lloyds.

At Leeds, September 6–9. DURHAM lost to YORKSHIRE by 228 runs.

DURHAM v SURREY

At Chester-le-Street, September 12–15. Durham won by 21 runs. Durham 24pts, Surrey 7pts. Toss: Durham.

A gripping climax ensured Durham's first-division status with a round to go (or so they thought, until events took a nasty turn ten days after the end of the season). Surrey entered the final session needing 113, with six wickets standing and Roy one shot from a second hundred in the game. Stokes had managed only 24 runs and no wickets up to that point, but Roy gloved the first ball after tea down the leg side to become the first of Stokes's four victims, before Onions claimed the last two, to finish with eight in the match. The opening day had belonged to Jennings, the first Durham player to score seven centuries in a season, and the sixth to carry his bat. After playing with calm orthodoxy, he reached three figures with a reverse paddle for four, and completed his second double of 2016 off the day's final delivery. Roy and Ansari added 164 for Surrey's fourth wicket under cloudless skies, and another 143 in the second innings, when they came together at 11 for three. In between, Sam Curran had taken a career-best seven for 58, including four important wickets in seven balls, to leave a gettable target of 281. He later made a fearless fifty, but could not prevent the final twist. This was Brian Hunt's last match as Durham scorer, after 41 years.

Close of play: first day, Durham 393-9 (Jennings 200, Onions 7); second day, Surrey 299-7 (S. M. Curran 10, Batty 3); third day, Durham 213-8 (Carse 0, Wood 0).

Durham

M. D. Stoneman c Foakes b Meaker	20	– lbw b S. M. Curran	92
K. K. Jennings not out	201	– b Meaker	11
S. G. Borthwick lbw b T. K. Curran	38	– c Foakes b S. M. Curran	12
J. T. A. Burnham c T. K. Curran b Meaker	15	– c Foakes b S. M. Curran	0
B. A. Stokes b Footitt	24	– c Sangakkara b S. M. Curran	0
*P. D. Collingwood c Sibley b Footitt	14	– c Burns b S. M. Curran	4
G. Clark c T. K. Curran b Footitt	0	– lbw b S. M. Curran	54
†S. W. Poynter c Roy b Footitt	0	– c Sangakkara b Footitt	19
B. A. Carse c Burns b T. K. Curran	32	– not out	21
M. A. Wood c Roy b Meaker	28	– c and b Footitt	5
G. Onions c Ansari b Footitt	14	– c Footitt b S. M. Curran	7
Lb 10, w 3, nb 2	15	B 5, lb 11, w 3, nb 2	21
1/35 (1) 2/105 (3) 3/128 (4) 4/165 (5) 5/218 (6) 6/226 (7) 7/232 (8) 8/311 (9) 9/372 (10) 10/401 (11) (98.4 overs)	401	1/40 (2) 2/77 (3) 3/77 (4) 4/77 (5) 5/83 (6) 6/192 (7) 7/209 (1) 8/213 (8) 9/223 (10) 10/246 (11) (60.3 overs)	246

T. K. Curran 20–2–78–2; S. M. Curran 16–4–55–0; Meaker 22–3–104–3; Footitt 24.4–3–90–5; Batty 6–1–24–0; Ansari 10–0–40–0. *Second innings*—T. K. Curran 10–1–37–0; S. M. Curran 18.3–3–58–7; Footitt 18–1–83–2; Meaker 10–1–37–1; Ansari 4–0–15–0.

Surrey

R. J. Burns c Poynter b Wood	15	– c Jennings b Onions	9
D. P. Sibley b Onions	31	– c Collingwood b Wood	0
K. C. Sangakkara lbw b Onions	48	– c Poynter b Wood	0
Z. S. Ansari c Borthwick b Jennings	48	– lbw b Borthwick	51
J. J. Roy lbw b Onions	120	– c Poynter b Stokes	96
†B. T. Foakes lbw b Wood	6	– c Borthwick b Stokes	20
S. M. Curran c Poynter b Onions	10	– not out	50
T. K. Curran b Onions	9	– c Poynter b Stokes	0
*G. J. Batty b Carse	29	– c Jennings b Stokes	12
S. C. Meaker not out	35	– c Collingwood b Onions	0
M. H. A. Footitt c Stoneman b Carse	0	– b Onions	4
B 4, lb 8, w 2, nb 2	16	B 4, lb 8, w 1, nb 4	17
1/24 (1) 2/99 (2) 3/100 (3) (109.1 overs)	367	1/1 (2) 2/1 (3) (74 overs)	259
4/264 (4) 5/276 (6) 6/276 (5)		3/11 (1) 4/154 (4)	
7/288 (8) 8/299 (7) 9/361 (9) 10/367 (11)		5/168 (5) 6/222 (6) 7/222 (8)	
		8/252 (9) 9/253 (10) 10/259 (11)	

Wood 21–0–64–2; Onions 31–6–90–5; Stokes 26–3–78–0; Carse 17.1–1–54–2; Jennings 4–0–22–1; Collingwood 5–0–17–0; Borthwick 5–0–30–0. *Second innings*—Wood 14–1–45–2; Onions 21–2–62–3; Stokes 21–6–54–4; Carse 8–1–52–0; Borthwick 10–2–34–1.

Umpires: N. A. Mallender and D. J. Millns.

At Southampton, September 20–23. DURHAM beat HAMPSHIRE by six wickets. *Durham condemn Hampshire to relegation, only for ECB sanctions to later reprieve them – at Durham's expense.*

ESSEX

That rising feeling

PAUL HISCOCK

After several near misses, Essex returned to the top flight for the first time since 2010, claiming the only available promotion spot and winning Division Two by 23 points. It was a triumph for the new coach, Chris Silverwood, whose man-management skills were a major factor: the dressing-room was a happier place than under the more autocratic Paul Grayson. For much of 2016, the atmosphere around Chelmsford was reminiscent of the 1980s glory days of Keith Fletcher's serial trophy-winners: there was a noticeable togetherness, and a refreshing air of enjoyment on the field.

The appointment of Ryan ten Doeschate as the Championship captain proved a great success. Free of IPL commitments, he spent the entire season with Essex, and thrived on the extra responsibility, enjoying his most productive season with the bat and scoring four centuries in his last nine matches. He will be in total charge in 2017, after Ravi Bopara gave up the limited-overs leadership after just one season to concentrate on his own game.

Ten Doeschate was one of four to make 1,000 first-class runs. Tom Westley was the first in the country to get there, and passed 2,000 in all formats, while opener Nick Browne had the distinction of scoring double-centuries home and away against Derbyshire, the first instance in the Championship against the same county since Yorkshire's Percy Holmes in 1922. Dan Lawrence, still a teenager, hit three stylish hundreds.

In all, eight different batsmen reached three figures in the Championship, the 18 centuries including three from Alastair Cook in the first four matches before he disappeared on national duty. The weight of runs was a tribute to Silverwood's former Yorkshire team-mate Anthony McGrath, who joined as assistant coach in the winter and installed a more ruthless approach. Arguably the only disappointment was Bopara, who for the second year running failed to reach a Championship hundred. A return to form would help Essex in Division One.

James Foster delivered another masterclass behind the stumps, as well as 677 runs. He made no secret of his wish to move up the order, but with Varun Chopra returning from Warwickshire, and Adam Wheater from Hampshire, Foster – who turns 37 in April – may have to stay at No. 8, from where he has organised so many rearguards. However, he showed no sign of relinquishing the gloves to Wheater.

With promotion achieved, Essex were not too perturbed by their patchy limited-overs form, reaching two quarter-finals but going no further. The batsmen have often struggled when the white ball spins, something Silverwood and McGrath will want to address in 2017.

Gareth Fuller, PA Photos

Dan Lawrence

Essex will face up to life without two trusted stalwarts of their seam attack: David Masters bowed out at 38, Graham Napier at 36. Between them they took more than 900 first-class wickets for the club, and 109 in 2016 alone. Napier enjoyed his most productive season with the ball – his 69 victims far exceeded his previous-best of 52 in 2014. Both cited wear and tear as the main reason for their retirements, and Napier had lined up a job at the Royal Hospital School in Ipswich. He showed his all-round talents against Sussex in August, on his club ground in Colchester, following a five-for with a six-filled century. Sadly, the Castle Ground won't be seen in 2017 either, partly because of the reduction in Championship fixtures.

The need to strengthen the pace bowling led to a reluctant farewell to New Zealander Jesse Ryder, who had performed with distinction for Essex, but was restricted by a calf problem. That allowed Silverwood to move for two high-quality international seamers, both left-armers. Neil Wagner, Ryder's feisty compatriot who did well for Lancashire last year, will cover the first half of the season, before being replaced by the exciting Pakistani Mohammad Amir. They will be backed up by Jamie Porter (from Leytonstone) who reached 50 Championship wickets for the second year running. The two Matts – Dixon from Australia and Quinn from New Zealand – had their moments, with Quinn snaffling 11 wickets against Gloucestershire at Cheltenham.

After letting go of Monty Panesar, Essex went through the summer without a frontline spinner: slow left-armer Ashar Zaidi, signed from Sussex, managed only two wickets but had more impact as a Twenty20 batsman. That problem has been addressed by off-spinner Simon Harmer, a Kolpak signing with five Tests for South Africa. Top-order batsman Jaik Mickleburgh was released after averaging 29 in nine seasons at the club.

The continued development at Chelmsford has been put on hold, but Essex have been in discussions with the London Olympic stadium, with a view to staging occasional Twenty20 matches there.

Championship attendance: 31,020.

ESSEX RESULTS

All first-class matches – Played 18: Won 7, Lost 3, Drawn 8.
County Championship matches – Played 16: Won 6, Lost 3, Drawn 7.

Specsavers County Championship, winners of Division 2;
NatWest T20 Blast, quarter-finalists; Royal London One-Day Cup, quarter-finalists.

COUNTY CHAMPIONSHIP AVERAGES, BATTING AND FIELDING

Cap		*Birthplace*	*M*	*I*	*NO*	*R*	*HS*	*100*	*Avge*	*Ct/St*
2005	†A. N. Cook§	*Gloucester*	7	11	4	643	142	3	91.85	8
2006	R. N. ten Doeschate††	*Port Elizabeth, SA*	15	21	3	1,157	145	4	64.27	12
2013	T. Westley	*Cambridge*	16	23	0	1,217	254	3	52.91	17
2015	†N. L. J. Browne	*Leytonstone‡*	16	25	3	1,046	255	2	47.54	13
	D. W. Lawrence	*Whipps Cross‡*	15	21	0	902	154	3	42.95	12
2001	J. S. Foster	*Whipps Cross‡*	15	20	3	677	113	1	39.82	48/1
2005	R. S. Bopara	*Forest Gate‡*	15	21	1	750	99	0	37.50	4
2013	J. C. Mickleburgh	*Norwich*	8	12	0	314	103	1	26.16	9
2014	†J. D. Ryder¶	*Masterton, NZ*	7	10	1	234	51	0	26.00	4
	†Ashar Zaidi	*Karachi, Pakistan*	3	5	0	120	37	0	24.00	0
2003	G. R. Napier	*Colchester‡*	14	15	2	298	124	1	22.92	2
2008	D. D. Masters	*Chatham*	9	10	5	105	47*	0	21.00	0
	J. A. Porter	*Leytonstone‡*	14	12	7	56	20*	0	11.20	7
	M. R. Quinn††	*Auckland, NZ*	4	6	1	29	10	0	5.80	1

Also batted: †A. P. Beard (*Chelmsford‡*) (2 matches) 0* (1 ct); V. Chopra (*Barking‡*) (2 matches) 1, 79, 25 (4 ct); M. W. Dixon†† (*Subiaco, Australia*) (3 matches) 8, 1, 14; T. C. Moore (*Basildon‡*) (1 match) 0, 4* (3 ct); †W. M. H. Rhodes (*Nottingham*) (4 matches) 1, 0, 3 (1 ct); K. S. Velani (*Newham‡*) (2 matches) 19, 22; †P. I. Walter (*Basildon‡*) (2 matches) 47, 28; A. J. A. Wheater (*Leytonstone‡*) (2 matches) 59, 18, 21 (6 ct).

‡ *Born in Essex.* § *ECB contract.* ¶ *Official overseas player.* †† *Other non-England-qualified.*

BOWLING

	Style	*O*	*M*	*R*	*W*	*BB*	*5I*	*Avge*
D. D. Masters	RFM	325.1	92	824	40	7-52	1	20.60
M. R. Quinn	RFM	142	24	473	22	7-76	1	21.50
G. R. Napier	RFM	451.3	96	1,460	63	5-59	4	23.17
R. S. Bopara	RM	336.3	65	1,110	42	5-49	2	26.42
J. A. Porter	RFM	456.2	74	1,613	55	5-46	2	29.32
R. N. ten Doeschate	RM	118	14	430	11	4-31	0	39.09

Also bowled: Ashar Zaidi (LM/SLA) 19.5–3–61–2; A. P. Beard (RFM) 54.2–6–219–4; N. L. J. Browne (LBG) 1–0–8–0; M. W. Dixon (RF) 84.1–12–386–9; D. W. Lawrence (OB) 25–2–129–3; T. C. Moore (RFM) 24–7–73–1; W. M. H. Rhodes (RFM) 87–23–278–9; J. D. Ryder (RM) 75–15–254–1; K. S. Velani (RM) 3–0–41–0; P. I. Walter (LM) 50–7–214–4; T. Westley (OB) 109.5–18–351–8.

LEADING ROYAL LONDON CUP AVERAGES (100 runs/4 wickets)

Batting	*Runs*	*HS*	*Avge*	*SR*	*Ct/St*
J. D. Ryder	435	131	54.37	92.16	4
J. S. Foster	160	75*	53.33	141.59	7/6
N. L. J. Browne	358	99	44.75	93.96	5
R. N. ten Doeschate	217	53	36.16	109.59	2
T. Westley	274	110	34.25	81.30	2
R. S. Bopara	219	74*	31.28	73.98	8
Ashar Zaidi	144	41	24.00	109.92	3

Bowling	*W*	*BB*	*Avge*	*ER*
R. N. ten Doeschate	8	2-25	23.00	7.07
G. R. Napier	12	3-50	23.33	6.22
R. S. Bopara	10	3-33	33.40	7.10
M. R. Quinn	9	4-71	34.22	6.41
Ashar Zaidi	6	3-33	37.16	5.06
D. D. Masters	8	2-16	37.37	3.93
D. W. Lawrence	6	3-35	42.50	5.54

LEADING NATWEST T20 BLAST AVERAGES (100 runs/20 overs)

Batting	*Runs*	*HS*	*Avge*	*SR*	*Ct*
Ashar Zaidi	363	59*	40.33	**168.83**	2
J. D. Ryder	214	52*	21.40	**129.69**	3
T. Westley	403	74*	31.00	**126.72**	9
D. W. Lawrence	229	36	25.44	**119.27**	6
R. N. ten Doeschate	233	58*	33.28	**116.50**	7
R. S. Bopara	283	81*	25.72	**115.51**	8

Bowling	*W*	*BB*	*Avge*	*ER*
Ashar Zaidi	5	2-16	38.00	**7.03**
D. W. Lawrence	10	2-11	18.50	**7.11**
R. S. Bopara	11	2-15	32.81	**7.52**
D. D. Masters	5	2-29	38.60	**8.04**
G. R. Napier	22	3-28	16.77	**8.51**
M. R. Quinn	16	4-35	29.37	**9.03**

FIRST-CLASS COUNTY RECORDS

Highest score for	343*	P. A. Perrin v Derbyshire at Chesterfield	1904
Highest score against	332	W. H. Ashdown (Kent) at Brentwood	1934
Leading run-scorer	30,701	G. A. Gooch (avge 51.77)	1973–97
Best bowling for	10-32	H. Pickett v Leicestershire at Leyton	1895
Best bowling against	10-40	E. G. Dennett (Gloucestershire) at Bristol	1906
Leading wicket-taker	1,610	T. P. B. Smith (avge 26.68)	1929–51
Highest total for	761-6 dec	v Leicestershire at Chelmsford	1990
Highest total against	803-4 dec	by Kent at Brentwood	1934
Lowest total for	20	v Lancashire at Chelmsford	2013
Lowest total against	14	by Surrey at Chelmsford	1983

LIST A COUNTY RECORDS

Highest score for	201*	R. S. Bopara v Leicestershire at Leicester	2008
Highest score against	158*	M. W. Goodwin (Sussex) at Chelmsford	2006
Leading run-scorer	16,536	G. A. Gooch (avge 40.93)	1973–97
Best bowling for	8-26	K. D. Boyce v Lancashire at Manchester	1971
Best bowling against	7-29	D. A. Payne (Gloucestershire) at Chelmsford	2010
Leading wicket-taker	616	J. K. Lever (avge 19.04)	1968–89
Highest total for	391-5	v Surrey at The Oval	2008
Highest total against	**324-8**	**by Glamorgan at Chelmsford**	**2016**
Lowest total for	57	v Lancashire at Lord's	1996
Lowest total against	41	by Middlesex at Westcliff-on-Sea	1972
	41	by Shropshire at Wellington	1974

TWENTY20 COUNTY RECORDS

Highest score for	152*	G. R. Napier v Sussex at Chelmsford	2008
Highest score against	153*	L. J. Wright (Sussex) at Chelmsford	2014
Leading run-scorer	2,782	M. L. Pettini (avge 26.75)	2003–15
Best bowling for	6-16	T. G. Southee v Glamorgan at Chelmsford	2011
Best bowling against	5-11	Mushtaq Ahmed (Sussex) at Hove	2005
Leading wicket-taker	**123**	**G. R. Napier (avge 24.74)**	**2003–16**
Highest total for	242-3	v Sussex at Chelmsford	2008
Highest total against	226-3	by Sussex at Chelmsford	2014
Lowest total for	74	v Middlesex at Chelmsford	2013
Lowest total against	82	by Gloucestershire at Chelmsford	2011

ADDRESS

County Ground, New Writtle Street, Chelmsford CM2 0PG; 01245 252420; administration@essexcricket.co.uk; www.essexcricket.org.uk.

OFFICIALS

Captain R. N. ten Doeschate
Head coach C. E. W. Silverwood
President D. J. Insole
Chairman J. F. Faragher

Chief executive D. W. Bowden
Chairman, cricket committee R. C. Irani
Head groundsman S. G. Kerrison
Scorer A. E. Choat

At Cambridge, March 31–April 2. ESSEX beat CAMBRIDGE MCCU by 523 runs. *Jaik Mickleburgh scores two centuries, as Essex achieve their largest victory by runs.*

ESSEX v GLOUCESTERSHIRE

At Chelmsford, April 10–13. Essex won by ten wickets. Essex 23pts, Gloucestershire 4pts. Toss: Gloucestershire. County debut: C. T. Bancroft. Championship debuts: M. W. Dixon; J. Shaw.

Essex made a fine start to the season, as did England's captain: Cook scored 140 runs for once out, batting with his usual calm authority. His first-innings 105 was his 52nd first-class hundred, but the first for Essex since April 2014. It soon emerged that his helmet did not meet new ECB safety regulations, which required a fixed grille and a smaller gap below the peak. After initial reluctance, Cook agreed to change his helmet for Essex's next game. On the opening day, only Gloucestershire's new captain Roderick showed application, surviving more than four hours for 88. Porter bowled tidily for four wickets, and Napier grabbed three in six balls. Then Cook added 222 with Westley, who on-drove with panache – his 121 included 22 fours – before Foster and Napier extended the lead to 123. Gloucestershire's goose was cooked when three wickets fell in the first four overs of their second innings. Roderick dug in again, but only some fireworks from Taylor, with five sixes from No. 8, staved off a three-day finish.

Close of play: first day, Essex 39-1 (Cook 17, Westley 19); second day, Essex 287-6 (Ryder 13, Foster 3); third day, Essex 34-0 (Browne 26, Cook 4).

Gloucestershire

C. T. Bancroft lbw b Dixon	7	– c Foster b Porter	0
C. D. J. Dent b Dixon	27	– c Westley b Dixon	3
I. A. Cockbain c Cook b Porter	24	– c Foster b Porter	0
*†G. H. Roderick not out	88	– c Cook b Napier	58
H. J. H. Marshall c Ryder b Porter	51	– b Porter	14
B. A. C. Howell lbw b Porter	0	– c ten Doeschate b Napier	21
K. Noema-Barnett c Lawrence b Ryder	5	– lbw b Bopara	21
J. M. R. Taylor b Napier	39	– c Porter b Napier	74
J. Shaw c Porter b Napier	0	– b Bopara	0
L. C. Norwell lbw b Napier	0	– c Westley b Bopara	1
T. R. G. Hampton c Foster b Porter	0	– not out	0
B 5, lb 9, w 1, nb 6	21	Lb 1, w 6, nb 16	23
1/30 (1) 2/42 (2) 3/70 (3) (77.3 overs)	262	1/0 (1) 2/0 (3) (56.4 overs)	215
4/143 (5) 5/143 (6) 6/164 (7)		3/8 (2) 4/25 (5)	
7/239 (8) 8/245 (9) 9/245 (10) 10/262 (11)		5/70 (6) 6/108 (7) 7/173 (4)	
		8/181 (9) 9/187 (10) 10/215 (8)	

Porter 19.3–5–59–4; Dixon 17–3–64–2; Ryder 17–7–36–1; Napier 17–4–57–3; Bopara 7–2–32–0. *Second innings*—Porter 15–2–53–3; Dixon 8–3–41–1; Ryder 8–1–31–0; Napier 11.4–3–36–3; Bopara 12–1–49–3; Westley 2–0–4–0.

Essex

N. L. J. Browne lbw b Norwell	1	– not out	55
A. N. Cook lbw b Taylor	105	– not out	35
T. Westley c Roderick b Taylor	121		
R. S. Bopara b Norwell	14		
D. W. Lawrence c Marshall b Shaw	11		
J. D. Ryder c Marshall b Shaw	15		
*R. N. ten Doeschate lbw b Shaw	4		
†J. S. Foster c Roderick b Norwell	34		
G. R. Napier c Bancroft b Hampton	33		
J. A. Porter not out	20		
M. W. Dixon c Dent b Shaw	8		
Lb 12, w 1, nb 6	19	B 4	4
1/2 (1) 2/224 (2) 3/246 (3) 4/267 (4) 5/271 (5) 6/277 (7) 7/298 (6) 8/355 (9) 9/355 (8) 10/385 (11) — (120.5 overs)	385	(no wkt, 26.4 overs)	94
110 overs: 355-8			

Norwell 34–7–81–3; Shaw 34.5–10–118–4; Noema-Barnett 17–3–64–0; Hampton 14–1–73–1; Howell 10–3–22–0; Taylor 11–5–15–2. *Second innings*—Norwell 3–0–10–0; Shaw 4–1–16–0; Taylor 10–3–17–0; Noema-Barnett 2.4–0–13–0; Hampton 7–0–34–0.

Umpires: J. H. Evans and M. A. Gough.

At Hove, April 17–20. ESSEX drew with SUSSEX.

ESSEX v NORTHAMPTONSHIRE

At Chelmsford, April 24–27. Essex won by an innings and 92 runs. Essex 23pts, Northamptonshire 1pt. Toss: uncontested.

Essex made it two out of two at home with another huge victory, this time against a side lacking several first-teamers through injury. Cook, dropped by Kleinveldt at slip off Azharullah when three, took 42 balls to reach double figures, but survived to share an opening stand of 105 with Browne. The top five all passed 50; only Sanderson, who kept a tight line, troubled the batsmen on the way to his first Championship five-for. Helped by 60 extras, Essex eventually declared at 441, although by then it was well into the third day: only ten overs were possible on the second, while there was ice on the covers before the start of the third. The chilly weather continued, the players staying on through a shower of sleet. When Northamptonshire batted, Masters swung the ball appreciably, and it was soon 14 for five; Rossington cracked 67 from 73 balls, but the next best was only 20, and the follow-on was quickly imposed. There was more resistance now – nine men made it into double figures, though only Duckett passed 35. But the seamers chipped away patiently, with the Championship captain ten Doeschate taking four in an innings for the first time in nearly three years.

Close of play: first day, Essex 335-3 (Bopara 57, Lawrence 44); second day, Essex 351-3 (Bopara 66, Lawrence 51); third day, Northamptonshire 148-4 (Levi 28, Azharullah 5).

Essex

N. L. J. Browne c Levi b Sanderson	60
A. N. Cook c Rossington b Gleeson	65
T. Westley b Sanderson	64
R. S. Bopara c Kleinveldt b Sanderson	76
D. W. Lawrence c Wakely b Azharullah	51
J. D. Ryder c Rossington b Kleinveldt	1
*R. N. ten Doeschate st Rossington b Sanderson	26
†J. S. Foster not out	36
G. R. Napier c Azharullah b Sanderson	2
B 4, lb 28, nb 28	60
1/105 (1) 2/185 (2) 3/247 (3) 4/351 (5) 5/352 (6) 6/390 (4) 7/413 (7) 8/441 (9) — (8 wkts dec, 122 overs)	441
110 overs: 364-5	

D. D. Masters and J. A. Porter did not bat.

Kleinveldt 29–6–57–1; Azharullah 32–6–102–1; Gleeson 23–3–96–1; Sanderson 24–5–108–5; Cobb 10–0–31–0; Libby 4–0–15–0.

Northamptonshire

J. D. Libby c Westley b Porter	4 – c Browne b Napier	18
B. M. Duckett c Porter b Masters	0 – lbw b Porter	58
*A. G. Wakely c Cook b Masters	0 – lbw b Porter	13
J. J. Cobb c ten Doeschate b Masters	2 – c Lawrence b Napier	15
R. E. Levi lbw b Porter	0 – c Lawrence b Porter	29
†A. M. Rossington not out	67 – (7) lbw b ten Doeschate	17
D. Murphy lbw b Napier	20 – (8) c Napier b ten Doeschate	9
R. K. Kleinveldt c Westley b Porter	11 – (9) not out	35
R. J. Gleeson lbw b Porter	6 – (10) c Porter b ten Doeschate	13
Azharullah b Porter	0 – (6) lbw b ten Doeschate	11
B. W. Sanderson b Napier	3 – b Napier	0
B 4, nb 2	6 Lb 6, nb 6	12
1/0 (2) 2/0 (3) 3/4 (1) 4/6 (5) 5/14 (4) 6/75 (7) 7/95 (8) 8/115 (9) 9/115 (10) 10/119 (11) (32.5 overs)	119 1/72 (1) 2/87 (2) 3/100 (3) 4/127 (4) 5/150 (5) 6/171 (7) 7/181 (8) 8/194 (6) 9/226 (10) 10/230 (11) (78.2 overs)	230

Porter 11–2–46–5; Masters 12–3–27–3; Napier 5.5–1–23–2; Ryder 4–1–19–0. *Second innings*—Porter 18–3–55–3; Masters 13–6–30–0; Napier 21.2–5–68–3; Ryder 12–0–40–0; ten Doeschate 14–6–31–4.

Umpires: M. Burns and D. J. Millns.

At Worcester, May 1–4. ESSEX drew with WORCESTERSHIRE.

At Chelmsford, May 8–10. ESSEX drew with SRI LANKANS (see Sri Lankan tour section).

ESSEX v DERBYSHIRE

At Chelmsford, May 15–18. Drawn. Essex 11pts, Derbyshire 8pts. Toss: uncontested. Championship debut: A. P. Beard.

Godleman's decision to bowl first on a flat track seemed strange – and stranger still when Essex waltzed past 500. Bopara just missed a fifty, and Westley missed out completely, but Browne settled in for 255, his maiden double-century. Playing resolutely straight, he faced 445 balls in 552 minutes, hitting 34 fours and a six, and put on 210 with the 18-year-old Lawrence, who reached three figures for the first time since making 161 in only his second match, in 2015. Derbyshire's reply began well – they were 143 for two on the third morning – but Bopara set them back, finishing with his first five-for since August 2006, and his best first-class figures. Ten Doeschate enforced the follow-on for the second time in two home games, but Derbyshire knuckled down on the benign pitch. The openers put on 76 before Chesney Hughes went off with a migraine, then Godleman and Rutherford took the score to 136. Essex were still hopeful at the start of the last day, but rain allowed only 22 overs before the final hour, and a truce was called after two more.

HIGHEST SCORES FOR ESSEX

343*	P. A. Perrin	v Derbyshire at Chesterfield	1904
286	J. R. Freeman	v Northamptonshire at Northampton	1921
277	C. P. McGahey	v Derbyshire at Leyton	1905
275	G. A. Gooch	v Kent at Chelmsford	1988
273	A. C. Russell	v Northamptonshire at Leyton	1921
271*	A. Flower	v Northamptonshire at Northampton	2006
263	S. G. Law	v Somerset at Chelmsford	1999
259	G. A. Gooch	v Middlesex at Chelmsford	1991
255	**N. L. J. Browne**	**v Derbyshire at Chelmsford**	**2016**
254	**T. Westley**	**v Worcestershire at Chelmsford**	**2016**

Close of play: first day, Essex 284-3 (Browne 154, Lawrence 51); second day, Derbyshire 124-2 (Rutherford 28, Madsen 7); third day, Derbyshire 150-1 (Rutherford 20, Taylor 6).

Essex

N. L. J. Browne c Rutherford b Thakor	255
J. C. Mickleburgh lbw b Palladino	24
T. Westley lbw b Palladino	0
R. S. Bopara lbw b Thakor	49
D. W. Lawrence b Hughes	116
J. D. Ryder st Poynton b Thakor	51
*R. N. ten Doeschate not out	15
†J. S. Foster lbw b Thakor	17
B 1, lb 4, w 2, nb 4	11
1/61 (2) 2/70 (3) 3/181 (4) 4/391 (5) 5/505 (6) 6/506 (1) 7/538 (8) (7 wkts dec, 148.4 overs)	538
110 overs: 340-3	

G. R. Napier, A. P. Beard and J. A. Porter did not bat.

Palladino 29–6–86–2; Cotton 22–8–57–0; Thakor 26.4–2–107–4; Taylor 24–4–67–0; Critchley 21–0–106–0; Madsen 17–2–65–0; Hughes 9–0–45–1.

Derbyshire

C. F. Hughes b Bopara	37	(2) not out	66
*B. A. Godleman b Beard	43	(1) b Beard	75
H. D. Rutherford c Beard b Bopara	49	c Foster b Bopara	68
W. L. Madsen c Foster b Bopara	12	(5) lbw b Napier	2
N. T. Broom b Westley	33	(6) not out	2
S. J. Thakor c Foster b ten Doeschate	5		
†T. Poynton c Foster b Bopara	8		
M. J. J. Critchley lbw b Bopara	7		
T. A. I. Taylor b Porter	25	(4) lbw b Porter	19
A. P. Palladino not out	24		
B. D. Cotton c ten Doeschate b Beard	19		
B 6, lb 6, w 2, nb 4	18	B 9, lb 9, w 5, nb 6	29
1/65 (2) 2/91 (1) 3/143 (4) 4/158 (3) 5/178 (6) 6/200 (5) 7/200 (7) 8/207 (8) 9/245 (9) 10/280 (11) (87.2 overs)	280	1/136 (1) 2/186 (4) 3/237 (3) 4/240 (5) (4 wkts, 71 overs)	261

In the second innings Hughes, when 26, retired ill at 76-0 and resumed at 186-2.

Porter 21–4–82–1; Beard 16.2–1–67–2; Napier 17–6–33–0; Westley 5–1–5–1; Bopara 18–6–49–5; ten Doeschate 10–1–32–1. *Second innings*—Porter 14–3–49–1; Napier 21–6–59–1; Beard 14–1–59–1; Ryder 3–1–10–0; Bopara 11–4–24–1; Westley 5–0–25–0; ten Doeschate 2–0–9–0; Lawrence 1–0–8–0.

Umpires: B. J. Debenham and I. J. Gould.

At Cardiff, May 22–25. ESSEX drew with GLAMORGAN.

At Northampton, May 28–31. ESSEX drew with NORTHAMPTONSHIRE.

ESSEX v LEICESTERSHIRE

At Chelmsford, June 19–22. Leicestershire won by four wickets. Leicestershire 20pts, Essex 5pts. Toss: uncontested.

Division leaders Essex suffered their first defeat of the season, outplayed by a resurgent Leicestershire, who wrapped up their second victory in successive visits to Chelmsford, despite the loss of the second day to rain. For once Essex's openers failed to shine and, although Westley and Bopara batted well, a total of 268 was below par. Three batsmen dragged on, including Bopara, a rare victim for Cosgrove's medium-pace. Robson dominated Leicestershire's reply, hitting 74 before falling to the persistent Masters. Porter suffered an attack of the yips, aborting his run-up four times in a row, before finally making it to the crease after a pep talk from Masters. His next ball trapped Horton, at which point his problems vanished. With Bopara claiming three wickets, Essex filched a narrow lead – but wasted it with some tame batting on the final day. McKay and Shreck reprised their steady first-innings bowling, and Westley's 25 was the highest score of a disappointing effort. Leicestershire needed 159 in 33 overs, and might have struggled if Robson had been caught by Bopara at square leg off Porter on seven. Instead he survived to make his second half-century of the match, and Leicestershire sneaked home, despite a late wobble of three wickets in 21 balls.

Close of play: first day, Essex 266-9 (Masters 14, Porter 4); second day, no play; third day, Essex 22-1 (Mickleburgh 12, Quinn 1).

Essex

N. L. J. Browne lbw b McKay	7	– b McKay	8
J. C. Mickleburgh b McKay	0	– c Eckersley b Raine	18
T. Westley b Shreck	57	– (4) lbw b Taylor	25
R. S. Bopara b Cosgrove	61	– (5) c Eckersley b Shreck	2
D. W. Lawrence c Taylor b Shreck	21	– (6) c Robson b Raine	22
J. D. Ryder b McKay	18	– (7) b McKay	21
*R. N. ten Doeschate c Eckersley b Dexter	42	– (8) c Dexter b McKay	17
†J. S. Foster c Eckersley b Shreck	21	– (9) b Shreck	3
D. D. Masters not out	14	– (10) lbw b Taylor	4
M. R. Quinn c Eckersley b Shreck	5	– (3) c Raine b McKay	10
J. A. Porter b McKay	5	– not out	0
B 2, lb 15	17	B 1, lb 2	3
1/1 (2) 2/14 (1) 3/90 (3) 4/132 (5) 5/169 (6) 6/195 (4) 7/232 (7) 8/244 (8) 9/250 (10) 10/268 (11) (86.3 overs)	268	1/18 (1) 2/38 (3) 3/39 (2) 4/60 (5) 5/66 (4) 6/101 (7) 7/123 (8) 8/127 (6) 9/133 (9) 10/133 (10) (61.3 overs)	133

McKay 16.3–2–47–4; Raine 18–7–34–0; Shreck 21–3–79–4; Taylor 18–4–63–0; Dexter 10–2–23–1; Cosgrove 3–0–5–1. *Second innings*—McKay 20–9–37–4; Raine 18–6–41–2; Dexter 4–2–5–0; Shreck 10–4–13–2; Taylor 9.3–2–34–2.

Leicestershire

P. J. Horton lbw b Porter	19	– c ten Doeschate b Bopara	15
A. J. Robson c Foster b Masters	74	– c ten Doeschate b Masters	56
N. J. Dexter b Quinn	33	– (6) not out	11
*M. J. Cosgrove c Westley b Masters	11	– c Mickleburgh b Masters	38
M. L. Pettini lbw b Bopara	36	– c ten Doeschate b Bopara	16
A. M. Ali c Westley b ten Doeschate	4	– (7) c Foster b Bopara	7
†E. J. H. Eckersley c Westley b Masters	7	– (8) not out	7
B. A. Raine c Foster b Bopara	13		
R. M. L. Taylor c Lawrence b Bopara	16	– (3) b Quinn	4
C. J. McKay c Lawrence b Porter	4		
C. E. Shreck not out	0		
Lb 6, nb 20	26	Lb 5	5
1/40 (1) 2/128 (3) 3/149 (4) 4/154 (2) 5/181 (6) 6/200 (7) 7/213 (5) 8/218 (8) 9/227 (10) 10/243 (9) (78 overs)	243	1/37 (1) 2/53 (3) 3/116 (4) 4/134 (5) 5/134 (2) 6/143 (7) (6 wkts, 31.1 overs)	159

Porter 16–1–61–2; Quinn 16–2–83–1; Masters 19–6–33–3; Bopara 21–8–43–3; ten Doeschate 6–1–17–1. *Second innings*—Porter 7–1–43–0; Masters 11.1–2–41–2; Quinn 5–0–27–1; Bopara 8–0–43–3.

Umpires: R. J. Evans and P. J. Hartley.

> "'I strongly believe this book is not my story, it is the story of what God has planned and realised through me.' Heavenly choirs sing out from every page."
> **Cricket Books in 2016, page 132**

ESSEX v KENT

At Chelmsford, July 3–6. Essex won by ten wickets. Essex 24pts, Kent 2pts. Toss: Essex. County debut: C. F. Jackson. Championship debut: K. Rabada.

Essex took a firm hold early on – Kent were 48 for four after being put in – and never let go. Only Blake showed much gumption against the seamers, while in the Essex reply four batsmen made it into the eighties, including Westley, who became the first to 1,000 first-class runs for the season. It was a chastening debut for the South African fast bowler Kagiso Rabada, though he persevered to take four wickets. Batting again 362 behind, Kent were contemplating a huge defeat at 128 for seven, only for Northeast to save face alongside Tredwell, whose career-best 124 was his fourth century, but first for six years. In 80 overs they added 222, a record for Kent's eighth wicket, beating 177 by Geraint Jones and Yasir Arafat against Warwickshire at Canterbury in 2007. Quinn, the promising New Zealander, finally ended the stand, and quickly added the last two wickets. Earlier, Porter had claimed his 100th first-class scalp when he had Cowdrey caught at point. Essex's victory meant they regained first place from Kent after a week off.

Close of play: first day, Essex 107-2 (Westley 16); second day, Essex 480-6 (ten Doeschate 77, Foster 3); third day, Kent 252-7 (Northeast 116, Tredwell 62).

HIGHEST FIRST-CLASS TOTALS WITHOUT A CENTURY

	HS		
609	87	Namibia v Uganda at Windhoek	2010-11
605	90	Madhya Pradesh v Haryana at Rajnandgaon	1998-99
603	89	Surrey v Gloucestershire at Bristol	2005
581	90	Nottinghamshire v Derbyshire at Derby	1899
580	88	Islamabad v Quetta at Islamabad	2006-07
575	95	Holkar v Bengal at Indore	1953-54
569-9 dec	98	Australians v Essex at Chelmsford	2001
569	**94**	**Essex v Kent at Chelmsford**	**2016**
560-9 dec	93	Essex v Sussex at Leyton	1933
558	92	Lord Londesborough's XI v Australians at Scarborough	1886

Kent

F. K. Cowdrey b Napier	3	– c Lawrence b Porter	15
S. R. Dickson c Foster b Porter	18	– c Cook b Napier	3
J. L. Denly c Foster b Bopara	5	– lbw b Porter	2
*S. A. Northeast c Foster b Quinn	5	– not out	166
D. I. Stevens lbw b Bopara	19	– b Bopara	25
A. J. Blake not out	89	– c Bopara b Quinn	2
A. J. Ball c Mickleburgh b Porter	4	– lbw b Bopara	8
†C. F. Jackson lbw b ten Doeschate	19	– c Quinn b Bopara	4
J. C. Tredwell b Porter	4	– c ten Doeschate b Quinn	124
K. Rabada b Lawrence	14	– c Foster b Quinn	5
M. E. Claydon c Mickleburgh b Napier	6	– c Bopara b Quinn	1
B 1, lb 12, nb 8	21	B 1, lb 8, nb 6	15
1/17 (1) 2/31 (3) 3/31 (2) 4/48 (4) 5/74 (5) 6/101 (7) 7/157 (8) 8/163 (9) 9/200 (10) 10/207 (11) (62.3 overs)	207	1/18 (2) 2/18 (1) 3/29 (3) 4/86 (5) 5/89 (6) 6/116 (7) 7/128 (8) 8/350 (9) 9/356 (10) 10/370 (11) (122 overs)	370

Porter 18–3–51–3; Napier 17.3–4–54–2; Bopara 13–3–42–2; Quinn 9–1–28–1; ten Doeschate 3–0–14–1; Lawrence 2–0–5–1. *Second innings*—Porter 27–6–84–2; Napier 27–5–79–1; Quinn 24–5–60–4; Bopara 23–5–58–3; Lawrence 2–0–15–0; ten Doeschate 10–2–33–0; Westley 9–2–32–0.

Essex

N. L. J. Browne c Northeast b Rabada	33	– not out	8
A. N. Cook lbw b Rabada	49	– not out	1
T. Westley c Jackson b Claydon	88		
R. S. Bopara c Dickson b Stevens	94		
J. C. Mickleburgh c Tredwell b Ball	24		
D. W. Lawrence c sub (M. D. Hunn) b Denly	82		
*R. N. ten Doeschate c Jackson b Claydon	91		
†J. S. Foster c Stevens b Denly	49		
G. R. Napier c Jackson b Rabada	12		
M. R. Quinn lbw b Rabada	6		
J. A. Porter not out	4		
B 4, lb 5, nb 28	37		
1/84 (1) 2/107 (2) 3/276 (3) 4/298 (4) 5/357 (5) 6/458 (6) 7/514 (7) 8/527 (9) 9/565 (10) 10/569 (8) (145.3 overs) 110 overs: 409-5	569	(no wkt, 1.4 overs)	9

Rabada 34–9–118–4; Stevens 30–7–94–1; Claydon 30–6–146–2; Tredwell 28–3–108–0; Ball 14–1–63–1; Denly 9.3–0–31–2. *Second innings*—Ball 1–0–8–0; Northeast 0.4–0–1–0.

Umpires: S. A. Garratt and D. J. Millns.

At Cheltenham, July 13–16. ESSEX lost to GLOUCESTERSHIRE by 61 runs. *Matt Quinn takes 11 wickets.*

ESSEX v SUSSEX

At Colchester, August 4–7. Drawn. Essex 11pts, Sussex 12pts. Toss: Essex. Championship debuts: J. C. Archer, D. Wiese.

A docile Castle Park pitch meant a draw was always likely, though it took fine centuries from ten Doeschate and Napier – playing his last first-class match on his home club ground – to ensure against an Essex defeat after they lost early wickets clearing a deficit of 90. Napier's innings followed a tenacious five-for when Sussex batted, while another all-rounder, Jordan, did his England prospects no harm. After taking the last four wickets of Essex's first innings, he batted for more than five hours for 131, his maiden century, and put on 140 for the seventh wicket with the Championship debutant Jofra Archer – who, like Jordan, was born in Barbados. As the match petered out, Brown removed his pads and bowled three undistinguished overs (substitute Christian Davis took the gloves). He did, however, procure a maiden first-class wicket when Napier holed out at long-on, aiming for a fifth six.

Close of play: first day, Essex 337-6 (Ashar Zaidi 7, Porter 2); second day, Sussex 291-6 (Jordan 59, Archer 60); third day, Essex 163-4 (ten Doeschate 42, Foster 16).

Essex

N. L. J. Browne c Brown b Archer	55	– c Joyce b Jordan	1
J. C. Mickleburgh b Magoffin	54	– lbw b Archer	12
T. Westley c Finch b Archer	0	– c Brown b Wiese	44
D. W. Lawrence c Wells b Archer	65	– lbw b Jordan	29
*R. N. ten Doeschate b Magoffin	83	– b Wells	109
†J. S. Foster lbw b Wiese	42	– lbw b Jordan	38
Ashar Zaidi c Brown b Jordan	12	– c Wells b Briggs	15
J. A. Porter lbw b Jordan	4		
G. R. Napier not out	8	– (8) c Magoffin b Brown	124
D. D. Masters c Brown b Jordan	0	– (9) not out	47
T. C. Moore b Jordan	0	– (10) not out	4
B 12, lb 4, w 2, nb 17	35	B 13, lb 18, nb 16	47
1/108 (1) 2/108 (3) 3/160 (2) (108.5 overs)	358	1/1 (1) (8 wkts dec, 126 overs)	470
4/243 (4) 5/320 (5) 6/334 (6)		2/41 (2) 3/88 (4)	
7/347 (7) 8/348 (8) 9/350 (10) 10/358 (11)		4/111 (3) 5/210 (6)	
		6/244 (7) 7/303 (5) 8/434 (8)	

Magoffin 22–3–76–2; Jordan 30.5–7–99–4; Archer 25–4–84–3; Wiese 14–4–25–1; Briggs 12–0–39–0; Wells 5–0–19–0. *Second innings*—Magoffin 18–4–40–0; Jordan 24–5–88–3; Archer 26–5–74–1; Wiese 17–2–71–1; Briggs 23–7–60–1; Wells 15–1–58–1; Brown 3–0–48–1.

Sussex

C. D. Nash c Foster b Masters	35
E. C. Joyce c Moore b Porter	92
L. W. P. Wells c Porter b Napier	0
*L. J. Wright c Foster b Masters	16
D. Wiese c Browne b Moore	13
†B. C. Brown c Moore b Napier	6
C. J. Jordan c Moore b Napier	131
J. C. Archer c Foster b Masters	73
D. R. Briggs lbw b Napier	49
H. Z. Finch c Foster b Napier	5
S. J. Magoffin not out	4
B 1, lb 15, nb 8	24
1/124 (1) 2/127 (3) (122.2 overs)	448
3/137 (2) 4/153 (5) 5/169 (6)	
6/173 (4) 7/313 (8) 8/405 (9)	
9/439 (10) 10/448 (7) 110 overs: 392-7	

Porter 25–2–98–1; Masters 26–4–74–3; Napier 29.2–3–114–5; Moore 24–7–73–1; Ashar Zaidi 8–1–22–0; ten Doeschate 9–0–39–0; Lawrence 1–0–12–0.

Umpires: N. G. C. Cowley and R. J. Evans.

At Derby, August 13–16. ESSEX beat DERBYSHIRE by an innings and 62 runs. *Nick Browne scores his second double-century of the season against Derbyshire.*

At Leicester, August 23–25. ESSEX beat LEICESTERSHIRE by an innings and ten runs.

ESSEX v WORCESTERSHIRE

At Chelmsford, August 31–September 2. Essex won by an innings and 161 runs. Essex 24pts, Worcestershire 2pts. Toss: Worcestershire. County debut: M. L. Cummins.

Another comprehensive Essex victory was set up by the 38-year-old Masters, who wrecked Worcestershire's first innings with three wickets in his sixth over. He added Mitchell and Whiteley to make it five for two in 33 balls and, after Rhodes and Cox had put on 94, finished with seven for 52. A total of 230 was soon put in perspective – though not before the scoreless Browne offered no shot at Leach's inswinger and departed lbw. But Cook, recently returned from England duty, played second fiddle in a stand of 153 with Westley, who reached 1,000 Championship runs for the season and looked particularly strong off his legs. On he purred, adding 213 with Bopara (who just missed a century) and 165 with ten Doeschate (who made sure of his, and also passed 1,000 in the Championship). Westley was finally out for a career-best 254, from 383 balls with 38 fours, after failing to beat D'Oliveira's direct hit from backward point. The total was Essex's highest against Worcestershire, surpassing 574 at New Road in 2005. Westley was not quite done: after a stubborn fifth-wicket stand between Rhodes and Whiteley held up their victory charge, he removed both with his off-breaks. Then Napier, mixing up his deliveries, mopped up with the 17th and last five-wicket haul of his career.

Close of play: first day, Essex 111-1 (Cook 43, Westley 58); second day, Essex 512-4 (Westley 238, ten Doeschate 77).

Worcestershire

*D. K. H. Mitchell lbw b Masters	15	– b Masters	19
B. L. D'Oliveira c ten Doeschate b Masters	20	– c Foster b Napier	25
T. C. Fell lbw b Masters	0	– c Browne b Rhodes	18
J. M. Clarke b Masters	0	– b Napier	22
G. H. Rhodes c Cook b Rhodes	59	– st Foster b Westley	41
R. A. Whiteley b Masters	6	– lbw b Westley	15
†O. B. Cox c Lawrence b Porter	63	– c Porter b Masters	35
J. Leach c Lawrence b Masters	34	– b Napier	1
E. G. Barnard not out	18	– c Westley b Napier	12
J. D. Shantry c Lawrence b Rhodes	0	– c ten Doeschate b Napier	18
M. L. Cummins b Masters	4	– not out	0
Lb 3, nb 8	11	Lb 4	4
1/35 (2) 2/35 (3) 3/35 (4) 4/36 (1) 5/48 (6) 6/142 (7) 7/200 (5) 8/214 (8) 9/215 (10) 10/230 (11) (68.2 overs)	230	1/44 (1) 2/44 (2) 3/76 (4) 4/85 (3) 5/136 (6) 6/141 (5) 7/152 (8) 8/178 (9) 9/200 (7) 10/210 (10) (57.1 overs)	210

Porter 12–3–53–1; Masters 21.2–7–52–7; Napier 16–4–50–0; Bopara 10–1–30–0; Rhodes 9–1–42–2. *Second innings*—Porter 9–1–39–0; Masters 18–6–61–2; Napier 16.1–4–59–5; Rhodes 5–0–22–1; Bopara 4–0–12–0; Westley 5–1–13–2.

Essex

N. L. J. Browne lbw b Leach	0
A. N. Cook c Whiteley b Barnard	66
T. Westley run out	254
R. S. Bopara c Whiteley b Shantry	99
D. W. Lawrence c D'Oliveira b Leach	1
*R. N. ten Doeschate not out	109
†J. S. Foster not out	37
B 5, lb 22, w 4, nb 4	35
1/1 (1) 2/154 (2) 3/367 (4) 4/368 (5) 5/533 (3) (5 wkts dec, 138 overs)	601
110 overs: 452-4	

W. M. H. Rhodes, G. R. Napier, D. D. Masters and J. A. Porter did not bat.

Cummins 28–3–114–0; Leach 29–3–107–2; Barnard 24–2–112–1; Shantry 34–4–135–1; Rhodes 17.2–1–80–0; D'Oliveira 0.4–0–3–0; Mitchell 5–0–23–0.

Umpires: N. L. Bainton and N. A. Mallender.

ESSEX v GLAMORGAN

At Chelmsford, September 12–15. Glamorgan won by 11 runs. Glamorgan 21pts, Essex 6pts. Toss: Glamorgan.

Essex collected the five points they needed to clinch the second division title, but some of the gloss was removed when they narrowly failed to chase down 264. They had looked set for another victory after reducing Glamorgan to 34 for five on the opening day, only for 18-year-old Kiran Carlson, in only his third match, to become their youngest first-class centurion, beating the record set by Mike Llewellyn in 1972. Carlson put on 133 for the eighth wicket with Morgan, before Essex slipped to 85 for five. But Wheater added 100 with ten Doeschate, who at 5.27 on the second day collected the single – and the bonus point – that sealed their title. He went on to complete his third home hundred in a row. Career-best figures for Meschede restricted the lead to 33, before Essex's seamers grabbed the initiative on the third afternoon, as Glamorgan declined from 127 for one to 163 for seven. Led by Wallace, however, the last three wickets took the total close to 300. Essex's chase started brightly, before three wickets went down in the nineties. Chopra made a tidy 79 in his first game for the club for seven years, after rejoining from Warwickshire, but Hogan and van der Gugten made regular inroads; Glamorgan's victory, completed with 19 balls to spare, meant they avoided the wooden spoon. The match began 90 minutes late because Glamorgan's kit van had been delayed by an accident on the nearby A12; the ECB refused a request to make up the overs lost.

Close of play: first day, Glamorgan 256-7 (Carlson 101, Morgan 51); second day, Essex 275-6 (ten Doeschate 109, Foster 33); third day, Glamorgan 293-9 (Wallace 75, Hogan 0).

Glamorgan

N. J. Selman b Porter	14	– lbw b Masters	9
*J. A. Rudolph c Westley b Napier	16	– b ten Doeschate	56
W. D. Bragg lbw b Napier	0	– c Foster b ten Doeschate	54
A. H. T. Donald b Napier	4	– b Porter	8
D. L. Lloyd c Chopra b Porter	0	– lbw b Bopara	25
K. S. Carlson c Foster b Masters	119	– c Foster b Bopara	1
C. A. J. Meschede c Porter b Napier	22	– c Foster b Porter	0
†M. A. Wallace b Bopara	29	– run out	78
A. O. Morgan b Porter	55	– lbw b Masters	18
T. van der Gugten not out	6	– c Bopara b Lawrence	32
M. G. Hogan c Chopra b Masters	0	– not out	0
Lb 6, w 2, nb 13	21	B 4, lb 5, nb 6	15
1/30 (2) 2/30 (3) 3/30 (1) 4/34 (5) 5/34 (4) 6/83 (7) 7/127 (8) 8/260 (9) 9/286 (6) 10/286 (11) (96.3 overs)	286	1/36 (1) 2/127 (2) 3/130 (3) 4/149 (4) 5/158 (6) 6/159 (7) 7/163 (5) 8/217 (9) 9/285 (10) 10/296 (8) (82.2 overs)	296

Porter 23–6–67–3; Masters 24.3–8–58–2; Napier 15–3–46–4; Bopara 23–3–63–1; ten Doeschate 5–0–33–0; Westley 5–0–10–0; Lawrence 1–0–3–0. *Second innings*—Porter 13–3–51–2; Masters 25.2–7–69–2; Bopara 20–3–93–2; Westley 14–1–41–0; ten Doeschate 7–1–20–2; Lawrence 3–1–13–1.

Essex

V. Chopra lbw b Meschede	1	– b Hogan	79
N. L. J. Browne c Wallace b Meschede	22	– c Bragg b van der Gugten	30
T. Westley c Wallace b Meschede	4	– lbw b Hogan	0
D. W. Lawrence c Donald b van der Gugten	9	– (5) b Hogan	30
R. S. Bopara st Wallace b Morgan	25	– (4) lbw b van der Gugten	1
A. J. A. Wheater c Selman b Morgan	59	– c and b Hogan	18
*R. N. ten Doeschate lbw b van der Gugten	117	– c Wallace b Hogan	23
†J. S. Foster c Rudolph b Meschede	64	– c Wallace b Meschede	23
G. R. Napier c Lloyd b Meschede	0	– lbw b van der Gugten	12
D. D. Masters c and b Hogan	4	– not out	19
J. A. Porter not out	0	– b van der Gugten	2
Lb 2, w 4, nb 8	14	Lb 15	15
1/16 (1) 2/21 (3) 3/34 (2) 4/63 (4) 5/85 (5) 6/185 (6) 7/289 (7) 8/296 (9) 9/319 (10) 10/319 (8) (92.5 overs)	319	1/92 (2) 2/93 (3) 3/98 (4) 4/138 (1) 5/147 (5) 6/187 (7) 7/200 (6) 8/223 (9) 9/229 (8) 10/252 (11) (87.5 overs)	252

Meschede 24.5–3–84–5; van der Gugten 24–3–99–2; Hogan 20–3–61–1; Morgan 19–4–55–2; Lloyd 2–0–9–0; Carlson 3–1–9–0. *Second innings*—Meschede 18–0–78–1; van der Gugten 29.5–5–56–4; Hogan 22–4–45–5; Morgan 11–1–27–0; Carlson 3–0–17–0; Lloyd 4–1–14–0.

Umpires: R. J. Evans and S. J. O'Shaughnessy.

At Canterbury, September 20–23. ESSEX drew with KENT.

GLAMORGAN

Croft's nursery of saplings

EDWARD BEVAN

Robert Croft's first year as coach had its moments, but was not helped by injuries to key players. Glamorgan endured a terrible season in the Championship, losing eight games – their most since 2007 – although three victories at least ensured they finished ahead of winless Derbyshire. Their limited-overs form was equally patchy: after winning their first three Royal London Cup games, Glamorgan lost the next four, while in the T20 Blast they scraped through to the quarter-finals, where a Cardiff crowd of over 10,000 watched Yorkshire bowl them out for 90.

The main problem in the four-day games was a knee injury to the South African Colin Ingram, who was outstanding in white-ball cricket – Player of the Tournament in the T20 Blast, in which he also won Sky's award for most sixes – but missed the entire Championship campaign. He returned home early for an operation. Chris Cooke, suffering from back trouble, played only seven Championship matches and missed a dozen one-day games.

Equally damaging was the fact that the captain Jacques Rudolph, who had enjoyed two productive years in all formats, endured a wretched summer, managing only 659 runs at 24 in the Championship. Rudolph, who turns 36 in May, was eventually reappointed for another season.

In contrast to 2015, when they had won four successive Championship matches by late June, Glamorgan's first victory did not come until July, over Derbyshire at Colwyn Bay. They had earlier wasted an opportunity against Gloucestershire: set 269 at Bristol, they reached 87 without loss, then all ten fell for 56. Glamorgan later beat Worcestershire and table-topping Essex, but an all-too-familiar collapse in the final match against Leicestershire epitomised a summer in which they collected just 34 batting points (only Derbyshire managed fewer). Needing 181 at Grace Road, Glamorgan were cruising at 144 for four before the last six wickets folded for just ten runs.

Will Bragg was alone in reaching 1,000 runs in the Championship, although Aneurin Donald fell 17 short. Glamorgan again lacked a solid opening combination, even if Nick Selman showed enough promise in his ten matches to suggest he could settle into the role. He made four successive ducks after carrying his bat for a maiden century against Northamptonshire at Swansea, but recovered to add another hundred, against Gloucestershire, in September. David Lloyd also made the first centuries of his career, and excelled as a Twenty20 opener, but lost form. Mark Wallace, dropped after the first Championship match, soon returned to tot up 611 runs, and 54 dismissals – only Warwickshire's Tim Ambrose made more. Early in 2017, Wallace – who made his debut for Glamorgan aged 17 in 1999 – announced his retirement to take up a post at the PCA.

Nigel French, PA Photos

Timm van der Gugten

The pace attack was in safe hands. Timm van der Gugten – born in Sydney but a Dutch international – was almost unknown when he was signed, but ended as Glamorgan's leading wicket-taker in Championship and Twenty20 cricket, and was named Player of the Year. Michael Hogan, now 35, was used as a third seamer, and underlined his commitment and fitness to take 49 wickets in the Championship, with a frugal economy-rate of 2.57. Hogan and van der Gugten sent down 950 overs between them, while Graham Wagg and Craig Meschede also made useful contributions. Wagg backed up 37 wickets for his seam bowling by frequently supplying important runs after the regular early setbacks, and finished with nearly 700.

At the start of the season, Andrew Salter had been Glamorgan's first-choice spinner, but he managed only seven expensive wickets in seven Championship appearances. After being hailed as one of the most promising young slow bowlers around – he was monitored by Peter Such, the ECB's national spin coach – Salter struggled for consistency. In Croft, though, he has the ideal mentor.

Croft himself described Glamorgan's season as "disappointing but encouraging", which seemed fair: not for many years have so many young Welsh-born players shone. The 19-year-old Donald hammered 234 against Derbyshire at Colwyn Bay, reaching 200 in 123 balls to match Ravi Shastri's world record for the fastest first-class double-century. Kiran Carlson, just 18, took five for 28 at Northampton on debut with his off-breaks, and hit 119 against Essex two matches later – Glamorgan's youngest first-class centurion. Lukas Carey, another 19-year-old, took seven wickets on his Championship debut, against Northamptonshire at Swansea. And Owen Morgan, a comparative veteran at 22, made a century after coming in as nightwatchman to help secure the win at Worcester.

Glamorgan said farewell to Dean Cosker, a loyal servant over 21 years. His accurate left-arm spin accounted for 597 first-class victims, and he became the first Glamorgan bowler to claim 100 in Twenty20 cricket. James Kettleborough and Dewi Penrhyn Jones were also released.

As debate continued over the future of domestic Twenty20 cricket, chief executive Hugh Morris remained hopeful that Cardiff would host one of the mooted city-based teams; two well-attended one-day internationals in 2016 backed up his optimism.

Championship attendance: 13,113.

GLAMORGAN RESULTS

All first-class matches – Played 17: Won 3, Lost 8, Drawn 6.
County Championship matches – Played 16: Won 3, Lost 8, Drawn 5.

Specsavers County Championship, 8th in Division 2;
NatWest T20 Blast, quarter-finalists; Royal London One-Day Cup, 7th in South Group.

COUNTY CHAMPIONSHIP AVERAGES, BATTING AND FIELDING

Cap		*Birthplace*	*M*	*I*	*NO*	*R*	*HS*	*100*	*Avge*	*Ct/St*
2016	C. B. Cooke	*Johannesburg, SA*	7	13	2	421	63	0	38.27	6
2013	G. G. Wagg	*Rugby*	13	22	3	693	106	1	36.47	5
2015	†W. D. Bragg	*Newport‡*	16	31	1	1,088	161*	2	36.26	10
	A. H. T. Donald	*Swansea‡*	16	30	1	983	234	1	33.89	12
	K. S. Carlson	*Cardiff‡*	4	8	1	227	119	1	32.42	1
	A. O. Morgan	*Swansea‡*	9	17	3	406	103*	1	29.00	3
2003	†M. A. Wallace	*Abergavenny‡*	14	26	4	611	78	0	27.77	53/1
	N. J. Selman	*Brisbane, Australia*	10	19	2	470	122*	2	27.64	7
	D. L. Lloyd	*St Asaph‡*	15	27	1	712	107	2	27.38	5
2014	†J. A. Rudolph¶	*Springs, SA*	15	29	2	659	87	0	24.40	10
	C. A. J. Meschede	*Johannesburg, SA*	13	22	4	431	78	0	23.94	3
	A. G. Salter	*Haverfordwest‡*	7	11	3	171	45*	0	21.37	5
	J. M. Kettleborough	*Huntingdon*	3	6	0	107	42	0	17.83	2
2013	M. G. Hogan††	*Newcastle, Aust.*	15	22	6	191	30	0	11.93	8
	T. van der Gugten††	*Hornsby, Australia*	13	20	4	159	36	0	9.93	2
	H. W. Podmore	*Hammersmith*	2	4	1	24	16*	0	8.00	0
	L. J. Carey	*Carmarthen‡*	3	5	1	12	11	0	3.00	1

Also batted: R. A. J. Smith (*Glasgow*) (1 match) 25, 0 (1 ct).

‡ *Born in Wales.* ¶ *Official overseas player.* †† *Other non-England-qualified.*

BOWLING

	Style	*O*	*M*	*R*	*W*	*BB*	*5I*	*Avge*
L. J. Carey	RFM	84.4	13	330	13	4-92	0	25.38
T. van der Gugten	RFM	450	72	1,458	56	5-52	5	26.03
M. G. Hogan	RFM	500.4	139	1,287	49	5-36	2	26.26
G. G. Wagg	SLA/LM	421	69	1,397	37	5-90	1	37.75
C. A. J. Meschede	RM	351.5	65	1,168	27	5-84	1	43.25
A. O. Morgan	SLA	232	34	740	13	2-37	0	56.92
D. L. Lloyd	RM	149.1	17	583	10	3-36	0	58.30

Also bowled: W. D. Bragg (RM) 9–1–29–0; K. S. Carlson (OB) 45–7–178–6; H. W. Podmore (RM) 54.3–5–225–6; J. A. Rudolph (LBG) 25.5–4–58–2; A. G. Salter (OB) 136–13–492–7; N. J. Selman (RM) 3–1–8–0; R. A. J. Smith (RM) 14–3–51–1.

LEADING ROYAL LONDON CUP AVERAGES (100 runs/4 wickets)

Batting

	Runs	*HS*	*Avge*	*SR*	*Ct*
C. A. Ingram	367	107	61.16	126.55	4
J. A. Rudolph	233	53	38.83	67.14	1
C. B. Cooke	150	80	37.50	113.63	4
W. D. Bragg	260	75	37.14	90.90	1
D. L. Lloyd	253	65	36.14	93.01	3
G. G. Wagg	152	52	21.71	107.04	6
A. H. T. Donald	109	53	15.57	77.30	4

Bowling

	W	*BB*	*Avge*	*ER*
C. A. Ingram	6	3-38	27.50	5.00
G. G. Wagg	11	2-48	37.36	6.30
M. G. Hogan	11	4-41	39.09	6.00
T. van der Gugten	7	3-33	43.42	6.44
C. A. J. Meschede	7	2-30	48.14	5.18

LEADING NATWEST T20 BLAST AVERAGES (100 runs/20 overs)

Batting	Runs	HS	Avge	SR	Ct/St
C. A. Ingram	502	101	41.83	**164.59**	10
D. L. Lloyd	382	97*	29.38	**129.49**	5
A. H. T. Donald	235	55	26.11	**128.41**	6
M. A. Wallace	180	69*	25.71	**108.43**	3/1
J. A. Rudolph	210	40*	21.00	**99.05**	6

Bowling	W	BB	Avge	ER
M. G. Hogan	16	4-28	17.25	**6.81**
D. A. Cosker	8	2-19	20.75	**6.82**
T. van der Gugten	19	4-14	14.10	**6.87**
C. A. J. Meschede	9	2-16	23.00	**7.34**
C. A. Ingram	9	4-32	18.11	**7.76**
G. G. Wagg	13	3-38	20.38	**8.50**

FIRST-CLASS COUNTY RECORDS

Highest score for	309*	S. P. James v Sussex at Colwyn Bay	2000
Highest score against	322*	M. B. Loye (Northamptonshire) at Northampton	1998
Leading run-scorer	34,056	A. Jones (avge 33.03)	1957–83
Best bowling for	10-51	J. Mercer v Worcestershire at Worcester	1936
Best bowling against	10-18	G. Geary (Leicestershire) at Pontypridd	1929
Leading wicket-taker	2,174	D. J. Shepherd (avge 20.95)	1950–72
Highest total for	718-3 dec	v Sussex at Colwyn Bay	2000
Highest total against	712	by Northamptonshire at Northampton	1998
Lowest total for	22	v Lancashire at Liverpool	1924
Lowest total against	33	by Leicestershire at Ebbw Vale	1965

LIST A COUNTY RECORDS

Highest score for	169*	J. A. Rudolph v Sussex at Hove	2014
Highest score against	268	A. D. Brown (Surrey) at The Oval	2002
Leading run-scorer	12,278	M. P. Maynard (avge 37.66)	1985–2005
Best bowling for	7-16	S. D. Thomas v Surrey at Swansea	1998
Best bowling against	7-30	M. P. Bicknell (Surrey) at The Oval	1999
Leading wicket-taker	356	R. D. B. Croft (avge 31.96)	1989–2012
Highest total for	429	v Surrey at The Oval	2002
Highest total against	438-5	by Surrey at The Oval	2002
Lowest total for	42	v Derbyshire at Swansea	1979
Lowest total against	59	by Combined Universities at Cambridge	1983
	59	by Sussex at Hove	1996

TWENTY20 COUNTY RECORDS

Highest score for	116*	I. J. Thomas v Somerset at Taunton	2004
Highest score against	117	M. J. Prior (Sussex) at Hove	2010
Leading run-scorer	1,578	J. Allenby (avge 33.57)	2010–14
Best bowling for	5-14	G. G. Wagg v Worcestershire at Worcester	2013
Best bowling against	6-5	A. V. Suppiah (Somerset) at Cardiff	2011
Leading wicket-taker	**100**	**D. A. Cosker (avge 30.32)**	**2003–16**
Highest total for	240-3	v Surrey at The Oval	2015
Highest total against	239-5	by Sussex at Hove	2010
Lowest total for	**90**	**v Yorkshire at Cardiff**	**2016**
Lowest total against	81	by Gloucestershire at Bristol	2011

ADDRESS

The SSE SWALEC, Sophia Gardens, Cardiff CF11 9XR; 029 2040 9380; info@glamorgancricket.co.uk; www.glamorgancricket.com.

OFFICIALS

Captain J. A. Rudolph
Head coach R. D. B. Croft
Head of talent development R. V. Almond
President A. Jones
Chairman B. J. O'Brien
Chief executive and director of cricket H. Morris
Head groundsman R. Saxton
Scorer/archivist A. K. Hignell

GLAMORGAN v CARDIFF MCCU

At Cardiff, April 11–13. Drawn. Toss: Glamorgan. First-class debut: R. D. Edwards. County debut: T. van der Gugten.

This match turned into extended middle practice after the first day was lost to rain. Glamorgan's top four all got starts, before maiden centuries for David Lloyd and Aneurin Donald – who, at 19, became the county's second-youngest first-class centurion, after Mike Llewellyn against Cambridge at Swansea in 1972. Wallace smacked a 28-ball half-century as Glamorgan continued briefly on the final day, when the students showed admirable resolve, losing only one wicket. Jeremy Lawlor, who had played in Glamorgan's final home Championship match of 2015 (when he suffered a pair), made an attractive 77, and shared an opening stand of 142 with Brad Scriven.

Close of play: first day, no play; second day, Glamorgan 444-7 (Meschede 27, Wallace 2).

Glamorgan

*J. A. Rudolph lbw b Thomson	29
J. M. Kettleborough c Herring b Turpin	32
W. D. Bragg b Thomson	38
C. B. Cooke c Lawlor b Turpin	44
D. L. Lloyd retired out	105
A. H. T. Donald retired out	105
G. G. Wagg c sub (C. R. Brown) b Rouse	43
C. A. J. Meschede not out	60
†M. A. Wallace not out	58
B 2, lb 5, nb 12	19
1/46 (2) 2/86 (1) 3/107 (3) 4/177 (4) 5/331 (5) 6/388 (6) 7/430 (7) (7 wkts dec, 107 overs)	533

M. G. Hogan and T. van der Gugten did not bat.

Westphal 19–4–105–0; Edwards 13–1–56–0; Turpin 16–2–63–2; Lawlor 8–1–38–0; Griffiths 18–3–94–0; Thomson 13.4–1–45–2; Brand 11.2–1–63–0; Rouse 8–0–62–1.

Cardiff MCCU

J. L. Lawlor c van der Gugten b Lloyd	77
B. R. M. Scriven not out	67
*N. Brand not out	16
Lb 3, w 1, nb 2	6
1/142 (1) (1 wkt dec, 58 overs)	166

†C. L. Herring, T. D. Rouse, G. C. Holmes, S. W. Griffiths, A. T. Thompson, R. D. Edwards, A. A. Westphal and J. R. Turpin did not bat.

Wagg 13–4–29–0; Hogan 12–1–35–0; van der Gugten 11–2–27–0; Meschede 9–2–31–0; Lloyd 12–3–40–1; Rudolph 1–0–1–0.

Umpires: I. D. Blackwell and A. G. Wharf.

GLAMORGAN v LEICESTERSHIRE

At Cardiff, April 17–20. Leicestershire won by ten wickets. Leicestershire 23pts, Glamorgan 5pts. Toss: Glamorgan. Championship debut: T. van der Gugten.

Aiming to avoid a fourth successive wooden spoon, Leicestershire finished Glamorgan off midway through the last day. Their varied seam attack did the damage: McKay and Shreck shared nine wickets in the first innings, while the lively Raine grabbed four in the second, as Glamorgan were bundled out for 191, setting a target of just 113. They had made 348 first time round, which proved below par on a benign pitch. Four batsmen made fifties, but the top score was Wagg's 64. After a solid start, Leicestershire lost three quick wickets – and it could have been worse, as three slip chances went begging in finger-numbing cold – before O'Brien shored up the reply with 93. McKay then thrashed a dozen boundaries to swell the lead to 79. Glamorgan quickly slipped to 29 for three and, although Rudolph and Donald put on 60, the seamers worked their way through, helped by two run-outs; O'Brien held five catches. Leicestershire knocked off the runs without alarm, Horton making a second half-century in his first Championship match since leaving Lancashire.

Close of play: first day, Leicestershire 15-0 (Horton 6, Robson 4); second day, Leicestershire 297-6 (White 42, Raine 8); third day, Glamorgan 172-8 (Wagg 19, Hogan 19).

Glamorgan

*J. A. Rudolph c O'Brien b McKay	6	– (2) c O'Brien b Shreck	39
J. M. Kettleborough lbw b McKay	18	– (1) c O'Brien b McKay	5
W. D. Bragg c Robson b McKay	50	– b McKay	0
C. B. Cooke c Naik b Shreck	56	– c O'Brien b Raine	8
A. H. T. Donald b McKay	1	– c O'Brien b Shreck	57
D. L. Lloyd c O'Brien b Dexter	59	– run out	18
G. G. Wagg c and b Shreck	64	– run out	33
C. A. J. Meschede c Cosgrove b McKay	44	– lbw b Raine	1
†M. A. Wallace lbw b McKay	9	– lbw b Raine	0
M. G. Hogan not out	21	– c O'Brien b Raine	23
T. van der Gugten c O'Brien b Shreck	11	– not out	1
Lb 7, nb 2	9	B 2, lb 2, nb 2	6
1/24 (2) 2/25 (1) 3/132 (4) 4/132 (3) 5/133 (5) 6/231 (6) 7/294 (7) 8/307 (9) 9/322 (8) 10/348 (11) (89.3 overs)	348	1/16 (1) 2/16 (3) 3/29 (4) 4/89 (2) 5/130 (6) 6/132 (5) 7/133 (8) 8/133 (9) 9/177 (10) 10/191 (7) (53.3 overs)	191

McKay 20–3–73–6; Raine 19–4–70–0; Dexter 16–6–55–1; Shreck 19.3–3–72–3; White 7–0–35–0; Naik 8–1–36–0. *Second innings*—McKay 13–4–38–2; Raine 16.3–4–57–4; Shreck 14–0–58–2; Dexter 2–0–8–0; White 8–2–26–0.

Leicestershire

P. J. Horton lbw b Meschede	67	– not out	64
A. J. Robson c Rudolph b Hogan	25	– not out	49
N. J. Dexter c Donald b Lloyd	4		
*M. J. Cosgrove c Wallace b Lloyd	0		
†N. J. O'Brien c Wallace b Wagg	93		
M. L. Pettini lbw b van der Gugten	27		
W. A. White lbw b Hogan	58		
B. A. Raine c Wallace b Meschede	22		
C. J. McKay c Kettleborough b Wagg	65		
J. K. H. Naik not out	26		
C. E. Shreck lbw b Rudolph	0		
B 8, lb 15, w 3, nb 14	40	Nb 2	2
1/89 (2) 2/99 (3) 3/99 (4) 4/142 (1) 5/224 (6) 6/280 (5) 7/324 (7) 8/353 (8) 9/421 (9) 10/427 (11) (132.2 overs) 110 overs: 370-8	427	(no wkt, 36.1 overs)	115

Hogan 31–6–78–2; Wagg 32–5–96–2; Meschede 24–5–91–2; van der Gugten 26–4–69–1; Lloyd 14–1–61–2; Rudolph 5.2–2–9–1. *Second innings*—Hogan 5–0–20–0; Meschede 6–1–16–0; van der Gugten 4–0–16–0; Wagg 12–1–36–0; Lloyd 9.1–2–27–0.

Umpires: S. A. Garratt and S. J. O'Shaughnessy.

At Derby, April 24–27. GLAMORGAN drew with DERBYSHIRE.

At Canterbury, May 1–4. GLAMORGAN lost to KENT by ten wickets.

GLAMORGAN v WORCESTERSHIRE

At Cardiff, May 8–11. Drawn. Glamorgan 5pts (after 1pt penalty), Worcestershire 11pts. Toss: Worcestershire. First-class debut: N. J. Selman. County debut: M. J. Santner.

There was no play after tea on the second day, which probably saved Glamorgan from their third Championship defeat of the season. They had lurched to 42 for four after Worcestershire amassed 456, mainly thanks to Brett D'Oliveira, who followed his father Damian and grandfather Basil in making a first-class double-century, a feat unmatched in first-class cricket. Only five families had previously provided three generations of centurions: the Townsends (Frank, Charles and David), Khans (Jahangir, Majid and Bazid), Mohammads (Hanif, Shoaib and Shehzar), Huttons (Len, Richard and Ben) and Gaekwads (Datta, Anshuman and Shatrunjay). A week after his maiden Championship hundred, D'Oliveira batted for 492 minutes, hit 32 fours from 359 balls, and shared a third-wicket stand of 253 with Clarke, whose attractive 133 was his third Championship century. When Glamorgan batted, Leach took two wickets in two balls in his second over, but the rain set in about an hour later. It was more frustration for Worcestershire, still without a Championship victory after four games, the first of which had been completely washed out.

Close of play: first day, Worcestershire 343-2 (D'Oliveira 152, Clarke 105); second day, Glamorgan 42-4 (Cooke 27, Donald 0); third day, no play.

Worcestershire

*D. K. H. Mitchell lbw b Meschede	3	M. J. Santner not out	23
B. L. D'Oliveira not out	202	B 5, lb 7, w 7, nb 10	29
M. M. Ali c Wallace b Wagg	55		—
J. M. Clarke c Wallace b Meschede	133	1/26 (1) (6 wkts dec, 120.2 overs)	456
T. Köhler-Cadmore c Rudolph b Wagg	10	2/134 (3) 3/387 (4)	
R. A. Whiteley c Wallace b Hogan	0	4/406 (5) 5/409 (6)	
†O. B. Cox c Bragg b Wagg	1	6/410 (7) 110 overs: 406-4	

J. Leach, E. G. Barnard and J. D. Shantry did not bat.

Meschede 24–3–99–2; van der Gugten 27–7–92–0; Wagg 25–7–103–3; Hogan 26.2–7–82–1; Lloyd 12–1–46–0; Selman 2–1–2–0; Rudolph 4–0–20–0.

Glamorgan

N. J. Selman lbw b Leach	4	A. H. T. Donald not out	0
†M. A. Wallace b Barnard	4	Nb 2	2
W. D. Bragg c Köhler-Cadmore b Leach	0		—
*J. A. Rudolph run out	5	1/8 (1) 2/8 (3) (4 wkts, 20 overs)	42
C. B. Cooke not out	27	3/8 (2) 4/40 (4)	

D. L. Lloyd, G. G. Wagg, C. A. J. Meschede, T. van der Gugten and M. G. Hogan did not bat.

Leach 8–4–15–2; Barnard 6–1–19–1; Shantry 6–3–8–0.

Umpires: J. W. Lloyds and P. R. Pollard.

At Bristol, May 15–18. GLAMORGAN lost to GLOUCESTERSHIRE by 125 runs.

GLAMORGAN v ESSEX

At Cardiff, May 22–25. Drawn. Glamorgan 10pts, Essex 10pts. Toss: uncontested.

Glamorgan remained rooted to the bottom of the table, with no wins out of six, despite a better all-round performance against the leaders. In an uncertain start, only Cooke made much headway against the seam movement of Napier, although Meschede and Salter later put on 79 for the eighth wicket. Twin 80s from Westley and Bopara ushered Essex towards a lead, but it was restricted by Timm van der Gugten, a Sydney-born seamer who has played for the Netherlands – and now claimed his maiden Championship five-for. Rudolph, forced to retire in the first innings after being hit on the finger by Napier, fell without scoring in the second, but the deficit was cleared without further loss. Out for a duck on the opening day, Bragg – often criticised for failing to convert fifties to hundreds – batted for more than seven hours, shared three successive century stands, and was on a career-best 161 when Rudolph's cautious declaration left Essex 334 in 70 overs. Glamorgan fancied their chances at 46 for three, but Browne survived more than three hours, and Ryder 98 minutes for 25. Verdayne Smith, a Jamaican schoolmaster, was standing under an exchange scheme with the West Indian board.

Close of play: first day, Essex 29-1 (Mickleburgh 10, Westley 14); second day, Essex 300-9 (ten Doeschate 43, Porter 4); third day, Glamorgan 295-3 (Bragg 119, Donald 44).

Glamorgan

*J. A. Rudolph lbw b Masters	27	– c Foster b Masters	0
†M. A. Wallace c Foster b Napier	27	– c Foster b Bopara	40
W. D. Bragg c Bopara b Napier	0	– not out	161
C. B. Cooke c Westley b Porter	63	– lbw b Masters	59
A. H. T. Donald b Masters	12	– c Foster b Napier	55
D. L. Lloyd lbw b Bopara	15	– c Browne b Masters	4
G. G. Wagg b Napier	7	– b Napier	25
C. A. J. Meschede c Foster b Porter	33	– c Mickleburgh b Westley	1
A. G. Salter not out	45	– c Browne b Westley	6
T. van der Gugten lbw b Napier	4		
M. G. Hogan b Napier	5		
B 7, lb 7, nb 8	22	B 5, lb 22, nb 8	35
1/43 (3) 2/96 (2) 3/101 (1) (75.4 overs)	260	1/2 (1) (8 wkts dec, 114.5 overs)	386
4/125 (5) 5/146 (4) 6/156 (6)		2/109 (2) 3/215 (4)	
7/164 (7) 8/243 (8) 9/248 (10) 10/260 (11)		4/332 (5) 5/342 (6)	
		6/379 (7) 7/380 (8) 8/386 (9)	

In the first innings Rudolph, when 27, retired hurt at 43-0 and resumed at 96-2.

Porter 14–0–66–2; Masters 19–3–46–2; Napier 20.4–3–82–5; Bopara 16–4–36–1; ten Doeschate 6–2–16–0. *Second innings*—Masters 36–8–95–3; Porter 20–4–54–0; Bopara 12–2–39–1; Napier 27–2–91–2; Ryder 3–1–15–0; Westley 14.5–1–55–2; ten Doeschate 2–0–10–0.

Essex

N. L. J. Browne lbw b Wagg	3	– lbw b Wagg	71
J. C. Mickleburgh b van der Gugten	33	– c Hogan b van der Gugten	4
T. Westley c Wallace b Hogan	80	– c Donald b van der Gugten	8
R. S. Bopara c Cooke b Hogan	80	– c Donald b Hogan	6
D. W. Lawrence lbw b Lloyd	13	– b Hogan	24
J. D. Ryder b Wagg	17	– not out	25
*R. N. ten Doeschate c Wallace b van der Gugten	48	– not out	22
†J. S. Foster lbw b van der Gugten	9		
G. R. Napier lbw b van der Gugten	5		
D. D. Masters b van der Gugten	6		
J. A. Porter not out	8		
Lb 3, nb 8	11		
1/3 (1) 2/69 (2) 3/162 (3) (115 overs)	313	1/12 (2) (5 wkts, 63 overs)	160
4/178 (5) 5/233 (4) 6/237 (6) 7/254 (8)		2/30 (3) 3/46 (4)	
8/272 (9) 9/288 (10) 10/313 (7) 110 overs: 297-9		4/78 (5) 5/122 (1)	

Van der Gugten 32–6–90–5; Wagg 26–4–90–2; Hogan 26–14–45–2; Meschede 21–10–50–0; Lloyd 6–0–17–1; Salter 4–1–18–0. *Second innings*—Wagg 17–4–49–1; van der Gugten 16–5–37–2; Meschede 6–3–9–0; Hogan 10–5–10–2; Lloyd 2–0–12–0; Salter 12–2–43–0.

Umpires: R. J. Bailey and V. M. Smith.

GLAMORGAN v KENT

At Cardiff, June 19–22. Drawn. Glamorgan 12pts, Kent 10pts. Toss: uncontested.

Glamorgan had beaten Kent twice in white-ball cricket the previous week, but the weather – which accounted for nearly 120 overs – scuppered hopes of a hat-trick. Three wickets from Claydon had helped reduce them to 137 for six, before Wagg and Meschede added 160 (a county seventh-wicket record in this fixture) at around five an over. Kent also made a poor start, dipping to 85 for five, and were bailed out in turn by Dickson, putting on 72 with Rouse, who temporarily retired hurt. Finally Tredwell inched Kent to within 69 of Glamorgan's total, but by then the third day was nearly over.

Van der Gugten claimed his second successive five-for, while Hogan's two wickets included his 200th in Championship cricket. Sam Billings had been expected to keep wicket for Kent, but was injured in the nets before the game; Rouse stepped in, but dislocated a finger on the second day, then broke it while batting on the third. Latham deputised briefly, before Callum Jackson arrived on the fourth day and caught Wallace, his opposite number.

Close of play: first day, Glamorgan 93-2 (Bragg 33, Cooke 42); second day, Kent 10-0 (Bell-Drummond 8, Latham 2); third day, Glamorgan 22-0 (Rudolph 7, Wallace 12).

Glamorgan

*J. A. Rudolph lbw b Stevens	6	– c Haggett b Claydon	11
†M. A. Wallace b Coles	0	– c sub (C. F. Jackson) b Coles	52
W. D. Bragg c Rouse b Claydon	35	– b Coles	22
C. B. Cooke c Latham b Claydon	46	– lbw b Claydon	17
A. H. T. Donald c Rouse b Claydon	9	– lbw b Tredwell	67
D. L. Lloyd c Tredwell b Haggett	26	– c Latham b Claydon	0
G. G. Wagg c Tredwell b Claydon	83	– not out	64
C. A. J. Meschede c Rouse b Haggett	78	– not out	23
A. G. Salter not out	20		
T. van der Gugten c Rouse b Haggett	4		
M. G. Hogan c Rouse b Claydon	20		
B 5, lb 9, nb 10	24	B 6, lb 11, w 2, nb 4	23
1/5 (2) 2/7 (1) 3/95 (3) 4/100 (4) 5/129 (5) 6/137 (6) 7/297 (7) 8/308 (8) 9/318 (10) 10/351 (11) (80 overs)	351	1/29 (1) 2/81 (3) 3/104 (2) 4/124 (4) 5/124 (6) 6/204 (5) (6 wkts dec, 73 overs)	279

Coles 20–2–96–1; Stevens 18–5–54–1; Claydon 23–4–106–5; Haggett 18–2–70–3; Tredwell 1–0–11–0. *Second innings*—Claydon 15–4–50–3; Stevens 12–3–28–0; Coles 16–3–47–2; Tredwell 12–1–64–1; Haggett 9–2–39–0; Denly 5–0–24–0; Latham 2–0–5–0; Dickson 1–0–4–0; Northeast 1–0–1–0.

Kent

D. J. Bell-Drummond c Bragg b van der Gugten	8
T. W. M. Latham b Wagg	29
J. L. Denly b van der Gugten	13
*S. A. Northeast c Wallace b Wagg	6
S. R. Dickson c Wallace b van der Gugten	75
D. I. Stevens b Meschede	14
†A. P. Rouse lbw b Hogan	65
C. J. Haggett c Wallace b van der Gugten	24
J. C. Tredwell not out	37
M. T. Coles c Bragg b Hogan	0
M. E. Claydon lbw b van der Gugten	0
B 5, lb 4, nb 2	11
1/10 (1) 2/34 (3) 3/56 (4) 4/57 (2) 5/85 (6) 6/205 (5) 7/216 (8) 8/271 (7) 9/273 (10) 10/282 (11) (88.3 overs)	282

Rouse, when 31, retired hurt at 157-5 and resumed at 205-6.

Van der Gugten 26.3–4–79–5; Hogan 19–8–24–2; Wagg 25–4–90–2; Meschede 12–1–48–1; Salter 6–0–32–0.

Umpires: S. C. Gale and R. T. Robinson.

At Hove, July 2–5. GLAMORGAN drew with SUSSEX.

> "One delicious over, costing 16, explained why: defended, reverse-swept, swept; defended, reverse-swept, swept. The immaculate execution showed Misbah as contemptuous of spin as Henry VIII of wives."
> England v Pakistan in 2016, First Test, page 300

At Newport, July 15. GLAMORGAN lost to PAKISTAN A by 123 runs (see Pakistan A tour section, page 702). *Ruaidhri Smith takes a hat-trick.*

GLAMORGAN v DERBYSHIRE

At Colwyn Bay, July 17–20. Glamorgan won by four wickets. Glamorgan 24pts, Derbyshire 3pts. Toss: Glamorgan.

The highlight of this game was a double-century by 19-year-old Aneurin Donald, who reached 200 in just 123 balls to match the record set by Ravi Shastri (a former Glamorgan player) for Bombay in the Ranji Trophy in 1984-85. After a sketchy start, Donald tucked in to the Derbyshire attack, reaching three successive landmarks – 100, 150 and 200 – with a six. He hit five cars parked in the ground, and a passing bus, becoming Glamorgan's youngest double-centurion (Mike Powell was 20 in 1997) and the eighth-youngest in English or Welsh first-class cricket. Despite that, 20-year-old seamer Will Davis stuck to his task and finished with a seven-for in his fourth first-class game. But Meschede and Owen Morgan, who made a tidy 40 in only his second Championship appearance, lifted the score past 500, which looked plenty when Derbyshire were bundled out for 177. They resisted stoutly in the follow-on, however, as both Chesney Hughes and Godleman made hundreds, and Critchley his first half-century since May 2015. Wallace matched Colin Metson's county record of nine dismissals in a game. Glamorgan needed 196 in 62 overs and, when Donald came down to earth with a duck, were in trouble at 85 for four – but Rudolph and Meschede, who ended the match with another bus-denting six, made sure of victory.

Close of play: first day, Glamorgan 481-8 (Meschede 54, Morgan 22); second day, Derbyshire 78-1 (Rutherford 32, Hughes 12); third day, Derbyshire 413-6 (Godleman 66, Critchley 12).

THE ROAD TO 200

How Aneurin Donald equalled the record for the fastest first-class double-century:

	Balls	*Mins*	*4*	*6*
50	38	54	8	1
100	80	115	15	4
150	104	165	21	7
200	**123**	**201**	**24**	**12**
234	136	220	26	15

Research: Andrew Hignell

Glamorgan

N. J. Selman c Hughes b Davis	57	– lbw b Thakor	26
†M. A. Wallace lbw b Palladino	4	– c Rutherford b Madsen	40
W. D. Bragg c Hosein b Davis	60	– b Palladino	5
*J. A. Rudolph c Madsen b Davis	0	– not out	51
A. H. T. Donald c Godleman b Palladino	234	– c Rutherford b Davis	0
D. L. Lloyd c Critchley b Palladino	30	– lbw b Madsen	30
G. G. Wagg b Davis	0	– c Madsen b Critchley	1
C. A. J. Meschede not out	66	– not out	36
A. G. Salter c Critchley b Davis	4		
A. O. Morgan lbw b Davis	40		
M. G. Hogan b Davis	7		
B 4, lb 10, nb 2	16	B 4, lb 3, nb 4	11
1/4 (2) 2/92 (1) 3/96 (4) 4/211 (3) 5/302 (6) 6/307 (7) 7/437 (5) 8/446 (9) 9/506 (10) 10/518 (11) (104.5 overs)	518	1/56 (1) 2/65 (3) 3/84 (2) 4/85 (5) 5/154 (6) 6/157 (7) (6 wkts, 45.4 overs)	200

Cotton 17–3–93–0; Palladino 25–3–79–3; Davis 25.5–2–146–7; Thakor 21–4–74–0; Madsen 7–0–35–0; Critchley 8–0–68–0; Hughes 1–0–9–0. *Second innings*—Cotton 8–2–29–0; Palladino 10–0–35–1; Davis 12–0–58–1; Thakor 4–0–16–1; Madsen 4.4–1–24–2; Critchley 7–1–31–1.

Derbyshire

H. D. Rutherford c Wallace b Meschede	26 – (2) c Wallace b Wagg	45
*B. A. Godleman lbw b Salter	24 – (5) c Wallace b Wagg	106
C. F. Hughes b Meschede	8 – c Wallace b Wagg	122
W. L. Madsen c Hogan b Meschede	9 – c Wallace b Salter	90
N. T. Broom c Wallace b Wagg	9 – (6) lbw b Hogan	3
S. J. Thakor c Wallace b Wagg	24 – (7) lbw b Lloyd	29
M. J. J. Critchley c Wallace b Lloyd	23 – (8) not out	70
†H. R. Hosein not out	27 – (1) c Wallace b Morgan	26
A. P. Palladino c Donald b Morgan	9 – c Hogan b Salter	7
W. S. Davis b Salter	6 – lbw b Morgan	0
B. D. Cotton b Hogan	0 – c Donald b Hogan	12
B 1, lb 3, nb 8	12 B 8, lb 5, w 3, nb 10	26
1/52 (1) 2/62 (2) 3/66 (3) 4/71 (4) 5/88 (5) 6/123 (6) 7/135 (7) 8/159 (9) 9/176 (10) 10/177 (11) (52 overs)	177 1/59 (1) 2/100 (2) 3/281 (3) 4/311 (4) 5/322 (6) 6/383 (7) 7/496 (5) 8/507 (9) 9/510 (10) 10/536 (11) (162.1 overs)	536

Wagg 9–0–51–2; Hogan 14–7–44–1; Meschede 12–3–33–3; Salter 6–0–15–2; Morgan 6–2–9–1; Lloyd 5–0–21–1. *Second innings*—Hogan 37.1–8–112–2; Meschede 19–1–92–0; Salter 39–3–122–2; Wagg 29–5–93–3; Morgan 23–4–48–2; Lloyd 14–1–52–1; Rudolph 1–0–4–0.

Umpires: N. G. C. Cowley and S. C. Gale.

GLAMORGAN v NORTHAMPTONSHIRE

At Swansea, August 3–6. Northamptonshire won by 251 runs. Northamptonshire 22pts, Glamorgan 4pts. Toss: Northamptonshire. First-class debut: L. J. Carey. County debut: L. J. Evans.

Set 347 in almost a day, Glamorgan collapsed for 95, with Sanderson grabbing a career-best seven for 22, the last four for none in 17 balls. On the first morning, Northamptonshire had stuttered to 38 for four, helped by three wickets for the 19-year-old debutant Lukas Carey, but recovered to 321 against an attack lacking two frontline seamers, Richard Gleeson and Steven Crook, rested ahead of the T20 Blast quarter-final. Making his only appearance of a loan spell from Warwickshire, Laurie Evans contributed an attractive 74, while 18-year-old Saif Zaib added a maiden half-century, and stand-in skipper Kleinveldt cracked seven sixes in his rapid 91. Selman led the reply with a maiden century, becoming the first to carry his bat for Glamorgan since the Australian Matthew Elliott in 2004. But with six others contributing just six runs between them, Northamptonshire led by 85, and extended that beyond 300 on the third day, as Evans again passed 70. Northamptonshire's first win of the season lifted them off the bottom – where they were replaced by Glamorgan.

Close of play: first day, Northamptonshire 108-4 (Evans 42, Murphy 29); second day, Glamorgan 139-5 (Selman 79, Salter 24); third day, Northamptonshire 230-7 (Terry 18, White 21).

Northamptonshire

B. M. Duckett c Smith b Carey	7 – (2) c Wallace b Carey	7
R. I. Newton c Wallace b van der Gugten	9 – (1) c Bragg b Carey	12
S. P. Terry lbw b Carey	6 – (8) c Wallace b van der Gugten	35
R. I. Keogh c Donald b Carey	12 – (3) c Rudolph b van der Gugten	36
L. J. Evans c Wallace b Lloyd	74 – (4) c Selman b van der Gugten	73
†D. Murphy c Donald b Smith	45 – (5) lbw b Carey	20
S. A. Zaib not out	65 – (6) c Wallace b Carey	6
*R. K. Kleinveldt c Wallace b Lloyd	91 – (7) c Morgan b van der Gugten	32
G. G. White c Rudolph b Lloyd	1 – b van der Gugten	33
Azharullah lbw b van der Gugten	4 – not out	2
B. W. Sanderson c and b van der Gugten	1	
B 1, lb 2, w 1, nb 2	6 B 1, lb 2, nb 2	5
1/11 (1) 2/24 (3) 3/24 (2) 4/38 (4) 5/135 (6) 6/170 (5) 7/300 (8) 8/303 (9) 9/319 (10) 10/321 (11) (86.4 overs)	321 1/20 (2) 2/21 (1) 3/96 (3) 4/140 (5) 5/150 (6) 6/191 (7) 7/191 (4) 8/248 (8) 9/261 (9) (9 wkts dec, 58.1 overs)	261

Van der Gugten 24.4–6–88–3; Carey 17–0–59–3; Lloyd 10–2–36–3; Morgan 8–1–38–0; Smith 14–3–51–1; Salter 10–1–42–0; Bragg 3–0–4–0. *Second innings*—van der Gugten 13.1–1–61–5; Carey 20–1–92–4; Bragg 4–1–12–0; Lloyd 3–1–17–0; Salter 3–0–9–0; Morgan 15–1–67–0.

Glamorgan

N. J. Selman not out	122	– c Murphy b Sanderson	0
†M. A. Wallace b Azharullah	22	– (7) not out	28
W. D. Bragg lbw b Sanderson	1	– c Murphy b Sanderson	2
*J. A. Rudolph c Murphy b Sanderson	0	– c Kleinveldt b Sanderson	8
A. H. T. Donald c Duckett b Azharullah	4	– c and b White	28
D. L. Lloyd c Keogh b Azharullah	0	– lbw b Sanderson	25
A. G. Salter lbw b Kleinveldt	24	– (8) c Evans b Sanderson	0
R. A. J. Smith c Evans b Sanderson	25	– (9) lbw b Sanderson	0
A. O. Morgan lbw b Keogh	24	– (2) b Kleinveldt	0
T. van der Gugten c Murphy b White	1	– c Duckett b Sanderson	1
L. J. Carey c Kleinveldt b White	0	– c Keogh b White	1
Lb 1, nb 12	13	B 1, lb 1	2
1/52 (2) 2/53 (3) 3/53 (4) (80 overs)	236	1/0 (1) 2/2 (3) 3/2 (2) (38 overs)	95
4/87 (5) 5/97 (6) 6/162 (7)		4/12 (4) 5/56 (5) 6/74 (6)	
7/198 (8) 8/235 (9) 9/236 (10) 10/236 (11)		7/74 (8) 8/78 (9) 9/80 (10) 10/95 (11)	

Sanderson 22–5–67–3; Kleinveldt 19–4–69–1; Azharullah 18–5–58–3; White 15–5–26–2; Keogh 6–1–15–1. *Second innings*—Sanderson 13–6–22–7; Kleinveldt 9–3–20–1; Azharullah 4–1–14–0; White 10–1–36–2; Keogh 2–1–1–0.

Umpires: S. A. Garratt and R. K. Illingworth.

At Worcester, August 13–16. GLAMORGAN beat WORCESTERSHIRE by five wickets. *Mark Wallace equals the county record of nine dismissals for the second time in three games.*

GLAMORGAN v SUSSEX

At Cardiff, August 23–26. Sussex won by two wickets. Sussex 21pts, Glamorgan 5pts. Toss: uncontested.

When Sussex slipped to 156 for seven on the final evening, needing 77 more from 17.2 overs, their first Championship defeat of the season looked on the cards. But Brown and Briggs put on a robust 55 in nine, then Garton helped complete the job with 20 balls to spare. Glamorgan paid for two anaemic batting performances. Only half-centuries from Wagg and Wallace – Nos 7 and 8 – got them as far as 252 in their first innings; then, after a decent start in their second, the last five wickets tumbled for 17. Sussex had threatened a big lead, reaching 232 for two, only for eight to fall for 51, during which Wagg took three for none in four balls. Nash, who shared a century opening stand with Joyce, batted calmly for six and a half hours for 132, and top-scored in the second innings too. Rain cut two sessions from the third day, but Glamorgan's collapse next morning set Sussex 233 from 62 overs.

Close of play: first day, Sussex 111-1 (Nash 62, Briggs 0); second day, Glamorgan 50-1 (Rudolph 24, Bragg 13); third day, Glamorgan 149-2 (Bragg 41, Lloyd 37).

Glamorgan

N. J. Selman b Magoffin	0 – (2) lbw b Magoffin	5
*J. A. Rudolph c Brown b Archer	7 – (1) lbw b Magoffin	47
W. D. Bragg c Wiese b Magoffin	14 – c Nash b Archer	42
D. L. Lloyd c Briggs b Wiese	14 – c Brown b Magoffin	47
A. H. T. Donald b Archer	24 – c Brown b Garton	59
C. A. J. Meschede c Briggs b Wiese	8 – lbw b Wiese	6
G. G. Wagg c and b Wiese	57 – c Archer b Briggs	20
†M. A. Wallace c Brown b Archer	61 – c Nash b Garton	0
A. O. Morgan not out	32 – not out	8
T. van der Gugten lbw b Archer	4 – c Garton b Briggs	1
M. G. Hogan c Archer b Garton	19 – c Davis b Archer	4
Lb 6, nb 6	12 B 5, lb 7, w 2, nb 10	24
1/0 (1) 2/18 (2) 3/41 (4) 4/45 (3) 5/56 (6) 6/106 (5) 7/150 (7) 8/212 (8) 9/219 (10) 10/252 (11) (60.1 overs)	252 1/10 (2) 2/77 (1) 3/154 (3) 4/168 (4) 5/202 (6) 6/246 (5) 7/246 (8) 8/254 (7) 9/256 (10) 10/263 (11) (77.1 overs)	263

Magoffin 13–5–48–2; Archer 21–4–91–4; Wiese 13–2–52–3; Garton 10.1–1–41–1; Briggs 3–1–14–0. *Second innings*—Magoffin 23–7–50–3; Archer 20.1–1–85–2; Wiese 17–3–60–1; Garton 10–4–34–2; Briggs 7–0–22–2.

Sussex

C. D. Nash b van der Gugten	132 – (2) c Wallace b Wagg	64
E. C. Joyce c Wallace b Meschede	47 – (1) lbw b van der Gugten	0
D. R. Briggs run out	36 – (9) c Meschede b van der Gugten	36
L. W. P. Wells b Meschede	24 – (3) lbw b Morgan	33
C. A. L. Davis c Wallace b Wagg	2 – (4) lbw b van der Gugten	12
*L. J. Wright c Wallace b Wagg	0 – (5) b van der Gugten	12
D. Wiese b Wagg	0 – (6) b van der Gugten	1
†B. C. Brown c Wallace b Hogan	3 – (7) not out	42
J. C. Archer c Selman b van der Gugten	6 – (8) c Wallace b Hogan	4
G. H. S. Garton not out	3 – not out	18
S. J. Magoffin b van der Gugten	16	
B 5, lb 3, nb 6	14 B 1, lb 9, nb 4	14
1/111 (2) 2/180 (3) 3/232 (4) 4/243 (5) 5/243 (6) 6/243 (7) 7/252 (8) 8/258 (1) 9/261 (9) 10/283 (11) (109.2 overs)	283 1/0 (1) 2/87 (3) 3/113 (4) 4/125 (2) 5/128 (6) 6/137 (5) 7/156 (8) 8/211 (9) (8 wkts, 58.4 overs)	236

Van der Gugten 26.2–5–61–3; Meschede 21–6–59–2; Hogan 23–7–39–1; Wagg 25–5–74–3; Morgan 13–2–32–0; Lloyd 1–0–10–0. *Second innings*—van der Gugten 19–2–73–5; Meschede 7–1–32–0; Wagg 12–0–45–1; Hogan 16.4–4–51–1; Morgan 4–0–25–1.

Umpires: N. G. C. Cowley and J. H. Evans.

At Northampton, August 31–September 2. GLAMORGAN lost to NORTHAMPTONSHIRE by 318 runs. *All 20 Glamorgan wickets fall to spinners.*

GLAMORGAN v GLOUCESTERSHIRE

At Cardiff, September 6–8. Gloucestershire won by ten wickets. Gloucestershire 22pts, Glamorgan 3pts. Toss: uncontested.

Glamorgan rounded off their home programme with a third successive defeat, the seventh of a disappointing season. They were once more let down by their batting, with the honourable exception of Selman, who made his second century of the summer. Of the others, only Donald passed 30 in the first innings, as Matt Taylor and Miles shared eight wickets. Gloucestershire built a big lead, thanks to Marshall's 22nd (and last) century for them, and his fourth-wicket partnership of 120 with England

Under-19 batsman George Hankins. Then Glamorgan misfired again, only Bragg lasting long; a tenth-wicket stand of 58 between Wallace and Hogan – captain in place of Jacques Rudolph, who had injured his neck and shoulder – was the highest of the innings. This time it was left-armer Payne's turn to take four wickets, to follow his highest score. Roderick atoned for his first-day duck, speeding along at more than four an over with Dent to complete victory well inside three days.

Close of play: first day, Gloucestershire 62-3 (Hankins 10, Marshall 11); second day, Gloucestershire 347-8 (Payne 58, Shaw 17).

Glamorgan

N. J. Selman b M. D. Taylor	101	– c Mustard b Payne	8
†M. A. Wallace lbw b Payne	5	– (9) not out	39
W. D. Bragg c Mustard b Shaw	13	– b Payne	52
D. L. Lloyd b M. D. Taylor	4	– c Mustard b M. D. Taylor	14
A. H. T. Donald c Payne b Miles	36	– c Marshall b J. M. R. Taylor	25
K. S. Carlson lbw b Miles	0	– c Mustard b Shaw	0
G. G. Wagg c and b Miles	29	– b J. M. R. Taylor	21
C. A. J. Meschede c Shaw b M. D. Taylor	0	– c J. M. R. Taylor b Payne	21
A. O. Morgan b M. D. Taylor	2	– (2) b Shaw	14
T. van der Gugten b Miles	24	– c Tavaré b Payne	4
*M. G. Hogan not out	0	– b J. M. R. Taylor	30
B 4, lb 2	6	B 2, lb 1, w 1	4
1/25 (2) 2/57 (3) 3/72 (4) 4/137 (5) 5/141 (6) 6/172 (1) 7/172 (8) 8/177 (9) 9/215 (10) 10/220 (7) (64.5 overs)	220	1/22 (2) 2/22 (1) 3/53 (4) 4/98 (5) 5/99 (6) 6/126 (7) 7/153 (8) 8/162 (3) 9/174 (10) 10/232 (11) (58.4 overs)	232

Payne 21–3–59–1; M. D. Taylor 15–2–56–4; Miles 14.5–2–44–4; Shaw 12–1–41–1; Marshall 2–0–14–0. *Second innings*—Payne 14–4–45–4; Shaw 10–3–44–2; M. D. Taylor 10–3–45–1; Miles 4–0–23–0; J. M. R. Taylor 19.4–5–70–3; Dent 1–0–2–0.

Gloucestershire

*G. H. Roderick c Selman b van der Gugten	0	– not out	56
C. D. J. Dent c Lloyd b Meschede	15	– not out	35
W. A. Tavaré lbw b Hogan	18		
G. T. Hankins c Wallace b Wagg	43		
H. J. H. Marshall lbw b Hogan	101		
†P. Mustard c Bragg b Hogan	11		
J. M. R. Taylor c Selman b van der Gugten	13		
C. N. Miles c Wagg b Carlson	34		
D. A. Payne not out	67		
J. Shaw c Wallace b Hogan	17		
M. D. Taylor c Wallace b Hogan	6		
B 23, lb 6, w 1, nb 8	38	W 1	1
1/1 (1) 2/36 (2) 3/38 (3) 4/158 (4) 5/214 (6) 6/215 (5) 7/231 (7) 8/291 (8) 9/347 (10) 10/363 (11) (130.1 overs) 110 overs: 305-8	363	(no wkt, 19.4 overs)	92

Van der Gugten 25–3–90–2; Wagg 29–5–69–1; Meschede 17–6–42–1; Hogan 25.1–12–36–5; Morgan 21–4–55–0; Carlson 13–2–42–1. *Second innings*—Wagg 6–0–19–0; van der Gugten 3–0–6–0; Hogan 2–0–6–0; Carlson 2–0–23–0; Morgan 3.4–0–25–0; Meschede 3–0–13–0.

Umpires: J. H. Evans and S. A. Garratt.

At Chelmsford, September 12–15. GLAMORGAN beat ESSEX by 11 runs. *Eighteen-year-old Kiran Carlson scores a maiden century.*

At Leicester, September 20–22. GLAMORGAN lost to LEICESTERSHIRE by 26 runs.

GLOUCESTERSHIRE

The post-Marshall Plan

ANDY STOCKHAUSEN

Many in last season's dressing-room were still at school when Hamish Marshall arrived at Bristol in May 2006. This year, the younger element will have to stand on their own feet after Marshall, a hugely influential and popular batsman, decided to call it a day and take his young family to his native New Zealand. During his decade at the club, he hit 9,298 first-class runs, as well as 5,512 in the limited-overs formats, but his absence will deprive Gloucestershire of much more. A senior figure with real authority, he had also become a mentor, a shoulder to cry on, a genuine leader – and an extension of the coaching staff. He was a wonderful ambassador for the county, and will be sorely missed.

The Championship resources were further depleted when Michael Klinger, their Australian former club captain, chose to concentrate on one-day cricket from 2017 because of family commitments. He was no slouch in the first-class game, but it is his record in white-ball cricket over four seasons with Gloucestershire that is most arresting: 1,798 List A runs at 78, plus 1,866 at 50 in Twenty20 matches. Klinger – at 36 a year younger than Marshall – agreed to stay at Nevil Road until the end of 2019.

The pair will be hard acts to follow, and plugging the gaps in the Championship batting represents the most pressing task. With that in mind, Gloucestershire signed one-time England wicketkeeper-batsman, Phil Mustard. A former Durham captain, he hit a hundred and three fifties in a productive loan spell in the second half of 2016. His keeping skills may also be useful, after captain Gareth Roderick's fragile fingers suffered one fracture too many, forcing him to become a specialist batsman. Cameron Bancroft, the Australia A opener who can also keep wicket, was invited back, despite poor returns in 2016.

Financial restraints prevent Gloucestershire from splashing out on high-profile recruits, and the emphasis will stay on promotion from within. There should be opportunities for graduates of the club's Academy, such as George Hankins. At Northampton in September, when still 19, he carved out a patient maiden hundred under intense pressure, suggesting he can emulate Chris Dent who was the only batsman to make 1,000 first-class runs other than Marshall.

Jack Taylor, already an aggressive limited-overs batsman, continued to advance in the four-day game – he made 860 first-class runs – and may move up to No. 6. Meanwhile teenage wicketkeeper-batsman James Bracey made his first-class debut at the end of the season, and is another pushing for a regular place. And there were encouraging signs that the left-arm seam of Matt Taylor – Jack's younger brother – was becoming increasingly dependable.

Gloucestershire, who briefly flirted with Championship promotion before falling away, finished sixth, masking the strides they had taken. After watching

Harry Trump, Getty Images

Craig Miles

his team lose their first four games at Bristol in 2015, head coach Richard Dawson had made a point of trying to improve performances there, with some success. While their 2015 record at Nevil Road had comprised four defeats and two draws, a year later they had one win (over Glamorgan), one defeat (by Kent) and four draws. Their Cheltenham form proved less predictable: they beat Essex, the only team to gain promotion, and lost to Leicestershire. The seam attack of David Payne, Craig Miles, Liam Norwell and Yorkshire loanee Josh Shaw all made progress, but the main issue was the unreliability of first-innings runs: in six out of eight home games, Gloucestershire trailed at the halfway stage. If they are to mount a sustained promotion bid in 2017, this needs to be ironed out.

In 2015, they had been Royal London champions, but couldn't put up a convincing defence. They contrived to lose their opening fixture to arch-rivals Somerset, whose last pair added 65 to snatch the game in the final over, and never properly recovered. They were not helped by the loss of Jack Taylor's off-spin after his action was ruled illegal for the second time in his career, and he played solely as a batsman for much of the season, upsetting the balance of the team. (He did return to bowling in the Championship with a remodelled delivery, with which he claimed eight wickets at 71.) Klinger failed in that game against Somerset, but against Hampshire he monstered an unbeaten 166, a Gloucestershire record against county opposition.

Gloucestershire made partial amends in Twenty20 cricket, continuing a trend of steady improvement that began in 2014. The ubiquitous Klinger hit more runs than anyone in the country – 548 at a strike-rate of 134 – while the unheralded medium-pacer Benny Howell claimed most wickets: 24 at 16 (and an economy-rate of 6.87). Together with Australian seamer Andrew Tye, who enjoyed his first stint at Nevil Road, the trio helped Gloucestershire to ten victories – no other side won more than eight group games – and first place in the southern division. Adept at finding ways to win even under pressure, they looked capable of going all the way. But in their home quarter-final they ran into Durham's Mark Wood, who grabbed two wickets in his first over. Jack Taylor's late heroics – 80 from 41 balls – could not prevent defeat.

Championship attendance: 25,502.

GLOUCESTERSHIRE RESULTS

All first-class matches – Played 17: Won 4, Lost 5, Drawn 8.
County Championship matches – Played 16: Won 4, Lost 5, Drawn 7.

Specsavers County Championship, 6th in Division 2;
NatWest T20 Blast, quarter-finalists; Royal London One-Day Cup, 8th in South Group.

COUNTY CHAMPIONSHIP AVERAGES, BATTING AND FIELDING

Cap		*Birthplace*	*M*	*I*	*NO*	*R*	*HS*	*100*	*Avge*	*Ct/St*
2013	M. Klinger¶	*Kew, Australia*	7	12	4	589	140	3	73.62	8
2016	†P. Mustard	*Sunderland*	6	10	2	447	107*	1	55.87	23
2010	†C. D. J. Dent	*Bristol‡*	16	29	3	1,243	180	3	47.80	17
2016	G. L. van Buuren††	*Pretoria, SA*	7	12	2	459	172*	2	45.90	4
2006	H. J. H. Marshall	*Warkworth, NZ*	16	26	0	1,022	135	4	39.30	13
2010	J. M. R. Taylor	*Banbury*	16	26	2	860	107*	2	35.83	10
2013	G. H. Roderick††	*Durban, SA*	14	25	3	725	102	1	32.95	25/2
2011	D. A. Payne	*Poole*	14	18	4	389	67*	0	27.78	9
2011	C. N. Miles	*Swindon*	13	20	4	407	60*	0	25.43	3
2016	G. T. Hankins	*Bath*	9	15	0	374	116	1	24.93	6
2016	C. T. Bancroft¶	*Attadale, Australia*	5	9	0	192	70	0	21.33	3
2011	I. A. Cockbain	*Liverpool*	4	7	0	147	67	0	21.00	1
2015	†K. Noema-Barnett††	*Dunedin, NZ*	8	12	0	245	84	0	20.41	6
2012	B. A. C. Howell	*Bordeaux, France*	5	7	1	113	41	0	18.83	0
2011	L. C. Norwell	*Bournemouth*	11	15	3	224	102	1	18.66	1
2013	M. D. Taylor	*Banbury*	5	8	5	42	9*	0	14.00	1
2014	W. A. Tavaré	*Bristol‡*	6	10	0	112	36	0	11.20	6
2016	J. Shaw	*Wakefield*	12	16	4	125	29	0	10.41	3

Also batted: †J. R. Bracey (*Bristol‡*) (cap 2016) (1 match) 2, 12; T. R. G. Hampton (*Kingston-upon-Thames*) (cap 2015) (1 match) 0, 0*.

‡ *Born in Gloucestershire.* ¶ *Official overseas player.* †† *Other non-England-qualified.*

BOWLING

	Style	*O*	*M*	*R*	*W*	*BB*	*5I*	*Avge*
L. C. Norwell	RFM	377.5	87	1,167	39	4-65	0	29.92
C. N. Miles	RFM	381	55	1,581	52	5-54	2	30.40
D. A. Payne	LFM	451.4	83	1,380	43	5-36	1	32.09
J. Shaw	RFM	326.5	59	1,258	34	5-79	1	37.00
M. D. Taylor	LM	143	15	543	13	4-56	0	41.76
J. M. R. Taylor	OB	293.5	52	998	22	4-16	0	45.36
K. Noema-Barnett	RM	192.4	43	551	11	3-56	0	50.09

Also bowled: I. A. Cockbain (RM) 2.5–0–20–0; C. D. J. Dent (SLA) 48.4–8–151–3; T. R. G. Hampton (RFM) 21–1–107–1; B. A. C. Howell (RM) 46.1–11–150–1; H. J. H. Marshall (RM) 9–0–58–0; G. L. van Buuren (SLA) 84–17–219–7.

LEADING ROYAL LONDON CUP AVERAGES (100 runs/4 wickets)

Batting	*Runs*	*HS*	*Avge*	*SR*	*Ct*
M. Klinger	337	166*	56.16	83.83	2
C. D. J. Dent	278	142	46.33	97.88	2
T. M. J. Smith	124	43*	41.33	68.13	3
H. J. H. Marshall	208	74	34.66	83.53	2
B. A. C. Howell	157	77	22.42	82.19	2
I. A. Cockbain	119	35	17.00	69.59	5

Bowling	*W*	*BB*	*Avge*	*ER*
B. A. C. Howell	10	2-32	27.60	4.91
L. C. Norwell	7	3-56	28.57	5.55
T. M. J. Smith	6	4-26	44.33	5.78
C. N. Miles	8	2-54	44.50	6.67
M. D. Taylor	6	2-33	53.66	5.64

LEADING NATWEST T20 BLAST AVERAGES (100 runs/18 overs)

Batting	Runs	HS	Avge	SR	Ct
J. M. R. Taylor	161	80	53.66	**167.70**	2
M. Klinger	548	101	49.81	**134.64**	7
I. A. Cockbain	499	73*	55.44	**132.36**	9
H. J. H. Marshall	298	90	21.28	**131.27**	5
B. A. C. Howell	150	37	18.75	**128.20**	4
C. D. J. Dent	193	45	38.60	**112.20**	5

Bowling	W	BB	Avge	ER
B. A. C. Howell	24	3-18	16.04	**6.87**
M. D. Taylor	15	3-16	21.00	**7.32**
T. M. J. Smith	12	2-13	27.25	**7.43**
G. L. van Buuren	6	3-19	23.00	**7.66**
A. J. Tye	18	3-16	23.38	**8.56**
K. Noema-Barnett	3	1-17	57.00	**9.00**
L. C. Norwell	3	1-32	103.33	**9.16**

FIRST-CLASS COUNTY RECORDS

Highest score for	341	C. M. Spearman v Middlesex at Gloucester	2004
Highest score against	319	C. J. L. Rogers (Northants) at Northamptonshire	2006
Leading run-scorer	33,664	W. R. Hammond (avge 57.05)	1920–51
Best bowling for	10-40	E. G. Dennett v Essex at Bristol	1906
Best bowling against	10-66	A. A. Mailey (Australians) at Cheltenham	1921
	10-66	K. Smales (Nottinghamshire) at Stroud	1956
Leading wicket-taker	3,170	C. W. L. Parker (avge 19.43)	1903–35
Highest total for	695-9 dec	v Middlesex at Gloucester	2004
Highest total against	774-7 dec	by Australians at Bristol	1948
Lowest total for	17	v Australians at Cheltenham	1896
Lowest total against	12	by Northamptonshire at Gloucester	1907

LIST A COUNTY RECORDS

Highest score for	177	A. J. Wright v Scotland at Bristol	1997
Highest score against	189*	J. G. E. Benning (Surrey) at Bristol	2006
Leading run-scorer	7,825	M. W. Alleyne (avge 26.89)	1986–2005
Best bowling for	7-29	D. A. Payne v Essex at Chelmsford	2010
Best bowling against	6-16	Shoaib Akhtar (Worcestershire) at Worcester	2005
Leading wicket-taker	393	M. W. Alleyne (avge 29.88)	1986–2005
Highest total for	401-7	v Buckinghamshire at Wing	2003
Highest total against	496-4	by Surrey at The Oval	2007
Lowest total for	49	v Middlesex at Bristol	1978
Lowest total against	48	by Middlesex at Lydney	1973

TWENTY20 COUNTY RECORDS

Highest score for	126*	M. Klinger v Essex at Bristol	2015
Highest score against	116*	C. L. White (Somerset) at Taunton	2006
Leading run-scorer	**2,633**	**H. J. H. Marshall (avge 27.71)**	**2006–16**
Best bowling for	5-24	D. A. Payne v Middlesex at Richmond	2015
Best bowling against	5-16	R. E. Watkins (Glamorgan) at Cardiff	2009
Leading wicket-taker	**66**	**B. A. C. Howell (avge 19.89)**	**2012–16**
Highest total for	254-3	v Middlesex at Uxbridge	2011
Highest total against	250-3	by Somerset at Taunton	2006
Lowest total for	68	v Hampshire at Bristol	2010
Lowest total against	97	by Surrey at The Oval	2010

ADDRESS

County Ground, Nevil Road, Bristol BS7 9EJ; 0117 910 8000; reception@glosccc.co.uk; www.gloscricket.co.uk.

OFFICIALS

Captain (first-class) G. H. Roderick
(limited-overs) M. Klinger
Head coach R. K. J. Dawson
Head of talent pathway T. H. C. Hancock

Chairman R. M. Cooke
Chief executive W. G. Brown
Head groundsman S. P. Williams
Scorer A. J. Bull

GLOUCESTERSHIRE v DURHAM MCCU

At Bristol, March 31–April 2. Drawn. Toss: Gloucestershire. First-class debuts: G. T. Hankins, J. Shaw; J. Clark, J. J. N. Dewes, J. E. Dunford, E. E. Kurtz.

Cockbain strode on to the stage in this curtain-raiser, collecting 213 runs – plus rhythm and confidence – across two innings. All told, three Gloucestershire team-mates hit fifties as the professionals enjoyed some batting practice. Not that they had it all their own way: seamer Will Phillips claimed three wickets before the county declared on 348 for seven, and Charlie Macdonell held up Gloucestershire's pace attack with a patient 91. At 248 for four, the students even eyed a lead, but eventually conceded a deficit of 60. Gloucestershire's fluent top order hastened a second declaration, but the victory charge was stalled by an obdurate 64 from Robert Gibson. No. 11 Jonathan Dewes – grandson of the late Test batsman John – helped him negotiate the last five overs.

Close of play: first day, Durham MCCU 39-0 (Kurtz 15, Clark 11); second day, Gloucestershire 94-0 (Dent 56, Cockbain 38).

Gloucestershire

I. A. Cockbain c Gibson b Dewes	84	– (2) not out	129
C. D. J. Dent c Dunford b Phillips	37	– (1) c Steel b Wood	56
G. T. Hankins b Jenkins	8	– c Clark b Dewes	34
*†G. H. Roderick c Dunford b Phillips	56		
H. J. H. Marshall lbw b Dewes	24		
B. A. C. Howell c Clark b Jenkins	43	– (4) not out	23
K. Noema-Barnett c Macdonell b Phillips	55		
C. N. Miles not out	6		
J. Shaw not out	12		
Lb 7, nb 16	23	B 1, nb 6	7
1/63 (2) 2/80 (3) 3/178 (4) 4/218 (1) 5/229 (5) 6/321 (6) 7/321 (7) (7 wkts dec, 91 overs)	348	1/99 (1) 2/175 (3) (2 wkts dec, 48 overs)	249

D. A. Payne and L. C. Norwell did not bat.

Jenkins 19–4–87–2; Wood 15–1–62–0; Phillips 17–7–45–3; Dewes 28–2–93–2; Steel 4–0–26–0; Macdonell 8–2–28–0. *Second innings*—Jenkins 11–1–71–0; Wood 12–2–58–1; Phillips 10–0–66–0; Dewes 13–0–38–1; Macdonell 2–0–15–0.

Durham MCCU

E. E. Kurtz c Howell b Miles	15	– run out	4
*J. Clark c Howell b Miles	32	– c Marshall b Miles	9
C. T. Steel c Miles b Norwell	27	– c Noema-Barnett b Miles	10
C. M. Macdonell run out	91	– c Roderick b Norwell	15
E. J. Pollock c Dent b Noema-Barnett	22	– c Roderick b Howell	13
R. A. M. Gibson c Shaw b Cockbain	44	– not out	64
W. H. Jenkins c Cockbain b Norwell	7	– b Noema-Barnett	9
W. D. B. Phillips lbw b Shaw	14	– c Roderick b Noema-Barnett	4
†J. E. Dunford c Marshall b Norwell	0	– lbw b Norwell	1
J. M. Wood c Roderick b Miles	14	– c Dent b Shaw	0
J. J. N. Dewes not out	3	– not out	4
B 1, lb 5, nb 13	19	B 4, lb 1, nb 10	15
1/39 (1) 2/66 (2) 3/104 (3) 4/158 (5) 5/248 (6) 6/257 (4) 7/259 (7) 8/259 (9) 9/275 (8) 10/288 (10) (92.2 overs)	288	1/11 (1) 2/26 (2) 3/27 (3) 4/46 (5) 5/69 (4) 6/105 (7) 7/117 (8) 8/118 (9) 9/138 (10) (9 wkts, 63 overs)	148

Payne 9.2–1–32–0; Norwell 21–4–63–3; Miles 14.2–4–41–3; Shaw 16–2–56–1; Noema-Barnett 19.4–7–37–1; Dent 8–1–30–0; Cockbain 4–0–23–1. *Second innings*—Norwell 15–3–41–2; Shaw 17–4–46–1; Noema-Barnett 13–4–16–2; Miles 9–3–19–2; Howell 4–2–15–1; Dent 5–2–6–0.

Umpires: M. Burns and J. H. Evans.

At Chelmsford, April 10–13. GLOUCESTERSHIRE lost to ESSEX by ten wickets.

GLOUCESTERSHIRE v DERBYSHIRE

At Bristol, April 17–20. Drawn. Gloucestershire 12pts, Derbyshire 8pts. Toss: Derbyshire. County debuts: A. Carter, L. J. Fletcher. Championship debut: N. T. Broom.

Liam Norwell, a career tailender, illuminated a drab stalemate by going well beyond his nightwatchman duties. Sent in just before the second-day close, he blossomed next morning, chancing his arm and upstaging Dent, his senior partner. In a performance that belied just 12 double-figure scores in 58 innings, Norwell surged to his first hundred in any form of cricket. "I'm still in shock," he said, after reaching his hundred from 120 deliveries. "I think my previous best was 98 in an Under-13 game for Redruth." Dent's more studied contribution – he faced 312 balls and batted almost seven hours – helped Gloucestershire sail on to 563, a lead of 119. Derbyshire had relied on patient innings from Hughes and Madsen, eventually stumped for 150; Norwell claimed four for 104, and Taylor a career-best four for 61. Having fallen four short of a hundred on the first day, Hughes made amends on the last, hitting 137 not out, as he and Rutherford ushered Derbyshire to safety. On this slow, gentle pitch, there was never much likelihood of a result.

Close of play: first day, Derbyshire 242-3 (Madsen 58, Broom 30); second day, Gloucestershire 110-1 (Dent 61, Norwell 2); third day, Gloucestershire 563.

Derbyshire

B. T. Slater c Taylor b Norwell	42	– run out	6
C. F. Hughes b Taylor	96	– not out	137
*H. D. Rutherford c Roderick b Norwell	1	– c Dent b Taylor	78
W. L. Madsen st Roderick b Taylor	150	– not out	27
N. T. Broom c Noema-Barnett b Norwell	32		
W. J. Durston b Payne	12		
S. J. Thakor c Dent b Payne	7		
†T. Poynton c Noema-Barnett b Norwell	53		
L. J. Fletcher c Shaw b Taylor	11		
B. D. Cotton c Bancroft b Taylor	11		
A. Carter not out	7		
Lb 19, w 1, nb 2	22	B 1, lb 4, w 5, nb 2	12
1/103 (1) 2/105 (3) 3/176 (2) 4/245 (5) 5/258 (6) 6/266 (7) 7/394 (8) 8/405 (9) 9/436 (10) 10/444 (4) (157.1 overs)	444	1/6 (1) 2/180 (3) (2 wkts dec, 76.5 overs)	260
110 overs: 276-6			

Payne 32–13–61–2; Norwell 35–7–104–4; Shaw 30–4–105–0; Noema-Barnett 33–8–91–0; Taylor 22.1–5–61–4; Howell 5–3–3–0. *Second innings*—Payne 10–1–32–0; Norwell 10–1–31–0; Shaw 8–1–39–0; Taylor 27–4–79–1; Dent 11–2–35–0; Noema-Barnett 8–3–19–0; Cockbain 2.5–0–20–0.

Gloucestershire

C. T. Bancroft b Thakor	41
C. D. J. Dent b Hughes	180
L. C. Norwell lbw b Hughes	102
I. A. Cockbain c Poynton b Fletcher	19
*†G. H. Roderick b Carter	5
H. J. H. Marshall c Carter b Durston	72
K. Noema-Barnett c Fletcher b Durston	58
J. M. R. Taylor c Slater b Hughes	18
B. A. C. Howell c Carter b Thakor	41
J. Shaw c Madsen b Durston	0
D. A. Payne not out	0
B 8, lb 6, w 3, nb 10	27
1/102 (1) 2/270 (3) 3/317 (4) 4/336 (5) 5/435 (2) 6/467 (6) 7/495 (8) 8/549 (7) 9/549 (10) 10/563 (9) (125.2 overs)	563
110 overs: 461-5	

Fletcher 21–6–54–1; Carter 26–4–84–1; Cotton 17–2–90–0; Thakor 15.2–1–82–2; Durston 27–1–149–3; Hughes 17–0–87–3; Madsen 2–1–3–0.

Umpires: N. G. B. Cook and A. G. Wharf.

GLOUCESTERSHIRE v WORCESTERSHIRE

At Bristol, April 24–27. Drawn. Gloucestershire 12pts, Worcestershire 13pts. Toss: uncontested. County debut: M. J. Henry. Championship debut: G. T. Hankins.

An eye-catching hundred from Ali denied Gloucestershire a first Championship win in Bristol since May 2014. Thanks to centuries from the in-form Dent and No. 8 Taylor, they had set Worcestershire 352 in 63 overs, and soon reduced them to 49 for three. But with the summer's first Test just three weeks away, Ali gave a reminder of his class, scoring a fluent unbeaten 136 – the last of the game's four scores in the 130s – from 144 balls, and sharing half-century stands with Köhler-Cadmore and Whiteley. On the opening day, Gloucestershire had sunk to 157 for five, before being revived by the New Zealand pair of Marshall and Noema-Barnett. The 19-year-old Joe Clarke responded with a brisk, career-best 135 as Worcestershire established a slender lead. Dent and Taylor – who reached three figures from his 96th ball – put Gloucestershire noses in front, adding 162 for the seventh wicket, but Ali held firm.

Close of play: first day, Gloucestershire 336-5 (Marshall 123, Noema-Barnett 84); second day, Worcestershire 297-5 (Clarke 103, Cox 59); third day, Gloucestershire 217-6 (Dent 81, Taylor 8).

Gloucestershire

C. T. Bancroft run out	15	– c Cox b Barnard	29
C. D. J. Dent c Köhler-Cadmore b Barnard	59	– not out	138
I. A. Cockbain lbw b Barnard	5	– c and b Leach	67
*†G. H. Roderick c Whiteley b Shantry	1	– lbw b Leach	0
H. J. H. Marshall c Cox b Henry	135	– b Henry	17
G. T. Hankins c Whiteley b Henry	18	– b Henry	5
K. Noema-Barnett c Whiteley b Shantry	84	– b Henry	0
J. M. R. Taylor c Whiteley b Henry	12	– c Köhler-Cadmore b Barnard	105
L. C. Norwell lbw b Shantry	9	– not out	5
J. Shaw not out	9		
D. A. Payne b Shantry	2		
B 14, lb 5, nb 12	31	B 4, lb 2, nb 10	16
1/37 (1) 2/56 (3) 3/57 (4) (114.2 overs)	380	1/49 (1) (7 wkts dec, 101 overs)	382
4/133 (2) 5/157 (6) 6/336 (7)		2/157 (3) 3/157 (4)	
7/348 (8) 8/369 (9) 9/369 (5)		4/190 (5) 5/204 (6)	
10/380 (11) 110 overs: 375-9		6/204 (7) 7/366 (8)	

Henry 31–4–89–3; Leach 21–3–70–0; Shantry 31.2–8–89–4; Barnard 20–2–67–2; Ali 8–2–32–0; D'Oliveira 3–0–14–0. *Second innings*—Henry 22–4–83–3; Leach 23–5–77–2; Shantry 26–6–82–0; Barnard 20–4–73–2; Ali 8–0–49–0; D'Oliveira 2–0–12–0.

Worcestershire

*D. K. H. Mitchell lbw b Payne	0	– b Norwell	8
B. L. D'Oliveira lbw b Noema-Barnett	40	– b Norwell	4
M. M. Ali c Roderick b Shaw	74	– not out	136
J. M. Clarke b Norwell	135	– b Shaw	8
T. Köhler-Cadmore b Shaw	0	– c Shaw b Norwell	25
R. A. Whiteley c Roderick b Noema-Barnett	8	– not out	21
†O. B. Cox c Roderick b Norwell	69		
J. Leach b Payne	0		
E. G. Barnard c Dent b Norwell	9		
M. J. Henry not out	42		
J. D. Shantry c Noema-Barnett b Payne	13		
Lb 14, w 1, nb 6	21	Lb 2, nb 6	8
1/0 (1) 2/120 (3) 3/128 (2) (98.2 overs)	411	1/10 (2) (4 wkts, 51.1 overs)	210
4/131 (5) 5/162 (6) 6/317 (7)		2/27 (1) 3/49 (4)	
7/318 (8) 8/331 (9) 9/370 (4) 10/411 (11)		4/123 (5)	

Payne 22.2–2–89–3; Norwell 28–4–112–3; Shaw 18–1–92–2; Noema-Barnett 22–4–79–2; Taylor 8–0–25–0. *Second innings*—Payne 14–0–56–0; Norwell 15–2–69–3; Shaw 12.1–3–42–1; Noema-Barnett 5–1–14–0; Taylor 5–0–27–0.

Umpires: I. D. Blackwell and M. J. Saggers.

At Canterbury, May 8–11. GLOUCESTERSHIRE drew with KENT.

GLOUCESTERSHIRE v GLAMORGAN

At Bristol, May 15–18. Gloucestershire won by 125 runs. Gloucestershire 21pts, Glamorgan 6pts. Toss: uncontested. County debut: G. L. van Buuren.

Gloucestershire's spinners took a combined seven for 31 from 16 overs to spark a startling turnaround on the final day – and give them the long-awaited Championship win at Nevil Road they had missed three weeks earlier. Pursuing 269, Glamorgan looked in control while openers Wallace and Rudolph were putting on 87. But slow left-armer Graeme van Buuren (who played for South Africa Under-19 before acquiring a UK passport) and seamer Miles grabbed three wickets each to leave the chase in tatters. Off-spinner Taylor finished things off with a career-best four for 16 as Glamorgan shed all ten for 56. A home victory had seemed improbable on the second day after Glamorgan earned a handy lead of 68: Lloyd just missed a hundred, while Wagg was on 55 when struck on the left arm by Miles. Gloucestershire were under pressure, but three half-centuries kept them in the game. Rain interrupted play with Glamorgan 142 for eight, but Taylor returned to claim the last two wickets. Van Buuren was twice dismissed by Netherlands international van der Gugten.

Close of play: first day, Glamorgan 82-1 (Rudolph 33, Bragg 45); second day, Gloucestershire 60-1 (Bancroft 35, van Buuren 22); third day, Gloucestershire 302-8 (Miles 23, Payne 9).

Gloucestershire

C. T. Bancroft b Wagg	5	– c Lloyd b Hogan	70
C. D. J. Dent lbw b Wagg	6	– c Donald b Podmore	3
G. L. van Buuren c Cooke b van der Gugten	33	– lbw b van der Gugten	22
*†G. H. Roderick c Salter b Podmore	12	– lbw b Hogan	67
H. J. H. Marshall lbw b Wagg	18	– c Salter b Hogan	58
G. T. Hankins b van der Gugten	56	– b van der Gugten	18
K. Noema-Barnett run out	1	– c sub (N. J. Selman) b Hogan	4
J. M. R. Taylor lbw b Hogan	24	– c Rudolph b Podmore	17
C. N. Miles not out	49	– not out	39
D. A. Payne b van der Gugten	39	– c Salter b van der Gugten	12
J. Shaw b Rudolph	1	– c Bragg b Podmore	9
B 3, lb 11, nb 4	18	B 4, lb 10, w 1, nb 2	17
1/10 (2) 2/11 (1) 3/43 (4) (67.3 overs)	262	1/22 (2) 2/60 (3) (122.3 overs)	336
4/69 (3) 5/85 (5) 6/110 (7)		3/117 (1) 4/200 (5)	
7/152 (8) 8/169 (6) 9/259 (10) 10/262 (11)		5/240 (6) 6/248 (4) 7/255 (7)	
		8/271 (8) 9/307 (10) 10/336 (11)	

Van der Gugten 15–2–49–3; Wagg 16–2–65–3; Hogan 16–5–41–1; Podmore 10–0–64–1; Salter 4–1–13–0; Lloyd 3–0–11–0; Rudolph 3.3–2–5–1. *Second innings*—Hogan 34–7–83–4; van der Gugten 34–4–106–3; Podmore 23.3–4–59–3; Salter 9–2–28–0; Rudolph 11–0–16–0; Lloyd 10–2–26–0; Bragg 1–0–4–0.

Glamorgan

*J. A. Rudolph run out	40	– c Marshall b van Buuren	36
†M. A. Wallace c van Buuren b Miles	0	– b van Buuren	50
W. D. Bragg c Roderick b Shaw	70	– c Taylor b van Buuren	5
C. B. Cooke c Hankins b Miles	30	– (5) c Bancroft b Miles	4
A. H. T. Donald st Roderick b van Buuren	7	– (6) c Marshall b Miles	4
D. L. Lloyd c van Buuren b Miles	99	– (7) c Roderick b Taylor	20
G. G. Wagg retired hurt	55	– (10) b Taylor	15
A. G. Salter c Roderick b Shaw	0	– (4) c Hankins b Miles	3
H. W. Podmore c Roderick b Shaw	3	– (8) b Taylor	1
T. van der Gugten not out	14	– (9) c Marshall b Taylor	0
M. G. Hogan c Marshall b Payne	0	– not out	1
Lb 4, w 2, nb 6	12	Lb 2, nb 2	4
1/1 (2) 2/97 (1) 3/137 (3) (99.4 overs)	330	1/87 (2) 2/94 (1) (49 overs)	143
4/150 (5) 5/167 (4) 6/272 (8)		3/97 (3) 4/98 (4)	
7/296 (9) 8/329 (6) 9/330 (11)		5/102 (5) 6/119 (6) 7/120 (8)	
		8/120 (9) 9/142 (10) 10/143 (7)	

In the first innings Wagg retired hurt at 271-5.

Payne 21.4–3–65–1; Miles 24–2–74–3; Shaw 16–3–90–3; Noema-Barnett 16–3–43–0; Taylor 5–1–7–0; van Buuren 17–2–47–1. *Second innings*—Payne 10–2–24–0; Miles 13–0–55–3; Noema-Barnett 4–0–21–0; van Buuren 10–5–15–3; Shaw 6–3–10–0; Taylor 6–3–16–4.

Umpires: R. K. Illingworth and G. D. Lloyd.

GLOUCESTERSHIRE v NORTHAMPTONSHIRE

At Bristol, May 22–25. Drawn. Gloucestershire 11pts, Northamptonshire 7pts. Toss: Northamptonshire. Championship debut: S. Prasanna.

Gloucestershire's quest for successive victories was stymied by Newton and Crook. Both reached a hundred on the last day as Northamptonshire overcame a first-innings deficit of 242 to end 157 ahead, the draw long since secure. Unbeaten on 58 on the third evening, Newton made his century from 208 balls; Crook was quicker about his business – getting there from 127 – and was still batting at the end, having shared an eighth-wicket stand of 101 with Gleeson, one of seven Northamptonians to hit 23 or more. A marathon six-and-a-half-hour innings of 140 from Klinger – who added 137 for the third wicket with Dent, and 76 for the ninth with Payne, before becoming the last of leg-spinner Seekkuge Prasanna's five victims – seemed to have made Gloucestershire's dominance complete after their seamers had skittled Northamptonshire for 176. The weather stole more than half the first day, but Miles and Shaw still had time to exploit a moving ball. It all seemed to add up to a home win, but Newton and Crook refused to buckle.

Close of play: first day, Northamptonshire 134-7 (Crook 43, Gleeson 0); second day, Gloucestershire 240-4 (Klinger 62); third day, Northamptonshire 120-3 (Newton 58, Levi 9).

Northamptonshire

B. M. Duckett c Roderick b Shaw	11	– c sub (C. J. W. Gregory) b Miles	4
R. I. Newton b Shaw	18	– b Payne	108
*A. G. Wakely c Klinger b Miles	4	– lbw b Noema-Barnett	14
R. I. Keogh c Klinger b Miles	5	– c Hankins b Taylor	30
R. E. Levi b Shaw	23	– c Roderick b Payne	23
†A. M. Rossington c Dent b Noema-Barnett	13	– c Payne b Noema-Barnett	39
S. P. Crook c Dent b Miles	60	– not out	103
S. Prasanna c Payne b Shaw	9	– c sub (C. J. W. Gregory) b Payne	26
R. J. Gleeson c Payne b Miles	10	– lbw b van Buuren	31
Azharullah c Payne b Miles	9	– not out	4
B. W. Sanderson not out	0		
B 3, lb 7, nb 4	14	B 4, lb 9, nb 4	17
1/27 (1) 2/32 (2) 3/39 (4) 4/40 (3) 5/59 (6) 6/110 (5) 7/134 (8) 8/161 (9) 9/167 (7) 10/176 (10) (52.4 overs)	176	1/5 (1) 2/28 (3) 3/99 (4) 4/144 (5) 5/204 (6) 6/246 (2) 7/294 (8) 8/395 (9) (8 wkts dec, 119 overs)	399

Payne 15–4–40–0; Miles 15.4–5–65–5; Shaw 19–2–52–4; Noema-Barnett 2–0–8–1; van Buuren 1–0–1–0. *Second innings*—Payne 21–2–72–3; Miles 28–5–109–1; Shaw 20–5–77–0; Noema-Barnett 22–7–48–2; van Buuren 16–3–48–1; Taylor 12–4–32–1.

Gloucestershire

*†G. H. Roderick lbw b Sanderson	40
C. D. J. Dent c Levi b Prasanna	93
G. L. van Buuren lbw b Gleeson	13
M. Klinger b Prasanna	140
H. J. H. Marshall c Wakely b Gleeson	0
G. T. Hankins b Sanderson	2
K. Noema-Barnett c Duckett b Prasanna	23
J. M. R. Taylor c Duckett b Prasanna	24
C. N. Miles c Duckett b Gleeson	0
D. A. Payne st Duckett b Prasanna	32
J. Shaw not out	8
B 20, lb 10, w 7, nb 6	43
1/76 (1) 2/100 (3) 3/237 (2) 4/240 (5) 5/243 (6) 6/301 (7) 7/328 (8) 8/331 (9) 9/407 (10) 10/418 (4) (134.4 overs)	418

110 overs: 328-7

Sanderson 28–6–72–2; Gleeson 34–6–94–3; Azharullah 19–2–42–0; Prasanna 27.4–6–97–5; Crook 22–4–65–0; Keogh 4–0–18–0.

Umpires: M. Burns and M. J. Saggers.

At Worcester, May 29–June 1. GLOUCESTERSHIRE beat WORCESTERSHIRE by five wickets.

At Leicester, June 27–30. GLOUCESTERSHIRE drew with LEICESTERSHIRE.

GLOUCESTERSHIRE v ESSEX

At Cheltenham, July 13–16. Gloucestershire won by 61 runs. Gloucestershire 21pts, Essex 6pts. Toss: uncontested.

Set 213, Essex crumpled in the face of sustained hostility from Norwell, Payne and Miles, who shot out the division leaders for 151. Miles also completed his first hat-trick in any cricket, spread across three overs – and three days. He had dismissed Foster from the last ball of the 81st over, ended the Essex innings (and the second day) by removing Quinn with the first of the 83rd, and bowled Bopara the moment he was introduced on a cloudy fourth morning. That reduced Essex to 59 for five, and Gloucestershire won half an hour after lunch. For much of the game, though, Essex had called the shots: Quinn, the New Zealand seamer, converted a career-best seven-for on the shortened first day into match figures of 11 for 163 (another career-best), and Lawrence hit a cultured 127 to help secure a lead of 78. Unsettled by Quinn's exemplary length, Gloucestershire had been indebted to half-centuries from Roderick and Miles for keeping their first innings afloat. Roderick reached three figures next time round and, aided by Dent and Klinger, threatened to set a substantial target, before a collapse of eight for 62 ceded the initiative. After almost 900 runs in three days, few foresaw Essex's limp finale.

Close of play: first day, Gloucestershire 218-8 (Miles 45, Norwell 7); second day, Essex 333; third day, Essex 16-1 (Browne 8, Porter 7).

Gloucestershire

*†G. H. Roderick lbw b Quinn	61	– lbw b Bopara	102
C. D. J. Dent c Westley b Porter	37	– b Bopara	72
G. L. van Buuren lbw b Quinn	13	– c Foster b Quinn	25
M. Klinger b Quinn	5	– not out	53
H. J. H. Marshall c Westley b Quinn	10	– lbw b Quinn	0
J. M. R. Taylor b Quinn	3	– c Lawrence b Napier	0
K. Noema-Barnett b Quinn	4	– c Browne b Quinn	10
C. N. Miles b Porter	58	– c ten Doeschate b Quinn	9
D. A. Payne c Mickleburgh b Quinn	26	– c Foster b Napier	0
L. C. Norwell c Browne b Porter	31	– c Foster b Napier	0
J. Shaw not out	0	– c Foster b Napier	7
B 4, lb 1, w 2	7	B 2, lb 7, w 1, nb 2	12
1/77 (2) 2/99 (3) 3/111 (4) 4/124 (1) 5/127 (5) 6/133 (7) 7/140 (6) 8/205 (9) 9/254 (8) 10/255 (10) (77.2 overs)	255	1/148 (2) 2/185 (3) 3/228 (1) 4/238 (5) 5/239 (6) 6/254 (7) 7/266 (8) 8/269 (9) 9/278 (10) 10/290 (11) (83.4 overs)	290

Porter 15.2–1–67–3; Quinn 26–6–76–7; Napier 22–4–68–0; Lawrence 1–0–3–0; Bopara 9–1–24–0; Ashar Zaidi 3–0–12–0; ten Doeschate 1–1–0–0. *Second innings*—Porter 21–4–70–0; Napier 22.4–6–62–4; Bopara 14–3–41–2; Quinn 24–3–87–4; Westley 1–0–6–0; ten Doeschate 1–0–15–0.

Essex

N. L. J. Browne c Dent b Payne	14 – lbw b Payne	27
J. C. Mickleburgh c Taylor b Shaw	34 – b Payne	1
T. Westley lbw b Shaw	24 – (4) c Noema-Barnett b Norwell	17
R. S. Bopara c Dent b Shaw	0 – (5) b Miles	3
D. W. Lawrence c Miles b Noema-Barnett	127 – (6) c Klinger b Miles	14
*R. N. ten Doeschate lbw b Shaw	52 – (7) c Roderick b Miles	25
Ashar Zaidi c Noema-Barnett b Norwell	21 – (8) b Norwell	37
†J. S. Foster c Marshall b Miles	47 – (9) c Roderick b Norwell	7
G. R. Napier c van Buuren b Noema-Barnett	0 – (10) c Roderick b Payne	0
M. R. Quinn c Norwell b Miles	0 – (11) not out	5
J. A. Porter not out	0 – (3) c Roderick b Norwell	7
B 4, lb 6, nb 4	14 B 4, lb 2, nb 2	8
1/14 (1) 2/53 (3) 3/57 (4) 4/80 (2) 5/182 (6) 6/221 (7) 7/304 (5) 8/304 (9) 9/333 (8) 10/333 (10) (82.1 overs)	333 1/7 (2) 2/16 (3) 3/52 (4) 4/52 (1) 5/59 (5) 6/82 (6) 7/97 (7) 8/124 (9) 9/125 (10) 10/151 (8) (43.3 overs)	151

Payne 13–2–68–1; Norwell 21–5–67–1; Miles 17.1–3–71–2; Shaw 17–2–72–4; Noema-Barnett 11–4–30–2; van Buuren 3–0–15–0. *Second innings*—Payne 15–3–40–3; Norwell 16.3–5–65–4; Miles 6–2–26–3; Shaw 5–2–14–0; Noema-Barnett 1–1–0–0.

Umpires: R. K. Illingworth and B. V. Taylor.

GLOUCESTERSHIRE v LEICESTERSHIRE

At Cheltenham, July 20–22. Leicestershire won by six wickets. Leicestershire 20pts, Gloucestershire 3pts. Toss: uncontested.

Gloucestershire would have replaced Essex at the top had they won, but they botched their first innings. Only Jack Taylor – playing as a specialist batsman while he remedied his action – reached 30, as Leicestershire's battery of pace bowlers, led by Raine, made hay on a slow pitch offering plenty of lateral movement. Robson then held firm for three and three-quarter hours, steering Leicestershire towards a handy lead of 35, despite five wickets for Payne. (Gloucestershire's donation of 43 extras in a low-scoring encounter made a difference, too.) The chances of a close finish receded with Klinger, his wicket sparking a slide from 155 for four to 167 for nine. The last pair added 48, taking Leicestershire's target to 181. They suffered two early setbacks either side of lunch, before Horton and Cosgrove, in the best of the conditions, guided them towards a three-day win with minimal fuss.

Close of play: first day, Leicestershire 122-5 (Robson 49, Eckersley 16); second day, Gloucestershire 133-4 (Klinger 43, Taylor 13).

Gloucestershire

W. A. Tavaré c Cosgrove b Jones	7 – (2) c Cosgrove b Shreck	18
†C. D. J. Dent c O'Brien b McKay	0 – (1) c Cosgrove b Dexter	34
G. L. van Buuren lbw b Raine	10 – b Raine	3
*M. Klinger c Cosgrove b Raine	25 – c O'Brien b Raine	54
H. J. H. Marshall b Shreck	19 – c Robson b Dexter	6
J. M. R. Taylor b Raine	51 – lbw b Raine	24
B. A. C. Howell lbw b Raine	27 – not out	20
C. N. Miles c O'Brien b Jones	0 – lbw b McKay	1
D. A. Payne c Robson b Dexter	16 – b McKay	0
L. C. Norwell c Jones b Dexter	9 – b McKay	3
J. Shaw not out	5 – c Horton b Shreck	29
B 1, lb 5, nb 8	14 Lb 16, w 1, nb 6	23
1/1 (2) 2/9 (1) 3/24 (3) 4/67 (4) 5/69 (5) 6/122 (7) 7/123 (8) 8/167 (6) 9/174 (9) 10/183 (10) (49.5 overs)	183 1/39 (2) 2/46 (3) 3/80 (1) 4/100 (5) 5/155 (4) 6/156 (6) 7/161 (8) 8/161 (9) 9/167 (10) 10/215 (11) (66.1 overs)	215

McKay 11–1–42–1; Jones 13–3–41–2; Raine 14–0–57–4; Shreck 7–0–26–1; Dexter 4.5–1–11–2. *Second innings*—McKay 17–4–43–3; Jones 11–0–44–0; Raine 15–3–54–3; Shreck 13.1–3–33–2; Dexter 10–2–25–2.

Leicestershire

P. J. Horton lbw b Payne	0	– lbw b van Buuren	73
A. J. Robson c Klinger b Miles	62	– c Tavaré b Payne	0
N. J. Dexter b Norwell	15	– b Norwell	3
*M. J. Cosgrove c Dent b Shaw	9	– c Tavaré b van Buuren	56
M. L. Pettini c Marshall b Shaw	1	– not out	18
†N. J. O'Brien lbw b Payne	6	– not out	11
E. J. H. Eckersley c Marshall b Miles	35		
C. J. McKay lbw b Payne	11		
B. A. Raine not out	33		
R. A. Jones lbw b Payne	3		
C. E. Shreck b Payne	0		
B 14, lb 14, w 1, nb 14	43	B 4, lb 14, nb 2	20
1/0 (1) 2/31 (3) 3/41 (4) 4/63 (5) (70.4 overs)	218	1/1 (2) (4 wkts, 54.3 overs)	181
5/86 (6) 6/159 (2) 7/168 (7)		2/16 (3) 3/124 (4)	
8/201 (8) 9/210 (10) 10/218 (11)		4/163 (1)	

Payne 19.4–5–36–5; Norwell 20–6–52–1; Miles 15–1–52–2; Shaw 14–5–44–2; Howell 2–1–6–0. *Second innings*—Payne 9–1–29–1; Norwell 15–5–42–1; Miles 10.3–2–39–0; Shaw 9–1–19–0; Howell 3–2–10–0; van Buuren 8–1–24–2.

Umpires: M. A. Gough and G. D. Lloyd.

At Hove, August 13–16. GLOUCESTERSHIRE lost to SUSSEX by an innings and two runs.

GLOUCESTERSHIRE v KENT

At Bristol, August 23–26. Kent won by an innings and 69 runs. Kent 24pts, Gloucestershire 2pts. Toss: uncontested. County debut: G. C. Viljoen.

A dominant partnership of 258 – Kent's highest for the fifth wicket in the Championship – buried Gloucestershire. Billings hit a career-best 171, and Stevens his first hundred of the season, as they scored at better than five an over. Rain ate into the third day, but their speed allowed a teatime declaration by Northeast – one of three others to make a half-century – at 533 for six. Armed with a lead of 312, Kent had four sessions to press for victory. Gloucestershire, undone by Hardus Viljoen, had again fallen short in their first innings. At the Wanderers in January, Viljoen had dismissed Alastair Cook with his first ball in Test cricket; now he marked his Kent debut with five for 55, including Marshall, the only Gloucestershire player to reach 50 on a feeble first day. Marshall did his utmost to thwart Kent in the second innings too: after Stevens reduced Gloucestershire to 34 for four, he alone batted with any confidence, hitting more than his team-mates combined and taking the game into the last session. He could not, however, deny Kent a maximum-points victory.

Close of play: first day, Gloucestershire 221; second day, Kent 346-4 (Billings 86, Stevens 121); third day, Gloucestershire 34-4 (Marshall 11, Mustard 0).

Gloucestershire

*G. H. Roderick lbw b Stevens	23	–	(2) c Tredwell b Viljoen	8
C. D. J. Dent b Stevens	0	–	(1) c and b Stevens	1
W. A. Tavaré b Gidman	20	–	b Stevens	0
M. Klinger lbw b Viljoen	10	–	c Coles b Stevens	10
H. J. H. Marshall lbw b Viljoen	58	–	lbw b Coles	118
†P. Mustard c Billings b Viljoen	38	–	c Dickson b Claydon	9
J. M. R. Taylor c Coles b Claydon	24	–	c Billings b Coles	22
C. N. Miles c Stevens b Viljoen	9	–	b Viljoen	15
D. A. Payne b Viljoen	1	–	b Tredwell	14
L. C. Norwell c Dickson b Coles	8	–	c Billings b Viljoen	24
M. D. Taylor not out	4	–	not out	7
B 9, lb 9, nb 8	26		B 10, lb 3, w 2	15
1/6 (2) 2/41 (1) 3/59 (4) 4/67 (3) 5/149 (6) 6/189 (7) 7/200 (5) 8/208 (9) 9/217 (10) 10/221 (8) (94.2 overs)	221		1/5 (1) 2/13 (2) 3/13 (3) 4/34 (4) 5/69 (6) 6/115 (7) 7/158 (8) 8/191 (9) 9/214 (5) 10/243 (10) (86.3 overs)	243

Coles 18–2–45–1; Stevens 20–5–30–2; Claydon 19–5–36–1; Viljoen 22.2–5–55–5; Gidman 7–2–19–1; Tredwell 7–4–18–0; Denly 1–1–0–0. *Second innings*—Viljoen 22.3–4–66–3; Stevens 19–6–47–3; Gidman 4–1–12–0; Claydon 12–3–31–1; Coles 17–6–49–2; Tredwell 11–5–20–1; Denly 1–0–5–0.

Kent

D. J. Bell-Drummond c Mustard b M. D. Taylor	65
S. R. Dickson lbw b Payne	0
J. L. Denly c Mustard b Norwell	6
*S. A. Northeast c Klinger b M. D. Taylor	54
†S. W. Billings c Miles b Norwell	171
D. I. Stevens c Klinger b Miles	140
W. R. S. Gidman not out	58
J. C. Tredwell not out	22
B 2, lb 6, w 3, nb 6	17
1/5 (2) 2/28 (3) 3/126 (1) 4/141 (4) 5/399 (6) 6/490 (5) (6 wkts dec, 119.4 overs)	533
110 overs: 479-5	

M. T. Coles, G. C. Viljoen and M. E. Claydon did not bat.

Payne 23–2–83–1; Norwell 27–7–88–2; M. D. Taylor 25–3–89–2; Miles 23–4–119–1; J. M. R. Taylor 15–0–100–0; Marshall 3–0–21–0; Dent 3.4–0–25–0.

Umpires: P. K. Baldwin and A. G. Wharf.

At Derby, August 31–September 3. GLOUCESTERSHIRE drew with DERBYSHIRE.

At Cardiff, September 6–8. GLOUCESTERSHIRE beat GLAMORGAN by ten wickets.

At Northampton, September 12–15. GLOUCESTERSHIRE lost to NORTHAMPTONSHIRE by 114 runs.

GLOUCESTERSHIRE v SUSSEX

At Bristol, September 20–23. Drawn. Gloucestershire 8pts, Sussex 12pts. Toss: uncontested. First-class debut: J. R. Bracey.

Early on the fourth day, Gloucestershire were 99 for five in their second innings, still 107 behind. But Marshall – playing his 160th and final first-class match for Gloucestershire – and Mustard put on 135 to help save a game in which Sussex had made most of the running, not that there was much at stake. Marshall, who was about to move back to his native New Zealand after 11 seasons at Bristol, took his aggregate for the county across all three formats to 14,810. Mustard then shared fifty stands with Jack Taylor and Miles to bank the draw. Back on a rain-affected opening day, when there was generous sideways movement, Gloucestershire lurched to 97 for seven; Dent and Payne then added

114. In the Sussex reply, fifties for Nash and Wells, plus 42 from Salt (caught Mustard), were followed by an unbeaten hundred from Brown, making light of a spirited performance from Shaw, who took a maiden five-for – and more rain interruptions. Sussex gained a commanding lead of 206 but, despite Briggs's second five-for since leaving Hampshire, they couldn't translate it into victory.

Close of play: first day, Gloucestershire 201-7 (Dent 86, Payne 48); second day, Sussex 208-4 (Salt 29, Brown 13); third day, Gloucestershire 88-3 (Dent 47, Shaw 0).

Gloucestershire

*G. H. Roderick b Jordan	0	– b Jordan	9
C. D. J. Dent c and b Archer	90	– c Brown b Briggs	55
J. R. Bracey b Magoffin	2	– lbw b Briggs	12
G. T. Hankins b Robinson	2	– lbw b Briggs	6
H. J. H. Marshall lbw b Magoffin	14	– (6) c Nash b Briggs	77
†P. Mustard c Brown b Magoffin	4	– (7) not out	90
J. M. R. Taylor b Robinson	5	– (8) c Haines b Archer	33
C. N. Miles c Brown b Archer	20	– (9) not out	16
D. A. Payne c and b Jordan	56		
J. Shaw b Archer	5	– (5) lbw b Briggs	2
M. D. Taylor not out	5		
B 6, lb 14, nb 6	26	B 17, lb 8, nb 12	37
1/1 (1) 2/6 (3) 3/12 (4) (79.1 overs)	229	1/25 (1) (7 wkts dec, 111 overs)	337
4/38 (5) 5/42 (6) 6/68 (7)		2/74 (3) 3/86 (4)	
7/97 (8) 8/211 (2) 9/223 (10) 10/229 (9)		4/92 (5) 5/99 (2) 6/234 (6) 7/287 (8)	

Magoffin 22–11–36–3; Jordan 23.1–9–67–2; Robinson 15–5–52–2; Archer 14–5–39–3; Haines 1–1–0–0; Briggs 4–0–15–0. *Second innings*—Magoffin 17–3–48–0; Jordan 20–2–66–1; Archer 25–6–67–1; Briggs 39–10–93–5; Wells 6–0–23–0; Robinson 4–0–15–0.

Sussex

C. D. Nash c Mustard b Shaw	66
T. J. Haines c Mustard b Shaw	1
L. W. P. Wells c M. D. Taylor b Shaw	75
F. J. Hudson-Prentice b Shaw	9
P. D. Salt c Mustard b Miles	42
*†B. C. Brown not out	118
C. J. Jordan lbw b Miles	19
O. E. Robinson c Mustard b Miles	20
J. C. Archer lbw b J. M. R. Taylor	39
D. R. Briggs lbw b Shaw	3
S. J. Magoffin b Miles	12
B 14, lb 6, w 5, nb 6	31
1/4 (2) 2/118 (1) (128.5 overs)	435
3/128 (4) 4/186 (3) 5/238 (5)	
6/278 (7) 7/325 (8) 8/410 (9)	
9/419 (10) 10/435 (11) 110 overs: 376-7	

Payne 28–5–81–0; Shaw 24–4–79–5; Miles 26.5–5–109–4; M. D. Taylor 30–4–90–0; J. M. R. Taylor 17–3–50–1; Dent 3–0–6–0.

Umpires: P. K. Baldwin and M. J. Saggers.

HAMPSHIRE

A sense of perspective

PAT SYMES

Overshadowing a dreadful season were the death of Hamza Ali and a serious illness for Michael Carberry. Ali, a promising and whole-hearted seamer who had made his first-class debut in April, drowned in June. A month later, former England opener Carberry revealed he was receiving treatment for cancer. In January came news that he had undergone a successful operation, and hoped to take part in the 2017 season.

Beside these events, on-field performances barely seemed to matter. A long list of injuries meant Hampshire never fielded a first-choice team, and unusually they failed to qualify for the knockout stages of either limited-overs tournament. They also failed in their last-ditch attempt to escape the relegation zone in the Championship.

But on October 3 they received a huge stroke of good fortune: Durham's dire financial predicament was punished with relegation, allowing Hampshire, who finished eighth, to stay up by default. It was not the route they would have chosen, and it could not hide a poor summer: they won only ten of their 39 first-team matches, the lowest for 19 years, and used 29 players in an attempt to halt the decline. It didn't help that their respected coach, Dale Benkenstein, quit halfway through, to spend more time with his family in South Africa. In November, it was announced that Craig White, the former England all-rounder who had replaced Benkenstein on a temporary basis, would take over permanently.

The summer had begun with a buzz of optimism, particularly about the bowling. England left-armer Reece Topley had arrived from Essex and would pair up with Fidel Edwards, whose 45 wickets at 20 had done so much to ensure an eleventh-hour Division One survival in 2015. There was also Gareth Berg, who had taken 42, plus South African Ryan McLaren. But Berg was injured on the pre-season tour of Barbados and did not play until June; Topley broke a hand in April in his only game and a month later was ruled out for the season with a stress fracture of the back; and Edwards fractured an ankle in a kick-about at Headingley, also in April. Chris Wood played three times before requiring knee surgery, and young off-spinner Brad Taylor ruptured ankle ligaments tripping on the Rose Bowl steps.

In other circumstances, there would have been satisfaction at England's selection of captain James Vince and Liam Dawson, but their absences simply exposed weaknesses. Will Smith was the only player to appear in all Championship matches, while Sean Ervine in his benefit year reached 1,000 first-class runs for the first time, despite missing four games through injury. No one else made 900, though all-rounder McLaren was a rare success, with 869 runs and 32 wickets; it was a blow when he chose to join Lancashire for 2017. The bowling was stretched by the loss of so many components, and

Harry Trump, Getty Images

Sean Ervine

Gareth Batty, whose Surrey side beat Hampshire by an innings in July, was critical of the workload asked of teenage leg-spinner Mason Crane. He claimed 35 first-class wickets, more than anyone.

Hampshire hoped the experienced West Indian Tino Best might be a like-for-like replacement for Edwards (who later signed up for 2017). But, after taking 14 wickets in six matches – and being penalised for hurling the ball at Essex's Ashar Zaidi in a Twenty20 game – Best was quietly discarded. The season's nadir came in a humiliating innings defeat by Middlesex. After being penalised for a slow over-rate, Hampshire left Merchant Taylors' School one point worse off than when they arrived. It was no surprise they had fewest bowling points in their division, nor that they won only two matches, both against Nottinghamshire, who finished last. As in 2015, Hampshire prolonged their fight for survival until the last afternoon, and it was ironic that defeat by Durham should, at least temporarily, have sent them down.

In recent years, Hampshire have won a reputation as a powerful one-day side. But their expertise deserted them. After ten matches in the T20 Blast, long their strongest format, they had four points: two from a victory over Kent; two from no-results. Darren Sammy was drafted in alongside Shahid Afridi, but neither contributed much. In the Royal London Cup, where Ervine assumed the captaincy, they were slightly less woeful. They won half their matches, but overall it was the worst limited-overs season for many a summer. The return of Australia's George Bailey on a two-year deal should stiffen the batting, as should the signing of Rilee Rossouw, who – like seamer Kyle Abbott – opted to join Hampshire on a Kolpak deal, at the expense of an international future with South Africa.

Under new groundsman Karl McDermott, the Rose Bowl pitch lost something of its traditional first-morning bite. There were several big scores, though Hampshire could not blame the square for winning just five matches at home all summer. Supporters instead raised their eyebrows at some unusual management decisions. Adam Wheater made 802 Championship runs at 47, including an unbeaten 204 at Edgbaston, but – unhappy at being supplanted behind the stumps by Lewis McManus – was allowed to rejoin Essex.

With another narrow escape behind them, Hampshire have another, unexpected, chance to rebuild. There is no shortage of youthful talent: as well as Topley, who should be fit again, they have Tom Alsop, whose century against Surrey was a highlight of a pleasing first full season, plus Brad Wheal – capable of real pace – Crane, McManus and Taylor. But they will have to make do without stalwart seamer James Tomlinson, who announced his retirement by thanking all the batsmen who had been kind enough to get out to him.

Championship attendance: 24,885.

HAMPSHIRE RESULTS

All first-class matches – Played 17: Won 2, Lost 4, Drawn 11.
County Championship matches – Played 16: Won 2, Lost 4, Drawn 10.

Specsavers County Championship, 8th in Division 1 (but not relegated);
NatWest T20 Blast, 8th in South Group; Royal London One-Day Cup, 5th in South Group.

COUNTY CHAMPIONSHIP AVERAGES, BATTING AND FIELDING

Cap		*Birthplace*	*M*	*I*	*NO*	*R*	*HS*	*100*	*Avge*	*Ct/St*
2005	†S. M. Ervine	*Harare, Zimbabwe*	12	21	4	1,050	158*	4	61.76	9
	†R. McLaren¶	*Kimberley, SA*	15	24	9	832	100	1	55.46	6
2016	A. J. A. Wheater	*Leytonstone*	12	21	4	802	204*	2	47.17	16/1
2006	†J. H. K. Adams	*Winchester‡*	14	25	0	897	99	0	35.88	13
	L. D. McManus	*Poole*	10	13	1	425	132*	1	35.41	20/6
2013	L. A. Dawson	*Swindon*	12	20	1	644	116	1	33.89	2
2013	J. M. Vince	*Cuckfield*	8	14	0	473	119	1	33.78	5
	†T. P. Alsop	*Wycombe*	12	20	0	655	117	1	32.75	12
2015	W. R. Smith	*Luton*	16	28	0	827	210	1	29.53	11
2006	†M. A. Carberry	*Croydon*	8	15	1	411	107	1	29.35	4
2016	G. K. Berg	*Cape Town, SA*	10	13	3	288	56	0	28.80	3
2008	†J. A. Tomlinson	*Winchester‡*	6	9	4	75	23*	0	15.00	2
	†G. M. Andrew	*Yeovil*	6	7	1	85	25	0	14.16	2
	M. S. Crane	*Shoreham-by-Sea*	12	17	4	101	22	0	7.76	4
	B. T. J. Wheal††	*Durban, SA*	8	9	4	37	14	0	7.40	1
	T. L. Best††	*St Michael, Barb.*	6	8	1	49	23*	0	7.00	3

Also batted: A. Carter (*Lincoln*) (2 matches) 4, 4 (1 ct); F. H. Edwards†† (*St Peter, Barbados*) (2 matches) 4; R. J. W. Topley (*Ipswich*) (1 match) 15; †D. J. Wainwright (*Pontefract*) (1 match) 35*, 1*; J. J. Weatherley (*Winchester‡*) (1 match) 4, 9; C. P. Wood (*Basingstoke‡*) (2 matches) 31, 6.

‡ *Born in Hampshire.* ¶ *Official overseas player.* †† *Other non-England-qualified.*

BOWLING

	Style	*O*	*M*	*R*	*W*	*BB*	*5I*	*Avge*
J. A. Tomlinson	LFM	151.3	40	483	14	4-74	0	34.50
B. T. J. Wheal	RFM	211	36	720	20	6-51	1	36.00
G. K. Berg	RFM	251.2	73	694	19	6-56	1	36.52
R. McLaren	RFM	382	81	1,242	32	5-104	1	38.81
T. L. Best	RFM	136.5	20	554	14	5-90	1	39.57
L. A. Dawson	SLA	306.5	56	877	20	4-100	0	43.85
M. S. Crane	LBG	372	49	1,409	31	3-19	0	45.45

Also bowled: T. P. Alsop (SLA) 10–0–66–2; G. M. Andrew (RFM) 129–25–439–7; A. Carter (RFM) 42–8–126–6; F. H. Edwards (RFM) 45–6–247–3; S. M. Ervine (RFM) 61–10–216–2; W. R. Smith (OB) 126.1–20–401–5; J. M. Vince (RM) 15.2–1–72–2; D. J. Wainwright (SLA) 31–4–112–2; C. P. Wood (LFM) 51–19–139–3.

LEADING ROYAL LONDON CUP AVERAGES (100 runs/4 wickets)

Batting	*Runs*	*HS*	*Avge*	*SR*	*Ct/St*
L. A. Dawson	359	100*	71.80	118.87	5
T. P. Alsop	327	116	54.50	86.50	2
A. J. A. Wheater	238	90	47.60	88.14	2/1
R. McLaren	136	46*	45.33	106.25	0
S. M. Ervine	219	53	36.50	102.81	4
W. R. Smith	225	84	32.14	73.77	3
J. H. K. Adams	221	92	31.57	84.35	3
G. M. Andrew	152	70*	30.40	138.18	3

Bowling	*W*	*BB*	*Avge*	*ER*
R. McLaren	10	4-42	18.20	4.91
B. T. J. Wheal	7	4-38	20.42	5.01
G. K. Berg	11	4-25	27.72	5.25
L. A. Dawson	8	2-42	37.75	4.25
M. S. Crane	9	4-80	38.77	6.34
G. M. Andrew	7	2-32	45.00	6.63

LEADING NATWEST T20 BLAST AVERAGES (125 runs/15 overs)

Batting	Runs	HS	Avge	SR	Ct/St
Shahid Afridi	191	35	17.36	**160.50**	3
L. A. Dawson	299	76*	29.90	**126.16**	7
M. A. Carberry	154	54	25.66	**120.31**	1
S. M. Ervine	127	56	11.54	**117.59**	2
T. P. Alsop	143	85	20.42	**117.21**	3
A. J. A. Wheater	148	39	16.44	**116.53**	3/2

Bowling	W	BB	Avge	ER
Shahid Afridi	9	3-33	30.44	**6.22**
L. A. Dawson	19	5-17	15.57	**6.72**
B. T. J. Wheal	5	3-43	25.80	**8.06**
G. M. Andrew	8	2-19	22.25	**8.90**
T. L. Best	4	2-38	64.50	**9.49**

FIRST-CLASS COUNTY RECORDS

Highest score for	316	R. H. Moore v Warwickshire at Bournemouth	1937
Highest score against	303*	G. A. Hick (Worcestershire) at Southampton	1997
Leading run-scorer	48,892	C. P. Mead (avge 48.84)	1905–36
Best bowling for	9-25	R. M. H. Cottam v Lancashire at Manchester	1965
Best bowling against	10-46	W. Hickton (Lancashire) at Manchester	1870
Leading wicket-taker	2,669	D. Shackleton (avge 18.23)	1948–69
Highest total for	714-5 dec	v Nottinghamshire at Southampton	2005
Highest total against	742	by Surrey at The Oval	1909
Lowest total for	15	v Warwickshire at Birmingham	1922
Lowest total against	23	by Yorkshire at Middlesbrough	1965

LIST A COUNTY RECORDS

Highest score for	177	C. G. Greenidge v Glamorgan at Southampton	1975
Highest score against	203	A. D. Brown (Surrey) at Guildford	1997
Leading run-scorer	12,034	R. A. Smith (avge 42.97)	1983–2003
Best bowling for	7-30	P. J. Sainsbury v Norfolk at Southampton	1965
Best bowling against	7-22	J. R. Thomson (Middlesex) at Lord's	1981
Leading wicket-taker	411	C. A. Connor (avge 25.07)	1984–98
Highest total for	371-4	v Glamorgan at Southampton	1975
Highest total against	358-6	by Surrey at The Oval	2005
Lowest total for	43	v Essex at Basingstoke	1972
Lowest total against	61	by Somerset at Bath	1973
	61	by Derbyshire at Portsmouth	1990

TWENTY20 COUNTY RECORDS

Highest score for	124*	M. J. Lumb v Essex v Southampton	2009
Highest score against	116*	L. J. Wright (Sussex) at Southampton	2014
Leading run-scorer	**2,842**	**M. A. Carberry (avge 31.23)**	**2006–16**
Best bowling for	5-14	A. D. Mascarenhas v Sussex at Hove	2004
Best bowling against	**5-13**	**R. F. Higgins (Middlesex) at Southampton**	**2016**
Leading wicket-taker	119	D. R. Briggs (avge 19.40)	2010–15
Highest total for	225-2	v Middlesex at Southampton	2006
Highest total against	220-4	by Somerset at Taunton	2010
Lowest total for	85	v Sussex at Southampton	2008
Lowest total against	67	by Sussex at Hove	2004

ADDRESS

The Ageas Bowl, Botley Road, West End, Southampton SO30 3XH; 023 8047 2002; enquiries@ageasbowl.com; www.ageasbowl.com.

OFFICIALS

Captain J. M. Vince
Cricket operations manager T. M. Tremlett
Director of cricket G. W. White
First-team coach C. White
Head of player development C. R. M. Freeston

President N. E. J. Pocock
Chairman R. G. Bransgrove
Chief executive D. Mann
Head groundsman K. McDermott
Scorer K. R. Baker

HAMPSHIRE v CARDIFF MCCU

At Southampton, April 4–6. Drawn. Toss: Hampshire. First-class debuts: Hamza Ali, J. J. Weatherley; G. C. Holmes, A. G. Milton, J. R. Turpin.

Alex Thomson, a 22-year-old off-spinner who had played for Staffordshire, removed six Hampshire batsmen in the first innings and one in the second. The fifth bowler used after stand-in captain Ervine chose to bat, Thomson had gone wicketless in his two previous first-class games, but now found unexpected turn on an early-season pitch. Hampshire youngsters Alsop and Joe Weatherley put on 166 for the first wicket before falling to Thomson in successive overs. Cardiff opener Jeremy Lawlor, who had played for Glamorgan in 2015, struck a confident 81, while Sean Griffiths made 65 from 59 balls, including four sixes. Thomson dismissed Wood when Hampshire, leading by 111, batted again. Ervine set Cardiff 238, but rain returned to prevent a conclusion.

Close of play: first day, Hampshire 270-5 (Wheater 41, McManus 13); second day, Cardiff MCCU 258-9 (Westphal 28, Turpin 0).

Hampshire

T. P. Alsop c Herring b Thomson	82		
J. J. Weatherley c Westphal b Thomson	83		
*S. M. Ervine c Holmes b Thomson	9	– (1) c Thomson b Turpin	31
R. McLaren c and b Westphal	10	– (2) c Herring b Turpin	27
C. P. Wood lbw b Thomson	24	– (3) c Lawlor b Thomson	35
†A. J. A. Wheater c sub (H. Allen) b Thomson	48		
L. D. McManus b Thomson	68		
B. J. Taylor c Turpin b Westphal	36		
M. S. Crane not out	1	– (4) not out	24
Lb 2, w 2, nb 4	8	B 4, w 5	9
1/166 (2) 2/171 (1) 3/190 (3) 4/192 (4) 5/250 (5) 6/277 (6) 7/358 (8) 8/369 (7) (8 wkts dec, 86.5 overs)	369	1/57 (1) 2/73 (2) 3/126 (3) (3 wkts dec, 30.4 overs)	126

B. T. J. Wheal and Hamza Ali did not bat.

Westphal 18–2–60–2; Leverock 9–3–33–0; Griffiths 21–3–84–0; Turpin 8–1–45–0; Thomson 29.5–3–138–6; Holmes 1–0–7–0. *Second innings*—Westphal 7–1–21–0; Turpin 10–2–44–2; Thomson 8.4–0–38–1; Griffiths 3–0–11–0; Holmes 2–0–8–0.

Cardiff MCCU

J. L. Lawlor c McManus b Wheal	81	– not out	33
*B. R. M. Scriven c Wheater b Hamza Ali	20	– lbw b Crane	23
C. L. Herring b Wheal	0	– not out	14
A. G. Milton c Ervine b Crane	12		
G. C. Holmes lbw b Crane	0		
†T. N. Cullen b Crane	12		
S. W. Griffiths c Hamza Ali b Taylor	65		
A. T. Thomson c McLaren b Hamza Ali	18		
A. A. Westphal not out	28		
K. S. Leverock b Taylor	14		
J. R. Turpin not out	0		
B 2, lb 6	8	Lb 4, p 5	9
1/41 (2) 2/42 (3) 3/71 (4) 4/71 (5) 5/131 (1) 6/133 (6) 7/168 (8) 8/241 (7) 9/258 (10) (9 wkts dec, 73 overs)	258	1/44 (2) (1 wkt, 22 overs)	79

Wood 9–1–45–0; Wheal 13–3–21–2; Hamza Ali 12–3–47–2; McLaren 5–2–7–0; Crane 21–4–70–3; Taylor 9–3–19–2; Weatherley 4–0–41–0. *Second innings*—Wheal 5–2–8–0; Hamza Ali 5–1–12–0; Wood 3–0–11–0; Crane 6–2–19–1; Taylor 3–0–20–0.

Umpires: D. J. Millns and B. V. Taylor.

HAMPSHIRE v WARWICKSHIRE

At Southampton, April 10–13. Drawn. Hampshire 8pts (after 1pt penalty), Warwickshire 12pts. Toss: uncontested. County debut: R. J. W. Topley.

Bell had no hesitation in choosing to bowl on a green pitch, and his decision was vindicated when Hampshire were flummoxed by swing: Barker took five early wickets as they lurched to 59 for six. Then, in improving conditions, McLaren led a tail-end recovery that spilled over on to the third day – the second was a washout – and edged Hampshire past 200. In his first Championship innings following his omission from England's tour of South Africa, Bell looked in supreme form. He began watchfully, but his tempo increased, and he finished with a seven-hour 174; it was his sixth century (including four hundreds for England) in 14 innings at the Rose Bowl, and he added 151 for the sixth wicket with Woakes. Warwickshire led by 158, though less than two and a half sessions remained. They had a glimmer of hope when Hampshire were five down for 112, but Dawson's patience ensured a draw. It was an inauspicious Hampshire debut for Reece Topley: unable to bowl after breaking his right hand while batting, he was later diagnosed with a stress fracture of the back, and missed the rest of the season.

Close of play: first day, Hampshire 189-8 (McLaren 84, Tomlinson 15); second day, no play; third day, Warwickshire 283-6 (Bell 130).

Hampshire

M. A. Carberry c Ambrose b Barker	3	– c Chopra b Barker	18
T. P. Alsop c Ambrose b Barker	1	– c Hain b Rankin	24
*J. M. Vince c Hain b Rankin	25	– lbw b Clarke	21
W. R. Smith c Hain b Barker	0	– lbw b Patel	3
L. A. Dawson lbw b Barker	20	– not out	50
S. M. Ervine lbw b Barker	4	– c Ambrose b Barker	22
†A. J. A. Wheater lbw b Clarke	7	– not out	34
R. McLaren b Clarke	85		
R. J. W. Topley b Woakes	15		
J. A. Tomlinson not out	23		
F. H. Edwards c Barker b Clarke	4		
B 4, lb 9, nb 2	15	B 8, lb 5	13
1/4 (1) 2/5 (2) 3/17 (4) 4/50 (3) (79.2 overs)	202	1/24 (1) (5 wkts, 71.5 overs)	185
5/54 (6) 6/59 (5) 7/87 (7) 8/138 (9)		2/59 (2) 3/66 (4)	
9/190 (8) 10/202 (11)		4/76 (3) 5/112 (6)	

Barker 18–5–53–5; Woakes 16–7–35–1; Rankin 16–1–39–1; Clarke 22.2–8–43–3; Patel 7–2–19–0. *Second innings*—Barker 15–5–33–2; Clarke 13–2–37–1; Patel 30.5–16–53–1; Rankin 11–0–43–1; Westwood 2–0–6–0.

Warwickshire

V. Chopra lbw b Edwards	8
I. J. Westwood lbw b Edwards	2
*I. R. Bell c Vince b Tomlinson	174
I. J. L. Trott c Ervine b Vince	27
S. R. Hain c Wheater b McLaren	25
†T. R. Ambrose c Alsop b Tomlinson	11
C. R. Woakes lbw b Edwards	66
R. Clarke c Wheater b McLaren	7
K. H. D. Barker not out	21
J. S. Patel b Dawson	1
W. B. Rankin c Vince b Tomlinson	0
B 8, lb 2, nb 8	18
1/3 (2) 2/10 (1) (106.4 overs)	360
3/59 (4) 4/108 (5) 5/132 (6)	
6/283 (7) 7/304 (8) 8/355 (3)	
9/359 (10) 10/360 (11)	

Edwards 22–4–102–3; Tomlinson 21.4–3–79–3; McLaren 23–3–70–2; Vince 4–0–14–1; Dawson 27–7–53–1; Smith 8–2–30–0; Alsop 1–0–2–0.

Umpires: S. J. O'Shaughnessy and M. J. Saggers.

At Leeds, April 17–20. HAMPSHIRE drew with YORKSHIRE.

HAMPSHIRE v MIDDLESEX

At Southampton, May 1–4. Drawn. Hampshire 11pts, Middlesex 12pts. Toss: uncontested. County debut: T. L. Best.

A freak accident on the first day ended Voges's involvement in the game. The ball had gone for a boundary to third man, and substitute fielder Ollie Rayner sent in a high return. Simpson, the Middlesex keeper, was unable to take it, and it struck Voges on the back of the head. He fell to the ground, and was later taken to hospital with concussion. Under ECB guidelines on head injuries he was obliged to remain out of action for six days. On a pitch of variable bounce, Hampshire had reached a respectable total thanks to Carberry's first Championship century since September 2014. Rain knocked a hole in the second day – only 42 overs were possible – but Malan and Simpson added 182 for the fourth wicket to guide Middlesex towards a small lead. Already without several key bowlers, Hampshire lost Wood to a knee injury, which might have explained Vince's excessive caution: Middlesex were not tempted by a target of 266 in a session. Although the fiery Best, hastily signed to strengthen the bowling, struck early, the match dawdled to inevitable stalemate.

Close of play: first day, Hampshire 315-7 (Dawson 87, Best 8); second day, Middlesex 84-3 (Malan 40, Simpson 9); third day, Hampshire 76-1 (Adams 16, Vince 28).

Hampshire

M. A. Carberry c sub (O. P. Rayner) b Harris	107	– lbw b Murtagh	15
J. H. K. Adams c Compton b Murtagh	5	– c sub (J. E. C. Franklin) b Finn	70
*J. M. Vince c Voges b Roland-Jones	25	– c Robson b Roland-Jones	38
W. R. Smith c sub (J. E. C. Franklin) b Roland-Jones	24	– lbw b Murtagh	14
L. A. Dawson c Simpson b Finn	89	– b Finn	19
†A. J. A. Wheater lbw b Murtagh	25	– not out	57
R. McLaren lbw b Roland-Jones	9	– not out	46
C. P. Wood lbw b Harris	6		
T. L. Best not out	23		
M. S. Crane b Murtagh	0		
J. A. Tomlinson lbw b Finn	0		
B 2, lb 7, nb 14	23	B 13, lb 8, w 6, nb 4	31
1/11 (2) 2/72 (3) 3/128 (4) 4/228 (1) 5/286 (6) 6/297 (7) 7/306 (8) 8/318 (5) 9/331 (10) 10/336 (11) (104 overs)	336	1/22 (1) 2/103 (3) 3/132 (4) 4/185 (5) 5/186 (2) (5 wkts dec, 88 overs)	290

Murtagh 27–9–64–3; Finn 22–3–79–2; Harris 19–5–69–2; Roland-Jones 23–2–87–3; Stirling 13–2–28–0. *Second innings*—Murtagh 16–7–39–2; Finn 20–4–59–2; Harris 16–2–47–0; Roland-Jones 17–4–52–1; Stirling 12–0–34–0; Gubbins 7–0–38–0.

Middlesex

S. D. Robson c Carberry b Tomlinson	5	– (2) c Wheater b Best	0
N. R. T. Gubbins c Wheater b McLaren	26	– (1) lbw b Tomlinson	5
N. R. D. Compton c Adams b McLaren	1	– not out	14
D. J. Malan c McLaren b Crane	121	– not out	24
†J. A. Simpson c Wheater b Tomlinson	65		
P. R. Stirling b McLaren	13		
J. A. R. Harris lbw b Tomlinson	57		
T. S. Roland-Jones b McLaren	4		
T. J. Murtagh not out	39		
S. T. Finn c Best b Tomlinson	5		
*A. C. Voges absent hurt			
B 18, lb 3, nb 4	25	B 6, lb 4, nb 2	12
1/11 (1) 2/25 (3) 3/58 (2) 4/240 (4) 5/242 (5) 6/273 (6) 7/279 (8) 8/347 (7) 9/361 (10) (104.5 overs)	361	1/5 (2) 2/19 (1) (2 wkts, 15 overs)	55

Best 19–1–93–0; Tomlinson 20.3–4–74–4; Wood 16.2–5–39–0; McLaren 24–4–74–4; Crane 25–7–60–1. *Second innings*—Best 6–2–18–1; Tomlinson 5–3–13–1; Crane 2–0–10–0; Smith 2–0–4–0.

Umpires: N. G. C. Cowley and R. T. Robinson.

At Manchester, May 8–11. HAMPSHIRE lost to LANCASHIRE by an innings and 94 runs.

HAMPSHIRE v NOTTINGHAMSHIRE

At Southampton, May 22–25. Hampshire won by 69 runs. Hampshire 21pts, Nottinghamshire 3pts. Toss: uncontested.

Hampshire fashioned a win that lifted them off the foot of the table, despite being without captain James Vince, away on Test duty, and several injured bowlers. Early in the final session, though, the game was in the balance. With Patel and Christian well set (Christian was playing only his second Championship match, six years after his first, for Hampshire), Nottinghamshire were 222 for five, needing 83 from 26 overs. Then Best tore through Christian's defences and in the same over bounced out Hutton. With Read unable to bat after Best broke his left hand in the first innings, Hampshire required just two wickets. Nineteen-year-old leg-spinner Crane grabbed them in two balls: Patel caught at slip, Gurney at point. Nottinghamshire had lost four for 13 in 21 deliveries. On a pitch of unreliable bounce, Alsop – a year older than Crane – had ushered Hampshire towards a couple of batting points after the weather disrupted the first day. Wessels, who later kept in place of Read, limited Nottinghamshire's deficit to 81, then Will Smith top-scored as Hampshire battled Gurney – his match figures of nine for 136 were a career-best – en route to a declaration. Jake Ball, temporarily released by England between the Leeds and Chester-le-Street Tests, was replaced by Hutton for days three and four.

Close of play: first day, Hampshire 149-4 (Ervine 38, Alsop 32); second day, Nottinghamshire 99-5 (Wessels 22, Read 8); third day, Hampshire 189-8 (McLaren 32, Crane 6).

Hampshire

M. A. Carberry c Christian b Ball	19	– c Wessels b Gurney	0
J. H. K. Adams c and b Fletcher	30	– c Christian b Fletcher	16
*W. R. Smith lbw b Ball	16	– c Taylor b Patel	61
L. A. Dawson lbw b Fletcher	0	– b Gurney	2
S. M. Ervine b Fletcher	42	– lbw b Gurney	45
T. P. Alsop c Read b Gurney	72	– c Wessels b Gurney	7
†A. J. A. Wheater c Read b Gurney	19	– c Mullaney b Fletcher	1
R. McLaren c Wessels b Gurney	10	– lbw b Gurney	43
T. L. Best lbw b Gurney	0	– lbw b Patel	0
M. S. Crane c Read b Patel	10	– not out	13
J. A. Tomlinson not out	21	– not out	16
B 1, lb 10, w 4, nb 16	31	B 4, lb 6, w 3, nb 6	19
1/45 (1) 2/60 (2) 3/60 (4) 4/84 (3) 5/156 (5) 6/199 (7) 7/232 (6) 8/234 (8) 9/235 (9) 10/270 (10) (104.2 overs)	270	1/9 (1) 2/21 (2) 3/24 (4) 4/102 (5) 5/112 (6) 6/115 (7) 7/165 (3) 8/165 (9) 9/201 (8) (9 wkts dec, 75 overs)	223

Ball 30–7–66–2; Fletcher 28–8–60–3; Gurney 26–3–61–4; Christian 6–1–31–0; Patel 6.2–1–19–1; Mullaney 8–1–22–0. *Second innings*—Fletcher 16–4–35–2; Gurney 24–1–75–5; Christian 6–0–27–0; Patel 16–3–50–2; Mullaney 5–3–10–0; Hutton 7–3–16–0; Libby 1–1–0–0.

Nottinghamshire

S. J. Mullaney c McLaren b Best	0 – c Adams b McLaren	20
J. D. Libby run out	2 – c Wheater b Best	4
M. J. Lumb c Adams b McLaren	32 – lbw b Best	9
B. R. M. Taylor c Wheater b McLaren	28 – c Best b Crane	71
M. H. Wessels c Ervine b Dawson	72 – c Wheater b McLaren	6
S. R. Patel c Smith b McLaren	3 – c Ervine b Crane	65
*†C. M. W. Read not out	8 – absent hurt	
D. T. Christian b Crane	14 – (7) b Best	31
B. A. Hutton c Adams b Crane	8 – (8) c Crane b Best	0
L. J. Fletcher b Crane	0 – (9) not out	3
H. F. Gurney b Best	16 – (10) c Carberry b Crane	0
B 2, lb 2, nb 2	6 B 13, lb 7, w 1, p 5	26
1/0 (1) 2/8 (2) 3/53 (3) 4/68 (4) 5/72 (6) 6/149 (8) 7/173 (9) 8/173 (5) 9/189 (10) 10/189 (11) (72.5 overs)	189 1/7 (2) 2/21 (3) 3/50 (1) 4/68 (5) 5/176 (4) 6/222 (7) 7/222 (8) 8/235 (6) 9/235 (10) (63.3 overs)	235

Hutton replaced J. T. Ball, who left to join England's Test squad.

In the first innings Read, when 8, retired hurt at 99-5 and resumed at 189-9.

Best 16.5–5–44–2; Tomlinson 19–7–56–0; McLaren 15–6–24–3; Crane 10–4–19–3; Ervine 9–3–23–0; Dawson 3–0–19–1. *Second innings*—Best 14–3–47–4; Tomlinson 11–5–20–0; McLaren 16–6–37–2; Crane 17.3–2–70–3; Dawson 2–0–19–0; Ervine 3–0–17–0.

Umpires: N. G. B. Cook and G. D. Lloyd.

At Northwood, May 29–June 1. HAMPSHIRE lost to MIDDLESEX by an innings and 116 runs. *Hampshire make a net loss of one point after being docked two for a slow over-rate.*

HAMPSHIRE v SOMERSET

At Southampton, June 26–29. Drawn. Hampshire 8pts, Somerset 13pts. Toss: Hampshire.

Somerset were on course for a comprehensive win until bad light and rain ended the match on the third afternoon; Hampshire, four down in their second innings, still trailed by 82. Will Smith had taken first use of a bland strip and, at 184 for three, his decision seemed sound. Then Jamie Overton found movement where previously there had been none, claiming five wickets as Hampshire lost six for 11 in eight overs. Somerset soon put a total of 219 into perspective. In his first Championship match of the season, Myburgh – who had briefly been based at the Rose Bowl in 2011 – shared a third-wicket stand of 167 with Hildreth, each making a century. McLaren did his best to slow Somerset's progress, claiming the only five-for of his 13-month stint at Southampton. But, with the bowlers tiring, Craig Overton and Davies added 82 in 64 balls for the ninth wicket, and Rogers declared 255 ahead. Gregory removed Adams for a duck, and later accounted for Smith and Dawson, but Somerset were frustrated, first by spirited batting, then by rain.

Close of play: first day, Somerset 66-1 (Trescothick 33, Myburgh 29); second day, Hampshire 18-1 (Smith 11, Alsop 7); third day, Hampshire 173-4 (Carberry 37, Ervine 34).

Hampshire

J. H. K. Adams c Trescothick b C. Overton	61	– (2) b Gregory	0
*W. R. Smith c Gregory b C. Overton	32	– (1) b Gregory	33
T. P. Alsop lbw b Allenby	37	– c Trescothick b Trego	53
M. A. Carberry c Rogers b J. Overton	29	– not out	37
L. A. Dawson b Allenby	15	– c Trescothick b Gregory	3
S. M. Ervine c Davies b J. Overton	0	– not out	34
R. McLaren not out	24		
†L. D. McManus b J. Overton	0		
G. K. Berg lbw b J. Overton	0		
M. S. Crane lbw b J. Overton	1		
T. L. Best c Rogers b C. Overton	9		
B 1, lb 8, nb 2	11	B 5, lb 6, nb 2	13
1/89 (2) 2/118 (1) 3/166 (3) (66.4 overs)	219	1/0 (2) (4 wkts, 64.4 overs)	173
4/184 (5) 5/184 (4) 6/189 (6)		2/89 (3) 3/113 (1)	
7/189 (8) 8/191 (9) 9/195 (10) 10/219 (11)		4/121 (5)	

C. Overton 13.4–2–52–3; Gregory 13–2–54–0; J. Overton 16–3–42–5; Leach 2–0–8–0; Allenby 17–7–38–2; Trego 5–2–16–0. *Second innings*—C. Overton 12–3–21–0; Gregory 13–4–26–3; J. Overton 9.4–1–35–0; Leach 17–3–36–0; Allenby 5–1–23–0; Trego 6–2–19–1; Myburgh 2–1–2–0.

Somerset

M. E. Trescothick c Ervine b McLaren	42
*C. J. L. Rogers c McManus b McLaren	0
J. G. Myburgh c Best b Crane	110
J. C. Hildreth lbw b McLaren	152
J. Allenby lbw b McLaren	22
P. D. Trego c Ervine b Crane	5
L. Gregory lbw b McLaren	18
C. Overton not out	35
J. Overton c Berg b Best	8
†R. C. Davies not out	52
B 9, lb 16, w 1, nb 4	30
1/4 (2) 2/88 (1) (8 wkts dec, 100 overs)	474
3/255 (3) 4/308 (5)	
5/325 (6) 6/367 (7) 7/376 (4) 8/392 (9)	

M. J. Leach did not bat.

Best 20–3–63–1; McLaren 23–4–104–5; Berg 21–3–91–0; Ervine 5–0–18–0; Dawson 6–0–33–0; Crane 25–2–140–2.

Umpires: S. C. Gale and P. J. Hartley.

At Chester-le-Street, July 3–6. HAMPSHIRE drew with DURHAM.

At Birmingham, July 10–13. HAMPSHIRE drew with WARWICKSHIRE.

HAMPSHIRE v SURREY

At Southampton, July 17–20. Surrey won by an innings and 13 runs. Surrey 23pts, Hampshire 5pts. Toss: Surrey.

In this bottom-of-the-table contest, Surrey ran riot after opting to bat on an immaculate surface. There were three centuries, including Batty's first since 2006, plus a near-miss from Sibley, who shared an opening stand of 208 with Burns. Next day, Batty and Foakes added an unbeaten 222, an eighth-wicket record both for Surrey and against Hampshire. Depleted by injuries and international call-ups, Hampshire asked Crane, their 19-year-old leg-spinner, to toil through 51 overs in increasing heat, which Batty said was too many. They were ragged and after 163 overs in the field, 184 for five when McManus – whose glovework had ousted Wheater from behind the stumps – came in. His previous three innings had brought five runs, but he held fast for a maiden hundred, reached during a tenth-wicket stand of 96 with Wheal. But it wasn't enough to prevent the follow-on, and Hampshire had 84 overs to survive. Thanks to resistance from Will Smith and McLaren, as well as more cussedness from McManus, they came close. But Batty claimed six wickets – the 14th Surrey player

MOST EXPENSIVE FIRST-CLASS ANALYSES FOR HAMPSHIRE

47–7–213–4	S. D. Udal (OB)	v Surrey at The Oval	2002
51–4–210–3	**M. S. Crane (LBG)**	**v Surrey at Southampton (Rose Bowl)**	**2016**
55–5–202–7	*A. S. Kennedy (RM)	v Middlesex at Lord's	1919
62–13–192–4	C. B. Llewellyn (LM)	v Sussex at Hove	1903
41–3–190–4	G. Brown (RM)	v Kent at Southampton (Northlands Road)	1926
44.1–7–187–5	C. B. Llewellyn (LM)	v Kent at Tonbridge	1901
55–8–183–2	S. D. Udal (OB)	v Essex at Colchester	1995
54.1–8–181–6	A. S. Kennedy (RM)	v Yorkshire at Southampton (Northlands Road)	1912
40–3–181–2	O. W. Herman (RFM)	v Cambridge University at Portsmouth	1947
42–5–179–4	C. P. Mead (SLA)	v Surrey at The Oval	1909

* *Kennedy claimed all seven wickets to fall in the Middlesex innings.*

to combine a century and a six-for – to guide his side to an innings victory. Hampshire stayed bottom; Surrey leapfrogged Nottinghamshire into seventh.

Close of play: first day, Surrey 332-4 (Finch 56, Davies 21); second day, Hampshire 73-2 (Alsop 29, McLaren 31); third day, Hampshire 398-9 (McManus 117, Wheal 9).

Surrey

R. J. Burns c Ervine b Crane	122
D. P. Sibley b Berg	99
Z. S. Ansari st McManus b Crane	5
A. J. Finch lbw b McLaren	86
J. J. Roy lbw b Berg	0
S. M. Davies lbw b Berg	25
†B. T. Foakes not out	141
S. M. Curran st McManus b Crane	16
*G. J. Batty not out	110
B 2, lb 21, nb 10	33
1/208 (1) 2/231 (3) 3/271 (2) 4/283 (5) 5/339 (6) 6/384 (4) 7/415 (8) (7 wkts dec, 163 overs)	637
110 overs: 376-5	

S. C. Meaker and M. H. A. Footitt did not bat.

Berg 30–8–85–3; Andrew 22–1–110–0; McLaren 24–3–95–1; Wheal 25–2–80–0; Crane 51–4–210–3; Smith 10–1–29–0; Alsop 1–0–5–0.

Hampshire

J. H. K. Adams c Meaker b Footitt	5	– (2) c Foakes b Meaker	16
*W. R. Smith b Footitt	0	– (1) b Batty	28
T. P. Alsop c Roy b Sibley	32	– c Foakes b Batty	5
R. McLaren lbw b Sibley	31	– c Sibley b Batty	59
A. J. A. Wheater c Davies b Footitt	59	– b Meaker	0
S. M. Ervine run out	52	– c Finch b Batty	5
†L. D. McManus not out	132	– lbw b Batty	35
G. K. Berg b Batty	40	– lbw b Meaker	38
G. M. Andrew c Roy b Curran	19	– c Davies b Batty	0
M. S. Crane b Batty	1	– c Foakes b Meaker	0
B. T. J. Wheal run out	14	– not out	1
B 7, lb 25, nb 6	38	Lb 12, nb 2	14
1/4 (2) 2/5 (1) 3/73 (4) 4/82 (3) 5/184 (5) 6/195 (6) 7/247 (8) 8/318 (9) 9/327 (10) 10/423 (11) (132.3 overs)	423	1/26 (2) 2/31 (3) 3/100 (1) 4/107 (5) 5/112 (6) 6/121 (4) 7/198 (7) 8/198 (9) 9/198 (8) 10/201 (10) (77.3 overs)	201
110 overs: 381-9			

Curran 22–4–67–1; Footitt 22–6–62–3; Meaker 28.3–8–73–0; Batty 32–13–78–2; Sibley 23–2–103–2; Burns 3–1–7–0; Finch 2–1–1–0. *Second innings*—Footitt 18–7–55–0; Curran 9–3–29–0; Meaker 17.3–3–40–4; Batty 26–12–51–6; Sibley 7–4–14–0.

Umpires: M. Burns and J. W. Lloyds.

HAMPSHIRE v LANCASHIRE

At Southampton, August 4–7. Drawn. Hampshire 9pts, Lancashire 7pts. Toss: Hampshire. First-class debut: S. Mahmood.

Once again, batting first led to riches, if not, in this instance, victory. In Hampshire's first Championship match since the departure of their coach, Dale Benkenstein, Will Smith called correctly, then dug in for 455 balls spread over nine and a half hours; dropped on 70, he eventually fell for a career-best 210, having put on 191 with Adams for the first wicket, and 129 with McLaren for the fifth. When he declared on 548 for six, Smith effectively gave his bowlers two days and 25 overs to dismiss Lancashire twice. If that never seemed likely on this surface, Hampshire did achieve the first part of their strategy by imposing the follow-on, despite half-centuries from four of the top five piloting Lancashire to 300 for three. Trouble was, it had taken Hampshire 156 overs to bowl them out and, although they enjoyed a lead of 161, they had less than two sessions to take another ten wickets. Dawson and Crane had found turn in the first innings, claiming three victims each, and Dawson managed three more, but Hameed – passing 50 for the sixth time in eight innings – comfortably steered Lancashire to safety.

Close of play: first day, Hampshire 276-1 (Smith 99, Alsop 50); second day, Lancashire 70-1 (Hameed 39, Procter 21); third day, Lancashire 310-4 (Croft 41, Kerrigan 3).

Hampshire

*W. R. Smith c Kerrigan b Croft	210
J. H. K. Adams c Croft b Clark	88
T. P. Alsop lbw b Smith	50
L. A. Dawson b Clark	20
A. J. A. Wheater c Croft b Kerrigan	29
R. McLaren not out	81
†L. D. McManus c Moores b Mahmood	18
G. K. Berg not out	5
B 21, lb 11, w 7, nb 8	47
	—
1/191 (2) 2/280 (3) 3/319 (4) 4/363 (5) 5/492 (1) 6/525 (7) (6 wkts dec, 165 overs)	548
110 overs: 316-2	

G. M. Andrew, M. S. Crane and B. T. J. Wheal did not bat.

Jarvis 31–11–73–0; Mahmood 33–5–121–1; Smith 17–5–55–1; Clark 23–7–63–2; Kerrigan 35–5–101–1; Procter 12–4–41–0; Croft 12–0–52–1; Livingstone 2–0–10–0.

Lancashire

T. C. Smith c McManus b Berg	4		
H. Hameed b Berg	89	– not out	57
L. A. Procter lbw b Smith	54	– c Alsop b Dawson	5
A. N. Petersen b Dawson	98	– c Andrew b Dawson	4
*S. J. Croft st McManus b Crane	78	– (1) c Andrew b Dawson	22
S. C. Kerrigan c McManus b Crane	3		
L. S. Livingstone b McLaren	1	– (5) not out	13
J. Clark c McLaren b Crane	11		
†T. J. Moores b Dawson	18		
K. M. Jarvis c Smith b Dawson	6		
S. Mahmood not out	0		
B 12, lb 11, nb 2	25	Lb 1	1
	—		—
1/12 (1) 2/131 (3) 3/216 (2) 4/300 (4) 5/311 (6) 6/320 (7) 7/333 (8) 8/371 (9) 9/383 (10) 10/387 (5) (156.3 overs)	387	1/37 (1) 2/47 (3) 3/61 (4) (3 wkts, 52 overs)	102
110 overs: 283-3			

Berg 21–6–61–2; McLaren 30–10–58–1; Dawson 31–6–63–3; Wheal 24–4–58–0; Crane 35.3–9–87–3; Andrew 13–4–37–0; Smith 2–2–0–1. *Second innings*—McLaren 4–2–6–0; Dawson 18–8–22–3; Berg 5–4–3–0; Crane 15–3–48–0; Andrew 2–1–2–0; Wheal 6–1–16–0; Smith 2–1–4–0.

Umpires: N. A. Mallender and R. T. Robinson.

At Nottingham, August 13–16. HAMPSHIRE beat NOTTINGHAMSHIRE by 176 runs.

At Taunton, August 23–26. HAMPSHIRE drew with SOMERSET. *Sean Ervine hits twin hundreds for Hampshire.*

HAMPSHIRE v YORKSHIRE

At Southampton, August 31–September 3. Drawn. Hampshire 9pts, Yorkshire 10pts. Toss: Yorkshire.

Yorkshire arrived without their England quintet – Bairstow, Plunkett, Rashid, Root and Willey – yet would have been the likelier winners had the weather not swallowed more than 120 overs. Gale eventually set Hampshire 298 from 70 overs and, when the elements forced an early finish with almost 40 unbowled, they were four down: a source of frustration for Yorkshire in their quest for a third successive title, and of relief for Hampshire, battling relegation. After huge first-innings scores in the Rose Bowl's previous two matches, Gale might have expected another, but Berg, with disconcerting seam movement, took a career-best six for 56 to keep them under 300. Hampshire were handily placed at 199 for four, but on the second day, still under cloud cover, Sidebottom and Brooks swung the ball, and Yorkshire gained a lead of 59. Lyth and Ballance built on that advantage, if not speedily, but Gale's declaration was scuppered by the rain.

Close of play: first day, Yorkshire 275-9 (Brooks 29, Sidebottom 8); second day, Yorkshire 69-1 (Lyth 37, Ballance 17); third day, Yorkshire 143-2 (Ballance 46, Gale 19).

Yorkshire

A. Lyth c Smith b McLaren	24	– c Ervine b Wheal	56
A. Z. Lees c Smith b Wheal	10	– b Wheal	12
G. S. Ballance c McManus b Berg	10	– b Berg	72
*A. W. Gale c McManus b McLaren	26	– c McManus b Wheal	19
J. S. Lehmann c Adams b Berg	58	– not out	35
T. T. Bresnan b Berg	56	– c Berg b Carter	27
†A. J. Hodd b Berg	17	– not out	1
Azeem Rafiq c McManus b Berg	5		
S. A. Patterson c Alsop b Crane	7		
J. A. Brooks not out	34		
R. J. Sidebottom b Berg	9		
B 5, lb 10, nb 10	25	B 2, lb 6, nb 8	16
1/22 (2) 2/39 (1) 3/57 (3) (88.2 overs)	281	1/39 (2) (5 wkts dec, 64 overs)	238
4/119 (4) 5/143 (5) 6/216 (6)		2/101 (1) 3/143 (4)	
7/221 (7) 8/224 (8) 9/234 (9) 10/281 (11)		4/189 (3) 5/235 (6)	

McLaren 20–3–76–2; Wheal 19–4–64–1; Berg 24.2–5–56–6; Carter 9–1–27–0; Ervine 5–0–13–0; Crane 11–1–30–1. *Second innings*—McLaren 17–1–60–0; Berg 22–8–60–1; Wheal 19–5–79–3; Carter 4–0–23–1; Ervine 2–0–8–0.

Hampshire

J. H. K. Adams c Lees b Patterson	23	– (2) c Lyth b Brooks	30
W. R. Smith lbw b Brooks	1	– (1) lbw b Sidebottom	4
T. P. Alsop lbw b Sidebottom	3	– c Azeem Rafiq b Brooks	18
*J. M. Vince c Lyth b Bresnan	60	– c Bresnan b Brooks	16
S. M. Ervine c Hodd b Sidebottom	80	– not out	10
R. McLaren c Hodd b Sidebottom	26	– not out	4
†L. D. McManus c Azeem Rafiq b Brooks	6		
G. K. Berg c Hodd b Brooks	0		
M. S. Crane not out	8		
B. T. J. Wheal b Brooks	0		
A. Carter b Brooks	4		
Lb 9, nb 2	11	Lb 2	2
1/14 (2) 2/17 (3) 3/38 (1) (64.2 overs)	222	1/8 (1) (4 wkts, 31.4 overs)	84
4/145 (4) 5/199 (5) 6/208 (7)		2/50 (3) 3/59 (2)	
7/210 (6) 8/212 (8) 9/214 (10) 10/222 (11)		4/74 (4)	

Sidebottom 19–6–45–3; Brooks 17.2–7–53–5; Bresnan 10–1–49–1; Patterson 10–2–39–1; Azeem Rafiq 8–0–27–0. *Second innings*—Sidebottom 8.4–1–36–1; Brooks 9–3–24–3; Bresnan 6–3–9–0; Patterson 6–3–9–0; Azeem Rafiq 2–1–4–0.

Umpires: N. G. B. Cook and N. G. C. Cowley.

At The Oval, September 6–9. HAMPSHIRE drew with SURREY.

HAMPSHIRE v DURHAM

At Southampton, September 20–23. Durham won by six wickets. Durham 22pts, Hampshire 7pts. Toss: uncontested.

On the last afternoon of the season – at the intangible moment when victory became impossible – Hampshire's relegation was confirmed. In 2015, they had miraculously grasped Division One survival at the eleventh hour, and for much of the first two days it looked as if they might pull another rabbit from the hat. History, however, did not repeat itself – at least not on the pitch. But on October 3, ten days after Stokes hit Durham's winning boundary, there came a *deus ex machina* in the form of an edict from Lord's: Durham, who had been bailed out of unsustainable debt by the ECB, would be relegated as part of a many-layered punishment. The beneficiaries (pending possible legal action by Division Two runners-up Kent) were Hampshire, whose eighth place now brought redemption. They had begun the game unsure whether a win would be enough, but full batting points – five of the top six made half-centuries – plus low scores in the Warwickshire–Lancashire match at Edgbaston simplified the equation: victory would spell safety. Hampshire had pinned their hopes on a sandy pitch taking spin, and first-innings wickets for Pringle and Borthwick bore this out. When Durham subsided to 186 for seven, still 225 behind, the plan was going swimmingly. Richardson, though, was in no mind to oblige: despite two Championship fifties all summer, he coaxed 175 from the last three wickets, before being marooned on 99. Leading by 50, Hampshire were in danger of being hoist with their own petard: all nine wickets to fall went to Durham's spin pair, with Pringle collecting a career-best seven for 107. Vince set 296 in a minimum of 78 overs, and turned to Dawson as soon as the eighth. But the three home spinners had little impact, and Stoneman and Borthwick – in their last innings before both joined Surrey – added 162 for the second wicket. Durham won with ten minutes remaining, spreading despair round the Rose Bowl. For ten days.

Close of play: first day, Hampshire 370-6 (Dawson 47, McManus 6); second day, Durham 242-7 (Richardson 50, Carse 30); third day, Hampshire 176-7 (McManus 41, Crane 1).

Hampshire

J. H. K. Adams b Borthwick	53	– (2) c Onions b Borthwick	30
W. R. Smith c Pringle b Carse	90	– (1) c Jennings b Pringle	30
T. P. Alsop lbw b Pringle	1	– c Collingwood b Pringle	0
*J. M. Vince run out	92	– b Pringle	13
S. M. Ervine c Collingwood b Pringle	50	– c Stoneman b Pringle	16
L. A. Dawson lbw b Onions	62	– c Pringle b Borthwick	39
R. McLaren lbw b Pringle	13	– lbw b Pringle	0
†L. D. McManus c Pringle b Borthwick	24	– c Richardson b Pringle	67
G. K. Berg c Collingwood b Onions	0	– (10) not out	36
M. S. Crane b Onions	4	– (9) c Borthwick b Pringle	1
B. T. J. Wheal not out	4	– not out	5
B 6, lb 6, nb 6	18	B 1, lb 5, nb 2	8

1/111 (1) 2/116 (3) 3/218 (2) (109.1 overs) 411
4/275 (4) 5/323 (5) 6/352 (7)
7/397 (6) 8/401 (9) 9/407 (10) 10/411 (8)

1/50 (2) (9 wkts dec, 63 overs) 245
2/50 (3) 3/70 (4)
4/85 (1) 5/108 (5) 6/108 (7)
7/165 (6) 8/177 (9) 9/218 (8)

Rushworth 13–2–33–0; Onions 17–2–41–3; Pringle 31–0–153–3; Carse 9–1–35–1; Stokes 13–2–47–0; Borthwick 24.1–2–81–2; Stoneman 2–1–9–0. *Second innings*—Rushworth 3–0–19–0; Onions 8–1–24–0; Pringle 28–6–107–7; Borthwick 12–0–57–2; Stokes 10–1–28–0; Carse 2–1–4–0.

Durham

M. D. Stoneman c Adams b Dawson	28	– c Alsop b Dawson	137
K. K. Jennings lbw b Berg	1	– lbw b Crane	25
S. G. Borthwick c McManus b Wheal	15	– lbw b Crane	88
G. Clark c McManus b Dawson	58	– st McManus b Crane	8
B. A. Stokes c McLaren b Wheal	50	– not out	23
*P. D. Collingwood c McManus b Crane	0	– not out	6
†M. J. Richardson not out	99		
R. D. Pringle c Adams b Wheal	0		
B. A. Carse c Smith b Dawson	45		
G. Onions c Alsop b Wheal	38		
C. Rushworth lbw b Dawson	0		
B 7, lb 3, w 5, nb 2, p 10	27	B 8, lb 2	10
1/2 (2) 2/39 (3) 3/49 (1) 4/136 (4) (116 overs)	361	1/75 (2) (4 wkts, 78 overs)	297
5/137 (6) 6/183 (5) 7/186 (8)		2/237 (1) 3/254 (4)	
8/265 (9) 9/351 (10) 10/361 (11) 110 overs: 335-8		4/282 (3)	

McLaren 9–2–24–0; Berg 15–5–36–1; Wheal 16–3–39–4; Dawson 33–4–100–4; Smith 13–4–32–0; Crane 30–3–110–1. *Second innings*—Berg 5–2–14–0; Wheal 5–0–22–0; Dawson 25–4–75–1; Smith 14–2–31–0; Crane 27–2–126–3; McLaren 2–0–19–0.

Umpires: M. Burns and N. G. B. Cook.

KENT

The only one was Essex

MARK PENNELL

Sometimes things just don't go your way – and in 2016 little fell right for Kent. They began by visiting a soggy Worcester, and left without ever taking the field. Eventually, after some intelligent cricket, they finished as runners-up – but in the only year it did not confer promotion since the splitting of the Championship in 2000. And in October, when Durham's punishment for unsustainable debt included relegation from Division One, the ECB chose to reprieve Hampshire, eighth in the upper tier, rather than reward Kent. Legal action was considered, but it came to naught.

The rain that blighted that opening fixture hardly went away: Kent lost more Championship cricket than any county bar Northamptonshire, though they were luckier in the limited-overs games. Yet despite Sam Northeast rarely getting the same team twice – either because of injury or selection policy – his side emerged as the likeliest to displace Essex.

Kent were hampered by the success of two of their younger players. The wicketkeeper-batsman Sam Billings missed chunks of the season, either at the IPL or with England's one-day and Lions squads, while opener Daniel Bell-Drummond was also called up by the Lions. A hand injury prevented him from reaching 1,000 first-class runs; he made 953 at 68.

They also had to cope without former captain Rob Key, who swapped his role as Kent anchorman for Sky Sports pundit. In came the affable New Zealand Test opener Tom Latham, the first of the summer's three overseas locums. He hit useful runs – beginning with three Championship half-centuries – but never a hundred. Sean Dickson suffered a spasmodic second season. At Leicester in April, he became the first Kent batsman since 1872 to be out handled the ball; a month later, he carried his bat for an unbeaten 207 at Derby. He failed to reach 20 in ten of his next 15 innings, but managed four fifties.

Northeast still has no double to his name, though in 2016 he came close: his five Championship hundreds were 189, 191, 166 not out, 190 and 178 not out. He ended the summer top of the averages with 1,402 runs at 82; in all three formats, he made 2,138. His captaincy grew in stature, and he was a near-unanimous choice as Player of the Season, though there were frustrations: failure to gain promotion, and a mystifying lack of international recognition.

Unlike Northeast, Billings *had* attracted attention, and in the spring Adam Rouse deputised behind the stumps. He did well, claiming 31 first-class dismissals before injuring a finger against Glamorgan, which required surgery. Callum Jackson stepped in for Billings later in the summer.

While the experienced pair of regular No. 3 Joe Denly and all-rounderDarren Stevens had so-so returns, both did enough to gain contract extensions. Will Gidman, another all-rounder, who arrived on loan from Nottinghamshire, gave the four-day side a balance it had lacked through the absence of several bowlers. Calum Haggett, Matt Hunn, Adam Ball and Adam Riley all played six games or fewer. Two youngsters, left-arm spinner Imran Qayyum and seamer Hugh Bernard, earned first-class debuts, with modest success.

Lee Warren, Gallo Images/Getty Images

Hardus Viljoen

Kent's attack leaned on veterans Mitch Claydon, with 50 first-class wickets, and Stevens, with 39. However, Matt Coles claimed the Bowler of the Season award for 40 wickets in 11 matches. He would have played more had he not been suspended, first for two games by the ECB, then for a month by Kent after he broke the team curfew at Cardiff. Some argued his indiscipline cost the title; it certainly denied him the chance to partner South Africa firebrand Kagiso Rabada, whose mid-season arrival coincided with Coles's second ban. They played only a single Twenty20 game together.

If Rabada's figures – seven wickets at 33 – were not startling, he and Gidman instilled a confidence in a Championship side who strode through the second half of the summer. Gidman's batting was reliability itself: his first three innings were unbeaten half-centuries and, by the time he was dismissed, he had again passed fifty; he added a fifth, also unbeaten, in his seventh innings. Kent were delighted he made his move permanent.

Gidman's debut had marked the start of a glorious August that contained big wins over Worcestershire, Gloucestershire and Sussex. At the heart of the last two was Hardus Viljoen, another South African, and the most successful of Kent's three overseas players. He claimed 20 wickets in four matches, and helped keep the pressure on Essex; he joined Derbyshire for 2017. But, in the penultimate game, against Northamptonshire, all hopes of promotion were shattered in a Ben Duckett-inspired hammering.

Kent's white-ball cricket, notable in 2015 for its innovative batting and canny bowling, seemed to lack self-belief, and they finished well short of the T20 Blast knockouts. Fabian Cowdrey, his slow bowling so effective in 2015, was temporarily sidelined by appendicitis, while Alex Blake lost his thunderous batting form. A late rally took Kent second in their Royal London Cup group, but they lost a home quarter-final to Yorkshire. After five trophyless seasons, head coach Jimmy Adams returned home to become West Indies' director of cricket, and helped arrange Kent's participation in the West Indian domestic Nagico Super50 competition in January and February 2017. Adams was replaced by his assistant, Matt Walker, with South African fast-bowling icon Allan Donald the new No. 2. Simon Willis left to head up Sri Lanka's Academy after 24 years on the playing or coaching staff.

Retirement apartments on the Old Dover Road side of the ground should be completed during 2017; the Colin Blythe Memorial will then be reinstated – in time for the centenary of his death in November.

Championship attendance: 28,893.

KENT RESULTS

All first-class matches – Played 16: Won 5, Lost 2, Drawn 9. Abandoned 1.
County Championship matches – Played 15: Won 5, Lost 2, Drawn 8. Abandoned 1.

Specsavers County Championship, 2nd in Division 2;
NatWest T20 Blast, 7th in South Group; Royal London One-Day Cup, quarter-finalists.

COUNTY CHAMPIONSHIP AVERAGES, BATTING AND FIELDING

Cap		Birthplace	M	I	NO	R	HS	100	Avge	Ct/St
	†W. R. S. Gidman	*High Wycombe*	5	7	4	362	99*	0	120.66	5
2012	S. A. Northeast	*Ashford‡*	15	22	6	1,337	191	5	83.56	5
2015	D. J. Bell-Drummond	*Lewisham‡*	12	19	5	747	124	1	53.35	1
2005	D. I. Stevens	*Leicester*	14	16	0	782	140	2	48.87	8
2015	S. W. Billings	*Pembury‡*	7	7	0	329	171	1	47.00	25/1
	†T. W. M. Latham¶	*Christchurch, NZ*	6	9	1	374	90	0	46.75	9
	S. R. Dickson††	*Johannesburg, SA*	14	20	3	675	207*	1	39.70	8
2008	J. L. Denly	*Canterbury‡*	15	21	2	733	206*	1	38.57	7
	†A. J. Blake	*Farnborough‡*	7	10	3	268	89*	0	38.28	4
2012	†M. T. Coles	*Maidstone‡*	10	9	0	273	70	0	30.33	5
2007	†J. C. Tredwell	*Ashford‡*	11	12	2	291	124	1	29.10	14
	A. P. Rouse	*Harare, Zimbabwe*	6	6	0	164	65	0	27.33	28/1
	A. J. Ball	*Greenwich‡*	4	6	0	141	66	0	23.50	2
	†C. J. Haggett	*Taunton*	6	5	1	87	33*	0	21.75	1
	G. C. Viljoen¶	*Witbank, SA*	4	4	0	80	63	0	20.00	1
2016	†M. E. Claydon	*Fairfield, Australia*	14	15	3	187	55	0	15.58	1
	C. F. Jackson	*Eastbourne*	3	4	0	61	38	0	15.25	9

Also batted: H. R. Bernard (*Canterbury‡*) (1 match) 14; F. K. Cowdrey (*Canterbury‡*) (1 match) 3, 15; M. D. Hunn (*Colchester*) (4 matches) 32*, 3, 0* (2 ct); Imran Qayyum (*Ealing*) (2 matches) 0, 0* (1 ct); †K. Rabada¶ (*Johannesburg, SA*) (2 matches) 14, 5, 6; A. E. N. Riley (*Sidcup‡*) (3 matches) 5*, 32*.

‡ *Born in Kent.* ¶ *Official overseas player.* †† *Other non-England-qualified.*

BOWLING

	Style	O	M	R	W	BB	5I	Avge
G. C. Viljoen	RFM	103.5	12	385	20	5-55	1	19.25
M. T. Coles	RFM	291.5	51	1,059	37	5-116	1	28.62
D. I. Stevens	RM	401.1	104	1,131	37	4-74	0	30.56
M. E. Claydon	RFM	399.4	75	1,519	48	5-42	2	31.64
C. J. Haggett	RM	158.4	30	529	15	4-15	0	35.26
J. C. Tredwell	OB	299	61	921	22	4-45	0	41.86

Also bowled: A. J. Ball (LFM) 42–2–159–3; H. R. Bernard (RFM) 22–3–105–3; J. L. Denly (LBG) 66.3–4–222–3; S. R. Dickson (RM) 1–0–4–0; W. R. S. Gidman (RFM) 44–15–123–4; M. D. Hunn (RFM) 87–8–335–8; Imran Qayyum (SLA) 78.2–14–283–6; T. W. M. Latham (RM) 2–0–5–0; S. A. Northeast (OB) 1.4–0–2–0; K. Rabada (RF) 77–21–232–7; A. E. N. Riley (OB) 26–1–146–0.

LEADING ROYAL LONDON CUP AVERAGES (100 runs/4 wickets)

Batting	Runs	HS	Avge	SR	Ct/St
A. J. Blake	202	66*	67.33	106.31	8
J. L. Denly	428	105	61.14	77.81	1
D. J. Bell-Drummond	332	91	41.50	86.23	4
S. A. Northeast	274	66*	34.25	83.03	5
D. I. Stevens	195	61	32.50	82.27	3
S. W. Billings	218	106*	31.14	117.20	10/1
M. T. Coles	114	91	28.50	156.16	5

Bowling	W	BB	Avge	ER
C. F. Hartley	4	2-23	16.25	4.06
M. T. Coles	24	6-56	17.41	5.21
W. R. S. Gidman	6	3-28	26.66	4.70
D. I. Stevens	7	2-14	35.28	4.04
F. K. Cowdrey	4	2-38	36.75	5.65
J. C. Tredwell	8	3-55	43.12	5.14
M. E. Claydon	6	2-42	57.33	5.44

LEADING NATWEST T20 BLAST AVERAGES (125 runs/18 overs)

Batting	*Runs*	*HS*	*Avge*	*SR*	*Ct/St*
D. J. Bell-Drummond	379	112*	54.14	**148.04**	1
S. A. Northeast	462	75	33.00	**145.28**	3
D. I. Stevens	168	33	15.27	**137.70**	2
J. L. Denly	378	75	27.00	**129.89**	6
T. W. M. Latham	128	48	21.33	**120.75**	3
S. W. Billings	164	55*	14.90	**115.49**	5/2
A. J. Blake	198	37	24.75	**115.11**	8

Bowling	*W*	*BB*	*Avge*	*ER*
K. Rabada	6	2-31	27.00	**6.75**
F. K. Cowdrey	8	3-18	22.25	**7.73**
M. T. Coles	8	4-27	29.37	**7.83**
J. C. Tredwell	8	3-32	51.75	**8.62**
M. E. Claydon	10	3-25	38.40	**9.14**
D. I. Stevens	11	4-31	33.81	**9.45**
D. A. Griffiths	13	2-22	33.61	**9.60**

FIRST-CLASS COUNTY RECORDS

Highest score for	332	W. H. Ashdown v Essex at Brentwood	1934
Highest score against	344	W. G. Grace (MCC) at Canterbury	1876
Leading run-scorer	47,868	F. E. Woolley (avge 41.77)	1906–38
Best bowling for	10-30	C. Blythe v Northamptonshire at Northampton	1907
Best bowling against	10-48	C. H. G. Bland (Sussex) at Tonbridge	1899
Leading wicket-taker	3,340	A. P. Freeman (avge 17.64)	1914–36
Highest total for	803-4 dec	v Essex at Brentwood	1934
Highest total against	676	by Australians at Canterbury	1921
Lowest total for	18	v Sussex at Gravesend	1867
Lowest total against	16	by Warwickshire at Tonbridge	1913

LIST A COUNTY RECORDS

Highest score for	146	A. Symonds v Lancashire at Tunbridge Wells	2004
Highest score against	167*	P. Johnson (Nottinghamshire) at Nottingham	1993
Leading run-scorer	7,814	M. R. Benson (avge 31.89)	1980–95
Best bowling for	8-31	D. L. Underwood v Scotland at Edinburgh	1987
Best bowling against	6-5	A. G. Wharf (Glamorgan) at Cardiff	2004
Leading wicket-taker	530	D. L. Underwood (avge 18.93)	1963–87
Highest total for	384-6	v Berkshire at Finchampstead	1994
Highest total against	371-8	by Somerset at Taunton	2014
Lowest total for	60	v Somerset at Taunton	1979
Lowest total against	60	by Derbyshire at Canterbury	2008

TWENTY20 COUNTY RECORDS

Highest score for	114	S. A. Northeast v Somerset at Taunton	2015
Highest score against	151*	C. H. Gayle (Somerset) at Taunton	2015
Leading run-scorer	**3,015**	**D. I. Stevens (avge 28.99)**	**2005–16**
Best bowling for	5-17	Wahab Riaz v Gloucestershire at Beckenham	2011
Best bowling against	5-17	G. M. Smith (Essex) at Chelmsford	2012
Leading wicket-taker	**115**	**J. C. Tredwell (avge 27.57)**	**2003–16**
Highest total for	231-7	v Surrey at The Oval	2015
Highest total against	224-7	by Somerset at Taunton	2015
Lowest total for	72	v Hampshire at Southampton	2011
Lowest total against	82	by Somerset at Taunton	2010

ADDRESS

St Lawrence Ground, Old Dover Road, Canterbury CT1 3NZ; 01227 456886; kent@ecb.co.uk; www.kentcricket.co.uk.

OFFICIALS

Captain S. A. Northeast
Head coach 2016 J. C. Adams
2017 M. J. Walker
Assistant coach 2017 A. A. Donald
High performance director J. R. Weaver
President C. J. C. Rowe

Chairman G. M. Kennedy
Chief executive J. A. S. Clifford
Chairman, cricket committee G. W. Johnson
Head groundsman S. Williamson
Scorer L. A. R. Hart

KENT v LOUGHBOROUGH MCCU

At Canterbury, April 5–7. Drawn. Toss: Kent. First-class debut: C. J. Nurse. County debut: A. P. Rouse.

Three gloomy days allowed little more than 150 overs, but that was time enough for two young batsmen to score centuries. Bell-Drummond, who during the winter had played for England Lions against Pakistan A, hit a maiden double-hundred, adding 148 for the seventh wicket with Coles, and enabling Kent to declare on 393 for seven. Coles and Stevens quickly reduced Loughborough to 19 for four, then 59 for five, before captain Michael Burgess and wicketkeeper Charlie Lowen organised a recovery. Basil Akram, an all-rounder who had hit 160 for Loughborough against Surrey a week earlier, ensured their work did not go to waste: aided by Sam Grant, he made an unbeaten century from No. 8 to thwart the experienced Kent attack for over three hours.

Close of play: first day, Loughborough MCCU 2-2 (Gamble 0, White 0); second day, Loughborough MCCU 19-3 (White 12, Kumar 0).

Kent

D. J. Bell-Drummond not out	206	M. T. Coles c White b Cook	60
S. R. Dickson c Burgess b Cook	26		
A. J. Ball lbw b Cook	0	Lb 12, w 2, nb 4	18
*S. A. Northeast c Lowen b Akram	65		
D. I. Stevens lbw b Akram	0	1/60 (2) (7 wkts dec, 80.1 overs)	393
A. J. Blake st Lowen b Nurse	17	2/60 (3) 3/181 (4)	
†A. P. Rouse b Gamble	1	4/187 (5) 5/242 (6) 6/245 (7) 7/393 (8)	

J. C. Tredwell, M. E. Claydon and M. D. Hunn did not bat.

Gamble 18–3–63–1; Grant 15–0–89–0; Cook 17.1–3–64–3; Akram 10–1–32–2; Nurse 11–0–58–1; Kumar 9–0–75–0.

Loughborough MCCU

Hasan Azad lbw b Coles	0	S. E. Grant b Hunn	52
C. O. Thurston c Blake b Stevens	2	C. J. Nurse not out	4
R. N. Gamble c Rouse b Coles	4		
R. G. White lbw b Coles	30	B 1, lb 2, nb 12	15
N. R. Kumar c Rouse b Stevens	0		
*M. G. K. Burgess b Claydon	51	1/0 (1) 2/2 (2) (8 wkts dec, 74 overs)	313
†C. T. Lowen b Claydon	55	3/18 (3) 4/19 (5)	
B. M. R. Akram not out	100	5/59 (4) 6/121 (6) 7/165 (7) 8/295 (9)	

S. J. Cook did not bat.

Coles 18–6–75–3; Stevens 14–2–41–2; Tredwell 1–1–0–0; Claydon 17–1–81–2; Hunn 15–0–71–1; Ball 9–2–42–0.

Umpires: B. J. Debenham and M. J. Saggers.

At Worcester, April 10–13. WORCESTERSHIRE v KENT. Abandoned.

> "He is unencumbered by modesty, real or false. 'Who wouldn't want to be me?' he asks on page six. 'Don't get me wrong. It's good fun being me,' he adds two pages later."
> Cricket Books in 2016, page 124

At Leicester, April 24–27. KENT drew with LEICESTERSHIRE.

KENT v GLAMORGAN

At Canterbury, May 1–4. Kent won by ten wickets. Kent 24pts, Glamorgan 5pts. Toss: Glamorgan. First-class debuts: H. R. Bernard; H. W. Podmore. County debut: T. W. M. Latham.

On a pitch offering pace and carry, Kent crushed Glamorgan with half a day to spare – despite dropping five catches. It was an encouraging Championship debut for New Zealand batsman Tom Latham, who in both innings passed 50 en route to a century opening stand with Bell-Drummond. After opting to bat, Glamorgan scored briskly, but wickets fell regularly, and by the first-day close Kent's reply to 260 had reached 124 without loss. Boosted by three more fifties, they went on to 488 – a lead of 228. Glamorgan fared better second time around: Lloyd hit his first Championship century, and Wagg his fourth, in a stand worth 215, a county sixth-wicket record against Kent. Claydon and Coles both ended with six scalps, while Stevens (who turned 40 the day before the game) took five, and Hugh Bernard, on debut, three. Kent's target was 187, which posed few problems – other than knowing when it had been reached. The teams had shaken hands and were walking off when the scorers alerted the umpires that one more run was needed. This did not delay Kent for long: Bell-Drummond hit the next delivery, from Harry Podmore, for four. Coles was later reported for throwing the ball near an opposing batsman "in an inappropriate and dangerous manner" and, because of past infringements, suspended for a fortnight.

AND FOR OUR NEXT TRICK...

Two century opening stands by the same pair in a first-class match for Kent:

C. J. Burnup/E. Humphreys	v South Africans at Beckenham	1901
W. H. Ashdown/A. E. Fagg	v Glam at Cardiff (Arms Park)	1935
A. E. Fagg/A. H. Phebey	v Glos at Gloucester (Wagon Works)	1954
L. Potter/N. R. Taylor	v Indians at Canterbury	1982
N. J. Dexter/J. L. Denly	v Camb UCCE at Cambridge	2006
D. J. Bell-Drummond/T. W. M. Latham	**v Glam at Canterbury**	**2016**

Close of play: first day, Kent 124-0 (Bell-Drummond 62, Latham 48); second day, Glamorgan 16-1 (Kettleborough 8, Bragg 6); third day, Kent 22-0 (Bell-Drummond 13, Latham 7).

Glamorgan

J. M. Kettleborough c Rouse b Coles	0	– c Rouse b Claydon	42
*J. A. Rudolph c Rouse b Claydon	4	– c Rouse b Stevens	0
W. D. Bragg b Claydon	14	– b Bernard	51
†C. B. Cooke c Rouse b Coles	45	– (5) c Latham b Coles	4
A. H. T. Donald c Dickson b Bernard	37	– (4) c Latham b Coles	38
D. L. Lloyd lbw b Coles	4	– c Rouse b Claydon	107
G. G. Wagg c Dickson b Stevens	40	– lbw b Stevens	106
C. A. J. Meschede c Northeast b Bernard	63	– b Stevens	0
A. G. Salter c Rouse b Claydon	25	– c Latham b Stevens	19
H. W. Podmore lbw b Claydon	4	– not out	16
M. G. Hogan not out	0	– c Rouse b Coles	1
B 6, lb 1, w 1, nb 16	24	B 8, lb 1, w 1, nb 20	30
1/0 (1) 2/22 (3) 3/44 (2) 4/91 (4) 5/103 (6) 6/124 (5) 7/194 (7) 8/242 (8) 9/260 (9) 10/260 (10) (64.5 overs)	260	1/2 (2) 2/80 (3) 3/134 (1) 4/147 (5) 5/156 (4) 6/371 (6) 7/372 (8) 8/377 (7) 9/407 (9) 10/414 (11) (94.3 overs)	414

Coles 9.5–3–26–3; Stevens 22–6–68–1; Claydon 16–4–59–4; Bernard 13–1–68–2; Riley 4–1–32–0. *Second innings*—Claydon 26–4–127–2; Stevens 27–7–79–4; Bernard 9–2–37–1; Coles 19.3–2–80–3; Riley 13–0–82–0.

Kent

D. J. Bell-Drummond c Cooke b Meschede	84 – not out	86
T. W. M. Latham c Donald b Hogan	53 – not out	79
J. L. Denly b Hogan	58	
*S. A. Northeast b Meschede	46	
S. R. Dickson c Kettleborough b Hogan	3	
D. I. Stevens c Salter b Meschede	58	
†A. P. Rouse c Donald b Podmore	22	
M. T. Coles b Hogan	29	
M. E. Claydon c Lloyd b Wagg	55	
A. E. N. Riley not out	32	
H. R. Bernard c Cooke b Podmore	14	
B 8, lb 8, w 8, nb 10	34	B 8, lb 11, nb 6 25
1/131 (2) 2/165 (1) 3/246 (3) 4/254 (5) 5/260 (4) 6/338 (7) 7/356 (6) 8/402 (8) 9/457 (9) 10/488 (11)	(111.2 overs) 488 110 overs: 481-9	(no wkt, 48.4 overs) 190

Hogan 29–6–91–4; Meschede 23–4–105–3; Wagg 22–4–95–1; Podmore 13.2–0–73–2; Salter 16–0–67–0; Lloyd 8–1–41–0. *Second innings*—Hogan 8–2–37–0; Meschede 8–3–11–0; Wagg 5–1–20–0; Salter 13–1–47–0; Podmore 7.4–1–29–0; Lloyd 7–1–27–0.

Umpires: R. J. Bailey and N. G. B. Cook.

KENT v GLOUCESTERSHIRE

At Canterbury, May 8–11. Drawn. Kent 12pts, Gloucestershire 10pts. Toss: Gloucestershire.

Gloucestershire escaped with a draw after Kent failed to hammer home their advantage. A combination of rain, tenacious batting and the loss of two key bowlers – Matt Coles was suspended, while off-spinner Riley strained his side after sending down five overs in the first innings – stymied Kent's ambitions. Claydon and Stevens, soon had Gloucestershire in trouble at 14 for four. But they rallied thanks to Marshall's 28th first-class century. All the same, they conceded a 141-run deficit after Northeast's career-best 189 and assorted other contributions, including Latham's third half-century in a row, and 32 from Hunn, who walloped the last three balls of an interrupted third day for six – and allowed an overnight declaration. Showers on the final morning ate up 33 overs to dent Kent's chances. Although Gloucestershire were six down going into the final hour, Taylor and Payne increased their modest lead, and ensured stalemate. Kent batsman Sean Dickson missed the game after a wound in his left hand needed eight stitches: he had been trying to mend a fan with a modelling knife when he slipped.

Close of play: first day, Gloucestershire 296-9 (Payne 22, Shaw 0); second day, Kent 304-3 (Northeast 154, Blake 45); third day, Kent 478-8 (Haggett 33, Hunn 32).

Gloucestershire

C. T. Bancroft c Rouse b Stevens	7 – c Latham b Stevens	18
C. D. J. Dent lbw b Claydon	1 – c Blake b Haggett	27
I. A. Cockbain c Rouse b Claydon	0 – c Rouse b Hunn	32
*†G. H. Roderick c Rouse b Stevens	1 – lbw b Haggett	11
H. J. H. Marshall c Latham b Claydon	112 – c Rouse b Hunn	20
G. T. Hankins b Haggett	45 – c Rouse b Haggett	12
K. Noema-Barnett b Hunn	24 – c Rouse b Claydon	11
J. M. R. Taylor c and b Stevens	52 – not out	46
C. N. Miles c Stevens b Haggett	20 – b Stevens	1
D. A. Payne not out	46 – not out	20
J. Shaw c Rouse b Haggett	17	
B 8, lb 2, nb 2	12	B 2, lb 3, nb 8 13
1/3 (2) 2/5 (3) 3/9 (1) 4/14 (4) 5/101 (6) 6/142 (7) 7/254 (8) 8/254 (5) 9/293 (9) 10/337 (11)	(107 overs) 337	1/39 (1) 2/53 (2) 3/75 (4) 4/111 (3) 5/122 (5) 6/132 (6) 7/155 (7) 8/158 (9) (8 wkts, 58 overs) 211

Claydon 27–4–97–3; Stevens 27–8–68–3; Haggett 26–7–66–3; Hunn 22–3–82–1; Riley 5–0–14–0. *Second innings*—Claydon 17–1–88–1; Stevens 20–2–58–2; Haggett 13–4–27–3; Hunn 8–0–33–2.

Kent

D. J. Bell-Drummond b Payne	0	M. E. Claydon b Taylor	8
T. W. M. Latham c and b Noema-Barnett	90	M. D. Hunn not out	32
J. L. Denly b Payne	0	B 9, lb 6, nb 4	19
*S. A. Northeast b Shaw	189		—
A. J. Blake c Dent b Miles	45	1/0 (1) 2/6 (3) (8 wkts dec, 126 overs)	478
D. I. Stevens c Cockbain b Shaw	54	3/210 (2) 4/314 (5)	
†A. P. Rouse c Roderick b Miles	8	5/376 (4) 6/393 (7)	
C. J. Haggett not out	33	7/413 (6) 8/424 (9) 110 overs: 397-6	

A. E. N. Riley did not bat.

Payne 30–5–76–2; Miles 31–2–146–2; Shaw 23–4–84–2; Taylor 16–0–92–1; Noema-Barnett 26–3–65–1.

Umpires: R. J. Evans and R. A. Kettleborough.

At Northampton, May 15–18. KENT drew with NORTHAMPTONSHIRE.

At Derby, May 22–25. KENT beat DERBYSHIRE by seven wickets.

KENT v LEICESTERSHIRE

At Canterbury, May 29–June 1. Drawn. Kent 8pts, Leicestershire 8pts. Toss: Leicestershire.

Rain and bad light, which wiped out the last seven sessions, condemned this match to a draw. It had been building nicely, with Leicestershire recovering from 19 for three to make 341, thanks largely to a stand of 218 in 52 overs between Cosgrove and Pettini, a county fourth-wicket record against Kent. Stevens claimed four for 74, but the weather – and the doggedness of Bell-Drummond – meant he had no chance to bat against his old employers. (Leicestershire fielded three ex-Kent players: Dexter, O'Brien and Shreck.) Just before tea on the second day, with the clouds filling in, the hosts were 117 for two, and Bell-Drummond had taken his first-class average for the season to 128. Come the end of the match, they had lost the equivalent of more than ten days' Championship play.

Close of play: first day, Leicestershire 340-8 (McKay 16, Sykes 11); second day, Kent 117-2 (Bell-Drummond 65, Northeast 5); third day, no play.

Leicestershire

P. J. Horton c Billings b Stevens	9	C. J. McKay c Billings b Stevens	16
A. J. Robson c Bell-Drummond b Coles	0	J. S. Sykes not out	12
N. J. Dexter lbw b Stevens	1	C. E. Shreck c Hunn b Coles	0
*M. J. Cosgrove run out	119	B 1, lb 20, nb 6	27
M. L. Pettini c Billings b Denly	97		—
†N. J. O'Brien lbw b Hunn	31	1/9 (1) 2/9 (2) 3/19 (3) (98.3 overs)	341
E. J. H. Eckersley c Billings b Stevens	11	4/237 (5) 5/266 (4) 6/280 (6)	
B. A. Raine c Billings b Coles	18	7/290 (7) 8/320 (8) 9/340 (9) 10/341 (11)	

Coles 23.3–6–94–3; Stevens 24–6–74–4; Haggett 11–2–41–0; Hunn 16–2–45–1; Tredwell 16–3–44–0; Denly 8–1–22–1.

Kent

D. J. Bell-Drummond not out	65
T. W. M. Latham lbw b McKay	9
J. L. Denly lbw b Raine	32
*S. A. Northeast not out	5
B 1, lb 4, w 1	6
1/15 (2) 2/103 (3) (2 wkts, 44 overs)	117

S. R. Dickson, D. I. Stevens, †S. W. Billings, C. J. Haggett, J. C. Tredwell, M. T. Coles and M. D. Hunn did not bat.

McKay 11–4–23–1; Raine 11–5–20–1; Dexter 11–3–30–0; Shreck 11–2–39–0.

Umpires: P. R. Pollard and A. G. Wharf.

At Cardiff, June 19–22. KENT drew with GLAMORGAN.

KENT v DERBYSHIRE

At Canterbury, June 26–29. Drawn. Kent 10pts, Derbyshire 12pts. Toss: uncontested.

A high-scoring draw briefly took Kent top, though for much of the time Derbyshire looked the stronger. Kent had slipped to 166 for six on a sound surface, only for Northeast and Ball to bail them out with a stand of 150. Northeast's six-hour career-best 191 seemed to have made good the absence of Daniel Bell-Drummond and Calum Haggett, both injured, and Matt Coles – omitted for out-of-hours misdemeanours during Kent's previous Championship match, in Cardiff. Against a weakened attack, Derbyshire batted deep into the third day and, thanks to Madsen and Thakor – familiar thorns in Kentish sides after hitting Championship hundreds in the corresponding game a month earlier – declared 195 ahead. Kent might have been vulnerable in their second innings, though three half-centuries had more than cleared the arrears when rain arrived on the last afternoon. Palladino had bowled 11 miserly overs, but was unable to add to his four first-innings victims.

Close of play: first day, Kent 354-7 (Northeast 173, Tredwell 11); second day, Derbyshire 291-3 (Madsen 73, Broom 15); third day, Kent 32-0 (Latham 12, Dickson 16).

Kent

T. W. M. Latham lbw b Davis	14	– c sub (R. P. Hemmings) b Madsen	74
S. R. Dickson run out	15	– c Poynton b Cotton	22
J. L. Denly c Poynton b Davis	24	– b Broom	64
*S. A. Northeast c Madsen b Hughes	191	– not out	70
A. J. Blake lbw b Palladino	11	– not out	1
D. I. Stevens c Hughes b Davis	30		
†S. W. Billings b Palladino	4		
A. J. Ball lbw b Palladino	66		
J. C. Tredwell c Rutherford b Thakor	12		
M. E. Claydon c Poynton b Palladino	4		
M. D. Hunn not out	0		
B 2, lb 4, nb 2	8	Lb 7	7
1/30 (1) 2/34 (2) 3/71 (3) 4/90 (5) 5/161 (6) 6/166 (7) 7/316 (8) 8/365 (9) 9/370 (10) 10/379 (4) (105.2 overs)	379	1/39 (2) 2/142 (1) 3/235 (3) (3 wkts, 74 overs)	238

Cotton 18–4–49–0; Palladino 29–6–76–4; Davis 20.3–1–86–3; Thakor 17–1–65–1; Madsen 8.3–1–34–0; Hughes 7.2–0–36–1; Slater 5–0–27–0. *Second innings*—Cotton 11–2–25–1; Palladino 11–4–11–0; Hughes 19–0–82–0; Madsen 17–3–51–1; Slater 4–0–28–0; Thakor 4–1–9–0; Broom 6–0–17–1; Rutherford 2–0–8–0.

Derbyshire

H. D. Rutherford c Blake b Tredwell	65	B. D. Cotton b Hunn	7
*B. A. Godleman c Latham b Claydon	33	W. S. Davis not out	0
C. F. Hughes c and b Tredwell	83	B 7, lb 14, w 1, nb 12	34
W. L. Madsen lbw b Hunn	163		—
N. T. Broom lbw b Claydon	26	1/75 (2) (9 wkts dec, 162.4 overs)	574
B. T. Slater b Tredwell	19	2/139 (1) 3/251 (3)	
S. J. Thakor c Northeast b Stevens	123	4/309 (5) 5/353 (6)	
†T. Poynton c Hunn b Stevens	8	6/497 (4) 7/539 (8)	
A. P. Palladino not out	13	8/560 (7) 9/573 (10)	110 overs: 392-5

Claydon 30–4–114–2; Stevens 33–8–81–2; Tredwell 48.4–5–153–3; Ball 10–1–34–0; Hunn 22–3–95–2; Denly 19–0–76–0.

Umpires: N. L. Bainton and S. J. O'Shaughnessy.

At Chelmsford, July 3–6. KENT lost to ESSEX by ten wickets. *Sam Northeast and James Tredwell add 222, a Kent record for the eighth wicket.*

KENT v SUSSEX

At Tunbridge Wells, July 17–20. Drawn. Kent 11pts, Sussex 8pts. Toss: Kent.

On a two-paced but largely docile pitch at The Nevill, Kent's batsmen made hay. There were four half-centuries in their 575, as well as another huge score for Northeast, whose purple patch extended to 622 in five innings at an average of 207; his 190 here followed an unbeaten 166 against Essex and 191 against Derbyshire, and took him past 1,000 first-class runs for the season. Despite the heat, he played – for reasons of superstition – in a short-sleeved sweater. Slow left-armer Briggs did manage five wickets, but at a cost of 169, and a couple of other Sussex bowlers became unwilling centurions. Two of Kent's attack were making home Championship debuts: Kagiso Rabada generated pace and excitement with his three for 81, while Imran Qayyum, a left-arm spinner, found life trickier. New Zealand batsman Taylor hit a classy maiden century for Sussex, but could not prevent the follow-on, 242 behind, at the start of day four. However, Kent lacked the firepower – or perhaps stamina – to roll Sussex over in three sessions, and instead Finch (patiently) and Taylor (more expansively) made important sixties.

Close of play: first day, Kent 310-3 (Northeast 75, Stevens 51); second day, Sussex 69-1 (Nash 48, Wells 7); third day, Sussex 333.

Kent

S. R. Dickson c Beer b Whittingham	81	M. E. Claydon b Magoffin	4
A. J. Ball c Taylor b Jordan	0	I. Qayyum not out	0
J. L. Denly c Taylor b Whittingham	78		
*S. A. Northeast c and b Magoffin	190	B 7, lb 8, w 1, nb 20	36
D. I. Stevens c Beer b Briggs	63		—
A. J. Blake lbw b Briggs	61	1/2 (2) 2/164 (1) (158.3 overs)	575
J. C. Tredwell c Wells b Briggs	18	3/199 (3) 4/330 (5) 5/457 (6)	
†C. F. Jackson c and b Briggs	38	6/489 (7) 7/559 (4) 8/568 (9)	
K. Rabada b Briggs	6	9/573 (10) 10/575 (8)	110 overs: 360-4

Magoffin 26–4–86–2; Jordan 33–4–106–1; Whittingham 26–2–107–2; Briggs 49.3–7–169–5; Beer 21–3–79–0; Finch 2–0–9–0; Nash 1–0–4–0.

Sussex

C. D. Nash lbw b Rabada	55	– (2) c Northeast b Qayyum	18
H. Z. Finch b Claydon	3	– (1) c Blake b Tredwell	66
L. W. P. Wells b Claydon	22	– c and b Qayyum	22
L. R. P. L. Taylor not out	142	– c Denly b Tredwell	68
*L. J. Wright c Jackson b Rabada	60	– lbw b Tredwell	38
†B. C. Brown lbw b Rabada	5	– not out	25
C. J. Jordan c Tredwell b Stevens	7	– not out	7
W. A. T. Beer run out	5		
D. R. Briggs c Jackson b Tredwell	8		
S. J. Magoffin lbw b Qayyum	1		
S. G. Whittingham lbw b Tredwell	0		
B 4, lb 9, nb 12	25	B 7, nb 4	11
1/29 (2) 2/82 (1) 3/105 (3) 4/219 (5) 5/229 (6) 6/251 (7) 7/273 (8) 8/309 (9) 9/332 (10) 10/333 (11) (127.1 overs)	333	1/54 (2) 2/96 (3) 3/153 (1) 4/214 (4) 5/237 (5) (5 wkts, 91 overs)	255
110 overs: 291-7			

Rabada 28–8–81–3; Stevens 20–5–48–1; Claydon 23–7–47–2; Tredwell 40.1–14–91–2; Qayyum 12–5–45–1; Ball 4–0–8–0. *Second innings*—Rabada 15–4–33–0; Stevens 6–3–15–0; Tredwell 30–11–76–3; Claydon 12–4–36–0; Qayyum 25–3–80–2; Denly 3–0–8–0.

Umpires: N. G. B. Cook and V. K. Sharma.

KENT v WORCESTERSHIRE

At Canterbury, August 3–6. Kent won by ten wickets. Kent 23pts, Worcestershire 4pts. Toss: Kent.

Lingering irritation over the early-season washout at New Road spurred Kent to a dominant victory. Canterbury Week began at noon, an hour later than usual, because of the previous day's Royal London Cup game at Hove and, not long after tea, Kent bowled Worcestershire out for 211. After missing three Championship games for disciplinary reasons, Coles claimed a couple of wickets, while Claydon, capped during the match, took five for 42, his best since leaving Durham in 2013; Billings became the second Kent keeper, after Steve Marsh, to make seven dismissals in an innings. Half-centuries for Dickson, Stevens and Gidman – making his Championship debut for Kent after joining on loan from Nottinghamshire – secured a lead of 240; the biggest partnership was the 75 added by Will Gidman and No. 11 Claydon. Only a dogged maiden fifty from George Rhodes, son of Worcestershire coach Steve, averted an innings defeat. Kent's 23 points propelled them from fifth to first, until the following day, when Essex pulled ahead again.

Close of play: first day, Kent 55-0 (Bell-Drummond 30, Dickson 19); second day, Kent 397-9 (Gidman 54, Claydon 13); third day, Worcestershire 213-6 (Cox 35).

Worcestershire

*D. K. H. Mitchell c Billings b Coles	16	– lbw b Gidman	43
G. H. Rhodes c Billings b Claydon	16	– b Gidman	55
T. C. Fell c Billings b Coles	34	– lbw b Tredwell	32
J. M. Clarke c Coles b Tredwell	69	– run out	10
T. Köhler-Cadmore c Billings b Claydon	3	– b Claydon	17
R. A. Whiteley c Gidman b Claydon	6	– b Tredwell	15
†O. B. Cox c Billings b Claydon	5	– c Tredwell b Coles	39
J. Leach c Billings b Gidman	16	– c Billings b Stevens	3
E. G. Barnard b Tredwell	25	– c Gidman b Stevens	17
K. J. Abbott c Billings b Claydon	3	– st Billings b Stevens	10
C. A. J. Morris not out	0	– not out	4
B 6, lb 4, nb 8	18	B 2, nb 4	6
1/24 (1) 2/70 (3) 3/103 (2) 4/111 (5) 5/121 (6) 6/127 (7) 7/149 (8) 8/198 (9) 9/205 (10) 10/211 (4) (73.1 overs)	211	1/94 (2) 2/105 (1) 3/122 (4) 4/142 (5) 5/162 (3) 6/213 (6) 7/220 (7) 8/220 (8) 9/234 (10) 10/251 (9) (93.3 overs)	251

Coles 19–6–61–2; Stevens 17–5–49–0; Claydon 17–5–42–5; Gidman 13–5–36–1; Tredwell 6.1–1–9–2; Denly 1–0–4–0. *Second innings*—Coles 22–7–48–1; Stevens 12.3–3–31–3; Claydon 14–2–41–1; Tredwell 27–7–88–2; Gidman 9–3–21–2; Denly 9–1–20–0.

Kent

D. J. Bell-Drummond c Whiteley b Abbott	37	– not out 2
S. R. Dickson b Barnard	79	– not out 4
J. L. Denly b Morris	21	
*S. A. Northeast c Clarke b Barnard	1	
†S. W. Billings c Cox b Morris	33	
D. I. Stevens c Clarke b Leach	81	
A. J. Blake c Whiteley b Leach	9	
W. R. S. Gidman not out	75	
J. C. Tredwell c Cox b Barnard	9	
M. T. Coles c Clarke b Rhodes	41	
M. E. Claydon b Rhodes	46	
B 9, lb 8, nb 2	19	B 4, nb 4 8
1/74 (1) 2/115 (3) 3/130 (4) 4/169 (2) 5/209 (5) 6/243 (7) 7/290 (6) 8/325 (9) 9/376 (10) 10/451 (11) — (129.3 overs)	451	(no wkt, 1.5 overs) 14
110 overs: 381-9		

Abbott 31–9–93–1; Leach 30–4–87–2; Barnard 27–4–97–3; Morris 18–3–72–2; Rhodes 21.3–3–83–2; Mitchell 2–1–2–0. *Second innings*—Morris 1–0–5–0; Mitchell 0.5–0–5–0.

Umpires: B. V. Taylor and A. G. Wharf.

At Bristol, August 23–26. KENT beat GLOUCESTERSHIRE by an innings and 69 runs.

At Hove, August 31–September 2. KENT beat SUSSEX by an innings and 127 runs.

KENT v NORTHAMPTONSHIRE

At Beckenham, September 6–8. Northamptonshire won by ten wickets. Northamptonshire 23pts, Kent 4pts. Toss: uncontested.

After winning three games by convincing margins, Kent came a cropper on a sporting September pitch. They lost not simply the match, but any realistic hope of the single promotion place. Inserted by Northamptonshire, they were bundled out for 230. Though Kent's strong batting line-up had struggled for timing, Duckett hit a confident, match-defining 208. It did him no harm that Andrew Strauss, director of England cricket, had dropped in to the County Ground. Quick on his feet, and displaying immaculate placement, Duckett pierced the field at will, deploying top-hand control that Colin Cowdrey would have admired. In an innings spanning 251 balls, he hit 26 fours, including reverse pulls, sweeps and savage cuts. Trailing by 154, Kent were blown away by Kleinveldt, and staggered to the second-day close on a calamitous 15 for four. Billings, who had been on drinks duty with the England Twenty20 side, joined next morning – Jackson made way – but fortunes barely

---

ALL OR NOTHING

A double-century and a pair against the same team in the same season:

C. A. Roach	West Indies v England	1929-30
E. R. T. Holmes	Surrey v Derbyshire	1935
K. D. Mackay	Queensland v New South Wales	1955-56
M. S. Atapattu	Sri Lanka v England	2000-01
J. S. Foster	Essex v Leicestershire	2004
J. H. Kallis	South Africa v Sri Lanka	2011-12
J. L. Denly	**Kent v Northamptonshire**	**2016**

changed: Northeast's early wicket left them 22 for five. There was resistance from the nightwatchman, Viljoen, but Northamptonshire sped home.

Close of play: first day, Northamptonshire 31-0 (Duckett 19, Newton 8); second day, Kent 15-4 (Viljoen 9).

Kent

D. J. Bell-Drummond c Murphy b Sanderson	20	– c Murphy b Kleinveldt	0
S. R. Dickson c Wakely b Keogh	63	– lbw b Kleinveldt	3
J. L. Denly c Murphy b Crook	0	– (4) b Kleinveldt	0
*S. A. Northeast c Murphy b Azharullah	9	– (6) c Murphy b Sanderson	1
D. I. Stevens c Keogh b Azharullah	0	– (8) c Wakely b Keogh	44
W. R. S. Gidman c Kleinveldt b White	51	– (9) c Murphy b Kleinveldt	16
†C. F. Jackson c sub (S. A. Zaib) b Crook	0		
J. C. Tredwell lbw b Kleinveldt	12	– (5) c Murphy b Kleinveldt	1
M. T. Coles c Levi b Kleinveldt	52	– (10) b Keogh	7
M. E. Claydon not out	4	– (11) not out	4
G. C. Viljoen c White b Kleinveldt	4	– (3) c Duckett b Crook	63
S. W. Billings (did not bat)		– (7) b Crook	39
B 1, lb 6, w 2, nb 6	15	B 4, nb 2	6
1/59 (1) 2/66 (3) 3/85 (4) 4/85 (5) 5/117 (2) 6/122 (7) 7/146 (8) 8/201 (6) 9/224 (9) 10/230 (11) (82.2 overs)	230	1/0 (1) 2/7 (2) 3/7 (4) 4/15 (5) 5/22 (6) 6/106 (3) 7/113 (7) 8/155 (9) 9/169 (10) 10/184 (8) (56.4 overs)	184

Billings replaced Jackson after being released from the England Twenty20 squad.

Kleinveldt 20.2–3–70–3; Sanderson 21–6–40–1; Azharullah 15–4–46–2; Crook 10–5–7–2; Keogh 12–1–44–1; White 4–1–16–1. *Second innings*—Kleinveldt 21–2–53–5; Sanderson 19–2–55–1; Azharullah 6–0–34–0; White 3–1–9–0; Crook 5–0–24–2; Keogh 2.4–1–5–2.

Northamptonshire

B. M. Duckett c Tredwell b Coles	208	– not out	12
R. I. Newton c Jackson b Claydon	14	– not out	15
*A. G. Wakely c Gidman b Coles	73		
R. I. Keogh c Tredwell b Claydon	18		
R. E. Levi c Tredwell b Claydon	6		
†D. Murphy c Denly b Viljoen	16		
S. P. Crook c Jackson b Viljoen	7		
R. K. Kleinveldt c Stevens b Viljoen	5		
G. G. White c Jackson b Stevens	12		
Azharullah c Jackson b Stevens	0		
B. W. Sanderson not out	1		
B 10, lb 4, w 2, nb 8	24	B 4	4
1/57 (2) 2/228 (3) 3/261 (4) 4/267 (5) 5/347 (1) 6/362 (7) 7/368 (8) 8/371 (6) 9/378 (10) 10/384 (9) (97.4 overs)	384	(no wkt, 4.3 overs)	31

Coles 18–0–79–2; Stevens 13.4–3–32–2; Viljoen 24–1–91–3; Tredwell 18–2–71–0; Denly 3–0–9–0; Claydon 16–0–73–3; Gidman 5–0–15–0. *Second innings*—Coles 2.3–1–15–0; Tredwell 2–0–12–0.

Umpires: N. L. Bainton and J. W. Lloyds.

KENT v ESSEX

At Canterbury, September 20–23. Drawn: Kent 13pts, Essex 10pts. Toss: uncontested.

Kent finished second in the division, behind Essex, to secure the runners-up cheque – and nothing else. In any other year, both would have been promoted, but the reduction of Division One to eight teams for 2017 left Kent where they were. After a first-day washout, Denly and Northeast set them on their way, then Stevens struck his seventh hundred against Essex. There was a hard-earned five for 124 for Dixon, while the 38-year-old Masters, in his farewell appearance at his old stomping ground, took two as Kent reached 441, their fifth batting point clinching the runners-up spot. Claydon picked up his 50th wicket of the season when he had Browne caught behind and, at 267 for nine, Essex looked unlikely to avert the follow-on; Masters and Dixon did so, just. When Kent batted again, 149 to the good, Northeast made an unbeaten 178, the fifth time he had reached 150 in 2016 – a Kent record in the Championship – and enough to take him top of the first-class averages. Towards the end, he took 30 off an over from Velani. Masters bowled the final over of the game, a maiden, before Essex were presented with the Division Two trophy.

Close of play: first day, no play; second day, Kent 389-7 (Stevens 107, Coles 24); third day, Essex 289-9 (Masters 7, Dixon 12).

Kent

D. J. Bell-Drummond c Chopra b Rhodes	32	– lbw b Masters	0
S. R. Dickson c Wheater b Dixon	16	– c Chopra b Rhodes	14
J. L. Denly c Wheater b Dixon	74	– c Browne b Dixon	9
*S. A. Northeast b Rhodes	56	– not out	178
†S. W. Billings lbw b Bopara	16	– c Wheater b Rhodes	2
D. I. Stevens c Rhodes b Dixon	136	– c Wheater b Masters	18
W. R. S. Gidman c Wheater b Dixon	0	– not out	63
J. C. Tredwell lbw b Dixon	39		
M. T. Coles c Wheater b Masters	32		
G. C. Viljoen c Westley b Masters	10		
M. E. Claydon not out	4		
B 4, lb 10, w 2, nb 10	26	Lb 2, nb 2	4
1/44 (1) 2/50 (2) 3/159 (4) 4/204 (5) 5/208 (3) 6/208 (7) 7/316 (8) 8/403 (9) 9/427 (10) 10/441 (6) (108.1 overs)	441	1/0 (1) 2/13 (3) 3/36 (2) 4/40 (5) 5/103 (6) (5 wkts dec, 67 overs)	288

Masters 29–8–74–2; Walter 14–1–72–0; Rhodes 18–3–80–2; Dixon 28.1–3–124–5; Bopara 14–0–68–1; Westley 5–1–9–0. *Second innings*—Masters 17–9–32–2; Dixon 15–2–65–1; Rhodes 12–4–34–2; Walter 5–1–30–0; Westley 4–0–22–0; Bopara 5–0–30–0; Lawrence 6–0–29–0; Velani 2–0–36–0; Browne 1–0–8–0.

Essex

V. Chopra lbw b Stevens	25
N. L. J. Browne c Billings b Claydon	36
*T. Westley c Dickson b Claydon	8
R. S. Bopara c Billings b Viljoen	22
D. W. Lawrence c Denly b Tredwell	88
†A. J. A. Wheater c Dickson b Coles	21
K. S. Velani c Tredwell b Viljoen	22
W. M. H. Rhodes c Tredwell b Viljoen	3
P. I. Walter b Tredwell	28
D. D. Masters not out	8
M. W. Dixon c Claydon b Coles	14
B 2, w 5, nb 10	17
1/51 (1) 2/68 (3) 3/73 (2) 4/137 (4) 5/169 (6) 6/206 (7) 7/214 (8) 8/265 (5) 9/267 (9) 10/292 (11) (82.4 overs)	292

Coles 14.4–0–70–2; Stevens 20–9–45–1; Viljoen 14–1–69–3; Claydon 14–1–61–2; Gidman 5–4–6–0; Tredwell 10–3–22–2; Denly 5–1–17–0.

Umpires: R. J. Evans and G. D. Lloyd.

LANCASHIRE

Spring success averts autumn fall

PAUL EDWARDS

When Lancashire won three of their first five Championship games and travelled to Leeds sitting on top of Division One, some wondered whether Steven Croft's team might emulate Glen Chapple's title-winning side of 2011. More realistic supporters suspected the primary benefit from points gained in April and May would be avoiding relegation in September.

Yorkshire's comfortable victory at Headingley swiftly justified that view, and the rest of the season confirmed it. Lancashire won none of their remaining ten matches, and lost three. On the fifth anniversary of their Championship triumph at Taunton, they were scraping together nine points from a home draw against Middlesex. Defeat by Warwickshire on the last day of the season left Lancashire's hope of avoiding a hat-trick of instant relegations seemingly dependent on Hampshire's failure to beat Durham. Few knew that the eighth-placed side in Division One would not be going down, and those who did were not telling.

The most encouraging aspect of the season was the emergence of three talented young batsmen – Haseeb Hameed, Liam Livingstone and Rob Jones – and the development of bowlers Tom Bailey and Matt Parkinson. To escape relegation while blooding a clutch of exciting freshmen was a respectable feat. But Ashley Giles, Lancashire's respected director of cricket, would not oversee the progress of this young squad; in December, he decided to return to Warwickshire. Chapple was appointed coach, with Mark Chilton his assistant.

Hameed's achievements in his first full season went far beyond those expected of a 19-year-old opener. Possessing a calm assurance not shown by a Lancastrian batsman since Mike Atherton, he became only the second teenager to score four centuries in a Championship season, after Warwickshire's Sam Hain in 2014. By June, Hameed was a strong candidate for a Lions tour; in September, he was chosen for Test tours of Bangladesh and India, where he made an accomplished debut before breaking a finger. No one was greatly surprised. If Hameed's statistics – 1,198 Championship runs at a tad under 50 – were remarkable enough, it was his composure and technique which really impressed the old pros.

Livingstone scored 70 on first-class debut, against Nottinghamshire, and an unbeaten century in the next game, at Taunton. His clean, fearless hitting in all formats earned him selection for the Lions squad, and suggested he was a cricketer in the modern mould. He also held 26 catches, mostly at slip, and could bowl useful leg-spin. Jones first appeared in August, and scored 106 against Middlesex in his third match.

Former South African international Alviro Petersen was the one batsman apart from Hameed to pass 1,000 runs. His contribution was predictable; what could not have been foreseen was that Luke Procter, who had played only three limited-overs game in 2015, would take to the No. 3 spot with gritty relish, frequently scoring runs when Lancashire most needed them, and partnering Hameed in several important stands.

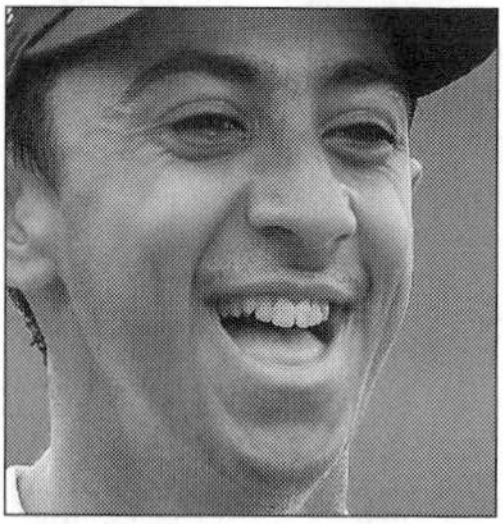

Haseeb Hameed

As well as captaining the side and playing in every match, Croft kept wicket for half the Championship campaign after Alex Davies suffered a recurrence of a knee problem. Croft deputised competently, but looked exhausted by September. It was a heavy burden to lead a faltering team badly affected by injuries. A variety of issues restricted Tom Smith, who had missed most of 2015, to eight Championship games (he was eventually forced to retire), while a back complaint kept Bailey out of seven mid-season matches.

Lancashire had one of the best seam attacks in England in April and May, when Kyle Jarvis was operating with Jimmy Anderson and Neil Wagner. But Test calls limited Anderson to half a game for the rest of the season and, once Wagner joined New Zealand's tour of southern Africa in July, Jarvis was often left to carry the load. He did an excellent job without complaint, and 51 wickets were less than he deserved. Slow left-armer Simon Kerrigan claimed 35 wickets, and at times looked to be recapturing his old control. Parkinson's leg-spin claimed five for 49 on debut against Warwickshire.

The team were unimpressive in the limited-overs competitions. The defence of the NatWest Blast T20 title got off to a poor start; not until their final two games did they record successive wins, and by then it was too late. The absence of Australian all-rounder James Faulkner was keenly felt, though he signed up to return for the 2017 competition. But there was a poignant reminder of Lancashire's Twenty20 triumph when seamers George Edwards and Gavin Griffiths were told their contracts would not be renewed. A year earlier, both had played in the final at Edgbaston. Nathan Buck, another seamer, left for Northamptonshire. Opener Luis Reece was also released, though some fans argued he had not been given a chance.

Lancashire won only two of their Royal London One-Day Cup games and finished bottom of a North Group in which the nine teams were separated by just three points. One of the chief aims was to improve their limited-overs fortunes, and they made a step towards this by signing South African all-rounder Ryan McLaren, who had spent the 2015 season with Hampshire, as the new overseas player. McLaren's responsibilities seem certain to increase after Cricket South Africa handed Petersen a two-year ban for involvement in a domestic match-fixing scandal. South African wicketkeeper-batsman Dane Vilas and the veteran West Indian Shivnarine Chanderpaul, who is 43 in August, both joined on Kolpak deals.

Championship attendance: 40,836.

LANCASHIRE RESULTS

All first-class matches – Played 16: Won 3, Lost 5, Drawn 8.
County Championship matches – Played 16: Won 3, Lost 5, Drawn 8.

Specsavers County Championship, 7th in Division 1;
NatWest T20 Blast, 5th in North Group; Royal London One-Day Cup, 9th in North Group.

COUNTY CHAMPIONSHIP AVERAGES, BATTING AND FIELDING

Cap		*Birthplace*	*M*	*I*	*NO*	*R*	*HS*	*100*	*Avge*	*Ct/St*
	L. S. Livingstone	*Barrow-in-Furness*	15	23	7	815	108*	2	50.93	26
2016	H. Hameed	*Bolton‡*	16	27	3	1,198	122	4	49.91	6
2016	A. N. Petersen††	*Port Elizabeth, SA*	15	24	1	1,134	191	3	49.30	8
	R. P. Jones	*Warrington*	4	7	2	212	106*	1	42.40	3
	†L. A. Procter	*Oldham‡*	16	25	1	822	137	2	34.25	5
2010	†T. C. Smith	*Liverpool‡*	8	13	0	417	87	0	32.07	9
	N. L. Buck	*Leicester*	3	4	2	63	27*	0	31.50	0
	A. L. Davies	*Darwen‡*	5	6	0	187	55	0	31.16	17/1
2010	S. J. Croft	*Blackpool‡*	16	25	1	713	100	1	29.70	30
	J. Clark	*Whitehaven*	7	10	1	225	84*	0	25.00	1
	A. M. Lilley	*Tameside‡*	4	7	1	129	45	0	21.50	1
2013	S. C. Kerrigan	*Preston‡*	13	18	7	225	48	0	20.45	6
2015	K. R. Brown	*Bolton‡*	10	17	0	337	61	0	19.82	6
2015	K. M. Jarvis††	*Harare, Zimbabwe*	16	23	4	338	57	0	17.78	3
	T. E. Bailey	*Preston‡*	6	9	1	91	53	0	11.37	0
	†N. Wagner¶	*Pretoria, SA*	9	12	0	111	37	0	9.25	2
2003	†J. M. Anderson§	*Burnley‡*	4	4	1	14	8	0	4.66	1
	M. W. Parkinson	*Bolton‡*	4	5	1	16	9	0	4.00	1

Also batted: J. C. Buttler§ (*Taunton*) (1 match) 16, 26 (1 ct); †T. J. Lester (*Blackpool‡*) (2 matches) 0*, 1; S. Mahmood (*Birmingham*) (1 match) 0*; †T. J. Moores (*Brighton*) (2 matches) 25, 35, 18 (7 ct).

‡ Born in Lancashire. § ECB contract. ¶ Official overseas player. †† Other non-England-qualified.

BOWLING

	Style	*O*	*M*	*R*	*W*	*BB*	*5I*	*Avge*
J. M. Anderson	RFM	137.5	46	307	15	3-29	0	20.46
T. C. Smith	RFM	133	31	374	15	5-25	1	24.93
T. E. Bailey	RFM	215.4	51	592	22	5-110	2	26.90
N. Wagner	LFM	286.4	52	937	32	6-66	2	29.28
K. M. Jarvis	RFM	545.2	130	1,673	51	6-70	2	32.80
M. W. Parkinson	LBG	114.1	23	363	10	5-49	1	36.30
S. C. Kerrigan	SLA	498.4	106	1,326	35	6-86	2	37.88
J. Clark	RM	132	23	456	11	3-20	0	41.45
L. A. Procter	RFM	152.5	28	505	10	3-14	0	50.50

Also bowled: N. L. Buck (RFM) 63–12–210–2; S. J. Croft (RFM/OB) 46–7–155–2; H. Hameed (LBG) 2–0–3–0; T. J. Lester (LFM) 29–3–119–0; A. M. Lilley (OB) 105.3–21–333–8; L. S. Livingstone (LBG) 51–7–166–1; S. Mahmood (RFM) 33–5–121–1.

LEADING ROYAL LONDON CUP AVERAGES (100 runs/4 wickets)

Batting	*Runs*	*HS*	*Avge*	*SR*	*Ct*
S. J. Croft	249	78	41.50	81.63	6
L. A. Procter	198	63*	39.60	85.34	0
L. S. Livingstone	189	98	31.50	88.31	1
A. N. Petersen	177	73*	29.50	70.80	2
K. R. Brown	149	51	24.83	76.41	3
T. C. Smith	130	56	21.66	64.03	2

Bowling	*W*	*BB*	*Avge*	*ER*
K. M. Jarvis	6	4-31	20.16	5.11
N. L. Buck	8	3-45	26.75	5.94
T. C. Smith	7	3-45	27.28	5.45
S. D. Parry	9	3-43	31.66	5.18
J. Clark	6	2-37	36.66	5.64
S. Mahmood	5	3-55	52.00	5.90

LEADING NATWEST T20 BLAST AVERAGES (100 runs/18 overs)

Batting	*Runs*	*HS*	*Avge*	*SR*	*Ct/St*
J. C. Buttler	166	57	41.50	**204.93**	5/1
J. Clark	111	31*	22.20	**146.05**	5
L. S. Livingstone	247	55	27.44	**144.44**	5
A. N. Petersen	455	103*	45.50	**140.43**	4
M. J. Guptill	125	72	25.00	**131.57**	5
K. R. Brown	289	62*	26.27	**124.56**	3
S. J. Croft	199	36	28.42	**112.42**	6

Bowling	*W*	*BB*	*Avge*	*ER*
S. J. Croft	6	2-24	30.00	**6.92**
N. L. Buck	12	4-26	17.16	**7.35**
A. M. Lilley	8	2-21	25.75	**7.77**
S. D. Parry	12	5-13	29.08	**8.11**
J. Clark	9	2-28	33.55	**8.62**
G. A. Edwards	16	3-33	20.93	**9.57**

FIRST-CLASS COUNTY RECORDS

Highest score for	424	A. C. MacLaren v Somerset at Taunton	1895
Highest score against	315*	T. W. Hayward (Surrey) at The Oval	1898
Leading run-scorer	34,222	E. Tyldesley (avge 45.20)	1909–36
Best bowling for	10-46	W. Hickton v Hampshire at Manchester	1870
Best bowling against	10-40	G. O. B. Allen (Middlesex) at Lord's	1929
Leading wicket-taker	1,816	J. B. Statham (avge 15.12)	1950–68
Highest total for	863	v Surrey at The Oval	1990
Highest total against	707-9 dec	by Surrey at The Oval	1990
Lowest total for	25	v Derbyshire at Manchester	1871
Lowest total against	20	by Essex at Chelmsford	2013

LIST A COUNTY RECORDS

Highest score for	162*	A. R. Crook v Buckinghamshire at Wormsley	2005
Highest score against	186*	C. G. Greenidge (West Indians) at Liverpool	1984
Leading run-scorer	11,969	N. H. Fairbrother (avge 41.84)	1982–2002
Best bowling for	6-10	C. E. H. Croft v Scotland at Manchester	1982
Best bowling against	8-26	K. D. Boyce (Essex) at Manchester	1971
Leading wicket-taker	480	J. Simmons (avge 25.75)	1969–89
Highest total for	381-3	v Hertfordshire at Radlett	1999
Highest total against	360-9	by Hampshire at Manchester	2014
Lowest total for	59	v Worcestershire at Worcester	1963
Lowest total against	52	by Minor Counties at Lakenham	1998

TWENTY20 COUNTY RECORDS

Highest score for	**103***	**A. N. Petersen v Leicestershire at Leicester**	**2016**
Highest score against	108*	I. J. Harvey (Yorkshire) at Leeds	2004
Leading run-scorer	**2,908**	**S. J. Croft (avge 30.93)**	**2006–16**
Best bowling for	**5-13**	**S. D. Parry v Worcestershire at Manchester**	**2016**
Best bowling against	5-21	J. Allenby (Leicestershire) at Manchester	2008
Leading wicket-taker	**108**	**S. D. Parry (avge 23.44)**	**2009–16**
Highest total for	231-4	v Yorkshire at Manchester	2015
Highest total against	**207-8**	**by Leicestershire at Leicester**	**2016**
Lowest total for	91	v Derbyshire at Manchester	2003
Lowest total against	**53**	**by Worcestershire at Manchester**	**2016**

ADDRESS

Emirates Old Trafford, Talbot Road, Manchester M16 0PX; 0161 282 4000; enquiries@lccc.co.uk; www.lccc.co.uk.

OFFICIALS

Captain S. J. Croft
Cricket director/Head coach 2016 A. F. Giles
Head coach 2017 G. Chapple
Assistant head coach 2017 M. J. Chilton
President Sir Howard Bernstein

Chairman M. A. Cairns
Chief executive D. Gidney
Head groundsman M. Merchant
Scorer C. Rimmer

At Cambridge, April 11–13. LANCASHIRE drew with CAMBRIDGE MCCU.

LANCASHIRE v NOTTINGHAMSHIRE

At Manchester, April 17–20. Lancashire won by eight wickets. Lancashire 22pts, Nottinghamshire 3pts. Toss: Nottinghamshire. First-class debut: L. S. Livingstone. County debut: N. Wagner.

Lancashire strolled home on the final morning after Nottinghamshire – who never really recovered from 98 for six on the opening day – underperformed twice with the bat. New Zealand's left-arm seamer Neil Wagner claimed 11 for 111, the second-best return on debut for Lancashire, behind Cec Parkin's 14 for 99 against Leicestershire in 1914. Croft later said the team's bowling was the best he had seen in his 12 years at the club. But coach Ashley Giles was just as pleased with the way his batsmen ground out a 90-run lead against an attack containing four internationals, plus Ball, who would soon become a fifth. They owed much of that lead to Liam Livingstone, already a regular in the Twenty20 side, who showed refreshing willingness to play his shots in a vital ninth-wicket stand of 69 with Jarvis. On the third day, Wagner's accuracy and mean bouncers again proved too much for Nottinghamshire. Lancashire knocked off a target of 86 with little fuss; Procter hit three successive fours off Patel, then ended the match in the same over with a six to midwicket, while his name was chanted by a party of children from Altrincham Preparatory School.

Close of play: first day, Lancashire 25-1 (Hameed 6, Procter 17); second day, Lancashire 311-8 (Livingstone 63, Jarvis 36); third day, Nottinghamshire 175.

Nottinghamshire

S. J. Mullaney c Davies b Jarvis	19	– b Anderson	21
G. P. Smith c Livingstone b Wagner	17	– c Croft b Kerrigan	41
M. J. Lumb lbw b Jarvis	14	– lbw b Wagner	19
B. R. M. Taylor b Wagner	3	– c Livingstone b Jarvis	14
M. H. Wessels lbw b Wagner	27	– lbw b Anderson	16
S. R. Patel lbw b Jarvis	11	– c Livingstone b Wagner	18
*†C. M. W. Read c Kerrigan b Wagner	52	– not out	25
S. C. J. Broad b Kerrigan	43	– c Hameed b Wagner	4
J. T. Ball c Davies b Wagner	33	– b Wagner	5
J. M. Bird c Davies b Wagner	1	– lbw b Wagner	0
H. F. Gurney not out	6	– c Davies b Anderson	2
B 9, lb 1, nb 6	16	B 3, lb 5, nb 2	10
1/31 (1) 2/48 (3) 3/56 (2) 4/63 (4) 5/98 (6) 6/98 (5) 7/172 (8) 8/229 (9) 9/231 (10) 10/242 (7) (74.2 overs)	242	1/52 (1) 2/76 (2) 3/93 (4) 4/99 (3) 5/133 (5) 6/142 (6) 7/155 (8) 8/167 (9) 9/167 (10) 10/175 (11) (84.5 overs)	175

Anderson 16–4–40–0; Jarvis 18–6–72–3; Wagner 20.2–7–66–6; Procter 8–1–34–0; Kerrigan 12–4–20–1. *Second innings*—Anderson 22.5–9–29–3; Jarvis 16–7–24–1; Wagner 19–2–45–5; Kerrigan 26–5–64–1; Livingstone 1–0–5–0.

Lancashire

K. R. Brown lbw b Ball	0	– lbw b Ball	8
H. Hameed c Read b Ball	18	– c Wessels b Ball	9
L. A. Procter c Mullaney b Gurney	33	– not out	35
A. N. Petersen c and b Broad	48	– not out	31
*S. J. Croft c Read b Mullaney	15		
†A. L. Davies lbw b Ball	55		
L. S. Livingstone lbw b Ball	70		
N. Wagner c Taylor b Broad	1		
J. M. Anderson c Read b Broad	6		
K. M. Jarvis c Mullaney b Patel	37		
S. C. Kerrigan not out	13		
B 4, lb 20, nb 12	36	Lb 5	5
1/0 (1) 2/57 (3) 3/57 (2) 4/117 (5) 5/156 (4) 6/228 (6) 7/229 (8) 8/249 (9) 9/318 (7) 10/332 (10) (121.1 overs) 110 overs: 304-8	332	1/8 (1) 2/27 (2) (2 wkts, 17 overs)	88

Ball 26–5–63–4; Broad 22–9–57–3; Gurney 17–8–40–1; Bird 23–3–58–0; Patel 17.1–2–57–1; Mullaney 16–5–33–1. *Second innings*—Ball 6–1–29–2; Broad 7–1–25–0; Patel 3–0–24–0; Bird 1–0–5–0.

Umpires: R. K. Illingworth and N. A. Mallender.

At Taunton, May 1–4. LANCASHIRE drew with SOMERSET.

LANCASHIRE v HAMPSHIRE

At Manchester, May 8–11. Lancashire won by an innings and 94 runs. Lancashire 23pts, Hampshire 1pt. Toss: Hampshire. County debut: G. M. Andrew.

The last time Kerrigan had taken a Division One five-wicket haul was September 2011, when he went on to nine for 51 to beat Hampshire at Liverpool – a key moment in winning the Championship. His five for 59 here made Lancashire leaders for a couple of hours; while comparisons were premature, their cricket possessed a rare brio, exemplified by Croft's athletic stop and throw to run out Vince on the first morning. Procter, whose first-team record in 2015 consisted of three limited-overs games, claimed three wickets on the opening day, and by the close had put Lancashire in the lead. He advanced to a career-best 137 in six and a half hours, which helped extend their advantage to 347. Though Best took five wickets in 37 deliveries, his explosions of joy did not mark a shift in the match's balance. Rain shortened the third day but, when play resumed, a pitch that had offered pace and bounce to the seamers helped the spinners, particularly Kerrigan, whose rhythm and control were back to their best. Vince was dismissed by Anderson early on the final morning; next day, both were named in England's Test squad for Headingley.

Close of play: first day, Lancashire 157-1 (Hameed 41, Procter 48); second day, Hampshire 22-1 (Carberry 15, Vince 7); third day, Hampshire 76-2 (Vince 39, Smith 13).

Hampshire

M. A. Carberry c Davies b Wagner	16	– c Davies b Anderson	16
J. H. K. Adams c Brown b Anderson	5	– c Brown b Anderson	0
*J. M. Vince run out	0	– c Wagner b Anderson	47
W. R. Smith c Davies b Procter	18	– lbw b Jarvis	45
L. A. Dawson lbw b Wagner	0	– c Croft b Kerrigan	18
†A. J. A. Wheater b Procter	32	– lbw b Kerrigan	47
R. McLaren c Croft b Anderson	4	– c Anderson b Kerrigan	15
G. M. Andrew c Davies b Jarvis	3	– c Hameed b Kerrigan	21
T. L. Best c Livingstone b Anderson	11	– lbw b Livingstone	6
M. S. Crane not out	10	– c Livingstone b Kerrigan	3
J. A. Tomlinson b Procter	0	– not out	6
Lb 6, nb 4	10	B 8, lb 9, nb 12	29
1/13 (2) 2/14 (3) 3/34 (1) 4/34 (5) 5/57 (4) 6/63 (7) 7/66 (8) 8/83 (9) 9/105 (6) 10/109 (11) (48.3 overs)	109	1/3 (2) 2/23 (1) 3/88 (3) 4/125 (5) 5/160 (4) 6/208 (6) 7/219 (7) 8/230 (9) 9/246 (8) 10/253 (10) (120 overs)	253

Anderson 17–5–42–3; Jarvis 14–4–27–1; Procter 8.3–3–14–3; Wagner 9–3–20–2. *Second innings*—Anderson 24–14–29–3; Jarvis 22–9–44–1; Kerrigan 36–17–59–5; Wagner 21–5–68–0; Procter 5–1–17–0; Livingstone 10–2–19–1; Croft 2–2–0–0.

Lancashire

K. R. Brown lbw b Andrew	40
H. Hameed c Vince b Crane	62
L. A. Procter c Dawson b Best	137
A. N. Petersen c Carberry b Best	81
*S. J. Croft c Vince b Best	12
†A. L. Davies c Carberry b Crane	17
L. S. Livingstone b Best	0
N. Wagner st Wheater b Crane	37
J. M. Anderson b Best	0
K. M. Jarvis b Dawson	6
S. C. Kerrigan not out	21
B 4, lb 14, w 9, nb 16	43
1/53 (1) 2/226 (2) (124.2 overs)	456

3/349 (4) 4/365 (5) 5/374 (3)
6/378 (7) 7/398 (6) 8/408 (9)
9/430 (10) 10/456 (8) 110 overs: 374-5

Best 20–1–90–5; Tomlinson 15–3–59–0; McLaren 20–6–54–0; Andrew 11–2–22–1; Crane 31.2–4–116–3; Dawson 27–4–97–1.

Umpires: M. A. Gough and N. J. Llong.

At Chester-le-Street, May 15–18. LANCASHIRE lost to DURHAM by 73 runs.

LANCASHIRE v SURREY

At Manchester, May 22–24. Lancashire won by an innings and 96 runs. Lancashire 23pts, Surrey 3pts. Toss: Surrey.

In another echo of 2011, Lancashire won their opening three home Championship games – and victory put them firmly on top of the table. It was a triumph for Jarvis, who followed six for 70, his best figures in England, with five more for a career-best match analysis of 11 for 119. The game followed a now familiar pattern: Croft lost the toss, and the visitors were quickly bowled out before Lancashire established a match-winning lead. Surrey's first-day plight would have been even worse but for Burns, who batted throughout their innings for 92. In reply, Tom Smith scored 59 on his first first-class appearance for 13 months, and Petersen reached his third hundred in nine innings against Surrey (for three counties). Jarvis and Kerrigan shared a last-wicket stand of 63, stretching the lead to 203 – far more than they eventually needed. Burns had been concussed fielding at short leg and played no further part, while Steven Davies, who had been ill, was not allowed to come in until after lunch on the third day. Despite never having batted higher than No. 7 in a first-class game, Tom Curran was promoted to open and made a defiant 53 – with no support. Like Burns, he was last out, as Surrey crumbled inside 38 overs. It would be Lancashire's last victory of the season.

Close of play: first day, Lancashire 16-0 (Smith 7, Hameed 5); second day, Lancashire 342-9 (Jarvis 15, Kerrigan 4).

Surrey

R. J. Burns lbw b Wagner	92	– absent hurt	
A. Harinath c Davies b Bailey	5	– c Davies b Bailey	16
K. C. Sangakkara lbw b Jarvis	0	– c Jarvis b Wagner	8
S. M. Davies c Davies b Jarvis	0	– (7) c Davies b Bailey	5
J. J. Roy c Procter b Jarvis	2	– (4) lbw b Jarvis	9
†B. T. Foakes b Jarvis	13	– (5) c Davies b Jarvis	0
J. E. Burke c Livingstone b Jarvis	31	– (6) c Livingstone b Jarvis	0
T. K. Curran c Davies b Jarvis	10	– (1) c Procter b Wagner	53
*G. J. Batty c Smith b Wagner	21	– (8) b Jarvis	3
M. W. Pillans b Wagner	0	– (9) lbw b Jarvis	4
S. C. Meaker not out	3	– (10) not out	2
B 1, lb 9, nb 4	14	B 5, lb 2	7
1/15 (2) 2/20 (3) 3/20 (4) (61.1 overs)	191	1/27 (2) 2/46 (3) (37.3 overs)	107
4/26 (5) 5/40 (6) 6/104 (7)		3/62 (4) 4/62 (5) 5/62 (6)	
7/114 (8) 8/182 (9) 9/182 (10) 10/191 (1)		6/67 (7) 7/80 (8) 8/84 (9) 9/107 (1)	

Bailey 16–4–32–1; Jarvis 22–3–70–6; Wagner 14.1–3–52–3; Smith 9–2–27–0. *Second innings*—Bailey 12–6–22–2; Jarvis 15–4–49–5; Kerrigan 7–3–12–0; Wagner 3.3–1–17–2.

Lancashire

T. C. Smith lbw b Batty	59	K. M. Jarvis c Foakes b Meaker	35
H. Hameed b Meaker	44	S. C. Kerrigan not out	32
L. A. Procter b Curran	2		
A. N. Petersen c Foakes b Meaker	105	B 4, lb 21	25
*S. J. Croft lbw b Curran	42		
†A. L. Davies c sub (M. P. Dunn) b Meaker	13	1/99 (1) 2/106 (3) (117.4 overs)	394
L. S. Livingstone c Foakes b Curran	23	3/115 (2) 4/263 (4) 5/281 (5)	
T. E. Bailey run out	1	6/292 (6) 7/293 (8) 8/319 (7)	
N. Wagner lbw b Batty	13	9/331 (9) 10/394 (10) 110 overs: 353-9	

Curran 35–10–85–3; Pillans 25–5–86–0; Meaker 24.4–3–78–4; Burke 10–3–45–0; Batty 23–5–75–2.

Umpires: R. J. Evans and R. T. Robinson.

At Leeds, May 29–June 1. LANCASHIRE lost to YORKSHIRE by 175 runs.

LANCASHIRE v WARWICKSHIRE

At Manchester, June 20–23. Drawn. Lancashire 11pts, Warwickshire 10pts. Toss: uncontested. First-class debut: M. W. Parkinson.

A game that demonstrated the burgeoning abilities of Lancashire youngsters ended with Warwickshire's old hands Bell and Trott securing the draw. After a wet first morning, Croft's only century of the season, and his 143-run partnership with Brown, had set up a respectable total, before an eventful second afternoon dominated by 19-year-old leg-spinner Matt Parkinson. His opening over was interrupted by a loud buzzing from the PA system, disturbing Trott and prompting an early tea; on Parkinson's return, he removed Trott and Chopra. Extracting spin and displaying exemplary control, he made it five on debut next day, though not before Ambrose and Barker – joining forces at 94 for six – had taken their stand to 125, a Warwickshire record for the seventh wicket against Lancashire. Barker then made an impact with the ball, striking three times in 15 deliveries; Lancashire were soon five down and just 149 ahead. But Hameed, also 19, and Livingstone repaired the damage, and Hameed reached a maiden hundred on the final morning, before Clarke grabbed three in four balls. Livingstone, who had passed 50 five times in his ten Championship innings, completed his second century with a six and a four in Clarke's next over (taking 115 balls to Hameed's 291). Croft challenged Warwickshire to score 312 in a minimum of 72 overs, but the gauntlet was ignored.

Close of play: first day, Lancashire 196-4 (Croft 82, Brown 41); second day, Warwickshire 202-6 (Ambrose 48, Barker 57); third day, Lancashire 170-5 (Hameed 81, Livingstone 39).

Lancashire

T. C. Smith c Ambrose b Barker	2 – c Patel b Rankin	19
H. Hameed lbw b Clarke	0 – lbw b Clarke	103
L. A. Procter st Ambrose b Patel	36 – c Chopra b Barker	21
A. N. Petersen c Hain b Patel	25 – c Clarke b Barker	5
*†S. J. Croft c Ambrose b Clarke	100 – c Ambrose b Barker	0
K. R. Brown lbw b Barker	61 – c Ambrose b Patel	1
L. S. Livingstone not out	34 – not out	106
A. M. Lilley c and b Rankin	12 – c Ambrose b Clarke	0
N. Wagner c Ambrose b Hannon-Dalby	5 – b Clarke	0
K. M. Jarvis lbw b Rankin	8 – not out	3
M. W. Parkinson b Patel	9	
B 3, lb 9, nb 4	16 B 2, lb 2, nb 4	8
1/6 (1) 2/6 (2) 3/46 (4) (103.1 overs)	308 1/52 (1) (8 wkts dec, 94 overs)	266
4/91 (3) 5/234 (6) 6/236 (5)	2/87 (3) 3/103 (4)	
7/253 (8) 8/277 (9) 9/289 (10) 10/308 (11)	4/103 (5) 5/104 (6)	
	6/241 (2) 7/241 (8) 8/241 (9)	

Barker 19–8–40–2; Clarke 18–3–45–2; Hannon-Dalby 9–0–46–1; Patel 30.1–6–87–3; Rankin 24–4–67–2; Trott 3–0–11–0. *Second innings*—Barker 23–5–62–3; Clarke 16–3–54–3; Patel 38–15–92–1; Rankin 10–1–27–1; Hannon-Dalby 7–0–27–0.

Warwickshire

V. Chopra c Croft b Parkinson	59	– lbw b Parkinson	48
A. R. I. Umeed c Smith b Jarvis	18	– c Croft b Jarvis	17
*I. R. Bell c Livingstone b Jarvis	0	– not out	55
I. J. L. Trott c Livingstone b Parkinson	3	– not out	50
S. R. Hain c Croft b Smith	8		
†T. R. Ambrose not out	70		
R. Clarke lbw b Smith	0		
K. H. D. Barker c Croft b Smith	64		
J. S. Patel c Wagner b Parkinson	19		
W. B. Rankin b Parkinson	0		
O. J. Hannon-Dalby b Parkinson	6		
B 5, lb 9, nb 2	16	B 12, lb 7, nb 6	25
1/54 (2) 2/54 (3) 3/73 (4) 4/90 (1) 5/94 (5) 6/94 (7) 7/219 (8) 8/253 (9) 9/253 (10) 10/263 (11) (78.1 overs)	263	1/52 (2) 2/84 (1) (2 wkts, 72 overs)	195

Wagner 17–1–68–0; Jarvis 19–3–63–2; Parkinson 23.1–6–49–5; Smith 12–4–30–3; Lilley 4–0–26–0; Livingstone 3–0–13–0. *Second innings*—Wagner 10–0–34–0; Jarvis 10–2–22–1; Parkinson 31–10–74–1; Lilley 18–6–36–0; Livingstone 3–0–10–0.

Umpires: J. H. Evans and G. D. Lloyd.

At Lord's, June 26–29. LANCASHIRE drew with MIDDLESEX.

At Nottingham, July 3–6. LANCASHIRE drew with NOTTINGHAMSHIRE.

LANCASHIRE v DURHAM

At Southport, July 16–19. Durham won by two wickets. Durham 21pts, Lancashire 4pts. Toss: Lancashire. First-class debut: T. J. Moores. Championship debut: A. J. Hickey.

By the time Rushworth's cover-driven four secured Durham's victory on the final evening, this contest was being hailed as an example of county cricket's virtues. Then Collingwood (who said he wished all county games could be played on pitches as good as this) and his team chose to stay another night: they played on the outfield with Peter and Tom Crew, two Southport & Birkdale juniors, before leading a sing-song with club members. Pictures spread of Stokes batting against an 11-year-old, less than 72 hours before appearing in the Manchester Test, an illustration of how the professional game can reconnect with its roots. The match itself was closely fought, fuelling Lancashire's resentment that Anderson was withdrawn after two days, whereas Stokes played all four: both were recovering from injuries, both took part at Old Trafford. Rushworth's accuracy had

Paul Collingwood

Bad light, start play: Ben Stokes faces a schoolboy as the shadows lengthen.

restricted the Lancashire batsmen on the first day, before eight Durham batsmen reached double figures to carve out a vital 87-run lead. However, Procter's fine hundred, backed up by Hameed and Tom Moores (the son of Lancashire's former coach, Peter, on loan from Nottinghamshire because of a wicketkeeping crisis) meant Durham needed 247 on the final day. Jennings and Burnham broke the back of the task, only for Tom Smith's four wickets in 29 balls to put the match in the hazard again. But Stokes added 48 with Championship debutant Adam Hickey, pulling Kerrigan over the railway line for three sixes before being run out four short of victory.

Close of play: first day, Durham 88-3 (Borthwick 37); second day, Lancashire 59-1 (Hameed 24, Procter 22); third day, Lancashire 333.

Lancashire

T. C. Smith c Stokes b Rushworth	0	– c Richardson b Onions	1
H. Hameed c Jennings b Coughlin	10	– c sub (J. T. A. Benton) b Stokes	53
L. A. Procter c Richardson b Coughlin	30	– c Burnham b Borthwick	122
A. N. Petersen run out	51	– lbw b Borthwick	17
*S. J. Croft c and b Rushworth	54	– c Borthwick b Hickey	20
K. R. Brown c Jennings b Onions	0	– c Jennings b Hickey	5
†T. J. Moores c Richardson b Jennings	25	– run out	35
K. M. Jarvis c and b Jennings	2	– b Borthwick	0
S. C. Kerrigan c Richardson b Rushworth	11	– c Richardson b Stokes	19
M. W. Parkinson b Rushworth	0	– (11) c Burnham b Stokes	0
J. M. Anderson not out	0		
N. L. Buck (did not bat)		– (10) not out	27
B 8, lb 4, w 1, nb 8	21	B 5, lb 14, w 1, nb 14	34
1/0 (1) 2/26 (2) 3/92 (3) 4/103 (4) (70.1 overs)	204	1/3 (1) 2/117 (2) (118.4 overs)	333
5/105 (6) 6/146 (7) 7/168 (8)		3/160 (4) 4/193 (5)	
8/195 (9) 9/197 (10) 10/204 (5)		5/209 (6) 6/279 (3) 7/283 (7)	
		8/286 (8) 9/313 (9) 10/333 (11)	

Buck replaced Anderson, who had left to join England's Test squad.

Rushworth 16.1–6–30–4; Onions 16–4–49–1; Coughlin 13–5–31–2; Stokes 14–3–37–0; Hickey 4–0–19–0; Jennings 7–1–26–2. *Second innings*—Rushworth 15–6–39–0; Onions 19–4–45–1; Stokes 19.4–7–50–3; Borthwick 29–1–98–3; Coughlin 16–2–45–0; Hickey 20–4–37–2.

Durham

M. D. Stoneman c Moores b Procter	40	– lbw b Jarvis	1
K. K. Jennings c Croft b Anderson	2	– c Moores b Smith	82
S. G. Borthwick b Kerrigan	64	– c Petersen b Smith	28
J. T. A. Burnham c Croft b Procter	7	– lbw b Kerrigan	52
B. A. Stokes c and b Parkinson	21	– run out	36
†M. J. Richardson c Croft b Jarvis	28	– c Moores b Smith	3
*P. D. Collingwood c Moores b Anderson	50	– lbw b Smith	4
P. Coughlin b Jarvis	26	– c Moores b Smith	5
A. J. Hickey c Moores b Anderson	0	– not out	21
C. Rushworth c Procter b Parkinson	30	– not out	4
G. Onions not out	15		
B 1, lb 4, w 1, nb 2	8	B 3, lb 4, nb 4	11
1/7 (2) 2/76 (1) 3/88 (4) 4/131 (5) 5/149 (3) 6/169 (6) 7/240 (8) 8/241 (9) 9/250 (7) 10/291 (10) (95 overs)	291	1/6 (1) 2/47 (3) 3/170 (4) 4/170 (2) 5/175 (6) 6/183 (7) 7/195 (8) 8/243 (5) (8 wkts, 77.2 overs)	247

Anderson 22–7–58–3; Jarvis 23–4–89–2; Smith 6–0–28–0; Kerrigan 21–5–47–1; Procter 12–4–31–2; Croft 2–1–3–0; Parkinson 9–0–30–2. *Second innings*—Jarvis 14.2–4–48–1; Buck 4–0–26–0; Smith 16–4–25–5; Kerrigan 31–5–97–1; Parkinson 10–1–32–0; Croft 2–0–12–0.

Umpires: R. J. Bailey and R. A. Kettleborough.

At Southampton, August 4–7. LANCASHIRE drew with HAMPSHIRE.

LANCASHIRE v YORKSHIRE

At Manchester, August 13–16. Drawn. Lancashire 11pts, Yorkshire 10pts. Toss: Lancashire. County debut: J. S. Lehmann.

Haseeb Hameed became the first Lancastrian to score two hundreds in a Roses match – and only the third on either side. Thanks to him, Lancashire dominated the game – but it might have been stolen from them on the final afternoon. Challenged to score 367 from 71 overs, they proceeded coolly to 188 without loss, before Yorkshire agreed to a draw, needing a further 179 off 19. The odds did not favour them, but the refusal to risk a few wickets attempting a chase against a tired attack seemed cautious. On the opening day Hameed had scored his third hundred in six games; though he was one of six to fall after tea, next day Clark and Jarvis shared Lancashire's first century stand for the last wicket against Yorkshire. Both scored career-bests, and Jarvis then claimed four wickets to help secure a 134-run lead, despite Gale making only his second half-century of 2016. Hameed reached another hundred, in 124 balls, 65 fewer than his first; on the way, at 19 years 212 days he became the fifth-youngest batsman to score 1,000 Championship runs in an English season, after Arthur Fagg, Keith Fletcher, Denis Compton and Sachin Tendulkar. "Hameed is one of the best young batsmen I've seen in a long time," said Gale.

HUNDRED IN EACH INNINGS OF A ROSES MATCH

126	111*	P. Holmes (Yorkshire) at Manchester	1920
125*	132	E. I. Lester (Yorkshire) at Manchester	1948
114	**100**	**H. Hameed (Lancashire) at Manchester**	**2016**

Close of play: first day, Lancashire 299-7 (Clark 4); second day, Yorkshire 136-2 (Lees 62, Gale 36); third day, Lancashire 70-0 (Smith 35, Hameed 30).

Lancashire

T. C. Smith lbw b Sidebottom	46	– c Hodd b Bresnan	87
H. Hameed c and b Bresnan	114	– not out	100
L. A. Procter c Hodd b Bresnan	79		
A. N. Petersen b Brooks	32	– (3) c and b Rashid	2
*†S. J. Croft c Bresnan b Brooks	13	– (4) c Hodd b Bresnan	3
L. S. Livingstone c Hodd b Sidebottom	0	– (5) not out	31
S. C. Kerrigan c Hodd b Brooks	2		
J. Clark not out	84		
A. M. Lilley c Hodd b Patterson	45		
N. L. Buck lbw b Bresnan	1		
K. M. Jarvis lbw b Rashid	57		
B 4, lb 11, nb 6	21	B 4, lb 1, nb 4	9
1/86 (1) 2/238 (3) 3/247 (2) 4/268 (5) 5/279 (6) 6/286 (7) 7/299 (4) 8/386 (9) 9/387 (10) 10/494 (11) (133 overs)	494	1/168 (1) 2/172 (3) 3/177 (4) (3 wkts dec, 44 overs)	232
110 overs: 387-9			

Sidebottom 24–6–81–2; Brooks 23–3–81–3; Bresnan 24–4–80–3; Patterson 26–8–69–1; Rashid 32–2–149–1; Lyth 4–1–19–0. *Second innings*—Sidebottom 9–0–52–0; Brooks 4–0–25–0; Bresnan 11–1–60–2; Rashid 16–1–68–1; Patterson 4–1–22–0.

Yorkshire

A. Lyth lbw b Jarvis	25	– not out	63
A. Z. Lees lbw b Jarvis	85	– not out	114
J. A. Leaning c Livingstone b Smith	7		
*A. W. Gale c Kerrigan b Smith	83		
J. S. Lehmann b Jarvis	46		
A. U. Rashid c Hameed b Kerrigan	16		
T. T. Bresnan lbw b Jarvis	7		
†A. J. Hodd c Livingstone b Kerrigan	43		
S. A. Patterson b Buck	20		
J. A. Brooks not out	6		
R. J. Sidebottom c Croft b Kerrigan	3		
B 9, lb 4, nb 6	19	B 10, lb 1	11
1/38 (1) 2/55 (3) 3/185 (2) 4/237 (4) 5/272 (6) 6/272 (5) 7/283 (7) 8/341 (8) 9/357 (9) 10/360 (11) (134.5 overs)	360	(no wkt, 52 overs)	188
110 overs: 290-7			

Jarvis 25–5–70–4; Buck 25–5–65–1; Smith 14–3–38–2; Clark 15–2–46–0; Lilley 15–5–31–0; Kerrigan 38.5–7–91–3; Livingstone 2–1–6–0. *Second innings*—Jarvis 13–2–39–0; Kerrigan 11–3–33–0; Buck 10–2–43–0; Clark 5–0–28–0; Lilley 8–1–20–0; Livingstone 5–0–14–0.

Umpires: P. K. Baldwin and D. J. Millns.

At The Oval, August 23–26. LANCASHIRE lost to SURREY by ten wickets.

LANCASHIRE v SOMERSET

At Manchester, August 31–September 3. Drawn. Lancashire 10pts, Somerset 10pts. Toss: Lancashire.

Even before rain washed out the final day, Somerset's late challenge for the County Championship was being frustrated by the Old Trafford pitch, which seemed made to break bowlers' hearts once the ball had lost its shine. Petersen batted more than five hours, sharing century partnerships with Livingstone and Croft to help avert the follow-on. Nevertheless, Rogers had reason to be optimistic as his team returned to the West Country for the final run-in. Three of his players had made career-bests. Though he was dropped in the gully on 32, Abell batted beautifully for 135 before he was one of four dismissed in seven deliveries by Bailey on the first evening. The following day Trego, who scored at a run a ball, and Davies extended their stand for Somerset's eighth wicket to 236, a county record, beating 217 by Roelof van der Merwe and Craig Overton against Hampshire at Taunton only six days before. For the bowlers, rain was a merciful release.

Close of play: first day, Somerset 339-7 (Trego 49, Davies 8); second day, Lancashire 138-2 (Livingstone 20, Petersen 25); third day, Lancashire 422-9 (Bailey 17, Lester 0).

Somerset

M. E. Trescothick c Kerrigan b Clark	60	†R. C. Davies b Bailey	86
T. B. Abell c Croft b Bailey	135	T. D. Groenewald not out	17
*C. J. L. Rogers c Croft b Clark	47	B 5, lb 9, w 1, nb 2	17
J. C. Hildreth c Petersen b Bailey	27		—
J. Allenby c Petersen b Bailey	1	1/134 (1) (8 wkts dec, 138 overs)	553
P. D. Trego not out	154	2/227 (3) 3/267 (4)	
L. Gregory lbw b Bailey	0	4/273 (5) 5/274 (2) 6/274 (7)	
C. Overton b Jarvis	9	7/287 (8) 8/523 (9) 110 overs: 394-7	

M. J. Leach did not bat.

Bailey 34–6–111–5; Jarvis 26–4–113–1; Lester 19–2–73–0; Kerrigan 24–1–113–0; Procter 13–1–49–0; Clark 21–4–67–2; Livingstone 1–0–13–0.

Lancashire

R. P. Jones run out	34	S. C. Kerrigan c Hildreth b Gregory	0
H. Hameed c Davies b Groenewald	56	T. J. Lester not out	0
L. S. Livingstone c Davies b Leach	57		
A. N. Petersen c Trescothick b Groenewald	155	B 9, lb 8	17
*†S. J. Croft c Allenby b Leach	58		—
L. A. Procter lbw b Overton	2	1/87 (2) 2/96 (1) (9 wkts, 148 overs)	422
J. Clark c Davies b Gregory	16	3/213 (3) 4/370 (4)	
T. E. Bailey not out	17	5/370 (5) 6/387 (6) 7/404 (7)	
K. M. Jarvis b Gregory	10	8/414 (9) 9/414 (10) 110 overs: 333-3	

Overton 25–3–70–1; Gregory 23–4–74–3; Groenewald 26–3–73–2; Leach 40–11–105–2; Allenby 22–3–32–0; Trego 11–0–47–0; Rogers 1–0–4–0.

Umpires: M. Burns and P. J. Hartley.

LANCASHIRE v MIDDLESEX

At Manchester, September 12–15. Drawn. Lancashire 9pts, Middlesex 11pts. Toss: Lancashire.

A draw had seemed unlikely when Roland-Jones reduced Lancashire to six for four, then 32 for five, in reply to Middlesex's 327. But Rob Jones mounted a recovery, adding 106 with a disciplined Livingstone and 92 with Bailey. In only his fourth first-class innings, Jones reached a maiden century in six and a half hours, lifting a six over long-on off Rayner; his uninhibited celebration was later named Lancashire's champagne moment of the season. At 20, he was their youngest player to carry his bat since Cyril Washbrook in 1935. Second time round, Malan and Simpson batted with control and enterprise, though Kerrigan returned his best innings and match figures for three years. Franklin challenged Lancashire to score 309 in 44 overs and Buttler, in his first Championship game since 2014, opened with three fours and a six in eight balls. His dismissal, however, brought Hameed to the wicket, a sure sign the chase had been abandoned. Middlesex finished nine points ahead of Yorkshire, who would meet them at Lord's the following week, and ten clear of Somerset, while a draw at Edgbaston would in all likelihood guarantee Lancashire safety.

Close of play: first day, Middlesex 258-3 (Malan 49, Eskinazi 4); second day, Lancashire 102-5 (Jones 42, Livingstone 31); third day, Middlesex 72-4 (Malan 20, Simpson 7).

Middlesex

S. D. Robson c Livingstone b Kerrigan	77	– (2) lbw b Kerrigan	26
N. R. T. Gubbins c Petersen b Jarvis	69	– (1) c Livingstone b Jarvis	0
N. R. D. Compton b Jarvis	56	– lbw b Kerrigan	10
D. J. Malan b Bailey	53	– c Buttler b Kerrigan	87
S. S. Eskinazi b Jarvis	4	– lbw b Kerrigan	4
†J. A. Simpson c Croft b Bailey	5	– b Procter	74
*J. E. C. Franklin not out	31	– (8) c Croft b Kerrigan	0
O. P. Rayner c Livingstone b Kerrigan	6	– (9) not out	9
T. S. Roland-Jones b Kerrigan	17	– (7) c Jones b Kerrigan	12
T. J. Murtagh c Jones b Croft	4	– not out	7
S. T. Finn b Kerrigan	2		
Lb 1, nb 2	3	B 8, lb 3	11
1/127 (2) 2/151 (1) 3/248 (3) 4/262 (4) 5/262 (5) 6/272 (6) 7/285 (8) 8/313 (9) 9/322 (10) 10/327 (11) (119.4 overs) 110 overs: 302-7	327	1/11 (1) 2/36 (2) 3/39 (3) 4/55 (5) 5/206 (4) 6/218 (7) 7/218 (8) 8/225 (6) (8 wkts dec, 85 overs)	240

Bailey 31–9–72–2; Jarvis 29–8–70–3; Lester 10–1–46–0; Kerrigan 23.4–4–80–4; Procter 16–5–39–0; Croft 10–1–19–1. *Second innings*—Bailey 16–8–26–0; Jarvis 15–5–36–1; Kerrigan 30–5–86–6; Croft 6–2–25–0; Livingstone 7–3–15–0; Procter 11–1–41–1.

Lancashire

R. P. Jones not out	106	– not out	25
H. Hameed c Rayner b Roland-Jones	0	– (3) not out	25
L. A. Procter c Eskinazi b Murtagh	1		
A. N. Petersen c Simpson b Roland-Jones	3		
*S. J. Croft b Roland-Jones	0		
†J. C. Buttler c Simpson b Roland-Jones	16	– (2) c Compton b Finn	26
L. S. Livingstone c Rayner b Finn	53		
T. E. Bailey c Robson b Finn	53		
K. M. Jarvis c Compton b Finn	0		
S. C. Kerrigan lbw b Finn	10		
T. J. Lester b Rayner	1		
B 1, lb 5, nb 10	16	B 4	4
1/0 (2) 2/3 (3) 3/6 (4) 4/6 (5) 5/32 (6) 6/138 (7) 7/230 (8) 8/230 (9) 9/254 (10) 10/259 (11) (98.5 overs)	259	1/26 (2) (1 wkt, 26 overs)	80

Murtagh 23–10–51–1; Roland-Jones 23–8–54–4; Finn 21–5–71–4; Franklin 3–1–5–0; Rayner 25.5–7–62–1; Malan 3–1–10–0. *Second innings*—Roland-Jones 7–2–20–0; Finn 7–2–20–1; Rayner 9–3–30–0; Franklin 3–1–6–0.

Umpires: M. A. Gough and A. G. Wharf.

At Birmingham, September 20–23. LANCASHIRE lost to WARWICKSHIRE by 237 runs. *An abject defeat threatens to relegate Lancashire, but Durham beat Hampshire.*

LEICESTERSHIRE

Foxes emerge from their hole

PAUL JONES

A glance at the Division Two table might not immediately suggest it, but Leicestershire made considerable progress in 2016. They had held the wooden spoon for three years, so four victories and seventh place came as welcome relief. There was the odd glitch – a horrible collapse for 43 at home to Worcestershire sticks in the memory – but on the whole Leicestershire were solid, and even challenged for promotion. After a dozen games, they were second, 23 points behind Essex, who then beat them at Grace Road in August, ending the dream. Leicestershire lost, drew and won their last three matches, which was a fair reflection of the season: they were closely matched to the bulk of Division Two.

Their progress was built around the arrival of three seasoned professionals: Neil Dexter from Middlesex, Paul Horton from Lancashire, and Mark Pettini from Essex. Each came eager for more red-ball cricket, and played in every match. They scored 2,560 first-class runs between them, with seven centuries, while Dexter's 958 was his best Championship season. Only Mark Cosgrove, the captain, scored more: 1,279, including five centuries, at just shy of 50.

Ned Eckersley showed in patches what an attractive strokemaker he can be. He had struggled for form since 2013, and missed the first five games while he recovered from a broken finger sustained pre-season. On his return, he hit 624 Championship runs at an average of 39, including a golden run in August of three consecutive centuries; he was the third Leicestershire player to achieve the feat, after Ben Smith, in 2001, and Stewie Dempster, who did it twice, in 1937 and 1938. Later that month, he signed a new contract to keep him until 2018. Eckersley will also have the chance to establish himself as first-choice wicketkeeper after the management decided not to offer a new deal to Niall O'Brien. Despite being contracted until September, he left abruptly in August, having scored 2,816 first-class runs in his four years with the club.

The bowling unit was again spearheaded by the Australian seamer Clint McKay, who for the second year running claimed more than 50 wickets, at 22 runs apiece. He was sorely missed when a calf injury ruled him out of the home game with Essex. McKay had excellent support from the veteran Charlie Shreck and, if Ben Raine's 35 wickets did not quite match his 59 of 2015, the shortfall was made up by Dexter's medium-pace. His 29 victims – another season's best – completed an encouraging first summer. Richard Jones made his loan move from Warwickshire permanent, but Ollie Freckingham was released despite his team-mates voting him Player of the Year.

The major concern was the slow bowling. Off-spinner Rob Sayer was developing, but not yet capable of running through the opposition. Slow left-armer James Sykes has still to make the progress Leicestershire had hoped for, although time is on his side, while injuries prevented Jigar Naik reaching his full potential; he was released after 11 seasons at the club. It was a disappointing departure for a popular and talented player, though he may flourish elsewhere if he enjoys better fortune with injuries. Leicestershire signed left-arm spinner Callum Parkinson, who took seven wickets when he played for Derbyshire at Grace Road.

Stephen Pond, Getty Images

Neil Dexter

Another area that urgently needs improvement is white-ball cricket: Leicestershire failed to progress to the knockouts in either competition. They appeared to have a squad capable of challenging in T20, particularly with McKay and the explosive Pakistan batsman Umar Akmal. With floodlights installed at Grace Road, the stage was set for the club to bid for a fourth T20 crown. But they finished bottom of their group with just four wins. The 50-over story was little better. Two victories – the first since 2014 – were welcome, though qualification remained a long way off. Fans will hope that a new captain can change the team's fortunes: in 2017, McKay will lead them in limited-overs matches, replacing Pettini. Dynamic Pakistani opener Sharjeel Khan has signed for the T20 Blast.

There was change in the coaching set-up, too. Andrew McDonald, the elite performance director, and former Leicestershire all-rounder, decided in August to return to Australia at the end of the season. He was keen to be closer to his family, and has taken up coaching roles with Victoria and the Melbourne Renegades. His work with chief executive Wasim Khan over the past two seasons helped turn Leicestershire's form around and restored pride in their performances. He leaves a considerable hole.

South African Pierre de Bruyn, who joined last season as Second XI coach, stepped into the top job, while Graeme Welch, who resigned as Derbyshire's elite performance director in June, arrived as his assistant. Welch's experience of the domestic game adds to the considerable knowledge in the dressing-room, and should help ensure Leicestershire build on the foundations McDonald put in place.

De Bruyn's real test will come in the four-day game, where they should be nothing less than competitive. And if their key men find their touch, Leicestershire can emerge as genuine contenders for promotion.

Championship attendance: 12,703.

LEICESTERSHIRE RESULTS

All first-class matches – Played 17: Won 4, Lost 4, Drawn 9.
County Championship matches – Played 16: Won 4, Lost 4, Drawn 8.

Specsavers County Championship, 7th in Division 2;
NatWest T20 Blast, 9th in North Group; Royal London One-Day Cup, 8th in North Group.

COUNTY CHAMPIONSHIP AVERAGES, BATTING AND FIELDING

Cap		*Birthplace*	*M*	*I*	*NO*	*R*	*HS*	*100*	*Avge*	*Ct*
2012	W. A. White	*Derby*	4	4	2	103	58	0	51.50	1
2015	†M. J. Cosgrove††	*Elizabeth, Australia*	16	27	1	1,279	146	5	49.19	10
	†N. J. O'Brien	*Dublin, Ireland*	9	14	3	432	93	0	39.27	30
2013	E. J. H. Eckersley	*Oxford*	11	18	2	624	117	3	39.00	29
	N. J. Dexter	*Johannesburg, SA*	16	27	1	958	136	3	36.84	4
	P. J. Horton	*Sydney, Australia*	16	28	2	908	117*	2	34.92	8
	M. L. Pettini	*Brighton*	16	26	2	694	142*	2	28.91	3
	A. J. Robson	*Darlinghurst, Aust.*	16	28	1	732	84	0	27.11	14
	R. A. Jones	*Stourbridge*	6	9	2	127	33	0	18.14	2
	R. J. Sayer	*Huntingdon*	2	4	2	36	32*	0	18.00	0
	†B. A. Raine	*Sunderland*	14	19	1	321	64	0	17.83	2
2015	C. J. McKay¶	*Melbourne, Aust.*	15	20	1	300	65	0	15.78	0
	†R. M. L. Taylor	*Northampton*	3	4	0	50	21	0	12.50	2
	L. J. Hill	*Leicester‡*	2	4	0	46	36	0	11.50	0
	D. Klein††	*Lichtenbeurg, SA*	2	4	1	31	16*	0	10.33	0
	A. M. Ali	*Leicester‡*	4	7	0	71	30	0	10.14	1
	†H. E. Dearden	*Bury*	2	4	0	36	16	0	9.00	2
	C. E. Shreck	*Truro*	16	20	12	51	20	0	6.37	6

Also batted: Z. J. Chappell (*Grantham*) (2 matches) 7, 10, 0; J. K. H. Naik (*Leicester‡*) (cap 2013) (2 matches) 26*, 8* (2 ct); †J. S. Sykes (*Hinchingbrooke*) (1 match) 12*; T. J. Wells (*Grantham*) (1 match) 18, 0.

‡ *Born in Leicestershire.* ¶ *Official overseas player.* †† *Other non-England-qualified.*

BOWLING

	Style	*O*	*M*	*R*	*W*	*BB*	*5I*	*Avge*
C. J. McKay	RFM	411.1	78	1,260	56	6-73	1	22.50
W. A. White	RFM	64.1	13	225	10	4-24	0	22.50
N. J. Dexter	RM	261.5	50	824	29	5-52	1	28.41
B. A. Raine	RFM	338	77	1,108	35	5-66	1	31.65
C. E. Shreck	RFM	442.3	85	1,455	44	4-33	0	33.06

Also bowled: A. M. Ali (OB) 3–1–21–0; Z. J. Chappell (RFM) 20.2–2–98–3; M. J. Cosgrove (RM) 29.4–2–112–3; E. J. H. Eckersley (OB) 2–0–7–0; P. J. Horton (RM) 13–3–43–2; R. A. Jones (RFM) 115–20–446–7; D. Klein (LFM) 44–5–211–9; J. K. H. Naik (OB) 30–6–67–0; A. J. Robson (LBG) 8–1–32–0; R. J. Sayer (OB) 67–6–273–4; R. M. L. Taylor (LM) 48.3–9–187–2.

LEADING ROYAL LONDON CUP AVERAGES (100 runs/4 wickets)

Batting	*Runs*	*HS*	*Avge*	*SR*	*Ct/St*
N. J. O'Brien	164	82	54.66	100.00	3/2
K. J. O'Brien	203	89	50.75	105.72	0
M. J. Cosgrove	194	91	48.50	97.48	3
M. L. Pettini	165	92	33.00	73.00	1
L. J. Hill	112	55	22.40	95.72	2

Bowling	*W*	*BB*	*Avge*	*ER*
R. M. L. Taylor	5	4-58	18.80	5.87
C. S. Delport	4	2-41	22.75	4.78
K. J. O'Brien	5	2-48	38.80	6.06
R. J. Sayer	4	1-31	39.75	4.54
N. J. Dexter	4	4-22	42.25	5.63
B. A. Raine	5	3-62	59.80	6.36

LEADING NATWEST T20 BLAST AVERAGES (100 runs/15 overs)

Batting	*Runs*	*HS*	*Avge*	*SR*	*Ct*
L. J. Hill	187	31*	37.40	**155.83**	3
C. S. Delport	178	68	29.66	**142.40**	1
M. J. Cosgrove	294	66*	26.72	**141.34**	3
M. L. Pettini	331	76	30.09	**124.43**	5
Umar Akmal	134	52*	33.50	**121.81**	2
K. J. O'Brien	115	29	16.42	**111.65**	4

Bowling	*W*	*BB*	*Avge*	*ER*
C. J. McKay	13	3-20	20.53	**6.30**
N. J. Dexter	6	2-16	35.33	**7.31**
K. J. O'Brien	7	3-27	25.14	**7.82**
B. A. Raine	13	3-7	23.84	**8.69**
R. M. L. Taylor	3	1-19	50.33	**9.74**

FIRST-CLASS COUNTY RECORDS

Highest score for	309*	H. D. Ackerman v Glamorgan at Cardiff	2006
Highest score against	355*	K. P. Pietersen (Surrey) at The Oval	2015
Leading run-scorer	30,143	L. G. Berry (avge 30.32)	1924–51
Best bowling for	10-18	G. Geary v Glamorgan at Pontypridd	1929
Best bowling against	10-32	H. Pickett (Essex) at Leyton	1895
Leading wicket-taker	2,131	W. E. Astill (avge 23.18)	1906–39
Highest total for	701-4 dec	v Worcestershire at Worcester	1906
Highest total against	761-6 dec	by Essex at Chelmsford	1990
Lowest total for	25	v Kent at Leicester	1912
Lowest total against	24	by Glamorgan at Leicester	1971
	24	by Oxford University at Oxford	1985

LIST A COUNTY RECORDS

Highest score for	201	V. J. Wells v Berkshire at Leicester	1996
Highest score against	201*	R. S. Bopara (Essex) at Leicester	2008
Leading run-scorer	8,216	N. E. Briers (avge 27.66)	1975–95
Best bowling for	6-16	C. M. Willoughby v Somerset at Leicester	2005
Best bowling against	6-21	S. M. Pollock (Warwickshire) at Birmingham	1996
Leading wicket-taker	308	K. Higgs (avge 18.80)	1972–82
Highest total for	406-5	v Berkshire at Leicester	1996
Highest total against	**376-3**	**by Yorkshire at Leicester**	**2016**
Lowest total for	36	v Sussex at Leicester	1973
Lowest total against	62	by Northamptonshire at Leicester	1974
	62	by Middlesex at Leicester	1998

TWENTY20 COUNTY RECORDS

Highest score for	111	D. L. Maddy v Yorkshire at Leeds	2004
Highest score against	**103***	**A. N. Petersen (Lancashire) at Leicester**	**2016**
Leading run-scorer	1,455	P. A. Nixon (avge 21.71)	2003–*11*
Best bowling for	5-13	A. B. McDonald v Nottinghamshire at Nottingham	2010
Best bowling against	5-21	J. A. Brooks (Yorkshire) at Leeds	2013
Leading wicket-taker	69	C. W. Henderson (avge 26.95)	2004–12
Highest total for	221-3	v Yorkshire at Leeds	2004
Highest total against	225-2	by Durham at Chester-le-Street	2010
Lowest total for	90	v Nottinghamshire at Nottingham	2014
Lowest total against	72	by Derbyshire at Derby	2013

ADDRESS

County Ground, Grace Road, Leicester LE2 8AD; 0116 283 2128; enquiries@leicestershireccc.co.uk; www.leicestershireccc.co.uk.

OFFICIALS

Captain M. J. Cosgrove
(limited-overs) **2016** M. L. Pettini
(limited-overs) **2017** C. J. McKay
Elite perf director 2016 A. B. McDonald
Head coach 2017 P. de Bruyn
Elite development coach 2016 K. J. Piper
Academy director A. P. Siddall
Assistant coach 2017 G. Welch
President D. W. Wilson
Chairman P. R. Haywood
Chief executive W. G. Khan
Operations manager P. Atkinson
Head groundsman A. Ward
Scorer P. J. Rogers

At Loughborough, April 11–13. LEICESTERSHIRE drew with LOUGHBOROUGH MCCU.

At Cardiff, April 17–20. LEICESTERSHIRE beat GLAMORGAN by ten wickets.

LEICESTERSHIRE v KENT

At Leicester, April 24–27. Drawn. Leicestershire 13pts, Kent 10pts. Toss: Kent.

This was a game with a sprinkling of the bizarre. Facing the eighth delivery of the match, Dickson kept out a Raine yorker, then stooped to push the ball away with his right glove after it had bounced back towards the stumps. Wicketkeeper O'Brien appealed immediately and, after the umpires consulted, Dickson became the 62nd player in first-class cricket to be out handled the ball, the sixth in county cricket, and the second for Kent, after George Bennett against Sussex 144 years earlier.

HANDLED THE BALL IN FIRST-CLASS CRICKET IN ENGLAND

J. Grundy	MCC v Kent at Lord's	1857
G. Bennett	Kent v Sussex at Hove	1872
C. W. Wright	Nottinghamshire v Gloucestershire at Bristol	1893
A. W. Nourse	South Africans v Sussex at Hove	1907
Khalid Ibadulla	Warwickshire v Hampshire at Coventry	1963
A. H. M. Rees	Glamorgan v Middlesex at Lord's	1965
G. A. Gooch	England v Australia at Manchester	1993
K. M. Krikken	Derbyshire v Indians at Derby	1996
C. A. Pujara	Derbyshire v Leicestershire at Derby	2014
S. R. Dickson	**Kent v Leicestershire at Leicester**	**2016**

Later, the weather lost its bearings too, as hail and snow battered the ground, forcing several stoppages, and ultimately a draw. Some fine batting, however, shone through the gloom. Bell-Drummond compiled a high-class century, including 20 fours, to haul Kent's total towards respectability. In reply, Cosgrove and new signing Dexter hit beautiful hundreds to build a healthy lead. Leicestershire eventually declared 137 ahead. That left them a possible 45 overs to force an unlikely win; two quick wickets for McKay were all they managed.

Close of play: first day, Kent 227-7 (Haggett 6, Coles 1); second day, Kent 233-8 (Haggett 7, Claydon 5); third day, Leicestershire 174-2 (Dexter 57, Cosgrove 99).

Kent

D. J. Bell-Drummond lbw b Dexter	124	– lbw b McKay	4
S. R. Dickson handled the ball	0	– not out	34
J. L. Denly b White	14	– c Horton b McKay	9
*S. A. Northeast b Shreck	4	– not out	31
D. I. Stevens c Cosgrove b White	0		
A. J. Blake c O'Brien b McKay	26		
†A. P. Rouse c Robson b McKay	38		
C. J. Haggett b Chappell	13		
M. T. Coles c O'Brien b McKay	1		
M. E. Claydon c Cosgrove b Chappell	24		
A. E. N. Riley not out	5		
B 1, lb 12, nb 2	15	Lb 4, w 3	7
1/4 (2) 2/42 (3) 3/47 (4) 4/48 (5) 5/105 (6) 6/212 (7) 7/222 (1) 8/227 (9) 9/255 (10) 10/264 (8) (81.5 overs)	264	1/9 (1) 2/25 (3) (2 wkts, 26 overs)	85

McKay 22–4–66–3; Raine 13–4–40–0; Shreck 19–8–54–1; White 10–2–37–2; Chappell 10.5–2–44–2; Dexter 7–2–10–1. *Second innings*—McKay 6–0–19–2; Raine 5–1–12–0; Shreck 7–0–26–0; Chappell 1.2–0–2–0; White 4.4–1–18–0; Cosgrove 1–0–1–0; Robson 1–0–3–0.

Leicestershire

P. J. Horton c Rouse b Stevens	3	Z. J. Chappell c Blake b Coles	7
A. J. Robson c Rouse b Coles	0	C. E. Shreck not out	17
N. J. Dexter lbw b Stevens	131		
*M. J. Cosgrove b Claydon	122	B 5, lb 11, nb 12	28
M. L. Pettini b Claydon	2		—
†N. J. O'Brien b Stevens	25	1/3 (2) 2/15 (1) (9 wkts dec, 88 overs)	401
W. A. White not out	42	3/232 (4) 4/236 (5)	
B. A. Raine b Coles	24	5/305 (6) 6/308 (3)	
C. J. McKay b Claydon	0	7/353 (8) 8/360 (9) 9/373 (10)	

Coles 24–2–95–3; Stevens 26–6–110–3; Claydon 19–1–99–3; Haggett 15–4–63–0; Riley 4–0–18–0.

Umpires: R. J. Evans and S. C. Gale.

At Hove, May 1–4. LEICESTERSHIRE drew with SUSSEX.

LEICESTERSHIRE v NORTHAMPTONSHIRE

At Leicester, May 8–11. Drawn. Leicestershire 11pts, Northamptonshire 8pts. Toss: uncontested.

Leicestershire continued their encouraging start to the season, but heavy weather again thwarted a push for victory. After Northamptonshire had chosen to bowl on a temptingly green pitch, Dexter fell within two runs of a second successive century at Grace Road as Leicestershire ended day one on 311 for five. But they could add only 21 the next morning, and ball dominated bat throughout day two when, all told, 21 wickets fell. All-rounder White was particularly effective, dismantling Northamptonshire's batting with four for 24 to give Leicestershire a commanding 181-run lead. Cosgrove mulled over enforcing the follow-on but, with signs of uneven bounce, opted to bat again rather than risk a chase. It didn't work out, as Leicestershire stumbled to 132 for six, before rain washed out the third day and the first two sessions of the fourth. Play finally resumed at 4.30, but bad light intervened after only seven of the scheduled 24 overs.

Close of play: first day, Leicestershire 311-5 (O'Brien 15, Raine 0); second day, Leicestershire 132-6 (O'Brien 48); third day, no play.

Leicestershire

P. J. Horton lbw b Kleinveldt	12	– lbw b Kleinveldt	10
A. J. Robson lbw b Stone	56	– c Kleinveldt b Sanderson	25
N. J. Dexter lbw b Azharullah	98	– b Stone	0
*M. J. Cosgrove c Kleinveldt b Libby	47	– lbw b Sanderson	32
M. L. Pettini c Duckett b Kleinveldt	23	– c Levi b Sanderson	1
†N. J. O'Brien lbw b Stone	17	– not out	48
B. A. Raine c and b Sanderson	0		
A. M. Ali b Stone	0	– (7) c Rossington b Sanderson	7
W. A. White not out	3		
C. J. McKay b Sanderson	8		
C. E. Shreck b Stone	8		
B 36, lb 10, w 8, nb 6	60	B 6, lb 1, nb 2	9
	—		—
1/12 (1) 2/155 (2) 3/247 (3) (103.4 overs)	332	1/14 (1) (6 wkts dec, 39 overs)	132
4/272 (4) 5/305 (5) 6/312 (7)		2/21 (3) 3/60 (2)	
7/313 (8) 8/314 (6) 9/323 (10) 10/332 (11)		4/62 (5) 5/79 (4) 6/132 (7)	

Kleinveldt 22–5–41–2; Stone 20.4–3–56–4; Azharullah 20–5–62–1; Sanderson 24–5–71–2; Crook 9–1–36–0; Cobb 3–0–7–0; Libby 5–2–13–1. *Second innings*—Kleinveldt 11–3–21–1; Stone 9–0–39–1; Sanderson 8–0–36–4; Azharullah 7–2–20–0; Libby 4–0–9–0.

Northamptonshire

J. D. Libby c O'Brien b White	32 – not out	14
B. M. Duckett lbw b Raine	2 – b McKay	0
*A. G. Wakely b Raine	17 – not out	16
J. J. Cobb c O'Brien b McKay	30	
R. E. Levi c O'Brien b Dexter	19	
†A. M. Rossington not out	35	
S. P. Crook c Ali b Dexter	0	
R. K. Kleinveldt c Horton b Dexter	4	
O. P. Stone b White	4	
Azharullah c Horton b White	0	
B. W. Sanderson lbw b White	0	
Lb 3, w 5	8	
1/8 (2) 2/44 (3) 3/59 (1) 4/93 (4) 5/126 (5) 6/126 (7) 7/136 (8) 8/143 (9) 9/145 (10) 10/151 (11) (46.3 overs)	151 1/1 (2) (1 wkt, 7 overs)	30

McKay 11–4–15–1; Raine 12–2–53–2; Shreck 11–3–41–0; White 8.3–2–24–4; Dexter 4–0–15–3. *Second innings*—McKay 4–0–20–1; Raine 3–1–10–0.

Umpires: P. K. Baldwin and P. J. Hartley.

At Leicester, May 13–15. LEICESTERSHIRE drew with SRI LANKANS (see Sri Lankan tour section).

LEICESTERSHIRE v WORCESTERSHIRE

At Leicester, May 22–24. Worcestershire won by seven wickets. Worcestershire 21pts, Leicestershire 6pts. Toss: uncontested.

For once it wasn't the weather that undermined Leicestershire, but a horrendous batting collapse. Having gained a handy first-innings lead of 42, they crumbled against testing seam bowling on a challenging pitch to 43 all out in 25 overs, their second-lowest Championship total since 1968. Henry and Leach – whose match figures of nine for 109 were a career-best – took four each as they bowled unchanged; only O'Brien reached double figures, while eight men failed to pass two. Cosgrove described his side's efforts – in their first defeat of the season – as "unacceptable". The slump was typified by Pettini's failed attempt to steal a quick single from a misfield, with his side already reeling on 11 for three. It left Worcestershire needing only 86; despite three wickets from McKay, they got there with ease. Earlier, Leicestershire's top order helped lift them to 243 for three, but Leach chipped away to earn a five-for, before Henry's unbeaten 49 from No. 9 ensured Worcestershire stayed in touch.

Close of play: first day, Leicestershire 253-4 (Pettini 45, O'Brien 3); second day, Worcestershire 249-8 (Henry 30, Shantry 8).

LOWEST LEICESTERSHIRE TOTALS SINCE WORLD WAR TWO

33	v Glamorgan at Ebbw Vale	1965
34	v Essex at Southend	2011
36	v Derbyshire at Loughborough	1965
37	v Lancashire at Leicester	1960
39	v Kent at Gillingham	1958
40	v Sussex at Hove	1960
40	v Glamorgan at Leicester	1965
41	v Somerset at Leicester	1957
42	v Lancashire at Hinckley	1955
42	v Sussex at Leicester	1960
43	v Northamptonshire at Peterborough	1968
43	**v Worcestershire at Leicester**	**2016**

Leicestershire

P. J. Horton lbw b Henry	89	– c Köhler-Cadmore b Henry	2
A. J. Robson c Cox b Morris	50	– lbw b Leach	2
N. J. Dexter lbw b Shantry	50	– c D'Oliveira b Leach	0
*M. J. Cosgrove lbw b Henry	4	– b Henry	0
M. L. Pettini c Mitchell b Leach	49	– run out	7
†N. J. O'Brien lbw b Leach	13	– c Whiteley b Leach	17
A. M. Ali c Cox b Leach	21	– run out	2
T. J. Wells c Mitchell b Shantry	18	– lbw b Leach	0
B. A. Raine b Leach	5	– c Cox b Henry	1
C. J. McKay c Köhler-Cadmore b Leach	0	– b Henry	6
C. E. Shreck not out	0	– not out	0
Lb 10, w 5, nb 2	17	Lb 6	6
1/141 (2) 2/149 (1) 3/157 (4) 4/243 (3) 5/259 (5) 6/268 (6) 7/311 (8) 8/311 (7) 9/311 (10) 10/316 (9) (106.1 overs)	316	1/2 (1) 2/3 (3) 3/4 (4) 4/11 (5) 5/15 (2) 6/26 (7) 7/30 (8) 8/31 (9) 9/43 (6) 10/43 (10) (25 overs)	43

Henry 30–10–75–2; Leach 28.1–7–99–5; Morris 18–3–75–1; Shantry 23–8–45–2; D'Oliveira 6–1–10–0; Mitchell 1–0–2–0. *Second innings*—Henry 13–3–27–4; Leach 12–7–10–4.

Worcestershire

*D. K. H. Mitchell lbw b Dexter	25	– c O'Brien b McKay	18
B. L. D'Oliveira b Dexter	47	– c O'Brien b McKay	20
J. M. Clarke c O'Brien b Shreck	16	– (4) not out	5
A. N. Kervezee lbw b McKay	11	– (5) not out	29
T. Köhler-Cadmore lbw b Raine	44		
R. A. Whiteley b Shreck	2	– (3) c Shreck b McKay	4
†O. B. Cox b McKay	49		
J. Leach b Raine	6		
M. J. Henry not out	49		
J. D. Shantry c Horton b Raine	10		
C. A. J. Morris run out	0		
B 1, lb 14	15	B 4, lb 8	12
1/51 (1) 2/78 (3) 3/94 (2) 4/111 (4) 5/126 (6) 6/203 (5) 7/203 (7) 8/215 (8) 9/261 (10) 10/274 (11) (75.3 overs)	274	1/22 (1) 2/38 (3) 3/57 (2) (3 wkts, 15.5 overs)	88

McKay 22.3–2–80–2; Raine 21–4–69–3; Shreck 16–3–61–2; Dexter 15–4–49–2; Ali 1–1–0–0. *Second innings*—McKay 7–0–28–3; Dexter 3–0–14–0; Shreck 4.5–1–31–0; Raine 1–0–3–0.

Umpires: N. G. C. Cowley and B. V. Taylor.

At Canterbury, May 29–June 1. LEICESTERSHIRE drew with KENT.

At Chelmsford, June 19–22. LEICESTERSHIRE beat ESSEX by four wickets.

LEICESTERSHIRE v GLOUCESTERSHIRE

At Leicester, June 27–30. Drawn. Leicestershire 8pts, Gloucestershire 12pts. Toss: uncontested.

Gloucestershire shaded the bonus points, but bad weather left both sides frustrated; rain stole half the second day, all of the third, and a session of the last. The only complete day was evenly matched: Norwell, bowling in conditions suiting his seamers, thoroughly tested the Leicestershire batsmen, while Dexter's century held the innings together. But, after all the rain, Gloucestershire were still in their first innings on the last afternoon. With Leicestershire's bowlers some way below full throttle, the batsmen enjoyed themselves, and centuries from Dent and van Buuren saw them to maximum batting points.

Close of play: first day, Leicestershire 252-7 (Dexter 107, McKay 8); second day, Gloucestershire 69-0 (Roderick 23, Dent 34); third day, no play.

Leicestershire

P. J. Horton lbw b Payne	5
A. J. Robson b Payne	2
N. J. Dexter c Dent b Norwell	136
*M. J. Cosgrove c Payne b Noema-Barnett	54
M. L. Pettini c Roderick b Norwell	5
A. M. Ali b Miles	30
†E. J. H. Eckersley lbw b Noema-Barnett	5
R. M. L. Taylor lbw b Noema-Barnett	21
C. J. McKay c Payne b Norwell	55
R. A. Jones c Roderick b Norwell	5
C. E. Shreck not out	0
B 1, lb 11, nb 4	16
1/7 (2) 2/18 (1) 3/119 (4) 4/130 (5) 5/188 (6) 6/211 (7) 7/243 (8) 8/329 (3) 9/334 (9) 10/334 (10) (114.1 overs)	334
110 overs: 329-7	

Payne 25–3–75–2; Norwell 32.1–8–72–4; Miles 21–6–89–1; Howell 5–1–12–0; Noema-Barnett 23–6–56–3; van Buuren 8–2–18–0.

Gloucestershire

*†G. H. Roderick c Robson b Jones	46
C. D. J. Dent lbw b Dexter	165
G. L. van Buuren not out	121
M. Klinger not out	45
B 15, lb 7, w 2, nb 2	26
1/138 (1) 2/315 (2) (2 wkts, 89.1 overs)	403

H. J. H. Marshall, K. Noema-Barnett, J. M. R. Taylor, B. A. C. Howell, C. N. Miles, D. A. Payne and L. C. Norwell did not bat.

McKay 19–2–88–0; Jones 20–6–75–1; Shreck 18.1–5–69–0; Taylor 11–1–47–0; Dexter 16–1–62–1; Ali 2–0–21–0; Cosgrove 3–0–19–0.

Umpires: N. G. C. Cowley and S. A. Garratt.

At Worcester, July 3–6. LEICESTERSHIRE lost to WORCESTERSHIRE by three wickets.

At Cheltenham, July 20–22. LEICESTERSHIRE beat GLOUCESTERSHIRE by six wickets.

LEICESTERSHIRE v DERBYSHIRE

At Leicester, August 4–7. Drawn. Leicestershire 11pts, Derbyshire 11pts. Toss: Leicestershire. First-class debuts: A. J. Mellor, C. F. Parkinson.

Eckersley became only the second Leicestershire batsman to score two hundreds in a first-class match more than once, following Maurice Hallam, who did it three times between 1959 and 1965. Eckersley's first pair of centuries had come in a heavy defeat by Worcestershire in 2013, but his efforts in this game, where no team-mate reached 50, ensured a draw. Replying to 380, Derbyshire slipped to 174 for six before the tail helped them reach 362, with No. 11 Callum Parkinson adding an unbeaten 48 on debut, to figures of four for 90 with his left-arm spin. His twin brother Matt, a leg-spinner, had made his own debut for Lancashire in June. Leicestershire wobbled to 103 for five on the third evening, but Eckersley steered them to safety, and they eventually declared on 294 for nine, leaving 38 overs to force an unlikely win. Two wickets in the first three overs raised hopes, but Madsen and former Leicestershire all-rounder Thakor added an unbeaten 61 for the fifth wicket.

Close of play: first day, Leicestershire 300-7 (Eckersley 73, Raine 10); second day, Derbyshire 199-6 (A. L. Hughes 40, Mellor 6); third day, Leicestershire 109-5 (O'Brien 2, Eckersley 4).

Leicestershire

P. J. Horton c Mellor b Parkinson	42 – c Broom b Palladino	1
A. J. Robson c Madsen b Milnes	4 – b Milnes	0
N. J. Dexter c Mellor b Thakor	44 – lbw b Milnes	16
*M. J. Cosgrove b Parkinson	14 – b Thakor	49
M. L. Pettini lbw b Thakor	13 – lbw b Parkinson	32
†N. J. O'Brien lbw b Madsen	40 – c Mellor b Parkinson	35
E. J. H. Eckersley c Godleman b Parkinson	117 – c Palladino b C. F. Hughes	104
C. J. McKay b Parkinson	40 – b Parkinson	13
B. A. Raine c Mellor b A. L. Hughes	33 – b Broom	13
R. A. Jones b Broom	8 – not out	22
C. E. Shreck not out	0 – not out	1
B 10, lb 5, nb 10	25 B 5, lb 3	8
1/6 (2) 2/95 (3) 3/114 (4) (125.4 overs)	380 1/1 (2) (9 wkts dec, 107 overs)	294
4/121 (1) 5/138 (5) 6/206 (6)	2/1 (1) 3/30 (3)	
7/289 (8) 8/347 (9) 9/362 (10)	4/103 (4) 5/103 (5) 6/174 (6)	
10/380 (7) 110 overs: 340-7	7/210 (8) 8/265 (9) 9/276 (7)	

Palladino 30–13–60–0; Milnes 27–4–94–1; Thakor 14–0–59–2; Parkinson 33.4–4–90–4; A. L. Hughes 9–0–34–1; Madsen 10–2–19–1; Broom 2–1–9–1. *Second innings*—Milnes 14–2–51–2; Palladino 20–3–51–1; Parkinson 37–7–88–3; Thakor 13–2–34–1; Madsen 15–6–23–0; A. L. Hughes 4–0–26–0; Broom 3–1–11–1; C. F. Hughes 1–0–2–1.

Derbyshire

B. T. Slater b Raine	15 – lbw b Shreck	24
*B. A. Godleman b McKay	12 – b Raine	0
C. F. Hughes b Raine	11 – c Shreck b McKay	1
W. L. Madsen c Cosgrove b Shreck	76 – not out	42
N. T. Broom c Raine b Shreck	30 – c Pettini b Shreck	1
S. J. Thakor lbw b McKay	0 – not out	31
A. L. Hughes b Jones	48	
†A. J. Mellor b Raine	27	
T. P. Milnes c O'Brien b Raine	24	
A. P. Palladino c O'Brien b Raine	46	
C. F. Parkinson not out	48	
B 10, lb 13, nb 2	25 Lb 5	5
1/25 (2) 2/29 (1) 3/40 (3) (109.1 overs)	362 1/4 (2) 2/5 (3) (4 wkts, 30 overs)	104
4/122 (5) 5/124 (6) 6/174 (4)	3/41 (1) 4/43 (5)	
7/224 (7) 8/250 (8) 9/289 (9) 10/362 (10)		

McKay 22–6–48–2; Jones 13–1–61–1; Raine 24.1–3–66–5; Dexter 16–1–79–0; Shreck 28–8–68–2; Cosgrove 1–0–1–0; Horton 5–2–16–0. *Second innings*—McKay 6–1–32–1; Raine 8–2–16–1; Jones 5–0–10–0; Shreck 7–2–14–2; Eckersley 1–0–5–0; Horton 1–0–8–0; Cosgrove 2–0–14–0.

Umpires: R. J. Bailey and M. Burns.

At Northampton, August 13–16. LEICESTERSHIRE drew with NORTHAMPTONSHIRE. *Leicestershire move up to second.*

LEICESTERSHIRE v ESSEX

At Leicester, August 23–25. Essex won by an innings and ten runs. Essex 24pts, Leicestershire 3pts. Toss: uncontested. Championship debut: D. Klein.

Nineteen-year-old Dan Lawrence's century inspired Essex to an innings win that all but extinguished Leicestershire's fleeting promotion hopes. There was further disappointment after the match: elite performance director Andrew McDonald announced he would be returning to Australia at the end of the season to lead Melbourne Renegades in the Big Bash League, and Victoria in the state competitions. Leicestershire had begun poorly, losing two wickets in the first over, and – despite fifties from Robson and Cosgrove – were all out on the first evening for 238. Porter collected four for 50. They fought back, as Essex slipped to 68 for five, all but one for South African left-arm seamer Dieter Klein, making his debut in the absence of the injured Clint McKay. But they could not sustain the pressure. Lawrence compiled a vital 154 and shared century stands with ten Doeschate and Foster to take Essex to a commanding total. Leicestershire were punch-drunk, and crumbled to a crushing defeat; Porter took another four, while Masters enjoyed his return to his old club with four of his own.

Close of play: first day, Essex 13-2 (Browne 2, Westley 1); second day, Essex 368-8 (Lawrence 123, Napier 18).

Leicestershire

P. J. Horton lbw b Porter	1	– c Foster b Masters	2
A. J. Robson b Napier	52	– c Cook b Napier	21
N. J. Dexter lbw b Porter	0	– c Foster b Porter	44
*M. J. Cosgrove b Rhodes	71	– lbw b Masters	27
M. L. Pettini b Masters	7	– c Foster b Porter	6
†E. J. H. Eckersley b Westley	11	– c sub (K. S. Velani) b Porter	12
L. J. Hill lbw b Bopara	36	– c Foster b Masters	0
B. A. Raine c Foster b Porter	17	– run out	16
R. A. Jones c ten Doeschate b Napier	11	– c Foster b Porter	19
D. Klein b Porter	15	– not out	16
C. E. Shreck not out	0	– lbw b Masters	0
Lb 13, nb 4	17	B 2, lb 3, w 1, nb 6	12
1/2 (1) 2/2 (3) 3/131 (2) (84.1 overs)	238	1/7 (1) 2/53 (2) (49.3 overs)	175
4/143 (5) 5/155 (4) 6/172 (6)		3/88 (4) 4/99 (5)	
7/191 (8) 8/222 (7) 9/232 (9) 10/238 (10)		5/115 (6) 6/116 (7) 7/116 (3)	
		8/141 (8) 9/174 (9) 10/175 (11)	

Porter 14.1–3–50–4; Masters 17–4–35–1; Napier 18–3–50–2; Bopara 14–3–38–1; Rhodes 16–4–41–1; Westley 5–2–11–1. *Second innings*—Porter 15–2–49–4; Masters 15.3–5–39–4; Napier 10–3–47–1; Rhodes 4–2–8–0; Bopara 5–1–27–0.

Essex

N. L. J. Browne b Klein	2
A. N. Cook b Klein	4
J. A. Porter c Eckersley b Klein	0
T. Westley c Horton b Klein	35
R. S. Bopara b Shreck	11
D. W. Lawrence c Cosgrove b Raine	154
*R. N. ten Doeschate c Eckersley b Raine	86
†J. S. Foster c Eckersley b Jones	54
W. M. H. Rhodes c Cosgrove b Jones	0
G. R. Napier c Dexter b Shreck	31
D. D. Masters not out	2
B 10, lb 11, w 5, nb 18	44
1/10 (2) 2/12 (3) (117.2 overs)	423
3/13 (1) 4/60 (5) 5/68 (4)	
6/193 (7) 7/323 (8) 8/323 (9)	
9/407 (10) 10/423 (6) 110 overs: 400-8	

Raine 22.2–5–78–2; Klein 26–4–107–4; Jones 18–5–69–2; Shreck 31–8–88–2; Dexter 19–0–57–0; Cosgrove 1–0–3–0.

Umpires: N. G. B. Cook and B. V. Taylor.

LEICESTERSHIRE v SUSSEX

At Leicester, September 6–7. Sussex won by an innings and 59 runs. Sussex 22pts, Leicestershire 3pts. Toss: uncontested. Championship debut: P. D. Salt.

If the innings defeat by Essex had sobered Leicestershire up, another one here felt more like a nasty hangover. Sussex needed only two days, and 313 runs, to earn a big victory. Sensing a helpful pitch, they chose to bowl, removed Horton first ball, and ran through Leicestershire for 135; Magoffin and Archer took nine between them as only four batsmen made double figures. When the Sussex openers reached 82 without loss, the die looked cast, though Leicestershire rallied: Dexter followed up his fifty with a five-for to reduce Sussex to 156 for seven. But Brown and Robinson survived until the close, then upped the tempo next morning, putting on 133 in all. Leicestershire resumed 178 behind, and soon wilted. Only three reached double figures this time, as the Sussex seamers buffed their averages.

Close of play: first day, Sussex 182-7 (Brown 28, Robinson 8).

Leicestershire

P. J. Horton c Brown b Magoffin	0	– c Nash b Magoffin	7
A. J. Robson b Archer	18	– c Nash b Magoffin	0
N. J. Dexter b Archer	52	– lbw b Archer	9
*M. J. Cosgrove lbw b Magoffin	4	– lbw b Wiese	10
M. L. Pettini b Archer	7	– b Robinson	2
†E. J. H. Eckersley c Magoffin b Wiese	19	– lbw b Wiese	31
L. J. Hill b Magoffin	1	– b Wiese	9
C. J. McKay c Wiese b Magoffin	0	– c Wiese b Archer	9
Z. J. Chappell b Magoffin	10	– b Archer	0
B. A. Raine c Brown b Archer	2	– c Wiese b Robinson	25
C. E. Shreck not out	2	– not out	0
B 8, lb 12	20	B 8, w 3, nb 6	17
1/0 (1) 2/55 (2) 3/66 (4) (51 overs)	135	1/5 (2) 2/17 (1) (47.1 overs)	119
4/90 (5) 5/99 (3) 6/100 (7)		3/17 (3) 4/25 (5)	
7/100 (8) 8/114 (9) 9/121 (10) 10/135 (6)		5/29 (4) 6/59 (7) 7/75 (8)	
		8/81 (9) 9/117 (6) 10/119 (10)	

Magoffin 18–5–50–5; Robinson 11–4–23–0; Archer 15–6–31–4; Wiese 7–4–11–1. *Second innings*—Magoffin 15–4–32–2; Archer 14–3–31–3; Robinson 9.1–3–28–2; Wiese 9–3–20–3.

Sussex

C. D. Nash b Dexter	65	O. E. Robinson c Shreck b Horton	81
E. C. Joyce b Shreck	24	J. C. Archer b Chappell	11
L. W. P. Wells c Robson b Shreck	8	S. J. Magoffin not out	2
F. J. Hudson-Prentice c Eckersley b Dexter	15	B 6, lb 2, w 6	14
C. Cachopa c Eckersley b Dexter	15		
*†B. C. Brown c Robson b Horton	71	1/82 (2) 2/100 (1) 3/100 (3) (72.1 overs)	313
P. D. Salt lbw b Dexter	2	4/129 (5) 5/132 (4) 6/146 (7)	
D. Wiese lbw b Dexter	5	7/156 (8) 8/289 (6) 9/302 (9) 10/313 (10)	

McKay 13–0–52–0; Raine 10–0–46–0; Shreck 22–0–95–2; Chappell 8.1–0–52–1; Dexter 14–4–52–5; Cosgrove 1–0–2–0; Horton 4–1–6–2.

Umpires: N. G. C. Cowley and S. C. Gale.

At Derby, September 12–15. LEICESTERSHIRE drew with DERBYSHIRE.

LEICESTERSHIRE v GLAMORGAN

At Leicester, September 20–22. Leicestershire won by 26 runs. Leicestershire 19pts, Glamorgan 3pts. Toss: uncontested.

After successive innings defeats at home, Leicestershire were desperate to remind their supporters of their early-season progress. At 64 for nine on the first morning, however, a win looked inconceivable. They eventually scraped together 96, with van der Gugten claiming a Championship-best five for 52 – and the extra runs were to prove vital. Though Glamorgan took the lead only three wickets down, they then collapsed themselves, before Leicestershire closed a frenetic day on almost equal terms at 78 without loss. Careful knocks from Robson and Dexter helped them to 213 for three, before van der Gugten picked up four more to leave a target of 181 – far from straightforward on a seaming pitch. Shortly after lunch on day three, Glamorgan had the task in hand at 144 for four, but Shreck and McKay bowled beautifully to polish off the last six for ten runs and claim a dramatic win.

Close of play: first day, Leicestershire 78-0 (Horton 28, Robson 42); second day, Glamorgan 11-1 (Rudolph 9, Morgan 0).

Leicestershire

P. J. Horton lbw b van der Gugten	25	– c Selman b Meschede	41
A. J. Robson c Selman b Hogan	4	– c Bragg b Carey	72
N. J. Dexter b Meschede	10	– b van der Gugten	73
*M. J. Cosgrove c and b van der Gugten	2	– b Meschede	35
†E. J. H. Eckersley c Wallace b van der Gugten	6	– c Morgan b Hogan	12
M. L. Pettini c Wallace b van der Gugten	0	– b van der Gugten	1
H. E. Dearden b van der Gugten	5	– lbw b van der Gugten	16
C. J. McKay not out	17	– lbw b van der Gugten	10
B. A. Raine c Rudolph b Carey	1	– c and b Hogan	6
D. Klein lbw b Carey	0	– lbw b Hogan	0
C. E. Shreck c Carlson b Hogan	20	– not out	0
Lb 1, w 1, nb 4	6	B 4, lb 12, w 1	17
1/8 (2) 2/37 (3) 3/41 (1) 4/49 (5) 5/49 (6) 6/52 (4) 7/55 (7) 8/64 (9) 9/64 (10) 10/96 (11) (29.3 overs)	96	1/123 (1) 2/123 (2) 3/198 (4) 4/213 (5) 5/222 (6) 6/256 (7) 7/272 (8) 8/283 (9) 9/283 (10) 10/283 (3) (94.3 overs)	283

Van der Gugten 12–0–52–5; Hogan 6.3–3–10–2; Meschede 6–2–13–1; Carey 5–1–20–2. *Second innings*—van der Gugten 26.3–6–81–4; Hogan 25–11–55–3; Meschede 17–1–57–2; Morgan 8–1–21–0; Carlson 4–0–9–0; Carey 14–5–44–1.

Glamorgan

N. J. Selman c Horton b Raine	24	– lbw b Klein	2
*J. A. Rudolph b McKay	10	– c Horton b Klein	15
W. D. Bragg c Eckersley b Shreck	23	– (4) c Dearden b Shreck	65
A. H. T. Donald b Dexter	32	– (5) c Robson b Shreck	23
K. S. Carlson not out	74	– (6) lbw b McKay	22
C. A. J. Meschede c Eckersley b Dexter	9	– (7) lbw b McKay	0
†M. A. Wallace c Eckersley b Dexter	2	– (8) c Eckersley b Shreck	0
A. O. Morgan b Klein	0	– (3) b Klein	9
T. van der Gugten lbw b Klein	0	– lbw b Shreck	0
M. G. Hogan c Dexter b McKay	14	– c Eckersley b McKay	1
L. J. Carey b McKay	0	– not out	0
B 4, lb 1, nb 6	11	B 4, lb 7, nb 6	17
1/16 (2) 2/63 (3) 3/63 (1) 4/124 (4) 5/144 (6) 6/152 (7) 7/153 (8) 8/155 (9) 9/191 (10) 10/199 (11) (42.2 overs)	199	1/4 (1) 2/17 (2) 3/36 (3) 4/89 (5) 5/144 (6) 6/144 (7) 7/145 (8) 8/145 (9) 9/154 (10) 10/154 (4) (39.3 overs)	154

Klein 11–1–58–2; McKay 7.2–2–12–3; Shreck 9–1–44–1; Raine 8–1–44–1; Dexter 7–0–36–3. *Second innings*—Klein 7–0–46–3; McKay 15–4–42–3; Shreck 11.3–0–33–4; Raine 3–0–10–0; Dexter 3–1–12–0.

Umpires: S. A. Garratt and B. V. Taylor.

MIDDLESEX

Profits soar at house of Fraser

KEVIN HAND

The end was sweet: Middlesex were crowned county champions late on the final evening of the season. There were 28 balls remaining when, in front of an animated crowd, Toby Roland-Jones bowled Ryan Sidebottom to complete a hat-trick and clinch a first title since 1993.

In truth, as stand-in captain James Franklin admitted, Middlesex rather limped over the line, finishing with two of their least impressive performances. It helped that Yorkshire were also gunning for the title, so were open to the final-day negotiations which allowed Middlesex to nip past them and Somerset. But their consistency – they were unbeaten in the Championship – meant they were worthy winners. And contrasting victories over Yorkshire, beaten by an innings at Scarborough for the first time in the Championship, and Somerset, sealed with a last-over six, showed the spirit of a tight-knit squad.

When Angus Fraser took over as managing director of cricket in 2009, he admitted Middlesex were in "a bit of a mess". He wanted people who were proud to play for them, and eventually he found them. In his first two seasons they only just avoided the wooden spoon, but the second division title in 2011 was followed by improvement. In 2015, they finished second, and were the only county to beat Yorkshire, the champions.

In 2016, Middlesex hardly faltered. Roland-Jones was the star at Scarborough, where he transformed a match seemingly destined for a draw with a rapid half-century and three wickets. Others stepped up too. After a quiet 2015, Sam Robson began with 231 and 106 against Warwickshire, and an unbeaten 114 in the next home game, against Nottinghamshire, to become the first Middlesex batsman to score three successive hundreds at Lord's since Mike Gatting in 1995. Robson added 99 in his next innings there, but went off the boil and failed to reach 1,000 for the season. His opening partner, left-hander Nick Gubbins, had no such problems. A maiden century, against Somerset, was quickly followed by his first double, and 125 in the decider redeemed Middlesex's sticky start. Gubbins finished with 1,409 Championship runs – only Durham's Keaton Jennings made more – and looked certain to play for England sooner than later. Shrewd judges at Lord's were even tipping him as a Test captain.

Franklin took charge when Adam Voges was unable to return after injuring a hamstring during Australia's mid-season tour of Sri Lanka. Fraser's decision not to sign an overseas replacement raised eyebrows, but he was rewarded by the form of Stevie Eskinazi, another to collect a maiden century. He averaged over 40, as did Franklin, Dawid Malan and wicketkeeper John Simpson, who enjoyed one of his best seasons as a batsman. His finest hour came at Taunton, where he smashed that match-winning six with two balls (and two wickets) to

Nick Gubbins

spare. The result, celebrated wildly, assumed even greater significance as the season wore on: Middlesex finished just four points ahead of Somerset.

The pace attack was in good hands. Roland-Jones led the way with 54 wickets, but not far behind was the dependable Tim Murtagh. Arguably his best performance came on a dozy Lord's pitch, when he finished with five for 53 from 30 miserly overs after Somerset had reached 230 for two. Murtagh's Championship celebrations were slightly hampered by the need to catch an evening flight to join his Ireland team-mates in South Africa, though nothing could remove the smile from his face. Since crossing the river from Surrey in 2006, he has taken 557 first-class wickets for Middlesex at 25 apiece.

Off-spinner Ollie Rayner passed 50 Championship wickets for the first time, earning an England Lions call-up – along with Gubbins and Roland-Jones – for the winter trip to the UAE where Gubbins became captain after Jennings joined the Test team in India.

Middlesex's white-ball form also picked up. They reached the knockout stage of the T20 Blast for the first time since winning the competition in 2008, but lost to eventual champions Northamptonshire. Progress beyond the group stage of the Royal London Cup remained elusive, but signing up Daniel Vettori to coach the Twenty20 side showed Fraser was thinking beyond the four-day game.

The Championship title had looked remote: the first eight games produced seven draws and a win, and the run-in featured matches on four Test grounds – Edgbaston, Trent Bridge and Old Trafford, before the visit of Yorkshire. There were draws in the first five games at Lord's, where Middlesex players and supporters have long grumbled about docile pitches: they are prepared by MCC, who have historically been immune to suggestions that the tracks might be more bowler-friendly. There are signs, though, of greater co-operation between owner and tenant: as part of the ambitious Lord's rebuilding programme, Fraser has been given an office in the Pavilion, rather than in the block (admittedly much upgraded from the draughty shed the county occupied in the 1970s) beside the tennis court and museum.

The last Middlesex Championship had come under the captaincy of Gatting, now an influential member of their executive board. He and his old team-mate Fraser shared an embrace in the dressing-room after the title was secured – then got down to the business of planning a repeat.

Championship attendance: 62,258.

MIDDLESEX RESULTS

All first-class matches – Played 16: Won 6, Drawn 10.
County Championship matches – Played 16: Won 6, Drawn 10.

Specsavers County Championship, winners of Division 1;
NatWest T20 Blast, quarter-finalists; Royal London One-Day Cup, 6th in South Group.

COUNTY CHAMPIONSHIP AVERAGES, BATTING AND FIELDING

Cap		*Birthplace*	*M*	*I*	*NO*	*R*	*HS*	*100*	*Avge*	*Ct/St*
2016	A. C. Voges¶	*Perth, Australia*	6	6	1	388	160*	1	77.60	5
	G. J. Bailey¶	*Launceston, Aust.*	3	5	1	284	110*	1	71.00	2
2016	†N. R. T. Gubbins	*Richmond*	16	24	1	1,409	201*	4	61.26	6
2013	S. D. Robson	*Paddington, Aust.*	14	21	1	899	231	3	44.95	16
	S. S. Eskinazi††	*Johannesburg, SA*	9	15	1	609	157	2	43.50	4
2011	†J. A. Simpson	*Bury*	16	23	5	779	100*	1	43.27	45/1
2010	†D. J. Malan	*Roehampton*	15	23	1	951	147	3	43.22	6
2015	†J. E. C. Franklin††	*Wellington, NZ*	14	19	4	641	99	0	42.73	10
2015	J. A. R. Harris	*Morriston*	7	9	3	203	78	0	33.83	2
2016	P. R. Stirling	*Belfast, N. Ireland*	9	7	1	199	85	0	33.16	3
2012	T. S. Roland-Jones	*Ashford‡*	15	14	3	319	79*	0	29.00	4
2006	N. R. D. Compton	*Durban, SA*	10	17	1	436	131	1	27.25	9
2008	†T. J. Murtagh	*Lambeth*	14	12	4	168	47	0	21.00	4
2015	O. P. Rayner	*Fallingbostel, Ger.*	13	13	3	100	26	0	10.00	18
2009	S. T. Finn§	*Watford*	8	7	1	50	22*	0	8.33	1

Also batted: J. K. Fuller†† (*Cape Town, SA*) (3 matches) 93, 36 (3 ct); R. H. Patel (*Harrow‡*) (1 match) 4*; H. W. Podmore (*Hammersmith‡*) (3 matches) 2*, 21 (1 ct).

‡ *Born in Middlesex.* § *ECB contract.* ¶ *Official overseas player.*
†† *Other non-England-qualified.*

BOWLING

	Style	*O*	*M*	*R*	*W*	*BB*	*5I*	*Avge*
H. W. Podmore	RM	90	21	240	11	4-54	0	21.81
O. P. Rayner	OB	444.5	108	1,202	51	6-79	3	23.56
T. S. Roland-Jones	RFM	482.2	95	1,524	54	6-54	2	28.22
T. J. Murtagh	RFM	457.2	116	1,227	43	5-53	1	28.53
S. T. Finn	RFM	259	41	912	31	4-54	0	29.41
J. K. Fuller	RFM	100	17	393	12	5-70	1	32.75
J. A. R. Harris	RFM	228.2	34	807	16	3-67	0	50.43
J. E. C. Franklin	LFM	205	39	646	11	3-26	0	58.72

Also bowled: N. R. T. Gubbins (LBG) 7–0–38–0; D. J. Malan (LBG) 29–4–87–2; R. H. Patel (SLA) 37–7–94–3; P. R. Stirling (OB) 53–6–138–0; A. C. Voges (SLA) 15–0–65–0.

LEADING ROYAL LONDON CUP AVERAGES (100 runs/4 wickets)

Batting	*Runs*	*HS*	*Avge*	*SR*	*Ct/St*
B. B. McCullum	228	110	76.00	128.08	0
P. R. Stirling	348	125*	49.71	91.33	1
E. J. G. Morgan	219	103*	43.80	85.54	2
N. R. T. Gubbins	227	89	28.37	93.03	3
J. E. C. Franklin	149	55	24.83	94.90	2
D. J. Malan	124	70	24.80	72.09	0
J. A. Simpson	124	33	20.66	64.58	6/2

Bowling	*W*	*BB*	*Avge*	*ER*
T. S. Roland-Jones	13	4-40	16.46	5.05
J. E. C. Franklin	12	3-25	20.83	4.76
J. A. R. Harris	4	2-19	29.75	5.66
O. P. Rayner	6	2-40	41.00	4.64
J. K. Fuller	6	3-53	43.00	6.73
T. J. Murtagh	4	2-28	50.50	5.31

LEADING NATWEST T20 BLAST AVERAGES (125 runs/18 overs)

Batting	Runs	HS	Avge	SR	Ct/St
P. R. Stirling	266	60	26.60	**154.65**	5
B. B. McCullum	132	87*	33.00	**148.31**	3
D. J. Malan	368	93	36.80	**147.79**	3
J. A. Simpson	243	54	22.09	**142.10**	8/3
E. J. G. Morgan	220	59*	36.66	**122.90**	6
G. J. Bailey	225	76	28.12	**109.75**	5

Bowling	W	BB	Avge	ER
N. A. Sowter	11	2-29	23.63	**7.22**
T. S. Roland-Jones	17	3-24	16.88	**7.35**
J. E. C. Franklin	6	1-3	35.16	**7.44**
J. K. Fuller	14	3-24	22.85	**8.17**
H. W. Podmore	5	2-27	43.40	**10.09**

FIRST-CLASS COUNTY RECORDS

Highest score for	331*	J. D. B. Robertson v Worcestershire at Worcester	1949
Highest score against	341	C. M. Spearman (Gloucestershire) at Gloucester	2004
Leading run-scorer	40,302	E. H. Hendren (avge 48.81)	1907–37
Best bowling for	10-40	G. O. B. Allen v Lancashire at Lord's	1929
Best bowling against	9-38	R. C. Robertson-Glasgow (Somerset) at Lord's	1924
Leading wicket-taker	2,361	F. J. Titmus (avge 21.27)	1949–82
Highest total for	642-3 dec	v Hampshire at Southampton	1923
Highest total against	850-7 dec	by Somerset at Taunton	2007
Lowest total for	20	v MCC at Lord's	1864
Lowest total against	31	by Gloucestershire at Bristol	1924
	31	by Glamorgan at Cardiff	1997

LIST A COUNTY RECORDS

Highest score for	163	A. J. Strauss v Surrey at The Oval	2008
Highest score against	163	C. J. Adams (Sussex) at Arundel	1999
Leading run-scorer	12,029	M. W. Gatting (avge 34.96)	1975–98
Best bowling for	7-12	W. W. Daniel v Minor Counties East at Ipswich	1978
Best bowling against	6-27	J. C. Tredwell (Kent) at Southgate	2009
Leading wicket-taker	491	J. E. Emburey (avge 24.68)	1975–95
Highest total for	367-6	v Sussex v Hove	2015
Highest total against	368-2	by Nottinghamshire at Lord's	2014
Lowest total for	23	v Yorkshire at Leeds	1974
Lowest total against	41	by Northamptonshire at Northampton	1972

TWENTY20 COUNTY RECORDS

Highest score for	129	D. T. Christian v Kent at Canterbury	2014
Highest score against	119	K. J. O'Brien (Gloucestershire) at Uxbridge	2011
Leading run-scorer	**2,628**	**D. J. Malan (avge 34.12)**	**2006–16**
Best bowling for	5-13	M. Kartik v Essex at Lord's	2007
	5-13	**R. F. Higgins v Hampshire at Hove**	**2016**
Best bowling against	6-24	T. J. Murtagh (Surrey) at Lord's	2005
Leading wicket-taker	54	N. J. Dexter (avge 25.25)	2008–15
Highest total for	221-2	v Sussex at Hove	2015
Highest total against	254-3	by Gloucestershire at Uxbridge	2011
Lowest total for	92	v Surrey at Lord's	2013
Lowest total against	74	by Essex at Chelmsford	2013

ADDRESS

Lord's Cricket Ground, London NW8 8QN; 020 7289 1300; enquiries@middlesexccc.com; www.middlesexccc.com.

OFFICIALS

Captain J. E. C. Franklin
Managing director of cricket A. R. C. Fraser
Head coach R. J. Scott
Twenty20 coach D. L. Vettori
Academy director A. J. Coleman
President A. H. Latchman
Chairman M. O'Farrell
Secretary/chief executive R. J. Goatley
Head groundsman M. J. Hunt
Scorer D. K. Shelley

At Oxford, April 11–13. OXFORD MCCU v MIDDLESEX. Abandoned.

MIDDLESEX v WARWICKSHIRE

At Lord's, April 17–20. Drawn. Middlesex 12pts, Warwickshire 11pts. Toss: uncontested.

Sam Robson put a disappointing 2015 emphatically behind him, becoming the first to score a double and single century in the same match for Middlesex. But on a slow, low pitch it was not enough to conjure their first Lord's victory over Warwickshire since 1983, as Trott replied with a double-hundred of his own. Robson started by doing most of the scoring in an opening stand of 180 with Gubbins, whose dismissal by Wright, the former Middlesex seamer. was followed by a first-baller for Compton. In all Robson grafted for 482 minutes, hit 30 fours and a six in his highest score, and surpassed Bill Edrich's 225 at Edgbaston in 1947, Middlesex's previous best against these opponents. Replying to a healthy 452, Warwickshire slipped to 173 for six on the third morning, but Trott remained resolute and, thanks to a stand of 143 for the seventh wicket with Barker, they even managed a slender lead. With little chance of a result, Middlesex batted out time. Robson's 337 runs in the match was a county record, beating 331 by Jack Robertson (in 1949) and Paul Weekes (1996). All the Warwickshire players had a trundle, and Voges missed out on a century when the 11th, wicketkeeper Ambrose, took his maiden first-class wicket in his 198th match.

Close of play: first day, Middlesex 317-4 (Robson 175, Simpson 31); second day, Warwickshire 146-4 (Trott 62, Ambrose 6); third day, Middlesex 76-2 (Robson 35, Compton 34).

Middlesex

S. D. Robson c Bell b Patel	231	– (2) st Ambrose b Patel	106
N. R. T. Gubbins c Clarke b Wright	68	– (1) c Chopra b Barker	6
N. R. D. Compton c Hain b Wright	0	– (4) lbw b Clarke	44
D. J. Malan b Barker	15	– (3) c Chopra b Barker	0
*A. C. Voges b Barker	21	– c Barker b Ambrose	92
†J. A. Simpson c Ambrose b Clarke	52	– lbw b Patel	13
J. E. C. Franklin c Clarke b Hannon-Dalby	3	– not out	30
J. A. R. Harris lbw b Patel	12		
T. S. Roland-Jones c Bell b Patel	18		
T. J. Murtagh b Patel	1		
S. T. Finn not out	22		
Lb 9	9	B 4, lb 1, nb 8	13
1/180 (2) 2/180 (3) 3/211 (4) 4/263 (5) 5/370 (6) 6/377 (7) 7/405 (1) 8/409 (8) 9/415 (10) 10/452 (9) (131.5 overs)	452	1/14 (1) 2/20 (3) 3/91 (4) 4/196 (2) 5/222 (6) 6/304 (5) (6 wkts dec, 102.5 overs)	304
110 overs: 370-4			

Barker 25–3–78–2; Wright 24–5–77–2; Clarke 26–4–79–1; Patel 20.5–2–80–4; Hannon-Dalby 28–4–104–1; Trott 8–2–25–0. *Second innings*—Barker 13–4–27–2; Wright 14–1–52–0; Clarke 16–3–41–1; Patel 20–2–56–2; Hannon-Dalby 14–1–42–0; Trott 10–1–30–0; Westwood 2–0–8–0; Bell 7–2–15–0; Hain 4–0–16–0; Chopra 2–0–12–0; Ambrose 0.5–0–0–1.

Warwickshire

V. Chopra b Murtagh	57
I. J. Westwood c Compton b Finn	0
*I. R. Bell b Murtagh	14
I. J. L. Trott not out	219
S. R. Hain b Finn	2
†T. R. Ambrose b Roland-Jones	6
R. Clarke lbw b Roland-Jones	2
K. H. D. Barker lbw b Murtagh	81
J. S. Patel c Voges b Harris	30
C. J. C. Wright b Harris	7
O. J. Hannon-Dalby c Murtagh b Finn	30
B 10, lb 8, nb 2	20
1/0 (2) 2/31 (3) 3/108 (1) 4/117 (5) 5/161 (6) 6/173 (7) 7/316 (8) 8/381 (9) 9/401 (10) 10/468 (11) (112.2 overs)	468
110 overs: 441-9	

Murtagh 22–5–68–3; Finn 23.2–3–110–3; Roland-Jones 20–4–81–2; Harris 23–3–76–2; Franklin 7–0–42–0; Voges 9–0–45–0; Malan 8–0–28–0.

Umpires: P. J. Hartley and R. A. Kettleborough.

At Chester-le-Street, April 24–27. MIDDLESEX drew with DURHAM.

At Southampton, May 1–4. MIDDLESEX drew with HAMPSHIRE.

MIDDLESEX v NOTTINGHAMSHIRE

At Lord's, May 8–11. Drawn. Middlesex 9pts, Nottinghamshire 10pts. Toss: Nottinghamshire.

The loss of the last two days condemned Middlesex to their fourth draw of the season – although another placid pitch meant a positive result might have been elusive anyway. After Nottinghamshire chose to bat first, Mullaney departed in the first over, but Hales and Lumb put on 107 for the third wicket in 23, and later Patel and Read propelled the score towards 300. However, the batsmen were kept in check by Roland-Jones, who ended the innings quickly on the second morning. Middlesex stuttered, losing three for nine, before Robson calmed things down with his third century in three innings at Lord's in 2016. Displaying astute judgment of which balls to hit, he had put on 154 with Simpson – who struck 11 fours and also clattered Patel through a window on the middle tier of the Pavilion – when rain brought an early close on the second afternoon; dismal weather meant no more play was possible.

Close of play: first day, Nottinghamshire 345-7 (Patel 86, Hutton 23); second day, Middlesex 203-3 (Robson 114, Simpson 66); third day, no play.

Nottinghamshire

S. J. Mullaney lbw b Murtagh	4
A. D. Hales b Roland-Jones	73
G. P. Smith c Rayner b Roland-Jones	29
M. J. Lumb lbw b Rayner	78
M. H. Wessels lbw b Roland-Jones	0
S. R. Patel c Malan b Roland-Jones	86
*†C. M. W. Read c Compton b Finn	38
S. C. J. Broad c Compton b Finn	7
B. A. Hutton not out	28
J. T. Ball b Murtagh	4
H. F. Gurney b Roland-Jones	0
Lb 3, nb 4	7
1/4 (1) 2/61 (3) 3/168 (2) (100 overs)	354
4/168 (5) 5/208 (4) 6/279 (7)	
7/291 (8) 8/346 (6) 9/351 (10) 10/354 (11)	

Murtagh 23–6–80–2; Finn 22–3–89–2; Roland-Jones 22–2–61–5; Franklin 12–2–45–0; Rayner 19–5–64–1; Stirling 2–0–12–0.

Middlesex

S. D. Robson not out	114
N. R. T. Gubbins b Broad	11
N. R. D. Compton lbw b Hutton	3
D. J. Malan c Read b Hutton	0
†J. A. Simpson not out	66
Lb 5, nb 4	9
1/40 (2) 2/49 (3) (3 wkts, 62.2 overs)	203
3/49 (4)	

*J. E. C. Franklin, P. R. Stirling, O. P. Rayner, T. S. Roland-Jones, T. J. Murtagh and S. T. Finn did not bat.

Ball 12–0–42–0; Broad 12–3–27–1; Hutton 14–2–47–2; Gurney 11.2–5–32–0; Patel 5–0–30–0; Mullaney 8–1–20–0.

Umpires: R. J. Bailey and B. V. Taylor.

At The Oval, May 15–18. MIDDLESEX drew with SURREY.

MIDDLESEX v SOMERSET

At Lord's, May 22–25. Drawn. Middlesex 9pts, Somerset 10pts. Toss: Somerset.

There were centuries for Middlesex players old and new – while Robson fell one short of four in four innings at Lord's – but still no positive result. First to three figures was Rogers, his ninth hundred here but first since he moved to Taunton. He and Hildreth put on 136, then – after Murtagh made three quick strikes – Trego and Gregory added 113 for the sixth wicket. Middlesex's openers replied with 198, before Robson fell in the 67th over. But Gubbins, who had been out in the nineties three times before – at The Oval the previous week, and twice against Somerset – finally ticked off his maiden first-class hundred, though the latter stages were painful to watch after some attractive strokeplay earlier on. Middlesex dipped to 252 for five, but the Ireland opener Stirling, down at No. 7, settled in for more than three hours; his highest Championship score of 85 helped secure a handy lead. There was little room for manoeuvre when Somerset started their second innings on the final morning, and Hildreth made sure that some early wickets – and, later, three in 11 balls for Rayner – were inconsequential.

Close of play: first day, Somerset 219-2 (Rogers 104, Hildreth 60); second day, Middlesex 139-0 (Robson 67, Gubbins 65); third day, Middlesex 407-9 (Harris 11, Murtagh 4).

Somerset

M. E. Trescothick lbw b Roland-Jones	8	– c Simpson b Murtagh	5
T. B. Abell c Simpson b Roland-Jones	41	– lbw b Murtagh	9
*C. J. L. Rogers c Simpson b Murtagh	109	– c Simpson b Rayner	12
J. C. Hildreth lbw b Murtagh	68	– not out	85
J. Allenby c Rayner b Murtagh	0	– c Rayner b Harris	6
P. D. Trego b Murtagh	65	– c Harris b Rayner	58
L. Gregory c Simpson b Rayner	49	– c Franklin b Rayner	0
†R. C. Davies c Franklin b Murtagh	7	– b Rayner	0
C. Overton b Roland-Jones	0	– not out	19
M. J. Leach c Voges b Rayner	4		
T. D. Groenewald not out	7		
B 1, lb 17	18	Lb 6, nb 2	8
1/9 (1) 2/94 (2) 3/230 (3) 4/230 (5) 5/233 (4) 6/346 (6) 7/356 (8) 8/357 (9) 9/367 (7) 10/376 (10) (130.2 overs) 110 overs: 308-5	376	1/9 (2) 2/16 (1) 3/36 (3) 4/57 (5) 5/156 (6) 6/156 (7) 7/158 (8) (7 wkts, 62 overs)	202

Murtagh 30–13–53–5; Roland-Jones 27–5–69–3; Rayner 28.2–5–75–2; Harris 23–3–80–0; Franklin 19–1–69–0; Malan 1–0–4–0; Voges 2–0–8–0. *Second innings*—Murtagh 15–6–33–2; Roland-Jones 13–2–50–0; Rayner 21–4–56–4; Harris 13–1–57–1.

Middlesex

S. D. Robson b Leach	99
N. R. T. Gubbins c Trescothick b Allenby	109
D. J. Malan c Trescothick b Allenby	5
*A. C. Voges lbw b Groenewald	18
†J. A. Simpson lbw b Groenewald	10
J. E. C. Franklin c Allenby b Leach	23
P. R. Stirling lbw b Leach	85
O. P. Rayner lbw b Leach	26
J. A. R. Harris not out	17
T. S. Roland-Jones c Rogers b Allenby	2
T. J. Murtagh b Leach	14
B 6, lb 3, nb 6	15
1/198 (1) 2/213 (3) 3/234 (2) 4/243 (4) 5/252 (5) 6/301 (6) 7/372 (8) 8/395 (7) 9/402 (10) 10/423 (11) (141 overs) 110 overs: 321-6	423

Groenewald 29–9–66–2; Gregory 22–1–102–0; Overton 26–5–92–0; Allenby 21–6–51–3; Trego 13–2–26–0; Leach 30–8–77–5.

Umpires: N. L. Bainton and M. A. Gough.

MIDDLESEX v HAMPSHIRE

At Northwood, May 29–June 1. Middlesex won by an innings and 116 runs. Middlesex 24pts, Hampshire –1pt (after 2pt penalty). Toss: Middlesex. Championship debut: J. J. Weatherley.

Merchant Taylors' had previously been a soggy outpost, with five of the eight days' Championship cricket scheduled there washed out. But now Middlesex celebrated the move away from Lord's by emphatically ending a run of six draws. They shrugged off an unpromising start – the openers gone inside seven overs – to rack up an imposing total against an injury-hit attack. Malan batted fluently for 147, his second hundred of the season against Hampshire, and put on 279 in 70 overs with Voges, who motored on next morning alongside Simpson, whose second fifty took just 35 balls. Hampshire found batting rather more difficult, as Murtagh and Roland-Jones exploited uneven bounce to share eight wickets; they soon followed on, and lost 13 in all on the second day. Only an hour's play was possible on the third, but the pacy Fuller – with five wickets in his first Championship match for Middlesex – wrapped up victory next day, despite a staunch effort from Adams, who battled 227 minutes for 78. Best completed a second successive pair, and departed to some choice words from fielders unimpressed by an earlier beamer to Voges. Hampshire lost two points for a slow over-rate, so finished in the red.

Close of play: first day, Middlesex 342-3 (Voges 128, Simpson 28); second day, Hampshire 62-3 (Adams 21, Dawson 17); third day, Hampshire 100-4 (Adams 47, Weatherley 4).

Middlesex

S. D. Robson c Adams b Best	2
N. R. T. Gubbins c Smith b Tomlinson	4
D. J. Malan c Ervine b Dawson	147
*A. C. Voges not out	160
†J. A. Simpson not out	100
B 14, lb 17, w 5, nb 18	54
1/6 (2) (3 wkts dec, 115.2 overs)	467
2/14 (1) 3/293 (3) 110 overs: 414-3	

J. E. C. Franklin, P. R. Stirling, O. P. Rayner, T. S. Roland-Jones, J. K. Fuller and T. J. Murtagh did not bat.

Best 22–3–95–1; Tomlinson 22.2–4–77–1; McLaren 27–5–77–0; Ervine 8–2–34–0; Dawson 22–2–89–1; Crane 14–1–64–0.

Hampshire

M. A. Carberry c Simpson b Murtagh	4	– (3) c Rayner b Fuller	21
J. H. K. Adams b Murtagh	19	– lbw b Franklin	78
*W. R. Smith c Franklin b Murtagh	12	– (1) c Simpson b Murtagh	0
S. M. Ervine c Simpson b Murtagh	31	– b Fuller	1
L. A. Dawson c Robson b Fuller	21	– c Robson b Murtagh	23
J. J. Weatherley c Gubbins b Rayner	4	– b Roland-Jones	9
†A. J. A. Wheater c Simpson b Roland-Jones	22	– c Voges b Fuller	25
R. McLaren not out	10	– not out	33
T. L. Best c Murtagh b Roland-Jones	0	– c Malan b Fuller	0
M. S. Crane c Voges b Roland-Jones	0	– c sub (R. G. White) b Fuller	21
J. A. Tomlinson c Franklin b Roland-Jones	5	– c Franklin b Rayner	2
Lb 3	3	Lb 1, nb 6	7
1/6 (1) 2/32 (3) 3/43 (2) (51.4 overs)	131	1/0 (1) 2/30 (3) (77 overs)	220
4/77 (5) 5/89 (6) 6/116 (7)		3/38 (4) 4/72 (5)	
7/120 (4) 8/123 (9) 9/123 (10) 10/131 (11)		5/109 (6) 6/162 (2) 7/162 (7)	
		8/162 (9) 9/202 (10) 10/220 (11)	

Murtagh 17–4–33–4; Roland-Jones 17.4–5–49–4; Franklin 8–6–9–0; Fuller 7–0–34–1; Rayner 2–1–3–1. *Second innings*—Murtagh 15–4–28–2; Roland-Jones 17–2–53–1; Franklin 16–4–42–1; Fuller 18–3–70–5; Rayner 8–3–14–1; Stirling 3–0–12–0.

Umpires: J. W. Lloyds and N. A. Mallender.

MIDDLESEX v LANCASHIRE

At Lord's, June 26–29. Drawn. Middlesex 11pts, Lancashire 9pts. Toss: Lancashire.

This match was destined for a draw long before rain consigned it to a watery grave. On another timid Lord's track, over 900 runs were scored for the loss of only 15 wickets. First to tuck in was Hameed, who was close to adding to his maiden century of three days previously when he edged to slip, where Robson juggled but held on. Petersen made no such mistake, though, and looked set for his fourth double-hundred next day until he scooped a return catch to the persistent Roland-Jones. He hit only ten fours (and two sixes) in 408 minutes. A run-a-ball 58 from Livingstone ushered Lancashire towards 500, and then it was Middlesex's turn. Gubbins, who had scored his own maiden hundred in the previous match at Lord's, settled in with Stevie Eskinazi, playing his second first-class match, and first of the season. The close friends put on 208 before Eskinazi was out for a composed 106, but the left-handed Gubbins flowed on, reaching his first double-century after more than seven hours. He got there with ten runs off the final three balls of the third day – just as well, as no play was possible on the fourth.

Close of play: first day, Lancashire 298-3 (Petersen 105, Croft 34); second day, Middlesex 146-1 (Gubbins 71, Eskinazi 43); third day, Middlesex 419-5 (Gubbins 201, Stirling 2).

Lancashire

T. C. Smith lbw b Franklin	17	K. M. Jarvis c Robson b Rayner	14
H. Hameed c Robson b Roland-Jones	89	M. W. Parkinson not out	4
L. A. Procter c Rayner b Murtagh	45		
A. N. Petersen c and b Roland-Jones	191	B 4, lb 3, nb 4	11
*†S. J. Croft c Simpson b Rayner	46		—
K. R. Brown c Fuller b Rayner	21	1/36 (1) 2/101 (3) (145.5 overs)	513
L. S. Livingstone c Fuller b Roland-Jones	58	3/198 (2) 4/326 (5) 5/368 (6)	
J. Clark lbw b Roland-Jones	3	6/471 (7) 7/477 (4) 8/490 (8)	
N. Wagner c Malan b Rayner	14	9/498 (9) 10/513 (10)	110 overs: 334-4

Murtagh 32–5–98–1; Roland-Jones 31–4–122–4; Fuller 25–3–92–0; Franklin 19–3–64–1; Rayner 35.5–6–120–4; Malan 3–0–10–0.

Middlesex

S. D. Robson c Livingstone b Parkinson	21	P. R. Stirling not out	2
N. R. T. Gubbins not out	201	B 10, lb 5, nb 8	23
S. S. Eskinazi c Smith b Jarvis	106		—
D. J. Malan c Smith b Wagner	24	1/59 (1) 2/267 (3) (5 wkts, 111 overs)	419
†J. A. Simpson b Clark	1	3/308 (4) 4/309 (5)	
*J. E. C. Franklin c Croft b Jarvis	41	5/404 (6)	110 overs: 409-5

O. P. Rayner, T. S. Roland-Jones, J. K. Fuller and T. J. Murtagh did not bat.

Jarvis 25–4–101–2; Wagner 29–5–83–1; Parkinson 26–5–110–1; Smith 9–1–27–0; Clark 17–3–60–1; Livingstone 4–0–15–0; Procter 1–0–8–0.

Umpires: P. K. Baldwin and N. G. B. Cook.

At Scarborough, July 3–6. MIDDLESEX beat YORKSHIRE by an innings and four runs. *Middlesex go top.*

At Taunton, July 10–13. MIDDLESEX beat SOMERSET by two wickets. *Middlesex chase down 302 in 45.4 overs.*

MIDDLESEX v SURREY

At Lord's, August 4–7. Drawn. Middlesex 10pts, Surrey 13pts. Toss: Surrey.

An off-colour performance nearly resulted in Middlesex's first defeat of the season – but they were rescued by the Antipodean pair of Bailey, who made an attacking century in his first red-ball match at Lord's, and Franklin. They came together at 82 for five, the target beyond the horizon, and survived 51 overs, adding 174. Surrey had seized the upper hand on the first day, when Roy followed Burns's tidy 88 with a forthright century; the lower order, shepherded by Foakes, took the total to 415. Middlesex's batsmen then found various ways of getting out. Only Gubbins pressed on, until Simpson hunkered down for 58 from 153 balls. Surrey led by 122 and, although they lost four for nought in 13 balls, a seventh-wicket stand of 127 between Foakes – with his second unbeaten sixty of the match – and Sam Curran stretched the lead close to 400. The Currans then removed the Middlesex openers cheaply, before Ansari weighed in with an incisive spell.

Close of play: first day, Surrey 384-8 (Foakes 53, Batty 4); second day, Middlesex 249-5 (Simpson 52, Franklin 16); third day, Surrey 234-6 (Foakes 50, S. M. Curran 71).

Surrey

R. J. Burns c Bailey b Harris	88	– b Roland-Jones	39
D. P. Sibley lbw b Murtagh	3	– c Simpson b Harris	7
Z. S. Ansari lbw b Murtagh	1	– lbw b Roland-Jones	0
A. J. Finch lbw b Franklin	37	– lbw b Roland-Jones	0
J. J. Roy c Compton b Roland-Jones	110	– b Rayner	37
S. M. Davies lbw b Rayner	38	– c Compton b Rayner	20
†B. T. Foakes not out	63	– not out	65
S. M. Curran b Franklin	20	– st Simpson b Rayner	71
T. K. Curran lbw b Harris	26	– not out	17
*G. J. Batty lbw b Roland-Jones	23		
S. C. Meaker lbw b Harris	1		
Lb 5	5	Lb 9, w 1	10
1/3 (2) 2/23 (3) 3/70 (4) (110.2 overs)	415	1/47 (1) (7 wkts dec, 85 overs)	266
4/188 (1) 5/271 (6) 6/287 (5) 7/319 (8)		2/47 (3) 3/47 (2)	
8/373 (9) 9/406 (10) 10/415 (11) 110 overs: 415-9		4/47 (4) 5/107 (6) 6/108 (5) 7/235 (8)	

Murtagh 28–8–100–2; Roland-Jones 27–2–118–2; Harris 22.2–1–98–3; Franklin 13–0–42–2; Rayner 20–4–52–1. *Second innings*—Murtagh 18–5–23–0; Roland-Jones 16–2–44–3; Rayner 23–6–72–3; Harris 15–3–65–1; Franklin 13–0–53–0.

Middlesex

S. S. Eskinazi lbw b T. K. Curran	8	– lbw b T. K. Curran	13
N. R. T. Gubbins b Ansari	82	– c T. K. Curran b S. M. Curran	5
N. R. D. Compton b Meaker	11	– st Foakes b Ansari	22
D. J. Malan c Sibley b Ansari	31	– c Foakes b Ansari	29
G. J. Bailey lbw b Batty	37	– not out	110
†J. A. Simpson lbw b S. M. Curran	58	– lbw b Ansari	4
*J. E. C. Franklin b S. M. Curran	17	– b Ansari	70
J. A. R. Harris c Davies b T. K. Curran	9	– not out	11
T. S. Roland-Jones lbw b S. M. Curran	7		
O. P. Rayner c Foakes b S. M. Curran	8		
T. J. Murtagh not out	9		
B 8, lb 1, w 1, nb 6	16	B 4, lb 6, nb 4	14
1/14 (1) 2/45 (3) 3/125 (4) (91.3 overs)	293	1/18 (1) (6 wkts, 91 overs)	278
4/134 (2) 5/204 (5) 6/251 (7)		2/26 (2) 3/71 (3)	
7/266 (6) 8/274 (9) 9/278 (8) 10/293 (10)		4/78 (4) 5/82 (6) 6/256 (7)	

T. K. Curran 21–3–66–2; S. M. Curran 14.3–3–60–4; Ansari 24–6–61–2; Meaker 13–2–65–1; Batty 18–5–30–1; Sibley 1–0–2–0. *Second innings*—T. K. Curran 11–3–39–1; S. M. Curran 15–5–39–1; Meaker 15–2–75–0; Ansari 29–3–63–4; Sibley 3–0–6–0; Batty 18–5–46–0.

Umpires: G. D. Lloyd and D. J. Millns.

MIDDLESEX v DURHAM

At Lord's, August 13–15. Middlesex won by an innings and 80 runs. Middlesex 22pts, Durham 2pts. Toss: Durham.

After five draws at Lord's, Middlesex finally had their prayers answered, with MCC preparing an inviting green pitch. Then, to general surprise – there were clouds around too – Collingwood chose to bat. Riding their luck, the Durham openers put on 74, before four wickets went down for no runs in 17 balls; it would have been five had Eskinazi at slip not dropped Richardson first ball, off Rayner. Durham reached 200 thanks only to handy thirties from Coughlin and Wood, but that soon looked insignificant, as Gubbins and Compton booked in for bed (ending the first evening at 100 for one) and breakfast (taking their partnership to 247 next day). Gubbins was shelled by keeper Richardson, while his partner offered two slip chances. This was Compton's second match back after a break following the Sri Lanka Tests in June; his previous-best score of a troubled season was 44. Franklin and Roland-Jones thumped 100 for the eighth wicket in less than 14 overs, before a declaration left Durham facing a dizzying deficit of 332. They made another useful start, but Rayner removed Stoneman with a superb return catch, and finished with nine wickets in the match – his best haul at Lord's – as Durham narrowly failed to see out the third day. Middlesex ended this round of matches 26 points clear at the top, though second-placed Yorkshire had a game in hand.

Close of play: first day, Middlesex 100-1 (Gubbins 42, Compton 10); second day, Middlesex 408-6 (Franklin 10, Rayner 3).

Durham

M. D. Stoneman c Simpson b Franklin	46	– c and b Rayner	25
K. K. Jennings lbw b Franklin	27	– lbw b Rayner	45
S. G. Borthwick b Rayner	0	– lbw b Franklin	12
J. T. A. Burnham run out	0	– b Murtagh	30
†M. J. Richardson c Malan b Murtagh	17	– lbw b Rayner	2
*P. D. Collingwood c Compton b Podmore	9	– b Podmore	22
P. Coughlin lbw b Rayner	39	– c Gubbins b Rayner	37
A. J. Hickey c Simpson b Franklin	7	– c Simpson b Podmore	0
M. A. Wood c Stirling b Rayner	36	– c Eskinazi b Malan	33
C. Rushworth c Roland-Jones b Rayner	15	– (11) not out	9
G. Onions not out	0	– (10) c Roland-Jones b Rayner	34
B 3, lb 5	8	B 2, lb 1	3
1/74 (1) 2/74 (2) 3/74 (3) (59.3 overs)	204	1/55 (1) 2/82 (2) (71.5 overs)	252
4/74 (4) 5/101 (5) 6/105 (6)		3/82 (3) 4/107 (5)	
7/130 (8) 8/170 (7) 9/198 (10) 10/204 (9)		5/125 (4) 6/159 (6) 7/161 (8)	
		8/194 (7) 9/222 (9) 10/252 (10)	

Murtagh 15–2–54–1; Roland-Jones 14–3–62–0; Podmore 10–3–37–1; Franklin 12–5–26–3; Rayner 8.3–2–17–4. *Second innings*—Murtagh 14–6–39–1; Roland-Jones 17–4–70–0; Rayner 21.5–5–85–5; Franklin 6–2–21–1; Malan 5–0–15–1; Podmore 8–1–19–2.

Middlesex

S. S. Eskinazi b Onions	42	T. J. Murtagh c sub (R. D. Pringle) b Borthwick	12
N. R. T. Gubbins c Borthwick b Wood	145	B 4, lb 12, w 1	17
N. R. D. Compton b Onions	131		
D. J. Malan c Richardson b Onions	5	1/77 (1) (9 wkts dec, 151.4 overs)	536
P. R. Stirling c Jennings b Hickey	43	2/324 (2) 3/335 (4)	
†J. A. Simpson c Borthwick b Coughlin	14	4/338 (3) 5/363 (6) 6/401 (5)	
*J. E. C. Franklin not out	56	7/410 (8) 8/510 (9)	
O. P. Rayner b Wood	5	9/536 (10)	110 overs: 344-4
T. S. Roland-Jones c Burnham b Hickey	66		

H. W. Podmore did not bat.

Rushworth 21–5–52–0; Onions 31–5–104–3; Wood 29–5–91–2; Coughlin 21–3–72–1; Borthwick 34.4–4–133–1; Hickey 15–1–68–2.

Umpires: M. Burns and A. G. Wharf.

At Birmingham, August 31–September 3. MIDDLESEX drew with WARWICKSHIRE.

At Nottingham, September 6–9. MIDDLESEX beat NOTTINGHAMSHIRE by five wickets.

At Manchester, September 12–15. MIDDLESEX drew with LANCASHIRE.

MIDDLESEX v YORKSHIRE

At Lord's, September 20–23. Middlesex won by 61 runs. Middlesex 17pts (after 4pt penalty), Yorkshire 7pts. Toss: uncontested.

In a pulsating finish to the Championship, the top two locked horns, and the match went deep into the final hour, ending with only 28 balls left. Honours had been roughly even over the first three days on another mild-mannered pitch, but Somerset's rapid victory over relegated Nottinghamshire at Taunton meant a draw was of no use to either side here. After a spell of declaration bowling, which drew criticism (despite once being a regular feature of the county game), Yorkshire were set 240 in 40 overs – and, after looking in with a chance at 153 for four in the 30th, they collapsed. Roland-Jones started the slide by removing Bresnan after his second fine innings of the match, and rounded things off in front of an appreciative audience with a hat-trick as Middlesex clinched their first Championship title for 23 years. Crucial in the captains' negotiations – which took so long that Gale was stopped from bowling when he retook the field – was Yorkshire's agreement to keep swinging for victory, even if wickets fell. Middlesex lost four points for a dilatory over-rate, but still finished four in front of Somerset. The match drew the biggest crowds for Championship cricket at Lord's since May 1966: in all, 21,595 attended over the four days, and 7,408 on the last. The early exchanges had been less frenetic. Gubbins grafted to his fourth century of the season, underpinning a total in which no one else reached 50, as Brooks took six for 65. Then a Yorkshire side lacking Jonny Bairstow (refused permission to play by England) and Adil Rashid (family reasons) made a hesitant start, Roland-Jones ripping out three quick wickets, all for ducks. But Bresnan, from the unaccustomed heights of No. 5, shared hundred stands with Hodd and Azeem Rafiq. Sidebottom then helped Bresnan add 56 for the last wicket, including an extra bonus point – eventually collected after an hour's break for rain with the score stuck on 349 for nine. It proved pivotal on the final day, as it meant Yorkshire could still pass Somerset and claim the title themselves, so were receptive to Middlesex's target talks. After 455 minutes, Bresnan was left high and dry with 142, his sixth first-class century (five of them unbeaten). It lifted Yorkshire to a lead of 120, and two quick strikes on the third evening raised their hopes further. But Gubbins and Malan settled in next morning, batting calmly until the afternoon, by when it was apparent some contrivance would be necessary. Lyth and Lees – who looked embarrassed to claim his first two senior wickets – donated runs until the agreed target was reached, setting up the exciting finale.

Close of play: first day, Middlesex 208-5 (Gubbins 120, Franklin 21); second day, Yorkshire 235-6 (Bresnan 72, Azeem Rafiq 20); third day, Middlesex 81-2 (Gubbins 39, Malan 37).

Middlesex

S. D. Robson lbw b Brooks	0	– (2) c Lees b Sidebottom	0
N. R. T. Gubbins c Lyth b Bresnan	125	– (1) c and b Azeem Rafiq	93
N. R. D. Compton lbw b Brooks	8	– b Brooks	1
D. J. Malan b Willey	22	– c Brooks b Lees	116
S. S. Eskinazi b Brooks	12	– not out	78
†J. A. Simpson lbw b Bresnan	15	– b Lees	31
*J. E. C. Franklin c Hodd b Bresnan	48	– c and b Lyth	30
O. P. Rayner not out	15		
T. S. Roland-Jones c Lyth b Brooks	7		
T. J. Murtagh c Gale b Brooks	0		
S. T. Finn c Lyth b Brooks	6		
B 4, lb 6, nb 2	12	B 1, lb 6, w 1, nb 2	10
1/11 (1) 2/33 (3) 3/57 (4) (108.3 overs)	270	1/1 (2) (6 wkts dec, 93.5 overs)	359
4/97 (5) 5/154 (6) 6/229 (2)		2/2 (3) 3/200 (1)	
7/244 (7) 8/254 (9) 9/258 (10) 10/270 (11)		4/265 (4) 5/303 (6) 6/359 (7)	

Sidebottom 22–12–29–0; Brooks 23.3–2–65–6; Willey 16–1–71–1; Patterson 17–9–32–0; Bresnan 23–7–48–3; Azeem Rafiq 7–1–15–0. *Second innings*—Sidebottom 13–0–36–1; Brooks 15–5–48–1; Bresnan 12–3–33–0; Patterson 14–5–40–0; Willey 10–3–21–0; Azeem Rafiq 18–3–46–1; Lyth 7.5–0–77–1; Lees 4–0–51–2.

Yorkshire

A. Lyth b Finn	43	– c Robson b Roland-Jones	13
A. Z. Lees b Roland-Jones	0	– c Gubbins b Murtagh	20
G. S. Ballance c Rayner b Roland-Jones	0	– (4) c Robson b Finn	30
*A. W. Gale c Rayner b Roland-Jones	0	– (6) b Roland-Jones	22
T. T. Bresnan not out	142	– lbw b Roland-Jones	55
†A. J. Hodd lbw b Roland-Jones	64	– (7) b Roland-Jones	17
D. J. Willey lbw b Murtagh	22	– (3) c Eskinazi b Murtagh	11
Azeem Rafiq b Murtagh	65	– c Simpson b Roland-Jones	4
S. A. Patterson c Rayner b Finn	11	– b Finn	2
J. A. Brooks c Gubbins b Murtagh	0	– not out	0
R. J. Sidebottom b Rayner	23	– b Roland-Jones	0
Lb 14, nb 6	20	Lb 4	4
1/14 (2) 2/32 (3) 3/32 (4) (116.3 overs)	390	1/27 (1) 2/39 (2) (35.2 overs)	178
4/53 (1) 5/169 (6) 6/204 (7) 7/318 (8)		3/48 (3) 4/98 (4)	
8/333 (9) 9/334 (10) 10/390 (11) 110 overs: 363-9		5/153 (5) 6/160 (6) 7/174 (8)	
		8/178 (9) 9/178 (7) 10/178 (11)	

Murtagh 32–4–96–3; Roland-Jones 29–5–73–4; Franklin 9–1–32–0; Finn 30–4–105–2; Rayner 16.3–1–70–1. *Second innings*—Murtagh 8–1–28–2; Roland-Jones 12.2–0–54–6; Rayner 5–0–32–0; Finn 10–0–60–2.

Umpires: R. J. Bailey and R. T. Robinson.

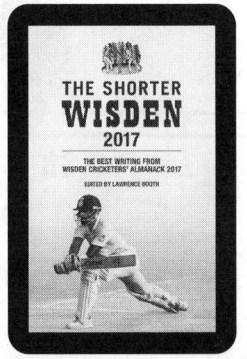

NORTHAMPTONSHIRE

Master Blasters

ANDREW RADD

It was a scenario familiar to anyone with a grasp of Northamptonshire's history: they battled financial oblivion, but made do with limited resources, and won a trophy against the odds. In August, two days after losing a Royal London Cup quarter-final against Surrey in a last-ball thriller, they won the NatWest T20 Blast for the second time in four years. An open-top bus trip followed, from Wantage Road to a civic reception at Northampton Guildhall. And even if rain dampened spirits, the parade went on. Northamptonshire won their last three Championship matches – their best run-in since 2003 – to finish fifth in Division Two.

With money scant – chairman Gavin Warren admitted he was "counting every loo roll" – the squad was shallow: just 16 full-time players competed on all fronts. It was a struggle initially, with a Championship win not coming until their 11th game, against Glamorgan in August. The captain, Alex Wakely, took some grief from supporters, though they were not helped by a combination of unresponsive pitches at Northampton and dismal weather – they lost more Championship overs than any county. But white-ball success – the product of excellent recruitment, and the tactical nous of Wakely and the coach, David Ripley – kept the fans happy, and the late four-day surge came as a pleasant surprise.

Then there was Ben Duckett. Rarely has an individual dominated a Northamptonshire season as he did in 2016. He began in unpromising fashion with a second-ball duck against Oxford MCCU, but in the first Championship match he made 282 not out against Sussex, denied a triple-century only by rain. He never looked back: Duckett, aged only 21, scored 2,258 runs in the three competitions, plus two sparkling one-day centuries for England Lions, one of them a double. His 1,338 was the highest Championship aggregate for Northamptonshire since David Sales's 1,384 in 2007.

His extraordinary summer was crowned by a stack of awards – he became the first to win both the PCA's Player and Young Player accolades in the same year – and selection for England's tour to Bangladesh and India. He also agreed to stay at Northamptonshire until the end of 2018. Duckett's signature was a potent symbol of the club's determination to keep hold of talent developed by the youth system, rather than feed wealthier counties. For the Wantage Road faithful, it ranked alongside the T20 victory as the year's best news.

But it wasn't a one-man show. South African Rory Kleinveldt does not conform to everyone's image of the modern athlete, yet his performances answered all the jibes. Time and again Kleinveldt – described by Ripley as "a Steelback to the core" – produced runs, wickets and tight overs when it

Josh Cobb

mattered. His 128 off 63 balls in the Royal London group match against Nottinghamshire at Trent Bridge, bringing his side within striking distance of a seemingly impossible target, ranks among Northamptonshire's most spectacular one-day innings.

Kleinveldt agreed a one-year extension, while fellow seamers Richard Gleeson and Ben Sanderson both made longer-term commitments, and Nathan Buck joined from Lancashire. Sanderson celebrated with a career-best eight for 73 on the final day of the Championship to sink Gloucestershire; he ended with 55 wickets, five times as many as his previous best haul. Gleeson's contract was his first full-time deal, after he had plugged away for Cumberland until the age of 27. He generated genuine pace and was outstanding in the T20 group stages – with the best economy-rate of any regular bowler in the competition – only to miss out on Finals Day through injury. Their achievements repaid Northamptonshire's faith in ambitious players who are eager for a chance in county cricket (or second chance in Sanderson's case – he was released by Yorkshire in 2011). And their contracts cushioned the blow of Olly Stone's departure for Warwickshire.

For once, the familiar platitudes about "a squad effort" rang true: almost everyone made a telling contribution. Josh Cobb celebrated his three-year contract with the match award in the T20 final, taking Durham apart with 80 from 48 deliveries. Rob Keogh scored a maiden one-day hundred and, at home to Glamorgan in the Championship, spun his way to nine for 52, Northamptonshire's sixth-best figures, and 13 in the match. Slow left-armer Graeme White, who claimed the other seven wickets in that game, was named the PCA's Player of the Year in the Royal London Cup, and took a T20 hat-trick for good measure. Wakely supplemented his immense value as leader with useful runs in all formats, and opening batsman Rob Newton finished the season strongly to average 50 in the Championship. Monty Panesar returned to the fold after seven years, eager to rebuild his career, but his continuing shoulder problems limited opportunities.

There was significant activity off the field, too. At the pre-season AGM the chairman, Gavin Warren, and the board of directors proposed turning the club into a limited company, with the aim of attracting major investment. Concerns were raised (not least by former *Wisden* editor Matthew Engel, a Northamptonshire life member) about the long-term security of the County Ground, but the change of status was backed by 86% of the members at an EGM in September. Supporters could buy shares for £250, but at the end of the 2017 season Northamptonshire will no longer be a members' club after nearly 140 years. A county that have been no strangers to the financial cliff-edge is hoping for a less anxious future.

Championship attendance: 20,356.

NORTHAMPTONSHIRE RESULTS

All first-class matches – Played 16: Won 4, Lost 3, Drawn 9. Abandoned 1.
County Championship matches – Played 15: Won 4, Lost 3, Drawn 8. Abandoned 1.

Specsavers County Championship, 5th in Division 2;
NatWest T20 Blast, winners; Royal London One-Day Cup, quarter-finalists.

COUNTY CHAMPIONSHIP AVERAGES, BATTING AND FIELDING

Cap		*Birthplace*	*M*	*I*	*NO*	*R*	*HS*	*100*	*Avge*	*Ct/St*
2016	†B. M. Duckett	*Farnborough, Kent*	14	24	2	1,338	282*	4	60.81	9/1
	R. I. Newton	*Taunton*	10	19	3	810	202*	3	50.62	4
	J. D. Libby	*Plymouth*	5	7	1	293	102	1	48.83	1
	A. M. Rossington	*Edgware*	12	17	4	556	138*	1	42.76	11/3
2013	S. P. Crook	*Modbury, Australia*	10	15	3	484	145	2	40.33	1
2012	A. G. Wakely	*Hammersmith*	12	19	3	630	104	1	39.37	11
	†S. A. Zaib	*High Wycombe*	3	5	1	127	65*	0	31.75	3
	R. I. Keogh	*Dunstable*	11	17	0	519	154	1	30.52	3/1
	R. E. Levi††	*Johannesburg, SA*	10	14	0	427	104	1	30.50	11
2016	R. K. Kleinveldt¶	*Cape Town, SA*	11	15	2	391	97	0	30.07	11
	D. Murphy	*Welwyn Garden City*	11	17	4	355	60*	0	27.30	33/2
	R. J. Gleeson	*Blackpool*	6	6	2	89	31	0	22.25	1
	J. J. Cobb	*Leicester*	6	8	0	160	49	0	20.00	0
	S. Prasanna¶	*Balapitiya, SL*	2	4	0	70	31	0	17.50	2
	G. G. White	*Milton Keynes*	5	5	0	73	33	0	14.60	3
2006	†M. S. Panesar	*Luton*	3	4	2	28	17*	0	14.00	2
2015	Azharullah	*Burewala, Pakistan*	12	15	3	72	14*	0	6.00	1
	B. W. Sanderson	*Sheffield*	14	15	3	58	19	0	4.83	1

Also batted: C. A. Barrett†† (*Johannesburg, SA*) (2 matches) 114*, 4* (3 ct); L. J. Evans (*Lambeth*) (1 match) 74, 73 (2 ct); O. P. Stone (*Norwich*) (3 matches) 4, 60, 19 (3 ct); S. P. Terry (*Southampton*) (2 matches) 54, 6, 35 (1 ct).

¶ *Official overseas player.* †† *Other non-England-qualified.*

BOWLING

	Style	*O*	*M*	*R*	*W*	*BB*	*5I*	*Avge*
B. W. Sanderson	RFM	408.5	95	1,157	55	8-73	4	21.03
G. G. White	SLA	107	24	281	13	6-44	1	21.61
R. I. Keogh	OB	242.2	42	828	31	9-52	1	26.70
R. K. Kleinveldt	RFM	302.1	60	930	26	5-53	1	35.76
Azharullah	RFM	277.2	46	987	25	6-68	1	39.48
R. J. Gleeson	RFM	147.5	25	505	10	4-105	0	50.50
S. P. Crook	RFM	139.2	18	578	10	2-7	0	57.80

Also bowled: C. A. Barrett (RFM) 20–0–100–2; J. J. Cobb (OB) 39–6–94–0; B. M. Duckett (OB) 0.5–0–8–0; J. D. Libby (OB) 21–3–71–2; D. Murphy (OB) 5–0–40–1; M. S. Panesar (SLA) 112–16–425–5; S. Prasanna (LBG) 53.2–13–165–9; A. M. Rossington (RM) 2–0–12–0; O. P. Stone (RFM) 87.4–8–282–6; A. G. Wakely (RM) 5–1–12–0; S. A. Zaib (SLA) 32–2–174–5.

LEADING ROYAL LONDON CUP AVERAGES (150 runs/4 wickets)

Batting	*Runs*	*HS*	*Avge*	*SR*	*Ct/St*
R. K. Kleinveldt	285	128	95.00	160.11	0
B. M. Duckett	443	121	63.28	98.88	0
S. P. Crook	207	52*	51.75	107.25	1
R. I. Keogh	321	134	45.85	103.54	2
J. J. Cobb	337	88	42.12	91.32	3
A. M. Rossington	287	97	41.00	100.34	4/2
A. G. Wakely	235	71	29.37	84.83	4

Bowling	*W*	*BB*	*Avge*	*ER*
G. G. White	18	6-37	17.50	4.77
R. J. Gleeson	13	5-47	22.46	5.29
J. J. Cobb	7	3-53	31.71	5.84
Azharullah	12	5-43	36.66	6.28
R. K. Kleinveldt	4	1-18	64.25	5.58

LEADING NATWEST T20 BLAST AVERAGES (100 runs/18 overs)

Batting	Runs	HS	Avge	SR	Ct/St
R. E. Levi	269	61	24.45	**151.97**	6
B. M. Duckett	477	84	43.36	**141.54**	3
A. M. Rossington	317	85	22.64	**140.26**	7/5
A. G. Wakely	286	64	35.75	**134.90**	4
J. J. Cobb	464	80	35.69	**128.17**	7
S. P. Crook	163	43	16.30	**113.98**	10

Bowling	W	BB	Avge	ER
R. J. Gleeson	14	3-12	16.00	**5.97**
S. Prasanna	12	3-24	21.41	**6.94**
M. A. Ashraf	7	3-17	23.57	**7.50**
G. G. White	13	4-20	24.46	**7.57**
R. K. Kleinveldt	15	3-14	19.73	**7.82**
J. J. Cobb	6	2-21	32.66	**8.46**
Azharullah	8	2-27	41.87	**8.48**
S. P. Crook	9	3-28	29.55	**8.86**

FIRST-CLASS COUNTY RECORDS

Highest score for	331*	M. E. K. Hussey v Somerset at Taunton	2003
Highest score against	333	K. S. Duleepsinhji (Sussex) at Hove	1930
Leading run-scorer	28,980	D. Brookes (avge 36.13)	1934–59
Best bowling for	10-127	V. W. C. Jupp v Kent at Tunbridge Wells	1932
Best bowling against	10-30	C. Blythe (Kent) at Northampton	1907
Leading wicket-taker	1,102	E. W. Clark (avge 21.26)	1922–47
Highest total for	781-7 dec	v Nottinghamshire at Northampton	1995
Highest total against	673-8 dec	by Yorkshire at Leeds	2003
Lowest total for	12	v Gloucestershire at Gloucester	1907
Lowest total against	33	by Lancashire at Northampton	1977

LIST A COUNTY RECORDS

Highest score for	172*	W. Larkins v Warwickshire at Luton	1983
Highest score against	**184**	**M. J. Lumb (Nottinghamshire) at Nottingham**	**2016**
Leading run-scorer	11,010	R. J. Bailey (avge 39.46)	1983–99
Best bowling for	7-10	C. Pietersen v Denmark at Brøndby	2005
Best bowling against	7-35	D. E. Malcolm (Derbyshire) at Derby	1997
Leading wicket-taker	251	A. L. Penberthy (avge 30.45)	1989–2003
Highest total for	**425**	**v Nottinghamshire at Nottingham**	**2016**
Highest total against	**445-8**	**by Nottinghamshire at Nottingham**	**2016**
Lowest total for	41	v Middlesex at Northampton	1972
Lowest total against	56	by Leicestershire at Leicester	1964
	56	by Denmark at Brøndby	2005

TWENTY20 COUNTY RECORDS

Highest score for	111*	L. Klusener v Worcestershire at Kidderminster	2007
Highest score against	116*	G. A. Hick (Worcestershire) at Luton	2004
Leading run-scorer	**1,768**	**A. G. Wakely (avge 27.20)**	**2009–16**
Best bowling for	6-21	A. J. Hall v Worcestershire at Northampton	2008
Best bowling against	5-6	P. D. Collingwood (Durham) at Chester-le-Street	2011
Leading wicket-taker	73	D. J. Willey (avge 19.45)	2009–15
Highest total for	224-5	v Gloucestershire at Milton Keynes	2005
Highest total against	227-6	by Worcestershire at Kidderminster	2007
Lowest total for	47	v Durham at Chester-le-Street	2011
Lowest total against	86	by Worcestershire at Worcester	2006

ADDRESS

County Ground, Abington Avenue, Northampton NN1 4PR; 01604 514455; reception@nccc.co.uk; www.northantscricket.com.

OFFICIALS

Captain A. G. Wakely
Head coach D. Ripley
Academy coach P. Rowe
President Lord Naseby

Chairman G. G. Warren
Chief executive R. Payne
Head groundsman C. Harvey
Scorer A. C. Kingston

At Oxford, April 5–7. NORTHAMPTONSHIRE drew with OXFORD MCCU.

NORTHAMPTONSHIRE v SUSSEX

At Northampton, April 10–13. Drawn. Northamptonshire 9pts, Sussex 6pts. Toss: uncontested. County debuts: J. D. Libby; L. R. P. L. Taylor. Championship debut: G. H. S. Garton.

Heavy rain cost Duckett his chance of becoming only the sixth batsman to make a triple-century for Northamptonshire. Despite hitting an unbeaten 282, he was left crestfallen after play was impossible on the last two days. "Words cannot describe how gutted I feel," he said. Sussex's decision to bowl first soon looked like folly: the pitch offered negligible help to the seamers, and meant more work for the two spinners, Briggs and Wells, than they might have expected on the opening day of the Championship. Duckett shared century stands for the first two wickets with Libby (on a month-long loan from Nottinghamshire) and his captain Wakely. He unerringly punished any width, and looked as if his luck was in: he survived a couple of streaky drives over the slips before reaching 50, and was dropped twice on the second day. Then came the rain. His 367-ball innings lasted eight and a half hours, included 38 fours and two sixes, and was the highest score for Northamptonshire against Sussex, beating Rob Bailey's 204 not out at Northampton in 1990. George Garton, an 18-year-old on Championship debut, bowled Levi and Rossington in successive overs, and later added Kleinveldt.

Close of play: first day, Northamptonshire 296-2 (Duckett 178, Cobb 9); second day, Northamptonshire 481-7 (Duckett 282, Gleeson 2); third day, no play.

Northamptonshire

J. D. Libby lbw b Magoffin	42
B. M. Duckett not out	282
*A. G. Wakely lbw b Briggs	51
J. J. Cobb c Brown b Robinson	24
R. E. Levi b Garton	11
†A. M. Rossington b Garton	0
D. Murphy c Taylor b Shahzad	31
R. K. Kleinveldt c Brown b Garton	13
R. J. Gleeson not out	2
B 6, lb 6, nb 8, p 5	25
	—
1/130 (1) 2/253 (3) 3/343 (4) 4/369 (5) 5/371 (6) 6/435 (7) 7/461 (8) (7 wkts, 135 overs)	481
110 overs: 396-5	

Azharullah and B. W. Sanderson did not bat.

Magoffin 22–8–53–1; Robinson 20–1–74–1; Shahzad 24–2–95–1; Garton 21–1–93–3; Briggs 36–5–107–1; Wells 12–0–42–0.

Sussex

E. C. Joyce, L. W. P. Wells, L. R. P. L. Taylor, M. W. Machan, H. Z. Finch, *†B. C. Brown, O. E. Robinson, A. Shahzad, G. H. S. Garton, D. R. Briggs, S. J. Magoffin.

Umpires: R. A. Kettleborough and B. V. Taylor.

At Chelmsford, April 24–27 NORTHAMPTONSHIRE lost to ESSEX by an innings and 92 runs.

NORTHAMPTONSHIRE v DERBYSHIRE

At Northampton, May 1–4. Drawn. Northamptonshire 13pts, Derbyshire 10pts. Toss: Derbyshire.

Another sluggish pitch, and the loss of most of the second day to rain, ruled out a positive result. Only the spectacular batting of Kleinveldt brought proceedings to life. Between hundreds from Libby and Levi, Kleinveldt clubbed 97 off 69 balls, taking advantage of a short boundary towards the West Stand to smite three sixes and 13 fours. Carter came in for particular punishment – one of his overs went for 24. A draw was already certain when a moment of controversy marred the final afternoon. Godleman, on 63, stood his ground after Libby claimed a low catch at deep point. Following a lengthy consultation, the umpires ruled in the batsman's favour – prompting a protest from Northamptonshire's captain, Wakely, and coach, David Ripley, who said it set "a difficult precedent". Libby enjoyed a measure of revenge when Godleman, attempting to cut his occasional off-spin, hit his own wicket, after sharing a double-century opening stand with Chesney Hughes.

Close of play: first day, Derbyshire 275-8 (Thakor 60, Fletcher 2); second day, Northamptonshire 66-0 (Libby 28, Duckett 36); third day, Northamptonshire 438-7 (Levi 84, White 23).

Derbyshire

C. F. Hughes st Rossington b Sanderson	39	– (2) not out	109
*B. A. Godleman c Rossington b Sanderson	32	– (1) hit wkt b Libby	94
H. D. Rutherford c Rossington b Kleinveldt	35	– not out	6
W. L. Madsen lbw b Azharullah	11		
N. T. Broom b Kleinveldt	4		
W. J. Durston c Rossington b Kleinveldt	0		
S. J. Thakor not out	83		
†T. Poynton c Levi b Azharullah	10		
A. P. Palladino b White	49		
L. J. Fletcher b Azharullah	3		
A. Carter c White b Azharullah	17		
B 14, lb 10, w 1, nb 16	41	B 7, lb 3, nb 10	20
1/56 (2) 2/101 (1) 3/117 (3) (89.2 overs)	324	1/215 (1) (1 wkt dec, 60.4 overs)	229
4/129 (5) 5/133 (6) 6/133 (4)			
7/161 (8) 8/266 (9) 9/276 (10) 10/324 (11)			

Kleinveldt 23–4–90–3; Azharullah 21.2–3–95–4; Sanderson 15–3–53–2; Cobb 10–4–18–0; White 18–4–31–1; Libby 1–0–3–0; Crook 1–0–10–0. *Second innings*—Kleinveldt 9–2–31–0; Azharullah 8–1–27–0; Cobb 16–2–38–0; Sanderson 8–2–27–0; White 7–0–41–0; Crook 5–0–20–0; Libby 7–1–31–1; Duckett 0.4–0–4–0.

Northamptonshire

J. D. Libby lbw b Durston	102
B. M. Duckett c Durston b Carter	60
*A. G. Wakely lbw b Thakor	35
J. J. Cobb c Broom b Thakor	0
R. E. Levi b Palladino	104
S. P. Crook b Thakor	1
†A. M. Rossington c Durston b Fletcher	19
R. K. Kleinveldt c Rutherford b Palladino	97
G. G. White c Hughes b Carter	23
Azharullah c Durston b Carter	6
B. W. Sanderson not out	0
B 10, lb 5, nb 8	23
1/109 (2) 2/191 (3) (124 overs)	470
3/205 (4) 4/207 (1) 5/208 (6)	
6/249 (7) 7/389 (8) 8/442 (9)	
9/454 (10) 10/470 (5) 110 overs: 409-7	

Fletcher 20–5–49–1; Palladino 31–3–104–2; Thakor 18–2–65–3; Carter 21–0–114–3; Durston 28–4–99–1; Hughes 4–0–21–0; Madsen 2–0–3–0.

Umpires: R. J. Evans and M. J. Saggers.

At Leicester, May 8–11. NORTHAMPTONSHIRE drew with LEICESTERSHIRE.

NORTHAMPTONSHIRE v KENT

At Northampton, May 15–18. Drawn. Northamptonshire 11pts, Kent 11pts. Toss: Kent. First-class debut: I. Qayyum.

Groundsman Paul Marshall left more grass on the pitch, but the story was the same – bat dominating ball, before the weather intervened. Panesar, making his first appearance since 2009 for the county where his career began, received a warm welcome from the Northamptonshire supporters and celebrated his first wicket – a return catch to remove Northeast – with characteristic ebullience. But he also spilled a sharp caught-and-bowled chance offered on 22 by Denly, who took full advantage to record his maiden double-century. Northamptonshire replied with a fine collective effort: five batsmen struck fifties in a series of hefty partnerships, and last pair Stone and Panesar added 49 to bring the lead above 100. But Kent lost just one wicket on the third evening, and rain allowed only 11 overs on the final day.

Close of play: first day, Kent 300-7 (Denly 126, Claydon 10); second day, Northamptonshire 206-3 (Cobb 19, Levi 11); third day, Kent 88-1 (Bell-Drummond 45, Denly 18).

Kent

D. J. Bell-Drummond c Kleinveldt b Azharullah	47	– not out	69
T. W. M. Latham run out	2	– b Panesar	24
J. L. Denly not out	206	– c Stone b Keogh	36
*S. A. Northeast c and b Panesar	49	– not out	0
S. R. Dickson c Wakely b Keogh	14		
D. I. Stevens c Libby b Kleinveldt	21		
†A. P. Rouse c Wakely b Kleinveldt	6		
C. J. Haggett c Rossington b Panesar	2		
M. E. Claydon st Rossington b Panesar	16		
M. D. Hunn b Keogh	3		
I. Qayyum c Rossington b Kleinveldt	0		
B 9, lb 11, nb 10	30	B 1, lb 1	2
1/15 (2) 2/117 (1) 3/202 (4) 4/229 (5) 5/259 (6) 6/275 (7) 7/289 (8) 8/321 (9) 9/389 (10) 10/396 (11) (115.5 overs) 110 overs: 358-8	396	1/54 (2) 2/126 (3) (2 wkts, 40 overs)	131

Kleinveldt 17.5–4–53–3; Stone 25–0–75–0; Azharullah 22–4–78–1; Panesar 40–8–122–3; Keogh 11–0–48–2. *Second innings*—Panesar 19–4–60–1; Kleinveldt 5–1–15–0; Stone 5–0–19–0; Keogh 8–2–24–1; Azharullah 3–0–11–0.

Northamptonshire

J. D. Libby c Rouse b Haggett	81
B. M. Duckett c Dickson b Stevens	7
*A. G. Wakely c Rouse b Haggett	87
J. J. Cobb c Stevens b Qayyum	40
R. E. Levi c Stevens b Claydon	23
†A. M. Rossington c Rouse b Claydon	78
R. I. Keogh b Hunn	9
R. K. Kleinveldt lbw b Hunn	71
O. P. Stone c Denly b Qayyum	60
Azharullah c Latham b Qayyum	8
M. S. Panesar not out	17
B 9, lb 8	17
1/8 (2) 2/164 (3) 3/187 (1) 4/224 (5) 5/283 (4) 6/310 (7) 7/380 (6) 8/430 (8) 9/449 (10) 10/498 (9) (140.2 overs) 110 overs: 395-7	498

Claydon 31–11–79–2; Stevens 13–2–54–1; Qayyum 41.2–6–158–3; Hunn 19–0–80–2; Haggett 35–8–105–2; Denly 1–0–5–0.

Umpires: I. D. Blackwell and J. W. Lloyds.

At Bristol, May 22–25. NORTHAMPTONSHIRE drew with GLOUCESTERSHIRE.

NORTHAMPTONSHIRE v ESSEX

At Northampton, May 28–31. Drawn. Northamptonshire 11pts, Essex 12pts. Toss: uncontested. Championship debut: M. R. Quinn.

Essex were well placed to push for another resounding victory, only for rain to halt their charge on the final day. They built their strong position on two substantial partnerships: an opening stand of 195 between Browne (dropped twice by Duckett at first slip, on five and 27) and Mickleburgh; then a rapid 215 in 32 overs, full of skilful running, between ten Doeschate and Foster – a record for any seventh wicket against Northamptonshire. The hosts cracked under scoreboard pressure on the third evening, stumbling to 56 for four by the close. Nightwatchman Sanderson was quickly removed next morning by Bopara, his seventh scalp of the match, before the weather intervened with Northamptonshire still 121 in arrears. Duckett had shone on the first day with another stylish innings, sharing three-figure partnerships with Newton and Keogh to guide his team to 344 for two. But Bopara hit back, striking three times in eight deliveries with the second new ball to reach 200 first-class wickets, and Northamptonshire's total fell short of expectations.

Close of play: first day, Northamptonshire 376-5 (Cobb 49, Murphy 3); second day, Essex 274-2 (Westley 44, Bopara 30); third day, Northamptonshire 56-4 (Rossington 10, Sanderson 1).

Northamptonshire

R. I. Newton c sub (K. S. Velani) b Bopara	75	– lbw b Quinn	0
B. M. Duckett b Bopara	189	– c Browne b Ashar Zaidi	33
R. I. Keogh c Foster b Lawrence	41	– lbw b Bopara	10
*J. J. Cobb lbw b Bopara	49	– b Quinn	0
A. M. Rossington c Mickleburgh b Bopara	4	– not out	20
S. P. Crook c Westley b Bopara	0	– (7) not out	1
†D. Murphy c Mickleburgh b Quinn	9		
O. P. Stone c Browne b Quinn	19		
R. J. Gleeson not out	27		
B. W. Sanderson c Foster b Beard	1	– (6) lbw b Bopara	2
M. S. Panesar b Ashar Zaidi	5		
B 2, lb 15, w 2, nb 6	25	Lb 4, w 1, nb 4	9
1/167 (1) 2/279 (3) 3/344 (2) 4/350 (5) 5/362 (6) 6/378 (4) 7/400 (7) 8/411 (8) 9/423 (10) 10/444 (11) (114.5 overs) 110 overs: 423-9	444	1/9 (1) 2/36 (3) 3/37 (4) 4/51 (2) 5/73 (6) (5 wkts, 25 overs)	75

Beard 19–3–73–1; Quinn 27–4–86–2; Napier 7–1–24–0; Bopara 27–6–95–5; Ashar Zaidi 7.5–1–27–1; ten Doeschate 11–0–45–0; Westley 8–0–36–0; Lawrence 8–1–41–1. *Second innings*—Quinn 11–3–26–2; Beard 5–1–20–0; Bopara 8–1–25–2; Ashar Zaidi 1–1–0–1.

Essex

N. L. J. Browne c Stone b Gleeson	88
J. C. Mickleburgh c Murphy b Gleeson	103
T. Westley c Murphy b Gleeson	69
R. S. Bopara lbw b Crook	58
D. W. Lawrence run out	12
*R. N. ten Doeschate run out	145
Ashar Zaidi c and b Stone	35
†J. S. Foster c Panesar b Gleeson	113
A. P. Beard not out	0
M. R. Quinn c Murphy b Crook	3
Lb 6, nb 8	14
1/195 (2) 2/200 (1) 3/322 (3) 4/335 (4) 5/357 (5) 6/422 (7) 7/637 (6) 8/637 (8) 9/640 (10) (9 wkts dec, 149.2 overs) 110 overs: 377-5	640

G. R. Napier did not bat.

Stone 28–5–93–1; Gleeson 30–5–105–4; Sanderson 33–5–130–0; Panesar 22–0–133–0; Crook 22.2–5–94–2; Keogh 14–0–79–0.

Umpires: N. L. Bainton and G. D. Lloyd.

At Arundel, June 22–25. NORTHAMPTONSHIRE drew with SUSSEX.

At Chesterfield, July 4–7. DERBYSHIRE v NORTHAMPTONSHIRE. Abandoned.

NORTHAMPTONSHIRE v WORCESTERSHIRE

At Northampton, July 10–12. Worcestershire won by 311 runs. Worcestershire 21pts, Northamptonshire 3pts. Toss: Worcestershire. First-class debut: G. H. Rhodes.

After Northamptonshire's heaviest defeat by runs since 2011, their supporters were left dismayed. Despite good limited-overs form, they were still without a win in the Championship. They had begun well enough, as Azharullah helped reduce Worcestershire to 54 for five. But Whiteley and Cox engineered a recovery, and Leach struck an unbeaten fifty before joining forces with Henry to demolish Northamptonshire's batting; the last seven were swept away for 52. D'Oliveira hit 81 to extend the lead, before Whiteley's three sixes on the third morning hastened a declaration. Northamptonshire needed 454 to win or – more realistically – to bat five sessions to draw. But a slipshod display, rounded off by last man Panesar's run-out, allowed Worcestershire to close the gap on leaders Essex to a point. Henry earned his first five-for in the Championship, in his final four-day game before flying off to a New Zealand training camp.

Close of play: first day, Northamptonshire 64-3 (Rossington 30, Levi 11); second day, Worcestershire 181-4 (Fell 36, Barnard 0).

Worcestershire

*D. K. H. Mitchell b Azharullah	1	– lbw b Prasanna	47
B. L. D'Oliveira c Prasanna b Azharullah	4	– st Murphy b Keogh	81
T. C. Fell b Sanderson	37	– lbw b Sanderson	45
J. M. Clarke c sub (S. A. Zaib) b Azharullah	4	– b Keogh	0
T. Köhler-Cadmore c Murphy b Azharullah	6	– lbw b Prasanna	0
R. A. Whiteley b Crook	66	– (7) c Prasanna b Crook	45
†O. B. Cox c Levi b Sanderson	74	– (8) not out	20
J. Leach not out	51	– (9) b Crook	0
G. H. Rhodes lbw b Sanderson	14	– (10) not out	31
E. G. Barnard b Prasanna	2	– (6) c Murphy b Panesar	34
M. J. Henry b Prasanna	13		
Lb 3, w 2	5	B 5, lb 8, w 2, nb 6	21
1/2 (1) 2/11 (2) 3/33 (4) (76.4 overs)	277	1/104 (1) (8 wkts dec, 83 overs)	324
4/49 (5) 5/54 (3) 6/183 (6)		2/177 (2) 3/177 (4)	
7/202 (7) 8/222 (9) 9/227 (10) 10/277 (11)		4/180 (5) 5/197 (3)	
		6/271 (6) 7/281 (7) 8/282 (9)	

Sanderson 19–4–52–3; Azharullah 15–5–68–4; Crook 11–0–63–1; Prasanna 17.4–3–54–2; Panesar 13–1–35–0; Keogh 1–0–2–0. *Second innings*—Azharullah 10–0–62–0; Sanderson 16–3–34–1; Crook 13–0–65–2; Panesar 18–3–75–1; Prasanna 8–4–14–2; Keogh 18–2–61–2.

Northamptonshire

R. I. Newton c Köhler-Cadmore b Leach	15	– (2) c Cox b Henry	11
*B. M. Duckett lbw b Leach	4	– (1) c Whiteley b D'Oliveira	10
R. I. Keogh c Cox b Leach	4	– b Henry	9
A. M. Rossington c Cox b Henry	55	– c Cox b Leach	3
R. E. Levi c Cox b Henry	27	– lbw b Henry	6
S. P. Crook c Mitchell b Leach	0	– c Mitchell b Leach	33
†D. Murphy c D'Oliveira b Leach	23	– c Leach b Henry	0
S. Prasanna c Mitchell b Henry	4	– c Rhodes b Henry	31
Azharullah lbw b D'Oliveira	7	– not out	14
B. W. Sanderson lbw b D'Oliveira	4	– c Cox b Rhodes	12
M. S. Panesar not out	1	– run out	5
B 1, lb 1, nb 2	4	B 1, lb 5, nb 2	8
1/4 (2) 2/18 (3) 3/35 (1) (45.1 overs)	148	1/14 (1) 2/28 (3) (35.3 overs)	142
4/96 (5) 5/96 (6) 6/114 (4)		3/31 (4) 4/37 (2)	
7/118 (8) 8/130 (9) 9/136 (10) 10/148 (7)		5/50 (5) 6/62 (7) 7/81 (6)	
		8/115 (8) 9/129 (10) 10/142 (11)	

Henry 17–4–52–3; Leach 18.1–3–70–5; Barnard 6–1–18–0; Rhodes 1–0–3–0; D'Oliveira 3–1–3–2. *Second innings*—Henry 14–3–36–5; Leach 11–1–49–2; D'Oliveira 3.3–0–18–1; Barnard 4–0–29–0; Rhodes 3–0–4–1.

Umpires: V. K. Sharma and A. G. Wharf.

At Swansea, August 3–6. NORTHAMPTONSHIRE beat GLAMORGAN by 251 runs. *Northamptonshire's first win of the season.*

NORTHAMPTONSHIRE v LEICESTERSHIRE

At Northampton, August 13–16. Drawn. Northamptonshire 10pts, Leicestershire 11pts. Toss: Leicestershire.

Despite declaring 122 behind on the third afternoon, Northamptonshire could not persuade Leicestershire to make a game of it – when a win would have put them only 12 points behind leaders

Essex. The final day became an exercise in futility. A docile pitch didn't help: first-innings hundreds from Cosgrove, Pettini and Eckersley (who became the third Leicestershire batsman to score three in a row, after two against Derbyshire), plus a ninth-wicket stand of 123, a record in this fixture, sent them over 500. Sanderson's persistence earned him six wickets. Newton bolstered the reply with his first double-hundred, hitting 29 fours and sharing a century partnership with Crook, who batted with a runner after a calf injury. The declaration might have brought the game to life, but Leicestershire killed it. Left-arm spinner Zaib ended the opening stand of 184 with his maiden first-class wicket, and – as Leicestershire continued after lunch – went on to pouch four more, including Horton for 99, in a 26-over spell. As if to relieve the tedium, wicketkeeper Murphy came on to bowl, and earned a maiden first-class wicket of his own, spoiling Eckersley's sequence. Leicestershire's pointless declaration came an over later.

Close of play: first day, Leicestershire 330-5 (Pettini 109, Eckersley 15); second day, Northamptonshire 142-4 (Newton 69); third day, Leicestershire 49-0 (Horton 24, Robson 23).

Leicestershire

P. J. Horton c Rossington b Sanderson	22	– c Kleinveldt b Zaib	99
A. J. Robson c Kleinveldt b Sanderson	10	– c Newton b Zaib	84
N. J. Dexter c Murphy b Sanderson	16	– lbw b Zaib	33
*M. J. Cosgrove c Newton b Azharullah	111	– c Newton b Zaib	5
M. L. Pettini c Zaib b Sanderson	117	– st Keogh b Zaib	24
†N. J. O'Brien lbw b Gleeson	5	– not out	36
E. J. H. Eckersley c Wakely b Keogh	107	– c Wakely b Murphy	1
C. J. McKay c Murphy b Sanderson	6		
R. J. Sayer b Sanderson	0	– (8) not out	4
B. A. Raine c Rossington b Keogh	64		
C. E. Shreck not out	3		
B 14, lb 16, w 4, nb 24	58	Lb 4, w 2	6
1/41 (1) 2/50 (2) 3/61 (3) 4/279 (4) 5/292 (6) 6/348 (5) 7/356 (8) 8/356 (9) 9/479 (10) 10/519 (7) (144.2 overs) 110 overs: 368-8	519	1/184 (2) 2/189 (1) 3/203 (4) 4/247 (5) 5/266 (3) 6/275 (7) (6 wkts dec, 58 overs)	292

Kleinveldt 26–3–98–0; Sanderson 30–10–58–6; Azharullah 29–1–107–1; Gleeson 26–5–91–1; Keogh 24.2–2–94–2; Crook 3–0–15–0; Zaib 6–0–26–0. *Second innings*—Sanderson 7–3–14–0; Gleeson 2–0–11–0; Keogh 14–3–54–0; Zaib 26–2–148–5; Wakely 2–0–9–0; Rossington 2–0–12–0; Murphy 5–0–40–1.

Northamptonshire

†D. Murphy c Eckersley b McKay	5	– not out	36
R. I. Newton not out	202	– b Raine	22
*A. G. Wakely c O'Brien b Sayer	11	– not out	53
R. I. Keogh b Dexter	50		
Azharullah c Eckersley b Sayer	4		
A. M. Rossington c Eckersley b McKay	26		
S. A. Zaib c Eckersley b Dexter	43		
R. K. Kleinveldt run out	12		
S. P. Crook not out	31		
B 2, lb 5, nb 6	13	B 4, lb 3	7
1/14 (1) 2/32 (3) 3/123 (4) 4/142 (5) 5/184 (6) 6/265 (7) 7/296 (8) (7 wkts dec, 124 overs) 110 overs: 332-7	397	1/31 (2) (1 wkt, 38 overs)	118

R. J. Gleeson and B. W. Sanderson did not bat.

McKay 23.4–2–78–2; Raine 21–5–65–0; Shreck 28–5–88–0; Sayer 30–4–113–2; Dexter 19–2–35–2; Cosgrove 2.2–0–11–0. *Second innings*—Raine 9–2–25–1; Sayer 12–0–48–0; Shreck 9–3–18–0; Dexter 2–1–1–0; Robson 5–1–17–0; Eckersley 1–0–2–0.

Umpires: N. L. Bainton and J. H. Evans.

At Worcester, August 23–26. NORTHAMPTONSHIRE lost to WORCESTERSHIRE by two wickets.

NORTHAMPTONSHIRE v GLAMORGAN

At Northampton, August 31–September 2. Northamptonshire won by 318 runs. Northamptonshire 21pts, Glamorgan 3pts. Toss: Northamptonshire. First-class debut: K. S. Carlson.

A dry, worn pitch offered plenty of help for the spinners, but another dazzling display from Duckett proved it was no minefield. He looked a class apart, scoring more runs than the entire Glamorgan team put together, as Northamptonshire recorded their second-highest victory by runs (they beat Worcestershire by 356 at Northampton in 1921). Kiran Carlson, an 18-year-old off-spinner on first-class debut, had shone for Glamorgan on the opening day, taking five as Northamptonshire slumped from 140 without loss to 269 all out. And yet he was comfortably overshadowed. As the turn grew more pronounced, Keogh ripped his off-breaks to blow Glamorgan away with nine for 52,

TOP SPIN

All 20 wickets taken by spinners in a Championship match in the last 50 years:

Yorks	v Leics at Leicester	R. Illingworth 11, D. Wilson 5, G. A. Cope 4	1967
Middx	v Glos at Lord's	P. H. Edmonds 14, J. E. Emburey 6	1977
Essex	v Kent at Canterbury	R. E. East 9, D. L. Acfield 11	1981
Glos	v Surrey at Cheltenham	J. H. Childs 8, D. A. Graveney 10, Sadiq Mohammad 2	1981
Kent	v Leics at Dartford	R. P. Davis 10, M. M. Patel 10	1990
Northants	v Leics at Northampton	J. F. Brown 4, M. S. Panesar 8, G. P. Swann 8	2001
Northants	v Yorks at Northampton	J. F. Brown 10, M. S. Panesar 10	2005
Northants	**v Glam at Northampton**	**R. I. Keogh 13, G. G. White 7**	**2016**

the sixth-best figures in Northamptonshire's history; he had previously taken 36 wickets in 44 first-class matches. Duckett, who had top-scored in the first innings, then put on a masterclass, hitting three sixes and 25 fours in a 159-ball 185, and passing 1,000 Championship runs for the season. White's left-arm spin did most of the damage in Glamorgan's second collapse with a career-best six for 44, as he and Keogh hogged all 20 wickets.

Close of play: first day, Glamorgan 23-0 (Selman 8, Rudolph 10); second day, Glamorgan 0-0 (Morgan 0, Rudolph 0).

Northamptonshire

B. M. Duckett b Carlson	80	– c Hogan b van der Gugten	185
R. I. Newton b Wagg	78	– c Wallace b Hogan	25
*A. G. Wakely c Bragg b Lloyd	33	– lbw b Wagg	14
R. I. Keogh b van der Gugten	5	– run out	40
S. A. Zaib c Rudolph b Morgan	13	– (6) c Lloyd b Wagg	0
†D. Murphy c Wagg b Carlson	23	– (7) not out	8
S. P. Crook b Carlson	0	– (5) c Bragg b Wagg	30
R. K. Kleinveldt b Carlson	11	– b Morgan	1
C. A. Barrett not out	4		
G. G. White c Wagg b Carlson	4		
B. W. Sanderson c Wallace b Morgan	9		
Lb 4, w 1, nb 4	9	Lb 1, w 1	2
1/140 (1) 2/185 (2) 3/203 (3) (82.3 overs)	269	1/113 (2) (7 wkts dec, 58.4 overs)	305
4/207 (4) 5/230 (5) 6/230 (7)		2/143 (3) 3/243 (4)	
7/244 (8) 8/251 (6) 9/256 (10) 10/269 (11)		4/271 (1) 5/275 (6) 6/302 (5) 7/305 (8)	

Wagg 15–2–38–1; van der Gugten 16–4–56–1; Hogan 16–1–57–0; Lloyd 13–2–49–1; Morgan 8.3–1–37–2; Carlson 14–3–28–5. *Second innings*—van der Gugten 10–0–62–1; Carlson 6–1–50–0; Morgan 14.4–0–81–1; Hogan 12–3–39–1; Wagg 16–0–72–3.

Glamorgan

N. J. Selman c Zaib b Keogh	9	– (3) not out	30
*J. A. Rudolph c Crook b White	37	– b White	11
W. D. Bragg lbw b Keogh	1	– (4) lbw b Keogh	3
D. L. Lloyd b Keogh	8	– (5) st Murphy b White	16
A. H. T. Donald c Barrett b Keogh	6	– (6) b White	22
K. S. Carlson c Barrett b Keogh	1	– (7) c Murphy b Keogh	10
G. G. Wagg c Zaib b Keogh	4	– (8) c Barrett b White	1
†M. A. Wallace not out	25	– (9) b White	0
A. O. Morgan lbw b Keogh	7	– (1) lbw b White	22
T. van der Gugten c Murphy b Keogh	4	– c Newton b Keogh	0
M. G. Hogan b Keogh	12	– b Keogh	5
B 5, lb 5	10	B 5, lb 5, nb 2	12
1/26 (1) 2/28 (3) 3/52 (4) 4/60 (5) 5/71 (6) 6/75 (7) 7/77 (2) 8/104 (9) 9/110 (10) 10/124 (11) (42.5 overs)	124	1/22 (2) 2/45 (1) 3/52 (4) 4/69 (5) 5/99 (6) 6/116 (7) 7/117 (8) 8/121 (9) 9/122 (10) 10/132 (11) (62.5 overs)	132

Kleinveldt 8–3–10–0; Sanderson 3–1–5–0; Keogh 18.5–3–52–9; White 13–3–47–1. *Second innings*—Keogh 30.5–14–73–4; Kleinveldt 2–2–0–0; Sanderson 2–0–5–0; White 28–8–44–6.

Umpires: P. K. Baldwin and A. G. Wharf.

At Beckenham, September 6–8. NORTHAMPTONSHIRE beat KENT by ten wickets.

NORTHAMPTONSHIRE v GLOUCESTERSHIRE

At Northampton, September 12–15. Northamptonshire won by 114 runs. Northamptonshire 22pts, Gloucestershire 5pts. Toss: uncontested.

Sanderson's career-best eight-wicket haul delivered a third successive victory for Northamptonshire, and sent their supporters home for the winter in good spirits. Set 442, Gloucestershire lost two wickets on the third evening, before reaching 286 for five thanks to a maiden century from Hankins. With 27 overs remaining, a draw was in sight, but the second new ball helped Sanderson make the decisive breakthrough. On the opening day, Newton and Wakely hit hundreds to take Northamptonshire to 322 for six at stumps, before Payne pegged them back. He took four in 11 balls in the morning, and notched a spirited half-century in the evening to restrict the lead to 65. Duckett looked on course for a fifth first-class hundred of the season before splicing Matt Taylor to point, and walked off to a generous ovation in recognition of his memorable summer. It was left to Levi, with a rapid 95, to seize the initiative and set up the win.

Close of play: first day, Northamptonshire 322-6 (Crook 27, Murphy 3); second day, Northamptonshire 44-0 (Duckett 31, Newton 11); third day, Gloucestershire 35-2 (Dent 10, Norwell 4).

Northamptonshire

B. M. Duckett c Mustard b Norwell	5	– c Hankins b M. D. Taylor	70
R. I. Newton c Mustard b Norwell	130	– c Dent b M. D. Taylor	47
*A. G. Wakely lbw b J. M. R. Taylor	104	– c Tavaré b Payne	19
R. I. Keogh c Mustard b Miles	8	– c Mustard b Payne	13
R. E. Levi c Roderick b Norwell	28	– run out	95
A. M. Rossington c Mustard b Miles	11	– lbw b J. M. R. Taylor	24
S. P. Crook c Mustard b Payne	27	– c Mustard b Payne	46
†D. Murphy not out	7	– c Dent b Payne	36
R. K. Kleinveldt c J. M. R. Taylor b Payne	0	– not out	0
Azharullah c Marshall b Payne	0	– c Roderick b Miles	3
B. W. Sanderson b Payne	0	– c Roderick b Miles	6
Lb 2, nb 4	6	B 6, lb 8, w 1, nb 2	17
1/11 (1) 2/207 (3) 3/230 (4) 4/279 (5) 5/279 (2) 6/317 (6) 7/322 (7) 8/322 (9) 9/326 (10) 10/326 (11) (99 overs)	326	1/116 (2) 2/125 (1) 3/150 (3) 4/155 (4) 5/228 (6) 6/304 (5) 7/367 (8) 8/367 (7) 9/370 (10) 10/376 (11) (86.1 overs)	376

Payne 23–7–57–4; Norwell 22–6–55–3; Miles 19–6–58–2; M. D. Taylor 18–0–88–0; J. M. R. Taylor 11–1–51–1; Dent 6–2–15–0. *Second innings*—Norwell 17–1–79–0; Payne 18–2–75–4; M. D. Taylor 12–0–45–2; Miles 18.1–2–84–2; J. M. R. Taylor 13–0–53–1; Dent 8–0–26–0.

Gloucestershire

*G. H. Roderick c Murphy b Kleinveldt	18	– c Murphy b Sanderson	19
C. D. J. Dent c Murphy b Kleinveldt	9	– c Levi b Sanderson	58
W. A. Tavaré c Kleinveldt b Keogh	36	– c Levi b Sanderson	0
G. T. Hankins c Rossington b Azharullah	8	– (5) b Sanderson	116
H. J. H. Marshall b Azharullah	38	– (6) lbw b Sanderson	0
†P. Mustard c Murphy b Keogh	19	– (7) c Levi b Sanderson	79
J. M. R. Taylor c Kleinveldt b Sanderson	35	– (8) lbw b Sanderson	5
C. N. Miles b Crook	3	– (9) c Levi b Sanderson	10
D. A. Payne c Wakely b Keogh	56	– (10) c sub (S. A. Zaib) b Kleinveldt	1
L. C. Norwell not out	13	– (4) c Murphy b Kleinveldt	14
M. D. Taylor c Duckett b Keogh	2	– not out	5
B 12, lb 8, nb 4	24	B 5, lb 11, nb 4	20
1/17 (2) 2/30 (1) 3/53 (4) 4/106 (5) 5/134 (3) 6/143 (6) 7/158 (8) 8/210 (7) 9/255 (9) 10/261 (11) (79.3 overs)	261	1/27 (1) 2/27 (3) 3/48 (4) 4/151 (2) 5/151 (6) 6/286 (5) 7/296 (8) 8/314 (9) 9/315 (10) 10/327 (7) (96.5 overs)	327

Kleinveldt 17–4–54–2; Sanderson 18–7–31–1; Azharullah 16–3–55–2; Crook 11–2–34–1; Keogh 17.3–1–67–4. *Second innings*—Kleinveldt 25–4–99–2; Sanderson 29.5–9–73–8; Keogh 19–7–49–0; Azharullah 11–1–26–0; Crook 12–1–64–0.

Umpires: S. C. Gale and M. J. Saggers.

NOTTINGHAMSHIRE

Notts undone

JON CULLEY

The warning signs had been there in 2015, when Nottinghamshire found themselves bottom of Division One at the end of June. The crisis was apparently solved by adding former England coach Peter Moores to the backroom staff, and his presence invigorated the dressing-room: Nottinghamshire finished third. When the pattern recurred in 2016, there was no instant remedy. It took longer to sink to the bottom – 12 matches instead of eight – but that allowed less recovery time, and there was a sense of irreversible decline. After one win, in the opening fixture, Nottinghamshire suffered nine defeats, including five of their last six games; relegation, after nine seasons in the top division, was confirmed with one to go.

A change in the hierarchy was announced immediately. Moores was elevated from coaching consultant to head coach, replacing Mick Newell, who remained director of cricket, having combined the two roles since 2003. Newell had his critics among members, and some of the players he signed were not successful, but most improved the side, many significantly. His dual role asked questions of him, and winning the County Championship twice – in 2005 and 2010 – was no small achievement. Only in the last couple of seasons did the workload take its toll. He insisted that no blame should attach to his successor: "It is not Peter's team that has been relegated. This is my team and relegation goes on my CV."

The change should enable Moores (who had also won the Championship twice, with Sussex and Lancashire) to put his own stamp on the side, leaving Newell to focus on management, recruitment and developing local players through closer relationships with schools and clubs.

Little would change in the short term, although some, chiefly batsmen, were thankful their contracts were not up for review. In Division One, no side accrued more bowling points than Nottinghamshire, but no one had so few batting points. Only twice did they pick up the maximum five; in half their matches, it was one or none.

Brendan Taylor struggled, and Riki Wessels lost his place: 166 of his 489 Championship runs came in one match (against Durham, when Taylor scored 219 of his 759). Michael Lumb and Samit Patel had middling seasons, and Chris Read – who missed four games after breaking his hand – failed to reach 500 Championship runs for only the third time since 2000. Steven Mullaney alone topped 1,000; his 165 against Somerset in July was the highest first-class score.

Little was seen of Alex Hales because of international call-ups – and then there was the loss of James Taylor. This was difficult to quantify, since he was on the verge of becoming an England regular too, but there was no doubt his sudden enforced retirement in April, because of a life-threatening heart disorder, had a profound impact on his colleagues.

Tim Goode, PA Photos

Steven Mullaney

Jake Ball confirmed his enormous potential, taking 49 wickets at 23 in 11 Championship matches and making his Test debut against Pakistan at Lord's. His commitment to gym work paid off in pace and stamina, and his performances against defending champions Yorkshire in May and future champions Middlesex in September – when he took a hat-trick in his first over – were especially impressive.

Left-armer Harry Gurney bowled well at times, but overseas players Jackson Bird and Imran Tahir were disappointing; Australia's Peter Siddle, who had signed a two-year contract before a stress fracture ruled him out, was due to return in 2017. Of the bowlers who had broken through the previous season, Brett Hutton levelled off a little, and Luke Wood was hampered by back problems. Matthew Carter, the tall off-spinner who had collected ten wickets in his debut match at Taunton in 2015, managed only three in three appearances. Will Gidman didn't get a look-in, and left for Kent in July, initially on loan.

For a while, it seemed white-ball cricket might provide consolation. Runs came much more easily, particularly for Lumb and Wessels. After losing their first two fixtures in the NatWest T20 Blast, Nottinghamshire won nine in a row to head the North Group (despite four abandoned games) and reach the semi-final, assisted by overseas players Dan Christian and Andre Russell. In the Royal London Cup, the county scored 860 in their first two matches. In a total of 445 against Northamptonshire, Wessels and Lumb combined in a stand of 342, an all-wicket one-day record in England (for seven weeks); then they put on 178 out of 415 against Warwickshire. Yet Nottinghamshire stumbled in the matches that mattered most, losing to Northamptonshire on Twenty20 finals day at Edgbaston, and failing to qualify for the 50-over quarter-finals after finishing with three defeats.

Thankfully, relegation in cricket does not bring dire financial consequences. For Nottinghamshire it was a blow to pride and prestige. Yet it offered a chance to step back, allowing youngsters such as Jake Libby, Billy Root and Tom Moores to build form and confidence in a more forgiving environment. With Siddle available, reinforced by Ball, Hales and Stuart Broad when not required by England, Nottinghamshire could be a formidable force in the second tier.

Championship attendance: 49,584.

NOTTINGHAMSHIRE RESULTS

All first-class matches – Played 17: Won 2, Lost 9, Drawn 6.
County Championship matches – Played 16: Won 1, Lost 9, Drawn 6.

Specsavers County Championship, 9th in Division 1;
NatWest T20 Blast, semi-finalists; Royal London One-Day Cup, 6th in North Group.

COUNTY CHAMPIONSHIP AVERAGES, BATTING AND FIELDING

Cap		*Birthplace*	*M*	*I*	*NO*	*R*	*HS*	*100*	*Avge*	*Ct/St*
2013	S. J. Mullaney	*Warrington*	16	30	2	1,009	165	3	36.03	19
2015	B. R. M. Taylor††	*Harare, Zimbabwe*	13	24	2	759	114	2	34.50	10
2008	S. R. Patel	*Leicester*	16	28	0	957	124	2	34.17	12
2008	†S. C. J. Broad§	*Nottingham‡*	4	6	0	191	55	0	31.83	3
	J. D. Libby	*Plymouth*	11	21	0	627	144	1	29.85	3
1999	C. M. W. Read	*Paignton*	12	21	4	492	101	1	28.94	33/2
2012	†M. J. Lumb	*Johannesburg, SA*	16	29	0	817	108	1	28.17	6
2014	M. H. Wessels	*Marogudoore, Aust.*	12	21	2	489	159*	1	25.73	21/2
2016	D. T. Christian¶	*Camperdown, Aust.*	3	5	1	96	31	0	24.00	2
	G. P. Smith	*Leicester*	7	12	0	257	54	0	21.41	3
	B. A. Hutton	*Doncaster*	12	19	3	337	74	0	21.06	3
	†T. J. Moores	*Brighton*	4	7	0	123	41	0	17.57	0
2015	Imran Tahir¶	*Lahore, Pakistan*	7	12	4	127	25	0	15.87	3
	†L. Wood	*Sheffield*	3	5	1	55	27	0	13.75	2
2014	L. J. Fletcher	*Nottingham‡*	6	10	2	88	32	0	11.00	3
2016	J. T. Ball	*Mansfield‡*	11	17	1	153	33	0	9.56	3
2016	J. M. Bird¶	*Paddington, Aust.*	5	8	0	51	23	0	6.37	1
	M. Carter	*Lincoln*	3	5	1	20	8	0	5.00	2
2014	H. F. Gurney	*Nottingham‡*	13	21	9	56	16	0	4.66	1

Also batted: A. D. Hales§ (*Hillingdon*) (cap 2011) (2 matches) 36, 34, 73; †W. T. Root (*Sheffield*) (1 match) 10, 66*.

‡ *Born in Nottinghamshire.* § *ECB contract.* ¶ *Official overseas player.*
†† *Other non-England-qualified.*

BOWLING

	Style	*O*	*M*	*R*	*W*	*BB*	*5I*	*Avge*
J. T. Ball	RFM	343	64	1,133	49	6-57	3	23.12
S. C. J. Broad	RFM	116	35	312	10	3-50	0	31.20
L. J. Fletcher	RFM	183.1	48	469	15	4-25	0	31.26
H. F. Gurney	LFM	412.5	76	1,304	41	6-61	2	31.80
S. R. Patel	SLA	351.5	64	1,147	32	4-71	0	35.84
Imran Tahir	LBG	288.4	51	930	25	7-112	1	37.20
J. M. Bird	RFM	157.3	27	558	15	4-56	0	37.20
B. A. Hutton	RM	268.3	47	1,027	26	3-54	0	39.50
S. J. Mullaney	RM	139.5	36	430	10	3-54	0	43.00

Also bowled: M. Carter (OB) 76–8–316–3; D. T. Christian (RFM) 15–1–80–1; J. D. Libby (OB) 4–1–8–0; W. T. Root (OB) 2–0–5–0; L. Wood (LM) 80–13–297–4.

LEADING ROYAL LONDON CUP AVERAGES (100 runs/4 wickets)

Batting	*Runs*	*HS*	*Avge*	*SR*	*Ct*
M. J. Lumb	482	184	68.85	107.82	1
M. H. Wessels	453	146	64.71	110.48	3
S. J. Mullaney	189	89*	63.00	106.77	3
D. T. Christian	328	94	46.85	117.14	3
C. M. W. Read	119	59	29.75	125.26	7
S. R. Patel	176	55	29.33	104.76	3
G. P. Smith	171	73	24.42	81.42	2
B. R. M. Taylor	136	44	22.66	84.47	3

Bowling	*W*	*BB*	*Avge*	*ER*
H. F. Gurney	19	5-51	19.78	5.82
D. T. Christian	6	3-44	29.00	6.00
J. T. Ball	6	2-47	40.83	6.44
S. J. Mullaney	8	3-81	43.25	6.34
L. J. Fletcher	6	2-52	61.83	6.21
S. R. Patel	6	2-51	66.83	6.57

LEADING NATWEST T20 BLAST AVERAGES (100 runs/18 overs)

Batting	*Runs*	*HS*	*Avge*	*SR*	*Ct*
D. T. Christian	327	56	40.87	**159.51**	3
M. J. Lumb	269	69*	24.45	**141.57**	0
M. H. Wessels	420	80*	42.00	**139.53**	11
G. P. Smith	264	52*	29.33	**125.11**	3
S. R. Patel	143	58	17.87	**106.71**	3

Bowling	*W*	*BB*	*Avge*	*ER*
S. R. Patel	16	4-20	19.50	**6.50**
Imran Tahir	6	3-13	26.66	**6.95**
S. J. Mullaney	12	3-12	23.16	**7.65**
J. T. Ball	9	2-18	32.00	**8.00**
L. J. Fletcher	2	1-30	76.50	**8.19**
H. F. Gurney	17	4-20	20.11	**8.30**

FIRST-CLASS COUNTY RECORDS

Highest score for	312*	W. W. Keeton v Middlesex at The Oval	1939
Highest score against	345	C. G. Macartney (Australians) at Nottingham	1921
Leading run-scorer	31,592	G. Gunn (avge 35.69)	1902–32
Best bowling for	10-66	K. Smales v Gloucestershire at Stroud	1956
Best bowling against	10-10	H. Verity (Yorkshire) at Leeds	1932
Leading wicket-taker	1,653	T. G. Wass (avge 20.34)	1896–1920
Highest total for	791	v Essex at Chelmsford	2007
Highest total against	781-7 dec	by Northamptonshire at Northampton	1995
Lowest total for	13	v Yorkshire at Nottingham	1901
Lowest total against	16	by Derbyshire at Nottingham	1879
	16	by Surrey at The Oval	1880

LIST A COUNTY RECORDS

Highest score for	**184**	**M. J. Lumb v Northants at Nottingham**	**2016**
Highest score against	191	D. S. Lehmann (Yorkshire) at Scarborough	2001
Leading run-scorer	11,237	R. T. Robinson (avge 35.33)	1978–99
Best bowling for	6-10	K. P. Evans v Northumberland at Jesmond	1994
Best bowling against	7-41	A. N. Jones (Sussex) at Nottingham	1986
Leading wicket-taker	291	C. E. B. Rice (avge 22.60)	1975–87
Highest total for	**445-8**	**v Northamptonshire at Nottingham**	**2016**
Highest total against	**425**	**by Northamptonshire at Nottingham**	**2016**
Lowest total for	57	v Gloucestershire at Nottingham	2009
Lowest total against	43	by Northamptonshire at Northampton	1977

TWENTY20 COUNTY RECORDS

Highest score for	97	M. H. Wessels v Durham at Chester-le-Street	2015
Highest score against	111	W. J. Durston (Derbyshire) at Nottingham	2010
Leading run-scorer	**2,832**	**S. R. Patel (avge 27.23)**	**2003–16**
Best bowling for	5-22	G. G. White v Lancashire at Nottingham	2013
Best bowling against	5-13	A. B. McDonald (Leicestershire) at Nottingham	2010
Leading wicket-taker	**124**	**S. R. Patel (avge 24.49)**	**2003–16**
Highest total for	220-4	v Leicestershire at Leicester	2014
Highest total against	209-4	by Yorkshire at Leeds	2015
Lowest total for	91	v Lancashire at Manchester	2006
Lowest total against	90	by Leicestershire at Nottingham	2014

ADDRESS

County Cricket Ground, Trent Bridge, Nottingham NG2 6AG; 0115 982 3000; administration@nottsccc.co.uk; www.nottsccc.co.uk.

OFFICIALS

Captain (Championship/one-day) C. M. W. Read
(Twenty20) D. T. Christian
Director of cricket M. Newell
Head coach 2017 P. Moores
President P. Wynne-Thomas

Chairman R. Tennant
Chief executive L. J. Pursehouse
Chairman, cricket committee W. Taylor
Head groundsman S. Birks
Scorer R. Marshall

At Cambridge, April 5–7. NOTTINGHAMSHIRE beat CAMBRIDGE MCCU by 517 runs.
Nottinghamshire achieve their second-biggest win by runs.

NOTTINGHAMSHIRE v SURREY

At Nottingham, April 10–13. Nottinghamshire won by three wickets. Nottinghamshire 24pts, Surrey 4pts. Toss: uncontested. County debuts: J. M. Bird; R. Rampaul.

Nottinghamshire began the season by beating promoted Surrey – though victory was overshadowed by news that James Taylor, their England batsman, had been forced to retire because of a heart condition. With Alex Hales resting after international duty, Mullaney scored the first century of the Championship season, at a run a ball (narrowly beating Northamptonshire's Ben Duckett), and enabled his side to amass 446 on the first day. Surrey's decision to bowl had looked reasonable in conditions aiding swing and seam, but their youngsters perhaps tried too hard, while West Indian seamer Ravi Rampaul, apparently not fully fit, was flattered by five wickets on his county debut. The Nottinghamshire attack were more disciplined. Their own debutant seamer, Australia's Jackson Bird, made Surrey follow on, but Ball was the pick, returning the second five-wicket haul of his career. A century from Harinath, backed up by Sangakkara's 83, meant Nottinghamshire needed 169 in two sessions. They slipped from 72 without loss to 100 for five – Tom Curran took three for nought in seven balls – before Ball struck the winning boundary. It would remain their only Championship victory of the season.

Close of play: first day, Surrey 7-0 (Burns 4, Harinath 3); second day, Surrey 14-0 (Burns 6, Harinath 8); third day, Surrey 297-5 (Harinath 114, S. M. Curran 0).

Nottinghamshire

S. J. Mullaney c Foakes b Rampaul	113	– lbw b Rampaul	42
G. P. Smith c Sangakkara b T. K. Curran	9	– c Foakes b T. K. Curran	54
M. J. Lumb lbw b Footitt	24	– c Foakes b T. K. Curran	2
B. R. M. Taylor c Sangakkara b T. K. Curran	20	– c Roy b T. K. Curran	0
M. H. Wessels c Foakes b Rampaul	81	– c Foakes b T. K. Curran	0
S. R. Patel c S. M. Curran b T. K. Curran	85	– c Sangakkara b Rampaul	6
*†C. M. W. Read not out	63	– lbw b Rampaul	22
B. A. Hutton b Footitt	0	– not out	14
J. T. Ball b Rampaul	21	– not out	9
J. M. Bird c Burns b Rampaul	2		
H. F. Gurney b Rampaul	0		
B 1, lb 10, w 1, nb 16	28	B 6, lb 2, w 1, nb 14	23
1/43 (2) 2/91 (3) 3/147 (4) 4/201 (1) 5/308 (5) 6/401 (6) 7/402 (8) 8/442 (9) 9/446 (10) 10/446 (11) (91.4 overs)	446	1/72 (1) 2/85 (3) 3/85 (4) 4/91 (5) 5/100 (6) 6/136 (7) 7/152 (2) (7 wkts, 42.4 overs)	172

T. K. Curran 23–2–98–3; Footitt 19–4–98–2; S. M. Curran 18–1–92–0; Rampaul 16.4–1–93–5; Batty 10–1–38–0; Harinath 5–0–16–0. *Second innings*—T. K. Curran 16–2–58–4; Footitt 11.4–0–49–0; Rampaul 15–0–57–3.

Surrey

R. J. Burns c Read b Bird	8 – lbw b Ball	17
A. Harinath c Wessels b Bird	23 – c Wessels b Bird	137
K. C. Sangakkara c Mullaney b Hutton	32 – c Read b Ball	83
S. M. Davies c Wessels b Gurney	8 – c Read b Ball	0
J. J. Roy lbw b Ball	28 – lbw b Hutton	37
†B. T. Foakes c Read b Gurney	38 – c and b Patel	26
S. M. Curran b Hutton	20 – lbw b Ball	28
T. K. Curran lbw b Bird	35 – lbw b Gurney	8
*G. J. Batty c Smith b Patel	15 – lbw b Ball	6
R. Rampaul lbw b Bird	0 – not out	13
M. H. A. Footitt not out	0 – c Taylor b Hutton	5
B 8, lb 4, nb 6	18 B 9, lb 14, nb 6	29
1/21 (1) 2/42 (2) 3/71 (4) 4/85 (3) 5/131 (5) 6/170 (6) 7/174 (7) 8/221 (9) 9/222 (10) 10/225 (8) (67.1 overs)	225 1/25 (1) 2/167 (3) 3/167 (4) 4/233 (5) 5/288 (6) 6/341 (7) 7/353 (2) 8/360 (9) 9/366 (8) 10/389 (11) (99.4 overs)	389

Ball 13–2–45–1; Bird 17.1–4–56–4; Gurney 15–4–43–2; Hutton 15–4–51–2; Mullaney 4–0–13–0; Patel 3–1–5–1. *Second innings*—Bird 26–5–63–1; Ball 23–2–98–5; Gurney 22–3–85–1; Hutton 15.4–3–76–2; Patel 13–4–44–1.

Umpires: D. J. Millns and R. T. Robinson.

At Manchester, April 17–20. NOTTINGHAMSHIRE lost to LANCASHIRE by eight wickets.

NOTTINGHAMSHIRE v YORKSHIRE

At Nottingham, May 1–4. Drawn. Nottinghamshire 10pts, Yorkshire 10pts. Toss: uncontested. County debut: D. J. Willey.

An enthralling match – shown live on Sky TV – came down to the final delivery, as the advantage fluctuated between sides fielding thirteen internationals. Nottinghamshire started the last day five down and just 122 in front, before Read's 25th first-class century and Broad's 44-ball fifty set Yorkshire 320 in 53 overs. A magnificent hundred from Lees kept the rate in hand: with 93 needed from 61 deliveries, and seven wickets in hand, victory seemed possible. Then Ball had Bairstow caught at deep cover, Gurney grabbed four in consecutive overs and, when Broad trapped Patterson, his only victim of the game, Yorkshire had lost six for 26; Brooks survived two balls to draw. After Nottinghamshire were bowled out on a rain-shortened opening day, Ball removed Lyth with the first delivery of Yorkshire's reply, adding Ballance and Root with successive balls in his fourth over. The resilient Lees scored 92 before becoming Read's 900th dismissal for Nottinghamshire early on the third day, and Yorkshire took a lead of 29. Hales batted determinedly for two and a half hours, and a counter-attacking 51 from Patel helped set up the dramatic conclusion.

Close of play: first day, Nottinghamshire 261; second day, Yorkshire 170-4 (Lees 91, Gale 21); third day, Nottinghamshire 151-5 (Patel 51, Read 13).

Nottinghamshire

S. J. Mullaney c Lees b Patterson	78	– lbw b Willey	2
A. D. Hales c Root b Brooks	36	– b Brooks	34
G. P. Smith b Brooks	0	– b Patterson	17
M. J. Lumb lbw b Brooks	49	– c Lyth b Patterson	9
M. H. Wessels c Root b Plunkett	12	– b Plunkett	15
S. R. Patel lbw b Rashid	16	– c Root b Brooks	51
*†C. M. W. Read c Bairstow b Brooks	5	– c Rashid b Patterson	101
S. C. J. Broad run out	36	– c Lyth b Brooks	55
J. T. Ball c Brooks b Rashid	7	– b Willey	22
J. M. Bird lbw b Rashid	4	– lbw b Patterson	23
H. F. Gurney not out	8	– not out	3
Lb 9, w 1	10	B 8, lb 6, w 2	16
1/77 (2) 2/89 (3) 3/132 (1) 4/163 (5) 5/195 (6) 6/201 (4) 7/214 (7) 8/225 (9) 9/238 (10) 10/261 (8) (69.2 overs)	261	1/2 (1) 2/28 (3) 3/47 (4) 4/75 (2) 5/98 (5) 6/151 (6) 7/255 (8) 8/289 (9) 9/341 (10) 10/348 (7) (100.3 overs)	348

Willey 14–3–54–0; Brooks 16–4–74–4; Patterson 17.2–4–48–1; Plunkett 10–1–38–1; Rashid 11–3–29–3; Lyth 1–0–9–0. *Second innings*—Willey 21–5–68–2; Brooks 23–6–69–3; Plunkett 13–1–52–1; Patterson 23.3–8–57–4; Rashid 17–1–79–0; Root 3–0–9–0.

Yorkshire

A. Lyth lbw b Ball	0	– c Read b Ball	4
A. Z. Lees c Read b Gurney	92	– c Bird b Gurney	107
G. S. Ballance c Read b Ball	7	– c Mullaney b Patel	43
J. E. Root c Wessels b Ball	0	– c Smith b Ball	27
†J. M. Bairstow lbw b Gurney	29	– c Broad b Ball	35
*A. W. Gale c Mullaney b Ball	44	– (8) lbw b Gurney	2
A. U. Rashid c Ball b Patel	19	– (9) not out	1
L. E. Plunkett c Smith b Bird	51	– (6) c Lumb b Gurney	11
D. J. Willey c Read b Bird	18	– (7) lbw b Gurney	5
S. A. Patterson c Ball b Patel	1	– lbw b Broad	1
J. A. Brooks not out	0	– not out	4
Lb 25, nb 4	29	B 1, lb 11, w 3, nb 2	17
1/0 (1) 2/24 (3) 3/24 (4) 4/107 (5) 5/173 (2) 6/216 (6) 7/250 (7) 8/279 (9) 9/284 (10) 10/290 (8) (76.2 overs)	290	1/4 (1) 2/120 (3) 3/173 (4) 4/227 (5) 5/234 (2) 6/247 (6) 7/251 (8) 8/252 (7) 9/253 (10) (9 wkts, 53 overs)	257

Ball 18–4–57–4; Broad 14–3–48–0; Bird 17.2–1–76–2; Gurney 16–0–60–2; Patel 11–2–24–2. *Second innings*—Ball 15–1–68–3; Broad 11–2–60–1; Gurney 16–3–53–4; Bird 6–0–34–0; Patel 5–0–30–1.

Umpires: M. A. Gough and R. A. Kettleborough.

At Lord's, May 8–11. NOTTINGHAMSHIRE drew with MIDDLESEX.

NOTTINGHAMSHIRE v WARWICKSHIRE

At Nottingham, May 15–18. Warwickshire won by 53 runs. Warwickshire 23pts, Nottinghamshire 7pts. Toss: Warwickshire.

Warwickshire's winning margin looked comfortable – but an astonishing century by Samit Patel had threatened an extraordinary upset. Murky conditions had delayed the fourth day until 2.45, and soon Nottinghamshire were 25 for five, after Barker struck twice in two balls. Patel averted the hat-trick, then smashed 124 off 82 deliveries, with 12 fours and eight sixes, mixing aggression and technique. His 68-ball hundred remained the season's fastest, and he scored 71% of Nottinghamshire's total (only Cyril Sewell had contributed a higher proportion from No. 7, with 78% of Gloucestershire's

80 at Hove in 1913). Warwickshire steadily picked off his partners, with Taylor the only other batsman to reach double figures, and were never close to defeat. Yet, wary of Patel's flashing blade – twice he hit Jeetan Patel for three sixes in an over – they had nine on the boundary when he finally miscued a skyer. On the first day Woakes, acting-captain for the injured Ian Bell, had rescued Warwickshire from 60 for five, adding 167 with Barker, an eighth-wicket record in this fixture; both reached centuries. But Lumb's 20th hundred – his first for almost three years – set up a slender lead before Fletcher, summoned from a loan spell at Derbyshire to cover Jake Ball's England call-up, helped ensure a target of 227.

Close of play: first day, Warwickshire 372-9 (Patel 15, Wright 2); second day, Nottinghamshire 316-7 (Hutton 35, Fletcher 0); third day, Nottinghamshire 21-3 (Smith 8, Taylor 1).

Warwickshire

V. Chopra c Wessels b Bird	3	– c Read b Fletcher	82
I. J. Westwood lbw b Fletcher	1	– c Patel b Fletcher	1
I. J. L. Trott c Hutton b Bird	68	– lbw b Patel	59
L. J. Evans c Read b Fletcher	4	– run out	4
S. R. Hain lbw b Fletcher	0	– c Read b Bird	9
†T. R. Ambrose lbw b Mullaney	14	– lbw b Fletcher	16
*C. R. Woakes c Read b Bird	121	– not out	20
R. Clarke c Wessels b Patel	9	– lbw b Patel	0
K. H. D. Barker c Read b Gurney	113	– c Read b Fletcher	6
J. S. Patel c Fletcher b Gurney	15	– b Patel	6
C. J. C. Wright not out	3	– c Fletcher b Patel	20
B 7, lb 6, w 1, nb 8	22	Lb 3, nb 10	13
1/5 (1) 2/5 (2) 3/13 (4) 4/17 (5) 5/60 (6) 6/117 (3) 7/161 (8) 8/328 (7) 9/368 (9) 10/373 (10) (98 overs)	373	1/26 (2) 2/103 (3) 3/149 (4) 4/159 (5) 5/180 (1) 6/185 (6) 7/186 (8) 8/193 (9) 9/202 (10) 10/236 (11) (67 overs)	236

Bird 24–6–81–3; Fletcher 20–6–70–3; Hutton 19–1–89–0; Gurney 17–1–64–2; Mullaney 7–2–27–1; Patel 11–3–29–1. *Second innings*—Bird 16–2–76–1; Fletcher 16–6–25–4; Hutton 5–0–34–0; Gurney 6–0–27–0; Patel 24–6–71–4.

Nottinghamshire

S. J. Mullaney c Ambrose b Woakes	56	– c Clarke b Barker	0
G. P. Smith c Clarke b Barker	26	– b Barker	8
M. J. Lumb c Clarke b Patel	108	– c Chopra b Barker	8
B. R. M. Taylor c Ambrose b Barker	16	– (5) c Ambrose b Wright	26
M. H. Wessels lbw b Clarke	6	– (6) lbw b Barker	0
S. R. Patel c Chopra b Clarke	26	– (7) c Hain b Wright	124
*†C. M. W. Read c Ambrose b Woakes	23	– (8) c Wright b Patel	0
B. A. Hutton c Evans b Clarke	59	– (9) c Ambrose b Patel	2
L. J. Fletcher b Clarke	29	– (4) c Chopra b Woakes	4
J. M. Bird c Patel b Wright	9	– b Wright	1
H. F. Gurney not out	3	– not out	0
B 5, lb 11, nb 6	22		
1/41 (2) 2/139 (1) 3/178 (4) 4/189 (5) 5/256 (6) 6/266 (3) 7/315 (7) 8/361 (8) 9/374 (10) 10/383 (9) (109 overs)	383	1/0 (1) 2/14 (3) 3/19 (4) 4/25 (2) 5/25 (6) 6/114 (5) 7/115 (8) 8/119 (9) 9/154 (10) 10/173 (7) (36.4 overs)	173

Barker 25–6–75–2; Woakes 23–2–108–2; Wright 20–4–68–1; Clarke 24–5–72–4; Patel 17–6–44–1. *Second innings*—Barker 11–2–38–4; Woakes 8–1–33–1; Clarke 4–0–33–0; Wright 7.4–0–23–3; Patel 6–1–46–2.

Umpires: R. J. Evans and D. J. Millns.

At Southampton, May 22–25. NOTTINGHAMSHIRE lost to HAMPSHIRE by 69 runs.

NOTTINGHAMSHIRE v DURHAM

At Nottingham, May 28–31. Drawn. Nottinghamshire 12pts, Durham 12pts. Toss: Nottinghamshire.

Nottinghamshire were leading by 376 when bad weather ended play on the final afternoon. It rendered academic the argument that Mullaney, deputising for Chris Read – who broke his hand against Hampshire – should have declared. His reluctance allowed Brendan Taylor, who had overhauled his technique after a poor run, to become the first Nottinghamshire batsman to score a century in each innings since Russell Warren in 2003. Coming in on the first morning when Rushworth and Onions had reduced his side to 27 for three, Taylor combined diligently with Patel to put on 168 for the fifth wicket, before Wessels (with an unbeaten 159), and Hutton (a career-best 74), added 197 for the seventh. But the plan to bat Durham out of the game was foiled by a superb 188 from Borthwick, advertising his England ambitions with some lovely shots in the second-highest score of his career. He also demonstrated that his leg-spin remained a potent second string, taking eight wickets in all. With Carse and then Onions injured, Taylor had licence to play with more freedom in his second hundred, which was full of improvisation and completed off only 79 balls.

Close of play: first day, Nottinghamshire 353-6 (Wessels 46, Hutton 33); second day, Durham 193-4 (Borthwick 59, Collingwood 38); third day, Nottinghamshire 104-1 (Libby 33, Smith 21).

Nottinghamshire

*S. J. Mullaney c Weighell b Rushworth	2	– lbw b Borthwick	43
J. D. Libby b Rushworth	19	– c Borthwick b Rushworth	42
G. P. Smith c Collingwood b Onions	5	– lbw b Onions	21
M. J. Lumb c Borthwick b Weighell	22	– c and b Borthwick	52
B. R. M. Taylor c Rushworth b Weighell	114	– not out	105
S. R. Patel b Borthwick	84	– c Richardson b Borthwick	10
†M. H. Wessels not out	159	– not out	7
B. A. Hutton c sub (G. Clark) b Borthwick	74		
J. T. Ball c Onions b Borthwick	10		
J. M. Bird b Borthwick	11		
H. F. Gurney c Collingwood b Borthwick	0		
B 14, lb 7, w 1, nb 12	34	B 1, lb 7, w 1	9
1/14 (1) 2/27 (2) 3/27 (3) 4/93 (4) (144.4 overs)	534	1/66 (1) (5 wkts, 64 overs)	289
5/261 (5) 6/291 (6) 7/488 (8)		2/105 (3) 3/141 (2)	
8/500 (9) 9/528 (10) 10/534 (11) 110 overs: 389-6		4/238 (4) 5/264 (6)	

Rushworth 32–8–94–2; Onions 32–6–114–1; Carse 7–0–41–0; Weighell 30–5–73–2; Collingwood 11–5–23–0; Borthwick 13.4–0–79–5; Pringle 17–0–77–0; Jennings 2–0–12–0. *Second innings*—Rushworth 15–3–27–1; Onions 13.2–2–54–1; Weighell 3–0–28–0; Borthwick 17–2–73–3; Pringle 8.4–1–51–0; Collingwood 6–0–39–0; Stoneman 1–0–9–0.

Durham

M. D. Stoneman c Patel b Bird	39
K. K. Jennings c Patel b Bird	26
S. G. Borthwick not out	188
J. T. A. Burnham lbw b Bird	0
†M. J. Richardson b Bird	17
*P. D. Collingwood c Mullaney b Gurney	40
R. D. Pringle c Wessels b Ball	34
W. J. Weighell lbw b Gurney	22
B. A. Carse c Wessels b Hutton	47
C. Rushworth c Wessels b Hutton	2
G. Onions b Gurney	4
B 2, lb 13, w 1, nb 12	28
1/72 (2) 2/75 (1) 3/75 (4) 4/121 (5) 5/198 (6) 6/282 (7) 7/316 (8) 8/408 (9) 9/423 (10) 10/447 (11) (109.5 overs)	447

Ball 22–3–95–1; Gurney 26.5–2–125–3; Bird 27–6–109–4; Hutton 19–1–70–2; Patel 15–5–33–0.

Umpires: N. G. B. Cook and S. A. Garratt.

At The Oval, June 19–22. NOTTINGHAMSHIRE lost to SURREY by 228 runs.

At Birmingham, June 26–29. NOTTINGHAMSHIRE drew with WARWICKSHIRE.

NOTTINGHAMSHIRE v LANCASHIRE

At Nottingham, July 3–6. Drawn. Nottinghamshire 13pts, Lancashire 9pts. Toss: Lancashire.

Nottinghamshire threatened a second Championship win – against the leaders – but were denied by some stout Lancashire resistance. Hameed looked every inch a future Test batsman as he battled two established international bowlers: Broad, briefly back at Trent Bridge ahead of the Pakistan series, and leg-spinner Imran Tahir, newly arrived from South Africa's Caribbean tour. Hameed's vigil of six and a half hours brought him 122, and his 151-run partnership with Tom Smith was Lancashire's first century opening stand of the season. Neither side was helped by a surface so unresponsive that wicketkeeper Wessels was able to stand up to Broad. Nottinghamshire led by 198 on first innings: all their top nine reached 30, though no one passed Patel's 67. Despite Hameed's efforts, they sniffed a chance when Lancashire were effectively 51 for five at tea on the last day, but Croft blocked heroically for more than three hours, assisted by Brown and Clark, and the draw was agreed with 11 overs to go.

Close of play: first day, Lancashire 273-9 (Jarvis 17, Parkinson 3); second day, Nottinghamshire 303-5 (Patel 51, Wessels 25); third day, Lancashire 128-0 (Smith 66, Hameed 58).

Lancashire

T. C. Smith st Wessels b Imran Tahir	70	– c Mullaney b Gurney	71
H. Hameed c Lumb b Hutton	16	– c Wessels b Hutton	122
L. A. Procter b Imran Tahir	48	– lbw b Broad	13
A. N. Petersen c Wessels b Broad	11	– b Broad	4
*†S. J. Croft lbw b Imran Tahir	9	– not out	34
K. R. Brown c Wessels b Gurney	36	– (7) c Taylor b Imran Tahir	12
L. S. Livingstone c Patel b Broad	33	– (6) c Lumb b Hutton	2
J. Clark c and b Broad	1	– b Gurney	11
N. Wagner b Gurney	0		
K. M. Jarvis not out	20	– (9) not out	4
M. W. Parkinson lbw b Imran Tahir	3		
B 12, lb 9, nb 8	29	B 4, lb 11, nb 16	31
1/34 (2) 2/118 (3) 3/133 (4) 4/154 (5) 5/199 (1) 6/239 (6) 7/250 (8) 8/251 (9) 9/253 (7) 10/276 (11) (97.5 overs)	276	1/151 (1) 2/209 (3) 3/213 (4) 4/231 (2) 5/233 (6) 6/261 (7) 7/287 (8) (7 wkts, 134 overs)	304

Broad 25–7–50–3; Gurney 22–6–53–2; Hutton 8–1–42–1; Mullaney 12–5–27–0; Imran Tahir 27.5–3–81–4; Patel 3–2–2–0. *Second innings*—Broad 25–10–45–2; Gurney 29–9–82–2; Imran Tahir 45–12–93–1; Hutton 19–4–48–2; Patel 11–4–12–0; Mullaney 3–2–4–0; Libby 2–0–5–0.

Nottinghamshire

*S. J. Mullaney b Jarvis	43
J. D. Libby c Croft b Wagner	54
G. P. Smith lbw b Jarvis	30
M. J. Lumb c and b Clark	43
B. R. M. Taylor c Smith b Clark	37
S. R. Patel c Croft b Smith	67
†M. H. Wessels c Livingstone b Smith	62
S. C. J. Broad b Parkinson	46
B. A. Hutton b Wagner	46
Imran Tahir c Livingstone b Wagner	7
H. F. Gurney not out	12
B 9, lb 5, w 1, nb 12	27
1/86 (1) 2/124 (2) 3/136 (3) 4/210 (5) 5/241 (4) 6/346 (6) 7/369 (7) 8/448 (8) 9/459 (10) 10/474 (9) (128.1 overs)	474
110 overs: 400-7	

Wagner 33.1–5–107–3; Jarvis 31–7–108–2; Smith 20–2–70–2; Clark 21–1–84–2; Parkinson 15–1–68–1; Procter 8–1–23–0.

Umpires: M. J. Saggers and A. G. Wharf.

NOTTINGHAMSHIRE v SOMERSET

At Nottingham, July 17–20. Somerset won by ten wickets. Somerset 23pts, Nottinghamshire 6pts. Toss: Nottinghamshire.

Somerset swept to their second win of the season, after Nottinghamshire squandered a strong start. It was built around a magnificent double-century from the 40-year-old Trescothick, whose powers seemed undiminished: he was on the field throughout, in sometimes baking heat. His century – the first in his 17 matches at Trent Bridge – equalled Harold Gimblett's record of 49 hundreds for Somerset; he went on to equal Viv Richards's county record of six doubles, and passed 1,000 runs in the season a few minutes later. Trescothick was last out after eight hours and 11 minutes, having shared century stands with Myburgh, Rogers (who ticked off 25,000 first-class runs) and Allenby, and helped Somerset to a lead of 36. He also became the seventh victim for Imran Tahir, whose figures were the best for a Nottinghamshire overseas player since fellow leg-spinner Stuart MacGill in 2004. Nottinghamshire had finished day one on 311 for four, after Mullaney and Libby shared an opening stand of 196. Next morning, Mullaney equalled his first-class best of 165, but his dismissal sparked a cascade of six for 85. Their second innings was feeble, subsiding from 74 for two to 135 all out. Trescothick and Myburgh steered Somerset home inside 17 overs.

Close of play: first day, Nottinghamshire 311-4 (Mullaney 161, Fletcher 1); second day, Somerset 244-3 (Trescothick 117, Leach 1); third day, Nottinghamshire 58-2 (Libby 24, Taylor 22).

Nottinghamshire

S. J. Mullaney c Davies b Overton	165	– lbw b Overton	11
J. D. Libby c Allenby b Groenewald	90	– b Overton	44
M. J. Lumb c Davies b Leach	10	– b Allenby	0
B. R. M. Taylor c Overton b Leach	21	– lbw b Allenby	28
M. H. Wessels lbw b Allenby	3	– c Trescothick b Allenby	0
L. J. Fletcher lbw b Allenby	32	– (8) b Gregory	0
S. R. Patel c Hildreth b Overton	15	– (6) c Hildreth b Gregory	35
*†C. M. W. Read lbw b Leach	15	– (7) hit wkt b Gregory	9
B. A. Hutton c Davies b Overton	9	– absent hurt	
Imran Tahir not out	15	– (9) b Leach	7
H. F. Gurney c Davies b Overton	0	– (10) not out	0
B 5, lb 12, w 1, nb 8	26	W 1	1
1/196 (2) 2/231 (3) 3/295 (4) (130.3 overs)	401	1/20 (1) 2/21 (3) (66.2 overs)	135
4/309 (5) 5/316 (1) 6/336 (7)		3/74 (4) 4/74 (5)	
7/377 (6) 8/377 (8) 9/401 (9)		5/86 (2) 6/98 (7)	
10/401 (11) 110 overs: 354-6		7/98 (8) 8/135 (9) 9/135 (6)	

Gregory 17–2–85–0; Groenewald 23–5–51–1; Overton 25.3–9–54–4; Trego 7–1–30–0; Allenby 22–4–44–2; Leach 36–2–120–3. *Second innings*—Overton 21–8–37–2; Groenewald 14–6–27–0; Allenby 14–6–23–3; Leach 5–0–21–1; Gregory 12.2–2–27–3.

Somerset

M. E. Trescothick c Taylor b Imran Tahir	218	– not out	37
J. G. Myburgh b Imran Tahir	54	– not out	58
*C. J. L. Rogers c Read b Gurney	48		
J. C. Hildreth b Gurney	5		
M. J. Leach c Patel b Imran Tahir	1		
J. Allenby b Patel	63		
P. D. Trego c Taylor b Imran Tahir	5		
L. Gregory lbw b Imran Tahir	0		
C. Overton c sub (G. P. Smith) b Imran Tahir	5		
†R. C. Davies c Mullaney b Imran Tahir	2		
T. D. Groenewald not out	0		
B 12, lb 12, w 2, nb 10	36	B 4, lb 1	5
1/123 (2) 2/224 (3) 3/234 (4) (127.4 overs)	437	(no wkt, 16.5 overs)	100
4/257 (5) 5/379 (6) 6/400 (7)			
7/410 (8) 8/426 (9) 9/436 (10)			
10/437 (1) 110 overs: 404-6			

Fletcher 23–5–62–0; Gurney 28–5–85–2; Hutton 15–1–82–0; Imran Tahir 36.4–7–112–7; Patel 22–5–69–1; Mullaney 3–1–3–0. *Second innings*—Fletcher 6–2–15–0; Gurney 2–0–13–0; Mullaney 2.5–0–22–0; Imran Tahir 4–1–42–0; Patel 2–0–3–0.

Umpires: N. L. Bainton and S. J. O'Shaughnessy.

NOTTINGHAMSHIRE v HAMPSHIRE

At Nottingham, August 13–16. Hampshire won by 176 runs. Hampshire 22pts, Nottinghamshire 4pts. Toss: Hampshire. County debut: A. Carter.

Hampshire arrived as the only team below Nottinghamshire, but beat them for the second time in 2016 to create a glimmer of hope of escaping relegation. Left-arm seamer Wood claimed three of Hampshire's top four in his first Championship game of the season after back problems, though Wheater's tenth century led a recovery to 319. On a flat pitch, Nottinghamshire's reply was poor: only Read passed 39. Andy Carter – who had left Trent Bridge for Derby in the winter but had just signed a short-term deal with Hampshire – took three in 12 balls at the start of the second day. The visitors led by 74, which Adams and Alsop built on in a handsome stand of 160. Will Smith declared on the third evening, setting an unlikely 468. He was briefly concerned as Mullaney, who made his fourth century of the season, added 162 with Taylor. But once Mullaney fell, Nottinghamshire lost five for 17 either side of tea, three to 19-year-old seamer Wheal, who wrapped up the match by bowling Read and Gurney in four deliveries and finished with a career-best six for 51.

Close of play: first day, Nottinghamshire 39-1 (Mullaney 10, Ball 14); second day, Hampshire 106-1 (Adams 68, Alsop 10); third day, Nottinghamshire 42-2 (Mullaney 18).

Hampshire

J. H. K. Adams b Wood	8	– (2) c Read b Ball	99
*W. R. Smith lbw b Wood	12	– (1) lbw b Gurney	20
T. P. Alsop lbw b Patel	17	– lbw b Imran Tahir	93
L. A. Dawson c Lumb b Wood	54	– b Patel	69
A. J. A. Wheater c Libby b Imran Tahir	102	– c and b Imran Tahir	2
R. McLaren lbw b Gurney	16	– not out	71
†L. D. McManus c Read b Mullaney	56	– c Mullaney b Patel	0
G. K. Berg not out	28	– c Read b Imran Tahir	17
M. S. Crane b Ball	0	– not out	5
B. T. J. Wheal lbw b Imran Tahir	0		
A. Carter b Ball	4		
Lb 7, w 1, nb 14	22	B 1, lb 4, nb 12	17
1/13 (1) 2/26 (2) 3/91 (3) 4/98 (4) 5/157 (6) 6/280 (7) 7/304 (5) 8/305 (9) 9/306 (10) 10/319 (11) (83 overs)	319	1/42 (1) 2/202 (2) 3/246 (3) 4/252 (5) 5/332 (4) 6/332 (7) 7/367 (8) (7 wkts dec, 104 overs)	393

Ball 18–5–66–2; Wood 14–3–53–3; Gurney 15–5–54–1; Mullaney 9–0–36–1; Patel 12–1–35–1; Imran Tahir 15–0–68–2. *Second innings*—Ball 21–4–77–1; Wood 14–1–56–0; Gurney 15–1–47–1; Imran Tahir 31–2–111–3; Patel 23–3–97–2.

Nottinghamshire

S. J. Mullaney b Carter	20	– c Berg b Wheal	137
J. D. Libby lbw b McLaren	11	– c Alsop b Carter	9
J. T. Ball c Wheater b Carter	14	– (9) lbw b Wheal	1
M. H. Wessels c Crane b Carter	4	– (3) c Smith b Crane	11
M. J. Lumb c McManus b Carter	39	– (4) c McManus b Wheal	17
B. R. M. Taylor c Crane b Berg	6	– (5) c Adams b Crane	58
S. R. Patel lbw b Wheal	4	– (6) c McManus b Wheal	0
*†C. M. W. Read not out	70	– (7) b Wheal	23
L. Wood c Adams b McLaren	27	– (8) c McLaren b Crane	0
Imran Tahir c Carter b Dawson	25	– not out	15
H. F. Gurney lbw b Dawson	0	– b Wheal	4
B 8, lb 15, nb 2	25	B 1, lb 9, nb 6	16
1/19 (2) 2/44 (3) 3/48 (4) 4/57 (1) 5/84 (6) 6/91 (7) 7/145 (5) 8/193 (9) 9/245 (10) 10/245 (11) (75 overs)	245	1/21 (2) 2/42 (3) 3/83 (4) 4/245 (1) 5/245 (6) 6/259 (5) 7/259 (8) 8/262 (9) 9/287 (7) 10/291 (11) (94 overs)	291

McLaren 17–2–80–2; Berg 9–5–18–1; Carter 14–1–52–4; Dawson 20–4–36–2; Wheal 12–4–20–1; Crane 3–0–16–0. *Second innings*—Berg 8–3–27–0; McLaren 10–3–23–0; Carter 15–6–24–1; Dawson 16–2–61–0; Crane 26–2–95–3; Wheal 19–4–51–6.

Umpires: R. J. Evans and M. J. Saggers.

At Scarborough, August 23–26. NOTTINGHAMSHIRE lost to YORKSHIRE by 305 runs.

At Chester-le-Street, August 31–September 3. NOTTINGHAMSHIRE drew with DURHAM.

NOTTINGHAMSHIRE v MIDDLESEX

At Nottingham, September 6–9. Middlesex won by five wickets. Middlesex 20pts, Nottinghamshire 4pts. Toss: uncontested.

A match that ended with Nottinghamshire's relegation, after nine top-level seasons, began with the news that former England coach Peter Moores, a consultant at Trent Bridge since June 2015, had been appointed head coach. On the field, Nottinghamshire succumbed to their eighth defeat, but at least put up a fight. That was chiefly down to Ball, who took a hat-trick in his opening over, and claimed nine wickets in only his second Championship match since June. Their batting, though, remained frail, and had needed an attractive century from Patel to lift them to 241. Then, after Middlesex slipped to nought for three, Nottinghamshire's bowlers allowed them to grab a lead of six, with Gubbins making a five-hour 75. Nottinghamshire subsided from 106 for one to 240 all out on the third day, against ordinary bowling from the leaders, who needed only 235 to win. This time, Ball dismissed Gubbins with his first delivery, and soon reduced them to 25 for three. But Compton's patience and technique broke Nottinghamshire's spirits, and fifties from Simpson and Franklin completed victory by mid-afternoon.

Close of play: first day, Middlesex 9-3 (Gubbins 3, Malan 4); second day, Nottinghamshire 24-0 (Mullaney 20, Libby 4); third day, Middlesex 48-3 (Compton 26, Eskinazi 5).

Nottinghamshire

S. J. Mullaney c Rayner b Finn	22	– lbw b Rayner	64
J. D. Libby c Robson b Murtagh	5	– c Simpson b Roland-Jones	18
T. J. Moores b Finn	16	– c Finn b Rayner	28
M. J. Lumb c Gubbins b Rayner	23	– c Simpson b Finn	16
B. R. M. Taylor c Gubbins b Roland-Jones	30	– lbw b Finn	17
S. R. Patel c Malan b Finn	100	– b Roland-Jones	36
*†C. M. W. Read c Murtagh b Rayner	24	– c Rayner b Finn	0
B. A. Hutton c Simpson b Finn	10	– not out	32
J. T. Ball c Simpson b Rayner	1	– lbw b Rayner	4
Imran Tahir c Eskinazi b Murtagh	5	– c Roland-Jones b Rayner	16
H. F. Gurney not out	1	– run out	1
Lb 2, nb 2	4	Lb 6, nb 2	8
1/11 (2) 2/35 (3) 3/56 (1) (86.2 overs)	241	1/62 (2) 2/106 (1) (77.4 overs)	240
4/87 (4) 5/117 (5) 6/166 (7)		3/121 (3) 4/141 (4)	
7/204 (8) 8/219 (9) 9/237 (6) 10/241 (10)		5/162 (5) 6/164 (7) 7/193 (6)	
		8/200 (9) 9/230 (10) 10/240 (11)	

Murtagh 19.2–5–46–2; Roland-Jones 14–3–59–1; Finn 22–4–54–4; Franklin 9–1–25–0; Rayner 20–7–46–3; Malan 2–0–9–0. *Second innings*—Murtagh 12–3–35–0; Roland-Jones 17–5–49–2; Finn 18.4–1–57–3; Franklin 4–2–10–0; Rayner 26–1–83–4.

Middlesex

S. D. Robson c Mullaney b Ball	0	– (2) b Ball	2
N. R. T. Gubbins c Read b Hutton	75	– (1) c Read b Ball	0
O. P. Rayner lbw b Ball	0		
N. R. D. Compton lbw b Ball	0	– (3) run out	63
D. J. Malan lbw b Hutton	13	– (4) lbw b Ball	11
S. S. Eskinazi b Imran Tahir	35	– (5) c Read b Ball	30
†J. A. Simpson b Hutton	27	– (6) not out	58
*J. E. C. Franklin c Imran Tahir b Ball	40	– (7) not out	54
T. S. Roland-Jones c and b Ball	17		
T. J. Murtagh not out	6		
S. T. Finn b Imran Tahir	10		
B 3, lb 5, w 2, nb 14	24	B 4, lb 7, nb 6	17
1/0 (1) 2/0 (3) 3/0 (4) 4/39 (5) 5/81 (6) 6/138 (7) 7/197 (2) 8/227 (8) 9/234 (9) 10/247 (11) (95.1 overs)	247	1/0 (1) 2/13 (2) 3/25 (4) 4/92 (5) 5/146 (3) (5 wkts, 74 overs)	235

Ball 21–6–66–5; Hutton 18–3–54–3; Gurney 16–8–27–0; Imran Tahir 25.1–4–61–2; Patel 15–6–31–0. *Second innings*—Ball 20–7–54–4; Hutton 9–2–19–0; Gurney 16–3–49–0; Imran Tahir 20–5–61–0; Patel 9–0–41–0.

Umpires: M. Burns and D. J. Millns.

At Taunton, September 20–22. NOTTINGHAMSHIRE lost to SOMERSET by 325 runs.

SOMERSET

Who wants seconds?

RICHARD LATHAM

For the second time in seven seasons, Somerset were helpless television viewers as their quest for a first Championship reached an epic climax. In 2010, having drawn with Durham, they had watched as Nottinghamshire secured the bonus point they needed to steal the trophy. This time the agony was prolonged. On the third evening of the final round of matches, Somerset completed an emphatic win (over Nottinghamshire, as it happened) and next morning the players joined many supporters at Taunton to watch the final day of the game at Lord's between Middlesex and Yorkshire, the other title contenders. It was heartbreaking: early in the afternoon, a draw looked possible, which would have seen Somerset achieve their dream. But the captains agreed to contrive a result, and Toby Roland-Jones's hat-trick sealed it for Middlesex. For the fourth time this century, Somerset had to settle for the runners-up spot.

While some claimed foul play – Middlesex were fed runs to hasten a declaration – Somerset sportingly swallowed their disappointment. Andy Nash, the club chairman, opened his address to the disconsolate fans with an anguished cry – "Bugger!" – before offering his congratulations to Middlesex, and conceding that Somerset would have done the same. Matthew Maynard, the director of cricket (who earned a two-year contract extension), and Marcus Trescothick, the longest-serving player, both agreed.

There was despondency but, in winning five of their last seven games, Somerset had demonstrated spirit in spades, and given much hope for 2017 and beyond. It will be a future with a new captain: Chris Rogers announced his retirement at the age of 39, after scoring a century in each innings in the final game. It took him past 1,000 runs in his only season with Somerset, and to a first-class aggregate of 25,470, including 76 hundreds. The promising young batsman Tom Abell will replace him as captain, while the South African opener Dean Elgar takes over as overseas player, though he is likely to join his countrymen on their England tour for much of the late summer. Rogers will still be seen at Taunton for much of the season, as batting coach and player mentor.

Trescothick, now into his forties, signed a one-year contract towards the end of a season that brought 1,353 first-class runs at an average of 52. The consistent James Hildreth, awarded a benefit in 2017, also passed the 1,000 mark, as did 35-year-old Peter Trego, for the first time in his career. Craig Overton (*see Errata, page 1506*), who may inherit Trego's mantle of gung-ho all-rounder, notched a maiden first-class century, against Hampshire.

Many of those runs came on pitches at Taunton that were far from the batting paradise of previous years. Often green in the middle and worn at the ends – especially in the second half of the season – they offered real encouragement to the spinners. And Taunton-born left-armer Jack Leach had, the talent to capitalise. He claimed 65 Championship wickets at under 22 each to earn the Player of the Year accolade and a place on the Lions' tour to the United Arab Emirates. There was widespread surprise in December when it emerged that he had not been called up to the senior squad in India because a routine test at Loughborough had revealed a kink in his action. After undergoing remedial work in the UAE, Leach was confident it was no longer an issue. The final two home games also saw the emergence of 19-year-old Devonian off-spinner Dom Bess, whose 13 wickets at ten each marked him as a player of huge potential.

Harry Trump, Getty Images

Jack Leach

Tim Groenewald was the most successful seamer, with 37 Championship scalps, while Craig Overton bowled better than his 34 suggested. He took on greater responsibility after his twin brother Jamie was ruled out of the second half of the season with a stress fracture of the back, sustained during an extraordinary home loss to Middlesex, who hit 302 inside 46 overs. Young wicketkeeper Ryan Davies had a testing first full season, but showed promise with the bat, particularly in the later games. In 2017, he will benefit from the competition provided by a more experienced Davies, Steven, who signed from Surrey. After giving up keeping in 2014, he is keen to return to the role to revive his international career. Alex Barrow, another keeper, was released.

Somerset improved as a 50-over team, reaching the semi-finals of the Royal London Cup after finishing top of their group and annihilating Worcestershire in the quarter-final at Taunton. Jim Allenby, the white-ball captain, made 423 runs at 42, while Mahela Jayawardene averaged 60 from five appearances. Lewis Gregory showed maturity to pick up 17 wickets, and Roelof van der Merwe again proved a capable spinner. But they lost to eventual winners Warwickshire, after failing to deal with Jeetan Patel's off-spin, which claimed five lbws.

The NatWest T20 Blast was a huge disappointment. After winning two of their first four matches, Somerset lost the last seven, and finished bottom. Chris Gayle was unable to reproduce the feats of the previous season – he scored 177 in five outings, compared with 328 in three in 2015 – while Jayawardene, for all his skills, looked uncomfortable. The team rarely managed challenging totals. Jamie Overton looked strong before his injury, taking 14 wickets, but a major rethink on tactics and personnel is required.

The season's champagne moment came in that final Championship match against Nottinghamshire. Hildreth was on seven when a yorker from Jake Ball broke his ankle. He took painkillers and battled on, improvising shots on one leg and using a runner to reach an incredible century. It summed up the determination which characterised much of Somerset's cricket.

Championship attendance: 43,573.

SOMERSET RESULTS

All first-class matches – Played 17: Won 6, Lost 1, Drawn 10.
County Championship matches – Played 16: Won 6, Lost 1, Drawn 9.

Specsavers County Championship, 2nd in Division 1;
NatWest T20 Blast, 9th in South Group; Royal London One-Day Cup, semi-finalists.

COUNTY CHAMPIONSHIP AVERAGES, BATTING AND FIELDING

Cap		*Birthplace*	*M*	*I*	*NO*	*R*	*HS*	*100*	*Avge*	*Ct/St*
	J. G. Myburgh††	*Pretoria, SA*	3	5	1	234	110	1	58.50	0
1999	†M. E. Trescothick	*Keynsham‡*	16	27	3	1,239	218	4	51.62	33
2007	J. C. Hildreth	*Milton Keynes*	16	23	2	1,012	166	4	48.19	9
2007	P. D. Trego	*Weston-super-Mare‡*	16	24	2	1,047	154*	2	47.59	5
	†C. J. L. Rogers¶	*Kogarah, Australia*	16	25	2	1,010	132	3	43.91	8
2016	T. D. Groenewald	*Pietermaritzburg, SA*	12	16	12	138	26*	0	34.50	1
2015	L. Gregory	*Plymouth*	12	16	4	329	73*	0	27.41	3
	J. Allenby	*Perth, Australia*	12	17	0	446	63	0	26.23	20
	T. B. Abell	*Taunton‡*	13	22	1	538	135	2	25.61	10
2016	C. Overton	*Barnstaple*	13	19	2	435	138	1	25.58	11
	J. Overton	*Barnstaple*	6	9	2	161	51	0	23.00	1
	R. C. Davies	*Thanet*	15	19	1	380	86	0	21.11	27/6
	R. E. van der Merwe††	*Johannesburg, SA*	7	10	1	180	102*	1	20.00	3
	†M. J. Leach	*Taunton‡*	15	16	4	121	27*	0	10.08	5

Also batted: A. W. R. Barrow (*Bath‡*) (1 match) 10, 21 (2 ct); D. M. Bess (*Exeter*) (2 matches) 9, 25, 41 (4 ct); J. H. Davey†† (*Aberdeen, Scotland*) (1 match) 10 (1 ct).

‡ *Born in Somerset.* ¶ *Official overseas player.* †† *Other non-England-qualified.*

BOWLING

	Style	*O*	*M*	*R*	*W*	*BB*	*5I*	*Avge*
D. M. Bess	OB	59.5	20	136	13	6-28	2	10.46
M. J. Leach	SLA	526.3	117	1,422	65	6-42	5	21.87
J. Overton	RFM	133.3	27	382	17	5-42	1	22.47
T. D. Groenewald	RFM	347.2	85	1,005	37	5-90	2	27.16
R. E. van der Merwe	SLA	203.4	40	614	22	4-45	0	27.90
J. Allenby	RM	243.2	57	598	21	4-67	0	28.47
L. Gregory	RFM	276.5	61	894	29	4-58	0	30.82
C. Overton	RFM	380.5	83	1,168	34	4-54	0	34.35

Also bowled: T. B. Abell (RM) 1–0–11–0; J. H. Davey (RM) 20–3–79–2; J. G. Myburgh (OB) 5–1–22–0; C. J. L. Rogers (LBG) 1–0–4–0; P. D. Trego (RFM) 149.3–35–429–5.

LEADING ROYAL LONDON CUP AVERAGES (100 runs/4 wickets)

Batting	*Runs*	*HS*	*Avge*	*SR*	*Ct*
D. P. M. D. Jayawardene	240	117*	60.00	96.00	2
T. B. Abell	141	106	47.00	80.57	2
J. Allenby	423	81	42.30	93.79	3
P. D. Trego	321	104	40.12	86.29	3
J. G. Myburgh	240	81	40.00	102.12	2
J. C. Hildreth	194	48	24.25	78.86	2
L. Gregory	152	69	19.00	80.85	3
R. E. van der Merwe	110	41	18.33	113.40	7

Bowling	*W*	*BB*	*Avge*	*ER*
L. Gregory	17	4-23	22.11	5.69
R. E. van der Merwe	14	3-51	23.07	5.22
T. D. Groenewald	15	3-30	24.40	5.96
J. Overton	4	2-47	25.25	6.73
P. D. Trego	8	3-33	30.75	5.12
M. T. C. Waller	5	2-36	48.20	6.17
C. Overton	8	3-60	48.87	5.43

LEADING NATWEST T20 BLAST AVERAGES (100 runs/14 overs)

Batting	Runs	HS	Avge	SR	Ct
C. H. Gayle	177	52	35.40	**166.98**	2
P. D. Trego	257	63	19.76	**158.64**	3
R. E. van der Merwe	190	59	38.00	**155.73**	6
J. G. Myburgh	218	86*	24.22	**139.74**	0
D. P. M. D. Jayawardene	239	51	26.55	**131.31**	1
L. Gregory	196	37*	24.50	**128.10**	4
J. Allenby	328	91	27.33	**117.14**	4

Bowling	W	BB	Avge	ER
J. H. Davey	6	3-20	17.16	**7.35**
R. E. van der Merwe	6	3-16	47.00	**7.42**
M. T. C. Waller	12	4-33	24.16	**7.94**
L. Gregory	9	2-25	36.44	**8.55**
J. Overton	14	4-22	22.92	**9.30**
Yasir Arafat	3	1-35	68.33	**10.88**

FIRST-CLASS COUNTY RECORDS

Highest score for	342	J. L. Langer v Surrey at Guildford	2006
Highest score against	424	A. C. MacLaren (Lancashire) at Taunton	1895
Leading run-scorer	21,142	H. Gimblett (avge 36.96)	1935–54
Best bowling for	10-49	E. J. Tyler v Surrey at Taunton	1895
Best bowling against	10-35	A. Drake (Yorkshire) at Weston-super-Mare	1914
Leading wicket-taker	2,165	J. C. White (avge 18.03)	1909–37
Highest total for	850-7 dec	v Middlesex at Taunton	2007
Highest total against	811	by Surrey at The Oval	1899
Lowest total for	25	v Gloucestershire at Bristol	1947
Lowest total against	22	by Gloucestershire at Bristol	1920

LIST A COUNTY RECORDS

Highest score for	184	M. E. Trescothick v Gloucestershire at Taunton	2008
Highest score against	167*	A. J. Stewart (Surrey) at The Oval	1994
Leading run-scorer	7,374	M. E. Trescothick (avge 36.87)	1993–2014
Best bowling for	8-66	S. R. G. Francis v Derbyshire at Derby	2004
Best bowling against	7-39	A. Hodgson (Northamptonshire) at Northampton	1976
Leading wicket-taker	309	H. R. Moseley (avge 20.03)	1971–82
Highest total for	413-4	v Devon at Torquay	1990
Highest total against	383-7	by Kent at Taunton	2014
Lowest total for	58	v Essex at Chelmsford	1977
	58	v Middlesex at Southgate	2000
Lowest total against	60	by Kent at Taunton	1979

TWENTY20 COUNTY RECORDS

Highest score for	151*	C. H. Gayle v Kent at Taunton	2015
Highest score against	122*	J. J. Roy (Surrey) at The Oval	2015
Leading run-scorer	**2,663**	**J. C. Hildreth (avge 23.56)**	**2004–16**
Best bowling for	6-5	A. V. Suppiah v Glamorgan at Cardiff	2011
Best bowling against	**5-17**	**L. A. Dawson (Hampshire) at Southampton**	**2016**
Leading wicket-taker	137	A. C. Thomas (avge 20.17)	2008–15
Highest total for	250-3	v Gloucestershire at Taunton	2006
Highest total for	227-4	by Gloucestershire at Bristol	2006
	227-7	by Kent at Taunton	2015
Lowest total for	82	v Kent at Taunton	2010
Lowest total against	73	by Warwickshire at Taunton	2013

ADDRESS

County Ground, St James's Street, Taunton TA1 1JT; 0845 337 1875; enquiries@somersetcountycc.co.uk; www.somersetcountycc.co.uk.

OFFICIALS

Captain 2016 C. J. L. Rogers
2017 T. B. Abell
(limited-overs) J. Allenby
Director of cricket M. P. Maynard
Assistant coach J. I. D. Kerr
Academy director S. D. Snell

President R. Parsons
Chairman A. J. Nash
Chief executive G. W. Lavender
Chairman, cricket committee V. J. Marks
Head groundsman S. Lee
Scorer G. A. Stickley

At Chester-le-Street, April 10–13. SOMERSET drew with DURHAM.

At Taunton Vale, April 17–19 (not first-class). **Drawn.** ‡**Somerset 370-6 dec** (78 overs) (T. B. Abell 101, P. D. Trego 115; J. R. Turpin 3-54) **and 480-9 dec** (86.2 overs) (M. E. Trescothick 100, C. J. L. Rogers 56, J. C. Hildreth 96, R. C. Davies 66, C. Overton 69; J. R. Turpin 3-49); **Cardiff MCCU 118** (56 overs) (C. Overton 3-27, L. Gregory 3-19) **and 143-8** (50 overs) (T. D. Groenewald 3-5). *A ninth-wicket stand of 70* between Andrew Westphal and James Turpin blunted a first-choice Somerset attack and saved the game for Cardiff. Craig Overton had smashed six sixes in a 37-ball 69 to set up a second declaration after Marcus Trescothick became Somerset's third centurion of the match, but they could not press home their advantage.*

At The Oval, April 24–27. SOMERSET drew with SURREY.

SOMERSET v LANCASHIRE

At Taunton, May 1–4. Drawn. Somerset 9pts, Lancashire 11pts. Toss: Lancashire.

Winter drainage work had led to concerns about the bowlers' run-ups, which meant the use of a dead pitch on the town side of the ground – and a match that always looked like a draw. Lancashire's No. 7 Liam Livingstone – author of a 138-ball 350 in a club game for Nantwich the previous season – marshalled the tail superbly to reach his maiden first-class century, after Petersen, formerly of Somerset, and Croft had laid a solid foundation. Hildreth then continued where he had left off in 2015, with an artful hundred against the most testing bowling of the match; Anderson produced a triple-wicket maiden, and it needed an eighth-wicket stand of 139 between Hildreth and Jamie Overton to avert meltdown. Despite that, Somerset followed on, 180 behind, before 40-year-old Trescothick's 60th first-class century, and an unbroken third-wicket stand of 168 with Rogers, saw them to safety.

Close of play: first day, Lancashire 295-4 (Croft 71, Davies 32); second day, Somerset 14-0 (Trescothick 4, Abell 9); third day, Somerset 0-0 (Groenewald 0, Trescothick 0).

Lancashire

K. R. Brown lbw b Leach	47
H. Hameed c Abell b Leach	29
L. A. Procter lbw b Groenewald	26
A. N. Petersen lbw b C. Overton	83
*S. J. Croft c Davies b van der Merwe	94
†A. L. Davies c Davies b Groenewald	32
L. S. Livingstone not out	108
N. Wagner st Davies b van der Merwe	13
J. M. Anderson c Trescothick b C. Overton	8
K. M. Jarvis c Rogers b van der Merwe	34
S. C. Kerrigan not out	11
B 5, lb 1, nb 2	8
1/56 (2) 2/87 (1) (9 wkts dec, 151 overs)	493
3/125 (3) 4/250 (4)	
5/295 (6) 6/354 (5) 7/386 (8)	
8/399 (9) 9/479 (10) 110 overs: 323-5	

C. Overton 31–9–97–2; Trego 8–1–36–0; Groenewald 28–14–50–2; J. Overton 30–4–105–0; Leach 31–7–112–2; van der Merwe 23–3–87–3.

Somerset

M. E. Trescothick c and b Jarvis	5	– (2) not out 129
T. B. Abell lbw b Kerrigan	29	– (3) c and b Kerrigan 10
*C. J. L. Rogers c Brown b Anderson	55	– (4) not out 75
J. C. Hildreth c Jarvis b Wagner	130	
R. E. van der Merwe lbw b Anderson	0	
P. D. Trego lbw b Anderson	0	
†R. C. Davies st Davies b Kerrigan	22	
C. Overton b Jarvis	4	
J. Overton c Davies b Wagner	51	
M. J. Leach c Croft b Kerrigan	7	
T. D. Groenewald not out	0	– (1) b Jarvis 5
B 5, lb 3, nb 2	10	B 8, lb 2 10
1/15 (1) 2/76 (2) 3/102 (3) 4/102 (5) 5/102 (6) 6/143 (7) 7/150 (8) 8/289 (9) 9/307 (10) 10/313 (4) (98.2 overs)	313	1/13 (1) 2/61 (3) (2 wkts dec, 86 overs) 229

Anderson 21–3–72–3; Jarvis 16–3–56–2; Kerrigan 34–6–63–3; Wagner 19.2–1–89–2; Procter 6–1–13–0; Croft 1–0–7–0; Livingstone 1–0–5–0. *Second innings*—Anderson 15–4–37–0; Jarvis 11–3–26–1; Wagner 11–4–25–0; Kerrigan 30–11–71–1; Croft 9–1–27–0; Livingstone 9–0–31–0; Hameed 1–0–2–0.

Umpires: J. H. Evans and A. G. Wharf.

At Birmingham, May 8–11. SOMERSET drew with WARWICKSHIRE.

SOMERSET v YORKSHIRE

At Taunton, May 15–18. Drawn. Somerset 12pts, Yorkshire 9pts. Toss: uncontested.

Yorkshire coach Jason Gillespie described the decision to field first in glorious sunshine as a "no-brainer", only for Somerset to dominate from the start. On a pitch offering little for the bowlers, Hildreth helped himself to a big hundred, passing 13,000 first-class runs for Somerset, while Trescothick, Rogers and Trego all made it into the nineties, if not out of them. (The only other instance in the Championship came for Hampshire against Middlesex in 1919: Basil Melle, George Brown and Ledger Hill.) Following a declaration at 562 for seven, Yorkshire struggled against the discipline of Groenewald and the fire of Jamie Overton, much the quickest bowler in the match. Only the efforts of Lyth, who survived a sharp caught-and-bowled chance to Groenewald on two to record his third century at Taunton, and a last-wicket stand of 74 between Patterson and Brooks, provided any meaningful resistance. Yorkshire followed on, but that partnership – which used up more than 20 overs – eventually cost Somerset. Though they reduced the visitors to 99 for six on the final afternoon, still 152 behind, Leaning and Plunkett hung on for a draw; Gillespie accepted his team had been outplayed.

Close of play: first day, Somerset 342-4 (Hildreth 68, Trego 7); second day, Yorkshire 127-1 (Lyth 80, Rhodes 6); third day, Yorkshire 306-9 (Patterson 32, Brooks 34).

THREE NINETIES IN A FIRST-CLASS INNINGS

Sussex (592) v Cambridge University at Hove	1895
Hampshire (446-9 dec) v Middlesex at Southampton	1919
Kent (486-9 dec) v Oxford University at Oxford	1931
Hyderabad (486-8 dec) v Mysore at Secunderabad	1946-47
Barbados (406-6 dec†) v Leeward Islands at Basseterre	1966-67
Delhi (437-4 dec) v Jammu & Kashmir at Delhi	1989-90
Bengal (525) v Maharashtra at Calcutta	1997-98
Multan (567-5 dec) v Customs at Okara	2007-08
Matabeleland Tuskers (461-9 dec) v Mid West Rhinos at Kwekwe	2014-15
Hyderabad (522†) v Andhra at Visakhapatnam	2014-15
Somerset (562-7 dec) v Yorkshire at Taunton	**2016**

† *Includes one score of 90 or more not out.*

Somerset

M. E. Trescothick c and b Rashid	97	L. Gregory not out	7
T. B. Abell b Patterson	8	B 11, lb 7, w 5, nb 2	25
*C. J. L. Rogers c Hodd b Rashid	91		
J. C. Hildreth c and b Rashid	166	1/30 (2) (7 wkts dec, 138.2 overs)	562
J. Allenby c Ballance b Rhodes	51	2/178 (1) 3/247 (3)	
P. D. Trego c Hodd b Rashid	94	4/332 (5) 5/531 (6)	
J. Overton c Lees b Patterson	23	6/544 (4) 7/562 (7) 110 overs: 387-4	

†R. C. Davies, M. J. Leach and T. D. Groenewald did not bat.

Brooks 25–2–106–0; Plunkett 19–1–87–0; Patterson 27.2–8–80–2; Rhodes 21–2–70–1; Lyth 12–1–41–0; Rashid 34–2–160–4.

Yorkshire

A. Lyth c Allenby b Gregory	106	– b Overton	18
A. Z. Lees c Trego b Overton	33	– b Overton	11
W. M. H. Rhodes c Overton b Trego	15	– c Abell b Leach	18
G. S. Ballance c Davies b Groenewald	37	– c Leach b Overton	18
*A. W. Gale c Allenby b Leach	8	– c Leach b Groenewald	13
J. A. Leaning c Davies b Gregory	17	– not out	29
A. U. Rashid run out	0	– c Allenby b Groenewald	0
L. E. Plunkett c Davies b Groenewald	4	– not out	20
†A. J. Hodd b Groenewald	0		
S. A. Patterson b Overton	32		
J. A. Brooks not out	38		
B 6, lb 5, nb 10	21	Lb 9, w 5	14
1/103 (2) 2/145 (3) 3/172 (1) (113.1 overs)	311	1/19 (1) (6 wkts, 71.4 overs)	141
4/189 (5) 5/226 (6) 6/232 (7)		2/45 (3) 3/49 (2)	
7/232 (4) 8/232 (9) 9/237 (8)		4/69 (5) 5/88 (4) 6/99 (7)	
10/311 (10) 110 overs: 306-9			

Gregory 21–9–55–2; Groenewald 20–4–54–3; Overton 27.1–7–87–2; Leach 27–10–64–1; Allenby 6–0–15–0; Trego 12–3–25–1. *Second innings*—Groenewald 15–5–32–2; Gregory 14–4–32–0; Leach 21–8–33–1; Overton 17–7–26–3; Trego 4–1–3–0; Allenby 0.4–0–6–0.

Umpires: S. J. O'Shaughnessy and B. V. Taylor.

At Lord's, May 22–25. SOMERSET drew with MIDDLESEX.

SOMERSET v SURREY

At Taunton, May 28–30. Somerset won by one wicket. Somerset 19pts, Surrey 5pts. Toss: Surrey.

This was Championship cricket at its dramatic best, as two days of Surrey domination were upended by a nail-biting Somerset victory late on the third evening. On a turning pitch which had helped Batty claim ten victims with his off-breaks and go past 600 in first-class cricket, last pair Leach and Groenewald came together with 31 required. After Brown put down Leach at slip, they avoided expansive shot-making, taking more than 12 overs to tie the scores, with every scurried single loudly cheered.They then jangled the nerves for another 11 balls, before Groenewald cover-drove the winning run well into the extra half-hour to send the home balcony into raptures. Batty's efforts, particularly while taking seven wickets in nine overs to earn Surrey a first-innings lead of 162, did not go unnoticed: Somerset's left-armer Leach later said he had studied his "sense of theatre", claiming eight wickets in the match and going for less than two an over. Jamie Overton took four of his own as Surrey collapsed to 138, including the last three during a rapid spell. Trescothick passed 24,000 first-class runs in making 56 as Somerset inched towards a memorable win.

Close of play: first day, Surrey 236-8 (Foakes 17, Pillans 22); second day, Surrey 94-6 (Foakes 14, Ansari 26).

Surrey

R. J. Burns c Trescothick b C. Overton	14	– b Leach	8
A. Harinath c Trescothick b Allenby	32	– c Trescothick b C. Overton	13
K. C. Sangakkara c and b Groenewald	45	– c Davies b C. Overton	3
G. C. Wilson lbw b Allenby	12	– b J. Overton	11
S. M. Davies lbw b Leach	49	– c Hildreth b Leach	7
Z. S. Ansari c Trescothick b Leach	37	– (8) c Davies b J. Overton	38
†B. T. Foakes b C. Overton	31	– (6) c Rogers b Leach	14
T. K. Curran c Allenby b Leach	0	– (7) c C. Overton b Leach	5
*G. J. Batty lbw b Leach	0	– b J. Overton	17
M. W. Pillans not out	34	– b J. Overton	0
S. C. Meaker c C. Overton b Groenewald	1	– not out	7
B 8, lb 1	9	B 10, w 1, nb 4	15
1/26 (1) 2/70 (2) 3/90 (4) 4/111 (3) 5/196 (5) 6/201 (6) 7/201 (8) 8/201 (9) 9/255 (7) 10/264 (11) (91.5 overs)	264	1/17 (2) 2/25 (1) 3/27 (3) 4/38 (5) 5/44 (4) 6/51 (7) 7/94 (6) 8/117 (9) 9/117 (10) 10/138 (8) (69.1 overs)	138

C. Overton 18–4–66–2; Groenewald 21.5–6–62–2; J. Overton 11–1–37–0; Allenby 16–3–38–2; Trego 6–1–18–0; Leach 19–6–34–4. *Second innings*—Groenewald 7–3–16–0; C. Overton 17–6–25–2; Leach 31–10–63–4; J. Overton 11.1–3–18–4; Allenby 3–0–6–0.

Somerset

M. E. Trescothick lbw b Batty	12	– c Foakes b Meaker	56
T. B. Abell lbw b Meaker	25	– c Foakes b Curran	7
*C. J. L. Rogers c Pillans b Batty	19	– lbw b Curran	28
J. C. Hildreth b Meaker	5	– c Foakes b Meaker	0
J. Allenby c Sangakkara b Meaker	9	– lbw b Meaker	56
P. D. Trego lbw b Batty	12	– lbw b Batty	44
C. Overton c Burns b Batty	0	– c Davies b Batty	8
†R. C. Davies c Meaker b Batty	4	– lbw b Batty	5
J. Overton b Batty	1	– c Foakes b Meaker	29
M. J. Leach b Batty	1	– not out	24
T. D. Groenewald not out	5	– not out	18
Lb 1, w 6, nb 2	9	B 5, lb 16, w 5	26
1/46 (2) 2/48 (1) 3/53 (4) 4/73 (3) 5/89 (6) 6/89 (7) 7/93 (8) 8/96 (5) 9/97 (10) 10/102 (9) (29 overs)	102	1/46 (2) 2/92 (1) 3/92 (4) 4/127 (3) 5/207 (6) 6/219 (7) 7/225 (5) 8/237 (8) 9/270 (9) (9 wkts, 84 overs)	301

Curran 6–2–8–0; Pillans 4–1–22–0; Meaker 10–0–39–3; Batty 9–0–32–7. *Second innings*—Curran 16–1–69–2; Pillans 7–0–27–0; Batty 33–7–83–3; Meaker 19–0–79–4; Ansari 9–1–22–0.

Umpires: J. H. Evans and B. V. Taylor.

At Southampton, June 26–29. SOMERSET drew with HAMPSHIRE.

At Taunton, July 3–5. SOMERSET drew with PAKISTANIS (see Pakistan tour section).

SOMERSET v MIDDLESEX

At Taunton, July 10–13. Middlesex won by two wickets. Middlesex 23pts, Somerset 3pts. Toss: uncontested.

"I'm almost speechless," said Simpson, the Middlesex wicketkeeper, whose swipe over square leg sealed an enthralling match with two balls to spare, and condemned Somerset to their only defeat of the season. "The elation when that ball went for six was unbelievable." Somerset's enterprise had helped produce the spectacle: shortly before play Rogers, their captain, gambled on moving to a green-tinged pitch. With Middlesex deprived of Tim Murtagh (back injury), he reasoned that a seam battle would suit his own side, and – on a lively surface – fought his way to a half-century in a total of 236. Middlesex slipped to 212 for eight in reply, only for Harris and Fuller, with a career-best 93, to add 162, a ninth-wicket record in this fixture. As the pitch flattened, the match took another turn, Trescothick and Trego scoring hundreds to set up a declaration. Middlesex needed 302 in 46 overs, and looked out of it at 185 for five from 34. But Fuller, promoted to No. 7, swung the contest again: he crashed an 18-ball 36 out of a sixth-wicket stand of 86 in less than eight overs – one from Craig Overton cost 23. Three more wickets fell, but Simpson celebrated his 28th birthday in dramatic style. Jamie Overton had been restricted to 21 balls in the first innings by a back injury; scans revealed a stress fracture, which ended his season.

Close of play: first day, Middlesex 51-1 (Gubbins 31, Eskinazi 7); second day, Middlesex 361-8 (Harris 69, Fuller 84); third day, Somerset 348-6 (Trego 115, Barrow 7).

Somerset

M. E. Trescothick b Harris	35	– c Simpson b Harris	124
J. G. Myburgh c Simpson b Fuller	0	– b Podmore	12
*C. J. L. Rogers c Simpson b Podmore	57	– c Bailey b Podmore	0
J. C. Hildreth lbw b Fuller	19	– c Franklin b Rayner	11
J. Allenby c Simpson b Podmore	44	– c Fuller b Podmore	38
P. D. Trego c Simpson b Podmore	4	– c Franklin b Fuller	138
C. Overton c Simpson b Harris	0	– c Simpson b Harris	2
†A. W. R. Barrow c Rayner b Harris	10	– c Simpson b Fuller	21
J. Overton c Robson b Podmore	14	– (10) c Simpson b Fuller	5
M. J. Leach c Rayner b Fuller	12	– (9) not out	27
T. D. Groenewald not out	9	– not out	26
B 8, lb 7, w 1, nb 16	32	B 4, lb 9, w 3, nb 26	42
1/6 (2) 2/77 (1) 3/115 (4) (67 overs)	236	1/16 (2) (9 wkts dec, 134 overs)	446
4/133 (3) 5/153 (6) 6/154 (7)		2/18 (3) 3/59 (4)	
7/172 (8) 8/211 (9) 9/213 (5) 10/236 (10)		4/126 (5) 5/307 (1) 6/315 (7)	
		7/381 (8) 8/396 (6) 9/404 (10)	

Harris 18–2–67–3; Fuller 20–7–72–3; Podmore 21–4–54–4; Franklin 8–1–28–0. *Second innings*—Fuller 30–4–125–3; Podmore 34–7–89–3; Harris 33–3–114–2; Rayner 29–9–72–1; Franklin 7–1–32–0; Malan 1–0–1–0.

Middlesex

S. D. Robson lbw b C. Overton	0	– (2) c Barrow b Groenewald	22
N. R. T. Gubbins c Trescothick b Allenby	67	– (1) c Allenby b Groenewald	76
S. S. Eskinazi c Hildreth b C. Overton	7	– (9) c C. Overton b Groenewald	11
D. J. Malan b Trego	10	– (3) c C. Overton b Groenewald	32
G. J. Bailey c C. Overton b Allenby	71	– b Groenewald	4
†J. A. Simpson c Barrow b Allenby	0	– not out	79
*J. E. C. Franklin b Allenby	5	– (4) lbw b Allenby	28
O. P. Rayner c Allenby b C. Overton	12	– b Leach	0
J. A. R. Harris c Allenby b Groenewald	78	– (10) not out	2
J. K. Fuller c Allenby b Groenewald	93	– (7) c Trego b Leach	36
H. W. Podmore not out	2		
B 13, lb 22, w 1	36	B 1, lb 6, w 5	12
1/0 (1) 2/51 (3) 3/74 (4) (119.4 overs)	381	1/32 (2) (8 wkts, 45.4 overs)	302
4/115 (2) 5/117 (6) 6/133 (7) 7/177 (8)		2/108 (3) 3/150 (1)	
8/212 (5) 9/374 (10) 10/381 (9) 110 overs: 353-8		4/155 (5) 5/185 (4)	
		6/271 (7) 7/271 (8) 8/292 (9)	

C. Overton 30–7–86–3; Groenewald 30.4–3–97–2; J. Overton 3.3–1–8–0; Allenby 26–5–67–4; Trego 15.3–3–41–1; Leach 12–2–38–0; Myburgh 2–0–9–0. *Second innings*—C. Overton 10–0–94–0; Groenewald 19–3–90–5; Leach 5–0–36–2; Myburgh 1–0–11–0; Allenby 10.4–1–64–1.

Umpires: S. A. Garratt and D. J. Millns.

At Nottingham, July 17–20. SOMERSET beat NOTTINGHAMSHIRE by ten wickets.

SOMERSET v DURHAM

At Taunton, August 4–6. Somerset won by 39 runs. Somerset 19pts, Durham 3pts. Toss: Somerset.

Undaunted by the Middlesex defeat, Somerset produced an even spicier pitch in pursuit of a win. Seventeen wickets fell on the first day: Somerset folded against seam for 184, before their left-arm spinners, Leach and van der Merwe, got to work, eventually sharing nine as Durham finished five runs ahead. It was the cue for another Somerset collapse. After seven balls, they were none for three; soon, it was 33 for six. But quick late-order runs meant Durham, unbeaten in 2016, needed 176. A half-century from Stoneman – the only one of the match – got them going, and they began the third day needing only 46, with five wickets in hand. But in 17 minutes Somerset blew away the Durham tail, Leach and van der Merwe exploiting the vicious turn to earn another four each. In all, the last seven wickets had fallen for 18 in 64 balls. The gamble had worked, lifting Somerset above Durham into second place and kindling hopes of a first Championship title.

Close of play: first day, Durham 154-7 (Hickey 25, Wood 11); second day, Durham 130-5 (Poynter 7, Onions 0).

Somerset

M. E. Trescothick c Borthwick b Rushworth	6	– c Borthwick b Rushworth	0
T. B. Abell c Poynter b Onions	0	– c Poynter b Onions	0
*C. J. L. Rogers c Stoneman b Coughlin	30	– lbw b Rushworth	0
J. C. Hildreth b Wood	34	– c Muchall b Onions	8
J. Allenby c Poynter b Coughlin	11	– c Borthwick b Wood	15
P. D. Trego b Wood	16	– lbw b Onions	0
R. E. van der Merwe c Borthwick b Wood	0	– b Onions	47
C. Overton b Rushworth	42	– b Hickey	38
†R. C. Davies c Stoneman b Onions	31	– c Borthwick b Hickey	49
M. J. Leach not out	12	– b Wood	0
T. D. Groenewald c Hickey b Rushworth	2	– not out	20
		Lb 3	3
1/6 (2) 2/6 (1) 3/61 (3) 4/77 (4) 5/81 (5) 6/82 (7) 7/115 (6) 8/166 (9) 9/170 (8) 10/184 (11) (41.1 overs)	184	1/0 (1) 2/0 (3) 3/0 (2) 4/21 (4) 5/21 (6) 6/33 (5) 7/105 (7) 8/117 (8) 9/128 (10) 10/180 (9) (40.5 overs)	180

Rushworth 10.1–0–47–3; Onions 14–1–65–2; Coughlin 10–0–48–2; Wood 7–1–24–3. *Second innings*—Rushworth 7–1–28–2; Onions 14–2–50–4; Wood 7–0–51–2; Borthwick 3–0–26–0; Hickey 8.5–1–19–2; Coughlin 1–0–3–0.

Durham

M. D. Stoneman c Trescothick b Leach	35	– b van der Merwe	57
*K. K. Jennings c Trescothick b van der Merwe	14	– lbw b Overton	0
S. G. Borthwick c Hildreth b van der Merwe	16	– c Hildreth b Overton	9
M. J. Richardson c Allenby b Leach	0	– lbw b Leach	33
†S. W. Poynter c Rogers b van der Merwe	7	– (6) lbw b Leach	12
P. Coughlin b Overton	30	– (8) c Allenby b Leach	0
G. J. Muchall lbw b Leach	13	– (5) c Trescothick b van der Merwe	17
A. J. Hickey not out	36	– (9) not out	0
M. A. Wood c Allenby b Leach	27	– (10) c Trescothick b van der Merwe	1
C. Rushworth lbw b van der Merwe	0	– (11) c Allenby b van der Merwe	0
G. Onions lbw b Leach	4	– (7) lbw b Leach	0
Lb 7	7	B 6, lb 1	7
1/38 (1) 2/58 (3) 3/65 (2) 4/69 (4) 5/73 (5) 6/102 (7) 7/141 (6) 8/181 (9) 9/182 (10) 10/189 (11) (61.3 overs)	189	1/1 (2) 2/19 (3) 3/88 (4) 4/118 (1) 5/127 (5) 6/130 (7) 7/130 (8) 8/135 (6) 9/136 (10) 10/136 (11) (44.4 overs)	136

Overton 11–4–30–1; Groenewald 4–2–14–0; Allenby 2–0–10–0; Leach 19.3–2–69–5; van der Merwe 25–7–59–4. *Second innings*—Overton 8–0–31–2; Groenewald 2–0–7–0; van der Merwe 17.4–3–45–4; Leach 17–3–46–4.

Umpires: P. K. Baldwin and M. J. Saggers.

SOMERSET v HAMPSHIRE

At Taunton, August 23–26. Drawn. Somerset 13pts, Hampshire 10pts. Toss: Hampshire. County debut: D. J. Wainwright.

Twin centuries from Ervine brought Hampshire a hard-earned draw. His first came in the face of another spin onslaught: Leach and van der Merwe were bowling in tandem by the 19th over, and winkled out nine between them. Despite that, Hampshire battled to 338, even becalming the slow bowlers while Ervine and McLaren were sharing a century stand for the fifth wicket. Somerset's reply produced a return to form for the 22-year-old Abell, whose second full season of Championship cricket had been disappointing. His 79 in tough conditions helped them to 257 for five by the end of the second day, but the pitch flattened out overnight: only two wickets fell on the third, which finished with Craig Overton three short of his maiden first-class century. He feared a declaration, but got there within four balls next morning (van der Merwe reached his first Somerset hundred two overs later). Overton finally perished going for his ninth six, ending a county-record stand of 217 for the eighth wicket (which survived for six days), and prompting Rogers to declare at 587 for eight. Ervine's second century of the match – he was dropped three times – and 96 from Adams took Hampshire to safety.

Close of play: first day, Hampshire 281-6 (McManus 41, Berg 12); second day, Somerset 257-5 (Allenby 37, Gregory 1); third day, Somerset 534-7 (van der Merwe 91, Overton 97).

Hampshire

*W. R. Smith b van der Merwe	16	– (2) lbw b Leach	0
J. H. K. Adams b Gregory	8	– (1) c Trescothick b Leach	96
S. M. Ervine lbw b Leach	103	– b Overton	106
J. M. Vince b Leach	0	– c Leach b van der Merwe	13
A. J. A. Wheater lbw b van der Merwe	21	– c Davies b van der Merwe	0
R. McLaren c Abell b Leach	61	– not out	32
†L. D. McManus b Leach	43		
G. K. Berg lbw b van der Merwe	22		
D. J. Wainwright not out	35	– (7) not out	1
M. S. Crane c Trescothick b Leach	2		
B. T. J. Wheal c Trescothick b Leach	3		
B 20, lb 4	24	B 3, lb 3	6
1/16 (2) 2/56 (1) 3/61 (4) (119.5 overs)	338	1/6 (2) (5 wkts, 96 overs)	254
4/92 (5) 5/210 (6) 6/244 (3) 7/288 (7)		2/165 (3) 3/191 (4)	
8/298 (8) 9/303 (10) 10/338 (11) 110 overs: 306-9		4/191 (5) 5/251 (1)	

Overton 17–3–37–0; Gregory 13–3–34–1; Allenby 10–2–21–0; Leach 40.5–4–108–6; van der Merwe 36–5–99–3; Trego 3–0–15–0. *Second innings*—Gregory 7–3–17–0; Overton 11–5–22–1; Leach 38–10–111–2; van der Merwe 27–8–54–2; Allenby 13–1–44–0.

Somerset

M. E. Trescothick c Crane b Wainwright	36
T. B. Abell lbw b Wainwright	79
*C. J. L. Rogers st McManus b Crane	11
J. C. Hildreth lbw b Smith	40
J. Allenby c McManus b McLaren	56
P. D. Trego c Smith b McLaren	42
L. Gregory c Ervine b Crane	61
R. E. van der Merwe not out	102
C. Overton c Adams b Crane	138
B 7, lb 8, w 1, nb 6	22
1/87 (1) (8 wkts dec, 137.4 overs)	587
2/112 (3) 3/150 (2)	
4/183 (4) 5/252 (6) 6/300 (5)	
7/370 (7) 8/587 (9) 110 overs: 416-7	

†R. C. Davies and M. J. Leach did not bat.

McLaren 22–3–100–2; Berg 12–1–46–0; Crane 30.4–3–143–3; Wainwright 31–4–112–2; Smith 28–2–92–1; Wheal 14–0–79–0.

Umpires: R. J. Evans and J. W. Lloyds.

At Manchester, August 31–September 3. SOMERSET drew with LANCASHIRE.

SOMERSET v WARWICKSHIRE

At Taunton, September 6–8. Somerset won by 31 runs. Somerset 19pts, Warwickshire 3pts. Toss: Somerset. First-class debut: M. Lamb. Championship debut: D. M. Bess.

Another fruity pitch produced an all-action contest, which ended early on the third morning. Anticipating turn later on, Somerset had chosen to bat, but – as Barker and Wright nipped the ball around – slipped to 28 for three, lost three wickets on 36, and were all out for 95 in an extended first session. After lunch, 19-year-old off-spinner Dom Bess, on Championship debut, bowled Somerset back into contention. He took six for 28, including Trott and Bell with successive deliveries, as 21 wickets fell on the opening day. It was enough to trigger a visit from ECB pitch liaison officer Tony Pigott, who decided the surface was less to blame than the batsmen. Rogers's half-century lifted Somerset to 141 for four, before he became the third of Patel's five victims. The carnage continued as Warwickshire, needing 184 for victory, slipped to 61 for eight, Leach ripping through the middle order. A battling stand of 86 between Clarke and Wright made Somerset sweat into the third morning but, after Gregory made the breakthrough, Leach took his sixth to complete an extraordinary victory. Trescothick held the final catch at leg gully. His seven in the match equalled the county record for an outfielder and took him past Jack White's Somerset record of 393.

Close of play: first day, Somerset 41-1 (Trescothick 19, Rogers 7); second day, Warwickshire 131-8 (Clarke 42, Wright 38).

Somerset

M. E. Trescothick lbw b Wright	2	– b Patel	25
T. B. Abell c Mellor b Wright	20	– lbw b Poysden	15
*C. J. L. Rogers c Clarke b Barker	1	– b Patel	58
J. C. Hildreth c Bell b Barker	9	– lbw b Wright	1
P. D. Trego b Barker	4	– lbw b Patel	31
L. Gregory c Mellor b Clarke	4	– lbw b Patel	11
R. E. van der Merwe c Clarke b Barker	0	– b Barker	22
†R. C. Davies c and b Clarke	16	– c Patel b Poysden	3
D. M. Bess c Mellor b Clarke	9	– c Hain b Poysden	25
M. J. Leach b Patel	14	– b Patel	2
T. D. Groenewald not out	10	– not out	0
Lb 2, nb 4	6	B 16, lb 2	18
1/7 (1) 2/8 (3) 3/28 (4) 4/36 (2) 5/36 (5) 6/36 (7) 7/46 (6) 8/66 (9) 9/69 (8) 10/95 (10) (30.1 overs)	95	1/31 (2) 2/70 (1) 3/75 (4) 4/130 (5) 5/141 (3) 6/160 (6) 7/169 (8) 8/190 (7) 9/211 (9) 10/211 (10) (74.3 overs)	211

Barker 14–7–33–4; Wright 8–0–28–2; Clarke 8–0–32–3; Patel 0.1–0–0–1. *Second innings*— Barker 12–4–24–1; Patel 34.3–10–86–5; Poysden 12–0–52–3; Wright 15–3–31–1; Clarke 1–1–0–0.

Warwickshire

I. J. Westwood c Trescothick b Bess	34 – c Rogers b Groenewald	3
†A. J. Mellor c Bess b Groenewald	20 – c Abell b Leach	22
I. J. L. Trott c Trescothick b Bess	10 – st Davies b Leach	4
*I. R. Bell c and b Bess	0 – c Trescothick b Leach	1
S. R. Hain c Trescothick b Groenewald	9 – c Trescothick b Bess	0
M. Lamb b Leach	1 – b Leach	1
R. Clarke c Davies b Bess	19 – not out	55
K. H. D. Barker c and b Bess	1 – c Trescothick b Bess	2
J. S. Patel c Abell b Bess	16 – lbw b Leach	1
C. J. C. Wright b Leach	9 – c Davies b Gregory	45
J. E. Poysden not out	1 – c Trescothick b Leach	0
W 1, nb 2	3 B 15, lb 3	18
1/31 (2) 2/62 (3) 3/62 (4) (49.2 overs)	123 1/10 (1) 2/20 (3) (58 overs)	152
4/67 (1) 5/72 (6) 6/82 (5)	3/32 (4) 4/33 (5)	
7/89 (8) 8/107 (7) 9/114 (9) 10/123 (10)	5/34 (6) 6/49 (2) 7/56 (8)	
	8/61 (9) 9/147 (10) 10/152 (11)	

Gregory 2–0–21–0; Groenewald 11–4–26–2; Leach 18.2–4–48–2; Bess 16–4–28–6; van der Merwe 2–2–0–0. *Second innings*—Groenewald 6–1–17–1; Gregory 5–0–12–1; Leach 25–9–42–6; Bess 11–3–31–2; van der Merwe 11–3–32–0.

Umpires: S. J. O'Shaughnessy and M. J. Saggers.

At Leeds, September 12–14. SOMERSET beat YORKSHIRE by ten wickets.

SOMERSET v NOTTINGHAMSHIRE

At Taunton, September 20–22. Somerset won by 325 runs. Somerset 23pts, Nottinghamshire 3pts. Toss: Somerset.

An extraordinary hundred from Hildreth, and a century in each innings by Rogers, the departing captain, brought an emphatic victory – and so nearly the Championship. Hildreth was on seven on the opening morning when a yorker from Ball hit his right ankle. An X-ray later revealed it was broken but, with the aid of a runner, he hit 135, and put on 269 with Rogers, a third-wicket record in this fixture. Maximum batting points looked a certainty, only for five wickets to fall on 322, as Ball ended the day with six. Bess helped Somerset reach 365 next morning, before picking up five wickets to earn his side a first-innings lead of 227. Rogers declined the follow-on, instead crafting a 76th first-class hundred to extend the advantage to 540. He was only the third player to score twin centuries in his final first-class match, after William Lambert in 1817 and Leonard Baichan in 1982-83. Nottinghamshire, already relegated, put up little resistance, and victory came at 5pm on the third day; it shot Somerset to the top of the table, and encouraged dreams of a first title. "My overriding feeling is one of immense pride in my team," said Rogers. "We were favourites to go down at the start of the season, and look where we are now." But events at Lord's next day, where Middlesex and Yorkshire – both chasing the title themselves – contrived a finish, meant Somerset missed out again.

Close of play: first day, Somerset 322-9 (Bess 0); second day, Somerset 105-2 (Rogers 31, Davies 24).

Somerset

M. E. Trescothick c Read b Ball	25	–	c Mullaney b Carter	39
T. B. Abell c Libby b Ball	8	–	lbw b Hutton	10
*C. J. L. Rogers c Mullaney b Ball	132	–	not out	100
J. C. Hildreth c Read b Hutton	135			
P. D. Trego lbw b Ball	9	–	b Patel	55
L. Gregory b Imran Tahir	2	–	(7) not out	20
R. E. van der Merwe lbw b Imran Tahir	0			
C. Overton c Patel b Ball	0	–	(6) c Imran Tahir b Patel	21
†R. C. Davies c Mullaney b Ball	0	–	(4) st Read b Patel	59
D. M. Bess c Lumb b Patel	41			
M. J. Leach not out	2			
B 1, lb 8, nb 2	11		B 4, lb 1, nb 4	9
1/32 (1) 2/33 (2) 3/302 (3) (110.5 overs)	365		1/30 (2) (5 wkts dec, 57 overs)	313
4/308 (4) 5/322 (6) 6/322 (5)			2/60 (1) 3/173 (4)	
7/322 (8) 8/322 (7) 9/322 (9)			4/251 (5) 5/281 (6)	
10/365 (10) 110 overs: 365-9				

Ball 26–9–57–6; Hutton 20–4–62–1; Imran Tahir 22–5–92–2; Carter 17–2–63–0; Patel 20.5–3–61–1; Mullaney 5–1–21–0. *Second innings*—Ball 14–0–71–0; Hutton 8–1–38–1; Patel 15–1–95–3; Carter 16–1–88–1; Imran Tahir 2–0–11–0; Root 2–0–5–0.

Nottinghamshire

S. J. Mullaney c Abell b Gregory	5	–	c Trego b van der Merwe	18
J. D. Libby c Abell b Bess	42	–	run out	26
T. J. Moores c Gregory b Bess	10	–	run out	4
M. J. Lumb c and b Bess	29	–	lbw b van der Merwe	31
S. R. Patel st Davies b Leach	12	–	lbw b Overton	37
W. T. Root c Abell b Leach	10	–	not out	66
*†C. M. W. Read run out	4	–	lbw b Leach	0
B. A. Hutton c Overton b Bess	2	–	b Leach	0
M. Carter c Overton b Leach	0	–	c Trescothick b van der Merwe	5
J. T. Ball lbw b Bess	2	–	st Davies b Leach	11
Imran Tahir not out	16	–	c Trego b Leach	6
Lb 4, nb 2	6		B 8, lb 1, nb 2	11
1/9 (1) 2/38 (3) 3/91 (2) (64.5 overs)	138		1/48 (1) 2/53 (2) (63.2 overs)	215
4/92 (4) 5/108 (5) 6/117 (7)			3/55 (3) 4/112 (4)	
7/120 (6) 8/120 (9) 9/120 (8) 10/138 (10)			5/138 (5) 6/149 (7) 7/149 (8)	
			8/190 (9) 9/207 (10) 10/215 (11)	

Overton 9–1–24–0; Gregory 6–3–10–1; Bess 22.5–10–43–5; Leach 21–6–42–3; van der Merwe 6–0–15–0. *Second innings*—Overton 10–2–30–1; Gregory 2–1–13–0; Trego 2–1–1–0; Bess 10–3–34–0; Leach 21.2–5–69–4; van der Merwe 18–4–59–3.

Umpires: N. A. Mallender and A. G. Wharf.

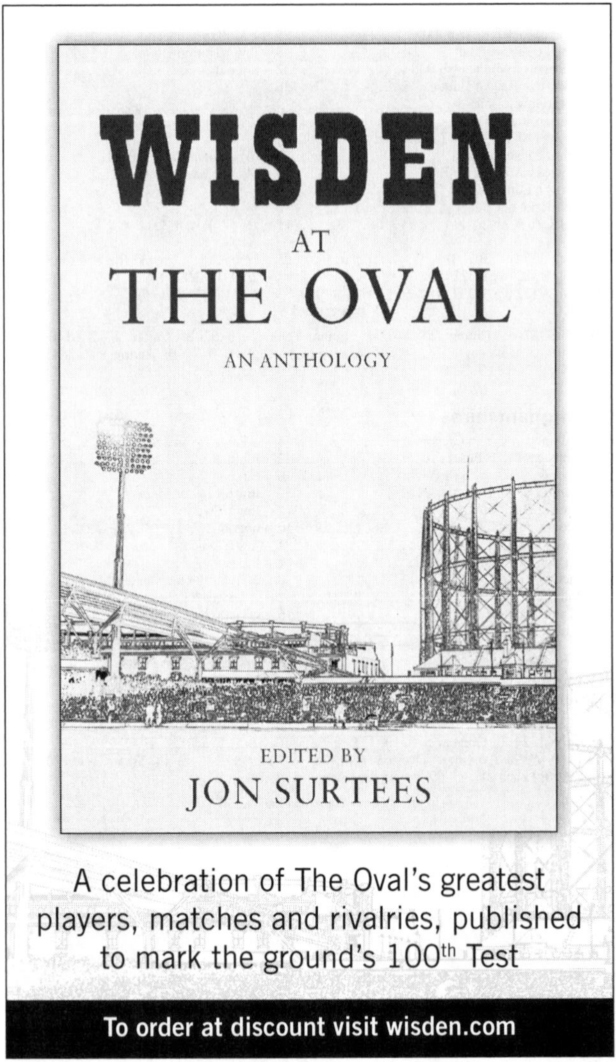
WISDEN
AT
THE OVAL
AN ANTHOLOGY
EDITED BY
JON SURTEES
A celebration of The Oval's greatest players, matches and rivalries, published to mark the ground's 100th Test
To order at discount visit wisden.com

SURREY

Adjusting to altitude

RICHARD SPILLER

Demolition by Warwickshire in the Royal London Cup final ended Surrey's season on a low note, yet they deserved credit for a midsummer revival which had driven them to Lord's for the second year running. That they were able to sit back and watch the struggle for survival in the Championship underlined the strides they had made.

Things looked miserable in early July: fresh from promotion, Surrey had suffered five defeats in nine Championship games, Royal London qualification seemed unlikely, and the Twenty20 Blast had not taken off. The change in fortunes – even if the T20 knockouts proved beyond them – said much for their resilience, and fifth place in the Championship was a solid achievement.

Once again Surrey had to battle an injury crisis among the bowlers, a phenomenon so regular it could be included in the fixture list. Conceding 446 on the opening day at Trent Bridge on the way to defeat confirmed misgivings about the pace attack, which deepened when new signing Mark Footitt missed two months with a side strain. They were already without Jade Dernbach, who had stress fractures of the back, and Stuart Meaker, who paid an eye-watering price for not wearing a box in the nets.

Defeats by Yorkshire and Lancashire – in between some fighting draws – were followed by the last two Somerset wickets adding 64 to snatch victory at Taunton. Instant relegation looked probable. But Surrey beat fellow strugglers Nottinghamshire, and finally came to terms with Division One as they ground out a vital win over Hampshire at the Rose Bowl. The better of a draw at Lord's against Middlesex, then victories over Warwickshire and Lancashire made them confident of staying up with two matches left.

Head coach Michael Di Venuto – who had arrived just before the start of the season after Graham Ford had rejoined Sri Lanka – earned his stripes under early fire, alongside director of cricket Alec Stewart. Shaky batting caused most concern at first. The overseas pair Kumar Sangakkara and Aaron Finch (who deputised while Sangakkara played in the Caribbean T20 competition) led the way. But until Rory Burns hit form, the top order lacked solidity. Arun Harinath, capped in May, and Dominic Sibley had their moments, but Jason Roy's four-day returns were patchy, although he dominated in white-ball games. It made sense when Durham's Mark Stoneman and Scott Borthwick were lured south for 2017.

Steven Davies offered regular middle-order contributions in the Championship and 50-over games, but his desire to reclaim the wicketkeeping gloves was blocked by Ben Foakes, who excelled either side of the stumps. Though often left with the tail, Foakes flourished, especially in the run to the Royal London final. At the end of the season Davies accepted an offer from

John Walton, PA Photos

Rory Burns

Somerset, while Gary Wilson – acting-captain in 2014, and the regular keeper then and the following year – joined Derbyshire. Aneesh Kapil and second-team coach Alistair Brown also departed.

Just as in 2015, Sam Curran's youthful exuberance, zippy left-arm swingers and audacious batting helped transform Surrey's fortunes – once he had finished his A-levels. Footitt recaptured his best form late on, finally giving Surrey a juicy new-ball attack with the speedy Meaker, whose revival after three injury-hit years was one of the most heartening aspects of the season. Tom Curran found wickets more elusive in the first division, but worked hard; Kolpak signing Ravi Rampaul enjoyed early success, but was restricted to five Championship outings. Matt Dunn's persistent hamstring problem ruined his summer, while South African Matt Pillans had four outings at the height of the injury crisis, but failed to pick up a wicket.

Gareth Batty had to take on even greater responsibility given the regular absences through injury of his fellow spinner Zafar Ansari, and made the most of it to earn a Test recall after 11 years. He bowled as well as ever, although his conservative captaincy irked some. Ansari had trouble with his left thumb (a hangover from serious injury late in 2015) and his back, but also earned a winter tour spot, despite never finding his best touch. Injuries to Dernbach and 41-year-old Azhar Mahmood hit the T20 campaign badly, although the batting was patchy too (they failed to reach 120 three times). Overseas all-rounders Dwayne Bravo and Chris Morris added more stardust than substance.

Losing three of the first four Royal London games did not augur well, but Dernbach's return was crucial. A rain-affected run-dash at Lord's stole a spot in the quarter-final, in which Sangakkara's magnificent unbeaten 130 conjured a one-wicket victory at Northampton, before Yorkshire were narrowly overcome at Headingley.

Surrey opposed both the cut in Championship matches and the introduction of a city-based T20 competition. They continued to develop The Oval, the new Peter May Stand adding 1,500 seats to make 26,000 overall, while a £1.5m profit underlined the club's commercial expertise. Surrey contributed ten players to England's various winter selections, putting right a recent shortage – something Stewart had pinpointed when he returned in 2013.

Championship attendance: 43,893.

SURREY RESULTS

All first-class matches – Played 17: Won 4, Lost 6, Drawn 7.
County Championship matches – Played 16: Won 4, Lost 6, Drawn 6.

Specsavers County Championship, 5th in Division 1;
NatWest T20 Blast, 5th in South Group; Royal London One-Day Cup, finalists.

COUNTY CHAMPIONSHIP AVERAGES, BATTING AND FIELDING

Cap		*Birthplace*	*M*	*I*	*NO*	*R*	*HS*	*100*	*Avge*	*Ct/St*
2015	†K. C. Sangakkara¶	*Matale, SL*	12	22	1	1,039	171	1	49.47	10
	A. J. Finch¶	*Colac, Australia*	4	6	0	292	110	1	48.66	2
2016	B. T. Foakes	*Colchester*	15	24	6	759	141*	1	42.16	43/3
2014	†R. J. Burns	*Epsom‡*	16	30	2	1,144	122	2	40.85	15
	†S. M. Curran	*Northampton*	9	14	2	472	96	0	39.33	3
2014	J. J. Roy	*Durban, SA*	11	19	0	745	120	2	39.21	9
2011	†S. M. Davies	*Bromsgrove*	15	26	2	923	117	1	38.45	10
2016	†A. Harinath	*Sutton‡*	11	21	1	707	137	1	35.35	5
	D. P. Sibley	*Epsom‡*	7	13	2	377	99	0	34.27	6
2014	†Z. S. Ansari	*Ascot*	10	17	1	439	53	0	27.43	5
2011	G. J. Batty	*Bradford*	16	25	4	478	110*	1	22.76	4
2016	T. K. Curran	*Cape Town, SA*	15	26	1	427	54	0	17.08	5
	M. W. Pillans††	*Durban, SA*	4	6	1	73	34*	0	14.60	1
2012	S. C. Meaker	*Pietermaritzburg, SA*	11	15	6	126	41	0	14.00	5
	†R. Rampaul††	*Preysal, Trinidad*	5	7	4	33	13*	0	11.00	2
	J. E. Burke	*Plymouth*	3	5	0	38	31	0	7.60	0
2014	G. C. Wilson	*Dundonald, N. Ire.*	2	4	0	27	12	0	6.75	1
	M. H. A. Footitt	*Nottingham*	8	11	3	49	16	0	6.12	3

Also batted: †M. P. Dunn (*Egham‡*) (2 matches) 6*, 5*, 2.

‡ *Born in Surrey.* ¶ *Official overseas player.* †† *Other non-England-qualified.*

BOWLING

	Style	*O*	*M*	*R*	*W*	*BB*	*5I*	*Avge*
R. Rampaul	RFM	128.5	13	510	21	5-85	2	24.28
M. H. A. Footitt	LFM	248.3	44	913	34	7-62	3	26.85
S. M. Curran	LFM	215	49	752	27	7-58	2	27.85
S. C. Meaker	RF	298.5	42	1,145	37	4-40	0	30.94
G. J. Batty	OB	434.1	93	1,280	41	7-32	2	31.21
Z. S. Ansari	SLA	236.4	39	691	22	6-36	1	31.40
T. K. Curran	RFM	445.4	87	1,494	33	4-58	0	45.27

Also bowled: J. E. Burke (RFM) 37.3–4–184–4; R. J. Burns (RM) 3–1–7–0; M. P. Dunn (RFM) 39–5–188–1; A. J. Finch (SLA) 3–1–10–0; A. Harinath (OB) 18.2–1–59–0; M. W. Pillans (RFM) 93–15–332–0; D. P. Sibley (LBG) 36–6–133–2.

LEADING ROYAL LONDON CUP AVERAGES (100 runs/4 wickets)

Batting

	Runs	*HS*	*Avge*	*SR*	*Ct/St*
B. T. Foakes	330	90	47.14	101.53	13/1
K. C. Sangakkara	278	130*	46.33	90.84	5
R. J. Burns	311	70*	44.42	84.97	4
J. J. Roy	387	93*	43.00	102.65	8
S. M. Davies	396	104	39.60	91.45	3
S. M. Curran	178	57	29.66	94.17	3
Z. S. Ansari	129	62	25.80	78.18	1

Bowling

	W	*BB*	*Avge*	*ER*
J. W. Dernbach	15	4-39	13.66	4.57
R. Rampaul	6	4-47	16.66	5.40
G. J. Batty	14	5-41	22.21	4.96
S. C. Meaker	17	3-47	24.29	6.25
T. K. Curran	12	3-26	27.66	5.35
S. M. Curran	5	1-34	54.60	5.21

LEADING NATWEST T20 BLAST AVERAGES (100 runs/18 overs)

Batting	Runs	HS	Avge	SR	Ct
K. C. Sangakkara	227	72	28.37	**165.69**	1
J. J. Roy	495	120*	45.00	**164.45**	8
A. J. Finch	259	79	43.16	**144.69**	3
T. K. Curran	145	32	18.12	**126.08**	5
D. P. Sibley	247	74*	49.40	**119.90**	1
Z. S. Ansari	104	34*	20.80	**115.55**	1
R. J. Burns	105	22	10.50	**109.37**	3
S. M. Curran	134	32	13.40	**100.75**	3

Bowling	W	BB	Avge	ER
Z. S. Ansari	8	2-12	27.37	**7.30**
T. K. Curran	8	3-21	40.62	**7.76**
D. J. Bravo	5	2-3	31.20	**7.86**
S. M. Curran	11	2-23	28.00	**7.89**
J. W. Dernbach	9	3-32	21.33	**8.00**
G. J. Batty	6	2-25	45.00	**8.14**
C. H. Morris	5	2-21	36.00	**8.18**

FIRST-CLASS COUNTY RECORDS

Highest score for	357*	R. Abel v Somerset at The Oval	1899
Highest score against	366	N. H. Fairbrother (Lancashire) at The Oval	1990
Leading run-scorer	43,554	J. B. Hobbs (avge 49.72)	1905–34
Best bowling for	10-43	T. Rushby v Somerset at Taunton	1921
Best bowling against	10-28	W. P. Howell (Australians) at The Oval	1899
Leading wicket-taker	1,775	T. Richardson (avge 17.87)	1892–1904
Highest total for	811	v Somerset at The Oval	1899
Highest total against	863	by Lancashire at The Oval	1990
Lowest total for	14	v Essex at Chelmsford	1983
Lowest total against	16	by MCC at Lord's	1872

LIST A COUNTY RECORDS

Highest score for	268	A. D. Brown v Glamorgan at The Oval	2002
Highest score against	180*	T. M. Moody (Worcestershire) at The Oval	1994
Leading run-scorer	10,358	A. D. Brown (avge 32.16)	1990–2008
Best bowling for	7-30	M. P. Bicknell v Glamorgan at The Oval	1999
Best bowling against	7-15	A. L. Dixon (Kent) at The Oval	1967
Leading wicket-taker	409	M. P. Bicknell (avge 25.21)	1986–2005
Highest total for	496-4	v Gloucestershire at The Oval	2007
Highest total against	429	by Glamorgan at The Oval	2002
Lowest total for	64	v Worcestershire at Worcester	1978
Lowest total against	44	by Glamorgan at The Oval	1999

TWENTY20 COUNTY RECORDS

Highest score for	122*	J. J. Roy v Somerset at The Oval	2015
Highest score against	106*	S. B. Styris (Essex) at Chelmsford	2010
Leading run-scorer	**2,464**	**J. J. Roy (avge 31.18)**	**2008–16**
Best bowling for	6-24	T. J. Murtagh v Middlesex at Lord's	2005
Best bowling against	4-9	D. J. Willey (Northamptonshire) at Birmingham	2013
Leading wicket-taker	**82**	**Azhar Mahmood (avge 23.52)**	**2003–16**
Highest total for	224-5	v Gloucestershire at Bristol	2006
Highest total against	240-3	by Glamorgan at The Oval	2015
Lowest total for	88	v Kent at The Oval	2012
Lowest total against	68	by Sussex at Hove	2007

ADDRESS

The Oval, Kennington, London SE11 5SS; 0844 375 1845; enquiries@surreycricket.com; www.surreycricket.com.

OFFICIALS

Captain G. J. Batty
Director of cricket A. J. Stewart
Head coach M. J. Di Venuto
Assistant head coach S. N. Barnes
Academy director G. T. J. Townsend

President 2016 P. I. Pocock
2017 D. P. Stewart
Chairman R. W. Thompson
Chief executive R. A. Gould
Head groundsman L. E. Fortis
Scorer K. R. Booth

SURREY v LOUGHBOROUGH MCCU

At The Oval, March 31–April 2. Drawn. Toss: Loughborough MCCU. First-class debuts: S. J. Cook, O. J. P. Haley, C. T. Lowen, C. O. Thurston. County debut: M. H. A. Footitt.

When Loughborough slipped to 92 for five in response to 397, Surrey looked set for an emphatic victory – but No. 7 Basil Akram (earlier the biggest danger with the ball) made a stylish maiden century. He put on 183 for the sixth wicket with Charlie Lowen, and ended up with 160. Akram, a 23-year-old from Essex formerly on Hampshire's books, had previously made only 37 first-class runs, but added another hundred in the next game. It all meant the students ended only 38 behind Surrey, for whom Davies had timed the ball sweetly. He repeated the dose on the final day, completing his second century of the match as Surrey enjoyed a fine early-season pitch. Akram was at it again, too, grabbing three more wickets.

Close of play: first day, Loughborough MCCU 45-2 (Hasan Azad 18, Kumar 14); second day, Surrey 31-1 (Burns 12, Davies 2).

Surrey

R. J. Burns lbw b Akram	27	– c Thurston b Cook	77
A. Harinath st Lowen b Kumar	70		
S. M. Davies c Gamble b Akram	115	– c Kumar b Akram	109
G. C. Wilson c White b Kumar	72	– lbw b Akram	65
†B. T. Foakes not out	72	– c Lowen b Gamble	5
S. M. Curran b Akram	12	– (2) lbw b Kumar	15
J. E. Burke (did not bat)		– (6) lbw b Akram	4
T. K. Curran (did not bat)		– (7) lbw b Haley	8
*G. J. Batty (did not bat)		– (8) not out	27
M. P. Dunn (did not bat)		– (9) not out	5
B 8, lb 8, w 1, nb 12	29	B 6, lb 4, w 1, nb 10	21
1/47 (1) 2/178 (2) 3/246 (3) 4/364 (4) 5/397 (6) — (5 wkts dec, 80.2 overs)	397	1/28 (2) 2/159 (1) 3/257 (3) 4/268 (5) 5/273 (6) 6/292 (4) 7/308 (7) — (7 wkts, 71.1 overs)	336

M. H. A. Footitt did not bat.

Gamble 13–2–61–0; Grant 12–3–68–0; Akram 16.2–2–74–3; Cook 14–3–51–0; Kumar 15–0–63–2; Haley 10–0–64–0. *Second innings*—Gamble 14–0–77–1; Grant 14.1–1–64–0; Kumar 13–0–46–1; Hasan Azad 1–0–2–0; Akram 10–1–50–3; Cook 13–2–63–1; Haley 6–1–24–1.

Loughborough MCCU

C. O. Thurston c Burns b T. K. Curran	13
Hasan Azad lbw b Footitt	18
R. G. White c Burke b Footitt	0
N. R. Kumar b Dunn	30
*†M. G. K. Burgess c Wilson b T. K. Curran	26
C. T. Lowen c Foakes b Burke	66
B. M. R. Akram c S. M. Curran b Footitt	160
O. J. P. Haley c Foakes b T. K. Curran	8
R. N. Gamble b Footitt	10
S. E. Grant not out	0
S. J. Cook c and b T. K. Curran	0
Lb 11, w 1, nb 16	28
1/18 (1) 2/19 (3) 3/45 (2) 4/92 (4) 5/92 (5) 6/275 (6) 7/327 (8) 8/352 (9) 9/359 (7) 10/359 (11) — (89.4 overs)	359

T. K. Curran 23.4–6–71–4; Footitt 21–6–78–4; S. M. Curran 11–1–32–0; Dunn 13–0–74–1; Burke 11–2–48–1; Batty 10–0–45–0.

Umpires: R. J. Bailey and T. Lungley.

At Nottingham, April 10–13. SURREY lost to NOTTINGHAMSHIRE by three wickets.

SURREY v SOMERSET

At The Oval, April 24–27. Drawn. Surrey 13pts, Somerset 12pts. Toss: Surrey.

Conditions which would have suited Shackleton – the polar explorer, not the Hampshire seamer – reduced the chances of a result. Sangakkara set the tone with 171, his 56th first-class century, at virtually a run a ball. With Burns and Roy also reaching 80, Surrey seemed set to top 500, only to lose their last six for 69. Trescothick also enjoyed an even-paced pitch, unleashing some assured drives on the way to his 59th hundred, during which he passed Peter Wight (16,965) to become Somerset's second-highest run-scorer, behind Harold Gimblett. Yet they still looked likely to follow on, before Gregory and Overton made forthright contributions. Rampaul became the first Surrey bowler to claim five-fors in both his first two matches since left-armer McIvor Jackson in 1903. A total of 66 overs were lost on the middle two days, the third including a snowstorm which briefly blanketed the outfield. With Footitt absent because of a side strain, Batty left Somerset 292 in just 42 overs – and, as the ball started turning sharply, probably regretted his conservatism.

Close of play: first day, Surrey 394-5 (Ansari 28, Foakes 0); second day, Somerset 99-1 (Trescothick 68, Rogers 6); third day, Somerset 353.

Surrey

R. J. Burns c and b van der Merwe	80	– c Davies b Overton	6
A. Harinath lbw b Overton	9	– c Davies b Gregory	10
K. C. Sangakkara c Overton b Groenewald	171	– c Leach b Overton	71
S. M. Davies c Trego b Groenewald	7	– st Davies b Leach	26
J. J. Roy lbw b Gregory	85	– c Rogers b Leach	19
Z. S. Ansari c Trescothick b Groenewald	53	– lbw b Gregory	14
†B. T. Foakes c Davies b Groenewald	8	– not out	13
T. K. Curran run out	7	– b Overton	6
*G. J. Batty run out	12	– b Gregory	4
R. Rampaul not out	4		
M. H. A. Footitt c van der Merwe b Groenewald	5		
B 9, lb 11, nb 2	22	B 5, lb 4, w 1, nb 2	12
1/26 (2) 2/213 (1) 3/248 (4) 4/313 (3) 5/394 (5) 6/419 (7) 7/429 (8) 8/444 (9) 9/453 (6) 10/463 (11) (109.5 overs)	463	1/18 (2) 2/18 (1) 3/71 (4) 4/109 (5) 5/153 (6) 6/166 (3) 7/176 (8) 8/181 (9) (8 wkts dec, 53.3 overs)	181

Overton 28–5–114–1; Gregory 25–7–69–1; Leach 10–0–41–0; Groenewald 23.5–4–94–5; Trego 9–1–44–0; van der Merwe 13–2–70–1; Abell 1–0–11–0. *Second innings*—Overton 14–1–55–3; Gregory 10.3–1–24–3; Groenewald 9–1–33–0; Leach 13–2–34–2; van der Merwe 7–0–26–0.

Somerset

M. E. Trescothick b Batty	127	– c Roy b Ansari	12
T. B. Abell c Harinath b Footitt	19	– c Burns b Rampaul	0
*C. J. L. Rogers b Rampaul	11	– b Ansari	24
J. C. Hildreth c Foakes b Rampaul	10	– not out	40
R. E. van der Merwe lbw b Ansari	4	– b Ansari	2
P. D. Trego c Foakes b Rampaul	41	– not out	34
†R. C. Davies c Ansari b Rampaul	5		
L. Gregory not out	47		
C. Overton c Ansari b Rampaul	44		
M. J. Leach lbw b Batty	9		
T. D. Groenewald c Foakes b Batty	1		
B 4, lb 12, w 1, nb 18	35	B 8, lb 2	10
1/63 (2) 2/111 (3) 3/133 (4) 4/156 (5) 5/231 (6) 6/233 (1) 7/239 (7) 8/317 (9) 9/345 (10) 10/353 (11) (98.3 overs)	353	1/0 (2) 2/22 (1) 3/54 (3) 4/62 (5) (4 wkts, 35 overs)	122

Curran 22–7–67–0; Footitt 20.4–5–78–1; Rampaul 24–3–85–5; Ansari 17.2–1–56–1; Batty 14.3–0–51–3. *Second innings*—Curran 6–2–22–0; Rampaul 5–1–18–1; Ansari 13–3–43–3; Batty 11–1–29–0.

Umpires: P. K. Baldwin and R. K. Illingworth.

SURREY v DURHAM

At The Oval, May 1–4. Drawn. Surrey 11pts, Durham 12pts. Toss: Surrey. County debut: M. W. Pillans.

Durham gave up hope of a fifth consecutive victory over Surrey only with six overs remaining. It was quite a turnaround: handicapped by losing the toss on a pitch grassy in the middle but shaved at the ends, Durham should have been facing a mammoth total. Harinath, Davies and Roy all sparkled, but spurned centuries, and there were four wickets for Stokes, who bowled unchanged on the second morning. When Durham batted, Borthwick played some attractive shots after a century opening stand, then Jack Burnham weighed in with his maiden first-class hundred. He launched Ansari on to the first floor of the pavilion, then drove crisply to take command against an attack which looked increasingly disheartened, not least when Ansari took a blow on his left thumb. Collingwood ensured a substantial Durham lead with a typically workmanlike century, while Mathew Pillans – a fast bowler who had played 31 first-class games in South Africa – went wicketless on his county debut. Surrey were soon in trouble, as Stokes claimed three wickets in a hostile ten-over spell, but Foakes and Tom Curran used up 28 overs.

Close of play: first day, Surrey 371-7 (Foakes 17, Batty 0); second day, Durham 156-2 (Borthwick 20, Burnham 21); third day, Durham 543-7 (Collingwood 75, Carse 3).

Surrey

R. J. Burns b Stokes	15	– c Richardson b Stokes	28
A. Harinath c Stoneman b Rushworth	96	– lbw b Stokes	18
K. C. Sangakkara b Carse	26	– c Borthwick b Stokes	14
S. M. Davies c Jennings b Rushworth	87	– c Richardson b Pringle	32
J. J. Roy c Carse b Onions	64	– c Borthwick b Carse	34
Z. S. Ansari c Richardson b Stokes	41		
†B. T. Foakes c Richardson b Carse	38	– (6) not out	36
T. K. Curran c Richardson b Carse	0	– (7) c Richardson b Rushworth	54
*G. J. Batty b Stokes	40	– (8) not out	17
M. W. Pillans c Borthwick b Stokes	15		
M. P. Dunn not out	6		
B 4, lb 17, nb 8	29	B 4, lb 4, w 1, nb 2	11
1/39 (1) 2/91 (3) 3/226 (4) (119.4 overs)	457	1/41 (2) (6 wkts, 75 overs)	244
4/233 (2) 5/345 (5) 6/365 (6)		2/58 (1) 3/65 (3)	
7/366 (8) 8/409 (7) 9/430 (10)		4/117 (4) 5/139 (5) 6/222 (7)	
10/457 (9) 110 overs: 422-8			

Rushworth 22–3–82–2; Onions 17–4–52–1; Stokes 33.4–6–117–4; Pringle 12–2–48–0; Carse 23–3–91–3; Borthwick 12–1–46–0. *Second innings*—Rushworth 7–1–24–1; Onions 9–3–29–0; Pringle 8–4–20–1; Stokes 21–3–69–3; Borthwick 27–5–80–0; Carse 3–0–14–1.

Durham

M. D. Stoneman lbw b Batty	57
K. K. Jennings b Ansari	53
S. G. Borthwick lbw b Batty	77
J. T. A. Burnham c Harinath b Curran	135
B. A. Stokes c and b Ansari	12
†M. J. Richardson c Foakes b Dunn	68
*P. D. Collingwood not out	106
R. D. Pringle c and b Curran	37
B. A. Carse not out	30
B 5, lb 13, w 6, nb 8	32
1/114 (2) (7 wkts dec, 153 overs)	607
2/118 (1) 3/263 (3)	
4/282 (5) 5/373 (4)	
6/469 (6) 7/526 (8) 110 overs: 405-5	

C. Rushworth and G. Onions did not bat.

Curran 30–3–105–2; Dunn 22–3–109–1; Pillans 31–3–136–0; Ansari 39.5–7–131–2; Batty 30–5–108–2; Harinath 0.1–0–0–0.

Umpires: S. J. O'Shaughnessy and B. V. Taylor.

At Leeds, May 8–11. SURREY lost to YORKSHIRE by an innings and 20 runs.

SURREY v MIDDLESEX

At The Oval, May 15–18. Drawn. Surrey 9pts, Middlesex 10pts. Toss: Middlesex.

Rain had the last word in the first London derby for three years, washing out the final day of a match Middlesex dominated from the start. Their openers had taken advantage of Surrey's depleted attack, which also lost Rampaul to a hamstring strain on the first afternoon. Gubbins seemed set for a maiden century before falling to a combination of Harinath and Curran, both capped during lunch. When the bowlers finally straightened their lines on a relaid pitch with little pace or bounce, they reaped the benefit: from 238 for two, Middlesex lost seven for 89, before Roland-Jones and Murtagh (both products of Surrey clubs) punished a tiring attack. Tom Curran, once again a willing workhorse, finished with four for 113. Then Rayner, who had claimed 15 wickets in that last meeting in 2013, enjoyed the conditions again, picking up six for 79 against impatient opponents. But Foakes resisted for almost five hours, watched by around 4,500 pupils from more than 100 local schools, and took Surrey to within a boundary of saving the follow-on. Burns and Harinath matched his studious example, and had cut the deficit to 55 before the premature end.

Close of play: first day, Middlesex 298-7 (Franklin 11, Harris 5); second day, Surrey 134-6 (Foakes 22, Curran 0); third day, Surrey 98-0 (Burns 57, Harinath 37).

Middlesex

S. D. Robson st Foakes b Batty	53
N. R. T. Gubbins c Harinath b Curran	91
D. J. Malan c Foakes b Burke	58
*A. C. Voges lbw b Burke	47
†J. A. Simpson lbw b Batty	12
J. E. C. Franklin b Batty	32
P. R. Stirling b Curran	7
O. P. Rayner lbw b Curran	6
J. A. R. Harris b Curran	9
T. S. Roland-Jones not out	44
T. J. Murtagh b Burke	24
B 2, lb 5, w 1, nb 4	12
1/126 (1) 2/166 (2) 3/238 (3) 4/257 (4) 5/270 (5) 6/281 (7) 7/289 (8) 8/323 (9) 9/327 (6) 10/395 (11) (125.3 overs)	395
110 overs: 328-9	

Curran 35–7–113–4; Rampaul 10.5–2–47–0; Pillans 26–6–61–0; Batty 35–7–96–3; Burke 15.3–1–65–3; Harinath 3.1–0–6–0.

Surrey

R. J. Burns c Malan b Rayner	19	– not out	57
A. Harinath lbw b Rayner	20	– not out	37
K. C. Sangakkara c Murtagh b Rayner	14		
S. M. Davies c Stirling b Murtagh	10		
J. J. Roy c Robson b Malan	47		
†B. T. Foakes not out	59		
J. E. Burke lbw b Roland-Jones	1		
T. K. Curran c Simpson b Harris	8		
*G. J. Batty lbw b Rayner	38		
M. W. Pillans c Harris b Rayner	20		
R. Rampaul lbw b Rayner	0		
Lb 6	6	B 4	4
1/40 (1) 2/41 (2) 3/62 (3) 4/69 (4) 5/129 (5) 6/130 (7) 7/151 (8) 8/213 (9) 9/237 (10) 10/242 (11) (114.3 overs)	242	(no wkt, 45 overs)	98
110 overs: 226-8			

Murtagh 22–3–42–1; Roland-Jones 21–8–33–1; Harris 22–7–56–1; Rayner 36.3–7–79–6; Franklin 7–2–13–0; Malan 3–1–5–1; Stirling 1–1–0–0; Voges 2–0–8–0. *Second innings*—Murtagh 5–1–13–0; Roland-Jones 9–2–22–0; Rayner 11–4–12–0; Franklin 6–0–14–0; Harris 7–2–21–0; Voges 2–0–4–0; Malan 3–2–5–0; Stirling 2–1–3–0.

Umpires: P. K. Baldwin and N. J. Llong.

At Manchester, May 22–24. SURREY lost to LANCASHIRE by an innings and 96 runs.

At Taunton, May 28–30. SURREY lost to SOMERSET by one wicket.

SURREY v NOTTINGHAMSHIRE

At The Oval, June 19–22. Surrey won by 228 runs. Surrey 22pts, Nottinghamshire 3pts. Toss: Surrey.

The groundwork for Surrey's first win since returning to Division One – which lifted them off the bottom of the table – was laid on the first day, when they grafted to 299 for eight on a pitch designed to turn later; they reached 323 next morning. Such riches had looked unlikely at 172 for six, before an unusually subdued Davies put on 112 in 33 overs with Tom Curran. Ball's control and bounce caused problems, but his efforts were squandered by Nottinghamshire's batsmen on the third day, after most of the second had been rained off. Patel was run out after a mix-up, then the anchorman Lumb deceived by Batty – a flatter, quicker ball going straight on after the previous one had turned. Batty cleaned up to give Surrey a lead of 141, before Harinath shared useful stands with Burns and Sangakkara. A more typical Davies knock – 45 from 29 balls – swelled the advantage to 385. Batty declared overnight, and Nottinghamshire were soon in trouble again. Libby and Taylor put on 90, but four wickets tumbled for five runs as the spinners got to work. Ansari, on the way to his only five-for of the season, had Taylor stumped for 68, and in all the last eight wickets used up only 74 deliveries.

Close of play: first day, Surrey 299-8 (Batty 11, Meaker 4); second day, Nottinghamshire 82-2 (Lumb 23, Taylor 13); third day, Surrey 244-5 (Davies 45).

Surrey

R. J. Burns c Wessels b Ball	4	– c Patel b Ball	34
A. Harinath c Wessels b Patel	73	– c Patel b Hutton	83
K. C. Sangakkara b Mullaney	29	– c Carter b Hutton	49
G. C. Wilson c Gurney b Carter	2	– c Carter b Hutton	2
S. M. Davies b Hutton	82	– not out	45
Z. S. Ansari lbw b Gurney	0		
†B. T. Foakes c Wessels b Ball	22		
T. K. Curran b Ball	52	– (6) c Libby b Patel	21
*G. J. Batty c Wessels b Ball	28		
S. C. Meaker c and b Patel	6		
R. Rampaul not out	0		
B 5, lb 19, w 1	25	B 2, lb 6, nb 2	10
1/18 (1) 2/91 (3) 3/98 (4) 4/137 (2) 5/138 (6) 6/172 (7) 7/284 (8) 8/284 (5) 9/321 (9) 10/323 (10) (102.1 overs)	323	1/59 (1) 2/151 (3) 3/159 (4) 4/194 (2) 5/244 (6) (5 wkts dec, 62.2 overs)	244

Ball 26–2–85–4; Gurney 20–3–61–1; Hutton 16–3–52–1; Carter 16–2–56–1; Mullaney 4–3–1–1; Patel 20.1–5–44–2. *Second innings*—Ball 9–3–18–1; Gurney 7–1–14–0; Patel 13.2–2–59–1; Carter 16–2–63–0; Mullaney 4–0–21–0; Hutton 13–3–61–3.

Nottinghamshire

*S. J. Mullaney b Ansari	34	– b Rampaul	5
J. D. Libby lbw b Rampaul	10	– c Rampaul b Ansari	33
M. J. Lumb b Batty	48	– c Wilson b Batty	11
B. R. M. Taylor lbw b Rampaul	21	– st Foakes b Ansari	68
†M. H. Wessels c Foakes b Curran	5	– c Foakes b Ansari	0
S. R. Patel run out	12	– c Burns b Ansari	2
D. T. Christian not out	19	– c Foakes b Meaker	11
B. A. Hutton c Harinath b Batty	8	– c Curran b Meaker	8
M. Carter c Rampaul b Batty	8	– not out	5
J. T. Ball b Meaker	8	– lbw b Ansari	1
H. F. Gurney c Meaker b Batty	0	– c Batty b Ansari	0
B 6, lb 3	9	Lb 4, w 5, nb 4	13
1/28 (2) 2/50 (1) 3/95 (4) 4/120 (5) 5/132 (6) 6/135 (3) 7/159 (8) 8/173 (9) 9/181 (10) 10/182 (11) (59.4 overs)	182	1/13 (1) 2/29 (3) 3/119 (2) 4/119 (5) 5/123 (6) 6/124 (4) 7/140 (7) 8/151 (8) 9/157 (10) 10/157 (11) (48.3 overs)	157

Curran 14–4–53–1; Rampaul 12–3–26–2; Ansari 14–1–43–1; Meaker 8–1–28–1; Batty 11.4–3–23–4. *Second innings*—Curran 9–1–28–0; Rampaul 13–3–31–1; Batty 7–3–23–1; Meaker 8–1–35–2; Ansari 11.3–3–36–6.

Umpires: N. L. Bainton and N. G. B. Cook.

SURREY v WARWICKSHIRE

At Guildford, July 2–4. Warwickshire won by ten wickets. Warwickshire 23pts, Surrey 4pts. Toss: Surrey. County debut: A. J. Finch.

Warwickshire completed their third win in five Championship matches at Woodbridge Road, with more than a day to spare. The pitch had been left bare at either end to encourage Surrey's slow men, but it was the visiting off-spinner Patel who took best advantage, with five wickets in each innings. Austalia's Aaron Finch had marked his Surrey debut with a first-ball six and a 90-ball hundred on the first afternoon, but received little help from his new team-mates. They were given a lesson in application by Trott, who tucked the ball into gaps, and enjoyed the short square boundaries. He shared century stands with Bell and Ambrose, and later Barker clouted 11 fours as the advantage grew to 176, though Footitt and Sam Curran persevered to share seven wickets. The lead proved almost enough. Burns, in his second adhesive innings of the match, put on 102 with Ansari, but after that only Davies made it into double figures as the seamers gave Patel good support. Finch's first match for Surrey proved expensive. One of his sixes shattered tiles on the roof of the cafe in nearby Dapdune Wharf: a fortnight later, the National Trust presented Guildford CC with a bill for £250.

Close of play: first day, Warwickshire 12-0 (Chopra 7, Umeed 3); second day, Warwickshire 345-6 (Clarke 16, Barker 10).

Surrey

R. J. Burns lbw b Patel	45	– b Patel	68
A. Harinath c Ambrose b Barker	15	– c Ambrose b Barker	0
Z. S. Ansari lbw b Barker	11	– c Hain b Patel	40
A. J. Finch c Clarke b Patel	110	– c Ambrose b Clarke	7
S. M. Davies c Ambrose b Clarke	13	– c Umeed b Rankin	44
S. M. Curran c Clarke b Rankin	15	– c Ambrose b Clarke	0
†B. T. Foakes run out	23	– lbw b Patel	1
T. K. Curran b Patel	1	– c Clarke b Patel	9
*G. J. Batty c Chopra b Patel	4	– c Ambrose b Rankin	4
S. C. Meaker not out	3	– b Patel	0
M. H. A. Footitt st Ambrose b Patel	16	– not out	0
B 3, lb 12, nb 2	17	Lb 2, nb 2	4
1/35 (2) 2/79 (1) 3/95 (3) 4/144 (5) 5/180 (6) 6/243 (4) 7/245 (8) 8/251 (9) 9/252 (7) 10/273 (11) (74 overs)	273	1/5 (2) 2/107 (1) 3/112 (3) 4/122 (4) 5/122 (6) 6/123 (7) 7/149 (8) 8/170 (9) 9/177 (10) 10/177 (5) (72.2 overs)	177

Barker 18–5–56–2; Clarke 16–3–55–1; Patel 17–2–62–5; Rankin 17–2–58–1; Trott 2–0–5–0; Poysden 4–0–22–0. *Second innings*—Barker 13–6–20–1; Clarke 17–4–46–2; Patel 29–8–61–5; Rankin 10.2–2–32–2; Poysden 3–0–16–0.

Warwickshire

V. Chopra c Foakes b Footitt	42	– not out	1
A. R. I. Umeed b Meaker	18	– not out	4
*I. R. Bell c S. M. Curran b Batty	66		
I. J. L. Trott lbw b S. M. Curran	123		
S. R. Hain c Burns b Meaker	0		
†T. R. Ambrose c Ansari b S. M. Curran	53		
R. Clarke c Foakes b S. M. Curran	17		
K. H. D. Barker c Harinath b Footitt	65		
J. S. Patel c Burns b Footitt	31		
J. E. Poysden not out	7		
W. B. Rankin c Batty b Footitt	3		
B 4, lb 8, w 2, nb 10	24		
1/39 (2) 2/82 (1) 3/198 (3) 4/204 (5) 5/315 (4) 6/322 (6) 7/359 (7) 8/435 (9) 9/440 (8) 10/449 (11) — (118.5 overs)	449	(no wkt, 0.5 overs)	5
110 overs: 396-7			

T. K. Curran 30–9–92–0; Footitt 19.5–4–57–4; Meaker 20–1–86–2; S. M. Curran 16–3–58–3; Ansari 12–1–43–0; Batty 20–0–92–1; Finch 1–0–9–0. *Second innings*—T. K. Curran 0.5–0–5–0.

Umpires: I. J. Gould and N. J. Llong.

SURREY v YORKSHIRE

At The Oval, July 11–14. Drawn. Surrey 10pts, Yorkshire 13pts. Toss: Surrey.

The loss of more than 140 overs on the first two days made this a battle for bonus points, although Surrey – low on confidence and nursing several injuries – were grateful Yorkshire batted as long as they did, leaving them less than two sessions to survive. Finch alone had found much freedom when Surrey embarked on an innings that, thanks to the rain, stretched until lunch on the third day. Lyth then tucked in for his fourth double-century: he batted for 395 minutes and faced 291 balls, but broke loose occasionally to smite five sixes, and 17 fours. Taking advantage of Batty's reluctance to post a third man, he put on 150 with Gale and 91 with Patterson, the nightwatchman. The cast changed confusingly: Ansari went off with a back strain, Davies deputised for the unwell Foakes behind the stumps, and when umpire Neil Bainton was taken ill on the final afternoon he was replaced at square leg by the former Surrey bowler Tony Pigott, now ECB pitch liaison officer.

Close of play: first day, Surrey 95-2 (Ansari 35, Finch 34); second day, Surrey 164-5 (Davies 29, Foakes 14); third day, Yorkshire 207-3 (Lyth 116, Patterson 5).

Surrey

R. J. Burns lbw b Willey	8	– c and b Azeem Rafiq	14
D. P. Sibley c Hodd b Patterson	17	– not out	54
Z. S. Ansari b Willey	40	– not out	24
A. J. Finch c Leaning b Patterson	52		
J. J. Roy c Hodd b Willey	0		
S. M. Davies lbw b Bresnan	56		
†B. T. Foakes c Lyth b Patterson	14		
S. M. Curran not out	59		
T. K. Curran lbw b Rashid	6		
*G. J. Batty lbw b Rashid	0		
S. C. Meaker c Lyth b Azeem Rafiq	4		
B 2, lb 7, nb 2	11	B 8, nb 6	14
1/13 (1) 2/36 (2) 3/121 (3) 4/121 (4) 5/121 (5) 6/164 (7) 7/239 (6) 8/254 (9) 9/254 (10) 10/267 (11) — (82.3 overs)	267	1/20 (1) — (1 wkt, 38 overs)	106

Bresnan 10–4–22–1; Willey 18–3–59–3; Plunkett 9–2–26–0; Patterson 18–5–58–3; Rashid 14–2–47–2; Azeem Rafiq 13.3–2–46–1. *Second innings*—Bresnan 2–0–10–0; Willey 3–1–6–0; Rashid 13–1–37–0; Lyth 3–1–11–0; Azeem Rafiq 11–5–12–1; Plunkett 1–0–1–0; Leaning 4–1–7–0; Hodd 1–0–14–0.

Yorkshire

A. Lyth c Davies b Meaker	202	†A. J. Hodd c Burns b T. K. Curran	5
A. Z. Lees b S. M. Curran	15	Azeem Rafiq not out	0
J. A. Leaning b Meaker	0		
*A. W. Gale c Davies b T. K. Curran	61	B 6, lb 3, w 6	15
S. A. Patterson b Ansari	51		—
A. U. Rashid c Finch b Ansari	16	1/28 (2) 2/47 (3) (106.2 overs)	407
T. T. Bresnan lbw b Batty	3	3/197 (4) 4/288 (5)	
L. E. Plunkett run out	37	5/324 (6) 6/330 (7) 7/388 (8)	
D. J. Willey c S. M. Curran b Meaker	2	8/400 (1) 9/406 (10) 10/407 (9)	

T. K. Curran 19–2–73–2; S. M. Curran 11–2–58–1; Meaker 11.2–1–66–3; Ansari 34–8–98–2; Batty 31–4–103–1.

Umpires: N. L. Bainton and M. J. Saggers.

At Southampton, July 17–20. SURREY beat HAMPSHIRE by an innings and 13 runs. *Ben Foakes and Gareth Batty put on 222* for the eighth wicket, a county record.*

At Lord's, August 4–7. SURREY drew with MIDDLESEX.

At Birmingham, August 13–16. SURREY beat WARWICKSHIRE by 226 runs.

SURREY v LANCASHIRE

At The Oval, August 23–26. Surrey won by ten wickets. Surrey 23pts, Lancashire 4pts. Toss: Lancashire. First-class debut: R. P. Jones.

Lancashire's victory at Old Trafford in May had sent them top, and Surrey bottom, but a fine all-round performance from the hosts emphasised how things had changed: Surrey's victory kept them third. A juicy pitch encouraged their seamers, and Lancashire's batsmen looked uncomfortable almost throughout. They were disconcerted by late movement from Sam Curran and Meaker's pace on the first day, yet threatened 300 thanks to a vigorous counter-attack from Clark. He hit ten fours in his 56, and put on a last-wicket partnership of 48 with Buck. Burns and Sibley replied with an opening stand of 160 before Lilley's off-spin pegged Surrey back. But they zoomed ahead thanks to 96 from Sam Curran, who missed a maiden century when he top-edged a return catch to Lilley two balls after carting him for a third six. Trailing by 193, Lancashire made it as far as 167 for two, only for Footitt to claim three for three in 28 balls en route to a career-best seven for 62. Surrey knocked off their target of 38 on the final morning, as Burns reached 1,000 Championship runs for the season with the winning boundary.

Close of play: first day, Surrey 50-0 (Burns 33, Sibley 10); second day, Surrey 354-6 (S. M. Curran 28, T. K. Curran 0); third day, Lancashire 203-8 (Jarvis 7, Buck 5).

Lancashire

L. A. Procter lbw b S. M. Curran	5	– lbw b Footitt	76
H. Hameed c Foakes b Meaker	26	– c Foakes b Footitt	17
L. S. Livingstone c Foakes b T. K. Curran	37	– c Davies b Meaker	13
A. N. Petersen b S. M. Curran	17	– c Sibley b Footitt	56
*†S. J. Croft c Foakes b S. M. Curran	12	– c Sangakkara b Footitt	0
R. P. Jones b S. M. Curran	25	– lbw b Batty	10
J. Clark c Sangakkara b Meaker	56	– b Batty	1
A. M. Lilley c Foakes b Meaker	38	– c Burns b Footitt	3
K. M. Jarvis c Footitt b T. K. Curran	6	– c Meaker b Footitt	14
N. L. Buck not out	24	– c Burns b Footitt	11
S. C. Kerrigan c Foakes b Footitt	25	– not out	12
B 5, lb 3, w 4, nb 4	16	B 2, lb 5, nb 10	17
1/15 (1) 2/51 (2) 3/81 (4) 4/99 (3) 5/99 (5) 6/184 (7) 7/198 (6) 8/231 (9) 9/239 (8) 10/287 (11) (79 overs)	287	1/49 (2) 2/89 (3) 3/167 (4) 4/167 (5) 5/178 (1) 6/188 (6) 7/189 (7) 8/193 (8) 9/211 (10) 10/230 (9) (72.4 overs)	230

T. K. Curran 19–3–51–2; S. M. Curran 17–4–61–4; Meaker 20–3–83–3; Footitt 16–1–56–1; Batty 7–0–28–0. *Second innings*—T. K. Curran 11–1–37–0; S. M. Curran 5–2–11–0; Footitt 20.4–4–62–7; Meaker 9–0–46–1; Batty 27–5–67–2.

Surrey

R. J. Burns c Croft b Jarvis	88	– not out	28
D. P. Sibley b Jarvis	56	– not out	11
K. C. Sangakkara c Hameed b Buck	67		
A. Harinath lbw b Lilley	21		
S. M. Davies c Kerrigan b Lilley	59		
†B. T. Foakes lbw b Procter	14		
S. M. Curran c and b Lilley	96		
T. K. Curran c Jones b Lilley	25		
*G. J. Batty lbw b Kerrigan	16		
S. C. Meaker not out	8		
M. H. A. Footitt b Lilley	9		
B 9, lb 5, w 1, nb 6	21		
1/160 (2) 2/163 (1) 3/208 (4) 4/285 (3) 5/317 (6) 6/348 (5) 7/418 (8) 8/453 (7) 9/463 (9) 10/480 (11) (143.3 overs) 110 overs: 350-6	480	(no wkt, 9.1 overs)	39

Jarvis 25–7–90–2; Buck 24–5–76–1; Clark 15–2–58–0; Lilley 36.3–7–130–5; Kerrigan 30–7–76–1; Procter 10–1–30–1; Livingstone 2–1–5–0; Hameed 1–0–1–0. *Second innings*—Lilley 4–0–20–0; Kerrigan 4.1–0–14–0; Livingstone 1–0–5–0.

Umpires: S. J. O'Shaughnessy and M. J. Saggers.

SURREY v HAMPSHIRE

At The Oval, September 6–9. Drawn. Surrey 9pts, Hampshire 12pts. Toss: uncontested.

Surrey batted through the fourth day to ensure their first division status, while Hampshire's failure to press home their advantage left them stuck in the relegation zone. Sangakkara survived almost four hours, countering a marathon spell from slow left-armer Dawson, who made the occasional ball misbehave from the Vauxhall End. Surrey had also lasted through a murky first day – the lights were on throughout, and 16 overs lopped off at the end – with Burns making a typically neat and determined century, while the others had problems against the pacy Wheal. The sun shone when Hampshire batted: 20-year-old Tom Alsop made the most of some narrow escapes

– and erratic early bowling – to post a maiden century, then Ervine and McLaren put on 186 for the sixth wicket, a county record in this fixture. Berg smashed 42 from 27 balls as Hampshire romped to a lead of 253, but they never threatened to bowl Surrey out a second time.

Close of play: first day, Surrey 260-6 (Foakes 47, T. K. Curran 3); second day, Hampshire 213-3 (Alsop 117, Ervine 30); third day, Surrey 23-0 (Burns 11, Sibley 12).

Surrey

R. J. Burns c Alsop b Wheal	101	– c Alsop b Dawson	18
D. P. Sibley c McManus b Berg	11	– c McManus b Wheal	44
K. C. Sangakkara c McManus b Andrew	26	– not out	84
A. Harinath c Wheal b McLaren	9	– c McManus b Ervine	57
S. M. Davies c Smith b Wheal	32	– not out	29
†B. T. Foakes b McLaren	48		
S. M. Curran c Alsop b Dawson	17		
T. K. Curran c McManus b Wheal	17		
*G. J. Batty not out	41		
S. C. Meaker c Alsop b Wheal	8		
M. H. A. Footitt c McLaren b Dawson	0		
B 2, lb 11, nb 6	19	B 5, lb 7, nb 4	16
1/23 (2) 2/69 (3) 3/96 (4) (103.5 overs)	329	1/49 (1) (3 wkts, 82.4 overs)	248
4/144 (5) 5/220 (1) 6/255 (7)		2/91 (2) 3/191 (4)	
7/266 (6) 8/302 (8) 9/326 (10) 10/329 (11)			

Berg 22–6–52–1; McLaren 21–8–49–2; Wheal 22–2–100–4; Andrew 17–3–63–1; Dawson 16.5–3–36–2; Smith 1–0–3–0; Ervine 4–1–13–0. *Second innings*—Berg 5–3–4–0; McLaren 9–3–23–0; Wheal 13–3–45–1; Dawson 36–8–95–1; Smith 8.4–0–29–0; Andrew 9–3–29–0; Ervine 2–0–11–1.

Hampshire

W. R. Smith c Foakes b Footitt	49
J. H. K. Adams c Foakes b T. K. Curran	8
T. P. Alsop c Foakes b Footitt	117
*J. M. Vince c Foakes b Footitt	4
S. M. Ervine not out	158
L. A. Dawson c sub (J. W. Dernbach) b Footitt	8
R. McLaren c Meaker b Footitt	100
†L. D. McManus c Foakes b Batty	39
G. K. Berg c Batty b Footitt	42
G. M. Andrew b Meaker	25
B. T. J. Wheal not out	10
B 3, lb 10, w 3, nb 6	22
1/23 (2) (9 wkts dec, 154.5 overs)	582
2/115 (1) 3/125 (4)	
4/213 (3) 5/229 (6) 6/415 (7) 7/480 (8)	
8/528 (9) 9/572 (10) 110 overs: 369-5	

T. K. Curran 33–10–97–1; S. M. Curran 23–6–88–0; Footitt 34–4–161–6; Meaker 29.5–6–105–1; Batty 35–7–118–1.

Umpires: P. J. Hartley and A. G. Wharf.

At Chester-le-Street, September 12–15. SURREY lost to DURHAM by 21 runs.

SUSSEX

All eyes on Andrew's conversion

BRUCE TALBOT

The emergence of three young fast bowlers with huge potential offered supporters some solace, even if there was no escaping the fact that 2016 was a year of anticlimax and underachievement.

Sussex had been expected to mount a strong challenge for a prompt return to the first division, but by mid-August they had won only once. Three victories in the last six games lifted them to fourth, though in one-day cricket – an avowed target for new coach Mark Davis and captain Luke Wright – they never gained momentum. For the third time in four years, they failed to reach the knockout stages of the Twenty20 competition, while their wretched form in the Royal London Cup continued: not since August 2014 have they won a 50-over match; last season's sole victory came in a shortened game.

It was a tough first season for Davis. The days of Sussex having the financial clout to compete for top players were long gone. However, there was evidence that the county's emphasis on developing their own players was bearing fruit. George Garton and Stuart Whittingham, both Academy products, and Barbados-born Jofra Archer, who started the year playing for Horsham in the Sussex League, were given a run – and took 51 wickets in their combined 16 Championship appearances. At the start of the season, Wright reckoned Garton and Whittingham were two or three years away from a regular first-team place, but they were thrown in the deep end – and proved natural swimmers.

Archer took five wickets on debut, against the Pakistanis, while 19-year-old left-armer Garton struck with his first first-class delivery – and went on to play for the Lions. Archer had raw pace and, fitness permitting, he should have a bright future; Chris Jordan was happy to play a mentoring role to his fellow Bajan. Meanwhile, Abidine Sakande, another exciting fast bowler from the Academy, signed a two-year contract. The youngsters should lessen Sussex's reliance on Steve Magoffin, who took 62 Championship wickets; Archer and Danny Briggs, next on the list, took 23.

The strides taken by the young seamers reflected well on bowling coach Jon Lewis. If only Sussex could have employed a full-time batting equivalent! Murray Goodwin had gained the respect of the players, but in early June he left because of business commitments, and was not replaced.

Tom Haines, a 17-year-old batsman who had been in the Sussex system since he was ten, showed promise, but others spurned their chances, including Craig Cachopa, who was released. It meant the club depended heavily on their experienced campaigners. Chris Nash benefited from some winter coaching by Gary Kirsten to compile 1,256 Championship runs; the 38-year-old Ed Joyce also passed 1,000, despite missing four games. In December, he was awarded

Ben Brown

a Category A contract by Cricket Ireland, which meant he could continue with Sussex when international committments allowed.

At times, Luke Wells and Ben Brown batted well, and Brown made a good job of combining three roles: leading the side (in Wright's absence), keeping wicket and batting in the middle order. He passed 50 seven times, often digging Sussex out of trouble.

Back and wrist injuries limited Wright to six Championship appearances, and his runs were missed. When fit, he led the side enthusiastically, but was acutely aware that Sussex needed to strengthen the batting. In November, recent South Africa Test player Stiaan van Zyl – a batsman who can bowl – signed a three-year Kolpak deal; the following month, Laurie Evans joined from Warwickshire, also on a three-year contract.

Sussex's Twenty20 campaign began with two wins. The second, over Somerset, included the highlight of the summer: Tymal Mills hurling 90mph thunderbolts down the Hove slope and making Chris Gayle look a novice. Nash hit his maiden 20-over hundred in the same game, but Sussex won only three more – and criminally lost to Hampshire when, with Ross Taylor established, they failed to make five off the last over. Despite that, Taylor and the South African David Wiese proved good overseas signings; Wiese will play as a Kolpak in 2017. Bangladesh left-armer Mustafizur Rahman, scheduled to arrive in May, did not make his debut until July 21, when he produced a match-winning performance at Chelmsford; Sussex's patience appeared to have paid off. But a shoulder injury ruled him out after his second game – one reason the Royal London Cup never got going. Garton bowled threateningly, and batsman Harry Finch looked good before his season was ended by a broken thumb, though Sussex had seen enough to extend his contract. Wells, Whittingham and Phil Salt agreed new deals, and Nash was awarded a testimonial for 2017.

In September, Zac Toumazi announced he was stepping down after four years as a highly regarded chief executive. Two months later, his replacement made headlines: former England rugby fly-half Rob Andrew – who had resigned as the RFU's director of professional rugby in April 2016 – would start in January. He hit a first-class hundred for Cambridge University against Nottinghamshire in 1984, but the move raised eyebrows. It remains to be seen whether Davis and Wright, who enjoy a good relationship, can build a partnership with Andrew.

Championship attendance: 27,301.

SUSSEX RESULTS

All first-class matches – Played 18: Won 4, Lost 2, Drawn 12.
County Championship matches – Played 16: Won 4, Lost 2, Drawn 10.

Specsavers County Championship, 4th in Division 2;
NatWest T20 Blast, 6th in South Group; Royal London One-Day Cup, 9th in South Group.

COUNTY CHAMPIONSHIP AVERAGES, BATTING AND FIELDING

Cap		*Birthplace*	*M*	*I*	*NO*	*R*	*HS*	*100*	*Avge*	*Ct*
2014	C. J. Jordan§	*Lowlands, Barbados*	5	7	2	323	131	1	64.60	6
2009	†E. C. Joyce	*Dublin, Ireland*	12	17	1	1,026	250	3	64.12	3
2008	C. D. Nash	*Cuckfield‡*	15	24	1	1,256	144	3	54.60	20
2014	B. C. Brown	*Crawley‡*	16	22	5	854	159*	3	50.23	40
	L. R. P. L. Taylor¶	*Lower Hutt, NZ*	8	11	1	478	142*	1	47.80	6
2016	†L. W. P. Wells	*Eastbourne‡*	15	21	1	859	181	4	42.95	6
	O. E. Robinson	*Margate*	11	14	4	389	81	0	38.90	4
	†M. W. Machan	*Brighton‡*	7	9	0	249	66	0	27.66	6
2007	L. J. Wright	*Grantham*	6	8	0	213	60	0	26.62	0
	H. Z. Finch	*Hastings‡*	7	9	2	175	66	0	25.00	5
	J. C. Archer††	*Bridgetown, Barb.*	6	8	0	195	73	0	24.37	4
	D. Wiese¶	*Roodepoort, SA*	6	9	2	153	70*	0	21.85	7
	D. R. Briggs	*Newport, IoW*	11	13	3	197	49	0	19.70	5
	A. Shahzad	*Huddersfield*	7	8	1	109	26	0	15.57	1
	P. D. Salt	*Bodelwyddan*	3	4	0	61	42	0	15.25	0
	Craig Cachopa††	*Welkom, SA*	3	5	0	68	34	0	13.60	3
	†G. H. S. Garton	*Brighton‡*	4	5	2	36	18*	0	12.00	1
	F. J. Hudson-Prentice	*Haywards Heath‡*	4	6	0	69	20	0	11.50	0
2013	†S. J. Magoffin††	*Corinda, Australia*	16	16	4	122	23*	0	10.16	4
	S. G. Whittingham	*Derby*	6	4	2	20	8*	0	10.00	1

Also batted: W. A. T. Beer (*Crawley‡*) (2 matches) 12*, 5 (2 ct); C. A. L. Davis (*Milton Keynes*) (2 matches) 0, 2, 12 (2 ct); †T. J. Haines (*Crawley‡*) (2 matches) 0, 11, 1 (1 ct); †L. J. Hatchett (*Shoreham-by-Sea‡*) (2 matches) 3, 17 (1 ct).

‡ *Born in Sussex.* § *ECB contract.* ¶ *Official overseas player.* †† *Other non-England-qualified.*

BOWLING

	Style	*O*	*M*	*R*	*W*	*BB*	*5I*	*Avge*
S. J. Magoffin	RFM	523.1	144	1,249	62	5-32	5	20.14
D. Wiese	RFM	152.2	34	456	19	4-18	0	24.00
J. C. Archer	RFM	212.1	45	705	23	4-31	0	30.65
S. G. Whittingham	RFM	153.4	18	576	18	4-58	0	32.00
G. H. S. Garton	LFM	88.1	9	352	10	3-93	0	35.20
C. J. Jordan	RFM	201	38	678	17	4-36	0	39.88
A. Shahzad	RFM	184.5	25	673	16	3-34	0	42.06
D. R. Briggs	SLA	345.5	64	1,061	23	5-93	2	46.13
O. E. Robinson	RM/OB	267.3	46	910	19	4-110	0	47.89

Also bowled: W. A. T. Beer (LBG) 48.3–5–164–1; B. C. Brown (RM) 3–0–48–1; H. Z. Finch (RFM) 11–1–44–1; T. J. Haines (RM) 4–1–8–0; L. J. Hatchett (LFM) 41–6–182–6; M. W. Machan (OB) 1–0–3–0; C. D. Nash (OB) 6–0–24–0; L. W. P. Wells (LBG) 153–13–558–9.

LEADING NATWEST T20 BLAST AVERAGES (100 runs/15 overs)

Batting	*Runs*	*HS*	*Avge*	*SR*	*Ct*
M. W. Machan	247	41*	30.87	**149.69**	12
C. J. Jordan	110	45*	27.50	**135.80**	5
C. D. Nash	308	112*	28.00	**133.91**	3
L. R. P. L. Taylor	394	93*	56.28	**133.10**	6
L. J. Wright	285	83	28.50	**131.94**	6
P. D. Salt	151	33	18.87	**123.77**	3

Bowling	*W*	*BB*	*Avge*	*ER*
C. J. Jordan	12	3-18	18.33	**7.25**
W. A. T. Beer	9	2-23	30.11	**7.63**
T. S. Mills	15	3-15	19.73	**7.65**
A. Shahzad	11	3-26	18.45	**8.12**
J. C. Archer	5	2-39	27.80	**9.26**
D. R. Briggs	7	3-24	34.57	**9.68**

LEADING ROYAL LONDON CUP AVERAGES (100 runs/4 wickets)

Batting	Runs	HS	Avge	SR	Ct/St
H. Z. Finch	236	87*	39.33	66.29	2
L. R. P. L. Taylor	113	54	37.66	94.95	0
B. C. Brown	207	62	34.50	82.80	9/1
E. C. Joyce	187	73	31.16	72.76	3
L. J. Wright	249	65	31.12	96.51	2
P. D. Salt	127	81	25.40	85.23	1
C. J. Jordan	154	55	22.00	94.47	5
C. D. Nash	107	69*	17.83	72.29	0

Bowling	W	BB	Avge	ER
J. C. Archer	7	5-42	19.42	4.66
C. J. Jordan	13	5-28	23.69	5.25
G. H. S. Garton	10	3-40	26.90	6.40
D. R. Briggs	6	2-45	39.16	4.89
W. A. T. Beer	7	2-34	42.28	5.10
A. Shahzad	6	2-34	59.83	5.79

FIRST-CLASS COUNTY RECORDS

Highest score for	344*	M. W. Goodwin v Somerset at Taunton	2009
Highest score against	322	E. Paynter (Lancashire) at Hove	1937
Leading run-scorer	34,150	J. G. Langridge (avge 37.69)	1928–55
Best bowling for	10-48	C. H. G. Bland v Kent at Tonbridge	1899
Best bowling against	9-11	A. P. Freeman (Kent) at Hove	1922
Leading wicket-taker	2,211	M. W. Tate (avge 17.41)	1912–37
Highest total for	742-5 dec	v Somerset at Taunton	2009
Highest total against	726	by Nottinghamshire at Nottingham	1895
Lowest total for	19	v Surrey at Godalming	1830
	19	v Nottinghamshire at Hove	1873
Lowest total against	18	by Kent at Gravesend	1867

LIST A COUNTY RECORDS

Highest score for	163	C. J. Adams v Middlesex at Arundel	1999
Highest score against	198*	G. A. Gooch (Essex) at Hove	1982
Leading run-scorer	7,969	A. P. Wells (avge 31.62)	1981–96
Best bowling for	7-41	A. N. Jones v Nottinghamshire at Nottingham	1986
Best bowling against	8-21	M. A. Holding (Derbyshire) at Hove	1988
Leading wicket-taker	370	R. J. Kirtley (avge 22.35)	1995–2010
Highest total for	399-4	v Worcestershire at Horsham	2011
Highest total against	377-9	by Somerset at Hove	2003
Lowest total for	49	v Derbyshire at Chesterfield	1969
Lowest total against	36	by Leicestershire at Leicester	1973

TWENTY20 COUNTY RECORDS

Highest score for	153*	L. J. Wright v Essex at Chelmsford	2014
Highest score against	152*	G. R. Napier (Essex) at Chelmsford	2008
Leading run-scorer	**3,031**	**L. J. Wright (avge 32.59)**	**2004–16**
Best bowling for	5-11	Mushtaq Ahmed v Essex at Hove	2005
Best bowling against	5-14	A. D. Mascarenhas (Hampshire) at Hove	2004
Leading wicket-taker	77	C. J. Liddle (avge 22.68)	2008–15
	77	M. H. Yardy (avge 28.02)	2004–15
Highest total for	**242-5**	**v Gloucestershire at Bristol**	**2016**
Highest total against	242-3	by Essex at Chelmsford	2008
Lowest total for	67	v Hampshire at Hove	2004
Lowest total against	85	by Hampshire at Southampton	2008

ADDRESS

County Ground, Eaton Road, Hove BN3 3AN; 0844 264 0202; info@sussexcricket.co.uk; www.sussexcricket.co.uk.

OFFICIALS

Captain L. J. Wright
Director of cricket K. Greenfield
Head coach M. J. G. Davis
Academy director C. D. Hopkinson

Chief executive 2016 Z. Toumazi
2017 C. R. Andrew
Chairman, cricket committee J. R. T. Barclay
Head groundsman A. Mackay
Scorer M. J. Charman

SUSSEX v LEEDS/BRADFORD MCCU

At Hove, April 5–7. Drawn. Toss: Sussex. First-class debuts: G. H. S. Garton; C. S. Harwood. County debut: D. R. Briggs.

Eighteen-year-old left-arm seamer George Garton marked his first-class debut by taking a wicket with his first ball, which Henry Thompson edged behind. He became the second Sussex player to do so, after Henry Stubberfield against Surrey at Hove in 1857 (when John Wisden opened the bowling for Sussex). "I was just hoping it wouldn't be hit for four," said Garton. But in the main the bowlers toiled on an easy-paced pitch: only eight wickets fell in three days. After opting to bat, Sussex were 129 for four, before Brown and Finch hit hundreds in an unbroken partnership of 258. It was Finch's first in senior cricket and, after the declaration, Billy Root followed suit, before rain ended the game.

Close of play: first day, Sussex 387-4 (Brown 126, Finch 135); second day, Leeds/Bradford MCCU 192-2 (Root 84, Davis 38).

Sussex

E. C. Joyce c Harwood b Ogden	33
L. W. P. Wells c Thompson b Lilley	3
M. W. Machan lbw b Ogden	42
*L. J. Wright c sub (L. P. Weston) b Harwood	29
†B. C. Brown not out	126
H. Z. Finch not out	135
B 8, lb 6, w 1, nb 4	19
1/15 (2) 2/76 (1) 3/87 (3) 4/129 (4) (4 wkts dec, 101 overs)	387

O. E. Robinson, A. Shahzad, L. J. Hatchett, G. H. S. Garton and D. R. Briggs did not bat.

Lilley 18–5–53–1; Ashraf 21–3–51–0; Harwood 18–0–103–1; Ogden 21–0–88–2; Watkinson 23–0–78–0.

Leeds/Bradford MCCU

S. F. G. Bullen lbw b Briggs	56
H. L. Thompson c Brown b Garton	4
W. T. Root c Joyce b Finch	133
*C. A. L. Davis c and b Briggs	65
G. F. B. Scott not out	16
L. Watkinson not out	0
Lb 12, nb 4	16
1/26 (2) 2/115 (1) 3/257 (4) 4/290 (3) (4 wkts, 88 overs)	290

†A. M. Gowers, A. E. Lilley, A. Ogden, M. A. Ashraf and C. S. Harwood did not bat.

Robinson 15–2–41–0; Hatchett 13–4–30–0; Shahzad 13–1–52–0; Garton 18–1–68–1; Briggs 15–2–41–2; Wells 12–0–37–0; Finch 2–0–9–1.

Umpires: N. L. Bainton and I. D. Blackwell.

At Northampton, April 10–13. SUSSEX drew with NORTHAMPTONSHIRE.

SUSSEX v ESSEX

At Hove, April 17–20. Drawn. Sussex 12pts, Essex 11pts. Toss: Sussex.

All eyes were on Cook's head: in defiance of new ECB safety guidelines, the England captain had caused turbulence by using his old helmet in Essex's first match, against Gloucestershire. Here he complied, wearing an approved model with a narrower, fixed gap between peak and grille. And though there were teething pains – he lasted just five balls in the first innings, and was dropped on one in the second – he adjusted, batting six hours to save the game with a determined hundred. The first day had begun with a memorial ceremony for Sussex bowler Matt Hobden, who had died in January: a willow tree was planted at the Sea End. Nash, batting with Hobden's name and number on his back, provided his own tribute with his 20th first-class hundred. Westley led the reply to keep Essex in touch, before Napier and Porter – nag and foal – bowled marathon spells on the third evening to give them a sniff of victory. When they eventually ran out of steam, however, Sussex's last pair added crucial runs. Porter finally removed Shahzad on the final morning to earn his maiden five-for, and Essex were still on course for a target of 329 in 91 overs when Cook and Ryder compiled a century stand for the fifth wicket. But Wells struck twice with his leg-spin to reverse the momentum, and it was Sussex who ended up pressing for victory.

Close of play: first day, Sussex 355-8 (Shahzad 24, Briggs 6); second day, Essex 252-7 (ten Doeschate 32, Napier 13); third day, Sussex 282-9 (Shahzad 18, Magoffin 22).

Sussex

C. D. Nash lbw b ten Doeschate	119	– (2) lbw b Napier	92
E. C. Joyce c Foster b ten Doeschate	61	– (1) b Napier	10
M. W. Machan c and b Westley	35	– c Foster b Napier	47
L. R. P. L. Taylor c Foster b Napier	12	– c Westley b Porter	22
L. W. P. Wells c Ryder b Westley	25	– lbw b Porter	11
*†B. C. Brown lbw b Napier	0	– lbw b Porter	8
O. E. Robinson lbw b Napier	51	– b Porter	19
A. Shahzad b Porter	24	– c Ryder b Porter	23
G. H. S. Garton b Bopara	1	– b Napier	0
D. R. Briggs not out	11	– lbw b Napier	9
S. J. Magoffin b Porter	0	– not out	23
Lb 7, w 2, nb 12	21	B 2, lb 11, w 1, nb 10	24
1/188 (2) 2/191 (1) 3/216 (4) 4/248 (3) 5/249 (6) 6/289 (5) 7/340 (7) 8/343 (9) 9/360 (8) 10/360 (11) (97 overs)	360	1/23 (1) 2/120 (3) 3/165 (4) 4/199 (5) 5/209 (6) 6/227 (2) 7/231 (7) 8/232 (9) 9/242 (10) 10/288 (8) (70.2 overs)	288

Porter 20–2–83–2; Dixon 12–1–66–0; Ryder 17–2–51–0; Napier 23–7–61–3; Bopara 8–1–38–1; Westley 10–6–20–2; ten Doeschate 7–0–34–2. *Second innings*—Porter 26.2–4–82–5; Napier 24–3–92–5; Dixon 4–0–26–0; Ryder 4–0–20–0; Bopara 7–0–41–0; ten Doeschate 5–0–14–0.

Essex

N. L. J. Browne c and b Robinson	15	– lbw b Magoffin	3
A. N. Cook c Nash b Magoffin	1	– not out	127
T. Westley c Robinson b Briggs	86	– lbw b Robinson	16
R. S. Bopara c Brown b Garton	17	– c Machan b Shahzad	28
D. W. Lawrence c Brown b Magoffin	11	– lbw b Shahzad	22
J. D. Ryder c Joyce b Shahzad	51	– b Wells	35
*R. N. ten Doeschate c Briggs b Robinson	51	– c Machan b Wells	4
†J. S. Foster b Garton	14	– lbw b Shahzad	5
G. R. Napier lbw b Shahzad	45	– not out	6
J. A. Porter not out	6		
M. W. Dixon lbw b Briggs	1		
B 4, lb 9, w 1, nb 8	22	B 6, lb 10, nb 4	20
1/5 (2) 2/58 (1) 3/77 (4) 4/106 (5) 5/189 (3) 6/191 (6) 7/219 (8) 8/308 (7) 9/319 (9) 10/320 (11) (105.2 overs)	320	1/4 (1) 2/32 (3) 3/80 (4) 4/128 (5) 5/231 (6) 6/241 (7) 7/251 (8) (7 wkts, 90.4 overs)	266

Magoffin 22–5–52–2; Robinson 22–4–74–2; Shahzad 20–3–66–2; Garton 16–1–60–2; Briggs 23.2–9–52–2; Wells 2–0–3–0. *Second innings*—Magoffin 18–5–40–1; Robinson 13–5–28–1; Garton 6–1–23–0; Briggs 24–6–58–0; Shahzad 20.4–2–68–3; Wells 9–0–33–2.

Umpires: P. K. Baldwin and R. T. Robinson.

SUSSEX v LEICESTERSHIRE

At Hove, May 1–4. Drawn. Sussex 6pts, Leicestershire 12pts. Toss: Sussex.

New recruits Horton and Pettini scored maiden hundreds for Leicestershire, but last-day defiance from Nash denied them victory. He had spent five weeks of the winter at the Cape Town academy run by former South Africa opener Gary Kirsten, and his innings of 144 – the longest of his career, from 315 balls – evoked Kirsten's grit. Nash rescued Sussex after a first-innings capitulation in which they lost their last seven for 33 against bowling that was disciplined rather than threatening. Horton unfussily strengthened Leicestershire's position, then Pettini twisted the knife with an unbeaten 142 that vindicated his decision to leave Essex: this was his highest Championship score since 2006.

The loss of 53 overs to rain on the second day delayed the declaration, but Sussex – resuming 310 behind – still had four sessions to survive. Despite eight bowlers having a try, Nash's rearguard with Joyce, who passed 17,000 first-class runs, and Taylor ensured survival.

Close of play: first day, Leicestershire 140-2 (Horton 71, Cosgrove 20); second day, Leicestershire 300-4 (Pettini 42, O'Brien 7); third day, Sussex 113-0 (Joyce 62, Nash 45).

Sussex

C. D. Nash c Robson b Raine	4	– (2) c O'Brien b Raine	144
E. C. Joyce c O'Brien b White	56	– (1) c O'Brien b White	69
M. W. Machan lbw b Raine	4	– c O'Brien b Shreck	13
L. R. P. L. Taylor c O'Brien b Shreck	35	– lbw b McKay	62
L. W. P. Wells c White b McKay	23	– lbw b Dexter	23
*†B. C. Brown c O'Brien b White	1	– lbw b Shreck	16
O. E. Robinson c O'Brien b White	1	– not out	25
A. Shahzad run out	0	– not out	6
G. H. S. Garton c O'Brien b Raine	14		
D. R. Briggs not out	6		
S. J. Magoffin c Naik b Raine	0		
B 8, lb 10, w 1	19	B 4, lb 5, nb 10	19
1/11 (1) 2/23 (3) 3/96 (4) (58 overs)	163	1/136 (1) (6 wkts, 127 overs)	377
4/130 (5) 5/140 (2) 6/142 (7)		2/164 (3) 3/257 (4)	
7/142 (8) 8/143 (6) 9/163 (9) 10/163 (11)		4/302 (5) 5/342 (2) 6/356 (6)	

McKay 13–4–27–1; Raine 15–8–30–4; White 10–3–25–3; Dexter 6–0–16–0; Shreck 12–1–42–1; Naik 2–0–5–0. *Second innings*—McKay 31–5–99–1; Raine 26–6–87–1; Shreck 26–8–62–2; White 16–3–60–1; Naik 20–5–26–0; Dexter 5–1–24–1; Robson 1–0–5–0; Horton 2–0–5–0.

Leicestershire

P. J. Horton c Brown b Garton	100
A. J. Robson b Magoffin	1
N. J. Dexter lbw b Robinson	28
*M. J. Cosgrove b Garton	80
M. L. Pettini not out	142
†N. J. O'Brien c Brown b Magoffin	55
W. A. White b Wells	0
B. A. Raine b Wells	3
C. J. McKay c Nash b Magoffin	0
J. K. H. Naik not out	8
B 8, lb 15, w 4, nb 29	56
1/7 (2) 2/107 (3) (8 wkts dec, 137 overs)	473
3/221 (1) 4/270 (4)	
5/413 (6) 6/414 (7)	
7/420 (8) 8/423 (9) 110 overs: 385-4	

C. E. Shreck did not bat.

Magoffin 28–8–58–3; Robinson 18–1–73–1; Shahzad 20–5–62–0; Garton 25–1–101–2; Briggs 22–1–89–0; Wells 24–1–67–2.

Umpires: I. J. Gould and N. J. Llong.

At Derby, May 8–11. SUSSEX drew with DERBYSHIRE.

At Worcester, May 15–18. SUSSEX drew with WORCESTERSHIRE.

SUSSEX v DERBYSHIRE

At Hove, May 28–31. Sussex won by ten wickets. Sussex 24pts, Derbyshire 2pts. Toss: Sussex.

Play did not begin until 4pm but, as soon as it did, a Sussex win looked likely: Chesney Hughes, who took guard as the division's top scorer, edged Magoffin to slip second ball. The seamers continued to make the most of friendly conditions, taking all ten in short time, though they were helped by a number of poor shots: Thakor apart, Derbyshire's batsmen failed to apply themselves. Their bowlers fared little better, battered into submission by Joyce and Wells, who – having added 310 at Derby three weeks earlier – took advantage of fairer weather to make chanceless hundreds. After Sussex declared, Robinson's four wickets drove them on. He opened the bowling with seam to account for the hapless Hughes, then turned to off-spin to have Godleman caught behind, before reverting to pace to take two more. Thakor once again showed gumption and, helped by Palladino and Cotton's tail-end swiping, ensured Sussex batted again – though not for long. Joyce, who hit the winning single had already replaced Hughes as Division Two's leading scorer.

Close of play: first day, Derbyshire 142-9 (Thakor 44, Cotton 0); second day, Sussex 342-4 (Wells 104); third day, Derbyshire 195-6 (Thakor 58, Critchley 9).

Derbyshire

C. F. Hughes c Nash b Magoffin	0	– (2) lbw b Robinson	11
*B. A. Godleman c Wells b Shahzad	17	– (1) c Brown b Robinson	49
H. D. Rutherford b Whittingham	13	– c Nash b Magoffin	3
W. L. Madsen c Finch b Whittingham	10	– lbw b Whittingham	23
N. T. Broom c Nash b Shahzad	22	– c Nash b Robinson	7
S. J. Thakor not out	47	– c Brown b Whittingham	81
†T. Poynton b Shahzad	1	– run out	29
M. J. J. Critchley c Machan b Whittingham	3	– c Brown b Magoffin	20
T. A. I. Taylor c Machan b Magoffin	14	– c Taylor b Robinson	9
A. P. Palladino c Nash b Magoffin	0	– not out	29
B. D. Cotton c Brown b Magoffin	5	– b Shahzad	26
B 8, lb 6, nb 4	18	B 4, lb 4, nb 12	20
1/0 (1) 2/33 (3) 3/43 (4) (43.3 overs)	150	1/44 (2) 2/47 (3) (94.1 overs)	307
4/71 (2) 5/82 (5) 6/84 (7)		3/79 (4) 4/97 (1)	
7/97 (8) 8/141 (9) 9/141 (10) 10/150 (11)		5/106 (5) 6/185 (7) 7/211 (8)	
		8/238 (6) 9/256 (9) 10/307 (11)	

Magoffin 12.3–5–23–4; Robinson 10–3–26–0; Whittingham 9–0–52–3; Shahzad 11–2–34–3; Wells 1–0–1–0. *Second innings*—Magoffin 19–6–44–2; Robinson 30–3–110–4; Whittingham 14–2–76–2; Shahzad 6.1–2–12–1; Wells 21–6–38–0; Machan 1–0–3–0; Nash 3–0–16–0.

Sussex

C. D. Nash b Madsen	65	– (2) not out	0
E. C. Joyce c Hughes b Madsen	106	– (1) not out	5
L. W. P. Wells c Poynton b Cotton	104		
L. R. P. L. Taylor c Poynton b Taylor	54		
M. W. Machan c Rutherford b Taylor	6		
H. Z. Finch c Poynton b Palladino	16		
*†B. C. Brown b Critchley	61		
O. E. Robinson not out	16		
A. Shahzad c Broom b Critchley	7		
B 1, lb 1, nb 10	12	Nb 6	6
1/113 (1) 2/248 (2) (8 wkts dec, 109.5 overs)	447	(no wkt, 0.3 overs)	11
3/336 (4) 4/342 (5)			
5/342 (3) 6/395 (6) 7/437 (7) 8/447 (9)			

S. J. Magoffin and S. G. Whittingham did not bat.

Cotton 22–4–84–1; Taylor 19–4–103–2; Thakor 10–2–39–0; Palladino 18–3–53–1; Critchley 19.5–1–101–2; Madsen 21–1–65–2. *Second innings*—Cotton 0.3–0–11–0.

Umpires: M. J. Saggers and V. M. Smith.

SUSSEX v NORTHAMPTONSHIRE

At Arundel, June 22–25. Drawn. Sussex 6pts, Northamptonshire 13pts. Toss: uncontested. County debut: S. P. Terry.

Sussex probably enjoy the annual pilgrimage to Arundel less than their supporters. Their last Championship win at the Castle Ground came in 2012 and, had rain not nabbed swathes from the second and fourth days, this game might well have ended in Northamptonshire victory. Put in under glowering skies, Sussex were bundled out for 178, largely by Azharullah, who harnessed the conditions in an expert display of swing bowling. By contrast, Sussex hit too short a length and, when the sun came out and the pitch reverted to its familiar slow and low self, several of their batsmen cashed in – not least Rossington, who made a career-best 138 not out from 121 balls. His unbroken stand of 199 with Murphy was a Northamptonshire record for the sixth wicket in this fixture. Sussex trailed by 300, but Nash and Joyce survived 24 overs on the third evening to raise a century partnership next morning. Between the last-day downpours, Northamptonshire concentrated almost as much on avoiding an over-rate penalty as on forcing a win.

Close of play: first day, Northamptonshire 43-1 (Duckett 32, Wakely 10); second day, Northamptonshire 142-2 (Wakely 46, Keogh 10); third day, Sussex 70-0 (Joyce 28, Nash 36).

Sussex

C. D. Nash c Murphy b Gleeson	75	– (2) b Keogh	53
E. C. Joyce b Azharullah	10	– (1) lbw b Sanderson	60
L. W. P. Wells c Murphy b Azharullah	5	– not out	16
H. Z. Finch lbw b Azharullah	0	– not out	9
*L. J. Wright lbw b Azharullah	14		
M. W. Machan c Murphy b Azharullah	30		
†B. C. Brown c Murphy b Azharullah	4		
O. E. Robinson c Terry b Sanderson	5		
A. Shahzad c Gleeson b Keogh	20		
S. J. Magoffin c Murphy b Sanderson	7		
S. G. Whittingham not out	4		
Lb 2, nb 2	4	B 1, lb 2, nb 4	7
1/42 (2) 2/56 (3) 3/56 (4) 4/87 (5) 5/133 (6) 6/139 (7) 7/146 (8) 8/146 (1) 9/155 (10) 10/178 (9) (51.1 overs)	178	1/110 (2) 2/124 (1) (2 wkts, 57.5 overs)	145

Gleeson 17–1–57–1; Azharullah 16–1–68–6; Sanderson 14–4–32–2; White 3–0–18–0; Keogh 1.1–0–1–1. *Second innings*—Sanderson 18–4–44–1; Azharullah 5–2–12–0; Gleeson 15.5–5–51–0; Keogh 10–3–19–1; Wakely 3–1–3–0; White 6–1–13–0.

Northamptonshire

B. M. Duckett c Nash b Shahzad	72
R. I. Newton b Robinson	0
*A. G. Wakely c Brown b Robinson	46
R. I. Keogh c Brown b Shahzad	75
S. P. Terry c Machan b Finch	54
†D. Murphy not out	60
A. M. Rossington not out	138
B 15, lb 12, nb 6	33
1/22 (2) 2/118 (1) 3/144 (3) 4/263 (5) 5/279 (4) (5 wkts dec, 116 overs) 110 overs: 426-5	478

G. G. White, R. J. Gleeson, Azharullah and B. W. Sanderson did not bat.

Magoffin 27–7–65–0; Robinson 27–5–111–2; Whittingham 20–2–89–0; Shahzad 24–4–91–2; Finch 8–1–30–1; Wells 10–0–65–0.

Umpires: B. J. Debenham and S. J. O'Shaughnessy.

SUSSEX v GLAMORGAN

At Hove, July 2–5. Drawn. Sussex 11pts, Glamorgan 9pts. Toss: Glamorgan. County debut: A. O. Morgan.

A turgid pitch was a throwback to a decade earlier, when Mushtaq Ahmed's leg-breaks would propel Sussex to victory. How they could have done with him now as they struggled to dismantle Glamorgan's second innings. There was no lack of effort: Whittingham, in particular, ran in quickly and found swing, but Sussex's slow bowlers made slow progress, despite a lead of 217. Lloyd's second Championship hundred of the season helped Glamorgan pick their way to a draw. On the third day, after Joyce had laid the foundations with a stylish century of his own, more than 600 schoolchildren rapturously greeted big hundreds from Wells and Brown. They added 294, an all-wicket record for Sussex against Glamorgan, before Wright declared at 552 for five, another record against these opponents. But leg-spinner Beer, playing only his second home Championship game, eight years after his first, was unable to match Mushtaq's impact. Glamorgan were hampered by injuries to Hogan, who suffered concussion after ducking into a Whittingham bouncer, and skipper Rudolph, struck on the left hand, also by Whittingham; it meant they used five substitutes, including their 46-year-old coach, Robert Croft.

Close of play: first day, Glamorgan 291-7 (Rudolph 76, Morgan 15); second day, Sussex 227-3 (Wells 41, Wright 17); third day, Glamorgan 30-1 (Wallace 9, Morgan 9).

Glamorgan

N. J. Selman lbw b Whittingham	52	– lbw b Magoffin	7
†M. A. Wallace c Brown b Whittingham	20	– c Taylor b Whittingham	9
W. D. Bragg c Nash b Magoffin	29	– (4) run out	33
*J. A. Rudolph c Shahzad b Whittingham	87	– (7) c Brown b Briggs	38
A. H. T. Donald b Beer	37	– b Shahzad	44
D. L. Lloyd lbw b Magoffin	37	– not out	102
G. G. Wagg c Taylor b Shahzad	7	– (8) not out	1
C. A. J. Meschede c Nash b Magoffin	0		
A. O. Morgan c Brown b Whittingham	15	– (3) b Briggs	36
T. van der Gugten not out	12		
M. G. Hogan retired hurt	19		
B 8, lb 7, w 1, nb 4	20	B 17, lb 12, nb 8	37
1/41 (2) 2/106 (1) 3/112 (3) (112.1 overs)	335	1/16 (1) (6 wkts, 97.3 overs)	307
4/173 (5) 5/242 (6) 6/259 (7)		2/30 (2) 3/80 (3)	
7/271 (8) 8/296 (9) 9/309 (4) 110 overs: 324-9		4/108 (4) 5/194 (5) 6/287 (7)	

In the first innings Hogan retired hurt at 335-9.

Magoffin 26–5–54–3; Shahzad 24–1–95–1; Whittingham 26.1–3–58–4; Briggs 20–4–58–0; Beer 12–1–39–1; Nash 2–0–4–0; Wells 2–0–12–0. *Second innings*—Magoffin 14–3–42–1; Whittingham 23–7–58–1; Shahzad 16–2–55–1; Briggs 26–7–62–2; Beer 15.3–1–46–0; Wells 3–0–15–0.

Sussex

C. D. Nash c Wallace b Morgan	37
E. C. Joyce b van der Gugten	106
L. W. P. Wells c and b Morgan	181
L. R. P. L. Taylor lbw b Wagg	4
*L. J. Wright b Wagg	19
†B. C. Brown not out	159
W. A. T. Beer not out	12
B 12, lb 6, w 2, nb 14	34
1/133 (1) (5 wkts dec, 158 overs)	552
2/176 (2) 3/181 (4)	
4/239 (5) 5/533 (3) 110 overs: 322-4	

A. Shahzad, D. R. Briggs, S. J. Magoffin and S. G. Whittingham did not bat.

Wagg 31–4–98–2; van der Gugten 28–2–92–1; Morgan 42–4–137–2; Meschede 29–3–88–0; Lloyd 17–0–79–0; Hogan 10–1–31–0; Bragg 1–0–9–0.

Umpires: P. K. Baldwin and R. A. Kettleborough.

At Hove, July 8–10. SUSSEX drew with PAKISTANIS (see Pakistani tour section).

At Tunbridge Wells, July 17–20. SUSSEX drew with KENT.

At Colchester, August 4–7. SUSSEX drew with ESSEX.

SUSSEX v GLOUCESTERSHIRE

At Hove, August 13–16. Sussex won by an innings and two runs. Sussex 24pts, Gloucestershire 6pts. Toss: Gloucestershire. Championship debut: C. A. L. Davis.

Sussex strolled to victory, only their second of the season, and their first by an innings against Gloucestershire for 32 years. On the opening day they reduced their opponents, who had opted to bat, to 34 for four, before Klinger organised a recovery. His shot selection was impeccable, though Sussex were convinced he had been caught by the debutant, Christian Davis, at point on 29. There were handy fifties, too, from Mustard, Miles and Extras, but on a flat pitch a total of 367 was no more than par. Worse, they had lost Norwell, struck on the head by Jordan and unfit to take further part in the game. (Van Buuren also collided with a boundary board, injured his shoulder and lost a tooth.) Matt Taylor claimed four wickets, his left-arm pace posing more of a threat than his brother Jack's remodelled off-spin, but generally the Gloucestershire attack wilted; Wells and Brown, as they had in the last Championship match here, hit hundreds. Armed with a lead of 160, Sussex pressed home their advantage. The Taylors saw out the extra half-hour on the third day, before Magoffin – back to his best – wrapped things up next morning.

Close of play: first day, Gloucestershire 332-7 (Klinger 106, Miles 56); second day, Sussex 326-4 (Wells 102, Wiese 38); third day, Gloucestershire 149-8 (J. M. R. Taylor 52, M. D. Taylor 4).

Gloucestershire

W. A. Tavaré b Magoffin	2	– lbw b Magoffin	0
C. D. J. Dent c Brown b Magoffin	11	– c Brown b Jordan	16
G. L. van Buuren c Brown b Magoffin	4	– (8) lbw b Jordan	1
*M. Klinger not out	129	– c Brown b Wiese	8
H. J. H. Marshall c Jordan b Archer	6	– c Davis b Briggs	23
†P. Mustard b Briggs	71	– c Jordan b Briggs	19
J. M. R. Taylor c Jordan b Magoffin	29	– b Magoffin	56
B. A. C. Howell c Brown b Wiese	0	– (3) b Jordan	4
C. N. Miles b Magoffin	56	– c Joyce b Jordan	2
L. C. Norwell retired hurt	5	– absent hurt	
M. D. Taylor b Wiese	4	– (10) not out	9
B 18, lb 16, nb 16	50	B 9, lb 1, nb 10	20
1/8 (1) 2/18 (3) 3/19 (2) 4/34 (5) 5/167 (6) 6/229 (7) 7/233 (8) 8/333 (9) 9/367 (11) (107 overs)	367	1/4 (1) 2/13 (3) 3/26 (2) 4/46 (4) 5/81 (5) 6/102 (6) 7/106 (8) 8/112 (9) 9/158 (7) (54.5 overs)	158

In the first innings Norwell retired hurt at 353-8.

Magoffin 28–8–73–5; Jordan 26–2–104–0; Archer 17–7–54–1; Wiese 20–4–67–2; Briggs 16–3–35–1. *Second innings*—Magoffin 9.5–4–18–2; Jordan 16–6–36–4; Wiese 7–3–10–1; Archer 11–2–37–0; Briggs 9–0–35–2; Wells 2–1–12–0.

Sussex

C. D. Nash c Klinger b M. D. Taylor	66
E. C. Joyce b Miles	25
L. W. P. Wells lbw b M. D. Taylor	120
C. A. L. Davis c J. M. R. Taylor b M. D. Taylor	0
*L. J. Wright c J. M. R. Taylor b Miles	54
D. Wiese c sub (T. M. J. Smith) b M. D. Taylor	47
†B. C. Brown lbw b Dent	113
C. J. Jordan b Dent	52
J. C. Archer run out	0
D. R. Briggs not out	4
S. J. Magoffin c sub (T. M. J. Smith) b Howell	0
B 8, lb 8, w 2, nb 28	46
1/59 (2) 2/138 (1) 3/140 (4) 4/256 (5) 5/335 (6) 6/369 (3) 7/516 (8) 8/517 (9) 9/524 (7) 10/527 (11) (132.1 overs)	527
110 overs: 442-6	

M. D. Taylor 33–3–130–4; Miles 31–2–128–2; Howell 21.1–1–97–1; J. M. R. Taylor 34–6–111–0; van Buuren 1–0–1–0; Dent 8–2–21–2; Marshall 4–0–23–0.

Umpires: G. D. Lloyd and B. V. Taylor.

At Cardiff, August 23–26. SUSSEX beat GLAMORGAN by two wickets.

SUSSEX v KENT

At Hove, August 31–September 2. Kent won by an innings and 127 runs. Kent 24pts, Sussex 2pts. Toss: uncontested. First-class debut: T. J. Haines.

Kent's first win at Hove since 1992 was as conclusive as any in the long history of this fixture. They had the better of the conditions, twice bowling under heavy cloud cover, but Sussex offered flimsy resistance. While Gidman, the Kent No. 7, faced 240 balls, almost as many as the entire Sussex team managed in either innings. Brown, captaining in the absence of the injured Luke Wright, was alone in reaching 50; if he had hoped for a dry pitch that turned, he instead got a seamer-friendly surface with uneven bounce. With eight others either injured or unavailable, Sussex had drafted in 17-year-old opener Tom Haines from Hurstpierpoint College, but like his new colleagues he struggled against an unforgiving attack who twice shared the wickets around. Fifteen fell on the first day, despite conditions easing in the afternoon; on the second, in late-summer sunshine, Kent batted around the obdurate Gidman. He missed a century after placing too much faith in last man Claydon – almost the only thing that went wrong for Kent, who sauntered to victory with five sessions to spare.

Close of play: first day, Kent 211-5 (Stevens 12, Gidman 1); second day, Sussex 42-2 (Nash 19).

YOUNGEST FIRST-CLASS DEBUTANTS FOR SUSSEX SINCE 1945

Yrs	*Days*			
16	205	J. R. T. Barclay	v Jamaica at Hove	1970
16	228	Nawab of Pataudi jnr	v Somerset at Bristol (Imperial Ground)	1957
17	52	D. L. Bates	v Scotland at Hove	1950
17	108	A. S. M. Oakman	v Northamptonshire at Northampton	1947
17	158	M. A. Buss	v Oxford University at Hove	1961
17	186	S. J. Still	v Nottinghamshire at Nottingham	1975
17	190	G. Potter	v Cambridge University at Cambridge	1949
17	233	J. M. Parks	v Cambridge University at Horsham	1949
17	253	M. T. Robinson	v Lancashire at Eastbourne	1947
17	**308**	**T. J. Haines**	**v Kent at Hove**	**2016**

Sussex

C. D. Nash run out	16	– c Tredwell b Viljoen	23
T. J. Haines c Tredwell b Stevens	0	– c Billings b Viljoen	11
L. W. P. Wells c Billings b Stevens	1	– (4) c Coles b Viljoen	23
F. J. Hudson-Prentice lbw b Coles	5	– (5) c Gidman b Coles	20
C. Cachopa c Gidman b Viljoen	19	– (6) c Billings b Coles	34
*†B. C. Brown c Viljoen b Claydon	54	– (7) b Stevens	19
D. Wiese c Billings b Viljoen	4	– (8) not out	9
O. E. Robinson c Billings b Viljoen	32	– (9) c Denly b Coles	6
D. R. Briggs c Northeast b Coles	8	– (10) lbw b Claydon	4
A. Shahzad c Denly b Claydon	26	– (3) c Billings b Claydon	3
S. J. Magoffin not out	0	– c Billings b Claydon	8
B 1, lb 2, nb 12	15	B 10, lb 2, w 7, nb 10	29
1/2 (2) 2/4 (3) 3/9 (4) 4/41 (1) 5/54 (5) 6/70 (7) 7/126 (8) 8/135 (9) 9/180 (6) 10/180 (10) (40.5 overs)	180	1/39 (2) 2/42 (3) 3/59 (1) 4/87 (4) 5/116 (5) 6/149 (7) 7/159 (6) 8/172 (9) 9/181 (10) 10/189 (11) (41.5 overs)	189

Coles 13–2–32–2; Stevens 11–3–36–2; Viljoen 12–1–70–3; Claydon 3.5–0–25–2; Gidman 1–0–14–0. *Second innings*—Coles 12–2–72–3; Stevens 10–2–30–1; Viljoen 9–0–34–3; Claydon 10.5–2–41–3.

Kent

D. J. Bell-Drummond c Brown b Magoffin	20
S. R. Dickson c Brown b Magoffin	8
J. L. Denly c Wiese b Magoffin	48
*S. A. Northeast c Nash b Shahzad	44
†S. W. Billings lbw b Wiese	64
D. I. Stevens b Magoffin	79
W. R. S. Gidman not out	99
J. C. Tredwell b Shahzad	13
M. T. Coles c Robinson b Briggs	70
G. C. Viljoen c Cachopa b Robinson	3
M. E. Claydon c sub (P. D. Salt) b Magoffin	11
B 14, lb 15, nb 8	37
1/19 (2) 2/54 (1) 3/101 (3) 4/151 (4) 5/206 (5) 6/306 (6) 7/351 (8) 8/466 (9) 9/479 (10) 10/496 (11) (132.5 overs)	496
110 overs: 405-7	

Magoffin 34.5–6–88–5; Robinson 25–2–77–1; Shahzad 19–2–95–2; Wiese 31–5–90–1; Haines 3–0–8–0; Briggs 15–1–77–1; Wells 5–0–32–0.

Umpires: S. A. Garratt and S. J. O'Shaughnessy.

At Leicester, September 6–7. SUSSEX beat LEICESTERSHIRE by an innings and 59 runs.

SUSSEX v WORCESTERSHIRE

At Hove, September 12–14. Worcestershire won by 11 runs. Worcestershire 22pts, Sussex 4pts. Toss: Worcestershire.

Worcestershire coach Steve Rhodes said neither side deserved to lose, and it was hard to disagree. Two overseas seam bowlers, Cummins and Magoffin, dominated a fluctuating contest on a pitch of pace and carry. But, with Sussex 45 from victory, Cummins swept away the tail with a burst of four for 16 to finish with career-best figures of 12 for 166, bringing Worcestershire victory by 11 runs. Magoffin, meanwhile, passed 50 wickets for the fifth successive season en route to his fourth ten-wicket haul. At the halfway mark, Worcestershire enjoyed a handy lead of 77, thanks mainly to Cummins's seven-for. It would have been better still, had Jordan and Archer – papering over the cracks of a frail Sussex line-up that included just four specialist batsmen – not added 97 for the eighth wicket. The Worcestershire second innings was a patchy affair: 95% of the runs from the bat came from Fell, Clarke and Cox, and there was a second successive pair for Köhler-Cadmore. Set 272, Sussex lurched to 113 for six, before Wiese and Jordan doubled the score – only for the last word to go to Cummins.

Close of play: first day, Sussex 50-4 (Brown 14); second day, Sussex 13-1 (Hudson-Prentice 8).

Worcestershire

*D. K. H. Mitchell c Brown b Magoffin	75	– c Cachopa b Magoffin	0
B. L. D'Oliveira c Wiese b Jordan	6	– c Nash b Magoffin	1
T. C. Fell lbw b Magoffin	0	– c Brown b Magoffin	85
J. M. Clarke c Brown b Jordan	39	– c Briggs b Wiese	31
G. H. Rhodes c Jordan b Magoffin	24	– lbw b Wiese	6
T. Köhler-Cadmore lbw b Briggs	0	– lbw b Archer	0
†O. B. Cox c Archer b Wiese	69	– lbw b Magoffin	56
J. Leach c Jordan b Magoffin	8	– b Wiese	0
E. G. Barnard c Cachopa b Robinson	30	– not out	2
M. L. Cummins b Magoffin	25	– b Magoffin	0
C. A. J. Morris not out	5	– b Wiese	0
B 5, lb 12, nb 8	25	B 9, nb 4	13
1/10 (2) 2/11 (3) 3/108 (4) 4/165 (1) 5/166 (6) 6/166 (5) 7/178 (8) 8/253 (9) 9/296 (10) 10/306 (7) (80.2 overs)	306	1/0 (1) 2/1 (2) 3/69 (4) 4/75 (5) 5/76 (6) 6/189 (3) 7/192 (7) 8/192 (8) 9/193 (10) 10/194 (11) (55 overs)	194

Magoffin 19–7–38–5; Jordan 15–3–60–2; Wiese 6.2–0–32–1; Archer 18–2–83–0; Robinson 12–2–39–1; Briggs 10–2–37–1. *Second innings*—Magoffin 15–5–32–5; Jordan 13–0–52–0; Archer 6–0–29–1; Wiese 11–4–18–4; Briggs 7–1–39–0; Robinson 3–0–15–0.

Sussex

C. D. Nash lbw b Leach	23	– c Cox b Leach	5
F. J. Hudson-Prentice c Cox b Cummins	0	– b Leach	20
C. Cachopa b Cummins	0	– b Leach	0
*†B. C. Brown c Köhler-Cadmore b Leach	26	– lbw b Cummins	17
O. E. Robinson lbw b Cummins	11	– run out	42
P. D. Salt b Cummins	0	– c Clarke b Morris	17
C. J. Jordan not out	57	– (8) c Cox b Cummins	50
D. Wiese b Cummins	4	– (7) not out	70
J. C. Archer c Mitchell b Cummins	46	– c Mitchell b Cummins	16
D. R. Briggs c Cox b Cummins	22	– c D'Oliveira b Cummins	1
S. J. Magoffin c Fell b Barnard	13	– b Cummins	0
B 9, lb 10, nb 8	27	B 8, lb 12, nb 2	22
1/9 (2) 2/11 (3) 3/25 (1) 4/50 (5) 5/50 (6) 6/66 (4) 7/71 (8) 8/168 (9) 9/206 (10) 10/229 (11) (46 overs)	229	1/13 (1) 2/13 (3) 3/42 (4) 4/42 (2) 5/96 (6) 6/113 (5) 7/227 (8) 8/246 (9) 9/260 (10) 10/260 (11) (60.3 overs)	260

Cummins 19–3–84–7; Leach 11–0–57–2; Barnard 11–0–55–1; Morris 2–1–10–0; D'Oliveira 3–0–4–0. *Second innings*—Cummins 17.3–0–82–5; Leach 18–2–71–3; Barnard 7–0–30–0; Morris 12–3–37–1; D'Oliveira 6–1–20–0.

Umpires: N. L. Bainton and I. J. Gould.

At Bristol, September 20–23. SUSSEX drew with GLOUCESTERSHIRE.

WARWICKSHIRE

A trophy, but no triumph

PAUL BOLTON

For most counties, a season containing a victorious Lord's final would be considered a success. Not Warwickshire: three weeks after they won the Royal London One-Day Cup, Dougie Brown left – apparently by mutual consent – to end a 27-year association as stalwart all-rounder, Second XI coach, Academy director and, finally, director of cricket. Ashley Giles and Jim Troughton, the coach–captain combination that had guided Warwickshire to the Championship in 2012, were reunited as Brown's replacement. Lancashire were paid compensation for Giles, who had spent two years as director of cricket at Old Trafford. Troughton was promoted from assistant to first-team coach.

Perhaps Brown was a victim of his achievements as a player: he was part of the 1994 side that came within a match of completing a clean sweep of four domestic trophies. That remains the standard by which all Warwickshire teams are judged, though he did contribute to his own downfall. The 2015 season had finished amid murmurings of dressing-room discontent, and in January 2016 Varun Chopra resigned as captain. Chopra, who had led Warwickshire to the Natwest T20 Blast in 2014, wanted flexibility to spend more time with his wife in London – but it was denied. And, when he was not offered a new contract, he grew disconsolate. In August, he announced he would be rejoining Essex – having left in 2009 – and played two matches for them on loan.

Warwickshire's decision to overlook Chopra for white-ball cricket lacked any logic. He played just one Twenty20 match, when summoned as a late replacement for the ill Sam Hain, and made an unbeaten 97 – Warwickshire's highest score of the season – to set up victory over Durham.

Hain prospered in limited-overs games, but struggled in the Championship, hitting a solitary century, against Hampshire in July. Yet the management showed patience with him, which meant frustration for Laurie Evans. Although he remained an integral part of the one-day team, Evans played only twice for Warwickshire in the Championship either side of a loan spell with Northamptonshire in August (when he was recalled after one match). Even in Warwickshire's last two fixtures, when a specialist batsman was required to replace Chopra, Evans was not selected, and chose to head for Sussex.

Failure to develop talented youngsters into first-team regulars also counted against Brown. It is damning that the last Academy player to win a county cap was Chris Woakes, whose first-class debut came in 2006. Plenty have come and gone since then, and more left in 2016: batsmen Freddie Coleman and Jonathon Webb, and seamers Richard Jones – who joined Leicestershire – and Recordo Gordon.

Warwickshire used 26 players across all formats, and the churn did little for cohesion. Only 11 appeared in all three competitions, while four wicketkeepers

Keith Barker

were employed, including Luke Ronchi and Matthew Wade, overseas recruits who contributed little to a disappointing Twenty20 campaign. Warwickshire needed to win one of their last three group matches to secure a quarter-final place, but lost them all, to make it six defeats out of seven, and ensure another Edgbaston Finals Day without the hosts.

Success in the 50-over competition, in which Hain and Jonathan Trott excelled, salvaged some pride, but could not disguise shortcomings in the Championship. Warwickshire briefly looked like title contenders when they beat Surrey at Guildford in July, but ended the summer scrapping to avoid relegation. Survival was only assured with a last-day victory over Lancashire.

The form of Trott, after two harrowing years, was heartening, and he finished as the leading run-scorer in the Championship, with 975. But the rest of the batting again looked fragile, even Ian Bell. After he was dropped by England for the tour of South Africa in 2015-16, Warwickshire made him captain, and looked forward to having him available for his first full county season since 2003. It was not the boon they expected: he began with a century against Hampshire but, despite never looking out of form, made only three more fifties. Andy Umeed, an opening batsman from Glasgow, hit a century in his first Championship innings, then 64 runs in his next nine, and was dropped.

Jeetan Patel was once again the outstanding performer, taking 102 wickets with his off-breaks in all cricket, and winning the PCA's Most Valuable Player award for the second time in three seasons. His form – which won him a recall to New Zealand's Test side after a three-year absence – helped cover for a depleted pace attack. Chris Wright and Boyd Rankin missed games through injury, while Woakes was called up by England during the match against Durham after he took nine for 36 in the first innings. Keith Barker performed admirably, collecting 59 at 23 apiece, while Rikki Clarke gave splendid support; his 42 compensated for diminishing returns with the bat. Olly Stone will add an edge, joining from Northamptonshire.

Off the pitch, Neil Snowball made a favourable impression in his first year as chief executive. He was a vocal supporter of a city-based T20 competition, perhaps unsurprisingly since Warwickshire had rebranded themselves as Birmingham Bears in 2014. Yet selling T20 cricket to a fickle public remained a challenge for the marketing department: most matches at Edgbaston were played in a stadium two-thirds empty, and only the derby against Worcestershire and the last match, against Nottinghamshire, attracted a five-figure crowd. Giles and Troughton must produce cricket that brings the punters back. But regenerating an ageing squad, and uniting the dressing-room, will have to come first.

Championship attendance: 22,808.

WARWICKSHIRE RESULTS

All first-class matches – Played 17: Won 3, Lost 4, Drawn 10.
County Championship matches – Played 16: Won 3, Lost 4, Drawn 9.

Specsavers County Championship, 6th in Division 1;
NatWest T20 Blast, 6th in North Group; Royal London One-Day Cup, winners.

COUNTY CHAMPIONSHIP AVERAGES, BATTING AND FIELDING

Cap		*Birthplace*	*M*	*I*	*NO*	*R*	*HS*	*100*	*Avge*	*Ct/St*
2005	I. J. L. Trott	*Cape Town, SA*	16	24	2	975	219*	2	44.31	3
2009	C. R. Woakes§	*Birmingham‡*	5	7	1	252	121	1	42.00	1
2007	T. R. Ambrose	*Newcastle, Australia*	14	19	4	599	104	1	39.93	53/4
2012	V. Chopra	*Barking*	14	22	2	694	107	1	34.70	18
2001	I. R. Bell§	*Walsgrave‡*	15	22	2	678	174	1	33.90	7
2013	†K. H. D. Barker	*Manchester*	16	22	3	608	113	1	32.00	7
2008	†I. J. Westwood	*Birmingham‡*	10	16	1	367	127	1	24.46	3
	†A. J. Mellor	*Stoke-on-Trent*	3	5	1	93	27	0	23.25	4
	S. R. Hain	*Hong Kong*	15	21	1	455	135	1	22.75	19
2011	R. Clarke	*Orsett*	15	20	3	384	74	0	22.58	30
2012	J. S. Patel¶	*Wellington, NZ*	16	21	5	298	31	0	18.62	8
	A. R. I. Umeed	*Glasgow, Scotland*	6	10	1	165	101	1	18.33	4
2013	C. J. C. Wright	*Chipping Norton*	9	15	2	207	45	0	15.92	2
	†O. J. Hannon-Dalby	*Halifax*	7	9	3	39	30	0	6.50	0
	L. J. Evans	*Lambeth*	2	4	0	26	9	0	6.50	3
2013	†W. B. Rankin††	*Londonderry, N. Ire.*	7	6	1	22	16*	0	4.40	2
	†J. E. Poysden	*Shoreham-by-Sea*	5	4	2	8	7*	0	4.00	0

Also batted: M. R. Adair (*Belfast, N. Ireland*) (1 match) 32; M. Lamb (Wolverhampton) (1 match) 1, 1.

‡ *Born in Warwickshire.* § *ECB contract.* ¶ *Official overseas player.*
†† *Other non-England-qualified.*

BOWLING

	Style	*O*	*M*	*R*	*W*	*BB*	*5I*	*Avge*
C. R. Woakes	RFM	128.1	30	409	23	9-36	1	17.78
J. E. Poysden	LBG	80.4	7	323	15	5-53	1	21.53
K. H. D. Barker	LFM	522.1	153	1,365	59	5-53	1	23.13
J. S. Patel	OB	616.4	168	1,658	69	5-32	4	24.02
C. J. C. Wright	RFM	265.2	51	776	30	4-41	0	25.86
R. Clarke	RFM	415.3	99	1,179	42	4-20	0	28.07
W. B. Rankin	RFM	169.2	23	514	18	3-33	0	28.55

Also bowled: M. R. Adair (RFM) 15–4–47–0; T. R. Ambrose (OB) 1.5–1–0–1; I. R. Bell (RM) 8–2–17–0; V. Chopra (LBG) 2–0–12–0; S. R. Hain (RM) 6–0–24–0; O. J. Hannon-Dalby (RFM) 153–26–524–8; I. J. L. Trott (RM) 58–7–203–3; I. J. Westwood (OB) 5–0–16–0.

LEADING ROYAL LONDON CUP AVERAGES (100 runs/4 wickets)

Batting	*Runs*	*HS*	*Avge*	*SR*	*Ct/St*
I. J. L. Trott	515	118	85.83	86.12	3
L. J. Evans	257	70*	64.25	116.81	7
S. R. Hain	540	107	60.00	84.24	4
T. R. Ambrose	357	86	59.50	98.89	5/3
I. R. Bell	310	94*	51.66	94.22	4
W. T. S. Porterfield	269	92	44.83	71.73	4

Bowling	*W*	*BB*	*Avge*	*ER*
W. B. Rankin	6	4-66	17.16	5.15
J. S. Patel	22	5-43	20.31	4.84
A. Javid	10	4-42	21.20	5.04
R. O. Gordon	6	2-49	25.16	5.26
R. Clarke	13	5-26	31.07	4.86
C. J. C. Wright	8	2-61	34.50	5.30
J. E. Poysden	4	3-46	38.50	5.31
O. J. Hannon-Dalby	9	2-27	41.66	5.59

LEADING NATWEST T20 BLAST AVERAGES (100 runs/18 overs)

Batting	Runs	HS	Avge	SR	Ct/St
M. S. Wade	108	74	21.60	**158.82**	1/1
L. Ronchi	112	53	22.40	**149.33**	5
I. R. Bell	489	80	40.75	**130.74**	6
S. R. Hain	371	92*	33.72	**120.84**	9
L. J. Evans	179	52*	17.90	**111.87**	5
W. T. S. Porterfield	190	61*	27.14	**109.82**	3

Bowling	W	BB	Avge	ER
R. Clarke	15	3-22	17.86	**6.45**
J. S. Patel	11	3-23	28.18	**6.96**
A. Javid	4	1-12	39.00	**8.21**
O. J. Hannon-Dalby	12	2-29	29.33	**8.25**
R. O. Gordon	6	2-21	32.83	**8.95**

FIRST-CLASS COUNTY RECORDS

Highest score for	501*	B. C. Lara v Durham at Birmingham	1994
Highest score against	322	I. V. A. Richards (Somerset) at Taunton	1985
Leading run-scorer	35,146	D. L. Amiss (avge 41.64)	1960–87
Best bowling for	10-41	J. D. Bannister v Comb. Services at Birmingham	1959
Best bowling against	10-36	H. Verity (Yorkshire) at Leeds	1931
Leading wicket-taker	2,201	W. E. Hollies (avge 20.45)	1932–57
Highest total for	810-4 dec	v Durham at Birmingham	1994
Highest total against	887	by Yorkshire at Birmingham	1896
Lowest total for	16	v Kent at Tonbridge	1913
Lowest total against	15	by Hampshire at Birmingham	1922

LIST A COUNTY RECORDS

Highest score for	206	A. I. Kallicharran v Oxfordshire at Birmingham	1984
Highest score against	172*	W. Larkins (Northamptonshire) at Luton	1983
Leading run-scorer	11,254	D. L. Amiss (avge 33.79)	1963–87
Best bowling for	7-32	R. G. D. Willis v Yorkshire at Birmingham	1981
Best bowling against	6-27	M. H. Yardy (Sussex) at Birmingham	2005
Leading wicket-taker	396	G. C. Small (avge 25.48)	1980–99
Highest total for	392-5	v Oxfordshire at Birmingham	1984
Highest total against	**415-5**	**by Nottinghamshire at Nottingham**	**2016**
Lowest total for	59	v Yorkshire at Leeds	2001
Lowest total against	56	by Yorkshire at Birmingham	1995

TWENTY20 COUNTY RECORDS

Highest score for	158*	B. B. McCullum v Derbyshire at Birmingham	2015
Highest score against	100*	I. J. Harvey (Gloucestershire) at Birmingham	2003
Leading run-scorer	1,911	I. J. L. Trott (avge 39.81)	2003–14
Best bowling for	5-19	N. M. Carter v Worcestershire at Birmingham	2005
Best bowling against	5-25	D. J. Pattinson (Nottinghamshire) at Birmingham	2011
Leading wicket-taker	**93**	**J. S. Patel (avge 21.79)**	**2009–16**
Highest total for	242-2	v Derbyshire at Birmingham	2015
Highest total against	215-6	by Durham at Birmingham	2010
Lowest total for	73	v Somerset at Taunton	2013
Lowest total against	96	by Northamptonshire at Northampton	2011
	96	by Gloucestershire at Cheltenham	2013

ADDRESS

County Ground, Edgbaston, Birmingham B5 7QU; 0844 635 1902; info@edgbaston.com; www.edgbaston.com.

OFFICIALS

Captain I. R. Bell
Director of cricket 2016 D. R. Brown
Sport director 2017 A. F. Giles
First-team coach J. O. Troughton
Elite development manager P. Greetham
President Earl of Aylesford
Chairman N. Gascoigne
Chief executive N. Snowball
Chairman, cricket committee J. H. Dodge
Head groundsman G. Barwell
Scorer M. D. Smith

WARWICKSHIRE v LEEDS/BRADFORD MCCU

At Birmingham, March 31–April 2. Drawn. Toss: Leeds/Bradford MCCU. First-class debuts: A. M. Gowers, A. Ogden.

It looked like a mismatch: one side contained six Test players, the other boasted just 41 first-class appearances, 21 of those by former Yorkshire squad member Moin Ashraf. But, until bad weather wiped out the last day, this proved a competitive affair. Chopra and Westwood gave Warwickshire their best start to a first-class innings since April 2014, sharing 152 before both falling to the combination of Liam Watkinson's medium-pace and debutant Ash Gowers' tidy glovework. In reply, maiden first-class half-centuries for Billy Root, younger brother of England's Joe, and Alex Lilley, another former Yorkshire player, pushed Leeds/Bradford past the follow-on target, and made the game safe.

Close of play: first day, Leeds/Bradford MCCU 30-1 (Bullen 14, Root 12); second day, Warwickshire 45-1 (Trott 29, Woakes 16).

Warwickshire

V. Chopra c Gowers b Watkinson	86		
I. J. Westwood st Gowers b Watkinson	75		
*I. R. Bell b Lilley	25		
I. J. L. Trott c Scott b Ogden	47	– (2) not out	29
S. R. Hain c Ashraf b Ogden	2	– (1) c and b Lilley	0
†T. R. Ambrose st Gowers b Watkinson	54		
C. R. Woakes not out	17	– (3) not out	16
R. Clarke not out	24		
B 1, lb 1, w 4, nb 14	20		
1/152 (2) 2/191 (3) 3/209 (1) 4/215 (5) 5/288 (4) 6/322 (6) (6 wkts dec, 85 overs)	350	1/0 (1) (1 wkt, 8.1 overs)	45

K. H. D. Barker, C. J. C. Wright and W. B. Rankin did not bat.

Lilley 18–1–50–1; Ashraf 16–4–41–0; Ogden 15–1–80–2; Davis 5–0–33–0; Watkinson 29–1–132–3; Root 2–0–12–0. *Second innings*—Lilley 4–1–17–1; Ashraf 3–0–24–0; Ogden 1.1–0–4–0.

Leeds/Bradford MCCU

S. F. G. Bullen c Clarke b Woakes	18
H. L. Thompson c Chopra b Woakes	4
W. T. Root b Barker	62
*C. A. L. Davis run out	36
G. F. B. Scott c Ambrose b Barker	5
L. P. Weston c Ambrose b Rankin	22
L. Watkinson c Trott b Rankin	16
†A. M. Gowers c Woakes b Trott	38
A. E. Lilley not out	51
A. Ogden c sub (O. J. Hannon-Dalby) b Barker	24
B 2, lb 11, nb 2	15
1/14 (2) 2/53 (1) 3/115 (4) 4/129 (5) 5/148 (3) 6/161 (6) 7/180 (7) 8/235 (8) 9/291 (10) (9 wkts dec, 86.3 overs)	291

M. A. Ashraf did not bat.

Barker 18.3–3–61–3; Woakes 21–4–58–2; Rankin 12–0–42–2; Clarke 15–4–44–0; Wright 15–3–57–0; Westwood 2–0–3–0; Trott 3–0–13–1.

Umpires: N. G. B. Cook and S. C. Gale.

At Southampton, April 10–13. WARWICKSHIRE drew with HAMPSHIRE.

At Lord's, April 17–20. WARWICKSHIRE drew with MIDDLESEX.

WARWICKSHIRE v YORKSHIRE

At Birmingham, April 24–27. Drawn. Warwickshire 13pts, Yorkshire 11pts. Toss: Yorkshire.

Bleak weather blighted the first two days, costing the match 88 overs and any chance of a result. Yorkshire's decision to bat appeared bold on a pitch tinged with green, but the diligence of Ballance and Leaning helped them overcome a stuttering start. Rashid and Patterson, who was effective, if skittish, during a career-best unbeaten 63, continued the recovery between stoppages for rain, sleet and bad light. Chopra led Warwickshire's reply with a stylish century, his first in nearly a year, and was ably supported by four ex-England men: Bell, Trott, Ambrose and Clarke all made fifties to secure maximum batting points and set up the declaration. But Yorkshire survived the early loss of their openers to bat out the remaining overs, the last of which was delivered by Ambrose, bowling off-spin, with Trott keeping wicket.

Close of play: first day, Yorkshire 177-4 (Ballance 50, Leaning 50); second day, Yorkshire 368-9 (Patterson 62, Sidebottom 6); third day, Warwickshire 205-2 (Chopra 101, Trott 38).

Yorkshire

A. Lyth c Bell b Rankin	19	– lbw b Patel	8
A. Z. Lees b Clarke	19	– c Woakes b Rankin	20
G. S. Ballance c Ambrose b Barker	68	– not out	21
*A. W. Gale b Barker	5	– not out	13
†J. M. Bairstow b Woakes	20		
J. A. Leaning c Ambrose b Woakes	51		
A. U. Rashid b Woakes	63		
L. E. Plunkett c Ambrose b Clarke	26		
S. A. Patterson not out	63		
J. A. Brooks c Ambrose b Barker	2		
R. J. Sidebottom c Clarke b Woakes	15		
B 19, lb 7, w 2	28	B 5, lb 4, nb 2	11
1/46 (2) 2/50 (1) 3/56 (4) (108 overs)	379	1/19 (1) (2 wkts dec, 22 overs)	73
4/85 (5) 5/187 (6) 6/209 (3)		2/37 (2)	
7/252 (8) 8/343 (7) 9/352 (10) 10/379 (11)			

Barker 28–6–101–3; Woakes 28–6–87–4; Clarke 20–7–46–2; Rankin 24–2–93–1; Patel 8–2–26–0. *Second innings*—Rankin 6–1–18–1; Patel 9–1–24–1; Barker 3–0–12–0; Hain 2–0–8–0; Bell 1–0–2–0; Ambrose 1–1–0–0.

Warwickshire

V. Chopra c Lyth b Patterson	107
I. J. Westwood b Brooks	4
*I. R. Bell c Lyth b Rashid	59
I. J. L. Trott c Lees b Lyth	74
S. R. Hain st Bairstow b Lyth	15
†T. R. Ambrose not out	61
C. R. Woakes c Lyth b Rashid	15
R. Clarke c and b Rashid	51
K. H. D. Barker b Rashid	18
J. S. Patel b Patterson	9
W. B. Rankin not out	16
B 6, lb 8	14
1/18 (2) (9 wkts dec, 117 overs)	443
2/150 (3) 3/220 (1) 4/253 (5)	
5/270 (4) 6/305 (7) 7/387 (8)	
8/410 (9) 9/423 (10) 110 overs: 410-7	

Sidebottom 5.3–1–19–0; Brooks 24–3–105–1; Patterson 25.3–4–80–2; Plunkett 24–1–79–0; Rashid 31–4–127–4; Lyth 7–1–19–2.

Umpires: N. G. C. Cowley and J. W. Lloyds.

WARWICKSHIRE v SOMERSET

At Birmingham, May 8–11. Drawn. Warwickshire 8pts, Somerset 10pts. Toss: Somerset.

This game was marred by a parlous pitch: 18 wickets fell on the second day and numerous batsmen were hit, including Gregory, struck on the head when a ball from Rankin reared off a length. The umpires reported the surface to the ECB, while Warwickshire argued that wild variations in weather before the match – from snow to extreme heat – had led to dryness and cracking; the board decided Warwickshire were not at fault. Somerset capitalised while the pitch was at its best, Abell showing an unflappable temperament against a strong attack to compile his second hundred. And Trego was game as ever, hitting a pair of half-centuries to leave Somerset favourites before rain washed out the last two days. Warwickshire, with the exception of Chopra, had struggled against the pace of the Overton twins. They avoided the follow-on, but only just, when last man Patel lashed Gregory to the cover boundary.

Close of play: first day, Warwickshire 27-2 (Chopra 11, Trott 12); second day, Warwickshire 4-0 (Chopra 0, Westwood 4); third day, no play.

Somerset

M. E. Trescothick b Barker	12	– c Barker b Woakes	14
T. B. Abell lbw b Trott	104	– c Ambrose b Barker	2
*C. J. L. Rogers c Ambrose b Barker	0	– c Hain b Rankin	16
J. C. Hildreth c Hain b Rankin	38	– b Woakes	0
J. Allenby c Trott b Barker	7	– c Clarke b Rankin	17
P. D. Trego lbw b Woakes	94	– c Hain b Patel	51
L. Gregory b Woakes	1	– lbw b Rankin	9
†R. C. Davies c Clarke b Rankin	4	– c Rankin b Barker	12
C. Overton c Chopra b Trott	13	– b Woakes	19
J. Overton not out	12	– not out	18
M. J. Leach c Chopra b Woakes	0	– c Ambrose b Clarke	5
Lb 5, w 1, nb 4	10	B 5, lb 8, nb 2	15
1/28 (1) 2/28 (3) 3/84 (4) 4/117 (5) 5/227 (2) 6/228 (7) 7/238 (8) 8/265 (9) 9/295 (6) 10/295 (11) (86.3 overs)	295	1/17 (2) 2/23 (1) 3/23 (4) 4/53 (5) 5/88 (3) 6/104 (7) 7/125 (8) 8/151 (6) 9/164 (9) 10/178 (11) (46.5 overs)	178

Barker 19–7–54–3; Woakes 20.3–6–65–3; Rankin 15–4–43–2; Clarke 11–1–51–0; Patel 11–1–51–0; Trott 10–1–26–2. *Second innings*—Barker 12–2–39–2; Woakes 12–2–45–3; Clarke 7.5–0–27–1; Rankin 8–1–33–3; Patel 7–0–21–1.

Warwickshire

V. Chopra lbw b J. Overton	56	– not out	0
I. J. Westwood lbw b Gregory	3	– not out	4
W. B. Rankin c Hildreth b C. Overton	1		
I. J. L. Trott c C. Overton b Gregory	14		
S. R. Hain lbw b Gregory	12		
†T. R. Ambrose c Davies b Allenby	3		
*I. R. Bell c Allenby b Trego	7		
C. R. Woakes lbw b C. Overton	22		
R. Clarke lbw b J. Overton	12		
K. H. D. Barker c Davies b J. Overton	0		
J. S. Patel not out	9		
B 4, lb 7, nb 2	13		
1/6 (2) 2/15 (3) 3/30 (4) 4/60 (5) 5/75 (6) 6/88 (7) 7/121 (1) 8/135 (9) 9/135 (10) 10/152 (8) (49.4 overs)	152	(no wkt, 2 overs)	4

C. Overton 11.4–1–42–2; Gregory 15–4–50–3; Allenby 9–3–11–1; Trego 6–1–14–1; J. Overton 8–0–24–3. *Second innings*—C. Overton 1–1–0–0; Gregory 1–0–4–0.

Umpires: I. J. Gould and N. A. Mallender.

At Nottingham, May 15–18. WARWICKSHIRE beat NOTTINGHAMSHIRE by 53 runs.

WARWICKSHIRE v DURHAM

At Birmingham, May 22–25. Durham won by four wickets. Durham 19pts, Warwickshire 6pts. Toss: uncontested. County debut: A. R. I. Umeed.

Durham weathered a Woakes storm to end a sequence of four heavy defeats at Edgbaston. Bowling what Collingwood described as 90mph leg-breaks, Woakes took nine for 36 to record his county's best figures since Jack Bannister's ten for 41 against Combined Services in 1959 at Birmingham's old Mitchells & Butlers ground. "It's amazing when you are in rhythm like that, you don't really think about anything," said Woakes. "I'm not sure I have ever bowled as well." Scotland international Andy Umeed also enjoyed a memorable match, composing a measured hundred on debut after a late call-up. He had been driving home to Glasgow for the weekend before being told of his selection, and boarded a plane in time to help Warwickshire to their first century opening stand in the Championship in two years. After Woakes's burst, Durham were 123 behind, but when he was summoned by England at the end of the second day to replace the injured Ben Stokes for the Second Test against Sri Lanka at Chester-le-Street, the momentum shifted. James Weighell claimed his maiden five-for as Warwickshire slipped to 114, and nine wickets in only his fourth first-class match. That left Durham needing 238 and, without Woakes to worry about, Jennings marshalled them home with an unflustered century.

Close of play: first day, Warwickshire 273-8 (Patel 8, Wright 7); second day, Warwickshire 15-2 (Umeed 3, Chopra 8); third day, Durham 154-4 (Jennings 88, Collingwood 26).

Warwickshire

V. Chopra lbw b Weighell	71	– (4) lbw b McCarthy	34
A. R. I. Umeed c McCarthy b Onions	101	– c Richardson b Weighell	7
*I. R. Bell c Borthwick b Carse	38	– (5) lbw b Weighell	15
I. J. L. Trott c Richardson b Carse	1	– (6) c Collingwood b Carse	26
S. R. Hain c Richardson b Weighell	4	– (7) b Weighell	6
†T. R. Ambrose c Borthwick b Weighell	6	– (8) c Stoneman b Weighell	0
C. R. Woakes c Jennings b Weighell	4	– (1) b Onions	4
K. H. D. Barker c Richardson b Carse	10	– (9) c Borthwick b Onions	6
J. S. Patel c Stoneman b Onions	27	– (10) not out	9
C. J. C. Wright b Onions	24	– (3) b Onions	0
O. J. Hannon-Dalby not out	1	– c McCarthy b Weighell	0
B 8, lb 12, w 2, nb 4	26	B 1, lb 6	7
1/120 (1) 2/195 (3) 3/201 (4) 4/222 (5) 5/242 (2) 6/244 (6) 7/255 (7) 8/259 (8) 9/311 (9) 10/313 (10) (92.4 overs)	313	1/4 (1) 2/4 (3) 3/22 (2) 4/46 (5) 5/79 (4) 6/95 (7) 7/95 (6) 8/101 (8) 9/103 (9) 10/114 (11) (37.5 overs)	114

J. E. Poysden replaced Woakes, who left to join England's Test squad.

Onions 22.4–4–69–3; Weighell 27–4–97–4; McCarthy 15–0–48–0; Carse 23–3–70–3; Collingwood 5–1–9–0. *Second innings*—Onions 12–2–36–3; Weighell 14.5–6–33–5; Carse 7–2–16–1; McCarthy 4–0–22–1.

Durham

M. D. Stoneman b Woakes	36	– lbw b Wright	23
K. K. Jennings b Hannon-Dalby	29	– b Patel	113
S. G. Borthwick c Ambrose b Woakes	24	– b Wright	4
J. T. A. Burnham b Woakes	15	– c Umeed b Wright	0
†M. J. Richardson c Ambrose b Woakes	14	– c Patel b Wright	8
*P. D. Collingwood c Barker b Woakes	2	– lbw b Patel	44
R. D. Pringle c Ambrose b Woakes	19	– not out	19
W. J. Weighell c Umeed b Woakes	11	– not out	6
B. A. Carse c Ambrose b Woakes	0		
B. J. McCarthy c Hain b Woakes	14		
G. Onions not out	5		
B 8, lb 8, w 5	21	B 8, lb 11, nb 2	21
1/62 (2) 2/92 (1) 3/97 (3) 4/112 (4) 5/116 (6) 6/145 (5) 7/162 (7) 8/162 (9) 9/163 (8) 10/190 (10) (71.4 overs)	190	1/67 (1) 2/77 (3) 3/79 (4) 4/87 (5) 5/198 (2) 6/227 (6) (6 wkts, 79.4 overs)	238

Barker 19–3–67–0; Woakes 20.4–6–36–9; Patel 3–2–3–0; Hannon-Dalby 17–6–43–1; Wright 12–4–25–0. *Second innings*—Barker 20–5–62–0; Wright 22–4–72–4; Patel 20.4–6–44–2; Hannon-Dalby 10–1–26–0; Poysden 7–3–15–0.

Umpires: R. K. Illingworth and A. G. Wharf.

At Manchester, June 20–23. WARWICKSHIRE drew with LANCASHIRE.

WARWICKSHIRE v NOTTINGHAMSHIRE

At Birmingham. June 26–29. Drawn. Warwickshire 11pts, Nottinghamshire 8pts. Toss: Nottinghamshire.

Rain came 25 minutes after lunch on the third day, saving Nottinghamshire from probable defeat. They had batted after winning the toss, but struggled on a blameless pitch: only Libby, who survived 53 overs for 59, showed much application against the aggressive Rankin and Clarke. Ambrose claimed six victims, the last a stumping to end the innings at 152 and earn Patel a 600th first-class wicket. Ambrose and Clarke then hit season's-best seventies to help Warwickshire recover from a stuttering start. Ball had done the early damage but, after fellow seamer Fletcher went off with a groin strain, he had little support. By the end of the second day, Ball had delivered 23 overs out of 79, and developed a sore elbow, which prevented him bowling on the third, when Warwickshire pushed on to 311. Nottinghamshire lost two wickets, and were still 78 behind when the weather intervened.

Close of play: first day, Nottinghamshire 125-6 (Christian 16, Hutton 6); second day, Warwickshire 283-8 (Adair 19, Patel 10); third day, Nottinghamshire 81-2 (Mullaney 38, Taylor 5).

Nottinghamshire

*S. J. Mullaney b Clarke	6	– not out	38
J. D. Libby c Ambrose b Rankin	59	– c Clarke b Barker	1
M. J. Lumb lbw b Patel	10	– lbw b Patel	32
B. R. M. Taylor c Patel b Barker	14	– not out	5
†M. H. Wessels c Ambrose b Rankin	3		
S. R. Patel c Ambrose b Rankin	6		
D. T. Christian c Ambrose b Clarke	21		
B. A. Hutton c Ambrose b Clarke	12		
L. J. Fletcher not out	13		
M. Carter c Hain b Patel	2		
J. T. Ball st Ambrose b Patel	0		
B 1, lb 3, nb 2	6	B 1, lb 4	5
1/19 (1) 2/49 (3) 3/76 (4) 4/81 (5) 5/101 (6) 6/110 (2) 7/133 (7) 8/136 (8) 9/152 (10) 10/152 (11) (76 overs)	152	1/3 (2) 2/70 (3) (2 wkts, 28.3 overs)	81

Barker 20–5–45–1; Clarke 18–7–24–3; Adair 12–4–29–0; Rankin 21–4–42–3; Patel 5–3–8–3. *Second innings*—Barker 6–3–14–1; Clarke 5.3–1–12–0; Rankin 6–1–14–0; Adair 3–0–18–0; Patel 8–4–18–1.

Warwickshire

V. Chopra c Hutton b Ball	2
A. R. I. Umeed c Mullaney b Ball	0
*I. R. Bell c Mullaney b Ball	10
I. J. L. Trott lbw b Hutton	18
S. R. Hain c Wessels b Carter	39
†T. R. Ambrose c Mullaney b Patel	72
R. Clarke c Hutton b Ball	74
K. H. D. Barker st Wessels b Mullaney	21
M. R. Adair c Taylor b Hutton	32
J. S. Patel not out	19
W. B. Rankin c Taylor b Christian	2
B 4, lb 10, nb 8	22
1/2 (1) 2/11 (2) 3/28 (3) 4/48 (4) 5/117 (5) 6/181 (6) 7/236 (8) 8/264 (7) 9/302 (9) 10/311 (11) (86.1 overs)	311

Ball 23–3–76–4; Fletcher 10.1–3–23–0; Hutton 17–3–66–2; Christian 3–0–22–1; Carter 11–1–46–1; Patel 14–1–44–1; Mullaney 8–2–20–1.

Umpires: J. W. Lloyds and B. V. Taylor.

At Guildford, July 2–4. WARWICKSHIRE beat SURREY by ten wickets.

WARWICKSHIRE v HAMPSHIRE

At Birmingham, July 10–13. Drawn. Warwickshire 10pts, Hampshire 11pts. Toss: Hampshire.

Warwickshire needed firepower on a placid pitch, but Rankin's sore back forced him out of the match after his first over. It left them with just two frontline seamers; Trott was pressed into 17 overs, allowing Dawson and Wheater to capitalise. Despite losing their last five wickets for nine, Hampshire reached their highest total at Edgbaston. Wheater, still smarting at losing the gloves to McManus, struck his maiden double-century and went past 5,000 first-class runs while batting with Ervine, who reached 10,000 in the same stand. Warwickshire slipped to 11 for two in reply but, after the third day was washed out, centuries from Hain and Ambrose secured the draw. Hain had totalled only 203 in his previous 20 first-class innings going back a year, but relieved the pressure, reaching three figures with a pulled six. Hampshire batsman Michael Carberry had been left out of the match after feeling unwell, and was later diagnosed with cancer. The news came more than five years after doctors found blood clots on one of his lungs. "Carbs has beaten serious illness before," said Rod Bransgrove, the Hampshire chairman. "And we will be doing all we can to make sure he does the same again."

Close of play: first day, Hampshire 304-4 (Wheater 89, Crane 1); second day, Warwickshire 131-3 (Trott 59, Hain 20); third day, no play.

Hampshire

J. H. K. Adams c Bell b Patel	14
*W. R. Smith lbw b Barker	21
T. P. Alsop c Patel b Poysden	50
L. A. Dawson lbw b Barker	116
A. J. A. Wheater not out	204
M. S. Crane b Trott	22
S. M. Ervine c Hain b Patel	75
†L. D. McManus c Clarke b Patel	0
G. K. Berg lbw b Poysden	4
G. M. Andrew b Poysden	2
B. T. J. Wheal lbw b Poysden	0
B 2, lb 9, nb 12	23
1/35 (2) 2/63 (1) 3/144 (3) 4/299 (4) 5/378 (6) 6/522 (7) 7/522 (8) 8/527 (9) 9/531 (10) 10/531 (11) — (140.4 overs)	531
110 overs: 364-4	

Barker 29–8–92–2; Clarke 30–7–97–0; Patel 48–12–160–3; Rankin 1–0–5–0; Poysden 15.4–1–85–4; Trott 17–1–81–1.

Warwickshire

V. Chopra b Andrew	39
A. R. I. Umeed b Andrew	0
*I. R. Bell b Berg	5
I. J. L. Trott st McManus b Berg	68
S. R. Hain c Adams b Crane	135
†T. R. Ambrose c Dawson b Crane	104
R. Clarke not out	11
K. H. D. Barker not out	4
B 20, lb 7, w 1, nb 4	32
1/4 (2) 2/11 (3) 3/78 (1) 4/155 (4) 5/378 (6) 6/380 (5) — (6 wkts, 110 overs)	398

J. S. Patel, J. E. Poysden and W. B. Rankin did not bat.

Berg 22–1–71–2; Andrew 25–2–72–2; Wheal 17–4–67–0; Dawson 21–4–72–0; Ervine 5–0–15–0; Crane 18–2–65–2; Smith 2–0–9–0.

Umpires: R. J. Bailey and P. K. Baldwin.

At Leeds, August 4–6. WARWICKSHIRE lost to YORKSHIRE by 48 runs.

WARWICKSHIRE v SURREY

At Birmingham, August 13–16. Surrey won by 226 runs. Surrey 21pts, Warwickshire 4pts. Toss: Surrey.

The dressing-rooms after the match told the story: Surrey banged their bats and gave a hearty rendition of their team song, while Warwickshire locked themselves in for an hour-long post-mortem. It had, though, begun evenly: Patel took four wickets on a turning pitch as Surrey made a modest 252 on the first day. When Warwickshire replied, Sam Curran's career-best five-for, including three for two in 18 balls, was counterbalanced by Barker's attacking half-century, which narrowed the deficit to five. But a fluent 88 from Sangakkara – in his first Championship match for two months after a stint playing in, and winning, the Caribbean Premier League – tilted the match Surrey's way. Davies and Sam Curran rammed home the advantage by flaying 102 in 17 overs for the seventh wicket. Warwickshire showed little interest in chasing 396, but could not hold out against an attack hungry to avenge their mauling at Guildford six weeks earlier.

Close of play: first day, Surrey 252; second day, Surrey 33-1 (Burns 14, Meaker 4); third day, Warwickshire 2-1 (Chopra 2, Wright 0).

Surrey

R. J. Burns lbw b Patel	50	– lbw b Hannon-Dalby	49
D. P. Sibley c Westwood b Patel	33	– c Westwood b Patel	11
K. C. Sangakkara c Clarke b Patel	47	– (4) c Ambrose b Barker	88
Z. S. Ansari c Evans b Hannon-Dalby	8	– (5) c Ambrose b Wright	28
J. J. Roy c Ambrose b Clarke	16	– (6) c Clarke b Barker	36
†S. M. Davies c Bell b Patel	38	– (7) c Patel b Wright	42
S. M. Curran c Ambrose b Clarke	8	– (8) c Ambrose b Wright	62
T. K. Curran c Evans b Clarke	4	– (9) c Ambrose b Wright	0
*G. J. Batty lbw b Barker	27	– (10) not out	11
S. C. Meaker c Chopra b Wright	7	– (3) c Ambrose b Patel	41
M. H. A. Footitt not out	3	– c Barker b Patel	7
Lb 4, w 1, nb 6	11	B 2, lb 8, w 3, nb 2	15
1/62 (2) 2/110 (1) 3/146 (4) 4/146 (3) 5/202 (5) 6/202 (6) 7/214 (7) 8/219 (8) 9/249 (10) 10/252 (9) (90.2 overs)	252	1/28 (2) 2/87 (1) 3/147 (3) 4/208 (5) 5/262 (6) 6/263 (4) 7/365 (7) 8/365 (9) 9/380 (8) 10/390 (11) (106.3 overs)	390

Barker 19.2–5–58–1; Wright 15–2–50–1; Clarke 19–9–46–3; Hannon-Dalby 11–3–36–1; Patel 26–9–58–4. *Second innings*—Barker 19–6–42–2; Wright 21–3–75–4; Clarke 14–2–64–0; Patel 36.3–8–126–3; Hannon-Dalby 16–4–73–1.

Warwickshire

V. Chopra c Roy b T. K. Curran	8	– c Davies b Footitt	17
I. J. Westwood c Roy b Meaker	45	– lbw b T. K. Curran	0
I. J. L. Trott c Sangakkara b Meaker	13	– (4) c Davies b Meaker	9
*I. R. Bell c Sibley b S. M. Curran	43	– (5) c Burns b Batty	32
L. J. Evans c Burns b S. M. Curran	9	– (6) b Ansari	9
†T. R. Ambrose c Burns b S. M. Curran	0	– (7) not out	27
R. Clarke lbw b S. M. Curran	1	– (8) b S. M. Curran	17
K. H. D. Barker c Sibley b S. M. Curran	62	– (9) c Davies b Meaker	2
J. S. Patel c Roy b Footitt	29	– (10) c Burns b Footitt	16
C. J. C. Wright not out	18	– (3) run out	24
O. J. Hannon-Dalby b T. K. Curran	1	– lbw b Batty	0
B 4, lb 9, w 1, nb 4	18	B 4, lb 6, w 2, nb 4	16
1/18 (1) 2/58 (3) 3/85 (2) 4/99 (5) 5/99 (6) 6/101 (7) 7/196 (4) 8/197 (8) 9/236 (9) 10/247 (11) (78.5 overs)	247	1/1 (2) 2/37 (3) 3/48 (1) 4/52 (4) 5/77 (6) 6/111 (5) 7/142 (8) 8/147 (9) 9/168 (10) 10/169 (11) (78 overs)	169

T. K. Curran 20.5–10–61–2; S. M. Curran 19–6–44–5; Footitt 14–3–45–1; Meaker 17–2–62–2; Ansari 8–1–22–0. *Second innings*—T. K. Curran 7–2–13–1; S. M. Curran 11–3–32–1; Meaker 16–5–44–2; Footitt 10–2–17–2; Ansari 11–4–18–1; Batty 21–8–27–2; Sibley 2–0–8–0.

Umpires: N. G. C. Cowley and R. T. Robinson.

At Chester-le-Street, August 23–26. WARWICKSHIRE drew with DURHAM.

WARWICKSHIRE v MIDDLESEX

At Birmingham, August 31–September 3. Drawn. Warwickshire 8pts, Middlesex 9pts. Toss: Middlesex. County debut: A. J. Mellor.

Bad weather restricted the final day to less than an hour after tea, and frustrated Middlesex's victory push. The pitch was worn – it was used for Twenty20 finals day and a Royal London Cup semi-final – and helped leg-spinner Poysden pick up a maiden five-wicket haul on the first day to keep Middlesex to 242. Warwickshire calmly reached 122 for two, before a bizarre run-out sparked an implosion. Rayner bowled, then dived as Bell pushed towards mid-on. He failed to stop the ball, but did block the path of Westwood, the non-striker, as he set off for a run. Westwood was sent back, and Roland-Jones's direct hit had him short. The umpires consulted, but decided the obstruction had been unintentional. The last eight wickets fell for 50, as Rayner – who had opened the bowling to no reward – hoovered up the final five. Despite a pessimistic weather forecast, Middlesex made cautious progress towards a declaration, particularly against the accuracy of Barker and Wright; Robson's 74 took 218 balls. Warwickshire lost three before stumps on the third day, but only Wright, the nightwatchman, on the abbreviated last.

Close of play: first day, Warwickshire 1-0 (Chopra 0, Westwood 1); second day, Middlesex 63-0 (Gubbins 41, Robson 20); third day, Warwickshire 74-3 (Bell 12, Wright 10).

Middlesex

S. D. Robson c Chopra b Wright	1	– (2) c Chopra b Patel	74
N. R. T. Gubbins c and b Wright	2	– (1) lbw b Patel	46
N. R. D. Compton c Chopra b Wright	33	– b Barker	1
D. J. Malan c Clarke b Poysden	57	– c Mellor b Patel	17
S. S. Eskinazi b Poysden	49	– b Poysden	53
†J. A. Simpson c Hain b Poysden	5	– not out	37
*J. E. C. Franklin lbw b Poysden	29	– (8) c Clarke b Poysden	5
O. P. Rayner b Poysden	12	– (9) not out	1
T. S. Roland-Jones c Hain b Patel	12	– (7) b Poysden	21
H. W. Podmore c Clarke b Wright	21		
R. H. Patel not out	4		
Lb 7, nb 10	17	B 5, lb 3, nb 4	12
1/3 (1) 2/6 (2) 3/100 (3) 4/126 (4) 5/134 (6) 6/190 (7) 7/191 (5) 8/210 (8) 9/223 (9) 10/242 (10) (91.1 overs)	242	1/69 (1) 2/76 (3) 3/99 (4) 4/196 (2) 5/213 (5) 6/251 (7) 7/263 (8) (7 wkts dec, 86 overs)	267

Barker 15–4–20–0; Wright 16.1–2–41–4; Clarke 14–6–25–0; Trott 7–2–22–0; Patel 18–3–74–1; Poysden 21–2–53–5. *Second innings*—Barker 14–6–23–1; Wright 14–0–36–0; Patel 29–4–92–3; Poysden 18–1–80–3; Clarke 11–0–28–0.

Warwickshire

V. Chopra c Simpson b Podmore	14	– c Robson b Roland-Jones	9
I. J. Westwood run out	81	– lbw b Rayner	28
I. J. L. Trott c Robson b Roland-Jones	4	– lbw b Patel	8
*I. R. Bell c Simpson b Patel	19	– not out	25
S. R. Hain c Franklin b Patel	0	– (6) not out	21
†A. J. Mellor not out	18		
R. Clarke lbw b Rayner	0		
K. H. D. Barker c Simpson b Rayner	22		
J. S. Patel b Rayner	0		
C. J. C. Wright c Robson b Rayner	8	– (5) lbw b Rayner	22
J. E. Poysden c Podmore b Rayner	0		
B 2, lb 2, nb 2	6	B 5, lb 2	7
1/33 (1) 2/49 (3) 3/122 (2) 4/122 (5) 5/127 (4) 6/128 (7) 7/152 (8) 8/152 (9) 9/172 (10) 10/172 (11) (74.5 overs)	172	1/20 (1) 2/37 (3) 3/55 (2) 4/89 (5) (4 wkts, 50.4 overs)	120

Roland-Jones 14–5–33–1; Rayner 26.5–9–49–5; Podmore 12–3–26–1; Franklin 3–0–6–0; Patel 19–4–54–2. *Second innings*—Roland-Jones 10–4–16–1; Podmore 5–3–15–0; Patel 18–3–40–1; Rayner 17.4–4–42–2.

Umpires: D. J. Millns and M. J. Saggers.

At Taunton, September 6–8. WARWICKSHIRE lost to SOMERSET by 31 runs.

WARWICKSHIRE v LANCASHIRE

At Birmingham, September 20–23. Warwickshire won by 237 runs. Warwickshire 20pts, Lancashire 3pts. Toss: uncontested.

Both teams were worried about relegation; both survived, though in contrasting circumstances. Warwickshire knew they were safe by the last afternoon, when they completed their only home victory of the season; Lancashire could not relax until Hampshire lost to Durham three hours later (though it was Durham who were eventually demoted following the ECB's intervention). The pitch was low and seamer-friendly, and Warwickshire adapted better. Hain's application in their first innings had hauled them up towards 219, before four wickets for Barker – who had begun at the Lancashire Academy – put them in control. Then Ambrose's 59, backed by a series of cameos, allowed Warwickshire to declare on the third evening, setting 347. Despite the diligence of nightwatchman Kerrigan, who extended his shift beyond lunch, Lancashire crumbled in dismal fashion. Clarke had Croft caught at short leg with his first ball, and went on to fillet the lower order. "At the moment we all feel pretty crap," said Ashley Giles, the Lancashire head coach. "But time is a healer."

Close of play: first day, Lancashire 14-0 (Jones 2, Hameed 4); second day, Warwickshire 12-0 (Westwood 6, Mellor 6); third day, Lancashire 28-3 (Hameed 11, Kerrigan 0).

Warwickshire

I. J. Westwood lbw b Bailey	0	– lbw b Clark	34
A. J. Mellor c Livingstone b Bailey	27	– lbw b Bailey	6
I. J. L. Trott c Croft b Clark	25	– b Lilley	42
*I. R. Bell lbw b Jarvis	37	– b Jarvis	31
S. R. Hain lbw b Procter	52	– lbw b Lilley	30
†T. R. Ambrose run out	0	– not out	59
R. Clarke lbw b Clark	16	– lbw b Kerrigan	20
K. H. D. Barker b Clark	22	– lbw b Lilley	23
J. S. Patel c Hameed b Bailey	26	– not out	23
C. J. C. Wright c Croft b Bailey	4		
O. J. Hannon-Dalby not out	0		
B 1, lb 7, nb 2	10	B 4, lb 5, w 2	11
1/0 (1) 2/43 (2) 3/80 (3) (84.4 overs)	219	1/13 (2) (7 wkts dec, 83 overs)	279
4/105 (4) 5/105 (6) 6/142 (7)		2/74 (1) 3/110 (3)	
7/182 (5) 8/190 (8) 9/214 (10) 10/219 (9)		4/148 (4) 5/152 (5)	
		6/196 (7) 7/234 (8)	

Bailey 19.4–4–52–4; Jarvis 19–5–54–1; Procter 12–3–39–1; Clark 9–4–20–3; Kerrigan 22–5–32–0; Lilley 3–0–14–0. *Second innings*—Bailey 23–4–62–1; Jarvis 17–5–50–1; Procter 3–0–17–0; Clark 6–0–30–1; Kerrigan 17–2–55–1; Lilley 17–2–56–3.

Lancashire

R. P. Jones lbw b Wright	8	– lbw b Barker	4
H. Hameed lbw b Clarke	17	– c Clarke b Wright	27
L. A. Procter c Ambrose b Barker	1	– lbw b Patel	7
K. R. Brown lbw b Wright	1	– c Ambrose b Wright	4
*†S. J. Croft b Barker	45	– (6) c Hain b Clarke	1
L. S. Livingstone c Barker b Hannon-Dalby	21	– (7) c Trott b Patel	7
J. Clark b Barker	34	– (8) b Clarke	8
A. M. Lilley b Patel	4	– (9) not out	27
T. E. Bailey c Bell b Patel	0	– (10) b Clarke	1
K. M. Jarvis b Barker	3	– (11) c Westwood b Clarke	4
S. C. Kerrigan not out	0	– (5) c Clarke b Patel	10
B 11, lb 1, nb 6	18	B 3, lb 4, nb 2	9
1/35 (2) 2/35 (1) 3/37 (4) 4/39 (3) 5/79 (6) 6/134 (5) 7/145 (8) 8/149 (9) 9/149 (7) 10/152 (10) (64.5 overs)	152	1/4 (1) 2/17 (3) 3/26 (4) 4/51 (2) 5/57 (6) 6/64 (7) 7/73 (5) 8/77 (8) 9/83 (10) 10/109 (11) (60.5 overs)	109

Barker 20.5–8–30–4; Wright 14–7–30–2; Patel 16–1–42–2; Clarke 6–2–24–1; Hannon-Dalby 8–1–14–1. *Second innings*—Barker 12–3–28–1; Wright 14–8–8–2; Patel 24–11–46–3; Clarke 10.5–3–20–4.

Umpires: P. J. Hartley and D. J. Millns.

WORCESTERSHIRE

New direction at New Road?

JOHN CURTIS

Three days after the end of an up-and-down season, Steve Rhodes, Worcestershire's director of cricket, informed Daryl Mitchell he would no longer be captain. Mitchell, an Academy product who had done the job for six of his 11 years in the first team, said he was "deeply hurt" by the decision, but conceded he had not always been at his best.

Worcestershire had hoped Mitchell could recapture the form of 2014, when his runs drove a successful promotion campaign. But it wasn't to be: after the opening match, at home to Kent, was washed out, Worcestershire were always playing catch-up. Their first win – at Leicestershire – took six games, by which time Essex were holding fast to the lone promotion spot. Three victories in the last four matches brought Worcestershire level on wins with the leaders, but they were never going to overtake them.

Above all, they struggled to bowl sides out, mainly because their pace attack – so incisive during the previous two seasons – fired on too few cylinders. Charlie Morris laboured after remodelling his action, while the potency of Jack Shantry – whose highlight came with the bat, during a ferocious century from No. 10 against Gloucestershire – was reduced by flatter pitches, partly a result of the new toss rule. Their combined tally of 29 Championship wickets at an average of 55 – compared with 101 at 29 a year earlier – meant 20-year-old Ed Barnard had to shoulder greater responsibility; he finished as the second-highest wicket-taker, with 31, but each cost 43. It was left to Joe Leach, the new captain for 2017, to carry the attack: he was Division Two's leading wicket-taker, with 65, and was voted Player of the Year by team-mates for the second year in a row.

While New Zealand fast bowler Matt Henry's haul of 27 wickets in six games was a decent return, his replacement, the South African Kyle Abbott, was less successful. He had been earmarked for the second half of the summer, but was restricted to two Championship appearances through injury and international calls, picking up one wicket for 249. West Indian Miguel Cummins arrived for three games and took 15. The signing of Australian all-rounder John Hastings for the majority of 2017 should add much-needed bite. Worcestershire also lacked an experienced frontline spinner. In 2014, Saeed Ajmal's 63 wickets from only nine matches were crucial to promotion. Yet their leading slow bowler in 2016 was Brett D'Oliveira, whose leg-spin picked up 16 wickets at 47 each.

Of the top six batsmen, only 20-year-old Joe Clarke, who had earned an England Lions call the previous winter, performed well. In his first full season, he was Worcestershire's top run-scorer, with 1,206 in the Championship and five hundreds, three more than any of his colleagues, with two during

Stu Forster, Getty Images

Joe Clarke

imposing chases against Leicestershire and Northamptonshire. Clarke wanted to play for England by 2018, and was again recognised by the Lions for their 2016-17 winter programme.

An encouraging story of a different kind was the return of Tom Fell midway through the season. In October 2015, he had undergone surgery for testicular cancer. He recovered quickly, and spent the winter playing grade cricket in Perth. But, in March 2016, doctors discovered the cancer had spread to his lymph nodes. Fell had chemotherapy, which finished in May, and by July he was back in the Championship team, beginning with a half-century against Leicestershire. A few weeks later, he made a hundred in the Royal London Cup against Lancashire at New Road, earning a standing ovation.

For others – notably Mitchell, D'Oliveira and Tom Köhler-Cadmore – it was a season of two halves. D'Oliveira started with a flurry of runs, including a double-hundred away to Glamorgan, while Köhler-Cadmore also looked as if his talent was set to flourish. Both tailed off alarmingly.

Mitchell's graph went the other way: he put a difficult start behind him to finish second in the run-charts to Clarke, hitting two centuries in a match for the third time, against Northamptonshire. Ross Whiteley was a disappointment at No. 6, failing to convert several promising starts, and was eventually dropped. It was often left to wicketkeeper Ben Cox – "Mr Reliable" according to Rhodes – and Leach to rescue precarious positions.

Worcestershire won four of their first five group matches in the NatWest Twenty20 Blast, but could not reach the knockouts. Their excellent start came despite losing New Zealand spinner Mitchell Santner to a broken finger in the opening game against Durham. But the run-in contained some substandard performances, not least when they were bowled out for 53 at Old Trafford – their lowest T20 score. Consolation might have come in the Royal London Cup, but Somerset routed them in the quarter-finals at Taunton.

In the boardroom, lifelong fan and local businessman Tom Scott was confirmed as David Leatherdale's permanent successor as chief executive. One of his main tasks was to ensure the club's finances maintained steady growth. The players could do with similar improvement.

Championship attendance: 27,052.

WORCESTERSHIRE RESULTS

All first-class matches – Played 16: Won 7, Lost 4, Drawn 5. Abandoned 1.
County Championship matches – Played 15: Won 6, Lost 4, Drawn 5. Abandoned 1.

Specsavers County Championship, 3rd in Division 2;
NatWest T20 Blast, 8th in North Group; Royal London One-Day Cup, quarter-finalists.

COUNTY CHAMPIONSHIP AVERAGES, BATTING AND FIELDING

Colours		*Birthplace*	*M*	*I*	*NO*	*R*	*HS*	*100*	*Avge*	*Ct/St*
2007	†M. M. Ali§	*Birmingham*	3	4	1	273	136*	1	91.00	0
2015	J. M. Clarke	*Shrewsbury*	15	26	1	1,206	194	5	48.24	6
2016	M. J. Henry¶	*Christchurch, NZ*	6	6	2	180	49*	0	45.00	1
2012	J. Leach	*Stafford*	15	21	5	583	107*	1	36.43	4
2009	O. B. Cox	*Wordsley‡*	15	23	2	757	75	0	36.04	32/2
2013	T. C. Fell	*Hillingdon*	8	16	1	530	85	0	35.33	4
2005	D. K. H. Mitchell	*Badsey‡*	15	27	2	873	107*	2	34.92	13
2012	B. L. D'Oliveira	*Worcester‡*	14	25	1	763	202*	2	31.79	8
2016	G. H. Rhodes	*Birmingham*	6	11	2	274	59	0	30.44	2
2014	T. Köhler-Cadmore	*Chatham*	13	21	1	561	169	2	28.05	18
2013	†R. A. Whiteley	*Sheffield*	13	22	2	542	71	0	27.10	12
2015	E. G. Barnard	*Shrewsbury*	14	20	4	430	73	0	26.87	5
2009	†J. D. Shantry	*Shrewsbury*	11	12	4	210	106	1	26.25	4
2009	A. N. Kervezee	*Walvis Bay, Nam.*	4	7	1	151	41	0	25.16	1
2014	C. A. J. Morris	*Hereford*	7	9	6	32	11	0	10.66	1
2016	†M. L. Cummins¶	*St Michael, Barb.*	3	4	1	29	25	0	9.66	0

Also batted: K. J. Abbott¶ (*Empangeni, SA*) (colours 2016) (2 matches) 5, 3, 10; †M. J. Santner¶ (*Hamilton, NZ*) (colours 2016) (1 match) 23*.

‡ *Born in Worcestershire.* § *ECB contract.* ¶ *Official overseas player.*

BOWLING

	Style	*O*	*M*	*R*	*W*	*BB*	*5I*	*Avge*
M. L. Cummins	RF	96.2	12	377	15	7-84	2	25.13
M. J. Henry	RFM	234	48	716	27	5-36	1	26.51
J. Leach	RFM	495.4	74	1,786	65	5-60	5	27.47
E. G. Barnard	RFM	358.2	66	1,351	31	4-62	0	43.58
B. L. D'Oliveira	LBG	259.1	30	761	16	4-80	0	47.56
C. A. J. Morris	RFM	144.1	26	563	11	2-35	0	51.18
J. D. Shantry	LFM	358.2	87	1,039	18	4-89	0	57.72

Also bowled: K. J. Abbott (RFM) 75–17–249–1; M. M. Ali (OB) 42–5–161–1; J. M. Clarke (LBG) 2–0–22–0; T. C. Fell (OB) 2.2–1–10–0; A. N. Kervezee (OB) 33–9–89–1; D. K. H. Mitchell (RM) 30.5–6–92–3; G. H. Rhodes (OB) 64.5–5–263–3.

LEADING ROYAL LONDON CUP AVERAGES (100 runs/4 wickets)

Batting	*Runs*	*HS*	*Avge*	*SR*	*Ct*
T. C. Fell	252	116*	84.00	95.09	2
A. N. Kervezee	138	77	46.00	104.54	0
D. K. H. Mitchell	215	64	43.00	72.88	2
J. Leach	162	63	27.00	100.62	5
T. Köhler-Cadmore	209	119	26.12	91.26	1
R. A. Whiteley	121	61	24.20	93.79	1
J. M. Clarke	102	44	20.40	75.00	2

Bowling	*W*	*BB*	*Avge*	*ER*
K. J. Abbott	4	3-56	28.00	5.60
G. H. Rhodes	5	2-34	32.40	5.78
E. G. Barnard	9	3-45	34.11	5.68
J. Leach	9	3-79	38.33	5.64
J. D. Shantry	4	2-10	40.75	3.99
D. K. H. Mitchell	4	1-15	46.25	5.38
B. L. D'Oliveira	5	2-9	47.20	4.64

LEADING NATWEST T20 BLAST AVERAGES (100 runs/18 overs)

Batting	*Runs*	*HS*	*Avge*	*SR*	*Ct*
O. B. Cox	234	59*	58.50	**156.00**	6
T. Köhler-Cadmore	323	127	24.84	**148.16**	7
R. A. Whiteley	226	42*	22.60	**141.25**	4
D. K. H. Mitchell	215	61	21.50	**132.71**	4
B. L. D'Oliveira	353	62*	35.30	**126.97**	6
J. M. Clarke	227	69*	20.63	**120.10**	2
A. N. Kervezee	122	52*	15.25	**107.96**	4

Bowling	*W*	*BB*	*Avge*	*ER*
D. K. H. Mitchell	3	1-15	45.33	**7.41**
B. L. D'Oliveira	6	2-20	41.83	**8.36**
J. D. Shantry	4	1-22	72.75	**8.55**
E. G. Barnard	7	2-43	35.71	**8.87**
J. Leach	20	5-33	20.10	**9.27**
M. J. Henry	7	3-15	46.42	**9.70**

FIRST-CLASS COUNTY RECORDS

Highest score for	405*	G. A. Hick v Somerset at Taunton	1988
Highest score against	331*	J. D. B. Robertson (Middlesex) at Worcester	1949
Leading run-scorer	34,490	D. Kenyon (avge 34.18)	1946–67
Best bowling for	9-23	C. F. Root v Lancashire at Worcester	1931
Best bowling against	10-51	J. Mercer (Glamorgan) at Worcester	1936
Leading wicket-taker	2,143	R. T. D. Perks (avge 23.73)	1930–55
Highest total for	701-6 dec	v Surrey at Worcester	2007
Highest total against	701-4 dec	by Leicestershire at Worcester	1906
Lowest total for	24	v Yorkshire at Huddersfield	1903
Lowest total against	30	by Hampshire at Worcester	1903

LIST A COUNTY RECORDS

Highest score for	180*	T. M. Moody v Surrey at The Oval	1994
Highest score against	158	W. Larkins (Northamptonshire) at Luton	1982
	158	R. A. Smith (Hampshire) at Worcester	1996
Leading run-scorer	16,416	G. A. Hick (avge 44.60)	1985–2008
Best bowling for	7-19	N. V. Radford v Bedfordshire at Bedford	1991
Best bowling against	7-15	R. A. Hutton (Yorkshire) at Leeds	1969
Leading wicket-taker	370	S. R. Lampitt (avge 24.52)	1987–2002
Highest total for	404-3	v Devon at Worcester	1987
Highest total against	399-4	by Sussex at Horsham	2011
Lowest total for	58	v Ireland v Worcester	2009
Lowest total against	45	by Hampshire at Worcester	1988

TWENTY20 COUNTY RECORDS

Highest score for	**127**	**T. Köhler-Cadmore v Durham at Worcester**	**2016**
Highest score against	141*	C. L. White (Somerset) at Worcester	2006
Leading run-scorer	**1,890**	**M. M. Ali (avge 24.86)**	**2007–16**
Best bowling for	5-28	D. K. H. Mitchell v Northants at Northampton	2014
Best bowling against	6-21	A. J. Hall (Northamptonshire) at Northampton	2008
Leading wicket-taker	**90**	**J. D. Shantry (avge 26.92)**	**2010–16**
Highest total for	227-6	v Northamptonshire at Kidderminster	2007
Highest total against	229-4	by Lancashire at Worcester	2014
Lowest total for	**53**	**v Lancashire at Manchester**	**2016**
Lowest total against	93	by Gloucestershire at Bristol	2008

ADDRESS

County Ground, New Road, Worcester WR2 4QQ; 01905 748474; info@wccc.co.uk; www.wccc.co.uk.

OFFICIALS

Captain 2016 D. K. H. Mitchell
2017 J. Leach
Director of cricket S. J. Rhodes
Academy coach E. J. Wilson
President N. Gifford

Chairman S. Taylor
Chief executive T. Scott
Head groundsman T. R. Packwood
Scorer S. Drinkwater/D. E. Pugh

At Oxford, March 31–April 2. WORCESTERSHIRE beat OXFORD MCCU by 482 runs. *Worcestershire's biggest victory by runs.*

WORCESTERSHIRE v KENT

At Worcester, April 10–13. Abandoned. Worcestershire 5pts, Kent 5pts.

Heavy rain on the eve of the match, and further downpours on the first and third days, left the outfield like "jelly blancmange", according to groundsman Tim Packwood. It meant only the seventh Championship washout at New Road since 1901, and the third in the last ten years. Given the conditions and the high water table, an ECB Cricket Discipline Commission were satisfied Worcestershire had done all they could.

At Bristol, April 24–27. WORCESTERSHIRE drew with GLOUCESTERSHIRE.

WORCESTERSHIRE v ESSEX

At Worcester, May 1–4. Drawn. Worcestershire 12pts, Essex 12pts. Toss: Essex.

Brett D'Oliveira became the third generation of his family to score a Championship century for Worcestershire after grandfather Basil, who made his first – also against Essex at New Road – in 1965, and father Damian, who made his in 1983. D'Oliveira got there with a two into the covers off Napier, from his 134th ball. Earlier, Cook had continued his fine form, striking a third Championship hundred in four matches, and sharing a stand of 222 with fellow centurion Westley. But the loss of 102 overs to rain on the first two days meant a draw was always likely. Leach took five on the third morning, including four in 23 balls and a superb one-handed return catch to dismiss Cook, but Essex declared on 451 for nine. Worcestershire built their reply on an opening stand of 179 between D'Oliveira and Mitchell, before five wickets fell for 43. But Köhler-Cadmore – the game's fourth century-maker – and the lower order rallied to secure maximum batting points with an over to spare.

Close of play: first day, Essex 144-1 (Cook 53, Westley 70); second day, Essex 335-2 (Cook 130, Bopara 48); third day, Worcestershire 226-5 (Köhler-Cadmore 13, Cox 2).

Essex

N. L. J. Browne c Cox b Henry	15	– c Köhler-Cadmore b Barnard	8
A. N. Cook c and b Leach	142	– not out	48
T. Westley lbw b Henry	125	– b Ali	20
R. S. Bopara b Leach	48	– not out	12
D. W. Lawrence c Köhler-Cadmore b Leach	0		
J. D. Ryder lbw b Leach	0		
*R. N. ten Doeschate lbw b Barnard	28		
†J. S. Foster not out	51		
G. R. Napier c Henry b Shantry	16		
D. D. Masters c Barnard b Leach	1		
B 4, lb 6, w 2, nb 8, p 5	25	Lb 1, nb 6	7
1/16 (1) 2/238 (3) (9 wkts dec, 113.4 overs)	451	1/28 (1) (2 wkts dec, 36 overs)	95
3/344 (4) 4/346 (5)		2/59 (3)	
5/346 (6) 6/359 (2) 7/432 (7)			
8/449 (9) 9/451 (10) 110 overs: 414-6			

J. A. Porter did not bat.

Henry 23–5–90–2; Leach 27.4–3–115–5; Shantry 29–9–87–1; Ali 11–0–52–0; Barnard 16–5–70–1; D'Oliveira 7–0–22–0. *Second innings*—Henry 4–2–6–0; Leach 3–0–16–0; Ali 15–3–28–1; Barnard 5–2–16–1; D'Oliveira 9–0–28–0.

Worcestershire

*D. K. H. Mitchell b Napier	66
B. L. D'Oliveira c Ryder b Porter	128
M. M. Ali c Foster b Napier	8
J. M. Clarke c Cook b Masters	2
T. Köhler-Cadmore not out	119
R. A. Whiteley lbw b Napier	0
†O. B. Cox c Lawrence b Napier	24
J. Leach c Cook b Porter	23
M. J. Henry c Lawrence b Masters	34
Lb 1, nb 6	7
1/179 (1) (8 wkts dec, 110.2 overs)	411

2/189 (3) 3/194 (4) 4/221 (2) 5/222 (6) 6/283 (7) 7/353 (8) 8/411 (9) — 110 overs: 405-7

E. G. Barnard and J. D. Shantry did not bat.

Porter 28–5–83–2; Masters 21.2–6–58–2; Napier 29–5–127–4; Ryder 7–2–32–0; ten Doeschate 14–0–53–0; Bopara 2–0–16–0; Westley 9–1–41–0.

Umpires: M. Burns and N. A. Mallender.

At Cardiff, May 8–11. WORCESTERSHIRE drew with GLAMORGAN.

WORCESTERSHIRE v SUSSEX

At Worcester, May 15–18. Drawn. Worcestershire 13pts, Sussex 9pts. Toss: Worcestershire.

Worcestershire controlled proceedings, only to be denied by a last-day rearguard. Following on, Sussex lost four wickets in clearing a deficit of 213, but contributions down the order – including a maiden Championship fifty from Harry Finch, before he became Mitchell's first first-class victim since 2013 – led them to safety. A second successive opening century stand at New Road from Mitchell and D'Oliveira had laid the foundations for some superb strokeplay from Clarke, followed by a post-tea onslaught by Köhler-Cadmore and Whiteley. In reply, Nash passed 10,000 first-class runs, but Sussex struggled against Worcestershire's seamers. Second time round, Wells's attritional 11 off 110 balls and nightwatchman Hatchett's fourth-morning defiance used up precious time, but last pair Robinson and Whittingham still needed to survive eight overs before the teams shook hands.

Close of play: first day, Worcestershire 382-4 (Köhler-Cadmore 43, Whiteley 54); second day, Sussex 192-6 (Brown 49, Robinson 9); third day, Sussex 137-3 (Taylor 16, Hatchett 1).

Worcestershire

*D. K. H. Mitchell c Magoffin b Whittingham	43
B. L. D'Oliveira c Finch b Wells	99
J. M. Clarke c and b Wells	82
A. N. Kervezee b Whittingham	29
T. Köhler-Cadmore lbw b Magoffin	51
R. A. Whiteley b Magoffin	71
†O. B. Cox c Nash b Hatchett	30
J. Leach c Nash b Whittingham	26
E. G. Barnard c Whittingham b Wells	14
M. J. Henry c Machan b Robinson	11
J. D. Shantry not out	1
B 17, lb 15, nb 2	34
1/113 (1) 2/190 (2) (121.2 overs)	491

3/244 (4) 4/281 (3) 5/401 (5) 6/408 (6) 7/455 (8) 8/467 (7) 9/484 (9) 10/491 (10) — 110 overs: 419-6

Magoffin 29–8–56–2; Robinson 26.2–3–109–1; Whittingham 19–1–86–3; Hatchett 22–1–103–1; Wells 25–3–105–3.

Sussex

C. D. Nash lbw b Henry	36	– (2) b Shantry	26
E. C. Joyce b Barnard	31	– (1) c Köhler-Cadmore b Barnard	74
L. W. P. Wells c Shantry b Leach	16	– c Köhler-Cadmore b Henry	11
L. R. P. L. Taylor lbw b Leach	11	– b Henry	62
M. W. Machan lbw b D'Oliveira	36	– (6) c Cox b Leach	66
H. Z. Finch c Köhler-Cadmore b Shantry	3	– (7) c and b Mitchell	57
*†B. C. Brown c Cox b Barnard	55	– (8) lbw b Henry	29
O. E. Robinson not out	51	– (9) not out	29
L. J. Hatchett c D'Oliveira b Barnard	3	– (5) b Leach	17
S. J. Magoffin b Leach	20	– c Leach b Henry	16
S. G. Whittingham b D'Oliveira	8	– not out	8
B 1, lb 4, w 1, nb 2	8	B 14, lb 1, w 1	16
1/58 (2) 2/72 (1) 3/94 (3) 4/97 (4) 5/116 (6) 6/172 (5) 7/204 (7) 8/208 (9) 9/251 (10) 10/278 (11) (97.2 overs)	278	1/54 (2) 2/105 (3) 3/131 (1) 4/183 (5) 5/231 (4) 6/286 (6) 7/346 (7) 8/364 (8) 9/396 (10) (9 wkts, 144 overs)	411

Henry 23–6–57–1; Leach 19–1–73–3; Shantry 18–6–25–1; Barnard 20–4–67–3; D'Oliveira 16.2–1–45–2; Kervezee 1–0–6–0. *Second innings*—Leach 29–5–77–2; Shantry 19–4–61–1; Henry 31–3–122–4; Barnard 22–6–42–1; D'Oliveira 25–5–45–0; Kervezee 15–5–39–0; Mitchell 3–0–10–1.

Umpires: S. A. Garratt and M. A. Gough.

At Leicester, May 22–24. WORCESTERSHIRE beat LEICESTERSHIRE by seven wickets.

WORCESTERSHIRE v GLOUCESTERSHIRE

At Worcester, May 29–June 1. Gloucestershire won by five wickets. Gloucestershire 23pts, Worcestershire 7pts. Toss: uncontested.

A remarkable century from Shantry at No. 10 was not enough to save Worcestershire, after Roderick's declaration paved the way for a thrilling chase. Köhler-Cadmore had engineered a first-day recovery from 34 for five to 297 for eight when Shantry reached the crease. But once Köhler-Cadmore had gone for 169, his fourth hundred in five innings in all cricket at New Road, the carnage really began: Shantry moved past 50 with the first of six sixes, including five in nine deliveries off Miles. Fourteen balls later, he had completed the second century of his career. In a last-wicket stand of 69, Morris went scoreless. Gloucestershire were in danger of following on at 230 for six, but van Buuren's maiden ton for the county, and his rollicking stand of 134 in 33 overs with Miles, allowed Roderick's enterprising third-day declaration, 75 behind. Miles and Norwell shared nine wickets to set up a target of 315 in 70 overs, and then came Gloucestershire's reward. The chase wobbled when wickets fell either side of tea, but Klinger and Taylor took centre stage, targeting the short boundary towards the pavilion to plunder 179 in 24 overs. Taylor finished with 107 off 72 balls, including 11 fours and six sixes, as the visitors triumphed with more than 12 overs to spare.

Close of play: first day, Worcestershire 341-8 (Köhler-Cadmore 153, Shantry 26); second day, Gloucestershire 226-5 (van Buuren 104, Taylor 3); third day, Worcestershire 151-5 (Whiteley 20, Cox 7).

Worcestershire

*D. K. H. Mitchell lbw b Payne	0	– c Marshall b Miles	55
B. L. D'Oliveira lbw b Payne	10	– lbw b Norwell	3
J. M. Clarke c Dent b Norwell	3	– b Norwell	0
A. N. Kervezee c Dent b Payne	2	– c Klinger b Taylor	39
T. Köhler-Cadmore c Roderick b Norwell	169	– b Norwell	18
R. A. Whiteley b Shaw	3	– c Payne b Miles	71
†O. B. Cox c Dent b Miles	75	– c Roderick b Norwell	18
J. Leach c Taylor b Miles	4	– c van Buuren b Miles	4
E. G. Barnard lbw b Norwell	50	– c Hankins b Miles	7
J. D. Shantry b Norwell	106	– c Roderick b Miles	0
C. A. J. Morris not out	0	– not out	4
B 8, lb 7, nb 2	17	B 6, lb 10, w 2, nb 2	20
1/0 (1) 2/3 (3) 3/26 (4) 4/31 (2) 5/34 (6) 6/189 (7) 7/205 (8) 8/297 (9) 9/370 (5) 10/439 (10) (113.1 overs)	439	1/16 (2) 2/20 (3) 3/82 (1) 4/122 (5) 5/130 (4) 6/196 (7) 7/201 (8) 8/215 (9) 9/215 (10) 10/239 (6) (56.3 overs)	239
110 overs: 434-9			

Payne 25–3–92–3; Norwell 29.1–9–70–4; Shaw 15–1–65–1; Miles 17–1–124–2; van Buuren 17–4–35–0; Taylor 10–1–38–0. *Second innings*—Payne 8–2–21–0; Norwell 17–2–70–4; Miles 12.3–1–54–5; Shaw 6–0–43–0; Taylor 10–3–20–1; van Buuren 3–0–15–0.

Gloucestershire

*†G. H. Roderick lbw b D'Oliveira	60	– c Kervezee b Barnard	30
C. D. J. Dent b Shantry	5	– c Köhler-Cadmore b Leach	5
G. L. van Buuren not out	172	– c Cox b Morris	42
M. Klinger lbw b Shantry	8	– not out	102
H. J. H. Marshall c Whiteley b Leach	34	– c Barnard b Kervezee	10
G. T. Hankins c Cox b Barnard	8	– lbw b Leach	1
J. M. R. Taylor lbw b D'Oliveira	6	– not out	107
C. N. Miles not out	60		
B 4, lb 4, w 1, nb 2	11	B 12, lb 9, nb 2	23
1/16 (2) 2/136 (1) 3/147 (4) 4/191 (5) 5/208 (6) 6/230 (7) (6 wkts dec, 112 overs)	364	1/9 (2) 2/60 (1) 3/109 (3) 4/133 (5) 5/141 (6) (5 wkts, 57.4 overs)	320
110 overs: 354-6			

D. A. Payne, J. Shaw and L. C. Norwell did not bat.

Leach 24–4–77–1; Shantry 27–3–56–2; D'Oliveira 24–5–77–2; Barnard 20–4–76–1; Morris 11–0–53–0; Kervezee 5–1–12–0; Mitchell 1–0–5–0. *Second innings*—Leach 14–1–70–2; Shantry 13–2–60–0; Barnard 9–1–43–1; Morris 9–0–62–1; Kervezee 5–1–12–1; D'Oliveira 7.4–0–52–0.

Umpires: S. C. Gale and S. J. O'Shaughnessy.

At Derby, June 20–23. WORCESTERSHIRE drew with DERBYSHIRE.

WORCESTERSHIRE v LEICESTERSHIRE

At Worcester, July 3–6. Worcestershire won by three wickets. Worcestershire 21pts, Leicestershire 5pts (after 1pt penalty). Toss: Leicestershire.

Clemency from the umpires helped Worcestershire chase 366 on the last afternoon. Clarke was unhappy when given out lbw to Raine on 31, believing he had got an inside edge. As he walked off, the umpires consulted – and agreed there had been two noises. Recalled, Clarke went on to a match-winning 123 to help Worcestershire squeak home with ten balls to spare. Leicestershire captain Cosgrove was furious, but his side had not helped themselves: they dropped Whiteley three times during a fifth-wicket stand of 142 with Clarke. Earlier, Dexter and Eckersley had steered Leicestershire's first innings over 400, and despite Fell's half-century – in his first game after undergoing chemotherapy for testicular cancer – Worcestershire were in danger of following on at

193 for seven by the second-day close. The lower order, led by Leach, kept them afloat, but Horton, who passed 1,000 runs, and Cosgrove hit hundreds. They added 264, a third-wicket record for Leicestershire against Worcestershire, to set up a challenging declaration. After the hosts slipped to 73 for four, there looked to be only one winner, but Clarke's reprieve changed the mood, and a stand of 108 in 17 overs with Leach, making a second half-century of the game, helped secure victory.

Close of play: first day, Leicestershire 299-7 (Eckersley 40, Raine 6); second day, Worcestershire 193-7 (Leach 2); third day, Leicestershire 172-2 (Horton 75, Cosgrove 58).

Leicestershire

P. J. Horton c Köhler-Cadmore b Barnard	3	– not out	117
A. J. Robson c Cox b Barnard	50	– c D'Oliveira b Leach	15
N. J. Dexter c Cox b Leach	109	– st Cox b Leach	2
*M. J. Cosgrove c Cox b D'Oliveira	28	– lbw b Shantry	146
M. L. Pettini run out	16		
†E. J. H. Eckersley not out	92		
R. M. L. Taylor c Shantry b D'Oliveira	9		
C. J. McKay lbw b Barnard	19		
B. A. Raine c and b D'Oliveira	25		
R. A. Jones b Barnard	33		
C. E. Shreck lbw b D'Oliveira	0		
B 2, lb 11, nb 10	23	B 15, lb 5, w 1, nb 6	27
1/31 (1) 2/110 (2) 3/164 (4) 4/205 (5) 5/230 (3) 6/251 (7) 7/282 (8) 8/337 (9) 9/406 (10) 10/407 (11) (125 overs)	407	1/39 (2) 2/43 (3) 3/307 (4) (3 wkts dec, 76 overs)	307
110 overs: 334-7			

Abbott 29–5–110–0; Leach 22–4–101–1; Barnard 20–4–62–4; Shantry 20–10–32–0; D'Oliveira 30–3–80–4; Mitchell 4–1–9–0. *Second innings*—Abbott 15–3–46–0; Shantry 14–4–61–1; Barnard 8–0–31–0; D'Oliveira 21–4–78–0; Leach 14–1–54–2; Mitchell 3–1–17–0; Fell 1–1–0–0.

Worcestershire

*D. K. H. Mitchell run out	52	– c Eckersley b McKay	32
B. L. D'Oliveira c Jones b McKay	18	– c Dexter b McKay	16
T. C. Fell c Eckersley b Raine	61	– c Eckersley b Shreck	10
J. M. Clarke b Dexter	34	– run out	123
T. Köhler-Cadmore lbw b Shreck	8	– c and b Shreck	5
R. A. Whiteley lbw b McKay	5	– c Robson b Shreck	71
†O. B. Cox c Robson b Cosgrove	2	– b Shreck	9
J. Leach c Shreck b McKay	90	– not out	64
E. G. Barnard c Taylor b Cosgrove	42	– not out	11
J. D. Shantry not out	13		
K. J. Abbott c Robson b McKay	5		
B 6, lb 11, nb 2	19	B 18, lb 10	28
1/38 (2) 2/135 (1) 3/140 (3) 4/170 (5) 5/187 (6) 6/191 (7) 7/193 (4) 8/293 (9) 9/341 (8) 10/349 (11) (103.1 overs)	349	1/50 (1) 2/59 (2) 3/67 (3) 4/73 (5) 5/215 (6) 6/237 (7) 7/345 (4) (7 wkts, 73.2 overs)	369

McKay 24.1–7–59–4; Jones 12–1–67–0; Raine 16–4–61–1; Dexter 15–5–41–1; Shreck 24–6–58–1; Taylor 7–2–25–0; Robson 1–0–7–0; Cosgrove 4–0–14–2. *Second innings*—McKay 21–1–81–2; Raine 9–0–60–0; Shreck 22–2–104–4; Jones 6–2–28–0; Dexter 9–2–36–0; Cosgrove 3.2–0–14–0; Taylor 3–0–18–0.

Umpires: G. D. Lloyd and J. W. Lloyds.

At Northampton, July 10–12. WORCESTERSHIRE beat NORTHAMPTONSHIRE by 311 runs.

At Worcester, July 29–30 (not first-class). WORCESTERSHIRE drew with PAKISTANIS (see Pakistan tour section)

At Canterbury, August 3–6. WORCESTERSHIRE lost to KENT by ten wickets.

WORCESTERSHIRE v GLAMORGAN

At Worcester, August 13–16. Glamorgan won by five wickets. Glamorgan 21pts, Worcestershire 3pts. Toss: uncontested.

Owen Morgan cover-drove his 242nd ball for four to become the second Glamorgan nightwatchman to score a century after Eifion Jones in 1968. It also secured the victory that lifted his side off the foot of the table. Poor shot selection on the first day saw Worcestershire bundled out for 163, only for Glamorgan to struggle in return, despite Bragg's 98. Thanks to Wallace – demoted from No. 2 in the previous game to No. 9 here, after Rudolph decided he wanted to open again – the tail carved out a healthy lead. Worcestershire batted with greater application second time round, and Clarke was denied a century only by a stunning one-handed grab on the boundary by Carey off Wagg, who went on to collect five wickets. With four second-innings catches, Wallace finished with nine dismissals, equalling for the second time in a month Colin Metson's county record. Glamorgan's progress towards a target of 277 was careful, until Donald made a brisk 57 in a fifth-wicket stand of 99 with Morgan. Leach, with eight wickets and 108 runs, did not deserve to be on the losing side.

Close of play: first day, Glamorgan 118-5 (Bragg 75, Morgan 10); second day, Worcestershire 150-2 (Fell 65, Clarke 32); third day, Glamorgan 16-1 (Rudolph 7, Morgan 9).

Worcestershire

*D. K. H. Mitchell c Wallace b Wagg	9	– c Meschede b Carey	33
B. L. D'Oliveira b Carey	4	– c Wallace b Wagg	16
T. C. Fell c Wagg b Hogan	16	– c Wallace b Wagg	65
J. M. Clarke c Wallace b Meschede	4	– c Carey b Wagg	98
T. Köhler-Cadmore c Wallace b Hogan	0	– c Wallace b Hogan	0
R. A. Whiteley c Rudolph b Meschede	40	– c Wallace b Wagg	37
†O. B. Cox c Donald b Wagg	16	– lbw b Meschede	9
J. Leach c Meschede b Hogan	43	– not out	65
E. G. Barnard c Wallace b Hogan	0	– lbw b Wagg	16
J. D. Shantry c Wallace b Carey	4	– b Morgan	29
C. A. J. Morris not out	8	– lbw b Morgan	11
Lb 13, w 4, nb 2	19	B 2, lb 10, w 2	14
1/10 (2) 2/22 (1) 3/30 (3) 4/30 (5) 5/37 (4) 6/74 (7) 7/140 (6) 8/144 (9) 9/148 (8) 10/163 (10) (57.4 overs)	163	1/29 (2) 2/55 (1) 3/151 (3) 4/152 (5) 5/256 (4) 6/256 (6) 7/279 (7) 8/308 (9) 9/364 (10) 10/393 (11) (138.1 overs)	393

Wagg 17–6–37–2; Carey 13.4–3–52–2; Hogan 15–4–44–4; Meschede 12–3–17–2. *Second innings*—Meschede 27–5–63–1; Carey 15–3–63–1; Hogan 26–5–72–1; Wagg 33–6–90–5; Morgan 35.1–9–83–2; Selman 1–0–6–0; Rudolph 1–0–4–0.

Glamorgan

N. J. Selman b Leach	0 – c Cox b Leach	0
*J. A. Rudolph c Mitchell b Morris	11 – c Fell b D'Oliveira	25
W. D. Bragg b Barnard	98 – (4) st Cox b Morris	46
D. L. Lloyd c Whiteley b Shantry	8 – (5) lbw b Leach	0
A. H. T. Donald b Leach	8 – (6) c Cox b Leach	57
C. A. J. Meschede c Shantry b Barnard	0 – (7) not out	17
A. O. Morgan b Leach	21 – (3) not out	103
G. G. Wagg c D'Oliveira b Leach	46	
†M. A. Wallace not out	67	
M. G. Hogan b Leach	4	
L. J. Carey b Barnard	11	
Lb 2, nb 4	6	B 6, lb 17, w 1, nb 6 30
1/0 (1) 2/54 (2) 3/75 (4) 4/88 (5) 5/105 (6) 6/134 (7) 7/161 (3) 8/236 (8) 9/240 (10) 10/280 (11) (77.2 overs)	280	1/0 (1) 2/59 (2) 3/147 (4) 4/150 (5) 5/249 (6) (5 wkts, 87.1 overs) 278

Leach 22–1–106–5; Barnard 12.2–2–57–3; Morris 13–2–46–1; Shantry 23–2–59–1; D'Oliveira 6–2–8–0; Mitchell 1–0–2–0. *Second innings*—Leach 21–4–66–3; Barnard 19–6–49–0; D'Oliveira 20–1–54–1; Shantry 16–4–51–0; Morris 10.1–2–34–1; Mitchell 1–0–1–0.

Umpires: S. A. Garratt and P. J. Hartley.

WORCESTERSHIRE v NORTHAMPTONSHIRE

At Worcester, August 23–26. Worcestershire won by two wickets. Worcestershire 19pts, Northamptonshire 5pts. Toss: Worcestershire. Championship debut: C. A. Barrett.

Worcestershire achieved their best chase at New Road, knocking off a target of 401 in 80 overs with one to spare. The thrilling finish needed help from the captains: after a rain-hit third day, Worcestershire declared 350 behind, before Northamptonshire sent them back in nine overs later. Mitchell led the pursuit with his second hundred of the game, and Worcestershire were cruising during his stand of 232 with fellow centurion Clarke, who went past 1,000 first-class runs for the first time. Sanderson removed both in a three-wicket burst, but Whiteley and Cox hit back with 78 in nine overs. After they fell in the space of three balls, Leach saw in victory. Northamptonshire had batted for a day and a half in making their highest score at New Road; their third centurion, Championship debutant Chad Barrett, a South African-born 27-year-old, struck the highest score by a Northamptonshire No. 10. His stand of 145 with Crook – whose own 145 was a career-best – was also a ninth-wicket record in this fixture. Earlier, Keogh hit a season's-best 154. Mitchell led a strong reply with his first Championship hundred for 13 months; his next century, which took him past 10,000 first-class runs, would not have to wait as long.

HIGHEST SUCCESSFUL RUN-CHASES BY WORCESTERSHIRE

449-9 (*set 446*)	v Somerset at Bath	1996
404-8 (*401*)	**v Northamptonshire at Worcester**	**2016**
376-7 (*373*)	v Surrey at Worcester	1961
373-9 (*373*)	v Derbyshire at Worcester	2002
369-7 (*366*)	**v Leicestershire at Worcester**	**2016**

Worcestershire's highest fourth-innings score is 467 for nine, chasing 517 against Derbyshire at Kidderminster in 1995.

Close of play: first day, Northamptonshire 345-6 (Crook 84, Murphy 7); second day, Worcestershire 153-1 (Mitchell 86, Fell 61); third day, Worcestershire 195-3 (Mitchell 102, Rhodes 6).

Northamptonshire

R. I. Newton c Morris b Barnard	2	– not out	27
B. M. Duckett c Rhodes b Leach	26	– c Mitchell b Shantry	6
*A. G. Wakely c Cox b Barnard	25	– not out	15
R. I. Keogh run out	154		
A. M. Rossington c Mitchell b Shantry	7		
R. E. Levi c Clarke b Morris	33		
S. P. Crook c Barnard b D'Oliveira	145		
†D. Murphy c Mitchell b Barnard	7		
R. K. Kleinveldt lbw b Leach	8		
C. A. Barrett not out	114		
B. W. Sanderson c Barnard b Leach	19		
Lb 7, nb 4	11	Nb 2	2
1/17 (1) 2/29 (2) 3/93 (3) 4/118 (5) 5/172 (6) 6/331 (4) 7/346 (8) 8/361 (9) 9/506 (7) 10/551 (11) (144.1 overs) 110 overs: 399-8	551	1/7 (2) (1 wkt dec, 9.2 overs)	50

Leach 29.1–1–121–3; Barnard 30–7–117–3; Shantry 23–6–80–1; Morris 25–7–93–1; D'Oliveira 26–0–88–1; Rhodes 10–0–41–0; Mitchell 1–0–4–0. *Second innings*—Shantry 3–1–6–1; Morris 3–0–12–0; Clarke 2–0–22–0; Fell 1.2–0–10–0.

Worcestershire

*D. K. H. Mitchell not out	107	– c sub (G. G. White) b Sanderson	103
B. L. D'Oliveira c Levi b Sanderson	0	– c Murphy b Kleinveldt	1
T. C. Fell c Murphy b Sanderson	66	– b Kleinveldt	22
J. M. Clarke c Duckett b Barrett	6	– lbw b Sanderson	125
G. H. Rhodes not out	7	– c Wakely b Sanderson	5
R. A. Whiteley (did not bat)		– b Barrett	45
†O. B. Cox (did not bat)		– c Wakely b Keogh	34
J. Leach (did not bat)		– not out	33
E. G. Barnard (did not bat)		– c Murphy b Sanderson	8
J. D. Shantry (did not bat)		– not out	4
B 1, lb 10, nb 4	15	B 5, lb 5, nb 14	24
1/8 (2) 2/160 (3) 3/189 (4) (3 wkts dec, 59.1 overs)	201	1/12 (2) 2/36 (3) 3/268 (1) 4/274 (5) 5/275 (4) 6/353 (6) 7/355 (7) 8/391 (9) (8 wkts, 79 overs)	404

C. A. J. Morris did not bat.

Kleinveldt 16–5–48–0; Sanderson 20–5–54–2; Barrett 11–0–29–1; Keogh 7–0–33–0; Crook 5–0–22–0; Duckett 0.1–0–4–0. *Second innings*—Sanderson 17–0–74–4; Kleinveldt 22–2–101–2; Barrett 9–0–71–1; Keogh 21–1–89–1; Crook 10–0–59–0.

Umpires: S. C. Gale and G. D. Lloyd.

At Chelmsford, August 31–September 2. WORCESTERSHIRE lost to ESSEX by an innings and 161 runs.

At Hove, September 12–14. WORCESTERSHIRE beat SUSSEX by 11 runs.

WORCESTERSHIRE v DERBYSHIRE

At Worcester, September 20–23. Worcestershire won by nine wickets. Worcestershire 23pts, Derbyshire 3pts. Toss: uncontested. First-class debut: G. T. G. Cork.

Derbyshire seemed to be heading towards a draw, only to lose their last five for 11 and leave a simple target. It was a predictable end to a dismal campaign: for the first time since 1924, they finished a Championship season without a win. Clarke's runs had them under pressure from the first morning: he was in by the 13th over, and stayed until the last before lunch on the second day, when he was caught on the boundary for a career-best 194. Leach continued, hitting his first century for three years, before backing it up with a five-wicket haul to confirm Worcestershire's dominance. Only Hosein, with a maiden hundred, and debutant Greg Cork – son of Dominic – offered much resistance, and Derbyshire followed on, 227 in arrears. They soon slipped to 74 for four, but Madsen's sixth Championship century of the season – the most for Derbyshire since Chris Rogers in 2009 – and another impressive knock from Hosein appeared to have dug them out of a hole. Mitchell, however, took two wickets in two overs, D'Oliveira two in two balls, and Worcestershire needed just 40.

Close of play: first day, Worcestershire 255-6 (Clarke 117, Leach 5); second day, Derbyshire 15-0 (Slater 7, Godleman 8); third day, Derbyshire 15-1 (Godleman 5, Hughes 10).

Worcestershire

*D. K. H. Mitchell lbw b Cotton	67	– not out	28
B. L. D'Oliveira b Milnes	0	– c Godleman b Milnes	0
T. C. Fell c Hughes b Milnes	24	– not out	15
J. M. Clarke c Hughes b Madsen	194		
G. H. Rhodes c Hosein b Cotton	16		
T. Köhler-Cadmore b Palladino	9		
†O. B. Cox c Wood b Cotton	5		
J. Leach not out	107		
E. G. Barnard not out	32		
B 10, lb 9, nb 2	21		
1/0 (2) 2/36 (3) 3/145 (1) 4/204 (5) 5/232 (6) 6/246 (7) 7/403 (4) — (7 wkts dec, 137 overs) — 110 overs: 350-6	475	1/1 (2) — (1 wkt, 9.3 overs)	43

M. L. Cummins and C. A. J. Morris did not bat.

Palladino 33–7–91–1; Milnes 30–8–90–2; Cotton 20–3–63–3; Cork 17–2–70–0; Davis 16–1–73–0; Hughes 14–5–41–0; Madsen 7–1–28–1. *Second innings*—Milnes 5–1–14–1; Davis 4.3–1–29–0.

Derbyshire

B. T. Slater c Köhler-Cadmore b Morris	25	– c Fell b Leach	0
*B. A. Godleman c Cox b Leach	11	– c Barnard b Cummins	16
T. A. Wood lbw b Leach	0	– (5) c Cox b Barnard	10
W. L. Madsen lbw b Cummins	5	– lbw b Morris	100
†H. R. Hosein c Mitchell b Leach	108	– (6) c Fell b D'Oliveira	59
A. L. Hughes c Köhler-Cadmore b Morris	4	– (3) c Köhler-Cadmore b Leach	12
T. P. Milnes c Cox b Leach	16	– b Mitchell	36
G. T. G. Cork c Clarke b Leach	49	– b Mitchell	4
A. P. Palladino lbw b Barnard	8	– lbw b Cummins	4
W. S. Davis b Barnard	0	– lbw b D'Oliveira	0
B. D. Cotton not out	13	– not out	1
B 3, lb 5, w 1	9	B 7, lb 6, w 5, nb 6	24
1/20 (2) 2/20 (3) 3/27 (4) 4/59 (1) 5/68 (6) 6/103 (7) 7/199 (8) 8/222 (9) 9/222 (10) 10/248 (5) — (85.3 overs)	248	1/1 (1) 2/19 (3) 3/29 (2) 4/74 (5) 5/198 (4) 6/255 (7) 7/261 (8) 8/261 (6) 9/261 (10) 10/266 (9) — (80.5 overs)	266

Cummins 14–2–40–1; Leach 19.3–5–60–5; Barnard 20–5–61–2; Morris 12–2–35–2; Rhodes 5–1–21–0; D'Oliveira 12–2–17–0; Mitchell 3–0–6–0. *Second innings*—Cummins 17.5–4–57–2; Leach 17–2–48–2; Morris 10–3–29–1; D'Oliveira 13–3–26–2; Barnard 12–2–57–1; Rhodes 7–0–31–0; Mitchell 4–3–5–2.

Umpires: N. G. C. Cowley and S. C. Gale.

YORKSHIRE

Third time unlucky

DAVID WARNER

Yorkshire began the season contemplating the prospect of scooping all of county cricket's prizes, including a third successive Championship. But, when coach Jason Gillespie said his final farewell, there was no new silverware in his swag bag, and Yorkshire had lost some of the zing that had seen them at their strongest in almost half a century. Yet Gillespie returned to Australia with his reputation greatly enhanced, after five seasons in which he guided Yorkshire to promotion, then runners-up in Division One, followed by two Championship titles and, finally, third place. His record of 36 wins and only seven defeats in 80 matches speaks for itself.

A spate of injuries to fast bowlers, and disappointing form from several top-order batsmen, including captain Andrew Gale, eventually handed the Championship to Middlesex, who had become their bogey side. An enthralling match at Lord's turned against Yorkshire in the final hours of the season, setting the seal on a triumph generously acknowledged by Gillespie and Gale.

David Willey's arrival from Northamptonshire meant Yorkshire had seven quality fast bowlers, plus Matthew Fisher who, at 18, had already touched 90mph. But Fisher's summer was wrecked by a hamstring tear in Dubai, in a warm-up for the champions' fixture against MCC; he suffered two similar injuries trying to regain full fitness. Tim Bresnan damaged his left Achilles tendon in the match itself, and missed the first five Championship fixtures, while in the second game Ryan Sidebottom sustained an ankle injury, exacerbated during a game of football, which kept him out until August. Willey suffered an abdominal strain early on; between that and call-ups to England's limited-overs side, he managed only four Championship appearances. Rather than having a surfeit of resources, Yorkshire found themselves overstretched.

Bresnan and Sidebottom were magnificent on their return – in Bresnan's case not only with the ball. His batting reached new heights and regularly dug Yorkshire out of trouble, never more so than in the final joust with Middlesex, when his remarkable unbeaten 142 brought an unlikely seventh bonus point to keep them in the hunt until the last afternoon.

Despite the bowling setbacks, Yorkshire might still have won a third consecutive Championship title – for the first time since Brian Close's team in 1968 – if they had not been let down by their specialist batsmen. Time and again, they lost several wickets for a pittance, leaving the rest to fight hard. As Gillespie ruefully reflected, they could not go on expecting to get out of fixes of their own making.

Openers Alex Lees and Adam Lyth were the only two to exceed 1,000 runs – Lyth led from the front in all formats – but too often they were unable to click together, opening a gate which the likes of Jack Leaning and Gale were unable to shut tight. Leaning, the Cricket Writers' Young Player of the Year in 2015, simply could not get going at first-class level. Neither could Gale: he still provided strong leadership, but mustered only 525 runs at 21 in 15 Championship matches. It left this honest cricketer pondering his future as captain and player. He initially decided to continue, before events took an unexpected turn in November. Although Gale was not one of the 16 applicants for Gillespie's job, it was offered to him by director of cricket Martyn Moxon; he accepted, and hung up his boots. His first major decision was to appoint Gary Ballance as captain, leaving last year's one-day skipper, Lees, to concentrate on his batting. Ballance will have Australia's Peter Handscomb in the middle order in 2017.

Daniel Smith, Getty Images

Jack Brooks

In terms of wickets, Jack Brooks was streets ahead of anyone else, reaching 60 in the Championship for the third consecutive season and, as ever, Steven Patterson was superb. Yorkshire stayed in contention until the last lap, when they were unable to field their preferred team at Lord's. Australian batsman Jake Lehmann, son of Darren, signed as overseas player in August after brief spells from Kane Williamson and Travis Head, but was ordered home by South Australia after scoring a splendid century in the penultimate match against Somerset; Adil Rashid declined to play because of a family illness and the need to rest before England's tour to Bangladesh; and England ruled out Jonny Bairstow, saying he too needed a break, though he was ready and willing.

Yorkshire's failure to land a one-day trophy was as disappointing as missing out on Championship glory, although they fought back from abysmal starts to make it to the semi-finals in both limited-overs tournaments. In the NatWest T20 Blast, three defeats were followed by two no-results before they discovered better form – aided by two one-run victories. But in the semi-final against Durham only Lyth batted convincingly, and in the Royal London Cup they were knocked out by Surrey. Yorkshire have yet to master one-day cricket.

The good-news story was the comeback of off-spinning all-rounder Azeem Rafiq, plucked from league cricket for a second chance after his services had been dispensed with two years earlier. He responded with 15 wickets in the Blast, while giving away only seven an over; his courageous batting in the Championship helped turn the tables on Nottinghamshire at Scarborough – where he scored 74 after coming in at 51 for six – and did much to bring about the dramatic conclusion at Lord's.

Championship attendance: 65,337.

YORKSHIRE RESULTS

All first-class matches – Played 18: Won 5, Lost 4, Drawn 9.
County Championship matches – Played 16: Won 5, Lost 3, Drawn 8.

Specsavers County Championship, 3rd in Division 1;
NatWest T20 Blast, semi-finalists; Royal London One-Day Cup, semi-finalists.

COUNTY CHAMPIONSHIP AVERAGES, BATTING AND FIELDING

Cap		*Birthplace*	*M*	*I*	*NO*	*R*	*HS*	*100*	*Avge*	*Ct/St*
2011	J. M. Bairstow§	*Bradford‡*	4	6	0	533	246	2	88.83	5/1
	†J. S. Lehmann¶	*Melbourne, Aust.*	5	8	1	384	116	1	54.85	2
2006	T. T. Bresnan	*Pontefract‡*	11	19	4	722	142*	1	48.13	12
2013	L. E. Plunkett§	*Middlesbrough‡*	8	13	3	449	126	1	44.90	3
2010	†A. Lyth	*Whitby‡*	16	30	2	1,133	202	4	40.46	25
2014	†A. Z. Lees	*Halifax‡*	16	30	1	1,165	132	3	40.17	12
2012	†G. S. Ballance§	*Harare, Zimbabwe*	13	25	2	780	132	2	33.91	8
2016	Azeem Rafiq	*Karachi, Pakistan*	6	8	2	201	74	0	33.50	5
2008	A. U. Rashid§	*Bradford‡*	10	16	2	393	88	0	28.07	7
2013	J. A. Brooks	*Oxford*	14	20	11	250	48	0	27.77	4
2016	A. J. Hodd	*Chichester*	12	18	3	391	96*	0	26.06	35/3
2008	†A. W. Gale	*Dewsbury‡*	15	26	1	525	83	0	21.00	2
	†W. M. H. Rhodes	*Nottingham*	2	4	0	73	20	0	18.25	1
2016	J. A. Leaning	*Bristol*	9	15	2	233	51	0	17.92	8
2012	S. A. Patterson	*Beverley‡*	15	20	1	300	63*	0	15.78	0
2016	†D. J. Willey	*Northampton*	4	5	0	58	22	0	11.60	0
	K. S. Williamson¶	*Tauranga, NZ*	2	4	0	42	28	0	10.50	3
2000	†R. J. Sidebottom	*Huddersfield‡*	9	11	3	75	23	0	9.37	1

Also batted: B. O. Coad (*Harrogate‡*) (1 match) 17*; †T. M. Head¶ (*Adelaide*) (1 match) 54, 2; J. E. Root§ (*Sheffield‡*) (cap 2012) (2 matches) 0, 27, 213 (5 ct); J. Shaw (*Wakefield‡*) (1 match) 24 (1 ct).

‡ *Born in Yorkshire.* § *ECB contract.* ¶ *Official overseas player.*

BOWLING

	Style	*O*	*M*	*R*	*W*	*BB*	*5I*	*Avge*
R. J. Sidebottom	LFM	245	63	657	31	5-51	1	21.19
J. A. Brooks	RFM	432.2	105	1,501	60	6-65	3	25.01
S. A. Patterson	RFM	440.5	138	1,146	39	6-56	1	29.38
T. T. Bresnan	RFM	297.1	71	934	31	5-36	1	30.12
A. U. Rashid	LBG	293.2	36	1,083	32	4-17	0	33.84
L. E. Plunkett	RFM	172.1	23	602	10	2-46	0	60.20

Also bowled: Azeem Rafiq (OB) 99.3–24–275–3; G. S. Ballance (LBG) 1–0–11–0; B. O. Coad (RFM) 35–10–108–1; T. M. Head (OB) 4–1–16–0; A. J. Hodd (LBG) 1–0–14–0; J. A. Leaning (RFM) 10–2–27–0; A. Z. Lees (LBG) 4–0–51–2; A. Lyth (RM) 79–10–322–7; W. M. H. Rhodes (RFM) 41–5–137–3; J. E. Root (OB) 18–3–49–2; J. Shaw (RFM) 29–3–119–2; D. J. Willey (LFM) 102–23–334–9; K. S. Williamson (OB) 18–2–59–2.

LEADING ROYAL LONDON CUP AVERAGES (100 runs/4 wickets)

Batting	*Runs*	*HS*	*Avge*	*SR*	*Ct*
T. M. Head	277	175	69.25	105.32	1
T. T. Bresnan	361	95*	60.16	81.85	2
A. Lyth	439	136	48.77	114.92	3
G. S. Ballance	213	80	42.60	80.68	2
J. A. Leaning	195	131*	32.50	94.20	2
D. J. Willey	123	27	20.50	83.67	2
A. Z. Lees	134	32	14.88	62.91	7

Bowling	*W*	*BB*	*Avge*	*ER*
K. Carver	5	3-5	11.00	4.23
A. U. Rashid	10	3-23	23.00	5.54
L. E. Plunkett	12	4-52	23.25	4.57
D. J. Willey	11	3-34	32.81	5.74
T. T. Bresnan	10	2-22	33.50	5.40
S. A. Patterson	9	2-30	35.00	5.16
Azeem Rafiq	6	2-46	44.83	6.72

LEADING NATWEST T20 BLAST AVERAGES (125 runs/15 overs)

Batting	*Runs*	*HS*	*Avge*	*SR*	*Ct*
A. Lyth	312	87	26.00	**152.19**	10
D. J. Willey	272	79	27.20	**148.63**	5
J. A. Leaning	272	64	27.20	**145.45**	4
T. T. Bresnan	180	29*	20.00	**138.46**	8
A. Z. Lees	294	59	22.61	**123.01**	4
K. S. Williamson	209	65	34.83	**121.51**	2

Bowling	*W*	*BB*	*Avge*	*ER*
Azeem Rafiq	15	2-21	18.46	**7.07**
S. A. Patterson	7	3-23	16.71	**7.46**
D. J. Willey	9	2-28	23.77	**7.68**
T. T. Bresnan	21	3-15	16.80	**8.02**
L. E. Plunkett	13	2-22	25.38	**8.11**
A. U. Rashid	15	4-26	19.06	**8.17**

FIRST-CLASS COUNTY RECORDS

Highest score for	341	G. H. Hirst v Leicestershire at Leicester	1905
Highest score against	318*	W. G. Grace (Gloucestershire) at Cheltenham	1876
Leading run-scorer	38,558	H. Sutcliffe (avge 50.20)	1919–45
Best bowling for	10-10	H. Verity v Nottinghamshire at Leeds	1932
Best bowling against	10-37	C. V. Grimmett (Australians) at Sheffield	1930
Leading wicket-taker	3,597	W. Rhodes (avge 16.02)	1898–1930
Highest total for	887	v Warwickshire at Birmingham	1896
Highest total against	681-7 dec	by Leicestershire at Bradford	1996
Lowest total for	23	v Hampshire at Middlesbrough	1965
Lowest total against	13	by Nottinghamshire at Nottingham	1901

LIST A COUNTY RECORDS

Highest score for	191	D. S. Lehmann v Nottinghamshire at Scarborough	2001
Highest score against	177	S. A. Newman (Surrey) at The Oval	2009
Leading run-scorer	8,699	G. Boycott (avge 40.08)	1963–86
Best bowling for	7-15	R. A. Hutton v Worcestershire at Leeds	1969
Best bowling against	7-32	R. G. D. Willis (Warwickshire) at Birmingham	1981
Leading wicket-taker	308	C. M. Old (avge 18.96)	1967–82
Highest total for	411-6	v Devon at Exmouth	2004
Highest total against	375-4	by Surrey at Scarborough	1994
Lowest total for	54	v Essex at Leeds	2003
Lowest total against	23	by Middlesex at Leeds	1974

TWENTY20 COUNTY RECORDS

Highest score for	109	I. J. Harvey v Derbyshire at Leeds	2005
Highest score against	111	D. L. Maddy (Leicestershire) at Leeds	2004
Leading run-scorer	2,260	A. W. Gale (avge 25.39)	2004–15
Best bowling for	5-16	R. M. Pyrah v Durham at Scarborough	2011
Best bowling against	4-9	C. K. Langeveldt (Derbyshire) at Leeds	2008
Leading wicket-taker	108	R. M. Pyrah (avge 21.43)	2005–15
Highest total for	**223-6**	**v Durham at Leeds**	**2016**
Highest total against	231-4	by Lancashire at Manchester	2015
Lowest total for	90-9	v Durham at Chester-le-Street	2009
Lowest total against	**90**	**by Glamorgan at Cardiff**	**2016**

ADDRESS

Headingley Cricket Ground, Leeds LS6 3BU; 0843 504 3099; cricket@yorkshireccc.com; www.yorkshireccc.com.

OFFICIALS

Captain 2016 A. W. Gale
(limited-overs) **2016** A. Z. Lees
2017 G. S. Ballance
Director of cricket M. D. Moxon
First-team coach 2016 J. N. Gillespie
2017 A. W. Gale

Director of cricket development I. M. Dews
President J. H. Hampshire
Chairman S. J. Denison
Chief executive M. A. Arthur
Head groundsman A. Fogarty
Scorer J. T. Potter

At Abu Dhabi, March 20–23. YORKSHIRE lost to MCC by four wickets (see MCC section).

At Leeds, April 11–13 (not first-class). **Drawn.** ‡**Leeds/Bradford MCCU 225-8** (74.4 overs) (H. L. Thompson 64, L. P. Weston 68*; J. A. Brooks 3-36, K. Carver 3-58) **v Yorkshire.** *County debut:* J. Read. *Each side chose from 12 players in a game which – as the last of the students' fixtures against the counties – lacked first-class status, taking the gloss off half-centuries from Henry Thompson and Logan Weston against the county champions. Joe Root's brother, Billy, was caught and bowled for a five-ball duck by Jack Brooks who, like left-arm spinner Karl Carver, collected three wickets. Bad light ended play shortly after tea on the first day, and it never resumed.*

YORKSHIRE v HAMPSHIRE

At Leeds, April 17–20. Drawn. Yorkshire 12pts, Hampshire 10pts. Toss: uncontested.

After two days, Yorkshire had Hampshire five down and trailing by 452 – but if they expected an easy win they were mistaken. Hampshire's injury-hit attack had reduced Yorkshire to 41 for three before Bairstow reproduced the spectacular form that had brought 1,108 runs in nine Championship matches in 2015. He hit a career-best 246 off 270 balls, sharing double-century stands with Lyth and Plunkett. On the second morning he advanced by 102 in 70 balls, while Plunkett reached 94 in 73, completing a maiden Championship hundred after lunch. Wood pulled up mid-over with a bad knee, and Dawson was restricted to three overs by a stomach bug. But Hampshire played with discipline next day. Vince scored an elegant century, Ervine a courageous one after Plunkett struck his left index finger, and the ninth-wicket pair saved the follow-on. Playing football in the final day's warm-up, Edwards broke his ankle; though Wood returned, coach Dale Benkenstein and video analyst Joe Maiden joined twelfth man Mason Crane as substitutes. But the fit bowlers rose to the occasion; having struggled to 43 for four, Yorkshire had to bat out time.

Close of play: first day, Yorkshire 270-5 (Bairstow 107, Rashid 7); second day, Hampshire 141-5 (Vince 76, Ervine 7); third day, Hampshire 450-8 (McLaren 55, Wood 28).

Yorkshire

A. Lyth lbw b Ervine	111	– c Wheater b McLaren	15
A. Z. Lees c Vince b Tomlinson	7	– lbw b Tomlinson	1
G. S. Ballance c Wheater b Wood	12	– c Alsop b Tomlinson	4
*A. W. Gale c Wheater b McLaren	0	– c Wheater b Wood	46
†J. M. Bairstow c Tomlinson b Alsop	246	– c Wheater b McLaren	5
J. A. Leaning c Wheater b Wood	1	– b Smith	18
A. U. Rashid c Wheater b Tomlinson	34	– c Smith b Tomlinson	22
L. E. Plunkett b Smith	126	– not out	27
S. A. Patterson lbw b Alsop	5	– c Tomlinson b Vince	1
J. A. Brooks not out	13	– not out	15
B 5, lb 12, w 3, nb 18	38	B 1, lb 20, nb 8	29
1/16 (2) 2/36 (3) (9 wkts dec, 118 overs)	593	1/3 (2) (8 wkts dec, 68.3 overs)	183
3/41 (4) 4/246 (1)		2/13 (3) 3/35 (1)	
5/249 (6) 6/348 (7) 7/575 (5)		4/43 (5) 5/116 (4) 6/120 (6)	
8/575 (8) 9/593 (9) 110 overs: 526-6		7/148 (7) 8/156 (9)	

R. J. Sidebottom did not bat.

Edwards 23–2–145–0; Tomlinson 21–4–74–2; Wood 18.4–6–79–2; McLaren 19–4–85–1; Dawson 3–0–7–0; Ervine 12–4–32–1; Vince 1.2–0–15–0; Smith 12–0–80–1; Alsop 8–0–59–2. *Second innings*—Tomlinson 16–7–31–3; Wood 16–8–21–1; Vince 10–1–43–1; McLaren 10–2–26–2; Smith 16.3–5–41–1.

Hampshire

M. A. Carberry c Lees b Plunkett	19	R. McLaren not out	55
T. P. Alsop lbw b Sidebottom	1	C. P. Wood c Lyth b Sidebottom	31
*J. M. Vince lbw b Patterson	119	Lb 9, w 1, nb 4	14
W. R. Smith lbw b Brooks	11		—
L. A. Dawson lbw b Sidebottom	16	1/9 (2) (9 wkts dec, 152.4 overs)	453
J. A. Tomlinson c Leaning b Plunkett	2	2/34 (1) 3/66 (4)	
S. M. Ervine c Bairstow b Sidebottom	123	4/125 (5) 5/128 (6) 6/203 (3) 7/346 (8)	
†A. J. A. Wheater c Ballance b Patterson	62	8/391 (7) 9/453 (10) 110 overs: 306-6	

F. H. Edwards did not bat.

Sidebottom 27.4–10–80–4; Brooks 32–11–103–1; Plunkett 25–6–75–2; Patterson 31–8–75–2; Rashid 32–4–85–0; Lyth 4–2–15–0; Ballance 1–0–11–0.

Umpires: S. C. Gale and N. J. Llong.

At Birmingham, April 24–27. YORKSHIRE drew with WARWICKSHIRE.

At Nottingham, May 1–4. YORKSHIRE drew with NOTTINGHAMSHIRE.

YORKSHIRE v SURREY

At Leeds, May 8–11. Yorkshire won by an innings and 20 runs. Yorkshire 24pts, Surrey 5pts. Toss: Surrey.

Root and Bairstow prepared for the Headingley Test by rewriting the record books and setting up Yorkshire's first win of the season. Late on, Root also led the side when Gale was hit on the knee; his first decision was to bowl himself, and he broke Surrey's backbone by dismissing Sangakkara and Davies after their second century partnership of the match. On the opening day, Davies had scored his first Championship hundred for a year, before Surrey's last six toppled for 66. Yorkshire, in turn, were 45 for three next morning, but Root and Bairstow were in a class of their own as they piled up 372 – the county's fifth-highest stand for any wicket and their biggest at Headingley. They also beat the club record against Surrey: 340 between Ted Wainwright and George Hirst at The Oval in 1899. Root's 213 from 242 balls was his sixth century for Yorkshire (and fifth over 150); Bairstow's 198 was his 15th, including seven in his last 13 matches. After a rain-wrecked third day Yorkshire declared, 227 ahead. Willey was off with an abdominal injury but, once Root had intervened, Patterson followed up with three wickets, and the champions were back on top of the table.

Close of play: first day, Yorkshire 15-0 (Lyth 6, Lees 5); second day, Yorkshire 486-5 (Root 190, Rashid 21); third day, Yorkshire 557-6 (Rashid 60, Plunkett 4).

HIGHEST PARTNERSHIPS FOR YORKSHIRE

555 for 1st	P. Holmes (224*)/H. Sutcliffe (313)	v Essex at Leyton	1932
554 for 1st	J. T. Brown (300)/J. Tunnicliffe (243)	v Derbys at Chesterfield	1898
378 for 1st	J. T. Brown (311)/J. Tunnicliffe (147)	v Sussex at Sheffield	1897
375 for 1st	A. Lyth (230)/A. Z. Lees (138)	v Northants at Northampton	2014
372 for 4th	**J. E. Root (213)/J. M. Bairstow (198)**	**v Surrey at Leeds**	**2016**
366* for 7th	J. M. Bairstow (219*)/T. T. Bresnan (169*)	v Durham at Chester-le-Street	2015
362 for 1st	M. D. Moxon (213)/M. P. Vaughan (183)	v Glam at Cardiff	1996
358 for 4th	D. S. Lehmann (339)/M. J. Lumb (98)	v Durham at Leeds	2006
351 for 1st	G. Boycott (184)/M. D. Moxon (168)	v Worcs at Worcester	1985

Surrey

R. J. Burns c Bairstow b Willey	12	– lbw b Brooks	8
A. Harinath c Ballance b Plunkett	12	– c Root b Plunkett	21
K. C. Sangakkara c Lees b Plunkett	73	– c Ballance b Root	61
S. M. Davies c Plunkett b Patterson	117	– lbw b Root	52
J. J. Roy c Root b Brooks	1	– c Rashid b Brooks	4
†B. T. Foakes c Lees b Patterson	45	– b Patterson	21
J. E. Burke lbw b Willey	6	– lbw b Brooks	0
T. K. Curran b Brooks	32	– b Patterson	22
*G. J. Batty lbw b Willey	0	– c Bairstow b Patterson	0
R. Rampaul c Bairstow b Brooks	12	– not out	4
M. P. Dunn not out	5	– lbw b Plunkett	2
Lb 13, nb 2	15	B 7, lb 5	12
1/14 (1) 2/38 (2) 3/160 (3) 4/161 (5) 5/264 (4) 6/273 (6) 7/309 (7) 8/309 (9) 9/321 (8) 10/330 (10) (91.4 overs)	330	1/14 (1) 2/34 (2) 3/138 (3) 4/143 (5) 5/151 (4) 6/152 (7) 7/194 (8) 8/194 (9) 9/205 (6) 10/207 (11) (73.1 overs)	207

Willey 20–7–55–3; Brooks 18.4–3–73–3; Plunkett 18–2–77–2; Patterson 21–6–53–2; Rashid 10–1–42–0; Root 3–0–17–0; Lyth 1–1–0–0. *Second innings*—Brooks 20–6–65–3; Plunkett 14.1–4–46–2; Patterson 9–5–15–3; Rashid 18–5–46–0; Root 12–3–23–2.

Yorkshire

A. Lyth lbw b Rampaul	13
A. Z. Lees c Foakes b Curran	16
G. S. Ballance b Rampaul	8
J. E. Root c Batty b Rampaul	213
†J. M. Bairstow c Sangakkara b Burke	198
*A. W. Gale c Foakes b Rampaul	18
A. U. Rashid not out	60
L. E. Plunkett not out	4
B 7, lb 10, w 4, nb 6	27
1/27 (1) 2/41 (3) 3/45 (2) 4/417 (5) 5/452 (6) 6/547 (4) (6 wkts dec, 111.2 overs)	557
110 overs: 551-6	

D. J. Willey, S. A. Patterson and J. A. Brooks did not bat.

Curran 31–0–139–1; Rampaul 32.2–0–153–4; Burke 12–0–74–1; Dunn 17–2–79–0; Batty 9–1–58–0; Harinath 10–1–37–0.

Umpires: S. A. Garratt and A. G. Wharf.

At Taunton, May 15–18. YORKSHIRE drew with SOMERSET.

YORKSHIRE v LANCASHIRE

At Leeds, May 29–June 1. Yorkshire won by 175 runs. Yorkshire 22pts, Lancashire 3pts. Toss: uncontested.

Yorkshire's emphatic Roses win – only their second in home Championship games since 1992 – pulled them level with Lancashire at the top of the table. Returning after a calf injury, Bresnan brought balance, most importantly contributing 69 on the opening day, when he and Rashid stopped Yorkshire falling apart with a stand of 136. Rashid scored more than anyone else in the match, though his return of seven wickets owed something to fortune. Patterson's plucky 45 secured a third batting point before he collected his 300th first-class wicket, Brown, caught by the newly capped Hodd. Lancashire were soon 92 for seven, and conceded a lead of 112. Lyth was the sole top-five batsman on either side to reach 40 as Yorkshire extended that; Lancashire were handicapped as a side strain prevented Bailey bowling. They were already missing both wicketkeepers, Alex Davies (injured) and Jos Buttler (rested); Croft gamely stood in, held six catches and conceded only two byes. But his side crumbled again in dreary conditions: most of the last two days were played under floodlights.

Close of play: first day, Yorkshire 301-9 (Patterson 41); second day, Yorkshire 77-3 (Lyth 44, Patterson 0); third day, Lancashire 41-1 (Hameed 16, Procter 6).

Yorkshire

A. Lyth c Croft b Bailey	4	– b Wagner	48
A. Z. Lees c Brown b Jarvis	0	– c Croft b Smith	17
J. A. Leaning c Smith b Jarvis	10	– c Smith b Wagner	4
G. S. Ballance c Smith b Jarvis	0	– c Croft b Wagner	8
*A. W. Gale lbw b Wagner	36	– (6) c Hameed b Wagner	7
A. U. Rashid c Procter b Kerrigan	88	– (7) c Croft b Kerrigan	34
T. T. Bresnan c Croft b Wagner	69	– (8) c Livingstone b Procter	29
L. E. Plunkett c Procter b Jarvis	3	– (9) c Petersen b Kerrigan	57
†A. J. Hodd c Livingstone b Wagner	40	– (10) not out	15
S. A. Patterson c Smith b Wagner	45	– (5) c Croft b Smith	1
J. A. Brooks not out	3	– b Procter	5
B 1, lb 7, nb 2	10	B 1, lb 6, nb 4	11
1/4 (1) 2/6 (2) 3/14 (4) (97.1 overs)	308	1/41 (2) 2/54 (3) (84.2 overs)	236
4/29 (3) 5/74 (5) 6/210 (6)		3/70 (4) 4/81 (1)	
7/215 (8) 8/226 (7) 9/301 (9) 10/308 (10)		5/89 (5) 6/89 (6) 7/130 (8)	
		8/204 (7) 9/221 (9) 10/236 (11)	

Bailey 17–2–48–1; Jarvis 20–5–74–4; Smith 16–2–54–0; Wagner 24.1–5–75–4; Kerrigan 20–3–49–1. *Second innings*—Wagner 24–3–71–4; Jarvis 23–5–72–0; Smith 14–8–20–2; Kerrigan 11–1–36–2; Procter 12.2–1–30–2.

Lancashire

T. C. Smith c Ballance b Patterson	26	– c Plunkett b Patterson	15
H. Hameed c Lyth b Bresnan	17	– c Hodd b Rashid	20
L. A. Procter lbw b Brooks	6	– c Bresnan b Lyth	16
A. N. Petersen lbw b Brooks	8	– lbw b Bresnan	24
*†S. J. Croft c Leaning b Bresnan	14	– b Bresnan	5
K. R. Brown c Hodd b Patterson	0	– c Ballance b Bresnan	51
L. S. Livingstone not out	60	– c Plunkett b Rashid	24
T. E. Bailey c Hodd b Plunkett	0	– c Hodd b Rashid	2
N. Wagner lbw b Rashid	12	– c Hodd b Bresnan	2
K. M. Jarvis st Hodd b Rashid	33	– lbw b Rashid	0
S. C. Kerrigan lbw b Rashid	6	– not out	0
B 5, lb 5, nb 4	14	B 4, lb 10	14
1/46 (1) 2/56 (2) 3/59 (3) (60.4 overs)	196	1/28 (1) 2/55 (2) (86.4 overs)	173
4/68 (4) 5/69 (6) 6/91 (5)		3/55 (3) 4/71 (5)	
7/92 (8) 8/126 (9) 9/174 (10) 10/196 (11)		5/98 (4) 6/161 (7) 7/169 (8)	
		8/172 (9) 9/173 (6) 10/173 (10)	

Bresnan 14–2–50–2; Brooks 17–7–39–2; Patterson 14–6–22–2; Plunkett 10–1–38–1; Rashid 5.4–0–37–3. *Second innings*—Bresnan 22–9–36–4; Brooks 17–8–43–0; Patterson 15–5–26–1; Plunkett 14–4–29–0; Rashid 14.4–7–17–4; Lyth 4–0–8–1.

Umpires: M. Burns and P. J. Hartley.

At Chester-le-Street, June 20–23. YORKSHIRE drew with DURHAM.

At Leeds, June 26–29. YORKSHIRE drew with PAKISTAN A (see Pakistan A tour section).

YORKSHIRE v MIDDLESEX

At Scarborough, July 3–6. Middlesex won by an innings and four runs. Middlesex 21pts, Yorkshire 4pts. Toss: Yorkshire.

After drifting for three days the game exploded into life, and a remarkable victory put Middlesex on top of Division One. It was only Yorkshire's third defeat in the competition since the start of 2014 – all by Middlesex – and their first innings defeat in 143 Championship matches at North Marine Road. Though Ballance reached his first Championship century since August, Yorkshire's measured progress earned just three batting points, later matched by the visitors. The unflappable Eskinazi batted six hours 40 minutes for a career-best 157, adding 172 with Franklin before both fell to Brooks in a flurry of wickets on the third evening. Middlesex started the final day on 470 for eight, hoping to stretch a 64-run lead to three figures. Instead, Roland-Jones and Murtagh launched a violent assault of 107 in 58 balls, hitting eight sixes between them, including six in seven deliveries. Roland-Jones, dropped at fine leg on 18, finished unbeaten on 79 from 51. The total of 577 was a record between these teams, and invigorated Middlesex's four-man attack, who rushed Yorkshire to defeat. Next day Roland-Jones, who also took six wickets, was named in England's Test squad for the first time, while Ballance was recalled.

Close of play: first day, Yorkshire 291-5 (Ballance 106, Rhodes 12); second day, Middlesex 130-2 (Eskinazi 19, Bailey 19); third day, Middlesex 470-8 (Roland-Jones 14, Murtagh 7).

Yorkshire

A. Lyth c Simpson b Murtagh	0	– c Franklin b Roland-Jones	23
A. Z. Lees c Rayner b Murtagh	63	– c Simpson b Rayner	26
K. S. Williamson c Simpson b Franklin	28	– c Simpson b Roland-Jones	4
G. S. Ballance c and b Franklin	132	– c Simpson b Finn	3
*A. W. Gale lbw b Roland-Jones	7	– c Simpson b Rayner	7
T. T. Bresnan b Murtagh	63	– b Murtagh	39
W. M. H. Rhodes b Roland-Jones	20	– c Simpson b Finn	20
†A. J. Hodd c Robson b Roland-Jones	37	– c Rayner b Murtagh	6
Azeem Rafiq c Simpson b Franklin	0	– not out	8
S. A. Patterson b Finn	13	– c Rayner b Roland-Jones	3
J. A. Brooks not out	19	– c Robson b Murtagh	6
B 4, lb 14, nb 6	24	B 5, lb 7, nb 10	22
1/0 (1) 2/85 (3) 3/111 (2) 4/131 (5) 5/257 (6) 6/300 (7) 7/334 (4) 8/334 (9) 9/371 (10) 10/406 (8) (127.5 overs) 110 overs: 332-6	406	1/41 (1) 2/47 (3) 3/63 (2) 4/63 (4) 5/89 (5) 6/136 (7) 7/144 (6) 8/147 (8) 9/156 (10) 10/167 (11) (69 overs)	167

Murtagh 31–4–100–3; Roland-Jones 29.5–7–88–3; Finn 30–8–90–1; Franklin 21–6–62–3; Rayner 15–6–44–0; Stirling 1–0–4–0. *Second innings*—Murtagh 18–4–44–3; Finn 15–2–54–2; Roland-Jones 17–5–34–3; Rayner 19–9–23–2.

Middlesex

S. D. Robson c Rhodes b Brooks	40
N. R. T. Gubbins lbw b Rhodes	43
S. S. Eskinazi c Williamson b Brooks	157
G. J. Bailey c Bresnan b Rhodes	62
†J. A. Simpson c Bresnan b Brooks	15
*J. E. C. Franklin c Williamson b Brooks	99
P. R. Stirling c Bresnan b Brooks	5
O. P. Rayner c Lees b Williamson	0
T. S. Roland-Jones not out	79
T. J. Murtagh c and b Lyth	47
S. T. Finn c Azeem Rafiq b Lyth	0
B 10, lb 5, w 1, nb 14	30
1/87 (1) 2/94 (2) 3/215 (4) 4/256 (5) 5/428 (3) 6/436 (7) 7/439 (8) 8/454 (6) 9/577 (10) 10/577 (11) (148.4 overs) 110 overs: 338-4	577

Bresnan 35–11–112–0; Brooks 37–12–137–5; Patterson 29–3–119–0; Azeem Rafiq 21–5–99–0; Rhodes 20–3–67–2; Lyth 2.4–0–9–2; Williamson 4–0–19–1.

Umpires: J. H. Evans and P. J. Hartley.

At The Oval, July 11–14. YORKSHIRE drew with SURREY.

YORKSHIRE v WARWICKSHIRE

At Leeds, August 4–6. Yorkshire won by 48 runs. Yorkshire 21pts, Warwickshire 3pts. Toss: Yorkshire. Championship debut: T. M. Head.

An exciting three-day win propelled Yorkshire from sixth to third. Plunkett and Willey were left out in favour of Sidebottom and Brooks – recovered from injuries to ankle and quad respectively – on their most effective ground; they responded with five wickets apiece, while Rashid twice sucked in the tail with his leg-spin. On a dry pitch that turned, Patel also bowled splendidly to finish with six for 104 off 61 overs, an extraordinary effort at Headingley. But several factors tilted the game towards Yorkshire. Gale won a vital toss, and the Australian Travis Head scored a polished fifty on Championship debut, before Patterson and Sidebottom shared a last-wicket stand of 53, crucial in a low-scoring match. Between destructive bursts from Sidebottom and Brooks, Lees almost carried his bat for an understated 70, helping raise the target to 229. Things just did not go Warwickshire's way: when Trott and Ambrose threatened to win, Leaning took an astonishing catch, diving to his right at third slip; Clarke, outstanding with bat and ball, probably got a nick on to his pad; and Hain had to bat at No. 7 after crashing into a concrete terrace while fielding and damaging his shoulder.

Close of play: first day, Yorkshire 252-9 (Patterson 35, Sidebottom 11); second day, Yorkshire 78-5 (Lees 39, Rashid 3).

Yorkshire

A. Lyth c Ambrose b Hannon-Dalby	24	– c Chopra b Clarke	20
A. Z. Lees lbw b Clarke	10	– c Ambrose b Wright	70
T. M. Head c Umeed b Barker	54	– c Chopra b Clarke	2
*A. W. Gale c Ambrose b Barker	14	– c Clarke b Patel	1
J. A. Leaning c Clarke b Barker	42	– b Clarke	3
A. U. Rashid c Clarke b Patel	6	– (7) c Hain b Patel	17
T. T. Bresnan c Patel b Hannon-Dalby	28	– (8) c Barker b Patel	5
†A. J. Hodd lbw b Patel	7	– (9) c Ambrose b Wright	8
S. A. Patterson c Trott b Wright	38	– (6) lbw b Clarke	0
J. A. Brooks b Barker	5	– not out	9
R. J. Sidebottom not out	13	– c Clarke b Patel	0
B 6, lb 8, nb 2	16	B 5, lb 8, nb 2	15
1/18 (2) 2/57 (1) 3/90 (4) 4/109 (3) 5/130 (6) 6/190 (5) 7/199 (7) 8/199 (8) 9/204 (10) 10/257 (9) (98.3 overs)	257	1/43 (1) 2/50 (3) 3/53 (4) 4/68 (5) 5/68 (6) 6/99 (7) 7/115 (8) 8/134 (9) 9/141 (2) 10/150 (11) (65.3 overs)	150

Barker 22–8–55–4; Wright 20.3–5–53–1; Clarke 11–2–41–1; Patel 32–8–55–2; Hannon-Dalby 13–2–39–2. *Second innings*—Barker 9–2–23–0; Wright 6–1–18–2; Patel 29.3–11–49–4; Clarke 20–5–45–4; Hannon-Dalby 1–0–2–0.

Warwickshire

V. Chopra lbw b Sidebottom	23	– (2) lbw b Brooks	4
A. R. I. Umeed c Leaning b Brooks	0	– (1) lbw b Sidebottom	0
I. J. L. Trott c and b Brooks	3	– c and b Brooks	59
*I. R. Bell c Rashid b Patterson	2	– lbw b Brooks	0
S. R. Hain c Bresnan b Sidebottom	48	– (7) c Lyth b Rashid	34
†T. R. Ambrose c Hodd b Patterson	11	– (5) c Leaning b Sidebottom	36
R. Clarke not out	50	– (6) lbw b Patterson	21
K. H. D. Barker lbw b Rashid	20	– lbw b Rashid	2
J. S. Patel c Sidebottom b Rashid	7	– st Hodd b Rashid	4
C. J. C. Wright b Rashid	0	– lbw b Rashid	8
O. J. Hannon-Dalby c Hodd b Sidebottom	0	– not out	1
B 10, lb 5	15	B 4, lb 7	11
1/4 (2) 2/26 (1) 3/26 (3) 4/40 (4) 5/80 (6) 6/112 (5) 7/163 (8) 8/175 (9) 9/178 (10) 10/179 (11) (52 overs)	179	1/0 (1) 2/14 (2) 3/14 (4) 4/105 (5) 5/109 (3) 6/141 (6) 7/145 (8) 8/157 (9) 9/167 (10) 10/180 (7) (68.3 overs)	180

Sidebottom 15–1–41–3; Brooks 11–5–28–2; Bresnan 3–0–14–0; Patterson 10–3–30–2; Lyth 4–0–19–0; Rashid 9–0–32–3. *Second innings*—Sidebottom 11–2–30–2; Brooks 17–3–48–3; Bresnan 7–2–14–0; Patterson 12–4–21–1; Rashid 13.3–1–29–4; Head 4–1–16–0; Lyth 4–0–11–0.

Umpires: J. H. Evans and S. J. O'Shaughnessy.

At Manchester, August 13–16. YORKSHIRE drew with LANCASHIRE.

YORKSHIRE v NOTTINGHAMSHIRE

At Scarborough, August 23–26. Yorkshire won by 305 runs. Yorkshire 21pts, Nottinghamshire 3pts. Toss: uncontested. County debut: T. J. Moores.

When Yorkshire slipped to 51 for six on the first morning, relegation favourites Nottinghamshire were threatening a shock. But the form book eventually held true, and Yorkshire's crushing win left them only five points behind leaders Middlesex. Mullaney did the early damage – a run-out and three wickets in 23 deliveries – but it was repaired by an admirable 132-run stand between Azeem Rafiq and Hodd, who ran out of partners four short of a maiden century for Yorkshire. No such recovery rescued Nottinghamshire from 61 for six; they could not even reach three figures. There was some chuntering among a crowd of almost 5,000 when Ballance, acting-captain because of Gale's bad back, waived the follow-on, but it did not matter. Though a deluge wiped out more than half the third day, Ballance had time to complete a hundred before declaring 451 ahead. Bresnan was virtually unplayable, enjoying career-best innings and match returns, before Sidebottom and Brooks mopped up the last four in 21 balls after lunch. Nottinghamshire's only comfort was some fine batting from Tom Moores, son of their coaching consultant Peter, and making his debut for them after a short spell at Lancashire.

Close of play: first day, Nottinghamshire 38-2 (Mullaney 15); second day, Yorkshire 200-4 (Ballance 75, Bresnan 0); third day, Nottinghamshire 61-3 (Moores 41, Taylor 3).

Yorkshire

A. Lyth run out	12	– c and b Wood	41
A. Z. Lees c Taylor b Mullaney	13	– lbw b Hutton	30
*G. S. Ballance lbw b Fletcher	1	– not out	101
J. S. Lehmann c Patel b Mullaney	5	– c Wood b Patel	35
J. A. Leaning c Patel b Hutton	5	– st Read b Patel	15
T. T. Bresnan lbw b Mullaney	10	– not out	35
†A. J. Hodd not out	96		
Azeem Rafiq lbw b Patel	74		
S. A. Patterson lbw b Imran Tahir	2		
J. A. Brooks b Hutton	48		
R. J. Sidebottom lbw b Hutton	0		
Lb 12, w 2, nb 2	16	Lb 3, w 1, nb 2	6
1/21 (1) 2/26 (2) 3/36 (4) 4/36 (3) 5/51 (6) 6/51 (5) 7/183 (8) 8/192 (9) 9/280 (10) 10/282 (11) (81.3 overs)	282	1/72 (2) 2/76 (1) 3/137 (4) 4/194 (5) (4 wkts dec, 73.2 overs)	263

Wood 9–0–35–0; Fletcher 18–5–43–1; Mullaney 16–6–54–3; Hutton 14.3–2–67–3; Imran Tahir 13–1–48–1; Patel 11–1–23–1. *Second innings*—Mullaney 8–0–40–0; Fletcher 16–1–57–0; Wood 18–4–67–1; Hutton 16.2–6–53–1; Imran Tahir 4–1–10–0; Patel 11–0–33–2.

Nottinghamshire

S. J. Mullaney lbw b Sidebottom	25	– c Leaning b Brooks	2
J. D. Libby lbw b Brooks	0	– c Lehmann b Bresnan	9
T. J. Moores c Lyth b Bresnan	23	– c Lyth b Bresnan	41
M. J. Lumb c Hodd b Sidebottom	0	– c Hodd b Bresnan	0
B. R. M. Taylor b Patterson	14	– c Lees b Brooks	38
S. R. Patel c Bresnan b Sidebottom	4	– c Hodd b Bresnan	5
*†C. M. W. Read c Lees b Brooks	7	– c Lehmann b Bresnan	1
B. A. Hutton c Lyth b Brooks	5	– c Hodd b Sidebottom	20
L. Wood c Hodd b Bresnan	7	– not out	16
L. J. Fletcher c Leaning b Bresnan	6	– b Brooks	0
Imran Tahir not out	2	– c Lees b Brooks	0
Lb 1	1	B 8, lb 4, nb 2	14
1/0 (2) 2/38 (3) 3/41 (4) 4/48 (1) 5/52 (6) 6/61 (7) 7/79 (8) 8/79 (5) 9/87 (9) 10/94 (10) (37.1 overs)	94	1/3 (1) 2/34 (2) 3/34 (4) 4/61 (3) 5/77 (6) 6/83 (7) 7/130 (8) 8/130 (5) 9/130 (10) 10/146 (11) (57.3 overs)	146

Sidebottom 12–3–21–3; Brooks 11–1–41–3; Patterson 7–3–16–1; Bresnan 7.1–1–15–3. *Second innings*—Sidebottom 16–5–37–1; Brooks 13.3–4–35–4; Patterson 15–8–26–0; Bresnan 12–2–36–5; Azeem Rafiq 1–1–0–0.

Umpires: M. Burns and N. A. Mallender.

At Southampton, August 31–September 3. YORKSHIRE drew with HAMPSHIRE.

YORKSHIRE v DURHAM

At Leeds, September 6–9. Yorkshire won by 228 runs. Yorkshire 23pts, Durham 4pts. Toss: uncontested.

Apart from the second afternoon, when Durham advanced to 205 for four, Yorkshire dominated this game; the only niggle was not going quite fast enough to secure the fifth batting point which would have put them joint top with Middlesex. But they were happy to reach 460 on a pitch whose early moisture Durham's bowlers would have better exploited with a fuller length. Lees led the way with a century that made him the first Yorkshireman to reach 1,000 Championship runs in 2016; in the second innings, Lyth also achieved the landmark, with a six that brought up his hundred, and Brooks joined in when he dismissed Stoneman a second time, his 50th Championship wicket of the season. Brooks and Sidebottom bowled explosively, though Yorkshire never seriously considered enforcing the follow-on. Gale's declaration left Durham 421 to win, and it was all over by mid-afternoon. Collingwood had taken the gloves for much of Yorkshire's first innings after Richardson injured a finger, though he returned on the second day, and Patterson missed part of the third day because his father was ill.

Close of play: first day, Yorkshire 341-5 (Bresnan 11, Hodd 22); second day, Durham 205-4 (Burnham 34, Clark 17); third day, Durham 39-3 (Borthwick 7, Onions 2).

Yorkshire

A. Lyth c Jennings b Onions	2	– not out	114
A. Z. Lees c and b Pringle	132	– c Richardson b Pringle	88
G. S. Ballance c Collingwood b McCarthy	71	– b Pringle	20
*A. W. Gale b Onions	17		
J. S. Lehmann c Pringle b Rushworth	58		
T. T. Bresnan b Rushworth	22		
†A. J. Hodd c Collingwood b McCarthy	31		
Azeem Rafiq st Richardson b Borthwick	45		
S. A. Patterson b McCarthy	4		
J. A. Brooks b Collingwood	36		
R. J. Sidebottom not out	7		
B 21, lb 12, nb 2	35	Lb 3	3
1/5 (1) 2/168 (3) 3/190 (4) 4/277 (2) 5/308 (5) 6/355 (6) 7/392 (7) 8/397 (9) 9/444 (8) 10/460 (10) — (121.1 overs) 110 overs: 392-7	460	1/185 (2) 2/225 (3) — (2 wkts dec, 50.4 overs)	225

Rushworth 27–5–101–2; Onions 34–8–101–2; Collingwood 12.1–0–39–1; McCarthy 20–1–103–3; Pringle 7–4–14–1; Jennings 13–6–30–0; Borthwick 8–0–39–1. *Second innings*—Rushworth 6–0–27–0; Onions 11–0–37–0; Pringle 13.4–0–69–2; Borthwick 14–0–74–0; McCarthy 6–0–15–0.

Durham

M. D. Stoneman c Lyth b Brooks	38	– c Gale b Brooks	10
K. K. Jennings c Hodd b Patterson	40	– c Hodd b Brooks	8
S. G. Borthwick c Lyth b Patterson	53	– lbw b Sidebottom	9
J. T. A. Burnham b Sidebottom	49	– lbw b Patterson	9
*P. D. Collingwood b Bresnan	6	– (6) lbw b Sidebottom	9
G. Clark lbw b Brooks	25	– (7) c Hodd b Bresnan	25
†M. J. Richardson c Lyth b Brooks	4	– (8) c Bresnan b Sidebottom	33
R. D. Pringle lbw b Brooks	1	– (9) not out	57
B. J. McCarthy c Hodd b Bresnan	10	– (10) c Lyth b Bresnan	3
G. Onions b Sidebottom	19	– (5) c Ballance b Sidebottom	6
C. Rushworth not out	0	– b Brooks	6
B 10, lb 8, nb 2	20	B 5, lb 6, nb 6	17
1/56 (1) 2/113 (2) 3/154 (3) 4/165 (5) 5/227 (6) 6/235 (4) 7/235 (7) 8/236 (8) 9/265 (9) 10/265 (10) — (94.1 overs)	265	1/17 (1) 2/18 (2) 3/31 (4) 4/49 (5) 5/56 (3) 6/63 (6) 7/112 (7) 8/149 (8) 9/171 (10) 10/192 (11) — (63.2 overs)	192

Sidebottom 22.1–6–55–2; Brooks 19–2–76–4; Bresnan 21–9–49–2; Patterson 15–4–35–2; Azeem Rafiq 13–4–19–0; Lyth 4–0–13–0. *Second innings*—Sidebottom 15–3–34–4; Brooks 15.2–4–55–3; Patterson 16–5–41–1; Bresnan 12–3–44–2; Azeem Rafiq 5–2–7–0.

Umpires: R. J. Evans and G. D. Lloyd.

YORKSHIRE v SOMERSET

At Leeds, September 12–14. Somerset won by ten wickets. Somerset 23pts, Yorkshire 3pts. Toss: Yorkshire.

Somerset inflicted Yorkshire's first defeat at Headingley since April 2013 – only the second there in Jason Gillespie's five-year reign as coach – to enter the final round one point behind them and ten behind Middlesex. It looked inevitable once they demolished Yorkshire for 145. There was some assistance from a previously used pitch, and plenty of movement in hot and humid weather, but Gale would not blame conditions for their lowest first-innings total since May 2014. Somerset bowled intelligently – Overton and Allenby deserved their six cheap wickets – and fielded brilliantly, while Yorkshire were poor on the first evening, when Trescothick and Rogers put on 107. The attack picked up, but the damage had been done. Sidebottom swung the ball for his best figures of 2016, but Somerset batted with responsibility. Gregory pepped them up in a career-best 73 after Trego completed 1,000 first-class runs in a season for the first time. By the second evening, Yorkshire's position was near-hopeless: three down and still 188 behind. On the third day Jake Lehmann, son of Darren, showed he was a chip off the old block in a sparkling 116, his final innings before being summoned home by South Australia. But Leach's skilful left-arm spin hoovered up the last six wickets to seal the victory that gave Somerset hope of their first Championship title.

Close of play: first day, Somerset 107-1 (Trescothick 45, Rogers 58); second day, Yorkshire 57-3 (Lyth 27, Lehmann 15).

Yorkshire

A. Lyth c Davies b Allenby	14	– c Davies b Overton	49
A. Z. Lees c Allenby b Overton	0	– c Allenby b Gregory	9
G. S. Ballance c Gregory b Overton	3	– b Groenewald	1
*A. W. Gale c Davies b Overton	29	– b Groenewald	2
J. S. Lehmann c Hildreth b Trego	31	– lbw b Leach	116
A. U. Rashid c Overton b Allenby	1	– st Davies b Leach	16
T. T. Bresnan not out	38	– b Leach	4
†A. J. Hodd b Allenby	0	– c Abell b Leach	1
L. E. Plunkett c Allenby b Groenewald	10	– c Trescothick b Leach	73
J. A. Brooks b Groenewald	7	– c and b Leach	0
R. J. Sidebottom c Davies b Gregory	3	– not out	2
B 5, lb 2, nb 2	9	B 7, lb 4, nb 2	13
1/1 (2) 2/19 (3) 3/39 (1) (61.2 overs)	145	1/22 (2) 2/23 (3) (96.3 overs)	286
4/86 (5) 5/87 (4) 6/95 (6)		3/37 (4) 4/99 (1)	
7/97 (8) 8/112 (9) 9/122 (10) 10/145 (11)		5/126 (6) 6/156 (7) 7/162 (8)	
		8/263 (5) 9/265 (10) 10/286 (9)	

Overton 15–3–32–3; Gregory 7.2–0–32–1; Allenby 15–8–16–3; Groenewald 12–1–43–2; Leach 2–1–1–0; Trego 10–5–14–1. *Second innings*—Overton 16–1–57–1; Gregory 18–5–41–1; Groenewald 18–6–55–2; Allenby 7–0–27–0; Leach 24.3–4–64–6; Trego 13–4–31–0.

Somerset

M. E. Trescothick b Plunkett	73	– not out	37
T. B. Abell lbw b Brooks	0	– not out	7
*C. J. L. Rogers c Lyth b Sidebottom	63		
J. C. Hildreth b Sidebottom	2		
J. Allenby lbw b Rashid	50		
P. D. Trego c Hodd b Sidebottom	46		
L. Gregory not out	73		
C. Overton lbw b Rashid	38		
†R. C. Davies c Bresnan b Sidebottom	9		
M. J. Leach b Sidebottom	1		
T. D. Groenewald st Hodd b Rashid	13		
Lb 21, w 1	22		
1/0 (2) 2/123 (3) 3/125 (4) (98.3 overs)	390	(no wkt, 10.3 overs)	44
4/164 (1) 5/228 (6) 6/257 (5)			
7/358 (8) 8/369 (9) 9/375 (10) 10/390 (11)			

Sidebottom 22–7–51–5; Brooks 19–1–84–1; Bresnan 17–1–74–0; Plunkett 15–0–54–1; Rashid 22.3–2–99–3; Lyth 3–0–7–0. *Second innings*—Sidebottom 3–0–10–0; Brooks 5–3–24–0; Lyth 2.3–0–10–0.

Umpires: R. A. Kettleborough and J. W. Lloyds.

At Lord's, September 20–23. YORKSHIRE lost to MIDDLESEX by 61 runs. *Chasing 240 in 40 overs to win a third successive Championship, Yorkshire yield the title to Middlesex.*

NATWEST T20 BLAST IN 2016

REVIEW BY NEVILLE SCOTT

1 Northamptonshire *2 Durham* *3= Nottinghamshire, Yorkshire*

Against the background hoopla of a finals day conducted, as usual, with all the class and dignity of a Donald Trump rally in Alabama, it was the tone of true cricket that triumphed. At its best, most often between national sides, Twenty20 can be very good, largely because these teams have the depth in batting, and the wicket-taking bowling, to change a match. It is this compelling potential for the narrative to shift that has long been the abiding essence of cricket. But in England's domestic competition, games are too often mundane and predictable, damp squibs that sullenly puncture the hype. Not so on a squally, miserable day at Edgbaston, where incisive bowling, intelligent captaincy and team cohesion defined three superb games. As Alex Wakely, the winning Northamptonshire captain, reflected: "It's not all about superstars."

Indeed, it is not. The four teams on show owed far less than many rivals to imported talent, and the two finalists – Wakely's Steelbacks and a Durham side that had only once before advanced beyond the quarters – were the two most financially straitened counties. The entire quartet emerged from the North Group, leaving richer clubs from the South-East, and their capacity crowds, behind. Previews spoke of the "northern powerhouse finale", though Northampton is hardly Trondheim. What was on offer was professional rigour, as the best of English Twenty20 continues its passage from power batting alone to clear analysis.

In 2013, David Ripley, Northamptonshire's outstanding, unsung coach, had prepared for his first full campaign with a team that in the two previous seasons had lost 18 matches and won just three. They have now appeared in three of the last four finals, winning twice. Ripley's well-upholstered side still turn up looking like a village XI who have stopped en route for pasties, yet they play with the tactical nous of Napoleon. Beyond biffing, they grasp the key moments of battle, forever a prime virtue in the longer game. "We get a lot of stick for being big boys," observed Graeme White, their left-arm spinner. "But we don't half take some catches."

The single most significant moment was precisely such a catch. Andre Russell, who had arrived from the Caribbean two days earlier, was racing along in Nottinghamshire's reply in the first semi-final. As famous for missing drugs tests as for hammering sixes, he attempted his fourth in 18 balls, but was held on the boundary by Rob Keogh, sprinting and diving full length. Nottinghamshire fell to an eight-run defeat against a side lacking Richard Gleeson, an unknown seamer from Cumberland who was the competition's meanest regular bowler – and a typical Ripley recruit. Gleeson was cruelly injured with finals day in sight.

It was tighter still for Durham. Eschewing containment, they set fields for attacking bowling at decisive junctures, seizing their semi against Yorkshire

Gareth Copley, Getty Images

Oops, we did it again: Rob Keogh and Rory Kleinveldt celebrate Northamptonshire's triumph.

by seven runs. And, in the most enthralling few minutes of the day, Mark Wood – summoning searing pace – so unsettled Joe Root that it brought his downfall next over. It was classic cricket.

Wood and Ben Stokes had only recently returned for Durham after injury. But the inclusion in the two more fancied teams of five England players released for the occasion, and of Russell, proved less than a blessing. If their selection was inevitable, it arguably unsettled tight-knit squads. All four teams who lost the quarter-finals fielded a greater percentage of imported talent through the competition than Northamptonshire or Durham, whose men had grown together, learning each other's games.

Keaton Jennings, Durham's left-handed South African-born opener, made 88, taking his side to 153 for eight in the climax. Now in a fifth season with his mother's native county, his Twenty20-best before May had been one not out. Jennings's innings of old-school resolve was the highest on any finals day, and looked match-winning when Northamptonshire slipped to nine for three. But Wakely bedded in, and Josh Cobb's 80 from 48 balls was perhaps the one batting performance of the day to supply the full T20 flair, outshining even Ben Duckett's 84 from 47 against Nottinghamshire.

If the finals, with such varied virtues, were outstanding, the quarters typified so much of the rest. In the midsummer referendum, Britain had opted out of Europe; for their part, Glamorgan turned their back on Wales. In marked contrast to the nation's successful football team, nurtured from meagre home resources, 58% of their appearances were by imports raised in the southern hemisphere. More veldt than valleys, they lost to Yorkshire by 90 runs after catastrophic batting failure. Despite a bravura late effort from Jack Taylor,

Gloucestershire had long surrendered their game with Durham after top-order chaos. Middlesex, granting half their overall appearances to players brought up overseas, were hammered at Northampton. Only Essex threatened to win, chasing 163 against Nottinghamshire. But from 76 for one in the 11th over, they lost four in 14 balls from Samit Patel, seeking big shots without focus, in a slide to 123 all out.

In the 98 (of 126) group-stage games that escaped rain interference, first-innings scores brought the following results:

93–152 runs: P31 W4 L27
153–186: P43 W20 L23
187–225: P24 W20 L4

If there has been a slow improvement in the tightness of matches, about half could still be predicted at the midway stage. And one familiar indicator applied again: in around three-quarters of fixtures, the side with the higher score at the second wicket's fall won the game. Further assessment is intrinsically more subjective. But perhaps 55 of the 98 matches seemed essentially walkovers, and 22 were nailbiters. In the other 21, some smaller chance of a tense finish remained after 15 overs of the reply.

Jason Roy hit two of the season's eight hundreds, though Varun Chopra, granted only one Warwickshire game, and Glamorgan's David Lloyd both made unbeaten 97s before their sides' innings ended early. Roy's 187-run stand with Aaron Finch in the final group round ushered Surrey to victory over Kent, and equalled the second-highest partnership in domestic T20; but for rain at Chelmsford that night, it would probably have secured Surrey a quarter-final. Instead Essex, able to lose yet still needing 183 to advance on net run-rate, took a point for a no-result without having to bat against Glamorgan.

The ECB, betraying their addiction to commercial-speak, used to talk of "appointments to view" in the fixture schedules. This seemed to imply some mysterious role for estate agents; in fact it meant only that certain games were played on Fridays. But play in 2017 will be shifted, en bloc, to the school holidays: squatter's rights to high summer, perhaps? With barely a pause, the entire 133-match programme takes place on 40 days and 40 nights, a wilderness indeed for those trying to learn how to bowl (or counter) Test-quality spin at precisely the time when dry pitches once let slow bowlers take the stage. Between July 12 and August 28, there will be a single Championship round.

Claims that this helps embrace a new, youthful audience would be more convincing if clubs attempted to put the young into active contact with the recreational game, promoting participation more than passive consumption. As for the ECB's other aim, to introduce a new tournament of eight city-based teams, plans soon stalled once specifics (who would run such sides, who select them, how might player auctions actually work) were faced. It was agreed in September, with only Surrey, Sussex and Kent dissenting, to investigate possibilities, but wider opposition fast emerged. Change may not now come until 2020, when current media contracts run out. Yet Colin Graves, the ECB chairman, is so ardently committed to the idea that intense political machination, for the ownership – even soul – of the game, looks certain.

Whatever the schedule, T20 remains crucially influenced by rain. Of 23 matches in the North Group between June 10 and July 3 (more than a third of the total), 13 were either no-results or subject to DLS. Scores plummeted, and the flavour of games changed completely.

Worcestershire's 53 all out against Lancashire was the second-lowest total in competition history, with Stephen Parry claiming five for 13. Ryan Higgins (Zimbabwe-born but Berkshire-raised) replicated those figures for Middlesex a month later; only two home-grown bowlers, Tim Murtagh and Paul Collingwood, had returned better domestic analyses. But two Durham seamers, Barry McCarthy (on competition debut) and Usman Arshad, equalled the fourth-most expensive returns, each conceding 63.

In between, both claimed three wickets to beat Lancashire, one week after McCarthy's unfortunate start. On the same dubious Old Trafford pitch, Warwickshire later missed the quarters by failing to reach a target of 125. Durham were last-gasp beneficiaries that night – things would be less kind in the final as the Birmingham rain fell.

Prize money

£256,060 for winners: NORTHAMPTONSHIRE.
£123,934 for runners-up: DURHAM.
£30,212 for losing semi-finalists: NOTTINGHAMSHIRE, YORKSHIRE.
£4,500 for losing quarter-finalists: ESSEX, GLAMORGAN, GLOUCESTERSHIRE, MIDDLESEX.
Match-award winners received £2,500 in the final, £1,000 in the semi-finals, £500 in the quarter-finals and £225 in the group games.

FINAL GROUP TABLES

	North Group	*Played*	*Won*	*Lost*	*No-result*	*Points*	*NRR*
1	NOTTINGHAMSHIRE	14	8	2	4	20	0.74
2	NORTHAMPTONSHIRE	14	7	5	2	16	0.27
3	YORKSHIRE	14	7	5	2	16	0.22
4	DURHAM	14	6	6	2	14	–0.05
5	Lancashire	14	6	7	1	13	0.20
6	Warwickshire	14	6	7	1	13	–0.22
7	Derbyshire	14	5	7	2	12	0.02
8	Worcestershire	14	5	7	2	12	–0.86
9	Leicestershire	14	4	8	2	10	–0.18

	South Group	*Played*	*Won*	*Lost*	*No-result*	*Points*	*NRR*
1	GLOUCESTERSHIRE	14	10	3	1	21	0.52
2	GLAMORGAN	14	8	3	3	19	1.01
3	MIDDLESEX	14	7	6	1	15	0.40
4	ESSEX	14	7	6	1	15	0.17
5	Surrey	14	7	7	0	14	0.15
6	Sussex	14	5	6	3	13	–0.05
7	Kent	14	6	8	0	12	–0.64
8	Hampshire	14	4	8	2	10	–0.69
9	Somerset	14	3	10	1	7	–0.66

Where counties finished equal on points, positions were decided by (a) net run-rate, (b) most points in head-to-head matches, and (c) drawing lots.

NATWEST T20 BLAST AVERAGES

BATTING (300 runs at SR of 125)

		M	*I*	*NO*	*R*	*HS*	*100*	*50*	*Avge*	***SR***	*4*	*6*
1	†Ashar Zaidi (*Essex*)	15	11	2	363	59*	0	3	40.33	**168.83**	21	23
2	†C. A. Ingram (*Glam*)	14	14	2	502	101	1	4	41.83	**164.59**	42	29
3	J. J. Roy (*Surrey*)	12	12	1	495	120*	2	2	45.00	**164.45**	66	13
4	D. T. Christian (*Notts*)	13	11	3	327	56	0	3	40.87	**159.51**	17	23
5	†A. Lyth (*Yorks*)	12	12	0	312	87	0	2	26.00	**152.19**	39	12
6	T. Köhler-Cadmore (*Worcs*)	13	13	0	323	127	1	1	24.84	**148.16**	33	15
7	D. J. Bell-Drummond (*Kent*)	9	9	2	379	112*	1	2	54.14	**148.04**	47	4
8	†D. J. Malan (*Middx*)	13	12	2	368	93	0	4	36.80	**147.79**	37	15
9	S. A. Northeast (*Kent*)	14	14	0	462	75	0	4	33.00	**145.28**	40	15
10	†H. D. Rutherford (*Derbys*)	12	12	1	343	71*	0	2	31.18	**142.91**	36	12
11	†B. M. Duckett (*Northants*)	14	14	3	477	84	0	3	43.36	**141.54**	64	7
12	A. N. Petersen (*Lancs*)	12	12	2	455	103*	1	2	45.50	**140.43**	32	13
13	A. M. Rossington (*Northants*)	15	15	1	317	85	0	3	22.64	**140.26**	38	11
14	M. H. Wessels (*Northants*)	13	12	2	420	80*	0	3	42.00	**139.53**	43	15
15	†M. D. Stoneman (*Durham*)	17	15	1	356	82*	0	2	25.42	**137.45**	37	8
16	M. Klinger (*Glos*)	15	14	3	548	101	1	4	49.81	**134.64**	58	16
17	C. D. Nash (*Sussex*)	13	12	1	308	112*	1	0	28.00	**133.91**	34	10
18	L. R. P. L. Taylor (*Sussex*)	10	10	3	394	93*	0	3	56.28	**133.10**	30	17
19	I. A. Cockbain (*Glos*)	15	14	5	499	73*	0	3	55.44	**132.36**	43	13
20	I. R. Bell (*Warwicks*)	14	13	1	489	80	0	5	40.75	**130.74**	46	16
21	J. L. Denly (*Kent*)	14	14	0	378	75	0	3	27.00	**129.89**	32	16
22	D. L. Lloyd (*Glam*)	14	14	1	382	97*	0	2	29.38	**129.49**	47	8
23	J. J. Cobb (*Northants*)	15	15	2	464	80	0	5	35.69	**128.17**	43	18
24	B. L. D'Oliveira (*Worcs*)	13	13	3	353	62*	0	1	35.30	**126.97**	25	10
25	T. Westley (*Essex*)	15	14	1	403	74*	0	1	31.00	**126.72**	53	3

BOWLING (10 wickets, economy-rate 7.60)

		Style	*O*	*Dots*	*R*	*W*	*BB*	*4I*	*Avge*	*SR*	***ER***
1	R. J. Gleeson (*Northants*)	RFM	37.3	124	224	14	3-12	0	16.00	16.07	**5.97**
2	D. W. Steyn (*Glam*)	RF	18.3	61	113	11	4-18	1	10.27	10.09	**6.10**
3	C. J. McKay (*Leics*)	RFM	42.2	120	267	13	3-20	0	20.53	19.53	**6.30**
4	C. Rushworth (*Durham*)	RFM	46.0	135	297	19	3-14	0	15.63	14.52	**6.45**
4	R. Clarke (*Warwicks*)	RFM	41.3	128	268	15	3-22	0	17.86	16.60	**6.45**
6	S. R. Patel (*Notts*)	SLA	48.0	96	312	16	4-20	1	19.50	18.00	**6.50**
7	L. A. Dawson (*Hants*)	SLA	44.0	90	296	19	5-17	2	15.57	13.89	**6.72**
8	M. G. Hogan (*Glam*)	RFM	40.3	94	276	16	4-28	1	17.25	15.18	**6.81**
9	M. J. J. Critchley (*Derbys*)	LBG	37.5	71	259	11	3-36	0	23.54	20.63	**6.84**
10	B. A. C. Howell (*Glos*)	RFM	56.0	120	385	24	3-18	0	16.04	14.00	**6.87**
11	T. van der Gugten (*Glam*)	RFM	39.0	115	268	19	4-14	2	14.10	12.31	**6.87**
12	S. Prasanna (*Northants*)	LBG	37.0	71	257	12	3-24	0	21.41	18.50	**6.94**
13	J. S. Patel (*Warwicks*)	OB	44.3	84	310	11	3-23	0	28.18	24.27	**6.96**
14	Azeem Rafiq (*Yorks*)	OB	39.1	88	277	15	2-21	0	18.46	15.66	**7.07**
15	D. W. Lawrence (*Essex*)	LBG	26.0	56	185	10	2-11	0	18.50	15.60	**7.11**
16	N. A. Sowter (*Middx*)	LBG	36.0	70	260	11	2-29	0	23.63	19.63	**7.22**
17	C. J. Jordan (*Sussex*)	RFM	30.2	70	220	12	3-18	0	18.33	15.16	**7.25**
18	M. D. Taylor (*Glos*)	LFM	43.0	101	315	15	3-16	0	21.00	17.20	**7.32**
19	T. S. Roland-Jones (*Middx*)	RFM	39.0	96	287	17	3-24	0	16.88	13.76	**7.35**
19	N. L. Buck (*Lancs*)	RFM	28.0	74	206	12	4-26	1	17.16	14.00	**7.35**
21	S. G. Borthwick (*Durham*)	LBG	50.4	97	373	18	4-18	1	20.72	16.88	**7.36**
22	T. M. J. Smith (*Glos*)	SLA	44.0	69	327	12	2-13	0	27.25	22.00	**7.43**
23	R. S. Bopara (*Essex*)	RM	48.0	81	361	11	2-15	0	32.81	26.18	**7.52**
24	G. G. White (*Northants*)	SLA	42.0	73	318	13	4-20	1	24.46	19.38	**7.57**

LEADING WICKETKEEPERS

Dismissals	M	
14 (12 ct, 2 st)	14	P. Mustard (*Durham, Glos*)
12 (10 ct, 2 st)	6	C. B. Cooke (*Glam*)
12 (7 ct, 5 st)	15	A. M. Rossington (*N'hants*)
11 (9ct, 2 st)	10	B. T. Foakes (*Surrey*)
11 (8ct, 3 st)	15	J. A. Simpson (*Middx*)
9 (6ct, 3st)	8	C. M. W. Read (*Notts*)
8 (3ct, 5 st)	12	A. J. Hodd (*Yorks*)

LEADING FIELDERS

Ct	M	
12	11	M. W. Machan (*Sussex*)
10	12	A. Lyth (*Yorks*)
10	17	M. J. Richardson (*Durham*)
10	14	C. A. Ingram (*Glam*)
10	15	S. P. Crook (*Northants*)
9	9	R. I. Keogh (*Northants*)
9	13	S. R. Hain (*Warwicks*)
9	15	I. A. Cockbain (*Glos*)
9	15	T. Westley (*Essex*)

NORTH GROUP

DERBYSHIRE

At Derby, June 3 (floodlit). **Derbyshire won by four wickets. Leicestershire 120** (20 overs) (N. J. Dexter 34; J. D. S. Neesham 3-26, S. J. Thakor 3-17); ‡**Derbyshire 123-6** (18 overs). *MoM:* J. D. S. Neesham. *Attendance:* 3,279. *On the day Graeme Welch, Derbyshire's elite performance director, handed in his resignation, and white-ball captain Wes Durston was ruled out for a month through injury, victory was a fillip. Seamers Jimmy Neesham and Shiv Thakor shared six wickets to dismiss Leicestershire for 120, though Derbyshire – barely in better shape at 54-5 than Leicestershire were at 53-6 – needed a calming stand of 49 in eight overs between Neesham and Alex Hughes, the stand-in captain.*

At Derby, June 17 (floodlit). **Warwickshire won by four wickets. Derbyshire 141-7** (20 overs) (H. D. Rutherford 33, W. L. Madsen 38); ‡**Warwickshire 145-6** (20 overs) (I. R. Bell 67). *MoM:* I. R. Bell. *Attendance:* 2,404. *Warwickshire almost blew their chase after restricting Derbyshire to an unimposing 141. Ian Bell's 67 had set them on their way but, needing ten off the final over, they lost two wickets to leave the scores level as new man Ateeq Javid faced the last. Undeterred, he punched a low full toss from Neesham to the long-on boundary.*

At Derby, June 24 (floodlit). **Nottinghamshire won by seven wickets. Derbyshire 114** (19.3 overs) (H. F. Gurney 4-20); ‡**Nottinghamshire 120-3** (14.3 overs) (M. H. Wessels 35*, D. T. Christian 38*). *MoM:* H. F. Gurney. *Attendance:* 3,973. *Disciplined bowling from Nottinghamshire – Harry Gurney took a format-best 4-20 – coupled with erratic Derbyshire batting meant a one-sided contest. Set 115 on a blameless pitch, Nottinghamshire won with 33 balls to spare.*

At Chesterfield, July 3. **Derbyshire v Northamptonshire. Abandoned.**

At Derby, July 10. **Yorkshire won by one run. Yorkshire 166-6** (20 overs) (D. J. Willey 33, K. S. Williamson 65); ‡**Derbyshire 165-8** (20 overs) (H. D. Rutherford 44, N. T. Broom 37, C. F. Hughes 35; A. U. Rashid 3-20). *MoM:* A. U. Rashid. *Attendance:* 3,879. *Derbyshire responded well to Yorkshire's 166, which had been led by Kane Williamson's 65, but had to rebuild after a fine spell from Adil Rashid. They needed 17 from 12 balls, only to lose four for nine to render Matt Critchley's six off the last irrelevant. The game had been moved to Derby after a sodden outfield at Chesterfield prevented play on any of the five other days of the festival.*

At Derby, July 13 (floodlit). **Derbyshire won by six wickets. Lancashire 167-9** (20 overs) (A. N. Petersen 79, L. M. Reece 32; J. D. S. Neesham 4-35); ‡**Derbyshire 170-4** (18.4 overs) (H. D. Rutherford 47, W. J. Durston 51). *MoM:* J. D. S. Neesham. *Attendance:* 2,383. *Alviro Petersen's outstanding 79 off 49 balls set the foundation for a stiffer target, but Lancashire's final three overs added just 14 for the loss of six wickets; Neesham took three in the last – a fourth fell to a run-out – to claim a Twenty20-best 4-35. The switch in momentum was picked up by Derbyshire openers Hamish Rutherford and Durston, who put on 75 in 38 balls, and helped keep the chances of a quarter-final place alive.*

At Derby, July 22 (floodlit). **Derbyshire won by 29 runs. Derbyshire 192-5** (20 overs) (H. D. Rutherford 64, W. L. Madsen 50*); ‡**Worcestershire 163** (17.5 overs) (B. L. D'Oliveira 44; M. J. J. Critchley 3-36). *MoM:* H. D. Rutherford. *Attendance:* 2,429. *In a must-win match for both sides, Rutherford's dynamic strokeplay at the top of the innings, and Wayne Madsen's at the end, sped Derbyshire to 192. Brett D'Oliveira took the fight to them, before becoming one of three victims for leg-spinner Critchley.*

Derbyshire away matches

May 21: beat Lancashire by nine wickets.
May 27: lost to Northamptonshire by three wickets.
June 10: no result v Nottinghamshire.
June 19: lost to Yorkshire by one run (DLS).
July 1: beat Worcestershire by seven wickets.
July 8: lost to Leicestershire by nine wickets.
July 29: lost to Durham by 13 runs.

DURHAM

At Chester-le-Street, June 1 (floodlit). **Durham won by 66 runs. Durham 178-7** (20 overs) (P. D. Collingwood 44*; S. R. Patel 3-14); ‡**Nottinghamshire 112** (19.2 overs) (M. H. Wessels 38; P. Coughlin 3-25, B. J. McCarthy 3-27). *MoM:* P. D. Collingwood. *Attendance:* 3,022. *Paul Collingwood went in at 111-6 in the 15th over and walloped 44* off 22 balls. On a bitterly cold night, the slow-medium variations of Keaton Jennings and Collingwood then stifled Nottinghamshire, who threw away wickets in frustration; Paul Coughlin and Barry McCarthy were a little costlier, but finished with three wickets apiece. Earlier, Samit Patel's 3-14 had ensured Durham's innings stalled in the middle.*

At Chester-le-Street, June 24 (floodlit). **Durham won by six runs** (DLS). **Yorkshire 134** (19.3 overs) (A. Z. Lees 43, J. A. Leaning 48; C. Rushworth 3-14); ‡**Durham 68-3** (9.5 overs). *MoM:* C. Rushworth. *Attendance:* 5,757. *Yorkshire were undone by the accuracy of Chris Rushworth, who accounted for both Adam Lyth and Kane Williamson in his opening spell (3–15–9–2), and went on to a career-best 3-14. For Durham, Ben Stokes, playing solely as a batsman after a knee operation, made only five before being athletically caught by Williamson at short extra. Even so, home noses were just ahead when a storm broke. The game was watched by the king and queen of Lesotho, in Durham to celebrate a 30-year partnership with the diocese.*

At Chester-le-Street, June 30 (floodlit). **No result. Worcestershire 103-5** (14.1 overs) (J. M. Clarke 36) **v** ‡**Durham.** *County debut:* K. J. Abbott (Worcestershire). *Rain stopped play in the 15th over. Jennings had smothered Worcestershire with 4–9–18–2.*

At Chester-le-Street, July 10. **Durham won by five wickets. Leicestershire 146-6** (20 overs) (L. J. Hill 31*; S. G. Borthwick 4-18); ‡**Durham 147-5** (18.3 overs) (P. Mustard 75*, G. J. Muchall 32; C. J. McKay 3-21). *MoM:* S. G. Borthwick. *Attendance:* 3,497. *Leicestershire slipped into gear only for their last two overs, which yielded 38; Lewis Hill raced to 31* from 15 balls. Scott Borthwick had taken four Twenty20 wickets for the first time, pipping Phil Mustard – whose 75* came from 50 deliveries – to the match award.*

At Chester-le-Street, July 15 (floodlit). **Durham won by six wickets. Northamptonshire 149-5** (20 overs) (J. J. Cobb 68, B. M. Duckett 48*); ‡**Durham 153-4** (18.3 overs) (M. D. Stoneman 40, P. Mustard 40, K. K. Jennings 36*; S. Prasanna 3-24). *MoM:* K. K. Jennings. *Attendance:* 3,147. *Jennings rode to the rescue with 36* off 24 balls after Durham, needing 150, slipped from 77-0 to 89-4; leg-spinner Seekkuge Prasanna grabbed three. For Northamptonshire, Josh Cobb had made 68 off 51 balls, sharing a third-wicket stand of 95 with Duckett, whose 48* did not quite have his customary fluency.*

At Chester-le-Street, July 22 (floodlit). **Lancashire won by four runs. Lancashire 176-3** (20 overs) (A. N. Petersen 42, K. R. Brown 41, L. S. Livingstone 43*); ‡**Durham 172-5** (20 overs) (M. D. Stoneman 36, C. S. MacLeod 45; S. Mahmood 3-31). *MoM:* S. Mahmood. *Attendance:* 4,241. *Liam Livingstone and Saqib Mahmood were released from England Lions duty – and both played their part. Livingstone reeled off ramps and scoops in his 43* from 24 balls, while Mahmood, generating real pace, hit the stumps three times in four deliveries. His first victim was Calum MacLeod, just when he was threatening to take Durham home.*

At Chester-le-Street, July 29 (floodlit). **Durham won by 13 runs. Durham 193-2** (20 overs) (M. D. Stoneman 82*, C. S. MacLeod 83); ‡**Derbyshire 180-9** (20 overs) (W. J. Durston 44, N. T. Broom

68; S. G. Borthwick 3-33). *MoM:* C. S. MacLeod. *Attendance:* 3,519. *County debut:* A. J. Mellor (Derbyshire). *Mark Stoneman and MacLeod put on a Durham-record 141 for the second wicket, helping them clinch – and deny Derbyshire – a quarter-final spot. Stoneman's 82 came from 56 balls, MacLeod's 83 from 50. Although Neil Broom made a brisk 68, Derbyshire lost wickets too regularly to sustain their early pace.*

Durham away matches

May 20: lost to Worcestershire by 38 runs.
May 27: beat Lancashire by six wickets.
June 3: lost to Warwickshire by nine wickets.
June 4: lost to Leicestershire by six wickets.
June 17: lost to Northamptonshire by 26 runs.
July 1: no result v Nottinghamshire.
July 20: lost to Yorkshire by 49 runs.

LANCASHIRE

At Manchester, May 21. **Derbyshire won by nine wickets. Lancashire 131-7** (19 overs) (S. J. Croft 31); ‡**Derbyshire 132-1** (13.4 overs) (W. J. Durston 30, H. D. Rutherford 71*). *MoM:* H. D. Rutherford. *Attendance:* 3.054. *County debut:* J. D. S. Neesham (Derbyshire). *In a game reduced to 19 overs a side, the county with fewest Twenty20 wins thrashed the county with most, as Lancashire's trophy defence began badly. Tom Smith returned after missing most of the 2015 season with a back injury, but no one could master a Derbyshire attack led by Jimmy Neesham, who took two wickets on debut. Hamish Rutherford's 40-ball 71* exposed the inadequacy of Lancashire's score.*

At Manchester, May 27 (floodlit). **Durham won by six wickets. Lancashire 149-8** (20 overs) (M. J. Guptill 72; U. Arshad 3-30, B. J. McCarthy 3-23); ‡**Durham 151-4** (15 overs) (P. Mustard 46, G. Clark 36, M. J. Richardson 34*). *MoM:* P. Mustard. *Attendance:* 5,114. *County debut:* M. J. Guptill (Lancashire). *Martin Guptill's fine innings on debut was eclipsed by an even more ferocious assault from Phil Mustard, who fell for 46 to just his 18th ball. His demolition of poor bowling helped Durham swipe 43 from their first two overs, which made the pursuit of a weak total straightforward.*

At Manchester, June 3 (floodlit). **Lancashire won by 26 runs. Lancashire 204-7** (20 overs) (K. R. Brown 54, L. S. Livingstone 55; T. T. Bresnan 3-24); ‡**Yorkshire 178-7** (20 overs) (J. E. Root 92*; G. A. Edwards 3-33). *MoM:* L. S. Livingstone. *Attendance:* 15,868. *A compelling Roses game featured two remarkable innings: Liam Livingstone scorched what was then Lancashire's quickest Twenty20 fifty, off 21 balls, while Yorkshire's attempt to score at more than ten an over was sustained almost single-handedly by Joe Root. His career-best 92* came from 51 balls, but the control of Lancashire's three spinners determined the outcome.*

At Manchester, June 10 (floodlit). **Lancashire won by nine wickets** (DLS). **Leicestershire 131-3** (14 overs) (M. J. Cosgrove 66*); ‡**Lancashire 77-1** (6.1 overs) (J. Clark 31*). *MoM:* J. Clark. *Attendance:* 3,780. *County debut:* C. S. Delport (Leicestershire). *Jordan Clark and Jos Buttler scored 35 from 11 balls to secure a Lancashire victory in a rain-splattered game: a heavy shower delayed the start and reduced the match to a 14-over affair, though Mark Cosgrove's 66* gave Leicestershire hope. More rain left Lancashire needing 74 from seven, which proved gettable.*

At Manchester, June 16 (floodlit). **Lancashire v Northamptonshire. Abandoned.**

At Manchester, June 24 (floodlit). **Lancashire won by 96 runs. Lancashire 149-5** (20 overs) (A. N. Petersen 68*); ‡**Worcestershire 53** (13.5 overs) (N. L. Buck 3-12, S. D. Parry 5-13). *MoM:* S. D. Parry. *Attendance:* 5,000. *County debut:* T. J. Moores (Lancashire). *Alviro Petersen's relative caution – he took 54 balls over 68* – steered Lancashire to a modest total, yet it was enough to bring their second-largest victory by runs. Stephen Parry claimed their best Twenty20 figures as Worcestershire collapsed for 53, their lowest score: only Brett D'Oliveira (16) made double figures. Wicketkeeper Tom Moores – on loan from Nottinghamshire – took a leg-side catch to dismiss Tom Köhler-Cadmore from the first ball of Worcestershire's reply.*

At Manchester, July 29 (floodlit). **Lancashire won by 30 runs.** ‡**Lancashire 124-5** (20 overs) (T. J. Moores 39*, J. Clark 31*); **Warwickshire 94-8** (20 overs) (S. Mahmood 3-12). *MoM:* T. J. Moores. *Attendance:* 10,263. *The upshot of an intriguing game on a slow pitch was the elimination of both teams. A win would have seen Warwickshire progress, but they were undone by Lancashire's four* *spinners – and the accuracy of Saqib Mahmood. Lancashire, whose graphene-thin chances of qualification were scuppered by other results, had recovered from 59-5 in the 14th thanks to a counter-attack from Moores and Clark.*

Lancashire away matches

June 4: lost to Nottinghamshire by two wickets.
June 19: lost to Warwickshire by 18 runs (DLS).
July 1: lost to Yorkshire by five runs.
July 8: beat Worcestershire by seven wickets.
July 13: lost to Derbyshire by six wickets.
July 15: lost to Leicestershire by nine runs.
July 22: beat Durham by four runs.

LEICESTERSHIRE

At Leicester, May 20 (floodlit). **Northamptonshire won by five wickets** (DLS). **Leicestershire 178-5** (20 overs) (M. L. Pettini 43, Umar Akmal 52*); ‡**Northamptonshire 168-5** (17.5 overs) (R. E. Levi 61, B. M. Duckett 37*). *MoM:* R. E. Levi. *Attendance:* 3,250. *County debut:* S. Prasanna (Northamptonshire). *In the first match played under permanent floodlights at Grace Road, Umar Akmal thrashed a rapid 52* to leave Northamptonshire a stiff challenge, later revised to 164 in 18 overs. But Richard Levi's brutal 61 from 29 balls gave them the advantage, and Seekkuge Prasanna, on debut, sealed victory with a first-ball six off the game's penultimate delivery.*

At Leicester, June 4 (floodlit). **Leicestershire won by six wickets. Durham 120-9** (20 overs) (K. K. Jennings 42; B. A. Raine 3-24); ‡**Leicestershire 123-4** (16.3 overs) (N. J. O'Brien 33*). *MoM:* B. A. Raine. *Attendance:* 3,140. *An unbroken fifth-wicket stand of 57* between Akmal and Niall O'Brien completed a Leicestershire victory set up by their bowlers. Durham's top five were all gone within 26 balls and, though Calum MacLeod and Keaton Jennings put on 58, the damage had been done.*

At Leicester, June 17 (floodlit). **Leicestershire v Worcestershire. Abandoned.**

At Leicester, June 24 (floodlit). **Warwickshire won by eight wickets. Leicestershire 125-7** (20 overs) (Umar Akmal 31); ‡**Warwickshire 126-2** (15.3 overs) (I. R. Bell 36*, L. J. Evans 52*). *MoM:* L. J. Evans. *Attendance:* 2,873. *Leicestershire never recovered from 25-4, as the Warwickshire seamers applied a chokehold. Their eventual 125 proved inadequate; Laurie Evans helped himself to 52* from 29 balls.*

At Leicester, July 8 (floodlit). **Leicestershire won by nine wickets. Derbyshire 158** (19.5 overs) (N. T. Broom 59, J. D. S. Neesham 45; B. A. Raine 3-43, C. J. McKay 3-20); ‡**Leicestershire 164-1** (15.5 overs) (M. L. Pettini 71*, M. J. Cosgrove 52, C. S. Delport 38*). *MoM:* M. L. Pettini. *Attendance:* 2,739. *County debut:* F. Behardien (Leicestershire). *Mark Pettini and Mark Cosgrove put on 106 for the first wicket in ten overs to help Leicestershire brush aside 159. Clint McKay's 3-20 had left Derbyshire short of runs, despite Neil Broom's 59 and a belligerent 45 from Jimmy Neesham.*

At Leicester, July 12 (floodlit). **Leicestershire v Nottinghamshire. Abandoned.**

At Leicester, July 15 (floodlit). **Leicestershire won by nine runs. Leicestershire 207-3** (20 overs) (M. L. Pettini 76, C. S. Delport 68); ‡**Lancashire 198-4** (20 overs) (A. N. Petersen 103*, S. J. Croft 36). *MoM:* M. L. Pettini. *Attendance:* 2,675. *Leicestershire's highest T20 total at Grace Road – built around a stand of 140 in 12 overs between Pettini and Cameron Delport, who hit six sixes – proved enough. Despite a 52-ball 103 from Alviro Petersen, holders Lancashire were on the brink.*

Leicestershire away matches

May 27: beat Yorkshire by 54 runs.
June 3: lost to Derbyshire by four wickets.
June 10: lost to Lancashire by nine wickets (DLS).
June 26: lost to Northamptonshire by six wickets.
July 10: lost to Durham by five wickets.
July 17: lost to Warwickshire by 28 runs.
July 29: lost to Nottinghamshire by eight wickets (DLS).

NORTHAMPTONSHIRE

At Northampton, May 27 (floodlit). **Northamptonshire won by three wickets. Derbyshire 195-7** (20 overs) (W. J. Durston 47, C. F. Hughes 46, T. Poynton 37*); ‡**Northamptonshire 197-7** (19.4 overs) (R. E. Levi 58, J. J. Cobb 35, S. P. Crook 33*; A. Carter 3-34). *MoM:* R. E. Levi.

Attendance: 3,350. *Richard Levi's 28-ball half-century powered Northamptonshire's highest successful T20 chase at home. He boosted them to 77-1 in the powerplay and, though two wickets fell in the last over, a no-ball brought victory. Rapid forties from Wes Durston and Chesney Hughes had given Derbyshire a crackling start, before the loss of four wickets in 11 balls.*

At Northampton, June 3 (floodlit). **Northamptonshire won by seven wickets.** ‡**Worcestershire 144-6** (20 overs) (D. K. H. Mitchell 44*); **Northamptonshire 147-3** (16.3 overs) (R. E. Levi 44, J. J. Cobb 56*). *MoM:* J. J. Cobb. *Attendance:* 3,361. *A straightforward Northamptonshire win was marred by a freak injury to their fast bowler Olly Stone. Leaping in the air to celebrate the dismissal of Moeen Ali, he landed heavily and suffered knee damage, ending his season. Worcestershire's 144 looked modest and, after another Levi burst, Josh Cobb proved it so, hitting his first six into one of the bars, and finishing the game with his third.*

At Northampton, June 17 (floodlit). **Northamptonshire won by 26 runs. Northamptonshire 161-9** (20 overs) (J. J. Cobb 68; P. Coughlin 5-42); ‡**Durham 135-8** (20 overs) (P. D. Collingwood 38; M. A. Ashraf 3-17). *MoM:* J. J. Cobb. *Attendance:* 3,875. *County debut:* M. A. Ashraf (Northamptonshire). *Paul Coughlin took a hat-trick with the last three balls of Northamptonshire's innings – the second for Durham in the competition, after Paul Collingwood's against the same opposition in 2011. It completed a triple-wicket maiden, brought Coughlin his first Twenty20 five-for, and left Durham needing 162. But they never recovered after sliding to 9-4, three of them to former Yorkshire seamer Moin Ashraf on debut for Northamptonshire. Cobb chipped in with two to back up his brisk 68.*

At Northampton, June 26. **Northamptonshire won by six wickets. Leicestershire 149-5** (20 overs) (M. L. Pettini 56; R. J. Gleeson 3-20); ‡**Northamptonshire 152-4** (17.5 overs) (A. M. Rossington 50, J. J. Cobb 57). *MoM:* J. J. Cobb. *Attendance:* 4,393. *Adam Rossington and Cobb helped Northamptonshire to an easy win with a second-wicket stand of 89 in ten overs. Earlier, Mark Pettini hit 56, but Richard Gleeson made life difficult for Leicestershire. He took 3-20 and delivered a last-over beamer, which struck Paul Horton in the ribs and forced him to retire hurt.*

At Northampton, July 8 (floodlit). **Nottinghamshire won by six wickets. Northamptonshire 122** (18.2 overs) (R. E. Levi 35; Imran Tahir 3-13, S. J. Mullaney 3-12); ‡**Nottinghamshire 123-4** (17 overs) (M. J. Lumb 38, D. T. Christian 56). *MoM:* Imran Tahir. *Attendance:* 6,114. *Leg-spinner Imran Tahir enjoyed a successful T20 debut for Nottinghamshire – his fifth county – sharing 6-25 with Steven Mullaney as Northamptonshire collapsed from 60-1 to 122. Gleeson removed Riki Wessels and ran out Greg Smith early in the reply, but Michael Lumb and Dan Christian added 79; Nottinghamshire extended their unbeaten run against Northamptonshire to 15 matches in all competitions.*

At Northampton, July 19 (floodlit). **Northamptonshire won by 74 runs. Northamptonshire 200-5** (20 overs) (R. E. Levi 31, A. M. Rossington 85, A. G. Wakely 53*); ‡**Warwickshire 126** (17.5 overs) (I. R. Bell 62; R. K. Kleinveldt 3-14, S. Prasanna 3-26, G. G. White 4-20). *MoM:* A. M. Rossington. *Attendance:* 5,221. *Northamptonshire's near-perfect display secured them a quarter-final place. Rossington laid the foundations, and Alex Wakely built on them, hitting three sixes in a fierce 23-ball 53 to swell the target to 201. Ian Bell unfurled some sumptuous strokes in reply but, after a solid start, Warwickshire lost all ten for 62. Graeme White's hat-trick, spread over two overs, went unnoticed until announced over the PA system.*

At Northampton, July 29 (floodlit). **Yorkshire won by 14 runs.** ‡**Yorkshire 177-5** (20 overs) (A. Z. Lees 59, J. A. Leaning 64); **Northamptonshire 163-7** (20 overs) (B. M. Duckett 41, A. G. Wakely 64; T. T. Bresnan 3-15). *MoM:* J. A. Leaning. *Attendance:* 6,428. *Both sides were happy with the outcome: victory booked Yorkshire a place in the last eight, while Northamptonshire, by exceeding 159, secured a lucrative home quarter-final. Yorkshire had struggled until Jack Leaning provided acceleration with 64 off 29 balls, including five sixes. Tim Bresnan's outstanding spell then put Northamptonshire behind the required rate, but a format-best knock from Wakely – also with five sixes – made sure of the secondary target.*

Northamptonshire away matches

May 20: beat Leicestershire by five wickets (DLS).
June 10: lost to Worcestershire by three wickets.
June 16: no result v Lancashire.
July 1: beat Warwickshire by eight wickets (DLS).
July 3: no result v Derbyshire.
July 15: lost to Durham by six wickets.
July 22: lost to Yorkshire by 75 runs.

NOTTINGHAMSHIRE

At Nottingham, May 20 (floodlit). **Warwickshire won by six wickets. Nottinghamshire 179-7** (20 overs) (M. H. Wessels 52, G. P. Smith 43, D. T. Christian 34; J. S. Patel 3-23); ‡**Warwickshire 185-4** (19.4 overs) (S. R. Hain 92*). *MoM:* S. R. Hain. *Attendance:* 10,423. *County debut:* L. Ronchi (Warwickshire). *After Riki Wessels and Greg Smith put on 83 in 8.3 overs for the third wicket, an explosion from Dan Christian left Warwickshire a daunting target. They scored only one run from the first two overs, but opener Sam Hain, on T20 debut, wrested control with 92* from 54 balls.*

At Nottingham, June 4. **Nottinghamshire won by two wickets. Lancashire 184-4** (20 overs) (K. R. Brown 47, J. C. Buttler 56*); ‡**Nottinghamshire 185-8** (19.4 overs) (M. J. Lumb 53, M. H. Wessels 58; G. A. Edwards 3-38). *MoM:* M. H. Wessels. *Attendance:* 10,749. *After Jos Buttler's 56* off 29 balls left Nottinghamshire needing 185, they reached 100-0 in the ninth over. A collapse to 168-8 made it tight, but Lancashire incurred a six-run penalty for failing to start the last over on time, which brought the task down from 15. After Sam Wood hit the second ball for six, the rest was simple.*

At Nottingham, June 10 (floodlit). **Nottinghamshire v Derbyshire. Abandoned.**

At Nottingham, July 1 (floodlit). **Nottinghamshire v ‡Durham. Abandoned.**

At Nottingham, July 9. **Nottinghamshire won by nine wickets. Worcestershire 124-8** (20 overs) (O. B. Cox 37*); ‡**Nottinghamshire 128-1** (12.2 overs) (M. H. Wessels 80*, G. P. Smith 32*). *MoM:* M. H. Wessels. *Attendance:* 8,484. *Disciplined and penetrative bowling proved too much for every Worcestershire batsman bar Ben Cox, and Nottinghamshire romped home. Wessels finished on 80* from 35 balls, hitting seven sixes, including three in Ed Barnard's only over.*

At Nottingham, July 15 (floodlit). **Nottinghamshire won by three wickets.** ‡**Yorkshire 160-7** (20 overs) (A. Lyth 39, K. S. Williamson 39, T. M. Head 40; H. F. Gurney 3-16); **Nottinghamshire 162-7** (19.4 overs) (G. P. Smith 32, S. R. Patel 58, C. M. W. Read 35*). *MoM:* C. M. W. Read. *Attendance:* 12,595. *County debut:* T. M. Head (Yorkshire). *Samit Patel and Chris Read rescued Nottinghamshire's chase from a wobbly 102-6 in the 14th over to all but guarantee a quarter-final place. Earlier, Travis Head had smashed four sixes on Yorkshire debut before becoming one of the outstanding Harry Gurney's three victims.*

At Nottingham, July 29 (floodlit). **Nottinghamshire won by eight wickets** (DLS). **Leicestershire 170-4** (18 overs) (M. J. Cosgrove 53, F. Behardien 48*, L. J. Hill 30); ‡**Nottinghamshire 146-2** (10.3 overs) (M. J. Lumb 69*, D. T. Christian 54*). *MoM:* D. T. Christian. *Attendance:* 12,810. *Pursuing a revised 141 from 14 overs, Nottinghamshire sprinted to an eighth win from eight completed T20 matches. Christian launched six sixes in a 16-ball 54*, matching Alex Hales's fastest half-century for Nottinghamshire. Michael Lumb was hardly slower: he took one more ball to reach the mark, and whacked 26 off seamer Richard Jones in the fourth over of the chase.*

Nottinghamshire away matches

June 1: lost to Durham by 66 runs.
June 17: no result v Yorkshire.
June 18: beat Worcestershire by four wickets.
June 24: beat Derbyshire by seven wickets.
July 8: beat Northamptonshire by six wickets.
July 12: no result v Leicestershire.
July 22: beat Warwickshire by six wickets.

WARWICKSHIRE

At Birmingham, May 27 (floodlit). **Worcestershire won by five wickets. Warwickshire 155-7** (20 overs) (I. R. Bell 66); ‡**Worcestershire 161-5** (19.1 overs) (A. N. Kervezee 40, B. L. D'Oliveira 62*). *MoM:* B. L. D'Oliveira. *Attendance:* 13,007. *Brett D'Oliveira played decisive hands in both innings as Worcestershire earned their first T20 win at Edgbaston in five years. First, he conceded 17 from four overs of leg-spin, then he biffed a format-best 62*, finishing the game with a six.*

At Birmingham, June 3 (floodlit). **Warwickshire won by nine wickets. Durham 154-9** (20 overs) (R. D. Pringle 33, P. D. Collingwood 40*; C. R. Woakes 3-25); ‡**Warwickshire 155-1** (17.4 overs) (V. Chopra 97*, I. R. Bell 35). *MoM:* V. Chopra. *Attendance:* 6,894. *Former captain Varun Chopra had been omitted from Warwickshire's white-ball teams in 2016, but was a late call-up here for the ill Sam Hain; he vented his frustration by stroking a competition-best 97*. It ensured a comfortable* *win, but proved his only limited-overs appearance of the year. Earlier, Chris Woakes's 3-25 kept Durham below par.*

At Birmingham, June 10 (floodlit). **Warwickshire v ‡Yorkshire. Abandoned.** *After three defeats, Yorkshire claimed their first point.*

At Birmingham, June 19. **Warwickshire won by 18 runs** (DLS). **Warwickshire 144-9** (20 overs) (L. Ronchi 53; N. L. Buck 4-26); ‡**Lancashire 39-4** (6.3 overs). *MoM:* L. Ronchi. *Attendance:* 7,279. *Luke Ronchi hit the only half-century of his brief stint with Warwickshire before falling to Nathan Buck, who finished with competition-best figures in his first T20 match for Lancashire. The target looked gettable, but Lancashire started hesitantly and, two deliveries after Jos Buttler fell for a second-ball duck, rain came with them well behind the rate.*

At Birmingham, July 1 (floodlit). **Northamptonshire won by eight wickets** (DLS). **Warwickshire 86-8** (16 overs) (A. Javid 34*; R. J. Gleeson 3-12); ‡**Northamptonshire 89-2** (12.3 overs) (J. J. Cobb 39*). *MoM:* R. J. Gleeson. *Attendance:* 7,058. *Northamptonshire won the toss in a 17-over contest and had Warwickshire 19-4 inside four overs, three to Gleeson, who finished with a competition-best 3-12. Ateeq Javid battled to 34*, but only he and Rikki Clarke made double figures, and 86 was never defendable.*

At Birmingham, July 17. **Warwickshire won by 28 runs. Warwickshire 186-4** (20 overs) (S. R. Hain 79, I. R. Bell 57); ‡**Leicestershire 158-9** (20 overs) (M. J. Cosgrove 42). *MoM:* S. R. Hain. *Attendance:* 7,829. *Warwickshire's opening stand of 125 in 13 overs between Hain and Ian Bell set up an intimidating total. While they perhaps should have made 200, Clarke's parsimony (2-17) ensured 186 was enough.*

At Birmingham, July 22 (floodlit). **Nottinghamshire won by six wickets. Warwickshire 172-2** (20 overs) (I. R. Bell 80, W. T. S. Porterfield 61*); ‡**Nottinghamshire 173-4** (19.1 overs) (M. J. Lumb 34, M. H. Wessels 37, G. P. Smith 52*, D. T. Christian 37; K. H. D. Barker 3-34). *MoM:* G. P. Smith. *Attendance:* 10,129. *Warwickshire, who needed only one win from their last three matches to make the knockouts, suffered a second timid defeat in four days. After a slow start, a stand of 116 between Bell and William Porterfield had helped them recover to 172. Nottinghamshire's openers managed 68 from eight overs and, after they both fell in the ninth, Greg Smith took charge to secure a home quarter-final.*

Warwickshire away matches

May 20: beat Nottinghamshire by six wickets.
June 17: beat Derbyshire by four wickets.
June 24: beat Leicestershire by eight wickets.
July 8: lost to Yorkshire by two runs.
July 15: lost to Worcestershire by five wickets.
July 19: lost to Northamptonshire by 74 runs.
July 29: lost to Lancashire by 30 runs.

WORCESTERSHIRE

At Worcester, May 20. **Worcestershire won by 38 runs. Worcestershire 225-6** (20 overs) (T. Köhler-Cadmore 127, B. L. D'Oliveira 39*); ‡**Durham 187-8** (20 overs) (P. Mustard 64, G. Clark 32; J. Leach 5-33). *MoM:* T. Köhler-Cadmore. *Attendance:* 2,170. *Hours after Tom Fell had been given the all-clear to return to cricket following chemotherapy, his close friend Tom Köhler-Cadmore smashed a 54-ball 127, the highest T20 score for Worcestershire, surpassing Graeme Hick's 116* in 2004. It helped them to a daunting 225, their biggest total at New Road. Joe Leach then returned format-best figures of 5-33 as Durham fell short, despite Phil Mustard's rapid 64. Mitchell Santner made an impressive T20 debut for Worcestershire with 2-29, but broke a finger in the field and did not play again.*

At Worcester, June 2. **Worcestershire won by seven wickets.** ‡**Yorkshire 173-6** (20 overs) (A. Z. Lees 46, L. E. Plunkett 34*; J. Leach 3-33); **Worcestershire 174-3** (19.1 overs) (J. M. Clarke 34, A. N. Kervezee 52*, B. L. D'Oliveira 34*). *MoM:* J. Leach. *Attendance:* 3,061. *After Leach had ripped out their middle order, Yorkshire were listing at 112-6, before Tim Bresnan and Liam Plunkett smashed 61 off the last three overs – one of Ed Barnard's cost 30. But Worcestershire recovered their composure, and Alexei Kervezee organised the chase with a calm 52*.*

At Worcester, June 10. **Worcestershire won by three wickets. Northamptonshire 169-7** (20 overs) (B. M. Duckett 50; J. Leach 3-26); ‡**Worcestershire 170-7** (19.3 overs) (T. Köhler-Cadmore 60,

B. L. D'Oliveira 37, O. B. Cox 42*; B. W. Sanderson 3-34). *MoM:* O. B. Cox. *Attendance:* 2,733. *In funereal light and constant drizzle, Ben Cox's inventive 42 off 24 balls brought Worcestershire a tense victory. They needed nine from Azharullah's last over and – with a reverse paddle, a pull and a push into the covers – Cox got them. Earlier, another impressive performance from Leach had helped restrict Northamptonshire, before Köhler-Cadmore's 60 set up Cox's finishing act.*

At Worcester, June 18. **Nottinghamshire won by four wickets. Worcestershire 164-5** (20 overs) (T. Köhler-Cadmore 30, M. M. Ali 40, J. M. Clarke 69*); ‡**Nottinghamshire 167-6** (18.5 overs) (M. H. Wessels 36, D. T. Christian 53*, A. D. Russell 41). *MoM:* A. D. Russell. *Attendance:* 3,245. *County debut:* A. D. Russell (Nottinghamshire). *After his first two games had been washed out, Andre Russell starred on his Nottinghamshire debut. First, he shared 4-50 with Steven Mullaney to check Worcestershire's progress; only Joe Clarke, with a maiden T20 half-century, showed fluency. Later, Russell shared a stand of 64 in six overs with Dan Christian – who hit a third fifty in four white-ball innings – to tip the balance after Brett D'Oliveira's two wickets in two balls had reduced Nottinghamshire to 95-5.*

At Worcester, July 1. **Derbyshire won by seven wickets. Worcestershire 185-7** (20 overs) (O. B. Cox 59*, M. J. Henry 35*; A. L. Hughes 3-23); ‡**Derbyshire 188-3** (18.5 overs) (W. J. Durston 32, H. D. Rutherford 37, C. F. Hughes 43*, W. L. Madsen 59*). *MoM:* W. L. Madsen. *Attendance:* 2,634. *After playing Durham the night before, Worcestershire had not returned home until 3.30am, and batted as if half asleep, as Alex Hughes collected a format-best 3-23. Cox kept them competitive, helping add 62 off the last four overs, and finishing with a personal-best 59*. But, from 91-3, Chesney Hughes and Wayne Madsen guided Derbyshire to victory with an unbroken 97*. Worcestershire wore a one-off yellow kit, later auctioned to raise money for cancer charities in support of Fell and scorer Dawn Pugh.*

At Worcester, July 8. **Lancashire won by seven wickets. Worcestershire 198** (19.4 overs) (B. L. D'Oliveira 30, R. A. Whiteley 38, O. B. Cox 44); ‡**Lancashire 200-3** (18.1 overs) (A. N. Petersen 34, J. C. Buttler 57, K. R. Brown 62*). *MoM:* J. C. Buttler. *Attendance:* 3,363. *Despite breaking a thumb while keeping, Jos Buttler cracked Lancashire's fastest T20 half-century, from just 20 balls, to give their chase a rollicking start. Matt Henry suffered particular torment, conceding three consecutive sixes, and finishing with 3–5–57–0. After that, there was no hurry, and Karl Brown's 62* completed the formalities. Cox's 21-ball 44 seemed to have given Worcestershire's total a formidable look.*

At Worcester, July 15. **Worcestershire won by five wickets. Warwickshire 164** (19.3 overs) (S. R. Hain 46, M. S. Wade 74; M. J. Henry 3-15, G. H. Rhodes 4-13); ‡**Worcestershire 166-5** (19.2 overs) (D. K. H. Mitchell 61, R. A. Whiteley 42*; R. Clarke 3-22). *MoM:* R. A. Whiteley. *Attendance:* 4,330. *Thanks to a second-wicket stand of 103 between Sam Hain and Matthew Wade, Warwickshire were 129-1 in the 13th over. But they lost their last nine for 35; George Rhodes picked up three in an over, and Henry signed off before returning to New Zealand duty with 3-15. Worcestershire slipped to 23-3, but Daryl Mitchell steadied the ship with 61, before Ross Whiteley's 20-ball 42* ensured a victory that maintained slim hopes of the quarter-finals.*

Worcestershire away matches

May 27: beat Warwickshire by five wickets.
June 3: lost to Northamptonshire by seven wickets.
June 17: no result v Leicestershire.
June 24: lost to Lancashire by 96 runs.
June 30: no result v Durham.
July 9: lost to Nottinghamshire by nine wickets.
July 22: lost to Derbyshire by 29 runs.

YORKSHIRE

At Leeds, May 27 (floodlit). **Leicestershire won by 54 runs. Leicestershire 174-7** (20 overs) (B. A. Raine 48, N. J. O'Brien 39); ‡**Yorkshire 120** (18.4 overs) (W. M. H. Rhodes 45; B. A. Raine 3-7, K. J. O'Brien 3-27). *MoM:* B. A. Raine. *Attendance:* 6,133. *Raine ended play (seamer Ben, that is) with figures of 3.4–15–7–3, after earlier dampening Yorkshire spirits with the highest score of the match. The O'Brien brothers backed him up: Kevin allied a brisk 21 to three wickets, while Niall's 39 included four sixes but no fours. Leicestershire hit no sixes until the 14th over, but eight more followed. Only Will Rhodes passed 17 in a weak reply.*

At Leeds, June 17 (floodlit). **Yorkshire v Nottinghamshire. Abandoned.**

At Leeds, June 19. **Yorkshire won by one run** (DLS). **Derbyshire 153-9** (20 overs) (S. J. Thakor 30; T. T. Bresnan 3-22); ‡**Yorkshire 67-3** (9 overs) (A. Lyth 30). *MoM:* Azeem Rafiq. *Attendance:* 7,114. *Off-spinner Azeem Rafiq, re-signed after being released in 2014, roared back with two wickets and two catches to set up Yorkshire's first win of the season. It came when rain ended play with them just one ahead on DLS, although – with four of England's current ODI squad on display – they were favourites by then. Kane Williamson captained as Alex Lees, the regular one-day skipper, stood down to accommodate the in-form Adam Lyth. Yorkshire's players wore black armbands in memory of Jo Cox, the Batley & Spen MP who had been murdered a few days earlier.*

At Leeds, July 1 (floodlit). **Yorkshire won by five runs. Yorkshire 141-7** (18 overs) (N. L. Buck 3-25); ‡**Lancashire 136** (17.4 overs) (L. S. Livingstone 36; S. A. Patterson 3-23). *MoM:* Azeem Rafiq. *Attendance:* 15,396. *Eight clean-as-a-whistle catches, all but one on the boundary, set up a narrow Yorkshire victory in a game reduced to 18 overs each. Three were held by Lyth, the most spectacular a sprawling effort at deep backward square to send back Jordan Clark. The decisive over was the 11th: after Liam Livingstone struck Karl Carver for three successive sixes, he and Steven Croft fell to the last two deliveries, leaving Lancashire wobbling at 87-5.*

At Leeds, July 8 (floodlit). **Yorkshire won by two runs.** ‡**Yorkshire 156-6** (20 overs) (K. S. Williamson 48, G. S. Ballance 33); **Warwickshire 154** (20 overs) (I. R. Bell 30, W. T. S. Porterfield 48, L. J. Evans 37). *MoM:* K. S. Williamson. *Attendance:* 7,082. *County debut:* M. S. Wade (Warwickshire). *Warwickshire seemed to be sailing to victory at 141-4 in the 18th, needing only 16 from 13 balls. But William Porterfield went for 48, and panic set in. Six wickets tumbled, including three run-outs in the final over, one off the last delivery: with four needed to tie, Ateeq Javid lifted Tim Bresnan over mid-on – but Lyth acrobatically prevented the ball from crossing the rope, and Javid was caught short after a frantic mix-up.*

At Leeds, July 20 (floodlit). **Yorkshire won by 49 runs.** ‡**Yorkshire 223-6** (20 overs) (A. Lyth 87, D. J. Willey 32, T. M. Head 34, J. A. Leaning 32); **Durham 174-8** (20 overs) (U. Arshad 43; K. Carver 3-40). *MoM:* A. Lyth. *Attendance:* 8,076. *A fast and furious start brought 64 from 4.4 overs before David Willey was out, but Lyth charged to a career-best 87 from 54 balls, and Yorkshire to their best T20 total (previously 213-7 against Worcestershire in 2010), and the second-highest of the tournament. The target proved beyond Durham.*

At Leeds, July 22 (floodlit). **Yorkshire won by 75 runs.** ‡**Yorkshire 215-6** (20 overs) (D. J. Willey 74, A. Z. Lees 35, J. A. Leaning 30); **Northamptonshire 140** (15.2 overs) (B. M. Duckett 51, S. P. Crook 43). *MoM:* D. J. Willey. *Attendance:* 7,841. *Yorkshire's renaissance continued as they passed 200 for the second time in three days. Willey led the way against his former county, his 46-ball 74 containing six sixes and five fours. Ben Duckett hit back with five fours in Bresnan's second over, but when he was stumped off Adil Rashid – released earlier in the day by England – Northamptonshire declined rapidly, not helped by Richard Levi's inability to bat after injuring his shoulder taking a superb diving catch to dismiss Lees.*

Yorkshire away matches

June 2: lost to Worcestershire by seven wickets.
June 3: lost to Lancashire by 26 runs.
June 10: no result v Warwickshire.
June 24: lost to Durham by six runs (DLS).
July 10: beat Derbyshire by one run.
July 15: lost to Nottinghamshire by three wickets.
July 29: beat Northamptonshire by 14 runs.

SOUTH GROUP

ESSEX

At Chelmsford, May 20 (floodlit). **Surrey won by eight runs. Surrey 170-8** (20 overs) (K. C. Sangakkara 32, Azhar Mahmood 42, T. K. Curran 32; M. R. Quinn 4-35); ‡**Essex 162** (19.4 overs) (T. Westley 46, R. N. ten Doeschate 36, Ashar Zaidi 30; Azhar Mahmood 4-38, T. K. Curran 3-21). *MoM:* Azhar Mahmood. *Attendance:* 4,878. *County debuts:* Ashar Zaidi, M. R. Quinn, Wahab Riaz (Essex). *Surrey were 77-5 at the halfway stage, but Azhar Mahmood, who faced 22 balls, and Tom Curran put on 65 for the seventh wicket in seven overs. They then shared seven wickets to keep Essex in check.*

At Chelmsford, June 10 (floodlit). **Middlesex won by 17 runs.** ‡**Middlesex 173-8** (20 overs) (D. J. Malan 34, P. R. Stirling 30, E. J. G. Morgan 59*; G. R. Napier 3-40); **Essex 156-8** (20 overs) (R. N. ten Doeschate 58*; M. J. McClenaghan 4-33). *MoM:* E. J. G. Morgan. *Attendance:* 4,519. *Eoin Morgan bided his time before opening his shoulders as 23 came from the last over of Middlesex's innings. Essex again fell short, despite Ryan ten Doeschate's gallant half-century, with Mitchell McClenaghan grabbing three late wickets in seven balls. One of the banks of floodlights failed during Essex's innings, although it seemed to affect the nearby fielders as much as the batsmen.*

At Chelmsford, June 16 (floodlit). **Gloucestershire won by eight wickets. Essex 153-8** (20 overs) (T. Westley 45); ‡**Gloucestershire 154-2** (16.5 overs) (M. Klinger 78, H. J. H. Marshall 42). *MoM:* M. Klinger. *Attendance:* 2,824. *Essex batted without much sparkle, and were consigned to a third successive home defeat by a classy opening stand of 126 in 13.3 overs between the Antipodean pair of Michael Klinger and Hamish Marshall.*

At Chelmsford, June 24 (floodlit). **Essex won by five wickets.** ‡**Hampshire 135-8** (20 overs) (M. A. Carberry 34; G. R. Napier 3-31); **Essex 136-5** (18.5 overs) (Ashar Zaidi 52; L. A. Dawson 3-24). *MoM:* Ashar Zaidi. *Attendance:* 5,148. *County debut:* P. I. Walter (Essex). *Hampshire floundered after making 45-0 in the powerplay, and Essex finally won at home thanks to Ashar Zaidi's 30-ball half-century. Their captain Ravi Bopara was handed three penalty points by the ECB after a petulant display on being given lbw second ball by umpire Neil Bainton. In a bad-tempered match, Hampshire's Tino Best hurled the ball too close to Zaidi, conceding four overthrows and leading to a three-point penalty of his own.*

At Chelmsford, July 1 (floodlit). **Essex won by 50 runs. Essex 204-3** (20 overs) (T. Westley 33, R. S. Bopara 81*, Ashar Zaidi 54*); ‡**Kent 154-9** (20 overs) (A. J. Blake 37; P. I. Walter 3-26). *MoM:* R. S. Bopara. *Attendance:* 4,358. *An Essex record fourth-wicket stand of 131 in ten overs between Bopara and Zaidi set up a formidable total. Kent never got close, with left-arm seamer Paul Walter taking three wickets, including Joe Denly with his second delivery. Graham Napier had earlier completed a hat-trick of sorts: after wickets with his last two balls in the previous match, against Surrey, he had Sam Northeast caught behind with his first here.*

At Chelmsford, July 21 (floodlit). **Sussex won by 24 runs. Sussex 200-6** (20 overs) (L. J. Wright 32, P. D. Salt 33, C. J. Jordan 45*); ‡**Essex 176-8** (20 overs) (D. W. Lawrence 36, R. S. Bopara 32; Mustafizur Rahman 4-23). *MoM:* Mustafizur Rahman. *Attendance:* 4,953. *County debut:* Mustafizur Rahman (Sussex). *After the start was delayed for a few minutes by scoreboard failure, some consistent batting gave Sussex a solid base. Chris Jordan, who slapped five sixes, oversaw the addition of 66 in the last four overs. The slippery Bangladesh seamer Mustafizur Rahman, in his first county match, set Essex back by dismissing Bopara early on, then returned to claim three wickets in six balls.*

At Chelmsford, July 29 (floodlit). **No result. Glamorgan 184-5** (20 overs) (C. A. Ingram 101) **v** ‡**Essex.** *Colin Ingram's second century in a week – he batted for 56 balls and clattered seven sixes – came to nothing when heavy rain set in between innings. One point took Essex into the last eight.*

Essex away matches

June 1: beat Glamorgan by seven wickets.
June 3: lost to Somerset by seven wickets.
June 25: beat Surrey by eight wickets.
July 8: beat Hampshire by three runs.
July 17: lost to Gloucestershire by 30 runs.
July 22: beat Kent by 33 runs.
July 28: beat Middlesex by five wickets.

GLAMORGAN

At Cardiff, June 1 (floodlit). **Essex won by seven wickets. Glamorgan 140-6** (20 overs) (A. H. T. Donald 51); ‡**Essex 143-3** (16.2 overs) (J. D. Ryder 42, T. Westley 41, R. N. ten Doeschate 30*). *MoM:* J. D. Ryder. *Attendance:* 3,233. *County debut:* D. W. Steyn (Glamorgan). *Aneurin Donald put on 56 for the third wicket with Colin Ingram, but a mid-innings lull, with no boundary for more than eight overs, meant a modest target. Jesse Ryder started with a flurry of fours, and Essex sailed home, with Glamorgan's bowlers – even the debutant Dale Steyn – making little impression.*

At Cardiff, June 3 (floodlit). **Glamorgan won by five wickets. Hampshire 141** (18.3 overs) (A. J. A. Wheater 39, Shahid Afridi 32; D. W. Steyn 3-22, M. G. Hogan 4-28); ‡**Glamorgan 143-5** (16.1 overs) (C. A. Ingram 43, A. H. T. Donald 55). *MoM:* A. H. T. Donald. *Attendance:* 6,165.

After Steyn and Michael Hogan scuppered Hampshire, Ingram and Donald – whose 55 came from 27 balls – effectively ensured victory with a stand of 94 in 8.3 overs after Glamorgan had stuttered to 9-2. Hampshire's overseas import Darren Sammy endured a miserable evening, going for 18 in his only over and dropping a straightforward catch in the deep.

At Cardiff, June 17 (floodlit). **Glamorgan won by 55 runs** (DLS). **Glamorgan 175-4** (16 overs) (D. L. Lloyd 97*, C. A. Ingram 60); ‡**Kent 121** (15.5 overs) (A. J. Blake 30, M. T. Coles 31; D. W. Steyn 4-18, M. G. Hogan 3-12). *MoM:* D. L. Lloyd. *Attendance:* 2,870. *After an early shower, the match was reduced to 16 overs a side, and Kent's eventual target increased to 177. David Lloyd's explosive 49-ball innings – he clouted ten fours and four sixes – and his second-wicket stand of 132 in 9.1 overs with the consistent Ingram, set up a total that proved beyond Kent, especially with Steyn striking in each of his four overs.*

At Cardiff, June 24 (floodlit). **Glamorgan won by nine wickets.** ‡**Surrey 110** (19.2 overs); **Glamorgan 114-1** (15.5 overs) (J. A. Rudolph 40*, C. A. Ingram 73*). *MoM:* D. A. Cosker. *Attendance:* 4,735. *Despite losing Lloyd for a duck in the first over of the chase, Glamorgan cantered to their fifth win out of six thanks to a stand of 114* between Jacques Rudolph and Ingram, and completed the double over lacklustre Surrey. Wicketkeeper Chris Cooke equalled the competition record with five dismissals, while Dean Cosker (2-23) became the first Glamorgan bowler to take 100 Twenty20 wickets.*

At Cardiff, July 7 (floodlit). **Glamorgan won by 46 runs. Glamorgan 159-8** (20 overs) (D. L. Lloyd 81; K. M. D. N. Kulasekara 4-28); ‡**Sussex 113** (18.3 overs) (T. van der Gugten 4-17). *MoM:* D. L. Lloyd. *Attendance:* 2,705. *The Australian tearaway Shaun Tait failed to strike in his first game of the season, but his presence seemed to inspire Glamorgan's other seamers – especially Timm van der Gugten, who reduced to Sussex to 22-3 – as they shared all ten wickets. Earlier, another rapid knock from Lloyd, who faced 55 balls, ensured a competitive total.*

At Cardiff, July 10. **Gloucestershire won by nine wickets.** ‡**Glamorgan 119-6** (20 overs) (G. G. Wagg 32*; G. L. van Buuren 3-19); **Gloucestershire 120-1** (16.1 overs) (M. Klinger 56*, I. A. Cockbain 53*). *MoM:* M. Klinger. *Attendance:* 3,758. *Gloucestershire replaced Glamorgan at the top of the table with an easy win on a slow pitch. The home batsmen struggled against the turn extracted by left-arm spinners Tom Smith (3–11–13–2) and Graeme van Buuren, but Gloucestershire's Michael Klinger and Ian Cockbain had no such problems against the seamers, adding 97*.*

At Cardiff, July 22 (floodlit). **Glamorgan won by seven wickets. Somerset 152** (19.3 overs) (J. C. Hildreth 39; C. A. Ingram 3-20); ‡**Glamorgan 156-3** (18 overs) (C. A. Ingram 54, A. H. T. Donald 44*). *MoM:* C. A. Ingram. *Attendance:* 7,542. *Somerset's batsmen let themselves down with some poor shot selection, allowing Glamorgan to stroll to the victory that confirmed their quarter-final place. Ingram, with his fourth fifty of the competition, put on 76 with Aneurin Donald, who followed his Championship double-century five days earlier with another rumbustious innings.*

Glamorgan away matches

May 26: beat Surrey by eight wickets.
June 10: beat Gloucestershire by six wickets.
June 15: no result v Somerset.
July 8: beat Middlesex by nine wickets.
July 14: lost to Hampshire by 25 runs.
July 28: no result v Sussex.
July 29: no result v Essex.

GLOUCESTERSHIRE

At Bristol, May 20 (floodlit). **Sussex won by one run** (DLS). **Sussex 242-5** (20 overs) (C. D. Nash 30, B. C. Brown 43, L. R. P. L. Taylor 93*, M. W. Machan 31); ‡**Gloucestershire 83-1** (7.3 overs) (M. Klinger 42*). *MoM:* L. R. P. L. Taylor. *Attendance:* 2,759. *County debut:* C. J. Liddle (Gloucestershire). *Rain denied Gloucestershire a proper tilt at victory beneath Bristol's new permanent floodlights. When play was abandoned they were 83-1, narrowly behind on DLS – had they not donated six penalty runs for a slow over-rate, they would have sneaked home. Sussex had* *made 242, founded on Ross Taylor's 48-ball 93*. David Payne's 4–2–62–0 were the worst figures for Gloucestershire in Twenty20 cricket.*

HIGHEST TWENTY20 TOTALS IN ENGLAND

254-3	Gloucestershire	v Middlesex at Uxbridge	2011
250-3	Somerset	v Gloucestershire at Taunton	2006
248-6	Australia	v England at Southampton	2013
242-2	Warwickshire	v Derbyshire at Birmingham	2015
242-3	Essex	v Sussex at Chelmsford	2008
242-5	**Sussex**	**v Gloucestershire at Bristol**	**2016**
240-3	Glamorgan	v Surrey at The Oval	2015
239-5	Sussex	v Glamorgan at Hove	2010
235-5	Somerset	v Middlesex at Taunton	2011

At Bristol, June 10 (floodlit). **Glamorgan won by six wickets. Gloucestershire 168-8** (20 overs) (I. A. Cockbain 37, K. Noema-Barnett 37); ‡**Glamorgan 172-4** (18.5 overs) (C. A. Ingram 64, A. H. T. Donald 48*). *MoM:* C. A. Ingram. *Attendance:* 2,603. *Colin Ingram, who faced 30 balls for his 64, and Aneurin Donald shared a third-wicket stand of 89 to help Glamorgan home with time to spare. Gloucestershire's Australian fast bowler Andrew Tye struggled in wet conditions, and he was removed from the attack after his third over included two beamers.*

At Bristol, June 17 (floodlit). **Gloucestershire won by four wickets. Somerset 158-5** (20 overs) (C. H. Gayle 40); ‡**Gloucestershire 160-6** (19.5 overs) (M. Klinger 60; R. E. van der Merwe 3-16). *MoM:* M. Klinger. *Attendance:* 10,588. *Gloucestershire won a thrilling derby with one ball to spare, but it had begun slowly: Somerset's Chris Gayle saw out a maiden from Matt Taylor, and did not get off the mark until his ninth ball. In all, though, he smashed 40 from 26. In Gloucestershire's reply, Michael Klinger hit 60 from 43 – after Yasir Arafat had removed Hamish Marshall with the first delivery. Klinger departed at 128-6, but the seventh-wicket pair held firm.*

At Bristol, July 6 (floodlit). **Gloucestershire won by six wickets.** ‡**Surrey 151-9** (20 overs) (A. J. Finch 31, D. P. Sibley 32; M. D. Taylor 3-31, A. J. Tye 3-16); **Gloucestershire 152-4** (19 overs) (I. A. Cockbain 73*, C. D. J. Dent 39). *MoM:* I. A. Cockbain. *Attendance:* 2,828. *County debut:* C. H. Morris (Surrey). *Tye laid the foundations of Gloucestershire's fifth consecutive victory by claiming 3-16, including fellow Australian Aaron Finch, as Surrey never got going. Ian Cockbain's 73* settled it with an over to spare.*

At Bristol, July 8 (floodlit). **Kent won by three runs. Kent 148-7** (20 overs) (J. L. Denly 51; B. A. C. Howell 3-29); ‡**Gloucestershire 145-8** (20 overs) (M. Klinger 42, B. A. C. Howell 37). *MoM:* J. L. Denly. *Attendance:* 3,544. *An eventful final over began with Gloucestershire needing 16, but the ball slipped from Mitch Claydon's hand, and he was ordered out of the attack for a second beamer. David Griffiths took over, and kept things tight. But with the requirement nine from two, he also sent down a high full toss. Benny Howell, who had earlier claimed 3-29, survived being caught – but was run out trying to filch a second run. Norwell could manage only two from Griffiths's last two balls. Klinger had contributed 42 to the chase before being stumped off a wide. Kent's modest-looking 148 on a true pitch had owed much to 51 from Joe Denly.*

At Cheltenham, July 17. **Gloucestershire won by 30 runs. Gloucestershire 212-1** (20 overs) (M. Klinger 95*, H. J. H. Marshall 43, I. A. Cockbain 69*); ‡**Essex 182-9** (20 overs) (D. W. Lawrence 35; B. A. C. Howell 3-28). *MoM:* M. Klinger. *Attendance:* 4,896. *Klinger showed brutal efficiency in his 57-ball 95*, putting on 75 with Marshall and 137* with Cockbain, who thumped 69* from 35. Essex lurched to 58-5, with Howell grabbing three wickets as Gloucestershire – in front of a sell-out festival crowd – extended their lead at the top of the table.*

At Bristol, July 29 (floodlit). **Gloucestershire won by four wickets.** ‡**Middlesex 156-5** (20 overs) (J. A. Simpson 40*; B. A. C. Howell 3-18); **Gloucestershire 162-6** (19.3 overs) (I. A. Cockbain 42, J. M. R. Taylor 44*). *MoM:* J. M. R. Taylor. *Attendance:* 4,251. *Both counties had already qualified, but produced a tense finish. Howell's customary three-for made him the leading wicket-taker in the tournament, with 23, and limited Middlesex to 156. Gloucestershire required 24 from the last two overs, and were powered home by Jack Taylor, who hit three sixes en route to 44* from 23 balls.*

Gloucestershire away matches

May 20: beat Middlesex by four wickets.
June 3: beat Kent by seven wickets.
June 16: beat Essex by eight wickets.
June 25: no result v Hampshire.
June 26: beat Sussex by 11 runs.
July 1: beat Somerset by seven wickets.
July 10: beat Glamorgan by nine wickets.

HAMPSHIRE

At Southampton, June 2 (floodlit). **Hampshire won by nine runs. Hampshire 158-8** (20 overs) (M. A. Carberry 54; M. T. Coles 4-27); **‡Kent 149** (19.3 overs) (D. J. Bell-Drummond 64, J. L. Denly 31; Shahid Afridi 3-33). *MoM:* Shahid Afridi. *Attendance:* 6,031. *County debut:* D. J. G. Sammy. *Darren Sammy, on Hampshire debut, and Shahid Afridi both took wickets with consecutive balls as Kent's promising pursuit of a modest target crumbled. They were ideally placed at 75-0 in the tenth over, and still favourites at 112-3 in the 15th, but seven fell for 37.*

At Southampton, June 17 (floodlit). **Hampshire v Sussex. Abandoned.**

At Southampton, June 25. **Gloucestershire v ‡Hampshire. Abandoned.**

At Southampton, July 8 (floodlit). **Essex won by three runs. ‡Essex 153-6** (20 overs) (T. Westley 33, Ashar Zaidi 47); **Hampshire 150-7** (20 overs) (J. M. Vince 62). *MoM:* Ashar Zaidi. *Attendance:* 8,127. *Ravi Bopara bowled the last over, with Hampshire eight from victory. The equation became four from two balls shortly after Lewis McManus, who had scurried to 17 from 11, was caught at deep midwicket; Gareth Andrew could score from neither. Ashar Zaidi had starred with bat (a busy 47 containing only three boundaries) and ball (4–11–16–2). Hampshire, with one win and seven defeats in ten fixtures, were bottom of the group.*

At Southampton, July 14 (floodlit). **Hampshire won by 25 runs. Hampshire 167-6** (20 overs) (L. A. Dawson 76*, J. J. Weatherley 43; G. G. Wagg 3-38); **‡Glamorgan 142-7** (20 overs) (M. A. Wallace 45; L. A. Dawson 4-23). *MoM:* L. A. Dawson. *Attendance:* 4,199. *County debut:* G. T. Griffiths (Hampshire). *A sparkling all-round performance by Liam Dawson prevented Glamorgan from going top. He hit a maiden Twenty20 fifty in his 57th innings, then snatched 4-23 as Glamorgan, who were 51-0 after seven overs, made a mess of their reply. Shortly before the game, Michael Carberry revealed he had been diagnosed with cancer.*

At Southampton, July 22 (floodlit). **Middlesex won by 43 runs. ‡Middlesex 181-6** (20 overs) (G. J. Bailey 76, J. A. Simpson 54; B. T. J. Wheal 3-43); **Hampshire 138** (19.1 overs) (S. M. Ervine 36; J. K. Fuller 3-24, R. F. Higgins 5-13). *MoM:* G. J. Bailey. *Attendance:* 7,104. *Going into this match, off-spinner Ryan Higgins, the sixth bowler used by Middlesex, had taken one senior wicket – the night before. Now he claimed 5-13, the joint-best return of the tournament (with Lancashire's Stephen Parry) to wreck Hampshire's reply to a useful Middlesex total. Their mainstay had been George Bailey, whose 76 was a Twenty20 best, in his 129th innings. Hampshire must have been impressed: they signed him for 2017.*

At Southampton, July 29 (floodlit). **Hampshire won by 83 runs. ‡Hampshire 181-3** (20 overs) (T. P. Alsop 85, J. Goodwin 32); **Somerset 98** (15.2 overs) (J. Allenby 40; L. A. Dawson 5-17). *MoM:* L. A. Dawson. *Attendance:* 8,567. *County debuts:* J. Goodwin (Hampshire); B. G. F. Green, O. R. T. Sale (Somerset). *Five made their Twenty20 debuts – and three their senior debuts – as the group's bottom clubs scrapped to avoid last place. Tom Alsop took advantage of a weakened Somerset to record his first fifty in the format, while Dawson grabbed a Twenty20-best 5-17. All five Hampshire batsmen passed 12; only Jim Allenby did for Somerset.*

Hampshire away matches

May 27: lost to Middlesex by 69 runs.
June 3: lost to Glamorgan by five wickets.
June 8: lost to Kent by eight runs.
June 9: lost to Surrey by 80 runs.
June19: lost to Somerset by six wickets.
June 24: lost to Essex by five wickets.
July 15: beat Sussex by one run.

KENT

At Canterbury, May 20 (floodlit). **Kent won by eight wickets.** ‡**Somerset 197-7** (20 overs) (J. Allenby 91, P. D. Trego 57; F. K. Cowdrey 3-18); **Kent 200-2** (17.2 overs) (D. J. Bell-Drummond 83*, J. L. Denly 75). *MoM:* D. J. Bell-Drummond. *Attendance:* 4,562. *County debut:* M. A. Leask (Somerset). *Daniel Bell-Drummond and Joe Denly shared an opening stand of 150, at the time a Kent all-wicket record, as they romped to a demanding target. Earlier, Jim Allenby and Peter Trego put on 124 for Somerset's second, but once left-arm spinner Fabian Cowdrey ended the alliance, the innings fell away: no one else made ten.*

At Beckenham, June 3. **Gloucestershire won by seven wickets. Kent 144-7** (20 overs) (S. A. Northeast 35; A. J. Tye 3-18); ‡**Gloucestershire 146-3** (19.2 overs) (H. J. H. Marshall 56, I. A. Cockbain 37). *MoM:* A. J. Tye. *Attendance:* 3,367. *In chill, gloomy conditions, Kent's batting misfired on a tricky surface. Sam Northeast managed 35, but Andrew Tye undermined the innings with a canny 3-18. By the time Hamish Marshall fell at 132-3, the result was clear – unlike conditions at Worsley Bridge Road, where poor light prevented Kent from using their quicker bowlers at the death.*

At Canterbury, June 8 (floodlit). **Kent won by eight runs. Kent 193-3** (20 overs) (D. J. Bell-Drummond 35, J. L. Denly 59, S. A. Northeast 38, S. W. Billings 55*); ‡**Hampshire 185-9** (20 overs) (S. M. Ervine 56, Shahid Afridi 35, D. J. G. Sammy 30). *MoM:* S. W. Billings. *Attendance:* 3,069. *Despite a true pitch, and a short boundary to the Old Dover Road, David Griffiths helped Kent defend a large but gettable total. He dismissed Hampshire's overseas all-rounders, Darren Sammy and Shahid Afridi, and conceded just five from the final over when 14 were needed. Fifties from Denly and Sam Billings (from 27 balls) had given Kent something to play with, though Hampshire might have fared better without four run-outs.*

At Canterbury, June 24 (floodlit). **Middlesex won by 40 runs.** ‡**Middlesex 210-6** (20 overs) (B. B. McCullum 87*, D. J. Malan 60; D. I. Stevens 4-31); **Kent 170-7** (20 overs) (S. A. Northeast 41, F. K. Cowdrey 71; T. S. Roland-Jones 3-24). *MoM:* B. B. McCullum. *Attendance:* 5,085. *Brendon McCullum ushered Middlesex to a formidable 210-6, though he was never at his most fluent – Dawid Malan outscored him in their century opening stand. It might have been more had Darren Stevens not skittled the middle order. Northeast larruped 41, and Cowdrey a career-best 71 from 42 balls, but Kent fell well short.*

At Canterbury, June 30 (floodlit). **Kent won by ten runs.** ‡**Kent 166-6** (20 overs) (T. W. M. Latham 48, J. L. Denly 44, A. J. Blake 36*); **Sussex 156-4** (20 overs) (L. R. P. L. Taylor 49, M. W. Machan 30*). *MoM:* K. Rabada. *Attendance:* 3,238. *County debuts:* K. Rabada (Kent); K. M. D. N. Kulasekara (Sussex). *South Africa firebrand Kagiso Rabada took two important wickets on debut as Kent held on for a tense win. Batting was awkward on a two-paced pitch and, despite Kent reaching 97-0 in the 12th over, no one broke free. Sussex lost Chris Nash and Luke Wright to Rabada's pace, but the turning point came when Cowdrey (2–4–8–2) trapped Ross Taylor for 49. On a beautiful evening, Sussex's innings was twice halted: after a 17-minute delay for the sun shining into the eyes of the batsman at the Nackington Road End, another ten minutes were lost when the reflection from the window of the Sky commentary box affected the Pavilion End.*

At Tunbridge Wells, July 15. **Kent won by eight wickets.** ‡**Surrey 180-8** (20 overs) (J. J. Roy 52; J. C. Tredwell 3-32); **Kent 181-2** (19.4 overs) (D. J. Bell-Drummond 112*, S. A. Northeast 57). *MoM:* D. J. Bell-Drummond. *Attendance:* 4,999. *A full house lapped up a victory that took Kent third. Denly fell to his first ball, but Bell-Drummond, returning after a hand injury, reached his maiden Twenty20 hundred from his 58th. He and Northeast added 151 – an all-wicket Kent record. Jason Roy had earlier raced to fifty but, though six other Surrey batsmen made starts, none passed 25.*

At Canterbury, July 22 (floodlit). **Essex won by 33 runs.** ‡**Essex 190-2** (20 overs) (T. Westley 74*, R. S. Bopara 51*); **Kent 157** (19.2 overs) (D. I. Stevens 33; G. R. Napier 3-29). *MoM:* T. Westley. *Attendance:* 6,003. *Essex held their nerve in front of a passionate crowd to extinguish Kent's hopes of qualifying. Ravi Bopara and Tom Westley made the most of some uninspiring bowling to build a third-wicket stand of 119*. Kent were never up with the rate.*

Kent away matches

June 2: lost to Hampshire by nine runs.
June 10: lost to Sussex by four wickets.
June 17: lost to Glamorgan by 55 runs (DLS).
July 1: lost to Essex by 50 runs.
July 7: beat Somerset by 12 runs.
July 8: beat Gloucestershire by three runs.
July 29: lost to Surrey by 37 runs.

MIDDLESEX

At Uxbridge, May 27. **Middlesex won by 69 runs. Middlesex 195-6** (20 overs) (D. J. Malan 93); ‡**Hampshire 126** (15.1 overs) (A. J. A. Wheater 30, L. A. Dawson 46). *MoM:* D. J. Malan. *Attendance:* 3,115. *County debut:* J. K. Fuller (Middlesex). *Dawid Malan fell just short of a third Twenty20 century, but his solo effort – 93 from 48 balls, with 70 in boundaries – was more than enough for a depleted Hampshire. They were not helped when the unsuspecting Shahid Afridi was run out in the eighth over by a bullet-like throw from the boundary by James Fuller.*

At Merchant Taylors' School, Northwood, June 2. **Gloucestershire won by four wickets.** ‡**Middlesex 159-9** (20 overs) (P. R. Stirling 60, A. C. Voges 52*); **Gloucestershire 163-6** (19.5 overs) (I. A. Cockbain 40, C. D. J. Dent 45, B. A. C. Howell 37). *MoM:* B. A. C. Howell. *Attendance:* 1,949. *County debuts:* B. B. McCullum (Middlesex); A. J. Tye (Gloucestershire). *Gloucestershire scrambled to their target in near darkness. Brendon McCullum got off the mark for Middlesex with a six, but was out fifth ball without addition. Paul Stirling's 43-ball 60 was the game's highest score before he became the second of Benny Howell's victims.*

At Lord's, June 16 (floodlit). ‡**Middlesex v Sussex. Abandoned.**

At Lord's, June 23 (floodlit). **Middlesex won by four runs. Middlesex 92-3** (9 overs) (D. J. Malan 53*); ‡**Somerset 88-6** (9 overs). *MoM:* D. J. Malan. *Attendance:* 19,175. *In a match reduced to nine overs a side by rain, Malan shrugged off the loss of three wickets for five runs to reach his half-century with a six off the last ball. It proved crucial: Somerset struggled to recover after Fuller removed both their openers in the third over.*

At Richmond, July 8. **Glamorgan won by nine wickets. Middlesex 144-8** (20 overs) (E. J. G. Morgan 58, R. F. Higgins 57*); ‡**Glamorgan 145-1** (16.3 overs) (D. L. Lloyd 49, M. A. Wallace 69*). *MoM:* M. A. Wallace. *Attendance:* 4,322. *Eoin Morgan and Ryan Higgins both passed 50, but Middlesex's total was below par on this small club ground. Glamorgan sailed past them with ease, Colin Ingram (19*) completing the formalities with three successive sixes after David Lloyd and Mark Wallace put on 125.*

At Lord's, July 21 (floodlit). **Middlesex won by five wickets.** ‡**Surrey 196-6** (20 overs) (J. J. Roy 50, A. J. Finch 78); **Middlesex 200-5** (19.1 overs) (P. R. Stirling 34, E. J. G. Morgan 42, G. J. Bailey 55, J. A. Simpson 43; J. W. Dernbach 3-33). *MoM:* G. J. Bailey. *Attendance:* 27,218. *Middlesex had never scored 200 to win a T20 game, but did so now with something to spare, thanks to the experience of Morgan and the Australian George Bailey. Surrey had started well, but were slowed by leg-spinner Nathan Sowter (2-29). Middlesex seamer Harry Podmore was removed from the attack for a second beamer, and the over was completed by Higgins.*

At Lord's, July 28 (floodlit). **Essex won by five wickets. Middlesex 126-5** (16 overs) (D. J. Malan 68*); ‡**Essex 132-5** (15.3 overs) (D. W. Lawrence 36, Ashar Zaidi 59*). *MoM:* Ashar Zaidi. *Attendance:* 26,336. *Middlesex's hopes of a home quarter-final were dashed by Ashar Zaidi, who hammered five sixes in his 24-ball 59* after it looked as if Malan's patient innings had set the bar high enough in a match reduced to 16 overs a side by rain. Zaidi had coloured his bat black, which was later ruled illegal by MCC; he said he was trying to publicise charities working in Syria.*

Middlesex away matches

June 10: beat Essex by 17 runs.
June 17: lost to Surrey by 29 runs.
June 24: beat Kent by 40 runs.
July 1: lost to Sussex by seven wickets.
July 15: beat Somerset by five wickets.
July 22: beat Hampshire by 22 runs.
July 29: lost to Gloucestershire by four wickets.

SOMERSET

At Taunton, June 3. **Somerset won by seven wickets. Essex 178-7** (20 overs) (T. Westley 40, R. N. ten Doeschate 47, Ashar Zaidi 31); ‡**Somerset 181-3** (17.5 overs) (C. H. Gayle 49, J. Allenby 37*, P. D. Trego 34, L. Gregory 37*). *MoM:* L. Gregory. *Attendance:* 7,543. *Chris Gayle marked his return to Taunton with a 23-ball 49, including a six carrying more than 100 yards, into the car park. He got the headlines, but it was economical bowling from Lewis Gregory and Max Waller – restricting Essex to a modest total, for Taunton – that set up victory.*

At Taunton, June 10. **Somerset won by six wickets.** ‡**Surrey 186-4** (20 overs) (D. P. Sibley 74*, K. C. Sangakkara 37); **Somerset 189-4** (19.2 overs) (C. H. Gayle 31, J. G. Myburgh 86*, R. E. van der Merwe 39*). *MoM:* J. G. Myburgh. *Attendance:* 7,216. *After Gayle had plundered three successive sixes off fellow West Indian Ravi Rampaul, the less heralded Johann Myburgh took over: he hit five sixes and put on 87* with Roelof van der Merwe to finish the job. Surrey's 186 was built around Dom Sibley, who batted through for 74*.*

At Taunton, June 15. **Somerset v Glamorgan. Abandoned.**

At Taunton, June 19. **Somerset won by six wickets. Hampshire 133** (18.3 overs) (L. A. Dawson 46; J. Overton 4-22, M. T. C. Waller 4-33); ‡**Somerset 136-4** (15.4 overs) (C. H. Gayle 52, D. P. M. D. Jayawardene 45*). *MoM:* M. T. C. Waller. *Attendance:* 7,543. *On a lively pitch under heavy skies, Hampshire were put to the sword by Jamie Overton and Waller, who shared 8-55. Shahid Afridi and Darren Sammy were kept back to Nos 8 and 9, but could not revive the innings. Spectators who braved the weather were then treated to the contrasting delights of Gayle and Mahela Jayawardene in a 67-run partnership, as Somerset breezed to their target.*

At Taunton, July 1. **Gloucestershire won by seven wickets. Somerset 167-7** (20 overs) (P. D. Trego 32, D. P. M. D. Jayawardene 41; M. D. Taylor 3-16); ‡**Gloucestershire 168-3** (19.2 overs) (M. Klinger 101, I. A. Cockbain 41; J. Overton 3-33). *MoM:* M. Klinger. *Attendance:* 7,233. *Gayle had headed back to Jamaica, and with him went Somerset's winning habit. Michael Klinger's 67-ball century led Gloucestershire to a last-over win, after Matt Taylor's career-best 3-16 had kept the target within bounds.*

At Taunton, July 7. **Kent won by 12 runs.** ‡**Kent 187-5** (20 overs) (J. L. Denly 35, S. A. Northeast 75); **Somerset 175-9** (20 overs) (P. D. Trego 63; D. I. Stevens 3-30). *MoM:* S. A. Northeast. *Attendance:* 7,471. *Kent captain Sam Northeast crashed 75 off 42 balls, before Darren Stevens blunted the reply with 3-30. Peter Trego's belligerent half-century was not enough to prevent Somerset falling to their eighth limited-overs loss in a row against Kent; they now languished second bottom of the South Group.*

At Taunton, July 15. **Middlesex won by five wickets.** ‡**Somerset 137** (19.3 overs) (J. Allenby 64; T. S. Roland-Jones 3-24); **Middlesex 141-5** (19.1 overs) (E. J. G. Morgan 43). *MoM:* J. K. Fuller. *Attendance:* 7,328. *A fifth successive defeat left Taunton restless after Somerset collapsed from 97-2 to 136 all out. The denouement could scarcely have been more dispiriting: in the penultimate over, a no-ball for not having enough fielders in the circle handed Middlesex a free hit, which disappeared for four. John Simpson won it with a six, two days after finishing the Championship match here in the same fashion.*

Somerset away matches

May 20: lost to Kent by eight wickets.
June 1: lost to Sussex by 48 runs.
June 17: lost to Gloucestershire by four wickets.
June 23: lost to Middlesex by four runs.
July 8: lost to Surrey by 15 runs.
July 22: lost to Glamorgan by seven wickets.
July 29: lost to Hampshire by 83 runs.

SURREY

At The Oval, May 26 (floodlit). **Glamorgan won by eight wickets.** ‡**Surrey 93** (17.2 overs) (T. van der Gugten 4-14); **Glamorgan 96-2** (12.2 overs) (D. L. Lloyd 31, J. A. Rudolph 34*). *MoM:* T. van der Gugten. *Attendance:* 15,944. *Four wickets for Timm van der Gugten set up Glamorgan's fourth* *successive T20 victory at The Oval, completed so quickly that the floodlights barely made an impression. Surrey's innings was ruined when they slipped from 28-0 to 32-4 in 13 deliveries, and later Azhar Mahmood retired hurt with a calf injury after facing three balls.*

At The Oval, June 9 (floodlit). **Surrey won by 80 runs.** ‡**Surrey 188-5** (20 overs) (D. P. Sibley 67, K. C. Sangakkara 72); **Hampshire 108** (16.3 overs) (L. D. McManus 41, G. M. Andrew 31). *MoM:* D. P. Sibley. *Attendance:* 16,940. *Dom Sibley, in his first T20 match, hit 67 from 49 balls, sharing a second-wicket stand of 114 with Kumar Sangakkara, and then took two wickets with his leg-breaks. Hampshire slipped to 59-6 after nine overs, and never got to grips with an exacting target.*

At The Oval, June 17 (floodlit). **Surrey won by 29 runs. Surrey 173-7** (20 overs) (J. J. Roy 35, Z. S. Ansari 34*; O. P. Rayner 3-23); ‡**Middlesex 144** (19.3 overs) (J. E. C. Franklin 39; R. Rampaul 3-21). *MoM:* Z. S. Ansari. *Attendance:* 21,456. *A burst of 46 in the last 3.5 overs from the eighth-wicket pair Zafar Ansari and Tom Curran (22*), after the earlier batsmen were troubled by Ollie Rayner's off-spin, proved decisive in Surrey's 150th Twenty20 match. Taking the pace off the ball was important as Middlesex's chase stalled: only James Franklin made more than 16, with Ansari (2-16) to the fore again.*

At The Oval, June 25. **Essex won by eight wickets. Surrey 117-9** (20 overs) (S. M. Curran 32; G. R. Napier 3-28); ‡**Essex 121-2** (16.5 overs) (J. D. Ryder 52*, R. S. Bopara 36*). *MoM:* J. D. Ryder. *Attendance:* 13,470. *Surrey's batsmen managed only seven boundaries, as a spin-heavy attack – Dan Lawrence led the way with 2-11 – kept the brakes on. Jesse Ryder and Ravi Bopara then sauntered to victory with a stand of 76*, untroubled by a brief stoppage for rain.*

At The Oval, July 8 (floodlit). **Surrey won by 15 runs. Surrey 154-8** (20 overs) (A. J. Finch 51; J. H. Davey 3-20); ‡**Somerset 139-6** (20 overs) (D. P. M. D. Jayawardene 36, L. Gregory 31; J. W. Dernbach 3-32). *MoM:* A. J. Finch. *Attendance:* 20,662. *Aaron Finch's 26-ball blast set up a decent total, despite three wickets from the nagging Josh Davey. Somerset were then throttled by excellent death bowling from Jade Dernbach and Tom Curran.*

At The Oval, July 22 (floodlit). **Surrey won by six wickets. Sussex 153-6** (20 overs) (C. D. Nash 39, C. Cachopa 45); ‡**Surrey 154-4** (18.2 overs) (J. J. Roy 36, D. P. Sibley 40). *MoM:* C. H. Morris. *Attendance:* 21,491. *Sussex looked set for a big score, but managed only 18 in the last four overs as the foundations laid by Chris Nash and Craig Cachopa were undermined by the seamers – Dernbach finished with 2-25 and Chris Morris 2-21. Surrey were faltering at 116-4 in the 15th over, but Ben Foakes and Morris responded with a rapid partnership of 38*.*

At The Oval, July 29 (floodlit). **Surrey won by 37 runs.** ‡**Surrey 212-4** (20 overs) (J. J. Roy 120*, A. J. Finch 79); **Kent 175-7** (20 overs) (D. J. Bell-Drummond 31, S. A. Northeast 59, W. R. S. Gidman 30*). *MoM:* J. J. Roy. *Attendance:* 22,065. *Jason Roy crashed 15 fours and three sixes in his brilliant 62-ball knock (his second hundred of the tournament) and his opening stand with Aaron Finch amounted to 187. Kent started brightly, but three quick wickets left them 111-6 in the 14th over. However, Surrey's win was academic: they already knew a quarter-final place was beyond them after five defeats away from The Oval, where they won five.*

HIGHEST TWENTY20 OPENING PARTNERSHIPS IN THE UK

192	K. J. O'Brien and H. J. H. Marshall	Glos v Middx at Uxbridge	2011
187	D. J. Malan and P. R. Stirling	Middx v Sussex at Hove	2015
187	**J. J. Roy and A. J. Finch**	**Surrey v Kent at The Oval**	**2016**
175	V. S. Solanki and G. A. Hick	Worcs v Northants at Kidderminster	2007
169	M. L. Pettini and A. N. Cook	Essex v Surrey at The Oval	2009
167	B. J. Hodge and D. L. Maddy	Leics v Yorks at Leeds	2004
160	V. Chopra and B. B. McCullum	Warwicks v Derbys at Birmingham	2015
156	M. Klinger and H. J. H. Marshall	Glos v Somerset at Taunton	2015
156	**C. D. Nash and L. J. Wright**	**Sussex v Somerset at Hove**	**2016**
150	**D. J. Bell-Drummond and J. L. Denly**	**Kent v Somerset at Canterbury**	**2016**

Surrey away matches

May 20: beat Essex by eight runs.
June 3: beat Sussex by 23 runs.
June 10: lost to Somerset by six wickets.
June 24: lost to Glamorgan by nine wickets.
July 6: lost to Gloucestershire by six wickets.
July 15: lost to Kent by eight wickets.
July 21: lost to Middlesex by five wickets.

SUSSEX

At Hove, June 1 (floodlit). **Sussex won by 48 runs. Sussex 222-3** (20 overs) (C. D. Nash 112*, L. J. Wright 83); ‡**Somerset 174** (19.4 overs) (D. P. M. D. Jayawardene 51, R. E. van der Merwe 59; D. Wiese 4-38). *MoM:* C. D. Nash. *Attendance:* 4,953. *County debuts:* D. Wiese (Sussex); D. P. M. D. Jayawardene (Somerset). *Chris Nash, dropped on nought and 17, reached his first T20 century (from 59 balls) after putting on 156 for the first wicket with Luke Wright, back with a bang after injury. Nash, though, was in danger of being overshadowed by Tymal Mills. Tearing down the slope with the wind at his back, he bowled at 90mph and more – too fast for Chris Gayle, who was yorked for five. South African international David Wiese took four wickets on his first appearance for Sussex.*

At Hove, June 3 (floodlit). **Surrey won by 23 runs.** ‡**Surrey 205-4** (20 overs) (J. J. Roy 109, K. C. Sangakkara 54, D. J. Bravo 30); **Sussex 182-5** (20 overs) (L. J. Wright 34, L. R. P. L. Taylor 51, C. J. Jordan 30*). *MoM:* J. J. Roy. *Attendance:* 5,748. *County debut:* D. J. Bravo (Surrey). *Jason Roy mixed muscle and improvisation to make 109 from 67 deliveries. Kumar Sangakkara and Dwayne Bravo lent good support, while Mills this time proved expensive (4–5–55–1). Nash fell for four, giving Sam Curran a wicket on his 18th birthday, and Sussex were never really in contention.*

At Hove, June 10 (floodlit). **Sussex won by four wickets. Kent 140** (20 overs) (S. A. Northeast 53; T. S. Mills 3-15, C. J. Jordan 3-18); ‡**Sussex 143-6** (19.3 overs) (L. R. P. L. Taylor 62; M. E. Claydon 3-25). *MoM:* L. R. P. L. Taylor. *Attendance:* 5,205. *A slow pitch produced an excellent derby, not settled until Wiese hit successive boundaries in the last over. Sussex owed much to their seam attack. Chris Jordan was inventive, Mills bowled with gusto and control, and Ajmal Shahzad gave the Kent batsmen no freedom: the three had combined figures of 10–36–40–6. Mitch Claydon then made life awkward for Sussex, but Ross Taylor guided them most of the way home.*

At Arundel, June 26. **Gloucestershire won by 11 runs. Gloucestershire 184-4** (20 overs) (H. J. H. Marshall 90, I. A. Cockbain 37; A. Shahzad 3-26); ‡**Sussex 173-9** (20 overs) (L. J. Wright 71, M. W. Machan 31; M. D. Taylor 3-29). *MoM:* H. J. H. Marshall. *Attendance:* 5,612. *A healthy crowd saw Gloucestershire continue to thrive at outgrounds: they had already won at Northwood and Beckenham (and would do so at Cheltenham). Hamish Marshall, who hit 90 off 55 balls, added 120 for the second wicket with Ian Cockbain to ensure a tricky target on another slow surface. Wright led the chase, but when he fell Sussex needed 63 from 31 deliveries, and left-armer Matt Taylor helped close out the game with three wickets in five.*

At Hove, July 1 (floodlit). **Sussex won by seven wickets. Middlesex 146** (17.4 overs) (P. R. Stirling 52, N. R. T. Gubbins 32; D. R. Briggs 3-24); ‡**Sussex 147-3** (18.2 overs) (L. R. P. L. Taylor 33*, M. W. Machan 41*). *MoM:* D. R. Briggs. *Attendance:* 5,211. *County debut:* G. J. Bailey (Middlesex). *Thanks to Paul Stirling's muscular hitting, Middlesex thrashed 71 in the powerplay, but his dismissal four balls later – to a smart catch by wicketkeeper Craig Cachopa – sent them into a tailspin. Slow bowlers Danny Briggs and Will Beer applied a tourniquet as Middlesex lost nine for 75. Taylor and Matt Machan then supervised the later stages of the chase.*

At Hove, July 15 (floodlit). **Hampshire won by one run.** ‡**Hampshire 134-9** (20 overs); **Sussex 133-8** (20 overs) (C. D. Nash 32, L. R. P. L. Taylor 46*; G. T. Griffiths 3-33). *MoM:* B. T. J. Wheal. *Attendance:* 5,591. *Brad Wheal bowled a superb last over, conceding just four singles – but Sussex should have won at a canter. A desperately slow pitch inhibited strokeplayers on both sides, and Sussex managed only 31 runs from the start of the fifth over to the end of the 11th. A flurry of boundaries brought the requirement down to 28 from six, with seven wickets in hand. Taylor, though, struggled to gain the strike, and defeat dented Sussex's hopes of making the knockouts. Hampshire were already resigned to missing finals day for the first time in eight years.*

At Hove, July 28 (floodlit). **No result. Glamorgan 101** (13.2 overs) (G. H. S. Garton 4-16); **‡Sussex 30-1** (4.1 overs). *After dismissing Glamorgan with four balls unused – the game had become a 14-over contest – Sussex were victory-bound when rain returned. They made it back out, but for only one of the six balls required for a result. Against a side already through to the quarter-finals, Sussex bowled superbly, especially 19-year-old left-arm seamer George Garton. Glamorgan were gifted 26 extras – twice as many as their highest scorer – and Sussex rued the time lost to bowling 13 extra deliveries.*

FIVE CATCHES BY A FIELDER IN A TWENTY20 MATCH

M. Ilahi	Jammu & Kashmir v Delhi at Delhi	2010-11
J. M. Vince	Hampshire v Leeward Islands at North Sound	2010-11
J. L. Ontong	Cape Cobras v Knights at Cape Town	2014-15
K. V. A. Adikari	Chilaw v Bloomfield at Colombo (SSC)	2014-15
P. G. Fulton	Canterbury v Northern Districts at Hamilton	2015-16
M. W. Machan	**Sussex v Glamorgan at Hove**	**2016**

Sussex away matches

May 20: beat Gloucestershire by one run (DLS).
June 16: no result v Middlesex.
June 17: no result v Hampshire.
June 30: lost to Kent by ten runs.
July 7: lost to Glamorgan by 46 runs.
July 21: beat Essex by 24 runs.
July 22: lost to Surrey by six wickets.

QUARTER-FINALS

At Nottingham, August 8. **Nottinghamshire won by 39 runs. Nottinghamshire 162-7** (20 overs) (M. H. Wessels 36, G. P. Smith 50; R. N. ten Doeschate 3-19); **‡Essex 123** (18.4 overs) (J. D. Ryder 47; S. R. Patel 4-20). *MoM:* S. R. Patel. *Attendance:* 13,515. *After losing four consecutive quarter-finals between 2011 and 2014, Nottinghamshire made their first finals day since 2010. Despite Greg Smith's 50, their total had looked inadequate on a good pitch, particularly after Jesse Ryder led Essex to 65-0 off seven overs. He bludgeoned ten fours in reaching 47 but, when he was run out at the non-striker's end, the match turned. Samit Patel bowled brilliantly to take 4-20, including three wickets in four balls, as all ten fell for 58.*

At Northampton, August 9. **Northamptonshire won by seven wickets. ‡Middlesex 132-7** (20 overs) (P. R. Stirling 35, G. J. Bailey 46; R. K. Kleinveldt 3-24); **Northamptonshire 135-3** (18.1 overs) (A. M. Rossington 67*). *MoM:* R. K. Kleinveldt. *Attendance:* 5,817. *Northamptonshire's victory, which sent them to finals day for the third time in four seasons, belonged to their attack. Rory Kleinveldt bowled Dawid Malan second ball of the match and, together with Seekkuge Prasanna and Richard Gleeson, squeezed the life from Middlesex. It still might have been close had Ben Duckett been dismissed when he offered a chance to cover on three, but he added 58 with Adam Rossington in an unhurried chase.*

At Bristol, August 10 (floodlit). **Durham won by 19 runs. ‡Durham 180-5** (20 overs) (M. D. Stoneman 61, K. K. Jennings 36, M. J. Richardson 37); **Gloucestershire 161** (19 overs) (J. M. R. Taylor 80). *MoM:* M. J. Richardson. Attendance: 5,531. *Chris Rushworth and Mark Wood paved the way for a Durham victory, each claiming two wickets with the new ball as Gloucestershire's top order for once failed. Jack Taylor came in at 49-5, and brought a glimmer of hope with a career-best 41-ball 80, but the game was up when he became the fourth home batsman to be run out. Durham's openers, Mark Stoneman and Keaton Jennings, had put on 96, before Michael Richardson – who would later despatch Michael Klinger with a breathtaking catch behind the stumps – also weighed in. A good day for Durham was not so good for their captain: Paul Collingwood bowled three legitimate balls and two full tosses over waist height, which forced him from the attack with figures of 0.3–0–22–0.*

At Cardiff, August 11 (floodlit). **Yorkshire won by 90 runs.** ‡**Yorkshire 180-8** (20 overs) (D. J. Willey 79, A. Z. Lees 36; C. A. Ingram 4-32); **Glamorgan 90** (13 overs) (A. U. Rashid 4-26). *MoM:* D. J. Willey. *Attendance:* 10,084. *David Willey launched Yorkshire's innings with a violent 38-ball assault, which included six sixes and seven fours, before Colin Ingram pegged them back to give Glamorgan an outside chance of a first appearance at Twenty20 finals day since 2004. But David Lloyd was bowled by the first ball of the chase, then the prolific Ingram fell in the fifth over, and at 37-6 in the ninth the result was clear. To the disappointment of a big crowd, Glamorgan were sent packing for 90, their lowest T20 total.*

FINALS DAY REPORTS BY RICHARD GIBSON

SEMI-FINALS

NORTHAMPTONSHIRE v NOTTINGHAMSHIRE

At Birmingham, August 20. Northamptonshire won by eight runs. Toss: Nottinghamshire.

The portents for Northamptonshire were bad: they had not beaten Nottinghamshire in the Twenty20 – there had been two ties in 2010 – nor indeed in any competition since 2006. Nottinghamshire, meanwhile, boasted nine internationals, including West Indies all-rounder Andre Russell, who flew in for only his third appearance for them; Northamptonshire had two. They were also missing injured seamer Richard Gleeson, the tournament's most economical regular bowler. And when they slumped to 15 for three, defeat seemed inevitable. But Duckett embarked on a scintillating Twenty20-best 84 from 47 balls, and with Wakely put on 123; no one else passed seven. Nottinghamshire, who had won their last nine completed games in the tournament, then staggered to 15 for three themselves, only for Russell – who had tweaked a calf in the field – to grab back the initiative in an 18-ball 39, ended spectacularly by Keogh's full-length grab at deep midwicket. Crook collected three wickets as Nottinghamshire fell behind, and Broad's attempts to waste time – which might have taken the innings past its cut-off point, costing Northamptonshire six penalty runs – fell flat. In the end, continuity of selection and team spirit overcame big-name flair, which was not lost on Wakely. "Greg Smith was one of Notts' best players all year, and he's not playing," he said.

Man of the Match: B. M. Duckett. *Attendance* (for all three matches on finals day): 23,893.

Northamptonshire

		B	4/6
1 R. E. Levi *lbw b 6*	3	5	0
2 †A. M. Rossington *run out*	1	1	0
3 J. J. Cobb *c 8 b 11*	7	10	0/1
4 B. M. Duckett *b 10*	84	47	12/2
5 *A. G. Wakely *run out*	53	45	4
6 R. K. Kleinveldt *c 2 b 6*	0	2	0
7 S. P. Crook *c 2 b 6*	1	2	0
8 R. I. Keogh *c 7 b 10*	4	7	0
9 G. G. White *not out*	0	2	0
10 B. W. Sanderson *not out*	1	1	0
Lb 2, w 1, nb 4	7		
6 overs: 47-3 (20 overs)	161-8		

1/4 2/15 3/15 4/138 5/139 6/141 7/151 8/160

11 Azharullah did not bat.

Russell 4–9–20–3; Gurney 4–9–34–1; Ball 4–11–24–2; Broad 2–3–18–0; Patel 4–6–42–0; Mullaney 2–0–21–0.

Nottinghamshire

		B	4/6
1 M. J. Lumb *c 7 b 10*	2	6	0
2 A. D. Hales *b 6*	0	2	0
3 M. H. Wessels *c 7 b 9*	24	21	3
4 *D. T. Christian *c 3 b 11*	2	7	0
5 S. R. Patel *c and b 7*	21	21	2
6 A. D. Russell *c 8 b 6*	39	18	4/3
7 S. J. Mullaney *c 4 b 7*	10	6	0/1
8 †C. M. W. Read *c 9 b 7*	30	20	4
9 S. C. J. Broad *c 2 b 10*	11	11	1
10 J. T. Ball *not out*	2	5	0
11 H. F. Gurney *not out*	5	4	1
Lb 4, w 1, nb 2	7		
6 overs: 38-3 (20 overs)	153-9		

1/4 2/5 3/15 4/45 5/90 6/92 7/107 8/141 9/147

Sanderson 4–12–21–2; Kleinveldt 4–10–24–2; Azharullah 4–9–41–1; White 3–6–28–1; Crook 4–13–28–3; Cobb 1–1–7–0.

Umpires: D. J. Millns and R. T. Robinson. Third umpire: A. G. Wharf.

Sliced and diced: Joe Root is worked over by Mark Wood.

DURHAM v YORKSHIRE

At Birmingham, August 20. Durham won by seven runs. Toss: Durham.

Seldom do three successive dot balls become the talking point of a Twenty20 contest, but Wood's dramatic welcome to Root thrilled even the traditionalists. He beat his England colleague twice on the outside edge, and in between cut him in half. "It looked as if I had my hands and feet on backwards," said Root. "I couldn't get settled." He soon top-edged a crab-like pull off Rushworth, and Yorkshire were 30 for two. Suddenly, Durham's 157 – a stop–start innings, amid persistent squalls – felt bigger. It had owed much to Stokes, on his return from a calf tear: rusty at first, he exploited the spinners' inability to grip a wet ball, slog-sweeping both Rashid and Root for six. Yet until Stokes held Lees at deep midwicket in the tenth over of the Yorkshire reply to make it 75 for three, it looked as if his batting would be in vain. Then Collingwood gambled, opting to give Wood his third over, the 12th of the innings. His first ball, a yorker, speared through Bairstow's prod; his third, to Ballance, flew to Collingwood at leg gully. Lyth and Leaning added 34 in five overs, but Rushworth's slower ball did for Lyth on 64. Two more wickets for Wood in the 19th confirmed career-best figures of four for 25, victory for Durham – and the Man of the Match champagne for that rarest of breeds, the teetotal fast bowler.

Man of the Match: M. A. Wood.

"He recited his speeches without notes, having fine-tuned them on long walks with his otterhound, Hotspur."
Obituaries, page 175

Durham

		B	4/6
1 M. D. Stoneman *b 9*	25	20	4
2 K. K. Jennings *st 5 b 11*	11	13	1
3 B. A. Stokes *c 8 b 11*	56	36	4/3
4 †M. J. Richardson *lbw b 10*	29	23	4/1
5 J. T. A. Burnham *c 5 b 8*	17	15	1/1
6 R. D. Pringle *b 9*	10	9	1
7 *P. D. Collingwood *not out*	2	3	0
8 U. Arshad *not out*	1	1	0
Lb 4, w 1	5		

6 overs: 39-1 (20 overs) 156-6

1/31 2/47 3/119 4/128 5/144 6/154

9 S. G. Borthwick, 10 M. A. Wood and 11 C. Rushworth did not bat.

Willey 4–10–25–0; Bresnan 4–11–29–1; Azeem Rafiq 4–9–34–2; Plunkett 4–12–22–2; Rashid 2–3–22–1; Root 2–3–20–0.

Yorkshire

		B	4/6
1 A. Lyth *c 1 b 11*	64	42	6/2
2 D. J. Willey *c 7 b 11*	3	5	0
3 J. E. Root *c 5 b 11*	7	10	1
4 *A. Z. Lees *c 3 b 9*	22	16	3/1
5 †J. M. Bairstow *b 10*	3	6	0
6 G. S. Ballance *c 7 b 10*	0	2	0
7 J. A. Leaning *c 6 b 8*	19	19	2
8 T. T. Bresnan *b 10*	9	7	0/1
9 L. E. Plunkett *b 10*	9	4	2
10 A. U. Rashid *not out*	5	4	0
11 Azeem Rafiq *not out*	6	5	0
Lb 1, w 1	2		

6 overs: 43-2 (20 overs) 149-9

1/21 2/30 3/75 4/86 5/86 6/120 7/122 8/138 9/139

Rushworth 4–12–19–3; Wood 4–14–25–4; Arshad 4–3–42–1; Pringle 2–5–17–0; Borthwick 4–7–31–1; Jennings 2–2–14–0.

Umpires: N. A. Mallender and A. G. Wharf. Third umpire: R. T. Robinson.

FINAL

DURHAM v NORTHAMPTONSHIRE

At Birmingham, August 20 (floodlit). Northamptonshire won by four wickets. Toss: Durham.

Amid all the talk of a money-spinning Twenty20 city revolution, the final was contested by two paupers – and it provided one of the richest stories of the season. Northamptonshire showed what could be achieved with canny recruitment, attentive planning and freedom of expression, becoming the tournament's second multiple winners (after three-times champions Leicestershire). There may never be a franchise at Wantage Road, but they have T20 down to a T.

"People are always on our backs, hammering us down, talking about our being 'units', overweight, all that kind of stuff," said Wakely, their captain. "But I genuinely believe this group of players is as talented as there is. I couldn't be more proud. I love the club to bits. It's a pretty simple formula: if you have a happy changing-room, you perform."

As if to emphasise the point, it was Cobb – affectionately known as Tuckshop – who proved the match-winner, 24 hours after signing a new contract. Discontent had triggered a move from Leicestershire two years earlier, but such was his drive now that he put off knee surgery to be here, skipping training for six weeks and surviving on painkillers to preserve himself for matches.

Circumstances had made it hard for either side to maintain composure. Rain compressed the scheduling so much that Collingwood arrived for the toss straight from the semi-final press conference, denying him time to fill in an official team sheet. He sought to apply scoreboard pressure by batting first once more, but Northamptonshire proved spoilers.

Stokes began in fifth gear, only for Sanderson – Richard Gleeson's replacement – to apply the brakes by switching his angle of attack. Going round the wicket, he persuaded Stokes to clump a slower delivery straight to Keogh, diving forward in the deep. It was Keogh's second significant catch of the day – and one of five wickets for Sanderson. With others departing, it was left to Jennings – who had been making his name in the four-day game – to put a par score on the board. He showed brain and brawn, and late, straight sixes sped him towards a 58-ball 88, the highest score on finals day.

Northamptonshire tried to see off Wood's thunderbolts. But Rossington was taken at slip from his first ball, and Levi run out, after edging into the cordon, from his second. When the demise of Duckett reduced them to nine for three in the next over, they were reeling for the second time in the day.

But under head coach David Ripley's tutelage they had become adept at escaping adversity. Wakely batted with sobriety, forging another century stand, this time with Cobb, who claimed a second match award in the final. The first, for Leicestershire in 2011, Cobb said, had been for "a few long hops". Here, he downed Durham with his ability to hit a long ball: the momentum changed when he effectively took 12 off one delivery from Arshad – a no-ball hauled for six, followed by a free-hit four.

By nine o'clock, with the rain at its heaviest, Northamptonshire had reached 100 – almost home, most definitely hosed. Cobb eventually fell for 80 from 48 balls, and they took their time completing the job, but nothing could douse the elation of their remarkable triumph.

Man of the Match: J. J. Cobb. *Most Valuable Player:* C. A. Ingram (Glamorgan).

Durham

		B	4/6
1 M. D. Stoneman *c and b 11*	3	6	0
2 K. K. Jennings *c 3 b 8*	88	58	5/4
3 B. A. Stokes *c 6 b 10*	18	8	4
4 †M. J. Richardson *c 2 b 7*	4	8	0
5 J. T. A. Burnham *run out*	0	3	0
6 *P. D. Collingwood *c 7 b 10*	9	11	0
7 R. D. Pringle *c 3 b 10*	2	7	0
8 S. G. Borthwick *c 2 b 8*	10	12	0
9 U. Arshad *not out*	4	5	0
10 M. A. Wood *not out*	5	3	1
Lb 4, w 4, nb 2	10		
6 overs: 40-2 (20 overs)	153-8		

1/16 2/34 3/43 4/49 5/89 6/104 7/140 8/144

11 C. Rushworth did not bat.

Sanderson 4–11–31–3; Kleinveldt 4–8–40–2; Azharullah 4–9–21–1; Crook 4–10–26–1; Cobb 1–0–9–0; White 3–4–22–0.

Northamptonshire

		B	4/6
1 R. E. Levi *run out*	2	3	0
2 †A. M. Rossington *c 8 b 10*	2	4	0
3 J. J. Cobb *c 4 b 11*	80	48	10/3
4 B. M. Duckett *lbw b 11*	4	5	1
5 *A. G. Wakely *run out*	43	39	3/2
6 R. I. Keogh *not out*	16	11	2
7 S. P. Crook *run out*	0	3	0
8 R. K. Kleinveldt *not out*	2	3	0
Lb 1, w 3, nb 2	6		
6 overs: 46-3 (19.1 overs)	155-6		

1/4 2/4 3/9 4/129 5/148 6/149

9 G. G. White, 10 B. W. Sanderson and 11 Azharullah did not bat.

Rushworth 4–11–22–2; Wood 4–12–25–1; Arshad 3.1–4–41–0; Jennings 4–6–34–0; Borthwick 4–11–32–0.

Umpires: N. A. Mallender and R. T. Robinson. Third umpire: D. J. Millns.

WINNERS

		Man of the Match
2003	SURREY beat Warwickshire by nine wickets at Nottingham.	J. Ormond
2004	LEICESTERSHIRE beat Surrey by seven wickets at Birmingham.	B. J. Hodge
2005	SOMERSET beat Lancashire by seven wickets at The Oval.	G. C. Smith
2006	LEICESTERSHIRE beat Nottinghamshire by four runs at Nottingham.	D. L. Maddy
2007	KENT beat Gloucestershire by four wickets at Birmingham.	R. McLaren
2008	MIDDLESEX beat Kent by three runs at Southampton.	O. A. Shah
2009	SUSSEX beat Somerset by 63 runs at Birmingham.	D. R. Smith
2010	HAMPSHIRE beat Somerset by virtue of losing fewer wickets at Soton.	N. D. McKenzie
2011	LEICESTERSHIRE beat Somerset by 18 runs at Birmingham.	J. J. Cobb
2012	HAMPSHIRE beat Yorkshire by ten runs at Cardiff.	D. A. Miller
2013	NORTHAMPTONSHIRE beat Surrey by 102 runs (D/L) at Birmingham.	D. J. Willey
2014	WARWICKSHIRE beat Lancashire by four runs at Birmingham.	L. J. Evans
2015	LANCASHIRE beat Northamptonshire by 13 runs at Birmingham.	A. L. Davies
2016	NORTHAMPTONSHIRE beat Durham by four wickets at Birmingham.	J. J. Cobb

ROYAL LONDON ONE-DAY CUP IN 2016

REVIEW BY JAMES GINGELL

1 Warwickshire 2 Surrey 3= Somerset, Yorkshire

One-day cricket was the future once, but Twenty20 stole its crown. As the shortest format heads for cities, schedules will grow tighter and the future murkier. It's difficult to see where there will be room or affection – among players or fans – for the awkward middle child of the county game.

Andrew Strauss, England's director of cricket, knew this, even as he helped draw up plans for an arriviste city competition. But he also knew, in the short term at least, that a thriving one-day scene remained critical to the future of the English game. Hosting the Champions Trophy in 2017 and the World Cup in 2019 presented a challenge as much as an opportunity: a vibrant and successful England side could energise the public and bring cricket to the front pages; another enervating campaign, as in every World Cup since they made the final in 1992, would cast the format further into the shadows. Strauss needed to galvanise the players from the lower ranks and unearth diamonds to gleam in global tournaments. He needed to inspire enthusiasm for a domestic one-day competition that, at times, has appeared a wearying vacuity.

In May, he announced plans to democratise England recognition: the PCA's Most Valuable Player algorithm would be used to identify the best eight performers, who would then take part in a North v South series in the UAE in March 2017, attended by England selectors. Strauss said it would deliver a "shot in the arm" to the flagging 50-over game, and give players from unfashionable counties a fair chance.

When the season began, Worcestershire's Tom Fell was having chemotherapy after testicular cancer was found to have spread to his lymph nodes. He returned in July to hit a hundred against Lancashire, and averaged 118 in the group stages to drag Worcestershire into the knockout rounds. Fell didn't have the time to force himself into the North v South game, but Matt Coles, Kent's muscular seamer, did. He topped the bowling charts with 24 wickets at 17, including a six-for at Southampton. Coles will be glad of the chance to regain favour: along with Ben Stokes, he was sent home from an England Lions tour in 2013 for poor behaviour. Northamptonshire's slow left-armer Graeme White also earned a call, after taking 18 wickets at 18, the best average of any spinner who bowled more than 13 overs.

Some from England's past reminded us they could still play, too. The 36-year-old Michael Lumb began with three hundreds in three innings, the first two buttressing successive Nottinghamshire scores of over 400 at home. Bowlers would have been forgiven phantom ailments on the way to Trent Bridge: seven of the ten worst figures in this year's competition were recorded at Cardus's lotus land for batting. After four innings, Lumb had 422 runs, but he failed to score more than 20 in the remaining rounds, and Nottinghamshire did not progress. Essex's evergreen keeper, the 36-year-old James Foster, also

Julian Finney, Getty Images

Reversing the trend: Jonathan Trott swept Warwickshire to victory.

flourished. His 50-ball 75 to force a tie against Somerset was described by team-mate Graham Napier – also aged 36 – as "possibly the best one-day knock I've ever seen".

Holders Gloucestershire – one of Strauss's sackcloth counties – flopped. Their captain, Michael Klinger, said their 2015 win "could be the start of something special", but their title defence was far from it. They began with a heart-stopping loss – a last-wicket partnership of 63 between Jamie Overton and Tim Groenewald proving just enough for Somerset – then succumbed next day to Glamorgan. They won only two matches in all, slumping to eighth in the southern group.

The wealthier counties simply waited for the paupers to punch themselves out. Surrey were determined to exorcise the ghost of the previous year's final, but appeared haunted in their first two games. They lost narrowly to Kent and emphatically to Somerset, before picking up momentum. Jade Dernbach was their engine, claiming 15 wickets at 14, many with crafty variations at the death. A rain-affected win over Middlesex in their last group game at Lord's saw them through to the quarter-finals, where they squeaked past Northamptonshire by one wicket. Rory Kleinveldt's hard-hitting 76 had left Surrey needing 276 and, when 12 off the last over became ten off four balls, it seemed the match was slipping away. But Kumar Sangakkara produced the moment of the tournament, lurching towards silly point and flicking Azharullah's blameless delivery over the wicketkeeper and into the sightscreen for six; a carve for four off the last ball brought him to a magnificent 130.

Getting past Yorkshire in the semi-final was rather more comfortable: Steven Davies's responsible hundred and Ben Foakes's 90 took them to a total they easily protected. As Surrey captain Gareth Batty celebrated dismissing his counterpart Alex Lees with a slider through the gate – arms aloft and shrieking like the kraken – it was tempting to think redemption was written in the fates. As it was, Surrey were to meet a new nemesis in the final.

While contemporary trends call for power hitters, 360-degree daring and impossibly disguised slower balls, Warwickshire reasoned that smart batting and disciplined bowling would never go out of fashion. With little fuss, they progressed from the northern group, where the top five were separated on net run-rate (Durham were unluckily eliminated after their last game, at Manchester, was rained off). Jonathan Trott, pragmatic and efficient, was Warwickshire's emblem. He made 227 runs in the knockout games – including a decisive hundred against Essex in the quarters – at an anachronistic strike-rate of 80, the only concession to modernity the occasional (very controlled) reverse sweep. In eight innings across the whole tournament, he averaged 86 and struck a solitary six; Brendon McCullum whacked ten in three for Middlesex.

Warwickshire were the earnest pros; Surrey had the tattoos, spunk and muscle

Trott's apprentice, the 21-year-old Sam Hain, was the only man to make more runs (540), many of them modestly driven with pleasing economy. They let their spinners take the headlines, particularly Jeetan Patel, whose aggressive off-breaks claimed more wickets than anyone but Coles. In the knockouts he raised his game to take ten at ten apiece, including five lbws to cripple Somerset in the semi-finals, each met with a pumped fist and an ursine snarl.

The final threw two sides into sharp relief: Warwickshire were the earnest and resourceful pros, all tucked-in shirts and mucking in. Surrey had the tattoos, spunk and muscle. They also had Jason Roy – in electric form for England all summer – and international call-ups Batty and Zafar Ansari. They were the modern way. But as soon as they lost Roy to a spectacular catch from Laurie Evans, their batsmen looked twitchy, and floundered on a pockmarked surface. They knew the game was up. Even Batty, the marching martinet, puffed out his cheeks in resignation; afterwards, he spouted platitudes and preached progress, but the fire had gone from his eyes.

Trott appeared calm from afar, but close-ups revealed a clenched jaw. In 2014, just ten months after leaving the Ashes tour, he had played in the inaugural Royal London Cup final, and made two as Warwickshire folded to Durham. He was determined this would be his day. He never hurried – there was no need to – and with clips and dabs and checked drives took Warwickshire to a comprehensive victory. Some redemption for him, but none for Surrey.

Prize money

£154,000 for winners: WARWICKSHIRE.
£72,000 for runners-up: SURREY.
£23,150 for losing semi-finalists: SOMERSET, YORKSHIRE.
There was no financial reward for winning individual matches.

FINAL GROUP TABLES

	North Group	Played	Won	Lost	Tied	No result	Points	NRR
1	NORTHAMPTONSHIRE	8	4	3	0	1	9	0.78
2	WARWICKSHIRE	8	4	3	0	1	9	0.74
3	YORKSHIRE	8	4	3	0	1	9	0.60
4	WORCESTERSHIRE	8	4	3	0	1	9	0.04
5	Durham	8	4	3	0	1	9	–0.63
6	Nottinghamshire	8	3	4	0	1	7	0.23
7	Derbyshire	8	2	3	0	3	7	–0.34
8	Leicestershire	8	2	3	0	3	7	–0.49
9	Lancashire	8	2	4	0	2	6	–1.33

	South Group	Played	Won	Lost	Tied	No result	Points	NRR
1	SOMERSET	8	6	1	1	0	13	–0.09
2	KENT	8	5	3	0	0	10	0.59
3	ESSEX	8	4	2	1	1	10	–0.12
4	SURREY	8	4	3	0	1	9	0.99
5	Hampshire	8	4	4	0	0	8	0.39
6	Middlesex	8	4	4	0	0	8	0.12
7	Glamorgan	8	3	4	0	1	7	–0.32
8	Gloucestershire	8	2	5	0	1	5	–0.71
9	Sussex	8	1	7	0	0	2	–0.68

Where two or more counties finished with an equal number of points, the positions were decided by (a) most wins (b) net run-rate.

ROYAL LONDON ONE-DAY CUP AVERAGES

BATTING (280 runs at 45.00)

		M	I	NO	R	HS	100	50	Avge	SR	4	6
1	R. K. Kleinveldt (*Northants*)	6	5	2	285	128	1	1	95.00	160.11	28	14
2	I. J. L. Trott (*Warwicks*)	8	7	1	515	118	3	2	85.83	86.12	50	1
3	†B. T. Slater (*Derbys*)	6	6	2	328	148*	2	1	82.00	84.97	39	2
4	L. A. Dawson (*Hants*)	8	8	3	359	100*	1	3	71.80	118.87	23	6
5	†M. J. Lumb (*Notts*)	8	7	0	482	184	3	0	68.85	107.82	54	11
6	M. H. Wessels (*Notts*)	8	7	0	453	146	2	2	64.71	110.48	54	15
7	†B. M. Duckett (*Northants*)	8	7	0	443	121	1	3	63.28	98.88	56	5
8	†C. A. Ingram (*Glam*)	8	7	1	367	107	1	2	61.16	126.55	19	19
9	J. L. Denly (*Kent*)	9	9	2	428	105	2	1	61.14	77.81	41	7
10	T. T. Bresnan (*Yorks*)	9	8	2	361	95*	0	3	60.16	81.85	21	8
11	S. R. Hain (*Warwicks*)	10	10	1	540	107	2	3	60.00	84.24	54	5
12	†B. A. Godleman (*Derbys*)	6	6	1	298	91	0	3	59.60	82.32	29	5
13	T. R. Ambrose (*Warwicks*)	10	8	2	357	86	0	4	59.50	98.89	32	6
14	M. Klinger (*Glos*)	8	7	1	337	166*	1	1	56.16	83.83	37	6
15	†T. P. Alsop (*Hants*)	7	7	1	327	116	1	2	54.50	86.50	31	2
16	†J. D. Ryder (*Essex*)	9	8	0	435	131	2	3	54.37	92.16	43	8
17	I. R. Bell (*Warwicks*)	10	8	2	310	94*	0	3	51.66	94.22	23	4
18	P. R. Stirling (*Middx*)	8	8	1	348	125*	2	1	49.71	91.33	37	7
19	†A. Lyth (*Yorks*)	10	9	0	439	136	2	1	48.77	114.92	41	18
20	B. T. Foakes (*Surrey*)	9	8	1	330	90	0	3	47.14	101.53	28	5
21	D. T. Christian (*Notts*)	8	7	0	328	94	0	4	46.85	117.14	23	14
22	R. I. Keogh (*Northants*)	9	8	1	321	134	1	2	45.85	103.54	34	2

BOWLING (10 wickets at 30.00)

		Style	*O*	*M*	*R*	*W*	*BB*	*4I*	*Avge*	*SR*	*ER*
1	J. W. Dernbach (*Surrey*)	RFM	44.5	1	205	15	4-39	2	13.66	17.93	4.57
2	T. S. Roland-Jones (*Middx*)	RFM	42.2	3	214	13	4-40	1	16.46	19.53	5.05
3	M. T. Coles (*Kent*)	RFM	80.1	4	418	24	6-56	2	17.41	20.04	5.21
4	G. G. White (*Northants*)	SLA	66	3	315	18	6-37	1	17.50	22.00	4.77
5	R. McLaren (*Hants*)	RFM	37	2	182	10	4-42	1	18.20	22.20	4.91
6	H. F. Gurney (*Notts*)	LFM	64.3	0	376	19	5-51	1	19.78	20.36	5.82
7	J. S. Patel (*Warwicks*)	OB	92.1	3	446	22	5-43	1	20.27	25.13	4.83
8	J. E. C. Franklin (*Middx*)	LFM	52.3	0	250	12	3-25	0	20.83	26.25	4.76
9	A. Javid (*Warwicks*)	OB	42	0	212	10	4-42	1	21.20	25.20	5.04
10	L. Gregory (*Somerset*)	RFM	66	1	376	17	4-23	1	22.11	23.29	5.69
11	G. J. Batty (*Surrey*)	OB	62.4	1	311	14	5-41	1	22.21	26.85	4.96
12	R. J. Gleeson (*Northants*)	RFM	55.1	2	292	13	5-47	2	22.46	25.46	5.29
13	A. U. Rashid (*Yorks*)	LBG	41.3	1	230	10	3-23	0	23.00	24.90	5.54
14	R. E. van der Merwe (*Somerset*)	SLA	61.5	1	323	14	3-51	0	23.07	26.50	5.22
15	L. E. Plunkett (*Yorks*)	RFM	61	1	279	12	4-52	1	23.25	30.50	4.57
16	G. R. Napier (*Essex*)	RFM	45	2	280	12	3-50	0	23.33	22.50	6.22
17	C. J. Jordan (*Sussex*)	RFM	58.4	3	308	13	5-28	1	23.69	27.07	5.25
18	S. C. Meaker (*Surrey*)	RFM	66	1	413	17	3-47	0	24.29	23.29	6.25
19	T. D. Groenewald (*Somerset*)	RFM	61.2	2	366	15	3-30	0	24.40	24.53	5.96
20	B. D. Cotton (*Derbys*)	RFM	47.2	4	258	10	4-43	1	25.80	28.40	5.45
21	S. J. Thakor (*Derbys*)	RM	41	2	268	10	3-36	0	26.80	24.60	6.53
22	G. H. S. Garton (*Sussex*)	LFM	42	0	269	10	3-40	0	26.90	25.20	6.40
23	B. A. C. Howell (*Glos*)	RFM	56.1	1	276	10	2-32	0	27.60	33.70	4.91
24	T. K. Curran (*Surrey*)	RFM	62	2	332	12	3-26	0	27.66	31.00	5.35
25	G. K. Berg (*Hants*)	RFM	58	1	305	11	4-25	2	27.72	31.63	5.25

NORTH GROUP

DERBYSHIRE

At Derby, June 7 (day/night). **Derbyshire won by seven wickets. Durham 216** (46.3 overs) (R. D. Pringle 125); ‡**Derbyshire 218-3** (41.4 overs) (B. T. Slater 119). *Attendance:* 572. *In his first 50-over match for Derbyshire, opener Ben Slater moved his team to the brink of victory with a smart hundred before becoming the very first victim for Mark Stoneman's off-breaks. Ryan Pringle was the only Durham player to emerge with credit – he came in at 58-6 and struck a belligerent 125, dwarfing his previous best of 35.*

At Chesterfield, June 12. **No result. Derbyshire 0-0** (1 over) **v** ‡**Yorkshire.**

At Derby, July 27 (day/night). **Lancashire won by 27 runs.** ‡**Lancashire 281-8** (50 overs) (L. S. Livingstone 98, S. J. Croft 68); **Derbyshire 254-9** (50 overs) (B. A. Godleman 91; K. M. Jarvis 4-31). *Attendance:* 1,100. *Liam Livingstone fell short of a maiden List A hundred, but his 98 helped Lancashire to an imposing total on a sluggish surface. Tight bowling – particularly from Kyle Jarvis – kept Derbyshire in check, but they were in the hunt at 177-2. Then, in consecutive overs, Wayne Madsen was caught and Billy Godleman bowled to spark a collapse.*

At Derby, August 1 (day/night). **No result.** ‡**Derbyshire 260-6** (50 overs) (B. A. Godleman 66, N. T. Broom 90); **Leicestershire 0-0** (0.2 overs). *Attendance:* 883. *Neither side was able to reach the quarter-finals, and rain brought a premature end. Neil Broom's 90, his highest score in the competition, provided the highlight.*

Derbyshire away matches

June 5: beat Worcestershire by seven wickets.
June 15: no result v Warwickshire.
July 24: lost to Nottinghamshire by 65 runs.
July 31: lost to Northamptonshire by seven wickets.

DURHAM

At Chester-le-Street, June 12. **Worcestershire won by seven wickets.** Reduced to 22 overs a side. **Durham 90** (21.1 overs); ‡**Worcestershire 91-3** (19.1 overs). *Attendance:* 633. *Durham were inserted on a seaming pitch in a game reduced by rain to 22 overs a side and stumbled to 90 all out, with nine batsmen failing to make double figures. Chris Rushworth reduced Worcestershire's chase to 31-3, but a composed stand of 60* between Alexei Kervezee and Brett D'Oliveira carried them home.*

At Chester-le-Street, June 15 (day/night). **Durham won by two wickets** (DLS). ‡**Nottinghamshire 274-5** (42 overs) (M. J. Lumb 105, D. T. Christian 57); **Durham 253-8** (37 overs) (P. D. Collingwood 69, M. J. Richardson 64; H. F. Gurney 5-51). *Attendance:* 1,070. *When Michael Richardson holed out for a one-day best 64, it gave Harry Gurney his fifth wicket and left Durham with two balls to score nine. But Keaton Jennings planted a full toss high over midwicket for six, then belted the final ball wide of mid-off for four. It was harsh on Michael Lumb, who had earlier battled through three rain delays in Nottinghamshire's first 13 overs to make a third hundred in three innings (having not scored a domestic one-day century since 2009). Durham had more luck with the weather, and Paul Collingwood's sprightly 69 set them on their way towards a revised target of 252 from 37 overs.*

At Gosforth, July 27. **Durham won by four wickets. Warwickshire 292-7** (50 overs) (S. R. Hain 107, T. R. Ambrose 86); ‡**Durham 296-6** (47.4 overs) (M. D. Stoneman 56, S. G. Borthwick 66, P. D. Collingwood 53). *Attendance:* 1,533. *Durham were in a mess after the last three days had brought a hammering at Northampton and news of senior departures: Phil Mustard to Gloucestershire on loan, and skipper Mark Stoneman, at the season's end, to Surrey. Collingwood assumed the one-day captaincy and hit a 33-ball 53, as Durham overcame Warwickshire's 292. On a superb pitch, Sam Hain's second hundred of the competition looked to have ensured a mammoth Warwickshire score. But excellent death bowling from Usman Arshad (3-50) kept their total within reach. The game marked the 150th anniversary of host club, South Northumberland.*

At Chester-le-Street, July 31. **Durham won by 15 runs.** ‡**Durham 281-7** (50 overs) (S. G. Borthwick 84, M. J. Richardson 53); **Yorkshire 266-8** (50 overs) (T. T. Bresnan 92). *Attendance:* 3,878. *Yorkshire – without four England players – didn't look capable of overhauling Durham's 281 until Bresnan's spirited 92 brought them within 28. But when he fell to the last ball of the 48th over, and only one run came off the next, from Mark Wood, the task drifted beyond them. Earlier, Collingwood had tweaked a calf muscle while batting with Scott Borthwick, who made a composed 84. The captaincy hot potato passed to Jennings, who cleverly shuffled his bowlers.*

Durham away matches

June 5: beat Leicestershire by 11 runs.
June 7: lost to Derbyshire by seven wickets.
July 24: lost to Northamptonshire by 170 runs.
August 1: no result v Lancashire.

LANCASHIRE

At Manchester, June 5. **Lancashire won by 42 runs.** ‡**Lancashire 296-8** (50 overs) (M. J. Guptill 50, J. C. Buttler 91, S. J. Croft 67; W. B. Rankin 4-66); **Warwickshire 254-9** (50 overs) (I. J. L. Trott 66, I. R. Bell 73). *Attendance:* 2,033. *Jos Buttler's inventive 91 from 73 balls helped Lancashire post a total about 30 runs above par. Despite having signed in 2014, he was making his List A debut for them, and shared a 122-run fourth-wicket stand with Steven Croft, his skipper. Croft later took four catches, three of them diving efforts off Stephen Parry, whose accuracy helped keep Warwickshire at bay on a testing pitch.*

At Blackpool, June 12. **No result. Lancashire 157-1** (33 overs) (A. N. Petersen 73*, L. A. Procter 63*) v ‡**Nottinghamshire.** *Attendance:* 2,627. *Rain set in at 1pm, with Lancashire building a large total.*

At Manchester, June 15 (day/night). **Yorkshire won by 242 runs** (DLS). ‡**Yorkshire 325-7** (47 overs) (A. Lyth 136); **Lancashire 84** (17.3 overs). *Attendance:* 2,749. *Adam Lyth's second Royal London Cup hundred in two days set up his side's biggest List A win, and Lancashire's biggest loss. In 92 balls he hit 12 fours and seven sixes to race to a career-best 136. After rain, Lancashire began competently in chasing a revised 327, before losing all their wickets for 45 inside 12 overs; Martin*

Guptill's 45 was the only double-figure score. Yorkshire used just four bowlers, including 20-year-old slow left-armer Karl Carver, who took 3-5.

At Manchester, August 1 (day/night). **No result.** Reduced to 24 overs a side. ‡**Lancashire 39-0** (7 overs) **v Durham.** *Attendance:* 2,180. *Lancashire had no chance of reaching the quarter-finals, and rain scuppered Durham's hopes.*

Lancashire away matches

June 8: lost to Northamptonshire by 76 runs.
July 26: lost to Leicestershire by 131 runs.
July 27: beat Derbyshire by 27 runs.
July 31: lost to Worcestershire by four wickets.

LEICESTERSHIRE

At Leicester, June 5. **Durham won by 11 runs. Durham 340-6** (50 overs) (M. D. Stoneman 93, P. Mustard 88, S. G. Borthwick 63; R. M. L. Taylor 4-58); ‡**Leicestershire 329-9** (50 overs) (K. J. O'Brien 89, M. J. Cosgrove 63; J. Harrison 4-40). *Attendance:* 970. *Durham began with a first-wicket stand of 180 in 28 overs between Mark Stoneman and Phil Mustard which set up a big total. Despite Kevin O'Brien's 89 from 84 deliveries, Leicestershire fell just short; left-arm seamer Jamie Harrison took 4-40.*

At Leicester, July 24. **Yorkshire won by 191 runs.** ‡**Yorkshire 376-3** (50 overs) (T. M. Head 175, J. A. Leaning 131*); **Leicestershire 185** (33.3 overs) (L. J. Hill 55). *Attendance:* 1,432. *Yorkshire ran amok to make 376-3, their highest List A score against a first-class county, beating 352-6 against Nottinghamshire at Scarborough in 2001. Travis Head crashed 22 boundaries in a 139-ball 175, and Jack Leaning five sixes in 131* from 110. Ben Raine came in for particular punishment, leaking 88 from nine overs. Leicestershire dribbled to 185.*

At Leicester, July 26. **Leicestershire won by 131 runs. Leicestershire 307-8** (50 overs) (M. L. Pettini 92, M. J. Cosgrove 91); ‡**Lancashire 176** (39.3 overs) (T. C. Smith 56; N. J. Dexter 4-22). *Attendance:* 795. *County debut:* D. Klein (Leicestershire). *Leicestershire recorded their first one-day win since August 2014, against a struggling Lancashire. Mark Pettini and Mark Cosgrove hit nineties, and Neil Dexter thumped consecutive sixes off Stephen Parry to lift them over 300. Dexter then claimed 4-22 with his seamers as Lancashire folded.*

At Leicester, July 31. **Leicestershire won by eight runs.** ‡**Leicestershire 279** (50 overs) (M. L. Pettini 50, N. J. O'Brien 82); **Nottinghamshire 271-9** (50 overs) (L. Wood 52). *Attendance:* 1,104. *Leicestershire survived a scare to complete back-to-back wins, after Niall O'Brien's 82 had given them a competitive 279. Nottinghamshire's chase was listing at 204-8 in the 44th over, before No. 9 Luke Wood, on List A debut, raced to 52 from 31 balls to bring the task down to 13 off the last. But Cameron Delport yorked him second ball to swing the game back Leicestershire's way.*

Leicestershire away matches

June 7: lost to Warwickshire by nine wickets.
June 12: no result v Northamptonshire.
June 15: no result v Worcestershire.
August 1: no result v Derbyshire.

NORTHAMPTONSHIRE

At Northampton, June 8 (day/night). **Northamptonshire won by 76 runs. Northamptonshire 287-8** (50 overs) (B. M. Duckett 98, R. I. Keogh 66); ‡**Lancashire 211** (43.3 overs) (K. R. Brown 51, L. A. Procter 52; G. G. White 6-37). *Attendance:* 2,226. *Graeme White's left-arm spin harvested figures of 6-37, the best of his career – and of this tournament – to help Northamptonshire to a comfortable victory. Batting first, they were in trouble at 37-3, but Ben Duckett and Rob Keogh ensured a competitive total with a stand of 137. Lancashire had a chance at 86-2 in the 17th, but lost three wickets in four overs – including Jos Buttler – and never recovered.*

At Northampton, June 12. **No result.** Reduced to 19 overs a side. **Northamptonshire 12-0** (2 overs) **v** ‡**Leicestershire.** *Attendance:* 1,587.

At Northampton, July 24. **Northamptonshire won by 170 runs. Northamptonshire 355-6** (50 overs) (J. J. Cobb 56, R. I. Keogh 134, R. I. Newton 65); ‡**Durham 185** (35.3 overs) (Azharullah 5-43).

Attendance: 2,525. *Northamptonshire were without Duckett, away with England Lions, but Keogh filled his shoes – and his own boots. He stepped up to No. 3 and hit 134 from 110 balls, his maiden one-day century. At the end of the innings Rory Kleinveldt (32*) hit six of his 13 deliveries for four to give Northamptonshire's total a daunting look. Azharullah then took five to wreck Durham.*

RUNS BY THE DUCKETT-FUL

Most List A runs in a calendar month:

Runs		*Month*	*Inns*	*NO*	*HS*	*100*	*Avge*
741	Sami Aslam (Baluchistan/National Bank) . .	Jan 2015	11	0	120	3	67.36
668	H. Masakadza (Mountaineers/Zimbabwe) . .	Oct 2009	10	2	178	2	83.50
650	**B. M. Duckett (Northants/Eng Lions)**. . . .	**Jul 2016**	**7**	**2**	**220***	**2**	**130.00**
633	Salim Elahi (Habib Bank)	Apr 1999	8	1	172	3	90.42
608	N. J. Astle (New Zealand/Canterbury).	Jan 2000	10	1	122	2	67.55
606	G. A. Gooch (Essex/England)	May 1990	9	2	112*	2	86.57
600	T. M. Moody (Warwickshire)	May 1991	8	2	128*	4	100.00

At Northampton, July 31. **Northamptonshire won by seven wickets.** ‡**Derbyshire 272-7** (50 overs) (B. T. Slater 148*; R. J. Gleeson 4-66); **Northamptonshire 278-3** (42 overs) (J. J. Cobb 88, B. M. Duckett 70, R. I. Keogh 63*). *Attendance:* 2,093. *Northamptonshire closed in on the quarter-finals despite the best efforts of Ben Slater, who batted throughout the innings for 148*. It was his second hundred of the tournament, and Derbyshire's highest List A innings against first-class opposition. He could only watch from the other end, though, as Richard Gleeson's burst of three wickets in six balls destroyed hopes of amassing 300. Fluent fifties from Josh Cobb, Duckett and Keogh set Northamptonshire on course for an easy win.*

Northamptonshire away matches

June 6: lost to Nottinghamshire by 20 runs.
June 14: lost to Yorkshire by two wickets.
July 26: lost to Warwickshire by eight wickets.
July 27: beat Worcestershire by 23 runs.

NOTTINGHAMSHIRE

At Nottingham, June 6 (day/night). **Nottinghamshire won by 20 runs.** ‡**Nottinghamshire 445-8** (50 overs) (M. J. Lumb 184, M. H. Wessels 146); **Northamptonshire 425** (48.2 overs) (A. M. Rossington 97, R. K. Kleinveldt 128). *Attendance:* 2,313. *It was not a day to be a bowler. Michael Lumb blasted 184, Nottinghamshire's highest one-day score, and shared an opening stand of 342 with Riki Wessels, the biggest for any wicket in one-day cricket in England. That set up a total of 445, the second highest in all List A cricket, behind Surrey's 496-4 against Gloucestershire at The Oval in 2007. Remarkably, Northamptonshire fought back, claiming eight for 102, before continuing the butchery themselves; by the end, six bowlers had conceded over 80. Adam Rossington made a rapid 97, before his departure brought Rory Kleinveldt to the crease with a runner for a sore calf. But Kleinveldt barely needed him, clubbing nine sixes and ten fours in a brutal maiden one-day century. Until he fell in the 45th over, a stunning win was on. "I've never seen anything like it", said David Ripley, Northamptonshire's head coach.*

At Nottingham, June 8 (day/night). **Nottinghamshire won by 36 runs. Nottinghamshire 415-5** (50 overs) (M. J. Lumb 133, M. H. Wessels 76, G. P. Smith 73, D. T. Christian 94); ‡**Warwickshire 379** (49.3 overs) (S. R. Hain 69, I. J. L. Trott 100, I. R. Bell 60, T. R. Ambrose 73). *Attendance:* 2,552. *For the second time in three days, Nottinghamshire passed 400, the second team to do so in consecutive one-day matches, after South Africa in the 2015 World Cup (408-5 v West Indies and 411-4 v Ireland). Lumb smashed another hundred (this time his opening stand with Wessels was worth 178), and Dan Christian five sixes in a 47-ball 94, before falling in the last over going for his sixth. Having conceded their highest one-day score, Warwickshire reached their own record total against a first-class county, but Jonathan Trott's 100 – which included his only six of the tournament – was not enough to force a win.*

HIGHEST RUN-RATE IN A FULL-LENGTH LIST A GAME

Runs/over	*Runs*	*Overs*		
9.44	718	76	Sussex (399-4) v Worcs (319) at Horsham	2011
8.84	**870**	**98.2**	**Notts (445-8) v Northants (425) at Nottingham**	**2016**
8.73	872	99.5	Australia (434-4) v South Africa (438-9) at Johannesburg	2005-06
8.73	735	84.1	Surrey (496-4) v Glos (239) at The Oval	2007
8.68	867	99.5	Surrey (438-5) v Glam (429) at The Oval	2002
8.63	662	76.4	Worcs (376-6) v Surrey (286) at The Oval	2010
8.57	673	78.3	Sussex (336-5) v Kent (337-7) at Canterbury	2013
8.38	827	98.4	India A (433-3) v South Africa A (394) at Pretoria	2013
8.25	825	100.0	India (414-7) v Sri Lanka (411-8) at Rajkot	2009-10
8.24	815	98.5	Central D (417-6) v Northern D (398) at Hamilton	2012-13

At Sookholme, July 24. **Nottinghamshire won by 65 runs. Nottinghamshire 340-7** (50 overs) (M. H. Wessels 114, C. M. W. Read 59); ‡**Derbyshire 275** (45.1 overs) (B. T. Slater 51). *Attendance:* 4,649. *Lumb finally failed, but opening partner Wessels covered for him with an 85-ball 114, before powerful hitting from Steven Mullaney (39*) and Chris Read lifted Nottinghamshire to an imposing total. They defended it comfortably, as Harry Gurney maintained his excellent form with three more wickets.*

At Nottingham, August 1 (day/night). **Worcestershire won by 35 runs** (DLS). **Nottinghamshire 284-8** (50 overs) (M. H. Wessels 50, S. R. Patel 55, D. T. Christian 54); ‡**Worcestershire 138-1** (24 overs) (D. K. H. Mitchell 61*, T. C. Fell 63*). *Attendance:* 3,029. *A third consecutive defeat ended Nottinghamshire's interest. In pursuit of 285, Worcestershire began in gloom, and lost Tom Köhler-Cadmore in the first over. But Daryl Mitchell put on 130 with Tom Fell and, when the rain came, Worcestershire had enough for victory.*

Nottinghamshire away matches

June 12: no result v Lancashire.
June 15: lost to Durham by two wickets (DLS).
July 27: lost to Yorkshire by two wickets.
July 31: lost to Leicestershire by eight runs.

WARWICKSHIRE

At Birmingham, June 7 (day/night). **Warwickshire won by nine wickets. Leicestershire 237** (49 overs) (K. J. O'Brien 77, R. M. L. Taylor 62); ‡**Warwickshire 243-1** (41 overs) (W. T. S. Porterfield 75, S. R. Hain 105*). *Attendance:* 1,324. *In his third List A match Warwickshire's Sam Hain pulled the last ball of the 41st over for six to complete both a cakewalk and his century. After being inserted, Leicestershire slipped to 134-6, before Rob Taylor's 62 from No. 9 gave them hope. But Hain's opening stand of 169 in 29 overs with William Porterfield made the chase a formality.*

At Birmingham, June 15 (day/night). **Warwickshire v Derbyshire. Abandoned.**

At Birmingham, July 24. **Warwickshire won by eight wickets.** ‡**Worcestershire 115** (38.2 overs) (R. Clarke 5-26); **Warwickshire 119-2** (22.4 overs) (T. R. Ambrose 54*). *Attendance:* 3,029. *Worcestershire chose to bat but soon regretted it. Rikki Clarke removed Tom Köhler-Cadmore in his first over and bowled ten unchanged to record a career-best 5-26. Ed Barnard and Ben Cox put on 70 for the eighth wicket to drag them past 100, but Warwickshire coasted home.*

At Birmingham, July 26. **Warwickshire won by eight wickets. Northamptonshire 254-9** (50 overs) (J. J. Cobb 50, A. G. Wakely 70); ‡**Warwickshire 257-2** (48 overs) (W. T. S. Porterfield 92, S. R. Hain 88). *Attendance:* 1,667. *Another huge opening stand – this time 180 in 33 overs – between Hain and Porterfield helped Warwickshire to another comfortable win. Northamptonshire had been looking strong on 101-1 after 20 overs but, after Josh Cobb was run out for 50, they lost three quick wickets, including Ben Duckett and Rob Keogh, both to Jeetan Patel. Captain Alex Wakely rallied, but it wasn't enough.*

Warwickshire away matches

June 5: lost to Lancashire by 42 runs.
June 8: lost to Nottinghamshire by 36 runs.
July 27: lost to Durham by four wickets.
August 1: beat Yorkshire by 114 runs (DLS).

WORCESTERSHIRE

At Worcester, June 5. **Derbyshire won by seven wickets.** ‡**Worcestershire 295** (49.4 overs) (A. N. Kervezee 77, R. A. Whiteley 61; B. D. Cotton 4-43); **Derbyshire 298-3** (48.1 overs) (B. A. Godleman 61, H. D. Rutherford 104, W. L. Madsen 69*). *Attendance:* 1,721. *The players took cover from a swarm of bees during Worcestershire's innings, but the home side were still stung: Hamish Rutherford's 74-ball hundred brought Derbyshire victory with 11 deliveries to spare. Derbyshire's other centurion was relieved: leg-spinner Matt Critchley's ten overs cost 101, the worst figures in this year's tournament.*

At Worcester, June 15. **Worcestershire v Leicestershire. Abandoned.**

At Worcester, July 27. **Northamptonshire won by 23 runs. Northamptonshire 319-7** (50 overs) (B. M. Duckett 86, A. M. Rossington 87, S. P. Crook 52*); ‡**Worcestershire 296** (49.5 overs) (T. Köhler-Cadmore 119, T. C. Fell 54; R. J. Gleeson 5-47). *Attendance:* 2,576. *Ben Duckett's 86 helped Northamptonshire set a winning total and lifted his white-ball aggregate to 631 in seven innings. At 193-1 in the 33rd over, Worcestershire looked on course to achieve their highest successful chase. But after Richard Gleeson bowled Tom Fell, they lost their way, and Tom Köhler-Cadmore's first one-day hundred came in vain; Gleeson mopped up to record 5-47, his first five-for in senior cricket.*

At Worcester, July 31. **Worcestershire won by four wickets.** ‡**Lancashire 267-7** (50 overs) (S. J. Croft 78); **Worcestershire 268-6** (47.4 overs) (T. C. Fell 116*). *Attendance:* 2,576. *After a mid-innings wobble, in which Joe Clarke and Brett D'Oliveira departed in successive Stephen Parry overs, Tom Fell hit his first hundred since returning from chemotherapy to earn a standing ovation – and Worcestershire a win. Lancashire, who needed victory to stay in the tournament, had opted to bat, but struggled to get away; D'Oliveira's leg-spin conceded just 27 in ten overs.*

Worcestershire away matches

June 7: beat Yorkshire by seven wickets.
June 12: beat Durham by seven wickets.
July 24: lost to Warwickshire by eight wickets.
August 1: beat Nottinghamshire by 35 runs (DLS).

YORKSHIRE

At Leeds, June 7 (day/night). **Worcestershire won by seven wickets.** ‡**Yorkshire 170** (45.2 overs); **Worcestershire 171-3** (25.3 overs) (J. Leach 63). *Attendance:* 2,530. *Yorkshire elected to bat, but crumbled to 170 all out. Joe Leach opened the bowling, taking 2-30, then opened the batting, smashing 63 from 35 balls to help seal the chase inside 26 overs. The List A debut of off-spinning all-rounder George Rhodes (son of Steve, and grandson of Nottinghamshire's Billy), meant Worcestershire had two third-generation county cricketers on show, the other being Brett D'Oliveira; both took two wickets.*

At Scarborough, June 14. **Yorkshire won by two wickets. Northamptonshire 310-7** (50 overs) (B. M. Duckett 121, A. G. Wakely 71); ‡**Yorkshire 314-8** (47.3 overs) (A. Lyth 125, G. S. Ballance 80). *Attendance:* 1,680. *Adam Lyth's blitz helped Yorkshire win their first one-day match of the season. Northamptonshire, boosted by Ben Duckett's maiden one-day century, made it difficult, but Lyth was up to the challenge, unleashing eight sixes, battering the fish and chip van in a 75-ball 125. Yorkshire looked friable, losing three for three, before David Willey smacked his third six against his former club to settle the issue.*

At Scarborough, July 27. **Yorkshire won by two wickets. Nottinghamshire 251-9** (50 overs) (D. T. Christian 52, S. J. Mullaney 89*); ‡**Yorkshire 254-8** (49.4 overs) (T. T. Bresnan 95*). *Attendance:* 4,949. *Soon after the start of a topsy-turvy game, it seemed as if Nottinghamshire, 46-5, would be* *routed. But Dan Christian and Steven Mullaney – who took 18 from the last over – gave them a chance. Yorkshire then slipped to 50-4, before Adil Rashid and Tim Bresnan pulled things round with 97. Three wickets for Christian shifted the balance again, but Yorkshire scrambled home with two balls to go; Bresnan ended five short of a maiden one-day century.*

At Leeds, August 1 (day/night). **Warwickshire won by 114 runs** (DLS). ‡**Warwickshire 283-6** (50 overs) (I. J. L. Trott 118); **Yorkshire 167** (37.4 overs) (T. M. Head 53; A. Javid 4-42). *Attendance:* 4,092. *Jonathan Trott's artful hundred helped set up a thumping Warwickshire win, and a home quarter-final. He was out at the beginning of the 45th over, but a late assault led by Laurie Evans – who made a 30-ball 48* – brought 66 off the last five. Yorkshire had their target reduced by two after an over was lost to rain, but capitulated to the spin of Ateeq Javid and Jeetan Patel, who claimed 7-76 between them.*

Yorkshire away matches

June 12: no result v Derbyshire.
June 15: beat Lancashire by 242 runs (DLS).
July 24: beat Leicestershire by 191 runs.
July 31: lost to Durham by 15 runs.

SOUTH GROUP

ESSEX

At Chelmsford, June 12. **Tied** (DLS). **Somerset 179-8** (29 overs) (A. J. Hose 77, J. Allenby 68); ‡**Essex 176-9** (29 overs) (J. S. Foster 75*; L. Gregory 4-23). *Attendance:* 1,335. *Going into the final four overs of an extraordinary rain-reduced match, Essex – their last pair at the crease – required 38 to reach a revised 177. James Foster took responsibility: he shielded No. 11 Matt Quinn while chipping away to leave 16 off the last, delivered by Lewis Gregory, whose first five overs had brought him 4-13. With two balls left, Foster still needed eight, but launched a towering six over cow corner and scrambled a bye to earn a thrilling tie; he ended on 75* from 50 balls, Quinn on 0* from four. For Somerset, only Adam Hose and Jim Allenby reached double figures, and the bowlers gave away 15 extras, including five byes in the last over.*

At Chelmsford, June 15. **Essex won by five wickets. Kent 285-8** (50 overs) (M. T. Coles 91); ‡**Essex 289-5** (49.1 overs) (J. D. Ryder 50, R. S. Bopara 74*). *Attendance:* 1,493. *Essex thought they had the game won when seamer Quinn and left-arm spinner Ashar Zaidi took three wickets each to reduce Kent to 135-7. But out strode Matt Coles to blast a 52-ball 91 and help post a tricky 285. He couldn't quite follow it up with the ball, though, as a century stand by Ravi Bopara and Ryan ten Doeschate (45) broke the back of the Essex chase.*

At Chelmsford, July 24. **Surrey won by 66 runs.** ‡**Surrey 313-8** (50 overs) (J. J. Roy 55, S. M. Davies 82, R. J. Burns 52); **Essex 247** (41.2 overs) (J. D. Ryder 131; J. W. Dernbach 4-41). *Attendance:* 2,709. *A trio of solid fifties, together with some late dash from Ben Foakes (45), lifted Surrey to a challenging 313. In reply, Essex lost regular wickets, before a stand of 91 in 12 overs for the sixth between hard-hitting left-handers Jesse Ryder and Zaidi reduced the task to 111 off 17. But Jade Dernbach removed both in consecutive overs, and Essex soon subsided.*

At Chelmsford, July 26. **Essex won by four wickets.** ‡**Glamorgan 324-8** (50 overs) (D. L. Lloyd 62, C. A. Ingram 107); **Essex 325-6** (49.1 overs) (N. L. J. Browne 99, J. D. Ryder 50, R. S. Bopara 59). *Attendance:* 2,140. *Despite a scintillating hundred from Colin Ingram that included six sixes, Glamorgan failed to protect a demanding total. Nick Browne led the reply, though he missed out on a maiden one-day century when he slipped turning for a second. With 35 needed from the last four overs, there was work to do, but Foster made it look easy, clubbing 26 from 12 balls to see Essex home.*

Essex away matches

June 5: beat Hampshire by three wickets.
June 6: beat Sussex by five wickets.
July 31: lost to Middlesex by four runs.
August 2: no result v Gloucestershire.

GLAMORGAN

At Cardiff, June 6 (day/night). **Glamorgan won by 52 runs. Glamorgan 289** (49.5 overs) (J. A. Rudolph 53, W. D. Bragg 75); ‡**Gloucestershire 237** (47.1 overs) (M. Klinger 52, B. A. C. Howell 77). *Attendance:* 1,034. *Glamorgan looked to have squandered the platform laid by Jacques Rudolph and William Bragg when four wickets fell for 23 to leave them 179-5. But Graham Wagg (49) gave them some late-innings oomph. Much depended on Michael Klinger but, once he went for 52, Gloucestershire struggled – particularly against Timm van der Gugten, who took 3-33. Despite a rousing 77 from Benny Howell, they came up short.*

At Cardiff, June 8 (day/night). **Glamorgan won by 84 runs.** ‡**Glamorgan 302-6** (50 overs) (A. H. T. Donald 53, C. B. Cooke 80, G. G. Wagg 52); **Sussex 218** (42.4 overs) (L. J. Wright 65; M. G. Hogan 4-41). *Attendance:* 1,080. *Glamorgan didn't look capable of 300 after dawdling to 109-3 in 26 overs. But 193 came from the next 24, thanks to swift fifties from Aneurin Donald, Chris Cooke and Wagg. Sussex dropped four catches, and were scarcely sharper with the bat. Only Luke Wright scored fluently and, when he was caught in the deep, their innings folded.*

At Cardiff, June 14 (day/night). **Middlesex won by 28 runs. Middlesex 294-7** (50 overs) (B. B. McCullum 110, D. J. Malan 70); ‡**Glamorgan 266** (48.2 overs) (C. A. Ingram 85). *Attendance:* 882. *When Middlesex reached 176-0 in 26 overs, they were eyeing 350. But Michael Hogan removed both openers, including Brendon McCullum for an 85-ball 110, and Middlesex were restricted to 294. With Ingram again running hot, Glamorgan looked well placed at 227-4 in the 42nd, before Cooke became one of Dawid Malan's two victims, and the last six wickets fell for 39.*

At Swansea, July 31. **Hampshire won by 186 runs.** ‡**Hampshire 316-5** (50 overs) (W. R. Smith 84, L. A. Dawson 100*); **Glamorgan 130** (32 overs) (R. McLaren 4-42, G. K. Berg 4-25). *Attendance:* 1,460. *Hampshire's acting-captain Liam Dawson smashed the last ball of the innings for six to go to a 68-ball century, as 40 came from the final two overs. It set up a crushing victory. Ryan McLaren trapped David Lloyd lbw with the first ball of the reply and, with Gareth Berg, reduced Glamorgan to 29-6. There was no way back.*

Glamorgan away matches

June 12: beat Kent by three wickets (DLS).
July 24: lost to Somerset by 33 runs (DLS).
July 26: lost to Essex by four wickets.
August 1: no result v Surrey.

GLOUCESTERSHIRE

At Bristol, June 8 (day/night). **Middlesex won by seven wickets** (DLS). **Gloucestershire 254-8** (50 overs) (G. H. Roderick 64, H. J. H. Marshall 74); ‡**Middlesex 211-3** (31.3 overs) (P. R. Stirling 125*). *Attendance:* 1,220. *Paul Stirling's forthright 87-ball hundred, his ninth in List A cricket, swept Middlesex to their revised target of 208 in 35 overs. Gareth Roderick and Hamish Marshall had mustered half-centuries after Toby Roland-Jones removed three of the top four, but Gloucestershire fell short of a competitive total.*

At Bristol, June 14 (day/night). **Gloucestershire won by ten runs. Gloucestershire 352-3** (50 overs) (C. D. J. Dent 142, M. Klinger 166*); ‡**Hampshire 342-8** (50 overs) (T. P. Alsop 50, S. M. Ervine 53, L. A. Dawson 57, G. M. Andrew 70*). *Attendance:* 852. *Openers Michael Klinger and Chris Dent put on 242 to help Gloucestershire to their first win. Klinger, happy to play second fiddle while Dent blazed to 142 from 116 balls, took 115 to reach his own hundred. But he exploded into life in the last ten overs, carting 66 from his next 35 to reach a career-best 166*. Hampshire gave the chase a good crack, but none of their four half-centurions could kick on.*

At Cheltenham, July 24. **Gloucestershire won by 51 runs. Gloucestershire 242-8** (50 overs); ‡**Sussex 191** (45.4 overs) (H. Z. Finch 87*; T. M. J. Smith 4-26). *Attendance:* 4,328. *Tom Smith played a leading role with bat and ball as Gloucestershire concluded the Cheltenham Festival with a comfortable victory (though this would prove their last win of the tournament). He struck 43* to* *help them reach 242, before claiming 4-26 from his ten overs; Sussex collapsed, despite Harry Finch's 87*.*

At Bristol, August 2 (day/night). **Gloucestershire v ‡Essex. Abandoned.**

Gloucestershire away matches

June 5: lost to Somerset by one wicket.
June 6: lost to Glamorgan by 52 runs.
July 27: lost to Surrey by 165 runs.
July 31: lost to Kent by seven wickets.

HAMPSHIRE

At Southampton, June 5. **Essex won by three wickets. Hampshire 310-4** (50 overs) (T. P. Alsop 83*, A. J. A. Wheater 90, L. A. Dawson 70*); **‡Essex 314-7** (49.3 overs) (T. Westley 110, J. D. Ryder 71). *Attendance:* 2,344. *Hampshire had never failed to defend more than 300 in 50-over cricket, but James Foster ended that record with a 19-ball 36*. Liam Dawson's 70 from 52 looked to have given Hampshire a winning score, but Tom Westley and Jesse Ryder put on 143 for the second wicket, and Foster completed the job in the last over.*

At Southampton, June 15 (day/night). **Hampshire won by six runs. Hampshire 289-8** (50 overs) (T. P. Alsop 116, S. M. Ervine 50); **‡Surrey 283-9** (50 overs) (Z. S. Ansari 62, B. T. Foakes 72; G. K. Berg 4-64). *Attendance:* 1,450. *Twenty-year-old opener Tom Alsop followed up fifties in his first two innings of the tournament with a maiden one-day century to set up a tight win. After a partnership of 130 between Zafar Ansari and Ben Foakes, Surrey needed just 16 from 13 balls, but Gareth Berg removed both Curran brothers and Gareth Batty in four to keep them at bay.*

At Southampton, July 26 (day/night). **Kent won by five wickets. Hampshire 229** (47.5 overs) (A. J. A. Wheater 63; M. T. Coles 6-56); **‡Kent 231-5** (43.3 overs) (D. J. Bell-Drummond 91, J. L. Denly 105; B. T. J. Wheal 4-38). *Attendance:* 2,261. *Kent openers Daniel Bell-Drummond and Joe Denly made victory certain with a stand of 203, though there was still time for five wickets to fall. Matt Coles had taken 6-56 against his old club, including a brilliant caught and bowled to remove Ryan McLaren.*

At Southampton, August 2 (day/night). **Somerset won by five runs. ‡Somerset 250-9** (50 overs) (D. P. M. D. Jayawardene 55, J. Allenby 69); **Hampshire 245** (50 overs) (J. H. K. Adams 50, W. R. Smith 59). *Attendance:* 1,805. *Top-placed Somerset confirmed their qualification for the quarter-finals with their sixth win. Hampshire needed 251 to join them, and a six off the last would have got them there, but Brad Wheal instead gave Tim Groenewald a return catch.*

Hampshire away matches

June 7: beat Middlesex by five wickets (DLS).
June 14: lost to Gloucestershire by ten runs.
July 27: beat Sussex by nine runs.
July 31: beat Glamorgan by 186 runs.

KENT

At Beckenham, June 5. **Kent won by one wicket. ‡Surrey 255-8** (50 overs) (K. C. Sangakkara 58); **Kent 260-9** (49.5 overs) (D. J. Bell-Drummond 56, A. J. Blake 66*). *Attendance:* 2,389. *Alex Blake played the most responsible innings of his eight-year Kent career to earn a one-wicket win with one ball to spare. For Surrey, only Kumar Sangakkara had adjusted to an unusually slow Beckenham pitch, posting 58 in a workmanlike 255. In reply, Kent slipped from 111-1 to 115-5, then 147-6, before No. 8 Blake took control, avoiding the big shot until the fifth ball of the last over, which he clubbed over deep extra cover.*

At Canterbury, June 12. **Glamorgan won by three wickets** (DLS). **Kent 290-3** (42 overs) (J. L. Denly 104*, S. W. Billings 106*); **‡Glamorgan 294-7** (40.5 overs) (D. L. Lloyd 65, W. D. Bragg 52, C. A. Ingram 95*). *Attendance:* 1,464. *Rumbustious centuries from Joe Denly and Sam Billings came in vain as Glamorgan won a rain-affected match. Billings reached his with a six on to the players' balcony from his 53rd ball. Glamorgan's target was revised to 293 in 42 overs and, inspired by Colin Ingram's elegant 53-ball 95*, they paced the chase adroitly.*

At Canterbury, June 14. **Kent won by 95 runs.** Reduced to 30 overs a side. **Kent 231-6** (30 overs) (D. J. Bell-Drummond 68, S. A. Northeast 64); ‡**Somerset 136** (24.2 overs). *Attendance:* 1,263. *Kent made light of tricky conditions to sweep Somerset aside. Daniel Bell-Drummond and Sam Northeast scored sixties to help Kent to a creditable 231-6 in 30 overs, and Somerset never got to grips with the rate.*

At Canterbury, July 31. **Kent won by seven wickets. Gloucestershire 200** (49.2 overs); ‡**Kent 203-3** (41.2 overs) (J. L. Denly 82*). *Attendance:* 2,793. *Brisk seamer Charlie Hartley was the pick of the Kent attack with 2-23, including Hamish Marshall, leg-before to a full off-cutter, as Gloucestershire crumbled. Denly coasted home with 82* off 124 balls.*

Kent away matches

June 15: lost to Essex by five wickets.
July 24: lost to Middlesex by six wickets.
July 26: beat Hampshire by five wickets.
August 2: beat Sussex by seven wickets.

MIDDLESEX

At Radlett, June 7. **Hampshire won by five wickets** (DLS). **Middlesex 295-8** (50 overs) (B. B. McCullum 74, E. J. G. Morgan 52; M. S. Crane 4-80); ‡**Hampshire 204-5** (25.3 overs) (L. A. Dawson 68*)*:* 1,256. *The day after delivering the Cowdrey Lecture at Lord's, Brendon McCullum blazed 74 in 56 balls to put Middlesex in a strong position. But heavy rain reduced the Hampshire target to 202 in 26 overs, and Liam Dawson's 40-ball 68 saw them home.*

At Lord's, July 24. **Middlesex won by six wickets.** ‡**Kent 238-7** (50 overs) (S. R. Dickson 99, D. I. Stevens 61); **Middlesex 239-4** (44.5 overs) (P. R. Stirling 112, E. J. G. Morgan 103*). *Attendance:* 3,608. *County debut:* W. R. S. Gidman (Kent). *Kent opener Sean Dickson fell a run short of a maiden one-day century, then watched as Eoin Morgan and Paul Stirling cantered to hundreds and a Middlesex win.*

At Lord's, July 31. **Middlesex won by four runs. Middlesex 219-8** (50 overs) (J. E. C. Franklin 55); ‡**Essex 215-9** (50 overs) (N. L. J. Browne 79; T. S. Roland-Jones 4-40). *Attendance:* 6,103. *Dan Lawrence's occasional leg-breaks (3-35) helped restrict Middlesex to 219, which looked paltry when Essex reached 100-1. But Toby Roland-Jones took three in three overs to lead a fightback in which five fell for 45. Essex needed 11 off the last, from James Franklin, but managed only six.*

At Lord's, August 2 (day/night). **Surrey won by five wickets** (DLS). **Middlesex 101-8** (16 overs); ‡**Surrey 105-5** (15.2 overs). *Attendance:* 2,243. *Middlesex's batsmen struggled through persistent rain to a total they could not defend. DLS set Surrey 102 in 16 overs and, though they lost early wickets, the weather eased enough for Ben Foakes and Zafar Ansari to share a match-winning stand of 66 in nine overs. Surrey went through; Middlesex went out.*

Middlesex away matches

June 8: beat Gloucestershire by seven wickets (DLS).
June 12: lost to Sussex by 31 runs.
June 14: beat Glamorgan by 28 runs.
July 26: lost to Somerset by four wickets.

SOMERSET

At Taunton, June 5. **Somerset won by one wicket. Gloucestershire 260** (50 overs) (C. D. J. Dent 100); ‡**Somerset 263-9** (49.3 overs) (J. G. Myburgh 81). *Attendance:* 4,296. *When Somerset lost their ninth wicket, they needed 62. But a rousing last-wicket stand between Jamie Overton and Tim Groenewald snatched victory with three balls to spare. Holders Gloucestershire had much to ponder, despite Chris Dent's first one-day hundred since 2013.*

At Taunton, July 24. **Somerset won by 33 runs** (DLS). **Somerset 322-7** (50 overs) (J. Allenby 53, P. D. Trego 80); ‡**Glamorgan 279** (45.2 overs). *Attendance:* 4,757. *Peter Trego's 80 off 76 balls helped Somerset to a commanding total, which they easily protected. Glamorgan were 167-3 facing a revised target of 313 in 47 overs, but scoreboard pressure told.*

At Taunton, July 26. **Somerset won by four wickets. Middlesex 296-9** (50 overs) (P. R. Stirling 58, N. R. T. Gubbins 89); ‡**Somerset 297-6** (49 overs) (P. D. Trego 104, L. Gregory 69). *Attendance:*

4,596. *Nick Gubbins hit three sixes in his 89 to give Middlesex a competitive score. But Trego was the hero again, taking 2-27 before making a 106-ball hundred.*

At Taunton, July 30. **Somerset won by ten runs.** ‡**Somerset 237** (48.1 overs) (T. B. Abell 106; J. C. Archer 5-42); **Sussex 227-9** (50 overs). *Attendance:* 4,712. *Tom Abell replaced the injured Johann Myburgh, and stood out with a maiden one-day century. Barbadian seamer Jofra Archer claimed his first one-day five-for in only his third game. Sussex fancied their chances, but Groenewald ripped out three of the top six, and Somerset romped to their fourth home win out of four.*

Somerset away matches

June 8: beat Surrey by eight wickets (DLS).
June 12: tied with Essex (DLS).
June 14: lost to Kent by 95 runs.
August 2: beat Hampshire by five runs.

SURREY

At The Oval, June 8 (day/night). **Somerset won by eight wickets** (DLS). ‡**Surrey 163-6** (24 overs) (R. J. Burns 51*); **Somerset 180-2** (23.1 overs) (J. G. Myburgh 76, J. Allenby 71). *Attendance:* 2,951. *Chasing a revised 180 in 24 overs, Somerset were all but guaranteed victory by an opening stand of 155 in 18 between Johann Myburgh and Jim Allenby. Surrey's acting-captain Rory Burns had chosen to bat, and only his 34-ball 51* gave them any chance.*

At Guildford, June 14. **Surrey won by six wickets** (DLS). **Sussex 239** (43.3 overs) (C. J. Jordan 55; R. Rampaul 4-47); ‡**Surrey 235-4** (33.4 overs) (R. J. Burns 70*, B. T. Foakes 61*). *Attendance:* 1,252. *Surrey's first win came after Burns and Ben Foakes joined forces at 99-4 and raced to a revised 235 off 43 overs. Chris Jordan's fifty had revived Sussex from 100-5, but their total always looked flimsy.*

At The Oval, July 27 (day/night). **Surrey won by 165 runs.** ‡**Surrey 323-8** (50 overs) (S. M. Davies 79, R. J. Burns 50, S. M. Curran 57); **Gloucestershire 158** (33.2 overs) (H. J. H. Marshall 55; G. J. Batty 5-41). *Attendance:* 4,136. *County debut:* P. Mustard (Gloucestershire). *Surrey exacted revenge for the previous year's final. Sam Curran's first one-day half-century, and a seventh-wicket partnership of 89 in 13 overs with brother Tom, put them in charge; then Jade Dernbach – who had taken a hat-trick in that final – demolished Gloucestershire's top three. Five wickets from Gareth Batty completed the rout, despite Hamish Marshall's resistance.*

At The Oval, August 1 (day/night). **No result. Surrey 157-1** (19 overs) (J. J. Roy 93*) **v** ‡**Glamorgan.** *Attendance:* 4,661. *Rain cut short Jason Roy's blistering 67-ball display.*

Surrey away matches

June 5: lost to Kent by one wicket.
June 15: lost to Hampshire by six runs.
July 24: beat Essex by 66 runs.
August 2: beat Middlesex by five wickets (DLS).

SUSSEX

At Hove, June 6 (day/night). **Essex won by five wickets. Sussex 271** (50 overs) (E. C. Joyce 73, L. J. Wright 50, L. R. P. L. Taylor 50; M. R. Quinn 4-71); ‡**Essex 275-5** (49 overs) (J. D. Ryder 100). *Attendance:* 1,280. *Essex left themselves 80 off the last nine overs, only for Jesse Ryder to race from 50 to 100 in 38 balls. By the time he fell, the line was in sight. Having been 133-1, Sussex were set for 300-plus, but none of their three half-centurions could provide a telling score.*

At Hove, June 12. **Sussex won by 31 runs. Sussex 222-7** (32 overs) (P. D. Salt 81, L. R. P. L. Taylor 54); ‡**Middlesex 191** (30.4 overs) (C. J. Jordan 5-28). *Attendance:* 1,368. *In a game reduced to 32 overs a side Chris Jordan bowled superbly to set up Sussex's first List A win since August 2014. Teenager Philip Salt's 81 ensured a competitive total, and Jordan – whose yorkers were particularly effective – took 5-28 to ensure it was protected.*

At Hove, July 27 (day/night). **Hampshire won by nine runs. Hampshire 268-9** (50 overs) (J. H. K. Adams 92); ‡**Sussex 259-6** (50 overs) (C. D. Nash 69*, B. C. Brown 62). *Attendance:* 1,474. *With Sussex chasing 269, Chris Nash and wicketkeeper Ben Brown gave them hope with a fifth-wicket* *partnership of 125 in 17 overs. But their ponderous top order had left them too much to do. Earlier, Jimmy Adams hit a stylish 92 for Hampshire, and Ryan McLaren a muscular 46 off 39 balls.*

At Hove, August 2 (day/night). **Kent won by seven wickets. Sussex 182-8** (43 overs) (H. Z. Finch 54; M. T. Coles 4-39); ‡**Kent 184-3** (31.5 overs) (S. A. Northeast 66*, S. W. Billings 55). *Attendance:* 1,364. *County debut:* C. A. L. Davis (Sussex). *Matt Coles's 4-39 meant Sussex fell below par in a 43-over contest, before Sam Northeast and Sam Billings hit attractive fifties to send Kent into the quarter-finals; Sussex sank to the bottom for the second year in succession.*

Sussex away matches

June 8: lost to Glamorgan by 84 runs.
June 14: lost to Surrey by six wickets (DLS).
July 24: lost to Gloucestershire by 51 runs.
July 30: lost to Somerset by ten runs.

QUARTER-FINALS

At Taunton, August 17. **Somerset won by nine wickets.** ‡**Worcestershire 210** (42.5 overs) (M. M. Ali 81, D. K. H. Mitchell 64); **Somerset 214-1** (36.5 overs) (D. P. M. D. Jayawardene 117*, J. Allenby 81). *Attendance:* 5,884. *A stand of 113 between Moeen Ali and Daryl Mitchell had given Worcestershire hope of a competitive score, only for Peter Trego to remove both on his way to 3-33. Mahela Jayawardene had barely shone for Somerset all summer, but in his last game for the county hit his 21st List A century to ease them into the semi-finals.*

At Birmingham, August 17. **Warwickshire won by 70 runs.** ‡**Warwickshire 283-7** (50 overs) (I. J. L. Trott 101, T. R. Ambrose 60, L. J. Evans 70*); **Essex 213** (42.1 overs) (T. Westley 61, R. N. ten Doeschate 53). *Attendance:* 2,767. *After an hour-long dressing-room lock-in that followed a Championship defeat by Surrey the previous day, Warwickshire gained a clinical win. Jonathan Trott's third century in five innings in the competition set up a late blast from Laurie Evans, before Warwickshire's three spinners throttled the chase. On a dry pitch that had been used for the Test against Pakistan earlier in the month, they returned combined figures of 24.1–0–108–8.*

At Northampton, August 18 (day/night). **Surrey won by one wicket.** ‡**Northamptonshire 276** (49 overs) (J. J. Cobb 66, R. K. Kleinveldt 76*; J. W. Dernbach 4-39); **Surrey 279-9** (50 overs) (K. C. Sangakkara 130*). *Attendance:* 3,421. *With 12 needed from Azharullah's final over, and last man Jade Dernbach for company, Kumar Sangakkara paddled a six over the wicketkeeper off the third ball, and laced the last through backward point to take Surrey home in a breathless finish. Northamptonshire had struggled until Rory Kleinveldt smashed three sixes and seven fours in a hectic 62-ball knock. When Surrey dipped from 207-4 to 250-9 in reply, that looked like a match-winning effort, but Sangakkara remained cool.*

At Canterbury, August 18 (day/night). **Yorkshire won by 11 runs. Yorkshire 256-9** (50 overs) (A. Lyth 88); ‡**Kent 245** (47.5 overs) (D. I. Stevens 54, A. J. Blake 50; L. E. Plunkett 4-52). *Attendance:* 4,927. *Not for the first time, the Vikings invaded Kent and left with the spoils. Despite fielding eight England players, Yorkshire's batting struggled, and their modest 256, underpinned by a dogged 88 from Adam Lyth and a scratchy 45 from Joe Root, appeared under par. But their attack rode to their rescue, bowling out Kent in the 48th over; David Willey and Liam Plunkett shared 7-86.*

SEMI-FINALS

YORKSHIRE v SURREY

At Leeds, August 28. Surrey won by 19 runs. Toss: Yorkshire. County debut: O. J. D. Pope.

Davies won the match award for an outstanding century, but it was Meaker who unlocked the door to Lord's. In the space of nine fast and straight deliveries, he captured three wickets for two runs to reduce Yorkshire from 75 for two to 81 for five; despite a fighting 68 from Bresnan, who added 80 with Waite, there was no way back. Batty led Surrey shrewdly against his native county, and his canny bowling accounted for his opposite number, Lees, just when he was starting to make an impact. All he got wrong was the toss but, after Surrey were an uncertain 61 for three, Davies and

Foakes shared a hundred partnership speckled with beautifully timed strokes. Shortly after the game, Jason Gillespie informed Yorkshire he would be standing down as coach at the end of the season to return to Australia.

Man of the Match: S. M. Davies. *Attendance:* 4,836.

Surrey

S. M. Davies c Rhodes b Waite	104	T. K. Curran not out	2
D. P. Sibley lbw b Brooks	0		
K. C. Sangakkara c Azeem Rafiq b Bresnan	4	Lb 2, w 3	5
R. J. Burns c Patterson b Waite	12		—
†B. T. Foakes c Brooks b Bresnan	90	1/3 (2) 2/8 (3) (7 wkts, 50 overs)	255
S. M. Curran b Waite	18	3/61 (4) 4/191 (1)	
O. J. D. Pope run out	20	5/214 (6) 6/249 (5) 7/255 (7)	10 overs: 38-2

*G. J. Batty, S. C. Meaker and J. W. Dernbach did not bat.

Bresnan 10–0–52–2; Brooks 10–1–42–1; Patterson 10–0–53–0; Waite 10–1–48–3; Rhodes 4–0–24–0; Azeem Rafiq 6–0–34–0.

Yorkshire

A. Lyth c Sibley b Dernbach	4	S. A. Patterson c Sangakkara b T. K. Curran	0
*A. Z. Lees b Batty	26	J. A. Brooks not out	1
G. S. Ballance c Foakes b Meaker	32		
†J. M. Bairstow c Sibley b Meaker	13	Lb 11, w 9, nb 2	22
J. A. Leaning b Meaker	3		—
T. T. Bresnan c Sibley b Dernbach	68	1/10 (1) 2/54 (2) 3/75 (4) (48.5 overs)	236
M. J. Waite c Batty b S. M. Curran	38	4/80 (3) 5/81 (5) 6/161 (7)	
W. M. H. Rhodes run out	23	7/207 (8) 8/231 (9) 9/234 (10)	
Azeem Rafiq c Burns b T. K. Curran	6	10/236 (6)	10 overs: 43-1

Dernbach 9.5–0–45–2; S. M. Curran 10–0–47–1; Batty 10–0–37–1; T. K. Curran 9–0–35–2; Meaker 10–0–61–3.

Umpires: P. J. Hartley and J. W. Lloyds. Third umpire: N. G. B. Cook.

WARWICKSHIRE v SOMERSET

At Birmingham, August 29. Warwickshire won by eight runs. Toss: Warwickshire.

Patel's best one-day figures sent Warwickshire to their fourth Lord's final in seven seasons. His first wicket set the mould: two balls after being hoisted into the stands by Trego, Patel upped his pace by 5mph and rapped his prey on the pad as he played across the line. Four more batsmen went in similar fashion, the last of them Davies, whose departure after a rapid 46 – though he was hit outside the line of off – seemed to extinguish Somerset's hopes. Warwickshire had built their total on meaty partnerships for the first two wickets, before late acceleration from Bell brought him into the nineties, and his team to a winning score.

Man of the Match: J. S. Patel. *Attendance:* 5,030.

Warwickshire

I. J. L. Trott c and b van der Merwe	44	R. Clarke not out	8
S. R. Hain c Overton b Gregory	86	B 1, lb 3, w 3, nb 4	11
*I. R. Bell not out	94		—
†T. R. Ambrose c Waller b van der Merwe	22	1/90 (1) 2/178 (2) (4 wkts, 50 overs)	284
L. J. Evans c Trego b Overton	19	3/227 (4) 4/274 (5)	10 overs: 51-0

A. Javid, J. S. Patel, C. J. C. Wright, O. J. Hannon-Dalby and J. E. Poysden did not bat.

Overton 9–0–51–1; Allenby 9–1–38–0; Gregory 8–0–46–1; van der Merwe 10–0–62–2; Groenewald 4–0–23–0; Trego 3–0–19–0; Waller 7–0–41–0.

Somerset

J. G. Myburgh c Ambrose b Wright 11	T. D. Groenewald not out 30
*J. Allenby lbw b Hannon-Dalby 22	M. T. C. Waller not out 10
P. D. Trego lbw b Patel 58	
T. B. Abell c sub (A. J. Mellor) b Wright . . 35	B 1, lb 5, w 4, nb 2 12
J. C. Hildreth c Bell b Hannon-Dalby 43	
L. Gregory lbw b Patel 4	1/17 (1) 2/44 (2) (9 wkts, 50 overs) 276
R. E. van der Merwe lbw b Patel 5	3/119 (4) 4/145 (3)
C. Overton lbw b Patel 0	5/153 (6) 6/161 (7) 7/161 (8)
†R. C. Davies lbw b Patel 46	8/232 (5) 9/234 (9) 10 overs: 49-2

Clarke 8–0–49–0; Wright 9–0–61–2; Hannon-Dalby 10–0–41–2; Poysden 10–0–58–0; Patel 10–0–43–5; Javid 3–0–18–0.

Umpires: R. J. Bailey and D. J. Millns. Third umpire: A. G. Wharf.

FINAL

SURREY v WARWICKSHIRE

JAMES GINGELL

At Lord's, September 17. Warwickshire won by eight wickets. Toss: Surrey.

At the end of a summer of placid Lord's pitches and violent batting, here was something for the bowlers. Pewter skies hung heavily over a surface that looked queasy from the season's boundary binges. Conditions were ripe for seam and nip, so it was a surprise when Batty decided Surrey would bat. Perhaps he feared a repeat of the previous year's final against Gloucestershire, when they froze in pursuit. But the change in strategy bore no fruit: they failed again, and failed worse.

Earlier in the year, Surrey had signed Durham's Mark Stoneman and Scott Borthwick for 2017. If that was a tacit admission of batting vulnerability, this was a public confession, as they crumbled to a score they had no hope of defending. Openers Roy and Davies began perkily enough, driving and clipping their way to 41 after six overs. But everything changed in the ninth, when Roy advanced at

LOWEST TOTALS BATTING FIRST IN LORD'S COUNTY FINALS

Total (overs)				
108 (36.4)	Derbys	Lancashire won by nine wickets	NatWest Trophy	1998
117 (46.3)	Derbys	Hampshire won by seven wickets	Benson & Hedges Cup	1988
118 (60)	Lancs	Kent won by four wickets	Gillette Cup	1974
127 (48)	Warwicks	Sussex won by eight wickets	Gillette Cup	1964
130 (50.1)	Notts	Somerset won by nine wickets	Benson & Hedges Cup	1982
136 (40.1)	**Surrey**	**Warwickshire won by eight wickets**	**Royal London Cup**	**2016**
136-9 (55)	Yorks	Leicestershire won by five wickets	Benson & Hedges Cup	1972

Wright and flailed a front-foot pull. It was a shot that had earned him runs all summer; but the ball didn't quite come on, he didn't quite middle it, and it didn't quite evade Evans's outstretched claw at midwicket. Evans had begun his county career at Surrey, and had spent time earlier in the season on loan at Northamptonshire, but this earned him a place in Warwickshire lore.

Davies was next, sleepwalking past a wide from Javid and – after Ambrose swiftly stumped him – back to a Surrey dressing-room for the last time before joining Somerset. Under suffocating pressure from excellent bowling, Burns and Sangakkara knuckled down, recalibrating Surrey's ambitions to 200 or so. But they stalled as they tried to engage lower gears. When the spidery Hannon-Dalby found Sangakkara's edge with the score on 99, it sparked a disastrous collapse: their last eight fell for 37. The Warwickshire crowd were bloodthirsty, and Woakes finally sated them, euthanising the innings on 136 at the start of the 41st over.

Before the game, Batty had talked up the death bowling of Dernbach and Tom Curran. But as soon as Trott took two fours off the first over, it was clear the match wouldn't get that far;

Warwickshire made it home inside 31, with barely a moistened brow. Trott – one of the last peaceful negotiators in an era of batting warfare – glowered under his helmet, but was serene in all other senses, smothering the bowling with a masterful, matt-finish 82 from 100 balls. When he pulled and punched consecutive fours off Sam Curran, the trophy was won. As the Warwickshire balcony erupted, he took time to return to his crease and drag a spike across his guard, his assiduousness extending even beyond the tournament's end.

Man of the Match: I. J. L. Trott. *Attendance:* 20,656.

Surrey

J. J. Roy c Evans b Wright	24
S. M. Davies st Ambrose b Javid	23
K. C. Sangakkara c Ambrose b Hannon-Dalby	21
R. J. Burns b Patel	40
†B. T. Foakes lbw b Hannon-Dalby	0
Z. S. Ansari c Evans b Patel	0
S. M. Curran b Javid	13
T. K. Curran run out	4
*G. J. Batty b Woakes	0
S. C. Meaker not out	0
J. W. Dernbach b Woakes	7
Lb 1, w 3	4
1/45 (1) 2/50 (2) 3/99 (3) 4/101 (5) 5/102 (6) 6/118 (7) 7/129 (8) 8/129 (9) 9/129 (4) 10/136 (11) (40.1 overs)	136
10 overs: 46-1	

Clarke 3–0–24–0; Woakes 9.1–2–24–2; Wright 6–1–17–1; Javid 5–0–15–2; Hannon-Dalby 8–0–27–2; Patel 9–1–28–2.

Warwickshire

I. J. L. Trott not out	82
S. R. Hain c S. M. Curran b Ansari	12
*I. R. Bell c Foakes b Meaker	17
†T. R. Ambrose not out	22
Lb 3, w 1	4
1/45 (2) 2/89 (3) (2 wkts, 30.2 overs)	137
10 overs: 40-0	

L. J. Evans, C. R. Woakes, R. Clarke, A. Javid, J. S. Patel, C. J. C. Wright and O. J. Hannon-Dalby did not bat.

Dernbach 6–0–27–0; S. M. Curran 4.2–0–20–0; T. K. Curran 4–0–14–0; Meaker 4–0–25–1; Ansari 8–0–33–1; Batty 4–0–15–0.

Umpires: D. J. Millns and R. T. Robinson. Third umpire: R. J. Bailey.

PAKISTAN A AND SRI LANKA A IN ENGLAND IN 2016

JAMES GINGELL

The A teams of Pakistan and Sri Lanka came to England, following their seniors in path and, to a large extent, performance. The Pakistanis fared better, but both were overwhelmed by an impressive England Lions side during the end-of-tour tri-series.

Few from the Sri Lankan ranks pressed claims for promotion, as they struggled badly in English conditions, winning only two matches all tour. They brought a callow squad, ten of them playing first-class cricket in England for the first time – though eight of the 14 used in the first-class games had international experience. Roshen Silva managed to shine from the gloom, scoring 314 runs at an average of 62, including a hundred against Durham. But on blameless pitches he had little support from his batting colleagues: Mahela Udawatte was the next highest run-scorer with 178 at 35.

The batsmen's shortcomings were masked in the first four-day game against Pakistan A at Leicester, where the bowlers, particularly the willing 18-year-old seamer Asitha Fernando, skittled the Pakistanis to claim an unlikely win. For the second match, Niroshan Dickwella and Dhananjaya de Silva were drafted in from the full Test squad. But the game followed a similar pattern and this time the Pakistanis, left to chase 148, made no mistake. The Sri Lankans enjoyed themselves more in the limited-overs game against Derbyshire, where de Silva's hundred helped them to an emphatic win. But they could not take any momentum into the tri-series, losing every match.

Despite their defeat at Grace Road, Pakistan's crop of rising stars looked better equipped for international cricket. Skipper Babar Azam led the way with a sixty in both four-day games against Sri Lanka A, before adding a hundred in the comfortable one-day win over Glamorgan. Among the bowlers, Hasan Ali's medium-pace stood out, as he took 14 first-class wickets at 20, while Mir Hamza proved that Pakistan's wellspring of quality left-arm seamers runs deep: he claimed 11 at 26. All-rounder Mohammad Nawaz also caught the eye. He scored a hundred and two fifties, and his left-arm darts provided control and penetration.

PAKISTAN A TOURING PARTY

*Babar Azam (fc/50), Abdul Rehman Muzammil (fc/50), Azizullah (fc/50), Bilawal Bhatti (fc/50), Fakhar Zaman (fc/50), Hasan Ali (fc/50), Jahid Ali (fc/50), Mir Hamza (fc/50), Mohammad Abbas (fc/50), Mohammad Asghar (fc/50), Mohammad Hasan (fc/50), Mohammad Nawaz (fc/50), Saud Shakil (fc/50), Shadab Khan (fc/50), Sharjeel Khan (fc/50), Umar Siddiq (fc/50). *Coach:* Basit Ali.

SRI LANKA A TOURING PARTY

*S. M. A. Priyanjan (fc/50), K. I. C. Asalanka (fc/50), D. M. de Silva (fc/50), D. P. D. N. Dickwella (fc/50), M. N. M. Dilshad (50), A. M. Fernando (fc/50), M. V. T. Fernando (fc), P. L. S. Gamage (fc/50), M. D. U. S. Jayasundera (fc/50), N. G. R. P. Jayasuriya (fc), S. S. Pathirana (fc/50), A. K. Perera (fc/50), N. L. T. C. Perera (50), P. B. B. Rajapaksa (50), C. A. K. Rajitha (fc/50), R. L. B. Rambukwella (fc/50), M. B. Ranasinghe (fc/50), P. A. D. L. R. Sandakan (50), A. R. S. Silva (fc), M. L. Udawatte (fc/50), K. D. K. Vithanage (50), M. S. Warnapura (fc). *Coach:* D. A. Gunawardene.

De Silva and Dickwella were added to the party following their release from the Test squad.

DURHAM v SRI LANKA A

At Chester-le-Street, June 26–29. Drawn. Toss: Sri Lanka A. First-class debut: J. Coughlin, A. J. Hickey. County debuts: G. S. Randhawa, G. S. Sandhu.

Paul Coughlin captained Durham, opened the bowling and then brought on his 18-year-old brother Josh, who was making his debut. Sri Lanka A looked like they were fluffing their lines at 119 for five, before Silva led the recovery with a measured 109. Former Middlesex left-arm seamer Gurjit Sandhu, a triallist here, collected four wickets. In reply, Muchall's 70 took Durham to 177 for four, only for six to fall for 28, the last four in five balls to skiddy left-armer Vishwa Fernando – including Wood, playing as a batsman as he recovered from his ankle operations. Sri Lanka A sensed victory, but the last day and a half were lost to rain.

Close of play: first day, Sri Lanka A 273-6 (Silva 103, Jayasuriya 30); second day, Sri Lanka A 24-0 (Jayasundera 16, Warnapura 7); third day, Sri Lanka A 143-2 (Udawatte 45, Silva 43).

Sri Lanka A

M. D. U. S. Jayasundera lbw b Sandhu	1	– lbw b J. Coughlin	23
M. S. Warnapura lbw b Pringle	34	– b Pringle	27
M. L. Udawatte c Poynter b Sandhu	26	– not out	45
A. R. S. Silva lbw b P. Coughlin	109	– not out	43
*S. M. A. Priyanjan c Muchall b P. Coughlin	15		
†M. B. Ranasinghe b Randhawa	2		
S. S. Pathirana c Randhawa b Sandhu	51		
N. G. R. P. Jayasuriya c P. Coughlin b Sandhu	31		
P. L. S. Gamage not out	43		
M. V. T. Fernando b J. Coughlin	20		
C. A. K. Rajitha c Poynter b P. Coughlin	4		
B 2, lb 13, w 2	17	B 4, lb 1	5
1/15 (1) 2/52 (2) 3/76 (3) 4/112 (5) 5/119 (6) 6/199 (7) 7/279 (8) 8/291 (4) 9/325 (10) 10/353 (11) (114.2 overs)	353	1/39 (1) 2/59 (2) (2 wkts, 52 overs)	143

P. Coughlin 22.2–5–65–3; Sandhu 23–1–70–4; J. Coughlin 16–6–35–1; Pringle 22–4–56–1; Randhawa 21–4–60–1; Hickey 9–0–47–0; Muchall 1–0–5–0. *Second innings*—Sandhu 12–1–34–0; J. Coughlin 10–6–10–1; Pringle 11–2–34–1; Muchall 6–1–19–0; Randhawa 7–0–27–0; Hickey 6–1–14–0.

Durham

A. J. Hickey c Pathirana b Jayasuriya	28
P. Mustard b Fernando	38
G. J. Muchall lbw b Jayasuriya	70
C. S. MacLeod b Gamage	7
R. D. Pringle b Gamage	0
†S. W. Poynter lbw b Gamage	29
M. A. Wood b Fernando	17
*P. Coughlin not out	4
G. S. Randhawa b Fernando	0
J. Coughlin b Fernando	0
G. S. Sandhu lbw b Fernando	0
B 2, lb 8, nb 2	12
1/67 (2) 2/91 (1) 3/121 (4) 4/127 (5) 5/177 (3) 6/199 (6) 7/201 (7) 8/201 (9) 9/201 (10) 10/205 (11) (54.1 overs)	205

Gamage 15–1–49–3; Fernando 11.1–2–37–5; Rajitha 7–0–47–0; Jayasuriya 10–2–32–2; Pathirana 11–1–30–0.

Umpires: I. D. Blackwell and J. H. Evans.

YORKSHIRE v PAKISTAN A

At Leeds, June 26–29. Drawn. Toss: Pakistan A. First-class debuts: H. C. Brook, E. Callis, R. Gibson, J. Read.

A Yorkshire side including four first-class debutants emerged with credit against more experienced opponents. Eliot Callis, a 21-year-old opener from Doncaster, stood out with a composed 84 after Mir Hamza – the pick of the Pakistan A seamers – uprooted Lees's off stump with an unplayable delivery. Azeem Rafiq, making his return to first-class cricket after two years in the wilderness, also shone for the hosts. He made 48 from No. 7, before taking three quick wickets with his off-breaks. Pakistan A wicketkeeper Mohammad Hasan fell for 98, having sacrificed runs while shielding No. 10 Mohammad Asghar. Their lead was 111, but more defiance from Callis – and a last-day washout – blunted their charge.

Close of play: first day, Yorkshire 243-8 (Shaw 7, Carver 12); second day, Pakistan A 341-8 (Mohammad Hasan 88, Mohammad Asghar 11); third day, Yorkshire 57-0 (Callis 30, Lees 17).

Yorkshire

E. Callis b Bilawal Bhatti	84	– not out	30
*A. Z. Lees b Mir Hamza	17	– not out	17
H. C. Brook b Mir Hamza	0		
J. A. Leaning lbw b Hasan Ali	33		
W. M. H. Rhodes c Mohammad Asghar b Mir Hamza	9		
R. Gibson lbw b Mohammad Asghar	0		
Azeem Rafiq lbw b Mohammad Nawaz	48		
†J. Read b Hasan Ali	14		
J. Shaw not out	7		
K. Carver c Sharjeel Khan b Hasan Ali	13		
B. O. Coad c Mohammad Hasan b Mir Hamza	1		
B 7, lb 5, w 1, nb 7	20	B 5, lb 2, nb 3	10
1/19 (2) 2/19 (3) 3/91 (4) 4/123 (5) 5/124 (6) 6/189 (1) 7/222 (8) 8/222 (7) 9/245 (10) 10/246 (11) (75.4 overs)	246	(no wkt, 18.2 overs)	57

Mir Hamza 19.4–5–53–4; Hasan Ali 18–4–69–3; Bilawal Bhatti 15–2–46–1; Mohammad Asghar 16–3–50–1; Sharjeel Khan 1–1–0–0; Mohammad Nawaz 6–1–16–1. *Second innings*—Mir Hamza 9–2–31–0; Hasan Ali 4.2–1–8–0; Bilawal Bhatti 5–2–11–0.

Pakistan A

Sharjeel Khan c Carver b Coad	25
Jahid Ali c Read b Azeem Rafiq	64
Fakhar Zaman c Read b Carver	49
*Babar Azam c Read b Rhodes	45
Umar Siddiq lbw b Azeem Rafiq	0
Mohammad Nawaz c sub (J. C. Wainman) b Azeem Rafiq	0
†Mohammad Hasan c Lees b Shaw	98
Bilawal Bhatti c Read b Gibson	0
Hasan Ali c Rhodes b Shaw	41
Mohammad Asghar c Callis b Shaw	15
Mir Hamza not out	1
B 8, lb 4, nb 7	19
1/29 (1) 2/142 (3) 3/160 (2) 4/170 (5) 5/174 (6) 6/214 (4) 7/215 (8) 8/305 (9) 9/356 (10) 10/357 (7) (98.4 overs)	357

Shaw 16.4–5–58–3; Coad 18–6–57–1; Rhodes 16–3–37–1; Gibson 12–1–42–1; Azeem Rafiq 20–7–60–3; Carver 16–3–91–1.

Umpires: G. D. Lloyd and T. Lungley.

PAKISTAN A v SRI LANKA A

First A-Team Test

At Leicester, July 3–6. Sri Lanka A won by 33 runs. Toss: Pakistan A. First-class debut: A. M. Fernando.

Asitha Fernando took five for 33 on first-class debut to snatch victory in an absorbing contest, as Pakistan A faltered in pursuit of 154. The target, on a good pitch, might have looked straightforward. But ball had dominated bat throughout: just three players passed 50, and there was only one hundred partnership, between Udawatte and Silva on the first day. And, after slow left-armer Pathirana had helped reduce the Pakistanis to 38 for five by the third evening, the task looked mountainous. Asitha Fernando finished the job – his whippy seamers had been Sri Lanka's most effective weapon at the Under-19 World Cup earlier in the year, and now he demonstrated the mettle for red-ball cricket, taking four of the last five wickets. For Pakistan A, Mohammad Nawaz enhanced his prospects of a senior call-up, top-scoring with 68 in the first innings, and claiming six victims with his left-arm spin.

Close of play: first day, Pakistan A 20-0 (Sharjeel Khan 13, Jahid Ali 4); second day, Pakistan A 271-8 (Mohammad Nawaz 62, Azizullah 0); third day, Pakistan A 38-5 (Jahid Ali 16, Azizullah 2).

Sri Lanka A

M. D. U. S. Jayasundera b Hasan Ali	17	– lbw b Mohammad Nawaz	10
M. S. Warnapura c Fakhar Zaman b Azizullah	1	– b Azizullah	15
M. L. Udawatte c Mohammad Hasan b Hasan Ali	64	– lbw b Azizullah	9
A. R. S. Silva c Mohammad Hasan b Mir Hamza	48	– c Sharjeel Khan b Bilawal Bhatti	17
*S. M. A. Priyanjan lbw b Hasan Ali	12	– c Umar Siddiq b Mir Hamza	9
†M. B. Ranasinghe c Bilawal Bhatti b Mohammad Nawaz	33	– c Sharjeel Khan b Mohammad Nawaz	26
S. S. Pathirana c Azizullah b Babar Azam	45	– not out	21
N. G. R. P. Jayasuriya b Mir Hamza	10	– lbw b Mohammad Nawaz	7
P. L. S. Gamage c Sharjeel Khan b Hasan Ali	2	– lbw b Mohammad Nawaz	0
M. V. T. Fernando b Mohammad Nawaz	14	– lbw b Azizullah	0
A. M. Fernando not out	1	– b Azizullah	0
B 28, lb 13, w 6, nb 5	52	B 8, lb 9	17
1/4 (2) 2/46 (1) 3/150 (3) 4/163 (5) 5/183 (4) 6/256 (7) 7/281 (8) 8/283 (6) 9/297 (9) 10/299 (10) (79.5 overs)	299	1/21 (3) 2/51 (2) 3/57 (4) 4/77 (5) 5/81 (1) 6/118 (6) 7/130 (8) 8/130 (9) 9/131 (10) 10/131 (11) (62.5 overs)	131

In the second innings Jayasundera, when 4, retired hurt at 10-0 and resumed at 57-3.

Mir Hamza 19–4–51–2; Azizullah 16–5–37–1; Bilawal Bhatti 12–2–55–0; Hasan Ali 17–1–63–4; Mohammad Nawaz 11.5–1–35–2; Babar Azam 4–0–17–1. *Second innings*—Mir Hamza 13–4–19–1; Hasan Ali 10–7–13–0; Azizullah 11.5–7–21–4; Bilawal Bhatti 15–6–30–1; Mohammad Nawaz 12–1–31–4; Babar Azam 1–1–0–0.

Pakistan A

Sharjeel Khan c Gamage b Priyanjan	42	– b M. V. T. Fernando	5
Jahid Ali c Ranasinghe b A. M. Fernando	15	– c Ranasinghe b A. M. Fernando	38
Fakhar Zaman b A. M. Fernando	0	– b M. V. T. Fernando	4
*Babar Azam lbw b Pathirana	61	– lbw b A. M. Fernando	1
Umar Siddiq b Priyanjan	39	– b Pathirana	5
Mohammad Nawaz lbw b M. V. T. Fernando	68	– (8) b Pathirana	10
†Mohammad Hasan c Ranasinghe b Pathirana	3	– (9) lbw b A. M. Fernando	24
Bilawal Bhatti c Ranasinghe b Gamage	5	– (6) c sub (A. K. Perera) b Pathirana	0
Hasan Ali lbw b Jayasuriya	22	– (10) b A. M. Fernando	8
Azizullah c Ranasinghe b Gamage	0	– (7) c Ranasinghe b A. M. Fernando	11
Mir Hamza not out	0	– not out	1
B 11, lb 8, w 3	22	B 10, lb 1, w 2	13
1/56 (2) 2/56 (3) 3/68 (1) 4/154 (4) 5/190 (5) 6/193 (7) 7/212 (8) 8/248 (9) 9/271 (10) 10/277 (6) (88 overs)	277	1/5 (1) 2/13 (3) 3/21 (4) 4/35 (5) 5/35 (6) 6/73 (2) 7/78 (7) 8/91 (8) 9/115 (9) 10/120 (10) (46.5 overs)	120

Gamage 21–3–68–2; M. V. T. Fernando 16–2–46–1; A. M. Fernando 14–4–42–2; Jayasuriya 11–2–23–1; Priyanjan 8–1–25–2; Pathirana 18–3–54–2. *Second innings*—A. M. Fernando 9.5–1–33–5; M. V. T. Fernando 12–2–28–2; Pathirana 14–5–27–3; Gamage 6–2–17–0; Jayasuriya 4–2–3–0; Priyanjan 1–0–1–0.

Umpires: N. L. Bainton and S. C. Gale.

PAKISTAN A v SRI LANKA A

Second A-Team Test

At Worcester, July 10–13. Pakistan A won by eight wickets. Toss: Sri Lanka A. First-class debut: Shadab Khan.

An unbroken stand of 111 between Babar Azam and Saud Shakil guided Pakistan A to a share of the series: they raced to a target of 148 in 23 overs with 23 balls to spare. The Pakistanis had dominated from the start, as Sri Lanka A – having opted to bat – struggled against the angles and movement of Mir Hamza and Hasan Ali, who took seven between them. Pakistan A then showed how good the pitch was: Shakeel led the way with the first of two impressive half-centuries, and – rounding off a powerful display – No. 9 Hasan hit an unbeaten 50 from 37 balls. Their lead was 211, but time was against them: much of the third day was lost to rain, and a last-wicket stand of 49 between Ranasinghe and Asitha Fernando ate up valuable overs on the fourth. But Hasan claimed his seventh wicket of the game, before Pakistan A hurried home, to the delight of a small but vociferous crowd.

Close of play: first day, Pakistan A 47-1 (Jahid Ali 15, Saud Shakil 25); second day, Pakistan A 370-7 (Mohammad Hasan 57); third day, Sri Lanka A 83-2 (de Silva 44, Gamage 0).

Sri Lanka A

D. M. de Silva c Saud Shakil b Azizullah	5	– lbw b Hasan Ali	88
M. D. U. S. Jayasundera b Mir Hamza	53	– c Abdul Rehman Muzammil b Mohammad Nawaz	25
M. L. Udawatte b Hasan Ali	26	– b Azizullah	8
A. R. S. Silva c Mohammad Hasan b Mir Hamza	57	– (5) c sub (Fakhar Zaman) b Shadab Khan	40
*S. M. A. Priyanjan c Jahid Ali b Shadab Khan	36	– (6) c Mohammad Hasan b Shadab Khan	66
†D. P. D. N. Dickwella c Jahid Ali b Hasan Ali	35	– (7) c Hasan Ali b Shadab Khan	5
M. B. Ranasinghe c Mohammad Hasan b Mir Hamza	0	– (8) not out	54
S. S. Pathirana c Abdul Rehman Muzammil b Mir Hamza	19	– (9) lbw b Hasan Ali	10
P. L. S. Gamage c Babar Azam b Hasan Ali	4	– (4) c Mohammad Hasan b Shadab Khan	21
M. V. T. Fernando b Azizullah	8	– b Hasan Ali	0
A. M. Fernando not out	0	– c Sharjeel Khan b Hasan Ali	2
B 2, lb 3, nb 2	7	B 28, lb 4, nb 7	39
1/13 (1) 2/54 (3) 3/112 (2) 4/160 (5) 5/206 (4) 6/214 (7) 7/220 (6) 8/226 (9) 9/246 (8) 10/250 (10) (69.5 overs)	250	1/62 (2) 2/83 (3) 3/142 (1) 4/166 (4) 5/268 (5) 6/275 (6) 7/284 (7) 8/309 (9) 9/309 (10) 10/358 (11) (93.2 overs)	358

Mir Hamza 19–3–62–4; Azizullah 17.5–5–43–2; Hasan Ali 16–3–70–3; Babar Azam 1–0–2–0; Mohammad Nawaz 8–0–37–0; Shadab Khan 8–0–31–1. *Second innings*—Azizullah 17–3–59–1; Mir Hamza 25–5–70–0; Hasan Ali 18.2–2–67–4; Mohammad Nawaz 16–4–41–1; Shadab Khan 17–2–89–4.

> "The closest thing to a security breach came when three old ladies on a tuk-tuk slipped their way into the convoy en route to the one-day warm-up at Fatullah. By the end of the tour, Reg Dickason had proved an unlikely Bangladeshi hero."
> **Bangladesh v England in 2016-17, page 326**

Pakistan A

Sharjeel Khan c Ranasinghe b M. V. T. Fernando	4	– c sub (A. K. Perera) b M. V. T. Fernando	19
Jahid Ali c Dickwella b A. M. Fernando	43		
Saud Shakil c Silva b M. V. T. Fernando	86	– (4) not out	51
*Babar Azam lbw b Gamage	31	– (2) not out	66
Abdul Rehman Muzammil c Udawatte b de Silva	14		
Mohammad Nawaz b de Silva	52	– (3) c Silva b M. V. T. Fernando	8
†Mohammad Hasan st Dickwella b Gamage	73		
Shadab Khan c Udawatte b Pathirana	48		
Hasan Ali not out	50		
Azizullah not out	15		
B 9, lb 15, w 9, nb 12	45	W 4	4
1/4 (1) 2/107 (2) 3/168 (4) 4/180 (3) 5/222 (5) 6/287 (6) 7/370 (8) 8/410 (7) (8 wkts dec, 117 overs)	461	1/25 (1) 2/37 (3) (2 wkts, 19.1 overs)	148

Mir Hamza did not bat.

M. V. T. Fernando 30–5–104–2; A. M. Fernando 23–2–85–1; Gamage 26–5–115–2; Pathirana 22–1–79–1; de Silva 10–1–28–2; Priyanjan 5–1–17–0; Jayasundera 1–0–9–0. *Second innings*—M. V. T. Fernando 5–0–38–2; A. M. Fernando 2–0–24–0; Gamage 3–0–21–0; Pathirana 5–0–41–0; de Silva 3–0–17–0; Priyanjan 1.1–0–7–0.

Umpires: B. J. Debenham and G. D. Lloyd.

At Derby, July 15. **Sri Lanka A won by seven wickets. Derbyshire 281-7** (43 overs) (B. T. Slater 124; P. A. D. L. R. Sandakan 5-40); ‡**Sri Lanka A 284-3** (32.2 overs) (D. P. D. N. Dickwella 67, D. M. de Silva 119). *Two recruits from the Test squad, Niroshan Dickwella and Dhananjaya de Silva, showed their class with an opening stand of 161 in 17 overs to propel the Sri Lankans to a blistering victory. Earlier, Ben Slater made a career-best 124, but Derbyshire were kept in check by Lakshan Sandakan, who claimed his first five-for with his enchanting left-arm wrist-spin.*

At Newport, July 15. **Pakistan A won by 123 runs. Pakistan A 327-9** (50 overs) (Abdul Rehman Muzammil 65, Babar Azam 119, Mohammad Nawaz 55; R. A. J. Smith 4-76); ‡**Glamorgan 204** (45.2 overs) (W. D. Bragg 61, A. G. Salter 51). *County debuts:* K. S. Carlson, J. R. Murphy. *All the action came in the second half of Pakistan A's innings. First, Babar Azam and Mohammad Nawaz smashed 105 in 11 overs for the sixth wicket to lift them past 300. Then Scottish international Ruaidhri Smith cleaned up the tail with a hat-trick in the last over. After that the game ran out of steam, with Glamorgan unable to break the shackles of Nawaz and Mohammad Abbas. It was the first senior match at Spytty Park.*

ENGLAND LIONS v PAKISTAN A v SRI LANKA A IN 2016

1 England Lions 2 Pakistan A 3 Sri Lanka A

Here was a tournament to suggest England's white-ball manifesto – gung-ho belligerence from first to last – was trickling down to the lower levels. Batsmen jostled to present themselves as the brightest pupil in finishing school, and a sequence of stellar performances followed as England Lions triumphed.

Northamptonshire's low-slung left-hander Ben Duckett set the tone, destroying a useful Pakistan A attack with an unbeaten 163 from 104 balls. Dawid Malan of Middlesex followed suit in the next game, plundering 185 not out against Sri Lanka A. Not to be outdone, Kent's Sam Billings scorched his home ground at Canterbury, deploying all his wristy wizardry on his way to 175. That meant that three of the four highest innings for England Lions or

England A had come in three games (Ravi Bopara's unbeaten 168 against West Indies A in 2010 was the other).

But, with the Lions having secured the tournament, the best was yet to come: Daniel Bell-Drummond and Duckett blitzed an extraordinary unbroken stand of 367 against a Sri Lanka A attack including six internationals. Bell-Drummond blazed to 171 from 139 balls, and Duckett hit 220 from 131 to reset Malan's short-lived record. The partnership was the second-highest in all white-ball cricket, while Duckett's innings had been bettered in England only by Ali Brown's, 268 for Surrey against Glamorgan at The Oval in 2002. Duckett ended the series with 448 runs at a strike-rate of 140. His heroics persuaded even Andy Flower, the Lions coach, to depart from his usual reticence and describe him as a "very talented man". The Lions, meanwhile, became the first side to register five individual scores of 150-plus in a List A series or tournament.

Mark Wood made a strong return after ankle surgery. He played three of the four games, collecting eight wickets at under ten. And the Curran brothers, Tom and Sam, continued their rapid rise, opening the bowling together and collecting two wickets each in the series-clinching game against Pakistan A.

There was little to cheer for Sri Lanka A, soundly beaten in all four games, but the Pakistanis could take succour from some encouraging batting performances. Sharjeel Khan scored a century and ended up as the competition's third-top run-scorer with 253, while Jahid Ali made a fifty and a fine century against a strong England attack. Ultimately, though, no one had an answer to the Lions' pyrotechnics.

At Cheltenham, July 18. **Pakistan A won by eight wickets. Sri Lanka A 199** (37.5 overs) (Mohammad Abbas 3-50, Mohammad Asghar 4-41); ‡**Pakistan A 200-2** (33.5 overs) (Fakhar Zaman 74, Sharjeel Khan 90). *Babar Azam's bowlers vindicated his decision to bowl, dismantling the fragile Sri Lankan line-up. Left-arm spinner Mohammad Asghar strangled the scoring, and only Angelo Perera's 35 provided any resistance. Pakistan A's openers galloped towards the target, putting on 155 inside 24 overs. Burly left-hander Sharjeel Khan led the way, slugging four sixes in a 74-ball 90.*

At Cheltenham, July 19. **England Lions won by seven wickets. Pakistan A 244** (46 overs) (Sharjeel Khan 125; T. K. Curran 4-39, M. A. Wood 3-27); ‡**England Lions 248-3** (36.2 overs) (B. M. Duckett 163*). *Ben Duckett gave notice of his talent with a brilliant 163* to give England Lions the perfect start. His masterly effort, which took just 104 balls and included 24 fours and four sixes, rendered a modest target minuscule. Earlier, Sharjeel had given Pakistan A some hope of a defendable total with a pugnacious 125 that included seven sixes. But Tom Curran and Mark Wood shared seven scalps, and the last six fell for 53.*

At Northampton, July 21. **England Lions won by 88 runs** (DLS). ‡**England Lions 393-5** (50 overs) (D. J. Bell-Drummond 52, D. J. Malan 185*, B. M. Duckett 61, S. W. Billings 68); **Sri Lanka A 164-4** (30 overs) (D. P. D. N. Dickwella 51). *A second magisterial performance from an England Lions left-hander delivered a second emphatic win. This time it was captain Dawid Malan's turn: he launched eight sixes in a career-best 126-ball 185*, putting on 83 with Daniel Bell-Drummond, 118 with Duckett, and 117 with Sam Billings to lever the Lions towards a mammoth score. Niroshan Dickwella led a plucky counter-attack, racing to a 36-ball 50, but four quick wickets for Toby Roland-Jones and Wood slowed Sri Lanka A down, and they were well behind when rain came.*

At Northampton, July 22. **Pakistan A won by four wickets.** ‡**Sri Lanka A 254** (46.5 overs) (P. B. B. Rajapaksa 56; Shadab Khan 3-51); **Pakistan A 258-6** (48.1 overs) (Jahid Ali 77, Babar Azam 73; P. L. S. Gamage 3-43). *A careful third-wicket stand of 139 between Jahid Ali and Babar was enough for Pakistan A. They had no need to rush their chase, after the Sri Lankans again failed to post a* *competitive total, in which five batsmen reached 34, but none made more than Bhanuka Rajapaksa's 56. By the time Lahiru Gamage snared Jahid and Babar in consecutive overs, the Pakistanis could sense the finishing line.*

At Canterbury, July 24. **England Lions won by 56 runs. England 324-8** (50 overs) (S. W. Billings 175, L. S. Livingstone 64; Bilawal Bhatti 4-62); ‡**Pakistan A 268** (48.2 overs) (Jahid Ali 103, Babar Azam 55; M. A. Wood 3-44). *The bustling seam of Bilawal Bhatti reduced the Lions to 49-4, but that merely set the stage for another spectacular innings. Billings treated his home crowd to a virtuoso display of 360-degree hitting – including a left-handed pull for six – on his way to a career-best 175 off 139 balls, with 21 fours and four sixes. The Curran brothers then took two quick wickets each to stymie Pakistan A's reply, though Jahid's calm hundred gave them a fighting chance. But scoreboard pressure told, as the last seven wickets fell for 60 runs, handing England Lions the series.*

HIGHEST LIST A PARTNERSHIPS

372	for 2nd	C. H. Gayle & M. N. Samuels, West Indies v Zimbabwe at Canberra	2014-15
367*	for 1st	M. N. van Wyk & C. S. Delport, Dolphins v Knights at Bloemfontein	2014-15
367*	**for 2nd**	**D. J. Bell-Drummond & B. M. Duckett, England Lions v Sri Lanka A at Canterbury**	**2016**
342	**for 1st**	**M. J. Lumb & M. H. Wessels, Notts v Northants at Nottingham**	**2016**
331	for 2nd	S. R. Tendulkar & R. S. Dravid, India v New Zealand at Hyderabad	1999-2000
326*	for 1st	Ghulam Ali & Sohail Jaffar, PIA v ADBP, Sialkot	2000-01
321	for 1st	J. A. Raval & J. M. How, Central Districts v Northern Districts	2012-13
318	for 2nd	S. C. Ganguly & R. S. Dravid, India v Sri Lanka at Taunton	1999
311	for 1st	A. J. Wright & N. J. Trainor, Glos v Scotland at Bristol	1997
309*	for 3rd	T. S. Curtis & T. M. Moody, Worcs v Surrey at The Oval	1994
303*	for 3rd	A. Barrow & H. R. Fotheringham, Natal v SA African XI	1975-76
302	for 2nd	M. E. Trescothick & C. Kieswetter Somerset v Glos at Taunton	2008

At Canterbury, July 25. **England Lions won by 140 runs.** ‡**England Lions 425-1** (50 overs) (D. J. Bell-Drummond 171*, B. M. Duckett 220*); **Sri Lanka A 285** (47.3 overs) (D. P. D. N. Dickwella 60, A. K. Perera 69; G. H. S. Garton 4-43). *Another day, another display of electrifying batting. After Bell-Drummond and Duckett came together at 58-1 in the 12th over, mayhem ensued. Bell-Drummond scored his first limited-overs hundred, hitting 15 fours and four sixes, going on to 171* from 139 balls; Duckett hammered 29 fours and four sixes, in his 220* from 131; their 367-run partnership fell five short of the all-wicket record; and the Lions became the first side to score over 400 in List A cricket while losing only one wicket. There was one other centurion: Tissara Perera sent down ten overs for 101. In reply, Sri Lanka started brightly, moving to 105 without loss. By then, however, the required rate had climbed towards nine, and the bowlers – particularly left-arm seamer George Garton – showed good control to squeeze them out.*

England Lions 8pts, Pakistan A 4pts, Sri Lanka A 0pts.

THE UNIVERSITIES IN 2016

CAMBRIDGE MCCU v ESSEX

At Cambridge, March 31–April 2. Essex won by 523 runs. Toss: Cambridge MCCU. First-class debuts: S. Bardolia, B. J. Bryant, H. J. Palmer, A. C. Waghorn. County debut: M. W. Dixon.

Essex cashed in on some friendly bowling and, after waiving the follow-on – a decision which allowed Mickleburgh to canter to his second hundred of the match, on day two – they led by 701 as the third morning dawned. This seemed like overkill, as the students had managed only 124 in their first innings. Even that could have been worse: they were 56 for eight before a maiden first-class

BIGGEST WINS BY RUNS IN ENGLISH FIRST-CLASS CRICKET

Runs		
562	Australia (701 and 327) beat England (321 and 145) at The Oval	1934
541	Notts (396-3 dec and 408-9 dec) beat Durham MCCU (142 and 121) at Nottingham	2013
524	Zimbabweans (568 and 258-2 dec) beat Glos (167 and 135) at Gloucester	2000
523	**Essex (416-4 dec and 409-7 dec) beat Camb MCCU (124 and 178) at Cambridge**	**2016**
522	Leics (353-6 dec and 361-3 dec) beat Camb U (127 and 65) at Cambridge	1984
517	**Notts (530-8 dec and 170-5 dec) beat Camb MCCU (52 and 131) at Cambridge**	**2016**
483	Surrey (494 and 492-9 dec) beat Leicestershire (361 and 142) at The Oval	2002
482	**Worcs (345-9 dec and 451-3 dec) beat Oxford MCCU (190 and 124) at Oxford**	**2016**
470	Sussex (309 and 307-5 dec) beat Glos (66 and 80) at Hove	1913
470	Hants (286 and 440-3 dec) beat Essex (121 and 135) at Southampton	2014

The highest margin in all first-class cricket is 685, by New South Wales (235 and 761-8 dec, including 452 by Don Bradman) over Queensland (227 and 84) at Sydney in 1929-30.*

half-century from No. 9 Alastair Allchin, who had played for Essex's youth teams. They did a little better second time round, with Adil Arif just missing a maiden fifty of his own, but the margin was still the heaviest defeat by runs in a first-class game for a Cambridge side: Leicestershire beat the University by 522 at Fenner's in 1984. It was Essex's biggest victory, too.

Close of play: first day, Cambridge MCCU 24-1 (Palmer 15, Bardolia 2); second day, Essex 409-7 (ten Doeschate 47, Dixon 0).

Essex

N. L. J. Browne c Tetley b Allchin	87	– c Tetley b Barton	101
J. C. Mickleburgh c Tetley b Patel	125	– retired out	102
T. Westley retired out	110		
R. S. Bopara c Arif b Allchin	3	– (3) b Waghorn	30
D. W. Lawrence not out	35	– (4) retired out	76
*R. N. ten Doeschate not out	22	– (5) not out	47
C. J. Taylor (did not bat)		– (6) c Barton b Waghorn	1
G. R. Napier (did not bat)		– (7) c Bryant b Waghorn	6
J. A. Porter (did not bat)		– (8) c Tetley b Patel	4
M. W. Dixon (did not bat)		– (9) not out	0
B 12, lb 8, nb 14	34	B 7, lb 9, w 19, nb 7	42
1/168 (1) 2/301 (2) 3/312 (4) 4/357 (3) (4 wkts dec, 85 overs)	416	1/236 (1) 2/236 (2) 3/325 (3) 4/363 (4) 5/368 (6) 6/404 (7) 7/409 (8) (7 wkts dec, 66 overs)	409

†J. S. Foster did not bat.

Allchin 25–3–117–2; Barton 18–4–54–0; Patel 15–1–90–1; Arif 15–0–73–0; Waghorn 12–0–62–0. *Second innings*—Allchin 14–1–82–0; Barton 15–1–77–1; Waghorn 16–1–79–3; Arif 5–1–23–0; Patel 11–0–93–1; Bryant 5–0–39–0.

Cambridge MCCU

J. B. Abbott b Porter	5	– lbw b Dixon	4
H. J. Palmer c Lawrence b Napier	21	– b ten Doeschate	32
S. Bardolia b Dixon	4	– c Bopara b Porter	0
B. J. Bryant c Napier b Porter	10	– lbw b Dixon	5
*H. R. C. Ellison b Napier	0	– c Taylor b Dixon	22
A. T. Arif lbw b Napier	0	– c Bopara b Napier	49
†J. W. Tetley c Browne b Napier	2	– c sub (M. H. Cross) b ten Doeschate	9
A. R. Patel c ten Doeschate b Dixon	5	– c sub (M. H. Cross) b Porter	13
A. T. A. Allchin not out	59	– c sub (M. H. Cross) b Bopara	32
A. C. Waghorn lbw b Napier	6	– not out	0
A. P. Barton b Taylor	6	– b Bopara	0
Lb 4, nb 2	6	B 9, lb 2, w 1	12
1/16 (1) 2/27 (3) 3/42 (2) 4/42 (4) 5/42 (5) 6/43 (6) 7/46 (7) 8/56 (8) 9/104 (10) 10/124 (11) (40.3 overs)	124	1/15 (1) 2/20 (3) 3/26 (4) 4/58 (5) 5/73 (2) 6/99 (7) 7/139 (8) 8/145 (6) 9/178 (9) 10/178 (11) (48.5 overs)	178

Porter 11–3–30–2; Dixon 12–4–16–2; Napier 7–2–29–5; Bopara 5–0–27–0; ten Doeschate 3–0–12–0; Taylor 2.3–0–6–1. *Second innings*—Porter 11–3–40–2; Dixon 11–5–35–3; Napier 12–2–50–1; ten Doeschate 5–2–15–2; Bopara 8.5–2–26–2; Westley 1–0–1–0.

Umpires: P. R. Pollard and R. T. Robinson.

At Bristol, March 31–April 2. DURHAM MCCU drew with GLOUCESTERSHIRE.

At Birmingham, March 31–April 2. LEEDS/BRADFORD MCCU drew with WARWICKSHIRE.

At The Oval, March 31–April 2. LOUGHBOROUGH MCCU drew with SURREY. *Loughborough's Basil Akram hits 160 and takes six wickets in the match.*

OXFORD MCCU v WORCESTERSHIRE

At Oxford, March 31–April 2. Worcestershire won by 482 runs. Toss: Worcestershire. First-class debuts: C. M. Dickinson, Hassam Mushtaq, M. J. Laidman; J. C. Tongue.

Oxford started brightly, restricting Worcestershire to 190 for six, despite an attractive century from the 19-year-old Clarke, younger than most of his opponents. But Leach made 37, and Barnard and Shantry put on 84 for the ninth wicket in 15 overs. Jack Grundy's first fifty helped Oxford reach 190, but an opening stand of 286 between Mitchell and D'Oliveira – who followed his grandfather Basil and father Damian in scoring first-class centuries for Worcestershire – stretched the lead over the horizon. A lunchtime declaration on the third day, 606 ahead, left the students 66 overs to survive. They so nearly made it: the tenth-wicket pair hung on for seven, before D'Oliveira's leg-spin winkled out Abi Sakande – a 6ft 5in fast bowler who later played for Sussex – with a dozen balls left. It was Worcestershire's biggest victory by runs (previously 342 against Gloucestershire in 1901), and the heaviest defeat for an Oxford side (the University lost to Sussex by 396 in 1935).

Close of play: first day, Oxford MCCU 22-2 (Dickinson 3, Grundy 2); second day, Worcestershire 234-0 (Mitchell 116, D'Oliveira 102).

Worcestershire

*D. K. H. Mitchell b Sakande	41	– c Leach b Weller	155
B. L. D'Oliveira lbw b Weller	3	– c Laidman b Weller	122
J. M. Clarke b Hassam Mushtaq	119		
A. N. Kervezee b Grundy	0	– (3) st Laidman b Hassam Mushtaq	59
T. Köhler-Cadmore c Leach b Bodenstein	19	– (4) not out	68
R. A. Whiteley c Paternott b Grundy	13	– (5) not out	26
†O. B. Cox b Grundy	4		
J. Leach c Laidman b Hassam Mushtaq	37		
E. G. Barnard not out	38		
J. D. Shantry b Lake	45		
B 9, lb 10, w 3, nb 4	26	B 15, lb 2, w 4	21
1/13 (2) 2/68 (1) 3/73 (4) 4/139 (5) 5/183 (6) 6/190 (7) 7/260 (8) 8/261 (3) 9/345 (10) (9 wkts dec, 83.3 overs)	345	1/286 (1) 2/307 (2) 3/408 (3) (3 wkts dec, 77 overs)	451

J. C. Tongue did not bat.

Weller 12–0–52–1; Bodenstein 12–2–51–1; Sakande 15–2–54–1; Grundy 15–4–41–3; McIver 13–1–59–0; Hassam Mushtaq 12–0–52–2; Lake 4.3–1–17–1. *Second innings*—Weller 15–2–74–2; Bodenstein 10–0–44–0; Sakande 4–0–20–0; Hassam Mushtaq 10–0–85–1; Grundy 6–0–32–0; McIver 25–0–138–0; Lake 7–0–41–0.

Oxford MCCU

S. G. Leach c Clarke b Tongue	6	– c Köhler-Cadmore b Leach	11
†M. J. Laidman c Mitchell b Tongue	10	– c Mitchell b Kervezee	30
C. M. Dickinson c Cox b Barnard	30	– c Cox b Leach	6
J. O. Grundy c Cox b Tongue	53	– (9) c Cox b Barnard	5
L. C. Paternott lbw b Shantry	0	– (4) lbw b Barnard	20
J. N. McIver c D'Oliveira b Shantry	19	– (5) not out	27
M. B. Lake c Cox b Shantry	0	– (6) b D'Oliveira	1
C. J. Bodenstein c Cox b Barnard	34	– (7) c Köhler-Cadmore b D'Oliveira	5
*S. D. Weller lbw b Shantry	17	– (8) c Whiteley b Tongue	8
Hassam Mushtaq lbw b Shantry	7	– lbw b Kervezee	6
A. Sakande not out	0	– lbw b D'Oliveira	4
B 4, lb 8, nb 2	14	B 1	1
1/7 (1) 2/18 (2) 3/54 (3) 4/55 (5) 5/93 (6) 6/93 (7) 7/164 (4) 8/164 (8) 9/177 (10) 10/190 (9) (59.1 overs)	190	1/17 (1) 2/23 (3) 3/55 (4) 4/73 (2) 5/74 (6) 6/82 (7) 7/96 (8) 8/102 (9) 9/113 (10) 10/124 (11) (64 overs)	124

Leach 13–3–30–0; Tongue 15–4–35–3; Shantry 15.1–5–46–5; Barnard 12–4–53–2; D'Oliveira 4–0–14–0. *Second innings*—Shantry 11–6–29–0; Leach 11–4–26–2; Barnard 12–6–19–2; Tongue 10–3–14–1; Kervezee 12–4–24–2; D'Oliveira 8–3–11–3.

Umpires: S. A. Garratt and R. J. Warren.

At Southampton, April 4–6. CARDIFF MCCU drew with HAMPSHIRE.

CAMBRIDGE MCCU v NOTTINGHAMSHIRE

At Cambridge, April 5–7. Nottinghamshire won by 517 runs. Toss: Cambridge MCCU. First-class debuts: D. Brierley, T. G. L. Colverd, C. J. Emerton.

This match was overshadowed by the events which led to the sudden retirement of the England batsman James Taylor. He felt ill while warming up before the second day, and was driven back to Nottingham, where the cause of a racing pulse – sometimes at above 250 beats per minute – was diagnosed as a rare and incurable heart disease. Taylor, who had won seven Test caps, ended his first-class career at the age of 26. Events on the field, where Cambridge received another thumping, seemed insignificant. Nottinghamshire had cruised to 530 for eight on the first day, with centuries for Mullaney and Wessels. Dropped by Ben Bryant in the covers off Josh Arksey on nought, Wessels pillaged 143 from 125 balls before retiring. What turned out to be Taylor's final innings had brought just ten runs when he edged a slip catch off medium-pacer Connor Emerton, whose first-class career had got off to an eventful start: he fell over trying to deliver his first ball, and play was briefly held up while he received treatment. Cambridge were bundled out for 52 and, after a second declaration from Read, were set 648. They battled to 83 for four, but the last six tumbled for 48, with left-arm seamer Luke Wood taking a maiden first-class five-for.

Close of play: first day, Nottinghamshire 530-8 (Wood 25, Ball 18); second day, Nottinghamshire 170-5 (Gurney 27).

Nottinghamshire

S. J. Mullaney c Bryant b Arksey	139		
B. R. M. Taylor c Palmer b Allchin	3	– (1) lbw b Allchin	0
M. J. Lumb lbw b Emerton	13	– (2) b Allchin	12
J. W. A. Taylor c Colverd b Emerton	10		
M. H. Wessels retired out	143		
S. R. Patel c Barton b Arksey	39	– (3) c Ellison b Arksey	62
*†C. M. W. Read c Bryant b Arksey	80		
B. A. Hutton run out	30	– (4) c Colverd b Arksey	44
L. Wood not out	25	– (5) c Colverd b Arksey	22
J. T. Ball not out	18		
H. F. Gurney (did not bat)		– (6) not out	27
B 1, lb 14, w 1, nb 14	30	Lb 2, w 1	3
1/43 (2) 2/78 (3) 3/110 (4) 4/263 (1) 5/362 (5) 6/370 (6) 7/474 (8) 8/494 (7) (8 wkts dec, 98 overs)	530	1/0 (1) 2/42 (2) 3/92 (3) 4/136 (5) 5/170 (4) (5 wkts dec, 36 overs)	170

Allchin 22–4–87–1; Barton 24–2–126–0; Arif 9–0–68–0; Emerton 19–0–100–2; Arksey 23–4–132–3; Ellison 1–0–2–0. *Second innings*—Allchin 13–5–41–2; Barton 2–0–5–0; Emerton 10–1–65–0; Arif 1–0–9–0; Arksey 9–1–41–3; Ellison 1–0–7–0.

Cambridge MCCU

†J. W. Tetley c Read b Wood	6	– c Read b Ball	6
H. J. Palmer c Patel b Hutton	10	– c Wessels b Wood	31
*H. R. C. Ellison c Read b Ball	8	– lbw b Hutton	14
B. J. Bryant c Hutton b Ball	0	– c Read b Gurney	3
A. T. Arif c B. R. M. Taylor b Ball	7	– c Read b Gurney	8
T. G. L. Colverd lbw b Gurney	3	– lbw b Wood	18
D. Brierley c Mullaney b Hutton	0	– lbw b Wood	12
A. T. A. Allchin c Gurney b Hutton	3	– lbw b Wood	9
C. J. Emerton lbw b Hutton	3	– run out	1
J. B. T. Arksey not out	2	– not out	12
A. P. Barton lbw b Gurney	0	– b Wood	8
B 1, lb 8, w 1	10	Lb 2, nb 7	9
1/7 (1) 2/22 (3) 3/22 (4) 4/35 (5) 5/39 (6) 6/41 (2) 7/44 (7) 8/47 (8) 9/51 (9) 10/52 (11) (23 overs)	52	1/7 (1) 2/32 (3) 3/35 (4) 4/47 (5) 5/83 (6) 6/92 (2) 7/105 (7) 8/107 (9) 9/113 (8) 10/131 (11) (43.5 overs)	131

Ball 6–2–21–3; Wood 7–2–13–1; Gurney 6–3–3–2; Hutton 4–2–6–4. *Second innings*—Wood 11.5–2–40–5; Ball 6–2–15–1; Hutton 4–1–15–1; Gurney 8–0–19–2; Mullaney 9–1–24–0; Patel 5–0–16–0.

Umpires: P. K. Baldwin and R. J. Evans.

At Chester-le-Street, April 5–7. DURHAM MCCU drew with DURHAM.

At Canterbury, April 5–7. LOUGHBOROUGH MCCU drew with KENT. *Basil Akram scores 100*, and finishes his season with a first-class average of 260.*

OXFORD MCCU v NORTHAMPTONSHIRE

At Oxford, April 5–7. Drawn. Toss: Oxford MCCU. First-class debut: B. M. Broughton.

Oxford bucked the trend of heavy home defeats for the MCCUs, helped by the loss of the last day to rain. Their first innings had been respectable, with Steve Leach, Calvin Dickinson and Jack McIver all making tidy half-centuries. Dickinson was born in South Africa but educated at nearby St Edward's School, where he broke the individual record in 2015 with an innings of 181. From 192 for three, Oxford lost six for 17, but then McIver and Johny Marsden shared a last-wicket stand of 62. Northamptonshire's reply started badly when Sam Weller inflicted a duck on Duckett, but honours were roughly even at the end of the second day.

Close of play: first day, Oxford MCCU 201-7 (McIver 19, Weller 0); second day, Northamptonshire 167-3 (Cobb 49, Rossington 50).

Oxford MCCU

S. G. Leach lbw b Stone	63
M. J. Laidman c Rossington b Stone	15
C. M. Dickinson c Rossington b Stone	62
L. C. Paternott c Newton b White	16
J. N. McIver b Gleeson	51
M. B. Lake c Rossington b Gleeson	1
B. M. Broughton lbw b Gleeson	0
†E. J. Ellis lbw b White	1
*S. D. Weller c Rossington b Cobb	2
J. O. Grundy b Stone	0
J. Marsden not out	27
B 10, lb 8, w 3, nb 12	33
1/57 (2) 2/153 (3) 3/154 (1) 4/192 (4) 5/193 (6) 6/193 (7) 7/198 (8) 8/208 (9) 9/209 (10) 10/271 (5) (84.1 overs)	271

Azharullah 14–1–61–0; Stone 19–3–57–4; Gleeson 18.1–7–33–3; Sanderson 12–3–47–0; White 15–3–36–2; Cobb 6–1–19–1.

Northamptonshire

R. I. Newton c Lake b Grundy	17
B. M. Duckett lbw b Weller	0
*A. G. Wakely c Ellis b Grundy	48
J. J. Cobb not out	49
†A. M. Rossington not out	50
W 1, nb 2	3
1/1 (2) 2/34 (1) 3/110 (3) (3 wkts, 49 overs)	167

D. Murphy, G. G. White, O. P. Stone, R. J. Gleeson, Azharullah and B. W. Sanderson did not bat.

Weller 5–0–20–1; Marsden 16–3–68–0; Grundy 14–3–38–2; McIver 14–2–41–0.

Umpires: N. G. C. Cowley and P. R. Pollard.

At Hove, April 5–7. LEEDS/BRADFORD MCCU drew with SUSSEX.

At Cambridge, April 11–13 (not first-class). **Drawn. Lancashire 290-7 dec** (85.2 overs) (H. Hameed 59, S. J. Croft 103*; J. B. T. Arksey 3-69); ‡**Cambridge MCCU 224** (87.2 overs) (J. W. Tetley 76; J. M. Anderson 3-29, K. M. Jarvis 3-58). *After crushing defeats in their two first-class games, Cambridge held their own, thanks in part to a second-day washout. They had bowled well to restrict Lancashire on the first, with skipper Steven Croft's century compensating for six batsmen falling between 12 and 27. And the students batted through the final day without too much bother, wicketkeeper Joe Tetley surviving nearly three hours, despite the Test experience of Lancashire's new-ball pair: James Anderson, in his first appearance against an MCCU side since 2008, and Zimbabwe's Kyle Jarvis.*

At Cardiff, April 11–13. CARDIFF MCCU drew with GLAMORGAN.

At Derby, April 11–13 (not first-class). DURHAM MCCU drew with DERBYSHIRE.

At Loughborough, April 11–13 (not first-class). **Drawn. Leicestershire 254-9 dec** (82 overs) (P. J. Horton 57, A. M. Ali 62; S. Cook 4-38) **and 201-4 dec** (39 overs) (A. J. Robson 59, M. J. Cosgrove 59); **‡Loughborough MCCU 262-8 dec** (76.5 overs) (N. R. Kumar 59, B. M. R. Akram 87; C. E. Shreck 3-45). *County debuts:* N. J. Dexter, P. J. Horton, M. L. Pettini. *Loughborough traded blows with their neighbours, but all three days lost time to rain. Sam Cook took the first four wickets as Leicestershire slipped to 97-4, before Aadil Ali made a sedate 62. On the third morning the students had the satisfaction of pinching a narrow lead. Once again their batting hero was Basil Akram: after centuries in Loughborough's first two matches, he looked set for another, before holing out at long-on for 87. This match, originally scheduled for Grace Road, was switched to the university ground after rebuilding work overran.*

At Oxford, April 11–13 (not first-class). OXFORD MCCU v MIDDLESEX. Abandoned.

At Leeds, April 11–13 (not first-class). LEEDS/BRADFORD MCCU drew with YORKSHIRE.

At Taunton Vale, April 17–19 (not first-class). CARDIFF MCCU drew with SOMERSET. *Set 733, Cardiff finished at 143-8.*

THE UNIVERSITY MATCHES IN 2016

At Oxford, May 20. **Oxford University won by 38 runs. ‡Oxford University 151-4** (20 overs) (M. S. T. Hughes 75*, O. J. Jones 34); **Cambridge University 113-6** (20 overs) (J. B. Abbott 44). *MoM:* M. S. T. Hughes. *After two quick wickets went down, Matt Hughes steadied Oxford's innings. Cambridge also had a bad start – 6-2 after 14 balls – and were never really on terms, despite 44 from skipper Jamie Abbott. Oxford made the score in the Varsity Twenty20 match 3–3 since the first in 2008 (two were abandoned and one a no-result).*

At Lord's, July 1. **Oxford University won by 43 runs. Oxford University 192-9** (40 overs) (D. A. Escott 32; C. J. Emerton 3-50); **‡Cambridge University 140** (34.1 overs) (A. D. Dalgleish 77; O. J. Jones 3-10, J. Marsden 3-26). *Rain forced a late start – and a reduction to 40 overs – and Oxford scrambled to 192. In reply, Angus Dalgleish hit 77 from 70 balls – but only Abbott of the other Cambridge batsmen reached double figures, and they fell well short. Oxford's fourth consecutive victory gave them a 13–9 lead in Varsity one-day games.*

OXFORD UNIVERSITY v CAMBRIDGE UNIVERSITY

At Oxford, July 5–8. Oxford University won by 103 runs. Toss: Oxford. First-class debuts: B. Bishnoi, M. J. Dawes, D. A. Escott, R. A. Heywood; A. D. Dalgleish.

Oxford completed a clean sweep, although this third leg was agonisingly close. After some dogged batting throughout the order, Cambridge's last pair came together with 25 minutes left, and had only five more to survive when Connor Emerton was caught by Tom Claughton, the son of Oxford's 1978 captain John, off the bowling of the 2016 skipper Johny Marsden. It ended a rearguard that had begun before tea on the third day, and lasted more than 141 overs. The second wicket did not go

---

A CENTURY AND A FIVE-FOR ON FIRST-CLASS DEBUT

M. Jahangir Khan (108 and 7-42)	Muslims v Hindus at Lahore	1928-29
Majid Khan (111* and 6-67)	Lahore B v Khairpur at Lahore	1961-62
Imran Bucha (120 and 5-40)	Servis Industries v Lahore B at Lahore	1976-77
D. A. Escott (125 and 6-71)	**Oxford U v Cambridge U at Oxford**	**2016**

Jahangir and Majid Khan were father and son.

down until after lunch on the fourth – in the 72nd over – with Singapore-born Darshan Chohan surviving four and a half hours, and Patrick Tice, the Irish wicketkeeper, making 41 in 257 minutes. But after they were separated Oxford chipped away patiently, 19-year-old freshman Dan Escott taking six successive wickets with his leg-breaks before Marsden finished things off. The previous day Escott had led the batting, stroking a fine 125: he was only the fourth man on first-class debut to combine five wickets in an innings with a century (and the first outside Lahore). Earlier, Matt Hughes had matched his 116 in the previous year's Varsity Match, before becoming one of five victims for Avish Patel's leg-spin. Cambridge then stumbled to nine for four, but Jamie Abbott and Angus Dalgleish repaired some of the damage in a stand of 89.

Close of play: first day, Oxford University 267; second day, Oxford University 44-0 (Escott 23, Heywood 14); third day, Cambridge University 96-1 (Chohan 50, Tice 5).

Oxford University

D. A. Escott c Abbott b Patel	36	– c sub (I. S. Khan) b Waghorn	125
R. A. Heywood b Crichard	13	– c Tice b Dalgleish	21
M. S. T. Hughes lbw b Patel	116	– b Dalgleish	76
M. J. Winter c and b Dalgleish	27	– (6) not out	1
O. J. Jones lbw b Patel	8	– (4) c Dalgleish b Waghorn	45
B. Bishnoi b Patel	0	– (5) b Patel	16
J. S. D. Gnodde c Bardolia b Dalgleish	27	– not out	0
T. H. Claughton c Chohan b Dalgleish	2		
†S. A. Westaway b Patel	7		
*J. Marsden lbw b Crichard	7		
M. J. Dawes not out	0		
B 4, lb 6, nb 14	24	B 11, lb 14, w 1, nb 6	32
1/17 (2) 2/150 (1) 3/199 (3) 4/211 (5) 5/211 (6) 6/231 (4) 7/241 (8) 8/254 (9) 9/266 (7) 10/267 (10) (93.2 overs)	267	1/62 (2) 2/233 (3) 3/280 (1) 4/311 (5) 5/311 (4) (5 wkts dec, 72 overs)	316

Crichard 22.2–8–60–2; Waghorn 11–2–44–0; Emerton 5.2–1–18–0; Dalgleish 20.4–5–49–3; Patel 34–8–86–5. *Second innings*—Crichard 18–3–69–0; Waghorn 14–1–60–2; Patel 20–1–79–1; Dalgleish 16–1–63–2; Abbott 4–0–20–0.

Cambridge University

T. G. L. Colverd lbw b Marsden	3	– c Westaway b Marsden	36
D. Chohan lbw b Jones	2	– c Gnodde b Claughton	83
*J. B. Abbott c Jones b Marsden	53	– (4) b Marsden	11
A. G. Hearne c Gnodde b Jones	0	– (5) lbw b Escott	19
S. Bardolia c and b Marsden	1	– (6) c and b Escott	20
A. D. Dalgleish lbw b Dawes	41	– (7) lbw b Escott	9
A. R. Patel lbw b Hughes	8	– (8) c Westaway b Escott	31
†P. J. A. Tice lbw b Marsden	19	– (3) c Westaway b Escott	41
R. J. Crichard not out	27	– c Heywood b Escott	21
C. J. Emerton c Westaway b Gnodde	6	– c Claughton b Marsden	6
A. C. Waghorn lbw b Marsden	4	– not out	0
B 3, lb 6, w 5, nb 4	18	B 13, lb 6, nb 2	21
1/3 (2) 2/7 (1) 3/8 (4) 4/9 (5) 5/98 (6) 6/113 (7) 7/131 (3) 8/144 (8) 9/173 (10) 10/182 (11) (80 overs)	182	1/87 (1) 2/148 (2) 3/170 (4) 4/200 (3) 5/207 (5) 6/227 (7) 7/242 (6) 8/281 (8) 9/294 (9) 10/298 (10) (141.4 overs)	298

Jones 22–7–46–2; Marsden 17–6–41–5; Dawes 20–10–26–1; Gnodde 9–1–33–1; Claughton 2–0–11–0; Hughes 10–1–16–1. *Second innings*—Jones 20–7–39–0; Marsden 23.4–2–51–3; Dawes 11–2–25–0; Hughes 6–2–5–0; Gnodde 42–19–72–0; Escott 31–9–71–6; Claughton 8–5–16–1.

Umpires: P. R. Pollard and R. J. Warren. K. Coburn replaced Warren on the fourth day.

This was the 171st University Match, a first-class fixture dating back to 1827. Cambridge have won 59 and Oxford 56, with 56 drawn. It was played at Lord's until 2000.

MCC UNIVERSITIES CHAMPIONSHIP

	Played	*Won*	*Lost*	*1st-inns wins*	*1st-inns losses*	*Drawn*	*Bonus points*	*Points*
Loughborough (3)	5	0	0	3	0	2	40	80
Oxford (4)	5	0	0	2	1	2	40	70
Leeds/Bradford (2)	5	1	0	0	1	3	32	64
Durham (6)	5	0	0	2	1	2	30	60
Cardiff (1)	5	0	0	1	2	2	34	54
Cambridge (5)	5	0	1	0	3	1	27	32

Outright win = 17pts; first-innings win in a drawn match = 10pts; no result on first innings = 5pts; abandoned = 5pts.

WINNERS

2001	Loughborough
2002	Loughborough
2003	Loughborough
2004	Oxford
2005	Loughborough
2006	Oxford
2007	Cardiff/Glamorgan
2008	Loughborough
2009	Leeds/Bradford
2010	Durham
2011	Cardiff
2012	Cambridge
2013	Leeds/Bradford
2014	Loughborough
2015	Cardiff
2016	Loughborough

MCC UNIVERSITIES CHALLENGE FINAL

At Lord's, June 21. **Oxford MCCU won by 37 runs. Oxford MCCU 267-9** (50 overs) (M. B. Lake 89, B. M. Broughton 90; G. K. R. McKinley 3-46); ‡**Loughborough MCCU 230** (47.5 overs) (C. O. Thurston 72; M. B. Lake 3-36, S. R. Green 3-28). *Oxford's successful season continued, as they tweaked the noses of table-toppers (and 2015 Challenge winners) Loughborough. Malcolm Lake, a Zimbabwe-born left-hander, held the early batting together with 89; the next four all failed to reach double figures (including a golden duck for Nasser Hussain's nephew Reece) after Oxford were put in. But Bruno Broughton took up the cudgels, and lifted the score to an imposing 267. With Charlie Thurston going well, Loughborough breezed past 100 in the 19th over, and looked on course at 194-4 in the 39th. But slow left-armer Steven Green took three wickets in nine balls and, with medium-pacer Lake chipping in, the last six fell for only 36.*

MCC IN 2016

STEVEN LYNCH

The redevelopment of Lord's continued to occupy MCC's officials and committee members. The first phase involved the new Warner Stand, which was used in the second half of the season, although the facilities were incomplete. It was finished over the winter, and due to be officially opened on May 3, the day of the club's AGM.

The next project, before work starts on refurbishing the Allen and Tavern Stands, is a new scorers' box, to replace the one beneath the Father Time weathervane in the Tavern. With the traditional scorers these days joined by analysts, internet inputters and operators for the electronic scoreboards, the new box needed to accommodate a dozen people. It will also include an old-fashioned manual scoreboard, so spectators will be able to keep up even when the electronic screens are showing something else.

The new Warner Stand includes more room for match-day personnel, such as ICC officials, security staff and the public address announcer. MCC's cricket office has been moved from the basement of the Pavilion to the old secretariat suite on the second floor, with a new bridge to the adjacent Warner Stand: telephone enquiries about the current score will no longer require someone to stand on a waste-paper basket and squint between the members standing outside the Bowlers' Bar. The Secretary's office has moved to the old Middlesex Room in the Allen Stand.

As part of the annual financial review, it was reluctantly decided that support for the MCC Universities scheme would be halved from 2017, to £275,000; MCC's overall spending on the project has been around £6.5m. Happily, some of the shortfall will be taken up by a sponsorship deal with Deloittes, and it is hoped the scheme will continue to flourish.

Notable deaths during the year included the elegant batsman Martin Crowe, who was first seen at Lord's as a precocious teenager on a New Zealand board scholarship in 1981, scored Test hundreds there in 1986 and 1994, and later served on the world cricket committee. Early in 2017 came news of the passing of the former England captain Rachael Heyhoe Flint, one of MCC's first female members and the first woman to be elected to the main committee.

During 2016, touring parties visited South Africa, Oman and Bahrain, the Netherlands and the USA, and a women's team also visited the US. At home, MCC played 465 out-matches, of which 163 were won, 86 drawn, one tied, 95 lost, and 120 abandoned or cancelled. Women's teams had 32, winning 12, drawing two and losing nine, with nine abandoned.

MCC v YORKSHIRE

At Abu Dhabi, March 20–23, 2016. MCC won by four wickets. Toss: Yorkshire.

This was the seventh edition of the traditional season-opener to be hosted in Abu Dhabi, but the first to use a red ball. Following a second successive Championship title, Yorkshire had persuaded MCC to revert to tradition after being dissatisfied with the visibility and durability of the pink ball the previous year. They agreed, though not for the same reason: MCC were content that the pink ball's viability had been proved by the day/night Test in Australia in November 2015. In the event, Yorkshire fell to only their fifth first-class defeat since 2011, as an MCC side captained by Ian Bell chased 256 on the final day. In his first competitive match since being omitted from the tour of South Africa, Bell stroked a composed 66 to set up victory. Given 78 overs to reach their target, MCC had overcome the early losses of Browne and Burns, and were grateful for Bell's partnership of 84 with Westley. Yorkshire had been restricted to 275 in their first innings, despite a century from Ballance – another England discard – and runs down the order from Rhodes. In reply, half-centuries from Burns, Foakes and Clarke helped MCC establish a lead of 24. On a pitch offering assistance to spinners, Tredwell and Patel then shared six wickets to keep Yorkshire below 280 once more. CHRIS STOCKS

Close of play: first day, MCC 0-0 (Harris 0, Browne 0); second day, MCC 282-6 (Foakes 83, Clarke 56); third day, Yorkshire 239-7 (Rhodes 41, Patterson 5).

Yorkshire

A. Lyth c Patel b Clarke	13	– lbw b Tredwell	7
A. Z. Lees lbw b Ball	0	– b Patel	86
G. S. Ballance lbw b Patel	105	– b Harris	9
*A. W. Gale c Foakes b Tredwell	23	– lbw b Patel	23
J. A. Leaning b Tredwell	6	– c Clarke b Tredwell	13
T. T. Bresnan c Foakes b Tredwell	3	– c Harris b Tredwell	6
W. M. H. Rhodes c Foakes b Clarke	95	– c Foakes b Onions	43
†A. J. Hodd b Ball	9	– lbw b Ball	44
S. A. Patterson b Onions	0	– b Onions	5
J. A. Brooks lbw b Onions	0	– st Foakes b Patel	25
K. Carver not out	4	– not out	12
B 3, lb 7, w 5, nb 2	17	B 1, lb 5	6
1/0 (2) 2/21 (1) 3/64 (4) (92.2 overs)	275	1/21 (1) 2/60 (3) (107 overs)	279
4/82 (5) 5/88 (6) 6/213 (3)		3/108 (4) 4/137 (5)	
7/233 (8) 8/234 (9) 9/234 (10) 10/275 (7)		5/147 (2) 6/147 (6) 7/227 (8)	
		8/241 (7) 9/242 (9) 10/279 (10)	

Onions 14–4–39–2; Ball 14–3–41–2; Clarke 14.2–3–39–2; Harris 13–2–48–0; Tredwell 25–8–53–3; Patel 8–2–28–1; Westley 4–0–17–0. *Second innings*—Onions 12–2–32–2; Ball 11–1–44–1; Tredwell 40–13–79–3; Clarke 8–1–23–0; Harris 13–0–43–1; Patel 23–4–52–3.

MCC

J. A. R. Harris c Leaning b Patterson	4	– (8) not out	0
N. L. J. Browne c Rhodes b Bresnan	2	– c Lees b Lyth	13
R. J. Burns c Hodd b Bresnan	51	– (1) run out	27
*I. R. Bell c Patterson b Carver	44	– (3) c Lees b Carver	66
S. R. Patel lbw b Bresnan	5	– c Ballance b Leaning	22
T. Westley c Hodd b Patterson	22	– (4) st Hodd b Carver	58
†B. T. Foakes b Carver	91	– (6) not out	32
R. Clarke lbw b Bresnan	58	– (7) st Hodd b Leaning	33
J. T. Ball st Hodd b Carver	1		
J. C. Tredwell not out	2		
G. Onions b Carver	3		
B 5, lb 8, w 1, nb 2	16	B 4, lb 2	6
1/2 (2) 2/14 (1) 3/103 (3) (97.2 overs)	299	1/29 (2) (6 wkts, 67.4 overs)	257
4/109 (4) 5/114 (5) 6/151 (6)		2/54 (1) 3/138 (4)	
7/290 (7) 8/292 (9) 9/296 (8) 10/299 (11)		4/173 (5) 5/199 (3) 6/246 (7)	

Brooks 14–6–37–0; Bresnan 19–5–58–4; Patterson 16–6–32–2; Carver 30.2–10–106–4; Rhodes 11–2–41–0; Lyth 7–2–12–0. *Second innings*—Bresnan 2–0–5–0; Brooks 13–1–45–0; Patterson 9–1–27–0; Rhodes 6–1–25–0; Lyth 8–1–31–1; Carver 25–7–88–2; Leaning 4.4–1–30–2.

Umpires: N. A. Mallender and D. J. Millns.

THE MINOR COUNTIES IN 2016

PHILIP AUGUST

For the first time, both Minor County finals were held at a single venue, and Wormsley drew good crowds in August sunshine. It was arranged by Geoff Evans, who died in September at his home by the Otter Estuary in Devon. Evans had been MCCA secretary since 2001, and a highly respected administrator with a deep love of the game.

Berkshire were unbeaten in the Western Division, and went on to become Minor County champions for the fifth time. Newcomer Oli Wilkin led the way, hitting 576 runs – including twin hundreds against Herefordshire – and taking 15 wickets with his seamers. Experienced slow left-armer Chris Peploe gave control: he bowled 274 overs with an economy-rate just over two, and took 35 wickets, the second-biggest haul in the competition. **Cornwall** were in the running until they met the league leaders at the end of July. Berkshire bowled them out for 92, then racked up 325 for six, before rain washed out the last two days.

Herefordshire enjoyed an excellent season under new captain Matthew Pardoe, who topped the batting averages. They took the knockout Trophy at Wormsley, and third place in a Championship season that included a thrilling tie against Devon. **Shropshire** won their penultimate game against Cheshire by 70 runs, but forfeited 24 points for fielding an ineligible player, and finished fourth. David Wainwright had a superb summer, taking 32 wickets with his left-arm spin, and scoring 444 runs.

An inexperienced **Devon** side endured an up-and-down year, collecting just eight batting points, and no draws. Josh and Zak Bess – their cousin Dom, the Somerset off-spinner, occasionally made it a family trio – had strong seasons, and a two-day win in the last game, against Cornwall, was the highlight. Ed Young took over as captain of **Wiltshire** mid-season and, with the introduction of younger players, oversaw improved performances with two victories in their last three games.

Cheshire lost four and won two, as selection difficulties proved hard to overcome, even for enthusiastic new captain Lee Dixon. **Dorset** chose to leave their long-standing home ground at Dean Park in Bournemouth, and had a poor season with the bat: they picked up just six bonus points and, in the last match against Oxfordshire, were bowled out for 96 and 84 to lose by 327 runs. **Oxfordshire** gave opportunities to a number of young players, but could not match the heights of the previous season, when they reached the final. Former Middlesex and Sussex seamer Chad Keegan retired; his contributions as player and mentor will be greatly missed. **Wales Minor Counties** finished bottom of the division with just one win, a two-day victory against Devon in the first match. In the next, they bowled Berkshire out for 98, but rain scotched a conclusion.

Lincolnshire became Eastern Division champions after a comprehensive win in their last match, against Staffordshire. In mid-season Adam Tillcock, who had been released by Nottinghamshire in 2015, enjoyed a golden spell: against Norfolk, he remained undefeated in innings of 153 and 50 (to go with six wickets), and in the next game scored 165 and 69 against Cumberland. He was the competition's top-scorer, with 720 runs at 80. **Northumberland** matched Lincolnshire's points total, but came second on net runs per wicket. Openers Jack Jessop and Matthew Whaley shared a county-record stand of 240 (beating the mark set in 1955) against Hertfordshire and, in the same match, captain Jacques du Toit hammered 105 from 57 balls.

Kadeer Ali scored four centuries for **Staffordshire**, including two in the game against Bedfordshire, and deep into the season they had hopes of the double. But a last-day washout against Suffolk in their penultimate match, and a below-par performance in the Trophy final, put paid to their aspirations. Lewis Bruce took the **Cambridgeshire** captaincy following a knee injury for Paul McMahon, and was well supported by player/coach Ben Smith who, in consecutive matches, scored 151 and 168 (both not out). James Spelman stood down from one-day cricket, but remained a force for **Norfolk** in the Championship with two centuries, while captain Chris Brown and Ben France shouldered the bowling burden, sending down 387 overs between them for 63 wickets. Brown, a veteran of 94 Minor County Championship matches since 2000, took 38 of them, at 15 apiece, to top the bowling charts and win the Frank Edwards Trophy (it took his career haul to 464).

Leg-spinner Mattie McKiernan claimed 33 in his debut season for **Cumberland** and, with slow left-armer Toby Bulcock, left many a batting line-up in a daze. Three **Hertfordshire** youngsters scored their maiden centuries – Joe Cooke, Reece Hussain and Steven Gale – while Tanveer Sikandar made a wonderful rearguard 188 to thwart Staffordshire.

Tom Huggins's last innings before retirement was 168 not out for **Suffolk**, which left him as the highest scorer in three-day Championship cricket. He also finished with 185 wickets. For the fifth season in six, **Bedfordshire** failed to win a match. Runs came from Ben Howgego – who won his second Wilfred Rhodes Trophy for best batsman – Andy Reynoldson and Luke Thomas, but they lacked support. A young **Buckinghamshire** side were also winless, labouring with an attack lacking penetration: Michael Payne was their leading wicket-taker, with 12.

The knockout Trophy featured Mervyn Westfield playing for Suffolk. In 2009, he took £6,000 to bowl badly for Essex against Durham; he served eight weeks in prison and was banned for five years from 2012. The ECB allowed him to return before the expiry of his ban in recognition of his work with a PCA anti-corruption programme. He played three games in the group stages, and took seven wickets.

Nick Archer, former captain of Staffordshire, was appointed MCCA chairman following the retirement of John Pickup, after 21 years. And Phil Caley, who had captained Suffolk, became the new secretary. They will need to decide how to resolve the issue of player availability in June, particularly when those in school are taking exams, and whether the Twenty20 competition should be reintroduced.

MINOR COUNTIES CHAMPIONSHIP IN 2016

	Eastern Division	P	W	L	T	D	Bonus points Batting	Bonus points Bowling	Total points	NRPW
1	LINCOLNSHIRE (4)	6	5	0	0	1	23	21	126†	19.26
2	Northumberland (5)	6	5	0	0	1	19	23	126	11.90
3	Staffordshire (3)	6	2	1	0	3	21	22	87	8.57
4	Norfolk (9)	6	2	3	0	1	13	24	73	0.95
5	Cambridgeshire (8)	6	2	1	0	3	9	20	73	0.82
6	Cumberland (1)	6	1	3	0	2	15	23	62	–4.03
7	Hertfordshire (6)	6	1	2	0	3	16	17	61	–10.86
8	Suffolk (10)	6	1	3	0	2	5	24	53	–6.61
9	Bedfordshire (7)	6	0	3	0	3	15	17	44	–7.88
10	Buckinghamshire (2)	6	0	3	0	3	11	17	40	–15.11

	Western Division	P	W	L	T	D	Bonus points Batting	Bonus points Bowling	Total points	NRPW
1	BERKSHIRE (2)	6	4	0	0	2	18	22	112	15.89
2	Cornwall (4)	6	3	2	0	1	16	22	90	0.13
3	Herefordshire (5)	6	2	2	1	1	13	23	80	–0.57
4	Shropshire (3)	6	4	2	0	0	12	21	73*	1.84
5	Devon (10)	6	2	3	1	0	8	24	72	–0.99
6	Wiltshire (7)	6	2	3	0	1	13	22	71	2.18
7	Cheshire (9)	6	2	4	0	0	11	24	65†	–5.11
8	Dorset (8)	6	2	3	0	1	6	23	63†	–5.24
9	Oxfordshire (1)	6	2	3	0	1	12	18	62‡	–10.86
10	Wales Minor Counties (6)	6	1	2	0	3	10	23	61	2.01

Win = 16pts; tie = 8pts; draw = 4pts. NRPW is net runs per wicket (runs per wicket for, less runs per wicket against).

* *Deducted 24pts for fielding an ineligible player.*

† *Deducted 2pts for slow over-rate.*

‡ *Deducted 4pts for slow over-rate.*

LEADING AVERAGES IN 2016

BATTING (375 runs at 45.00)

		M	I	NO	R	HS	100	50	Avge	Ct
1	M. G. Pardoe *(Herefordshire)*	4	7	2	428	167*	1	2	85.60	4
2	B. H. N. Howgego *(Bedfordshire)*	5	9	1	643	165	3	3	80.37	0
3	A. D. Tillcock *(Lincolnshire)*	7	12	3	720	165	3	3	80.00	1
4	H. R. H. Darby *(Oxfordshire)*	4	8	2	407	166	1	2	67.83	2
5	K. Ali *(Staffordshire)*	6	12	2	593	135	4	0	59.30	0
6	Tanveer Sikandar *(Hertfordshire)*	5	9	0	533	188	1	2	59.22	4
7	C. J. Louth *(Lincolnshire)*	5	10	2	471	125	2	1	58.87	4
8	A. M. Reynoldson *(Bedfordshire)*	6	10	2	465	97	0	4	58.12	7
9	J. du Toit *(Northumberland)*	5	7	0	396	105	2	2	56.57	5
10	D. J. Wainwright *(Shropshire)*	6	10	2	444	95	0	3	55.50	6
11	M. J. Hill *(Staffordshire)*	6	8	1	386	122	1	2	55.14	3
12	T. B. Huggins *(Suffolk)*	5	9	1	440	168*	1	2	55.00	5
13	S. S. E. Gumbs *(Buckinghamshire)*	6	10	0	541	156	2	3	54.10	5
14	S. W. Griffiths *(Wales)*	5	8	0	420	126	1	3	52.50	3
15	O. Wilkin *(Berkshire)*	7	12	1	576	163	2	0	52.36	3
16	Tahir Afridi *(Wiltshire)*	6	10	2	412	71*	0	4	51.50	2
17	B. F. Smith *(Cambridgeshire)*	6	10	2	400	168*	2	0	50.00	9
18	B. L. Wadlan *(Cornwall)*	6	9	0	436	191	2	1	48.44	1
19	J. A. Tattersall *(Lincolnshire)*	6	12	1	521	88	0	5	47.36	4
20	R. C. J. Aucott *(Shropshire)*	6	10	2	378	89	0	4	47.25	1

BOWLING (20 wickets at 30.00)

		Style	*O*	*M*	*R*	*W*	*BB*	*5I*	*Avge*
1	C. Brown *(Norfolk)*	OB	203.1	46	583	38	7-47	4	15.34
2	T. M. Nugent *(Berkshire)*	RFM	177.1	50	518	31	7-40	2	16.70
3	C. T. Peploe *(Berkshire)*	SLA	274.2	91	586	35	7-66	4	16.74
4	B. Roberts *(Wales)*	RFM	97.5	16	360	20	4-28	0	18.00
5	A. C. F. Wyatt *(Shropshire)*	RFM	175.2	28	580	32	6-69	3	18.12
6	J. S. Dawborn *(Cambridgeshire)*	RFM	145.4	37	381	21	5-51	1	18.14
7	S. R. J. Thomson *(Dorset)*	OB	146	30	473	26	6-35	3	18.19
8	O. F. McGee *(Northumberland)*	SLA	158.2	32	420	23	4-40	0	18.26
9	D. J. Wainwright *(Shropshire)*	SLA	233.2	46	646	32	5-30	3	20.18
10	A. C. Libby *(Cornwall)*	SLA	186	45	628	30	6-45	2	20.93
11	A. J. Willerton *(Lincolnshire)*	RM	176.1	38	496	23	4-31	0	21.56
12	T. Bulcock *(Cumberland)*	SLA	247	67	630	28	6-46	1	22.50
13	M. H. McKiernan *(Cumberland)*	LBG	264.5	56	751	33	7-114	5	22.75
14	J. M. King *(Wiltshire)*	OB	115.4	25	480	21	5-55	1	22.85
15	P. I. Burgoyne *(Herefordshire)*	OB	157.5	33	602	26	7-58	2	23.15
16	N. H. Davies *(Wales)*	SLA	164.1	46	475	20	5-26	1	23.75
17	B. J. France *(Norfolk)*	RM	184.4	41	602	25	5-65	2	24.08
18	G. Wade *(Northumberland)*	RFM	158.5	26	536	22	4-51	0	24.36
19	D. A. Woods *(Cheshire)*	SLA	218.2	52	689	27	6-100	2	25.51
20	S. E. Rippington *(Cambridgeshire)*	LM	164.3	35	549	21	4-22	0	26.14
21	G. M. Smith *(Cornwall)*	RFM/OB	183.4	42	529	20	5-43	1	26.45

CHAMPIONSHIP FINAL

At Wormsley, August 28–31. ‡**Berkshire won by 28 runs. Berkshire 332** (89.3 overs) (E. D. Woods 142*, C. T. Peploe 73; D. S. Lucas 4-47) **and 237** (76.1 overs) (S. R. Davison 51; A. J. Willerton 4-45, D. D. A. Brown 4-56); **Lincolnshire 284** (90 overs) (J. A. Tattersall 71; C. T. Peploe 5-101) **and 257** (123.4 overs) (D. D. A. Brown 51, M. Carter 59; C. T. Peploe 5-74). *Berkshire slipped to 70-6 on the first day, before 17-year-old Euan Woods staged a recovery, hitting 142* (improving his best in the Minor Counties Championship by 105), and hauling them to 332. Thanks to a five-for by Chris Peploe, Berkshire resumed with a lead of 48 and, despite another top-order collapse, set Lincolnshire 286. After they fell to 127-7 on the third evening, the pace slowed, and spectators might have nodded off were it not for the voluble Berkshire fielders. The tension grew, though, as Matthew Carter – who had two front teeth removed during the match, after he was struck in the field by a stray return throw – brought the target within range. But Peploe finally snared him, finishing with ten in the match and ending an epic Lincolnshire innings.*

TROPHY FINAL

At Wormsley, August 24. **Herefordshire won by 56 runs.** ‡**Herefordshire 258-9** (50 overs) (D. G. Ball 85; S. Kelsall 3-29); **Staffordshire 202** (44.4 overs) (P. J. Wilshaw 50, M. J. Hill 50; W. J. M. Barrett 4-25). *Herefordshire won the toss and batted, perhaps in part to avoid fielding when the sun was strongest: this was the hottest day of the year. David Ball held the innings together with 85, yet Staffordshire would have felt the target was within range, even if the pitch lacked pace. After captain Kadeer Ali fell early to a lifter, Peter Wilshaw and Michael Hill put on 76 for the fifth wicket. It looked as if it would be close, but three went down for three, and the last six for 57; left-arm seamer Will Barrett finished with four wickets.*

SECOND ELEVEN CHAMPIONSHIP IN 2016

	North Division	P	W	L	D	A	Bonus points Bat	Bonus points Bowl	Pen	Total points
1	Durham (2)	9	5	1	3	0	23	30	0	148
2	Lancashire (3)	9	4	0	3	2	17	25	0	131
3	MCC Universities (9)	9	2	1	6	0	26	31	0	119
4	Worcestershire (8)	9	3	3	3	0	25	28	0	116
5	Yorkshire (7)	9	2	3	4	0	13	32	0	97
6	Warwickshire (5)	9	0	0	8	1	27	23	0	95
7	Nottinghamshire (1)	9	2	4	2	1	17	29	0	93
8	Derbyshire (6)	9	1	2	5	1	18	25	0	89
9	Leicestershire (4)	9	1	3	4	1	21	24	0	86
10	Northamptonshire (10)	9	0	3	4	2	14	20	0	64

	South Division	P	W	L	D	A	Bonus points Bat	Bonus points Bowl	Pen	Total points
1	Middlesex (1)	9	5	1	2	1	22	27	0	144
2	Sussex (7)	9	4	2	2	1	24	25	0	128
3	MCCYC (10)	9	2	1	6	0	21	26	0	109
4	Kent (3)	9	3	3	3	0	18	26	0	107
5	Glamorgan (9)	9	2	2	4	1	22	27	0	106
6	Essex (8)	9	2	2	5	0	21	29	–1.5	105.5
7	Surrey (4)	9	2	3	4	0	23	30	–2	103
8	Hampshire (6)	9	1	2	6	0	29	21	0	96
9	Somerset (2)	9	1	3	5	0	29	25	0	95
10	Gloucestershire (5)	9	1	4	3	1	11	21	0	68

Win = 16pts; draw/abandoned = 5pts. All penalties were for slow over-rates.

LEADING AVERAGES, 2016

BATTING (420 runs)

		M	I	NO	Runs	HS	100	Avge	Ct/St
1	C. A. L. Davis (*MCCU, Sussex*)	5	7	1	469	258*	2	78.16	6
2	C. M. Dickinson (*Essex, MCCU*)	6	10	1	689	185	1	76.55	12/1
3	T. D. Rouse (*Somerset*)	4	6	0	450	175	2	75.00	5
4	G. J. Harte (*MCCYC, Sussex*)	10	14	6	585	199	1	73.12	3
5	J. R. Murphy (*Glamorgan*)	7	9	3	428	139	2	71.33	2
6	N. Brand (*Glamorgan, MCCU*)	5	8	0	554	162	2	69.25	2
7	J. M. Kettleborough (*Glamorgan*)	6	10	1	617	209*	2	68.55	4
8	N. J. Selman (*Glamorgan*)	5	8	1	470	124	3	67.14	2
9	A. J. Hose (*Somerset*)	8	14	2	644	120*	2	53.66	5
10	J. E. Burke (*Surrey*)	7	10	2	429	127*	1	53.62	6
11	T. J. Moores (*Lancashire, Notts*)	7	12	2	444	139	1	44.40	12/1
12	A. Hepburn (*Worcestershire*)	8	14	1	567	149	2	43.61	4
13	G. Fatouros (*Kent*)	8	13	1	496	105*	2	41.33	3
14	K. S. Velani (*Essex*)	8	11	0	451	116	2	41.00	8
15	O. E. Westbury (*Worcestershire*)	7	13	0	499	137	1	38.38	1
16	R. Gibson (*Yorkshire*)	8	15	2	486	162*	1	37.38	8
17	J. H. Barrett (*Glos, MCCYC, Notts*)	10	18	2	586	107	2	36.62	5
18	J. B. Harris (*MCCYC*)	9	14	1	466	73	0	35.84	2
19	H. E. Dearden (*Hampshire, Leics*)	10	15	0	534	132	1	35.60	7
20	M. H. Azad (*MCCU*)	9	16	1	478	123	1	31.86	8
21	T. F. Smith (*Glam, MCCYC, Sussex*)	11	17	1	461	106	2	28.81	3
22	B. J. Curran (*MCCYC, Notts, Surrey*)	9	17	2	432	74	0	28.80	7

BOWLING (18 wickets)

		Style	*O*	*M*	*R*	*W*	*BB*	*5I*	*Avge*
1	S. D. Parry (*Lancashire*)	SLA	92.5	30	204	18	6-38	2	11.33
2	A. T. E. Hazeldine (*MCCYC, Somerset*)	LFM	83.2	15	291	20	5-37	1	14.55
3	S. G. Whittingham (*Sussex*)	RFM	73.2	15	264	18	6-69	1	14.66
4	G. S. Virdi (*Surrey*)	OB	118.5	24	367	21	5-37	2	17.47
5	G. T. Griffiths (*Hampshire, Lancashire*)	RFM	125.1	27	390	22	5-77	1	17.72
6	G. S. Randhawa (*Durham, Derbyshire*)	SLA	239.5	61	674	37	7-69	2	18.21
7	B. O. Coad (*Yorkshire*)	RFM	147.1	40	418	20	6-57	2	20.90
8	P. Joshi (*Glamorgan, Warwickshire*)	RFM	144.4	42	444	20	5-42	1	22.20
9	B. M. Kitt (*Nottinghamshire*)	RFM	204	40	685	30	4-37	0	22.83
10	G. S. Sandhu (*Durham, Leicestershire*)	LFM	132.2	30	431	18	4-41	0	23.94
11	A. E. Lilley (*MCCU*)	LM	216.1	59	555	23	4-40	0	24.13
12	J. C. Wainman (*Yorkshire*)	LM	166.5	28	615	24	5-24	2	25.62
13	H. R. Bernard (*Kent*)	RFM	142	17	574	20	4-78	0	28.70
14	M. D. Hunn (*Kent*)	RFM	159.3	30	546	19	6-93	1	28.73
15	A. S. S. Nijjar (*Essex*)	SLA	159.2	27	608	20	4-23	0	30.40
16	C. J. Russell (*Worcestershire*)	RFM	183.3	36	684	22	5-90	2	31.09
17	J. N. McIver (*MCCU*)	OB	235	45	778	22	5-90	2	35.36
18	M. Carter (*Nottinghamshire*)	OB	241.4	70	651	18	5-43	1	36.16

SECOND ELEVEN CHAMPIONSHIP FINAL

At Chester-le-Street, September 6–8. **Durham won by an innings and 117 runs. Durham 504** (126.5 overs) (C. T. Steel 95, P. Coughlin 231, E. J. Hurst 36, Extras 74; J. A. R. Harris 3-118, J. K. Fuller 3-110); ‡**Middlesex 202** (67.5 overs) (J. A. R. Harris 53*, R. H. Patel 31; U. Arshad 4-35) **and 185** (45.2 overs) (P. R. Stirling 86, M. K. Anderson 45; L. Trevaskis 6-31).

SECOND ELEVEN TROPHY FINAL

At Manchester, August 25. **Lancashire won by ten wickets** (DLS). **Somerset 209** (44 overs) (A. W. R. Barrow 34, D. M. Bess 32; S. D. Parry 3-22); ‡**Lancashire 77-0** (18 overs) (K. R. Brown 37*, L. M. Reece 35*).

SECOND ELEVEN TWENTY20 FINAL

At Arundel, July 14. **Middlesex won by two wickets.** ‡**Somerset 161-7** (20 overs) (T. D. Rouse 30, G. A. Bartlett 58). **Middlesex 162-8** (19.5 overs) (R. G. White 53, A. Rath 35).

LEAGUE CRICKET IN 2016

A crown for Thornes

GEOFFREY DEAN

Which is the best club in Yorkshire? A new league structure allowed a definitive answer, as the four premier competitions threw forth a contender to decide a champion of champions (though the representatives from the North Yorkshire and South Durham League were runners-up Marske, not winners Barnard Castle: Durham-based clubs were excluded from the play-offs). In the October final, held at the Sheikh Zayed Stadium in Abu Dhabi, thanks to financial input from the Yorkshire Cricket Board, Wakefield Thornes beat Pudsey St Lawrence. A 110-ball century by David Toft helped Wakefield to 296 and, although Mark Robertshaw's 112 kept Pudsey in touch, they fell short at the death.

Tom Froggett, the victorious captain, said his side had aimed for nothing more than mid-table respectability. Yet they won Yorkshire League South by 48 points. "Fourteen years ago, this club were in the doldrums, struggling to turn out a second team, and with no junior division," Froggett said. "Now we have four senior teams, our seconds got promoted, and we have Under-9s through to Under-17s."

Finchampstead also exceeded expectations: a year after promotion they won their last 13 games to take the Home Counties League. They secured the title in the penultimate round, when Andy House hammered 228 off 148 balls against Slough.

"It was one of those days when everything clicked," said House. "At the start of the season, we were thinking about just staying up. But we started winning a few games, and kept building momentum."

Swardeston, a Norfolk village with under 700 inhabitants, romped to the East Anglian League title for the fifth successive year, and beat Tunbridge Wells and Sandiacre in the NatWest Club Twenty20 final. They had the chance of an unprecedented treble when they reached the final of the Royal London 50-over Club Championship, but lost to South Northumberland. "I think it is pretty amazing what we are doing for a little club in Norfolk," said Swardeston captain Mark Thomas. "We see some of our players pushing into first-class cricket. Matthew Taylor, a young leg-spinner, and Lewis Denmark, a young batsman, have a lot to offer."

Two of the most competitive leagues had first-time winners: Berkswell won the Birmingham League, the oldest title of them all, and Leigh the Liverpool & District Competition. Berkswell completed their triumph after skittling 2015 champions Shrewsbury for 81, and trouncing them by nine wickets; Leigh beat Wallasey at home by the same margin to prompt jubilant scenes. Elsewhere, Colwyn Bay's Shrikant Mundhe became the first in the league to take ten wickets in a match, against Birkenhead Park.

In the Surrey Championship, the top two – Sunbury and Reigate Priory – met in a winner-takes-all final match. Andy Delmont's unbeaten 118 helped Reigate to 255 for four, then Sunbury reached 81 for three off 16.5 overs before rain came. In another 19 balls, Duckworth-Lewis would have been deployed, but there was no further play, and the draw favoured Sunbury.

It was even tighter in the Hertfordshire League: in the final round, Bishop's Stortford needed a maximum-points victory, and defeat for leaders Radlett, who were playing bottom club Botany Bay. Radlett did indeed lose, but rain deprived Bishop's Stortford of full bonus points, despite a comfortable win. They were left level with Radlett, who were crowned champions by virtue of having one more victory.

The Swalec League had a nailbiting conclusion, too. Leaders Newport knew victory against Port Talbot Town on the last Saturday would guarantee them the trophy, but lost by one wicket after making only 151. Cardiff had it in their hands. But, having totalled 190 against Neath, they could not take all ten wickets, and a draw was not enough – Newport edged it by two points.

Chester-le-Street won the North East League for the first time since 2010, while St Just won their eighth Cornwall League title since 2004. Hartley wrapped up their fifth Kent League crown in six years, while Roffey won the Sussex League for the third successive season. And 46-year-old Dan Goldstraw became the first Southern League player to reach 500 wickets, when he picked up two against Portsmouth in the first division.

Chris Aspin writes: Following year-long talks, the Lancashire League decided, for the first time since 1896, to admit new clubs for 2017. Darwen, a founder member of the Northern League, were invited, as were two from the Ribblesdale League: Clitheroe and Great Harwood. The decision met with some opposition, and Ramsbottom considered joining the new Greater Manchester competition before the members voted to stay. The expansion is part of the league executive's plan to establish two divisions of 12 teams. They need seven more, and have asked for applications from clubs within ten miles of the present boundary.

In 2016, Ramsbottom and Burnley dominated a disrupted league – with a record 50 rain-affected games – and both were in the running on a dramatic last day. A win would have been enough for Ramsbottom, but they slumped to 54 for eight chasing 79. The ninth wicket fell with the scores level, before an edged boundary by No. 11 Mark Dentith delivered victory, and their sixth trophy, off the penultimate ball. Burnley finished five points behind, though they did win the Worsley Cup for a record fourth year in a row, beating Haslingden in the final by six wickets. In the first round against Bacup, Burnley pro Chris Holt hit 103 and took seven for 25.

The two leading clubs also had the season's outstanding individuals. Ramsbottom's South African professional Daryn Smit headed the batting averages with 774 runs at 86, and took 69 wickets at eight each. For Burnley, Vishal Tripathi made 959 runs – the season's highest – including an unbeaten 140 against Church. His brother Bharat, the captain, was the league's leading amateur bowler with 51 wickets at just under ten. And former county batsman

David Brown amassed 758 runs, including 162 not out off 145 balls against Nelson; that innings, and Burnley's 321 for three, were club records. Against Bacup, Brown hit Matt Thompson for six sixes in one over, which also included a wide.

Shaun von Berg from Rishton took most wickets – 75 at nine – and hit 955 runs, but lacked support. Graham Knowles, the Haslingden opener who first played for the club in 1988, hit 112 in the home game against Bacup to record his 14th century, a league record. East Lancashire's Andries Gous, a rare wicketkeeping pro, made an unbeaten 141 off 99 balls against Enfield and put on 175 with Sharrukh Khan, the highest eighth-wicket partnership in Worsley Cup history. Russell Bradley, the Nelson keeper, completed six dismissals in the cup clash with Todmorden, matched by Rawtenstall's Nick Payne in a league game against Burnley.

In December, Moorhouse's brewery from Burnley developed a new beer in honour of Colne stalwart Peter Little, who had died earlier that month. The beer – called Chumpy, Little's nickname – was served at his wake, and proved so popular that local pubs expressed an interest in stocking it.

The Pennine League was a new two-tier competition, formed from 24 Central Lancashire and Saddleworth League clubs. After snow delayed the start, it proved a success, if ill-disciplined. During August, seven players were banned for a total of 25 matches, mostly because of umpire abuse. And on the last day of the Championship season, the game between Friarmere and Moorside was abandoned in the seventh over after a send-off escalated; one Friarmere player was banned for four matches, another for eight. "Umpires are leaving the game in droves," said former Test official and Pennine League president John Holder. "Before the start of the season, we talk to the captains, explaining what is required from them and their players, but we still get problems."

It was also a rain-hit season: 71 games were lost to weather, including Friarmere's game against Micklehurst, which ended after 31 overs when Jake Cauldwell, Micklehurst's opening bowler, slipped and was seriously injured. In the end, Walsden clinched the Premier League, just two points ahead of Saddleworth. They also won the Lees Wood Cup, beating Rochdale in the final by five runs; Umesh Karunaratne, the Walsden pro, took a five-for to help restrict the target to a gettable 188. He ended the season with 70 wickets at just under 12, topping the bowling averages, while Milnrow's Rudi Second, from Bloemfontein, was the stand-out batsman: he hit 1,072 runs at 76.

Heyside won the Championship to earn promotion. They scored 287 for six against Moorside, as professional Bilal Khiljee and Jon-Ross Campbell hit big hundreds, and shared a second-wicket stand of 199. Khiljee then took five for 16 to help dismiss Moorside for 167 and secure a 120-run victory. Heyside won by an even bigger margin when they piled up 305 for six against Oldham, then skittled them for 38.

Stayley also gained promotion. On the way, Pakistani fast bowler Hamza Nadeem took eight for 16 against Uppermill, including a hat-trick. Uppermill had more luck against Hollinwood: Girvacques de Jager, their South African overseas amateur, smashed 98 off 41 balls, including ten sixes and an over which yielded 34. In the cup fixture between the clubs, he hit 128 as Uppermill reached 377 for seven, and won by 102 runs.

Mel Whittle, the Peter Pan of league cricket, who in years gone by had invigorated the fortunes of Oldham and Crompton (see *Wisden 2011*, page 705 and *Wisden 2016*, page 782), joined struggling Hollinwood in mid-season to beef up their attack. At the age of 69, he picked up 12 wickets at 14, with a best of five for 48 against Micklehurst.

ECB PREMIER LEAGUE TABLES IN 2016

Birmingham & District League

		P	*W*	*L*	*Pts*
1	**Berkswell**	**22**	**14**	**1**	**363**
2	Kidderminster Victoria	22	13	5	312
3	Shrewsbury	22	10	7	276
4	Knowle & Dorridge	22	10	6	276
5	Kenilworth Wardens	22	6	6	264
6	Ombersley	22	9	7	257
7	Wolverhampton	22	8	7	246
8	Barnt Green	22	7	8	232
9	Walsall	22	6	10	227
10	West Bromwich Dartmouth	22	5	10	217
11	Walmley	22	5	12	177
12	Leamington	22	1	15	102

Bradford Premier League

		P	*W*	*L*	*Pts*
1	**Pudsey St Lawrence**	**22**	**14**	**5**	**295**
2	Hanging Heaton	22	13	5	291
3	Farsley	22	11	5	265
4	New Farnley	22	10	7	224
5	Woodlands	22	9	8	223
6	Cleckheaton	22	8	8	210
7	Bradford & Bingley	22	8	9	204
8	Pudsey Congs	22	7	10	201
9	Lightcliffe	22	5*	10	182
10	East Bierley	22	6	11	173
11	Morley	22	5*	11	164
12	Scholes	22	5	12	159

* *Plus one tie.*

Cheshire County League Premier Division

		P	*W*	*L*	*Pts*
1	**Alderley Edge**	**22**	**13**	**3**	**386**
2	Bowdon	22	12	4	361
3	Hyde	22	10	4	340
4	Chester Boughton Hall	22	10	4	331
5	Neston	22	7	8	275
6	Cheadle	22	8	7	274
7	Bramhall	22	6	6	266
8	Toft	22	5	7	249
9	Timperley	22	5	11	246
10	Macclesfield	22	4	7	246
11	Nantwich	22	5	10	242
12	Urmston	22	2	16	141

Cornwall Premier Division

		P	*W*	*L*	*Pts*
1	**St Just**	**18**	**12**	**3**	**278**
2	Truro	18	11	6	266
3	Penzance	18	11	5	247
4	Helston	18	9	7	228
5	St Austell	18	7*	7	210
6	Werrington	18	7	7	200
7	Falmouth	18	7	6	184
8	Grampound Road	18	5*	9	183
9	Redruth	18	5	8	172
10	Newquay	18	0	16	79

* *Plus one tie.*

Derbyshire Premier League

		P	*W*	*L*	*Pts*
1	**Swarkestone**	**22**	**12**	**2**	**391**
2	Ockbrook & Borrowash	22	10	5	358
3	Sandiacre Town	22	9	4	353
4	Spondon	22	7	6	301
5	Ticknall	22	8	4	293
6	Eckington	22	7	8	273
7	Rolleston	22	3	7	261
8	Denby	22	4	4	245
9	Cutthorpe	22	4	6	240
10	Chesterfield	22	3	7	238
11	Lullington Park	22	4	9	193
12	Quarndon	22	1	10	165

Devon League Premier Division

		P	*W*	*L*	*Pts*
1	**Sidmouth**	**18**	**13**	**3**	**288**
2	Exeter	18	11	4	255
3	Heathcoat	18	10	5	241
4	Exmouth	18	8	7	211
5	North Devon	18	7	8	207
6	Torquay	18	7	7	203
7	Bovey Tracey	18	7	8	193
8	Plymouth	18	6	9	181
9	Cornwood	18	5	9	169
10	Brixham	18	1	15	72

East Anglian Premier League

		P	W	L	Pts
1	**Swardeston**	**22**	**14**	**4**	**448**
2	Cambridge Granta	22	9	5	340
3	Copdock & Old Ipswichian	22	7	3	331
4	Norwich	22	10	7	325
5	Vauxhall Mallards	22	8	4	321
6	Frinton-on-Sea	22	6	7	285
7	Sudbury	22	6	10	280
8	Burwell	22	5	10	260
9	Bury St Edmunds	22	4	7	253
10	Great Witchingham	22	4	6	235
11	Horsford	22	4	8	230
12	Woolpit	22	3	9	207

Essex League Premier Division

		P	W	L	Pts
1	**Wanstead & Snaresbrook**	**18**	**13**	**3**	**308**
2	Brentwood	18	10	3	263
3	Chelmsford	18	9	6	235
4	Hornchurch	18	8	7	231
5	Shenfield	18	7	7	223
6	Colchester & East Essex	18	6	7	210
7	Ilford	18	7	7	199
8	Chingford	18	5	9	169
9	Buckhurst Hill	18	4	11	158
10	South Woodford	18	3	12	118

Hertfordshire League Premier Division

		P	W	L	Pts
1	**Radlett**	**18**	**11**	**3**	**382**
2	Bishop's Stortford	18	10	3	382
3	Welwyn Garden City	18	9	2	354
4	Harpenden	18	8	3	324
5	Hertford	18	7	8	293
6	Totteridge Millhillians	18	6	9	259
7	North Mymms	18	4	8	248
8	Potters Bar	18	5	8	243
9	Botany Bay	18	4	10	199
10	Sawbridgeworth	18	3	13	188

Home Counties Premier League Division One

		P	W	L	Pts
1	**Finchampstead**	**18**	**13**	**2**	**329**
2	Henley	18	11	2	294
3	High Wycombe	18	9	5	273
4	Banbury	18	9	3	264
5	Slough	18	6	4	244
6	Tring Park	18	6	7	213
7	Burnham	18	6	8	175
8	Great and Little Tew	18	4	9	175
9	Reading	18	2	13	143
10	Harefield	18	1	14	121

Kent League Premier Division

		P	W	L	Pts
1	**Hartley Country Club**	**18**	**13**	**3**	**269**
2	Blackheath	18	11	5	236
3	Tenterden	18	9	6	218
4	Bexley	18	9	7	201
5	Beckenham	18	8	8	198
6	Sevenoaks Vine	18	7	7	198
7	Lordswood	18	7	8	181
8	Tunbridge Wells	18	6	10	178
9	Bromley	18	5	10	168
10	Dartford	18	2	13	101

Leics and Rutland League Premier Division

		P	W	L	Pts
1	**Kibworth**	**22**	**12**	**2**	**415**
2	Loughborough Town	22	11	3	333
3	Lutterworth	22	7	4	321
4	Leicester Ivanhoe	22	6	7	311
5	Sileby Town	22	6	6	308
6	Syston Town	22	6	5	303
7	Barkby United	22	7	5	302
8	Barrow Town	22	5	5	278
9	Rothley Park	22	5	7	274
10	Market Harborough	22	5	7	259
11	Hinckley Town	22	4	10	224
12	Earl Shilton Town	22	0	13	143

Lincolnshire Cricket Board Premier League

		P	W	L	Pts
1	**Bracebridge Heath**	**22**	**7**	**2**	**286**
2	Grantham	22	10	3	261
3	Sleaford	22	4	5	258
4	Market Deeping	22	7	4	253
5	Lindum	22	10	5	250
6	Bourne	22	8	6	224
7	Louth	22	5	5	219
8	Woodhall Spa	22	4	5	215
9	Boston	22	4	6	206
10	Skegness	22	4	9	175
11	Nettleham	22	3	10	159
12	Grimsby Town	22	3	9	157

Liverpool & District Competition

		P	W	L	Pts
1	**Leigh**	**22**	**14**	**3**	**364**
2	Formby	22	12	4	345
3	Ormskirk	22	12	4	335
4	Northern	22	12	6	324
5	Bootle	22	11	5	320
6	Wallasey	22	8	10	259
7	New Brighton	22	7	10	254
8	Rainhill	22	8	9	246
9	Lytham	22	6	9	227
10	Colwyn Bay	22	6	11	215
11	Rainford	22	4	14	163
12	Birkenhead Park	22	3	18	143

Middlesex County League Division One

		P	W	L	Pts
1	**Teddington**	**18**	**12**	**2**	**137**
2	North Middlesex	18	11	6	126
3	Richmond	18	11	5	125
4	Southgate	18	9	8	111
5	Ealing	18	8	7	103
6	Hampstead	18	7	6	88
7	Stanmore	18	6	10	70
8	Shepherd's Bush	18	6	12	67
9	Twickenham	18	5	9	62
10	Eastcote	18	3	13	33

Northamptonshire League Premier Division

		P	W	L	Pts
1	**Old Northamptonians**	**22**	**15**	**0**	**370**
2	Peterborough Town	22	13	4	324
3	Finedon Dolben	22	13	4	321
4	Rushden Town	22	13	5	307
5	Rushton	22	12	4	304
6	Wollaston	22	8	7	230
7	Brixworth	22	5	12	191
8	Stony Stratford	22	3	11	189
9	Northampton Saints	22	3	12	182
10	Horton House	22	5	11	178
11	Oundle Town	22	3	10	151
12	Wellingborough Town	22	1	14	118

North East Premier Division

		P	W	L	Pts
1	**Felling**	**22**	**9**	**2**	**378**
2	Sacriston	22	10	0	374
3	Willington	22	9	5	341
4	Burnmoor	22	8	3	316
5	Boldon	22	8	6	302
6	Mainsforth	22	8	8	258
7	Brandon	22	5	8	241
8	Washington	22	6	8	224
9	Seaham Harbour	22	4	8	224
10	Sunderland	22	5	8	223
11	Blaydon	22	3	7	171
12	Tudhoe	22	1	13	143

Northern Premier League

		P	W	L	Pts
1	**Leyland**	**24**	**14**	**2**	**267**
2	Blackpool	24	14	3	256
3	Fleetwood	24	13*	6	245
4	Barrow	24	10	6	209
5	Chorley	24	9	8	205
6	Netherfield	24	9	8	193
7	Preston	24	8	12	171
8	Kendal	24	7	8	170
9	St Annes	24	7	12	159
10	Penrith	24	4	8	147
11	Darwen	24	6*	11	143
12	Morecambe	24	3	11	121
13	Lancaster	24	5	14	105

* *Plus one tie.*

N. Staffs and S. Cheshire League Premier Division

		P	W	L	Pts
1	**Porthill Park**	**22**	**9**	**1**	**304**
2	J & G Meakin	22	7	4	289
3	Stone	22	9	4	280
4	Longton	22	8	5	273
5	Checkley	22	9	7	272
6	Ashcombe Park	22	7	6	226
7	Betley	22	6	12	212
8	Leek	22	5	6	211
9	Hem Heath	22	5	9	197
10	Whitmore	22	4	7	193
11	Knypersley	22	4	7	181
12	Moddershall	22	3	8	181

North Wales League Premier Division

		P	W	L	Pts
1	**Llandudno**	**22**	**17**	**2**	**239**
2	Menai Bridge	22	14	5	208
3	Bangor	22	13	6	195
4	Connah's Quay	22	11	8	163
5	Denbigh	22	9	6	153
6	Mochdre	22	9	9	152
7	Gresford	22	8	10	147
8	Llanrwst	22	7	10	138
9	Hawarden Park	22	5	12	124
10	Brymbo	22	5	14	117
11	Pontblyddyn	22	5	12	114
12	Pwllheli	22	4	13	95

N. Yorkshire and S. Durham Premier Division

		P	W	L	Pts
1	**Barnard Castle**	**24**	**13**	**2**	**405**
2	Great Ayton	24	12	5	362
3	Marske	24	12	6	359
4	Darlington	24	10	4	350
5	Richmondshire	24	10	6	348
6	Seaton Carew	24	8	5	286
7	Middlesbrough	24	7	7	279
8	Guisborough	24	7	8	273
9	Hartlepool	24	5	13	238
10	Norton	24	4	8	235
11	Stokesley	24	4	12	220
12	Normanby Hall	24	4	11	220
13	Billingham Synthonia	24	4	13	204

Nottinghamshire Cricket Board Premier League

		P	W	L	Pts
1	**Cuckney**	**22**	**9**	**2**	**307**
2	Plumtree	22	10	4	293
3	West Indian Cavaliers	22	9	2	277
4	Notts CCC Academy	22	5	5	242
5	Mansfield Hosiery Mills	22	6	4	226
6	Kimberley Institute	22	3	7	224
7	Caythorpe	22	5	5	209
8	Clifton Village	22	5	8	207
9	Radcliffe-on-Trent	22	5	8	202
10	Hucknall	22	2	8	190
11	Welbeck	22	3	6	186
12	Ordsall Bridon	22	3	6	181

Southern Premier League

		P	W	L	Pts
1	**Havant**	**18**	**10**	**1**	**272**
2	Burridge	18	11	2	259
3	Bashley (Rydal)	18	8*	3	240
4	South Wilts	18	7	4	199
5	Lymington	18	6*	5	188
6	Alton	18	5	6	165
7	New Milton	18	6	8	174
8	St Cross Symondians	18	5	9	160
9	Hampshire Academy	18	3	10	145
10	Ventnor	18	1	14	84

* *Plus one tie.*

Surrey Championship Premier Division

		P	W	L	Pts
1	**Sunbury**	**18**	**13**	**1**	**303**
2	Reigate Priory	18	12	3	288
3	Weybridge	18	10	6	266
4	Wimbledon	18	10	6	238
5	Normandy	18	9	8	230
6	Ashtead	18	8	7	205
7	Guildford	18	6	11	171
8	East Molesey	18	5	11	159
9	Sutton	18	5	10	147
10	Beddington	18	1	16	72

Sussex League Premier Division

		P	W	L	Pts
1	**Roffey**	**19**	**14**	**2**	**445**
2	Cuckfield	19	12	3	426
3	Bexhill	19	10	5	368
4	Horsham	19	10	6	352
5	Hastings & St Leonards	19	9	7	328
6	East Grinstead	19	7	6	315
7	Preston Nomads	19	6	7	276
8	Brighton & Hove	19	6	10	241
9	Billingshurst	19	3	13	190
10	Sussex Development XI	10	1	6	190*
11	Worthing	19	1	14	129

* *Played only ten games; their points were obtained by multiplying by 1.9.*

Swalec Premier League Division One

		P	W	L	Pts
1	**Newport**	**18**	**7**	**1**	**251**
2	Cardiff	18	5	1	249
3	Port Talbot Town	18	6	3	224
4	Bridgend Town	18	3	3	203
5	Ammanford	18	5	6	199
6	Neath	18	5	0	190
7	Pontarddulais	18	4	6	175
8	Mumbles	18	4	8	174
9	Ynysygerwn	18	2	7	140
10	Swansea	18	2	8	135

West of England Premier League

		P	W	L	Pts
1	**Bath**	**18**	**9†**	**3**	**277**
2	Frocester	18	11*	3	267
3	Corsham	18	8*	6	232
4	Potterne	18	8	6	216
5	Bristol	18	8	7	211
6	Bridgwater	18	8	8	210
7	Downend	18	7	8	202
8	Clevedon	18	5	9	200
9	Taunton St Andrews	18	6	9	196
10	Taunton	18	2	13	145

* *Plus one tie.*
† *Plus two ties.*

Yorkshire League North

		P	W	L	Pts
1	**Harrogate**	**22**	**14**	**3**	**162**
2	York	22	13	4	154
3	Yorkshire Academy	22	9	3	143
4	Sheriff Hutton Bridge	22	7	5	118
5	Driffield Town	22	7	7	109
6	Woodhouse Grange	22	4	5	100
7	Acomb	22	6	6	97
8	Stamford Bridge	22	5	6	97
9	Hull	22	5	7	96
10	Scarborough	22	4	9	77
11	Castleford	22	3	10	60
12	Dunnington	22	1	13	37

Yorkshire League South

		P	W	L	Pts
1	**Wakefield Thornes**	**22**	**16***	**2**	**216**
2	Appleby Frodingham	22	11*	5	164
3	Whitley Hall	22	11	8	150
4	Wickersley Old Village	22	10	6	150
5	Sheffield Collegiate	22	9	5	144
6	Cleethorpes	22	8	7	126
7	Aston Hall	22	7	8	122
8	Barnsley	22	8	9	122
9	Sheffield & Phoenix Utd	22	6	9	108
10	Treeton	22	6	9	104
11	Doncaster Town	22	5	13	90
12	Rotherham Town	22	1	17	36

The following leagues do not have ECB Premier League status:

LANCASHIRE LEAGUE TABLES IN 2016

Lancashire League

		P	*W*	*L*	*Pts*
1	**Ramsbottom**	**26**	**16**	**1**	**222**
2	Burnley	26	17	3	217
3	Lowerhouse	26	11*	7	164
4	Nelson	26	11*	8	162
5	Haslingden	26	9	7	153
6	Todmorden	26	11	8	152
7	East Lancashire	26	8*	7	148
8	Church	26	10	10	142
9	Enfield	26	7	10	128
10	Rishton	26	6*	13	123
11	Accrington	26	7	13	121
12	Colne	26	7	15	121
13	Rawtenstall	26	6	12	104
14	Bacup	26	4	16	79

* *Plus one tie.*

Pennine Cricket League – Premiership

		P	*W*	*L*	*Pts*
1	**Walsden**	**22**	**13**	**2**	**76**
2	Saddleworth	22	13	2	74
3	Littleborough	22	11	3	66
4	Norden	22	9	4	60
5	Crompton	22	8	4	56
6	Rochdale	22	8	5	55
7	Greenfield	22	8	7	52
8	Glodwick	22	7	8	47
9	Austerlands	22	7	7	47
10	Monton & Weaste	22	6	8	44
11	Royton	22	5	6	41
12	Middleton	22	2	12	21

OTHER LEAGUE WINNERS IN 2016

Airedale & Wharfedale	Beckwithshaw
Bolton League	Farnworth
Cambs & Hunts	Eaton Socon
Greater Manchester League	Egerton
Huddersfield	Delph & Dobcross
NEPL Division One	Felling
Norfolk Alliance	Brooke
North Essex	Frinton
North Lancs & Cumbria	Workington
Northumberland & Tyneside Senior	Ashington
Pembrokeshire	Haverfordwest
Quaid-e-Azam	Keighley RZM
Ribblesdale	Clitheroe
Shropshire	Sentinel
South Wales Association	Ammanford
Thames Valley	Kew
Two Counties	Mildenhall
Warwickshire	Bedworth
Worcestershire	Worcester Nomads
York Senior	Clifton Alliance

ECB CITY CUP IN 2016

JAMES GINGELL

The former Almanack editor Scyld Berry launched the Wisden City Cup in 2009, with the goal of reviving cricket in Britain's inner cities. "Where it differed from other projects," he wrote in the 2010 edition, "was that it offered a fast-track opportunity to the top." Since then the competition has twice changed its name, most recently to the ECB City Cup – suggesting that the tournament is taken seriously by the Establishment. David Graveney, then the national performance manager, certainly held an interest: he watched semi-finals day at Dunstable.

One who caught his eye was a 19-year-old slow-left armer playing for Luton. Shaan Ahmedzai came to England from Afghanistan in 2011, and is a member of Monty Panesar's old club, Luton Town & Indians; the pair trained and played together in 2015 while Panesar sought to reboot his career. Despite a superb all-round performance, Ahmedzai wasn't able to drag Luton through. South London needed one off the last ball to tie and progress by virtue of losing fewer wickets, and they made it thanks to a missed throw – when there was time to walk the ball to the stumps.

Manchester won the final at Grace Road, making up for their runners-up disappointment in 2015. On the same day, Ahmedzai was turning heads in the indoor school, where the Club Cricket Conference were running a trial to identify spinners not affiliated with first-class clubs. Previous finds have included Imran Qayyum, who now has a contract with Kent. In 2016, the former Kent and England left-armer Min Patel picked Ahmedzai among his top three, who were due to travel to Mumbai in March for a coaching clinic at the Global Cricket School. He was also invited to net with Northamptonshire in December and is applying to university – "hopefully Bradford, or somewhere I can play good cricket" – to study computer science.

Ahmedzai's story is a qualified success: he is an exceptional case, and has a long way to go to reach the top. Yet the opportunity he has been given is validation of the ECB City Cup's existence. Gulfraz Riaz, the development manager for the Club Cricket Conference, rams this message home. "There is not a chance in hell of an Academy director being brave enough to go to his CEO and say: 'Listen, I've just seen this 19-year-old Asian lad in the parks – I think we should sign him up.' The first thing they would say back is, 'How have you missed him? I pay you 50 grand a year!'"

FINAL

At Leicester, September 18. **Manchester won by 64 runs.** ‡**Manchester 155-9** (20 overs) (Agha Mustafa Durrani 56, Gurman Bains 36; Ihsaan Syed-Hussain 4-27); **South London 91** (15.4 overs) (Ejaz Din 3-28). *Manchester's openers thrashed 83 from ten overs, before three run-outs, plus four wickets for Ihsaan Syed-Hussain, put the brakes on; only one other batsman made double figures. South London's chase looked feasible, but Ejaz Din made things tricky, and teenage spin pair Bilal Tariq and Adam Masood shared 3-42 to send the cup north.*

ROYAL LONDON CLUB CHAMPIONSHIP AND NATWEST CLUB T20 IN 2016

PAUL EDWARDS

An old order reasserted itself in 2016: the finals of the Royal London Club Championship and the NatWest Club T20 featured clubs well used to such occasions. Swardeston even managed to reach both and, after Joe Gatting took three for none to finish the T20 final, added a cup to their East Anglia Premier League title. South Northumberland denied them a treble, and became the third club to win the national club championship – in its 48th year – on three separate occasions.

Despite the familiarity of the winners, much progress was made by sides that had not entered the 45-over competition for some years. Weybridge were the prime example, defeating Blackheath, the 2015 champions, and Havant, before losing to Swardeston by one run in the semi-final. The willingness of clubs to re-engage is to be applauded. Many teams enter knowing they will probably survive only a round or two; they do so to blood youngsters, some of whom may not be available on Saturdays but can gain valuable senior experience filling in for team-mates whose family commitments prevent them playing two games each weekend. The best players also get an opportunity to test themselves against unfamiliar opponents on different grounds.

Good weather helped with organisation in 2016: there were very few wet Sundays, and so little disruption to packed fixture lists. "Cricket is an easy game to administer when the sun's shining," said the ECB's Aaron Campbell. The ECB are reviewing all their competitions, and it is possible that the Twenty20 tournament – which has been open to clubs from 32 leagues – may be expanded. However, Campbell insists this will not detract from the well-established longer-form competition: "The teams that take part treat it with the greatest respect."

ROYAL LONDON CLUB CHAMPIONSHIP FINAL

SOUTH NORTHUMBERLAND v SWARDESTON

At Northampton, September 18. South Northumberland won by 75 runs. Toss: South Northumberland.

Swardeston needed 160 to become the first club to win both national knockout competitions in the same year, but were wrecked by high-class bowling. In the second over of the chase, they were eight for three, and thoughts of recovery were snuffed out by David Rutherford – who finished with four wickets – and off-spinner Lee Crozier; only two Swardeston players made double figures. Former Australia Test player Marcus North, who captained South Northumberland, paid tribute to his attack as he collected the cup. Such pleasures had seemed unlikely at the halfway point. North had offered glimpses of his pedigree in making a fluent 41, and adding 72 for the third wicket with Adam Heather, but leg-spinner Matt Taylor, with four for 28, chipped away at the middle order to leave a modest target. Still, South Northumberland roared back, and gained some measure of revenge for their defeat by Swardeston in the final of the 2010 Twenty20 tournament.

Man of the Match: D. J. Rutherford.

South Northumberland

†R. Peyton c Gatting b Eccles	1	D. J. Rutherford c Oxley b Eccles	14
A. T. Heather run out	30	J. R. Wightman run out	12
J. D. Craigs b Eccles	0	L. J. Crozier not out	0
*M. J. North c J. G. Taylor b Thomas	41	B 4, lb 1, w 5, nb 2	12
J. A. Graham lbw b M. Taylor	21		
J. N. Miller c Gatting b M. Taylor	1	1/1 (1) 2/1 (3) 3/73 (4) (44.5 overs)	159
S. Humble lbw b M. Taylor	14	4/84 (2) 5/89 (6) 6/118 (7)	
M. A. Craigs b M. Taylor	13	7/119 (5) 8/135 (8) 9/156 (9) 10/159 (10)	

Oxley 7–1–31–0; Eccles 8.5–2–26–3; Gatting 5–1–18–0; Thomas 8–1–25–1; M. Taylor 9–0–28–4; Walker 7–0–26–0.

Swardeston

P. A. Lambert c M. A. Craigs b Humble	0	*M. W. Thomas not out	13
J. G. Taylor lbw b Humble	8	M. P. Eccles c North b Rutherford	8
†S. K. Gray lbw b Wightman	5	T. R. S. Oxley c M. A. Craigs b Rutherford	0
J. S. Gatting b Wightman	0	Lb 1, w 6, nb 2	9
L. R. K. Denmark c North b Rutherford	34		
J. D. Reynolds b Rutherford	4	1/0 (1) 2/8 (3) 3/8 (4) (23.4 overs)	84
M. Taylor b Crozier	3	4/30 (2) 5/44 (6) 6/61 (7)	
G. W. Walker lbw b Crozier	0	7/61 (8) 8/63 (5) 9/73 (10) 10/84 (11)	

Humble 6–3–10–2; Wightman 5–0–32–2; Rutherford 6.4–0–17–4; Crozier 6–1–24–2.

Umpires: J. R. Tomsett and N. H. Wheatley.

WINNERS 2005–2016

2005	Horsham	2011	Shrewsbury
2006	South Northumberland	2012	York
2007	Bromley	2013	West Indian Cavaliers
2008	Kibworth	2014	Sandiacre Town
2009	Chester-le-Street	2015	Blackheath
2010	South Northumberland	2016	South Northumberland

A full list of winners 1969 to 2004 appears in Wisden 2005, page 941.

NATWEST CLUB T20

First semi-final At Derby, September 6. **Sandiacre Town won by eight wickets. ‡Bramhall 156-4** (20 overs) (A. West 42); **Sandiacre Town 160-2** (18 overs) (D. J. Birch 73, J. Chapman 45).

Second semi-final At Derby, September 6. **Swardeston won by 23 runs. Swardeston 167-9** (18 overs) (L. R. K. Denmark 39; F. A. W. Florey 4-26, P. Sadler 3-39); **‡Tunbridge Wells 144** (19.5 overs) (M. W. Thomas 3-21).

Final At Derby, September 6. **Swardeston won by 65 runs. Swardeston 148-5** (20 overs) (L. R. K. Denmark 69*); **‡Sandiacre Town 83** (16.1 overs) (J. S. Gatting 3-0).

WINNERS

2008	South Northumberland	2013	Wimbledon
2009	Bournemouth	2014	Chester Boughton Hall
2010	Swardeston	2015	Ealing
2011	Ealing	2016	Swardeston
2012	Wimbledon		

DAVIDSTOW VILLAGE CUP IN 2016

BENJ MOOREHEAD

The question of what qualifies as a village has vexed *The Cricketer* – long-time tournament organisers – for many years. In 2000, a Bristol court upheld the decision to expel Usk Cricket Club from the competition. Usk's population was only just over 2,000, but it did not *look* like a village: it had a town council, a mayor, a prison and a dozen or so pubs.

Usk may now be welcomed with open arms. For most of its life the competition had drawn close to 1,000 clubs from across the UK. But, as former villages have surrendered to urban sprawl, there has been a rapid decline. This is a busier generation of cricketers, too, and fitting in a 40-over Sunday cup alongside a Saturday league is demanding.

A season in which just 286 clubs signed up for the Village Cup led to radical changes, announced in October. The population threshold for any village wishing to participate was doubled from 5,000 to 10,000. Just as daringly, the requirement that it is "surrounded on all sides by open countryside" – enshrined in the constitution since the first National Village Championship in 1972 – was erased. Traditionalists may wonder if the competition has become the Market Town Cup in all but name, though the organisers would argue they had little choice but to cast the net wider. The Village Cup depends on a headline sponsor, which in turn requires a competition with a profile; Davidstow Cheddar's four-year deal ended after the 2016 final, replaced by Gunn & Moore.

Times may have changed, but the attraction of the tournament – an adventure into the unknown, with the lure of a Lord's final – still burns brightly. Miskin Manor (Glamorgan) battled through successive matches by one wicket, five runs and two runs, to meet Sibton Park (Kent) in the semi-finals. Sibton had themselves squeezed through, by one run against 2012 champions Reed, and by six in the quarter-final against Dinton, for whom Darren Gough's 18-year-old son Brennan opened the batting. Miskin brought 300 fans from South Wales to Kent, but it was Sibton who progressed from another gripping encounter, winning by nine runs after an outstanding catch on the long-on boundary turned the match. Vintage village fare.

By contrast, Sessay (North Yorkshire), champions in 2010, bulldozed their way through the top half of the draw, despite six of their seven games being on the road. They had a 550-mile round trip to Pembrokeshire for the semi-final against Carew, but it was worth it: playing in front of 600 spectators, and enjoying teas at £1 each, they won by seven wickets.

The final was a mixed occasion for Sibton's Ben Allon, easily the outstanding player of 2016. A bruiser of an all-rounder, he topped the batting and bowling charts (with 377 runs and 21 wickets), but his medium-pacers were a feast for the Sessay batsmen in the final, who set up a rout with a record score. A brilliant counter-attacking half-century gave Allon at least a memory to take back to Kent, if not the trophy.

FINAL

SESSAY v SIBTON PARK

At Lord's, September 4. Sessay won by 119 runs. Toss: Sessay.

Simon Mason, owner of a gardening shop in Thirsk, hit 138 – the highest score in Village Cup finals – as Sessay romped to their second trophy in seven summers. Viv Richards had made the same score during the 1979 World Cup final at Lord's, but needed 157 balls to Mason's 110. On a green-tinged pitch, Sessay had bravely chosen to bat and, though the openers fell cheaply, Mason was quickly into his stride, swatting the first of the match's 15 sixes. He repeated the shot to go to his hundred, and added 156 in less than 19 overs with Nick Harrison, whose fifty was a mixture of deft touches and punishing drives. Jacob Spencer then led a frenzied assault as 140 came from the last ten, and Sessay ran up the highest total in a Village final. Sibton's trials were summed up by 17-year-old Harry Wren, whose first two deliveries cost ten wides. And when their chase slipped from 51 for one to 55 for five, the trophy was heading to Yorkshire, for the tenth time. The last rites were delayed by Ben Allon, whose nine overs had gone for 83, but hit four sixes in a row, and seven in all.

Man of the Match: S. R. Mason.

Sessay

*M. Wilkie b Lewis	9
M. C. Till b Lewis	16
S. R. Mason b Allon	138
N. J. Harrison c Bishop c Murrell	69
J. K. Spencer not out	48
N. J. Thorne run out	1
T. A. Hall not out	1
B 2, lb 3, w 20	25
1/16 (1) 2/73 (2) 3/229 (4) 4/265 (3) 5/272 (6) (5 wkts, 40 overs)	307

†C. J. Till, L. Carver, S. M. Peirse and S. J. Langstaff did not bat.

Rowe 9–1–54–0; Lewis 9–1–37–2; Allon 9–1–83–1; Dunham 4–0–35–0; Murrell 8–0–80–1; H. J. Wren 1–0–13–0.

Sibton Park

T. C. Bishop c Harrison b Peirse	25
G. P. Bingham lbw b Peirse	11
T. R. Dunham c Harrison b Peirse	9
B. J. Allon c and b M. C. Till	70
†S. R. R. Hickmott b Wilkie	0
H. J. Wren b Wilkie	2
J. C. Woodward b Langstaff	19
M. S. Wren c Peirse b M. C. Till	20
*S. W. Rowe c Spencer b Carver	14
S. Murrell lbw b M. C. Till	0
T. D. Lewis not out	1
Lb 2, w 15	17
1/23 (2) 2/51 (3) 3/52 (1) 4/53 (5) 5/55 (6) 6/127 (7) 7/154 (4) 8/176 (8) 9/177 (10) 10/188 (9) (36.5 overs)	188

Peirse 9–1–21–3; Hall 5–0–37–0; Wilkie 4–0–31–2; Carver 5.5–1–45–1; Langstaff 9–0–36–1; M. C. Till 4–0–16–3.

Umpires: Rev. Canon S. Jones and K. Saunders.

RECENT WINNERS

2000	Elvaston (Derbyshire)
2001	Ynystawe (Glamorgan)
2002	Shipton-under-Wychwood (Oxfordshire)
2003	Shipton-under-Wychwood (Oxfordshire)
2004	Sully Centurions (Glamorgan)
2005	Sheriff Hutton Bridge (Yorkshire)
2006	Houghton Main (Yorkshire)
2007	Woodhouse Grange (Yorkshire)
2008	Valley End (Surrey)
2009	Glynde & Beddingham (Sussex)
2010	Sessay (Yorkshire)
2011	Woodhouses (Lancashire)
2012	Reed (Hertfordshire)
2013	Cleator (Cumberland)
2014	Woodhouse Grange (Yorkshire)
2015	Woodhouse Grange (Yorkshire)
2016	Sessay (Yorkshire)

A list of winners from the start of the competition in 1972 appears in Wisden 2005, *page 944*.

DISABILITY CRICKET IN 2016

PAUL EDWARDS

At the England team awards in May, a photo was taken of three cricketers holding their prizes: Joe Root and Anya Shrubsole were joined by Callum Flynn, the Disability Cricketer of the Year, epitomising the inclusive ethos the ECB had been so concerned to promote. In 2015, Flynn had helped the physical disability team win a five-team tournament in Bangladesh – which only underlined how difficult it was to follow that success in 2016.

England's Deaf side had been to Dubai to play in a quadrangular competition in March and, in the final, lost to Pakistan, whom they had beaten in the group stages. In October, England's Physical Disability team also travelled to Dubai, also reached the final (though this time it was a tri-series), and also lost to Pakistan. During the match, Liam Thomas dived to prevent a boundary in the outfield and, though the impact of the fall detached his prosthetic leg, he managed to return the ball before attending to repairs. The clip of Thomas's no-nonsense reaction went viral. "That incident gave the disabled game a global presence it didn't necessarily have before," said Ian Martin, the ECB's

Chris Whiteoak/ECB

Standing tall: Callum Flynn climbs into a cut shot.

head of disability cricket. "It took a mishap for that to come about, but you have to appreciate such publicity while you can."

There is always more work to do in disability cricket. The fact that each country assesses eligibility slightly differently has long needed addressing. The impartial investigation undertaken by sports scientist Emma Foden should help; she aims to establish a classification system which will apply to all five nations playing disabled cricket.

In the autumn David Gavrilovic received an ECB Outstanding Service to Cricket Award for his tireless work on behalf of the blind game over many years. Gavrilovic, who is also the vice-chairman of British Blind Sport, is the second chairman of Blind Cricket in England and Wales to earn the award, following his late predecessor Dave Townley. "As much as I love playing cricket," said Gavrilovic, "I also get a great sense of pride and satisfaction from being able to organise events and competitions that enable so many blind and partially sighted cricketers of any age to take part in this great sport. Receiving this award is the second proudest moment in my career, only surpassed by playing for England."

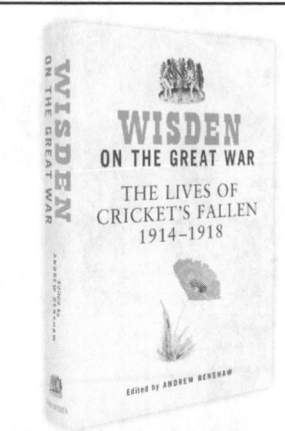

ENGLAND UNDER-19 v SRI LANKA UNDER-19 IN 2016

JAMES GINGELL

Under-19 Tests (2): England 0, Sri Lanka 1
Under-19 one-day internationals (3): England 0, Sri Lanka 3

When Sri Lanka's senior team came to England in May, they looked as callow as they were cold, and returned home winless. Their juniors arrived in July, and seemed determined to restore national pride. It took them a while to warm up – they followed on in the rain-affected draw at Cambridge – but they dominated after that, winning all the remaining matches.

Captain Charith Asalanka led with authority and hit three fifties, but he was outshone by two of his charges. Lahiru Kumara, a strapping seamer from Kandy, bowled quicker than any Sri Lankan all summer, with a sharp indipper to boot. At Northampton, he provided a match-winning burst, and by the end of the year he was touring southern Africa with the Test team, castling Hashim Amla and earning nicks from Quinton de Kock.

Avishka Fernando, whose 95 had helped see off England in the quarter-finals of the Under-19 World Cup in February, was a man apart in the one-day series. He smashed two hundreds from the top of the order, and impressed the national selectors enough to earn an ODI debut against Australia later in the year – despite not having played a single senior match.

Much was made of England's first loss at home in youth Tests since 2010, also against Sri Lanka. Yet the natural churn of players and the scarcity of matches – there had been only five at home, all drawn, between those two defeats – means each cohort deserve their own assessment, independent of the recent past. That said, this lot looked a little green. They were without a host of eligible players: Jack Burnham (Durham) – the top run-scorer at the World Cup – Sam Curran (Surrey), George Garton (Sussex) and Dan Lawrence (Essex) had all graduated to county first teams, while Matt Fisher (Yorkshire), the speediest young gun around, was injured.

Fourteen were given their youth international debuts. By comparison, Sri Lanka, who had recently played South Africa in three Tests (all drawn) and three 50-over games (all won), blooded just one. Olly Westbury, the Worcestershire Academy opener who signed a professional contract later in the year, gave England's most eye-catching performance: in the First Test he hit 196, and shared a massive stand with the match's other centurion, Somerset's George Bartlett.

Six of England's squad made first-class debuts during the summer, including George Hankins of Gloucestershire, who did most to threaten Sri Lanka's run in the one-day series. Aaron Beard, the Essex seamer, was another: he had already claimed four for 62 in his first first-class innings, against the senior Sri Lankans in May. But he took the same number in two Tests and two one-dayers against the Under-19s, which rather summed things up.

SQUADS

England *M. D. E. Holden (Middlesex), E. Barnes (Yorkshire), G. A. Bartlett (Somerset), A. P. Beard (Essex), D. M. Bess (Somerset), J. M. Blatherwick (Nottinghamshire), H. C. Brook (Yorkshire), J. Coughlin (Durham), J. J. Dell (Worcestershire), B. G. F. Green (Somerset), G. T. Hankins (Gloucestershire), J. I. McCoy (Hampshire), Z. A. Malik (Worcestershire), T. J. Moores (Nottinghamshire), G. D. Panayi (Warwickshire), O. J. D. Pope (Surrey), J. C. Tongue (Worcestershire), B. J. Twohig (Yorkshire), G. S. Virdi (Surrey), O. E. Westbury (Worcestershire). *Coach:* A. Hurry.

Sri Lanka *K. I. C. Asalanka, S. Ashan, K. N. A. Bandara, J. K. Z. Daniel, P. W. H. de Silva, T. R. Dilshan, W. I. A. Fernando, D. M. Jayalath, P. A. K. P. Jayawickrama, C. B. R. L. S. Kumara, V. N. G. N. K. Nirmal, P. Nissanka, T. L. H. W. N. K. Prasan, B. A. D. N. Silva, M. Silva. *Coach:* R. L. Dias.

ENGLAND v SRI LANKA

First Under-19 Test Match

At Cambridge, July 26–29. Drawn. Toss: England Under-19.

Olly Westbury hit 196, but the weather prevented England taking advantage of an imposing first innings. An opener from Dudley and the classical school of crease occupation, Westbury batted throughout the first day, and put on 231 with George Bartlett, who made his own century in zippier time. Next day, Surrey keeper Ollie Pope propelled England to 500 with a smart 78, but rain delayed the declaration until tea, and returned periodically. Off-spinner Amar Virdi, also of Surrey, took five to force Sri Lanka to follow on, 165 behind, though by then the game was into the last day. Dilan Jayalath and captain Charith Asalanka, who passed 50 for the second time in the match, put on 112 for the second wicket to douse dim hopes of a result, and the deficit was cleared for the loss of only three.

Close of play: first day, England Under-19 355-4 (Westbury 157, Pope 10); second day, Sri Lanka Under-19 96-2 (Asalanka 55, Fernando 13); third day, Sri Lanka Under-19 235-6 (Bandara 21, Daniel 1).

England Under-19

O. E. Westbury c Fernando b Silva	196
*M. D. E. Holden b Kumara	5
G. T. Hankins c Nissanka b Ashan	28
G. A. Bartlett c Asalanka b Kumara	131
J. J. Dell b Daniel	1
†O. J. D. Pope c Kumara b Daniel	78
J. Coughlin c Fernando b Daniel	14
E. Barnes not out	5
A. P. Beard run out	7
G. D. Panayi run out	2
B 6, lb 10, w 13, nb 4	33
1/20 (2) (9 wkts dec, 131 overs)	500

2/85 (3) 3/316 (4) 4/327 (5) 5/453 (1) 6/481 (6) 7/484 (7) 8/492 (9) 9/500 (10)

G. S. Virdi did not bat.

Kumara 35–5–104–2; Dilshan 21–0–89–0; Daniel 23–4–91–3; Silva 36–0–136–1; Ashan 6–0–21–1; Asalanka 6–0–29–0; Bandara 4–0–14–0.

Sri Lanka Under-19

P. Nissanka c Pope b Panayi	5	– c Pope b Beard	8
D. M. Jayalath c Panayi b Virdi	22	– not out	77
*K. I. C. Asalanka c Bartlett b Barnes	81	– c Pope b Panayi	70
W. I. A. Fernando c Hankins b Coughlin	45	– lbw b Panayi	12
S. Ashan c Pope b Virdi	51	– not out	9
K. N. A. Bandara c Holden b Beard	21		
†V. N. G. N. K. Nirmal c Pope b Coughlin	3		
J. K. Z. Daniel c Beard b Virdi	62		
B. A. D. N. Silva c Holden b Virdi	33		
C. B. R. L. S. Kumara b Virdi	3		
T. R. Dilshan not out	1		
B 4, lb 3, w 1	8	B 5, lb 1	6
1/7 (1) 2/52 (2) 3/131 (3) 4/173 (4) 5/223 (5) 6/228 (7) 7/235 (6) 8/325 (9) 9/332 (8) 10/335 (10) (104 overs)	335	1/26 (1) 2/138 (3) 3/152 (4) (3 wkts, 39 overs)	182

Beard 21–7–59–1; Panayi 15–2–59–1; Coughlin 21–7–45–2; Barnes 19–1–83–1; Virdi 26–4–77–5; Holden 2–0–5–0. *Second innings*—Beard 4–1–12–1; Panayi 10–0–62–2; Barnes 3–0–30–0; Virdi 15–3–33–0; Holden 7–0–39–0.

Umpires: J. W. Lloyds and S. J. O'Shaughnessy.

ENGLAND v SRI LANKA

Second Under-19 Test Match

At Northampton, August 3–6. Sri Lanka won by seven wickets. Toss: Sri Lanka.

Lahiru Kumara had taken time to adapt to English conditions. He left Fenner's with just two wickets and, on the first morning here, bowled ten overs in two spells for no reward, as England cantered to 91 without loss. By the end of his third spell, though, he had five victims – including two hooking to long leg – on his way to seven in the innings, and 11 in the match; both were bests for Sri Lanka in Under-19 Tests. England captain Max Holden watched the afternoon carnage from the other end. He was on 44 as the first wicket fell, yet made his hundred only during a last-wicket stand of 48; he carried his bat for 111 out of 208. Next day, Sri Lanka looked to be squandering their advantage when the English seamers, led by George Panayi, reduced them to 153 for six. But Vithanage Nirmal hit 80 not out, putting on 95 with Jehan Daniel, and dragging the lead up to 99. Kumara bowled Holden before the close, and England could muster a target of only 94 on the third day. It was swallowed up in the 11th over, Asalanka leading the charge with 40 off 18 balls.

Close of play: first day, Sri Lanka Under-19 48-1 (Fernando 10, Asalanka 20); second day, England Under-19 24-1 (Westbury 18, Hankins 0).

England Under-19

O. E. Westbury lbw b Kumara	45	– run out	41
*M. D. E. Holden not out	111	– b Kumara	1
G. T. Hankins c Jayawickrama b Kumara	0	– lbw b Jayawickrama	20
G. A. Bartlett c Jayawickrama b Kumara	1	– c Jayalath b Kumara	26
J. J. Dell lbw b Kumara	0	– c Jayalath b Jayawickrama	0
†O. J. D. Pope c Nirmal b Kumara	0	– lbw b Jayawickrama	23
J. I. McCoy lbw b de Silva	0	– b Kumara	0
E. Barnes b Kumara	16	– not out	18
A. P. Beard b Prasan	9	– c Kumara b Asalanka	26
G. D. Panayi b Kumara	2	– c Fernando b Asalanka	0
G. S. Virdi c Prasan b Daniel	16	– c Nirmal b Kumara	5
B 5, lb 1, w 1, nb 1	8	B 22, lb 9, w 1	32
1/91 (1) 2/93 (3) 3/97 (4) 4/98 (5) 5/102 (6) 6/107 (7) 7/124 (8) 8/140 (9) 9/160 (10) 10/208 (11) (82.2 overs)	208	1/19 (2) 2/83 (3) 3/89 (1) 4/89 (5) 5/125 (4) 6/137 (7) 7/137 (6) 8/185 (9) 9/185 (10) 10/192 (11) (66.4 overs)	192

Kumara 28–5–82–7; Prasan 15–4–33–1; Daniel 11.2–3–27–1; Jayawickrama 17–3–29–0; Ashan 4–0–18–0; de Silva 4–1–6–1; Asalanka 3–0–7–0. *Second innings*—Kumara 21.4–4–52–4; Prasan 14–5–37–0; de Silva 6–1–14–0; Daniel 4–1–8–0; Jayawickrama 18–8–38–3; Ashan 1–0–8–0; Asalanka 2–0–4–2.

Sri Lanka Under-19

D. M. Jayalath c Pope b Panayi	9	– c Bartlett b Barnes	9
W. I. A. Fernando c Hankins b Barnes	49	– lbw b Panayi	20
*K. I. C. Asalanka c and b Panayi	33	– c Bartlett b Panayi	40
P. W. H. de Silva c Pope b Beard	5	– not out	20
S. Ashan b Panayi	0	– not out	1
K. N. A. Bandara c Hankins b Barnes	25		
†V. N. G. N. K. Nirmal not out	80		
J. K. Z. Daniel c Hankins b Virdi	52		
T. L. H. W. N. K. Prasan c Virdi b Holden	20		
C. B. R. L. S. Kumara c Hankins b Beard	4		
P. A. K. P. Jayawickrama c Virdi b Barnes	8		
B 9, lb 13	22	B 1, w 2, nb 1	4
1/13 (1) 2/73 (3) 3/78 (4) 4/79 (5) 5/130 (2) 6/153 (6) 7/248 (8) 8/285 (9) 9/292 (10) 10/307 (11) (84 overs)	307	1/30 (1) 2/34 (2) 3/77 (3) (3 wkts, 10.2 overs)	94

Beard 18–1–78–2; Panayi 14–2–51–3; Virdi 21–4–69–1; Barnes 13–2–38–3; McCoy 9–1–35–0; Holden 9–3–14–1. *Second innings*—Beard 2–0–17–0; Barnes 3–0–21–1; Panayi 3.2–0–25–2; Virdi 1–0–18–0; McCoy 1–0–12–0.

Umpires: N. G. B. Cook and P. J. Hartley.

First Under-19 one-day international At Wormsley, August 10. **Sri Lanka won by 108 runs.** ‡**Sri Lanka 257-7** (50 overs) (K. I. C. Asalanka 70, S. Ashan 60*); **England 149** (40.3 overs) (B. A. D. N. Silva 3-28). *Chasing 258, England survived the threat of the pacy Kumara, though his five overs cost just nine. But from 96-2 they collapsed against the spinners, who shared seven wickets. Asalanka picked up two with his off-breaks, having earlier hit a patient 70, to set up a late charge from Shammu Ashan.*

Second Under-19 one-day international At Chelmsford, August 13. **Sri Lanka won by one wicket.** ‡**England 315-8** (50 overs) (T. J. Moores 70, G. T. Hankins 98, G. A Bartlett 85; C. B. R. L. S. Kumara 4-56); **Sri Lanka 318-9** (49.1 overs) (W. I. A. Fernando 117, S. Ashan 77*; B. G. F. Green 3-77). *Three Millfield old boys reached 70 to help England set 316, but while George Hankins just missed a hundred – middling a cut to point – Avishka Fernando made no such mistake during the chase. He stormed to 117 in 96 balls as Sri Lanka reached 229-3 in the 36th over. A direct hit from Dom Bess, England's most economical bowler for the second game in a row, ended Fernando's fireworks and, after two more run-outs, Sri Lanka were nine down and two short of victory. But Ashan drove the first ball of the last over through the covers to seal the series.*

Third Under-19 one-day international At Canterbury, August 16 (day/night). **Sri Lanka won by 24 runs.** ‡**Sri Lanka 300** (49.1 overs) (D. M. Jayalath 67, W. I. A. Fernando 138; B. G. F. Green 3-59); **England 276-9** (G. T. Hankins 79, O. J. Pope 87; P. W. H. de Silva 3-39). *This game was broadcast by Sky Sports, and England were undone by the two players who had vanquished them during the previous televised match between the sides – at the World Cup quarter-final in February. Fernando zoomed to his second century of the series, then Wanindu Hasaranga de Silva, a leg-spinning all-rounder from Galle, took 3-39. Hankins and Ollie Pope hit half-centuries, but there wasn't enough oomph from the rest.*

YOUTH CRICKET IN 2016

JAMES GINGELL

Every year, it seems, brings a new prophecy of cricketing doom. Clubs are closing, while fans are greying, or staying away. England players can sit at restaurants relatively untroubled by autograph hunters. Children would rather play football, or computer games. An inexorable decline is in motion.

But there is hope. In 2011, Cricket Australia had the same problem. A complacent Establishment – assuming themselves the guardians of the nation's favourite sport – were jolted into action by figures showing cricket was, in fact, only the sixth-most popular game among children aged 9–16. There was a danger of losing the next generation of spectators, and players. As part of their response, CA invested heavily in the Big Bash League, and targeted their marketing, broadcasting and social media strategy not towards established fans and party people – as the IPL had done – but the casual viewer and families. Since then, the number of cricketers in Australia under the age of 12 has doubled.

One of the architects of that success was Matt Dwyer, whose responsibility was to link the BBL to children. He helped make sure that boys and girls who saw the games on television had the opportunity to imitate their idols. With funding from the government, CA provided support for children to go to their local club, put on their favourite team's vibrant kit, and hit their first six or take their first catch.

Since the summer of 2015 Dwyer, as loquacious as he is passionate, has been working for the ECB as director of participation and growth. He is optimistic of effecting something similar here. "I saw how quickly you can change the trajectory of the game," he said. "And I'd love to go on that journey again." In November 2016, the ECB announced they would double their investment in the Chance to Shine charity, to £2.5m a year from 2017–21. According to Dwyer, that money will be used to shift focus towards younger children: "Insights tell us that three out of four of adult players were playing before the age of 12." Cricket is complex, certainly more so than most sports. Understanding the game – its rules, traditions and strategies – is the first step to loving it. And, like learning languages, it's best to get in early. The overall aim is to "win the battle of the playground". A similar competition to the BBL, with the appropriate marketing, would help.

In the meantime, the ECB have launched the All Stars cricket programme for under nines. It provides resources and equipment for clubs (around 3,500 have expressed an interest) to run a programme of 45-minute sessions that teach basic skills. "The message to parents is: 'We know you're busy, but we're going to give your kids a brilliant time,'" said Dwyer. Over three to four years, children would then slowly be introduced to soft-ball cricket, and finally the full game. A similar approach in Australia has not only seen participation increase, but quality too: the number of extras in colts cricket has halved compared to five years ago.

THE 2016 BUNBURY FESTIVAL

On July 18, three months after a heart problem forced him to retire from cricket, James Taylor presented the caps at the opening ceremony of the 30th Bunbury Festival, at Radley College. In 2005, he had been a Bunbury himself – leading the Midlands side at Newquay – and he went on to make his England debut in 2011. In November 2016, Haseeb Hameed became the 76th player to tread the same path. While it is hard to judge how many of the current crop will become international stars, there are certainly a few to watch over the coming years.

A combination of wonderful weather, with temperatures over 30°C, and immaculate pitches, meant a week dominated by batsmen. Sam Young, from Millfield School and the Somerset Academy, stood out, hitting 121 from 117 balls against London & the East to help South & West take the 50-over title for the second year running. His style reminded onlookers of Alex Hales: an aggressive opener, full of flair and daring, unafraid to give the bowlers a chance. The South & West won two of their three matches, falling only to the Midlands, by a run.

The week's other centurion was Sam Dorsey from Swinton High School in Greater Manchester. Coming in at No. 3 against London & the East, he hit 104 not out, and finished the week with 201 runs at an average of 67; his exploits earned him the Gray-Nicolls Man of the Series award.

The Twenty20 final was dominated by two all-rounders. London & the East asked the Midlands to bat, and Dan Mousley blasted 44 from 30 balls to help rack up 170. Mousley's off-spin then claimed two for 17 to splinter the reply, before No. 8 Sean Sullivan cracked an unbeaten 48. It rounded off a strong individual display – his seamers had taken two for 22 – but it wasn't enough to prevent a Midlands victory.

The best of Bunbury were invited to a three-day game at the end of August at Loughborough, where the South (combining London & the East and South & West) squeaked home by one wicket to cap a remarkable comeback. In reply to Midlands & the North's 226, they had slumped to 150 all out after Louis Botes took seven wickets. A hundred from captain Jack Haynes (adding to his first-innings 63) extended the deficit and, soon after he was run out, he declared to set the South 341. A hefty opening partnership between Ben Charlesworth and Rahul Sheemar gave them hope, all-rounder Lewis Goldsworthy's 73 kept the faith, and the tail finished the job. Earlier, Kent keeper Jordan Cox had taken eight catches in Midlands & the North's first innings. It earned him the admiration of ECB's national performance manager David Graveney: he made sure Cox received a framed scorecard and the match ball, and selected him as one of 14 to tour Sri Lanka at Easter for four limited-overs matches. Haynes, a member of the Worcestershire Academy, was chosen to lead the side.

SCHOOLS CRICKET IN 2016

REVIEW BY DOUGLAS HENDERSON

What glorious cricket weather it was! But how sad it didn't arrive until the autumn term. Those with long memories of schools cricket know May is often wet, and September lovely. So it was in 2016, when spring resembled late winter more than early summer.

Fixtures at the start of the autumn term would doubtless appeal to those parents, reportedly more prevalent in or near London, who are unhappy with the amount of time summer cricket takes up – time that they believe should be devoted to exam preparation. There is truth, though, in the proverbial wisdom that all work and no play makes Jack a dull boy – and probably hinders his academic performance too. Exams loom large over most of the traditional season, and are one reason why headmasters and directors of studies now try to make Twenty20 the norm, even for major schools fixtures on Saturdays.

Encouragingly, the ECB have been promoting September cricket. For most schools, this is unlikely to involve regular first-teamers, who will be needed for rugby or football – sports that have the luxury of long seasons largely untroubled by exams, weather or parental pressure. Autumn-term cricket would primarily be for those who enjoy the game, yet are unable to pursue it in the examination term (formerly known as the cricket season). There may be other problems to overcome, since many schools press their main ground into service for other sports. A rugby pitch certainly demands grass that would be too long for a cricket outfield. But some enterprising schools have circumvented the issue by hiring local club grounds.

In 2016, the weather was disruptive, though mercifully not as much as in 2012, when the qualification for inclusion in the schools' averages had to be reduced to reflect the paucity of cricket. If that wasn't necessary this time, there were still hundreds of matches abandoned without a ball bowled, and hundreds more where rain prevented a positive result.

One upshot was that A. J. Woodland (known by his initials) of St Edward's, Oxford, was alone in scoring 1,000 runs. A year earlier, ten had reached the mark. In all, he made 1,026 at an average of 85, including five centuries, and was one of only two to hit a double-hundred, along with Sam Evison of Stamford. Four batsmen averaged over 100: George Groenland of Wellingborough, and Tom Banton (formerly of Bromsgrove but now at King's College, Taunton) did so from at least six completed innings; Jadon Buckeridge of Portsmouth Grammar School and Arjan Bath of King Henry VIII's were both dismissed only once.

Similarly, only one bowler reached 40 wickets. Oliver Mann from King's, Canterbury, is a seamer, and his achievement all the more remarkable since ECB regulations prohibit faster bowlers from delivering prolonged spells. Mann totalled 43, while Felsted's Ben Waring – a slow left-armer who was named Wisden Schools Cricketer of the Year in 2015 after taking 68 wickets – found conditions less helpful, and finished with 33. All told, 15 bowlers took

A. J. Woodland of St Edward's School, Oxford: the tenth Wisden Schools Cricketer of the Year.

at least 30 wickets, while 30 managed ten or more at a cost of under ten. Oliver Rhys-Jones, from the Harvey School, claimed nine at just 4.88.

George Lavelle of Merchant Taylors', Crosby, was the leading wicketkeeper-batsman, and for the second year running made more stumpings than catches. He has two more years at school, and is an exciting prospect.

The National Schools T20 Cup remains a popular competition (though 20-over matches do not contribute to any of the statistics recorded here). Four strong schools made it to finals day at Arundel, where the weather might have been kinder. Millfield edged past a powerful Cranleigh side in the first semi-final, then Felsted comfortably beat Sedbergh, who fell away after rocketing to 61 for one in six overs. In the final, Millfield chose to bat and, in a formidable display of clean hitting, raced to 224 for four, thanks to two breathtaking innings: a 50-ball 93 from Josh McCoy, with eight sixes and six fours, and a 48-ball 79 from George Bartlett, with two sixes and nine fours. Felsted began well, but couldn't keep up with the rate.

The most astonishing batting performance of the year came in a three-day Under-17 fixture between Hampshire and Somerset at Basingstoke. Somerset captain Fin Trenouth, a highly capable wicketkeeper who moved from Clifton College to Millfield for his sixth-form years, hit a mammoth 332 not out from 302 balls, with 13 sixes and 33 fours. The next-highest score in a total of 477 was 84.

There was another extraordinary performance in an Under-13 game in Yorkshire. Oli Tomalin of St Olave's (the junior school of St Peter's, York) took all ten wickets for seven runs in just 23 balls. He began with a hat-trick from the innings' first three deliveries, missed out with the next, before removing batsmen with the last two balls of an astounding over. All ten were bowled – a feat famously achieved by John Wisden in 1850 (see the note on page 1240). Almost as remarkable were the efforts of Henry Wines, a 14-year-old exchange student recently arrived at Haileybury from the Sydney suburbs. Despite not being considered a frontline bowler, he scattered the Aldenham Twenty20 batting line-up, finishing with eight for 15 from four overs of highly skilled leg-spin.

WISDEN SCHOOLS CRICKETERS OF THE YEAR

2007	Jonny Bairstow	St Peter's School, York
2008	James Taylor	Shrewsbury School
2009	Jos Buttler	King's College, Taunton
2010	Will Vanderspar	Eton College
2011	Daniel Bell-Drummond	Millfield School
2012	Thomas Abell	Taunton School
2013	Tom Köhler-Cadmore	Malvern College
2014	Dylan Budge	Woodhouse Grove
2015	Ben Waring	Felsted School
2016	**A. J. Woodland**	**St Edward's School, Oxford**

If there were fewer gargantuan totals in 2016, the biggest was still huge. Led by captain and Hong Kong international Anshuman Rath, who hit 171 from 102 balls, Harrow made 442 against Hampton. In reply, Hampton set off at breakneck speed before the spinners wrested back control, steering Harrow to victory by 117 runs. Their 442 is believed the highest by a school in overs cricket, surpassing the 427 made by Caterham in 2014.

One other effect of the dreich weather was that it made the selection of the Wisden Schools Cricketer of the Year trickier than usual. Had Sam Curran played more for Wellington and less for Surrey, he might have made a convincing case. Others were called up for Second XIs or representative age-group sides. But, for his ability to overcome unhelpful conditions and score runs for his school by the sackful, the winner for 2016 is A. J. Woodland, of St Edward's, Oxford.

AJ is a meticulous and assured left-handed opener who has the ability to concentrate for hour upon hour – some have noticed a similarity to Alastair Cook. He also possesses an excellent technique and, according to Richard Howitt, master in charge of cricket at St Edward's, is a delight to coach. Fast between the wickets, and a good judge of a single, he has an instinctive knowledge about how to construct – and pace – his innings. In 2016, AJ made over 1,200 runs, across all formats, including a school-record unbeaten 204 against Abingdon. In the same match, he and his opening partner Ben Charlesworth put on 310, another record. Other strings to his bow include fastish outswing bowling (and occasional off-spin), as well as lightning reactions either in the cordon or at backward point. As Howitt said: "AJ turned matches – and heads – with his batting, bowling and fielding."

Douglas Henderson is editor of Schools Cricket Online.

Schools who wish to be considered for inclusion should email Wisden at almanack@wisden.com. State schools and girls' schools are especially welcome.

MCC Schools v ESCA

At Lord's, September 6. **ESCA won by 52 runs.** ‡**ESCA 263-8** (50 overs) (W. E. L. Buttleman 104, B. Claydon 63; T. R. A. Scriven 3-48); **MCC Schools 211** (42.5 overs) (A. S. B. Bramley 50, H. R. C. Came 38; T. J. Price 4-36, A. Nazir 3-51).

MCC *†B. J. Worcester (*Woodhouse Grove School*), A. S. B. Bramley (*The Leys School*), H. R. C. Came (*Bradfield College*), T. J. Haines (*Hurstpierpoint College*), H. J. Hankins (*Beechen Cliff School*), T. W. Hartley (*Merchant Taylors', Crosby*), H. A. Jordan (*The Windsor Boys' School*), F. S. Organ (*Canford School*), T. R. A. Scriven (*Magdalen College School*), R. S. Wijeratne (*Harrow School*), A. J. Woodland (*St Edward's School, Oxford*).

ESCA *†G. I. D. Lavelle (*Merchant Taylors', Crosby*), B. M. J. Allison (*Chelmsford College*), T. R. Bevan (*Millfield*), W. E. L. Buttleman (*Felsted School*), B. Claydon (*Long Road Sixth Form College*), J. G. T. Crawley (*Shrewsbury School*), A. Nazir (*Harrow School*), R. A. Parker-Cole (*Worksop College*), L. A. Patterson-White (*Worksop College*), T. J. Price (*Magdalen College School*), R. M. Yates (*Warwick School*).

Full coverage of the 2016 Eton v Harrow match can be found at wisden.com.

The following tables cover only those schools listed in the Schools A–Z section.

SCHOOLS AVERAGES

BEST BATTING AVERAGES (5 completed innings)

		I	*NO*	*Runs*	*HS*	*100*	*Avge*
1	G. Groenland (*Wellingborough School*)	13	7	763	142*	2	127.16
2	T. Banton (*King's College, Taunton*)	7	1	667	188	3	111.16
3	H. M. Rollings (*Ardingly College*)	7	1	576	188	2	96.00
4	B. J. Worcester (*Woodhouse Grove School*)	10	3	637	135*	3	91.00
5	A. J. Woodland (*St Edward's School, Oxford*)	18	6	1,026	204*	5	85.50
6	S. C. Nightingale (*Ratcliffe College*)	9	3	486	161*	2	81.00
7	F. S. Organ (*Canford School*)	9	1	647	142*	3	80.87
8	N. A. Hammond (*King's School, Worcester*)	10	0	797	144	5	79.70
9	M. A. Mniszko (*The Leys School*)	11	3	623	104	2	77.87
10	N. A. Chattha (*King Henry VIII School*)	8	3	384	96*	0	76.80
11	O. J. D. Pope (*Cranleigh School*)	18	6	904	120	3	75.33
12	N. J. Tilley (*Reed's School*)	11	3	597	123	2	74.62
13	B. J. Graff (*Westminster School*)	11	4	511	102*	1	73.00
14	W. J. Heywood (*King's School, Canterbury*)	21	9	874	106	1	72.83
15	G. I. D. Lavelle (*Merchant Taylors', Crosby*)	9	3	435	122	1	72.50
16	T. J. Haines (*Hurstpierpoint College*)	6	0	405	187	1	67.50
17	T. Snell (*Ratcliffe College*)	9	4	337	99	0	67.40
18	J. A. Price (*Sir Thomas Rich's School*)	11	3	534	113	3	66.75
19	R. K. Claassen (*Queen's College, Taunton*)	11	3	532	105*	1	66.50
20	R. M. Yates (*Warwick School*)	11	2	592	116	2	65.77
21	T. R. A. Scriven (*Magdalen College School*)	9	2	459	139	3	65.57
22	B. Lynch (*King's College, Taunton*)	9	3	393	104	1	65.50
23	N. G. Solomon (*St Paul's School*)	13	4	588	105*	1	65.33
24	A. D. Thomas (*Merchant Taylors', Northwood*)	12	1	716	110	2	65.09
25	W. J. Hodgson (*King's, Macclesfield*)	11	4	454	93*	0	64.85
26	S. H. G. Evison (*Stamford School*)	10	1	579	202*	2	64.33
27	H. M. E. Bailey (*Bishop's Stortford College*)	13	6	440	78*	0	62.85
28	J. J. O'Riordan (*Tonbridge School*)	13	4	563	128	1	62.55

Two other batsmen averaged over 100, but from fewer than five completed innings: J. P. Buckeridge (Portsmouth GS) 152.00; and A. S. Bath (King Henry VIII School) 151.00.

MOST RUNS

		I	*NO*	*Runs*	*HS*	*100*	*Avge*
1	A. J. Woodland (*St Edward's School, Oxford*)	18	6	1,026	204*	5	85.50
2	O. J. D. Pope (*Cranleigh School*)	18	6	904	120	3	75.33
3	Z. Crawley (*Tonbridge School*)	17	1	897	141	3	56.06
4	W. J. Heywood (*King's School, Canterbury*)	21	9	874	106	1	72.83
5	M. K. O'Riordan (*Tonbridge School*)	17	1	833	117*	4	52.06
6	A. Rath (*Harrow School*)	19	2	826	171	3	48.58
7	N. A. Hammond (*King's School, Worcester*)	10	0	797	144	5	79.70
8	G. Groenland (*Wellingborough School*)	13	7	763	142*	2	127.16
9	O. B. S. Tikare (*King's School, Canterbury*)	21	3	729	84	0	40.50
10	A. D. Thomas (*Merchant Taylors', Northwood*)	12	1	716	110	2	65.09
11	S. O. Blain (*Stewart's Melville College*)	19	3	707	100*	1	44.18
12	H. C. Brook (*Sedbergh School*)	15	0	698	198	2	46.53
13	C. A. Nicholls (*Berkhamsted School*)	16	2	680	124	2	48.57
14	J. J. S. Hennessey (*KCS, Wimbledon*)	21	2	673	87	0	35.42
15	T. Banton (*King's College, Taunton*)	7	1	667	188	3	111.16
16	C. W. T. Mack (*Haberdashers' Aske's*)	16	2	665	100*	1	47.50
17	E. W. Beard (*Rugby School*)	17	4	652	113	1	50.15
18	R. S. Wijeratne (*Harrow School*)	17	3	650	145*	2	46.42
19	F. S. Organ (*Canford School*)	9	1	647	142*	3	80.87
20	A. R. I. Sweet (*RGS, Guildford*)	14	0	645	107	2	46.07
21	H. D. Williams (*Epsom College*)	16	1	642	122	3	42.80
22	B. J. Worcester (*Woodhouse Grove School*)	10	3	637	135*	3	91.00
23	O. M. Heazel (*Haileybury*)	14	2	632	104*	1	52.66
24	G. F. Reid (*Harrow School*)	17	0	627	96	0	36.88
25	H. R. C. Came (*Bradfield College*)	13	3	624	123	2	62.40
26	M. A. Mniszko (*The Leys School*)	11	3	623	104	2	77.87
27	B. J. Lee (*Stowe School*)	16	0	622	117	1	38.87
28	W. Legg (*Oratory School*)	13	1	620	116	1	51.66
29	T. J. Hill (*Trent College*)	15	5	611	122*	1	61.10
30	C. T. Harvey (*Repton School*)	13	0	606	96	0	46.61
31	T. R. Wyatt (*Trent College*)	13	2	605	144*	2	55.00
32	J. W. Jamieson-Black (*Cheltenham College*)	15	2	604	130*	2	46.46
	B. G. Charlesworth (*St Edward's School, Oxford*)	15	2	604	110	2	46.46
34	J. J. Dell (*Cheltenham College*)	14	3	601	101*	1	54.63

BEST BOWLING AVERAGE (10 wickets)

		O	*M*	*Runs*	*W*	*BB*	*Avge*
1	B. J. Davidson (*Stewart's Melville College*)	26	3	87	17	5-13	5.11
2	T. Benson (*Latymer Upper School*)	51	6	121	21	3-6	5.76
3	T. D. Bracey (*Dr Challoner's GS*)	34	8	87	14	4-19	6.21
4	C. E. Home (*Wrekin College*)	36	10	91	14	6-23	6.50
5	N. B. Patel (*Queen Mary's GS*)	15.5	1	83	12	3-10	6.91
6	B. R. Day (*Chislehurst & Sidcup GS*)	20	4	70	10	3-16	7.00
7	B-J. Smith (*St Lawrence College*)	29.3	6	102	14	7-13	7.28
8	H. A. Tagg (*Eastbourne College*)	20	5	74	10	5-34	7.40
9	T. E. Anderson (*The Perse School*)	38	5	107	14	3-9	7.64
10	H. G. E. West (*Fettes College*)	50	12	134	17	4-16	7.88
11	L. J. H. Webber (*Bloxham School*)	44	5	87	11	6-14	7.90
12	J. L. Haynes (*Malvern College*)	71.5	8	182	23	5-12	7.91
13	T. Loten (*Pocklington School*)	68.2	16	169	21	4-5	8.04
14	O. J. Hunt (*St John's School, Leatherhead*)	78	10	140	17	4-13	8.23
15	C. A. Phipps (*Stewart's Melville College*)	25	3	84	10	5-16	8.40
16	J. B. Nordin (*St Edmund's School, Canterbury*)	26.3	3	138	16	4-11	8.62
17	M. R. James (*St John's School, Leatherhead*)	92	8	165	19	5-41	8.68
18	S. A. Harvey (*Aldenham School*)	23	4	87	10	4-21	8.70
19	P. J. G. Carter (*Sir Thomas Rich's School*)	32	2	114	13	4-12	8.76

		O	M	Runs	W	BB	Avge
20	M. I. C. Hay-Smith (*Stewart's Melville College*)	28	8	88	10	4-17	8.80
21	J. E. Miles (*Clayesmore School*)	36	11	97	11	5-17	8.81
22	J. S. Amor (*Rossall School*)	51.5	7	178	20	6-2	8.90
23	M. A. G. Hancock (*Stewart's Melville College*)	51	2	205	23	5-20	8.91
24	B. Anderson (*Kirkham GS*)	28.2	1	117	13	4-15	9.00
	J. Furnival (*Ellesmere College*)	32	8	90	10	5-5	9.00
	R. Thomas (*Shebbear College*)	16	0	90	10	5-13	9.00
27	J. R. Percival (*Glasgow Academy*)	29	2	129	14	4-29	9.21
28	A. Gonella (*RGS, Guildford*)	44	8	132	14	4-39	9.42
29	B. J. Thompson (*Clayesmore School*)	49	5	177	18	4-15	9.83
30	J. L. S. Clark (*King's College, Taunton*)	67	8	218	22	5-0	9.90

O. H. Rhys-Jones (The Harvey School) took nine wickets at 4.88.

MOST WICKETS

		O	M	Runs	W	BB	Avge
1	O. J. D. Mann (*King's School, Canterbury*)	144.5	9	560	43	5-37	13.02
2	J. A. Curtis (*St Edward's School, Oxford*)	156	12	601	38	5-20	15.81
3	C. D. S. Wood (*St Peter's School, York*)	140	27	411	37	5-36	11.10
	C. R. D. Terry (*Cranleigh School*)	113.4	15	489	37	6-27	13.21
5	T. H. S. Pettman (*Tonbridge School*)	150	21	586	35	4-48	16.74
6	B. A. Waring (*Felsted School*)	171	41	487	33	7-65	14.75
	G. A. V. Betts (*KCS, Wimbledon*)	136.3	21	564	33	4-15	17.09
	H. J. Millett (*Dulwich College*)	120	9	589	33	5-35	17.84
9	A. R. Amin (*Merchant Taylors', Northwood*)	107	18	326	32	5-10	10.18
10	S. Shah (*RGS, Worcester*)	123	19	480	31	6-40	15.48
	D. J. Lloyd (*Shrewsbury School*)	146.3	18	481	31	5-7	15.51
	J. S. Charles (*Charterhouse*)	174.3	24	648	31	6-46	20.90
13	P. B. O'Brien (*Epsom College*)	87	7	443	30	6-23	14.76
	K. K. Tahirkheli (*Sedbergh School*)	136.3	15	513	30	5-9	17.10
	O. D. Clarke (*Stowe School*)	181	19	578	30	5-13	19.26
16	L. R. Henderson (*Durham School*)	84	15	295	29	6-71	10.17
	T. W. Nightingale (*Lancing College*)	89.2	6	366	29	5-11	12.62
	K. D. Shirvani (*Winchester College*)	120	20	376	29	3-24	12.96
	W. M. Edwards (*Sutton Valence School*)	88.4	15	389	29	4-29	13.41
	A. Ragutharan (*Forest School*)	91.1	15	440	29	6-58	15.17
	A. S. Jawanda (*RGS, Worcester*)	150.3	20	512	29	7-24	17.65
	S. Jhala (*Bedford School*)	125	10	558	29	5-26	19.24
23	D. A. Patel (*Merchant Taylors', Northwood*)	105	12	340	28	5-23	12.14
	A. M. C. Russell (*St Paul's School*)	106.4	16	381	28	4-32	13.60
	A. E. C. Dahl (*Cranleigh School*)	109	16	402	28	4-10	14.35
	S. Marsh (*Christ's Hospital*)	97	5	428	28	7-33	15.28
	M. S. Chelvam (*KCS, Wimbledon*)	104.1	4	484	28	4-34	17.28
	W. E. Rogers (*Uppingham School*)	141.1	7	616	28	4-32	22.00

OUTSTANDING SEASONS (minimum 7 matches)

	P	W	L	T	D	A	%W
St George's College, Weybridge	9	8	1	0	0	3	88.88
Eton College	16	14	1	0	1	2	87.50
Clayesmore School	7	6	0	0	1	0	85.71
St Paul's School	14	12	2	0	0	0	85.71
Cranleigh School	20	17	3	0	0	2	85.00
King's College, Taunton	13	11	1	0	1	2	84.61
St Edmund's School, Canterbury	9	7	2	0	0	0	77.77
Tonbridge School	17	13	2	1	1	3	76.47
Ellesmere College	8	6	2	0	0	3	75.00
Woodhouse Grove School	12	9	2	0	1	5	75.00
Felsted School	15	11	2	0	2	1	73.33

	P	*W*	*L*	*T*	*D*	*A*	*%W*
Fettes College	11	8	1	0	2	1	72.72
Mount Kelly	11	8	3	0	0	1	72.72
St John's School, Leatherhead	11	8	3	0	0	2	72.72
Worksop College	11	8	3	0	0	6	72.72
Glasgow Academy	7	5	2	0	0	1	71.42
St Lawrence College	7	5	2	0	0	1	71.42
Stonyhurst College	7	5	1	0	1	0	71.42
Birkenhead School	10	7	0	0	3	1	70.00
King Henry VIII School	10	7	2	0	1	1	70.00
Watford Grammar School for Boys	10	7	3	0	0	3	70.00

SCHOOLS A–Z

In the results line, A = abandoned without a ball bowled. An asterisk indicates captain. The qualification for the averages (which exclude Twenty20 and overseas tour games) is 150 runs or ten wickets. Counties have been included for all schools. Since cricket does not follow the current complex system of administrative division, *Wisden* adheres to the county boundaries in existence before the dissolution of Middlesex in 1965. Those schools affected by the boundary changes of the last 50 years – such as Sedbergh, which was removed from Yorkshire and handed to Cumbria – are listed under their former county.

Abingdon School *Oxfordshire* P15 W3 L8 D4

Master i/c J. M. Golding **Coach** Dr C. J. Burnand

The first team were in need of rebuilding, but those promoted from the Under-15s looked exciting prospects. Max Mortimer carried the bowling attack, while Alex Ling showed his destructive ability as a batsman.

Batting *C. F. I. Graney 224 at 22.40; M. J. Mortimer 234 at 21.27; A. P. Ling 267 at 20.53; T. L. Dingwall 248 at 17.71.

Bowling A. P. Ling 12 at 19.66; M. J. Mortimer 18 at 27.16; J. J. Gooder 11 at 32.90.

Aldenham School *Hertfordshire* P13 W2 L9 T1 D1 A7

Masters i/c C. S. Irish and M. I. Yeabsley **Coach** D. G. Goodchild

In a difficult season badly affected by weather, there were only two wins – against Haberdashers' and Highgate; seven games were abandoned. The captain, Daniel Murphy, was the leading run-scorer, and Umer Zeeshan-Lohya took 15 wickets.

Batting S. Iqbal 210 at 35.00; D. T. Travers 211 at 23.44; *D. S. G. Murphy 237 at 19.75; G. T. Ellingham 151 at 15.10.

Bowling S. A. Harvey 10 at 8.70; U. Zeeshan-Lohya 15 at 11.66; Y. H. Khan 11 at 16.45.

Alleyn's School *Surrey* P9 W5 L3 D1

Master i/c R. N. Ody **Coach** P. E. Edwards

The first team were superbly led by Jonty West, who carried through his fine batting form from 2015. Slow left-armer Ben Swanson took 21 wickets.

Batting J. J. Keeling 274 at 45.66; B. J. C. Clinch 155 at 31.00; *J. C. West 214 at 26.75.

Bowling B. Swanson 21 at 11.38.

Ampleforth College *Yorkshire* P14 W6 L5 D3 A1

Master i/c R. W. Pineo **Coach** G. D. Thurman

After an excellent pre-season trip to Sri Lanka, the summer did not go quite as planned: mistakes towards the end of matches were especially costly. James Ainscough captained with maturity.

Batting B. M. B. Fawcett 554 at 50.36; B. E. Fitzherbert 277 at 25.18; A. G. Campion 228 at 20.72; *J. O. Ainscough 278 at 19.85; M. P. Blakiston-Houston 192 at 19.20.

Bowling S. A. MacLellan 18 at 14.83; B. E. Fitzherbert 14 at 15.92; B. M. B. Fawcett 15 at 26.53; J. O. Ainscough 15 at 30.40.

Ardingly College *Sussex* P11 W3 L5 T1 D2 A1

Master i/c N. J. Tester **Coach** M. Nash

In a year which hinted at a promising future, Harry Rollings shone. He displayed immense skill in two commanding centuries, and his 188 against Sussex Martlets was a school record.

Batting H. M. Rollings 576 at 96.00; B. J. G. Harris 201 at 25.12; T. G. R. Clark 166 at 23.71.

Bowling *S. J. Rattle 17 at 16.76; J. B. Walker 11 at 25.45.

Bancroft's School *Essex* P18 W11 L7 A1

Master i/c C. G. Greenidge

Results were good, if perhaps flattered by weakened opposition: some parents pressured exam candidates not to play cricket. Year 12 batsmen Will Hopkins, Tom Oliver and Angad Nijjar, plus opening bowler Haaris Sohoye, led the way.

Batting W. F. T. Hopkins 392 at 39.20; T. N. Oliver 533 at 38.07; A. Nijjar 450 at 34.61; A. K. Agedah 241 at 30.12; *F. D. Edwards 236 at 23.60.

Bowling A. Nijjar 14 at 12.28; H. Sohoye 20 at 13.55; D. V. Solanki 13 at 15.61.

Bede's School *Sussex* P10 W3 L7 A1

Master i/c A. P. Wells **Coach** N. J. Lenham

A young first team, including several from Years 9 and 10, struggled for wins, but competed well and learned much from a challenging season.

Batting D. Rawlins 484 at 44.00; J. Billings 352 at 32.00.

Bowling D. G. Wilson 18 at 14.00; N. J. Beck 16 at 19.00; S. N. Lenham 13 at 22.61; Z. M. Cisotti 12 at 22.66.

Bedford Modern School *Bedfordshire* P14 W6 L4 D4 A3

Master i/c P. J. Woodroffe

Todd Pitkin led the side superbly and topped the batting, while the performances of seamers James Taylor and Robert Bassin, and off-spinners Advait Vaidya and Sam Pitkin, pointed to a bright future.

Batting *T. B. Pitkin 438 at 31.28; M. J. Taylor 263 at 29.22; W. R. D. Hardwick 331 at 27.58; H. A. Evans 188 at 18.80; M. S. Rodgers 179 at 17.90; E. J. Else 153 at 12.75.

Bowling J. H. Taylor 11 at 15.09; S. A. Pitkin 16 at 18.37; A. Vaidya 15 at 19.13; U. Subhani 10 at 21.10; H. A. Evans 10 at 26.30.

Bedford School *Bedfordshire* P14 W7 L3 D4 A2

Master i/c I. G. S. Steer

The accomplished leadership of Ben Slawinski and the left-arm wrist-spin of Shiv Jhala proved pivotal in Bedford's seven victories. Sixteen-year-old Emilio Gay, who hit a wonderful 145 against Tonbridge, was the leading batsman.

Batting E. N. Gay 567 at 43.61; J. A. Duxbury 432 at 43.20; S. Tomlinson-Patel 311 at 38.87; S. Jhala 315 at 31.50; *B. Slawinski 263 at 21.91; R. Sheemar 262 at 21.83.

Bowling R. Sheemar 13 at 16.92; S. Jhala 29 at 19.24; B. Slawinski 27 at 19.25; W. A. Comfort 18 at 22.61; E. J. Wingfield 12 at 26.58.

Berkhamsted School *Hertfordshire* P16 W4 L8 D4 A2

Master i/c G. R. A. Campbell **Coaches** D. J. Gibson and B. R. Mahoney

In a year that improved as the season progressed, captain and wicketkeeper Charlie Nicholls led by example, scoring 680 runs, including hundreds against Merchant Taylors' and Haberdashers'. Harvey Robertson also demonstrated his all-round ability, contributing 21 wickets and 299 runs.

Batting C. A. Nicholls 680 at 48.57; H. J. Robertson 299 at 23.00; J. D. Fosberry 246 at 20.50.

Bowling H. J. Robertson 21 at 17.00; O. Holdroyd 12 at 19.66; J. Woodley 15 at 21.53; M. Skelton 16 at 23.00; H. Smart 13 at 28.15.

Birkenhead School *Cheshire* P10 W7 D3 A1

Master i/c R. L. Lytollis **Coach** G. J. Rickman

The first team recorded a rare win against Manchester Grammar School, and a hard-earned draw against MCC; outside the National T20, they were unbeaten. Dominic Smith, James O'Neill and Ashley Watkins all passed 300 runs.

Batting *D. I. Smith 335 at 47.85; A. Watkins 320 at 45.71; A. J. N. Rabot 237 at 39.50; J. O'Neill 306 at 34.00; L. Filer 232 at 33.14.

Bowling The leading bowler was A. Watkins, who claimed nine wickets at 15.66.

Bishop's Stortford College *Hertfordshire* P13 W7 L5 D1

Master i/c M. Drury **Coach** N. D. Hughes

Victories against Haileybury, Chigwell and RGS Colchester made this the most successful season in recent years. Tom Baucher's tactical acumen caught the eye, while Harry Bailey played several match-winning innings.

Batting H. M. E. Bailey 440 at 62.85; A. Bassingthwaighte 351 at 35.10; *T. A. Baucher 263 at 26.30; A. J. Portas 227 at 22.70; J. S. Hawkins 174 at 21.75.

Bowling T. B. Radley 13 at 16.00; H. M. E. Bailey 10 at 18.70; A. M. Sewell 12 at 20.83; T. A. Baucher 10 at 21.30.

Bloxham School *Oxfordshire* P16 W5 L10 D1 A5

Master i/c B. G. A. Richmond **Coaches** D. D. Finch and P. D. Atkins

With the core of 2015's steady first team now gone, some younger cricketers had the chance to show what they could do – and they did well, recording one more win than the year before.

Batting *O. J. Morgan 456 at 41.45; J. F. Beever 270 at 33.75; T. J. Staveley-Parker 193 at 21.44.

Bowling L. J. H. Webber 11 at 7.90.

Bradfield College *Berkshire* P15 W6 L5 D4 A4

Master i/c M. S. Hill **Coach** J. R. Wood

Pre-season preparation was disrupted by rain, leaving the batsmen short of confidence: not until half-term was there any fluency in the top six. Harry Came, who averaged 62 for a second consecutive summer, and Gus Atkinson, a fearsome quick bowler, will be sorely missed.

Batting *H. R. C. Came 624 at 62.40; A. A. P. Atkinson 337 at 33.70; C. O. Gwynn 160 at 14.54.

Bowling A. A. P. Atkinson 26 at 13.88; C. O. Gwynn 18 at 17.16; H. R. C. Came 17 at 21.88; O. T. F. Cox 10 at 26.50; S. D. Waddington 12 at 27.66.

Bradford Grammar School *Yorkshire* P16 W6 L9 D1 A3

Master i/c A. G. Smith **Coach** S. A. Kellett

The season started and finished well, but in between too many games were lost through inconsistent batting. Impressive innings from Scott van Berckel and Robbie Williams lit up the summer, while captain Yusuf Khan was the pick of the bowlers.

Batting S. M. van Berckel 308 at 28.00; R. G. Williams 339 at 26.07; W. Iqbal 266 at 24.18; O. J. Croudson 182 at 18.20; W. E. Heard 183 at 16.63.

Bowling *M. Y. Khan 24 at 18.75; M. S. Farooq 17 at 22.41; H. Arshad 11 at 24.81; M. Patel 12 at 26.25.

Brentwood School *Essex* P17 W7 L6 D4 A4

Master i/c S. Salisbury **Coach** G. O. Jones

A few individual performances stood out in a year of mixed results: opening pair Kieran Emmanuel and Rishi Patel dominated most attacks, while Steve Heywood's pace and Tom Wingrove's left-arm spin lent danger and variety to the bowling.

Batting R. K. Patel 403 at 36.63; S. C. Heywood 371 at 33.72; K. Emmanuel 431 at 28.73; M. S. Bell 393 at 28.07; J. S. Meadows 181 at 22.62; M. A. Fox 283 at 20.21.

Bowling T. A. Wingrove 21 at 17.71; O. F. Valentini 17 at 18.82; J. S. Meadows 14 at 21.71; S. C. Heywood 16 at 23.18; M. S. Bell 11 at 30.18; R. K. Patel 10 at 34.10.

Brighton College *Sussex* P16 W5 L6 T2 D3 A1

Master i/c M. P. Smethurst **Coach** J. E. Anyon

Brighton continued their progress under captain Will Wright, recording one more win than in 2015. Off-spinner Will Longley and Dominic Sear both took 15 wickets.

Batting M. S. Smith 347 at 34.70; A. J. Bone 273 at 24.81; D. J. Sear 297 at 22.84; *W. R. Wright 292 at 20.85; C. J. S. May 208 at 18.90; T. A. Walker 170 at 18.88; T. H. Chalmers 199 at 18.09.

Bowling J. Z. Montfort-Bebb 14 at 19.35; D. J. Sear 15 at 24.33; J. A. D'Orsaneo 10 at 27.90; T. A. Walker 10 at 32.10; W. S. Longley 15 at 34.13.

Bristol Grammar School *Gloucestershire* P15 W4 L9 D2 A3

Master i/c K. R. Blackburn

In a summer when batsmen struggled, Year 10 students Matty Brewer and Sujan Canagarajah provided much-needed stability. The bowling was stronger, led by seamers Jude Hazelgrove and James Nightingale.

Jono Jamieson-Black scored most runs and took most wickets for Cheltenham; Cranleigh captain Ollie Pope hit 904 runs at 75.

Batting B. C. Miller 222 at 22.20; S. Canagarajah 238 at 21.63; *R. N. Panchal 206 at 20.60; M. J. M. Brewer 179 at 16.27.
Bowling J. T. Hazelgrove 16 at 18.93; J. D. K. Nightingale 10 at 22.10.

Bromsgrove School *Worcestershire* P6 W5 L1 A5

Master i/c D. J. Fallows
The first team recorded memorable victories against Shrewsbury, Stowe, Clifton, MCC and Monmouth, and the Under-12, Under-14 and Under-15 teams all became county champions.
Batting H. F. Moberley 194 at 32.33; J. Bewick 152 at 25.33.
Bowling J. M. Smith 12 at 11.50.

Bryanston School *Dorset* P9 W6 L2 D1 A4

Master i/c S. J. Turrill **Coach** P. J. Norton
Captain and outstanding wicketkeeper Oliver Thomas helped the team develop into a strong unit, with wins over MCC, Portsmouth Grammar School and Ryde. With almost all the first team returning, 2017 should be exciting.
Batting O. A. Morris 295 at 42.14; H. G. Clarke 299 at 33.22; F. J. Turrill 154 at 25.66.
Bowling A. F. Chetwood 11 at 11.45; H. J. C. Maclean 13 at 11.84; H. G. Clarke 16 at 13.75; F. J. Turrill 13 at 17.00.

Canford School *Dorset* P11 W7 L4 A3

Master i/c S. L. Ives
Canford's successful season was based on a number of excellent performances, though captain Felix Organ stood out for his three centuries.
Batting *F. S. Organ 647 at 80.87; M. W. Mallinson 162 at 54.00; J. M. Leslie-Smith 154 at 22.00.
Bowling B. J. Howard-Allen 12 at 16.08; F. S. Organ 13 at 16.53; J. E. L. Moores 10 at 18.30.

Charterhouse *Surrey* P17 W3 L11 D3 A1

Master i/c M. P. Bicknell
A disappointing season brought only three wins. The batting was often a concern, with no one reaching 350 runs, while losing George Barlow to a back injury was a blow; all eight games in his absence ended in defeat. Jonny Charles, the captain, took 31 wickets.

Batting C. S. Peplow 150 at 37.50; F. J. D. Gratton 224 at 37.33; L. E. A. Clayton 307 at 27.90; G. C. H. Barlow 257 at 23.36; H. N. Gilbey 341 at 18.94; J. G. Hunter-Lees 255 at 17.00; *J. S. Charles 171 at 12.21; A. J. Kaul 192 at 11.29.
Bowling G. C. H. Barlow 21 at 17.80; J. S. Charles 31 at 20.90; T. A. Batchelor 11 at 25.54; T. G. A. M. Brown 18 at 31.88; F. J. D. Gratton 11 at 43.90.

Cheadle Hulme School *Cheshire* P11 W3 L6 T1 D1 A4

Master i/c S. Burnage **Coach** G. J. Clinton
The first team enjoyed a season full of humour, if modest success (despite the all-round efforts of captain James Scott). The future looks rosier, with Cheshire Cup victories for the Under-14 and Under-13 teams.
Batting *J. S. A. Scott 295 at 32.77.
Bowling D. W. Ray 12 at 18.83.

Cheltenham College *Gloucestershire* P16 W6 L7 D3 A5

Master i/c M. K. Coley **Coach** M. P. Briers
Josh Dell led the batting averages and earned selection for the England Under-19 squad to play Sri Lanka, having already represented Worcestershire Seconds. But the season's best performance came against Haileybury: Jono Jamieson-Black took seven for 43 and scored 109.
Batting *J. J. Dell 601 at 54.63; J. W. Jamieson-Black 604 at 46.46; J. K. Palmer 496 at 38.15; M. W. Ward 465 at 31.00; D. J. Ward 172 at 19.11; J. C. Soames 227 at 18.91.
Bowling M. H. Dymoke 23 at 13.86; J. W. Jamieson-Black 26 at 14.57; G. D. Mech 12 at 24.00; B. L. Frisby 11 at 26.36; J. T. Warner 13 at 27.38.

Chigwell School *Essex* P16 W4 L12

Master i/c F. A. Griffith **Coach** V. Chopra
The best moment of a mixed season came in the last match, when Jamie Colton, Sonal Ohrie, Tom Clapham and Matthew Koczan finished off their school careers in style – with a win against MCC.
Batting A. Gupta 498 at 41.50; J. W. Colton 200 at 20.00; H. S. Gard 185 at 18.50; T. S. Clapham 155 at 12.91.
Bowling R. Chahal 10 at 19.90; H. S. Gard 11 at 20.18; C. A. Redhead 10 at 21.70.

Chislehurst & Sidcup Grammar School *Kent* P4 W3 L1 A4

Master i/c R. A. Wallbridge **Coach** D. L. Pask
The squad were relieved when they got a game: as many fell victim to the weather as survived. Emily Thompson and Phoebe Franklin were selected for Kent Ladies, while Ollie Robinson played for Kent Second XI and for London and East of England Under-17s.
Batting The leading batsman was L. D. Buttery, who hit 115 runs at 38.33.
Bowling B. R. Day 10 at 7.00.

Christ College, Brecon *Breconshire* P9 W1 L7 T1

Master i/c T. J. Trumper **Coach** R. F. Evans
In a lean season, old hands James Newey, the captain, and Alex Ryan provided support to a young team. The highlight came at the end of the season, when a strong – and triumphant – Trinity Grammar School visited from Sydney for the annual T20 competition.
Batting A. M. D. Ryan 189 at 27.00.
Bowling A. M. D. Ryan 10 at 23.00.

Christ's Hospital *Sussex* P16 W8 L5 D3 A1

Master i/c H. P. Holdsworth **Coaches** T. E. Jesty and D. H. Messenger
Under the leadership of Alex Walker, the first team won the Martin Berrill Sports League for the first time, going unbeaten against Caterham, City of London Freemen's, Seaford College and Worth. Prospects look good: only two of the 2016 team are moving on.
Batting W. E. Freeman 474 at 39.50; *A. Walker 185 at 23.12; E. J. R. Swinn-Ward 193 at 21.44; A. P. Burgess 252 at 21.00.
Bowling S. A. Hannon 15 at 13.13; A. Walker 14 at 14.85; S. Marsh 28 at 15.28; W. A. Thwaites 17 at 18.00; A. P. Burgess 15 at 20.73.

Churcher's College *Hampshire* P10 W6 L3 D1

Master i/c R. Maier

Facing a string of new opponents, including Lord Wandsworth College, City of London Freemen's and Reigate Grammar, Churcher's enjoyed another fine season, with six hard-fought victories.

Batting F. McMillan 450 at 50.00; B. I. Crane 218 at 27.25.

Bowling K. D. Kelson 13 at 13.69; E. Garrett 11 at 14.27; J. McMillan 11 at 15.00.

City of London Freemen's School *Surrey* P14 W3 L9 D2 A3

Master i/c A. E. Buhagiar **Coach** N. M. Stewart

Stalwart batsman Tom Abraham left, after 56 first-team appearances. But, with encouraging debuts for Year 9 Jack Hamilton and Year 10 Tom Youngman, there is cause for optimism.

Batting *B. D. Sidwell 337 at 42.12; L. Butcher 339 at 28.25; J. Symonds 245 at 24.50; E. England 163 at 18.11; T. Abraham 157 at 17.44.

Bowling J. Symonds 10 at 19.80; L. Butcher 11 at 20.27; T. Youngman 10 at 21.90; L. Hunter 11 at 23.09; O. Graham 12 at 25.58.

Clayesmore School *Dorset* P7 W6 D1

Master i/c D. O. Conway

Despite spells of wet weather, the 2016 season proved most successful. Led by Oliver Perrin, and able to call on Will Hendy's experience, Clayesmore earned six wins in attacking style.

Batting *O. W. C. R. Perrin 215 at 71.66; W. A. Hendy 172 at 43.00; M. K. Meredith 187 at 26.71.

Bowling J. E. Miles 11 at 8.81; B. J. Thompson 18 at 9.83.

Clifton College *Gloucestershire* P12 W7 L3 D2 A3

Master i/c J. C. Bobby **Coach** J. R. A. Williams

In another excellent season for Clifton, there were outstanding wins against Cheltenham, Rugby and – in the National T20 – King's College, Taunton. All-rounder Louie Shaw led by example, and gained a place in the Somerset Academy.

Batting P. Sisodiya 263 at 43.83; V. Lakhani 403 at 40.30; *L. J. P. Shaw 298 at 33.11.

Bowling L. J. P. Shaw 23 at 13.95; V. Lakhani 17 at 16.05; F. A. P. Cole 17 at 16.82.

Cranleigh School *Surrey* P20 W17 L3 A2

Master i/c A. P. Forsdike **Coach** S. D. Welch

After leading the first team to a school-record 17 wins, Ollie Pope left with his head held high – and a Surrey contract. He scored more than 2,000 runs over three summers.

Batting *O. J. D. Pope 904 at 75.33; O. W. Trower 395 at 35.90; A. E. C. Dahl 282 at 35.25; L. Bedford 507 at 33.80; F. D. C. Austin 442 at 29.46; M. P. Subba Row 211 at 17.58.

Bowling C. R. D. Terry 37 at 13.21; A. E. C. Dahl 28 at 14.35; E. J. Tristem 14 at 15.28; S. J. A. Dickson 27 at 16.18; N. M. A. Lubbock 16 at 18.76; H. S. J. Watkinson 11 at 19.63; M. P. Subba Row 17 at 21.37.

Culford School *Suffolk* P12 W8 L2 D2 A1

Master i/c A. M. Northcote

Culford enjoyed the best year in their recent history, with Freddie Statham leading the side to eight commanding wins.

Batting A. Oxley 276 at 46.00; C. Holt 263 at 26.30; A. Dhesi 261 at 26.10; F. Allum 245 at 24.50.

Bowling B. Whittaker 10 at 13.80; D. Corbett 17 at 17.70; *F. Statham 13 at 19.30.

Dame Allan's School *Northumberland* P5 W2 L3 A4

Master i/c J. A. Benn

The season was blighted by weather but, in the one start he got, captain Zach Place showed his skill; Chris Todd, the efficient vice-captain, really did get the players organised.

Batting The leading batsman was *Z. Place, who hit 103 runs at 34.33.

Bowling The leading bowler was P. J. Holliday, who claimed six wickets at 5.50.

Dauntsey's School *Wiltshire* P14 W9 L3 D2 A2

Master i/c A. J. Palmer **Coach** J. R. Ayling

An inexperienced side exceeded expectations, earning memorable wins against Winchester and MCC. Three performances stood out: Archie Ayling and Fergus Hooke took hat-tricks in the same match, against Hampshire Collegiate, while Rahul Patel's 151 not out is the school's third-highest individual score.

Batting R. N. Patel 441 at 40.09; W. J. Thomas 275 at 22.91; H. G. E. Janes 213 at 17.75; H. E. Baker 178 at 14.83.
Bowling F. Hooke 13 at 12.23; *O. D. Jackson 16 at 13.81; A. J. Ayling 16 at 14.62; N. M. Cannon 16 at 17.87; H. M. J. Cox 10 at 19.80.

Denstone College *Staffordshire* P14 W4 L9 D1 A2
Master i/c T. A. H. Williams **Coach** S. M. Guy
With nine defeats, Denstone certainly gained experience during a difficult summer; eight members of the team return for 2017, including captain Josh Russell.
Batting *J. J. Russell 598 at 42.71; S. S. Nawale 247 at 35.28; E. M. R. Barlow 349 at 34.90; L. S. Davis 223 at 27.87; M. A. Webber 220 at 16.92.
Bowling W. J. Godfrey 12 at 23.16; C. W. Willis 17 at 27.05; N. Joyale 11 at 28.81; E. M. R. Barlow 15 at 30.26; B. E. S. Wakefield 11 at 32.09; A. D. Billington 12 at 36.66.

Dr Challoner's Grammar School *Buckinghamshire* P7 W3 L2 D2 A5
Master i/c N. J. S. Buchanan
Opening batsman Dan Ogden dominated many an opposition attack, but could do little about the weather: five games were lost to rain.
Batting D. Ogden 244 at 40.66; S. G. Walsh 166 at 33.20.
Bowling T. D. Bracey 14 at 6.21; S. Sritharan 10 at 12.10.

Dollar Academy *Clackmannanshire* P14 W7 L6 D1 A1
Master i/c J. G. A. Frost
The first team enjoyed a number of excellent run-chases, including a four-wicket win over Strathallan School, and a tense victory over Merchiston Castle, where they protected a first innings of 79.
Batting L. J. L. Peterson 152 at 30.40; B. R. I. Pearson 181 at 20.11; M. K. Shepherd 208 at 18.90; *H. A. M. Warr 181 at 18.10.
Bowling M. K. Shepherd 13 at 14.15; L. McLaren 13 at 19.92; H. A. M. Warr 11 at 25.09.

Dover College *Kent* P4 W1 L3 A8
Master i/c G. R. Hill
Under captain Jack May, inclusivity was the theme for the season. Eight players took wickets, and the fielding was stronger than the batting.
Batting The leading batsman was B. Lewis, who hit 122 runs at 30.50.
Bowling The leading bowlers were J. J. Kennedy and R. P. Sewell, who both claimed four wickets at 10.75.

Downside School *Somerset* P10 W1 L7 D2
Master i/c H. P. Pike **Coach** A. C. Thomas
In a season of gloomy weather, a superb (and lone) win against Bryanston shone brightest. Lawrie Graham captained strongly, and drew notable performances from Hugo Morgan and Oliver Church.
Batting H. J. Morgan 151 at 30.20; O. G. Church 153 at 21.85; *L. C. Graham 157 at 15.70.
Bowling The leading bowler was H. H. Ross, who claimed six wickets at 32.16.

Dulwich College *Surrey* P16 W7 L7 D2
Master i/c D. C. Shirazi **Coach** C. W. J. Athey
Seven wins and seven defeats added up to a mixed year, but 509 runs from 16-year-old Jake Scarisbrick and 33 wickets for off-spinner Harry Millett – in his debut season – suggested a successful future.
Batting J. H. Scarisbrick 509 at 36.35; M. B. P. Faulkner 154 at 25.66; S. G. Fetherston 347 at 23.13; E. E. Bettridge 161 at 23.00; W. T. Johnson 276 at 21.23; R. G. Marchant 166 at 15.09.
Bowling F. G. Allocca 20 at 16.45; H. J. Millett 33 at 17.84; W. T. Johnson 12 at 20.83; *N. X. Corbett 15 at 30.26; J. W. H. Simpson 13 at 30.76.

Durham School *County Durham* P13 W8 L2 D3 A4
Master i/c M. B. Fishwick
Luke Henderson, the captain, enjoyed a fine all-round summer. He took most wickets and came second among the batsmen, behind Josh O'Brien, who earned the most improved player award.
Batting J. A. O'Brien 524 at 52.40; *L. R. Henderson 462 at 46.20; D. T. Scott 225 at 32.14; C. M. Fyfe 236 at 26.22.
Bowling L. R. Henderson 29 at 10.17; D. T. Scott 16 at 17.75.

Eastbourne College *Sussex* P15 W10 L3 D2 A4

Master i/c R. S. Ferley **Coach** A. C. Waller

The batting of the captain, Giles Robinson, who hit three fine hundreds, steered the team to ten wins.
Batting *G. S. Robinson 501 at 50.10; B. S. Twine 361 at 45.12; W. T. Huchu 410 at 31.53; B. N. Evans 361 at 27.76; H. E. T. Lloyd 268 at 26.80; B. C. McIntosh 224 at 24.88.
Bowling H. A. Tagg 10 at 7.40; W. T. Huchu 18 at 15.55; B. N. Evans 14 at 18.64; B. S. Twine 15 at 24.80.

The Edinburgh Academy *Midlothian* P16 W8 L8

Master i/c R. W. Sales

An up-and-down season ended with excellent wins against Barnard Castle and Rossall School in the annual festival. Calum Clarkson headed the bowling charts, and played for Scotland Under-17s.
Batting *H. A. H. W. Simpson 390 at 30.00; H. J. O'Brien 175 at 17.50; C. H. Devine 175 at 14.58.
Bowling C. R. Clarkson 16 at 12.56; J. Mann 22 at 14.04; F. D. N. Carmichael 19 at 16.52; C. H. Devine 13 at 21.61.

Elizabeth College, Guernsey *Channel Islands* P9 W2 L6 D1 A1

Master i/c T. P. Eisenhuth

Only two victories across the season might suggest otherwise, but Elizabeth College's young squad could just have the talent to bring success to Guernsey cricket for years to come.
Batting N. C. Guilbert 483 at 53.66; *A. C. Stokes 135 at 19.28; N. M. Hutchinson 151 at 18.87.
Bowling N. J. Buckle 11 at 23.00.

Ellesmere College *Shropshire* P8 W6 L2 A3

Master i/c G. Owen **Coach** R. Jones

Against school sides, Ellesmere were unbeaten in games longer than 30 overs, only dipping in form when they came up against adults at the end of the season. Success was built on depth: no batsman scored more than 150 runs.
Batting The leading batsman was B. Gibbon, who hit 138 runs at 34.50.
Bowling J. Furnival 10 at 9.00; V. Bajaj 14 at 10.07.

Eltham College *Kent* P13 W4 L8 D1 A3

Master i/c J. N. Batty

Fifteen-year-old Sam Smith took over the captaincy, and remained firm during a tough season, leading the run-scoring and hitting a wonderful hundred against Reed's. Victories came against Bancroft's, Reigate Grammar School, John Fisher and the Old Boys.
Batting I. Turner 195 at 39.00; *S. Smith 362 at 36.20; J. O. M. Williams 339 at 28.25; D. J. Lester 201 at 22.33; A. J. L. Khanna 189 at 18.90; O. P. Davies 205 at 18.63.
Bowling T. Gallo 12 at 24.50; N. Smith 16 at 27.43.

Emanuel School *Surrey* P9 W2 L6 T1 A4

Master i/c P. A. King **Coach** M. G. Stear

Emanuel's results might not have been brilliant, but they tell only part of the story: a number of losses came in tight games.
Batting The leading batsman was H. A. L. Darlington, who hit 144 runs at 16.00.
Bowling C. W. Hughes 13 at 18.76.

Epsom College *Surrey* P17 W7 L5 D5 A1

Master i/c N. R. Taylor **Coach** M. Homes

In his last season, captain Harry Williams had an outstanding year, with 642 runs, three centuries and 24 wickets. Only Peter O'Brien – magnificent with the new ball – claimed more victims.
Batting *H. D. Williams 642 at 42.80; E. D. Hughes 365 at 33.18; B. E. Holder 227 at 22.70; I. Z. B. Braithwaite 191 at 19.10.
Bowling P. B. O'Brien 30 at 14.76; H. D. Williams 24 at 15.25; W. R. Onslow-Wyld 12 at 17.25; L. A. Head 15 at 21.40; B. E. Holder 11 at 24.09; A. J. Lawrence 11 at 29.81.

Eton College *Buckinghamshire* P16 W14 L1 D1 A2

Master i/c R. D. Oliphant-Callum **Coach** T. W. Roberts

In a fixture list full of high-quality opposition, Eton's results were excellent. Captain Alistair Russell, in his final year, kept beautifully and scored 515 runs. The only thing he couldn't do was take wickets – that was left mainly to Sam Ellison and Finn O'Brien, who both claimed more than 20.

All-rounder Harry Williams and bowling spearhead Peter O'Brien: Epsom's leading pair in 2016.

Batting *A. D. L. Russell 515 at 57.22; F. T. P. O'Brien 273 at 54.60; N. C. MacDonagh 470 at 52.22; T. R. W. Gnodde 272 at 38.85; J. H. R. I. Hardman 459 at 30.60; A. R. Treon 452 at 30.13; N. R. J. Harrington 343 at 26.38.
Bowling O. J. W. Rogers 17 at 15.76; S. B. R. Ellison 24 at 19.87; F. T. P. O'Brien 23 at 20.43; J. M. P. Takavarasha 17 at 23.41; J. H. R. I. Hardman 18 at 27.61; W. J. E. Whipple 18 at 27.66.

Felsted School *Essex* P15 W11 L2 D2 A1

Master i/c J. E. R. Gallian **Coaches** C. S. Knightley and N. J. Lockhart

Felsted could be proud of their year: they won the majority of their games and finished runners-up in the National T20 competition.
Batting C. S. Latham 369 at 92.25; J. M. Cox 484 at 53.77; *Y. A. Grant 547 at 45.58; A. A. Cox 361 at 36.10; S. R. Holland 241 at 34.42; W. E. L. Buttleman 300 at 27.27.
Bowling B. A. Waring 33 at 14.75; O. W. S. Hills 19 at 14.84; A. A. Cox 22 at 16.00; L. J. Chapman 24 at 16.50.

Fettes College *Midlothian* P11 W8 L1 D2 A1

Master i/c A. B. Russell

In Scotland, Fettes reigned supreme, winning every match and lifting the Scottish Schools T20 Cup. Player of the season George West finished in style, hitting 111 not out against The Leys to take his tally to 400.
Batting G. J. West 400 at 44.44; R. T. Mather 284 at 28.40; G. G. Conner 265 at 22.08.
Bowling H. G. E. West 17 at 7.88; C. A. Spilsbury 13 at 10.76; B. M. MacLeod 12 at 15.66; G. G. Conner 18 at 16.83; B. G. Sperling 13 at 17.46.

Forest School *Essex* P14 W8 L4 D2

Master i/c S. J. Foulds **Coach** J. S. Foster

Captain Christian Hall fostered excellent team spirit, and led his side to a successful year. He shone with bat and ball, while left-arm spinner Arunesh Ragutharan caught the eye as leading wicket-taker.
Batting C. Shekleton 448 at 49.77; *C. A. Hall 391 at 39.10; T. H. Kelsey 298 at 37.25; M. C. Lavery 231 at 21.00; J. Dennis 212 at 19.27; E. J. Risby 163 at 14.81.
Bowling O. Ashraf 15 at 12.66; C. A. Hall 26 at 14.76; A. Ragutharan 29 at 15.17; E. J. Risby 17 at 19.47; U. Ashraf 10 at 34.10.

Framlingham College *Suffolk* P11 W2 L5 D4 A1

Master i/c M. J. Marvell **Coach** S. D. Greenall

Results were encouraging, yet might have been even better: three defeats came in the final over. Jack Hobbs and Ben Boyden were in excellent form, and gained strong support from all-rounder Jonathan Hulley.

Batting J. L. Hobbs 454 at 50.44; B. A. M. Boyden 346 at 43.25; R. M. Taylor 226 at 28.25; *C. R. Greenhall 187 at 26.71.

Bowling J. S. P. Hulley 16 at 24.18; G. W. Heldreich 10 at 40.30.

George Heriot's School *Midlothian* P8 W4 L4

Master i/c E. L. Harrison

Much credit for the school's four wins goes to captain Sharav Senthil: competing school commitments made fielding the strongest team difficult, but he kept spirits high throughout.

Batting The leading batsman was G. H. Shand, who hit 106 runs at 21.20.

Bowling The leading bowler was P. Agarwal, who claimed eight wickets at 20.37.

George Watson's College *Midlothian* P17 W8 L6 T1 D2 A2

Master i/c M. J. Leonard **Coach** A. D. W. Patterson

Problems of availability meant results were up and down. But Oliver Brown captained well and batted positively, and gained useful support from Matthew Brian, who hit most runs.

Batting M. A. Brian 356 at 35.60; *O. J. Brown 317 at 28.81; F. M. Cousin 199 at 18.09; C. J. Macdonald 281 at 17.56; D. K. Arvind 170 at 14.16; P. M. Brown 173 at 13.30; M. K. Whitaker 163 at 12.53.

Bowling M. K. Whitaker 15 at 15.40; M. O. Bedford 10 at 21.70; C. Macleod 12 at 22.33; A. A. Sundaram 11 at 22.54; P. M. Brown 10 at 26.10; D. K. Arvind 10 at 29.70.

Giggleswick School *Yorkshire* P9 W4 L2 T1 D2 A1

Master i/c R. T. F. Bunday

Giggleswick's strength lay in the bowling, where John Davidson led the way. That he also topped the batting suggests a need for greater depth. However, 12 who played in the first team in 2016 will return, with greater experience.

Batting *J. J. Davidson 216 at 36.00.

Bowling J. J. Davidson 11 at 14.27; O. Whyte 11 at 14.90.

The Glasgow Academy *Lanarkshire* P7 W5 L2 A1

Master i/c P. J. W. Smith **Coach** V. Hariharan

A pre-season tour to Dubai fostered a strong *esprit de corps*, which in turn produced a fine season. With all players returning in 2017, results should get even better.

Batting *J. L. Oliver 272 at 90.66.

Bowling J. R. Percival 14 at 9.21.

The High School of Glasgow *Lanarkshire* P11 W3 L7 D1 A1

Master i/c D. N. Barrett **Coaches** N. R. Clarke and K. J. A. Robertson

Three excellent wins were easily outweighed by defeats, albeit some narrow ones.

Batting C. J. Coats 189 at 21.00.

Bowling The leading bowler was C. J. Coats, who took nine wickets at 27.44.

Glenalmond College *Perthshire* P8 W2 L5 D1 A4

Master i/c M. J. Davies

Despite good leadership from Harry Hartley-Metcalfe, and fine contributions with the bat from Kaleem Barreto and Jordan Chatt, this was a mixed season for Glenalmond, who claimed just two victories.

Batting K. A. Barreto 258 at 64.50; J. A. W. Chatt 181 at 45.25; T. A. Godfrey-Faussett 169 at 24.14.

Bowling R. W. P. Leader 10 at 14.10; *H. N. J. Hartley-Metcalfe 10 at 17.20.

Gordonstoun School *Morayshire* P11 W3 L5 D3 A2

Master i/c C. J. Barton **Coach** R. Denyer

Gordonstoun enjoyed a fantastic season, particularly their batsmen. Alex Hands made full use of dry conditions in north-east Scotland, scoring just shy of 400 runs, while Archie Houldsworth made his fifth *Wisden* appearance.

Dulwich's Harry Millett claimed 33 victims with his off-breaks, while Harrow captain Anshuman Rath hit 826 runs and took 21 wickets with his left-arm spin.

Batting A. J. I. Houldsworth 310 at 62.00; A. J. Hands 397 at 44.11; *M. I. S. Raheel 228 at 28.50; M. B. B. Rind 246 at 22.36; J. J. Congdon 177 at 22.12.
Bowling M. I. S. Raheel 14 at 24.14; M. B. B. Rind 10 at 39.10.

Gresham's School *Norfolk* P12 W4 L4 D4 A2

Master i/c A. Horsley **Coach** M. B. Loye
After a slow start, Gresham's finished with good wins against Norwich School and Framlingham College. Player of the season Tatenda Chiradza led both averages.
Batting T. Chiradza 370 at 37.00; *T. E. Sheridan 218 at 24.22; W. G. Buckingham 209 at 23.22; H. A. de Lucchi 213 at 19.36; W. W. Wright 167 at 16.70; A. Taylor 158 at 15.80.
Bowling T. Chiradza 20 at 12.50; D. S. Mazhawidza 22 at 15.40; W. W. Wright 11 at 25.54; K. Peters 18 at 28.55.

Haberdashers' Aske's Boys' School *Hertfordshire* P15 W6 L7 D2 A6

Master i/c S. D. Charlwood **Coaches** D. H. Kerry and J. P. Hewitt
The side played well in patches – notably in victories over Berkhamsted, St Albans and Exeter CC – but were prone to wobbles, particularly after half-term. Captain Ian Harris led by example, scoring 464 runs and topping the bowling averages.
Batting C. W. T. Mack 665 at 47.50; *I. M. Harris 464 at 29.00; A. R. C. Willis 417 at 26.06; J. H. Urban 334 at 22.26; N. Rasakulasuriar 255 at 18.21.
Bowling I. M. Harris 13 at 20.07; A. Chatterjee 19 at 22.15; C. W. T. Mack 14 at 26.71; N. Rasakulasuriar 16 at 28.18; S. A. Lakhani 19 at 30.52.

Haileybury *Hertfordshire* P15 W4 L10 D1

Master i/c D. L. S. van Bunge **Coach** C. Igolen-Robinson
Haileybury recorded four victories, two more than 2015, including fine wins against Stamford – where they chased a school-record 308 – and MCC. Even in the losses there were signs of improvement: routs the previous year became narrow defeats.
Batting *O. M. Heazel 632 at 52.66; F. J. R. Walker 492 at 44.72; B. W. Morris 238 at 19.83.
Bowling O. M. Heazel 25 at 17.36; H. F. E. Wines 18 at 32.05; J. C. Stibbs 16 at 39.75; H. G. Bradley 13 at 43.69.

Hampton School *Middlesex* P17 W9 L6 D2 A2

Master i/c A. M. Banerjee **Coach** C. P. Harrison
A young team produced some memorable performances, including a 19-run win over Dulwich, and victories over The King's School, Parramatta (New South Wales) and St David's Marist (Johannesburg). And with many of the juniors showing great promise, the future looks encouraging.

Batting C. R. Campbell 556 at 39.71; *C. J. Searle 459 at 35.30; T. M. Ryan 473 at 33.78; O. T. George 316 at 28.72; B. A. Gilbert 212 at 26.50; J. F. D. Wheeler 199 at 22.11; A. J. Lee 325 at 21.66.
Bowling L. O. Minshull 22 at 19.31; C. J. Searle 21 at 24.28; A. J. Lee 10 at 26.70; M. H. Starling 11 at 40.90; B. J. Dowse 13 at 43.38.

Harrow School *Middlesex* P21 W8 L9 D4 A1

Master i/c R. S. C. Martin-Jenkins **Coach** S. A. Jones

In a season dominated by the top four batsmen, the remarkable match against Hampton was the pinnacle: Harrow scored 442 for four in 50 overs, including Anshuman Rath's 101-ball 171. The spinners – Abdullah Nazir, Rahul Wijeratne and Rath – took most of the wickets, despite damp conditions.
Batting *A. Rath 826 at 48.58; R. S. Wijeratne 650 at 46.42; G. F. Reid 627 at 36.88; J. A. Jordache 534 at 31.41; H. H. Dicketts 219 at 24.33; H. E. J. Laing 150 at 16.66; A. P. Ferreira 181 at 12.92.
Bowling A. Nazir 23 at 20.60; R. S. Wijeratne 20 at 21.00; R. Shah 11 at 26.18; A. Rath 21 at 27.90; A. E. W. Maxwell 12 at 30.25; H. E. J. Laing 13 at 37.15.

The Harvey Grammar School *Kent* P5 W4 D1 A5

Master i/c S. Rowe **Coach** P. M. Castle

For the second successive season, weather severely curtailed the programme, but Oliver Rhys-Jones followed up on the promise of last year and became the leading wicket-taker.
Batting The leading batsman was *A. Leaver, who hit 136 runs at 34.00.
Bowling The leading bowler was O. H. Rhys-Jones, who claimed nine wickets at 4.88.

Highgate School *Middlesex* P8 W3 L5

Masters i/c A. G. Tapp and S. Patel

The form of Jack Bruce – who has played for Middlesex Seconds and is a member of their Academy – and Tom Waine helped the school to wins over Chigwell, Mill Hill and the XL Club.
Batting *J. M. Bruce 174 at 29.00; T. F. Waine 151 at 21.57.
Bowling J. M. Bruce 11 at 10.90; T. F. Waine 11 at 15.72.

Hurstpierpoint College *Sussex* P11 W5 L3 D3 A2

Master i/c N. J. K. Creed **Coaches** M. H. Yardy and P. G. Hudson

Thirteen wins from 22 fixtures in all cricket represented a very successful year. Tom Haines was the backbone of the batting, and he made his first-class debut for Sussex in August. Dan Doram, Jonty Jenner and Joe Gilligan all appeared for Sussex Seconds.
Batting T. J. Haines 405 at 67.50; T. L. Heath 179 at 44.75; R. J. M. Whyte 240 at 30.00; V. A. Lawson 175 at 25.00.
Bowling W. C. H. P. Collard 16 at 15.68; *J. J. Jenner 14 at 16.71; D. T. Doram 16 at 18.68.

Hymers College *Yorkshire* P16 W2 L12 T1 D1 A1

Master i/c G. Tipping

Hymers competed well, but were about 20 runs short in most games, and won only twice.
Batting C. J. Rawlins 303 at 21.64; T. G. Elstone 307 at 19.18; T. Wilson 249 at 19.15; A. R. F. Brocklesby 292 at 18.25; S. S. Khawar 168 at 14.00.
Bowling F. B. B. Dickenson 14 at 20.00; A. J. Juckes 19 at 20.21; H. R. Sweeting 12 at 35.00.

Ibstock Place School *Surrey* P13 W4 L7 D2 A2

Master i/c R. S. Brown

Ibstock Place's development continued with four wins, as well as two excellent draws for the mixed XI against Alleyn's and KCS, Wimbledon.
Batting *J. A. Welton 185 at 15.41.
Bowling J. A. Welton 12 at 23.83.

Ipswich School *Suffolk* P13 W5 L6 D2 A2

Master i/c A. K. Golding **Coach** R. E. East

Greater consistency might have yielded better results, but the team's exciting prospects – including Josh Rymell and Joe Macgregor – have the potential to make amends.

Batting J. S. Rymell 331 at 27.58; J. G. Stewart 254 at 25.40; J. L. H. Macgregor 305 at 23.46; S. L. Edmond 175 at 21.87; L. R. C. Froggatt 159 at 19.87; *J. A. C. Knight 199 at 18.09; J. S. W. Parry 150 at 16.66.

Bowling J. L. H. Macgregor 21 at 16.28; L. D. Totton 11 at 16.36; T. E. O. Phillips 12 at 19.16.

The John Fisher School *Surrey* P15 W6 L9 A5

Master i/c J. R. McCann **Coach** M. M. Cody

The first team had an up-and-down season: nine defeats were punctuated by notable wins against Emanuel, Wilson's and Wallington County Grammar School. Aidan Barton's superb captaincy, and the all-round skills of Harri Aravinthan, shone all summer.

Batting H. H. Aravinthan 467 at 58.37.

Bowling H. H. Aravinthan 18 at 10.72; L. A. Risolino 11 at 18.45; J. C. Roffey 10 at 20.20.

The John Lyon School *Middlesex* P14 W4 L8 D2 A1

Master i/c A. S. Ling **Coach** C. T. Peploe

Five wins from the first six games proved unsustainable and, when the batting faltered, so did results. Owen Marshall again bowled magnificently and improved his batting too, while the performances of Abhay Hirani and Zeshaan Mahmood gave encouragement.

Batting A. D. Hirani 187 at 26.71; O. J. Marshall 269 at 20.69; J. V. Gandhi 175 at 15.90; D. J. Maru 151 at 13.72.

Bowling O. J. Marshall 17 at 17.94; *K. D. Ghelani 14 at 18.71; Z. Mahmood 13 at 21.30.

The Judd School *Kent* P9 W5 L2 D2 A1

Master i/c D. W. Joseph

Under Chris Mingard's excellent leadership, the team earned five wins, a marked improvement from just one in 2015. Omkaar Divekar's batting and Callum Gallagher's all-round prowess were major factors.

Batting O. A. Divekar 173 at 34.60; C. J. Gallagher 172 at 34.40.

Bowling A. H. Reid-Dick 11 at 20.45; J. J. Wheeler 11 at 22.63; C. J. Gallagher 10 at 22.90.

Kimbolton School *Huntingdonshire* P14 W7 L7

Master i/c M. S. Gilbert **Coach** A. J. Tudor

Joshua Smith's 589 runs and 22 wickets stood out, but contributions throughout the team helped Kimbolton to seven wins. Harrison Peak hit 451 runs and took 13 wickets, while David Adesida, George Wilkinson, Cameron Carroll and Johnny Doyle all took at least ten.

Batting J. J. Smith 589 at 53.54; H. W. B. Peak 451 at 37.58; G. Wilkinson 169 at 15.36.

Bowling J. J. Smith 22 at 16.18; J. A. Doyle 10 at 17.70; C. J. W. Carroll 13 at 19.00; H. W. B. Peak 13 at 25.15; D. O. Adesida 14 at 26.00; G. Wilkinson 12 at 34.16.

King Edward VI School, Southampton *Hampshire* P9 W3 L4 D2

Master i/c D. Kent

The first team recorded dominant wins over Halliford and Churcher's, and a hard-earned draw against Lancing, but several narrow defeats left a tang of frustration. For results to improve, more runs will be needed.

Batting J. Fay 167 at 27.83.

Bowling J. Fay 13 at 12.84.

King Edward's School, Birmingham *Warwickshire* P16 W8 L6 D2 A4

Master i/c L. M. Roll **Coach** N. W. Round

A strong and varied bowling attack drove King Edward's to most of their eight wins. Tarush Gupta, the player of the season, held the batting together and kept smartly.

Batting T. Gupta 352 at 58.66; H. Ajaib 223 at 24.77; J. S. Ray 317 at 24.38; A. Hussain 290 at 24.16.

Bowling S. Sawlani 13 at 19.92; V. A. Sriram 15 at 20.86; *R. R. Gandhewar 13 at 21.30; K. S. Gangurde 12 at 23.08.

King Henry VIII School *Warwickshire* P10 W7 L2 D1 A1

Master i/c A. M. Parker

King Henry VIII began with seven straight wins, including victories over Bishop Vesey's, Ratcliffe and Solihull. Strong batting from Taran Toor, Arjan Bath and Sher Chattha regularly set difficult targets, and the suffocating spin of Luton Stonier and Rahul Trivedi often helped defend them.

Batting A. S. Bath 151 at 151.00; N. A. Chattha 384 at 76.80; A. C. Huxford 171 at 57.00; T. S. Toor 305 at 43.57.

Bowling L. G. Stonier 12 at 19.33.

King's College School, Wimbledon *Surrey* P22 W10 L10 T1 D1 A1

Master i/c J. S. Gibson **Coach** P. J. Scott

With a number of matches going to the last over – including a tie – this was an exciting season. Captain Jake Hennessey hit 673 runs in a strong batting team (nine players scored more than 150), while George Betts claimed 33 wickets.

Batting *J. J. S. Hennessey 673 at 35.42; F. A. H. Freeman 527 at 29.27; E. J. Hawkins-Hooker 333 at 25.61; A. G. Spencer 190 at 20.11; V. A. Bakker 238 at 18.30; O. C. D. Little 209 at 17.41; F. M. Bennett 203 at 15.61; S. H. Patel 287 at 15.10; W. G. Bennett 197 at 14.07.

Bowling A. Bond 20 at 15.20; V. A. Bakker 10 at 15.70; G. A. V. Betts 33 at 17.09; M. S. Chelvam 28 at 17.28; A. G. Spencer 19 at 22.68; O. C. D. Little 14 at 31.14.

King's College, Taunton *Somerset* P13 W11 L1 D1 A2

Master i/c P. D. Lewis **Coach** R. J. Woodman

In a brilliant season, King's College beat Exeter University for the first time, and lost only once, to a strong MCC side. Tom Banton was the outstanding player, with several big hundreds; Bradley Lynch also averaged over 65.

Batting T. Banton 667 at 111.16; *B. Lynch 393 at 65.50; E. J. Byrom 248 at 49.60; L. Machado 316 at 45.14; C. G. Harrison 229 at 38.16.

Bowling J. L. S. Clark 22 at 9.90; T. Banton 10 at 10.80; L. M. Tomkins 14 at 11.21.

King's School, Bruton *Somerset* P8 W2 L4 D2

Master i/c R. S. Hamilton

Despite a solid year for the batsmen – five players made 150 runs or more – it proved a difficult summer, with only two wins.

Batting R. J. Cadbury 234 at 33.42; *H. G. Woolway 186 at 31.00; M. Tomes-Smith 150 at 30.00; B. J. Latham 164 at 27.33; J. O. Hudson 156 at 26.00.

Bowling The leading bowler was A. M. Potter, who claimed nine wickets at 17.88.

The King's School, Canterbury *Kent* P17 W11 L3 D3 A1

Master i/c R. A. L. Singfield **Coach** M. A. Ealham

Oliver Tikare's strong team remained unbeaten until the last week of term. William Heywood was the outstanding batsman, with 874 runs, while seamer Oliver Mann again took most wickets: his 43 bettered his 2015 total by 20.

Batting W. J. Heywood 874 at 72.83; *O. B. S. Tikare 729 at 40.50; M. D. Barker 517 at 28.72; E. C. S. Solly 319 at 26.58; R. P. Heywood 181 at 25.85; R. J. Campbell 222 at 14.80.

Bowling O. J. D. Mann 43 at 13.02; W. J. Heywood 23 at 16.26; O. B. S. Tikare 17 at 20.11; G. W. R. Meddings 13 at 20.76; R. P. Heywood 14 at 23.21; M. D. Barker 13 at 26.84.

King's School, Chester *Cheshire* P10 W3 L5 D2 A4

Master i/c S. Neal **Coach** J. Potts

Fraser Smellie's temperament helped him become the outstanding batsman, while Shane Patel's left-arm spin asked difficult questions. These talented players deserved more cricket, but rain washed out four fixtures.

Batting *S. D. Rimmer 185 at 46.25; F. G. Smellie 251 at 41.83; M. J. Thompson 186 at 26.57.

Bowling S. Patel 14 at 11.28.

The King's School in Macclesfield *Cheshire* P16 W8 L5 D3 A2

Master i/c S. Moores **Coach** A. Kennedy

The first team improved with every game to end with eight wins, five more than in 2015. William Hodgson's superb leadership and batting deserve much credit.

Batting *W. J. Hodgson 454 at 64.85.
Bowling S. J. Buckingham 13 at 10.53; H. Elms 25 at 14.32; J. B. Bryning 17 at 18.82; J. A. Hodges 12 at 23.25.

King's School, Rochester *Kent* P12 W2 L9 D1 A3

Master i/c C. H. Page **Coaches** M. J. Hebden and J. Waite

Although the fielding was of a high standard, and the bowling well led by captain James Carslaw (who gained Under-17 county selection), the batting was rarely enough to force victory.
Batting *J. W. Carslaw 263 at 32.87; F. J. S. Hawes 152 at 13.81.
Bowling J. W. Carslaw 18 at 14.50; F. J. S. Hawes 13 at 18.84; O. Settle 11 at 27.90.

The King's School, Worcester *Worcestershire* P16 W10 L4 D2

Master i/c D. P. Iddon **Coach** A. A. D. Gillgrass

In a successful season, two stalwarts reached personal milestones: Nick Hammond took his aggregate to 2,800 first-team runs, including 12 centuries, while Henry Wilde reached 100 first-team wickets.
Batting *N. A. Hammond 797 at 79.70; J. G. Arnold 188 at 31.33; H. G. S. Armstrong 266 at 22.16; H. G. Annable 259 at 21.58.
Bowling H. C. Wilde 21 at 11.04; C. S. J. Stanley-Blakey 21 at 15.42; J. Ham 11 at 16.81; T. N. Whitworth 17 at 17.70.

Kingswood School, Bath *Somerset* P10 W5 L4 D1 A5

Master i/c J. O. Brown

Poor weather caused the abandonment of a third of the fixture list but, when the sun shone, the players took their chance. Charlie Brain topped the batting averages for the second year running, while Monty Keith claimed the only five-for of the season.
Batting C. O. Brain 282 at 47.00; T. A. Phillips 163 at 32.60.
Bowling M. A. K. Keith 19 at 11.10; T. A. Phillips 11 at 12.00; C. G. Walker 10 at 12.80; G. T. Postlethwaite 12 at 13.75.

Kirkham Grammar School *Lancashire* P9 W4 L4 T1

Master i/c J. R. Lyon

With the squad containing just three Year 13s, four wins represented a good season. The batting relied on Tyrell Maclean, Edward Bailey and wicketkeeper Kieran Wilkinson, while captain Ben Anderson's spin complemented opening bowler Sam Dugdale's pace and accuracy.
Batting T. A. Maclean 349 at 58.16; K. A. Wilkinson 217 at 31.00; E. J. Bailey 195 at 19.50.
Bowling *B. Anderson 13 at 9.00.

Lancing College *Sussex* P11 W6 L4 D1 A3

Master i/c R. J. Maru

Lancing coped well with losing key players, and were unbeaten in their last six games. William Fazakerley was player of the year, and earned a place in the Leicestershire Academy, as did fellow all-rounder Tom Nightingale.
Batting H. W. Smethurst 315 at 45.00; W. N. Fazakerley 327 at 40.87; T. W. Nightingale 320 at 26.66; *M. C. Clarke 218 at 21.80; F. Desjarlais 195 at 16.25.
Bowling W. N. Fazakerley 25 at 11.40; T. W. Nightingale 29 at 12.62; A. Symonds 12 at 20.33.

Latymer Upper School *Middlesex* P13 W6 L6 D1 A3

Master i/c G. S. Tidey **Coach** B. Taylor

Coruscating performances came throughout the season, with hat-tricks, five-fors and a fine century from Hari Badale. The first team enjoyed a good Under-19 cup run, but lost in the semi-finals on a bowl-out.
Batting *H. Badale 279 at 39.85.
Bowling T. Benson 21 at 5.76.

The Grammar School at Leeds *Yorkshire* P13 W3 L6 T1 D3 A4

Master i/c S. H. Dunn

After an undefeated season in 2015, difficulties with availability made wins harder to come by.
Batting E. B. Litvin 356 at 50.85; *O. F. J. Robinson 200 at 18.18.
Bowling J. C. M. Dracup 14 at 15.50; T. B. J. Burton 19 at 17.21; S. D. Winter 14 at 23.07.

Leicester Grammar School *Leicestershire* P8 W2 L4 D2 A4

Master i/c L. Potter

Despite seven of the previous year's first team having left, the school reached the final of the Leicestershire County Cup.

Batting J. Willmott 174 at 24.85.

Bowling L. F. Higham 10 at 15.70.

The Leys School *Cambridgeshire* P11 W7 L2 D2 A1

Master i/c R. I. Kaufman **Coach** W. J. Earl

In an excellent season for The Leys, Milan Mniszko was outstanding, scoring 623 runs at 77, while Andrew Bramley struck two magnificent hundreds.

Batting M. A. Mniszko 623 at 77.87; A. S. B. Bramley 420 at 42.00; H. J. Jarman 223 at 31.85; T. P. Cox 282 at 31.33; E. C. P. Fairey 257 at 25.70.

Bowling T. S. Waldock 13 at 18.07; A. S. B. Bramley 15 at 18.66; W. A. Latham 11 at 19.81; M. A. Mniszko 16 at 20.93; J. A. Gunn-Roberts 11 at 29.00.

Lord Wandsworth College *Hampshire* P12 W5 L4 D3 A1

Master i/c D. M. Beven **Coach** C. C. Hicks

The Lord Wandsworth boys will remember the season for wins against Epsom, Charterhouse and (in a T20) Radley, as well as the draw against MCC. Dan Scott grew into a fine all-round cricketer, topping both averages.

Batting D. A. Scott 184 at 61.33; B. M. Wetherell 221 at 44.20; *S. H. R. Culmer 212 at 42.40; C. J. Young 330 at 33.00; T. E. H. C. Williams 176 at 19.55.

Bowling D. A. Scott 15 at 20.93; O. H. Hewetson-Brown 14 at 24.35; W. P. Arnold 10 at 30.80.

Magdalen College School *Oxfordshire* P14 W7 L5 D2 A1

Master i/c D. Bebbington **Coach** A. J. Scriven

A summer of several significant wins was proof that MCS cricket is flourishing. Hampshire Academy player Tom Scriven led the batting (and struck three centuries), while all-rounder and vice-captain Tom Price claimed most wickets – and scored heavily too.

Batting *T. R. A. Scriven 459 at 65.57; T. J. Price 313 at 44.71; A. T. Spittles 348 at 29.00; A. Mayho 185 at 26.42; E. J. O. Smith 208 at 20.80; N. Devaney-Dykes 210 at 19.09.

Bowling T. J. Price 21 at 13.80; O. J. Price 14 at 17.57; E. J. O. Smith 13 at 22.92.

Malvern College *Worcestershire* P13 W7 L1 T1 D4 A5

Master i/c M. A. Hardinges **Coach** N. A. Brett

Five matches were lost to rain, but victories still abounded. Harrow, Millfield and Bromsgrove were beaten, and a six-wicket defeat of Wrekin – when Josh Haynes slammed a 34-ball hundred – delivered the Chesterton Cup.

Batting J. A. Haynes 418 at 38.00; *J. L. Haynes 424 at 35.33; M. Ahmed 219 at 24.33; W. D. Annetts 157 at 22.42.

Bowling J. L. Haynes 23 at 7.91; T. W. Strong 11 at 13.00; W. A. J. Sharp 10 at 16.70; J. F. Charters 10 at 22.50.

The Manchester Grammar School *Lancashire* P11 W6 L3 D2 A5

Master i/c M. Watkinson

Despite rain and exams, spirits remained high – and the first team prospered under the excellent captaincy of Josh Dooler, who maintained his fine all-round form from the 2015 season.

Batting O. G. F. Pooler 324 at 46.28; *J. Dooler 233 at 38.83; S. J. Perry 281 at 35.12; S. D. Povey 210 at 35.00.

Bowling J. Dooler 11 at 17.54; A. H. Makin 10 at 19.50.

Marlborough College *Wiltshire* P17 W11 L4 D2 A2

Master i/c M. P. L. Bush **Coach** M. W. Alleyne

A talented all-round team had a rewarding season. Highlights included thrilling one-wicket victories over MCC and St Edward's, Oxford, and dominant displays against Winchester and Sherborne. The college entered the National T20 Cup for the first time, and reached the last 16.

Wicketkeeper-batsman Andrew Thomas hit more than 700 runs for Merchant Taylors', Northwood; Billy Mead collected over 500 – plus 15 wickets – for Marlborough.

Batting S. W. Mead 569 at 37.93; M. P. K. Read 455 at 35.00; E. I. Samuel 409 at 34.08; W. P. Davies 176 at 25.14; D. H. Coulson 292 at 22.46; B. C. Wilson 198 at 16.50; J. N. A. Bunn 169 at 15.36.
Bowling *F. J. Gordon 25 at 18.16; J. N. A. Bunn 19 at 20.73; S. W. Mead 15 at 21.13; D. A. West 18 at 21.33; W. P. Davies 19 at 23.42; B. C. Wilson 12 at 25.66.

Merchant Taylors' School, Crosby *Lancashire* P17 W7 L5 D5

Master i/c S. P. Sutcliffe **Coach** J. Cole

In an encouraging summer, George Lavelle batted and kept wicket with skill – claiming five catches and nine stumpings – while Tom Hartley's spin was a constant threat. However, they played only nine matches each because of other cricket commitments. There were good wins over Gateshead and Bolton School, and an exciting draw at Lancaster RGS, where all four results were possible off the final ball.
Batting G. I. D. Lavelle 435 at 72.50; A. D. J. Rankin 258 at 23.45.
Bowling E. L. Brown 14 at 10.92; B. W. Aitchison 12 at 13.41; T. W. Hartley 18 at 14.00; T. E. Barker-Weinberger 16 at 16.87; E. Agarwal 11 at 25.36.

Merchant Taylors' School, Northwood *Hertfordshire* P15 W8 L4 T1 D2 A2

Master i/c T. Webley

Andrew Thomas scored sublime centuries against Haberdashers' Aske's and MCC. The school recorded some superb victories, and were North London champions of the National T20 Cup.
Batting *A. D. Thomas 716 at 65.09; J. Regan 515 at 46.81; A. R. Amin 502 at 45.63; A. L. Wijesuriya 386 at 42.88; O. A. Karim 423 at 35.25; N. Rawal 436 at 33.53.
Bowling A. R. Amin 32 at 10.18; D. A. Patel 28 at 12.14; M. T. N. Brown 14 at 14.92; A. K. Randev 17 at 17.76; K. A. Singh 16 at 18.56.

Merchiston Castle School *Midlothian* P13 W5 L7 T1 A1

Master i/c R. D. McCann

Angus Hinton had another outstanding year, averaging 58 with the bat and ably captaining a side containing many new faces.
Batting *A. M. M. Hinton 528 at 58.66.
Bowling C. T. Fullarton 16 at 13.81; J. M. Alexander 10 at 15.40; C. J. Fry 12 at 22.33.

Mill Hill School *Middlesex* P7 W3 L3 D1 A2

Master i/c I. J. F. Hutchinson **Coach** N. R. Hodgson

A talented group of cricketers enjoyed some great matches, with strong performances in all competitions. Against St Benedict's, the team chased down 251 for the loss of just two wickets.

Batting E. R. Bamber 228 at 76.00; W. G. Kilbourn 170 at 34.00.

Bowling W. G. Kilbourn 12 at 13.66; M. G. Thal 10 at 34.20.

Millfield School *Somerset* P15 W8 L3 D4 A5

Master i/c R. M. Ellison **Coach** C. D. Gange

The highlight of a rain-interrupted term was victory in the National T20 Cup. In September, the Under-17s won the School Sport 40/40, and the Under-15s their own National T20 competition. George Bartlett had a productive time with bat and ball. The first team, comprehensively beaten by Malvern and Tonbridge, discovered that any slip can be severely punished by strong sides.

Batting G. A. Bartlett 413 at 45.88; F. R. Trenouth 214 at 42.80; J. I. McCoy 374 at 41.55; J. Seward 271 at 33.87; D. A. Chesham 234 at 26.00; *T. C. Lace 173 at 24.71.

Bowling B. J. Currie 13 at 10.69; G. A. Bartlett 20 at 11.45; D. J. L. Clutterbuck 20 at 19.70; K. O. Hopper 11 at 24.90; J. I. McCoy 12 at 34.08.

Monkton Combe School *Somerset* P15 W6 L8 D1 A4

Master i/c S. P. J. Palmer **Coach** J. C. W. Arney

A good side underperformed, losing five games they should have won. A wet June, which ruined much of the season, didn't help. George Leakey, the skipper, took 27 wickets, taking his total for the first team to 68.

Batting B. J. J. Wells 490 at 35.00; T. M. B. Salmon 354 at 27.23; E. J. Halse 209 at 23.22; W. F. A. Bishop 217 at 19.72; W. G. K. Arney 187 at 14.38.

Bowling *G. A. Leakey 27 at 12.44; E. J. Halse 20 at 13.10; C. J. Wells 21 at 16.04; W. G. K. Arney 16 at 17.37; A. W. Parashar 12 at 22.16.

Monmouth School *Monmouthshire* P13 W3 L4 D6 A4

Master i/c A. J. Jones **Coach** G. I. Burgess

The batting of Hywel Rose lit up a summer badly affected by the weather. The first of his two fantastic centuries was 171, the third-highest score for the school. Lewis Devonald took six wickets in one match.

Batting B. R. Lander 384 at 48.00; *H. M. Rose 581 at 41.50; M. P. Kefalas 197 at 24.62; A. G. McIntyre 267 at 24.27.

Bowling L. M. Devonald 16 at 21.93; J. O. Sharpe 12 at 22.33; D. M. Sharp 12 at 25.58; A. G. Hamilton 12 at 33.66.

Mount Kelly College *Devon* P11 W8 L3 A1

Master i/c T. L. Honey **Coach** B. J. Worth

The first team, well led by Harry Williams, enjoyed their most successful season in recent memory. With Ben Grove, Tom Rogers and Oliver Allsop expected to return, there is optimism for the future.

Batting B. G. Grove 322 at 35.77; *H. S. Williams 238 at 34.00; O. R. M. Allsop 158 at 22.57.

Bowling T. J. Rogers 15 at 13.73; O. J. C. Wood 14 at 14.57; H. S. Williams 16 at 15.81.

New Hall School *Essex* P18 W9 L7 D2

Master i/c G. D. James **Coach** N. Hussain

An enthusiastic side took significant strides in an exciting season, whose highlight was winning the Castle Festival – thanks in part to maiden centuries from Julian Whetstone and James Berry.

Batting *J. M. Whetstone 554 at 36.93; B. T. Allison 273 at 30.33; J. D. Berry 288 at 26.18; C. G. Lockhart 364 at 26.00; S. S. Sullivan 253 at 25.30; G. P. Spires 153 at 12.75.

Bowling B. T. Allison 21 at 10.95; V. A. Gandhi 11 at 16.81; C. V. Limrick 16 at 22.00; J. Aggarwal 20 at 25.80; J. M. Whetstone 11 at 26.36; T. A. Clayton 10 at 29.30; G. P. Spires 12 at 29.50.

Newcastle under Lyme School *Staffordshire* P12 W3 L7 D2 A3

Master i/c G. M. Breen **Coach** K. J. Barnett

This was a disappointing season: in eight of their 12 matches, the school conceded more than 190. Yet there were compensations. In the victory over King's School, Chester, off-spinner Peter Vickers took a hat-trick, the fourth in the school's history; and against Old Newcastilians, Sam Dulson (100 not out) and Tom Cowling put on 112, a school record for the sixth wicket.

Batting S. E. Dulson 204 at 34.00; P. J. Vickers 197 at 28.14; *T. Y. Vickers 195 at 16.25; J. M. Pokora 152 at 15.20.
Bowling T. Y. Vickers 21 at 14.28; P. J. Vickers 20 at 16.50.

Norwich School *Norfolk* P10 W4 L3 D3 A1

Master i/c R. W. Sims
Batting proved the stronger suit, with Oscar Binny and Sam Hunt both hitting centuries – and making over 400 runs. The bowling was steady, but lacked real penetration.
Batting O. R. Binny 426 at 60.85; *S. S. E. T. Hunt 423 at 47.00; A. J. H. Cooper 283 at 31.44; T. A. Harris 290 at 29.00; W. P. Kidner 256 at 25.60.
Bowling O. R. Binny 10 at 16.30; G. H. Nolan 10 at 23.70; B. J. Carding 13 at 27.07.

Nottingham High School *Nottinghamshire* P10 L9 D1 A1

Master i/c M. Baker **Coach** L. Tennant
The backbone of the 2015 side had left, so this was always going to be a season of rebuilding. But several young players gained invaluable experience, and should look forward to 2017.
Batting H. Chaudry 169 at 24.14; D. Desai 184 at 20.44; *H. J. Smith 179 at 19.88; S. R. Menon 164 at 18.22.
Bowling The leading bowler was H. Chaudry, who claimed eight wickets at 23.12.

Oakham School *Rutland* P14 W6 L6 T1 D1 A2

Master i/c N. C. Johnson **Coach** F. C. Hayes
A young side with no outstanding batsman or bowler had an average season. There were 50-over victories against Repton, Bedford, Warwick, Stamford and Oundle, and defeats by Felsted, Brighton, Sedbergh and Wellington, plus a rain-affected draw against Wellingborough.
Batting D. N. Butchart 429 at 39.00; *L. W. James 432 at 33.23; H. Merriman 260 at 23.63; S. J. Wolstenholme 262 at 20.15; J. S. Lewis 153 at 15.30; W. J. Horrell 157 at 12.07.
Bowling W. Means 19 at 18.21; E. M. F. Tattersall 12 at 23.25; S. J. Wolstenholme 10 at 23.90; D. N. Butchart 14 at 28.78; N. T. Davies 11 at 33.27.

The Oratory School *Oxfordshire* P13 W7 L6

Master i/c S. C. B. Tomlinson
A total of seven wins was an excellent effort, with fine team performances. William Legg, a promising batsman, led by example.
Batting *W. Legg 620 at 51.66; M. C. Baker-Smith 340 at 42.50; O. H. Tong-Jones 380 at 38.00; M. Price 161 at 26.83.
Bowling C. L. Humphreys 24 at 13.33; W. Legg 14 at 18.00.

Oswestry School *Shropshire* P7 W1 L5 T1 A4

Master i/c D. Hollingsworth **Coach** T. L. N. Root
A young side, intelligently captained by Matthew Gale, ended a rain-affected season in encouraging style. The highlight was a tie against Rydal Penrhos.
Batting P. A. Derembwe 175 at 35.00.
Bowling *M. J. Gale 10 at 17.90; J. Wigley 12 at 18.33.

Oundle School *Northamptonshire* P16 W4 L7 D5

Master i/c J. P. Crawley **Coach** van der Merwe Genis
A challenging season – especially near the middle of term – included two victories in the Silk Trophy festival, Oundle's best showing since 2004.
Batting S. M. L. Fernandes 595 at 39.66; B. A. Curry 388 at 32.33; T. M. Curry 192 at 17.45; C. L. Fernandes 218 at 14.53; *T. E. P. Tusa 205 at 13.66.
Bowling F. J. Carr 10 at 27.60; A. W. L. Anstey 11 at 28.54; D. A. I. Russell 14 at 32.42; H. C. McLay 10 at 34.20.

The Perse School *Cambridgeshire* P12 W6 L2 D4 A3

Master i/c S. M. Park
Six wins and two defeats marked an improvement on the previous year. Highlights included excellent victories against Stamford School (when Michael Pepper hit 118, his maiden century) and Bishop's Stortford College.
Batting *M. K. S. Pepper 453 at 45.30; S. J. Abbasi 384 at 34.90; A. W. C. Lockie 213 at 16.38; Z. Akhter 150 at 13.63.

Bowling T. E. Anderson 14 at 7.64; F. P. Perkins 12 at 15.41; M. Chandaker 13 at 17.07; M. K. S. Pepper 11 at 19.00; Z. Akhter 11 at 19.81.

Pocklington School *Yorkshire* P11 W7 L3 D1

Master i/c D. Byas

Victories over St Peter's, Hymers and Silcoates – as well as retaining the festival trophy – were proof of a productive season for a young side. Tom Foster, who gained excellent support from the rest of the team, was a capable captain.

Batting J. Atkinson 273 at 30.33; T. Loten 225 at 28.12; C. Foster 210 at 21.00; *T. Foster 163 at 14.81.

Bowling T. Loten 21 at 8.04; J. Wraith 12 at 11.66; A. Harrison 10 at 12.00; L. Medley 15 at 17.93.

Portsmouth Grammar School *Hampshire* P12 W3 L9 A2

Master i/c S. J. Curwood **Coach** S. D. Lavery

The school year began in September 2015 with a dramatic one-wicket victory over Sedbergh in the final of the Under-17 National Cup. During the 2016 summer Dan Mugford was leading wicket-taker and run-scorer. There were also useful contributions from Jadon Buckeridge, Sam and Ben Caldera and Jay Hartard.

Batting J. P. Buckeridge 152 at 152.00; *J. C. Hartard 282 at 35.25; D. J. Mugford 282 at 28.20; S. G. Caldera 177 at 22.12; D. T. Wallis 161 at 20.12.

Bowling D. J. Mugford 13 at 22.07.

Prior Park College *Somerset* P12 W5 L6 D1 A2

Master i/c M. D. Bond **Coach** M. E. Knights

Several students from Years 10 and 11 made their debuts during a transitional season. Captain Nick Lees led from the front, opening the bowling and scoring runs from No. 6. Although more matches were lost than won, the season laid foundations for the future.

Batting J. J. Tonks 215 at 71.66; *N. G. Lees 170 at 28.33.

Bowling H. M. Doyle 19 at 12.73.

Queen Elizabeth Grammar School, Wakefield *Yorkshire* P10 W3 L6 D1 A4

Master i/c I. A. Wolfenden **Coach** C. Lawson

Four abandoned fixtures prevented any momentum, yet the first team managed several encouraging performances. Harry Graham, Amol Vani, George Thompson, Henry Longhurst and Alex Armstrong gave great service to cricket at the school.

Batting H. G. Duke 163 at 23.28; A. Vani 209 at 20.90; H. D. Thompson 163 at 16.30.

Bowling S. O. Russell 12 at 15.75; V. Patel 15 at 16.66; M. J. Flathers 11 at 23.81.

Queen Elizabeth's Hospital *Gloucestershire* P6 L5 D1 A5

Master i/c P. E. Joslin **Coach** D. Forder

A young side, led by Edgar Thornton, won no games, but did gain valuable experience.

Batting The leading batsman was E. W. T. Wilson, who hit 102 runs at 20.40.

Bowling The leading bowler was E. W. T. Wilson, who claimed six wickets at 23.66.

Queen Mary's Grammar School, Walsall *Staffordshire* P6 W4 L2 A4

Master i/c B. T. Gibbons **Coaches** T. E. Hodgson and M. Hingley

Despite the frustrations of fixtures lost to the weather, and exam pressure limiting availability, the team were competitive in every game. Several younger players, including Year 10 pupils Rohit Suglani, Seth Jordan and Arvind Sharma, performed encouragingly.

Batting The leading batsman was N. R. Blackwood, who hit 119 runs at 23.80.

Bowling N. B. Patel 12 at 6.91.

Queen's College, Taunton *Somerset* P14 W8 L3 D3

Master i/c A. V. Suppiah **Coach** A. G. Hamilton

Korie Joseph and Rudi Claassen scored centuries (against the XL Club and MCC), while Joe Gore, who has played for Somerset Seconds and is contracted to their Academy, took most wickets. There were victories over MCC, Blundell's, Exeter, Bristol GS and Taunton.

Batting R. K. Claassen 532 at 66.50; V. Singh 168 at 42.00; *K. B. Joseph 449 at 37.41; F. Hand 294 at 26.72; E. P. Trotman 255 at 25.50.

Bowling O. J. Carlson 17 at 12.05; A. C. Steenkamp 20 at 15.40; J. C. Gore 21 at 16.80; N. De Silva 15 at 24.86.

Radley College *Oxfordshire* P13 W5 L6 D2 A2

Master i/c S. H. Dalrymple **Coach** A. R. Wagner

There were notable wins against Harrow, Charterhouse and Abingdon, and an agonising three-run defeat by Eton. Archie Boscawen and Rory Betley led the batting, and Kit Morland the bowling. James Cunningham captained with growing confidence.

Batting A. H. Boscawen 373 at 33.90; S. D. T. Hoddinott 174 at 29.00; R. A. Betley 300 at 25.00; O. F. R. Martyn-Hemphill 252 at 21.00; C. M. Morland 197 at 19.70; *J. B. J. Cunningham 186 at 16.90.

Bowling C. M. Morland 25 at 15.68; J. B. J. Cunningham 16 at 21.12; T. P. J. Eden 12 at 23.00; J. A. Robinson 16 at 25.43; J. Folkestone 14 at 29.64.

Ratcliffe College *Leicestershire* P13 W6 L4 D3 A4

Master i/c E. O. Woodcock

Captain Sam Nightingale hit a school-record unbeaten 161, and gained useful batting support from Rion Senavirathna-Yapa, Ben Pole and Toby Snell, who was also the leading wicket-taker.

Batting *S. C. Nightingale 486 at 81.00; T. Snell 337 at 67.40; B. H. J. Pole 324 at 46.28; R. N. Senavirathna-Yapa 367 at 45.87.

Bowling J. E. Nightingale 13 at 14.38; T. Snell 17 at 15.41; T. A. Smith 10 at 27.20.

Reading Blue Coat School *Berkshire* P8 W3 L3 D2 A3

Master i/c G. C. Turner **Coach** P. D. Wise

From a squad of hard-working seniors, special mention goes to the captain, Thomas Halson, to James Kirkwood for his committed batting, as well as to bowlers Hamish Scott and Ben Cole.

Batting J. T. Kirkwood 278 at 55.60.

Bowling H. R. Scott 15 at 10.00; B. F. Cole 14 at 12.00.

Reed's School *Surrey* P15 W6 L4 T1 D4 A2

Master i/c M. R. Dunn **Coach** K. T. Medlycott

A young side, well led by bowling spearhead Mickey Strang, played excellent cricket. Baz Medlycott's off-spin picked up 25 wickets, while Jack Kenningham showed good pace. The outstanding batsman was Nathan Tilley.

Batting N. J. Tilley 597 at 74.62; H. G. D. Alderson 333 at 33.30; G. W. Griffiths 253 at 31.62; M. A. B. Mahne 209 at 26.12.

Bowling T. R. Clough 13 at 20.23; B. T. Medlycott 25 at 21.24; *R. M. D. Strang 15 at 22.20; J. D. Kenningham 15 at 25.26; N. J. Tilley 11 at 27.45.

Reigate Grammar School *Surrey* P16 W8 L8 A2

Master i/c P. R. Mann **Coach** J. E. Benjamin

Captain George Elliston helped an inexperienced side take significant strides in a tough season. There were excellent performances, though all players needed to perform more consistently.

Batting J. R. Randall 171 at 19.00; W. J. Elliston 191 at 17.36; J. B. Dodsworth 160 at 16.00; *G. A. Elliston 171 at 13.15.

Bowling T. H. T. Guise 12 at 14.08.

Repton School *Derbyshire* P16 W10 L3 D3 A2

Master i/c I. M. Pollock **Coaches** H. B. Dytham and J. A. Afford

The team went undefeated after May 7 thanks in part to Jack Bull, who claimed 27 wickets with an economy-rate of under three, and opener Callan Harvey, who passed 600 runs. Captain Joss Morgan came close to hitting 500 for the second year.

Batting E. J. Hibell 165 at 82.50; *J. L. Morgan 493 at 61.62; C. T. Harvey 606 at 46.61; J. H. Sookias 284 at 31.55; D. W. Glanville 369 at 30.75; S. O. Trotman 196 at 24.50.

Bowling J. W. Bull 27 at 13.48; C. T. Harvey 10 at 19.90; T. A. Buffin 14 at 20.35; B. J. Mann 17 at 22.94; S. O. Trotman 19 at 23.89; J. A. Bywater 12 at 35.00.

Rossall School *Lancashire* P8 W2 L6 A2

Master i/c O. S. P. Rogers **Coach** M. J. Kelly

Rossall endured a difficult season after the departure of several influential players in 2015. But the team played with enthusiasm – and in the spirit of the game. Bradley Gosling takes over as captain after a promising all-round season.

Batting B. N. Gosling 233 at 29.12.

Bowling J. S. Amor 20 at 8.90.

Royal Grammar School, Guildford *Surrey* P14 W7 L5 D2

Master i/c C. J. L. Sandbach

Captain Alex Sweet – outstanding with bat and ball – Duncan Ashworth and Tom Hartley will all be missed, though there is young talent coming through. Abhay Gonella looks an exciting prospect.

Batting *A. R. I. Sweet 645 at 46.07; A. Gonella 326 at 36.22; A. J. P. Curran 340 at 30.90; B. E. Thomas 349 at 26.84; M. H. James 264 at 24.00; H. S. M. Green 168 at 21.00; Z. D. E. Burrage 211 at 19.18.

Bowling A. Gonella 14 at 9.42; B. M. Shaw 16 at 22.00; A. R. I. Sweet 18 at 24.94; T. H. Hartley 18 at 26.16; D. J. R. Ashworth 10 at 32.50.

The Royal Grammar School, Worcester *Worcestershire* P17 W8 L7 D2 A2

Master i/c M. D. Wilkinson **Coach** P. J. Newport

Frail batting undermined decent bowling and fielding. Amar Jawanda captained maturely and, along with fellow Year 13s Suley Shah and Robbie Watts, should be proud of long first-team careers.

Batting *A. S. Jawanda 246 at 30.75; C. D. Turner 339 at 22.60; R. H. S. Williams 322 at 21.46; S. Shah 304 at 20.26; G. S. Cook 240 at 18.46; S. M. Hughes 203 at 12.68; J. J. Allen 154 at 10.26.

Bowling S. Shah 31 at 15.48; A. H. Cook 20 at 15.85; A. S. Jawanda 29 at 17.65; R. F. Watts 15 at 23.26; G. S. Cook 16 at 26.31.

Rugby School *Warwickshire* P16 W8 L4 D4 A1

Master i/c A. E. L. Thomson **Coach** M. J. Powell

Maia Bouchier, the first girl to represent Rugby's first team, scored 83 not out to seal a resounding eight-wicket victory over MCC; in a productive summer there were seven more wins. The traditional season finale against Marlborough brought a record-breaking unbroken tenth-wicket stand of 76 between Sam Pougatch and Saqlain Choudhary.

Batting E. W. Beard 652 at 50.15; F. D. W. McCreath 518 at 39.84; M. E. Bouchier 224 at 37.33; E. J. J. Robinson 326 at 32.60; H. J. R. Anton 228 at 25.33; H. E. Sutherland 177 at 25.28; W. J. Hatton 205 at 14.64.

Bowling W. J. Hardman 10 at 14.20; M. E. Bouchier 15 at 18.00; E. J. J. Robinson 23 at 20.08; F. D. W. McCreath 25 at 20.44; J. P. F. Fagan 21 at 23.00.

Rydal Penrhos *Denbighshire* P10 W2 L5 T1 D2

Master i/c M. T. Leach

Results did not properly reflect the improved performances of a team well captained by Jack Sissons.

Batting W. B. S. Sissons 379 at 47.37; *J. R. E. Sissons 332 at 41.50.

Bowling J. A. Jones 18 at 13.44; J. R. E. Sissons 10 at 22.20.

St Albans School *Hertfordshire* P10 W4 L2 D4 A1

Master i/c M. C. Ilott

A combination of poor performances and unkind weather meant the season never really got going. The captain, Alex Cook, shone intermittently, while Josh de Caires (whose father is Mike Atherton), Gus Laws-Mather and Charlie Scott all gave cause for optimism.

Batting *A. S. Cook 213 at 30.42; C. F. Scott 226 at 28.25; A. Laws-Mather 183 at 26.14; J. M. de Caires 156 at 26.00.

Bowling J. M. de Caires 15 at 14.26; A. Laws-Mather 11 at 18.72; C. V. Townsend 10 at 22.20.

St Benedict's School, Ealing *Middlesex* P23 W9 L12 T2

Master i/c K. Newell

The school retained the Middlesex Cup. All-rounder and captain Ben Chippendale concluded five full seasons in the first team. With only two regulars leaving, next season promises much.

Batting *B. D. P. Chippendale 494 at 32.93; S. J. L. Allen 528 at 31.05; S. M. Worrall 257 at 19.76; L. E. L. Campbell 170 at 15.45; J. M. L. Chippendale 182 at 14.00; F. G. Greenwood 174 at 12.42; T. A. Madden 162 at 10.12.

Bowling G. D. Johnson 22 at 16.81; S. J. F. Tsang 20 at 17.60; T. O. A. Morris 22 at 18.04; J. M. L. Chippendale 22 at 18.50; B. D. P. Chippendale 14 at 22.07; S. M. Worrall 10 at 22.70; G. D. Yates 13 at 27.53.

Dan Mullan, Getty Images

Maia Bouchier, the first girl to play for Rugby's first team, also turned out for Middlesex Women. Chris Wood, from St Peter's, York, enjoyed a stunning debut season, grabbing 37 wickets with his off-spin and, unlike former student Jonny Bairstow, hitting a century while still in Year 9.

St Edmund's School, Canterbury *Kent* P9 W7 L2

Master i/c A. R. Jones **Coach** H. L. Alleyne

With depth in batting and a range of bowling options, a young side won seven of their nine games. Several of the side have represented Kent, and the future looks encouraging.

Batting M. A. Nordin 154 at 30.80; H. C. Rutherford-Roberts 245 at 30.62; N. Farrar 172 at 28.66; *R. F. St John-Stevens 157 at 22.42.

Bowling J. B. Nordin 16 at 8.62; B. C. Mills 15 at 10.00.

St Edward's School, Oxford *Oxfordshire* P19 W12 L1 D6 A1

Master i/c S. J. O. Roche **Coaches** R. W. J. Howitt and D. P. Simpkins

An impressive season included victory in the John Harvey Cup for the fourth successive year. The captain, A. J. Woodland, hit 204 not out, one of five centuries, and totted up 1,207 runs (including Twenty20 games) – all school records. There were also two hundreds for Year 10 Ben Charlesworth, and 46 wickets (in all formats) for Jamie Curtis.

Batting *A. J. Woodland 1,026 at 85.50; B. G. Charlesworth 604 at 46.46; W. N. Deasy 315 at 45.00; B. L. Allen 438 at 33.69; W. J. Pickford 238 at 23.80; H. D. Ward 247 at 19.00.

Bowling R. H. M. Hipwell 11 at 11.81; H. D. Ward 27 at 15.33; T. E. R. Powell 23 at 15.47; J. A. Curtis 38 at 15.81; A. J. Woodland 12 at 19.08; B. G. Charlesworth 12 at 26.58.

St George's College, Weybridge *Surrey* P9 W8 L1 A3

Master i/c O. J. Clayson **Coach** R. Hall

Despite poor weather, the season proved most successful in the longer form of the game. Alex Bartlett led the team superbly, while Aman Behl, Will Jacks and Will Arkell all made major contributions. Charlie Brennen shows great promise.

Batting W. G. Jacks 388 at 48.50; W. B. G. Arkell 297 at 37.12; *A. J. Bartlett 196 at 32.66.

Bowling A. J. Bartlett 18 at 10.88; W. G. Jacks 19 at 11.15; W. B. G. Arkell 17 at 11.82.

St John's School, Leatherhead *Surrey* P11 W8 L3 A2

Master i/c D. J. Hammond

A young side, admirably led by Hayden Storey, enjoyed another summer of achievement. Retaining the festival trophy (also involving Brentwood, Colfe's and hosts Ipswich) ensured it finished on a high. The Under-14s won the county cup.

Batting B. B. A. Geddes 430 at 47.77; L. C. Trimming 308 at 34.22; M. R. James 254 at 28.22; S. Budinger 256 at 23.27; *H. D. Storey 182 at 20.22; M. P. Denley 182 at 18.20.

Bowling O. J. Hunt 17 at 8.23; M. R. James 19 at 8.68; S. Budinger 10 at 17.00.

St Lawrence College *Kent* P7 W5 L2 A1

Master i/c S. M. Simmons **Coach** T. Moulton

This rewarding summer felt like the end of an era, with Jake Smith (captain for two years), Brendan-James Smith, Ben Moulton and Rudy Hagemichael leaving after three years in the team. Smith took seven for 13 against King's, Rochester, and George Heming five for nought against Duke of York's.

Batting J. Valentine 175 at 35.00.

Bowling B-J. Smith 14 at 7.28.

St Paul's School *Surrey* P14 W12 L2

Master i/c N. E. Briers

The best set of results in living memory included victories against Merchant Taylors' (Northwood), Dulwich and Hampton. The team were top of the 50/40 League, and came sixth in the SOCS National Performance League.

Batting N. G. Solomon 588 at 65.33; *T. B. Powe 400 at 44.44; A. M. C. Russell 172 at 43.00; S. A. Turner 234 at 29.25; R. K. Soni 309 at 23.76; H. S. Mahajan 221 at 20.09.

Bowling A. M. C. Russell 28 at 13.60; E. M. Sharma 10 at 19.50; N. G. Solomon 18 at 20.16; T. B. Powe 13 at 22.23; A. Jenkyn-Jones 11 at 22.90.

St Peter's School, York *Yorkshire* P18 W9 L7 D2 A4

Master i/c G. J. Sharp **Coach** D. Foster

An emerging group of talented players gained plenty of experience, which should stand them in good stead for 2017, when Ted Patmore will be captain. Chris Wood's debut season could hardly have gone better.

Batting C. D. S. Wood 493 at 32.86; A. Liley 280 at 28.00; H. R. Contreras 403 at 25.18; T. J. Patmore 337 at 22.46; C. J. Burdass 247 at 22.45; S. C. Lodge 326 at 20.37; *T. R. Spearman 230 at 15.33.

Bowling C. D. S. Wood 37 at 11.10; H. R. Contreras 11 at 15.27; J. Black 16 at 16.00; T. J. Patmore 23 at 16.69; S. C. Lodge 17 at 18.00; T. R. Spearman 19 at 28.52.

Sedbergh School *Yorkshire* P17 W9 L5 D3 A7

Master i/c C. P. Mahon **Coach** M. P. Speight

Just one defeat against a school – by Shrewsbury – was the mark of a productive season. The first team reached finals day of the National T20 Cup, and won the BOWS Festival (beating Brighton, Oakham and Wellington). Harry Brook hit a school-record 198, against Durham.

Batting H. C. Brook 698 at 46.53; M. B. Silvester 423 at 30.21; J. C. H. Park-Johnson 271 at 22.58; C. W. G. Sanders 218 at 19.81; *A. C. Simpson 314 at 19.62; G. R. Cameron 229 at 19.08; M. G. Stables 292 at 18.25.

Bowling H. C. Brook 16 at 13.43; S. Barrett 16 at 15.18; K. K. Tahirkheli 30 at 17.10; C. W. G. Sanders 19 at 18.47; J. C. H. Park-Johnson 14 at 18.64; A. C. Simpson 13 at 23.23.

Sevenoaks School *Kent* P12 W7 L5 A2

Master i/c C. J. Tavaré **Coach** P. J. Hulston

Youth was no bar to achievement in 2016, when several close games were won by different players. Nick Bett prospered as batsman and bowler, while Year 9 Harry Houillon topped the batting averages.

Batting H. F. Houillon 160 at 53.33; N. M. Bett 177 at 19.66; P. D. Nickols 198 at 18.00.

Bowling R. L. Joseph 18 at 11.05; N. M. Bett 19 at 11.26; P. S. Wright 10 at 22.60; A. G. Sackville-West 10 at 25.40.

Shebbear College *Devon* P7 W3 L4 A2

Master i/c A. B. Bryan

The team relied heavily on the young captain Jabez Weale, especially his bowling. Carl Stanbury proved a useful batsman, as were Rivaldo Clarke from Barbados and Ismael Sheikh from South Africa.

Batting The leading batsman was R. Clarke, who hit 139 runs at 23.16.

Bowling R. Thomas 10 at 9.00; *J. Weale 10 at 11.00.

Sherborne School *Dorset* P14 W5 L7 D2 A2

Master i/c A. D. Nurton **Coach** C. J. Wake

The highlights of a challenging season were comprehensive wins against Millfield and Clifton College. A lack of runs meant victories elsewhere were hard to come by, despite spirited bowling from the younger members of the side.

Batting *W. R. H. Caldwell 214 at 42.80; T. J. I. Mason 238 at 23.80; G. J. R. Pope 173 at 21.62; H. S. Fisher 177 at 19.66.

Bowling B. E. G. J. Heber 13 at 19.15; T. C. Perkins 12 at 30.25.

Shiplake College *Oxfordshire* P13 W4 L8 D1

Master i/c J. H. Howorth **Coach** C. Ellison

A talented and dedicated team deserved better results. Harry Ibbitson again proved a capable captain, and topped the batting averages. Several younger players, such as left-arm spinner Ben Westbrook-Burr, showed great promise.

Batting *H. A. S. Ibbitson 294 at 32.66; M. Bridgman 237 at 23.70; C. W. Heppner-Logan 219 at 21.90.

Bowling Z. M. Heppner-Logan 12 at 17.58; A. Bradley 13 at 20.23; B. D. H. Westbrook-Burr 13 at 20.53; C. W. Heppner-Logan 12 at 21.58.

Shrewsbury School *Shropshire* P19 W11 L6 T1 D1 A6

Master i/c A. S. Barnard **Coach** A. P. Pridgeon

Poor weather, injuries and unavailability for other reasons all led to a disjointed, disappointing season. Compensations included a remarkable tie against Malvern, and captain George Panayi playing for England Under-19 against Sri Lanka.

Batting H. R. D. Adair 400 at 57.14; J. G. T. Crawley 290 at 36.25; *G. D. Panayi 279 at 31.00; G. T. Hargrave 150 at 25.00; D. J. Humes 173 at 24.71; D. J. Lloyd 197 at 24.62; G. W. Newton 386 at 22.70; G. A. Garrett 266 at 19.00.

Bowling C. P. J. Cooke 16 at 14.18; D. J. Lloyd 31 at 15.51; G. Newton 20 at 25.15; G. A. Garrett 17 at 25.47; P. J. Jacob 15 at 25.66; T. F. H. Brunskill 11 at 34.90.

Silcoates School *Yorkshire* P14 W8 L6 A4

Master i/c G. M. Roberts

A team benefiting from a blend of experience and youth enjoyed a prosperous season, including victory in the local derby against QEGS, Wakefield. Jonathan Donnelly, an excellent captain, played for Yorkshire Under-19s.

Batting M. O. Ingram 150 at 25.00; *J. M. Donnelly 215 at 23.88.

Bowling J. M. Donnelly 10 at 10.60; J. H. R. Holling 12 at 19.16.

Sir Thomas Rich's School *Gloucestershire* P13 W9 L3 D1 A3

Master i/c R. G. Williams **Coach** N. O'Neil

The high point of a productive summer was victory over Bristol Grammar. Sam Rideout captained a capable team in which Joel Price, who hit three centuries, and Haroon Shahzad stood out.

Batting J. A. Price 534 at 66.75; M. A. Cox 287 at 35.87; *S. M. Rideout 195 at 27.85.

Bowling P. J. G. Carter 13 at 8.76; H. Shahzad 22 at 12.63; O. S. Pearce 13 at 16.76; S. M. Rideout 10 at 23.50.

Solihull School *Warwickshire* P11 W4 L6 D1 A6

Master i/c D. L. Maddy **Coach** D. W. Smith

A young side, admirably led for a second year by Will Talbot-Davies, improved significantly over the summer. Two Under-13s made senior debuts, while Will Rigg and Ethan Brookes showed their quality – all sparking optimism for 2017.

Batting *W. G. Talbot-Davies 275 at 39.28; E. A. Brookes 226 at 32.28; W. E. Rigg 269 at 29.88; B. P. W. Watson 221 at 22.10.

Bowling A. D. Clay 12 at 19.83; O. J. Banks 12 at 20.33.

South Gloucestershire and Stroud College *Glos* P11 W6 L4 D1 A4

Master i/c S. G. Hinks

Benny Ellis was the leading batsman, with support from Dominic Hooper, Calum Burnstone and Ben Slade. Hooper and off-spinner George Drissell won Academy contracts with Gloucestershire. In all, six SGS College players had represented Gloucestershire Under-17s – captained by Slade – on their tour of Sri Lanka in February 2016.

Batting B. Ellis 426 at 47.33; D. Hooper 162 at 32.40; C. Burnstone 185 at 26.42; *B. Slade 196 at 21.77.
Bowling G. S. Drissell 14 at 13.42.

Stamford School *Lincolnshire* P10 W2 L8 A3

Master i/c C. A. R. Esson **Coach** D. W. Headley

Sam Evison equalled the school record with an unbeaten 202 against Haileybury, while his brother Joey, in Year 9, hit two centuries to earn selection for the Bunbury Festival. Sadly, individual brilliance did not translate into results.
Batting *S. H. G. Evison 579 at 64.33; J. D. M. Evison 434 at 48.22.
Bowling S. H. G. Evison 12 at 35.83.

Stewart's Melville College *Midlothian* P19 W13 L4 T1 D1 A2

Master i/c A. Ranson

Chris Miller led the college through another excellent summer. Scott Blain, who broke the school record for runs in a season, was one of six to reach 150 runs, while eight bowlers claimed ten wickets.
Batting S. O. Blain 707 at 44.18; M. A. G. Hancock 456 at 35.07; A. L. Appleton 166 at 20.75; P. G. F. Ritchie 233 at 19.41; *C. J. Miller 237 at 13.94; M. I. C. Hay-Smith 151 at 12.58.
Bowling B. J. Davidson 17 at 5.11; C. A. Phipps 10 at 8.40; M. I. C. Hay-Smith 10 at 8.80; M. A. G. Hancock 23 at 8.91; J. F. Blain 27 at 11.88; J. W. Stuart 15 at 12.46; A. L. Appleton 17 at 17.64; F. M. Bell 21 at 18.61.

Stonyhurst College *Lancashire* P7 W5 L1 D1

Master i/c G. Thomas **Coach** D. F. Haasbroek

In a spectacular turnaround from 2015, when all five games were lost, the first team improved in every respect, and were undefeated going into the last match. Josh Katz's match-winning 102 not out against Kirkham GS capped a wonderful sporting career at the college.
Batting J. G. Katz 242 at 60.50.
Bowling A. Chitnis 13 at 10.69; J. G. Katz 11 at 16.45.

Stowe School *Buckinghamshire* P18 W7 L5 D6 A6

Master i/c J. A. Knott **Coach** P. R. Arnold

Henry Hoare led the side well in a rainy summer, and hit a chanceless century in the two-day game against Magdalen College School. Top run-scorer Brandon Lee and leading wicket-taker Olly Clarke are available in 2017. Olly played for the Sussex Academy, and Year 11 wicketkeeper Adam King for Northamptonshire Seconds.
Batting B. J. Lee 622 at 38.87; B. T. Maynard 359 at 32.63; *H. J. Hoare 442 at 31.57; O. D. Clarke 332 at 27.66; A. E. King 305 at 20.33; A. E. N. Martin 155 at 14.09.
Bowling C. V. Leefe 18 at 14.38; O. D. Clarke 30 at 19.26; O. G. H. Woodward 13 at 29.46; H. J. Hoare 17 at 31.94; G. A. Markham 16 at 32.93.

Strathallan School *Perthshire* P14 W3 L11 A3

Master i/c G. S. R. Robertson **Coach** I. L. Philip

Despite discouraging results, the season contained several positives, such as the performances of all-rounders Alex Waller and Lisle Halkett. Injuries to Will Hardie, who turned out for Scotland Under-17s, robbed the team of an opening bat and left-arm spinner.
Batting W. W. Hardie 176 at 44.00; A. J. Waller 334 at 33.40; L. C. Halkett 294 at 32.66.
Bowling W. W. Hardie 12 at 16.33; A. J. Waller 15 at 18.20; L. C. Halkett 10 at 26.10.

Sutton Valence School *Kent* P14 W9 L2 D3 A2

Master i/c V. J. Wells

Captain Abdullah Adil contributed on two fronts in a fine season. With six senior players leaving, much will depend on batsmen James Bevan-Thomas and Jamie Drewe, left-arm spinner Will Edwards and fast bowler Elliot Aiken.
Batting *A. Adil 388 at 48.50; R. L. N. Jones 291 at 32.33; J. R. Bevan-Thomas 302 at 30.20; J. W. Drewe 278 at 25.27; T. H. Lennard 251 at 25.10.
Bowling W. M. Edwards 29 at 13.41; J. R. Deveson 15 at 14.73; A. Adil 15 at 15.20; E. P. A. Aiken 17 at 17.94.

Taunton School *Somerset* P14 W3 L9 T1 D1 A1

Master i/c D. A. Jessep

Results were mixed, but many of the team will return for at least one more season – and be better for their experience. Sam Whitefield, with 454 runs and 24 wickets was the most consistent player.

Batting E. Eminson 192 at 38.40; S. P. Whitefield 454 at 37.83; D. Court 252 at 22.90; M. Cave 151 at 13.72.

Bowling S. P. Whitefield 24 at 16.83; J. Houston 12 at 26.08; S. M. Horler 14 at 29.42.

Tiffin School *Surrey* P19 W12 L5 D2 A2

Master i/c M. J. Williams

This was a thoroughly pleasing year for Tiffin. An experienced side were well supported by an exceptional group of Under-15s. The contribution of those leaving after four years in the side has been immense.

Batting C. J. J. Fulton 486 at 44.18; K. K. Sachdeva 476 at 34.00; V. K. Samtani 201 at 22.33; *A. K. Rana 173 at 21.62.

Bowling Y. I. M. Jackson 27 at 11.11; B. A. Bhatti 27 at 11.18; D. L. S. Jones 19 at 13.89; K. K. Sachdeva 11 at 19.90.

Tonbridge School *Kent* P17 W13 L2 T1 D1 A3

Master i/c J. P. Arscott **Coach** I. Baldock

The major contributors to a rewarding season were Marcus O'Riordan (1,080 runs and six centuries), Zak Crawley (963 runs) and seamer Toby Pettman (45 wickets – figures in each case take three T20 games into account). Victories included Millfield, Eton, Harrow, MCC, Bedford and Dulwich; Tonbridge also won the Cowdrey Cup.

Batting J. J. O'Riordan 563 at 62.55; *Z. Crawley 897 at 56.06; M. K. O'Riordan 833 at 52.06; E. R. B. Hyde 520 at 43.33; A. J. Bissett 271 at 24.63; B. A. Earl 152 at 21.71; A. J. Moen 193 at 16.08.

Bowling T. H. S. Pettman 35 at 16.74; B. A. Earl 20 at 17.90; M. K. O'Riordan 23 at 27.08; C. V. Oster 13 at 29.23; J. J. O'Riordan 11 at 29.36.

Marcus O'Riordan and Toby Pettman, two mainstays of the Tonbridge attack; O'Riordan also scored 833 runs at 52.

Trent College *Derbyshire* P18 W12 L5 D1 A2
Master i/c S. A. J. Boswell **Coach** P. D. Johnson
Tom Hill captained a successful all-round side with great maturity and intelligence.
Batting *T. J. Hill 611 at 61.10; T. R. Wyatt 605 at 55.00; C. F. Gibson 356 at 29.66; M. J. Kimmitt 189 at 13.50.
Bowling M. Davis 21 at 16.42; R. Reza 14 at 18.92; C. F. Gibson 15 at 20.06; T. L. Naylor 18 at 20.27; J. R. Benstead 12 at 22.25; S. J. Riordan 15 at 26.73.

Trinity School, Croydon *Surrey* P19 W8 L8 D3 A2
Master i/c R. J. Risebro **Coach** I. D. K. Salisbury
Dominic Johnsen led a very young side exceptionally well and scored most runs, while George Jackson hit a superb 130 against Hampton in his first game back from injury. The nucleus of the squad are expected to return, and the prospects are exciting.
Batting G. L. Jackson 284 at 56.80; R. Hari 388 at 38.80; *D. J. Johnsen 524 at 32.75; A. H. Raza 353 at 29.41; A. W. E. Roberts 358 at 25.57; J. W. Blake 228 at 22.80; H. S. Neale-Smith 180 at 16.36; H. M. Weaver 191 at 13.64.
Bowling A. H. Raza 18 at 21.33; P. Peethamber 18 at 22.05; H. S. Neale-Smith 13 at 24.00; E. J. Lilley 14 at 27.92.

University College School *Middlesex* P11 W7 L4
Master i/c L. J. Greany **Coaches** M. G. Lane and A. Wilkes
The arrival of former England women's coach Mark Lane as cricket professional helped the team – at core very similar to the 2015 side – to go from strength to strength. The results were the best for many years. Daniel Grabinar thrived with bat and ball.
Batting D. A. Grabinar 222 at 24.66.
Bowling A. W. Beckham 18 at 11.83; J. Brettler 16 at 12.06; D. A. Grabinar 19 at 14.00.

Uppingham School *Rutland* P16 W4 L7 D5 A2
Master i/c T. Makhzangi **Coach** T. R. Ward
The season started with an 18-day tour to Sri Lanka in April. Harry Funnell later hit a maiden hundred in the defeat of Haileybury.
Batting *W. E. Rogers 408 at 37.09; J. H. Funnell 347 at 34.70; G. J. Loyd 368 at 33.45; G. M. Frankel 276 at 25.09; C. H. Bygott 146 at 24.33; S. R. Charlton 242 at 22.00; S. J. C. Wallis 267 at 19.07.
Bowling J. H. Funnell 22 at 19.90; W. E. Rogers 28 at 22.00; G. J. Loyd 17 at 24.23; S. R. Charlton 17 at 30.76; T. W. C. Bendall 11 at 34.81.

Warwick School *Warwickshire* P23 W13 L7 D3 A7
Master i/c S. R. G. Francis
The summer was marred only by defeats in the National T20 Cup and a local T20 final. Rob Yates scored runs despite the weight of expectation, while Oliver Richardson, bowling with aggression, claimed most wickets. Reuben Arnold and Jago Lynch left after three years' excellent service.
Batting R. M. Yates 592 at 65.77; *R. S. K. Arnold 493 at 30.81; O. H. Richardson 150 at 30.00; E. J. Briggs 272 at 22.66; M. Leatherdale 249 at 20.75; S. J. P. Forster 261 at 18.64; J. G. Lynch 203 at 16.91; F. P. Lowe 188 at 12.53.
Bowling O. H. Richardson 24 at 16.00; R. M. Yates 12 at 19.41; S. C. Thompson 12 at 23.25; E. J. Briggs 12 at 25.50; J. W. Talbot 18 at 26.00; C. Curtis 11 at 26.63; J. G. Lynch 16 at 28.37.

Watford Grammar School for Boys *Hertfordshire* P10 W7 L3 A3
Master i/c L. Samarasinghe **Coach** A. Needham
The first team had an outstanding year, winning seven of their ten games. One of the defeats came in the annual fixture against MCC, when the school – chasing 210 – lost from the last ball.
Batting E. Stock 316 at 39.50; T. Stock 161 at 32.20; S. Ahmed 172 at 21.50.
Bowling A. Gosrani 14 at 13.14; D. Arya 12 at 13.33; T. Stock 15 at 13.60; R. Curwen 10 at 23.00.

Wellingborough School *Northamptonshire* P14 W9 L2 D3 A2
Master i/c G. E. Houghton **Coach** D. J. Sales
The run-scoring of George Groenland and captain Ben Wall, who left having amassed a total of 2,114 runs, ensured another rewarding summer. The school won the Bablake Festival, and also defeated Stamford and Oundle.

Nigel French, PA Photos

Sam Curran's frequent appearances for Surrey reduced his availability for Wellington.

Batting G. Groenland 763 at 127.16; *B. T. Wall 487 at 54.11; S. J. Mulvey 333 at 47.57.
Bowling M. R. Chalcraft 16 at 18.93; G. Groenland 13 at 21.53; B. T. Wall 11 at 33.00.

Wellington College *Berkshire* P16 W6 L7 D3 A3

Master i/c D. M. Pratt **Coach** G. D. Franklin

There were good wins over Harrow, Radley, Charterhouse, Brighton College and Oakham School, but victories were outnumbered by defeats. Sam Curran's captaincy was well supported by Jhatha Subramanyan's leg-spin, as well as the batting of Jack Davies and Alex Shoff.

Batting *S. M. Curran 399 at 49.87; J. L. B. Davies 545 at 38.92; A. W. Shoff 432 at 33.23; J. S. Subramanyan 266 at 29.55; W. J. T. Bowcock 363 at 27.92; R. S. McMichael 196 at 24.50; S. J. Sweetland 234 at 18.00.

Bowling A. W. Shoff 15 at 13.86; J. S. Subramanyan 24 at 16.41; A. S. Dale 14 at 21.57; L. J. M. Methley 16 at 24.31.

Wells Cathedral School *Somerset* P10 W4 L3 D3 A2

Master i/c J. A. Boot **Coach** C. Vickery

Poor weather disrupted the season, though there were impressive wins against Prior Park and – by two runs – Bryanston. Other highlights included beating Millfield thirds and Warminster, as well as drawing against the XL Club.

Batting H. O. S. Connock 224 at 44.80; R. E. Moss 169 at 33.80; *L. W. Boot 161 at 20.12.
Bowling L. T. Howell 10 at 17.40.

Westminster School *Middlesex* P14 W7 L4 D3 A2

Master i/c J. D. Kershen **Coach** S. K. Ranasinghe

A young team won the London Schools Under-19 Cup for the fourth time. Barnaby Graff, the captain, ended five seasons in the first team with 1,700 runs and 82 wickets. Promising all-rounder Alex Vinen will aim to fill his shoes.

Batting *B. J. Graff 511 at 73.00; A. S. Vinen 210 at 23.33; D. F. Thomas du Toit 173 at 19.22.
Bowling B. J. Graff 23 at 12.17; W. D. C. Fryer 12 at 14.83; A. S. Vinen 18 at 25.16; J. R. U. Wilson 10 at 25.30.

Wilson's School *Surrey* P16 W4 L12 A1

Master i/c A. Parkinson **Coach** C. K. Bullen

A challenging season for a young team brought only four wins, though more application might have doubled that. Dan Moore led the batting, while George Kellingley claimed most wickets, followed by Curtis Rose and 15-year-old spinner Riley Jarrold.

Batting D. S. Moore 231 at 19.25; *C. E. A. Rose 191 at 15.91.

Bowling R. D. Jarrold 14 at 11.42; W. Honeyman 10 at 14.30; G. P. C. Kellingley 18 at 20.33; C. E. A. Rose 14 at 25.14; D. S. Moore 10 at 29.70.

Winchester College *Hampshire* P20 W6 L8 D6 A2

Master i/c G. J. Watson **Coach** P. N. Gover

Given the paucity of runs, a total of six wins was a fantastic result for a young side whose out-cricket was exceptional. All the bowlers return next year. Kehan Shirvani was emblematic of a side who always gave their best.

Batting K. D. Shirvani 219 at 24.33; S. G. Byers 327 at 20.43; W. N. A. Song 279 at 19.92; R. M. C. Quinault 354 at 19.66; A. G. Younger 262 at 15.41; A. F. J. Dodd 193 at 12.86.

Bowling F. J. Egleston 16 at 10.62; K. D. Shirvani 29 at 12.96; M. J. Otley 18 at 16.77; H. L. Adams 18 at 17.66; H. R. Vaughan 18 at 17.77; A. F. J. Dodd 18 at 24.44.

Wolverhampton Grammar School *Staffordshire* P11 W7 L4 A2

Master i/c T. King **Coach** N. H. Crust

A season dominated by exams and bad weather nevertheless contained some notable all-round performances. Year 10 batsman Archie O'Hara showed great potential.

Batting A. W. O'Hara 352 at 50.28; O. G. Singh 194 at 38.80; M. A. Evans 174 at 34.80; C. Singh 184 at 30.66; *A. R. Carey 171 at 28.50.

Bowling C. Singh 13 at 15.15; J. E. Timmins 10 at 20.70; K. Patel 10 at 21.40.

Woodbridge School *Suffolk* P7 W2 L3 D2 A4

Master i/c I. J. Simpson **Coach** D. A. Brous

A season brimming with opportunity was ruined by exams and rain (especially in cricket week). Excellent achievements included dismissing MCC for 168, as well as Oscar Beardwood's innings of 89, when he sacrificed a possible hundred to push for a win.

Batting O. Beardwood 175 at 35.00.

Bowling O. J. Whiting 12 at 14.91.

Woodhouse Grove School *Yorkshire* P12 W9 L2 D1 A5

Master i/c R. I. Frost **Coach** A. Sidebottom

Woodhouse Grove won 13 of 17 completed matches in all formats, and reached the North final of the National T20 Cup. Captain Bailey Worcester was outstanding, and represented Yorkshire at Under-19 level, as did Nicky Bulcock and Jibrael Malik. Meanwhile, Adbi H. Ahmed, a seamer, and his younger brother Ali – a spinner – show great promise.

Batting *B. J. Worcester 637 at 91.00; J. Malik 457 at 57.12; N. Elibox 240 at 30.00; J. G. Godfrey 198 at 28.28; N. G. J. Bulcock 187 at 20.77.

Bowling N. Elibox 21 at 11.95; A. H. Ahmed 11 at 16.09; A. Ahmed 15 at 16.20; H. W. Boggie 12 at 24.08; N. G. J. Bulcock 12 at 26.91.

Worksop College *Nottinghamshire* P11 W8 L3 A6

Master i/c N. J. Longhurst **Coach** I. C. Parkin

The summer was curtailed, yet successful. Despite losing the Shrewsbury Festival and MCC fixture to the weather, Worksop reached the last 16 of the National T20 Cup, and won the post-season Woodard Festival. Daniel McLean struck 370 runs, and Liam Patterson-White took 23 wickets.

Batting D. L. McLean 370 at 41.11; L. A. Patterson-White 192 at 38.40; K. Suresh 235 at 33.57; *T. G. Keast 184 at 26.28; N. A. Lowe 151 at 18.87.

Bowling L. A. Patterson-White 23 at 10.08; D. L. McLean 11 at 20.90; J. C. Holden 14 at 21.71; A. R. Shannon 10 at 26.00.

Worth School *Sussex* P15 W6 L4 D5 A5

Master i/c R. Chaudhuri

The summer, like the results, was mixed. The most influential players were bowlers Harnoop Kalsi and Akshay Ramani, and batsman Krishan Nayee. With many quality youngsters in the wings, the future looks promising.

Batting *M. J. Rivers 310 at 28.18; K. Nayee 356 at 25.42; N. K. Amin 269 at 24.45; G. O. Brien 191 at 17.36.
Bowling K. Nayee 16 at 12.18; A. M. Ramani 24 at 14.91; M. J. Rivers 17 at 16.76; H. S. Kalsi 23 at 18.13.

Wrekin College *Shropshire* P7 W4 L3 A4

Master i/c J. R. Mather **Coach** L. Swann

Rain denied several final-year cricketers the send-off they had hoped for. All-rounder Rupert Grainger impressed many in the National T20 Cup, while openers Harry Chandler and Charlie Home averaged over 60 for the first wicket.
Batting C. E. Home 201 at 67.00; *H. Chandler 189 at 47.25; R. T. J. Thomas 163 at 32.60.
Bowling C. E. Home 14 at 6.50.

Wycliffe College *Gloucestershire* P17 W4 L12 D1 A1

Master i/c M. J. Kimber **Coach** B. Gannon

In an enjoyable term, despite the results, captain Noah Cooper-Llanes and Tom Caesar were regularly in the runs, while leg-spinner Innes Pierce took most wickets.
Batting T. J. J. Caesar 414 at 29.57; *N. S. Cooper-Llanes 438 at 29.20; C. N. Trainor 243 at 24.30; O. Carey 249 at 22.63; W. L. Naish 170 at 17.00.
Bowling I. C. Pierce 20 at 23.90; O. Carey 13 at 30.23; A. A. Collins 10 at 30.50.

ARCHIVE OF SCHOOLS CRICKET IN WISDEN

The first *Wisden* to contain a detailed report on the previous summer's schools cricket appeared in 1888. The review spoke admiringly of a new addition to the Harrow team: "By far the best feature of the school's cricket was the batting of A. C. MacLaren, a very young cricketer, who played really superb cricket against Eton at Lord's, scoring 55 and 67… Not one of the other Harrow batsmen struck us as showing more than ordinary ability." F. S. Jackson, another Harrovian and future England captain, was commended for his "right hand fast" bowling.

Since then, every edition has devoted many pages to schools cricket, building into an archive of reviews, averages and scorecards that can be explored at www.schoolscricketonline.co.uk/wisden-archive. (The project is sponsored by the schools cricket committee of the HMC, an organisation representing a group of independent schools, though for many years *Wisden* has cast its net beyond the private sector.) The 2003 edition remarks on the prowess of a left-hander from Bedford School called Alastair Cook, while the 1985 volume recalls Mike Atherton's triumphant summer of '84, when he combined 1,013 runs with 61 wickets for his all-conquering leg-spin.

CRICKET IN IRELAND IN 2016

Greater Tests lie ahead

IAN CALLENDER

It was an indifferent year for Ireland, at least on the field. In 19 completed matches, they used 26 players (the most since 2008, when they were involved in county cricket's Friends Provident Trophy), had only one century-maker, collected no five-wicket hauls, and endured their worst win-rate since central contracts were introduced in 2009. The most positive news came elsewhere: in October, the ICC confirmed Ireland's Inter-Provincial Championship would, from 2017, be first-class. It was one more hurdle cleared on the path to the Test arena. Winning the Intercontinental Cup is another. Ireland beat Papua New Guinea and Hong Kong to maintain their 100% record after four games. They were due to meet second-placed Afghanistan in March 2017, when bonus points for a first-innings lead would be enough to keep them top, with two games to play. If they can stay there, they will earn a four-match series against the lowest-ranked Full Member, with Test status on the line.

It was a different story for Ireland in white-ball cricket, losing 12 of their 17 completed matches. An early Twenty20 defeat by Papua New Guinea (though they won the series in Townsville 2–1), and another in the UAE (1–1), were ominous, and a six-wicket hiding from Zimbabwe in their final warm-up before the World Twenty20 in March set the tone for a disastrous tournament. Ireland's five-wicket defeat by Oman – playing in their first global competition – was disappointing, and after a second-match washout, against Bangladesh, their exit was confirmed. But their worst performance was still to come: chasing 60 in a six-over bash against the Netherlands, they raced to 28 for one after two, but made only 19 more.

By their next Twenty20 game, in September, Ireland had made eight changes, handing debuts to five players, including left-arm seamer Josh Little who, at 16 years 309 days, was the second youngest to play for them in any format, and the second youngest of any nationality in T20Is (behind Waqas Khan, who appeared for Hong Kong in 2014 when still 15). But it did not change fortunes: Hong Kong won by 40 runs. Greg Thompson, who in 2004 had become the youngest Ireland player at 16, top-scored with 44.

In the summer, Ireland hosted two Full Members, each for a two-match series. Barry McCarthy, a 23-year-old seamer from Pembroke, made his debut against Sri Lanka in June, and took two early wickets, but an unbeaten century from Dinesh Chandimal guided the tourists to 303. In reply, William Porterfield's dismissal for 73 triggered a collapse. Sri Lanka won the second by 136 runs, giving Ireland their heaviest home defeat – for a couple of months. In August, Pakistan's left-arm spinner Imad Wasim took five for 14 as Ireland were dismissed for 82, to lose by 255 runs. There was no chance of redemption: the second game was rained off.

In between, Afghanistan shared a five-match series at Stormont. After the first was washed out, Ed Joyce, in his new role as opener, hit 105 and 160 – both unbeaten – in Ireland's two victories. The series was overshadowed by his run-out in the fourth game, which Afghanistan went on to win: Mohammad Nabi fielded the ball from well behind the boundary and, poker-faced, threw it back in, with Joyce well short. Sean Terry, son of England Test player Paul, made his debut in the series, but scored only 16 runs in three innings.

The highlight of the playing year was an invitation to take on South Africa and Australia in September, ahead of their bilateral series. Yet an understrength Ireland struggled; Joyce and Boyd Rankin were injured, while Niall O'Brien slipped in the shower and was also ruled out. McCarthy, who had taken 18 wickets in his first seven ODIs, was surprisingly left out, and South Africa piled up 354 for five. Ireland replied with 148. Two days later, they lost their last eight wickets for 77, before Australia reached their target of 199 for the loss of only one.

The women's team lost all four games at the World Twenty20, after which captain Isobel Joyce stepped down. Under Laura Delany, they recorded their first victories over South Africa, sharing the Twenty20 series 1–1, and losing the ODIs 3–1. In September, they also beat Bangladesh in a T20 at Bready, but lost the one-day series in sensational fashion. Needing 107 for victory, they were 52 without loss, before losing all ten for 44.

The Under-19s finished a respectable 13th at the World Cup in Bangladesh, after recording play-off victories against Canada and Scotland. Leinster Lightning, captained by John Anderson, won all three inter-provincial trophies for the second season running, without losing a match.

Winners of Irish Leagues and Cups
Irish Senior Cup Merrion. **Leinster League** Clontarf. **Leinster Senior Cup** YMCA. **Munster League** Cork County. **Munster Senior Cup** Co Galway. **Northern League** Instonians. **Northern Challenge Cup** Civil Service North. **North West League and Senior Cup** Donemana.

IRELAND v SRI LANKA

First one-day international At Malahide, June 16. **Sri Lanka won by 76 runs** (DLS). **Sri Lanka 303-7** (50 overs) (B. K. G. Mendis 51, L. D. Chandimal 100*); ‡**Ireland 216** (40.4 overs) (W. T. S. Porterfield 73, K. J. O'Brien 64; M. D. Shanaka 5-43). *ODI debuts:* B. J. McCarthy (Ireland); D. M. de Silva, B. K. G. Mendis, M. D. Shanaka (Sri Lanka). *Sri Lanka warmed up for their one-day series in England with a convincing victory in Dublin. Dinesh Chandimal's third ODI century propelled them past 300, after stands of 82 with Kusal Mendis, 88 with Angelo Mathews, and 61 in five overs with Dasun Shanaka, who marked his debut with 42 from 19 balls. A brief delay during Ireland's innings meant a revised target of 293 in 47 overs, but medium-pacer Shanaka became the 12th bowler – and second Sri Lankan, after Uwaisul Karnain in March 1984 – to take five wickets in his first ODI. Ireland were 211-6 in the 38th, but lost their last four for five runs.*

Second one-day international At Malahide, June 18. **Sri Lanka won by 136 runs. Sri Lanka 377-8** (50 overs) (M. D. K. J. Perera 135, M. D. Gunathilleke 63, S. Prasanna 95); ‡**Ireland 241** (45 overs) (A. R. McBrine 79; R. A. S. Lakmal 4-38). *Sri Lanka sprinted to a 2–0 series triumph, the highlight a helter-skelter 95 from Seekkuge Prasanna, who began with an ODI batting average of nine. Promoted to No. 3, he clattered nine sixes and five fours, and was in sight of one of Sri Lanka's most resonant records – Sanath Jayasuriya's 48-ball hundred against Pakistan in Singapore in April 1996 – when he missed his 46th, and was bowled by Tim Murtagh. That left them 308-1 in the 42nd over and, although Kusal Perera (who had earlier shared an opening partnership of 147 with Danushka Gunathilleke) followed two balls later for a fluent 135, Sri Lanka reached their fourth highest ODI total. Ireland slipped to 112-6, before Andy McBrine cuffed 79 from 64 – a maiden international half-century – to narrow the margin a little.*

Barry Chambers

Pushing the boundary: Mohammad Nabi fields the ball, moments before running out Ed Joyce.

IRELAND v AFGHANISTAN

IAN CALLENDER

One-day internationals (5): Ireland 2, Afghanistan 2

Afghanistan consolidated tenth place in the ICC's one-day rankings – two ahead of Ireland – in a controversial series in Belfast which boiled over in the fourth match. Mohammad Nabi fielded a ball with his feet behind the boundary, and Ed Joyce was run out for 12 while strolling back to his crease, confident he had scored a four. Nabi assured the umpires he had not been over the line, but photographs showed otherwise, and the ICC reprimanded him for conduct "contrary to the spirit of the game". Ireland had already squared the series thanks to Joyce's century; his unbeaten 160 in the last – he cited "extra motivation" after the Nabi incident – took his series average to 169.

AFGHANISTAN SQUAD

*Asghar Stanikzai, Afsar Zazai, Dawlat Zadran, Gulbadeen Naib, Hamid Hassan, Hamza Hotak, Imran Janat, Javed Ahmadi, Mirwais Ashraf, Mohammad Nabi, Mohammad Shahzad, Najibullah Zadran, Nasir Ahmadzai, Noor Ali Zadran, Rahmat Shah, Rashid Khan, Samiullah Shenwari, Shapoor Zadran, Yamin Ahmadzai. *Coach:* L. S. Rajput.

First one-day international At Belfast, July 10. **Ireland v Afghanistan. Abandoned.**

Second one-day international At Belfast, July 12. **Afghanistan won by 39 runs. Afghanistan 250** (49.2 overs) (Mohammad Shahzad 66, Najibullah Zadran 59; B. J. McCarthy 4-59, K. J. O'Brien 4-45); ‡**Ireland 211** (48.2 overs) (E. C. Joyce 62, K. J. O'Brien 35; Mohammad Nabi 3-45, Rashid Khan 3-28). *After Ed Joyce made 62, opening in an ODI for the first time in four years, Ireland looked in control at 160-3 in the 34th over. But the middle order were confounded by*

Mohammad Nabi's off-breaks and the leg-spin of 17-year-old Rashid Khan, and the last seven wickets tumbled for 51. Afghanistan had crumbled too, from 195-4 in the 39th; Barry McCarthy, the Dublin-born Durham seamer playing only his third ODI, took the last four wickets.

Third one-day international At Belfast, July 14. **Ireland won by six wickets.** **‡Afghanistan 236** (49.1 overs) (Mohammad Shahzad 81, Asghar Stanikzai 33, Mohammad Nabi 40; B. J. McCarthy 3-57, K. J. O'Brien 3-28); **Ireland 237-4** (47.3 overs) (E. C. Joyce 105*, K. J. O'Brien 75, P. R. Stirling 39*). *ODI debut:* S. P. Terry (Ireland). *Joyce's fourth ODI century – his third for Ireland, to go with 107 for England v Australia at Sydney in 2006-07 – anchored a series-squaring victory. He put on 144 for the fourth wicket with Kevin O'Brien, whose fifty was only the second in his last 22 white-ball innings. They might have been chasing a lower target: Asghar Stanikzai and Nabi were both dropped early on. Mohammad Shahzad had biffed his third successive half-century in ODIs, but Afghanistan made only 66 from their last 13 overs. Sean Terry, the son of the former Hampshire and England batsman Paul, made his international debut, courtesy of his Dublin-born mother.*

Fourth one-day international At Belfast, July 17. **Afghanistan won by 79 runs.** **‡Afghanistan 229-7** (50 overs) (Rahmat Shah 48, Mohammad Nabi 50, Rashid Khan 60*); **Ireland 150** (41 overs) (K. J. O'Brien 34, P. R. Stirling 31; Rashid Khan 4-21). *Afghanistan's victory was overshadowed by the run-out of Joyce. Nabi flicked the ball back, and assured the umpires he had not touched it outside the cover boundary, so the run-out stood. There was no TV coverage, but photographs were incriminating. Ireland never recovered, as Rashid followed a career-best 60* from 44 balls (he and Nabi had rescued Afghanistan from 109-6) with his best one-day figures.*

Fifth one-day international At Belfast, July 19. **Ireland won by 12 runs.** **Ireland 265-5** (50 overs) (E. C. Joyce 160*, G. C. Wilson 58); **‡Afghanistan 253-9** (50 overs) (Rahmat Shah 30, Asghar Stanikzai 32, Najibullah Zadran 54, Rashid Khan 40; K. J. O'Brien 3-57). *Joyce cracked his highest score in List A cricket to lift Ireland to a total that proved just beyond Afghanistan. Only Gary Wilson stayed with him for long, helping add 134 for the third wicket, although Stuart Poynter (12*) did share a late stand of 73* in 7.1 overs. Afghanistan dipped to 119-6, though Najibullah Zadran and Rashid kept them in touch, putting on 93 in 13.3 overs. But, with O'Brien taking three wickets, Ireland kept their noses in front, and the series was shared 2–2.*

IRELAND v PAKISTAN

First one-day international At Malahide, August 18. **Pakistan won by 255 runs.** **Pakistan 337-6** (47 overs) (Sharjeel Khan 152, Shoaib Malik 57*, Mohammad Nawaz 53; B. J. McCarthy 4-62); **‡Ireland 82** (23.4 overs) (Imad Wasim 5-14). *ODI debuts:* Hasan Ali, Mohammad Nawaz (Pakistan). *Ireland's sobering summer continued with another hammering, this time led by Sharjeel Khan, who belted 152 – his first international century – from 86 balls, with nine sixes and 16 fours. When he was out, it was 226-4 after 32 overs, with 15 left after a delayed start; Shoaib Malik and Mohammad Nawaz ensured another daunting target, piling on 105 for the sixth wicket. Paul Stirling fell to the second ball of the reply, and soon it was 55-6: Gary Wilson (21) inched the total to 81, but the last four wickets fell for just a single, to leave Ireland with their lowest total at home. Slow left-armer Imad Wasim took three in four balls to finish with 5-14, sealing Pakistan's biggest ODI win by runs.*

Second one-day international At Malahide, August 20. **Ireland v Pakistan. Abandoned.**

IRELAND v HONG KONG

First Twenty20 international At Bready, September 5. **Hong Kong won by 40 runs.** **‡Hong Kong 169-5** (20 overs) (Nizakat Khan 62, Babar Hayat 49); **Ireland 129** (19.3 overs) (K. J. O'Brien 32, G. J. Thompson 44; Aizaz Khan 3-10). *T20I debuts:* J. Little, J. Mulder, S. P. Terry, G. J. Thompson, L. Tucker (Ireland); Ehsan Khan, Shahid Wasif (Hong Kong). *Hong Kong upset an inexperienced home line-up: it was their second win in succession away to Ireland, after a five-run victory in the 2015 World Twenty20 Qualifier at Malahide. Nizakat Khan led the way with 62 from 43 balls, then captain Babar Hayat hit 49 from 31. Ireland made a poor start – 24-4 in the sixth – and although Kevin O'Brien and Greg Thompson put on 59 in seven overs, the rest could not finish the job. Medium-pacer Aizaz Khan returned 3–11–10–3.*

Second Twenty20 international At Bready, September 6. **Ireland v Hong Kong. Abandoned.** *MoS:* Nizakat Khan. *Hong Kong took the series when rain prevented any play.*

For Ireland's matches in the ICC World Twenty20, see page 793; for the Intercontinental Cup and the World Cricket League, see page 1141.

CRICKET IN SCOTLAND IN 2016

Dreich skies, bleak horizons

WILLIAM DICK

It was a year of too little cricket and too many departures. The national side had just 23 scheduled days in 2016, including a mere ten in the summer – half that of a decade earlier. For three of their most valued servants, it seemed the final straw.

In February, Craig Wright ended a 19-year association with Cricket Scotland, having been player, captain and, most recently, assistant coach. Wright appeared to have become disillusioned with the governance of international cricket, and called for a "bigger, healthier, more meritocratic game". In October, Andy Tennant, the former performance director, expressed fears that a group of players – as talented as any in the last quarter of a century – would wither on the vine, and left to take up a similar role with Scottish hockey.

In November, came the most damning announcement of all: Preston Mommsen, Scotland's captain and one of their leading batsmen, retired from international cricket at the age of 29 to pursue a business career. Mommsen, an outspoken champion of the Associate game, cited the absence of a stimulating fixture list. "What was there to keep me motivated?" he said. "I was spending far more time in the nets and the gym than I was between the stumps."

The last year of Mommsen's reign brought mixed results. In January, what would have been the first first-class match in Hong Kong was abandoned because of rain. The weather cleared for a World Cricket League game, which Hong Kong won by 109 runs, thanks to Harrow schoolboy Anshuman Rath's 98, before turning foul again to prevent the rematch. There were more showers when they met again at the World Twenty20 in India, but Scotland won by eight wickets, their first victory – at the 21st attempt – in global tournaments.

Back in Scotland, they lost a one-day international series to Afghanistan, then drew an Intercontinental Cup match against the UAE at Ayr, after rain had stolen another two days; the fixture had already been moved from Aberdeen because of drainage problems. But days later at Edinburgh, Scotland produced some of their most exhilarating cricket to record two victories over the UAE in the WCL. Their form continued with another win over Hong Kong to lift the Braidwood Cup. A feature of the upswing was the positivity of Scotland's batting, with Mommsen, Kyle Coetzer and Calum MacLeod all hitting centuries.

Despite the dearth of action, coach Grant Bradburn remained buoyant, talking up his players at every opportunity. But for how much longer will this ambitious and talented coach be content with so few big match days? Much may depend on whether Scotland win the WCL – they ended the year fourth – and with it, perhaps, a place in an expanded ODI Championship.

The women, meanwhile, had 16 matches against county opposition, won Division Three of the NatWest Twenty20 Cup, and beat the Netherlands to earn a place at the World Cup qualifier in early 2017. There was more success off the field, with Cricket Scotland winning the ICC's Best Overall Cricket Development Programme Award, while participation numbers at grassroots level continued to offer encouragement.

In domestic cricket, Eastern Knights beat Western Warriors and Caley Highlanders to win the regional Pro50 Cup and T20 Blitz competitions, before overcoming South Holland Seafarers in the North Sea Pro Series final. East also prevailed against west at club level: Carlton beat Clydesdale in the national Grand Final. Clydesdale consoled themselves by lifting the Scottish Cup for the first time since 1988, while Grange triumphed convincingly in the Murgitroyd Twenty20 competition.

Winners of Scottish Leagues and Cups
Eastern Premier Division Carlton. **Western Premier Division** Clydesdale. **National Champions** Carlton. **Scottish Cup** Clydesdale. **Murgitroyd Twenty20 Cup** Grange. **Women's National League** Carlton. **Women's Scottish Cup** George Watson's College.

SCOTLAND v AFGHANISTAN

First one-day international At Edinburgh, July 4, 2016. **No result. Afghanistan 283-4** (47.2 overs) (Rahmat Shah 100*, Najibullah Zadran 89*) **v ‡Scotland.** *ODI debuts:* C. D. de Lange, R. A. J. Smith (Scotland). *Afghanistan began their European tour with a bang, and were threatening to breach 300 when rain set in. Rahmat Shah made his first international hundred, and shared a fifth-wicket stand of 157* – an Afghan fifth-wicket record – with Najibullah Zadran, who faced only 53 balls and was in sight of his own maiden century. Scotland gave debuts to Con de Lange, a 35-year-old South African-born slow left-armer who formerly played for Northamptonshire, and Glamorgan all-rounder Ruaidhri Smith, 22.*

Second one-day international At Edinburgh, July 6, 2016. **Afghanistan won by 78 runs** (DLS). **‡Afghanistan 178-6** (37.2 overs) (Mohammad Shahzad 84); **Scotland 132** (27.1 overs). *After Mohammad Shahzad made 84 from 91 balls, Afghanistan were gearing up for the final assault when rain intervened. Scotland's target was revised upwards to 211 in 36 overs, but they lost Kyle Coetzer second ball. The other opener, Craig Wallace, clubbed 33 from 15, but 86-3 became 132 all out as the Afghan bowlers applied themselves well.*

SCOTLAND v HONG KONG

First Twenty20 international At Edinburgh, September 8, 2016. **No result. Scotland 153-6** (20 overs) (K. J. Coetzer 53); **‡Hong Kong 136-4** (18 overs). *ODI debuts:* M. R. J. Watt (Scotland); Ehsan Khan, Shahid Wasif, Tanveer Ahmed (Hong Kong). *Rain reduced this to a 21-over match, then lopped off another. The target was revised to 154 in 20, but only 18 were possible – not enough to constitute a game – before bad light ended play with Hong Kong needing 18 from 12 balls.*

Second Twenty20 international At Edinburgh, September 10, 2016. **Scotland won by 53 runs. ‡Scotland 266-7** (50 overs) (C. S. MacLeod 102, C. D. Wallace 52); **Hong Kong 213** (46.1 overs) (Babar Hayat 56; C. B. Sole 4-28). *Calum McLeod's fourth ODI hundred – his second in three matches – and sixth-wicket partnership of 116 with Wallace lifted Scotland to a total that proved beyond Hong Kong, although they were well placed at 139-2 in the 31st over, before Babar Hayat fell for 56. Seamer Chris Sole, whose father David captained Scotland's rugby team to the Five Nations Grand Slam in 1990, dismissed both openers and finished with four wickets.*

For Scotland's matches in the ICC World Twenty20, see page 793; for the Intercontinental Cup and the World Cricket League, see page 1441.

CRICKET IN THE NETHERLANDS IN 2016

Dry January as merry as it gets

DAVE HARDY

The year began well, with a four-wicket victory over the UAE in January – the Netherlands' first away win in the Intercontinental Cup since beating the same opposition in 2008. They won both 50-over matches too, thanks in large part to seamer Mudassar Bukhari, who picked up a combined eight for 45. It was a good start for the new chair of the KNCB, Betty Timmer, the first woman in the role.

But that was about as good as it got. At the World Twenty20 in India, the Netherlands failed to progress from the preliminary group. They lost to Bangladesh by eight runs and, after a washout against Oman, victory over Ireland in a six-over match was not enough. They fared little better during the Dutch summer: an ignominious two-day defeat by Afghanistan was followed by a 1–1 draw with Nepal in the 50-over World Cricket League. Tim Gruijters was recalled for those home games, more than two years after the acrimony of the 2014 World T20, when he was replaced in the squad by Wollongong-born Tom Cooper; Gruijters made four, nought and 44.

At the end of the season Anton Roux, head coach for almost three years, announced he was leaving to coach Otago Volts in New Zealand. Former England Test batsman Chris Adams took the role on an interim basis, before Ryan Campbell – who played two one-day internationals for Australia, and more recently represented Hong Kong at the World T20 – was confirmed as a permanent replacement. Soon after Roux's departure, Bukhari retired from four-day and 50-over cricket at the age of 32. He finished as the leading wicket-taker for the Netherlands in one-day internationals, taking his 57th in 2014, when they last had official status. He continues to be available in T20s, but was not selected for the Desert Challenge in the UAE in early 2017.

Using predominantly young home-grown players, Excelsior '20 of Schiedam, near Rotterdam, claimed the national *Topklasse*. Dosti United, who were runners-up, had the players with the best averages, though they were both South African: Stiaan van Zyl in the batting (73), Robbie Frylinck in the bowling (11). Eric Szwarczysnki, who plays for VRA on the outskirts of Amsterdam and is a veteran of 41 ODIs, hit the most runs, with 736. In 2017, the top two leagues will be expanded, from eight teams to ten, and Rotterdam club Punjab will play in the *Topklasse* for the first time.

In October, pace bowler Paul van Meekeren signed a two-year contract with Somerset, after joining on a short-term deal midway through the summer. Two Dutch women also played for counties in 2016: Sterre Kalis for Essex, and Miranda Veringmeier for Worcestershire. All three learned their trade in the Dutch system.

For the Netherlands' matches in the ICC World Twenty20, see page 793; the Intercontinental Cup, and the World Cricket League, see page 1141.

PART FIVE

Overseas Cricket

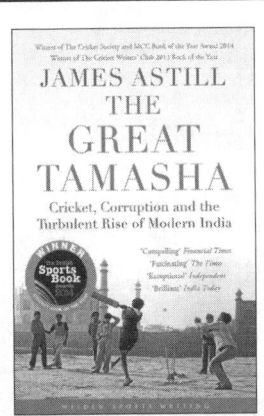

THE WORLD TWENTY20 IN 2015-16

REVIEW BY DILEEP PREMACHANDRAN

1 West Indies   2 England   3= India, New Zealand

For a previous generation of English cricketers, Eden Gardens in Kolkata meant the heartbreak of a World Cup final loss that turned on Mike Gatting's reverse sweep. Nearly three decades later, redemption appeared at hand: few expected West Indies to score 19 from the last over, not when the bowler was Ben Stokes, one of the competition's best operators at the death. And, while Marlon Samuels had batted well, he was now stranded at the non-striker's end. His partner, by contrast, was relatively unknown.

Before this game, Carlos Brathwaite had faced just 18 balls in the tournament. Delhi Daredevils had stumped up Rs42m (around £440,000) a month before the start of the World Twenty20, but his most eye-catching contribution in India had come during a warm-up game, also at Eden Gardens, where he smashed 33 from 14 balls to stun Australia. That was on March 13. Three weeks later, the stakes were infinitely higher. The harsher critics will say that – faced with such a powerful hitter – Stokes bowled it in the slot; the more charitable will argue he did little wrong. Either way, by the time Brathwaite was hitting his fourth successive six, TV commentator Ian Bishop was yelling: "Carlos Brathwaite! Carlos Brathwaite! Remember the name!" Thousands inside the ground, and millions watching at home, were unlikely to forget it.

It was a climax the tournament deserved, despite a slow-burn start in Nagpur and, in the Himalayan foothills, Dharamsala. And it said much about sport's

IBC/Getty Images

Sticking the boot in: Marlon Samuels revels in victory.

capacity to provide its own twists that the victors were a team who had briefly considered pulling out of the tournament, and who, on arrival in India, had no properly printed shirts. The West Indians had been engaged in a pay dispute with their board, whose president, Dave Cameron, was the subject of strong criticism from captain Darren Sammy at the post-match presentation. Sammy claimed his team had received a good luck message from the prime minister of Grenada but not from Cameron. The West Indies Cricket Board called Sammy's comments "inappropriate". (Four months later, he was replaced by Brathwaite.) Meanwhile, it emerged that a throwaway line in a pre-tournament column had also stoked their competitive fires. "West Indies are short of brains," wrote Mark Nicholas on ESPNcricinfo, "but have IPL history in their ranks." Sammy chose the eve of the final to air his disgust: "How could you describe people with no brains? Even animals have brains. We're not an object. That comment really set us off."

The final itself had plenty of needle, with West Indies' "Champion" celebrations – a dance deriving from a song of the same name written by all-rounder Dwayne Bravo – irking Joe Root; David Willey struck a sore nerve when he reprised the dance steps with England in the ascendancy. But it was the resumption of hostilities between Samuels and Stokes, who had clashed during England's tour of the Caribbean a year earlier, that proved ugliest. With victory almost assured after Brathwaite's third six, Samuels celebrated wildly in Stokes's face. Within an hour he was addressing a press conference with padded legs and booted feet on the table in front of him. A gracious victory it was not. Three weeks later, the ICC reprimanded the West Indians, saying "certain comments and actions were inappropriate, disrespectful and brought the event into disrepute".

A gracious victory it was not

None of this could obscure the fact that the best teams had reached the final. **West Indies**, with Chris Gayle rampaging to a 47-ball century (his only real contribution of the competition), had swatted England aside in their opening group game, and followed up with victories over Sri Lanka and South Africa. In the semi-final they were too powerful for India: Lendl Simmons broke hearts at the Wankhede not long after arriving in the country following an injury to Andre Fletcher, and there was a brutal cameo from Andre Russell as India's bowlers failed to back up Virat Kohli. Throughout, the 35-year-old Trinidadian leg-spinner Samuel Badree was outstanding, claiming nine wickets at 13 and conceding just 5.39 runs an over, a figure bettered among regular bowlers only by two other leggies – Sri Lanka's Jeffrey Vandersay (5.16) and South Africa's Imran Tahir (5.18).

England, despite a lack of IPL stars, had rebounded memorably from their early chastisement at the hands of Gayle, though midway through their game against South Africa, who had made 229, they appeared to be on their way out. But, after Jason Roy bludgeoned the new ball, Joe Root inspired England with an innings that underlined what Kohli was proving on a regular basis: orthodoxy does have a place in Twenty20 cricket – and it can be lethal. **South Africa** never quite recovered. Unconvincing in seeing off Afghanistan, they

Vivek Prakash, IDI/Getty Images

Pyrotechnician: Virat Kohli, who set the tournament alight, soaks up the adulation after India overcome Pakistan at Kolkata.

succumbed to West Indies on a tricky surface in Nagpur. Victory against a Sri Lankan side who had plummeted down the rankings since winning the tournament in 2014 was no more than a band-aid. **Sri Lanka** beat Afghanistan, just about, but did little else. With Kumar Sangakkara and Mahela Jayawardene gone, and captain Lasith Malinga pulling out with a knee injury, these were tough times. Angelo Mathews played a magnificent hand against England, but couldn't paper over flimsy displays from the top order.

Flying the flag for the Associates were **Afghanistan**. Having run Sri Lanka, South Africa and England close, they saved their best for the eventual champions. On a Nagpur pitch where the ball gripped, turned and occasionally spat, Mohammad Nabi's off-spin, Rashid Khan's leg-spin and Hamza Hotak's slow left-arm trickery were too much for West Indies – not that defeat stopped Gayle posing for a selfie with the delirious victors. The Afghans' competition had begun a good week before the rest, with a mini-qualifying round in Nagpur. They edged past Scotland, hammered Hong Kong, then – in the decider – routed Zimbabwe. For the **Zimbabweans** it was another reminder of their downward spiral since part-hosting the 50-over World Cup in 2003. **Scotland** had fallen repeatedly at ICC events. But, after 19 consecutive defeats, came a victory to savour, against **Hong Kong**.

The Scots also made headlines when captain Preston Mommsen questioned a format in which teams had to qualify twice for the main event – once in Ireland and Scotland in 2015, and again here. He was echoed by Peter Borren of the **Netherlands**, who were eliminated after a narrow defeat by Bangladesh

WORLD TWENTY20 NOTES AND QUOTES

Pakistan captain Shahid Afridi caused uproar back home when, on arrival in India, he said: "I've not enjoyed playing anywhere as much as I have in India. We have not got this much love even from Pakistan." Former captain Javed Miandad complained: "These cricketers should be ashamed of themselves for saying such a thing."

Doubts over the suitability of Delhi's Feroz Shah Kotla stadium meant it was confirmed as host of the first semi-final only a week beforehand. The Delhi & District Cricket Association had struggled to secure a clearance certificate from the South Delhi Municipal Corporation because of concerns over the safety of part of the R. P. Mehra Block, though journalists were still allowed to enter the stand, which housed the media centre.

Indian captain M. S. Dhoni's press conference after the semi-final defeat by West Indies took an unexpected twist when he invited Australian journalist Sam Ferris – who had asked whether he was "keen to continue playing" – to join him behind the microphones. Dhoni asked Ferris, a reporter for cricket.com.au, whether he wanted him to retire, and if he thought he was unfit; Ferris, clearly embarrassed, said no. Dhoni said he wished the question had been asked by an Indian journalist, "because I would have asked whether he has a son or a brother who is old enough to play and is a wicketkeeper. You fired the wrong ammunition at the wrong time."

Following his match award in the final, Marlon Samuels was asked why he thought Shane Warne – who had criticised his performance during the semi – had it in for him. "Maybe because my face is real and his face is not," he replied.

Two New Zealand radio presenters were temporarily suspended after Ben Stokes's mother – angered by comments about her son following the final – phoned in with a private complaint which was instead broadcast live. "I don't know whether they realise he was born and bred in New Zealand and quite frankly has family all over the country," said Deborah Stokes, who still lives in New Zealand with husband Ged. "And for those who listen to your station, for them to sit and listen to their cousin, their grandson, being bagged like that is absolutely unconscionable. I'm his mother and I'm totally brassed off. It's not about the cricket: it's about the personal attack on him. They called him arrogant and then they called him some sort of name. They don't know him. They wouldn't have a blooming clue." The presenters who duped her, Jeremy Wells and Matt Heath, of Radio Hauraki, were both reprimanded and taken off-air for a day.

Returning to Birmingham Airport on his own after the tournament, England all-rounder Moeen Ali was stopped and questioned by border officers, prompting him to tweet: "Have never been stopped at the airport when travelling with a team in uniform, but travel alone and get stopped for 40 minutes!! Joke". Former England cricketer Owais Shah responded: "Your beard might have something to do with it #sadreally". Airport officials confirmed Ali had been stopped on arrival in the UK, and pointed out that he had "exceeded his duty-free allowance" of £390 for personal gifts.

Lawrence Booth

and a washout against Oman. "It's a pretty emotional dressing-room," he said. "We sit here now after playing three hours of cricket against Bangladesh." A cameo from the 37-year-old Karachi-born Aamer Ali helped new boys **Oman** shock **Ireland**, who finished without a win and were left to rue a lack of batting oomph and dreadfully wayward bowling.

Bangladesh topped that group with no great fuss, and more was expected of them in the main draw. But they started sloppily against Pakistan, were edged out by Australia and – traumatically – by India, and thrashed by New Zealand. In left-arm seamer Mustafizur Rahman they had one of the most skilful bowlers on show, but the rest failed to build on the gains made at the 2015 World Cup. Their low point was India's great escape in Bangalore. A loss would have sent the hosts through the trap door, and – with two runs needed from Hardik Pandya's final three balls – Bangladesh were well placed to open it. But Mushfiqur Rahim and Mahmudullah, an experienced pair, suffered momentary lapses of reason. When tap-and-run would have been enough, both went for glory over midwicket – and both were caught in the deep. When M. S. Dhoni sprinted to the stumps to run out Mustafizur, denying Bangladesh a bye and a tie, India had sneaked home by a run. It was the most galling of chokes, and compounded the Bangladeshis' sense of injustice after two bowlers – seamer Taskin Ahmed and left-arm spinner Arafat Sunny – had been banned mid-tournament because of illegal actions.

Matthew Lewis, IDI/Getty Images

Strike force: Mustafizur Rahman spearheaded the Bangladesh attack.

That was one of three group games which India played with no margin for error, following a shellacking by New Zealand, whose spin trio of Nathan McCullum, Mitchell Santner and Ish Sodhi bowled them out for 79. Their next match had already been the subject of drama, as if India v Pakistan didn't already offer enough. Less than a fortnight earlier, the local Himachal Pradesh government had announced their reluctance to host the game in Dharamsala, in solidarity with the victims of a terror attack at the start of the year in Pathankot, just across the state border in Punjab. This extended to a reluctance to provide enough security to satisfy the Pakistani delegation. The ICC were incensed, and the BCCI – whose then secretary, Anurag Thakur, hails from Himachal Pradesh – were embarrassed. As a result, the entire caravanserai moved 1,000 miles east, to Eden Gardens. Once the game got under way, a perfectly paced half-century from Kohli had Sachin Tendulkar on his feet in the stands, and gave India their 11th win over their neighbours in 11 World Cup and World Twenty20 matches.

Not for the first time, **Pakistan** finished a global event in turmoil. Shahid Afridi's leadership was uninspiring, the batting little better; even the vaunted bowlers didn't produce the goods. Back home, debate raged about the effects of always playing on foreign soil, but word from within and outside the camp focused on poor fitness and a questionable work ethic. Afridi stepped down as Twenty20 captain, while Waqar Younis resigned as coach, having criticised Afridi's captaincy in a report inevitably leaked to the media.

New Zealand won every group match, including a close one against Australia, and earned respect for a brave selection policy based around their spinners: their established new-ball pair of Trent Boult and Tim Southee did not get a game. But, on a Delhi surface that favoured back-of-a-length seam bowling, they came a cropper in the semi-final against an England side who had played their previous two group games there. By contrast New Zealand, whose five matches took place at five different venues, were again left to reflect on their failure to win the big moments: nine World Cup semi-finals across the two limited-overs formats had now produced eight defeats.

Australia never got their combination right. David Warner, one of the most feared openers in the game, batted at No. 3 or 4. Usman Khawaja played some delightful cameos, but on their own they do not win tournaments, even in Twenty20. The young leg-spinner Adam Zampa, who went on to have a stunning IPL, was not fully trusted, and the lack of a coherent strategy cost the Australians dear in the winner-takes-all group match against India. Zampa bowled two overs for 11, and wasn't seen again; James Faulkner and Josh Hazlewood were given a pasting by Kohli.

Again, it was almost a one-man show: the next-highest score after Kohli's imperious unbeaten 82 was 21. He would play even better in the semi-final against West Indies, but – crucially, perhaps – **India** batted first in that game, when Kohli's great skill lay in his ability to gauge a chase. By the end of the competition, his record in successful Twenty20 international run-chases was staggering: 15 innings, nine undefeated, and an average of 122. So it felt incongruous that his outstanding tournament – he was dismissed only twice while scoring 273 runs – should end with his conceding the winning hit, as Russell belted a six over midwicket.

Until then, Dhoni's calmness under pressure had been impressive, especially against Bangladesh, but his lack of faith in Ravichandran Ashwin, his main spinner, was mystifying. Against West Indies, Pandya's four overs went for 43, yet – against batsmen who preferred seam – Ashwin bowled only two. Having retired from the Test side, and seen Kohli rejuvenate it, Dhoni may have wondered whether he would soon be stepping aside in the shorter formats too. If he struggled to find the big shots that once came so easily, then he was not the only Indian batsman to slip below par: Rohit Sharma averaged 17, while Yuvraj Singh appeared to be playing from memory; Shikhar Dhawan and Suresh Raina had a wretched time. For Kohli, a second successive World Twenty20 Man of the Tournament award was scant consolation.

Off the field, too, things could have been so much better for the hosts. The BCCI delayed naming the venues until December, which despite finger-pointing at the ICC made them chiefly responsible for the ensuing ticketing fiasco: there was no concrete information until late February, a fortnight before the first qualifying game. In Nagpur, tickets were sold at the old stadium in the heart of the city: fans arriving at the new one, ten miles away on the outskirts, couldn't buy any over the counter. Crowds spoiled by the razzmatazz and stardust of the IPL were also reluctant to attend matches not involving India, and many were played in front of echoing stands. Intense early-summer heat didn't help.

The knockout games were a different story, partly because the quality of the cricket was so high. And, even when India missed out on the final, the Kolkata crowd offered no shortage of decibels. Their mood ebbed and flowed like the

Pal Pillai, IDI/Getty Images

Christopher Lee, IDI/Getty Images

The turn of the screw: slow bowlers often gave least away, and two of the most miserly were West Indies' leg-spinner Samuel Badree and New Zealand left-armer Mitchell Santner.

game itself. At times, they cheered for England. But, mostly, the wall of sound was in favour of West Indies, historically the Indian fan's second team. By the time Brathwaite teed off, bedlam had descended. Stokes, on his haunches in despair in the middle of one of the sport's great venues, must have felt like a gladiator in the Colosseum. It was one of the enduring images of the tournament – Stokes consoled by his team-mates and watched by thousands, yet so very alone. Somewhere, Mike Gatting must have winced in sympathy.

WORLD TWENTY20 STATISTICS

Leading run-scorers

	M	*I*	*NO*	*R*	*HS*	*50*	*Avge*	*SR*	*4*	*6*
†Tamim Iqbal (B)	6	6	2	295	103*	2	73.75	142.51	24	14
V. Kohli (I)	5	5	3	273	89*	3	136.50	146.77	29	5
J. E. Root (E)	6	6	1	249	83	2	49.80	146.47	24	7
Mohammad Shahzad (Afg)	7	7	0	222	61	1	31.71	140.50	23	12
J. C. Buttler (E)	6	6	2	191	66*	1	47.75	159.16	13	12
J. J. Roy (E)	6	6	0	183	78	1	30.50	148.78	22	7
M. N. Samuels (WI)	6	6	1	181	85*	1	36.20	112.42	26	2
†Q. de Kock (SA)	4	4	0	153	52	1	38.25	142.99	18	6
Sabbir Rahman (B)	7	7	1	147	44	0	24.50	123.52	17	4
†U. T. Khawaja (A)	4	4	0	143	58	1	35.75	137.50	22	2
Asghar Stanikzai (Afg)	7	6	1	141	62	2	28.20	107.63	5	7
M. J. Guptill (NZ)	4	4	0	140	80	1	35.00	157.30	15	8
T. M. Dilshan (SL)	4	4	1	133	83*	1	44.33	123.14	13	5

The only centuries were Tamim Iqbal's 103 for Bangladesh v Oman at Dharamsala, and C. H. Gayle's 100* for West Indies v England at Mumbai.*

Best strike-rates

	SR	Runs		SR	Runs
†C. H. Gayle (WI)	194.82	113	M. J. Guptill (NZ)	157.30	140
Shahid Afridi (P)	183.67	90	S. R. Watson (A)	150.00	96
A. B. de Villiers (SA)	180.32	110	J. J. Roy (E)	148.78	183
†J-P. Duminy (SA)	172.91	83	†Najibullah Zadran (Afg)	147.14	103
Shoaib Malik (P)	165.51	96	V. Kohli (I)	146.77	273
J. C. Buttler (E)	159.16	191	J. E. Root (E)	146.47	249
L. M. P. Simmons (WI)	157.69	82	†N. L. T. C. Perera (SL)	145.45	80

Minimum 75 runs.

Leading wicket-takers

	Style	O	D	R	W	BB	4I	Avge	SR	ER
Mohammad Nabi (Afg)	OB	27	70	164	12	4-20	1	13.66	13.50	6.07
Rashid Khan (Afg)	LBG	28	69	183	11	3-11	0	16.63	15.27	6.53
I. S. Sodhi (NZ)	LBG	19.4	43	120	10	3-18	0	12.00	11.80	6.10
M. J. Santner (NZ)	SLA	18.1	55	114	10	4-11	1	11.40	10.90	6.27
Shakib Al Hasan (B)	SLA	23	52	166	10	4-15	1	16.60	13.80	7.21
D. J. Willey (E)	LFM	21	58	159	10	3-20	0	15.90	12.60	7.57
S. Badree (WI)	LBG	23	70	124	9	3-12	0	13.77	15.33	5.39
Mustafizur Rahman (B)	LFM	12	32	86	9	5-22	1	9.55	8.00	7.16
A. D. Russell (WI)	RFM	24	66	189	9	2-23	0	21.00	16.00	7.87
D. J. Bravo (WI)	RFM	24	49	190	9	3-37	0	21.11	16.00	7.91
J. P. Faulkner (A)	LFM	13.1	26	106	8	5-27	1	13.25	9.87	8.05
Al-Amin Hossain (B)	RFM	18	47	155	8	2-24	0	19.37	13.50	8.61

Most economical bowlers

	ER	Overs		ER	Overs
J. D. F. Vandersay (SL)	5.16	12	I. S. Sodhi (NZ)	6.10	19.4
Imran Tahir (SA)	5.18	16	H. M. R. K. B. Herath (SL)	6.18	16
S. Badree (WI)	5.39	23	Samiullah Shenwari (Afg)	6.27	22
G. D. Elliott (NZ)	5.76	13	A. Zampa (A)	6.27	11
A. Nehra (I)	5.94	19	M. J. Santner (NZ)	6.27	18.1
M. R. J. Watt (Scot)	6.00	12	Hamid Hassan (Afg)	6.29	13.3
Mohammad Nabi (Afg)	6.07	27	P. V. D. Chameera (SL)	6.36	11
Taskin Ahmed (B)	6.10	10	L. E. Plunkett (E)	6.37	16

Minimum 10 overs at less than 6.50 runs per over.

Leading wicketkeepers

	Dis	M		Dis	M
M. S. Dhoni (I)	8 (4ct, 4st)	5	Mushfiqur Rahim (B)	4 (2ct, 2st)	7
Q. de Kock (SA)	7 (5ct, 2st)	4	N. J. O'Brien (Ire)	3 (1ct, 2st)	3
L. Ronchi (NZ)	6 (2ct, 4st)	5	L. D. Chandimal (SL)	3 (2ct, 1st)	4
Mohammad Shahzad (Afg)	5 (1ct, 4st)	7	D. Ramdin (WI)	3 (2ct, 1st)	6
R. Mutumbami (Z)	4 (1ct, 3st)	3			

Leading fielders

	Ct	M		Ct	M
M. J. Guptill (NZ)	6	4	E. J. G. Morgan (E)	4	6
B. A. Stokes (E)	5	6	J. E. Root (E)	4	6
Sikandar Raza (Z)	4	3	Mahmudullah (B)	4	7
A. D. Hales (E)	4	5	Najibullah Zadran (Afg)	4	7
D. J. Bravo (WI)	4	6	Sabbir Rahman (B)	4	7

NATIONAL SQUADS

* *Captain.* ‡ *Did not play.*

Afghanistan *Asghar Stanikzai, Dawlat Zadran, Gulbadeen Naib, Hamid Hassan, Hamza Hotak, Karim Sadiq, Mohammad Nabi, Mohammad Shahzad, Najibullah Zadran, Noor Ali Zadran, Rashid Khan, Samiullah Shenwari, Shafiqullah Shinwari, Shapoor Zadran, Usman Ghani. *Coach:* Inzamam-ul-Haq.

Australia *S. P. D. Smith, A. C. Agar, N. M. Coulter-Nile, J. P. Faulkner, A. J. Finch, J. W. Hastings, J. R. Hazlewood, U. T. Khawaja, M. R. Marsh, G. J. Maxwell, P. M. Nevill, ‡A. J. Tye, D. A. Warner, S. R. Watson, A. Zampa. *Coach:* D. S. Lehmann.

Bangladesh *Mashrafe bin Mortaza, Abu Haider, Al-Amin Hossain, Arafat Sunny, Mahmudullah, Mithun Ali, Mushfiqur Rahim, Mustafizur Rahman, Nasir Hossain, ‡Nurul Hasan, Sabbir Rahman, Saqlain Sajib, Shakib Al Hasan, Shuvagata Hom, Soumya Sarkar, Tamim Iqbal, Taskin Ahmed. *Coach:* U. C. Hathurusinghe.

The bowling actions of Arafat Sunny and Taskin Ahmed were deemed illegal during the tournament; Saqlain Sajib and Shuvagata Hom replaced them.

England *E. J. G. Morgan, M. M. Ali, ‡S. W. Billings, J. C. Buttler, ‡L. A. Dawson, A. D. Hales, C. J. Jordan, L. E. Plunkett, A. U. Rashid, J. E. Root, J. J. Roy, B. A. Stokes, R. J. W. Topley, J. M. Vince, D. J. Willey. *Coach:* T. H. Bayliss.

S. T. Finn was originally selected, but injured his calf and was replaced by Plunkett.

Hong Kong *Tanvir Afzal, Adil Mehmood, Aizaz Khan, J. J. Atkinson, Babar Hayat, R. J. Campbell, ‡C. Carter, M. S. Chapman, Haseeb Amjad, Nadeem Ahmed, Nizakat Khan, A. Rath, K. D. Shah, ‡Waqas Barkat, ‡Waqas Khan. *Coach:* S. J. Cook.

India *M. S. Dhoni, R. Ashwin, J. J. Bumrah, S. Dhawan, ‡Harbhajan Singh, R. A. Jadeja, V. Kohli, ‡Mohammed Shami, ‡P. Negi, A. Nehra, M. K. Pandey, H. H. Pandya, A. M. Rahane, S. K. Raina, R. G. Sharma, Yuvraj Singh. *Coach:* R. J. Shastri.

Yuvraj Singh injured his ankle during the tournament, and was replaced by Pandey.

Ireland *W. T. S. Porterfield, ‡A. Balbirnie, G. H. Dockrell, A. R. McBrine, T. J. Murtagh, K. J. O'Brien, N. J. O'Brien, A. D. Poynter, ‡S. W. Poynter, W. B. Rankin, M. C. Sorensen, P. R. Stirling, ‡S. R. Thompson, G. C. Wilson, C. A. Young. *Coach:* J. G. Bracewell.

Netherlands *P. W. Borren, W. Barresi, B. N. Cooper, T. L. W. Cooper, M. A. A. Jamil, ‡V. J. Kingma, Mudassar Bukhari, S. J. Myburgh, ‡M. P. O'Dowd, ‡M. J. G. Rippon, P. M. Seelaar, L. V. van Beek, T. van der Gugten, R. E. van der Merwe, P. A. van Meekeren. *Coach:* A. Roux.

New Zealand *K. S. Williamson, C. J. Anderson, ‡T. A. Boult, G. D. Elliott, M. J. Guptill, M. J. McClenaghan, N. L. McCullum, A. F. Milne, C. Munro, H. M. Nicholls, L. Ronchi, M. J. Santner, I. S. Sodhi, ‡T. G. Southee, L. R. P. L. Taylor. *Coach:* M. J. Hesson.

Oman *Sultan Ahmed, Aamer Ali, Aamer Kaleem, Adnan Ilyas, M. S. Ansari, Bilal Khan, Jatinder Singh, Khawar Ali, A. V. Lalcheta, Mehran Khan, R. J. Ranpura, ‡Sufyan Mehmood, ‡V. S. Wategaonkar, Zeeshan Maqsood, ‡Zeeshan Siddiqui. *Coach:* L. R. D. Mendis.

Pakistan *Shahid Afridi, Ahmed Shehzad, ‡Anwar Ali, Imad Wasim, Khalid Latif, Mohammad Amir, Mohammad Hafeez, Mohammad Irfan, ‡Mohammad Nawaz, Mohammad Sami, Sarfraz Ahmed, Sharjeel Khan, Shoaib Malik, Umar Akmal, Wahab Riaz. *Coach:* Waqar Younis.

From the original selection, Babar Azam (broken arm) and Rumman Raees (hamstring injury) were replaced by Mohammad Sami and Sharjeel Khan. Shortly before the tournament the selectors replaced Iftikhar Ahmed and Khurram Manzoor with Ahmed Shehzad and Khalid Latif.

Scotland *P. L. Mommsen, R. D. Berrington, K. J. Coetzer, M. H. Cross, J. H. Davey, C. D. de Lange, A. C. Evans, M. A. Leask, M. W. Machan, C. S. MacLeod, G. T. Main, H. G. Munsey, S. M. Sharif, R. M. L. Taylor, M. R. J. Watt. *Coach:* G. E. Bradburn.

South Africa *F. du Plessis, K. J. Abbott, H. M. Amla, F. Behardien, Q. de Kock, A. B. de Villiers, J-P. Duminy, Imran Tahir, D. A. Miller, C. H. Morris, A. M. Phangiso, K. Rabada, R. R. Rossouw, D. W. Steyn, D. Wiese. *Coach:* R. C. Domingo.

Sri Lanka *A. D. Mathews, P. V. D. Chameera, L. D. Chandimal, T. M. Dilshan, H. M. R. K. B. Herath, D. S. N. F. G. Jayasuriya, C. K. Kapugedera, K. M. D. N. Kulasekara, R. A. S. Lakmal,

‡S. L. Malinga, N. L. T. C. Perera, ‡S. M. S. M. Senanayake, M. D. Shanaka, T. A. M. Siriwardene, H. D. R. L. Thirimanne, J. D. F. Vandersay. *Coach:* G. X. Ford.

The day before the team left for India, a new selection panel replaced D. P. D. N. Dickwella and Vandersay with Lakmal and Thirimanne, but Vandersay was recalled later when a persistent knee injury forced Malinga to withdraw. He had originally been named as captain, but stood down in favour of Mathews.

West Indies *D. J. G. Sammy, S. Badree, S. J. Benn, C. R. Brathwaite, D. J. Bravo, J. Charles, A. D. S. Fletcher, C. H. Gayle, ‡J. O. Holder, E. Lewis, ‡A. R. Nurse, D. Ramdin, A. D. Russell, M. N. Samuels, L. M. P. Simmons, J. E. Taylor. *Coach:* P. V. Simmons.

From the original selection, D. M. Bravo withdrew to concentrate on Test cricket, S. P. Narine pulled out to continue remedial work on his bowling action, K. A. Pollard pleaded a knee problem, and Simmons hurt his back. They were replaced by Brathwaite, Charles, Lewis and Nurse. Simmons was recalled for the semi-final after Fletcher tore a hamstring.

Zimbabwe *H. Masakadza, T. L. Chatara, ‡C. J. Chibhabha, E. Chigumbura, ‡T. S. Chisoro, W. P. Masakadza, ‡P. J. Moor, ‡T. Mupariwa, R. Mutumbami, T. Panyangara, V. Sibanda, Sikandar Raza, D. T. Tiripano, M. N. Waller, S. C. Williams. *Coach:* D. F. Whatmore.

A. G. Cremer (broken arm), L. M. Jongwe (thumb) and N. Madziva (eye) were all injured during pre-tournament warm-ups, and replaced by Chibhabha, Mupariwa and Tiripano.

PRELIMINARY STAGE

GROUP A

Sidharth Monga

At Dharamsala, March 9, 2016. **Bangladesh won by eight runs. Bangladesh 153-7** (20 overs) (Tamim Iqbal 83*; T. van der Gugten 3-21); ‡**Netherlands 145-7** (20 overs) (P. W. Borren 30). *MoM:* Tamim Iqbal. *Bangladesh made a nervous start, but Tamim Iqbal gave them a total they successfully defended on a slow pitch. It was hard to collar the Netherlands' tall bowlers, who prospered by banging the ball in. But Tamim, who survived a stumping chance off slow left-armer Roelof van der Merwe on 46, batted through to hit six of his side's ten fours and three of their six sixes. The Dutch batsmen found conditions similarly tough, though they kept themselves in the game, and needed 42 from 25 balls with seven wickets in hand. But Peter Borren top-edged a slog-sweep off Shakib Al Hasan, then Mashrafe bin Mortaza had van der Merwe caught behind in the next over, which cost only three; it also included a remarkable reprieve for Tom Cooper, whose inside edge hit off stump hard without dislodging a bail. Even so, 17 off the last, from seamer Taskin Ahmed, proved beyond the Netherlands. Both Taskin and slow left-armer Arafat Sunny were reported for suspect actions, and – ten days later – banned from bowling.*

At Dharamsala, March 9, 2016 (floodlit). **Oman won by two wickets.** ‡**Ireland 154-5** (20 overs) (G. C. Wilson 38; M. S. Ansari 3-37); **Oman 157-8** (19.4 overs) (Zeeshan Maqsood 38, Khawar Ali 34, Aamer Ali 32). *MoM:* Aamer Ali. *Oman, a team of ageing expats from India and Pakistan relying on spirit and surprise rather than orthodoxy and fitness, supplied the tournament's first feel-good story; Ireland, so often the giant-killers, were now the victims. Perhaps preoccupied with a slow pitch, and forgetting the problems posed by handling a dew-covered ball later on, Ireland chose to bat and managed a middling 154. Slow left-armer Ajay Lalcheta, whose stuttering action was hard to pick, began with a maiden, while Munis Ansari, whose slinging yorkers recalled Lasith Malinga, collected three wickets. Oman's openers started well, but 69-0 quickly became 90-5, with six overs to go. Aamer Ali, a jack-in-the-box 37-year-old marketing manager of an Indian restaurant in Muscat, got stuck in – and, with 14 needed off the last over, the dew kicked in too: Max Sorensen began with one that was no-balled on height and flashed to fine leg for four, then two more full-bungers slipped out. It didn't matter that Aamer was caught behind off the fourth legitimate ball, after clubbing 32 from 17: the next delivery – another high no-ball – nutmegged keeper Niall O'Brien, and sparked wild celebrations among the Omanis, who carried coach Duleep Mendis on their shoulders in gratitude.*

At Dharamsala, March 11, 2016. **Netherlands v Oman. Abandoned.** *Persistent rain left puddles on the outfield, and no play was possible. The Netherlands were eliminated – but Oman lived to fight another day.*

At Dharamsala, March 11, 2016 (floodlit). **No result. Bangladesh 94-2** (8 overs) (Tamim Iqbal 47) **v ‡Ireland.** *Ireland joined the Netherlands in being knocked out of the competition after only three days, when rain returned to play spoilsport following some heroic efforts from the groundstaff to set up a 12-over-a-side match. Tamim Iqbal continued his form, and Bangladesh were looking in good shape when the weather closed in.*

At Dharamsala, March 13, 2016. **Netherlands won by 12 runs. Netherlands 59-5** (6 overs) (G. H. Dockrell 3-7); **‡Ireland 47-7** (6 overs) (P. A. van Meekeren 4-11). *MoM:* P. A. van Meekeren. *More inclement weather did little to brighten up the sombre mood of two teams unhappy at the lack of opportunities for Associate sides. And the rain conspired to make this a six-over lottery. The pitch was tacky after its time under the covers, and the Netherlands were restricted to 59, despite swinging at everything. Paul Stirling got Ireland off to the ideal start, bringing the task down to 32 from four, with nine wickets in hand. But Paul van Meekeren, a tall seamer from Amsterdam, used the pitch cannily, banging in cutters halfway down. A stunning catch here, a top edge there – and a panicky Ireland lost the game in a trice.*

At Dharamsala, March 13, 2016 (floodlit). **Bangladesh won by 54 runs** (DLS). **Bangladesh 180-2** (20 overs) (Tamim Iqbal 103*, Sabbir Rahman 44); **‡Oman 65-9** (12 overs) (Shakib Al Hasan 4-15). *MoM:* Tamim Iqbal. *Tamim ensured Bangladesh would not slip up in the shoot-out for a place in the tournament proper. His 60-ball century was their first in T20 internationals, and made him the first Bangladeshi to score 1,000 runs in the format; he also topped the lists for Tests and ODIs. He made 233 runs in the three preliminary games, and would finish as the tournament's leading scorer, despite adding only 62 in the next phase. His main support came from Sabbir Rahman, who smacked 44 from 26 balls in a stand of 97. Still, 180 was not a conclusive total: with rain threatening, Oman needed to make 38-0 in the first five overs to ease ahead on DLS. Instead wickets tumbled, and when the rain finally came they were way adrift.*

GROUP B

Tim Wigmore

At Nagpur, March 8, 2016. **Zimbabwe won by 14 runs. Zimbabwe 158-8** (20 overs) (V. Sibanda 59, E. Chigumbura 30*); **‡Hong Kong 144-6** (20 overs) (J. J. Atkinson 53, Tanvir Afzal 31*). *MoM:* V. Sibanda. *T20I debut:* R. J. Campbell (Hong Kong). *There was no glitzy ceremony at the World Twenty20's opening match, and only a few hundred people in the VCA Stadium – not helped by the fact that tickets had to be bought online or at the old VCA Ground, ten miles away. Zimbabwe were soon 62-4: Hamilton Masakadza was run out, bat and foot over the crease but poised in mid-air, while Sean Williams dragged a cutter from Tanvir Afzal on to his stumps. The graceful Vusi Sibanda added 61 with Malcolm Waller but, after three more wickets in eight balls, it took three sixes from Elton Chigumbura to haul them past 150. Ryan Campbell, at 44 the oldest man to play in a Twenty20 international, bowled some economical off-spin on debut for Hong Kong (13 years after keeping wicket in two ODIs for Australia), but could not find his timing as opener. His side were 48-2 after ten overs, and played out 60 dot balls to Zimbabwe's 44, though James Atkinson battled to a fifty.*

At Nagpur, March 8, 2016 (floodlit). **Afghanistan won by 14 runs. ‡Afghanistan 170-5** (20 overs) (Mohammad Shahzad 61, Asghar Stanikzai 55*); **Scotland 156-5** (20 overs) (H. G. Munsey 41, K. J. Coetzer 40, M. W. Machan 36). *MoM:* Mohammad Shahzad. *Afghanistan repeated their victory over Scotland in the 50-over World Cup a year earlier. Mohammad Shahzad had fallen to the opening delivery of their previous World T20 campaign, in 2014, but this time his thunderous drive bisected the covers. He crashed consecutive sixes off Matt Machan and impudently moved across his stumps to flick Richie Berrington over fine leg. Shahzad's 61 – it was "a bit hot" for a century, he said – and more restrained batting from Asghar Stanikzai left Scotland needing 171. Their openers embraced the challenge: George Munsey reverse-swept with panache, and piled on 84 in 8.5 overs with Kyle Coetzer, who drove serenely. But Coetzer pulled a long hop to square leg, Munsey was lbw two balls later, and Scotland collapsed to 108-4. Against Afghanistan's four spinners, who delivered 15 overs for 100 runs, they struggled to meet the rate: Machan and Preston Mommsen ran hard but managed a solitary boundary in 50 balls.*

At Nagpur, March 10, 2016. **Zimbabwe won by 11 runs. ‡Zimbabwe 147-7** (20 overs) (S. C. Williams 53); **Scotland 136** (19.4 overs) (R. D. Berrington 36, P. L. Mommsen 31; W. P. Masakadza 4-28). *MoM:* W. P. Masakadza. *Hamilton Masakadza was run out again, this time crashing into*

Sibanda, who needed treatment for a cut chin. Sibanda picked out square leg a few minutes later. Scotland kept their grip, yielding a mere 19 in the last three overs, and it needed Williams's half-century to lift Zimbabwe towards 150. But in Scotland's opening over, from slow left-armer Wellington Masakadza, Munsey was stumped after reverse-sweeping two fours. Panic ensued: Matt Cross nicked his first delivery, Machan struck two fours then chipped to mid-on and, when Coetzer was snaffled one-handed by Sikandar Raza at cover, it was 20-4. Yet Berrington and Mommsen added 51 and, needing 55 from 35 balls with five wickets in hand, Scotland were hopeful, even after Masakadza collected two more in his final over. Berrington and Josh Davey reduced the equation to 24 off 13, but it was still too much.

At Nagpur, March 10, 2016 (floodlit). **Afghanistan won by six wickets. ‡Hong Kong 116-6** (20 overs) (Mohammad Nabi 4-20); **Afghanistan 119-4** (18 overs) (Mohammad Shahzad 41, Noor Ali Zadran 35). *MoM:* Mohammad Nabi. *Campbell (27) showed why Hong Kong had been so keen to select him: he started with a classical off-drive against Hamid Hassan, then smeared four more off-side boundaries with increasing authority. But in the sixth over, at 40-0, he top-edged a ball from Mohammad Nabi on to his helmet, and it trickled on to the stumps. Hong Kong floundered, collecting only three more fours, and failed to reach 120 as Nabi's flat off-spin snared four wickets. Shahzad launched another show of pyrotechnics, though he also gave Campbell the pleasure of his first wicket in international cricket (soon followed by his second, Nabi). The run-out of Noor Ali Zadran, after a brilliant throw from Babar Hayat in the deep, epitomised Hong Kong's spirit and zestful fielding, but Afghanistan waltzed to victory.*

At Nagpur, March 12, 2016. **Afghanistan won by 59 runs. ‡Afghanistan 186-6** (20 overs) (Mohammad Shahzad 40, Samiullah Shenwari 43, Mohammad Nabi 52; T. Panyangara 3-32); **Zimbabwe 127** (19.4 overs) (Rashid Khan 3-11). *MoM:* Mohammad Nabi. *Neither team in this shoot-out had reached the second stage of a World T20 competition before (this was Zimbabwe's fifth attempt, and Afghanistan's fourth). Afghanistan were favourites, having won all four previous T20Is against Zimbabwe, and Shahzad's brash unorthodoxy bore this out, as he blitzed 40 off 23 balls. His dismissal sparked a collapse of four wickets in 20 deliveries, but Samiullah Shenwari and Nabi (who should have been stumped on 20) added 98. Unobtrusive accumulation built up to fireworks as the Afghans blazed 88 in their last six overs. A target of 187 felt at least 30 too steep, and Zimbabwe were throttled: Rashid Khan showed off his googly to claim three victims, and the highest score was 17 from No. 10 Tinashe Panyangara. Their victory complete, each of the Afghans embraced their coach, the former Pakistan captain Inzamam-ul-Haq.*

At Nagpur, March 12, 2016 (floodlit). **Scotland won by eight wickets** (DLS). **‡Hong Kong 127-7** (20 overs) (M. S. Chapman 40); **Scotland 78-2** (8 overs). *MoM:* M. W. Machan. *A slog-sweep for six from Machan made history: after 19 defeats (and one abandonment) in World Cup and World T20 competitions since their debut in 1999, Scotland finally had a maiden win. They were already out of the tournament, but victory could scarcely have been more emphatic: after rain truncated the chase, Scotland cantered past a target of 76 from ten overs with two in hand. The triumph was rooted in their best bowling and fielding of the campaign. On a slow pitch, the spinners – Con de Lange, in his first game of the tournament, Machan and Mark Watt – collected 4-66 from their 12 overs, conceding only 18 in boundaries. They ensured another under-par Hong Kong total, despite Mark Chapman's nonchalant class.*

PRELIMINARY GROUP TABLES

Group A	*P*	*W*	*L*	*NR*	*Pts*	*NRR*
BANGLADESH	3	2	0	1	5	1.93
Netherlands	3	1	1	1	3	0.15
Oman	3	1	1	1	3	–1.52
Ireland	3	0	2	1	1	–0.68

Group B	*P*	*W*	*L*	*NR*	*Pts*	*NRR*
AFGHANISTAN	3	3	0	0	6	1.54
Zimbabwe	3	2	1	0	4	–0.56
Scotland	3	1	2	0	2	–0.13
Hong Kong	3	0	3	0	0	–1.01

SUPER TEN

GROUP ONE

ENGLAND v WEST INDIES

At Mumbai (Wankhede), March 16, 2016 (floodlit). West Indies won by six wickets. Toss: West Indies.

"Entertain me." When Chris Gayle walked out to begin West Indies' reply to England's more than respectable 182, a request from team-mate Sulieman Benn was ringing in his ears. An hour and a half later, Gayle had obliged, bludgeoning a 47-ball century and launching 11 sixes into Mumbai's night sky, many higher and longer than seemed reasonable. England had not bowled badly; they had simply walked into a hurricane. Or, as Morgan put it: "He did what he does." West Indies had looked vulnerable early in their chase: Charles flicked Willey to midwicket, and Samuels was fortunate to escape two impassioned pleas for leg-before in the same over. Samuels made the early running, while Gayle – deprived of the strike – ambled to 22 from 16 balls. It was the most illusory of precursors. He launched Rashid for two sixes over long-on, pulled Stokes for two more, and straight-drove Ali for three in a row. A pair of leg-side mows off Willey took him to 96. Moments later, Gayle was celebrating the joint-third-fastest hundred in Twenty20 internationals, and his 17th in all 20-over cricket. And he now had 98 sixes at this level, seven more than Brendon McCullum, the next-best. Only Jordan escaped punishment, mainly because he nailed his yorkers. But victory – West Indies' fourth out of four over England in World Twenty20s – came with 11 balls to spare. The England innings had been less memorable, though not without its merits. Root batted pleasantly until slapping Russell to mid-off, and Buttler connected with some blows; there were nine sixes in all, shared by five players. Gayle needed no such assistance, leaving England's semi-final hopes already swinging in the breeze of the Arabian Sea. LAWRENCE BOOTH

Man of the Match: C. H. Gayle.

England

		B	*4/6*
1 J. J. Roy *c 9 b 6*	15	15	2
2 A. D. Hales *b 10*	28	26	4
3 J. E. Root *c 11 b 6*	48	36	3/2
4 †J. C. Buttler *c 8 b 5*	30	20	0/3
5 *E. J. G. Morgan *not out*	27	14	1/2
6 B. A. Stokes *lbw b 5*	15	7	2/1
7 M. M. Ali *run out*	7	2	0/1
B 1, lb 1, w 10	12		
6 overs: 49-1 (20 overs)	182-6		

1/37 2/92 3/114 4/152 5/175 6/182

8 C. J. Jordan, 9 D. J. Willey, 10 A. U. Rashid and 11 R. J. W. Topley did not bat.

Taylor 3–9–30–0; Badree 4–7–34–0; Russell 4–11–36–2; Bravo 4–8–41–2; Benn 3–4–23–1; Brathwaite 2–2–16–0.

West Indies

		B	*4/6*
1 J. Charles *c 7 b 9*	0	2	0
2 C. H. Gayle *not out*	100	48	5/11
3 M. N. Samuels *c 9 b 10*	37	27	8
4 †D. Ramdin *c 10 b 7*	12	14	1
5 D. J. Bravo *c 2 b 11*	2	4	0
6 A. D. Russell *not out*	16	16	2
Lb 4, w 10, nb 2	16		
6 overs: 55-1 (18.1 overs)	183-4		

1/2 2/57 3/103 4/113

7 *D. J. G. Sammy, 8 C. R. Brathwaite, 9 S. Badree, 10 S. J. Benn and 11 J. E. Taylor did not bat.

Willey 3–9–33–1; Topley 2.1–7–22–1; Jordan 4–13–24–0; Stokes 3–7–42–0; Rashid 2–3–20–1; Ali 4–9–38–1.

Umpires: C. B. Gaffaney and R. J. Tucker. Third umpire: P. R. Reiffel.
Referee: D. C. Boon.

AFGHANISTAN v SRI LANKA

At Kolkata, March 17, 2016 (floodlit). Sri Lanka won by six wickets. Toss: Afghanistan.

Sri Lanka dropped three catches, resorted to some strange bowling changes, and produced an unconvincing display from the middle order – but Dilshan's 83 not out from 56 balls was enough to carry them home. Herath had helped reduce Afghanistan to 51 for four after 11 overs, but he was taken off with figures of two for 11 from three, and the innings recovered. Asghar Stanikzai, the captain, made a stuttering start – he was dropped on 34 as Thirimanne parried a slog-sweep over the midwicket boundary for six – but found fluency to put on 61 in 33 balls with Samiullah Shenwari. With 106 coming off the last ten overs, 153 for seven felt passable. But Dilshan hit his sixth ball over square leg for six, and scooped his seventh over fine leg for six more. He rarely looked ruffled, which was just as well: no one else in the top five reached 20, with Perera and Kapugedera both run out. Dilshan, though, continued to prosper square of the wicket, and the required rate remained in hand. Poor fielding from Afghanistan's boundary riders helped lubricate Sri Lanka's advance in the middle overs, and rapid runs from Mathews settled matters. FIDEL FERNANDO

Man of the Match: T. M. Dilshan.

Afghanistan

		B	4/6
1 †Mohammad Shahzad *c 11 b 6*	8	12	1
2 Noor Ali Zadran *b 10*	20	23	3
3 *Asghar Stanikzai *c 1 b 4*	62	47	3/4
4 Karim Sadiq *c 1 b 4*	0	7	0
5 Mohammad Nabi *lbw b 10*	3	4	0
6 Samiullah Shenwari *c 4 b 9*	31	14	3/2
7 Shafiqullah Shinwari *c 3 b 4*	5	7	0
8 Dawlat Zadran *not out*	5	3	0
9 Najibullah Zadran *not out*	12	3	1/1
Lb 1, w 6	7		
6 overs: 36-1 (20 overs)	153-7		

1/12 2/44 3/46 4/51 5/112 6/132 7/136

10 Rashid Khan and 11 Hamid Hassan did not bat.

Mathews 3–9–17–1; Kulasekara 4–9–43–1; Chameera 4–8–19–0; Herath 4–14–24–2; Perera 4–8–33–3; Siriwardene 1–0–16–0.

Sri Lanka

		B	4/6
1 †L. D. Chandimal *c 6 b 5*	18	17	2/1
2 T. M. Dilshan *not out*	83	56	8/3
3 H. D. R. L. Thirimanne *b 10*	6	13	1
4 N. L. T. C. Perera *run out*	12	8	0/1
5 C. K. Kapugedera *run out*	10	9	1
6 *A. D. Mathews *not out*	21	10	3/1
B 4, w 1	5		
6 overs: 41-1 (18.5 overs)	155-4		

1/41 2/58 3/85 4/113

7 T. A. M. Siriwardene, 8 D. S. N. F. G. Jayasuriya, 9 K. M. D. N. Kulasekara, 10 H. M. R. K. B. Herath and 11 P. V. D. Chameera did not bat.

Karim Sadiq 2–4–21–0; Hamid Hassan 3.5–6–38–0; Dawlat Zadran 3–7–31–0; Mohammad Nabi 4–9–25–1; Rashid Khan 4–11–27–1; Samiullah Shenwari 2–6–9–0.

Umpires: B. N. J. Oxenford and J. S. Wilson. Third umpire: R. A. Kettleborough.
Referee: B. C. Broad.

ENGLAND v SOUTH AFRICA

At Mumbai (Wankhede), March 18, 2016 (floodlit). England won by two wickets. Toss: England.

At the break between innings, England's tournament looked over almost before it had begun. Having felt the wrath of Chris Gayle two evenings earlier, their seamers had served up so many

HIGHEST SUCCESSFUL TWENTY20 RUN-CHASES

Total (Overs)		
236-6 (19.2)	West Indies v South Africa (231-7) at Johannesburg	2014-15
230-8 (19.4)	**England v South Africa (229-4) at Mumbai**	**2015-16**
226-3 (18.3)	Sussex v Essex (225-3) at Chelmsford	2014
224-5 (19.4)	Cape Cobras v Titans (222-4) at Centurion	2010-11
223-8 (20)	**Hobart Hurr. v Melb. Renegades (222-4) at Melbourne (Docklands)**	**2016-17**
220-4 (19)	Central Districts v Otago (219-4) at Dunedin	2005-06
220-4 (18)	Somerset v Hampshire (216-5) at Taunton	2010
217-3 (19)	**Warriors v Dolphins (216-5) at East London**	**2016-17**
217-7 (19.5)	Rajasthan Royals v Deccan Chargers (214-5) at Hyderabad	2007-08
215-7 (20)	Lahore Eagles v Sialkot Stallions (210) at Lahore	2004-05
215-8 (20)	Royal Challengers Bangalore v South Australia (214-2) at Bangalore	2011-12

Gareth Copley, Getty Images

Loft conversion: Joe Root goes aerial as England overhaul South Africa's 229.

freebies that their batsmen were obliged to make 230. Undeterred, Roy and Hales hit 44 off the first two overs, from Rabada and Steyn – and England began to believe. Wickets fell, but they stayed on top of the rate. And, with the hundred coming up in 7.3 overs, Root was playing a blinder. Morgan was outwitted by Duminy to make it 111 for four, but Root treated an equation of 112 off ten overs with serene disdain, pulling Duminy for six, then upper-cutting Morris for another. South Africa, who would eventually concede 20 in wides, were panicking, even more so when Steyn returned for an over which took his analysis to 2–0–35–0, the worst mauling of his Twenty20 career. With 44 needed off 27 balls, Buttler was stumped off the impressively tight Imran Tahir, who in a game of 39 fours and 22 sixes conceded none. And, by the time Root was caught at deep backward square for a sublime 83 from 44 deliveries, England were all but home; not even the frantic loss of two wickets with the scores level could dilute the euphoria. In reality, they could have been chasing even more. De Kock, who made a 21-ball fifty, equalling South Africa's quickest in the format, and Amla, who needed 25 for his, had begun with 96 in seven overs, and England were grateful for the relative tidiness of Ali and Rashid. Duminy, the third half-centurion of the innings, helped take 36 off the last two overs, at which point Morgan's team looked doomed. Then came spectacular redemption. LAWRENCE BOOTH

Man of the Match: J. E. Root.

South Africa

		B	4/6
1 H. M. Amla *lbw b 7*	58	31	7/3
2 †Q. de Kock *c 2 b 7*	52	24	7/3
3 A. B. de Villiers *c 5 b 10*	16	8	0/2
4 *F. du Plessis *c 1 b 9*	17	17	1
5 J-P. Duminy *not out*	54	28	3/3
6 D. A. Miller *not out*	28	12	2/2
B 2, w 2	4		
6 overs: 83-0 (20 overs)	229-4		

1/96 2/114 3/133 4/169

7 C. H. Morris, 8 K. J. Abbott, 9 K. Rabada, 10 D. W. Steyn and 11 Imran Tahir did not bat.

Willey 4–7–40–1; Topley 2–2–33–0; Ali 4–5–34–2; Jordan 3–2–49–0; Stokes 2–2–23–0; Rashid 4–8–35–1; Root 1–0–13–0.

England

		B	4/6
1 J. J. Roy *c 2 b 8*	43	16	5/3
2 A. D. Hales *lbw b 8*	17	7	4
3 B. A. Stokes *c 7 b 9*	15	9	1/1
4 J. E. Root *c 6 b 9*	83	44	6/4
5 *E. J. G. Morgan *b 5*	12	15	0
6 †J. C. Buttler *st 2 b 11*	21	14	1/1
7 M. M. Ali *not out*	8	10	1
8 C. J. Jordan *c 5 b 8*	5	3	1
9 D. J. Willey *run out*	0	0	0
10 A. U. Rashid *not out*	0	0	0
Lb 6, w 20	26		
6 overs: 89-3 (19.4 overs)	230-8		

1/48 2/71 3/87 4/111 5/186 6/219 7/229 8/229

11 R. J. W. Topley did not bat.

Rabada 4–7–50–2; Steyn 2–0–35–0; Abbott 3.4–8–41–3; Imran Tahir 4–3–28–1; Duminy 3–2–31–1; Morris 3–4–39–0.

Umpires: S. Ravi and P. R. Reiffel. Third umpire: R. J. Tucker.
Referee: D. C. Boon.

AFGHANISTAN v SOUTH AFRICA

At Mumbai (Wankhede), March 20, 2016. South Africa won by 37 runs. Toss: South Africa.

An onslaught from de Villiers proved the difference against a defiant Afghanistan, whose spirit was exemplified by their hard-hitting opener Mohammad Shahzad. Batting first in a contest they had to win, South Africa reached 90 for one in the tenth over, before Afghanistan's spinners stifled their progress. At 138 for three after 16, it took de Villiers's assault on leg-spinner Rashid Khan to restore confidence that their total would be safe: he smashed 29 in an over, including four sixes and a four, en route to 64 from 29 balls, a stamp of authority that ought to have put the Associates in their place. South Africa, however, had reckoned without the belligerence of Shahzad. Tearing into the new ball like Obelix faced with a Roman legion, he carted five sixes in the first three overs, reaching 32 before his opening partner Noor Ali Zadran had even faced a ball, and finished with 44 from 19. A canny spell of deck-hitting seam from Morris, who took a format-best four for 27, slowed the Afghan charge. But, with Noor Ali anchoring the chase, and Gulbadeen Naib and Samiullah Shenwari providing the impetus, their refusal to accept defeat was inspiring. Shahzad later caused hilarity by suggesting that the absence of Dale Steyn had hindered Afghanistan. "Steyn is not dangerous," he said. "This wicket is good to face a pacer – the ball is coming on to the bat. So, no, I am not happy that he was not playing." ANDREW MILLER

Man of the Match: C. H. Morris.

South Africa

		B	4/6
1 †Q. de Kock *c 1 b 10*	45	31	6/2
2 H. M. Amla *c 3 b 11*	5	5	1
3 *F. du Plessis *run out*	41	27	7/1
4 A. B. de Villiers *c 7 b 5*	64	29	4/5
5 J-P. Duminy *not out*	29	20	2/1
6 D. A. Miller *c 4 b 9*	19	8	2/1
7 D. Wiese *not out*	0	0	0
Lb 2, w 4	6		
6 overs: 66-1 (20 overs)	209-5		

1/25 2/90 3/97 4/173 5/203

8 C. H. Morris, 9 K. J. Abbott, 10 K. Rabada and 11 Imran Tahir did not bat.

Afghanistan

		B	4/6
1 †Mohammad Shahzad *b 8*	44	19	3/5
2 Noor Ali Zadran *st 1 b 11*	25	24	1/1
3 *Asghar Stanikzai *c 1 b 8*	7	6	0/1
4 Gulbadeen Naib *c 1 b 9*	26	18	3/1
5 Mohammad Nabi *c 4 b 11*	11	14	1
6 Samiullah Shenwari *c 7 b 9*	25	14	3
7 Najibullah Zadran *c 1 b 10*	12	8	1/1
8 Rashid Khan *b 8*	11	7	2
9 Dawlat Zadran *b 8*	0	2	0
10 Hamza Hotak *not out*	3	6	0
11 Shapoor Zadran *b 10*	1	2	0
Lb 1, w 6	7		
6 overs: 64-2 (20 overs)	172		

1/52 2/60 3/105 4/109 5/140 6/156 7/156 8/167 9/169

Hamza Hotak 3–6–25–1; Dawlat Zadran 3–6–46–1; Shapoor Zadran 3–6–28–1; Mohammad Nabi 4–11–35–1; Rashid Khan 4–5–51–0; Samiullah Shenwari 3–5–22–0.

Rabada 4–13–37–2; Abbott 4–12–36–2; Morris 4–15–27–4; Imran Tahir 4–7–24–2; Wiese 4–3–47–0.

Umpires: C. B. Gaffaney and P. R. Reiffel. Third umpire: S. Ravi.
Referee: D. C. Boon.

SRI LANKA v WEST INDIES

At Bangalore, March 20, 2016 (floodlit). West Indies won by seven wickets. Toss: West Indies.

One of Twenty20's delights is its propulsion of players into the limelight, few more so than the 35-year-old West Indian leg-spinner Samuel Badree. His CV included only a dozen first-class games for Trinidad, the last of them in 2009, yet his performance here was a reminder that, in the shortest format, he is a star. In his team's second pool match, a charged-up Badree was positive for West Indies, terminal for Sri Lanka. After Brathwaite won a terrible leg-before decision against Dilshan, Badree took three big wickets, conceded just 12 runs, and forced a run-out with the pressure of his dots: Sri Lanka were 47 for five, but Mathews and Perera rebuilt, and 122 wasn't terrible on a turning pitch on which both sets of spinners combined for an economy-rate of under five. With Gayle trying to shake off a hamstring twinge, Fletcher stepped in to open; unfortunately for Sri Lanka he also stepped up, crashing 22 from his first nine balls. Jeffrey Vandersay, another low-key leggie, tried to emulate Badree: his first two overs went for one run, and his four yielded 11. Siriwardene got rid of Samuels and Ramdin cheaply, and the target widened to 48 from 36 balls. But Fletcher was not to be denied, helping to loot 19 from a Siriwardene over, and finishing with five sixes from 64 balls as West Indies eased to only their second World Twenty20 win over Sri Lanka in seven attempts. "Today showed we aren't a one-man show," said Sammy. "We have 15 potential match-winners." GEOFF LEMON

Man of the Match: A. D. S. Fletcher.

Sri Lanka

		B	4/6
1 †L. D. Chandimal *run out*	16	18	1/1
2 T. M. Dilshan *lbw b 9*	12	10	1/1
3 H. D. R. L. Thirimanne *c 1 b 10*	5	7	1
4 C. K. Kapugedera *st 4 b 10*	6	10	1
5 *A. D. Mathews *c 4 b 7*	20	32	0
6 T. A. M. Siriwardene *c 6 b 10*	0	3	0
7 N. L. T. C. Perera *c 5 b 7*	40	29	5/1
8 K. M. D. N. Kulasekara *b 5*	7	8	0
9 H. M. R. K. B. Herath *run out*	3	3	0
10 J. D. F. Vandersay *not out*	0	1	0
11 P. V. D. Chameera *not out*	0	0	0
Lb 7, w 5, nb 1	13		
6 overs: 41-2 (20 overs)	122-9		

1/20 2/32 3/41 4/47 5/47 6/91 7/116 8/121 9/121

Russell 4–11–34–1; Badree 4–16–12–3; Benn 4–14–13–0; Brathwaite 4–9–36–1; Bravo 4–9–20–2.

West Indies

		B	4/6
1 A. D. S. Fletcher *not out*	84	64	6/5
2 J. Charles *b 10*	10	13	1
3 M. N. Samuels *st 1 b 6*	3	12	0
4 †D. Ramdin *b 6*	5	13	0
5 A. D. Russell *not out*	20	8	3/1
W 5	5		
6 overs: 39-1 (18.2 overs)	127-3		

1/39 2/54 3/72

6 C. H. Gayle, 7 D. J. Bravo, 8 *D. J. G. Sammy, 9 C. R. Brathwaite, 10 S. Badree and 11 S. J. Benn did not bat.

Mathews 1–1–13–0; Herath 4–11–27–0; Kulasekara 2–5–17–0; Vandersay 4–19–11–1; Siriwardene 4–10–33–2; Chameera 3–8–15–0; Perera 0.2–0–11–0.

Umpires: Aleem Dar and J. D. Cloete. Third umpire: S. D. Fry.
Referee: J. J. Crowe.

AFGHANISTAN v ENGLAND

At Delhi, March 23, 2016. England won by 15 runs. Toss: England.

For the second game in succession, England proved that Twenty20 can indeed ebb and flow. This time, they needed a flurry from Ali and Willey to bail them out, after Afghanistan's spinners had them floundering at 85 for seven. And, when Willey helped reduce the Afghans to 13 for three, it was tempting to wonder what all the fuss had been about. Yet England's ineptitude against slow bowling, on a sluggish surface offering less turn than expected, recalled ghosts of collapses past. From 42 for one, they surrendered three wickets in an over from off-spinner Mohammad Nabi – including Morgan, who lost his middle stump first ball offering no stroke, and Root, run out after Stokes did not respond to his call for a quick single. Buttler and Stokes, who failed to read Rashid Khan's googly, went in successive overs to leave England 57 for six in the tenth, and send Afghanistan's vociferous supporters wild. Ali, however, set about saving face. He put on 28 with the circumspect Jordan, then an unbeaten 57 in 33 balls with Willey. But it wasn't until the 19th over, bowled by slow left-armer Hamza Hotak and costing 25, that the mood changed. Chasing 143, Afghanistan lost the dangerous Mohammad Shahzad in the first over, trapped third ball by a Willey inswinger, and never recovered. The noose was tightened mid-innings by Rashid, while Plunkett – who had replaced Reece Topley – rattled through four overs for 12. England's only regret was Shafiqullah Shinwari's unbeaten 35 from No. 9, which deprived their net run-rate of a much-needed boost. LAWRENCE BOOTH

Man of the Match: M. M. Ali.

England

		B	4/6
1 J. J. Roy *b 10*	5	7	1
2 J. M. Vince *c and b 6*	22	18	4
3 J. E. Root *run out*	12	8	1/1
4 *E. J. G. Morgan *b 6*	0	1	0
5 B. A. Stokes *b 5*	7	8	1
6 †J. C. Buttler *c 6 b 7*	6	10	1
7 M. M. Ali *not out*	41	33	4/1
8 C. J. Jordan *c and b 5*	15	18	2
9 D. J. Willey *not out*	20	17	0/2
Lb 6, w 8	14		
6 overs: 42-4 (20 overs)	142-7		

1/16 2/42 3/42 4/42 5/50 6/57 7/85

10 L. E. Plunkett and 11 A. U. Rashid did not bat.

Hamza Hotak 4–10–45–1; Shapoor Zadran 4–8–34–0; Mohammad Nabi 4–13–17–2; Samiullah Shenwari 4–10–23–1; Rashid Khan 4–14–17–2.

Afghanistan

		B	4/6
1 †Mohammad Shahzad *lbw b 9*	4	3	1
2 Noor Ali Zadran *c and b 11*	17	19	0
3 *Asghar Stanikzai *c 3 b 8*	1	4	0
4 Gulbadeen Naib *c 5 b 9*	0	5	0
5 Rashid Khan *c 4 b 7*	15	20	1/1
6 Mohammad Nabi *c 8 b 11*	12	10	0/1
7 Samiullah Shenwari *c 3 b 5*	22	27	1
8 Najibullah Zadran *run out*	14	10	1/1
9 Shafiqullah Shinwari *not out*	35	20	4/2
10 Hamza Hotak *run out*	1	2	0
11 Shapoor Zadran *not out*	0	0	0
Lb 2, w 4	6		
6 overs: 28-3 (20 overs)	127-9		

1/4 2/12 3/13 4/35 5/39 6/64 7/85 8/94 9/108

Willey 4–12–23–2; Jordan 4–12–27–1; Plunkett 4–13–12–0; Ali 2–4–17–1; Rashid 3–9–18–2; Stokes 3–6–28–1.

Umpires: S. Ravi and R. J. Tucker. Third umpire: C. B. Gaffaney.
Referee: D. C. Boon.

SOUTH AFRICA v WEST INDIES

At Nagpur, March 25, 2016 (floodlit). West Indies won by three wickets. Toss: West Indies.

West Indies were cantering to victory at 66 for two from 11 overs, after South Africa's batsmen had failed to adjust from their riotous stay in Mumbai. But, instead of working the ball around on a typically grudging Nagpur surface, West Indies went for broke. Imran Tahir found himself on a hat-trick after Russell slogged to deep midwicket and Sammy was befuddled by his googly. And, when Samuels mistimed a slower ball from Morris to long-on, they were seven down, still needing ten off seven. But Brathwaite finally connected with a leg-side mow, carting the second ball of the last over from Rabada into the crowd at midwicket, and that was effectively that. South Africa had made a grim start: Amla was run out in the first over, du Plessis chipped Russell to mid-off, and Rossouw – in for the injured J-P. Duminy – went second ball to Gayle, bowling only his second over in Twenty20 internationals since December 2012. When de Villiers was bowled by Bravo's crafty slower one, and the left-handed Miller by a superb off-break from Gayle, it was 47 for five. De Kock and Wiese rallied in a stand of 50, and South Africa seemed back in it when Rabada curled a full-length delivery on to Gayle's off stump in the first over of the West Indian reply. Fletcher was run out at the non-striker's end by Rossouw's direct hit from point, but Charles kept his team ahead of the rate. In the end, West Indies were grateful for their batting depth. LAWRENCE BOOTH

Man of the Match: M. N. Samuels.

South Africa

		B	4/6
1 H. M. Amla *run out*	1	1	0
2 †Q. de Kock *b 6*	47	46	3/1
3 *F. du Plessis *c 11 b 6*	9	7	0/1
4 R. R. Rossouw *c 6 b 2*	0	2	0
5 A. B. de Villiers *b 5*	10	12	1
6 D. A. Miller *b 2*	1	4	0
7 D. Wiese *c 7 b 5*	28	26	2
8 C. H. Morris *not out*	16	17	2
9 A. M. Phangiso *run out*	4	5	0
B 4, w 2	6		
6 overers: 39-3 (20 overs)	122-8		

1/1 2/13 3/20 4/46 5/47 6/97 7/112 8/122

10 K. Rabada and 11 Imran Tahir did not bat.

Badree 3–9–22–0; Russell 4–11–28–2; Gayle 3–9–17–2; Brathwaite 2–3–11–0; Benn 4–8–20–0; Bravo 4–12–20–2.

West Indies

		B	4/6
1 J. Charles *c 3 b 7*	32	35	2/1
2 C. H. Gayle *b 10*	4	2	1
3 A. D. S. Fletcher *run out*	11	11	0/1
4 M. N. Samuels *c 5 b 8*	43	44	6
5 D. J. Bravo *c 7 b 9*	8	6	1
6 A. D. Russell *c 6 b 11*	4	8	0
7 *D. J. G. Sammy *b 11*	0	1	0
8 C. R. Brathwaite *not out*	10	10	0/1
9 †D. Ramdin *not out*	1	1	0
Lb 2, w 8	10		
6 overs: 37-2 (19.4 overs)	123-7		

1/5 2/34 3/66 4/87 5/100 6/100 7/113

10 S. Badree and 11 S. J. Benn did not bat.

Rabada 3.4–10–38–1; Morris 4–10–32–1; Imran Tahir 4–12–13–2; Wiese 4–11–19–1; Phangiso 4–11–19–1.

Umpires: I. J. Gould and R. A. Kettleborough. Third umpire: B. N. J. Oxenford.
Referee: B. C. Broad.

ENGLAND v SRI LANKA

At Delhi, March 26, 2016 (floodlit). England won by ten runs. Toss: Sri Lanka.

A claggy night in Delhi was illuminated by a Buttler blitzkrieg and some near-faultless work from England's seamers. Despite a classy rearguard from Mathews, it added up to a place in the semi-finals – a scenario that had seemed improbable halfway through their game against South Africa in Mumbai eight days earlier. Victory here was a reward for a canny innings of two phases: 99 for three in the first 15 overs as the top order, led by Roy, put the collapse against Afghanistan behind them; then 72 from the last five, as Buttler mixed reverse sweeps and ramps with sinewy muscle. As if punch-drunk, Sri Lanka staggered to 15 for four, with Willey again prominent, and Stokes running out Thirimanne, sent back by Mathews. Sri Lanka decided the spinners had to go: as Mathews added 80 in ten overs with Kapugedera, then 42 in 3.4 with Perera, Rashid and Ali disappeared for eight sixes, leaking 63 in four overs between them. Mathews tweaked a hamstring, and Jordan winkled out Perera, but Sri Lanka needed only 22 when Jordan began the 19th over. Amid tension thicker than the Delhi air, Root chose the moment to produce a spirit-soaring catch, diving to his left at mid-off to intercept a drive by Shanaka that would otherwise have reduced the equation to 13 off nine. Jordan then yorked Herath, finishing with a career-best four for 28, and leaving Stokes to defend 15 off the last over. With the hobbling Mathews unwilling to expose Vandersay, he could manage only a pair of twos. The holders were out; England, against the odds, were through. LAWRENCE BOOTH

Man of the Match: J. C. Buttler.

England

		B	4/6
1 J. J. Roy *lbw b 10*	42	39	3/2
2 A. D. Hales *lbw b 9*	0	4	0
3 J. E. Root *c 4 b 10*	25	24	4
4 †J. C. Buttler *not out*	66	37	8/2
5 *E. J. G. Morgan *run out*	22	16	1/1
6 B. A. Stokes *not out*	6	1	0/1
B 1, lb 5, w 3, nb 1	10		
6 overs: 38-1 (20 overs)	171-4		

1/4 2/65 3/88 4/162

7 M. M. Ali, 8 C. J. Jordan, 9 D. J. Willey, 10 L. E. Plunkett and 11 A. U. Rashid did not bat.

Sri Lanka

		B	4/6
1 †L. D. Chandimal *c 4 b 8*	1	3	0
2 T. M. Dilshan *c 2 b 9*	2	2	0
3 T. A. M. Siriwardene *c 5 b 9*	7	7	0/1
4 H. D. R. L. Thirimanne *run out*	3	5	0
5 *A. D. Mathews *not out*	73	54	3/5
6 C. K. Kapugedera *c 6 b 10*	30	27	2/1
7 N. L. T. C. Perera *c 9 b 8*	20	11	1/2
8 M. D. Shanaka *c 3 b 8*	15	9	2/1
9 H. M. R. K. B. Herath *b 8*	1	2	0
10 J. D. F. Vandersay *not out*	0	0	0
Lb 2, w 7	9		
6 overs: 34-4 (20 overs)	161-8		

1/3 2/4 3/15 4/15 5/95 6/137 7/155 8/157

11 P. V. D. Chameera did not bat.

Mathews 4–10–25–0; Herath 4–8–27–1; Vandersay 4–11–26–2; Siriwardene 1–2–9–0; Chameera 4–11–36–0; Perera 2–3–27–0; Shanaka 1–1–15–0.

Willey 4–13–26–2; Jordan 4–11–28–4; Plunkett 4–11–23–1; Stokes 4–12–19–0; Rashid 2–1–31–0; Ali 2–1–32–0.

Umpires: P. R. Reiffel and R. J. Tucker. Third umpire: C. B. Gaffaney.
Referee: J. J. Crowe.

AFGHANISTAN v WEST INDIES

At Nagpur, March 27, 2016 (floodlit). Afghanistan won by six runs. Toss: West Indies. Twenty20 international debut: E. Lewis.

An unforgettable day for Afghan cricket ended with Chris Gayle taking a selfie with the victors and dancing with Mohammad Shahzad. It was Afghanistan's first win over a top-eight nation – and would look even more impressive when West Indies went on to take the tournament. After Afghanistan had been put in, Shahzad briefly looked imperious, skipping down the track to launch Benn for six. But he and his colleagues were hapless against Badree. Only Najibullah Zadran, fusing power and unorthodoxy, inspired confidence. Afghanistan's 123 did not seem enough, but West Indies – already through to the semi-finals – had rested Gayle, and his replacement, the Trinidad left-hander Evin Lewis, made a seven-ball debut duck. In the sixth over, Charles played on to Hamid Hassan; three balls later, Fletcher retired hurt with a pulled hamstring; two after that, Samuels chopped a Rashid Khan googly on to his stumps. Ramdin and Bravo added a cautious 41, and West Indies needed 45 from six overs when Mohammad Nabi trapped Bravo. Tension grew as Hassan was called for bowling a second high full toss (though the batsman, Russell, was left rubbing his backside). Gulbadeen Naib finished off his over, and was then thumped for two sixes by Brathwaite, leaving Nabi to defend ten off the last. Brathwaite swung and missed at the first two balls, and was wonderfully caught by Najibullah in the deep off the third. Afghanistan's celebrations enthused everyone – except perhaps Phil Simmons, West Indies' coach, who was unamused by the willingness of his players to join in. TIM WIGMORE

Man of the Match: Najibullah Zadran.

Christopher Lee, IDI/Getty Images

Selfie-satisfied: Chris Gayle poses with the victorious Afghan team.

Afghanistan

		B	4/6
1 †Mohammad Shahzad *c 11 b 10*	24	22	2/1
2 Usman Ghani *b 10*	4	6	1
3 *Asghar Stanikzai *c 6 b 10*	16	22	0/1
4 Gulbadeen Naib *c 6 b 8*	8	14	0
5 Samiullah Shenwari *c 8 b 11*	1	3	0
6 Najibullah Zadran *not out*	48	40	4/1
7 Mohammad Nabi *c 4 b 7*	9	8	1
8 Shafiqullah Shinwari *c 3 b 7*	4	4	0
9 Rashid Khan *not out*	6	1	0/1
Lb 2, w 1	3		
6 overers: 33-2 (20 overs)	123-7		

1/8 2/33 3/50 4/52 5/56 6/90 7/103

10 Hamza Hotak and 11 Hamid Hassan did not bat.

Russell 4–14–23–2; Badree 4–16–14–3; Brathwaite 2–2–21–0; Benn 4–12–18–1; Bravo 4–9–28–0; Sammy 2–2–17–1.

West Indies

		B	4/6
1 J. Charles *b 11*	22	15	1/2
2 E. Lewis *c 9 b 10*	0	7	0
3 A. D. S. Fletcher *not out*	11	13	2
4 M. N. Samuels *b 9*	5	5	1
5 †D. Ramdin *st 1 b 9*	18	24	0
6 D. J. Bravo *lbw b 7*	28	29	1/1
7 A. D. Russell *run out*	7	9	0
8 *D. J. G. Sammy *c 5 b 4*	6	10	0
9 C. R. Brathwaite *c 6 b 7*	13	8	0/2
10 S. Badree *not out*	2	2	0
Lb 1, w 2, nb 2	5		
6 overs: 34-2 (20 overs)	117-8		

1/17 2/33 3/38 4/79 5/89 6/98 7/107 8/114

11 S. J. Benn did not bat.

Fletcher, when 10, retired hurt at 34-2 and resumed at 114-8.

Hamza Hotak 4–18–9–1; Mohammad Nabi 4–11–26–2; Hamid Hassan 2.4–8–19–1; Rashid Khan 4–7–26–2; Samiullah Shenwari 4–9–22–0; Gulbadeen Naib 1.2–4–14–1.

Umpires: Aleem Dar and B. N. J. Oxenford. Third umpire: R. A. Kettleborough.
Referee: B. C. Broad.

SOUTH AFRICA v SRI LANKA

At Delhi, March 28, 2016 (floodlit). South Africa won by eight wickets. Toss: South Africa.

South Africa coped better with the prospect of a dead game, though not before Steyn had taken another pummelling. Chandimal flicked him for four, hooked a six, then bashed him back over his head. But, with Sri Lanka 45 without loss in the fifth over, Phangiso hit the stumps twice in two balls. They remained in the game at 75 for two in the tenth, but the run-out of Siriwardene was the first of eight wickets to tumble for 45 in ten overs, as the leg-breaks and googlies of Imran Tahir and the nibbly seam of Behardien disrupted any fluency; and, following his hamstring injury against England, this time there was no Angelo Mathews to engineer a recovery. De Kock was soon run out, but tension faded as Amla and du Plessis put on an easy 60. Du Plessis, South Africa's captain, was given out leg-before by umpire Ravi after inside-edging an attempted ramp – and was later fined half his match fee for making clear his displeasure – but at least that gave the local de Villiers fanatics a glimpse of their hero. He wowed them with a flat six over midwicket, though Amla did most of the damage. When de Villiers lashed the final full toss between the stands and into the Delhi night, it was less a triumphant finale than an act of frustration with another poor South African tournament – and a symbol of how far Sri Lanka had fallen in the two years since becoming champions. GEOFF LEMON

Man of the Match: A. M. Phangiso.

Sri Lanka

		B	4/6
1 *†L. D. Chandimal *b 8*	21	20	2/1
2 T. M. Dilshan *lbw b 5*	36	40	4/1
3 H. D. R. L. Thirimanne *b 8*	0	1	0
4 T. A. M. Siriwardene *run out*	15	10	2
5 D. S. N. F. G. Jayasuriya *c 3 b 5*	1	3	0
6 C. K. Kapugedera *b 11*	4	7	0
7 N. L. T. C. Perera *c 5 b 10*	8	7	1
8 M. D. Shanaka *not out*	20	18	1/1
9 H. M. R. K. B. Herath *c 2 b 9*	2	5	0
10 J. D. F. Vandersay *b 9*	3	7	0
11 R. A. S. Lakmal *run out*	0	1	0
B 4, lb 2, w 2, nb 2	10		
6 overs: 47-2 (19.3 overs)	120		

1/45 2/45 3/75 4/78 5/85 6/85 7/96 8/109 9/120

Steyn 4–12–33–1; Abbott 3.3–10–14–2; Phangiso 4–12–26–2; Imran Tahir 4–12–18–1; Wiese 1–1–8–0; Behardien 3–8–15–2.

South Africa

		B	4/6
1 H. M. Amla *not out*	56	52	5/1
2 †Q. de Kock *run out*	9	6	2
3 *F. du Plessis *lbw b 11*	31	36	3
4 A. B. de Villiers *not out*	20	12	0/2
Lb 2, w 4	6		
6 overs: 34-1 (17.4 overs)	122-2		

1/15 2/75

5 F. Behardien, 6 D. A. Miller, 7 D. Wiese, 8 A. M. Phangiso, 9 K. J. Abbott, 10 D. W. Steyn and 11 Imran Tahir did not bat.

Jayasuriya 1–3–9–0; Lakmal 3.4–9–28–1; Herath 4–10–21–0; Vandersay 4–9–25–0; Shanaka 2–4–17–0; Perera 2–3–15–0; Siriwardene 1–1–5–0.

Umpires: S. Ravi and R. J. Tucker. Third umpire: P. R. Reiffel.
Referee: J. J. Crowe.

GROUP TWO

INDIA v NEW ZEALAND

At Nagpur, March 15, 2016 (floodlit). New Zealand won by 47 runs. Toss: New Zealand.

New Zealand stunned a sell-out crowd in Nagpur, which – having hosted some distinctly subdued first-round matches – was transformed for the opening game of the Super Tens. To general disbelief, India were humbled by spin: Santner, Sodhi and Nathan McCullum claimed nine for 44 in 11 overs, spectacularly vindicating New Zealand's decision to omit their usual new-ball pair of Trent Boult and Tim Southee. Emotions ran high before the start as the big screen played a tribute to Martin Crowe, who had died 12 days earlier. Guptill – one of his protégés – thundered the first ball, from Ashwin, for a straight six. But he fell lbw trying to sweep the second and, though Munro reverse-swept his second delivery for six more, New Zealand stuttered badly. That Anderson, normally a brazen hitter, took 42 balls over his 34 betrayed their struggles on a slow pitch offering significant turn, and it took a resourceful cameo from Ronchi to lift them to 126. But India were in for a shock. McCullum trapped Dhawan in the opening over, before Santner – who finished with four for 11, the best Twenty20 figures by a New Zealand spinner – removed Sharma and Raina in his first to make it 12 for three. Yuvraj Singh provided a return catch for McCullum, and then came the decisive blow as Kohli edged a sharp leg-break from Sodhi. That was 39 for five, which soon became 43 for seven, leaving Dhoni with far too much to do. India, who had never lost more than five wickets to spin in a Twenty20 innings, soon succumbed to their fifth defeat out of five by New Zealand in the format. Tim Wigmore

Man of the Match: M. J. Santner.

New Zealand

		B	4/6
1 M. J. Guptill *lbw b 9*	6	2	0/1
2 *K. S. Williamson *st 6 b 4*	8	16	1
3 C. Munro *c 7 b 10*	7	6	0/1
4 C. J. Anderson *b 11*	34	42	3
5 L. R. P. L. Taylor *run out*	10	14	1
6 M. J. Santner *c 6 b 8*	18	17	2
7 G. D. Elliott *run out*	9	12	0
8 †L. Ronchi *not out*	21	11	2/1
9 N. L. McCullum *not out*	0	0	0
B 4, lb 3, w 6	13		
6 overs: 33-2 (20 overs)	126-7		

1/6 2/13 3/35 4/61 5/89 6/98 7/114

10 A. F. Milne and 11 I. S. Sodhi did not bat.

Ashwin 4–11–32–1; Nehra 3–10–20–1; Bumrah 4–13–15–1; Raina 4–10–16–1; Jadeja 4–11–26–1; Pandya 1–1–10–0.

India

		B	4/6
1 R. G. Sharma *st 8 b 6*	5	7	0
2 S. Dhawan *lbw b 9*	1	3	0
3 V. Kohli *c 8 b 11*	23	27	2
4 S. K. Raina *c 1 b 6*	1	2	0
5 Yuvraj Singh *c and b 9*	4	5	1
6 *†M. S. Dhoni *c 9 b 6*	30	30	1/1
7 H. H. Pandya *lbw b 6*	1	7	0
8 R. A. Jadeja *c and b 11*	0	3	0
9 R. Ashwin *st 8 b 11*	10	20	0
10 A. Nehra *b 10*	0	4	0
11 J. J. Bumrah *not out*	0	2	0
W 3, nb 1	4		
6 overs: 29-4 (18.1 overs)	79		

1/5 2/10 3/12 4/26 5/39 6/42 7/43 8/73 9/79

McCullum 3–8–15–2; Anderson 3–7–18–0; Santner 4–16–11–4; Elliott 2–5–9–0; Milne 2.1–6–8–1; Sodhi 4–14–18–3.

Umpires: H. D. P. K. Dharmasena and R. K. Illingworth. Third umpire: M. Erasmus.
Referee: R. S. Madugalle.

BANGLADESH v PAKISTAN

At Kolkata, March 16, 2016. Pakistan won by 55 runs. Toss: Pakistan.

The stars aligned for Pakistan, whose batting came together seamlessly and emphatically. Ahmed Shehzad led the way, providing impetus with his customary boundaries through cover, midwicket and square leg, while Mohammad Hafeez – with whom he added 95 for the second wicket – ventured even bigger blows in a rapid 64. It was Shahid Afridi, though, who played the most devastating hand, pushing himself up to No. 4 and swinging from the start. Bangladesh eased him in with some hittable leg-side deliveries, but soon Afridi was clattering even the good ones over the ropes. In a 19-ball stay, he struck four fours and four sixes – the most memorable on bended knee over long-on, off Shakib Al Hasan. He was eventually out for 49 in the final over, having turned Pakistan's total from competitive to commanding: only once before, against the same opposition in Karachi in 2007-08, had they made more in a Twenty20 innings. Bangladesh's pursuit of 202 was limp. Soumya Sarkar was out in the first over, and charges from Tamim Iqbal and Sabbir Rahman were shut down by Afridi. Shakib hit an unbeaten 50 but, with team-mates faltering, he couldn't mount a meaningful challenge. FIDEL FERNANDO

Man of the Match: Shahid Afridi.

Pakistan

		B	4/6
1 Sharjeel Khan *b 9*	18	10	1/2
2 Ahmed Shehzad *c 5 b 3*	52	39	8
3 Mohammad Hafeez *c 2 b 9*	64	42	7/2
4 *Shahid Afridi *c 5 b 11*	49	19	4/4
5 Umar Akmal *c 4 b 11*	0	2	0
6 Shoaib Malik *not out*	15	9	2
7 Imad Wasim *not out*	0	0	0
Lb 1, w 1, nb 1	3		
6 overs: 55-1 (20 overs)	201-5		

1/26 2/121 3/163 4/175 5/198

8 †Sarfraz Ahmed, 9 Wahab Riaz, 10 Mohammad Amir and 11 Mohammad Irfan did not bat.

Bangladesh

		B	4/6
1 Tamim Iqbal *c 7 b 4*	24	20	0/2
2 Soumya Sarkar *b 10*	0	2	0
3 Sabbir Rahman *b 4*	25	19	5
4 Shakib Al Hasan *not out*	50	40	5/1
5 Mahmudullah *c 1 b 7*	4	5	0
6 †Mushfiqur Rahim *c 8 b 10*	18	21	3
7 Mithun Ali *c 10 b 11*	2	4	0
8 *Mashrafe bin Mortaza *not out*	15	9	2/1
Lb 4, w 4	8		
6 overs: 45-2 (20 overs)	146-6		

1/1 2/44 3/58 4/71 5/110 6/117

9 Arafat Sunny, 10 Al-Amin Hossain and 11 Taskin Ahmed did not bat.

Taskin Ahmed 4–10–32–2; Al-Amin Hossain 3–3–43–0; Arafat Sunny 4–9–34–2; Shakib Al Hasan 4–5–39–0; Mashrafe bin Mortaza 3–2–41–0; Sabbir Rahman 2–6–11–1.

Mohammad Amir 4–12–27–2; Mohammad Irfan 4–10–30–1; Wahab Riaz 4–12–31–0; Shahid Afridi 4–12–27–2; Shoaib Malik 2–4–14–0; Imad Wasim 2–4–13–1.

Umpires: I. J. Gould and R. A. Kettleborough. Third umpire: J. S. Wilson. Referee: B. C. Broad.

AUSTRALIA v NEW ZEALAND

At Dharamsala, March 18, 2016. New Zealand won by eight runs. Toss: New Zealand.

New Zealand ended a difficult 12 months against Australia with minor payback, replicating their win against India by defending a low total on a slow pitch. Khawaja aside, Australia blundered in pursuit of 143. From 44 without loss, they slipped to 66 for four, before Maxwell and Marsh helped reduce the requirement to 27 off three overs. But Sodhi completed a miserly spell of leg-spin, and McClenaghan undid Marsh and Agar with slower balls. Australia needed 19 off the last, bowled by Anderson, who immediately delivered the critical blow by removing Faulkner. They should have fared better after watching New Zealand's similarly death-or-glory approach yield equally middling results. There were exceptions: Guptill struck Agar – asked to bowl his left-arm spin in the third over, despite a lack of experience in the powerplay – for three sixes, and Munro's switch-hit late cut stood out for chutzpah. Zampa's sole over of leg-spin cost only three, exposing Smith's conservative reliance on the seamers. But, overall, Australia's efforts in the field were adequate: Watson and Faulkner bowled especially tightly, and two run-outs in the last over set the right tone for the break. The batting, though, could not maintain it. GEOFF LEMON

Man of the Match: M. J. McClenaghan.

New Zealand

		B	4/6
1 M. J. Guptill *c 5 b 8*	39	27	2/4
2 *K. S. Williamson *c 7 b 5*	24	20	4
3 C. Munro *c 8 b 6*	23	26	2
4 C. J. Anderson *c 7 b 5*	3	6	0
5 L. R. P. L. Taylor *c 6 b 2*	11	11	0/1
6 G. D. Elliott *run out*	27	20	3
7 †L. Ronchi *c 5 b 8*	6	7	0
8 M. J. Santner *run out*	1	1	0
9 A. F. Milne *not out*	2	2	0
B 4, w 2	6		
6 overs: 58-0 (20 overs)	142-8		

1/61 2/66 3/76 4/97 5/117 6/133 7/140 8/142

10 M. J. McClenaghan and 11 I. S. Sodhi did not bat.

Coulter-Nile 4–8–33–0; Watson 4–12–22–1; Agar 1–3–18–0; Faulkner 3–7–18–2; Zampa 1–3–3–0; Maxwell 3–7–18–2; Marsh 4–9–26–1.

Australia

		B	4/6
1 U. T. Khawaja *run out*	38	27	6
2 S. R. Watson *c 2 b 10*	13	12	1
3 *S. P. D. Smith *st 7 b 8*	6	7	1
4 D. A. Warner *c 1 b 8*	6	11	0
5 G. J. Maxwell *c 2 b 11*	22	23	2
6 M. R. Marsh *c 9 b 10*	24	23	0/2
7 A. C. Agar *c 5 b 10*	9	8	0/1
8 J. P. Faulkner *c 1 b 4*	2	4	0
9 N. M. Coulter-Nile *b 4*	1	2	0
10 †P. M. Nevill *not out*	7	2	0/1
11 A. Zampa *not out*	2	1	0
Lb 2, w 2	4		
6 overs: 50-1 (20 overs)	134-9		

1/44 2/51 3/62 4/66 5/100 6/121 7/123 8/124 9/132

Anderson 4–7–29–2; Milne 2–4–22–0; Elliott 2–3–17–0; McClenaghan 3–9–17–3; Santner 4–10–30–2; Williamson 1–3–3–0; Sodhi 4–11–14–1.

Umpires: M. Erasmus and N. J. Llong. Third umpire: R. K. Illingworth. Referee: R. S. Madugalle.

INDIA v PAKISTAN

At Kolkata, March 19, 2016 (floodlit). India won by six wickets. Toss: India.

India beat Pakistan for the 11th time in 11 World Cup matches – in both one-day and Twenty20 cricket – thanks to the classy calm of Kohli. But Pakistan were left to regret a tentative performance with the bat, after Ashwin tied their openers in knots, getting the new ball to jump and turn on a

Vivek Prakash, IDI/Getty Images

Six-shooters: Eden Gardens is in seventh heaven as India close in on victory over Pakistan.

damp surface in a game reduced to 18 overs a side by rain. Ahmed Shehzad and Sharjeel Khan battled through, but their stand of 38 consumed 46 deliveries, prompting Shahid Afridi to move himself up the order again. He struggled too, and only a partnership of 41 in four overs between Umar Akmal and Shoaib Malik lifted Pakistan towards a modest 118. India, in search of a fillip after defeat by New Zealand, began poorly: Mohammad Amir accounted for Rohit Sharma, and the 35-year-old Mohammad Sami cleaned up Dhawan and Raina with successive balls to make it 23 for three. Then came another run-chase masterclass from Kohli. He found admirable support from Yuvraj Singh during a fourth-wicket stand of 61 that first settled nerves, then decisively tilted the scales in India's favour. Dhoni helped do the rest, leaving Kohli – apparently playing on a different surface from everyone else – unbeaten with 55 from 37 balls. India's semi-final quest was back on track. R. Kaushik

Man of the Match: V. Kohli.

Pakistan

		B	*4/6*
1 Sharjeel Khan *c 7 b 4*	17	24	2
2 Ahmed Shehzad *c 8 b 11*	25	28	3
3 *Shahid Afridi *c 3 b 7*	8	14	1
4 Umar Akmal *c 6 b 8*	22	16	1/1
5 Shoaib Malik *c 9 b 10*	26	16	3/1
6 †Sarfraz Ahmed *not out*	8	6	1
7 Mohammad Hafeez *not out*	5	5	0
B 2, lb 3, w 1, nb 1	7		
5 overs: 24-0 (18 overs)	118-5		

1/38 2/46 3/60 4/101 5/105

8 Wahab Riaz, 9 Mohammad Sami, 10 Mohammad Amir and 11 Mohammad Irfan did not bat.

Nehra 4–11–20–1; Ashwin 3–9–12–0; Bumrah 4–10–32–1; Jadeja 4–12–20–1; Raina 1–3–4–1; Pandya 2–4–25–1.

India

		B	*4/6*
1 R. G. Sharma *c 5 b 10*	10	11	2
2 S. Dhawan *b 9*	6	15	1
3 V. Kohli *not out*	55	37	7/1
4 S. K. Raina *b 9*	0	1	0
5 Yuvraj Singh *c 9 b 8*	24	23	1/1
6 *†M. S. Dhoni *not out*	13	9	0/1
Lb 3, w 7, nb 1	11		
5 overs: 23-3 (15.5 overs)	119-4		

1/14 2/23 3/23 4/84

7 H. H. Pandya, 8 R. A. Jadeja, 9 R. Ashwin, 10 A. Nehra and 11 J. J. Bumrah did not bat.

Mohammad Amir 3–11–11–1; Mohammad Irfan 2.5–7–25–0; Mohammad Sami 2–6–17–2; Shahid Afridi 4–7–25–0; Shoaib Malik 2–3–22–0; Wahab Riaz 2–4–16–1.

Umpires: I. J. Gould and R. A. Kettleborough. Third umpire: B. N. J. Oxenford.
Referee: B. C. Broad.

AUSTRALIA v BANGLADESH

At Bangalore, March 21, 2016 (floodlit). Australia won by three wickets. Toss: Australia. Twenty20 international debut: Saqlain Sajib.

This was an opportunity missed for Bangladesh. Watson removed Soumya Sarkar in the second over, before returning in the sixth to account for Sabbir Rahman; he had two for two, and Bangladesh were pottering along at less than a run a ball. Mithun Ali and Shakib Al Hasan accelerated to add 37 but, as so often in this tournament, leg-spin provided the brake. The inexperienced Zampa bowled his full spell from the tenth over, dismissing Mithun in his first, Shuvagata Hom in his second, conceding only five singles in his third, and getting Shakib in his fourth. It added up to three for 23 and the match award. Mahmudullah ducked, weaved and chose his moments to pull and cut, finishing with an outstanding unbeaten 49 from 29 balls, to give Bangladesh what seemed a competitive total. Khawaja thought otherwise. He made a 45-ball 58, including three fours in a row off Shakib, with an elegance belying the format. Khawaja reduced the ask to 42 at six an over, though late wickets fell after he was bowled behind his legs. Maxwell's 26 from 15 kept the target easily in hand, and the result was not as close as the scoreline suggested. GEOFF LEMON

Man of the Match: A. Zampa.

Bangladesh

		B	*4/6*
1 Mithun Ali *c 2 b 11*	23	22	1/1
2 Soumya Sarkar *c 5 b 2*	1	6	0
3 Sabbir Rahman *c 7 b 2*	12	17	2
4 Shakib Al Hasan *c 10 b 11*	33	25	3/1
5 Shuvagata Hom *lbw b 11*	13	10	1/1
6 Mahmudullah *not out*	49	29	7/1
7 †Mushfiqur Rahim *not out*	15	11	2
Lb 7, w 3	10		
6 overs: 33-2 (20 overs)	156-5		

1/2 2/25 3/62 4/78 5/105

8 Saqlain Sajib, 9 *Mashrafe bin Mortaza, 10 Mustafizur Rahman and 11 Al-Amin Hossain did not bat.

Coulter-Nile 4–11–21–0; Watson 4–9–31–2; Hastings 3–9–24–0; Marsh 1–2–12–0; Maxwell 1–2–12–0; Zampa 4–9–23–3; Faulkner 3–4–26–0.

Australia

		B	*4/6*
1 U. T. Khawaja *b 11*	58	45	7/1
2 S. R. Watson *run out*	21	15	2/1
3 *S. P. D. Smith *b 10*	14	13	0/1
4 D. A. Warner *c and b 4*	17	9	1/1
5 G. J. Maxwell *st 7 b 4*	26	15	2/2
6 M. R. Marsh *c 4 b 10*	6	6	1
7 J. P. Faulkner *not out*	5	3	1
8 J. W. Hastings *c 2 b 4*	3	4	0
9 †P. M. Nevill *not out*	1	1	0
Lb 2, w 4	6		
6 overs: 51-0 (18.3 overs)	157-7		

1/62 2/95 3/115 4/119 5/135 6/148 7/152

10 N. M. Coulter-Nile and 11 A. Zampa did not bat.

Mashrafe bin Mortaza 1–3–9–0; Mahmudullah 2–1–22–0; Al-Amin Hossain 2–5–14–1; Mustafizur Rahman 4–12–30–2; Shakib Al Hasan 4–10–27–3; Saqlain Sajib 3.3–5–40–0; Shuvagata Hom 2–2–13–0.

Umpires: I. J. Gould and R. A. Kettleborough. Third umpire: Aleem Dar.
Referee: B. C. Broad.

NEW ZEALAND v PAKISTAN

At Mohali, March 22, 2016 (floodlit). New Zealand won by 22 runs. Toss: New Zealand.

New Zealand became the first to reach the semi-finals, after Pakistan failed to build on an electric start to their chase from Sharjeel Khan. He took three fours off Santner in the first over, two off Milne in the third, then three more, plus a six, off McClenaghan. It was breathtaking stuff: after four overs Sharjeel had 42 to Ahmed Shehzad's six, and Pakistan – needing 181 – had passed 50. But the momentum departed with Sharjeel: Shehzad and Umar Akmal, who had been vocal about his desire to move up the order, batted too slowly, and Shahid Afridi too briefly. After an opening stand worth

65 in 5.3 overs, only 93 came from the remaining 14.3, with no boundaries at all in the final five. "People will have to take a hard look at themselves," said their visibly agitated coach, Waqar Younis. On a bouncy track that brought welcome relief from the tournament's mainly sluggish surfaces, New Zealand had reached 60 in seven overs, as Guptill and Williamson recorded their eighth opening stand of 50-plus in their last ten Twenty20 international innings. Afridi briefly imposed himself on the contest by catching Williamson and dismissing Munro (he later snared Anderson to move to 39 wickets in World Twenty20s, beating Lasith Malinga's record). But Guptill took him for 27 runs from 14 balls faced and, by the time he was bowled in the 15th over for 80 of New Zealand's 127, he had allowed his team-mates to slog with abandon. Taylor obliged with a rapid unbeaten 36. Pakistan were reliant on results elsewhere for a place in the last four. GEOFF LEMON

Man of the Match: M. J. Guptill.

New Zealand

		B	4/6
1 M. J. Guptill *b 9*	80	48	10/3
2 *K. S. Williamson *c 5 b 11*	17	21	1
3 C. Munro *c 3 b 5*	7	6	1
4 C. J. Anderson *c 6 b 5*	21	14	3
5 L. R. P. L. Taylor *not out*	36	23	2/1
6 †L. Ronchi *c 6 b 9*	11	7	0/1
7 G. D. Elliott *not out*	1	1	0
Lb 4, w 3	7		
6 overs: 55-0 (20 overs)	180-5		

1/62 2/75 3/127 4/132 5/164

8 M. J. Santner, 9 A. F. Milne, 10 M. J. McClenaghan and 11 I. S. Sodhi did not bat.

Mohammad Amir 4–8–41–0; Mohammad Irfan 4–5–46–1; Mohammad Sami 4–14–23–2; Imad Wasim 4–6–26–0; Shahid Afridi 4–7–40–2.

Pakistan

		B	4/6
1 Sharjeel Khan *c 1 b 9*	47	25	9/1
2 Ahmed Shehzad *c 1 b 8*	30	32	3
3 Khalid Latif *c 7 b 8*	3	7	0
4 Umar Akmal *c 1 b 9*	24	26	0
5 *Shahid Afridi *c 4 b 11*	19	9	2/1
6 Shoaib Malik *not out*	15	13	0
7 †Sarfraz Ahmed *not out*	11	8	0
Lb 5, w 4	9		
6 overs: 66-1 (20 overs)	158-5		

1/65 2/79 3/96 4/123 5/140

8 Imad Wasim, 9 Mohammad Sami, 10 Mohammad Amir and 11 Mohammad Irfan did not bat.

Santner 4–12–29–2; Anderson 2–6–14–0; Milne 4–10–26–2; McClenaghan 4–5–43–0; Elliott 2–1–16–0; Sodhi 4–6–25–1.

Umpires: R. K. Illingworth and N. J. Llong. Third umpire: H. D. P. K. Dharmasena. Referee: R. S. Madugalle.

INDIA v BANGLADESH

At Bangalore, March 23, 2016 (floodlit). India won by one run. Toss: Bangladesh.

Years from now, Bangladesh will wonder how they allowed this match to get away. After restricting India's strong batting line-up to 146, they came within two runs of victory, only to lose wickets off the last three deliveries of the match, and fuel India's semi-final hopes. In a scrappy, error-prone encounter on a surface that changed considerably as the game progressed, the Bangladeshis had looked in control almost throughout. However, in Pandya's last over – which began with 11 needed – Mushfiqur Rahim and Mahmudullah, both vastly experienced, holed out in the deep when the requirement had come down to two from three balls. Then Dhoni completed a remarkable victory by sprinting up from behind the stumps to run out Mustafizur Rahman, trying to pinch a bye. India's total on a drying track was built around small contributions down the order, but there was no late flourish. Tamim Iqbal, dropped twice and the beneficiary of many a misfield, pepped up the chase with four fours in one Bumrah over. Bangladesh batted with intent to keep the target well in sight, and boundaries by Mushfiqur off the second and third balls of the last over seemed to have sealed the deal – but his clenched-fist celebrations came too soon, preceding a brain freeze which allowed India to escape to victory. R. KAUSHIK

Man of the Match: R. Ashwin.

India

		B	4/6
1 R. G. Sharma *c 3 b 10*	18	16	1/1
2 S. Dhawan *lbw b 4*	23	22	2/1
3 V. Kohli *b 9*	24	24	0/1
4 S. K. Raina *c 3 b 11*	30	23	1/2
5 H. H. Pandya *c 7 b 11*	15	7	2/1
6 *†M. S. Dhoni *not out*	13	12	1
7 Yuvraj Singh *c 11 b 6*	3	6	0
8 R. A. Jadeja *b 10*	12	8	2
9 R. Ashwin *not out*	5	2	1
Lb 2, w 1	3		

6 overs: 42-1 (20 overs) 146-7

1/42 2/45 3/95 4/112 5/112 6/117 7/137

10 A. Nehra and 11 J. J. Bumrah did not bat.

Mashrafe bin Mortaza 4–6–22–0; Shuvagata Hom 3–11–24–1; Al-Amin Hossain 4–10–37–2; Mustafizur Rahman 4–9–34–2; Shakib Al Hasan 4–7–23–1; Mahmudullah 1–2–4–1.

Bangladesh

		B	4/6
1 Tamim Iqbal *st 6 b 8*	35	32	5
2 Mithun Ali *c 5 b 9*	1	3	0
3 Sabbir Rahman *st 6 b 4*	26	15	3/1
4 Shakib Al Hasan *c 4 b 9*	22	15	0/2
5 *Mashrafe bin Mortaza *b 8*	6	5	0/1
6 Mahmudullah *c 8 b 5*	18	22	1
7 Soumya Sarkar *c 3 b 10*	21	21	1/1
8 †Mushfiqur Rahim *c 2 b 5*	11	6	2
9 Shuvagata Hom *not out*	0	1	0
10 Mustafizur Rahman *run out*	0	0	0
Lb 4, w 1	5		

6 overs: 45-1 (20 overs) 145-9

1/11 2/55 3/69 4/87 5/95 6/126 7/145 8/145 9/145

11 Al-Amin Hossain did not bat.

Nehra 4–8–29–1; Bumrah 4–6–32–0; Ashwin 4–12–20–2; Jadeja 4–13–22–2; Pandya 3–8–29–2; Raina 1–3–9–1.

Umpires: Aleem Dar and B. N. J. Oxenford. Third umpire: I. J. Gould.
Referee: B. C. Broad.

AUSTRALIA v PAKISTAN

At Mohali, March 25, 2016. Australia won by 21 runs. Toss: Australia.

Australia's batting finally clicked – and Pakistan's was found wanting once again. The result left the Australians facing a virtual quarter-final against India two days later at the same venue, and knocked the Pakistanis out. For coach Waqar Younis and captain Shahid Afridi, it was a subdued end to their tenures. A chaotic first six overs had yielded 52 for two: Mohammad Amir again began beautifully, Mohammad Sami was pummelled, and Wahab Riaz ripped through Khawaja and Warner. Smith, whose five previous Twenty20 innings against Pakistan had totalled just 28, did as he liked thereafter: running fours, pin-balling around the crease, changing the line to his liking. At his most outrageous, he took guard two feet outside off stump, watched Wahab follow him, then stepped further across to flick a four through square leg. Maxwell crashed a few, then came one last international display of Watson's best with the bat. He nailed three sixes from the fast bowlers – over long-on, extra cover and midwicket – to finish with an unbeaten 44 from 21 deliveries. Sami eventually leaked 53, second among Pakistan bowlers to his own 54, also against Australia, at the 2010 tournament in the West Indies. Chasing 194, Pakistan had only one feasible approach, but Hazlewood's three-over opening burst of one for 15 derailed them. Sharjeel Khan belted 30 but was out too soon, then Zampa slowed down Umar Akmal and Afridi, before picking up both. Shoaib Malik's lively 40 was redundant, while Faulkner helped himself to Australia's first Twenty20 five-for. Geoff Lemon

Man of the Match: J. P. Faulkner.

Australia

		B	4/6
1 U. T. Khawaja *b 9*	21	16	3/1
2 A. J. Finch *b 7*	15	16	1
3 D. A. Warner *b 9*	9	6	2
4 *S. P. D. Smith *not out*	61	43	7
5 G. J. Maxwell *c 2 b 7*	30	18	3/1
6 S. R. Watson *not out*	44	21	4/3
Lb 8, w 5	13		
6 overs: 52-2 (20 overs)	193-4		

1/28 2/42 3/57 4/119

7 J. P. Faulkner, 8 †P. M. Nevill, 9 N. M. Coulter-Nile, 10 A. Zampa and 11 J. R. Hazlewood did not bat.

Mohammad Amir 4–11–39–0; Mohammad Sami 4–6–53–0; Wahab Riaz 4–10–35–2; Shahid Afridi 4–5–27–0; Imad Wasim 4–5–31–2.

Pakistan

		B	4/6
1 Sharjeel Khan *b 7*	30	19	6
2 Ahmed Shehzad *c 9 b 11*	1	6	0
3 Khalid Latif *b 7*	46	41	4/1
4 Umar Akmal *b 10*	32	20	3/1
5 *Shahid Afridi *st 8 b 10*	14	7	0/2
6 Shoaib Malik *not out*	40	20	2/2
7 Imad Wasim *c 9 b 7*	0	1	0
8 †Sarfraz Ahmed *c 1 b 7*	2	3	0
9 Wahab Riaz *c 11 b 7*	0	1	0
10 Mohammad Sami *not out*	4	2	1
B 1, lb 1, w 1	3		
6 overs: 41-2 (20 overs)	172-8		

1/20 2/40 3/85 4/110 5/147 6/147 7/164 8/164

11 Mohammad Amir did not bat.

Hazlewood 4–11–26–1; Coulter-Nile 4–7–45–0; Faulkner 4–11–27–5; Watson 2–1–27–0; Zampa 4–6–32–2; Maxwell 2–4–13–0.

Umpires: H. D. P. K. Dharmasena and M. Erasmus. Third umpire: R. K. Illingworth. Referee: R. S. Madugalle.

BANGLADESH v NEW ZEALAND

At Kolkata, March 26, 2016. New Zealand won by 75 runs. Toss: New Zealand. Twenty20 international debut: H. M. Nicholls.

On a typical Eden Gardens turner New Zealand completed their fourth win out of four, condemning Bangladesh to their lowest Twenty20 total. Set 146 for a victory that might have provided a little consolation following their traumatic meltdown against India three days earlier, Bangladesh slipped from 29 for one to 70 all out, undercutting the 78 they made against the New Zealanders at Hamilton in February 2010. Shuvagata Hom alone spared them an even more embarrassing total, as Sodhi and Elliott shared the last six wickets; the only respite came when the floodlights stopped working for 11 minutes. New Zealand's own innings had been a typically pragmatic effort: at one stage, they managed just one boundary in 49 balls. But, despite a late flurry of wickets, a total of 145 for eight proved more than ample. The result – New Zealand's sixth successive win in the format, a national record – was hard luck on Bangladesh's nippy, whippy left-armer Mustafizur Rahman. His figures of five for 22, which remained the tournament's best, included four players bowled. In all, ten batsmen suffered that fate, by two the most in any Twenty20 international. LAWRENCE BOOTH

Man of the Match: K. S. Williamson.

New Zealand

		B	4/6
1 H. M. Nicholls *b 10*	7	11	1
2 *K. S. Williamson *b 10*	42	32	5/1
3 C. Munro *b 11*	35	33	1/2
4 L. R. P. L. Taylor *c 2 b 11*	28	24	2/1
5 C. J. Anderson *b 9*	0	3	0
6 G. D. Elliott *c 8 b 10*	9	7	1
7 †L. Ronchi *not out*	9	5	1
8 M. J. Santner *b 10*	3	3	0
9 N. L. McCullum *b 10*	0	1	0
10 M. J. McClenaghan *not out*	6	1	0/1
B 4, lb 1, w 1	6		
6 overs: 39-1 (20 overs)	145-8		

1/25 2/57 3/99 4/100 5/122 6/127 7/139 8/139

11 I. S. Sodhi did not bat.

Bangladesh

		B	4/6
1 Tamim Iqbal *run out*	3	8	0
2 Mithun Ali *b 10*	11	17	1
3 Sabbir Rahman *c 8 b 9*	12	18	1
4 Shakib Al Hasan *c 9 b 8*	2	6	0
5 Soumya Sarkar *st 7 b 11*	6	8	0
6 Mahmudullah *b 11*	5	8	0
7 †Mushfiqur Rahim *b 6*	0	2	0
8 Shuvagata Hom *not out*	16	17	2
9 *Mashrafe bin Mortaza *lbw b 6*	3	5	0
10 Mustafizur Rahman *c 7 b 6*	6	3	0/1
11 Al-Amin Hossain *b 11*	0	2	0
Lb 5, w 1	6		
6 overs: 30-2 (15.4 overs)	70		

1/4 2/29 3/31 4/38 5/43 6/44 7/48 8/59 9/65

Mashrafe bin Mortaza 3–6–21–1; Shuvagata Hom 3–5–16–0; Shakib Al Hasan 4–12–33–0; Mustafizur Rahman 4–11–22–5; Al-Amin Hossain 4–12–27–2; Mahmudullah 2–1–21–0.

McCullum 2–8–6–1; Anderson 2–6–7–0; Santner 3–9–16–1; McClenaghan 1–3–3–1; Elliott 4–17–12–3; Sodhi 3.4–7–21–3.

Umpires: J. D. Cloete and M. A. Gough. Third umpire: R. S. A. Palliyaguruge. Referee: A. J. Pycroft.

INDIA v AUSTRALIA

At Mohali, March 27, 2016. India won by six wickets. Toss: Australia.

Virat Kohli produced one champagne moment after another to send a packed crowd into raptures, and India into a semi-final against West Indies. His extraordinary unbeaten 82, off just 51 balls, sealed India's sixth successive Twenty20 win over Australia, who were consigned to an early flight home. And yet, despite failing to build on a frenetic start that yielded 53 in four overs, the Australians had set about defending their eventual 160 with disciplined bowling and outstanding fielding. Even with Kohli still there, India needed a gargantuan effort after they lost a hobbling Yuvraj Singh at the end of the 14th over: when Dhoni strode out, they still required 67, the track had become sluggish, and the soft ball hard to time. No one told Kohli. Batting as if on a shirtfront against schoolkids, he nipped, tucked and drove Australia into submission, and ran them ragged. When the equation boiled down to 39 off 18 deliveries, he went into fifth gear, pulling and square-driving Faulkner for four, then launching him over long-off for six. In the 19th over, Kohli eased Coulter-Nile for four fours, three of them through or over the covers. Largely a silent spectator until now, Dhoni slammed the winning boundary with five balls to spare, and Kohli slumped to his knees, physically and emotionally spent. Earlier, India's bowlers had dragged Australia's innings back, though Smith was unfortunate to be given out caught behind as he tried to cut Yuvraj. But they managed only 51 runs between the fifth over and the 14th. In his last international, Watson then helped reduce India to 49 for three, only for Kohli to play the innings of the tournament. R. KAUSHIK

Man of the Match: V. Kohli.

Australia

		B	4/6
1 U. T. Khawaja *c 6 b 10*	26	16	6
2 A. J. Finch *c 2 b 7*	43	34	3/2
3 D. A. Warner *st 6 b 9*	6	9	0
4 *S. P. D. Smith *c 6 b 5*	2	6	0
5 G. J. Maxwell *b 11*	31	28	1/1
6 S. R. Watson *not out*	18	16	2
7 J. P. Faulkner *c 3 b 7*	10	10	1
8 †P. M. Nevill *not out*	10	2	1/1
Lb 2, w 11, nb 1	14		
6 overs: 59-1 (20 overs)	160-6		

1/54 2/72 3/74 4/100 5/130 6/145

9 N. M. Coulter-Nile, 10 A. Zampa and 11 J. R. Hazlewood did not bat.

Nehra 4–13–20–1; Bumrah 4–7–32–1; Ashwin 2–2–31–1; Jadeja 3–8–20–0; Yuvraj Singh 3–6–19–1; Pandya 4–8–36–2.

India

		B	4/6
1 R. G. Sharma *b 6*	12	17	1
2 S. Dhawan *c 1 b 9*	13	12	1/1
3 V. Kohli *not out*	82	51	9/2
4 S. K. Raina *c 8 b 6*	10	7	1
5 Yuvraj Singh *c 6 b 7*	21	18	1/1
6 *†M. S. Dhoni *not out*	18	10	3
Lb 3, w 2	5		
6 overs: 37-2 (19.1 overs)	161-4		

1/23 2/37 3/49 4/94

7 H. H. Pandya, 8 R. A. Jadeja, 9 R. Ashwin, 10 A. Nehra and 11 J. J. Bumrah did not bat.

Hazlewood 4–8–38–0; Coulter-Nile 4–10–33–1; Watson 4–8–23–2; Faulkner 3.1–4–35–1; Maxwell 2–1–18–0; Zampa 2–6–11–0.

Umpires: H. D. P. K. Dharmasena and M. Erasmus. Third umpire: R. K. Illingworth. Referee: R. S. Madugalle.

SUPER TEN GROUP TABLES

Group One	*P*	*W*	*L*	*Pts*	*NRR*
WEST INDIES....	4	3	1	6	0.35
ENGLAND	4	3	1	6	0.14
South Africa......	4	2	2	4	0.65
Sri Lanka	4	1	3	2	−0.46
Afghanistan	4	1	3	2	−0.71

Group Two	*P*	*W*	*L*	*Pts*	*NRR*
NEW ZEALAND .	4	4	0	8	1.90
INDIA	4	3	1	6	−0.30
Australia.........	4	2	2	4	0.23
Pakistan	4	1	3	2	−0.09
Bangladesh.......	4	0	4	0	−1.80

SEMI-FINALS

ENGLAND v NEW ZEALAND

At Delhi, March 30, 2016 (floodlit). England won by seven wickets. Toss: England.

England's unexpectedly enjoyable tryst with Delhi continued with a ruthless win, earning a trip to Eden Gardens. If the headlines went to Roy, whose 44-ball 78 turned the chase into a stroll, then victory was set up by the seamers, who had limited New Zealand to 20 runs for the loss of five wickets in their last four overs. It was death bowling by asphyxiation. The New Zealanders had barely caught their breath when – with England chasing a modest 154 – Roy flashed and carved a quartet of fours in the first over, bowled by Anderson. McClenaghan's first over went for 13, as did Milne's second; after 4.2, England had 50, and Roy's maiden half-century at this level needed only 26 deliveries. By the time Hales lifted Santner to long-on in the ninth over, the score was 82, and the game all but over. Sodhi briefly threatened to reprise the tactic that had served New Zealand so well during their group games, when the spinners strangled opposition middle orders. He bowled Roy, advancing at – and playing round – a leg-break, then trapped Morgan first ball. But the Feroz Shah Kotla was the least spin-friendly of the five surfaces the New Zealanders had encountered, and England batted deep. Root and Buttler took 22 off Sodhi's final over to level the scores, before Buttler pulled Santner for the winning six with 17 balls to spare. Only when Munro was slashing and reverse-swatting his way to 46 had New Zealand looked in the game. But a promising ten-over total of 89 for one gave way to anticlimax. Williamson ballooned a return catch to Ali, who then held on at third man as Munro chased a wide one from Plunkett. And, from 133 for three after 16 overs, Jordan and Stokes – who found himself on a hat-trick after removing Ronchi and Anderson with low full tosses – took over. England, a figure of white-ball fun at the 50-over World Cup a year earlier, were laughing all the way to Kolkata. LAWRENCE BOOTH

Man of the Match: J. J. Roy.

New Zealand

		B	*4/6*
1 M. J. Guptill *c 5 b 9*	15	12	3
2 *K. S. Williamson *c and b 7*	32	28	3/1
3 C. Munro *c 7 b 10*	46	32	7/1
4 C. J. Anderson *c 8 b 6*	28	23	2/1
5 L. R. P. L. Taylor *c 4 b 8*	6	8	0
6 †L. Ronchi *c 9 b 6*	3	3	0
7 G. D. Elliott *not out*	4	6	0
8 M. J. Santner *c 8 b 6*	7	6	1
9 M. J. McClenaghan *run out*	1	2	0
B 1, lb 4, w 6	11		
6 overs: 51-1 (20 overs)	153-8		

1/17 2/91 3/107 4/134 5/139 6/139 7/150 8/153

10 A. F. Milne and 11 I. S. Sodhi did not bat.

England

		B	*4/6*
1 J. J. Roy *b 11*	78	44	11/2
2 A. D. Hales *c 3 b 8*	20	19	1/1
3 J. E. Root *not out*	27	22	3
4 *E. J. G. Morgan *lbw b 11*	0	1	0
5 †J. C. Buttler *not out*	32	17	2/3
Lb 1, w 1	2		
6 overs: 67-0 (17.1 overs)	159-3		

1/82 2/110 3/110

6 B. A. Stokes, 7 M. M. Ali, 8 C. J. Jordan, 9 D. J. Willey, 10 L. E. Plunkett and 11 A. U. Rashid did not bat.

Willey 2–4–17–1; Jordan 4–12–24–1; Plunkett 4–9–38–1; Rashid 4–8–33–0; Stokes 4–11–26–3; Ali 2–5–10–1.

Anderson 1–2–16–0; Milne 3–6–27–0; McClenaghan 3–5–24–0; Santner 3.1–8–28–1; Sodhi 4–5–42–2; Elliott 3–5–21–0.

Umpires: H. D. P. K. Dharmasena and R. J. Tucker. Third umpire: B. N. J. Oxenford.
Referee: D. C. Boon.

INDIA v WEST INDIES

At Mumbai (Wankhede), March 31, 2016 (floodlit). West Indies won by seven wickets. Toss: West Indies.

Sometimes a classic performance can be better remembered in a losing cause. Sometimes the finest margins decide contests. Both proved the case here, as Kohli played the perfect Twenty20 innings, then watched in disbelief as slivers of Indian boots helped West Indies chase their target. Simmons was twice reprieved by no-balls – by Ashwin, on 18, and Pandya, on 50 – and again, on 68, when Jadeja brushed the midwicket boundary rope, turning a catch into a six. Dew would hamper the side bowling second, but Kohli's second-innings average of 91 must also have helped persuade Sammy to ask India to bat. Kohli responded with 89 not out from 47 balls, despite hitting only one six and less than half his total in fours. His running was as exquisite as his strokeplay, creating scores where there should have been none. Including those he ran on behalf of Rahane – whose 35-ball 40 on a plum pitch felt unnecessarily cautious – and Dhoni, he interspersed orthodox pulls and drives with 15 twos and 36 singles; his 16th fifty in Twenty20 internationals moved him one clear at the top of the list, above Gayle and Brendon McCullum. West Indies were less beautiful but more brutal. At 19 for two after three overs, with Gayle bowled by a low full toss from Bumrah, it should have been settled. But Simmons, who had arrived in Mumbai only two days earlier after being recalled because Andre Fletcher had injured his hamstring against Afghanistan, shrugged off every near miss to keep swinging all the way to a career-best 82 not out. Charles bludgeoned 52 before falling to Kohli, then Russell launched four sixes, the destinations of which included the stadium's third tier and the press-box window. As he and Simmons, a Mumbai Indians regular in the IPL, added 80 in 6.3 overs, the Wankhede fell silent. West Indies were in the final. GEOFF LEMON

Man of the Match: L. M. P. Simmons.

India

		B	4/6
1 R. G. Sharma *lbw b 10*	43	31	3/3
2 A. M. Rahane *c 7 b 5*	40	35	2
3 V. Kohli *not out*	89	47	11/1
4 *†M. S. Dhoni *not out*	15	9	1
Lb 1, w 2, nb 2	5		
6 overs: 55-0 (20 overs)	192-2		

1/62 2/128

5 S. K. Raina, 6 M. K. Pandey, 7 H. H. Pandya, 8 R. A. Jadeja, 9 R. Ashwin, 10 A. Nehra and 11 J. J. Bumrah did not bat.

Russell 4–7–47–1; Badree 4–8–26–1; Brathwaite 4–5–38–0; Benn 4–3–36–0; Bravo 4–3–44–0.

West Indies

		B	4/6
1 J. Charles *c 1 b 3*	52	36	7/2
2 C. H. Gayle *b 11*	5	6	1
3 M. N. Samuels *c 2 b 10*	8	7	2
4 L. M. P. Simmons *not out*	82	51	7/5
5 A. D. Russell *not out*	43	20	3/4
Lb 4, nb 2	6		
6 overs: 44-2 (19.4 overs)	196-3		

1/6 2/19 3/116

6 †D. Ramdin, 7 D. J. Bravo, 8 *D. J. G. Sammy, 9 C. R. Brathwaite, 10 S. Badree and 11 S. J. Benn did not bat.

Nehra 4–14–24–1; Bumrah 4–11–42–1; Jadeja 4–5–48–0; Ashwin 2–5–20–0; Pandya 4–9–43–0; Kohli 1.4–4–15–1.

Umpires: I. J. Gould and R. A. Kettleborough. Third umpire: M. Erasmus.
Referee: B. C. Broad.

FINAL

ENGLAND v WEST INDIES

JONATHAN LIEW

At Kolkata, April 3, 2016 (floodlit). West Indies won by four wickets. Toss: West Indies.

On a sweltering evening at Eden Gardens, West Indies became the first team to win the World Twenty20 twice. But their victory felt unique for another reason: as far as anybody could remember, nobody had ever won a game, let alone a global final, quite like this. With six balls remaining, they required 19. But the night smelled faintly of possibility. Now, four consecutive sixes from Brathwaite off Stokes capsized a match that had seemed England's for the taking. By the time his third six levelled the scores, the West Indian players were embracing in the dugout. Stokes, whose death bowling had been so effective throughout England's journey to the final, was a broken man. The fourth six felt sadistically emphatic – like shooting a corpse between the eyeballs.

It was tempting to attribute this remarkable reversal to some unquantifiable outpouring of belief: the surging pride of the islands, the underdog spirit of a group of players chided and derided in equal measure. Yet it was simpler than that. To borrow the modern coach's parlance, West Indies simply executed their skills better when it mattered. This applied not merely to the final over, but to their all-round performance. Brathwaite's innings supplemented his three wickets with the ball, but it was not deemed enough to win the match award. For the second time in three finals, that honour went to Samuels, for his unbeaten 85, the highest score in a World T20 final, beating his own 78 in 2012.

Badree also had a claim. Striking with the second ball, as Roy stayed fatally back, and bowling his entire spell from the start, he wreathed the England top order in a pythonine grip, from which they were only partially able to escape. From 23 for three, Root and Buttler, who hit Benn for three sixes in five balls, jabbed the innings into life with a stand of 61. But three wickets in four deliveries – Root the last of them, caught at short fine leg attempting a scoop – left England 111 for seven, with nearly six overs remaining. Willey helped keep them in the game, though, and no team had overhauled more than their 155 for nine to win a World T20 final.

Ryan Pierse, Getty Images

Ryan Pierse, Getty Images

Cause and effect: Carlos Brathwaite launches another six to wrench the game West Indies' way; Ben Stokes is consoled by England coach Trevor Bayliss.

West Indies were more comfortable batting second, and had been grateful for Sammy's tenth successful call in a row at the toss, but any notions of complacency were soon banished. Root was handed the ball in the second over, a tactic designed to tempt Gayle. He went beyond the call of duty: Charles launched Root's first delivery high to long-on, and Gayle his third to long-off – both securely held by Stokes (the four openers in this game thus totalled six runs, a record low for any Twenty20 international). Samuels was given out on 27, caught behind off Plunkett, only for replays to show Buttler had taken it on the bounce. That allowed Samuels and Bravo to rebuild, but West Indies were falling dramatically behind the asking-rate: with six overs left, they required 70.

Tempers frayed. When they batted, England had been unimpressed by the West Indians' habit of performing Bravo's trademark "Champion" dance after every wicket, and by the send-off given to Root. Now Samuels and Stokes – a pair with a salty history – clashed again, a fracas that extended into a gloating post-match press conference, when Samuels mocked: "He doesn't learn." Samuels was fined 30% of his match fee.

Still, after Willey picked up two wickets in the 16th over – greeting the demise of Sammy with a Champion dance of his own – to make it 107 for six, and Jordan delivered a sumptuous set of yorkers to concede only eight runs in the 19th, England looked safe.

But Stokes's first ball was leg-sidish, and Brathwaite's well-timed hew cleared fine leg. The second was full on leg stump, a couple of inches from the blockhole, but those inches were sufficient for Brathwaite to get under the ball and muscle it high over long-on. The third was full and straight. Such was the adrenaline coursing through Brathwaite's biceps that, even though the ball did not remotely find the middle of his bat, it soared over long-off. And, before the fourth six had sailed into the crowd over midwicket, maroon shirts were flooding the field. Stokes slumped to his haunches. But, for West Indies, whose women's team had triumphed earlier in the day, the night smelled of victory.

Man of the Match: M. N. Samuels. *Man of the Tournament:* V. Kohli.

England

		B	4/6
1 J. J. Roy *b 10*	0	2	0
2 A. D. Hales *c 10 b 6*	1	3	0
3 J. E. Root *c 11 b 8*	54	36	7
4 *E. J. G. Morgan *c 2 b 10*	5	12	1
5 †J. C. Buttler *c 5 b 8*	36	22	1/3
6 B. A. Stokes *c 4 b 5*	13	8	1
7 M. M. Ali *c 9 b 5*	0	2	0
8 C. J. Jordan *not out*	12	13	1
9 D. J. Willey *c 1 b 8*	21	14	1/2
10 L. E. Plunkett *c 10 b 5*	4	4	0
11 A. U. Rashid *not out*	4	4	0
Lb 4, w 1	5		
6 overs: 33-3 (20 overs)	155-9		

1/0 2/8 3/23 4/84 5/110 6/110 7/111 8/136 9/142

Badree 4–14–16–2; Russell 4–12–21–1; Benn 3–3–40–0; Bravo 4–8–37–3; Brathwaite 4–8–23–3; Sammy 1–0–14–0.

West Indies

		B	4/6
1 J. Charles *c 6 b 3*	1	7	0
2 C. H. Gayle *c 6 b 3*	4	2	1
3 M. N. Samuels *not out*	85	66	9/2
4 L. M. P. Simmons *lbw b 9*	0	1	0
5 D. J. Bravo *c 3 b 11*	25	27	1/1
6 A. D. Russell *c 6 b 9*	1	3	0
7 *D. J. G. Sammy *c 2 b 9*	2	2	0
8 C. R. Brathwaite *not out*	34	10	1/4
Lb 3, w 6	9		
6 overs: 37-3 (19.4 overs)	161-6		

1/1 2/5 3/11 4/86 5/104 6/107

9 †D. Ramdin, 10 S. Badree and 11 S. J. Benn did not bat.

Willey 4–13–20–3; Root 1–3–9–2; Jordan 4–5–36–0; Plunkett 4–12–29–0; Rashid 4–6–23–1; Stokes 2.4–3–41–0.

Umpires: H. D. P. K. Dharmasena and R. J. Tucker. Third umpire: M. Erasmus.
Referee: R. S. Madugalle.

ICC WORLD TWENTY20 FINALS

		Man of the Match
2007-08	INDIA beat Pakistan by five runs at Johannesburg.	I. K. Pathan
2009	PAKISTAN beat Sri Lanka by eight wickets at Lord's.	Shahid Afridi
2010	ENGLAND beat Australia by seven wickets at Bridgetown.	C. Kieswetter
2012-13	WEST INDIES beat Sri Lanka by 36 runs at Colombo.	M. N. Samuels
2013-14	SRI LANKA beat India by six wickets at Mirpur.	K. C. Sangakkara
2015-16	WEST INDIES beat England by four wickets at Kolkata.	M. N. Samuels

ICC UNDER-19 WORLD CUP IN 2015-16

SIDHANTA PATNAIK

1 West Indies 2 India 3 Bangladesh

When the West Indies squad departed for the Under-19 World Cup in Bangladesh, the long-limbed Barbadian Chemar Holder was left at home. But, after Obed McCoy split the webbing in his left hand, Holder was summoned for the quarter-final, having impressed the selectors with a five-wicket haul for Combined Campuses and Colleges. And the new-ball partnership he formed with Alzarri Joseph – the tournament's fastest bowler, clocking 91mph – was crucial in the victories over Pakistan, Bangladesh and, in the final, India, as West Indies lifted their maiden title.

But there was more to their cricket than the pace duo's bounce, swing and accuracy. Skipper Shimron Hetmyer hit fifties in the quarter- and semi-finals, showcasing maturity and skill, particularly against spin. Left-handed opener Gidron Pope was compared to Chris Gayle, while seam-bowling all-rounders Shamar Springer and Keemo Paul added character, typified by Springer's chest-roll dance celebration, and shrewdness. Hetmyer's order when clutching the trophy at the presentation ceremony – "Everybody hold it!" – reflected the collective effort of a talented group.

There was controversy, too: Paul earned West Indies a place in the knockouts by Mankading Zimbabwe's No. 11 Richard Ngarava in the final over of their qualifying game, with three runs needed for victory. Harsh criticism flowed: on Twitter, England captain Eoin Morgan described their behaviour as "disgraceful", while his team-mate Jos Buttler, who had been Mankaded by Sri Lanka in 2014, called it "embarrassing". But the West Indian management insulated the teenagers from the bile, and they became a hit with the neutrals.

Australia were absent because of security concerns, and replaced by Ireland, runners-up in the qualifying tournament in Kuala Lumpur in October 2015. Throughout this absorbing competition, Associate nations usurped more established teams. Namibia beat South Africa, champions in 2014, to reach the quarter-finals, while Nepal joined them in the knockouts by defeating New Zealand. Afghanistan also shone, winning the plate competition ahead of Zimbabwe, South Africa and New Zealand. And the tournament's leading wicket-takers were all from the lesser nations: left-arm seamer Fritz Coetzee of Namibia, Nepalese leg-spinner Sandeep Lamichhane – who took a hat-trick against Ireland – and headband-wearing swing bowler Rory Anders (Ireland) led the way. It gave another nudge to the ICC: with a little encouragement, the line between bigger and smaller teams could be blurred.

Among the traditional powers, India remained undefeated until the final. Opening bowler Avesh Khan produced regular blocks of dots, and wicket-keeper Rishabh Panth hit the fastest youth one-day international fifty, off 18 balls, against Nepal. Their star, though, was Sarfaraz Khan, whose gutsy middle-order batting fetched him five fifties, and made him the tournament's second-highest run-scorer, behind England's Jack Burnham, who hit 420 at an average of 84, including a record three centuries. Sarfaraz's temperament, in his second World Cup, stood out: four of his five fifties were made with India in trouble at bowler-friendly Mirpur, including the final.

Bangladesh fought hard to finish third, and their success kept the atmosphere buzzing – a marked improvement on the previous competition, in the United Arab Emirates in 2014. The sound of 15,000 cheering Bangladesh in their first global semi-final was remarkable. Their captain, Mehedi Hasan, was Man of the Tournament for making four fifties – including two in the knockout games – and taking 12 wickets with wily off-breaks. His eloquence in front of the camera made him Bangladesh's poster boy.

Not everything was perfect. Inconsistent umpiring angered many sides, and a quarrel about the age of Raju Rijal, the Nepal captain, left a sour taste. "Medical experts tell you there is very little we can do to test the age of someone in a reliable fashion," said Dave Richardson, the ICC's chief executive. "To that extent, we have to rely quite heavily on documentation that is available, and the honesty and integrity of the participating players."

For the tournament's stars, the path to the top will be hard: from the 2014 edition, only South Africa's Kagiso Rabada made the transition to full international cricket. Rahul Dravid, the India coach, summed up the challenge: "In their long journeys as cricketers, they are going to face a lot of ups and downs. If we can learn some lessons from this, and if they can go on to become better cricketers and better people, that's really the purpose of the tournament."

For Kamindu Mendis, Sri Lanka's ambidextrous spinner, the lesson was the need to sustain mystery. Sarfaraz learned the importance of converting starts. Paul came to understand the value of phlegm under fire. Many grasped how to tackle spin, and many more discovered the pressure of a televised game. And, for Bangladesh, it was simply how thrilling things can be on home turf, with a fervent crowd blowing wind into your sails.

Group A

At Chittagong (ZAC), January 27, 2016. **Bangladesh won by 43 runs.** ‡**Bangladesh 240-7** (50 overs) (Nazmul Hossain 73; P. W. A. Mulder 3-42); **South Africa 197** (48.4 overs) (L. Smith 100; Mehedi Hasan 3-37, Mohammad Saifuddin 3-30). *MoM:* Nazmul Hossain. *Opener Liam Smith's round 100 proved a lone hand for the reigning champions, as no other South African passed 22. Bangladesh's bowlers – Mohammad Saifuddin arrowed in yorkers, while the spinners were parsimonious – built on the steady work of their batsmen, with Nazmul Hossain's 82-ball 73 the highlight. Bangladesh off-spinner Sanjit Saha was later reported for an illegal action, and subsequently banned from bowling in international cricket.*

At Cox's Bazar, January 29, 2016. **Namibia won by nine wickets.** ‡**Scotland 159** (36.3 overs) (M. van Lingen 3-19); **Namibia 162-1** (26 overs) (S. J. Loftie-Eaton 67*, N. Davin 52). *MoM:* S. J. Loftie-Eaton. *Jack Waller fell leg-before to Fritz Coetzee's first legal delivery of the game, and Scotland never properly recovered. They did reach 59-2, but six wickets fell for 38 – three to seamer Michael van Lingen – before the ninth and tenth scrambled 62. It was nothing like enough: S. J. Loftie-Eaton and Niko Davin put on 95, before captain Zane Green (39* off 42) completed the job with 24 overs to spare.*

At Cox's Bazar, January 31, 2016. **Bangladesh won by 114 runs. Bangladesh 256-6** (50 overs) (Nazmul Hossain 113*, Mehedi Hasan 51; M. A. Ghaffar 4-60); ‡**Scotland 142** (47.2 overs) (M. Azeem Dar 50; Mohammad Saifuddin 3-17, Saleh Ahmed 3-27). *MoM:* Nazmul Hossain. *From*

172, Bangladesh asserted themselves: Nazmul added 101 for the third wicket with Saif Hassan (49 from 108 balls) and 100 for the fourth with Mehedi Hasan. Scotland's openers put on 48, only for all ten to tumble for 94; Azeem Dar was last out for 50.

At Cox's Bazar (No. 2), January 31, 2016. **Namibia won by two wickets. ‡South Africa 136-9** (50 overs) (F. Coetzee 3-16, M. van Lingen 4-24); **Namibia 137-8** (39.4 overs) (L. Louwrens 58*). *MoM:* M. van Lingen. *Namibia stunned South Africa to earn a place in the last eight at the expense of the champions. "We have never had a side qualify for the quarter-finals, on any world stage, in any sport," said Andre Schmidlin, their manager. Lohan Louwrens supervised a tense chase, during which van Lingen walked for a catch behind after being given not out by umpire Enamul Haque. A sixth-wicket stand of 54 between Louwrens and Charl Brits eased Namibian nerves, though three late wickets threatened a twist. Earlier, South Africa collapsed to 60-8 against Coetzee (10–4–16–3) and van Lingen, before the last two wickets more than doubled the score. Namibia stumbled to 29-3, but Louwrens remained resolute.*

At Cox's Bazar, February 2, 2016. **Bangladesh won by eight wickets. Namibia 65** (32.5 overs); **‡Bangladesh 66-2** (16 overs). *MoM:* Saleh Ahmed. *Bangladesh topped the group with a crushing win inside 49 overs. Two days after their shock win over South Africa, only two Namibians reached double figures.*

At Cox's Bazar (No. 2), February 2, 2016. **South Africa won by ten wickets. Scotland 127** (45.4 overs); **‡South Africa 129-0** (29 overs) (L. Smith 64*, K. Verreynne 64*). *MoM:* K. Verreynne. *South Africa avoided a hat-trick of embarrassing defeats by making light work of Scotland. Set a feeble 128, they cantered home, with both Smith and wicketkeeper Kyle Verreynne making 64* from 87 balls.*

BANGLADESH 6pts, NAMIBIA 4pts, South Africa 2pts, Scotland 0pts.

Group B

At Sylhet, January 28, 2016. **Pakistan won by six wickets. Afghanistan 126** (41.2 overs) (Tariq Stanikzai 53; Hasan Mohsin 3-24, Shadab Khan 4-9); **‡Pakistan 129-4** (31.3 overs). *MoM:* Hasan Mohsin. *Hasan Mohsin, who had switched from leg-breaks to pace only six months earlier, grabbed three wickets to leave Afghanistan 29-3. A stand of 69 between Ikram Faizi (19) and Tariq Stanikzai restored some order, but Shadab Khan, the seventh Pakistan bowler (and still a leg-spinner), ran amok, claiming four victims in five overs. Mohsin then hit 28* to guide Pakistan home.*

At Sylhet (DS), January 28, 2016. **Sri Lanka won by 196 runs. ‡Sri Lanka 315-6** (50 overs) (W. M. K. Bandara 61, K. I. C. Asalanka 76, S. Ashan 74*, P. V. R. de Silva 51); **Canada 119** (39.2 overs). *MoM:* K. I. C. Asalanka. *Sri Lanka raced past 300 thanks to four half-centuries and a 13-ball 28 from Wanindu Hasaranga de Silva. In reply, seven Canadian batsman fell in single figures, with Arslan Khan (42*) alone passing 22. Four Sri Lankans claimed two wickets each.*

At Sylhet, January 30, 2016. **Sri Lanka won by 33 runs. ‡Sri Lanka 184** (48.1 overs) (K. I. C. Asalanka 71; Shamsurhman Karokhil 3-19); **Afghanistan 151** (44.5 overs) (P. H. K. D. Mendis 3-36). *MoM:* K. I. C. Asalanka. *The captain, Charith Asalanka, glued the Sri Lankan innings together in the face of some spirited Afghan bowling, especially from off-spinner Shamsurhman Karokhil. Asalanka, another off-spinner, then claimed 2-18 from his six overs, while Kamindu Mendis – who bowls finger-spin with either hand, according to need – took three. Karim Janat and Waheedullah Shafaq made forties, but victory for Sri Lanka took them into the quarters.*

At Sylhet (DS), January 30, 2016. **Pakistan won by seven wickets. ‡Canada 178** (48.3 overs) (B. S. Adhihetty 51; Hasan Khan 3-36); **Pakistan 180-3** (40.5 overs) (Zeeshan Malik 89*). *MoM:* Zeeshan Malik. *Pakistan also reached the quarter-finals with a comfortable win. Canada's 15-year-old opener Bhavindu Adhihetty ensured it was not a walkover, though Zeeshan Malik decided the contest for the favourites.*

At Sylhet, February 1, 2016. **Afghanistan won by four wickets. ‡Canada 147** (50 overs) (Muslim Musa 3-31, Shamsurhman Karokhil 3-21); **Afghanistan 149-6** (24.1 overs) (Tariq Stanikzai 56; M. R. Patel 3-17). *MoM:* Tariq Stanikzai. *Three of Canada's top four made ducks to leave them 31-4. They rebuilt slowly, and had reached 93-4 when leg-spinner Rashid Khan (10–1–20–2) broke through. Afghanistan sped towards a target of 148 and, at 89-2 in the 14th, seemed home and dry.*

Miraj Patel grabbed three wickets with his off-breaks – including Tariq Stanikzai, who made the game's only half-century – but could not alter the outcome.

At Mirpur, February 3, 2016. **Pakistan won by 23 runs. Pakistan 212** (48.4 overs) (Hasan Mohsin 86); ‡**Sri Lanka 189** (46.4 overs) (P. H. K. D. Mendis 68; Shadab Khan 3-31). *MoM:* Hasan Mohsin. *Needing another 66 at barely four an over – and with six wickets left – Sri Lanka were in the box seat. But they lost Kamindu Mendis for a steady 68, ending a fifth-wicket stand of 84 with Vishad Randika de Silva, who quickly followed for 46. No one else stayed long, and Pakistan topped the group. Earlier, they had relied on a run-a-ball 86 from Hasan Mohsin, whose medium-pace then accounted for the Sri Lankan openers.*

PAKISTAN 6pts, SRI LANKA 4pts, Afghanistan 2pts, Canada 0pts.

Group C

At Chittagong (MAA), January 27, 2016. **England won by 299 runs.** ‡**England 371-3** (50 overs) (D. W. Lawrence 174, J. T. A. Burnham 148); **Fiji 72** (27.3 overs) (S. Mahmood 3-2, S. M. Curran 3-22). *MoM:* D. W. Lawrence. *England ran riot against Fiji, who were making their debut at this level. Dan Lawrence and Jack Burnham piled on 303 for the second wicket – the first triple-century partnership in any Under-19 one-day international. Lawrence's 174 in 150 balls was England's highest innings (and only five short of the world Under-19 record), Burnham's 148 their third-highest, and their biggest total led to their biggest victory. Saqib Mahmood (5–4–2–3) and Sam Curran reduced Fiji to 17-6 in the ninth over, and only Peni Vuniwaga (36) got past ten.*

At Chittagong (ZAC), January 29, 2016. **England won by 61 runs.** ‡**England 282-7** (50 overs) (D. W. Lawrence 55, C. J. Taylor 59); **West Indies 221** (43.4 overs) (G. D. Pope 60, K. M. A. Paul 65; S. Mahmood 4-42). *MoM:* D. W. Lawrence. *West Indies provided England with stiffer opposition, but could not prevent them completing another straightforward win against the eventual champions. Most of England's top six contributed, with Curran scoring 39 in 36 balls before striking twice in his first over. Thanks to Gidron Pope and Keemo Paul, West Indies fought to 193-5, but lost their last five in four overs, Mahmood taking four in 11 deliveries.*

At Chittagong (MAA), January 29, 2016. **Zimbabwe won by seven wickets.** ‡**Fiji 81** (27.4 overs) (W. Madhevere 5-24, B. A. Mavuta 3-13); **Zimbabwe 84-3** (18.5 overs). *MoM:* W. Madhevere. *Fiji's novices made a better start in their second game – openers Jordan Dunham and Tadulala Veitacini reached 32 in eight overs – but ultimately survived only one more ball than against England, scoring nine more runs. The off-breaks of 15-year-old Wesley Madhevere and the leg-spin of his captain, Brandon Mavuta, ensured a simple target, which Zimbabwe knocked off with 31 overs to spare.*

At Chittagong (ZAC), January 31, 2016. **England won by 129 runs.** ‡**England 288-4** (50 overs) (D. W. Lawrence 59, M. D. E. Holden 51, J. T. A. Burnham 106*); **Zimbabwe 159** (43.4 overs) (J. Ives 91; S. Mahmood 4-39, C. J. Taylor 3-14). *MoM:* J. T. A. Burnham. *England completed their group games with a perfect record after another century from Burnham, who hit six sixes, while Curran smashed five fours in one over from pace bowler William Mashinge on his way to 32* in 16 balls. He and Mahmood removed Zimbabwe's top three for eight runs, before Jeremy Ives stopped the rot, last out for 91 to Mahmood, who took his tournament record to 11 wickets at 7.54.*

At Chittagong (MAA), January 31, 2016. **West Indies won by 262 runs. West Indies 340-7** (50 overs) (G. D. Pope 76, S. K. Springer 106, J. Goolie 66; C. T. Cokovaki 6-59); ‡**Fiji 78** (27.3 overs) (A. S. Joseph 3-15, G. D. Pope 4-24). *MoM:* G. D. Pope. *For the third time, Fiji failed to reach either three figures or the 29th over. Cakacaka Tikoisuva Cokovaki had claimed six of West Indies' seven wickets, but could not stop them sailing past 300; Shamar Springer struck 106 from 78 balls and added 157 with Jyd Goolie. Alzarri Joseph reduced Fiji to 13-4, and then Pope, who had put on 120 with fellow opener Tevin Imlach, collected 4-24 with his off-spin.*

At Chittagong (ZAC), February 2, 2016. **West Indies won by two runs. West Indies 226-9** (50 overs) (S. K. Springer 61; R. Magarira 3-28); ‡**Zimbabwe 224** (49 overs) (S. Snyder 52; A. S. Joseph 4-30). *MoM:* A. S. Joseph. *West Indies won the battle to reach the quarter-finals – but the Zimbabweans were in tears after a controversial finish. Their last pair needed three when non-striker Richard Ngarava was Mankaded by Paul, who ended the game with six balls unbowled. The* *third umpire confirmed the dismissal: Ngarava's bat was just on the crease. Zimbabwe had confined West Indies to 226 (left-arm wrist-spinner Rugare Magarira returned figures of 10–1–28–3) and Adam Keefe and Madhevere added 62 to take them to 209-6, with a real chance of qualifying. Springer dismissed both to set up the dramatic conclusion.*

ENGLAND 6pts, WEST INDIES 4pts, Zimbabwe 2pts, Fiji 0pts.

Group D

At Mirpur, January 28, 2016. **India won by 79 runs. India 268-9** (50 overs) (S. N. Khan 74, M. S. Washington Sundar 62; J. Little 3-52, R. J. Anders 3-35); **‡Ireland 189** (49.1 overs) (L. J. Tucker 57, W. T. McClintock 58; R. R. Batham 3-15). *MoM:* S. N. Khan. *India began sluggishly, losing Ishan Kishan without scoring and sliding to 55-4, before Sarfaraz Khan and Washington Sundar shouldered responsibility with a 110-run partnership. Ireland's chase was starved by the seamers – Aavesh Khan and Rahul Batham shared figures of 5-39 and they dribbled to 189 all out.*

At Fatullah, January 28, 2016. **Nepal won by 32 runs. Nepal 238-7** (50 overs) (N. G. Smith 3-58); **‡New Zealand 206** (47.1 overs) (G. D. Phillips 52; D. S. Airee 3-24). *MoM:* R. Rijal. *Nepal had history on their side: the only time they had played New Zealand, in the 2006 World Cup, they beat a team containing Martin Guptill and Tim Southee. Here they did it again. No Nepalese batsmen made 50, but they still managed a national-record 238, given late-order momentum by Khushal Bhurtel's 23-ball 35. New Zealand looked well set at 103-2 but, after opener Glenn Philips departed, they lost wickets regularly. Dipendra Airee extinguished the chase with three of them and a run-out, to spark jubilant celebrations.*

At Mirpur, January 30, 2016. **India won by 120 runs. India 258-8** (50 overs) (R. R. Panth 57, S. N. Khan 74; Z. N. Gibson 3-50); **‡New Zealand 138** (31.3 overs) (Aavesh Khan 4-32, M. K. Lomror 5-47). *MoM:* Aavesh Khan. *After another excellent innings from Sarfaraz, New Zealand needed 259, but their limp chase ended in the 32nd over, as did their chances of progressing. Aavesh reduced them to 16-4, before 16-year-old left-arm spinner Mahipal Lomror claimed a five-for to back up his 42-ball 45.*

At Fatullah, January 30, 2016. **Nepal won by eight wickets. ‡Ireland 131-9** (50 overs) (S. Lamichhane 5-27); **Nepal 132-2** (25.3 overs) (Y. S. Karki 61*). *MoM:* S. Lamichhane. *Nepal's spinners, led by 16-year-old leggie Sandeep Lamichhane, who took a hat-trick as part of a five-for (only the third in their history), mesmerised Ireland. Between them, they had figures of 36–8–78–7. Chasing 132, Nepal lost Sandeep Sunar to the first ball of the innings, but Yogendra Karki crashed 61* as they galloped into the quarter-finals.*

At Mirpur, February 1, 2016. **India won by seven wickets.** Reduced to 48 overs a side. **Nepal 169-8** (48 overs) (Aavesh Khan 3-34); **‡India 175-3** (18.1 overs) (R. R. Panth 78, I. P. Kishan 52). *MoM:* R. R. Panth. *Nepal's batsmen were strangled by Aavesh, their bowlers battered by Rishabh Panth: he scorched to the fastest youth ODI fifty, in 18 balls, and hit five sixes, including three in an over off Airee. After crashing 124 from the first nine overs, India breezed to the top of the group in the 19th.*

At Fatullah, February 1, 2016. **New Zealand won by four wickets.** Reduced to 48 overs a side. **Ireland 212** (47.5 overs) (J. B. Tector 56; R. Ravindra 3-36, J. L. Finnie 3-30); **‡New Zealand 213-6** (40.1 overs) (F. H. Allen 97, D. N. Phillips 58; R. J. Anders 4-32). *MoM:* F. H. Allen. *Jack Tector and Adam Dennison took Ireland to 100-1, but their platform crumbled: seven batsmen fell to spin, three with the score on 183. Rory Anders removed the top four to give the Irish a sniff, before Finn Allen and Dale Phillips put on 141 – New Zealand's highest fifth-wicket stand, beating 95 between Andrew de Boorder and Tim Southee, also against Ireland, in Colombo in 1996 – to condemn them to a third consecutive defeat.*

INDIA 6pts, NEPAL 4pts, New Zealand 2pts, Ireland 0pts.

Quarter-Finals

At Mirpur, February 5, 2016. **Bangladesh won by six wickets. ‡Nepal 211-9** (50 overs) (R. Rijal 72); **Bangladesh 215-4** (48.2 overs) (Zakir Hasan 75*, Mehedi Hasan 55*). *MoM:* Mehedi Hasan. *Bangladesh had some nervous moments before winning with ten balls to spare. Nepal's captain Raju*

Riyal – whose age had been queried ahead of the tournament by someone claiming to have been a Mumbai Under-15 team-mate ten years previously – took his side to a challenging total, then the hosts dipped to 98-4 in the 29th over. But Zakir Hasan and skipper Mehedi Hasan combined in a stand of 117, the turning point coming in the 38th, when Riyal failed to stump Mehedi.*

At Fatullah, February 6, 2016. **India won by 197 runs.** ‡**India 349-6** (50 overs) (R. R. Panth 111, S. N. Khan 76, A. K. Jaffer 64; F. Coetzee 3-78); **Namibia 152** (39 overs) (M. Dagar 3-25, Anmolpreet Singh 3-27). *MoM:* R. R. Panth. *Rishabh Panth's 96-ball 111 lifted India towards a total that was far too much for Namibia, whose fielding had buckled under pressure. They made a reasonable start (59-0 in the ninth over), then lost all ten for 93. "I think there were a few nerves in the dressing-room," said Namibia's captain Zane Green. "This was the first time we were playing on TV."*

At Mirpur, February 7, 2016. **Sri Lanka won by six wickets.** ‡**England 184** (49.2 overs) (P. W. H. de Silva 3-34); **Sri Lanka 186-4** (35.4 overs) (W. I. A. Fernando 95). *MoM:* W. I. A. Fernando. *England's campaign fizzled out in a disappointing batting display, which went wrong from the start: the lively seamer Asitha Fernando removed both openers cheaply. Apart from Fernando's six overs, the bowling came entirely from the spinners. Seven batsmen did make it into double figures, but only Essex's Callum Taylor (42) passed 26. Avishka Fernando then guided Sri Lanka into the semis with 95 from 96 balls.*

At Fatullah, February 8, 2016. **West Indies won by five wickets.** ‡**Pakistan 227-6** (50 overs) (Umair Masood 113, Salman Fayyaz 58*); **West Indies 229-5** (40 overs) (T. A. Imlach 54, S. O. Hetmyer 52). *MoM:* Umair Masood. *Pakistan did well to recover from 57-5, thanks to a sixth-wicket stand of 164 between Umair Masood and Salman Fayyaz. Barbadian fast bowler Chemar Holder, playing his first match of the tournament after being called up as a replacement, took the first two wickets and finished with 2-26. West Indies cantered past their target with ten overs in hand, led by their captain, Shemron Hetmyer, who crunched 52 from 42 balls.*

Semi-Finals

At Mirpur, February 9, 2016. **India won by 97 runs. India 267-9** (50 overs) (Anmolpreet Singh 72, S. N. Khan 59; A. M. Fernando 4-43); ‡**Sri Lanka 170** (42.4 overs) (M. Dagar 3-21). *MoM:* Anmolpreet Singh. *India swept to their fifth comfortable victory in a row, dismantling Sri Lanka for 170 after Anmolpreet Singh organised a commanding total; dropped in the covers when 32, he shared stands of 96 with Sarfaraz Khan and 70 with Washington Sundar (43). Sri Lanka's wicketkeeper Vishad Randika de Silva took five catches, and was instrumental in a run-out. India's slow left-armer Mayank Dagar's three wickets included Sri Lanka's top-scorer Kamindu Mendis for 39.*

At Mirpur, February 11, 2016. **West Indies won by three wickets.** ‡**Bangladesh 226** (50 overs) (Mehedi Hasan 60; K. M. A. Paul 3-20); **West Indies 230-7** (48.4 overs) (S. O. Hetmyer 60, S. K. Springer 62*; Saleh Ahmed 3-37). *MoM:* S. K. Springer. *West Indies looked certain winners after restricting Bangladesh to 226 on a slow pitch, then reaching 177-4 in the 38th over. But two wickets set nerves jangling, before Shamar Springer dragged his side over the line, scoring 34 of the last 49 runs, including successive fours off Mohammad Saifuddin to round off the victory.*

FINAL

INDIA v WEST INDIES

At Mirpur, February 14, 2016. West Indies won by five wickets. Toss: West Indies.

In the game's first over, Guyanese wicketkeeper Tevin Imlach spotted Rishabh Panth batting outside his crease. Unaware of the danger, Panth left Alzarri Joseph's fourth delivery, and Imlach – standing 20 yards back – underarmed the ball into the stumps. That set the tone: West Indies were sharper and harder throughout. Joseph and his new-ball partner Chemar Holder managed a combined return of 20–2–59–4, while the support bowlers sustained the pressure. Sarfaraz Khan made a steely

51 off 89 balls, but found little help, and was eighth out in the 39th over. Left-arm spinner Mayank Dagar, nephew of Virender Sehwag, then took three wickets in his first four overs to reduce West Indies to 77 for five. But Dagar's fielders could not take any more of the chances he created: Sarfaraz put down Keemo Paul, and Panth dropped Keacy Carty with 37 needed off 40 deliveries. Carty capitalised to make a 125-ball 52, and his 69-run stand with Paul took West Indies home with three balls to spare, triggering manic celebrations.

Man of the Match: K. U. Carty. *Man of the Tournament:* Mehedi Hasan (Bangladesh).

India Under-19

†R. R. Panth st Imlach b Joseph	1
*I. P. Kishan lbw b Joseph	4
Anmolpreet Singh c Imlach b Joseph	3
M. S. Washington Sundar c Joseph b John	7
S. N. Khan lbw b John	51
A. K. Jaffer c Paul b Springer	5
M. K. Lomror c Imlach b Holder	19
M. Dagar c Carty b John	8
R. R. Batham c Imlach b Paul	21
Aavesh Khan c John b Paul	1
K. K. Ahmed not out	2
B 2, lb 5, w 16	23
1/3 (1) 2/8 (3) 3/27 (2) 4/41 (4) 5/50 (6) 6/87 (7) 7/116 (8) 8/120 (5) 9/123 (10) 10/145 (9) (45.1 overs)	145
10 overs: 34-3	

Joseph 10–0–39–3; Holder 10–2–20–1; John 10–0–38–3; Springer 9–1–24–1; Paul 6.1–0–17–2.

West Indies Under-19

G. D. Pope c Ahmed b Aavesh Khan	3
†T. A. Imlach c Lomror b Ahmed	15
*S. O. Hetmyer c Jaffer b Dagar	23
K. U. Carty not out	52
S. K. Springer c Jaffer b Dagar	3
J. U. Goolie c and b Dagar	3
K. M. A. Paul not out	40
Lb 1, w 6	7
1/5 (1) 2/28 (2) 3/67 (3) 4/71 (5) 5/77 (6) (5 wkts, 49.3 overs)	146
10 overs: 29-2	

M. O. Frew, R. D. John, A. S. Joseph and C. K. Holder did not bat.

Aavesh Khan 10–1–29–1; Ahmed 9.3–2–32–1; Washington Sundar 9–1–18–0; Batham 3–0–12–0; Lomror 8–0–29–0; Dagar 10–1–25–3.

Umpires: R. J. Bailey and R. S. A. Palliyaguruge. Third umpire: M. D. Martell.
Referee: A. J. Pycroft.

UNDER-19 WORLD CUP WINNERS

1987-88	AUSTRALIA beat Pakistan by five wickets at Adelaide.
1997-98	ENGLAND beat New Zealand by seven wickets at Johannesburg.
1999-2000	INDIA beat Sri Lanka by six wickets at Colombo.
2001-02	AUSTRALIA beat South Africa by seven wickets at Lincoln.
2003-04	PAKISTAN beat West Indies by 25 runs at Dhaka.
2005-06	PAKISTAN beat India by 38 runs at Colombo.
2007-08	INDIA beat South Africa by 12 runs (D/L) at Kuala Lumpur.
2009-10	AUSTRALIA beat Pakistan by 25 runs at Lincoln.
2012	INDIA beat Australia by six wickets at Townsville.
2013-14	SOUTH AFRICA beat Pakistan by six wickets at Dubai.
2015-16	WEST INDIES beat India by five wickets at Mirpur.

Third-place Play-off

At Fatullah, February 13, 2016. **Bangladesh won by three wickets.** ‡**Sri Lanka 214** (48.5 overs) (K. I. C. Asalanka 76; Mehedi Hasan 3-28); **Bangladesh 218-7** (49.3 overs) (Mehedi Hasan 53). *MoM:* Mehedi Hasan. *The hosts clinched third place despite three run-outs in the second half of their chase.*

Fifth-place Play-off

Semi-finals At Fatullah, February 9, 2016. **Pakistan won by 122 runs. Pakistan 258-8** (50 overs) (Saif Badar 88, Hasan Mohsin 117; S. Lamichhane 3-53); ‡**Nepal 136** (43.5 overs) (P. Tamang 65*; Hasan Mohsin 4-42). *MoM:* Hasan Mohsin. *Nepal sniffed an upset when Pakistan's openers departed for ducks, but Hasan Mohsin put his side back on track, following his maiden century with his best bowling figures in youth ODIs.*

At Fatullah, February 10, 2016. **England won by 203 runs.** Reduced to 48 overs a side. **England 286-9** (48 overs) (T. J. Moores 85, J. T. A. Burnham 109; F. Coetzee 3-72); ‡**Namibia 83** (25.2 overs) (M. S. Crane 3-3). *MoM:* J. T. A. Burnham. *Jack Burnham's third century of the tournament – he faced 123 balls in all, and put on 170 for the second wicket with Tom Moores – set up a crushing victory.*

Final At Fatullah, February 12, 2016. **Pakistan won by seven wickets. England 264-7** (50 overs) (S. M. Curran 83); ‡**Pakistan 265-3** (43.1 overs) (Zeeshan Malik 93, Saif Badar 75*). *MoM:* Zeeshan Malik. *Burnham made only two, but still finished as the leading run-scorer with 420, which was 65 more than India's Sarfaraz Khan.*

Seventh-place Play-off

At Fatullah, February 11, 2016. **Namibia won by 15 runs.** Reduced to 45 overs a side. ‡**Namibia 225-9** (45 overs) (L. Louwrens 59, M. van Lingen 58; S. Lamichhane 3-35); **Nepal 210** (44.2 overs) (S. Dhamala 59; F. Coetzee 3-34, M. van Lingen 4-24). *MoM:* M. van Lingen. *Left-hander Michael van Lingen hit 58 from 36 balls, then took four wickets as Nepal collapsed from 166-4.*

Ninth-place Play-off

Quarter-finals At Cox's Bazar, February 4, 2016. **South Africa won by eight wickets.** ‡**Ireland 185-7** (50 overs) (L. J. Tucker 77*); **South Africa 187-2** (46 overs) (K. Verreynne 77). *MoM:* K. Verreynne.

At Cox's Bazar (No. 2), February 4, 2016. **New Zealand won by seven wickets.** ‡**Scotland 181-9** (50 overs) (R. M. ter Braak 3-34); **New Zealand 185-3** (27 overs) (G. D. Phillips 89). *MoM:* G. D. Phillips. *New Zealand's opener Glenn Phillips reached 53* from 22 balls, with 50 in boundaries; in all he faced 40 deliveries, and smacked 11 fours and six sixes.*

At Cox's Bazar, February 5, 2016. **Afghanistan won by 226 runs. Afghanistan 340-9** (50 overs) (Karim Janat 156, Perwez Malakzai 74; P. V. Vuniwaqa 3-41); ‡**Fiji 114** (31.2 overs) (Nijat Masood 3-6, Rashid Khan 3-16). *MoM:* Karim Janat. *Afghanistan's opener Karim Janat faced 132 balls, and hit 12 fours and six sixes. Fiji were 18-5 after ten overs, but finally made it past the 28th.*

At Cox's Bazar (No. 2), February 5, 2016. **Zimbabwe won by six wickets.** ‡**Canada 186-8** (50 overs) (J. Ives 3-30); **Zimbabwe 190-4** (31.4 overs) (S. Snyder 56). *MoM:* J. Ives.

Semi-finals At Cox's Bazar, February 8, 2016. **Zimbabwe won by eight wickets. South Africa 91** (39.5 overs) (R. Ngarava 4-10); ‡**Zimbabwe 94-2** (22 overs). *MoM:* R. Ngarava. *Zimbabwe tweaked their neighbours' noses: South Africa never recovered after crashing to 12-4.*

At Cox's Bazar (No. 2), February 9, 2016. **Afghanistan won by eight wickets.** ‡**New Zealand 135** (44.5 overs) (Shamsurhman Karokhil 3-37, Rashid Khan 3-30); **Afghanistan 137-2** (27.3 overs) (Tariq Stanikzai 50*). *MoM:* Tariq Stanikzai. *New Zealand scrambled 100 runs for the last four wickets after dipping to 35-6, but Afghanistan sailed home.*

Final At Cox's Bazar, February 12, 2016. **Afghanistan won by five wickets.** ‡**Zimbabwe 216-9** (50 overs) (R. Murray 53, W. T. Mashinge 66; Zia-ur-Rehman 3-33, Muslim Musa 3-38); **Afghanistan 218-5** (46.5 overs) (Tariq Stanikzai 106*, Rashid Khan 55*). *MoM:* Tariq Stanikzai. *Afghanistan won the Plate Championship for the nations ranked 9th–16th, recovering from 123-5 thanks to a stand of 95* between Tariq Stanikzai – who hit his first century in youth ODIs – and Rashid Khan.*

Eleventh-place Play-off

At Cox's Bazar (No. 2), February 12, 2016. **South Africa won by 138 runs. South Africa 288-6** (50 overs) (D. Foxcroft 117, R. Moonsamy 51, W. Makwetu 50*); ‡**New Zealand 150** (38.4 overs) (P. W. A. Mulder 4-14). *MoM:* D. Foxcroft.

Thirteenth-place Play-off

Semi-finals At Cox's Bazar, February 7, 2016. **Ireland won by six wickets. Canada 139** (48.2 overs) (R. J. Anders 4-21); ‡**Ireland 142-4** (34.3 overs) (B. S. Adhihetty 3-25). *MoM:* G. S. McClintock.

At Cox's Bazar (No. 2), February 8, 2016. **Scotland won by 76 runs. Scotland 225** (48.1 overs) (F. D. W. McCreath 60; C. T. Cokovaki 4-46); ‡**Fiji 149** (42.2 overs) (P. V. Vuniwaqa 80; C. L. Sloman 3-30, F. D. W. McCreath 3-48). *MoM:* F. D. W. McCreath.

Final At Cox's Bazar, February 10, 2016. **Ireland won by 95 runs. Ireland 235-7** (50 overs) (L. J. Tucker 59, W. T. McClintock 69; M. A. Ghaffar 3-49); ‡**Scotland 140** (44 overs) (F. B. Tucker 3-29, H. Tector 4-28). *MoM:* W. T. McClintock. *A fifth-wicket stand of 107 between Lorcan Tucker and William McClintock, followed by seven wickets for Fiachra Tucker and Harry Tector, gave Ireland bragging rights over their Gaelic neighbours.*

Fifteenth-place Play-off

At Cox's Bazar (No. 2), February 11, 2016. **Canada won by eight wickets. Fiji 83** (28 overs) (S. V. Patel 3-18, M. R. Patel 4-16); ‡**Canada 84-2** (20 overs). *MoM:* M. R. Patel. *As was traditional, Fiji were dismissed in the 28th over.*

Final rankings

1. West Indies 2. India 3. Bangladesh 4. Sri Lanka 5. Pakistan 6. England 7. Namibia 8. Nepal 9. Afghanistan 10. Zimbabwe 11. South Africa 12. New Zealand 13. Ireland 14. Scotland 15. Canada 16. Fiji.

AUSTRALIAN CRICKET IN 2016

The rollercoaster ride

DANIEL BRETTIG

"I am hurting. I need players that are willing to get in the battle and have some pride in playing for Australia and pride in the Baggy Green. At the moment it's not good enough, and I'm quite sick of saying it, to be honest with you." More than any match, innings or session, these words from Steve Smith at Hobart's Bellerive Oval in November were the pivot on which Australia's year turned. It had begun with their brief ascent to No. 1 in the Test rankings, veered wildly off course against supposedly modest Sri Lanka, then plummeted into humiliation against South Africa.

Until then, Smith had seemed a capable new captain, despite the odd misstep in his tactics or public words. But the innings defeat at Hobart, which surrendered the series to a well-drilled South Africa, pushed him to the limits;

AUSTRALIA IN 2016

	Played	*Won*	*Lost*	*Drawn/No result*
Tests	11	5	5	1
One-day internationals	29	17	11	1
Twenty20 internationals	12	6	6	–

DECEMBER } JANUARY	3 Tests (h) v West Indies	(see *Wisden 2016*, page 945)
	5 ODIs and 3 T20Is (h) v India	(page 840)
FEBRUARY	2 Tests and 3 ODIs (a) v New Zealand	(page 951)
MARCH	3 T20Is (a) v South Africa	(page 1010)
MARCH } APRIL	ICC World Twenty20 (in India)	(page 793)
MAY		
JUNE	Triangular ODI tournament (in West Indies) v WI and SA	(page 1081)
JULY } AUGUST	3 Tests, 5 ODIs and 2 T20Is (a) v Sri Lanka	(page 1055)
SEPTEMBER	1 ODI (in South Africa) v Ireland	(page 1017)
SEPTEMBER } OCTOBER	5 ODIs (a) v South Africa	(page 1018)
NOVEMBER	3 Tests (h) v South Africa	(page 850)
DECEMBER	3 ODIs (h) v New Zealand	(page 860)
DECEMBER } JANUARY	3 Tests and 5 ODIs (h) v Pakistan	(page 864)

For a review of Australian domestic cricket from the 2015-16 season, see page 881.

his anger and frustration brought to mind Allan Border during his "Captain Grumpy" phase in the mid-1980s. Border had threatened to resign depending on the result of a one-day series in New Zealand. And while Smith did not go that far, his high dudgeon was a harbinger of change. Chairman of selectors Rod Marsh had already convened an emergency meeting after the first day at Bellerive, where Australia were bundled out for 85, and resigned soon afterwards. Team performance chief Pat Howard and chief executive James Sutherland made hurried visits to Tasmania, both delivering terse announcements.

Howard, who was widely expected to leave Cricket Australia when his contract expired in June 2017, said coach Darren Lehmann needed to "reinvent" himself, just three months after he had signed a new deal keeping him in charge until after the 2019 World Cup and Ashes. Lehmann did not take kindly to this, but was part of the selection panel that chased a new direction in Marsh's wake.

Two batting debutants, 20-year-old Matt Renshaw and Peter Handscomb, were thrust into the day/night dead rubber at Adelaide, while the neat, softly spoken wicketkeeper Peter Nevill was sacrificed for the rougher-hewn Matthew Wade. Among the other casualties were Mitchell Marsh and Joe Burns, who had seemingly made their spots safe in New Zealand back in February. The Hobart debacle had hinged in part on losing the toss. At Wellington nine months earlier, Smith had been able to send Brendon McCullum's men in on a surface offering just the right amount of movement for Josh Hazlewood and Peter Siddle. Further fortune favoured Australia in that game when Adam Voges was bowled by a delivery from Doug Bracewell wrongly called a no-ball, before going on to his second double-century of the season; Usman Khawaja's hundred relied rather less on providence. Marsh struck the hammer blows with his muscular fast-medium, meaning McCullum went to Christchurch for his final Test unable to hope for anything more than a shared series. His blaze to the fastest of all Test centuries briefly threw Smith and his bowlers, but Australia's subsequent resilience seemed the stuff of a very decent side. Australia's players decamped to holidays and the IPL feeling pretty good about themselves, then victory in a one-day tri-series in the Caribbean against West Indies and South Africa – Justin Langer deputised as coach while Lehmann rested – maintained the sense of progress.

Then, in July, came the trip to Sri Lanka, who were not taken lightly, though they looked short of quality batting after the retirements of Mahela Jayawardene and Kumar Sangakkara. The tour began with the ICC's Test Championship mace being presented to Smith in secret – at the request of Sri Lanka Cricket, so as not to demoralise the hosts. All seemed rosy when Angelo Mathews's youngsters were bundled out on the first day at Pallekele, but it did not take long for Australia's veneer of superiority to be chipped away by Rangana Herath and his merry band of tweakers. Burns and Khawaja in particular looked lost, then Kusal Mendis smashed an inspired 167. Smith, Nevill and a hamstrung Steve O'Keefe battled to save the match, but – despite surviving 25 successive maidens – Australia lost. Having slipped off the summit, they were to find it was indeed a long way down.

Roaring back: David Warner, and Australia, came to life at the end of the year.

They were never in the Second Test at Galle, for all the best efforts of Mitchell Starc, and followed up with two dispirited collapses in Colombo. It seemed churlish that Smith and Lehmann highlighted the shortcomings of the spinners – Nathan Lyon and Jon Holland, O'Keefe's replacement – as much as the collective failures of the batsmen. And the batting would not instantly be set right on home turf.

After a limited-overs tour of South Africa that succeeded mainly in firming up the Proteas' plans for Australia's batsmen – and in building the confidence of South Africa's top six against a second-string attack – the sides met again in Perth. That it was not Brisbane spoke for CA's determination to build the case for day/night Tests, but the schedule change meant Faf du Plessis tossed up at a ground where his side had never lost, rather than at one where Australia habitually won.

Remarkably, the loss of Dale Steyn to a shoulder injury seemed to work in South Africa's favour, as Vernon Philander and Kagiso Rabada crashed into an uncertain middle order. Dean Elgar and J-P. Duminy then ensured the chase would be out of reach.

Cue Hobart's truth and consequence, that bottoming-out moment for Smith, and the injection of no fewer than five new faces for Adelaide. A staunch victory under the lights there was largely down to an outstanding innings from Khawaja, recalled after his Sri Lankan misadventures, and help from Renshaw the stolid, and Handscomb the dynamic. Their success ensured that Voges's Test average of 61, second only to Don Bradman, would stay that way: in February, he announced his retirement from international cricket.

Smith carried Adelaide's momentum through a home assignment against Pakistan who, for all their brilliance in England and brief rise to No. 1, have a truly abominable record Down Under – this was their fourth successive 3–0 defeat. Australia were made to sweat by Asad Shafiq in Brisbane, but bulldozed to victories at Melbourne and Sydney. Two rapid centuries for David Warner, his first in Tests since January, also helped – though he had been in remarkable form in 50-over cricket, scoring seven centuries in 2016, four more than anyone. Australia rounded out the year feeling optimistic again, but definitely chastened.

PHILLIP HUGHES'S DEATH: "NO ONE TO BLAME"

An inquest into the death of Australian batsman Phillip Hughes in November 2014, after he was hit on the neck by a bouncer from Sean Abbott during a Sheffield Shield match, concluded: "Neither the bowler nor anyone else was to blame for this tragic outcome." Michael Barnes, the New South Wales state coroner, found in November 2016 that a "minuscule misjudgement" by Hughes had led to the accident, but that "no failure to enforce the laws of the game contributed to his death". He advised Cricket Australia to continue trying to improve neck protection, although he admitted that even had Hughes been wearing a more modern helmet, there was no certainty it would have saved him.

Emotions ran high at the Sydney hearing, after testimony suggesting Hughes had been deliberately targeted with bouncers, as well as sledging from opponents. One former player said the NSW fast bowler Doug Bollinger had told him he regretted saying "I am going to kill you" earlier in Hughes's innings, although Bollinger denied this. Members of Hughes's family made their anger clear, and walked out. The coroner summed up: "Those who claim to love the game [should] reflect upon whether the practice of sledging is worthy of its participants. An outsider is left to wonder why such a beautiful game would need such an ugly underside."

AUSTRALIA v INDIA IN 2015-16

MELINDA FARRELL

One-day internationals (5): Australia 4, India 1
Twenty20 internationals (3): Australia 0, India 3

In the build-up to the World Twenty20, it was difficult to see the value of the 50-over component of an Indian tour tacked on to the end of a summer of Tests, seemingly in order to fulfil broadcasting requirements. Finding relevance for bilateral series remains one of cricket's great challenges. In the first year of a new World Cup cycle, one-day results and rankings can sit on the back burner, while the Twenty20 ladder is shaken up at a dizzying rate: India were eighth at the start of the series, but three victories took them top.

For Australia, the tour was not ideally timed. The Test Championship mace was within reach, provided they successfully negotiated the imminent two-match series in New Zealand, and the need to rest players and prepare for conditions across the Tasman made for a difficult balancing act.

For India, it was more straightforward. With no upcoming Test cricket, they could focus on the white-ball formats, and allow their players to settle and find form for the World Twenty20 at home: their 20-over side remained unchanged. In contrast, Australia's T20 campaign felt like an extended audition, with 19 players tried in the three games. The only reasonable conclusion was that the hosts considered preparation for the World Twenty20 more important than beating India.

The first T20 international also raised wider questions about how seriously the format is treated in Australia. Steve Smith was miked up for Channel Nine's coverage while at the crease, and was being interviewed by commentators in the over of his dismissal, though he was not speaking in the lead-up to the ball that got him. He was given a pointed send-off by Virat Kohli, who mimicked the chatter. And, while Smith didn't blame the broadcasters, his wicket sparked an Australian collapse.

This came a few days after Spidercam got in the way of a Kohli shot that was heading for the boundary – it became a dead ball instead of a four. It all led to suggestions the scales were sliding too far towards gimmickry as broadcasters looked for new ways to bring viewers closer to the action.

In terms of ratings and attendances, the tour was a bonanza for Cricket Australia. But, although bragging rights for the two series were split between the two countries, the tourists probably got more out of the matches. India did lose a high-scoring one-day series in which five Australians and four Indians made centuries, but they finished the Twenty20s in excellent form and, importantly, with a settled side. Kohli and Rohit Sharma, who both hit two hundreds during the 50-over matches, deservedly collected the series awards.

Australia were still dreaming of claiming top spot in all three rankings. But, while this tour confirmed their 50-over credentials, it exposed their muddled preparations for a tilt at the Twenty20 crown.

INDIAN TOURING PARTY

*M. S. Dhoni (50/20), R. Ashwin (50/20), Bhuvneshwar Kumar (50), J. J. Bumrah (50/20), R. Dhawan (50/20), S. Dhawan (50/20), Gurkeerat Singh (50/20), Harbhajan Singh (20), R. A. Jadeja (50/20), V. Kohli (50/20), Mohammed Shami (50), A. Nehra (20), M. K. Pandey (50), H. H. Pandya (20), A. R. Patel (50), A. M. Rahane (50/20), S. K. Raina (20), I. Sharma (50), R. G. Sharma (50/20), B. B. Sran (50), U. T. Yadav (50/20), Yuvraj Singh (20). *Coach:* R. J. Shastri.

Mohammed Shami injured his leg before the first warm-up match, and returned home. His replacement, Bhuvneshwar Kumar, broke his thumb during the fourth one-day international; Bumrah, who had arrived with the Twenty20 specialists, was included for the final ODI, and R. Dhawan replaced Bhuvneshwar in the T20 squad.

At Perth, January 8, 2016 (floodlit). **Indians won by 74 runs.** **‡Indians 192-4** (20 overs) (S. Dhawan 74, V. Kohli 74); **Western Australia XI 118-6** (20 overs) (T. R. Birt 74*). *The home team chose from 13 players, and the Indians from their entire squad of 15 (although the injured Mohammed Shami took no part). Shikhar Dhawan, who faced 46 balls, and Virat Kohli (44) piled on 149 for the second wicket in 14 overs. Only Travis Birt, who faced 60 and hit 11 of his side's 12 fours, passed 11 in the WA innings, in which newcomer Barinder Sran, a left-arm seamer from Punjab, took 2-24 in his four overs.*

At Perth, January 9, 2016 (day/night). **Indians won by 64 runs.** **‡Indians 249** (49.1 overs) (R. G. Sharma 67, M. K. Pandey 58; D. N. Porter 5-37); **Western Australia XI 185** (49.2 overs) (J. Morgan 50). *The Indians chose from 14 players, and WA from 12. The early loss of Shikhar Dhawan and Kohli reduced the tourists to 19-2, but Rohit Sharma and Ajinkya Rahane rebuilt carefully, putting on 88 in 16 overs. Seamer Drew Porter, who had not played for WA's senior team for more than four years, kept the total within bounds with five wickets. But the inexperienced WA batsmen struggled to make the most of starts – seven reached double figures, but only two passed 17.*

AUSTRALIA v INDIA

First One-Day International

At Perth, January 12, 2016. Australia won by five wickets. Toss: India. One-day international debuts: S. M. Boland, J. S. Paris; B. B. Sran.

There were three debutant fast bowlers at the WACA, but it was a retiree who made the biggest splash. Mitchell Johnson was ferried around the ground where he had enjoyed so much success, warm applause replacing the roars that so often greeted him. It was a reminder of what Australia – and cricket – had lost: not a single delivery topped 140kph. In a batsmen's match, Sharma feasted on a relatively green bowling attack, which included debutants Scott Boland and left-armer Joel Paris. He passed Viv Richards's 153 not out at Melbourne in 1979-80, previously the highest ODI score by a visiting batsman against Australia, and reached 1,000 runs against them in a record 19 innings (Brian Lara and Sachin Tendulkar needed 20). Sharma's partnership of 207 with Kohli was the cornerstone of a formidable, but not – as it turned out – unattainable target. India's own debutant, the left-arm seamer Barinder Sran, removed both openers in his first spell, but after that the bowling was largely impotent. Smith and Bailey, who put on 242, took a particular liking to the spin of Ashwin and Jadeja, bolting to individual centuries, and set up a record successful chase on the ground. Smith's 149 from 135 balls was the highest of his five one-day hundreds, and this was the first ODI to feature two double-century partnerships. It almost didn't, though: Bailey was reprieved first ball, when he gloved Sran down the leg side to Dhoni. Umpire Kettleborough said not out, but the Snickometer showed a clear spike, and there was a mark on Hot Spot. Never shy of a cheeky shot, Bailey reminded everyone why there was no DRS: "We're not the team that doesn't want it."

Man of the Match: S. P. D. Smith. *Attendance:* 15,004.

India

R. G. Sharma not out	171
S. Dhawan c Marsh b Hazlewood	9
V. Kohli c Finch b Faulkner	91
*†M. S. Dhoni c Boland b Faulkner	18
R. A. Jadeja not out	10
Lb 6, w 4	10
1/36 (2) 2/243 (3) 3/286 (4) (3 wkts, 50 overs)	309
10 overs: 52-1	

A. M. Rahane, M. K. Pandey, R. Ashwin, Bhuvneshwar Kumar, U. T. Yadav and B. B. Sran did not bat.

Hazlewood 10–0–41–1; Paris 8–0–53–0; Marsh 9–0–53–0; Boland 10–0–74–0; Faulkner 10–0–60–2; Maxwell 3–0–22–0.

Australia

A. J. Finch c and b Sran	8
D. A. Warner c Kohli b Sran	5
*S. P. D. Smith c Kohli b Sran	149
G. J. Bailey c Bhuvneshwar Kumar b Ashwin	112
G. J. Maxwell c Dhawan b Ashwin	6
M. R. Marsh not out	12
J. P. Faulkner not out	1
Lb 5, w 12	17
1/9 (1) 2/21 (2) 3/263 (4) 4/273 (5) 5/308 (3) (5 wkts, 49.2 overs)	310
10 overs: 40-2	

†M. S. Wade, S. M. Boland, J. R. Hazlewood and J. S. Paris did not bat.

Sran 9.2–0–56–3; Bhuvneshwar Kumar 9–0–42–0; Sharma 1–0–11–0; Yadav 10–0–54–0; Jadeja 9–0–61–0; Ashwin 9–0–68–2; Kohli 2–0–13–0.

Umpires: S. D. Fry and R. A. Kettleborough. Third umpire: M. D. Martell.
Referee: J. J. Crowe.

AUSTRALIA v INDIA

Second One-Day International

At Brisbane, January 15, 2016 (day/night). Australia won by seven wickets. Toss: India.

The speckled bowl of the Gabba replaced the concrete of the WACA, but otherwise this match could have been mistaken for the first. There was Rohit Sharma pummelling a century, with Kohli typically elegant in support. There was an apparently tricky target, a smidgen over 300. There was the Smith and Bailey show. And there was a record chase for the ground. While the result was virtually the same, though, there were some differences. This time Australia's openers made contributions, and this time the absence of DRS helped India: Sharma, on 89, feathered Paris to Wade, but was given not out. However, dropped catches and a missed run-out showed up the deficiencies in India's fielding. And, after Sharma and Kohli – this time with help from Rahane – provided a platform, India failed to build on it. The final ten overs produced only 75 runs, and six wickets – which turned the spotlight on their decision to play just five specialist batsmen. Australia, on the other hand, made the most of their batting depth, and again paced the chase to perfection. The required rate remained around a run a ball, and Bailey – who faced only 58 deliveries – chimed in with some explosive hitting.

Man of the Match: R. G. Sharma. *Attendance:* 28,851.

India

R. G. Sharma run out	124	U. T. Yadav not out	0
S. Dhawan c Wade b Paris	6		
V. Kohli run out	59	W 7	7
A. M. Rahane c Smith b Faulkner	89		
*†M. S. Dhoni c Maxwell b Boland	11	1/9 (2) 2/134 (3) (8 wkts, 50 overs)	308
M. K. Pandey c Paris b Faulkner	6	3/255 (1) 4/276 (5)	
R. A. Jadeja run out	5	5/298 (4) 6/302 (6)	
R. Ashwin c Boland b Hastings	1	7/306 (8) 8/308 (7)	10 overs: 47-1

I. Sharma and B. B. Sran did not bat.

Paris 8–0–40–1; Richardson 8–1–61–0; Hastings 8–0–46–1; Boland 10–0–64–1; Maxwell 6–0–33–0; Faulkner 10–0–64–2.

Australia

A. J. Finch c Rahane b Jadeja	71
S. E. Marsh c Kohli b I. Sharma	71
*S. P. D. Smith b Yadav	46
G. J. Bailey not out	76
G. J. Maxwell not out	26
Lb 7, w 11, nb 1	19
1/145 (1) 2/166 (2) (3 wkts, 49 overs)	309
3/244 (3)	10 overs: 40-0

†M. S. Wade, J. P. Faulkner, J. W. Hastings, S. M. Boland, K. W. Richardson and J. S. Paris did not bat.

Sran 9–1–51–0; I. Sharma 10–0–60–1; Yadav 10–0–74–1; Jadeja 9–0–50–1; Ashwin 10–0–60–0; Kohli 1–0–7–0.

Umpires: R. A. Kettleborough and M. D. Martell. Third umpire: S. D. Fry.
Referee: J. J. Crowe.

AUSTRALIA v INDIA

Third One-Day International

At Melbourne, January 17, 2016 (day/night). Australia won by three wickets. Toss: Australia. One-day international debuts: R. Dhawan, Gurkeerat Singh.

As the first two matches had each produced more than 600 runs, it was little surprise that both camps tinkered with their attacks. Hastings, a Victorian, made the most of his local knowledge to claim four wickets. But the prize scalp, Rohit Sharma, fell early to Richardson. Kohli's run-a-ball century whooshed him past 7,000 runs in his 161st ODI innings (five faster than A. B. de Villiers), while fifties for Shikhar Dhawan and Rahane ensured another competitive target, even though India failed to reach 300 for the first time in the series. Some sharp fielding was epitomised by a spectacular relayed boundary catch by Smith and Maxwell to dispose of Rahane. In contrast, the touring blues continued: the largely Indian-supporting crowd jeered Ishant Sharma for some sloppy ground fielding that also earned the ire of Kohli. India's selection change was arguably a mistake: they omitted Ravichandran Ashwin on a pitch offering turn, preferring seamer Rishi Dhawan, who failed to take a wicket on debut. And, although they did better in terms of wickets, a series of solid partnerships kept Australia's chase on track. It was marshalled by Maxwell, who fell for 96 with the scores level, having quietened his critics. Faulkner finished off yet another ground-record chase as Australia's 17th successive ODI victory on home soil – a record for any country – gave them an unassailable 3–0 lead.

Man of the Match: G. J. Maxwell. *Attendance:* 47,638.

India

R. G. Sharma c Wade b Richardson	6	R. Dhawan not out	3
S. Dhawan b Hastings	68		
V. Kohli c Bailey b Hastings	117	Lb 5, w 9	14
A. M. Rahane c Maxwell b Hastings	50		—
*†M. S. Dhoni c Maxwell b Hastings	23	1/15 (1) 2/134 (2) (6 wkts, 50 overs)	295
Gurkeerat Singh b Faulkner	8	3/243 (4) 4/265 (3)	
R. A. Jadeja not out	6	5/274 (6) 6/288 (5) 10 overs: 43-1	

U. T. Yadav, I. Sharma and B. B. Sran did not bat.

Richardson 10–0–48–1; Hastings 10–0–58–4; Faulkner 10–0–63–1; Boland 9–0–63–0; Maxwell 9–0–46–0; M. R. Marsh 2–0–12–0.

Australia

S. E. Marsh c Dhoni b I. Sharma	62	J. P. Faulkner not out	21
A. J. Finch c Dhoni b Yadav	21	J. W. Hastings not out	0
*S. P. D. Smith c Rahane b Jadeja	41	Lb 3, w 5, nb 1	9
G. J. Bailey st Dhoni b Jadeja	23		—
G. J. Maxwell c S. Dhawan b Yadav	96	1/48 (2) 2/112 (3) (7 wkts, 48.5 overs)	296
M. R. Marsh run out	17	3/150 (4) 4/167 (1)	
†M. S. Wade c S. Dhawan b I. Sharma	6	5/204 (6) 6/215 (7) 7/295 (5) 10 overs: 65-1	

S. M. Boland and K. W. Richardson did not bat.

Yadav 9.5–0–68–2; Sran 8–0–63–0; I. Sharma 10–0–53–2; R. Dhawan 6–0–33–0; Gurkeerat Singh 5–0–27–0; Jadeja 10–0–49–2.

Umpires: S. D. Fry and R. A. Kettleborough. Third umpire: M. D. Martell.
Referee: J. J. Crowe.

AUSTRALIA v INDIA

Fourth One-Day International

At Canberra, January 20, 2016 (day/night). Australia won by 25 runs. Toss: Australia.

The first three matches had all favoured the chasing side and – until the 38th over of the second innings – it appeared the sequence would extend to four. Batting first this time, Australia were again boosted by contributions from all the top five. Warner – who fell in the nineties for the first time in internationals, having notched 20 hundreds – and Finch, who made a run-a-ball 107, put on 187; Smith and Maxwell then accelerated when required. Such was the ferocity of the batting that three fielders and one umpire required treatment after being hit: Kettleborough, struck early by a Finch straight-drive, hobbled off at drinks, to be replaced by Paul Wilson. It prompted their colleague, John Ward, to call for a helmet, having been hospitalised by a blow on the head during a Ranji Trophy match at Natham seven weeks earlier. India responded with two quickfire centuries of their own, from Shikhar Dhawan and Kohli (his 25th in ODIs), and needed just 72 from 76 balls, before collapsing spectacularly. Richardson took five wickets for the first time, and in all the last nine tumbled for 46; it was only the second time, after India's defeat by South Africa at Nagpur in the 2011 World Cup, that any team had been bowled out after reaching 250 for one. The injury to

Mark Graham

Headstrong: umpire John Ward feels sufficiently threatened to wear a helmet.

Rahane, who suffered split webbing and came in at No. 7, may have unsettled the batting, but it was no excuse for India's implosion.

Man of the Match: K. W. Richardson. *Attendance:* 10,922.

Australia

D. A. Warner b I. Sharma	93
A. J. Finch c I. Sharma b Yadav	107
M. R. Marsh c Kohli b Yadav	33
*S. P. D. Smith c Gurkeerat Singh b I. Sharma	51
G. J. Maxwell c sub (M. K. Pandey) b I. Sharma	41
G. J. Bailey c R. G. Sharma b I. Sharma	10
J. P. Faulkner b Yadav	0
†M. S. Wade run out	0
J. W. Hastings not out	0
Lb 7, w 6	13
1/187 (1) 2/221 (2) 3/288 (3) 4/298 (4) 5/319 (6) 6/319 (7) 7/321 (8) 8/348 (5) — (8 wkts, 50 overs)	348
10 overs: 59-0	

K. W. Richardson and N. M. Lyon did not bat.

Yadav 10–1–67–3; Bhuvneshwar Kumar 8–0–69–0; I. Sharma 10–0–77–4; Gurkeerat Singh 3–0–24–0; R. Dhawan 9–0–53–0; Jadeja 10–0–51–0.

India

R. G. Sharma c Wade b Richardson	41
S. Dhawan c Bailey b Hastings	126
V. Kohli c Smith b Richardson	106
*†M. S. Dhoni c Wade b Hastings	0
Gurkeerat Singh c sub (S. E. Marsh) b Lyon	5
R. A. Jadeja not out	24
A. M. Rahane c Smith b Richardson	2
R. Dhawan c Warner b Richardson	9
Bhuvneshwar Kumar c Smith b Richardson	2
U. T. Yadav c Bailey b Marsh	2
I. Sharma c Wade b Marsh	0
W 5, nb 1	6
1/65 (1) 2/277 (2) 3/277 (4) 4/278 (3) 5/286 (5) 6/294 (7) 7/308 (8) 8/311 (9) 9/315 (10) 10/323 (11) — (49.2 overs)	323
10 overs: 80-1	

Lyon 10–0–76–1; Richardson 10–1–68–5; Hastings 10–0–50–2; Faulkner 7–0–48–0; Marsh 9.2–0–55–2; Maxwell 1–0–10–0; Smith 2–0–16–0.

Umpires: R. A. Kettleborough and J. D. Ward. Third umpire: P. Wilson.
Wilson replaced Kettleborough after 17 overs, and S. J. Nogajski replaced Wilson as third umpire.
Referee: J. J. Crowe.

AUSTRALIA v INDIA

Fifth One-Day International

At Sydney, January 23, 2016 (day/night). India won by six wickets. Toss: India. One-day international debut: J. J. Bumrah.

The final match may have been a dead rubber, but it was the most thrilling game of the series. It was no coincidence that it was played in the most interesting conditions, as wet weather before the game presented batsmen with the challenge of a moving ball. But while the conditions were more favourable to bowlers – the stiff-armed Jasprit Bumrah looked good on debut, after being drafted in from the Twenty20 squad to replace the injured Bhuvneshwar Kumar – it was a pair of maiden centuries that stood out. Warner lacked meaningful support until Mitchell Marsh joined him and pummelled his first international hundred. But Marsh was on the receiving end of an Indian counterpunch, led initially by Rohit Sharma and Shikhar Dhawan, and pressed home by a rousing partnership between Pandey and Dhoni. India required 13 off the final over, bowled by Marsh. A six from Dhoni and a four from Pandey, which brought up an outstanding one-day century in only his third innings, saved India from a whitewash. It was Australia's first ODI defeat at home for 20 matches (18 wins and a no-result), since losing to South Africa in November 2014.

Man of the Match: M. K. Pandey. *Attendance:* 33,710.
Man of the Series: R. G. Sharma.

Australia

A. J. Finch lbw b I. Sharma	6
D. A. Warner c Jadeja b I. Sharma	122
*S. P. D. Smith c R. G. Sharma b Bumrah	28
G. J. Bailey c I. Sharma b R. Dhawan	6
S. E. Marsh run out	7
M. R. Marsh not out	102
†M. S. Wade c Dhoni b Yadav	36
J. P. Faulkner b Bumrah	1
J. W. Hastings not out	2
B 4, lb 7, w 8, nb 1	20
1/6 (1) 2/64 (3) 3/78 (4) 4/117 (5) 5/235 (2) 6/320 (7) 7/323 (8) (7 wkts, 50 overs)	330
10 overs: 61-1	

S. M. Boland and N. M. Lyon did not bat.

I. Sharma 10–0–60–2; Yadav 8–0–82–1; Bumrah 10–0–40–2; R. Dhawan 10–0–74–1; Jadeja 10–0–46–0; Gurkeerat Singh 2–0–17–0.

India

R. G. Sharma c Wade b Hastings	99
S. Dhawan c S. E. Marsh b Hastings	78
V. Kohli c Wade b Hastings	8
M. K. Pandey not out	104
*†M. S. Dhoni c Warner b M. R. Marsh	34
Gurkeerat Singh not out	0
Lb 3, w 5	8
1/123 (2) 2/134 (3) 3/231 (1) 4/325 (5) (4 wkts, 49.4 overs)	331
10 overs: 68-0	

R. A. Jadeja, R. Dhawan, J. J. Bumrah, U. T. Yadav and I. Sharma did not bat.

Hastings 10–1–61–3; Boland 10–0–58–0; M. R. Marsh 9.4–0–77–1; Faulkner 10–0–54–0; Lyon 8–0–58–0; Smith 2–0–20–0.

Umpires: R. A. Kettleborough and P. Wilson. Third umpire: J. D. Ward.
Referee: J. J. Crowe.

AUSTRALIA v INDIA

First Twenty20 International

At Adelaide, January 26, 2016 (floodlit). India won by 37 runs. Toss: Australia. Twenty20 international debuts: T. M. Head; J. J. Bumrah, H. H. Pandya.

The switch in formats played to India's strengths, and exposed Australia's lack of a settled line-up less than two months ahead of the World Twenty20. After just one 20-over match in 2015, Australia turned to a mix of regulars and Big Bash successes, and even a wild thing as a wild card: fast bowler Shaun Tait was recalled for his first international in nearly five years. But, young or old, pace or spin, no one could contain the rampant Kohli. His brisk unbeaten 90 – his highest in the format – was well supported by Raina, and ensured Australia needed yet another record chase on home soil. Their batsmen, suffocated by the spin of Ashwin and Jadeja, failed to balance the need for quick runs with occupying the crease, and lost wickets at a disruptive rate. Smith's dismissal, which some blamed on his interaction with the TV commentators while in the middle, sparked a collapse. Bumrah's quirky action troubled the batsmen, and his fellow debutant, Hardik Pandya, recovered from a woeful opening over – which lasted 11 deliveries, with five wides – to finish with two for 37.

Man of the Match: V. Kohli. *Attendance:* 44,745.

India

		B	*4/6*
1 R. G. Sharma *c 8 b 6*	31	20	4/1
2 S. Dhawan *c 7 b 6*	5	8	0
3 V. Kohli *not out*	90	55	9/2
4 S. K. Raina *b 8*	41	34	3/1
5 *†M. S. Dhoni *not out*	11	3	1/1
Lb 3, w 7	10		
6 overs: 54-2 (20 overs)	188-3		

1/40 2/41 3/175

6 Yuvraj Singh, 7 H. H. Pandya, 8 R. A. Jadeja, 9 R. Ashwin, 10 J. J. Bumrah and 11 A. Nehra did not bat.

Tait 4–11–45–0; Richardson 4–5–41–0; Faulkner 4–3–43–1; Watson 4–11–24–2; Boyce 3–3–23–0; Head 1–1–9–0.

Australia

		B	*4/6*
1 *A. J. Finch *lbw b 9*	44	33	4/2
2 D. A. Warner *c 3 b 10*	17	9	2/1
3 S. P. D. Smith *c 3 b 8*	21	14	3
4 T. M. Head *lbw b 8*	2	5	0
5 C. A. Lynn *c 6 b 7*	17	16	0/1
6 S. R. Watson *c 11 b 9*	12	10	0/1
7 †M. S. Wade *c 8 b 7*	5	7	0
8 J. P. Faulkner *b 10*	10	7	0/1
9 K. W. Richardson *b 11*	9	7	1
10 C. J. Boyce *c 7 b 10*	3	6	0
11 S. W. Tait *not out*	1	3	0
Lb 2, w 8	10		
6 overs: 56-1 (19.3 overs)	151		

1/47 2/89 3/89 4/93 5/110 6/124 7/129 8/143 9/149

Nehra 4–12–30–1; Ashwin 4–8–28–2; Bumrah 3.3–10–23–3; Jadeja 4–8–21–2; Pandya 3–5–37–2; Yuvraj Singh 1–1–10–0.

Umpires: S. D. Fry and J. D. Ward. Third umpire: P. Wilson.
Referee: J. J. Crowe.

AUSTRALIA v INDIA

Second Twenty20 International

At Melbourne, January 29, 2016 (floodlit). India won by 27 runs. Toss: Australia. Twenty20 international debuts: S. M. Boland, N. M. Lyon, A. J. Tye.

Albert Einstein defined insanity as doing the same thing repeatedly and expecting different results. But Australia's revolving door, which threw out a vastly different team for this second match, merely resulted in a script that followed the first: India – with no changes – scored prolifically to set a formidable target that proved far too much. Sharma and Dhawan zoomed along, before Kohli doled out further punishment, offering little relief for Australia's hastily assembled attack. They had made six changes, fielding three format debutants, and only one man batted in the same position as in the previous game. That was Finch, who alone overcame an economical and incisive all-round performance by India's bowlers, though he received some support from his latest opening partner, Shaun Marsh. But, when Finch hobbled off with a hamstring twinge after being run out, it sparked a collective limp, as India claimed the series. Dhoni's two stumpings took him to 140 in all internationals, beating Kumar Sangakkara's record.

Man of the Match: V. Kohli. *Attendance:* 58,787.

India

		B	4/6
1 R. G. Sharma *run out*	60	47	5/2
2 S. Dhawan *c 3 b 4*	42	32	3/2
3 V. Kohli *not out*	59	33	7/1
4 *†M. S. Dhoni *c 5 b 9*	14	9	2
5 S. K. Raina *not out*	0	0	0
Lb 7, w 1, nb 1	9		
6 overs: 50-0 (20 overs)	184-3		

1/97 2/143 3/181

6 Yuvraj Singh, 7 H. H. Pandya, 8 R. A. Jadeja, 9 R. Ashwin, 10 J. J. Bumrah and 11 A. Nehra did not bat.

Watson 3–8–17–0; Hastings 3–7–35–0; Boland 4–9–30–0; Faulkner 3–3–35–0; Tye 4–7–28–1; Lyon 1–0–15–0; Maxwell 2–1–17–1.

Australia

		B	4/6
1 *A. J. Finch *run out*	74	48	8/2
2 S. E. Marsh *c 7 b 9*	23	23	2
3 C. A. Lynn *c 4 b 7*	2	4	0
4 G. J. Maxwell *st 4 b 6*	1	2	0
5 S. R. Watson *c and b 8*	15	11	2
6 †M. S. Wade *not out*	16	15	0/1
7 J. P. Faulkner *st 4 b 8*	10	7	0/1
8 J. W. Hastings *b 10*	4	6	0
9 A. J. Tye *b 10*	4	4	1
B 1, lb 2, w 5	8		
6 overs: 62-0 (20 overs)	157-8		

1/94 2/99 3/101 4/121 5/124 6/137 7/152 8/157

10 S. M. Boland and 11 N. M. Lyon did not bat.

Nehra 4–6–34–0; Bumrah 4–9–37–2; Jadeja 4–5–32–2; Ashwin 4–11–27–1; Pandya 2–4–17–1; Yuvraj Singh 2–6–7–1.

Umpires: S. D. Fry and P. Wilson. Third umpire: J. D. Ward.
Referee: J. J. Crowe.

AUSTRALIA v INDIA

Third Twenty20 International

At Sydney, January 31, 2016 (floodlit). India won by seven wickets. Toss: Australia. Twenty20 international debuts: C. T. Bancroft, U. T. Khawaja.

Australia shuffled the pack again: this time the selectors dealt five changes, including two more debutants. One alteration was forced by Finch's hamstring, which allowed Watson to captain in a T20 for the first time, in what turned out to be his final international in Australia. He responded magnificently, cracking an unbeaten 124 – the second-highest in 20-over internationals, after Finch's 156 against England at Southampton in 2013 – in the lead-up to the IPL auction and the World Twenty20. At last, Australia had a serious total to defend. But India weren't fussed: Sharma, Dhawan and Kohli calmly reduced the target to 51 with five overs remaining, before Raina and Yuvraj Singh grabbed the reins. It was an exhilarating finale. India needed 17 off Andrew Tye's final over, but Yuvraj thwacked a four and a six, then Raina finished things off with a last-ball four. Raina was only there at the death because of a missed stumping by newcomer Cameron Bancroft off the impressive leg-spin of Boyce; it was Raina's second ball, and he celebrated by hoisting the next for six. The

HIGHEST SCORES IN DEFEAT IN TWENTY20 CRICKET

151*	C. H. Gayle	Somerset v Kent at Taunton	2015
141*	C. L. White	Somerset v Worcestershire at Worcester	2006
129	D. T. Christian	Middlesex v Kent at Canterbury	2014
124*	**S. R. Watson**	**Australia v India at Sydney**	**2015-16**
123*	D. A. Warner	New South Wales v Royal Challengers Bangalore at Bangalore	2011-12
122*	C. H. Gayle	Jamaica v Guyana at Gros Islet	2012-13
122	**Babar Hayat**	**Hong Kong v Oman at Fatullah**	**2015-16**
122	**Sabbir Rahman**	**Rajshahi Kings v Barisal Bulls at Mirpur**	**2016-17**
120*	**D. A. Miller**	**Knights v Titans at Benoni**	**2016-17**
119	F. du Plessis	South Africa v West Indies at Johannesburg	2014-15
118	**S. P. Wakaskar**	**Railways v Delhi at Vadodara**	**2015-16**

recently retired Brad Haddin was critical of the experiment with part-timer Bancroft: "It's a specialist position, the same as a spinner or an opening bowler, so you pick your best wicketkeeper." It highlighted the difference between the sides: a stable India, in form and sure of individual roles, completing a whitewash over a mutable Australia, desperately seeking a winning formula.

Man of the Match: S. R. Watson. *Attendance:* 34,527.

Man of the Series: V. Kohli.

Australia

		B	*4/6*
1 U. T. Khawaja *c 6 b 11*	14	6	2
2 *S. R. Watson *not out*	124	71	10/6
3 S. E. Marsh *b 9*	9	12	1
4 G. J. Maxwell *c 4 b 5*	3	5	0
5 T. M. Head *b 8*	26	19	1/1
6 C. A. Lynn *c 8 b 10*	13	9	2
7 †C. T. Bancroft *not out*	0	0	0
Lb 2, w 4, nb 2	8		
6 overs: 57-1 (20 overs)	197-5		

1/16 2/69 3/75 4/168 5/193

8 A. J. Tye, 9 C. J. Boyce, 10 S. M. Boland and 11 S. W. Tait did not bat.

Nehra 4–9–32–1; Bumrah 4–7–43–1; Ashwin 4–6–36–1; Jadeja 4–7–41–1; Yuvraj Singh 2–3–19–1; Pandya 2–2–24–0.

India

		B	*4/6*
1 R. G. Sharma *c 2 b 9*	52	38	5/1
2 S. Dhawan *c 7 b 2*	26	9	4/1
3 V. Kohli *b 9*	50	36	2/1
4 S. K. Raina *not out*	49	25	6/1
5 Yuvraj Singh *not out*	15	12	1/1
B 1, w 7	8		
6 overs: 74-1 (20 overs)	200-3		

1/46 2/124 3/147

6 *†M. S. Dhoni, 7 H. H. Pandya, 8 R. A. Jadeja, 9 R. Ashwin, 10 J. J. Bumrah and 11 A. Nehra did not bat.

Tait 4–6–46–0; Boland 3–3–34–0; Watson 4–7–30–1; Tye 4–7–51–0; Boyce 4–10–28–2; Maxwell 1–1–10–0.

Umpires: S. D. Fry and J. D. Ward. Third umpire: P. Wilson.
Referee: J. J. Crowe.

AUSTRALIA v SOUTH AFRICA IN 2016-17

NEIL MANTHORP

Test matches (3): Australia 1, South Africa 2

South Africa won their third successive Test series in Australia, something they had never managed in their eight visits before 2008-09. They did so by producing some high-quality cricket in the first two matches, and wrapped things up by the time they had to play their first pink-ball Test, at Adelaide. It was unfortunate that, by then, the headlines focused on their captain, Faf du Plessis, spotted on TV applying saliva to the ball while sucking a sweet – technically, a breach of the Laws.

The incident was inevitably dubbed "Mintgate". In the circumstances, the hundred du Plessis made at Adelaide was a triumph, even though it couldn't prevent defeat. But to win the series without A. B. de Villiers, who missed the whole tour after an operation on his troublesome left elbow, and Dale Steyn, who broke his shoulder early in the First Test, was a remarkable effort.

South Africa were helped by a change in the scheduling. Australia usually start their home summers in Brisbane, where they have a fine record. But the Gabba had already been given a day/night match against Pakistan later in the season, so the series began in Perth. A superb second-innings effort, based on centuries from Dean Elgar and J-P. Duminy, consigned Australia to a shock defeat. Quinton de Kock then scored a hundred in a thumping victory at Hobart. The lone cloud on the batting horizon was the slump of Hashim Amla, who managed only 98 runs in five innings.

For the bowlers, the patient Kyle Abbott filled the gap left by Steyn, taking 13 wickets in the last two Tests, while Kagiso Rabada and Vernon Philander – back to his bouncy best – shared 27. The day/night Test in Adelaide was a rousing success, and convinced the previously sceptical South Africans – despite their defeat – that here was an experiment destined not just to survive, but thrive.

It was a sobering time for Australia, who called on 19 different players, including five debutants. One of them, 20-year-old Matt Renshaw, was born in England – which some locals thought even more embarrassing than being bowled out for 85 on the opening day at Hobart. Only Usman Khawaja managed a century, although an improved all-round performance at Adelaide, where the impressive new-ball pairing of Josh Hazlewood and Mitchell Starc claimed six wickets apiece, quietened the critics.

But most of the flak, after the Second Test at least, was aimed at du Plessis. When the footage first emerged, South Africa dismissed suggestions of ball-tampering as "laughable" and "a complete joke". The subsequent official charge by the ICC drew a closing of ranks. Four days after the Hobart match, Amla fronted a press conference at the MCG, backed up by the entire 30-man touring party in a PR exercise that backfired badly. Amla stumbled from one excuse to another, first claiming not to know anything about a practice which

Ryan Pierse, Getty Images

You beauty! Faf du Plessis shows his appreciation of Kagiso Rabada, one of his rampant seamers.

had been commonplace for years, then comparing sucking mints on the field to eating "nuts and biltong". He even asked whether players should be required to clean their teeth during breaks in play. He offered no explanation for why du Plessis had been filmed placing two fingers deep inside his mouth and then rubbing them on the ball: "Come on guys, we have to be realistic. He has done nothing wrong. It's ridiculous."

During the subsequent game against Victoria, the players openly toyed with jelly sweets and other confectionery, and conducted mock searches of each others' mouths. They may have thought it playful, but for the media it was a red rag. It didn't help when an Australian television news reporter was shoved out of the way by South African security officer, Zunaid Wadee, as the team arrived at Adelaide airport. Du Plessis, meanwhile, opened his mouth in front of the waiting snappers to reveal a large mint on his tongue. Whatever the tourists thought about the rights and wrongs of the regulations, they were showing scant respect for the officials charged with upholding them. Referee Andy Pycroft finally convened a disciplinary hearing, just under 48 hours before start of the pink-ball Test. Du Plessis was represented by a QC flown in from Melbourne, and by CSA's own lawyer, David Becker, via a video link. But he largely led his own defence, suggesting initially he did not know he was guilty of any wrongdoing, before changing his line to "everyone does it".

But he was found guilty, and fined his entire match fee, as well as three demerit points, the strongest sanction not to involve a suspension. Even so, CSA chief executive Haroon Lorgat appeared at the pre-match press conference to defend his captain, and said he would ask the ICC to clarify the "many grey areas" surrounding ball-shining, including the "academic and scientific debate".

David Richardson, the ICC chief executive, flew to Adelaide to explain the official stance. He admitted other teams used the tactic of shining the ball with artificial substances, and that it was "difficult to police", but pointed out that du Plessis had been caught in "obvious contravention of a clearly stated law of the game". Du Plessis contested the verdict, insisting: "I firmly believe I have done nothing wrong." The appeal was heard in Dubai shortly after the tour, and the punishment upheld by Michael Beloff QC, chairman of the ICC's Code of Conduct Commission. By then, the cricket had been almost forgotten.

SOUTH AFRICAN TOURING PARTY

*F. du Plessis, K. J. Abbott, H. M. Amla, T. Bavuma, S. C. Cook, Q. de Kock, J-P. Duminy, D. Elgar, K. A. Maharaj, M. Morkel, V. D. Philander, D. Pretorius, K. Rabada, R. R. Rossouw, T. Shamsi, D. W. Steyn, D. J. Vilas. *Coach:* R. C. Domingo.

Steyn broke his shoulder while bowling in the First Test, and was replaced by Pretorius.

TEST MATCH AVERAGES

AUSTRALIA – BATTING AND FIELDING

	T	*I*	*NO*	*R*	*HS*	*100*	*50*	*Avge*	*Ct/St*
†U. T. Khawaja	3	6	0	314	145	1	2	52.33	2
S. P. D. Smith	3	6	1	212	59	0	1	42.40	5
†D. A. Warner	3	6	0	236	97	0	1	39.33	1
P. M. Nevill	2	4	1	92	60*	0	1	30.66	7
†J. R. Hazlewood	3	5	2	58	29	0	0	19.33	0
†M. A. Starc	3	5	0	70	53	0	1	14.00	1
A. C. Voges	2	4	0	30	27	0	0	7.50	2
N. M. Lyon	3	5	0	27	13	0	0	5.40	1

Played in one Test: J. M. Bird 6; J. A. Burns 1, 0; C. J. Ferguson 3, 1; P. S. P. Handscomb 54, 1* (1 ct); †N. J. Maddinson 0; M. R. Marsh 0, 26 (1 ct); †S. E. Marsh 63, 15 (3 ct); J. M. Mennie 10, 0; †M. T. Renshaw 10, 34* (1 ct); P. M. Siddle 18*, 13; †M. S. Wade 4 (6 ct, 1 st).

BOWLING

	Style	*O*	*M*	*R*	*W*	*BB*	*5I*	*Avge*
J. R. Hazlewood	RFM	126.5	36	375	17	6-89	1	22.05
M. A. Starc	LF	120	21	422	14	4-71	0	30.14
P. M. Siddle	RFM	38	12	98	3	2-62	0	32.66
J. M. Bird	RFM	36	6	111	3	2-57	0	37.00
N. M. Lyon	OB	97	11	346	6	3-60	0	57.66

Also bowled: M. R. Marsh (RFM) 32–5–100–2; J. M. Mennie (RFM) 28–5–85–1; S. P. D. Smith (LBG) 2.1–0–8–1; A. C. Voges (SLA) 5–1–8–0; D. A. Warner (LBG) 1–0–5–0.

SOUTH AFRICA – BATTING AND FIELDING

	T	*I*	*NO*	*R*	*HS*	*100*	*50*	*Avge*	*Ct*
†Q. de Kock	3	5	0	281	104	1	2	56.20	11
F. du Plessis	3	5	1	206	118*	1	0	51.50	3
†J-P. Duminy	3	5	0	184	141	1	0	36.80	4
S. C. Cook	3	5	0	179	104	1	0	35.80	0
T. Bavuma	3	5	0	162	74	0	2	32.40	0
†D. Elgar	3	5	0	161	127	1	0	32.20	5
K. A. Maharaj	2	3	1	58	41*	0	0	29.00	0
V. D. Philander	3	5	0	136	73	0	1	27.20	1
H. M. Amla	3	5	0	98	47	0	0	19.60	5
†K. Rabada	3	4	2	24	11*	0	0	12.00	2
K. J. Abbott	2	3	0	20	17	0	0	6.66	0

Played in one Test: T. Shamsi 18*, 0*; D. W. Steyn 4.

BOWLING

	Style	*O*	*M*	*R*	*W*	*BB*	*5I*	*Avge*
K. J. Abbott	RFM	74.5	19	193	13	6-77	1	14.84
K. Rabada	RF	108.1	20	336	15	5-92	1	22.40
V. D. Philander	RFM	103.3	27	283	12	5-21	1	23.58
K. A. Maharaj	SLA	65.3	17	162	4	3-56	0	40.50

Also bowled: T. Bavuma (RM) 8–1–30–1; S. C. Cook (RM) 2–0–16–0; J-P. Duminy (OB) 24–1–84–1; D. Elgar (SLA) 2–0–11–0; T. Shamsi (SLC) 43.5–8–150–2; D. W. Steyn (RF) 12.4–3–51–1.

At Adelaide, October 22–23, 2016 (day/night). **Drawn.** ‡**South Africans 415** (89.5 overs) (H. M. Amla 51, J-P. Duminy 97, Q. de Kock 122) **and 181-5** (44 overs) (R. R. Rossouw 77); **Cricket Australia XI 103** (30.4 overs) (M. W. Short 57). *The South Africans chose from 16 players in this pink-ball warm-up, and the local team from 12. The tourists dominated, scoring at 4.6 an over on the first day, then skittling their inexperienced opponents on the second. J-P. Duminy just missed a century, but Quinton de Kock sprinted to 122 from 103 balls before retiring. He did not keep wicket next day: Harry Nielsen, the 21-year-old son of former Australian coach Tim, stood in and took four catches as the CA XI plummeted to 39-7. Matthew Short, the captain, saved some embarrassment – but no one else reached double figures as all five bowlers used took two wickets apiece.*

At Adelaide (Glenelg), October 27–28, 2016. **Drawn.** ‡**South Africans 489** (89.5 overs) (D. Elgar 117, F. du Plessis 102, Q. de Kock 99); **South Australia XI 435-8** (80.2 overs) (S. J. Raphael 91, T. P. Ludeman 167, J. L. Winter 63; K. A. Maharaj 3-59). *Both sides chose from 15 players. The South Africans again batted well, Dean Elgar and Faf du Plessis putting on 179. Both retired after reaching their centuries, then de Kock just missed another. This time the opposition matched them: skipper Sam Raphael opened with 91, before wicketkeeper Tim Ludeman caned the bowling, hitting eight sixes as well as 20 fours. In a left-arm spinners' shoot-out, Keshav Maharaj's orthodox stuff proved more effective than Tabraiz Shamsi's chinamen (11–2–87–0).*

AUSTRALIA v SOUTH AFRICA

First Test Match

At Perth, November 3–7, 2016. South Africa won by 177 runs. Toss: South Africa. Test debut: K. A. Maharaj.

South Africa emerged from various points of apparent hopelessness with a famous victory, their third in a row at the WACA. Australia, on the other hand, lost the opening Test of a home summer for the first time since November 1988, when West Indies won in Brisbane.

After choosing to bat, South Africa had crashed to 32 for four before recovering somewhat to 242. That still looked below par, especially once Australia galloped to 158 without loss an hour into the second day. But a bowling (and fielding) fightback brought about a stunning collapse: in 35 overs, all ten went down for 86. From then on, South Africa were not just in the contest – they dominated it. Perhaps the most extraordinary detail was that nine of the wickets fell after Steyn – who had dismissed Warner for 97 – had left the field (and the tour) with a broken bone in his shoulder.

But the game was sealed by Elgar and Duminy, who both made their fifth Test century during a third-wicket stand of 250, and were not separated until the 95th over of South Africa's second innings. De Kock – especially brutal on Lyon – and Philander added lively fifties, then the debutant Keshav Maharaj flogged three sixes. With a lead of 538, du Plessis called a halt. Australia needed to bat at least 140 overs against an attack containing just two frontline seamers and a tyro spinner. They did not come close.

The end could hardly have been more different from the beginning. Starc had removed Cook in the game's first over, then Hazlewood and Siddle found another three edges in quick succession. Du Plessis briefly fought back, and Bavuma and de Kock put on 71 before Shaun Marsh's outrageous short-leg catch accounted for Bavuma. But de Kock counter-attacked with glorious disregard for the situation, as the last five wickets all but tripled the score.

South Africa's recovery gave them a glimmer. But that faded as Warner got stuck in, sprinting to 73 out of 105 by the close. He and Shaun Marsh extended their stand next morning, before Warner – who had converted all 16 of his previous Test nineties into hundreds – sent an edge flying to Amla in the slips.

Then everything changed. After Steyn moped off, clutching his shoulder following a seemingly routine delivery, Khawaja was yorked by Rabada, and Smith given out lbw fourth ball by Aleem Dar, despite charging two metres down the track. Smith made no attempt to hide his disgust, and immediately reviewed, but the ball-tracker predicted a kiss on leg stump – either a dubious decision or a brilliant one. Regardless, it was a distinguished maiden Test wicket for slow left-armer Maharaj. Philander finally trapped Shaun Marsh for a gravelly 63, and brother Mitchell followed in his next over. Philander found some testing reverse swing, while Maharaj unveiled impressive control and flight. After losing six wickets in the session, Australia were all out at tea on the second day, just two ahead.

South Africa soon lost Cook, flicking to short midwicket, and Amla, cleaned up by a wonderful off-cutter from Hazlewood. But the damage was repaired in contrasting fashion by the third-wicket pair. Elgar, the workman, was content occasionally to lean on his shovel and watch Duminy, the craftsman, caress cover-drives. Elgar relied on clips and nudges against the quicks, but more expansive options against Lyon, who finished with none for 146; only Shane Warne and (in his only Test) Bryce McGain had endured worse wicketless figures for Australia.

After the lead swelled past 500, Cook and Bavuma volunteered their modest part-time seamers to aid the three-man attack, but it was Bavuma the fielder who manufactured the first breakthrough. Warner had pushed Rabada into the covers and set off for a single, but the diminutive Bavuma was already at full speed as the batsmen set off. Seven paces later he picked the ball up and – in mid-air, his feet higher than his head – threw the stumps down. It took less than two seconds, too quick for anyone to register what had happened. There were no celebrations: only when his team-mates – and the shell-shocked Warner – saw the big screen did it begin to sink in. It was fielding genius.

Shaun Marsh edged a Rabada snorter to slip four balls later, but South Africa then had to wait more than 30 overs, before Smith and Voges – after a high-class working-over from Rabada – edged behind. With Khawaja and Nevill standing firm, Australia had faint hopes of a draw. As lunch on the final day hove into view, and with Rabada and Philander approaching exhaustion but still required for the second new ball, du Plessis turned to Bavuma's extremely gentle medium-pacers for the 74th over. His first delivery was innocuous but straight – until it landed on a crack and deviated devilishly to trap Khawaja, on 84, in front: plumb, but also a no-ball.

However, South Africa were not to be denied. Three overs later, Duminy whipped a quicker one past Khawaja's defence. And Rabada completed a magnificent five-for with another lbw against Starc. Even so, it was still hard going for the exhausted bowlers, and du Plessis delayed taking the new ball until the 92nd over. Philander struck immediately – but Nevill and Hazlewood then put on 65, before Bavuma finally managed his moment of bowling glory, a leading edge popping up to cover. Australia's first defeat in 19 home Tests was completed before a delayed tea, when Lyon became the fifth leg-before victim of the innings.

Man of the Match: K. Rabada.

Close of play: first day, Australia 105-0 (Warner 73, S. E. Marsh 29); second day, South Africa 104-2 (Elgar 46, Duminy 34); third day, South Africa 390-6 (de Kock 16, Philander 23); fourth day, Australia 169-4 (Khawaja 58, M. R. Marsh 15).

South Africa

S. C. Cook c M. R. Marsh b Starc	0	– c S. E. Marsh b Siddle	12
D. Elgar c Nevill b Hazlewood	12	– c Starc b Hazlewood	127
H. M. Amla c Smith b Hazlewood	0	– b Hazlewood	1
J-P. Duminy c Nevill b Siddle	11	– c Nevill b Siddle	141
*F. du Plessis c Voges b Starc	37	– c Nevill b Starc	32
T. Bavuma c S. E. Marsh b Lyon	51	– c Khawaja b M. R. Marsh	8
†Q. de Kock c S. E. Marsh b Hazlewood	84	– c Voges b M. R. Marsh	64
V. D. Philander b Starc	10	– b Smith	73
K. A. Maharaj c Warner b Lyon	16	– not out	41
K. Rabada not out	11		
D. W. Steyn b Starc	4		
B 4, w 2	6	B 10, lb 13, w 17, nb 1	41
1/0 (1) 2/5 (3) 3/20 (2) 4/32 (4) 5/81 (5) 6/152 (6) 7/175 (8) 8/223 (9) 9/227 (7) 10/242 (11) (63.4 overs)	242	1/35 (1) 2/45 (3) 3/295 (4) 4/324 (2) 5/346 (6) 6/352 (5) 7/468 (7) 8/540 (8) (8 wkts dec, 160.1 overs)	540

Starc 18.4–2–71–4; Hazlewood 17–2–70–3; Siddle 12–3–36–1; M. R. Marsh 6–1–23–0; Lyon 10–1–38–2. *Second innings*—Starc 31–8–114–1; Hazlewood 37–11–107–2; Siddle 26–9–62–2; M. R. Marsh 26–4–77–2; Lyon 34–3–146–0; Voges 5–1–8–0; Smith 1.1–0–3–1.

Australia

D. A. Warner c Amla b Steyn	97	– (2) run out	35
S. E. Marsh lbw b Philander	63	– (1) c du Plessis b Rabada	15
U. T. Khawaja b Rabada	4	– lbw b Duminy	97
*S. P. D. Smith lbw b Maharaj	0	– c de Kock b Rabada	34
A. C. Voges c and b Rabada	27	– c de Kock b Rabada	1
M. R. Marsh lbw b Philander	0	– lbw b Rabada	26
†P. M. Nevill c Amla b Maharaj	23	– not out	60
M. A. Starc c du Plessis b Maharaj	0	– lbw b Rabada	13
P. M. Siddle not out	18	– lbw b Philander	13
J. R. Hazlewood c Duminy b Philander	4	– c Elgar b Bavuma	29
N. M. Lyon c Elgar b Philander	0	– lbw b Maharaj	8
Lb 3, nb 5	8	B 13, lb 11, w 4, nb 2	30
1/158 (1) 2/167 (3) 3/168 (4) 4/181 (2) 5/181 (6) 6/202 (5) 7/203 (8) 8/232 (7) 9/243 (10) 10/244 (11) (70.2 overs)	244	1/52 (2) 2/52 (1) 3/144 (4) 4/146 (5) 5/196 (6) 6/246 (3) 7/262 (8) 8/280 (9) 9/345 (10) 10/361 (11) (119.1 overs)	361

Steyn 12.4–3–51–1; Philander 19.2–2–56–4; Rabada 20–1–78–2; Maharaj 18.2–5–56–3. *Second innings*—Rabada 31–6–92–5; Philander 22–7–55–1; Duminy 17–1–51–1; Maharaj 40.1–10–94–1; Cook 2–0–16–0; Bavuma 7–1–29–1.

Umpires: Aleem Dar and N. J. Llong. Third umpire: R. A. Kettleborough.
Referee: A. J. Pycroft.

AUSTRALIA v SOUTH AFRICA

Second Test Match

At Hobart, November 12–15, 2016. South Africa won by an innings and 80 runs. Toss: South Africa. Test debuts: C. J. Ferguson, J. M. Mennie.

South Africa had previously conquered Australia in 22 Tests, but never quite like this – not even during the 4–0 whitewash at home in 1969-70. An innings win, their first in Australia, gave them a third successive series victory there, with a match to spare. By contrast, it was Australia's fifth defeat in a row, following the 3–0 whitewash in Sri Lanka. It was almost enough to overshadow a strange row about du Plessis's mint (see page 850).

The forecast for the first three days had varied between gloomy and cyclonic, but the cold front did not arrive as early as expected, and the match started under thunderous skies. To make things even more interesting, the pitch was generously grassed. Du Plessis was a relieved man when he won the toss: Australia were dismissed twice in just 93 overs – the equivalent of little more than a day.

Warner was out in the first over, Burns in the second, and Khawaja and Voges to successive balls in the ninth. Australia were 43 for six at lunch, and all out for 85 not long after, with Smith – who stormed off, shaking his head – unbeaten on 48. Of the rest, only Joe Mennie, the Victoria fast bowler, and with Callum Ferguson one of two new caps, made it into double figures. It was their lowest home total in 32 years.

In the batsmen's defence, Philander had rarely found more helpful conditions for his relentlessly questioning seam bowling, while Abbott, Dale Steyn's replacement, was not far behind. Everybody was either caught in the cordon, lbw or bowled – apart from Ferguson, run out by a direct hit from backward point by the reserve wicketkeeper, Dane Vilas, who had been on the field for only three balls (Philander had gone off following a collision as Smith scampered a leg-bye). Ferguson's departure dismayed his watching family, including his brother Lachlan, who had flown in from England – but trying to steal a second run at 17 for four was not a great decision. Philander returned to finish with five for 21.

Cook and Elgar then displayed solid defensive techniques, before Starc claimed three wickets in ten balls to burst open the top order. Hazlewood pinned du Plessis to make it 76 for four, raising hopes that Australia might reprise South Africa's great escape from Perth. But they were thwarted by Bavuma and de Kock, who kept things simple – ignoring the drive against anything but half-volleys, and leaving as many deliveries as they could. By the end of the first day they had taken their team 86 in front, and had a further 24 hours to plan, as rain washed out the second.

The reflection seemed to work. Bavuma was content to thwart and frustrate, while the elegant de Kock went for calculated risks, driving the seamers through the off side and lofting Lyon down the ground. After passing 50 for the fifth Test innings in a row, he reached his second century just before lunch, but was then beaten by a nip-backer from Hazlewood. After the interval, Bavuma's resistance ended with a leading edge to cover – a maiden scalp for the persevering Mennie – but Philander stretched the lead to 241.

Again Australia lost a wicket in the first over, Burns feathering a leg-side glance to de Kock. Warner's attempted flick off Abbott ricocheted off hip and elbow into the stumps, but at 121 for two by the close, with Khawaja and Smith comfortable, Australia seemed set to make South Africa work hard. Instead it was all over by lunch, their seamers producing as controlled a session of fast bowling as anyone could remember. So accurate was Philander that his first 30 deliveries were dots; it took Smith 40 minutes to score. And the wicket of Khawaja for 64, caught behind off Abbott, triggered one of Australia's more spectacular collapses, as eight wickets dominoed for 32 in 19 overs.

In a tale familiar to watchers of recent Ashes series in England, Australia's middle order failed to cope with lateral movement. Voges and Ferguson best illustrated the shattered confidence with half-hearted leaves against short deliveries which lobbed from bat or glove into the slips. Neither played in the next Test: Ferguson was dropped after one match, while the 37-year-old Voges (who might have been left out anyway, despite a Test average of 61) was concussed in a Sheffield Shield game. As the rout neared completion, Rabada took three wickets in seven balls, the last of them Smith, beaten for pace after batting two and a half hours. But it was Abbott who rounded off victory with the final two wickets to finish with nine all told, and the match award. At the press conference, Smith lamented: "I'm embarrassed to be sitting here, to be honest with you."

Man of the Match: K. J. Abbott.

Close of play: first day, South Africa 171-5 (Bavuma 38, de Kock 28); second day, no play; third day, Australia 121-2 (Khawaja 56, Smith 18).

Australia

D. A. Warner c de Kock b Philander	1	– (2) b Abbott	45
J. A. Burns lbw b Abbott	1	– (1) c de Kock b Abbott	0
U. T. Khawaja c Amla b Philander	4	– c de Kock b Abbott	64
*S. P. D. Smith not out	48	– c de Kock b Rabada	31
A. C. Voges c de Kock b Philander	0	– c Duminy b Abbott	2
C. J. Ferguson run out	3	– c Elgar b Rabada	1
†P. M. Nevill lbw b Rabada	3	– c Duminy b Rabada	6
J. M. Mennie b Philander	10	– lbw b Rabada	0
M. A. Starc c Duminy b Abbott	4	– c de Kock b Abbott	0
J. R. Hazlewood c Amla b Abbott	8	– not out	6
N. M. Lyon c de Kock b Philander	2	– c Philander b Abbott	4
Lb 1	1	Lb 1, nb 1	2
1/2 (1) 2/2 (2) 3/8 (3) (32.5 overs)	85	1/0 (1) 2/79 (2) (60.1 overs)	161
4/8 (5) 5/17 (6) 6/31 (7)		3/129 (3) 4/135 (5)	
7/59 (8) 8/66 (9) 9/76 (10) 10/85 (11)		5/140 (6) 6/150 (7) 7/150 (8)	
		8/151 (4) 9/151 (9) 10/161 (11)	

Philander 10.1–5–21–5; Abbott 12.4–3–41–3; Rabada 6–0–20–1; Maharaj 4–2–2–0. *Second innings*—Abbott 23.1–3–77–6; Philander 16–6–31–0; Duminy 1–0–8–0; Rabada 17–5–34–4; Maharaj 3–0–10–0.

South Africa

S. C. Cook c Nevill b Starc	23	K. A. Maharaj b Hazlewood	1
D. Elgar lbw b Starc	17	K. J. Abbott lbw b Hazlewood	3
H. M. Amla c Nevill b Hazlewood	47	K. Rabada not out	5
J-P. Duminy c Smith b Starc	1	B 3, lb 8, nb 1	12
*F. du Plessis lbw b Hazlewood	7		
T. Bavuma c Lyon b Mennie	74	1/43 (2) 2/44 (1) 3/46 (4) (100.5 overs)	326
†Q. de Kock b Hazlewood	104	4/76 (5) 5/132 (3) 6/276 (7)	
V. D. Philander c Nevill b Hazlewood	32	7/292 (6) 8/293 (9) 9/297 (10) 10/326 (8)	

Starc 24–1–79–3; Hazlewood 30.5–10–89–6; Mennie 28–5–85–1; Lyon 17–2–57–0; Smith 1–0–5–0.

Umpires: Aleem Dar and R. A. Kettleborough. Third umpire: N. J. Llong.
Referee: A. J. Pycroft.

At Melbourne, November 19, 2016 (day/night). **Victoria XI won by 53 runs. Victoria XI 258** (45.2 overs) (S. E. Gotch 53, M. W. Short 52, E. P. Gulbis 53; K. Rabada 3-37, T. Shamsi 4-72); ‡**South Africans 205-4** (50 overs) (H. M. Amla 81*). *The South Africans chose from 15 players, and Victoria from 12. A late burst from Evan Gulbis – 53 from 28 balls – propelled the home side to 258. Kagiso Rabada bowled only four overs, but Morne Morkel sent down nine in an unavailing bid to prove his fitness ahead of the Third Test. In a reversal of the previous warm-up game, Shamsi was now more effective, and claimed Maharaj's place for the pink-ball Test. The South African batsmen put practice under lights ahead of winning the match: Elgar retired after a leisurely 60-ball 40, and no one bettered Amla's strike-rate of 71.*

AUSTRALIA v SOUTH AFRICA

Third Test Match

At Adelaide, November 24–27, 2016 (day/night). Australia won by seven wickets. Toss: South Africa. Test debuts: P. S. P. Handscomb, N. J. Maddinson, M. T. Renshaw; T. Shamsi.

Desperate to avoid a sixth successive defeat, Australia's selectors handed out three more Baggy Greens, all to batsmen, bringing the number of players used in the series to 19, an Australian record for a three-match rubber. Against the odds – and to the barely disguised relief of Smith and his embattled employers, not to mention the fans – the new-look team won the pink-ball Test just as Adelaide's floodlights started to kick in on the fourth day.

Two of the debutants were at the crease when the winning runs were scored, the first such occurrence since September 1880 – in the first Test played in England – when Frank Penn and W. G. Grace finished the job against Australia at The Oval. In truth, the 20-year-old Yorkshire-born opener Matt Renshaw and Peter Handscomb played only minor roles. The impressive new-ball pair of Starc and Hazlewood shared a dozen wickets, while Khawaja responded to being pushed up to open with Australia's only hundred of the series.

They rarely ceded control once Starc removed Elgar in the seventh over, although there was a bravura century from du Plessis, who entered at 44 for three. He was accompanied to the crease by a cacophony of boos, following the Mintgate saga, but responded superbly on the ground where he had made a similarly phlegmatic debut four years earlier.

Hazlewood led a vastly improved bowling performance, in which the recalled Bird played the role of back-up seamer with conspicuous success. The best stand du Plessis was able to conjure was 51 with Cook, who on four had walked to within a yard of the boundary before the Starc delivery which had him lbw was judged a no-ball. Du Plessis did add 39 unlikely runs for the last wicket with the debutant Tabraiz Shamsi, before a cheeky late declaration: du Plessis had overheard the umpire telling Warner, who had been off the field, that he would not be able to bat until he had been back on for a few more minutes. It unsettled the Australians, who had to send Khawaja in first, but he and the debutant Renshaw survived 12 overs that night, as the pink ball stubbornly refused to move off the straight.

Khawaja's vigil would last 15 minutes short of eight hours spread across the first three days, the only obvious blemish coming when he ran out his captain, Smith, for a gritty 59. Handscomb batted deep in his crease, giving the quick bowlers a generous look at the stumps – then picked them off either side of the wicket when they excitedly bowled too full or too straight. His half-century was organised and assured.

Nic Maddinson, the third debutant, bagged a 12-ball duck, Wade (who had been recalled to keep wicket in place of Peter Nevill) edged behind, and finally Khawaja was trapped by Philander. But Starc knuckled down for two hours, as the lead grew from inconsequential to imposing. When Bird fell shortly after the left-arm unorthodox spinner Shamsi had claimed his maiden Test wicket, Australia were 124 in front.

Cook has few pretensions to elegance or grace, but he is a fighter, and he showed real determination. Wickets kept falling at the other end, however, and he was eventually last out, after six hours and 13 minutes. As in the first innings, meaningful partnerships were hard to come by, at least once Amla departed, having shown signs of a return to form in scoring 45. Australia's task was helped by Lyon, who had been punished in the first two Tests to the tune of two for 241: now he took three wickets, deceiving Duminy, then snaring Bavuma – caught on the sweep – and Abbott in six balls shortly before the end of the third day.

South Africa were effectively 70 for six when the fourth began. Cook was still there, but hopes that de Kock could continue his run of form were dashed when he missed a straight one in the fifth over. The tail cobbled together 49 more, with Cook just having time to reach his second Test hundred, before Starc penetrated his defences.

Australia needed only 127 to complete their second comfortable victory in two pink-ball Tests at Adelaide, and Warner ensured there would be no slip-ups, hurrying to 47 before Bavuma ran him out for the second time in the series. Khawaja was lbw on review to Shamsi's chinaman for a second-ball duck, but the fresh-faced Renshaw stoically blocked an unbeaten 34 from 137 balls. He ignored the crowd's calls to end the match with a flourish, leaving that to Handscomb's lazy flick through midwicket.

Man of the Match: U. T. Khawaja. *Man of the Series:* V. D. Philander.

Close of play: first day, Australia 14-0 (Khawaja 3, Renshaw 8); second day, Australia 307-6 (Khawaja 138, Starc 16); third day, South Africa 194-6 (Cook 81, de Kock 0).

South Africa

S. C. Cook c Smith b Starc	40	– b Starc	104
D. Elgar c Khawaja b Starc	5	– c Smith b Starc	0
H. M. Amla c Renshaw b Hazlewood	5	– c Wade b Hazlewood	45
J-P. Duminy c Wade b Hazlewood	5	– b Lyon	26
*F. du Plessis not out	118	– c Handscomb b Starc	12
T. Bavuma c Wade b Bird	8	– c Smith b Lyon	21
†Q. de Kock c Wade b Hazlewood	24	– (8) lbw b Bird	5
V. D. Philander c Wade b Hazlewood	4	– (9) lbw b Starc	17
K. J. Abbott lbw b Bird	17	– (7) lbw b Lyon	0
K. Rabada st Wade b Lyon	1	– c Wade b Hazlewood	7
T. Shamsi not out	18	– not out	0
B 3, lb 8, w 2, nb 1	14	Lb 10, nb 3	13
1/12 (2) 2/36 (3) 3/44 (4) (9 wkts dec, 76 overs) 4/95 (1) 5/117 (6) 6/149 (7) 7/161 (8) 8/215 (9) 9/220 (10)	259	1/1 (2) 2/82 (3) (85.2 overs) 3/131 (4) 4/154 (5) 5/190 (6) 6/194 (7) 7/201 (8) 8/235 (9) 9/250 (10) 10/250 (1)	250

Starc 23–5–78–2; Hazlewood 22–5–68–4; Bird 16–3–57–2; Lyon 15–1–45–1. *Second innings*—Starc 23.2–5–80–4; Hazlewood 20–8–41–2; Bird 20–3–54–1; Lyon 21–4–60–3; Warner 1–0–5–0.

Australia

U. T. Khawaja lbw b Philander	145	– (3) lbw b Shamsi	0
M. T. Renshaw c Elgar b Abbott	10	– (1) not out	34
D. A. Warner c Elgar b Abbott	11	– (2) run out	47
*S. P. D. Smith run out	59	– c de Kock b Abbott	40
P. S. P. Handscomb b Abbott	54	– not out	1
N. J. Maddinson b Rabada	0		
†M. S. Wade c de Kock b Philander	4		
M. A. Starc c and b Rabada	53		
J. R. Hazlewood not out	11		
N. M. Lyon c Amla b Shamsi	13		
J. M. Bird c du Plessis b Rabada	6		
B 3, lb 9, w 2, nb 3	17	Lb 4, nb 1	5
1/19 (2) 2/37 (3) 3/174 (4) (121.1 overs) 4/273 (5) 5/277 (6) 6/283 (7) 7/327 (1) 8/357 (8) 9/370 (10) 10/383 (11)	383	1/64 (2) (3 wkts, 40.5 overs) 2/64 (3) 3/125 (4)	127

Philander 29–5–100–2; Abbott 29–11–49–3; Rabada 25.1–4–84–3; Shamsi 29–4–101–1; Duminy 6–0–25–0; Elgar 2–0–11–0; Bavuma 1–0–1–0. *Second innings*—Abbott 10–2–26–1; Philander 7–2–20–0; Rabada 9–4–28–0; Shamsi 14.5–4–49–1.

Umpires: R. A. Kettleborough and N. J. Llong. Third umpire: Aleem Dar.
Referee: A. J. Pycroft.

AUSTRALIA v NEW ZEALAND IN 2016-17

MARK GEENTY

One-day internationals (3): Australia 3, New Zealand 0

A three-match series shoehorned into a six-day window might have appeared an inconvenience, but Steve Smith and David Warner were not fussed. Australia's batting giants flexed their muscles to devastating effect, helping their side regain the Chappell–Hadlee Trophy in a clean sweep.

In the 12 years since the trophy's inaugural match, in Melbourne, fitting it into Australia's packed schedule had proved troublesome – they hadn't played host since 2009. This resumption was partly a thank you to New Zealand for agreeing to participate in the first day/night Test, at Adelaide in November 2015, when Australia were keen to push the agenda. So it was fitting that these three one-dayers were wedged between two pink-ball Tests, against South Africa and Pakistan.

If that made Australia's preparation difficult, they did not help themselves. A few days before the series, Glenn Maxwell said that batting below his captain Matthew Wade in the Victoria team was "a little bit painful". Both men were in the Australia squad, but Maxwell was criticised for a lack of respect by Smith, the captain, fined by the senior leadership, and not selected; Wade played all three matches. Things were not ideal for New Zealand either. After celebrating a Test win over Pakistan in Hamilton, they crossed the Tasman Sea next morning, and had just two training sessions before the first match.

Whatever the scheduling issues, Australia coped much better. Their smallest winning margin was 68 runs at Sydney, where Smith took control with a superb 164. Then Warner, showing patience as well as power, hit back-to-back centuries at Canberra and Melbourne; he finished with 299 runs, the most for Australia in a bilateral series of three games or fewer. The Australians resisted the temptation to rest their Test new-ball duo, Mitchell Starc and Josh Hazlewood, who snared six wickets apiece. With the speedy Pat Cummins returning from injury to grab eight, their attack was sharp and clinical.

Martin Guptill's brilliant century at Sydney aside, New Zealand were well below their best. They badly missed the batting and on-field presence of Ross Taylor, recovering from eye surgery. In his absence, all-rounder Jimmy Neesham rose to No. 4 and acquitted himself well enough, before a Starc bouncer at Canberra badly bruised his forearm and ended his series. New Zealand's fielding was uncharacteristically ragged, and their bowlers wilted in the death overs of the first two matches. They dropped a place to No. 4 in the rankings, while Australia stayed top.

NEW ZEALAND TOURING PARTY

*K. S. Williamson, T. D. Astle, T. A. Boult, C. de Grandhomme, L. H. Ferguson, M. J. Guptill, M. J. Henry, T. W. M. Latham, C. Munro, J. D. S. Neesham, H. M. Nicholls, M. J. Santner, T. G. Southee, B-J. Watling. *Coach:* M. J. Hesson.

AUSTRALIA v NEW ZEALAND

First One-Day International

At Sydney, December 4, 2016 (day/night). Australia won by 68 runs. Toss: Australia. One-day international debut: L. H. Ferguson.

Like the big kid in his backyard playing against others half his size, Smith took ownership of the SCG. His 164 from 157 balls set a personal best, and a ground record, beating A. B. de Villiers's 162 against West Indies at the 2015 World Cup. Later, he grabbed one of the catches of the year – a full-stretch left-handed effort at gully off Watling's cut that ended with his face planted painfully in the dirt. New Zealand had begun well, removing Finch in the first over, before their debutant Lockie Ferguson – who topped 93mph with his second delivery – snared Warner. Australia were stumbling at 92 for four after 20 overs, but Smith tore away, adding 127 with Head, then 83 in six overs with Wade, and passing 1,000 one-day international runs in 2016. He was lucky to get there: on 14, Boult hit his pads, umpire Mick Martell said no, and New Zealand declined a review. Smith later said he glanced at his bat to give the impression he had edged the ball; technology would have overturned the decision. New Zealand needed 325, and Guptill's century was one of his best, the ball cracking off his bat like a rifle shot. He hit six sixes and lofted straight with ease, but his departure – for 114 from 102 balls – left them 185 for five from 33 overs, and no one else made 50.

Man of the Match: S. P. D. Smith.

Australia

D. A. Warner b Ferguson	24
A. J. Finch b Henry	0
*S. P. D. Smith c Munro b Boult	164
G. J. Bailey c Watling b Neesham	17
M. R. Marsh run out	1
T. M. Head c and b Boult	52
†M. S. Wade b Henry	38
P. J. Cummins not out	0
M. A. Starc c Watling b Neesham	11
A. Zampa not out	2
Lb 1, w 9, nb 5	15
1/1 (2) 2/47 (1) 3/89 (4) 4/92 (5) 5/219 (6) 6/302 (3) 7/311 (7) 8/322 (9) — (8 wkts, 50 overs)	324
10 overs: 47-2	

J. R. Hazlewood did not bat.

Henry 10–0–74–2; Boult 10–1–51–2; Ferguson 9–0–73–1; de Grandhomme 6–0–27–0; Santner 9–0–40–0; Neesham 6–0–58–2.

New Zealand

M. J. Guptill c sub (G. J. Maxwell) b Zampa	114
T. W. M. Latham b Hazlewood	2
*K. S. Williamson c Smith b Hazlewood	9
J. D. S. Neesham c Hazlewood b Starc	34
†B-J. Watling c Smith b Marsh	6
C. Munro c Bailey b Cummins	49
M. J. Santner c Warner b Zampa	0
C. de Grandhomme lbw b Hazlewood	6
M. J. Henry c Bailey b Cummins	27
L. H. Ferguson b Marsh	0
T. A. Boult not out	1
Lb 4, w 4	8
1/3 (2) 2/34 (3) 3/126 (4) 4/140 (5) 5/185 (1) 6/187 (7) 7/203 (8) 8/253 (9) 9/255 (6) 10/256 (10) — (44.2 overs)	256
10 overs: 44-2	

Starc 7–1–37–1; Hazlewood 10–0–49–3; Marsh 8.2–1–38–2; Cummins 9–0–62–2; Zampa 10–0–66–2.

Umpires: H. D. P. K. Dharmasena and M. D. Martell. Third umpire: P. Wilson.
Referee: R. B. Richardson.

AUSTRALIA v NEW ZEALAND

Second One-Day International

At Canberra, December 6, 2016 (day/night). Australia won by 116 runs. Toss: New Zealand.

In the previous six one-day internationals at Manuka Oval, where the pitch resembles tarmac, the team batting first had won. But, perhaps sensing tackiness in the surface after overnight rain, Williamson – in his 100th ODI – chose to bowl. The folly was cruelly exposed: Warner paced a hundred sensibly and, in a partnership of 145 with Smith, prepared Australia for lift-off. With New Zealand's bowlers increasingly demoralised – new-ball pair Henry and Boult managed one for 171 between them – Marsh blasted seven sixes in an unbeaten 76 off 40 deliveries, and 126 gushed from the final ten overs. Australia finished with 378, their third-highest total. Williamson tried to make amends, top-scoring with a run-a-ball 81 and, while he was adding 125 with Neesham for the third wicket, New Zealand weren't far off the pace. But such large chases have slim margins for error and, once that partnership ended, so did the contest. Starc and Cummins, with a career-best four for 41, raised their game, and the last eight tumbled for 85. The trophy – won by New Zealand at home in February – was heading back to Australia.

Man of the Match: D. A. Warner.

Australia

D. A. Warner c Williamson b de Grandhomme	119
A. J. Finch b Santner	19
*S. P. D. Smith c Santner b Southee	72
T. M. Head c Munro b Southee	57
M. R. Marsh not out	76
†M. S. Wade b Boult	11
G. J. Bailey not out	0
Lb 11, w 10, nb 3	24
1/68 (2) 2/213 (1) 3/248 (3) 4/319 (4) 5/357 (6) (5 wkts, 50 overs)	378
10 overs: 54-0	

J. P. Faulkner, M. A. Starc, P. J. Cummins and J. R. Hazlewood did not bat.

Henry 10–0–91–0; Boult 10–0–80–1; Santner 10–0–47–1; Southee 10–0–63–2; de Grandhomme 9–0–74–1; Neesham 1–0–12–0.

New Zealand

M. J. Guptill c Wade b Cummins	45
T. W. M. Latham c and b Hazlewood	4
*K. S. Williamson c Warner b Cummins	81
J. D. S. Neesham c Starc b Hazlewood	74
C. Munro c Marsh b Faulkner	11
C. de Grandhomme c Wade b Starc	12
M. J. Santner b Starc	2
†B-J. Watling c Warner b Faulkner	17
T. G. Southee c Bailey b Cummins	2
M. J. Henry c Faulkner b Cummins	7
T. A. Boult not out	2
Lb 1, w 4	5
1/40 (2) 2/52 (1) 3/177 (4) 4/191 (5) 5/229 (6) 6/232 (3) 7/236 (7) 8/243 (9) 9/254 (10) 10/262 (8) (47.2 overs)	262
10 overs: 53-2	

Starc 10–0–52–2; Hazlewood 9–1–42–2; Cummins 10–0–41–4; Head 7–0–31–0; Faulkner 8.2–0–69–2; Marsh 3–0–26–0.

Umpires: H. D. P. K. Dharmasena and P. Wilson. Third umpire: N. J. Llong.
Referee: R. B. Richardson.

AUSTRALIA v NEW ZEALAND

Third One-Day International

At Melbourne, December 9, 2016 (day/night). Australia won by 117 runs. Toss: Australia.

In 22 international innings at the MCG, Warner had not managed three figures. In his 23rd, he celebrated the end of that sequence with a signature leap, before going on to 156 off 128 balls. It was his seventh one-day international hundred of the year, and fourth in six innings. Williamson's quirky

MOST ODI HUNDREDS IN A CALENDAR YEAR

100s		*I*	*R*	*HS*	*Avge*	
9	S. R. Tendulkar (I)	33	1,894	143	65.31	1998
7	**D. A. Warner (A)**	**23**	**1,388**	**173**	**63.09**	**2016**
7	S. C. Ganguly (I)	32	1,579	144	56.39	2000
6	G. Kirsten (SA)	29	1,442	188*	57.68	1996
6	S. R. Tendulkar (I)	32	1,611	137	53.70	1996
6	R. Dravid (I)	43	1,761	153	46.34	1999

fields helped keep Australia in check. Yet Warner picked the right moments to attack, and provided the meat of their 264, before being run out off the final ball of the innings. His proportion of the total (59.09%) was the second-highest for Australia in a completed innings, behind Damien Martyn's 60.73% against New Zealand at Auckland in March 2000. On a tricky pitch where some deliveries stopped, Australia's 264 for eight proved far too many for New Zealand. With Jimmy Neesham missing, their middle order looked vulnerable, and Starc's reverse swing proved the point.

Man of the Match: D. A. Warner. *Man of the Series:* D. A. Warner.

Australia

D. A. Warner run out	156	M. A. Starc not out	0
A. J. Finch c Nicholls b Boult	3		
*S. P. D. Smith c Nicholls b Boult	0	Lb 5, w 11, nb 2	18
G. J. Bailey c Santner b de Grandhomme	23		—
M. R. Marsh b de Grandhomme	0	1/6 (2) 2/11 (3) (8 wkts, 50 overs)	264
T. M. Head b Santner	37	3/73 (4) 4/73 (5)	
†M. S. Wade c de Grandhomme b Santner	14	5/178 (6) 6/226 (7)	
J. P. Faulkner c Guptill b Boult	13	7/262 (8) 8/264 (1)	10 overs: 31-2

P. J. Cummins and J. R. Hazlewood did not bat.

Southee 10–2–45–0; Boult 10–1–49–3; Ferguson 8–0–50–0; Santner 9–0–43–2; de Grandhomme 10–0–50–2; Williamson 1–0–3–0; Munro 2–0–19–0.

New Zealand

M. J. Guptill c Bailey b Head	34	L. H. Ferguson not out	4
T. W. M. Latham c Faulkner b Cummins	28	T. A. Boult c Smith b Cummins	1
*K. S. Williamson lbw b Faulkner	13		
H. M. Nicholls b Starc	3	Lb 2, w 4	6
C. Munro b Starc	20		—
†B-J. Watling lbw b Head	8	1/44 (2) 2/74 (3) 3/79 (1) (36.1 overs)	147
C. de Grandhomme c Head b Hazlewood	11	4/83 (4) 5/98 (6) 6/113 (7)	
M. J. Santner lbw b Starc	15	7/126 (5) 8/139 (8) 9/143 (9)	
T. G. Southee c Warner b Faulkner	4	10/147 (11)	10 overs: 48-1

Starc 10–3–34–3; Hazlewood 7–1–22–1; Cummins 5.1–0–26–2; Faulkner 7–0–26–2; Head 7–0–37–2.

Umpires: N. J. Llong and M. D. Martell. Third umpire: H. D. P. K. Dharmasena.
Referee: R. B. Richardson.

AUSTRALIA v PAKISTAN IN 2016-17

ADAM COLLINS

Test matches (3): Australia 3, Pakistan 0
One-day internationals (5): Australia 4, Pakistan 1

It wasn't unreasonable to imagine Pakistan might win their first Test series in Australia. They had topped the rankings in August, while their hosts had just been ravaged by South Africa. Instead, the Australians dominated as their fans have come to expect: they hit huge scores and bowled with venom. Whether the ball was red, white or pink, Pakistan seldom had the answer.

The closeness of the First Test, at Brisbane, was not a sign of things to come. After being hammered for three and a half days, Pakistan staged a gallant revival, ending 40 short of what would have been the biggest successful fourth-innings chase in Tests. Asad Shafiq's brilliant hundred nearly stole the show, but Mitchell Starc pulled the curtain.

The rest of the tour was all Australia. In the Second Test, at Melbourne, Pakistan relinquished a game that should have been sodden beyond salvage. Double-centurion Azhar Ali was done a gross injustice by those around him, as a declaration ended in an innings defeat. In Sydney, their application was even worse, Younis Khan the man let down after a masterful hundred. They deserved to lose 3–0. Misbah-ul-Haq was composed as a leader, and all but decomposed as a batsman. Try as he might, there was no clobbering his way

Saeed Khan, Getty Images

Seaming in control: Josh Hazlewood's accuracy made him the series' top wicket-taker, with 15.

back into form. His leg-spinner Yasir Shah mirrored the side's fortunes: from No. 1 in the world to a mauling in Australia. He finished the Test series with eight wickets for 672. Despite some success at Brisbane, it took Mohammad Amir a month – and a change to the white ball – before he posed a reliable threat. Wahab Riaz's best was brilliant, but his no-balling was a factor in the defeat at Melbourne.

None of this diminished Australia's transformation after they had been humiliated by South Africa. Smith's two centuries earned him the series award, while David Warner's hundred before lunch at Sydney will be remembered for years. The pace bowling looked strong, too, as Starc and Josh Hazlewood – who went at less than two an over – picked up 29 wickets between them.

Even more encouraging for Australia was the form of the two new members of their top five. Rarely has a player looked as Test-ready as Peter Handscomb, who followed a hundred at Melbourne with another at Sydney, all with minimal fuss. The temperament of Matt Renshaw, meanwhile, was as impressive as his strokeplay, his first century achieved at the age of 20.

The one-day series briefly suggested a more resolute Pakistan, with disciplined bowling and careful batting. But after they won the second match, their resistance ended, unforced errors spread, and a pair of Warner hundreds secured a 4–1 thrashing. Pakistan seemed to be at the end of a cycle. Looking back, it had been more than a fling, if less than a marriage – and a relationship the cricket world were lucky to have.

PAKISTAN TOURING PARTY

*Misbah-ul-Haq (T), Asad Shafiq (T/50), Azhar Ali (T/50), Babar Azam (T/50), Hasan Ali (50), Imad Wasim (T/50), Imran Khan (T), Junaid Khan (50), Mohammad Amir (T/50), Mohammad Asghar (T), Mohammad Hafeez (50), Mohammad Nawaz (T/50), Mohammad Rizwan (T/50), Rahat Ali (T/50), Sami Aslam (T), Sarfraz Ahmed (T/50), Sharjeel Khan (T/50), Shoaib Malik (50), Sohail Khan (T), Wahab Riaz (T/50), Yasir Shah (T), Younis Khan (T/50). *Coach:* J. M. Arthur.

Mohammad Irfan was originally selected for the one-day series, but returned home after his mother died; Junaid Khan replaced him.

TEST MATCH AVERAGES

AUSTRALIA – BATTING AND FIELDING

	T	*I*	*NO*	*R*	*HS*	*100*	*50*	*Avge*	*Ct*
P. S. P. Handscomb	3	5	2	344	110	2	1	114.66	2
S. P. D. Smith	3	5	1	441	165*	2	2	110.25	9
†D. A. Warner	3	5	0	356	144	2	1	71.20	3
†M. T. Renshaw	3	4	0	271	184	1	1	67.75	4
†U. T. Khawaja	3	5	1	267	97	0	3	66.75	3
†M. A. Starc	3	3	0	110	84	0	1	36.66	0
†M. S. Wade	3	4	1	46	29	0	0	15.33	8
†N. J. Maddinson	2	3	0	27	22	0	0	9.00	2

Played in three Tests: †J. R. Hazlewood 8 (4 ct); N. M. Lyon 29, 12 (1 ct). Played in two Tests: J. M. Bird 19* (1 ct). Played in one Test: H. W. R. Cartwright 37; S. N. J. O'Keefe 0*.

BOWLING

	Style	O	M	R	W	BB	5I	Avge
J. R. Hazlewood	RFM	147.2	40	294	15	4-55	0	19.60
S. N. J. O'Keefe	SLA	37	7	103	4	3-53	0	25.75
J. M. Bird	RFM	90	19	292	10	3-23	0	29.20
M. A. Starc	LF	145.2	31	477	14	4-36	0	34.07
N. M. Lyon	OB	137	19	502	11	3-33	0	45.63

Also bowled: H. W. R. Cartwright (RM) 4–0–15–0; N. J. Maddinson (SLA) 6–0–27–0; S. P. D. Smith (LBG) 4–0–14–0.

PAKISTAN – BATTING AND FIELDING

	T	I	NO	R	HS	100	50	Avge	Ct
Azhar Ali	3	6	1	406	205*	1	2	81.20	1
Younis Khan	3	6	1	298	175*	1	1	59.60	1
Sarfraz Ahmed	3	6	2	226	72*	0	2	56.50	9
Asad Shafiq	3	6	0	239	137	1	1	39.83	5
†Mohammad Amir	3	6	0	118	48	0	0	19.66	0
Misbah-ul-Haq	3	6	0	76	38	0	0	12.66	2
†Sami Aslam	2	4	0	48	22	0	0	12.00	1
Yasir Shah	3	5	0	57	33	0	0	11.40	1
Babar Azam	3	6	0	68	23	0	0	11.33	2
Wahab Riaz	3	6	0	52	30	0	0	8.66	1

Played in one Test: Imran Khan 0, 0; Rahat Ali 4, 1* (1 ct); †Sharjeel Khan 4, 40; Sohail Khan 65, 10*.

BOWLING

	Style	O	M	R	W	BB	5I	Avge
Wahab Riaz	LF	100	14	400	11	4-89	0	36.36
Sohail Khan	RFM	31	7	131	3	3-131	0	43.66
Mohammad Amir	LFM	96	15	308	5	4-97	0	61.60
Yasir Shah	LBG	148.1	11	672	8	3-207	0	84.00

Also bowled: Asad Shafiq (LBG) 2–0–12–0; Azhar Ali (LBG) 36–0–207–2; Imran Khan (RFM) 33–6–154–2; Rahat Ali (LFM) 32–6–114–2.

At Cairns, December 8–10, 2016. **Pakistanis won by 201 runs.** ‡**Pakistanis 208** (84.5 overs) (Younis Khan 54; M. T. Steketee 3-47, C. Valente 4-36) **and 216-6 dec** (73 overs) (Azhar Ali 82); **Cricket Australia XI 114** (39.1 overs) (Mohammad Amir 3-15, Rahat Ali 3-26, Wahab Riaz 3-28) **and 109** (27.3 overs) (Mohammad Nawaz 3-31). *The Pakistani bowlers bared their teeth, taking all 20 in quick time. Mohammad Amir and Rahat Ali enjoyed themselves most, finishing with combined match figures of 10-78. Their batsmen weren't as dominant, but it hardly mattered.*

AUSTRALIA v PAKISTAN

First Test Match

At Brisbane, December 15–19, 2016 (day/night). Australia won by 39 runs. Toss: Australia.

During a grim, hail-interrupted penultimate afternoon, the only question was when Pakistan would be dismissed, especially with Younis Khan and Misbah-ul-Haq were out in quick succession. There was no talk of a threat to Test cricket's record run-chase, particularly as they had been so limp for most of the match. Yet Pakistan spluttered, then smashed, then crept their way to within touching distance of a miracle 490.

No one had factored in the persistence of Asad Shafiq and, in the final over of day four's madcap three-hour night session, he went to a thrilling hundred. Equally unexpected was the support he received from Mohammad Amir, Wahab Riaz and Yasir Shah, the three

MOST CENTURIES FROM No. 6

100 (total)		*T*	*R*	*HS*	*Avge*	*Span*
9 (10)	**Asad Shafiq (P)**	**46**	**2,753**	**137**	**44.40**	**2010-11–2016-17**
8 (26)	G. S. Sobers (WI)	42	2,614	174	53.34	1954-55–1973-74
7 (8)	A. W. Greig (E)	45	2,741	148	43.50	1972–1976-77
7 (11)	H. P. Tillekeratne (SL)	58	2,843	204*	47.38	1989-90–2003-04
7 (30)	S. Chanderpaul (WI)	40	2,528	147*	64.82	1993-94–2014
7 (41)	R. T. Ponting (A)	34	1,989	197	49.72	1995-96–2003-04
6 (11)	Asif Iqbal (P)	31	1,750	166	43.75	1964-65–1979-80
6 (15)	K. D. Walters (A)	34	1,869	250	47.92	1965-66–1980-81
6 (19)	C. H. Lloyd (WI)	40	2,114	161*	49.16	1967-68–1984-85
6 (22)	I. R. Bell (E)	31	1,623	140	60.11	2006–2015-16
6 (27)	A. R. Border (A)	48	2,556	153	52.16	1978-79–1993-94
6 (32)	S. R. Waugh (A)	66	3,165	177*	51.04	1985-86–2003-04

bowlers who helped add 229 in a series of gritty partnerships. The last of those began on the final day, consumed 22 overs, and eroded the target to 41, before Starc summoned an unplayable ball at Shafiq's throat. Finally he was gone for a personal-best 137, before Yasir ran himself out moments later to end the epic; it was the fourth biggest last-innings total, and the highest in Australia, beating 445 by India at Adelaide in 1977-78. The sight of the Pakistan fans weeping as they applauded their team reinforced the feeling that this had been the best of the sport.

The resistance had begun as Australia's bowlers tired on the fourth night of Brisbane's first floodlit Test. The session had been extended to make up time, and a frustrated Starc hurled abuse at Amir, who held his nerve until edging Bird two short of a maiden fifty. Pakistan were seven down, and Smith – who dropped two regulation catches – took the extra half-hour; David Saker, Australia's bowling coach, said afterwards he would have preferred the fast bowlers to put their feet up. As midnight approached, Wahab alternated gallant swings with theatrical leaves, in keeping with the chaotic theme, before falling in the last over.

Smith said his anxiety had been triggered with 60 required, as he contemplated the gravity of losing from a position of such strength. After winning the toss, he had enjoyed his 17th Test century as much as the locals – including those in the luxurious pool erected in the western corner of the Gabba – even if it required luck: he was dropped twice, while Amir failed to appeal when he was caught behind on 97.

Next day, Handscomb – whose partnership with Smith had been worth 172 – reached a maiden hundred in his second Test. It was met without the customary kiss of the helmet, a hint, perhaps, that he planned regular repeats; his patience and assured strokeplay square of the wicket suggested the same. Opener Renshaw had already hit 71, and their performances brought relief to the selectors who had invested in them after the horror of Hobart against South Africa a month earlier. Wahab and Amir – who finished with a four-for, his best Test figures since his return from exile – bounced back, and Smith was the first of six to fall for 57, but a flurry of boundaries from last pair Lyon and Bird ensured a healthy score.

As the lights went on, the pace trio of Starc, Hazlewood and Bird put on a clinic, finding Pakistan edges routinely to reduce them to 67 for eight; only Sarfraz Ahmed's unbeaten 59 dragged the innings into day three. Australia declined the follow-on, favouring rapid runs and recharged bowlers, and the middle order did as they pleased through 39 overs, before Pakistan lost two by the close. Azhar Ali's 71, controlled and defiant, looked futile, as did Younis Khan's twitchy half-century. This match won't be remembered for either, though, nor Starc's second-innings wickets. It will be for when the switch was flicked, and the miracle looked manageable. Not for the result, but the journey – for what nearly was.

Man of the Match: Asad Shafiq.

Close of play: first day, Australia 288-3 (Smith 110, Handscomb 64); second day, Pakistan 97-8 (Sarfraz Ahmed 31, Mohammad Amir 8); third day, Pakistan 70-2 (Azhar Ali 41, Younis Khan 0); fourth day, Pakistan 382-8 (Asad Shafiq 100, Yasir Shah 4).

Australia

M. T. Renshaw c Sarfraz Ahmed b Wahab Riaz	71	– (2) c Younis Khan b Rahat Ali	6
D. A. Warner lbw b Mohammad Amir	32	– (1) c Wahab Riaz b Mohammad Amir	12
U. T. Khawaja c Misbah-ul-Haq b Yasir Shah	4	– c Misbah-ul-Haq b Rahat Ali	74
*S. P. D. Smith c Sarfraz Ahmed b Wahab Riaz	130	– c Rahat Ali b Yasir Shah	63
P. S. P. Handscomb b Wahab Riaz	105	– not out	35
N. J. Maddinson c Sarfraz Ahmed b Wahab Riaz	1	– c Babar Azam b Wahab Riaz	4
†M. S. Wade c Azhar Ali b Mohammad Amir	7	– not out	1
M. A. Starc c Asad Shafiq b Mohammad Amir	10		
J. R. Hazlewood c Asad Shafiq b Mohammad Amir	8		
N. M. Lyon c Asad Shafiq b Yasir Shah	29		
J. M. Bird not out	19		
Lb 5, w 1, nb 7	13	B 2, lb 4, nb 1	7
1/70 (2) 2/75 (3) 3/151 (1) (130.1 overs)	429	1/12 (1) (5 wkts dec, 39 overs)	202
4/323 (4) 5/334 (6) 6/342 (7)		2/24 (2) 3/135 (4)	
7/354 (8) 8/380 (9) 9/380 (5) 10/429 (10)		4/188 (3) 5/199 (6)	

Mohammad Amir 31–7–97–4; Rahat Ali 22–5–74–0; Yasir Shah 43.1–6–129–2; Wahab Riaz 26–4–89–4; Azhar Ali 8–0–35–0. *Second innings*—Mohammad Amir 8–0–37–1; Rahat Ali 10–1–40–2; Yasir Shah 10–1–45–1; Wahab Riaz 7–1–47–1; Azhar Ali 4–0–27–0.

Pakistan

Sami Aslam c Wade b Bird	22	– c Renshaw b Starc	15
Azhar Ali c Khawaja b Starc	5	– c Wade b Starc	71
Babar Azam c Smith b Hazlewood	19	– c Smith b Lyon	14
Younis Khan c Wade b Hazlewood	0	– c Smith b Lyon	65
*Misbah-ul-Haq c Renshaw b Bird	4	– c Wade b Bird	5
Asad Shafiq c Khawaja b Starc	2	– c Warner b Starc	137
†Sarfraz Ahmed not out	59	– b Starc	24
Wahab Riaz c and b Hazlewood	1	– (9) c Smith b Bird	30
Yasir Shah c Khawaja b Starc	1	– (10) run out	33
Mohammad Amir c Wade b Bird	21	– (8) c Wade b Bird	48
Rahat Ali run out	4	– not out	1
Lb 3, w 1	4	Lb 5, w 2	7
1/6 (2) 2/43 (3) 3/43 (4) (55 overs)	142	1/31 (1) 2/54 (3) (145 overs)	450
4/48 (5) 5/54 (6) 6/56 (1)		3/145 (2) 4/165 (5)	
7/66 (8) 8/67 (9) 9/121 (10) 10/142 (11)		5/173 (4) 6/220 (7) 7/312 (8)	
		8/378 (9) 9/449 (6) 10/450 (10)	

Starc 18–2–63–3; Hazlewood 14–1–22–3; Bird 12–6–23–3; Lyon 11–2–31–0. *Second innings*—Starc 38–10–119–4; Hazlewood 42–11–99–0; Bird 33–6–110–3; Lyon 29–3–108–2; Maddinson 3–0–9–0.

Umpires: I. J. Gould and R. K. Illingworth. Third umpire: S. Ravi.
Referee: R. S. Madugalle.

AUSTRALIA v PAKISTAN

Second Test Match

At Melbourne, December 26–30, 2016. Australia won by an innings and 18 runs. Toss: Australia.

When the opposition declare on 443, and 141 overs have been lost to rain, and your own first innings ends just before lunch on the fifth day, you aren't meant to win. But, as The Strokes sang, this is the modern age: with a healthy dose of self-belief, Australia clinched the series with nearly an hour to spare. It was only the second time a side had declared and lost by an innings, after Australia themselves at Hyderabad in 2012-13.

They had begun the final day 22 ahead, with Smith – who resumed on 100 – believing a lead of 180 would be enough. Calculated walloping was required: Smith relied on invention, Starc on brutality. He clobbered seven sixes, a ground record in a Test innings, before holing out for 84. With phase one of the plan complete, phase two had the perfect start: Hazlewood bowled Sami Aslam before lunch, and Starc trapped Babar Azam first ball after it. Younis Khan then joined Azhar Ali – unbeaten for 580 minutes in Pakistan's first innings – and calmed things down. Enter Lyon, who woke to reports that he was bowling for his place, again. In the space of a session he secured his ticket to India: Younis and Asad Shafiq were caught via inside edges by Handscomb at short leg and, in between, Misbah-ul-Haq's second-ball sweep picked out backward square.

When Azhar was at last dismissed, lbw to Hazlewood at the beginning of the evening session, hopes of a draw evaporated, and masterful reverse swing from Bird and Starc secured victory. From Brisbane to Melbourne, Pakistan had regressed from nearly winning the unwinnable to abjectly losing the unlosable. They became the second country to lose by an innings having scored more than 400 batting first; England had done it four times, including twice earlier that month.

It all seemed unfair on Azhar. Through the first two and a half days, he had battled through one interruption after another, showing mental strength to complete a chanceless double-century, and passing 1,000 runs in the year along the way. Shafiq was the only other recognised batsman to reach 50, but Sohail Khan proved an unlikely partner on the third day, clobbering 65, with four sixes off Lyon. Soon after he fell, the parsimonious Hazlewood picked up Wahab, his 100th wicket in his 25th Test, and Misbah declared.

When Warner finally got his chance, in gorgeous conditions, he hit his first Test hundred at the MCG, and motored past 5,000 in all. It was high on fortune and low on fluency, but his 144 in 143 balls, and the 198 he added with Khawaja, put a dent in Pakistan's lead – and their confidence. Wahab overstepped ten times, including while yorking Warner on 81, the second in a hat-trick of no-balls. And Yasir Shah went at more than five an over, and conceded more than 200 for the second time in 2016.

Khawaja looked classy, but just missed a century when he edged Wahab early on day four. Handscomb, on home turf, hit another fifty, then Smith flowed to his century – a third in successive Tests at the MCG – before rain ended play on the fourth evening. Australia had their lead and, thanks to Pakistan's ineptitude and Starc's genius, they were back to doing what they do best: winning series at home.

Man of the Match: S. P. D. Smith.

Close of play: first day, Pakistan 142-4 (Azhar Ali 66, Asad Shafiq 4); second day, Pakistan 310-6 (Azhar Ali 139, Mohammad Amir 28); third day, Australia 278-2 (Khawaja 95, Smith 10); fourth day, Australia 465-6 (Smith 100, Starc 7).

> "Chappell could hit the ball safely only between the citrus and the almonds."
> Freaks of Nurture, page 115

Pakistan

Sami Aslam c Smith b Lyon	9	– b Hazlewood	2
Azhar Ali not out	205	– lbw b Hazlewood	43
Babar Azam c Smith b Hazlewood	23	– lbw b Starc	3
Younis Khan b Bird	21	– c Handscomb b Lyon	24
*Misbah-ul-Haq c Maddinson b Bird	11	– c Maddinson b Lyon	0
Asad Shafiq c Smith b Bird	50	– c Handscomb b Lyon	16
†Sarfraz Ahmed c Renshaw b Hazlewood	10	– b Starc	43
Mohammad Amir c Wade b Starc	29	– b Bird	11
Sohail Khan run out	65	– not out	10
Wahab Riaz c and b Hazlewood	1	– b Starc	0
Yasir Shah (did not bat)		– c Bird b Starc	0
B 4, lb 9, w 5, nb 1	19	B 4, lb 5, nb 2	11
1/18 (1) 2/60 (3) 3/111 (4) 4/125 (5) 5/240 (6) 6/268 (7) 7/317 (8) 8/435 (9) 9/443 (10) (9 wkts dec, 126.3 overs)	443	1/3 (1) 2/6 (3) 3/63 (4) 4/63 (5) 5/89 (6) 6/101 (2) 7/143 (8) 8/153 (7) 9/159 (10) 10/163 (11) (53.2 overs)	163

Starc 31–6–125–1; Hazlewood 32.3–11–50–3; Bird 34–5–113–3; Lyon 23–1–115–1; Smith 3–0–9–0; Maddinson 3–0–18–0. *Second innings*—Starc 15.2–4–36–4; Hazlewood 13–3–39–2; Bird 11–2–46–1; Lyon 14–4–33–3.

Australia

M. T. Renshaw b Yasir Shah	10
D. A. Warner c Sarfraz Ahmed b Wahab Riaz	144
U. T. Khawaja c Sarfraz Ahmed b Wahab Riaz	97
*S. P. D. Smith not out	165
P. S. P. Handscomb c Sami Aslam b Sohail Khan	54
N. J. Maddinson b Yasir Shah	22
†M. S. Wade c Asad Shafiq b Sohail Khan	9
M. A. Starc c Asad Shafiq b Sohail Khan	84
N. M. Lyon c and b Yasir Shah	12
B 1, lb 12, w 1, nb 13	27
1/46 (1) 2/244 (2) 3/282 (3) 4/374 (5) 5/433 (6) 6/454 (7) 7/608 (8) 8/624 (9) (8 wkts dec, 142 overs)	624

J. R. Hazlewood and J. M. Bird did not bat.

Mohammad Amir 33–6–91–0; Sohail Khan 31–7–131–3; Yasir Shah 41–2–207–3; Wahab Riaz 32–5–147–2; Azhar Ali 5–0–35–0.

Umpires: I. J. Gould and S. Ravi. Third umpire: R. K. Illingworth.
Referee: R. S. Madugalle.

AUSTRALIA v PAKISTAN

Third Test Match

At Sydney, January 3–7, 2017. Australia won by 220 runs. Toss: Australia. Test debuts: H. W. R. Cartwright; Sharjeel Khan.

After coming so close in Brisbane, and falling so fast in Melbourne, Pakistan's capitulation in Sydney had an inevitable air. So did Warner's century before lunch on the first day. He had threatened it before, stymied by dawdling over-rates. But on this picture-perfect Sydney morning, nothing would stand in his way. The SCG has grandstands named

TEST CENTURIES BEFORE LUNCH ON THE FIRST DAY

103*	V. T. Trumper (104)	Australia v England at Manchester	1902
112*	C. G. Macartney (151)	Australia v England at Leeds	1926
105*	D. G. Bradman (334)	Australia v England at Leeds	1930
108*	Majid Khan (112)	Pakistan v New Zealand at Karachi	1976-77
100*	**D. A. Warner (113)**	**Australia v Pakistan at Sydney**	**2016-17**

after two of the others to achieve the feat, Bradman and Trumper. Perhaps in time Warner will have one too.

Within six balls he had three boundaries, and a half-century before drinks, but this was no Twenty20 innings. His shot of choice was the back-foot punch, fed by Pakistan's seamers. The crowd realised they were watching something historic, and urged Renshaw to cede the strike for the session's final over. Warner worked his 78th ball into a gap and, thanks to a misfield at deep point, raced the last three runs. It was the fastest Test hundred at the SCG, beating his own record set a year earlier.

As Warner was applauded from the field, Renshaw trailed behind on 21, cool amid the frenzy. But after Warner guided a catch behind off Wahab Riaz, Renshaw took the lead; he worked his 201st delivery into the leg side for a maiden hundred, then raised his next 50 at nearly a run a ball. Khawaja had gone to a waft, and Smith to a Yasir Shah over-spinner, but Handscomb and Renshaw put together a swift century stand, and Australia slept on 365 for three.

The partnership finished early next morning, but Handscomb – the second Australian, after Herbie Collins in 1920-21, to hit at least a fifty in each of his first four Tests – cruised to his own century without alarm. At the other end, the Zimbabwe-born Hilton Cartwright's debut 37 was notable for his first delivery, a cover-driven four, and the comfort he showed throughout two hours at the crease. Handscomb eventually fell hit wicket to Wahab, as he gave himself room outside leg stump and dislodged the leg bail with the downswing of his cut. Despite regularly standing deep in his crease, it was his first such dismissal, but it was fitting it should happen here: no one looked capable of dismissing him without a helping hand. Only Wahab offered penetration, while Yasir went from bad to worse, picking up one for 167. Smith declared on 538, allowing Hazlewood to remove debutant Sharjeel Khan and Babar Azam before tea.

Azhar Ali and Younis Khan recovered, each passing 50 before stumps. But a run-out always threatened: one mix-up too many caught Azhar short, and Handscomb – replacing the ill Wade as wicketkeeper – finished the job. By the close, Pakistan were eight down, and 68 short of avoiding the follow-on. But Younis had survived the mess, and remained immaculate en route to a first hundred in Australia and his 34th in all, level with Sunil Gavaskar and Brian Lara. Uniquely, he now had centuries in all 11 countries to have hosted Tests.

After more rain, Hazlewood cleaned up the tail to leave Younis stranded on 175. The lead was 223, but Smith decided to bat again, and Australia put on a two-hour power show. Warner's 23-ball half-century was the second fastest in Tests, only two slower than Misbah-ul-Haq's against Australia at Abu Dhabi in 2014-15. Khawaja, elevated to open after Renshaw took blows to the head while batting and fielding, cashed in, while Smith and Handscomb produced Twenty20 knocks in all but name. Yasir's misery continued – one for 124 from 14 overs – and a target of 465 was remote. On the evidence of Melbourne, so was batting seven and a half hours for the draw. Sharjeel confirmed as much when he came out swinging, and fell to Lyon just before stumps.

Next morning, Hazlewood removed Azhar cheaply, then Younis was undone by Lyon's change of pace, 23 short of 10,000 Test runs. Misbah held on either side of lunch, but swiped once too often at O'Keefe, and finished with a series average of 12. Starc was too fast for Asad Shafiq, and the tail didn't last long; Sarfraz Ahmed's flayed unbeaten 72 acknowledged a foregone conclusion. Hazlewood ended it with his seventh wicket in the match, and 15th in the series, at 19 apiece.

When Pakistan rose to No. 1 in the world earlier in the year, few predicted this whitewash, their fourth in a row in Australia. Starting with West Indies in November, they had now lost six Tests in succession, their worst run. Australia had recently lost five in a row themselves, but a change in personnel had worked wonders. "When we all got together as a group for the first time," said Smith, "I felt a shift in attitude and energy and enthusiasm." They had turned their summer around.

Man of the Match: D. A. Warner. *Man of the Series:* S. P. D. Smith.

Close of play: first day, Australia 365-3 (Renshaw 167, Handscomb 40); second day, Pakistan 126-2 (Azhar Ali 58, Younis Khan 64); third day, Pakistan 271-8 (Younis Khan 136, Yasir Shah 5); fourth day, Pakistan 55-1 (Azhar Ali 11, Yasir Shah 3).

Australia

M. T. Renshaw b Imran Khan	184		
D. A. Warner c Sarfraz Ahmed b Wahab Riaz	113	– (1) b Wahab Riaz	55
U. T. Khawaja c Sarfraz Ahmed b Wahab Riaz	13	– (2) not out	79
*S. P. D. Smith c Sarfraz Ahmed b Yasir Shah	24	– (3) c Sarfraz Ahmed b Yasir Shah	59
P. S. P. Handscomb hit wkt b Wahab Riaz	110	– (4) not out	40
H. W. R. Cartwright b Imran Khan	37		
†M. S. Wade c Babar Azam b Azhar Ali	29		
M. A. Starc c sub (Mohammad Rizwan) b Azhar Ali	16		
S. N. J. O'Keefe not out	0		
B 5, lb 1, w 2, nb 4	12	B 3, lb 3, w 1, nb 1	8
1/151 (2) 2/203 (3) 3/244 (4) 4/386 (1) 5/477 (6) 6/516 (5) 7/532 (7) 8/538 (8) (8 wkts dec, 135 overs)	538	1/71 (1) 2/174 (3) (2 wkts dec, 32 overs)	241

J. R. Hazlewood and N. M. Lyon did not bat.

Mohammad Amir 24–2–83–0; Imran Khan 27–4–111–2; Wahab Riaz 28–4–89–3; Yasir Shah 40–2–167–1; Azhar Ali 14–0–70–2; Asad Shafiq 2–0–12–0. *Second innings*—Imran Khan 6–2–43–0; Yasir Shah 14–0–124–1; Wahab Riaz 7–0–28–1; Azhar Ali 5–0–40–0.

Pakistan

Azhar Ali run out	71	– c and b Hazlewood	11
Sharjeel Khan c Renshaw b Hazlewood	4	– c Warner b Lyon	40
Babar Azam lbw b Hazlewood	0	– (4) lbw b Hazlewood	9
Younis Khan not out	175	– (5) c Hazlewood b Lyon	13
*Misbah-ul-Haq c sub (J. M. Bird) b Lyon	18	– (6) c Lyon b O'Keefe	38
Asad Shafiq c Smith b O'Keefe	4	– (7) b Starc	30
†Sarfraz Ahmed c sub (J. M. Bird) b Starc	18	– (8) not out	72
Mohammad Amir c Warner b Lyon	4	– (10) run out	5
Wahab Riaz b Lyon	8	– c Wade b O'Keefe	12
Yasir Shah c Smith b Hazlewood	10	– (3) c sub (J. M. Bird) b O'Keefe	13
Imran Khan b Hazlewood	0	– c sub (J. M. Bird) b Hazlewood	0
B 3	3	Nb 1	1
1/6 (2) 2/6 (3) 3/152 (1) 4/178 (5) 5/197 (6) 6/239 (7) 7/244 (8) 8/264 (9) 9/315 (10) 10/315 (11) (110.3 overs)	315	1/51 (2) 2/55 (1) 3/67 (4) 4/82 (5) 5/96 (3) 6/136 (7) 7/188 (6) 8/202 (9) 9/224 (10) 10/244 (11) (80.2 overs)	244

Starc 26–7–77–1; Hazlewood 27.3–7–55–4; O'Keefe 20–3–50–1; Lyon 33–3–115–3; Cartwright 4–0–15–0. *Second innings*—Starc 17–2–57–1; Hazlewood 18.2–7–29–3; Lyon 27–6–100–2; O'Keefe 17–4–53–3; Smith 1–0–5–0.

Umpires: R. K. Illingworth and S. Ravi. Third umpire: I. J. Gould.
Referee: R. S. Madugalle.

At Brisbane (Allan Border Field), January 10, 2017. **Pakistanis won by 196 runs. Pakistanis 334-7** (50 overs) (Sharjeel Khan 62, Babar Azam 98, Umar Akmal 54; H. T. R. Y. Thornton 3-69, C. Green 3-59); ‡**Cricket Australia XI 138** (36.2 overs) (J. P. Inglis 70; Hasan Ali 3-18). *Babar Azam just missed out on a fourth consecutive List A hundred (after three against West Indies), as the Pakistanis racked up 334. Cricket Australia XI had no hope from 19-3, though Leeds-born Josh Inglis hit a 64-ball 70.*

AUSTRALIA v PAKISTAN

First One-Day International

At Brisbane, January 13, 2017 (day/night). Australia won by 92 runs. Toss: Australia. One-day international debuts: C. A. Lynn, B. Stanlake.

Pakistan had their opponents pinned, but let them back to their feet, and ended up being walked all over. Mohammad Amir, returning to form after a ragged end to the Tests, removed Warner and Smith in consecutive balls, and Australia slid to 78 for five, with keeper Mohammad Rizwan taking four catches. Wade began the rebuilding job, putting on 82 with Maxwell, then adding 108 with the tail. A leading edge from the final delivery was enough to raise his first one-day international hundred, at a run a ball. The target seemed gettable, but Pakistan were uncompetitive from the moment Azhar Ali's hamstring went ping. He remained for another seven deliveries – in which time Sharjeel Khan departed – but when he retired Pakistan were, in effect, 39 for two. Australia's quartet of seamers squeezed out regular breakthroughs, and no partnership surpassed the opening stand. Faulkner's bag of slower balls netted four wickets, and Cummins's extra pace three.

Man of the Match: M. S. Wade.

Australia

D. A. Warner b Mohammad Amir	7
T. M. Head c Mohammad Rizwan b Imad Wasim	39
*S. P. D. Smith c Mohammad Rizwan b Mohammad Amir	0
C. A. Lynn c Mohammad Rizwan b Hasan Ali	16
M. R. Marsh c Mohammad Rizwan b Imad Wasim	4
G. J. Maxwell c Mohammad Hafeez b Hasan Ali	60
†M. S. Wade not out	100
J. P. Faulkner c Mohammad Hafeez b Mohammad Nawaz	5
P. J. Cummins run out	15
M. A. Starc b Hasan Ali	10
B. Stanlake not out	1
Lb 1, w 9, nb 1	11
1/13 (1) 2/13 (3) 3/52 (4) 4/67 (2) 5/78 (5) 6/160 (6) 7/170 (8) 8/212 (9) 9/235 (10) (9 wkts, 50 overs)	268
10 overs: 61-3	

Mohammad Amir 10–0–54–2; Mohammad Hafeez 7–0–23–0; Hasan Ali 9–0–65–3; Wahab Riaz 6–0–42–0; Imad Wasim 10–0–35–2; Mohammad Nawaz 8–0–48–1.

Pakistan

*Azhar Ali c Warner b Faulkner	24
Sharjeel Khan c Maxwell b Faulkner	18
Mohammad Hafeez c Wade b Faulkner	4
Babar Azam c Smith b Cummins	33
Umar Akmal c Head b Starc	17
†Mohammad Rizwan c Marsh b Cummins	21
Imad Wasim c Warner b Marsh	29
Mohammad Nawaz b Starc	1
Mohammad Amir c Maxwell b Faulkner	8
Wahab Riaz c Starc b Cummins	6
Hasan Ali not out	1
B 4, lb 5, w 5	14
1/38 (2) 2/47 (3) 3/79 (5) 4/109 (4) 5/129 (6) 6/133 (8) 7/158 (7) 8/163 (1) 9/171 (9) 10/176 (10) (42.4 overs)	176
10 overs: 47-1	

Azhar Ali, when 12, retired hurt at 39-1 and resumed at 133-6.

Starc 8–0–34–2; Stanlake 3–0–13–0; Faulkner 7–1–32–4; Cummins 8.4–0–33–3; Head 10–0–28–0; Marsh 6–0–27–1.

Umpires: M. D. Martell and C. Shamshuddin. Third umpire: C. B. Gaffaney.
Referee: J. J. Crowe.

AUSTRALIA v PAKISTAN

Second One-Day International

At Melbourne, January 15, 2017 (day/night). Pakistan won by six wickets. Toss: Australia.

Pakistan achieved their first win of the tour, thanks mainly to their suffocating slow bowlers. As at Brisbane, Australia began by digging themselves a hole. From 41 for three, Smith rallied with 60 and a series of handy partnerships with the middle order, before being bowled from his 101st ball trying to up the tempo. On a slow surface, Pakistan's spin trio whipped through 24 overs, taking a collective three for 97. The chase began with Smith dropping acting-captain Mohammad Hafeez at slip in the first over. From there, the approach was low risk and, after a sturdy foundation of 68 with Sharjeel Khan, Hafeez continued past 50. Australia sniffed a chance when Babar Azam and Hafeez fell in quick succession, but Shoaib Malik calmly ended Pakistan's sequence of nine one-day international losses away to Australia, going back to 2004-05.

Man of the Match: Mohammad Hafeez.

Australia

U. T. Khawaja c Sharjeel Khan b Junaid Khan	17
D. A. Warner c Mohammad Rizwan b Junaid Khan	16
*S. P. D. Smith b Imad Wasim	60
M. R. Marsh c Imad Wasim b Mohammad Amir	0
T. M. Head c Mohammad Rizwan b Hasan Ali	29
G. J. Maxwell b Imad Wasim	23
†M. S. Wade b Shoaib Malik	35
J. P. Faulkner c Asad Shafiq b Mohammad Amir	19
M. A. Starc run out	3
P. J. Cummins c Mohammad Rizwan b Mohammad Amir	0
J. R. Hazlewood not out	0
Lb 7, w 11	18
1/31 (2) 2/40 (1) 3/41 (4) 4/86 (5) 5/128 (6) 6/193 (3) 7/199 (7) 8/207 (9) 9/212 (10) 10/220 (8) (48.2 overs)	220
10 overs: 49-3	

Mohammad Amir 9.2–0–47–3; Junaid Khan 8–0–40–2; Imad Wasim 10–0–37–2; Hasan Ali 7–0–29–1; Mohammad Hafeez 10–0–45–0; Shoaib Malik 4–0–15–1.

Pakistan

*Mohammad Hafeez c Hazlewood b Faulkner	72
Sharjeel Khan c Wade b Faulkner	29
Babar Azam c Hazlewood b Starc	34
Asad Shafiq c Wade b Starc	13
Shoaib Malik not out	42
Umar Akmal not out	18
Lb 6, w 7	13
1/68 (2) 2/140 (3) 3/142 (1) 4/195 (4) (4 wkts, 47.4 overs)	221
10 overs: 36-0	

†Mohammad Rizwan, Imad Wasim, Mohammad Amir, Hasan Ali and Junaid Khan did not bat.

Starc 10–1–45–2; Hazlewood 10–2–32–0; Cummins 10–1–48–0; Faulkner 9–0–35–2; Head 2.4–0–23–0; Marsh 6–0–32–0.

Umpires: C. B. Gaffaney and P. Wilson. Third umpire: C. Shamshuddin.
Referee: J. J. Crowe.

AUSTRALIA v PAKISTAN

Third One-Day International

At Perth, January 19, 2017 (day/night). Australia won by seven wickets. Toss: Australia. One-day international debut: P. S. P. Handscomb.

Chasing 264, Australia were 45 for two, and struggling against the seamers, particularly Mohammad Amir, who was moving the ball at pace as only a few can. When Handscomb, on his one-day international debut, nicked into the cordon on nought, Pakistan erupted, but Junaid Khan was found to have overstepped. Handscomb missed and edged and scrapped – when he did middle one off Junaid on ten, he was put down at point. The profligacy seemed to suck the life from the attack, and Australia seized the ascendancy. By the time Handscomb finally did go, for 82, his partnership of 183 with Smith had done the damage. Smith's eighth one-day international hundred never required the unconventional in order to keep pace. Earlier, Sharjeel Khan's 43-ball half-century had got Pakistan off to a brisk start, bolstered by Babar who, in his 21st ODI innings, became the joint fastest to 1,000 runs (matching Viv Richards, Kevin Pietersen, Jonathan Trott and Quinton de Kock). But they weren't able to accelerate, managing only 102 from the final 20 overs. Hazlewood did most to keep them in check, with three for 32.

Man of the Match: S. P. D. Smith.

Pakistan

*Mohammad Hafeez lbw b Hazlewood	4	†Mohammad Rizwan not out	14
Sharjeel Khan b Head	50	Mohammad Amir not out	4
Babar Azam c Handscomb b Hazlewood	84	Lb 7, w 8	15
Asad Shafiq c Khawaja b Head	5		—
Shoaib Malik c Wade b Stanlake	39	1/36 (1) 2/85 (2) (7 wkts, 50 overs)	263
Umar Akmal c Wade b Hazlewood	39	3/99 (4) 4/162 (5)	
Imad Wasim c Head b Cummins	9	5/222 (3) 6/244 (6) 7/246 (7) 10 overs: 50-1	

Hasan Ali and Junaid Khan did not bat.

Hazlewood 10–0–32–3; Stanlake 10–1–55–1; Cummins 10–1–42–1; Head 10–0–65–2; Faulkner 10–0–62–0.

Australia

D. A. Warner c Mohammad Rizwan b Junaid Khan	35	T. M. Head not out	23
U. T. Khawaja c Mohammad Rizwan b Mohammad Amir	9	B 1, lb 1, w 5, nb 1	8
*S. P. D. Smith not out	108		—
P. S. P. Handscomb c Mohammad Rizwan b Hasan Ali	82	1/44 (1) 2/45 (2) (3 wkts, 45 overs)	265
		3/228 (4) 10 overs: 45-2	

G. J. Maxwell, †M. S. Wade, J. P. Faulkner, P. J. Cummins, J. R. Hazlewood and B. Stanlake did not bat.

Mohammad Hafeez 6–1–30–0; Mohammad Amir 10–0–36–1; Junaid Khan 9–0–58–1; Hasan Ali 10–0–62–1; Imad Wasim 8–0–59–0; Shoaib Malik 2–0–18–0.

Umpires: S. D. Fry and C. Shamshuddin. Third umpire: C. B. Gaffaney.
Referee: J. J. Crowe.

AUSTRALIA v PAKISTAN

Fourth One-Day International

At Sydney, January 22, 2017 (day/night). Australia won by 86 runs. Toss: Australia.

Warner peppered the off-side boundary on his home ground once again, hitting a masterful hundred to set up a series-clinching win. He notched 50 inside 13 overs, dominating an opening stand of 92 with Khawaja, then put on 120 with Smith, who was dropped on 11 at gully by a sluggish Sharjeel Khan, part of a dreadful fielding display by Pakistan. Hasan Ali removed both in the 36th over, and went on to a maiden five-for, the only one of the series. But Head and Maxwell, mixing power with innovation, zoomed to half-centuries, and piled on 100 in 11 overs; both were dropped by rattled fielders, and Australia finished with their highest score against Pakistan, for a few days at least. Sharjeel's response was welcome viewing, blasting 74 from 47 balls, before being enticed to take on Zampa to the longer side of the ground. No one else could threaten the required rate.

Man of the Match: D. A. Warner.

Australia

U. T. Khawaja c Mohammad Rizwan b Hasan Ali	30	†M. S. Wade c Imad Wasim b Hasan Ali	5
D. A. Warner c Mohammad Rizwan b Hasan Ali	130	M. A. Starc not out	0
*S. P. D. Smith lbw b Hasan Ali	49	Lb 8, nb 2	10
T. M. Head c Shoaib Malik b Mohammad Amir	51	1/92 (1) 2/212 (2) 3/213 (3) 4/313 (4) 5/339 (6) 6/353 (5) (6 wkts, 50 overs)	353
G. J. Maxwell c Sharjeel Khan b Hasan Ali	78	10 overs: 63-0	

P. S. P. Handscomb, P. J. Cummins, A. Zampa and J. R. Hazlewood did not bat.

Mohammad Hafeez 9–0–54–0; Mohammad Amir 10–0–75–1; Junaid Khan 10–0–82–0; Hasan Ali 10–1–52–5; Imad Wasim 9–0–69–0; Shoaib Malik 2–0–13–0.

Pakistan

*Azhar Ali c Smith b Hazlewood	7	Mohammad Amir c Wade b Cummins	5
Sharjeel Khan c Warner b Zampa	74	Hasan Ali not out	8
Babar Azam c Hazlewood b Head	31	Junaid Khan b Hazlewood	0
Mohammad Hafeez c sub (J. P. Faulkner) b Zampa	40	Lb 5, w 4	9
Shoaib Malik c Warner b Head	47	1/15 (1) 2/88 (3) 3/119 (2) 4/183 (4) 5/215 (5) 6/218 (6) 7/245 (7) 8/252 (9) 9/267 (8) 10/267 (11) (43.5 overs)	267
Umar Akmal c Cummins b Starc	11	10 overs: 68-1	
†Mohammad Rizwan lbw b Zampa	10		
Imad Wasim c Wade b Hazlewood	25		

Starc 7–0–42–1; Hazlewood 8.5–0–54–3; Cummins 8–0–45–1; Head 10–0–66–2; Zampa 10–0–55–3.

Umpires: C. B. Gaffaney and M. D. Martell. Third umpire: C. Shamshuddin.
Referee: J. J. Crowe.

AUSTRALIA v PAKISTAN

Fifth One-Day International

At Adelaide, January 26, 2017 (day/night). Australia won by 57 runs. Toss: Australia.

It was some way to celebrate Australia Day. Driven by their marauding openers, Australia hit their highest score against Pakistan for the second time in four days. Warner smashed a ballistic 179, his 13th – and biggest – one-day international century, while Head clocked his first, on his home ground. It could have different if a diving Azhar Ali had held Warner at slip off the first ball of the match. Instead, just after the halfway mark, he had a century from 78 balls, his quickest in the format. Warner survived another drop – Mohammad Amir the culprit – while cantering past 150 and, soon after, Head joined the celebrations. In the 41st over, Warner tried one cut too many, ending the stand at 284, Australia's highest for any wicket, beating 260 by Warner and Smith against Afghanistan at the 2105 World Cup. The rest swung hard, and a round 100 came from the final ten. For a time, Sharjeel Khan kept Pakistan interested, with his third fifty of the series. He put on 130 for the second wicket with Babar Azam, who went on to a crisp century, the second by a Pakistani against Australia in Australia, after Zaheer Abbas at Sydney in 1981-82, but their tenth in Australia overall. They were defiant until the last, reaching 300 for the first time in the series, until Starc bowled Wahab Riaz to give him a fourth victim.

Man of the Match: D. A. Warner. *Man of the Series:* D. A. Warner.

Australia

D. A. Warner c Babar Azam b Junaid Khan	179
T. M. Head c Azhar Ali b Hasan Ali	128
*S. P. D. Smith c Wahab Riaz b Junaid Khan	4
G. J. Maxwell c Mohammad Hafeez b Mohammad Amir	13
†M. S. Wade c Shoaib Malik b Hasan Ali	8
P. S. P. Handscomb c Mohammad Hafeez b Wahab Riaz	1
J. P. Faulkner not out	18
M. A. Starc run out	6
P. J. Cummins not out	1
B 1, lb 4, w 6	11
1/284 (1) 2/288 (3) 3/323 (4) 4/336 (5) 5/342 (2) 6/351 (6) 7/367 (8) (7 wkts, 50 overs)	369
10 overs: 67-0	

A. Zampa and J. R. Hazlewood did not bat.

Mohammad Amir 10–0–71–1; Junaid Khan 10–0–61–2; Hasan Ali 9–0–100–2; Mohammad Hafeez 7–0–43–0; Wahab Riaz 10–0–62–1; Shoaib Malik 4–0–27–0.

Pakistan

*Azhar Ali lbw b Starc	6
Sharjeel Khan c Wade b Starc	79
Babar Azam c Head b Hazlewood	100
Mohammad Hafeez c Smith b Starc	3
Shoaib Malik retired hurt	10
Umar Akmal c Wade b Cummins	46
†Mohammad Rizwan c Starc b Cummins	6
Mohammad Amir c Maxwell b Faulkner	17
Wahab Riaz b Starc	17
Hasan Ali st Wade b Zampa	13
Junaid Khan not out	0
Lb 2, w 13	15
1/10 (1) 2/140 (2) 3/145 (4) 4/220 (3) 5/246 (7) 6/276 (6) 7/282 (8) 8/312 (10) 9/312 (9) (49.1 overs)	312
10 overs: 50-1	

Shoaib Malik retired hurt at 181-3.

Starc 9.1–1–42–4; Hazlewood 10–0–74–1; Cummins 10–0–60–2; Faulkner 9–0–60–1; Zampa 9–0–61–1; Head 2–0–13–0.

Umpires: S. D. Fry and C. Shamshuddin. Third umpire: C. B. Gaffaney.
Referee: J. J. Crowe.

KFC T20 BIG BASH LEAGUE IN 2015-16

WILL MACPHERSON

1 Sydney Thunder 2 Melbourne Stars

One number stood above all others in the Big Bash League's fifth edition: the 80,883 who attended the MCG on January 2 for the Melbourne derby. Here was proof, as if it were needed, of a competition that had found its place in Australia's sporting calendar. When this tournament's millionth paying customer turned up for the final, the figures felt seismic.

For the first time, the BBL was news on the front page as well as the back. Journeymen became household names. Devotees and newcomers oohed and aahed at skyscraping sixes. The swelling crowds took the competition into the world's top ten best-attended sports leagues – three behind the sixth-placed IPL – and it also gained bumper TV ratings, with more than a million viewers per match for the first time. None of this happened by accident. Cricket Australia had meticulously identified marquee fixtures and matched them against the most spectator-friendly dates. Traditions emerged: the citizens of Adelaide, for example, wondered what they used to do on New Year's Eve before the BBL.

There was even a bit of slapstick, when a blast from Dwayne Bravo ricocheted off non-striker Peter Nevill's bat, and bowler Adam Zampa's nose, on to the stumps; Nevill was less amused – he was short of his ground when the bails lit up. And there was headline-making controversy. When **Melbourne Renegades** batsman Chris Gayle asked Channel Ten reporter Mel McLaughlin out for a drink during a live pitch-side interview, adding a lascivious "Don't blush, baby," the BBL's family-friendly values were tested to the full. After a show of ambivalence, the Renegades fined Gayle $A10,000.

The on-field narratives were compelling, too: the triumph of perennial cellar-dwellers **Sydney Thunder**, under the leadership of the evergreen Mike Hussey, was an intoxicating tale, while **Melbourne Stars** won a semi-final, at the fifth attempt. But **Adelaide Strikers** lost theirs, to maintain the pool-stage curse: no team finishing top of the table had gone on to win the competition. The 2014-15 finalists **Sydney Sixers** were the tournament's flops. Their star-studded squad were beset by injury and international call-ups, while erstwhile coach Trevor Bayliss's horizontal demeanour was missed. They lost to cross-town rivals Thunder for the first time, on the opening night, and ended bottom. **Brisbane Heat**, reliant on Chris Lynn – he headed the run-charts with 378, over 200 more than his closest team-mate – lost their first four games, but recovered to beat both finalists, and finish above the Sixers and **Hobart Hurricanes**.

Under the former England fast-bowling coach David Saker, the Renegades lost every home game, including the BBL's first ten-wicket defeat, completed by Perth Scorchers openers Shaun Marsh and Michael Klinger. But the Renegades missed out on the semis only after losing the last of them, to the Strikers, despite Gayle's 12-ball half-century – the equal-fastest in all cricket.

The Stars skittled the Scorchers for 94 in Perth to earn a home semi-final, which they won, thanks to 62 off 36 balls from Kevin Pietersen, who enjoyed a superb tournament: his 323 runs were bettered only by Lynn and Usman Khawaja. It was the first time **Perth Scorchers** had failed to reach a BBL final; their title defence had been hampered by injury and international duty. And, although their bowlers – especially Jason Behrendorff, Andrew Tye and England's David Willey – ensured they remained competitive, their batting form deserted them when they needed it most.

The Strikers lost just one pool game, and pulled off a New Year's Eve heist against the Sixers along the way: before a packed Adelaide Oval, Travis Head took 45 from nine Sean Abbott balls to chase 177 with three deliveries to spare, a final six sealing victory, and his century. The Strikers' success, masterminded by new coach Jason Gillespie and 41-year-old skipper Brad Hodge, was built on the leg-spin of Adil Rashid and seamer Ben Laughlin's smart variations. Local lads Head, Alex Ross and Jake Lehmann, son of national coach Darren, shone with the bat. Lehmann struck his first ball of the tournament over long-off for six to complete a home victory over Hobart.

In the semis, the Strikers hosted the Thunder, who had lost four games after winning their first three – including a thrilling one-run victory over the Stars built on a fine century from Khawaja. It began a golden run of 345 in only four innings, with a lowest score of 62. Khawaja had been tempted to leave his franchise during the doldrums of a 19-game losing streak that stretched from December 2011 to January 2014, but was persuaded to stay by Hussey and the shrewd recruitment of experienced all-rounders. Another Khawaja special in the semi-final, an unbeaten 104, knocked off Adelaide's 159 with ease.

After all the preamble, the BBL had the showpiece the organisers craved: two virgin finalists, at the MCG, that millionth spectator and, neatly, a pair of brothers as captains: the Stars' David Hussey and the Thunder's Mike, in his last professional game in Australia – and on their mother Helen's birthday. Khawaja – who else? – made 70, which proved enough to trump Pietersen's 74, and complete Sydney Thunder's remarkable rise to the top.

KFC T20 BIG BASH LEAGUE, 2015-16

	Played	*Won*	*Lost*	*Points*	*Net run-rate*
ADELAIDE STRIKERS	8	7	1	14	0.54
MELBOURNE STARS	8	5	3	10	0.36
PERTH SCORCHERS	8	5	3	10	0.18
SYDNEY THUNDER	8	4	4	8	0.37
Melbourne Renegades	8	3	5	6	–0.04
Brisbane Heat	8	3	5	6	–0.20
Hobart Hurricanes	8	3	5	6	–0.95
Sydney Sixers	8	2	6	4	–0.33

Teams tied on points were separated on net run-rate.

First semi-final At Adelaide, January 21, 2016 (floodlit). **Sydney Thunder won by eight wickets.** ‡**Adelaide Strikers 159-7** (20 overs) (A. I. Ross 47; C. J. McKay 3-44); **Sydney Thunder 160-2** (17.4 overs) (U. T. Khawaja 104*, H. M. Nicholls 35*). *MoM:* U. T. Khawaja. *Attendance:* 48,699. *The Thunder had been the only team to beat the Strikers in the group stages – here they triumphed again. Without resorting to a single slog, Usman Khawaja blazed the ball all around Adelaide Oval,* *cantering to a brilliant match-winning century from only 59 deliveries. Earlier, seamer Clint McKay pegged the Strikers back, on his way to becoming the tournament's leading wicket-taker with 18.*

Second semi-final At Melbourne, January 22, 2016 (floodlit). **Melbourne Stars won by seven wickets. Perth Scorchers 139-7** (20 overs) (M. Klinger 44, A. C. Voges 52; D. J. Worrall 3-25); **‡Melbourne Stars 140-3** (18.1 overs) (M. P. Stoinis 44, K. P. Pietersen 62). *MoM:* K. P. Pietersen. *Attendance:* 30,174. *After a miserly bowling performance, the Stars were never hurried in reply. Kevin Pietersen – who looked imperious in a 36-ball 62 – and Marcus Stoinis began a partnership of 69 with a flurry of boundaries to break the Scorchers' spirits, before easing off as they neared the finishing line.*

FINAL

MELBOURNE STARS v SYDNEY THUNDER

At Melbourne, January 24, 2016 (floodlit). Sydney Thunder won by three wickets. Toss: Sydney Thunder.

The finale was a tale of pairs: two gun batsmen, two collapses and two captain Husseys, one victorious, one not. Pietersen made the early running with a superb 39-ball 74, but found little support. When Kallis yorked David Hussey, it sparked a slide of six for 45. The Thunder's own totem, Khawaja, allied force with finesse to race to another half-century, and make his side strong favourites at 86 for none by the end of the ninth. But, after the retiring Mike Hussey was bowled – and left the field to a standing ovation – they slipped to 146 for five. With nerves jangling, Rohrer had the final say, hoisting a towering straight six off Worrall to complete victory.

Man of the Match: U. T. Khawaja. *Attendance:* 47,672.

Man of the Tournament: C. A. Lynn (Brisbane Heat).

Melbourne Stars

		B	*4/6*
1 M. P. Stoinis *c 5 b 3*	5	8	1
2 L. J. Wright *b 3*	23	24	2/1
3 K. P. Pietersen *c and b 8*	74	39	4/5
4 †P. S. P. Handscomb *c 4 b 8*	9	9	1
5 *D. J. Hussey *b 2*	21	14	2/1
6 R. J. Quiney *c and b 5*	2	4	0
7 E. P. Gulbis *c 8 b 10*	16	11	3
8 A. Zampa *run out*	15	10	1
9 B. W. Hilfenhaus *not out*	0	1	0
10 D. J. Worrall *run out*	0	0	0
B 4, w 7	11		
6 overs: 43-1 (20 overs)	176-9		

1/6 2/50 3/85 4/131 5/139 6/144 7/176 8/176 9/176

11 M. A. Beer did not bat.

Russell 4–12–30–1; Watson 3–9–17–2; McKay 4–4–40–1; Kallis 3–8–24–1; Fawad Ahmed 2–3–24–0; Green 4–7–37–2.

Sydney Thunder

		B	*4/6*
1 U. T. Khawaja *c 10 b 5*	70	40	5/3
2 J. H. Kallis *c 3 b 8*	28	27	4
3 S. R. Watson *c 5 b 1*	6	7	0
4 *M. E. K. Hussey *b 8*	18	15	1
5 A. D. Russell *c 4 b 1*	10	8	0/1
6 B. J. Rohrer *not out*	13	9	0/1
7 A. C. Blizzard *run out*	16	7	2/1
8 C. J. Green *c 5 b 1*	8	5	1
9 †C. D. Hartley *not out*	0	0	0
Lb 3, w 8, nb 1	12		
6 overs: 62-0 (19.3 overs)	181-7		

1/86 2/94 3/123 4/142 5/146 6/163 7/172

10 C. J. McKay and 11 Fawad Ahmed did not bat.

Worrall 3.3–6–42–0; Hilfenhaus 2–2–21–0; Beer 3–10–25–0; Gulbis 2–2–19–0; Zampa 4–8–32–2; Stoinis 4–7–30–3; Hussey 1–2–9–1.

Umpires: S. D. Fry and S. J. Nogajski. Third umpire: G. C. Joshua.
Referee: R. W. Stratford.

BIG BASH FINALS

2011-12 SYDNEY SIXERS beat Perth Scorchers by seven wickets at Perth.
2012-13 BRISBANE HEAT beat Perth Scorchers by 34 runs at Perth.
2013-14 PERTH SCORCHERS beat Hobart Hurricanes by 39 runs at Perth.
2014-15 PERTH SCORCHERS beat Sydney Sixers by four wickets at Canberra.
2015-16 SYDNEY THUNDER beat Melbourne Stars by three wickets at Melbourne.

DOMESTIC CRICKET IN AUSTRALIA IN 2015-16

PETER ENGLISH

Cricket's on-field boundaries seem to shrink each year, but Australia's domestic horizons crossed international waters. A Sheffield Shield fixture headed abroad for the first time, with New South Wales and Western Australia meeting in New Zealand to help players prepare for the upcoming Test series. The schedule also included home fixtures in Mackay, Coffs Harbour and Alice Springs – more like an English backpacker's itinerary than a traditional summer programme.

The venue for the Shield final was also a first: South Australia hosted Victoria in the suburb of Glenelg. They had not reached the final for 20 years, so it was understandable that they had not reserved the Adelaide Oval, which was booked for Australian Rules football. A change in the points system, introduced the previous season – with bonuses for runs and wickets, and no reward for first-innings leads – helped them, and they headed the qualifying table, despite losing five of their ten matches. Victoria joined them in the final, thanks in part to being awarded six points for a game in Sydney which was called off because the outfield had not recovered from the football season. Needing only a draw, South Australia batted first, but their young side could not turn promising starts into substantial contributions, and Victoria raised their 30th Shield, and second in a row.

Victoria had a new coach in David Saker, who had returned home after five years supervising England's seamers, though he moved on to a similar role with Australia after just one season in charge; Andrew McDonald left Leicestershire to take over for 2016-17. Their campaign had a dramatic start when 23-year-old Travis Dean scored twin unbeaten centuries on debut. A third hundred in the Shield final took him to 807 runs at 44 in his first season. Chris Tremain and Scott Boland collected 69 wickets between them, while the recall of Cameron White provided a calm head in the closing stages.

Having finished bottom of the Shield five times in six years, **South Australia** were reborn, reaching two finals. Travis Head, who had assumed the captaincy in February 2015, aged 21, scored three hundreds in his 721 runs, plus a double in the one-day competition. Jake Lehmann, son of Darren, began his first full season with a double-century and added two more hundreds; Alex Ross also passed 600. Joe Mennie grabbed 51 wickets – remarkably, without a single five-wicket return – and Daniel Worrall claimed 44, including six for 96 in the final.

New South Wales finished third in a travel-weary season featuring four different home venues, including Lincoln in New Zealand, as well as the Bankstown Oval (on Cricket Australia's orders, after the outfield debacle at the SCG) and Coffs Harbour (in honour of the late Phillip Hughes, who had lived nearby). Only Kurtis Patterson, with 737 at 52, and Ed Cowan reached 500 Shield runs. They were more successful in the limited-overs arena, heading the one-day table and crushing South Australia in the final, while Sydney Thunder, boosted by Usman Khawaja's flood of 345 runs in four innings, won the Twenty20 Big Bash League.

For **Queensland**, James Hopes bowed out after 15 seasons, taking his 300th first-class wicket in his final game. Young batsmen Matt Renshaw and Sam Heazlett showed promise, as did all-rounder Jack Wildermuth. **Western Australia** waved goodbye to seamer Michael Hogan, still their leading wicket-taker with 37 at the age of 34, while Cameron Bancroft and Michael Klinger continued to bat responsibly.

It was mostly a season to forget for **Tasmania**, despite Ben Dunk topping the Shield run-list with 837, and Jackson Bird swinging to 40 wickets at 19. They finished far behind the pack in the Shield, and were the only side to lose to the Cricket Australia XI in the one-day tournament. This team, a development squad of players not used by their states, were despatched for 59 and 79 in their first two fixtures, before pipping Tasmania by three runs in the third game.

FIRST-CLASS AVERAGES, 2015-16

BATTING (500 runs)

	M	*I*	*NO*	*R*	*HS*	*100*	*Avge*	*Ct/St*
A. C. Voges (*Western Australia/Australia*)	10	14	4	1,057	269*	4	105.70	6
†U. T. Khawaja (*Queensland/Australia*)	5	7	1	536	174	3	89.33	1
S. P. D. Smith (*NSW/Australia*)	7	11	3	714	152*	3	89.25	13
†D. A. Warner (*NSW/Australia*)	7	12	1	925	253	4	84.09	7
†S. E. Marsh (*Western Australia/Australia*)	8	14	0	749	182	2	53.50	9
†K. R. Patterson (*Cricket Aus XI/NSW*)	10	17	3	737	129*	2	52.64	4
G. J. Bailey (*Tasmania*)	9	17	1	761	148*	3	47.56	8
M. Klinger (*Western Australia*)	10	16	3	617	202*	2	47.46	14
†B. R. Dunk (*Tasmania*)	10	19	1	837	190	4	46.50	8
C. T. Bancroft (*Western Australia*)	10	17	1	732	171	3	45.75	18/1
T. J. Dean (*Victoria*)	11	20	2	807	154*	3	44.83	6
†J. S. Lehmann (*South Australia*)	8	14	0	623	205	3	44.50	6
†C. D. Hartley (*Queensland*)	10	18	6	529	70*	0	44.08	35
P. S. P. Handscomb (*Victoria*)	11	19	1	784	137	3	43.55	21
†M. T. Renshaw (*Queensland*)	9	17	0	738	170	2	43.41	10
R. G. L. Carters (*Cricket Aus XI/NSW*)	9	15	0	643	209	1	42.86	16
†S. D. Heazlett (*Queensland*)	9	17	1	649	129	1	40.56	9
M. P. Stoinis (*Victoria*)	11	18	1	659	110	2	38.76	5
†E. J. M. Cowan (*New South Wales*)	9	17	3	509	107*	1	36.35	6
†T. M. Head (*South Australia*)	11	21	1	721	192	3	36.05	6
A. I. Ross (*South Australia*)	11	20	2	642	92*	0	35.66	12
†R. J. Quiney (*Victoria*)	10	18	1	557	85*	0	32.76	9
J. A. Burns (*Queensland/Australia*)	10	18	0	569	129	2	31.61	13
†M. J. Cosgrove (*South Australia*)	11	21	0	565	65	0	26.90	7

BOWLING (15 wickets, average 40.00)

	Style	*O*	*M*	*R*	*W*	*BB*	*5I*	*Avge*
M. A. Starc (*NSW/Australia*)	LF	118.2	25	392	21	5-28	1	18.66
J. M. Bird (*Tasmania*)	RFM	276.2	68	780	40	7-45	3	19.50
J. S. Paris (*Western Australia*)	LFM	212.3	50	685	35	6-23	2	19.57
S. M. Boland (*Victoria*)	RFM	282.4	84	691	33	7-31	2	20.93
C. P. Tremain (*Victoria*)	RFM	228.1	60	758	36	5-52	1	21.05
T. A. Copeland (*New South Wales*)	RFM	209.3	62	550	26	7-58	2	21.15
J. M. Mennie (*South Australia*)	RFM	429.5	108	1,082	51	4-50	0	21.21
J. D. Wildermuth (*Queensland*)	RFM	190.1	44	574	25	4-27	0	22.96
J. L. Pattinson (*Victoria/Australia*)	RFM	186	34	601	26	5-27	1	23.11
D. E. Bollinger (*New South Wales*)	LFM	221	64	634	27	4-74	0	23.48
S. N. J. O'Keefe (*NSW/Australia*)	SLA	191.3	43	482	20	4-38	0	24.10
M. R. Marsh (*W Australia/Australia*)	RFM	123.3	30	412	17	4-61	0	24.23
M. G. Hogan (*Western Australia*)	RFM	342.5	112	912	37	4-29	0	24.64
J. R. Hopes (*Queensland*)	RFM	313.2	94	714	28	4-32	0	25.50
J. R. Hazlewood (*NSW/Australia*)	RFM	230.4	50	670	26	6-70	1	25.76
D. J. Worrall (*South Australia*)	RFM	357.5	65	1,152	44	6-96	3	26.18
C. J. Sayers (*South Australia*)	RFM	306.1	85	889	32	7-46	1	27.78
P. R. George (*Queensland*)	RFM	204.1	50	579	20	3-39	0	28.95
H. P. Kingston (*Tasmania*)	RFM	125.1	23	525	18	4-61	0	29.16
P. M. Siddle (*Victoria/Australia*)	RFM	186	46	487	16	3-21	0	30.43
Fawad Ahmed (*Victoria*)	LBG	252.3	32	899	27	5-24	2	33.29
A. L. Fekete (*Tasmania*)	RFM	254.2	57	951	28	5-77	1	33.96
M. T. Steketee (*Queensland*)	RFM	267.3	64	850	23	4-52	0	36.95
M. J. Swepson (*Cricket Aus XI/Qld*)	LBG	164.5	18	645	17	3-64	0	37.94
S. A. Abbott (*New South Wales*)	RFM	246.4	45	804	21	3-51	0	38.28

Averages include the Sheffield Shield match between New South Wales and Western Australia played in New Zealand.

SHEFFIELD SHIELD, 2015-16

	Played	*Won*	*Lost*	*Drawn*	*Bonus points Batting*	*Bonus points Bowling*	*Points*
SOUTH AUSTRALIA	10	5	5	0	6.63	13	49.63
VICTORIA	10	5*	3	2	6.13	11	49.13
New South Wales	10	5	2*	3	5.57	9	47.57
Queensland	10	5	5	0	7.66	9	46.66
Western Australia	10	4	3	3	7.00	10	44.00
Tasmania	10	2	8	0	6.69	10.5	27.19†

* *Match awarded to Victoria because of an unsafe outfield in Sydney.*

† *2pts deducted for a slow over-rate.*

Outright win = 6pts; draw = 1pt. Bonus points awarded for the first 100 overs of each team's first innings: 0.01 batting points for every run over the first 200 runs; 0.5 bowling points for the fifth wicket taken and for every subsequent two.

At Adelaide, October 28–30, 2015 (day/night). **New South Wales won by 215 runs.** ‡**New South Wales 262-9 dec and 291-1 dec** (E. J. M. Cowan 107*, S. P. D. Smith 152*); **South Australia 120** (M. A. Starc 5-28) **and 218.** *New South Wales 8.12pts, South Australia 1.5pts. Pink balls were used in this round, with the third session played under lights. South Australia lost their top three for ducks on the first night and were 27-6 next day, with Mitchell Starc on his way to a Shield-best 5-28. But Ed Cowan and Steve Smith had no such problems: their second-wicket stand reached 160* overnight, and extended to 234* on the third day, when New South Wales won comfortably.*

At Hobart, October 28–31, 2015 (day/night). **Western Australia won by 162 runs. Western Australia 432-8 dec** (M. Klinger 202*, A. C. Agar 105) **and 136-4 dec;** ‡**Tasmania 189 and 217.** *Western Australia 8.16pts, Tasmania 0.5pts. Michael Klinger, with his fifth double-hundred but his first since leaving South Australia, and Ashton Agar, with a maiden century, added 214 for Western Australia's seventh wicket.*

At Melbourne, October 28–31, 2015 (day/night). **Victoria won by nine wickets.** ‡**Queensland 444** (S. O. Henry 141) **and 103; Victoria 319-3 dec** (T. J. Dean 154*, P. S. P. Handscomb 137) **and 230-1** (T. J. Dean 109*). *Victoria 7.69pts, Queensland 1.1pts. Travis Dean became the seventh player to score twin hundreds on first-class debut, and the first to be unbeaten in both; he was on the field for the entire match. In the first innings, he added 271 for Victoria's third wicket with Peter Handscomb; Matthew Wade declared 125 behind, then Queensland were rolled over inside 33 overs.*

At Sydney, November 6–7, 2015. **Victoria awarded match.** ‡**New South Wales 88-1 v Victoria.** *Victoria 6pts. Rain permitted only 34.2 overs on the first two days, and the match was abandoned on the third because parts of the outfield were unsafe. Ryan Carters was the only batsman dismissed – just as in his previous game, for Cricket Australia XI v New Zealanders at Sydney's Blacktown Sportspark, which was also abandoned after two days because of a deteriorating surface (see* Wisden 2016, *page 934).*

At Adelaide, November 6–9, 2015. **South Australia won by one wicket.** ‡**Western Australia 211 and 295** (C. T. Bancroft 111); **South Australia 191 and 317-9** (T. M. Head 114). *South Australia 7.5pts, Western Australia 1.61pts. South Australia had just over a day to score 316. Travis Head's maiden century helped them to 269-4; then they lost five for 39 before the last pair crossed the line.*

At Hobart, November 6–9, 2015. **Queensland won by three wickets.** ‡**Tasmania 433-8 dec** (B. R. Dunk 142, G. J. Bailey 148*) **and 168; Queensland 329-8 dec** (S. D. Heazlett 129) **and 274-7.** *Queensland 6.36pts, Tasmania 1.48pts. This turned out to be Tasmanian seamer Ben Hilfenhaus's last first-class game; he claimed the 387th wicket of a ten-year career, including a record 262 for Tasmania. Ben Dunk scored a maiden hundred, before 20-year-old left-hander Sam Heazlett made 129 on first-class debut. Queensland declared 104 behind and forced a win.*

At Sydney (Bankstown Oval), November 14–17, 2015. **Tasmania won by 223 runs.** ‡**Tasmania 295 and 313-7 dec** (B. R. Dunk 143*); **New South Wales 215 and 170.** *Tasmania 8.45pts, New South Wales 1.65pts. This game was moved from the SCG after the last there was called off. Dunk's match-winning 143* was a career-best.*

At Brisbane, November 14–17, 2015. **Queensland won by an innings and 14 runs. South Australia 203 and 235;** ‡**Queensland 452** (M. Labuschagne 112). *Queensland 8.51pts, South Australia*

0.53pts. Queensland wicketkeeper Chris Hartley held five catches in each innings (the fourth time he had made ten dismissals in a match) and became only the second player with 500 dismissals in Shield cricket after Darren Berry.

At Melbourne, November 14–17, 2015. **Drawn. ‡Victoria 423-7 dec and 238-7 dec; Western Australia 272** (Fawad Ahmed 5-105) **and 282-8** (W. G. Bosisto 108). *Victoria 3.75pts, Western Australia 1.51pts. Victoria's captain and wicketkeeper Wade broke his collarbone in the nets just before the start; reserve keeper Aaron Ayre was allowed to make his debut, while Peter Siddle deputised as captain. Dean was dismissed for the first time in his third first-class innings, for 84, taking his aggregate to 347.*

At Sydney, November 27–30, 2015. **New South Wales won by seven wickets. ‡Queensland 259 and 145; New South Wales 303** (N. J. Maddinson 112) **and 102-3.** *New South Wales 8.03pts, Queensland 1.82pts. Both teams wore black armbands to mark the anniversary of Phillip Hughes's death after he was struck on the neck while batting at this ground.*

At Hobart, November 27–30, 2015. **South Australia won by 302 runs. South Australia 600-7 dec** (C. J. Ferguson 213, J. S. Lehmann 205) **and 185** (J. M. Bird 5-69); **‡Tasmania 284** (B. R. Dunk 115, G. J. Bailey 112) **and 199.** *South Australia 9.97pts, Tasmania 0.84pts. Jake Lehmann converted his maiden hundred into 205, and Callum Ferguson scored his first double-century. Together, they added 378; the only higher fourth-wicket stand in Shield cricket was 462*, also for South Australia v Tasmania, by David Hookes and Wayne Phillips in 1986-87; their total of 600-7 remained the highest of this tournament. Tasmania's own fourth wicket added 167, but once Ben Dunk fell on the second evening, for his third century in successive games, the balance shifted towards the bowlers.*

At Perth, November 27–29, 2015. **Victoria won by 356 runs. Victoria 322 and 322-7 dec** (M. P. Stoinis 110); **‡Western Australia 186 and 102** (S. M. Boland 7-31). *Victoria 8.72pts, Western Australia 1.5pts. Victoria scored 322 in each innings; Western Australia totalled 288 over two, and succumbed to their heaviest defeat by runs in Shield cricket. Scott Boland claimed a career-best 11.2–1–31–7 – the tournament's best return – on the final day, when no home batsman passed 16.*

At Mackay, December 6–9, 2015. **New South Wales won by three wickets. ‡Queensland 342** (M. T. Renshaw 170; W. E. R. Somerville 5-110) **and 131-7 dec; New South Wales 260 and 217-7.** *New South Wales 6pts, Queensland 0.73pts. This was the second first-class match at the Ray Mitchell Oval in Harrup Park, following Queensland v Sri Lankans in November 1995. Nineteen-year-old Matt Renshaw hit a maiden hundred.*

At Melbourne, December 6–8, 2015. **South Australia won by eight wickets. Victoria 180** (D. J. Worrall 5-69) **and 163; ‡South Australia 199** (C. P. Tremain 5-52) **and 145-2.** *South Australia 7.5pts, Victoria 1.5pts. Sixteen wickets fell on the opening day, when Daniel Worrall claimed five for the first time. South Australia's win put them a fraction of a point behind leaders Victoria.*

At Perth, December 6–9, 2015. **Western Australia won by nine wickets. Tasmania 261 and 205** (J. S. Paris 6-23); **‡Western Australia 415** (A. C. Agar 106; A. L. Fekete 5-77) **and 52-1.** *Western Australia 8.34pts, Tasmania 1.11pts. Coming in at 219-5, Agar scored his second century of the season against Tasmania, helping Western Australia to a lead of 154. Joel Paris took 6-23 in his second first-class match.*

At Adelaide, February 3–6, 2016. **Queensland won by 173 runs. ‡Queensland 474-6 dec** (M. T. Renshaw 146, J. D. Wildermuth 100*) **and 258-8 dec; South Australia 315** (J. S. Lehmann 126) **and 244.** *Queensland 9.23pts, South Australia 1.65pts. Renshaw hit another hundred, with seven sixes in all, on the first day, and a maiden century from Jack Wildermuth took Queensland to what proved a match-winning total.*

At Lincoln (Bert Sutcliffe Oval), New Zealand, February 3–6, 2016. **Drawn. New South Wales 402 and 155-5; ‡Western Australia 491** (A. C. Voges 149). *New South Wales 2.57pts, Western Australia 2.57pts. This was the first Sheffield Shield match outside Australia, with the aim of preparing players for the Test series against New Zealand beginning the following week. Both sides passed 400; Adam Voges warmed up with his 30th first-class century, adding 157 for Western Australia's seventh wicket with Sam Whiteman (93). Cowan was hit on the helmet by a bouncer from Paris just before bad light ended the third day; he missed New South Wales's next game, in Perth.*

At Melbourne, February 3–5, 2016. **Victoria won by seven wickets. Tasmania 241** (B. J. Webster 107) **and 228; ‡Victoria 271 and 200-3.** *Victoria 8.21pts, Tasmania 1.91pts. At 19 years 55 days, Sam Harper became Victoria's youngest wicketkeeper; by the time his team had won two days later,* *he was also the youngest Australian to make nine dismissals in a match. Victoria required two full substitutes after Marcus Stoinis and James Pattinson left to join the tour of New Zealand.*

At Brisbane, February 14–17, 2016 (day/night). **Queensland won by seven wickets. ‡Tasmania 300** (B. J. Webster 106) **and 233; Queensland 376 and 158-3.** *Queensland 9.23pts, Tasmania 2.39pts. Cricket Australia decided in December to make this a second round of day/night matches. Beau Webster scored his second successive hundred in a losing cause. Hartley (70*) and James Hopes (94 in 60 balls) added 128 in 21 overs for Queensland's seventh wicket.*

At Adelaide, February 14–17, 2016 (day/night). **Victoria won by 218 runs. ‡Victoria 325-9 dec and 306-5 dec** (P. S. P. Handscomb 102); **South Australia 224** (S. M. Boland 5-38) **and 189** (Fawad Ahmed 5-24). *Victoria 8.75pts, South Australia 1.74pts. Victoria consolidated their position at the top of the table against South Australia, who started in second place.*

At Perth, February 14–17, 2016 (day/night). **Drawn. ‡New South Wales 316** (D. P. Hughes 124) **and 303-5** (K. R. Patterson 129*); **Western Australia 511-8 dec** (C. T. Bancroft 144, M. S. Harris 120). *Western Australia 2.86pts, New South Wales 1.94pts. Cameron Bancroft added 205 with Marcus Harris for Western Australia's third wicket, and 170 with Ashton Turner (96) for their fourth, but Kurtis Patterson ensured the draw.*

At Coffs Harbour, February 25–28, 2016. **New South Wales won by five wickets. South Australia 298** (J. S. Lehmann 122) **and 177** (T. A. Copeland 5-62); **‡New South Wales 211 and 267-5** (B. J. Rohrer 109*). *New South Wales 7.61pts, South Australia 2.48pts. The Phillip Hughes Tribute match, played by his two former states, was the first first-class fixture at Coffs Harbour, near Macksville, Hughes's home town on New South Wales's north coast.*

At Hobart, February 25–28, 2016. **Tasmania won by an innings and 136 runs. Victoria 165 and 265** (C. L. White 106); **‡Tasmania 566-8 dec** (B. R. Dunk 190, A. J. Doolan 119, G. J. Bailey 107). *Tasmania 9.09pts, Victoria 0.5pts. Bottom-placed Tasmania crushed leaders Victoria. Dunk, with his fourth century of the season, and Alex Doolan put on 294 for Tasmania's third wicket; George Bailey and Tom Triffitt (67) added 175 for the sixth, and a total of 566 left them 401 ahead. Wicketkeeper Triffitt followed up with six catches in Victoria's second innings, including Cameron White and Boland, who added 130 for the eighth wicket.*

At Perth, February 25–28, 2016. **Western Australia won by 24 runs. Western Australia 436-6 dec** (C. T. Bancroft 171) **and 291-5 dec** (S. E. Marsh 109, M. Klinger 102*); **‡Queensland 446-8 dec** (M. Labuschagne 103, C. A. Lynn 101) **and 257** (C. R. Hemphrey 102). *Western Australia 7.28pts, Queensland 1.18pts. This game featured six centuries. Bancroft shared stands of 116 with Harris and 205 with Shaun Marsh for Western Australia's first two wickets. Klinger reached three figures in just 84 balls. Set 282, Queensland were 207-3 but lost their last seven for 50 – four of them to Paris, a full substitute for Nathan Coulter-Nile, who left for Australia's trip to South Africa.*

At Brisbane, March 5–7, 2016. **Queensland won by 100 runs. Queensland 190 and 184; ‡Victoria 147 and 127.** *Queensland 7.5pts, Victoria 1.5pts. In a match producing only two fifties, Wildermuth claimed seven wickets in a three-day win which kept Queensland in second place behind Victoria going into the final round.*

At Hobart, March 5–7, 2016. **New South Wales won by seven wickets. Tasmania 242** (H. N. A. Conway 5-45) **and 177** (T. A. Copeland 7-58); **‡New South Wales 271** (K. R. Patterson 100; J. M. Bird 7-45) **and 150-3** (D. P. Hughes 100*). *New South Wales 8.21pts, Tasmania 1.92pts. Debutant seamer Harry Conway took five wickets on the first day. Jackson Bird hit back with a career-best 7-45, but Trent Copeland also took seven to set up a target of 149; both had ten in the match. Daniel Hughes sealed an 89-ball century and a three-day victory with four successive fours.*

At Perth, March 5–8, 2016. **South Australia won by one wicket. Western Australia 311** (H. W. R. Cartwright 139; D. J. Worrall 5-91) **and 192; ‡South Australia 230 and 275-9** (T. M. Head 134; J. S. Paris 5-87). *South Australia 7.8pts, Western Australia 2.35pts. Paris completed a hat-trick of sorts with his first ball, after he had wrapped up victory against Queensland with two in two. For the second time in the season, Head scored a century to help his team to a one-wicket win over Western Australia after trailing on first innings. Nick Benton, who had dislocated his shoulder, came in at 267-9 and hit the winning four; though South Australia were in fourth place, they were only six points behind Victoria, keeping their hopes alive.*

At Alice Springs, March 15–18, 2016. **Drawn. ‡New South Wales 341 and 178** (D. T. Christian 5-40); **Victoria 251** (M. P. Stoinis 107) **and 234-7.** *New South Wales 3.44pts, Victoria 2.51pts. Arriving at 242-8 in New South Wales's first innings, Nathan Lyon made 75 in 60 balls, with five* *sixes, including a maiden fifty in 36. Victoria were 56-6 on the fourth morning, 212 behind, and looked like squandering the lead they had enjoyed for most of the season. But White secured the draw with 97*, keeping New South Wales out of the final – though Victoria, half a point behind South Australia, lost the chance to stage the decider on this ground.*

At Brisbane, March 15–17, 2016. **Western Australia won by an innings and six runs. Queensland 147 and 227; ‡Western Australia 380.** *Western Australia 7.82pts, Queensland 1pt. Western Australian wicketkeeper Whiteman held six catches in Queensland's first innings, helping reduce them to 41-6. Hilton Cartwright (92) and Josh Nicholas (68*) put on 118 for Western Australia's ninth wicket. Chris Lynn smashed 80 in 46 balls with five sixes in Queensland's second innings, but defeat dashed their hopes of reaching the final. This was the last first-class match played by James Hopes, whose three wickets gave him 301, to go with 5,402 runs.*

At Adelaide (Glenelg Oval), March 15–16, 2016. **South Australia won by an innings and 78 runs. ‡Tasmania 91** (C. J. Sayers 7-46) **and 177; South Australia 346** (T. M. Head 192; J. M. Bird 5-81). *South Australia 8.96pts, Tasmania 1.5pts. Tasmania chose to bat and slumped to 18-4, then 91 all out, with Chadd Sayers collecting a career-best 7-46 (on his way to 10-77 in the match). By the end of the first day, South Australia were seven down but 148 in front. Head just missed a maiden double-hundred – he hit five sixes in 176 balls – but a two-day win meant South Australia leapt from fourth place to first, to claim home advantage in the final.*

FINAL

SOUTH AUSTRALIA v VICTORIA

At Adelaide (Glenelg Oval), March 26–30, 2016. Victoria won by seven wickets. Toss: South Australia.

Second-placed Victoria had to win to retain the Sheffield Shield, and their experience – plus another hundred for new star Travis Dean – paid off against South Australia's emerging side, who could not make the most of a flat pitch. Victoria were batting early on the second day; centuries from Dean and Handscomb, plus 78 from White, carried them to a 59-run lead, despite Worrall's career-best six, and Mennie's 50th wicket of the campaign. Slow left-armer Holland, in his second game of the season, then reduced South Australia's impatient top order to 76 for four. But Weatherald was approaching a maiden hundred when he skyed a catch off leg-spinner Fawad Ahmed, triggering a cascade of four for 11. Victoria breezed past a target of 193 on the final morning, when Stoinis reached his fifty with four consecutive sixes off Head; by then Sayers was injured and Worrall too sore to bowl. Victoria's coach, David Saker, had won the Shield in what was to be his only season in charge. Meanwhile, his assistant Mick Lewis was fined after scraping the ball in the gutter during South Australia's second innings.

Man of the Match: P. S. P. Handscomb.

Close of play: first day, South Australia 325-8 (Sayers 20, Worrall 5); second day, Victoria 269-4 (Handscomb 79, Boland 5); third day, South Australia 137-4 (Weatherald 72, Ross 30); fourth day, Victoria 95-2 (Stoinis 17, Handscomb 18).

South Australia

J. B. Weatherald c Wade b Christian	66	– c Handscomb b Fawad Ahmed	96
M. J. Cosgrove lbw b Tremain	42	– c Quiney b Holland	16
S. J. Raphael b Holland	29	– run out	8
*T. M. Head c White b Christian	21	– c Wade b Holland	1
J. S. Lehmann b Holland	14	– c Quiney b Holland	0
A. I. Ross b Boland	72	– c Christian b Holland	71
†A. T. Carey c Handscomb b Holland	50	– c Christian b Holland	0
J. M. Mennie c Wade b Fawad Ahmed	1	– c Wade b Fawad Ahmed	4
C. J. Sayers c Wade b Tremain	27	– (11) c Fawad Ahmed b Boland	10
D. J. Worrall b Tremain	9	– (9) not out	19
E. K. Opie not out	4	– (10) b Tremain	15
Lb 4, nb 1	5	Lb 2, w 4, p 5	11
1/90 (1) 2/131 (2) 3/162 (4) 4/162 (3) 5/185 (5) 6/288 (7) 7/290 (8) 8/318 (6) 9/329 (10) 10/340 (9) (93.3 overs)	340	1/48 (2) 2/63 (3) 3/76 (4) 4/76 (5) 5/197 (1) 6/197 (7) 7/206 (6) 8/208 (8) 9/230 (10) 10/251 (11) (102.5 overs)	251

Tremain 15.3–4–73–3; Boland 21–4–67–1; Stoinis 8–1–34–0; Christian 11–3–43–2; Holland 29–8–86–3; Fawad Ahmed 9–2–33–1. *Second innings*—Tremain 21–4–55–1; Boland 21.5–6–66–1; Holland 37–10–76–5; Fawad Ahmed 15–3–35–2; Christian 8–2–12–0.

Victoria

R. J. Quiney c Raphael b Worrall	23	– (2) lbw b Worrall	2
T. J. Dean c Carey b Opie	111	– (1) lbw b Mennie	54
M. P. Stoinis c Carey b Worrall	35	– c Worrall b Opie	72
P. S. P. Handscomb b Opie	112	– not out	61
*†M. S. Wade b Worrall	14	– not out	2
S. M. Boland lbw b Mennie	5		
C. L. White b Worrall	78		
D. T. Christian b Worrall	12		
C. P. Tremain lbw b Worrall	0		
J. M. Holland c Ross b Mennie	5		
Fawad Ahmed not out	0		
Lb 1, nb 3	4	Lb 1, nb 4	5
1/29 (1) 2/105 (3) 3/245 (2) 4/260 (5) 5/269 (6) 6/318 (4) 7/345 (8) 8/345 (9) 9/399 (10) 10/399 (7) (121.2 overs)	399	1/15 (2) 2/70 (1) 3/182 (3) (3 wkts, 51 overs)	196

Sayers 20–6–61–0; Worrall 34.2–8–96–6; Mennie 35–8–102–2; Opie 23–1–92–2; Head 9–1–47–0. *Second innings*—Worrall 14–3–62–1; Mennie 16–4–35–1; Opie 9–1–15–1; Lehmann 4–1–18–0; Head 8–0–65–0.

Umpires: M. D. Martell and P. Wilson. Third umpire: J. D. Ward.
Referee: S. R. Bernard.

SHEFFIELD SHIELD WINNERS

1892-93	Victoria	1924-25	Victoria	1958-59	New South Wales
1893-94	South Australia	1925-26	New South Wales	1959-60	New South Wales
1894-95	Victoria	1926-27	South Australia	1960-61	New South Wales
1895-96	New South Wales	1927-28	Victoria	1961-62	New South Wales
1896-97	New South Wales	1928-29	New South Wales	1962-63	Victoria
1897-98	Victoria	1929-30	Victoria	1963-64	South Australia
1898-99	Victoria	1930-31	Victoria	1964-65	New South Wales
1899-1900	New South Wales	1931-32	New South Wales	1965-66	New South Wales
1900-01	Victoria	1932-33	New South Wales	1966-67	Victoria
1901-02	New South Wales	1933-34	Victoria	1967-68	Western Australia
1902-03	New South Wales	1934-35	Victoria	1968-69	South Australia
1903-04	New South Wales	1935-36	South Australia	1969-70	Victoria
1904-05	New South Wales	1936-37	Victoria	1970-71	South Australia
1905-06	New South Wales	1937-38	New South Wales	1971-72	Western Australia
1906-07	New South Wales	1938-39	South Australia	1972-73	Western Australia
1907-08	Victoria	1939-40	New South Wales	1973-74	Victoria
1908-09	New South Wales	1940–46	*No competition*	1974-75	Western Australia
1909-10	South Australia	1946-47	Victoria	1975-76	South Australia
1910-11	New South Wales	1947-48	Western Australia	1976-77	Western Australia
1911-12	New South Wales	1948-49	New South Wales	1977-78	Western Australia
1912-13	South Australia	1949-50	New South Wales	1978-79	Victoria
1913-14	New South Wales	1950-51	Victoria	1979-80	Victoria
1914-15	Victoria	1951-52	New South Wales	1980-81	Western Australia
1915–19	*No competition*	1952-53	South Australia	1981-82	South Australia
1919-20	New South Wales	1953-54	New South Wales	1982-83	New South Wales*
1920-21	New South Wales	1954-55	New South Wales	1983-84	Western Australia
1921-22	Victoria	1955-56	New South Wales	1984-85	New South Wales
1922-23	New South Wales	1956-57	New South Wales	1985-86	New South Wales
1923-24	Victoria	1957-58	New South Wales	1986-87	Western Australia

1987-88	Western Australia	1997-98	Western Australia	2007-08	New South Wales
1988-89	Western Australia	1998-99	Western Australia*	2008-09	Victoria
1989-90	New South Wales	1999-2000	Queensland	2009-10	Victoria
1990-91	Victoria	2000-01	Queensland	2010-11	Tasmania
1991-92	Western Australia	2001-02	Queensland	2011-12	Queensland
1992-93	New South Wales	2002-03	New South Wales*	2012-13	Tasmania
1993-94	New South Wales	2003-04	Victoria	2013-14	New South Wales
1994-95	Queensland	2004-05	New South Wales*	2014-15	Victoria
1995-96	South Australia	2005-06	Queensland	2015-16	Victoria*
1996-97	Queensland*	2006-07	Tasmania		

New South Wales have won the title 46 times, Victoria 30, Western Australia 15, South Australia 13, Queensland 7, Tasmania 3.

The tournament was known as the Pura Milk Cup in 1999-2000, and the Pura Milk Cup from 2000-01 to 2007-08.

* *Second in table but won final. Finals were introduced in 1982-83.*

MATADOR BBQs ONE-DAY CUP, 2015-16

50-over league plus play-off and final

	Played	*Won*	*Lost*	*Bonus points*	*Points*	*Net run-rate*
NEW SOUTH WALES	6	5	1	6	26	2.24
VICTORIA	6	4	2	2	18	0.82
SOUTH AUSTRALIA	6	4	2	1	17	–0.43
Tasmania	6	3	3	2	14	0.38
Western Australia	6	2	4	2	10	0.46
Queensland	6	2	4	0	8	–0.67
Cricket Australia XI	6	1	5	0	4	–2.89

Win = 4pts; 1 bonus point for achieving victory with a run-rate 1.25 times that of the opposition, and 2 bonus pts for victory with a run-rate twice that of the opposition.

Play-off At Sydney (Drummoyne Oval), October 23, 2015 (day/night). **South Australia won by 56 runs. ‡South Australia 250-7** (50 overs); **Victoria 194** (46.4 overs). *South Australia's Alex Ross was stranded just short of a maiden century in all senior cricket, but his 104-ball 97* set a target of 251. Rob Quiney and Marcus Stoinis added 113 for Victoria's second wicket, but once they were separated their team fell away.*

Final At North Sydney, October 25, 2015. **New South Wales won by nine wickets. South Australia 221** (46.3 overs) (T. L. W. Cooper 105); **‡New South Wales 223-1** (29.5 overs). *MoM:* J. R. Hazlewood (NSW). *MoS:* M. A. Starc (NSW). *Callum Ferguson (61) and Tom Cooper piled up 154 for South Australia's third wicket, but their last seven went down for 30, and Josh Hazlewood finished with 3-28. Ed Cowan (88*) and Steve Smith (84* including six sixes) cruised to victory with 20 overs to spare in a second-wicket stand of 165*. It was New South Wales's third successive one-day final, but the first they had won since 2005-06.*

The KFC T20 Big Bash League has its own section *(page 878).*

BANGLADESH CRICKET IN 2016

Tigers' balm

UTPAL SHUVRO

On July 1, terrorists ambushed a cafe in Gulshan, the diplomatic hub of Dhaka, and killed 29 people. Many were concerned the attack would condemn Bangladesh to the fate of Pakistan – a land considered too dangerous for cricketing tourists – particularly as Australia had postponed a visit in 2015 because of safety concerns. But, after sending a delegation to inspect security provisions, the England management decided their October tour would go ahead. The news was greeted with joy.

In recent years, Bangladesh had established themselves as a formidable limited-overs force, especially at home. But their form in Test cricket lagged behind, largely because of its scarcity. When the England series began, they had not played with a red ball for 15 months, so no one was expecting much.

Their brilliant display in the First Test at Chittagong surprised everyone. It was a classic, possibly the best played in Bangladesh, and went punch for

BANGLADESH IN 2016

	Played	*Won*	*Lost*	*Drawn/No result*
Tests	2	1	1	–
One-day internationals	9	3	6	–
Twenty20 internationals	16	7	8	1

JANUARY	4 T20Is (h) v Zimbabwe	(page 891)
FEBRUARY / MARCH	Asia Cup (h)	(page 893)
MARCH / APRIL	ICC World Twenty20 (in India)	(page 793)
MAY		
JUNE		
JULY		
AUGUST		
SEPTEMBER / OCTOBER	3 ODIs (h) v Afghanistan	(page 900)
OCTOBER	2 Tests and 3 ODIs (h) v England	(page 323)
NOVEMBER		
DECEMBER / JANUARY	2 Tests, 3 ODIs and 3 T20Is (a) v New Zealand	(page 966)

For a review of Bangladesh domestic cricket from the 2015-16 season, see page 902.

punch throughout, until England prevailed by 22 runs on the final morning. Less than a week later at Mirpur, disappointment turned to jubilation: Bangladesh took ten wickets in the last session of the third day to win by 108 runs and square the series. It was their eighth victory from their 95 Tests, and their first against anyone other than Zimbabwe or West Indies. Mehedi Hasan, the off-spinner who had been Player of the Tournament at the Under-19 World Cup at home at the start of the year, immediately became a star. He opened the bowling in the first innings at Chittagong, took six wickets with exemplary control, and added two more six-fors at Mirpur. Tamim Iqbal backed him up with the bat, hitting 231 runs at 58, including the only hundred of the series.

The preceding one-dayers had been equally hard fought. Bangladesh had won their previous six series at home, their victims including Pakistan, India and South Africa. Had they not squandered a dominant position in the first match, it might have been seven. With 39 needed from 56 balls, they lost six for 17. Bangladesh won the second game, but lost a tense decider.

If the Test win at Mirpur was Bangladesh's high point in 2016, the World Twenty20 was its nadir. In preparation, the Asia Cup – which they hosted for the third time in a row – was transformed into a 20-over tournament, having been a 50-over competition since its inception in 1984. Bangladesh beat Sri Lanka and Pakistan to reach the final, only to be trounced by India. Sixteen days later, the teams met again in a World T20 group match at Bangalore. Bangladesh needed two off three balls to eliminate India from their own tournament. Instead, Mushfiqur Rahim and Mahmudullah perished in consecutive balls while trying to finish it in style; a frantic last-ball run-out denied them even a tie. New Zealand then condemned them to four defeats out of four.

There was more bad news. During the qualifier against the Netherlands, fast bowler Taskin Ahmed and left-arm spinner Arafat Sunny were reported for suspect actions. And, following tests in Chennai, they were suspended, despite an outcry from the Bangladesh management, who saw a conspiracy in the timing. After remedial work, the pair were cleared in September, though with different outcomes: Taskin returned to international cricket and starred in the one-day series against England, but Sunny was reported again during the Bangladesh Premier League in November.

The year's biggest controversy centred on the adoption of a new selection process. Previously, the three-member panel would consult the captain and coach, but had the freedom to choose the side. In May, the committee were expanded to include Chandika Hathurusinghe, the head coach, and two from the BCB: Akram Khan, the cricket operations chairman, and Khaled Mahmud, the team manager. Faruk Ahmed, the chief selector under the old system, resigned in June, citing concerns about board interference. He was replaced by former colleague Minhajul Abedin who, despite the ructions, will find comfort from having the players to compete with the red ball, as well as the white.

BANGLADESH v ZIMBABWE IN 2015-16

MOHAMMAD ISAM

Twenty20 internationals (4): Bangladesh 2, Zimbabwe 2

The Bangladesh Cricket Board announced they would be hosting four Twenty20 internationals against Zimbabwe just ten days before the first match at Khulna's Sheikh Abu Naser Stadium. Even that was a late switch from Sylhet, and the hurried nature of the series was illustrated by gaps in the stands where there had been no time to replace broken seats. Spectators had to sit on the floor.

This was not the first time Zimbabwe had visited Bangladesh in 2015-16. They had already met in November for three 50-over and two 20-over games, another hasty arrangement after Australia postponed their tour because of security concerns. And the November matches were originally part of a trip scheduled for January 2016, which would have included three Tests. But, as the ICC had abandoned responsibility for the Future Tours Programme in 2014, the BCB and Zimbabwe Cricket were free to chop and change; BCB president Nazmul Hassan apparently overruled the cricket committee's recommendation of playing a Test alongside these Twenty20s.

Bangladesh coach Chandika Hathurusinghe declared this would be a series for experimentation ahead of the Asia Cup and World Twenty20. His opposite number Dav Whatmore said the same: Bangladesh used 18 players, Zimbabwe 15. The matches were eventually tied 2–2 after Bangladesh had won the first two quite easily. Zimbabwe's Hamilton Masakadza stood apart, with 222 runs at a strike-rate of 145 – the first man to reach 200 in a bilateral Twenty20 series. Dropped a few months earlier and recalled only at the end of the year, he was appointed Zimbabwe's captain on their return home; Elton Chigumbura had stood down shortly after the win that levelled this series.

Bangladesh were jolted by the two defeats, but said they had succeeded in trying out potential players for the World Twenty20. Only one of those making their international debut here, left-arm seamer Abu Haider, eventually played in that tournament; the others proved that Bangladeshi Twenty20 cricket still needed more depth.

ZIMBABWEAN TOURING PARTY

*E. Chigumbura, C. J. Chibhabha, T. S. Chisoro, A. G. Cremer, L. M. Jongwe, N. Madziva, H. Masakadza, W. P. Masakadza, P. J. Moor, R. Mutumbami, T. Muzarabani, V. Sibanda, Sikandar Raza, B. V. Vitori, M. N. Waller, S. C. Williams. *Coach:* D. F. Whatmore.

First Twenty20 international At Khulna, January 15, 2016. **Bangladesh won by four wickets.** ‡**Zimbabwe 163-7** (20 overs) (V. Sibanda 46, H. Masakadza 79); **Bangladesh 166-6** (18.4 overs) (Sabbir Rahman 46). *MoM:* H. Masakadza. *T20I debuts:* Nurul Hasan, Shuvagata Hom (Bangladesh). *Bangladesh won with eight balls to spare, though their pursuit of 164 hit some snags: Tamim Iqbal, Sabbir Rahman and Mahmudullah all fell immediately after smashing sixes. Shakib Al Hasan calmly took Bangladesh to 161 with well-placed fours through third man and deep square leg off Luke Jongwe, whose next delivery went for five leg-side wides. Sabbir was Bangladesh's best batsman on* *a cool evening, adding 44 in five overs with Mushfiqur Rahim. Earlier, Hamilton Masakadza continued his good form from the series against Afghanistan in Sharjah, with 79 from 53 balls; he and Vusi Sibanda opened with 101, Zimbabwe's second-best T20 stand for any wicket. But a late collapse – five for 13 in the last 15 balls – cost them dearly; after Masakadza's run-out, Mustafizur Rahman and Al-Amin Hossain picked up two each.*

Second Twenty20 international At Khulna, January 17, 2016. **Bangladesh won by 42 runs.** ‡**Bangladesh 167-3** (20 overs) (Soumya Sarkar 43, Sabbir Rahman 43*); **Zimbabwe 125-8** (20 overs) (H. Masakadza 30; Sabbir Rahman 3-11). *MoM:* Sabbir Rahman. *Sabbir was back in the thick of things: after an unbeaten 43 from 30 balls, he collected three wickets (including Masakadza) in his 13 balls of leg-spin. The openers batted wildly to reach 45, before Sabbir rode out Mahmudullah's early dismissal and added 52 with Mushfiqur Rahim, who pulled a hamstring and retired hurt; 72 off the last seven overs gave Bangladesh a handy 167, while eight sixes equalled their record in a T20 innings. Masakadza and Sibanda began Zimbabwe's reply with 50, but they lost their way, four wickets falling in four overs. Masakadza, acting-captain as Elton Chigumbura was rested, again looked the most comfortable, but his 30 couldn't take Zimbabwe near their target. A sell-out crowd cheered as Bangladesh went 2–0 up.*

Third Twenty20 international At Khulna, January 20, 2016. **Zimbabwe won by 31 runs.** ‡**Zimbabwe 187-6** (20 overs) (V. Sibanda 44, S. C. Williams 32, M. N. Waller 49; Shakib Al Hasan 3-32); **Bangladesh 156-6** (20 overs) (Sabbir Rahman 50, Nurul Hasan 30*; A. G. Cremer 3-18). *MoM:* M. N. Waller. *T20I debuts:* Abu Haider, Mohammad Shahid, Mosaddek Hossain, Mukhtar Ali (Bangladesh). *Bangladesh made five changes, trying out four new players while Tamim and others sat out the game. Zimbabwe, still resting Chigumbura, made another bright start thanks to Sibanda's 33-ball 44, and this time the middle order kept up the run-rate. Malcolm Waller was the most brutal, hitting four sixes in his 49 from 23 deliveries. Debutant Abu Haider snatched two last-over wickets, but Zimbabwe scored 85 in the final seven to reach their third-highest T20 score. Although Sabbir maintained his form with a fifty, and put on 67 with Soumya Sarkar, Bangladesh mustered too few partnerships after that. Graeme Cremer's accurate leg-breaks extracted three key wickets to confirm Zimbabwe's first win.*

Fourth Twenty20 international At Khulna, January 22, 2016. **Zimbabwe won by 18 runs.** ‡**Zimbabwe 180-4** (20 overs) (H. Masakadza 93*, R. Mutumbami 32, M. N. Waller 36); **Bangladesh 162** (19 overs) (Mahmudullah 54; T. S. Chisoro 3-17, N. Madziva 4-34). *MoM:* H. Masakadza. *MoS:* H. Masakadza. *With Chigumbura back at the helm for what turned out to be the last time before he stepped down, Zimbabwe romped home to draw the series. Masakadza's whiplash bat-swing brought five sixes, most of them deep into the stands. His unbeaten 58-ball 93 was a Zimbabwean T20 record, bettering his own pair of 79s, a week earlier and against Canada in 2008-09. Richmond Mutumbami and Waller backed him up, and Bangladesh needed 181. They were soon 17-4. Neville Madziva topped and tailed the innings, while Tendai Chisoro dismissed the in-form Sabbir and Shakib. Imrul Kayes counter-attacked until caught at deep midwicket, and Mahmudullah, who put on 57 with Nurul Hasan, waged battle into the 16th over, when he was bowled by Chisoro.*

THE ASIA CUP IN 2015-16

MOHAMMAD ISAM

1 India 2 Bangladesh

After the role of the Asian Cricket Council was greatly reduced in 2015 – most functions were transferred to the ICC – some feared the biennial Asia Cup, the ACC's marquee event, would wither. However, the ICC chose to continue the tournament, at least in the medium term, if with some alterations.

The main change was that it would no longer be fixed as a 50-over competition. And because the World Twenty20 began two days after the final, it made sense for the 2016 edition of the Asia Cup to morph into a 20-over affair. It was won by a confident India, who warmed up nicely for the bigger event with five convincing victories. The original plan had been for the 2018 Asia Cup to revert to 50 overs a side – since the ICC had shifted the World T20 to a four-year cycle. But by May 2016 it looked increasingly likely that both tournaments would be played every two years, and that the 20-over structure might stick. In July, it was confirmed.

For 2016, a qualifying league was added, allowing four of the region's Associate Members to vie for a place at the main event. This preliminary stage was originally mooted as a discrete tournament to be hosted by the UAE in November 2015. However, it was postponed and moved to Bangladesh, where it became the curtain-raiser to the Asia Cup proper. Afghanistan were hot favourites to progress, only to slip up against the UAE in the opening game. They did beat Oman and Hong Kong, but so did the UAE, who therefore joined the regional giants.

Hong Kong's Babar Hayat terrorised Oman with his 60-ball 122, yet ended on the losing team. The game also included a Mankading incident, when Oman's Aamer Kaleem ran out Mark Chapman. The ICC requested that teams at the World T20 give a warning before attempting to run out a non-striker guilty of backing up too much. This was agreed, but not before some hesitation from Oman.

When the main tournament began, the green tinge of the Mirpur pitches soon became a concern. After India dismissed Pakistan for 83, M. S. Dhoni, the India captain, said the bowler-friendly surfaces devalued the competition as preparation for the World T20, and as a spectacle. As the games wore on, however, pitches became more brown than green, and in the final there was little help for the fast bowlers.

But what made the tournament tick were the full houses for the big games in Mirpur, where in the final the groundstaff might reasonably have been given the match award for their hard work after a massive storm struck 90 minutes before play was due to start.

Rather less satisfactory was the standard of umpiring. India's Virat Kohli and Pakistan's Mohammad Hafeez were both victims of erroneous lbw calls, while the Sri Lanka all-rounder Tissara Perera was wrongly given out stumped by Dhoni after the square-leg umpire chose not to seek guidance from the third official. Several caught-behind appeals were ignored, most notably in the India–Pakistan clash, prompting Dhoni to wonder whether the combination of a noisy crowd and the requirement for umpires to wear earpieces was impeding their ability to detect an edge.

India, on top of their game throughout, were clear and worthy winners. Their rejigged bowling attack proved especially influential: Ashish Nehra and Jasprit Bumrah provided power, and off-spinner Ravichandran Ashwin guile; Hardik Pandya looked a pace-bowling all-rounder of great promise. The batting was again led by Kohli, with telling contributions from others, including Shikhar Dhawan in the final. Driven by Sabbir Rahman – Player of the Tournament for 176 runs at a healthy rate on tricky pitches – Bangladesh could justifiably claim to be the second-best team. They beat both the confused Sri Lankans and a bedraggled Pakistan side, whose star was the rehabilitated Mohammad Amir: he claimed seven wickets and cost just five an over.

NATIONAL SQUADS

* *Captain.* ‡ *Did not play.*

Afghanistan *Asghar Stanikzai, Dawlat Zadran, ‡Fareed Ahmad, Gulbadeen Naib, Hamza Hotak, Karim Sadiq, ‡Mirwais Ashraf, Mohammad Nabi, Mohammad Shahzad, ‡Najeeb Tarakai, Najibullah Zadran, Noor Ali Zadran, Rashid Khan, ‡Rokhan Barakzai, Samiullah Shenwari, ‡Shafiqullah Shinwari, Shapoor Zadran, Usman Ghani, ‡Yamin Ahmadzai. *Coach:* Inzamam-ul-Haq.

Bangladesh *Mashrafe bin Mortaza, Abu Haider, Al-Amin Hossain, Arafat Sunny, Imrul Kayes, Mahmudullah, Mithun Ali, Mushfiqur Rahim, Mustafizur Rahman, Nasir Hossain, Nurul Hasan, Sabbir Rahman, Shakib Al Hasan, Soumya Sarkar, Tamim Iqbal, Taskin Ahmed. *Coach:* U. C. Hathurusinghe.

Mustafizur Rahman withdrew with a side strain after three games. Tamim Iqbal was absent for the birth of his first child, and played only in the last group game and the final.

Hong Kong *Tanvir Afzal, Adil Mehmood, Aizaz Khan, Babar Hayat, C. Carter, M. S. Chapman, Haseeb Amjad, Nadeem Ahmed, Nizakat Khan, A. Rath, K. D. Shah, ‡N. D. Shah, Tanveer Ahmed, ‡Waqas Barkat, Waqas Khan. *Coach:* S. J. Cook.

India *M. S. Dhoni, R. Ashwin, Bhuvneshwar Kumar, J. J. Bumrah, S. Dhawan, Harbhajan Singh, R. A. Jadeja, V. Kohli, ‡Mohammed Shami, P. Negi, A. Nehra, H. H. Pandya, A. M. Rahane, S. K. Raina, R. G. Sharma, Yuvraj Singh. *Coach:* R. J. Shastri.

Oman *Sultan Ahmed, Aamer Ali, Aamer Kaleem, Aaqib Sulehri, Adnan Ilyas, M. S. Ansari, Bilal Khan, Jatinder Singh, ‡Khawar Ali, A. V. Lalcheta, Mehran Khan, ‡Mohammad Nadeem, ‡R. J. Ranpura, Sufyan Mehmood, V. S. Wategaonkar, Zeeshan Maqsood, ‡Zeeshan Siddiqui. *Coach:* L. R. D. Mendis.

Pakistan *Shahid Afridi, Anwar Ali, Iftikhar Ahmed, ‡Imad Wasim, Khurram Manzoor, Mohammad Amir, Mohammad Hafeez, Mohammad Irfan, Mohammad Nawaz, Mohammad Sami, Sarfraz Ahmed, Sharjeel Khan, Shoaib Malik, Umar Akmal, Wahab Riaz. *Coach:* Waqar Younis.

Sri Lanka *S. L. Malinga, P. V. D. Chameera, L. D. Chandimal, D. P. D. N. Dickwella, T. M. Dilshan, H. M. R. K. B. Herath, D. S. N. F. G. Jayasuriya, C. K. Kapugedera, K. M. D. N. Kulasekara, A. D. Mathews, N. L. T. C. Perera, ‡S. M. S. M. Senanayake, M. D. Shanaka, T. A. M. Siriwardene, ‡J. D. F. Vandersay. *Coach:* G. X. Ford.

Malinga captained in Sri Lanka's first match but, after his knee injury flared up, the captaincy passed to Mathews and (for the last group game) Chandimal.

United Arab Emirates *Amjad Javed, Ahmed Raza, Fahad Tariq, Farhan Ahmed, Mohammad Kaleem, Mohammad Naveed, Mohammad Shehzad, Mohammad Usman, R. Mustafa, S. P. Patil, Qadeer Ahmed, Saqlain Haider, Shaiman Anwar, Usman Mushtaq, ‡Zaheer Maqsood. *Coach:* Aqib Javed.

QUALIFYING GROUP

At Fatullah, February 19, 2016. **United Arab Emirates won by 16 runs.** ‡**United Arab Emirates 176-4** (20 overs) (R. Mustafa 77; Rashid Khan 3-25); **Afghanistan 160** (19.5 overs) (Karim Sadiq 72; R. Mustafa 3-19). *A spirited all-round performance from Rohan Mustafa – who followed a 50-ball 77 with three cheap wickets for his off-spin – brought an upset. With just one team progressing to the competition proper, Afghanistan, for whom Karim Sadiq bashed 72 from 48 deliveries, now had to rely on the UAE slipping up.*

At Fatullah, February 19, 2016 (floodlit). **Oman won by five runs.** ‡**Oman 180-5** (20 overs) (Jatinder Singh 42, Aamer Ali 32*; Nadeem Ahmed 3-27); **Hong Kong 175-7** (20 overs) (Babar Hayat 122). *T20I debut:* V. S. Wategaonkar (Oman). *Babar Hayat dominated Hong Kong's reply: his 60-ball 122, the fourth-highest innings in T20Is, was 107 more than the next best. But his dismissal at long-off from the fourth ball of the last over spelt defeat. With all seven Omani batsmen reaching double figures, teamwork trumped individual excellence. There was controversy when Mark Chapman was Mankaded by Oman's Aamer Kaleem; Hong Kong coach Simon Cook called it a "cowardly act", while headline writers delighted in a case of Oman-kading.*

At Fatullah, February 20, 2016. **Afghanistan won by three wickets.** ‡**Oman 165-4** (20 overs) (Zeeshan Maqsood 52, Adnan Ilyas 54); **Afghanistan 168-7** (19.3 overs) (Noor Ali Zadran 63, Asghar Stanikzai 34; Bilal Khan 3-33, Mehran Khan 3-18). *With Afghanistan needing 21 from two overs, Samiullah Shenwari hit successive fours to bat the game their way. He holed out from the first ball of the final over, but No. 9 Dawlat Zadran promptly smashed two sixes. Oman had been 104-1 in the 14th, and might have eyed a beefier total. Mehran Khan then held the Afghan reply in check by conceding no boundaries in his 4–7–18–3.*

At Fatullah, February 21, 2016. **United Arab Emirates won by six wickets.** ‡**Hong Kong 146-7** (20 overs) (Babar Hayat 54; Mohammad Naveed 3-14); **United Arab Emirates 147-4** (18.3 overs) (Mohammad Shehzad 52, Mohammad Usman 41). *Hayat again proved the mainstay of the Hong Kong line-up and, once he had fallen for a 45-ball 54 at the start of the 16th over, the runs dried up; just 24 came from the last 30 balls, with seamer Mohammad Naveed giving nothing away. Mohammad Shehzad and Mohammad Usman added 79 for the third wicket to keep the UAE on track.*

At Mirpur, February 22, 2016. **Afghanistan won by 66 runs. Afghanistan 178-7** (20 overs) (Asghar Stanikzai 49, Najibullah Zadran 60*; Aizaz Khan 3-38); ‡**Hong Kong 112** (17.1 overs) (A. Rath 41; Mohammad Nabi 4-17). *MoM:* Mohammad Nabi. *T20I debuts:* Adil Mehmood, Tanveer Ahmed (Hong Kong). *A crushing win kept Afghanistan's hopes alive: Najibullah Zadran's career-best 60* from 35 balls propelled them to 178, with 23 flowing from the 19th over. At 79-1 in the tenth, Hong Kong were still in it. Then came the collapse: the top three aside, no one passed four, as nine wickets fell for 33.*

At Mirpur, February 22, 2016 (floodlit). **United Arab Emirates won by 71 runs. United Arab Emirates 172-6** (20 overs) (Mohammad Kaleem 50, Mohammad Shehzad 34, Mohammad Usman 46; Aamer Kaleem 4-36); ‡**Oman 101-8** (20 overs) (Zeeshan Maqsood 46). *MoM:* Mohammad Usman. *Any sort of win would have seen the UAE qualify, but they made it in style. Mohammad Kaleem and Mohammad Shehzad added 86 for the second wicket, and runs came at a lick throughout the innings. Zeeshan Maqsood was the only Omani to take up the fight.*

QUALIFYING GROUP TABLE

	Played	*Won*	*Lost*	*Points*	*Net run-rate*
UNITED ARAB EMIRATES	3	3	0	6	1.67
Afghanistan	3	2	1	4	0.95
Oman	3	1	2	2	–1.22
Hong Kong	3	0	3	0	–1.41

GROUP GAMES

At Mirpur, February 24, 2016 (floodlit). **India won by 45 runs. India 166-6** (20 overs) (R. G. Sharma 83, H. H. Pandya 31; Al-Amin Hossain 3-37); ‡**Bangladesh 121-7** (20 overs) (Sabbir Rahman 44; A. Nehra 3-23). *MoM:* R. G. Sharma. *Had Shakib Al Hasan held a catchable chance at* *point, India would have been 52-4, and the outcome might have been different. But the reprieved Rohit Sharma sped away, hitting the next three balls of the 11th over for four, six and four. Having meandered to 21 from 28, he crashed 62 from his next 26, scoring freely on both sides of the wicket and gaining help from Hardik Pandya, whose pugnacious 18-ball 31 included a memorable flicked six off Mustafizur Rahman. On a green-tinged pitch that offered plenty to the seamers – though little grip for Mustafizur's slower deliveries – Bangladesh's bowlers relinquished control, and 69 gushed from the last 30 balls. By contrast, the Indian attack stuck to their task: all enjoyed near-identical economy-rates, with four costing 23 runs and the fifth 25. Despite Sabbir Rahman's combative 44, the result was clear long before the end.*

At Mirpur, February 25, 2016 (floodlit). **Sri Lanka won by 14 runs. Sri Lanka 129-8** (20 overs) (L. D. Chandimal 50; Amjad Javed 3-25); ‡**United Arab Emirates 115-9** (20 overs) (S. P. Patil 37; S. L. Malinga 4-26, K. M. D. N. Kulasekara 3-10). *MoM:* S. L. Malinga. *Sri Lankan openers Tillekeratne Dilshan and Dinesh Chandimal put on 68 in nine overs. Despite reserves of wickets and time, Sri Lanka could add only 61 more. Amjad Javed took 3-25 with his outswingers, and was well supported by fellow medium-pacers Mohammad Naveed and Mohammad Shehzad. The UAE's target was a modest 130, but the pitch continued to help the bowlers, and Lasith Malinga and Nuwan Kulasekara swept the top four aside within four overs. Slow left-armer Rangana Herath picked up two to make it 47-6 after ten, before Swapnil Patil and the lower order salvaged some dignity without quite threatening an upset. Malinga, playing his first competitive match since hurting his knee in November, squashed the resistance. However, his injury flared up later, and he missed the remainder of this tournament and the World Twenty20 in India.*

At Mirpur, February 26, 2016 (floodlit). **Bangladesh won by 51 runs. Bangladesh 133-8** (20 overs) (Mithun Ali 47, Mahmudullah 36*); ‡**United Arab Emirates 82** (17.4 overs) (Mohammad Usman 30). *MoM:* Mahmudullah. *The UAE lost again, but only after they had given their opponents a scare. Mohammad Naveed claimed 2-12 from his four overs, while for the third match running slow left-armer Ahmed Raza conceded no boundaries. Bangladesh, who in the sixth over were sitting pretty at 46-0, lost wickets in clumps: near the end of their innings they lurched from 112-4 to 114-7, and they relied on Mahmudullah's late flourish to shepherd them to a decent score. For the second successive game the UAE lost an opener for a duck, and never gained any fluency against an experienced attack who shared the wickets around. Only three batsmen managed double figures as the UAE became the first team bowled out by Bangladesh in a chase.*

At Mirpur, February 27, 2016 (floodlit). **India won by five wickets. Pakistan 83** (17.3 overs) (H. H. Pandya 3-8); ‡**India 85-5** (15.3 overs) (V. Kohli 49; Mohammad Amir 3-18). *MoM:* V. Kohli. *T20I debut:* Khurram Manzoor (Pakistan). *A major draw of Asia Cups had long been the clash between India and Pakistan. But this encounter lost its sparkle once Pakistan had scored just 83 – the first time since 1985 they had been dismissed by India for under 100 in any format. Ashish Nehra made the breakthrough, before Jasprit Bumrah strangled the scoring: runs came from only two of his 18 balls. By the end of the eighth over – when Ravi Jadeja's rocket from the midwicket boundary caught Shahid Afridi comfortably short – they were in tatters at 42-6. Pandya ended with 3-8; just two batsmen, including the 29-year-old Khurram Manzoor, on Twenty20 international debut, reached double figures. Mohammad Amir fought back, claiming two victims in the first over with magnificent deliveries that swung in late, and another in the third. But, from the depths of 8-3, Virat Kohli weathered Amir's blitz with low and soft hands, adding 68 with a circumspect Yuvraj Singh. Despite a thick inside edge Kohli was given lbw on 49, though by then the outcome was settled.*

At Mirpur, February 28, 2016 (floodlit). **Bangladesh won by 23 runs.** ‡**Bangladesh 147-7** (20 overs) (Sabbir Rahman 80, Shakib Al Hasan 32; P. V. D. Chameera 3-30); **Sri Lanka 124-8** (20 overs) (L. D. Chandimal 37; Al-Amin Hossain 3-34). *MoM:* Sabbir Rahman. *Bangladesh, who lost both openers for ducks, were indebted to Sabbir Rahman for their first Twenty20 victory over Sri Lanka, after four defeats. He struck three leg-side sixes and ten fours, grabbing any opportunity to blast through midwicket or the covers. When he fell for 80 in the 16th over, he had scored 74% of his team's 108. He had, though, been partly guilty in the run-out of Mushfiqur Rahim, which left Bangladesh 26-3. Shakib helped add 82, but struggled for timing – unlike Mahmudullah, who walloped a 12-ball 23 – as they reached a competitive 147. Sri Lanka were given two early let-offs in the slips, but the boundaries dried up and, with five overs remaining, Sri Lanka needed 56. Angelo Mathews might have been the man for the job, but he laboured to a boundaryless 12 from 20 balls.*

At Mirpur, February 29, 2016 (floodlit). **Pakistan won by seven wickets.** ‡**United Arab Emirates 129-6** (20 overs) (Shaiman Anwar 46); **Pakistan 131-3** (18.4 overs) (Umar Akmal 50*, Shoaib

Malik 63*; Amjad Javed 3-36). *MoM:* Shoaib Malik. *T20I debut:* Mohammad Nawaz (Pakistan). *After their hiding by India two days earlier, Pakistan might have hoped for an easier affair. That seemed likely when their pace trio reduced the UAE to 12-3 in four overs; after 11, they had limped to 41-4. But Shaiman Anwar and the lower-middle order hacked, heaved, edged and blasted them to a respectable 129, despite Mohammad Amir sending down 21 dot balls. Pakistan then fell foul of*

CHEAPEST FOUR-OVER SPELLS IN T20 INTERNATIONALS

4–20–4–2	Aizaz Khan, Hong Kong v Nepal at Colombo (PSS)	2014-15
4–19–6–0	P. Utseya, Zimbabwe v Pakistan at King City	2008-09
4–21–6–1	C. B. Mpofu, Zimbabwe v Canada at King City	2008-09
4–20–6–2	R. W. Price, Zimbabwe v Canada at King City	2008-09
4–18–6–3	D. L. Vettori, New Zealand v Bangladesh at Hamilton	2009-10
4–20–6–4	S. J. Benn, West Indies v Zimbabwe at Port-of-Spain	2009-10
4–21–6–2	**Mohammad Amir, Pakistan v UAE at Mirpur**	**2015-16**
4–19–7–0	P. J. Ongondo, Kenya v Ireland at Belfast	2008
4–18–7–1	Aizaz Khan, Hong Kong v Nepal at Belfast	2015
4–21–7–4	**Mudassar Bukhari, Netherlands v UAE at Dubai**	**2015-16**

UAE captain Amjad Javed, whose medium-pace claimed three wickets in five legitimate deliveries and left them floundering at 17-3. Umar Akmal and Shoaib Malik read the situation intelligently: after realising the threat presented by the UAE attack, they waited until they were well set before going on the offensive. Between them, they hit nine fours and six sixes, and put on 114 for the fourth wicket – a Twenty20 international record until it was broken six days later by Australia's David Warner and Glenn Maxwell.*

At Mirpur, March 1, 2016 (floodlit). **India won by five wickets. Sri Lanka 138-9** (20 overs) (C. K. Kapugedera 30); ‡**India 142-5** (19.2 overs) (V. Kohli 56*, Yuvraj Singh 35). *MoM:* V. Kohli. *Once again, Nehra gave India an early breakthrough – a breach his colleagues soon exploited to reduce Sri Lanka to 57-4. The experienced Chamara Kapugedera, promoted to No. 4, managed 30, though at less than a run a ball, as he and Siriwardene put on 43 for the fifth wicket. Of greater concern to India was Tissara Perera, who hammered 17 from five deliveries – only to be given out from his sixth. Ravichandran Ashwin saw him advancing and bowled an off-side wide, neatly collected by M. S. Dhoni, who removed the bails. The square-leg umpire upheld the appeal without recourse to his off-field colleague; replays showed Perera had regained his ground. India lost their openers cheaply, but Kohli again came to the rescue. He struck 56* off 47 balls, sharing half-century stands with Suresh Raina and Yuvraj, who clattered three sixes. Victory guaranteed India a place in the final, while defending champions Sri Lanka were hanging by a thread.*

At Mirpur, March 2, 2016 (floodlit). **Bangladesh won by five wickets.** ‡**Pakistan 129-7** (20 overs) (Sarfraz Ahmed 58*, Shoaib Malik 41; Al-Amin Hossain 3-25); **Bangladesh 131-5** (19.1 overs) (Soumya Sarkar 48). *MoM:* Soumya Sarkar. *Bangladesh almost fluffed their lines in a compelling denouement. Ultimately, though, a cameo from Mahmudullah guided them home – and to the final. His 22* included an extraordinary back-foot driven six over extra cover, as well as the winning boundary to midwicket. It was sweet for Mahmudullah, who had been batting when Bangladesh lost the (50-over) 2012 Asia Cup final to Pakistan by two runs. Tension grew when Shakib was bowled trying to scoop Mohammad Amir; five down, Bangladesh needed 26 from 16 balls. Mashrafe bin Mortaza promptly blasted Amir down the ground, then somehow deflected the next, a full-blooded short ball, for another four. Earlier, Pakistan had recovered from 28-4 thanks to Sarfraz Ahmed, who made 58*, and Shoaib Malik. Opening bowler Al-Amin Hossain grabbed three wickets, while his partner Taskin Ahmed conceded just 14.*

At Mirpur, March 3, 2016 (floodlit). **India won by nine wickets.** ‡**United Arab Emirates 81-9** (20 overs) (Shaiman Anwar 43); **India 82-1** (10.1 overs) (R. G. Sharma 39). *MoM:* R. G. Sharma. *T20I debut:* P. Negi (India). *Nothing rested on this game, but as a test of India's bench strength it could hardly have gone better. Bhuvneshwar Kumar took the new ball, and did not concede a run until his third over; Harbhajan Singh was barely more expensive; debutant slow left-armer Pawan Negi took a wicket with his fifth delivery; and none of the six bowlers cost a run a ball. Relying heavily on Shaiman Anwar, the UAE dribbled to an inadequate 81. Sharma then made a*

LOWEST 20-OVER TOTALS IN TWENTY20 INTERNATIONALS

70	Bermuda v Canada at Belfast	2008
72	Nepal v Hong Kong at Colombo (PSS)	2014-15
79-7	†West Indies v Zimbabwe at Port-of-Spain	2009-10
81-9	**UAE v India at Mirpur**	**2015-16**
85-9	†Bangladesh v Pakistan at Mirpur	2011-12
85-8	†Ireland v West Indies at Kingston‡	2013-14
92-9	**PNG v Ireland at Townsville**	**2015-16**
93-8	Zimbabwe v South Africa at Hambantota	2012-13
96-9	West Indies v Ireland at Kingston‡	2013-14
96-9	Pakistan v Australia at Dubai	2014-15

† *Batting second.* ‡ *Same match.*

---

quickfire 39 before Shikhar Dhawan and Yuvraj Singh completed a simple win. It was the end of the road for the UAE who, after dominating the qualifying group, failed to find the batting strength to trouble classier opposition.

At Mirpur, March 4, 2016 (floodlit). **Pakistan won by six wickets. Sri Lanka 150-4** (20 overs) (L. D. Chandimal 58, T. M. Dilshan 75*); ‡**Pakistan 151-4** (19.2 overs) (Sharjeel Khan 31, Sarfraz Ahmed 38, Umar Akmal 48). *MoM:* Umar Akmal. *T20I debut:* Iftikhar Ahmed (Pakistan). *With neither side able to progress, there was little at stake bar confidence ahead of the World T20. Sri Lanka enjoyed a superb start, with openers Chandimal and Dilshan putting on 110 in 14 overs. Dilshan unfurled some trademark shots, including a reverse-Dilscoop, but was lucky to have been given three lives by Pakistan fielders; for the third time, he batted through all 20 overs. He finished on 75 – exactly half the Sri Lankan total – though none of the later batsmen could take advantage of an ideal platform. Pakistan lost an early wicket when Mohammad Hafeez popped a catch back to Shehan Jayasuriya in the fourth over. But Sharjeel Khan cracked five fours and a six in his rapid 31, and Sarfraz Ahmed and Umar Akmal took them to the brink of victory. However, it did not prevent the formation of a committee to examine Pakistan's selection process.*

FINAL GROUP TABLE

	Played	*Won*	*Lost*	*Points*	*Net run-rate*
INDIA	4	4	0	8	2.02
BANGLADESH	4	3	1	6	0.45
Pakistan	4	2	2	4	–0.29
Sri Lanka	4	1	3	2	–0.29
United Arab Emirates	4	0	4	0	–1.81

FINAL

BANGLADESH v INDIA

At Mirpur, March 6, 2016 (floodlit). India won by eight wickets. Toss: India.

An hour before the toss was due, a huge spring thunderstorm buffeted the ground, accompanied first by heavy dust and then torrential rain and lightning. The floodlights were turned off, and there were at least seven power failures. That the match survived as a 15-over affair was testimony to the tireless efforts of the groundstaff, as well as improved drainage. After India's disciplined attack prevented a quick getaway – Ashwin conceded just one four in his three overs, and Bumrah none – Bangladesh needed a late 13-ball 33 by Mahmudullah to keep them in the game. Sharma fell early, but Dhawan, whose tournament had been unexceptional, picked up boundaries at will, racing to his half-century from 35 balls and sharing a second-wicket stand worth 94 with Kohli. With two overs to go, India required 19; Dhoni swung Al-Amin Hossain for a beautifully timed four to cover and two massive sixes over midwicket, the second bringing India their sixth Asia Cup triumph, with seven balls to spare. It also confirmed their status as favourites for the looming World T20.

Man of the Match: S. Dhawan. *Man of the Series:* Sabbir Rahman.

Bangladesh

		B	4/6
1 Tamim Iqbal *lbw b 10*	13	17	2
2 Soumya Sarkar *c 7 b 11*	14	9	3
3 Sabbir Rahman *not out*	32	29	2
4 Shakib Al Hasan *c 10 b 9*	21	16	3
5 †Mushfiqur Rahim *run out*	4	5	0
6 *Mashrafe bin Mortaza *c 3 b 8*	0	1	0
7 Mahmudullah *not out*	33	13	2/2
W 3	3		
5 overs: 30-2 (15 overs)	120-5		

1/27 2/30 3/64 4/75 5/75

8 Nasir Hossain, 9 Al-Amin Hossain, 10 Abu Haider and 11 Taskin Ahmed did not bat.

Ashwin 3–8–14–1; Nehra 3–6–33–1; Bumrah 3–8–13–1; Jadeja 3–2–25–1; Pandya 3–4–35–0.

India

		B	4/6
1 R. G. Sharma *c 2 b 9*	1	5	0
2 S. Dhawan *c 2 b 11*	60	44	9/1
3 V. Kohli *not out*	41	28	5
4 *†M. S. Dhoni *not out*	20	6	1/2
5 overs: 33-1 (13.5 overs)	122-2		

1/5 2/99

5 S. K. Raina, 6 Yuvraj Singh, 7 H. H. Pandya, 8 R. A. Jadeja, 9 R. Ashwin, 10 J. J. Bumrah and 11 A. Nehra did not bat.

Taskin Ahmed 3–9–14–1; Al-Amin Hossain 2.5–6–30–1; Abu Haider 1–1–14–0; Shakib Al Hasan 2–2–26–0; Mashrafe bin Mortaza 2–4–16–0; Nasir Hossain 3–5–22–0.

Umpires: R. S. A. Palliyaguruge and Shozab Raza. Third umpire: Enamul Haque, snr. Referee: J. J. Crowe.

ASIA CUP WINNERS

1983-84	INDIA beat Pakistan by 54 runs at Sharjah.
1985-86	SRI LANKA beat Pakistan by five wickets in Colombo.
1988-89	INDIA beat Sri Lanka by six wickets at Dhaka.
1990-91	INDIA beat Sri Lanka by seven wickets at Calcutta.
1994-95	INDIA beat Sri Lanka by eight wickets at Sharjah.
1997	SRI LANKA beat India by eight wickets in Colombo.
2000	PAKISTAN beat Sri Lanka by 39 runs at Dhaka.
2004	SRI LANKA beat India by 25 runs in Colombo.
2008	SRI LANKA beat India by 100 runs at Karachi.
2010	INDIA beat Sri Lanka by 81 runs at Dambulla.
2011-12	PAKISTAN beat Bangladesh at Mirpur.
2013-14	PAKISTAN beat Bangladesh by two runs at Mirpur.
2015-16†	INDIA beat Bangladesh by eight wickets at Mirpur.

† *20-over matches, rather than 50.*

BANGLADESH v AFGHANISTAN IN 2016-17

UTPAL SHUVRO

One-day internationals (3): Bangladesh 2, Afghanistan 1

Starting with a victory over Zimbabwe in November 2014, Bangladesh had won five home one-day series in a row, their victims including Pakistan, India and South Africa. They had also reached the quarter-finals of the 2015 World Cup. In the context of such success, a visit from Afghanistan did not generate great excitement – even if it was the first bilateral series between the nations.

The scheduling did not help. By mid-August, England were still uncertain whether safety concerns would scupper their planned tour later in the year. The BCB were worried: having not played at all since the World T20 in February, they were desperate for cricket. An invitation was hastily sent to Afghanistan, who gladly accepted.

But on August 25, the ECB confirmed their tour would proceed. The Afghanistan series assumed real significance, since it became a dress rehearsal for the visit of England, whose board sought reassurance. That meant equally comprehensive security now, though a pitch invader threatened the calm in the third match, when he approached Bangladesh captain Mashrafe bin Mortaza at mid-on. He dealt with the situation impeccably: he gave the fan a hug, then ushered him off the field, while preventing the security guards from overzealous detainment.

The home side's rustiness and Afghanistan's habitual enthusiasm made for an engaging series. Bangladesh won the first game by coming back strongly in the death overs, but lost a low-scoring second. Their thumping victory in the decider was a momentous occasion: their 100th one-day win, in their 315th match.

The series also brought milestones for their biggest stars. Shakib Al Hasan became Bangladesh's highest one-day wicket-taker, passing Abdur Razzak's 207, to secure a treble: he already held the honour in Tests and Twenty20s. Before the series, Shakib also shared the national record for most ODI centuries (six) with Tamim Iqbal. But Tamim hit a seventh to achieve a feat unique in the modern game: most runs and most centuries for one country in all three formats.

AFGHANISTAN TOURING PARTY

*Asghar Stanikzai, Dawlat Zadran, Fareed Ahmad, Hamza Hotak, Hashmatullah Shahidi, Ihsanullah Janat, Karim Janat, Mirwais Ashraf, Mohammad Nabi, Mohammad Shahzad, Najibullah Zadran, Naveen-ul-Haq, Nawroz Mangal, Rahmat Shah, Rashid Khan, Samiullah Shenwari, Shabir Noori. *Coach:* L. S. Rajput.

At Fatullah, September 23. **Afghanistan won by 66 runs. Afghanistan 233** (49.2 overs) (Hashmatullah Shahidi 69); ‡**Bangladesh Cricket Board XI 167** (38.1 overs) (Mosaddek Hossain 76; Mohammad Nabi 4-24). *Both sides chose from 13 players. Afghanistan's spinners comfortably protected a meagre-looking 233 as Mohammad Nabi and Rashid Khan took 6-49 between them;*

eight Bangladeshis were removed in single figures. Earlier, Hashmatullah Shahidi batted for most of the Afghanistan innings for 69, laying a foundation for Mirwais Ashraf's 19-ball 32.

First one-day international At Mirpur, September 25, 2016 (day/night). **Bangladesh won by seven runs.** ‡**Bangladesh 265** (50 overs) (Tamim Iqbal 80, Mahmudullah 62; Dawlat Zadran 4-73); **Afghanistan 258** (50 overs) (Rahmat Shah 71, Hashmatullah Shahidi 72; Taskin Ahmed 4-59). *MoM:* Shakib Al Hasan. *ODI debut:* Naveen-ul-Haq (Afghanistan). *Afghanistan seemed to be cruising when they added 143 for the third wicket, to leave themselves needing 77 from the last ten. But Rahmat Shah charged at Shakib Al Hasan, took a wild swipe and was stumped; it was his 208th one-day international wicket, the most by a Bangladeshi, surpassing Abdur Razzak, another left-arm spinner. Shakib finished with 2-26, to back up a feisty 48. His control had given Bangladesh a chance, and Taskin Ahmed grabbed it. This was his first game after a ban for an illegal action, and he looked rusty: his first six overs brought 0-49. But he was trusted at the death, found his yorkers, and took four wickets in nine balls to clinch the match. Earlier, Bangladesh lost Soumya Sarkar in the first over, but Tamim Iqbal – dropped by Hashmatullah Shahidi at backward point on 30 – composed a restrained 80. Bangladesh reached 203-3, before seven fell for 62. Afghanistan had the momentum, but not the composure. In the 3,780th one-day international, this was the first instance of both teams being dismissed from the last ball of their allotted overs.*

Second one-day international At Mirpur, September 28, 2016 (day/night). **Afghanistan won by two wickets. Bangladesh 208** (49.2 overs); ‡**Afghanistan 212-8** (49.4 overs) (Asghar Stanikzai 57; Shakib Al Hasan 4-47). *MoM:* Mohammad Nabi. *ODI debut:* Mosaddek Hossain (Bangladesh). *Afghanistan stunned the Mirpur crowd with their second win over Bangladesh (their first had come in the 2014 Asia Cup). The bowlers set it up, as Bangladesh slid to 165-9. The top five all got starts, but none made fifty, and Rashid Khan's googlies and flippers proved lethal. Only Mosaddek Hossain's 45* on debut, including the lion's share of a 43-run stand with last man Rubel Hossain, dragged them over 200. Afghanistan's reply teetered at 63-4 after two wickets in three balls for Shakib, who was superb again, and one for the off-spin of Mosaddek – the first Bangladeshi to take a wicket with his first ball in ODIs. But Asghar Stanikzai and Mohammad Nabi shared a careful century stand to establish a strong position. There was still time for nerves: Stanikzai's impatient hoick ended a 95-ball 57, and left things to the tail. It got down to the last over, but Dawlat Zadran sliced his first ball to third man for the winning four.*

Third one-day international At Mirpur, October 1, 2016 (day/night). **Bangladesh won by 141 runs.** ‡**Bangladesh 279-8** (50 overs) (Tamim Iqbal 118, Sabbir Rahman 65); **Afghanistan 138** (33.5 overs). *MoM:* Tamim Iqbal. *MoS:* Tamim Iqbal. *A run-a-ball 118 from Tamim turned the decider into a procession. It was his seventh hundred in ODIs, a record for Bangladesh, who completed their 100th win in the format. Afghanistan had themselves to blame: Stanikzai dropped a sitter at mid-on when Tamim had only one. He added 140 with Sabbir Rahman, before Mahmudullah added late impetus with a 22-ball 32. Afghanistan's chase was all but dead in the 25th over, when Rahmat Shah fell for a slow 36 to leave them 88-6 and well behind the rate; they dribbled on for another eight overs. Left-arm spinner Mosharraf Hossain, making a comeback after eight years, did most of the damage with 3-24. He had missed 145 matches, the longest gap between appearances for Bangladesh.*

DOMESTIC CRICKET IN BANGLADESH IN 2015-16

UTPAL SHUVRO

It was a busy year, with a new format for the National Cricket League, the return of the Bangladesh Premier League, and familiar controversies in the Dhaka Premier League.

In the hope of making it more competitive, the first-class National Cricket League was split into two, with the eight teams divided on the previous year's standings. **Khulna** led Tier One for most of the season, and started the final round six points ahead of Dhaka Metropolis and seven ahead of Dhaka Division, which gave all three sides a chance. The two Dhaka teams were pitted against each other, but not a ball was bowled on the first three days of their match. (In a season badly affected by rain, only 30% of domestic first-class fixtures reached an outright result.) Khulna's game with Rangpur was also interrupted, but the inevitable draw was enough to ensure Khulna's fourth NCL title. Defending champions Rangpur were relegated, and **Barisal** promoted after heading Tier Two – a dramatic turnaround, as their fourth-round victory over Sylhet ended a winless streak of 26 first-class matches stretching back to 2011-12.

Khulna owed their success to their bowlers. Teenage off-spinner Mehedi Hasan took 30 wickets (a year later he would be tormenting England), and left-arm spinner Abdur Razzak 28; only Sanjamul Islam of second-tier Rajshahi managed more. Khulna's most successful batsmen were Imrul Kayes and Nurul Hasan, as low as Nos 12 and 13 in the list of leading run-scorers. Discarded Test batsman Shahriar Nafees came top with 715 at 79 for Barisal, boosted by twin centuries in the last round, when he followed 168 with 174 not out against Chittagong, the most runs for any batsman in a single NCL match.

The other first-class competition, the Bangladesh Cricket League, lost a bit of gloss as the top cricketers were preparing for the World Twenty20. **Central Zone** secured their second title, though a dramatic win for East Zone in the penultimate round had kept them in the hunt. Marshall Ayub topped the batting with 562 runs – one of three Central batsmen to pass 500 – and Razzak took another 38 wickets for South Zone, giving him 66 in all, the second season running in which he collected most first-class wickets. Out of favour with the selectors, Razzak overtook fellow left-arm spinner Enamul Haque junior (still playing for Sylhet and South Zone) as Bangladesh's leading first-class wicket-taker, ending the season with 428. Tushar Imran of Khulna and South Zone became the first Bangladeshi to score 8,000 first-class runs.

The franchise-based Twenty20 Bangladesh Premier League resumed after two seasons' absence, following a match-fixing scandal and pay disputes which wrecked its second edition in 2012-13. The winners of both earlier tournaments, Dhaka Gladiators, were banned because of alleged involvement in the corruption; after another round of bidding for franchises, one of three new teams, **Comilla Victorians**, became champions, led by Bangladesh's limited-overs captain, Mashrafe bin Mortaza.

The 50-over Dhaka Premier League remains Bangladesh's most popular domestic competition, and the main source of income for local cricketers. Like the BPL, it attracted an influx of foreign players – 32 across the 12 teams, 22 of them from India.

It also attracted its customary share of controversy. As well as washouts – blamed on careless groundstaff – and frequent last-minute changes of venue, umpires were accused of favouritism, usually towards Abahani, the most influential club. Tensions came to a head in their Super League match against Prime Doleshwar. After a stumping appeal was rejected there was a heated exchange with Abahani captain Tamim Iqbal – and both umpires walked off, claiming they were ill. There was no play on the reserve day; instead, the board formed a committee to investigate, and declared a no-result. Each team got one point. **Abahani** eventually won the league from Prime Doleshwar by two points, their 18th title, but first for five years.

FIRST-CLASS AVERAGES, 2015-16

BATTING (500 runs, average 30.00)

	M	*I*	*NO*	*R*	*HS*	*100*	*Avge*	*Ct/St*
Mosaddek Hossain (*Barisal/South Zone*)	6	10	1	734	200*	3	81.55	4
†Shahriar Nafees (*Barisal/South Zone*)	12	21	3	1,117	174*	3	62.05	9
Raqibul Hasan (*Dhaka/Central Zone*)	10	16	1	883	228	2	58.86	8
†Mominul Haque (*Chittagong/East Zone*)	11	16	0	899	239	2	56.18	6
Tasamul Haque (*Chittagong/East Zone*)	11	15	2	723	134*	2	55.61	10
†Zakir Hasan (*Sylhet/East Zone*)	9	14	3	609	137*	2	55.36	20/4
Shamsur Rahman (*Dhaka Metropolis/C Zone*)	12	22	1	1,086	144	5	51.71	10
Tanveer Haider (*Rangpur/Central Zone*)	12	17	2	759	129	3	50.60	12
Marshall Ayub (*Dhaka Metropolis/C Zone*)	12	22	3	959	141	4	50.47	13
Imtiaz Hossain (*Sylhet/East Zone*)	8	13	0	595	154	2	45.76	1
Farhad Hossain (*Rajshahi/North Zone*)	12	20	1	867	145	4	45.63	15
Sharifullah (*Dhaka Metropolis/Central Zone*)	12	17	2	681	113	1	45.40	5
Alok Kapali (*Sylhet/East Zone*)	12	19	1	792	154	3	44.00	11
†Nazmul Hossain (*Rajshahi/North Zone*)	9	17	1	701	126	2	43.81	7
Yasir Ali (*Chittagong/East Zone*)	10	14	1	520	91	0	40.00	10
Al-Amin (*Barisal/Central Zone*)	9	14	1	518	157	1	39.84	7
Dhiman Ghosh (*Rangpur/North Zone*)	12	18	3	590	101*	1	39.33	21/3
Anamul Haque (*Khulna/South Zone*)	8	14	0	530	100	1	37.85	9/6
Tushar Imran (*Khulna/South Zone*)	12	18	2	603	96	0	37.68	2
†Fazle Mahmud (*Barisal/South Zone*)	9	16	0	579	133	2	36.18	4
Naeem Islam (*Rangpur/North Zone*)	11	19	1	633	100	1	35.16	6
Farhad Reza (*Rajshahi/South Zone*)	12	18	2	561	86	0	35.06	13

BOWLING (15 wickets, average 40.00)

	Style	*O*	*M*	*R*	*W*	*BB*	*5I*	*Avge*
Mehedi Hasan jnr (*Khulna*)	OB	221.3	58	493	30	6-50	3	16.43
Abul Hasan (*Sylhet/East Zone*)	RFM	110	22	353	19	5-68	1	18.57
Sharifullah (*Dhaka Metro/C Zone*)	OB	224.2	52	621	27	4-21	0	23.00
Sujon Hawlader (*Rajshahi/South Zone*)	RM	150	40	431	17	4-83	0	25.35
Towhidul Islam (*Barisal/South Zone*)	RM	129	27	382	15	6-31	2	25.46
Mohammad Saifuddin (*Chittagong/EZ*)	RM	128.2	14	487	19	5-41	1	25.63
Tanveer Haider (*Rangpur/C Zone*)	LBG	219.3	29	736	28	4-62	0	26.28
Sanjamul Islam (*Rajshahi/North Zone*)	SLA	480.4	86	1,565	59	8-106	4	26.52
Mohammad Shahid (*Dhaka Metro/CZ*)	RFM	140	34	414	15	4-84	0	27.60
Shafaq Al Zabir (*Rajshahi/North Zone*)	LFM	155.2	26	506	17	4-95	0	29.76
Alok Kapali (*Sylhet/East Zone*)	LBG	189.1	32	572	18	5-70	1	31.77
Mohammad Sharif (*Dhaka/C Zone*)	RFM	257.4	39	934	29	6-105	1	32.20
Shuvagata Hom (*Dhaka/Central Zone*)	OB	189.1	46	524	16	3-36	0	32.75
Abdur Razzak (*Khulna/South Zone*)	SLA	732.5	166	2,225	66	7-58	5	33.71
Nabil Samad (*Chittagong*)	SLA	232.3	51	633	18	4-101	0	35.16
Abu Jayed (*Sylhet/East Zone*)	RFM	174.5	32	647	18	4-43	0	35.94
Sohag Gazi (*Barisal/South Zone*)	OB	527	100	1,503	41	5-112	2	36.65
Mosharraf Hossain (*Dhaka/C Zone*)	SLA	473	82	1,345	36	7-119	3	37.36

WALTON LED TV NATIONAL CRICKET LEAGUE, 2015-16

Tier One	*P*	*W*	*L*	*D*	*Pts*
Khulna	6	1	0	5	54
Dhaka Metropolis	6	1	0	5	44
Dhaka	6	1	1	4	43
Rangpur	6	0	2	4	39

Tier Two	*P*	*W*	*L*	*D*	*Pts*
Barisal	6	2	0	4	62
Rajshahi	6	2	1	3	54
Chittagong	6	0	2	4	38
Sylhet	6	1	2	3	37

Outright win = 10pts; draw = 3pts; first-innings lead = 1pt. First-innings bonus points were awarded as follows for the first 110 overs of each team's first innings: one batting point for the first

250 runs and then for 300, 350, 400 and 450; one bowling point for the third wicket taken and then for the sixth and ninth.

Barisal were promoted to Tier One, and Rangpur relegated.

Tier One

At Bogra, September 18–21, 2015. **Drawn. ‡Dhaka Metropolis 238** (Mahmudul Hasan 5-44); **Rangpur 266-5 dec.** *Dhaka Metropolis 4pts, Rangpur 8pts.*

At Khulna, September 18–21, 2015. **Drawn. ‡Dhaka 187 and 15-0; Khulna 340** (Mosharraf Hossain 7-119). *Khulna 9pts, Dhaka 6pts.*

At Bogra, October 3–6, 2015. **Dhaka won by eight wickets. ‡Dhaka 449** (Nadif Chowdhury 111) **and 55-2; Rangpur 248** (Mosharraf Hossain 6-82) **and 255** (Suhrawadi Shuvo 121). *Dhaka 17pts, Rangpur 2pts. In failing light, Dhaka raced to 55 in 4.2 overs, with Shuvagata Hom hitting 40 from 16 balls.*

At Mirpur, October 3–6, 2015. **Drawn. Khulna 455** (Mithun Ali 186); **‡Dhaka Metropolis 271** (Marshall Ayub 107; Mehedi Hasan jnr 6-61) **and 248-5** (Marshall Ayub 115*). *Dhaka Metropolis 6pts, Khulna 11pts. Marshall Ayub scored twin centuries to save Dhaka Metropolis from defeat, despite following on.*

At Fatullah (KSOA), October 10–13, 2015. **Dhaka Metropolis won by three wickets. ‡Dhaka 327** (Arafat Sunny 6-96) **and 115; Dhaka Metropolis 352** (Shamsur Rahman 138; Mosharraf Hossain 5-120) **and 93-7.** *Dhaka Metropolis 15pts, Dhaka 4pts.*

At Khulna, October 10–13, 2015. **Khulna won by 13 runs. ‡Khulna 211 and 208** (Sanjit Saha 7-64); **Rangpur 220** (Mehedi Hasan jnr 6-50) **and 186.** *Khulna 13pts, Rangpur 4pts. Opposing off-spinners Sanjit Saha and Mehedi Hasan took 11-101 and 10-103 respectively – and Khulna captain Abdur Razzak's left-arm spin claimed 8-174 to help his side to victory.*

At Fatullah (KSOA), October 17–20, 2015. **Drawn. ‡Khulna 117 and 506-7 dec** (Mehedi Hasan snr 104, Anamul Haque 100, Nurul Hasan 182*); **Dhaka 154 and 233-7.** *Dhaka 7pts, Khulna 6pts. Khulna's second-innings total was bigger than the other three put together. Nurul Hasan scored a career-best 182*, adding 153 for the fifth wicket with Anamul Haque and 154 for the sixth with Ziaur Rahman (89).*

At Khulna, October 17–20, 2015. **Drawn. ‡Dhaka Metropolis 242 and 352-7 dec** (Mehrab Hossain 109); **Rangpur 299 and 72-3.** *Dhaka Metropolis 6pts, Rangpur 8pts. All 11 Rangpur players bowled in Dhaka Metropolis's second innings.*

At Bogra, October 24–27, 2015. **Drawn. Rangpur 463** (Tariq Ahmed 102, Naeem Islam 100, Dhiman Ghosh 101*); **‡Dhaka 276 and 247-4.** *Dhaka 6pts, Rangpur 9pts.*

At Fatullah (KSOA), October 24–27, 2015. **Drawn. Dhaka Metropolis 399** (Shamsur Rahman 144, Mahmudullah 132; Mehedi Hasan jnr 5-96) **and 262; ‡Khulna 367** (Imrul Kayes 163) **and 84-2.** *Dhaka Metropolis 10pts, Khulna 8pts. Imrul Kayes hit seven sixes in his 163, helping Khulna enter the final round six points ahead of Dhaka Metropolis and seven ahead of Dhaka.*

At Cox's Bazar, October 31–November 3, 2015. **Drawn. ‡Dhaka Metropolis 286-3** (Shamsur Rahman 105) **v Dhaka.** *Dhaka 3pts, Dhaka Metropolis 3pts. The first three days were washed out, frustrating both teams' title ambitions. Shamsur Rahman and Mehdi Hasan, who retired hurt on 99, added 209 for Dhaka Metropolis's second wicket.*

At Chittagong (ZAC), October 31–November 3, 2015. **Drawn. Rangpur 344** (Tanveer Haider 105; Abdur Razzak 5-127); **‡Khulna 286-7 dec** (Imrul Kayes 107). *Khulna 7pts, Rangpur 8pts. Only seven overs survived the first two days. Imrul Kayes reached a century in 98 balls as Khulna became champions, and Rangpur – who had won the title the previous year – were relegated.*

Tier Two

At Fatullah (KSOA), September 18–21, 2015. **Drawn. Sylhet 352-8 dec; ‡Chittagong 36-0.** *Chittagong 3pts, Sylhet 3pts.*

At Rajshahi, September 18–21, 2015. **Drawn. ‡Barisal 302** (Mosaddek Hossain 122; Sanjamul Islam 6-123) **and 160; Rajshahi 93** (Towhidul Islam 6-31) **and 25-0.** *Rajshahi 6pts, Barisal 9pts. Mosaddek Hossain hit six sixes in his third century in successive first-class matches since May. Slow left-armer Sanjamul Islam took 10-172. Rajshahi's 93 was the tournament's lowest total, but they avoided defeat when the last two days were washed out.*

At Khulna, October 3–6, 2015. **Drawn. Barisal 527-9 dec** (Fazle Mahmud 103, Mosaddek Hossain 200*) **and 146-7; ‡Sylhet 400** (Imtiaz Hossain 127). *Barisal 9pts, Sylhet 6pts. Barisal's 527 was the highest total in this tournament. Mosaddek completed his third double-hundred since February, in 245 balls with seven sixes. Sylhet reached 267-1 before losing nine for 133; their top four totalled 363, their last seven 29.*

At Rajshahi, October 3–6, 2015. **Rajshahi won by seven wickets. ‡Chittagong 383** (Irfan Sukkur 102) **and 181; Rajshahi 308 and 260-3** (Junaid Siddique 102). *Rajshahi 15pts, Chittagong 7pts. Rajshahi openers Nazmul Hossain and Junaid Siddique shared first-wicket stands of 144 and 193.*

At Chittagong (ZAC), October 10–13, 2015. **Drawn. Chittagong 467-7 dec** (Tamim Iqbal 137, Tasamul Haque 107) **and 52-0; ‡Barisal 346.** *Chittagong 10pts, Barisal 6pts. Tamim Iqbal scored his first domestic century for three years.*

At Bogra, October 10–13, 2015. **Drawn. Sylhet 328** (Imtiaz Hossain 154) **and 267-7; ‡Rajshahi 380** (Farhad Hossain 145; Rahatul Ferdous 5-80). *Rajshahi 9pts, Sylhet 6pts.*

At Bogra, October 17–20, 2015. **Barisal won by 150 runs. Barisal 155 and 464-7 dec** (Salman Hossain 146, Al-Amin 157); **‡Sylhet 172 and 297** (Zakir Hasan 137*; Sohag Gazi 5-112). *Barisal 13pts, Sylhet 4pts. Salman Hossain, with a maiden century, and Al-Amin added 230 for Barisal's fourth wicket; off-spinner Sohag Gazi's eight wickets completed Barisal's first first-class win in almost four years (in which they had lost 17 and drawn nine).*

At Chittagong (ZAC), October 17–20, 2015. **Drawn. ‡Rajshahi 208** (Iftekhar Sajjad 5-63) **and 273-6** (Nazmul Hossain 101); **Chittagong 350** (Tasamul Haque 134*; Sanjamul Islam 8-106). *Chittagong 7pts, Rajshahi 4pts. Sanjamul Islam's 8-106 was the best return of the season.*

At Chittagong (ZAC), October 24–27, 2015. **Sylhet won by five wickets. ‡Chittagong 270 and 272; Sylhet 283 and 264-5.** *Sylhet 15pts, Chittagong 4pts.*

At Rajshahi, October 24–26, 2015. **Barisal won by eight wickets. Rajshahi 119** (Towhidul Islam 5-30, Salman Hossain 5-31) **and 259; ‡Barisal 311 and 69-2.** *Barisal 16pts, Rajshahi 3pts. Barisal's second win gave them a 16-point lead over Rajshahi, whom they had reduced to 36-7 on the first day. The groundsman later filed a complaint with the police, alleging that a club official (and colleague) had assaulted him after claiming he had overwatered the pitch.*

At Bogra, October 31–November 3, 2015. **Drawn. Barisal 489** (Shahriar Nafees 168, Fazle Mahmud 133) **and 303-6** (Shahriar Nafees 174*); **‡Chittagong 425** (Mominul Haque 239; Sohag Gazi 5-134). *Barisal 9pts, Chittagong 7pts. Shahriar Nafees and Fazle Mahmud put on 283 for Barisal's second wicket, and Shahriar added another hundred in the second innings. Mominul Haque hit a maiden double-century, and finished with the season's highest score.*

At Khulna, October 31–November 2, 2015. **Rajshahi won by ten wickets. Sylhet 176 and 242** (Rumman Ahmed 106); **‡Rajshahi 395** (Farhad Hossain 144, Hamidul Islam 105) **and 26-0.** *Rajshahi 17pts, Sylhet 3pts. Farhad Hossain and Hamidul Islam added 239 for Rajshahi's fourth wicket, helping set up a decisive win – but not enough to overtake Barisal.*

NATIONAL CRICKET LEAGUE WINNERS

†1999-2000	Chittagong	2004-05	Dhaka	2010-11	Rajshahi
2000-01	Biman Bangladesh Airlines	2005-06	Rajshahi	2011-12	Rajshahi
2001-02	Dhaka	2006-07	Dhaka	2012-13	Khulna
2002-03	Khulna	2007-08	Khulna	2013-14	Dhaka
2003-04	Dhaka	2008-09	Rajshahi	2014-15	Rangpur
		2009-10	Rajshahi	2015-16	Khulna

† *The National Cricket League was not first-class in 1999-2000.*

Dhaka and Rajshahi have won the title 5 times, Khulna 4 times, Biman Bangladesh Airlines, Chittagong and Rangpur 1.

BANGLADESH CRICKET LEAGUE, 2015-16

	P	*W*	*L*	*D*	*1st-inns points*	*Bonus points Batting*	*Bonus points Bowling*	*Pts*
Central Zone	6	1	0	5	5	15	16	61
East Zone	6	1	0	5	3	12	12	52
North Zone	6	1	2	3	2	7	18	46
South Zone	6	0	1	5	2	10	13	40

Outright win = 10pts; draw = 3pts; first-innings lead = 1pt. First-innings bonus points were awarded as follows for the first 110 overs of each team's first innings: one batting point for the first 250 runs and then for 300, 350, 400 and 450; one bowling point for the third wicket taken and then for the sixth and ninth.

At Bogra, January 12–15, 2016. **Drawn. Central Zone 394** (Tanveer Haider 129, Sharifullah 113; Abul Hasan 5-68) **and 168; ‡East Zone 355** (Liton Das 128, Alok Kapali 100) **and 183-5.** *Central Zone 9pts, East Zone 7pts. Liton Das and Alok Kapali added 210 for East Zone's fourth wicket.*

At Rajshahi, January 12–15, 2016. **North Zone won by 74 runs. North Zone 392** (Farhad Hossain 106, Ariful Haque 115) **and 182** (Abdur Razzak 7-58); **‡South Zone 344** (Sanjamul Islam 6-79) **and 156** (Taijul Islam 5-38). *North Zone 17pts, South Zone 5pts. Abdur Razzak took 11-220, to become the second Bangladeshi after his team-mate and fellow left-arm spinner Enamul Haque jnr to reach 400 first-class wickets – but it was North Zone's slow left-armers, Sanjamul Islam and Taijul Islam, who secured victory.*

At Rajshahi, January 19–22, 2016. **Drawn. Central Zone 381** (Shamsur Rahman 103; Abdur Razzak 5-134) **and 45-1; ‡South Zone 246.** *Central Zone 10pts, South Zone 6pts.*

At Bogra, January 19–22, 2016. **Drawn. East Zone 214; ‡North Zone 59-3 dec**. *East Zone 5pts, North Zone 6pts.*

At Cox's Bazar (No. 2), February 24–27, 2016. **Central Zone won by 202 runs. ‡Central Zone 260 and 329-7 dec** (Marshall Ayub 141; Farhad Hossain 5-49); **North Zone 168 and 219.** *Central Zone 15pts, North Zone 3pts. On the opening day, North Zone's Sanjamul reached 50 first-class wickets in the season. In Central Zone's second innings, Marshall Ayub and Zabid Hossain added 229 for the second wicket before Farhad Hossain grabbed three wickets in five balls (and five in 33). Mohammad Sharif then reduced North Zone to 27-4 chasing 422.*

At Cox's Bazar, February 24–27, 2016. **Drawn. ‡South Zone 262 and 353** (Iftekhar Sajjad 5-130); **East Zone 407** (Mominul Haque 112, Zakir Hasan 128*; Abdur Razzak 5-161) **and 112-4.** *East Zone 10pts, South Zone 5pts. Razzak's 5-161 took him to 50 first-class wickets in the season, two days after Sanjamul.*

At Cox's Bazar, March 1–4, 2016. **Drawn. ‡Central Zone 588-8 dec** (Raqibul Hasan 228, Tanveer Haider 110) **and 199-4** (Shamsur Rahman 125*); **East Zone 442.** *Central Zone 9pts, East Zone 6pts. Raqibul Hasan, who scored his second double-century, added 240 for Central Zone's fifth wicket with Tanveer Haider; left-arm spinner Rahatul Ferdous had figures of 54–6–224–3. Shamsur Rahman made his fifth century of the season.*

At Cox's Bazar (No. 2), March 1–4, 2016. **Drawn. ‡North Zone 296 and 390-7 dec** (Nazmul Hossain 126); **South Zone 341** (Sanjamul Islam 6-116) **and 182-2** (Shahriar Nafees 101*). *North Zone 7pts, South Zone 9pts. In South Zone's first innings, Tushar Imran's 96 made him the first Bangladeshi to 8,000 first-class runs; in their second, Shahriar Nafees's century took him past 1,000 in the season.*

At Cox's Bazar, March 7–10, 2016. **Drawn. ‡Central Zone 425** (Raqibul Hasan 114; Abdur Razzak 5-138) **and 292-6 dec; South Zone 312 and 109-4.** *Central Zone 10pts, South Zone 7pts. Shamsur Rahman's 61 in Central Zone's second innings helped him tick off 1,000 runs in the season, the second to get there.*

At Cox's Bazar (No. 2), March 7–10, 2016. **East Zone won by four wickets. East Zone 392** (Alok Kapali 154) **and 139-6; ‡North Zone 173** (Mohammad Saifuddin 5-41) **and 357** (Maisuqur Rahman 131; Alok Kapali 5-70). *East Zone 17pts, North Zone 3pts. East Zone needed 139 to win in the final session; despite slipping to 37-4 in the eighth over, they completed victory in 22.1 overs and moved ahead of North Zone into second place.*

At Mirpur, March 14–17, 2016. **Drawn. North Zone 378** (Farhad Hossain 131; Mohammad Sharif 6-105) **and 293-8 dec; ‡Central Zone 306 and 257-2** (Marshall Ayub 101*). *Central Zone 8pts, North Zone 10pts. Ayub reached his fourth century of the season, in 97 balls, to finish with 562 at 56 in the tournament; his team, Central Zone, won it for the second time.*

At Fatullah (KSOA Outer), March 14–17, 2016. **Drawn. ‡East Zone 442** (Alok Kapali 111) **and 189-0** (Liton Das 103*); **South Zone 601** (Mosaddek Hossain 152, Sohag Gazi 146). *East Zone 7pts, South Zone 8pts. South Zone opener Shahriar Nafees hit 90, the tenth time he had passed 50 in 2015-16; Mosaddek Hossain added 145 with Farhad Reza for the fifth wicket, and 137 for the seventh with Sohag Gazi, who hit six sixes and a hundred before lunch on the last day, to set up the season's highest total. Razzak's 38 wickets for South Zone gave him 66 in the season.*

BANGLADESH PREMIER LEAGUE, 2015-16

50-over league plus knockout

	Played	*Won*	*Lost*	*Points*	*Net run-rate*
COMILLA VICTORIANS	10	7	3	14	0.78
RANGPUR RIDERS	10	7	3	14	0.69
BARISAL BULLS	10	7	3	14	0.06
DHAKA DYNAMITES	10	4	6	8	−0.01
Sylhet Superstars	10	3	7	6	−0.71
Chittagong Vikings	10	2	8	4	−0.82

Preliminary finals 1st v 2nd: Comilla Victorians beat Rangpur Riders by 72 runs. **3rd v 4th:** Barisal Bulls beat Dhaka Dynamites by 18 runs. **Final play-off:** Barisal Bulls beat Rangpur Riders by five wickets.

Final At Mirpur, December 15, 2015 (floodlit). **Comilla Victorians won by three wickets. Barisal Bulls 156-4** (20 overs); **‡Comilla Victorians 157-7** (20 overs). *MoM:* Alok Kapali (Comilla). *Alok Kapali ran the winning single off the final delivery after hitting four fours in his previous five balls, to finish with 39* in 28.*

DHAKA PREMIER LEAGUE, 2015-16

50-over league plus Super League

Preliminary League	*Played*	*Won*	*Lost*	*Tied*	*NR/A*	*Points*	*NRR*
VICTORIA	11	7	3	1	0	15	0.37
MOHAMMEDAN	11	7	4	0	0	14	0.48
PRIME DOLESHWAR	11	7	4	0	0	14	0.38
ABAHANI	11	7	4	0	0	14	0.32
LEGENDS OF RUPGANJ	11	6	3	1	1	14	0.18
PRIME BANK	11	6	5	0	0	12	0.14
Kala Bagan Krira Chakra	11	6	5	0	0	12	−0.08
Gazi Group Cricketers	11	5	6	0	0	10	0.26
Sheikh Jamal Dhanmondi	11	5	6	0	0	10	−0.45
Brothers Union	11	4	6	0	1	9	−0.37
Cricket Coaching School	11	2	9	0	0	4	−0.64
Kala Bagan Cricket Academy	11	2	9	0	0	4	−0.74

Super League	*Played*	*Won*	*Lost*	*Tied*	*NR/A*	*Points*	*NRR*
Abahani	16	11	4	0	1	23	1.02
Prime Doleshwar	16	10	5	0	1	21	0.55
Legends of Rupganj	16	9	5	1	1	20	0.05
Victoria	16	9	6	1	0	19	0.02
Mohammedan	16	8	8	0	0	16	−0.21
Prime Bank	16	7	9	0	0	14	−0.06

The top six teams advanced to the Super League, carrying forward all their results from the Preliminary League and then playing the other five qualifiers again.

INDIAN CRICKET IN 2016

Top of the world, but shrouded in mist

DILEEP PREMACHANDRAN

India stormed to No. 1 in the Test rankings, helped by the resplendent form of their captain, Virat Kohli, and the exploits of the world's best all-rounder, Ravichandran Ashwin. The Twenty20 team enjoyed some memorable moments, including a clean sweep in Australia, although they were knocked out in the semi-finals, at home, in the only global competition of the year. Sixty IPL matches reached over 360 million people, and the Under-19s another World Cup final. It should have been a year to savour for Indian cricket.

Instead, the on-field highlights were often eclipsed by activity in the boardrooms and the Supreme Court, where the lawmakers finally lost patience with the BCCI's high-handedness and intransigence.

INDIA IN 2016

	Played	*Won*	*Lost*	*Drawn/No result*
Tests	12	9	–	3
One-day internationals	13	7	6	–
Twenty20 internationals	21	15	5	1

JANUARY	5 ODIs and 3 T20Is (a) v Australia	(page 840)
FEBRUARY	3 T20Is (h) v Sri Lanka	(page 912)
FEBRUARY–MARCH	Asia Cup (in Bangladesh)	(page 899)
MARCH–APRIL	ICC World Twenty20 (h)	(page 793)
MAY		
JUNE	3 ODIs and 3 T20Is (a) v Zimbabwe	(page 1109)
JULY–AUGUST	4 Tests (a) and 2 T20Is (in USA) v West Indies	(page 1090)
SEPTEMBER–OCTOBER	3 Tests and 5 ODIs (h) v New Zealand	(page 915)
NOVEMBER–DECEMBER–JANUARY–FEBRUARY	5 Tests, 3 ODIs and 3 T20Is (h) v England	(page 342)

For a review of Indian domestic cricket from the 2015-16 season, see page 931.

Ajay Aggarwal, *Hindustan Times*/Getty Images

Leaping lights: Virat Kohli and Ravichandran Ashwin celebrate more Indian success.

With Kohli scoring 655 runs, including a glorious double-hundred at the Wankhede, India thrashed England 4–0 to cap an unforgettable 12 months in which they won nine Tests out of 12, and lost none; West Indies (away) had already been beaten 2–0, and New Zealand (at home) 3–0. Anurag Thakur, then BCCI president, issued a triumphant tweet, promising: "We'll continue to nurture & promote new talent @BCCI."

"We" would do nothing of the sort. When the Supreme Court reconvened in the first week of 2017, Thakur and Ajay Shirke, the board secretary, were sacked for their failure to implement reforms suggested by a committee headed by Rajendra Mal Lodha, himself a former Supreme Court chief justice. In July 2016, the court had asked the BCCI to initiate changes; reminders and warnings followed. But with Thakur and Co reluctant to force state associations into accepting them, the court had its final say.

In one sweep, two generations of cricket administrators were swatted into history's dustbin. No longer could central ministers, or those over 70, hold BCCI posts. Anyone who had served more than nine years at state or national level was also out, though subsequent amendments suggested administrators would be allowed 18 years in total – nine with their states, nine at the board. The real death knell, however, was the "cooling-off" period of three years recommended after each three-year term in office. Thakur himself had been in charge at the Himachal Pradesh Cricket Association for nearly two decades. Tamil Nadu cricket was synonymous with N. Srinivasan, erstwhile ICC chairman and BCCI president, while Saurashtra orbited around Niranjan Shah. "If Supreme Court judges feel that BCCI could do better under retired judges, I wish them all the best," said a dishevelled Thakur in a social-media video. Gone were the dapper suit, pocket square and preening confidence; in their place was disbelief.

Confusion remained, however, about the road ahead. Having asked the *amicus curiae* to come up with a shortlist of interim administrators, the Supreme Court was perplexed to find it contained the names of two former players – Bishan Bedi and Farokh Engineer – both over 70. Less than a fortnight later, the court appointed Diana Edulji, Ramachandra Guha, Vikram Limaye and Vinod Rai – a former India women's captain, a historian who has written extensively on cricket, a banker and a one-time Comptroller and Auditor General.

The start of 2017 also saw the end of the M. S. Dhoni captaincy era. After nearly a decade in charge of the limited-overs teams, and two years after calling time on his 90-Test career, Dhoni handed the reins to Kohli in all three formats. Rumours were rife that the man who led India in 199 ODIs and 72 T20s – winning a World Cup, Champions Trophy and World T20 – had been pushed, as much because of his proximity to disgraced administrators as Kohli's readiness to take over. At Gahunje in January, Dhoni celebrated his return to the ranks with a punishing one-day century against England, his first in over three years.

Kohli couldn't stop scoring. He topped 1,000 Test runs in a calendar year for the first time (1,215 at 75), with three of his four centuries in excess of 200. And he was equally dominant in the white-ball formats, scoring 739 ODI runs at 92, and 641 from just 457 balls in Twenty20 internationals. He also smashed the IPL record for most in a season, with 973.

A bumper crop of 13 home Tests was the Thakur-led administration's affirmation of their commitment to the longest format, with six new venues – Indore, Rajkot, Visakhapatnam, Pune, Dharamsala and Ranchi (the last three against Australia in February and March 2017) – joining the usual suspects. As a consequence, India played only 13 ODIs, their lowest annual tally since 1995. They won 15 of their (record) 21 Twenty20 games, but lost the one that mattered most, to West Indies in the semi-final of the World T20. That tournament was bedevilled by administrative glitches – the India–Pakistan match was moved 2,000km at the eleventh hour, from Dharamsala to Kolkata, after the state government failed to provide security guarantees – but it was embraced by millions of fans. Their disappointment at India's defeat was partially assuaged by some superb entertainment.

As in 2014, Kohli was Player of the Tournament. After batting with great restraint to see off Pakistan on a tricky Eden Gardens pitch, he produced a masterclass to beat Australia, prompting Gideon Haigh to write: "Much as the marketers would like to take the cricket out of T20, Kohli keeps putting it back." That India got as far as they did was down to Dhoni's sense of calm against Bangladesh. With two needed from three balls, Mushfiqur Rahim and Mahmudullah both fell to slogs, before Dhoni – glove off in anticipation – sprinted to the stumps to run out Mustafizur Rahman and steal victory.

But there was far more to Indian cricket than canny leadership and exemplary batsmanship. Ashwin took 72 Test wickets at 23, collecting his 15th five-wicket haul since his golden spell began in June 2015. He also scored two Test hundreds in the West Indies to reinforce his claim as the sport's most valuable player; 43 Test wickets at 24 for Ravindra Jadeja's left-arm spin underlined India's invincibility at home.

Ashwin's evolution as a high-class off-spinner owed much to India's new coach. After his playing days finished in 2010, Anil Kumble had spent three years in cricket administration, before becoming a team mentor in the IPL. Invited to replace Ravi Shastri, who had enjoyed an excellent rapport with Kohli, Kumble (thought to be closer to the contemporary game than his predecessor) took to the job with characteristic composure and tenacity.

It helped that India had enviable strength in depth. Karun Nair hit a triple-century in only his third Test, against England in Chennai, while K. L. Rahul established himself at the top of the order. Jasprit Bumrah and Hardik Pandya added to the quick-bowling options, and Mohammed Shami was magnificent on his return from injury. Meanwhile, Parthiv Patel – who led unfancied Gujarat to a first Ranji Trophy – made a good impression after replacing the injured Wriddhaman Saha against England, and playing only his second Test in 12 years.

India changed their XI for every Test – Lord's 2014 was the last time they played the same side in consecutive matches – but this did not breed insecurity. Instead, it created a band of brothers happy to follow the captain's lead. Bigger tests await them, especially away from home, but for now the future seems golden. Off the field, by contrast, it remained – like Delhi on a winter morning – shrouded in mist.

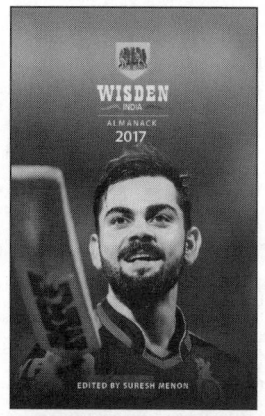

INDIA v SRI LANKA IN 2015-16

KARTHIK LAKSHMANAN

Twenty20 internationals (3): India 2, Sri Lanka 1

Series between India and Sri Lanka are not infrequent, but ones with context certainly are, and this tour formed a crucial part of preparations for the World Twenty20 in India the following month. India needed only fine-tuning: they were coming off the back of a 3–0 Twenty20 win in Australia, and had announced their tournament squad before this series began. They even had the luxury of resting Virat Kohli. By contrast, Sri Lanka looked unsure. Lasith Malinga and Angelo Mathews were injured, leaving the captaincy with Dinesh Chandimal. Their coach, Graham Ford, was just beginning his second stint in charge, two years after leaving for Surrey. And their squad was a muddle: three players had no Twenty20 experience at this level, and 36-year-old seamer Dilhara Fernando was back in international cricket for the first time since 2012.

The results varied with the conditions. Sri Lanka surprised many with a convincing victory in the first game in Gahunje, where the track was green enough for M. S. Dhoni to call it "English", and the visiting seamers, led by debutant Kasun Rajitha, knocked India over for 101. From there, the pitches became drier, and India exerted their force. In Ranchi, Shikhar Dhawan powered them towards a massive victory. Ravichandran Ashwin then wove his magic in Visakhapatnam to secure the series. The result reinforced India's position as the favourites for the World T20; Sri Lanka were left with more questions than answers.

SRI LANKAN TOURING PARTY

*L. D. Chandimal, P. V. D. Chameera, D. P. D. N. Dickwella, T. M. Dilshan, R. M. S. Eranga, C. R. D. Fernando, D. A. S. Gunaratne, M. D. Gunathilleke, C. K. Kapugedera, N. L. T. C. Perera, S. Prasanna, C. A. K. Rajitha, S. M. S. M. Senanayake, M. D. Shanaka, T. A. M. Siriwardene, J. D. F. Vandersay. *Coach:* G. X. Ford.

B. Fernando was originally selected, but injured a hamstring in training; Eranga replaced him. S. L. Malinga was out with a knee injury, so Chandimal led the side.

INDIA v SRI LANKA

First Twenty20 International

At Gahunje, February 9, 2016 (floodlit). Sri Lanka won by five wickets. Toss: Sri Lanka. Twenty20 international debuts: D. P. D. N. Dickwella, C. A. K. Rajitha.

Two Sri Lankan seamers, with just one Twenty20 international between them, stunned a star-studded Indian batting line-up to set up a thumping win. After Sri Lanka opted to field on a surprisingly verdant track, 22-year-old Kasun Rajitha made a dream start to his international career, dismissing Sharma and Rahane in his first over, and adding Dhawan in his third. Dasun Shanaka – a veteran of one cap – followed suit, rattling off Raina (playing his 50th T20I), Dhoni and Pandya in 11 balls to leave India tottering at 58 for seven. Ashwin made an unbeaten 31, but they were shot out for 101, their third lowest total in the format. India paid the price for being over-aggressive in conditions demanding patience; No. 10 Nehra faced more deliveries than seven of the top eight. Sri Lanka lost their openers cheaply, but the paltry target meant they needed only one decent partnership, and Chandimal and Kapugedera provided it.

Man of the Match: C. A. K. Rajitha.

India

		B	4/6
1 R. G. Sharma *c 10 b 11*	0	2	0
2 S. Dhawan *c 2 b 11*	9	13	0/1
3 A. M. Rahane *c 3 b 11*	4	4	1
4 S. K. Raina *b 6*	20	20	1/1
5 Yuvraj Singh *c and b 10*	10	14	0/1
6 *†M. S. Dhoni *c 1 b 6*	2	2	0
7 H. H. Pandya *lbw b 6*	2	6	0
8 R. A. Jadeja *lbw b 9*	6	9	0
9 R. Ashwin *not out*	31	24	5
10 A. Nehra *c 5 b 10*	6	19	0
11 J. J. Bumrah *run out*	0	0	0
B 2, lb 1, w 8	11		
6 overs: 40-3 (18.5 overs)	101		

1/0 2/5 3/32 4/49 5/51 6/53 7/58 8/72 9/100

Rajitha 4–13–29–3; Perera 3–14–10–0; Senanayake 3–10–18–1; Chameera 3.5–13–14–2; Shanaka 3–8–16–3; Prasanna 2–5–11–0.

Sri Lanka

		B	4/6
1 †D. P. D. N. Dickwella *c 2 b 10*	4	3	1
2 M. D. Gunathilleke *c 2 b 10*	9	18	0/1
3 *L. D. Chandimal *lbw b 4*	35	35	1/2
4 C. K. Kapugedera *lbw b 9*	25	26	4
5 T. A. M. Siriwardene *not out*	21	14	2/1
6 M. D. Shanaka *c 4 b 9*	3	8	0
7 S. Prasanna *not out*	3	4	0
Lb 3, w 2	5		
6 overs: 28-2 (18 overs)	105-5		

1/4 2/23 3/62 4/84 5/91

8 N. L. T. C. Perera, 9 S. M. S. M. Senanayake, 10 P. V. D. Chameera and 11 C. A. K. Rajitha did not bat.

Nehra 3–10–21–2; Bumrah 4–14–19–0; Jadeja 3–9–18–0; Pandya 3–11–18–0; Ashwin 3–9–13–2; Raina 2–6–13–1.

Umpires: V. A. Kulkarni and C. K. Nandan. Third umpire: A. K. Chaudhary.
Referee: J. J. Crowe.

INDIA v SRI LANKA

Second Twenty20 International

At Ranchi, February 12, 2016 (floodlit). India won by 69 runs. Toss: Sri Lanka.

The might of India's batting and spin bowling combined to level the series with a massive victory. Dhawan flayed the ball around the barren outfield on his way to a 22-ball half-century, his first in T20Is, as the openers raced to 75 from seven overs. Raina and Pandya took up the mantle, blasting 59 in a rollicking 26-ball partnership to push India towards 200. Perera claimed a late hat-trick – Sri Lanka's first in T20Is, and the fourth overall – but it made little difference. Dilshan, returning from a finger injury, dragged his foot out of his crease and was stumped from the first legal ball of the reply. It brought Ashwin the first of three scalps from four miserly overs and, as others chipped in, Sri Lanka were left miles short.

Man of the Match: S. Dhawan.

India

		B	4/6
1 R. G. Sharma *c and b 10*	43	36	2/1
2 S. Dhawan *c 4 b 10*	51	25	7/2
3 A. M. Rahane *c 2 b 9*	25	21	3
4 S. K. Raina *c 10 b 8*	30	19	5
5 H. H. Pandya *c 1 b 8*	27	12	1/2
6 *†M. S. Dhoni *not out*	9	5	1
7 Yuvraj Singh *c 9 b 8*	0	1	0
8 R. A. Jadeja *not out*	1	1	0
Lb 1, w 9	10		
6 overs: 70-0 (20 overs)	196-6		

1/75 2/122 3/127 4/186 5/186 6/186

9 R. Ashwin, 10 J. J. Bumrah and 11 A. Nehra did not bat.

Sri Lanka

		B	4/6
1 M. D. Gunathilleke *c 6 b 11*	2	7	0
2 T. M. Dilshan *st 6 b 9*	0	1	0
3 S. Prasanna *c 7 b 11*	1	4	0
4 *†L. D. Chandimal *st 6 b 8*	31	30	2
5 C. K. Kapugedera *c 5 b 8*	32	27	3/1
6 T. A. M. Siriwardene *not out*	28	20	1/1
7 M. D. Shanaka *c 4 b 9*	27	18	0/3
8 N. L. T. C. Perera *c 3 b 9*	0	1	0
9 S. M. S. M. Senanayake *lbw b 10*	0	2	0
10 P. V. D. Chameera *b 10*	0	3	0
11 C. A. K. Rajitha *not out*	3	7	0
W 3	3		
6 overs: 37-3 (20 overs)	127-9		

1/2 2/3 3/16 4/68 5/68 6/116 7/117 8/119 9/119

Rajitha 4–5–45–0; Perera 3–4–33–3; Senanayake 4–6–40–1; Chameera 4–7–38–2; Prasanna 3–2–21–0; Siriwardene 1–4–6–0; Shanaka 1–1–12–0.

Ashwin 4–12–14–3; Nehra 3–8–26–2; Yuvraj Singh 3–7–19–0; Jadeja 4–7–24–2; Raina 2–1–22–0; Bumrah 3–10–17–2; Pandya 1–1–5–0.

Umpires: A. K. Chaudhary and V. A. Kulkarni. Third umpire: C. K. Nandan. Referee: J. J. Crowe.

INDIA v SRI LANKA

Third Twenty20 International

At Visakhapatnam, February 14, 2016 (floodlit). India won by nine wickets. Toss: India. Twenty20 international debut: D. A. S. Gunaratne.

There had been signs of Sri Lankan weakness against spin in Ranchi, and here they were completely exposed. Ashwin, varying his pace beautifully, nipped out their top four in the first five overs, and finished with India's best Twenty20 figures. In ripe conditions, his spin partner Jadeja bowled 20 dots, also a national record, and shared three more wickets with Raina as Sri Lanka were shot out for 82. It was their lowest 20-over score, undercutting 87 against Australia at Bridgetown during the World T20 in 2010. India might have hoped for more batting time for their middle order, particularly Yuvraj Singh, who faced just 15 balls in the series, but the top three completed the job with minimal fuss. Ashwin finished the series with nine wickets at an average of 3.88 and an economy-rate of 3.18.

Man of the Match: R. Ashwin. *Man of the Series:* R. Ashwin.

Sri Lanka

		B	*4/6*
1 †D. P. D. N. Dickwella *st 5 b 9*	1	2	0
2 T. M. Dilshan *lbw b 9*	1	2	0
3 *L. D. Chandimal *c 7 b 9*	8	9	2
4 D. A. S. Gunaratne *c 4 b 9*	4	12	0
5 T. A. M. Siriwardene *b 11*	4	2	1
6 M. D. Shanaka *b 8*	19	24	1/2
7 S. Prasanna *run out*	9	7	2
8 N. L. T. C. Perera *c 8 b 4*	12	20	1
9 S. M. S. M. Senanayake *c 5 b 4*	8	16	0
10 P. V. D. Chameera *not out*	9	9	1
11 C. R. D. Fernando *b 10*	1	6	0
Lb 2, w 3, nb 1	6		
6 overs: 29-5 (18 overs)	82		

1/2 2/3 3/12 4/20 5/21 6/48 7/54 8/72 9/73

Ashwin 4–17–8–4; Nehra 2–8–17–1; Bumrah 3–11–10–1; Jadeja 4–20–11–1; Yuvraj Singh 1–3–15–0; Pandya 2–3–13–0; Raina 2–7–6–2.

India

		B	*4/6*
1 R. G. Sharma *lbw b 10*	13	13	1/1
2 S. Dhawan *not out*	46	46	5/1
3 A. M. Rahane *not out*	22	24	1
Lb 3	3		
6 overs: 35-1 (13.5 overs)	84-1		

1/29

4 S. K. Raina, 5 *†M. S. Dhoni, 6 Yuvraj Singh, 7 H. H. Pandya, 8 R. A. Jadeja, 9 R. Ashwin, 10 J. J. Bumrah and 11 A. Nehra did not bat.

Senanayake 4–13–22–0; Fernando 2–8–7–0; Chameera 2–5–14–1; Prasanna 1–3–3–0; Siriwardene 1–0–9–0; Gunaratne 2.5–5–22–0; Dilshan 1–2–4–0.

Umpires: A. K. Chaudhary and C. K. Nandan. Third umpire: V. A. Kulkarni. Referee: J. J. Crowe.

INDIA v NEW ZEALAND IN 2016-17

DILEEP PREMACHANDRAN

Test matches (3): India 3, New Zealand 0
One-day internationals (5): India 3, New Zealand 2

Before this series, there were many in India – such as Ravi Shastri, their team director until March – who thought New Zealand would present the toughest challenge of a 13-Test home season that included visits from England and Australia. In Kane Williamson, the captain, they had one of the world's best batsmen, as well as Ross Taylor, who had scored a hundred on their previous tour, in 2012. And their spinners had fresh memories of embarrassing India on an abrasive surface at Nagpur during the World Twenty20. For two days at Kanpur, New Zealand lived up to the hype, reaching 152 for one in reply to 318. After that, India wrested the initiative: whenever a game was in the balance, they found someone to tilt the scales.

New Zealand, though, were hamstrung by the failure of their batsmen. Williamson missed the Second Test at Kolkata through illness, and made only 135 runs, falling to Ravichandran Ashwin four times out of four; Taylor played in all three, and totalled a miserable 89, perhaps suffering from an eye complaint that later required surgery. Tom Latham made a half-century in every Test, but no one scored a hundred, and a collapse was never far away. Ashwin did most damage, with ten wickets in Kanpur, and a career-best 13 at Indore, while the support from Ravindra Jadeja, Mohammed Shami and Umesh Yadav was excellent. Bhuvneshwar Kumar took six for 76 at Kolkata, before a back strain ruled him out.

Cheteshwar Pujara had been criticised for his poor form and slow scoring in the West Indies earlier in the year. But here he averaged nearly 75 with a perfectly respectable strike-rate of 50, and was the leading scorer on pitches far from docile. Virat Kohli made little impression until he hit a double-hundred at Indore and put on 365 with Ajinkya Rahane to seal New Zealand's fate. By then, their bowling attack had run out of puff. After they lost Tim Southee to an ankle injury before the first match, the others toiled hard, but were thwarted by obduracy and class.

The one-day series was Kohli's. He began with an unbeaten 85 in a crushing victory at Dharamsala, and later scored 154 not out at Mohali to make a chase of 286 look like a parkland stroll. New Zealand relied on the consistency of Latham and, buoyed by the return of Southee, twice defended middling totals. Visakhapatnam became the decider, and Kohli hit 65 to end the series with 358 runs for three dismissals. Amit Mishra's five-for did the rest, as New Zealand wilted to 79 all out; he ended with 15 wickets at just over 14 each. None of the others put up eye-catching numbers but, with Ashwin, Jadeja and Shami rested after their Test exertions, the fringe players got their chance; few let themselves down. Hardik Pandya excelled on debut, Kedar Jadhav made an impression with pugnacious batting and clever off-spin, and Jasprit Bumrah was exceptionally frugal, particularly at the death, conceding a breath above four an over.

Even M. S. Dhoni, whose eponymous movie was playing in cinemas at the time, rolled back the years with 80 in Mohali. After he had quit Tests in 2014, there were now long gaps between his international appearances but, once he had shaken off the rust, he reminded all of his value. It was a good thing he did: after the Tests, the chorus was growing louder for Kohli to be handed the reins in all formats. As for New Zealand, this was a trip to forget, the gap between reputation and reality as wide as the Arabian Sea.

NEW ZEALAND TOURING PARTY

*K. S. Williamson (T/50), C. J. Anderson (50), T. A. Boult (T/50), D. A. J. Bracewell (T/50), M. D. Craig (T), A. P. Devcich (50), M. J. Guptill (T/50), M. J. Henry (T/50), T. W. M. Latham (T/50), J. D. S. Neesham (T/50), H. M. Nicholls (T), J. S. Patel (T), L. Ronchi (T/50), M. J. Santner (T/50), I. S. Sodhi (T/50), T. G. Southee (50), L. R. P. L. Taylor (T/50), N. Wagner (T), B-J. Watling (T/50). *Coach:* M. J. Hesson.

Southee was originally selected in both squads, but damaged his left ankle before the Test series; Henry provided cover, and remained for the ODIs. Craig suffered a side strain in the First Test, and was replaced by J. S. Patel.

TEST MATCH AVERAGES

INDIA – BATTING AND FIELDING

	T	*I*	*NO*	*R*	*HS*	*100*	*50*	*Avge*	*Ct*
W. P. Saha	3	3	2	112	58*	0	2	112.00	2
R. G. Sharma	3	5	2	238	82	0	3	79.33	2
C. A. Pujara	3	6	1	373	101*	1	3	74.60	1
A. M. Rahane	3	6	1	347	188	1	1	69.40	4
†R. A. Jadeja	3	5	3	129	50*	0	1	64.50	0
V. Kohli	3	6	0	309	211	1	0	51.50	3
M. Vijay	3	6	0	186	76	0	2	31.00	3
R. Ashwin	3	3	0	71	40	0	0	23.66	4
Mohammed Shami	3	3	0	15	14	0	0	5.00	2

Played in two Tests: U. T. Yadav 9. Played in one Test: Bhuvneshwar Kumar 5, 23; †S. Dhawan 1, 17; †G. Gambhir 29, 50; K. L. Rahul 32, 38.

BOWLING

	Style	*O*	*M*	*R*	*W*	*BB*	*5I*	*Avge*
Bhuvneshwar Kumar	RFM	27	6	76	6	5-48	1	12.66
R. Ashwin	OB	146.3	28	480	27	7-59	3	17.77
R. A. Jadeja	SLA	144	39	337	14	5-73	1	24.07
Mohammed Shami	RFM	75.1	10	243	8	3-46	0	30.37

Also bowled: R. G. Sharma (OB) 1–0–5–0; M. Vijay (OB) 13–0–40–0; U. T. Yadav (RF) 46–11–124–2.

NEW ZEALAND – BATTING AND FIELDING

	T	*I*	*NO*	*R*	*HS*	*100*	*50*	*Avge*	*Ct*
K. S. Williamson	2	4	0	135	75	0	1	33.75	0
L. Ronchi	3	6	0	200	80	0	1	33.33	1
†T. W. M. Latham	3	6	0	194	74	0	3	32.33	5
M. J. Guptill	3	6	0	159	72	0	1	26.50	3
†M. J. Santner	3	6	0	159	71	0	1	26.50	1
B-J. Watling	3	6	1	111	25	0	0	22.20	5
J. S. Patel	2	4	0	67	47	0	0	16.75	0
L. R. P. L. Taylor	3	6	0	89	36	0	0	14.83	4
M. J. Henry	2	4	1	33	18	0	0	11.00	2
†N. Wagner	2	4	2	15	10	0	0	7.50	0
T. A. Boult	3	6	2	16	6*	0	0	4.00	1

Played in one Test: †M. D. Craig 2, 1; †J. D. S. Neesham 71, 0; †H. M. Nicholls 1, 24 (1 ct); I. S. Sodhi 0, 17 (3 ct).

BOWLING

	Style	*O*	*M*	*R*	*W*	*BB*	*5I*	*Avge*
T. A. Boult	LFM	106.4	20	333	10	3-38	0	33.30
N. Wagner	LFM	66	17	196	5	2-42	0	39.20
M. J. Henry	RFM	82	12	254	6	3-46	0	42.33
J. S. Patel	OB	83	8	292	6	2-56	0	48.66
I. S. Sodhi	LBG	35	5	149	3	2-99	0	49.66
M. J. Santner	SLA	155.2	25	524	10	3-60	0	52.40

Also bowled: M. D. Craig (OB) 47–9–139–2; M. J. Guptill (OB) 4–0–17–0; J. D. S. Neesham (RFM) 22–1–80–0; K. S. Williamson (OB) 3–0–7–0.

At Delhi, September 16–18, 2016 (not first-class). **Drawn. New Zealanders 324-7** (75 overs) (T. W. M. Latham 55, K. S. Williamson 50) **and 235** (66.4 overs) (L. Ronchi 107); ‡**Mumbai 464-8** (114 overs) (K. R. Pawar 100, S. A. Yadav 103, S. D. Lad 100*). *Each side chose from 15 players. A Mumbai innings including three hundreds and 18 sixes (15 between centurions Suryakumar Yadav and Siddhesh Lad) allowed a declaration on the last morning, 140 ahead. Martin Guptill failed for a second time, but Luke Ronchi's 112-ball hundred ensured safety.*

INDIA v NEW ZEALAND

First Test Match

At Kanpur, September 22–26, 2016. India won by 197 runs. Toss: India.

The BCCI aren't renowned for planning ahead. If they were, perhaps India's 500th Test might have taken place somewhere other than Kanpur's Green Park, a historic but dilapidated venue. For two days, New Zealand threatened to spoil the occasion. But an extraordinary collapse on the third afternoon – when they lost their last five wickets for seven runs in 29 balls – handed India control, and Ashwin's mastery of drift and spin delivered an emphatic victory.

India had suffered their own malfunction on the opening day. Pujara added an authoritative 112 with Vijay, then chipped one back to Santner in uncharacteristically loose fashion. Three overs later, Kohli top-edged a pull off Wagner into an obvious leg-side trap. And, when the lower order succumbed to the second new ball, India had slid from 154 for one to 277 for nine. It needed Jadeja's use of the long handle to take them past 300 next morning. By the time rain washed out the final session on the second day, New Zealand were 152 for one, with Latham and Williamson holding firm against the spinners, despite the odd ball spitting out of the rough.

QUICKEST TO 200 TEST WICKETS

T		*Debut*	*200th wicket*
36	C. V. Grimmett (A)	1924-25	1935-36
37	**R. Ashwin (I)**	**2011-12**	**2016-17**
38	D. K. Lillee (A)	1970-71	1979-80
38	Waqar Younis (P)	1989-90	1995-96
39	D. W. Steyn (SA)	2004-05	2010

Two wonderful deliveries from Ashwin on the third morning transformed the mood. Latham went to his arm-ball and, after Jadeja thudded one into Taylor's pad, Ashwin bowled Williamson with a delivery that turned like a Muttiah Muralitharan special. Ronchi and Santner held India up, but the tail had no answer to Jadeja's zip and stump-challenging line; a triple-wicket maiden helped him finish with five for 73.

After conceding a 56-run lead, New Zealand needed early inroads. But a lively knock from Rahul stretched the advantage past 100, before Vijay and Pujara stitched together their second century partnership of the match. Neither reached three figures, but they allowed Sharma and Jadeja to throw the bat; they harassed the bowling to the tune of 100 runs in just 18.3 overs, swelling the target over 400.

In short time, Ashwin had another three scalps, all with a sense of familiarity. Guptill failed again, Latham was undone by a straight one, and Williamson beaten by a vicious off-break. It brought Ashwin his 200th Test wicket, in his 37th Test. And when Taylor dozily forgot to ground his bat and was run out, New Zealand were 56 for four.

Ronchi played with confidence while adding 102 with Santner but, fourth ball after drinks on the last morning, fell to an ugly heave across the line for 80. Santner persevered, lasting 179 deliveries before Ashwin squared him up with a peach that pitched well outside leg stump and rose to take the shoulder of the bat. He bowled Sodhi to earn a 19th five-for, then trapped Wagner leg-before to finish the match. It also brought Ashwin a fifth ten-wicket haul in Tests, bringing him level with Harbhajan Singh and behind only his coach Anil Kumble (eight) among Indian bowlers. A callus on his middle finger meant he used the carrom ball more than usual, but the results were just as effective.

Man of the Match: R. A. Jadeja.

Close of play: first day, India 291-9 (Jadeja 16, Yadav 8); second day, New Zealand 152-1 (Latham 56, Williamson 65); third day, India 159-1 (Vijay 64, Pujara 50); fourth day, New Zealand 93-4 (Ronchi 38, Santner 8).

India

K. L. Rahul c Watling b Santner	32	– c Taylor b Sodhi	38
M. Vijay c Watling b Sodhi	65	– lbw b Santner	76
C. A. Pujara c and b Santner	62	– c Taylor b Sodhi	78
*V. Kohli c Sodhi b Wagner	9	– c Sodhi b Craig	18
A. M. Rahane c Latham b Craig	18	– c Taylor b Santner	40
R. G. Sharma c Sodhi b Santner	35	– not out	68
R. Ashwin c Taylor b Boult	40		
†W. P. Saha b Boult	0		
R. A. Jadeja not out	42	– (7) not out	50
Mohammed Shami b Boult	0		
U. T. Yadav c Watling b Wagner	9		
B 5, lb 1	6	B 1, lb 8	9
1/42 (1) 2/154 (3) 3/167 (4) 4/185 (2) 5/209 (5) 6/261 (6) 7/262 (8) 8/273 (7) 9/277 (10) 10/318 (11) (97 overs)	318	1/52 (1) 2/185 (2) 3/214 (4) 4/228 (3) 5/277 (5) (5 wkts dec, 107.2 overs)	377

Boult 20–3–67–3; Wagner 15–4–42–2; Santner 23–2–94–3; Craig 24–6–59–1; Sodhi 15–3–50–1. *Second innings*—Boult 9–0–34–0; Santner 32.2–11–79–2; Craig 23–3–80–1; Wagner 16–5–52–0; Sodhi 20–2–99–2; Guptill 4–0–17–0; Williamson 3–0–7–0.

New Zealand

M. J. Guptill lbw b Yadav	21	– (2) c Vijay b Ashwin	0
T. W. M. Latham lbw b Ashwin	58	– (1) lbw b Ashwin	2
*K. S. Williamson b Ashwin	75	– lbw b Ashwin	25
L. R. P. L. Taylor lbw b Jadeja	0	– run out	17
L. Ronchi lbw b Jadeja	38	– c Ashwin b Jadeja	80
M. J. Santner c Saha b Ashwin	32	– c Sharma b Ashwin	71
†B-J. Watling c and b Ashwin	21	– lbw b Mohammed Shami	18
M. D. Craig lbw b Jadeja	2	– b Mohammed Shami	1
I. S. Sodhi lbw b Jadeja	0	– b Ashwin	17
T. A. Boult c Sharma b Jadeja	0	– not out	2
N. Wagner not out	0	– lbw b Ashwin	0
B 8, lb 5, nb 2	15	Lb 2, nb 1	3
1/35 (1) 2/159 (2) 3/160 (4) 4/170 (3) 5/219 (5) 6/255 (6) 7/258 (8) 8/258 (9) 9/258 (10) 10/262 (7) (95.5 overs)	262	1/2 (2) 2/3 (1) 3/43 (3) 4/56 (4) 5/158 (5) 6/194 (7) 7/196 (8) 8/223 (6) 9/236 (9) 10/236 (11) (87.3 overs)	236

Mohammed Shami 11–1–35–0; Yadav 15–5–33–1; Jadeja 34–7–73–5; Ashwin 30.5–7–93–4; Vijay 4–0–10–0; Sharma 1–0–5–0. *Second innings*—Mohammed Shami 8–2–18–2; Ashwin 35.3–5–132–6; Jadeja 34–17–58–1; Yadav 8–1–23–0; Vijay 2–0–3–0.

Umpires: R. A. Kettleborough and R. J. Tucker. Third umpire: A. K. Chaudhary.
Referee: D. C. Boon.

INDIA v NEW ZEALAND

Second Test Match

At Kolkata, September 30–October 3, 2016. India won by 178 runs. Toss: India.

Kane Williamson was out with fever, so Taylor led New Zealand, but the story was much the same. A sparky bowling effort on the first day came to nothing, as their batting failed under intense scrutiny.

Henry had made the early incisions on a well-grassed pitch, before Kohli sliced to gully to leave India tottering at 46 for three. Once again, though, Pujara shepherded a recovery, batting with the poise and patience of old, while despatching anything loose, and adding 141 with Rahane. In the evening, New Zealand clawed their way back, just as they had at Kanpur. Pujara miscued Wagner to short cover for 87, then off-spinner Jeetan Patel, in his first Test for four years after choosing to focus on the County Championship, struck twice, including Rahane for 77. With Ashwin also falling before stumps, it was New Zealand who started the second day with a spring in their step.

But India added 85 for the final three wickets – local lad Saha hitting a combative unbeaten 54 – before their seamers got to work. Mohammed Shami, another who spent his formative years on Kolkata's maidans, trapped Latham, before Bhuvneshwar Kumar had both Guptill and Nicholls playing on. New Zealand were 23 for three – and had lost their footing.

Ronchi led a brief counterattack, but fell to a questionable lbw decision last ball before a 90-minute rain delay. On resumption, the overcast conditions suited Bhuvneshwar's wobblers: he had Taylor edging to slip, before adding two more to earn the fourth five-wicket haul of his Test career, and leave New Zealand in dire trouble at 128 for seven by the second-day close. Patel infused life into the innings with a rollicking run-a-ball 47, but Shami's pacy reverse swing meant the deficit was 112. It was the first time since 2008 that Indian seamers had taken eight wickets in a Test innings at home.

Again, New Zealand's fast bowlers gave them a sniff, reducing India to 45 for four. And Boult didn't just remove Dhawan: he struck him twice on the left hand, leaving a fracture that ruled him out of the rest of the series. Kohli's footwork was precise and, despite an increasingly tricky pitch, he found the gaps with ease. A Boult delivery that skidded through at shin height sent him back for 45, but by then Sharma was in his element, hitting through the line on his way to 82. From 106 for six, his century partnership with Saha, who once more showed application, stretched the lead above 300 and, realistically, out of range: no team had chased more than 117 to win a Test at Eden Gardens.

Latham played another outstanding innings, and New Zealand went past 100 for the loss of Guptill. But from there the slide was swift. Jadeja and Ashwin struck before tea and, when Latham nicked one soon after, India sensed a four-day finish. His 74 was New Zealand's only half-century in the match. There was otherwise little resistance against the combination of spin and hooping swing, with Shami's delivery that straightened to take out Watling's off stump the pick. As their most famous ground fell into shadow, India took the last seven wickets for 56, securing a fourth straight series win.

Man of the Match: W. P. Saha.

Close of play: first day, India 239-7 (Saha 14, Jadeja 0); second day, New Zealand 128-7 (Watling 12, Patel 5); third day, India 227-8 (Saha 39, Bhuvneshwar Kumar 8).

India

S. Dhawan b Henry	1	– lbw b Boult	17
M. Vijay c Watling b Henry	9	– c Guptill b Henry	7
C. A. Pujara c Guptill b Wagner	87	– lbw b Henry	4
*V. Kohli c Latham b Boult	9	– lbw b Boult	45
A. M. Rahane lbw b Patel	77	– c Boult b Henry	1
R. G. Sharma c Latham b Patel	2	– c Ronchi b Santner	82
R. Ashwin lbw b Henry	26	– lbw b Santner	5
†W. P. Saha not out	54	– not out	58
R. A. Jadeja c Henry b Wagner	14	– c sub (J. D. S. Neesham) b Santner	6
Bhuvneshwar Kumar lbw b Santner	5	– c Nicholls b Wagner	23
Mohammed Shami c Henry b Boult	14	– c Latham b Boult	1
B 8, lb 10	18	B 10, lb 1, w 3	14
1/1 (1) 2/28 (2) 3/46 (4) 4/187 (3) 5/193 (6) 6/200 (5) 7/231 (7) 8/272 (9) 9/281 (10) 10/316 (11) (104.5 overs)	316	1/12 (2) 2/24 (3) 3/34 (1) 4/43 (5) 5/91 (4) 6/106 (7) 7/209 (6) 8/215 (9) 9/251 (10) 10/263 (11) (76.5 overs)	263

Boult 20.5–9–46–2; Henry 20–6–46–3; Wagner 20–5–57–2; Santner 23–5–83–1; Patel 21–3–66–2. *Second innings*—Boult 17.5–6–38–3; Henry 20–2–59–3; Wagner 15–3–45–1; Patel 8–0–50–0; Santner 16–2–60–3.

New Zealand

M. J. Guptill b Bhuvneshwar Kumar	13	– (2) lbw b Ashwin	24
T. W. M. Latham lbw b Mohammed Shami	1	– (1) c Saha b Ashwin	74
H. M. Nicholls b Bhuvneshwar Kumar	1	– c Rahane b Jadeja	24
*L. R. P. L. Taylor c Vijay b Bhuvneshwar Kumar	36	– lbw b Ashwin	4
L. Ronchi lbw b Jadeja	35	– b Jadeja	32
M. J. Santner lbw b Bhuvneshwar Kumar	11	– lbw b Mohammed Shami	9
†B-J. Watling lbw b Mohammed Shami	25	– b Mohammed Shami	1
M. J. Henry b Bhuvneshwar Kumar	0	– c Kohli b Jadeja	18
J. S. Patel c Mohammed Shami b Ashwin	47	– b Bhuvneshwar Kumar	2
N. Wagner lbw b Mohammed Shami	10	– not out	5
T. A. Boult not out	6	– c Vijay b Mohammed Shami	4
B 9, lb 4, w 5, nb 1	19		
1/10 (2) 2/18 (1) 3/23 (3) 4/85 (5) 5/104 (4) 6/122 (6) 7/122 (8) 8/182 (9) 9/187 (7) 10/204 (10) (53 overs)	204	1/55 (2) 2/104 (3) 3/115 (4) 4/141 (1) 5/154 (6) 6/156 (7) 7/175 (5) 8/178 (9) 9/190 (8) 10/197 (11) (81.1 overs)	197

Bhuvneshwar Kumar 15–2–48–5; Mohammed Shami 18–1–70–3; Jadeja 12–4–40–1; Ashwin 8–3–33–1. *Second innings*—Bhuvneshwar Kumar 12–4–28–1; Mohammed Shami 18.1–5–46–3; Ashwin 31–6–82–3; Jadeja 20–3–41–3.

Umpires: R. A. Kettleborough and R. J. Tucker. Third umpire: C. K. Nandan.
Referee: D. C. Boon.

INDIA v NEW ZEALAND

Third Test Match

At Indore, October 8–11, 2016. India won by 321 runs. Toss: India.

More than 18,000 turned up on the opening day of Indore's inaugural Test. And the enthusiasm continued for four days as India, powered by a mammoth first innings and Ashwin's bewitching skill, eased to a huge win. It was their second-biggest victory by runs in Tests, and completed only their fourth whitewash in series of three matches or more.

Kohli won another toss, and Gambhir – recalled in place of the injured Shikhar Dhawan – showed the folly of bowling short on a slow pitch, pulling Henry for two consecutive sixes in the fourth over. New Zealand chipped away, however, and had three wickets by drinks on the first afternoon, but would not get another until after tea on the second day. Kohli, determined to break a sequence of low scores, ground out a hundred, his only indulgence some crisp drives and punches through leg. Rahane struggled early on, as his hesitancy against short bowling was relentlessly targeted. The first 20 overs of the partnership yielded 48 runs, but the duo opened up in an evening session that brought 119.

Next day, they more than doubled their stand. While Kohli stuck to strokes along the carpet, Rahane was not shy to loft the spinners, and the partnership rose to an Indian fourth-wicket record of 365, beating Sachin Tendulkar and V. V. S. Laxman's 353 at Sydney in 2003-04. Kohli eventually fell after becoming the first Indian captain to register two double-hundreds, before Rahane was caught behind for a career-best 188, trying to up the tempo. Sharma then helped himself to an enterprising half-century, while Jadeja was warned for running across the danger area; a second offence brought a five-run penalty.

With 557 in their pocket, India gave New Zealand nine overs to survive on the second evening. The openers did so and, after Rahane dropped Guptill at gully next morning, they continued frustrating the bowlers with a partnership of 118, easily the highest first-wicket stand in the series. Just before lunch, Ashwin decided enough was enough. Latham was deceived in the flight and popped a return catch off the leading edge; after the break, it was a procession, with Ashwin calling the tune. Williamson, back after his illness, chopped on, and Taylor edged to slip for a duck. Ashwin had fortune on his side, too, deflecting a fierce straight-drive from Ronchi on to the stumps, with Guptill out of his crease; Ronchi could not atone, nicking the first ball of Ashwin's next over.

Neesham, out of the first two Tests with a rib injury, kept India at bay, putting on fifty stands with Watling and Santner, before he missed a sweep. It gave Ashwin his 20th five-wicket haul and soon – after another run-out at the non-striker's end, this time from a fumbled catch – he ended the innings. On the third evening, India were batting again with a lead of 258 on a surface where the cracks were becoming wider.

Gambhir retired hurt when he injured his right shoulder in a dive but, after Guptill had brilliantly run out Vijay with a reverse flick from cover, returned next morning to make a sprightly 50. The highlight, though, was another Pujara hundred, the second fifty compiled at a run a ball to hasten a declaration. Having shown plenty of fight throughout the series, New Zealand then wilted in the face of an ungettable target and, inevitably, Ashwin.

Yadav provided the early breakthrough, but Ashwin removed Williamson leg-before with a ripping off-break, and Taylor with one that sneaked under an ill-judged swat. As the collapse gathered pace, New Zealand lost their last seven for 51 to crumble within 45 overs; Ashwin finished with career-best figures for both an innings (seven for 59) and a match (13 for 140).

For Kohli and his team, it meant another day off, probably welcome after celebrations that included acquiring the Test championship mace. With ten more home Tests coming up, there seemed little danger of it slipping from the captain's grasp any time soon.

Man of the Match: R. Ashwin. *Man of the Series:* R. Ashwin.

Close of play: first day, India 267-3 (Kohli 103, Rahane 79); second day, New Zealand 28-0 (Guptill 17, Latham 6); third day, India 18-0 (Vijay 11, Pujara 1).

India

M. Vijay c Latham b Patel	10	run out	19
G. Gambhir lbw b Boult	29	c Guptill b Patel	50
C. A. Pujara b Santner	41	not out	101
*V. Kohli lbw b Patel	211	lbw b Patel	17
A. M. Rahane c Watling b Boult	188	not out	23
R. G. Sharma not out	51		
R. A. Jadeja not out	17		
B 4, lb 3, w 1, nb 2	10	B 4, lb 1, w 1	6
1/26 (1) 2/60 (2) 3/100 (3) 4/465 (4) 5/504 (5) (5 wkts dec, 169 overs)	557	1/34 (1) 2/110 (2) 3/158 (4) (3 wkts dec, 49 overs)	216

R. Ashwin, †W. P. Saha, Mohammed Shami and U. T. Yadav did not bat.

In the second innings Gambhir, when 6, retired hurt at 11-0 and resumed at 34-1.

Boult 32–2–113–2; Henry 35–3–127–0; Patel 40–5–120–2; Santner 44–4–137–1; Neesham 18–1–53–0. *Second innings*—Boult 7–0–35–0; Patel 14–0–56–2; Santner 17–1–71–0; Henry 7–1–22–0; Neesham 4–0–27–0.

New Zealand

M. J. Guptill run out	72	(2) lbw b Jadeja	29
T. W. M. Latham c and b Ashwin	53	(1) lbw b Yadav	6
*K. S. Williamson b Ashwin	8	lbw b Ashwin	27
L. R. P. L. Taylor c Rahane b Ashwin	0	b Ashwin	32
L. Ronchi c Rahane b Ashwin	0	b Ashwin	15
J. D. S. Neesham lbw b Ashwin	71	c Kohli b Jadeja	0
†B-J. Watling c Rahane b Jadeja	23	not out	23
M. J. Santner c Kohli b Jadeja	22	b Ashwin	14
J. S. Patel run out	18	b Ashwin	0
M. J. Henry not out	15	c Mohammed Shami b Ashwin	0
T. A. Boult c Pujara b Ashwin	0	c and b Ashwin	4
B 6, lb 5, w 1, p 5	17	B 2, nb 1	3
1/118 (2) 2/134 (3) 3/140 (4) 4/148 (1) 5/148 (5) 6/201 (7) 7/253 (8) 8/276 (6) 9/294 (9) 10/299 (11) (90.2 overs)	299	1/7 (1) 2/42 (3) 3/80 (4) 4/102 (5) 5/103 (6) 6/112 (2) 7/136 (8) 8/138 (9) 9/138 (10) 10/153 (11) (44.5 overs)	153

Mohammed Shami 13–1–40–0; Yadav 15–1–55–0; Ashwin 27.2–5–81–6; Jadeja 28–5–80–2; Vijay 7–0–27–0. *Second innings*—Mohammed Shami 7–0–34–0; Yadav 8–4–13–1; Ashwin 13.5–2–59–7; Jadeja 16–3–45–2.

Umpires: H. D. P. K. Dharmasena and B. N. J. Oxenford. Third umpire: C. Shamshuddin.
Referee: D. C. Boon.

> "Once again they had to battle an injury crisis among the bowlers, a phenomenon so regular it could be included in the fixture list."
> Surrey in 2016, page 583

INDIA v NEW ZEALAND

First One-Day International

At Dharamsala, October 16, 2016 (day/night). India won by six wickets. Toss: India. One-day international debut: H. H. Pandya.

Hardik Pandya was given his first one-day cap by Kapil Dev and, armed with the new ball ahead of Bumrah, performed a fair impression of the great man. There was early swing and seam movement, and Pandya – whose Twenty20 career had shown a fondness for the short delivery – made the most of it by pitching the ball up. Yadav chipped in with two scalps, including Taylor for a fourth duck in eight international innings. By the time part-time off-spinner Kedar Jadhav had picked up his first two ODI wickets in consecutive balls, New Zealand were 65 for seven. It took an innings of calm and class from Latham, and Southee's stroke-filled 55 (the highest by a New Zealand No. 10) to give them even a chance. They managed to get rid of Sharma and Rahane, the Mumbai pair, but Kohli demonstrated his mastery of the chase. A six into the sightscreen off Sodhi left him unbeaten on 85 as India romped home.

Man of the Match: H. H. Pandya.

CARRYING THE BAT IN A ONE-DAY INTERNATIONAL

G. W. Flower	84* (205)	Zimbabwe v England at Sydney	1994-94
Saeed Anwar	103* (219)	Pakistan v Zimbabwe at Harare	1994-95
N. V. Knight	125* (246)	England v Pakistan at Nottingham	1996
R. D. Jacobs	49* (110)	West Indies v Australia at Manchester	1999
D. R. Martyn	116* (191)	Australia v New Zealand at Auckland	1999-2000
H. H. Gibbs	59* (101†)	South Africa v Pakistan at Sharjah	1999-2000
A. J. Stewart	100* (192)	England v West Indies at Nottingham	2000
Javed Omar	33* (103)	Bangladesh v Zimbabwe at Harare	2000-01
Azhar Ali	81* (199)	Pakistan v Sri Lanka at Colombo (RPS)	2012
T. W. M. Latham	**79* (190)**	**New Zealand v India at Dharamsala**	**2016-17**

Figures in brackets show team's total.

† *One man retired hurt.*

New Zealand

M. J. Guptill c Sharma b Pandya	12	T. G. Southee c Pandey b Mishra	55
T. W. M. Latham not out	79	I. S. Sodhi lbw b Mishra	1
*K. S. Williamson c Mishra b Yadav	3		
L. R. P. L. Taylor c Dhoni b Yadav	0	B 2, lb 1, w 8	11
C. J. Anderson c Yadav b Pandya	4		—
†L. Ronchi c Yadav b Pandya	0	1/14 (1) 2/29 (3) 3/33 (4) (43.5 overs)	190
J. D. S. Neesham c and b Jadhav	10	4/43 (5) 5/48 (6) 6/65 (7)	
M. J. Santner c Dhoni b Jadhav	0	7/65 (8) 8/106 (9) 9/177 (10)	
D. A. J. Bracewell c Rahane b Mishra	15	10/190 (11) 10 overs: 42-3	

Yadav 8–0–31–2; Pandya 7–0–31–3; Bumrah 8–1–29–0; Jadhav 3–0–6–2; Patel 9–1–41–0; Mishra 8.5–0–49–3.

India

R. G. Sharma lbw b Bracewell	14	K. M. Jadhav not out	10
A. M. Rahane c Ronchi b Neesham	33	Lb 1, w 13	14
V. Kohli not out	85		—
M. K. Pandey c Williamson b Sodhi	17	1/49 (1) 2/62 (2) (4 wkts, 33.1 overs)	194
*†M. S. Dhoni run out	21	3/102 (4) 4/162 (5) 10 overs: 49-1	

A. R. Patel, H. H. Pandya, A. Mishra, U. T. Yadav and J. J. Bumrah did not bat.

Southee 9–0–57–0; Bracewell 8–2–44–1; Neesham 6–0–40–1; Sodhi 4.1–0–34–1; Santner 6–0–18–0.

Umpires: B. N. J. Oxenford and C. Shamshuddin. Third umpire: A. K. Chaudhary.
Referee: R. B. Richardson.

INDIA v NEW ZEALAND

Second One-Day International

At Delhi, October 20, 2016 (day/night). New Zealand won by six runs. Toss: India.

On a slow surface, Williamson's masterful 118 proved the difference. After Yadav had castled Guptill second ball, he added 120 with Latham, who continued his form with a run-a-ball 46. Williamson was especially strong on the leg side, which accounted for 73% of his runs, and New Zealand were set for a big total at 204 for three in the 41st over. But India came roaring back: Mishra dismissed Anderson and Williamson in quick succession, and Bumrah snipped off the tail; the last seven fell for 38. By contrast, their chase never gathered momentum: Kohli tickled one down the leg side to Ronchi, Rahane fell to a controversial low catch at fine leg, and Dhoni struggled for fluency. Jadhav's brisk 41 gave India a glimmer and, after he nicked behind, Pandya took them close with some clever strike rotation and clean hitting. But he fell to Boult, who had been rested in Dharamsala, and Southee yorked Bumrah to make sure India wouldn't get out of jail. It gave New Zealand their first win of the tour, and their first away to India in a one-day international since November 2003.

Man of the Match: K. S. Williamson.

New Zealand

M. J. Guptill b Yadav	0
T. W. M. Latham lbw b Jadhav	46
*K. S. Williamson c Rahane b Mishra	118
L. R. P. L. Taylor c Sharma b Mishra	21
C. J. Anderson lbw b Mishra	21
†L. Ronchi c Dhoni b Patel	6
M. J. Santner not out	9
A. P. Devcich c Patel b Bumrah	7
T. G. Southee b Bumrah	0
M. J. Henry b Bumrah	6
T. A. Boult not out	5
W 3	3
1/0 (1) 2/120 (2) 3/158 (4) 4/204 (5) 5/213 (3) 6/216 (6) 7/224 (8) 8/225 (9) 9/237 (10) — (9 wkts, 50 overs)	242
10 overs: 50-1	

Yadav 9–0–42–1; Pandya 9–0–45–0; Bumrah 10–0–35–3; Patel 10–0–49–1; Mishra 10–0–60–3; Jadhav 2–0–11–1.

India

R. G. Sharma c Ronchi b Boult	15
A. M. Rahane c Anderson b Southee	28
V. Kohli c Ronchi b Santner	9
M. K. Pandey run out	19
*†M. S. Dhoni c and b Southee	39
K. M. Jadhav c Ronchi b Henry	41
A. R. Patel c Santner b Guptill	17
H. H. Pandya c Santner b Boult	36
A. Mishra c sub (D. A. J. Bracewell) b Guptill	1
U. T. Yadav not out	18
J. J. Bumrah b Southee	0
Lb 5, w 8	13
1/21 (1) 2/40 (3) 3/72 (2) 4/73 (4) 5/139 (6) 6/172 (5) 7/180 (7) 8/183 (9) 9/232 (8) 10/236 (11) — (49.3 overs)	236
10 overs: 35-1	

Henry 10–0–51–1; Boult 10–2–25–2; Southee 9.3–0–52–3; Devcich 9–0–48–0; Santner 10–0–49–1; Guptill 1–0–6–2.

Umpires: A. K. Chaudhary and B. N. J. Oxenford. Third umpire: C. Shamshuddin.
Referee: R. B. Richardson.

INDIA v NEW ZEALAND

Third One-Day International

At Mohali, October 23, 2016 (day/night). India won by seven wickets. Toss: India.

Dropped catches lose matches. India were 23 for one chasing 286 when Taylor spilled Kohli at wide slip; he went on to a ground-record 154 not out, adding 151 with Dhoni and an unbeaten 97 with Pandey. New Zealand should have set a more challenging target: Latham's 61 anchored the innings, and they were 153 for two in the 29th. But Mishra deceived Taylor and Ronchi in the flight, Jadhav picked up two more, and they tumbled to 199 for eight. Neesham and Henry added 84, but New Zealand would have needed 300 to cause serious concern. India lost their openers cheaply, though the crowd were delighted when Dhoni walked to the middle, ahead of Pandey. He had promoted himself so he could bat with more freedom, and one six over long-off took him past 9,000 ODI runs; another, into the sightscreen, overhauled Sachin Tendulkar's national record of 195. Dhoni made 80, yet even his brilliance was eclipsed by Kohli. His hundred was his 26th in ODIs from 166 innings and raised his average in successful chases to 90.

Man of the Match: V. Kohli.

New Zealand

M. J. Guptill lbw b Yadav	27
T. W. M. Latham c Pandya b Jadhav	61
*K. S. Williamson lbw b Jadhav	22
L. R. P. L. Taylor st Dhoni b Mishra	44
C. J. Anderson c Rahane b Jadhav	6
†L. Ronchi st Dhoni b Mishra	1
J. D. S. Neesham c Jadhav b Yadav	57
M. J. Santner c Kohli b Bumrah	7
T. G. Southee b Yadav	13
M. J. Henry not out	39
T. A. Boult b Bumrah	1
W 7	7
1/46 (1) 2/80 (3) 3/153 (4) (49.4 overs)	285
4/160 (5) 5/161 (6) 6/169 (2)	
7/180 (8) 8/199 (9) 9/283 (7)	
10/285 (11) 10 overs: 64-1	

Yadav 10–0–75–3; Pandya 5–0–34–0; Bumrah 9.4–0–52–2; Jadhav 5–0–29–3; Patel 10–0–49–0; Mishra 10–0–46–2.

India

R. G. Sharma lbw b Southee	13
A. M. Rahane c Santner b Henry	5
V. Kohli not out	154
*†M. S. Dhoni c Taylor b Henry	80
M. K. Pandey not out	28
Lb 2, w 7	9
1/13 (2) 2/41 (1) (3 wkts, 48.2 overs)	289
3/192 (4) 10 overs: 45-2	

K. M. Jadhav, A. R. Patel, H. H. Pandya, A. Mishra, U. T. Yadav and J. J. Bumrah did not bat.

Henry 9.2–0–56–2; Boult 10–0–73–0; Southee 10–0–55–1; Santner 10–0–43–0; Neesham 9–0–60–0.

Umpires: B. N. J. Oxenford and C. Shamshuddin. Third umpire: A. K. Chaudhary.

INDIA v NEW ZEALAND

Fourth One-Day International

At Ranchi, October 26, 2016 (day/night). New Zealand won by 19 runs. Toss: New Zealand.

On a pitch of sharp turn and erratic bounce, both teams struggled, particularly once the ball lost its sheen. But New Zealand batted better, and took wickets at crucial moments. Winning the toss for the first time on tour helped, as did a 96-run opening stand. Latham fell short of another fifty, but Guptill, dropped on 29, continued to a powerful 72 studded with imperious drives. He departed at the halfway mark, and without him New Zealand were slowed by the spinners: only 99 came from the last 20 overs. India's two previous fixtures at this ground – Dhoni's home patch – had produced successful chases inspired by Kohli. While sharing a partnership of 79 with Rahane, he again looked in control, but once he edged a long hop from Sodhi to Watling – playing his first ODI in three and a half years – India lost their way. Neesham trapped Rahane, then bowled a struggling Dhoni (who faced 31 balls for 11) through the gate to leave an inexperienced lower order needing more than six an over. Akshar Patel combined nudging and slugging for 38, but Southee returned to flummox Pandey and Jadhav with slower balls, and the chase became a pursuit of shadows.

Man of the Match: M. J. Guptill.

New Zealand

M. J. Guptill c Dhoni b Pandya	72	M. J. Santner not out	17
T. W. M. Latham c Rahane b Patel	39	T. G. Southee not out	9
*K. S. Williamson c Dhoni b Mishra	41	Lb 3, w 13	16
L. R. P. L. Taylor run out	35		—
J. D. S. Neesham c Kohli b Mishra	6	1/96 (2) 2/138 (1) (7 wkts, 50 overs)	260
†B-J. Watling c Sharma b Kulkarni	14	3/184 (3) 4/192 (5)	
A. P. Devcich c Pandya b Yadav	11	5/217 (6) 6/223 (4) 7/242 (7)	10 overs: 80-0

I. S. Sodhi and T. A. Boult did not bat.

Yadav 10–1–60–1; Kulkarni 7–0–59–1; Pandya 5–0–31–1; Mishra 10–0–42–2; Patel 10–0–38–1; Jadhav 8–0–27–0.

India

A. M. Rahane lbw b Neesham	57	D. S. Kulkarni not out	25
R. G. Sharma c Watling b Southee	11	U. T. Yadav c Taylor b Boult	7
V. Kohli c Watling b Sodhi	45		
*†M. S. Dhoni b Neesham	11	Lb 3, w 9	12
A. R. Patel b Boult	38		—
M. K. Pandey c Latham b Southee	12	1/19 (2) 2/98 (3) (48.4 overs)	241
K. M. Jadhav lbw b Southee	0	3/128 (1) 4/135 (4) 5/154 (6)	
H. H. Pandya c Latham b Santner	9	6/154 (7) 7/167 (8) 8/205 (9)	
A. Mishra run out	14	9/207 (5) 10/241 (11)	10 overs: 50-1

Southee 9–0–40–3; Boult 9.4–1–48–2; Neesham 6–0–38–2; Santner 10–0–38–1; Sodhi 10–1–52–1; Devcich 4–0–22–0.

Umpires: A. K. Chaudhary and B. N. J. Oxenford. Third umpire: C. K. Nandan.
Referee: R. B. Richardson.

INDIA v NEW ZEALAND

Fifth One-Day International

At Visakhapatnam, October 29, 2016 (day/night). India won by 190 runs. Toss: India. One-day international debut: J. Yadav.

New Zealand had fought hard to level the series but, much as they did during the Tests, collapsed when it mattered most. India won the toss and, after Rahane miscued a flick, a run-a-ball partnership of 79 between Sharma and Kohli restored their equilibrium. But a pudding of a pitch made life difficult, as did Santner's parsimony: his ten overs cost just 36, to leave him with a series economy-rate of four. Harrying knocks from Jadhav and Patel lifted India to 269, but New Zealand were in the game – until their reply began. They lost their openers early to pace, and the dismissal of Williamson to a fine diving catch by Jadhav at long-off triggered chaos. Mishra had Taylor caught behind, bowled Watling with a googly and rattled Neesham's stumps with dramatic turn. Jayant Yadav, the debutant off-spinner, struck in his second over, before two more for Mishra gave him five for 18; he finished with 15 across the five matches, the most for any bowler against New Zealand in a bilateral one-day series. When Patel got one to scoot through Santner's defence, they were all out for 79 in 23.1 overs, their shortest innings in the format.

Man of the Match: A. Mishra. *Man of the Series:* A. Mishra.

India

A. M. Rahane c Latham b Neesham	20	J. Yadav not out	1
R. G. Sharma c Neesham b Boult	70		
V. Kohli c Guptill b Sodhi	65	B 1, lb 1, w 7	9
*†M. S. Dhoni lbw b Santner	41		
M. K. Pandey c Boult b Sodhi	0	1/40 (1) 2/119 (2) (6 wkts, 50 overs)	269
K. M. Jadhav not out	39	3/190 (4) 4/195 (5)	
A. R. Patel b Boult	24	5/220 (3) 6/266 (7) 10 overs: 45-1	

A. Mishra, U. T. Yadav and J. J. Bumrah did not bat.

Southee 10–0–56–0; Boult 10–0–52–2; Neesham 6–0–30–1; Santner 10–0–36–1; Sodhi 10–0–66–2; Anderson 4–0–27–0.

New Zealand

M. J. Guptill b U. T. Yadav	0	I. S. Sodhi c Rahane b Mishra	0
T. W. M. Latham c J. Yadav b Bumrah	19	T. A. Boult not out	1
*K. S. Williamson c Jadhav b Patel	27		
L. R. P. L. Taylor c Dhoni b Mishra	19	W 6	6
J. D. S. Neesham b Mishra	3		
†B-J. Watling b Mishra	0	1/0 (1) 2/28 (2) 3/63 (3) (23.1 overs)	79
C. J. Anderson lbw b J. Yadav	0	4/66 (4) 5/66 (6) 6/74 (7)	
M. J. Santner b Patel	4	7/74 (5) 8/74 (9) 9/76 (10)	
T. G. Southee st Dhoni b Mishra	0	10/79 (8) 10 overs: 46-2	

U. T. Yadav 4–0–28–1; Bumrah 5–0–16–1; Patel 4.1–0–9–2; Mishra 6–2–18–5; J. Yadav 4–0–8–1.

Umpires: C. K. Nandan and B. N. J. Oxenford. Third umpire: C. Shamshuddin.
Referee: R. B. Richardson.

THE VIVO INDIAN PREMIER LEAGUE IN 2015-16

ANAND VASU

1 Sunrisers Hyderabad 2 Royal Challengers Bangalore

This was meant to be the year the music of the cash registers died for the Indian Premier League. Its finances had always been sturdier than its morals, but the tournament had already lost two of its most popular teams to a damaging scandal before a ball was bowled: Chennai Super Kings and Rajasthan Royals, both banned for two years in July 2015 by India's Supreme Court because of their involvement in betting corruption, and replaced by **Gujarat Lions** and **Rising Pune Supergiants.**

With the Chennai and Rajasthan players released to auction, Gujarat and Pune had shades of the teams in exile. But only Gujarat competed, topping the points table at the end of the league phase, before falling to **Sunrisers Hyderabad** in the second qualifying final. Pune, led by M. S. Dhoni – until now synonymous with CSK yellow – avoided last place only thanks to a disastrous run from **Kings XI Punjab.**

The surprise of the tournament was the emergence of David Warner as an effective captain. Though not the most astute tactician, he inspired Hyderabad through example and exhortation, batting brilliantly and willing his players to do the same. In Hyderabad's maiden final, away to **Royal Challengers Bangalore**, he chose to bat – bucking the trend for chasing at the high-scoring M. Chinnaswamy Stadium – and crashed a 38-ball 69 to lift his season's tally to 848 at 60. Hyderabad posted 208 for seven, before their bowling attack, comfortably the best in the competition, took over. Banglaore had earlier beaten **Kolkata Knight Riders** in the Elminination Final.

Chris Gayle, A. B. de Villiers and the reinvented K. L. Rahul gave Bangalore serious firepower. They also had Virat Kohli, who came into the final boasting four hundreds and an average in the eighties. But they fell short by eight runs. Bhuvneshwar Kumar, who topped the wicket-taking list with 23, and Bangladeshi left-armer Mustafizur Rahman, with his probing cutters, were just too good.

The IPL has a habit of making household names of virtual unknowns. Pawan Negi, a left-arm spinner and lower-order tonker, was obscure even when he was selected for India's Asia Cup and World T20 squads a day before the IPL auction. But he became headline news when **Delhi Daredevils** picked him up for a staggering Rs85m (just over £1m). Negi, though, did not enjoy the confidence of his team's management: he played in just eight matches, scored 57 runs and took a solitary wicket. Soon after the IPL was over, India dropped him from their T20 squad after only one cap, against the UAE in the Asia Cup. He was out in the wilderness once more.

For 21-year-old Shreyas Iyer, another Delhi acquisition, the tournament proved a misery. Widely tipped for higher honours after terrific performances for Mumbai in the Ranji Trophy, he quickly became surplus to requirements, scoring 30 runs in six matches, including three ducks.

It was not only Indian players who found the going tough. Gayle was dropped by Bangalore early on after a run of poor form. South African David Miller, named captain of Punjab before the tournament, was replaced by Murali Vijay after overseeing five losses from their first six matches. And Glenn Maxwell, another Punjab player, failed to fire, save for a couple of cameos in losing causes.

The big gain for India was the emergence of Rahul, who went from being bracketed as a long-form specialist to an all-format regular in international cricket. He had to wait until Bangalore's third game, against **Mumbai Indians**, for his chance, replacing Gayle, who had returned to Jamaica for the birth of his first child. But with an upright, classical style – and keeping wicket to boot – Rahul hit four half-centuries to cement his place and win selection in India's white-ball squads. He soon forced his way back into the Test team as well, having been dropped in late 2015.

By the end of the tournament, which contained little off-field drama, the Chennai and Rajasthan sagas were all but forgotten. The IPL rarely manages to be in the news for its cricket alone, but in 2016 – once the games got under way, at any rate – it managed precisely that. For a competition that does not do low-key, it made for one of its least memorable years.

INDIAN PREMIER LEAGUE IN 2015-16

	Played	*Won*	*Lost*	*Points*	*Net run-rate*
GUJARAT LIONS	14	9	5	18	–0.37
ROYAL CHALLENGERS BANGALORE	14	8	6	16	0.93
SUNRISERS HYDERABAD	14	8	6	16	0.25
KOLKATA KNIGHT RIDERS	14	8	6	16	0.11
Mumbai Indians	14	7	7	14	–0.01
Delhi Daredevils	14	7	7	14	–0.16
Rising Pune Supergiants	14	5	9	10	0.02
Kings XI Punjab	14	4	10	8	–0.65

First qualifying final At Bangalore, May 24, 2016 (floodlit). **Royal Challengers Bangalore won by four wickets. Gujarat Lions 158** (20 overs) (D. R. Smith 73; S. R. Watson 4-29); ‡**Royal Challengers Bangalore 159-6** (18.2 overs) (A. B. de Villiers 79*, Iqbal Abdulla 33*; D. S. Kulkarni 4-14). *MoM:* A. B. de Villiers. *When Virat Kohli, who had 919 runs in the competition at 92, chopped on for a duck in the second over of the chase, Bangalore were rattled. Without their linchpin, they slipped to 29-5, as Dhawal Kulkarni bowled through to finish with 4-14. But A. B. de Villiers remained calm, lashing five sixes and adding 91* for the seventh wicket with Iqbal Abdulla to send them to the final. Gujarat had suffered their own poor start: their top three had burned out with the score on nine. Dwayne Smith's 73 gave them a foothold, but they now had to win the second qualifying final to avoid elimination.*

Elimination final At Delhi, May 25, 2016 (floodlit). **Sunrisers Hyderabad won by 22 runs. Sunrisers Hyderabad 162-8** (20 overs) (M. C. Henriques 31, Yuvraj Singh 44; Kuldeep Yadav 3-35); ‡**Kolkata Knight Riders 140-8** (20 overs) (M. K. Pandey 36; Bhavenshwar Kumar 3-19). *MoM:* M. C. Henriques. *Kolkata happily inserted Hyderabad – who had succeeded with six chases out of seven in IPL 2016 – and the slow surface produced a quiet start, before Yuvraj Singh hustled a 30-ball 44. Kolkata needed 163 but struggled for boundaries, and when Yusuf Pathan (who began the game with an average near Kohli's) holed out for two to make it 69-4, the asking-rate went over ten. Bhuvneshwar Kumar picked up three wickets as the noose tightened. Kolkata's exit meant the ninth IPL would have new champions.*

Second qualifying final At Delhi, May 27, 2016 (floodlit). **Sunrisers Hyderabad won by four wickets. Gujarat Lions 162-7** (20 overs) (B. B. McCullum 32, A. J. Finch 50); ‡**Sunrisers Hyderabad 163-6** (19.2 overs) (D. A. Warner 93*). *MoM:* D. A. Warner. *David Warner's superb 58-ball 93* supervised a tense chase and took Hyderabad to their first final. When they slipped to*

117-6, he was the only player to have scored more than 11, before Bipul Sharma finally provided support, carting 27 from 11 balls. Earlier, Aaron Finch had responded to a demotion to No. 5 with a bright 50. Despite 2-22 from Shivil Kaushik's leg-spin, it was not enough. Warner's innings brought his season's aggregate in chases to 468, an IPL record.

FINAL

ROYAL CHALLENGERS BANGALORE v SUNRISERS HYDERABAD

At Bangalore, May 29, 2016 (floodlit). Sunrisers Hyderabad won by eight runs. Toss: Sunrisers Hyderabad.

When Ben Cutting walked out to the middle for Hyderabad, their captain was stewing in the dug-out. Warner had elected to bat and knew he needed a big score to keep Bangalore at bay on their run-soaked home patch. It wasn't going well: despite his 69, Hyderabad were 158 for six with 17 deliveries remaining, and Kohli & Co were licking their lips. But Cutting long-handled 39 off 15 balls as 50 came in a frenzy. His three sixes off Watson's last over – one of which cleared the stadium – visibly energised Warner. Bangalore needed 209. Gayle and Kohli sizzled to 114 without loss after ten. Yet Warner urged his men on: in the space of 21 balls, the openers were gone and de Villiers had skyed a swipe. As the galacticos departed, Hyderabad's conviction strengthened, and boundaries grew rarer. Bhuvneshwar Kumar, the competition's best bowler, was entrusted with protecting 18 from the last, and conceded only nine. Bangalore had their third defeat in three finals; Hyderabad were champions at the first attempt.

Man of the Match: B. C. J. Cutting. *Man of the Tournament:* V. Kohli.

Sunrisers Hyderabad

		B	*4/6*
1 *D. A. Warner *c 9 b 10*	69	38	8/3
2 S. Dhawan *c 8 b 11*	28	25	3/1
3 M. C. Henriques *c 11 b 8*	4	5	0
4 Yuvraj Singh *c 5 b 8*	38	23	4/2
5 D. Hooda *c 2 b 10*	3	6	0
6 B. C. J. Cutting *not out*	39	15	3/4
7 †N. V. Ojha *run out*	7	4	1
8 B. Sharma *c 11 b 8*	5	3	1
9 Bhuvneshwar Kumar *not out*	1	1	0
B 1, lb 2, w 11	14		
6 overs: 59-0 (20 overs)	208-7		

1/63 2/97 3/125 4/147 5/148 6/158 7/174

10 B. B. Sran and 11 Mustafizur Rahman did not bat.

Aravind 4–9–30–2; Gayle 3–8–24–0; Watson 4–7–61–0; Chahal 4–5–35–1; Iqbal Abdulla 1–1–10–0; Jordan 4–9–45–3.

R Challengers Bangalore

		B	*4/6*
1 C. H. Gayle *c 8 b 6*	76	38	4/8
2 *V. Kohli *b 10*	54	35	5/2
3 A. B. de Villiers *c 3 b 8*	5	6	0
4 †K. L. Rahul *b 6*	11	9	1
5 S. R. Watson *c 3 b 11*	11	9	0/1
6 S. Baby *not out*	18	10	1/1
7 S. T. R. Binny *run out*	9	7	0/1
8 C. J. Jordan *run out*	3	4	0
9 Iqbal Abdulla *not out*	4	2	1
Lb 5, w 4	9		
6 overs: 59-0 (20 overs)	200-7		

1/114 2/140 3/148 4/160 5/164 6/180 7/194

10 S. Aravind and 11 Y. S. Chahal did not bat.

Bhuvneshwar Kumar 4–13–25–0; Sran 3–6–41–1; Cutting 4–7–35–2; Mustafizur Rahman 4–9–37–1; Henriques 3–5–40–0; Sharma 2–1–17–1.

Umpires: H. D. P. K. Dharmasena and B. N. J. Oxenford. Third umpire: A. K. Chaudhary. Referee: R. S. Madugalle.

IPL FINALS

2007-08 RAJASTHAN ROYALS beat Chennai Super Kings by three wickets at Mumbai.
2008-09 DECCAN CHARGERS beat Royal Challengers Bangalore by six runs at Johannesburg.
2009-10 CHENNAI SUPER KINGS beat Mumbai Indians by 22 runs at Mumbai.
2010-11 CHENNAI SUPER KINGS beat Royal Challengers Bangalore by 58 runs at Chennai.
2011-12 KOLKATA KNIGHT RIDERS beat Chennai Super Kings by five wickets at Chennai.
2012-13 MUMBAI INDIANS beat Chennai Super Kings by 23 runs at Kolkata.
2013-14 KOLKATA KNIGHT RIDERS beat Kings XI Punjab by three wickets at Bangalore.
2014-15 MUMBAI INDIANS beat Chennai Super Kings by 41 runs at Kolkata.
2015-16 SUNRISERS HYDERABAD beat Royal Challengers Bangalore by eight runs at Bangalore.

DOMESTIC CRICKET IN INDIA IN 2015-16

R. MOHAN

Concerns that the preparation of pitches to suit home teams was distorting Indian cricket came to the boil in 2015-16. Of 108 Ranji Trophy group matches scheduled for four days, nine finished in two, and a further 17 in three. Underprepared surfaces designed for spinners can also help accurate seamers; though they may have reduced Indian cricket's tendency to batathons, some felt the bias to home teams had taken on a devilish slant. Rahul Dravid, now running India's Under-19 team, made scathing remarks about "square turners where matches are finishing in two or three days", and suggested that neutral venues, already used for the knockout stages, would be fairer.

As a result, the BCCI decided to stage all Ranji games in 2016-17 on neutral grounds. But there were critics of the change, including Sachin Tendulkar, who was concerned that the fan base of the state teams would be weakened if all matches were played away from home.

In 2015-16, **Mumbai** notched up another Ranji Trophy, extending their record to 41 titles – exactly half the 82 tournaments played since its introduction in 1934-35, and one step nearer to New South Wales's 46 Sheffield Shields (though that competition began in 1892-93). Shreyas Iyer was outstanding, gathering 1,321 runs in 11 Ranji matches – 442 more than the next best aggregate, by his Mumbai team-mate Akhil Herwadkar, and second only to V. V. S. Laxman's Ranji record of 1,415 in 1999-2000. Iyer was not one of those young batsmen who have broken into the first-class ranks on the strength of their ability to score quickly in the IPL; rather, he earned an IPL contract following success in his maiden Ranji season, in 2014-15. He was third in the averages, with Himachal Pradesh's Paras Dogra top for the second year in a row.

It used to be believed that Indian cricket was strong when Mumbai were strong, but the competition has evened out, spreading talent across the country. **Karnataka**, champions for the previous two seasons, did not make it to the knockouts, while **Assam's** progress to a first semi-final was a Cinderella story. They had won promotion the previous season from Group C (which supplies only two quarter-finalists, while A and B get three each); but it was **Saurashtra**, bouncing back after relegation, who knocked them out in the semi-final.

Mumbai, however, enjoyed the greater big-match experience. Saurashtra held their own in the first two days of the final at Gahunje, but Mumbai's last-wicket pair were allowed to boost the first-innings lead from 33 to 136, and Saurashtra surrendered for 115 on a blameless pitch.

Back on home ground, at the Brabourne Stadium, Mumbai were confident of following up with their first Irani Cup victory over the **Rest of India** since 1997-98. After scoring 603 on a plumb surface, they waived the follow-on and left a target of 480. But the enterprising batting of Faiz Fazal, Karun Nair and Stuart Binny enabled the Rest to scale the peak, the third-highest successful run-chase in Indian history.

The first-class interzonal Duleep Trophy was knocked off the calendar altogether, after 54 years. But it was restored for 2016-17, as a three-team tournament with all sides picked by the national selectors rather than representing the traditional geographical zones.

The limited-overs tournaments tended to be played on better surfaces. Two seasoned hands, Parthiv Patel and R. P. Singh, headed **Gujarat's** campaign in the 50-over interstate competition, helping them to win their first Vijay Hazare Trophy. **Uttar Pradesh** were also new winners of the T20 equivalent, the Syed Mushtaq Ali Trophy.

Baroda, the team they beat in the final, had earlier played a memorable group match, when their all-rounder Hardik Pandya slammed five sixes and a four off one over from Delhi seamer Akash Sudan – who also bowled a wide which went for five (Pandya claimed he had nicked that, too). The over cost 39.

FIRST-CLASS AVERAGES, 2015-16

BATTING (600 runs, average 40.00)

	M	*I*	*NO*	*R*	*HS*	*100*	*Avge*	*Ct/St*
P. Dogra (*Himachal Pradesh*)	8	12	3	703	227	3	78.11	8
R. Paliwal (*Services*)	8	12	1	753	203	4	68.45	8
S. S. Iyer (*India A/Mumbai*)	13	21	0	1,414	200	4	67.33	14
U. A. Sharma (*Uttar Pradesh*)	6	11	1	607	215	1	60.70	7
I. Dev Singh (*Jammu & Kashmir*)	8	15	2	773	127	3	59.46	7
†P. Rohan Prem (*Kerala*)	8	14	2	705	208	3	58.75	4
S. A. Asnodkar (*Goa*)	8	14	1	762	232	3	58.61	4
K. K. Nair (*India A/Karnataka/Rest of India*)	9	14	1	757	126	2	58.23	5
†S. S. Tiwary (*Jharkhand*)	9	15	3	698	209*	1	58.16	14
Parvez Rasool (*Jammu & Kashmir*)	8	15	4	617	130	2	56.09	4
P. K. Panchal (*Gujarat*)	8	12	0	665	141	3	55.41	1
K. H. Devdhar (*Baroda*)	8	13	1	659	186	1	54.91	3
†H. S. Bhatia (*Madhya Pradesh*)	9	15	1	750	139	2	53.57	13
S. A. Yadav (*Mumbai*)	12	20	1	993	156	4	52.26	21
R. V. Uthappa (*Karnataka*)	9	15	0	763	160	3	50.86	4
†S. K. Kamat (*Goa*)	8	14	2	602	163	3	50.16	10
†A. A. Herwadkar (*Mumbai*)	12	20	0	970	192	3	48.50	16
G. H. Vihari (*Hyderabad*)	8	13	0	626	219	2	48.15	6
†S. D. Chatterjee (*Bengal/Rest of India*)	10	18	1	812	147	4	47.76	12
K. B. Arun Karthik (*Assam*)	10	19	2	802	151	3	47.17	20
†A. L. Menaria (*Rajasthan*)	8	15	2	612	150*	1	47.07	5
M. K. Tiwary (*Bengal*)	9	15	1	650	124	2	46.42	12
†U. Kaul (*Punjab*)	9	15	1	636	139	3	45.42	6
†F. Y. Fazal (*Vidarbha/Rest of India*)	9	17	1	714	127	3	44.62	7
N. V. Ojha (*India A/Madhya Pradesh/Rest*)	11	17	1	701	113	1	43.81	37/6
S. D. Lad (*Mumbai*)	12	20	1	817	150	1	43.00	4
S. P. Jackson (*Saurashtra/Rest of India*)	11	16	1	634	122	2	42.26	17
†S. P. Wakaskar (*Railways*)	8	16	0	649	185	1	40.56	1
†A. P. Tare (*Mumbai*)	11	18	2	640	137*	2	40.00	47/4

BOWLING (30 wickets, average 30.00)

	Style	*O*	*M*	*R*	*W*	*BB*	*5I*	*Avge*
R. Ashwin (*India*)	OB	164.4	56	345	31	7-66	4	11.12
R. A. Jadeja (*India A/Saurashtra/India*)	SLA	318.2	102	712	62	7-55	8	11.48
B. C. Mohanty (*Odisha*)	RFM	295.1	92	635	41	6-39	3	15.48
K. R. Makwana (*Saurashtra*)	OB	182	26	556	33	7-100	1	16.84
A. A. Sarwate (*Vidarbha*)	SLA	234.5	45	573	33	6-64	2	17.36
K. S. Monish (*Kerala*)	SLA	347.4	82	878	49	6-81	5	17.91
P. Sangwan (*Delhi*)	LM	251.3	66	583	32	7-38	1	18.21
K. Anureet Singh (*Railways*)	RFM	279	83	656	36	5-15	3	18.22
K. S. Das (*Assam/Rest of India*)	RM	388.3	113	980	53	7-21	5	18.49
A. K. Das (*Assam*)	RM	230	56	664	35	8-83	3	18.97
S. Nadeem (*Jharkhand*)	SLA	351.2	80	1,001	51	7-45	4	19.62
D. Pathania (*Services*)	RM	337.4	98	768	37	7-64	2	20.75
J. D. Unadkat (*Saurashtra/Rest of India*)	LFM	290.2	60	949	45	6-77	4	21.08
A. B. Dinda (*Bengal*)	RFM	295	77	810	36	7-19	1	22.50
J. S. Saxena (*Madhya Pradesh*)	OB	403.4	72	1,105	49	8-58	4	22.55
S. B. Pradhan (*Odisha*)	RM	239	57	697	30	5-27	1	23.23
P. P. Ojha (*Bengal*)	SLA	333.3	78	877	36	7-58	1	24.36
S. S. Mundhe (*Maharashtra*)	RM	265	56	771	30	6-62	1	25.70
M. Sharma (*Delhi*)	SLA	323.4	65	928	35	6-105	2	26.51
S. N. Thakur (*Mumbai*)	RFM	398.1	99	1,115	42	6-107	2	26.54
A. A. Wakhare (*Vidarbha*)	OB	475.2	106	1,305	49	6-58	4	26.63
I. C. Pandey (*India A/Madhya Pradesh*)	RFM	259	57	844	30	4-45	0	28.13

RANJI TROPHY, 2015-16

Group A	Played	Won	Lost	Drawn	1st-inns points	Bonus points	Points	NRR
VIDARBHA	8	4	2	2	4	1	29	0.04
BENGAL	8	2	0	6	16	0	28	0.11
ASSAM	8	3	2	3	7	1	26	–0.30
Delhi	8	3	1	4	6	1	25	0.21
Karnataka	8	2	1	5	11	1	24	0.33
Rajasthan	8	2	3	3	5	0	17	–0.31
Maharashtra	8	1	2	5	11	0	17	0.30
Odisha	8	1	3	4	6	0	12	0.01
Haryana	8	0	4	4	6	0	6	–0.40

Group B	Played	Won	Lost	Drawn	1st-inns points	Bonus points	Points	NRR
MUMBAI	8	4	0	4	10	1	35	0.85
PUNJAB	8	3	2	3	7	1	26	0.04
MADHYA PRADESH	8	3	2	3	5	1	24	–0.05
Gujarat	8	3	1	4	4	2	24	–0.09
Uttar Pradesh	8	2	1	5	9	0	21	–0.11
Tamil Nadu	8	2	2	4	6	0	18	–0.32
Baroda	8	2	3	3	3	2	17	–0.04
Railways	8	2	6	0	0	0	12	0.03
Andhra	8	0	4	4	10	0	10	–0.45

Group C	Played	Won	Lost	Drawn	1st-inns points	Bonus points	Points	NRR
SAURASHTRA	8	5	1	2	4	2	36	–0.06
JHARKHAND	8	4	2	2	4	3	31	0.08
Himachal Pradesh	8	3	1	4	10	2	30	1.01
Services	8	3	1	4	8	1	27	0.47
Kerala	8	2	2	4	12	1	25	0.08
Goa	8	1	1	6	12	0	18	–0.21
Jammu & Kashmir	8	0	3	5	9	0	9	–0.05
Hyderabad	8	0	2	6	8	0	8	–0.46
Tripura	8	0	5	3	3	0	3	–0.76

Outright win = 6pts; lead on first innings in a drawn match = 3pts; deficit on first innings in a drawn match = 1pt; no decision on first innings = 1pt. Teams tied on points were ranked on most wins, and then on net run-rate.

The top three teams from Groups A and B, and the top two from Group C, advanced to the quarter-finals. The bottom teams from Groups A and B (Haryana and Andhra) transferred to C for 2016-17, and were replaced by the Group C qualifiers (Saurashtra and Jharkhand).

Group A

At Guwahati (Barsapara), October 1–4, 2015. **Drawn. ‡Karnataka 187** (J. Syed Mohammad 7-44) **and 394-8 dec** (R. Samarth 131); **Assam 194 and 259-5** (K. B. Arun Karthik 115*). *Assam 3pts, Karnataka 1pt. Left-arm seamer Syed Mohammad took six of his career-best 7-44 in his first spell.*

At Gahunje, October 1–4, 2015. **Drawn. ‡Haryana 335** (H. Rana 157); **Maharashtra 570-6** (A. R. Bawne 172, C. G. Khurana 136*). *Maharashtra 3pts, Haryana 1pt. Himanshu Rana scored his second first-class century, on his 17th birthday. Ankit Bawne and Chirag Khurana added 246 for Maharashtra's sixth wicket.*

At Jaipur (Sawai Mansingh), October 1–4, 2015. **Drawn. Delhi 138** (D. L. Chahar 5-60) **and 437-9 dec** (S. Narwal 106*; N. B. Singh 7-87); **‡Rajasthan 240 and 186-3.** *Rajasthan 3pts, Delhi 1pt. No. 9 Sumit Narwal hit 106* in 94 balls to set a target of 336. Delhi coach Ajay Jadeja resigned during the match, saying the Association ignored his opinions.*

At Nagpur (VCA Stadium), October 1–4, 2015. **Drawn.** **‡Vidarbha 467** (A. D. Shanware 119, U. T. Yadav 128*); **Odisha 274** (G. B. Podder 148*) **and 230-6** (A. A. Wakhare 5-77). *Vidarbha 3pts, Odisha 1pt. Aditya Shanware scored 119 on first-class debut. Umesh Yadav hit 128 in 119 balls from No. 9 – his maiden century – including seven sixes.*

At Guwahati (Barsapara), October 8–11, 2015. **Assam won by an innings and 152 runs. Rajasthan 186** (K. S. Das 5-32) **and 84** (A. K. Das 5-39, K. S. Das 5-23); **‡Assam 422-9 dec** (K. B. Arun Karthik 151; K. Ajay Singh 5-116). *Assam 7pts.*

At Delhi (Feroz Shah Kotla), October 8–11, 2015. **Delhi won by ten wickets. Vidarbha 298** (I. Sharma 6-36) **and 98; ‡Delhi 302** (A. A. Wakhare 5-113) **and 96-0.** *Delhi 7pts.*

At Bangalore (Chinnaswamy), October 8–11, 2015. **Drawn. Bengal 312** (S. D. Chatterjee 145) **and 249-4** (M. K. Tiwary 103*); **‡Karnataka 537-9 dec** (S. A. Bhavane 119, K. K. Nair 126, R. Shreyas Gopal 139). *Karnataka 3pts, Bengal 1pt.*

At Cuttack (Barabati), October 8–11, 2015. **Drawn. Maharashtra 281 and 289-4 dec** (K. M. Jadhav 100*); **‡Odisha 267** (G. B. Podder 100; S. S. Mundhe 6-62) **and 129-5.** *Odisha 1pt, Maharashtra 3pts.*

At Kolkata (Eden Gardens), October 15–18, 2015. **Drawn. ‡Rajasthan 198 and 146-5; Bengal 282.** *Bengal 3pts, Rajasthan 1pt. Vineet Saxena carried his bat through Rajasthan's first innings for 66*.*

At Delhi (Feroz Shah Kotla), October 15–18, 2015. **Delhi won by four wickets. Haryana 195** (M. Sharma 5-57) **and 265** (M. Sharma 6-105); **‡Delhi 237 and 225-6.** *Delhi 6pts. Virender Sehwag returned to his old ground as Haryana's captain. Manan Sharma picked up 11-162.*

At Bangalore (Chinnaswamy), October 15–18, 2015. **Drawn. Karnataka 350** (M. K. Pandey 104) **and 331-3 dec** (R. Samarth 121*, K. K. Nair 101*); **‡Vidarbha 310 and 17-0.** *Karnataka 3pts, Vidarbha 1pt. Vidarbha seamer Shrikant Wagh was fined 60% of his fee after accusing the umpires of favouring Karnataka.*

At Cuttack (Barabati), October 15–17, 2015. **Odisha won by eight wickets. Assam 92** (B. C. Mohanty 5-24) **and 137** (S. B. Pradhan 5-27); **‡Odisha 88** (K. S. Das 7-21) **and 142-2.** *Odisha 6pts.*

At Delhi (Feroz Shah Kotla), October 22–25, 2015. **Drawn. Bengal 357** (S. D. Chatterjee 116) **and 217-5 dec; ‡Delhi 249 and 161-4.** *Delhi 1pt, Bengal 3pts. Both captains were fined – Delhi's Gautam Gambhir 70% of his fee, Bengal's Manoj Tiwary 40% – after Gambhir accused Tiwary of time-wasting, and Tiwary claimed Gambhir had insulted his parents.*

At Mysore (Srikantadatta Narasimha Raja Wadeyar), October 22–25, 2015. **Drawn. ‡Haryana 331** (V. Sehwag 136, J. Yadav 100; H. S. Sharath 5-48) **and 262-9 dec; Karnataka 221 and 202-8** (J. Yadav 6-65). *Karnataka 1pt, Haryana 3pts. Sehwag and Jayant Yadav added 206 for Haryana's third wicket; later in the innings, H. S. Sharath claimed a hat-trick in his career-best 5-48.*

At Jaipur (Sawai Mansingh), October 22–25, 2015. **Drawn. Rajasthan 318 and 334-5 dec** (A. L. Menaria 150*); **‡Maharashtra 409** (R. A. Tripathi 119) **and 23-0.** *Rajasthan 1pt, Maharashtra 3pts.*

At Nagpur (VCA Stadium), October 22–25, 2015. **Vidarbha won by three wickets. ‡Assam 206 and 160** (A. A. Sarwate 6-64); **Vidarbha 154 and 215-7.** *Vidarbha 6pts.*

At Rohtak, October 30–November 2, 2015. **Drawn. Bengal 329** (S. Rana 5-46) **and 211-8 dec; ‡Haryana 225 and 195-6.** *Haryana 1pt, Bengal 3pts. Debutant Rohit Sharma (78) and Yuzvendra Chahal (42) added 105 for the ninth wicket in Haryana's first innings.*

At Bhubaneswar (Kalinga), October 30–November 2, 2015. **Drawn. Delhi 311 and 193-9 dec** (B. C. Mohanty 6-39); **‡Odisha 217** (P. Sangwan 7-38) **and 88-3.** *Odisha 1pt, Delhi 3pts. The first first-class match at the Kalinga Institute of Industrial Technology Ground. Basant Mohanty took a hat-trick during a second-innings spell in which he claimed five wickets and a run-out inside five overs.*

At Jaipur (Sawai Mansingh), October 30–November 2, 2015. **Karnataka won by 92 runs. Karnataka 281** (A. V. Choudhary 5-77) **and 318-5 dec** (R. V. Uthappa 160); **‡Rajasthan 242 and 265** (P. I. Sharma 114). *Karnataka 6pts. Robin Uthappa's 160 came in 128 balls.*

At Nagpur (VCA Ground), October 30–November 2, 2015. **Vidarbha won by 82 runs. ‡Vidarbha 332** (F. Y. Fazal 120) **and 149** (A. A. Darekar 5-78); **Maharashtra 237 and 162** (A. A. Wakhare 6-58). *Vidarbha 6pts.*

At Kolkata (Jadavpur University), November 7–10, 2015. **Bengal won by 105 runs. Bengal 334** (S. D. Chatterjee 116) **and 164** (A. A. Wakhare 5-61); **‡Vidarbha 202** (P. P. Ojha 7-58) **and 191.**

Bengal 6pts. Wasim Jaffer, now playing for Vidarbha after 19 seasons with Mumbai, became the first player to reach 10,000 runs in the Ranji Trophy. Wicketkeeper Amol Ubarhande made six catches and a stumping in Bengal's first innings, and nine dismissals in the match.

At Delhi (Feroz Shah Kotla), November 7–8, 2015. **Delhi won by nine wickets. ‡Maharashtra 80** (N. Saini 6-32) **and 176; Delhi 230** (D. Shorey 104*; S. M. Fallah 5-45) **and 30-1.** *Delhi 6pts.*

At Rohtak, November 7–10, 2015. **Assam won by six wickets. ‡Haryana 168** (K. S. Das 6-56) **and 111** (A. K. Das 6-39); **Assam 120 and 160-4.** *Assam 6pts.*

At Mysore (Srikantadatta Narasimha Raja Wadeyar), November 7–10, 2015. **Karnataka won by an innings and 64 runs. ‡Odisha 232** (G. B. Podder 153) **and 104; Karnataka 400-9 dec** (R. V. Uthappa 148). *Karnataka 7pts.*

At Guwahati (Barsapara), November 15–18, 2015. **Assam won by five wickets. Delhi 149 and 172; ‡Assam 157 and 168-5.** *Assam 6pts. Assam's third win put them two points behind leaders Delhi.*

At Rohtak, November 15–18, 2015. **Drawn. ‡Odisha 529-6 dec** (N. B. Behera 255*, Ranjit Singh 112); **Haryana 216 and 250-4.** *Haryana 1pt, Odisha 3pts. Natraj Behera batted 11 hours 26 minutes for the highest score of the season, and added 282 for Odisha's second wicket with Ranjit Singh.*

At Gahunje, November 15–18, 2015. **Drawn. Bengal 528-8 dec** (S. D. Chatterjee 147) **and 100-1; ‡Maharashtra 406** (R. A. Tripathi 132). *Maharashtra 1pt, Bengal 3pts. Sudip Chatterjee's century was his fourth in six matches.*

At Nagpur (VCA Ground), November 15–18, 2015. **Vidarbha won by eight wickets. ‡Rajasthan 216 and 226** (A. A. Sarwate 5-58); **Vidarbha 247 and 199-2.** *Vidarbha 6pts. Umesh Yadav ended Rajasthan's first innings with a hat-trick. In the next, Ashok Menaria hit seven sixes in a 92-ball 76.*

At Kalyani, November 23–24, 2015. **Bengal won by 133 runs. ‡Bengal 142** (Dhiraj Kumar 5-58) **and 135** (B. C. Mohanty 5-16); **Odisha 107** (A. A. Gani 6-34) **and 37** (A. B. Dinda 7-19). *Bengal 6pts. The first first-class match in Kalyani lasted less than two days. Mohanty had figures of 17–9–16–5. Needing 171, Odisha collapsed for 37, only two more than their lowest total, against Bihar in 1958-59. Their coach called the pitch "a paddy field", and Odisha lodged a complaint.*

At Rohtak, November 23–26, 2015. **Rajasthan won by nine wickets. Haryana 112 and 324** (N. Saini 146; Pankaj Singh 5-85); **‡Rajasthan 279** (M. Sharma 5-56) **and 161-1** (P. R. Yadav 107*). *Rajasthan 6pts.*

At Hubli, November 23–26, 2015. **Drawn. Karnataka 542** (M. A. Agarwal 118, R. V. Uthappa 148); **‡Delhi 301 and 290-2** (D. Shorey 107*, N. Rana 132*). *Karnataka 3pts, Delhi 1pt. Mayank Agarwal and Uthappa, who scored his third successive century, put on 236 for Karnataka's second wicket. When Delhi followed on, Dhruv Shorey and Nitish Rana added 240* for their third. Delhi led the group, but four teams had a chance to overtake them as they sat out the last round.*

At Gahunje, November 23–26, 2015. **Drawn. Assam 298** (K. B. Arun Karthik 130) **and 135; ‡Maharashtra 196** (K. S. Das 6-73) **and 82-3.** *Maharashtra 1pt, Assam 3pts. Assam complained that the pitch was too dangerous to bat on.*

At Guwahati (Barsapara), December 1–4, 2015. **Drawn. Bengal 444-6 dec** (S. P. Goswami 112*); **‡Assam 143 and 143-8** (A. A. Gani 5-62). *Assam 1pt, Bengal 3pts. Thanks to Karnataka's defeat, a draw was enough to see both Assam and Bengal into the knockouts.*

At Gahunje, December 1–4, 2015. **Maharashtra won by 53 runs. Maharashtra 212 and 260; ‡Karnataka 180 and 239** (N. R. Dhumal 5-78). *Maharashtra 6pts. Maharashtra's only win was Karnataka's first defeat for three years, after a run of 37 first-class matches (34 in the Ranji Trophy); it ended their hopes of a third successive title.*

At Jaipur (Sawai Mansingh), December 1–3, 2015. **Rajasthan won by two wickets. Odisha 151** (A. V. Choudhary 6-27) **and 129; ‡Rajasthan 51** (A. C. Sahoo 6-33) **and 231-8.** *Rajasthan 6pts. Rajasthan won despite collapsing for their lowest first-class total in the first innings.*

At Nagpur (VCA Ground), December 1–4, 2015. **Vidarbha won by an innings and 31 runs. ‡Vidarbha 504-7 dec** (F. Y. Fazal 126, R. L. Jangid 110, A. A. Sarwate 103*); **Haryana 241 and 232** (R. Sharma 107; R. L. Jangid 7-59). *Vidarbha 7pts. Ravi Jangid, who shared a seventh-wicket stand of 212 with Aditya Sarwate, followed up a century by taking 11-103. Chahal delayed Vidarbha's victory with a 77-ball duck from No. 10. The result put Vidarbha on top of the group.*

Group B

At Vizianagram (Dr P. V. G. Raju), October 1–4, 2015. **Drawn. Andhra 244** (R. K. Bhui 103; B. S. Sandhu 5-53) **and 176-3; ‡Mumbai 237** (B. Ayyappa 6-71). *Andhra 3pts, Mumbai 1pt.*

At Mohali, October 1–4, 2015. **Punjab won by an innings and 126 runs. ‡Punjab 604-5 dec** (U. Kaul 112, Mandeep Singh 109, Gurkeerat Singh 201*, G. Khera 102*); **Railways 196** (B. B. Sran 6-61) **and 282** (V. Khanna 8-97). *Punjab 7pts. Four Punjab batsmen reached centuries: Uday Kaul and Mandeep Singh added 197 for the third wicket, and Gurkeerat Singh and Gitansh Khera 306* for the sixth. Gurkeerat's maiden double-century needed just 207 balls. In his first match since 2008-09, slow left-armer Varun Khanna took a career-best 8-97.*

At Chennai (Chidambaram), October 1–3, 2015. **Tamil Nadu won by seven runs. ‡Tamil Nadu 125 and 155** (B. A. Bhatt 6-58); **Baroda 159 and 114** (R. S. Shah 5-43). *Tamil Nadu 6pts. Needing 122, Baroda reached 111-6 before Rahil Shah spun out their last four in eight balls.*

At Moradabad, October 1–4, 2015. **Drawn. ‡Uttar Pradesh 686-7 dec** (Almas Saukat 128, Mohammad Saif 198, S. N. Khan 155); **Madhya Pradesh 528-7** (A. R. Shrivastava 169). *Uttar Pradesh 1pt, Madhya Pradesh 1pt. The first first-class match at Teerthanker Mahaveer University produced 1,214 runs for 14; Uttar Pradesh's 686 was their highest total. Almas Saukat scored 128 on debut; fellow teenagers Mohammad Saif and Sarfaraz Khan added 287 for the fourth wicket.*

At Vizianagram (Dr P. V. G. Raju), October 8–11, 2015. **Drawn. Gujarat 308** (P. A. Patel 122) **and 254-4; ‡Andhra 421** (K. Srikar Bharat 127; R. B. Kalaria 5-55). *Andhra 3pts, Gujarat 1pt.*

At Vadodara (Moti Bagh), October 8–10, 2015. **Baroda won by an innings and 113 runs. ‡Railways 166** (H. H. Pandya 5-61) **and 221; Baroda 500-8 dec** (D. Hooda 122; K. Anureet Singh 5-111). *Baroda 7pts.*

At Indore (Emerald HS), October 8–11, 2015. **Drawn. Tamil Nadu 596-9 dec** (J. Kousik 151, M. Rangarajan 131); **‡Madhya Pradesh 407** (J. S. Saxena 124). *Madhya Pradesh 1pt, Tamil Nadu 3pts. Jagadeesan Kousik and Malolan Rangarajan added 196 for Tamil Nadu's seventh wicket. In reply, Aditya Shrivastava (90) and Jalaj Saxena put on 213 for Madhya Pradesh's first.*

At Mumbai (Wankhede), October 8–11, 2015. **Mumbai won by an innings and 12 runs. Punjab 154 and 403** (Mandeep Singh 116; A. A. Herwadkar 6-52); **‡Mumbai 569-8 dec** (S. S. Iyer 200, A. P. Tare 137*). *Mumbai 7pts. Shreyas Iyer reached a 176-ball maiden double-century and added 233 for Mumbai's third wicket with Surya Yadav. Opener Akhil Herwadkar, whose occasional off-spin had previously claimed two first-class wickets, collected six to ensure an innings win.*

At Vizianagram (Dr P. V. G. Raju), October 15–18, 2015. **Drawn. Baroda 302 and 60-2; ‡Andhra 474-6 dec** (K. Srikar Bharat 144, R. K. Bhui 116, A. G. Pradeep 100). *Andhra 3pts, Baroda 1pt.*

At Mumbai (Bandra Kurla), October 15–18, 2015. **Mumbai won by one wicket. Tamil Nadu 434** (K. D. Karthik 167; V. V. Dabholkar 5-122) **and 95** (V. V. Dabholkar 7-53); **‡Mumbai 294** (S. D. Lad 150; M. Mohammed 5-86) **and 236-9.** *Mumbai 6pts. Tamil Nadu led by 140 on first innings, thanks to a 182-run stand between Dinesh Karthik and Rangarajan for their seventh wicket. But a second-innings collapse against slow left-armer Vishal Dabholkar, who finished with 12-175, meant Mumbai needed 236. After they slid from 202-4 to 232-9, last man Dabholkar hit the winning runs.*

At Mohali, October 15–18, 2015. **Drawn. Gujarat 467** (P. K. Panchal 105, P. A. Patel 113; Sarabjit Singh 5-133) **and 135-4; ‡Punjab 608** (M. Vohra 104, Yuvraj Singh 187; R. H. Bhatt 8-151). *Punjab 3pts, Gujarat 1pt. Punjab passed 600 for the second time in three games; Yuvraj Singh made his highest score, before becoming one of Rujul Bhatt's career-best 8-151.*

At Ghaziabad, October 15–18, 2015. **Railways won by 282 runs. Railways 375** (Ashish Singh 101) **and 229-4 dec; ‡Uttar Pradesh 264** (R. L. Mali 5-88) **and 58** (K. Anureet Singh 5-15). *Railways 6pts.*

At Ongole (C. S. R. Sarma), October 22–25, 2015. **Uttar Pradesh won by 56 runs. Uttar Pradesh 170 and 309; ‡Andhra 297 and 126** (A. Rajpoot 5-35). *Uttar Pradesh 6pts.*

At Vadodara (Reliance), October 22–25, 2015. **Drawn. ‡Mumbai 447** (S. S. Iyer 173) **and 202-5** (S. A. Yadav 100*); **Baroda 397** (D. S. Kulkarni 5-82). *Baroda 1pt, Mumbai 3pts. Iyer and Surya Yadav added 202 for the fourth wicket in Mumbai's first innings.*

At Patiala (Dhruve Pandove), October 22–25, 2015. **Drawn.** ‡**Madhya Pradesh 370** (A. R. Shrivastava 131; Sarabjit Singh 5-110) **and 314-6; Punjab 358** (U. Kaul 139; A. N. Sharma 5-122). *Punjab 1pt, Madhya Pradesh 3pts. Shrivastava scored his fourth hundred in his seventh first-class innings – making his career aggregate 740 at 123.*

At Delhi (Karnail Singh), October 22–24, 2015. **Gujarat won by an innings and 36 runs. Gujarat 387** (P. K. Panchal 141); ‡**Railways 234 and 117.** *Gujarat 7pts.*

At Vadodara (Moti Bagh), October 30–November 2, 2015. **Madhya Pradesh won by 87 runs.** ‡**Madhya Pradesh 269 and 288-6 dec** (R. M. Patidar 101); **Baroda 296** (M. N. Hirwani 5-60) **and 174.** *Madhya Pradesh 6pts. Rajat Patidar scored 101 on first-class debut.*

At Valsad, October 30–November 1, 2015. **Uttar Pradesh won by 155 runs.** ‡**Uttar Pradesh 273 and 257** (A. R. Patel 5-90); **Gujarat 100** (P. Kumar 5-16, Saurabh Kumar 5-37) **and 275** (Saurabh Kumar 5-106). *Uttar Pradesh 6pts.*

At Patiala (Dhruve Pandove), October 30–31, 2015. **Punjab won by seven wickets.** ‡**Andhra 80 and 133** (Gurkeerat Singh 5-38); **Punjab 147 and 67-3.** *Punjab 6pts. Punjab captain Gurkeerat's off-spin improved his career-best return twice in a two-day victory.*

At Delhi (Karnail Singh), October 30–November 2, 2015. **Tamil Nadu won by eight wickets. Tamil Nadu 328** (R. N. B. Indrajith 151; K. Anureet Singh 5-104) **and 77-2;** ‡**Railways 164** (A. A. Crist 6-60) **and 240.** *Tamil Nadu 6pts.*

At Valsad, November 7–10, 2015. **Gujarat won by an innings and 46 runs.** ‡**Gujarat 505** (P. K. Panchal 128; I. K. Pathan 6-47); **Baroda 252 and 207.** *Gujarat 7pts.*

At Gwalior, November 7–9, 2015. **Madhya Pradesh won by nine wickets.** ‡**Railways 256** (J. S. Saxena 8-96) **and 131** (J. S. Saxena 8-58); **Madhya Pradesh 276** (R. M. Patidar 113; K. V. Sharma 5-102) **and 112-1.** *Madhya Pradesh 6pts. Patidar scored his second century in his second first-class game. Saxena's off-spin claimed career-bests in each innings; 8-58 was the best return of the season, and 16-154 equalled Pradeep Sunderam (Rajasthan v Vidarbha, 1985-86) in Ranji history behind only Anil Kumble's 16-99 (Karnataka v Kerala, 1994-95).*

At Mumbai (Wankhede), November 7–10, 2015. **Drawn. Mumbai 610-9 dec** (S. S. Iyer 137, R. G. Sharma 113); ‡**Uttar Pradesh 440 and 140-1.** *Mumbai 3pts, Uttar Pradesh 1pt. Iyer reached his third century of the season in 81 balls, and faced 110 in all.*

At Chennai (Chidambaram), November 7–10, 2015. **Drawn.** ‡**Andhra 203; Tamil Nadu 164-7.** *Tamil Nadu 1pt, Andhra 1pt.*

At Vadodara (Moti Bagh), November 15–17, 2015. **Baroda won by an innings and 116 runs. Baroda 475** (K. H. Devdhar 186); ‡**Punjab 212 and 147.** *Baroda 7pts. Kedar Devdhar and Aditya Waghmode (96) opened Baroda's innings with 245.*

At Surat, November 15–18, 2015. **Gujarat won by 153 runs.** ‡**Gujarat 311 and 202-9 dec** (J. S. Saxena 6-60); **Madhya Pradesh 200 and 160** (R. P. Singh 5-33). *Gujarat 6pts.*

At Mumbai (Wankhede), November 15–18, 2015. **Mumbai won by six wickets.** ‡**Railways 217 and 408-4 dec** (S. P. Wakaskar 185, V. Cheluvaraj 133*); **Mumbai 331** (A. A. Herwadkar 145; K. V. Sharma 7-91) **and 295-4.** *Mumbai 6pts. Saurabh Wakaskar and Vairamudi Cheluvaraj added 253 for Railways' second wicket.*

At Kanpur (Modi), November 15–18, 2015. **Drawn. Uttar Pradesh 348 and 273-5 dec** (S. K. Raina 145*); ‡**Tamil Nadu 231 and 212-4.** *Uttar Pradesh 3pts, Tamil Nadu 1pt.*

At Indore (Holkar), November 23–25, 2015. **Mumbai won by three wickets.** ‡**Madhya Pradesh 240 and 201; Mumbai 162** (J. S. Saxena 5-66, A. N. Sharma 5-80) **and 283-7.** *Mumbai 6pts. Mumbai's highest successful run-chase away from home secured their place in the knockouts.*

At Delhi (Karnail Singh), November 23–25, 2015. **Railways won by 148 runs. Railways 182** (C. Sneha Kishore 5-76) **and 204** (B. Sudhakar 5-49); ‡**Andhra 114** (K. V. Sharma 5-30) **and 124.** *Railways 6pts.*

At Tirunelveli, November 23–26, 2015. **Drawn. Gujarat 195-2 dec v** ‡**Tamil Nadu.** *Tamil Nadu 1pt, Gujarat 1pt.*

At Kanpur (Modi), November 23–26, 2015. **Drawn. Punjab 272 and 295-7 dec** (U. Kaul 109*); ‡**Uttar Pradesh 226 and 204-6.** *Uttar Pradesh 1pt, Punjab 3pts.*

At Indore (Holkar), December 1–3, 2015. **Madhya Pradesh won by an innings and nine runs.** **‡Madhya Pradesh 279** (B. Ayyappa 5-66); **Andhra 56** (A. N. Sharma 6-17) **and 214** (A. N. Sharma 7-91). *Madhya Pradesh 7pts. Slow left-armer Ankit Sharma improved his career-best figures twice, to finish with 13-108. Madhya Pradesh sprang from sixth place to third – thanks to the bonus point for an innings win, they tied on points and wins with Gujarat, but went through on net run-rate.*

At Mumbai (Wankhede), December 1–4, 2015. **Drawn. Mumbai 531** (A. A. Herwadkar 192, S. A. Yadav 104) **and 227-6; ‡Gujarat 421** (B. H. Merai 166; S. N. Thakur 6-107). *Mumbai 3pts, Gujarat 1pt. Herwadkar and Yadav added 208 for Mumbai's third wicket. Gujarat, who started in second place, missed out on the knockouts after failing to secure first-innings points.*

At Natham, December 1–2, 2015. **Punjab won by 243 runs. ‡Punjab 206 and 174; Tamil Nadu 68** (Rajwinder Singh 6-29) **and 69** (Harbhajan Singh 7-37). *Punjab 6pts. Australian umpire John Ward – in India on an exchange scheme – was taken to hospital after being struck on the head. Tamil Nadu were bowled out for 68 and 69 in a two-day defeat which put Punjab in the quarter-finals. Harbhajan Singh claimed 10-67.*

At Greater Noida, December 1–4, 2015. **Drawn. ‡Baroda 321 and 258-3** (A. A. Waghmode 100*); **Uttar Pradesh 524** (U. A. Sharma 215). *Uttar Pradesh 3pts, Baroda 1pt. The first first-class game at Greater Noida. Umang Sharma converted a maiden century into a double, batting over ten hours to rescue Uttar Pradesh from 78-4; he put on 132 for the eighth wicket with Praveen Kumar (84).*

Group C

At Porvorim, October 1–4, 2015. **Drawn. Hyderabad 325; ‡Goa 425-7** (S. K. Kamat 109). *Goa 3pts, Hyderabad 1pt.*

At Srinagar, October 1–4, 2015. **Drawn. ‡Jammu & Kashmir 330 and 225; Kerala 485-8 dec** (S. Baby 151, S. V. Samson 101) **and 44-4.** *Jammu & Kashmir 1pt, Kerala 3pts.*

At Rajkot (Madhavrao Scindia), October 1–3, 2015. **Saurashtra won by an innings and 118 runs.** **‡Saurashtra 307; Tripura 103** (R. A. Jadeja 6-27) **and 86** (R. A. Jadeja 5-45). *Saurashtra 7pts. In his first Ranji game for nearly three years, Test left-arm spinner Ravindra Jadeja followed 91 in Saurashtra's innings by taking 11-72.*

At Delhi (Palam), October 1–3, 2015. **Services won by nine wickets. Jharkhand 45** (D. Pathania 6-19) **and 192** (D. Pathania 7-64); **‡Services 161 and 78-1.** *Services 6pts. Jharkhand collapsed for 45 on the first day as seamer Diwesh Pathania claimed 6-19, which became 13-83, on first-class debut.*

At Porvorim, October 8–11, 2015. **Drawn. Services 402 and 217-7 dec; ‡Goa 285** (S. A. Asnodkar 139; P. S. Poonia 5-60) **and 3-0.** *Goa 1pt, Services 3pts.*

At Dharamsala, October 8–11, 2015. **Himachal Pradesh won by ten wickets. Jammu & Kashmir 293** (Parvez Rasool 114*) **and 276; ‡Himachal Pradesh 554** (N. Gangta 203, B. Sharma 117*) **and 16-0.** *Himachal Pradesh 7pts. Nikhil Gangta made his first double-century, with seven sixes, and added 168 for Himachal Pradesh's seventh wicket with Bipul Sharma, whose 117* was his third century in successive innings since January.*

At Hyderabad (Uppal), October 8–11, 2015. **Drawn. ‡Kerala 401** (P. Rohan Prem 208; A. A. Bhandari 5-72); **Hyderabad 218** (K. S. Monish 6-91) **and 176-7** (K. S. Monish 5-73). *Hyderabad 1pt, Kerala 3pts. Rohan Prem scored a maiden double-hundred.*

At Rajkot (Madhavrao Scindia), October 8–9, 2015. **Saurashtra won by eight wickets. ‡Jharkhand 168** (R. A. Jadeja 6-71) **and 122** (R. A. Jadeja 7-55); **Saurashtra 205 and 86-2.** *Saurashtra 6pts. Jharkhand's 17-year-old opener Ishan Kishan hit eight sixes in a 69-ball 87 in their first innings – but Saurashtra won in two days as Jadeja collected 13-126.*

At Porvorim, October 15–17, 2015. **Goa won by nine wickets. ‡Tripura 61 and 245** (M. B. Murasingh 104; S. B. Jakati 5-54); **Goa 257 and 50-1.** *Goa 6pts.*

At Dharamsala, October 15–18, 2015. **Drawn. Hyderabad 434** (T. D. Agarwal 118, G. H. Vihari 101) **and 2-0; ‡Himachal Pradesh 707-8 dec** (A. Bains 161, R. D. Bist 220*, R. Dhawan 114). *Himachal Pradesh 3pts, Hyderabad 1pt. Tanmay Agarwal and Hanuma Vihari added 205 for Hyderabad's third wicket. Himachal Pradesh, who had never before reached 600, passed 700, the highest total of the season, with Robin Bist completing a maiden double-century.*

At Jammu (Gandhi), October 15–16, 2015. **Services won by nine wickets. Jammu & Kashmir 85** (R. R. Raj 7-38) **and 161** (M. Khalid Ahmed 7-61); ‡**Services 229 and 18-1.** *Services 6pts. Raushan Raj and Khalid Ahmed both collected career-bests in a two-day victory.*

At Perintalmanna, October 15–18, 2015. **Jharkhand won by 133 runs. Jharkhand 202 and 262** (K. S. Monish 5-66); ‡**Kerala 148** (V. R. Aaron 5-23) **and 183** (S. Nadeem 7-64). *Jharkhand 6pts. Kerala wicketkeeper Sanju Samson made eight dismissals in the match.*

At Dharamsala, October 22–25, 2015. **Drawn. Goa 324** (S. K. Kamat 163; R. Dhawan 6-108) **and 367-6 dec** (S. S. Kauthankar 101); ‡**Himachal Pradesh 376** (P. Dogra 167; P. Parameswaran 5-82) **and 125-2.** *Himachal Pradesh 3pts, Goa 1pt.*

At Rajkot (Khanderi), October 22–23, 2015. **Saurashtra won by 35 runs.** ‡**Saurashtra 102** (Mehdi Hasan 5-43) **and 215** (Mehdi Hasan 5-69); **Hyderabad 148** (R. A. Jadeja 6-75) **and 134** (R. A. Jadeja 7-60). *Saurashtra 6pts. Jadeja's 13-135 gave him 37 wickets in his first three Ranji games of the season, and six successive returns of five or more. Saurashtra won in two days again.*

At Delhi (Palam), October 22–25, 2015. **Drawn.** ‡**Kerala 322** (P. Rohan Prem 101) **and 176-3 dec; Services 319 and 43-4.** *Services 1pt, Kerala 3pts.*

At Agartala (Institute of Technology), October 22–25, 2015. **Drawn.** ‡**Jammu & Kashmir 428** (Parvez Rasool 130) **and 163-3 dec; Tripura 224 and 243-2** (A. S. Das 106*, Parvinder Singh 100*). *Tripura 1pt, Jammu & Kashmir 3pts. Mithun Manhas and Parvez Rasool put on 207 for the fourth wicket in Jammu & Kashmir's first innings; in the second, Bandeep Singh reached 50 in 15 balls, which equalled the Ranji record and was the joint-third-fastest in all first-class cricket.*

At Dharamsala, October 30–November 2, 2015. **Himachal Pradesh won by an innings and six runs. Tripura 285 and 270;** ‡**Himachal Pradesh 561-5 dec** (A. Bains 114, P. Chopra 101, P. Dogra 209*). *Himachal Pradesh 7pts. Ankush Bains and Prashant Chopra opened Himachal Pradesh's innings with 210, before Paras Dogra scored his sixth double-century.*

At Hyderabad (Uppal), October 30–November 2, 2015. **Drawn. Jammu & Kashmir 460** (M. Manhas 150; Anwar Ahmed 5-92) **and 56-2;** ‡**Hyderabad 280 and 329** (R. Punia 5-55). *Hyderabad 1pt, Jammu & Kashmir 3pts.*

At Jamshedpur, October 30–November 2, 2015. **Drawn.** ‡**Goa 302** (S. S. Quadri 6-97) **and 102-5 dec; Jharkhand 209** (S. B. Jakati 5-72) **and 105-6.** *Jharkhand 1pt, Goa 3pts.*

At Delhi (Palam), October 30–November 2, 2015. **Saurashtra won by four wickets. Services 254** (R. Paliwal 121; J. D. Unadkat 6-80) **and 311-6 dec** (R. Paliwal 103, Yashpal Singh 115*); ‡**Saurashtra 264** (M. Khalid Ahmed 5-74) **and 302-6.** *Saurashtra 6pts. Rajat Paliwal scored twin hundreds, while Yashpal Singh made 55* and 115* in his 100th first-class match – but Saurashtra still won their fourth game out of four in 2015-16.*

At Dharamsala, November 7–10, 2015. **Drawn. Himachal Pradesh 531** (P. Dogra 227); ‡**Services 448-8** (R. Paliwal 107, Yashpal Singh 115). *Himachal Pradesh 1pt, Services 1pt. Dogra compiled his seventh double-hundred – equalling Ajay Sharma's Ranji record – and second in a week, hitting eight sixes and adding 217 for Himachal Pradesh's fifth wicket with Gangta (98). Paliwal scored his third century in successive innings, and put on 219 for Services' fourth with Yashpal.*

At Jamshedpur, November 7–10, 2015. **Drawn.** ‡**Jharkhand 551-8 dec** (I. P. Kishan 109, Anand Singh 124); **Jammu & Kashmir 309 and 265-4** (I. Dev Singh 126). *Jharkhand 3pts, Jammu & Kashmir 1pt.*

At Perintalmanna, November 7–10, 2015. **Drawn.** ‡**Kerala 347** (P. Rohan Prem 118; R. K. Datta 5-50) **and 117-4 dec; Tripura 236** (S. Sandeep Warrier 6-69) **and 53-0.** *Kerala 3pts, Tripura 1pt.*

At Rajkot (Khanderi), November 7–10, 2015. **Drawn.** ‡**Goa 239** (D. W. Misal 106*) **and 299-7 dec** (S. A. Asnodkar 104); **Saurashtra 258** (R. R. Singh 5-70) **and 223-5.** *Saurashtra 3pts, Goa 1pt.*

At Porvorim, November 15–17, 2015. **Kerala won by an innings and 83 runs.** ‡**Kerala 441** (R. M. Fernandez 109, Fabid Ahmed 106); **Goa 191** (S. Sandeep Warrier 6-44) **and 167.** *Kerala 7pts.*

At Rajkot (Khanderi), November 15–18, 2015. **Drawn.** ‡**Himachal Pradesh 551** (P. Chopra 187, R. D. Bist 101); **Saurashtra 437** (J. N. Shah 142). *Saurashtra 1pt, Himachal Pradesh 3pts. Himachal Pradesh passed 500 for the fifth time in six matches.*

At Delhi (Palam), November 15–18, 2015. **Drawn. Services 353** (S. Chatterjee 156) **and 217-7 dec; ‡Hyderabad 272** (P. Akshath Reddy 125) **and 140-3.** *Services 3pts, Hyderabad 1pt.*

At Agartala (Institute of Technology), November 15–18, 2015. **Jharkhand won by an innings and 67 runs. Tripura 166** (R. A. Shukla 6-40) **and 161** (S. Nadeem 6-50); **‡Jharkhand 394-4 dec** (I. R. Jaggi 102*). *Jharkhand 7pts.*

At Hyderabad (Uppal), November 23–26, 2015. **Drawn. Hyderabad 548-5 dec** (G. H. Vihari 219); **‡Tripura 237 and 294-5** (Parvinder Singh 104*). *Hyderabad 3pts, Tripura 1pt. Vihari scored his third double-hundred, and put on 213 for the fourth wicket with Bavanaka Sandeep.*

At Jammu (Gandhi), November 23–26, 2015. **Drawn. Goa 552-5 dec** (A. S. Desai 106, S. A. Asnodkar 232, S. K. Kamat 105) **and 82-1; ‡Jammu & Kashmir 501** (I. Dev Singh 115, M. Manhas 135). *Jammu & Kashmir 1pt, Goa 3pts. Swapnil Asnodkar retired hurt on 62, but resumed to reach his third double-century, adding 213 for Goa's second wicket with Sagun Kamat.*

At Ranchi (Jharkhand SCA), November 23–24, 2015. **Jharkhand won by an innings and 71 runs. ‡Jharkhand 337** (S. P. Gautam 122; B. Sharma 6-59); **Himachal Pradesh 133** (S. Nadeem 7-45) **and 133.** *Jharkhand 7pts. On the first day, Jharkhand scored 306-4; on the next, 26 wickets fell for 297 as they completed a two-day win.*

At Perintalmanna, November 23–25, 2015. **Kerala won by 45 runs. ‡Kerala 166** (D. A. Jadeja 5-44) **and 105** (D. A. Jadeja 6-59); **Saurashtra 157** (K. S. Monish 6-81) **and 69** (K. S. Monish 5-46). *Kerala 6pts. Saurashtra needed only 115 for their fifth win, but lost their last nine for 53 on the third morning to suffer their first defeat. Karaparambil Monish finished with 11-127.*

At Hyderabad (Uppal), December 1–4, 2015. **Jharkhand won by ten wickets. Hyderabad 145 and 269** (R. A. Shukla 5-89); **‡Jharkhand 388-8 dec** (S. S. Tiwary 209*) **and 29-0.** *Jharkhand 7pts. Saurabh Tiwary scored his second double-century to help Jharkhand into the knockouts.*

At Jammu (Gandhi), December 1–3, 2015. **Saurashtra won by an innings and 63 runs. Jammu & Kashmir 138** (S. M. Sanandiya 5-53) **and 296** (I. Dev Singh 127; K. R. Makwana 7-100); **‡Saurashtra 497** (S. P. Jackson 121). *Saurashtra 7pts. Jaydev Unadkat (92) and Dharmendrasinh Jadeja (43*) put on 119 for Saurashtra's tenth wicket, extending their advantage to 359. Saurashtra wicketkeeper Sagar Jogiyani made eight dismissals as they sailed into the quarter-finals.*

At Perintalmanna, December 1–2, 2015. **Himachal Pradesh won by six wickets. ‡Kerala 103** (Rahul Singh 6-19) **and 83** (B. Sharma 6-33); **Himachal Pradesh 163 and 24-4.** *Himachal Pradesh 6pts. The match was completed in four sessions; Himachal needed only 24 to win, and knocked them off in 4.3 overs – though Monish bowled four men, three for ducks, for figures of 2–2–0–4. On the opening day another left-arm spinner, Rahul Singh, had taken a career-best 19.4–9–19–6.*

At Agartala (Maharaja Bir Bikram), December 1–4, 2015. **Services won by an innings and 62 runs. Services 512** (R. Paliwal 203); **‡Tripura 230 and 220.** *Services 7pts. Paliwal's fourth century in six innings became a maiden double; he added 239 for the sixth wicket with Devender Lohchab (95).*

Knockouts

Quarter-final At Valsad, February 3–6, 2016. **Assam won by 51 runs. Assam 323** (J. Syed Mohammad 121) **and 101** (B. B. Sran 5-43); **‡Punjab 137 and 236** (A. K. Das 8-83). *Arup Das's career-best 8-83 (and 11-124) ushered Assam into the Ranji semi-finals for the first time.*

Quarter-final At Mumbai (Brabourne), February 3–7, 2016. **Madhya Pradesh won by 355 runs. Madhya Pradesh 348** (V. Pratap Singh 5-76) **and 560-9 dec** (R. M. Patidar 137, H. S. Bhatia 139); **‡Bengal 121 and 432** (M. K. Tiwary 124, P. P. Shaw 118). *In the only quarter-final to reach the fifth day, Bengal were set 788. They managed 432, their highest fourth-innings total, but still went down to their second-heaviest defeat – also Madhya Pradesh's biggest victory – by runs.*

Quarter-final At Mysore (Srikantadatta Narasimha Raja Wadeyar), February 3–6, 2016. **Mumbai won by 395 runs. ‡Mumbai 416** (A. A. Herwadkar 107; S. Nadeem 5-140) **and 245** (S. S. Quadri 5-62); **Jharkhand 172 and 94** (Iqbal Abdulla 5-35, J. G. Bista 5-16). *Shreyas Iyer reached 1,000 runs in the season in Mumbai's first innings, and 1,000 in the tournament in the second. Jharkhand lost their last nine for 30 on the final day. Shahbaz Nadeem's 5-140 gave him 50 for the season.*

Quarter-final At Vizianagram (Dr P. V. G. Raju), February 3–5, 2016. **Saurashtra won by an innings and 85 runs. Vidarbha 151** (J. D. Unadkat 5-70) **and 139; ‡Saurashtra 375** (S. D. Jogiyani 130, S. P. Jackson 122; U. T. Yadav 5-81). *Jogiyani and Sheldon Jackson put on 206 for Saurashtra's fourth wicket, and Unadkat collected 9-105 in another efficient Saurashtra victory.*

Semi-final At Vadodara (Reliance), February 13–15, 2016. **Saurashtra won by ten wickets. Assam 234** (J. D. Unadkat 6-77) **and 139** (J. D. Unadkat 5-45); **‡Saurashtra 353** (C. A. Pujara 126) **and 24-0**. *Assam's dreams were ended by Saurashtra's seventh win – and sixth with at least a day to spare. Unadkat claimed 11-122, while Assam's Krishna Das took his 50th wicket of the season.*

Semi-final At Cuttack (Dhaneswar Rath), February 13–17, 2016. **Drawn.** Mumbai qualified for the final by virtue of their first-innings lead. **Mumbai 371** (C. R. Sakure 5-137) **and 426** (S. A. Yadav 115, A. P. Tare 109); **‡Madhya Pradesh 227** (B. S. Sandhu 5-43) **and 361-5** (N. V. Ojha 113, H. S. Bhatia 105). *Surya Yadav and Aditya Tare added 217 for Mumbai's fourth wicket in the second innings, when both were caught by Madhya Pradesh wicketkeeper Naman Ojha, who made eight dismissals – as well as 192 runs – in the match. Chasing 571, Madhya Pradesh made their highest fourth-innings total, but Mumbai's first-innings lead carried them into the final.*

Final At Gahunje, February 24–26, 2016. **Mumbai won by an innings and 21 runs. Saurashtra 235** (D. S. Kulkarni 5-42) **and 115** (S. N. Thakur 5-26); **‡Mumbai 371** (S. S. Iyer 117). *Iyer's fourth hundred of the tournament was also his 11th score of 50-plus, equalling the Ranji record. After he fell, Mumbai stumbled to 268-9, only 33 ahead. But Siddhesh Lad (88) and Balwinder Sandhu (34*) added 103 – a Mumbai tenth-wicket record – to extend the lead to 136 on the third day, when Saurashtra crumbled against seamer Shardul Thakur, to give Mumbai their 41st Ranji Trophy.*

RANJI TROPHY WINNERS

1934-35	Bombay	1962-63	Bombay	1990-91	Haryana
1935-36	Bombay	1963-64	Bombay	1991-92	Delhi
1936-37	Nawanagar	1964-65	Bombay	1992-93	Punjab
1937-38	Hyderabad	1965-66	Bombay	1993-94	Bombay
1938-39	Bengal	1966-67	Bombay	1994-95	Bombay
1939-40	Maharashtra	1967-68	Bombay	1995-96	Karnataka
1940-41	Maharashtra	1968-69	Bombay	1996-97	Mumbai
1941-42	Bombay	1969-70	Bombay	1997-98	Karnataka
1942-43	Baroda	1970-71	Bombay	1998-99	Karnataka
1943-44	Western India	1971-72	Bombay	1999-2000	Mumbai
1944-45	Bombay	1972-73	Bombay	2000-01	Baroda
1945-46	Holkar	1973-74	Karnataka	2001-02	Railways
1946-47	Baroda	1974-75	Bombay	2002-03	Mumbai
1947-48	Holkar	1975-76	Bombay	2003-04	Mumbai
1948-49	Bombay	1976-77	Bombay	2004-05	Railways
1949-50	Baroda	1977-78	Karnataka	2005-06	Uttar Pradesh
1950-51	Holkar	1978-79	Delhi	2006-07	Mumbai
1951-52	Bombay	1979-80	Delhi	2007-08	Delhi
1952-53	Holkar	1980-81	Bombay	2008-09	Mumbai
1953-54	Bombay	1981-82	Delhi	2009-10	Mumbai
1954-55	Madras	1982-83	Karnataka	2010-11	Rajasthan
1955-56	Bombay	1983-84	Bombay	2011-12	Rajasthan
1956-57	Bombay	1984-85	Bombay	2012-13	Mumbai
1957-58	Baroda	1985-86	Delhi	2013-14	Karnataka
1958-59	Bombay	1986-87	Hyderabad	2014-15	Karnataka
1959-60	Bombay	1987-88	Tamil Nadu	2015-16	Mumbai
1960-61	Bombay	1988-89	Delhi		
1961-62	Bombay	1989-90	Bengal		

Bombay/Mumbai have won the Ranji Trophy 41 times, Karnataka 8, Delhi 7, Baroda 5, Holkar 4, Bengal, Hyderabad, Madras/Tamil Nadu, Maharashtra, Railways and Rajasthan 2, Haryana, Nawanagar, Punjab, Uttar Pradesh and Western India 1.

IRANI CUP, 2015-16

Ranji Trophy Champions (Mumbai) v Rest of India

At Mumbai (Brabourne), March 6–10, 2016. **Rest of India won by four wickets.** ‡**Mumbai 603** (J. G. Bista 104, S. A. Yadav 156) **and 182; Rest of India 306 and 482-6** (F. Y. Fazal 127; Iqbal Abdulla 5-154). *Mumbai became the sixth team to lose after scoring 600. On the first day, 20-year-old Jay Bista scored 104 in 90 balls, his maiden century, out of 193 for the first wicket. Mumbai led the Rest (down to ten men after seamer Ankit Rajpoot hurt his knee) by 297, but waived the follow-on; Jayant Yadav and Jaydev Unadkat bowled them out cheaply to leave a target of 480. Faiz Fazal and Karun Nair – with his second ninety in the match – took the Rest past 300, and Sheldon Jackson (59*) steered them to the tenth-highest winning fourth-innings total.*

HIGHEST LOSING TOTALS IN A FIRST-CLASS MATCH

642	Essex lost to Glamorgan by four wickets at Chelmsford	2004
632	Northamptonshire lost to Essex by four wickets at Northampton	2002
614	New South Wales lost to Victoria by seven wickets at Sydney	1924-25
608-9 dec	Wellington lost to Northern Districts by three wickets at Hamilton	1998-99
604†	Maharashtra lost to Bombay by 354 runs at Poona	1948-49
603	**Mumbai lost to Rest of India by four wickets at Mumbai**	**2015-16**

† *Fourth innings. All other instances were in the first innings of the match.*

VIJAY HAZARE TROPHY, 2015-16

Four 50-over leagues plus knockout

Semi-final At Bangalore (Chinnaswamy), December 26, 2015. **Delhi won by six wickets. Himachal Pradesh 200-9** (50 overs); ‡**Delhi 201-4** (41.1 overs). *MoM:* U. Chand (Delhi).

Semi-final At Alur, December 26, 2015. **Gujarat won by 31 runs. Gujarat 248-8** (50 overs); ‡**Tamil Nadu 217** (47.3 overs) (A. Mukund 104*; A. R. Patel 6-43). *MoM:* A. R. Patel (Gujarat).

Final At Bangalore (Chinnaswamy), December 28, 2015 (day/night). **Gujarat won by 139 runs. Gujarat 273** (50 overs) (P. A. Patel 105); ‡**Delhi 134** (32.3 overs) (J. J. Bumrah 5-28). *MoM:* P. A. Patel and R. P. Singh (Gujarat). *Gujarat captain Parthiv Patel led them to their first Vijay Hazare Trophy, helped by R. P. Singh's four top-order wickets.*

DEODHAR TROPHY, 2015-16

50-over knockout for India A, India B and winner of Vijay Hazare Trophy

Final At Kanpur (Modi), January 29, 2016. **India A won by 87 runs.** ‡**India A 286-7** (50 overs) (F. Y. Fazal 100); **India B 199** (40.4 overs). *MoM:* F. Y. Fazal.

SYED MUSHTAQ ALI TROPHY, 2015-16

Four 20-over leagues, two super leagues plus final

Final At Mumbai (Wankhede), January 20, 2016 (floodlit). **Uttar Pradesh won by 38 runs. Uttar Pradesh 163-7** (20 overs); ‡**Baroda 125-7** (20 overs). *MoM:* S. K. Raina (Uttar Pradesh). *Uttar Pradesh captain Suresh Raina hit 47* in 37 balls to secure their first 20-over title.*

NEW ZEALAND CRICKET IN 2016

Life after McCullum

ANDREW ALDERSON

New Zealand fans had become accustomed to their team winning at home, and occasionally abroad, so there was dismay when results fell short in 2016. Brendon McCullum retired after the Australian series in February, and the rest of the year became a test of whether the team he left behind could continue the culture created during his time as captain. Performances were mixed. There were moments of brilliance, but overall New Zealand struggled to sustain the momentum built during the previous year's World Cup. That said, expectations were higher than ever, with the possible exception of the Richard Hadlee-inspired triumphs of the 1980s.

McCullum's final series came with an appropriate crescendo. Already the only player to hit 100 Test sixes, he reached 200 in one-day internationals

NEW ZEALAND IN 2016

	Played	*Won*	*Lost*	*Drawn/No result*
Tests	11	4	6	1
One-day internationals	18	10	7	1
Twenty20 internationals	10	8	2	–

DECEMBER / JANUARY	2 Tests, 5 ODIs and 2 T20Is (h) v Sri Lanka	(see *Wisden 2016*, page 1036)
JANUARY	2 ODIs and 3 T20Is (h) v Pakistan	(page 946)
FEBRUARY	2 Tests and 3 ODIs (h) v Australia	(page 951)
MARCH / APRIL	ICC World Twenty20 (in India)	(page 793)
MAY		
JUNE		
JULY / AUGUST	2 Tests (a) v Zimbabwe	(page 1112)
AUGUST	2 Tests (a) v South Africa	(page 1013)
SEPTEMBER / OCTOBER	3 Tests and 5 ODIs (a) v India	(page 915)
NOVEMBER	2 Tests (h) v Pakistan	(page 961)
DECEMBER	3 ODIs (a) v Australia	(page 860)
DECEMBER / JANUARY	2 Tests, 3 ODIs and 3 T20Is (h) v Bangladesh	(page 966)

For a review of New Zealand domestic cricket from the 2015-16 season, see page 973.

during February's Chappell–Hadlee Series. The First Test at Wellington was his 100th in a row from debut, a first by anyone, and he signed off at Christchurch by slamming the fastest Test century of all time, from just 54 balls. It seemed almost incidental that Australia won both Tests, although the Basin Reserve loss ended New Zealand's sequence of 13 without defeat at home, which equalled the national record. McCullum captained in 12 of those.

Shortly after his international retirement, he was invited to deliver the prestigious Cowdrey Lecture at Lord's, recognition of his influence on the game, and his role in the crusade against corruption. He used the forum to call for his former team-mate Lou Vincent to be shown clemency, after he had confessed to fixing and received 11 life bans.

The 2–0 Test victory over Pakistan in November – their first series win against them for 31 years – resonated. In the first session of the series, at Christchurch, the Zimbabwe-born seamer Colin de Grandhomme took six for 41, the best figures for New Zealand on debut. In the last, at Hamilton, New Zealand grabbed nine wickets to steal victory. That result came after two predictable wins in Zimbabwe, and struggles in South Africa and India. Securing inaugural Test series victories in both countries had been an optimistic aspiration, and remained so: a soggy draw at Durban was followed by five straight defeats.

The 50-over highlight was defending the Chappell–Hadlee Trophy at home. Matt Henry's caught-and-bowled from a ricochet off Mitchell Marsh's boot in the finale was the defining moment of a 2–1 win. The low point was losing the trophy in Australia during December. The media there labelled the series a distraction between the Tests against South Africa and Pakistan, and New Zealand's 3–0 surrender hardly altered their opinion. The result showed the team's vulnerability without Ross Taylor, who had undergone surgery to remove a growth on his left eye. It left Kane Williamson, the new captain, with too much to do.

New Zealand played ten 20-over internationals in 2016 and won eight, but the two defeats included the most important game – the World Twenty20 semi-final. They had looked as if they might lift their first international tournament since the 2000 ICC Knockout in Kenya, winning their four group matches, with the spin trio of Mitchell Santner, Ish Sodhi and Nathan McCullum (in his own international swansong) revelling in the conditions. But England trounced them in Delhi.

Coach Mike Hesson's contract was extended until the end of the 2019 World Cup, while Williamson looked comfortable in his new role. In his second Test in charge – a victory against Zimbabwe at Bulawayo – he became the first New Zealander to score a Test century against all nine possible opponents.

It was a momentous year for women's cricket in New Zealand. The White Ferns won their T20 series against Australia, but lost the subsequent 50-over Rose Bowl, then were knocked out of the World Twenty20 semi-finals by eventual winners West Indies. The captain Suzie Bates became the first woman to be named both ICC one-day international and Twenty20 player of the year.

Fifteen women were offered annual retainers of between $NZ20,000 and $34,000 (an advance on previous years), and there were opportunities to play

Martin Hunter, Getty Images

Man on the rise: Kane Williamson took on Pakistan, and the captaincy.

in the burgeoning T20 leagues in Australia and England. In November, New Zealand Cricket issued a mea culpa, admitting the women's game had been neglected for a generation. They commissioned an independent report – Women and Cricket, Cricket and Women – to examine the state of the sport. It revealed that only 10% of Kiwi cricketers were female, and 90% of them were under 12 (compared to 65% of males). Over half the country's clubs (58%) had no participation options for women. Increasing the number of women on provincial boards – there were five out of 43 by the end of the year – was earmarked as a start. "Women's cricket has been sidelined," admitted NZC's chief executive David White. "This is wrong, and we have a responsibility to put things right."

The board's annual report disclosed an operating loss of $2.16m for the 2015-16 financial year, an improvement on the budgeted $5m deficit, thanks to an increase in gate money and distributions from the ICC. Perhaps the most uplifting snippet was the announcement of a 19.4% increase in junior players since the 2015 World Cup.

There was sad news in March, when Martin Crowe succumbed to lymphoma, aged 53. Arguably New Zealand's finest batsman, and an innovative captain, he became a respected broadcaster and pundit. He also invented Cricket Max, a forerunner of Twenty20. Crowe collated many of his ideas and struggles in his 2013 autobiography, *Raw*, an exercise in catharsis as he fought the cancer. "I want to live a life that is fearless, that is without judgment or scrutiny, let alone have any negative emotions of hate, resentment or grievance," he wrote. "I am so tired of that life, of fighting, of ego, of trying to win opinion and of needing acceptance."

NEW ZEALAND v PAKISTAN IN 2015-16

ANDREW ALDERSON

Twenty20 internationals (3): New Zealand 2, Pakistan 1
One-day internationals (3): New Zealand 2, Pakistan 0

This brief tour formed part of the teams' preparations for the World Twenty20, although off-field developments threatened to overshadow it. The main interest centred on the international return of Pakistan's left-arm seamer Mohammad Amir, more than five years after he was banned for bowling deliberate no-balls in a Test at Lord's.

At first, some of his team-mates were reluctant to accept him back into the fold. Azhar Ali had to be persuaded not to resign as the one-day captain, while Mohammad Hafeez expressed reservations about playing with someone who had "damaged the pride and integrity of the country". Both missed the start of the pre-tour training camp, but were talked round by the Pakistan Cricket Board. There was also speculation that Amir might be denied an entry visa, but he made it to New Zealand without any drama.

Amir, still only 23, seemed to cope with the pressure. There were catcalls when he bowled, while spectators brandished wads of banknotes when he fielded near the boundary. New Zealand Cricket were embarrassed by the Wellington ground announcer playing a cash-register sound effect during one of his spells; NZC's chief executive David White was forced to apologise to the Pakistanis. Amir managed only one for 100 during the Twenty20s, but did better in the 50-over games, collecting five wickets and going for less than four an over.

New Zealand came from behind to win the T20 series, in which the pacy Adam Milne took eight wickets, while Trent Boult – newly installed at the top of the ODI rankings – claimed six in the two 50-over matches that escaped the weather.

New Zealand had other concerns. Thoughts were turning to life after Brendon McCullum, who had announced he would retire after the series against Australia. He featured only in the final one-day international, after resting his troublesome back, and bagged a golden duck. In his absence, Kane Williamson – the anointed successor – did a good job, leading the fightback after the loss of the first Twenty20 game.

Mitchell McClenaghan suffered a nasty injury in the first one-dayer, when he missed a pull at a short delivery from Anwar Ali: the ball went through the grille of his old-style helmet and fractured his left eye socket. Luckily, there was no permanent damage.

PAKISTAN TOURING PARTY

*Azhar Ali (50), Aamer Yamin (20), Ahmed Shehzad (50/20), Anwar Ali (50/20), Asad Shafiq (50), Babar Azam (50), Iftikhar Ahmed (20), Imad Wasim (50/20), Mohammad Amir (50/20), Mohammad Hafeez (50/20), Mohammad Irfan (50), Mohammad Rizwan (50/20), Rahat Ali (50), Saad Nasim

(20), Sarfraz Ahmed (50/20), Shahid Afridi (20), Shoaib Malik (50/20), Sohaib Maqsood (50/20), Umar Akmal (20), Umar Gul (20), Wahab Riaz (50/20), Zafar Gohar (50). *Coach:* Waqar Younis.

Shahid Afridi captained in the Twenty20s.

NEW ZEALAND v PAKISTAN

First Twenty20 International

At Auckland, January 15, 2016 (floodlit). Pakistan won by 16 runs. Toss: New Zealand. Twenty20 international debut: T. D. Astle.

At 89 for one in the tenth over, New Zealand looked on course for victory – but the loss of Munro, after belting six sixes, started a slide in which five wickets went down for 19. Williamson held things together, but his side's fate was sealed when he skewed the first ball of the final over to deep square. Mohammad Amir made a low-key return to international cricket, claiming the wicket of Henry with his last delivery, after having two catches dropped. Earlier, Mohammad Hafeez had anchored Pakistan's innings, which received late impetus from the middle order – especially Shahid Afridi, who went on to strike twice in his final over, a double-wicket maiden.

Man of the Match: Shahid Afridi.

Pakistan

		B	4/6
1 Mohammad Hafeez *c 8 b 10*	61	47	8/2
2 Ahmed Shehzad *c 5 b 10*	16	14	2/1
3 Sohaib Maqsood *c 6 b 7*	0	2	0
4 Shoaib Malik *c 5 b 7*	20	18	1/1
5 Umar Akmal *c 3 b 10*	24	14	1/1
6 *Shahid Afridi *c 2 b 11*	23	8	2/2
7 Imad Wasim *c 11 b 9*	18	9	1/1
8 †Sarfraz Ahmed *c 2 b 10*	2	3	0
9 Wahab Riaz *not out*	2	4	0
10 Umar Gul *not out*	1	1	0
B 1, w 3	4		
6 overs: 52-1 (20 overs)	171-8		

1/33 2/52 3/78 4/110 5/146 6/147 7/167 8/168

11 Mohammad Amir did not bat.

Henry 4–14–31–1; Boult 4–8–42–1; Milne 4–8–37–4; Anderson 1–2–18–0; Santner 4–11–14–2; Astle 3–4–28–0.

New Zealand

		B	4/6
1 M. J. Guptill *run out*	2	3	0
2 *K. S. Williamson *c 1 b 9*	70	60	6/1
3 C. Munro *b 9*	56	27	2/6
4 C. J. Anderson *c and b 7*	0	2	0
5 G. D. Elliott *b 6*	3	5	0
6 †L. Ronchi *c 2 b 6*	0	4	0
7 M. J. Santner *c 6 b 10*	0	4	0
8 T. D. Astle *b 10*	1	5	0
9 M. J. Henry *c 6 b 11*	10	5	2
10 A. F. Milne *not out*	2	2	0
11 T. A. Boult *c 6 b 9*	0	3	0
B 1, lb 7, w 3	11		
6 overs: 48-1 (20 overs)	155		

1/9 2/89 3/90 4/107 5/107 6/108 7/138 8/152 9/152

Mohammad Amir 4–10–31–1; Imad Wasim 4–11–18–1; Umar Gul 4–10–38–2; Shahid Afridi 4–11–26–2; Wahab Riaz 4–10–34–3.

Umpires: P. D. Jones and D. J. Walker. Third umpire: B. F. Bowden.
Referee: D. C. Boon.

NEW ZEALAND v PAKISTAN

Second Twenty20 International

At Hamilton, January 17, 2016 (floodlit). New Zealand won by ten wickets. Toss: Pakistan.

New Zealand squared the series in emphatic style, as Guptill and Williamson put on an unbroken 171, the highest partnership in Twenty20 internationals. It meant Pakistan's handy total – which had owed much to Umar Akmal's 22-ball half-century – was knocked off without loss. The previous record of 170 was set by South Africa's openers Graeme Smith and Loots Bosman against England at Centurion in November 2009. Williamson bewitched the bowlers by targeting, or feinting to target, the shorter 52-metre city-side boundary; he used the full dimensions of the crease as a market gardener might cultivate a small plot. Pakistan's bowlers could not settle on a line or length, and Mohammad Amir was scooped over short fine leg for one of Williamson's 11 fours. Guptill, who hit four sixes, drove through the line and pulled well, as New Zealand completed only the 12th ten-wicket victory in Twenty20 internationals. McClenaghan had earlier kept Pakistan quiet, conceding just eight runs from his first three overs.

Man of the Match: M. J. Guptill.

Pakistan

		B	4/6
1 Mohammad Hafeez *c 9 b 8*	19	23	2/1
2 Ahmed Shehzad *c 2 b 4*	9	8	1
3 Sohaib Maqsood *c 8 b 6*	18	23	1/1
4 Shoaib Malik *b 11*	39	30	5
5 Umar Akmal *not out*	56	27	4/4
6 *Shahid Afridi *c 2 b 10*	7	3	0/1
7 Imad Wasim *c 10 b 11*	8	4	0/1
8 †Sarfraz Ahmed *run out*	1	2	0
9 Wahab Riaz *not out*	0	0	0
B 1, lb 3, w 7	11		
6 overs: 34-1 (20 overs)	168-7		

1/29 2/34 3/67 4/130 5/137 6/161 7/163

10 Umar Gul and 11 Mohammad Amir did not bat.

Santner 3–9–29–1; Anderson 4–12–26–1; Milne 4–8–37–1; McClenaghan 4–13–23–2; Astle 1–1–13–0; Elliott 4–4–36–1.

New Zealand

		B	4/6
1 M. J. Guptill *not out*	87	58	9/4
2 *K. S. Williamson *not out*	72	48	11
Lb 6, w 6	12		
6 overs: 59-0 (17.4 overs)	171-0		

3 C. Munro, 4 C. J. Anderson, 5 L. R. P. L. Taylor, 6 G. D. Elliott, 7 †L. Ronchi, 8 M. J. Santner, 9 T. D. Astle, 10 A. F. Milne and 11 M. J. McClenaghan did not bat.

Umar Gul 2–5–18–0; Mohammad Amir 3–6–34–0; Imad Wasim 4–6–32–0; Shahid Afridi 4–9–38–0; Wahab Riaz 3–5–30–0; Shoaib Malik 1.4–4–13–0.

Umpires: B. F. Bowden and D. J. Walker. Third umpire: W. R. Knights.
Referee: D. C. Boon.

NEW ZEALAND v PAKISTAN

Third Twenty20 International

At Wellington (Westpac Stadium), January 22, 2016 (floodlit). New Zealand won by 95 runs. Toss: Pakistan.

One shellacking followed another, as Pakistan suffered their worst defeat by runs in Twenty20 internationals, sunk by the loss of three wickets in the first 15 balls, then three apiece for Milne and the canny Elliott. New Zealand had got to within a boundary of 200, led by Anderson, who took charge when Taylor retired with a side strain. After zooming to his highest score in the format, Anderson opened the bowling and took two early wickets, although Boult had started the rot with his first ball. Pakistan were out of it at 55 for five in the ninth over, with only Sarfraz Ahmed able to make much headway as New Zealand clinched the series.

Man of the Match: C. J. Anderson.

New Zealand

		B	4/6
1 M. J. Guptill *c 6 b 7*	42	19	6/2
2 *K. S. Williamson *c 4 b 10*	33	34	3/1
3 C. Munro *run out*	4	3	0
4 C. J. Anderson *not out*	82	42	6/4
5 L. R. P. L. Taylor *retired hurt*	6	4	1
6 G. D. Elliott *run out*	19	14	1/1
7 †L. Ronchi *c 6 b 10*	1	2	0
8 M. J. Santner *not out*	2	3	0
Lb 2, w 4, nb 1	7		
6 overs: 57-1 (20 overs)	196-5		

1/57 2/62 3/94 4/174 5/175

9 A. F. Milne, 10 M. J. McClenaghan and 11 T. A. Boult did not bat.

Taylor retired hurt at 110-3.

12th man: P. F. Younghusband; 13th man: M. J. Henry.

Pakistan

		B	4/6
1 Mohammad Hafeez *c 8 b 11*	2	4	0
2 Ahmed Shehzad *c 11 b 4*	8	6	1
3 Mohammad Rizwan *run out*	4	4	1
4 Shoaib Malik *c 10 b 4*	14	6	3
5 †Sarfraz Ahmed *c 9 b 6*	41	36	5
6 Umar Akmal *c 12 b 9*	5	13	0
7 *Shahid Afridi *c 13 b 6*	8	8	0/1
8 Imad Wasim *c 1 b 6*	0	1	0
9 Anwar Ali *c 7 b 9*	8	7	1
10 Wahab Riaz *c 7 b 9*	4	5	0
11 Mohammad Amir *not out*	1	7	0
Lb 2, w 4	6		
6 overs: 42-4 (16.1 overs)	101		

1/7 2/14 3/15 4/36 5/55 6/75 7/76 8/92 9/98

Anwar Ali 3–5–31–0; Mohammad Amir 4–7–35–0; Imad Wasim 4–3–42–0; Wahab Riaz 4–8–43–2; Shahid Afridi 4–10–27–1; Shoaib Malik 1–1–16–0.

Anderson 3–9–17–2; Boult 3–6–32–1; Milne 3.1–15–8–3; Santner 1–2–7–0; McClenaghan 3–8–15–0; Elliott 2–6–7–3; Munro 1–0–13–0.

Umpires: B. F. Bowden and D. J. Walker. Third umpire: W. R. Knights.
Referee: D. C. Boon.

NEW ZEALAND v PAKISTAN

First One-Day International

At Wellington (Basin Reserve), January 25, 2016. New Zealand won by 70 runs. Toss: Pakistan.

A New Zealand victory looked unlikely when they dipped to 99 for six in the 23rd over in the face of some fine pace bowling – but they were hauled to a respectable total by the 24-year-old Canterbury left-hander Henry Nicholls, who made his first international half-century in his sixth match, following the injury to Ross Taylor. Dropped by Mohammad Hafeez at slip off Anwar Ali when 15, Nicholls put on 79 with Santner, before Henry – who clouted four sixes – supervised a ninth-wicket stand of 73 which ended only when McClenaghan was struck a sickening blow by Anwar. He missed a pull, and the ball crashed through his helmet grille to fracture his left eye socket. Anwar claimed three wickets, as did Mohammad Amir, who was forced to leave the field not long after stopping a Santner drive with his left shin. Pakistan motored to 111 for two at halfway, against an attack lacking McClenaghan, but shortly afterwards Williamson flummoxed Hafeez, and the middle order found Boult and Elliott hard to get away. Sarfraz Ahmed briefly threatened a recovery, but the last three wickets could add only five runs. This was the first one-day international at Wellington's Basin Reserve for almost 11 years; recent matches had been played at the nearby Westpac Stadium.

Man of the Match: H. M. Nicholls.

New Zealand

M. J. Guptill c Wahab Riaz b Mohammad Irfan	11
T. W. M. Latham c Sarfraz Ahmed b Mohammad Amir	11
*K. S. Williamson b Anwar Ali	10
H. M. Nicholls b Anwar Ali	82
G. D. Elliott b Anwar Ali	0
C. J. Anderson c Sarfraz Ahmed b Mohammad Amir	10
†L. Ronchi c Sarfraz Ahmed b Mohammad Amir	5
M. J. Santner c Sarfraz Ahmed b Mohammad Irfan	48
M. J. Henry not out	48
M. J. McClenaghan retired hurt	31
T. A. Boult not out	4
B 4, lb 3, w 13	20
1/23 (1) 2/25 (2) 3/70 (3) 4/70 (5) 5/93 (6) 6/99 (7) 7/178 (8) 8/203 (4) — (8 wkts, 50 overs)	280
10 overs: 45-2	

McClenaghan retired hurt at 276-8.

Mohammad Irfan 10–0–43–2; Mohammad Amir 8.1–0–28–3; Anwar Ali 9.5–0–66–3; Wahab Riaz 10–0–67–0; Imad Wasim 8–0–47–0; Azhar Ali 4–0–22–0.

Pakistan

*Azhar Ali c Henry b Elliott	19
Ahmed Shehzad c Williamson b Elliott	13
Mohammad Hafeez c Henry b Williamson	42
Babar Azam c Nicholls b Anderson	62
Sohaib Maqsood c sub (A. F. Milne) b Elliott	10
†Sarfraz Ahmed c Anderson b Boult	30
Imad Wasim c Ronchi b Santner	1
Anwar Ali c Latham b Boult	16
Wahab Riaz not out	5
Mohammad Amir b Boult	0
Mohammad Irfan b Boult	0
Lb 2, w 10	12
1/33 (1) 2/37 (2) 3/118 (3) 4/142 (5) 5/168 (4) 6/170 (7) 7/205 (6) 8/206 (8) 9/210 (10) 10/210 (11) — (46 overs)	210
10 overs: 33-1	

Henry 8–0–43–0; Boult 9–1–40–4; Elliott 10–1–43–3; Anderson 9–1–35–1; Santner 8–0–36–1; Williamson 2–0–11–1.

Umpires: N. J. Llong and D. J. Walker. Third umpire: B. N. J. Oxenford.
Referee: D. C. Boon.

NEW ZEALAND v PAKISTAN

Second One-Day International

At Napier, January 28, 2016 (day/night). Abandoned.

Locals suggest that, if you want to break a drought in Hawke's Bay, you schedule a cricket match – and it worked. The umpires made five inspections of the saturated ground, before finally calling the game off at 6.22.

NEW ZEALAND v PAKISTAN

Third One-Day International

At Auckland, January 31, 2016. New Zealand won by three wickets (DLS). Toss: Pakistan.

New Zealand took the series, but it was a close-run thing. A shower interrupted their chase for an hour in the 36th over, with the score 210 for five, and when play resumed the revised target demanded another 53 from 45 balls. Six were still needed from the final over and, although Santner immediately drove Wahab Riaz for four, the tension was ratcheted up by two dot balls, before he finally threaded a pull through midwicket. Earlier Guptill and Williamson – both eventually defeated by Azhar Ali's rusty leg-spin – had put on 159 for the second wicket, beating the New Zealand record of 157 by Guptill and Brendon McCullum against Zimbabwe at Harare in October 2011. Here McCullum, returning after resting his back, was out first ball. Pakistan's total had also featured one big partnership, Mohammad Hafeez and Babar Azam (with a career-best 83) adding 134 for the third wicket. But the lively Milne mopped up three wickets in seven balls, while nine catches were taken in all, four by Guptill, which equalled the national record for a fielder.

Man of the Match: M. J. Guptill.

Pakistan

*Azhar Ali c Guptill b Henry	3
Ahmed Shehzad c Guptill b Boult	12
Mohammad Hafeez c Milne b Santner	76
Babar Azam c Guptill b Henry	83
Shoaib Malik c Ronchi b Boult	32
†Sarfraz Ahmed c Ronchi b Milne	41
Mohammad Rizwan run out	16
Wahab Riaz c Guptill b Anderson	11
Mohammad Amir c Ronchi b Milne	1
Rahat Ali c Ronchi b Milne	0
Mohammad Irfan not out	0
W 14, nb 1	15
(47.3 overs)	290

1/16 (2) 2/20 (1) 3/154 (3) 4/215 (5) 5/227 (4) 6/256 (7) 7/279 (8) 8/284 (9) 9/284 (10) 10/290 (6) 10 overs: 53-2

Boult 9–0–60–2; Henry 10–0–44–2; Anderson 4–0–26–1; Santner 5–0–56–1; Milne 9.3–0–49–3; Elliott 10–0–55–0.

New Zealand

M. J. Guptill c Mohammad Hafeez b Azhar Ali	82
*B. B. McCullum c Mohammad Irfan b Mohammad Amir	0
K. S. Williamson st Sarfraz Ahmed b Azhar Ali	84
H. M. Nicholls lbw b Mohammad Amir	5
G. D. Elliott c Babar Azam b Shoaib Malik	10
C. J. Anderson c Babar Azam b Mohammad Irfan	35
†L. Ronchi b Wahab Riaz	20
M. J. Santner not out	10
A. F. Milne not out	0
Lb 5, w 14	19
(7 wkts, 42.4 overs)	265

1/6 (2) 2/165 (1) 3/180 (3) 4/188 (4) 5/210 (5) 6/253 (7) 7/256 (6) 10 overs: 52-1

M. J. Henry and T. A. Boult did not bat.

Mohammad Irfan 8–0–60–1; Mohammad Amir 9–0–39–2; Rahat Ali 7–0–54–0; Wahab Riaz 8.4–0–51–1; Shoaib Malik 3–0–19–1; Azhar Ali 7–0–37–2.

Umpires: B. F. Bowden and N. J. Llong. Third umpire: B. N. J. Oxenford.
Referee: D. C. Boon.

NEW ZEALAND v AUSTRALIA IN 2015-16

GEOFF LEMON

One-day internationals (3): New Zealand 2, Australia 1
Test matches (2): New Zealand 0, Australia 2

Over the course of a year, New Zealand mastered the art of anticlimax – against Australia, at least. It started with the 50-over World Cup, where they scythed through everyone before being deflated by their rivals in the final. Then, in October 2015, they arrived in Australia for three Tests against a side hollowed out by retirements, and lost 2–0.

In February 2016, many believed the reciprocal tour would go New Zealand's way. They had home advantage, and could serve up green pitches of the kind that had exposed Australia in England. And Brendon McCullum's imminent retirement from international cricket at the end of the series seemed to load the contest with an emotional charge. It became a farewell tour: his last one-day international, his 100th Test, and his last Test, in his home city of Christchurch, where he signed off with one final blast.

Initially results went to plan, as New Zealand won the one-day Chappell–Hadlee Trophy, contested for the first time over a full series since 2009-10. That raised expectations of a Test challenge, only for Australia to take both matches at a canter. The supposed green mamba became a brown snakeskin purse: at Wellington and Christchurch, grass cover soon gave way to slower surfaces, on which Australia – who won both tosses, so avoiding the pitches at their liveliest – swelled their batting averages, and lowered their bowling. In a short series affording no margin for error, the New Zealanders took longer to adapt.

Still, the hosts will remember the series fondly for one reason. On the first day of the Second Test, McCullum walked to the wicket through a guard of honour, and walked off with the fastest Test century, a 54-ball convulsion that surpassed by two deliveries the previous record, held jointly by Viv Richards and Misbah-ul-Haq. In his best tradition, McCullum's innings was audacious, outrageous, and largely instinctive; like many an enterprise in its final days,

MOST SIXES IN INTERNATIONAL CRICKET

Sixes		*Tests*	*ODIs*	*T20Is*
476	**Shahid Afridi (P/World/Asia)**	**52**	**351**	**73**
434	**C. H. Gayle (WI/World)**	**98**	**238**	**98**
398	**B. B. McCullum (NZ)**	**107**	**200**	**91**
352	S. T. Jayasuriya (SL/Asia)	59	270	23
302	**M. S. Dhoni (I/Asia)**	**78**	**192**	**32**
292	**A. B. de Villiers (SA/Africa)**	**57**	**187**	**48**
264	S. R. Tendulkar (I)	69	195	0
262	A. C. Gilchrist (A/World)	100	149	13
254	J. H. Kallis (SA/World/Africa)	97	137	20

To December 31, 2016.

his philosophy was "everything must go". And so it went, in one of those displays that, decades hence, will have people reminiscing about where they were when they watched it. The fact that McCullum suffered his first home Test defeats as captain seemed incidental.

The series was notable for Australians as well. It was Steve Smith's first tour in charge, and success was a small step towards recovery from an Ashes-induced crisis of confidence. With one eye on tours of Sri Lanka and India, he was keen to gain assurance away from home. Recent inclusions, such as Joe Burns, Usman Khawaja and 36-year-old Adam Voges – who ended up averaging 161 over the course of the 2015-16 Test season – felt more settled, while Jackson Bird eventually justified his reintroduction to Test cricket. And, if all-rounder Mitchell Marsh's credentials at No. 6 remained unproven, his fast bowling took stride after stride.

The clean sweep also lifted Australia back to the top of the Test rankings, matching their position in one-day internationals. This double had been Cricket Australia's long-stated aim; based as it was over four years of results, it was vindication of more than just the present line-up. But, while Australia left satisfied, New Zealand faced a long wait before their next chance at neighbourhood success.

AUSTRALIAN TOURING PARTY

*S. P. D. Smith (T/50), G. J. Bailey (50), J. M. Bird (T), S. M. Boland (50), J. A. Burns (T), J. P. Faulkner (50), J. W. Hastings (50), J. R. Hazlewood (T/50), U. T. Khawaja (T/50), N. M. Lyon (T), M. R. Marsh (T/50), S. E. Marsh (T/50), G. J. Maxwell (50), P. M. Nevill (T), J. L. Pattinson (T), K. W. Richardson (50), C. J. Sayers (T), P. M. Siddle (T), M. P. Stoinis (50), A. C. Voges (T), M. S. Wade (50), D. A. Warner (T/50), A. Zampa (50). *Coach:* D. S. Lehmann (T), M. J. Di Venuto (50).

A. J. Finch was originally chosen for the one-day team, but injured his hamstring and was replaced by Khawaja. Faulkner injured his hamstring in the first ODI, and was replaced by Stoinis. Coach Lehmann was late joining the tour, because he had to undergo treatment for deep vein thrombosis.

NEW ZEALAND v AUSTRALIA

First One-Day International

At Auckland, February 3, 2016 (day/night). New Zealand won by 159 runs. Toss: Australia.

Eden Park may be small, but when – from the first ball of the fourth over, bowled by Richardson – Guptill hit his patented golf shot on to the stadium roof beyond long-on, spectators sensed it would be New Zealand's day. McCullum had already laced 20 off the previous over from Hazlewood, and the opening pair had 79 by the time he fell in the 11th, having become the third New Zealander – after Nathan Astle and Stephen Fleming – to pass 6,000 one-day international runs. Guptill went on to 90, his best score against Australia, from only 76 balls; Nicholls covered Williamson's eight-ball duck with a stylish 61; and, though the scoring slowed after Guptill was run out by Maxwell's direct hit from cover, Santner's calm intervention took the total past 300. It was more than enough, as Australia responded with the shortest completed innings in their one-day history, undercutting by six balls the 152 they faced against England at Edgbaston in 1977. Boult and Henry grabbed three wickets each, Williamson took a screaming catch to send back Maxwell for a duck, and Australia crashed to 41 for six. Wade and Faulkner put on 79, but in 24.2 overs it was done; Santner took wickets with both balls he bowled. During the World Cup a year earlier, Australia had been shot out here for 151; this time they couldn't make even that many. The Australians' mood was not improved when it emerged Faulkner would be flying home because of an injured right hamstring.

Man of the Match: M. J. Guptill.

New Zealand

M. J. Guptill run out	90
*B. B. McCullum b Faulkner	44
K. S. Williamson c S. E. Marsh b Hazlewood	0
H. M. Nicholls c Wade b M. R. Marsh	61
G. D. Elliott c Hastings b M. R. Marsh	21
C. J. Anderson c Richardson b Hastings	10
†L. Ronchi b Hazlewood	16
M. J. Santner not out	35
A. F. Milne c and b Faulkner	14
M. J. Henry not out	5
B 1, lb 3, w 7	11
1/79 (2) 2/81 (3) 3/181 (1) 4/205 (5) 5/231 (4) 6/234 (6) 7/263 (7) 8/290 (9) — (8 wkts, 50 overs)	307
10 overs: 71-0	

T. A. Boult did not bat.

Hazlewood 10–1–68–2; Richardson 10–1–64–0; Hastings 10–0–39–1; Faulkner 10–0–67–2; Maxwell 3–0–30–0; M. R. Marsh 7–0–35–2.

Australia

S. E. Marsh c Guptill b Henry	5
D. A. Warner lbw b Boult	12
*S. P. D. Smith b Henry	18
G. J. Bailey c Anderson b Henry	2
G. J. Maxwell c Williamson b Boult	0
M. R. Marsh c McCullum b Boult	0
†M. S. Wade c Nicholls b Anderson	37
J. P. Faulkner b Milne	36
J. W. Hastings c Guptill b Santner	8
K. W. Richardson c Williamson b Santner	19
J. R. Hazlewood not out	0
Lb 2, w 9	11
1/10 (1) 2/33 (3) 3/39 (2) 4/40 (4) 5/40 (5) 6/41 (6) 7/120 (7) 8/121 (8) 9/148 (10) 10/148 (9) — (24.2 overs)	148
10 overs: 47-6	

Boult 7–0–38–3; Henry 6–0–41–3; Milne 6–0–46–1; Anderson 4–1–14–1; Elliott 1–0–7–0; Santner 0.2–0–0–2.

Umpires: I. J. Gould and D. J. Walker. Third umpire: S. Ravi.
Referee: B. C. Broad.

NEW ZEALAND v AUSTRALIA

Second One-Day International

At Wellington (Westpac Stadium), February 6, 2016 (day/night). Australia won by four wickets. Toss: New Zealand. One-day international debut: A. Zampa.

Australia withstood the heat of Wellington's Cake Tin. McCullum's fiery start burned out – he made 28 of the first 35 runs in 4.2 overs – while Guptill failed to rise at the site of his World Cup double-century against West Indies. Williamson provided the first-half drive, then Santner and some late hitting by Milne lifted New Zealand to 281. But old-fashioned pitch-basher Hastings was frugal for the second game running, while Adam Zampa's leg-spin brought control and key wickets on his international debut. The chase featured Khawaja, whose recent form in all cricket had him inked in as opener for Earth in case a match was required against Mars. His effortless start with Warner – 122 from 16.2 overs with a sumptuous range of shots – should have sealed the pursuit. But Australia lost four for 22, and it was 197 for six once Warner had fallen for 98 and Milne reeled in an outrageous one-handed catch at deep midwicket to dispose of Wade, who sank to his knees. On a pitch that hadn't allowed fluency, Mitchell Marsh and Hastings now needed 85 in 17.3 overs. With sensible defence and the occasional biff, they saw off good bowling and harvested singles, until Hastings finished Australia's biggest chase in New Zealand (previously only 248) with two lashed fours. The series was level.

Man of the Match: M. R. Marsh.

New Zealand

M. J. Guptill c Khawaja b Marsh	31	M. J. Henry b Hazlewood	0
*B. B. McCullum b Boland	28	T. A. Boult not out	2
K. S. Williamson c Smith b Zampa	60		
H. M. Nicholls c Wade b Marsh	4	Lb 4, w 4	8
G. D. Elliott c Maxwell b Zampa	32		—
C. J. Anderson c Wade b Hazlewood	16	1/35 (2) 2/88 (1) (9 wkts, 50 overs)	281
†L. Ronchi c Marsh b Boland	19	3/95 (4) 4/158 (3)	
M. J. Santner not out	45	5/164 (5) 6/193 (7) 7/205 (6)	
A. F. Milne c Smith b Hazlewood	36	8/266 (9) 9/266 (10)	10 overs: 57-1

Hazlewood 10–0–61–3; Hastings 10–1–42–0; Boland 10–0–61–2; Zampa 10–0–57–2; Marsh 6–0–30–2; Maxwell 4–0–26–0.

Australia

U. T. Khawaja c and b Santner	50	J. W. Hastings not out	48
D. A. Warner lbw b Santner	98		
*S. P. D. Smith c Ronchi b Henry	2	Lb 2, w 6	8
G. J. Bailey b Henry	0		—
G. J. Maxwell b Boult	6	1/122 (1) 2/133 (3) (6 wkts, 46.3 overs)	283
M. R. Marsh not out	69	3/133 (4) 4/144 (5)	
†M. S. Wade c Milne b Santner	2	5/191 (2) 6/197 (7)	10 overs: 77-0

A. Zampa, J. R. Hazlewood and S. M. Boland did not bat.

Boult 9.3–0–66–1; Henry 10–0–57–2; Williamson 2–0–16–0; Milne 9–0–58–0; Santner 10–0–47–3; Elliott 3–0–20–0; Anderson 3–0–17–0.

Umpires: B. F. Bowden and S. Ravi. Third umpire: I. J. Gould.
Referee: B. C. Broad.

NEW ZEALAND v AUSTRALIA

Third One-Day International

At Hamilton, February 8, 2016 (day/night). New Zealand won by 55 runs. Toss: Australia.

A foot injury ruled out Santner, who had collected 80 unbeaten runs and five cheap wickets in the first two games, but his replacement was leg-spinner Sodhi, and the change did New Zealand no harm. McCullum had begun his farewell one-day international on 197 sixes, and – as if there was any doubt – reached 200 while slashing 47 from 27 balls; only Shahid Afridi, Sanath Jayasuriya and Chris Gayle had beaten him to it. Guptill and Elliott made fifties but, on a tacky, slowing surface, New Zealand's last six fell for 23 in five overs. Australia's seamers shared nine wickets, while Zampa again played an important containing role. Khawaja's serene strokeplay carried them to 75 for one in the 12th over but, when Bracewell had him caught behind, the innings stalled. The tall Sodhi bowled with bounce and turn, conceding seven from his first three overs, then removing Smith and Maxwell in three balls. Henry ended Bailey's resistance to leave Australia 153 for five, before controversially snaring Marsh, who drove a ball into his own boot and was given out, caught and bowled, on referral after the umpires glimpsed a replay on the big screen. What looked a simple chase now fell apart: Australia lost their last six for 38, and Seddon Park was covered in metallic blue confetti as a champion left one form of the game on a high. New Zealand celebrated their first one-day series win over Australia since 2006-07.

Man of the Match: I. S. Sodhi.

New Zealand

M. J. Guptill c Hastings b Zampa	59	M. J. Henry not out	0
*B. B. McCullum c Hastings b Marsh	47	I. S. Sodhi b Hastings	0
K. S. Williamson b Boland	18		
H. M. Nicholls c Smith b Hazlewood	18	Lb 6, w 9	15
G. D. Elliott c Maxwell b Marsh	50		—
C. J. Anderson c Khawaja b Hazlewood	27	1/84 (2) 2/123 (3) (45.3 overs)	246
†L. Ronchi c Boland b Marsh	5	3/131 (1) 4/171 (4) 5/223 (6)	
D. A. J. Bracewell b Hastings	2	6/237 (7) 7/237 (5) 8/246 (9)	
A. F. Milne lbw b Boland	5	9/246 (8) 10/246 (11) 10 overs: 84-1	

Hazlewood 10–0–45–2; Hastings 7.3–0–42–2; Boland 9–0–59–2; Marsh 6–0–34–3; Zampa 10–0–45–1; Maxwell 3–0–15–0.

Australia

U. T. Khawaja c Ronchi b Bracewell	44	J. R. Hazlewood not out	5
D. A. Warner c Elliott b Henry	16	S. M. Boland run out	2
*S. P. D. Smith lbw b Sodhi	21		
G. J. Bailey b Henry	33	Lb 2, w 2	4
G. J. Maxwell c McCullum b Sodhi	0		—
M. R. Marsh c and b Henry	41	1/39 (2) 2/75 (1) (43.4 overs)	191
†M. S. Wade c Guptill b Milne	17	3/94 (3) 4/94 (5) 5/153 (4)	
J. W. Hastings c Elliott b Anderson	6	6/164 (6) 7/179 (8) 8/184 (7)	
A. Zampa c McCullum b Anderson	2	9/184 (9) 10/191 (11) 10 overs: 67-1	

Henry 10–1–60–3; Milne 8.4–0–42–1; Anderson 6–1–16–2; Bracewell 6–0–15–1; Sodhi 8–0–31–2; Elliott 5–0–25–0.

Umpires: I. J. Gould and D. J. Walker. Third umpire: S. Ravi.
Referee: B. C. Broad.

NEW ZEALAND v AUSTRALIA

First Test Match

At Wellington (Basin Reserve), February 12–15, 2016. Australia won by an innings and 52 runs. Toss: Australia. Test debut: H. M. Nicholls.

Locals claim the Basin Reserve is the world's biggest roundabout and, over four days of gentle New Zealand summer, life burbled contentedly around the ground, with crowds circling like the traffic. There wasn't much to cheer on day one. It took Hazlewood less than four overs to tick off both openers with bounce and seam, before having McCullum caught at slip via his pad for a duck in his 100th Test. Either side of McCullum's dismissal, Siddle removed Williamson from an inside edge that was brilliantly caught by Nevill, then Test debutant Nicholls on the drive. Five for 34 in nine overs left New Zealand nowhere to go.

Anderson and Watling made it to lunch, but Watling followed up his sandwich with a peach from Hazlewood, and Bracewell came and went. Anderson's uncharacteristically watchful 38, from 87 balls, was wasted when he thrashed at Lyon, who quickly added Southee. At 137 for nine, Craig and Boult had licence to hit, and their 46 was the best stand of the innings. Siddle's first 11 overs had gone for 21, but Craig struck 16 from the next, while Boult affirmed his status as cricket's most entertaining last man in with three enormous driven sixes off Lyon. A smart boundary catch from Khawaja – stepping over the rope after parrying the ball in the air, then back into play to catch it – denied Boult a fourth.

New Zealand were briefly in the game as Southee sent back Australia's openers with five on the board. But Craig dropped Smith on 18 at second slip off Bracewell, and the third-wicket stand with Khawaja extended to 126. In the day's final over a nervy Voges, on seven, left a Bracewell inswinger, which took out off stump. Australia should have been four down and 37 behind – but umpire Richard Illingworth extended his arm for a no-ball. Replays showed Bracewell's entire heel behind the line, but there was no way to unscramble the omelette.

New Zealand could lament it, but Voges had the class to add 232. He returned on the second day like an old Soviet soldier in Eastern Europe: he shouldn't have been there, but his occupation was undeniable. Never did he look settled, and there was an edginess to his blocking and squeezing. But there was a bloody-mindedness, too, and it would not countenance dismissal.

By contrast, Khawaja's left-handed cover-drives were double cream. He had made an even hundred in fours by the time Boult swung a beauty into his pads; two balls later, Boult procured an acrobatic return catch off Marsh. By stumps Voges had taken his career average above Bradman's 99.94, and passed Sachin Tendulkar's record of 497 runs between dismissals. Never one for attention, Voges later said he was relieved to drop back to a mortal 97.46 after he was finally dislodged for 239, though by then he had extended Tendulkar's old record to 614.

In their previous two Tests at Wellington, New Zealand had recovered from deficits of 135 (to beat Sri Lanka) and 246 (to draw with India). But there would be no third escape. With 379 runs to play with – Australia's highest first-innings lead in New Zealand – Lyon had time to find rhythm. Latham yet again gave away a start, while Nicholls looked in good touch, but played across the line to Bird, the only wicket for the only Australian bowler to have a poor match.

When McCullum was nailed in the final over of the third day, the contest was as good as done. Southee boshed 48 next afternoon to claim the most Test sixes from No. 10 (nipping past Fred Trueman's 16), having already set the record for No. 9 (29, nine more than Michael Holding). Not to be left out, Boult claimed the record for No. 11, moving ahead of Courtney Walsh to 17. But humorous trivialities were all New Zealand could take from the game, their first innings defeat at home since England won here in 1996-97. McCullum's bandwagon had hit a bump.

Man of the Match: A. C. Voges.

Close of play: first day, Australia 147-3 (Khawaja 57, Voges 7); second day, Australia 463-6 (Voges 176, Siddle 29); third day, New Zealand 178-4 (Nicholls 31).

New Zealand

M. J. Guptill c Smith b Hazlewood	18	– (2) c Marsh b Lyon	45
T. W. M. Latham c Nevill b Hazlewood	6	– (1) c Khawaja b Lyon	63
K. S. Williamson c Nevill b Siddle	16	– c Nevill b Hazlewood	22
H. M. Nicholls c Nevill b Siddle	8	– b Bird	59
*B. B. McCullum c Warner b Hazlewood	0	– lbw b Marsh	10
C. J. Anderson c Khawaja b Lyon	38	– lbw b Marsh	0
†B-J. Watling c Nevill b Hazlewood	17	– b Lyon	10
D. A. J. Bracewell c Voges b Siddle	5	– lbw b Hazlewood	14
M. D. Craig not out	41	– not out	33
T. G. Southee c Hazlewood b Lyon	0	– c Khawaja b Lyon	48
T. A. Boult c Khawaja b Lyon	24	– b Marsh	12
B 4, lb 1, nb 5	10	B 2, lb 5, nb 4	11
1/17 (2) 2/38 (1) 3/44 (3) 4/47 (5) 5/51 (4) 6/88 (7) 7/97 (8) 8/137 (6) 9/137 (10) 10/183 (11) (48 overs)	183	1/81 (2) 2/121 (3) 3/157 (1) 4/178 (5) 5/185 (6) 6/214 (7) 7/218 (4) 8/242 (8) 9/301 (10) 10/327 (11) (104.3 overs)	327

Hazlewood 14–2–42–4; Bird 10–1–52–0; Siddle 12–5–37–3; Marsh 6–1–15–0; Lyon 6–0–32–3. *Second innings*—Hazlewood 29–7–75–2; Bird 19–4–51–1; Siddle 8–0–30–0; Marsh 17.3–2–73–3; Lyon 31–10–91–4.

Australia

J. A. Burns c Watling b Southee	0	N. M. Lyon c and b Anderson	3
D. A. Warner c Watling b Southee	5	J. M. Bird not out	3
U. T. Khawaja lbw b Boult	140		
*S. P. D. Smith c and b Craig	71	B 4, lb 3, w 2, nb 3	12
A. C. Voges c and b Craig	239		
M. R. Marsh c and b Boult	0	1/0 (1) 2/5 (2) (154.2 overs)	562
†P. M. Nevill c Watling b Anderson	32	3/131 (4) 4/299 (3)	
P. M. Siddle c Anderson b Bracewell	49	5/299 (6) 6/395 (7) 7/494 (8)	
J. R. Hazlewood c Southee b Bracewell	8	8/508 (9) 9/532 (10) 10/562 (5)	

Southee 31–5–87–2; Boult 33–6–101–2; Bracewell 33–4–127–2; Anderson 18–0–79–2; Craig 35.2–2–153–2; Williamson 4–0–8–0.

Umpires: R. K. Illingworth and R. A. Kettleborough. Third umpire: R. E. J. Martinesz. Referee: B. C. Broad.

NEW ZEALAND v AUSTRALIA

Second Test Match

At Christchurch, February 20–24, 2016. Australia won by seven wickets. Toss: Australia.

Hagley Oval exists as a Test venue only because the 2011 Christchurch earthquake damaged Lancaster Park, but it remains one of the few places in the city where the ravages of the disaster are not evident. Ten minutes' walk from the rubble and construction sites that make up the central business district, cricket fans find themselves in idyllic parkland, carpeted by oak saplings along a quiet creek, then emerge from the trees to find a ground like a saucer in the lushness, circled by green banks and with a tiny pavilion.

This was the setting for Brendon McCullum's last roll of the dice as a New Zealand cricketer. But the dice didn't simply land right: they produced the most remarkable streak of his hard-gambling career. On the list of fastest hundreds, Viv Richards, Misbah-ul-Haq and Adam Gilchrist had occupied the top three spots, all scored from the comfort of the third innings while setting a declaration. McCullum – whose only other Test innings here, against Sri Lanka in December 2014, had brought him 195 off 134 balls – walked out at

---

MOST TESTS IN SUCCESSION FROM DEBUT

		From	*To*
101†	**B. B. McCullum (New Zealand)**	**2003-04**	**2015-16**
98	A. B. de Villiers (South Africa)	2004-05	2014-15
96†	A. C. Gilchrist (Australia)	1999-2000	2007-08
94	R. Dravid (India/World)	1996	2005-06
84	S. R. Tendulkar (India)	1989-90	2001
79†	M. E. K. Hussey (Australia)	2005-06	2012-13
66	Kapil Dev (India)	1978-79	1984-85
64	I. A. Healy (Australia)	1988-89	1994-95
61	R. B. Kanhai (West Indies)	1957	1968-69
58†	J. R. Reid (New Zealand)	1949	1965
58†	A. W. Greig (England)	1972	1977

† *Entire Test career.*

32 for three, on the first morning of a Test, on a lively pitch, against fired-up bowlers… and went faster than them all. New Zealand's eventual defeat felt almost immaterial.

His second delivery he aimed at midwicket – and cleared slip. His fifth, the start of a Marsh over, was lofted straight for six, his 101st in Tests, one clear of Gilchrist's record. McCullum played a limbo-leaning cut for four two balls later, then immediately a cover-drive for four more. His trademark shot involves charging at fast bowlers, making room towards leg, and using that momentum and space to deploy either a diagonal carve over cover, or a flat-batted carve over point; either tends to carry for six. This time it was cover's turn. Marsh's over cost 21.

Williamson fell after lunch, and then came the moment. On 39, McCullum's slice to gully was superbly snared by a diving Marsh. Pattinson, in for the injured Peter Siddle, celebrated, but now it was Australia's turn to be informed of a no-ball – and this time the call was accurate.

McCullum needed no further invitation, pulling the next ball through Hazlewood behind square for four. On ESPNcricinfo, the commentary read: "No, Baz, no, this is not a free hit." His fifty came up outrageously, from 34 balls – a Bird bouncer so short McCullum leapt off the ground to reach it, swatting a forehand over the long-on fence. Hazlewood returned, having bowled ten overs for 11: he was about to bowl four more for 57, with McCullum making 49.

When he had 82 from 48 deliveries, with seven balls to break the record, he hooked at Hazlewood and missed, then ducked out of the way of the next delivery. Now, from successive balls, came a top edge for six, a pull-drive for four, another top edge, this time for four, and the signature shot over cover. The hundred had taken 54 balls, with 16 fours and four sixes. Euphoria was rolling through the Christchurch parkland.

THE BAZ-OOKA

Brendon McCullum reached his century in 54 balls, a Test record:

• 4 // • 1 // 6 • 4 4 6 1 // 2 • 4 • 4 • // 1 • //
• • • • wd • 1 // • 1 // • • • • 4 1 // • 6 [50* in 34 balls]
4 • • 4 // 4 4 • • 2 • // 4 4 2 4 // • • 6 4 4 4 [100* in 54 balls] // • • 4 1 // 1 // 6 1 4 1 // • 1 // 2 4 1 //
• • 2 6 4 • // 4 1 // 1 1 // W [145 in 79 balls]

Anderson played his forgotten part, as the pair put on 179 at a rate of 9.76 an over, the highest in Tests for any stand over 150. Between lunch and tea alone, New Zealand added 199. By then McCullum had departed for 145 from 79 balls, having slashed 21 fours and six sixes in four minutes over two hours. (Only Rodney Redmond before him had scored a century in his final Test for New Zealand, though in Redmond's case – against Pakistan at Auckland in 1972-73 – it was also his debut.) Anderson fell soon after, for 72 from 66, and Watling contributed a 57-ball 58. When New Zealand were dismissed for 370, they had scored so furiously that there was still time for Australia to face 20 overs before stumps, which they negotiated for the loss of Warner.

For the hosts, however, the magic ended there. Wagner would claim a career-best six-for with a sustained bouncer attack, but it took him a day and a half. Burns dug in for his most important century to date – passing Ian Redpath's unbeaten 159 at Auckland in 1973-74 as the highest Test score by an Australian opener in New Zealand – and Smith kept vigil during a third-wicket stand of 289. A stubborn 60 from Voges damaged his average but helped his team. It hardly mattered that Australia's last six fell for 67.

New Zealand began batting again before tea on the third day, 135 behind. From 105 for four, with McCullum making a 27-ball 25 (and adding one final six to his Test tally), Williamson and Anderson saw out 44 overs. Then, in the space of eight deliveries, Bird removed Anderson with the old ball and Williamson, for 97, with the new; Southee

Marty Melville, AFP/Getty Images

Aerial bombardment: Brendon McCullum powers his way to the fastest hundred in Tests.

followed in the same over. Henry smashed a maiden Test fifty, but Bird eventually claimed him and Boult to complete his first Test five-for.

Australia chased 201 with ease on the final day, finishing the series with the top four run-scorers and top three wicket-takers. But there remained little need for New Zealand memories to extend past day one.

Man of the Match: J. A. Burns.

Close of play: first day, Australia 57-1 (Burns 27, Khawaja 18); second day, Australia 363-4 (Voges 2, Lyon 4); third day, New Zealand 121-4 (Williamson 45, Anderson 9); fourth day, Australia 70-1 (Burns 27, Khawaja 19).

New Zealand

M. J. Guptill c Burns b Pattinson	18	– (2) c Nevill b Pattinson	0
T. W. M. Latham c Smith b Bird	4	– (1) c Nevill b Pattinson	39
K. S. Williamson c Smith b Marsh	7	– b Bird	97
H. M. Nicholls lbw b Hazlewood	7	– c Smith b Pattinson	2
*B. B. McCullum c Lyon b Pattinson	145	– c Warner b Hazlewood	25
C. J. Anderson c Voges b Lyon	72	– b Bird	40
†B-J. Watling c Burns b Bird	58	– c Burns b Pattinson	46
T. G. Southee c Hazlewood b Lyon	5	– c Smith b Bird	0
M. J. Henry c Khawaja b Lyon	21	– b Bird	66
N. Wagner c Nevill b Hazlewood	10	– not out	3
T. A. Boult not out	14	– c Pattinson b Bird	0
Lb 2, w 5, nb 2	9	B 2, lb 14, nb 1	17
1/21 (1) 2/23 (2) 3/32 (4) 4/74 (3) 5/253 (5) 6/266 (6) 7/273 (8) 8/297 (9) 9/333 (10) 10/370 (7) (65.4 overs)	370	1/8 (2) 2/66 (1) 3/72 (4) 4/105 (5) 5/207 (6) 6/210 (3) 7/210 (8) 8/328 (7) 9/335 (9) 10/335 (11) (111.1 overs)	335

Hazlewood 18–5–98–2; Pattinson 15–2–81–2; Bird 14.4–4–66–2; Marsh 8–1–62–1; Lyon 10–0–61–3. *Second innings*—Hazlewood 34–11–92–1; Pattinson 26–8–77–4; Bird 17.1–5–59–5; Lyon 17–3–42–0; Marsh 17–4–49–0.

Australia

D. A. Warner c Guptill b Boult	12	– (2) c Watling b Wagner	22
J. A. Burns c Guptill b Wagner	170	– (1) b Boult	65
U. T. Khawaja c McCullum b Boult	24	– c McCullum b Southee	45
*S. P. D. Smith c Guptill b Wagner	138	– not out	53
A. C. Voges c Latham b Wagner	60	– not out	10
N. M. Lyon c McCullum b Williamson	33		
M. R. Marsh c Nicholls b Wagner	18		
†P. M. Nevill c Watling b Wagner	13		
J. L. Pattinson c Boult b Anderson	1		
J. R. Hazlewood c McCullum b Wagner	13		
J. M. Bird not out	4		
B 9, lb 10	19	Lb 4, nb 2	6
1/25 (1) 2/67 (3) 3/356 (2) 4/357 (4) 5/438 (6) 6/464 (5) 7/483 (7) 8/484 (9) 9/496 (8) 10/505 (10) (153.1 overs)	505	1/49 (2) 2/113 (3) 3/179 (1) (3 wkts, 54 overs)	201

Southee 25–4–85–0; Boult 31–5–108–2; Henry 32–8–101–0; Anderson 22–2–66–1; Wagner 32.1–6–106–6; Williamson 7–0–17–1; McCullum 4–2–3–0. *Second innings*—Boult 17–1–60–1; Southee 7–2–30–1; Henry 9–1–33–0; Wagner 18–4–60–1; Anderson 3–0–14–0.

Umpires: R. A. Kettleborough and R. E. J. Martinesz. Third umpire: R. K. Illingworth.
Referee: B. C. Broad.

NEW ZEALAND v PAKISTAN IN 2016-17

ANDREW ALDERSON

Test matches (2): New Zealand 2, Pakistan 0

Three days before the series, an earthquake of magnitude 7.8 struck about 70 miles north of Christchurch, killing two people. Aftershocks forced the abandonment of the Plunket Shield match between Wellington and Central Districts at the Basin Reserve. The Pakistan team were traumatised. "We had just finished watching the India–England match," said Wasim Bari, the team manager. "The doors and windows were going from one side to another as if they were made of paper."

Their three-day practice match at Nelson a few days earlier had also been a washout. Pakistan had not lost any of their previous seven series, going back to August 2014, but their preparation here could hardly have been worse. The troubles continued: after they lost the First Test by a distance, captain Misbah-ul-Haq left the tour because of the death of his father-in-law. He later learned he would not have been able to play at Hamilton anyway: Pakistan's slow over-rate at Christchurch, his 50th Test as captain, had earned him a second warning (after the Oval Test in August) and a one-match ban.

New Zealand had their own uncertainties. They had suffered four consecutive Test losses in South Africa and India, so needed freshening up. Opener Jeet Raval and all-rounder Colin de Grandhomme made their Test debuts, while leg-spinner Todd Astle reappeared after a four-year hiatus (if only as cover for Mitchell Santner, who returned for the Second Test).

Born in Zimbabwe, the 30-year-old de Grandhomme – who moved to New Zealand in 2006 – was a surprise selection in the squad, let alone the playing XI; many had assumed he was merely back-up for Jimmy Neesham. But he was in form. He had made 144 not out to help Auckland beat Otago in October and, when he was selected, averaged 54 for the domestic first-class season. He had also enjoyed bowling success in 2015-16, when his disciplined medium-pace earned him 17 wickets at 25, and the nickname "De Groundhog". Raval, meanwhile, seemed the logical answer at the top of the order. Martin Guptill had struggled in India in October, and Raval had been quietly making his case in first-class cricket, averaging over 40 in seven of the previous eight seasons.

Contrasting wins, dictated by the first session at Christchurch and the last session at Hamilton, secured New Zealand's first series victory over Pakistan in 31 years. At Christchurch, winning the toss enabled their seamers to exploit a grassy wicket that had spent the first day sweating under the covers. Play eventually began on the second morning; by tea, Pakistan were all out. At Hamilton, all three results were available come the last evening, but a draw seemed most likely. Then, in a thrilling denouement, Pakistan collapsed with 8.5 overs remaining as New Zealand – and the light – closed in.

PAKISTAN TOURING PARTY

*Misbah-ul-Haq, Asad Shafiq, Azhar Ali, Babar Azam, Imran Khan, Mohammad Amir, Mohammad Nawaz, Mohammad Rizwan, Rahat Ali, Sami Aslam, Sarfraz Ahmed, Sharjeel Khan, Sohail Khan, Wahab Riaz, Yasir Shah, Younis Khan. *Coach:* J. M. Arthur.

At Nelson, November 11–13, 2016. **New Zealand A v Pakistanis. Abandoned.**

NEW ZEALAND v PAKISTAN

First Test Match

At Christchurch, November 17–20, 2016. New Zealand won by eight wickets. Toss: New Zealand. Test debut: C. de Grandhomme, J. A. Raval.

Colin de Grandhomme had to wait for his debut to begin, when the first day was washed out. Even so, it did not take him long to make an impression. Sporting a Movember moustache that would make Tom Selleck blanch, he was brought on in the ninth over, and with his 15th ball uprooted Azhar Ali's off stump. His swing and seam benefited from a thatch of grass as thick as his upper lip, and the batsmen had few answers. Pakistan were dismissed for 133 by tea; de Grandhomme finished with six for 41, the best figures by a New Zealander on debut, eclipsing Alex Moir's six for 155 against England at Christchurch in 1950-51.

Jeet Raval, the other debutant, got in on the act, snaffling three catches in the cordon; in the second innings he added a fourth, at deep midwicket, a record for a New Zealand fielder in his maiden Test. He also anchored the reply, reaching the second-day close on a disciplined 55, to take control of the match. The pitch remained lively, so he left where possible, scoring just one single between cover and point.

Raval failed to add to his score next morning, when New Zealand went from 104 for three to 200 all out before lunch. But Pakistan's batsmen failed again, dribbling to 80 for three after 50 overs, and were bundled out for 171 on the fourth morning. Wagner passed 100 wickets in his 26th Test, one more than the quickest New Zealander to the mark, Richard Hadlee. Respite came from Sohail Khan, who top-scored with 40 from No. 9, but the odds were stacked against a full recovery: he had taken guard after Pakistan had collapsed from 93 for three to 105 for seven.

New Zealand coach Mike Hesson said it was the best collective bowling performance he could remember, but Azhar added a caveat: "Maybe this was the most seam-friendly pitch I've played on in my international career," he said. Leg-spinner Yasir Shah, the world's No. 1 bowler as recently as July, failed to strike in either innings, the first blank of his 20-Test career. His counterpart Todd Astle, meanwhile, bowled just four overs on his return to Test cricket.

Raval and Williamson eased the hosts towards victory with an 85-run partnership, and de Grandhomme became the fourth New Zealander to pick up the match award on debut, after Stephen Fleming, Mathew Sinclair and Mark Craig. Hesson could be forgiven for breaking out the port and clipping cigars with fellow selector Gavin Larsen. "Colin's been a talented player for a long time," he said. "But we've been waiting for something to click, to show he's worked out how to play at first-class level." De Grandhomme, usually taciturn, offered a pearl that might have resonated with cricketers from any level. "You think you're going to quit," he said. "Then you find something to make you come back and want it more."

Close of play: first day, no play; second day, New Zealand 104-3 (Raval 55, Nicholls 29); third day, Pakistan 129-7 (Asad Shafiq 6, Sohail Khan 22).

Pakistan

Sami Aslam c Raval b Southee	19	– c Watling b de Grandhomme	7
Azhar Ali b de Grandhomme	15	– b Boult	31
Babar Azam c Taylor b de Grandhomme	7	– c Watling b Wagner	29
Younis Khan c Raval b de Grandhomme	2	– c Watling b Wagner	1
*Misbah-ul-Haq c Williamson b Boult	31	– c Boult b Southee	13
Asad Shafiq c Raval b de Grandhomme	16	– c Raval b Wagner	17
†Sarfraz Ahmed c Astle b Southee	7	– b Boult	2
Mohammad Amir b Boult	3	– c Astle b Boult	6
Sohail Khan c Latham b de Grandhomme	9	– c de Grandhomme b Southee	40
Yasir Shah not out	4	– not out	6
Rahat Ali c Watling b de Grandhomme	0	– c Latham b Southee	2
B 8, lb 12	20	B 5, lb 7, w 5	17
1/31 (2) 2/53 (1) 3/53 (3) 4/56 (4) 5/88 (6) 6/101 (7) 7/114 (8) 8/129 (9) 9/129 (5) 10/133 (11) (55.5 overs)	133	1/21 (1) 2/58 (3) 3/64 (4) 4/93 (5) 5/93 (2) 6/95 (7) 7/105 (8) 8/158 (9) 9/166 (6) 10/171 (11) (78.4 overs)	171

Southee 19–11–20–2; Boult 16–5–39–2; de Grandhomme 15.5–5–41–6; Wagner 5–0–13–0. *Second innings*—Boult 17–5–37–3; Southee 23.4–10–53–3; de Grandhomme 14–4–23–1; Wagner 20–6–34–3; Astle 4–0–12–0.

New Zealand

T. W. M. Latham lbw b Mohammad Amir	1	– c Asad Shafiq b Mohammad Amir	9
J. A. Raval c Sami Aslam b Mohammad Amir	55	– not out	36
*K. S. Williamson c Sami Aslam b Sohail Khan	4	– c Sami Aslam b Azhar Ali	61
L. R. P. L. Taylor c Sarfraz Ahmed b Rahat Ali	11		
H. M. Nicholls lbw b Sohail Khan	30	– (4) not out	0
C. de Grandhomme c Rahat Ali b Sohail Khan	29		
†B-J. Watling c Younis Khan b Rahat Ali	18		
T. D. Astle c Asad Shafiq b Rahat Ali	0		
T. G. Southee c Sarfraz Ahmed b Mohammad Amir	22		
N. Wagner c Asad Shafiq b Rahat Ali	21		
T. A. Boult not out	3		
Lb 1, w 1, nb 4	6	Nb 2	2
1/6 (1) 2/15 (3) 3/40 (4) 4/105 (5) 5/109 (2) 6/146 (6) 7/146 (8) 8/171 (7) 9/177 (9) 10/200 (10) (59.5 overs)	200	1/19 (1) 2/104 (3) (2 wkts, 31.3 overs)	108

Mohammad Amir 18–4–43–3; Sohail Khan 22–5–78–3; Rahat Ali 15.5–2–62–4; Yasir Shah 4–0–16–0. *Second innings*—Mohammad Amir 7–2–12–1; Sohail Khan 6–1–21–0; Rahat Ali 6–0–24–0; Yasir Shah 9.3–1–45–0; Azhar Ali 3–1–6–1.

Umpires: I. J. Gould and S. Ravi. Third umpire: S. D. Fry.
Referee: R. B. Richardson.

NEW ZEALAND v PAKISTAN

Second Test Match

At Hamilton, November 25–29, 2016. New Zealand won by 138 runs. Toss: Pakistan. Test debut: Mohammad Rizwan.

The wicket was verdant enough for Pakistan to drop Yasir Shah in favour of seamer Imran Khan. And, after they inserted New Zealand, Mohammad Amir's menacing movement vindicated the decision. Sami Aslam dropped Raval at first slip from the game's third ball, then clung on to remove Latham from the sixth. Yet, after rain shortened the first day to 21 overs, New Zealand scrapped to 271 all out by the second evening. Raval survived an action-replay drop on 40 – Aslam, off Amir – to reach the second 55 of his career, and Watling helped add 152 for the last five wickets.

Pakistan then slumped to 51 for five before the close, as New Zealand's seam attack got stuck in. With Trent Boult rested to nurse a knee niggle, Southee was the senior bowler, and took the first three, finishing with six for 80 on the third day. Babar Azam provided resistance: he hit a personal-best 90 not out, and cobbled together half-century stands with Sarfraz Ahmed, then Sohail Khan, to help Pakistan battle past 200.

> Then Sarfraz was run out by a missile

Latham stretched the lead with 80, but there was work to do when Taylor came out to bat at 107 for two. He almost missed this Test because of a growth on his left eye, for which he was scheduled to have surgery. But after a terrible run of form – he had averaged less than 15 in India – he passed 50, for the first time in 12 Test innings. And he marched on to his 16th Test century, leaving him one short of his late mentor Martin Crowe's national record. Two balls after the celebrations, Williamson called his men in, setting Pakistan 369 in a day and three overs.

Punditry on talkback radio and website forums surmised that caution had got the better of him; the highest fourth-innings chase in New Zealand was 345 by West Indies in 1968-69. But the pitch had not been subjected to the usual attrition – rain had also curtailed the third day – and now Aslam and stand-in captain Azhar Ali put on 131 in 60 overs, Pakistan's longest fourth-innings opening partnership.

Then the dominoes fell. Santner struck first, securing Azhar and Babar Azam either side of tea. Both drove at balls flighted outside off, both chopped on. After that, Pakistan needed 210 at better than one a ball. A draw appeared the logical outcome but, after showing intent by bumping Sarfraz up to No. 4, they lost wickets at a canter. Aslam bunted Southee to mid-off and ended on a Test-best 91, then Sarfraz was run out by a missile from de Grandhomme at fine leg. The chase looked gone; soon, so did the draw. Asad Shafiq fell for his fifth duck in 13 innings, then Southee – armed with the new ball – trapped Younis Khan lbw on review when he failed to offer a shot.

The last time New Zealand had achieved a series victory over Pakistan was February 14, 1985, at Dunedin, where Jeremy Coney and last man Ewen Chatfield hauled in 278. That afternoon, an Invercargill-bound train stopped for ten minutes, unscheduled, to watch history unfold across the tracks. This time, it was Hamilton, where – under an absconding sun – the crowd were huddling in blankets to ward off the chill of a westerly wind. As the gloom gathered and time grew short, Wagner ended the match with three for none in six balls, the last of them from an instinctive short-leg catch by Latham to remove Imran Khan.

Pakistan had lost nine wickets for 71 after tea, the worst last-session collapse in history. Azhar, who followed Misbah-ul-Haq in being fined for a slow over-rate, offered his excuses. "It's always difficult to make 350-plus in a day," he said. "But once you're 1–0 down, you want to make a result of it."

Close of play: first day, New Zealand 77-2 (Raval 35, Taylor 29); second day, Pakistan 76-5 (Babar Azam 34, Sarfraz Ahmed 9); third day, New Zealand 0-0 (Raval 0, Latham 0); fourth day, Pakistan 1-0 (Sami Aslam 1, Azhar Ali 0).

New Zealand

J. A. Raval c Mohammad Rizwan b Imran Khan	55 – lbw b Mohammad Amir	2
T. W. M. Latham c Sami Aslam b Mohammad Amir	0 – c Sarfraz Ahmed b Wahab Riaz	80
*K. S. Williamson c Sarfraz Ahmed b Sohail Khan	13 – c Sarfraz Ahmed b Imran Khan	42
L. R. P. L. Taylor c Sarfraz Ahmed b Sohail Khan	37 – not out	102
H. M. Nicholls c Sarfraz Ahmed b Wahab Riaz	13 – c Sarfraz Ahmed b Imran Khan	26
C. de Grandhomme c Sarfraz Ahmed b Imran Khan	37 – c Azhar Ali b Imran Khan	32
†B-J. Watling not out	49 – not out	15
M. J. Santner c Younis Khan b Sohail Khan	16	
T. G. Southee b Sohail Khan	29	
M. J. Henry c Sohail Khan b Mohammad Amir	15	
N. Wagner c Younis Khan b Imran Khan	1	
W 5, nb 1	6	Lb 6, w 6, nb 2 14

1/5 (2) 2/39 (3) 3/90 (4) (83.4 overs) 271
4/113 (1) 5/119 (5) 6/170 (6)
7/203 (8) 8/239 (9) 9/270 (10) 10/271 (11)

1/11 (1) (5 wkts dec, 85.3 overs) 313
2/107 (3) 3/159 (2)
4/219 (5) 5/254 (6)

Mohammad Amir 19–2–59–2; Sohail Khan 25–6–99–4; Imran Khan 20.4–5–52–3; Wahab Riaz 18–4–57–1; Azhar Ali 1–0–4–0. *Second innings*—Mohammad Amir 22–4–86–1; Sohail Khan 17–2–69–0; Imran Khan 20.3–4–76–3; Wahab Riaz 19–3–53–1; Azhar Ali 6–0–19–0; Asad Shafiq 1–0–4–0.

Pakistan

Sami Aslam c Raval b Southee	5 – c Williamson b Southee	91
*Azhar Ali c Watling b Southee	1 – b Santner	58
Babar Azam not out	90 – b Santner	16
Younis Khan c Watling b Southee	2 – (5) lbw b Southee	11
Asad Shafiq b Wagner	23 – (6) c Nicholls b Henry	0
Mohammad Rizwan c Henry b Wagner	0 – (7) not out	13
†Sarfraz Ahmed c Raval b Wagner	41 – (4) run out	19
Sohail Khan c Watling b Southee	37 – c Nicholls b de Grandhomme	8
Wahab Riaz lbw b de Grandhomme	0 – (10) c Watling b Wagner	0
Mohammad Amir c Raval b Southee	5 – (9) c Watling b Wagner	0
Imran Khan c Watling b Southee	6 – c Latham b Wagner	0
B 4, lb 1, nb 1	6	B 4, lb 3, w 6, nb 1 14

1/7 (1) 2/8 (2) 3/12 (4) (67 overs) 216
4/51 (5) 5/51 (6) 6/125 (7)
7/192 (8) 8/193 (9) 9/206 (10) 10/216 (11)

1/131 (2) 2/159 (3) (92.1 overs) 230
3/181 (1) 4/199 (4)
5/204 (6) 6/218 (5) 7/229 (8)
8/230 (9) 9/230 (10) 10/230 (11)

Southee 21–4–80–6; Henry 19–5–30–0; de Grandhomme 9–2–29–1; Wagner 14–2–59–3; Santner 4–0–13–0. *Second innings*—Southee 24–6–60–2; Henry 19–5–38–1; Wagner 20.1–4–57–3; Santner 16–2–49–2; de Grandhomme 12–5–17–1; Williamson 1–0–2–0.

Umpires: S. D. Fry and S. Ravi. Third umpire: I. J. Gould.
Referee: R. B. Richardson.

NEW ZEALAND v BANGLADESH IN 2016-17

ANDREW ALDERSON

One-day internationals (3): New Zealand 3, Bangladesh 0
Twenty20 internationals (3): New Zealand 3, Bangladesh 0
Tests (2): New Zealand 2, Bangladesh 0

Bangladesh were flying high after their maiden Test victory over England in October, while New Zealand had just been trounced in the Chappell–Hadlee Trophy by Australia. Yet whenever Bangladesh seemed set to turn a promising performance into victory, self-belief evaporated. They crumbled in both the second one-day international and the final Twenty20. Then came the First Test at Wellington, which broke Bangladeshi hearts, as well as records: Shakib Al Hasan hit a national-best 217, but their 595 for eight became the highest total to result in defeat.

In mitigation, they were shredded by injuries. The two captains – Mushfiqur Rahim and Mashrafe bin Mortaza – and experienced batsmen Imrul Kayes and Mominul Haque all missed games, and just four Bangladeshis began the Second Test with more than three caps. There were outstanding individual performances: Shakib finished with 170 more runs and nine more wickets than any of his team-mates, and Soumya Sarkar, who had batted no higher than No. 6 in his previous five Test innings, made 86 and 36 as an opener at Christchurch. But they could not swing the results.

New Zealand were not at their best, but their tenacity made up for it, and they ended up winning all eight internationals. Most of the senior players delivered, and fine cameos in the shorter formats came from less-established names, such as Neil Broom and Lockie Ferguson.

The timing of the tour posed a problem for New Zealand Cricket, as it competed for local interest with Australia's burgeoning Big Bash. NZC need a successful national team, to bring in the sponsors and television deals that fund development programmes and competitions. So the presence just across the Tasman of the BBL – with all its televisual magnetism – was disconcerting. The administrators had mostly kept a lid on any conflict by granting players no-objection certificates to take part in global Twenty20 leagues. But, as the Bangladesh series struggled for an audience, debate turned to whether that agreement could continue.

After eye surgery, Ross Taylor had been left out of the limited-overs squads, but showed good form for Central Districts the domestic T20 competition. With time ahead of the Tests, he applied for permission to play for Melbourne Renegades in the BBL. Coach Mike Hesson gave his blessing, but NZC chief executive David White blocked the move, citing a rule which limits players' travel before games. Taylor later found he had a slight side strain, which would have prevented his playing for the Renegades anyway, but he barely disguised his annoyance. He hit two fifties in the Tests, confirming his sight was clear, even if his future was less so.

BANGLADESH TOURING PARTY

*Mushfiqur Rahim (T/50/20), Ebadat Hossain (50), Imrul Kayes (T/50/20), Kamrul Islam (T), Mahmudullah (T/50/20), Mashrafe bin Mortaza (50/20), Mehedi Hasan (T/50), Mominul Haque (T/50), Mosaddek Hossain (50/20), Mustafizur Rahman (50/20), Nazmul Hossain (50), Nurul Hasan (T/50/20), Rubel Hossain (T/50/20), Sabbir Rahman (T/50/20), Shafiul Islam (50), Shakib Al Hasan (T/50/20), Shuvagata Hom (50/20), Soumya Sarkar (T/50/20), Subashis Roy (T/50/20), Taijul Islam (T/50/20), Tamim Iqbal (T/50/20), Tanveer Haider (50), Taskin Ahmed (T/50/20). *Coach:* U. C. Hathurusinghe.

Mashrafe bin Mortaza captained in the limited-overs matches.

At Whangarei, December 22, 2016. **New Zealand XI won by three wickets.** ‡**Bangladeshis 245-8** (43 overs); **New Zealand XI 247-7** (41.4 overs) (B. S. Smith 50, B. J. Horne 60*; Shakib Al Hasan 3-41). *The Bangladeshis chose from 13, the New Zealand XI from 12. After five months out with shoulder trouble, left-armer Mustafizur Rahman picked up 2-39, but couldn't stop Ben Horne shepherding the chase.*

First one-day international At Christchurch, December 26, 2016. **New Zealand won by 77 runs.** ‡**New Zealand 341-7** (50 overs) (T. W. M. Latham 137, C. Munro 87; Shakib Al Hasan 3-69); **Bangladesh 264** (44.5 overs) (Shakib Al Hasan 59, Mosaddek Hossain 50*; L. H. Ferguson 3-54, J. D. S. Neesham 3-36). *MoM:* T. W. M. Latham. *At 158-4, New Zealand weren't running away with it, until Tom Latham and Colin Munro – who each hit four sixes on their way to personal-bests – doubled the score. They finished with 341-7, a joint ground record (matching Scotland against the Netherlands in a World Cup qualifier in 2013-14), and the highest in matches between the sides. Despite the daunting target, Bangladeshi fans chanted, waved flags and raised a stuffed tiger. But after Jimmy Neesham removed three of the top four, they looked in trouble. Still, Shakib Al Hasan's swift 59 gave Bangladesh a foothold, and there was a glimmer until Mushfiqur Rahim strained a hamstring and retired hurt on 41. That ended a seventh-wicket partnership of 52 with Mosaddek Hossain, who continued to an ODI-best 50* from 44 balls.*

Second one-day international At Nelson, December 29, 2016. **New Zealand won by 67 runs. New Zealand 251** (50 overs) (N. T. Broom 109*; Mashrafe Mortaza 3-49); ‡**Bangladesh 184** (42.4 overs) (Imrul Kayes 59; K. S. Williamson 3-22). *MoM:* N. T. Broom. *ODI debuts:* Nurul Hasan, Subashis Roy, Tanveer Haider (Bangladesh). *In his first series for more than six years, Neil Broom hit his maiden one-day international century, but regular wickets reduced New Zealand's throttle on their way to 251. Captain Mashrafe bin Mortaza led an excellent bowling effort, galloping to the crease as if it was the finishing post in the Melbourne Cup, and claiming 3-49. And, after he had criticised his team's lethargic fielding at Christchurch, they chased the ball with extra intent. Bangladesh looked poised for victory until Williamson's occasional off-spin accounted for three wickets in five overs. Earlier, he had helped run out Sabbir Rahman, who lost a race with Imrul Kayes for the same crease. That ended a 75-run second-wicket partnership and, from 105-1, Bangladesh capitulated for 184.*

Third one-day international At Nelson, December 31, 2016. **New Zealand won by eight wickets.** ‡**Bangladesh 236-9** (50 overs) (Tamim Iqbal 59); **New Zealand 239-2** (41.2 overs) (K. S. Williamson 95*, N. T. Broom 97). *MoM:* K. S. Williamson. *A century opening stand gave Bangladesh the perfect start, until Imrul miscued a slog sweep off Mitchell Santner in the 22nd over: Broom sprinted back from short third man, flung out an arm, and clasped the ball. From there, the innings spluttered, with the three spinners, including Jeetan Patel – playing his first ODI since October 2009 – each going at less than four an over. As the squeeze came on, Shakib tried a quick single, but Luke Ronchi shed a glove and threw down the stumps at the non-striker's end. That left Bangladesh 168-5 and, despite a personal-best 44 from replacement keeper Nurul Hasan, their eventual 236 was inadequate. New Zealand's openers departed quickly – Martin Guptill to a hamstring strain – and Broom was dropped on nought. But, in his first international partnership with Williamson, he helped dismantle the bowling in a New Zealand all-wicket record stand against Bangladesh of 179 (beating 158 between Martin Crowe and John Wright at Sharjah in 1989-90). It was also their second-wicket best against any country, 20 more than Guptill and Williamson managed against Pakistan at Auckland in 2015-16. Broom just missed a second ODI century, but victory came soon after.*

First Twenty20 international At Napier, January 3, 2017 (floodlit). **New Zealand won by six wickets. ‡Bangladesh 141-8** (20 overs) (Mahmudullah 52; L. H. Ferguson 3-32); **New Zealand 143-4** (18 overs) (K. S. Williamson 73*, C. de Grandhomme 41*). *MoM:* K. S. Williamson. *T20I debuts:* T. C. Bruce, L. H. Ferguson, B. M. Wheeler (New Zealand). *On a pitch akin to asphalt, New Zealand's raw attack restricted Bangladesh to a below-par 141. Left-arm seamer Ben Wheeler opened the bowling, recorded 11 dot balls in his first three overs, and finished with 2-22. Lockie Ferguson became the second T20 debutant, after Australia's Michael Kasprowicz, to claim two wickets with his first two deliveries – one a full toss, one a beauty – before Mahmudullah averted the hat-trick by clamping down on a 90mph yorker. He risked whiplash avoiding the next, a ferocious bouncer, and made it to 52 before Ferguson got him in the last over. New Zealand's chase looked vulnerable at 62-4 in the 11th, but Williamson and Colin de Grandhomme cruised to their highest T20 international scores.*

Second Twenty20 international At Mount Maunganui, January 6, 2017. **New Zealand won by 47 runs. New Zealand 195-7** (20 overs) (C. Munro 101, T. C. Bruce 59*; Rubel Hossain 3-37); **‡Bangladesh 148** (18.1 overs) (Sabbir Rahman 48, Soumya Sarkar 39; I. S. Sodhi 3-36). *MoM:* C. Munro. *Colin Munro became the third New Zealander, after Brendon McCullum and Guptill, to score a T20 international century. He clonked seven sixes in his 54-ball knock, including three in an over from Mahmudullah costing 28, and put on 123 with Tom Bruce (59* off 39). Bangladesh's own fourth-wicket pair, Soumya Sarkar and Sabbir Rahman, managed 68 off 40, but the pressure was too much. Luke Ronchi's day started with a diamond duck, and his misfortune continued when he suffered a groin injury in the eighth over. It meant Bruce, who had last kept seriously at school, was given the gloves in his second international. In the 19th over, he took the catch that finished the match.*

Third Twenty20 international At Mount Maunganui, January 8, 2017. **New Zealand won by 27 runs. New Zealand 194-4** (20 overs) (K. S. Williamson 60, C. J. Anderson 94*; Rubel Hossain 3-31); **‡Bangladesh 167-6** (20 overs) (Soumya Sarkar 42, Shakib Al Hasan 41). *MoM:* C. J. Anderson. *T20I debut:* T. A. Blundell (New Zealand). *Corey Anderson, playing with the freedom of someone hammering tennis balls from the sand to the surf, hit ten sixes in a format best 94* off 41 deliveries, and helped complete the limited-overs whitewash. He put on 124 with Williamson, eclipsing the New Zealand fourth-wicket record set by Munro and Bruce in the previous match. Bangladesh had moments of control, and were 80-1 after eight, but Soumya Sarkar's departure, via a return catch to Ish Sodhi, was a tipping point. Later, Sodhi's googly bamboozled Mahmudullah, which seemed to sow uncertainty in the rest.*

MOST SIXES IN A TWENTY20 INTERNATIONAL INNINGS

14	A. J. Finch (A)	156 v England at Southampton	2013
13	R. E. Levi (SA)	117* v New Zealand at Hamilton	2011-12
11	C. H. Gayle (WI)	100* v England at Mumbai	2015-16
10	C. H. Gayle (WI)	117 v South Africa at Johannesburg	2007-08
10	**C. J. Anderson (NZ)**	**94* v Bangladesh at Mount Maunganui**	**2016-17**
9	L. E. Bosman (SA)	94 v England at Centurion	2009-10
9	M. N. Samuels (WI)	85* v Bangladesh at Dhaka	2012-13
9	**E. Lewis (WI)**	**100 v India at Lauderhill**	**2016**
9	**G. J. Maxwell (A)**	**145* v Sri Lanka at Pallekele**	**2016**

"'In terms of cricketing disasters this is right at the top of the tree,' Willis told viewers, raising the prospect of The Bob Willis Cricket Disaster Tree being an actual thing he keeps at home and gets down from the attic now and then."

Cricket in the Media, page 147

NEW ZEALAND v BANGLADESH

First Test Match

At Wellington, January 12–16, 2017. New Zealand won by seven wickets. Toss: New Zealand. Test debuts: Subashis Roy, Taskin Ahmed.

As the fans poured into the Basin Reserve on the final day, free admission seemed a likelier attraction than the prospect of a result. But, from 66 for three at the start of play, Bangladesh were all out for 160 soon after lunch, leaving New Zealand with a dash for victory.

Bangladesh's second innings was decimated by injuries. Opener Imrul Kayes retired hurt on the fourth evening with a thigh strain, while captain Mushfiqur Rahim, who badly damaged his right hand during his first-innings 159, would have preferred not to have returned to the crease. In desperate circumstances, he entered the fray on the last morning, and was peppered by the short ball, until Southee felled him with a blow behind the left ear. An ambulance rushed through the pickets and, after Mushfiqur was stabilised, sped to hospital for scans, which cleared him of danger. After Boult obliterated the tail, the same could not be said of Bangladesh.

New Zealand had 57 overs to knock off 217, and reached it with consummate ease. The result became a fait accompli after Williamson and Taylor put on 163 at more than six an over for the third wicket. Williamson's 15th century, completed in 89 balls, was the fourth fastest in the final innings of a Test. Yet it came without fluster or flamboyance, as he clipped the ball around at will. Among those to have batted 15 times or more in the fourth innings, Williamson's average of 66 was behind only Don Bradman's 73.

HIGHEST TOTALS IN TEST DEFEAT

595-8 dec	**Bangladesh v New Zealand at Wellington**	**2016-17**
586	Australia v England at Sydney	1894-95
574-8 dec	Pakistan v Australia at Melbourne	1972-73
556	Australia v India at Adelaide	2003-04
556	Bangladesh v West Indies at Mirpur	2012-13
551-6 dec	England v Australia at Adelaide	2006-07
547-8 dec	Sri Lanka v Australia at Colombo (SSC)	1992
538	Pakistan v England at Leeds	2006
532	India v Australia at Sydney	2007-08
526-7 dec	West Indies v England at Port-of-Spain	1967-68

The late drama masked an extraordinary three and a half days of batting, amid gales and rain. On the first evening, Shakib Al Hasan was dropped on four by Mitchell Santner, part of a shoddy fielding display from New Zealand. By the second, he had reached 217, Bangladesh's highest Test score, and put on 359 for the fifth wicket with Mushfiqur, an all-wicket record between the countries. Bangladesh declared at 595 for eight, their second highest total, behind 638 against Sri Lanka at Galle in 2012-13. But, after Shakib became the seventh player to record a double-century and a duck in the same Test, it would also become the highest innings to result in defeat.

Wagner plugged away with short stuff for four wickets, then Latham led the battle for parity with 177. Williamson, Nicholls and Santner – with a Test-best 73 – gave support. As New Zealand built to 539, Imrul took five catches deputising for Mushfiqur, a record for a substitute keeper; after his own injury, he did not reprise the role in the second innings. Sabbir Rahman was pressed into service, but was helpless as Bangladesh slid to a demoralising defeat.

Man of the Match: T. W. M. Latham.

Close of play: first day, Bangladesh 154-3 (Mominul Haque 64, Shakib Al Hasan 5); second day, Bangladesh 542-7 (Sabbir Rahman 10); third day, New Zealand 292-3 (Latham 119, Nicholls 35); fourth day, Bangladesh 66-3 (Mominul Haque 10).

Bangladesh

Tamim Iqbal lbw b Boult	56	– b Santner	25
Imrul Kayes c Boult b Southee	1	– not out	36
Mominul Haque c Watling b Southee	64	– c de Grandhomme b Wagner	23
Mahmudullah c Watling b Wagner	26	– c Watling b Wagner	5
Shakib Al Hasan b Wagner	217	– (6) c Williamson b Santner	0
*†Mushfiqur Rahim c Watling b Boult	159	– (8) retired hurt	13
Sabbir Rahman not out	54	– c Watling b Boult	50
Mehedi Hasan c Southee b Wagner	0	– (5) run out	1
Taskin Ahmed c Southee b Wagner	3	– b Boult	5
Kamrul Islam not out	6	– c de Grandhomme b Southee	1
Subashis Roy (did not bat)		– b Boult	0
B 2, lb 6, nb 1	9	Nb 1	1
1/16 (2) 2/60 (1) 3/145 (4) 4/160 (3) 5/519 (6) 6/536 (5) 7/542 (8) 8/566 (9) (8 wkts dec, 152 overs)	595	1/50 (1) 2/63 (4) 3/66 (5) 4/66 (6) 5/96 (3) 6/137 (9) 7/148 (10) 8/152 (7) 9/160 (11) (57.5 overs)	160

In the second innings Imrul Kayes, when 24, retired hurt at 46-0 and resumed at 148-7; Mushfiqur Rahim retired hurt at 114-5.

Boult 34–5–131–2; Southee 34–5–158–2; de Grandhomme 20–2–65–0; Wagner 44–8–151–4; Santner 17–2–62–0; Williamson 3–0–20–0. *Second innings*—Boult 13.5–3–53–3; Southee 13–5–34–1; Santner 16–5–36–2; Wagner 15–3–37–2.

New Zealand

J. A. Raval c Imrul Kayes b Kamrul Islam	27	– (2) c and b Mehedi Hasan	13
T. W. M. Latham lbw b Shakib Al Hasan	177	– (1) b Mehedi Hasan	16
*K. S. Williamson c Imrul Kayes b Taskin Ahmed	53	– not out	104
L. R. P. L. Taylor c Mahmudullah b Kamrul Islam	40	– c Mehedi Hasan b Subashis Roy	60
H. M. Nicholls c Mehedi Hasan b Shakib Al Hasan	53	– not out	4
C. de Grandhomme c Imrul Kayes b Subashis Roy	14		
†B-J. Watling c Imrul Kayes b Mahmudullah	49		
M. J. Santner b Subashis Roy	73		
T. G. Southee lbw b Mahmudullah	1		
N. Wagner c Imrul Kayes b Kamrul Islam	18		
T. A. Boult not out	4		
B 10, lb 3, w 16, nb 1	30	B 14, lb 6	20
1/54 (1) 2/131 (3) 3/205 (4) 4/347 (5) 5/366 (6) 6/398 (2) 7/471 (7) 8/473 (9) 9/504 (10) 10/539 (8) (148.2 overs)	539	1/32 (2) 2/39 (1) 3/202 (4) (3 wkts, 39.4 overs)	217

Mehedi Hasan 37–5–116–0; Subashis Roy 26.2–6–89–2; Taskin Ahmed 29–4–141–1; Kamrul Islam 26–4–87–3; Shakib Al Hasan 27–2–78–2; Mahmudullah 3–0–15–2. *Second innings*—Kamrul Islam 7–0–31–0; Mehedi Hasan 11.4–0–66–2; Shakib Al Hasan 10–0–30–0; Taskin Ahmed 6–0–38–0; Subashis Roy 5–0–32–1.

Umpires: M. Erasmus and P. R. Reiffel. Third umpire: N. J. Llong.
Referee: J. Srinath.

NEW ZEALAND v BANGLADESH

Second Test Match

At Christchurch, January 20–23, 2017. New Zealand won by nine wickets. Toss: New Zealand. Test debuts: Nazmul Hossain, Nurul Hasan.

During a washed-out third day, the covers leaked on a good length at the Port Hills end, and it needed a pair of industrial-strength blow-dryers – nicknamed the Sir Alex

Fergusons – to make the surface fit. There was no need to rush: New Zealand began the fourth day on 260 for seven in reply to Bangladesh's 289, and secured victory just after 7pm.

On the second evening, New Zealand had wobbled, as Shakib Al Hasan took three wickets in two overs. That threatened to undermine the century partnership put together by Taylor – who became the third New Zealander to 6,000 Test runs, after Stephen Fleming and Brendon McCullum – and Latham. But Nicholls remained until the close, and hit a Test-best 98 to help carve out a lead of 65. It proved the game's most important contribution.

The innings ended in bizarre fashion. Wagner had touched his bat behind the crease before leaping into another stride as keeper Nurul Hasan flicked the ball towards the stumps. At the moment the bails were dislodged, neither of Wagner's feet – nor his bat – was grounded, and he was run out. Coach Mike Hesson later called for Law 29 to be tinkered with.

The bowlers, meanwhile, channelled any sense of injustice into dissecting Bangladesh, as Boult, Southee and Wagner himself took three each. When Shakib guided to deep gully, Southee became the second fastest New Zealander to 200 Test scalps, in his 56th game, behind only Richard Hadlee (44). Fleeting resistance came from ninth-wicket pair Kamrul Islam and Taskin Ahmed, prompting a chorus of "Go Tigers, Go!" But the Bangladeshi line-up, deprived of Imrul Kayes, Mominul Haque and Mushfiqur Rahim, was cruelly exposed. New Zealand promoted de Grandhomme to No. 3, and he finished it with two sixes.

For the 22nd consecutive Test in New Zealand, going back to January 2011, the side winning the toss had bowled. Stand-in captain Tamim Iqbal fell early, before Soumya Sarkar hit a streaky maiden half-century, and put on 127 with Shakib for the third wicket at nearly five an over. But Sarkar's luck ran out on 86, and Boult and Southee took nine between them as Bangladesh subsided for 289. One of Southee's five included Shakib, held by Watling down the leg side, which took them one clear of Hadlee and Ian Smith as New Zealand's most prolific bowler–keeper combination, with 44. Their next victim was Rubel Hossain, the last Bangladeshi wicket to fall on tour. After their 595 for eight at Wellington, Bangladesh had lost 30 for 622.

Man of the Match: T. G. Southee.

Close of play: first day, Bangladesh 289; second day, New Zealand 260-7 (Nicholls 56, Southee 4); third day, no play.

Bangladesh

*Tamim Iqbal c Watling b Southee	5	– c Santner b Southee	8
Soumya Sarkar c de Grandhomme b Boult	86	– c Raval b de Grandhomme	36
Mahmudullah c Watling b Boult	19	– b Wagner	38
Shakib Al Hasan c Watling b Southee	59	– c de Grandhomme b Southee	8
Sabbir Rahman c Southee b Boult	7	– (6) c Watling b Wagner	0
Nazmul Hossain c Raval b Southee	18	– (5) b Boult	12
†Nurul Hasan c Watling b Boult	47	– c Watling b Wagner	0
Mehedi Hasan b Wagner	10	– c Latham b Boult	4
Taskin Ahmed c Williamson b Southee	8	– b Boult	33
Kamrul Islam lbw b Southee	2	– not out	25
Rubel Hossain not out	16	– c Watling b Southee	7
B 4, lb 2, w 5, nb 1	12	Lb 2	2
1/7 (1) 2/38 (3) 3/165 (2) 4/177 (5) 5/179 (4) 6/232 (6) 7/248 (8) 8/257 (9) 9/273 (7) 10/289 (10) (84.3 overs)	289	1/17 (1) 2/58 (2) 3/73 (4) 4/92 (3) 5/100 (6) 6/100 (7) 7/106 (5) 8/115 (8) 9/166 (9) 10/173 (11) (52.5 overs)	173

Boult 24–4–87–4; Southee 28.3–7–94–5; de Grandhomme 14–4–58–0; Wagner 18–1–44–1. *Second innings*—Boult 17–3–52–3; Southee 12.5–2–48–3; de Grandhomme 11–3–27–1; Wagner 12–3–44–3.

New Zealand

J. A. Raval b Kamrul Islam	16	– b Kamrul Islam	33
T. W. M. Latham c Nurul Hasan b Taskin Ahmed	68	– not out	41
*K. S. Williamson c Nurul Hasan b Kamrul Islam	2		
L. R. P. L. Taylor c sub (Taijul Islam) b Mehedi Hasan	77		
H. M. Nicholls b Mehedi Hasan	98		
M. J. Santner lbw b Shakib Al Hasan	29		
†B-J. Watling b Shakib Al Hasan	1		
C. de Grandhomme b Shakib Al Hasan	0	– (3) not out	33
T. G. Southee c Mehedi Hasan b Shakib Al Hasan	17		
N. Wagner run out	26		
T. A. Boult not out	7		
Lb 6, w 4, nb 3	13	B 1, w 1, nb 2	4
1/45 (1) 2/47 (3) 3/153 (2) 4/177 (4) 5/252 (6) 6/256 (7) 7/256 (8) 8/286 (9) 9/343 (5) 10/354 (10) (92.4 overs)	354	1/56 (1) (1 wkt, 18.4 overs)	111

Taskin Ahmed 22–2–86–1; Mehedi Hasan 19–3–59–2; Rubel Hossain 17–2–65–0; Kamrul Islam 19–4–78–2; Shakib Al Hasan 12.4–1–50–4; Soumya Sarkar 3–0–10–0. *Second innings*—Taskin Ahmed 5–0–21–0; Mehedi Hasan 6–0–27–0; Kamrul Islam 3–0–21–1; Shakib Al Hasan 4–0–28–0; Nazmul Hossain 0.4–0–13–0.

Umpires: N. J. Llong and P. R. Reiffel. Third umpire: M. Erasmus.
Referee: J. Srinath.

DOMESTIC CRICKET IN NEW ZEALAND IN 2015-16

MARK GEENTY

Auckland is New Zealand's cultural melting pot, holding one-third of the population. It is no surprise, then, that its team were crowned the best in the country, completing a Twenty20 and Plunket Shield double.

Though **Auckland** had collected four limited-overs trophies in the previous five seasons, their 23rd first-class title was their first for seven years. With captain Rob Nicol injured in the later stages, Michael Bates took charge in his final season, and clinched it with a round to spare. Despite them losing to Central Districts in Bates's farewell game – their only defeat – Auckland won six of their ten matches. **Canterbury** were chasing a third successive Shield – a feat not achieved since Auckland's dominance of the 1930s – but could not catch up, though they leapfrogged **Wellington**, beating them in the last round to finish runners-up.

Auckland had plenty of depth and a heavy South African influence, reflecting the regular drift across the Indian Ocean into the city's northern suburbs. Coach Mark O'Donnell, though New Zealand-born, had spent 14 years in South Africa and coached Gauteng to titles in the late 1990s. In early January, Auckland played a one-day match with a single native New Zealander, fast bowler Lockie Ferguson. Of the others, six were born in South Africa, two in India and one each in Zimbabwe and Hong Kong. Indian-born opener Jeet Raval was their batting anchor with 1,016 runs at 59, and his partner Michael Guptill-Bunce – cousin of international opener Martin Guptill – scored 859 at 45.

The domestic player of the year was another Indian-born batsman, Bharat Popli, who plundered 1,149 at 67 for **Northern Districts**, a sound launch pad for international honours, though his team finished fourth, with just two wins.

On largely flat surfaces, three of the Plunket Shield's top four wicket-takers were spinners: Central's Ajaz Patel had 43, Auckland's Tarun Nethula 39 and Canterbury's consistent Todd Astle 35. Leg-spinner Nethula, who had played five one-day internationals in 2012, was excellent in all formats and might have piqued the national selectors' interest again but for Ish Sodhi's late-season revival. The promising Ferguson was one of the few to bowl at a sharp clip, collecting 31 wickets for Auckland at 22.

The Twenty20 competition was a headache for New Zealand Cricket. The bulk of the Georgie Pie Super Smash was played in November at the request of Sky Television, but fickle spring weather meant spectators largely stayed away, even for finals weekend in mid-December. NZC said they would review the format of a competition intended to pull the crowds but struggling for attention between home internationals and the Australian Big Bash. But the tournament went just fine for Auckland, spurred on by international short-form specialists Colin Munro and Mitchell McClenaghan, who snatched the final away from Otago with three wickets in four balls on a drop-in pitch at a rugby ground in New Plymouth.

New Plymouth also hosted the 50-over final, at leafy Pukekura Park, where **Central Districts** relished the short boundaries to rack up 405 against Canterbury and win back-to-back Ford Trophies. Opener George Worker scored 159 in that match, and made his international debut on the tour of southern Africa in August, while Jesse Ryder returned to Central, initially only for white-ball cricket, and enjoyed himself with 506 one-day runs at 56, and a strike-rate of 122. Their team-mate Seth Rance was the leading one-day wicket-taker, with 19 at just 13.

Otago had a roller-coaster season, during which two of their favourite sons. Brendon and Nathan McCullum, retired from first-class and international cricket. After heading the league table in the Super Smash (but losing the final), they finished last in the Plunket Shield, with a single win; Nathan King resigned after only one season as head coach, amid reports of player unrest. South African Rob Walter was announced as King's successor after three years coaching Eastern Titans.

FIRST-CLASS AVERAGES, 2015-16

BATTING (500 runs, average 30.00)

	M	I	NO	R	HS	100	Avge	Ct/St
B. Popli (*Northern Districts*)	10	17	0	1,149	172	3	67.58	9
B. S. Smith (*Central Districts*)	9	17	2	917	244	3	61.13	6
†G. H. Worker (*Central Districts*)	6	11	1	610	210	3	61.00	8
K. J. McClure (*Canterbury*)	8	13	2	667	193*	2	60.63	9
†J. A. Raval (*New Zealand/Auckland*)	10	19	2	1,016	202*	4	59.76	15
N. T. Broom (*Otago*)	7	14	2	633	131*	2	52.75	8
†S. G. Borthwick (*Wellington*)	6	12	1	532	110*	2	48.36	4
W. A. Young (*C Districts/New Zealand A*)	10	18	1	799	85	0	47.00	7
B. S. Wilson (*Otago*)	10	20	1	886	126	3	46.63	10
M. L. Guptill-Bunce (*Auckland*)	10	19	0	859	189	2	45.21	6
B-J. Watling (*N Districts/New Zealand*)	9	15	1	630	176	1	45.00	26
T. A. Blundell (*Wellington*)	10	19	2	761	153	1	44.76	19/1
D. Cleaver (*Central Districts*)	8	16	2	626	151*	1	44.71	17/3
S. J. Murdoch (*Wellington*)	10	20	1	824	171	2	43.36	7
†D. R. Flynn (*Northern Districts*)	10	18	0	764	158	3	42.44	5
D. C. de Boorder (*New Zealand A/Otago*)	10	17	3	566	86*	0	40.42	36/1
R. R. O'Donnell (*Auckland*)	10	19	1	721	167	2	40.05	16
†L. J. Woodcock (*Wellington*)	10	20	1	739	131	2	38.89	4
T. C. Bruce (*Central Districts*)	10	19	2	654	166*	1	38.47	22
A. M. Ellis (*Canterbury*)	9	15	1	518	143	1	37.00	7
C. de Grandhomme (*Auckland*)	10	18	1	605	106*	1	35.58	7
D. J. Mitchell (*Northern Districts*)	10	18	2	568	100*	1	35.50	13
P. G. Fulton (*Canterbury*)	10	20	2	622	155*	1	34.55	19
T. L. Seifert (*Northern Districts*)	9	16	1	509	106	1	33.93	32/2
G. R. Hay (*Central Districts*)	10	19	1	585	127*	1	32.50	7

BOWLING (15 wickets, average 35.00)

	Style	O	M	R	W	BB	5I	Avge
A. M. Ellis (*Canterbury*)	RFM	274.2	90	613	33	5-52	1	18.57
L. H. Ferguson (*Auckland*)	RFM	224.1	48	686	31	5-37	3	22.12
M. J. McClenaghan (*Auckland*)	LFM	125.4	26	399	17	4-38	0	23.47
T. D. Astle (*New Zealand A/Canterbury*)	LBG	351.2	46	1,168	47	7-78	2	24.85
D. J. Grobbelaar (*Auckland*)	LM	202.2	38	635	25	3-27	0	25.40
T. G. Southee (*N Districts/New Zealand*)	RFM	209.3	40	613	24	5-56	1	25.54
C. de Grandhomme (*Auckland*)	RFM	162	39	438	17	4-31	0	25.76
S. C. Kuggeleijn (*Northern Districts*)	RFM	270.5	50	981	38	5-32	1	25.81
L. V. van Beek (*Canterbury*)	RFM	160.3	34	474	18	6-57	1	26.33
K. A. Jamieson (*Canterbury*)	RFM	175	34	574	21	5-47	1	27.33
N. A. Patel (*Central Districts*)	RM	227.3	47	744	27	5-71	2	27.55
J. D. Baker (*Northern Districts*)	RFM	310.1	89	925	33	5-63	1	28.03
N. Wagner (*NZ A/New Zealand/Otago*)	LFM	230.1	49	819	29	6-106	2	28.24
H. K. Bennett (*Canterbury*)	RFM	135	23	524	18	5-54	1	29.11
T. S. Nethula (*Auckland*)	LBG	315.1	44	1,137	39	6-132	3	29.15
D. A. J. Bracewell (*C Dists/N Zealand*)	RFM	238.3	47	731	25	5-60	2	29.24
M. D. Bates (*Auckland*)	LFM	204.1	50	584	19	5-48	1	30.73
A. P. Devcich (*Northern Districts*)	SLA	150.3	25	494	16	4-43	0	30.87
M. R. Quinn (*Auckland/New Zealand A*)	RFM	192.1	37	619	20	4-81	0	30.95
I. S. Sodhi (*New Zealand A/N Districts*)	LBG	199.2	18	850	27	7-102	2	31.48
J. S. Hunter (*Otago*)	RFM	160	32	501	15	4-47	0	33.40
A. Y. Patel (*Central Districts*)	SLA	399	69	1,449	43	6-117	3	33.69
J. S. Patel (*Wellington*)	OB	364.1	89	1,098	32	6-77	1	34.31

PLUNKET SHIELD, 2015-16

	Played	Won	Lost	Drawn	Bonus points Batting	Bonus points Bowling	Points	Net avge runs/wkt
Auckland	10	6	1	3	23	38	133	6.51
Canterbury	10	5	3	2	18	39	117	5.20
Wellington	10	5	3	2	23	25	108	–6.42
Northern Districts	10	2	4	4	25	38	87	4.61
Central Districts	10	2	5	3	27	34	85	–4.82
Otago	10	1	5	4	15	34	61	–7.39

Outright win = 12pts. Bonus points were awarded as follows for the first 110 overs of each team's first innings: one batting point for the first 200 runs and then for 250, 300 and 350; one bowling point for the third wicket taken and then for the fifth, seventh and ninth. Net average runs per wicket is calculated by subtracting average runs conceded per wicket from average runs scored per wicket.

At Auckland (Eden Park Outer Oval), October 15–18, 2015. **Auckland won by nine wickets. Canterbury 149 and 321; ‡Auckland 316 and 158-1.** *Auckland 18pts, Canterbury 3pts. Auckland started with a win over the reigning champions, after their opening bowlers Mitchell McClenaghan and Matt Quinn claimed seven wickets apiece.*

At Napier (Nelson Park), October 15–18, 2015. **Drawn. ‡Otago 352** (J. D. S. Neesham 131; D. A. J. Bracewell 5-67) **and 265-3** (N. T. Broom 131*); **Central Districts 650-8 dec** (B. S. Smith 244, G. H. Worker 129). *Central Districts 8pts, Otago 5pts. Central Districts reached 600 for the first time; their eventual 650 remained the highest total of the season. Ben Smith scored a maiden double-hundred, adding 234 for the fourth wicket with George Worker. He was the second Ben Smith to hit a double for Central, after the former Leicestershire and Worcestershire batsman in 2001-02. The match was drawn after Brad Wilson (83) and Neil Broom put on 204 for Otago's third wicket.*

At Hamilton, October 15–18, 2015. **Drawn. Wellington 267** (L. Ronchi 115; T. G. Southee 5-56) **and 409-9** (T. A. Boult 5-97); **‡Northern Districts 429** (D. R. Flynn 102; D. S. Hutchinson 5-116). *Northern Districts 7pts, Wellington 3pts. Dane Hutchinson ended Northern Districts' innings with a hat-trick, collecting five wickets for the first time, and later reached a career-best 48* during a last-wicket stand of 81 with Brent Arnel.*

At Nelson (Saxton Oval), October 23–26, 2015. **Wellington won by five wickets. Central Districts 385** (G. H. Worker 210) **and 273-8 dec** (B. S. Smith 117*); **‡Wellington 353-5 dec** (S. J. Murdoch 171) **and 307-5.** *Wellington 20pts, Central Districts 6pts. Worker hit six sixes in a maiden double-century, and added 134 for Central Districts' last wicket with Andrew Mathieson (12*). Set 306 in two sessions, Wellington won with 15 balls to spare.*

At Mount Maunganui, October 23–25, 2015. **Auckland won by three wickets. Northern Districts 124 and 206; ‡Auckland 98** (S. C. Kuggeleijn 5-32) **and 233-7.** *Auckland 16pts, Northern Districts 4pts. Auckland won in three days after being routed for 98; Scott Kuggeleijn claimed five.*

At Christchurch (Hagley Oval), October 24–27, 2015. **Canterbury won by 304 runs. Canterbury 293** (L. V. van Beek 111*) **and 350-2 dec** (P. G. Fulton 155*); **‡Otago 91 and 248** (B. S. Wilson 100; L. V. van Beek 6-57). *Canterbury 18pts, Otago 4pts. Jack Hunter trapped both Canterbury openers for ducks in the game's first over, but No. 9 Logan van Beek, grandson of Test player Sammy Guillen, completed a maiden century during a last-wicket stand of 104 with Will Williams (21). The pair then shared five wickets in Otago's collapse for 91. After Peter Fulton and Ken McClure (66*) had put on 216* for Canterbury's third wicket, van Beek added a career-best 6-57.*

At Auckland (Eden Park Outer Oval), December 17–20, 2015. **Drawn. Northern Districts 381** (B. Popli 116; L. H. Ferguson 5-61) **and 374-7 dec** (S. C. Kuggeleijn 104*); **‡Auckland 380 and 253-7.** *Auckland 8pts, Northern Districts 8pts. Set 376 for a third successive win, Auckland slid to 187-7 before Brad Cachopa's 89* ensured the draw.*

At Rangiora, December 17–20, 2015. **Canterbury won by 161 runs. Canterbury 320** (L. J. Carter 101) **and 310; ‡Central Districts 245 and 224** (T. D. Astle 5-50). *Canterbury 19pts, Central Districts 5pts. Leo Carter reached his maiden first-class century in the dressing-room, rather than on the pitch. On 99, he had run two, signalled as leg-byes, and was then caught without addition. Umpires Tony Gillies and Derek Walker later reviewed footage, ruled Carter had gloved the ball and awarded him the extra runs, which took his score to 101. Central Districts used four* *wicketkeepers: Dane Cleaver was injured in the third over, and Ben Smith took over, then substitutes Joel Harden and Ma'ava Ave deputised after he hurt a finger.*

At Wellington (Basin Reserve), December 17–20, 2015. **Wellington won by 92 runs. Wellington 328** (L. Ronchi 116*) **and 305-4 dec** (L. J. Woodcock 131, M. H. W. Papps 132); ‡**Otago 279-8 dec and 262** (J. S. Patel 6-77). *Wellington 18pts, Otago 6pts. Luke Woodcock and Michael Papps, who hit five sixes, shared an opening stand of 235 in Wellington's second innings. Jeetan Patel bowled them to victory as Otago's last six fell for 35.*

At Christchurch (Hagley Oval), February 5–8, 2016. **Auckland won by five wickets. Canterbury 294 and 222** (M. D. Bates 5-48); ‡**Auckland 279** (E. J. Nuttall 5-72) **and 239-5** (C. de Grandhomme 106*). *Auckland 18pts, Canterbury 6pts. Auckland trailed on first innings, but Michael Bates derailed Canterbury's second, and Colin de Grandhomme steered them to a third win.*

At Napier (McLean Park), February 5–8, 2016. **Northern Districts won by 284 runs. Northern Districts 268** (T. L. Seifert 106) **and 425-7 dec** (B. Popli 133, D. J. Mitchell 100*); ‡**Central Districts 256 and 153.** *Northern Districts 18pts, Central Districts 6pts. A 284-run win seemed unlikely when Northern Districts were floundering at 55-5 on the first morning, but Tim Seifert's maiden hundred, from No. 7, rallied them, and Central Districts were in similar trouble at 95-6. Bharat Popli and Daryl Mitchell helped extend a narrow lead to 437; Kuggeleijn claimed four wickets in each of Central's innings.*

At Queenstown, February 5–8, 2016. **Wellington won by 102 runs.** ‡**Wellington 348** (S. G. Borthwick 102; N. Wagner 5-101) **and 282-8 dec** (M. D. Craig 5-79); **Otago 240** (B. J. Arnel 5-59) **and 288.** *Wellington 19pts, Otago 4pts. Scott Borthwick of Durham made a century on his first-class debut in New Zealand to help Wellington pull level with Auckland at the top of the table.*

At Auckland (Colin Maiden Park), February 13–16, 2016. **Auckland won by an innings and 119 runs. Wellington 174 and 219;** ‡**Auckland 512-9 dec** (R. R. O'Donnell 167). *Auckland 19pts, Wellington 1pt. Auckland regained the upper hand over Wellington as Robbie O'Donnell's maiden century set up an innings win.*

At Nelson (Saxton Oval), February 13–16, 2016. **Drawn. Canterbury 204 and 339** (A. Y. Patel 6-152); ‡**Central Districts 168** (K. A. Jamieson 5-47) **and 278-9** (A. M. Ellis 5-52). *Central Districts 4pts, Canterbury 5pts. Andrew Ellis reduced Central Districts to 253-9 on the final day; captain Will Young (66*) and Seth Rance (20*) survived 50 balls for the draw.*

At Dunedin (University Oval), February 13–16, 2016. **Otago won by 61 runs. Otago 237 and 287** (I. S. Sodhi 7-102); ‡**Northern Districts 324 and 139.** *Otago 17pts, Northern Districts 7pts. Ish Sodhi's career-best 7-102 was the best return of the season, though a fourth-innings collapse meant he finished on the wrong side of Otago's only win.*

At Auckland (Eden Park Outer Oval), February 20–23, 2016. **Drawn. Auckland 277 and 431-8 dec** (J. A. Raval 202*); ‡**Otago 265 and 338-7** (B. S. Wilson 107). *Auckland 6pts, Otago 6pts. Jeet Raval batted throughout Auckland's second innings for his second double-hundred.*

At Napier (McLean Park), February 20–23, 2016. **Central Districts won by 87 runs. Central Districts 424-6 dec** (G. H. Worker 123, D. Cleaver 151*) **and 314-6 dec** (G. R. Hay 127*); ‡**Wellington 370-7 dec and 281.** *Central Districts 19pts, Wellington 6pts. Worker and Cleaver added 230 for Central Districts' sixth wicket.*

At Hamilton, February 20–23, 2016. **Canterbury won by eight wickets. Northern Districts 257 and 316;** ‡**Canterbury 485** (A. M. Ellis 143; I. S. Sodhi 5-167) **and 90-2.** *Canterbury 20pts, Northern Districts 5pts. McClure (96) and Ellis, who hit eight sixes, rescued Canterbury from 77-4 with a stand of 235.*

At Auckland (Eden Park Outer Oval), March 8–11, 2016. **Auckland won by 47 runs. Auckland 373** (M. L. Guptill-Bunce 112; A. Y. Patel 6-117) **and 425-6 dec** (J. A. Raval 139, R. R. O'Donnell 100; A. Y. Patel 5-148); ‡**Central Districts 416** (T. S. Nethula 6-132) **and 335** (T. S. Nethula 5-140). *Auckland 19pts, Central Districts 8pts. Two spinners shared 22 of the 36 wickets that fell for 1,549 runs: Central Districts' slow left-armer Ajaz Patel claimed 11-265, and Auckland leg-spinner Tarun Nethula 11-272.*

At Invercargill, March 8–11, 2016. **Canterbury won by five wickets. Otago 351** (N. T. Broom 117) **and 225-3 dec;** ‡**Canterbury 180 and 398-5** (K. J. McClure 193*). *Canterbury 16pts, Otago 7pts. McClure completed a maiden century, in his fifth first-class match, as he led Canterbury's last-day charge; victory prevented him converting it into a double.*

At Wellington (Basin Reserve), March 8–11, 2016. **Wellington won by three wickets. Northern Districts 438-8 dec and 291-3 dec** (D. R. Flynn 110); **‡Wellington 352-7 dec** (L. J. Woodcock 111) **and 378-7.** *Wellington 19pts, Northern Districts 7pts. Daniel Flynn hit 110 in 86 balls, and Anton Devcich 83* in 56 as Northern Districts set 378 in 76 overs; Wellington made it with one to spare.*

At Christchurch (Hagley Oval), March 15–18, 2016. **Wellington won by 54 runs. Wellington 206** (S. G. Borthwick 110*) **and 136** (H. K. Bennett 5-54); **‡Canterbury 159-2 dec and 129.** *Wellington 13pts, Canterbury 4pts. Wellington were 78-8 before a stand of 125 between Borthwick and Iain McPeake (interrupted by a second-day washout); 20 wickets fell on the final day.*

At Hamilton, March 15–18, 2016. **Northern Districts won by 115 runs. Northern Districts 458-6 dec** (D. R. Flynn 158, B. Popli 172) **and 332-7 dec; ‡Central Districts 293 and 382** (T. C. Bruce 166*). *Northern Districts 20pts, Central Districts 3pts. Flynn and Popli added 258 for Northern Districts' third wicket. Anton Devcich bowled them to victory with four in each innings, though Tom Bruce and Bevan Small (76) shared a seventh-wicket stand of 177.*

At Dunedin (University Oval), March 15–18, 2016. **Auckland won by ten runs. Auckland 255 and 139; ‡Otago 177 and 207** (L. H. Ferguson 5-68). *Auckland 18pts, Otago 4pts. Ryan Duffy carried his bat for 90* in Otago's first innings, when Auckland wicketkeeper Brad Cachopa held five catches. Auckland narrowly completed their sixth win.*

At Christchurch (Hagley Oval), March 23–26, 2016. **Drawn. Northern Districts 185 and 355; ‡Canterbury 258 and 78-6.** *Canterbury 6pts, Northern Districts 4pts. Northern Districts' Popli passed 1,000 runs for the season.*

At Dunedin (University Oval), March 23–26, 2016. **Drawn. Central Districts 258** (J. A. Duffy 5-96) **and 282-8 dec; ‡Otago 198** (N. A. Patel 5-72) **and 305-8** (R. M. Duffy 104). *Otago 4pts, Central Districts 6pts. Both sides were frustrated in their quest for a second win. Ryan Duffy helped Otago survive after they were set 343 in 84 overs.*

At Wellington (Basin Reserve), March 23–26, 2016. **Drawn. Auckland 152** (B. J. Arnel 5-51) **and 598** (M. L. Guptill-Bunce 189, D. J. Grobbelaar 101); **‡Wellington 236** (L. H. Ferguson 5-37) **and 308-8.** *Wellington 5pts, Auckland 4pts. Auckland made sure of the Plunket Shield with a draw, despite a first-day collapse. Their second innings took them past 500 against Wellington for the second time in six weeks, thanks to career-bests from Michael Guptill-Bunce (who shared an opening stand of 215 with Jeet Raval) and Donovan Grobbelaar. Brad Cachopa held six catches in Wellington's first innings.*

At Napier (McLean Park), March 30–April 2, 2016. **Central Districts won by four wickets. ‡Auckland 396** (J. A. Raval 147; D. A. J. Bracewell 5-60) **and 266** (N. A. Patel 5-71); **Central Districts 464** (B. S. Smith 161) **and 202-6** (T. S. Nethula 5-73). *Central Districts 20pts, Auckland 7pts. Raval's 147 took him past 1,000 runs in the season, but the new champions' campaign ended in their only defeat.*

At Whangarei (New Cobham Oval), March 30–April 2, 2016. **Drawn. ‡Otago 298** (B. S. Wilson 126; J. D. Baker 5-63) **and 172-3; Northern Districts 431** (B-J. Watling 176). *Northern Districts 7pts, Otago 4pts. Popli made his tenth score of 50-plus in his tenth match of the season, and added 199 for Northern Districts' third wicket with B-J. Watling.*

At Wellington (Basin Reserve), March 30–April 2, 2016. **Canterbury won by seven wickets. Canterbury 430-8 dec** (K. J. McClure 115) **and 108-3; ‡Wellington 201** (S. J. Murdoch 105) **and 333** (T. A. Blundell 153). *Canterbury 20pts, Wellington 4pts. Canterbury made Wellington follow on, then usurped them in second place when Andrew Ellis dashed to victory with a 25-ball 55* after the first two sessions of the final day were washed out. Their wicketkeeper Cam Fletcher made 23 dismissals in the last three matches, finishing with 41 in the season – behind Auckland's Brad Cachopa, whose 45 were a tournament record.*

PLUNKET SHIELD WINNERS

1921-22	Auckland	1926-27	Auckland	1931-32	Wellington
1922-23	Canterbury	1927-28	Wellington	1932-33	Otago
1923-24	Wellington	1928-29	Auckland	1933-34	Auckland
1924-25	Otago	1929-30	Wellington	1934-35	Canterbury
1925-26	Wellington	1930-31	Canterbury	1935-36	Wellington

1936-37	Auckland
1937-38	Auckland
1938-39	Auckland
1939-40	Auckland
1940–45	*No competition*
1945-46	Canterbury
1946-47	Auckland
1947-48	Otago
1948-49	Canterbury
1949-50	Wellington
1950-51	Otago
1951-52	Canterbury
1952-53	Otago
1953-54	Central Districts
1954-55	Wellington
1955-56	Canterbury
1956-57	Wellington
1957-58	Otago
1958-59	Auckland
1959-60	Canterbury
1960-61	Wellington
1961-62	Wellington
1962-63	Northern Districts
1963-64	Auckland
1964-65	Canterbury
1965-66	Wellington
1966-67	Central Districts
1967-68	Central Districts
1968-69	Auckland
1969-70	Otago
1970-71	Central Districts
1971-72	Otago
1972-73	Wellington
1973-74	Wellington
1974-75	Otago
1975-76	Canterbury
1976-77	Otago
1977-78	Auckland
1978-79	Otago
1979-80	Northern Districts
1980-81	Auckland
1981-82	Wellington
1982-83	Wellington
1983-84	Canterbury
1984-85	Wellington
1985-86	Otago
1986-87	Central Districts
1987-88	Otago
1988-89	Auckland
1989-90	Wellington
1990-91	Auckland
1991-92	Central Districts / Northern Districts
1992-93	Northern Districts
1993-94	Canterbury
1994-95	Auckland
1995-96	Auckland
1996-97	Canterbury
1997-98	Canterbury
1998-99	Central Districts
1999-2000	Northern Districts
2000-01	Wellington
2001-02	Auckland
2002-03	Auckland
2003-04	Wellington
2004-05	Auckland
2005-06	Central Districts
2006-07	Northern Districts
2007-08	Canterbury
2008-09	Auckland
2009-10	Northern Districts
2010-11	Canterbury
2011-12	Northern Districts
2012-13	Central Districts
2013-14	Canterbury
2014-15	Canterbury
2015-16	Auckland

Auckland have won the title outright 23 times, Wellington 20, Canterbury 18, Otago 13, Central Districts 8, Northern Districts 7. Central Districts and Northern Districts also shared the title once.

The tournament was known as the Shell Trophy from 1975-76 to 2000-01, and the State Championship from 2001-02 to 2008-09.

THE FORD TROPHY, 2015-16

50-over league plus knockout

	Played	*Won*	*Lost*	*Tied*	*NR/A*	*Bonus points*	*Points*	*Net run-rate*
CANTERBURY	8	5	1	0	2	3	27	1.04
CENTRAL DISTRICTS	8	4	2	0	2	2	22	0.47
OTAGO	8	3	3	1	1	2	18	0.72
AUCKLAND	8	4	4	0	0	1	17	–0.57
Northern Districts	8	3	5	0	0	1	13	–0.25
Wellington	8	1	5	1	1	0	8	–1.20

Preliminary finals 1st v 2nd: Central Districts beat Canterbury by two wickets. **3rd v 4th:** Otago beat Auckland by 125 runs (DLS). **Final play-off:** Canterbury v Otago – no result. Canterbury advanced to the final by virtue of their higher place in the table.

Final At New Plymouth (Pukekura Park), January 30, 2016. **Central Districts won by 156 runs.** ‡**Central Districts 405-6** (50 overs) (G. H. Worker 159); **Canterbury 249** (37.4 overs) (A. M. Ellis 101). *Central Districts retained their one-day title after running up a massive total – the fifth to reach 400 in 50-over cricket in New Zealand, all but one by Central Districts. George Worker smashed 159 in 151 balls, backed up by Tom Bruce, who reached a half-century in 16 balls, the fastest in List A cricket in New Zealand, and finished with a 23-ball 71; each hit seven sixes. Canterbury captain Andrew Ellis fought back from 33-3 with a maiden one-day hundred (76 balls), but they never got close.*

GEORGIE PIE SUPER SMASH, 2015-16

	Played	*Won*	*Lost*	*A*	*Points*	*NRR*
OTAGO.	10	6	3	1	26	0.98
AUCKLAND	10	5	3	2	24	–0.08
CANTERBURY . . .	10	5	4	1	22	0.25
Central Districts . . .	10	4	5	1	18	0.01
Northern Districts . .	10	4	5	1	18	–0.29
Wellington.	10	3	7	0	12	–0.82

Preliminary finals **1st v 2nd:** Otago v Auckland – no result. Otago advanced to the final by virtue of their higher place in the table. **Loser of 1st play-off v 3rd:** Auckland beat Canterbury by two runs (DLS).

Final At New Plymouth (Yarrow Stadium), December 13, 2015 (floodlit). **Auckland won by 20 runs.** ‡**Auckland 166-6** (20 overs); **Otago 146-9** (20 overs). *Auckland captain Rob Nicol batted through 19 overs to hit 77 in 54 balls, before Mitchell McClenaghan removed Otago's top three in the sixth over.*

STATE OF ORIGIN MATCH

At Wellington (Basin Reserve), February 28, 2016 (floodlit). **North Island won by six wickets.** ‡**South Island 126** (19.2 overs); **North Island 127-4** (13 overs). *Leg-spinner Ish Sodhi claimed four South wickets for 24, and George Worker knocked up 53 in 30 balls as North coasted home.*

PAKISTAN CRICKET IN 2016

On top – but not for long

OSMAN SAMIUDDIN

Pakistan lost more matches than they won in both Tests and one-day internationals in 2016. In Twenty20 cricket, they won one more than they lost, though only because of the largesse of West Indies, who were brushed aside with minimal resistance. The Test rankings briefly told a different, glorious, story, but it was a poor year for Pakistan, who finished with six defeats in a row, five of them in New Zealand or Australia. It was the first time New Zealand had beaten them in over 30 years, and their fourth successive whitewash in Australia, bringing to 12 the number of successive Test defeats there, the most for one country in another. Barring the occasional session – and a memorable chase at Brisbane, where Pakistan came within 40 of a target of 490 – their cricket was poor. Only Azhar Ali, who scored a triple-hundred against West Indies in Dubai and a double at Melbourne, both unbeaten, rose above the malaise.

PAKISTAN IN 2016

	Played	*Won*	*Lost*	*Drawn/No result*
Tests	11	4	7	–
One-day internationals	13	5	6	2
Twenty20 internationals	15	8	7	0

JANUARY	3 ODIs and 3 T20Is (a) v New Zealand	(page 946)
FEBRUARY	Asia Cup (in Bangladesh)	(page 893)
MARCH – APRIL	ICC World Twenty20 (in India)	(page 793)
MAY		
JUNE		
JULY – SEPTEMBER	4 Tests, 5 ODIs and 1 T20I (a) v England	(page 288)
	2 ODIs (a) v Ireland	(page 784)
OCTOBER	3 Tests, 3 ODIs and 3 T20Is (h) v West Indies (in the UAE)	(page 983)
NOVEMBER	2 Tests (a) v New Zealand	(page 961)
DECEMBER – JANUARY	3 Tests and 5 ODIs (a) v Australia	(page 864)

For a review of Pakistan domestic cricket from the 2015-16 season, see page 998.

AFP/Getty Images

Looking after No. 1: Islamabad United, led by Misbah-ul-Haq, win the first Pakistan Super League.

It was a far cry from the English summer when, for the first time since official rankings began, Pakistan became the No. 1 Test team in the world. It wasn't a long stay – 43 days in all – but what days they were, and what a sense of achievement coursed through them. This was a side led by a 42-year-old. They were composed of unfashionable, disciplined players. Their board were outside the Big Three. And despite making a home in one of the globe's most central locations, they had been mostly playing around the margins of the cricket world for six years. It was one of sport's great stories.

Pakistan reached the summit soon after a series-squaring win at The Oval in August, when Younis Khan put a middling run of form behind him with a resplendent double-century. For the first time in years, they had been a popular touring side, generating goodwill wherever they went. At Lord's, where leg-spinner Yasir Shah's ten wickets helped them win the First Test, Misbah-ul-Haq's push-up celebrations – repeated by the entire squad in homage to the soldiers who had knocked them into shape back home – provided one of the images of the year. So stable and prosperous was the environment Misbah and others had created that they were able to reintegrate Mohammad Amir, playing his first Test in six years following his ban for spot-fixing, without much drama. It was another compelling story. His performances were steady rather than spectacular, but physically he had lost nothing; even accounting for his youth, this was remarkable.

That, though, was pretty much it, and either side of the 2–2 draw in England were signs of erosion and decay. If time seemed to be catching up with the Test side, it had long ago overhauled the limited-overs teams. In 2016, the extent to which Pakistan lagged behind the modern white-ball game was as clear as day. The alarm bells began to ring at the World Twenty20, where Shahid Afridi led a side that looked so off the pace they should have come with an expiry date. Their batting lacked power and innovation; their bowling was better, but still not modern enough; and they were the worst fielding outfit bar none. To think that, for the first few editions of the event, Pakistan had been one of the sharpest sides around.

Starker still was the thumping they received in England, including the concession of a world-record 444 in Nottingham. There were plenty of reasons for the fall: the structure and format of domestic cricket, its lack of competitiveness, the quality of surfaces – all as well known as they are intractable. But one that has gained greater relevance has been the exclusion of Pakistan's players from the IPL's melting pot. Coach Mickey Arthur's determination to modernise Pakistan's white-ball cricket began to reap some rewards, with Babar Azam scoring three centuries in the 3–0 one-day win over West Indies. But there's no doubt they have missed out on the benefits of sharing dressing-rooms, ideas and skills with the world's finest talent, overseen by the best coaches.

To that end, the birth of the Pakistan Super League, staged in February 2016 in the UAE, felt like an important moment. Ever since the inaugural IPL in 2008, the Pakistan board had toyed with the idea of setting up a privately owned, franchise-based Twenty20 tournament. Their commitment to it had waxed and waned, depending on the administration. But, in PCB chairman Shaharyar Khan and Najam Sethi, head of the board's executive committee, plus a clutch of young professionals, they finally found the right mix of vision and vim.

The rights to five city-based teams (Karachi, Lahore, Islamabad, Peshawar and Quetta) were sold for over $US9m, and the leading Pakistani players – along with some of the world's best – thrown into a draft: hey presto, cricket had its next shiny T20 league! For just under three weeks, Dubai and Sharjah did their best to confirm the old joke about their being the best cities in Pakistan. It was a heady period, made all the sweeter by the fact that the board turned a profit of $2.6m – one of the main motivations behind the PSL.

Just as significant were the stories of Pakistani players interacting with foreign players, such as Brad Haddin and Kevin Pietersen, or older legends, such as Viv Richards. The PSL will not change Pakistan's fortunes overnight – and in February 2017 it was hit by a match-fixing scandal – but the fact that it existed at all was a start.

PAKISTAN v WEST INDIES IN 2016-17

OSMAN SAMIUDDIN

Test matches (3): Pakistan 2, West Indies 1
One-day internationals (3): Pakistan 3, West Indies 0
Twenty20 internationals (3): Pakistan 3, West Indies 0

There was a time when Pakistan v West Indies was the business class of rivalries – even if it made little sense to those outside cricketing circles. There were no economic or geopolitical threads to bind them. Neither housed a substantial diaspora of the other, so there was a lack of cultural familiarity. Were it not for cricket, Pakistan and West Indies could have existed quite happily without their destinies crossing. Yet Test series between them – though lacking the history of the Ashes, or the passion of India v Pakistan – were a dramatic upgrade on standard fare.

It was simply brilliant cricket that made the rivalry, particularly three encounters between the mid-1980s and early 1990s, magnificent battles for an unofficial world championship. But over the years a sharp decline in quality, especially West Indies', has led to a troubling question: what real reason is there – other than nostalgia – for them to be playing each other?

This was the first time in ten years Pakistan had hosted West Indies for a full tour. During that decade, few pined for their return and, with a great dark cloud of pointlessness hovering throughout, few rejoiced when they did. Instead, this series spoke volumes for the Future Tours Programme: an annoying obligation that, like family, you don't get to choose, just endure. The ICC can point to the ranking points at stake, yet nobody, except the No. 1 side and their fans, has much time for the league table.

There was the significance of Test cricket's second day/night game, the first in this series, at Dubai. Despite Azhar Ali's triple-century, the contest itself had little to recommend it, at least until the last two days, when Devendra Bishoo's eight-for and Darren Bravo's hundred nearly engineered a remarkable West Indies victory. Attendances throughout the series were pitiful, which came as no surprise: five-day cricket does not have a rich history in the UAE, where the supporters have grown up with Twenty20. When plans for a Test Cricket Fund were first drawn up, to support contests that would otherwise be unviable, it was conceived with this kind of series in mind.

West Indies were dismal during the limited-overs matches, whitewashed in both formats. They slipped to ninth in the 50-over rankings; if they are still there in September 2017, they will not qualify automatically for the World Cup in 2019. From afar, they seemed uninterested but, as administrative shenanigans continued, who could blame them? Phil Simmons, the popular coach who had won the World Twenty20 earlier in the year, had been sacked as the squad prepared to depart. The WICB cited "differences in culture and strategic approach" and, as a stopgap, replaced Simmons with Joel Garner, formerly the team manager.

Aamir Qureshi, Getty Images

Triple agent: Azhar Ali drives Pakistan to a mammoth score at Dubai.

Dwayne Bravo gave his glum assessment after the T20 series. "Basically the players were lost," he said. "The management looked lost… we were looking like schoolkids again. The team meetings had no sort of positive input. It was like we were just there."

For once, Pakistan enjoyed the greater stability, and carried out a long-overdue reboot of their white-ball game, with Babar Azam scoring a hundred in each of the three one-day internationals, and totalling a record 360. But they grew complacent as the Tests began, collapsing three times in six innings. The last two, in Sharjah, allowed a win for West Indies – as unlikely a result as there was in 2016. That averted a cross-format clean sweep, and provided the series with at least one unexpected memory.

WEST INDIES TOURING PARTY

*J. O. Holder (T/50/20), S. J. Benn (50), S. Badree (20), D. Bishoo (T), J. Blackwood (T), C. R. Brathwaite (T/50/20), K. C. Brathwaite (T/50), D. J. Bravo (20), D. M. Bravo (T/50), J. L. Carter (50), J. Charles (50/20), R. L. Chase (T), M. L. Cummins (T), S. O. Dowrich (T), A. D. S. Fletcher

(20), S. T. Gabriel (T/50), S. D. Hope (T), L. R. Johnson (T), A. S. Joseph (T/50), E. Lewis (50/20), S. P. Narine (50/20), A. R. Nurse (50), K. A. Pollard (50/20), N. Pooran (20), R. Powell (20), D. Ramdin (50), J. E. Taylor (20), M. N. Samuels (T/50/20), C. A. K. Walton (20), J. A. Warrican (T), K. O. K. Williams (20). *Interim coach:* J. Garner.

C. R. Brathwaite captained in the Twenty20 games. A. D. Russell was originally selected in the T20 squad, but withdrew for personal reasons; Williams replaced him.

TEST MATCH AVERAGES

PAKISTAN – BATTING AND FIELDING

	T	*I*	*NO*	*R*	*HS*	*100*	*50*	*Avge*	*Ct*
Azhar Ali	3	6	1	474	302*	1	2	94.80	1
Younis Khan	2	4	1	207	127	1	1	69.00	2
Misbah-ul-Haq	3	5	1	197	96	0	2	49.25	1
†Sami Aslam	3	6	0	281	90	0	3	46.83	1
Sarfraz Ahmed	3	4	0	164	56	0	2	41.00	7
Asad Shafiq	3	6	1	198	68	0	3	39.60	2
Zulfiqar Babar	2	3	2	16	15*	0	0	16.00	1
†Mohammad Nawaz	3	4	0	50	25	0	0	12.50	2
†Mohammad Amir	2	3	0	29	20	0	0	9.66	1
Yasir Shah	3	4	0	37	23	0	0	9.25	3
Wahab Riaz	2	3	0	10	5	0	0	3.33	0

Played in two Tests: Sohail Khan 1*, 26 (1 ct). Played in one Test: Babar Azam 69, 21 (1 ct); Rahat Ali 0*.

PAKISTAN – BATTING AND FIELDING

	T	*I*	*NO*	*R*	*HS*	*100*	*50*	*Avge*	*Ct*
Azhar Ali	3	6	1	474	302*	1	2	94.80	1
Younis Khan	2	4	1	207	127	1	1	69.00	2
Misbah-ul-Haq	3	5	1	197	96	0	2	49.25	1
†Sami Aslam	3	6	0	281	90	0	3	46.83	1
Sarfraz Ahmed	3	4	0	164	56	0	2	41.00	7
Asad Shafiq	3	6	1	198	68	0	3	39.60	2
Zulfiqar Babar	2	3	2	16	15*	0	0	16.00	1
†Mohammad Nawaz	3	4	0	50	25	0	0	12.50	2
†Mohammad Amir	2	3	0	29	20	0	0	9.66	1
Yasir Shah	3	4	0	37	23	0	0	9.25	3
Wahab Riaz	2	3	0	10	5	0	0	3.33	0

Played in two Tests: Sohail Khan 1*, 26 (1 ct). Played in one Test: Babar Azam 69, 21 (1 ct); Rahat Ali 0*.

WEST INDIES – BATTING AND FIELDING

	T	*I*	*NO*	*R*	*HS*	*100*	*50*	*Avge*	*Ct/St*
K. C. Brathwaite	3	6	2	328	142*	1	2	82.00	2
S. O. Dowrich	2	4	1	139	60*	0	1	46.33	2/2
†D. M. Bravo	3	6	0	273	116	1	1	45.50	3
J. O. Holder	3	5	2	123	40*	0	0	41.00	4
J. Blackwood	3	6	0	182	95	0	1	30.33	1
M. N. Samuels	3	6	0	143	76	0	1	23.83	0
R. L. Chase	3	6	0	135	50	0	1	22.50	1
†D. Bishoo	3	5	0	93	27	0	0	18.60	3
†L. R. Johnson	3	6	0	96	47	0	0	16.00	4
S. T. Gabriel	3	5	2	27	13	0	0	9.00	0
†M. L. Cummins	2	4	0	4	3	0	0	1.00	0

Played in one Test: S. D. Hope 11, 41 (2 ct); A. S. Joseph 6 (1 ct).

BOWLING

	Style	*O*	*M*	*R*	*W*	*BB*	*5I*	*Avge*
J. O. Holder	RFM	87.3	21	213	9	5-30	1	23.66
D. Bishoo	LBG	134.5	10	486	18	8-49	1	27.00
S. T. Gabriel	RFM	100.1	9	357	10	5-96	1	35.70
R. L. Chase	OB	93	9	309	3	1-47	0	103.00

Also bowled: J. Blackwood (OB) 1.3–0–8–0; K. C. Brathwaite (OB) 39–4–130–1; M. L. Cummins (RF) 59–3–219–1; A. S. Joseph (RFM) 30.5–8–98–2.

At Dubai, September 20, 2016. **West Indians won by 22 runs.** ‡**West Indians 166** (20 overs) (J. Charles 42, R. Powell 38, N. Pooran 47*; Mohammad Naveed 3-20, Ahmed Raza 3-20); **Emirates Cricket Board XI 144** (20 overs) (Mohammed Qasim 46, Shaiman Anwar 31; S. Badree 3-20). *Both teams chose from 15 players. Uncapped left-hander Nicolas Pooran came in with the West Indians 74-4 after ten overs, and got them to 166 with 47* from 23 balls. Still, when the reply reached 91-2, an embarrassing defeat looked on the cards. But Sunil Narine took two wickets in the 13th over to sap Emirati spirits, and Samuel Badree backed him up with 3-20.*

PAKISTAN v WEST INDIES

First Twenty20 International

At Dubai, September 23, 2016 (floodlit). Pakistan won by nine wickets. Toss: Pakistan. Twenty20 international debut: N. Pooran.

Imad Wasim's bowling set up a nine-wicket shellacking of the world champions. With a style that could have emerged only in the Twenty20 era – not so much a spinner as a slow left-arm in-dipper – he picked up three victims in his first two overs to set the course of the match. West Indies had endured their worst powerplay (25 for five), and slumped to 48 for eight before Dwayne Bravo and Taylor – the only two to make double figures – added 66. Wasim ended with five for 14, becoming only the second Pakistani to take a Twenty20 international five-for after Umar Gul, who did it twice. Under the new captaincy of Sarfraz Ahmed, a world removed from his stale predecessor Shahid Afridi, a pursuit of 116 was never an issue. Sharjeel Khan got them going before Babar Azam, elegantly and clinically, finished things off well ahead of time.

Man of the Match: Imad Wasim.

West Indies

		B	4/6
1 J. Charles *b 8*	7	7	1
2 E. Lewis *c 8 b 7*	1	3	0
3 †A. D. S. Fletcher *b 7*	2	6	0
4 M. N. Samuels *lbw b 7*	4	2	1
5 D. J. Bravo *c 6 b 11*	55	54	4/2
6 N. Pooran *c 5 b 10*	5	4	1
7 K. A. Pollard *b 7*	9	17	0
8 *C. R. Brathwaite *c 2 b 7*	0	2	0
9 S. P. Narine *run out*	1	4	0
10 J. E. Taylor *b 11*	21	21	2/1
11 S. Badree *not out*	1	1	0
Lb 2, w 5, nb 2	9		
6 overs: 25-5 (19.5 overs)	115		

1/3 2/11 3/15 4/17 5/22 6/47 7/47 8/48 9/114

Imad Wasim 4–13–14–5; Sohail Tanvir 3.5–10–26–2; Mohammad Nawaz 4–13–16–1; Hasan Ali 3–5–32–1; Shoaib Malik 1–2–5–0; Wahab Riaz 4–18–20–0.

Pakistan

		B	4/6
1 Sharjeel Khan *b 11*	22	18	3/1
2 Khalid Latif *not out*	34	32	4/1
3 Babar Azam *not out*	55	37	6/2
Lb 1, w 3, nb 1	5		
6 overs: 38-1 (14.2 overs)	116-1		

1/28

4 Shoaib Malik, 5 *†Sarfraz Ahmed, 6 Umar Akmal, 7 Imad Wasim, 8 Mohammad Nawaz, 9 Wahab Riaz, 10 Hasan Ali and 11 Sohail Tanvir did not bat.

Badree 4–14–27–1; Taylor 1–4–8–0; Narine 3–8–21–0; Bravo 2–3–16–0; Brathwaite 2.2–6–29–0; Pollard 2–2–14–0.

Umpires: Ahsan Raza and Shozab Raza. Third umpire: Ahmed Shahab.
Referee: A. J. Pycroft.

PAKISTAN v WEST INDIES

Second Twenty20 International

At Dubai, September 24, 2016 (floodlit). Pakistan won by 16 runs. Toss: West Indies.

It was difficult to square the performances of this West Indies with the one at the World Twenty20 final – when it felt as if no force on earth, let alone Ben Stokes's attempted yorkers, could stop them. This may as well have been a different team. Without being truly explosive, Khalid Latif, Shoaib Malik and Sarfraz Ahmed had played strong hands to ensure a par score. But in reply West Indies were never in contention. Imad Wasim, again, and Sohail Tanvir stymied their start – there were three wickets and 21 dot balls in the first six overs – and before long West Indies slumped to 89 for seven. Narine made an entertaining 17-ball 30 to make it appear close, but it wasn't.

Man of the Match: Sarfraz Ahmed.

Pakistan

		B	4/6
1 Sharjeel Khan *b 11*	2	5	0
2 Khalid Latif *run out*	40	36	3/1
3 Babar Azam *c 6 b 7*	19	18	2
4 Shoaib Malik *c 6 b 5*	37	28	3/1
5 *†Sarfraz Ahmed *not out*	46	32	5
6 Umar Akmal *not out*	1	1	0
Lb 10, w 5	15		
6 overs: 39-1 (20 overs)	160-4		

1/4 2/58 3/85 4/154

7 Imad Wasim, 8 Mohammad Nawaz, 9 Wahab Riaz, 10 Hasan Ali and 11 Sohail Tanvir did not bat.

Badree 4–9–24–1; Taylor 4–9–28–0; Narine 4–5–36–0; Bravo 4–4–38–1; Brathwaite 4–9–24–1.

West Indies

		B	4/6
1 J. Charles *c 6 b 7*	10	12	1
2 E. Lewis *c 1 b 11*	3	6	0
3 †A. D. S. Fletcher *b 10*	29	37	1/1
4 M. N. Samuels *c 5 b 11*	1	5	0
5 D. J. Bravo *b 8*	18	16	1/1
6 K. A. Pollard *c 5 b 10*	18	13	2
7 *C. R. Brathwaite *c 6 b 10*	8	6	1
8 N. Pooran *c 8 b 11*	4	6	1
9 S. P. Narine *c 6 b 9*	30	17	4/1
10 J. E. Taylor *not out*	10	4	2
W 7, nb 6	13		
6 overs: 20-3 (20 overs)	144-9		

1/12 2/15 3/19 4/45 5/82 6/83 7/89 8/119 9/144

11 S. Badree did not bat.

Imad Wasim 4–8–18–1; Sohail Tanvir 4–17–13–3; Mohammad Nawaz 3–6–19–1; Shoaib Malik 1–4–3–0; Hasan Ali 4–8–49–3; Wahab Riaz 4–9–42–1.

Umpires: Ahmed Shahab and Shozab Raza. Third umpire: Ahsan Raza.
Referee: A. J. Pycroft.

PAKISTAN v WEST INDIES

Third Twenty20 International

At Abu Dhabi, September 27, 2016 (floodlit). Pakistan won by eight wickets. Toss: Pakistan. Twenty20 international debuts: Rumman Raees; K. O. K. Williams.

On the slower surfaces and larger outfields of the UAE, the West Indian power-hitting game once more seemed hopelessly limited. They were even worse than in the first match, limping past 100 with only seven boundaries. Their top order continued to struggle against Imad Wasim's non-spinning left-arm spin – all three of his victims were bowled by straight deliveries – while Samuels used up 59 balls for 42. Shoaib Malik bowled the only two right-arm overs in West Indies' innings, and backed it up with 43 of the lowest-pressure runs he will ever score. A near-full stadium did not cavil at the lack of competition. This was Pakistan's first T20 in Abu Dhabi since February 2012, so any game would do.

Man of the Match: Imad Wasim. *Man of the Series:* Imad Wasim.

West Indies

		B	4/6
1 J. Charles *b 7*	5	5	0
2 †A. D. S. Fletcher *run out*	9	17	1
3 C. A. K. Walton *b 7*	0	1	0
4 M. N. Samuels *not out*	42	59	3
5 D. J. Bravo *b 7*	11	9	2
6 N. Pooran *c 4 b 8*	16	12	0/1
7 K. A. Pollard *not out*	16	17	0
Lb 3, w 1	4		
6 overs: 26-3 (20 overs)	103-5		

1/12 2/12 3/17 4/31 5/66

8 *C. R. Brathwaite, 9 S. P. Narine, 10 J. E. Taylor and 11 K. O. K. Williams did not bat.

Imad Wasim 4–11–21–3; Sohail Tanvir 4–11–22–0; Mohammad Nawaz 3–11–16–1; Mohammad Amir 4–9–20–0; Shoaib Malik 2–4–11–0; Rumman Raees 3–9–10–0.

Pakistan

		B	4/6
1 Sharjeel Khan *c 2 b 11*	11	13	2
2 Khalid Latif *b 11*	21	20	3
3 Babar Azam *not out*	27	24	1
4 Shoaib Malik *not out*	43	34	4/1
Lb 4, w 2	6		
6 overs: 40-2 (15.1 overs)	108-2		

1/36 2/40

5 *†Sarfraz Ahmed, 6 Umar Akmal, 7 Imad Wasim, 8 Mohammad Nawaz, 9 Rumman Raees, 10 Sohail Tanvir and 11 Mohammad Amir did not bat.

Taylor 2–6–19–0; Williams 4–13–15–2; Bravo 4–7–31–0; Narine 4–6–21–0; Brathwaite 1.1–2–18–0.

Umpires: Ahsan Raza and Shozab Raza. Third umpire: Ahmed Shahab.
Referee: A. J. Pycroft.

PAKISTAN v WEST INDIES

First One-Day International

At Sharjah, September 30, 2016 (day/night). Pakistan won by 111 runs (DLS). Toss: West Indies. One-day international debut: K. C. Brathwaite.

It might not quite match the Mohammad family, but the Akmals have been prolific providers of talent for Pakistan. First came brothers Kamran, Umar and Adnan; now their cousin, Babar Azam, arrived. Many believe he may trump them all. His maiden international hundred set up a comfortable Pakistan victory, in much the same temper as their T20 triumphs. Azam has all the shots – much like his kin – but it was the cold-bloodedness with which he reached his hundred that stood out; it is not a trait common among Pakistanis of recent vintage. Assistance came from Sharjeel Khan's burst at the top, and cameos from Sarfraz Ahmed and Imad Wasim lower down, though a floodlight failure for 80 minutes scuttled some momentum (and reduced the contest to 49 overs). West Indies did not so much reply as complete the formality of a loss, as relative newcomers Hasan Ali and Mohammad Nawaz shared seven wickets on a slow pitch.

Man of the Match: Babar Azam.

Pakistan

*Azhar Ali c Ramdin b Gabriel	0
Sharjeel Khan c Narine b Benn	54
Babar Azam c Pollard b C. R. Brathwaite	120
Shoaib Malik c Benn b Narine	6
†Sarfraz Ahmed c Ramdin b Holder	35
Mohammad Rizwan run out	11
Imad Wasim b C. R. Brathwaite	24
Mohammad Nawaz c Holder b C. R. Brathwaite	19
Wahab Riaz run out	0
Mohammad Amir not out	3
Hasan Ali not out	2
B 1, lb 3, w 5, nb 1	10
(9 wkts, 49 overs)	284

1/0 (1) 2/82 (2) 3/93 (4) 4/192 (5) 5/211 (6) 6/239 (3) 7/269 (7) 8/269 (9) 9/281 (8) 10 overs: 60-1

Gabriel 8–0–53–1; Holder 7–0–35–1; C. R. Brathwaite 10–0–54–3; Benn 10–0–46–1; Narine 10–0–58–1; Pollard 4–0–34–0.

West Indies

J. Charles c Sarfraz Ahmed b Mohammad Amir	20	C. R. Brathwaite b Mohammad Nawaz	15
K. C. Brathwaite c Sarfraz Ahmed b Hasan Ali	14	S. P. Narine c Imad Wasim b Hasan Ali	23
D. M. Bravo b Mohammad Nawaz	12	S. J. Benn not out	16
M. N. Samuels b Wahab Riaz	46	S. T. Gabriel b Hasan Ali	2
†D. Ramdin c Azhar Ali b Mohammad Nawaz	8	Lb 6, w 2, nb 1	9
K. A. Pollard c Sharjeel Khan b Mohammad Nawaz	9	1/27 (1) 2/41 (2) 3/54 (3) 4/89 (5) 5/99 (6) 6/103 (7) 7/125 (8) 8/135 (4) 9/166 (9) 10/175 (11) (38.4 overs)	175
*J. O. Holder b Imad Wasim	1	10 overs: 30-1	

Imad Wasim 8–0–36–1; Mohammad Amir 5–1–21–1; Hasan Ali 5.4–0–14–3; Wahab Riaz 6–0–27–1; Shoaib Malik 4–0–29–0; Mohammad Nawaz 10–0–42–4.

Umpires: Ahsan Raza and R. S. A. Palliyaguruge. Third umpire: S. Ravi.
Referee: A. J. Pycroft.

PAKISTAN v WEST INDIES

Second One-Day International

At Sharjah, October 2, 2016 (day/night). Pakistan won by 59 runs. Toss: Pakistan. One-day international debut: A. S. Joseph.

Over the last few years, 300 had become the new 250, but nobody told Pakistan. So a total of 337 felt like a foray into new territory, particularly on such a sluggish surface. Sharjeel Khan's 12-ball 24 screamed intent, and Babar Azam and Shoaib Malik heard it, putting on 169 for the third wicket. Malik was the aggressor, overcoming a slow outfield by going aerial – he hit six sixes, including three in an over off Benn. Azam carried on from the first game, except this time with better strike rotation. Sarfraz Ahmed's brisk 60 carried Pakistan to their highest total against West Indies, beating 307 for five at Perth in 2004-05. West Indies fought harder this time and, with Darren Bravo and Samuels in tandem, even entertained thoughts of a successful chase. But despite Pakistani profligacy – six chances went down – they fell comfortably short.

Man of the Match: Babar Azam.

Pakistan

*Azhar Ali lbw b Holder	9	Mohammad Rizwan not out	6
Sharjeel Khan c Holder b Joseph	24	Lb 2, w 12	14
Babar Azam c C. R. Brathwaite b Joseph	123	1/40 (1) 2/40 (2) 3/209 (4) 4/282 (3) 5/320 (6) (5 wkts, 50 overs)	337
Shoaib Malik c Bravo b Narine	90	10 overs: 55-2	
†Sarfraz Ahmed not out	60		
Imad Wasim b Holder	11		

Mohammad Nawaz, Wahab Riaz, Mohammad Amir and Hasan Ali did not bat.

Holder 8–1–51–2; Joseph 10–0–62–2; C. R. Brathwaite 8–0–60–0; Narine 8–0–39–1; Benn 8–0–61–0; K. C. Brathwaite 3–0–18–0; Pollard 5–0–44–0.

West Indies

J. Charles c Imad Wasim b Mohammad Amir	2	*J. O. Holder not out	31
K. C. Brathwaite run out	39	S. P. Narine not out	1
D. M. Bravo run out	61	Lb 8, w 9	17
M. N. Samuels b Wahab Riaz	57	1/3 (1) 2/92 (2) 3/127 (3) 4/194 (4) 5/209 (5) 6/231 (7) 7/273 (6) (7 wkts, 50 overs)	278
†D. Ramdin b Wahab Riaz	34	10 overs: 46-1	
K. A. Pollard c Shoaib Malik b Imad Wasim	22		
C. R. Brathwaite run out	14		

S. J. Benn and A. S. Joseph did not bat.

Imad Wasim 10–0–62–1; Mohammad Amir 9–0–49–1; Hasan Ali 9–0–56–0; Wahab Riaz 10–0–48–2; Shoaib Malik 5–2–16–0; Mohammad Nawaz 7–0–39–0.

Umpires: S. Ravi and Shozab Raza. Third umpire: R. S. A. Palliyaguruge.
Referee: A. J. Pycroft.

At Dubai, October 3–4, 2016 (not first-class). **Drawn.** ‡**West Indians 249-6** (70 overs) (L. R. Johnson 50, S. D. Hope 59) **and 173-7** (51 overs) (S. O. Dowrich 52*); **Emirates Cricket Board XI 117** (39.1 overs) **and 43-1** (15 overs). *Both teams chose from 15 players. When Miguel Cummins and Jonathan Carter reduced the Emiratis to 20-7 on the first evening – with five ducks – it looked as if two days might be enough for a result. But Rohan Mustafa top-scored with 44* from No. 9 to make the West Indians bat again; Shane Dowrich became their third half-centurion of the match.*

PAKISTAN v WEST INDIES

Third One-Day International

At Abu Dhabi, October 5, 2016 (day/night). Pakistan won by 136 runs. Toss: Pakistan. One-day international debut: E. Lewis.

If Babar Azam stole the headlines, Azhar Ali earned valuable breathing space. His spot had been under threat and, after nine runs in the first two games, criticism was growing. His method appeared out of place in white-ball cricket, but he responded with his third one-day hundred as Pakistan captain, more than any other. He put on 147 for the second wicket with Babar, who hit another assured century to become the highest run-scorer in a three-match series, and the third Pakistani to score three in a row. As in the other games, Pakistan's finish lacked power-hitters: just two boundaries came from the last ten overs. Other sides will exploit that weakness, but West Indies rendered it irrelevant. They were unable to work out another slow surface, and only Holder's strike-rate broke 100.

Man of the Match: Babar Azam. *Man of the Series:* Babar Azam.

MOST CONSECUTIVE 100s IN ONE-DAY INTERNATIONALS

100s			
4	K. C. Sangakkara (SL)	v Bangladesh, England, Australia, Scotland	2014-15
3	Zaheer Abbas (P)	v India (3)	1982-83
3	Saeed Anwar (P)	v Sri Lanka, West Indies, Sri Lanka	1993-94
3	H. H. Gibbs (SA)	v Kenya, India, Bangladesh	2002-03
3	A. B. de Villiers (SA)	v India (2), West Indies	2009-10
3	Q. de Kock (SA)	v India (3)	2013-14
3	L. R. P. L. Taylor (NZ)	v India (2), Pakistan	2013-14
3	**Babar Azam (P)**	**v West Indies (3)**	**2016-17**

Pakistan

*Azhar Ali b Holder	101
Sharjeel Khan c Joseph b Benn	38
Babar Azam b Pollard	117
Shoaib Malik c Ramdin b Narine	5
†Sarfraz Ahmed not out	24
Mohammad Rizwan lbw b Joseph	4
Imad Wasim c Bravo b Joseph	4
Mohammad Nawaz not out	4
Lb 7, w 3, nb 1	11
1/85 (2) 2/232 (1) 3/239 (4) 4/280 (3) 5/285 (6) 6/303 (7) — (6 wkts, 50 overs)	308
10 overs: 66-0	

Wahab Riaz, Sohail Khan and Hasan Ali did not bat.

Joseph 8–0–62–2; Gabriel 5–0–37–0; Brathwaite 4–0–22–0; Holder 10–0–63–1; Narine 10–0–47–1; Benn 10–0–51–1; Pollard 3–0–19–1.

West Indies

K. C. Brathwaite lbw b Shoaib Malik	32
E. Lewis b Sohail Khan	22
D. M. Bravo c Sarfraz Ahmed b Wahab Riaz	17
M. N. Samuels run out	13
†D. Ramdin run out	37
K. A. Pollard c Shoaib Malik b Mohammad Nawaz	11
*J. O. Holder b Imad Wasim	26
S. P. Narine st Sarfraz Ahmed b Mohammad Nawaz	0
S. J. Benn c Sohail Khan b Mohammad Nawaz	0
A. S. Joseph c Shoaib Malik b Wahab Riaz	2
S. T. Gabriel not out	1
B 1, lb 4, w 6	11
1/45 (2) 2/75 (1) 3/87 (3) 4/93 (4) 5/117 (6) 6/159 (7) 7/161 (8) 8/161 (9) 9/170 (10) 10/172 (5) (44 overs)	172
10 overs: 46-1	

Imad Wasim 8–0–29–1; Sohail Khan 7–0–34–1; Hasan Ali 6–1–13–0; Shoaib Malik 6–0–23–1; Mohammad Nawaz 9–0–40–3; Wahab Riaz 8–0–28–2.

Umpires: Ahsan Raza and R. S. A. Palliyaguruge. Third umpire: S. Ravi.
Referee: A. J. Pycroft.

At Sharjah, October 7–9, 2016 (day/night). **Drawn. ‡Pakistan Cricket Board Patron's XI 308** (103.4 overs) (Shan Masood 58, Ahmed Shehzad 52, Iftikhar Ahmed 63, Adnan Akmal 69; D. Bishoo 5-107) **and 26-3** (16 overs); **West Indians 297** (132.5 overs) (K. C. Brathwaite 55, D. M. Bravo 91, S. D. Hope 76; Shahzaib Ahmed 5-85). *West Indies needed competitive practice with a pink ball, and got it against a team containing eight Test players. Two leg-spinners enjoyed the conditions – Devendra Bishoo and Shahzaib Ahmed both collected five-fors – but the batsmen's caution ensured a draw. Shan Masood used 191 balls for his 58 and, in reply, Darren Bravo and Shai Hope faced 491 between them for 167.*

PAKISTAN v WEST INDIES

First Test Match

At Dubai, October 13–17, 2016 (day/night). Pakistan won by 56 runs. Toss: Pakistan. Test debuts: Babar Azam, Mohammad Nawaz.

It was hard to know what to make of cricket's second day/night Test. There was a triple-century, 17 wickets for leg-spin, a fourth-day collapse, and a valiant hundred in a big chase. Yet the public barely bothered: the first evening drew a crowd of around 600 and, even as Azhar Ali inched towards 300, the second day – a Friday, and therefore a public holiday – fared little better. The game sprang into life towards the end, though only a handful were there to watch it.

An hour into the fourth day, Pakistan were in control, dismissing West Indies for 357 to earn a lead of 222. Misbah-ul-Haq decided against the follow-on, reasoning his bowlers needed a rest after 124 overs in the field. But they were soon back at the coalface: Pakistan collapsed to 121 for eight by dinner and, soon after, left a target of 346. Bishoo was responsible, taking eight for 49 with his leg-spin, the best by a visiting bowler in Asia, beating Lance Klusener's eight for 64 at Calcutta in 1996-97. He bowled well, taking a couple with classic bits of deception on a pitch that belatedly gave prodigious, if slow,

---

BEST BOWLING IN AN INNINGS FOR WEST INDIES

9-95	J. M. Noreiga	v India at Port-of-Spain	1970-71
8-29	C. E. H. Croft	v Pakistan at Port-of-Spain	1976-77
8-38	L. R. Gibbs	v India at Bridgetown	1961-62
8-45	C. E. L. Ambrose	v England at Bridgetown	1989-90
8-49	**D. Bishoo**	**v Pakistan at Dubai**	**2016-17**
8-92	M. A. Holding	v England at The Oval	1976
8-104	A. L. Valentine	v England at Manchester	1950

turn. But Pakistan played him terribly: six of his wickets came from outright errors in the hunt for quick runs.

Bishoo outshone his counterpart, Yasir Shah, who had created his own bit of history earlier in the day. By bowling Miguel Cummins, he collected his 100th wicket in his 17th Test – the joint-second-fastest to the mark, one slower than George Lohmann. It was also his seventh Test five-for.

All told, West Indies handled him well: his seven victims in the game cost 234. But it was his one wicket on the final evening that sealed the match. Left-handed, lovely of shot, and bearing down on an unlikely target, Darren Bravo appeared to be fulfilling the prophecies written of him early in his career, when he was compared to Brian Lara. Then a loopy leg-break caught the inner half of his bat as he attempted another cover-drive. The ball went to the left of Yasir, who flew as if saving a penalty and grabbed it with both hands. Sixth out, with West Indies 83 short of their target, Bravo had faced 249 balls for his 116, and survived six-and-three-quarter hours; it was his eighth Test hundred, and his seventh outside the Caribbean. Holder, the captain, batted on manfully, and West Indies held out for their longest fourth innings in Asia, beating 105.1 overs at Calcutta in 1978-79. But two run-outs ended their resistance, and gave Pakistan a win in their 400th Test with only 12 overs left.

Nothing on three soporific days had hinted at a gripping finish. Misbah is rarely happy with the surfaces in the UAE, and this one did nothing to cheer him up. From ball one, it was slow, low and straight – not a friend to any bowler.

That rather dampened the magnitude of Azhar's triple-hundred – the fourth for Pakistan (following Hanif Mohammad in 1957-58, Inzamam-ul-Haq in 2002 and Younis Khan in 2008-09), and only the third against West Indies (following England's Andy Sandham in 1929-30, and Hanif). Dropped in the gully on 17 by Johnson off Cummins, he put on 215 with Sami Aslam – the highest opening stand in UAE Tests – 137 with Asad Shafiq, and 165 with debutant Babar Azam. Azhar's score, another UAE best, lasted 469 balls and almost 11 hours, buttressing a score of 579 for three, yet another record in the Emirates. He provided few frills, hitting only 23 fours and two sixes.

Fans in Sharjah had booed him during the one-day series – fallout from his leadership of a side that had been in sharp decline over the previous three years. But Tests are his natural habitat, and this mammoth effort provided great satisfaction, even if few were there to share it.

Man of the Match: Azhar Ali.

Close of play: first day, Pakistan 279-1 (Azhar Ali 146, Asad Shafiq 33); second day, West Indies 69-1 (Brathwaite 32, Bravo 14); third day, West Indies 315-6 (Dowrich 27, Holder 10); fourth day, West Indies 95-2 (Bravo 26, Samuels 4).

Pakistan

Sami Aslam b Chase	90	– c Blackwood b Bishoo	44
Azhar Ali not out	302	– lbw b Gabriel	2
Asad Shafiq c and b Bishoo	67	– lbw b Bishoo	5
Babar Azam c Holder b Bishoo	69	– b Bishoo	21
*Misbah-ul-Haq not out	29	– b Bishoo	15
†Sarfraz Ahmed (did not bat)		– st Dowrich b Bishoo	15
Mohammad Nawaz (did not bat)		– b Bishoo	0
Wahab Riaz (did not bat)		– c Brathwaite b Bishoo	5
Yasir Shah (did not bat)		– c and b Holder	2
Sohail Khan (did not bat)		– not out	1
Mohammad Amir (did not bat)		– b Bishoo	1
B 1, lb 9, w 1, nb 11	22	B 10, nb 2	12
1/215 (1) 2/352 (3) 3/517 (4) (3 wkts dec, 155.3 overs)	579	1/13 (2) 2/20 (3) 3/77 (4) 4/93 (1) 5/112 (5) 6/112 (7) 7/118 (8) 8/121 (9) 9/121 (6) 10/123 (11) (31.5 overs)	123

Gabriel 22–3–99–0; Cummins 25–2–99–0; Holder 25–4–73–0; Brathwaite 14–2–56–0; Bishoo 35–4–125–2; Chase 33–2–109–1; Blackwood 1.3–0–8–0. *Second innings*—Gabriel 7–1–23–1; Cummins 7–0–29–0; Bishoo 13.5–1–49–8; Holder 4–0–12–1.

West Indies

K. C. Brathwaite b Yasir Shah	32	– b Mohammad Amir	6
L. R. Johnson lbw b Yasir Shah	15	– lbw b Mohammad Amir	47
D. M. Bravo c Azhar Ali b Mohammad Nawaz	87	– c and b Yasir Shah	116
M. N. Samuels lbw b Sohail Khan	76	– c Sarfraz Ahmed b Mohammad Amir	4
J. Blackwood c Sarfraz Ahmed b Wahab Riaz	37	– lbw b Mohammad Nawaz	15
R. L. Chase c Babar Azam b Wahab Riaz	6	– b Yasir Shah	35
†S. O. Dowrich lbw b Yasir Shah	32	– b Wahab Riaz	0
*J. O. Holder b Yasir Shah	20	– not out	40
D. Bishoo b Mohammad Nawaz	17	– lbw b Mohammad Nawaz	3
M. L. Cummins b Yasir Shah	0	– run out	1
S. T. Gabriel not out	6	– run out	1
B 9, lb 8, w 1, nb 11	29	B 5, lb 7, w 5, nb 4	21

1/42 (2) 2/69 (1) 3/182 (4) (123.5 overs)	357	1/27 (1) 2/87 (2) (109 overs)	289
4/259 (5) 5/266 (6) 6/300 (3)		3/95 (4) 4/116 (5)	
7/325 (7) 8/346 (8) 9/351 (10) 10/357 (9)		5/193 (6) 6/194 (7) 7/263 (3)	
		8/276 (9) 9/277 (10) 10/289 (11)	

Mohammad Amir 22–6–54–0; Sohail Khan 16–2–56–1; Yasir Shah 43–15–121–5; Wahab Riaz 23.3–3–65–2; Mohammad Nawaz 16.5–5–38–2; Azhar Ali 2.3–1–6–0. *Second innings*—Mohammad Amir 23–5–63–3; Sohail Khan 10–1–22–0; Yasir Shah 41–6–113–2; Mohammad Nawaz 18–4–32–2; Wahab Riaz 17–1–47–1.

Umpires: R. K. Illingworth and P. R. Reiffel. Third umpire: M. A. Gough.
Referee: J. J. Crowe.

PAKISTAN v WEST INDIES

Second Test Match

At Abu Dhabi, October 21–25, 2016. Pakistan won by 133 runs. Toss: Pakistan.

Can a bowler take ten wickets to decide a Test, yet still be criticised? Yasir Shah's performance here invited the question. He earned the match award and sealed the series, but rarely looked like the player who had enchanted the world for two years.

The Sheikh Zayed Stadium has never been kind to bowlers, and again the surface was dull. Patience can be the key, lulling the batsmen to wooziness with sedative repetition. Most leg-spinners find such precision difficult yet, since his debut, Yasir's accuracy had set him apart. In his first series against Australia, in 2014-15, he had – according to analytics tool CricViz – landed 93% of deliveries in Dubai on a good length, and 74% in Abu Dhabi. But in this series, Yasir regressed: 29% in Dubai, and under 50% in Abu Dhabi.

It was difficult to recall how many of his wickets here (and in the previous match) were the result of genuinely good deliveries. In the second innings he outdid Chase, who was drawn by drift and beaten on the outside edge, and – with a skidder – Blackwood. But a more settled line-up may not have been so compliant in such unsparing conditions.

Even if West Indies had handled Yasir better, winning would have been a struggle. In the six years Pakistan have played Tests in Abu Dhabi, it has become their fortress: this

MOST PRODUCTIVE PARTNERSHIPS FOR PAKISTAN

	Runs	*I*	*High*	*Avge*	*Span*
Misbah-ul-Haq/Younis Khan	**3,205**	**52**	**218**	**69.67**	**2000-01–2016-17**
Mohammad Yousuf/Younis Khan	3,137	42	363	78.42	1999-2000–2009
Inzamam-ul-Haq/Mohammad Yousuf	3,013	57	259	56.84	1997-98–2007-08
Majid Khan/Sadiq Mohammad	2,325	42	195	59.61	1972-73–1980-81
Azhar Ali/Younis Khan	**2,585**	**46**	**250**	**56.19**	**2010-11–2016-17**
Mohsin Khan/Mudassar Nazar	2,189	56	157	40.53	1977-78–1986-87
Javed Miandad/Mudassar Nazar	2,117	28	451	75.60	1977-78–1988-89
Javed Miandad/Shoaib Mohammad	2,112	23	248	91.82	1984-85–1993-94
Javed Miandad/Zaheer Abbas	2,042	41	287	53.73	1976-77–1984-85

As at January 31, 2017.

was their fifth victory in nine Tests, with no losses. Their method is as predictable as it is successful. Misbah-ul-Haq wins the toss (here for the eighth time), and his batsmen carefully raise a withering score (here passing 400 in their first innings for the seventh).

This effort had familiar protagonists: Younis Khan made a record 13th hundred since turning 35, one more than Gooch, Dravid and Tendulkar. Younis and Misbah became the most productive Test pairing for Pakistan, before Asad Shafiq and Sarfraz Ahmed chipped in with pleasant fifties. Gabriel's muscular pace – touching the mid-90s – earned a deserving five-for, his first in Tests, but Pakistan had scoreboard pressure.

Sometimes the surface is too slow for the strategy to bear fruit, but this time the West Indian batting was co-operative enough. Seven of their top nine batted for at least an hour in the first innings, yet none reached 50, and they folded to 224. That simply added to the frustration: they had the technique to hang around, but not the temperament to last. After Misbah again ignored the follow-on, he watched his top three make fifties, and left West Indies attempting another escape act. But, despite Blackwood's 95, and their highest fourth-innings total against Pakistan, they finally yielded to Yasir on the last afternoon, leaving Misbah with ten series wins, the most by an Asian Test captain.

Man of the Match: Yasir Shah.

Close of play: first day, Pakistan 304-4 (Misbah-ul-Haq 90, Yasir Shah 0); second day, West Indies 106-4 (Bishoo 0, Blackwood 0); third day, Pakistan 114-1 (Azhar Ali 52, Asad Shafiq 5); fourth day, West Indies 171-4 (Blackwood 41, Chase 17).

Pakistan

Sami Aslam b Bishoo	6	– c Hope b Gabriel	50
Azhar Ali b Gabriel	0	– c Holder b Cummins	79
Asad Shafiq b Gabriel	68	– not out	58
Younis Khan c Chase b Brathwaite	127	– not out	29
*Misbah-ul-Haq lbw b Gabriel	96		
Yasir Shah c Bishoo b Holder	23		
†Sarfraz Ahmed b Gabriel	56		
Mohammad Nawaz b Holder	25		
Sohail Khan c Johnson b Holder	26		
Zulfiqar Babar c Hope b Gabriel	0		
Rahat Ali not out	0		
B 1, lb 15, nb 9	25	B 4, lb 3, w 1, nb 3	11
1/6 (2) 2/42 (1) 3/129 (3) 4/304 (4) 5/332 (5) 6/342 (6) 7/412 (7) 8/430 (8) 9/452 (9) 10/452 (10) (119.1 overs)	452	1/93 (1) 2/164 (2) (2 wkts dec, 67 overs)	227

Gabriel 23.1–1–96–5; Cummins 20–1–65–0; Holder 22–8–47–3; Bishoo 26–0–112–1; Chase 19–1–80–0; Brathwaite 9–0–36–1. *Second innings*—Gabriel 12–2–36–1; Cummins 7–0–26–1; Brathwaite 15–2–33–0; Bishoo 20–0–77–0; Holder 7–0–22–0; Chase 6–0–26–0.

West Indies

L. R. Johnson lbw b Rahat Ali	12	– (2) b Yasir Shah	9
D. M. Bravo lbw b Yasir Shah	43	– (3) c Mohammad Nawaz b Rahat Ali	13
K. C. Brathwaite run out	21	– (1) lbw b Mohammad Nawaz	67
M. N. Samuels c Sami Aslam b Rahat Ali	30	– c and b Yasir Shah	23
D. Bishoo b Sohail Khan	20	– (9) c Misbah-ul-Haq b Zulfiqar Babar	26
J. Blackwood c Sarfraz Ahmed b Rahat Ali	8	– (5) b Yasir Shah	95
R. L. Chase c Asad Shafiq b Yasir Shah	22	– (6) c Sarfraz Ahmed b Yasir Shah	20
†S. D. Hope b Yasir Shah	11	– (7) c Younis Khan b Zulfiqar Babar	41
*J. O. Holder not out	31	– (8) lbw b Yasir Shah	16
M. L. Cummins b Sohail Khan	3	– b Yasir Shah	0
S. T. Gabriel c Sohail Khan b Yasir Shah	13	– not out	7
B 2, lb 7, nb 1	10	B 4, lb 1	5
1/27 (1) 2/65 (2) 3/106 (4) 4/106 (3) 5/121 (6) 6/144 (5) 7/169 (7) 8/178 (8) 9/197 (10) 10/224 (11) (94.4 overs)	224	1/28 (2) 2/63 (3) 3/112 (4) 4/124 (1) 5/187 (6) 6/244 (5) 7/266 (8) 8/311 (7) 9/312 (10) 10/322 (9) (108 overs)	322

Rahat Ali 21–8–45–3; Sohail Khan 19–8–35–2; Zulfiqar Babar 21–6–39–0; Asad Shafiq 1–0–2–0; Yasir Shah 28.4–6–86–4; Mohammad Nawaz 4–1–8–0. *Second innings*—Sohail Khan 14–3–44–0; Rahat Ali 23–2–69–1; Yasir Shah 39–5–124–6; Zulfiqar Babar 22–5–51–2; Mohammad Nawaz 10–0–29–1.

Umpires: M. A. Gough and R. K. Illingworth. Third umpire: P. R. Reiffel.
Referee: J. J. Crowe.

PAKISTAN v WEST INDIES

Third Test Match

At Sharjah, October 30–November 3, 2016. West Indies won by five wickets. Toss: Pakistan.

In the Caribbean, this is supposed to be the age of Twenty20, of maroon shirts and superstars, of Gayle and Sammy and Russell. But in the year Carlos Brathwaite broke Ben Stokes in the World T20 final, one of the finest performances in West Indies' history came from a little-known namesake, clad in white.

Kraigg Brathwaite, as slight as Shivnarine Chanderpaul, had not played a single 20-over game, even domestically, and only a handful of one-day internationals; red-ball cricket is his niche. Here, against one of the world's best attacks, he was immovable, becoming the first opener to be unbeaten in both innings of a Test, and only the fifth West Indian to carry his bat (though Desmond Haynes did it three times). And he inspired his team to their first win in 14, their first under Holder, and only their second – to set against 56 defeats – outside the Caribbean against a top-eight nation since the turn of the millennium. It was the kind of heroism and history that deserved a grander stage than a dead rubber, in a low-key series, in front of empty, low-rise stands.

After the first-day discipline of the West Indian bowlers, Brathwaite batted eight hours for 142. For the first time in 14 Tests, West Indies had a first-innings lead. In the second, he stood firm while others wilted, refusing to believe – as many did – that his side would collapse in pursuit of a small target. Yet his presence in the game was somehow unobtrusive, lost amid the tenseness of battle. Over half his first-innings runs came in singles, mainly from nurdles and checked pushes all around the wicket. It was quiet accumulation in the finest tradition.

There were other heroes, not least the unstinting Gabriel, who got the Test off to a rollicking start with two wickets in the first over. His second victim, Asad Shafiq, was on his way to a second pair in five Tests (only the third top-six batsman to make two in a calendar year, after Mohinder Amarnath in 1983 and Mark Waugh in 1992). Bishoo was prominent as well, and between them they ensured Pakistan's first innings ended on an inadequate 281. Misbah-ul-Haq, leading them for a national-record 49th time in Tests, was one of four half-centurions.

Perhaps most heartening was the contribution of Holder, who had taken much criticism during his tenure. In his 20th Test, he picked up a maiden five-for to bring about a second-innings collapse. His medium-pace was never more than honest, but Pakistan continued their tradition of turning unassuming, and hitherto unsuccessful, bowlers into fleeting match-winners.

Finally, there was the wicketkeeper Dowrich, diminutive of stature but with the punch to make up for it. His counter-attacking vim complemented Brathwaite's gliding calm in partnerships that shaped both West Indian innings. In the first, their stand of 83 kept them in contention. In the second, when West Indies appeared to be choking at 67 for five in pursuit of 153, Dowrich hit 60 in an unbroken 87, including the last, slashed, four. It would have been fitting for Brathwaite to have the final say, yet it seems there will be no forgetting the name.

Man of the Match: K. C. Brathwaite. *Man of the Series:* Yasir Shah.

Close of play: first day, Pakistan 255-8 (Yasir Shah 1, Mohammad Amir 6); second day, West Indies 244-6 (Brathwaite 95, Holder 6); third day, Pakistan 87-4 (Azhar Ali 45, Sarfraz Ahmed 19); fourth day, West Indies 114-5 (Brathwaite 44, Dowrich 36).

Pakistan

Sami Aslam c Holder b Bishoo	74	– c Joseph b Holder	17
Azhar Ali c Brathwaite b Gabriel	0	– c Bravo b Bishoo	91
Asad Shafiq lbw b Gabriel	0	– c Bravo b Holder	0
Younis Khan c Johnson b Chase	51	– c Dowrich b Holder	0
*Misbah-ul-Haq c Dowrich b Bishoo	53	– c Bishoo b Chase	4
†Sarfraz Ahmed b Gabriel	51	– c Bravo b Bishoo	42
Mohammad Nawaz st Dowrich b Bishoo	6	– c Johnson b Bishoo	19
Wahab Riaz lbw b Bishoo	4	– (9) c Johnson b Holder	1
Yasir Shah b Joseph	12	– (10) lbw b Holder	0
Mohammad Amir b Joseph	20	– (8) run out	8
Zulfiqar Babar not out	1	– not out	15
Lb 4, w 1, nb 4	9	B 2, lb 1, w 6, nb 2	11
1/1 (2) 2/1 (3) 3/107 (4) 4/150 (1) 5/230 (5) 6/242 (7) 7/248 (6) 8/248 (8) 9/280 (10) 10/281 (9) (90.5 overs)	281	1/37 (1) 2/41 (3) 3/41 (4) 4/48 (5) 5/134 (6) 6/175 (7) 7/189 (2) 8/192 (8) 9/193 (9) 10/208 (10) (81.3 overs)	208

Gabriel 21–1–67–3; Joseph 16.5–5–57–2; Holder 12–4–29–0; Chase 20–5–47–1; Bishoo 21–3–77–4. *Second innings*—Gabriel 15–1–36–0; Joseph 14–3–41–0; Holder 17.3–5–30–5; Brathwaite 1–0–5–0; Chase 15–1–47–1; Bishoo 19–2–46–3.

West Indies

K. C. Brathwaite not out	142	– not out	60
L. R. Johnson lbw b Wahab Riaz	1	– lbw b Yasir Shah	12
D. M. Bravo c Mohammad Amir b Zulfiqar Babar	11	– c Sarfraz Ahmed b Yasir Shah	3
M. N. Samuels lbw b Yasir Shah	0	– c Zulfiqar Babar b Yasir Shah	10
J. Blackwood c Asad Shafiq b Mohammad Amir	23	– b Wahab Riaz	4
R. L. Chase c Younis Khan b Mohammad Amir	50	– c Mohammad Nawaz b Wahab Riaz	2
†S. O. Dowrich b Wahab Riaz	47	– not out	60
*J. O. Holder b Mohammad Amir	16		
D. Bishoo c Sarfraz Ahmed b Wahab Riaz	27		
A. S. Joseph c Yasir Shah b Wahab Riaz	6		
S. T. Gabriel c Sarfraz Ahmed b Wahab Riaz	0		
Lb 6, nb 8	14	Lb 2, nb 1	3
1/6 (2) 2/32 (3) 3/38 (4) 4/68 (5) 5/151 (6) 6/234 (7) 7/263 (8) 8/323 (9) 9/333 (10) 10/337 (11) (115.4 overs)	337	1/29 (2) 2/35 (3) 3/57 (4) 4/63 (5) 5/67 (6) (5 wkts, 43.5 overs)	154

Mohammad Amir 25–5–71–3; Wahab Riaz 26.4–1–88–5; Yasir Shah 26–2–80–1; Zulfiqar Babar 21–3–56–1; Mohammad Nawaz 11–2–20–0; Azhar Ali 6–0–16–0. *Second innings*—Mohammad Amir 9.5–0–43–0; Wahab Riaz 12–0–46–2; Yasir Shah 15–4–40–3; Zulfiqar Babar 3–1–3–0; Mohammad Nawaz 4–0–20–0.

Umpires: M. A. Gough and P. R. Reiffel. Third umpire: R. K. Illingworth.
Referee: J. J. Crowe.

DOMESTIC CRICKET IN PAKISTAN IN 2015-16

ABID ALI KAZI

The Pakistan Super League joined the proliferation of global Twenty20 franchise tournaments, and the first, in February 2016, was a success. But, like Pakistan's home internationals over the past seven seasons, it had to be played in the United Arab Emirates, where it was easier to ensure the safety of the competition's overseas players. The five franchises – Islamabad United, Karachi Kings, Lahore Qalandars, Peshawar Zalmi and Quetta Gladiators – selected their teams on a draft system, with each allowed five foreign recruits. England's Ravi Bopara and West Indian all-rounder Andre Russell were among the imports who flourished; Bopara's 329 runs were exceeded only by Umar Akmal, while Russell shared the bowling honours with Wahab Riaz. **Islamabad United**, led by Test captain Misbah-ul-Haq, became the first PSL champions, defeating Quetta Gladiators in the final by six wickets thanks to half-centuries from another West Indian, Dwayne Smith, and former Australia wicketkeeper Brad Haddin.

Misbah had already won one domestic tournament, when in January he guided **Sui Northern Gas** to their second successive Quaid-e-Azam Trophy. As usual, the Pakistan Cricket Board had changed the format: it was contested by both regional and departmental sides, as in the previous year, but a two-tier system was abandoned after a single season. Instead, it reverted to something very like the 2013-14 format, when it was a regional competition and the departmental sides competed separately for the President's Trophy. There were 16 first-class teams divided into two parallel leagues, followed by two Super Eight groups leading to a final. Ten sides from the previous season's Golden League and two from the Silver League were automatically included; the other four came through separate qualifying tournaments for the regional and departmental teams. These produced a new first-class regional team, the Federally Administered Tribal Areas (though Federal Areas had competed in Pentangular Cups during the past decade).

Sui Northern Gas and **United Bank** headed the two Super Eight groups and met in Karachi in a day/night final using pink balls, to prepare players for floodlit Tests. An 11-wicket haul from Bilawal Bhatti and fifties in both innings by Misbah ensured Sui Northern's victory, despite a fighting 98 by Younis Khan in United Bank's second innings. They dedicated victory to team-mate Ali Waqas, who had undergone a kidney transplant since appearing in the previous final, but hoped to return.

With the Quaid-e-Azam Trophy providing the only first-class cricket, and only the finalists playing as many as 11 first-class matches, no one reached 1,000 runs; the leading scorer was Asif Zakir of **Sui Southern Gas**, with 791 at 56, though Peshawar's Zohaib Khan headed the averages with 599 at 85. Only Mohammad Abbas of Khan Research Labs reached 50 wickets (he finished with 61 at 16), while Umar Gul topped the averages with 28 at 14 for Habib Bank. There were some one-sided games: 13 of the 69 Quaid-e-Azam matches were won by an innings, including three by an innings and 300 or more, and there were 17 totals under 100.

Mohammad Amir returned to first-class cricket after serving his ban for spot-fixing on the 2010 tour of England, and took 16 wickets in four games for Sui Southern Gas. The Water and Power Development Authority signed Salman Butt and Mohammad Asif, who had also been jailed for their role in the scandal, but were not allowed to play them in the Quaid-e-Azam, as they were still on a rehabilitation programme; they did make their comeback in January in the National One-Day Cup. This also involved the 16 Quaid-e-Azam teams, but the final was washed out: **National Bank** and **Islamabad** shared the title.

There was also a 50-over Pentangular competition for five provincial teams; **Khyber Pakhtunkhwa**, led by Younis, defeated Punjab by 151 runs. The regional sides had earlier taken part in a domestic T20 tournament, won by **Peshawar** in September.

FIRST-CLASS AVERAGES, 2015-16

BATTING (450 runs, average 35.00)

	M	*I*	*NO*	*R*	*HS*	*100*	*Avge*	*Ct/St*
Zohaib Khan (*Peshawar*)	7	9	2	599	154*	3	85.57	2
Kamran Akmal (*National Bank*)	7	9	1	480	140	2	60.00	31/4
Akbar-ur-Rehman (*National Bank*)	10	16	3	761	202	4	58.53	15
Mohammad Waqas (*Karachi Whites*)	7	13	2	625	164*	2	56.81	4
Asif Zakir (*Sui Southern Gas*)	10	16	2	791	115*	3	56.50	5
Khalid Latif (*Port Qasim Authority*)	7	11	3	450	172*	2	56.25	5
†Fawad Alam (*National Bank*)	8	14	2	672	224*	1	56.00	5
Younis Khan (*United Bank*)	6	10	0	519	197	1	51.90	5
†Umar Amin (*Sui Southern Gas*)	10	16	1	763	169	3	50.86	9
Abid Ali (*Islamabad*)	7	13	2	548	136	2	49.81	1
Faisal Iqbal (*Karachi Whites*)	7	11	1	490	176	2	49.00	4
†Saud Shakil (*Karachi Whites*)	10	16	3	635	121	3	48.84	4
Aamer Sajjad (*WAPDA*)	10	15	2	606	178	2	46.61	5
†Zain Abbas (*KRL*)	10	19	3	730	178	2	45.62	2
†Taufeeq Umar (*Sui Northern Gas*)	9	14	0	601	247	1	42.92	8
†Saad Ali (*Karachi Whites*)	9	13	1	508	104	1	42.33	9
†Awais Zia (*Sui Southern Gas*)	7	12	1	462	86	0	42.00	4
†Naeemuddin (*Sui Northern Gas*)	9	13	1	503	162	2	41.91	7
†Umar Siddiq (*United Bank*)	8	13	1	490	174	2	40.83	1
Jahid Ali (*Karachi Whites*)	10	17	0	675	155	1	39.70	13
†Umair Khan (*United Bank*)	10	16	1	567	100	1	37.80	9
Mohammad Saad (WAPDA)	10	15	1	526	125	1	37.57	12
Fawad Khan (*FATA*)	7	14	0	521	172	2	37.21	7
Saeed Bin Nasir (*United Bank*)	9	14	1	483	128	1	37.15	7

BOWLING (25 wickets, average 30.00)

	Style	*O*	*M*	*R*	*W*	*BB*	*5I*	*Avge*
Umar Gul (*Habib Bank*)	RFM	153	38	413	28	7-32	1	14.75
Azizullah (*Sui Northern Gas*)	RFM	190.2	50	502	33	6-36	2	15.21
Asad Ali (*Sui Northern Gas*)	RFM	241	51	686	44	6-28	3	15.59
Shehzad Azam (*Islamabad*)	RFM	202.4	54	578	35	6-38	2	16.51
Mohammad Abbas (*KRL*)	RFM	365.1	82	1,024	61	7-68	6	16.78
Aizaz Cheema (*Lahore Blues*)	RFM	299	82	747	44	6-30	4	16.97
Hasan Ali (*Islamabad*)	RFM	167.3	33	567	31	6-43	3	18.29
Ahmed Jamal (*National Bank*)	RFM	257	60	733	40	5-26	2	18.32
Ehsan Adil (*United Bank*)	RFM	301.5	69	891	48	6-61	2	18.56
Mir Hamza (*United Bank*)	LFM	243.5	68	651	35	5-30	2	18.60
Bilawal Bhatti (*Sui Northern Gas*)	RFM	202.2	38	635	33	8-56	1	19.24
Sadaf Hussain (*KRL*)	LFM	231.1	54	704	36	6-45	2	19.55
Waqas Maqsood (*WAPDA*)	LFM	236.4	47	740	36	6-31	2	20.55
Ahmed Bashir (*Lahore Blues*)	RFM	149.4	26	584	28	6-118	2	20.85
Amad Butt (*Habib Bank*)	RFM	170.1	40	572	27	5-34	1	21.18
Adnan Ghaus (*Sui Southern Gas*)	RFM	199.1	34	704	32	6-72	2	22.00
Zohaib Shera (*Port Qasim Authority*)	LFM	180.3	36	602	27	6-46	4	22.29
Asif Raza (*Lahore Whites*)	RFM	172.4	24	580	26	6-127	3	22.30
Zia-ul-Haq (*National Bank*)	LFM	246.3	54	749	33	6-40	1	22.69
Saad Altaf (*Rawalpindi*)	LFM	184.2	42	575	25	5-53	1	23.00
Taj Wali (*Peshawar*)	LFM	200.3	38	665	26	5-30	3	25.57
Mohammad Asghar (*National Bank*)	SLA	287	58	806	31	5-28	3	26.00
Babar Rehman (*Karachi Whites*)	RFM	204.4	31	787	29	4-75	0	27.13
Adeel Malik (*Karachi Whites*)	RFM	375.5	90	1,089	40	6-74	4	27.22
Zulfiqar Babar (*WAPDA*)	SLA	279	57	818	30	6-38	3	27.26
Tabish Khan (*Sui Southern Gas*)	RFM	229.4	63	690	25	4-59	0	27.60

QUAID-E-AZAM TROPHY, 2015-16

PRELIMINARY GROUPS

Pool A	P	W	L	D	Pts
SUI NORTHERN GAS	7	3	0	4	40
UNITED BANK	7	3	0	4	35
LAHORE BLUES	7	2	2	3	22
SUI SOUTHERN GAS	7	1	1	5	16
Peshawar	7	0	0	7	13
Port Qasim Authority	7	1	1	5	11
Islamabad	7	1	2	4	7
Hyderabad	7	0	5	2	6

Pool B	P	W	L	D	Pts
NATIONAL BANK	7	3	1	3	36
KRL	7	4	1	2	33
KARACHI WHITES	7	2	2	3	28
WAPDA	7	2	1	4	25
Habib Bank	7	2	1	4	22
Rawalpindi	7	1	2	4	12
Lahore Whites	7	0	4	3	9
FATA	7	1	3	3	6

SUPER EIGHT

Group A	P	W	L	D	Pts
SUI NORTHERN GAS	3	2	0	1	22
WAPDA	3	1	1	1	11
Lahore Blues	3	1	1	1	9
KRL	3	0	2	1	0

Group B	P	W	L	D	Pts
UNITED BANK	3	2	0	1	18
National Bank	3	2	1	0	15
Karachi Whites	3	0	1	2	3
Sui Southern Gas	3	0	2	1	3

FATA = Federally Administered Tribal Areas; KRL = Khan Research Laboratories; WAPDA = Water and Power Development Authority.

Outright win = 6pts; win by an innings = 1pt extra; lead on first innings in a won or drawn game = 3pts; draw after following on = 1pt; no result on first innings = 1pt.

The top four teams from the preliminary groups advanced to the Super Eight groups, but did not carry forward their earlier results. Hyderabad and Port Qasim Authority (the weakest departmental team) were relegated for 2016-17.

Pool A

At Hyderabad (Niaz), October 26–29, 2015. **Drawn. Hyderabad 402** (Azeem Ghumman 188) **and 268** (Azam Hussain 5-94); **‡Port Qasim Authority 382 and 192-3** (Shahzaib Hasan 100). *Hyderabad 3pts. Shahzaib Hasan rushed to 100 in 86 balls.*

At Islamabad (Diamond), October 26–29, 2015. **United Bank won by an innings and 120 runs. United Bank 399; ‡Islamabad 111** (Mir Hamza 5-30) **and 168.** *United Bank 10pts.*

At Lahore (Gaddafi), October 26–29, 2015. **Drawn. Lahore Blues 301 and 221; ‡Sui Southern Gas 256** (Asif Zakir 115*) **and 52-1.** *Lahore Blues 3pts. This was Mohammad Amir's first first-class match after his five-year ban for spot-fixing. He took five wickets in the match and scored a maiden fifty, helping Asif Zakir to rescue Sui Southern from 93-7 in a 130-run partnership.*

At Peshawar (Arbab Niaz), October 26–29, 2015. **Drawn. Peshawar 231 and 153-4; ‡Sui Northern Gas 411-5 dec** (Imran Butt 124, Naeemuddin 162). *Sui Northern Gas 3pts. Imran Butt and Naeemuddin put on 291 for Sui Northern's first wicket.*

At Hyderabad (Niaz), November 2–4, 2015. **Sui Southern Gas won by an innings and 379 runs. ‡Sui Southern Gas 529** (Babar Azam 167); **Hyderabad 80** (Mohammad Amir 5-29) **and 70** (Sohail Khan 7-33). *Sui Southern Gas 10pts. After Sui Southern scored 529, Hyderabad totalled 150 in two innings. Babar Azam had managed more than that single-handed, and put on 203 for the second wicket with Ali Asad (57). Sohail Khan's second-innings analysis was 9–1–33–7.*

At Islamabad (Diamond), November 2–5, 2015. **Drawn. Sui Northern Gas 182** (Hasan Ali 6-47) **and 127; ‡Islamabad 93 and 126-6.** *Sui Northern Gas 3pts.*

At Lahore (Gaddafi), November 2–5, 2015. **Port Qasim Authority won by 231 runs. Port Qasim Authority 230** (Aizaz Cheema 5-42) **and 287-8 dec; ‡Lahore Blues 101** (Zohaib Shera 6-46) **and 185.** *Port Qasim Authority 9pts.*

At Peshawar (Arbab Niaz), November 2–5, 2015. **Drawn. United Bank 324 and 58-0; ‡Peshawar 332-6 dec** (Akbar Badshah 106*). *Peshawar 3pts.*

At Hyderabad (Niaz), November 9–12, 2015. **Sui Northern Gas won by 153 runs. ‡Sui Northern Gas 331 and 303-8 dec; Hyderabad 271 and 210** (Imran Khalid 5-62). *Sui Northern Gas 9pts.*

At Islamabad (Diamond), November 9–12, 2015. **Drawn. Islamabad 326** (Abid Ali 136; Zohaib Shera 5-126); **‡Port Qasim Authority 114-2.** *Islamabad 1pt, Port Qasim Authority 1pt.*

At Lahore (Gaddafi), November 9–11, 2015. **United Bank won by an innings and 206 runs. United Bank 432-5 dec** (Umair Khan 100, Saeed Bin Nasir 128); **‡Lahore Blues 96 and 130.** *United Bank 10pts. Lahore Blues were 21-7 in their first innings; only Agha Salman (56) passed ten.*

At Peshawar (Arbab Niaz), November 9–12, 2015. **Drawn. Peshawar 246; ‡Sui Southern Gas 117-4.** *Peshawar 1pt, Sui Southern Gas 1pt.*

At Hyderabad (Niaz), November 16–19, 2015. **United Bank won by 263 runs. United Bank 259 and 392-9 dec** (Sajjad Hussain 5-72); **‡Hyderabad 197** (Mir Hamza 5-42) **and 191.** *United Bank 9pts.*

At Islamabad (Diamond), November 16–19, 2015. **Drawn. Sui Southern Gas 375** (Umar Amin 161, Asif Zakir 115; Hasan Ali 5-65) **and 216-8 dec; ‡Islamabad 325** (Abid Ali 131) **and 69-1.** *Sui Southern Gas 3pts. Umar Amin and Asif Zakir put on 264 for Sui Southern's fourth wicket.*

At Lahore (Gaddafi), November 16–19, 2015. **Drawn. Sui Northern Gas 445** (Adnan Akmal 148) **and 251-6 dec; ‡Lahore Blues 380** (Saad Nasim 104; Asad Ali 5-94) **and 262-6.** *Sui Northern Gas 3pts. Saad Nasim's 104 took only 90 balls, while Test captain Misbah-ul-Haq hit 58 in 40 in Sui Northern's second innings.*

At Peshawar (Arbab Niaz), November 16–19, 2015. **Drawn. ‡Port Qasim Authority 107** (Taj Wali 5-30) **and 416** (Khalid Latif 134); **Peshawar 490-4 dec** (Zohaib Khan 154*) **and 10-1.** *Peshawar 3pts. Left-armer Taj Wali took four wickets in four balls in Port Qasim Authority's first innings.*

At Islamabad (Diamond), November 23–26, 2015. **Islamabad won by nine wickets. ‡Hyderabad 279 and 200** (Shehzad Azam 6-38); **Islamabad 211** (Babar Khan 6-59) **and 272-1** (Ali Sarfraz 133*). *Islamabad 6pts.*

At Lahore (LCCA), November 23–26, 2015. **Drawn. Lahore Blues 267 and 328-5; ‡Peshawar 295** (Zohaib Khan 108). *Peshawar 3pts.*

At Faisalabad (Iqbal), November 23–25, 2015. **Sui Northern Gas won by an innings and 119 runs. Port Qasim Authority 119 and 69** (Azizullah 6-36); **‡Sui Northern Gas 307** (Azhar Ali 142; Zohaib Shera 6-84). *Sui Northern Gas 10pts.*

At Islamabad (Marghzar), November 23–26, 2015. **Drawn. ‡United Bank 514-8 dec; Sui Southern Gas 244 and 293-6.** *Sui Southern Gas 1pt, United Bank 3pts.*

At Islamabad (Diamond), November 30–December 2, 2015. **Lahore Blues won by 13 runs. Lahore Blues 188 and 159** (Hasan Ali 6-43); **‡Islamabad 169** (Bilawal Iqbal 5-40, Ahmed Bashir 5-66) **and 165.** *Lahore Blues 9pts. Islamabad needed 179 to win a low-scoring game, but fell just short. It was easily the closest result of the tournament.*

At Peshawar (Arbab Niaz), November 30–December 3, 2015. **Drawn. Peshawar 223** (Nasir Awais 5-44) **and 350-4** (Ashfaq Ahmed 157, Zohaib Khan 115); **‡Hyderabad 392** (Rizwan Ahmed 107; Taj Wali 5-85). *Hyderabad 3pts. Ashfaq Ahmed and Zohaib Khan shared a 270-run stand for Peshawar's third wicket.*

At Islamabad (Marghzar), November 30–December 3, 2015. **Drawn. United Bank 318** (Umar Siddiq 113; Zohaib Shera 6-80) **and 395-9 dec** (Umar Siddiq 174; Azam Hussain 5-91); **‡Port Qasim Authority 215** (Khalid Latif 172*; Ehsan Adil 6-61) **and 204-7.** *United Bank 3pts. Port Qasim Authority were 36-8 before Khalid Latif and Zohaib Shera (17) put on 154; Khalid made 80% of his side's total. Umar Siddiq scored twin centuries, adding 184 for the seventh wicket with Yasim Murtaza (85) in the second innings.*

ONE-MAN BANDS

Highest percentage of an all-out first-class total

%		*Score*	*Total*		
83.43	G. M. Turner . .	141*	169	Worcestershire v Glamorgan at Swansea	1977
81.56	G. Snyman	230	282	Namibia v Kenya at Sharjah	2007-08
80.00	**Khalid Latif** . .	**172***	**215**	**Port Qasim A v Utd Bank at Islamabad**	**2015-16**
79.84	V. S. Hazare . . .	309	387	The Rest v Hindus at Bombay (Brabourne) . . .	1943-44
79.24	W. G. Grace . . .	126	159	Utd S of England v Utd N of England at Hull .	1876
78.94	A. N. Hornby . .	45	57	MCC v Sussex at Lord's	1890
78.78	S. Nazir Ali . . .	52	66	Indians v Yorkshire at Harrogate	1932
78.75	C. O. H. Sewell	63*	80†	Gloucestershire v Sussex at Hove	1913
78.26	J. Noel	18	23	South Australia v Victoria at East Melbourne .	1882-83
78.04	H. R. Kingscote	32	41	Surrey v Kent at Sevenoaks	1828
77.00	B. Sutcliffe	385	500	Otago v Canterbury at Christchurch	1952-53

† *Two men absent.*

At Faisalabad (Iqbal), November 30–December 3, 2015. **Sui Northern Gas won by five wickets. Sui Southern Gas 124 and 303** (Umar Amin 106); ‡**Sui Northern Gas 256** (Adnan Ghaus 5-66) **and 172-5.** *Sui Northern Gas 9pts.*

At Hyderabad (Niaz), December 7–9, 2015. **Lahore Blues won by an innings and 184 runs. Hyderabad 122** (Aizaz Cheema 6-30) **and 118;** ‡**Lahore Blues 424-9 dec** (Waqas Saleem 192). *Lahore Blues 10pts.*

At Peshawar (Arbab Niaz), December 7–10, 2015. **Drawn. Islamabad 129** (Taj Wali 5-33) **and 96-1;** ‡**Peshawar 170** (Shehzad Azam 6-38). *Peshawar 3pts.*

At Islamabad (Diamond), December 7–10, 2015. **Drawn.** ‡**Port Qasim Authority 283; Sui Southern Gas 208-6.** *Port Qasim Authority 1pt, Sui Southern Gas 1pt. Sui Southern made sure of a place in the next stage.*

At Rawalpindi (Cricket), December 7–10, 2015. **Drawn.** ‡**United Bank 132** (Azizullah 5-33) **and 112-3; Sui Northern Gas 230** (Imran Khalid 113; Ehsan Adil 5-69). *Sui Northern Gas 3pts. The group's two leading teams were already through to the Super Eight.*

Pool B

At Sialkot (Jinnah), October 26–29, 2015. **Drawn. Habib Bank 404-5 dec** (Fakhar Zaman 205) **and 172-1 dec;** ‡**FATA 273** (Rehan Afridi 103) **and 114-3.** *Habib Bank 3pts. Fakhar Zaman scored a maiden double-century against the Federally Administered Tribal Areas team, who were making their first appearance in the Quaid-e-Azam Trophy and included six first-class debutants.*

At Karachi (National), October 26–29, 2015. **Drawn. Karachi Whites 438 and 83-1;** ‡**WAPDA 295.** *Karachi Whites 3pts. WAPDA wicketkeeper Bismillah Khan held seven catches in Karachi Whites' first innings.*

At Lahore (LCCA), October 26–29, 2015. **National Bank won by an innings and 12 runs. Lahore Whites 178 and 218;** ‡**National Bank 408** (Kamran Akmal 140). *National Bank 10pts.*

At Rawalpindi (Cricket), October 26–29, 2015. **Drawn. Rawalpindi 225 and 145-4;** ‡**KRL 203.** *Rawalpindi 3pts.*

At Karachi (National), November 2–5, 2015. **Drawn. Habib Bank 181 and 387-7 dec** (Nauman Anwar 199); ‡**Karachi Whites 292 and 125-3.** *Karachi Whites 3pts. Nauman Anwar scored a maiden hundred, but fell one short of making it a double.*

At Lahore (LCCA), November 2–5, 2015. **KRL won by ten wickets. Lahore Whites 163 and 81** (Mohammad Abbas 5-36); ‡**KRL 171 and 77-0.** *KRL 9pts.*

At Sialkot (Jinnah), November 2–5, 2015. **Drawn. FATA 257** (Fahim Ashraf 5-67) **and 106-2;** ‡**National Bank 457-6 dec** (Mohammad Nawaz 111, Kamran Akmal 137). *National Bank 3pts. Kamran Akmal's 137 was his third first-class century in successive innings, going back to December 2014.*

At Rawalpindi (Cricket), November 2–5, 2015. **Drawn. Rawalpindi 195** (Waqas Maqsood 5-58) **and 119-8; ‡WAPDA 307.** *WAPDA 3pts.*

At Karachi (National), November 9–12, 2015. **National Bank won by an innings and 23 runs. Karachi Whites 227** (Zia-ul-Haq 6-40) **and 215; ‡National Bank 465-4 dec** (Umar Waheed 125, Fawad Alam 224*, Akbar-ur-Rehman 103*). *National Bank 10pts. Fawad Alam scored his third double-century, adding 256 with Umar Waheed for National Bank's third wicket and 190* with Akbar-ur-Rehman for the fifth.*

At Sialkot (Jinnah), November 9–11, 2015. **KRL won by ten wickets. FATA 168 and 99** (Mohammad Abbas 5-54); **‡KRL 107** (Zeeshan Khan 5-58) **and 161-0.** *KRL 6pts. KRL completed their second successive ten-wicket victory.*

At Lahore (LCCA), November 9–12, 2015. **Drawn. Lahore Whites 344 and 139-4; ‡WAPDA 275** (Mohammad Saad 125). *Lahore Whites 3pts.*

At Rawalpindi (Cricket), November 9–12, 2015. **Drawn. Rawalpindi 183** (Amad Butt 5-34) **and 34-1; ‡Habib Bank 181.** *Rawalpindi 3pts.*

At Karachi (National), November 16–19, 2015. **Drawn. KRL 296** (Sohaib Khan 5-74) **and 328-5** (Zain Abbas 178); **‡Karachi Whites 424** (Saud Shakil 114*). *Karachi Whites 3pts.*

At Lahore (LCCA), November 16–18, 2015. **Habib Bank won by an innings and 56 runs. Lahore Whites 89** (Umar Gul 7-32) **and 186; ‡Habib Bank 331** (Asif Raza 5-91). *Habib Bank 10pts. Umar Gul ran through Lahore Whites' first innings, then scored 61 from No. 9.*

At Rawalpindi (Cricket), November 16–18, 2015. **National Bank won by an innings and 79 runs. National Bank 453** (Akbar-ur-Rehman 128); **‡Rawalpindi 236** (Ahmed Jamal 5-26) **and 138** (Fahim Ashraf 5-35). *National Bank 10pts. Fawad Alam (93) and Akbar-ur-Rehman added 206 for the fifth wicket.*

At Sialkot (Jinnah), November 16–18, 2015. **WAPDA won by an innings and four runs. ‡WAPDA 440** (Aamer Sajjad 178); **FATA 250** (Khushdil Shah 122) **and 186.** *WAPDA 10pts. FATA's Ibraheem Gul dismissed Bismillah Khan with the first ball of the match on his first-class debut.*

At Islamabad (National), November 23–26, 2015. **Habib Bank won by 51 runs. Habib Bank 278** (Mohammad Abbas 6-84) **and 133-8 dec; ‡KRL 99 and 261.** *Habib Bank 9pts.*

At Lahore (Gaddafi), November 23–26, 2015. **Drawn. FATA 314** (Fawad Khan 108; Saif-ur-Rehman 5-76) **and 276-8; ‡Lahore Whites 508-9 dec** (Sami Aslam 221, Usman Salahuddin 111). *Lahore Whites 3pts. FATA captain Fawad Khan hit 108 in 70 balls, with five sixes, before lunch on the first day. Sami Aslam scored a maiden double-century and added 240 for Lahore Whites' fourth wicket with Usman Salahuddin.*

At Sialkot (Jinnah), November 23–26, 2015. **Drawn. WAPDA 315** (Aamer Sajjad 100) **and 240-7 dec; ‡National Bank 201** (Azhar Attari 6-57) **and 244-4** (Akbar-ur-Rehman 102*). *WAPDA 3pts.*

At Rawalpindi (Cricket), November 23–26, 2015. **Rawalpindi won by 90 runs. Rawalpindi 172 and 218** (Adeel Malik 6-74); **‡Karachi Whites 209 and 91.** *Rawalpindi 6pts.*

At Sialkot (Jinnah), November 30–December 3, 2015. **Drawn. National Bank 326** (Umar Waheed 100) **and 199; ‡Habib Bank 188 and 136-4.** *National Bank 3pts.*

At Islamabad (National), November 30–December 3, 2015. **KRL won by five wickets. WAPDA 187** (Rahat Ali 6-40) **and 159** (Mohammad Abbas 6-51); **‡KRL 212** (Zulfiqar Babar 5-50) **and 136-5.** *KRL 9pts. WAPDA tried to include Salman Butt and Mohammad Asif, two of the players convicted of spot-fixing in 2010, but the match referee refused to accept them, as they had not completed their rehabilitation.*

At Lahore (Gaddafi), November 30–December 2, 2015. **Karachi Whites won by an innings and 160 runs. Karachi Whites 363** (Saad Ali 104; Asif Raza 6-127); **‡Lahore Whites 145** (Adeel Malik 5-42) **and 58** (Ghulam Mudassar 5-28, Abdullah Muqaddam 5-10). *Karachi Whites 10pts. A week after scoring 508, Lahore Whites were bowled out for 58, the lowest total of the season.*

At Rawalpindi (Cricket), November 30–December 2, 2015. **FATA won by four wickets. ‡Rawalpindi 163 and 105** (Razaullah Wazir 6-21); **FATA 89** (Yasir Arafat 5-33, Saad Altaf 5-53) **and 180-6.** *FATA 6pts. FATA completed their first win, despite slipping to 13-6 in their first innings, when their top four made ducks.*

At Faisalabad (Iqbal), December 7–10, 2015. **WAPDA won by 225 runs. WAPDA 212 and 240-5 dec; ‡Habib Bank 87** (Waqas Maqsood 6-31) **and 140** (Zulfiqar Babar 6-38). *WAPDA 9pts. WAPDA advanced to the Super Eight.*

At Karachi (National), December 7–10, 2015. **Karachi Whites won by three wickets. Karachi Whites 300** (Mohammad Waqas 137; Irfanullah Shah 6-76) **and 323-7** (Saud Shakil 116); **‡FATA 141 and 478** (Fawad Khan 172). *Karachi Whites 9pts. Jahid Ali (96) and Mohammad Waqas added 230 for Karachi Whites' second wicket, before nine fell for 49. When FATA followed on, Fawad Khan hit 172 in 165 balls, with nine sixes, but Karachi Whites passed a target of 320.*

At Sialkot (Jinnah), December 7–9, 2015. **KRL won by eight wickets. National Bank 138** (Sadaf Hussain 6-45) **and 167** (Mohammad Abbas 7-68); **‡KRL 176** (Ahmed Jamal 5-59) **and 130-2.** *KRL 9pts. KRL joined group leaders National Bank in the Super Eight.*

At Lahore (LCCA), December 7–10, 2015. **Drawn. Lahore Whites 201** (Haseeb Azam 6-74) **and 107; ‡Rawalpindi 183** (Asif Raza 5-74) **and 11-2.** *Lahore Whites 3pts.*

Super Eight Group I

At Karachi (National), December 14–17, 2015. **Drawn. KRL 208 and 361** (Zain Abbas 133; Asad Ali 5-84); **‡Sui Northern Gas 349** (Naeemuddin 108*) **and 193-8.** *Sui Northern Gas 3pts. Mohammad Abbas took his 50th first-class wicket of the season.*

At Karachi (NBP), December 14–17, 2015. **Drawn. ‡Lahore Blues 511** (Haris Nazar 103, Agha Salman 115, Raza Ali Dar 133); **WAPDA 315** (Haider Ali 5-68) **and 105-3.** *Lahore Blues 3pts, WAPDA 1pt.*

At Hyderabad (Niaz), December 20–22, 2015. **Lahore Blues won by five wickets. KRL 158** (Aizaz Cheema 5-53) **and 80** (Aizaz Cheema 5-28, Bilawal Iqbal 5-46); **‡Lahore Blues 122** (Mohammad Abbas 5-53, Sadaf Hussain 5-52) **and 119-5.** *Lahore Blues 6pts. Aizaz Cheema took ten wickets for the second time in three matches.*

At Karachi (UBL), December 20–23, 2015. **Sui Northern Gas won by three wickets. WAPDA 297 and 236; ‡Sui Northern Gas 310** (Zulfiqar Babar 6-102) **and 227-7.** *Sui Northern Gas 9pts. Azizullah finished off WAPDA's first innings with a hat-trick.*

At Karachi (UBL), December 28–30, 2015. **WAPDA won by an innings and 300 runs. WAPDA 500-9 dec** (Atiq-ur-Rehman 144); **‡KRL 116 and 84.** *WAPDA 10pts. KRL were a man short in both innings after Nayyer Abbas was injured while bowling.*

At Karachi (National), December 28–30, 2015. **Sui Northern Gas won by an innings and 325 runs. Lahore Blues 90** (Asad Ali 6-28) **and 97; ‡Sui Northern Gas 512** (Taufeeq Umar 247; Ahmed Bashir 6-118). *Sui Northern Gas 10pts. Both teams had a chance to reach the final, but Sui Northern became the third team to win by an innings and 300-plus in this tournament – Lahore Blues failed to reach three figures in either innings. Taufeeq Umar scored his second double-hundred, batting for eight hours 39 minutes; he added 219 with Hussain Talat (86) after Imran Butt was out in Sui Northern's first over.*

Super Eight Group II

At Hyderabad (Niaz), December 14–17, 2015. **Drawn. Karachi Whites 269** (Adnan Ghaus 6-72) **and 323-5 dec** (Mohammad Waqas 164*, Faisal Iqbal 107); **‡Sui Southern Gas 311** (Asif Zakir 107; Adeel Malik 5-101) **and 275-9.** *Sui Southern Gas 3pts.*

At Karachi (UBL), December 14–16, 2015. **United Bank won by 67 runs. ‡United Bank 268** (Mohammad Asghar 5-72) **and 103** (Mohammad Asghar 5-28); **National Bank 148 and 156** (Hammad Azam 5-39). *United Bank 9pts. National Bank's captain and wicketkeeper Kamran Akmal made five catches and one stumping in United Bank's first innings, and nine dismissals in the match.*

At Karachi (NBP), December 20–23, 2015. **Drawn. ‡United Bank 585-7 dec** (Younis Khan 197, Sohaib Maqsood 101); **Karachi Whites 597-9** (Jahid Ali 155, Faisal Iqbal 176, Saud Shakil 121; Yasim Murtaza 5-222). *Karachi Whites 3pts. Karachi Whites' 597-9 was the season's highest total*

– and United Bank's 585-7 the second highest. Both featured huge fourth-wicket partnerships: Younis Khan and Sohaib Maqsood put on 212 for United Bank; Jahid Ali (with a maiden century) and Faisal Iqbal 304 for Karachi. Left-armer Yasim Murtaza's full figures were 69–10–222–5.

At Karachi (National), December 20–23, 2015. **National Bank won by seven wickets. Sui Southern Gas 348** (Umar Amin 169) **and 226; ‡National Bank 457** (Akbar-ur-Rehman 202) **and 118-3.** *National Bank 9pts. Coming in at 17-3, Akbar-ur-Rehman scored his second double-hundred – and fourth century of the season – adding 183 for National Bank's fifth wicket with Kamran Akmal (92).*

At Karachi (NBP), December 28–31, 2015. **National Bank won by five wickets. Karachi Whites 276 and 131** (Mohammad Asghar 5-37); **‡National Bank 246** (Adeel Malik 5-59) **and 163-5.** *National Bank 6pts. National Bank started level on points with United Bank – but their failure to take first-innings points meant victory was not enough to qualify for the final.*

At Hyderabad (Niaz), December 28–30, 2015. **United Bank won by six wickets. ‡Sui Southern Gas 115 and 232; United Bank 218 and 130-4.** *United Bank 9pts. United Bank reached the final.*

Final At Karachi (National), January 3–6, 2016 (day/night). **Sui Northern Gas won by six wickets. ‡United Bank 208 and 189** (Bilawal Bhatti 8-56); **Sui Northern Gas 238 and 160-4.** *The match was played with pink balls, and partly under floodlights. Misbah-ul-Haq helped make sure of Sui Northerns' second successive Quaid-e-Azam with 85 and 60*, steering them to victory with a day to spare. Younis Khan's 98 in United Bank's second innings was the game's highest score, but their last six fell for 29 as Bilawal Bhatti claimed a career-best 8-56, and 11-95 in all – the best innings and match returns of the season.*

QUAID-E-AZAM TROPHY WINNERS

1953-54	Bahawalpur	1978-79	National Bank	1998-99	Peshawar
1954-55	Karachi	1979-80	PIA	1999-2000	PIA
1956-57	Punjab	1980-81	United Bank	2000-01	Lahore City Blues
1957-58	Bahawalpur	1981-82	National Bank	2001-02	Karachi Whites
1958-59	Karachi	1982-83	United Bank	2002-03	PIA
1959-60	Karachi	1983-84	National Bank	2003-04	Faisalabad
1961-62	Karachi Blues	1984-85	United Bank	2004-05	Peshawar
1962-63	Karachi A	1985-86	Karachi	2005-06	Sialkot
1963-64	Karachi Blues	1986-87	National Bank	2006-07	Karachi Urban
1964-65	Karachi Blues	1987-88	PIA	2007-08	Sui Northern Gas
1966-67	Karachi	1988-89	ADBP	2008-09	Sialkot
1968-69	Lahore	1989-90	PIA	2009-10	Karachi Blues
1969-70	PIA	1990-91	Karachi Whites	2010-11	Habib Bank
1970-71	Karachi Blues	1991-92	Karachi Whites	2011-12	PIA
1972-73	Railways	1992-93	Karachi Whites	2012-13	Karachi Blues
1973-74	Railways	1993-94	Lahore City	2013-14	Rawalpindi
1974-75	Punjab A	1994-95	Karachi Blues	2014-15	Sui Northern Gas
1975-76	National Bank	1995-96	Karachi Blues	2015-16	Sui Northern Gas
1976-77	United Bank	1996-97	Lahore City		
1977-78	Habib Bank	1997-98	Karachi Blues		

The competition has been contested sometimes by regional teams, sometimes by departments, and sometimes by a mixture of the two. Karachi teams have won the Quaid-e-Azam Trophy 20 times, PIA 7, National Bank 5, Lahore teams and United Bank 4, Sui Northern Gas 3, Bahawalpur, Habib Bank, Peshawar, Punjab, Railways and Sialkot 2, ADBP, Faisalabad and Rawalpindi 1.

COOL AND COOL PRESENTS NATIONAL ONE-DAY CUP, 2015-16

Two 50-over leagues plus knockout

Semi-final At Lahore (Gaddafi), January 26, 2016. **National Bank won by six wickets. United Bank 185** (48.5 overs) (Zia-ul-Haq 5-33); **‡National Bank 189-4** (41.4 overs). *MoM:* Zia-ul-Haq.

Semi-final At Lahore (Gaddafi), January 27, 2016. **Islamabad won by seven wickets. KRL 231-9** (50 overs); **‡Islamabad 232-3** (46 overs) (Shahid Yousuf 100*). *MoM:* Shahid Yousuf.

Final At Lahore (Gaddafi), January 29, 2016. **Islamabad v National Bank. Abandoned.** *The teams shared the trophy after a washout.*

COOL AND COOL PRESENTS HAIER PAKISTAN CUP, 2015-16

50-over league plus final

	Played	Won	Lost	Points	Net run-rate
KHYBER PAKHTUNKHWA	4	3	1	6	0.38
PUNJAB	4	2	2	4	0.60
Sind	4	2	2	4	0.16
Baluchistan	4	2	2	4	–0.55
Islamabad	4	1	3	2	–0.74

Final At Faisalabad (Iqbal), May 1, 2016 (day/night). **Khyber Pakhtunkhwa won by 151 runs.** ‡**Khyber Pakhtunkhwa 311-9** (50 overs) (Fakhar Zaman 115); **Punjab 160** (36.1 overs). *MoM:* Fakhar Zaman.

COOL AND COOL PRESENTS HAIER MOBILE T20 CUP, 2015-16

Four 20-over leagues (including two qualifiers) plus knockout

Semi-final At Rawalpindi (Cricket), September 14, 2015 (floodlit). **Karachi Blues won by eight runs.** ‡**Karachi Blues 189-8** (20 overs); **Multan 181-9** (20 overs). *MoM:* Abdul Ameer (Karachi).

Semi-final At Rawalpindi (Cricket), September 14, 2015 (floodlit). **Peshawar won by five wickets. Sialkot 169-7** (20 overs); ‡**Peshawar 170-5** (18.4 overs). *MoM:* Rafatullah Mohmand (Peshawar).

Final At Rawalpindi (Cricket), September 15, 2015 (floodlit). **Peshawar won by seven wickets. Karachi Blues 177-8** (20 overs); ‡**Peshawar 178-3** (18.5 overs). *MoM:* Mohammad Rizwan (Peshawar).

HBL PAKISTAN SUPER LEAGUE, 2015-16

20-over league plus knockout

	Played	Won	Lost	Points	Net run-rate
PESHAWAR ZALMI	8	6	2	12	0.57
QUETTA GLADIATORS	8	6	2	12	0.21
ISLAMABAD UNITED	8	4	4	8	–0.28
KARACHI KINGS	8	2	6	4	–0.03
Lahore Qalandars	8	2	6	4	–0.53

1st v 2nd At Dubai, February 19, 2016 (floodlit). **Quetta Gladiators won by one run. Quetta Gladiators 133** (19.3 overs); ‡**Peshawar Zalmi 132-9** (20 overs). *MoM:* Mohammad Nawaz (Quetta). *Kevin Pietersen scored a 38-ball 53 for Quetta.*

3rd v 4th At Dubai, February 20, 2016 (floodlit). **Islamabad United won by nine wickets. Karachi Kings 111-9** (20 overs) (Mohammad Sami 5-8); ‡**Islamabad United 115-1** (14.2 overs). *MoM:* Mohammad Sami (Islamabad). *Mohammad Sami smothered the Karachi batsmen, before fifties from Dwayne Smith and Brad Haddin saw Islamabad home.*

Final play-off At Dubai, February 21, 2016 (floodlit). **Islamabad United won by 50 runs. Islamabad United 176-3** (20 overs) (Sharjeel Khan 117); ‡**Peshawar Zalmi 126** (18 overs). *MoM:* Sharjeel Khan (Islamabad). *Sharjeel Khan hit 117 in 62 balls, with eight sixes.*

Final At Dubai, February 23, 2016 (floodlit). **Islamabad United won by six wickets. Quetta Gladiators 174-7** (20 overs); ‡**Islamabad United 175-4** (18.4 overs). *MoM:* D. R. Smith (Islamabad). *MoT:* R. S. Bopara (Karachi). *Kumar Sangakkara scored 55 in 32 balls for Quetta, but half-centuries from Smith and Haddin ensured the inaugural trophy went to Islamabad. Karachi's Ravi Bopara, though not playing in this game, was Man of the Tournament.*

SOUTH AFRICAN CRICKET IN 2016

Heading for the shires?

COLIN BRYDEN

Under Faf du Plessis, their third – and most impressive – captain of the year, South Africa's Test team ended 2016 on an upward trend. But as 2017 dawned, there was cause for grave concern about senior players leaving to pursue careers abroad. After the New Year Test against Sri Lanka, Kyle Abbott announced he had – five months earlier – signed a four-year Kolpak deal with Hampshire. His contract with Cricket South Africa was cancelled immediately. At the same time, one-day international batsman Rilee Rossouw confirmed he too was heading for Hampshire, on a three-year deal. They were soon followed by David Wiese, a Twenty20 regular, who joined the procession to the English South Coast after agreeing terms with Sussex, and Test keeper Dane Vilas, bound for Lancashire.

SOUTH AFRICA IN 2016

	Played	*Won*	*Lost*	*Drawn/No result*
Tests	9	5	2	2
One-day internationals	17	11	5	1
Twenty20 internationals	9	5	4	–

DECEMBER / JANUARY / FEBRUARY	4 Tests, 5 ODIs and 2 T20Is (h) v England	(see *Wisden 2016*, page 403)
MARCH / APRIL	3 T20Is (h) v Australia	(page 1010)
	ICC World Twenty20 (in India)	(page 793)
MAY		
JUNE	Triangular ODI tournament (in West Indies) v WI and Aus	(page 1081)
JULY		
AUGUST	2 Tests (h) v New Zealand	(page 1013)
SEPTEMBER / OCTOBER	1 ODI (h) v Ireland	(page 1017)
	5 ODIs (h) v Australia	(page 1018)
NOVEMBER	3 Tests (a) v Australia	(page 850)
DECEMBER / JANUARY / FEBRUARY	3 Tests, 5 ODIs, 3 T20Is (h) v Sri Lanka	(page 1024)

For a review of South African domestic cricket from the 2015-16 season, see page 1040.

These four were the latest of seven internationals to take the Kolpak route, the flurry explained by concerns – shared by employer and employee – that the Brexit vote might close the loophole. Batsman Stiaan van Zyl, seamer Hardus Viljoen and off-spinner Simon Harmer, all recent Test cricketers, opted for a guaranteed income in hard currency rather than the uncertainty of life on the fringes of the national team. CSA's immediate reaction was to threaten to make it harder for Kolpak players to gain contracts for the domestic season.

Such a restriction would add another layer of complexity to selection. The year had already seen racial transformation targets extended from domestic to international cricket. While domestic teams were obliged to field a minimum of six non-white players, of whom three must be black African, the requirement at international level is for two black Africans (with the numbers measured as an average across the season). This means five places for white players, though that could be increased for particular matches, as long as there was compensatory juggling in lesser games. Four black Africans and only four white players appeared in the victory over Ireland in September.

Du Plessis said the targets were one of many factors contributing to the exodus, while Haroon Lorgat, CSA chief executive, saw the player drain in terms of a worldwide mobility of skills. He insisted that the targets, introduced in September, were realistic, and that teams representing South Africa would always be picked on merit. CSA had agreed with the government on a barometer for measuring "representivity", but in May came a shock. The sports minister, Fikile Mbalula, announced that cricket, along with three other sports, would not be allowed to bid for major international events, such as the World Cup, because the Eminent Persons Group, set up to monitor transformation in sport, had determined it was changing too slowly. Whether this shot across the bows influenced the adoption of new targets was not revealed.

The year had started with South Africa losing their No. 1 spot in Tests when they lost at home to England. The full impact of a poor 2015 became clear later in the year, and by August South Africa were seventh. By January 2017, though, after beating Sri Lanka 3–0, they had climbed back to third.

Hashim Amla had resigned as captain during the England series. His reign had started promisingly, but in India in late 2015 he endured a torrid time, and he was replaced by A. B. de Villiers. After Stuart Broad bowled England to victory in Johannesburg in de Villiers's first Test in charge, he led South Africa to a consolation victory at Centurion. For that match, the selectors called up opener Stephen Cook, who made a century on debut. He had played in the same school team as Graeme Smith, who racked up 116 Tests before retiring in 2014. And back in 2002, Cook had been part of the Under-19 World Cup squad; Amla, his captain then, was now playing his 92nd Test.

Also at Centurion, Kagiso Rabada, aged 20, took 13 wickets with an electrifying display of fast bowling. Rabada and batsman Temba Bavuma established themselves as the first regular black African members of the Test team since Makhaya Ntini, although both had come through established cricket schools, and neither could be claimed as products of CSA's development system.

The first half of the year had more lows than highs. South Africa won both white-ball series against England, but were pipped 2–1 by Australia before the

Saeed Khan, AFP/Getty Images

Brains trust: Hashim Amla, Dean Elgar, Faf du Plessis and J-P. Duminy at Hobart, November 2016.

World T20 in India, where they failed to reach the knockouts. And they finished last in a triangular with West Indies and Australia in the Caribbean.

The revival started when they won a two-Test series against New Zealand, with du Plessis taking over as captain after de Villiers was ruled out with an elbow injury that required surgery. And it continued during a 5–0 one-day home sweep against Australia who, because of rotation and injuries, fielded a weakened attack. The major triumph was South Africa's third successive Test series win in Australia. Sri Lanka were then outplayed in a series that saw Amla return to form with a hundred in his 100th Test.

With de Villiers's absence stretching into 2017, he had announced before the Sri Lanka series that he would give up the Test captaincy. His recommendation that his old schoolmate du Plessis should be given the job on a long-term basis was accepted.

Stalwarts such as de Villiers, Dale Steyn, Morne Morkel and Vernon Philander all suffered injury during the year, but there was evidence of depth in the Test squad: seven batsmen – though not de Villiers – hit 12 centuries in nine Tests. The averages were headed by Quinton de Kock, a wicketkeeper-batsman in the Adam Gilchrist mould. Among the bowlers, Rabada established himself as a world star. Steyn's third major injury in a year put his future in doubt, but a pace attack of Philander, Abbott and Rabada, augmented by left-arm spinner Keshav Maharaj, proved a match-winning combination in Australia. It confirmed the seriousness of Abbott's defection, but there is a reasonable pool of young fast-bowling talent. De Villiers remains the one-day captain, and should be fully fit when South Africa embark on another quest for an ICC crown in the Champions Trophy in England in June.

SOUTH AFRICA v AUSTRALIA IN 2015-16

NEIL MANTHORP

Twenty20 internationals (3): South Africa 1, Australia 2

Australia's Twenty20 team looked like a work in progress when they landed for a three-game stopover en route to the World Twenty20 in India. They had lost their last four 20-over matches (one in Cardiff, three at home to India), while South Africa had won theirs (two in India, two at home to England).

South Africa seemed balanced, settled and confident, and captain Faf du Plessis was happy to say so. By contrast, Australia had an odd-looking squad: four opening batsmen, a stack of all-rounders, and few specialists. Steve Smith had captained the national Twenty20 side only once before, although he had led Sydney Sixers and Rajasthan Royals. There were many pieces of the jigsaw unplaced, and all 15 players got at least a game. Three of Australia's quartet of openers – Aaron Finch, Usman Khawaja and Shane Watson – took their turn at the job; David Warner dropped down to the middle order for the first time, and stayed there throughout the World Twenty20.

Finch, their previous T20 captain, said other teams would be targeting their top order with spinners, and pinpointed Imran Tahir as the danger man, although Smith suggested the 360-degree hitting of A. B. de Villiers posed the greater threat. "Hopefully the South African curators can make the pitches a little bit slow and turning," he added. "That would benefit both sides ahead of India."

The matches (each preceded by a women's fixture against West Indies) drew near-capacity crowds, buoyed by the forthcoming global event. Though South Africa won the first game, Australia fought back to take the series, and made considerable headway with their jigsaw. Du Plessis skimmed over some obvious shortcomings – particularly in the bowling – and pronounced his team ready for their return to India. In the event, neither would progress beyond the group stages.

AUSTRALIAN TOURING PARTY

*S. P. D. Smith, A. C. Agar, N. M. Coulter-Nile, J. P. Faulkner, A. J. Finch, J. W. Hastings, J. R. Hazlewood, U. T. Khawaja, M. R. Marsh, G. J. Maxwell, P. M. Nevill, A. J. Tye, D. A. Warner, S. R. Watson, A. Zampa. *Coach:* D. S. Lehmann.

SOUTH AFRICA v AUSTRALIA

First Twenty20 International

At Durban, March 4, 2016 (floodlit). South Africa won by three wickets. Toss: Australia. Twenty20 international debuts: P. M. Nevill, A. Zampa.

A flying start persuaded some of the Australians that unrelenting attack was the way to bat. But there was more in the pitch than they recognised. Wickets began to fall regularly, though Marsh shored up one end, ninth out in the 20th over. No team had won a Twenty20 international at Durban chasing as many as 158, but it still seemed below par – until South Africa were 95 for six. De Villiers steered their first ball straight to the keeper, Nevill, who also ran out du Plessis. Miller, however, was in belligerent mood, with trios of fours and sixes to ensure victory in front of his home crowd. Australia should have done better with the bat after Finch and Warner raced to 69 for one in the powerplay; Finch hit Duminy's first three deliveries for six in a solitary over costing 24. But both were dismissed carelessly soon after. Warner slapped Wiese to backward point, while Finch lifted a full toss straight to deep square leg. The men who followed showed no interest in consolidation – if they had, Australia might well have won.

Man of the Match: D. A. Miller.

Australia

		B	*4/6*
1 U. T. Khawaja *c 7 b 10*	9	10	1
2 A. J. Finch *c 10 b 11*	40	18	2/4
3 D. A. Warner *c 4 b 7*	20	11	3/1
4 *S. P. D. Smith *c 2 b 7*	6	17	0
5 G. J. Maxwell *c 3 b 8*	17	11	3
6 M. R. Marsh *c 6 b 9*	35	25	1/2
7 †P. M. Nevill *lbw b 11*	4	5	0
8 J. W. Hastings *b 11*	7	9	1
9 N. M. Coulter-Nile *b 10*	9	9	0/1
10 A. Zampa *not out*	5	5	0
11 A. J. Tye *not out*	0	0	0
B 2, lb 1, w 2	5		
6 overs: 69-1 (20 overs)	157-9		

1/23 2/69 3/71 4/91 5/97 6/104 7/114 8/149 9/154

Rabada 4–10–26–2; Abbott 4–10–32–1; Duminy 1–1–24–0; Morris 3–7–35–1; Wiese 4–12–16–2; Imran Tahir 4–11–21–3.

South Africa

		B	*4/6*
1 A. B. de Villiers *c 7 b 9*	0	1	0
2 †Q. de Kock *c and b 9*	7	8	1
3 *F. du Plessis *run out*	40	26	4/1
4 J-P. Duminy *c 2 b 11*	5	9	0
5 R. R. Rossouw *c 1 b 6*	19	14	2
6 D. A. Miller *not out*	53	35	3/3
7 D. Wiese *run out*	13	11	0/1
8 C. H. Morris *c 2 b 9*	8	9	1
9 K. J. Abbott *not out*	6	4	1
Lb 1, w 5, nb 1	7		
6 overs: 45-3 (19.2 overs)	158-7		

1/0 2/17 3/41 4/72 5/72 6/95 7/134

10 K. Rabada and 11 Imran Tahir did not bat.

Coulter-Nile 4–9–29–3; Hastings 4–11–29–0; Maxwell 1–1–16–0; Tye 3.2–4–40–1; Marsh 3–8–17–1; Zampa 4–8–26–0.

Umpires: S. George and A. T. Holdstock. Third umpire: B. P. Jele.
Referee: R. B. Richardson.

SOUTH AFRICA v AUSTRALIA

Second Twenty20 International

At Johannesburg, March 6, 2016 (floodlit). Australia won by five wickets. Toss: Australia. Twenty20 international debut: A. C. Agar.

There is no such thing as enough at the Wanderers: Australia's 205 was the fourth-highest winning chase in Twenty20 internationals, and the third of them on this ground. Warner, striking the ball as cleanly as ever, and Maxwell, at his opportunist, unorthodox best, shared a thrilling stand of 161, an all-wicket record for Australia and for any fourth wicket. They started cautiously but timed their charge well – until both fell in sight of the finish. Maxwell sliced to deep cover with 12 required from eight balls; Warner was clean bowled by Rabada at the start of the final over. But two wides meant that Faulkner, unable to find the boundary, could scramble twos instead. Marsh needed another two from the last delivery: Rabada produced a fine yorker, only to see him block it so powerfully into the pitch that it bounced back over the bowler's head, between long-on and long-off, enabling Australia to complete the runs comfortably. De Kock had provided early evidence that conditions were skewed towards batsmen, wristily manipulating a ball which neither seamed nor swung; du Plessis added the bulk of South Africa's runs, although his acceleration, including two fours and two sixes in the last over, was perhaps too late. But it seemed they had plenty when Australia slipped to 32 for three: Rabada flattened Finch's stumps with a yorker, while Steyn, in his first game since the Boxing Day Test, struck twice in his second over.

Man of the Match: D. A. Warner.

South Africa

		B	4/6
1 A. B. de Villiers *b 9*	13	9	1/1
2 †Q. de Kock *b 7*	44	28	8/1
3 *F. du Plessis *c 5 b 9*	79	41	5/5
4 J-P. Duminy *c 3 b 6*	14	12	1/1
5 D. A. Miller *c 5 b 11*	33	18	2/2
6 F. Behardien *c 11 b 7*	3	5	0
7 C. H. Morris *c 4 b 7*	3	5	0
8 D. Wiese *not out*	10	3	0/1
9 K. Rabada *not out*	0	0	0
Lb 1, w 3, nb 1	5		

6 overs: 62-1 (20 overs) 204-7

1/15 2/77 3/103 4/142 5/151 6/165 7/198

10 D. W. Steyn and 11 Imran Tahir did not bat.

Hazlewood 4–6–50–0; Hastings 4–11–42–2; Marsh 2–5–28–1; Maxwell 4–6–30–0; Faulkner 4–9–28–3; Agar 2–2–25–1.

Australia

		B	4/6
1 A. J. Finch *b 9*	2	4	0
2 S. R. Watson *c 4 b 10*	9	15	2
3 *S. P. D. Smith *c 9 b 10*	19	15	2/1
4 D. A. Warner *b 9*	77	40	6/5
5 G. J. Maxwell *c 1 b 7*	75	43	7/3
6 M. R. Marsh *not out*	2	1	0
7 J. P. Faulkner *not out*	7	4	0
Lb 4, w 8, nb 2	14		

6 overs: 36-3 (20 overs) 205-5

1/2 2/28 3/32 4/193 5/194

8 †P. M. Nevill, 9 J. W. Hastings, 10 J. R. Hazlewood and 11 A. C. Agar did not bat.

Rabada 4–12–25–2; Morris 4–9–39–1; Steyn 4–11–32–2; Wiese 4–5–58–0; Imran Tahir 4–5–47–0.

Umpires: S. George and A. T. Holdstock. Third umpire: B. P. Jele. Referee: R. B. Richardson.

SOUTH AFRICA v AUSTRALIA

Third Twenty20 International

At Cape Town, March 9, 2016 (floodlit). Australia won by six wickets. Toss: South Africa.

Amla's unbeaten 97, a career-best, helped South Africa reach the second-highest T20 total at Newlands, but Australia beat it to clinch the series. They always seemed in control of the asking-rate: Watson was ruthless in the powerplay and Steve Smith dominated the middle overs. Though he had a strike-rate of 156, Amla did miss a number of scoring opportunities as fatigue set in. Zampa, the 23-year-old leg-spinner, demonstrated outstanding control and an apparent ability to predict batsmen's movements. Khawaja and Watson opened with 76 at more than nine an over, before South Africa's leg-spinner, Imran Tahir, had both caught within four deliveries. But Smith was unperturbed, allowing Warner to play within himself – and a straightforward victory was wrapped up by Maxwell. A squirrel had wandered about the outfield for most of South Africa's innings, resisting attempts to lure it off with a trail of nuts.

Man of the Match: H. M. Amla. *Man of the Series:* D. A. Warner.

South Africa

		B	4/6
1 †Q. de Kock *c 9 b 10*	25	13	4/1
2 H. M. Amla *not out*	97	62	8/4
3 *F. du Plessis *c 7 b 2*	4	7	0
4 R. R. Rossouw *c 3 b 10*	16	21	1
5 D. A. Miller *c 1 b 7*	30	16	2/2
6 J-P. Duminy *not out*	1	1	0
Lb 3, w 2	5		

6 overs: 68-1 (20 overs) 178-4

1/47 2/74 3/121 4/171

7 D. Wiese, 8 K. J. Abbott, 9 K. Rabada, 10 D. W. Steyn and 11 Imran Tahir did not bat.

Coulter-Nile 4–9–36–2; Hastings 3–7–28–0; Watson 2–3–22–1; Faulkner 4–6–42–1; Zampa 4–10–23–0; Maxwell 3–3–24–0.

Australia

		B	4/6
1 U. T. Khawaja *c 2 b 11*	33	25	4/1
2 S. R. Watson *c 3 b 11*	42	27	2/3
3 *S. P. D. Smith *c 1 b 9*	44	26	2/2
4 D. A. Warner *run out*	33	27	3
5 G. J. Maxwell *not out*	19	10	2/1
6 M. R. Marsh *not out*	4	1	1
Lb 2, w 4	6		

6 overs: 51-0 (19.2 overs) 181-4

1/76 2/78 3/157 4/169

7 J. P. Faulkner, 8 †P. M. Nevill, 9 J. W. Hastings, 10 N. M. Coulter-Nile and 11 A. Zampa did not bat.

Steyn 4–12–30–0; Rabada 4–8–38–1; Abbott 3.2–5–32–0; Imran Tahir 4–6–38–2; Wiese 2–2–23–0; Duminy 2–1–18–0.

Umpires: S. George and A. T. Holdstock. Third umpire: B. P. Jele. Referee: R. B. Richardson.

SOUTH AFRICA v NEW ZEALAND IN 2016

NEIL MANTHORP

Test matches (2): South Africa 1, New Zealand 0

New Zealand arrived quietly confident of a first series win in South Africa. They had just dismantled Zimbabwe, which put nine days' Test cricket into their legs, whereas the South Africans had not played a Test for more than six months. With a tour of India looming, new skipper Kane Williamson and coach Mike Hesson were aware that the busiest nine months in New Zealand's history could define the game's profile back home.

South Africa, by contrast, had crashed from No. 1 in the rankings to an all-time low of seventh, and hopes they could prove this was just a temporary blip were not helped when A. B. de Villiers and Morne Morkel were ruled out by injury. Their absence, though, was mitigated by the return of the potent new-ball pairing of Dale Steyn and Vernon Philander.

The scheduling of the two Tests during the rugby season was unfamiliar. The first started on August 19, almost two months before the previous-earliest Test in South Africa. There was also official confirmation from Cricket South Africa shortly before the tour that racial quotas, which had existed at domestic level for over a decade and a half, would be introduced at national level as well. The actual numbers were not revealed, but South Africa's side in both Tests included six non-whites.

The first was at Durban, where the board failed to ensure adequate covering. Rain fell, and the last three and a half days were lost to a wet outfield. The conditions in Centurion were impeccable, justifying the gamble of reseeding the entire playing area, with cool-weather winter grass. It was soft, and a natural emerald-green – unlike the dead, tufty surface which had been spray-painted when these teams played a one-day international 12 months earlier. New Zealand's hopes were swept away, largely by the returning Steyn.

NEW ZEALAND TOURING PARTY

*K. S. Williamson, T. A. Boult, D. A. J. Bracewell, M. D. Craig, M. J. Guptill, M. J. Henry, T. W. M. Latham, H. M. Nicholls, J. A. Raval, L. Ronchi, M. J. Santner, I. S. Sodhi, T. G. Southee, L. R. P. L. Taylor, N. Wagner, B-J. Watling. *Coach:* M. J. Hesson.

SOUTH AFRICA v NEW ZEALAND

First Test Match

At Durban, August 19–23, 2016. Drawn. Toss: South Africa.

The meteorologists suggested there was nothing wrong with staging a Test in the Durban winter. But the decision backfired when a thunderstorm soaked Kingsmead on the second afternoon, and no further play was possible. The mistake lay not in the scheduling, but in the covering. It is not usual practice to protect the entire outfield in South Africa –

but it should have been done on this occasion, and could have been achieved with help from local clubs.

This was easily the earliest that a Test match had been played in the South African season: the first of the 1902-03 series against Australia – on their way back from England – had started in Johannesburg on October 11. The match was developing nicely when the storm struck. There was plenty of life in the pitch, which meant South Africa's total of 263 was better than it looked. Left-armers Boult and Wagner took three wickets apiece, while Amla top-scored with 53, which included ten fours. A wicket was rarely far away: the longest partnership lasted 22.4 overs, between du Plessis, captaining for the first time in a Test, and Bavuma, who survived for nearly two and a half hours.

When New Zealand's innings finally started, it was a fast bowler's paradise: low thundery clouds, the floodlights straining to pierce the gloom, and the Durban tide at its highest. The ball swung exotically. Steyn soon removed both openers, but Williamson and Taylor toughed it out before bad light intervened. When the storm arrived, it drenched an outfield which had been deeply scarified less than two months earlier. On the third morning the square and its immediate surrounds, including the run-ups, were bone dry under the covers – but large areas of the unprotected outfield, where the grass had not regrown, were little more than mud.

Close of play: first day, South Africa 236-8 (Rabada 14, Steyn 2); second day, New Zealand 15-2 (Williamson 2, Taylor 2); third day, no play; fourth day, no play.

South Africa

S. C. Cook c Watling b Boult	20
D. Elgar c Guptill b Bracewell	19
H. M. Amla c Watling b Boult	53
J-P. Duminy c Boult b Wagner	14
*F. du Plessis c Williamson b Wagner	23
T. Bavuma lbw b Santner	46
†Q. de Kock c Bracewell b Santner	33
V. D. Philander c Southee b Wagner	8
K. Rabada not out	32
D. W. Steyn b Southee	2
D. L. Piedt c Watling b Boult	9
Lb 4	4
1/33 (1) 2/41 (2) 3/102 (4) (87.4 overs)	263
4/106 (3) 5/160 (5) 6/208 (7)	
7/208 (6) 8/228 (8) 9/236 (10) 10/263 (11)	

Southee 23–3–80–1; Boult 21.4–5–52–3; Bracewell 16–6–53–1; Wagner 15–4–47–3; Santner 11–2–22–2; Guptill 1–0–5–0.

New Zealand

M. J. Guptill lbw b Steyn	7
T. W. M. Latham c Amla b Steyn	4
*K. S. Williamson not out	2
L. R. P. L. Taylor not out	2
1/7 (2) 2/12 (1) (2 wkts, 12 overs)	15

H. M. Nicholls, †B-J. Watling, M. J. Santner, D. A. J. Bracewell, T. G. Southee, N. Wagner and T. A. Boult did not bat.

Steyn 6–4–3–2; Philander 6–1–12–0.

Umpires: I. J. Gould and R. K. Illingworth. Third umpire: P. R. Reiffel.
Referee: A. J. Pycroft.

SOUTH AFRICA v NEW ZEALAND

Second Test Match

At Centurion, August 27–30, 2016. South Africa won by 204 runs. Toss: New Zealand.

After the Durban damp it was a relief that Centurion served up decent weather for a Test which South Africa won to pinch the series. The conditions nonetheless played a part: the pitch was juicier than usual, and the grass cover generous, while indentations created on the first day made for uneven bounce which became more exaggerated.

It was hardly surprising Williamson chose to bowl. Boult seamed some deliveries so much they looked like illusions, but he and the other fast bowlers also served up too many half-volleys, while short balls sat up, demanding to be cut or pulled. The opening stand was worth 100 by lunch, and – for only the second time – South Africa's top five all reached fifty. A total of 58 fours and three sixes between them was evidence of too many bad balls, though Wagner, born in nearby Pretoria, finished with five for 86. South Africa did have the rub of the green: video analysis revealed they played and missed on 56 occasions – around three times the average, according to New Zealand's coach Mike Hesson.

BOTH OPENERS OUT FIRST BALL IN A TEST INNINGS

P. S. McDonnell and A. C. Bannerman . .	Australia v England at Manchester.	1888
H. Sutcliffe and E. Paynter.	England v New Zealand at Christchurch	1932-33
Mohsin Khan and Mudassar Nazar	Pakistan v England at Leeds.	1982
M. S. Atapattu and S. T. Jayasuriya.	Sri Lanka v South Africa at Kandy.	2000
T. W. M. Latham and M. J. Guptill . . .	**New Zealand v South Africa at Centurion .**	**2016**

Research: Andrew Samson

On the second day, du Plessis grafted to a six-hour century, ensuring a formidable total. South Africa never accelerated, plugging away at around three an over, because they knew how precious every run was – and how unpredictable the pitch would become. When the declaration finally arrived after tea, most locals believed the only remaining question was the size of South Africa's victory.

New Zealand were soon in trouble at 26 for three, with Taylor's departure (to Bavuma's direct hit after running back from short leg) ending a sequence of 367 runs without dismissal. Williamson showed exemplary technique and judgment for almost five hours, and Nicholls also battled well, but others were less willing to get into line. Everyone was hit on the body or hands as New Zealand were all out 267 behind, though the follow-on was rejected: du Plessis was not going to risk batting last, especially with Steyn and Philander returning from long-term injuries.

South Africa's second innings started in unprecedented fashion, as de Kock hit his first four balls to the boundary, off Boult. He was the first wicketkeeper to open for them in a Test since Denis Lindsay in 1965, after Dean Elgar injured his ankle the day before the match. But things soon returned to normal and, with edges grasped and lbws upheld (Duminy went this way for the 19th time in 47 Test innings, a record percentage), it was soon 47 for four. Bavuma applied himself well, his unbeaten 40 occupying 173 minutes.

The eventual declaration set New Zealand 400, or an even unlikelier 140-odd overs to survive. Their slim chances of doing either disappeared when both openers fell to their first ball in the first over, from Steyn: Latham played on trying to shoulder arms, then Guptill edged to first slip. Soon it was seven for four, undercutting their 14 for four against England at Auckland in 1954-55 (when they were all out for 26). Despite a character-building 76 from Nicholls and an obdurate 32 from Watling, the end came with over a day to spare, Steyn finishing with five for 33. "It wasn't really a fair contest," he said. "The ball which got Taylor rolled, and Latham's was heading for his throat off a good length."

Richard Illingworth, the third umpire, also had a busy match. In all, 17 decisions were referred for review: South Africa had five of eight overturned, New Zealand two of nine. The tourists were unhappy that Latham's first-innings caught-behind was upheld, despite no sound or visible deviation. South Africa's win was their 17th in 22 Tests at Centurion, a record (77%) for any venue staging 20 or more matches.

Man of the Match: Q. de Kock.

Close of play: first day, South Africa 283-3 (Duminy 67, du Plessis 13); second day, New Zealand 38-3 (Williamson 15, Nicholls 4); third day, South Africa 105-6 (Bavuma 25, Philander 3).

South Africa

S. C. Cook c Williamson b Bracewell	56	– lbw b Boult	4
†Q. de Kock c Boult b Wagner	82	– c Williamson b Bracewell	50
H. M. Amla c Watling b Wagner	58	– c Guptill b Southee	1
J-P. Duminy c Watling b Southee	88	– lbw b Southee	0
*F. du Plessis not out	112	– c Taylor b Boult	6
T. Bavuma c Bracewell b Wagner	8	– not out	40
S. van Zyl c Taylor b Wagner	35	– c Watling b Wagner	5
V. D. Philander b Wagner	8	– b Southee	14
K. Rabada c Nicholls b Santner	7		
D. W. Steyn not out	13		
D. L. Piedt (did not bat)		– (9) not out	0
B 10, lb 4	14	B 4, lb 1, w 6, nb 1	12
1/133 (2) 2/151 (1) 3/246 (3) 4/317 (4) 5/342 (6) 6/426 (7) 7/442 (8) 8/463 (9) (8 wkts dec, 154 overs)	481	1/31 (1) 2/32 (3) 3/32 (4) 4/47 (5) 5/82 (2) 6/98 (7) 7/129 (8) (7 wkts dec, 47 overs)	132

Southee 35–5–114–1; Boult 35.4–7–107–0; Bracewell 30.2–9–98–1; Santner 14–1–62–1; Wagner 39–8–86–5. *Second innings*—Southee 16–6–46–3; Boult 14–3–44–2; Bracewell 7–2–19–1; Wagner 10–1–18–1.

New Zealand

M. J. Guptill c van Zyl b Philander	8	– (2) c Amla b Steyn	0
T. W. M. Latham c de Kock b Steyn	4	– (1) b Steyn	0
*K. S. Williamson c de Kock b Rabada	77	– c de Kock b Philander	5
L. R. P. L. Taylor run out	1	– lbw b Steyn	0
H. M. Nicholls lbw b Rabada	36	– c Rabada b Steyn	76
†B-J. Watling c de Kock b Steyn	8	– lbw b Piedt	32
M. J. Santner b Philander	0	– b Steyn	16
D. A. J. Bracewell lbw b Rabada	18	– lbw b Philander	30
T. G. Southee c de Kock b Piedt	8	– b Rabada	14
N. Wagner c de Kock b Steyn	31	– lbw b Rabada	3
T. A. Boult not out	0	– not out	0
B 5, lb 2, w 15, nb 1	23	B 10, lb 7, w 2	19
1/13 (1) 2/13 (2) 3/26 (4) 4/86 (5) 5/106 (6) 6/111 (7) 7/144 (8) 8/169 (9) 9/214 (10) 10/214 (3) (58.3 overs)	214	1/0 (1) 2/3 (2) 3/5 (4) 4/7 (3) 5/75 (6) 6/118 (7) 7/164 (8) 8/187 (9) 9/195 (10) 10/195 (5) (58.2 overs)	195

Steyn 20–3–66–3; Philander 15–1–43–2; Rabada 16.3–4–62–3; Piedt 7–0–36–1. *Second innings*—Steyn 16.2–4–33–5; Philander 14–4–34–2; Rabada 13–2–54–2; van Zyl 3–1–5–0; Piedt 12–3–52–1.

Umpires: I. J. Gould and P. R. Reiffel. Third umpire: R. K. Illingworth.
Referee: A. J. Pycroft.

IRELAND IN SOUTH AFRICA IN 2016-17

FIRDOSE MOONDA

In January 2015, the ICC announced that Ireland, along with Afghanistan, would join the ten Full Members in the qualification system for the 2019 World Cup. If they were ranked in the top eight by September 2017, they would be invited to the tournament without having to play any qualifiers. To take advantage of their status, Ireland must beat those above them in the standings. But they have played top-eight nations rarely, and most at home: only West Indies have hosted them outside World Cups. Here was a chance: one-off games against South Africa and Australia, big beasts with their mind on their own forthcoming series, and intent on blooding youngsters.

Ireland were without several key players – Ed Joyce and Boyd Rankin did not travel, while Niall O'Brien injured himself on tour – and were routed, taking only six wickets and not managing a single half-century. Their destroyers were two players with a point to prove: Temba Bavuma hit a hundred on one-day debut for South Africa, while Australia's Usman Khawaja made his case to depose Aaron Finch with a classy unbeaten 82. In the end, neither performance was enough to earn selection for the series that followed – though sufficient to keep Ireland down at 12th.

IRELAND SQUAD

*W. T. S. Porterfield, J. Anderson, P. K. D. Chase, G. H. Dockrell, A. R. McBrine, B. J. McCarthy, T. J. Murtagh, K. J. O'Brien, N. J. O'Brien, S. W. Poynter, P. R. Stirling, S. P. Terry, G. C. Wilson, C. A. Young. *Coach:* J. G. Bracewell.

N. J. O'Brien hit his head slipping in the bathroom the day before the South Africa match, and took no part in either game.

First one-day international At Benoni, September 25, 2016. **South Africa won by 206 runs.** **South Africa 354-5** (50 overs) (Q. de Kock 82, T. Bavuma 113, J-P. Duminy 52, F. Behardien 50); ‡**Ireland 148** (30.5 overs) (J-P. Duminy 4-16). *MoM:* T. Bavuma. *ODI debuts:* T. Bavuma, A. L. Phehlukwayo, D. Pretorius (South Africa). *Temba Bavuma was deployed as an opener, despite having done the job only twice in List A cricket. It proved a masterstroke: after putting on 159 in 24 overs with de Kock, he became the second South African to score a century on ODI debut, after Colin Ingram in 2010-11. A 22-ball 50 from Farhaan Behardien completed a towering total. William Porterfield fell to the second ball of the reply, and Ireland never recovered, losing their last seven for 71; J-P. Duminy was gifted a career-best 4-16.*

Second one-day international At Benoni, September 27, 2016. **Australia won by nine wickets.** ‡**Ireland 198** (43.5 overs); **Australia 199-1** (30.1 overs) (U. T. Khawaja 82*, S. P. D. Smith 59*). *MoM:* U. T. Khawaja. *ODI debut:* D. J. Worrall (Australia). *Ireland began strongly against a second-string Australian attack, reaching 121-2 in the 24th over. But when John Anderson was lbw to Scott Boland, it sparked a mid-innings collapse that included the first-ball run-out of Sean Terry, who wandered out of his crease after a leg-before shout. Ireland tumbled to 198, though it was their highest score against Australia. It didn't help when Peter Chase spilled Usman Khawaja on eight, and he made Ireland pay, combining with Steve Smith in a second-wicket stand of 126*.*

SOUTH AFRICA v AUSTRALIA IN 2016-17

FIRDOSE MOONDA

One-day internationals (5): South Africa 5, Australia 0

Victory in a one-day series would not normally rank among most teams' proudest moments, but for South Africa this felt different. Never before had Australia lost 5–0 – in any format. And if they were weakened by injuries and rotation, South Africa had issues of their own to overcome. They had to cope without A. B. de Villiers, their captain and brightest star, who was recovering from surgery on his left elbow; Faf du Plessis stood in. And their triumph came in the first series governed by Cricket South Africa's strict transformation policy. Over the course of a season, the national side now had to include an average of at least six non-white players, of whom at least two should be black African.

AUSTRALIA'S HEAVIEST ONE-DAY SERIES DEFEATS

5–0	**in South Africa**	**2016-17**	4–1	v South Africa	2008-09
*4–0	in England	2012	3–0	in England	1997
4–1	in West Indies	1994-95	3–0	in New Zealand	2006-07

* *One game abandoned.*

South Africa met that target, and unearthed new talent in the process. The biggest success was fast-bowling all-rounder Andile Phehlukwayo, a graduate of the Under-19 World Cup-winning squad of 2014, and the top wicket-taker here. And, while Dale Steyn and Kagiso Rabada were underwhelming, the supporting cast suggested strength in depth. Leg-spinner Imran Tahir faced competition from chinaman bowler Tabraiz Shamsi, while Kyle Abbott pushed for a more regular place.

By contrast, Australia's attack looked threadbare. Mitchell Starc and Josh Hazlewood were rested, and Nathan Coulter-Nile, Pat Cummins and James Faulkner were ruled out with injuries. They travelled with three newcomers, and their inexperience showed: Joe Mennie, Chris Tremain and Daniel Worrall were tormented by South Africa's batting.

Centuries in the first three games from Quinton de Kock, du Plessis and David Miller, who at long last seemed to be living up to his potential as a finisher, sealed the series. And then a final hundred, from fringe player Rilee Rossouw, sealed the whitewash. He had come into the squad only when de Villiers was ruled out, but made himself indispensable, scoring 311 runs at 78 in a range of roles. He was second only to David Warner, whose sensational 173 in the last match brought his tally to 386 – the most for Australia in a one-day series of five games or fewer. It was a heroic effort, but even that could not bring his side a win.

AUSTRALIAN TOURING PARTY

*S. P. D. Smith, G. J. Bailey, S. M. Boland, A. J. Finch, J. W. Hastings, T. M. Head, U. T. Khawaja, M. R. Marsh, J. M. Mennie, C. P. Tremain, M. S. Wade, D. A. Warner, D. J. Worrall, A. Zampa. *Coach:* D. S. Lehmann.

S. E. Marsh was originally selected, but withdrew because a broken finger – sustained during the Sri Lanka tour – had not healed; Khawaja replaced him. J. P. Faulkner was also named, but did not travel after straining a calf muscle.

SOUTH AFRICA v AUSTRALIA

First One-Day International

At Centurion, September 30, 2016. South Africa won by six wickets. Toss: South Africa.

De Kock's imperious 178 from 113 balls made a mockery of Australia's 294. It was the second-highest one-day score *for* South Africa, behind Gary Kirsten's undefeated 188 against the UAE at the 1996 World Cup, and the highest by anyone *in* South Africa, beating Herschelle Gibbs's 175 during the famous chase against the Australians at Johannesburg in March 2006. Having witnessed much of the innings from the non-striker's end, stand-in captain du Plessis declared: "Quinton played one of the best one-day knocks you will ever see." South Africa were fearing a tougher challenge after Australia raced to 88 for one in 12 overs. Phehlukwayo's first had gone for 16, but he trusted his slower balls, and removed Finch and Smith in his second to stall progress; following his debut against Ireland five days earlier, he now finished with four for 44. The innings spluttered to 192 for six in the 29th over, but Bailey and Hastings ensured South Africa would not have it easy. Instead, de Kock and Rossouw – replacing Hashim Amla, who was ill – carted 145 from the first 17 overs. And, when Rossouw was trapped by Zampa for a 45-ball 63, de Kock grew more savage, slamming 94 of the 123 he put on with du Plessis. Though he fell aiming for his 12th six, he had all but completed the rout.

Man of the Match: Q. de Kock.

Australia

D. A. Warner c Phehlukwayo b Parnell	40	D. J. Worrall not out		6
A. J. Finch c Parnell b Phehlukwayo	33	S. M. Boland not out		3
*S. P. D. Smith lbw b Phehlukwayo	8			
G. J. Bailey c Miller b Steyn	74	Lb 5, w 8		13
M. R. Marsh c de Kock b Phehlukwayo	31			
T. M. Head st de Kock b Imran Tahir	18	1/64 (1) 2/88 (2)	(9 wkts, 50 overs)	294
†M. S. Wade run out	5	3/90 (3) 4/131 (5)		
J. W. Hastings c Behardien b Phehlukwayo	51	5/172 (6) 6/192 (7) 7/271 (8)		
A. Zampa c Miller b Steyn	12	8/278 (4) 9/286 (9)	10 overs: 64-1	

Steyn 10–0–65–2; Rabada 10–0–63–0; Parnell 8–0–56–1; Phehlukwayo 10–1–44–4; Imran Tahir 10–0–46–1; Behardien 2–0–15–0.

South Africa

†Q. de Kock c Head b Boland	178	F. Behardien not out		5
R. R. Rossouw lbw b Zampa	63	W 4		4
*F. du Plessis b Boland	26			
J-P. Duminy c Head b Boland	9	1/145 (2) 2/268 (3)	(4 wkts, 36.2 overs)	295
D. A. Miller not out	10	3/280 (4) 4/280 (1)	10 overs: 87-0	

W. D. Parnell, A. L. Phehlukwayo, D. W. Steyn, K. Rabada and Imran Tahir did not bat.

Worrall 7.2–0–50–0; Hastings 7–0–52–0; Boland 7–0–67–3; Marsh 8–0–66–0; Head 2–0–16–0; Zampa 5–0–44–1.

Umpires: B. P. Jele and J. S. Wilson. Third umpire: N. J. Llong.
Referee: B. C. Broad.

SOUTH AFRICA v AUSTRALIA

Second One-Day International

At Johannesburg, October 2, 2016. South Africa won by 142 runs. Toss: Australia. One-day international debuts: J. M. Mennie, C. P. Tremain.

South Africa bullied the bowling on a flat, fast pitch to set up their second-biggest victory over Australia by runs; they had won by 196 at Cape Town in March 2006. Du Plessis's sixth ODI hundred provided the bulk of their 361, while the tourists' inexperienced seamers bore the brunt of the assault: Joe Mennie conceded 82, the most by an Australian on debut, and Chris Tremain 78, which equalled the old record (held by Steve Smith). The in-form Rossouw, retained as opener despite Hashim Amla's availability, relentlessly pierced the off side until departing in the 25th over. Then, du Plessis and Duminy, who required only 58 balls for his 82, combined power and placement to put on 150 at more than eight an over. Australia needed a similar partnership to get close, but the biggest they managed was 69 for the sixth wicket, and by then they were out of it. Despite the efforts of Head – who scored his first international half-century – wickets fell too frequently. Australia hit six sixes to South Africa's four, but 142 fewer runs.

Man of the Match: F. du Plessis.

South Africa

†Q. de Kock c Tremain b Hastings	22
R. R. Rossouw c sub (D. J. Worrall) b Hastings	75
*F. du Plessis c Smith b Marsh	111
J-P. Duminy b Marsh	82
D. A. Miller c Zampa b Hastings	26
F. Behardien c Warner b Tremain	13
W. D. Parnell not out	8
A. L. Phehlukwayo not out	13
Lb 1, w 10	11
1/70 (1) 2/146 (2) 3/296 (4) 4/308 (3) 5/334 (6) 6/347 (5) (6 wkts, 50 overs)	361
10 overs: 66-0	

D. W. Steyn, K. Rabada and Imran Tahir did not bat.

Tremain 10–0–78–1; Mennie 10–0–82–0; Hastings 10–0–57–3; Marsh 10–0–68–2; Zampa 8–0–54–0; Head 2–0–21–0.

Australia

A. J. Finch c Behardien b Rabada	1
D. A. Warner c Miller b Duminy	50
*S. P. D. Smith c de Kock b Steyn	14
G. J. Bailey b Parnell	9
M. R. Marsh c de Kock b Parnell	19
T. M. Head lbw b Rabada	51
†M. S. Wade c Duminy b Parnell	33
J. W. Hastings c Miller b Phehlukwayo	23
J. M. Mennie b Imran Tahir	1
A. Zampa b Phehlukwayo	8
C. P. Tremain not out	0
Lb 4, w 6	10
1/3 (1) 2/29 (3) 3/55 (4) 4/87 (5) 5/114 (2) 6/183 (6) 7/185 (7) 8/204 (9) 9/213 (8) 10/219 (10) (37.4 overs)	219
10 overs: 54-2	

Steyn 7–0–37–1; Rabada 7–0–31–2; Parnell 7–0–40–3; Phehlukwayo 6.4–0–59–2; Imran Tahir 7–1–31–1; Duminy 3–0–17–1.

Umpires: S. George and N. J. Llong. Third umpire: J. S. Wilson.
Referee: B. C. Broad.

SOUTH AFRICA v AUSTRALIA

Third One-Day International

At Durban, October 5, 2016. South Africa won by four wickets. Toss: Australia.

Miller was on 26 in the 31st over of South Africa's daunting chase when he tweaked his groin. Five balls later, Duminy – the only other specialist batsman left – fell to Hastings, the target still 155 away. Already under severe pressure after being dropped from the tour of the Caribbean in June, Miller finished with an extraordinary unbeaten 118 from 79 balls; because of his injury, it would be his last contribution to the series. He shared an unbroken 107 in 70 with Phehlukwayo, who completed the chase – the second-highest in ODIs – in the last over, with a fearless reverse sweep off Zampa. With the series on the line, Australia's senior batsmen had stood up: Warner and Smith scored a century each, before a late charge produced 65 off the last five overs. Steyn's ten overs leaked 96, the most by a South African; Rabada's figures were barely healthier. The reply began with atypical aggression from Amla, who had returned to the top of the order, and familiar belligerence from de Kock. A score of 140 for one soon became 179 for four, but Miller's magic secured South Africa's first one-day bilateral series win over Australia since early 2009.

Man of the Match: D. A. Miller.

Australia

D. A. Warner c Duminy b Imran Tahir 117	†M. S. Wade not out 17
A. J. Finch c Rabada b Imran Tahir. 53	Lb 3, w 8 11
*S. P. D. Smith b Steyn. 108	——
G. J. Bailey c du Plessis b Phehlukwayo. . . 28	1/110 (2) 2/234 (1) (6 wkts, 50 overs) 371
M. R. Marsh c Miller b Steyn 2	3/280 (4) 4/300 (5)
T. M. Head c and b Rabada. 35	5/325 (3) 6/371 (6) 10 overs: 88-0

J. W. Hastings, A. Zampa, C. P. Tremain and D. J. Worrall did not bat.

Steyn 10–0–96–2; Rabada 10–0–86–1; Pretorius 6–0–42–0; Imran Tahir 10–0–54–2; Phehlukwayo 8–0–58–1; Duminy 6–0–32–0.

South Africa

†Q. de Kock c Worrall b Tremain 70	A. L. Phehlukwayo not out 42
H. M. Amla lbw b Hastings. 45	
*F. du Plessis c Warner b Head. 33	Lb 3, w 8 11
R. R. Rossouw lbw b Zampa. 18	——
J-P. Duminy c Finch b Hastings 20	1/66 (2) 2/140 (3) (6 wkts, 49.2 overs) 372
D. A. Miller not out. 118	3/164 (1) 4/179 (4)
D. Pretorius c Warner b Marsh 15	5/217 (5) 6/265 (7) 10 overs: 77-1

D. W. Steyn, K. Rabada and Imran Tahir did not bat.

Tremain 10–0–65–1; Worrall 9–0–78–0; Hastings 10–0–79–2; Marsh 10–0–61–1; Zampa 7.2–1–55–1; Head 3–0–31–1.

Umpires: A. T. Holdstock and J. S. Wilson. Third umpire: N. J. Llong.
Referee: B. C. Broad.

SOUTH AFRICA v AUSTRALIA

Fourth One-Day International

At Port Elizabeth, October 9, 2016. South Africa won by six wickets. Toss: Australia.

South Africa produced a show of strength as their reserve attack ran through Australia. Abbott found early seam movement to dismiss the openers, before left-arm wrist-spinner Shamsi spun through Smith and Head in three balls. Marsh countered with 50 but, when he nicked Abbott behind, Australia crumbled to 167 – their lowest score in 11 one-day internationals at St George's Park. Six batsmen fell lbw, equalling the record for an ODI innings. Despite his gritty half-century, Wade further jeopardised respectability: after quarrelling with Shamsi, he hung out his elbow while running past him. Contact was minimal, but the umpires intervened; both were fined 25% of their match fee, and earned a demerit point (part of the ICC's new disciplinary system). So swift was Australia's demise that the reply began before lunch, and Tremain quickly snared the openers. But South Africa were never in real danger. Du Plessis, badly dropped at point by Zampa off Hastings on 16, anchored the chase with 69, and the runs were ticked off with time to spare.

Man of the Match: K. J. Abbott.

Australia

A. J. Finch b Abbott	2	C. P. Tremain not out	23
D. A. Warner b Abbott	6	S. M. Boland lbw b Phangiso	0
*S. P. D. Smith lbw b Shamsi	21		
G. J. Bailey lbw b Pretorius	1	W 3	3
M. R. Marsh c de Kock b Abbott	50		—
T. M. Head lbw b Shamsi	0	1/2 (1) 2/9 (2) 3/12 (4) (36.4 overs)	167
†M. S. Wade lbw b Phangiso	52	4/49 (3) 5/49 (6) 6/111 (5)	
J. W. Hastings lbw b Shamsi	4	7/116 (8) 8/121 (9) 9/167 (7)	
A. Zampa b Abbott	5	10/167 (11)	10 overs: 30-3

Abbott 8–0–40–4; Pretorius 7–1–33–1; Shamsi 10–1–36–3; Phehlukwayo 5–1–28–0; Phangiso 4.4–0–17–2; Duminy 2–0–13–0.

South Africa

H. M. Amla lbw b Tremain	4	F. Behardien not out	12
†Q. de Kock c Zampa b Tremain	18	Lb 3, w 4	7
*F. du Plessis c Head b Marsh	69		—
J-P. Duminy c Marsh b Zampa	25	1/8 (1) 2/29 (2) (4 wkts, 35.3 overs)	168
R. R. Rossouw not out	33	3/85 (4) 4/140 (3)	10 overs: 35-2

D. Pretorius, A. L. Phehlukwayo, K. J. Abbott, A. M. Phangiso and T. Shamsi did not bat.

Tremain 10–0–48–2; Boland 10–2–36–0; Hastings 4–0–27–0; Zampa 6.3–0–32–1; Marsh 5–0–22–1.

Umpires: A. T. Holdstock and N. J. Llong. Third umpire: J. S. Wilson.
Referee: B. C. Broad.

SOUTH AFRICA v AUSTRALIA

Fifth One-Day International

At Cape Town, October 12, 2016. South Africa won by 31 runs. Toss: South Africa.

With Australia chasing 328, Warner almost did it by himself. He struck a remarkable 136-ball 173, as seven of his team-mates failed to reach double figures; of the Australians' 35 boundaries, he hit 24. At the end of it all, South Africa had their whitewash, though they were sluggish at first: after deciding to bat, they slipped to 52 for three after 11. Rossouw and Duminy steadied them, putting on 178 as Australia struggled to exert pressure during the middle overs. Mennie finally removed Duminy in the 39th over, but Rossouw completed a hundred, and Miller chipped in with 39 from 29 balls. Australia reached 72 for none, but Finch couldn't find fluency, and was bowled in Imran Tahir's first over for a 40-ball 19; Smith departed in the same fashion two deliveries later. As wickets continued

---

HIGHEST ODI SCORE IN A LOSING CAUSE

194*	C. K. Coventry	Zimbabwe v Bangladesh at Bulawayo	2009
181*	M. L. Hayden	Australia v New Zealand at Hamilton	2006-07
175	‡S. R. Tendulkar	India v Australia at Hyderabad	2009-10
173	**‡D. A. Warner**	**Australia v South Africa at Cape Town**	**2016-17**
171*	R. G. Sharma	India v Australia at Perth	2015-16
167*	R. A. Smith	England v Australia at Birmingham	1993
164	R. T. Ponting	Australia v South Africa at Johannesburg	2005-06
160*	T. M. Dilshan	Sri Lanka v India at Hobart	2011-12
160	‡T. M. Dilshan	Sri Lanka v India at Rajkot	2009-10
156	G. J. Bailey	Australia v India at Nagpur	2013-14
156	K. J. Coetzer	Scotland v Bangladesh at Nelson	2014-15

‡ *Second innings of the match.*

to fall and the run-rate rose, Warner soldiered on, becoming the first to pass 1,000 ODI runs in 2016. He had been dropped on 11, when de Kock dived across Amla at slip, but everything else came out of the middle. Until he fell in the 48th over, there was a glimmer of hope. Only Damien Martyn, who made 116 out of 191 at Auckland in March 2000, had scored a higher percentage of runs in a completed one-day innings for Australia (60.7% to Warner's 58.4%). Du Plessis was left glowing with pride. "Whatever was thrown at us, we had the answers," he said. "We were just too good for them."

Man of the Match: D. A. Warner. *Man of the Series:* R. R. Rossouw.

South Africa

†Q. de Kock c Marsh b Boland	12	K. J. Abbott c Wade b Tremain	0
H. M. Amla b Mennie	25	D. W. Steyn not out	6
*F. du Plessis b Mennie	11	B 6, lb 5, w 8	19
R. R. Rossouw c Marsh b Tremain	122		—
J-P. Duminy c Bailey b Mennie	73	1/37 (1) 2/37 (2) (8 wkts, 50 overs)	327
D. A. Miller c Smith b Tremain	39	3/52 (3) 4/230 (5)	
A. L. Phehlukwayo b Boland	11	5/281 (4) 6/306 (7)	
K. Rabada not out	9	7/308 (6) 8/309 (9) 10 overs: 52-2	

Imran Tahir did not bat.

Tremain 10–0–64–3; Boland 10–0–68–2; Mennie 10–2–49–3; Marsh 7–0–53–0; Head 8–0–49–0; Zampa 5–0–33–0.

Australia

D. A. Warner run out	173	A. Zampa not out	6
A. J. Finch b Imran Tahir	19	S. M. Boland run out	4
*S. P. D. Smith b Imran Tahir	0		
G. J. Bailey b Phehlukwayo	2	Lb 7, w 7, nb 1	15
M. R. Marsh b Rabada	35		—
T. M. Head c de Kock b Abbott	35	1/72 (2) 2/72 (3) 3/75 (4) (48.2 overs)	296
†M. S. Wade c de Kock b Abbott	7	4/139 (5) 5/229 (6) 6/248 (7)	
J. M. Mennie c Miller b Rabada	0	7/249 (8) 8/261 (9) 9/288 (1)	
C. P. Tremain run out	0	10/296 (11) 10 overs: 60-0	

Abbott 10–1–48–2; Rabada 9–0–84–2; Steyn 9.2–0–56–0; Imran Tahir 10–1–42–2; Phehlukwayo 9–1–51–1; Duminy 1–0–8–0.

Umpires: S. George and J. S. Wilson. Third umpire: N. J. Llong.
Referee: B. C. Broad.

SOUTH AFRICA v SRI LANKA IN 2016-17

TELFORD VICE

Test matches (3): South Africa 3, Sri Lanka 0
Twenty20 internationals (3): South Africa 1, Sri Lanka 2
One-day internationals (5): South Africa 5, Sri Lanka 0

Paul Harris, these days a pundit as pithy as his slow left-arm bowling was unflashy, nailed it. As South Africa's one-day series triumph beckoned, he said: "It's a bit boring, because these Sri Lankans are rubbish. They just don't cut it in these conditions. Their best player at the moment is rain." Yet not nearly enough of it fell to spare the Sri Lankans what became routine hidings. In the figurative sense, it poured. In the Tests, Dean Elgar, J-P. Duminy, Quinton de Kock, Hashim Amla and Stephen Cook all scored hundreds; Sri Lanka had only three half-centuries, from Angelo Mathews, Kusal Mendis and Dimuth Karunaratne.

The brightening star of Kagiso Rabada rose still further in the Tests, where he claimed 19 wickets at 17. But the most dominant bowler was Vernon Philander, who showed all the mastery that had almost been taken for granted before an ankle injury sidelined him from November 2015 until August 2016. He took 17 wickets at 14, figures that did not flatter him.

For Sri Lanka, Suranga Lakmal – rangy and raw-boned, with a compelling edge to his bowling – made even soaked-in-seam South Africans take notice, and was rewarded with a dozen wickets. But their portly champion, Rangana Herath, was taken out of the equation by South Africa's ploy of leaving more grass than usual on the pitches. The surfaces were not unfair, but they were covered well enough to limit Herath's left-arm spin to six pricy wickets.

That was also the trend in the one-day internationals, although there was a difference of opinion. After the first match, at Port Elizabeth, A. B. de Villiers likened the pitch to Hambantota, where South Africa had clinched their first ODI series win in Sri Lanka, in 2014. But Sanath Jayasuriya, Sri Lanka's chief selector, told Cricbuzz a different story: "In ODIs, you generally get wickets that are good for batting. Port Elizabeth is the slowest wicket in South Africa, but this time they left a lot of grass."

Excuses missed the point, and the South Africans recognised in their visitors their own plight from a year before, when there still didn't seem to be life after Graeme Smith, Jacques Kallis and Mark Boucher. Replace those names with Muttiah Muralitharan, Mahela Jayawardene and Kumar Sangakkara, and the point is made. The hosts had little trouble winning the Test series 3–0, even less the one-dayers 5–0, and in between hardly cared a jot that they lost the Twenty20s 2–1 – but they couldn't quite find the empathy to put an arm around Sri Lanka's shoulder and say: "Don't worry – things will come right."

An important part of the reason they did so well was Faf du Plessis's appointment as captain, in the wake of de Villiers's resignation two weeks before the Test series, which he missed to recover from elbow surgery. As a leader of men, du Plessis invited comparisons with Mike Brearley, but he is a better player, and should have been made captain when Graeme Smith retired in March 2014.

But not even du Plessis could stop Kyle Abbott from taking up a Kolpak deal with Hampshire – one he had signed five months earlier. Abbott hid that fact from the dressing-room, and even said after the First Test that South Africa was "where you want to play your cricket". Less than a week later, after his signing had been exposed in the English media, he said: "I need to pay bills, I need to buy groceries." Look out for him at Waitrose.

SRI LANKAN TOURING PARTY

*A. D. Mathews (T/20), J. R. M. V. S. Bandara (T/50), P. V. D. Chameera (T), L. D. Chandimal (T/50/20), D. M. de Silva (T/50/20), P. C. de Silva (50), S. N. T. de Silva (20), D. P. D. N. Dickwella (50/20), A. N. P. R. Fernando (T/20), D. A. S. Gunaratne (50/20), M. D. Gunathilleke (20), H. M. R. K. B. Herath (T), F. D. M. Karunaratne (T), K. M. D. N. Kulasekara (50/20), C. B. R. L. S. Kumara (T/50), R. A. S. Lakmal (T/50/20), L. D. Madushanka (50), B. K. G. Mendis (T/50/20), S. S. Pathirana (50/20), M. D. K. Perera (T), M. D. K. J. Perera (T), S. Prasanna (20), P. A. D. L. R. Sandakan (50/20), J. K. Silva (T), W. U. Tharanga (T/50/20), I. Udana (20), J. D. F. Vandersay (50), D. S. Weerakkody (50). *Coach:* G. X. Ford.

Mathews missed the ODIs with an ankle injury; Tharanga captained instead. The day before the 50-over series started, S. N. T. de Silva, Prasanna and Udana were replaced by Bandara, Kumara and Vandersay.

TEST MATCH AVERAGES

SOUTH AFRICA – BATTING AND FIELDING

	T	*I*	*NO*	*R*	*HS*	*100*	*50*	*Avge*	*Ct/St*
†D. Elgar	3	5	0	308	129	1	2	61.60	3
†J-P. Duminy	3	5	0	273	155	1	1	54.60	3
†Q. de Kock	3	5	0	270	101	1	1	54.00	15/1
K. A. Maharaj	2	3	2	52	32*	0	0	52.00	0
F. du Plessis	3	5	1	199	67*	0	1	49.75	4
H. M. Amla	3	5	0	231	134	1	0	46.20	3
S. C. Cook	3	5	0	216	117	1	1	43.20	4
V. D. Philander	3	4	1	48	20	0	0	16.00	2
†K. Rabada	3	3	2	8	8	0	0	8.00	2
T. Bavuma	3	5	0	21	10	0	0	4.20	3

Played in two Tests: K. J. Abbott 0, 16 (1 ct). Played in one Test: D. Olivier 3; †W. D. Parnell 23 (1 ct).

BOWLING

	Style	*O*	*M*	*R*	*W*	*BB*	*5I*	*Avge*
D. Olivier	RFM	18	5	57	5	3-38	0	11.40
V. D. Philander	RFM	92	23	248	17	5-45	1	14.58
W. D. Parnell	LFM	21.1	3	89	6	4-51	0	14.83
K. Rabada	RF	87	18	326	19	6-55	1	17.15
K. A. Maharaj	SLA	67.3	14	212	7	3-86	0	30.28
K. J. Abbott	RFM	64.5	16	156	5	3-63	0	31.20

Also bowled: J-P. Duminy (OB) 4–0–9–0.

SRI LANKA – BATTING AND FIELDING

	T	*I*	*NO*	*R*	*HS*	*100*	*50*	*Avge*	*Ct*
A. D. Mathews	3	6	0	178	59	0	1	29.66	4
†W. U. Tharanga	2	4	1	88	26*	0	0	29.33	2
B. K. G. Mendis	3	6	0	138	58	0	1	23.00	6
†F. D. M. Karunaratne	3	6	0	128	50	0	1	21.33	3
D. M. de Silva	3	6	0	125	43	0	0	20.83	1
J. K. Silva	3	6	0	117	48	0	0	19.50	1
†H. M. R. K. B. Herath	3	6	1	81	35*	0	0	16.20	0
L. D. Chandimal	3	6	0	85	30	0	0	14.16	15
R. A. S. Lakmal	3	6	1	68	31	0	0	13.60	0
A. N. P. R. Fernando	3	6	2	21	8*	0	0	5.25	0
†C. B. R. L. S. Kumara	2	4	1	14	9	0	0	4.66	0

Played in one Test: P. V. D. Chameera 19, 0 (1 ct); †M. D. K. J. Perera 7, 6.

BOWLING

	Style	*O*	*M*	*R*	*W*	*BB*	*5I*	*Avge*
C. B. R. L. S. Kumara	RFM	62.1	3	291	11	6-122	1	26.45
R. A. S. Lakmal	RFM	121.5	25	370	12	5-63	1	30.83
A. N. P. R. Fernando	RFM	89.3	16	301	7	4-78	0	43.00
H. M. R. K. B. Herath	SLA	88.1	9	288	6	2-48	0	48.00

Also bowled: P. V. D. Chameera (RF) 29–1–153–1; D. M. de Silva (OB) 37–1–170–2; A. D. Mathews (RFM) 54–14–129–2.

At Potchefstroom, December 18–20, 2016 (not first-class). ‡**Sri Lankans 373** (98.5 overs) (F. D. M. Karunaratne 71, J. K. Silva 80, B. K. G. Mendis 51, D. M. de Silva 62; D. Olivier 4-54, G. F. Linde 3-85) **and 212-5** (47.1 overs) (M. D. K. J. Perera 51, W. U. Tharanga 50, L. D. Chandimal 60); **South African Invitation XI 289** (69.5 overs) (J. L. du Plooy 142; A. N. P. R. Fernando 3-41, C. B. R. L. S. Kumara 3-36). *Sri Lanka's batsmen made the most of their only warm-up match: seven reached half-centuries, and the one to miss out, Angelo Mathews, batted an hour for 37 in the second innings after a duck in the first. He also had figures of 7–2–15–2 from his first spell for more than three months. Leus du Plooy, who hit 25 fours, dominated the Invitation XI's innings; no one else reached 30. The home side chose from 13 players, and the Sri Lankans from 15.*

SOUTH AFRICA v SRI LANKA

First Test Match

At Port Elizabeth, December 26–30, 2016. Toss: South Africa. South Africa won by 206 runs.

St George's Park seemed set to offer Sri Lanka their best opportunity of the series – until it emerged that enough grass had been left on the pitch to take Herath out of the equation. He was the only bowler the hosts felt could threaten them, as he had done at Durban in December 2011, when his nine wickets earned what is still Sri Lanka's only Test win in South Africa. But this time his left-arm spin yielded only three wickets in nearly 45 overs – not that anyone else was able to rise far enough above the conditions.

Events at Port Elizabeth tend to be shaped by the wind. If it comes in off the sea, and over the main scoreboard – an easterly – wickets fall. If it blows from beyond the Grandstand – a westerly – the pitch dries faster, and runs trickle off the bat more easily. Regardless, both batting and bowling at this grinch of a ground is hard work, which invariably makes for absorbing play. And David Boon, the match referee, made it a little bit harder on the first day by ordering the band to tone down their brassy garrulousness.

South Africa were reminded of the local challenges when their batsmen were made to look ordinary by Sri Lanka's seamers, led by Lakmal. Six of the top seven batted for over an hour and a half, and all reached 20, but no one passed 63. Cook put on 104 with Elgar – South Africa's first hundred opening partnership here since Barry Richards and Eddie Barlow managed 157 against Australia in March 1970. The other half-centurion, Duminy, seemed as irked with Boon as he was with himself for the ill-considered sweep that helped Herath trap him in front. "I love the band," he said, "especially when they're shouting: 'JP, *jou lekker ding* [you good thing]'."

The next day the wind barrelled in from over the scoreboard. With it went South Africa's four remaining wickets, allowing Lakmal to complete his first five-for in his 32nd Test, and seven of Sri Lanka's. Early on the third day, the visitors were dismissed for 205, and trailed by 81. Philander's alchemy of accuracy and awkward angles proved particularly poisonous. De Silva was the most patient of the batsmen, but he needed to spend longer than his two hours if Sri Lanka were to stay in the fight.

Philander's alchemy of accuracy and awkward angles proved particularly poisonous

What was required was the innings Cook played later that day, a monument to those blessed with more substance than style. He compiled 117, having put on another century stand with Elgar. After du Plessis and de Kock hit brisk sixties, the declaration set Sri Lanka 488. By the close, despite the openers digging in for more than 32 overs, they were 240 for five. Mathews was their last hope, but he was dismissed for 58 in the third over of the fifth day, and South Africa wrapped things up after 70 minutes, Rabada and Maharaj splitting six wickets.

Man of the Match: S. C. Cook.

Close of play: first day, South Africa 267-6 (de Kock 25, Philander 6); second day, Sri Lanka 181-7 (de Silva 43, Chameera 7); third day, South Africa 351-5 (du Plessis 41, de Kock 42); fourth day, Sri Lanka 240-5 (Mathews 58, de Silva 9).

South Africa

S. C. Cook c Chandimal b Lakmal	59	– c Chandimal b Chameera	117
D. Elgar c Chandimal b Lakmal	45	– c Mathews b Lakmal	52
H. M. Amla c Chandimal b Lakmal	20	– lbw b Fernando	48
J-P. Duminy lbw b Herath	63	– c Mathews b de Silva	25
*F. du Plessis c Karunaratne b Lakmal	37	– not out	67
T. Bavuma lbw b Herath	3	– c Mendis b de Silva	8
†Q. de Kock b Fernando	37	– lbw b Herath	69
V. D. Philander c Chameera b Fernando	13		
K. A. Maharaj c Chandimal b Lakmal	0		
K. J. Abbott run out	0		
K. Rabada not out	0		
Lb 3, w 1, nb 5	9	B 5, lb 2, w 3, nb 10	20
1/104 (1) 2/105 (2) 3/178 (3) (98.5 overs)	286	1/116 (2) (6 wkts dec, 90.5 overs)	406
4/213 (4) 5/225 (6) 6/253 (5)		2/221 (3) 3/245 (1)	
7/276 (8) 8/276 (9) 9/281 (10) 10/286 (7)		4/267 (4) 5/277 (6) 6/406 (7)	

Lakmal 27–9–63–5; Fernando 21.5–5–66–2; Mathews 13–5–26–0; Chameera 14–1–68–0; Herath 20–4–48–2; de Silva 3–0–12–0. *Second innings*—Lakmal 18–2–64–1; Fernando 14–0–65–1; Mathews 4–0–10–0; Chameera 15–0–85–1; Herath 24.5–1–84–1; de Silva 15–0–91–2.

Sri Lanka

F. D. M. Karunaratne b Abbott	5	– run out	43
J. K. Silva lbw b Philander	16	– lbw b Rabada	48
M. D. K. J. Perera c de Kock b Philander	7	– c de Kock b Maharaj	6
B. K. G. Mendis c de Kock b Abbott	0	– c de Kock b Rabada	58
*A. D. Mathews c Elgar b Rabada	39	– lbw b Abbott	59
†L. D. Chandimal lbw b Philander	28	– c Rabada b Maharaj	8
D. M. de Silva c de Kock b Philander	43	– lbw b Abbott	22
H. M. R. K. B. Herath lbw b Maharaj	24	– c and b Philander	3
P. V. D. Chameera c Amla b Abbott	19	– c de Kock b Rabada	0
R. A. S. Lakmal c Abbott b Philander	4	– not out	19
A. N. P. R. Fernando not out	8	– b Maharaj	4
Lb 4, w 5, nb 3	12	B 4, lb 3, w 3, nb 1	11
1/10 (1) 2/19 (3) 3/22 (4) 4/61 (2) 5/94 (5) 6/121 (6) 7/157 (8) 8/181 (7) 9/185 (10) 10/205 (9) (64.5 overs)	205	1/87 (1) 2/93 (3) 3/118 (2) 4/193 (4) 5/225 (6) 6/246 (5) 7/258 (7) 8/258 (8) 9/274 (9) 10/281 (11) (96.3 overs)	281

Philander 20–7–45–5; Abbott 21.5–4–63–3; Rabada 13–3–63–1; Maharaj 10–3–30–1. *Second innings*—Philander 22–5–65–1; Abbott 20–6–38–2; Rabada 21–4–77–3; Maharaj 30.3–7–86–3; Duminy 3–0–8–0.

Umpires: Aleem Dar and B. N. J. Oxenford.
Third umpire: R. J. Tucker. S. George replaced Tucker on the second day
Referee: D. C. Boon.

SOUTH AFRICA v SRI LANKA

Second Test Match

At Cape Town, January 2–5, 2017. Toss: Sri Lanka. South Africa won by 282 runs.

Kyle Abbott's Kolpak defection hove into the public consciousness in reports from England on the first evening. Once there, it hung over proceedings like the noxious clouds caused by Cape Town's bushfires, and dominated the aftermath of South Africa's crushing victory; Abbott went wicketless, and was dropped.

The batting heroes were Elgar, who scored a century high on discipline, and de Kock, whose own hundred was a paean to the profanity of mad left-handers everywhere. With the ball, Rabada was alight with malevolence during a return of ten for 92 – the best match figures for South Africa against Sri Lanka, and the best in a Cape Town Test since readmission, passing Saeed Ajmal's ten for 147 for Pakistan in 2012-13.

Put in, the South Africans had slumped to 66 for three shortly before lunch. That they were still at the crease by the close, having lost only three more wickets while adding 231 more runs, was due in no small part to Elgar's cussedness. Until the sixth over before the close, he had withstood the probing impertinence of Lakmal and the 19-year-old Kumara. Elgar, who left the ball impeccably, had added 103 for the sixth wicket with de Kock, as South Africa surged towards 400 with the help of nuggety efforts by Philander and Maharaj. In just his third Test, Kumara finished with six for 122; only Muttiah Muralitharan, with six for 39 at Durban in 2000-01, had better innings figures for Sri Lanka in South Africa. Herath, meanwhile, moved to 356 Test wickets, one more than Chaminda Vaas and behind only Murali on Sri Lanka's all-time list.

But individual pleasure quickly gave way to general despondency: Sri Lanka were dismissed for 110, their second-lowest total against South Africa, though they were spared the indignity of following on, perhaps because next day's forecast was for warmth and no cloud cover. Their answer to Philander's precision and Rabada's fire was misplaced aggression: no one came to terms with the conditions, nor escaped the twenties. Having been 56 for one, they lost nine for 54.

South Africa were already a commanding 317 ahead by the second-day close, but batted on until 45 minutes before tea on the third, to set a target of 507. Philander and Rabada then picked off Sri Lanka's top four before stumps, which came with Mathews and Chandimal standing firm. Both, along with Tharanga, were cleared away in the space of three overs next morning, as the scale of the hiding became obvious. South Africa's bowlers made expert snipers, but the tourists, with their penchant for big, loose shots when they should have been thinking small and tight, were sitting ducks. The carnage, and a series win, was complete 15 minutes before lunch, leaving du Plessis to purr: "It was pretty much a perfect performance."

Man of the Match: K. Rabada.

Close of play: first day, South Africa 297-6 (de Kock 68, Abbott 16); second day, South Africa 35-0 (Cook 15, Elgar 19); third day, Sri Lanka 130-4 (A. D. Mathews 29, Chandimal 28).

South Africa

S. C. Cook c Mendis b Lakmal	0	– c Karunaratne b Lakmal	30
D. Elgar c Mendis b Lakmal	129	– c Mathews b Herath	55
H. M. Amla b Kumara	29	– c Chandimal b Lakmal	0
J-P. Duminy c Mendis b Kumara	0	– lbw b Lakmal	30
*F. du Plessis c Mathews b Herath	38	– c Chandimal b Lakmal	41
T. Bavuma c Tharanga b Kumara	10	– run out	0
†Q. de Kock c Chandimal b Kumara	101	– c Chandimal b Kumara	29
K. J. Abbott c Chandimal b Herath	16		
V. D. Philander c Chandimal b Kumara	20	– not out	15
K. A. Maharaj not out	32	– (8) not out	20
K. Rabada c Chandimal b Kumara	8		
Lb 3, w 5, nb 1	9	W 1, nb 3	4
1/0 (1) 2/66 (3) 3/66 (4) 4/142 (5) 5/169 (6) 6/272 (2) 7/303 (8) 8/336 (7) 9/376 (9) 10/392 (11) (116 overs)	392	1/64 (1) 2/64 (3) 3/110 (2) 4/136 (4) 5/137 (6) 6/170 (5) 7/192 (7) (7 wkts dec, 51.5 overs)	224

Lakmal 27–4–93–2; Fernando 15.4–3–46–0; Mathews 17–3–41–0; Kumara 25–1–122–6; Herath 23.2–4–57–2; de Silva 8–0–30–0. *Second innings*—Lakmal 19.5–2–69–4; Fernando 11–0–46–0; Kumara 12–0–62–1; de Silva 3–0–15–0; Herath 6–0–32–1.

Sri Lanka

F. D. M. Karunaratne c Bavuma b Rabada	24	– b Philander	6
J. K. Silva b Rabada	11	– c Cook b Rabada	29
B. K. G. Mendis c Duminy b Maharaj	11	– c Elgar b Philander	4
D. M. de Silva lbw b Maharaj	16	– lbw b Rabada	22
*A. D. Mathews c du Plessis b Rabada	2	– c de Kock b Rabada	49
†L. D. Chandimal c de Kock b Rabada	4	– c Cook b Rabada	30
W. U. Tharanga not out	26	– c de Kock b Rabada	12
H. M. R. K. B. Herath lbw b Philander	1	– not out	35
R. A. S. Lakmal c Amla b Philander	0	– c de Kock b Rabada	10
C. B. R. L. S. Kumara b Philander	4	– st de Kock b Maharaj	9
A. N. P. R. Fernando c du Plessis b Philander	0	– b Philander	5
Lb 5, w 5, nb 1	11	B 6, lb 5, nb 2	13
1/31 (2) 2/56 (3) 3/56 (1) 4/60 (5) 5/78 (4) 6/78 (6) 7/100 (8) 8/100 (9) 9/110 (10) 10/110 (11) (43 overs)	110	1/11 (1) 2/25 (3) 3/66 (2) 4/69 (4) 5/144 (6) 6/165 (7) 7/166 (5) 8/178 (9) 9/211 (10) 10/224 (11) (62 overs)	224

Philander 12–4–27–4; Abbott 8–3–9–0; Rabada 12–2–37–4; Maharaj 11–1–32–2. *Second innings*—Abbott 15–3–46–0; Philander 14–1–48–3; Rabada 17–3–55–6; Maharaj 16–3–64–1.

Umpires: Aleem Dar and R. J. Tucker. Third umpire: B. N. J. Oxenford.
Referee: D. C. Boon.

SOUTH AFRICA v SRI LANKA

Third Test Match

At Johannesburg, January 12–14, 2017. Toss: South Africa. South Africa won by an innings and 118 runs. Test debut: D. Olivier.

With the series decided at Newlands, all that remained to be discovered – from a South African perspective, at least – was whether Amla could deliver a performance befitting his 100th Test. The question was prickly. One of the greatest batsmen of the age, and as close to a deity as any South African sportsman can become, he had gone 13 innings without a century, and ten without even a fifty, a period in which he had twice been dismissed for ducks and twice for one, and watched his average dip below 50 for the first time in four years. This constituted something akin to a crisis – to everyone except Amla.

Happily, then, du Plessis won the toss, and batted on a Wanderers pitch full of Jo'burg jive. More happily, Mathews had Cook leg-before early in the second hour. Most happily, the Amla who came out to bat was the Amla the cricket world has come to know, respect and love. The crowd was small, which was less an insult to him than a nod to the pulling power of golfer Rory McIlroy, who was playing in the South African Open at nearby Glendower. But the fans who did show up were rewarded by a performance from Amla at his most mesmerising – once he had overcome an hour and more of fragility, anyway.

His fluency grew: one day and seven minutes after he had taken guard, he was stunningly caught by Chandimal – diving in front of first slip – for 134, his 26th Test century. He explained why he had declined to attend a pre-match press conference, which had been scheduled to mark his centenary: "There have been some frustrations after not getting runs over the last couple of games, and not contributing to the team's success. I wanted my focus to be as pure as possible, with no side attractions or razzmatazz." And it worked: Amla was the eighth player to score a hundred in his 100th Test, and the second South African, after Graeme Smith at The Oval in 2012.

Almost lost in the hoopla was a fine 155 from Duminy, who put on 292 for the third wicket with Amla, South Africa's biggest stand for any wicket against Sri Lanka, beating 205 by Alviro Petersen and Jacques Kallis at Newlands five years earlier. Though the last eight fell for 89, with four wickets apiece for Pradeep Fernando and Kumara, the Sri Lankans were still faced with 426. By lunch on the third day, they were following on again, a disheartening 295 behind, after another inept batting display, in which Parnell – playing only his second Test in almost seven years – and debutant seamer Duanne Olivier took two wickets apiece. They fared better in their second innings, but only just, and their evisceration was over before stumps, with Parnell adding another four.

Sri Lanka had lost 16 wickets in a day, a national record, pipping the 15 to fall on the third day at Bangalore in January 1994. In all, they had faced just 88.1 overs, as they slid to the 3–0 whitewash that had looked on the cards since the second day of the series.

Man of the Match: J-P. Duminy. *Man of the Series:* D. Elgar.

Close of play: first day, South Africa 338-3 (Amla 125, Olivier 0); second day, Sri Lanka 80-4 (A. D. Mathews 11, Chandimal 3).

South Africa

S. C. Cook lbw b Mathews	10
D. Elgar c Karunaratne b Kumara	27
H. M. Amla c Chandimal b Fernando	134
J-P. Duminy c Mendis b Kumara	155
D. Olivier c Chandimal b Mathews	3
*F. du Plessis c Mendis b Fernando	16
T. Bavuma c Silva b Fernando	0
†Q. de Kock c de Silva b Kumara	34
V. D. Philander c Chandimal b Fernando	0
W. D. Parnell c Tharanga b Kumara	23
K. Rabada not out	0
B 11, lb 8, w 4, nb 1	24
1/45 (1) 2/45 (2) 3/337 (4) 4/346 (5) 5/364 (6) 6/364 (7) 7/367 (3) 8/378 (9) 9/425 (10) 10/426 (8) (124.1 overs)	426

Lakmal 30–8–81–0; Fernando 27–8–78–4; Mathews 20–6–52–2; Kumara 25.1–2–107–4; Herath 14–0–67–0; de Silva 8–1–22–0.

Sri Lanka

F. D. M. Karunaratne c de Kock b Philander	0	– b Rabada	50
J. K. Silva c de Kock b Rabada	13	– c de Kock b Rabada	0
B. K. G. Mendis c Duminy b Rabada	41	– b Parnell	24
D. M. de Silva c Bavuma b Philander	10	– c du Plessis b Olivier	12
*A. D. Mathews c de Kock b Rabada	19	– c du Plessis b Olivier	10
†L. D. Chandimal c de Kock b Philander	5	– c Amla b Philander	10
W. U. Tharanga c Elgar b Olivier	24	– c Duminy b Parnell	26
H. M. R. K. B. Herath c Cook b Olivier	8	– c Bavuma b Parnell	10
R. A. S. Lakmal c Rabada b Parnell	4	– c Philander b Parnell	31
C. B. R. L. S. Kumara not out	1	– c Cook b Olivier	0
A. N. P. R. Fernando c and b Parnell	4	– not out	0
Lb 2	2	Lb 2, w 1, nb 1	4
1/0 (1) 2/47 (2) 3/62 (3) 4/70 (4) 5/90 (6) 6/100 (5) 7/108 (8) 8/126 (9) 9/126 (7) 10/131 (11) (45.4 overs)	131	1/2 (2) 2/39 (3) 3/59 (4) 4/87 (5) 5/108 (6) 6/108 (1) 7/134 (8) 8/177 (7) 9/177 (10) 10/177 (9) (42.3 overs)	177

Philander 14–5–28–3; Parnell 10.4–2–38–2; Olivier 9–3–19–2; Rabada 12–3–44–3. *Second innings*—Philander 10–1–35–1; Rabada 12–3–50–2; Parnell 10.3–1–51–4; Olivier 9–2–38–3; Duminy 1–0–1–0.

Umpires: B. N. J. Oxenford and R. J. Tucker. Third umpire: Aleem Dar.
Referee: D. C. Boon.

SOUTH AFRICA v SRI LANKA

First Twenty20 International

At Centurion, January 20, 2017 (floodlit). South Africa won by 19 runs. Toss: Sri Lanka. Twenty20 international debuts: T. B. de Bruyn, M. Mosehle, L. T. Ngidi, A. L. Phehlukwayo, J. T. Smuts; S. N. T. de Silva.

After rain reduced the match to ten overs a side, South Africa rattled up 126 for five at better than two a ball. Miller smacked 40 off 18, and Behardien – captaining for the first time, after Faf du Plessis was rested – contributed an unbeaten 31, helping Miller add 51 off 23 deliveries for the fourth wicket. The Sri Lankan attack were run ragged, and only seamer Gunaratne conceded fewer than a dozen an over. Even so, while Dickwella and Dhananjaya de Silva hustled and bustled through an opening stand of 59 in five overs, the visitors were in the contest. The illusion was shattered in the sixth, when Imran Tahir removed both. But a rain-streaked night ultimately belonged to Lungi Ngidi, a 20-year-old fast bowler, and one of five format debutants in a new-look South African side. Having been carted for two boundaries in his first over, he dismissed Prasanna and Mendis in the eighth, conceding only four singles, as Sri Lanka's challenge faded.

Man of the Match: L. T. Ngidi.

South Africa

		B	4/6
1 J. T. Smuts *c 8 b 10*	13	8	1/1
2 H. G. Kuhn *lbw b 9*	10	6	2
3 T. B. de Bruyn *c 8 b 5*	19	10	2/1
4 D. A. Miller *c 10 b 9*	40	18	3/3
5 *F. Behardien *not out*	31	18	3/1
6 †M. Mosehle *run out*	6	1	0/1
7 W. D. Parnell *not out*	0	0	0
Lb 1, w 5, nb 1	7		
6 overs: 37-2 (10 overs)	126-5		

1/15 2/30 3/54 4/105 5/125

8 A. L. Phehlukwayo, 9 A. M. Phangiso, 10 Imran Tahir and 11 L. T. Ngidi did not bat.

Mathews 2–0–29–0; Kulasekara 2–5–27–2; Lakmal 1–2–18–1; Gunaratne 2–2–12–0; Prasanna 1–1–14–1; Fernando 2–2–25–0.

Sri Lanka

		B	4/6
1 D. P. D. N. Dickwella *c 3 b 10*	43	19	6/2
2 D. M. de Silva *b 10*	27	16	2/2
3 *A. D. Mathews *c 3 b 7*	6	8	0
4 S. N. T. de Silva *c 2 b 9*	0	1	0
5 S. Prasanna *c 6 b 11*	12	3	0/2
6 B. K. G. Mendis *c 10 b 11*	1	2	0
7 †L. D. Chandimal *not out*	6	5	1
8 D. A. S. Gunaratne *not out*	10	6	0/1
Lb 2	2		
6 overs: 40-0 (10 overs)	107-6		

1/59 2/73 3/74 4/88 5/90 6/91

9 K. M. D. N. Kulasekara, 10 R. A. S. Lakmal and 11 A. N. P. R. Fernando did not bat.

Ngidi 2–6–12–2; Parnell 2–4–23–1; Phehlukwayo 2–2–23–0; Imran Tahir 2–4–23–2; Phangiso 2–4–24–1.

Umpires: S. George and A. T. Holdstock. Third umpire: B. P. Jele.
Referee: R. B. Richardson.

SOUTH AFRICA v SRI LANKA

Second Twenty20 International

At Johannesburg, January 22, 2017. Sri Lanka won by three wickets. Toss: South Africa. Twenty20 international debut: P. A. D. L. R. Sandakan.

After more than a month on tour without a win, Sri Lanka finally broke their duck. Lakshan Sandakan, a wispy 5ft 6in left-arm wrist-spinner, and Isuru Udana, an intense left-arm seamer with fine control of his changes of pace, took seven wickets between them to dismiss South Africa for their lowest Twenty20 score against Sri Lanka. No one reached 30, and no partnership lasted six overs. Sandakan became the first Sri Lankan to claim a wicket with his first delivery in Twenty20 internationals when his chinaman had Mangaliso Mosehle caught behind. A pitch more Wankhede than Wanderers played its part in the South Africans' travails, but the bigger truth was that, for once, the Sri Lankans showed some fight. Mathews then batted through five partnerships for his unbeaten 54, hammering Jon-Jon Smuts, a hapless off-spinner, for two sixes in three balls to win the match, after Sri Lanka's seventh wicket had fallen with nine still required. But victory came at a price: Mathews twisted an ankle, ending his tour. After trapping Gunaratne, Imran Tahir revealed his T-shirt depicting Junaid Jamshed, a Pakistani celebrity who had died in a plane crash the previous month; Tahir earned a reprimand from the ICC.

Man of the Match: A. D. Mathews.

South Africa

		B	4/6
1 J. T. Smuts *c 11 b 9*	4	8	1
2 H. G. Kuhn *st 4 b 11*	29	20	1/2
3 T. B. de Bruyn *c 2 b 10*	7	6	1
4 †M. Mosehle *c 4 b 11*	11	10	2
5 D. A. Miller *c 5 b 2*	11	14	1
6 *F. Behardien *c 4 b 10*	27	22	2
7 W. D. Parnell *c 5 b 11*	3	7	0
8 A. L. Phehlukwayo *c 4 b 11*	0	2	0
9 A. M. Phangiso *c 6 b 10*	13	19	1
10 Imran Tahir *b 9*	1	6	0
11 L. T. Ngidi *not out*	2	3	0
Lb 2, w 3	5		
6 overs: 41-2 (19.3 overs)	113		

1/5 2/13 3/41 4/57 5/68 6/74 7/74 8/107 9/109

Mathews 2–7–11–0; Kulasekara 3–11–10–2; Udana 2.3–9–13–3; Prasanna 3–4–24–0; Sandakan 4–11–23–4; Gunaratne 4–6–27–0; D. M. de Silva 1–3–3–1.

Sri Lanka

		B	4/6
1 D. P. D. N. Dickwella *c 4 b 11*	22	15	5
2 D. M. de Silva *c 5 b 11*	2	6	0
3 B. K. G. Mendis *b 11*	4	2	1
4 †L. D. Chandimal *c 4 b 11*	22	28	0
5 *A. D. Mathews *not out*	54	50	1/3
6 D. A. S. Gunaratne *lbw b 10*	3	5	0
7 S. Prasanna *c 10 b 1*	2	5	0
8 S. N. T. de Silva *c 6 b 7*	3	6	0
9 K. M. D. N. Kulasekara *not out*	0	1	0
B 3, lb 2, w 2	7		
6 overs: 38-3 (19.4 overs)	119-7		

1/11 2/15 3/35 4/86 5/93 6/97 7/105

10 I. Udana and 11 P. A. D. L. R. Sandakan did not bat.

Ngidi 4–11–19–4; Parnell 3–9–16–1; Phehlukwayo 2–3–22–0; Imran Tahir 4–11–14–1; Phangiso 4–8–24–0; Smuts 2.4–8–19–1.

Umpires: A. T. Holdstock and B. P. Jele. Third umpire: S. George.
Referee: R. B. Richardson.

SOUTH AFRICA v SRI LANKA

Third Twenty20 International

At Cape Town, January 25, 2017 (floodlit). Sri Lanka won by five wickets. Toss: South Africa. Twenty20 international debut: D. Paterson.

Sri Lanka won a series of any description in South Africa for the first time in nine attempts with a sturdy all-round performance – despite the return of de Villiers from the elbow injury that had kept him away from national duty since June. He showed little signs of rust in his 63 but, aside from Reeza Hendricks's 41, did not get solid enough support, and South Africa needed Mosehle's unbeaten 32 off 15 balls to push them to a decent total. It wasn't decent enough, however, to stop the Sri Lankans scrambling home with a ball to spare, thanks in part to Dickwella batting into the 16th over for 68. His dismissal, by Imran Tahir, who removed Dhananjaya de Silva in the same over, started a slide of three for 26. But the heads of Prasanna and Gunaratne proved sufficiently cool, although Gunaratne had to apologise to the umpires for snatching a souvenir stump with the scores level. He drilled the next ball into the covers for the winning single.

Man of the Match: D. P. D. N. Dickwella. *Man of the Series:* D. P. D. N. Dickwella.

South Africa

		B	4/6
1 J. T. Smuts *lbw b 5*	19	14	3
2 R. R. Hendricks *st 3 b 11*	41	34	4
3 A. B. de Villiers *c 2 b 9*	63	44	2/3
4 D. A. Miller *c 11 b 7*	1	4	0
5 *F. Behardien *run out*	6	6	0
6 †M. Mosehle *not out*	32	15	1/3
7 W. D. Parnell *not out*	3	3	0
Lb 2, w 2	4		
6 overs: 48-1 (20 overs)	169-5		

1/36 2/107 3/117 4/133 5/135

8 A. L. Phehlukwayo, 9 D. Paterson, 10 Imran Tahir and 11 L. T. Ngidi did not bat.

S. N. T. de Silva 1–2–10–0; Kulasekara 4–5–30–1; Udana 4–3–49–0; Prasanna 3–5–21–1; Sandakan 4–7–23–1; Gunaratne 4–7–34–1.

Sri Lanka

		B	4/6
1 D. P. D. N. Dickwella *c 5 b 10*	68	51	10/1
2 W. U. Tharanga *c 5 b 7*	20	11	4
3 *†L. D. Chandimal *b 10*	5	5	0
4 D. M. de Silva *st 6 b 10*	19	27	0
5 S. Prasanna *not out*	37	16	3/3
6 B. K. G. Mendis *run out*	2	3	0
7 D. A. S. Gunaratne *not out*	11	6	2
B 2, lb 3, w 3	8		
6 overs: 48-2 (19.5 overs)	170-5		

1/36 2/45 3/116 4/118 5/142

8 S. N. T. de Silva, 9 K. M. D. N. Kulasekara, 10 I. Udana and 11 P. A. D. L. R. Sandakan did not bat.

Ngidi 2–6–13–0; Paterson 3.5–7–38–0; Parnell 4–6–42–1; Imran Tahir 4–11–18–3; Phehlukwayo 4–12–32–0; Smuts 2–2–22–0.

Umpires: S. George and B. P. Jele. Third umpire: A. T. Holdstock.
Referee: R. B. Richardson.

SOUTH AFRICA v SRI LANKA

First One-Day International

At Port Elizabeth, January 28, 2017. South Africa won by eight wickets. Toss: South Africa. One-day international debut: D. S. Weerakkody.

The teams returned to the scene of the First Test – and faithfully reprised their performances. South Africa's bowlers were again too hot for Sri Lanka's batsmen, even on another slow pitch, and victory was again achieved with time to spare. Put in, the Sri Lankans were limited to 181 by Parnell, who removed both openers cheaply, and Imran Tahir, who struck three times in four overs after Mendis and Chandimal had added 72 for the third wicket; Tahir did not concede a boundary, and went for only 26 runs, the tightest ten overs of his ODI career. Mendis alone passed 28, while six of his team-mates failed to reach double figures. Amla then put on 71 with de Kock and 60 with du Plessis. The rout was completed by an unbroken stand of 54 at better than a run a ball between du Plessis and de Villiers.

Man of the Match: Imran Tahir.

Sri Lanka

D. P. D. N. Dickwella lbw b Parnell	1
D. S. Weerakkody c Amla b Parnell	5
B. K. G. Mendis lbw b Imran Tahir	62
†L. D. Chandimal b Imran Tahir	22
*W. U. Tharanga c Duminy b Imran Tahir	6
D. M. de Silva c du Plessis b Parnell	28
D. A. S. Gunaratne run out	10
K. M. D. N. Kulasekara c de Kock b Rabada	17
J. D. F. Vandersay lbw b Morris	8
R. A. S. Lakmal b Morris	3
P. A. D. L. R. Sandakan not out	2
Lb 5, w 12	17
1/1 (1) 2/14 (2) 3/86 (4) 4/99 (3) 5/102 (5) 6/126 (7) 7/155 (8) 8/170 (9) 9/170 (6) 10/181 (10) (48.3 overs)	181

10 overs: 37-2

Rabada 10–1–35–1; Parnell 10–1–48–3; Morris 9.3–1–29–2; Phehlukwayo 7–0–31–0; Imran Tahir 10–0–26–3; Duminy 2–0–7–0.

South Africa

†Q. de Kock c Weerakkody b Sandakan	34
H. M. Amla c and b Gunaratne	57
F. du Plessis not out	55
*A. B. de Villiers not out	30
Lb 2, w 2, p 5	9
1/71 (1) (2 wkts, 34.2 overs)	185
2/131 (2) 10 overs: 43-0	

J-P. Duminy, D. A. Miller, C. H. Morris, W. D. Parnell, A. L. Phehlukwayo, K. Rabada and Imran Tahir did not bat.

Kulasekara 5–0–20–0; Lakmal 6–1–29–0; de Silva 2–0–9–0; Vandersay 7–0–51–0; Sandakan 8–0–35–1; Gunaratne 5–0–19–1; Mendis 1.2–0–15–0.

Umpires: B. P. Jele and R. A. Kettleborough. Third umpire: R. K. Illingworth.
Referee: R. B. Richardson.

SOUTH AFRICA v SRI LANKA

Second One-Day International

At Durban, February 1, 2017 (day/night). South Africa won by 121 runs. Toss: Sri Lanka.

Tharanga erred by bowling first on a pitch that became more difficult for batting, but that was the least of Sri Lanka's problems. Top of the list was their bowlers' failure to stop du Plessis and Miller from scoring centuries in an innings in which no one else made more than 26. There was no mistaking du Plessis's alloy of grit and calm, but Miller showed his game had developed from its wham-bam beginnings, deflecting deliveries he would normally have tried to muscle over the boundary. While du Plessis, who was dropped at slip by Dhananjaya de Silva off Sandakan on 63, faced 120 balls in total, Miller needed only 98 for his unbeaten 117, and carted six sixes. Their fifth-wicket stand was worth 117. Then scintillating catches by du Plessis, leaping one-handed in the covers, and de Villiers, over his shoulder as he ran towards the boundary from mid-off, helped hurry Sri Lanka out inside 38 overs. Just as spectacular was Duminy's direct hit to account for Gunaratne, when he had only one stump to aim at from backward point. Sri Lanka had plenty of starts, but no finishers, with Imran Tahir's variations again proving tough to get away.

Man of the Match: F. du Plessis.

South Africa

H. M. Amla lbw b Lakmal	15
†Q. de Kock c Lakmal b D. M. de Silva	17
F. du Plessis c Mendis b Kulasekara	105
*A. B. de Villiers c Chandimal b Sandakan	3
J-P. Duminy c D. M. de Silva b Pathirana	11
D. A. Miller not out	117
C. H. Morris c Mendis b Lakmal	26
W. D. Parnell not out	2
Lb 5, w 6	11
1/19 (1) 2/65 (2) (6 wkts, 50 overs)	307
3/71 (4) 4/108 (5)	
5/225 (3) 6/285 (7) 10 overs: 62-1	

A. L. Phehlukwayo, K. Rabada and Imran Tahir did not bat.

Kulasekara 10–0–76–1; Lakmal 7–0–54–2; D. M. de Silva 8–0–42–1; P. C. de Silva 4–0–23–0; Sandakan 10–0–51–1; Pathirana 4–0–19–1; Gunaratne 7–0–37–0.

Sri Lanka

D. P. D. N. Dickwella c du Plessis b Parnell	25
*W. U. Tharanga c de Villiers b Parnell	26
B. K. G. Mendis c du Plessis b Phehlukwayo	20
†L. D. Chandimal c de Kock b Morris	36
D. M. de Silva st de Kock b Imran Tahir	1
D. A. S. Gunaratne run out	18
P. C. de Silva c sub (F. Behardien) b Duminy	14
S. S. Pathirana c Parnell b Duminy	26
K. M. D. N. Kulasekara c du Plessis b Rabada	12
R. A. S. Lakmal not out	2
P. A. D. L. R. Sandakan lbw b Imran Tahir	0
Lb 1, w 5	6
1/45 (1) 2/52 (2) 3/74 (3) (37.5 overs)	186

4/75 (5) 5/119 (6) 6/132 (4) 7/152 (7) 8/181 (8) 9/184 (9) 10/186 (11)

10 overs: 56-2

Rabada 8–0–47–1; Parnell 6–0–34–2; Morris 6–0–27–1; Imran Tahir 8.5–1–26–2; Phehlukwayo 4–0–21–1; Duminy 5–0–30–2.

Umpires: S. George and R. K. Illingworth. Third umpire: R. A. Kettleborough.
Referee: R. B. Richardson.

SOUTH AFRICA v SRI LANKA

Third One-Day International

At Johannesburg, February 4, 2017 (day/night). South Africa won by seven wickets. Toss: South Africa. One-day international debuts: C. B. R. L. S. Kumara, L. D. Madushanka.

The game's unlikely hero was Pierre Hefer, who was watching on television at home when a swarm of bees buzzed the Wanderers and refused to budge, halting play midway through the Sri Lankan innings. As Hefer, an amateur bee-keeper, looked on, the groundstaff tried – and failed – to shoo them into a wheelie-bin with fire extinguishers. So Hefer donned his white overalls, gloves and boots, loaded trays of honey and beeswax into his car, and drove the five miles from his home to the ground. Once there, he talked his way in, with neither a ticket nor accreditation. Thanks to his efforts, the delay was limited to just over an hour. The Sri Lankans probably wished Hefer had never turned on his TV. Put in, they had struggled to come to terms with the bowling, and crashed from 60 without loss to 163 all out; Dickwella's plucky 74 was the only highlight. Dwaine Pretorius, a strapping fast bowler in only his fourth ODI, proved particularly problematic, taking three for 19 from seven overs. With the result never in doubt, South Africa were unfazed by losing de Kock, du Plessis and Amla before reaching 100. De Villiers's steady 60 not out completed the job, taking his ODI average at the Wanderers to 100 from 11 innings, and giving South Africa a 3–0 lead with two to play – their seventh successive one-day series win at home.

Man of the Match: D. Pretorius.

Sri Lanka

D. P. D. N. Dickwella c de Kock b Pretorius	74
*W. U. Tharanga c Pretorius b Rabada	31
B. K. G. Mendis c Amla b Phehlukwayo	4
†L. D. Chandimal c Morris b Phehlukwayo	4
D. M. de Silva c Amla b Morris	16
D. A. S. Gunaratne c Pretorius b Rabada	2
S. S. Pathirana b Imran Tahir	18
L. D. Madushanka c du Plessis b Pretorius	0
R. A. S. Lakmal c Behardien b Pretorius	0
C. B. R. L. S. Kumara c Rabada b Imran Tahir	5
P. A. D. L. R. Sandakan not out	0
Lb 3, w 6	9
1/60 (2) 2/79 (3) 3/89 (4) (39.2 overs)	163

4/115 (5) 5/125 (6) 6/149 (1) 7/149 (8) 8/155 (9) 9/158 (7) 10/163 (10)

10 overs: 54-0

Rabada 7–0–39–2; Morris 8–0–38–1; Pretorius 7–2–19–3; Duminy 3–0–17–0; Phehlukwayo 5–0–26–2; Imran Tahir 9.2–2–21–2.

South Africa

†Q. de Kock b Kumara	8
H. M. Amla run out	34
F. du Plessis c de Silva b Madushanka	24
*A. B. de Villiers not out	60
J-P. Duminy not out	28
Lb 1, w 8, nb 1	10
1/23 (1) 2/58 (3) 3/92 (2) (3 wkts, 32 overs)	164
10 overs: 52-1	

F. Behardien, C. H. Morris, D. Pretorius, A. L. Phehlukwayo, K. Rabada and Imran Tahir did not bat.

Lakmal 6–1–23–0; Kumara 8–0–49–1; Madushanka 4–0–15–1; Sandakan 6–0–33–0; Pathirana 7–0–35–0; de Silva 1–0–8–0.

Umpires: A. T. Holdstock and R. A. Kettleborough. Third umpire: R. K. Illingworth. Referee: R. B. Richardson.

SOUTH AFRICA v SRI LANKA

Fourth One-Day International

At Cape Town, February 7, 2017 (day/night). South Africa won by 40 runs. Toss: South Africa.

Sri Lanka delivered their best performance of the series in a match that had no bearing on its outcome. That didn't seem likely when South Africa rattled up 367 for five, the highest total at Newlands (they had made 354 twice, against Kenya in 2001-02 and England in 2009-10) and, for all of three days, their highest against Sri Lanka (previously 339 for five at Hambantota in 2014). Du Plessis hit 185 – the second highest one-day score for South Africa, after Gary Kirsten's unbeaten 188 against the United Arab Emirates at Rawalpindi during the 1996 World Cup. After facing 141 balls, hitting 16 fours and three sixes, and sharing century stands with de Kock and de Villiers, du Plessis perished in the last over, trying to hit Madushanka down the ground. Sri Lanka's highest total of the series until now had been only one more than du Plessis managed here, yet they gave South Africa a scare. Dickwella and Tharanga began with 139 in 16 overs and, at 203 for one in the 28th, they were in the hunt. Tharanga fell for a 90-ball 119, including seven sixes – his first ODI hundred since July 2013 – and a maiden half-century from left-hander Sandun Weerakkody took them 307 for four in the 44th. Anything was possible. But Imran Tahir struck twice in the next, though – after proving unhittable in the first three games – he finished with the most expensive ten-over analysis of his ODI career. Parnell returned to mop up the tail, with Sri Lanka having restored at least a little pride.

Man of the Match: F. du Plessis.

South Africa

H. M. Amla c Gunaratne b Kumara	1
†Q. de Kock c Tharanga b Pathirana	55
F. du Plessis c Gunaratne b Madushanka	185
*A. B. de Villiers b Pathirana	64
J-P. Duminy c Mendis b Kumara	20
F. Behardien not out	36
W. D. Parnell not out	1
W 4, nb 1	5
1/3 (1) 2/103 (2) 3/240 (4) 4/287 (5) 5/361 (3) (5 wkts, 50 overs)	367
10 overs: 59-1	

D. Pretorius, K. Rabada, Imran Tahir and T. Shamsi did not bat.

Kulasekara 10–0–74–0; Kumara 7–0–73–2; Madushanka 10–0–69–1; de Silva 3–0–18–0; Sandakan 8–0–62–0; Pathirana 10–0–55–2; Gunaratne 2–0–16–0.

Sri Lanka

†D. P. D. N. Dickwella c Behardien b Pretorius	58
*W. U. Tharanga c Duminy b Parnell	119
B. K. G. Mendis c de Kock b Parnell	29
D. S. Weerakkody c Parnell b Imran Tahir	58
D. M. de Silva lbw b Rabada	5
D. A. S. Gunaratne c Amla b Rabada	38
K. M. D. N. Kulasekara lbw b Imran Tahir	1
S. S. Pathirana c de Kock b Pretorius	1
L. D. Madushanka c Pretorius b Parnell	6
C. B. R. L. S. Kumara not out	1
P. A. D. L. R. Sandakan b Parnell	1
Lb 7, w 3	10
1/139 (1) 2/203 (3) (48.1 overs)	327

3/216 (2) 4/228 (5) 5/307 (6)
6/308 (7) 7/317 (4) 8/325 (8)
9/325 (9) 10/327 (11) 10 overs: 100-0

Parnell 9.1–0–58–4; Pretorius 8–0–55–2; Duminy 1–0–12–0; Rabada 9–1–50–2; Imran Tahir 10–0–76–2; Shamsi 10–0–60–0; Behardien 1–0–9–0.

Umpires: A. T. Holdstock and R. K. Illingworth. Third umpire: R. A. Kettleborough.
Referee: R. B. Richardson.

SOUTH AFRICA v SRI LANKA

Fifth One-Day International

At Centurion, February 10, 2017 (day/night). South Africa won by 88 runs. Toss: Sri Lanka.

Chasing a second consecutive 5–0 win in home one-day series after they had seen off Australia in October, South Africa began with a towering 384 for six. De Kock and Amla got things going with 187 in 26 overs, de Kock hitting 16 fours from 87 balls and scoring his fourth one-day international hundred in six innings at Centurion. Amla also enjoys the place – this was his fifth in 12 – and picked up fluency, lasting into the 49th over for his 154. He faced 134 balls, hitting 15 fours and, uncharacteristically for a player who tends to value poise over power, five sixes. Sri Lanka fell some way short but, for the first time in the series, were not bowled out, and could celebrate Gunaratne's maiden ODI century. He put on 93 for the sixth wicket with Pathirana, and an unbroken 97 for the ninth with Lakmal, Sri Lanka's fast-bowling find of the tour. They might have managed more had Morris not kept his head amid the hitting to take a career-best four for 31.

Man of the Match: H. M. Amla. *Man of the Series:* F. du Plessis.

South Africa

†Q. de Kock c Weerakkody b Lakmal	109
H. M. Amla c Mendis b Madushanka	154
F. du Plessis c Lakmal b Madushanka	41
*A. B. de Villiers c Kumara b Vandersay	14
J-P. Duminy c Dickwella b Lakmal	10
F. Behardien c Gunaratne b Lakmal	32
C. H. Morris not out	3
W. D. Parnell not out	1
B 4, lb 5, w 10, nb 1	20
1/187 (1) 2/250 (3) (6 wkts, 50 overs)	384

3/271 (4) 4/309 (5)
5/371 (2) 6/379 (6) 10 overs: 71-0

A. L. Phehlukwayo, K. Rabada and Imran Tahir did not bat.

Lakmal 10–0–71–3; Kumara 7–0–60–0; Madushanka 8–0–70–2; de Silva 4–0–24–0; Pathirana 6–1–43–0; Vandersay 10–0–61–1; Gunaratne 5–0–46–0.

Sri Lanka

†D. P. D. N. Dickwella c de Villiers b Parnell	39
*W. U. Tharanga c Rabada b Morris	7
B. K. G. Mendis c de Villiers b Morris	1
D. S. Weerakkody c Rabada b Parnell	10
D. M. de Silva b Imran Tahir	11
D. A. S. Gunaratne not out	114
S. S. Pathirana c de Villiers b Morris	56
L. D. Madushanka run out	7
J. D. F. Vandersay b Morris	7
R. A. S. Lakmal not out	20
B 4, lb 9, w 11	24
1/25 (2) 2/43 (3) 3/55 (1) 4/70 (4) 5/82 (5) 6/175 (7) 7/183 (8) 8/199 (9) (8 wkts, 50 overs)	296
10 overs: 73-4	

C. B. R. L. S. Kumara did not bat.

Rabada 10–0–55–0; Morris 10–1–31–4; Parnell 7–0–51–2; Imran Tahir 10–0–57–1; Duminy 5–0–28–0; Phehlukwayo 7–1–44–0; Behardien 1–0–17–0.

Umpires: S. George and R. A. Kettleborough. Third umpire: R. K. Illingworth.
Referee: R. B. Richardson.

DOMESTIC CRICKET IN SOUTH AFRICA IN 2015-16

COLIN BRYDEN

The taint of corruption returned in 2015-16 when Cricket South Africa announced they were charging an individual with contriving to fix elements of the latest Ram Slam T20 challenge. In January 2016, Gulam Bodi – who had last appeared the previous season, for the Lions – was banned from all cricketing activity for 20 years after confessing he had attempted to approach players on behalf of betting syndicates. CSA believed they had caught him before any fixing took place, but five players were later banned after admitting breaches of the anti-corruption code. The best known was Alviro Petersen, banned for two years; former Test wicketkeeper Thami Tsolekile got 12, Pumelela Matshikwe and Ethy Mbhalati ten, and Jean Symes seven. Four played for the Lions franchise; the exception was Mbhalati, part of the Titans team which had recently won two trophies.

The sport's growing popularity in the Afrikaans-speaking community, the excellent facilities at a custom-built stadium and sound administration have all boosted the **Titans**, based at Centurion near Pretoria. Their latest titles, in the first-class Sunfoil Series and the T20 Challenge, put them ahead of their nearest rivals, the Cape Cobras; of 37 tournaments since the franchise system began in 2004, they have won or shared 13, to the Cobras' 11. Like the Cobras, they have succeeded despite providing significant numbers of players to the national team.

At first glance, the Titans' four-day triumph was achieved with comfort: they won six of their ten matches and finished almost 24 points clear. Yet their character was tested in the last two rounds. They fought their way to a draw against the Lions by batting for ten and a half hours after following on; then, they left the Cobras a target of just 136, but bowled them out for 125. Heino Kuhn was the competition's leading run-scorer, with 1,126 at 62, and left-handers Dean Elgar and Qaasim Adams also averaged above 50. Left-arm wrist-spinner Tabraiz Shamsi and fast bowler Marchant de Lange took 79 wickets between them. Earlier, the Titans had established a T20 tournament record by winning eight games in a row; they beat the Dolphins in the final.

The Johannesburg-based **Lions** finished second in the four-day competition and won the Momentum One-Day Cup, in which Petersen hit five centuries in six innings. Captain Stephen Cook scored freely, but the Lions would see less of him after he finally made his Test debut, at the age of 33, and scored 115 against England. Fast bowler Hardus Viljoen was the tournament's leading wicket-taker with 47, and all-rounder Dwaine Pretorius was one of the country's most improved players.

The **Knights**, who play in Bloemfontein and Kimberley, punched above their weight in the Sunfoil Series, finishing third with five wins; Duanne Olivier led a strong attack. They were less successful in white-ball cricket. The **Cape Cobras** topped the one-day log but lost the final to the Lions. They were beaten by the Dolphins in the T20 semi and had a poor four-day campaign. The batting of wicketkeeper Dane Vilas, and the all-round form of Wayne Parnell in the second half, lit up an otherwise forgettable season.

Durban's **Dolphins** recruited Kevin Pietersen for their T20 campaign; he hit 401 in seven innings, including two centuries, at a strike-rate of 172. But they lost the final to the Titans, and finished fifth in the other tournaments; coach Lance Klusener was sacked, and David Miller and Kyle Abbott left. The under-resourced **Warriors** finished bottom of the Sunfoil Series but performed respectably in the limited-overs formats. Sisanda Magala was a consistent bowler in all formats.

In the provincial competitions, **KwaZulu-Natal Inland** won their first three-day title plus the CSA Provincial T20 league, and reached the final of another 20-over tournament, the Africa T20 Cup, which they lost to **Northerns**. The CSA Provincial 50-over Challenge was won by **Gauteng**.

FIRST-CLASS AVERAGES, 2015-16

BATTING (600 runs, average 35.00)

	M	*I*	*NO*	*R*	*HS*	*100*	*Avge*	*Ct/St*
†K. Nipper (*KwaZulu-Natal Inland*)	8	13	5	794	151*	3	99.25	6
D. Smit (*KwaZulu-Natal/Dolphins*)	16	20	6	1,081	156*	3	77.21	49/3
M. Z. Hamza (*Western Province*)	10	17	3	830	156	3	59.28	8
D. J. Vilas (*SA A/Cape Cobras/South Africa*)	10	17	3	829	216*	2	59.21	27/2
H. G. Kuhn (*Northerns/Titans*)	11	22	2	1,159	151*	4	57.95	17
P. J. Malan (*Western Province*)	9	17	3	778	177*	3	55.57	12
K. D. Petersen (*Boland/Cape Cobras*)	10	18	4	742	124	2	53.00	10/1
S. C. Cook (*N West/SA A/Lions/South Africa*)	13	23	2	1,073	168*	4	51.09	15
†D. Elgar (*Titans/South Africa*)	10	19	1	892	173	3	49.55	8
†V. B. van Jaarsveld (*Dolphins*)	9	13	0	640	122	2	49.23	3
†D. A. Hendricks (*Gauteng/Lions*)	13	22	2	972	167	4	48.60	12
†M. Q. Adams (*Northerns/Lions/Titans*)	11	20	3	780	167	2	45.88	15
†E. M. Moore (*Eastern Province/Warriors*)	11	18	3	676	144	2	45.06	3
†I. Khan (*KwaZulu-Natal Inland/Dolphins*)	14	22	2	888	146*	4	44.40	5
A. K. Markram (*Northerns*)	10	16	0	702	182	2	43.87	9
M. D. Walters (*Border/Warriors*)	11	19	3	690	117*	2	43.12	3
†K. R. Smuts (*Eastern Province/Warriors*)	11	16	1	625	109	3	41.66	5
H. Klaasen (*Northerns/Titans*)	10	19	2	690	187	2	40.58	32/1
†S. J. Erwee (*KwaZulu-Natal Inland/Dolphins*)	12	18	1	683	200*	2	40.17	13
†O. A. Ramela (*SA A/W Prov/Cape Cobras*)	10	18	0	713	109	2	39.61	2
T. G. Mokoena (*Easterns/Titans*)	17	32	3	1,121	217	3	38.65	15
H. E. van der Dussen (*Lions/North West*)	11	17	0	652	135	2	38.35	6
T. B. de Bruyn (*Titans*)	9	17	1	602	150*	2	37.62	7
J. F. Smith (*Western Province/Cape Cobras*)	11	18	1	618	121	2	36.35	9
†J. L. du Plooy (*Free State/Knights*)	11	19	1	632	181	1	35.11	11

BOWLING (30 wickets, average 30.00)

	Style	*O*	*M*	*R*	*W*	*BB*	*5I*	*Avge*
D. Olivier (*Free State/Knights*)	RFM	301	70	863	63	5-17	6	13.69
C. J. Alexander (*KZN Inland/Dolphins*)	RFM	201.3	42	657	43	6-60	4	15.27
P. Fojela (*Border*)	RFM	191.4	40	565	36	6-91	2	15.69
P. E. Kruger (*Northern Cape*)	RM	151.3	28	495	30	5-16	3	16.50
E. L. Hawken (*Northerns/Titans*)	RF	281.4	95	705	42	5-23	3	16.78
G. I. Hume (*KwaZulu-Natal Inland*)	RFM	287.2	86	715	40	5-45	1	17.87
C. P. Savage (*KwaZulu-Natal/Dolphins*)	RF	245.5	56	699	37	5-62	1	18.89
R. R. Richards (*Northerns/Titans*)	LFM	385.2	85	1,117	58	7-40	1	19.25
T. Shamsi (*Easterns/Titans*)	SLC	352.5	78	1,100	57	7-63	6	19.29
G. R. Rabie (*South Western Districts*)	RFM	322.5	86	839	43	5-44	3	19.51
G. A. Stuurman (*South Western Districts*)	RM	251.3	67	656	33	7-85	2	19.87
D. Pretorius (*Lions*)	RFM	287	93	769	36	6-66	1	21.36
A. A. Nortje (*Eastern Province/Warriors*)	RF	237.4	51	709	32	5-34	2	22.15
D. M. Dupavillon (*KZN/Dolphins*)	RF	271.5	49	909	41	5-18	3	22.17
S. R. Harmer (*Warriors*)	OB	282	79	695	31	8-60	1	22.41
M. W. Pillans (*KZN Inland/Dolphins*)	RFM	208.3	47	673	30	5-33	1	22.43
K. J. Dudgeon (*Gauteng*)	RFM	209	47	696	31	6-36	2	22.45
L. B. Williams (*W Province/Cape Cobras*)	RFM	264.2	53	903	40	7-75	3	22.57
S. H. Jamison (*Gauteng/Lions*)	RFM	196.1	36	725	30	6-70	1	24.16
G. C. Viljoen (*Lions/South Africa*)	RFM	353.5	67	1,176	48	6-44	4	24.50
M. de Lange (*Easterns/S Africa A/Titans*)	RF	260.5	43	1,044	42	7-76	1	24.85
D. Stanley (*Easterns*)	LFM	211.3	42	779	31	4-46	0	25.12
D. L. Piedt (*WP/Cape Cobras/S Africa*)	OB	405	84	1,387	51	7-106	3	27.19

Averages include CSA Provincial Three-Day Challenge matches played in Namibia.

SUNFOIL SERIES, 2015-16

					Bonus points		
	Played	*Won*	*Lost*	*Drawn*	*Batting*	*Bowling*	*Points*
Titans	10	6	1	3	37.20	36	133.20
Lions	10	4	2	4	32.30	37	109.30
Knights	10	5	5	0	23.04	36	109.04
Cape Cobras	10	3	5	2	28.84	34	92.84
Dolphins	10	3	3	3†	28.54	29	92.54
Warriors	10	2	7	0†	21.04	25	71.04

† *Plus one match abandoned.*

Outright win = 10pts; abandoned = 5pts. Bonus points awarded for the first 100 overs of each team's first innings: one batting point for the first 150 runs and 0.02 of a point for every subsequent run; one bowling point for the third wicket taken and for every subsequent two.

At Cape Town, December 17–19, 2015. **Knights won by an innings and 102 runs.** ‡**Cape Cobras 146** (S. C. van Schalkwyk 5-45) **and 243; Knights 491-9 dec** (W. L. Coetsee 103). *Knights 18.02pts, Cape Cobras 2pts. Six batsmen passed 50 for Knights, helping set up their innings win.*

At Johannesburg, December 17–20, 2015. **Lions won by 79 runs.** ‡**Lions 214** (C. P. Savage 5-62) **and 316-8 dec; Dolphins 141 and 310** (I. Khan 101; G. C. Viljoen 6-113). *Lions 16.28pts, Dolphins 4pts. Dolphins wicketkeeper Daryn Smit held ten catches. Hardus Viljoen claimed 10-157.*

At Centurion, December 17–20, 2015. **Titans won by 66 runs. Titans 369** (H. G. Kuhn 141; B. D. Walters 5-49) **and 171;** ‡**Warriors 209 and 265.** *Titans 18.2pts, Warriors 4.18pts. Heino Kuhn scored 141 out of 215-3 – his first three partners totalled six.*

At Kimberley, December 27–29, 2015. **Dolphins won by 63 runs.** ‡**Dolphins 306** (D. Smit 123*) **and 106; Knights 257** (R. S. Second 122; K. A. Maharaj 5-54) **and 92** (Imran Tahir 8-42). *Dolphins 17.46pts, Knights 7.14pts. Needing 156 to win, Knights were dismissed for 92; Imran Tahir's career-best 8-42, the best return of the season, gave him 12-133 in the match.*

At Johannesburg, December 27–30, 2015. **Lions won by 203 runs. Lions 291 and 294-4 dec** (S. C. Cook 168*); ‡**Warriors 163** (G. C. Viljoen 6-44) **and 219.** *Lions 17.82pts, Warriors 5.26pts. Viljoen picked up 10-123 to give him 20 wickets in the first two games of the season.*

At Benoni, December 27–29, 2015. **Titans won by ten wickets.** ‡**Titans 362** (Q. de Kock 117) **and 66-0; Cape Cobras 107** (T. Shamsi 5-22) **and 320** (T. Shamsi 7-63). *Titans 19.24pts, Cape Cobras 4pts. Left-arm wrist-spinner Tabraiz Shamsi's 12-85 was the best match return of this tournament.*

At Paarl, January 7–10, 2016. **Drawn.** ‡**Cape Cobras 570-4 dec** (J-P. Duminy 260*, D. J. Vilas 216*); **Lions 252** (S. C. Cook 118; R. J. Peterson 5-62) **and 287-9** (D. Pretorius 101). *Cape Cobras 9.04pts, Lions 4.04pts. J-P. Duminy and Vilas both reached a second double-century as they added 393* for Cape Cobras' fifth wicket. Lions' last pair held out for 14.2 overs to draw.*

At Pietermaritzburg, January 7–10, 2016. **Dolphins v ‡Warriors. Abandoned.** *Dolphins 5pts, Warriors 5pts.*

At Bloemfontein, January 7–9, 2016. **Knights won by five wickets.** ‡**Titans 141** (D. Olivier 5-42) **and 187; Knights 76** (N. E. Mbhalati 5-29) **and 255-5.** *Knights 14pts, Titans 4pts. Ethy Mbhalati had figures of 6.4–0–29–5 on the first day, when 21 wickets fell. Knights wanted 253 to win, and got there despite Marchant de Lange grabbing three in an over at 245-2.*

At Kimberley, January 14–16, 2016. **Lions won by 45 runs.** ‡**Lions 264** (L. M. G. Masekela 7-38) **and 94** (M. P. Siboto 7-44); **Knights 221 and 92.** *Lions 17.02pts, Knights 5.42pts. Knights needed 138 after bowling out Lions for 94 – but were dismissed in double figures for the third match running.*

At Benoni, January 14–17, 2016. **Titans won by four wickets. Dolphins 357 and 255** (I. Khan 107); ‡**Titans 440** (H. G. Kuhn 129, T. B. de Bruyn 123; K. A. Maharaj 5-103) **and 175-6.** *Titans 19.28pts, Dolphins 6.14pts. Kuhn followed a century with 62 as Titans won with 19 balls to spare.*

At Port Elizabeth, January 14–16, 2016. **Cape Cobras won by 148 runs.** ‡**Cape Cobras 325** (S. R. Harmer 8-60) **and 130; Warriors 129 and 178** (R. K. Kleinveldt 5-30). *Cape Cobras 17.74pts,*

Warriors 3pts. Off-spinner Simon Harmer claimed a career-best 8-60 in Cobras' first innings, but Rory Kleinveldt reduced Warriors to 18-5 in reply on his way to nine in the match.

At Durban, January 21–24, 2016. **Drawn. ‡Dolphins 405; Cape Cobras 216** (K. A. Maharaj 5-62) **and 361-6** (O. A. Ramela 107). *Dolphins 7.9pts, Cape Cobras 5.32pts. Omphile Ramela's century saved Cobras as they followed on.*

At Potchefstroom, January 21–24, 2016. **Drawn. ‡Titans 294** (F. Behardien 108; D. Pretorius 6-66) **and 169-8** (G. C. Viljoen 6-75); **Lions 295** (A. N. Petersen 203). *Lions 7.9pts, Titans 7.88pts. Alviro Petersen reached a third double-hundred; last out after coming in at 3-2, he made 68% of the total.*

At East London, January 21–24, 2016. **Knights won by four wickets. ‡Warriors 252** (M. P. Siboto 6-54) **and 226** (M. Y. Vallie 105); **Knights 270 and 212-6.** *Knights 16.7pts, Warriors 5.04pts. Knights' victory kept them in touch with Titans and Lions – 7.32 points separated the top three.*

At Potchefstroom, March 3–6, 2016. **Lions won by an innings and 78 runs. ‡Lions 580-7 dec** (S. C. Cook 150, D. A. Hendricks 160); **Cape Cobras 258 and 244.** *Lions 19.1pts, Cape Cobras 4.16pts. Stephen Cook added 261 for Lions' second wicket with Dominic Hendricks.*

At Centurion, March 3–5, 2016. **Titans won by 359 runs. ‡Titans 277** (D. Olivier 5-53) **and 368-2 dec** (H. G. Kuhn 151*, T. B. de Bruyn 150*); **Knights 122 and 164** (M. de Lange 7-76). *Titans 17.54pts, Knights 4pts. Kuhn and Theunis de Bruyn added 254* for Titans' third wicket.*

At East London, March 3–6, 2016. **Dolphins won by an innings and 54 runs. ‡Dolphins 450-8 dec** (M. N. van Wyk 122); **Warriors 209** (D. M. Dupavillon 5-49) **and 187.** *Dolphins 18.12pts, Warriors 3.18pts. Dolphins declared at the start of the third day, on which Warriors lost 17 wickets.*

At Paarl, March 10–12, 2016. **Cape Cobras won by an innings and 12 runs. ‡Warriors 217** (M. Y. Vallie 104) **and 175; Cape Cobras 404** (W. D. Parnell 111*). *Cape Cobras 17.82pts, Warriors 4.34pts. Cape Cobras were 293-8 before Wayne Parnell reached a maiden century during a ninth-wicket stand of 111 with Tshepo Moreki (22).*

At Durban, March 10–13, 2016. **Drawn. Titans 451-8 dec** (M. Q. Adams 123*) **and 208-4 dec; ‡Dolphins 306-4 dec** (S. J. Erwee 108) **and 336-6** (V. B. van Jaarsveld 122). *Dolphins 7.12pts, Titans 6.94pts. Grant Mokoena was the first to 1,000 runs for the season. With Dolphins chasing 354, Andile Phehlukwayo and Keshav Maharaj hit 58* in six overs before bad light thwarted them.*

At Johannesburg, March 10–13, 2016. **Knights won by ten wickets. Lions 144 and 218; ‡Knights 248 and 117-0.** *Knights 16.96pts, Lions 4pts. Duanne Olivier's seven wickets made him the first bowler to take 50 first-class wickets in the season.*

At Pietermaritzburg, March 18–21, 2016. **Drawn. ‡Lions 516-5 dec** (H. E. van der Dussen 135, D. A. Hendricks 167); **Dolphins 259-9.** *Dolphins 4.18pts, Lions 8.58pts. Stephen Cook of Lions and Daryn Smith of Dolphins both completed 1,000 runs for the season.*

At Bloemfontein, March 18–21, 2016. **Knights won by three wickets. ‡Cape Cobras 337** (D. J. Vilas 157) **and 291** (O. A. Ramela 109); **Knights 372** (W. L. Coetsee 149; D. L. Piedt 5-106) **and 259-7.** *Knights 18.44pts, Cape Cobras 8.02pts. Vilas came in at 83-4 and steered Cobras to 334-7; Werner Coetsee then emulated him by taking Knights from 67-5 to 363-8.*

At Port Elizabeth, March 18–21, 2016. **Titans won by eight wickets. ‡Warriors 282** (S. Seyibokwe 101; T. Shamsi 7-93) **and 256** (T. Shamsi 5-80); **Titans 399** (D. Elgar 130, M. Q. Adams 167) **and 145-2.** *Titans 19.24pts, Warriors 6.64pts. Shamsi collected 12 wickets again, including nine lbws. This was Warriors' ninth consecutive defeat since March 2015, excluding one abandoned.*

MOST LBWs BY ONE BOWLER IN A MATCH

9	Kabir Khan	Peshawar v Karachi Blues at Peshawar	1991-92
9	M. C. Ilott	Essex v Northamptonshire at Luton	1995
9	**T. Shamsi**	**Titans v Warriors at Port Elizabeth**	**2015-16**
8	C. W. Flanagan	Canterbury v Auckland at Rangiora	1993-94
8	Mohammad Zahid	Pakistan v New Zealand at Rawalpindi (*on Test debut*)	1996-97
8	W. P. U. J. C. Vaas	Sri Lanka v West Indies at Colombo (SSC)	2001-02
8	Tabish Khan	Karachi Whites v KRL at Karachi (NBP)	2011-12

At Cape Town, March 31–April 2, 2016. **Cape Cobras won by nine wickets. Dolphins 183** (W. D. Parnell 7-51) **and 139** (W. D. Parnell 5-54); ‡**Cape Cobras 252** (C. J. Alexander 5-62) **and 74-1.** *Cape Cobras 17.04pts, Dolphins 5.66pts. Parnell took a career-best 7-51 in Dolphins' first innings, and 12-105 in the match. His team-mate Andrew Puttick passed 10,000 first-class runs.*

At Kimberley, March 31–April 1, 2016. **Warriors won by nine wickets. Knights 128 and 131** (A. A. Nortje 5-34); ‡**Warriors 165** (D. Olivier 5-61) **and 95-1.** *Warriors 15.3pts, Knights 4pts. Malusi Siboto had figures of 19–13–19–4 in Warriors' first innings – but their luck finally changed as they won a low-scoring game in two days.*

At Centurion, March 31–April 3, 2016. **Drawn.** ‡**Lions 609** (D. Pretorius 118, B. C. Fortuin 116; T. Shamsi 5-183); **Titans 230 and 385-6** (D. Elgar 173; P. Matshikwe 6-58). *Titans 5.6pts, Lions 10.56pts. Lions recovered from 156-5 to pass 500 for the third time in four matches; their eventual 609 was the highest total of the tournament. They made Titans follow on, 379 behind, but lost the chance to cut their lead to under three points, as Titans batted ten and a half hours for the draw. Shamsi took his 50th first-class wicket of the season, while Kuhn reached 1,000 runs.*

At Paarl, April 7–9, 2016. **Titans won by ten runs. Titans 164** (W. D. Parnell 5-62) **and 256** (H. G. Kuhn 127; D. L. Piedt 7-106); ‡**Cape Cobras 285 and 125** (R. R. Richards 7-40). *Titans 15.28pts, Cape Cobras 7.7pts. Titans secured the title, despite trailing by 121 and leaving a target of just 136; Rowan Richards's career-best 7-40 routed Cobras to ensure they ended the campaign with their sixth, and unlikeliest, win. Off-spinner Dane Piedt's 7-106 took him past 50 wickets for the season.*

At Durban, April 7–10, 2016. **Dolphins won by 118 runs. Dolphins 375** (V. B. van Jaarsveld 106; D. du Preez 5-44) **and 224-3 dec** (I. Khan 106*); ‡**Knights 218** (C. J. Alexander 6-60) **and 263.** *Dolphins 16.96pts, Knights 4.36pts. Dolphins deprived Knights of second place, although their wicketkeeper Rudi Second scored two half-centuries and made his 50th dismissal of the season.*

At Port Elizabeth, April 7–9, 2016. **Warriors won by an innings and 101 runs. Lions 68** (S. S. B. Magala 6-24) **and 206;** ‡**Warriors 375** (G. C. Viljoen 5-139). *Warriors 19.1pts, Lions 4pts. Lions followed the tournament's highest total with its lowest when they crashed for 68 on the opening day, dashing their title hopes; Warriors' second win came too late to lift them out of bottom place.*

CHAMPIONS

1889-90	Transvaal
1890-91	Kimberley
1892-93	Western Province
1893-94	Western Province
1894-95	Transvaal
1896-97	Western Province
1897-98	Western Province
1902-03	Transvaal
1903-04	Transvaal
1904-05	Transvaal
1906-07	Transvaal
1908-09	Western Province
1910-11	Natal
1912-13	Natal
1920-21	Western Province
1921-22	Transvaal Natal Western Province
1923-24	Transvaal
1925-26	Transvaal
1926-27	Transvaal
1929-30	Transvaal
1931-32	Western Province
1933-34	Natal
1934-35	Transvaal
1936-37	Natal
1937-38	Natal Transvaal
1946-47	Natal
1947-48	Natal
1950-51	Transvaal
1951-52	Natal
1952-53	Western Province
1954-55	Natal
1955-56	Western Province
1958-59	Transvaal
1959-60	Natal
1960-61	Natal
1962-63	Natal
1963-64	Natal
1965-66	Natal Transvaal
1966-67	Natal
1967-68	Natal
1968-69	Transvaal
1969-70	Transvaal Western Province
1970-71	Transvaal
1971-72	Transvaal
1972-73	Transvaal
1973-74	Natal
1974-75	Western Province
1975-76	Natal
1976-77	Natal
1977-78	Western Province
1978-79	Transvaal

1979-80	Transvaal
1980-81	Natal
1981-82	Western Province
1982-83	Transvaal
1983-84	Transvaal
1984-85	Transvaal
1985-86	Western Province
1986-87	Transvaal
1987-88	Transvaal
1988-89	Eastern Province
1989-90	{ Eastern Province Western Province
1990-91	Western Province
1991-92	Eastern Province
1992-93	Orange Free State
1993-94	Orange Free State
1994-95	Natal
1995-96	Western Province
1996-97	Natal
1997-98	Free State
1998-99	Western Province
1999-2000	Gauteng
2000-01	Western Province
2001-02	KwaZulu-Natal
2002-03	Easterns
2003-04	Western Province
2004-05	{ Dolphins Eagles
2005-06	{ Dolphins Titans
2006-07	Titans
2007-08	Eagles
2008-09	Titans
2009-10	Cape Cobras
2010-11	Cape Cobras
2011-12	Titans
2012-13	Cape Cobras
2013-14	Cape Cobras
2014-15	Lions
2015-16	Titans

Transvaal/Gauteng have won the title outright 25 times, Natal/KwaZulu-Natal 21, Western Province 18, Cape Cobras and Titans 4, Orange Free State/Free State 3, Eastern Province 2, Eagles, Easterns, Kimberley and Lions 1. The title has been shared seven times as follows: Transvaal 4, Natal and Western Province 3, Dolphins 2, Eagles, Eastern Province and Titans 1.

The tournament was the Currie Cup from 1889-90 to 1989-90, the Castle Cup from 1990-91 to 1995-96, the SuperSport Series from 1996-97 to 2011-12, and the Sunfoil Series from 2012-13.

From 1971-72 to 1990-91, the non-white South African Cricket Board of Control (later the South African Cricket Board) organised their own three-day tournaments. These are now recognised as first-class (see *Wisden 2006*, pages 79–80). A list of winners appears in *Wisden 2007*, page 1346.

SUNFOIL THREE-DAY CUP, 2015-16

Pool A	*P*	*W*	*L*	*D*	*Pts*
W PROVINCE . . .	10	5	3	2	127.44
North West.	10	5	2	3	113.74
KwaZulu-Natal . . .	10	4	2	4	103.24
Northerns	10	3	2	5	102.60
SW Districts.	10	3	3	4	90.52
Northern Cape	10	3	5	2	86.38
Border	10	2	3	5	76.82

Pool B	*P*	*W*	*L*	*D*	*Pts*
KZN INLAND. . . .	10	4	0	6	117.16
Eastern Province . .	10	4	2	4	116.10
Easterns	10	3	4	3	106.88
Gauteng	10	2	5	3	90.40‡
Free State	10	3	3	4	86.70†
Boland	10	2	2	6	81.30
Namibia	10	1	8	1	47.60

† *2pts deducted for slow over-rate.* ‡ *4pts deducted for slow over-rate.*

Outright win = 10pts. Bonus points awarded for the first 100 overs of each team's first innings; one batting point for the first 150 runs and 0.02 of a point for every subsequent run; one bowling point for the third wicket taken and for every subsequent two.

The teams were divided into pools of seven. Each played the other six in their pool, plus four teams from the other; all results counted towards the final table. The two pool leaders met in a final.

Pool A

At Kimberley, October 8–10, 2015. **Western Province won by 275 runs.** ‡**Western Province 367-7 dec** (M. Z. Hamza 156) **and 191-3 dec** (P. J. Malan 100*); **Northern Cape 167 and 116** (G. F. Linde 5-20). *Western Province 19.34pts, Northern Cape 4.34pts. Zubayr Hamza and Jason Smith added 225 for Western Province's fifth wicket.*

At Potchefstroom, October 15–17, 2015. **North West won by nine wickets. Border 156** (D. Klein 5-50) **and 306;** ‡**North West 351** (P. Fojela 5-55) **and 113-1.** *North West 19.02pts, Border 5.12pts.*

At East London, October 29–31, 2015. **Western Province won by 100 runs. Western Province 192 and 236; ‡Border 135 and 193.** *Western Province 15.84pts, Border 4pts.*

At Chatsworth, October 29–31, 2015. **KwaZulu-Natal won by an innings and 75 runs. KwaZulu-Natal 362** (J. D. Vandiar 114; G. A. Stuurman 7-85); **‡South Western Districts 118 and 169.** *KwaZulu-Natal 17.98pts, South Western Districts 3pts.*

At Oudtshoorn, November 5–7, 2015. **North West won by three wickets. ‡South Western Districts 122 and 259** (N. B. Hornbuckle 142); **North West 272** (M. N. Piedt 5-86) **and 111-7** (G. R. Rabie 5-48). *North West 17.44pts, South Western Districts 4pts.*

At Kimberley, November 19–21, 2015. **Drawn. ‡Border 216** (P. E. Kruger 5-42) **and 209-8; Northern Cape 260.** *Northern Cape 7.2pts, Border 6.32pts. Warren Bell was out obstructing the field in Northern Cape's first innings, only the second instance in South African first-class cricket.*

At Centurion, November 19–21, 2015. **Drawn. Northerns 243** (G. R. Rabie 5-61) **and 329-5 dec** (H. Klaasen 116, S. Naidoo 104*); **‡South Western Districts 359** (L. L. Mnyanda 135) **and 64-2.** *Northerns 6.86pts, South Western Districts 9.18pts.*

At Durban, November 26–28, 2015. **Drawn. KwaZulu-Natal 313** (D. Smit 156*); **‡North West 132** (D. M. Dupavillon 5-45) **and 211-6.** *KwaZulu-Natal 8.26pts, North West 4pts.*

At Kimberley, December 10–12, 2015. **KwaZulu-Natal won by eight wickets. ‡KwaZulu-Natal 422** (B. S. Makhanya 192) **and 30-2; Northern Cape 218 and 233.** *KwaZulu-Natal 20.44pts, Northern Cape 6.36pts.*

At Pretoria (Irene Villagers), December 10–12, 2015. **North West won by 134 runs. North West 144 and 274; ‡Northerns 172 and 112** (P. Matshikwe 6-17). *North West 14pts, Northerns 5.44pts. The first first-class match at Irene Villagers CC.*

At Centurion, January 5–7, 2016. **Drawn. ‡Border 359** (M. Marais 109) **and 187-1** (M. D. Walters 107*); **Northerns 456** (G. L. van Buuren 147; P. Fojela 6-91). *Northerns 9.02pts, Border 8.02pts. Marco Marais hit five sixes in his career-best 109, and added 152 for Border's seventh wicket with debutant Avumile Mnci (41). Another newcomer, Lungi Ngidi, dismissed Border opener Martin Walters with his first ball in first-class cricket.*

At Potchefstroom, January 7–9, 2016. **Drawn. ‡North West 538-8 dec** (B. C. Fortuin 194, F. J. Lubbe 106) **and 45-0; Western Province 520** (M. C. Kleinveldt 173, J. F. Smith 121). *North West 8.08pts, Western Province 7.78pts. Maiden centuries from Bjorn Fortuin and Edrich Lubbe, who added 238 for North West's sixth wicket, helped them reach their highest total – but career-bests from Matthew Kleinveldt and Jason Smith meant Western Province almost matched it. No other team got to 500 in this tournament.*

At Chatsworth, January 14–16, 2016. **Drawn. KwaZulu-Natal 163** (E. L. Hawken 5-23); **‡Northerns 145-4.** *KwaZulu-Natal 2.26pts, Northerns 4pts.*

At Cape Town, January 14–16, 2016. **Western Province won by 119 runs. ‡Western Province 329-7 dec and 217-3 dec; South Western Districts 212** (N. B. Hornbuckle 105; J. F. Smith 6-49) **and 215.** *Western Province 18.58pts, South Western Districts 5.24pts.*

At Oudtshoorn, January 21–22, 2016. **South Western Districts won by an innings and 14 runs. South Western Districts 299** (S. E. Avontuur 142); **‡Border 119 and 166.** *South Western Districts 17.98pts, Border 4pts.*

At Cape Town, January 21–23, 2016. **Northerns won by an innings and 122 runs. Northerns 499** (A. K. Markram 182, L. J. Kgoatle 123); **‡Western Province 214 and 163.** *Northerns 19.32pts, Western Province 5.28pts. Northerns No. 8 Lerato Kgoatle reached a maiden century in 97 balls and added 116 for the ninth wicket with Rowan Richards.*

At Kimberley, February 18–20, 2016. **South Western Districts won by two wickets. Northern Cape 130 and 153** (G. A. Stuurman 5-45); **‡South Western Districts 179 and 107-8.** *South Western Districts 15.58pts, Northern Cape 4pts.*

At East London, March 10–12, 2016. **Drawn. Border 267-5 v ‡KwaZulu-Natal.** *Border 3.34pts, KwaZulu-Natal 2pts.*

At Potchefstroom, March 10–12, 2016. **Drawn. Northern Cape 267 and 353-9 dec; ‡North West 249** (A. J. Malan 107) **and 221-7** (P. E. Kruger 5-16). *North West 6.98pts, Northern Cape 7.34pts.*

At Kimberley, March 18–20, 2016. **Northern Cape won by one wicket. Northerns 185 and 161; ‡Northern Cape 155 and 192-9.** *Northern Cape 15.1pts, Northerns 5.7pts. Chasing 192, Northern Cape were 164-9, but Kagisho Mohale (32*) and Reece Williams (6*) took them over the line with 28* in seven overs. Richards took his 50th first-class wicket of the season.*

At Rondebosch, March 18–20, 2016. **Western Province won by ten wickets. Western Province 403-9 dec** (S. A. Engelbrecht 162*) **and 68-0; ‡KwaZulu-Natal 214 and 253.** *Western Province 20.06pts, KwaZulu-Natal 6.28pts. On the opening day, Western Province's No. 9 George Linde hit 64 in 35 balls, with six sixes.*

Pool B

At Benoni, October 8–10, 2015. **Drawn. ‡Easterns 445-6 dec** (E. H. Kemm 101, T. G. Mokoena 217) **and 170-5; Eastern Province 495-9 dec** (K. R. Smuts 109, A. J. N. Price 124). *Easterns 9.9pts, Eastern Province 9.2pts. Grant Mokoena's maiden double-hundred was the highest score of the tournament; he and Ernest Kemm added 250 for Easterns' third wicket – but Eastern Province took first-innings lead.*

At Windhoek (Wanderers Affies Park), October 8–10, 2015. **Boland won by eight wickets. ‡Namibia 225 and 203** (G. A. Edmeades 6-66); **Boland 256** (B. M. Scholtz 5-66) **and 173-2.** *Boland 17.12pts, Namibia 6.5pts. The first first-class match at the former Windhoek Afrikaans Primary School ground.*

At Johannesburg, October 22–24, 2015. **Drawn. Gauteng 353-9 dec** (M. Y. Cook 154) **and 210-3 dec; ‡Boland 268 and 186-9.** *Gauteng 9.06pts, Boland 7.36pts.*

At Bloemfontein, November 5–7, 2015. **Drawn. KwaZulu-Natal Inland 82 and 377-7 dec** (D. J. van Wyk 153*, K. Nipper 118); **‡Free State 258.** *Free State 7.16pts, KwaZulu-Natal Inland 4pts.*

At Windhoek (Wanderers), November 12–14, 2015. **Free State won by an innings and 66 runs. ‡Free State 420-8 dec** (J. L. du Plooy 181); **Namibia 86** (D. Olivier 5-29) **and 268.** *Free State 18.88pts, Namibia 2pts.*

At Pietermaritzburg, November 26–28, 2015. **KwaZulu-Natal Inland won by nine wickets. KwaZulu-Natal Inland 271** (I. Khan 146*) **and 38-1; ‡Eastern Province 47** (C. J. Alexander 5-15) **and 259** (E. M. Moore 119). *KwaZulu-Natal Inland 17.42pts, Eastern Province 4pts. Imraan Khan carried his bat through KZN Inland's first innings. There were five ducks and no one passed 12 as Eastern Province's first innings folded for the lowest total of the season.*

At Paarl, December 10–12, 2015. **Drawn. Easterns 418-9 dec** (E. H. Kemm 136; Z. C. Qwabe 5-99); **‡Boland 351-9 dec** (G. A. Edmeades 166). *Boland 6.82pts, Easterns 7.4pts.*

At Port Elizabeth, December 10–12, 2015. **Eastern Province won by an innings and 21 runs. Eastern Province 311** (B. M. Scholtz 5-86); **‡Namibia 132** (A. E. Kula 5-42) **and 158** (N. Sigwili 5-33). *Eastern Province 18.22pts, Namibia 4pts.*

At Bloemfontein, December 17–19, 2015. **Easterns won by 149 runs. ‡Easterns 357** (G. M. Thomson 131) **and 159; Free State 161** (T. Shamsi 5-30) **and 206.** *Easterns 19.14pts, Free State 5.22pts. Grant Thomson and Thando Bula (84) added 221 for Easterns' fourth wicket.*

At Windhoek (Wanderers), January 7–9, 2016. **Gauteng won by ten wickets. ‡Gauteng 300-5 dec** (Y. Valli 130*, J. Symes 105) **and 6-0; Namibia 77 and 228** (R. A. H. Pitchers 100). *Gauteng 18pts, Namibia 2pts.*

At Port Elizabeth, January 21–23, 2016. **Drawn. ‡Free State 264 and 277-4** (P. Botha 109*); **Eastern Province 384.** *Eastern Province 8.24pts, Free State 6.28pts. Leus du Plooy (96) and Patrick Botha added 207 for Free State's fourth wicket.*

At Pietermaritzburg, January 21–23, 2016. **Drawn. Gauteng 253 and 163-7; ‡KwaZulu-Natal Inland 417** (L. N. Mosena 105). *KwaZulu-Natal Inland 10.18pts, Gauteng 7.06pts. Kushen Kishun (96) and Graham Hume (57) added 138 for the eighth wicket.*

At Paarl, February 11–13, 2016. **Eastern Province won by an innings and 93 runs. Boland 205** (K. R. Smuts 7-36) **and 144** (K. R. Smuts 6-35); **‡Eastern Province 442** (K. R. Smuts 108). *Eastern Province 19.52pts, Boland 5.1pts. Kelly Smuts became the third player to score a century and take* *four in four balls in the same game, after Kevan James for Hampshire v Indians in 1996, and Mahmudullah for Central Zone v North Zone in Bangladesh in 2013-14. He finished with 13-71.*

At Benoni, February 11–13, 2016. **Drawn. Easterns 404** (T. G. Mokoena 144, W. Coulentianos 100) **and 207-5 dec; ‡KwaZulu-Natal Inland 305 and 134-9.** *Easterns 10.08pts, KwaZulu-Natal Inland 8.1pts.*

At Port Elizabeth, February 18–20, 2016. **Drawn. Eastern Province 347** (K. R. Smuts 109) **and 177-3 dec; ‡Gauteng 222** (A. E. Kula 6-61) **and 109-2.** *Eastern Province 8.94pts, Gauteng 6.44pts.*

At Johannesburg, February 25–27, 2016. **Free State won by seven wickets. Gauteng 227** (D. P. Conway 103) **and 221; ‡Free State 259** (A. G. S. Gous 107; S. H. Jamison 6-70) **and 190-3.** *Free State 17.18pts, Gauteng 6.54pts.*

At Pietermaritzburg, February 25–26, 2016. **KwaZulu-Natal Inland won by an innings and 119 runs. Namibia 179 and 118** (C. J. Alexander 5-13); **‡KwaZulu-Natal Inland 416-1 dec** (D. J. van Wyk 152, S. J. Erwee 200*). *KwaZulu-Natal Inland 19.72pts, Namibia 1.58pts. Sarel Erwee converted his maiden century into a double after an opening stand of 306 with Divan van Wyk.*

At Benoni, March 3–4, 2016. **Easterns won by an innings and 155 runs. ‡Namibia 140 and 110** (C. J. Dala 5-24); **Easterns 405-7 dec** (J. Snyman 144, W. Coulentianos 171). *Easterns 20.1pts, Namibia 3pts. Jurie Snyman and Wesley Coulentianos added 270 for Easterns' fourth wicket. Namibia suffered their third innings defeat of the tournament, and the second to be over in two days.*

At Bloemfontein, March 10–12, 2016. **Drawn. Free State 222 and 283** (H. H. Paulse 5-57); **‡Boland 339** (K. D. Petersen 124) **and 38-2.** *Free State 5.44pts, Boland 8.24pts.*

At Paarl, March 18–20, 2016. **KwaZulu-Natal Inland won by six wickets. Boland 188 and 230** (G. I. Hume 5-45); **‡KwaZulu-Natal Inland 252 and 170-4.** *KwaZulu-Natal Inland 17.04pts, Boland 5.76pts.*

At Johannesburg, March 18–20, 2016. **Gauteng won by an innings and 14 runs. Easterns 256** (K. J. Dudgeon 5-51) **and 145; ‡Gauteng 415-6 dec** *Gauteng 20.3pts, Easterns 5.12pts. Easterns' last two batsmen, Junior Dala (79*) and Kofi Apea-Adu (31), put on 113 in the first innings.*

Cross Pool

At Durban, October 8–10, 2015. **Drawn. KwaZulu-Natal Inland 230** (A. Myoli 5-46) **and 220-6 dec; ‡KwaZulu-Natal 192 and 54-0.** *KwaZulu-Natal 5.84pts, KwaZulu-Natal Inland 6.6pts.*

At Walvis Bay, October 15–17, 2015. **Drawn. ‡Namibia 325** (S. J. Baard 114) **and 131-7; South Western Districts 382-9 dec** *Namibia 6.88pts, South Western Districts 8.5pts. The first first-class match at Sparta CC.*

At Bloemfontein, October 22–23, 2015. **Northern Cape won by three wickets. Free State 58** (J. Coetzee 5-13) **and 134** (P. E. Kruger 5-18); **‡Northern Cape 107** (D. Olivier 5-17) **and 86-7** (D. Olivier 5-21). *Northern Cape 14pts, Free State 4pts. Six Free State batsmen were out for ducks in the first innings, five of them to Jandre Coetzee, in the lowest total of the tournament.*

At Pietermaritzburg, October 22–23, 2015. **KwaZulu-Natal Inland won by an innings and 88 runs. North West 91** (K. Nipper 6-29) **and 140; ‡KwaZulu-Natal Inland 319** (D. Klein 5-72). *KwaZulu-Natal Inland 18.38pts, North West 4pts.*

At Oudtshoorn, October 22–24, 2015. **Drawn. Eastern Province 311 and 45-1; ‡South Western Districts 459-5 dec** (L. L. Mnyanda 188). *South Western Districts 7pts, Eastern Province 5.12pts.*

At Pretoria (L. C. de Villiers Oval), October 29–31, 2015. **Northerns won by nine wickets. Easterns 240 and 268-9 dec; ‡Northerns 424-7 dec** (A. K. Markram 157) **and 88-1.** *Northerns 20.48pts, Easterns 5.8pts. Aiden Markram and Graeme van Buuren (78) put on 202 for the fourth wicket.*

At Johannesburg, November 5–7, 2015. **Northerns won by five wickets. Gauteng 220 and 148** (E. L. Hawken 5-41); **‡Northerns 187** (K. J. Dudgeon 6-36) **and 182-5.** *Northerns 15.74pts, Gauteng 6.4pts.*

At Cape Town, November 5–7, 2015. **Drawn. Western Province 183 and 341-9 dec** (J. F. Smith 119); **‡Boland 131** (M. B. Njoloza 5-30) **and 340-9** (G. A. Edmeades 100; L. B. Williams 7-75).

Western Province 5.66pts, Boland 4pts. Lizaad Williams took 11-106 but not the 12th needed to win. Six of his 11 were caught by wicketkeeper Taariq Chiecktey, who made nine catches in all.

At East London, November 12–14, 2015. **Border won by three wickets. Eastern Province 162** (T. Mnyaka 5-47) **and 138; ‡Border 135 and 169-7.** *Border 14pts, Eastern Province 5.24pts.*

At Benoni, November 12–14, 2015. **KwaZulu-Natal won by ten wickets. KwaZulu-Natal 380** (D. Smit 123*) **and 44-0; ‡Easterns 141 and 277.** *KwaZulu-Natal 19.6pts, Easterns 4pts.*

At Johannesburg, November 12–14, 2015. **North West won by seven wickets. Gauteng 313** (D. A. Hendricks 142*; J. N. Diseko 5-68) **and 131; ‡North West 231 and 214-3.** *North West 16.62pts, Gauteng 8.26pts. Dominic Hendricks carried his bat through Gauteng's first innings.*

At Pretoria (L. C. de Villiers Oval), November 12–14, 2015. **Drawn. KwaZulu-Natal Inland 420-9 dec** (K. Nipper 151*) **and 173-7 dec; ‡Northerns 291** (T. P. Kaber 101; M. W. Pillans 5-33) **and 125-6.** *Northerns 6.82pts, KwaZulu-Natal Inland 9.84pts.*

At Potchefstroom, November 19–21, 2015. **Easterns won by 100 runs. Easterns 380-8 dec** (T. G. Mokoena 102, T. A. Bula 106) **and 124-5 dec; ‡North West 177 and 227.** *Easterns 18.24pts, North West 2.54pts.*

At Paarl, November 26–28, 2015. **Drawn. ‡Boland 220** (E. L. Hawken 5-43) **and 227-2** (K. D. Petersen 118*); **Northerns 475** (H. Klaasen 187, R. Moonsamy 122; G. A. Edmeades 5-126). *Boland 4.4pts, Northerns 9.22pts.*

At Cape Town, November 26–28, 2015. **Western Province won by 62 runs. Western Province 411-4 dec** (P. J. Malan 135, M. Z. Hamza 103*) **and 201-6 dec; ‡Gauteng 356-9 dec** (D. A. Hendricks 151*; L. B. Williams 6-51) **and 194** (M. B. Njoloza 5-32). *Western Province 19.58pts, Gauteng 6.12pts.*

At East London, December 3–5, 2015. **Border won by an innings and 125 runs. Namibia 68** (T. Mnyaka 5-14) **and 159** (A. Gqamane 7-65); **‡Border 352-6 dec** (G. V. J. Koopman 103, D. L. Brown 103*). *Border 19.04pts, Namibia 2pts.*

At Oudtshoorn, December 10–12, 2015. **Drawn. Free State 204 and 153-8 dec** (G. R. Rabie 5-44); **‡South Western Districts 116 and 9-0.** *South Western Districts 3pts, Free State 5.98pts.*

At Port Elizabeth, January 7–9, 2016. **Eastern Province won by ten wickets. Northern Cape 240** (A. A. Nortje 5-76) **and 155; ‡Eastern Province 350-9 dec** (M. L. Price 135, E. M. Moore 144; D. S. Rosier 5-41) **and 46-0.** *Eastern Province 19pts, Northern Cape 6.8pts. Michael Price and Ed Moore put on 240 for Eastern Province's first wicket; only one team-mate reached double figures.*

At Windhoek (Wanderers), January 14–16, 2016. **Namibia won by 137 runs. ‡Namibia 182 and 254-8 dec; Northern Cape 133** (S. F. Burger 5-26) **and 166** (B. M. Scholtz 8-33). *Namibia 15.64pts, Northern Cape 4pts. Bernard Scholtz secured Namibia's only win with the tournament's best return.*

At Paarl, January 21–22, 2016. **Boland won by seven wickets. ‡KwaZulu-Natal 117** (F. D. Adams 6-42) **and 147; Boland 137 and 129-3.** *Boland 14pts, KwaZulu-Natal 4pts.*

At Potchefstroom, February 11–13, 2016. **North West won by an innings and 79 runs. Free State 151 and 228** (A. G. S. Gous 100); **‡North West 458-8 dec** (H. E. van der Dussen 132, R. H. Frenz 126). *North West 21.06pts, Free State 4.02pts. Debutant Jean-Pierre le Roux dismissed Free State opener Bokang Mosena with his first delivery in first-class cricket. Rassie van der Dussen and Richardt Frenz added 255 for North West's second wicket.*

At Oudtshoorn, February 11–13, 2016. **South Western Districts won by eight wickets. Gauteng 211 and 146; ‡South Western Districts 252** (B. I. Louw 103; Z. Pongolo 5-53) **and 107-2.** *South Western Districts 17.04pts, Gauteng 6.22pts.*

At East London, February 18–20, 2016. **Drawn. Boland 325-8 dec; ‡Border 252-9.** *Border 6.04pts, Boland 8.5pts.*

At Bloemfontein, February 18–20, 2016. **Free State won by four wickets. Western Province 387-3 dec** (P. J. Malan 177*, M. Z. Hamza 118) **and 170-8 dec; ‡Free State 277-8 dec** (L. B. Williams 5-68) **and 285-6** (A. J. Pienaar 109). *Free State 14.54pts, Western Province 8.26pts.*

At Durban, February 18–20, 2016. **KwaZulu-Natal won by an innings and 91 runs. KwaZulu-Natal 229** (B. M. Scholtz 5-64); **‡Namibia 49** (R. J. Engelbrecht 5-18) **and 89** (D. M. Dupavillon

5-18). *KwaZulu-Natal 16.58pts, Namibia 4pts. Namibia were bowled out for fewer than 90 in both innings – the fourth and fifth time they had been dismissed in double figures in their last six matches.*

At Benoni, February 25–27, 2016. **Northern Cape won by ten wickets. Easterns 255 and 48** (R. C. Williams 5-16); ‡**Northern Cape 262** (S. von Berg 5-77) **and 44-0.** *Northern Cape 17.24pts, Easterns 7.1pts. Only Wesley Marshall (15) passed nine as Easterns collapsed in 15.1 overs.*

At Port Elizabeth, March 3–5, 2016. **Eastern Province won by nine wickets. Western Province 253** (S. A. Engelbrecht 113) **and 118** (E. O'Reilly 5-30); ‡**Eastern Province 331** (D. J. White 160) **and 43-1.** *Eastern Province 18.62pts, Western Province 7.06pts.*

At Pietermaritzburg, March 3–5, 2016. **Drawn. Border 247 and 262-4 dec** (M. D. Walters 117*); ‡**KwaZulu-Natal Inland 194** (S. T. Ndwandwa 6-59) **and 304-8** (K. Nipper 125). *KwaZulu-Natal Inland 5.88pts, Border 6.94pts.*

Final At Rondebosch, March 31–April 3, 2016. **KwaZulu-Natal Inland won by 46 runs.** ‡**KwaZulu-Natal Inland 268** (M. Gqadushe 116; G. F. Linde 5-55) **and 162; Western Province 137 and 247.** *KwaZulu-Natal Inland won their maiden first-class title, in their tenth season.*

MOMENTUM ONE-DAY CUP, 2015-16

50-over league plus knockout

	Played	*Won*	*Lost*	*NR*	*Bonus points*	*Points*	*Net run-rate*
CAPE COBRAS	10	7	3	0	5	33	0.56
LIONS	10	5	3	2	2	26	0.28
WARRIORS	10	5	4	1	1	23	0.22
Knights	10	4	6	0	2	18	−0.55
Dolphins	10	4	6	0	2	16‡	−0.40
Titans	10	3	6	1	2	15†	−0.04

† *1pt deducted for slow over-rate.* ‡ *2pts deducted for slow over-rate.*

Play-off At Johannesburg, February 24, 2016 (day/night). **Lions won by eight wickets** (DLS). **Warriors 202-8** (41 overs); ‡**Lions 174-2** (29 overs). *MoM:* D. A. Hendricks (Lions). *Lions' target was revised to 174 in 32 overs. Dominic Hendricks hit 70* in 56 balls and added 128* for their third wicket with Rassie van der Dussen (83*).*

Final At Cape Town, February 28, 2016. **Lions won by eight wickets. Cape Cobras 169** (42 overs); ‡**Lions 171-2** (33.4 overs). *MoM:* S. C. Cook (Lions). *Cobras' fifth successive final ended in defeat: Stephen Cook saw Lions to their first outright one-day title with 77*, supported by a run-a-ball 55 from Alviro Petersen.*

RAM SLAM T20 CHALLENGE, 2015-16

	Played	*Won*	*Lost*	*NR*	*Bonus points*	*Points*	*Net run-rate*
TITANS	10	8	2	0	3	35	1.10
DOLPHINS	10	5	4	1	0	22	−0.29
CAPE COBRAS	10	5	5	0	0	20	−0.18
Warriors	10	4	5	1	0	18	−0.51
Lions	10	4	6	0	0	16	−0.46
Knights	10	3	7	0	2	14	0.29

Play-off At Durban, December 9, 2015 (floodlit). **Dolphins won by five runs.** ‡**Dolphins 178-3** (20 overs); **Cape Cobras 173-8** (20 overs). *MoM:* R. E. Levi (Cobras) and A. L. Phehlukwayo (Dolphins). *Richard Levi hit 85 in 43 balls but once he fell, at 132-3, Cobras ran out of venom.*

Final At Centurion, December 12, 2015 (floodlit). **Titans won by seven wickets. Dolphins 159-5** (20 overs); ‡**Titans 161-3** (16.5 overs). *MoM:* M. Mosehle and H. Davids (both Titans). *Mangaliso Mosehle hit seven sixes in his 39-ball 87 as Titans coasted home.*

CSA PROVINCIAL 50-OVER CHALLENGE, 2015-16

50-over league plus final

Pool A	P	W	L	T	NR	Pts
NORTH WEST	6	4	1	1	0	20
Western Province	6	3	1	1	1	19
SW Districts	6	4	2	0	0	17
Northerns	6	3	3	0	0	15
Northern Cape	6	3	3	0	0	14
Border	6	1	3	0	2	8
KwaZulu-Natal	6	0	5	0	1	2

Pool B	P	W	L	Pts
GAUTENG	6	4	2	19
Eastern Province	6	4	2	19
KZ-Natal Inland	6	3	3	15
Boland	6	3	3	14
Namibia	6	3	3	12
Free State	6	2	4	9
Easterns	6	2	4	8

Gauteng qualified for the final because their net run-rate was 0.83 to Eastern Province's 0.39.

Final At Potchefstroom, April 9, 2016. **Gauteng won by seven wickets. North West 224-8** (50 overs); ‡**Gauteng 230-3** (46.2 overs). *Devon Conway and Neels Bergh completed victory by adding 102* in 19 overs.*

AFRICA T20 CUP, 2015-16

20-over league plus semi-finals and final

Pool A	P	W	L	NR	Pts
NORTHERNS	3	2	0	1	10
Easterns	3	1	1	1	6
Zimbabwe Pres XI	3	1	1	1	6
Western Province	3	0	2	1	2

Pool B	P	W	L	Pts
KZN INLAND	3	3	0	14
Boland	3	1	2	5
Border	3	1	2	4
North West	3	1	2	4

Pool C	P	W	L	NR	Pts
KWAZULU-NTL	3	2	1	0	10
Eastern Province	3	2	1	0	9
Northern Cape	3	2	1	0	8
Namibia	3	0	3	0	0

Pool D	P	W	L	Pts
FREE STATE	3	3	0	14
SW Districts	3	1	2	4
Gauteng	3	1	2	4
Kenya	3	1	2	4

Teams tied on points were separated on net run-rate, except in Pool B, where Border finished ahead of North West by virtue of winning their head-to-head match.

Semi-final At Bloemfontein, October 3, 2015. **Northerns won by 35 runs. Northerns 180-4** (20 overs); ‡**KwaZulu-Natal 145-9** (20 overs).

Semi-final At Bloemfontein, October 3, 2015. **KwaZulu-Natal Inland won by four runs.** ‡**KwaZulu-Natal Inland 139-5** (20 overs); **Free State 135-7** (20 overs).

Final At Bloemfontein, October 4, 2015. **Northerns won by seven wickets.** ‡**KwaZulu-Natal Inland 103-8** (20 overs); **Northerns 107-3** (18 overs). *Mat Pillans reduced Northerns to 25-3 before Qaasim Adams scored a match-winning 50*.*

CSA PROVINCIAL T20, 2015-16

20-over league

	Played	Won	Lost	Bonus points	Points	Net run-rate
KwaZulu-Natal Inland	4	4	0	2	18	1.46
Eastern Province	4	4	0	1	17	1.61
Free State	4	3	1	3	15	1.71
Western Province	4	3	1	2	14	0.26
Northerns	4	3	1	1	13	0.68
South Western Districts	4	2	2	1	9	−0.23
Border	4	2	2	0	8	0.04
KwaZulu-Natal	4	2	2	0	8	0.00
North West	4	2	2	0	8	−0.64
Northern Cape	4	2	2	0	8	−0.68
Easterns	4	1	3	0	4	−0.93
Namibia	4	0	4	0	0	−0.50
Gauteng	4	0	4	0	0	−1.67
Boland	4	0	4	0	0	−1.68

SRI LANKA CRICKET IN 2016

Old faces, young guns

SA'ADI THAWFEEQ

Perhaps the most important step taken by Sri Lanka Cricket's board during the year came soon after Thilanga Sumathipala's election in January, when they reinstated Graham Ford as head coach. He had done the job in 2012 and 2013, before joining Surrey. In his absence, the influential figures of Kumar Sangakkara and Mahela Jayawardene had retired from international cricket – Tillekeratne Dilshan followed in September – and the task of rebuilding the national team was daunting. Ford was given a contract that would keep him in place until after the 2019 World Cup.

SRI LANKA IN 2016

	Played	*Won*	*Lost*	*Drawn/No result*
Tests	9	5	3	1
One-day internationals	19	6	9	4
Twenty20 internationals	16	3	13	–

DECEMBER / JANUARY	2 Tests, 5 ODIs and 2 T20Is (a) v New Zealand	(see *Wisden 2016*, page 1036)
FEBRUARY	3 T20Is (a) v India	(page 912)
FEBRUARY / MARCH	Asia Cup (in Bangladesh)	(page 893)
MARCH / APRIL	ICC World Twenty20 (in India)	(page 793)
MAY / JUNE / JULY	3 Tests, 5 ODIs, 1 T20I (a) v England	(page 259)
	2 ODIs (a) v Ireland	(page 784)
AUGUST / SEPTEMBER	3 Tests, 5 ODIs, 2 T20Is (h) v Australia	(page 1055)
OCTOBER / NOVEMBER	2 Tests (a) v Zimbabwe	(page 1117)
NOVEMBER	Triangular ODI tournament (in Zimbabwe) v Zim and WI	(page 1122)
DECEMBER / JANUARY / FEBRUARY	3 Tests, 5 ODIs, 3 T20Is (a) v South Africa	(page 1024)

For a review of Sri Lankan domestic cricket from the 2015-16 season, see page 1070.

Lakruwan Wanniarachchi, AFP/Getty Images

He's the man! Rangana Herath is flanked by Dinesh Chandimal and Angelo Mathews, as Sri Lanka celebrate whitewashing Australia.

The start of his second tenure was not straightforward, with disappointing performances in both the Asia Cup and the World Twenty20 (which they had won in 2014). Then came a dismal tour of England – admittedly in challenging, early-summer conditions. But in August, Angelo Mathews's men stunned everyone, cleaning up Australia in a 3–0 Test whitewash. It was a humiliation for the tourists, who never came to terms with the left-arm spin of Rangana Herath: his 28 wickets cost 12 each. And the two heaviest scorers were the promising youngsters Dhananjaya de Silva (then aged 24) and Kusal Mendis (21), whose monumental 176 in the First Test at Pallekele – Sri Lanka had been dismissed for 117 on the opening day – set up the series.

Sri Lanka followed this with two rather more predictable Test victories in Zimbabwe. Mathews and vice-captain Dinesh Chandimal were injured, so the captaincy passed to Herath, much the most experienced player in a youthful side; this time he claimed 19 wickets at 15. However, after a run of five Test wins, it was the Sri Lankans' turn to suffer a whitewash, in South Africa. They lost the Boxing Day game at Port Elizabeth by 206 runs, then at Cape Town and Johannesburg by widening margins. It was hard to take, but facing top-quality fast bowling on pitches offering pace and bounce was a great learning opportunity.

Sumathipala's SLC also ran into some skirmishes with the selection committee, overseen since April 2015 by former Test seamer Kapila Wijegunawardene. One issue was fast bowler Lasith Malinga. SLC thought he should captain the Twenty20 side, despite worries over the state of his left knee; the selectors believed otherwise. Wijegunawardene and his fellow selectors were replaced overnight by an ad hoc committee, headed by former Sri Lanka captain Aravinda de Silva and also including Sangakkara. The new selectors chose the team for the defence of the World T20 title in India, and named Mathews as captain after Malinga – uncertain of his future – stepped down. He remained part of the squad, but returned home without playing a match, after his knee flared up again. Sri Lanka won only once in the tournament, against Afghanistan.

Then, in April – a year after he had resigned – former captain Sanath Jayasuriya was restored as chairman of selectors. He and his new committee picked the squad to tour England, with Jayasuriya claiming Sri Lanka had "the best bowling side in the world". Subsequent events, with a likely 3–0 Test defeat averted only by rain at Lord's, did not quite bear him out.

Aravinda de Silva, though no longer an official selector, was retained by SLC as "an advisor of cricket affairs", and helped maintain a long-standing link between Sri Lanka and Kent. Ford, former national coach Paul Farbrace, and de Silva himself had all spent time there and, during the year, two more arrived from Canterbury: Simon Willis as high performance manager, and Nick Lee as trainer. South African wicketkeeper-batsman Nic Pothas was appointed fielding coach. In other developments, Chaminda Vaas became SLC's fast-bowling consultant, Hemantha Devapriya coach of the women's team, Avishka Gunawardene coach of Sri Lanka A, and Roy Dias supervised the Under-19s. Dias's charges enjoyed singular success, doing what their seniors could not, and winning handsomely in England.

Elsewhere, SLC managed to overturn the ban imposed on Kusal Perera for a doping charge. Fast-bowling coach Anusha Samaranayake was cleared of match-fixing allegations, but Test batsman Kithuruwan Vithanage did receive a year's suspension from all forms of cricket for his part in a public brawl in Colombo.

SRI LANKA v AUSTRALIA IN 2016

DANIEL BRETTIG

Test matches (3): Sri Lanka 3, Australia 0
One-day internationals (5): Sri Lanka 1, Australia 4
Twenty20 internationals (2): Sri Lanka 0, Australia 2

A day before the series began, Dave Richardson, the ICC's chief executive, arrived in Kandy to hand the Test Championship mace to Steve Smith. At the last minute, it was decided the presentation would take place away from the media – when the master of ceremonies arrived at the Australian team hotel, he was told he had nothing to do. The reason was that Sri Lanka Cricket were worried a public occasion would be demoralising, and underline the gulf between Smith's men at No. 1, and the young home team at No. 7.

Little more than three weeks later, those concerns appeared ludicrous. Australia could not cope with a skilful and varied spin attack, nor mount cogent support for their excellent spearhead Mitchell Starc, and received a 3–0 hiding. By the end of the Test series, the SLC top brass had gone from low profile to ubiquitous, and remained so during the limited-overs matches (even though Australia won). Cameras regularly found Thilanga Sumathipala, the SLC president, sitting in his box, and there were plenty of guest commentary appearances by administrative luminaries. A series that started as a secret had become a big-ticket item.

As much as anything, this was thanks to Australian frailty. They had arrived with a veneer of confidence after an undefeated Test summer at home and in New Zealand. But after their batsmen failed to exploit Sri Lanka's cheap dismissal on the first day of the series, that veneer cracked. The tour became another chapter in the litany of recent Australian underperformance in Asia. A whitewash here made it nine defeats in a row across three series, dating back to early 2013, when a side led by Michael Clarke lost 4–0 in India. While that tour was infamous for internal strife and the homework affair, supposedly happier teams touring the UAE (2–0 to Pakistan in late 2014) and now Sri Lanka fared no better.

Of the three, this was perhaps the most humiliating: India and Pakistan had fielded teams with far more experience, while Sri Lanka had floundered in recent series, losing first in New Zealand, then in England. But their assuredness grew exponentially once Australia's unfamiliarity with the conditions, their opponents – Lakshan Sandakan and Kusal Mendis in particular – and the pitches, became clear. There were traces of paranoia: the tourists felt the surfaces had been made to order, and Rod Marsh, the chairman of selectors, invited the Australian press corps for a personal tour of the pitch on the eve of the Colombo Test. Oddly enough, coach Darren Lehmann said afterwards it had been the best strip of the series. It suggested the demons lay not in the turf but in the mind, as illustrated by the number of Australian batsmen beaten by straight balls from the ageless Rangana Herath.

This is not to downplay Sri Lanka's achievement. Herath had been widely predicted to perform well, but it was the unexpected brilliance of others that made victory possible: Mendis's match-changing innings in Pallekele was of the highest quality; Dilruwan Perera was the dominant spinner on a helpful Galle surface; and Dhananjaya de Silva's partnership with Dinesh Chandimal in Colombo, after Sri Lanka had slipped to 26 for five, showed a resilience the Australians could only envy. The final result was that Smith gave up the Championship mace less than two months after receiving it. The next presentation ceremony, to Pakistan, was a far more public affair.

AUSTRALIAN TOURING PARTY

*S. P. D. Smith (T/50), G. J. Bailey (50/20), J. M. Bird (T), S. M. Boland (50/20), J. A. Burns (T), N. M. Coulter-Nile (T/50), J. P. Faulkner (50/20), A. J. Finch (50/20), J. W. Hastings (50/20), J. R. Hazlewood (T/50), T. M. Head (50/20), M. C. Henriques (T/50/20), J. M. Holland (T), U. T. Khawaja (T/50/20), C. A. Lynn (20), N. M. Lyon (T/50), M. R. Marsh (T), S. E. Marsh (T/50/20), G. J. Maxwell (20), P. M. Nevill (T/20), S. N. J. O'Keefe (T), M. A. Starc (T/50/20), A. C. Voges (T), M. S. Wade (50/20), D. A. Warner (T/50/20), A. Zampa (50/20). *Coach:* D. S. Lehmann.

Smith returned home to rest after the second ODI; Warner assumed the captaincy. O'Keefe injured a hamstring in the First Test and was replaced by Holland. Coulter-Nile sustained a back injury, and returned to Australia. Shaun Marsh and Finch each broke a finger during the ODI series, and Lynn dislocated a shoulder in training. Their places in the T20 squad were taken by Khawaja, Bailey and Wade.

TEST MATCH AVERAGES

SRI LANKA – BATTING AND FIELDING

	T	*I*	*NO*	*R*	*HS*	*100*	*50*	*Avge*	*Ct/St*
D. M. de Silva	3	6	1	325	129	1	1	65.00	1
B. K. G. Mendis	3	6	0	296	176	1	1	49.33	6
L. D. Chandimal	3	6	0	250	132	1	0	41.66	1/1
A. D. Mathews	3	6	0	152	54	0	1	25.33	4
†M. D. K. J. Perera	3	6	0	148	49	0	0	24.66	6/3
†H. M. R. K. B. Herath	3	6	1	119	35	0	0	23.80	1
J. K. Silva	3	6	0	133	115	1	0	22.16	2
M. D. K. Perera	3	6	0	116	64	0	1	19.33	1
P. A. D. L. R. Sandakan	3	5	3	33	19*	0	0	16.50	1
†F. D. M. Karunaratne	3	6	0	41	22	0	0	6.83	2

Played in one Test: A. N. P. R. Fernando 0, 10*; M. V. T. Fernando 0*, 0; R. A. S. Lakmal 5, 4*.

BOWLING

	Style	*O*	*M*	*R*	*W*	*BB*	*5I*	*Avge*
H. M. R. K. B. Herath	SLA	145	41	357	28	7-64	3	12.75
P. A. D. L. R. Sandakan	SLC	71.4	12	207	9	4-58	0	23.00
M. D. K. Perera	OB	131	20	372	15	6-70	1	24.80

Also bowled: D. M. de Silva (OB) 26–8–63–2; A. N. P. R. Fernando (RFM) 22–9–52–2; M. V. T. Fernando (LFM) 2–0–16–1; R. A. S. Lakmal (RFM) 13–0–54–1; A. D. Mathews (RFM) 10–3–24–0.

AUSTRALIA – BATTING AND FIELDING

	T	*I*	*NO*	*R*	*HS*	*100*	*50*	*Avge*	*Ct/St*
S. P. D. Smith	3	6	0	247	119	1	1	41.16	10
†D. A. Warner	3	6	0	163	68	0	1	27.16	0
M. R. Marsh	3	6	0	163	53	0	1	27.16	2
A. C. Voges	3	6	0	118	47	0	0	19.66	2
†M. A. Starc	3	6	1	69	26	0	0	13.80	1
†U. T. Khawaja	2	4	0	55	26	0	0	13.75	2
P. M. Nevill	3	6	0	51	24	0	0	8.50	10/1
J. A. Burns	2	4	0	34	29	0	0	8.50	3
N. M. Lyon	3	6	0	44	17	0	0	7.33	1
†J. R. Hazlewood	3	6	2	12	7	0	0	3.00	0
J. M. Holland	2	4	3	1	1	0	0	1.00	0

Played in one Test: M. C. Henriques 4, 4; †S. E. Marsh 130, 23 (1 ct); S. N. J. O'Keefe 23, 4.

BOWLING

	Style	*O*	*M*	*R*	*W*	*BB*	*5I*	*Avge*
M. A. Starc	LF	103.2	28	364	24	6-50	3	15.16
S. N. J. O'Keefe	SLA	26.4	6	74	3	2-32	0	24.66
N. M. Lyon	OB	154	23	511	16	4-123	0	31.93
J. R. Hazlewood	RFM	84.4	19	229	7	3-21	0	32.71
J. M. Holland	SLA	82	13	274	5	2-72	0	54.80

Also bowled: M. C. Henriques (RFM) 2–0–9–0; M. R. Marsh (RFM) 35–4–118–2; S. P. D. Smith (LBG) 8–0–32–0; A. C. Voges (SLA) 4.4–0–18–0; D. A. Warner (LBG) 1–0–10–0.

At Colombo (PSO), July 18–20, 2016. **Australians won by an innings and 162 runs.** ‡**Sri Lankan XI 229** (57.2 overs) (D. A. S. Gunaratne 58, T. A. M. Siriwardene 53; S. N. J. O'Keefe 5-43) **and 83** (20.5 overs) (S. N. J. O'Keefe 5-21); **Australians 474** (132.3 overs) (J. A. Burns 72, S. P. D. Smith 57, S. N. J. O'Keefe 78*; D. S. N. F. G. Jayasuriya 5-110). *Australia's spinners looked in fine fettle, running through the Sri Lankan XI on the third day. Nathan Lyon picked up two wickets, but Steve O'Keefe led the way. In the 11th over he zipped one on to Asela Gunaratne's off stump to earn his 200th first-class scalp; ten overs later, he trapped last man Dilhara Fernando, his tenth wicket of the match, following his 78* in a strong Australian innings.*

SRI LANKA v AUSTRALIA

First Test Match

At Pallekele, July 26–30, 2016. Sri Lanka won by 106 runs. Toss: Sri Lanka. Test debuts: D. M. de Silva, P. A. D. L. R. Sandakan.

The Pallekele Test followed the script for one day, before twisting violently as it became clear Australia could not handle the Sri Lankan spinners. Their failure to set up a decisive first-innings lead left the door open, and Kusal Mendis barged through with a knock that would define the match – and the series.

As Lakshan Sandakan and Dhananjaya de Silva were handed debuts, there was much discussion of how an inexperienced Sri Lanka might wilt. When play began, the prediction seemed prudent: Hazlewood, Lyon and O'Keefe – whose low-slung left-arm spin looked ideally suited to the conditions – all delivered exacting spells to cover for a rusty Starc. Sri Lanka's first innings was over soon after lunch, and their 117 looked puny on a pitch that offered few threats to attentive and patient batsmen.

There was surprise when Australia's openers played around straight balls from Pradeep Fernando and Herath, but by the time rain ended play Khawaja and Smith had taken the tourists more than halfway to parity. A moment of early-morning arrogance from Smith changed the tone of the match: aiming an unsightly heave at Herath's second ball of the day, he missed and was stumped. Khawaja was pinned in front soon after, and from there wickets fell steadily to leave Australia only 86 in front. Sandakan's left-arm wrist-spin flummoxed the tail, after he claimed his first Test wicket with a lovely wrong'un to deceive Mitchell Marsh.

One substantial innings or partnership would have put the match out of Sri Lanka's reach. But though five men reached 20, no one scored more than Voges' 47, giving the hosts the chance to seize the initiative. Initially they were unsteady, losing four before gaining a lead. But Mendis found a willing ally in Chandimal, and their century stand – coupled with a hamstring strain that ruled O'Keefe out of the rest of the series – gave Sri Lanka the upper hand. De Silva helped add another priceless 71, and Herath's customary late-innings biffing pushed the target up to 268. Mendis's hundred, sealed with a six off Lyon, was his first in Tests, an innings full of calm and command. He had hinted at his ability during the torrid England tour earlier in the summer, but few expected him to bloom so soon. His 176 was a ground record.

Australia were quickly in difficulty as the memory of their first-innings struggles clouded thinking. Time was not short, but Warner and Khawaja were out trying to up the rate; Burns was entirely unprepared for Sandakan's sharp spin back from Starc's footmarks. Smith pared his game down almost purely to leg-side deflections but, when Voges bunted a return catch to Herath, the game looked finished. All that remained was an extraordinary period of dead-bat defiance. After O'Keefe hit a four in the 63rd over to take Australia to 161 for eight, there followed 154 consecutive deliveries without a run, including Nevill's wicket, beating England's record of 92 against West Indies at Lord's in 1950.

They blocked in the hope of late-afternoon rain, but it did not arrive, and when Herath eventually dismissed O'Keefe – for a 98-ball four – Sri Lanka clinched only their second Test win over Australia (after Kandy in September 1999), and Smith's first defeat as captain. While Mendis basked in glory, Sandakan took pride in collecting the best debut figures by a chinaman bowler in Tests, with his first-innings four for 58. By the end, the Australians' strut had disappeared, replaced by uncertainty about the opposition, and a persecution complex about the conditions.

Man of the Match: B. K. G. Mendis.

Close of play: first day, Australia 66-2 (Khawaja 25, Smith 28); second day, Sri Lanka 6-1 (Silva 2, Karunaratne 0); third day, Sri Lanka 282-6 (Mendis 169, M. D. K. Perera 5); fourth day, Australia 83-3 (Smith 26, Voges 9).

Sri Lanka

F. D. M. Karunaratne lbw b Starc	5	– (3) lbw b Starc	0
J. K. Silva c Voges b Hazlewood	4	– lbw b O'Keefe	7
B. K. G. Mendis lbw b Hazlewood	8	– (4) c Nevill b Starc	176
†L. D. Chandimal c Nevill b Hazlewood	15	– (6) lbw b Marsh	42
*A. D. Mathews c Smith b O'Keefe	15	– c Burns b Lyon	9
D. M. de Silva c Burns b Lyon	24	– (7) c Khawaja b Lyon	36
M. D. K. J. Perera b Lyon	20	– (1) lbw b Starc	4
M. D. K. Perera lbw b Lyon	0	– lbw b Hazlewood	12
H. M. R. K. B. Herath lbw b Starc	6	– c sub (M. C. Henriques) b Hazlewood	35
P. A. D. L. R. Sandakan not out	19	– b Starc	9
A. N. P. R. Fernando c Smith b O'Keefe	0	– not out	10
Lb 1	1	B 1, lb 12	13
1/6 (1) 2/15 (3) 3/18 (2) 4/43 (5) 5/67 (4) 6/87 (6) 7/87 (8) 8/94 (7) 9/100 (9) 10/117 (11) (34.2 overs)	117	1/6 (1) 2/6 (3) 3/45 (2) 4/86 (5) 5/203 (6) 6/274 (7) 7/290 (4) 8/314 (8) 9/323 (10) 10/353 (9) (93.4 overs)	353

Starc 11–1–51–2; Hazlewood 10–4–21–3; O'Keefe 10.2–3–32–2; Lyon 3–0–12–3. *Second innings*—Starc 19–4–84–4; Hazlewood 18.4–3–59–2; O'Keefe 16.2–3–42–1; Lyon 27–2–108–2; Warner 1–0–10–0; Voges 1.4–0–3–0; Marsh 9–1–33–1; Smith 1–0–1–0.

Australia

J. A. Burns b Herath	3	– b Sandakan	29
D. A. Warner b Fernando	0	– b Herath	1
U. T. Khawaja lbw b Herath	26	– lbw b M. D. K. Perera	18
*S. P. D. Smith st Chandimal b Herath	30	– lbw b Herath	55
A. C. Voges c Mendis b Fernando	47	– c and b Herath	12
M. R. Marsh b Sandakan	31	– lbw b Herath	25
†P. M. Nevill c M. D. K. J. Perera b Herath	2	– c Chandimal b de Silva	9
S. N. J. O'Keefe c Mendis b Sandakan	23	– (10) b Herath	4
M. A. Starc c M. D. K. J. Perera b Sandakan	11	– (8) c and b Sandakan	0
N. M. Lyon lbw b Sandakan	17	– (9) lbw b Sandakan	8
J. R. Hazlewood not out	2	– not out	0
B 4, lb 7	11		
1/3 (2) 2/7 (1) 3/69 (4) 4/70 (3) 5/130 (6) 6/137 (7) 7/160 (5) 8/179 (9) 9/190 (8) 10/203 (10) (79.2 overs)	203	1/2 (2) 2/33 (3) 3/63 (1) 4/96 (5) 5/139 (6) 6/140 (4) 7/141 (8) 8/157 (9) 9/161 (7) 10/161 (10) (88.3 overs)	161

Fernando 16–6–36–2; Herath 25–8–49–4; M. D. K. Perera 14–1–43–0; Sandakan 21.2–3–58–4; Mathews 3–1–6–0. *Second innings*—Fernando 6–3–16–0; Herath 33.3–16–54–5; M. D. K. Perera 13–3–30–1; Sandakan 25–8–49–3; de Silva 11–7–12–1.

Umpires: R. A. Kettleborough and S. Ravi. Third umpire: C. B. Gaffaney.
Referee: B. C. Broad.

SRI LANKA v AUSTRALIA

Second Test Match

At Galle, August 4–6. Sri Lanka won by 229 runs. Toss: Sri Lanka. Test debuts: M. V. T. Fernando; J. M. Holland.

A Sri Lanka Cricket sign outside the stadium read "Breakfast in Kandy, Lunch in Galle, Dinner in Colombo". And Sri Lanka's spinners showed their appetite once more, chewing Australia up and spitting them out inside three days. Galle pitches have always turned extravagantly, but this one did not offer the same treacherous, variable bounce as when Australia last visited, in 2011. Then, an away victory was forged through the doughty batting of Michaels Hussey and Clarke, and the tireless bowling of Shane Watson and Ryan Harris. This time, however, only Starc's 11 wickets were worth plucking from a wreckage in which no Australian passed 42.

Sri Lanka's batsmen did not command the field – but they did enough. After Karunaratne flicked the game's first delivery, from Starc, to square leg, their middle order provided the bulk of a first-innings 281 that was no more than decent. They went after the spinners – Lyon and the debutant left-armer Jon Holland – allowing neither to settle, nor exploit the turning surface. Between them, they leaked 142 from 33 overs. Holland, having hurriedly renewed his passport, bowled too full and lacked the assurance of his recent displays for Victoria in the Sheffield Shield.

In reply, Burns pulled left-arm seamer Vishwa Fernando's second ball in Test cricket to square leg; but his next over was his last in the game, and he was dropped for the final match. Warner was positive until he edged an off-break to slip just before the close. The next morning was pure chaos. Khawaja was crooked and late on a straight ball, Smith missed a cut off the stumps, and the rest fell away with frightening speed. Herath, who completed a hat-trick (only Sri Lanka's second, after Nuwan Zoysa against Zimbabwe at Harare in 1999-2000) when he trapped Starc lbw on review, and shared the spoils with Dilruwan Perera, bewitching batsmen who lacked plans or comprehension.

Sri Lanka's second innings followed a similar pattern to the first. They were brittle against Starc – his searing pace and swing yielding his best innings (six for 50) and match figures (11 for 94) – but bold against the spinners, who struggled once more, despite the ripe conditions. Dilruwan Perera, enjoying a superb match, punched his way to a half-century from No. 8, and helped build an intimidating lead.

Having lasted barely 33 overs in the first innings, Australia now faced a purely theoretical target of 413 on a worn pitch. A mid-match team meeting had resulted in a change of tack, exemplified by Voges's rash of reverse sweeps and Smith's sallies down the wicket. But these brainwaves extended the second innings only to 50 overs, all delivered by spinners, and by early afternoon on the third day Sri Lanka were rejoicing in a series win. Dilruwan Perera's ten included a straight one that Khawaja courteously allowed to flatten his off stump, summing up the addled Australian mind.

Only weeks before, Mathews had been facing serious criticism of his team and leadership in England. Now he was asked for his opinion of the abject Australians. "They look a bit lost when it comes to our spinners," he said.

Man of the Match: M. D. K. Perera.

Close of play: first day, Australia 54-2 (Khawaja 11); second day, Australia 25-3 (Warner 22, Smith 1).

Sri Lanka

F. D. M. Karunaratne c Burns b Starc	0	– (2) c Marsh b Starc	7
J. K. Silva c Nevill b Starc	5	– (1) c Smith b Hazlewood	2
M. D. K. J. Perera c Smith b Lyon	49	– b Lyon	35
B. K. G. Mendis c Nevill b Starc	86	– c Nevill b Starc	7
*A. D. Mathews c Nevill b Marsh	54	– b Lyon	47
†L. D. Chandimal c Khawaja b Hazlewood	5	– c Nevill b Starc	13
D. M. de Silva lbw b Holland	37	– c Nevill b Starc	34
M. D. K. Perera lbw b Lyon	16	– b Starc	64
H. M. R. K. B. Herath b Starc	14	– b Holland	26
P. A. D. L. R. Sandakan b Starc	1	– not out	0
M. V. T. Fernando not out	0	– c Voges b Starc	0
B 4, lb 10	14	Lb 1, w 1	2
1/0 (1) 2/9 (2) 3/117 (3) 4/184 (4) 5/199 (6) 6/224 (5) 7/259 (8) 8/265 (7) 9/274 (10) 10/281 (9) (73.1 overs)	281	1/5 (1) 2/9 (2) 3/31 (4) 4/79 (3) 5/98 (6) 6/121 (5) 7/172 (7) 8/233 (9) 9/237 (8) 10/237 (11) (59.3 overs)	237

Starc 16.1–7–44–5; Hazlewood 15–3–51–1; Lyon 18–1–78–2; Marsh 9–0–30–1; Holland 15–0–64–1. *Second innings*—Starc 12.3–1–50–6; Hazlewood 9–3–13–1; Lyon 19–2–80–2; Holland 10–1–69–1; Voges 1–0–4–0; Marsh 4–1–7–0; Smith 4–0–13–0.

Australia

J. A. Burns c M. D. K. J. Perera b Fernando	0	– (2) c de Silva b Herath	2
D. A. Warner c Mathews b M. D. K. Perera	42	– (1) lbw b M. D. K. Perera	41
U. T. Khawaja b M. D. K. Perera	11	– (4) b M. D. K. Perera	0
*S. P. D. Smith b Herath	5	– (5) c Silva b M. D. K. Perera	30
A. C. Voges c Karunaratne b Herath	8	– (6) b M. D. K. Perera	28
M. R. Marsh c Karunaratne b Sandakan	27	– (7) lbw b Sandakan	18
†P. M. Nevill lbw b Herath	0	– (8) run out	24
M. A. Starc lbw b Herath	0	– (9) b Herath	26
N. M. Lyon c Mendis b M. D. K. Perera	4	– (3) c Silva b M. D. K. Perera	0
J. R. Hazlewood c Mathews b M. D. K. Perera	3	– c and b M. D. K. Perera	7
J. M. Holland not out	0	– not out	0
B 5, lb 1	6	Lb 7	7
1/0 (1) 2/54 (2) 3/59 (3) 4/59 (4) 5/80 (5) 6/80 (7) 7/80 (8) 8/85 (9) 9/89 (10) 10/106 (6) (33.2 overs)	106	1/3 (2) 2/10 (3) 3/10 (4) 4/61 (1) 5/80 (5) 6/119 (7) 7/123 (6) 8/164 (9) 9/181 (10) 10/183 (8) (50.1 overs)	183

Fernando 2–0–16–1; Herath 11–2–35–4; M. D. K. Perera 15–4–29–4; Mathews 3–1–13–0; de Silva 2–1–7–0; Sandakan 0.2–0–0–1. *Second innings*—Herath 19.1–1–74–2; M. D. K. Perera 23–5–70–6; Sandakan 6–1–30–1; de Silva 2–0–2–0.

Umpires: C. B. Gaffaney and R. A. Kettleborough. Third umpire: S. Ravi.
Referee: B. C. Broad.

SRI LANKA v AUSTRALIA

Third Test Match

At Colombo (SSC), August 13–17. Sri Lanka won by 163 runs. Toss: Sri Lanka.

Australia were far more competitive than in Galle, but still surrendered in dramatic fashion on the final day. It gave Sri Lanka a 3–0 sweep, and more laurels for Herath, who finished with two more five-fors, to take him to seventh on the all-time list with 26. There had been moments, particularly when Smith and the recalled Shaun Marsh were in the ascendant, when Australia's prospects looked brighter. But all came crashing down in the end, maintaining their diabolical form in Asia.

Mathews won his third consecutive toss and gave his batsmen first use of a pitch widely predicted to crumble. Within 17 overs the innings looked sickly, as Starc and Lyon worked in concert to reduce the hosts to 26 for five. But the series had shown that Australia were not so good at pressing home advantages, nor Sri Lanka so good at ceding them, as many

MOST WICKETS AGAINST AUSTRALIA IN A THREE-TEST SERIES

Wkts		*Balls*	*Avge*	
33	R. J. Hadlee (NZ)	1,017	12.15	1985-86
32	Harbhajan Singh (I)	1,071	17.03	2000-01
28	**H. M. R. K. B. Herath (SL)**	**870**	**12.75**	**2016**
28	M. Muralitharan (SL)	1,255	23.17	2003-04
25	C. B. Llewellyn (SA)	796	17.92	1902-03
24	R. Peel (E)	442	7.54	1888
24	M. A. Holding (WI)	843	14.33	1981-82
24	T. Richardson (E)	876	18.29	1896
23	A. Kumble (I)	1,146	18.08	1997-98
22	Abdul Qadir (P)	1,275	25.54	1982-83

Hadlee and Holding were playing in Australia; all others were at home. Kumble also took 24 wickets in Australia in 2003-04, when he missed one Test of a four-match series.

had thought. And now Chandimal and de Silva combined for a tremendous stand of 211, blunting all, including an improved Holland. Even after de Silva exited for a beautifully crafted maiden Test hundred, Australia's frustrations continued, as Chandimal helped the last four add another precious 118.

By now, Sri Lanka were opening the bowling with spin at each end, though Australia were spared Herath until the eighth over; he had spent time off the field after a blow amidships while batting. Shaun Marsh and Smith each hit a century in a well-constructed alliance of 246, easily Australia's best of the series. But after Lakmal – Sri Lanka's fastest bowler here, though only the fifth used – coaxed Marsh to drag on, Herath began tearing through the ranks. Smith was the first of his six victims in a decline of nine for 112 when he was induced down the wicket and stumped by Kusal Perera, keeping in place of the tired Chandimal. Despite their start, Australia led by merely 24.

Their selectors had felt Joe Burns and Usman Khawaja needed to be replaced by fresher minds. But while Shaun Marsh proved a smart choice, the all-rounder Moises Henriques did not look technically or mentally ready. Meanwhile, Kaushal Silva displayed fortitude for the Australians to admire. Following scores of four, seven, five, two and nought, he crafted a handsome hundred to help Sri Lanka to a healthy lead. There was assistance down the order, and Mathews had the luxury of declaring early on the final morning, setting a healthy target of 324.

Warner made a sprightly start, but an Australian collapse seemed inevitable – and this time they slid from 77 without loss to 160 all out. Familiar dismissals added to the gallery of the grotesque: Smith missed a cut, while Voges played around another straight delivery. At least Warner provided variety, allowing Dilruwan Perera to bowl him behind his pads without offering a shot.

The SSC crowd swelled in anticipation of victory, and were chanting Herath's name at the moment he sealed it with his 13th wicket in the match – the best haul for Sri Lanka against Australia, beating Muttiah Muralitharan's 11 for 212 at Galle in 2003-04. He now had more fourth-innings five-fors (eight) than any bowler in history (Muralitharan and Shane Warne took seven each), and it lifted his series haul to 28; fellow spinners Dilruwan Perera and Sandakan claimed another 24 between them. Smith was left to reflect on a first series defeat as Test captain, and the continuing Asian malaise. "It's been a very tough series again," he said. "What we are doing isn't working." He wasn't kidding.

Man of the Match: H. M. R. K. B. Herath. *Man of the Series:* H. M. R. K. B. Herath.

Close of play: first day, Sri Lanka 214-5 (Chandimal 64, de Silva 116); second day, Australia 141-1 (S. E. Marsh 64, Smith 61); third day, Sri Lanka 22-1 (Karunaratne 8, Silva 6); fourth day, Sri Lanka 312-8 (de Silva 44, Lakmal 0).

Sri Lanka

J. K. Silva c Smith b Starc	0	– (3) c Smith b Holland	115
F. D. M. Karunaratne b Starc	7	– st Nevill b Lyon	22
M. D. K. J. Perera c Smith b Lyon	16	– (4) c Nevill b Holland	24
B. K. G. Mendis c Smith b Starc	1	– (5) lbw b Starc	18
*A. D. Mathews c Starc b Lyon	1	– (6) c Smith b Lyon	26
†L. D. Chandimal c Nevill b Starc	132	– (7) lbw b Lyon	43
D. M. de Silva c S. E. Marsh b Lyon	129	– (8) not out	65
M. D. K. Perera c Lyon b Holland	16	– (1) lbw b Starc	8
H. M. R. K. B. Herath retired hurt	33	– c Smith b Lyon	5
R. A. S. Lakmal c M. R. Marsh b Starc	5	– not out	4
P. A. D. L. R. Sandakan not out	4		
B 4, lb 7	11	B 8, lb 3, w 1, nb 5	17
1/2 (1) 2/21 (3) 3/23 (2) 4/24 (5) 5/26 (4) 6/237 (7) 7/267 (8) 8/348 (6) 9/355 (10) (141.1 overs)	355	1/8 (1) 2/44 (2) 3/69 (4) 4/98 (5) 5/156 (6) 6/246 (7) 7/276 (3) 8/297 (9) (8 wkts dec, 99.3 overs)	347

In the first innings Herath retired hurt at 340-7.

Starc 25.1–11–63–5; Hazlewood 18–4–52–0; Lyon 50–11–110–3; Holland 37–8–69–1; M. R. Marsh 10–1–45–0; Smith 1–0–5–0. *Second innings*—Starc 19.3–4–72–2; Lyon 37–7–123–4; Holland 20–4–72–2; Hazlewood 14–2–33–0; Smith 2–0–13–0; M. R. Marsh 3–1–3–0; Henriques 2–0–9–0; Voges 2–0–11–0.

Australia

D. A. Warner c M. D. K. J. Perera b de Silva	11	– (2) b M. D. K. Perera	68
S. E. Marsh b Lakmal	130	– (1) c Mendis b M. D. K. Perera	23
*S. P. D. Smith st M. D. K. J. Perera b Herath	119	– b Herath	8
A. C. Voges lbw b Herath	22	– lbw b Herath	1
M. C. Henriques st M. D. K. J. Perera b Herath	4	– run out	4
M. R. Marsh c Mendis b Herath	53	– c M. D. K. J. Perera b Herath	9
†P. M. Nevill lbw b M. D. K. Perera	14	– c Mathews b Herath	2
M. A. Starc not out	9	– c M. D. K. J. Perera b Herath	23
N. M. Lyon c Mendis b M. D. K. Perera	3	– lbw b Herath	12
J. R. Hazlewood b Herath	0	– st M. D. K. J. Perera b Herath	0
J. M. Holland c Mathews b Herath	1	– not out	0
B 4, lb 9	13	B 4, lb 6	10
1/21 (1) 2/267 (2) 3/275 (3) 4/283 (5) 5/316 (4) 6/353 (7) 7/367 (6) 8/376 (9) 9/377 (10) 10/379 (11) (125.1 overs)	379	1/77 (1) 2/100 (3) 3/102 (4) 4/114 (2) 5/115 (5) 6/123 (6) 7/140 (7) 8/157 (8) 9/159 (10) 10/160 (9) (44.1 overs)	160

M. D. K. Perera 44–4–129–2; de Silva 7–0–27–1; Herath 38.1–11–81–6; Sandakan 19–0–70–0; Lakmal 13–0–54–1; Mathews 4–1–5–0. *Second innings*—Herath 18.1–3–64–7; M. D. K. Perera 22–3–71–2; de Silva 4–0–15–0.

Umpires: C. B. Gaffaney and S. Ravi. Third umpire: R. A. Kettleborough.
Referee: B. C. Broad.

LIMITED-OVERS INTERNATIONAL REPORTS BY ADAM COLLINS

SRI LANKA v AUSTRALIA

First One-Day International

At Colombo (RPS), August 21, 2016 (day/night). Australia won by three wickets. Toss: Australia. One-day international debuts: M. A. Aponso, P. A. D. L. R. Sandakan.

For Australia's batsmen, further trial by spin was predictable, but they displayed considerable patience to counter a turning pitch and earn a battling victory. Predictable too was Starc's excellence: following 24 wickets in the Tests, he crashed into Kusal Perera's stumps in the opening over. Then, after patient fifties from Mendis and Chandimal, he deceived de Silva with a neat slower ball to become the fastest to 100 one-day international scalps, in his 52nd game, one fewer than Saqlain Mushtaq of Pakistan; 37 of his victims had been bowled. Faulkner's four for 38, his best ODI return, restricted the target to 228. After dark, Sri Lanka spun the ball markedly, not least debutant slow left-armer Amila Aponso, who also bowled with impressive control. But Australia's batsmen did not panic as they had in the Tests, and fifties for Finch and Smith, who faced 92 balls, brought them a much-needed fillip. Kusal Perera kept wicket after Chandimal was hit in the ribs by Henriques.

Man of the Match: J. P. Faulkner.

Sri Lanka

M. D. K. J. Perera b Starc	1	M. D. K. Perera c Hazlewood b Faulkner	10
T. M. Dilshan c Smith b Henriques	22	M. A. Aponso not out	2
B. K. G. Mendis c Head b Faulkner	67	B 1, w 2	3
†L. D. Chandimal not out	80		
*A. D. Mathews c Head b Faulkner	0	1/3 (1) 2/45 (2) (8 wkts, 50 overs)	227
D. M. de Silva c Bailey b Starc	2	3/124 (3) 4/124 (5)	
T. A. M. Siriwardene c Finch b Starc	19	5/132 (6) 6/173 (7)	
N. L. T. C. Perera c Wade b Faulkner	21	7/209 (8) 8/224 (9) 10 overs: 43-1	

P. A. D. L. R. Sandakan did not bat.

Starc 10–1–32–3; Hazlewood 10–0–56–0; Faulkner 10–1–38–4; Henriques 9–0–48–1; Zampa 7–0–34–0; Head 4–0–18–0.

Australia

D. A. Warner c M. D. K. J. Perera b N. L. T. C. Perera	8
A. J. Finch c Mathews b Aponso	56
*S. P. D. Smith c sub (M. D. Gunathilleke) b M. D. K. Perera	58
†M. S. Wade c Dilshan b Sandakan	26
G. J. Bailey c Sandakan b M. D. K. Perera	39
M. C. Henriques c sub (M. D. Gunathilleke) b Sandakan	6
T. M. Head st M. D. K. J. Perera b M. D. K. Perera	10
J. P. Faulkner not out	5
M. A. Starc not out	5
B 2, lb 1, w 12	15
1/40 (1) 2/79 (2) 3/128 (4) 4/190 (3) 5/202 (6) 6/216 (5) 7/222 (7) (7 wkts, 46.5 overs)	228
10 overs: 61-1	

A. Zampa and J. R. Hazlewood did not bat.

Mathews 7–0–33–0; Dilshan 3.5–0–25–0; N. L. T. C. Perera 5–1–25–1; Aponso 10–1–27–1; Siriwardene 6–0–34–0; M. D. K. Perera 10–0–48–3; Sandakan 5–0–33–2.

Umpires: Aleem Dar and R. E. J. Martinesz. Third umpire: M. A. Gough.
Referee: J. Srinath.

SRI LANKA v AUSTRALIA

Second One-Day International

At Colombo (RPS), August 24, 2016 (day/night). Sri Lanka won by 82 runs. Toss: Sri Lanka.

Just as the Australians appeared to have adjusted to spin, their troubles resurfaced in a series-levelling thrashing. They had begun well enough, as Starc and Lyon, sharing the new ball, sent back the openers in a hurry. After Mendis and Chandimal added 125, Zampa trapped both with top-spinners, and grabbed a third when de Silva picked out cover to make it 158 for five. But Mathews and Kusal Perera changed the trajectory of the match with a pair of brisk half-centuries in a stand of 103. Sri Lanka were set for 300, until Faulkner took a hat-trick, and the innings ended with seven balls unused. Australia's mission was tricky; when Warner nicked behind in the second over, and Finch chopped on in the fourth, it appeared impossible. Aponso snared Smith with his second delivery, and his four for 18 seized control. Wade resisted with 76, but the next best was Head's 31. After the match, Smith returned home for a scheduled break, with Warner assuming the captaincy for the rest of the tour.

Man of the Match: A. D. Mathews.

Sri Lanka

M. D. Gunathilleke b Starc	2
T. M. Dilshan b Lyon	10
B. K. G. Mendis lbw b Zampa	69
†L. D. Chandimal lbw b Zampa	48
*A. D. Mathews c Henriques b Faulkner	57
D. M. de Silva c Smith b Zampa	7
M. D. K. J. Perera lbw b Faulkner	54
N. L. T. C. Perera b Faulkner	12
S. Prasanna not out	2
M. D. K. Perera b Starc	5
M. A. Aponso b Starc	2
B 4, lb 7, w 9	20
1/12 (1) 2/12 (2) 3/137 (4) 4/146 (3) 5/158 (6) 6/261 (7) 7/279 (5) 8/279 (8) 9/286 (10) 10/288 (11) (48.5 overs)	288
10 overs: 59-2	

Starc 9.5–0–53–3; Lyon 9–0–49–1; Faulkner 9–0–45–3; Head 4–0–41–0; Zampa 10–0–42–3; Finch 2–0–7–0; Henriques 5–0–40–0.

Australia

D. A. Warner c Chandimal b N. L. T. C. Perera	1	M. A. Starc c and b Mathews	0
A. J. Finch b N. L. T. C. Perera	4	A. Zampa c Dilshan b Aponso	5
*S. P. D. Smith c M. D. K. Perera b Aponso	30	N. M. Lyon not out	4
G. J. Bailey b Aponso	27	B 1, lb 3, w 7	11
†M. S. Wade c Gunathilleke b N. L. T. C. Perera	76	1/3 (1) 2/16 (2) 3/41 (3) 4/102 (4) 5/118 (6) 6/182 (5) 7/184 (7) 8/185 (9) 9/202 (10) 10/206 (8) (47.2 overs)	206
M. C. Henriques st Chandimal b Prasanna	4		
T. M. Head c Dilshan b Mathews	31		
J. P. Faulkner lbw b Aponso	13	10 overs: 42-3	

Mathews 6–0–17–2; N. L. T. C. Perera 5–0–33–3; Aponso 9.2–0–18–4; Prasanna 8–1–48–1; M. D. K. Perera 10–0–43–0; Dilshan 5–0–23–0; de Silva 4–0–20–0.

Umpires: M. A. Gough and R. R. Wimalasiri. Third umpire: Aleem Dar.
Referee: J. Srinath.

SRI LANKA v AUSTRALIA

Third One-Day International

At Dambulla, August 28, 2016 (day/night). Australia won by two wickets. Toss: Sri Lanka.

Warner's temporary elevation to the job commonly described as the second-most important in Australia – after the Prime Minister – brought immediate returns. He continued Smith's rotten luck at the toss, though, and soon Dilshan, playing his 330th and last ODI because of pressure from the selectors, was firing off a flurry of boundaries. A packed crowd were loving it, but the fun ended when he popped a Zampa full toss to midwicket. He finished on 10,290 runs, made across three decades, and enjoyed the long walk from the arena, arms aloft. The innings spluttered, and Chandimal was the only other to get out of the teens; he ticked over to three figures, before being last to fall, with the score 226. Aponso was introduced in the fourth over, and Finch took him on, but lost the mini-battle, while Mathews forced false strokes from Warner and Marsh. At 44 for three, Australia were in familiar trouble, before Bailey took over, adding 62 with Head and 81 with Wade. Late wickets obliged the tail to close the game, but Warner had the perfect start, and Australia a 2–1 lead.

Man of the Match: G. J. Bailey.

Sri Lanka

M. D. Gunathilleke b Starc	5	M. D. K. Perera c Warner b Hastings	17
T. M. Dilshan c Bailey b Zampa	42	M. A. Aponso not out	1
B. K. G. Mendis c Warner b Hazlewood	4	Lb 10, w 8	18
L. D. Chandimal c Zampa b Faulkner	102	1/6 (1) 2/23 (3) 3/96 (2) 4/103 (5) 5/133 (6) 6/154 (7) 7/165 (8) 8/178 (9) 9/217 (10) 10/226 (4) (49.2 overs)	226
*A. D. Mathews lbw b Zampa	2		
D. M. de Silva c Marsh b Faulkner	12		
†M. D. K. J. Perera b Starc	11		
N. L. T. C. Perera c Marsh b Hastings	9		
S. Prasanna c Bailey b Zampa	3	10 overs: 53-2	

Starc 10–0–42–2; Hazlewood 10–0–51–1; Hastings 10–1–41–2; Faulkner 9.2–0–44–2; Zampa 10–0–38–3.

Australia

*D. A. Warner c Dilshan b Mathews	10	M. A. Starc c Prasanna b de Silva	12
A. J. Finch lbw b Aponso	30	A. Zampa not out	5
S. E. Marsh c Chandimal b Mathews	1		
G. J. Bailey b Prasanna	70	Lb 6, w 6	12
T. M. Head b M. D. K. Perera	36		
†M. S. Wade st M. D. K. J. Perera b M. D. K. Perera	42	1/31 (1) 2/42 (2) (8 wkts, 46 overs)	227
J. P. Faulkner c M. D. K. Perera b Aponso	4	3/44 (3) 4/106 (5) 5/187 (6) 6/204 (4)	
J. W. Hastings not out	5	7/206 (7) 8/222 (9) 10 overs: 45-3	

J. R. Hazlewood did not bat.

Mathews 7–0–30–2; N. L. T. C. Perera 2–0–18–0; Aponso 10–0–44–2; M. D. K. Perera 10–0–45–2; Dilshan 4–0–24–0; Prasanna 9–0–39–1; de Silva 4–0–21–1.

Umpires: Aleem Dar and R. E. J. Martinesz. Third umpire: M. A. Gough.
Referee: J. Srinath.

SRI LANKA v AUSTRALIA

Fourth One-Day International

At Dambulla, August 31, 2016 (day/night). Australia won by six wickets. Toss: Sri Lanka. One-day international debut: W. I. A. Fernando.

Journeyman seamer Hastings claimed a career-best six wickets to help Australia seal the series. His opening partner Starc set the tone: faced with 18-year-old debutant Avishka Fernando – picked to replace Tillekeratne Dilshan, despite not having played a single senior game – he pinned him in front in the first over. Sri Lanka slipped to 31 for three, before de Silva, given a first chance to open, counterpunched to a maiden ODI fifty in a stand of 84 with Mathews. But the captain retired hurt after tearing his calf, and minutes later de Silva miscued a pull off Hastings, who ripped through the lower order to leave Australia 213 to win. They had ground to victory in the previous fixture; here they sprinted, winning with 19 overs to spare. Finch hit his first four balls, from Aponso, for four, and brought up a formidable half-century from 18 deliveries, matching Simon O'Donnell and Glenn Maxwell as the quickest for Australia in an ODI. Bailey continued the ballistics, roaring to 20 from five, before settling down.

Man of the Match: J. W. Hastings.

Sri Lanka

D. M. de Silva c Finch b Hastings	76	M. D. K. Perera c Wade b Hastings	18
W. I. A. Fernando lbw b Starc	0	M. A. Aponso not out	1
B. K. G. Mendis c Wade b Hastings	1		
†L. D. Chandimal c Wade b Boland	5	B 4, lb 2, w 15	21
*A. D. Mathews c Bailey b Hastings	40		
A. K. Perera c Wade b Zampa	7	1/1 (2) 2/18 (3) (50 overs)	212
M. D. K. J. Perera c Warner b Head	6	3/31 (4) 4/121 (1) 5/130 (6)	
N. L. T. C. Perera c Finch b Hastings	13	6/134 (7) 7/165 (8) 8/199 (10)	
S. S. Pathirana c Faulkner b Hastings	24	9/200 (9) 10/212 (5) 10 overs: 32-3	

Mathews, when 28, retired hurt at 115-3 and resumed at 199-8.

Starc 10–1–51–1; Hastings 10–0–45–6; Boland 10–1–36–1; Faulkner 10–0–39–0; Zampa 8–0–30–1; Head 2–0–5–1.

Australia

*D. A. Warner b Pathirana	19	†M. S. Wade not out	8
A. J. Finch lbw b Pathirana	55	B 1, lb 1, w 2, nb 1	5
U. T. Khawaja lbw b Pathirana	0		
G. J. Bailey not out	90	1/74 (2) 2/74 (3) (4 wkts, 31 overs)	217
T. M. Head lbw b M. D. K. Perera	40	3/97 (1) 4/197 (5) 10 overs: 109-3	

J. P. Faulkner, J. W. Hastings, M. A. Starc, A. Zampa and S. M. Boland did not bat.

N. L. T. C. Perera 3–1–24–0; Aponso 8–0–59–0; M. D. K. Perera 7–0–69–1; Pathirana 8–0–37–3; de Silva 4–0–21–0; A. K. Perera 1–0–5–0.

Umpires: M. A. Gough and R. S. A. Palliyaguruge. Third umpire: Aleem Dar.
Referee: J. Srinath.

SRI LANKA v AUSTRALIA

Fifth One-Day International

At Pallekele, September 4, 2016 (day/night). Australia won by five wickets. Toss: Sri Lanka.

It might have been a dead rubber, but Australia were relentless, and Warner's first century as captain completed a 4–1 win. He was challenged by Sri Lanka's spinners, and received some luck from the officials, but remained calm to ease his side towards their target. For a time, it seemed they would be chasing more, after Sri Lanka withstood Starc's early onslaught to reach 73 without loss. But Warner shuffled his bowlers cleverly and, when de Silva holed out on 34, it set a damaging pattern: four players made it to 30, but none to 40. Australia needed 196 and soon lost Wade (elevated to open in place of Finch, who had broken a finger in the slips) and Khawaja to Dilruwan Perera. At 44 for two, Warner appeared to tickle a sweep to leg slip, but he survived to share a century stand with Bailey, whose 270 runs at 67 earned him the series award.

Man of the Match: D. A. Warner. *Man of the Series:* G. J. Bailey.

Sri Lanka

D. M. de Silva c Starc b Faulkner	34
M. D. Gunathilleke b Zampa	39
B. K. G. Mendis c Wade b Hastings	33
*L. D. Chandimal c Wade b Starc	1
W. U. Tharanga c Zampa b Head	15
†M. D. K. J. Perera lbw b Head	14
M. D. Shanaka b Zampa	13
S. S. Pathirana c Faulkner b Boland	32
M. D. K. Perera b Starc	5
R. A. S. Lakmal b Starc	0
M. A. Aponso not out	0
Lb 2, w 6, nb 1	9
1/73 (1) 2/77 (2) 3/78 (4) 4/121 (3) 5/129 (5) 6/145 (6) 7/165 (7) 8/184 (9) 9/184 (10) 10/195 (8) (40.2 overs)	195
10 overs: 58-0	

Starc 9–0–40–3; Hastings 7–1–30–1; Boland 6.2–0–28–1; Faulkner 7–0–30–1; Zampa 6–0–43–2; Head 5–0–22–2.

Australia

*D. A. Warner c and b de Silva	106
†M. S. Wade c M. D. K. J. Perera b M. D. K. Perera	3
U. T. Khawaja c Gunathilleke b M. D. K. Perera	6
G. J. Bailey lbw b M. D. K. Perera	44
T. M. Head c Lakmal b de Silva	13
J. P. Faulkner not out	8
J. W. Hastings not out	8
B 2, lb 2, w 7	11
1/11 (2) 2/25 (3) 3/157 (4) 4/179 (5) 5/189 (1) (5 wkts, 43 overs)	199
10 overs: 31-2	

A. J. Finch, M. A. Starc, A. Zampa and S. M. Boland did not bat.

Lakmal 8–1–30–0; M. D. K. Perera 10–1–51–3; Pathirana 10–0–36–0; Shanaka 2–0–10–0; Aponso 6–0–33–0; de Silva 7–0–35–2.

Umpires: Aleem Dar and R. S. A. Palliyaguruge. Third umpire: M. A. Gough.
Referee: J. Srinath.

SRI LANKA v AUSTRALIA

First Twenty20 International

At Pallekele, September 6, 2016 (floodlit). Australia won by 85 runs. Toss: Sri Lanka. Twenty20 international debut: S. S. Pathirana.

With Aaron Finch ruled out because of his broken finger, Maxwell asked to fill the opening vacancy. And, despite a poor year in which he had lost his 50-over spot, he blasted a maiden Twenty20 century, as Australia cruised to victory. His 65-ball 145 was the second-highest innings at this level, bettered only by Finch's 156 against England at the Rose Bowl in 2013. Head followed Maxwell's lead, clocking 45 in 18 balls at the death, including a six off the penultimate delivery to bring up the format's highest total, overtaking Sri Lanka's own 260 against Kenya at Johannesburg during the 2007 World Twenty20; Australia also equalled the highest score in all 20-over cricket (Royal Challengers Bangalore made 263 for five against Pune Warriors in the 2013 IPL). Defending that monolith posed no problems, especially after Dilshan chopped on in the first over. A brisk half-century from Chandimal could only limit the damage.

Man of the Match: G. J. Maxwell.

Australia

		B	*4/6*
1 G. J. Maxwell *not out*	145	65	14/9
2 *D. A. Warner *b 9*	28	16	5
3 U. T. Khawaja *c 6 b 8*	36	22	2/2
4 T. M. Head *c 3 b 6*	45	18	4/3
B 4, lb 2, w 2, nb 1	9		
6 overs: 73-1 (20 overs)	263-3		

1/57 2/154 3/263

5 M. C. Henriques, 6 G. J. Bailey, 7 J. P. Faulkner, 8 †P. M. Nevill, 9 M. A. Starc, 10 A. Zampa and 11 S. M. Boland did not bat.

Senanayake 4–7–49–1; Lakmal 4–6–51–0; Rajitha 3–3–46–0; N. L. T. C. Perera 4–5–58–1; de Silva 1–1–8–0; Pathirana 4–4–45–1.

Sri Lanka

		B	*4/6*
1 †M. D. K. J. Perera *c 9 b 11*	4	6	1
2 T. M. Dilshan *b 9*	4	3	1
3 D. M. de Silva *b 7*	12	8	1
4 *L. D. Chandimal *c 5 b 11*	58	43	6/1
5 B. K. G. Mendis *c 1 b 5*	22	13	2/2
6 N. L. T. C. Perera *c 11 b 10*	7	7	1
7 C. K. Kapugedera *c 6 b 9*	43	25	3/3
8 S. S. Pathirana *c 4 b 11*	2	2	0
9 S. M. S. M. Senanayake *not out*	6	6	1
10 R. A. S. Lakmal *c and b 9*	1	2	0
11 C. A. K. Rajitha *not out*	0	5	0
B 8, lb 8, w 3	19		
6 overs: 56-3 (20 overs)	178-9		

1/9 2/15 3/45 4/76 5/94 6/138 7/142 8/174 9/177

Starc 4–12–26–3; Boland 4–14–26–3; Faulkner 4–8–38–1; Henriques 2–3–24–1; Zampa 4–8–27–1; Maxwell 2–2–21–0.

Umpires: R. E. J. Martinesz and R. R. Wimalasiri. Third umpire: R. S. A. Palliyaguruge. Referee: J. Srinath.

SRI LANKA v AUSTRALIA

Second Twenty20 International

At Colombo (RPS), September 9, 2016 (floodlit). Australia won by four wickets. Toss: Sri Lanka.

Sri Lanka won another toss to give Dilshan the stage for his final international fixture. He received a guard of honour walking out, and generous applause when returning in the second over as man and crowd bade each other farewell. De Silva made a controlled 62, but only he and Kusal Perera reached double figures, as Faulkner and Zampa picked up six for 35 between them. Maxwell tore after the target, registering an 18-ball half-century – equalling the Australian Twenty20 international record he already shared with Warner – to bring his side to 92 for none after eight overs. Dilshan was determined to get something from his last game, and his two wickets – including one from his final delivery – were part of a late slump of six for 27, but Sri Lanka never had enough.

Man of the Match: G. J. Maxwell. *Man of the Series:* G. J. Maxwell.

Sri Lanka

		B	*4/6*
1 †M. D. K. J. Perera *c 1 b 4*	22	18	4
2 T. M. Dilshan *c 1 b 9*	1	3	0
3 D. M. de Silva *c 4 b 10*	62	50	5
4 *L. D. Chandimal *c and b 4*	4	5	0
5 B. K. G. Mendis *lbw b 11*	5	7	1
6 C. K. Kapugedera *c 1 b 11*	7	12	0
7 N. L. T. C. Perera *c 7 b 11*	0	2	0
8 S. S. Pathirana *c and b 9*	6	5	1
9 S. Prasanna *c 6 b 4*	7	11	0
10 S. M. S. M. Senanayake *not out*	7	8	0
11 R. A. S. Lakmal *not out*	0	0	0
Lb 1, w 5, nb 1	7		
6 overs: 46-2 (20 overs)	128-9		

1/9 2/44 3/51 4/58 5/76 6/76 7/86 8/114 9/125

Starc 4–9–32–1; Hastings 4–9–23–2; Maxwell 1–0–16–0; Faulkner 4–10–19–3; Zampa 4–11–16–3; Henriques 3–5–21–0.

Australia

		B	*4/6*
1 *D. A. Warner *c 7 b 8*	25	24	3
2 G. J. Maxwell *b 9*	66	29	7/4
3 M. C. Henriques *st 1 b 8*	1	3	0
4 J. P. Faulkner *run out*	1	2	0
5 M. S. Wade *c 4 b 2*	14	23	0
6 U. T. Khawaja *lbw b 2*	6	15	0
7 T. M. Head *not out*	9	10	0/1
8 †P. M. Nevill *not out*	3	1	0
Lb 1, w 4	5		
6 overs: 75-0 (17.5 overs)	130-6		

1/93 2/97 3/98 4/99 5/113 6/120

9 J. W. Hastings, 10 M. A. Starc and 11 A. Zampa did not bat.

Lakmal 2–7–15–0; Senanayake 4–9–36–0; Pathirana 2.5–9–23–2; N. L. T. C. Perera 1–1–19–0; Prasanna 4–15–16–1; de Silva 2–2–12–0; Dilshan 2–6–8–2.

Umpires: R. E. J. Martinesz and R. S. A. Palliyaguruge. Third umpire: R. R. Wimalasiri. Referee: J. Srinath.

DOMESTIC CRICKET IN SRI LANKA IN 2015-16

SA'ADI THAWFEEQ

For the second season running, there was a new winner of the Premier League, Sri Lanka's main first-class tournament. Technically, **Tamil Union** had won twice before, but their last title was in 1950-51, which was 38 years before the competition gained first-class status. They headed their preliminary group, with two victories, then rampaged through the Super Eight stage, winning all four of their remaining matches.

They secured the title in the last game, against **Galle** – who had been relegated from the competition in 2013, but looked as if they might become champions in their first season back when they took a first-innings lead of 152. But Tamil Union's captain, Test seamer Suranga Lakmal, seized four wickets, despite a fractured finger; Galle collapsed for 126, and a century from Dhananjaya de Silva set the Tamils on the road to victory. Tharanga Paranavitana, the season's leading batsman with 953 at 79, eased them home with six wickets to spare. De Silva not only scored 868 runs for Tamil Union, but was also their most successful bowler, taking 34 wickets at 14 with his off-breaks; leg-spinner Jeewan Mendis claimed 32.

Galle's slow bowlers Suraj Randiv and Gayan Sirisoma shared 96 wickets, while Lakshan Sandakan, a left-arm wrist-spinner for Colombo, was the tournament's leading wicket-taker for the second time in three seasons, with 52. The top 14 in the list were all spinners, eight of them slow left-armers. But, with suspicions that they owed much of their success to helpful domestic pitches, Sri Lanka's search for a match-winner to succeed Rangana Herath continued. Herath turned 38 in March and had dodgy knees; Tharindu Kaushal, who had taken most first-class wickets across the previous two seasons, had suffered a setback in September 2015 when his doosra was declared illegal, and struggled in the subsequent series against West Indies, though he was to take 42 wickets for Nondescripts. Sandakan made his Test debut against Australia in July.

Minod Bhanuka Ranasinghe and Udara Jayasundera, two promising left-handed openers, scored triple-centuries in the Premier League. Ranasinghe made 342 for Sinhalese against Badureliya – and was later on the fielding side when Jayasundera made 318 for Ragama.

The previous season's surprise winners, Ports Authority, were relegated after finishing last in the Plate competition, which they unsuccessfully challenged in court. Burgher, the winners of the non-first-class Emerging Trophy Tournament, took their place in 2016-17.

There were two limited-overs competitions contested by the same 14 teams as the Premier League. **Nondescripts** won the 50-over final, after Farveez Maharoof took a hat-trick in the first over of Colts' innings. In the Premier T20 tournament, the **Army** claimed their first major trophy when they beat Tamil Union. In the group rounds, there was some sensational hitting in two centuries from Sinhalese all-rounder Dasun Shanaka. Against Saracens, he blazed 16 sixes in a 46-ball 123, as his team raced to 251 for six; only Chris Gayle has hit more sixes in a Twenty20 innings, with 17 for Royal Challengers Bangalore in the 2013 IPL. A week earlier, Shanaka had struck 12 sixes and ten fours in an unbeaten 48-ball 131 against Galle – and, two days before that, ten sixes in a first-class 108.

The interim committee which had been running Sri Lanka Cricket had planned a provincial first-class competition to follow the Premier League. But once Thilanga Sumathipala was re-elected SLC president, a decade after being ousted, those plans were dropped. There was a T20 provincial tournament in February, contested by sides representing Colombo, Galle, Hambantota, Kandy and Kurunegala; it was won by **Colombo Commandos**. Sumathipala's administration did introduce a ten-team Super Under-19 Provincial Tournament, intended to function as a link between school and senior cricket. It was won by **North Western Province**, who led on first innings in the final against Southern Province.

FIRST-CLASS AVERAGES, 2015-16

BATTING (500 runs)

	M	*I*	*NO*	*R*	*HS*	*100*	*Avge*	*Ct/St*
†N. T. Paranavitana (*Tamil Union*)	10	17	5	953	150*	3	79.41	11
†M. D. U. S. Jayasundera (*Ragama*)	7	11	0	808	318	2	73.45	7
†F. D. M. Karunaratne (*Sri Lanka/Sinhalese*)	10	16	3	935	186	3	71.92	16
J. K. Silva (*Sri Lanka/Sinhalese*)	7	10	1	631	225	2	70.11	8
†M. B. Ranasinghe (*Sinhalese*)	10	15	1	901	342	3	64.35	25/3
†M. L. Udawatte (*Moors*)	9	14	0	894	212	3	63.85	7
†B. K. E. L. Milantha (*Ragama*)	10	15	1	883	191	3	63.07	4/4
†W. U. Tharanga (*Nondescripts*)	9	15	2	803	172	3	61.76	11
G. K. Amarasinghe (*Saracens*)	7	11	1	607	217	3	60.70	1
A. R. S. Silva (*Ragama*)	10	14	2	678	225*	2	56.50	7
D. M. de Silva (*Tamil Union*)	10	17	1	868	150	3	54.25	11
D. A. S. Gunaratne (*Army*)	9	15	3	642	160	2	53.50	10
L. P. C. Silva (*Galle*)	10	18	1	881	158*	3	51.82	16
H. Dumindu (*Colts*)	9	13	2	560	118	2	50.90	11
†J. Mubarak (*Nondescripts*)	9	14	1	654	197	1	50.30	5
†B. M. A. J. Mendis (*Tamil Union*)	9	13	1	574	132	3	47.83	9
†K. G. N. Randika (*Galle*)	10	18	2	749	135*	2	46.81	8
†M. L. R. Buddika (*Galle*)	10	18	0	794	193	2	44.11	8
P. A. R. P. Perera (*Colts*)	9	12	0	526	96	0	43.83	6
H. E. Vithana (*Galle*)	9	16	2	612	112	1	43.71	13
W. S. R. Samarawickrama (*Colts*)	9	13	0	565	117	2	43.46	13/2
N. M. N. P. Nawela (*Badureliya*)	9	15	0	617	119	1	41.13	9
†D. S. Weerakkody (*Nondescripts*)	9	14	1	534	130	1	41.07	10/3
T. M. N. Sampath (*Galle*)	10	18	0	620	100	1	34.44	10

BOWLING (20 wickets, average 30.00)

	Style	*O*	*M*	*R*	*W*	*BB*	*5I*	*Avge*
D. M. de Silva (*Tamil Union*)	OB	155.5	23	484	34	6-33	1	14.23
E. M. C. D. Edirisinghe (*Nondescripts*)	SLA	197.5	23	578	34	7-57	3	17.00
K. P. Gajasinghe (*Moors*)	OB	97.3	16	350	20	4-34	0	17.50
B. M. A. J. Mendis (*Tamil Union*)	LBG	198	36	655	32	5-63	1	20.46
M. A. Aponso (*Ragama*)	SLA	342.1	69	986	47	7-130	3	20.97
Ali Khan (*Colts*)	RFM	93.5	11	433	20	6-98	1	21.65
N. G. R. P. Jayasuriya (*Colts*)	SLA	229	42	840	38	7-56	4	22.10
S. Prasanna (*Army*)	LBG	219	43	693	31	7-55	2	22.35
P. A. D. L. R. Sandakan (*Colombo*)	SLC	355.4	45	1,206	52	5-67	2	23.19
M. A. Liyanapathiranage (*Chilaw Marians*)	OB	297.2	58	865	37	9-142	2	23.37
S. A. D. U. Indrasiri (*Bloomfield*)	SLA	318.1	50	1,024	43	5-57	5	23.81
N. V. R. Perera (*Moors*)	LFM	142	19	504	21	5-52	1	24.00
P. C. de Silva (*Moors*)	SLA	160.4	24	538	22	7-70	1	24.45
N. C. Komasaru (*Ports Authority*)	SLA	189.5	41	590	24	6-29	1	24.58
S. K. C. Randunu (*Bloomfield*)	SLA	182.2	19	716	29	5-70	1	24.68
P. M. Pushpakumara (*Moors*)	SLA	299	56	976	39	8-41	3	25.02
R. M. G. K. Sirisoma (*Galle*)	SLA	361.4	58	1,171	46	7-51	3	25.45
C. A. K. Rajitha (*Badureliya*)	RFM	127.5	5	596	23	7-86	3	25.91
M. S. D. Fernando (*Ragama*)	OB	156.5	24	574	22	4-39	0	26.09
K. M. C. Bandara (*Ports Authority*)	LFM	188.4	19	868	33	9-68	2	26.30
S. Randiv (*Galle*)	OB	393.2	50	1,425	50	8-111	4	28.50
M. D. K. Perera (*Sri Lanka/Colts*)	OB	282.2	46	826	28	4-35	0	29.50
S. S. Pathirana (*Colombo*)	SLA	337.3	44	1,333	45	5-32	2	29.62
P. H. T. Kaushal (*Sri Lanka/Nondescripts*)	OB	360.1	39	1,275	43	6-87	3	29.65

Averages do not include India's tour in August 2015.

AIA PREMIER LEAGUE TOURNAMENT, 2015-16

Group A	P	W	L	D	Pts
TAMIL UNION	6	2	0	4	59.415
MOORS SC	6	2	0	3*	47.565
COLOMBO CC	6	1	2	3	44.485
RAGAMA CC	6	1	1	4	38.370
Chilaw Marians CC	6	0	1	5	32.590
Ports Authority	6	1	1	4	22.830
Saracens SC	6	0	2	3*	19.920

Group B	P	W	L	D	Pts
GALLE CC	6	1	0	5	60.585
COLTS CC	6	1	0	4*	51.515
NONDESCRIPTS CC	6	2	0	3*	48.755
SINHALESE SC	6	1	0	5	39.375
Bloomfield	6	1	0	5	34.660
Army SC	6	0	2	4	23.365
Badureliya SC	6	0	4	2	13.485

Super Eight	P	W	L	D	Pts
Tamil Union	7	4	0	3	82.785
Moors SC	7	3	1	3	70.195
Ragama CC	7	1	2	4	61.790
Galle CC	7	2	1	4	60.440
Sinhalese SC	7	2	1	4	57.890
Colts CC	7	1	3	2*	54.420
Colombo CC	7	1	5	1	35.415
Nondescripts CC	7	1	2	3*	33.490

Plate	P	W	L	D	Pts
Bloomfield	5	1	0	4	52.935
Saracens SC	5	0	1	4	38.865
Army SC	5	1	1	3	35.320
Chilaw Marians CC	5	0	0	5	32.125
Badureliya SC	5	0	0	5	22.910
Ports Authority	5	0	0	5	20.135

* *One match abandoned.*

The top four teams from each group advanced to the Super Eight, carrying forward their results against fellow qualifiers, then played the other four qualifiers. The bottom three from each group entered the Plate competition, run on the same principles. The bottom-placed Plate team were relegated, and replaced by the winners of the Emerging Trophy Tournament.

Outright win = 12pts; win by an innings = 2pts extra; lead on first innings in a drawn game = 8pts. Bonus points were awarded as follows: 0.1pt for each wicket taken and 0.005pt for each run scored, up to 400 runs per innings.

Group A

At Colombo (CCC), December 4–6, 2015. **Drawn. Colombo 117** (N. T. Gamage 7-50); **‡Tamil Union 57-0.** *Colombo 0.585pts, Tamil Union 1.285pts. All first-round matches were ruined by rain.*

At Colombo (Moors), December 4–6, 2015. **Drawn. Ragama 250** (B. K. E. L. Milantha 144; P. M. Pushpakumara 5-87); **‡Moors 116-5.** *Moors 1.58pts, Ragama 1.75pts.*

At Moratuwa (Tyronne Fernando), December 4–6, 2015. **Drawn. ‡Saracens 44-1 v Ports Authority.** *Ports Authority 0.1pts, Saracens 0.22pts.*

At Katunayake (FTZ), December 11–13, 2015. **Drawn. Ports Authority 230; ‡Chilaw Marians 255-5.** *Chilaw Marians 10.275pts, Ports Authority 1.65pts.*

At Maggona, December 11–13, 2015. **Colombo won by 79 runs. Colombo 171 and 260** (M. A. Aponso 6-65); **‡Ragama 121** (S. S. Pathirana 5-35) **and 231.** *Colombo 16.155pts, Ragama 3.76pts. Sachith Pathirana hit a 52-ball 80 with eight sixes in Colombo's second innings.*

At Colombo (Moors), December 11–13, 2015. **Moors v Saracens. Abandoned.**

At Katunayake (FTZ), December 18–20, 2015. **Drawn. ‡Chilaw Marians 193** (P. A. D. L. R. Sandakan 5-67) **and 134-6; Colombo 265-9 dec.** *Chilaw Marians 2.535pts, Colombo 10.925pts.*

At Mattegoda, December 18–20, 2015. **Drawn. Ports Authority 144-9 dec; ‡Ragama 26-0.** *Ports Authority 0.72pts, Ragama 1.03pts. The first first-class match at the Army Ground in Mattegoda.*

At Colombo (PSO), December 18–20, 2015. **Drawn. Moors 203; ‡Tamil Union 255.** *Tamil Union 10.275pts, Moors 2.015pts.*

At Moratuwa (Tyronne Fernando), December 26–28, 2015. **Drawn. ‡Colombo 263 and 109** (D. H. A. Isanka 5-51); **Saracens 164 and 192-6.** *Colombo 11.46pts, Saracens 3.78pts.*

At Colombo (Moors), December 26–28, 2015. **Moors won by 92 runs. Moors 201 and 195** (D. Hettiarachchi 7-101); **‡Chilaw Marians 137** (S. C. Serasinghe 5-17) **and 167.** *Moors 15.98pts,*

Chilaw Marians 3.52pts. Saliya Saman Jeewantha hit 87 in Chilaw Marians' second innings, including eight sixes.

At Colombo (Colts), December 26–28, 2015. **Tamil Union won by nine wickets. Ports Authority 183 and 102** (D. M. de Silva 6-33); **‡Tamil Union 227 and 60-1.** *Tamil Union 15.435pts, Ports Authority 2.525pts.*

At Katunayake (FTZ), January 2–4, 2016. **Drawn. ‡Saracens 405-9 dec** (A. A. S. Silva 102*; P. L. S. Gamage 5-149); **Chilaw Marians 400** (W. C. A. Ganegama 133). *Chilaw Marians 2.9pts, Saracens 11pts. Alankara Silva and Rajith Priyan (64) put on 143 for Saracens' eighth wicket.*

At Colombo (CCC), January 2–3, 2016. **Ports Authority won by nine wickets. ‡Colombo 92** (N. C. Komasaru 6-29) **and 126; Ports Authority 128** (S. S. Pathirana 5-32) **and 93-1.** *Ports Authority 15.105pts, Colombo 2.19pts. Ports Authority beat group leaders Colombo in two days.*

At Colombo (PSO), January 2–4, 2016. **Drawn. ‡Tamil Union 426 and 134-1; Ragama 559** (M. D. U. S. Jayasundera 100, B. K. E. L. Milantha 191). *Tamil Union 3.67pts, Ragama 11.1pts. Udara Jayasundera and Lahiru Milantha opened Ragama's innings with a stand of 229.*

At Katunayake (FTZ), January 8–10, 2016. **Drawn. ‡Ragama 257** (D. E. T. Rathnayake 103*) **and 156-3; Chilaw Marians 344** (M. A. Aponso 7-130). *Chilaw Marians 11.02pts, Ragama 3.065pts.*

At Colombo (CCC), January 8–10, 2016. **Drawn. Moors 392** (M. L. Udawatte 212) **and 137-2; ‡Ports Authority 306.** *Moors 11.645pts, Ports Authority 2.73pts. Mahela Udawatte scored a maiden double-century.*

At Mattegoda, January 8–10, 2016. **Tamil Union won by seven wickets. ‡Saracens 237 and 113; Tamil Union 305 and 46-3.** *Tamil Union 15.755pts, Saracens 3.05pts. Tamil Union wicketkeeper Manoj Sarathchandra made nine dismissals in the match (six caught, three stumped).*

At Maggona, January 14–15, 2016. **Ragama won by an innings and 159 runs. Ragama 333** (A. R. S. Silva 145); **‡Saracens 76 and 98.** *Ragama 17.665pts, Saracens 1.87pts. A two-day victory lifted Ragama from sixth place to fourth to enter the Super Eight. In Saracens' first innings only Mohomad Aslam (27) passed eight; he also scored nearly half their second-innings runs, with 48.*

At Colombo (CCC), January 15–16, 2016. **Moors won by 235 runs. ‡Moors 201 and 268** (M. L. Udawatte 120); **Colombo 79** (P. M. Pushpakumara 8-41) **and 155** (P. M. Pushpakumara 5-78). *Moors 16.345pts, Colombo 3.17pts. Both teams qualified for the Super Eight, though Colombo lost in two days, again. Slow left-armer Malinda Pushpakumara took 13-119 (including 11.2–2–41–8).*

At Colombo (PSO), January 15–17, 2016. **Drawn. ‡Tamil Union 419** (D. M. de Silva 150, N. T. Paranavitana 117; M. A. Liyanapathiranage 9-142) **and 399-6** (N. T. Paranavitana 150*, B. M. A. J. Mendis 123); **Chilaw Marians 148.** *Tamil Union 12.995pts, Chilaw Marians 2.34pts. Tamil Union led the table after Tharanga Paranavitana scored twin hundreds. Chilaw Marians were squeezed out of the Super Eight, despite off-spinner Maduka Liyanapathiranage's 9-142 – he was on course for all ten, but the last man was run out off his bowling – and 11-274 in the match.*

Group B

At Panagoda, December 4–6, 2015. **Drawn. ‡Army 287-6** (D. A. S. Gunaratne 124*) **v Badureliya.** *Army 1.435pts, Badureliya 0.6pts.*

At Colombo (Bloomfield), December 4–6, 2015. **Drawn. Colts 24-2 v ‡Bloomfield.** *Bloomfield 0.2pts, Colts 0.12pts.*

At Colombo (NCC), December 4–6, 2015. **Drawn. Nondescripts 7-0 v ‡Sinhalese.** *Nondescripts 0.035pts. Rain permitted only 16 deliveries.*

At Panagoda, December 11–13, 2015. **Drawn. ‡Army 119 and 57-2; Colts 123** (G. D. Bandara 5-46). *Army 1.88pts, Colts 9.815pts.*

At Galle, December 11–13, 2015. **Drawn. ‡Galle 298** (M. L. R. Buddika 137; P. H. T. Kaushal 6-104) **and 204-8 dec; Nondescripts 136** (R. M. G. K. Sirisoma 7-51) **and 113-5.** *Galle 12.01pts, Nondescripts 3.045pts.*

At Colombo (SSC), December 11–13, 2015. **Drawn. Sinhalese 341-9 dec** (M. B. Ranasinghe 127); **‡Bloomfield 248-5.** *Sinhalese 2.205pts, Bloomfield 2.14pts.*

At Maggona, December 18–20, 2015. **Drawn. Badureliya 221** (S. A. D. U. Indrasiri 5-57) **and 86-7; ‡Bloomfield 296** (P. D. Dias 143*; B. M. D. K. Mendis 5-88). *Badureliya 2.535pts, Bloomfield 11.18pts.*

At Galle, December 18–20, 2015. **Drawn. ‡Galle 406-5 dec** (K. G. N. Randika 135*); **Army 201** (S. Randiv 8-111) **and 232-5.** *Galle 11.5pts, Army 2.665pts. Suraj Randiv took 8-111 in the Army's first innings and 10-201 in all. Seekkuge Prasanna hit 76 in 31 balls in their second, with eight sixes.*

At Colombo (NCC), December 18–20, 2015. **Nondescripts v Colts. Abandoned.**

At Colombo (Bloomfield), December 26–28, 2015. **Drawn. ‡Galle 401-8 dec** (T. M. N. Sampath 100, K. G. N. Randika 106*) **and 135-6; Bloomfield 270** (S. Randiv 5-113). *Bloomfield 2.75pts, Galle 11.675pts.*

At Colombo (NCC), December 26–28, 2015. **Nondescripts won by an innings and 103 runs. ‡Nondescripts 499-7 dec** (D. P. D. N. Dickwella 137, M. F. Maharoof 106*); **Badureliya 247** (R. J. I. Udayanga 107; P. H. T. Kaushal 5-87) **and 149.** *Nondescripts 18pts, Badureliya 2.68pts.*

At Colombo (SSC), December 26–28, 2015. **Drawn. Army 270 and 203-6 dec; ‡Sinhalese 133** (N. K. Liyanapathirana 5-30, S. Prasanna 5-32) **and 149-5.** *Sinhalese 3.01pts, Army 11.865pts. Prasanna claimed a hat-trick in Sinhalese's first innings, for figures of 6.1–0–32–5.*

At Panagoda, January 2–4, 2016. **Nondescripts won by nine wickets. Army 190** (E. M. C. D. Edirisinghe 7-57) **and 92** (E. M. C. D. Edirisinghe 6-48); **‡Nondescripts 228 and 59-1.** *Nondescripts 15.435pts, Army 2.51pts. Chamikara Edirisinghe claimed 13-105, the season's best match figures.*

At Maggona, January 2–3, 2016. **Colts won by an innings and 46 runs. ‡Colts 344; Badureliya 134** (N. G. R. P. Jayasuriya 5-25) **and 164** (N. G. R. P. Jayasuriya 5-58). *Colts 17.72pts, Badureliya 2.49pts. Slow left-armer Prabath Jayasuriya wrapped up Badureliya's first innings with a hat-trick, and made it four in four with the first delivery of the follow-on.*

At Colombo (SSC), January 2–4, 2016. **Drawn. Galle 376** (L. P. C. Silva 108; M. D. Shanaka 6-69) **and 201; ‡Sinhalese 399** (M. D. Shanaka 108). *Sinhalese 11.995pts, Galle 3.885pts. Dasun Shanaka hit ten sixes in his 108.*

At Maggona, January 8–10, 2016. **Sinhalese won by an innings and 121 runs. ‡Badureliya 254 and 209; Sinhalese 584-2 dec** (F. D. M. Karunaratne 121, M. B. Ranasinghe 342, R. T. M. Wanigamuni 107*). *Sinhalese 18pts, Badureliya 2.515pts. Left-arm seamer Binura Fernando ended Badureliya's first innings with a hat-trick. Minod Bhanuka Ranasinghe (previous best 128) made 342 in 320 balls, the season's highest, including 200 from 35 fours and ten sixes. He put on 279 for Sinhalese's first wicket with Dimuth Karunaratne, 305 for the second with Ramesh Wanigamuni.*

At Colombo (Bloomfield), January 8–10, 2016. **Drawn. Nondescripts 365 and 283-4** (D. P. D. N. Dickwella 117); **‡Bloomfield 235.** *Bloomfield 2.575pts, Nondescripts 12.24pts. Nondescripts ended their group programme sure of a place in the Super Eight.*

At Colombo (Colts), January 8–10, 2016. **Drawn. Galle 376** (L. P. C. Silva 136, H. E. Vithana 112; H. I. A. Jayaratne 5-41) **and 127-5; ‡Colts 444** (A. J. A. D. D. L. A. Jayasinghe 141; R. M. G. K. Sirisoma 6-127). *Colts 11.5pts, Galle 3.515pts.*

At Colombo (Bloomfield), January 15–17, 2016. **Bloomfield won by eight wickets. ‡Army 212** (S. A. D. U. Indrasiri 5-72) **and 150; Bloomfield 194 and 169-2.** *Bloomfield 15.815pts, Army 3.01pts.*

At Galle, January 15–17, 2016. **Galle won by an innings and 101 runs. ‡Badureliya 160 and 233** (R. M. G. K. Sirisoma 6-90); **Galle 494-7 dec** (M. L. R. Buddika 193). *Galle 18pts, Badureliya 2.665pts. Galle's decisive win meant they headed the group.*

At Colombo (SSC), January 15–17, 2016. **Drawn. Colts 225 and 387; ‡Sinhalese 214 and 219-3** (F. D. M. Karunaratne 101*). *Sinhalese 4.165pts, Colts 12.36pts. Both entered the Super Eight.*

Super Eight

At Colombo (PSO), February 11–13, 2016. **Colts won by an innings and 153 runs. Colts 529** (H. Dumindu 118, M. D. K. Perera 137*); **‡Colombo 221** (N. G. R. P. Jayasuriya 5-64) **and 155** (N. G. R. P. Jayasuriya 7-56). *Colts 18pts, Colombo 2.88pts. Coming in at 338-6, Dilruwan Perera scored a career-best 137* in 114 balls, with eight sixes. Jayasuriya took 12-120 in the match.*

At Colombo (SSC), February 11–14, 2016. **Galle won by five wickets. Ragama 344** (H. D. R. L. Thirimanne 153; T. C. B. Fernando 5-57) **and 252; ‡Galle 209** (M. A. Aponso 5-37) **and 388-5** (L. P. C. Silva 158*). *Galle 16.985pts, Ragama 4.48pts. Lahiru Thirimanne and Roshen Silva (77) put on 214 for Ragama's fourth wicket. Debutant Thissa Sanjeewa Bandara took a wicket with his first ball in Galle's innings. But Chamara Silva and Navindu Nirmal (69*) won the game with a sixth-wicket stand of 175*.*

At Colombo (Colts), February 11–14, 2016. **Moors won by 23 runs. Moors 228 and 261** (S. C. Serasinghe 102; E. M. C. D. Edirisinghe 5-64); **‡Nondescripts 255 and 211.** *Moors 16.445pts, Nondescripts 4.33pts.*

At Colombo (Moors), February 11–14, 2016. **Tamil Union won by 314 runs. Tamil Union 238** (K. T. H. Ratnayake 6-89) **and 538-7 dec** (N. T. Paranavitana 132, B. M. A. J. Mendis 103); **‡Sinhalese 167 and 295.** *Tamil Union 17.19pts, Sinhalese 4.01pts. Ramith Rambukwella hit six sixes in a 29-ball 66 at the end of Tamil Union's second innings, adding 100 in 56 with Jeewan Mendis.*

At Colombo (Colts), February 18–20, 2016. **Galle won by 194 runs. ‡Galle 344 and 202; Colombo 202** (S. Randiv 5-70) **and 150.** *Galle 16.73pts, Colombo 3.76pts.*

At Colombo (SSC), February 18–21, 2016. **Ragama won by 92 runs. Ragama 264 and 358-8 dec** (B. K. E. L. Milantha 141); **‡Colts 276** (W. S. R. Samarawickrama 103; K. P. C. M. Peiris 5-69) **and 254.** *Ragama 17.11pts, Colts 4.45pts.*

At Colombo (Bloomfield), February 18–21, 2016. **Sinhalese won by eight wickets. ‡Sinhalese 544-8 dec** (J. K. Silva 211) **and 119-2; Moors 302 and 360.** *Sinhalese 16.595pts, Moors 4.31pts. Kaushal Silva reached a maiden double-century, adding 232 with Kavindu Kulasekara (90) for Sinhalese's fourth wicket.*

At Colombo (RPS), February 18–21, 2016. **Tamil Union won by 169 runs. Tamil Union 369** (B. M. A. J. Mendis 132) **and 275-6 dec; ‡Nondescripts 282** (W. U. Tharanga 111; R. M. S. Eranga 5-63) **and 193.** *Tamil Union 17.22pts, Nondescripts 3.975pts.*

At Colombo (Colts), February 25–28, 2016. **Sinhalese won by 52 runs. ‡Sinhalese 595-6 dec** (J. K. Silva 225, M. B. Ranasinghe 120, K. Kulasekara 104*) **and 237-4 dec; Colombo 430** (H. U. K. Madushanka 5-82) **and 350** (R. K. Chandraguptha 140; K. T. H. Ratnayake 5-106). *Sinhalese 17.185pts, Colombo 4.75pts. Kaushal Silva scored his second double-hundred in a row; he put on 222 for Sinhalese's third wicket with Ranasinghe and 181 for the fourth with Kulasekara.*

At Colombo (Moors), February 25–28, 2016. **Tamil Union won by five wickets. ‡Colts 218** (B. M. A. J. Mendis 5-63) **and 338** (H. Dumindu 112*); **Tamil Union 255 and 304-5** (D. M. de Silva 113). *Tamil Union 16.795pts, Colts 4.28pts.*

At Colombo (RPS), February 25–28, 2016. **Drawn. ‡Galle 300 and 234-5; Moors 579-9 dec** (I. S. S. Samarasooriya 108, M. L. Udawatte 205). *Galle 3.57pts, Moors 11.5pts. Udawatte scored his second double-century and added 222 for Moors' third wicket with Sachithra Serasinghe (89).*

At Colombo (PSO), February 25–28, 2016. **Drawn. ‡Nondescripts 417** (D. S. Weerakkody 130; S. Nanayakkare 6-80) **and 312-3** (W. U. Tharanga 139); **Ragama 647** (A. R. S. Silva 225*). *Nondescripts 4.56pts, Ragama 11.3pts. Ragama's 647 was their highest total, and the highest of the season – for a week. Roshen Silva completed a maiden double, and added 132 for the eighth wicket with Sahan Nanayakkare; off-spinner Tharindu Kaushal conceded 223 in his 67 overs.*

At Colombo (Moors), March 3–6, 2016. **Nondescripts won by 316 runs. ‡Nondescripts 510** (J. Mubarak 197, W. U. Tharanga 172; P. A. D. L. R. Sandakan 5-146) **and 309-6 dec; Colombo 312 and 191** (P. H. T. Kaushal 6-87). *Nondescripts 17.545pts, Colombo 4.115pts. Jehan Mubarak and Upul Tharanga added 323 for the fifth wicket. Lakshan Sandakan reached 50 wickets in the season.*

At Colombo (NCC), March 3–6, 2016. **Moors won by an innings and 31 runs. ‡Colts 266** (W. S. R. Samarawickrama 117; N. V. R. Perera 5-52) **and 300** (P. C. de Silva 7-70); **Moors 597** (S. D. Withanawasam 128; Ali Khan 6-98). *Moors 18pts, Colts 3.83pts. Victory pushed Moors into the runners-up spot. No. 7 Shanuka Dulaj Withanawasam steered them past 500, adding 103 for the seventh wicket with Malinda Pushpakumara, and 136 for the eighth with Sanitha de Mel.*

At Colombo (Colts), March 3–5, 2016. **Tamil Union won by six wickets. ‡Galle 343 and 126; Tamil Union 191** (S. Randiv 6-70) **and 279-4** (D. M. de Silva 124). *Tamil Union 16.35pts, Galle 3.745pts. In a fight between the Super Eight's top two, Galle took a first-innings lead of 152 – despite Jeewan Mendis, who hit 82 including eight sixes in Tamil Union's reply – but Test seamers Suranga*

Lakmal, bowling with a broken finger, and Shaminda Eranga routed them for 126 in their second innings. Opener Dhananjaya de Silva scored a brisk 124 to help Tamil Union reach a target of 279 and claim their maiden first-class title. Randiv finished the season with 50 first-class wickets.

At Colombo (RPS), March 3–6, 2016. **Drawn. Ragama 665** (M. D. U. S. Jayasundera 318, H. D. R. L. Thirimanne 135) **and 238; ‡Sinhalese 362 and 26-1.** *Ragama 12.29pts, Sinhalese 3.94pts. For the second week in a row, Ragama hit their record total, also the biggest of the season; they finished in third place. Udara Jayasundera reached his third double-hundred, and converted it into his first triple; he added 267 for the third wicket with Thirimanne.*

CHAMPIONS

1988-89	Nondescripts CC / Sinhalese SC	1996-97	Bloomfield C&AC	2006-07	Colombo CC
1989-90	Sinhalese SC	1997-98	Sinhalese SC	2007-08	Sinhalese SC
1990-91	Sinhalese SC	1998-99	Bloomfield C&AC	2008-09	Colts CC
1991-92	Colts CC	1999-2000	Colts CC	2009-10	Chilaw Marians
1992-93	Sinhalese SC	2000-01	Nondescripts CC	2010-11	Bloomfield C & AC
1993-94	Nondescripts CC	2001-02	Colts CC	2011-12	Colts CC
1994-95	Bloomfield C&AC / Sinhalese SC	2002-03	Moors SC	2012-13	Sinhalese SC
1995-96	Colombo CC	2003-04	Bloomfield C&AC	2013-14	Nondescripts CC
		2004-05	Colts CC	2014-15	Ports Authority CC
		2005-06	Sinhalese SC	2015-16	Tamil Union

Sinhalese have won the title outright 7 times, Colts 6, Bloomfield 4, Nondescripts 3, Colombo 2, Chilaw Marians, Moors, Ports Authority and Tamil Union 1. Sinhalese have shared it twice, Bloomfield and Nondescripts once each.

The tournament was known as the Lakspray Trophy from 1988-89 to 1989-90, the P. Saravanamuttu Trophy from 1990-91 to 1997-98, and the Premier League from 1998-99.

Plate

At Panagoda, February 19–21, 2016. **Drawn. Badureliya 197** (K. M. C. Bandara 5-63) **and 267-7 dec; ‡Ports Authority 211** (C. A. K. Rajitha 5-86) **and 143-5.** *Badureliya 3.82pts, Ports Authority 11.47pts.*

At Katunayake (FTZ), February 19–21, 2016. **Drawn. ‡Saracens 492-9 dec** (G. K. Amarasinghe 217; S. A. D. U. Indrasiri 5-153) **and 127-1; Bloomfield 228.** *Bloomfield 2.14pts, Saracens 11.635pts. Gamindu Kanishka Amarasinghe retired hurt soon after completing a maiden double-century, having added 254 for Saracens' second wicket with Sangeeth Cooray (85); he resumed but was out in the next over.*

RESUMING AFTER RETIRING ON A DOUBLE-HUNDRED

	Retired	Final score		
Imtiaz Ahmed	263*	300*	PM's XI v Commonwealth XI at Bombay	1950-51
G. A. Gooch	222*	239	England XI v Jamaica at Kingston	1989-90
H. G. Kuhn	214*	216	Titans v Dolphins at Pietermaritzburg. . . .	2006-07
G. K. Amarasinghe	**210***	**217**	**Bloomfield v Saracens at Katunayake . .**	**2015-16**

At Colombo (CCC), February 19–21, 2016. **Drawn. Chilaw Marians 306 and 125-2; ‡Army 286** (D. Hettiarachchi 7-110). *Chilaw Marians 11.155pts, Army 2.63pts.*

At Katunayake (FTZ), February 26–28, 2016. **Drawn. Chilaw Marians 242** (C. A. K. Rajitha 7-86) **and 290** (C. A. K. Rajitha 5-94); **‡Badureliya 385** (N. M. N. P. Nawela 119; M. A. Liyanapathiranage 5-113) **and 81-3.** *Badureliya 12.33pts, Chilaw Marians 3.96pts. Kasun Rajitha took 12-180.*

At Panagoda, February 26–28, 2016. **Drawn. ‡Bloomfield 477-9 dec** (E. M. D. Y. Munaweera 114, P. D. Dias 108, L. D. Madushanka 130); **Ports Authority 214** (S. A. D. U. Indrasiri 5-70) **and 251-9** (S. K. C. Randunu 5-70). *Bloomfield 11.9pts, Ports Authority 3.225pts. Deshan Dias and Lahiru Madushanka, who scored a maiden century, put on 231 for Bloomfield's sixth wicket.*

At Colombo (Bloomfield), February 26–28, 2016. **Army won by seven wickets. ‡Army 272 and 95-3; Saracens 113** (W. R. Palleguruge 5-14) **and 253.** *Army 15.835pts, Saracens 3.13pts. The Army were 157-9 before Janith Silva and Ravindra Palleguruge added 115, reaching maiden fifties.*

At Panagoda, March 4–6, 2016. **Drawn. Saracens 374** (G. K. Amarasinghe 102) **and 382** (G. K. Amarasinghe 178); **‡Badureliya 304** (S. S. M. Perera 6-99) **and 21-1.** *Badureliya 3.625pts, Saracens 12.88pts. Amarasinghe scored twin hundreds.*

At Katunayake (FTZ), March 4–6, 2016. **Drawn. ‡Chilaw Marians 346** (N. A. N. N. Perera 115) **and 221-9** (S. A. D. U. Indrasiri 5-70); **Bloomfield 447** (M. S. Warnapura 100; D. Hettiarachchi 6-133). *Bloomfield 11.9pts, Chilaw Marians 3.835pts. A draw with second-placed Chilaw Marians was enough for Bloomfield to win the Plate. Shasheen Fernando (76) and Nimesh Perera, who hit 115 in 65 balls with nine sixes, added 150 for Chilaw Marians' eighth wicket.*

At Colombo (CCC), March 4–6, 2016. **Drawn. Army 202** (K. M. C. Bandara 9-68) **and 496** (D. A. S. Gunaratne 160); **‡Ports Authority 131** (S. Prasanna 7-55) **and 207-4.** *Army 12.41pts, Ports Authority 3.69pts. Left-arm seamer Chaminda Bandara's 9-68 was the best return of the season; he finished with 12-185.*

AIA PREMIER LIMITED-OVERS TOURNAMENT, 2015-16

Two 50-over leagues plus knockout

Semi-final At Colombo (RPS), December 23, 2015. **Colts won by five wickets. Bloomfield 133** (42 overs) (N. G. R. P. Jayasuriya 5-19); **‡Colts 137-5** (27.4 overs).

Semi-final At Colombo (RPS), December 24, 2015. **Nondescripts won by 121 runs. Nondescripts 208** (48.2 overs) (C. R. D. Fernando 5-30); **‡Sinhalese 87** (26.1 overs) (E. M. C. D. Edirisinghe 6-18). *Nondescripts coasted into the final after Chamikara Edirisinghe collected a career-best 6-18.*

Final At Colombo (RPS), December 30, 2015. **Nondescripts won by 77 runs. ‡Nondescripts 255-8** (50 overs) (M. D. K. Perera 6-28); **Colts 178** (45 overs). *Farveez Maharoof took a hat-trick in the first over of Colts' innings; though Hashan Dumindu and Angelo Jayasinghe added 105 for the fourth wicket, Nondescripts claimed the title with five overs in hand.*

AIA PREMIER T20 TOURNAMENT, 2015-16

20-over league plus knockout

Semi-final At Colombo (RPS), January 23, 2016. **Tamil Union won by three wickets. Nondescripts 178-9** (20 overs); **‡Tamil Union 182-7** (18.5 overs). *Tillekeratne Dilshan hit 95* in 55 balls to take Tamil Union into the final.*

Semi-final At Colombo (RPS), January 23, 2016. **Army won by five wickets. Sinhalese 144** (20 overs); **‡Army 145-5** (17.4 overs).

Final At Colombo (RPS), January 24, 2016. **Army won by five wickets. Tamil Union 164-9** (20 overs); **‡Army 170-5** (17 overs). *Dilshan scored 85 in 57 balls before Tamil Union folded against Janaka Sampath Perera; Asela Gunaratne's 65* guided the Army to their first major title.*

SUPER T20 PROVINCIAL TOURNAMENT, 2015-16

20-over league plus knockout

Semi-final At Colombo (RPS), February 3, 2016. **Colombo Commandos won by six wickets. Hambantota Troopers 164** (20 overs); **‡Colombo Commandos 169-4** (16 overs).

Semi-final At Colombo (RPS), February 3, 2016. **Galle Guardians won by six wickets. Kurunegala Warriors 121** (20 overs); **‡Galle Guardians 125-4** (17.2 overs).

Final At Colombo (RPS), February 5, 2016 (floodlit). **Colombo Commandos won by eight wickets. Galle Guardians 143-7** (20 overs); **‡Colombo Commandos 147-2** (16.4 overs). *MoM:* R. M. S. Eranga (Colombo). *MoS:* D. M. de Silva (Colombo). *Shaminda Eranga took 4-27 in Galle's innings, and Shehan Jayasuriya led Colombo's run-chase with 62*.*

WEST INDIES CRICKET IN 2016

Parties and politics

VANEISA BAKSH

By early April, West Indies had completed an extraordinary trifecta. First, they won the Under-19 World Cup in Mirpur, beating hot favourites India by five wickets in the February final. Then, on a Kolkatan Sunday in April, came a glorious double: the women's team, led by Stafanie Taylor, won the World Twenty20 – again beating the favourites, Australia – before the men followed suit in a breathtaking finale against England. Carlos Brathwaite's four consecutive sixes brought Ben Stokes to his knees, and 66,000 spectators at Eden Gardens to their feet. West Indies cricket had stirred it up. The Caribbean was exhilarated.

But the celebrations could not mask the reality. A stage built for euphoria became a pulpit of frustration as captain Darren Sammy lost his trademark

WEST INDIES IN 2016

	Played	*Won*	*Lost*	*Drawn/No result*
Tests	8	1	4	3
One-day internationals	14	4	9	1
Twenty20 internationals	11	6	4	1

DECEMBER / JANUARY	3 Tests (a) v Australia	(see *Wisden 2016*, page 945)
FEBRUARY		
MARCH / APRIL	ICC World Twenty20 (in India)	(page 793)
MAY		
JUNE	Triangular ODI tournament (h) v Australia and South Africa	(page 1081)
JULY / AUGUST	4 Tests (h) and 2 T20Is (in USA) v India	(page 1090)
SEPTEMBER / OCTOBER	3 Tests, 3 ODIs and 3 T20Is (a) v Pakistan (in UAE)	(page 983)
NOVEMBER	Triangular ODI tournament (in Zimbabwe) v Zim and SL	(page 1122)
DECEMBER		

For a review of West Indies domestic cricket from the 2015-16 season, see page 1101.

composure at the post-match interview, and slammed the West Indies Cricket Board for their mismanagement. He revealed his team had arrived in India without uniforms, and had not heard a message of good luck from the WICB throughout the tournament. Predictably, Sammy soon got the sack, and was replaced by Brathwaite in August.

Under the obdurate leadership of Dave Cameron, the WICB faced public petitions for dissolution, backed by calls from big-name ex-players and the Caribbean Community. But all were snubbed; the board were more concerned with removing dissenting voices. Players such as Chris Gayle and Kieron Pollard questioned selection policy and hinted at victimisation. The highly regarded coach, Phil Simmons, was sacked due to "differences in culture and strategic approach". The prime minister of Grenada, Dr Keith Mitchell, flared up. "The board have become an extremely inflexible and autocratic unit in which power and control dominate," he said. "Cricket development and performance appear to be low on the board's list of priorities." He was echoing the venerated broadcaster and writer, Tony Cozier, who until his death in May was writing columns on the ills of West Indies cricket.

In June, Clive Lloyd resigned as a selector; in August, Courtney Walsh followed suit. In September, former board officials – including past presidents Pat Rousseau and Ken Gordon – called for a forensic audit of the WICB. The board saw this as an allegation of wrongdoing, and considered legal action. In November, Carlos Brathwaite and Marlon Samuels declined central contracts, as did Darren Bravo. It emerged that he had been offered reduced terms which, despite his finishing second in the Test batting averages for 2016, Cameron said was due to poor performance; only Kraigg Brathwaite scored more Test runs for West Indies in 2016 than Bravo. On Twitter, Bravo called Cameron a "big idiot", and was swiftly removed from the squad altogether.

Later that month, the WICB decided to withhold No-Objection Certificates from cricketers intent on playing in overseas T20 leagues, unless the host boards coughed up 20% of their contract. Cricket South Africa and Cricket Australia opposed the move, saying it had not been accepted by the ICC. In December, director of cricket Richard Pybus opted not to renew his contract, and was replaced by former Test captain Jimmy Adams. And in January, Johnny Grave, former commercial director of the PCA in England, was appointed the board's chief executive. Soon after, Stuart Law, the Australian batsman who had been in charge of

Aamir Qureshi, Getty Images

Staying power: Kraigg Brathwaite became the first Test opener to be not out in both innings, during West Indies' victory at Sharjah.

Bangladesh and Sri Lanka, signed a two year deal as coach. Through it all, the Cameron administration remained unmoved.

Cricket continued, despite the shenanigans. After a poorly attended tri-series with Australia and South Africa, the Caribbean Premier League came to town, and proved that T20 is the most appealing format in the region. The atmosphere was festive, the cricket spectacular.

Then came the Indians, who slaughtered an inexperienced West Indies by an innings in the First Test. In the Second, Roston Chase's heroics brought a hard-earned draw; he became the second West Indian, after Garry Sobers at The Oval 50 years earlier, to pull off a century and a five-wicket haul in the same match. But any hopes of a comeback were dashed in St Lucia, and drenched in Trinidad. After 22 overs of the first day, play was ended by torrential rain and, despite blistering sunshine for the rest of the game, never restarted; according to the officials, the outfield was too hazardous. The Queen's Park Oval management and the Trinidad & Tobago Cricket Board were reprimanded by the ICC, but received no penalty.

Elsewhere, it was more of the same. In October, West Indies played Pakistan in the UAE and lost 8–1 across the formats. Their only victory – their first in 14 Tests – was thanks to Kraigg Brathwaite, who became the first opener to remain unbeaten in both innings of a Test. West Indies A lost an unofficial Test series against Sri Lanka A 2–1. The women's team lost 3–2 to England, then flew out to India, where they went down 3–0 (though they did grab the T20s 3–0).

As the losses mounted, so did proposals for prising the WICB's hands off West Indies cricket. Some advocated fan boycotts; some urged the Caribbean governments to refuse WICB access to their cricket stadiums; others planned to petition the ICC to withdraw their recognition of the board. In 2016, political turmoil was not limited to politics.

WEST INDIES TRI-SERIES IN 2016

NICK SADLEIR

1 Australia 2 West Indies 3 South Africa

This tournament – combining separately planned visits by Australia and South Africa – was finely balanced from start to finish, offering fascinating matches in a range of testing conditions. The teams drew blood from each other on a slow wicket in Providence, and continued their struggle for ascendancy on the postage-stamp-sized Warner Park in Basseterre. But, on the quicker surface of Bridgetown's Kensington Oval, it was Australia who finally prevailed.

Spinners dominated the early skirmishes, but the pitches were still good enough for four excellent centuries to be made. All the sides had won and lost two when they arrived for the last qualifying round in Barbados. South Africa topped the standings on bonus points but, after a rained-off game against Australia, and a 100-run thrashing by West Indies, they were on their way home.

After dropping out of the world's top eight in September 2015, West Indies had failed to qualify for the 2017 Champions Trophy, sparking concerns about the future of 50-over cricket in the Caribbean. But, despite missing a raft of big names – including Dwayne Bravo, Chris Gayle, Andre Russell and Darren Sammy, who had ruled themselves out by preferring Australia's BBL to their own domestic 50-over competition – the hosts were worthy of second place.

Their success was partly thanks to two returnees. Sunil Narine had been absent since being reported for a crooked arm during the one-day series with Sri Lanka in November 2015 – when he was ranked as the best white-ball bowler in the world. With a remodelled action, he had an immediate impact: a career-best six-for against South Africa. Kieron Pollard, who had not played a one-day international for 19 months, underlined his value with strong all-round performances.

South Africa lacked batting depth, managing a big score only once, when they blitzed 343 for four against West Indies in Basseterre. There were some positives: debutant left-arm wrist-spinner Tabraiz Shamsi showed promise, while Imran Tahir's seven for 45 in that Basseterre game was a national record. But, after their premature departure, doubts swirled around the future of head coach Russell Domingo. Already under pressure after recent failures in Test and Twenty20 cricket, he blamed his side's struggles on a heavy workload.

Australia – coached by Justin Langer while Darren Lehmann rested – entered the tournament as the world's top-ranked team, and shuffled their 16 players to suit conditions. Josh Hazlewood was particularly impressive, taking 11 wickets at a little over 20, including a decisive five in the final. They lost twice in qualifying, but their professionalism shone through.

Despite West Indies' victory at the World T20, crowds were disappointing. The conclusion was worrying: 50-over cricket is joining Test cricket in generating dwindling interest in the Caribbean.

NATIONAL SQUADS

West Indies *J. O. Holder, S. J. Benn, C. R. Brathwaite, D. M. Bravo, J. L. Carter, J. Charles, A. D. S. Fletcher, S. T. Gabriel, S. P. Narine, A. R. Nurse, K. A. Pollard, D. Ramdin, M. N. Samuels, J. E. Taylor. *Coach:* P. V. Simmons.

Taylor was dropped from the squad before the matches in Bridgetown.

Australia *S. P. D. Smith, G. J. Bailey, S. M. Boland, N. M. Coulter-Nile, J. P. Faulkner, A. J. Finch, J. R. Hazlewood, T. M. Head, U. T. Khawaja, N. M. Lyon, M. R. Marsh, G. J. Maxwell, M. A. Starc, M. S. Wade, D. A. Warner, A. Zampa. *Coach:* J. L. Langer.

J. W. Hastings was originally selected but withdrew because of an ankle injury and was replaced by Boland. Warner flew home after breaking his finger at Basseterre.

South Africa *A. B. de Villiers, K. J. Abbott, H. M. Amla, F. Behardien, Q. de Kock, J-P. Duminy, F. du Plessis, D. Elgar, Imran Tahir, M. Morkel, C. H. Morris, W. D. Parnell, A. M. Phangiso, K. Rabada, R. R. Rossouw, T. Shamsi. *Coach:* R. C. Domingo.

Rossouw injured his shoulder against Australia at Providence and was replaced by Elgar.

WEST INDIES v SOUTH AFRICA

At Providence, Guyana, June 3, 2016 (day/night). West Indies won by four wickets. West Indies 4pts. Toss: South Africa.

Narine decimated South Africa's batting on an extremely slow pitch: the normally free-scoring top-order could not manage a boundary in 137 balls during the middle overs. De Villiers fell to a return catch by Taylor, then Narine took control on his return to international cricket after a ban for an illegal action. With his variations apparently intact, he bewitched the South Africans, claiming six for 27 – the best one-day international figures by a West Indian slow bowler, beating his own five for 27 against New Zealand at Basseterre in 2012. The last seven wickets fell for just 28. Spin continued to cause problems, as West Indies slipped to 76 for four in the 26th over, before Pollard saved the day. As Darren Bravo knuckled down, crawling to 30 from 69 balls, Pollard clubbed three sixes down the ground from his first five deliveries. He finished with six in all – the only sixes of the game – and an unbeaten run-a-ball 67 as West Indies eased home.

Man of the Match: S. P. Narine.

South Africa

†Q. de Kock b Brathwaite	30	K. Rabada not out	1
H. M. Amla lbw b Narine	20	Imran Tahir lbw b Narine	0
R. R. Rossouw c Brathwaite b Narine	61		
*A. B. de Villiers c and b Taylor	31	Lb 1, w 4	5
J-P. Duminy b Holder	23		
F. Behardien lbw b Narine	0	1/52 (1) 2/52 (2) 3/130 (4) (46.5 overs)	188
C. H. Morris lbw b Narine	9	4/160 (3) 5/160 (6) 6/172 (5)	
K. J. Abbott b Brathwaite	5	7/181 (7) 8/181 (8) 9/185 (9)	
A. M. Phangiso c Holder b Narine	3	10/188 (11)	10 overs: 52-1

Taylor 7–0–36–1; Holder 10–1–37–1; Brathwaite 8–0–35–2; Narine 9.5–0–27–6; Benn 10–0–41–0; Pollard 2–0–11–0.

West Indies

J. Charles b Imran Tahir	31	*J. O. Holder not out	10
A. D. S. Fletcher b Imran Tahir	11		
D. M. Bravo lbw b Phangiso	30	Lb 13, w 9, nb 1	23
M. N. Samuels lbw b Phangiso	1		
†D. Ramdin c de Villiers b Duminy	10	1/37 (2) 2/52 (1) (6 wkts, 48.1 overs)	191
K. A. Pollard not out	67	3/53 (4) 4/76 (5)	
C. R. Brathwaite c Behardien b Phangiso	8	5/150 (3) 6/174 (7)	10 overs: 34-0

S. J. Benn, S. P. Narine and J. E. Taylor did not bat.

Abbott 10–1–26–0; Rabada 9–1–34–0; Morris 7–0–22–0; Imran Tahir 10–0–41–2; Phangiso 10–1–40–3; Duminy 1.1–0–12–1; Behardien 1–0–3–0.

Umpires: R. K. Illingworth and J. S. Wilson. Third umpire: N. J. Llong.
Referee: J. J. Crowe.

WEST INDIES v AUSTRALIA

At Providence, Guyana, June 5, 2016 (day/night). Australia won by six wickets. Australia 5pts. Toss: Australia.

Australia justified their status as tournament favourites, as their spinners skittled West Indies for 116 – their third-lowest one-day total in the Caribbean. Put in, they had been 50 for one, but Marsh saw off Bravo, and Starc – who, on his return from foot surgery, had already removed Fletcher in the first over – found trademark swing to get rid of Charles. Then the slow bowlers took charge: offering subtle variations in angle and pace, Lyon, Zampa and Maxwell took a combined seven for 58 to leave West Indies in dire straits. A large Sunday crowd – agitated by the lack of Guyanese representation – found little to cheer, as Australia knocked off the target in the 26th over. Narine had removed Smith and Maxwell in the 20th, and continued to pose a threat, but Warner carried over his IPL form to hold the chase together and earn Australia a bonus point. "We played some horrible shots," admitted Holder, the West Indies captain.

Man of the Match: N. M. Lyon.

West Indies

J. Charles b Starc	22
A. D. S. Fletcher c Maxwell b Starc	4
D. M. Bravo c Zampa b Marsh	19
M. N. Samuels lbw b Lyon	10
†D. Ramdin lbw b Maxwell	12
K. A. Pollard c Warner b Lyon	0
C. R. Brathwaite c Finch b Zampa	21
*J. O. Holder b Zampa	1
S. J. Benn c and b Lyon	3
S. P. Narine st Wade b Zampa	5
J. E. Taylor not out	5
Lb 3, w 9, nb 2	14
1/6 (2) 2/50 (3) 3/59 (1) 4/70 (4) 5/70 (6) 6/85 (5) 7/88 (8) 8/91 (9) 9/111 (10) 10/116 (7) (32.3 overs)	116
10 overs: 48-1	

Starc 9–0–37–2; Hazlewood 3–0–13–0; Lyon 10–2–39–3; Marsh 3–1–5–1; Zampa 5.3–0–16–3; Maxwell 2–1–3–1.

Australia

D. A. Warner not out	55
A. J. Finch lbw b Holder	19
U. T. Khawaja c Holder b Benn	27
*S. P. D. Smith lbw b Narine	6
G. J. Maxwell b Narine	0
M. R. Marsh not out	9
Lb 1	1
1/44 (2) 2/85 (3) 3/92 (4) 4/92 (5) (4 wkts, 25.4 overs)	117
10 overs: 54-1	

†M. S. Wade, M. A. Starc, A. Zampa, N. M. Lyon and J. R. Hazlewood did not bat.

Narine 10–2–36–2; Taylor 3–0–20–0; Benn 6–0–21–1; Holder 3–0–21–1; Brathwaite 3–0–14–0; Fletcher 0.4–0–4–0.

Umpires: G. O. Brathwaite and N. J. Llong. Third umpire: R. K. Illingworth.
Referee: J. J. Crowe.

AUSTRALIA v SOUTH AFRICA

At Providence, Guyana, June 7, 2016 (day/night). South Africa won by 47 runs. South Africa 5pts. Toss: South Africa. One-day international debut: T. Shamsi.

Behardien dragged the South African innings to a modest 189, yet it was enough to set up a surprising bonus-point win. A superbly controlled spell by Hazlewood had given Australia the upper hand, and the pressure told: Amla's suicidal run-out sparked a collapse from 81 for two to 112 for six, exposing South Africa's long tail. But Behardien, playing for his place, fought his way to 62 to give his bowlers something to defend. Rabada and Parnell – in his first international since July 2015 – took up the challenge with three quick wickets, before the slow bowlers asphyxiated the chase. The inclusion of left-arm wrist-spinner Tabraiz Shamsi, who snared Maxwell in his first over and looked dangerous throughout, meant this was the first time South Africa had picked three specialist spinners, since March 2011. The decision was vindicated as Australia slipped to 90 for eight in the 23rd over. And, when Finch fell to Phangiso for 72 out of a total of 113, it all but ensured that the three teams would leave South America with one win each. South Africa fielded a record eight non-white players, but a series-ending shoulder injury to Rossouw, sustained while diving to prevent a boundary, cast a shadow over their victory.

Man of the Match: F. Behardien.

South Africa

H. M. Amla run out	35
†Q. de Kock lbw b Hazlewood	18
R. R. Rossouw lbw b Lyon	7
*A. B. de Villiers b Coulter-Nile	22
J-P. Duminy b Coulter-Nile	13
F. Behardien b Maxwell	62
W. D. Parnell b Hazlewood	2
A. M. Phangiso c Hazlewood b Zampa	9
K. Rabada not out	15
Imran Tahir c Coulter-Nile b Maxwell	0
T. Shamsi not out	0
Lb 1, w 5	6
1/29 (2) 2/41 (3) 3/81 (1) 4/97 (4) 5/104 (5) 6/112 (7) 7/149 (8) 8/188 (6) 9/188 (10) (9 wkts, 50 overs)	189
10 overs: 43-2	

Hazlewood 10–3–20–2; Coulter-Nile 10–2–38–2; Lyon 10–0–40–1; Zampa 10–0–46–1; Marsh 4–0–18–0; Finch 3–0–11–0; Maxwell 3–0–15–2.

Australia

D. A. Warner lbw b Parnell	1
A. J. Finch c de Villiers b Phangiso	72
U. T. Khawaja b Rabada	2
*S. P. D. Smith lbw b Parnell	8
G. J. Maxwell lbw b Shamsi	3
M. R. Marsh c de Kock b Imran Tahir	8
†M. S. Wade c de Kock b Rabada	2
N. M. Coulter-Nile b Rabada	0
A. Zampa lbw b Imran Tahir	0
N. M. Lyon lbw b Phangiso	30
J. R. Hazlewood not out	11
Lb 5	5
1/1 (1) 2/10 (3) 3/21 (4) 4/47 (5) 5/72 (6) 6/83 (7) 7/85 (8) 8/90 (9) 9/113 (2) 10/142 (10) (34.2 overs)	142
10 overs: 38-3	

Rabada 7–1–13–3; Parnell 6–1–23–2; Imran Tahir 8–0–39–2; Phangiso 5.2–0–26–2; Shamsi 8–1–36–1.

Umpires: R. K. Illingworth and J. S. Wilson. Third umpire: N. J. Llong.
Referee: J. J. Crowe.

AUSTRALIA v SOUTH AFRICA

At Basseterre, St Kitts, June 11, 2016 (day/night). Australia won by 36 runs. Australia 4pts. Toss: Australia.

At a ground which shares his name, Warner struck his first one-day international hundred outside Australia, and his sixth in all – only to fracture his left index finger as he tried to catch Duminy, ruling him out for the rest of the tournament. Punishing anything wide, he put on 136 for the second wicket with Khawaja, before a feisty half-century from Smith propelled Australia to 288. In reply, du Plessis – returning after a finger injury – looked in excellent touch, adding 105 with Amla to make South Africa favourites at 140 for one in the 26th over. But, once the Australians found reverse swing, batting became more difficult. Starc, Hazlewood and leg-spinner Zampa claimed three wickets each and South Africa lost their last seven for 42 inside ten overs, prompting de Villiers to lament a string of soft dismissals, and taking Australia top of the table.

Man of the Match: D. A. Warner.

Australia

D. A. Warner c Amla b Parnell	109	J. P. Faulkner not out	1
A. J. Finch b Imran Tahir	13		
U. T. Khawaja c Amla b Phangiso	59	Lb 2, w 3, nb 4	9
*S. P. D. Smith not out	52		
G. J. Bailey lbw b Imran Tahir	11	1/48 (2) 2/184 (1) (6 wkts, 50 overs)	288
M. R. Marsh c Behardien b Abbott	10	3/196 (3) 4/217 (5)	
†M. S. Wade lbw b Rabada	24	5/240 (6) 6/274 (7)	10 overs: 48-1

A. Zampa, M. A. Starc and J. R. Hazlewood did not bat.

Abbott 10–2–50–1; Rabada 8–0–66–1; Imran Tahir 9–0–45–2; Parnell 7–0–34–1; Duminy 7–0–39–0; Phangiso 9–0–52–1.

South Africa

†Q. de Kock c Faulkner b Hazlewood	19	K. Rabada not out	3
H. M. Amla c Smith b Hazlewood	60	Imran Tahir run out	6
F. du Plessis c Bailey b Starc	63		
*A. B. de Villiers b Hazlewood	39	Lb 8, w 2	10
J-P. Duminy c sub (G. J. Maxwell) b Zampa	41		
F. Behardien lbw b Zampa	4	1/35 (1) 2/140 (2) (47.4 overs)	252
W. D. Parnell c Marsh b Zampa	3	3/177 (3) 4/210 (4) 5/221 (6)	
K. J. Abbott b Starc	1	6/236 (5) 7/237 (8) 8/239 (7)	
A. M. Phangiso c sub (G. J. Maxwell) b Starc	3	9/240 (9) 10/252 (11)	10 overs: 50-1

Starc 10–0–43–3; Hazlewood 9.4–0–52–3; Faulkner 7–0–32–0; Marsh 9–0–52–0; Zampa 10–0–52–3; Finch 2–0–13–0.

Umpires: N. J. Llong and J. S. Wilson. Third umpire: R. K. Illingworth.
Referee: J. J. Crowe.

WEST INDIES v AUSTRALIA

At Basseterre, St Kitts, June 13, 2016 (day/night). West Indies won by four wickets. West Indies 4pts. Toss: West Indies. One-day international debut: T. M. Head.

West Indies organised their chase comfortably to enjoy their first one-day win against Australia in eight games spread across four years. Victory had looked distant while Khawaja – promoted to open in the absence of the injured David Warner – was putting on 170 with Smith for the second wicket. But after Smith was caught and bowled aiming an ugly heave at a Brathwaite leg-cutter, the scoring-rate was squeezed, and Khawaja – attempting a third – was eventually run out two short of a maiden century in the format. Bailey picked up the baton with a bright fifty, but a middle order including debutant Travis Head otherwise failed to fire. Charles and Fletcher then attacked the new ball and rode their luck – both were badly dropped by Khawaja – to put on 74 inside ten overs. Bravo consolidated with Samuels, who then satisfied his craving for the dramatic, striking three successive sixes off Zampa in the 41st over to all but seal the match. It prompted Wade to challenge his hubris, first in heated word, then in deed, running Samuels out for 92 with a smart pick-up as he ambled a leg-bye. Coulter-Nile – in for the rested Mitchell Starc – claimed two wickets in three balls, but the West Indians completed victory with 26 to spare.

Man of the Match: M. N. Samuels.

Australia

U. T. Khawaja run out	98	J. P. Faulkner not out	4
A. J. Finch c Benn b Holder	0	N. M. Coulter-Nile not out	1
*S. P. D. Smith c and b Brathwaite	74	Lb 2, w 9	11
G. J. Bailey c Ramdin b Pollard	55		
M. R. Marsh c Holder b Brathwaite	16	1/1 (2) 2/171 (3) (7 wkts, 50 overs)	265
T. M. Head c Ramdin b Pollard	1	3/196 (1) 4/245 (5)	
†M. S. Wade b Holder	5	5/249 (6) 6/257 (7) 7/259 (4)	10 overs: 40-1

A. Zampa and J. R. Hazlewood did not bat.

Holder 10–0–44–2; Taylor 5–0–31–0; Narine 10–0–44–0; Brathwaite 10–0–60–2; Benn 9–0–52–0; Pollard 6–0–32–2.

West Indies

J. Charles lbw b Zampa	48
A. D. S. Fletcher c Bailey b Faulkner	27
D. M. Bravo c Wade b Zampa	39
M. N. Samuels run out	92
†D. Ramdin b Coulter-Nile	29
K. A. Pollard not out	16
*J. O. Holder c Wade b Coulter-Nile	0
C. R. Brathwaite not out	3
Lb 3, w 9	12
1/74 (2) 2/85 (1) 3/167 (3) 4/240 (4) 5/254 (5) 6/254 (7) (6 wkts, 45.4 overs)	266
10 overs: 74-1	

S. J. Benn, S. P. Narine and J. E. Taylor did not bat.

Hazlewood 9–0–46–0; Coulter-Nile 9.4–0–67–2; Faulkner 6–0–31–1; Head 6–0–29–0; Marsh 8–0–30–0; Zampa 7–0–60–2.

Umpires: G. O. Brathwaite and R. K. Illingworth. Third umpire: N. J. Llong.
Referee: J. J. Crowe.

WEST INDIES v SOUTH AFRICA

At Basseterre, St Kitts, June 15, 2016 (day/night). South Africa won by 139 runs. South Africa 5pts. Toss: West Indies.

Imran Tahir took seven for 45 – the best figures for South Africa in one-day internationals, beating Rabada's six for 16 against Bangladesh at Mirpur in 2015 – as West Indies got nowhere near the biggest total of the competition. Amla had led the charge, racing to his 23rd ODI hundred in an opening stand of 182 with de Kock. Morris, promoted to No. 3, and du Plessis then combined beauty with brutality: 105 came in the final ten overs, as the bowling wilted. West Indies had never successfully chased more than 300, though their openers gave them another decent start, putting on 69 in nine overs. But Fletcher swung Tahir to deep midwicket, and Shamsi – rivalling his fellow spinner for celebratory exuberance – removed Charles and Ramdin to make it 121 for four. The innings did not truly disintegrate, however, until Tahir returned for his third spell. He collected three wickets in an over, and four in nine balls, and finished the match in his next over, giving him the third-best analysis by a spinner in ODIs, behind Shahid Afridi (seven for 12 for Pakistan against West Indies at Providence in 2013) and Muttiah Muralitharan (seven for 30 for Sri Lanka against India at Sharjah in 2000-01).

Man of the Match: Imran Tahir.

South Africa

H. M. Amla c Narine b Pollard	110
†Q. de Kock b Taylor	71
C. H. Morris c sub (J. L. Carter) b Brathwaite	40
F. du Plessis not out	73
*A. B. de Villiers c Charles b Pollard	27
J-P. Duminy not out	10
B 4, lb 2, w 4, nb 2	12
1/182 (1) 2/185 (2) 3/245 (3) 4/309 (5) (4 wkts, 50 overs)	343
10 overs: 52-0	

F. Behardien, W. D. Parnell, K. Rabada, Imran Tahir and T. Shamsi did not bat.

Taylor 8–0–72–1; Holder 6–0–51–0; Narine 10–0–46–0; Brathwaite 10–0–69–1; Benn 7–0–35–0; Pollard 9–0–64–2.

West Indies

A. D. S. Fletcher c Behardien b Imran Tahir	21
J. Charles c du Plessis b Shamsi	49
D. M. Bravo b Parnell	11
M. N. Samuels c de Kock b Imran Tahir	24
†D. Ramdin c Morris b Shamsi	11
K. A. Pollard c Behardien b Imran Tahir	20
*J. O. Holder lbw b Imran Tahir	19
C. R. Brathwaite b Imran Tahir	0
S. P. Narine not out	18
S. J. Benn c Shamsi b Imran Tahir	0
J. E. Taylor b Imran Tahir	16
B 1, lb 2, w 10, nb 2	15
1/69 (1) 2/82 (2) 3/90 (3) 4/121 (5) 5/128 (4) 6/169 (7) 7/169 (8) 8/170 (6) 9/182 (10) 10/204 (11) (38 overs)	204
10 overs: 74-1	

Parnell 6–0–43–1; Rabada 7–0–46–0; Imran Tahir 9–0–45–7; Morris 7–0–26–0; Shamsi 9–0–41–2.

Umpires: G. O. Brathwaite and N. J. Llong. Third umpire: R. K. Illingworth.
Referee: J. J. Crowe.

AUSTRALIA v SOUTH AFRICA

At Bridgetown, Barbados, June 19, 2016 (day/night). No result. Australia 2pts, South Africa 2pts. Toss: Australia.

Like his 100th Test, at Bangalore the previous November, de Villiers's 200th one-day international for South Africa was ruined by the weather. Starc's single over was followed by three hours' rain, but – just as play seemed possible, and with the outfield sufficiently dry – the groundstaff spilled water on the pitch. The points were shared, leaving both sides needing to win their last group match, against West Indies, to reach the final.

South Africa

†Q. de Kock not out	5
H. M. Amla not out	0
W 3	3
(no wkt, 1 over)	8

F. du Plessis, *A. B. de Villiers, J-P. Duminy, F. Behardien, C. H. Morris, W. D. Parnell, K. Rabada, M. Morkel and Imran Tahir did not bat.

Starc 1–0–8–0.

Australia

U. T. Khawaja, A. J. Finch, *S. P. D. Smith, G. J. Bailey, M. R. Marsh, G. J. Maxwell, †M. S. Wade, J. P. Faulkner, M. A. Starc, J. R. Hazlewood, S. M. Boland.

Umpires: H. D. P. K. Dharmasena and J. S. Wilson. Third umpire: R. A. Kettleborough.
Referee: J. J. Crowe.

WEST INDIES v AUSTRALIA

At Bridgetown, Barbados, June 21, 2016 (day/night). Australia won by six wickets. Australia 4pts. Toss: Australia. One-day international debut: S. T. Gabriel.

Samuels made an outstanding hundred in vain, as Maxwell stole the show to book Australia a place in the final. Left out for a couple of games, he began cautiously, but a switch-hit six over point off Narine was the start of a 13-ball assault that brought 32 runs, as Australia raced home with eight deliveries to spare. Earlier, Starc – who before now had been rested for alternate games – looked fresh in making light work of the openers. West Indies were listing at 31 for three before a sublime partnership of 192 between Samuels and Ramdin restored their equilibrium. Samuels was dropped by Wade on 65 – part of an uncharacteristically poor fielding display by the Australians – but was otherwise faultless on his way to a tenth ODI hundred, passing 5,000 runs in the format. Australia then slipped to 99 for three, before Smith and Marsh put on 122. But, when Smith was run out for 78, the asking-rate had crept past eight. Enter Maxwell, who took 14 off three balls from Brathwaite, and left his partner, Marsh, "literally speechless".

Man of the Match: M. N. Samuels.

West Indies

J. Charles c Smith b Starc	0
A. D. S. Fletcher c Marsh b Starc	9
D. M. Bravo c Smith b Hazlewood	15
M. N. Samuels c Marsh b Faulkner	125
†D. Ramdin b Starc	91
K. A. Pollard c Marsh b Boland	20
C. R. Brathwaite b Boland	7
*J. O. Holder c Marsh b Faulkner	1
S. P. Narine not out	1
Lb 4, w 9	13
1/0 (1) 2/29 (3) 3/31 (2) 4/223 (5) 5/247 (6) 6/269 (7) 7/274 (8) 8/282 (4) (8 wkts, 50 overs)	282
10 overs: 36-3	

S. J. Benn and S. T. Gabriel did not bat.

Starc 10–1–51–3; Hazlewood 10–3–40–1; Faulkner 10–0–56–2; Boland 10–0–69–2; Marsh 5–0–36–0; Finch 3–0–16–0; Maxwell 2–0–10–0.

Australia

U. T. Khawaja c Ramdin b Gabriel	17	G. J. Maxwell not out	46
A. J. Finch c Samuels b Brathwaite	16	B 3, lb 4, w 6	13
*S. P. D. Smith run out	78		—
G. J. Bailey c Pollard b Benn	34	1/35 (2) 2/35 (1) (4 wkts, 48.4 overs)	283
M. R. Marsh not out	79	3/99 (4) 4/221 (3)	10 overs: 60-2

†M. S. Wade, J. P. Faulkner, M. A. Starc, J. R. Hazlewood and S. M. Boland did not bat.

Holder 2–0–20–0; Gabriel 9–1–43–1; Brathwaite 9–0–62–1; Benn 10–0–47–1; Narine 10–0–49–0; Pollard 5.4–0–42–0; Fletcher 3–0–13–0.

Umpires: G. O. Brathwaite and R. A. Kettleborough. Third umpire: H. D. P. K. Dharmasena. Referee: J. J. Crowe.

WEST INDIES v SOUTH AFRICA

At Bridgetown, Barbados, June 24, 2016 (day/night). West Indies won by 100 runs. West Indies 5pts. Toss: South Africa.

A magnificent, counter-attacking hundred from Bravo meant West Indies qualified for the final at South Africa's expense. The hosts had crashed to 21 for four against the searing pace of Rabada, who found Charles's edge and yorked both Samuels and Ramdin. Morkel nearly added Bravo, whose top-edged hook was parried over the rope for six by Parnell. A short rain break three balls later allowed West Indies to draw breath and, on resumption, Bravo and Pollard nullified Imran Tahir and savaged the seamers to put on a match-shaping 156 – a West Indies record for the fifth wicket, beating 154 by Carl Hooper and Shivnarine Chanderpaul against Pakistan at Sharjah in February 2002. Holder and Brathwaite chipped in, and South Africa needed 286 to qualify. Instead, they were hobbled by Gabriel – who bowled consistently over 90mph on his way to three for 17 – and Narine. From 65 for six, there was no way back, leaving de Villiers to insist that the players, and not South Africa's coach Russell Domingo, deserved the blame.

Man of the Match: D. M. Bravo.

West Indies

J. Charles c Morris b Rabada	4	S. J. Benn c Duminy b Morris	5
A. D. S. Fletcher c de Kock b Parnell	8	S. T. Gabriel run out	2
D. M. Bravo c du Plessis b Morris	102		
M. N. Samuels b Rabada	0	Lb 5, w 17, nb 2	24
†D. Ramdin b Rabada	4		—
K. A. Pollard c du Plessis b Morkel	62	1/12 (2) 2/12 (1) 3/12 (4) (49.5 overs)	285
*J. O. Holder c de Kock b Morris	40	4/21 (5) 5/177 (6) 6/210 (3)	
C. R. Brathwaite not out	33	7/264 (7) 8/266 (9) 9/275 (10)	
S. P. Narine run out	1	10/285 (11)	10 overs: 40-4

Rabada 10–1–31–3; Parnell 9.5–0–63–1; Morkel 9–0–68–1; Morris 10–0–63–3; Imran Tahir 10–0–40–0; Duminy 1–0–15–0.

South Africa

H. M. Amla lbw b Narine	16	M. Morkel not out	32
†Q. de Kock c Ramdin b Gabriel	6	Imran Tahir c Ramdin b Brathwaite	29
F. du Plessis lbw b Gabriel	3		
*A. B. de Villiers c Ramdin b Gabriel	2	B 8, w 5	13
F. Behardien c Charles b Brathwaite	35		—
J-P. Duminy c Benn b Holder	5	1/16 (2) 2/24 (3) 3/28 (4) (46 overs)	185
C. H. Morris c Pollard b Narine	7	4/35 (1) 5/51 (6) 6/65 (7)	
W. D. Parnell c sub (J. L. Carter) b Narine	28	7/96 (5) 8/118 (8) 9/134 (9)	
K. Rabada run out	9	10/185 (11)	10 overs: 32-3

Holder 10–1–33–1; Gabriel 5–1–17–3; Narine 10–0–28–3; Brathwaite 10–2–39–2; Benn 10–0–51–0; Fletcher 1–0–9–0.

Umpires: G. O. Brathwaite and H. D. P. K. Dharmasena. Third umpire: R. A. Kettleborough. Referee: J. J. Crowe.

FINAL TABLE

	Played	Won	Lost	No result	Bonus points	Points	Net run-rate
AUSTRALIA	6	3	2	1	1	15	0.38
WEST INDIES	6	3	3	0	1	13	–0.46
South Africa	6	2	3	1	2	12	0.15

Win = 4pts. 1 bonus pt awarded for achieving victory with a run-rate 1.25 times that of the opposition.

FINAL

WEST INDIES v AUSTRALIA

At Bridgetown, Barbados, June 26, 2016 (day/night). Australia won by 58 runs. Toss: Australia.

Mitchell Marsh's spell of three for six decided the contest – and backed up Smith's pre-match claim that "Australia always step up in finals" – after Wade's resourceful knock had set a defendable score. Australia's top five all made starts without settling, as the odd ball misbehaved and the spinners extracted purchase. At 173 for six in the 37th over, a modest total seemed likely, before Wade skilfully shepherded the total towards 270 for nine. He was particularly productive through the leg side, belting three sixes between long-on and midwicket, including the last ball of the innings, from Brathwaite. West Indies' chase began promisingly, but Hazlewood removed Fletcher, and Marsh – preferred to James Faulkner – left them in tatters at 72 for four, accounting for Bravo, Samuels and Charles in consecutive overs. The damage proved irrevocable, and Hazlewood mopped up the tail for his second ODI five-for. It was the first major 50-over final West Indies had reached since 2006, but the crowd went home disappointed.

Man of the Match: M. R. Marsh. *Man of the Series:* J. R. Hazlewood.

Australia

U. T. Khawaja c Ramdin b Holder 14
A. J. Finch c Samuels b Pollard 47
*S. P. D. Smith c Samuels b Gabriel 46
G. J. Bailey b Brathwaite 22
M. R. Marsh b Benn 32
G. J. Maxwell lbw b Gabriel 4
†M. S. Wade not out 57
M. A. Starc st Ramdin b Narine 17
N. M. Coulter-Nile c Bravo b Holder 15
A. Zampa run out 5
J. R. Hazlewood not out 0

B 1, lb 2, w 8 11

1/28 (1) 2/69 (2) 3/120 (4) 4/152 (3) 5/156 (6) 6/173 (5) 7/211 (8) 8/238 (9) 9/264 (10) (9 wkts, 50 overs) 270

10 overs: 55-1

Holder 10–1–51–2; Gabriel 7–0–58–2; Brathwaite 8–2–32–1; Pollard 5–0–33–1; Narine 10–1–55–1; Benn 10–0–38–1.

West Indies

A. D. S. Fletcher c Smith b Hazlewood 9
J. Charles lbw b Marsh 45
D. M. Bravo c Wade b Marsh 6
M. N. Samuels c Bailey b Marsh 6
†D. Ramdin b Hazlewood 40
K. A. Pollard c Hazlewood b Zampa 20
*J. O. Holder c Finch b Coulter-Nile 34
C. R. Brathwaite b Hazlewood 14
S. P. Narine c Smith b Hazlewood 23
S. J. Benn c Maxwell b Hazlewood 2
S. T. Gabriel not out 1

Lb 2, w 9, nb 1 12

1/49 (1) 2/62 (3) 3/68 (4) 4/72 (2) 5/105 (6) 6/148 (7) 7/185 (8) 8/194 (5) 9/211 (9) 10/212 (10) (45.4 overs) 212

10 overs: 48-0

Starc 8–0–32–0; Hazlewood 9.4–1–50–5; Coulter-Nile 8–0–46–1; Marsh 10–1–32–3; Zampa 10–0–50–1.

Umpires: R. A. Kettleborough and J. S. Wilson. Third umpire: H. D. P. K. Dharmasena.
Referee: J. J. Crowe.

WEST INDIES v INDIA IN 2016

ANAND VASU

Test matches (4): West Indies 0, India 2
Twenty20 internationals (2): West Indies 1, India 0

India managed two Test wins in the West Indies for the first time – but so low have local expectations sunk that this was hardly a surprise. Indeed, probably only the weather saved the hosts from a worse beating.

On previous visits, India had often struggled on fast, bouncy pitches, and won only five of their 45 Tests. But the days of West Indies perming four ferocious fast bowlers from six or seven have long gone – although youngsters Alzarri Joseph and Miguel Cummins looked promising. The surfaces, though, are slower and lower than in the heyday of Malcolm Marshall and Co, while the home batsmen are not disciplined enough to compete in the five-day format. To compound matters, West Indies again had to do without several star one-day performers, on duty for English counties in the T20 Blast.

This Indian team had long been touchy on the subject of pitches, with critics cavilling that tracks at home were tailored for their spinners. Ever since being installed as captain, Virat Kohli had stressed the need to perform outside India too, setting the ball rolling with a 2–1 win in Sri Lanka late in 2015.

In truth, India were stretched on only one of the 13 days' Test cricket on this tour, when West Indies surrendered just two wickets on the final day of the Second Test in Jamaica to escape with a draw. They were led by a feisty century from Barbadian Roston Chase, who had made his debut in the previous match. In Jamaica, he also claimed a five-for with his off-spin, a rare double.

But that was the only time West Indies passed 250 in six attempts. Jason Holder had tried his best since assuming the leadership, but was still too raw a player – and too defensive and unimaginative a captain – to lift an inexperienced bunch. He was not helped by selectorial confusion: seam-bowling all-rounder Carlos Brathwaite, who had hit fifties in his first two Tests, played only once in this series, was sent in at No. 9… and made another half-century. It was hardly a surprise when coach Phil Simmons, no great admirer of the WICB, was relieved of his duties shortly after the series, with the board citing "differences in culture and strategic approach".

In contrast, Kohli was ultra-aggressive, and led from the front in the First Test in Antigua with an authoritative double-century, the first by an Indian captain overseas. After that, the other batsmen followed his example. K. L. Rahul's 158 in Jamaica was his third century in just six Tests (he made another in the first Twenty20 international). Ravichandran Ashwin, pushed up to No. 6, added two hundreds, while wicketkeeper Wriddhaman Saha cemented his place with a maiden ton in St Lucia, where his stand of 213 with Ashwin rescued India from 126 for five.

India never had to wait too long for a collapse. They were patient when required, and Kohli had all bases covered: pace, bounce, swing – conventional

Randy Brooks, Getty Images

Smiles all-round: Ravichandran Ashwin celebrates his hundred in St Lucia.

and reverse – and three types of spin. Ashwin's rise continued apace, as he took 17 wickets with his varied off-breaks.

It wasn't all good news. The Indians were far from happy in the final Test, in Trinidad, where inadequate covers and poor drainage – not to mention the ridiculous absence of a Super Sopper – meant no play was possible after a truncated first day. A 3–0 win would have kept them at No. 1 in the ICC Test rankings, but 2–0 gave Pakistan a chance to nip ahead.

The tour finished with the latest attempt to wake cricket's supposed sleeping giant, the American audience. Two Twenty20 internationals were played in Florida, and the first provided a feast of runs – 489 (easily a record for the format), with M. S. Dhoni's Indian side falling just a couple short of a huge target of 246 after a brutal hundred from West Indies' latest find, Evin Lewis. But the second match was an embarrassment, and must have mystified any watching locals. The start was delayed by 40 minutes as the broadcasters struggled with the satellite connection, which meant that when a thunderstorm hit – showing up some more inadequate covering – there had not been enough overs to constitute a match.

INDIAN TOURING PARTY

*V. Kohli (T/20), R. Ashwin (T/20), Bhuvneshwar Kumar (T/20), S. T. R. Binny (T/20), J. J. Bumrah (20), S. Dhawan (T/20), M. S. Dhoni (20), R. A. Jadeja (T/20), A. Mishra (T/20), Mohammed Shami (T/20), C. A. Pujara (T), A. M. Rahane (T/20), K. L. Rahul (T/20), W. P. Saha (T), I. Sharma (T), R. G. Sharma (T/20), S. N. Thakur (T), M. Vijay (T), U. T. Yadav (T/20). *Coach:* A. Kumble.

Dhoni captained in the Twenty20 matches.

TEST MATCH AVERAGES

WEST INDIES – BATTING AND FIELDING

	T	*I*	*NO*	*R*	*HS*	*100*	*50*	*Avge*	*Ct/St*
R. L. Chase	4	6	1	190	137*	1	0	38.00	0
S. O. Dowrich	4	6	1	168	74	0	2	33.60	6/1
K. C. Brathwaite	4	7	1	200	74	0	2	33.33	5
J. O. Holder	4	6	1	132	64*	0	1	26.40	2
†M. L. Cummins	3	3	2	26	24*	0	0	26.00	0
M. N. Samuels	4	7	1	152	50	0	1	25.33	1
J. Blackwood	4	6	0	146	63	0	2	24.33	1
†D. Bishoo	3	3	0	69	45	0	0	23.00	0
†D. M. Bravo	4	7	0	139	59	0	1	19.85	3
R. Chandrika	2	4	0	53	31	0	0	13.25	2
†L. R. Johnson	2	3	0	32	23	0	0	10.66	2
S. T. Gabriel	4	5	1	32	15	0	0	8.00	1

Played in one Test: C. R. Brathwaite 0, 51*; A. S. Joseph 0, 0.

BOWLING

	Style	*O*	*M*	*R*	*W*	*BB*	*5I*	*Avge*
M. L. Cummins	RF	59.2	13	189	9	6-48	1	21.00
A. S. Joseph	RFM	28	6	92	3	3-69	0	30.66
R. L. Chase	OB	114.1	17	334	8	5-121	1	41.75
S. T. Gabriel	RFM	75	17	230	5	2-65	0	46.00
K. C. Brathwaite	OB	44.5	3	165	3	3-65	0	55.00
D. Bishoo	LBG	78	6	270	4	3-163	0	67.50

Also bowled: C. R. Brathwaite (RFM) 25–5–80–0; J. O. Holder (RFM) 86.2–24–239–1.

INDIA – BATTING AND FIELDING

	T	*I*	*NO*	*R*	*HS*	*100*	*50*	*Avge*	*Ct/St*
A. M. Rahane	4	4	2	243	108*	1	1	121.50	3
K. L. Rahul	3	3	0	236	158	1	1	78.66	6
V. Kohli	4	4	0	251	200	1	0	62.75	6
R. Ashwin	4	4	0	235	118	2	0	58.75	0
W. P. Saha	4	4	0	205	104	1	0	51.25	9/2
†S. Dhawan	3	4	0	138	84	0	1	34.50	3
Mohammed Shami	4	3	2	17	17*	0	0	17.00	1

Played in four Tests: I. Sharma 0. Played in three Tests: C. A. Pujara 16, 46 (3 ct). Played in two Tests: Bhuvneshwar Kumar 0 (1 ct); A. Mishra 53, 21; R. G. Sharma 9, 41 (3 ct); M. Vijay 7; U. T. Yadav 19. Played in one Test: †R. A. Jadeja 6, 16 (1 ct).

BOWLING

	Style	*O*	*M*	*R*	*W*	*BB*	*5I*	*Avge*
Bhuvneshwar Kumar	RFM	41.4	17	59	6	5-33	1	9.83
R. A. Jadeja	SLA	29.3	10	47	3	2-20	0	15.66
R. Ashwin	OB	131	29	394	17	7-83	2	23.17
Mohammed Shami	RFM	93	20	284	11	4-66	0	25.81
U. T. Yadav	RF	49	15	149	5	4-41	0	29.80
I. Sharma	RFM	84	18	257	8	2-30	0	32.12
A. Mishra	LBG	69.5	16	232	6	2-43	0	38.66

At Basseterre, St Kitts, July 9–10, 2016 (not first-class). **Drawn.** ‡**Indians 258-6 dec** (93 overs) (K. L. Rahul 50, S. Dhawan 51, R. G. Sharma 54*); **West Indies Cricket Board President's XI 281-7** (87 overs) (R. Chandrika 69, S. D. Hope 118*, J. A. Warrican 50*; A. Mishra 4-67). *The teams chose from 12 players. After the Indians got in some batting practice on the first day – the first three all retired out – two men competing for a place in the West Indies Test side shared a century stand on the second. Shai Hope batted all day for a leisurely century, but it was opener Rajendra Chandrika who earned the vacant spot after making 69 from 142 balls. Indian Leg-spinner Amit Mishra's four wickets sealed a Test recall.*

At Basseterre, St Kitts, July 14–16, 2016 (not first-class). **Drawn.** ‡**West Indies Cricket Board President's XI 180** (62.5 overs) (R. Ashwin 3-62, R. A. Jadeja 3-16) **and 223-6** (86 overs) (J. Blackwood 51; R. Ashwin 3-59); **Indians 364** (105.4 overs) (K. L. Rahul 64, V. Kohli 51, R. A. Jadeja 56; R. R. S. Cornwall 5-118). *Both sides chose from 13 players. After the Indian spinners demolished the President's XI for 180, almost all their batsmen contributed – everyone made double figures except Shikhar Dhawan, who was out for nine. Rahkeem Cornwall, a well-built off-spinner from Antigua, took five wickets. The President's XI had to bat out the last day to draw – and did so on a sluggish pitch, with Jermaine Blackwood surviving for three hours, and Vishaul Singh and Montcin Hodge for almost two apiece.*

WEST INDIES v INDIA

First Test Match

At North Sound, Antigua, July 21–24, 2016. India won by an innings and 92 runs. Toss: India. Test debut: R. L. Chase.

India have traditionally failed to get going at the start of a tour, when conditions are still alien. But this time they hit the ground running, and coasted to a thumping victory. It helped that Kohli won a crucial toss, allowing his batsmen to bed down while the pitch was at its best.

Dhawan, under pressure for his place, weathered a sharp early burst from Gabriel, then feasted on the rest of an insipid attack. He missed out on a hundred, failing to connect with a sweep at Bishoo, and the other batsmen were tied down. But Kohli had no such problems: he toyed with the bowling after reaching his 12th Test century, mixing confident straight-drives with assured hits through cover. Bishoo winkled out two more wickets with long hops, but Kohli found an able ally in Ashwin, promoted to No. 6 for the first time to enable India to play an extra bowler.

By the end of the first day, Kohli – who had spent the eve of the Test chatting to Viv Richards, at the stadium that bears his name – had reached 143, and Ashwin had got his eye in. Next day Kohli motored to his maiden first-class double-century, and dropped to the ground to kiss the turf. Almost immediately, he chopped Gabriel into his stumps. But Ashwin was not about to give his wicket away and, with a little help from the lower order, brought up his third Test hundred. Batting may be the second string to his bow, but the time he spent in the middle gave him valuable insight into how the pitch might play when it was his turn to bowl.

After India allowed themselves the rare luxury of an overseas declaration, at 566 for eight, West Indies' initial response was anything but promising. Kraigg Brathwaite showed it was possible to occupy the crease, even if runs did not come at a fast clip, but none of his top-order colleagues displayed the determination, technique or appetite required to resist a disciplined attack.

Mohammed Shami, returning to Test cricket after a knee injury had kept him out for a year, was excellent with new ball and old, picking up four wickets as West Indies stumbled to 243; they got that far only thanks to a maiden fifty from Dowrich (playing his third Test but keeping for the first time), who put on 69 for the eighth wicket with Holder. India led by 323, but Kohli resisted the temptation to bat, feeling his bowlers were fresh enough to get stuck in again. It meant West Indies followed on in a home Test for the first time in ten years.

The fast men had done the hard yards in the first innings, but spin came to the fore in the second. Ashwin ran amok with his perfectly flighted off-spin, but the West Indians seemed to have even less stomach for a battle, slipping to 132 for eight before Carlos Brathwaite and Bishoo showed some gumption. But it wasn't enough to deny India their first innings victory in the Caribbean, and their biggest win anywhere outside Asia. Ashwin finished with his fourth seven-for in Tests, but his first abroad – which, allied to his century, made the match award a simple task.

Man of the Match: R. Ashwin.

Close of play: first day, India 302-4 (Kohli 143, Ashwin 22); second day, West Indies 31-1 (K. C. Brathwaite 11, Bishoo 0); third day, West Indies 21-1 (Chandrika 9, Bravo 10).

India

M. Vijay c K. C. Brathwaite b Gabriel	7
S. Dhawan lbw b Bishoo	84
C. A. Pujara c K. C. Brathwaite b Bishoo	16
*V. Kohli b Gabriel	200
A. M. Rahane c Bravo b Bishoo	22
R. Ashwin c Gabriel b K. C. Brathwaite	113
†W. P. Saha st Dowrich b K. C. Brathwaite	40
A. Mishra c Holder b K. C. Brathwaite	53
Mohammed Shami not out	17
B 6, lb 2, nb 6	14
1/14 (1) 2/74 (3) 3/179 (2) 4/236 (5) 5/404 (4) 6/475 (7) 7/526 (6) 8/566 (8) (8 wkts dec, 161.5 overs)	566

U. T. Yadav and I. Sharma did not bat.

Gabriel 21–5–65–2; Holder 24–4–83–0; C. R. Brathwaite 25–5–80–0; Chase 34–3–102–0; Bishoo 43–1–163–3; K. C. Brathwaite 14.5–1–65–3.

West Indies

K. C. Brathwaite c Saha b Yadav	74	– lbw b Sharma	2
R. Chandrika c Saha b Mohammed Shami	16	– c Saha b Ashwin	31
D. Bishoo st Saha b Mishra	12	– (10) c Pujara b Ashwin	45
D. M. Bravo c Saha b Mohammed Shami	11	– (3) c Rahane b Yadav	10
M. N. Samuels c Saha b Mohammed Shami	1	– (4) b Ashwin	50
J. Blackwood c Rahane b Mohammed Shami	0	– (5) c Kohli b Ashwin	0
R. L. Chase c Kohli b Yadav	23	– (6) c sub (K. L. Rahul) b Ashwin	8
†S. O. Dowrich not out	57	– (7) lbw b Mishra	9
*J. O. Holder c Saha b Yadav	36	– (8) b Ashwin	16
C. R. Brathwaite b Yadav	0	– (9) not out	51
S. T. Gabriel b Mishra	2	– b Ashwin	4
B 4, lb 2, w 2, nb 3	11	Nb 5	5
1/30 (2) 2/68 (3) 3/90 (4) 4/92 (5) 5/92 (6) 6/139 (7) 7/144 (1) 8/213 (9) 9/213 (10) 10/243 (11) (90.2 overs)	243	1/2 (1) 2/21 (3) 3/88 (2) 4/92 (5) 5/101 (4) 6/106 (6) 7/120 (7) 8/132 (8) 9/227 (10) 10/231 (11) (78 overs)	231

Sharma 20–7–44–0; Yadav 18–8–41–4; Mohammed Shami 20–4–66–4; Ashwin 17–5–43–0; Mishra 15.2–4–43–2. *Second innings*—Sharma 11–2–27–1; Mohammed Shami 10–3–26–0; Yadav 13–4–34–1; Ashwin 25–8–83–7; Mishra 19–3–61–1.

Umpires: Aleem Dar and I. J. Gould. Third umpire: G. O. Brathwaite.
Referee: R. S. Madugalle.

ALL-ROUND GOOD GUYS

A century and a five-for in the same Test, for West Indies or India:

M. H. Mankad (184 and 5-196).......	India v England at Lord's..................	1952
D. S. Atkinson (219 and 5-56)........	West Indies v Australia at Bridgetown.......	1954-55
O. G. Smith (100 and 5-60)..........	West Indies v India at Delhi................	1959-60
P. R. Umrigar (172* and 5-107)......	India v West Indies at Port-of-Spain.........	1961-62
G. S. Sobers (104 and 5-63)..........	West Indies v India at Kingston.............	1961-62
G. S. Sobers (174 and 5-41)..........	West Indies v England at Leeds.............	1966
R. Ashwin (103 and 5-156)..........	India v West Indies at Mumbai..............	2011-12
R. Ashwin (113 and 7-83)..........	**India v West Indies at North Sound.......**	**2016**
R. L. Chase (137* and 5-121).......	**West Indies v India at Kingston...........**	**2016**

There have been 23 instances by players from other countries, five of them by I. T. Botham (England).

WEST INDIES v INDIA

Second Test Match

At Kingston, Jamaica, July 30–August 3, 2016. Drawn. Toss: West Indies. Test debut: M. L. Cummins.

When India arrived in Kingston, it seemed only the impending arrival of tropical storm Earl might derail them. The weather did interrupt after they claimed a lead of 304, but once the last session of the third day and most of the fourth were washed out, India were hit by a different sort of storm. Led by Roston Chase, in only his second Test, West Indies saved the game with panache, scoring 340 runs on the final day.

Things had looked more ominous for them at the start, when Holder won the toss and inexplicably decided to bat on a damp surface. West Indies were soon seven for three and, although Samuels and Blackwood applied themselves, adding 81 in 20 overs, the innings was done and dusted before tea for 196. Even that needed a feisty tenth-wicket stand between last man Gabriel and the debutant Miguel Cummins.

Fast bowler Cummins made little impression, though, and India were only 70 behind, for the loss of Dhawan, by the end of a hectic first day. They stretched their legs on the second, galloping into the lead with no further damage. Pujara and Kohli both fell in the forties, but Rahul and Rahane went on to sparkling centuries. Rahul, playing only because Murali Vijay hurt his thumb during the First Test, batted with confidence and freedom, and gambolled to 158. After he departed, Rahane – who, like Rahul, launched three sixes – put on 98 with Saha to help India declare at 500 after lunch on the third day. Chase's off-breaks brought him a maiden Test five-for, and he also ran out Pujara with a direct hit from square leg.

Now the weather took a hand. West Indies could not start their second innings that day, and faced only 15.5 overs on the fourth, when they contrived to lose four wickets. The final day dawned bright, and most expected India to wrap things up – but they reckoned without Chase, who batted for almost six hours, faced 269 deliveries, and became the first West Indian since Garry Sobers 50 years earlier to score a hundred and take a five-for in the same Test. After warming up with a stand of 93 with Blackwood, whose 63 came from 54 balls, Chase put on 144 for the sixth wicket with Dowrich, who worked the ball deftly into the gaps before an unfortunate lbw decision (he inside-edged Mishra) sent him on his way for a Test-best 74. Finally, Chase – the latest Test player to emerge from Combermere School in Barbados – joined his captain, Holder, in an unbroken alliance eventually worth 103, taking the hosts to Sabina Park's first draw in 16 Tests.

Man of the Match: R. L. Chase.

Close of play: first day, India 126-1 (Rahul 75, Pujara 18); second day, India 358-5 (Rahane 42, Saha 17); third day, India 500-9 dec; fourth day, West Indies 48-4 (Blackwood 3).

West Indies

K. C. Brathwaite c Pujara b Sharma	1	– c Rahul b Mishra	23
R. Chandrika c Rahul b Mohammed Shami	5	– b Sharma	1
D. M. Bravo c Kohli b Sharma	0	– c Rahul b Mohammed Shami	20
M. N. Samuels c Rahul b Ashwin	37	– b Mohammed Shami	0
J. Blackwood lbw b Ashwin	62	– c Pujara b Ashwin	63
R. L. Chase c Dhawan b Mohammed Shami	10	– not out	137
†S. O. Dowrich c Saha b Ashwin	5	– lbw b Mishra	74
*J. O. Holder c Rahul b Ashwin	13	– not out	64
D. Bishoo c Dhawan b Ashwin	12		
M. L. Cummins not out	24		
S. T. Gabriel c Kohli b Mishra	15		
W 2, nb 10	12	Lb 2, w 1, nb 3	6
1/4 (1) 2/4 (3) 3/7 (2) 4/88 (5) 5/115 (4) 6/127 (7) 7/131 (6) 8/151 (9) 9/158 (8) 10/196 (11) (52.3 overs)	196	1/5 (2) 2/41 (1) 3/41 (4) 4/48 (3) 5/141 (5) 6/285 (7) (6 wkts, 104 overs)	388

Sharma 10–1–53–2; Mohammed Shami 10–3–23–2; Ashwin 16–2–52–5; Yadav 6–1–30–0; Mishra 10.3–3–38–1. *Second innings*—Sharma 18–3–56–1; Mohammed Shami 19–3–82–2; Mishra 25–6–90–2; Yadav 12–2–44–0; Ashwin 30–4–114–1.

India

K. L. Rahul c Dowrich b Gabriel	158
S. Dhawan c Bravo b Chase	27
C. A. Pujara run out	46
*V. Kohli c Chandrika b Chase	44
A. M. Rahane not out	108
R. Ashwin lbw b Bishoo	3
†W. P. Saha lbw b Holder	47
A. Mishra c Chandrika b Chase	21
Mohammed Shami b Chase	0
U. T. Yadav c Holder b Chase	19
B 8, lb 3, w 6, nb 10	27
1/87 (2) 2/208 (3) 3/277 (1) 4/310 (4) 5/327 (6) 6/425 (7) 7/458 (8) 8/458 (9) 9/500 (10) (9 wkts dec, 171.1 overs)	500

I. Sharma did not bat.

Gabriel 28–8–62–1; Cummins 26.4–4–87–0; Holder 34.2–12–72–1; Chase 36.1–4–121–5; Bishoo 35–5–107–1; Brathwaite 11–0–40–0.

Umpires: Aleem Dar and I. J. Gould. Third umpire: N. Duguid.
Referee: R. S. Madugalle.

WEST INDIES v INDIA

Third Test Match

At Gros Islet, St Lucia, August 9–13, 2016. India won by 237 runs. Toss: West Indies. Test debut: A. S. Joseph.

India had never previously won two Tests in a series in the Caribbean, and had been shaken by West Indies' rearguard at Sabina Park. But things returned to script in St Lucia, where another big first innings set up a series-clinching triumph. India's start was less certain, though. They had made two surprising decisions, preferring Dhawan and Rohit Sharma to Murali Vijay, who was fit again, and Cheteshwar Pujara. Neither reached double figures as Gabriel and the lively 19-year-old debutant Alzarri Joseph struck quickly. Rahul made a defiant 50 but, when Rahane fell for 35, West Indies were on top at 126 for five.

Ashwin changed all that, in partnership with Saha. They batted cautiously for the rest of the first day and half the next, eventually adding 213, India's best for the sixth wicket against West Indies, beating 170 by Sunil Gavaskar and Ravi Shastri at Madras in 1983-84. It was Ashwin's fourth Test century – all against West Indies – but Saha's first, in 14 matches spread over six years; it seemed to cement his place as M. S. Dhoni's successor as India's Test keeper.

The last five wickets tumbled for 14, both Joseph and Cummins finishing with three, and West Indies began well enough, reaching 107 for one by the end of the second day, before rain obliterated the third. When play resumed, Ashwin removed Brathwaite after more than four hours, but at 202 for three a draw looked likely – before West Indies outdid India's collapse with an even more calamitous effort. Bhuvneshwar Kumar, in his first Test for 19 months, got the ball swinging after lunch, and blew away the middle order, as seven wickets tumbled for 23.

From nowhere, India had a lead of 128, and more than doubled that by stumps, with Rahane and Rohit Sharma going well. After 60 runs in nine overs on the final morning – Cummins ending with six of the seven wickets to fall – Kohli declared for the third Test in a row, setting West Indies 346 in 79 overs. They never got close. Mohammed Shami started the rot, removing Johnson for a duck, and three balls later Kumar trapped Brathwaite. Darren Bravo resisted for three hours, but West Indies were bundled out in less than 48 overs.

Man of the Match: R. Ashwin.

Close of play: first day, India 234-5 (Ashwin 75, Saha 46); second day, West Indies 107-1 (Brathwaite 53, Bravo 18); third day, no play; fourth day, India 157-3 (Rahane 51, R. G. Sharma 41).

India

K. L. Rahul c Brathwaite b Chase	50	– c Brathwaite b Cummins	28
S. Dhawan c Dowrich b Gabriel	1	– lbw b Chase	26
*V. Kohli c Bravo b Joseph	3	– lbw b Cummins	4
A. M. Rahane b Chase	35	– not out	78
R. G. Sharma c Dowrich b Joseph	9	– lbw b Cummins	41
R. Ashwin c Blackwood b Cummins	118	– (8) c Brathwaite b Cummins	1
†W. P. Saha c Dowrich b Joseph	104	– (6) c Dowrich b Cummins	14
R. A. Jadeja c Dowrich b Cummins	6	– (7) c Samuels b Cummins	16
Bhuvneshwar Kumar c Johnson b Gabriel	0		
Mohammed Shami not out	0		
I. Sharma c Johnson b Cummins	0		
B 7, lb 8, w 2, nb 10	27	B 1, lb 2, nb 6	9
1/9 (2) 2/19 (3) 3/77 (1) 4/87 (5) 5/126 (4) 6/339 (7) 7/351 (8) 8/353 (9) 9/353 (6) 10/353 (11) (129.4 overs)	353	1/49 (1) 2/58 (3) 3/72 (2) 4/157 (5) 5/181 (6) 6/213 (7) 7/217 (8) (7 wkts dec, 48 overs)	217

Gabriel 23–4–84–2; Joseph 24–6–69–3; Cummins 21.4–8–54–3; Holder 19–7–34–0; Chase 33–9–70–2; Brathwaite 9–1–27–0. *Second innings*—Gabriel 3–0–19–0; Joseph 4–0–23–0; Cummins 11–1–48–6; Holder 9–1–50–0; Chase 11–1–41–1; Brathwaite 10–1–33–0.

West Indies

K. C. Brathwaite c Saha b Ashwin	64	– lbw b Bhuvneshwar Kumar	4
L. R. Johnson run out	23	– c R. G. Sharma b Mohammed Shami	0
D. M. Bravo c Jadeja b I. Sharma	29	– c R. G. Sharma b Mohammed Shami	59
M. N. Samuels b Bhuvneshwar Kumar	48	– b I. Sharma	12
J. Blackwood c Kohli b Bhuvneshwar Kumar	20	– (6) st Saha b Jadeja	1
R. L. Chase c Rahane b Jadeja	2	– (5) b I. Sharma	10
†S. O. Dowrich c Dhawan b Bhuvneshwar Kumar	18	– c Kohli b Mohammed Shami	5
*J. O. Holder lbw b Bhuvneshwar Kumar	2	– run out	1
A. S. Joseph c Rahul b Bhuvneshwar Kumar	0	– c Mohammed Shami b Ashwin	0
M. L. Cummins c Saha b Ashwin	0	– not out	2
S. T. Gabriel not out	0	– c Bhuvneshwar Kumar b Jadeja	11
B 13, lb 2, w 2, nb 2	19	Lb 2, nb 1	3
1/59 (2) 2/129 (3) 3/135 (1) 4/202 (5) 5/203 (4) 6/205 (6) 7/212 (8) 8/212 (9) 9/221 (10) 10/225 (7) (103.4 overs)	225	1/4 (2) 2/4 (1) 3/35 (4) 4/64 (5) 5/68 (6) 6/84 (7) 7/88 (8) 8/95 (3) 9/95 (9) 10/108 (11) (47.3 overs)	108

Bhuvneshwar Kumar 23.4–10–33–5; Mohammed Shami 17–3–58–0; Ashwin 26–7–52–2; I. Sharma 13–2–40–1; Jadeja 24–9–27–1. *Second innings*—Bhuvneshwar Kumar 12–6–13–1; Mohammed Shami 11–2–15–3; I. Sharma 7–0–30–2; Ashwin 12–2–28–1; Jadeja 5.3–1–20–2.

Umpires: N. J. Llong and R. J. Tucker. Third umpire: G. O. Brathwaite.
Referee: R. S. Madugalle.

WEST INDIES v INDIA

Fourth Test Match

At Port-of-Spain, Trinidad, August 18–22, 2016. Drawn. Toss: West Indies.

A match supposed to celebrate 125 years of the Queen's Park Cricket Club descended into embarrassment for both them and the West Indian board when only 22 overs were possible, all on the first day. A sharp shower had sent the players off and – with the groundstaff slow bringing on the covers – parts of the outfield were soaked. Then a clogged drain at one end of the ground prevented water from seeping away, even after a day of bright sunshine. To make matters worse, no Super Sopper was available.

Although it was the rainy season in Trinidad – a time when no Test had been attempted before – it should have been possible to get some play. Instead, the second day was called off, after which the Indians did not even bother turning up, relying on periodic updates from the umpires, who finally put everyone out of their misery at 9.30 on the fifth morning. The referee, Ranjan Madugalle, criticised the ground management as "poor", and the ICC later issued an official warning (jointly with Durban, which staged a similarly soggy Test at almost the same time).

India had to settle for a series win – their sixth in succession over West Indies – but were unhappy at not being able to push for a third victory, which would have taken them top of the Test rankings. Instead, Pakistan grabbed the No. 1 spot, before India overhauled them with victory at home against New Zealand.

Ashwin, who took one of the two wickets to fall, was deprived of the chance of equalling the Australian leg-spinner Clarrie Grimmett's record of reaching 200 in 36 Tests, ending this match with 193. He had to be content with his sixth Man of the Series award, beating the Indian record held (from many more matches) by Virender Sehwag and Sachin Tendulkar.

Man of the Series: R. Ashwin.

Close of play: first day, West Indies 62-2 (Brathwaite 32, Samuels 4); second day, no play; third day, no play; fourth day, no play.

West Indies

K. C. Brathwaite not out	32
L. R. Johnson c R. G. Sharma b I. Sharma .	9
D. M. Bravo b Ashwin	10
M. N. Samuels not out.	4
Lb 6, nb 1	7
1/31 (2) 2/48 (3) (2 wkts, 22 overs)	62

J. Blackwood, R. L. Chase, †S. O. Dowrich, *J. O. Holder, D. Bishoo, M. L. Cummins and S. T. Gabriel did not bat.

Bhuvneshwar Kumar 6–1–13–0; Mohammed Shami 6–2–14–0; I. Sharma 5–3–7–1; Ashwin 5–1–22–1.

India

M. Vijay, K. L. Rahul, C. A. Pujara, *V. Kohli, A. M. Rahane, R. G. Sharma, R. Ashwin, †W. P. Saha, Bhuvneshwar Kumar, Mohammed Shami, I. Sharma.

Umpires: N. J. Llong and R. J. Tucker. Third umpire: N. Duguid.
Referee: R. S. Madugalle.

TWENTY20 INTERNATIONAL REPORTS BY PETER DELLA PENNA

WEST INDIES v INDIA

First Twenty20 International

At Lauderhill, Florida, August 27, 2016. West Indies won by one run. Toss: India.

India may have won the Test series, but World Twenty20 champions West Indies were the favourites when two rather different teams convened in the unfamiliar surroundings of Florida. Most of West Indies' short-format specialists returned and, although Chris Gayle pulled out on the morning of the match with a recurrence of a back injury, the batting was nonetheless led by a hard-hitting left-hander: Evin Lewis, a 25-year-old Trinidadian, spanked a 48-ball century, which included nine sixes. He took advantage of a strong wind blowing across the Central Broward ground, as his opening stand with the equally explosive Charles piled up 126 in 9.3 overs. When 200 came up in the 16th, a record total was on the cards – but three wickets fell in Bumrah's final over of the innings. Still, 245 was the third-highest in T20 internationals at the time (Australia hit a record 263 less than a fortnight later). Yet India came within a whisker in front of an appreciative crowd made up largely of expats. After two early wickets, Rahul cracked a maiden T20 century, completing his set in all three international formats in just 15 games. His stand of 89 with Sharma set India on course, then a hundred partnership with Dhoni left eight required from the last over. But Dwayne Bravo was equal to the task. Dhoni needed two from the final delivery – but sliced to third man, where Samuels (who had dropped a sitter from the first ball of the over) held on. West Indies had won by the odd run in 489 – an international record, beating 467 by South Africa and West Indies at Johannesburg in January 2015.

Man of the Match: E. Lewis.

West Indies

		B	4/6
1 J. Charles *b 10*	79	33	6/7
2 E. Lewis *c 8 b 6*	100	49	5/9
3 A. D. Russell *lbw b 6*	22	12	1/2
4 K. A. Pollard *b 11*	22	15	0/2
5 *C. R. Brathwaite *run out*	14	10	1/1
6 D. J. Bravo *not out*	1	1	0
7 L. M. P. Simmons *b 11*	0	1	0
8 M. N. Samuels *not out*	1	1	0
W 4, nb 2	6		
6 overs: 78-0 (20 overs)	245-6		

1/126 2/204 3/205 4/236 5/244 6/244

9 †A. D. S. Fletcher, 10 S. P. Narine and 11 S. Badree did not bat.

Mohammed Shami 4–5–48–1; Bhuvneshwar Kumar 4–7–43–0; Bumrah 4–7–47–2; Ashwin 4–10–36–0; Jadeja 3–6–39–2; Binny 1–0–32–0.

India

		B	4/6
1 R. G. Sharma *c 1 b 4*	62	28	4/4
2 A. M. Rahane *c 6 b 3*	7	7	1
3 V. Kohli *c 9 b 6*	16	9	3
4 K. L. Rahul *not out*	110	51	12/5
5 *†M. S. Dhoni *c 8 b 6*	43	25	2/2
Lb 2, w 4	6		
6 overs: 67-2 (20 overs)	244-4		

1/31 2/48 3/137 4/244

6 R. A. Jadeja, 7 S. T. R. Binny, 8 R. Ashwin, 9 Bhuvneshwar Kumar, 10 Mohammed Shami and 11 J. J. Bumrah did not bat.

Russell 4–6–53–1; Badree 2–3–25–0; Bravo 4–5–37–2; Narine 3–4–50–0; Brathwaite 4–3–47–0; Pollard 3–4–30–1.

Umpires: N. Duguid and J. S. Wilson. Third umpire: L. S. Reifer.
Referee: R. S. Madugalle.

WEST INDIES v INDIA

Second Twenty20 International

At Lauderhill, Florida, August 28, 2016. No result. Toss: India.

The ground was bathed in sunshine at 10am, but the start was held up for 40 minutes as the satellite feed – essential for the voracious primetime audience in India – was not working. The hold-up probably cost their side victory. They had knocked West Indies over for 143, spinners Ashwin and Mishra sharing five for 35 after some intelligent full bowling from the seamers nullified the stiff crosswind exploited by the batsmen in the first match. But a brief thunderstorm drove the players off two overs into the reply, and inadequate covers and poor drainage prevented a resumption. Had the match begun on time India would have received the five overs necessary for a result. It was all rather confusing for the American audience – and embarrassing for the organisers, who had earlier kept a sizeable crowd in the dark about the delayed start. Dhoni, for one, thought the match should have resumed: "Frankly, I've played under worse conditions."

West Indies

		B	*4/6*
1 J. Charles *c 2 b 9*	43	25	5/2
2 E. Lewis *c 9 b 10*	7	6	1
3 M. N. Samuels *c 5 b 11*	5	10	0
4 L. M. P. Simmons *st 5 b 7*	19	19	3
5 †A. D. S. Fletcher *b 11*	3	9	0
6 K. A. Pollard *lbw b 7*	13	8	1/1
7 A. D. Russell *c 3 b 8*	13	15	0/1
8 D. J. Bravo *b 9*	3	6	0
9 *C. R. Brathwaite *b 9*	18	10	2/1
10 S. P. Narine *not out*	9	7	0/1
11 S. Badree *b 10*	1	4	0
Lb 4, w 4, nb 1	9		
6 overs: 54-2 (19.4 overs)	143		

1/24 2/50 3/76 4/76 5/92 6/98 7/111 8/123 9/133

Bhuvneshwar Kumar 4–11–36–1; Mohammed Shami 2.4–5–31–2; Mishra 4–12–24–3; Jadeja 2–7–11–0; Ashwin 3–8–11–2; Bumrah 4–13–26–2.

India

		B	*4/6*
1 R. G. Sharma *not out*	10	8	0/1
2 A. M. Rahane *not out*	4	4	0
B 1	1		
(2 overs)	15-0		

3 V. Kohli, 4 K. L. Rahul, 5 *†M. S. Dhoni, 6 R. A. Jadeja, 7 R. Ashwin, 8 Bhuvneshwar Kumar, 9 A. Mishra, 10 Mohammed Shami and 11 J. J. Bumrah did not bat.

Russell 1–4–7–0; Badree 1–1–7–0.

Umpires: L. S. Reifer and J. S. Wilson. Third umpire: N. Duguid.
Referee: R. S. Madugalle.

DOMESTIC CRICKET IN THE WEST INDIES IN 2015-16

HAYDN GILL

On the face of it, the second season of the WICB Professional Cricket League looked rather like the first. Although it was designed to raise standards, the batting statistics remained poor, and failed to allay concerns over a general decline. But there was also evidence that the new system – six franchises drawing on a pool of 90 players contracted on a year-round basis – was beginning to bear fruit. A handful performed outstandingly to earn international selection, and others suggested their turn was just around the corner.

For the second year running, **Guyana** became champions after winning eight of their ten games, during a battle for the title with **Barbados** in which the other four sides never competed. The previous season, Windward Islands had been close behind Barbados; this time, there was a 57-point chasm between second and third. Even more worrying was the fact that, from the 30 matches, there were 25 outright results, the same as the previous year. No team ever reached 500; there were only eight totals of 400 or more (up from six), 33 under 200 (down from 35), and an identical 26 centuries. At least in 2014-15 there had been one double-hundred and three double-century stands; this time, there was none of either.

Some, however, made the most of their opportunities – notably Roston Chase, a tall 23-year-old batting all-rounder, who followed his 534 runs for Barbados the previous season with 710 at 59, plus 23 wickets with his handy off-spin. Selected for West Indies' home series against India, he scored a match-saving unbeaten 137 in his second Test. His team-mate Shai Hope, who had broken into the Test side a year earlier, headed the averages with 538 at 67. Two Guyanese batsmen also attracted attention. Their captain, Leon Johnson, was the season's leading scorer, earning a Test recall with 807 at 57; fellow left-hander Vishaul Singh batted solidly to accumulate 712 at 50, making his case to be next in line.

In another season dominated by spinners, 20-year-old slow left-armer Gudakesh Motie emerged to grab 40 wickets at 13 in his seven matches for Guyana, while Jon-Russ Jaggesar, a year younger, claimed 23 in five for Trinidad & Tobago. Miguel Cummins of Barbados was the only fast bowler to feature in the top ten of the wicket-takers' list: his 33 at 20 apiece led to a Test debut and a brief stint with Worcestershire. Another fast bowler, 19-year-old Antiguan Alzarri Joseph, was the spearhead of the West Indies team that won the Under-19 World Cup in February; either side of that tournament, he appeared for Leeward Islands, capturing 24 wickets at 21, and within six months graduated from the youth team to the senior West Indies ranks.

Despite Joseph's efforts, and 48 wickets from well-built off-spinner Rahkeem Cornwall, **Leeward Islands** had a dreadful season – bottom of the league for the second year running and bottom of their group in the Nagico Super50 tournament, while their Twenty20 representatives, the St Kitts & Nevis Patriots, were bottom of the T20 Caribbean Premier League. **Windward Islands** went out in the knockout stages of both limited-overs competitions.

Jamaica were the best of the also-rans in the Professional Cricket League, where left-arm spinner Nikita Miller was the leading wicket-taker with 65. As Jamaica Tallawahs, they became the first team to lift the CPL trophy twice, dismissing Guyana Amazon Warriors cheaply in the final, before Chris Gayle struck a rapid fifty.

Earlier, **Trinidad & Tobago** retained the Super50 title, comfortably defeating Barbados on home turf (all matches were played in Trinidad, Tobago or St Kitts). Each side played six zonal games, up from three, and an ICC Americas team (drawn primarily from the USA and Canada) replaced West Indies Under-19, but – like them – never won.

FIRST-CLASS AVERAGES, 2015-16

BATTING (300 runs, average 20.00)

	M	*I*	*NO*	*R*	*HS*	*100*	*Avge*	*Ct/St*
S. D. Hope (*Barbados*)	6	9	1	538	162	2	67.25	9
K. C. Brathwaite (*Barbados*)	7	12	1	676	123	3	61.45	9
R. L. Chase (*Barbados*)	10	16	4	710	136*	1	59.16	4
†L. R. Johnson (*Guyana*)	10	17	3	807	111*	2	57.64	17
†V. A. Singh (*Guyana*)	10	16	2	712	150	3	50.85	4
M. V. Hodge (*Leeward Islands*)	5	9	1	401	149*	1	50.12	5
†E. Lewis (*Trinidad & Tobago*)	5	9	0	442	104	1	49.11	8
†D. S. Smith (*Windward Islands*)	8	15	0	719	127	2	47.93	15
J. N. Hamilton (*Leeward Islands*)	7	13	2	442	130*	1	40.18	20
†J. L. Carter (*Barbados*)	7	11	1	396	100*	1	39.60	17
D. C. Thomas (*Jamaica*)	6	11	1	373	122	1	37.30	5
S. S. J. Brooks (*Barbados*)	10	16	1	534	111	1	35.60	6
†N. Deonarine (*Trinidad & Tobago*)	9	15	1	494	91*	0	35.28	10
K. A. Hope (*Trinidad & Tobago*)	10	18	2	553	77	0	34.56	6
N. E. Bonner (*Leeward Islands*)	7	14	1	449	89	0	34.53	4
†J. D. Campbell (*Jamaica*)	10	20	2	583	135	1	32.38	6
R. Chandrika (*Guyana*)	7	12	0	371	146	1	30.91	1
†T. Chanderpaul (*Guyana*)	6	11	0	327	81	0	29.72	12
K. Y. G. Ottley (*Trinidad & Tobago*)	10	16	2	404	99*	0	28.85	11
†Y. Cariah (*Trinidad & Tobago*)	9	15	2	374	70	0	28.76	6
A. M. McCarthy (*Jamaica*)	10	19	0	520	121	1	27.36	15
T. Theophile (*Windward Islands*)	10	19	2	453	83*	0	26.64	16
S. Katwaroo (*Trinidad & Tobago*)	10	15	0	357	71	0	23.80	19/5
K. A. Edwards (*Jamaica*)	8	15	0	346	93	0	23.06	2
O. Peters (*Leeward Islands*)	10	19	1	411	60	0	22.83	18
S. W. Ambris (*Windward Islands*)	10	18	2	348	89	0	21.75	17/1
I. Khan (*Trinidad & Tobago*)	10	15	1	304	82	0	21.71	3

BOWLING (15 wickets, average 30.00)

	Style	*O*	*M*	*R*	*W*	*BB*	*5I*	*Avge*
G. Motie (*Guyana*)	SLA	251	79	540	40	6-20	4	13.50
K. A. Stoute (*Barbados*)	RFM	200	64	421	26	4-12	0	16.19
N. O. Miller (*Jamaica*)	SLA	546.3	145	1,097	65	8-67	4	16.87
R. L. Chase (*Barbados*)	OB	178.5	57	397	23	5-27	2	17.26
J. A. Warrican (*Barbados*)	SLA	195.5	52	509	28	6-102	2	18.17
V. Permaul (*Guyana*)	SLA	351.4	116	751	40	5-25	4	18.77
S. J. Benn (*Barbados*)	SLA	138.2	34	360	19	6-55	1	18.94
M. Matthew (*Windward Islands*)	RFM	187.5	64	357	18	6-81	2	19.83
S. A. Jacobs (*Guyana*)	OB	167.4	43	380	19	4-35	0	20.00
M. L. Cummins (*Barbados*)	RF	247.1	74	683	33	5-47	1	20.69
A. S. Joseph (*Leeward Islands*)	RFM	141.3	22	504	24	7-46	2	21.00
K. R. Mayers (*Windward Islands*)	RM	133.5	38	373	17	5-83	1	21.94
J. L. Jaggesar (*Trinidad & Tobago*)	OB	191	37	518	23	8-58	1	22.52
R. R. S. Cornwall (*Leeward Islands*)	OB	432.2	121	1,085	48	7-131	5	22.60
S. Shillingford (*Windward Islands*)	OB	307.3	52	870	34	6-107	3	25.58
J. D. Campbell (*Jamaica*)	OB	180.2	28	527	20	7-73	2	26.35
L. A. S. Sebastien (*Windward Islands*)	OB	366	69	977	37	7-58	3	26.40
R. A. Reifer (*Guyana*)	LM	211.3	54	606	22	4-35	0	27.54
I. Khan (*Trinidad & Tobago*)	LBG	405.1	68	1,237	44	7-90	1	28.11
R. R. Emrit (*Trinidad & Tobago*)	RFM	163.1	49	459	16	3-44	0	28.68
D. K. Jacobs (*Jamaica*)	LBG	361.1	66	1,034	35	5-50	3	29.54
A. R. Nurse (*Barbados*)	OB	151	35	503	17	5-65	1	29.58

Averages do not include India's tour in July and August, 2016.

WICB PROFESSIONAL CRICKET LEAGUE, 2015-16

					Bonus points		
	Played	*Won*	*Lost*	*Drawn*	*Batting*	*Bowling*	*Points*
Guyana Jaguars	10	8	0	2	18	29	149
Barbados Pride	10	7	1	2	22	30	142
Jamaica Scorpions	10	4	6	0	11	26	85
Trinidad & Tobago Red Force	10	3	5	2	14	25	81
Windward Islands Volcanoes	10	2	6	2	12	22	64
Leeward Islands Hurricanes	10	1	7	2	7	25	50

Win = 12pts; draw = 3pts. Bonus points were awarded as follows for the first 110 overs of each team's first innings: one batting point for the first 200 runs and then for 250, 300, 350 and 400; one bowling point for the third wicket taken and then for the sixth and ninth.

At Bridgetown (Kensington Oval), Barbados, November 6–9, 2015. **Barbados won by ten wickets. Barbados 373** (K. C. Brathwaite 119) **and 4-0; ‡Jamaica 189 and 187.** *Barbados 17pts, Jamaica 1pt. Seamer Kevin Stoute had figures of 15–5–12–4 in Jamaica's first innings.*

At Providence, Guyana, November 6–9, 2015. **Guyana won by 104 runs. ‡Guyana 362** (R. Chandrika 146; S. Shillingford 6-107) **and 95** (S. Shillingford 5-36); **Windward Islands 228 and 125.** *Guyana 18pts, Windward Islands 3pts. Set up by Rajindra Chandrika's maiden century, Guyana won the opening match in their defence of the title, despite being bowled out for 95 in the second innings; Windwards off-spinner Shane Shillingford collected 11-143.*

At Basseterre, St Kitts, November 6–8, 2015. **Trinidad & Tobago won by an innings and 23 runs. Trinidad & Tobago 325; ‡Leeward Islands 118 and 184.** *Trinidad & Tobago 17pts, Leeward Islands 2pts. When Leewards followed on, No. 9 Gavin Tonge hit 41 in 18 balls, but could not make Trinidad & Tobago bat again.*

At Bridgetown (Kensington Oval), Barbados, November 13–16, 2015. **Drawn. ‡Barbados 300** (S. S. J. Brooks 111) **and 243-5 dec; Trinidad & Tobago 246 and 182-4.** *Barbados 8pts, Trinidad & Tobago 6pts.*

At Providence, Guyana, November 13–16, 2015. **Guyana won by an innings and 35 runs. Guyana 419-9 dec** (V. A. Singh 150; A. S. Joseph 5-99); **‡Leeward Islands 85** (G. Motie 6-20) **and 299** (G. Motie 5-85). *Guyana 17pts, Leeward Islands 2pts. After Vishaul Singh and the 41-year-old Shivnarine Chanderpaul boosted Guyana with 171 for the fourth wicket, there were five ducks in Leewards' first innings, and they followed on again, 334 behind. Slow left-armer Gudakesh Motie took 11-105 in his second first-class match.*

At Kingston, Jamaica, November 13–15, 2015. **Jamaica won by 30 runs. ‡Jamaica 259** (L. A. S. Sebastien 7-58) **and 128** (M. Matthew 5-31, S. Shillingford 5-57); **Windward Islands 212 and 145** (N. O. Miller 5-46). *Jamaica 17pts, Windward Islands 4pts. Jamaica collapsed to 25-7 in their second innings before Nikita Miller and Damion Jacobs added 76. Miller also finished with nine wickets after Windwards, who reached 126-4 chasing 176, lost their last six for 19.*

At Providence, Guyana, November 20–23, 2015. **Guyana won by nine wickets. ‡Guyana 337** (V. A. Singh 121) **and 43-1; Barbados 104 and 272** (G. Motie 6-79). *Guyana 18pts, Barbados 3pts. Vishaul completed his second successive century – and hit more runs than Barbados managed between them in their first innings, when Tino Best top-scored with 19 at No. 10. Motie took 9-98 in all, giving him 20 in two games.*

At Port-of-Spain, Trinidad, November 20–23, 2015. **Jamaica won by six wickets. ‡Trinidad & Tobago 271** (J. L. Solozano 110) **and 175** (J. D. Campbell 7-73); **Jamaica 291** (A. M. McCarthy 121; I. Khan 7-90) **and 156-4.** *Jamaica 16pts, Trinidad & Tobago 5pts.*

At Roseau, Dominica, November 20–21, 2015. **Windward Islands won by eight wickets. Leeward Islands 24-7 dec and 170** (L. A. S. Sebastien 5-76); **‡Windward Islands 140** (A. S. Joseph 7-46) **and 56-2.** *Windward Islands 14pts, Leeward Islands 3pts. Leeward Islands declared on 24-7 after 18.3 overs on the first morning, prompted by concerns over the state of the pitch. Alzarri Joseph took a career-best seven in 12 overs in Windwards' reply. The match finished inside two days and, at 128.3 overs, was the fourth-shortest first-class game in the West Indies.*

At Kingston, Jamaica, December 4–6, 2015. **Jamaica won by three wickets. ‡Leeward Islands 164** (S. S. Cottrell 5-38) **and 228; Jamaica 243 and 150-7** (R. R. S. Cornwall 5-39). *Jamaica 16pts, Leeward Islands 3pts. Jamaica's third successive victory.*

At Port-of-Spain, Trinidad, December 4–7, 2015. **Guyana won by an innings and 49 runs. ‡Trinidad & Tobago 210** (C. D. Barnwell 5-32) **and 216** (V. Permaul 5-62); **Guyana 475** (A. B. Fudadin 102). *Guyana 17pts, Trinidad & Tobago 2pts. Trinidad & Tobago's ninth-wicket pair, Marlon Richards and debutant Uthman Muhammad, scored 53 each and added 108, more than half their first innings. Guyana's 475 was the highest total of the season, and led to their fourth win.*

At St George's, Grenada, December 4–7, 2015. **Barbados won by 181 runs. ‡Barbados 296 and 261-7 dec; Windward Islands 179 and 197** (S. J. Benn 6-55). *Barbados 16pts, Windward Islands 2pts.*

At Bridgetown (Kensington Oval), Barbados, December 11–13, 2015. **Barbados won by ten wickets. Barbados 368** (R. L. Chase 136*) **and 1-0; ‡Leeward Islands 170** (A. R. Nurse 5-65) **and 198.** *Barbados 19pts, Leeward Islands 3pts. In Leewards' second innings, Tonge hit six sixes in a 17-ball 39 to make Barbados bat again. They needed a single to complete their second ten-wicket victory of the season, and Leewards' fifth successive defeat; it came from a Tonge no-ball.*

At Kingston, Jamaica, December 11–14, 2015. **Guyana won by 117 runs. Guyana 189** (N. O. Miller 6-46) **and 282; ‡Jamaica 146** (V. Permaul 5-25) **and 208** (G. Motie 6-33). *Guyana 15pts, Jamaica 3pts.*

At Gros Islet, St Lucia, December 11–14, 2015. **Drawn. Windward Islands 306 and 198-8; ‡Trinidad & Tobago 382.** *Windward Islands 6pts, Trinidad & Tobago 7pts. Yannick Otley was stranded on 99* in Trinidad & Tobago's innings.*

At North Sound, Antigua, February 11–14, 2016. **Leeward Islands won by 85 runs. Leeward Islands 155** (D. K. Jacobs 5-50) **and 368-8 dec** (J. N. Hamilton 130*); **‡Jamaica 158** (R. R. S. Cornwall 5-74) **and 280** (R. R. S. Cornwall 7-131). *Leeward Islands 15pts, Jamaica 3pts. Off-spinner Rahkeem Cornwall collected 12-205, the best match return of the season, to secure Leewards' only win. His team-mate Orlando Peters held seven catches, four of them off Cornwall.*

At Bridgetown (Kensington Oval), Barbados, February 12–15, 2016. **Barbados won by an innings and 56 runs. ‡Windward Islands 250** (M. L. Cummins 5-47) **and 144; Barbados 450-5 dec** (K. C. Brathwaite 117, S. D. Hope 162). *Barbados 19pts, Windward Islands 3pts. Keddy Lesporis was out handled the ball in Windwards' first innings. Shai Hope's 162 was the highest score of the season; he added 168 with Kraigg Brathwaite, to set up Barbados's third victory in a row.*

At Providence, Guyana, February 12–15, 2016. **Guyana won by 105 runs. ‡Guyana 237** (V. A. Singh 104*) **and 244-4 dec** (L. R. Johnson 111*); **Trinidad & Tobago 179** (V. Permaul 5-65) **and 197.** *Guyana 16pts, Trinidad & Tobago 3pts. Guyana's sixth win in six; they led the table by 19 points from Barbados.*

At Bridgetown (Kensington Oval), Barbados, February 19–22, 2016. **Drawn. ‡Barbados 274 and 320-4 dec** (S. D. Hope 114*, J. L. Carter 100*); **Guyana 190** (R. L. Chase 5-27) **and 252-7** (R. L. Chase 5-77). *Barbados 8pts, Guyana 6pts. Hope and Jonathan Carter, whose 100* came in 104 balls, added 161* for Barbados's fifth wicket to set a target of 405. Off-spinner Roston Chase finished with 10-104 in the match, and Guyana were seven down with 20 overs to go, but survived.*

At Kingston, Jamaica, February 19–22, 2016. **Trinidad & Tobago won by eight wickets. ‡Jamaica 225 and 155** (J. L. Jaggesar 8-58); **Trinidad & Tobago 206** (N. O. Miller 7-69) **and 178-2** (E. Lewis 104). *Trinidad & Tobago 16pts, Jamaica 4pts. Off-spinner Jon-Russ Jaggesar's 8-58 was the best return of the season; his 11-111 gave him 18 wickets in his first two first-class games.*

At Charlotte Amalie, St Thomas, US Virgin Islands, February 19–22, 2016. **Drawn. ‡Leeward Islands 327** (K. R. Mayers 5-83) **and 171-8; Windward Islands 389** (K. A. R. Hodge 105). *Leeward Islands 8pts, Windward Islands 9pts. Cornwall hit 97 in 95 balls, with ten fours and six sixes, in Leewards' first innings.*

At Kingston, Jamaica, February 26–28, 2016. **Barbados won by six wickets. ‡Jamaica 177** (J. P. Greaves 5-41) **and 157; Barbados 217** (N. O. Miller 8-67) **and 118-4.** *Barbados 16pts, Jamaica 3pts. Miller's 8-67 took him past 50 wickets in the season, and he finished with 10-105, but could not prevent a fourth successive defeat for Jamaica.*

At Couva, Trinidad, February 26–29, 2016. **Trinidad & Tobago won by nine wickets. Leeward Islands 225 and 287; ‡Trinidad & Tobago 406** (R. R. S. Cornwall 5-88) **and 111-1.** *Trinidad & Tobago 18pts, Leeward Islands 3pts.*

At Gros Islet, St Lucia, February 26–28, 2016. **Guyana won by six wickets. Windward Islands 216** (R. R. Beaton 5-43) **and 161; ‡Guyana 339** (L. R. Johnson 107; M. Matthew 6-81) **and 39-4.** *Guyana 18pts, Windward Islands 4pts.*

At North Sound, Antigua, March 11–14, 2016. **Drawn. ‡Leeward Islands 430** (M. V. Hodge 149*); **Guyana 190 and 222-8.** *Leeward Islands 9pts, Guyana 5pts. In his first game in the West Indies since being dropped by the national side in 2014 – and after a flirtation with baseball – Kieran Powell scored 55 in 54 balls opening for Leewards. Their wicketkeeper Jahmar Hamilton caught eight in the match, and Cornwall had second-innings figures of 40–25–34–3; following on 240 behind, Guyana were 186-8 before Chanderpaul, down the order because of injury, batted for an hour and a half to secure the draw.*

At Couva, Trinidad, March 11–14, 2016. **Barbados won by seven wickets. Barbados 396** (K. C. Brathwaite 123) **and 74-3; ‡Trinidad & Tobago 226 and 240** (J. A. Warrican 5-54). *Barbados 17pts, Trinidad & Tobago 3pts. While Guyana hung on for a draw in Antigua, second-placed Barbados's victory narrowed the gap to seven points; there was one round left.*

At Arnos Vale, St Vincent, March 11–14, 2016. **Jamaica won by nine wickets. ‡Jamaica 445** (J. D. Campbell 135, D. C. Thomas 122) **and 143-1; Windward Islands 233** (D. K. Jacobs 5-95) **and 350** (D. S. Smith 126; J. D. Campbell 5-106). *Jamaica 19pts, Windward Islands 2pts. Jamaica's Paul Palmer (82) and Devon Thomas shared the season's highest stand – 178 for the sixth wicket.*

At Providence, Guyana, March 18–20, 2016. **Guyana won by an innings and 55 runs. ‡Guyana 420** (S. O. Hetmyer 107; D. K. Jacobs 5-131); **Jamaica 231 and 134** (V. Permaul 5-36). *Guyana 19pts, Jamaica 3pts. Guyana made sure of the title with an innings victory. A maiden hundred for Shimron Hetmyer, who had just captained West Indies to the Under-19 World Cup, backed up by half-centuries from Chandrika and captain Leon Johnson – the season's leading scorer, with 807 – gave them plenty to bowl at. Slow left-armers Motie and Veerasammy Permaul worked through Jamaica's batting twice, with a day to spare.*

At Basseterre, St Kitts, March 18–20, 2016. **Barbados won by an innings and 93 runs. ‡Leeward Islands 119 and 224** (J. A. Warrican 6-102); **Barbados 436** (R. R. S. Cornwall 5-155). *Barbados 19pts, Leeward Islands 2pts. Barbados completed a third straight victory, in three days – but it was not enough to overtake Guyana.*

At Couva, Trinidad, March 18–21, 2016. **Windward Islands won by seven wickets. ‡Trinidad & Tobago 211 and 243** (L. A. S. Sebastien 5-63); **Windward Islands 289** (D. S. Smith 127) **and 169-3.** *Windward Islands 17pts, Trinidad & Tobago 4pts. Devon Smith, with his second successive century and sixth fifty in seven innings, and Tyrone Theophile (75) shared the largest opening partnership of the season – 163.*

REGIONAL CHAMPIONS

1965-66	Barbados	1980-81	Combined Islands	1996-97	Barbados
1966-67	Barbados	1981-82	Barbados	1997-98	Leeward Islands / Guyana
1967-68	No competition	1982-83	Guyana		
1968-69	Jamaica	1983-84	Barbados	1998-99	Barbados
1969-70	Trinidad	1984-85	Trinidad & Tobago	1999-2000	Jamaica
1970-71	Trinidad	1985-86	Barbados	2000-01	Barbados
1971-72	Barbados	1986-87	Guyana	2001-02	Jamaica
1972-73	Guyana	1987-88	Jamaica	2002-03	Barbados
1973-74	Barbados	1988-89	Jamaica	2003-04	Barbados
1974-75	Guyana	1989-90	Leeward Islands	2004-05	Jamaica
1975-76	Trinidad / Barbados	1990-91	Barbados	2005-06	Trinidad & Tobago
		1991-92	Jamaica	2006-07	Barbados
1976-77	Barbados	1992-93	Guyana	2007-08	Jamaica
1977-78	Barbados	1993-94	Leeward Islands	2008-09	Jamaica
1978-79	Barbados	1994-95	Barbados	2009-10	Jamaica
1979-80	Barbados	1995-96	Leeward Islands	2010-11	Jamaica

2011-12	Jamaica	2013-14	Barbados	2015-16	Guyana
2012-13	Barbados	2014-15	Guyana		

Barbados have won the title outright 21 times, Jamaica 12, Guyana 7, Trinidad/Trinidad & Tobago 4, Leeward Islands 3, Combined Islands 1. Barbados, Guyana, Leeward Islands and Trinidad have also shared the title.

The tournament was known as the Shell Shield from 1965-66 to 1986-87, the Red Stripe Cup from 1987-88 to 1996-97, the President's Cup in 1997-98, the Busta Cup from 1998-99 to 2001-02, the Carib Beer Cup from 2002-03 to 2007-08, the Headley–Weekes Trophy from 2008-09 to 2012-13, the President's Trophy in 2013-14, and the WICB Professional Cricket League from 2014-15.

NAGICO REGIONAL SUPER50, 2015-16

50-over league plus knockout

Zone A	*P*	*W*	*L*	*A*	*Pts*
TRINIDAD & TOBAGO	6	4	1	1	22
BARBADOS	6	4	2	0	18
Jamaica	6	3	3	0	14
ICC Americas	6	0	5	1	2

Zone B	*P*	*W*	*L*	*NR*	*Pts*
WINDWARD ISLANDS	6	4	1	1	18
GUYANA	6	4	2	0	18
Campus/Colleges	6	1	3	2	9
Leeward Islands	6	1	4	1	6

Semi-final At Port-of-Spain, Trinidad, January 20, 2016 (day/night). **Trinidad & Tobago won by 54 runs. Trinidad & Tobago 259-9** (50 overs); ‡**Guyana 205** (48.3 overs). *MoM:* D. M. Bravo (T&T). *Darren Bravo hit 95, including five sixes.*

Semi-final At Port-of-Spain, Trinidad, January 21, 2016 (day/night). **Barbados won by seven wickets.** ‡**Windward Islands 175** (45.4 overs); **Barbados 179-3** (44.3 overs). *MoM:* S. J. Benn (Barbados). *Sulieman Benn reduced Windwards to 95-5, collecting 4-26, and Kraigg Brathwaite booked Barbados's place in the final with 80*.*

Final At Port-of-Spain, Trinidad, January 23, 2016 (day/night). **Trinidad & Tobago won by 72 runs. Trinidad & Tobago 270-7** (50 overs); ‡**Barbados 198** (42.5 overs). *MoM:* D. M. Bravo (T&T). *Bravo now scored 97, falling in the 49th over – and finished the tournament with 274 in just three games. Trinidad & Tobago's third successive final produced their second successive title.*

CARIBBEAN PREMIER LEAGUE, 2016

20-over league plus knockout

	Played	*Won*	*Lost*	*NR/A*	*Points*	*Net run-rate*
GUYANA AMAZON WARRIORS	10	7	3	0	14	0.12
JAMAICA TALLAWAHS	10	6	3	1	13	0.70
ST LUCIA ZOUKS	10	6	4	0	12	0.33
TRINBAGO KNIGHT RIDERS	10	5	5	0	10	–0.06
Barbados Tridents	10	3	6	1	7	–0.26
St Kitts & Nevis Patriots	10	2	8	0	4	–0.77

1st v 2nd At Basseterre, St Kitts, August 3, 2016 (floodlit). **Guyana Amazon Warriors won by four wickets. Jamaica Tallawahs 146-8** (20 overs); ‡**Guyana Amazon Warriors 150-6** (19.4 overs). *MoM:* Sohail Tanvir (Guyana). *Sohail Tanvir took 2-24 and hit 21* in 13 balls.*

3rd v 4th At Basseterre, St Kitts, August 4, 2016 (floodlit). **Trinbago Knight Riders won by five wickets. St Lucia Zouks 164-8** (20 overs); ‡**Trinbago Knight Riders 165-5** (18.3 overs). *MoM:* B. B. McCullum (Trinbago). *Brendon McCullum led the chase with 49* in 41 balls.*

Final play-off At Basseterre, St Kitts, August 5, 2016 (floodlit). **Jamaica Tallawahs won by 19 runs** (DLS). **Jamaica Tallawahs 195-7** (20 overs) (A. D. Russell 100); ‡**Trinbago Knight Riders 110-7** (12 overs). *MoM:* A. D. Russell (Jamaica). *Andre Russell smashed 11 sixes in a 44-ball 100. Trinbago's DLS target was 130 in 12 overs; from 67-1 they lost six for 36, three to Shakib Al Hasan.*

Final At Basseterre, St Kitts, August 7, 2016 (floodlit). **Jamaica Tallawahs won by nine wickets. Guyana Amazon Warriors 93** (16.1 overs); ‡**Jamaica Tallawahs 95-1** (12.5 overs). *MoM:* Imad Wasim (Jamaica). *MoS:* A. D. Russell. *Jamaica won their second CPL title, while Guyana's third final ended in a third defeat. Imad Wasim grabbed 3-21 as Guyana's last six fell for 23; Chris Gayle saw Jamaica most of the way home with 54 in 27 balls.*

ZIMBABWE CRICKET IN 2016

Time for a hot Streak

LIAM BRICKHILL

It was a year of recession for Zimbabwe. Amid a shrinking fixture list, their successes came mostly at the expense of lower-ranked teams, though a narrow Twenty20 victory over an inexperienced India at Harare in June was followed in November by a place in the final of the home tri-series at Bulawayo. Zimbabwe neither rose to triumph nor sank to ignominy, treading water throughout. Adopting austerity, they travelled less often, and began to look beyond the core of senior players who had carried them through much of the last decade.

They played four Tests in 2016, after none in 2015, but fewer internationals overall (27, compared with 42 the previous year). But they lost all four of those Tests, and what solace they could find was limited to Twenty20: a 2–2 draw in Bangladesh, edgy wins over Hong Kong and Scotland during the World T20

ZIMBABWE IN 2016

	Played	*Won*	*Lost*	*Drawn/No result*
Tests	4	–	4	–
One-day internationals	11	3	6	2
Twenty20 internationals	12	5	7	–

DECEMBER / JANUARY	5 ODIs and 2 T20Is (a) v Afghanistan (in UAE)	(see *Wisden 2016*, page 1194)
JANUARY	4 T20Is (a) v Bangladesh	(page 891)
FEBRUARY		
MARCH / APRIL	ICC World Twenty20 (in India)	(page 793)
MAY		
JUNE	3 ODIs and 3 T20Is (h) v India	(page 1109)
JULY / AUGUST	2 Tests (h) v New Zealand	(page 1112)
SEPTEMBER		
OCTOBER / NOVEMBER	2 Tests (h) v Sri Lanka	(page 1117)
NOVEMBER	Triangular ODI tournament (h) v SL and WI	(page 1122)
DECEMBER		

For a review of Zimbabwe domestic cricket from the 2015-16 season, see page 1125.

in India, then a two-run win over the Indians after Neville Madziva defended eight off the last over, with M. S. Dhoni on strike.

Their overall World T20 experience, however, when they were knocked out by Afghanistan – who earlier in the year had beaten them 3–2 in a one-day series in Sharjah – was offered by Zimbabwe Cricket chairman Tavengwa Mukuhlani as grounds for coach Dav Whatmore's dismissal in May. Yet the acrimonious nature of his parting suggested the troubles extended beyond the boundary. And many felt he had not been given a fair crack of the whip. Between his appointment at the end of 2014 and his sacking, Zimbabwe did not play a single Test; this lack of matches meant that, shortly before Whatmore went, the ICC announced they had temporarily lost their Test ranking. By the time Zimbabwe took on New Zealand at Bulawayo in July, they had gone a whopping 619 days without Test cricket. They were predictably rusty, losing that game by an innings and 117, and the second by 254 runs.

The ugliness around Whatmore's dismissal lent an extra layer of melancholy to Zimbabwe's abysmal one-day series defeat by India a month earlier, when they were bowled out three times while totalling just 417; India lost three wickets for 428 runs. Something had to change, and the chalice was handed to Heath Streak in September; former South African stars Makhaya Ntini and Lance Klusener completed the coaching staff. Streak's appointment came after former captain Tatenda Taibu had started his dual role as convenor of selectors and a development officer, and the new faces brought a fresh energy. In October, Zimbabwe rallied to take their two Tests against Sri Lanka into the fifth day, though both were lost by heavy margins; in November, a win and a tie against West Indies lifted them into the tri-series final, where the Sri Lankans won again.

But Zimbabwe's political and economic crises are likely to get worse before they get better. The country and its cricket team still need drastic change. Yet when the opportunity to lobby for a new direction in world cricket came up, with the tabling of a two-tier Test system, Zimbabwe voted against a proposition that would have brought greater context to their long-form fixtures. The board's managing director Wilfred Mukondiwa insisted their commitment to Test cricket remained "as unquestionable and as strong as ever", but the reality is that Tests are making less financial sense for Zimbabwe, and the trend is likely to continue. Survival is all that counts, and that depends on qualification for the 2019 World Cup. Limited-overs cricket and short tours will provide Zimbabwe's subsistence for the foreseeable future.

That future seems as uncertain as ever under Streak and captain Graeme Cremer, yet there were some grounds for hope, and Zimbabwe's year was bookended by two unlikely comebacks. In their first match of 2016, they recovered from 49 for seven to beat Afghanistan, while in late November they fought back from 89 for seven to overcome West Indies under rainy Matabeleland skies. Amid ups and downs, smiles and frowns, matches such as these were a reminder of the character Zimbabwe's cricketers can draw on when the mood takes them.

ZIMBABWE v INDIA IN 2016

NEIL MANTHORP

One-day internationals (3): Zimbabwe 0, India 3
Twenty20 internationals (3): Zimbabwe 1, India 2

For the past decade India had made several flying visits to Zimbabwe: this was their fourth since 2010. The aim was to keep the Zimbabwean administrators' noses just above the financial floodwater, in return for their loyal vote at ICC meetings, which had helped maintain the BCCI's grip on the game's global affairs.

But changes at the ICC removed that dynamic – this was the last of the quid pro quo tours, with no further visit scheduled for another three years – so the Indian board sought a better, more sensible objective for six essentially meaningless games. All but one of India's most senior cricketers were rested, and the squad assembled almost entirely from those who had excelled in the IPL, in order to broaden the base of players, particularly fast bowlers, with international experience. Meanwhile, a Test was replaced by three Twenty20 internationals.

The result was 16 limited-overs specialists – only K. L. Rahul had been selected for the Test series which followed in the Caribbean – but the biggest surprise was M. S. Dhoni's decision to make himself available to lead the next generation. The news delighted Zimbabwean Indians, whose small but vocal community chanted his name and called for selfies at every opportunity. It was a happy squad (once they had moved from their original hotel into Harare's best).

Only Zimbabwe's interim coach, the former South African pace bowler Makhaya Ntini, was upset by the arrival of an A-team. "If you send us a team that is not your strongest team, we're going to put them under the carpet," he said. Ntini had been promoted to head coach when Dav Whatmore was sacked at the end of May, while Graeme Cremer replaced Hamilton Masakadza, who had lasted just four months as captain.

But apart from the dreamlike win in the first T20 international, it was Zimbabwe who were swept aside. They were so dire in the one-day internationals that they claimed only three wickets across the three games – Indian seamer Jasprit Bumrah alone took nine – and their highest total was just 168, compared with 170 in the T20 victory. Only half India's squad were required to bat more than once but, of those who did, opener Rahul was the undoubted star, with 265 runs at 88 during the two series.

INDIAN TOURING PARTY

*M. S. Dhoni, J. J. Bumrah, Y. S. Chahal, R. Dhawan, F. Y. Fazal, K. M. Jadhav, D. S. Kulkarni, Mandeep Singh, K. K. Nair, M. K. Pandey, A. R. Patel, K. L. Rahul, A. T. Rayudu, B. B. Sran, J. D. Unadkat, J. Yadav. *Coach:* S. B. Bangar.

First one-day international At Harare, June 11, 2016. **India won by nine wickets. Zimbabwe 168** (49.5 overs) (E. Chigumbura 41; J. J. Bumrah 4-28); ‡**India 173-1** (42.3 overs) (K. L. Rahul 100*, A. T. Rayudu 62*). *MoM:* K. L. Rahul. *ODI debuts:* Y. S. Chahal, K. K. Nair, K. L. Rahul (India). *Rahul became the first Indian to score a century on ODI debut, though he cut things fine. On a slow, low surface, Ambati Rayudu was often becalmed in their stand of 162*, but less so Rahul. After accumulating just seven fours in a slick innings, he was on 94, with India needing two for victory. Rahul saw his chance: taking half a step down the wicket, he launched Hamilton Masakadza's gentle medium-pace on to the players' balcony at long-on. Earlier, Jasprit Bumrah deserved his career-best 4-28, while slow left-armer Axar Patel and leg-spinner Yuzvendra Chahal strangled the middle order, though Zimbabwe's batsmen were as careless as their bowlers were toothless. Craig Ervine and Sikandar Raza settled briefly before gifting their wickets, leaving Elton Chigumbura to prop up the tail.*

Second one-day international At Harare, June 13, 2016. **India won by eight wickets. Zimbabwe 126** (34.3 overs) (V. Sibanda 53; Y. S. Chahal 3-25); ‡**India 129-2** (26.5 overs) (K. L. Rahul 33, K. K. Nair 39, A. T. Rayudu 41*). *MoM:* Y. S. Chahal. *Zimbabwe's chances were even worse than usual when they were reduced to ten men: all-rounder Sean Williams hurt his hand during catching practice after the toss and took no part. Still, at 106-3 after 25 overs, a respectable score beckoned. Vusi Sibanda had struck the ball as crisply as ever during a neat fifty, adding 67 with Sikandar Raza; the field was spread and the pitch flat. Then both lobbed catches to long-on, with Chigumbura lbw in between; Chahal's leg-breaks had claimed three wickets in eight deliveries and, by the 35th over, Zimbabwe had lost their last six for 20. Chasing only 127, openers Rahul and Karun Nair were perhaps the victims of boredom against insipid bowling, but Rayudu's fluency grew, before Manish Pandey hit his only ball for four.*

Third one-day international At Harare, June 15, 2016. **India won by ten wickets.** ‡**Zimbabwe 123** (42.2 overs) (V. Sibanda 38; J. J. Bumrah 4-22); **India 126-0** (21.5 overs) (K. L. Rahul 63*, F. Y. Fazal 55*). *MoM:* K. L. Rahul. *MoS:* K. L. Rahul. *ODI debut:* F. Y. Fazal (India). *Zimbabwe saved the worst until last. Thanks largely to Chamu Chibhabha and Sibanda, they reached 104-3: then six wickets crashed for six in 24 balls, four of them to Bumrah, who improved on his career-best four days earlier. The unusual angles created by his upright, wide-of-the-crease style were too much for the batsmen; they were just as baffled by Patel's changes of pace (rather than any appreciable turn) as he conceded just 16 off ten overs. Rahul, who keeps wicket for his IPL team, held a couple of sharp chances at slip, and Dhawal Kulkarni made a direct-hit run-out off his own bowling. India coasted home inside 22 overs. Faiz Fazal scored an efficient 55* on international debut, aged 30; the only tourist with no IPL contract, he had been called up from Durham's Hetton Lyons in the North East Premier League.*

First Twenty20 international At Harare, June 18, 2016. **Zimbabwe won by two runs. Zimbabwe 170-6** (20 overs) (M. N. Waller 30, E. Chigumbura 54*); ‡**India 168-6** (20 overs) (Mandeep Singh 31, M. K. Pandey 48). *MoM:* E. Chigumbura. *T20I debuts:* Y. S. Chahal, R. Dhawan, Mandeep Singh, K. L. Rahul, J. D. Unadkat (India). *Twenty20 may be unpredictable, but nobody gave Zimbabwe a chance after the one-day thrashings – still less when India wanted eight off the last over, with M. S. Dhoni at the crease. But he made a mess of it. Zimbabwe's 170 owed everything to Chigumbura, whose 26-ball 54* included seven sixes and a solitary four (the boundaries had been considerably shortened). Opening bowlers Jaydev Unadkat and Rishi Dhawan bowled poor lengths, conceding 85 in their eight overs – twice as many as Bumrah and Patel. Though Rahul was bowled first ball, Pandey seemed in full control until, needing 28 from 17, he drove to deep cover. Patel smashed two sixes and a four off his first eight deliveries, bringing it down to eight off six. But Neville Madziva produced the over of his life. Patel holed out to his second ball and, when Dhoni and Dhawan kept walking way outside off stump attempting to hit through leg, he matched them with wide yorkers, though one prompted an absurd call of wide by umpire Russell Tiffin. Dhoni needed four from the final delivery, but ran just one as his searing slap-drive went straight to deep backward point, triggering Zimbabwean delirium.*

Second Twenty20 international At Harare, June 20, 2016. **India won by ten wickets.** ‡**Zimbabwe 99-9** (20 overs) (P. J. Moor 31; B. B. Sran 4-10, J. J. Bumrah 3-11); **India 103-0** (13.1 overs) (K. L. Rahul 47*, Mandeep Singh 52*). *MoM:* B. B. Sran. *T20I debuts:* D. S. Kulkarni, B. B. Sran (India). *Normal service was resumed with another crushing, one-sided Indian victory. Left-armer Barinder Sran, who had begun his sporting career as a boxer, knocked the stuffing out of Zimbabwe's batting in an extraordinary opening spell of 3–13–9–4, including three wickets in his third over, from which there was no recovery. Bumrah was hardly less impressive with 3-11 from his four overs, and Peter Moor was the only batsman who could hold his head high. Sran's swing and Bumrah's bounce were* *beyond Zimbabwean ken. Chasing only 100, Rahul and Mandeep Singh were never remotely challenged, and completed India's first ten-wicket win in Twenty20 cricket with 41 balls to spare.*

Third Twenty20 international At Harare, June 22, 2016. **India won by three runs. India 138-6** (20 overs) (K. M. Jadhav 58; D. T. Tiripano 3-20); ‡**Zimbabwe 135-6** (20 overs). *MoM:* K. M. Jadhav. *MoS:* B. B. Sran. *Another awkwardly slow surface made timing difficult but produced a low-scoring thriller – which nearly led to a home series win. Chigumbura needed four off the final ball, from Sran, but was caught at cover off a wide full toss. Somehow Zimbabwe, nervously prodding and poking, seemed half a dozen runs behind the rate throughout the chase. Only when they required 32 from the final two overs did they show much urgency: Timycen Maruma hit Bumrah for six, then managed another in the final over. But Sran, defending 21, could afford to bowl a wide and a no-ball and concede 17. After Zimbabwe put India in, Kedar Jadhav's composed 58 from 42 balls offset the loss of three wickets in the first five overs.*

ZIMBABWE v NEW ZEALAND IN 2016

TELFORD VICE

Test matches (2): Zimbabwe 0, New Zealand 2

Imagine The Oval, the SCG, or the Wanderers being denied Test cricket for almost five years. And imagine the ground being besieged by political protesters and almost as many riot police. There you have a sense of the atmosphere at Bulawayo.

Arrests outside the gates during the first over of the Second Test were followed by more after the 36th, when sections of the crowd stood up, waved flags and sang the national anthem to lament the 36 years of Robert Mugabe's reign. Hunter S. Thompson would have revelled in the scene, but the fear and loathing clouded an otherwise bright morning for Zimbabwe's cricket-minded folk.

By then, New Zealand had romped to the First Test by an innings. It was Zimbabwe's tenth defeat in 12 since their previous Test in Bulawayo, including five games in Harare (bypassed this time because its political activism was even stronger). And yet the memory of their two victories, against Bangladesh and Pakistan in 2013, was cause for something close to hope: in their history, they had now won 11 Tests out of 98; two out of 12 suggested improvement.

That optimism told of what it is to be a Zimbabwe cricket fan, to magnify pinpricks of brightness in the gloom – the feisty 40, or the miserly five overs before tea – rather than trip the light fantastic. So, in these parts, they ignored the eventual series whitewash, and toasted the centuries by Sean Williams and Craig Ervine, one brave, the other stoic. And they marvelled at Graeme Cremer in his first Test series as captain.

New Zealand came from another world. While Zimbabwe had been subsisting on Test crumbs for five years, the New Zealanders had played 43 Tests, and won 14. That they added two more successes here surprised no one. They did have their own challenges: Kane Williamson was at the Test helm for the first time, steering his side into an uncertain future without Brendon McCullum and Daniel Vettori. But six centuries, including two each by Tom Latham and Ross Taylor, bristling pace bowling epitomised by Neil Wagner, and even an off-spinning cameo by Martin Guptill told of a team continuing their rise."When you replace the likes of Dan and Brendon, you don't expect the same output straightaway," said Mike Hesson, their New Zealand coach. But, sometimes, you get it anyway.

NEW ZEALAND TOURING PARTY

*K. S. Williamson, T. A. Boult, D. A. J. Bracewell, M. D. Craig, M. J. Guptill, M. J. Henry, T. W. M. Latham, H. M. Nicholls, J. A. Raval, L. Ronchi, M. J. Santner, I. S. Sodhi, T. G. Southee, L. R. P. L. Taylor, N. Wagner, B-J. Watling. *Coach:* M. J. Hesson.

At Harare, July 22–24, 2016 (not first-class). **New Zealanders won by 259 runs**. ‡**New Zealanders 345-7 dec** (90 overs) (M. J. Guptill 74, H. M. Nicholls 52, B-J. Watling 61, I. S. Sodhi 54*) **and**

201-7 dec (51.5 overs) (M. J. Santner 51); **Zimbabwe A 114** (49.5 overs) (S. C. Williams 55; I. S. Sodhi 4-18) **and 173** (61.5 overs). *Both teams chose from 15 players. Three New Zealanders retired out on the opening day and four second time round. Zimbabwe were effectively 0-3 after seven balls of their first innings: captain Tino Mawoyo was struck on the thumb by Tim Southee (which ruled him out of the First Test) and the next two made ducks. Later in the innings, players had to lie down as a swarm of bees crossed the field.*

ZIMBABWE v NEW ZEALAND

First Test Match

At Bulawayo, July 28–31, 2016. New Zealand won by an innings and 117 runs. Toss: Zimbabwe. Test debuts: C. J. Chibhabha, M. T. Chinouya, P. S. Masvaure.

Pretoria-born Neil Wagner was a lusty but lacking left-arm slinger when he left for New Zealand in 2008. And, when he returned to play a Test against his native South Africa five years later, his accent was all that seemed to have changed. But now Wagner landed in Africa reborn as a bodyline bruiser.

The fierce bounce he generated was a feat in itself, given the Queens Sports Club's reputation for pitches more suited to picnicking than pace bowling. And there had been signs that the wicket would be flatter than ever: two days before the match, an already heavy roller was loaded fore and aft with concrete railway sleepers. But Wagner rose above those challenges as surely as his deliveries steepled towards ribs and heads, and took a career-best six for 41. An hour before the close, Zimbabwe were all out for 164. It could have been worse: four wickets fell at 72, before a stand of 85 between debutant Prince Masvaure and No. 10 Donald Tiripano.

By stumps next evening, New Zealand were 151 ahead with six wickets in hand; Latham's fourth Test century was in the bank and Taylor's 14th in the making. Watling's sixth followed on the third day, as Williamson finally declared 412 ahead soon after tea. All the centurions batted within themselves, as is the way of New Zealanders who are not Glenn Turner, Martin Crowe or Brendon McCullum. To call their efforts characterless would be cruel, but their runs did not so much flow as trickle, the product of diligence more than dash. Latham's 105 stood out, but only because he achieved it in the city where his father, Rod, had scored his only Test century almost 24 years previously.

Williams (flu) and wicketkeeper Chakabva (tonsillitis) were not at the ground for the entire second day; Chari took the gloves and held three catches. But, as Zimbabwe shambled in the shadow of their enormous deficit, both were urgently summoned. By the time Williams completed the five-minute drive from his home to the ground, they were four down. Wagner removed Sikandar Raza before Cremer and Ervine nursed Zimbabwe to stumps without further calamity. As darkness fell, Williams returned home to care for his wife, Chantelle, who had caught his bug. During a febrile night, she fainted and suffered what she believed was a seizure; Williams dared close his eyes only at 5am. Considering all this, his resolve – in only his third Test – was remarkable.

A naturally enterprising batsman, Williams had been unable to take the fight to the bowlers in the first innings because of a stupefying dose of cough mixture and, in the absence of DRS, a poor umpiring decision – caught off his helmet from one of Wagner's bumpers. Second time around, he was clearly still suffering, taking every opportunity to rest on all fours. But when he was upright he stood tall and, after stroking 20 boundaries, mustered the energy to run two off Sodhi to go to his maiden Test century. To top it off, it was also Zimbabwe's fastest hundred, at 106 balls, beating Neil Johnson's record against Pakistan at Peshawar in November 1998 by a single delivery. He was ninth out as New Zealand wrapped up the game by tea, but Williams had proved himself an emblem of Zimbabwean defiance.

Man of the Match: L. R. P. L. Taylor.

Close of play: first day, New Zealand 32-0 (Guptill 14, Latham 16); second day, New Zealand 315-4 (Taylor 38, Sodhi 5); third day, Zimbabwe 121-5 (Ervine 49, Cremer 14).

Zimbabwe

B. B. Chari c Guptill b Southee	4	– (3) b Boult	5
C. J. Chibhabha c Latham b Wagner	15	– (1) c Taylor b Boult	7
H. Masakadza c and b Santner	15	– (2) c Taylor b Southee	4
C. R. Ervine st Watling b Santner	13	– c Watling b Boult	50
S. C. Williams c Sodhi b Wagner	1	– (8) c Williamson b Santner	119
Sikandar Raza c Latham b Wagner	22	– c Latham b Wagner	37
P. S. Masvaure lbw b Southee	42	– (5) lbw b Boult	0
†R. W. Chakabva c Watling b Wagner	0	– (9) b Southee	11
*A. G. Cremer c Nicholls b Wagner	0	– (7) lbw b Sodhi	33
D. T. Tiripano not out	49	– c Watling b Wagner	14
M. T. Chinouya b Wagner	1	– not out	0
Lb 2	2	B 6, lb 9	15
1/4 (1) 2/35 (2) 3/35 (3) 4/36 (5) 5/72 (4) 6/72 (6) 7/72 (8) 8/72 (9) 9/157 (7) 10/164 (11) (77.5 overs)	164	1/7 (2) 2/12 (3) 3/17 (1) 4/17 (5) 5/86 (6) 6/124 (4) 7/242 (7) 8/277 (9) 9/285 (8) 10/295 (10) (79 overs)	295

Southee 17–8–28–2; Boult 11–5–23–0; Santner 14–5–16–2; Wagner 20.5–8–41–6; Sodhi 15–3–54–0. *Second innings*—Southee 15–3–68–2; Boult 17–3–52–4; Wagner 17–1–62–2; Santner 17–6–32–1; Sodhi 12–1–66–1; Williamson 1–1–0–0.

New Zealand

M. J. Guptill c Ervine b Chibhabha	40
T. W. M. Latham c Chari b Masakadza	105
*K. S. Williamson c Masakadza b Cremer	91
L. R. P. L. Taylor not out	173
H. M. Nicholls c Chari b Tiripano	18
I. S. Sodhi c Chari b Chinouya	11
†B-J. Watling c sub (T. Muzarabani) b Sikandar Raza	107
B 15, w 4, nb 12	31
1/79 (1) 2/235 (2) 3/272 (3) 4/299 (5) 5/323 (6) 6/576 (7) (6 wkts dec, 166.5 overs)	576

M. J. Santner, T. G. Southee, N. Wagner and T. A. Boult did not bat.

Chinouya 26–6–79–1; Tiripano 28–4–82–1; Masvaure 10–0–38–0; Cremer 53–4–187–1; Sikandar Raza 25.5–4–106–1; Chibhabha 15–1–44–1; Masakadza 9–1–25–1.

Umpires: M. A. Gough and P. R. Reiffel. Third umpire: L. Rusere.
Referee: D. C. Boon.

ZIMBABWE v NEW ZEALAND

Second Test Match

At Bulawayo, August 6–10, 2016. New Zealand won by 254 runs. Toss: New Zealand. Test debut: P. J. Moor.

"Jeez, he's an old 26-year-old," said Taylor in describing the precocious Williamson. Early on the second morning – the day before he had turned 26 – he became the youngest to complete a set of centuries against every Test nation, the first New Zealander, and the 13th overall. Only the PA announcer could spoil the mood, telling a sparse crowd: "We'd like to wish a very happy birthday to the Australian captain, Kane Williamson."

His knock was sandwiched by hundreds from Latham and Taylor – who went past Martin Crowe's 5,444 to become New Zealand's third-highest Test run-scorer – and established complete dominance. The partnerships mounted as Zimbabwe toiled: this was the first time in a New Zealand Test innings that three pairs had put on 150. By the time they'd had enough, eight bowlers had been tried, sharing only four wickets. The declaration came like an angel of mercy.

Could it be that this pitch was even flatter than the one prepared for the First Test? Somehow, it could. Mawoyo, who had missed the first match with a bruised right thumb, and Chibhabha guided them to the second-day close without loss, registering Zimbabwe's first opening partnership over 50 in nearly five years. But, next morning, Mawoyo edged Southee on to his stumps, and Zimbabwe were soon back in familiar territory at 147 for

BATSMEN WITH TEST HUNDREDS AGAINST NINE TEAMS

Years	*Days*		*Tests taken*	*Season*
25	**365**	**K. S. Williamson (NZ)**	**50**	**2016**
30	38	K. C. Sangakkara (SL)	69	2007-08
31	115	R. T. Ponting (A)	104	2005-06
31	231	S. R. Tendulkar (I)	119	2004-05
31	270	D. P. M. D. Jayawardene (SL)	101	2008-09
31	341	R. Dravid (I)	86	2004-05
34	135	M. S. Atapattu (SL)	80	2004-05
34	148	A. C. Gilchrist (A)	84	2005-06
34	329	G. Kirsten (SA)	84	2002-03
36	24	B. C. Lara (WI)	116	2004-05
36	79	J. H. Kallis (SA)	150	2011-12
36	327	Younis Khan (P)	92	2014-15
38	47	S. R. Waugh (A)	161	2003

M. L. Hayden (A) scored centuries against eight national Test teams plus the ICC World XI in 73 Tests by 2005-06, when he was 33 years and 350 days old, but never made one against Bangladesh.

five. At least "Slug" was there. Whatever the origins of Ervine's nickname, it was apt for a maiden century whose slowness gave Zimbabwe hope. Steadfast support came from debutant keeper Peter Moor in a stand of 148 that ended five overs before stumps on the third day. After that, Ervine had little help, and was last out, with Zimbabwe 220 runs behind.

Williamson did not enforce the follow-on, giving his bowlers a rest after ten hours in the field. Instead, New Zealand built their lead to 386, thanks to brisk half-centuries by Williamson and Taylor. Zimbabwe welcomed more patience from Mawoyo, who consumed 92 balls for his 35. But, after he and Sikandar Raza were removed in successive overs to end the day's play, their fate was all but sealed.

New Zealand still had to work hard and think creatively. Unimpressed with his seamers, Williamson tossed the ball to Guptill to try his off-breaks. Despite a meagre Test record – he had taken only five wickets in 41 games – he ripped the ball square in Bulawayo's dust, dismissing Ervine, Williams and the obdurate Cremer to claim career-best figures of three for 11. After Sodhi had Chinouya popping a catch to short cover, New Zealand could celebrate, their future seemingly safe in the hands of their new captain.

Man of the Match: K. S. Williamson. *Man of the Series:* N. Wagner.

Close of play: first day, New Zealand 329-2 (Williamson 95); second day, Zimbabwe 55-0 (Mawoyo 20, Chibhabha 31); third day, Zimbabwe 305-6 (Ervine 115, Cremer 2); fourth day, Zimbabwe 58-3 (Tiripano 0).

New Zealand

M. J. Guptill lbw b Tiripano	87	– (2) c Nyumbu b Chinouya	11
T. W. M. Latham c and b Williams	136	– (1) c Moor b Tiripano	13
*K. S. Williamson c Ervine b Chinouya	113	– not out	68
L. R. P. L. Taylor not out	124	– not out	67
H. M. Nicholls lbw b Cremer	15		
†B-J. Watling not out	83		
B 12, lb 3, w 1, nb 8	24	Lb 4, w 3	7
1/169 (1) 2/329 (2) 3/369 (3) 4/389 (5) (4 wkts dec, 150 overs)	582	1/24 (1) 2/26 (2) (2 wkts dec, 36 overs)	166

M. J. Santner, I. S. Sodhi, T. G. Southee, N. Wagner and T. A. Boult did not bat.

Tiripano 25–4–102–1; Chinouya 22–6–64–1; Chibhabha 12–2–45–0; Cremer 36–2–147–1; Nyumbu 34–3–107–0; Williams 13–0–62–1; Sikandar Raza 4–0–17–0; Masvaure 4–0–23–0. *Second innings*—Chinouya 9–2–45–1; Tiripano 6–1–14–1; Chibhabha 3–0–22–0; Cremer 11–0–59–0; Nyumbu 7–0–22–0.

Zimbabwe

T. M. K. Mawoyo b Southee	26	– lbw b Boult	35
C. J. Chibhabha c Williamson b Santner	60	– c Guptill b Wagner	21
Sikandar Raza c Williamson b Wagner	3	– lbw b Southee	0
C. R. Ervine c Wagner b Sodhi	146	– (5) c Watling b Guptill	27
P. S. Masvaure b Santner	2	– (6) c Taylor b Sodhi	11
S. C. Williams lbw b Sodhi	16	– (7) c Williamson b Guptill	11
†P. J. Moor c Guptill b Sodhi	71	– (8) lbw b Sodhi	1
*A. G. Cremer lbw b Boult	8	– (9) lbw b Guptill	1
D. T. Tiripano lbw b Wagner	3	– (4) lbw b Santner	22
J. C. Nyumbu c Santner b Sodhi	8	– not out	0
M. T. Chinouya not out	0	– c Williamson b Sodhi	0
B 12, lb 6, nb 1	19	B 1, lb 2	3
1/65 (1) 2/83 (3) 3/107 (2) 4/115 (5) 5/147 (6) 6/295 (7) 7/319 (8) 8/327 (9) 9/352 (10) 10/362 (4) (143.4 overs)	362	1/45 (2) 2/58 (1) 3/58 (3) 4/97 (4) 5/112 (5) 6/130 (7) 7/131 (8) 8/132 (9) 9/132 (6) 10/132 (11) (68.4 overs)	132

Southee 28–14–73–1; Boult 27–13–45–1; Santner 35–8–105–2; Wagner 31–8–61–2; Sodhi 21.4–9–60–4; Guptill 1–1–0–0. *Second innings*—Southee 14–7–35–1; Boult 12–4–26–1; Wagner 12–5–23–1; Santner 12–4–15–1; Sodhi 11.4–5–19–3; Guptill 7–4–11–3.

Umpires: M. A. Gough and P. R. Reiffel. Third umpire: T. J. Matibiri.
Referee: D. C. Boon.

ZIMBABWE v SRI LANKA IN 2016-17

TRISTAN HOLME

Test matches (2): Zimbabwe 0, Sri Lanka 2

This was a series that largely followed expectations, though it did at least offer a few souvenirs. The opening game was Zimbabwe's 100th Test, 24 years after their first. Even Bangladesh had played 95 in 16, a reminder of the hardship Zimbabwe had endured, not least their two suspensions from Test cricket. In a further nod to the past, Heath Streak – captain, dissident, exile, and assistant coach – was appointed head coach three weeks before the series. But he was focused only on the future, and spoke of his desire to change Zimbabwe's survivalist mentality. "I think in the past we've just been happy to compete," he said. "We're not happy with that any more."

Things did not begin well: in the first innings of the series, Zimbabwe put down six catches, which set the tone. And while there was more purpose about their batting, they were unable to match the heavy totals racked up by the Sri Lankans, who scored five centuries to Zimbabwe's one – Graeme Cremer's first in Tests. Nevertheless, they might have saved the first match had DRS been in use. Six of the seven incorrect calls favoured Sri Lanka, who earned ten lbws to Zimbabwe's none. After a similar experience against New Zealand, the need for change was obvious.

In fact, Zimbabwe Cricket had wanted DRS throughout the series, but did not inform the ICC in time for the First Test. For the Second, slow-motion cameras were flown in from South Africa, and Marais Erasmus brought in as third umpire. So it was that DRS made its debut in Zimbabwe (if in its barest form, without Hot Spot or Snickometer).

With Angelo Mathews and Dinesh Chandimal among five players missing through injury, Sri Lanka tested their depth ahead of the trip to South Africa in December and January. The signs were good: Kusal Perera and Asela Gunaratne scored maiden Test centuries, Dhananjaya de Silva grabbed his second, and 19-year-old Lahiru Kumara bowled with pace and aggression.

Yet the series was sealed by an old hand: captaining Sri Lanka for the first time in his 17-year career, Rangana Herath picked up 13 wickets in the Second Test with his left-arm spin, becoming the third – after Muttiah Muralitharan and Dale Steyn – to collect five-wicket hauls against all nine opponents.

> "A group of Donald Trumps were booed as they took their seats, the loudest abuse coming from a group of Mexican sombreros."
>
> England v Sri Lanka in 2016, First Test, page 270

SRI LANKAN TOURING PARTY

*H. M. R. K. B. Herath, D. M. de Silva, D. P. D. N. Dickwella, P. L. S. Gamage, D. A. S. Gunaratne, F. D. M. Karunaratne, C. B. R. L. S. Kumara, R. A. S. Lakmal, H. U. K. Madushanka, B. K. G. Mendis, M. D. K. Perera, M. D. K. J. Perera, P. A. D. L. R. Sandakan, J. K. Silva. *Coach:* G. X. Ford.

Captain A. D. Mathews was originally selected, but had not recovered sufficiently from a torn calf. L. D. Chandimal, the vice-captain, was also absent (with a broken thumb), so Herath led the team.

ZIMBABWE v SRI LANKA

First Test Match

At Harare, October 29–November 2, 2016. Sri Lanka won by 225 runs. Toss: Sri Lanka. Test debuts: C. T. Mumba; D. A. S. Gunaratne, C. B. R. L. S. Kumara.

Zimbabwe marked their 100th Test with a performance like many of the previous 99: short on luck, long on pluck. Hindered by a number of poor umpiring decisions, they lost by a wide margin, though a mere 45 balls remained when the final wicket fell.

They did, however, contribute to their downfall. In the first innings, they dropped half a dozen catches, including Kusal Perera, who went on to a maiden Test hundred, from just 104 balls, and Tharanga, who took his time over his second century, more than ten years after his first. It was the longest gap between Test centuries since the Second World War. Further reprieves came from umpires Simon Fry and Ian Gould, who turned down four appeals – mistakenly, to judge from replays. With DRS absent, all Zimbabwe could do was soldier on. And though they bowled a side out for the first time in three Tests – having taken just 12 wickets in two matches against New Zealand – they conceded 537.

A positive second-wicket partnership between Mawoyo and Masakadza brought optimism, but 88 for one at the second-day close became 139 for six next morning. As Cremer – who had a Test average of ten – walked out, it looked grim, but he batted more than four hours for his maiden Test hundred. He played only one shot with relish, a push through extra cover that yielded seven of his ten fours, and wicketkeeper Moor provided the force in a partnership of 132. They proved that survival was not a difficult task on a friendly surface, and Tiripano got the message, helping add another 92 after Moor became teenager Lahiru Kumara's first Test victim. Still, Cremer nearly ran out of partners. He had 99 when the ninth wicket fell, and needed last man Mpofu to survive one ball from Herath, before clipping a full toss from Mendis into the leg side. "I hadn't got 50 in Test cricket," said Cremer, "and I don't even have a five-for yet, so it was quite special."

Despite the excitement, Zimbabwe conceded a heavy first-innings lead, which became unbridgable after Karunaratne hit a century in the second. Some luck finally came their way when a downpour on the fourth day shortened the third session to 23 balls. Herath declared overnight with a lead of 411, leaving Zimbabwe 98 overs to bat out.

The first two hours brought just one wicket, but another umpiring blunder – Mawoyo, given out lbw to a ball that would have missed leg – sparked a dread procession, as three fell with the score on 74. That Zimbabwe got so close to surviving was once again due to Cremer, who extended his time at the crease past seven hours. It was a shock when, with less than 11 overs remaining, he leapt down the track to Herath and was stumped. "I blame myself for losing this game," he said. Without him, Zimbabwe would have lost far earlier.

Man of the Match: A. G. Cremer.

Close of play: first day, Sri Lanka 317-4 (Tharanga 13, de Silva 10); second day, Zimbabwe 88-1 (Mawoyo 41, Masakadza 33); third day, Sri Lanka 5-0 (Karunaratne 1, Silva 3); fourth day, Sri Lanka 247-6 (Gunaratne 16, M. D. K. Perera 1).

Sri Lanka

F. D. M. Karunaratne c Mawoyo b Cremer	56	– c and b Mpofu	110
J. K. Silva c Williams b Waller	94	– b Mumba	7
†M. D. K. J. Perera c Waller b Cremer	110	– c Masakadza b Waller	17
B. K. G. Mendis c Moor b Cremer	34	– c Cremer b Mumba	19
W. U. Tharanga not out	110	– c Moor b Mumba	1
D. M. de Silva c Williams b Cremer	25	– c Waller b Mumba	64
D. A. S. Gunaratne c Cremer b Williams	54	– not out	16
M. D. K. Perera run out	23	– not out	1
*H. M. R. K. B. Herath c Waller b Mumba	7		
R. A. S. Lakmal c Tiripano b Mpofu	7		
C. B. R. L. S. Kumara c Moor b Mpofu	0		
B 10, lb 7	17	B 6, lb 5, nb 1	12
1/123 (1) 2/198 (2) 3/282 (4) (155 overs)	537	1/17 (2) (6 wkts dec, 61.5 overs)	247
4/307 (3) 5/351 (6) 6/450 (7)		2/72 (3) 3/111 (4)	
7/498 (8) 8/512 (9) 9/536 (10) 10/537 (11)		4/117 (5) 5/211 (1) 6/241 (6)	

Mpofu 31–6–96–2; Mumba 24–2–101–1; Tiripano 26–7–71–0; Cremer 42–6–142–4; Masakadza 9–3–31–0; Williams 17–2–54–1; Waller 6–0–25–1. *Second innings*—Mpofu 16–2–42–1; Cremer 14–0–67–0; Mumba 11.5–2–50–4; Tiripano 8–0–33–0; Waller 5–0–17–1; Williams 1–0–5–0; Masakadza 6–1–22–0.

Zimbabwe

T. M. K. Mawoyo c Gunaratne b Lakmal	45	– lbw b M. D. K. Perera	37
B. B. Chari lbw b Herath	5	– b Kumara	10
H. Masakadza c Karunaratne b Lakmal	33	– lbw b Lakmal	20
C. R. Ervine lbw b M. D. K. Perera	12	– lbw b M. D. K. Perera	0
S. C. Williams c Gunaratne b Herath	10	– c de Silva b Herath	40
M. N. Waller lbw b M. D. K. Perera	22	– lbw b Lakmal	0
†P. J. Moor c M. D. K. Perera b Kumara	79	– lbw b Kumara	7
*A. G. Cremer not out	102	– st M. D. K. J. Perera b Herath	43
D. T. Tiripano lbw b Mendis	46	– lbw b Herath	0
C. T. Mumba b Herath	1	– not out	10
C. B. Mpofu b Lakmal	2	– b M. D. K. Perera	0
B 4, lb 4, w 7, nb 1	16	B 5, lb 13, w 1	19
1/21 (2) 2/92 (1) 3/92 (3) (107.5 overs)	373	1/31 (2) 2/68 (1) (90.3 overs)	186
4/111 (5) 5/134 (4) 6/139 (6)		3/74 (4) 4/74 (3)	
7/271 (7) 8/363 (9) 9/366 (10) 10/373 (11)		5/74 (6) 6/100 (7) 7/139 (5)	
		8/145 (9) 9/183 (8) 10/186 (11)	

Lakmal 21.5–3–69–3; Kumara 22–3–90–1; Herath 37–5–97–3; M. D. K. Perera 18–1–66–2; Gunaratne 3–0–23–0; de Silva 2–0–10–0; Mendis 4–0–10–1. *Second innings*—Lakmal 24–6–43–2; Herath 30–13–38–3; Kumara 19–3–45–2; M. D. K. Perera 15.3–4–34–3; Mendis 2–1–8–0.

Umpires: S. D. Fry and I. J. Gould. Third umpire: T. J. Matibiri.
Referee: B. C. Broad.

ZIMBABWE v SRI LANKA

Second Test Match

At Harare, November 6–10, 2016. Sri Lanka won by 257 runs. Toss: Zimbabwe.

The first use of DRS in Zimbabwe saved the hosts from some poor decisions, but Herath's hatful ensured a 2–0 win for the Sri Lankans. Zimbabwe figured their best chance stood with their seamers, so Cremer requested a grassy surface, and was happy to bowl first. But Carl Mumba limped off with knee pain after the first over – only to return in the tenth – and the others wasted the first hour. It was left to part-timer Masakadza, who picked up two in six balls as Sri Lanka let their guard down. After Silva and Mendis fell in quick succession, they found themselves 112 for four, and under pressure for the first time in the series.

Just 44 runs dribbled from 18 overs after lunch, and Tharanga dug in for 79 before becoming the first player given out on review in Zimbabwe, when cameras caught a nick into his pad that ballooned to Masakadza at slip. De Silva, known as the "Ice Man" according to Sri Lanka coach Graham Ford, carried on the rebuilding job; he went to a hundred with a rolled pull off Mpofu, and brought his side to the close on a comfortable 290 for five.

Next day, Sri Lanka asserted their authority, as Gunaratne's maiden Test century ensured Zimbabwe conceded 500 in an innings for the fifth straight match; another four dropped catches did not help their cause. But they began their reply strongly. In the second over, Chari hit his first ball for six, lofting Herath over long-on, then struck the next two for four. Then, after Mawoyo and Masakadza had fallen to Herath with the score on 17, Chari repeated the shot to bring up his maiden Test fifty. He finished the day on 60, as did Ervine.

Thereafter, it was all about Herath. He picked up another three victims on the third day, completing five-wicket hauls against all nine Test opponents. Having done the damage, he opted against the follow-on and, though Zimbabwe's bowling improved, fifties from Karunaratne and Kusal Perera allowed a declaration midway through the fourth day. By stumps he had another five-for, and returned on the final morning to scoop up the remaining three, and finish with the best innings (eight for 63) and match figures (13 for 152) in Zimbabwe.

Herath shrugged off the feat with typical modesty, but his opposite number was in awe. "His control was exceptional," said Cremer. "He doesn't look like he's doing a lot, but he's got subtle variations that, as a batsman, you don't pick up."

Man of the Match: H. M. R. K. B. Herath. *Man of the Series:* F. D. M. Karunaratne.

Close of play: first day, Sri Lanka 290-5 (de Silva 100, Gunaratne 13); second day, Zimbabwe 126-2 (Chari 60, Ervine 60); third day, Sri Lanka 102-4 (Karunaratne 54, Gunaratne 6); fourth day, Zimbabwe 180-7 (Ervine 65, Tiripano 0).

Sri Lanka

F. D. M. Karunaratne c Williams b Masakadza	26	– lbw b Mpofu	88
J. K. Silva lbw b Mpofu	37	– c Waller b Mumba	6
†M. D. K. J. Perera c Mumba b Masakadza	4	– (7) c Williams b Cremer	62
B. K. G. Mendis c Moor b Tiripano	26	– (3) c Mpofu b Mumba	0
W. U. Tharanga c Masakadza b Cremer	79	– (4) lbw b Cremer	17
D. M. de Silva c and b Cremer	127	– (5) c Chari b Mumba	9
D. A. S. Gunaratne st Moor b Williams	116	– (6) lbw b Tiripano	39
M. D. K. Perera lbw b Cremer	34	– c Masakadza b Cremer	2
*H. M. R. K. B. Herath c Moor b Tiripano	27	– b Cremer	4
R. A. S. Lakmal b Tiripano	0	– not out	21
C. B. R. L. S. Kumara not out	7		
B 9, lb 8, w 2, nb 2	21	B 6, lb 4	10
1/62 (1) 2/66 (3) 3/84 (2) 4/112 (4) 5/255 (5) 6/342 (6) 7/396 (8) 8/471 (9) 9/471 (10) 10/504 (7) (144.4 overs)	504	1/14 (2) 2/16 (3) 3/44 (4) 4/84 (5) 5/153 (6) 6/198 (1) 7/201 (8) 8/211 (9) 9/258 (7) (9 wkts dec, 81.4 overs)	258

Mumba 23–4–80–0; Tiripano 32–4–91–3; Mpofu 23–4–92–1; Masakadza 13–4–34–2; Cremer 40–1–136–3; Williams 8.4–1–31–1; Waller 5–0–23–0. *Second innings*—Mpofu 21–8–51–1; Mumba 19–4–67–3; Cremer 21.4–2–91–4; Tiripano 11–4–14–1; Williams 6–0–21–0; Chari 1–0–3–0; Masakadza 2–1–1–0.

Zimbabwe

T. M. K. Mawoyo lbw b Herath	3 – c de Silva b Herath	15
B. B. Chari b Herath	80 – b Herath	8
H. Masakadza c de Silva b Herath	0 – lbw b Herath	10
C. R. Ervine c Karunaratne b Lakmal	64 – c de Silva b Herath	72
S. C. Williams lbw b M. D. K. Perera	58 – c Mendis b Kumara	45
M. N. Waller c Silva b Herath	18 – c M. D. K. J. Perera b de Silva	0
†P. J. Moor lbw b M. D. K. Perera	33 – c Mendis b Herath	20
*A. G. Cremer c Karunaratne b M. D. K. Perera	3 – b Herath	5
D. T. Tiripano c Herath b Lakmal	3 – not out	16
C. T. Mumba lbw b Herath	2 – lbw b Herath	1
C. B. Mpofu not out	0 – lbw b Herath	20
B 2, lb 6	8 B 12, lb 6, w 3	21
1/17 (1) 2/17 (3) 3/134 (4) 4/173 (2) 5/210 (6) 6/253 (5) 7/265 (8) 8/268 (7) 9/272 (10) 10/272 (9) (82.1 overs)	272 1/16 (2) 2/32 (3) 3/39 (1) 4/113 (5) 5/114 (6) 6/166 (7) 7/176 (8) 8/195 (4) 9/201 (10) 10/233 (11) (58 overs)	233

Lakmal 21.1–5–55–2; Herath 26–4–89–5; Kumara 14–0–60–0; M. D. K. Perera 18–2–51–3; Gunaratne 2–0–5–0; de Silva 1–0–4–0. *Second innings*—Lakmal 15–2–58–0; Herath 23–6–63–8; M. D. K. Perera 8–1–42–0; Kumara 9–0–42–1; de Silva 3–0–10–1.

Umpires: S. D. Fry and I. J. Gould. Third umpire: M. Erasmus.
Referee: B. C. Broad.

ZIMBABWE TRI-SERIES IN 2016-17

LIAM BRICKHILL

1 Sri Lanka 2 Zimbabwe 3 West Indies

This triangular series between some of international cricket's lesser lights twinkled with possibility. Sri Lanka were weakened by injuries to senior players, and West Indies beset by the seemingly unending quarrels between the board and team, so for once Zimbabwe had the most experienced side on show. This probably helped them win the tight moments: they conjured an unlikely tie in the first match against West Indies, then won the tense, rain-affected return fixture to make sure they reached the final of their own party.

However, that was the end of the good news. Sri Lanka played streetwise cricket, under their experienced stand-in captain Upul Tharanga, and were too strong in the final. They ran out worthy winners, although they were helped by having the best of the conditions. After the match, the Zimbabwean seamer Brian Vitori – having just returned from remedial work on his action – was reported again.

The first two matches were played under gloomy skies in Harare, before the circus – and the bad weather – moved south to Bulawayo. Only one game was rained off, but three others were interrupted. It all added to the drama of a hard-fought series which included a one-run victory, as well as that tie.

West Indies should have won both, dropped three points and missed out on the final, which also harmed their chances of picking up the ranking points necessary to qualify directly for the next World Cup. Their personnel problems got worse, too: Darren Bravo was sent home mid-series for tweeting that the West Indian board president Dave Cameron – who had spoken about why Bravo was offered a reduced contract – was a "big idiot".

For Zimbabwean fans, the series permitted brief respite from the country's financial and political problems. Under new coach Heath Streak, there were promising debuts for batsman Tarisai Musakanda and seamer Carl Mumba. The tour was also notable for the spirit in which the teams competeted. Suranga Lakmal's occasional bluster aside, there was hardly a cross moment.

NATIONAL SQUADS

Zimbabwe *A. G. Cremer, B. B. Chari, C. J. Chibhabha, E. Chigumbura, T. S. Chisoro, C. R. Ervine, H. Masakadza, P. J. Moor, C. B. Mpofu, C. T. Mumba, T. K. Musakanda, T. Panyangara, Sikandar Raza, D. T. Tiripano, B. V. Vitori, M. N. Waller, S. C. Williams. *Coach:* H. H. Streak.

Sri Lanka *W. U. Tharanga, D. M. de Silva, D. P. D. N. Dickwella, A. N. P. R. Fernando, D. A. S. Gunaratne, D. S. N. F. G. Jayasuriya, K. M. D. N. Kulasekara, C. B. L. R. S. Kumara, R. A. S. Lakmal, B. K. G. Mendis, S. S. Pathirana, M. D. K. J. Perera, P. A. D. L. R. Sandakan, M. D. Shanaka, J. D. F. Vandersay. *Coach:* G. X. Ford.

West Indies *J. O. Holder, S. J. Benn, D. Bishoo, C. R. Brathwaite, K. C. Brathwaite, D. M. Bravo, J. L. Carter, J. Charles, M. L. Cummins, S. O. Dowrich, S. T. Gabriel, S. D. Hope, E. Lewis, J. N. Mohammed, S. P. Narine, A. R. Nurse, R. Powell. *Acting-coach:* H. W. D. Springer.

A. S. Joseph and M. N. Samuels were originally selected, then replaced by Cummins and Dowrich after West Indies' series against Pakistan. Bravo was sent home for insubordination, and replaced by Mohammed. Narine returned home for personal reasons, and was replaced by Bishoo.

At Harare, November 14, 2016. **Sri Lanka won by eight wickets. Zimbabwe 154** (41.3 overs) (P. J. Moor 47, A. G. Cremer 31*; D. A. S. Gunaratne 3-21); ‡**Sri Lanka 155-2** (24.3 overs) (D. M. de Silva 78*, D. P. D. N. Dickwella 41). *Sri Lanka 5pts. MoM:* D. M. de Silva. *ODI debuts:* C. T. Mumba (Zimbabwe); D. A. S. Gunaratne (Sri Lanka). *Put in on an unusually green pitch, under swing-friendly cloud, Zimbabwe were soon in trouble at 50-6. They recovered slightly, thanks to Peter Moor's adventurous batting – he heaved four leg-side sixes – and some late grit from skipper Graeme Cremer, but the target was still a modest one. It didn't help that, when Dhananjaya de Silva feathered the first ball of the chase to Moor, bowler Tinashe Panyangara had overstepped. De Silva pulled the free hit for four, and never looked back as Sri Lanka zoomed to a bonus-point victory.*

At Harare, November 16, 2016. **West Indies won by 62 runs. West Indies 227** (49.2 overs) (S. D. Hope 47, J. L. Carter 54, R. Powell 44); ‡**Sri Lanka 165** (43.1 overs) (D. S. N. F. G. Jayasuriya 31, S. S. Pathirana 45; S. T. Gabriel 3-31, A. R. Nurse 3-46). *West Indies 5pts. MoM:* J. O. Holder. *ODI debuts:* S. D. Hope, A. R. Nurse, R. Powell (West Indies). *Jason Holder showed his bowlers the way, starting with a spell of 5–0–12–2, while Shannon Gabriel worked up high speed. Sri Lanka dipped to 79-6 and, with debutant off-spinner Ashley Nurse picking up three wickets, West Indies claimed the bonus point. Their innings had also been a bit of a struggle, before Jonathan Carter made a cultured 54 and Rovman Powell, another debutant, unveiled some powerful hitting in a 29-ball 44. But from 209-5 in the 45th over, the last five wickets mustered only 18.*

At Bulawayo, November 19, 2016. **Tied.** ‡**Zimbabwe 257** (50 overs) (C. R. Ervine 92, Sikandar Raza 77; C. R. Brathwaite 4-48); **West Indies 257-8** (50 overs) (K. C. Brathwaite 78, S. D. Hope 101). *Zimbabwe 2pts, West Indies 2pts. MoM:* S. D. Hope. *Donald Tiripano hadn't bowled since the tenth over, but was recalled for the last, with West Indies needing four to win – and conceded just three. It allowed Zimbabwe to pinch a tie from a game they had seemed bound to lose 30 minutes earlier, when West Indies were 220-2 in the 45th, after Hope's first international century. But Carter was run out trying to steal a bye to win from the last ball, the third wicket to go down in that tumultuous final over. Zimbabwe had stumbled too, after Craig Ervine and Sikandar Raza put on 144 for the third wicket in 25 overs, but eventually reached their highest one-day total of the year. Local umpire Russell Tiffin – overseeing his 150th ODI – had also stood in the last tie in Zimbabwe, against New Zealand at Bulawayo in October 1997.*

At Bulawayo, November 21, 2016. **No result.** ‡**Zimbabwe 55-2** (13.3 overs) **v Sri Lanka.** *Zimbabwe 2pts, Sri Lanka 2pts.No play was possible after a downpour in the 14th over.*

At Bulawayo, November 23, 2016. **Sri Lanka won by one run. Sri Lanka 330-7** (50 overs) (D. M. de Silva 58, D. P. D. N. Dickwella 94, B. K. G. Mendis 94; J. O. Holder 3-57); ‡**West Indies 329-9** (50 overs) (E. Lewis 148, J. O. Holder 45*). *Sri Lanka 4pts. MoM:* B. K. G. Mendis. *Chasing a mountainous target, West Indies got their fingertips to the summit – but had them prised off in the final over for the second match running. This time it was a maiden ODI century from bruising left-hander Evin Lewis that set up the chase, and when he was run out in the 41st over the target had been reduced to 69 from 57 balls. Holder held firm, but Sri Lanka's seamers – expensive earlier – chipped away at the other end. Twin career-best 94s from Niroshan Dickwella and Kusal Mendis (who slammed five sixes) had set up a towering total as Sri Lanka passed 300 in an ODI in Zimbabwe for the first time. The aggregate of 659 runs was a record for any ODI in the country, beating 657 by New Zealand (328-5) and Zimbabwe (329-9) at Bulawayo in October 2011.*

At Bulawayo, November 25, 2016. **Zimbabwe won by five runs (DLS).** ‡**Zimbabwe 218-8** (49 overs) (Sikandar Raza 76*, T. S. Chisoro 42*; D. Bishoo 3-30, A. R. Nurse 3-27); **West Indies 124-5** (27.3 overs) (J. L. Carter 43*). *Zimbabwe 4pts. MoM:* T. S. Chisoro. *After spinners Nurse and Devendra Bishoo took three wickets apiece, Sikandar Raza orchestrated a remarkable comeback, as Zimbabwe recovered from 89-7 to reach 218. Sikandar, who hit just three fours from 103 balls, put on 38 with Tiripano, then 91* – a national ninth-wicket record – with Tendai Chisoro. West Indies' reply also had a poor start. The openers fell quickly, as Cremer began with spin from both ends in the drizzle. Carter and Holder (22*) were putting things right when the rain intensified, with West Indies just short of the par score – and a point short of the final.*

SRI LANKA 11pts, ZIMBABWE 8pts, West Indies 7pts.

FINAL

ZIMBABWE v SRI LANKA

At Bulawayo, November 27, 2016. Sri Lanka won by six wickets. Toss: Zimbabwe. One-day international debut: T. K. Musakanda.

This was a match of two distinct halves, each with their own weather and batting conditions. In gusting early rain, Zimbabwe inexplicably decided to bat, and were trussed up by the spinners, who shared eight wickets. Tarisai Musakanda, making his debut, top-scored with a boisterous 36, but Zimbabwe could muster only 160, which never looked enough – especially when the clouds parted and the weather mellowed to provide near-ideal conditions for batting in the afternoon. To their credit, Zimbabwe's bowlers never let the runs come easily, with Vitori – recalled after remedial work on his action – picking up three early wickets (sadly for him, he was reported again after the match). The top order had been undone by their rush to get at the bowling, but skipper Tharanga ground his way towards the target. At one point he had 28 from 78 balls, before hitting Chisoro for three successive fours; not long after, he crashed Sikandar Raza for four and six to seal the win. An energised crowd, numbering around 3,000, never lost their voices, even as defeat loomed. After a large, unwieldy trophy was handed over to the happy Sri Lankans, the Zimbabwean squad went across to the busy side of the ground, adjacent to the old clubhouse, to thank the Bulawayo faithful for their support.

Man of the Match: B. K. G. Mendis. *Man of the Series:* B. K. G. Mendis.

Zimbabwe

H. Masakadza lbw b Kulasekara	10
†P. J. Moor c Pathirana b Lakmal	1
T. K. Musakanda c de Silva b Vandersay	36
C. R. Ervine c and b Vandersay	25
Sikandar Raza lbw b Pathirana	5
S. C. Williams c de Silva b Gunaratne	35
M. N. Waller c and b Pathirana	14
*A. G. Cremer c Mendis b Vandersay	9
D. T. Tiripano not out	10
T. S. Chisoro c Dickwella b Gunaratne	5
B. V. Vitori lbw b Gunaratne	0
Lb 3, w 6, nb 1	10
1/8 (2) 2/19 (1) 3/72 (4) 4/85 (3) 5/89 (5) 6/108 (7) 7/133 (8) 8/155 (6) 9/160 (10) 10/160 (11) (36.3 overs)	160
10 overs: 43-2	

Kulasekara 7–0–30–1; Lakmal 6–0–23–1; Pathirana 7–0–26–2; Shanaka 2–0–18–0; Vandersay 10–0–50–3; Gunaratne 4.3–0–10–3.

Sri Lanka

D. M. de Silva lbw b Vitori	0
M. D. K. J. Perera c Waller b Vitori	14
†D. P. D. N. Dickwella b Vitori	16
B. K. G. Mendis c Williams b Cremer	57
*W. U. Tharanga not out	57
D. A. S. Gunaratne not out	16
Lb 2, w 4	6
1/1 (1) 2/29 (3) 3/42 (2) 4/117 (4) (4 wkts, 37.3 overs)	166
10 overs: 56-3	

M. D. Shanaka, S. S. Pathirana, K. M. D. N. Kulasekara, R. A. S. Lakmal and J. D. F. Vandersay did not bat.

Vitori 9–0–52–3; Tiripano 2–0–14–0; Chisoro 8–0–31–0; Cremer 10–2–32–1; Williams 6–1–22–0; Sikandar Raza 2.3–0–13–0.

Umpires: R. K. Illingworth and T. J. Matibiri. Third umpire: M. A. Gough.
Referee: J. Srinath.

DOMESTIC CRICKET IN ZIMBABWE IN 2015-16

JOHN WARD

On the plus side, there were no pay disputes between Zimbabwe Cricket and the players in 2015-16. But there was little else to cheer in a disorganised season of low standards and poorly motivated teams.

During one of Zimbabwe's busiest international programmes, the administrators tried to arrange domestic matches when the leading players were free, but were frustrated by changes in the national schedule, coach Dav Whatmore's preference for training camps over match practice, and some players' reluctance to play domestic cricket at all. The fixture list was often revised at short notice. Financial constraints meant the Logan Cup and Pro50 Championship were both reduced from nine rounds to six, and Mountaineers, based in Mutare, had to play home first-class fixtures 165 miles away in Harare. With the Test venues in Harare and Bulawayo claiming to be overworked, many games were played on club grounds with poor facilities. None of the 12 Logan Cup matches was drawn; only seven reached the fourth day. A drought was one reason – weather rarely intervened – but another was the low quality of batsmanship, especially when the internationals were missing. Coaches bemoaned a lack of application, rather than ability. There was more good bowling than batting, on slow but rarely difficult pitches.

Mashonaland Eagles won an unprecedented hat-trick of trophies. They were not consistent, but raised their game when it mattered. After two humiliating defeats in their first three matches, they were bottom of the Logan Cup log, but three successive victories brought them the crown. They retained the Pro50 title, winning five games, while bad weather ended the sixth. The Twenty20 tournament (staged in Bulawayo after a two-year gap caused by player strikes and lack of funding) typified Mashonaland's season: they finished second in the qualifying table, with three wins to Mountaineers' six, tied the final and triumphed by a single run in the eliminator over. Tino Mutombodzi showed more confidence in his second stint as captain. Only Regis Chakabva reached a century – twice – but six bowlers managed ten wickets at less than 23 in the Logan Cup; Tanyaradzwa Munyaradzi took 24 at 15.

Defending champions **Matabeleland Tuskers** might have come last but for a one-wicket win over Mid West Rhinos in their final match, when opener Nkosana Mpofu batted more than eight hours for 117 out of 288 for nine. Mpofu had the temperament for a crisis, but scored only one other fifty. His side led on first innings in all six games, but lost three. Craig Ervine made two double-centuries in his three matches – both against Mountaineers – while Keith Dabengwa played a valuable stabilising role. The bowling rarely had real bite, although Tawanda Mupariwa turned in some startling new-ball spells.

Strengthened by Vusi Sibanda and Wellington Masakadza (rejoining his brothers), **Mountaineers** looked the most powerful side, with or without their internationals. Yet they were lethargic and seemed to lack motivation, especially when Sibanda and Hamilton Masakadza were absent. Having to play away from home was probably a factor. They needed one victory in their last two games to win the Logan Cup, but lost both. The batting rarely performed, though Shingi Masakadza, the only brother not required by Zimbabwe, had a good all-round season, and Donald Tiripano often bowled superbly.

Mid West Rhinos finished last, thanks to that one-wicket defeat by Matabeleland Tuskers. They suffered severely from international call-ups, but frequently put up a good fight. Rhinos had one of cricket's most entertaining opening pairs: Bothwell Chapungu and Tendai Maruma attacked with an audacity bordering on recklessness, often scoring more than a run a ball. Former Under-19 internationals Tarisai Musakanda and pace bowler Carl Mumba were both selected for Zimbabwe in 2016.

The latest financial crisis in Zimbabwe Cricket made it unlikely that domestic standards would improve in the near future. The game is in serious trouble, with no solutions in sight; what ZC can achieve is greater efficiency and stability in what cricket there is.

FIRST-CLASS AVERAGES, 2015-16

BATTING (200 runs)

	M	*I*	*NO*	*R*	*HS*	*100*	*Avge*	*Ct/St*
M. N. Waller (*Zimbabwe A*)	1	2	0	256	138	2	128.00	1
†C. R. Ervine (*Matabeleland Tuskers*)	3	5	0	477	215	2	95.40	0
†R. P. Burl (*Zim A/Mashonaland Eagles*)	3	6	2	279	78	0	69.75	1
P. J. Moor (*Zimbabwe A/Mid West Rhinos*)	5	10	1	563	129*	3	62.55	9
R. W. Chakabva (*Zim A/Mashonaland Eagles*)	6	11	0	586	175	4	53.27	14/1
V. Sibanda (*Zimbabwe A/Mountaineers*)	6	11	1	422	140	1	42.20	7
N. R. Waller (*Mashonaland Eagles*)	4	7	1	242	78	0	40.33	5
T. K. Musakanda (*Mid West Rhinos*)	5	10	1	351	66	0	39.00	8
†K. M. Dabengwa (*Matabeleland Tuskers*)	6	11	2	344	90	0	38.22	7
†N. Mpofu (*Matabeleland Tuskers*)	6	11	1	378	117*	1	37.80	2
T. P. Maruma (*Mid West Rhinos*)	6	12	1	398	86*	0	36.18	1
F. Mutizwa (*Mountaineers*)	6	11	2	313	61	0	34.77	12
K. O. Maunze (*Mashonaland Eagles*)	4	7	0	241	96	0	34.42	3
H. Masakadza (*Zimbabwe A/Mountaineers*)	5	10	0	316	67	0	31.60	6
†B. M. Chapungu (*Mid West Rhinos*)	6	12	0	328	118	1	27.33	2
S. W. Masakadza (*Mountaineers*)	6	10	0	242	86	0	24.20	5
B. B. Chari (*Zim A/Matabeleland Tuskers*)	7	13	0	271	128	1	20.84	2
J. Gumbie (*Zimbabwe A/Mashonaland Eagles*)	7	13	1	239	70	0	19.91	16/4

BOWLING (10 wickets)

	Style	*O*	*M*	*R*	*W*	*BB*	*5I*	*Avge*
G. T. Aliseni (*Mashonaland Eagles*)	RFM	44.2	9	125	11	4-36	0	11.36
C. T. Mumba (*Mid West Rhinos*)	RFM	132.3	36	314	23	4-20	0	13.65
W. P. Masakadza (*Mountaineers*)	SLA	57.1	13	150	10	3-14	0	15.00
T. Munyaradzi (*Mashonaland Eagles*)	RM	107.2	19	371	24	4-23	0	15.45
T. Muzarawetu (*Mashonaland Eagles*)	RM	76	18	246	14	4-32	0	17.57
L. M. Jongwe (*Matabeleland Tuskers*)	RFM	57	13	188	10	4-58	0	18.80
Mohammad Shahid (*Bangladesh A*)	RFM	64.1	19	196	10	5-45	1	19.60
T. Mupariwa (*Matabeleland Tuskers*)	RFM	113	26	377	18	5-33	2	20.94
T. Muzarabani (*Mashonaland Eagles*)	RFM	88.5	20	274	13	4-21	0	21.07
T. N. Garwe (*Zim A/Mashonaland Eagles*)	RFM	172.1	41	543	25	5-41	1	21.72
D. T. Tiripano (*Zimbabwe A/Mountaineers*)	RFM	156.3	34	457	21	4-34	0	21.76
S. W. Masakadza (*Mountaineers*)	RFM	168.4	32	557	25	5-50	1	22.28
H. T. Chikomba (*Mashonaland Eagles*)	SLA	79.3	17	290	13	4-32	0	22.30
M. T. Chinouya (*Mid West Rhinos*)	RFM	115.1	36	282	12	3-17	0	23.50
C. B. Mpofu (*Matabeleland Tuskers*)	RFM	73.5	12	262	11	3-27	0	23.81
T. S. Chisoro (*Mid West Rhinos*)	LFM	97	20	291	12	5-53	1	24.25
J. C. Nyumbu (*Matabeleland Tuskers*)	OB	138.4	16	524	20	4-63	0	26.20
V. M. Nyauchi (*Zimbabwe A/Mountaineers*)	RFM	185.2	51	497	18	3-23	0	27.61
T. M. Mboyi (*Matabeleland Tuskers*)	RM	81.2	14	290	10	5-46	1	29.00
N. M'shangwe (*Zimbabwe A/Mountaineers*)	LBG	191	21	768	17	3-20	0	45.17

LOGAN CUP, 2015-16

	Played	*Won*	*Lost*	*Drawn*	*1st-inns points*	*Points*
Mashonaland Eagles	6	4	2	0	2	26
Matabeleland Tuskers	6	3	3	0	6	24
Mountaineers	6	3	3	0	3	21
Mid West Rhinos	6	2	4	0	1	13

Win = 6pts; draw = 2pts; lead on first innings = 1pt.

At Harare (Country Club), November 25–27, 2015. **Mashonaland Eagles won by 60 runs. ‡Mashonaland Eagles 88** (T. Mupariwa 5-33) **and 233; Matabeleland Tuskers 138 and 123.** *Mashonaland Eagles 6pts, Matabeleland Tuskers 1pt. Mashonaland Eagles began by losing their top four for ducks. They were 47-9 but scraped 88 thanks to 37* from No. 10 Taurai Muzarabani. But Tino Mutombodzi scored 72 in the second innings, and left Matabeleland Tuskers a target of 184; Trevor Garwe's 4-40 secured an unlikely win.*

At Kwekwe, November 25–27, 2015. **Mountaineers won by 56 runs. Mountaineers 233 and 207** (N. Madziva 5-37); **‡Mid West Rhinos 165 and 219** (P. J. Moor 129*). *Mountaineers 7pts. Mid West Rhinos needed 276, and Peter Moor hit six sixes in a career-best 129* – but was stranded when the last seven fell for nine, three to Wellington Masakadza's left-arm spin and four to Donald Tiripano's pace. The last six batsmen scored a single between them.*

At Harare (Country Club), December 5–7, 2015. **Mid West Rhinos won by 142 runs. ‡Mid West Rhinos 296 and 100; Mashonaland Eagles 165** (T. S. Chisoro 5-53) **and 89.** *Mid West Rhinos 7pts. For the second game running, Mashonaland Eagles were 47-9 and bowled out for under 90. Muzarabani (demoted to No. 11) saved some face again, hitting 33 in 17 balls, when none of his team-mates had managed more than eight – but it was too little, too late.*

At Bulawayo (Queens), December 5–8, 2015. **Matabeleland Tuskers won by three wickets. ‡Mountaineers 244** (V. Sibanda 140) **and 295; Matabeleland Tuskers 386** (C. R. Ervine 203) **and 154-7.** *Matabeleland Tuskers 7pts. Vusi Sibanda hit 140 on first-class debut for Mountaineers, followed by 90. But Craig Ervine secured a decisive advantage with his maiden double-hundred.*

At Harare (Old Hararians), December 15–17, 2015. **Mountaineers won by nine wickets. ‡Mashonaland Eagles 104 and 128** (S. W. Masakadza 5-50); **Mountaineers 213 and 22-1.** *Mountaineers 7pts. Two more collapses by Mashonaland Eagles left Mountaineers needing only 20 to win; a match aggregate of 467 for 31 was the season's lowest. In Mashonaland's second innings, Cephas Zhuwao retired hurt at 1-0; the next three batsmen were dismissed in five balls, and he resumed at 16-4.*

At Bulawayo (Athletic Club), December 15–18, 2015. **Mid West Rhinos won by seven wickets. ‡Matabeleland Tuskers 310 and 161; Mid West Rhinos 288** (T. Mupariwa 5-95) **and 184-3.** *Mid West Rhinos 6pts, Matabeleland Tuskers 1pt. With Mid West Rhinos chasing 184, Bothwell Chapungu and Tendai Maruma opened with 74 at eight an over; Maruma finished on 86* from 87 balls.*

At Bulawayo (Queens), January 8–11, 2016. **Mashonaland Eagles won by 88 runs. ‡Mashonaland Eagles 237** (M. M. Mabuza 5-36) **and 234** (D. S. A. Bell 5-51); **Matabeleland Tuskers 279 and 104.** *Mashonaland Eagles 6pts, Matabeleland Tuskers 1pt. After two defeats, Mashonaland Eagles were seven down in their second innings and only 137 ahead when debutant Deven Bell took his fifth wicket, but Zhuwao's career-best 82 helped extend that to 192. Then it was their turn to inflict a collapse: Gerald Aliseni collected seven wickets in the match, and Tanyaradzwa Munyaradzi eight.*

At Harare (Old Hararians), January 8–11, 2016. **Mountaineers won by eight wickets. ‡Mid West Rhinos 280** (T. Mufudza 5-85) **and 165; Mountaineers 370** (I. Kaia 102) **and 76-2.** *Mountaineers 7pts. In Mid West Rhinos' second-innings 165, Tendai Maruma made 65, Tarisai Musakanda 59 and the next best was eight from Extras. Tinashe Kamunhukamwe batted as a full substitute for Mountaineers on the final day, after Sibanda was called up by Zimbabwe.*

At Harare (Sports Club), February 23–26, 2016. **Matabeleland Tuskers won by an innings and 50 runs. Mountaineers 136** (T. M. Mboyi 5-46) **and 281** (T. Maruma 106*); **‡Matabeleland Tuskers 467-6 dec** (C. R. Ervine 215). *Matabeleland Tuskers 7pts. Ervine scored his second double-century of the season, both against Mountaineers; no one else managed one. He added 141 for Matabeleland's third wicket with Nkosana Mpofu and 184 for the fifth with Keith Dabengwa to set up the highest total of the tournament. Timycen Maruma retired on 54 in the second innings, then returned to complete an unbeaten century, but could not avert an innings defeat.*

At Kwekwe, February 23–25, 2016. **Mashonaland Eagles won by an innings and 143 runs. Mashonaland Eagles 445** (R. W. Chakabva 175); **‡Mid West Rhinos 124 and 178.** *Mashonaland Eagles 7pts. Heavily depleted by injuries and international calls, Mid West Rhinos suffered a crushing loss which meant they were the only team who entered the final round unable to take the title. Zhuwao and Kudzai Maunze shared the tournament's only century opening partnership, before Regis Chakabva steered Mashonaland past 400, sharing further three-figure stands with Maunze and Nathan Waller. Mashonaland dismissed Rhinos twice inside 81 overs.*

At Harare (Sports Club), March 2–5, 2016. **Mashonaland Eagles won by five wickets. Mountaineers 192 and 268; ‡Mashonaland Eagles 359** (R. W. Chakabva 103) **and 102-5.** *Mashonaland Eagles 7pts. Mashonaland Eagles, who started two points behind leaders Mountaineers, put them in and reduced them to 72-7, before Shingi Masakadza hit five sixes in a 72-ball 86. But Chakabva's second successive century, again backed up by fifties from Maunze and Waller, meant Mashonaland led by 167. It required a seventh-wicket century stand between Forster Mutizwa and Masakadza to clear that deficit; Mashonaland needed only 102 to collect their third trophy in 2016.*

At Bulawayo (Athletic Club), March 2–5, 2016. **Matabeleland Tuskers won by one wicket. Mid West Rhinos 170 and 291** (B. M. Chapungu 118); **‡Matabeleland Tuskers 174** (B. A. Mavuta 6-45) **and 288-9** (N. Mpofu 117*). *Matabeleland Tuskers 7pts. Scheduled for Kwekwe, this game was moved after the dates were changed twice. Leg-spinner Brandon Mavuta took 6-45, the tournament's best return, on debut; another debutant, seamer Charlton Tshuma, took seven for Matabeleland Tuskers. Chapungu (with a run-a-ball maiden hundred) and Maruma opened the second innings with 92 at seven an over. Needing 288, Matabeleland stumbled to 158-7; Chris Mpofu joined Nkosana Mpofu and scored a maiden fifty as they added 96. Nkosana batted throughout the innings for 117* off 352 balls, completing victory in a last-wicket stand of 32* with Tshuma.*

LOGAN CUP WINNERS

1993-94	Mashonaland U24	2001-02	Mashonaland	2009-10	Mashonaland Eagles
1994-95	Mashonaland	2002-03	Mashonaland	2010-11	Matabeleland Tuskers
1995-96	Matabeleland	2003-04	Mashonaland	2011-12	Matabeleland Tuskers
1996-97	Mashonaland	2004-05	Mashonaland	2012-13	Matabeleland Tuskers
1997-98	Mashonaland	2005-06	*No competition*	2013-14	Mountaineers
1998-99	Matabeleland	2006-07	Easterns	2014-15	Matabeleland Tuskers
1999-2000	Mashonaland	2007-08	Northerns	2015-16	Mashonaland Eagles
2000-01	Mashonaland	2008-09	Easterns		

Mashonaland/Northerns/Mashonaland Eagles have won the title 12 times, Matabeleland/Matabeleland Tuskers 6, Easterns/Mountaineers 3, Mashonaland Under-24 1.

PRO50 CHAMPIONSHIP, 2015-16

50-over league

	Played	*Won*	*Lost*	*No result*	*Bonus points*	*Points*	*Net run-rate*
Mashonaland Eagles	6	5	0	1	3	25	1.09
Mountaineers	6	3	2	1	1	15	0.13
Matabeleland Tuskers	6	2	4	0	0	8	−0.91
Mid West Rhinos	6	1	5	0	1	5	0.01

DOMESTIC TWENTY20, 2015-16

20-over league plus final and third-place play-off

	Played	*Won*	*Lost*	*Bonus points*	*Points*	*Net run-rate*
MOUNTAINEERS	6	6	0	3	27	2.69
MASHONALAND EAGLES	6	3	3	0	12	−1.32
Mid West Rhinos	6	2	4	1	9	−0.23
Matabeleland Tuskers	6	1	5	0	4	−1.15

Third-place play-off At Bulawayo (Queens), February 13, 2016. **Mid West Rhinos won by 18 runs. Mid West Rhinos 150-5** (20 overs); **‡Matabeleland Tuskers 132-6** (20 overs).

Final At Bulawayo (Queens), February 13, 2016. **Mashonaland Eagles won an eliminator over, following a tie. ‡Mountaineers 167-6** (20 overs); **Mashonaland Eagles 167-6** (20 overs). *MoT:* H. Masakadza. *When these sides met two days earlier, Hamilton Masakadza had hit 162* in 71 balls for Mountaineers, the second-highest score in all Twenty20 cricket. This time, he scored 66 in 42 – but Cephas Zhuwao replied for Mashonaland Eagles with 71 in 48, including seven sixes. In the eliminator over, Mashonaland scored 17-1 (all to Zhuwao) and Mountaineers 16-0.*

INTERNATIONAL RESULTS IN 2016

TEST MATCHES

	Tests	*Won*	*Lost*	*Drawn*	*% won*	*% lost*	*% drawn*
India	12	9	0	3	**75.00**	0.00	25.00
Sri Lanka	9	5	3	1	**55.55**	33.33	11.11
South Africa	9	5	2	2	**55.55**	22.22	22.22
Bangladesh	2	1	1	0	**50.00**	50.00	0.00
Australia	11	5	5	1	**45.45**	45.45	9.09
New Zealand	11	4	6	1	**36.36**	54.54	9.09
Pakistan	11	4	7	0	**36.36**	63.63	0.00
England	17	6	8	3	**35.29**	47.05	17.64
West Indies	8	1	4	3	**12.50**	50.00	37.50
Zimbabwe	4	0	4	0	**0.00**	100.00	0.00
Totals	47	40	40	7	**85.10**	85.10	14.89

ONE-DAY INTERNATIONALS

(Full Member matches only)

	ODIs	*Won*	*Lost*	*Tied*	*NR*	*% won*	*% lost*
England	18	11	5	1	1	**67.64**	32.35
South Africa	16	10	5	0	1	**66.66**	33.33
Australia	28	16	11	0	1	**59.25**	40.74
New Zealand	18	10	7	0	1	**58.82**	41.17
India	13	7	6	0	0	**53.84**	46.15
Pakistan	10	4	6	0	0	**40.00**	60.00
West Indies	14	4	9	1	0	**32.14**	67.85
Sri Lanka	17	4	9	1	3	**32.14**	67.85
Zimbabwe	8	1	5	1	1	**21.42**	78.57
Bangladesh	6	1	5	0	0	**16.66**	83.33
Totals	74	68	68	2	4		

The following teams also played official one-day internationals in 2016, some against Full Members (not included in the table above): Hong Kong (P6 W3 L2 NR1); Scotland (P7 W3 L2 NR2); Afghanistan (P12 W5 L6 NR1); Papua New Guinea (P3 W1 L2); Ireland (P9 W2 L7); United Arab Emirates (P2 L2). The % won and lost excludes no-results; ties are counted as half a win.

TWENTY20 INTERNATIONALS

(Full Member matches only)

	T20Is	*Won*	*Lost*	*NR*	*% won*	*% lost*
New Zealand	10	8	2	0	**80.00**	20.00
India	20	14	5	1	**73.68**	26.31
West Indies	10	6	3	1	**66.66**	33.33
Pakistan	14	7	7	0	**50.00**	50.00
Australia	12	6	6	0	**50.00**	50.00
South Africa	8	4	4	0	**50.00**	50.00
England	9	4	5	0	**44.44**	55.55
Zimbabwe	7	3	4	0	**42.85**	57.14
Bangladesh	12	4	8	0	**33.33**	66.66
Sri Lanka	14	1	13	0	**7.14**	92.85
Totals	58	57	57	1		

The following teams also played official T20 internationals in 2016, some against Full Members (not included in the table above): Afghanistan (P15 W11 L4); Netherlands (P5 W2 L2 NR1); Scotland (P7 W3 L4); Oman (P6 W2 L3 NR1); Ireland (P9 W3 L5 NR1); United Arab Emirates (P14 W5 L9); Papua New Guinea (P3 W1 L2); Hong Kong (P9 W2 L7). The % won and lost excludes no-results.

MRF TYRES ICC TEAM RANKINGS

TEST CHAMPIONSHIP (as at January 23, 2017)

		Matches	*Points*	*Rating*
1	India	35	4,208	120
2	Australia	44	4,797	109
3	South Africa	33	3,528	107
4	England	50	5,071	101
5	New Zealand	41	4,011	98
6	Pakistan	36	3,494	97
7	Sri Lanka	39	3,578	92
8	West Indies	30	2,077	69
9	Bangladesh	18	1,116	62
10	Zimbabwe	10	48	5

ONE-DAY CHAMPIONSHIP (as at December 31, 2016)

		Matches	*Points*	*Rating*
1	Australia	54	6,506	120
2	South Africa	52	6,024	116
3	India	53	5,891	111
4	New Zealand	52	5,771	111
5	England	54	5,804	107
6	Sri Lanka	60	6,056	101
7	Bangladesh	33	3,019	91
8	Pakistan	51	4,555	89
9	West Indies	37	3,168	86
10	Afghanistan	26	1,341	52
11	Zimbabwe	50	2,409	48
12	Ireland	20	834	42

TWENTY20 CHAMPIONSHIP (as at December 31, 2016)

		Matches	*Points*	*Rating*
1	New Zealand	21	2,683	128
2	India	28	3,441	123
3	South Africa	25	2,986	119
4	West Indies	22	2,547	116
5	England	23	2,644	115
6	Australia	21	2,391	114
7	Pakistan	34	3,852	113
8	Sri Lanka	28	2,632	94
9	Afghanistan	30	2,473	82
10	Bangladesh	25	1,828	73
11	Netherlands	17	1,073	63
12	Zimbabwe	26	1,614	62
13	Scotland	16	975	61
14	Hong Kong	19	832	44
15	UAE	20	847	42
16	Oman	9	352	39
17	Ireland	17	596	35
	Papua New Guinea (*insufficient matches to achieve a ranking*)	6	410	68

The ratings are based on all Test series, one-day and T20 internationals completed since May 1, 2013.

MRF TYRES ICC PLAYER RANKINGS

Introduced in 1987, the rankings have been backed by various sponsors, and were taken over by the ICC in January 2005. They rank cricketers on a scale up to 1,000 on their performance. The rankings take into account playing conditions, quality of opposition, and result. In August 1998, a similar set of rankings for one-day internationals was launched, and Twenty20 rankings were added in October 2011.

The leading players in the Test rankings on January 23, 2017, were:

Rank	*Batsmen*	*Points*	*Rank*	*Bowlers*	*Points*
1	S. P. D. Smith (A)	933	1	R. Ashwin (I)	887
2	V. Kohli (I)	875	2	R. A. Jadeja (I)	879
3	J. E. Root (E)	848	3	J. R. Hazlewood (A)	860
4	K. S. Williamson (NZ)	823	4	H. M. R. K. B. Herath (SL)	827
5	D. A. Warner (A)	812	5	K. Rabada (SA)	821
6	H. M. Amla (SA)	787	6	D. W. Steyn (SA)	819
7	Azhar Ali (P)	779	7	J. M. Anderson (E)	810
8	Younis Khan (P)	772	8	S. C. J. Broad (E)	803
9	Q. de Kock (SA)	760	9	V. D. Philander (SA)	798
10	A. B. de Villiers (SA)	755	10	M. A. Starc (A)	770

The leading players in the one-day international rankings on December 31, 2016, were:

Rank	*Batsmen*	*Points*	*Rank*	*Bowlers*	*Points*
1	A. B. de Villiers (SA)	861	1	T. A. Boult (NZ)	718
2	V. Kohli (I)	848	2	Imran Tahir (SA)	712
3	D. A. Warner (A)	846	3	S. P. Narine (WI)	711
4	Q. de Kock (SA)	779	4	M. A. Starc (A)	705
5	K. S. Williamson (NZ)	770	5	A. U. Rashid (E)	655
6	H. M. Amla (SA)	748	6	Shakib Al Hasan (B)	643
7	J. E. Root (E)	747	7	M. J. Henry (NZ)	641
8	M. J. Guptill (NZ)	735	8	K. Rabada (SA)	628
9	R. G. Sharma (I)	728	9	A. R. Patel (I)	624
10	S. P. D. Smith (A)	725	10	J. R. Hazlewood (A)	619
				Mohammad Nabi (Afg)	619

The leading players in the Twenty20 international rankings on December 31, 2016, were:

Rank	*Batsmen*	*Points*	*Rank*	*Bowlers*	*Points*
1	V. Kohli (I)	820	1	Imran Tahir (SA)	740
2	A. J. Finch (A)	771	2	J. J. Bumrah (I)	735
3	G. J. Maxwell (A)	763	3	S. Badree (WI)	723
4	M. J. Guptill (NZ)	754	4	Imad Wasim (P)	718
5	F. du Plessis (SA)	741	5	Rashid Khan (Afg)	706
6	K. S. Williamson (NZ)	719	6	R. Ashwin (I)	684
7	J. E. Root (E)	708	7	J. P. Faulkner (A)	672
8	A. D. Hales (E)	705	8	K. J. Abbott (SA)	671
9	Mohammad Shahzad (Afg)	687	9	A. F. Milne (NZ)	655
10	H. Masakadza (Z)	657	10	S. P. Narine (WI)	653

TEST AVERAGES IN CALENDAR YEAR 2016

BATTING (400 runs)

	T	*I*	*NO*	*R*	*HS*	*100*	*50*	*Avge*	*SR*	*Ct/St*
V. Kohli (I)	12	18	2	1,215	235	4	2	75.93	60.41	14
S. P. D. Smith (A)	11	18	3	1,079	165*	4	5	71.93	58.73	29
†Q. de Kock (SA)	8	13	2	695	129*	2	5	63.18	78.61	34
Azhar Ali (P)	11	22	3	1,198	302*	3	4	63.05	46.63	7
L. R. P. L. Taylor (NZ)	9	15	5	606	173*	3	1	60.60	64.67	10
K. L. Rahul (I)	7	9	0	539	199	2	1	59.88	62.02	9
J. M. Bairstow (E)	17	29	4	1,470	167*	3	8	58.80	58.21	66/4
F. du Plessis (SA)	8	13	3	567	118*	2	2	56.70	48.37	4
D. M. de Silva (SL)	6	12	1	615	129	2	2	55.90	54.56	5
C. A. Pujara (I)	11	16	1	836	124	3	4	55.73	48.43	6
K. C. Brathwaite (WI)	8	14	3	613	142*	1	5	55.72	42.04	7
A. M. Rahane (I)	10	15	3	653	188	2	2	54.41	47.69	10
J. E. Root (E)	17	32	2	1,477	254	3	10	49.23	60.70	26
H. M. Amla (SA)	9	15	0	729	201	2	3	48.60	51.30	9
S. C. Cook (SA)	7	12	0	575	117	3	2	47.91	46.29	2
†U. T. Khawaja (A)	10	16	0	753	145	2	4	47.06	54.28	13
K. S. Williamson (NZ)	10	18	2	753	113	1	6	47.06	53.40	10
†M. M. Ali (E)	17	29	6	1,078	155*	4	5	46.86	53.79	7
†B. A. Stokes (E)	12	21	1	904	258	2	3	45.20	66.76	9
R. Ashwin (I)	12	14	0	612	118	2	4	43.71	48.15	5
B-J. Watling (NZ)	11	17	4	554	107	1	2	42.61	49.42	30/1
†A. N. Cook (E)	17	33	3	1,270	130	2	7	42.33	51.90	17
T. Bavuma (SA)	9	15	3	505	102*	1	3	42.08	47.91	3
†D. A. Warner (A)	11	19	1	748	144	2	2	41.55	86.87	4
A. C. Voges (A)	8	13	1	457	239	1	1	38.08	49.40	6
Younis Khan (P)	10	19	1	673	218	2	2	37.38	50.48	12
M. Vijay (I)	10	15	0	550	136	2	2	36.66	42.56	6
Asad Shafiq (P)	11	21	1	733	137	2	5	36.65	53.89	11
†Sami Aslam (P)	9	18	1	618	91	0	6	36.35	39.11	6
L. D. Chandimal (SL)	7	13	0	458	132	2	0	35.23	42.64	11/2
†J-P. Duminy (SA)	7	12	0	419	141	1	2	34.91	55.57	4
B. K. G. Mendis (SL)	9	18	1	589	176	1	3	34.64	65.15	15
Sarfraz Ahmed (P)	11	19	2	562	59*	0	3	33.05	70.33	36
†T. W. M. Latham (NZ)	11	20	0	658	136	2	5	32.90	45.69	12
Misbah-ul-Haq (P)	10	18	1	543	114	1	4	31.94	47.96	5
†D. M. Bravo (WI)	8	14	0	445	116	1	2	31.78	41.05	6
†D. Elgar (SA)	8	13	0	403	127	1	1	31.00	43.85	9
C. R. Woakes (E)	12	21	5	493	66	0	2	30.81	44.49	6
J. K. Silva (SL)	9	18	0	534	115	1	3	29.66	41.98	4
†F. D. M. Karunaratne (SL)	9	18	1	498	110	1	3	29.29	49.11	7
A. D. Hales (E)	10	19	0	537	94	0	5	28.26	44.71	8

BOWLING (10 wickets)

	Style	*O*	*M*	*R*	*W*	*BB*	*5I*	*Avge*	*SR*
D. W. Steyn (SA)	RF	55	14	153	11	5-33	1	13.90	30.00
Bhuvneshwar Kumar (I)	RFM	85.4	24	195	13	5-33	2	15.00	39.53
Mehedi Hasan (B)	OB	109.2	12	297	19	6-77	3	15.63	34.52
Shakib Al Hasan (B)	SLA	81	19	221	12	5-85	1	18.41	40.50
K. J. Abbott (SA)	RFM	137.4	38	340	18	6-77	1	18.88	45.88
H. M. R. K. B. Herath (SL)	SLA	412.2	89	1,079	57	8-63	5	18.92	43.40
N. Wagner (NZ)	LFM	320.1	74	863	41	6-41	3	21.04	46.85
V. D. Philander (SA)	RFM	180.3	45	482	22	5-21	2	21.90	49.22

	Style	O	M	R	W	BB	5I	Avge	SR
M. A. Starc (A)	LF	325.4	71	1,129	50	6-50	3	22.58	39.08
K. Rabada (SA)	RF	281.2	50	1,074	46	7-112	4	23.34	36.69
J. M. Anderson (E)	RFM	394.1	103	973	41	5-16	3	23.73	57.68
R. Ashwin (I)	OB	584.4	102	1,721	72	7-59	8	23.90	48.72
R. A. Jadeja (I)	SLA	463.4	116	1,056	43	7-48	2	24.55	64.69
M. D. K. Perera (SL)	OB	190.3	28	565	23	6-70	1	24.56	49.69
C. R. Woakes (E)	RFM	339.2	78	1,042	41	6-70	2	25.41	49.65
B. A. Stokes (E)	RFM	279.2	46	852	33	5-73	1	25.81	50.78
S. C. J. Broad (E)	RFM	463.4	117	1,275	48	6-17	1	26.56	57.95
Mohammed Shami (I)	RFM	271.1	52	779	29	4-66	0	26.86	56.10
J. R. Hazlewood (A)	RFM	426	111	1,170	42	6-89	1	27.85	60.85
I. Sharma (I)	RFM	115	26	316	11	2-30	0	28.72	62.72
J. M. Bird (A)	RFM	186.5	39	631	21	5-59	1	30.04	53.38
I. S. Sodhi (NZ)	LBG	95.2	23	348	11	4-60	0	31.63	52.00
T. G. Southee (NZ)	RFM	298.4	88	859	27	6-80	1	31.81	66.37
T. A. Boult (NZ)	LFM	359	82	1,027	31	4-52	0	33.12	69.48
M. Morkel (SA)	RF	105.2	24	332	10	3-36	0	33.20	63.20
A. N. P. R. Fernando (SL)	RFM	153.5	35	499	15	4-107	0	33.26	61.53
Sohail Khan (P)	RFM	247.4	44	880	26	5-68	2	33.84	57.15
D. Bishoo (WI)	LBG	212.5	16	756	22	8-49	1	34.36	58.04
Wahab Riaz (P)	LF	270	25	999	29	5-88	1	34.44	55.86
R. A. S. Lakmal (SL)	RFM	212	35	665	19	5-63	1	35.00	66.94
A. U. Rashid (E)	LBG	287.1	23	1,070	30	4-52	0	35.66	57.43
N. M. Lyon (A)	OB	438	69	1,490	41	4-91	0	36.34	64.09
Yasir Shah (P)	LBG	538.2	82	1,780	46	6-72	4	38.69	70.21
Mohammad Amir (P)	LFM	380.2	74	1,165	30	4-97	0	38.83	76.06
S. T. Gabriel (WI)	RFM	175.1	26	587	15	5-96	1	39.13	70.06
M. J. Santner (NZ)	SLA	278.2	53	838	21	3-60	0	39.90	79.52
Rahat Ali (P)	LFM	203.5	35	721	18	4-62	0	40.05	67.94
M. L. Cummins (WI)	RF	118.2	16	408	10	6-48	1	40.80	71.00
A. Mishra (I)	LBG	145.4	28	507	11	2-43	0	46.09	79.45
S. T. Finn (E)	RFM	235.1	33	793	17	3-26	0	46.64	83.00
J. O. Holder (WI)	RFM	177.5	46	467	10	5-30	1	46.70	106.70
U. T. Yadav (I)	RF	238.5	49	737	15	4-41	0	49.13	95.53
M. M. Ali (E)	OB	532	83	1,962	37	5-57	1	53.02	86.27
R. L. Chase (WI)	OB	207.1	26	643	11	5-121	1	58.45	113.00
A. G. Cremer (Z)	LBG	217.4	15	829	13	4-91	0	63.76	100.46

MOST DISMISSALS BY A WICKETKEEPER

Dis		T	
70	(66ct, 4st)	17	J. M. Bairstow (E)
36	(36ct)	11	Sarfraz Ahmed (P)
34	(34ct)	8	Q. de Kock (SA)
31	(30ct, 1st)	11	B-J. Watling (NZ)
27	(26ct, 1st)	8	P. M. Nevill (A)
19	(17ct, 2st)	9	W. P. Saha (I)

MOST CATCHES IN THE FIELD

Ct	T	
29	11	S. P. D. Smith (A)
26	17	J. E. Root (E)
17	17	A. N. Cook (E)
14	12	V. Kohli (I)
13	9	B. K. G. Mendis (SL)
13	10	U. T. Khawaja (A)
12	10	Younis Khan (P)

Mendis made two further catches when deputising as wicketkeeper.

ONE-DAY INTERNATIONAL AVERAGES IN CALENDAR YEAR 2016

BATTING (350 runs)

	M	*I*	*NO*	*R*	*HS*	*100*	*50*	*Avge*	*SR*	*4*	*6*
V. Kohli (I)	10	10	2	739	154*	3	4	92.37	100.00	62	8
†E. C. Joyce (Ire)	7	7	2	366	160*	2	1	73.20	81.33	37	4
†D. A. Warner (A)	23	23	1	1,388	173	7	4	63.09	105.47	148	22
R. G. Sharma (I)	10	10	1	564	171*	2	2	62.66	95.27	46	19
A. D. Hales (E)	14	13	1	743	171	3	4	61.91	101.36	86	12
J. E. Root (E)	15	14	1	796	125	2	6	61.23	91.81	71	8
Babar Azam (P)	11	11	0	656	123	3	2	59.63	95.21	58	6
L. D. Chandimal (SL)	14	13	2	656	102	2	6	59.63	77.72	37	6
J. C. Buttler (E)	16	13	3	573	105	1	5	57.30	129.93	50	21
†Q. de Kock (SA)	17	17	2	857	178	3	3	57.13	108.61	91	26
Sarfraz Ahmed (P)	11	11	2	492	105	1	3	54.66	92.83	41	1
S. P. D. Smith (A)	26	25	2	1,154	164	3	7	50.17	89.18	102	15
†B. A. Stokes (E)	13	12	2	490	101	1	4	49.00	105.60	37	18
F. du Plessis (SA)	15	14	2	578	111	1	4	48.16	97.96	59	5
A. D. Mathews (SL)	13	12	1	520	95	0	5	47.27	83.20	35	7
†R. R. Rossouw (SA)	10	10	1	413	122	1	3	45.88	93.43	49	3
†Tamim Iqbal (B)	9	9	0	407	118	1	2	45.22	73.73	44	2
J. J. Roy (E)	17	17	2	647	162	2	2	43.13	108.01	65	12
M. R. Marsh (A)	23	21	6	642	102*	1	4	42.80	96.10	60	15
M. J. Guptill (NZ)	18	18	1	727	114	2	4	42.76	99.86	74	28
K. S. Williamson (NZ)	18	18	1	699	118	1	5	41.11	81.75	73	8
†Sharjeel Khan (P)	9	9	0	368	152	1	2	40.88	143.19	49	15
†U. T. Khawaja (A)	12	11	1	399	98	0	4	39.90	90.68	37	8
H. M. Amla (SA)	14	14	1	511	127	2	2	39.30	88.86	58	3
B. K. G. Mendis (SL)	17	16	1	569	94	0	7	37.93	91.47	71	9
Mohammad Shahzad (Afg)	12	12	0	453	84	0	3	37.75	88.82	55	7
M. N. Samuels (WI)	10	10	0	374	125	1	2	37.40	92.34	30	11
†J-P. Duminy (SA)	16	14	2	444	82	0	3	37.00	89.15	38	6
G. J. Bailey (A)	27	25	3	808	112	1	5	36.72	79.21	59	11
†T. W. M. Latham (NZ)	14	14	1	461	137	1	2	35.46	89.34	40	7
†T. M. Head (A)	15	14	0	416	57	0	3	29.71	86.12	40	5
A. J. Finch (A)	25	23	0	655	107	1	5	28.47	94.10	72	19
†M. S. Wade (A)	29	23	3	518	76	0	3	25.90	95.22	32	14
†M. D. K. J. Perera (SL)	17	16	0	376	135	1	1	23.50	83.74	43	3

BOWLING (15 wickets)

	Style	*O*	*M*	*R*	*W*	*BB*	*4I*	*Avge*	*SR*	*ER*
A. Mishra (I)	LBG	44.5	2	215	15	5-18	1	14.33	17.93	4.79
J. J. Bumrah (I)	RFM	68.3	4	249	17	4-22	2	14.64	24.17	3.63
Rashid Khan (Afg)	LBG	104	5	429	22	4-21	1	19.50	28.36	4.12
M. A. Starc (A)	LF	113.5	7	512	26	3-32	0	19.69	26.26	4.49
A. C. Evans (Scot)	RFM	54.5	1	313	15	4-41	2	20.86	21.93	5.70
Mohammad Nabi (Afg)	OB	91	6	361	17	3-26	0	21.23	32.11	3.96
Mirwais Ashraf (Afg)	RFM	82.2	5	331	15	3-20	0	22.06	32.93	4.02
B. J. McCarthy (Ire)	RFM	66.2	3	417	18	4-59	2	23.16	22.11	6.28
K. J. Abbott (SA)	RFM	75	6	357	15	4-40	1	23.80	30.00	4.76
J. W. Hastings (A)	RFM	131.2	4	700	29	6-45	2	24.13	27.17	5.32
Mashrafe bin Mortaza (B)	RFM	81.4	4	366	15	4-29	1	24.40	32.66	4.48
Imran Tahir (SA)	LBG	131	2	675	27	7-45	1	25.00	29.11	5.15
J. R. Hazlewood (A)	RFM	137.2	10	656	26	5-50	1	25.23	31.69	4.77
Dawlat Zadran (Afg)	RFM	97.2	5	513	20	4-73	1	25.65	29.20	5.27
T. A. Boult (NZ)	LFM	130	6	694	27	4-40	1	25.70	28.88	5.33

	Style	*O*	*M*	*R*	*W*	*BB*	*4I*	*Avge*	*SR*	*ER*
R. A. S. Lakmal (SL)	RFM	88.2	4	443	16	4-38	1	27.68	33.12	5.01
M. J. Henry (NZ)	RFM	101.2	2	610	22	5-40	1	27.72	27.63	6.01
A. Zampa (A)	LBG	155.2	2	834	30	3-16	0	27.80	31.06	5.36
A. U. Rashid (E)	LBG	158.2	0	822	29	4-43	2	28.34	32.75	5.19
S. P. Narine (WI)	OB	97.5	3	429	15	6-27	1	28.60	39.13	4.38
J. O. Holder (WI)	RFM	114	4	584	20	3-57	0	29.20	34.20	5.12
K. Rabada (SA)	RF	118.5	6	655	22	4-45	1	29.77	32.40	5.51
J. P. Faulkner (A)	LFM	140.4	1	766	24	4-38	1	31.91	35.16	5.44
L. E. Plunkett (E)	RFM	90	0	515	15	3-44	0	34.33	36.00	5.72
C. R. Brathwaite (WI)	RFM	110	4	623	18	4-48	1	34.61	36.66	5.66
M. J. Santner (NZ)	SLA	134.2	2	626	18	3-47	0	34.77	44.77	4.66
C. R. Woakes (E)	RFM	115.3	8	618	17	4-41	1	36.35	40.76	5.35
U. T. Yadav (I)	RF	88.5	2	581	15	3-67	0	38.73	35.53	6.54
M. R. Marsh (A)	RFM	147.2	3	846	21	3-32	0	40.28	42.09	5.74
S. M. Boland (A)	RFM	119.2	3	725	16	3-67	0	45.31	44.75	6.07

MOST DISMISSALS BY A WICKETKEEPER

Dis		*M*	
25	(24ct, 1st)	29	M. S. Wade (A)
21	(17ct, 4st)	16	J. C. Buttler (E)
19	(17ct, 2st)	13	L. Ronchi (NZ)
17	(13ct, 4st)	13	M. S. Dhoni (I)
16	(15ct, 1st)	17	Q. de Kock (SA)
15	(11ct, 4st)	11	Sarfraz Ahmed (P)
14	(11ct, 3st)	11	L. D. Chandimal (SL)

Chandimal made one further catch in three one-day internationals when not keeping wicket.

MOST CATCHES IN THE FIELD

Ct	*M*	
19	26	S. P. D. Smith (A)
17	27	G. J. Bailey (A)
13	23	D. A. Warner (A)
11	23	M. R. Marsh (A)
10	15	F. Behardien (SA)

TWENTY20 INTERNATIONAL AVERAGES IN CALENDAR YEAR 2016

BATTING (250 runs, strike-rate 110.00)

	M	*I*	*NO*	*R*	*HS*	*100*	*50*	*Avge*	*SR*	*4*	*6*
G. J. Maxwell (A)	11	11	2	435	145*	1	2	48.33	**174.69**	41	21
M. J. Guptill (NZ)	9	9	1	392	87*	0	4	49.00	**171.92**	40	23
†Najibullah Zadran (Afg)	14	12	7	312	60*	0	2	62.40	**166.84**	22	16
Mohammad Shahzad (Afg)	15	15	1	520	118*	1	1	37.14	**152.94**	59	25
†C. Munro (NZ)	10	9	1	264	56	0	2	33.00	**152.60**	16	19
J. C. Buttler (E)	10	10	4	366	73*	0	3	61.00	**151.23**	24	20
S. R. Watson (A)	9	9	3	298	124*	1	0	49.66	**150.50**	25	14
Babar Hayat (HK)	9	9	1	294	122	1	1	36.75	**150.00**	27	12
H. M. Amla (SA)	7	7	3	308	97*	0	4	77.00	**146.66**	32	11
J. E. Root (E)	9	9	1	297	83	0	2	37.12	**142.78**	29	9
V. Kohli (I)	15	13	7	641	90*	0	7	106.83	**140.26**	70	9
Mahmudullah (B)	16	14	5	275	54	0	1	30.55	**139.59**	22	10
H. Masakadza (Z)	12	12	1	411	93*	0	3	37.36	**137.45**	41	21
J. Charles (WI)	11	11	0	261	79	0	2	23.72	**137.36**	24	14
†Tamim Iqbal (B)	11	11	2	368	103*	1	1	40.88	**135.79**	32	17
†Sharjeel Khan (P)	12	12	0	258	59	0	1	21.50	**135.78**	38	9
R. G. Sharma (I)	18	18	1	497	83	0	4	29.23	**131.48**	45	19
Shoaib Malik (P)	15	13	6	370	63*	0	1	52.85	**131.20**	36	10

	M	I	NO	R	HS	100	50	Avge	SR	4	6
Sabbir Rahman (B)	16	16	3	463	80	0	2	35.61	**127.54**	46	13
M. N. Waller (Z)	12	12	1	277	49*	0	0	25.18	**127.06**	17	10
F. du Plessis (SA)	9	9	1	268	79	0	1	33.50	**126.41**	23	8
Umar Akmal (P)	14	12	3	269	56*	0	2	29.88	**123.96**	15	12
Asghar Stanikzai (Afg)	15	14	1	308	62	0	2	23.69	**121.25**	19	16
K. S. Williamson (NZ)	10	10	2	383	72*	0	3	47.87	**118.94**	42	5
T. M. Dilshan (SL)	14	14	2	299	83*	0	2	24.91	**118.18**	36	6
†Rohan Mustafa (UAE)	14	14	0	288	77	0	2	20.57	**118.03**	30	12
†S. Dhawan (I)	14	14	2	301	60	0	2	25.08	**117.57**	35	10
†Shakib Al Hasan (B)	16	16	5	260	50*	0	1	23.63	**113.53**	22	6
Shaiman Anwar (UAE)	14	14	1	352	60	0	2	27.07	**112.10**	26	14
†Mohammad Usman (UAE)	14	14	3	281	49*	0	0	25.54	**111.95**	27	11

BOWLING (12 wickets, 30 overs)

	Style	O	Dots	R	W	BB	4I	Avge	SR	ER
Mohammad Naveed (UAE)	RM	55.4	196	292	19	3-14	0	15.36	17.57	**5.24**
Imad Wasim (P)	SLA	38	76	232	15	5-14	1	15.46	15.20	**6.10**
Mustafizur Rahman (B)	LFM	31.5	97	195	16	5-22	1	12.18	11.93	**6.12**
M. J. Santner (NZ)	SLA	30.1	90	188	15	4-11	1	12.53	12.06	**6.23**
Rashid Khan (Afg)	LBG	59	151	371	23	3-11	0	16.13	15.39	**6.28**
R. Ashwin (I)	OB	59	155	372	23	4-8	1	16.17	15.39	**6.30**
Nadeem Ahmed (HK)	OB	32	91	203	13	3-23	0	15.61	14.76	**6.34**
Imran Tahir (SA)	LBG	36	76	235	16	4-21	1	14.68	13.50	**6.52**
J. J. Bumrah (I)	RFM	79.3	227	527	28	3-11	0	18.82	17.03	**6.62**
R. A. Jadeja (I)	SLA	59	149	413	17	2-11	0	24.29	20.82	**7.00**
A. Nehra (I)	LFM	53	152	372	18	3-23	0	20.66	17.66	**7.01**
Mohammad Nabi (Afg)	OB	54	128	380	21	4-17	2	18.09	15.42	**7.03**
Shakib Al Hasan (B)	SLA	55.4	124	412	20	4-15	1	20.60	16.70	**7.40**
Rohan Mustafa (UAE)	OB	39.3	81	311	12	3-19	0	25.91	19.75	**7.87**
Amjad Javed (UAE)	RM	43	99	341	22	3-25	0	15.50	11.72	**7.93**
Al-Amin Hossain (B)	RFM	41.5	116	334	22	3-25	0	15.18	11.40	**7.98**
Mohammad Shehzad (UAE)	RM	41.1	86	332	12	3-34	0	27.66	20.58	**8.06**
H. H. Pandya (I)	RFM	44.3	108	360	15	3-8	0	24.00	17.80	**8.08**
Wahab Riaz (P)	LF	40.3	106	330	13	3-18	0	25.38	18.69	**8.14**
D. J. Bravo (WI)	RFM	38	68	312	12	3-37	0	26.00	19.00	**8.21**
J. P. Faulkner (A)	LFM	36.1	65	311	17	5-27	1	18.29	12.76	**8.59**
K. Rabada (SA)	RF	31.2	81	271	13	2-25	0	20.84	14.46	**8.64**
C. J. Jordan (E)	RFM	34.4	76	304	12	4-28	1	25.33	17.33	**8.76**

MOST DISMISSALS BY A WICKETKEEPER

Dis		M	
27	(16ct, 11st)	21	M. S. Dhoni (I)
12	(2ct, 10st)	15	Mohammad Shahzad (Afg)
11	(7ct, 4st)	10	L. Ronchi (NZ)
11	(8ct, 3st)	11	S. P. Patil (UAE)
10	(8ct, 2st)	11	L. D. Chandimal (SL)

Chandimal made two further catches in five Twenty20 internationals when not keeping wicket.

MOST CATCHES IN THE FIELD

Ct	M	
12	16	Sabbir Rahman (B)
12	16	Soumya Sarkar (B)
10	16	H. H. Pandya (I)
9	9	M. J. Guptill (NZ)
9	15	Mohammad Nabi (Afg)
9	16	Mahmudullah (B)

OTHER FIRST-CLASS TOURS IN 2016

SOUTH AFRICA A IN ZIMBABWE IN 2016

South Africa A, captained by Stephen Cook, travelled to Zimbabwe in July for two four-day representative matches. They had the better of the first, but ran out of time to force victory, then made no mistake in the second with a crushing innings win. For Zimbabwe A, the hard-hitting left-hander Prince Masvaure made 88 not out in the first match, 146 in the second, and a Test debut a fortnight later.

At Harare, July 9–12, 2016. **Drawn.** **‡South Africa A 455-6 dec** (S. C. Cook 78, T. B. de Bruyn 52, S. van Zyl 73, O. A. Ramela 101*, D. Pretorius 89; S. W. Masakadza 3-83) **and 171-3 dec** (S. C. Cook 30, T. B. de Bruyn 50, S. van Zyl 43*); **Zimbabwe A 269** (T. M. K. Mawoyo 30, B. B. Chari 98, T. Maruma 44, C. T. Mutombodzi 35; D. Pretorius 3-38, D. L. Piedt 3-82) **and 192-1** (T. M. K. Mawoyo 79*, P. S. Masvaure 88*). *Tino Mawoyo and Prince Masvaure batted through most of the final day to force a draw, putting on 177*.*

At Bulawayo (Queens), July 15–18, 2016. **South Africa A won by an innings and 81 runs.** **‡South Africa A 570-6 dec** (S. C. Cook 143, H. G. Kuhn 108, O. A. Ramela 30, S. van Zyl 133*, M. Q. Adams 63, D. J. Vilas 48, Extras 39; N. M'shangwe 3-144); **Zimbabwe A 356** (P. S. Masvaure 146, C. R. Ervine 59; D. Olivier 3-63, A. L. Phehlukwayo 5-62) **and 133** (K. A. Maharaj 3-37, D. L. Piedt 4-19). *Stephen Cook and Heino Kuhn opened with a stand of 203 in 46 overs.*

INDIA A AND SOUTH AFRICA A IN AUSTRALIA IN 2016

India, captained by Manish Pandey in one-day games and Naman Ojha in first-class matches, and South Africa, led by Stephen Cook and Heino Kuhn, spent a month in tropical Queensland. After Australia A won both four-day games against the South Africans, the teams were joined by the Australian National Performance Squad for a four-way one-day competition. India A emerged victorious, then played two four-dayers against Australia A, who won the first. The three centuries in the first-class matches were all scored by home batsmen: Peter Handscomb and Hilton Cartwright, who would both win Test caps in the season that followed, and Marcus Stoinis, already an Australian limited-overs representative.

At Brisbane (Allan Border Field), July 30–August 2, 2016. **Australia A won by 197 runs.** **‡Australia A 396** (C. T. Bancroft 34, K. R. Patterson 74, M. P. Stoinis 120, S. M. Whiteman 40, J. M. Mennie 50*; V. D. Philander 3-52) **and 248-7 dec** (C. T. Bancroft 71, M. T. Renshaw 94, G. J. Maxwell 38; D. Olivier 3-28, S. S. B. Magala 3-50); **South Africa A 284** (D. Elgar 56, S. van Zyl 85, D. J. Vilas 60*; C. P. Tremain 5-75) **and 163** (D. Elgar 37, A. L. Phehlukwayo 55; J. M. Mennie 5-38). *MoM:* J. M. Mennie.

At Townsville, August 6–9, 2016. **Australia A won by ten wickets.** **‡South Africa A 304** (S. C. Cook 53, O. A. Ramela 82, A. L. Phehlukwayo 31; J. M. Mennie 5-61, M. J. Swepson 3-55) **and 180** (D. Elgar 35, D. J. Vilas 36; M. P. Stoinis 3-24, M. J. Swepson 4-33); **Australia A 402** (K. R. Patterson 92, P. S. P. Handscomb 137; A. L. Phehlukwayo 3-70, D. L. Piedt 3-99) **and 85-0** (K. R. Patterson 50*, C. T. Bancroft 32*). *MoM:* P. S. P. Handscomb. *Joe Mennie, the South Australia seamer who made his Test debut later in the year, took his second five-for in successive matches.*

At Townsville, August 13, 2016. **Australia National Performance Squad won by 17 runs.** **Australia National Performance Squad 243-8** (50 overs) (S. D. Heazlett 101, A. J. Nair 40); **‡South Africa A 226** (48.4 overs) (M. Q. Adams 78, S. S. B. Magala 35; D. J. M. Moody 3-44, D. M. K. Grant 4-31). *MoM:* S. D. Heazlett. *Queenslander Sam Heazlett's century set up victory for the National Performance Squad.*

At Townsville, August 14, 2016. **Australia A won by eight wickets.** **India A 55** (15.4 overs) (C. P. Tremain 5-25, D. J. Worrall 4-26); **‡Australia A 56-2** (17.1 overs). *MoM:* C. P. Tremain. *With Victoria seamer Chris Tremain taking three wickets in his third over, India A plummeted to 27-7 in the sixth, and the match finished well before the scheduled meal break.*

At Townsville, August 16, 2016. **Australia National Performance Squad won by 12 runs** (DLS). **Australia National Performance Squad 231-9** (49 overs) (H. W. R. Cartwright 81, M. G. Neser 31, S. A. Abbott 44; C. P. Tremain 5-47); **‡Australia A 177-7** (28 overs) (M. P. Stoinis 42, C. A.

Lynn 42, C. T. Bancroft 37*; H. W. R. Cartwright 3-26). *MoM:* H. W. R. Cartwright. *Australia A's target was revised to 190 in 28 overs.*

At Townsville, August 17, 2016. **India A won by three wickets. South Africa A 230-8** (50 overs) (T. B. de Bruyn 40, D. A. Miller 90, M. Q. Adams 52; D. S. Kulkarni 4-37); ‡**India A 234-7** (48.4 overs) (M. K. Pandey 100*). *MoM:* M. K. Pandey. *India A did much better with the bat in their second match: Manish Pandey completed victory – and his hundred – with a four off Aaron Phangiso.*

At Townsville, August 20, 2016. **South Africa A won by eight wickets.** ‡**Australia A 107** (37.2 overs) (K. W. Richardson 34*; D. Paterson 3-13, T. Shamsi 3-25); **South Africa A 108-2** (21 overs) (T. B. de Bruyn 57*). *MoM:* D. Paterson. *Australia A reached three figures only thanks to No. 9 Kane Richardson, who was dropped twice on the way to 34*.*

At Townsville, August 21, 2016. **India A won by 86 runs. India A 304-7** (50 overs) (K. K. Nair 72, S. S. Iyer 45, M. K. Pandey 31, K. M. Jadhav 45, S. V. Samson 54); ‡**Australia National Performance Squad 218** (46 overs) (H. W. R. Cartwright 65, S. D. Heazlett 60; J. D. Unadkat 3-43, D. S. Kulkarni 3-38). *MoM:* S. V. Samson.

At Mackay, August 24, 2016. **Australia A v Australia National Performance Squad. Abandoned.**

At Mackay, August 25, 2016. **No result. India A 140-4** (35.2 overs) (M. K. Pandey 47, K. M. Jadhav 41*) v ‡**South Africa A.**

At Mackay, August 27, 2016. **India A won by six wickets. Australia National Performance Squad 207-8** (50 overs) (M. T. Renshaw 31, S. B. Harper 72, M. W. Short 30, C. D. Hinchliffe 43; V. R. Aaron 3-58); ‡**India A 208-4** (38.2 overs) (S. S. Iyer 62, K. M. Jadhav 93*; T. J. O'Donnell 4-28). *MoM:* K. M. Jadhav. *India A made sure of a place in the final, despite four wickets for left-arm seamer Tom O'Donnell, the 19-year-old son of former Australian all-rounder Simon.*

At MacKay, August 28, 2016. **Australia A won by eight wickets. South Africa A 134** (42.1 overs) (K. Zondo 40; C. J. Boyce 4-21); ‡**Australia A 136-2** (18.5 overs) (C. A. Lynn 56*, G. J. Maxwell 46*). *MoM:* G. J. Maxwell.

At Mackay, August 30, 2016. **Australia A won by one run. Australia A 322-6** (50 overs) (K. R. Patterson 115, N. J. Maddinson 118); ‡**India A 321-8** (50 overs) (Mandeep Singh 56, M. K. Pandey 110, S. V. Samson 87). *MoM:* N. J. Maddinson. *Kurtis Patterson and Nic Maddinson added 230 for the second wicket in 35 overs, but Pandey led a strong reply, putting on 157 for the fifth with Sanju Samson in less than 20. With two balls left, India A needed three to win – but Samson was caught off Richardson for 87, then Shardul Thakur run out scrambling for a second. Australia A's victory put them into the final.*

At Mackay, August 31, 2016. **South Africa A won by five wickets.** ‡**Australia National Performance Squad 287-7** (50 overs) (C. P. Jewell 62, S. D. Heazlett 73, M. W. Short 44); **South Africa A 288-5** (46.3 overs) (R. R. Hendricks 31, D. A. Miller 124*, M. Q. Adams 44, D. J. Vilas 45*). *MoM:* D. A. Miller.

Third-place play-off At Mackay, September 3, 2016. **South Africa A won by nine wickets.** ‡**Australia National Performance Squad 207** (48.3 overs) (S. D. Heazlett 35*, S. B. Harper 60, M. W. Short 70); **South Africa A 209-1** (38.2 overs) (H. G. Kuhn 37, T. B. de Bruyn 90*, D. A. Miller 72*). *MoM:* T. B. de Bruyn.

Final At Mackay, September 4, 2016. **India A won by 57 runs.** ‡**India A 266-4** (50 overs) (Mandeep Singh 95, S. S. Iyer 41, M. K. Pandey 61); **Australia A 209** (44.5 overs) (C. T. Bancroft 34, N. J. Maddinson 31, P. S. P. Handscomb 43, A. I. Ross 34; Y. S. Chahal 4-34). *MoM:* Mandeep Singh. *India A won the four-team one-day tournament: Pandey, their captain, top-scored with 359 runs; South Africa A's David Miller came next, with 322 at 110. Australia A's Chris Tremain took 13 wickets.*

At Brisbane (Allan Border Field), September 8–11, 2016. **Australia A won by three wickets.** ‡**India A 230** (A. A. Herwadkar 34, F. Y. Fazal 48, M. K. Pandey 77; D. J. M. Moody 3-26, M. J. Swepson 4-78) **and 156** (J. Yadav 46; D. J. Worrall 3-43, D. J. M. Moody 3-64, C. J. Sayers 3-21); **Australia A 228** (J. A. Burns 78, P. S. P. Handscomb 87; V. R. Aaron 3-41, J. Yadav 3-44) **and 161-7** (C. T. Bancroft 58*, B. J. Webster 30; S. N. Thakur 3-42). *MoM:* P. S. P. Handscomb. *Pink balls were used in this match and the next.*

At Brisbane (Allan Border Field), September 15–18, 2016. **Drawn. India A 169** (H. H. Pandya 79; K. W. Richardson 4-37, J. M. Bird 3-53) **and 158-4** (A. A. Herwadkar 82*, S. V. Samson 34*; J. M.

Holland 3-59); ‡**Australia A 435** (N. J. Maddinson 81, B. J. Webster 79, H. W. R. Cartwright 117, S. M. Whiteman 51; S. N. Thakur 5-101, J. Yadav 3-95). *MoM:* H. W. R. Cartwright. *No play was possible on the final day.*

PAKISTAN A IN ZIMBABWE IN 2016-17

Pakistan A visited Zimbabwe in September and October, under the captaincy of Sohaib Maqsood. They won the 50-over series 3–2, and had the better of two four-day games, winning the second. Left-hander Fakhar Zaman hit 180 in the second match, and 311 in the series. Two 17-year-old slow bowlers – off-spinner Mohammad Asghar and leg-spinner Shadab Khan – both claimed 13 wickets in the two first-class matches, with Shadab adding a maiden century.

At Harare, September 26, 2016. **Pakistan A won by six wickets. Zimbabwe A 197** (48.3 overs) (T. K. Musakanda 51, Sikandar Raza 40; Ehsan Adil 3-37, Mohammad Asghar 3-36); ‡**Pakistan A 199-4** (45 overs) (Umar Amin 86*, Saud Shakil 32).

At Harare, September 28, 2016. **Pakistan A won by 188 runs. Pakistan A 339-2** (50 overs) (Fakhar Zaman 180, Umar Amin 83*); ‡**Zimbabwe A 151** (33 overs) (T. K. Musakanda 40, N. Madziva 47; Mohammad Asghar 5-41). *Fakhar Zaman hit 21 fours and four sixes, and put on 206 for the second wicket with Umar Amin.*

At Harare, September 30, 2016. **Zimbabwe A won by 105 runs. Zimbabwe A 297-5** (50 overs) (T. K. Musakanda 99*, M. N. Waller 72, E. Chigumbura 31, Sikandar Raza 50*); ‡**Pakistan A 192** (43.1 overs) (Fakhar Zaman 31, Umar Amin 32, Sohaib Maqsood 56, Saad Ali 31; Sikandar Raza 3-49, T. S. Chisoro 4-36). *Tarisai Musakanda missed out on a maiden century when he lost the strike in the final over.*

At Harare, October 3, 2016. **Pakistan A won by nine runs. Pakistan A 310-5** (50 overs) (Zain Abbas 108, Fakhar Zaman 81, Umar Amin 52; V. M. Nyauchi 3-55); ‡**Zimbabwe A 301-9** (50 overs) (B. B. Chari 53, M. N. Waller 74, E. Chigumbura 67, Sikandar Raza 37).

At Harare, October 5, 2016. **Zimbabwe A won by three wickets.** ‡**Pakistan A 274-6** (50 overs) (Sohaib Maqsood 53, Saad Ali 86*, Shadab Khan 40; Sikandar Raza 3-31); **Zimbabwe A 277-7** (49.5 overs) (B. B. Chari 41, R. W. Chakabva 86, M. N. Waller 86; Fahim Ashraf 3-43).

At Bulawayo (Queens), October 9–12, 2016. **Drawn.** ‡**Zimbabwe A 444** (H. Masakadza 32, C. R. Ervine 34, M. N. Waller 37, P. J. Moor 157, R. Mutumbami 38, A. G. Cremer 54; Mohammad Asghar 3-112, Shadab Khan 4-114) **and 219-5 dec** (C. R. Ervine 38, Sikandar Raza 40, M. N. Waller 87*; Mohammad Asghar 4-81); **Pakistan A 358** (Zain Abbas 137, Sohaib Maqsood 54, Saad Ali 62, Fahim Ashraf 61*; C. B. Mpofu 3-61, A. G. Cremer 4-82) **and 72-0** (Fakhar Zaman 40*, Zain Abbas 31*). *Peter Moor hit eight sixes in a career-best 157.*

At Bulawayo (Queens), October 15–18, 2016. **Pakistan A won by eight wickets.** ‡**Zimbabwe A 346** (B. B. Chari 118, S. C. Williams 112, E. Chigumbura 32, B. V. Vitori 30*; Mohammad Asghar 3-131, Shadab Khan 4-84) **and 202** (T. K. Musakanda 87, S. C. Williams 42; Mohammad Asghar 3-61, Shadab Khan 5-82); **Pakistan A 512** (Zain Abbas 78, Umar Amin 30, Jahid Ali 32, Sohaib Maqsood 41, Saad Ali 97, Saifullah Bangash 42, Shadab Khan 132, Mohammad Asghar 31; B. V. Vitori 3-112) **and 38-2**. *Brian Chari and Sean Williams put on 199 for the third wicket, but Zimbabwe A were swamped by a consistent batting display, including a maiden century from No. 8 for Shadab Khan, who also took nine wickets in the match. In Pakistan A's first innings, Jahid Ali was out obstructing the field after deliberately blocking a fielder's throw with his bat.*

WEST INDIES A IN SRI LANKA IN 2016-17

Sri Lanka A had the upper hand in the first-class games, winning 2–1, but West Indies – captained by Jason Mohammed, after Sharmarh Brooks led in the unofficial Tests – swept the one-dayers 3–0, thanks to some fine batting displays. Rahkeem Cornwall, a well-upholstered off-spinner from Antigua, took 23 wickets in the three first-class matches.

At Colombo (RPS), October 4–7, 2016. **Sri Lanka A won by seven wickets.** ‡**West Indies A 276** (K. O. A. Powell 36, S. S. J. Brooks 65, V. A. Singh 96, K. A. J. Roach 45*; D. A. S. Gunaratne 3-27) **and 175** (V. A. Singh 46, G. Moti-Kanhai 34; P. A. D. L. R. Sandakan 4-51); **Sri Lanka A 386** (F. D. M. Karunaratne 131, M. D. K. J. Perera 87, D. P. D. N. Dickwella 59, D. A. S. Gunaratne 38; R. R. S. Cornwall 8-108) **and 67-3** (F. D. M. Karunaratne 39*). *Dimuth Karunaratne and Kusal*

Perera shared an opening stand of 167, before off-spinner Rahkeem Cornwall – who opened the bowling with Kemar Roach – claimed career-best figures.

At Pallekele, October 11–14, 2016. **West Indies A won by 333 runs. West Indies A 509-9 dec** (R. Chandrika 84, S. O. Hetmyer 48, V. A. Singh 161, J. N. Hamilton 99, K. A. J. Roach 39; K. I. C. Asalanka 4-104) **and 216-3 dec** (R. Chandrika 68, S. S. J. Brooks 53*, J. N. Hamilton 56*); **‡Sri Lanka A 245** (F. D. M. Karunaratne 68, D. P. D. N. Dickwella 88, D. A. S. Gunaratne 46; R. R. S. Cornwall 6-91) **and 147** (K. I. C. Asalanka 34, J. D. F. Vandersay 47). *Left-hander Vishaul Singh made his highest score, and put on 188 for the fourth wicket with wicketkeeper Jahmar Hamilton. Cornwall took another seven wickets as West Indies A squared the series in convincing style.*

At Dambulla, October 18–21, 2016. **Sri Lanka A won by 138 runs. ‡Sri Lanka A 318** (D. S. Weerakkody 79, M. D. K. J. Perera 69, K. I. C. Asalanka 46, A. R. S. Silva 49; D. E. Johnson 4-65, R. R. S. Cornwall 3-93) **and 257-6 dec** (D. S. Weerakkody 48, D. A. S. Gunaratne 69, A. R. S. Silva 44, M. D. Shanaka 33*; R. R. S. Cornwall 4-87); **West Indies A 243** (S. O. Hetmyer 94, S. S. J. Brooks 54; H. U. K. Madushanka 3-45, P. A. D. L. R. Sandakan 3-54) **and 194** (R. Chandrika 30, K. O. A. Powell 44, S. S. J. Brooks 46; P. A. D. L. R. Sandakan 3-61, J. D. F. Vandersay 6-47). *Cornwall finished the unofficial Tests with 23 wickets, including his 100th first-class scalp – but two undistinguished batting displays cost his side the series.*

At Dambulla, October 24–25, 2016. **West Indies A won by 165 runs. ‡West Indies A 267-6** (50 overs) (K. A. Hope 81, J. N. Mohammed 58, R. Powell 55); **Sri Lanka A 102** (32.3 overs) (R. R. Beaton 3-26, J-R. L. Jaggesar 4-29). *Sri Lanka struggled against Ronsford Beaton, a seamer from tiny Montserrat, and the Trinidadian off-spinner Jon-Russ Jaggesar.*

At Kurunegala, October 27, 2016. **West Indies A won by 109 runs. ‡West Indies A 347-9** (50 overs) (C. A. K. Walton 70, K. A. Hope 107, A. B. Fudadin 57, R. Powell 52; D. S. N. F. G. Jayasuriya 4-54); **Sri Lanka A 238** (42.1 overs) (D. S. N. F. G. Jayasuriya 119, K. I. C. Asalanka 44, M. D. Shanaka 32; R. Powell 3-44). *Kyle Hope, the 17-year-old brother of Test batsman Shai, put on 111 for the first wicket with Chadwick Walton, and 109 for the second with Asad Fudadin. West Indies A went on to clinch the series, despite the all-round efforts of Shehan Jayasuriya.*

At Colombo (RPS), October 30, 2016. **West Indies A won by eight runs** (DLS). **‡West Indies A 305-5** (47 overs) (C. A. K. Walton 36, J. N. Mohammed 105*, A. M. McCarthy 102); **Sri Lanka A 248-7** (38 overs) (M. D. Gunathilleke 58, T. A. M. Siriwardene 35, M. D. Shanaka 33*, S. S. Pathirana 34). *Centuries for Jason Mohammed and Andre McCarthy, who put on 163 for the fourth wicket, set up a big West Indian total. Sri Lanka A's target was revised to 257 in 38 overs, but they fell just short of a consolation victory.*

THE ICC INTERCONTINENTAL CUP IN 2016

The big fish in the Associate world fared well in the middle part of the three-year cycle of the ICC's first-class competition. Ireland won both their matches to maintain a 100% record, while Afghanistan claimed two clinical innings victories to move second. Both sides were eyeing the prize on offer to the eventual winners: a play-off in 2018 against the bottom-ranked Full Member nation, with the promise of Test cricket – starting against England at Lord's – should they win. What was shaping up as the crunch match, between the two leaders, was scheduled to take place in India in March 2017, and the tournament finishes later in the year. The Netherlands briefly pinched top spot, but were set back by losing inside two days to Afghanistan, while Papua New Guinea secured a joyous victory over Namibia in their first first-class match on home soil, in Port Moresby. Hong Kong ran Ireland close in Belfast, where Nizakat Khan made 123, but Scotland continued to be hamstrung by the weather: they bowled only 66 overs – and didn't bat – in the competition all year.

INTERCONTINENTAL CUP TABLE

	P	*W*	*L*	*D*	*A*	*1st-inns lead*	*Pts*
Ireland	4	4	0	0	0	4	80
Afghanistan	4	3	0	1	0	2	61
Netherlands	4	2	2	0	0	3	46
Papua New Guinea	4	2	2	0	0	2	40
Hong Kong	4	1	2	0	1	1	30
Scotland	4	0	1	2	1	1	30
Namibia	4	1	3	0	0	1	20
United Arab Emirates	4	0	3	1	0	0	7

As at December 31, 2016.

Win = 14pts. Tie = 7pts. Draw with more/less than ten hours lost to weather = 7/3pts. First-innings lead = 6pts. Tie on first innings = 3pts. Abandoned = 10pts.

At Mong Kok, January 21–24, 2016. **Hong Kong v Scotland. Abandoned.** *Hong Kong 10pts, Scotland 10pts. The temperature fell as low as 4°C at a soggy Mission Road ground.*

At Abu Dhabi, January 21–23, 2016. **Netherlands won by four wickets. ‡United Arab Emirates 164** (V. J. Kingma 3-37, M. J. G. Rippon 4-45) **and 276** (Shaiman Anwar 148; M. A. A. Jamil 3-55); **Netherlands 315** (S. J. Myburgh 62, P. W. Borren 96; Farhan Ahmed 4-78, Ahmed Raza 6-112) **and 128-6** (Zaheer Maqsood 3-26). *Netherlands 20pts. First-class debuts:* Farhan Ahmed, Mohammad Kaleem, Mohammad Shehzad, Mohammad Usman, Qadeer Ahmed, Saqlain Haider (UAE). *The Netherlands made heavy weather of a target of 126, but a win sent them top. That they needed as many was down to Shaiman Anwar, whose 148 was his second first-class century, after 106 for Sialkot in Pakistan's Quaid-e-Azam Trophy more than 13 years earlier. He rescued the UAE from 80-5, putting on 144 with wicketkeeper Saqlain Haider (49), before seamer Quirijn Gunning removed both in six balls. Skipper Peter Borren's 96 had given the Dutch a big lead, despite seven lbws, and six wickets for the UAE's captain, slow left-armer Ahmed Raza.*

At Townsville, January 31–February 3, 2016. **Ireland won by 145 runs. Ireland 289** (N. J. O'Brien 63; N. Vanua 5-59) **and 244-5 dec** (E. C. Joyce 58, K. J. O'Brien 75*); **‡Papua New Guinea 188** (A. Vala 120; T. J. Murtagh 4-33, W. B. Rankin 3-21) **and 200** (W. B. Rankin 3-31). *Ireland 20pts. All-round consistency gave Ireland the points – and restored them to the top of the table – although the stand-out performance came from Asad Vala, who made 120 out of 188, with only seven fours, in PNG's first innings. Ireland were wobbling at 129-5 in their second innings, before Kevin O'Brien and Andy McBrine (40*) put on 115*. Their new-ball pair, Tim Murtagh and Boyd Rankin, both took six wickets, Murtagh's haul including his 600th in first-class cricket.*

At Greater Noida, India, April 10–12, 2016. **Afghanistan won by an innings and 36 runs.** ‡**Namibia 172** (Mohammad Nabi 5-25, Zahir Khan 3-31) **and 126** (Dawlat Zadran 3-7, Zahir Khan 5-31); **Afghanistan 334** (Mohammad Shahzad 139; Z. Groenewald 3-84, G. Snyman 4-78). *Afghanistan 20pts. MoM:* Mohammad Shahzad. *Afghanistan's opener Mohammad Shahzad suppressed his usual aggression for four and a half hours, and his 139 set up an innings victory. Zahir Khan, a 17-year-old chinaman bowler, took eight wickets, including his maiden five-for. No one reached 50 for Namibia, who suffered 11 lbws. This was only the second first-class match at the Greater Noida Sports Complex in Uttar Pradesh, after a Ranji Trophy game in December 2015.*

At Voorburg, July 29–30, 2016. **Afghanistan won by an innings and 36 runs. Netherlands 117** (Dawlat Zadran 4-32, Yamin Ahmadzai 5-29) **and 159** (M. J. G. Rippon 80; Dawlat Zadran 3-45, Zahir Khan 4-29); ‡**Afghanistan 312** (Rahmat Shah 51, Hashmatullah Shahidi 83; M. J. G. Rippon 5-79). *Afghanistan 20pts. First-class debuts:* S. Snater (Netherlands); Ihsanullah Janat (Afghanistan). *Another innings victory meant Afghanistan leapfrogged Ireland (by a point) and the Netherlands (by 15) at the top. The Dutch were hustled out soon after lunch on the first day, with opening bowlers Dawlat Zadran and Yamin Ahmadzai sharing nine wickets. Afghanistan stretched their lead to 195 next day, despite five wickets for Michael Rippon's chinamen. He then made a career-best 80 in the second innings, but they slipped away, and the match was over inside two days.*

At Ayr, August 9–12, 2016. **Drawn. United Arab Emirates 212-5** (Shaiman Anwar 78, Rameez Shahzad 74*) v ‡**Scotland.** *Scotland 7pts, United Arab Emirates 7pts. First-class debuts:* C. B. Sole, M. R. J. Watt (Scotland); Mohammad Qasim (UAE). *Only 59 overs were possible on the first day, seven on the second, and none on the third or fourth.*

At Belfast, August 30–September 2, 2016. **Ireland won by 70 runs.** ‡**Ireland 316** (W. T. S. Porterfield 88, G. C. Wilson 95; Tanvir Afzal 4-63, Nadeem Ahmed 4-73) **and 230** (J. Anderson 59; Tanvir Afzal 3-53, Nadeem Ahmed 3-65); **Hong Kong 237** (Nizakat Khan 69, A. Rath 73*; G. H. Dockrell 3-46, P. K. D. Chase 3-50) **and 239** (Nizakat Khan 123; T. J. Murtagh 4-29). *Ireland 20pts. First-class debuts:* Ehsan Shah, N. D. Shah, Tanveer Ahmed, Waqas Khan (Hong Kong). *Ireland maintained their 100% record in the competition – and regained top spot – with another victory, although they were held up by Nizakat Khan, who followed 69 with his maiden first-class century.*

At Port Moresby, October 16–19, 2016. **Papua New Guinea won by 199 runs.** ‡**Papua New Guinea 311** (A. Vala 144*; B. M. Scholtz 5-105) **and 189** (V. V. Morea 61; J. J. Smit 3-42, B. M. Scholtz 6-65); **Namibia 146** (S. F. Burger 52*; N. Vanua 3-39, L. Siaka 3-16) **and 155** (N. Vanua 3-23, L. Siaka 4-38). *Papua New Guinea 20pts. First-class debuts:* D. Bau (PNG). *Papua New Guinea celebrated their first first-class match on home soil, at Port Moresby's Amini Park, with a thumping victory. (See* Wisden 2012, *page 1198.) Vala's 144* – his third century in four first-class matches – raised his average to 93. In reply Namibia slumped to 57-7, then in their second innings (chasing 355) were 91-8. Lega Siaka, who had not previously claimed a first-class wicket, took 7-54 in the match. Vala was captaining PNG, as Jack Vare had a knee injury.*

ICC WORLD CRICKET LEAGUE CHAMPIONSHIP IN 2016

Winning the first division of the ICC's ambitious World Cricket League – like the Intercontinental Cup, run on a three-year cycle and ending in 2017 – offers admittance to the 2018 World Cup Qualifier. Afghanistan and Ireland, already through because of previous results, were not included. Four of the remaining teams have official one-day international status, and three – Papua New Guinea, Hong Kong and Scotland – led the way, along with the Netherlands, who lost that cachet early in 2014, after the previous World Cup qualifying tournament. But the UAE, who that year had regained ODI status, were languishing at the bottom of this table by the end of 2016. PNG, whose unfettered batting was epitomised by left-hander Asad Vala, were top, level on points with the Dutch, but with more wins.

WORLD CRICKET LEAGUE CHAMPIONSHIP TABLE

	P	*W*	*L*	*T*	*NR*	*Pts*	*NRR*
Papua New Guinea	8	6	2	0	0	12	0.03
Netherlands	8	5	1	0	2	12	1.55
Hong Kong	8	5	2	0	1	11	1.35
Scotland	8	4	1	0	3	11	0.24
Kenya	8	4	4	0	0	8	0.01
Nepal	8	3	5	0	0	6	−0.50
Namibia	8	1	7	0	0	2	−0.50
United Arab Emirates	8	1	7	0	0	2	−1.31

As at December 31, 2016.

Win = 2pts. Tie/no result = 1pt. Where teams were level on points, standings are decided by (a) most wins, (b) net run-rate. Only Scotland's matches against Hong Kong and the UAE in 2016 were official one-day internationals.

At Mong Kok, January 26, 2016. **Hong Kong won by 109 runs. Hong Kong 259** (49.1 overs) (A. Rath 97, Nizakat Khan 94; A. C. Evans 4-41); ‡**Scotland 150** (39.1 overs) (C. S. MacLeod 58; Tanvir Afzal 3-20, Nadeem Ahmed 4-26). *MoM:* A. Rath. *ODI debuts:* Ishtiaq Muhammad (Hong Kong); B. T. J. Wheal (Scotland). *Victory in their first official ODI at home took Hong Kong top. Opener Anshuman Rath – just 18 and about to captain Harrow – put on 170 with Nizakat Khan, but the last seven went down for 34. Scotland slid to 17-3 in gloomy conditions, and never recovered.*

At Abu Dhabi, January 27, 2016. **Netherlands won by seven wickets. United Arab Emirates 112** (36 overs) (Mohammad Shehzad 37, Saqlain Haider 33*; Mudassar Bukhari 6-24); ‡**Netherlands 114-3** (20.3 overs) (M. R. Swart 60*). *Seamer Mudassar Bukhari's best List A figures demolished the UAE for 112, and left a simple target.*

At Mong Kok, January 28–29, 2016. **Hong Kong v Scotland. Abandoned.** *Scotland's watery trip to Hong Kong continued – of six scheduled days' international cricket, they played only one.*

At Abu Dhabi, January 29, 2016. **Netherlands won by six runs. Netherlands 216** (49.4 overs) (W. Barresi 42, R. E. van der Merwe 31, P. M. Seelaar 49, M. J. G. Rippon 34; A. M. Guruge 3-41); ‡**United Arab Emirates 210** (49.3 overs) (Shaiman Anwar 71, Mohammad Usman 52; T. van der Gugten 3-44). *The Netherlands went top after winning their second match in the UAE, but this was much closer: the middle order bailed them out from 34-4, then their bowlers did the same after the UAE reached 159-3 in the 38th. Timm van der Gugten disposed of Shaiman Anwar and Saqlain Haider, and of the rest only Rohan Mustafa (27) made it into double figures.*

At Kirtipur, April 16, 2016. **Nepal won by five wickets.** ‡**Namibia 195-9** (50 overs) (S. F. Burger 38; B. Regmi 3-40); **Nepal 197-5** (47.1 overs) (S. Vesawkar 50*, B. Bhandari 40*, Extras 34). *Namibia's batting was unimpressive: eight reached double figures, but the top score was Sarel Burger's 38 from 77 balls. Nepal wobbled from 82-2 to 113-5, but Sharad Vesawkar and Binod Bhandari took them home with a stand of 84*. Nepal blooded a 15-year-old leg-spinner, Sandeep Lamichhane, who removed Namibia's No. 3 Pikky Ya France.*

At Kirtipur, April 18, 2016. **Nepal won by three wickets. Namibia 239-9** (50 overs) (S. J. Baard 51, Z. E. Green 47, S. F. Burger 43*, J-P. Kotze 32); ‡**Nepal 240-7** (49.5 overs) (S. Vesawkar 74*, P. Khadka 103; S. F. Burger 3-38). *For once Namibia made a decent start, openers Stephan Baard and Zane Green putting on 95 but, soon after they were parted by Lamichhane, it was 114-5. Another diligent innings from Burger, plus 32 in 11 balls from wicketkeeper J-P. Kotze, lifted the total to 239. Nepal made a watchful start, and it was 37-2 in the 14th over when Vesawkar was joined by his captain, Paras Khadka, who scythed a century in 89 balls, including seven sixes. When he was out, after a stand of 167 in 28 overs, Nepal needed only 36 from 52 deliveries – but Burger weighed in with three quick wickets, and it went down to the final over.*

At Port Moresby, May 28, 2016. **Papua New Guinea won by six wickets.** ‡**Kenya 188** (47 overs) (I. A. Karim 73*, R. R. Patel 39, Gurdeep Singh 33; C. A. Soper 5-27); **Papua New Guinea 191-4** (34.3 overs) (V. V. Morea 53, A. Vala 69*). *Irfan Karim carried his bat for Kenya, who were 172-5 before Chad Soper took the last five wickets, all bowled, in 19 deliveries.*

At Port Moresby, May 30, 2016. **Papua New Guinea won by 21 runs.** ‡**Papua New Guinea 249-6** (50 overs) (V. V. Morea 102*, S. Bau 66, J. B. Reva 43*; C. O. Obuya 4-42); **Kenya 228** (47.5 overs) (R. N. Patel 95, R. R. Patel 33, C. O. Obuya 38; N. Vanua 3-47, J. B. Reva 4-31). *Vani Morea batted through PNG's innings for his maiden List A century, adding 124 for the third wicket with Sese Bau and 73* for the seventh with John Reva. With Rushab (R. N.) Patel well set, Kenya looked on course, but they fell behind the rate and, from 210-3 in the 45th, lost seven for 18 in 21 balls.*

At Amstelveen, August 13, 2016. **Netherlands won by seven wickets. Nepal 94** (38.1 overs) (T. van der Gugten 3-21, M. J. G. Rippon 3-21); ‡**Netherlands 96-3** (16.5 overs) (S. J. Myburgh 33*, W. Barresi 37). *Anil Mandal (20) top-scored in an underwhelming Nepal innings.*

At Edinburgh, August 14, 2016. **Scotland won by 98 runs. Scotland 327-5** (50 overs) (K. J. Coetzer 127, P. L. Mommsen 111*; Mohammad Shehzad 3-61); ‡**United Arab Emirates 229** (43.3 overs) (R. Mustafa 43, Mohammad Usman 34, Amjad Javed 32; A. C. Evans 4-41). *ODI debuts:* Mohammad Usman, Rameez Shahzad (UAE). *Hundreds from Kyle Coetzer and Preston Mommsen powered Scotland to their second-highest ODI total, after 341-9 against Canada at Christchurch in 2013-14. The UAE were never on terms, although eight men reached double figures.*

At Amstelveen, August 15, 2016. **Nepal won by 19 runs. Nepal 217-9** (50 overs) (G. Malla 39, P. Khadka 84, S. Pun 45; M. J. G. Rippon 4-35); ‡**Netherlands 198** (48.3 overs) (M. P. O'Dowd 35, R. E. van der Merwe 56, T. G. J. Gruijters 44, T. van der Gugten 36). *Nepal turned the tables after their disappointing display two days earlier; skipper Khadka made 84, and put on 118 for the fourth wicket with Sagar Pun. Khadka then claimed two early wickets with his seamers as the Dutch declined to 21-3. Max O'Dowd dropped anchor for 95 balls, and put on 82 with Roelof van der Merwe, but the tail was left with too much to do.*

At Edinburgh, August 16, 2016. **Scotland won by seven wickets.** ‡**United Arab Emirates 228** (45.4 overs) (Shaiman Anwar 63, Mohammad Usman 43, Rameez Shahzad 33; S. M. Sharif 3-25, C. B. Sole 3-51); **Scotland 229-3** (47.4 overs) (C. S. MacLeod 103, P. L. Mommsen 80*). *ODI debut:* C. B. Sole (Scotland). *Shaiman Anwar was the backbone of a decent UAE effort, but the Scots were rarely troubled; Calum MacLeod hit his third ODI century, and put on 165 for the third wicket with Mommsen.*

At Port Moresby, October 21, 2016. **Papua New Guinea won by five wickets.** ‡**Namibia 273-4** (50 overs) (W. van Vuuren 60, J-P. Kotze 30, C. G. Williams 109*, S. F. Burger 34*); **Papua New Guinea 274-5** (48 overs) (L. Siaka 70, S. Bau 76, D. Bau 80*). *Craig Williams smacked 109* from 89 balls, with five sixes, to propel Namibia to a decent total despite Mahuru Dai's frugal mid-innings spell of 10–0–24–1. Lega Siaka provided early impetus in the chase, then the Bau brothers – Sese and Dogodo – put on 126 for the fifth wicket.*

At Port Moresby, October 23, 2016. **Papua New Guinea won by six wickets.** ‡**Namibia 212** (50 overs) (S. J. Baard 54, N. R. P. Scholtz 61*; N. Vanua 3-38, W. T. Gavera 3-39); **Papua New Guinea 213-4** (48 overs) (V. V. Morea 67, A. Vala 55, S. Bau 40*). *PNG's second win in three days took them top. Non-striker Zane Green was run out without facing, while trying for a third off the game's first ball. Nicolaas Scholtz, who faced 88 balls after coming in at No. 7, ensured PNG needed more than 200 – but again they chased well. Morea and Vala put on 100 for the third wicket, before the Bau brothers finished the job.*

At Nairobi (Gymkhana), November 18, 2016. **Kenya won by three wickets** (DLS). **Hong Kong 222** (46.2 overs) (K. D. Shah 34, A. Rath 90, Shahid Wasif 44; N. M. Odhiambo 3-14, R. R. Patel 5-16); ‡**Kenya 201-7** (40.5 overs) (I. A. Karim 67, D. M. Gondaria 45). *A fifth-wicket stand of 105 between Rath and Shahid Wasif took Hong Kong to 191-4 after 37 overs, but six wickets tumbled for 31, to leave an inviting target that was barely affected by a downpour after 35 overs; the new requirement was 200 in 43.*

At Nairobi (Gymkhana), November 20, 2016. **Hong Kong won by 39 runs** (DLS). **Hong Kong 148-4** (25.1 overs) (C. J. Carter 41, Babar Hayat 78; L. N. Oluoch 3-29); ‡**Kenya 133** (23 overs) (I. A. Karim 33, A. A. Obanda 39; Nadeem Ahmed 3-23, Ehsan Khan 3-12, Tanveer Ahmed 3-20). *A late start meant a 31-over game, and Babar Hayat's 78 revitalised Hong Kong following an early wicket. But they were stalled at 148-4 when more rain fell, and the target became 173 from 25. Karim and Alex Obanda started with 79 in 12.4, but with captain Rakep Patel falling first ball to off-spinner Ehsan Khan – who finished with 4–0–12–3 – Kenya lost their way, not helped by three wickets in four deliveries for Tanveer Ahmed's medium-pace.*

CRICKET IN AFGHANISTAN IN 2016

Aiming high

SHAHID HASHMI

The growing passion for cricket in Afghanistan was evident on a chilly December morning. To mark the opening of a new ground at Khost, near the Pakistan border, the Afghanistan Cricket Board organised a Twenty20 exhibition featuring their biggest stars. They hoped the stadium, built with the help of a $US1m grant from the German government, would help increase the profile of the game in the area. The early signs were good: the capacity was 10,000, but three times that number turned up. So overwhelmed were staff at the gates that the start was delayed, and the game reduced to ten overs a side.

The fourth edition of the Shpageeza Twenty20 tournament also showed progress. For the first time it featured foreign players, including Pakistan's Umar Akmal and Zimbabwe's Sikandar Raza. Many were impressed: "I have no words to praise Afghanistan and the development of cricket here," said Pakistani international Awais Zia. "We will come again and again."

The national team had success, too. At the World T20 in India, they thrashed Zimbabwe to reach the Super Ten phase, where they lit up the tournament. Against South Africa, the burly wicketkeeper-batsman Mohammad Shahzad launched a thrilling opening salvo, clubbing 22 runs in one Kyle Abbott over; little wonder he was voted Associate Player of the Year in December. Afghanistan also gave England a fright, reducing them to 57 for six. And they were the only side to beat West Indies, the eventual champions. The pictures of Chris Gayle dancing with the Afghan players after the match were wonderful souvenirs.

In June, former India batsman Lalchand Rajput was named coach in place of Inzamam-ul-Haq, who returned to Pakistan to head up their selection committee. A month later, Shafiq Stanikzai, the chief executive of the ACB, set him a target of breaking into the top six of the one-day international rankings by 2019, and the top three of both white-ball formats by 2025. Rajput's reign began with two away ODI series: a win over Scotland, and a draw with Ireland. And, after hammering the Netherlands in the Intercontinental Cup, they stretched Bangladesh to a decider. But it remains to be seen how realistic Stanikzai's ambitions are, even if Afghanistan ended the year by whitewashing the UAE in a Twenty20 series.

Support for the top Associates has grown at the ICC. There are plans to increase the number of Test nations, which could include Afghanistan and Ireland by 2019. Both nations were also granted $500,000 in October to help fill their schedule with bilateral series. They need to play more ODIs to have a chance of direct entry to the World Cup in 2019, as only the top eight in the rankings by September 2017 automatically qualify. For Afghanistan, arranging a first tour of the Caribbean was a step in the right direction: in 2017, they will play West Indies in eight limited-overs internationals.

For Afghanistan's matches in the ICC World Twenty20, see page 793; the Asia Cup, see page 893; the Intercontinental Cup and the World Cricket League, see page 1141; and their first-class match against England Lions in the UAE, see page 1152.

CRICKET IN HONG KONG IN 2016

Marketing blitz

ALVIN SALLAY

What's in a name? For this cricketing outpost, plenty. Cricket Hong Kong believed it was time for a rebranding, so they dropped "Association" from their title. With the change seemed to come a renewed enthusiasm for developing the game.

The T20 Blitz began life in May 2016, with former Australia captain Michael Clarke playing for the Kowloon Cantons. Although it was mostly washed out (only three of the seven games reached a conclusion), it had significant commercial potential; Shahid Afridi, Darren Sammy and Kumar Sangakkara are among those who have signed up for the second edition. In August, it was also announced the Hong Kong Sixes would return in 2017, ending a five-year absence caused by a funding shortage. At the same time, they outlined a commitment to tie down a major sponsor and secure the long-term future of the event, and end its dependence on government money.

For the national team, the year began by hosting Scotland. The tour was supposed to include Hong Kong's first home first-class match, but rain forced an abandonment at the Mission Road Ground. Even so, their main focus remained the 50-over World Cricket League Championship. Hong Kong finished 2016 in third and, if they remain in the top four by September 2017, will join the four lowest-ranked Full Members in a qualifying tournament for the 2019 World Cup.

In February, the Asia Cup qualifiers in Bangladesh were an unmitigated disaster: Hong Kong lost three out of three, to Oman, the UAE and Afghanistan. Things didn't get better at the World T20 in India the following month, with defeat by Scotland, Afghanistan and Zimbabwe. Next came a trip to Europe in late summer. Against Ireland, Hong Kong lost an ICC Intercontinental Cup match by 70 runs, despite Nizakat Khan's century. He finished the year with 722 runs across all formats – second only to Babar Hayat's 865 – and in December had his leg-spin cleared, after a ban in 2015. Hong Kong grabbed the Twenty20 series at Bready (population: 100) in Co. Tyrone, with a little help from the weather. They bowled Ireland out for 129 to win the first match by 40 runs, before the second fell victim to the elements.

Gloomy skies hung over Edinburgh, too, and the first game was washed out, before Scotland exacted revenge for their defeat earlier in the year. Hong Kong concluded the year by winning two out of three one-day internationals against table-toppers Papua New Guinea at home, before sharing another 50-over series against Kenya in Nairobi, where both games were decided by DLS.

HONG KONG v SCOTLAND

First Twenty20 international At Mong Kok, January 30, 2016. **Hong Kong won by nine wickets. Scotland 66-7** (10 overs); **‡Hong Kong 72-1** (6.2 overs). *MoM:* Babar Hayat. *T20I debut:* B. T. J. Wheal (Scotland). *After a delayed start reduced the overs available to ten apiece, Scotland began well – but three run-outs slowed them, and the eventual target was picked off easily by Hong Kong. Jamie Atkinson started with 20 from seven balls; Babar Hayat finished things off with 26* from 14.*

Second Twenty20 international At Mong Kok, January 31, 2016. **Scotland won by 37 runs. Scotland 161-9** (20 overs) (K. J. Coetzer 70; Haseeb Amjad 3-21, Nadeem Ahmed 3-23); **‡Hong Kong 124** (18.4 overs) (Tanvir Afzal 56; B. T. J. Wheal 3-20, R. D. Berrington 3-22). *MoM:* K. J. Coetzer. *Scotland squared the series thanks to Kyle Coetzer's uncompromising 70 from 40 balls, with six sixes. By the ninth over Hong Kong were 33-6 and, although Tanvir Afzal hammered seven sixes in his 22-ball 56, it was not enough.*

HONG KONG v PAPUA NEW GUINEA

First one-day international At Mong Kok, November 4, 2016. **Hong Kong won by 106 runs. ‡Hong Kong 269** (49.4 overs) (Babar Hayat 77); **Papua New Guinea 163** (38.2 overs). *MoM:* Babar Hayat. *ODI debuts:* D. Bau, S. Bau, H. Hiri, C. A. Soper (PNG). *When Mahuru Dai's third wicket reduced Hong Kong to 111-6 in the 28th over, PNG seemed to be on top – but with captain Hayat solid at one end, Afzal spanked 47 from 32 balls, Aizaz Khan added 44 from 46, and the eventual total was a good one. PNG motored to 100-2 in the 18th, but 19-year-old slow left-armer Anshuman Rath (3-22) set them back.*

Second one-day international At Mong Kok, November 6, 2016. **Papua New Guinea won by 14 runs. ‡Papua New Guinea 201** (45.5 overs) (A. Vala 70; Nadeem Ahmed 4-50); **Hong Kong 187** (48.1 overs) (C. A. Soper 6-41). *MoM:* C. A. Soper. *ODI debuts:* K. J. Christie (Hong Kong); J. B. Reva (PNG). *Seamer Chad Soper led the way with six wickets as PNG squared the series, the most important strike coming in the third over when he caught and bowled Hayat for a duck. Shahid Wasif's career-best 45 kept Hong Kong in the hunt, but Soper took two wickets in the 48th to settle the issue. Earlier, Asad Vala's 70 – and his stand of 78 with Sese Bau (40) – ensured a reasonable target, although the tail added only 30 from 67 balls after Vala was stumped in the 35th over. Hong Kong's wicketkeeper Jamie Atkinson had also stumped both openers, off slow left-armer Nadeem Khan, who took the new ball. Hong Kong medium-pacer Kyle Christie endured a chastening debut: his only over went for 18, then he fell without scoring.*

Third one-day international At Mong Kok, November 8, 2016. **Hong Kong won by seven wickets** (DLS). **‡Papua New Guinea 244-7** (50 overs) (M. D. Dai 76*); **Hong Kong 181-3** (33.3 overs) (Babar Hayat 82*, A. Rath 52*). *MoM:* A. Rath. *MoS:* Babar Hayat. *PNG made their highest total of the series, propelled by Dai's 76* from 62, but Hong Kong prevailed 2–1, chasing down a revised target of 178 in 38 overs with 27 balls to spare. They owed much to a partnership of 120* between Hayat – whose 82* was his highest score in ODIs – and Rath, who had earlier taken 3-25.*

For Hong Kong's matches in the ICC World Twenty20, see page 793; the Asia Cup, see page 893; the Intercontinental Cup and the World Cricket League, see page 1141.

> "Others later picked up the bat and ran with it. But he created the bat."
>
> Obituaries, page 176

CRICKET IN OMAN IN 2016

Two nations

PAUL BIRD

Oman's qualification for their first global competition – the World Twenty20 in India in March – was a phenomenal achievement. And better was to come: in their first match they beat Ireland by two wickets with two balls to spare. During that game, Zeeshan Maqsood took the catch of the tournament, a flying one-handed grab to send back Paul Stirling. It was a symbol of how far Omani cricket had progressed in the three years since the first grass pitch was opened at the national stadium in Al Amerat (by the end of 2016, there would be a second, built next door). But, after an abandonment against the Netherlands, Oman were soundly beaten by a Tamim Iqbal-inspired Bangladesh, and returned home.

Perhaps the players should have been welcomed as heroes. Yet while cricket remains the country's most successful sport at international level, two-thirds of the population are not interested. Apart from applause at Indian schools, and feasts hosted by prominent South Asians, there was little fanfare. Writing about the state of the Omani game on ESPNcricinfo, Sharda Ugra told of "a packed seasonal schedule running from September to April, an eight-division corporate league featuring 92 clubs, 30 school teams, 40-odd Level I and II qualified umpires, and a youth development programme". But there are few indigenous players, and even fewer at management level; cricket is played predominantly by South Asian immigrants, of which there are around 750,000. Among the Omani squad at the World T20, only seamer Sufyan Mehmood was born in the country.

Support from the government increased in 2016, and sponsorship from the telecommunications company Omantel has made a difference. The continued health of the game, though, relies on captivating the indigenous youth. Despite this, the governing body of Omani cricket often fail to provide Arabic speakers for school visits.

Regardless, success on the field continued. Under new captain Ajay Lalcheta, they were promoted to the World Cricket League Division 4 in May. Then, in November, they were promoted again, after finishing runners-up to the USA in Los Angeles. The best players found themselves in demand overseas. Jatinder Singh, Munis Ansari and Zeeshan negotiated contracts with league teams in the UK and Ireland. But, as the 2016 squad had an average age of 32, an injection of youth may be needed.

For Oman's matches in the ICC World Twenty20, see page 793; the Asia Cup, see page 893; the Intercontinental Cup and the World Cricket League, see page 1141.

CRICKET IN PAPUA NEW GUINEA IN 2016

Home improvements

ANDREW NIXON

Papua New Guinea continued their redevelopment of Amini Park in Port Moresby, aiming for it to become fit enough – in the eyes of the ICC – to host one-day internationals in time for Scotland's visit in 2017. As a mark of their progress, they were granted permission to play their first home Intercontinental Cup match and, in October, beat Namibia by 199 runs, thanks to an unbeaten century from stand-in captain Asad Vala. Earlier in the year, he had scored a hundred during the defeat by Ireland at Townsville, Queensland, and after four first-class games his average stood at 93; PNG ended 2016 fourth in the table.

Between May and October, Amini Park also hosted its first World Cricket League Championship games, and PNG won all four. Later, they travelled to Hong Kong for three one-day internationals – ending a two-year gap without any – and lost 2–1, yet still finished 2016 top. Remaining there may allow them to join Ireland and Afghanistan in the ODI Championship. In any case, a top-four finish would allow them entry to the World Cup qualifying tournament in 2018, and give them a chance of playing their first official internationals against Test nations (though they did welcome the West Indians to Amini Park in 1975-76 as part of their tour of Australia).

Unlike the men, PNG's women had a regional tournament, and won all four matches in Samoa – including two against Japan – to reach the World Cup qualifier in Sri Lanka in February 2017. Two of their stars were also picked for the BBL – a joint initiative between Cricket Australia and the ICC: Konio Oala was selected by Sydney Thunder, and Ravina Oa by Adelaide Strikers.

While PNG are one of a handful of Associates where cricket is a mainstream sport, they have flown under the radar, lacking the high-profile wins of Ireland, the romance of Afghanistan, or the market potential of the USA. It helps that ICC funding goes further in a country with a low cost of living. But it doesn't always go far enough: PNG had to turn down an invitation to the Desert T20 Challenge in the UAE early in 2017 because they couldn't afford the flights – a reminder that, even for the top Associates, money can still be an issue.

PAPUA NEW GUINEA v IRELAND IN AUSTRALIA

First Twenty20 international At Townsville, February 6, 2016. **Ireland won by five wickets. Papua New Guinea 92-9** (20 overs); **‡Ireland 97-5** (12.1 overs) (G. C. Wilson 45; N. Vanua 3-26). *T20I debuts:* S. Bau, H. Hiri, N. Pokana (PNG). *Ireland's globe-trotting team scooted to victory in northern Queensland, overhauling PNG's modest total with ease, despite three wickets for seamer Norman Vanua.*

Second Twenty20 international At Townsville, February 7, 2016. **Ireland won by seven runs** (DLS). **Ireland 96-5** (11 overs) (W. T. S. Porterfield 30, S. W. Poynter 35; P. Raho 3-11); **‡Papua New Guinea 89-9** (11 overs) (M. C. Sorensen 3-17, G. H. Dockrell 3-18). *T20I debut:* P. Raho (PNG). *Rain made this an 11-over match, and three wickets for medium-pacer Pipi Raho – all caught* *by Lega Siaka – kept Ireland in check. PNG slipped from 41-2 to 63-9, before two sixes from Vanua (26*) narrowed the margin of defeat.*

Third Twenty20 international At Townsville, February 9, 2016. **Papua New Guinea won by 11 runs.** ‡**Papua New Guinea 116-8** (20 overs) (T. J. Murtagh 3-23); **Ireland 105** (19.1 overs) (C. A. Soper 3-13). *PNG scrapped to 116, their biggest partnership 48 for the fourth wicket between Sese Bau (25) and Chris Amini (24). But it proved enough, to the PNG players' delight: Chad Soper removed the openers cheaply, and returned at the death to have Tim Murtagh caught by skipper Asad Vala. His opposite number was Gary Wilson, playing his 200th match of all kinds for Ireland.*

For Papua New Guinea's matches in the Intercontinental Cup and the World Cricket League, see page 1411.

CRICKET IN THE UNITED ARAB EMIRATES IN 2016

The off-spinning Englishwoman

PAUL RADLEY

After spending years working out how to fund it, the Emirates Cricket Board took a step towards professionalism in July, when they announced their first batch of central contracts. Eight players went full-time, while four more – including the captain Amjad Javed, a cargo loader for Emirates Airlines – were handed part-time retainers. It followed qualification for the main part of the Twenty20 Asia Cup in Bangladesh: three rousing wins against fellow Associates had put the UAE through to face the likes of Virat Kohli and Shahid Afridi in front of a live audience of thousands, and a TV audience of millions.

But the satisfaction was only fleeting. The UAE played 14 T20 internationals in 2016, and lost nine, while both their 50-over internationals, in Scotland, ended in defeat. The year finished with three thrashings by the England Lions, by which time the UAE were bottom in both the one-day World Cricket League and the four-day Intercontinental Cup.

Off the field, the picture was equally depressing. Aqib Javed, the former Pakistan seamer who oversaw qualification for both the 50-over and T20 World Cups during a broadly successful four years as the UAE's head coach, quit in May. He was settled in Dubai, but opted to return home to take charge of the Lahore Qalandars in the Pakistan Super League. The process of replacing him was muddled. Two former England internationals, Paul Franks and Owais Shah, filled the breach temporarily, but could not arrest the slide. In January 2017, former Warwickshire coach Dougie Brown was appointed.

In the search for players, the selectors – former captains Khurram Khan and Mohammad Tauqir, plus the Emirati businessman Waleed Bukhatir – were happy to explore all available options. A nationwide talent hunt attracted thousands, including bankers, computer programmers and lorry drivers – and, at the Dubai event, 26-year-old Justyne Smagacz, an off-spinning Englishwoman who works in PR.

At the elite end, two former Pakistan Test players featured in the selection discussions. Riaz Afridi, a burly pace bowler, was a star of Pakistan's age-group cricket, and won a Test cap against Zimbabwe in 2004-05. After falling from favour he relocated to Dubai and, still only 32, had been earmarked for one of the first central contracts by Aqib. But that did not happen, and his prospects were further harmed when the company side for which he played domestic cricket were disbanded.

Hasan Raza, down in the books as the youngest Test cricketer, is also in the frame. Supposedly only 14 when he made the first of his seven appearances for Pakistan as a middle-order batsman in October 1996, he now lives in Sharjah, and will be eligible for the UAE in 2017.

NETHERLANDS AND SCOTLAND IN THE UAE

At Dubai (ICC Academy), February 3, 2016. **Netherlands won by 84 runs. Netherlands 157-5** (20 overs) (S. J. Myburgh 35, W. Barresi 48, P. W. Borren 43); ‡**United Arab Emirates 73** (16.4 overs) (Mohammad Usman 49*; Mudassar Bukhari 4-7, M. J. G. Rippon 3-8). *MoM:* Mudassar Bukhari. *T20I debuts:* Fahad Tariq, Farhan Ahmed, Mohammad Kaleem, Mohammad Usman (UAE); Sikander Zulfiqar (Netherlands). *Wesley Barresi and captain Peter Borren put on 77 in eight overs as the Netherlands went past 150, than an inexperienced UAE side collapsed to 21-7. The debutant Mohammad Usman fought hard, but no one else managed double figures: medium-pacer Mudassar Bukhari finished with 4–21–7–4, including two old-fashioned wicket-maidens.*

At Dubai (ICC Academy), February 4, 2016. **United Arab Emirates won by nine runs.** ‡**United Arab Emirates 148-8** (20 overs) (Amjad Javed 76; S. M. Sharif 4-24); **Scotland 139-9** (20 overs) (P. L. Mommsen 56). *MoM:* Amjad Javed. *T20I debut:* Saqlain Haider (UAE). *Skipper Amjad Javed's 42-ball 76, with five sixes, led the UAE to a competitive score. Scotland looked on course at 102-4 after 14 overs, but collected only 37 more from the last six, with just three boundaries.*

At Dubai (ICC Academy), February 5, 2016. **Scotland won by 37 runs.** ‡**Scotland 140-5** (20 overs) (K. J. Coetzer 30, M. W. Machan 43, R. D. Berrington 42); **Netherlands 103** (18.2 overs) (B. N. Cooper 32; M. R. J. Watt 5-27). *MoM:* M. R. J. Watt. *T20I debut:* V. J. Kingma (Netherlands). *Now it was the Netherlands' turn to collapse: after Stephan Myburgh fell to the first ball of the chase, they made it to 55-1, before nine wickets tumbled for 48, with slow left-armer Mark Watt recording his maiden international five-for. Earlier, Scotland were only 53-3 after ten, before Matt Machan and Richie Berrington injected some urgency by adding 74 in 46 balls. This match completed these teams' preparations for the World Twenty20 in India in March.*

UNITED ARAB EMIRATES v IRELAND

First Twenty20 international At Abu Dhabi, February 14, 2016. **Ireland won by 34 runs. Ireland 134-8** (20 overs) (N. J. O'Brien 38; Amjad Javed 3-41); ‡**United Arab Emirates 100** (19.2 overs) (K. J. O'Brien 3-14). *Ireland swapped the Barrier Reef for barrier cream against desert sun, and slumped to 19-4 after five overs. But the O'Brien brothers put on 55 in eight, and the tail conjured 44 from the last four. The UAE also made a bad start – 15-3 in the fourth – and never recovered. Kevin O'Brien added three wickets to his earlier 23.*

Second Twenty20 international At Abu Dhabi, February 16, 2016. **United Arab Emirates won by five runs.** ‡**United Arab Emirates 133-7** (20 overs) (S. P. Patil 31; W. B. Rankin 3-17); **Ireland 128-9** (20 overs) (W. T. S. Porterfield 72). *T20I debut:* Usman Mushtaq (UAE). *The UAE dented Ireland's World Twenty20 preparations with a narrow victory, despite skipper William Porterfield's 72 from 60 balls. Ireland were in charge at 91-1 in the 13th, but then lost eight for 25.*

ENGLAND LIONS IN THE UNITED ARAB EMIRATES IN 2016-17

PAUL RADLEY

50-over matches (3): UAE 0, England Lions 3

The England Lions captain Keaton Jennings had an exciting time in December. He made two centuries, a week – and 1,250 miles – apart. The first, for England Lions in their opening match against the UAE, came in front of almost no spectators in Dubai. Seven days later, in the hustle and bustle of Mumbai's Wankhede, he added a second, in his first Test innings.

Even though he was not around by the time the Lions' tour finished, Jennings was right to suggest it "couldn't have gone much better". He was told of his promotion the day before things got under way in Dubai, and played in the first two matches before boarding the flight to India. By then, the series was already wrapped up, with Tom Curran taking five wickets in the second game. Jennings's evenly paced 101 not out in a run-chase in the opener had given the tourists an advantage they never looked likely to surrender, against a UAE side that have lost their way since qualifying for the 2015 World Cup. They had actually beaten the Lions in a 50-over match in January 2016, but didn't threaten a repeat.

The tour was rounded off by a hard-fought four-day game against Afghanistan, which the Lions won to preserve their 100% tour record. They were indebted to the Surrey wicketkeeper Ben Foakes, who rescued the first innings with 70, and added an undefeated 89 in the second.

ENGLAND LIONS SQUAD

*K. K. Jennings (Durham), T. P. Alsop (Hampshire), D. J. Bell-Drummond (Kent), J. M. Clarke (Worcestershire), S. M. Curran (Surrey), T. K. Curran (Surrey), L. A. Dawson (Hampshire), B. T. Foakes (Surrey), J. K. Fuller (Middlesex), N. R. T. Gubbins (Middlesex), T. G. Helm (Middlesex), M. J. Leach (Somerset), L. S. Livingstone (Lancashire), S. C. Meaker (Surrey), C. Overton (Somerset), O. P. Rayner (Middlesex), T. S. Roland-Jones (Middlesex), T. Westley (Essex). *Coach:* A. Flower.

After Jennings joined the England team in India, Gubbins captained in the third 50-over match, and Roland-Jones in the four-day game against Afghanistan. J. T. Ball (Nottinghamshire) was originally selected, but was added to the Test squad after an injury to J. M. Anderson. Dawson travelled to the UAE, but was called up as a reinforcement for the Test team in India.

At Dubai (Sports City), December 1, 2016. **England Lions won by eight wickets. United Arab Emirates 174** (45.3 overs) (Rohan Mustafa 33, Ghulam Shabbir 33, Mohammad Shehzad 38; S. C. Meaker 4-38); ‡**England Lions 175-2** (33.1 overs) (D. J. Bell-Drummond 40, K. K. Jennings 101*). *MoM:* K. K. Jennings.

At Dubai (Sports City), December 3, 2016. **England Lions won by 100 runs. England Lions 190** (47.3 overs) (T. P. Alsop 44, T. K. Curran 40, J. K. Fuller 35); ‡**United Arab Emirates 90** (29.2 overs) (Rohan Mustafa 45; T. K. Curran 5-16, M. J. Leach 3-7). *MoM:* T. K. Curran.

At Dubai (Sports City), December 5, 2016. **England Lions won by 16 runs. England Lions 223-8** (50 overs) (J. M. Clarke 42, S. M. Curran 40; Qadeer Ahmed 3-48); ‡**United Arab Emirates 207** (48.1 overs) (Rohan Mustafa 40, Adnan Mufti 69; O. P. Rayner 3-27, C. Overton 3-29). *MoM:* C. Overton.

At Abu Dhabi, December 7–10, 2016. **England Lions won by 48 runs.** ‡**England Lions 279** (96.4 overs) (T. Westley 84, B. T. Foakes 70; Yamin Ahmadzai 3-40, Rashid Khan 4-48) **and 210**

(84 overs) (N. R. T. Gubbins 53, B. T. Foakes 89*; Rashid Khan 8-74); **Afghanistan 273** (92.5 overs) (Rahmat Shah 33, Asghar Stanikzai 51, Hashmatullah Shahidi 40, Mohammad Nabi 51; T. S. Roland-Jones 6-73) **and 168** (49 overs) (Asghar Stanikzai 43, Rashid Khan 52; T. K. Curran 3-54, S. M. Curran 3-13). *Rashid Khan, the 18-year-old leg-spinner who had caught the eye at the World Twenty20 in India, had a first-class debut to remember for Afghanistan, but still ended up on the losing side. He took 12 wickets, including eight in the Lions' second innings, then provided some late defiance in the run-chase, after Afghanistan dipped to 76-7 in pursuit of 217. The Lions finished with four wins out of four in the UAE, thanks to canny seam bowling from skipper Toby Roland-Jones, whose six-for gave his side a slender first-innings lead, and a perky double from the Surrey wicketkeeper Ben Foakes. First he shared a fifth-wicket stand of 125 with his former Essex team-mate Tom Westley, making his first appearance of the tour after sitting out the one-dayers. Then he rescued the second innings with 89*, after Nick Gubbins and Sam Curran fell to successive balls from Rashid, to make it 134-6.*

UNITED ARAB EMIRATES v AFGHANISTAN

First Twenty20 international At Dubai (ICC Academy), December 14, 2016. **Afghanistan won by 11 runs.** ‡**Afghanistan 161-6** (20 overs) (Mohammad Shahzad 38, Najibullah Zadran 31*; Mohammad Shehzad 3-34); **United Arab Emirates 150-7** (20 overs) (Shaiman Anwar 34, Rameez Shahzad 49; Karim Janat 3-31). *MoM:* Karim Janat. *T20I debuts:* Ghulam Shabbir, Mohammad Qasim, Rameez Shahzad (UAE); Fareed Ahmed, Karim Janat (Afghanistan). *Afghanistan had too much firepower, first cracking 55 from the last three overs – Najibullah Zadran hit 26* from ten balls – then restricting the UAE to 41-3 in their first seven. Karim Janat, making his debut aged 18, took all three wickets, to follow a quick 25. Shaiman Anwar put on 65 with another debutant, Rameez Shahzad – whose father Shahzad Altaf played two ODIs for the UAE in 1996 – but the asking-rate kept growing. Afghanistan's Mohammad Shahzad was dismissed by the UAE's Mohammad Shehzad.*

Second Twenty20 international At Dubai (Sports City), December 16, 2016. **Afghanistan won by five wickets.** ‡**United Arab Emirates 179-4** (20 overs) (Rohan Mustafa 43, Shaiman Anwar 60, Rameez Shahzad 47*); **Afghanistan 183-5** (19.4 overs) (Mohammad Shahzad 31, Najibullah Zadran 55*; Amjad Javed 3-40). *MoM:* Najibullah Zadran. *T20I debuts:* Atif Ali Khan (UAE); Hazratullah Zazai (Afghanistan). *Afghanistan looked out of it at 116-5 after 14 – but Najibullah Zadran had other ideas, pummelling 55* from 24 balls to take his side home in the last over: Mohammad Nabi contributed 13* to their stand of 67*. Earlier, the UAE had made their highest T20 total, Shaiman putting on 67 in 32 balls with Rameez, who this time hit 47* from 19.*

Third Twenty20 international At Dubai (ICC Academy), December 18, 2016. **Afghanistan won by 44 runs.** ‡**Afghanistan 189-5** (20 overs) (Mohammad Shahzad 44, Najeeb Tarakai 40, Samiullah Shenwari 39); **United Arab Emirates 145-8** (20 overs) (Rohan Mustafa 58, Shaiman Anwar 56; Mohammad Nabi 3-30, Rashid Khan 3-14). *MoM:* Rashid Khan. *T20I debuts:* Imran Haider, Mohammad Shanil (UAE). *Afghanistan were 95-1, and the UAE 91-1 – but the Afghans powered to 189, with Samiullah Shenwari needing just 22 balls for his 39, while the Emiratis managed only 54 more as the slow men applied the brakes. Off-spinner Nabi and leg-spinner Rashid Khan had combined figures of 6-44, as Afghanistan swept the series 3–0.*

For the UAE's matches in the Asia Cup, see page 893; the Intercontinental Cup and the World Cricket League, see page 1141.

CRICKET ROUND THE WORLD IN 2016

COMPILED BY JAMES COYNE AND TIMOTHY ABRAHAM

ICC WORLD CRICKET LEAGUE

Ten years after the formation of the World Cricket League, the ICC's global 50-over ladder, the USA finally hosted a tournament. WCL Division Four was held at the Leo Magnus Cricket Complex in Los Angeles, and clips from each game – most memorably a leaping one-handed catch by USA wicketkeeper Akeem Dodson to remove Bermuda's Tre Manders – brought the event to life on social media like no Associate event before. Mick Jagger even turned up on the last day, at a ground where he had played the odd celebrity game.

ICC chief executive David Richardson had said the USA should be qualifying for major global tournaments – partly because of its considerable player base, but also because of the commercial opportunities American involvement would bring. So it was handy that they won Division Four, taking a small step closer to the World Cup, even if they sneaked promotion on net run-rate. After three wins, they were pegged back by some excellent death bowling from Denmark (temporarily captained by former England bowler Amjad Khan), then lost by one run to Jersey who, mid-injury crisis, drafted in 46-year-old team manager Tony Carlyon for the play-off against Italy; also in the side was his 15-year-old son, Harrison. In the final, the USA beat Oman by 13 runs. If a home victory was an encouraging sign of the winds of change, there were some unwelcome gusts too. The Bermuda v Jersey game ground to a halt when the sightscreen blew over; it took so long to sort things out it became a 45-over affair, and DLS tables were consulted.

For Oman, who were missing some of their 2016 World Twenty20 squad because of stricter WCL eligibility rules, it was the second time in six months they had topped the group stage, only to lose the final to the hosts – underlining the value of home advantage in Associate events. In May, Jersey had pipped Oman to the Division Five title, with Vanuatu, Tanzania and Nigeria relegated to regional tournaments. Sue Redfern and Jacqueline Williams (third umpire) presided over Oman's game against Nigeria: the first pair of female officials in an ICC men's match.

Absent from Division Five were Suriname, winners of the last Division Six tournament – later scrapped for cost reasons – in September 2015. Vanuatu, supported by Botswana, claimed Suriname had imported several Guyanese players without satisfying the 183-day residency requirement, prompting a five-month ICC investigation. Suriname forfeited their Division Five slot, and an ICC grant of $US25,000. JAMES COYNE

BOLIVIA

The need to deliver a heavy ball has an entirely different meaning at La Paz's High Altitude CC. At 3,640 metres, it is the highest capital city in the world, bringing with it unique challenges for cricketers. The lack of oxygen can leave players, particularly newcomers, gasping for air after a quick single. The atmosphere is so thin that, if a batsman middles a shot, the ball is often lost outside the postage-stamp ground. Supplies are dwindling. "We need somebody to design us a special cricket ball," explained Vimal Menon, the club's chief organiser. "Preferably a ball that is heavier – to cope with the thin air – but still feels, looks and plays like a normal ball. Maybe Dukes and NASA's scientists could get together to help us!" Since the early 2000s, cricket has been played sporadically on the not wholly satisfactory sports field at the American Cooperative School, the institution favoured by the diplomats and expats living in the upmarket part of La Paz. However, the equipment was collecting dust in the British Embassy until High Altitude were formed in 2013. The Condors, as they are informally known, include a hotchpotch of expats: New Zealander Alistair Matthew organises bicycle tours on the infamous El Camino de la Muerte – the Road of Death – while Englishman Thomas Lynch runs Nemo's Bar on the shores of Lake Titicaca, necessitating a 12-hour round trip by bus for each game. There is also a sprinkling of Bolivians. Finding a level plot of land is difficult. A possible site near the spectacular Valle de la Luna has been identified, which would mean an even higher altitude. That might have some upsides for the club's seamers, though. "I'm in my forties, and with the altitude I already feel like I'm bowling the same pace as I was in my twenties," joked Menon. "So maybe I'll feel like a teenager again at the new ground!" TIMOTHY ABRAHAM

BRAZIL

In 2016, Rio de Janeiro made history by staging a national cricket championship and an ICC-recognised regional tournament (oh, and the Olympic Games). The scale of those competitions was modest, the quality patchy and the participants largely foreign, but their very existence was testament to the progress made in rebuilding the sporting infrastructure of a city once home to the gilded age of Brazilian cricket.

In the mid-19th century, relations between Brazil's aristocracy and Britain's empire were close enough for the expanse of grass outside Princess Isabel's palace in the Laranjeiras district to become the country's first cricket ground; by 1872, it was the official home of the new Rio Cricket Club. Even though the first football match was not played in Brazil for another 22 years, it somehow grabbed the popular imagination, while cricket withered along with the monarchy (replaced by a republic in 1889) and British influence.

Nowadays Rio CC exists in name only. Despite moving across Guanabara Bay to unfashionable Niterói, cricket could not escape its upstart rival. Regular cricket matches ended in the 1990s, and all the playing areas are now football pitches. Even taking unofficial friendlies into account, the last confirmed runs were scored there in 2012. Yet cricket is now enjoying a resurgence, if in a different form and at a new venue.

The Carioca Cricket Club were founded in 2011 by a group of British boozers at the Pavão Azul (Blue Peacock) bar. The focus was fun rather than tradition, and the self-deprecatingly low expectations encapsulated by the CCC logo: Christ the Redeemer in umpire's coat signalling a wide. Since then, the club have lived down to those expectations – apart from a shock Brazil championship win in 2013 against perennial favourites São Paulo. But they have built such a reputation as tournament (and party) hosts that they can be considered the headquarters of cricket in Latin America.

There are stronger nations (Argentina) and stronger cities (São Paulo), but it is hard to match the facilities or hospitality of the CCC. With sponsorship from beauty products firm Granado, they now boast a clubhouse with a corrugated roof, already punctured by several sixes. There is a small tiered stand for spectators, a net and a bowling machine. The location is the São Fernando Polo (& Cricket) Club in Itaguaí, often referred to as "the corridor of sun certainty" – inappropriately, given the frequency of storms. There is space for four pitches, and the ground is sufficiently far from habitation to avoid complaints about raucous parties.

Despite such attractions, cricket has not gripped the locals. More than 150 years after the first match in Rio, it is still a nascent sport. But that hasn't stopped the dogged organisers: chairman Tobias Hanbury, president Craig Allison and captain Oliver Ballhatchet have rallied a mix of expat businessmen, teachers, diplomats, journalists and engineers. There is only one regular Brazilian player, Felipe Lima de Melo, but it is hoped the number will increase.

In October, the club hosted the four-day South American Cricket Championship, an ICC-recognised event with nine national teams that has run since 1997, although there has been a Brazil v Argentina fixture for more than a century. Chile won the men's trophy, Brazil the women's. Back in April, the domestic tournament featured teams from São Paulo (champions for seven of the past eight years), Curitiba, Brasilia and Minas Gerais, where former Kent Cricket Board batsman and current Brazil captain Matthew Featherstone organises a training programme in local schools.

The standard ranges from semi-professional to inebriated geriatric, but while individual performances have included a double hat-trick by Asanka Bandara, that is hardly the point. Any club that have "Sand, sea, sungas and sledging" as their motto are in no rush to burnish averages or supplant football. Cricket, Carioca style, is serious first and foremost about having fun. JONATHAN WATTS

BRITISH INDIAN OCEAN TERRITORY

These days, the only cricket played in these 55 islands is when British or American troops take a bat and tennis ball to one of the sandy beaches. The Chagos Archipelago is midway between Africa and Indonesia, and covers a little over 20 square miles. The French used it as a leper colony – sufferers ate the local turtles in the mistaken belief they offered a cure – before the British took charge in the 19th century. The main island, Diego Garcia, became a military base during the Second World War, and the Foreign and Commonwealth Office say the atoll's cricket field, on a patch of land by the meteorological station, was probably created then. On September 25, 1979, an Ashes match took place between Naval Party 1002 and the visiting Royal

Australian Air Force. "The Brits, swilling Courage Ale, defeated the devotees of Swan Lager by an unspecified, but impressive score," read one account. Annual games began between British troops and the crew of the *Pacific Marlin*, a patrol vessel. The British also played Mauritian employees at least twice. The only traceable photo of cricket, taken in the late 1980s after a game between the Royal Navy and the USS *Jason*, shows players in full whites and pads, plus the odd bottle of beer. Although officially a British territory, Diego Garcia is leased by the American military and off-limits to tourists, and the cricket pitch no longer exists. The FCO say the island "doesn't have a cleared area large enough" – but there is a nine-hole golf course. Either way, the native Chagos islanders wouldn't be able to play: they were removed between 1968 and 1973 to make way for the US base, and in November 2016 the UK government announced they could not return. OWEN AMOS

COOK ISLANDS

Davis Teinaki, new chief executive of the Cook Islands Cricket Association, has a long-term goal of building an indoor facility to allow more cricket outside the traditional season. The Cooks' international aspirations, however, have been put on hold. The ICC have advised East Asia–Pacific members to shift their "disproportionate focus on international activities and high performance", towards building "grassroots interests and participation". But a country with a scattered population of around 15,000, where cricket lags behind both rugby codes, is unable to meet ICC requirements to establish age-group leagues. The islands are therefore excluded from official international tournaments. CHRIS DRURY

COSTA RICA

The cradle of Costa Rican cricket is Limón Province, where enthusiasm for George Headley and Learie Constantine was so high among West Indian fruit workers of the 1920s and 1930s that as many as 46 teams sprang up beside the railway lines of the Caribbean coast. Football has long since taken over, but bats and balls are coming out of hibernation. With ICC Americas cutting back most of their Affiliate tournaments in recent years, the Costa Rican Cricket Federation (Fedecric) have stepped up the countrywide grassroots development programme, centred on Limón. From 2008 to 2014, the number of schools playing cricket in Limón Province leapt from ten to 100; participants in the Standford Barton inter-schools tournaments from five to 45; and young people who had a cricket experience from 50 to 5,000. Fedecric have held courses, and run week-long sleepover camps for boys, girls and teachers at EARTH University in Guacimo, supported by the British and Trinidadian embassies. In 2016, a total of 23 PE teachers, all members of the recently formed Costa Rican Women's Cricket Association, took part in coaching clinics directed by Ann Browne-John, a former Trinidad & Tobago and West Indies cricketer. The level of enthusiasm for women's cricket, under the inspired leadership of new board member Trudy Poyser, has the potential to revitalise the game in Limón Province, and provide a social uplift in Puerto Limón – a city of crumbling grandeur. T. RICHARD ILLINGWORTH

GERMANY

Germany's *Cricketwunder* – as it was christened by *Stuttgarter Zeitung* – rides the wave of immigration from Afghanistan and Pakistan. Some of the personal stories are harrowing, while the experience of Arif Jamal (see *Wisden 2016*, page 1205) is being turned into a film, provisionally titled *Rites of Passage*, written by Berlin-based O'neil Sharma – an assistant director on Quentin Tarantino's *Inglourious Basterds*. There are dizzying numbers of new cricketers in Germany, and the infrastructure is coming under enormous pressure. In 2011, there were around 1,500 active players in 70 sides; by October 2016, the Deutscher Cricket Bund were reporting more than 6,000 in 300 teams, excluding the unaudited numbers in informal tape-ball matches. "The big breakthrough will be in five or six years' time, when recent refugees will be eligible to play for Germany in ICC tournaments," said Brian Mantle, the DCB managing director. Moneygram – the cash transfer company – have become the board's main sponsor. To combat a chronic pitch shortage, the DCB have invested in around 30 coconut mats – bought from an unwitting German manufacturer in Eifel – which, laid over wooden boards, can provide a decent surface. Already, the national team were good enough to win the rain-hit ICC Europe Division Two in Sweden, putting them one promotion from a return to the World Cricket League and a place in the next World Twenty20 Qualifier. Once official playing numbers reach 10,000, the DCB will be eligible for funding from the German Olympic Committee. It is sorely needed: even after the surge in players, the ICC contribution for 2017 has gone up by just $US10,000. There seems no immediate prospect of Germany being treated as a special case, like Afghanistan or the USA. "What really matters," said Mantle, "is the ICC and the IOC getting cricket in the Olympic Games." JAMES COYNE

ITALY

A former Italy Under-19 captain was deported for allegedly plotting an attack in support of ISIS. Aftab Farooq, 26, born in Pakistan, was recorded talking about possible gun or bomb attacks in Milan and Bergamo. Farooq's family moved to Milan when he was ten. They appealed against his deportation, and the case was passed to the European Court of Human Rights.

MALAWI

The Blantyre Sports Club ground is ringed on one side by trees inhabited by monkeys, and on the other by an elevated clubhouse and bar, giving it a captivating, if dilapidated, colonial charm. Cricket has a long history here, though it has been plagued by infighting and maladministration: the Malawi Cricket Union's failure to account for $US80,000 earmarked for development led to their suspension from the ICC in 2011. However, there is a new board with a fresh and transparent grassroots approach. More than 4,000 schoolchildren are taking part in training programmes organised by local coaches. Malawi are also returning to regional international tournaments. In May 2015, the men's side – coached by former Ireland all-rounder Andre Botha – took part in a triangular series with Mozambique and Zambia. Malawi captain Gift Kansonkho was the leading run-scorer, and 19-year-old off-spinner Tyler House the most promising player, but Mozambique edged the final. Last August, the Under-19 women's team made their international debut, narrowly losing to Zambia and Mozambique, before being outclassed by a team from Gauteng. Against Mozambique, all-rounder Lydia Dimba won the match award for a classy 35 and three for 19. In 2017, a group of players will visit the Tuks Cricket Centre in Pretoria for a week-long training camp, and men's and women's vice-captains Gershom Ntambalika and Mary Mabvuka will spend three months at the Perth Cricket Academy. BEN GWILLIAM

Ben Gwilliam is a board member of the Malawi Cricket Union.

MONGOLIA

During the spring thaw, Battulga Gombo made a pilgrimage to Burkhan Khaldun, the holiest mountain in Mongolia, and said to be the birthplace – and burial ground – of Genghis Khan. Battulga sought the blessing of lamas (Buddhist monks) to press on with the construction of the country's first cricket ground. In 2014, the Mongolia Amateur Cricket Association, headed by Battulga, had secured land in the Ulan Bator National Park, in the shadow of another sacred mountain, and set about raising $US121,000 to install an artificial wicket, grass outfield, pavilion, nets and groundsman's hut. In Mongolia, disturbing such land can be a serious matter. But the monks gave their approval. Despite temperatures of minus 25°C, a successful fundraising dinner and auction was held in January 2016, and in April the British Embassy's Steppe Inn – essentially a pub – hosted an exhibition by artist Emma Trenchard. She presented a remarkable set of paintings of Mongolian animals playing cricket: among them *The Marmot Umpire, The Batting Yak*, and *The Padded Argali*. In May, the hard graft began. Doug Graham provided heavy equipment to level the playing area and bring in topsoil. A team of volunteers, including William Hurd, who had flown over especially from England, removed countless stones by hand. Matting was laid on top of a concrete base and, in September, the ground held a grand opening match, attended by 120 people, including the British, Australian and Indian ambassadors, and governors of local schools. It was encouraging to see Mongolian boys scoring runs and taking wickets from day one. Six weekends of matches and training sessions were held – with more than 100 children introduced to the game – before the freeze returned in mid-October. MACA received from friends of Battulga in Melbourne a generous donation of more than 300kg of cricket gear, which they intended to distribute to local schools. MACA will also train ten PE teachers. The aim is to make cricket accessible

Putting the bat into Ulan Bator? A net session at the Mongolian Friendship Cricket Ground.

to young Mongolians from impoverished backgrounds, not least in Ulan Bator's *ger* districts – *gers* are also known as yurts – inhabited mainly by rural immigrants to the city. ADAM HOQUE

NIGERIA

Cricket clings on in embattled north-east Nigeria, in the face of atrocities perpetrated by Boko Haram. The sport had fallen dormant in Borno State around 1980, but was resurrected in 2006 for the Nigerian university games, held at Maiduguri. A lecturer, Sadiq Saidu El-Buba, found a playing space, which allowed students – including women and girls who, in this predominantly Muslim area, play in hijabs – to get a game. The sexes play alongside each other, and Sadiq hopes there will soon be enough for two teams. The students rely on a kitbag despatched by Kwesi Sagoe, former president of the Nigerian Cricket Federation, who also helped train the keenest players, and encouraged Borno to field teams in the National Sports Festival. However, cricket – which in West Africa carries colonial baggage – was unlikely to meet with approval from Boko Haram (which roughly translates as "Western education is forbidden"). Their insurgency caused the North-East Women's Cricket Championships to be cancelled in 2014, and the region could not send a representative side to Abuja for the national competition. JAMES COYNE

SWEDEN

Sweden is one of cricket's fastest developing nations. This is partly thanks to funding from the government, who have grasped the value of the game in integrating an increasingly multicultural society – and insulated the country

EUROPEAN NATIVE CRICKET SIXES

Going Native

VLADIMIR NINKOVIĆ

Crouching at the striker's end as Poland's Adam Krasinski runs in is an intimidating prospect. He may be only 17, but he is two metres tall, and probably the best native bowler I've faced. He is one of the Warsaw Hussars, a team of Poles who learned cricket while living in England, and have since toured South London and Surrey.

Being an indigenous cricketer in Continental Europe is not easy. Most of us started playing quite late, and so – unlike the British freelance journalists or middle-aged Indian IT professionals we frequently come up against – picked up no skills in our youth. In the past, many European countries shied away from developing grassroots cricket, and preferred the short-term gains of using the best available expats. This made cricket harder to sell to the mainstream population, and the sport remained on the fringes. It was a vicious circle.

Native players and officials are key to the game's sustainable development. They establish contacts with national sports authorities, appear in the local media (since they speak the local language) and promote cricket in schools; it is also with them that young domestic players identify. Native cricketers tend to be experienced sportsmen who are prepared to take the sport seriously. This especially holds true in the ex-socialist countries, where success at team sports was the fruit of a strict approach to training. So I was excited about a Native Cricket Sixes tournament organised by Warsaw Hussars, and involving teams from Poland, Estonia and Serbia.

The Hussars' ground, in the village of Stare Babice, about eight miles from Warsaw, is part of a well-maintained sports complex, and the artificial wicket has even bounce. Serbia had Boško Didanović (a hot prospect), Tijana Anić (girls' team captain), and 14-year-old Jovan Reb. Poland included Adam Krasinski and Kuba Blazejczyk, batsmen Robert Grzedowski and Piotr Sochaj, and the talented Stas Krasinski (just 12). The pick of the Estonians were wicketkeeper Marko Vaik and seamer Kalle Vislapuu, with an excellent female bowler, Annemari Vessik. The matches between the A teams were tightly contested: Poland won, with Estonia second, and Serbia third. The organisers are planning an 11-a-side Twenty20 version for 2017.

Vladimir Ninković is the general secretary of the Serbian Cricket Federation.

from the recent reduction of ICC funds for Affiliate nations. In May 2015, the Svenska Cricket Förbundet were incorporated into the Swedish Sports Confederation, raising the profile of a sport that has long struggled for attention. The federation now have an office, an annual grant of 1m kroner (£90,000), and greater reach. Clubs have secured land and grants from local councils, thus increasing the number of grounds available in a rapidly expanding national league. Stockholm City Council paid for a new, two-pitch ground in Skarpnäck, in the south of the city, which last August hosted the ICC Europe Division Two. Sweden, who are coached by former Yorkshire and England A left-arm seamer Paul Hutchison – he doubles up as kit supplier through his company, Romwear – came second and were promoted. Because of the rising numbers of South Asians, participation has soared over the last two years, and there are now at least 2,500 players in more than 50 clubs. Cricket regularly features in the news, and Afghanistan-born national captain, Azam Khalil, starred in a TV documentary about the changing role of cricket in a diverse society. Ethnic Swedes are joining clubs too, and the SCF have worked hard to take cricket into schools. TIM BROOKS

TAIWAN

Mellow Lin, a 21-year-old wicketkeeper, is so taken by cricket that in August she moved to Hong Kong to enrol in the Michael Clarke Academy and play for one of the local teams. She hopes to return to Taiwan to build up the cricket scene. Taiwanese cricket is currently played on a ten-metre stretch of green carpet laid down on the dirt of a softball diamond. There is a drive to expand women's cricket and boost local involvement, which has resulted in the birth of the Taiwan Darling Daredevils and the Chung Jung University teams. This in turn inspired a tour from one of Hong Kong's oldest clubs, Craigengower CC, in 2015. Local teams played matches against men's side Craigengower Hung See, and women's team Craigengower Fung Wong. DUANE CHRISTIE

TURKEY

There are fewer cricketers in Turkey (population 80m) than in Todmorden (15,481 at the last count). But that may be about to change. In November, Haluk Bey, my boss in a computer company where I teach English ushered about 30 of us on to a bus on an unseasonably warm, late autumnal day in Istanbul. It turned out Bey had bought bats, balls and stumps from Amazon – and we were going to play cricket. We found the only flat piece of land in the Belgrade Forest, where balls were chucked at heads, bats were held baseball-style, and fielders slunk about looking for a place for a quiet smoke. After ten overs, my side had amassed 35 runs. Play was interrupted by guards, who asked us to move to another piece of forest – beaten earth which looked more subcontinental than Home Counties – but our opponents knocked off the target comfortably. Everyone declared cricket a fine game, and Haluk his intention to make it a regular event. Turkey, ICC Affiliate Members since 2008, are currently suspended for having rival governing bodies and failing to submit an approved budget. Pakistanis feature prominently both in the national side and a league, based around Bilkent University in Ankara. ROB LEWIS

USA

Time was when the suspension of a nation's governing body for 18 months might have caused their cricket to wither. But, though the USA Cricket Association had been excluded from the ICC since June 2015, there followed a period of considerable progress for the American game. The caretaker administration, led by ICC Americas, began 2016 by sending a mixed squad of US and Canadian players to the Nagico Super50 tournament in the West Indies. Later, three Americans were drafted into Caribbean Premier League squads, with Timroy Allen and Ali Khan, who had been off the USA radar a year earlier, earning junior contracts.

City-based combines – aimed at identifying talent at men's, women's and junior levels – were organised throughout spring and summer. For the men, these trials informed the choice of a 30-strong national squad to prepare for Division Four of the WCL. Ricardo Powell, the ex-West Indies batsman, headed a new selection panel, while former Sri Lanka Test wicketkeeper Pubudu Dassanayake was coach. After two failed attempts to have the USA host a WCL event, ICC Americas made no mistake this time; the USA gained promotion after winning the tournament in Los Angeles.

The women's national team, dormant since 2012, were re-formed in time for the inaugural tour of North America by MCC Women, who included Charlotte Edwards and Claire Taylor. The home talent was modest, but the players did enough to convince the ICC that the USA should return to international events. The last ICC Americas Women's Championship was back in 2013, but the USA were given a wild-card to the ICC Europe Qualifier for 2017.

There was also renewed interest in the USA as a neutral venue. First came the CPL, which staged six games at Florida's Central Broward Regional Park at the end of July. A month later, India and West Indies played a pair of Twenty20 internationals there, the first in the USA for four years. What some saw as the USA's favoured status was rumoured to have caused the head of an unnamed Associate Member to stand up at June's ICC annual conference in Edinburgh and jokingly volunteer the suspension of his board – if it brought his country similar increases in support and investment.

USACA's status remained in limbo. The ICC had set a December deadline for the ratification of a new constitution laying out major reforms, particularly to the board's structure. The deadline passed, though the ICC and USACA – still headed by controversial long-serving president Gladstone Dainty – said they had reached a consensus on progress towards a final agreement.

The rival American Cricket Federation slipped into near anonymity. Their National Championship was quietly scaled down to a small event featuring two teams from New England and two from Washington DC. They have no significant funding and, without the presence of several of their administrators on ICC advisory committees, might have folded. Whenever the ICC decide to relinquish their hold on US cricket, it seems the USACA will remain in charge, if with reduced power. Precisely who features in a revamped board of directors remains to be seen. PETER DELLA PENNA

GLOBAL TOURNAMENTS

ICC WORLD CRICKET LEAGUE

	Date	*Winner*	*Runners-up*	*Others*
Division Four	Oct–Nov	USA	Oman	Denmark, Bermuda, Jersey, Italy
Division Five	May	Jersey	Oman	Guernsey, Vanuatu, Tanzania, Nigeria

REGIONAL T20 TOURNAMENTS

	Date	*Winner*	*Runners-up*	*Others*
Europe Division Two	Aug	Germany	Sweden	Spain, Israel, Isle of Man, Gibraltar
East Asia Cup	Nov	South Korea	Japan	Hong Kong, China
South American Ch'ships	Oct	Chile	Argentina	Peru, Brazil, Colombia, Mexico

WOMEN'S TOURNAMENTS

	Date	*Winner*	*Runners-up*	*Others*
2017 World Cup Africa Qualifier	Apr	Zimbabwe	Kenya	Uganda, Tanzania
2017 World Cup Asia Qualifier	Oct	Thailand	Nepal	China, Hong Kong
2017 World Cup East Asia–Pacific Qualifier	Jul	PNG	Samoa	Japan
2017 World Cup Europe Qualifier	Jul	Scotland	Netherlands	–
Twenty20 Asia Cup	Nov–Dec	India	Pakistan	Sri Lanka, Bangladesh, Thailand, Nepal
South American Championships	Oct	Brazil	Argentina	Peru

PART SIX

Women's Cricket

WOMEN'S INTERNATIONAL CRICKET IN 2016

MELINDA FARRELL

If a tree falls in a forest and no one is around to hear it, does it make a sound? The question could once have been the motto for women's cricket. Until recently, the most outstanding batting, bowling or fielding performances by female players had largely been the stuff of legend, imagined from scorecards or – when available – basic match reports. The broadcasting of women's internationals has been sporadic, so it was encouraging that, in 2016, as the women's game marched towards full professionalism, a much wider audience could judge the talent for themselves.

Following the hugely successful Women's Big Bash League in Australia, the fifth Women's World Twenty20 (held in conjunction with the men's) brought elite female cricketers to an unprecedented audience: 13 of the 23 matches were broadcast, and the ICC estimated the tournament drew 24.5m viewers in India, and a worldwide audience of more than a billion.

West Indies became the first team apart from Australia, England or New Zealand to win a world final in either format. Cricket Australia have streaked ahead of other boards in terms of investment, while England have scrambled to allocate resources to keep up. But West Indies, led by the outstanding Stafanie Taylor and bursting with raw talent, battled gamely against India, then bested the in-form New Zealand to enter the final against Australia – a team they had never beaten in the T20 format, and who were aiming for a fourth straight title.

West Indies' victory and the commercial success of the tournament had a knock-on effect. The WICB expanded their central contract system, a move mirrored by other boards, including South Africa and New Zealand. The ECB extended central contracts to two years, and introduced a "rookie" contract for players on the fringe of the national side, in an attempt to create a secondary layer of professionals. In Australia, New South Wales became the first women's domestic team to offer full-time contracts.

England's performance at the WWT20, where they lost to Australia in the semi-final, led to a shake-up and the forced retirement of captain Charlotte Edwards. She had played for England for 20 years, and her axing was a bold move by coach Mark Robinson, who favoured handing responsibility to younger players and a new captain, Heather Knight. It seemed to work: England won 13 of their next 15 games, with clean sweeps against Pakistan and Sri Lanka bookending a 3–2 victory in a competitive one-day series in the West Indies.

Those results took England to second place, behind Australia, as the inaugural ICC Women's Championship concluded in November. Along with New Zealand and West Indies, they qualified automatically for the 2017 World Cup. India, South Africa – who managed some impressive wins against the top sides – Pakistan and Sri Lanka joined other nations in a tournament to settle the final four qualifiers.

CHARLOTTE EDWARDS STEPS DOWN

As one door closes…

VITHUSHAN EHANTHARAJAH

"I know you can't do it for ever, and I know there's always a time to go." That is about as much of an admission of weakness as you are likely to get from Charlotte Edwards, and it came a few weeks after she announced her retirement from international cricket. England Women's head coach Mark Robinson had seen the beginning of the summer as the time for change, and Edwards was prepared to relinquish the captaincy. But Robinson and Clare Connor, head of women's cricket at the ECB, wanted a clean break; Edwards stepped down.

After 20 years of England duty – and more than ten as captain, during which she led her side to victory in a World Cup, a World Twenty20, and won the Ashes four times – that was that. The 2016 World T20 provided a snapshot of the problem. Edwards was the tournament's second highest scorer, while only one other England player (Tammy Beaumont) passed 100 runs. Their wickets routinely set off collapses, though it wasn't until the semi-final against Australia that the problem caught up with them. It was Edwards's 309th and final game for her country, leaving her with 10,273 international runs – of which her tallies in ODIs (5,992) and Twenty20s (2,605) were world records. Only Jan Brittin scored more than her 1,676 Test runs. In all Edwards made 80 scores of 50-plus, including 13 hundreds.

England, it was felt, needed to evolve, to match Australia's tenacity and West Indies' explosiveness. And they needed to do it without the safety blanket of Edwards. That last part was crucial: from the start of Robinson's tenure, he urged the players to get fitter and expand their game. In his first meeting with Edwards, at Lord's, he asked why – with the abundance of medium-pacers in women's cricket – a player of her class was not looking to lap-sweep through the often vacant backward square leg. Fast forward to the final World T20 group game against Pakistan, where Edwards played the shot with relish in an unbeaten 77 from 61 balls. Robinson urged his players to raise their game, and Edwards did just that.

For Robinson, her ability was never an issue: "I have worked with three players who were just on another level: Murray Goodwin, Mahela Jayawardene and Lottie. That belief in their skills, where no total is beyond them. It's such a rare trait." Had 2016 been an Ashes summer, Robinson admits Edwards would not have gone when she did.

She could have slunk into the shadows, out of harm's way and into an administrative or ambassadorial role. Instead, she took commentary positions with Sky and the BBC, as England shellacked a weak Pakistan; who knows how many runs Edwards would have hit. The team were moving on – but she had unfinished business.

Returning to domestic cricket with a point to prove, she was relentless. In July, she led Kent to their third NatWest Twenty20 Cup. At the end of the season, a seventh County Championship followed. But her most notable victory came in the inaugural Kia Super League. As captain of the Southern Vipers, she guided them to four group wins out of five. The final, in the end, was a formality: the Vipers won by seven wickets after Edwards and Suzie Bates put on 78 for the first wicket in response to Western Storm's 140. As Edwards put it: "You couldn't have made up my summer."

The Women's Championship gave arguably the fairest indication of rankings international cricket had seen. This was the final year of the inaugural competition, envied by those wanting meaningful context for men's bilateral series (in February 2017, the ICC announced plans for a male equivalent).

That no team from the subcontinent qualified directly for the World Cup was a concern. Despite India claiming their first bilateral series victory over Australia – they won two of three Twenty20 games there – clinching a 3–0 one-day win at home to West Indies, and taking the Asia Cup for the sixth time, they were hampered by politics, when the BCCI refused to let them play in Pakistan. They forfeited all six Championship points on offer, when four points would have seen them qualify ahead of West Indies.

For Sri Lanka and Pakistan it was a bleak year, with no victories until the Asia Cup. There is a danger that the gap between the weaker countries and the front runners will widen, as the domestic structures and pay scales of England and Australia, in particular, continue to improve.

And therein lies one of the biggest challenges. As the women's game heads into the first World Cup of the modern era, contested by many players who are now fully professional, how can it develop and maintain genuine competition, while showcasing the best talent to a rapidly widening audience? There are eyes and ears in the forest now. They expect an entertaining show.

ICC WOMEN'S CHAMPIONSHIP, 2014–2016

In 2014, the ICC introduced a Women's Championship as a qualifying tournament for the next World Cup, and to create a more meaningful programme for the leading teams. Each of the eight sides who had contested the 2012-13 World Cup played each other in three ODIs over two and a half years (they could arrange more games if they chose, but only the designated three carried points). The first Championship ended in November 2016, and the top four teams – Australia, England, New Zealand and West Indies – qualified directly for the 2017 World Cup, to be held in England. The bottom four were to meet six regional qualifiers, in a further tournament in Sri Lanka in February 2017, to settle the remaining four World Cup places. India, who finished three points behind West Indies, might well have qualified above them had they played their series against Pakistan; the ICC ruled it was the BCCI's fault this did not happen, and awarded Pakistan the six points.

FINAL QUALIFYING TABLE

	Played	*Won*	*Lost*	*No result*	*Points*	*Net run-rate*
AUSTRALIA	21	18	3	0	36	0.98
ENGLAND	21	14	6	1	29	1.04
NEW ZEALAND	21	13	8	0	26	0.44
WEST INDIES	21	11	10	0	22	0.12
India	21	9	11*	1	19	–0.48
South Africa	21	8	12	1	17	–0.23
Pakistan	21	7*	14	0	14	–1.12
Sri Lanka	21	2	18	1	5	–1.53

Win = 2pts; no result = 1pt.

* *India failed to meet Pakistan; the three games were awarded to Pakistan, along with six points. India were credited with no runs in 50 overs in each game for net run-rate purposes.*

LEADING WOMAN CRICKETER IN THE WORLD IN 2016

Ellyse Perry

RAF NICHOLSON

It might have been thought that Ellyse Perry – named Australia's most marketable athlete, male or female, in 2013 – could do little more to enhance her reputation. But, in 2016, she did. Across 14 one-day internationals, she hit 732 runs at 81, improving her highest score twice in successive innings, with 93 and 95 (both unbeaten) against South Africa in November. In Twenty20 internationals, she twice equalled her best (55 not out) and in one of those games, against India in January, collected a career-best four for 12. She captained the Sydney Sixers, runners-up in the inaugural Women's Big Bash League; reached a fourth successive World Twenty20 final; and won the National Cricket League final with New South Wales.

If consistency is the mark of greatness, Perry raised the bar: her run of 17 fifties in 23 ODI innings since the start of 2014 has never been bettered by man or woman. She was the leading scorer in the last two Ashes – at home in 2013-14, and in England in 2015 – and no one took more wickets. The 2015 series was a career highlight: "It's nice to have played more of a role with the bat in the last couple of years, but it's far more enjoyable when you're celebrating a series victory as a team." Her ultimate aim is to "contribute equally with bat and ball".

Though in recent years her batting has brought fame, Perry began as a bowler, the spearhead of the attack. On debut against New Zealand in July 2007, aged 16, she became Australia's youngest international cricketer. In 2010, she was the leading wicket-taker when they won the World Twenty20 in the Caribbean, and claimed three for 18 in the final. She was vital in Australia's hat-trick of titles – two more WWT20s, one World Cup – between 2012 and 2014, and will for ever be remembered for the 2013 World Cup final against West Indies when, with an injured ankle, she limped in for ten overs and took three for 19.

Born in the Sydney suburb of Wahroonga, Perry learned multiple sports in the backyard with her father, Mark, still one of her coaches. At Pymble Ladies' College she was captain in sports, athletics and cricket, and she became the first woman to represent Australia at World Cups in two sports when she played for the Matildas football team in 2011. She still plays for Sydney FC.

But cricket has come to dominate her life, thanks largely to its professionalisation: Perry now earns over $A100,000, thanks to her Cricket Australia contract, the WBBL and New South Wales's recent move to make players fully professional. She identifies this as the key development of the year, "particularly how successful the WBBL was, and how many more opportunities there have been for female cricketers". It would be hard to argue that her status as one of Australia's best-paid sportswomen is undeserved.

ICC WOMEN'S WORLD TWENTY20 IN 2015-16

KRITIKA NAIDU

1 West Indies 2 Australia 3= England, New Zealand

Change swept through women's cricket on a memorable afternoon in Kolkata, as a sprightly West Indies were crowned World Twenty20 champions for the first time. They had dethroned the mighty Australians – winners of the last three tournaments – in the first final since the competition's inception in 2009 to feature a team other than Australia, England or New Zealand. This edition boasted 13 televised matches, four half-centuries in the final (no previous final had featured any), growing audiences and media interest, and – usually – competitive cricket.

But it wasn't all rainbows and butterflies. Given that good crowds turned up whenever women's matches preceded the men's, double-headers were inexplicably few, which seemed especially wasteful when both teams from one country were playing in different cities on the same day. The absence of a broadcaster in ten group games meant third-umpire replays were unavailable. Security concerns delayed the arrival of Pakistan, who missed out on their warm-up matches, while India squandered a chance to drive the sport's development at home by failing to progress beyond the group stages. Too many pitches proved unappealingly sluggish, and the big-ticket sides, England and Australia, were both below par.

West Indies, by contrast, satisfied the desire of their captain, Stafanie Taylor, to play fearless cricket. Britney Cooper's bold 61 was the defining contribution to their semi-final win over New Zealand, and a blazing 66 from 18-year-old Hayley Matthews did the same job in the final. Before that, Deandra Dottin's all-round prowess helped oust **India**, who had begun high on confidence having recently won a series in Australia for the first time in any format, then whitewashed Sri Lanka. Billboards featured women players alongside the men, but the pressure got to Mithali Raj's team. Following a big win over Bangladesh, their batting and fielding grew scratchy, and they emerged on the wrong side of three nail-biters: by two runs, two wickets, and three runs.

India's spinners were effective, but then most were. Slow pitches thwarted strokeplay, resulting in low scores and tense denouements, though both Raj and England coach Mark Robinson were critical of conditions which, they felt, did not play to women cricketers' strengths. A lack of pace once the new ball had softened meant sixes proved in shorter supply than during the 2014 tournament in Bangladesh, dropping from 57 to 43. Only in the final did the batsmen encounter a track to encourage adventure.

Despite that, England captain Charlotte Edwards became the first player of either gender to pass 2,500 runs in Twenty20 internationals. She and Tammy Beaumont covered for a stumbling middle order as **England** scraped past India and West Indies in the pool stages, but they couldn't offset a collapse in the

Gareth Copley, Getty Images

Up and running: Hayley Matthews gives West Indies the perfect start to their chase in the final.

semi-final against Australia, when they needed only 45 off 42 balls with nine wickets in hand. Robinson blamed his team's poor running between the wickets on a lack of fitness, prompting awkward questions about why England had handed out so few new caps in the previous three years. In May came an unexpected development: the 36-year-old Edwards – second only to Stafanie Taylor in the competition's run-scoring list – was forced into international retirement, after two decades at the highest level.

Sana Mir, in her last tournament as Twenty20 captain, led **Pakistan** to within touching distance of the knockouts, and went home with a tale for the grandchildren: a rain-affected two-run win in Delhi over India, who had no answers to the guile of Anam Amin, a left-arm spinner spotted at a college match in Lahore two years earlier. **Sri Lanka** again failed to reach the last four, and **South Africa** – semi-finalists in 2014 – were also a let-down. They beat only an inexperienced **Ireland**, whose squad included three players aged 16 or younger. **Bangladesh** managed their highest score batting second, against England, but – like Ireland – exited without a win.

Leigh Kasperek's journey from her native Scotland, for whom she played as a teenager, to **New Zealand** was worth the miles: she ended as joint-leading wicket-taker, claiming nine at ten apiece, including three to help reduce Australia to four for four in the group stages. Suzie Bates clubbed New Zealand to the tournament's highest total, 177 against Ireland, and their unbeaten run to the knockouts oozed authority. It was a shock when West Indies narrowly defended 143 against them in the semi-final.

Nerves were palpable in West Indies' maiden final as Elyse Villani and Meg Lanning cashed in on full tosses and fumbles. Both made half-centuries; Villani finished fifth in the run charts, and Lanning third. But a star was born when Matthews launched an audacious counter-attack, striking three big sixes in a 45-ball 66. Taylor was an expert second fiddle, as West Indies chased down **Australia's** 148. Their success told of a narrowing gap between the traditional powerhouses of the women's game and the rest.

Australian media were quick to attribute Matthews's feat to her recent stint in their inaugural Big Bash, though she had managed only one innings of substance for Hobart Hurricanes. Taylor, however, claimed to have benefited from her time with Sydney Thunder. "It allowed me to know the bowlers a lot better," she said after making 59 in the final, to finish with 246 runs, comfortably the most. While Australia's women were welcomed home with a significant pay rise, the West Indians secured a greater prize: a sense of restored pride in Caribbean cricket, strengthened when Darren Sammy's team won the men's event a few hours later.

NATIONAL SQUADS

** Captain. ‡ Did not play.*

Australia *M. M. Lanning, K. M. Beams, A. J. Blackwell, ‡N. J. Carey, L. R. Cheatle, ‡S. J. Coyte, R. M. Farrell, ‡H. L. Ferling, A. J. Healy, J. L. Jonassen, B. L. Mooney, E. A. Osborne, E. A. Perry, M. L. Schutt, E. J. Villani. *Coach:* M. P. Mott.

G. M. Harris was originally selected, but had to withdraw with deep vein thrombosis. She was replaced by Carey, who was also a non-playing reinforcement in the previous tournament.

Bangladesh *Jahanara Alam, Ayasha Rahman, Fahima Khatun, Farzana Haque, Khadija Tul Kobra, Lata Mondal, Nahida Akter, Nigar Sultana, Panna Ghosh, Ritu Moni, Rumana Ahmed, Salma Khatun, Sanjida Islam, ‡Shaila Sharmin, Sharmin Akter. *Coach:* J. C. Gamage.

England *C. M. Edwards, T. T. Beaumont, K. H. Brunt, G. A. Elwiss, ‡N. E. Farrant, L. S. Greenway, R. L. Grundy, J. L. Gunn, D. Hazell, ‡A. E. Jones, H. C. Knight, L. A. Marsh, N. R. Sciver, A. Shrubsole, S. J. Taylor, D. N. Wyatt. *Coach:* M. A. Robinson.

Hazell injured her leg during the tournament, and was replaced by Marsh.

India *M. D. Raj, E. Bisht, R. S. Gayakwad, J. N. Goswami, H. Kaur, V. Krishnamurthy, S. S. Mandhana, ‡N. Niranjana, S. S. Pandey, A. A. Patil, ‡D. B. Sharma, ‡M. D. Thirush Kamini, V. R. Vanitha, S. Verma, P. Yadav. *Coach:* P. Rau.

Ireland *I. M. H. C. Joyce, C. C. Dalton, L. Delany, K. J. Garth, ‡J. Gray, C. N. I. M. Joyce, S. M. Kavanagh, A. J. Kenealy, G. H. Lewis, R. A. Lewis, ‡K. McKenna, C. J. Metcalfe, L. K. O'Reilly, C. M. A. Shillington, M. V. Waldron. *Coach:* A. Hamilton.

New Zealand *S. W. Bates, E. M. Bermingham, S. F. M. Devine, L. M. Kasperek, ‡F. C. Leydon-Davis, S. J. McGlashan, K. J. Martin, ‡T. M. M. Newton, M. J. G. Nielsen, K. T. Perkins, A. M. Peterson, R. H. Priest, ‡H. M. Rowe, A. E. Satterthwaite, L-M. M. Tahuhu. *Coach:* H. M. Tiffen.

Pakistan *Sana Mir, Aliya Riaz, Anam Amin, Asmavia Iqbal, ‡Ayesha Zafar, Bismah Maroof, ‡Diana Baig, Iram Javed, Javeria Khan, Muneeba Ali, Nahida Khan, Nain Abidi, Nida Dar, Sadia Yousuf, Sidra Ameen, Sidra Nawaz. *Coach:* Mohtashim Rasheed.

Sania Khan was originally selected, but broke her right thumb shortly before the tournament and was replaced by Diana Baig. Javeria Khan was injured while batting in the first match, and replaced by Ayesha Zafar.

South Africa *M. du Preez, T. Chetty, M. Daniels, D. Devnarain, Y. Fourie, S. Ismail, M. Kapp, A. Khaka, ‡O. Kirsten, M. Klaas, L. Lee, M. M. Letsoalo, S. Luus, C. L. Tryon, D. van Niekerk. *Coach:* H. K. Moreeng.

Sri Lanka *H. A. S. D. Siriwardene, N. N. D. de Silva, M. D. N. Hansika, A. C. Jayangani, K. A. D. A. Kanchana, ‡H. I. H. Karunaratne, L. E. Kaushalya, B. M. S. M. Kumari, B. Y. A. Mendis, K. D. U. Prabodhani, O. U. Ranasinghe, I. Ranaweera, H. M. D. Samarawickrama, M. A. A. Sanjeewani, M. A. D. D. Surangika, W. P. M. Weerakkody. *Coach:* S. K. L. de Silva.

Siriwardene injured her leg during the tournament, and was replaced by Sanjeewani; Jayangani took over the captaincy.

West Indies *S. R. Taylor, M. R. Aguilleira, S. A. Campbelle, S. S. Connell, B. Cooper, D. J. S. Dottin, A. S. S. Fletcher, S. C. King, ‡Kycia A. Knight, Kyshona A. Knight, H. K. Matthews, A. Mohammed, S. L. Quintyne, ‡S. C. Selman, ‡T. D. Smartt. *Coach:* V. C. Drakes.

Group A

At Delhi, March 15, 2016 (floodlit). **New Zealand won by seven wickets.** ‡**Sri Lanka 110-8** (20 overs) (B. Y. A. Mendis 30, M. A. D. D. Surangika 37); **New Zealand 111-3** (15.5 overs) (S. W. Bates 37). *PoM:* S. W. Bates. *Before now, these teams had met in nine ODIs and six T20 internationals. New Zealand had won the lot and, though Sri Lanka began encouragingly, the apple cart was not to be upset. From 82-1 in the 13th over they suffered a calamitous demise: the remaining 43 (boundary-less) balls brought seven wickets, including three run-outs, for 28. New Zealand coasted to 64-0 in the tenth and, after a brief wobble, sped home with 25 deliveries unneeded.*

At Mohali, March 18, 2016 (floodlit). **New Zealand won by 93 runs.** ‡**New Zealand 177-3** (20 overs) (S. W. Bates 82, S. F. M. Devine 47); **Ireland 84-5** (20 overs). *PoM:* S. W. Bates. *A punishing 82 in 60 balls from Suzie Bates left Ireland to climb a mountain that proved beyond them. She put on 104 inside 13 overs with Sophie Devine, and finished the match as the format's second-highest scorer – on 2,063 – behind England's Charlotte Edwards. Ireland stuttered to 29-3 in the ninth over, and barely sped up. Leigh Kasperek's four overs of off-spin cost just ten.*

At Nagpur, March 18, 2016 (floodlit). **Australia won by six wickets.** ‡**South Africa 102-6** (20 overs) (D. van Niekerk 45, T. Chetty 34); **Australia 105-4** (18.3 overs) (A. J. Blackwell 42*, M. M. Lanning 30*). *PoM:* M. M. Lanning. *Twice South Africa seemed on top: at 72-0 in the 13th over, and later when Shabnim Ismail helped reduce Australia to 9-3. Twice, however, the defending champions fought back. Openers Dane van Niekerk and Trish Chetty aside, there was little in the South African arsenal, and their eventual 102-6 was poor, given a reliable pitch. Athletic fielding and disciplined bowling – Lauren Cheatle and Ellyse Perry both claimed 2-13 – stymied the scoring. After missing much of the South African innings with illness, Meg Lanning batted at No. 6.*

At Mohali, March 20, 2016 (floodlit). **Sri Lanka won by 14 runs.** ‡**Sri Lanka 129-7** (20 overs) (A. C. Jayangani 34, W. P. M. Weerakkody 32, L. E. Kaushalya 35*; C. J. Metcalfe 4-15); **Ireland 115-8** (20 overs) (B. M. S. M. Kumari 3-24). *PoM:* C. J. Metcalfe. *T20I debut:* H. M. D. Samarawickrama (Sri Lanka). *Sri Lanka were given a scare, but clung on for their first win of the tournament. From 45-0, they lost five for 14, as Ciara Metcalfe finished with a career-best 4-15, only for Eshani Kaushalya to chip in with 35* from 28 balls. Ireland lost two early wickets to Sugandika Kumari, then recovered to 87-3 with five overs to go. But Isobel Joyce, whose four overs had earlier gone for only 11, became the first of three run-out victims, and the lower order fell away.*

At Nagpur, March 21, 2016. **New Zealand won by six wickets.** ‡**Australia 103-8** (20 overs) (E. A. Perry 42; L. M. Kasperek 3-13); **New Zealand 104-4** (16.2 overs) (R. H. Priest 34). *PoM:* L. M. Kasperek. *Australia endured a terrible start: after four overs, they were 4-4. Off-spinner Kasperek snatched three, while Lanning, having opted to bat on a turning pitch, was run out for a duck. Bates persisted with spin – slow left-armer Morna Nielsen had figures of 4–21–4–0 – and it needed a skittish 42 from Perry to yank Australia towards 100. Rachel Priest hit 34 off 27, allowing New Zealand to ride the loss of a few wickets. Victory effectively put them in the semis.*

At Chennai, March 23, 2016 (floodlit). **South Africa won by 67 runs.** ‡**South Africa 156-5** (20 overs) (T. Chetty 35, L. Lee 30*); **Ireland 89-9** (20 overs) (C. M. A. Shillington 34; S. Luus 5-8). *PoM:* S. Luus. *Ireland sniffed an upset when South Africa creaked to 84-4 in the 14th over, but the last 38 balls produced 72 runs: the final over of the innings – which had to be completed by Isobel Joyce after Lucy O'Reilly was taken off for a second high full toss – cost 23 in all. Ireland then floundered against the leg-spin of Suné Luus, who returned the second-best figures in all women's T20 internationals, after Amy Satterthwaite's 6-17 for New Zealand v England at Taunton in August 2007.*

At Delhi, March 24, 2016. **Australia won by nine wickets.** ‡**Sri Lanka 123-8** (20 overs) (A. C. Jayangani 38, M. A. D. D. Surangika 38); **Australia 125-1** (17.4 overs) (E. J. Villani 53*, M. M. Lanning 56*). *PoM:* E. J. Villani. *A stroll-in-the-park stand of 98* between Elyse Villani (53* off 39 balls) and Lanning (56* off 53) brushed Sri Lanka aside with 14 deliveries to spare, and helped Australia put behind them horror starts of 9-3 against South Africa and 4-4 against New Zealand. The Sri Lankans ought to have pushed them harder after reaching 75-1 in the 11th over, but had to settle for 123-8. It was nothing like enough.*

At Delhi, March 26, 2016. **Australia won by seven wickets. Ireland 91-7** (20 overs) (M. L. Schutt 3-29); ‡**Australia 92-3** (13.2 overs) (E. J. Villani 43). *PoM:* M. L. Schutt. *Australia's bowlers ruled the roost: medium-pacer Rene Farrell claimed 2-11 in her four overs, while spinners Jess Jonassen and Kristen Beams conceded just 14 apiece in theirs. Alyssa Healy and Lanning departed for single figures, but Villani ensured Ireland slipped to their fourth defeat out of four.*

At Bangalore, March 26, 2016 (floodlit). **New Zealand won by seven wickets. South Africa 99** (19.3 overs) (S. F. M. Devine 3-16, L. M. Kasperek 3-19); ‡**New Zealand 100-3** (14.3 overs). *PoM:* S. F. M. Devine. *A merciless all-round display from New Zealand ended South Africa's hopes of a semi-final – and guaranteed Australia's qualification instead. The South Africans had a platform of sorts at 90-5 with 14 balls to spare, only to lose five for nine. Chasing 100, New Zealand were never stretched, especially after Bates and Priest began with 57 at better than a run a ball.*

At Bangalore, March 28, 2016. **Sri Lanka won by ten runs.** ‡**Sri Lanka 114-7** (20 overs) (A. C. Jayangani 52); **South Africa 104-7** (20 overs). *PoM:* A. C. Jayangani. *With only pride to play for, South Africa seemed to be cruising to a consolation victory at 50-0 after nine overs – but then lost three for two in eight balls, and never regained the initiative as left-armers Kumari (2-24) and Udeshika Prabodhani (2-13) applied the brakes. Earlier, skipper Chamari Atapattu Jayangani's 49-ball 52 – her maiden half-century in the format – was twice as many as anyone else managed in the game.*

Group B

At Bangalore, March 15, 2016. **India won by 72 runs. India 163-5** (20 overs) (M. D. Raj 42, V. R. Vanitha 38, H. Kaur 40, V. Krishnamurthy 36*); ‡**Bangladesh 91-5** (20 overs). *PoM:* H. Kaur. *India's victory seemed inevitable almost from the start. Vellaswamy Vanitha hammered seven fours in a 24-ball 38, and Mithali Raj five in a 35-ball 42. But the real damage was done by Harmanpreet Kaur and Veda Krishnamurthy, who both hit two sixes as India passed their previous best of 151-5, also against Bangladesh, in the same tournament two years earlier. The Bangladeshis never suggested they would get close.*

At Chennai, March 16, 2016 (floodlit). **West Indies won by four runs. West Indies 103-8** (20 overs) (S. R. Taylor 40; Anam Amin 4-16); ‡**Pakistan 99-5** (20 overs) (A. Mohammed 3-25). *PoM:* Anam Amin. *T20I debut:* Muneeba Ali (Pakistan). *In a low-scoring match, West Indies owed much to Stafanie Taylor's 40; slow left-armers Anam Amin and Sadia Yousuf pinned them down and there were three ducks, including Deandra Dottin. Javeria Khan took no further part in the tournament after a bouncer from Shamilia Connell in Pakistan's first over broke her right thumb. They advanced to 40-0, before off-spinner Anisa Mohammed struck three times in five deliveries. Sana Mir and Asmavia Iqbal steered them to 97-4, needing seven from three balls, but Mohammed caught Sana off Dottin and the chase fizzled out.*

At Bangalore, March 17, 2016. **England won by 36 runs.** ‡**England 153-7** (20 overs) (C. M. Edwards 60; Jahanara Alam 3-32); **Bangladesh 117-6** (20 overs) (Nigar Sultana 35, Salma Khatun 32*). *PoM:* C. M. Edwards. *Despite being pegged back by Bangladesh's captain, the bustling medium-pacer Jahanara Alam, England reached a decent total thanks to their own skipper: Edwards* *made 60 from 51 balls. Katherine Brunt struck in the first over of the chase, a wicket maiden, and Bangladesh became hopelessly bogged down, managing only 43-3 by halfway. Nigar Sultana and Salma Khatun put on 64 for the fifth wicket, but didn't threaten victory.*

At Delhi, March 19, 2016. **Pakistan won by two runs** (DLS). **India 96-7** (20 overs); ‡**Pakistan 77-6** (16 overs). *PoM:* Anam Amin. *Once again Pakistan tied down a supposedly stronger team – but this time the nail-biting finish went their way. India were 7-2 after the six powerplay overs, which were bowled by Anam Amin and seamer Asmavia Iqbal, and featured 30 dot balls, six singles and a wide. Only Veda Krishnamurthy (24) passed 16 as they failed to reach three figures. Pakistan opener Sidra Ameen scored a run-a-ball 26, which took them halfway to victory: 48-2 after nine overs. Indian hopes were reviving as the later batsmen lost their nerve – until a storm ended play, with Pakistan just ahead.*

At Chennai, March 20, 2016 (floodlit). **West Indies won by 49 runs.** ‡**West Indies 148-4** (20 overs) (H. K. Matthews 41, S. R. Taylor 40; Nahida Akter 3-27); **Bangladesh 99** (18.3 overs) (S. R. Taylor 3-13). *PoM:* S. R. Taylor. *An opening stand of 67 in 11.4 overs between Hayley Matthews and Taylor set up a decent score, although three wickets for 16-year-old slow left-armer Nahida Akter kept the runs down. Bangladesh made a brisk start, but then Taylor, Matthews (2-16) and Dottin (2-17) tightened things up; from 55-2, seven wickets tumbled for 27.*

At Dharamsala, March 22, 2016. **England won by two wickets. India 90-8** (20 overs) (H. C. Knight 3-15); ‡**England 92-8** (19 overs) (E. Bisht 4-21). *PoM:* H. C. Knight. *For the second time running India could not make 100, yet almost clung on to win on a turning pitch. Heather Knight struck in the first over, and her off-breaks claimed two more victims; only Harmanpreet (26) got India to 90. Tammy Beaumont and Sarah Taylor advanced to 42-1 before Harmanpreet dismissed them with successive balls; left-arm spinner Ekta Bisht, whose first delivery of the tournament had removed Edwards, then grabbed three wickets in five, plus a run-out. England would have been 88-9 had Harmanpreet not dropped Anya Shrubsole, who promptly hit the winning four.*

At Dharamsala, March 24, 2016 (floodlit). **England won by one wicket.** ‡**West Indies 108-4** (20 overs) (S. R. Taylor 35); **England 109-9** (20 overs) (C. M. Edwards 30, T. T. Beaumont 31; A. S. S. Fletcher 3-12, S. L. Quintyne 3-19). *PoM:* T. T. Beaumont. *England came within a whisker of losing a game they were bossing until – having knocked off more than half the target of 109 – they lost Beaumont, their first wicket, for a hard-hitting 31. Edwards went six balls later, and with her pretty much every scrap of nous. When Rebecca Grundy arrived with two balls remaining, England had crashed from 59-0 to 106-9 in 70 deliveries. Dottin then conceded West Indies' only wide of the innings, before Grundy stole a single to level the scores, leaving Natalie Sciver, on 19, to face the last. She threw the bat, missed, and ran; wicketkeeper Merissa Aguilleira threw the ball, missed, and despaired. Earlier, West Indies had struggled for fluency against stifling seam from Shrubsole and Jenny Gunn, whose eight overs cost 26.*

At Delhi, March 24, 2016. **Pakistan won by nine wickets.** ‡**Bangladesh 113-9** (20 overs) (Farzana Haque 36); **Pakistan 114-1** (16.3 overs) (Sidra Ameen 53*, Bismah Maroof 43*). *PoM:* Sidra Ameen. *Pakistan secured another win in Delhi, while Bangladesh suffered their fourth defeat. They had chosen to bat, making a respectable 113, despite four run-outs, but had no answer to Sidra Ameen, who struck Pakistan's only fifty of the tournament, and Bismah Maroof, who hit leg-spinner Rumana Ahmed for three successive fours. A stand of 99 saw Pakistan home with 21 balls to spare.*

At Mohali, March 27, 2016. **West Indies won by three runs. West Indies 114-8** (20 overs) (S. R. Taylor 47, D. J. S. Dottin 45; A. A. Patil 3-16, H. Kaur 4-23); ‡**India 111-9** (20 overs) (D. J. S. Dottin 3-16). *PoM:* D. J. S. Dottin. *The ability of Taylor and Dottin to milk India's five-pronged spin attack proved crucial: from the 18 overs delivered by the slow bowlers Taylor and Dottin filched 42 singles. West Indies' other seven batsmen managed a combined 18 runs. India's reply was more of a team affair, though no one could stamp their authority on it. Twenty were needed from 12 balls, then 12 from nine, but India ran out of steam, and were eliminated; West Indies were notionally dependent on the outcome of the England v Pakistan game.*

At Chennai, March 27, 2016 (floodlit). **England won by 68 runs.** ‡**England 148-5** (20 overs) (C. M. Edwards 77*, T. T. Beaumont 37; Nida Dar 3-21); **Pakistan 80** (17.5 overs) (L. A. Marsh 3-12). *PoM:* C. M. Edwards. *England headed Group B after a fourth straight victory, with Pakistan well short of the 149 in 18.1 overs they needed to enter the semis. When Edwards hit the game's first delivery for four, she became the first player, man or woman, to amass 2,500 runs in Twenty20 internationals. She batted throughout England's innings, hit ten fours in 61 balls, and shared stands* *of 68 with Beaumont (including 55 in the powerplay), plus 59 with Danni Wyatt. Brunt dismissed the in-form Sidra Ameen for nought in Pakistan's first over; they succumbed for this competition's lowest completed total.*

GROUP TABLES

Group A	Played	Won	Lost	Points	Net run-rate
NEW ZEALAND	4	4	0	8	2.43
AUSTRALIA	4	3	1	6	0.61
Sri Lanka	4	2	2	4	–0.24
South Africa	4	1	3	2	0.17
Ireland	4	0	4	0	–2.81

Group B	Played	Won	Lost	Points	Net run-rate
ENGLAND	4	4	0	8	1.41
WEST INDIES	4	3	1	6	0.68
Pakistan	4	2	2	4	–0.67
India	4	1	3	2	0.79
Bangladesh	4	0	4	0	–2.30

Semi-finals

At Delhi, March 30, 2016. **Australia won by five runs. Australia 132-6** (20 overs) (M. M. Lanning 55); ‡**England 127-7** (20 overs) (C. M. Edwards 31, T. T. Beaumont 32). *PoM:* M. M. Lanning. *England's paper-like middle order folded in sight of victory as Australia qualified for their fourth successive World Twenty20 final. Needing 45 off seven overs and with nine wickets in hand, England panicked horribly, losing six for 28 on a sluggish pitch; a target of 13 off the last, bowled by Farrell, proved beyond them. Their running between the wickets had been equally culpable, not least while openers Edwards and Beaumont were putting on 67 in ten overs: coach Mark Robinson later lambasted his side for their lack of fitness. Australia's gettable 132 centred on Lanning's 50-ball 55, while a mercurial England performance in the field was summed up when Brunt's throw from mid-on struck Sciver on the side of the head as she returned to her mark.*

At Mumbai (Wankhede), March 31, 2016. **West Indies won by six runs. West Indies 143-6** (20 overs) (B. Cooper 61; S. F. M. Devine 4-22); ‡**New Zealand 137-8** (20 overs) (S. J. McGlashan 38; S. R. Taylor 3-26). *PoM:* B. Cooper. *A solid all-round performance ensured West Indies broke the hegemony of England, Australia and New Zealand, who had contested all four previous finals. The New Zealanders, meanwhile, aped their menfolk by falling in the semi after sailing through the group stages. Nielsen maintained tight control, despite the Wankhede – staging its first women's T20 international – giving little help to her left-arm spin. Her fellow slow bowlers were less frugal, and Britney Cooper crashed a 48-ball 61 to set a demanding target. At 42-1 after the powerplay, and at 107-3 ten overs later, New Zealand were well placed, but two wickets in the 17th, from Taylor, gave new batsmen too much to do.*

FINAL

AUSTRALIA v WEST INDIES

At Kolkata, April 3, 2016. West Indies won by eight wickets. Toss: Australia.

A rollicking 66 from Hayley Matthews, who had turned 18 barely a fortnight earlier, inspired West Indies to an unexpected win – a triumph replicated a few hours later by their men. Matthews put on 120 for the first wicket with Taylor, her captain, and hit three sixes in 45 balls; after 12 single-figure dismissals in 18 previous Twenty20 international innings, it was her maiden half-century. Taylor fell with five needed, but West Indies – whose highest chase had been 140, against England at Arundel in 2012 – scrambled home. A first Twenty20 win over Australia in nine attempts deprived Lanning's team of a fourth straight title. And, while both Lanning and Villani made 52, the Australians were left to rue a dismal final over bowled by Dottin: they scored only a single and lost two wickets. Matthews built on the mood swing, setting up a famous day for Caribbean cricket.

Player of the Match: H. K. Matthews. *Player of the Tournament:* S. R. Taylor.

Australia

		B	4/6
1 †A. J. Healy *c and b 1*	4	5	0
2 E. J. Villani *c 2 b 3*	52	37	9
3 *M. M. Lanning *lbw b 11*	52	49	8
4 E. A. Perry *lbw b 3*	28	23	0/2
5 A. J. Blackwell *not out*	3	5	0
6 E. A. Osborne *run out*	0	1	0
7 J. L. Jonassen *not out*	0	0	0
B 4, lb 2, w 3	9		

6 overs: 54-1 (20 overs) 148-5

1/15 2/92 3/134 4/147 5/147

8 B. L. Mooney, 9 M. L. Schutt, 10 R. M. Farrell and 11 K. M. Beams did not bat.

Connell 2–4–15–0; Matthews 2–5–13–1; Taylor 3–4–26–0; Dottin 4–13–33–2; Fletcher 1–3–9–0; Mohammed 4–9–19–1; Quintyne 4–6–27–0.

West Indies

		B	4/6
1 H. K. Matthews *c 5 b 11*	66	45	6/3
2 *S. R. Taylor *c 7 b 10*	59	57	6
3 D. J. S. Dottin *not out*	18	12	2
4 B. Cooper *not out*	3	3	0
Lb 2, w 1	3		

6 overs: 45-0 (19.3 overs) 149-2

1/120 2/144

5 S. C. King, 6 †M. R. Aguilleira, 7 S. A. Campbelle, 8 S. L. Quintyne, 9 S. S. Connell, 10 A. S. S. Fletcher and 11 A. Mohammed did not bat.

Jonassen 4–10–26–0; Perry 3.3–9–27–0; Schutt 3–8–26–0; Farrell 4–5–35–1; Beams 4–4–27–1; Osborne 1–0–6–0.

Umpires: Aleem Dar and R. K. Illingworth. Third umpire: N. J. Llong.
Referee: A. J. Pycroft.

WOMEN'S WORLD T20 WINNERS

2009	ENGLAND (86-4) beat New Zealand (85) by six wickets at Lord's.
2010	AUSTRALIA (106-8) beat New Zealand (103-6) by three runs at Bridgetown.
2012-13	AUSTRALIA (142-4) beat England (138-9) by four runs at Colombo (RPS).
2013-14	AUSTRALIA (106-4) beat England (105-8) by six wickets at Mirpur.
2015-16	WEST INDIES (149-2) beat Australia (148-5) by eight wickets at Kolkata.

WOMEN'S INTERNATIONAL SERIES IN 2016

AUSTRALIA v INDIA IN 2015-16

Twenty20 internationals (3): Australia 1, India 2
One-day internationals (3): Australia 2, India 1

The teams took it in turns to claim a 2–0 lead before losing the dead rubber, though India emerged the happier after securing their first bilateral series victory over Australia, in the Twenty20s. Meg Lanning, Ellyse Perry and Mithali Raj – three of the biggest names on the world stage – all contributed during the course of several close-fought games.

First Twenty20 international At Adelaide, January 26, 2016. **India won by five wickets. Australia 140-5** (20 overs) (B. L. Mooney 36, A. J. Healy 41*); ‡**India 141-5** (18.4 overs) (V. Krishnamurthy 35, H. Kaur 46). *PoM:* H. Kaur. *T20I debuts:* B. L. Mooney, N. E. Stalenburg (Australia). *India pulled off their highest successful chase, beating 128-7 against New Zealand at Bangalore in 2015. Harmanpreet Kaur got them most of the way there, with 46 from 31 balls, after Alyssa Healy had given Australia something to defend with 41* from just 15.*

Second Twenty20 international At Melbourne, January 29, 2016. **India won by ten wickets** (DLS). **Australia 125-8** (18 overs) (M. M. Lanning 49); ‡**India 69-0** (9.1 overs) (M. D. Raj 37*). *PoM:* J. N. Goswami. *T20I debut:* L. R. Cheatle (Australia). *India celebrated their first series win over Australia in any format. Mithali Raj and Smriti Mandhana had taken them to 52-0 in the eighth over when the weather – which had already reduced the game to 18 overs a side – revised their target to 66 in ten. They swept past it with five balls to spare. Earlier, Meg Lanning had sped to 49 from 39 deliveries, only to be run out at the non-striker's end when Kaur deflected a straight-drive from Jess Jonassen on to the stumps.*

Third Twenty20 international At Sydney, January 31, 2016. **Australia won by 15 runs. Australia 136-5** (20 overs) (B. L. Mooney 34, E. A. Perry 55*); ‡**India 121-8** (20 overs) (E. A. Perry 4-12). *PoM:* E. A. Perry. *PoS:* J. N. Goswami (India). *T20I debut:* D. B. Sharma (India). *Ellyse Perry almost single-handedly prevented a clean sweep, equalling her highest score with 55* from 41 balls, then following up with a career-best 4-12 to stymie India's middle order.*

First one-day international At Canberra, February 2, 2016 (day/night). **Australia won by 101 runs.** ‡**Australia 276-6** (50 overs) (M. M. Lanning 43, E. A. Perry 90, A. J. Blackwell 114; S. S. Pandey 3-32); **India 175** (46.5 overs) (H. Kaur 42; E. A. Perry 4-45). *PoM:* A. J. Blackwell. *ODI debut:* G. M. Harris (Australia). *Another all-round tour de force from Perry gave Australia an early lead in the 50-over series. After putting on 180 for the third wicket with Alex Blackwell – whose 114 off 112 balls was the highest of her three ODI hundreds – Perry opened the bowling and claimed 4-45 as India fell comfortably short. No one made more than Kaur's 42.*

Second one-day international At Hobart, February 5, 2016 (day/night). **Australia won by six wickets.** ‡**India 252-8** (50 overs) (S. S. Mandhana 102, M. D. Raj 58, S. S. Pandey 33*; E. A. Perry 3-54); **Australia 253-4** (46.4 overs) (N. E. Bolton 77, M. M. Lanning 61, E. A. Perry 31). *PoM:* S. S. Mandhana. *Australia took instant revenge for the T20 series after openers Nicole Bolton and Lanning broke the back of their chase, adding 138 in 22.3 overs. India had looked set for more than 252 after Mandhana – with a maiden ODI hundred – and Raj had overcome the first-ball loss of Thirush Kamini to put on 150. But the last 19 overs yielded only 102 as the bowlers fought back.*

Third one-day international At Hobart, February 7, 2016. **India won by five wickets.** ‡**Australia 231-7** (50 overs) (E. A. Perry 50, A. J. Blackwell 60, J. L. Jonassen 32*; S. S. Pandey 3-50); **India 234-5** (47 overs) (S. S. Mandhana 55, M. D. Raj 89). *PoM:* M. D. Raj. *It was India's turn to avert a whitewash, thanks to Mandhana's lively 55 and Raj's steady 89. Australia had been pegged back by the seam of Shikha Pandey after Perry and Blackwell had put on 99 for the third wicket.*

Women's Championship: Australia 4pts, India 2pts.

SOUTH AFRICA v ENGLAND IN 2015-16

One-day internationals (3): South Africa 1, England 2
Twenty20 internationals (3): South Africa 1, England 2

With the World Twenty20 starting in March, the fixtures were split evenly between 50- and 20-over games, so all six internationals had a clear context. The three ODIs counted towards the Women's Championship, whose main prize was automatic qualification for the 2017 World Cup for the top four teams, while the shorter games allowed new coach Mark Robinson to gauge progress just before a global tournament.

South Africa were not the strongest opponents. They had not beaten England since February 2004, and in the intervening 12 years had lost 15 ODIs and 11 Twenty20s against them. But there was a suspicion England might be past their best – and South Africa on the rise. The visitors extended their run to 16 with a convincing rain-affected win at Benoni, but tripped up at Centurion, where strong home batting made light of a stiff target. Heather Knight then came good in the decider to give England the series.

The second series echoed the first, although the opener at Paarl, where England defended a modest total, was the only one of the six internationals not won by the chasing team. In the next, at Cape Town, indifferent bowling and fielding from England – plus powerful batting from Dané van Niekerk and South Africa captain Mignon du Preez – led to defeat. And then, just as before, the decider went convincingly to the tourists, so repeating the not-entirely-satisfactory scoreline of 2–1. In one other respect the series were twins: when Anya Shrubsole did well, England did well. In the four victories, her combined figures were 28–3–117–12. But in the two defeats her 13 wicketless overs cost 90.

South Africa's upper order was often a match for their opponents, while the form of England's Sarah Taylor in the Twenty20s was little short of perfect: 200 runs at a strike-rate of 139 and an average of precisely 100.

ENGLAND TOURING PARTY

*C. M. Edwards (Kent), T. T. Beaumont (Kent), K. H. Brunt (Yorkshire), K. L. Cross (Lancashire), G. A. Elwiss (Staffordshire), N. E. Farrant (Kent), L. S. Greenway (Kent), R. L. Grundy (Warwickshire), J. L. Gunn (Nottinghamshire), D. Hazell (Yorkshire), A. E. Jones (Warwickshire), H. C. Knight (Berkshire), N. R. Sciver (Surrey), A. Shrubsole (Somerset), S. J. Taylor (Sussex), L. Winfield (Yorkshire), D. N. Wyatt (Nottinghamshire). *Coach:* M. A. Robinson.

Brunt injured her back in the second ODI; she was replaced by Farrant for the T20Is.

First one-day international At Benoni, February 7, 2016. **England won by seven wickets** (DLS). ‡**South Africa 196** (49.2 overs) (T. Chetty 90, M. du Preez 38; A. Shrubsole 4-29); **England 150-3** (28.3 overs) (A. E. Jones 34, C. M. Edwards 33, S. J. Taylor 41*). *PoM:* A. Shrubsole. *ODI debut:* L. Wolvaardt (South Africa). *The England innings was interrupted first by rain, then thunder and lightning, but brisk batting from opener Amy Jones (34 from 27 balls) and wicketkeeper Sarah Taylor (41 from 44) steered them to a revised target of 150 in 35 overs with more than six to spare. South Africa had made 196, though at 119-1 in the 31st had seemed on course for more. But Anya Shrubsole ended a 93-run partnership between Trisha Chetty and Mignon du Preez, and quickly snatched a couple more to leave them 137-4. After that, the South Africans meandered towards inadequacy.*

Second one-day international At Centurion, February 12, 2016. **South Africa won by five wickets.** ‡**England 262-9** (50 overs) (C. M. Edwards 45, H. C. Knight 61, D. N. Wyatt 40; S. Ismail 3-32); **South Africa 265-5** (48.5 overs) (L. Wolvaardt 55, T. Chetty 66, M. Kapp 44, L. Lee 69). *PoM:* L. Lee. *South Africa defeated England for the first time since 2004 when they overhauled an apparently testing target. An opening stand of 113 between Laura Wolvaardt and Chetty gave them an ideal start, and they were not deflected by losing three for 21 in five overs: Marizanne Kapp and Lizelle Lee added 112 at eight an over to take them to the brink. Earlier, England had stumbled to 16-3. Charlotte Edwards and Heather Knight repaired some damage, as did a circumspect Lydia Greenway (23 from 48); the last ten overs brought 94, but on a true surface the earlier failings proved critical. Katherine Brunt suffered back spasms and limped out of the tour.*

Third one-day international At Johannesburg, February 14, 2016. **England won by five wickets. South Africa 196-9** (50 overs) (T. Chetty 31, L. Lee 74; A. Shrubsole 3-35); ‡**England 198-5** (43.5 overs) (H. C. Knight 67*, G. A. Elwiss 61). *PoM:* H. C. Knight. *PoS:* H. C. Knight. *The deciding game ebbed and flowed, before the cool heads of Knight and Georgia Elwiss swept England towards victory. South Africa had lost Wolvaardt without a run on the board, then rallied through a fifty partnership between Chetty and du Preez. Next came a lurch to 85-6 as Shrubsole picked up her second and third wickets. Lee, a thorn in England's side two days earlier, left her mark again, hitting 74. When England subsided to 38-3, in reply to 196, South Africa were nicely placed, only for Knight to calm nerves, first in a stand of 53 with Edwards, then 97 with the more aggressive Elwiss.*

Women's Championship: England 4pts, South Africa 2pts.

First Twenty20 international At Paarl, February 18, 2016. **England won by 15 runs. England 147-7** (20 overs) (S. J. Taylor 74*); ‡**South Africa 132-6** (20 overs) (D. van Niekerk 52, T. Chetty 46; A. Shrubsole 3-25). *PoM:* S. J. Taylor. *England relied on the hard-hitting Taylor, whose 74* came from 51 balls, to hide their deficiencies: no one else reached 20. Then openers Dané van Niekerk and Chetty put on 96, the fourth best for any South African wicket – giving Chetty a hand in nine of their 13 highest stands. But there were 52 needed, and only 31 balls left. The pressure told, and no one else found any footing. Shrubsole's fine form continued.*

Second Twenty20 international At Cape Town, February 19, 2016. **South Africa won by 17 runs** (DLS). **England 156-6** (20 overs) (C. M. Edwards 34, S. J. Taylor 66); ‡**South Africa 145-3** (17.2 overs) (D. van Niekerk 63, M. du Preez 47*). *PoM:* D. van Niekerk. *After 12 T20I defeats (and a no-result) against England, South Africa turned the tables. England made nine more than the day before, but were fallible in the field, reprieving van Niekerk on six and 22. Play was briefly interrupted at 108-2, with South Africa well placed, despite having just lost van Niekerk for her second successive half-century. On the resumption, du Preez and Kapp maintained the momentum and, when rain ended the game 16 balls early, were 17 ahead on DLS. Earlier, England had again leant on Taylor, who this time received a little more support.*

Third Twenty20 international At Johannesburg, February 21, 2016. **England won by four wickets. South Africa 131-4** (20 overs) (M. du Preez 39, L. Lee 69*); ‡**England 133-6** (15.3 overs) (S. J. Taylor 60; S. Ismail 3-27). *PoM:* S. J. Taylor. *PoS:* S. J. Taylor. *Taylor continued to be England's guiding light: she made her third fifty in a row, and became only the third person – after Charlotte Edwards and Brendon McCullum – to hit 2,000 runs in T20Is. She fell with England 17 short, but still with plenty of time, so Shabnim Ismail's two late wickets made little difference. South Africa had suffered a dreadful start, tumbling to 6-3, with Shrubsole coming within an inside-edge of a hat-trick. Du Preez and Lee, who went on to a career-best 69*, rebuilt steadily but, from 49-3 after ten, a demanding total was beyond them.*

INDIA v SRI LANKA IN 2015-16

One-day internationals (3): India 3, Sri Lanka 0
Twenty20 internationals (3): India 3, Sri Lanka 0

The series began with India and Sri Lanka at the bottom of the Women's Championship table; Sri Lanka remained rooted in eighth place, but India's easy dominance in the one-day games briefly lifted them into the top half. India went on to complete another series sweep in the T20Is, before hosting the Women's World Twenty20 in March – when they would manage a single win to Sri Lanka's two. India's Smriti Mandhana scored 190 runs across the six tour matches, and captain Mithali Raj 156 for two dismissals, while off-spinner Deepti Sharma collected 12 one-day wickets at 5.25.

First one-day international At Ranchi, February 15, 2016. **India won by 107 runs. India 245-6** (50 overs) (S. S. Mandhana 55, M. D. Raj 49, H. Kaur 50); ‡**Sri Lanka 138** (45.2 overs) (W. P. M. Weerakkody 69; P. Yadav 4-22). *PoM:* S. S. Mandhana. *Led by Smriti Mandhana's third fifty in successive innings, India's top order gave them a solid total. Only opener Prasadini Weerakkody got past 18 in Sri Lanka's reply. She batted nearly 38 overs for her 69 before becoming one of leg-spinner Poonam Yadav's four victims; the last seven went for 16 runs.*

Second one-day international At Ranchi, February 17, 2016. **India won by six wickets.** ‡**Sri Lanka 178-9** (50 overs) (W. P. M. Weerakkody 37, M. A. D. D. Surangika 43*; D. B. Sharma 4-23);

India 179-4 (43.1 overs) (S. S. Mandhana 46, M. D. Raj 53*, H. Kaur 41; B. M. S. M. Kumari 4-39). *PoM:* D. B. Sharma. *Sri Lanka just about survived their 50 overs, with No. 7 Dilani Manodara Surangika holding out, despite a career-best 4-23 for off-spinner Deepti Sharma. Mandhana hit a run-a-ball 46, and Mithali Raj steered India to their target with nearly seven overs to go; slow left-armer Sugandika Kumari claimed all four wickets to fall.*

Third one-day international At Ranchi, February 19, 2016. **India won by seven wickets.** ‡**Sri Lanka 112** (38.2 overs) (D. B. Sharma 6-20); **India 114-3** (29.3 overs) (V. Krishnamurthy 61*). *PoM:* D. B. Sharma. *ODI debuts:* P. Bose (India), H. I. H. Karunaratne (Sri Lanka). *Sharma improved her career-best for the second game running, backed up by left-arm spinner Preeti Bose's 8–4–8–2 on debut, as Sri Lanka crumbled. India were 18-2 after Kumari trapped Punam Raut and ran out Mandhana, but Veda Krishnamurthy made it 3–0 with 20 overs in hand.*

Women's Championship: India 6pts, Sri Lanka 0pts.

First Twenty20 international At Ranchi, February 22, 2016. **India won by 34 runs.** ‡**India 130-6** (20 overs) (S. S. Mandhana 35, H. Kaur 36; B. M. S. M. Kumari 3-28); **Sri Lanka 96-7** (20 overs) (M. A. D. D. Surangika 41*; A. A. Patil 3-14). *PoM:* A. A. Patil. *T20I debut:* H. I. H. Karunaratne (Sri Lanka). *Kumari continued to thrive, dismissing India's top three. But Anuja Patel lifted them to 130 with 22* in 17 balls, then reduced Sri Lanka to 18-3 with her off-spin. They could not break three figures, though Surangika remained unbeaten for 19 overs.*

Second Twenty20 international At Ranchi, February 24, 2016. **India won by five wickets.** ‡**Sri Lanka 107-8** (20 overs) (E. Bisht 3-22, P. Yadav 3-17); **India 108-5** (19 overs) (M. D. Raj 51*, A. A. Patil 34; I. Ranaweera 3-10). *PoM:* M. D. Raj. *Sri Lanka got to 84-2 before losing six for 17 in 17 balls, including three in an over from Ekta Bisht. Her fellow slow left-armer Inoka Ranaweera hit back, striking three times in successive overs as India limped to 27-4, but Raj, who batted throughout the innings, and Patil added 77 in 11 overs to make sure of the series.*

Third Twenty20 international At Ranchi, February 26, 2016. **India won by nine wickets.** ‡**Sri Lanka 89-9** (20 overs) (E. Bisht 3-17); **India 91-1** (13.5 overs) (V. R. Vanitha 34, S. S. Mandhana 43*). *PoM:* S. S. Mandhana. *Bisht claimed another three wickets as Sri Lanka staggered to 46-7; they were in danger of succumbing for the lowest total in women's T20Is until Eshani Kaushalya (25*) and Ama Kanchana (17) added 39. Vellaswamy Vanitha and Mandhana knocked up 64 before being separated in the ninth over, and there were six left when India wrapped up the series.*

NEW ZEALAND v AUSTRALIA IN 2015-16

One-day internationals (3): New Zealand 1, Australia 2
Twenty20 internationals (3): New Zealand 2, Australia 1

After pinching the first match, New Zealand missed the chance to close the gap at the top of the table, as Australia won the next two at the Bay Oval. Meg Lanning, their captain, scored hundreds in the last two games, and her New Zealand counterpart Suzie Bates also made a century in the decider, a unique double. Lanning finished the series with 246 runs, and Bates 214, while the consistent Ellyse Perry collected 150 – although she was less impressive with the ball, finishing with one for 138 from 28 overs. Australia's slow left-armer Jess Jonassen took nine wickets. The teams followed up with three Twenty20 games, preparation for the World Twenty20 in March. This time New Zealand made sure of the series, before Australia claimed a consolation win at New Plymouth.

First one-day international At Mount Maunganui, February 20, 2016. **New Zealand won by nine runs. New Zealand 202-9** (50 overs) (S. W. Bates 43, A. E. Satterthwaite 72; G. M. Harris 3-32, J. L. Jonassen 3-32); ‡**Australia 193** (49.4 overs) (B. L. Mooney 53, E. A. Perry 51; L-M. M. Tahuhu 3-34, E. M. Bermingham 3-38). *PoM:* A. E. Satterthwaite. *ODI debuts:* T. M. M. Newton (New Zealand); B. L. Mooney (Australia). *After Amy Satterthwaite's 88-ball 72 set up New Zealand's total, Australia looked on course during an opening stand of 69 in 17 overs between Nicole Bolton (27) and the debutant wicketkeeper Beth Mooney. But Erin Bermingham struck three times with her leg-breaks as Australia declined to 156-7. Lea Tahuhu crucially removed Ellyse Perry for a fighting 51, and Australia finished ten short; all their wickets fell to catches.*

Second one-day international At Mount Maunganui, February 22, 2016. **Australia won by eight wickets. New Zealand 206-9** (50 overs) (S. W. Bates 61, S. F. M. Devine 67, K. J. Martin 39; J. L. Jonassen 5-50); ‡**Australia 210-2** (41 overs) (M. M. Lanning 114*, E. A. Perry 64*). *PoM:* M. M. Lanning. *New Zealand nosedived to 5-2 when Rachel Priest and Satterthwaite fell to successive balls from Megan Schutt. But Suzie Bates and Sophie Devine put on 73, before slow left-armer Jess Jonassen twirled her way through the rest. Their total was four up on the previous match, but Mooney's early departure was the end of the good news for New Zealand: Meg Lanning and Perry demolished the target in a bouncy partnership of 147*. Lanning squared the series with successive fours off Bates, shortly after reaching her seventh ODI hundred.*

Third one-day international At Mount Maunganui, February 24, 2016. **Australia won by six wickets. New Zealand 243-5** (50 overs) (S. W. Bates 110, A. E. Satterthwaite 44, S. J. McGlashan 46); ‡**Australia 244-4** (48.4 overs) (M. M. Lanning 127, E. A. Perry 35, A. J. Blackwell 50*). *PoM:* M. M. Lanning. *Bates's seventh ODI century, and partnerships of 87 with Satterthwaite and 101 with Sara McGlashan, hoisted New Zealand to their highest score of the series – but it still wasn't enough. Bolton fell for a duck in Australia's second over, but that only brought Lanning to the crease. She purred to her second hundred in three days, adding 129 for the fourth wicket with Alex Blackwell, before falling to off-spinner Leigh Kasperek with just four required to retain the Rose Bowl trophy; Alyssa Healy smacked the only delivery she faced in the series to the boundary. It was the first time both captains had scored centuries in a women's ODI.*

Women's Championship: Australia 4pts, New Zealand 2pts.

First Twenty20 international At Wellington, February 28, 2016. **New Zealand won by four wickets. Australia 113-7** (20 overs) (M. M. Lanning 30; L. M. Kasperek 4-7); ‡**New Zealand 114-6** (18.3 overs) (S. W. Bates 33). *PoM:* L. M. Kasperek. *Australia reached 54-1 before Kasparek grabbed four in ten balls – including Lanning and Perry, both stumped by Priest – and it was 71-6 when Tahuhu had Elyse Villani caught behind. New Zealand were well ahead of the asking-rate when Bates fell at 75-3; despite a wobble, Katey Martin ensured victory with nine balls to spare.*

Second Twenty20 international At Wellington, March 1, 2016. **New Zealand won by five wickets. Australia 116-6** (20 overs) (E. A. Perry 55*; L. M. Kasperek 3-26); ‡**New Zealand 117-5** (19.3 overs) (S. W. Bates 54, A. E. Satterthwaite 34). *PoM:* S. W. Bates. *Australia made another disappointing total after Morna Nielsen removed both openers by the third over, and Tahuhu made it 13-3. Though Perry hit back with 55*, Kasparek picked up three more, and New Zealand needed only 117. Bates saw them to 107 before they lost three in 14 balls, but they sealed the series win.*

Third Twenty20 international At New Plymouth, March 4, 2016. **Australia won by 17 runs. Australia 145-7** (20 overs) (E. A. Perry 43); ‡**New Zealand 128-8** (20 overs) (S. W. Bates 54, S. J. McGlashan 35). *PoM:* E. A. Perry. *At last Australia set a proper target, thanks to Perry. New Zealand were hoping for a whitewash when Bates and McGlashan took them to 72-1 from 11 overs – but no one else reached double figures. Bates was finally dismissed for her fourth fifty in six games (she averaged 59 across the tour) as Perry struck twice in the penultimate over.*

SOUTH AFRICA v WEST INDIES IN 2015-16

One-day internationals (3): South Africa 1, West Indies 2
Twenty20 internationals (3): South Africa 2, West Indies 1

This was a last chance for fringe players to impress before the World Twenty20, but West Indies merely confirmed a reliance on their twin totems. Across six games, Deandra Dottin and Stafanie Taylor scored nearly 40% of the runs off the bat, and took nearly 30% of the wickets (excluding run-outs). They carried the team to victory in the ODI series but, in the deciding T20I, that dependence became a vulnerability: after they were dismissed, the West Indian chase imploded. South Africa, meanwhile, looked to Trisha Chetty for steadiness at the top of the order – she scored 153 runs during the one-dayers – and Shabnim Ismail for fire with the ball. Her seven T20 wickets, at an average of eight, were crucial to South Africa's two wins.

First one-day international At East London, February 24, 2016. **West Indies won by 16 runs.** ‡**West Indies 214-7** (50 overs) (H. K. Matthews 56, B. Cooper 55*); **South Africa 198** (48.5 overs) (T. Chetty 47, M. Kapp 69*, S. Ismail 34; D. J. S. Dottin 5-34). *PoM:* D. J. S. Dottin. *After Britney*

Cooper's first international fifty, South Africa needed 215, and were looking strong at 82-2 in the 23rd over. But Deandra Dottin removed Trisha Chetty for 47, and Lizelle Lee next ball, to induce a collapse to 120-7. Dottin – one of eight bowlers juggled by West Indies – went on to her first five-for in ODIs, which ensured victory, despite Marizanne Kapp's 69.*

Second one-day international At East London, February 27, 2016 (day/night). **West Indies won by 57 runs.** ‡**West Indies 232** (49.1 overs) (S. R. Taylor 79, D. J. S. Dottin 61; S. E. Luus 3-34); **South Africa 175** (45.3 overs) (T. Chetty 51). *PoM:* S. R. Taylor. *Stafanie Taylor won the toss and crafted a 135-run third-wicket stand with Dottin. West Indies' last five fell for 26, but still they made 232. South Africa began solidly but couldn't change gears from 85-1, as Taylor shuffled her options cannily: only Anisa Mohammed completed ten overs – her 2-29 included the key wicket of Chetty.*

Third one-day international At East London, February 29, 2016. **South Africa won by 35 runs.** ‡**South Africa 235-6** (50 overs) (T. Chetty 55, M. du Preez 43, M. Kapp 39, D. van Niekerk 55); **West Indies 200-8** (50 overs) (S. L. Quintyne 40, M. R. Aguilleira 40). *PoM:* T. Chetty. *Another fifty from Chetty built a solid platform, and Dané van Niekerk's 48-ball 55, including three sixes, lifted South Africa out of range. In reply, only Dottin went at more than a run a ball and, when she departed for 25 at halfway to leave West Indies 96-4, the chase fizzled out.*

Women's Championship: West Indies 4pts, South Africa 2pts.

First Twenty20 international At Durban, March 4, 2016. **South Africa won by 11 runs.** ‡**South Africa 125-6** (20 overs) (L. Lee 35); **West Indies 114-6** (20 overs) (D. J. S. Dottin 40; S. Ismail 3-12). *PoM:* S. Ismail. *T20I debut:* O. Kirsten (South Africa). *South Africa's 125 looked vulnerable before Shabnim Ismail's three wickets in seven balls reduced West Indies to 16-4. Then Dottin smote four sixes and put on 72 for the fifth wicket with Stacy-Ann King to leave West Indies needing 39 from the last five. Van Niekerk's leg-spin snared them both in the next over, setting up South Africa's first T20I win over West Indies, at the tenth attempt.*

Second Twenty20 international At Johannesburg, March 6, 2016. **West Indies won by 45 runs. West Indies 143-6** (20 overs) (S. R. Taylor 63; S. Ismail 3-25); ‡**South Africa 98** (18.4 overs). *PoM:* S. R. Taylor. *T20I debut:* L. Goodall (South Africa). *Mignon du Preez soon regretted fielding. A burst from Ismail removed the openers, but Taylor muscled a 53-ball 63 to help West Indies to 143. South Africa lacked firepower and, as the asking-rate spiralled, lost their last six for 24.*

Third Twenty20 international At Cape Town, March 9, 2016. **South Africa won by four runs.** ‡**South Africa 119-3** (20 overs) (M. du Preez 32, L. Lee 33*); **West Indies 115-8** (20 overs). *PoM:* L. Lee. *The series looked to be West Indies' when they were 81-3 in the 15th over, needing another 39, with Dottin well set. But after she holed out to long-on, her team crumbled to 97-8. Ismail was entrusted to protect 12 from the last, and conceded only seven. Earlier, two late sixes from Lee had given South Africa something to defend, after slow progress from the top order.*

ENGLAND v PAKISTAN IN 2016

MARTIN DAVIES

One-day internationals (3): England 3, Pakistan 0
Twenty20 internationals (3): England 3, Pakistan 0

England came into this series with more trepidation than was warranted, given the relative strengths of the teams. Since their defeat in the World Twenty20 semi-final in March, long-serving captain Charlotte Edwards and Lydia Greenway – with 534 caps between them – had been encouraged to retire by the head coach, Mark Robinson, while Sarah Taylor had withdrawn from the team to work on anxiety issues. After losing series to New Zealand and Australia, England were only sixth in the ICC Women's Championship table, one place above Pakistan. They needed to be in the top four in November to guarantee qualification for the 2017 World Cup.

As it was, they achieved three one-day wins with consummate ease and some style, climbing up to third. New captain Heather Knight made a perfect start, with a fifty and five wickets in the first match, while opener Tammy Beaumont, recalled by Robinson at the start of 2016, seemed transformed. She had scored just 207 runs at 17 in 16 one-day innings up to 2014; now, in consecutive games, she advanced to a maiden international fifty, century and 150, racking up 342 runs at 171, a record for any woman in a three-match series. She and Lauren Winfield proved a formidable opening combination, putting on 235 in the second one-day match, at Worcester, and two century stands in the Twenty20 series. Despite lasting only one ball in the first game, Winfield had identical figures in each format: 166 runs at 55. Those starts helped England reach their highest 50-over total – 378 for five at Worcester – followed by their biggest in 20-over cricket, 187 for five at Bristol. The Twenty20 series was another whitewash.

Pakistan had punched above their weight in the World Twenty20, but were outclassed here. Their spin attack were nullified by good pitches and short straight boundaries; the fielding was sluggish; and the batting lacked both firepower and the ability to rotate the strike. Statistically at least, they improved: their first two one-day totals exceeded their previous best against England, and they passed 100 in all the Twenty20 games, which they had managed against them only once before – but they were well short every time.

PAKISTANI TOURING PARTY

*Sana Mir, Aimen Anwar, Anam Amin, Asmavia Iqbal, Bismah Maroof, Iram Javed, Javeria Khan, Maham Tariq, Muneeba Ali, Nahida Khan, Nain Abidi, Nida Dar, Sadia Yousuf, Sania Khan, Sidra Ameen, Sidra Nawaz. *Coach:* Mohtashim Rasheed.

Bismah Maroof led the team in the T20Is.

First one-day international At Leicester, June 20–21. **England won by seven wickets. Pakistan 165** (45.4 overs) (Sidra Ameen 52; H. C. Knight 5-26); ‡**England 166-3** (31.5 overs) (T. T. Beaumont 70, H. C. Knight 50*). *PoM:* H. C. Knight. *Heather Knight's debut as England captain was a triumph. After a first-day washout, she won the toss, claimed five wickets for the first time in ODIs and followed up with 50* – the first woman to combine a five-for with a fifty in a limited-overs international – as England cruised to victory with 18 overs in hand. Pakistan's innings had drifted from wicket to wicket. The first of the series was Katherine Brunt's 100th in ODIs, but opener Sidra Ameen combined straight-bat defence with a more agricultural approach in a maiden half-century, though only one of her team-mates reached 20. Lauren Winfield fell to the first ball of England's reply. But once Knight joined Tammy Beaumont, all nerves were shrugged aside. Beaumont reached a maiden fifty as she and Knight added 96, and Nat Sciver completed their win with a run-a-ball 27.*

Second one-day international At Worcester, June 22. **England won by 212 runs. England 378-5** (50 overs) (L. Winfield 123, T. T. Beaumont 104, N. R. Sciver 80); ‡**Pakistan 166** (47.4 overs) (Bismah Maroof 61; A. Shrubsole 4-19). *PoM:* T. T. Beaumont and L. Winfield. *Asked to bat, Winfield and Beaumont scored maiden centuries during a chanceless opening stand of 235 (England's third highest in ODIs) to set them on course for a mammoth 378-5 – their biggest ODI total, beating 376-2 in 1997-98, also against Pakistan. They piled on 132 in the last ten overs, with Sciver scoring 80 off 33 balls, before being run out off the final delivery. Only West Indies' Deandra Dottin had hit more than Sciver's six sixes in an innings, and England's total of 11 was a world record. Pakistan could offer little in response, though they hung on into the 48th over. Left-hander Bismah Maroof became the first Pakistani to score ten one-day fifties, before Anya Shrubsole mopped up the tail. A second win meant England bounced up to third place in the Women's Championship.*

Third one-day international At Taunton, June 27. **England won by 202 runs.** ‡**England 366-4** (50 overs) (L. Winfield 43, T. T. Beaumont 168*, G. A. Elwiss 77, N. R. Sciver 48); **Pakistan 164** (44.5 overs) (Bismah Maroof 33, Sidra Nawaz 47; K. H. Brunt 5-30, L. A. Marsh 3-29). *PoM:* T. T. Beaumont. *ODI debut:* A. Hartley (England). *Beaumont completed a dream series with 168* in 144 balls, the second highest for England in ODIs, after Charlotte Edwards's 173* v Ireland in 1997-98; she was the first Englishwoman to score consecutive one-day centuries. The batters took full advantage of some woeful fielding – Beaumont was dropped on two and 64 – to amass another huge total. Beaumont put on 166 with Georgia Elwiss and 119 in just nine overs with Sciver, who hit 48 in 22 balls off a shell-shocked attack. Pakistan were 22-3 before Bismah Maroof and keeper Sidra Nawaz added 74, the tourists' best stand of the series. Brunt ended the game with four for three in 12 balls; nine wickets in the series lifted her to second in the ICC rankings.*

Women's Championship: England 6pts, Pakistan 0pts.

First Twenty20 international At Bristol, July 3. **England won by 68 runs.** ‡**England 187-5** (20 overs) (L. Winfield 74, T. T. Beaumont 82); **Pakistan 119-7** (20 overs) (Asmavia Iqbal 35). *PoM:* T. T. Beaumont. *T20I debut:* S. Ecclestone (England). *Beaumont and Winfield carried on with a T20I all-wicket England record stand of 147. Only Charlotte Edwards (92* v Australia in 2013-14) had scored more than Beaumont's 82 in 53 balls for England; Winfield contributed 74 in 45. They powered England to their highest T20I total – far too many for Pakistan to chase down – despite three wickets (one a run-out) in successive deliveries in the final over. The home seamers took pace off the ball, while off-spinner Danielle Hazell and 17-year-old slow left-armer Sophie Ecclestone kept things tight, conceding only 39 in their eight overs. Some late hitting from Asmavia Iqbal lifted Pakistan to 119, their best T20I score against England.*

Second Twenty20 international At Southampton, July 5. **England won by 35 runs.** ‡**England 138-7** (20 overs) (F. C. Wilson 43*); **Pakistan 103** (19.4 overs). *PoM:* F. C. Wilson. *T20I debut:* Aimen Anwar (Pakistan). *On a sticky wicket, England's batting looked under pressure for the first time. Beaumont suffered her only failure in either series, trapped by debutant seamer Aimen Anwar for five, while spinners Bismah Maroof and Sadia Yousuf claimed two apiece. But Fran Wilson's battling 43* off 39 balls – in her first international for five and a half years – helped England to 138. In response Pakistan batted positively, though no one could pass 23. Medium-pacer Jenny Gunn finished with figures of 4–20–7–2.*

Third Twenty20 international At Chelmsford, July 7 (floodlit). **England won by 57 runs.** ‡**England 170-5** (20 overs) (L. Winfield 63, T. T. Beaumont 55); **Pakistan 113-7** (20 overs) (Bismah Maroof 35). *PoM:* L. Winfield. *T20I debut:* A. Hartley (England). *England completed a 6–0 whitewash across the two series. Winfield and Beaumont shared their third century opening partnership in five games – 108 in 12.3 overs – to set up the innings. Pakistan did well to restrict them to 170, though Sadia Yousuf conceded 16 to Danni Wyatt and Wilson in the last over. But the tourists showed little interest in chasing the target. Only captain Bismah Maroof made more than 23, before becoming one of two victims for debutant slow left-armer Alex Hartley.*

IRELAND v SOUTH AFRICA IN 2016

Twenty20 internationals (2): Ireland 1, South Africa 1
One-day internationals (4): Ireland 1, South Africa 3

Outside the framework of the ICC Women's Championship, the South Africans visited Dublin. They had much the better of the ODIs until the final match, but Ireland had given a good account of themselves in the T20 games, and could have won both. As it was, they recorded one victory in each format, their first against South Africa. For the tourists, leg-spinner Suné Luus collected 16 wickets in the six matches, and 17-year-old Laura Wolvaardt suggested a bright future with a century in the third one-day international.

First Twenty20 international At Dublin (Claremont Road), August 1 (floodlit). **South Africa won by four wickets. Ireland 140-4** (20 overs) (C. M. A. Shillington 30, I. M. H. C. Joyce 31*, K. J. Garth 30*); ‡**South Africa 144-6** (20 overs) (M. du Preez 55). *T20I debut:* L. Wolvaardt (South Africa). *South Africa needed three off the final ball; captain Dinesha Devnarain ran two to level the scores, and Ireland donated four more in overthrows to surrender the match. They owed their highest total on home soil to Isobel Joyce and Kim Garth, who added 61* in the last eight overs. South Africa were in trouble when Mignon du Preez was run out, with 28 needed off 15 deliveries. But Devnarain's 11-ball 21 and Ireland's misfield settled the outcome.*

Second Twenty20 international At Dublin (Claremont Road), August 3 (floodlit). **Ireland won by 20 runs. Ireland 115-7** (20 overs) (C. M. A. Shillington 48); ‡**South Africa 95** (19.3 overs). *Ireland beat South Africa for the first time, at the 23rd attempt. Clare Shillington and 15-year-old Gaby Lewis (26) opened with 78, but the innings tailed off, with four run-outs. There were four more in the South Africa innings – equalling the T20I record of eight, in the women's game between New Zealand and South Africa at Taunton in 2007.*

First one-day international At Dublin (Anglesea Road), August 5. **South Africa won by 89 runs. South Africa 283-7** (50 overs) (L. Wolvaardt 55, S. E. Luus 52, C. L. Tryon 92, Extras 31; K. J. Garth 3-61); ‡**Ireland 194** (44.5 overs) (K. J. Garth 72*; S. E. Luus 6-36). *ODI debuts:* C. C. Dalton,

G. H. Lewis (Ireland); O. Kirsten (South Africa). *Suné Luus dominated the game with a maiden fifty and a career-best 6-36 – the second woman to combine a half-century and five wickets in the same ODI, after Heather Knight for England v Pakistan a few weeks before. She added 142 for South Africa's sixth wicket with Chloe Tryon, who hit six sixes in a 68-ball 92, to set up their highest total in official ODIs. Ireland slumped to 56-5 before Garth, with a maiden half-century, gave them respectability.*

Second one-day international At Dublin (Claremont Road), August 7. **South Africa won by 68 runs.** ‡**South Africa 272-6** (50 overs) (L. Wolvaardt 35, T. Chetty 49, M. du Preez 116*, C. L. Tryon 53); **Ireland 204** (48.2 overs) (C. M. A. Shillington 41, M. V. Waldron 43*). *Du Preez made 116* in 98 balls, her highest ODI score, and put on 89 for the sixth wicket with Tryon to ensure another solid total; Ireland's top order collapsed again, to 55-5, before another recovery.*

Third one-day international At Dublin (Malahide), August 9. **South Africa won by 67 runs.** ‡**South Africa 260-6** (50 overs) (L. Wolvaardt 105, T. Chetty 95); **Ireland 193** (45 overs) (I. M. H. C. Joyce 57, K. J. Garth 51*; S. E. Luus 5-32). *ODI debuts:* U. Raymond-Hoey (Ireland); L. Goodall (South Africa). *Laura Wolvaardt, aged 17, became the second-youngest woman to score an international hundred, after 16-year-old Mithali Raj – and the youngest South African of either sex. She and Chetty, who made a career-best 95, put on 192, South Africa's highest opening stand in women's ODIs. Luus's five wickets gave her 13 in three games, as Ireland went 3–0 down.*

Fourth one-day international At Dublin (Vineyard), August 11. **Ireland won by seven wickets.** ‡**South Africa 143** (46.4 overs) (A. Steyn 43, C. L. Tryon 30; K. J. Garth 3-27, C. J. Metcalfe 3-23); **Ireland 146-3** (36.1 overs) (I. M. H. C. Joyce 62*). *Ireland completed their first 50-over win over South Africa, after 12 defeats and a no-result. Garth's medium-pace and Ciara Metcalfe's leg-breaks bowled out the tourists inside 47 overs; needing only 144, Ireland were steered to victory by Isobel Joyce with time to spare.*

IRELAND v BANGLADESH IN 2016

Twenty20 internationals (2): Ireland 1, Bangladesh 0
One-day internationals (3): Ireland 0, Bangladesh 1

September did not prove a good time for Bangladesh to visit Northern Ireland – only the last of their five internationals was not shortened by rain, and that one had been added to the programme after the earlier washouts. Of the matches played to a conclusion, the teams claimed one apiece.

First Twenty20 international At Bready, September 5. **Ireland won by six runs. Ireland 54-8** (10 overs) (Khadija Tul Kobra 3-5); ‡**Bangladesh 48-6** (10 overs). *Rain reduced the game to ten overs a side, and only one player on each team reached double figures: Clare Shillington (26) and Farzana Haque (24). Bangladesh needed ten off the last over, bowled by 16-year-old Lucy O'Reilly, with Farzana still in, but O'Reilly claimed a hat-trick of sorts – an lbw, a run-out and a stumping – and conceded just three.*

Second Twenty20 international At Bready, September 6. **Ireland v Bangladesh. Abandoned.**

First one-day international At Bready, September 8. **Ireland v Bangladesh. Abandoned.**

Second one-day international At Belfast (Instonians), September 9. **No result. Ireland 68-0** (18 overs) (C. N. I. M. Joyce 37*) **v** ‡**Bangladesh.** *ODI debut:* M. F. Kendal (Ireland). *The match was first reduced to 47 overs a side, then washed out altogether after 70 minutes, in which time Cecelia Joyce and newcomer Meg Kendal (26*) had put on 68*.*

Third one-day international At Belfast (Instonians), September 10. **Bangladesh won by ten runs.** ‡**Bangladesh 106** (40.1 overs) (Sanjida Islam 33; A. J. Kenealy 4-32); **Ireland 96** (37.5 overs) (C. N. I. M. Joyce 35; Rumana Ahmed 3-20). *Bangladesh looked finished when Amy Kenealy had them reeling on 25-5, with a career-best four wickets. But 33 from opener Sanjida Islam, some late-order runs and 23 in wides helped them into three figures. Kendal and Cecelia Joyce then shared another half-century opening stand, before Khadija Tul Kobra claimed two in two balls; leg-spinner Rumana Ahmed went one better with Bangladesh's first international hat-trick, all lbw, as Ireland's last six went for 12 runs.*

SRI LANKA v AUSTRALIA IN 2016-17

One-day internationals (4): Australia 4, Sri Lanka 0
Twenty20 international (1): Australia 1, Sri Lanka 0

This was women against girls, as Australia won all five matches at a canter, inducing a Sri Lankan batting collapse in each. Leg-spinner Kristen Beams claimed 13 wickets in the four-match one-day series at just 5.92 apiece, while seamer Holly Ferling took ten at 9.90. Sri Lanka managed a single half-century all told, while none of their bowlers took more than the six wickets managed by Chamari Atapattu Jayangani.

First one-day international At Dambulla, September 18, 2016. **Australia won by four wickets.** ‡**Sri Lanka 76** (24.5 overs) (I. Ranaweera 32*; H. L. Ferling 3-4, K. M. Beams 3-16); **Australia 79-6** (15.4 overs) (I. Ranaweera 3-20). *PoM:* H. L. Ferling. *ODI debuts:* S. I. P. Fernando, H. I. S. Mendis (Sri Lanka). *Sri Lanka made a catastrophic start, slipping to 3-5 against Holly Ferling (who finished with 4–2–4–3) and Megan Schutt (4–2–5–2), with all five gone for ducks. When Imalka Mendis followed for a single, the first of three victims for the leg-spin of Kristen Beams, it was 20-6; soon, Sri Lanka were 38-8, and did well to reach 76. Australia themselves slid from 45-1 to 50-5, before sealing victory with almost 35 overs to spare, despite five dismissals for wicketkeeper Prasadini Weerakkody. This match was not part of the ICC Women's Championship.*

Second one-day international At Dambulla, September 20, 2016. **Australia won by 78 runs.** ‡**Australia 254-8** (50 overs) (N. E. Bolton 64, E. J. Villani 45, A. J. Blackwell 56*; A. C. Jayangani 3-31); **Sri Lanka 176-9** (50 overs) (P. R. C. S. Kumarihami 68*, Extras 50; K. M. Beams 4-15). *PoM:* K. M. Beams. *ODI debut:* H. M. D. Samarawickrama (Sri Lanka). *Another Sri Lankan collapse – this time to 35-5, including three ducks – made the result a foregone conclusion. Beams collected a career-best 4-15 from ten overs, while No. 3 Chamari Polgampola Kumarihami held firm, but Australia's margin of victory would have been even larger had they not conceded 41 in wides, a national record. Half-centuries from Nicole Bolton and Alex Blackwell had set up a testing total.*

Third one-day international At Colombo (RPS), September 23, 2016. **Australia won by nine wickets. Sri Lanka 102** (36.5 overs) (W. P. M. Weerakkody 31; J. L. Jonassen 3-1); ‡**Australia 104-1** (27.3 overs) (N. E. Bolton 35, E. J. Villani 48*). *PoM:* J. L. Jonassen. *For once, Sri Lanka got off to a solid start. But it was horribly illusory: from 50-0, they cascaded to 102 all out, as Jess Jonassen returned 4–3–1–3 with her left-arm spin. Bolton and Elyse Villani, whose 48* was a second career-best in four days, confirmed Australia's series victory with an opening stand of 89.*

Fourth one-day international At Colombo (RPS), September 25, 2016. **Australia won by 137 runs.** ‡**Australia 268-3** (50 overs) (N. E. Bolton 113, M. M. Lanning 43, E. A. Perry 77*); **Sri Lanka 131** (45.5 overs) (W. P. M. Weerakkody 33; H. L. Ferling 3-30, R. M. Farrell 3-17, K. M. Beams 4-26). *PoM:* N. E. Bolton. *Australia completed a 4–0 rout after Bolton's second ODI hundred and a run-a-ball 77* from Ellyse Perry took them beyond Sri Lanka's reach. Beams completed a dominant series with four more wickets, and there were three each for Ferling and Rene Farrell, as Sri Lanka plummeted from 69-1 to 131 all out.*

Women's Championship: Australia 6pts, Sri Lanka 0pts.

Twenty20 international At Colombo (RPS), September 27, 2016. **Australia won by ten wickets. Sri Lanka 59-8** (20 overs) (K. M. Beams 3-11); ‡**Australia 63-0** (8.1 overs) (E. J. Villani 34*). *PoM:* K. M. Beams. *Australia finished their trip with a record victory, romping home with 71 balls to spare (New Zealand had 70 left when they beat Pakistan at Basseterre during the 2010 World Twenty20). Beams had taken her tour tally to 16 wickets as Sri Lanka inched their way to 59-8.*

SOUTH AFRICA v NEW ZEALAND IN 2016-17

One-day internationals (7): South Africa 2, New Zealand 5

South Africa had taken significant strides over the previous year, defeating England twice and West Indies three times when they visited in 2015-16. A seven-match one-day series against New Zealand gave them a chance to discover whether those improvements had been consolidated. The answer was a vague "yes, but…" Against opponents they had never beaten in ODIs, they won twice, though there were also one or two wallopings. Mignon du Preez had passed the captaincy to Dané van Niekerk, who in one purple patch made scores of 78, 48 and 36, all unbeaten. She did have to cope without two regulars: Shabnim Ismail and Trisha Chetty had been suspended by Cricket South Africa for "unbecoming or detrimental conduct". The star of the series, though, was New Zealand's Amy Satterthwaite. She hit 344 runs at 68, and added 11 wickets at 15.

First one-day international At Kimberley, October 8, 2016. **New Zealand won by 12 runs. New Zealand 127** (40.1 overs) (E. M. Bermingham 33; A. Khaka 3-27); ‡**South Africa 115** (42.2 overs) (L. Wolvaardt 33, D. van Niekerk 37; L-M. M. Tahuhu 3-41, A. E. Satterthwaite 4-13). *PoM:* A. E. Satterthwaite. *When South Africa were 115-5 – with 12.2 overs to make the 13 that would bring their first one-day victory over New Zealand – the result seemed beyond doubt. But on a tricky pitch and under leaden skies, batting had never been comfortable. New captain Dané van Niekerk was bowled by Amy Satterthwaite, sending the South African innings into a tailspin: the last five fell for no addition in 28 balls. While Satterthwaite and Lea Tahuhu collected seven victims, Morna Nielsen conceded just nine runs from ten overs. Fourteen players failed to reach double figures.*

Second one-day international At Kimberley, October 11, 2016. **South Africa won by four wickets. New Zealand 222-8** (50 overs) (S. W. Bates 66, R. H. Priest 31, A. E. Satterthwaite 47; M. Kapp 3-41); ‡**South Africa 226-6** (49.1 overs) (L. Lee 42, M. du Preez 80; M. J. G. Nielsen 5-39). *PoM:* M. du Preez. *After botching their chance of a historic win three days earlier, South Africa made amends, relying on a run-a-ball 42 from Lizelle Lee and a more measured 80 from Mignon du Preez. The only bowler to cause them real problems was Nielsen, bowling left-arm spin, who took 5-39. At 140-1 in the 31st over, New Zealand had been on course for a more challenging total than their eventual 222, but Marizanne Kapp's medium-pace kept them in check.*

Third one-day international At Kimberley, October 13, 2016. **New Zealand won by nine wickets.** ‡**South Africa 188-9** (50 overs) (L. Lee 36, M. Kapp 32, D. van Niekerk 78*; H. R. Huddleston 5-25); **New Zealand 190-1** (33.1 overs) (S. W. Bates 82*, A. E. Satterthwaite 89*). *PoM:* H. R. Huddleston. *In the 1,000th women's ODI, New Zealand clicked into gear after a couple of unconvincing performances. They lost the toss but, with only four South Africans making double figures, restricted them to 188. Seamer Holly Huddleston took a career-best 5-25 as the innings – after van Niekerk oversaw a recovery from 55-4 – dribbled away. Rachel Priest was bowled by Ayabonga Khaka in the fifth over, but thereafter it was plain sailing for Suzie Bates (88 balls) and Satterthwaite (97). New Zealand moved joint second in the Women's Championship.*

Women's Championship: New Zealand 4pts, South Africa 2pts.

Fourth one-day international At Paarl, October 17, 2016. **New Zealand won by eight wickets. South Africa 194** (49 overs) (D. Devnarain 42, D. van Niekerk 48*; A. E. Satterthwaite 3-33); ‡**New Zealand 196-2** (28.2 overs) (R. H. Priest 86, A. E. Satterthwaite 81*). *PoM:* A. E. Satterthwaite. *Satterthwaite maintained her magnificent form, this time excelling with ball and bat. First she brought the South African innings to an abrupt halt, when the last four wickets fell for two runs in her eighth over (two were run-outs). Then she and Priest added 139 for New Zealand's second wicket at seven an over.*

Fifth one-day international At Paarl, October 19, 2016. **New Zealand won by 95 runs.** ‡**New Zealand 208-8** (50 overs) (N. C. Dodd 52, A. E. Satterthwaite 42, K. T. Perkins 34, S. R. H. Curtis 42*); **South Africa 113** (35.5 overs) (M. du Preez 62; E. M. Bermingham 3-28, S. W. Bates 3-17). *PoM:* N. C. Dodd. *New Zealand secured the series with a thumping win, despite languishing on 10-3 after nine overs. Natalie Dodd held firm for 52 from 107 balls, while the middle order upped the tempo to reach 208. When South Africa's reply stood at 28-4 – effectively 28-5, since Kapp had retired with concussion – the game was up, though du Preez battled on, adding 55 with Suné Luus.*

Sixth one-day international At Paarl, October 22, 2016. **South Africa won by five wickets. New Zealand 130** (33.3 overs) (K. J. Martin 65*; M. M. Klaas 3-32); ‡**South Africa 131-5** (37.4 overs) (M. du Preez 44, D. van Niekerk 36*). *PoM:* M. M. Klaas. *ODI debut:* S. Jafta (South Africa). *In a game reduced to 39 overs a side, South Africa's seamers sliced through their opponents to ensure a modest task for the home batting. Masabata Klaas led the way with a career-best 3-32 and, without a fighting 65* from Katey Martin, New Zealand would have faced ignominy. The experienced pair of du Preez and van Niekerk, captains past and present, steered South Africa to victory.*

Seventh one-day international At Paarl, October 24, 2016. **New Zealand won by 126 runs.** ‡**New Zealand 273-7** (50 overs) (A. E. Satterthwaite 53, K. J. Martin 81, M. L. Green 46); **South Africa 147** (45.5 overs) (E. M. Bermingham 3-18). *PoM:* K. J. Martin. *After the hiccup of the last ODI, New Zealand's dependable middle order powered them to success. Satterthwaite hit 53 – her fifth score of 40 or more in seven innings – while Martin showed she was still in the groove with 81 from 72 balls. A target of 274 required a couple of South Africans to score heavily but, although many enjoyed starts, none progressed beyond 22, perplexed either by Erin Bermingham's leg-breaks or Satterthwaite's off-spin.*

WEST INDIES v ENGLAND IN 2016-17

MARTIN DAVIES

One-day internationals (5): West Indies 2, England 3

On their one-day tour of Jamaica in October 2016, England overcame Hurricane Matthew, a low and slow turner at the Trelawny Stadium, and a cabbage patch of an outfield at Sabina Park to record a confidence-boosting 3–2 win. The last three matches, all staged in Kingston, were part of the ICC Women's Championship, and England took four of the six points on offer – not quite enough to guarantee an automatic place at the 2017 World Cup, though one win in Sri Lanka in November would complete that goal. Two points for West Indies meant they slipped to third in the table, a point behind England, but they were hopeful of clinching qualification in their next series, in India. The outcome confirmed Australia as winners of the Championship trophy with a round to go.

This was Heather Knight's first tour as England captain, and she had to manage without her vice-captain, quick bowler Anya Shrubsole, who strained her side in a warm-up game and was eventually sent home after further problems with neck pains. In her absence, Katherine Brunt led the pace attack, and finished with ten wickets. But she was outshone by left-arm spinner Alex Hartley, who took 13 in the five games, a one-day series record for England, including four in the decider.

West Indies captain Stafanie Taylor was the leading run-scorer, with 216 including three fifties – ahead of England's Lauren Winfield (168) and Nat Sciver (155), who each scored two – but the rest of the batting struggled. All-rounder Deandra Dottin never reached 30, though her seam bowling claimed ten wickets, including a match-winning four for 19 in the second game, while Afy Fletcher's accurate leg-spin picked up nine.

ENGLAND TOURING PARTY

*H. C. Knight (Berkshire), T. T. Beaumont (Kent), K. H. Brunt (Yorkshire), S. Ecclestone (Lancashire), G. A. Elwiss (Sussex), J. L. Gunn (Warwickshire), A. Hartley (Middlesex), D. Hazell (Yorkshire), A. E. Jones (Warwickshire), B. A. Langston (Yorkshire), L. A. Marsh (Kent), N. R. Sciver (Surrey), A. Shrubsole (Somerset), L. Winfield (Yorkshire), D. N. Wyatt (Sussex). *Coach:* M. A. Robinson.

Shrubsole left the tour after being injured in a practice match.

First one-day international At Trelawny Greenfields, Jamaica, October 8, 2016. **England won by five runs.** ‡**England 149** (49.1 overs) (D. N. Wyatt 44; D. J. S. Dottin 3-21); **West Indies 144** (44.2 overs) (K. H. Brunt 3-24, A. Hartley 3-26). *PoM:* D. N. Wyatt. *ODI debuts:* E. M. Giddings (West Indies); S. Ecclestone (England). *On a hot and humid day and a sticky, spinning pitch, both teams struggled for runs. Deandra Dottin reduced England to 47-3, which became 62-5 before Danni Wyatt and Amy Jones added 45. But they were bowled out for a meagre 149, and West Indies openers Hayley Matthews and Shaquana Quintyne were going along nicely at 53-0. Then both fell in successive overs from 17-year-old left-arm spinner Sophie Ecclestone, while captain Stafanie Taylor retired with a leg injury. Though she returned at 81-4, she was one of three wickets to fall at*

100, along with Dottin. Shemaine Campbelle got West Indies back in the game, backed up by Afy Fletcher. But Laura Marsh broke through, and Katherine Brunt trapped their last two, leaving Campbelle stranded on 24.*

Second one-day international At Trelawny Greenfields, Jamaica, October 10, 2016. **West Indies won by 38 runs.** ‡**West Indies 148** (50 overs) (S. R. Taylor 56; A. Hartley 4-31); **England 110** (41.4 overs) (A. S. S. Fletcher 3-20, D. J. S. Dottin 4-19). *PoM:* D. J. S. Dottin. *The same pitch produced another low-scoring game, which West Indies won after sweeping away England's last six for three runs. Taylor chose to bat, and scored more than twice as many as anyone on either side, but wickets tumbled around her, slow left-armer Alex Hartley taking three in ten balls; Taylor herself was eventually caught trying to hit Brunt over the top. England needed a measured approach to knock off 149, but their batters got in, only to get themselves out. They were 93-3 before Fletcher's leg-spin claimed three in three overs, and 109-6 at the start of the 40th over, in which Dottin grabbed three; she finished the game in her next over, with England in tatters.*

Third one-day international At Kingston, Jamaica, October 14, 2016. **England won by 112 runs.** ‡**England 220** (49.5 overs) (L. Winfield 79, N. R. Sciver 58; S. L. Quintyne 3-36); **West Indies 108** (35.4 overs). *PoM:* L. Winfield. *The teams moved on to Kingston for the three Women's Championship games. The first went decisively England's way, thanks to a thoroughly professional performance and their highest total of the tour. Lauren Winfield and Nat Sciver made half-centuries as they added 95 in 18 overs for the fourth wicket, helped by poor fielding – though, after England had passed 200, spinners Quintyne and Matthews collected five for 12 in the last three overs. England bowled straight and caught well, as Jenny Gunn, Hartley and Marsh picked up two wickets each; no one passed Quintyne's 21 and West Indies were all out with 14 overs to spare.*

Fourth one-day international At Kingston, Jamaica, October 16, 2016. **West Indies won by 42 runs.** ‡**West Indies 223-6** (50 overs) (S. L. Quintyne 41, S. R. Taylor 85, M. R. Aguilleira 32); **England 181** (44.2 overs) (L. Winfield 51, T. T. Beaumont 57, H. C. Knight 36; S. R. Taylor 3-22). *PoM:* S. R. Taylor. *Taylor had a perfect day from the moment she won the toss: 85 runs, three wickets, two run-outs and a series-levelling win, after more fragility from England's middle order. Taylor occupied the crease for most of West Indies' innings, sharing solid partnerships with Quintyne and Merissa Aguilleira. But openers Winfield and Tammy Beaumont responded to a challenging target of 224 with an untroubled 95 and, after Beaumont sent a simple return catch to Taylor, Heather Knight joined Winfield to help steer England to 133-1. Then three wickets fell for four runs – two of them run-outs. Knight persevered until another crazy run-out heralded a second collapse, of four for four. There was no way back from 165-8. Taylor completed victory with the fifth run-out of the innings (one short of England's record, against Australia at Southampton in 1998).*

Fifth one-day international At Kingston, Jamaica, October 19, 2016. **England won by five wickets.** ‡**West Indies 155** (47.1 overs) (S. R. Taylor 57; K. H. Brunt 3-35, A. Hartley 4-24); **England 158-5** (38.5 overs) (T. T. Beaumont 34, N. R. Sciver 58*). *PoM:* A. Hartley. *PoS:* A. Hartley and S. R. Taylor. *The previous four matches had been won by the team winning the toss and batting, so West Indies had no hesitation in sticking to that formula. But only Taylor, with her third fifty in four innings, got on top of the bowling, and Hartley's career-best 4-24 ripped the heart out of their innings. Tied down by her nagging line and length, Dottin, Aguilleira and Campbelle were all caught on the leg side, before Hartley added Taylor, neatly stumped by Jones to make it 137-7. England needed only 156, and a third-wicket stand of 56 between Knight and Sciver broke the back of the chase; though wickets continued to fall, Sciver held her nerve to lead England over the line, and secure a 3–2 series win.*

Women's Championship: England 4pts, West Indies 2pts.

PAKISTAN v INDIA IN 2016-17

Three Women's Championship games which should have been played between Pakistan and India between August 1 and October 31, 2016, never took place. In November, the ICC ruled that the Indian authorities were responsible for this failure, and awarded Pakistan two points for each of the three games, crediting India with no runs in 50 overs in each game for net run-rate purposes.

Women's Championship: Pakistan 6pts, India 0pts.

NEW ZEALAND v PAKISTAN IN 2016-17

One-day internationals (5): New Zealand 5, Pakistan 0
Twenty20 international (1): New Zealand 1, Pakistan 0

New Zealand whitewashed Pakistan in all six games, including the last three 50-over matches, which formed part of the Women's Championship, thus making sure of their place in the 2017 World Cup. Amy Satterthwaite became the first woman to score centuries in three successive one-day international innings, finishing with 393 for two dismissals, well ahead of her captain Suzie Bates's 236; five home bowlers collected at least five one-day wickets, compared with one Pakistani.

First one-day international At Lincoln, November 9, 2016. **New Zealand won by eight wickets. Pakistan 156** (49 overs) (Nain Abidi 49, Asmavia Iqbal 49*; L-M. M. Tahuhu 3-37); ‡**New Zealand 157-2** (23 overs) (S. W. Bates 64, S. R. H. Curtis 55*). *PoM:* L-M. M. Tahuhu. *ODI debut:* A. C. Kerr (New Zealand). *New Zealand used fewer than half their overs in their dash to victory; Suzie Bates and Sam Curtis opened with 100 in 13.3, and Curtis went on to a maiden fifty. Earlier, Lea Tahuhu reduced Pakistan to 90-6, before Asmavia Iqbal supervised the addition of 66 for the last four.*

Second one-day international At Lincoln, November 11, 2016. **New Zealand won by 60 runs** (DLS). ‡**New Zealand 309-4** (50 overs) (S. W. Bates 32, A. E. Satterthwaite 137*, K. J. Martin 65, S. F. M. Devine 34); **Pakistan 142-4** (34.2 overs) (Nahida Khan 33, Nain Abidi 45, Bismah Maroof 30*). *PoM:* A. E. Satterthwaite. *Amy Satterthwaite hit a career-best 137* in 117 balls, adding 150 for New Zealand's third wicket with Katey Martin, before lifting them past 300. Pakistan's reply was interrupted, then ended, by rain, but they were well behind the retrospective target of 203.*

Third one-day international At Lincoln, November 13, 2016. **New Zealand won by eight wickets.** ‡**Pakistan 263-6** (50 overs) (Ayesha Zafar 30, Javeria Khan 73, Bismah Maroof 91*); **New Zealand 267-2** (44.2 overs) (S. W. Bates 74, A. E. Satterthwaite 115*, K. J. Martin 50*). *PoM:* A. E. Satterthwaite. *This was the first match of the series to count towards the Women's Championship. Javeria Khan and Bismah Maroof put on 117, a third-wicket record for Pakistan, to help them to their best total of the tour. But New Zealand easily overtook it, as Satterthwaite scored a second century. She added 102 for the second wicket with Bates and 105* for the third with Martin, and finished with 115* in 101 balls.*

Fourth one-day international At Nelson, November 17, 2016. **New Zealand won by seven wickets. Pakistan 158** (48.1 overs) (Ayesha Zafar 52, Javeria Khan 30, Sana Mir 31; H. R. Huddleston 4-20); ‡**New Zealand 162-3** (22.3 overs) (S. W. Bates 66, S. F. M. Devine 54). *PoM:* H. R. Huddleston. *Three days after an earthquake in the South Island killed two people, the teams wore black armbands and observed a minute's silence. New Zealand's victory ensured World Cup qualification; they coasted past 159 inside 23 overs, with Bates hurrying to her third fifty of the series. Pakistan reached 107-1 before losing nine for 51, with four for Holly Huddleston.*

Fifth one-day international At Nelson, November 19, 2016. **New Zealand won by five wickets.** ‡**Pakistan 220** (49.5 overs) (Ayesha Zafar 50, Nahida Khan 31, Javeria Khan 50; A. C. Kerr 4-42, T. M. M. Newton 5-31); **New Zealand 223-5** (38.3 overs) (A. E. Satterthwaite 123; Sadia Yousuf 3-49). *PoM:* T. M. M. Newton. *Satterthwaite, acting-captain as Bates rested, became the first woman to score three centuries in successive ODI innings (she had not batted in the last game); she smashed a 99-ball 123, which was 100 more than New Zealand's next highest, to guarantee a clean sweep. In Pakistan's innings, 16-year-old leg-spinner Amelia Kerr and seamer Thamsyn Newton took nine between them; neither had managed more than one in any previous ODI.*

Women's Championship: New Zealand 6pts, Pakistan 0pts.

Twenty20 international At Nelson, November 21, 2016. **New Zealand won by 14 runs.** ‡**New Zealand 118-9** (20 overs); **Pakistan 104** (20 overs) (L-M. M. Tahuhu 3-17, A. C. Kerr 3-16). *PoM:* L-M.M. Tahuhu. *T20I debut:* A. C. Kerr (New Zealand). *Iram Javed removed Bates with the first ball of the match, Asmavia added Rachel Priest in the next over, and New Zealand were soon having to fight back from 36-4. Their 118 turned out to be enough to collect a sixth win. Tahuhu claimed three wickets and a run-out to leave Pakistan on 22-4, and Kerr made that 60-8 before No. 10 Aliya Riaz knocked up 28* in 22 balls, the highest score of the match.*

SRI LANKA v ENGLAND IN 2016-17

One-day internationals (4): Sri Lanka 0, England 4

England made sure of their place in the 2017 World Cup, winning all four one-day internationals – the last three counted towards the Women's Championship – by comfortable margins, although they were in some difficulty in the final game after dipping to 58 for six. On pitches receptive to spin, their slow bowlers outperformed their hosts: Danielle Hazell took nine wickets at 12 apiece, and her fellow off-spinner Laura Marsh eight at ten. Sri Lanka's captain Inoka Ranaweera, a slow left-armer, also claimed eight wickets – but conceded more than five an over, while the English pair went for less than three. Natalie Sciver, who chipped in with four wickets, led the batting with 185 runs, one of four England players to pass 100. Sri Lanka had none – their highest individual score was just 35 – and hit only two sixes to England's ten. Although World Cup qualification had never really been in doubt, it was a relief for it to be rubber-stamped. "We have the best fans in the world," said Heather Knight, their captain. "So to get the opportunity to play in a World Cup on home soil is really exciting."

ENGLAND TOURING PARTY

*H. C. Knight (Berkshire), T. T. Beaumont (Kent), K. H. Brunt (Yorkshire), G. A. Elwiss (Sussex), J. L. Gunn (Warwickshire), A. Hartley (Middlesex), D. Hazell (Yorkshire), A. E. Jones (Warwickshire), B. A. Langston (Yorkshire), L. A. Marsh (Kent), N. R. Sciver (Surrey), F. C. Wilson (Middlesex), L. Winfield (Yorkshire), D. N. Wyatt (Sussex). *Coach:* M. A. Robinson.

First one-day international At Colombo (SSC), November 9, 2016. **England won by eight wickets.** ‡**Sri Lanka 168-7** (50 overs); **England 171-2** (29.3 overs) (L. Winfield 33, T. T. Beaumont 41, H. C. Knight 45*, N. R. Sciver 47*). *ODI debut:* B. A. Langston (England). *Sri Lanka's top five all passed 20, but no one exceeded Dilani Manodara Surangika's 27, which meant England's target was relatively straightforward. Lauren Winfield and Tammy Beaumont opened with a stand of 77, then Heather Knight and Nat Sciver added 82* from 79 balls. This match did not count towards the Women's Championship.*

Second one-day international At Colombo (RPS), November 12, 2016. **England won by 122 runs. England 295** (50 overs) (L. Winfield 51, H. C. Knight 53, N. R. Sciver 51, G. A. Elwiss 46; K. A. D. A. Kanchana 3-49, I. Ranaweera 3-48); ‡**Sri Lanka 173** (48.5 overs) (G. W. H. M. Perera 35, M. D. N. Hansika 32, P. R. C. S. Kumarihami 33; D. Hazell 3-38). *Put in, England were given mid-innings oomph by Sciver, who faced only 27 balls for her 51, and hit nine fours and a six. Georgia Elwiss added 46 from 36 later on, then Danielle Hazell (29) pushed the total towards 300. Sri Lanka made a reasonable start, but 50-0 became 66-4, and the target was never in sight after that. Their innings included five lbws. Opener Hasini Perera top-scored with 35 from 90 balls, despite retiring hurt after the second over and resuming later. England's comfortable victory ensured their place in the World Cup, to be staged at home in 2017.*

Third one-day international At Colombo (RPS), November 15, 2016. **England won by five wickets.** ‡**Sri Lanka 161** (49.4 overs); **England 162-5** (29.3 overs) (T. T. Beaumont 78, F. C. Wilson 30). *England's slow bowlers kept the brakes on, with Hazell, Laura Marsh and Alex Hartley combining for 26–4–72–6. Beaumont, who hit three sixes, supervised the chase with a run-a-ball 78, before falling six short of the victory that clinched the series.*

Fourth one-day international At Colombo (RPS), November 17–18, 2016. **England won by 162 runs.** ‡**England 240-9** (50 overs) (N. R. Sciver 77, D. Hazell 45, L. A. Marsh 36*; S. I. P. Fernando 3-28, I. Ranaweera 3-38); **Sri Lanka 78** (33.1 overs) (W. P. M. Weerakkody 32; D. Hazell 3-21, L. A. Marsh 4-21). *England marched to a 4–0 clean sweep, skittling Sri Lanka for 78 on the reserve day after bad weather, their three spinners this time returning 24.1–3–55–8. The previous day, England had stuttered to 58-6 – Beaumont, Danni Wyatt and Fran Wilson all bagged ducks – against the off-breaks of the recalled Inoshi Priyadharshani Fernando, and skipper Inoka Ranaweera's left-arm slows. But Sciver (whose seam-up later brought her figures of 5–1–9–2) put on 104 with Hazell, and the last four wickets added 182 in all.*

Women's Championship: England 6pts, Sri Lanka 0pts.

INDIA v WEST INDIES IN 2016-17

One-day internationals (3): India 3, West Indies 0
Twenty20 internationals (3): India 0, West Indies 3

The sides traded clean sweeps but, while India's one-day success earned them six points in the Women's Championship, it did them little good: the ICC confirmed they would be penalised for failing to play Pakistan, and would have to go through a further qualifying competition to enter the 2017 World Cup. Meanwhile, one 50-over win would have guaranteed West Indies' World Cup place, but after losing all three they had to wait until South Africa's failure to win in Australia ensured they would go through. Veda Krishnamurthy was the mainstay of India's batting, scoring three fifties across the six games, while Harmanpreet Kaur was dismissed only once in making 171 runs in the T20Is. Rajeshwari Gayakwad claimed nine ODI wickets with her left-arm spin at under ten apiece. In the country where she had lifted the World Twenty20 title in April, West Indies captain Stafanie Taylor made 181 runs in the 20-over games.

First one-day international At Mulapadu, November 10, 2016. **India won by six wickets.** ‡**West Indies 131** (42.4 overs) (M. R. Aguilleira 42*; E. Bisht 3-14, R. S. Gayakwad 4-21); **India 133-4** (39.1 overs) (M. D. Raj 46*, V. Krishnamurthy 52*). *A stand of 97* for India's fifth wicket between captain Mithali Raj and Veda Krishnamurthy settled the match after 14 wickets had fallen for 167. West Indies had been unpicked by Rajeshwari Gayakwad, who took a career-best 4-21, with only wicketkeeper Melissa Aguilleira showing any grit. Shakera Selman (9–4–11–2) helped reduce India to 36-4, but no more wickets fell.*

Second one-day international At Mulapadu, November 13, 2016. **India won by five wickets. West Indies 153-7** (50 overs) (D. J. S. Dottin 63); ‡**India 154-5** (38 overs) (S. S. Mandhana 44, D. B. Sharma 32, M. D. Raj 45). *Thirush Kamini became the first woman to be given out obstructing the field in an international. Sent back by non-striker Smriti Mandhana, she was hit by a shy at the stumps, prompting an appeal from West Indies, who believed she had changed her course; eventually, the umpires agreed. But it did not prevent India from claiming the series. Set a modest 154, they were boosted by a second-wicket stand of 63 between Mandhana and Deepti Sharma, whose ten overs of off-spin had cost just 19. Raj then scored 45 from 51 balls to power them home. For West Indies, only Deandra Dottin made any headway with the bat.*

Third one-day international At Mulapadu, November 16, 2016. **India won by 15 runs. India 199-6** (50 overs) (V. Krishnamurthy 71, D. P. Vaidya 32*); ‡**West Indies 184** (49.1 overs) (H. K. Matthews 44, K. A. Knight 55; R. S. Gayakwad 4-34). *ODI debuts:* S. K. Parida, D. P. Vaidya (India). *India's clean sweep meant West Indies had to wait on other results before finding out whether they had qualified automatically for the 2017 World Cup. At 166-4 in the 45th over, they were on course to secure the win they needed to sidestep the play-offs, but Aguilleira became the first of three run-out victims, and Kycia Knight fell for 55, one of four wickets for Gayakwad. In all, the last six tumbled for 18. India's 199 had centred on Krishnamurthy's classy 71 from 79 balls.*

Women's Championship: India 6pts, West Indies 0pts.

First Twenty20 international At Mulapadu, November 18, 2016. **West Indies won by six wickets.** ‡**India 150-4** (20 overs) (V. Krishnamurthy 50, H. Kaur 68*); **West Indies 154-4** (19.1 overs) (S. R. Taylor 90; S. S. Pandey 3-31). *T20I debuts:* P. Bose, N. M. Parween (India). *Taylor's aggressive 51-ball 90 eased West Indies to victory with five balls to spare, despite three wickets for Shikha Pandey. India had recovered from 28-2 thanks to half-centuries from Krishnamurthy and Harmanpreet Kaur (68* from 50 balls).*

Second Twenty20 international At Mulapadu, November 20, 2016. **West Indies won by 31 runs. West Indies 137-5** (20 overs) (S. R. Taylor 47*, D. J. S. Dottin 35); ‡**India 106** (18.1 overs) (H. Kaur 43; D. J. S. Dottin 3-24, A. Mohammed 3-23). *T20I debut:* S. Meghana. *West Indies secured the series after India lost their last six wickets for 33. There were three each for Anisa Mohammed and Dottin, who earlier bashed 35 from 21 balls. Taylor batted throughout West Indies' innings, scoring 47 from 45.*

Third Twenty20 international At Mulapadu, November 22, 2016. **West Indies won by 15 runs.** ‡**West Indies 139-4** (20 overs) (H. K. Matthews 47, S. R. Taylor 44*); **India 124-3** (20 overs)

(V. Krishnamurthy 31*, H. Kaur 60*). *A curious display from Krishnamurthy, who failed to hit a four in her 40-ball 31*, left India short – and handed West Indies a 3–0 win. She and Kaur, whose 60* from 51 deliveries (including three sixes) went to waste, had rebuilt India's chase from 32-3, which included the first-ball run-out of opener Vellaswamy Vanitha. But Hayley Matthews's belligerent 47 from 22 had given West Indies enough to play with.*

AUSTRALIA v SOUTH AFRICA IN 2016-17

One-day internationals (5): Australia 4, South Africa 0

England's defeat of West Indies in October had already guaranteed Australia the ICC Women's Championship, and qualification for the 2017 World Cup. But there was no complacency: with a seventh straight series win here, they finished the competition on a high. Ellyse Perry was their heartbeat, hitting fifties in all four games she played (making it 17 from 23 ODI innings since January 2014) and averaging 156. She was also Australia's top wicket-taker, with seven. South Africa had a chance to secure their own passage to the World Cup, but finished the series sixth in the final standings. They had won none of their 13 one-day games against Australia (though they tied one here). To reach the World Cup, they needed to progress from a further qualifying competition in February.

First one-day international At Canberra, November 18, 2016 (day/night). **Australia won by two wickets.** ‡**South Africa 226-5** (50 overs) (L. Lee 38, S. E. Luus 52, M. du Preez 37); **Australia 230-8** (49.5 overs) (E. A. Perry 93*; S. E. Luus 3-52). *PoM:* E. A. Perry. *ODI debut:* A. E. Bosch (South Africa). *Australia needed 26 from three overs with three wickets left, but Ellyse Perry hit 16 from the 48th, bowled by Suné Luus, and the winning four from the penultimate ball to finish on 93*. It was a supreme solo effort – no one else managed more than Alyssa Healy's 28 – and spoiled the good work of Luus, who had taken three wickets to back up a gritty fifty.*

Second one-day international At Canberra, November 20, 2016 (day/night). **Australia won by 65 runs** (DLS). ‡**Australia 278-4** (50 overs) (M. M. Lanning 134, E. A. Perry 95*; A. Khaka 3-55); **South Africa 119-5** (31.2 overs) (S. E. Luus 60*). *PoM:* M. M. Lanning. *Meg Lanning hit 134 to equal Charlotte Edwards's record of nine ODI centuries (though in 51 innings to Edwards's 169), and put on 224 with Perry, who came within five of a maiden hundred. A shower initially reduced South Africa's target to 241 off 38, but they were well behind the rate when more rain came.*

Third one-day international At North Sydney, November 23, 2016 (day/night). **Australia won by nine wickets.** ‡**South Africa 173-8** (32 overs) (L. Lee 102, M. du Preez 36; G. M. Harris 3-31); **Australia 174-1** (27.1 overs) (N. E. Bolton 77*, M. M. Lanning 80*). *PoM:* L. Lee. *In a game reduced to 32 overs, Lizelle Lee's 89-ball hundred – her first in international cricket – gave South Africa a platform for a late-innings assault. Instead, they collapsed from 143-2 to 173-8. Australia lost Elyse Villani in the first over of the reply, before Nicole Bolton and Lanning led a procession with a series-sealing stand of 161*.*

Women's Championship: Australia 6pts, South Africa 0pts.

Fourth one-day international At Coffs Harbour, November 27, 2016 (day/night). **Tied.** ‡**Australia 242** (49.5 overs) (N. E. Bolton 63, E. A. Perry 69, A. J. Blackwell 35; D. van Niekerk 3-52, S. E. Luus 4-37); **South Africa 242** (50 overs) (M. Kapp 66, D. van Niekerk 81; J. L. Jonassen 3-37). *PoM:* D. van Niekerk. *ODI debuts:* T. M. McGrath, A. Wellington (Australia). *When Masabata Klaas hit the penultimate ball for four to bring South Africa level, she looked to have broken their Australian hoodoo. But her final swipe found Beth Mooney at midwicket, who smartly ran her out. It was a cruel end after Marizanne Kapp and Dané van Niekerk had revitalised the chase from 40-4 with a stand of 144. Australia's 242 had relied on sixties from Bolton and Perry, while seven fell to leg-spinners van Niekerk and Luus.*

Fifth one-day international At Coffs Harbour, November 29, 2016 (day/night). **Australia won by 43 runs. Australia 260-9** (50 overs) (N. E. Bolton 43, M. M. Lanning 42, E. A. Perry 56, J. L. Jonassen 39; M. R. Daniels 3-53, S. E. Luus 3-56); ‡**South Africa 217** (48.3 overs) (L. Lee 44, S. E. Luus 31, M. du Preez 31, C. L. Tryon 32; E. A. Perry 3-52). *PoM:* E. A. Perry. *Chasing 261, South Africa's openers put on 66 in 13 overs. But with Lee's departure, for a 43-ball 44, went the thrust, and they were miles behind when the last wicket fell. Perry followed her run-a-ball 56 with 3-52, while Jess Jonassen and Grace Harris clogged things up with a combined 20–1–56–3.*

WOMEN'S TWENTY20 ASIA CUP IN 2016-17

1 India 2 Pakistan

This was the sixth Women's Asia Cup, but the second to be played in a Twenty20 format. India, Pakistan, Sri Lanka and Bangladesh were joined by Nepal and hosts Thailand, but the 15 fixtures involving the latter two teams did not have full international status. India won all five qualifying matches, plus the final against Pakistan; it was the sixth time they had claimed the trophy. Mithali Raj's batting dominated the tournament: she scored 220 runs in four innings, all of them against full-status sides.

At Bangkok (Terdthai), November 26, 2016. **India won by 64 runs. India 118-6** (20 overs) (M. D. Raj 49*, S. S. Mandhana 41); ‡**Bangladesh 54** (18.2 overs) (P. Yadav 3-13). *PoM:* M. D. Raj. *T20I debut:* M. Joshi (India). *Bangladesh's 54 was the lowest total in women's T20Is – for four days. Poonam Yadav took a career-best 3-13, and Ekta Bisht conceded only two runs in 2.2 overs.*

At Bangkok (Asian IoT), November 27, 2016. **Pakistan won by eight wickets.** ‡**Sri Lanka 112-8** (20 overs) (A. C. Jayangani 31); **Pakistan 113-2** (18.2 overs) (Javeria Khan 56*). *PoM:* Javeria Khan. *Javeria Khan ensured a comfortable win with 56* in 52 balls.*

At Bangkok (Asian IoT), November 29, 2016. **India won by five wickets. Pakistan 97-7** (20 overs) (Nain Abidi 37*; E. Bisht 3-20); ‡**India 98-5** (19.2 overs) (M. D. Raj 36). *PoM:* H. Kaur. *Pakistan suffered their only defeat of the qualifying round. They never got going against the spin of Bisht and Anuja Patil and, although they bowled economically, Harmanpreet Kaur completed India's victory with 26* in 22 balls.*

At Bangkok (Asian IoT), November 30, 2016. **Pakistan won by nine wickets.** ‡**Bangladesh 44** (15.3 overs) (Sana Mir 3-5); **Pakistan 45-1** (9.5 overs). *PoM:* Sana Mir. *For the second time in the tournament, Bangladesh scored the lowest total in women's official T20Is. (It was not the worst total of this tournament, however; Nepal were bowled out for fewer on three occasions, their nadir being 21.) Only two players passed five, and Sana Mir took 3-5 in 18 deliveries. Javeria Khan (26*) led Pakistan to their target inside ten overs.*

At Bangkok (Asian IoT), December 1, 2016. **India won by 52 runs.** ‡**India 121-4** (20 overs) (M. D. Raj 62); **Sri Lanka 69-9** (20 overs) (P. Bose 3-14, E. Bisht 3-8). *PoM:* M. D. Raj. *Mithali Raj hit 62 in 59 balls. Between them, Preeti Bose and Bisht claimed 6-22 in their eight overs.*

At Bangkok (Terdthai), December 3, 2016. **Sri Lanka won by seven wickets. Bangladesh 93-3** (20 overs) (Sanjida Islam 35); ‡**Sri Lanka 97-3** (19 overs) (A. C. Jayangani 39). *PoM:* A. C. Jayangani. *Chamari Atapattu Jayangani dismissed both Bangladesh openers and took Sri Lanka most of the way to victory with 39 in 25 balls.*

India 10pts, Pakistan 8pts, Sri Lanka 6pts, Bangladesh 4pts, Thailand 2pts, Nepal 0pts.

Final At Bangkok (Asian IoT), December 4, 2016. **India won by 17 runs.** ‡**India 121-5** (20 overs) (M. D. Raj 73*); **Pakistan 104-6** (20 overs). *PoM:* M. D. Raj. *PoT:* M. D. Raj. *Raj batted throughout India's innings for a career-best 73* in 65 balls; the match's next highest score was 25, by Pakistan captain Bismah Maroof, but once she was out they quickly fell behind the required rate.*

MRF TYRES ICC WOMEN'S RANKINGS

TEAM RANKINGS (as at December 31, 2016)

		Matches	Points	Rating
1	Australia	48	6,172	129
2	England	47	5,742	122
3	New Zealand	53	6,263	118
4	West Indies	52	5,607	108
5	India	37	3,964	107
6	South Africa	55	5,002	91
7	Pakistan	47	3,629	77
8	Sri Lanka	45	2,998	67
9	Bangladesh	17	726	43
10	Ireland	22	838	38

The ratings are based on all women's Tests, one-day and Twenty20 internationals played since October 1, 2013.

PLAYER RANKINGS

In October 2008, the ICC launched a set of rankings for women cricketers, on the same principles as those for men, based on one-day international performance. Twenty20 rankings were added in September 2012. There are no Test rankings.

The leading players in the women's one-day international rankings on December 31, 2016, were:

Rank	*Batsmen*	*Points*	*Rank*	*Bowlers*	*Points*
1	M. M. Lanning (*Australia*)	804	1	J. N. Goswami (*India*)	687
2	E. A. Perry (*Australia*)	721	2	S. R. Taylor (*West Indies*)	636
3	M. D. Raj (*India*)	715	3	K. H. Brunt (*England*)	606
4	S. W. Bates (*New Zealand*)	701	4	M. Kapp (*South Africa*)	594
5	A. E. Satterthwaite (*NZ*)	689	5	A. Mohammed (*West Indies*)	577
6	S. R. Taylor (*West Indies*)	687	6	J. L. Jonassen (*Australia*)	574
7	A. J. Blackwell (*Australia*)	621	7	E. A. Perry (*Australia*)	547
8	D. J. S. Dottin (*West Indies*)	583	8	M. J. G. Nielsen (*New Zealand*)	544
9	H. Kaur (*India*)	573	9	Sana Mir (*Pakistan*)	539
10	Bismah Maroof (*Pakistan*)	545	10	R. S. Gayakwad (*India*)	527

The leading players in the women's Twenty20 international rankings on December 31, 2016, were:

Rank	*Batsmen*	*Points*	*Rank*	*Bowlers*	*Points*
1	S. R. Taylor (*West Indies*)	684	1	M. J. G. Nielsen (*New Zealand*)	655
2	M. M. Lanning (*Australia*)	662	2	A. Shrubsole (*England*)	632
3	S. W. Bates (*New Zealand*)	652	3	E. A. Perry (*Australia*)	621
4	D. J. S. Dottin (*West Indies*)	613	4	A. Mohammed (*West Indies*)	616
5	M. D. Raj (*India*)	609	5	D. Hazell (*England*)	603
6	S. J. Taylor (*England*)	597	6	M. L. Schutt (*Australia*)	578
7	H. Kaur (*India*)	550	7	H. K. Matthews (*West Indies*)	573
8	Bismah Maroof (*Pakistan*)	543	8	S. Ismail (*South Africa*)	567
9	S. F. M. Devine (*New Zealand*)	537	9	Anam Amin (*Pakistan*)	566
10	M. du Preez (*South Africa*)	531	9	J. L. Jonassen (*Australia*)	566

WOMEN'S ONE-DAY INTERNATIONAL AVERAGES IN CALENDAR YEAR 2016

BATTING (250 runs)

	M	*I*	*NO*	*R*	*HS*	*100*	*50*	*Avge*	*SR*	*Ct/St*
†A. E. Satterthwaite (NZ)	15	14	4	853	137*	3	4	85.30	95.62	11
E. A. Perry (A).	14	13	4	732	95*	0	9	81.33	77.78	4
M. M. Lanning (A).	15	15	3	761	134	3	2	63.41	93.14	11
M. D. Raj (I).	9	8	2	378	89	0	3	63.00	65.51	1
T. T. Beaumont (E)	12	12	1	611	168*	2	3	55.54	86.05	3
N. R. Sciver (E)	12	12	3	495	80	0	5	55.00	112.24	6
K. J. Martin (NZ).	15	13	6	375	81	0	4	53.57	84.84	6/1
S. W. Bates (NZ)	14	13	1	632	110	1	6	52.66	82.07	9
H. C. Knight (E).	14	14	5	464	67*	0	4	51.55	72.16	13
T. Chetty (SA)	10	10	0	506	95	0	5	50.60	68.01	6/4
A. J. Blackwell (A)	15	11	3	383	114	1	3	47.87	84.54	8
N. E. Bolton (A).	15	15	1	589	113	1	4	42.07	71.56	4
†Bismah Maroof (P).	8	8	2	250	91*	0	2	41.66	70.82	3
S. S. Mandhana (I)	8	8	0	320	102	1	2	40.00	85.56	2
S. R. Taylor (WI).	10	10	0	356	85	0	4	35.60	60.75	5
L. Wolvaardt (SA)	10	9	0	318	105	1	2	35.33	58.99	2
D. van Niekerk (SA)	17	17	4	453	81	0	3	34.84	69.37	12
L. Winfield (E).	14	14	0	461	123	1	3	32.92	72.37	6
M. du Preez (SA)	22	22	1	641	116*	1	2	30.52	67.97	5
M. Kapp (SA).	16	16	5	326	69*	0	2	29.63	68.48	3
L. Lee (SA)	18	18	0	494	102	1	2	27.44	97.05	9/2
D. J. S. Dottin (WI)	11	11	0	300	63	0	2	27.27	66.66	6
†W. P. M. Weerakkody (SL) . .	11	11	0	265	69	0	1	24.09	59.68	12/7
G. A. Elwiss (E).	13	12	1	260	77	0	2	23.63	79.75	5
S. E. Luus (SA)	22	21	4	399	60*	0	3	23.47	59.73	15
†C. L. Tryon (SA)	16	16	2	306	92	0	2	21.85	92.72	3

BOWLING (10 wickets, average 26.00)

	Style	*O*	*M*	*R*	*W*	*BB*	*4I*	*Avge*	*SR*	*ER*
D. B. Sharma (I).	RM	51.3	3	136	13	6-20	2	10.46	23.76	2.64
A. Shrubsole (E).	RFM	53.4	6	193	13	4-19	2	14.84	24.76	3.59
K. H. Brunt (E).	RFM	98.1	10	314	21	5-30	1	14.95	28.04	3.19
D. Hazell (E)	OB	58.1	7	180	12	3-21	0	15.00	29.08	3.09
A. Hartley (E).	SLA	76	6	274	17	4-24	2	16.11	26.82	3.60
H. R. Huddleston (NZ).	RM	64.2	3	255	15	5-25	2	17.00	25.73	3.96
R. S. Gayakwad (I).	SLA	83.2	12	295	17	4-21	2	17.35	29.41	3.54
D. J. S. Dottin (WI)	RFM	68.3	1	314	18	5-34	2	17.44	22.83	4.58
H. L. Ferling (A)	RFM	55.1	4	241	13	3-4	0	18.53	25.46	4.36
L. A. Marsh (E)	OB	106.4	9	335	18	4-21	1	18.61	35.55	3.14
S. S. Pandey (I)	RM	64	6	246	13	3-32	0	18.92	29.53	3.84
K. M. Beams (A)	LBG	103.5	14	345	18	4-15	2	19.16	34.61	3.32
J. L. Jonassen (A).	SLA	108	13	397	20	5-50	1	19.85	32.40	3.67
G. M. Harris (A).	OB	65	4	224	11	3-31	0	20.36	35.45	3.44
S. E. Luus (SA)	LBG	149.2	3	755	37	6-36	3	20.40	24.21	5.05
H. C. Knight (E).	OB	88.5	10	351	17	5-26	1	20.64	31.35	3.95
A. S. S. Fletcher (WI).	LBG	78	7	249	12	3-20	0	20.75	39.00	3.19
E. M. Bermingham (NZ)	LBG	80.1	6	272	13	3-18	0	20.92	37.00	3.39
I. Ranaweera (SL)	SLA	56	3	285	13	3-20	0	21.92	25.84	5.08
A. E. Satterthwaite (NZ)	OB	110.5	11	404	18	4-13	1	22.44	36.94	3.64
E. A. Perry (A).	RFM	102	5	488	20	4-45	1	24.40	30.60	4.78
L-M. M. Tahuhu (NZ)	RFM	113	10	442	18	3-34	0	24.55	37.66	3.91
A. Khaka (SA).	RM	121.3	10	552	22	3-27	0	25.09	33.13	4.54

WOMEN'S BIG BASH LEAGUE IN 2015-16

MELINDA FARRELL

1 Sydney Thunder 2 Sydney Sixers 3= Hobart Hurricanes, Perth Scorchers

The inaugural Women's Big Bash League could hardly have been more successful. Impressive crowds and unprecedented viewing figures changed the landscape for women's sport in Australia – and women's cricket worldwide.

In many ways, the conditions were perfectly set. Five years into the thriving men's BBL, the eight city-based teams had been established as household names, on which the women could piggyback. Female players were added to existing marketing strategies, and profiles of men and women appeared side by side on websites. The fledgling competition, which featured 59 matches to the men's 35, had a low-key start: early games were held at outgrounds and squeezed into a couple of weekends before the men's tournament began. Some teams played three times in two days, or even four in three, reflecting the fact that many players were not fully professional.

Once the women's league aligned with the men's, the exposure lifted significantly, with Channel Ten broadcasting several matches in double-headers with the BBL; Cricket Australia injected around $A500,000 to cover the extra costs. Games were initially shown on Ten's secondary free-to-air channel, One, but figures were good enough for them to promote the Melbourne derby between the **Stars** and the **Renegades** to the main channel. It was a hit: the national television audience averaged 372,000, and peaked at over 400,000, while the crowd in the ground rose to 13,000 by the finish. Ten decided to broadcast both semi-finals on top of the scheduled eight matches.

In the first semi-final, league leaders **Sydney Thunder** strangled the fourth-placed **Perth Scorchers** out of a low-scoring game. The following day the **Hobart Hurricanes** – who had exceeded expectations by finishing second, ably captained by England's Heather Knight – met the **Sydney Sixers**, who had recovered remarkably after losing their first six games, winning the next eight, and making it nine in a rain-marred semi.

The all-Sydney final – staged in Melbourne – was scrappy, but tense and exciting, and came down to the final over: the Thunder scrambled across the line, a few hours before their men's team made it a double. Led by the experienced Alex Blackwell, the Thunder had been the league's pace-setters, despite looking thin on star power compared with some sides – though West Indies captain Stafanie Taylor scored 372 for them. The Player of the Tournament was Meg Lanning, who ran up 560 for the Melbourne Stars, while England's Charlotte Edwards made 462 for the Scorchers; the Thunder's Rene Farrell was the leading wicket-taker with 26, followed by Veronica Pyke, a 34-year-old seamer from Hobart, with 22 for the Hurricanes.

The skills possessed by these players were not really shown off in the final – but that couldn't detract from a tournament that surpassed all expectations, and set the benchmark for women's domestic cricket.

WOMEN'S BIG BASH LEAGUE, 2015-16

20-over league plus semi-finals and final

	Played	*Won*	*Lost*	*Points*	*Net run-rate*
SYDNEY THUNDER	14	9	5	18	0.35
HOBART HURRICANES	14	8	6	16	0.19
SYDNEY SIXERS	14	8	6	16	−0.07
PERTH SCORCHERS	14	7	7	14	0.16
Melbourne Stars	14	7	7	14	0.03
Brisbane Heat	14	7	7	14	−0.09
Adelaide Strikers	14	6	8	12	−0.13
Melbourne Renegades	14	4	10	8	−0.46

Semi-final At Adelaide, January 21, 2016. **Sydney Thunder won by eight runs.** ‡**Sydney Thunder 118-6** (20 overs) (A. J. Blackwell 39; R. M. Farrell 3-20); **Perth Scorchers 110-9** (20 overs). *PoM:* A. J. Blackwell. *Despite 39 from Alex Blackwell, the Thunder's total looked below par. But after a strong start from Elyse Villani, the Scorchers lost their momentum.*

Semi-final At Melbourne, January 22, 2016. **Sydney Sixers won by ten wickets** (DLS). ‡**Hobart Hurricanes 86-8** (14 overs) (L. C. Sthalekar 3-9); **Sydney Sixers 55-0** (6.2 overs) (A. J. Healy 32*). *PoM:* L. C. Sthalekar. *Persistent rain curtailed the match; the target was 55 from eight overs, but Alyssa Healy and Ellyse Perry (22*) needed just 6.2 to stretch the Sixers' winning run to nine.*

FINAL

SYDNEY SIXERS v SYDNEY THUNDER

At Melbourne, January 24, 2016. Sydney Thunder won by three wickets. Toss: Sydney Sixers.

Ellyse Perry chose to bat, but contributed only eight as the Sixers scraped to 115, aided by clumsy fielding, though Erin Osborne's off-spin claimed three victims. Rachael Haynes and Stafanie Taylor made a slow but steady start to the reply, and the Thunder appeared to be cruising towards victory, with Alex Blackwell going strong. Then a late collapse – five in 13 balls, three of them run out – threatened to derail the chase. But they too were helped by fielding blunders; it summed up the match when the winning runs came from a bye off a wide.

Player of the Match: E. A. Osborne. *Player of the Tournament:* M. M. Lanning (Melbourne Stars).

Sydney Sixers

		B	*4/6*
1 †A. J. Healy *lbw b 10*	19	20	0
2 *E. A. Perry *c 1 b 7*	8	13	1
3 A. Gardner *st 8 b 6*	20	16	4
4 S. J. McGlashan *lbw b 7*	20	21	2
5 M. Kapp *c and b 6*	7	7	1
6 L. C. Sthalekar *c 1 b 10*	1	2	0
7 S. E. Aley *c 8 b 6*	7	15	0
8 A. R. Reakes *not out*	23	18	2
9 K. Sutherland *not out*	7	8	0
W 3	3		
6 overs: 35-1 (20 overs)	115-7		

1/18 2/43 3/51 4/59 5/60 6/75 7/94

10 E. A. Leys and 11 L. E. M. Smith did not bat.

Farrell 4–11–22–2; Cheatle 4–13–15–0; Carey 4–6–36–0; Gibson 4–12–21–2; Osborne 4–10–21–3.

Sydney Thunder

		B	*4/6*
1 R. L. Haynes *run out*	37	50	1
2 S. R. Taylor *c 3 b 7*	27	35	3
3 N. E. Stalenburg *b 7*	0	1	0
4 *A. J. Blackwell *b 5*	30	23	3
5 N. J. Carey *run out*	1	1	0
6 E. A. Osborne *run out*	1	1	0
7 R. M. Farrell *c 10 b 2*	1	4	0
8 †C. J. Koski *not out*	5	3	0
9 L. R. Cheatle *not out*	0	0	0
B 2, lb 5, w 6, nb 1	14		
6 overs: 26-0 (19.3 overs)	116-7		

1/54 2/56 3/100 4/107 5/107 6/109 7/113

10 M. L. Gibson and 11 B. W. Vakarewa did not bat.

Kapp 4–19–11–1; Perry 3.3–10–22–1; Aley 4–12–19–2; Sthalekar 3–2–24–0; Reakes 1–1–10–0; Smith 4–6–23–0.

Umpires: A. J. Barrow and S. A. J. Craig. Third umpire: G. J. Davidson.
Referee: D. Cox.

KIA SUPER LEAGUE IN 2016

KALIKA MEHTA

1 Southern Vipers   2 Western Storm   3 Loughborough Lightning

At the end of the 2015 summer, after a decisive Ashes defeat, there were calls for sweeping changes to the English women's domestic game. Fears that not only Australia, but traditionally second-tier countries – such as West Indies, India and Pakistan – were getting stronger, while England regressed, were compounded in March, after a semi-final exit at the World Twenty20.

Nevertheless, some eyebrows were raised when the ECB announced a six-team Twenty20 Super League, intended to mirror the Women's Big Bash League in Australia – and to reinvent women's cricket in England. Six franchise hosts were chosen: Hampshire (partnered by other southern counties and Southampton Solent University), Lancashire, Loughborough University, the South-West (a collaboration between Somerset, Gloucestershire and Exeter University), Surrey and Yorkshire. Each assembled a squad of 15, which could include three overseas players, four with England contracts, three from the England Academy and the rest from the development programme.

As the hosts were announced, players allocated and fixtures released, there seemed more questions than answers. The tournament ran from the end of July to mid-August – clashing with the Olympics, two men's Tests with Pakistan and the start of the football season. Clare Connor, the ECB director of women's cricket, said that improving the game was too important to wait for "the right time". But some overseas players were perplexed by the decision not to seek television coverage, even for the final. They were won over by a £2,000 fee for foreign signings, on top of the £150 per match (plus expenses) paid to everyone; there was no sweetener for the domestic players.

Given the negativity, many expected the worst. But over 15,000 attended the 15 group games, and 1,350 came to Chelmsford for finals day. Worries about the quality of cricket soon vanished. While some overseas players struggled to adapt to conditions, West Indies captain Stafanie Taylor entertained the crowds with her big hitting and clever spin for Western Storm. Among the home players, 18-year-old opener Emma Lamb was one of Lancashire Thunder's successes, while Linsey Smith, 21, sometimes outbowled her fellow left-arm spinner, New Zealand's Morna Nielsen, for Southern Vipers.

The tournament ended with the familiar sight of Charlotte Edwards lifting a trophy. Leading the Vipers after her reluctant international retirement in May, she had made an unfortunate start: she collided with team-mate Fi Morris while fielding in their first game, against Surrey Stars, and new concussion protocol ruled her out of the rest of that match, plus the next. When Edwards finally did bat, against Yorkshire Diamonds, Katherine Brunt removed her first ball.

However, **Southern Vipers**, or "Mum's Army", were packed with experience, including three New Zealanders – national captain Suzie Bates, Sara McGlashan and Nielsen – plus former England players Arran Brindle and

Lydia Greenway. They lost only once, to **Western Storm**, who met them in the final; Bates and Brindle played key roles in the Vipers' seven-wicket win.

While there was room for improvement, the league exposed domestic talent – despite no TV coverage – to a wider audience, most importantly England coach Mark Robinson. As the debate over the men's domestic T20 competition raged on, the women were laying the foundations for a franchise model.

KIA SUPER LEAGUE, 2016

20-over league plus play-off and final

	Played	*Won*	*Lost*	*Bonus points*	*Points*	*Net run-rate*
SOUTHERN VIPERS	5	4	1	3	11	1.43
WESTERN STORM	5	4	1	1	9	0.83
LOUGHBOROUGH LIGHTNING	5	3	2	2	8	0.17
Surrey Stars	5	2	3	1	5	–0.27
Yorkshire Diamonds	5	1	4	1	3	–0.36
Lancashire Thunder	5	1	4	0	2	–1.72

Play-off At Chelmsford, August 21. **Western Storm won by five wickets. Loughborough Lightning 124-7** (20 overs) (E. A. Perry 64*; S. R. Taylor 3-31); ‡**Western Storm 128-5** (19.3 overs) (S. R. Taylor 34, H. C. Knight 52). *Ellyse Perry hit the only two sixes of the match in her 48-ball 64*, but Sophie Luff ran out two Joneses – Amy and Evelyn – in three deliveries as Loughborough Lightning slipped to 99-6. Heather Knight led Western Storm's chase with 52 in 43 balls, falling with the scores level; Georgia Hennessy hit the next delivery for four.*

FINAL

SOUTHERN VIPERS v WESTERN STORM

At Chelmsford, August 21. Southern Vipers won by seven wickets. Toss: Southern Vipers.

The teams who had dominated the inaugural Kia Super League won the first prize money handed out for an English women's domestic tournament. Charlotte Edwards's Southern Vipers picked up £25,000, while Western Storm, led by her successor as England captain, Heather Knight, collected £15,000. Edwards had chosen to bowl, but New Zealand's Rachel Priest and West Indies captain Stafanie Taylor started strongly, reaching 74 in the 11th over. Arran Brindle choked the scoring-rate, however, and the Vipers were left with a target of 141. Edwards and Suzie Bates shared another big opening stand – 78 inside ten overs – and, despite two run-outs, Lydia Greenway hit the winning four with seven balls to spare.

Western Storm

		B	*4/6*
1 S. R. Taylor *c 2 b 8*	35	28	3/1
2 †R. H. Priest *c 5 b 1*	57	55	8/1
3 *H. C. Knight *c 11 b 8*	6	9	0
4 F. C. Wilson *not out*	16	13	1
5 L. Lee *c 1 b 10*	6	8	0
6 S. N. Luff *b 1*	2	4	0
7 G. M. Hennessy *not out*	9	3	2
Lb 2, w 7	9		
6 overs: 34-0 (20 overs)	140-5		

1/74 2/102 3/107 4/123 5/131

8 A. Shrubsole, 9 F. R. Davies, 10 J. M. Dibble and 11 C. O'Keefe did not bat.

Farrant 4–12–17–1; Nielsen 4–10–26–0; Bates 4–7–37–2; Smith 3–8–27–0; George 1–1–16–0; Brindle 4–9–15–2.

Southern Vipers

		B	*4/6*
1 S. W. Bates *run out*	52	46	7
2 *C. M. Edwards *b 10*	24	18	3/1
3 G. L. Adams *run out*	15	17	2
4 S. J. McGlashan *not out*	21	19	2
5 L. S. Greenway *not out*	17	13	3
Lb 2, w 12	14		
6 overs: 43-0 (18.5 overs)	143-3		

1/78 2/84 3/104

6 †C. E. Rudd, 7 M. J. G. Nielsen, 8 A. Brindle, 9 L. C. N. Smith, 10 N. E. Farrant and 11 K. L. George did not bat.

Davies 3.5–9–30–0; Knight 2–3–17–0; Shrubsole 3–7–26–0; Taylor 4–11–24–0; Hennessy 2–5–17–0; Dibble 4–10–27–1.

Umpires: R. J. Warren and C. M. Watts.

ENGLISH DOMESTIC CRICKET IN 2016

The new franchise-based Kia Super League attracted all the attention, but it was business as usual on the county front. After the northern interruption of 2015, when Yorkshire broke the stranglehold of Kent and Sussex on the County Championship, Kent claimed a double triumph by winning the Championship (now known as the Royal London Women's One-Day Cup) and the NatWest Women's Twenty20 Cup. In both, there was an unexpected challenge from Warwickshire, who in July entered the final weekend of the Twenty20 competition, heading Division One by five points. Kent needed to win both their remaining matches and hope Warwickshire lost both theirs; they met in the final game, which Kent won by seven wickets.

Kent had the 50-over Royal London One-Day Cup sewn up by the end of August, with a round to spare. Again, they secured the title by beating Warwickshire, who had been ahead of them when the tournament paused to accommodate the Super League, but lost two of their last three games, which allowed Sussex to squeeze into second. It was Kent's seventh Championship title in 11 seasons, and the second time they had combined it with the Twenty20 Cup. And it was the third trophy of 2016 for Charlotte Edwards, forced to retire from the England side but keeping herself busy leading Kent and Super League champions Southern Vipers. Kent dropped only one batting point in eight games, and claimed maximum bowling points every time; they had three of the division's top five wicket-takers.

Lancashire continued to yo-yo between the top tiers, winning Division Two for the second time in three years to go back up along with Nottinghamshire, also relegated in 2015, while newly promoted Somerset and Staffordshire came straight down again, along with Surrey. Only unbeaten Derbyshire came up from Division Three, as more teams were relegated than promoted, to achieve a new structure for the competition. In 2017, there would be two top divisions of eight teams each, while the remaining 20 sides were spread across four regional groups. The ECB abandoned plans for a 50-over version of the Super League. Yorkshire won the Under-17 County Cup and (for the fourth time running) the Under-13 Cup, while Staffordshire and Hampshire shared the Under-17 Cup. The national final of the Regional Leagues was won by Finchley Gunns, the Southern League champions, who beat Walmley from the Midlands.

Earlier in the season, Oxford won two exceptionally one-sided Varsity matches: their openers shared stands of 173 in the Twenty20 match and 206 in the longer game; their bowlers restricted Cambridge to under 60 in both.

NATWEST WOMEN'S TWENTY20 CUP IN 2016

Division One: Kent 20pts, Warwickshire 17, Middlesex 14, Berkshire 12, Lancashire 12, Yorkshire 10, Sussex 10, Nottinghamshire 9.

Division Two: Somerset 20pts, Surrey 18, Wales 17, Worcestershire 16, Essex 13, Hampshire 12, Staffordshire 9, Durham 1.

Division Three: Scotland 32pts, Derbyshire 28, Devon 24, Northamptonshire 16, Oxfordshire 13, Cheshire 13, Hertfordshire 8, Cornwall 8, Shropshire 0.

Division Four: *Group A:* Suffolk 24pts, Norfolk 12, Cambridgeshire 0; *Group B:* Gloucestershire 18, Wiltshire 10, Buckinghamshire 10, Dorset 2; *Group C:* Leicestershire 24, Northumberland 12, Cumbria 8, Lincolnshire 4.

To create two primary divisions of nine teams each in 2017, the top two in Divisions Two and Three were promoted, while the bottom team in Division One (and no one in Division Two) were relegated; Divisions Three and Four were reorganised into three regional groups.

ROYAL LONDON WOMEN'S ONE-DAY CUP IN 2016

50-over league

Division One

						Bonus Points			
	Played	*Won*	*Lost*	*NR*	*A*	*Batting*	*Bowling*	*Points*	*Avge pts*
Kent	8	7	1	0	0	31	32	133	16.62
Sussex	8	4	2	1	1	22	19	81	13.50
Warwickshire	8	4	2	0	2	18	22	80	13.33
Yorkshire	8	4	2	0	2	16	18	74	12.33
Berkshire	8	3	4	0	1	21	26	77	11.00
Middlesex	8	4	3	0	1	19	17	76	10.85
Somerset	8	2	5	1	0	11	18	49	7.00
Surrey	8	1	7	0	0	21	22	53	6.62
Staffordshire	8	1	4	2	1	11	9	30	6.00

Division Two

						Bonus Points			
	Played	*Won*	*Lost*	*NR*	*A*	*Batting*	*Bowling*	*Points*	*Avge pts*
LANCASHIRE	7	4	1	1	1	15	20	75	15.00
NOTTINGHAMSHIRE	7	5	1	0	1	20	18	88	14.66
Hampshire	7	5	2	0	0	19	26	95	13.57
Devon	7	4	3	0	0	22	22	84	12.00
Wales	7	3	2	1	1	13	17	60	12.00
Worcestershire	7	2	4	0	1	16	16	52	8.66
Leicestershire	7	1	4	2	0	11	13	34	6.80
Essex	7	0	7	0	0	15	17	32	4.57

Division Three

						Bonus Points			
	Played	*Won*	*Lost*	*NR*	*A*	*Batting*	*Bowling*	*Points*	*Avge pts*
DERBYSHIRE	8	6	0	1	1	23	22	105	17.50
Durham	8	6	1	1	0	19	23	102	14.57
Gloucestershire	8	5	1	0	2	17	20	87	14.50
Northamptonshire	8	3	2	1	2	12	13	55	11.00
Oxfordshire	8	3	4	0	1	19	23	72	10.28
Netherlands	8	3	4	1	0	22	20	72	10.28
Scotland	8	3	4	1	0	19	20	69	9.85
Cheshire	8	1	6	1	0	13	10	33	4.71
Norfolk	8	0	8	0	0	14	13	27	3.37

Division Four

North and East: Hertfordshire avge pts 17.25, Suffolk 13.75, Northumberland 12.00, Lincolnshire 10.25, Cumbria 9.33, Cambs & Hunts 4.60.

South and West: Shropshire avge pts 17.33, Cornwall 9.50, Dorset 8.66, Wiltshire 7.66, Buckinghamshire 7.33.

Win = 10pts. Up to four batting and four bowling points are available to each team in each match. Final points are divided by the number of matches played (excluding no results and abandoned games) to calculate the average number of points.

To create two primary divisions of eight teams each in 2017, the top two in Division Two plus the top team in Division Three were promoted, while the bottom three in Division One and the bottom two in Division Two were relegated; Divisions Three and Four were reorganised into four regional groups. Cheshire withdrew from the competition.

DIVISION ONE AVERAGES

BATTING (170 runs)

	M	*I*	*NO*	*R*	*HS*	*100*	*50*	*Avge*	*SR*	*Ct/St*
D. N. Wyatt (*Sussex*)	6	6	2	244	120*	1	1	61.00	89.37	4
K. E. White (*Surrey*)	8	8	1	337	98*	0	3	48.14	53.66	3/4
H. C. Knight (*Berks*)	7	7	0	308	92	0	4	44.00	73.68	6
G. L. Adams (*Sussex*)	5	4	0	175	75	0	2	43.75	84.95	1
T. T. Beaumont (*Kent*)	8	8	1	292	72	0	2	41.71	83.90	5
S. W. Bates (*Kent*)	6	6	1	206	75	0	2	41.20	94.93	4
C. E. Rudd (*Berks*)	7	7	1	198	79	0	1	33.00	66.22	3/5
N. R. Sciver (*Surrey*)	7	7	0	190	65	0	2	27.14	100.00	3
†L. S. Greenway (*Kent*)	8	7	0	174	69	0	1	24.85	62.14	8

BOWLING (12 wickets)

	Style	*O*	*M*	*R*	*W*	*BB*	*4I*	*Avge*	*SR*	*ER*
C. V. E. Pape (*Kent*)	RM	37.1	6	99	14	3-9	0	7.07	15.92	2.66
K. C. Thompson (*Yorks*)	SLA	44.3	11	92	12	6-10	1	7.66	22.25	2.06
M. S. Belt (*Kent*)	OB	48.2	6	127	16	5-8	1	7.93	18.12	2.62
G. A. Elwiss (*Sussex*)	RFM	47.3	10	155	15	6-17	2	10.33	19.00	3.26
N. E. Farrant (*Kent*)	LM	50	11	162	15	6-16	2	10.80	20.00	3.24
H. R. Huddleston (*Middx*)	RM	51	6	134	12	3-9	0	11.16	25.50	2.62
L. A. Marsh (*Kent*)	RFM/OB	58	11	168	12	3-28	0	14.00	29.00	2.89
C. R. Scutt (*Surrey*)	LM	52.4	4	227	14	5-30	2	16.21	22.57	4.31
H. V. Jones (*Surrey*)	RM	59.5	4	270	13	4-31	2	20.76	27.61	4.51

NATIONAL KNOCKOUT CUP REGIONAL LEAGUE FINAL IN 2016

At Bishop's Stortford, September 18. **Finchley won by five wickets. Walmley 176-9** (45 overs) (E. V. Smart 44, Extras 33; S. I. R. Dunkley 5-41); ‡**Finchley 179-5** (39 overs) (N. D. Dattani 92*, B. L. Morgan 37). *Sophia Dunkley's leg-spin reduced Walmley to 111-7, before No. 9 Anisha Patel helped extend Finchley's target to 177. Their captain, left-hander Naomi Dattani, batted throughout the chase to complete victory with six overs to spare.*

THE UNIVERSITY MATCHES IN 2016

At Oxford, May 20. **Oxford University won by 162 runs. Oxford University 204-2** (20 overs) (S. Kelly 102*, C. M. Gough 52, Extras 32); ‡**Cambridge University 42** (16.4 overs) (S. L. Moore 3-4, I. N. Brown 3-8). *In a double-header with the men's Varsity T20 match, Sian Kelly (61 balls) and Tina Gough shared an opening stand of 173. Cambridge then collapsed embarrassingly – Extras top-scored with 16, and Kate Gibson was next, with nine. Kelly had scored 127* in the 2015 fixture.*

At Lord's (Nursery), July 1. **Oxford University won by 148 runs.** ‡**Oxford University 206-0 dec** (25 overs) (S. Kelly 118*, C. M. Gough 71*); **Cambridge University 58-7** (30 overs) (S. T. Attrill 4-11). *Played on the Nursery ground while the men were on the main square, this game was reduced from 50 overs to 30 – but, with more rain threatening, Oxford's captain Imogen Brown declared after 25, reasoning they had enough after Kelly (who laced 21 of her 81 balls to the short boundaries) and Gough hurtled to 206-0. Cambridge limped to 58-7, half the runs coming in extras. Sarah Attrill's loopy medium-pacers claimed four wickets, and Gibson top-scored again… with 14.*

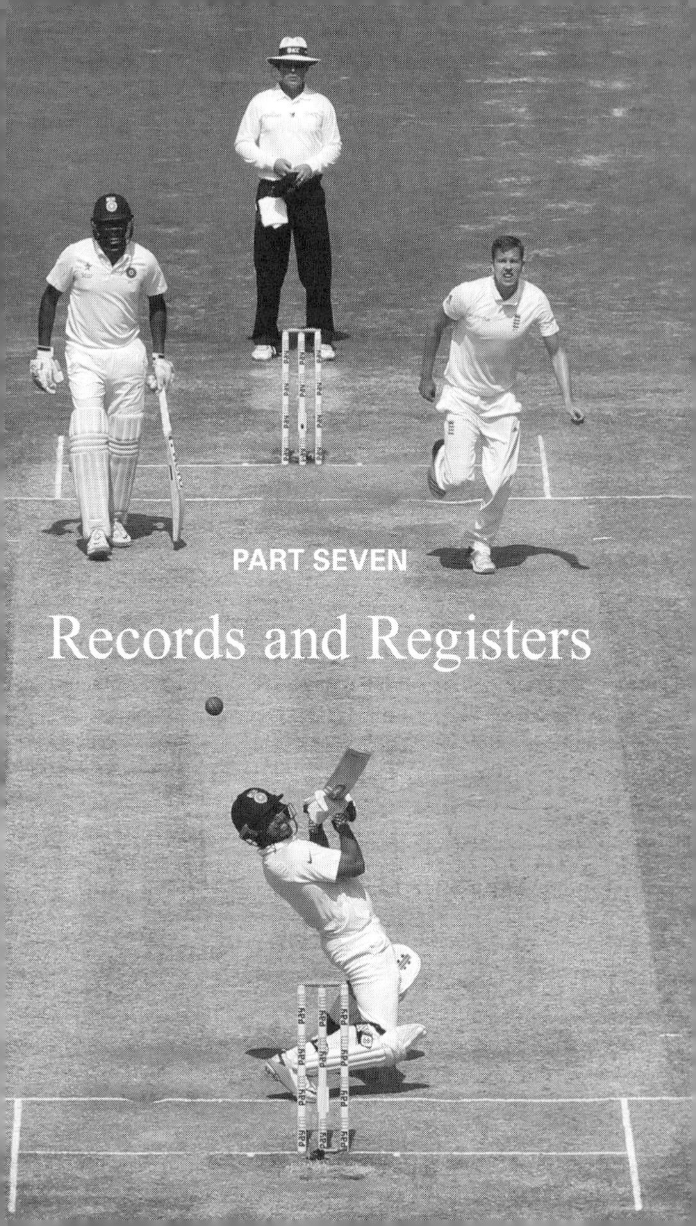

PART SEVEN

Records and Registers

FEATURES OF 2016

This section covers the calendar year. Some of the features listed occurred in matches reported in *Wisden 2016* and some will be reported in *Wisden 2018*; these items are indicated by [W16] or [W18].

A dagger (†) indicates a national record.

Double-Hundreds (90)

	Mins	*Balls*	*4*	*6*		
359*	964	723	45	1	S. B. Gohel	Gujarat v Orissa at Jaipur. [W18]
351*	717	521	37	5	S. M. Gugale	Maharashtra v Delhi at Mumbai. [W18]
342		320	35	10	M. B. Ranasinghe	Sinhalese v Badureliya at Maggona.
318		448	34	1	M. D. U. S. Jayasundera	Ragama v Sinhalese at Colombo.
314*	776	460	32	0	‡P. K. Panchal	Gujarat v Punjab at Belagavi. [W18]
308	514	326	42	9	R. R. Pant	Delhi v Maharashtra at Mumbai. [W18]
304*	662	453	39	0	S. K. Kamat	Goa v Services at Cuttack. [W18]
303*	565	381	32	4	K. K. Nair	India v England (5th Test) at Chennai.
302*	658	469	23	3	‡Azhar Ali	Pakistan v West Indies (1st Test) at Dubai.
300*	654	420	32	0	Hamza Ghanchi	Karachi Whites v Nat. Bank at Karachi. [W18]
293*	598	354	25	6	D. Hooda	Baroda v Punjab at Delhi. [W18]
282*	513	367	38	2	‡B. M. Duckett	Northamptonshire v Sussex at Northampton.
273	418	336	21	14	I. P. Kishan	Jharkhand v Delhi at Thumba. [W18]
260*	570	409	23	2	J-P. Duminy	Cape Cobras v Lions at Paarl.
260	692	520	29	0	Sarmad Bhatti	Islamabad v Peshawar at Lahore. [W18]
260	526	370	26	4	Yuvraj Singh	Punjab v Baroda at Delhi. [W18]
258*	674	500	18	2	A. R. Bawne	Maharashtra v Delhi at Mumbai. [W18]
258	335	198	30	11	B. A. Stokes	England v SA (2nd Test) at Cape Town. [W16]
256*	541	363	28	0	C. A. Pujara	India Blue v India Red at Greater Noida. [W18]
255	552	445	34	1	‡N. L. J. Browne	Essex v Derbyshire at Chelmsford.
254	617	406	27	0	‡J. E. Root	England v Pakistan (2nd Test) at Manchester.
254	506	383	38	0	T. Westley	Essex v Worcestershire at Chelmsford.
250*		425	22	4	S. Baby	Kerala v Services at Delhi. [W18]
250	434	327	34	2	E. C. Joyce	Sussex v Derbyshire at Derby.
250	481	340	39	0	Khurram Manzoor	Karachi Blues v United Bank at Karachi. [W18]
246	364	270	29	3	J. M. Bairstow	Yorkshire v Hampshire at Leeds.
239	504	364	30	3	A. C. Voges	Australia v NZ (1st Test) at Wellington.
237	359	241	25	7	P. Chopra	Himachal Pradesh v Haryana at Valsad. [W18]
235	515	340	25	1	‡V. Kohli	India v England (4th Test) at Mumbai.
235	682	462	24	2	R. Samarth	Karnataka v Jharkhand at Greater Noida. [W18]
234	220	136	26	15	A. H. T. Donald	Glamorgan v Derbyshire at Colwyn Bay.
233*	664	482	17	4	G. H. Vihari	Andhra v Tripura at Valsad. [W18]
232	623	434	28	2	‡P. K. Panchal	Gujarat v Mumbai at Hubli. [W18]
231	482	345	30	1	S. D. Robson	Middlesex v Warwickshire at Lord's.
229*	562	417	22	2	‡N. L. J. Browne	Essex v Derbyshire at Derby.
228	459	338	19	2	Raqibul Hasan	Central Zone v East Zone at Cox's Bazar.
227	548	442	20	0	N. Saini	Haryana v Goa at Ghaziabad. [W18]
225*		361	18	1	A. R. S. Silva	Ragama v Nondescripts at Colombo.
225*	467	328	25	3	S. P. Goswami	Bengal v Madhya Pradesh at Delhi. [W18]
225		318	27	1	‡J. K. Silva	Sinhalese v Colombo at Colombo.
225	598	406	34	0	Asif Ali	FATA v National Bank at Lahore. [W18]
225	481	374	30	4	S. S. Kauthankar	Goa v Haryana at Ghaziabad. [W18]
225	467	332	24	0	J. L. Ontong	Cape Cobras v Dolphins at Paarl. [W18]
225	518	364	21	2	G. B. Podder	Orissa v Assam at Hyderabad. [W18]
224	562	386	20	2	M. Vohra	Punjab v Baroda at Delhi. [W18]
222*	285	212	25	6	Sohaib Maqsood	Utd Bank v Sui Southern Gas at Sialkot. [W18]
221*	578	416	23	0	‡K. K. Jennings	Durham v Yorkshire at Chester-le-Street.
219*	422	289	31	0	I. J. L. Trott	Warwickshire v Middlesex at Lord's.
218	491	355	32	1	M. E. Trescothick	Somerset v Nottinghamshire at Nottingham.

	Mins	*Balls*	*4*	*6*		
218	451	308	31	4	Younis Khan.	Pakistan v England (4th Test) at The Oval.
217		378	26	2	G. K. Amarasinghe	Saracens v Bloomfield at Katunayake.
217	387	270	25	5	J. N. Shah	Saurashtra v Maharashtra at Vizianagram. [W18]
216*	371	250	20	3	D. J. Vilas.	Cape Cobras v Lions at Paarl.
216*	403	274	25	4	H. S. Bhatia	Madhya Prad. v Uttar Prad. at Hyderabad. [W18]
215	467	317	21	2	C. R. Ervine	Matabele Tuskers v Mountaineers at Harare.
215		56	23	1	P. S. P. Handscomb	Victoria v New South Wales at Sydney. [W18]
213	391	242	22	1	‡J. E. Root	Yorkshire v Surrey at Leeds.
212		302	19	3	‡M. L. Udawatte. . . .	Moors v Ports Authority at Colombo.
211*	489	350	23	1	‡P. J. Malan	W Province v Namibia at Walvis Bay. [W18]
211		313	23	1	‡J. K. Silva.	Sinhalese v Moors at Colombo.
211	536	366	20	0	‡V. Kohli	India v New Zealand (3rd Test) at Indore.
210	574	455	28	0	W. R. Smith	Hampshire v Lancashire at Southampton.
208	345	251	26	0	‡B. M. Duckett.	Northamptonshire v Kent at Beckenham.
207*	497	362	24	2	S. R. Dickson	Kent v Derbyshire at Derby.
206*	334	246	26	2	D. J. Bell-Drummond	Kent v Loughborough MCCU at Canterbury.
206*	423	315	25	2	J. L. Denly	Kent v Northamptonshire at Northampton.
205*	580	364	20	0	‡Azhar Ali	Pakistan v Australia (2nd Test) at Melbourne.
205		333	20	0	‡M. L. Udawatte. . . .	Moors v Galle at Colombo.
204*	373	234	27	3	A. J. A. Wheater. . .	Hampshire v Warwickshire at Birmingham.
204*	527	391	19	2	‡P. J. Malan	Western Province v Boland at Paarl. [W18]
204	449	328	25	2	B. A. Godleman . . .	Derbyshire v Worcestershire at Derby.
203*	465	332	22	3	B. P. Sandeep	Hyderabad v Services at Mumbai. [W18]
203*	499	366	29	1	L. J. Woodcock . . .	Wellington v Auckland at Auckland. [W18]
203	320	252	34	2	A. N. Petersen.	Lions v Titans at Potchefstroom.
202*	443	311	28	0	J. A. Raval	Auckland v Otago at Auckland.
202*	492	359	32	0	B. L. D'Oliveira . . .	Worcestershire v Glamorgan at Cardiff.
202*	481	347	29	0	R. I. Newton	Northants v Leicestershire at Northampton.
202*		311	33	2	A. J. Doolan	Tasmania v Western Australia at Perth. [W18]
202	395	291	17	5	A. Lyth	Yorkshire v Surrey at The Oval.
202	770	538	25	0	K. M. Gandhi	Tamil Nadu v Gujarat at Belagavi. [W18]
201*	444	329	23	3	N. R. T. Gubbins . .	Middlesex v Lancashire at Lord's.
201*	398	287	31	0	‡K. K. Jennings	Durham v Surrey at Chester-le-Street.
201*	488	334	21	0	M. C. Juneja	Gujarat v Baroda at Jaipur. [W18]
201	707	477	27	0	H. M. Amla	SA v England (2nd Test) at Cape Town. [W16]
201	495	343	24	3	Nasir Hossain	Rangpur v Sylhet at Sylhet. [W18]
200*	401	310	23	0	S. J. Erwee	KZN Inland v Namibia at Pietermaritzburg.
200*	476	380	23	3	Asif Zakir	Sui Southern Gas v WAPDA at Sialkot. [W18]
200*		364	14	1	Imam-ul-Haq	Habib Bank v WAPDA at Karachi. [W18]
200	375	283	24	0	‡V. Kohli	India v West Indies (1st Test) at North Sound.
200	284	202	37	1	Ahsan Ali	National Bank v FATA at Lahore. [W18]

‡ *Kohli scored three double-hundreds, while Azhar Ali, Browne, Duckett, Jennings, Malan, Panchal, Root, Silva and Udawatte each scored two.*

Hundred on First-Class Debut

101	S. P. Amonkar.	Goa v Services at Cuttack. [W18]
140	Ashutosh Singh	Chhattisgarh v Tripura at Ranchi. [W18]
140	W. P. D. P. Dharmasiri .	Kurunegala Youth v Navy at Kurunegala. [W18]
125	D. A. Escott.	Oxford University v Cambridge University at Oxford.
109*	M. H. P. Gunathilake . .	Kurunegala Youth v Navy at Kurunegala. [W18]
120	Guntashveer Singh	Haryana v Himachal Pradesh at Valsad. [W18]
123*	N. Jagadeesan	Tamil Nadu v Madhya Pradesh at Cuttack. [W18]
110	S. F. Khan	Rajasthan v Orissa at Patiala. [W18]
120	M. M. Madushanka. . . .	Navy v Kurunegala Youth at Kurunegala. [W18]
126	Rizwan Hussain	Lahore Whites v KRL at Lahore. [W18]

105*	W. S. C. Sadamal	Navy v Kurunegala Youth at Kurunegala. [W18]
107	T. D. T. N. Siriwardene	Kalutara Town v Kalutara PCC at Maggona. [W18]
117	M. S. Trunkwala	Maharashtra v Saurashtra at Vizianagram. [W18]
115*	A. S. Yadav	Orissa v Rajasthan at Patiala. [W18]

Three or More Hundreds in Successive Innings

A. C. Voges (Australia/WA).	269*	‡v West Indies (1st Test) at Hobart. [W16]
	106*	‡v West Indies (2nd Test) at Melbourne. [W16]
	149	v New South Wales at Lincoln.
	239	v New Zealand (1st Test) at Wellington.
A. P. Agathangelou (SW Districts)	109 and 199*	v Easterns at Benoni. [W18]
	115*	v KZN Inland at Pietermaritzburg. [W18]
E. J. H. Eckersley (Leicestershire)	117 and 104	v Derbyshire at Leicester.
	107	v Northamptonshire at Northampton.
J. C. Mickleburgh (Essex).	125 and 102	v Cambridge MCCU at Cambridge.
	109	v Sri Lankans at Chelmsford.

‡ *Voges's first two innings were in the calendar year 2015.*

Hundred in Each Innings of a Match

T. D. Agarwal	119	103*	Hyderabad v Jammu & Kashmir at Vadodara. [W18]
A. P. Agathangelou	109	199*	South Western Districts v Easterns at Benoni. [W18]
G. K. Amarasinghe	102	178	Saracens v Badureliya at Panagoda.
S. G. Borthwick.	134	103*	Durham v Lancashire at Chester-le-Street.
D. P. Conway	175*	122*	Gauteng v Namibia at Johannesburg. [W18]
S. M. Davies	115	109	Surrey v Loughborough MCCU at The Oval.
A. R. Easwaran	142	110*	Bengal v Uttar Pradesh at Jaipur. [W18]
E. J. H. Eckersley	117	104	Leicestershire v Derbyshire at Leicester.
S. M. Ervine	103	106	Hampshire v Somerset at Taunton.
H. Hameed	114	100*	Lancashire v Yorkshire at Manchester.
K. K. Jennings.	116	105*	Durham v Somerset at Chester-le-Street.
A. N. Khare.	106	117*	Chhattisgarh v Jammu & Kashmir at Gwalior. [W18]
J. C. Mickleburgh	125	102	Essex v Cambridge MCCU at Cambridge.
D. W. Misal.	106	119	Goa v Himachal Pradesh at Mumbai. [W18]
D. K. H. Mitchell	107*	103	Worcestershire v Northamptonshire at Worcester.
R. R. Pant	117	135	Delhi v Jharkhand at Thumba. [W18]
N. T. Paranavitana.	117	150*	Tamil Union v Chilaw Marians at Colombo.
S. D. Robson	231	106	Middlesex v Warwickshire at Lord's.
C. J. L. Rogers.	132	100*	Somerset v Nottinghamshire at Taunton.
Salman Butt.	125	105*	WAPDA v Habib Bank at Karachi. [W18]
Tasamul Haque	104	100*	Chittagong v Rajshahi at Chittagong. [W18]
B. R. M. Taylor.	114	105*	Nottinghamshire v Durham at Nottingham.
B. S. Wilson	111	117*	Otago v Central Districts at Nelson.

Carrying Bat through Completed Innings

K. C. Brathwaite	142*	West Indies (337) v Pakistan (3rd Test) at Sharjah.
S. R. Dickson.	207*	Kent (412) v Derbyshire at Derby.
R. M. Duffy	90*	Otago (177) v Auckland at Dunedin.
S. B. Gohel	359*	Gujarat (641) v Orissa at Jaipur. [W18]
K. K. Jennings	201*	Durham (401) v Surrey at Chester-le-Street.
R. P. Jones	106*	Lancashire (259) v Middlesex at Manchester.
N. J. Selman.	122*	Glamorgan (236) v Northamptonshire at Swansea.
D. S. Smith.	86*	Windward Is (142) v Trinidad & Tobago at Port-of-Spain. [W18]
Umair Khan	101*	United Bank (285) v Karachi Blues at Karachi. [W18]
Zahid Mansoor.	179*	WAPDA (332) v Sui Southern Gas at Sialkot. [W18]

Hundred before Lunch

J. M. Bairstow . .	107* to 209*	Yorkshire v Hampshire at Leeds (2nd day).
Sohag Gazi	21* to 146	South Zone v East Zone at Fatullah (4th day).
B. A. Stokes. . . .	74* to 204*	England v South Africa (2nd Test) at Cape Town (2nd day). W16

Fast Double-Hundred

A. H. T. Donald	123 balls	Glamorgan v Derbyshire at Colwyn Bay.

Donald equalled R. J. Shastri's world record for Bombay v Baroda at Bombay in 1984-85.

Most Sixes in an Innings

15	A. H. T. Donald (234).	Glamorgan v Derbyshire at Colwyn Bay.
14	I. P. Kishan (273)	Jharkhand v Delhi at Thumba. W18
13	P. A. S. S. Jeewantha (129)	Badureliya v Sinhalese at Colombo. W18
13	B. A. King (194).	Jamaica v Leeward Islands at Basseterre. W18
13	R. R. Pant (135)	Delhi v Jharkhand at Thumba. W18
11	B. A. Stokes (258)	England v South Africa (2nd Test) at Cape Town. W16

Most Runs in Boundaries

	4	*6*		
222	42	9	R. R. Pant (308)	Delhi v Maharashtra at Mumbai. W18
200	35	10	M. B. Ranasinghe (342)	Sinhalese v Badureliya at Maggona.

Longest Innings

Mins		
964	S. B. Gohel (359*)	Gujarat v Orissa at Jaipur. W18
776	P. K. Panchal (314*)	Gujarat v Punjab at Belagavi. W18
770	K. M. Gandhi (202)	Tamil Nadu v Gujarat at Belagavi. W18
717	S. M. Gugale (351*).	Maharashtra v Delhi at Mumbai. W18
707	H. M. Amla (201).	South Africa v England (2nd Test) at Cape Town. W16
692	Sarmad Bhatti (260).	Islamabad v Peshawar at Lahore. W18
682	R. Samarth (235)	Karnataka v Jharkhand at Greater Noida. W18
674	A. R. Bawne (258*)	Maharashtra v Delhi at Mumbai. W18
664	G. H. Vihari (233*)	Andhra v Tripura at Valsad. W18
662	S. K. Kamat (304*)	Goa v Services at Cuttack. W18

Unusual Dismissals

Handled the Ball

S. R. Dickson (0)	Kent v Leicestershire at Leicester.
M. Z. Hamza (10).	Cape Cobras v Knights at Bloemfontein. W18
K. Lesporis (22)	Windward Islands v Barbados at Bridgetown.

Obstructing the Field

Jahid Ali (32)	Pakistan A v Zimbabwe A at Bulawayo.

First-Wicket Partnership of 100 in Each Innings

168	236	N. L. J. Browne/J. C. Mickleburgh, Essex v Cambridge MCCU at Cambridge.
131	190*	D. J. Bell-Drummond/T. W. M. Latham, Kent v Glamorgan at Canterbury.
123	100*	M. E. Trescothick/J. G. Myburgh, Somerset v Nottinghamshire at Nottingham.
140	113	B. M. Duckett/R. I. Newton, Northamptonshire v Glamorgan at Northampton.
212	118	M. A. Agarwal/G. Gambhir, India Blue v India Green at Greater Noida. W18
227	133	H. D. Rutherford/B. S. Wilson, Otago v Central Districts at Nelson. W18
113	124*	E. M. Moore/M. L. Price, Eastern Province v Boland at Port Elizabeth. W18
104	116	S. C. Cook/D. Elgar, South Africa v Sri Lanka (1st Test) at Port Elizabeth.

Highest Wicket Partnerships

First Wicket

306 D. J. van Wyk/S. J. Erwee, KwaZulu-Natal Inland v Namibia at Pietermaritzburg.

303 Imam-ul-Haq/Fakhar Zaman, Habib Bank v WAPDA at Karachi. [W18]

286 D. K. H. Mitchell/B. L. D'Oliveira, Worcestershire v Oxford MCCU at Oxford.

279 F. D. M. Karunaratne/M. B. Ranasinghe, Sinhalese v Badureliya at Maggona.

Second Wicket

343 Hamza Ghanchi/Behram Khan, Karachi Whites v National Bank at Karachi. [W18]

310 E. C. Joyce/L. W. P. Wells, Sussex v Derbyshire at Derby.

305 M. B. Ranasinghe/R. T. M. Wanigamuni, Sinhalese v Badureliya at Maggona.

303 Y. Valli/D. P. Conway, Gauteng v Namibia at Johannesburg. [W18]

292 U. U. Bose/S. K. Patel, Tripura v Services at Guwahati. [W18]

Third Wicket

594*† S. M. Gugale/A. R. Bawne, Maharashtra v Delhi at Mumbai. [W18]

343 M. Vohra/Yuvraj Singh, Punjab v Baroda at Delhi. [W18]

294 B. R. Dunk/A. J. Doolan, Tasmania v Victoria at Hobart.

289 J. A. Burns/S. P. D. Smith, Australia v New Zealand (2nd Test) at Christchurch.

279 D. J. Malan/A. C. Voges, Middlesex v Hampshire at Northwood.

Fourth Wicket

372 J. E. Root/J. M. Bairstow, Yorkshire v Surrey at Leeds.

365 V. Kohli/A. M. Rahane, India v New Zealand (3rd Test) at Indore.

325* Sohaib Maqsood/Akbar-ur-Rehman, United Bank v Sui Southern Gas at Sialkot. [W18]

271 S. D. Chatterjee/M. K. Tiwary, Bengal v Mumbai at Nagpur. [W18]

270 J. Snyman/W. Coulentianos, Easterns v Namibia at Benoni.

Fifth Wicket

393*† J-P. Duminy/D. J. Vilas, Cape Cobras v Lions at Paarl.

323 J. Mubarak/W. U. Tharanga, Nondescripts v Colombo at Colombo.

309 B. A. King/D. C. Thomas, Jamaica v Leeward Islands at Basseterre. [W18]

294 L. W. P. Wells/B. C. Brown, Sussex v Glamorgan at Hove.

279 Asif Ali/Abdul Aziz, FATA v National Bank at Lahore. [W18]

Sixth Wicket

399† B. A. Stokes/J. M. Bairstow, England v South Africa (2nd Test) at Cape Town. [W16]

257* S. Baby/A. R. Chandran, Kerala v Services at Delhi. [W18]

253† L. R. P. L. Taylor/B-J. Watling, New Zealand v Zimbabwe (1st Test) at Bulawayo.

Seventh Wicket

258 Sarmad Bhatti/Zohaib Ahmed, Islamabad v Peshawar at Lahore. [W18]

227 J. M. Bairstow/L. E. Plunkett, Yorkshire v Hampshire at Leeds.

215 R. N. ten Doeschate/J. S. Foster, Essex v Northamptonshire at Northampton.

Eighth Wicket

267 B. P. Sandeep/C. V. Milind, Hyderabad v Services at Mumbai. [W18]

241 V. Kohli/J. Yadav, India v England (4th Test) at Mumbai.

236 P. D. Trego/R. C. Davies, Somerset v Lancashire at Manchester.

222 S. A. Northeast/J. C. Tredwell, Kent v Essex at Chelmsford.

222* B. T. Foakes/G. J. Batty, Surrey v Hampshire at Southampton.

217 R. E. van der Merwe/C. Overton, Somerset v Hampshire at Taunton.

200* S. D. Lad/A. M. Nayar, Mumbai v Madhya Pradesh at Naya Raipur. [W18]

Ninth Wicket

174 M. D. Shanaka/H. M. R. K. B. Herath, Sri Lankans v Leicestershire at Leicester.

163* S. Beigh/Aamir Aziz, Jammu & Kashmir v Services at Jaipur. [W18]

162 J. A. R. Harris/J. K. Fuller, Middlesex v Somerset at Taunton.

150 P. W. H. de Silva/L. D. Madushanka, Colombo v Colts at Colombo. [W18]

Tenth Wicket

119*	S. P. Goswami/S. S. Ghosh, Bengal v Madhya Pradesh at Delhi. W18
115	A. J. C. Silva/W. R. Palleguruge, Army v Saracens at Colombo.
113	C. J. Dala/K. Apea-Adu, Easterns v Gauteng at Johannesburg.
107	J. Clark/K. M. Jarvis, Lancashire v Yorkshire at Manchester.
103	S. D. Lad/B. S. Sandhu, Mumbai v Saurashtra at Gahunje.
102*	Rameez Aziz/Yamin Ahmadzai, Habib Bank v Karachi Blues at Karachi. W18

Most Wickets in an Innings

9-36	C. R. Woakes	Warwickshire v Durham at Birmingham.
9-38	R. M. G. K. Sirisoma	Panadura v Police at Panadura. W18
9-41	N. O. Miller	Jamaica v Trinidad & Tobago at Kingston. W18
9-52	R. I. Keogh	Northamptonshire v Glamorgan at Northampton.
9-68	K. M. C. Bandara	Ports Authority v Army at Colombo.
9-142	M. A. Liyanapathiranage	Chilaw Marians v Tamil Union at Colombo.
8-30	R. Frylinck	Dolphins v Lions at Potchefstroom. W18
8-33	B. M. Scholtz	Namibia v Northern Cape at Windhoek.
8-36	W. W. A. K. R. Fernando	Police v Kurunegala Youth at Katunayake. W18
8-41	P. M. Pushpakumara	Moors v Colombo at Colombo.
8-44	Sameen Gul	United Bank v Habib Bank at Multan. W18
8-46	Mohammad Abbas	KRL v Karachi Whites at Karachi. W18
8-46	R. M. G. K. Sirisoma	Panadura v Navy at Welisara. W18
8-48	H. M. T. I. Herath	Kurunegala Youth v Police at Katunayake. W18
8-49	D. Bishoo	West Indies v Pakistan (1st Test) at Dubai.
8-53	S. B. Jakati	Goa v Andhra at Dhanbad. W18
8-56	Bilawal Bhatti	Sui Northern Gas v United Bank at Karachi.
8-58	J. L. Jaggesar	Trinidad & Tobago v Jamaica at Kingston.
8-60	S. R. Harmer	Warriors v Cape Cobras at Port Elizabeth.
8-63	H. M. R. K. B. Herath	Sri Lanka v Zimbabwe (2nd Test) at Harare.
8-63	Khalid Usman	WAPDA v Lahore Blues at Lahore. W18
8-67	N. O. Miller	Jamaica v Barbados at Kingston.
8-73	B. W. Sanderson	Northamptonshire v Gloucestershire at Northampton.
8-73	A. A. Sanklecha	Maharashtra v Assam at Chennai. W18
8-74	K. A. Jamieson	Canterbury v Auckland at Rangiora. W18
8-74	Rashid Khan	Afghanistan v England Lions at Abu Dhabi. W18
8-83	A. K. Das	Assam v Punjab at Valsad.
8-102	I. C. Pandey	Madhya Pradesh v Punjab at Rohtak. W18
8-102	Tahir Khan	PIA v KRL at Abbottabad. W18
8-108	R. R. S. Cornwall	West Indies A v Sri Lanka A at Colombo.

Most Wickets in a Match

14-62	R. Frylinck	Dolphins v Lions at Potchefstroom. W18
14-93	Mohammad Abbas	KRL v Karachi Whites at Karachi. W18
14-94	A. A. Sanklecha	Maharashtra v Vidarbha at Kolkata. W18
14-95	O. E. G. Baartman	South Western Districts v KwaZulu-Natal at Oudtshoorn. W18
13-71	K. R. Smuts	Eastern Province v Boland at Paarl.
13-88	Irfanullah Shah	FATA v Rawalpindi at Rawalpindi. W18
13-105	E. M. C. D. Edirisinghe	Nondescripts v Army at Panagoda.
13-119	P. M. Pushpakumara	Moors v Colombo at Colombo.
13-125	R. I. Keogh	Northamptonshire v Glamorgan at Northampton.
13-140	R. Ashwin	India v New Zealand (3rd Test) at Indore.
13-144	K. Rabada	South Africa v England (4th Test) at Centurion. W16
13-145	H. M. R. K. B. Herath	Sri Lanka v Australia (3rd Test) at Colombo.
13-152	H. M. R. K. B. Herath	Sri Lanka v Zimbabwe (2nd Test) at Harare.
13-157	K. A. Maharaj	Dolphins v Warriors at East London. W18
13-160	R. M. G. K. Sirisoma	Panadura v Kalutara Town at Panadura. W18
13-198	R. M. G. K. Sirisoma	Panadura v Navy at Welisara. W18

Outstanding Innings Analyses

3–3–0–4	A. A. Bhandari	Hyderabad v Himachal Pradesh at Guwahati. [W18]

Four Wickets in Four Balls

N. G. R. P. Jayasuriya	Colts v Badureliya at Maggona.
K. R. Smuts	Eastern Province v Boland at Paarl.

Hat-Tricks (10)

J. T. Ball	Nottinghamshire v Middlesex at Nottingham.
R. K. Datta	Tripura v Himachal Pradesh at Kalyani. [W18]
B. Fernando	Sinhalese v Badureliya at Maggona.
H. M. R. K. B. Herath	Sri Lanka v Australia (2nd Test) at Galle.
N. G. R. P. Jayasuriya	Colts v Badureliya at Maggona.
M. C. Kleinveldt	Western Province v Namibia at Walvis Bay. [W18]
C. N. Miles	Gloucestershire v Essex at Cheltenham.
T. I. Ntuli	Free State v Namibia at Bloemfontein. [W18]
T. S. Roland-Jones	Middlesex v Yorkshire at Lord's.
K. R. Smuts	Eastern Province v Boland at Paarl.

Wicket with First Ball in First-Class Career

M. A. T. S. Bandara	Ragama v Galle at Colombo.
E. M. K. K. R. Ekanayake	Kurunegala Youth v Kalutara PCC at Maggona. [W18]
G. H. S. Garton	Sussex v Leeds/Bradford MCCU at Hove.
J. P. le Roux	North West v Free State at Potchefstroom.
L. T. Ngidi	Northerns v Border at Centurion.
S. S. A. H. Nirmal	Kalutara Town v Panadura at Panadura. [W18]
O. R. Thomas	Jamaica v Windward Islands at Kingston. [W18]

Hundred and Four Wickets in Four Balls in the Same Match

K. R. Smuts	Eastern Province v Boland at Paarl.

Match Double (100 runs and 10 wickets)

K. R. Smuts	108; 7-36, 6-35	Eastern Province v Boland at Paarl.

Most Wicketkeeping Dismissals in an Innings

7 (7ct)	S. W. Billings	Kent v Worcestershire at Canterbury.
7 (6ct, 1st)	H. Klaasen	Titans v Warriors at Port Elizabeth. [W18]
7 (7ct)	Mohammad Hasan	Karachi Whites v Sui Northern Gas at Karachi. [W18]
7 (6ct, 1st)	R. S. Second	Knights v Warriors at Port Elizabeth. [W18]
6 (5ct, 1st)	L. Abeyratne	Colombo v Galle at Colombo.
6 (5ct, 1st)	T. R. Ambrose	Warwickshire v Nottinghamshire at Birmingham.
6 (5ct, 1st)	M. Azharuddeen	Kerala v Andhra at Guwahati. [W18]
6 (6ct)	J. M. Bairstow	England v South Africa (3rd Test) at Johannesburg. [W16]
6 (6ct)	B. Cachopa	Auckland v Wellington at Wellington.
6 (6ct)	M. C. Christensen	Eastern Province v Northerns at Centurion. [W18]
6 (5ct, 1st)	I. Dev Singh	Jammu & Kashmir v Chhattisgarh at Gwalior. [W18]
6 (6ct)	S. B. Harper	Victoria v Tasmania at Melbourne.
6 (6ct)	S. B. Harper	Victoria v South Australia at Melbourne. [W18]
6 (6ct)	Jamal Anwar	Habib Bank v United Bank at Multan. [W18]
6 (6ct)	Mohammad Waqas	Karachi Blues v WAPDA at Karachi. [W18]
6 (6ct)	N. V. Ojha	Madhya Pradesh v Mumbai at Cuttack.
6 (5ct, 1st)	N. V. Ojha	Madhya Pradesh v Gujarat at Nagothane. [W18]
6 (6ct)	K. S. T. Perera	Badureliya v Saracens at Panagoda.

6 (5ct, 1st)	W. P. Saha	India v West Indies (1st Test) at North Sound.
6 (4ct, 2st)	Shehzar Mohammad	PIA v FATA at Sialkot. [W18]
6 (6ct)	T. I. F. Triffitt	Tasmania v Victoria at Hobart.
6 (6ct)	Umar Siddiq	United Bank v WAPDA at Sialkot. [W18]
6 (6ct)	N. J. van den Bergh	Lions v Titans at Potchefstroom.
6 (5ct, 1st)	M. S. Wade	Victoria v Queensland at Melbourne. [W18]
6 (6ct)	S. M. Whiteman	Western Australia v Queensland at Brisbane.

Most Wicketkeeping Dismissals in a Match

11 (11ct)	Mohammad Hasan	Karachi Whites v Sui Northern Gas at Karachi. [W18]
11 (10ct, 1st)	R. S. Second	Knights v Warriors at Port Elizabeth. [W18]
10 (10ct)	Mohammad Waqas	Karachi Blues v WAPDA at Karachi. [W18]
9 (9ct)	J. M. Bairstow	England v South Africa (3rd Test) at Johannesburg. [W16]
9 (9ct)	J. M. Bairstow	England v Sri Lanka (1st Test) at Leeds.
9 (8ct, 1st)	S. W. Billings	Kent v Worcestershire at Canterbury.
9 (9ct)	S. B. Harper	Victoria v Tasmania at Melbourne.
9 (9ct)	Kamran Akmal	WAPDA v Karachi Blues at Karachi. [W18]
9 (9ct)	M. Rawat	Railways v Bengal at Dharamsala. [W18]
9 (6ct, 3st)	D. M. Sarathchandra	Tamil Union v Saracens at Mattegoda.
9 (9ct)	J. A. Simpson	Middlesex v Somerset at Taunton.
9 (9ct)	Umar Siddiq	United Bank v WAPDA at Sialkot. [W18]
9 (9ct)	M. A. Wallace	Glamorgan v Derbyshire at Colwyn Bay.
9 (9ct)	M. A. Wallace	Glamorgan v Worcestershire at Worcester.
9 (9ct)	Zulfiqar Jan	KRL v Sui Northern Gas at Faisalabad. [W18]
9 (8ct, 1st)	Zulfiqar Jan	KRL v Habib Bank at Karachi. [W18]

Most Catches in an Innings in the Field

5	J. L. Carter	Barbados v Guyana at Providence. [W18]
5	A. C. Voges	Western Australia v Queensland at Perth. [W18]
5	Zohaib Khan	Habib Bank v Karachi Blues at Karachi. [W18]

Most Catches in a Match in the Field

7	O. Peters	Leeward Islands v Jamaica at North Sound.
7	M. E. Trescothick	Somerset v Warwickshire at Taunton.
6	J. L. Carter	Barbados v Guyana at Bridgetown.
6	J. L. Carter	Barbados v Leeward Islands at Basseterre.
6	L. S. Livingstone	Lancashire v Durham at Chester-le-Street.
6	M. H. W. Papps	Wellington v Auckland at Wellington.
6	A. K. Perera	Nondescripts v Army at Panagoda.
6	S. P. D. Smith	Australia v Sri Lanka (3rd Test) at Colombo.
6	A. C. Voges	Western Australia v Queensland at Perth. [W18]
6	D. S. Weerakkody	Nondescripts v Bloomfield at Colombo. [W18]

No Byes Conceded in Total of 500 or More

A. Bains	Himachal Pradesh v Tripura (549) at Kalyani. [W18]
O. B. Cox	Worcestershire v Northamptonshire (551) at Worcester.
Faizan Khan	National Bank v Karachi Whites (628-5 dec) at Karachi. [W18]
Faizan Khan	National Bank v KRL (503-9 dec) at Rawalpindi. [W18]
Farhan Khan	Lahore Whites v Sui Northern Gas (545-9 dec) at Lahore. [W18]
Farhan Khan	Lahore Whites v Karachi Whites (500-8 dec) at Lahore. [W18]
G. Khera	Punjab v Baroda (529) at Delhi. [W18]
M. Mosehle	Lions v Knights (572) at Kimberley. [W18]
D. Murphy	Northamptonshire v Essex (640-9 dec) at Northampton.
W. P. Saha	Bengal v Madhya Pradesh (560-9 dec) at Mumbai.
W. S. R. Samarawickrama	Colts v Moors (597) at Colombo.

Sarfraz Ahmed	Pakistan v England (589-8 dec) (2nd Test) at Manchester.
D. J. Vilas	Cape Cobras v Warriors (525-7 dec) at Cape Town. W18
M. S. Wade	Victoria v Tasmania (566-8 dec) at Hobart.
S. M. Whiteman	Western Australia v South Australia (505-9 dec) at Perth. W18

Highest Innings Totals

759-7 dec	India v England (5th Test) at Chennai.
715-8	Islamabad v Peshawar at Lahore. W18
707	India Blue v India Green at Greater Noida. W18
702-7	Karachi Blues v United Bank at Karachi. W18
693-6 dec	India Blue v India Red at Greater Noida. W18
670	Punjab v Baroda at Delhi. W18
665	Ragama v Sinhalese at Colombo.
657-8 dec	Saurashtra v Maharashtra at Vizianagram. W18
647	Ragama v Nondescripts at Colombo.
641	Gujarat v Orissa at Jaipur. W18
640-9 dec	Essex v Northamptonshire at Northampton.
637-7 dec	Surrey v Hampshire at Southampton.
635-2 dec	Maharashtra v Delhi at Mumbai. W18
631	India v England (4th Test) at Mumbai.

Lowest Innings Totals

36	Himachal Pradesh v Hyderabad at Guwahati. W18
43	Leicestershire v Worcestershire at Leicester.
48‡	Easterns v Northern Cape at Benoni.
49‡	Namibia v KwaZulu-Natal at Durban.
49	Kalutara PCC v Ports Authority at Panagoda. W18
52	Cambridge MCCU v Nottinghamshire at Cambridge.
57	Titans v Knights at Centurion. W18
59	Vidarbha v Maharashtra at Kolkata. W18
64‡	Windward Islands v Jamaica at Kingston. W18
68	Lions v Warriors at Port Elizabeth.
69	Assam v Rajasthan at Visakhapatnam. W18
69	Northern Cape v Border at East London. W18

‡ *One batsman absent hurt.*

Highest Fourth-Innings Totals

482-6	Rest of India v Mumbai at Mumbai (set 480).
450	Pakistan v Australia (1st Test) at Brisbane (set 490).
432	Bengal v Madhya Pradesh at Mumbai (set 788).
404-8	Worcestershire v Northamptonshire at Worcester (set 401).

Match Aggregate of 1,500 Runs

1,612 for 30	Sinhalese (595-6 dec and 237-4 dec) v Colombo (430 and 350) at Colombo.
1,573 for 35	Mumbai (603 and 182) v Rest of India (306 and 482-6) at Mumbai.
1,549 for 36	Auckland (373 and 425-6 dec) v Central Districts (416 and 335) at Auckland.

Matches Dominated by Batting (1,200 runs at 80 runs per wicket)

1,283-12 (106.91) Maharashtra (635-2 dec and 58-0) v Delhi (590) at Mumbai. W18

Six Individual Fifties in an Innings

Tamil Union (538-7 dec) v Sinhalese at Colombo.
Moors (597) v Colts at Colombo.
Mumbai (603) v Rest of India at Mumbai.
Durham (607-7 dec) v Surrey at The Oval.
Essex (640-9 dec) v Northamptonshire at Northampton.

Large Margin of Victory

Essex (416-4 dec and 409-7 dec) beat Cambridge MCCU (124 and 178) at Cambridge by 523 runs.
Notts (530-8 dec and 170-5 dec) beat Cambridge MCCU (52 and 131) at Cambridge by 517 runs.
Worcestershire (345-9 dec and 451-3 dec) beat Oxford MCCU (190 and 124) at Oxford by 482 runs.

Victory Losing Only One Wicket

Namibia (179 and 118) lost to KwaZulu-Natal Inland (416-1 dec) at Pietermaritzburg.

Eleven Bowlers in an Innings

Warwickshire v Middlesex (304-6 dec) at Lord's.

Most Extras in an Innings

	b	*lb*	*w*	*nb*	
60	4	28	0	28	Essex (441-8 dec) v Northamptonshire at Chelmsford.
60	36	10	8	6	Leicestershire (332) v Northamptonshire at Leicester.
58	14	16	4	24	Leicestershire (519) v Northamptonshire at Northampton.
56	8	15	4	29	Leicestershire (473-8 dec) v Sussex at Hove.
54	14	17	5	18	Middlesex (467-3 dec) v Hampshire at Northwood.
52	28	13	6	5	Sri Lanka A (299) v Pakistan A at Leicester.
50	18	16	0	16	Gloucestershire (367) v Sussex at Hove.
50	16	10	11	13	WAPDA (342) v Karachi Blues at Karachi. [W18]

Career Aggregate Milestones

25,000 runs	C. J. L. Rogers.
15,000 runs	H. M. Amla, P. D. Collingwood.
10,000 runs	S. Badrinath, R. S. Bopara, S. M. Davies, S. M. Ervine, Fawad Alam, P. G. Fulton, P. J. Horton, M. Kaif, D. K. H. Mitchell, C. D. Nash, S. R. Patel, C. A. Pujara, A. G. Puttick.
500 wickets	A. Mishra, N. Wagner.
500 dismissals	Adnan Akmal, N. J. O'Brien.
500 catches in the field	M. E. Trescothick.

RECORDS

Compiled by Philip Bailey

This section covers

- first-class records to December 31, 2016 (page 1225).
- List A one-day records to December 31, 2016 (page 1253).
- List A Twenty20 records to December 31, 2016 (page 1256).
- Test records to January 23, 2017, the end of the New Zealand v Bangladesh series (page 1258).
- Test records series by series (page 1291).
- one-day international records to December 31, 2016 (page 1331).
- Twenty20 international records to December 31, 2016 (page 1341).
- miscellaneous other records to December 31, 2016 (page 1346).
- women's Test records, one-day international and Twenty20 international records to December 31, 2016 (page 1351).

The sequence

- Test series records begin with those involving England, arranged in the order their opponents entered Test cricket (Australia, South Africa, West Indies, New Zealand, India, Pakistan, Sri Lanka, Zimbabwe, Bangladesh). Next come all remaining series involving Australia, then South Africa – and so on until Zimbabwe v Bangladesh records appear on page 1328.

Notes

- Unless otherwise stated, all records apply only to first-class cricket. This is considered to have started in 1815, after the Napoleonic War.
- mid-year seasons taking place outside England are given simply as 2015, 2016, etc.
- (E), (A), (SA), (WI), (NZ), (I), (P), (SL), (Z) or (B) indicates the nationality of a player or the country in which a record was made.
- in career records, dates in italic indicate seasons embracing two different years (i.e. non-English seasons). In these cases, only the first year is given, e.g. *2015* for 2015-16.

See also

- up-to-date records on www.wisdenrecords.com.
- Features of 2016 (page 1206).

CONTENTS

FIRST-CLASS RECORDS

BATTING RECORDS

Highest Individual Innings 1225
Double-Hundred on Debut 1225
Two Separate Hundreds on Debut. 1226
Two Double-Hundreds in a Match 1226
Triple-Hundred and Hundred in a Match 1226
Double-Hundred and Hundred in a Match 1226
Two Separate Hundreds in a Match Most Times 1226
Five Hundreds or More in Succession. 1227
Most Hundreds in a Season. 1227
Most Double-Hundreds in a Career. 1227

Most Hundreds in a Career . . . 1228
Most Runs in a Season . . . 1228
2,000 Runs in a Season Most Times . . . 1229
1,000 Runs in a Season Most Times . . . 1229
Highest Aggregates outside England . . . 1229
Leading Batsmen in an English Season . . . 1230
Most Runs . . . 1231
Highest Career Average . . . 1232
Fast Scoring . . . 1233
Most Runs in a Day by One Batsman . . . 1234
Longest Innings . . . 1234
1,000 Runs in May . . . 1234
1,000 Runs in April and May . . . 1234
Most Runs Scored off an Over . . . 1235
Most Sixes in an Innings . . . 1235
Most Sixes in a Match . . . 1236
Most Sixes in a Season . . . 1236
Most Boundaries in an Innings . . . 1236
Partnerships over 500 . . . 1236
Highest Partnerships for each Wicket . . . 1237
Unusual Dismissals . . . 1238

BOWLING RECORDS

Ten Wickets in an Innings . . . 1239
Outstanding Bowling Analyses . . . 1240
Most Wickets in a Match . . . 1240
Four Wickets with Consecutive Balls . . . 1241
Hat-Tricks . . . 1241
250 Wickets in a Season . . . 1242
100 Wickets in a Season Most Times . . . 1242
100 Wickets in a Season outside England . . . 1243
Leading Bowlers in an English Season . . . 1243
Most Wickets . . . 1243

ALL-ROUND RECORDS

Remarkable All-Round Matches . . . 1245
Hundred and Hat-Trick . . . 1245
The Double . . . 1245

WICKETKEEPING RECORDS

Most Dismissals in an Innings . . . 1246
Wicketkeepers' Hat-Tricks . . . 1246
Most Dismissals in a Match . . . 1247
100 Dismissals in a Season . . . 1247
Most Dismissals . . . 1247

FIELDING RECORDS

Most Catches in an Innings . . . 1248
Most Catches in a Match . . . 1248
Most Catches in a Season . . . 1248
Most Catches . . . 1248

TEAM RECORDS

Highest Innings Totals . . . 1249
Highest Fourth-Innings Totals . . . 1249
Most Runs in a Day (One Side) . . . 1249
Most Runs in a Day (Both Sides) . . . 1249
Highest Aggregates in a Match . . . 1250

Lowest Innings Totals 1250
Lowest Totals in a Match 1250
Lowest Aggregate in a Completed Match 1251
Largest Victories 1251
Tied Matches 1251
Matches Completed on First Day 1252
Shortest Completed Matches 1252

LIST A ONE-DAY RECORDS

Batting Records 1253
Bowling Records 1254
Wicketkeeping and Fielding Records 1254
Team Records 1255

LIST A TWENTY20 RECORDS

Batting Records 1256
Bowling Records 1257
Wicketkeeping and Fielding Records 1257
Team Records 1257

TEST RECORDS

BATTING RECORDS

Highest Individual Innings 1258
Hundred on Test Debut 1258
Two Separate Hundreds in a Test 1260
Most Double-Hundreds 1261
Most Hundreds 1261
Most Hundreds against One Team 1261
Most Ducks 1261
Carrying Bat through Test Innings 1261
Most Runs in a Series 1262
Most Runs in a Calendar Year 1263
Most Runs 1263
Most Runs for Each Country 1264
Highest Career Average 1265
Best Career Strike-Rates 1265
Highest Percentage of Team's Runs over Career 1266
Fastest Fifties 1266
Fastest Hundreds 1267
Fastest Double-Hundreds 1267
Fastest Triple-Hundreds 1267
Most Runs Scored off an Over 1267
Most Runs in a Day 1268
Most Sixes in a Career 1268
Slowest Individual Batting 1268
Slowest Hundreds 1268
Partnerships over 400 1269
Highest Partnerships for each Wicket 1269
Highest Partnerships for each Country 1271
Unusual Dismissals 1273

BOWLING RECORDS

Most Wickets in an Innings 1273
Outstanding Bowling Analyses 1274
Wicket with First Ball in Test Cricket 1274
Hat-Tricks 1275
Four Wickets in Five Balls 1275

Most Wickets in a Test 1275
Most Balls Bowled in a Test 1275
Most Wickets in a Series 1276
Most Wickets in a Calendar Year 1276
Most Wickets 1276
Most Wickets for Each Country 1277
Best Career Averages 1278
Best Career Strike-Rates 1278
Best Career Economy-Rates 1278
Highest Percentage of Team's Wickets over Career 1279

ALL-ROUND RECORDS

Hundred and Five Wickets in an Innings 1279
Hundred and Five Dismissals in an Innings 1280
100 Runs and Ten Wickets in a Test 1280
2,000 Runs and 200 Wickets 1280

WICKETKEEPING RECORDS

Most Dismissals in an Innings 1281
Most Stumpings in an Innings 1281
Most Dismissals in a Test 1281
Most Dismissals in a Series 1282
Most Dismissals 1282

FIELDING RECORDS

Most Catches in an Innings 1282
Most Catches in a Test 1283
Most Catches in a Series 1283
Most Catches 1283

TEAM RECORDS

Highest Innings Totals 1283
Highest Fourth-Innings Totals 1284
Most Runs in a Day 1284
Most Wickets in a Day 1284
Highest Aggregates in a Test 1285
Lowest Innings Totals 1285
Fewest Runs in a Full Day's Play 1285
Lowest Aggregates in a Completed Test 1286
Largest Victories 1286
Tied Tests 1286
Most Consecutive Test Victories 1286
Most Consecutive Tests without Victory 1286
Whitewashes 1287

PLAYERS

Youngest Test Players 1287
Oldest Players on Test Debut 1287
Oldest Test Players 1288
Most Test Appearances 1288
Most Consecutive Test Appearances 1288
Most Tests as Captain 1289

UMPIRES

Most Tests 1289

TEST SERIES

Summary of Tests 1290
England v Australia 1291
England v South Africa 1296
England v West Indies 1298
England v New Zealand 1299
England v India 1300
England v Pakistan 1301
England v Sri Lanka 1302
England v Zimbabwe 1302
England v Bangladesh 1303
Australia v South Africa 1303
Australia v West Indies 1304
Australia v New Zealand 1305
Australia v India 1306
Australia v Pakistan 1307
Australia v Sri Lanka 1308
Australia v Zimbabwe 1309
Australia v Bangladesh 1309
Australia v ICC World XI 1309
South Africa v West Indies 1310
South Africa v New Zealand 1310
South Africa v India 1311
South Africa v Pakistan 1312
South Africa v Sri Lanka 1312
South Africa v Zimbabwe 1313
South Africa v Bangladesh 1314
West Indies v New Zealand 1314
West Indies v India 1315
West Indies v Pakistan 1316
West Indies v Sri Lanka 1316
West Indies v Zimbabwe 1317
West Indies v Bangladesh 1318
New Zealand v India 1318
New Zealand v Pakistan 1319
New Zealand v Sri Lanka 1320
New Zealand v Zimbabwe 1321
New Zealand v Bangladesh 1321
India v Pakistan 1322
India v Sri Lanka 1323
India v Zimbabwe 1323
India v Bangladesh 1324
Pakistan v Sri Lanka 1324
Pakistan v Zimbabwe 1325
Pakistan v Bangladesh 1326
Sri Lanka v Zimbabwe 1326
Sri Lanka v Bangladesh 1327
Zimbabwe v Bangladesh 1328
Test Grounds 1328

ONE-DAY INTERNATIONAL RECORDS

Summary of One-Day Internationals 1331
Results Summary of One-Day Internationals 1332
Highest Individual Innings 1332
Most Hundreds 1333
Most Runs 1333
Best Career Strike-Rates by Batsmen 1334
Fast Scoring 1334
Highest Partnership for each Wicket 1335
Best Bowling Analyses 1335

Hat-Tricks 1335
Most Wickets. . . . 1336
Best Career Strike-Rates by Bowlers 1336
Best Career Economy-Rates 1337
Most Dismissals in an Innings. . . . 1337
Most Dismissals. . . . 1337
Most Catches in an Innings 1338
Most Catches 1338
Highest Innings Totals. . . . 1338
Highest Totals Batting Second 1338
Highest Match Aggregates 1339
Lowest Innings Totals 1339
Largest Victories 1339
Tied Matches 1339
Most Appearances 1340
Most Matches as Captain. . . . 1340
World Cup Finals 1340

TWENTY20 INTERNATIONAL RECORDS

Results Summary of Twenty20 Internationals 1341
Batting Records 1341
Bowling Records 1343
Wicketkeeping and Fielding Records 1344
Team Records 1345
Most Appearances 1345
World Twenty20 Finals. . . . 1345

MISCELLANEOUS RECORDS

Large Attendances. . . . 1346
Lord's Cricket Ground 1346
Highest Individual Scores in Minor Cricket 1347
Highest Partnerships in Minor Cricket 1347
Most Wickets with Consecutive Balls in Minor Cricket. . . . 1347
Ten Wickets for No Runs in Minor Cricket 1347
Nought All Out in Minor Cricket 1348
Most Dismissals in an Innings in Minor Cricket. . . . 1348
Record Hit 1348
Throwing the Cricket Ball. . . . 1348
Most County Championship Appearances 1348
Most Consecutive County Championship Appearances 1349
Most County Championship Appearances by Umpires 1349
Most Seasons on First-Class Umpires' List. . . . 1349

WOMEN'S TEST AND OTHER INTERNATIONAL RECORDS

Test Batting Records 1351
Test Bowling Records 1351
Test Wicketkeeping Records. . . . 1351
Test Team Records 1352
One-Day International Records. . . . 1352
World Cup Winners 1354
Twenty20 International Records 1354
World Twenty20 Winners 1355

NOTES ON RECORDS

No limits in limited-overs

ROB SMYTH

There are limits in white-ball cricket, but only on the number of overs. The modern batsman thinks anything can be achieved, usually with good reason; as a consequence the record books have become one never-ending rewrite. In 2016, the extreme rebranding of English white-ball cricket reached a peak when they hit 444 for three against Pakistan at Nottingham in late August, by one run the highest score in one-day international history, with Alex Hales contributing an England-record 171. It was also the third highest List A score of all time. The second highest had come on the same ground two months earlier: Nottinghamshire's 445 for eight against Northamptonshire (who replied with 425).

In Twenty20, Australia went one better than England. Not only did their 263 for three against Sri Lanka at Pallekele break the international record, it also equalled the highest total in any Twenty20 match (Royal Challengers Bangalore had made 263 for five during the 2013 IPL).

With such relentless power hitting, a degree of crossover into Test cricket is inevitable and, by the end of his career, Brendon McCullum was almost playing Test20 cricket. In his final appearance, against Australia in Christchurch, he smashed the fastest hundred in Test history, from 54 balls. Who writes your records?

There is still plenty to be said for the long game, however. Ask Swapnil Gugale and Ankit Bawne: they added an unbroken 594 for Maharashtra against Delhi, the second highest partnership for any wicket in first-class cricket. Or Alastair Cook, who became the first Englishman to reach 10,000 Test runs, then the first to 11,000. Younis Khan began 2017 in sight of becoming the first Pakistani to score 10,000, while the four batsmen regularly described as the best of their generation – Virat Kohli, Joe Root, Steve Smith and Kane Williamson – could all pass 5,000 this year. James Anderson needs 33 wickets to become the first Englishman to 500 in Tests. But, for most bowlers, record-breaking increasingly means being the victim rather than the perpetrator.

ROLL OF DISHONOUR

The following players have either been banned after being found guilty of some form of corruption, or have admitted to some form of on-field corruption:

Amit Singh (I), Ata-ur-Rehman (P), M. Azharuddin (I), A. Bali (I), G. H. Bodi (SA), A. Chandila (I), A. A. Chavan (I), P. Cleary (A), W. J. Cronje (SA), Danish Kaneria (P), H. H. Gibbs (SA), C. L. Hall (A), Irfan Ahmed (HK), A. Jadeja (I), H. N. K. Jensen (NZ), J. Logan (A), K. S. Lokuarachchi (SL), P. Matshikwe (SA), N. E. Mbhalati (SA), M. D. Mishra (I), Mohammad Amir (P), Mohammad Ashraful (B), Mohammad Asif (P), Naved Arif (P), M. O. Odumbe (Ken), A. N. Petersen (SA), M. Prabhakar (I), Salim Malik (P), Salman Butt (P), M. N. Samuels (WI), H. N. Shah (I), Shariful Haque (B), Ajay Sharma (I), S. Sreesanth (I), S. J. Srivastava (I), T. P. Sudhindra (I), J. Symes (SA), S. K. Trivedi (I), T. L. Tsolekile (SA), L. Vincent (NZ), M. S. Westfield (E), H. S. Williams (SA), A. R. Yadav (I).

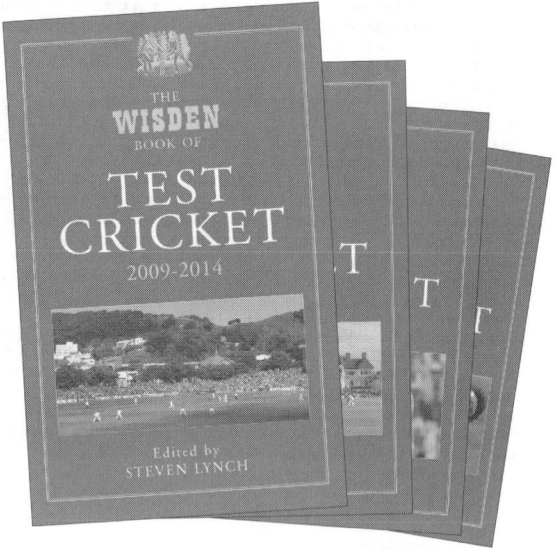

FIRST-CLASS RECORDS

This section covers first-class cricket to December 31, 2016. Bold type denotes performances in the calendar year 2016 or, in career figures, players who appeared in first-class cricket in that year.

BATTING RECORDS

HIGHEST INDIVIDUAL INNINGS

In all first-class cricket, there have been **213** individual scores of 300 or more. The highest are:

501*	B. C. Lara	Warwickshire v Durham at Birmingham	1994
499	Hanif Mohammad	Karachi v Bahawalpur at Karachi	1958-59
452*	D. G. Bradman	NSW v Queensland at Sydney	1929-30
443*	B. B. Nimbalkar	Maharashtra v Kathiawar at Poona	1948-49
437	W. H. Ponsford	Victoria v Queensland at Melbourne	1927-28
429	W. H. Ponsford	Victoria v Tasmania at Melbourne	1922-23
428	Aftab Baloch	Sind v Baluchistan at Karachi	1973-74
424	A. C. MacLaren	Lancashire v Somerset at Taunton	1895
405*	G. A. Hick	Worcestershire v Somerset at Taunton	1988
400*	B. C. Lara	West Indies v England at St John's	2003-04
394	Naved Latif	Sargodha v Gujranwala at Gujranwala	2000-01
390	S. C. Cook	Lions v Warriors at East London	2009-10
385	B. Sutcliffe	Otago v Canterbury at Christchurch	1952-53
383	C. W. Gregory	NSW v Queensland at Brisbane	1906-07
380	M. L. Hayden	Australia v Zimbabwe at Perth	2003-04
377	S. V. Manjrekar	Bombay v Hyderabad at Bombay	1990-91
375	B. C. Lara	West Indies v England at St John's	1993-94
374	D. P. M. D. Jayawardene	Sri Lanka v South Africa at Colombo (SSC)	2006
369	D. G. Bradman	South Australia v Tasmania at Adelaide	1935-36
366	N. H. Fairbrother	Lancashire v Surrey at The Oval	1990
366	M. V. Sridhar	Hyderabad v Andhra at Secunderabad	1993-94
365*	C. Hill	South Australia v NSW at Adelaide	1900-01
365*	G. S. Sobers	West Indies v Pakistan at Kingston	1957-58
364	L. Hutton	England v Australia at The Oval	1938
359*	V. M. Merchant	Bombay v Maharashtra at Bombay	1943-44
359*	**S. B. Gohel**	**Gujarat v Orissa at Jaipur**	**2016-17**
359	R. B. Simpson	NSW v Queensland at Brisbane	1963-64
357*	R. Abel	Surrey v Somerset at The Oval	1899
357	D. G. Bradman	South Australia v Victoria at Melbourne	1935-36
356	B. A. Richards	South Australia v Western Australia at Perth	1970-71
355*	G. R. Marsh	Western Australia v South Australia at Perth	1989-90
355*	K. P. Pietersen	Surrey v Leicestershire at The Oval	2015
355	B. Sutcliffe	Otago v Auckland at Dunedin	1949-50
353	V. V. S. Laxman	Hyderabad v Karnataka at Bangalore	1999-2000
352	W. H. Ponsford	Victoria v NSW at Melbourne	1926-27
352	C. A. Pujara	Saurashtra v Karnataka at Rajkot	2012-13
351*	**S. M. Gugale**	**Maharashtra v Delhi at Mumbai**	**2016-17**
351	K. D. K. Vithanage	Tamil Union v Air Force at Katunayake	2014-15
350	Rashid Israr	Habib Bank v National Bank at Lahore	1976-77

A fuller list can be found in Wisdens *up to 2011.*

DOUBLE-HUNDRED ON DEBUT

227	T. Marsden	Sheffield & Leicester v Nottingham at Sheffield	1826
207	N. F. Callaway†	New South Wales v Queensland at Sydney	1914-15
240	W. F. E. Marx	Transvaal v Griqualand West at Johannesburg	1920-21
200*	A. Maynard	Trinidad v MCC at Port-of-Spain	1934-35
232*	S. J. E. Loxton	Victoria v Queensland at Melbourne	1946-47

215*	G. H. G. Doggart	Cambridge University v Lancashire at Cambridge . . .	1948
202	J. Hallebone	Victoria v Tasmania at Melbourne	1951-52
230	G. R. Viswanath	Mysore v Andhra at Vijayawada.	1967-68
260	A. A. Muzumdar	Bombay v Haryana at Faridabad.	1993-94
209*	A. Pandey	Madhya Pradesh v Uttar Pradesh at Bhilai	1995-96
210*	D. J. Sales	Northamptonshire v Worcestershire at Kidderminster	1996
200*	M. J. Powell	Glamorgan v Oxford University at Oxford.	1997
201*	M. C. Juneja	Gujarat v Tamil Nadu at Ahmedabad	2011-12
213	Jiwanjot Singh	Punjab v Hyderabad at Mohali	2012-13

† *In his only first-class innings. He was killed in action in France in 1917.*

TWO SEPARATE HUNDREDS ON DEBUT

148	and 111	A. R. Morris	New South Wales v Queensland at Sydney	1940-41
152	and 102*	N. J. Contractor	Gujarat v Baroda at Baroda	1952-53
132*	and 110	Aamer Malik	Lahore A v Railways at Lahore	1979-80
130	and 100*	Noor Ali	Afghanistan v Zimbabwe XI at Mutare	2009
158	and 103*	K. H. T. Indika	Police v Seeduwa Raddoluwa at Colombo (Police)	2010-11
126	and 112	V. S. Awate	Maharashtra v Vidarbha at Nagpur.	2012-13
154*	and 109*	T. J. Dean	Victoria v Queensland at Melbourne	2015-16

TWO DOUBLE-HUNDREDS IN A MATCH

A. E. Fagg	244	202*	Kent v Essex at Colchester.	1938

TRIPLE-HUNDRED AND HUNDRED IN A MATCH

G. A. Gooch.	333	123	England v India at Lord's.	1990
K. C. Sangakkara	319	105	Sri Lanka v Bangladesh at Chittagong	2013-14

DOUBLE-HUNDRED AND HUNDRED IN A MATCH

In addition to Fagg, Gooch and Sangakkara, there have been **61** further instances of a batsman scoring a double-hundred and a hundred in the same first-class match. The most recent are:

V. Sibanda.	209	116*	Zimbabwe XI v Kenya at Kwekwe	2009-10
Y. K. Pathan	108	210*	West Zone v South Zone at Hyderabad.	2009-10
S. M. Ervine	208	160	Southern Rocks v MW Rhinos at Masvingo . .	2009-10
C. J. L. Rogers.	200	140*	Derbyshire v Surrey at The Oval.	2010
M. R. Ramprakash	223	103*	Surrey v Middlesex at The Oval	2010
N. V. Ojha.	219*	101*	India A v Australia A at Brisbane	2014
S. D. Robson.	**231**	**106**	**Middlesex v Warwickshire at Lord's**.	**2016**

Zaheer Abbas achieved the feat four times, for Gloucestershire between 1976 and 1981, and was not out in all eight innings. M. R. Hallam did it twice for Leicestershire, in 1959 and 1961; N. R. Taylor twice for Kent, in 1990 and 1991; G. A. Gooch for England in 1990 (see above) and Essex in 1994; M. W. Goodwin twice for Sussex, in 2001 and 2007; and C. J. L. Rogers for Northamptonshire in 2006 and for Derbyshire in 2010.

TWO SEPARATE HUNDREDS IN A MATCH MOST TIMES

R. T. Ponting	8	J. B. Hobbs.	6	M. L. Hayden.	5
Zaheer Abbas	8	G. M. Turner	6	G. A. Hick	5
W. R. Hammond	7	C. B. Fry.	5	**C. J. L. Rogers**	5
M. R. Ramprakash	7	G. A. Gooch.	5		

W. Lambert scored 107 and 157 for Sussex v Epsom at Lord's in 1817, a feat not repeated until W. G. Grace's 130 and 102 for South of the Thames v North of the Thames at Canterbury in 1868.*

FIVE HUNDREDS OR MORE IN SUCCESSION

D. G. Bradman (1938-39)	6	B. C. Lara (1993-94–1994)	5
C. B. Fry (1901)	6	P. A. Patel (2007–2007-08)	5
M. J. Procter (1970-71)	6	E. D. Weekes (1955-56)	5
M. E. K. Hussey (2003)	5		

Bradman also scored four hundreds in succession twice, in 1931-32 and 1948–1948-49; W. R. Hammond did it in 1936-37 and 1945–1946, and H. Sutcliffe in 1931 and 1939.

T. W. Hayward (Surrey v Nottinghamshire and Leicestershire), D. W. Hookes (South Australia v Queensland and New South Wales) and V. Sibanda (Zimbabwe XI v Kenya and Mid West v Southern Rocks) are the only players to score two hundreds in each of two successive matches. Hayward scored his in six days, June 4–9, 1906.

The most fifties in consecutive innings is ten – by E. Tyldesley in 1926, by D. G. Bradman in the 1947-48 and 1948 seasons and by R. S. Kaluwitharana in 1994-95.

MOST HUNDREDS IN A SEASON

D. C. S. Compton (1947)	18	W. R. Hammond (1937)	13
J. B. Hobbs (1925)	16	T. W. Hayward (1906)	13
W. R. Hammond (1938)	15	E. H. Hendren (1923)	13
H. Sutcliffe (1932)	14	E. H. Hendren (1927)	13
G. Boycott (1971)	13	E. H. Hendren (1928)	13
D. G. Bradman (1938)	13	C. P. Mead (1928)	13
C. B. Fry (1901)	13	H. Sutcliffe (1928)	13
W. R. Hammond (1933)	13	H. Sutcliffe (1931)	13

Since 1969 (excluding G. Boycott – above)

G. A. Gooch (1990)	12	M. R. Ramprakash (1995)	10
S. J. Cook (1991)	11	M. R. Ramprakash (2007)	10
Zaheer Abbas (1976)	11	G. M. Turner (1970)	10
G. A. Hick (1988)	10	Zaheer Abbas (1981)	10
H. Morris (1990)	10		

The most outside England is nine by V. Sibanda in Zimbabwe (2009-10), followed by eight by D. G. Bradman in Australia (1947-48), D. C. S. Compton (1948-49), R. N. Harvey and A. R. Morris (both 1949-50) all three in South Africa, M. D. Crowe in New Zealand (1986-87), Asif Mujtaba in Pakistan (1995-96), V. V. S. Laxman in India (1999-2000) and M. G. Bevan in Australia (2004-05).

The most double-hundreds in a season is six by D. G. Bradman (1930), five by K. S. Ranjitsinhji (1900) and E. D. Weekes (1950), and four by Arun Lal (1986-87), C. B. Fry (1901), W. R. Hammond (1933 and 1934), E. H. Hendren (1929-30), V. M. Merchant (1944-45), C. A. Pujara (2012-13) and G. M. Turner (1971-72).

MOST DOUBLE-HUNDREDS IN A CAREER

D. G. Bradman	37	W. H. Ponsford	13	G. Boycott	10
W. R. Hammond	36	J. T. Tyldesley	13	R. Dravid	10
E. H. Hendren	22	P. Holmes	12	M. W. Gatting	10
M. R. Ramprakash	17	Javed Miandad	12	S. M. Gavaskar	10
H. Sutcliffe	17	J. L. Langer	12	J. Hardstaff jnr	10
C. B. Fry	16	**K. C. Sangakkara**	**12**	V. S. Hazare	10
G. A. Hick	16	R. B. Simpson	12	B. J. Hodge	10
J. B. Hobbs	16	**Younis Khan**	**12**	D. P. M. D. Jayawardene	10
C. G. Greenidge	14	J. W. Hearne	11	**C. A. Pujara**	**10**
K. S. Ranjitsinhji	14	L. Hutton	11	I. V. A. Richards	10
G. A. Gooch	13	D. S. Lehmann	11	A. Shrewsbury	10
W. G. Grace	13	V. M. Merchant	11	R. T. Simpson	10
B. C. Lara	13	**C. J. L. Rogers**	**11**	G. M. Turner	10
C. P. Mead	13	A. Sandham	11	Zaheer Abbas	10

MOST HUNDREDS IN A CAREER

(100 or more)

		Total	Total Inns	100th 100 Season	Inns	400+	300+	200+
1	J. B. Hobbs	197	1,315	1923	821	0	1	16
2	E. H. Hendren	170	1,300	1928-29	740	0	1	22
3	W. R. Hammond	167	1,005	1935	680	0	4	36
4	C. P. Mead	153	1,340	1927	892	0	0	13
5	G. Boycott	151	1,014	1977	645	0	0	10
6	H. Sutcliffe	149	1,088	1932	700	0	1	17
7	F. E. Woolley	145	1,532	1929	1,031	0	1	9
8	G. A. Hick	136	871	1998	574	1	3	16
9	L. Hutton	129	814	1951	619	0	1	11
10	G. A. Gooch	128	990	1992-93	820	0	1	13
11	W. G. Grace	126	1,493	1895	1,113	0	3	13
12	D. C. S. Compton	123	839	1952	552	0	1	9
13	T. W. Graveney	122	1,223	1964	940	0	0	7
14	D. G. Bradman	117	338	1947-48	295	1	6	37
15	I. V. A. Richards	114	796	1988-89	658	0	1	10
	M. R. Ramprakash	114	764	2008	676	0	1	17
17	Zaheer Abbas	108	768	1982-83	658	0	0	10
18	A. Sandham	107	1,000	1935	871	0	1	11
	M. C. Cowdrey	107	1,130	1973	1,035	0	1	3
20	T. W. Hayward	104	1,138	1913	1,076	0	1	8
21	G. M. Turner	103	792	1982	779	0	1	10
	J. H. Edrich	103	979	1977	945	0	1	4
23	L. E. G. Ames	102	951	1950	916	0	0	9
	E. Tyldesley	102	961	1934	919	0	0	7
	D. L. Amiss	102	1,139	1986	1,081	0	0	3

In the above table, 200+, 300+ and 400+ include all scores above those figures.

G. A. Gooch's record includes his century in South Africa in 1981-82, which is no longer accepted by the ICC. Zaheer Abbas and G. Boycott scored their 100th hundreds in Test matches.

Current Players

The following who played in 2016 have scored 40 or more hundreds.

C. J. L. Rogers	76	Younis Khan	55	E. C. Joyce	45
S. Chanderpaul	73	I. R. Bell	51	Misbah-ul-Haq	43
M. E. Trescothick	63	Wasim Jaffer	51	A. N. Petersen	42
A. N. Cook	56	J. A. Rudolph	49	V. Sehwag	42
K. C. Sangakkara	56	H. M. Amla	46	S. C. Cook	40

MOST RUNS IN A SEASON

	Season	I	NO	R	HS	100	Avge
D. C. S. Compton	1947	50	8	3,816	246	18	90.85
W. J. Edrich	1947	52	8	3,539	267*	12	80.43
T. W. Hayward	1906	61	8	3,518	219	13	66.37
L. Hutton	1949	56	6	3,429	269*	12	68.58
F. E. Woolley	1928	59	4	3,352	198	12	60.94
H. Sutcliffe	1932	52	7	3,336	313	14	74.13
W. R. Hammond	1933	54	5	3,323	264	13	67.81
E. H. Hendren	1928	54	7	3,311	209*	13	70.44
R. Abel	1901	68	8	3,309	247	7	55.15

3,000 in a season has been surpassed on 19 other occasions (a full list can be found in Wisden *1999 and earlier editions). W. R. Hammond, E. H. Hendren and H. Sutcliffe are the only players to achieve the feat three times. K. S. Ranjitsinhji was the first batsman to reach 3,000 in a season, with 3,159 in 1899. M. J. K. Smith (3,245 in 1959) and W. E. Alley (3,019 in 1961) are the only players except those listed above to have reached 3,000 since World War II.*

W. G. Grace scored 2,739 runs in 1871 – the first batsman to reach 2,000 in a season. He made ten hundreds including two double-hundreds, with an average of 78.25 in all first-class matches.

The highest aggregate in a season since the reduction of County Championship matches in 1969 is 2,755 by S. J. Cook (42 innings) in 1991, and the last batsman to achieve 2,000 was M. R. Ramprakash (2,026 in 2007).

2,000 RUNS IN A SEASON MOST TIMES

J. B. Hobbs	17	F. E. Woolley	13	C. P. Mead	11
E. H. Hendren	15	W. R. Hammond	12	T. W. Hayward	10
H. Sutcliffe	15	J. G. Langridge	11		

Since the reduction of County Championship matches in 1969, G. A. Gooch is the only batsman to have reached 2,000 runs in a season five times.

1,000 RUNS IN A SEASON MOST TIMES

Includes overseas tours and seasons

W. G. Grace	28	A. Jones	23	G. Gunn	20
F. E. Woolley	28	T. W. Graveney	22	T. W. Hayward	20
M. C. Cowdrey	27	W. R. Hammond	22	G. A. Hick	20
C. P. Mead	27	D. Denton	21	James Langridge	20
G. Boycott	26	J. H. Edrich	21	J. M. Parks	20
J. B. Hobbs	26	G. A. Gooch	21	M. R. Ramprakash	20
E. H. Hendren	25	W. Rhodes	21	A. Sandham	20
D. L. Amiss	24	D. B. Close	20	M. J. K. Smith	20
W. G. Quaife	24	K. W. R. Fletcher	20	C. Washbrook	20
H. Sutcliffe	24	M. W. Gatting	20		

F. E. Woolley reached 1,000 runs in 28 consecutive seasons (1907–1938), C. P. Mead in 27 (1906–1936).

Outside England, 1,000 runs in a season has been reached most times by D. G. Bradman (in 12 seasons in Australia).

Three batsmen have scored 1,000 runs in a season in each of four different countries: G. S. Sobers in West Indies, England, India and Australia; M. C. Cowdrey and G. Boycott in England, South Africa, West Indies and Australia.

HIGHEST AGGREGATES OUTSIDE ENGLAND

	Season	*I*	*NO*	*R*	*HS*	*100*	*Avge*
In Australia							
D. G. Bradman	1928-29	24	6	1,690	340*	7	93.88
In South Africa							
J. R. Reid	1961-62	30	2	1,915	203	7	68.39
In West Indies							
E. H. Hendren	1929-30	18	5	1,765	254*	6	135.76
In New Zealand							
M. D. Crowe	1986-87	21	3	1,676	175*	8	93.11
In India							
C. G. Borde	1964-65	28	3	1,604	168	6	64.16

	Season	I	NO	R	HS	100	Avge
In Pakistan							
Saadat Ali	1983-84	27	1	1,649	208	4	63.42
In Sri Lanka							
R. P. Arnold	1995-96	24	3	1,475	217*	5	70.23
In Zimbabwe							
V. Sibanda	2009-10	26	4	1,612	215	9	73.27
In Bangladesh							
Liton Das	2014-15	17	1	1,232	175	5	77.00

In more than one country, the following aggregates of over 2,000 runs have been recorded:

M. Amarnath (P/I/WI)	1982-83	34	6	2,234	207	9	79.78
J. R. Reid (SA/A/NZ)	1961-62	40	2	2,188	203	7	57.57
S. M. Gavaskar (I/P)	1978-79	30	6	2,121	205	10	88.37
R. B. Simpson (I/P/A/WI)	1964-65	34	4	2,063	201	8	68.76
M. H. Richardson (Z/SA/NZ)	2000-01	34	3	2,030	306	4	65.48

The only other player to hit ten centuries in an overseas season is V. V. S. Laxman, in India and Australia in 1999-2000.

LEADING BATSMEN IN AN ENGLISH SEASON

(Qualification: 8 completed innings)

Season	Leading scorer	Runs	Avge	Top of averages	Runs	Avge
1946	D. C. S. Compton	2,403	61.61	W. R. Hammond	1,783	84.90
1947	D. C. S. Compton	3,816	90.85	D. C. S. Compton	3,816	90.85
1948	L. Hutton	2,654	64.73	D. G. Bradman	2,428	89.92
1949	L. Hutton	3,429	68.58	J. Hardstaff	2,251	72.61
1950	R. T. Simpson	2,576	62.82	E. D. Weekes	2,310	79.65
1951	J. D. Robertson	2,917	56.09	P. B. H. May	2,339	68.79
1952	L. Hutton	2,567	61.11	D. S. Sheppard	2,262	64.62
1953	W. J. Edrich	2,557	47.35	R. N. Harvey	2,040	65.80
1954	D. Kenyon	2,636	51.68	D. C. S. Compton	1,524	58.61
1955	D. J. Insole	2,427	42.57	D. J. McGlew	1,871	58.46
1956	T. W. Graveney	2,397	49.93	K. Mackay	1,103	52.52
1957	T. W. Graveney	2,361	49.18	P. B. H. May	2,347	61.76
1958	P. B. H. May	2,231	63.74	P. B. H. May	2,231	63.74
1959	M. J. K. Smith	3,245	57.94	V. L. Manjrekar	755	68.63
1960	M. J. K. Smith	2,551	45.55	R. Subba Row	1,503	55.66
1961	W. E. Alley	3,019	56.96	W. M. Lawry	2,019	61.18
1962	J. H. Edrich	2,482	51.70	R. T. Simpson	867	54.18
1963	J. B. Bolus	2,190	41.32	G. S. Sobers	1,333	47.60
1964	T. W. Graveney	2,385	54.20	K. F. Barrington	1,872	62.40
1965	J. H. Edrich	2,319	62.67	M. C. Cowdrey	2,093	63.42
1966	A. R. Lewis	2,198	41.47	G. S. Sobers	1,349	61.31
1967	C. A. Milton	2,089	46.42	K. F. Barrington	2,059	68.63
1968	B. A. Richards	2,395	47.90	G. Boycott	1,487	64.65
1969	J. H. Edrich	2,238	69.93	J. H. Edrich	2,238	69.93
1970	G. M. Turner	2,379	61.00	G. S. Sobers	1,742	75.73
1971	G. Boycott	2,503	100.12	G. Boycott	2,503	100.12
1972	Majid Khan	2,074	61.00	G. Boycott	1,230	72.35
1973	G. M. Turner	2,416	67.11	G. M. Turner	2,416	67.11
1974	R. T. Virgin	1,936	56.94	C. H. Lloyd	1,458	63.39
1975	G. Boycott	1,915	73.65	R. B. Kanhai	1,073	82.53
1976	Zaheer Abbas	2,554	75.11	Zaheer Abbas	2,554	75.11
1977	I. V. A. Richards	2,161	65.48	G. Boycott	1,701	68.04

Season	*Leading scorer*	*Runs*	*Avge*	*Top of averages*	*Runs*	*Avge*
1978	D. L. Amiss	2,030	53.42	C. E. B. Rice	1,871	66.82
1979	K. C. Wessels	1,800	52.94	G. Boycott	1,538	102.53
1980	P. N. Kirsten	1,895	63.16	A. J. Lamb	1,797	66.55
1981	Zaheer Abbas	2,306	88.69	Zaheer Abbas	2,306	88.69
1982	A. I. Kallicharran	2,120	66.25	G. M. Turner	1,171	90.07
1983	K. S. McEwan	2,176	64.00	I. V. A. Richards	1,204	75.25
1984	G. A. Gooch	2,559	67.34	C. G. Greenidge	1,069	82.23
1985	G. A. Gooch	2,208	71.22	I. V. A. Richards	1,836	76.50
1986	C. G. Greenidge	2,035	67.83	C. G. Greenidge	2,035	67.83
1987	G. A. Hick	1,879	52.19	M. D. Crowe	1,627	67.79
1988	G. A. Hick	2,713	77.51	R. A. Harper	622	77.75
1989	S. J. Cook	2,241	60.56	D. M. Jones	1,510	88.82
1990	G. A. Gooch	2,746	101.70	G. A. Gooch	2,746	101.70
1991	S. J. Cook	2,755	81.02	C. L. Hooper	1,501	93.81
1992	P. D. Bowler	2,044	65.93	Salim Malik	1,184	78.93
	M. A. Roseberry	2,044	56.77			
1993	G. A. Gooch	2,023	63.21	D. C. Boon	1,437	75.63
1994	B. C. Lara	2,066	89.82	J. D. Carr	1,543	90.76
1995	M. R. Ramprakash	2,258	77.86	M. R. Ramprakash	2,258	77.86
1996	G. A. Gooch	1,944	67.03	S. C. Ganguly	762	95.25
1997	S. P. James	1,775	68.26	G. A. Hick	1,524	69.27
1998	J. P. Crawley	1,851	74.04	J. P. Crawley	1,851	74.04
1999	S. G. Law	1,833	73.32	S. G. Law	1,833	73.32
2000	D. S. Lehmann	1,477	67.13	M. G. Bevan	1,124	74.93
2001	M. E. K. Hussey	2,055	79.03	D. R. Martyn	942	104.66
2002	I. J. Ward	1,759	62.82	R. Dravid	773	96.62
2003	S. G. Law	1,820	91.00	S. G. Law	1,820	91.00
2004	R. W. T. Key	1,896	79.00	R. W. T. Key	1,896	79.00
2005	O. A. Shah	1,728	66.46	M. E. K. Hussey	1,074	76.71
2006	M. R. Ramprakash	2,278	103.54	M. R. Ramprakash	2,278	103.54
2007	M. R. Ramprakash	2,026	101.30	M. R. Ramprakash	2,026	101.30
2008	S. C. Moore	1,451	55.80	T. Frost	1,003	83.58
2009	M. E. Trescothick	1,817	75.70	M. R. Ramprakash	1,350	90.00
2010	M. R. Ramprakash	1,595	61.34	J. C. Hildreth	1,440	65.45
2011	M. E. Trescothick	1,673	79.66	I. R. Bell	1,091	90.91
2012	N. R. D. Compton	1,494	99.60	N. R. D. Compton	1,494	99.60
2013	C. J. L. Rogers	1,536	51.20	S. M. Katich	1,097	73.13
2014	A. Lyth	1,619	70.39	J. E. Root	1,052	75.14
2015	J. C. Hildreth	1,758	56.70	J. M. Bairstow	1,226	72.11
2016	**K. K. Jennings**	**1,602**	**64.08**	**S. A. Northeast**	**1,402**	**82.47**

The highest average recorded in an English season was 115.66 (2,429 runs, 26 innings) by D. G. Bradman in 1938.

In 1953, W. A. Johnston averaged 102.00 from 17 innings, 16 not out.

MOST RUNS

Dates in italics denote the first half of an overseas season; i.e. *1945* denotes the 1945-46 season.

		Career	*R*	*I*	*NO*	*HS*	*100*	*Avge*
1	J. B. Hobbs	1905–1934	61,237	1,315	106	316*	197	50.65
2	F. E. Woolley	1906–1938	58,969	1,532	85	305*	145	40.75
3	E. H. Hendren	1907–1938	57,611	1,300	166	301*	170	50.80
4	C. P. Mead	1905–1936	55,061	1,340	185	280*	153	47.67
5	W. G. Grace	1865–1908	54,896	1,493	105	344	126	39.55
6	W. R. Hammond	1920–1951	50,551	1,005	104	336*	167	56.10
7	H. Sutcliffe	1919–1945	50,138	1,088	123	313	149	51.95
8	G. Boycott	1962–1986	48,426	1,014	162	261*	151	56.83
9	T. W. Graveney	1948–*1971*	47,793	1,223	159	258	122	44.91
10	G. A. Gooch	1973–2000	44,846	990	75	333	128	49.01

		Career	R	I	NO	HS	100	Avge
11	T. W. Hayward	1893–1914	43,551	1,138	96	315*	104	41.79
12	D. L. Amiss	1960–1987	43,423	1,139	126	262*	102	42.86
13	M. C. Cowdrey	1950–1976	42,719	1,130	134	307	107	42.89
14	A. Sandham	1911–*1937*	41,284	1,000	79	325	107	44.82
15	G. A. Hick	*1983*–2008	41,112	871	84	405*	136	52.23
16	L. Hutton	1934–1960	40,140	814	91	364	129	55.51
17	M. J. K. Smith	1951–1975	39,832	1,091	139	204	69	41.84
18	W. Rhodes	1898–1930	39,802	1,528	237	267*	58	30.83
19	J. H. Edrich	1956–1978	39,790	979	104	310*	103	45.47
20	R. E. S. Wyatt	1923–1957	39,405	1,141	157	232	85	40.04
21	D. C. S. Compton	1936–1964	38,942	839	88	300	123	51.85
22	E. Tyldesley	1909–1936	38,874	961	106	256*	102	45.46
23	J. T. Tyldesley	1895–1923	37,897	994	62	295*	86	40.66
24	K. W. R. Fletcher	1962–1988	37,665	1,167	170	228*	63	37.77
25	C. G. Greenidge	1970–1992	37,354	889	75	273*	92	45.88
26	J. W. Hearne	1909–1936	37,252	1,025	116	285*	96	40.98
27	L. E. G. Ames	1926–1951	37,248	951	95	295	102	43.51
28	D. Kenyon	1946–1967	37,002	1,159	59	259	74	33.63
29	W. J. Edrich	1934–1958	36,965	964	92	267*	86	42.39
30	J. M. Parks	1949–1976	36,673	1,227	172	205*	51	34.76
31	M. W. Gatting	1975–1998	36,549	861	123	258	94	49.52
32	D. Denton	1894–1920	36,479	1,163	70	221	69	33.37
33	G. H. Hirst	1891–1929	36,323	1,215	151	341	60	34.13
34	I. V. A. Richards	*1971*–1993	36,212	796	63	322	114	49.40
35	A. Jones	1957–1983	36,049	1,168	72	204*	56	32.89
36	W. G. Quaife	1894–1928	36,012	1,203	185	255*	72	35.37
37	R. E. Marshall	*1945*–1972	35,725	1,053	59	228*	68	35.94
38	M. R. Ramprakash	1987–2012	35,659	764	93	301*	114	53.14
39	G. Gunn	1902–1932	35,208	1,061	82	220	62	35.96

Some works of reference provide career figures which differ from those in this list, owing to the exclusion or inclusion of matches recognised or not recognised as first-class by Wisden. *A fuller list can be found in* Wisdens *up to 2011.*

Current Players with 20,000 Runs

	Career	R	I	NO	HS	100	Avge
S. Chanderpaul	*1991–2016*	25,919	579	105	303*	73	54.68
C. J. L. Rogers	*1998*–2016	25,470	554	40	319	76	49.55
M. E. Trescothick	1993–2016	24,884	620	34	284	63	42.46

HIGHEST CAREER AVERAGE

(Qualification: 10,000 runs)

Avge		Career	I	NO	R	HS	100
95.14	D. G. Bradman	*1927–1948*	338	43	28,067	452*	117
71.22	V. M. Merchant	*1929–1951*	229	43	13,248	359*	44
67.46	Ajay Sharma	*1984–2000*	166	16	10,120	259*	38
65.18	W. H. Ponsford	*1920–1934*	235	23	13,819	437	47
64.99	W. M. Woodfull	*1921–1934*	245	39	13,388	284	49
58.24	A. L. Hassett	*1932–1953*	322	32	16,890	232	59
58.19	V. S. Hazare	*1934–1966*	365	45	18,621	316*	60
57.84	S. R. Tendulkar	*1988–2013*	490	51	25,396	248*	81
57.83	D. S. Lehmann	1987–2007	479	33	25,795	339	82
57.32	M. G. Bevan	*1989–2006*	400	66	19,147	216	68
57.22	A. F. Kippax	*1918–1935*	256	33	12,762	315*	43
56.94	**C. A. Pujara**	***2005–2016***	**227**	**32**	**11,104**	**352**	**36**
56.83	G. Boycott	1962–1986	1,014	162	48,426	261*	151
56.55	C. L. Walcott	*1941–1963*	238	29	11,820	314*	40

Avge		*Career*	*I*	*NO*	*R*	*HS*	*100*
56.51	**Fawad Alam**	***2003–2016***	**215**	**35**	**10,172**	**296***	**25**
56.37	K. S. Ranjitsinhji	1893–1920	500	62	24,692	285*	72
56.22	R. B. Simpson	*1952–1977*	436	62	21,029	359	60
56.10	W. R. Hammond	1920–1951	1,005	104	50,551	336*	167
56.02	M. D. Crowe	*1979–1995*	412	62	19,608	299	71
55.90	R. T. Ponting	*1992*–2013	494	62	24,150	257	82
55.51	L. Hutton	1934–1960	814	91	40,140	364	129
55.34	E. D. Weekes	*1944*–1964	241	24	12,010	304*	36
55.33	R. Dravid	*1990–2011*	497	67	23,794	270	68
55.11	S. V. Manjrekar	*1984–1997*	217	31	10,252	377	31

G. A. Headley scored 9,921 runs, average 69.86, between 1927-28 and 1954.

FASTEST FIFTIES

Minutes			
11	C. I. J. Smith (66)	Middlesex v Gloucestershire at Bristol	1938
13	Khalid Mahmood (56)	Gujranwala v Sargodha at Gujranwala	2000-01
14	S. J. Pegler (50)	South Africans v Tasmania at Launceston	1910-11
14	F. T. Mann (53)	Middlesex v Nottinghamshire at Lord's	1921
14	H. B. Cameron (56)	Transvaal v Orange Free State at Johannesburg	1934-35
14	C. I. J. Smith (52)	Middlesex v Kent at Maidstone	1935

The number of balls taken to achieve fifties was rarely recorded until recently. C. I. J. Smith's two fifties (above) may have taken only 12 balls each. Khalid Mahmood reached his fifty in 15 balls.

Fifties scored in contrived circumstances and with the bowlers' compliance are excluded from the above list, including the fastest of them all, in 8 minutes (13 balls) by C. C. Inman, Leicestershire v Nottinghamshire at Nottingham, 1965, and 10 minutes by G. Chapple, Lancashire v Glamorgan at Manchester, 1993.

FASTEST HUNDREDS

Minutes			
35	P. G. H. Fender (113*)	Surrey v Northamptonshire at Northampton	1920
40	G. L. Jessop (101)	Gloucestershire v Yorkshire at Harrogate	1897
40	Ahsan-ul-Haq (100*)	Muslims v Sikhs at Lahore	1923-24
42	G. L. Jessop (191)	Gentlemen of South v Players of South at Hastings	1907
43	A. H. Hornby (106)	Lancashire v Somerset at Manchester	1905
43	D. W. Hookes (107)	South Australia v Victoria at Adelaide	1982-83
44	R. N. S. Hobbs (100)	Essex v Australians at Chelmsford	1975

The fastest recorded authentic hundred in terms of balls received was scored off 34 balls by D. W. Hookes (above). Research of the scorebook has shown that P. G. H. Fender scored his hundred from between 40 and 46 balls. He contributed 113 to an unfinished sixth-wicket partnership of 171 in 42 minutes with H. A. Peach.

E. B. Alletson (Nottinghamshire) scored 189 out of 227 runs in 90 minutes against Sussex at Hove in 1911. It has been estimated that his last 139 runs took 37 minutes.

Hundreds scored in contrived circumstances and with the bowlers' compliance are excluded, including the fastest of them all, in 21 minutes (27 balls) by G. Chapple, Lancashire v Glamorgan at Manchester, 1993, 24 minutes (27 balls) by M. L. Pettini, Essex v Leicestershire at Leicester, 2006, and 26 minutes (36 balls) by T. M. Moody, Warwickshire v Glamorgan at Swansea, 1990.

FASTEST DOUBLE-HUNDREDS

Minutes			
113	R. J. Shastri (200*)	Bombay v Baroda at Bombay	1984-85
120	G. L. Jessop (286)	Gloucestershire v Sussex at Hove	1903
120	C. H. Lloyd (201*)	West Indians v Glamorgan at Swansea	1976
130	G. L. Jessop (234)	Gloucestershire v Somerset at Bristol	1905
131	V. T. Trumper (293)	Australians v Canterbury at Christchurch	1913-14

Shastri faced 123 balls, which was matched by A. H. T. Donald for Glamorgan v Derbyshire at Colwyn Bay in 2016.

FASTEST TRIPLE-HUNDREDS

Minutes			
181	D. C. S. Compton (300)	MCC v North Eastern Transvaal at Benoni	1948-49
205	F. E. Woolley (305*)	MCC v Tasmania at Hobart	1911-12
205	C. G. Macartney (345)	Australians v Nottinghamshire at Nottingham	1921
213	D. G. Bradman (369)	South Australia v Tasmania at Adelaide	1935-36

MOST RUNS IN A DAY BY ONE BATSMAN

390*	B. C. Lara	Warwickshire v Durham at Birmingham	1994
345	C. G. Macartney	Australians v Nottinghamshire at Nottingham	1921
334	W. H. Ponsford	Victoria v New South Wales at Melbourne	1926-27
333	K. S. Duleepsinhji	Sussex v Northamptonshire at Hove	1930
331*	J. D. Robertson	Middlesex v Worcestershire at Worcester	1949
325*	B. A. Richards	South Australia v Western Australia at Perth	1970-71

These scores do not necessarily represent the complete innings. See pages 1225.

*There have been another **14** instances of a batsman scoring 300 in a day, most recently 319 by R. R. Rossouw, Eagles v Titans at Centurion in 2009-10 (see* Wisden *2003, page 278, for full list).*

LONGEST INNINGS

Hrs	*Mins*			
16	55	R. Nayyar (271)	Himachal Pradesh v Jammu&Kashmir at Chamba	1999-2000
16	10	Hanif Mohammad (337)	Pakistan v West Indies at Bridgetown	1957-58
		Hanif believed he batted 16 hours 39 minutes.		
16	**4**	**S. B. Gohel (359*)**	**Gujarat v Orissa at Jaipur**	**2016-17**
15	7	V. A. Saxena (257)	Rajasthan v Tamil Nadu at Chennai	2011-12
14	38	G. Kirsten (275)	South Africa v England at Durban	1999-2000
14	32	K. K. Nair (328)	Karnataka v Tamil Nadu at Mumbai	2014-15
13	58	S. C. Cook (390)	Lions v Warriors at East London	2009-10
13	56	A. N. Cook (263)	England v Pakistan at Abu Dhabi	2015-16
13	43	T. Kohli (300*)	Punjab v Jharkhand at Jamshedpur	2012-13
13	41	S. S. Shukla (178*)	Uttar Pradesh v Tamil Nadu at Nagpur	2008-09
13	32	A. Chopra (301*)	Rajasthan v Maharashtra at Nasik	2010-11

1,000 RUNS IN MAY

	Runs	*Avge*
W. G. Grace, May 9 to May 30, 1895 (22 days)	1,016	112.88
Grace was 46 years old.		
W. R. Hammond, May 7 to May 31, 1927 (25 days)	1,042	74.42
Hammond scored his 1,000th run on May 28, thus equalling Grace's record of 22 days.		
C. Hallows, May 5 to May 31, 1928 (27 days)	1,000	125.00

1,000 RUNS IN APRIL AND MAY

	Runs	*Avge*
T. W. Hayward, April 16 to May 31, 1900	1,074	97.63
D. G. Bradman, April 30 to May 31, 1930	1,001	143.00
On April 30 Bradman was 75 not out.		
D. G. Bradman, April 30 to May 31, 1938	1,056	150.85
Bradman scored 258 on April 30, and his 1,000th run on May 27.		
W. J. Edrich, April 30 to May 31, 1938	1,010	84.16
Edrich was 21 not out on April 30. All his runs were scored at Lord's.		
G. M. Turner, April 24 to May 31, 1973	1,018	78.30
G. A. Hick, April 17 to May 29, 1988	1,019	101.90
Hick scored a record 410 runs in April, and his 1,000th run on May 28.		

MOST RUNS SCORED OFF AN OVER

(All instances refer to six-ball overs)

36	G. S. Sobers	off M. A. Nash, Nottinghamshire v Glamorgan at Swansea (six sixes)	1968
36	R. J. Shastri	off Tilak Raj, Bombay v Baroda at Bombay (six sixes)	1984-85
34	E. B. Alletson	off E. H. Killick, Nottinghamshire v Sussex at Hove (46604446; including two no-balls)	1911
34	F. C. Hayes	off M. A. Nash, Lancashire v Glamorgan at Swansea (646666)	1977
34†	A. Flintoff	off A. J. Tudor, Lancashire v Surrey at Manchester (64444660; including two no-balls)	1998
34	C. M. Spearman	off S. J. P. Moreton, Gloucestershire v Oxford UCCE at Oxford (666646) *Moreton's first over in first-class cricket.*	2005
32	I. T. Botham	off I. R. Snook, England XI v Central Districts at Palmerston North (466466)	1983-84
32	P. W. G. Parker	off A. I. Kallicharran, Sussex v Warwickshire at Birmingham (466664)	1982
32	I. R. Redpath	off N. Rosendorff, Australians v Orange Free State at Bloemfontein (666644)	1969-70
32	C. C. Smart	off G. Hill, Glamorgan v Hampshire at Cardiff (664664)	1935
32	Khalid Mahmood	off Naved Latif, Gujranwala v Sargodha at Gujranwala (666662)	2000-01

† *Altogether 38 runs were scored off this over, the two no-balls counting for two extra runs each under ECB regulations.*

The following instances have been excluded because of the bowlers' compliance: 34 – M. P. Maynard off S. A. Marsh, Glamorgan v Kent at Swansea, 1992; 34 – G. Chapple off P. A. Cottey, Lancashire v Glamorgan at Manchester, 1993; 34 – F. B. Touzel off F. J. J. Viljoen, Western Province B v Griqualand West at Kimberley, 1993-94. Chapple scored a further 32 off Cottey's next over.

There were 35 runs off an over received by A. T. Reinholds off H. T. Davis, Auckland v Wellington at Auckland 1995-96, but this included 16 extras and only 19 off the bat.

In a match against KwaZulu-Natal at Stellenbosch in 2006-07, W. E. September (Boland) conceded 34 in an over: 27 to M. Bekker, six to K. Smit, plus one no-ball.

In a match against Canterbury at Christchurch in 1989-90, R. H. Vance (Wellington) deliberately conceded 77 runs in an over of full tosses which contained 17 no-balls and, owing to the umpire's understandable miscalculation, only five legitimate deliveries.

The greatest number of runs scored off an eight-ball over is 34 (40446664) by R. M. Edwards off M. C. Carew, Governor-General's XI v West Indians at Auckland, 1968-69.

MOST SIXES IN AN INNINGS

23	C. Munro (281)	Auckland v Central Districts at Napier	2014-15
16	A. Symonds (254*)	Gloucestershire v Glamorgan at Abergavenny	1995
16	G. R. Napier (196)	Essex v Surrey at Croydon	2011
16	J. D. Ryder (175)	New Zealanders v Australia A at Brisbane	2011-12
16	Mukhtar Ali (168)	Rajshahi v Chittagong at Savar	2013-14
15	J. R. Reid (296)	Wellington v Northern Districts at Wellington	1962-63
15	Ziaur Rahman (152*)	South Zone v Central Zone at Mirpur	2012-13
15	H. G. Kumara (200*)	Saracens v Air Force at Katunayake	2014-15
15	K. P. Pietersen (355*)	Surrey v Leicestershire at The Oval	2015
15	**A. H. T. Donald (234)**	**Glamorgan v Derbyshire at Colwyn Bay**	**2016**

There have been ***nine*** *further instances of 14 or more sixes in an innings.*

An expanded and regularly updated online version of the Records can be found at www.wisdenrecords.com

MOST SIXES IN A MATCH

23	C. Munro (281)	Auckland v Central Districts at Napier	2014-15
21	**R. R. Pant (117, 131)**	**Delhi v Jharkhand at Thumba**	**2016-17**
20	A. Symonds (254*, 76)	Gloucestershire v Glam at Abergavenny	1995
17	W. J. Stewart (155, 125)	Warwickshire v Lancashire at Blackpool	1959
17	K. P. S. P. Karunanayake (52, 150*)	Army v Ports Authority at Colombo (CCC)	2014-15

MOST SIXES IN A SEASON

80	I. T. Botham	1985
66	A. W. Wellard	1935
57	A. W. Wellard	1936
57	A. W. Wellard	1938
51	A. W. Wellard	1933
49	I. V. A. Richards	1985
48	A. W. Carr	1925
48	J. H. Edrich	1965
48	A. Symonds	1995

MOST BOUNDARIES IN AN INNINGS

	4/6			
72	62/10	B. C. Lara (501*)	Warwickshire v Durham at Birmingham	1994
68	68/–	P. A. Perrin (343*)	Essex v Derbyshire at Chesterfield	1904
65	64/1	A. C. MacLaren (424)	Lancashire v Somerset at Taunton	1895
64	64/–	Hanif Mohammad (499)	Karachi v Bahawalpur at Karachi	1958-59
57	52/5	J. H. Edrich (310*)	England v New Zealand at Leeds	1965
57	52/5	Naved Latif (394)	Sargodha v Gujranwala at Gujranwala	2000-01
56	54/2	K. M. Jadhav (327)	Maharashtra v U. Pradesh at Gahunje	2012-13
55	55/–	C. W. Gregory (383)	NSW v Queensland at Brisbane	1906-07
55	53/2	G. R. Marsh (355*)	W. Australia v S. Australia at Perth	1989-90
55	51/3†	S. V. Manjrekar (377)	Bombay v Hyderabad at Bombay	1990-91
55	52/3	D. S. Lehmann (339)	Yorkshire v Durham at Leeds	2006
55	54/1	D. K. H. Mitchell (298)	Worcestershire v Somerset at Taunton	2009
55	54/1	S. C. Cook (390)	Lions v Warriors at East London	2009-10
55	47/8	R. R. Rossouw (319)	Eagles v Titans at Centurion	2009-10

† *Plus one five.* ‡ *Plus three fives.*

PARTNERSHIPS OVER 500

624	for 3rd	K. C. Sangakkara (287)/D. P. M. D. Jayawardene (374), Sri Lanka v South Africa at Colombo (SSC)	2006
594*	**for 3rd**	**S. M. Gugale (351*)/A. R. Bawne (258*), Maharashtra v Delhi at Mumbai**	**2016-17**
580	for 2nd	Rafatullah Mohmand (302*)/Aamer Sajjad (289), WAPDA v Sui Southern Gas at Sheikhupura	2009-10
577	for 4th	V. S. Hazare (288)/Gul Mahomed (319), Baroda v Holkar at Baroda	1946-47
576	for 2nd	S. T. Jayasuriya (340)/R. S. Mahanama (225), Sri Lanka v India at Colombo (RPS)	1997-98
574*	for 4th	F. M. M. Worrell (255*)/C. L. Walcott (314*), Barbados v Trinidad at Port-of-Spain	1945-46
561	for 1st	Waheed Mirza (324)/Mansoor Akhtar (224*), Karachi Whites v Quetta at Karachi	1976-77
555	for 1st	P. Holmes (224*)/H. Sutcliffe (313), Yorkshire v Essex at Leyton	1932
554	for 1st	J. T. Brown (300)/J. Tunnicliffe (243), Yorks v Derbys at Chesterfield	1898
539	for 3rd	S. D. Jogiyani (282)/R. A. Jadeja (303*), Saurashtra v Gujarat at Surat	2012-13
523	for 3rd	M. A. Carberry (300*)/N. D. McKenzie (237), Hants v Yorks at Southampton	2011
520*	for 5th	C. A. Pujara (302*)/R. A. Jadeja (232*), Saurashtra v Orissa at Rajkot	2008-09
503	for 1st	R. G. L. Carters (209)/A. J. Finch (288*), Cricket Australia XI v New Zealanders at Sydney	2015-16
502*	for 4th	F. M. M. Worrell (308*)/J. D. C. Goddard (218*), Barbados v Trinidad at Bridgetown	1943-44
501	for 3rd	A. N. Petersen (286)/A. G. Prince (261), Lancs v Glam at Colwyn Bay	2015

HIGHEST PARTNERSHIPS FOR EACH WICKET

irst Wicket

51	Waheed Mirza/Mansoor Akhtar, Karachi Whites v Quetta at Karachi	1976-77
55	P. Holmes/H. Sutcliffe, Yorkshire v Essex at Leyton	1932
54	J. T. Brown/J. Tunnicliffe, Yorkshire v Derbyshire at Chesterfield	1898
03	R. G. L. Carters/A. J. Finch, Cricket Australia XI v New Zealanders at Sydney	2015-16
90	E. H. Bowley/J. G. Langridge, Sussex v Middlesex at Hove	1933

econd Wicket

80	Rafatullah Mohmand/Aamer Sajjad, WAPDA v Sui S. Gas at Sheikhupura	2009-10
76	S. T. Jayasuriya/R. S. Mahanama, Sri Lanka v India at Colombo (RPS)	1997-98
30	D. Elgar/R. R. Rossouw, Eagles v Titans at Centurion	2009-10
75	Zahir Alam/L. S. Rajput, Assam v Tripura at Gauhati	1991-92
65*	J. A. Jameson/R. B. Kanhai, Warwicks v Gloucestershire at Birmingham	1974

hird Wicket

24	K. C. Sangakkara/D. P. M. D. Jayawardene, Sri Lanka v SA at Colombo (SSC)	2006
94*	**S. M. Gugale/A. R. Bawne, Maharashtra v Delhi at Mumbai**	**2016-17**
39	S. D. Jogiyani/R. A. Jadeja, Saurashtra v Gujarat at Surat	2012-13
23	M. A. Carberry/N. D. McKenzie, Hampshire v Yorks at Southampton	2011
01	A. N. Petersen/A. G. Prince, Lancashire v Glamorgan at Colwyn Bay	2015

ourth Wicket

77	V. S. Hazare/Gul Mahomed, Baroda v Holkar at Baroda	1946-47
74*	C. L. Walcott/F. M. M. Worrell, Barbados v Trinidad at Port-of-Spain	1945-46
02*	F. M. M. Worrell/J. D. C. Goddard, Barbados v Trinidad at Bridgetown	1943-44
70	A. I. Kallicharran/G. W. Humpage, Warwicks v Lancs at Southport	1982
62*	D. W. Hookes/W. B. Phillips, South Australia v Tasmania at Adelaide	1986-87

ifth Wicket

20*	C. A. Pujara/R. A. Jadeja, Saurashtra v Orissa at Rajkot	2008-09
94	Marshall Ayub/Mehrab Hossain, Central Zone v East Zone at Bogra	2012-13
79	Misbah-ul-Haq/Usman Arshad, Sui N. Gas v Lahore Shalimar at Lahore	2009-10
64*	M. E. Waugh/S. R. Waugh, New South Wales v Western Australia at Perth	1990-91
23	Mosaddek Hossain/Al-Amin, Barisal v Rangpur at Savar	2014-15

ixth Wicket

87*	G. A. Headley/C. C. Passailaigue, Jamaica v Lord Tennyson's XI at Kingston	1931-32
28	W. W. Armstrong/M. A. Noble, Australians v Sussex at Hove	1902
17	W. P. Saha/L. R. Shukla, Bengal v Assam at Kolkata	2010-11
11	R. M. Poore/E. G. Wynyard, Hampshire v Somerset at Taunton	1899
99	**B. A. Stokes/J. M. Bairstow, England v South Africa at Cape Town**	**2015-16**

eventh Wicket

60	Bhupinder Singh jnr/P. Dharmani, Punjab v Delhi at Delhi	1994-95
71	M. R. Marsh/S. M. Whiteman, Australia A v India A at Brisbane	2014
66*	J. M. Bairstow/T. T. Bresnan, Yorkshire v Durham at Chester-le-Street	2015
47	D. St E. Atkinson/C. C. Depeiza, West Indies v Australia at Bridgetown	1954-55
47	Farhad Reza/Sanjamul Islam, Rajshahi v Chittagong at Savar	2013-14

Eighth Wicket

433	A. Sims and V. T. Trumper, A. Sims' Aust. XI v Canterbury at Christchurch	1913-1
392	A. Mishra/J. Yadav, Haryana v Karnataka at Hubli	2012-1
332	I. J. L. Trott/S. C. J. Broad, England v Pakistan at Lord's	201
313	Wasim Akram/Saqlain Mushtaq, Pakistan v Zimbabwe at Sheikhupura	1996-9
292	R. Peel/Lord Hawke, Yorkshire v Warwickshire at Birmingham	189

Ninth Wicket

283	A. Warren/J. Chapman, Derbyshire v Warwickshire at Blackwell	191
268	J. B. Commins/N. Boje, South Africa A v Mashonaland at Harare	1994-9
261	W. L. Madsen/T. Poynton, Derbyshire v Northants at Northampton	201
251	J. W. H. T. Douglas/S. N. Hare, Essex v Derbyshire at Leyton	192
249*†	A. S. Srivastava/K. Seth, Madhya Pradesh v Vidarbha at Indore	2000-0

† *276 unbeaten runs were scored for this wicket in two separate partnerships; after Srivastav retired hurt, Seth and N. D. Hirwani added 27.*

Tenth Wicket

307	A. F. Kippax/J. E. H. Hooker, New South Wales v Victoria at Melbourne	1928-2
249	C. T. Sarwate/S. N. Banerjee, Indians v Surrey at The Oval	194
239	Aqeel Arshad/Ali Raza, Lahore Whites v Hyderabad at Lahore	2004-0
235	F. E. Woolley/A. Fielder, Kent v Worcestershire at Stourbridge	190
233	Ajay Sharma/Maninder Singh, Delhi v Bombay at Bombay	1991-9

There have been only 13 last-wicket stands of 200 or more.

UNUSUAL DISMISSALS

Handled the Ball

There have been **63** instances in first-class cricket. The most recent are:

W. S. A. Williams	Canterbury v Otago at Dunedin	2012-1
E. Lewis	Trinidad & Tobago v Leeward Islands at Port-of-Spain	2013-1
C. A. Pujara	Derbyshire v Leicestershire at Derby	201
I. Khan	Dolphins v Lions at Johannesburg	2014-1
K. Lesporis	**Windward Islands v Barbados at Bridgetown**	**2015-1**
S. R. Dickson	**Kent v Leicestershire at Leicester**	**201**
M. Z. Hamza	**Cape Cobras v Knights at Bloemfontein**	**2016-1**

Obstructing the Field

There have been **26** instances in first-class cricket. T. Straw of Worcestershire was given out fo obstruction v Warwickshire in both 1899 and 1901. The most recent are:

Riaz Kail	Abbottabad v Quetta at Abbottabad	2009-1
M. R. Ramprakash	Surrey v Gloucestershire at Cheltenham	201
Z. E. Surkari	Canada v Afghanistan at King City	201
Nasir Ahmadzai	Afghanistan v Zimbabwe A at Harare	201
W. E. Bell	Northern Cape v Border at Kimberley	2015-1
Jahid Ali	**Pakistan A v Zimbabwe A at Bulawayo**	**2016-1**

lit the Ball Twice

here have been **21** instances in first-class cricket. The last occurrence in England involved J. H. ing of Leicestershire v Surrey at The Oval in 1906. The most recent are:

.ziz Malik	Lahore Division v Faisalabad at Sialkot	1984-85
ıved Mohammad	Multan v Karachi Whites at Sahiwal	1986-87
hahid Pervez	Jammu & Kashmir v Punjab at Srinagar	1986-87
.li Naqvi	PNSC v National Bank at Faisalabad	1998-99
. George	Tamil Nadu v Maharashtra at Pune	1998-99
Iaqsood Raza	Lahore Division v PNSC at Sheikhupura	1999-2000
). Mahajan	Jammu & Kashmir v Bihar at Jammu	2005-06

'imed Out

here have been **five** instances in first-class cricket:

.. Jordaan	Eastern Province v Transvaal at Port Elizabeth (SACB match)	1987-88
I. Yadav	Tripura v Orissa at Cuttack	1997-98
'. C. Drakes	Border v Free State at East London	2002-03
.. J. Harris	Nottinghamshire v Durham UCCE at Nottingham	2003
:. A. Austin	Combined Campuses & Colleges v Windward Is at Arnos Vale	2013-14

BOWLING RECORDS

TEN WICKETS IN AN INNINGS

ı the history of first-class cricket, there have been **80** instances of a bowler taking all ten wickets in n innings, plus a further three instances of ten wickets in 12-a-side matches. Occurrences since the 'econd World War:

	O	*M*	*R*		
V. E. Hollies (Warwickshire)	20.4	4	49	v Notts at Birmingham	1946
. M. Sims (East)	18.4	2	90	v West at Kingston	1948
'. E. Bailey (Essex)	39.4	9	90	v Lancashire at Clacton	1949
K. Graveney (Glos.)	18.4	2	66	v Derbyshire at Chesterfield	1949
:. Berry (Lancashire)	36.2	9	102	v Worcestershire at Blackpool	1953
. P. Gupte (President's XI)	24.2	7	78	v Combined XI at Bombay	1954-55
. C. Laker (Surrey)	46	18	88	v Australians at The Oval	1956
. C. Laker (England)	51.2	23	53	v Australia at Manchester	1956
ǰ. A. R. Lock (Surrey)	29.1	18	54	v Kent at Blackheath	1956
<. Smales (Nottinghamshire)	41.3	20	66	v Gloucestershire at Stroud	1956
'. M. Chatterjee (Bengal)	19	11	20	v Assam at Jorhat	1956-57
. D. Bannister (Warwickshire)	23.3	11	41	v Comb. Services at Birmingham†	1959
\. J. G. Pearson (Cambridge U.)	30.3	8	78	v Leics at Loughborough	1961
I. I. Thomson (Sussex)	34.2	19	49	v Warwickshire at Worthing	1964
'. J. Allan (Queensland)	15.6	3	61	v Victoria at Melbourne	1965-66
. J. Brayshaw (W. Australia)	17.6	4	44	v Victoria at Perth	1967-68
'hahid Mahmood (Karachi Whites)	25	5	58	v Khairpur at Karachi	1969-70
:. E. Hemmings (International XI)	49.3	14	175	v West Indies XI at Kingston	1982-83
'. Sunderam (Rajasthan)	22	5	78	v Vidarbha at Jodhpur	1985-86
;. T. Jefferies (W. Province)	22.5	7	59	v Orange Free State at Cape Town	1987-88
mran Adil (Bahawalpur)	22.5	3	92	v Faisalabad at Faisalabad	1989-90
ǰ. P. Wickremasinghe (Sinhalese)	19.2	5	41	v Kalutara PCC at Colombo (SSC)	1991-92
ł. L. Johnson (Middlesex)	18.5	6	45	v Derbyshire at Derby	1994
Naeem Akhtar (Rawalpindi B)	21.3	10	28	v Peshawar at Peshawar	1995-96
\. Kumble (India)	26.3	9	74	v Pakistan at Delhi	1998-99

	O	M	R		
D. S. Mohanty (East Zone)	19	5	46	v South Zone at Agartala	2000-01
O. D. Gibson (Durham)	17.3	1	47	v Hampshire at Chester-le-Street	2007
M. W. Olivier (Warriors)	26.3	4	65	v Eagles at Bloemfontein	2007-08
Zulfiqar Babar (Multan)	39.4	3	143	v Islamabad at Multan	2009-10

* *W. E. Hollies bowled seven and had three lbw. The only other instance of a bowler achieving the feat without the direct assistance of a fielder came in 1850 when J. Wisden bowled all ten, for North v South at Lord's.*

† *Mitchells & Butlers Ground.*

OUTSTANDING BOWLING ANALYSES

	O	M	R	W		
H. Verity (Yorkshire)	19.4	16	10	10	v Nottinghamshire at Leeds	1932
G. Elliott (Victoria)	19	17	2	9	v Tasmania at Launceston	1857-58
Ahad Khan (Railways)	6.3	4	7	9	v Dera Ismail Khan at Lahore	1964-65
J. C. Laker (England)	14	12	2	8	v The Rest at Bradford	1950
D. Shackleton (Hampshire)	11.1	7	4	8	v Somerset at Weston-s-Mare	1955
E. Peate (Yorkshire)	16	11	5	8	v Surrey at Holbeck	1883
K. M. Dabengwa (Westerns)	4.4	3	1	7	v Northerns at Harare	2006-07
F. R. Spofforth (Australians)	8.3	6	3	7	v England XI at Birmingham	1884
W. A. Henderson (NE Transvaal)	9.3	7	4	7	v OFS at Bloemfontein	1937-38
Rajinder Goel (Haryana)	7	4	4	7	v Jammu & Kashmir at Chandigarh	1977-78
N. W. Bracken (NSW)	7	5	4	7	v South Australia at Sydney	2004-05
V. I. Smith (South Africans)	4.5	3	1	6	v Derbyshire at Derby	1947
S. Cosstick (Victoria)	21.1	20	1	6	v Tasmania at Melbourne	1868-69
Israr Ali (Bahawalpur)	11	10	1	6	v Dacca U. at Bahawalpur	1957-58
A. D. Pougher (MCC)	3	3	0	5	v Australians at Lord's	1896
G. R. Cox (Sussex)	6	6	0	5	v Somerset at Weston-s-Mare	1921
R. K. Tyldesley (Lancashire)	5	5	0	5	v Leicestershire at Manchester	1924
P. T. Mills (Gloucestershire)	6.4	6	0	5	v Somerset at Bristol	1928

MOST WICKETS IN A MATCH

19-90	J. C. Laker	England v Australia at Manchester	1956
17-48†	C. Blythe	Kent v Northamptonshire at Northampton	1907
17-50	C. T. B. Turner	Australians v England XI at Hastings	1888
17-54	W. P. Howell	Australians v Western Province at Cape Town	1902-03
17-56	C. W. L. Parker	Gloucestershire v Essex at Gloucester	1925
17-67	A. P. Freeman	Kent v Sussex at Hove	1922
17-89	W. G. Grace	Gloucestershire v Nottinghamshire at Cheltenham	1877
17-89	F. C. L. Matthews	Nottinghamshire v Northants at Nottingham	1923
17-91	H. Dean	Lancashire v Yorkshire at Liverpool	1913
17-91†	H. Verity	Yorkshire v Essex at Leyton	1933
17-92	A. P. Freeman	Kent v Warwickshire at Folkestone	1932
17-103	W. Mycroft	Derbyshire v Hampshire at Southampton	1876
17-106	G. R. Cox	Sussex v Warwickshire at Horsham	1926
17-106†	T. W. J. Goddard	Gloucestershire v Kent at Bristol	1939
17-119	W. Mead	Essex v Hampshire at Southampton	1895
17-137	W. Brearley	Lancashire v Somerset at Manchester	1905
17-137	J. M. Davison	Canada v USA at Fort Lauderdale	2004
17-159	S. F. Barnes	England v South Africa at Johannesburg	1913-14
17-201	G. Giffen	South Australia v Victoria at Adelaide	1885-86
17-212	J. C. Clay	Glamorgan v Worcestershire at Swansea	1937

† *Achieved in a single day.*

H. Arkwright took 18-96 for MCC v Gentlemen of Kent in a 12-a-side match at Canterbury in 1861.

There have been ***58*** *instances of a bowler taking 16 wickets in an 11-a-side match, the most recent being 16-100 by J. U. Chaturanga for Singha v Antonians at Gampaha, 2010-11.*

FOUR WICKETS WITH CONSECUTIVE BALLS

here have been **44** instances in first-class cricket. R. J. Crisp achieved the feat twice, for Western rovince in 1931-32 and 1933-34. A. E. Trott took four in four balls and another hat-trick in the me innings for Middlesex v Somerset in 1907, his benefit match. Occurrences since 2007:

abish Khan	Karachi Whites v ZTBL at Karachi	2009-10
amran Hussain	Habib Bank v Lahore Shalimar at Lahore	2009-10
. Wagner	Otago v Wellington at Queenstown	2010-11
halid Usman	Abbottabad v Karachi Blues at Karachi	2011-12
ahmudullah	Central Zone v North Zone at Savar	2013-14
. C. Thomas	Somerset v Sussex at Taunton	2014
aj Wali	Peshawar v Port Qasim Authority at Peshawar	2015-16
. G. R. P. Jayasuriya	**Colts v Badureliya at Maggona**	**2015-16**
. R. Smuts	**Eastern Province v Boland at Paarl**	**2015-16**

n their match with England at The Oval in 1863, Surrey lost four wickets in the course of a four-all over from G. Bennett.

Sussex lost five wickets in the course of the final (six-ball) over of their match with Surrey at astbourne in 1972. P. I. Pocock, who had taken three wickets in his previous over, captured four ore, taking in all seven wickets with 11 balls, a feat unique in first-class matches. (The eighth icket fell to a run-out.)

In 1996, K. D. James took four in four balls for Hampshire against Indians at Southampton and cored a century, a feat later emulated by Mahmudullah and Smuts.

HAT-TRICKS

ouble Hat-Trick

esides Trott's performance, which is mentioned in the preceding section, the following instances re recorded of players having performed the hat-trick twice in the same match, Rao doing so in the ame innings.

. Shaw	Nottinghamshire v Gloucestershire at Nottingham	1884
. J. Matthews	Australia v South Africa at Manchester	1912
. W. L. Parker	Gloucestershire v Middlesex at Bristol	1924
. O. Jenkins	Worcestershire v Surrey at Worcester	1949
. S. Rao	Services v Northern Punjab at Amritsar	1963-64
min Lakhani	Combined XI v Indians at Multan	1978-79

ive Wickets in Six Balls

. H. Copson	Derbyshire v Warwickshire at Derby	1937
. A. Henderson	NE Transvaal v Orange Free State at Bloemfontein	1937-38
. I. Pocock	Surrey v Sussex at Eastbourne	1972
asir Arafat	Rawalpindi v Faisalabad at Rawalpindi	2004-05
. Wagner	Otago v Wellington at Queenstown	2010-11

asir Arafat's five wickets were spread across two innings and interrupted only by a no-ball. Wagner as the first to take five wickets in a single over.

ost Hat-Tricks

. V. P. Wright	7	R. G. Barlow	4	T. G. Matthews	4
. W. J. Goddard	6	Fazl-e-Akbar	4	M. J. Procter	4
. W. L. Parker	6	A. P. Freeman	4	T. Richardson	4
. Haigh	5	J. T. Hearne	4	F. R. Spofforth	4
. W. C. Jupp	5	J. C. Laker	4	F. S. Trueman	4
. E. G. Rhodes	5	G. A. R. Lock	4		
. A. Tarrant	5	G. G. Macaulay	4		

Hat-Trick on Debut

There have been **18** instances in first-class cricket. Occurrences since 2000:

S. M. Harwood	Victoria v Tasmania at Melbourne	2002-0
P. Connell	Ireland v Netherlands at Rotterdam	200
A. Mithun	Karnataka v Uttar Pradesh at Meerut	2009-1
Zohaib Shera	Karachi Whites v National Bank at Karachi	2009-1

R. R. Phillips (Border) took a hat-trick in his first over in first-class cricket (v Eastern Province c Port Elizabeth, 1939-40) having previously played in four matches without bowling.

250 WICKETS IN A SEASON

	Season	*O*	*M*	*R*	*W*	*Avg*
A. P. Freeman	1928	1,976.1	423	5,489	304	18.0
A. P. Freeman	1933	2,039	651	4,549	298	15.2
T. Richardson	1895‡	1,690.1	463	4,170	290	14.3
C. T. B. Turner	1888†	2,427.2	1,127	3,307	283	11.6
A. P. Freeman	1931	1,618	360	4,307	276	15.6
A. P. Freeman	1930	1,914.3	472	4,632	275	16.8
T. Richardson	1897‡	1,603.4	495	3,945	273	14.4
A. P. Freeman	1929	1,670.5	381	4,879	267	18.2
W. Rhodes	1900	1,553	455	3,606	261	13.8
J. T. Hearne	1896‡	2,003.1	818	3,670	257	14.2
A. P. Freeman	1932	1,565.5	404	4,149	253	16.3
W. Rhodes	1901	1,565	505	3,797	251	15.1

† *Indicates 4-ball overs.* ‡ *5-ball overs.*

In four consecutive seasons (1928–1931), A. P. Freeman took 1,122 wickets, and in eight consecutiv seasons (1928–1935), 2,090 wickets. In each of these eight seasons he took over 200 wickets.

T. Richardson took 1,005 wickets in four consecutive seasons (1894–1897).

The earliest date by which any bowler has taken 100 in an English season is June 12, achieved b J. T. Hearne in 1896 and C. W. L. Parker in 1931, when A. P. Freeman did it on June 13.

100 WICKETS IN A SEASON MOST TIMES

(Includes overseas tours and seasons)

W. Rhodes	23	C. W. L. Parker	16	G. H. Hirst	1
D. Shackleton	20	R. T. D. Perks	16	A. S. Kennedy	1
A. P. Freeman	17	F. J. Titmus	16		
T. W. J. Goddard	16	J. T. Hearne	15		

D. Shackleton reached 100 wickets in 20 successive seasons – 1949–1968.

Since the reduction of County Championship matches in 1969, D. L. Underwood (five times) and J. K. Lever (four times) are the only bowlers to have reached 100 wickets in a season more thar twice. The highest aggregate in a season since 1969 is 134 by M. D. Marshall in 1982.

The most instances of 200 wickets in a season is eight by A. P. Freeman, who did it in eigh successive seasons – 1928 to 1935 – including 304 in 1928. C. W. L. Parker did it five times, T. W. J. Goddard four times, and J. T. Hearne, G. A. Lohmann, W. Rhodes, T. Richardson, M. W. Tate and H. Verity three times each.

The last bowler to reach 200 wickets in a season was G. A. R. Lock (212 in 1957).

An expanded and regularly updated online version of the Records can be found at www.wisdenrecords.com

100 WICKETS IN A SEASON OUTSIDE ENGLAND

V		Season	Country	R	Avge
16	M. W. Tate	1926-27	India/Ceylon	1,599	13.78
13	Kabir Khan	1998-99	Pakistan	1,706	15.09
07	Ijaz Faqih	1985-86	Pakistan	1,719	16.06
06	C. T. B. Turner	1887-88	Australia	1,441	13.59
06	R. Benaud	1957-58	South Africa	2,056	19.39
05	Murtaza Hussain	1995-96	Pakistan	1,882	17.92
04	S. F. Barnes	1913-14	South Africa	1,117	10.74
04	Sajjad Akbar	1989-90	Pakistan	2,328	22.38
03	Abdul Qadir	1982-83	Pakistan	2,367	22.98

LEADING BOWLERS IN AN ENGLISH SEASON

(Qualification: 10 wickets in 10 innings)

eason	Leading wicket-taker	Wkts	Avge	Top of averages	Wkts	Avge
946	W. E. Hollies	184	15.60	A. Booth	111	11.61
947	T. W. J. Goddard	238	17.30	J. C. Clay	65	16.44
948	J. E. Walsh	174	19.56	J. C. Clay	41	14.17
949	R. O. Jenkins	183	21.19	T. W. J. Goddard	160	19.18
950	R. Tattersall	193	13.59	R. Tattersall	193	13.59
951	R. Appleyard	200	14.14	R. Appleyard	200	14.14
952	J. H. Wardle	177	19.54	F. S. Trueman	61	13.78
953	B. Dooland	172	16.58	C. J. Knott	38	13.71
954	B. Dooland	196	15.48	J. B. Statham	92	14.13
955	G. A. R. Lock	216	14.49	R. Appleyard	85	13.01
956	D. J. Shepherd	177	15.36	G. A. R. Lock	155	12.46
957	G. A. R. Lock	212	12.02	G. A. R. Lock	212	12.02
958	G. A. R. Lock	170	12.08	H. L. Jackson	143	10.99
959	D. Shackleton	148	21.55	J. B. Statham	139	15.01
960	F. S. Trueman	175	13.98	J. B. Statham	135	12.31
961	J. A. Flavell	171	17.79	J. A. Flavell	171	17.79
962	D. Shackleton	172	20.15	C. Cook	58	17.13
963	D. Shackleton	146	16.75	C. C. Griffith	119	12.83
964	D. Shackleton	142	20.40	J. A. Standen	64	13.00
965	D. Shackleton	144	16.08	H. J. Rhodes	119	11.04
966	D. L. Underwood	157	13.80	D. L. Underwood	157	13.80
967	T. W. Cartwright	147	15.52	D. L. Underwood	136	12.39
968	R. Illingworth	131	14.36	O. S. Wheatley	82	12.95
969	R. M. H. Cottam	109	21.04	A. Ward	69	14.82
970	D. J. Shepherd	106	19.16	Majid Khan	11	18.81
971	L. R. Gibbs	131	18.89	G. G. Arnold	83	17.12
972	T. W. Cartwright	98	18.64	I. M. Chappell	10	10.60
	B. Stead	98	20.38			
973	B. S. Bedi	105	17.94	T. W. Cartwright	89	15.84
974	A. M. E. Roberts	119	13.62	A. M. E. Roberts	119	13.62
975	P. G. Lee	112	18.45	A. M. E. Roberts	57	15.80
976	G. A. Cope	93	24.13	M. A. Holding	55	14.38
977	M. J. Procter	109	18.04	R. A. Woolmer	19	15.21
978	D. L. Underwood	110	14.49	D. L. Underwood	110	14.49
979	D. L. Underwood	106	14.85	J. Garner	55	13.83
	J. K. Lever	106	17.30			
980	R. D. Jackman	121	15.40	J. Garner	49	13.93
981	R. J. Hadlee	105	14.89	R. J. Hadlee	105	14.89
982	M. D. Marshall	134	15.73	R. J. Hadlee	61	14.57
983	J. K. Lever	106	16.28	Imran Khan	12	7.16
	D. L. Underwood	106	19.28			
984	R. J. Hadlee	117	14.05	R. J. Hadlee	117	14.05

Season	*Leading wicket-taker*	*Wkts*	*Avge*	*Top of averages*	*Wkts*	*Avge*
1985	N. V. Radford	101	24.68	R. M. Ellison	65	17.2
1986	C. A. Walsh	118	18.17	M. D. Marshall	100	15.0
1987	N. V. Radford	109	20.81	R. J. Hadlee	97	12.6
1988	F. D. Stephenson	125	18.31	M. D. Marshall	42	13.1
1989	D. R. Pringle	94	18.64	T. M. Alderman	70	15.6
	S. L. Watkin	94	25.09			
1990	N. A. Foster	94	26.61	I. R. Bishop	59	19.0
1991	Waqar Younis	113	14.65	Waqar Younis	113	14.6
1992	C. A. Walsh	92	15.96	C. A. Walsh	92	15.9
1993	S. L. Watkin	92	22.80	Wasim Akram	59	19.2
1994	M. M. Patel	90	22.86	C. E. L. Ambrose	77	14.4
1995	A. Kumble	105	20.40	A. A. Donald	89	16.0
1996	C. A. Walsh	85	16.84	C. E. L. Ambrose	43	16.6
1997	A. M. Smith	83	17.63	A. A. Donald	60	15.6
1998	C. A. Walsh	106	17.31	V. J. Wells	36	14.2
1999	A. Sheriyar	92	24.70	Saqlain Mushtaq	58	11.3
2000	G. D. McGrath	80	13.21	C. A. Walsh	40	11.4
2001	R. J. Kirtley	75	23.32	G. D. McGrath	40	15.6
2002	M. J. Saggers	83	21.51	C. P. Schofield	18	18.3
	K. J. Dean	83	23.50			
2003	Mushtaq Ahmed	103	24.65	Shoaib Akhtar	34	17.0
2004	Mushtaq Ahmed	84	27.59	D. S. Lehmann	15	17.4
2005	S. K. Warne	87	22.50	M. Muralitharan	36	15.0
2006	Mushtaq Ahmed	102	19.91	Naved-ul-Hasan	35	16.7
2007	Mushtaq Ahmed	90	25.66	Harbhajan Singh	37	18.5
2008	J. A. Tomlinson	67	24.76	M. Davies	41	14.6
2009	Danish Kaneria	75	23.69	G. Onions	69	19.9
2010	A. R. Adams	68	22.17	J. K. H. Naik	35	17.6
2011	D. D. Masters	93	18.13	T. T. Bresnan	29	17.6
2012	G. Onions	72	14.73	G. Onions	72	14.7
2013	G. Onions	73	18.92	T. A. Copeland	45	18.2
2014	M. H. A. Footitt	84	19.19	G. R. Napier	52	15.6
2015	C. Rushworth	90	20.54	R. J. Sidebottom	43	18.0
2016	**G. R. Napier**	**69**	**22.30**	**J. M. Anderson**	**45**	**17.0**
	J. S. Patel	**69**	**24.02**			

MOST WICKETS

Dates in italics denote the first half of an overseas season; i.e. *1970* denotes the 1970-71 season.

		Career	*W*	*R*	*Avg*
1	W. Rhodes	1898–1930	4,187	69,993	16.7
2	A. P. Freeman	1914–1936	3,776	69,577	18.4
3	C. W. L. Parker	1903–1935	3,278	63,817	19.4
4	J. T. Hearne	1888–1923	3,061	54,352	17.7
5	T. W. J. Goddard	1922–1952	2,979	59,116	19.8
6	W. G. Grace	1865–1908	2,876	51,545	17.9
7	A. S. Kennedy	1907–1936	2,874	61,034	21.2
8	D. Shackleton	1948–1969	2,857	53,303	18.6
9	G. A. R. Lock	1946–*1970*	2,844	54,709	19.2
10	F. J. Titmus	1949–1982	2,830	63,313	22.3
11	M. W. Tate	1912–1937	2,784	50,571	18.1
12	G. H. Hirst	1891–1929	2,739	51,282	18.7
13	C. Blythe	1899–1914	2,506	42,136	16.8

Some works of reference provide career figures which differ from those in this list, owing to the exclusion or inclusion of matches recognised or not recognised as first-class by Wisden. *A fuller list can be found in* Wisdens *up to 2011.*

urrent Players with 750 Wickets

	Career	*W*	*R*	*Avge*
M. R. K. B. Herath	*1996–2016*	983	24,514	24.93
Hettiarachchi	*1994–2016*	903	21,024	23.28
ısir Arafat	*1997–2016*	787	18,910	24.02
Weerakoon	*1995–2016*	783	16,919	21.60
M. Anderson	2002–*2016*	777	20,556	26.45
ırbhajan Singh	*1997–2015*	777	22,418	28.85
ıran Tahir	*1997–2016*	771	20,474	26.55

ALL-ROUND RECORDS

REMARKABLE ALL-ROUND MATCHES

. E. Walker	20*	108	10-74	4-17	England v Surrey at The Oval	1859
'. G. Grace	104		2-60	10-49	MCC v Oxford University at Oxford	1886
. Giffen	271		9-96	7-70	South Australia v Victoria at Adelaide	1891-92
. J. T. Bosanquet	103	100*	3-75	8-53	Middlesex v Sussex at Lord's	1905
. H. Hirst	111	117*	6-70	5-45	Yorkshire v Somerset at Bath	1906
. D. Stephenson	111	117	4-105	7-117	Notts v Yorkshire at Nottingham	1988

. M. Grace, for MCC v Gentlemen of Kent in a 12-a-side match at Canterbury in 1862, scored 192 ıd took 5-77 and 10-69.*

HUNDRED AND HAT-TRICK

. Giffen, Australians v Lancashire at Manchester	1884
'. E. Roller, Surrey v Sussex at The Oval	1885
'. B. Burns, Worcestershire v Gloucestershire at Worcester	1913
. W. C. Jupp, Sussex v Essex at Colchester	1921
E. S. Wyatt, MCC v Ceylonese at Colombo (Victoria Park)	1926-27
. N. Constantine, West Indians v Northamptonshire at Northampton	1928
. E. Davies, Glamorgan v Leicestershire at Leicester	1937
. M. Merchant, Dr C. R. Pereira's XI v Sir Homi Mehta's XI at Bombay	1946-47
I. J. Procter, Gloucestershire v Essex at Westcliff-on-Sea	1972
I. J. Procter, Gloucestershire v Leicestershire at Bristol	1979
. D. James, Hampshire v Indians at Southampton	1996
E. C. Franklin, Gloucestershire v Derbyshire at Cheltenham	2009
ɔhag Gazi, Barisal v Khulna at Khulna	2012-13
ɔhag Gazi, Bangladesh v New Zealand at Chittagong	2013-14
Iahmudullah, Central Zone v North Zone at Savar	2013-14
. R. Smuts, Eastern Province v Boland at Paarl	**2015-16**

W. E. Roller is the only player to combine 200 with a hat-trick.

K. D. James, Mahmudullah and K. R. Smuts all combined 100 with four wickets in four balls Mahmudullah's split between two innings).

THE DOUBLE

he double was traditionally regarded as 1,000 runs and 100 wickets in an English season. The feat ecame exceptionally rare after the reduction of County Championship matches in 1969.

Remarkable Seasons

	Season	*R*	*W*		*Season*	*R*	*W*
. H. Hirst	1906	2,385	208	J. H. Parks	1937	3,003	101

1,000 Runs and 100 Wickets

W. Rhodes	16	W. G. Grace	8	F. J. Titmus	
G. H. Hirst	14	M. S. Nichols	8	F. E. Woolley	
V. W. C. Jupp	10	A. E. Relf	8	G. E. Tribe	
W. E. Astill	9	F. A. Tarrant	8		
T. E. Bailey	8	M. W. Tate	8†		

† *M. W. Tate also scored 1,193 runs and took 116 wickets on the 1926-27 MCC tour of India an Ceylon.*

R. J. Hadlee (1984) and F. D. Stephenson (1988) are the only players to perform the feat since th reduction of County Championship matches in 1969. A complete list of those performing the fea before then may be found on page 202 of the 1982 Wisden. *T. E. Bailey (1959) was the last playe to achieve 2,000 runs and 100 wickets in a season; M. W. Tate (1925) the last to reach 1,000 run and 200 wickets. Full lists may be found in* Wisdens *up to 2003.*

Wicketkeeper's Double

The only wicketkeepers to achieve 1,000 runs and 100 dismissals in a season were L. E. G. Ame (1928, 1929 and 1932, when he scored 2,482 runs) and J. T. Murray (1957).

WICKETKEEPING RECORDS

MOST DISMISSALS IN AN INNINGS

9 (8ct, 1st)	Tahir Rashid	Habib Bank v PACO at Gujranwala	1992-9
9 (7ct, 2st)	W. R. James*	Matabeleland v Mashonaland CD at Bulawayo	1995-9
8 (all ct)	A. T. W. Grout	Queensland v Western Australia at Brisbane	1959-6
8 (all ct)†	D. E. East	Essex v Somerset at Taunton	198
8 (all ct)	S. A. Marsh‡	Kent v Middlesex at Lord's	199
8 (6ct, 2st)	T. J. Zoehrer	Australians v Surrey at The Oval	199
8 (7ct, 1st)	D. S. Berry	Victoria v South Australia at Melbourne	1996-9
8 (7ct, 1st)	Y. S. S. Mendis	Bloomfield v Kurunegala Y at Colombo (Bloomfield)	2000-0
8 (7ct, 1st)	S. Nath§	Assam v Tripura at Guwahati	2001-0
8 (all ct)	J. N. Batty¶	Surrey v Kent at The Oval	200
8 (all ct)	Golam Mabud	Sylhet v Dhaka at Dhaka	2005-0
8 (all ct)	A. Z. M. Dyili	Eastern Province v Free State at Port Elizabeth	2009-1
8 (all ct)	D. C. de Boorder	Otago v Wellington at Wellington	2009-1
8 (all ct)	R. S. Second	Free State v North West at Bloemfontein	2011-1
8 (all ct)	T. L. Tsolekile	South Africa A v Sri Lanka A at Durban	201

There have been ***105*** *further instances of seven dismissals in an innings. R. W. Taylor achieved th feat three times, and G. J. Hopkins, Kamran Akmal, I. Khaleel, S. A. Marsh, K. J. Piper, Shahi Hossain, T. L. Tsolekile and Wasim Bari twice. Khaleel did it twice in the same match. Marsh's an Tsolekile's two instances both included one of eight dismssals – see above. H. Yarnold made si stumpings and one catch in an innings for Worcestershire v Scotland at Dundee in 1951. A fuller lis can be found in* Wisdens *before 2004.*

* *W. R. James also scored 99 and 99 not out.*
† *The first eight wickets to fall.*
‡ *S. A. Marsh also scored 108 not out.*
§ *On his only first-class appearance.*
¶ *J. N. Batty also scored 129.*

WICKETKEEPERS' HAT-TRICKS

W. H. Brain, Gloucestershire v Somerset at Cheltenham, 1893 – three stumpings off successive ball from C. L. Townsend.

G. O. Dawkes, Derbyshire v Worcestershire at Kidderminster, 1958 – three catches off successive balls from H. L. Jackson.

R. C. Russell, Gloucestershire v Surrey at The Oval, 1986 – three catches off successive balls fro C. A. Walsh and D. V. Lawrence (2).

MOST DISMISSALS IN A MATCH

4 (11ct, 3st)	I. Khaleel	Hyderabad v Assam at Guwahati	2011-12
3 (11ct, 2st)	W. R. James*	Matabeleland v Mashonaland CD at Bulawayo	1995-96
2 (8ct, 4st)	E. Pooley	Surrey v Sussex at The Oval	1868
2 (9ct, 3st)	D. Tallon	Queensland v New South Wales at Sydney	1938-39
2 (9ct, 3st)	H. B. Taber	New South Wales v South Australia at Adelaide	1968-69
2 (all ct)	P. D. McGlashan	Northern Districts v Central Districts at Whangarei	2009-10
2 (11ct, 1st)	T. L. Tsolekile	Lions v Dolphins at Johannesburg	2010-11
2 (all ct)	Kashif Mahmood	Lahore Shalimar v Abbottabad at Abbottabad	2010-11
2 (all ct)	R. S. Second	Free State v North West at Bloemfontein	2011-12

W. R. James also scored 99 and 99 not out.

100 DISMISSALS IN A SEASON

28 (79ct, 49st)	L. E. G. Ames	1929	104 (82ct, 22st)	J. T. Murray	1957
22 (70ct, 52st)	L. E. G. Ames	1928	102 (69ct, 33st)	F. H. Huish	1913
10 (63ct, 47st)	H. Yarnold	1949	102 (95ct, 7st)	J. T. Murray	1960
07 (77ct, 30st)	G. Duckworth	1928	101 (62ct, 39st)	F. H. Huish	1911
07 (96ct, 11st)	J. G. Binks	1960	101 (85ct, 16st)	R. Booth	1960
04 (40ct, 64st)	L. E. G. Ames	1932	100 (91ct, 9st)	R. Booth	1964

. E. G. Ames achieved the two highest stumping totals in a season: 64 in 1932, and 52 in 1928.

MOST DISMISSALS

ates in italics denote the first half of an overseas season; i.e. *1914* denotes the 1914-15 season.

		Career	*M*	*Ct*	*St*
R. W. Taylor	1,649	1960–1988	639	1,473	176
J. T. Murray	1,527	1952–1975	635	1,270	257
H. Strudwick	1,497	1902–1927	675	1,242	255
A. P. E. Knott	1,344	1964–1985	511	1,211	133
R. C. Russell	1,320	1981–2004	465	1,192	128
F. H. Huish	1,310	1895–1914	497	933	377
B. Taylor	1,294	1949–1973	572	1,083	211
S. J. Rhodes	1,263	1981–2004	440	1,139	124
D. Hunter	1,253	1888–1909	548	906	347

urrent Players with 500 Dismissals

		Career	*M*	*Ct*	*St*
,047	C. M. W. Read	*1997*–2016	334	995	52
841	Kamran Akmal	*1997–2016*	219	778	63
834	J. S. Foster	2000–2016	273	775	59
763	M. A. Wallace	1999–2016	264	707	56
667	P. Mustard	2002–2016	195	648	19
590	T. R. Ambrose	2001–2016	210	553	37
589	Zulfiqar Jan	*1999–2016*	161	560	29
560	C. D. Hartley	*2003–2016*	128	543	17
521	N. J. O'Brien	2004–2016	168	474	47
507	Adnan Akmal	*2003–2016*	148	478	29

ome of these figures include catches taken in the field.

FIELDING RECORDS

excluding wicketkeepers

MOST CATCHES IN AN INNINGS

7	M. J. Stewart	Surrey v Northamptonshire at Northampton	195
7	A. S. Brown	Gloucestershire v Nottinghamshire at Nottingham	196
7	R. Clarke	Warwickshire v Lancashire at Liverpool	201

MOST CATCHES IN A MATCH

10	W. R. Hammond†	Gloucestershire v Surrey at Cheltenham	192
9	R. Clarke	Warwickshire v Lancashire at Liverpool	201
8	W. B. Burns	Worcestershire v Yorkshire at Bradford	190
8	F. G. Travers	Europeans v Parsees at Bombay	1923-2
8	A. H. Bakewell	Northamptonshire v Essex at Leyton	192
8	W. R. Hammond	Gloucestershire v Worcestershire at Cheltenham	193
8	K. J. Grieves	Lancashire v Sussex at Manchester	195
8	C. A. Milton	Gloucestershire v Sussex at Hove	195
8	G. A. R. Lock	Surrey v Warwickshire at The Oval	195
8	J. M. Prodger	Kent v Gloucestershire at Cheltenham	196
8	P. M. Walker	Glamorgan v Derbyshire at Swansea	197
8	Masood Anwar	Rawalpindi v Lahore Division at Rawalpindi	1983-8
8	M. C. J. Ball	Gloucestershire v Yorkshire at Cheltenham	199
8	J. D. Carr	Middlesex v Warwickshire at Birmingham	199
8	G. A. Hick	Worcestershire v Essex at Chelmsford	200
8	Naved Yasin	State Bank v Bahawalpur Stags at Bahawalpur	2014-1
8	A. M. Rahane	India v Sri Lanka at Galle	2015-1

† *Hammond also scored a hundred in each innings.*

MOST CATCHES IN A SEASON

78	W. R. Hammond	1928
77	M. J. Stewart	1957
73	P. M. Walker	1961
71	P. J. Sharpe	196
70	J. Tunnicliffe	190

The most catches by a fielder since the reduction of County Championship matches in 1969 is 59 by G. R. J. Roope in 1971.

MOST CATCHES

Dates in italics denote the first half of an overseas season; i.e. *1970* denotes the 1970-71 season.

		Career	*M*
1,018	F. E. Woolley	1906–1938	979
887	W. G. Grace	1865–1908	879
830	G. A. R. Lock	1946–*1970*	654
819	W. R. Hammond	1920–1951	634
813	D. B. Close	1949–1986	786
784	J. G. Langridge	1928–1955	574
764	W. Rhodes	1898–1930	1,107
758	C. A. Milton	1948–1974	620
754	E. H. Hendren	1907–1938	833

*The most catches by a current player is **513** by **M. E. Trescothick** between 1993 and 2016 (including two taken while deputising as wicketkeeper).*

TEAM RECORDS

HIGHEST INNINGS TOTALS

1,107	Victoria v New South Wales at Melbourne	1926-27
1,059	Victoria v Tasmania at Melbourne	1922-23
952-6 dec	Sri Lanka v India at Colombo (RPS)	1997-98
951-7 dec	Sind v Baluchistan at Karachi	1973-74
944-6 dec	Hyderabad v Andhra at Secunderabad	1993-94
918	New South Wales v South Australia at Sydney	1900-01
912-8 dec	Holkar v Mysore at Indore	1945-46
912-6 dec†	Tamil Nadu v Goa at Panjim	1988-89
910-6 dec	Railways v Dera Ismail Khan at Lahore	1964-65
903-7 dec	England v Australia at The Oval	1938
900-6 dec	Queensland v Victoria at Brisbane	2005-06

† *Tamil Nadu's total of 912-6 dec included 52 penalty runs from their opponents' failure to meet the required bowling rate.*

The highest total in a team's second innings is 770 by New South Wales v South Australia at Adelaide in 1920-21.

HIGHEST FOURTH-INNINGS TOTALS

654-5	England v South Africa at Durban *After being set 696 to win. The match was left drawn on the tenth day.*	1938-39
604	Maharashtra (*set 959 to win*) v Bombay at Poona	1948-49
576-8	Trinidad (*set 672 to win*) v Barbados at Port-of-Spain	1945-46
572	New South Wales (*set 593 to win*) v South Australia at Sydney	1907-08
541-7	West Zone (*won*) v South Zone at Hyderabad	2009-10
529-9	Combined XI (*set 579 to win*) v South Africans at Perth	1963-64
518	Victoria (*set 753 to win*) v Queensland at Brisbane	1926-27
513-9	Central Province (*won*) v Southern Province at Kandy	2003-04
507-7	Cambridge University (*won*) v MCC and Ground at Lord's	1896
506-6	South Australia (*won*) v Queensland at Adelaide	1991-92
503-4	South Zone (*won*) v England A at Gurgaon	2003-04
502-6	Middlesex (*won*) v Nottinghamshire at Nottingham	1925
502-8	Players (*won*) v Gentlemen at Lord's	1900
500-7	South African Universities (*won*) v Western Province at Stellenbosch	1978-79

MOST RUNS IN A DAY (ONE SIDE)

721	Australians (721) v Essex at Southend (1st day)	1948
651	West Indians (651-2) v Leicestershire at Leicester (1st day)	1950
649	New South Wales (649-7) v Otago at Dunedin (2nd day)	1923-24
645	Surrey (645-4) v Hampshire at The Oval (1st day)	1909
644	Oxford U. (644-8) v H. D. G. Leveson Gower's XI at Eastbourne (1st day)	1921
640	Lancashire (640-8) v Sussex at Hove (1st day)	1937
636	Free Foresters (636-7) v Cambridge U. at Cambridge (1st day)	1938
625	Gloucestershire (625-6) v Worcestershire at Dudley (2nd day)	1934

MOST RUNS IN A DAY (BOTH SIDES)

(excluding the above)

685	North (169-8 and 255-7), South (261-8 dec) at Blackpool (2nd day)	1961
666	Surrey (607-4), Northamptonshire (59-2) at Northampton (2nd day)	1920
665	Rest of South Africa (339), Transvaal (326) at Johannesburg (1st day)	1911-12
663	Middlesex (503-4), Leicestershire (160-2) at Leicester (2nd day)	1947
661	Border (201), Griqualand West (460) at Kimberley (1st day)	1920-21
649	Hampshire (570-8), Somerset (79-3) at Taunton (2nd day)	1901

HIGHEST AGGREGATES IN A MATCH

Runs	*Wkts*		
2,376	37	Maharashtra v Bombay at Poona	1948-49
2,078	40	Bombay v Holkar at Bombay	1944-45
1,981	35	South Africa v England at Durban	1938-39
1,945	18	Canterbury v Wellington at Christchurch	1994-95
1,929	39	New South Wales v South Australia at Sydney	1925-26
1,911	34	New South Wales v Victoria at Sydney	1908-09
1,905	40	Otago v Wellington at Dunedin	1923-24

In Britain

Runs	*Wkts*		
1,815	28	Somerset v Surrey at Taunton	2002
1,808	20	Sussex v Essex at Hove	1993
1,795	34	Somerset v Northamptonshire at Taunton	2001
1,723	31	England v Australia at Leeds	1948
1,706	23	Hampshire v Warwickshire at Southampton	1997

LOWEST INNINGS TOTALS

12†	Oxford University v MCC and Ground at Oxford	1877
12	Northamptonshire v Gloucestershire at Gloucester	1907
13	Auckland v Canterbury at Auckland	1877-78
13	Nottinghamshire v Yorkshire at Nottingham	1901
14	Surrey v Essex at Chelmsford	1983
15	MCC v Surrey at Lord's	1839
15†	Victoria v MCC at Melbourne	1903-04
15†	Northamptonshire v Yorkshire at Northampton	1908
15	Hampshire v Warwickshire at Birmingham *Following on, Hampshire scored 521 and won by 155 runs.*	1922
16	MCC and Ground v Surrey at Lord's	1872
16	Derbyshire v Nottinghamshire at Nottingham	1879
16	Surrey v Nottinghamshire at The Oval	1880
16	Warwickshire v Kent at Tonbridge	1913
16	Trinidad v Barbados at Bridgetown	1942-43
16	Border v Natal at East London (first innings)	1959-60
17	Gentlemen of Kent v Gentlemen of England at Lord's	1850
17	Gloucestershire v Australians at Cheltenham	1896
18	The Bs v England at Lord's	1831
18†	Kent v Sussex at Gravesend	1867
18	Tasmania v Victoria at Melbourne	1868-69
18†	Australians v MCC and Ground at Lord's	1896
18	Border v Natal at East London (second innings)	1959-60
18†	Durham MCCU v Durham at Chester-le-Street	2012

† *One man absent.*

At Lord's in 1810, The Bs, with one man absent, were dismissed by England for 6.

LOWEST TOTALS IN A MATCH

34	(16 and 18) Border v Natal at East London	1959-60
42	(27† and 15†) Northamptonshire v Yorkshire at Northampton	1908

† *Northamptonshire batted one man short in each innings.*

LOWEST AGGREGATE IN A COMPLETED MATCH

Runs	*Wkts*		
85	11†	Quetta v Rawalpindi at Islamabad	2008-09
105	31	MCC v Australians at Lord's	1878

† *Both teams forfeited their first innings.*

The lowest aggregate in a match in which the losing team was bowled out twice since 1900 is 157 for 22 wickets, Surrey v Worcestershire at The Oval, 1954.

LARGEST VICTORIES

Largest Innings Victories

Inns and 851 runs	Railways (910-6 dec) v Dera Ismail Khan at Lahore	1964-65
Inns and 666 runs	Victoria (1,059) v Tasmania at Melbourne	1922-23
Inns and 656 runs	Victoria (1,107) v New South Wales at Melbourne	1926-27
Inns and 605 runs	New South Wales (918) v South Australia at Sydney	1900-01
Inns and 579 runs	England (903-7 dec) v Australia at The Oval	1938
Inns and 575 runs	Sind (951-7 dec) v Baluchistan at Karachi	1973-74
Inns and 527 runs	New South Wales (713) v South Australia at Adelaide	1908-09
Inns and 517 runs	Australians (675) v Nottinghamshire at Nottingham	1921

Largest Victories by Runs Margin

685 runs	New South Wales (235 and 761-8 dec) v Queensland at Sydney	1929-30
675 runs	England (521 and 342-8 dec) v Australia at Brisbane	1928-29
638 runs	New South Wales (304 and 770) v South Australia at Adelaide	1920-21
609 runs	Muslim Comm. Bank (575 and 282-0 dec) v WAPDA at Lahore	1977-78

Victory Without Losing a Wicket

Lancashire (166-0 dec and 66-0) beat Leicestershire by ten wickets at Manchester	1956
Karachi A (277-0 dec) beat Sind A by an innings and 77 runs at Karachi	1957-58
Railways (236-0 dec and 16-0) beat Jammu & Kashmir by ten wickets at Srinagar	1960-61
Karnataka (451-0 dec) beat Kerala by an innings and 186 runs at Chikmagalur	1977-78

*There have been **30** wins by an innings and 400 runs or more, the most recent being an innings and 413 runs by Dhaka v Barisal at Mirpur in 2014-15.*

*There have been **23** wins by 500 runs or more, the most recent being **523 runs by Essex v Cambridge MCCU** and **517 runs by Nottinghamshire v Cambridge MCCU, both at Cambridge in 2016** in consecutive matches.*

*There have been **33** wins by a team losing only one wicket, the most recent being by **KwaZulu-Natal Inland v Namibia at Pietermaritzburg in 2015-16**.*

TIED MATCHES

Since 1948, a tie has been recognised only when the scores are level with all the wickets down in the fourth innings. There have been **34** instances since then, including two Tests (see Test record section); Sussex have featured in five of those, Essex and Kent in four each.

The most recent instances are:

Somerset v West Indies A at Taunton	†2002
Warwickshire v Essex at Birmingham	2003
Worcestershire v Zimbabweans at Worcester	2003
Habib Bank v WAPDA at Lahore	2011-12
Border v Boland at East London	2012-13

† *Somerset (453) made the highest total to tie a first-class match.*

MATCHES COMPLETED ON FIRST DAY

(Since 1946)

Derbyshire v Somerset at Chesterfield, June 11	1947
Lancashire v Sussex at Manchester, July 12	1950
Surrey v Warwickshire at The Oval, May 16	1953
Somerset v Lancashire at Bath, June 6 (H. F. T. Buse's benefit)	1953
Kent v Worcestershire at Tunbridge Wells, June 15	1960
Griqualand West v Easterns at Kimberley, March 10	2010-11

SHORTEST COMPLETED MATCHES

Balls		
121	Quetta (forfeit and 41) v Rawalpindi (forfeit and 44-1) at Islamabad	2008-09
350	Somerset (35 and 44) v Middlesex (86) at Lord's	1899
352	Victoria (82 and 57) v Tasmania (104 and 37-7) at Launceston	1850-51
372	Victoria (80 and 50) v Tasmania (97 and 35-2) at Launceston	1853-54

An expanded and regularly updated online version of the Records can be found at www.wisdenrecords.com

LIST A ONE-DAY RECORDS

List A is a concept intended to provide an approximate equivalent in one-day cricket of first-class status. It was introduced by the Association of Cricket Statisticians and Historians and is now recognised by the ICC, with a separate category for Twenty20 cricket. Further details are available at stats.acscricket.com/ListA/Description.html. List A games comprise:

(a) One-day internationals.
(b) Other international matches (e.g. A-team internationals).
(c) Premier domestic one-day tournaments in Test-playing countries.
(d) Official tourist matches against the main first-class teams (e.g. counties, states and Board XIs).

The following matches are excluded:

(a) Matches originally scheduled as less than 40 overs per side (e.g. Twenty20 games).
(b) World Cup warm-up games.
(c) Tourist matches against teams outside the major domestic competitions (e.g. universities).
(d) Festival games and pre-season friendlies.

This section covers one-day cricket to December 31, 2016. Bold type denotes performances in the calendar year 2016 or, in career figures, players who appeared in List A cricket in that year.

BATTING RECORDS

HIGHEST INDIVIDUAL INNINGS

268	A. D. Brown	Surrey v Glamorgan at The Oval	2002
264	R. G. Sharma	India v Sri Lanka at Kolkata	2014-15
248	S. Dhawan	India A v South Africa A at Pretoria	2013
237*	M. J. Guptill	New Zealand v West Indies at Wellington	2014-15
229*	B. R. Dunk	Tasmania v Queensland at Sydney	2014-15
222*	R. G. Pollock	Eastern Province v Border at East London	1974-75
222	J. M. How	Central Districts v Northern Districts at Hamilton	2012-13
220*	**B. M. Duckett**	**England Lions v Sri Lanka A at Canterbury**	**2016**
219	V. Sehwag	India v West Indies at Indore	2011-12
215	C. H. Gayle	West Indies v Zimbabwe at Canberra	2014-15
209	R. G. Sharma	India v Australia at Bangalore	2013-14
207	Mohammad Ali	Pakistan Customs v DHA at Sialkot	2004-05
206	A. I. Kallicharran	Warwickshire v Oxfordshire at Birmingham	1984
204*	Khalid Latif	Karachi Dolphins v Quetta Bears at Karachi	2008-09
203	A. D. Brown	Surrey v Hampshire at Guildford	1997
202*	A. Barrow	Natal v SA African XI at Durban	1975-76
202*	P. J. Hughes	Australia A v South Africa A at Darwin	2014
202	T. M. Head	South Australia v Western Australia at Sydney	2015-16
201*	R. S. Bopara	Essex v Leicestershire at Leicester	2008
201	V. J. Wells	Leicestershire v Berkshire at Leicester	1996
200*	S. R. Tendulkar	India v South Africa at Gwalior	2009-10

MOST RUNS

	Career	*M*	*I*	*NO*	*R*	*HS*	*100*	*Avge*
G. A. Gooch	1973–1997	614	601	48	22,211	198*	44	40.16
G. A. Hick	*1983*–2008	651	630	96	22,059	172*	40	41.30
S. R. Tendulkar	*1989–2011*	551	538	55	21,999	200*	60	45.54
K. C. Sangakkara	***1997–2016***	**519**	**491**	**52**	**18,908**	**169**	**37**	**43.07**
I. V. A. Richards	1973–1993	500	466	61	16,995	189*	26	41.96
R. T. Ponting	*1992*–2013	456	445	53	16,363	164	34	41.74
C. G. Greenidge	1970–1992	440	436	33	16,349	186*	33	40.56
S. T. Jayasuriya	*1989–2011*	557	542	25	16,128	189	31	31.19
A. J. Lamb	1972–1995	484	463	63	15,658	132*	19	39.14
D. L. Haynes	1976–1996	419	416	44	15,651	152*	28	42.07
S. C. Ganguly	*1989–2011*	437	421	43	15,622	183	31	41.32

	Career	M	I	NO	R	HS	100	Avge
K. J. Barnett	1979–2005	527	500	54	15,564	136	17	34.89
D. P. M. D. Jayawardene	***1995–2016***	**546**	**509**	**51**	**15,364**	**163***	**21**	**33.54**
R. Dravid	*1992*–2011	449	416	55	15,271	153	21	42.30
M. G. Bevan	*1989–2006*	427	385	124	15,103	157*	13	57.86

HIGHEST PARTNERSHIP FOR EACH WICKET

367*	for 1st	M. N. van Wyk/C. S. Delport, Dolphins v Knights at Bloemfontein	2014-15
372	for 2nd	C. H. Gayle/M. N. Samuels, West Indies v Zimbabwe at Canberra	2014-15
309*	for 3rd	T. S. Curtis/T. M. Moody, Worcestershire v Surrey at The Oval	1994
276	for 4th	Mominul Haque/A. R. S. Silva, Prime Doleshwar v Abahani at Bogra	2013-14
267*	for 5th	Minhazul Abedin/Khaled Mahmud, Bangladeshis v Bahawalpur at Karachi	1997-98
267*	for 6th	G. D. Elliott/L. Ronchi, New Zealand v Sri Lanka at Dunedin	2014-15
203*	for 7th	S. H. T. Kandamby/H. M. R. K. B. Herath, Sri Lanka A v South Africa A at Benoni	2008-09
203	for 8th	Shahid Iqbal/Haaris Ayaz, Karachi Whites v Hyderabad at Karachi	1998-99
155	for 9th	C. M. W. Read/A. J. Harris, Notts v Durham at Nottingham	2006
128	for 10th	A. Ashish Reddy/M. Ravi Kiran, Hyderabad v Kerala at Secunderabad	2014-15

BOWLING RECORDS

BEST BOWLING ANALYSES

8-15	R. L. Sanghvi	Delhi v Himachal Pradesh at Una	1997-98
8-19	W. P. U. J. C. Vaas	Sri Lanka v Zimbabwe at Colombo (SSC)	2001-02
8-20*	D. T. Kottehewa	Nondescripts v Ragama at Colombo (Moors)	2007-08
8-21	M. A. Holding	Derbyshire v Sussex at Hove	1988
8-26	K. D. Boyce	Essex v Lancashire at Manchester	1971
8-30	G. D. R. Eranga	Burgher v Army at Colombo (Colts)	2007-08
8-31	D. L. Underwood	Kent v Scotland at Edinburgh	1987
8-43	S. W. Tait	South Australia v Tasmania at Adelaide	2003-04
8-52	K. A. Stoute	West Indies A v Lancashire at Manchester	2010
8-66	S. R. G. Francis	Somerset v Derbyshire at Derby	2004

* *Including two hat-tricks.*

MOST WICKETS

	Career	M	B	R	W	BB	4I	Avge
Wasim Akram	*1984*–2003	594	29,719	19,303	881	5-10	46	21.91
A. A. Donald	*1985–2003*	458	22,856	14,942	684	6-15	38	21.84
M. Muralitharan	*1991–2010*	453	23,734	15,270	682	7-30	29	22.39
Waqar Younis	*1988–2003*	412	19,841	15,098	675	7-36	44	22.36
J. K. Lever	1968–1990	481	23,208	13,278	674	5-8	34	19.70
J. E. Emburey	1975–2000	536	26,399	16,811	647	5-23	26	25.98
I. T. Botham	1973–1993	470	22,899	15,264	612	5-27	18	24.94

WICKETKEEPING AND FIELDING RECORDS

MOST DISMISSALS IN AN INNINGS

8	(all ct)	D. J. S. Taylor	Somerset v Combined Universities at Taunton	1982
8	(5ct, 3st)	S. J. Palframan	Boland v Easterns at Paarl	1997-98
8	(all ct)	D. J. Pipe	Worcestershire v Hertfordshire at Hertford	2001
7	(6ct, 1st)	R. W. Taylor	Derbyshire v Lancashire at Manchester	1975
7	(4ct, 3st)	Rizwan Umar	Sargodha v Bahawalpur at Sargodha	1991-92

7	(all ct)	A. J. Stewart	Surrey v Glamorgan at Swansea	1994
7	(all ct)	I. Mitchell	Border v Western Province at East London	1998-99
7	(6ct, 1st)	M. K. P. B. Kularatne	Galle v Colts at Colombo (Colts)	2001-02
7	(5ct, 2st)	T. R. Ambrose	Warwickshire v Middlesex at Birmingham	2009
7	(3ct, 4st)	W. A. S. Niroshan	Chilaw Marians v Saracens at Katunayake	2009-10
7	(all ct)	M. Rawat	Railways v Madhya Pradesh at Nagpur	2011-12
7	(all ct)	H. C. Madushan	Badureliya v Colombo at Colombo (CCC)	2013-14
7	(6ct, 1st)	P. A. Patel	West Zone v Central Zone at Visakhapatnam	2013-14
7	(all ct)	D. J. Vilas	Cape Cobras v Knights at Kimberley	2014-15

MOST CATCHES IN AN INNINGS IN THE FIELD

5	V. J. Marks	Combined Universities v Kent at Oxford	1976
5	J. M. Rice	Hampshire v Warwickshire at Southampton	1978
5	A. J. Kourie	Transvaal v Western Province at Johannesburg	1979-80
5	J. N. Rhodes	South Africa v West Indies at Bombay	1993-94
5	J. W. Wilson	Otago v Auckland at Dunedin	1993-94
5	K. C. Jackson	Boland v Natal at Durban	1995-96
5	Mohammad Ramzan	PNSC v PIA at Karachi	1998-99
5	Amit Sharma	Punjab v Jammu & Kashmir at Ludhiana	1999-2000
5	B. E. Young	South Australia v Tasmania at Launceston	2001-02
5	Hasnain Raza	Bahawalpur v Pakistan Customs at Karachi	2002-03
5	D. J. Sales	Northamptonshire v Essex at Northampton	2007
5	L. N. Mosena	Free State v North West at Bloemfontein	2007-08
5	A. R. McBrine	Ireland v Sri Lanka A at Belfast	2014

TEAM RECORDS

HIGHEST INNINGS TOTALS

496-4	(50 overs)	Surrey v Gloucestershire at The Oval	2007
445-8	**(50 overs)**	**Nottinghamshire v Northamptonshire at Nottingham**	**2016**
444-3	**(50 overs)**	**England v Pakistan at Nottingham**	**2016**
443-9	(50 overs)	Sri Lanka v Netherlands at Amstelveen	2006
439-2	(50 overs)	South Africa v West Indies at Johannesburg	2014-15
438-4	(50 overs)	South Africa v India at Mumbai	2014-15
438-5	(50 overs)	Surrey v Glamorgan at The Oval	2002
438-9	(49.5 overs)	South Africa v Australia at Johannesburg	2005-06
434-4	(50 overs)	Australia v South Africa at Johannesburg	2005-06
433-3	(50 overs)	India A v South Africa A at Pretoria	2013
429	(49.5 overs)	Glamorgan v Surrey at The Oval	2002
425-1	**(50 overs)**	**England Lions v Sri Lanka A at Canterbury**	**2016**
425	**(48.2 overs)**	**Northamptonshire v Nottinghamshire at Nottingham**	**2016**

LOWEST INNINGS TOTALS

18	(14.3 overs)	West Indies Under-19 v Barbados at Blairmont	2007-08
19	(10.5 overs)	Saracens v Colts at Colombo (Colts)	2012-13
23	(19.4 overs)	Middlesex v Yorkshire at Leeds	1974
30	(20.4 overs)	Chittagong v Sylhet at Dhaka	2002-03
31	(13.5 overs)	Border v South Western Districts at East London	2007-08
34	(21.1 overs)	Saurashtra v Mumbai at Mumbai	1999-2000
35	(18 overs)	Zimbabwe v Sri Lanka at Harare	2003-04
35	(20.2 overs)	Cricket Coaching School v Abahani at Fatullah	2013-14
35	(15.3 overs)	Rajasthan v Railways at Nagpur	2014-15
36	(25.4 overs)	Leicestershire v Sussex at Leicester	1973
36	(18.4 overs)	Canada v Sri Lanka at Paarl	2002-03
38	(15.4 overs)	Zimbabwe v Sri Lanka at Colombo (SSC)	2001-02
39	(26.4 overs)	Ireland v Sussex at Hove	1985
39	(15.2 overs)	Cape Cobras v Eagles at Paarl *(one man absent)*	2008-09
39	(24.4 overs)	Namibia v United Arab Emirates at Sharjah	2013-14

LIST A TWENTY20 RECORDS

This section covers Twenty20 cricket to December 31, 2016. Bold type denotes performances in the calendar year 2016 or, in career figures, players who appeared in Twenty20 cricket in that year.

BATTING RECORDS

HIGHEST INDIVIDUAL INNINGS

175*	C. H. Gayle	RC Bangalore v Pune Warriors at Bangalore	2012-13
162*	**H. Masakadza**	**Mountaineers v Mashonaland Eagles at Bulawayo**	**2015-16**
158*	B. B. McCullum	Kolkata Knight Riders v RC Bangalore at Bangalore	2007-08
158*	B. B. McCullum	Warwickshire v Derbyshire at Birmingham	2015
156	A. J. Finch	Australia v England at Southampton	2013
153*	L. J. Wright	Sussex v Essex at Chelmsford	2014
152*	G. R. Napier	Essex v Sussex at Chelmsford	2008
151*	C. H. Gayle	Somerset v Kent at Taunton	2015
145*	**G. J. Maxwell**	**Australia v Sri Lanka at Pallekele**	**2016**
145	L. P. van der Westhuizen	Namibia v Kenya at Windhoek	2011-12

MOST RUNS

	Career	*M*	*I*	*NO*	*R*	*HS*	*100*	*Avge*	*SR*
C. H. Gayle	**2005–*2016***	**277**	**272**	**37**	**9,777**	**175***	**18**	**41.60**	**150.29**
B. J. Hodge	**2003–*2016***	**265**	**251**	**57**	**7,170**	**106**	**2**	**36.95**	**131.53**
B. B. McCullum	***2004–2016***	**254**	**250**	**25**	**7,073**	**158***	**7**	**31.43**	**137.76**
D. A. Warner	***2006–*2016**	**222**	**221**	**22**	**6,921**	**135***	**5**	**34.77**	**143.58**
Shoaib Malik	***2004–2016***	**257**	**241**	**67**	**6,630**	**95***	**0**	**38.10**	**123.41**
K. A. Pollard	**2006–*2016***	**339**	**304**	**90**	**6,592**	**89***	**0**	**30.80**	**152.09**
V. Kohli	***2006–*2016**	**206**	**193**	**38**	**6,461**	**113**	**4**	**41.68**	**133.07**
D. R. Smith	***2005–2016***	**275**	**268**	**22**	**6,408**	**110***	**3**	**26.04**	**127.37**
S. K. Raina	***2006–2015***	**242**	**228**	**37**	**6,326**	**109***	**3**	**33.12**	**139.00**
R. G. Sharma	***2006–*2016**	**236**	**225**	**39**	**6,209**	**109***	**3**	**33.38**	**131.68**
L. J. Wright	**2004–*2016***	**257**	**237**	**25**	**6,070**	**153***	**6**	**28.63**	**146.12**

HIGHEST PARTNERSHIP FOR EACH WICKET

201	for 1st	P. J. Ingram/J. M. How, C. Dist. v Wellington at New Plymouth	2011-12
229	**for 2nd**	**V. Kohli/A. B. de Villiers, RC Bangalore v Gujarat Lions at Bangalore**	**2015-16**
162	for 3rd	Abdul Razzaq/Nasir Jamshed, Lahore Lions v Quetta Bears at Lahore	2009
202*	for 4th	M. C. Juneja/A. Malik, Gujarat v Kerala at Indore	2012-13
150	**for 5th**	**H. M. Amla/D. J. Bravo, Trinbago NR v Barb. Tridents at Port-of-Spain**	**2016**
126*	for 6th	C. S. MacLeod/J. W. Hastings, Durham v Northants at Chester-le-Street	2014
107*	**for 7th**	**L. Abeyratne/P. S. R. Anurudhda, Colombo v Chilaw Marians at Colombo (Colts)**	**2015-16**
120	for 8th	Azhar Mahmood/I. Udana, Wayamba v Uva at Colombo (RPS)	2012
64	for 9th	K. Magage/H. S. M. Zoysa, Burgher v Panadura at Colombo (SSC)	2011-12
63	**for 10th**	**G. D. Elliott/Zulfiqar Babar, Quetta Glad. v Peshawar Zalmi at Sharjah**	**2015-16**

BOWLING RECORDS

BEST BOWLING ANALYSES

6-5	A. V. Suppiah	Somerset v Glamorgan at Cardiff	2011
6-6	Shakib Al Hasan	Barbados v Trinidad & Tobago at Bridgetown	2013
6-7	S. L. Malinga	Melbourne Stars v Perth Scorchers at Perth	2012-13
6-8	B. A. W. Mendis	Sri Lanka v Zimbabwe at Hambantota	2012-13
6-9	P. Fojela	Border v Easterns at East London	2014-15
6-14	Sohail Tanvir	Rajasthan Royals v Chennai Superstars at Jaipur	2007-08
6-14	D. Punia	Services v Haryana at Delhi	2014-15
6-15	S. R. Abeywardene	Panadura v Air Force at Colombo (BRC)	2005-06

MOST WICKETS

	Career	*M*	*B*	*R*	*W*	*BB*	*4I*	*Avge*	*ER*
D. J. Bravo	***2005–2016***	**344**	**6,535**	**8,784**	**367**	**5-23**	**9**	**23.93**	**8.06**
S. L. Malinga	***2004–2015***	**221**	**4,835**	**5,393**	**299**	**6-7**	**12**	**18.03**	**6.69**
Yasir Arafat	***2005–2016***	**226**	**4,702**	**6,344**	**281**	**4-5**	**10**	**22.57**	**8.09**
A. C. Thomas	*2003*–2015	225	4,558	5,739	263	5-24	5	21.82	7.55
Saeed Ajmal	***2004–2016***	**183**	**4,114**	**4,418**	**260**	**4-14**	**8**	**16.99**	**6.44**
Azhar Mahmood	**2003–2016**	**230**	**4,825**	**6,143**	**258**	**5-24**	**4**	**23.81**	**7.63**
Shahid Afridi	**2004–*2016***	**235**	**5,082**	**5,619**	**257**	**5-7**	**7**	**21.86**	**6.63**
D. P. Nannes	*2007–2014*	215	4,624	5,719	257	5-31	9	22.25	7.42
Shakib Al Hasan	***2006–2016***	**223**	**4,719**	**5,315**	**255**	**6-6**	**8**	**20.84**	**6.75**

WICKETKEEPING AND FIELDING RECORDS

MOST DISMISSALS IN AN INNINGS

7 (all ct)	E. F. M. U. Fernando	Lankan v Moors at Colombo (Bloomfield)	2005-06

MOST CATCHES IN AN INNINGS IN THE FIELD

5	Manzoor Ilahi	Jammu & Kashmir v Delhi at Delhi	2010-11
5	J. M. Vince	Hampshire v Leeward Islands at North Sound	2010-11
5	J. L. Ontong	Cape Cobras v Knights at Cape Town	2014-15
5	A. K. V. Adikari	Chilaw Marians v Bloomfield at Colombo (SSC)	2014-15
5	P. G. Fulton	Canterbury v Northern Districts at Hamilton	2015-16
5	**M. W. Machan**	**Sussex v Glamorgan at Hove**	**2016**

TEAM RECORDS

HIGHEST INNINGS TOTALS

263-3	**(20 overs)**	**Australia v Sri Lanka at Pallekele**	**2016**
263-5	(20 overs)	RC Bangalore v Pune Warriors at Bangalore	2012-13
260-6	(20 overs)	Sri Lanka v Kenya at Johannesburg	2007-08
254-3	(20 overs)	Gloucestershire v Middlesex at Uxbridge	2011
251-6	**(20 overs)**	**Sinhalese v Saracens at Colombo (Colts)**	**2015-16**
250-3	(20 overs)	Somerset v Gloucestershire at Taunton	2006

LOWEST INNINGS TOTALS

30	(11.1 overs)	Tripura v Jharkhand at Dhanbad	2009-10
39	(10.3 overs)	Netherlands v Sri Lanka at Chittagong	2013-14
44	(12.5 overs)	Leeward Islands v Trinidad & Tobago at North Sound	2011-12
44	(14.4 overs)	Boland v North West at Potchefstroom	2014-15
44	**(12.1 overs)**	**Assam v Delhi at Vadodara**	**2015-16**
44	**(10.4 overs)**	**Khulna Titans v Rangpur Riders at Mirpur**	**2016-17**

TEST RECORDS

This section covers all Tests up to January 23, 2017. Bold type denotes performances since January 1, 2016, or, in career figures, players who have appeared in Test cricket since that date.

BATTING RECORDS

HIGHEST INDIVIDUAL INNINGS

400*	B. C. Lara	West Indies v England at St John's	2003-04
380	M. L. Hayden	Australia v Zimbabwe at Perth	2003-04
375	B. C. Lara	West Indies v England at St John's	1993-94
374	D. P. M. D. Jayawardene	Sri Lanka v South Africa at Colombo (SSC)	2006
365*	G. S. Sobers	West Indies v Pakistan at Kingston	1957-58
364	L. Hutton	England v Australia at The Oval	1938
340	S. T. Jayasuriya	Sri Lanka v India at Colombo (RPS)	1997-98
337	Hanif Mohammad	Pakistan v West Indies at Bridgetown	1957-58
336*	W. R. Hammond	England v New Zealand at Auckland	1932-33
334*	M. A. Taylor	Australia v Pakistan at Peshawar	1998-99
334	D. G. Bradman	Australia v England at Leeds	1930
333	G. A. Gooch	England v India at Lord's	1990
333	C. H. Gayle	West Indies v Sri Lanka at Galle	2010-11
329*	M. J. Clarke	Australia v India at Sydney	2011-12
329	Inzamam-ul-Haq	Pakistan v New Zealand at Lahore	2002
325	A. Sandham	England v West Indies at Kingston	1929-30
319	V. Sehwag	India v South Africa at Chennai	2007-08
319	K. C. Sangakkara	Sri Lanka v Bangladesh at Chittagong	2013-14
317	C. H. Gayle	West Indies v South Africa at St John's	2004-05
313	Younis Khan	Pakistan v Sri Lanka at Karachi	2008-09
311*	H. M. Amla	South Africa v England at The Oval	2012
311	R. B. Simpson	Australia v England at Manchester	1964
310*	J. H. Edrich	England v New Zealand at Leeds	1965
309	V. Sehwag	India v Pakistan at Multan	2003-04
307	R. M. Cowper	Australia v England at Melbourne	1965-66
304	D. G. Bradman	Australia v England at Leeds	1934
303*	**K. K. Nair**	**India v England at Chennai**	**2016-17**
302*	**Azhar Ali**	**Pakistan v West Indies at Dubai**	**2016-17**
302	L. G. Rowe	West Indies v England at Bridgetown	1973-74
302	B. B. McCullum	New Zealand v India at Wellington	2013-14

*There have been **63** further instances of 250 or more runs in a Test innings.*

The highest innings for the countries not mentioned above are:

266	D. L. Houghton	Zimbabwe v Sri Lanka at Bulawayo	1994-95
217	**Shakib Al Hasan**	**Bangladesh v New Zealand at Wellington**	**2016-17**

HUNDRED ON TEST DEBUT

C. Bannerman (165*)	Australia v England at Melbourne	1876-77
W. G. Grace (152)	England v Australia at The Oval	1880
H. Graham (107)	Australia v England at Lord's	1893
†K. S. Ranjitsinhji (154*)	England v Australia at Manchester	1896
†P. F. Warner (132*)	England v South Africa at Johannesburg	1898-99
†R. A. Duff (104)	Australia v England at Melbourne	1901-02
§R. E. Foster (287)	England v Australia at Sydney	1903-04
G. Gunn (119)	England v Australia at Sydney	1907-08
†R. J. Hartigan (116)	Australia v England at Adelaide	1907-08
†H. L. Collins (104)	Australia v England at Sydney	1920-21
W. H. Ponsford (110)	Australia v England at Sydney	1924-25

A. A. Jackson (164)	Australia v England at Adelaide	1928-29
†G. A. Headley (176)	West Indies v England at Bridgetown	1929-30
J. E. Mills (117)	New Zealand v England at Wellington	1929-30
Nawab of Pataudi snr (102)	England v Australia at Sydney	1932-33
B. H. Valentine (136)	England v India at Bombay	1933-34
†L. Amarnath (118)	India v England at Bombay	1933-34
†P. A. Gibb (106)	England v South Africa at Johannesburg	1938-39
S. C. Griffith (140)	England v West Indies at Port-of-Spain	1947-48
A. G. Ganteaume (112)	West Indies v England at Port-of-Spain	1947-48
†J. W. Burke (101*)	Australia v England at Adelaide	1950-51
P. B. H. May (138)	England v South Africa at Leeds	1951
R. H. Shodhan (110)	India v Pakistan at Calcutta	1952-53
B. H. Pairaudeau (115)	West Indies v India at Port-of-Spain	1952-53
†O. G. Smith (104)	West Indies v Australia at Kingston	1954-55
A. G. Kripal Singh (100*)	India v New Zealand at Hyderabad	1955-56
C. C. Hunte (142)	West Indies v Pakistan at Bridgetown	1957-58
C. A. Milton (104*)	England v New Zealand at Leeds	1958
†A. A. Baig (112)	India v England at Manchester	1959
Hanumant Singh (105)	India v England at Delhi	1963-64
Khalid Ibadulla (166)	Pakistan v Australia at Karachi	1964-65
B. R. Taylor (105)	New Zealand v India at Calcutta	1964-65
K. D. Walters (155)	Australia v England at Brisbane	1965-66
J. H. Hampshire (107)	England v West Indies at Lord's	1969
†G. R. Viswanath (137)	India v Australia at Kanpur	1969-70
G. S. Chappell (108)	Australia v England at Perth	1970-71
‡§L. G. Rowe (214, 100*)	West Indies v New Zealand at Kingston	1971-72
A. I. Kallicharran (100*)	West Indies v New Zealand at Georgetown	1971-72
R. E. Redmond (107)	New Zealand v Pakistan at Auckland	1972-73
†F. C. Hayes (106*)	England v West Indies at The Oval	1973
†C. G. Greenidge (107)	West Indies v India at Bangalore	1974-75
†L. Baichan (105*)	West Indies v Pakistan at Lahore	1974-75
G. J. Cosier (109)	Australia v West Indies at Melbourne	1975-76
S. Amarnath (124)	India v New Zealand at Auckland	1975-76
Javed Miandad (163)	Pakistan v New Zealand at Lahore	1976-77
†A. B. Williams (100)	West Indies v Australia at Georgetown	1977-78
†D. M. Wellham (103)	Australia v England at The Oval	1981
†Salim Malik (100*)	Pakistan v Sri Lanka at Karachi	1981-82
K. C. Wessels (162)	Australia v England at Brisbane	1982-83
W. B. Phillips (159)	Australia v Pakistan at Perth	1983-84
¶M. Azharuddin (110)	India v England at Calcutta	1984-85
D. S. B. P. Kuruppu (201*)	Sri Lanka v New Zealand at Colombo (CCC)	1986-87
†M. J. Greatbatch (107*)	New Zealand v England at Auckland	1987-88
M. E. Waugh (138)	Australia v England at Adelaide	1990-91
A. C. Hudson (163)	South Africa v West Indies at Bridgetown	1991-92
R. S. Kaluwitharana (132*)	Sri Lanka v Australia at Colombo (SSC)	1992-93
D. L. Houghton (121)	Zimbabwe v India at Harare	1992-93
P. K. Amre (103)	India v South Africa at Durban	1992-93
†G. P. Thorpe (114*)	England v Australia at Nottingham	1993
G. S. Blewett (102*)	Australia v England at Adelaide	1994-95
S. C. Ganguly (131)	India v England at Lord's	1996
†Mohammad Wasim (109*)	Pakistan v New Zealand at Lahore	1996-97
Ali Naqvi (115)	Pakistan v South Africa at Rawalpindi	1997-98
Azhar Mahmood (128*)	Pakistan v South Africa at Rawalpindi	1997-98
M. S. Sinclair (214)	New Zealand v West Indies at Wellington	1999-2000
†Younis Khan (107)	Pakistan v Sri Lanka at Rawalpindi	1999-2000
Aminul Islam (145)	Bangladesh v India at Dhaka	2000-01
†H. Masakadza (119)	Zimbabwe v West Indies at Harare	2001
T. T. Samaraweera (103*)	Sri Lanka v India at Colombo (SSC)	2001
Taufeeq Umar (104)	Pakistan v Bangladesh at Multan	2001-02
†Mohammad Ashraful (114)	Bangladesh v Sri Lanka at Colombo (SSC)	2001-02
V. Sehwag (105)	India v South Africa at Bloemfontein	2001-02
L. Vincent (104)	New Zealand v Australia at Perth	2001-02
S. B. Styris (107)	New Zealand v West Indies at St George's	2002

J. A. Rudolph (222*)	South Africa v Bangladesh at Chittagong	2003
‡Yasir Hameed (170, 105)	Pakistan v Bangladesh at Karachi	2003
†D. R. Smith (105*)	West Indies v South Africa at Cape Town	2003-04
A. J. Strauss (112)	England v New Zealand at Lord's	2004
M. J. Clarke (151)	Australia v India at Bangalore	2004-05
†A. N. Cook (104*)	England v India at Nagpur	2005-06
M. J. Prior (126*)	England v West Indies at Lord's	2007
M. J. North (117)	Australia v South Africa at Johannesburg	2008-09
†Fawad Alam (168)	Pakistan v Sri Lanka at Colombo (PSS)	2009
†I. J. L. Trott (119)	England v Australia at The Oval	2009
Umar Akmal (129)	Pakistan v New Zealand at Dunedin	2009-10
†A. B. Barath (104)	West Indies v Australia at Brisbane	2009-10
A. N. Petersen (100)	South Africa v India at Kolkata	2009-10
S. K. Raina (120)	India v Sri Lanka at Colombo (SSC)	2010
K. S. Williamson (131)	New Zealand v India at Ahmedabad	2010-11
†K. A. Edwards (110)	West Indies v India at Roseau	2011
S. E. Marsh (141)	Australia v Sri Lanka at Pallekele	2011-12
Abul Hasan (113)	Bangladesh v West Indies at Khulna	2012-13
†F. du Plessis (110*)	South Africa v Australia at Adelaide	2012-13
H. D. Rutherford (171)	New Zealand v England at Dunedin	2012-13
S. Dhawan (187)	India v Australia at Mohali	2012-13
R. G. Sharma (177)	India v West Indies at Kolkata	2013-14
†J. D. S. Neesham (137*)	New Zealand v India at Wellington	2013-14
S. van Zyl (101*)	South Africa v West Indies at Centurion	2014-15
A. C. Voges (130*)	Australia v West Indies at Roseau	2015
S. C. Cook (115)	South Africa v England at Centurion	2015-16
K. K. Jennings (112)	**England v India at Mumbai**	**2016-17**

† *In his second innings of the match.*
‡ *L. G. Rowe and Yasir Hameed are the only batsmen to score a hundred in each innings on debut.*
§ *R. E. Foster (287, 19) and L. G. Rowe (214, 100*) are the only batsmen to score 300 on debut.*
¶ *M. Azharuddin is the only batsman to score hundreds in each of his first three Tests.*

L. Amarnath and S. Amarnath were father and son.
Ali Naqvi and Azhar Mahmood achieved the feat in the same innings.
Only Bannerman, Houghton and Aminul Islam scored hundreds in their country's first Test.

TWO SEPARATE HUNDREDS IN A TEST

Triple-Hundred and Hundred in a Test

G. A. Gooch (England)	333 and 123 v India at Lord's	1990
K. C. Sangakkara (Sri Lanka)	319 and 105 v Bangladesh at Chittagong	2013-14

The only instances in first-class cricket. M. A. Taylor (Australia) scored 334 and 92 v Pakistan at Peshawar in 1998-99.*

Double-Hundred and Hundred in a Test

K. D. Walters (Australia)	242 and 103 v West Indies at Sydney	1968-69
S. M. Gavaskar (India)	124 and 220 v West Indies at Port-of-Spain	1970-71
†L. G. Rowe (West Indies)	214 and 100* v New Zealand at Kingston	1971-72
G. S. Chappell (Australia)	247* and 133 v New Zealand at Wellington	1973-74
B. C. Lara (West Indies)	221 and 130 v Sri Lanka at Colombo (SSC)	2001-02

† *On Test debut.*

Two Hundreds in a Test

There have been **81** instances of a batsman scoring two separate hundreds in a Test, including the seven listed above. The most recent was by A. M. Rahane for India v South Africa at Delhi in 2015-16.

S. M. Gavaskar (India), R. T. Ponting (Australia) and D. A. Warner (Australia) all achieved the feat three times. C. L. Walcott scored twin hundreds twice in one series, for West Indies v Australia in 1954-55. L. G. Rowe and Yasir Hameed both did it on Test debut.

MOST DOUBLE-HUNDREDS

D. G. Bradman (A)	12	M. S. Atapattu (SL)	6	**Younis Khan (P)**	**6**
K. C. Sangakkara (SL)	11	Javed Miandad (P)	6	R. Dravid (I)	5
B. C. Lara (WI)	9	R. T. Ponting (A)	6	G. C. Smith (SA)	5
W. R. Hammond (E)	7	V. Sehwag (I)	6		
D. P. M. D. Jayawardene (SL)	7	S. R. Tendulkar (I)	6		

M. J. Clarke (Australia) scored four double-hundreds in the calendar year 2012.

MOST HUNDREDS

S. R. Tendulkar (I)	51	M. J. Clarke (A)	28	I. R. Bell (E)	22
J. H. Kallis (SA)	45	A. R. Border (A)	27	G. Boycott (E)	22
R. T. Ponting (A)	41	G. C. Smith (SA)	27	M. C. Cowdrey (E)	22
K. C. Sangakkara (SL)	38	**H. M. Amla (SA)**	**26**	W. R. Hammond (E)	22
R. Dravid (I)	36	G. S. Sobers (WI)	26	D. C. Boon (A)	21
S. M. Gavaskar (I)	34	Inzamam-ul-Haq (P)	25	**A. B. de Villiers (SA)**	**21**
D. P. M. D. Jayawardene (SL)	34	G. S. Chappell (A)	24	R. N. Harvey (A)	21
B. C. Lara (WI)	34	Mohammad Yousuf (P)	24	G. Kirsten (SA)	21
Younis Khan (P)	**34**	I. V. A. Richards (WI)	24	A. J. Strauss (E)	21
S. R. Waugh (A)	32	Javed Miandad (P)	23	K. F. Barrington (E)	20
S. Chanderpaul (WI)	30	J. L. Langer (A)	23	P. A. de Silva (SL)	20
A. N. Cook (E)	**30**	K. P. Pietersen (E)	23	G. A. Gooch (E)	20
M. L. Hayden (A)	30	V. Sehwag (I)	23	M. E. Waugh (A)	20
D. G. Bradman (A)	29	M. Azharuddin (I)	22		

*The most hundreds for New Zealand is 17 by M. D. Crowe, the most for Zimbabwe is 12 by A. Flower, and the most for Bangladesh is 8 by **Tamim Iqbal**.*

MOST HUNDREDS AGAINST ONE TEAM

D. G. Bradman	19	Australia v England	K. C. Sangakkara	10	Sri Lanka v Pakistan
S. M. Gavaskar	13	India v West Indies	G. S. Sobers	10	West Indies v England
J. B. Hobbs	12	England v Australia	S. R. Waugh	10	Australia v England
S. R. Tendulkar	11	India v Australia			

MOST DUCKS

	0s	*Inns*		*0s*	*Inns*
C. A. Walsh (WI)	43	185	M. S. Atapattu (SL)	22	156
C. S. Martin (NZ)	36	104	S. R. Waugh (A)	22	260
G. D. McGrath (A)	35	138	S. J. Harmison (E/World)	21	86
S. K. Warne (A)	34	199	M. Ntini (SA)	21	116
M. Muralitharan (SL/World)	33	164	Waqar Younis (P)	21	120
Zaheer Khan (I)	29	127	**J. M. Anderson (E)**	**21**	**168**
M. Dillon (WI)	26	68	M. S. Panesar (E)	20	68
C. E. L. Ambrose (WI)	26	145	B. S. Bedi (I)	20	101
Danish Kaneria (P)	25	84	**S. C. J. Broad (E)**	**20**	**145**
D. K. Morrison (NZ)	24	71	D. L. Vettori (NZ/World)	20	174
B. S. Chandrasekhar (I)	23	80	M. A. Atherton (E)	20	212
I. Sharma (I)	**23**	**101**			

CARRYING BAT THROUGH TEST INNINGS

(Figures in brackets show team's total)

A. B. Tancred	26*	(47)	South Africa v England at Cape Town	1888-89
J. E. Barrett	67*	(176)†	Australia v England at Lord's	1890
R. Abel	132*	(307)	England v Australia at Sydney	1891-92
P. F. Warner	132*	(237)†	England v South Africa at Johannesburg	1898-99

W. W. Armstrong	159*	(309)	Australia v South Africa at Johannesburg	1902-03
J. W. Zulch	43*	(103)	South Africa v England at Cape Town	1909-10
W. Bardsley	193*	(383)	Australia v England at Lord's	1926
W. M. Woodfull	30*	(66)§	Australia v England at Brisbane	1928-29
W. M. Woodfull	73*	(193)‡	Australia v England at Adelaide	1932-33
W. A. Brown	206*	(422)	Australia v England at Lord's	1938
L. Hutton	202*	(344)	England v West Indies at The Oval	1950
L. Hutton	156*	(272)	England v Australia at Adelaide	1950-51
Nazar Mohammad¶	124*	(331)	Pakistan v India at Lucknow	1952-53
F. M. M. Worrell	191*	(372)	West Indies v England at Nottingham	1957
T. L. Goddard	56*	(99)	South Africa v Australia at Cape Town	1957-58
D. J. McGlew	127*	(292)	South Africa v New Zealand at Durban	1961-62
C. C. Hunte	60*	(131)	West Indies v Australia at Port-of-Spain	1964-65
G. M. Turner	43*	(131)	New Zealand v England at Lord's	1969
W. M. Lawry	49*	(107)	Australia v India at Delhi	1969-70
W. M. Lawry	60*	(116)‡	Australia v England at Sydney	1970-71
G. M. Turner	223*	(386)	New Zealand v West Indies at Kingston	1971-72
I. R. Redpath	159*	(346)	Australia v New Zealand at Auckland	1973-74
G. Boycott	99*	(215)	England v Australia at Perth	1979-80
S. M. Gavaskar	127*	(286)	India v Pakistan at Faisalabad	1982-83
Mudassar Nazar¶	152*	(323)	Pakistan v India at Lahore	1982-83
S. Wettimuny	63*	(144)	Sri Lanka v New Zealand at Christchurch	1982-83
D. C. Boon	58*	(103)	Australia v New Zealand at Auckland	1985-86
D. L. Haynes	88*	(211)	West Indies v Pakistan at Karachi	1986-87
G. A. Gooch	154*	(252)	England v West Indies at Leeds	1991
D. L. Haynes	75*	(176)	West Indies v England at The Oval	1991
A. J. Stewart	69*	(175)	England v Pakistan at Lord's	1992
D. L. Haynes	143*	(382)	West Indies v Pakistan at Port-of-Spain	1992-93
M. H. Dekker	68*	(187)	Zimbabwe v Pakistan at Rawalpindi	1993-94
M. A. Atherton	94*	(228)	England v New Zealand at Christchurch	1996-97
G. Kirsten	100*	(239)	South Africa v Pakistan at Faisalabad	1997-98
M. A. Taylor	169*	(350)	Australia v South Africa at Adelaide	1997-98
G. W. Flower	156*	(321)	Zimbabwe v Pakistan at Bulawayo	1997-98
Saeed Anwar	188*	(316)	Pakistan v India at Calcutta	1998-99
M. S. Atapattu	216*	(428)	Sri Lanka v Zimbabwe at Bulawayo	1999-2000
R. P. Arnold	104*	(231)	Sri Lanka v Zimbabwe at Harare	1999-2000
Javed Omar	85*	(168)†‡	Bangladesh v Zimbabwe at Bulawayo	2000-01
V. Sehwag	201*	(329)	India v Sri Lanka at Galle	2008
S. M. Katich	131*	(268)	Australia v New Zealand at Brisbane	2008-09
C. H. Gayle	165*	(317)	West Indies v Australia at Adelaide	2009-10
Imran Farhat	117*	(223)	Pakistan v New Zealand at Napier	2009-10
R. Dravid	146*	(300)	India v England at The Oval	2011
T. M. K. Mawoyo	163*	(412)	Zimbabwe v Pakistan at Bulawayo	2011-12
D. A. Warner	123*	(233)	Australia v New Zealand at Hobart	2011-12
C. A. Pujara	145*	(312)	India v Sri Lanka at Colombo (SSC)	2015-16
D. Elgar	118*	(214)	South Africa v England at Durban	2015-16
K. C. Brathwaite	**142***	**(337)**	**West Indies v Pakistan at Sharjah**	**2016-17**

† *On debut.* ‡ *One man absent.* § *Two men absent.* ¶ *Father and son.*

G. M. Turner (223) holds the record for the highest score by a player carrying his bat through a Test innings. He was also the youngest at 22 years 63 days old when he first did it in 1969.*

D. L. Haynes, who is alone in achieving this feat on three occasions, also opened the batting and was last man out in each innings for West Indies v New Zealand at Dunedin, 1979-80.

MOST RUNS IN A SERIES

	T	*I*	*NO*	*R*	*HS*	*100*	*Avge*		
D. G. Bradman	5	7	0	974	334	4	139.14	A v E	1930
W. R. Hammond	5	9	1	905	251	4	113.12	E v A	1928-29
M. A. Taylor	6	11	1	839	219	2	83.90	A v E	1989
R. N. Harvey	5	9	0	834	205	4	92.66	A v SA	1952-53

	T	*I*	*NO*	*R*	*HS*	*100*	*Avge*		
I. V. A. Richards. . .	4	7	0	829	291	3	118.42	WI v E	1976
C. L. Walcott	5	10	0	827	155	5	82.70	WI v A	1954-55
G. S. Sobers	5	8	2	824	365*	3	137.33	WI v P	1957-58
D. G. Bradman	5	9	0	810	270	3	90.00	A v E	1936-37
D. G. Bradman	5	5	1	806	299*	4	201.50	A v SA	1931-32

MOST RUNS IN A CALENDAR YEAR

	T	*I*	*NO*	*R*	*HS*	*100*	*Avge*	*Year*
Mohammad Yousuf (P).	11	19	1	1,788	202	9	99.33	2006
I. V. A. Richards (WI).	11	19	0	1,710	291	7	90.00	1976
G. C. Smith (SA).	15	25	2	1,656	232	6	72.00	2008
M. J. Clarke (A).	11	18	3	1,595	329*	5	106.33	2012
S. R. Tendulkar (I).	14	23	3	1,562	214	7	78.10	2010
S. M. Gavaskar (I)	18	27	1	1,555	221	5	59.80	1979
R. T. Ponting (A).	15	28	5	1,544	207	6	67.13	2005
R. T. Ponting (A).	11	18	3	1,503	257	6	100.20	2003

M. Amarnath reached 1,000 runs in 1983 on May 3, in his ninth Test of the year.

The only case of 1,000 in a year before World War II was C. Hill of Australia: 1,060 in 1902.

M. L. Hayden (Australia) scored 1,000 runs in each year from 2001 to 2005.

MOST RUNS

		T	*I*	*NO*	*R*	*HS*	*100*	*Avge*
1	S. R. Tendulkar (India)	200	329	33	15,921	248*	51	53.78
2	R. T. Ponting (Australia).	168	287	29	13,378	257	41	51.85
3	J. H. Kallis (South Africa/World) .	166	280	40	13,289	224	45	55.37
4	R. Dravid (India/World)	164	286	32	13,288	270	36	52.31
5	K. C. Sangakkara (Sri Lanka)	134	233	17	12,400	319	38	57.40
6	B. C. Lara (West Indies/World) . .	131	232	6	11,953	400*	34	52.88
7	S. Chanderpaul (West Indies)	164	280	49	11,867	203*	30	51.37
8	D. P. M. D. Jayawardene (SL) . . .	149	252	15	11,814	374	34	49.84
9	A. R. Border (Australia)	156	265	44	11,174	205	27	50.56
10	**A. N. Cook (England)**	**140**	**253**	**15**	**11,057**	**294**	**30**	**46.45**
11	S. R. Waugh (Australia)	168	260	46	10,927	200	32	51.06
12	S. M. Gavaskar (India)	125	214	16	10,122	236*	34	51.12
13	**Younis Khan (Pakistan)**	**115**	**207**	**19**	**9,977**	**313**	**34**	**53.06**
14	G. C. Smith (South Africa/Wld) . .	117	205	13	9,265	277	27	48.25
15	G. A. Gooch (England)	118	215	6	8,900	333	20	42.58
16	Javed Miandad (Pakistan)	124	189	21	8,832	280*	23	52.57
17	Inzamam-ul-Haq (Pakistan/World)	120	200	22	8,830	329	25	49.60
18	V. V. S. Laxman (India)	134	225	34	8,781	281	17	45.97
19	M. J. Clarke (Australia).	115	198	22	8,643	329*	28	49.10
20	M. L. Hayden (Australia)	103	184	14	8,625	380	30	50.73
21	V. Sehwag (India/World)	104	180	6	8,586	319	23	49.34
22	I. V. A. Richards (West Indies). . .	121	182	12	8,540	291	24	50.23
23	A. J. Stewart (England)	133	235	21	8,463	190	15	39.54
24	D. I. Gower (England).	117	204	18	8,231	215	18	44.25
25	K. P. Pietersen (England)	104	181	8	8,181	227	23	47.28
26	G. Boycott (England)	108	193	23	8,114	246*	22	47.72
27	**A. B. de Villiers (South Africa)** .	**106**	**176**	**16**	**8,074**	**278***	**21**	**50.46**
28	G. S. Sobers (West Indies)	93	160	21	8,032	365*	26	57.78
29	M. E. Waugh (Australia).	128	209	17	8,029	153*	20	41.81
30	**H. M. Amla (South Africa)**	**100**	**169**	**13**	**7,799**	**311***	**26**	**49.99**
31	M. A. Atherton (England).	115	212	7	7,728	185*	16	37.69
32	I. R. Bell (England).	118	205	24	7,727	235	22	42.69
33	J. L. Langer (Australia).	105	182	12	7,696	250	23	45.27
34	M. C. Cowdrey (England).	114	188	15	7,624	182	22	44.06
35	C. G. Greenidge (West Indies) . . .	108	185	16	7,558	226	19	44.72

		T	I	NO	R	HS	100	Avge
36	Mohammad Yousuf (Pakistan) . . .	90	156	12	7,530	223	24	52.29
37	M. A. Taylor (Australia)	104	186	13	7,525	334*	19	43.49
38	C. H. Lloyd (West Indies)	110	175	14	7,515	242*	19	46.67
39	D. L. Haynes (West Indies)	116	202	25	7,487	184	18	42.29
40	D. C. Boon (Australia)	107	190	20	7,422	200	21	43.65
41	G. Kirsten (South Africa)	101	176	15	7,289	275	21	45.27
42	W. R. Hammond (England)	85	140	16	7,249	336*	22	58.45
43	C. H. Gayle (West Indies)	103	182	11	7,214	333	15	42.18
44	S. C. Ganguly (India)	113	188	17	7,212	239	16	42.17
45	S. P. Fleming (New Zealand)	111	189	10	7,172	274*	9	40.06
46	G. S. Chappell (Australia)	87	151	19	7,110	247*	24	53.86
47	A. J. Strauss (England)	100	178	6	7,037	177	21	40.91
48	D. G. Bradman (Australia)	52	80	10	6,996	334	29	99.94
49	S. T. Jayasuriya (Sri Lanka)	110	188	14	6,973	340	14	40.07
50	L. Hutton (England)	79	138	15	6,971	364	19	56.67

MOST RUNS FOR EACH COUNTRY

ENGLAND

A. N. Cook **11,057**
G. A. Gooch 8,900
A. J. Stewart 8,463
D. I. Gower 8,231
K. P. Pietersen 8,181
G. Boycott 8,114

AUSTRALIA

R. T. Ponting 13,378
A. R. Border 11,174
S. R. Waugh 10,927
M. J. Clarke 8,643
M. L. Hayden 8,625
M. E. Waugh 8,029

SOUTH AFRICA

J. H. Kallis† 13,206
G. C. Smith† 9,253
A. B. de Villiers **8,074**
H. M. Amla **7,799**
G. Kirsten 7,289
H. H. Gibbs 6,167

† *J. H. Kallis also scored 44 and 39* and G. C. Smith 12 and 0 for the World XI v Australia (2005-06 Super Series Test).*

WEST INDIES

B. C. Lara† 11,912
S. Chanderpaul 11,867
I. V. A. Richards 8,540
G. S. Sobers 8,032
C. G. Greenidge 7,558
C. H. Lloyd 7,515

† *B. C. Lara also scored 5 and 36 for the World XI v Australia (2005-06 Super Series Test).*

NEW ZEALAND

S. P. Fleming 7,172
B. B. McCullum **6,453**
L. R. P. L. Taylor **6,015**
M. D. Crowe 5,444
J. G. Wright 5,334
K. S. Williamson **4,807**

INDIA

S. R. Tendulkar 15,921
R. Dravid† 13,265
S. M. Gavaskar 10,122
V. V. S. Laxman 8,781
V. Sehwag† 8,503
S. C. Ganguly 7,212

† *R. Dravid also scored 0 and 23 and V. Sehwag 76 and 7 for the World XI v Australia (2005-06 Super Series Test).*

PAKISTAN

Younis Khan 9,977	Inzamam-ul-Haq† 8,829	Salim Malik. 5,768
Javed Miandad. 8,832	Mohammad Yousuf. . . 7,530	Zaheer Abbas. 5,062

† *Inzamam-ul-Haq also scored 1 and 0 for the World XI v Australia (2005-06 Super Series Test).*

SRI LANKA

K. C. Sangakkara . . . 12,400	S. T. Jayasuriya 6,973	M. S. Atapattu 5,502
D. P. M. D. Jayawardene 11,814	P. A. de Silva. 6,973	T. M. Dilshan. 5,492

ZIMBABWE

A. Flower. 4,794	A. D. R. Campbell. . . . 2,858	H. H. Streak. 1,990
G. W. Flower. 3,457	G. J. Whittall 2,207	**H. Masakadza 1,794**

BANGLADESH

Tamim Iqbal 3,443	Habibul Bashar 3,026	Mohammad Ashraful . 2,737
Shakib Al Hasan 3,213	**Mushfiqur Rahim . . . 2,922**	Javed Omar 1,720

HIGHEST CAREER AVERAGE

(Qualification: 20 innings)

Avge		*T*	*I*	*NO*	*R*	*HS*	*100*
99.94	D. G. Bradman (A)	52	80	10	6,996	334	29
61.87	**A. C. Voges (A)**	**20**	**31**	**7**	**1,485**	**269***	**5**
60.97	R. G. Pollock (SA)	23	41	4	2,256	274	7
60.83	G. A. Headley (WI)	22	40	4	2,190	270*	10
60.73	H. Sutcliffe (E)	54	84	9	4,555	194	16
60.15	**S. P. D. Smith (A)**	**50**	**92**	**13**	**4,752**	**215**	**17**
59.23	E. Paynter (E)	20	31	5	1,540	243	4
58.67	K. F. Barrington (E)	82	131	15	6,806	256	20
58.61	E. D. Weekes (WI)	48	81	5	4,455	207	15
58.45	W. R. Hammond (E).	85	140	16	7,249	336*	22
57.78	G. S. Sobers (WI)	93	160	21	8,032	365*	26
57.40	K. C. Sangakkara (SL)	134	233	17	12,400	319	38
56.94	J. B. Hobbs (E)	61	102	7	5,410	211	15
56.68	C. L. Walcott (WI)	44	74	7	3,798	220	15
56.67	L. Hutton (E).	79	138	15	6,971	364	19
55.37	J. H. Kallis (SA/World)	166	280	40	13,289	224	45
55.00	E. Tyldesley (E)	14	20	2	990	122	3

S. G. Barnes (A) scored 1,072 runs at 63.05 from 19 innings.

BEST CAREER STRIKE-RATES

(Runs per 100 balls. Qualification: 1,000 runs)

SR		*T*	*I*	*NO*	*R*	*100*	*Avge*
88.37	**T. G. Southee (NZ)**.	**56**	**84**	**6**	**1,300**	**0**	**16.66**
86.97	Shahid Afridi (P)	27	48	1	1,716	5	36.51
82.22	V. Sehwag (I).	104	180	6	8,586	23	49.34
81.98	A. C. Gilchrist (A).	96	137	20	5,570	17	47.60
78.80	**D. A. Warner (A)**.	**60**	**111**	**4**	**5,261**	**18**	**49.16**
76.49	G. P. Swann (E).	60	76	14	1,370	0	22.09

SR		*T*	*I*	*NO*	*R*	*100*	*Avge*
74.04	**Sarfraz Ahmed (P)**	**33**	**58**	**12**	**1,948**	**3**	**42.34**
72.40	**Q. de Kock (SA)**	**16**	**25**	**3**	**1,123**	**3**	**51.04**
70.28	M. Muralitharan (SL)	133	164	56	1,261	0	11.67
67.88	D. J. G. Sammy (WI)	38	63	2	1,323	1	21.68
65.98	Umar Akmal (P)	16	30	2	1,003	1	35.82
65.54	T. M. Dilshan (SL)	87	145	11	5,492	16	40.98
65.13*	S. T. Jayasuriya (SL)	110	188	14	6,973	14	40.07

* *The above figures are complete except for Jayasuriya, who played one innings for which the balls faced are not recorded. Comprehensive data on balls faced has been available only in recent decades, and its introduction varied from country to country. Among earlier players for whom partial data is available, Kapil Dev (India) had a strike-rate of 80.91 and I. V. A. Richards (West Indies) 70.19 in those innings which were fully recorded.*

HIGHEST PERCENTAGE OF TEAM'S RUNS OVER TEST CAREER

(Qualification: 20 Tests)

	Tests	*Runs*	*Team Runs*	*% of Team Runs*
D. G. Bradman (Australia)	52	6,996	28,810	24.28
G. A. Headley (West Indies)	22	2,190	10,239	21.38
B. C. Lara (West Indies)	131	11,953	63,328	18.87
L. Hutton (England)	79	6,971	38,440	18.13
J. B. Hobbs (England)	61	5,410	30,211	17.90
A. D. Nourse (South Africa)	34	2,960	16,659	17.76
E. D. Weekes (West Indies)	48	4,455	25,667	17.35
B. Mitchell (South Africa)	42	3,471	20,175	17.20
H. Sutcliffe (England)	54	4,555	26,604	17.12
K. C. Sangakkara (Sri Lanka)	134	12,400	72,779	17.03
B. Sutcliffe (New Zealand)	42	2,727	16,158	16.87

The percentage shows the proportion of a team's runs scored by that player in all Tests in which he played, including team runs in innings in which he did not bat.

FASTEST FIFTIES

Minutes			
24	Misbah-ul-Haq	Pakistan v Australia at Abu Dhabi	2014-15
27	Mohammad Ashraful	Bangladesh v India at Mirpur	2007
28	J. T. Brown	England v Australia at Melbourne	1894-95
29	S. A. Durani	India v England at Kanpur	1963-64
30	E. A. V. Williams	West Indies v England at Bridgetown	1947-48
30	B. R. Taylor	New Zealand v West Indies at Auckland	1968-69

The fastest fifties in terms of balls received (where recorded) are:

Balls			
21	Misbah-ul-Haq	Pakistan v Australia at Abu Dhabi	2014-15
23	**D. A. Warner**	**Australia v Pakistan at Sydney**	**2016-17**
24	J. H. Kallis	South Africa v Zimbabwe at Cape Town	2004-05
25	S. Shillingford	West Indies v New Zealand at Kingston	2014
26	Shahid Afridi	Pakistan v India at Bangalore	2004-05
26	Mohammad Ashraful	Bangladesh v India at Mirpur	2007
26	D. W. Steyn	South Africa v West Indies at Port Elizabeth	2014-15

An expanded and regularly updated online version of the Records can be found at www.wisdenrecords.com

FASTEST HUNDREDS

Minutes			
70	J. M. Gregory	Australia v South Africa at Johannesburg	1921-22
74	Misbah-ul-Haq	Pakistan v Australia at Abu Dhabi	2014-15
75	G. L. Jessop	England v Australia at The Oval	1902
78	R. Benaud	Australia v West Indies at Kingston	1954-55
80	J. H. Sinclair	South Africa v Australia at Cape Town	1902-03
81	I. V. A. Richards	West Indies v England at St John's	1985-86
86	B. R. Taylor	New Zealand v West Indies at Auckland	1968-69

The fastest hundreds in terms of balls received (where recorded) are:

Balls			
54	**B. B. McCullum**	**New Zealand v Australia at Christchurch**	**2016-17**
56	I. V. A. Richards	West Indies v England at St John's	1985-86
56	Misbah-ul-Haq	Pakistan v Australia at Abu Dhabi	2014-15
57	A. C. Gilchrist	Australia v England at Perth	2006-07
67	J. M. Gregory	Australia v South Africa at Johannesburg	1921-22
69	S. Chanderpaul	West Indies v Australia at Georgetown	2002-03
69	D. A. Warner	Australia v India at Perth	2011-12
70	C. H. Gayle	West Indies v Australia at Perth	2009-10

FASTEST DOUBLE-HUNDREDS

Minutes			
214	D. G. Bradman	Australia v England at Leeds	1930
217	N. J. Astle	New Zealand v England at Christchurch	2001-02
223	S. J. McCabe	Australia v England at Nottingham	1938
226	V. T. Trumper	Australia v South Africa at Adelaide	1910-11
234	D. G. Bradman	Australia v England at Lord's	1930
240	W. R. Hammond	England v New Zealand at Auckland	1932-33

The fastest double-hundreds in terms of balls received (where recorded) are:

Balls			
153	N. J. Astle	New Zealand v England at Christchurch	2001-02
163	**B. A. Stokes**	**England v South Africa at Cape Town**	**2015-16**
168	V. Sehwag	India v Sri Lanka at Mumbai (BS)	2009-10
182	V. Sehwag	India v Pakistan at Lahore	2005-06
186	B. B. McCullum	New Zealand v Pakistan at Sharjah	2014-15
194	V. Sehwag	India v South Africa at Chennai	2007-08

FASTEST TRIPLE-HUNDREDS

Minutes			
288	W. R. Hammond	England v New Zealand at Auckland	1932-33
336	D. G. Bradman	Australia v England at Leeds	1930

The fastest triple-hundred in terms of balls received (where recorded) is:

Balls			
278	V. Sehwag	India v South Africa at Chennai	2007-08

MOST RUNS SCORED OFF AN OVER

28	B. C. Lara (466444)	off R. J. Peterson	WI v SA at Johannesburg	2003-04
28	G. J. Bailey (462466)	off J. M. Anderson	A v E at Perth	2013-14
27	Shahid Afridi (666621)	off Harbhajan Singh	P v I at Lahore	2005-06
26	C. D. McMillan (444464)	off Younis Khan	NZ v P at Hamilton	2000-01
26	B. C. Lara (406664)	off Danish Kaneria	WI v P at Multan	2006-07
26	M. G. Johnson (446066)	off P. L. Harris	A v SA at Johannesburg	2009-10
26	B. B. McCullum (466046)	off R. A. S. Lakmal	NZ v SL at Christchurch	2014-15

MOST RUNS IN A DAY

309	D. G. Bradman	Australia v England at Leeds	1930
295	W. R. Hammond	England v New Zealand at Auckland	1932-33
284	V. Sehwag	India v Sri Lanka at Mumbai	2009-10
273	D. C. S. Compton	England v Pakistan at Nottingham	1954
271	D. G. Bradman	Australia v England at Leeds	1934

MOST SIXES IN A CAREER

B. B. McCullum (NZ)	**107**
A. C. Gilchrist (A)	100
C. H. Gayle (WI)	98
J. H. Kallis (SA/World)	97
V. Sehwag (I/World)	91
B. C. Lara (WI)	88
C. L. Cairns (NZ)	87
I. V. A. Richards (WI)	84
A. Flintoff (E/World)	82
M. L. Hayden (A)	82
K. P. Pietersen (E)	81
M. S. Dhoni (I)	78
Misbah-ul-Haq (P)	**73**
R. T. Ponting (A)	73
C. H. Lloyd (WI)	70

SLOWEST INDIVIDUAL BATTING

0	in 101 minutes	G. I. Allott, New Zealand v South Africa at Auckland	1998-99
4*	in 110 minutes	Abdul Razzaq, Pakistan v Australia at Melbourne	2004-05
6	in 137 minutes	S. C. J. Broad, England v New Zealand at Auckland	2012-13
9*	in 184 minutes	Arshad Khan, Pakistan v Sri Lanka at Colombo (SSC)	2000
18	in 194 minutes	W. R. Playle, New Zealand v England at Leeds	1958
19*	in 217 minutes	M. D. Crowe, New Zealand v Sri Lanka at Colombo (SSC)	1983-84
25	in 289 minutes	H. M. Amla, South Africa v India at Delhi	2015-16
35	in 332 minutes	C. J. Tavaré, England v India at Madras	1981-82
43	in 354 minutes	A. B. de Villiers, South Africa v India at Delhi	2015-16
60	in 390 minutes	D. N. Sardesai, India v West Indies at Bridgetown	1961-62
62	in 408 minutes	Ramiz Raja, Pakistan v West Indies at Karachi	1986-87
68	in 458 minutes	T. E. Bailey, England v Australia at Brisbane	1958-59
86	in 474 minutes	Shoaib Mohammad, Pakistan v West Indies at Karachi	1990-91
99	in 505 minutes	M. L. Jaisimha, India v Pakistan at Kanpur	1960-61
104	in 529 minutes	S. V. Manjrekar, India v Zimbabwe at Harare	1992-93
105	in 575 minutes	D. J. McGlew, South Africa v Australia at Durban	1957-58
114	in 591 minutes	Mudassar Nazar, Pakistan v England at Lahore	1977-78
120*	in 609 minutes	J. J. Crowe, New Zealand v Sri Lanka at Colombo (CCC)	1986-87
136*	in 675 minutes	S. Chanderpaul, West Indies v India at St John's	2001-02
163	in 720 minutes	Shoaib Mohammad, Pakistan v New Zealand at Wellington	1988-89
201*	in 777 minutes	D. S. B. P. Kuruppu, Sri Lanka v NZ at Colombo (CCC)	1986-87
275	in 878 minutes	G. Kirsten, South Africa v England at Durban	1999-2000
337	in 970 minutes	Hanif Mohammad, Pakistan v West Indies at Bridgetown	1957-58

SLOWEST HUNDREDS

557 minutes	Mudassar Nazar, Pakistan v England at Lahore	1977-78
545 minutes	D. J. McGlew, South Africa v Australia at Durban	1957-58
535 minutes	A. P. Gurusinha, Sri Lanka v Zimbabwe at Harare	1994-95
516 minutes	J. J. Crowe, New Zealand v Sri Lanka at Colombo (CCC)	1986-87
500 minutes	S. V. Manjrekar, India v Zimbabwe at Harare	1992-93
488 minutes	P. E. Richardson, England v South Africa at Johannesburg	1956-57

The slowest hundred for any Test in England is 458 minutes (329 balls) by K. W. R. Fletcher, England v Pakistan, The Oval, 1974.

The slowest double-hundred in a Test was scored in 777 minutes (548 balls) by D. S. B. P. Kuruppu for Sri Lanka v New Zealand at Colombo (CCC), 1986-87, on his debut.

PARTNERSHIPS OVER 400

624	for 3rd	K. C. Sangakkara (287)/ D. P. M. D. Jayawardene (374)	SL v SA	Colombo (SSC)	2006
576	for 2nd	S. T. Jayasuriya (340)/R. S. Mahanama (225)	SL v I	Colombo (RPS)	1997-98
467	for 3rd	A. H. Jones (186)/M. D. Crowe (299)	NZ v SL	Wellington	1990-91
451	for 2nd	W. H. Ponsford (266)/D. G. Bradman (244)	A v E	The Oval	1934
451	for 3rd	Mudassar Nazar (231)/Javed Miandad (280*)	P v I	Hyderabad	1982-83
449	for 4th	A. C. Voges (269*)/S. E. Marsh (182)	A v WI	Hobart	2015-16
446	for 2nd	C. C. Hunte (260)/G. S. Sobers (365*)	WI v P	Kingston	1957-58
438	for 2nd	M. S. Atapattu (249)/K. C. Sangakkara (270)	SL v Z	Bulawayo	2003-04
437	for 4th	D. P. M. D. Jayawardene (240)/ T. T. Samaraweera (231)	SL v P	Karachi	2008-09
429*	for 3rd	J. A. Rudolph (222*)/H. H. Dippenaar (177*)	SA v B	Chittagong	2003
415	for 1st	N. D. McKenzie (226)/G. C. Smith (232)	SA v B	Chittagong	2007-08
413	for 1st	V. Mankad (231)/Pankaj Roy (173)	I v NZ	Madras	1955-56
411	for 4th	P. B. H. May (285*)/M. C. Cowdrey (154)	E v WI	Birmingham	1957
410	for 1st	V. Sehwag (254)/R. Dravid (128*)	I v P	Lahore	2005-06
405	for 5th	S. G. Barnes (234)/D. G. Bradman (234)	A v E	Sydney	1946-47

415 runs were added for the third wicket for India v England at Madras in 1981-82 by D. B. Vengsarkar (retired hurt), G. R. Viswanath and Yashpal Sharma. 408 runs were added for the first wicket for India v Bangladesh at Mirpur in 2007 by K. D. Karthik (retired hurt), Wasim Jaffer (retired hurt), R. Dravid and S. R. Tendulkar.

HIGHEST PARTNERSHIPS FOR EACH WICKET

First Wicket

415	N. D. McKenzie (226)/G. C. Smith (232)	SA v B	Chittagong	2007-08
413	V. Mankad (231)/Pankaj Roy (173)	I v NZ	Madras	1955-56
410	V. Sehwag (254)/R. Dravid (128*)	I v P	Lahore	2005-06
387	G. M. Turner (259)/T. W. Jarvis (182)	NZ v WI	Georgetown	1971-72
382	W. M. Lawry (210)/R. B. Simpson (201)	A v WI	Bridgetown	1964-65

Second Wicket

576	S. T. Jayasuriya (340)/R. S. Mahanama (225)	SL v I	Colombo (RPS)	1997-98
451	W. H. Ponsford (266)/D. G. Bradman (244)	A v E	The Oval	1934
446	C. C. Hunte (260)/G. S. Sobers (365*)	WI v P	Kingston	1957-58
438	M. S. Atapattu (249)/K. C. Sangakkara (270)	SL v Z	Bulawayo	2003-04
382	L. Hutton (364)/M. Leyland (187)	E v A	The Oval	1938

Third Wicket

624	K. C. Sangakkara (287)/ D. P. M. D. Jayawardene (374)	SL v SA	Colombo (SSC)	2006
467	A. H. Jones (186)/M. D. Crowe (299)	NZ v SL	Wellington	1990-91
451	Mudassar Nazar (231)/Javed Miandad (280*)	P v I	Hyderabad	1982-83
429*	J. A. Rudolph (222*)/H. H. Dippenaar (177*)	SA v B	Chittagong	2003
397	Qasim Omar (206)/Javed Miandad (203*)	P v SL	Faisalabad	1985-86

Fourth Wicket

449	A. C. Voges (269*)/S. E. Marsh (182)	A v WI	Hobart	2015-16
437	D. P. M. D. Jayawardene (240)/ T. T. Samaraweera (231)	SL v P	Karachi	2008-09
411	P. B. H. May (285*)/M. C. Cowdrey (154)	E v WI	Birmingham	1957
399	G. S. Sobers (226)/F. M. M. Worrell (197*)	WI v E	Bridgetown	1959-60
388	W. H. Ponsford (181)/D. G. Bradman (304)	A v E	Leeds	1934

Fifth Wicket

405	S. G. Barnes (234)/D. G. Bradman (234)	A v E	Sydney	1946-47
385	S. R. Waugh (160)/G. S. Blewett (214)	A v SA	Johannesburg	1996-97
376	V. V. S. Laxman (281)/R. Dravid (180)	I v A	Kolkata	2000-01
359	**Shakib Al Hasan (217)/Mushfiqur Rahim (159)**	**B v NZ**	**Wellington**	**2016-17**
338	G. C. Smith (234)/A. B. de Villiers (164)	SA v P	Dubai	2013-14

Sixth Wicket

399	**B. A. Stokes (258)/J. M. Bairstow (150*)**	**E v SA**	**Cape Town**	**2015-16**
352	B. B. McCullum (302)/B-J. Watling (124)	NZ v I	Wellington	2013-14
351	D. P. M. D. Jayawardene (275)/ H. A. P. W. Jayawardene (154*)	SL v I	Ahmedabad	2009-10
346	J. H. Fingleton (136)/D. G. Bradman (270)	A v E	Melbourne	1936-37

Seventh Wicket

347	D. St E. Atkinson (219)/C. C. Depeiza (122)	WI v A	Bridgetown	1954-55
308	Waqar Hassan (189)/Imtiaz Ahmed (209)	P v NZ	Lahore	1955-56
280	R. G. Sharma (177)/R. Ashwin (124)	I v WI	Kolkata	2013-14
259*	V. V. S. Laxman (143*)/M. S. Dhoni (132*)	I v SA	Kolkata	2009-10
248	Yousuf Youhana (203)/Saqlain Mushtaq (101*)	P v NZ	Christchurch	2000-01

Eighth Wicket

332	I. J. L. Trott (184)/S. C. J. Broad (169)	E v P	Lord's	2010
313	Wasim Akram (257*)/Saqlain Mushtaq (79)	P v Z	Sheikhupura	1996-97
256	S. P. Fleming (262)/J. E. C. Franklin (122*)	NZ v SA	Cape Town	2005-06
253	N. J. Astle (156*)/A. C. Parore (110)	NZ v A	Perth	2001-02
246	L. E. G. Ames (137)/G. O. B. Allen (122)	E v NZ	Lord's	1931

Ninth Wicket

195	M. V. Boucher (78)/P. L. Symcox (108)	SA v P	Johannesburg	1997-98
190	Asif Iqbal (146)/Intikhab Alam (51)	P v E	The Oval	1967
184	Mahmudullah (76)/Abul Hasan (113)	B v WI	Khulna	2012-13
180	J-P. Duminy (166)/D. W. Steyn (76)	SA v A	Melbourne	2008-09
163*	M. C. Cowdrey (128*)/A. C. Smith (69*)	E v NZ	Wellington	1962-63

Tenth Wicket

198	J. E. Root (154*)/J. M. Anderson (81)	E v I	Nottingham	2014
163	P. J. Hughes (81*)/A. C. Agar (98)	A v E	Nottingham	2013
151	B. F. Hastings (110)/R. O. Collinge (68*)	NZ v P	Auckland	1972-73
151	Azhar Mahmood (128*)/Mushtaq Ahmed (59)	P v SA	Rawalpindi	1997-98
143	D. Ramdin (107*)/T. L. Best (95)	WI v E	Birmingham	2012

HIGHEST PARTNERSHIPS FOR EACH COUNTRY

ENGLAND

359	for 1st	L. Hutton (158)/C. Washbrook (195)	v SA	Johannesburg	1948-49
382	for 2nd	L. Hutton (364)/M. Leyland (187)	v A	The Oval	1938
370	for 3rd	W. J. Edrich (189)/D. C. S. Compton (208) . . .	v SA	Lord's	1947
411	for 4th	P. B. H. May (285*)/M. C. Cowdrey (154) . . .	v WI	Birmingham	1957
254	for 5th	K. W. R. Fletcher (113)/A. W. Greig (148) . . .	v I	Bombay	1972-73
399	**for 6th**	**B. A. Stokes (258)/J. M. Bairstow (150*) . . .**	**v SA**	**Cape Town**	**2015-16**
197	for 7th	M. J. K. Smith (96)/J. M. Parks (101*).	v WI	Port-of-Spain	1959-60
332	for 8th	I. J. L. Trott (184)/S. C. J. Broad (169).	v P	Lord's	2010
163*	for 9th	M. C. Cowdrey (128*)/A. C. Smith (69*)	v NZ	Wellington	1962-63
198	for 10th	J. E. Root (154*)/J. M. Anderson (81)	v I	Nottingham	2014

AUSTRALIA

382	for 1st	W. M. Lawry (210)/R. B. Simpson (201).	v WI	Bridgetown	1964-65
451	for 2nd	W. H. Ponsford (266)/D. G. Bradman (244). . .	v E	The Oval	1934
315	for 3rd	R. T. Ponting (206)/D. S. Lehmann (160)	v WI	Port-of-Spain	2002-03
449	for 4th	A. C. Voges (269*)/S. E. Marsh (182)	v WI	Hobart	2015-16
405	for 5th	S. G. Barnes (234)/D. G. Bradman (234)	v E	Sydney	1946-47
346	for 6th	J. H. Fingleton (136)/D. G. Bradman (270) . . .	v E	Melbourne	1936-37
217	for 7th	K. D. Walters (250)/G. J. Gilmour (101)	v NZ	Christchurch	1976-77
243	for 8th	R. J. Hartigan (116)/C. Hill (160).	v E	Adelaide	1907-08
154	for 9th	S. E. Gregory (201)/J. McC. Blackham (74) . .	v E	Sydney	1894-95
163	for 10th	P. J. Hughes (81*)/A. C. Agar (98).	v E	Nottingham	2013

SOUTH AFRICA

415	for 1st	N. D. McKenzie (226)/G. C. Smith (232).	v B	Chittagong	2007-08
315*	for 2nd	H. H. Gibbs (211*)/J. H. Kallis (148*).	v NZ	Christchurch	1998-99
429*	for 3rd	J. A. Rudolph (222*)/H. H. Dippenaar (177*) .	v B	Chittagong	2003
308	for 4th	H. M. Amla (208)/A. B. de Villiers (152).	v WI	Centurion	2014-15
338	for 5th	G. C. Smith (234)/A. B. de Villiers (164).	v P	Dubai	2013-14
271	for 6th	A. G. Prince (162*)/M. V. Boucher (117)	v B	Centurion	2008-09
246	for 7th	D. J. McGlew (255*)/A. R. A. Murray (109) . .	v NZ	Wellington	1952-53
150	for 8th	N. D. McKenzie (103)/S. M. Pollock (111) . . .	v SL	Centurion	2000-01
		G. Kirsten (130)/M. Zondeki (59).	v E	Leeds	2003
195	for 9th	M. V. Boucher (78)/P. L. Symcox (108)	v P	Johannesburg	1997-98
107*	for 10th	A. B. de Villiers (278*)/M. Morkel (35*).	v P	Abu Dhabi	2010-11

WEST INDIES

298	for 1st	C. G. Greenidge (149)/D. L. Haynes (167). . . .	v E	St John's	1989-90
446	for 2nd	C. C. Hunte (260)/G. S. Sobers (365*).	v P	Kingston	1957-58
338	for 3rd	E. D. Weekes (206)/F. M. M. Worrell (167). . .	v E	Port-of-Spain	1953-54
399	for 4th	G. S. Sobers (226)/F. M. M. Worrell (197*). . .	v E	Bridgetown	1959-60
322	for 5th†	B. C. Lara (213)/J. C. Adams (94)	v A	Kingston	1998-99
282*	for 6th	B. C. Lara (400*)/R. D. Jacobs (107*).	v E	St John's	2003-04
347	for 7th	D. St E. Atkinson (219)/C. C. Depeiza (122) . .	v A	Bridgetown	1954-55
148	for 8th	J. C. Adams (101*)/F. A. Rose (69)	v Z	Kingston	1999-2000
161	for 9th	C. H. Lloyd (161*)/A. M. E. Roberts (68)	v I	Calcutta	1983-84
143	for 10th	D. Ramdin (107*)/T. L. Best (95).	v E	Birmingham	2012

† *344 runs were added between the fall of the 4th and 5th wickets: P. T. Collins retired hurt when he and Lara had added 22 runs.*

NEW ZEALAND

387	for 1st	G. M. Turner (259)/T. W. Jarvis (182)	v WI	Georgetown	1971-72
297	for 2nd	B. B. McCullum (202)/K. S. Williamson (192)	v P	Sharjah	2014-15
467	for 3rd	A. H. Jones (186)/M. D. Crowe (299)	v SL	Wellington	1990-91
271	for 4th	L. R. P. L. Taylor (151)/J. D. Ryder (201)	v I	Napier	2008-09
222	for 5th	N. J. Astle (141)/C. D. McMillan (142)	v Z	Wellington	2000-01
365*	for 6th	K. S. Williamson (242*)/B-J. Watling (142*)	v SL	Wellington	2014-15
225	for 7th	C. L. Cairns (158)/J. D. P. Oram (90)	v SA	Auckland	2003-04
256	for 8th	S. P. Fleming (262)/J. E. C. Franklin (122*)	v SA	Cape Town	2005-06
136	for 9th	I. D. S. Smith (173)/M. C. Snedden (22)	v I	Auckland	1989-90
151	for 10th	B. F. Hastings (110)/R. O. Collinge (68*)	v P	Auckland	1972-73

INDIA

413	for 1st	V. Mankad (231)/Pankaj Roy (173)	v NZ	Madras	1955-56
370	for 2nd	M. Vijay (167)/C. A. Pujara (204)	v A	Hyderabad	2012-13
336	for 3rd†	V. Sehwag (309)/S. R. Tendulkar (194*)	v P	Multan	2003-04
365	**for 4th**	**V. Kohli (211)/A. M. Rahane (188)**	**v NZ**	**Indore**	**2016-17**
376	for 5th	V. V. S. Laxman (281)/R. Dravid (180)	v A	Kolkata	2000-01
298*	for 6th	D. B. Vengsarkar (164*)/R. J. Shastri (121*)	v A	Bombay	1986-87
280	for 7th	R. G. Sharma (177)/R. Ashwin (124)	v WI	Kolkata	2013-14
241	**for 8th**	**V. Kohli (235)/J. Yadav (104)**	**v E**	**Mumbai**	**2016-17**
149	for 9th	P. G. Joshi (52*)/R. B. Desai (85)	v P	Bombay	1960-61
133	for 10th	S. R. Tendulkar (248*)/Zaheer Khan (75)	v B	Dhaka	2004-05

† *415 runs were scored for India's 3rd wicket v England at Madras in 1981-82, in two partnerships: D. B. Vengsarkar and G. R. Viswanath put on 99 before Vengsarkar retired hurt, then Viswanath and Yashpal Sharma added a further 316.*

PAKISTAN

298	for 1st	Aamir Sohail (160)/Ijaz Ahmed snr (151)	v WI	Karachi	1997-98
291	for 2nd	Zaheer Abbas (274)/Mushtaq Mohammad (100)	v E	Birmingham	1971
451	for 3rd	Mudassar Nazar (231)/Javed Miandad (280*)	v I	Hyderabad	1982-83
350	for 4th	Mushtaq Mohammad (201)/Asif Iqbal (175)	v NZ	Dunedin	1972-73
281	for 5th	Javed Miandad (163)/Asif Iqbal (166)	v NZ	Lahore	1976-77
269	for 6th	Mohammad Yousuf (223)/Kamran Akmal (154)	v E	Lahore	2005-06
308	for 7th	Waqar Hassan (189)/Imtiaz Ahmed (209)	v NZ	Lahore	1955-56
313	for 8th	Wasim Akram (257*)/Saqlain Mushtaq (79)	v Z	Sheikhupura	1996-97
190	for 9th	Asif Iqbal (146)/Intikhab Alam (51)	v E	The Oval	1967
151	for 10th	Azhar Mahmood (128*)/Mushtaq Ahmed (59)	v SA	Rawalpindi	1997-98

SRI LANKA

335	for 1st	M. S. Atapattu (207*)/S. T. Jayasuriya (188)	v P	Kandy	2000
576	for 2nd	S. T. Jayasuriya (340)/R. S. Mahanama (225)	v I	Colombo (RPS)	1997-98
624	for 3rd	K. C. Sangakkara (287)/ D. P. M. D. Jayawardene (374)	v SA	Colombo (SSC)	2006
437	for 4th	D. P. M. D. Jayawardene (240)/ T. T. Samaraweera (231)	v P	Karachi	2008-09
280	for 5th	T. T. Samaraweera (138)/T. M. Dilshan (168)	v B	Colombo (PSS)	2005-06
351	for 6th	D. P. M. D. Jayawardene (275)/ H. A. P. W. Jayawardene (154*)	v I	Ahmedabad	2009-10
223*	for 7th	H. A. P. W. Jayawardene (120*)/ W. P. U. J. C. Vaas (100*)	v B	Colombo (SSC)	2007
170	for 8th	D. P. M. D. Jayawardene (237)/ W. P. U. J. C. Vaas (69)	v SA	Galle	2004
118	for 9th	T. T. Samaraweera (83)/B. A. W. Mendis (78)	v I	Colombo (PSS)	2010
79	for 10th	W. P. U. J. C. Vaas (68*)/M. Muralitharan (43)	v A	Kandy	2003-04

ZIMBABWE

164	for 1st	D. D. Ebrahim (71)/A. D. R. Campbell (103)	v WI	Bulawayo	2001
160	for 2nd	Sikandar Raza (82)/H. Masakadza (81)	v B	Chittagong	2014-15
194	for 3rd	A. D. R. Campbell (99)/D. L. Houghton (142)	v SL	Harare	1994-95
269	for 4th	G. W. Flower (201*)/A. Flower (156)	v P	Harare	1994-95
277*	for 5th	M. W. Goodwin (166*)/A. Flower (100*)	v P	Bulawayo	1997-98
165	for 6th	D. L. Houghton (121)/A. Flower (59)	v I	Harare	1992-93
154	for 7th	H. H. Streak (83*)/A. M. Blignaut (92)	v WI	Harare	2001
168	for 8th	H. H. Streak (127*)/A. M. Blignaut (91)	v WI	Harare	2003-04
87	for 9th	P. A. Strang (106*)/B. C. Strang (42)	v P	Sheikhupura	1996-97
97*	for 10th	A. Flower (183*)/H. K. Olonga (11*)	v I	Delhi	2000-01

BANGLADESH

312	for 1st	Tamim Iqbal (206)/Imrul Kayes (150)	v P	Khulna	2014-15
232	for 2nd	Shamsur Rahman (106)/Imrul Kayes (115)	v SL	Chittagong	2013-14
157	for 3rd	Tamim Iqbal (70)/Mominul Haque (126*)	v NZ	Mirpur	2013-14
167	for 4th	Naeem Islam (108)/Shakib Al Hasan (89)	v WI	Mirpur	2012-13
359	**for 5th**	**Shakib Al Hasan (217)/ Mushfiqur Rahim (159)**	**v NZ**	**Wellington**	**2016-17**
191	for 6th	Mohammad Ashraful (129*)/ Mushfiqur Rahim (80)	v SL	Colombo (PSS)	2007
145	for 7th	Shakib Al Hasan (87)/Mahmudullah (115)	v NZ	Hamilton	2009-10
113	for 8th	Mushfiqur Rahim (79)/Naeem Islam (38)	v E	Chittagong	2009-10
184	for 9th	Mahmudullah (76)/Abul Hasan (113)	v WI	Khulna	2012-13
69	for 10th	Mohammad Rafique (65)/Shahadat Hossain (3*)	v A	Chittagong	2005-06

UNUSUAL DISMISSALS

Handled the Ball

W. R. Endean	South Africa v England at Cape Town	1956-57
A. M. J. Hilditch	Australia v Pakistan at Perth	1978-79
Mohsin Khan	Pakistan v Australia at Karachi	1982-83
D. L. Haynes	West Indies v India at Bombay	1983-84
G. A. Gooch	England v Australia at Manchester	1993
S. R. Waugh	Australia v India at Chennai	2000-01
M. P. Vaughan	England v India at Bangalore	2001-02

Obstructing the Field

L. Hutton	England v South Africa at The Oval	1951

There have been no cases of Hit the Ball Twice or Timed Out in Test cricket.

BOWLING RECORDS

MOST WICKETS IN AN INNINGS

10-53	J. C. Laker	England v Australia at Manchester	1956
10-74	A. Kumble	India v Pakistan at Delhi	1998-99
9-28	G. A. Lohmann	England v South Africa at Johannesburg	1895-96
9-37	J. C. Laker	England v Australia at Manchester	1956
9-51	M. Muralitharan	Sri Lanka v Zimbabwe at Kandy	2001-02
9-52	R. J. Hadlee	New Zealand v Australia at Brisbane	1985-86
9-56	Abdul Qadir	Pakistan v England at Lahore	1987-88
9-57	D. E. Malcolm	England v South Africa at The Oval	1994
9-65	M. Muralitharan	Sri Lanka v England at The Oval	1998

9-69	J. M. Patel	India v Australia at Kanpur	1959-60
9-83	Kapil Dev	India v West Indies at Ahmedabad	1983-84
9-86	Sarfraz Nawaz	Pakistan v Australia at Melbourne	1978-79
9-95	J. M. Noreiga	West Indies v India at Port-of-Spain	1970-71
9-102	S. P. Gupte	India v West Indies at Kanpur	1958-59
9-103	S. F. Barnes	England v South Africa at Johannesburg	1913-14
9-113	H. J. Tayfield	South Africa v England at Johannesburg	1956-57
9-121	A. A. Mailey	Australia v England at Melbourne	1920-21
9-127	H. M. R. K. B. Herath	Sri Lanka v Pakistan at Colombo (SSC)	2014

There have been ***75*** *instances of eight wickets in a Test innings.*

The best bowling figures for the countries not mentioned above are:

8-39	Taijul Islam	Bangladesh v Zimbabwe at Mirpur	2014-15
8-109	P. A. Strang	Zimbabwe v New Zealand at Bulawayo	2000-01

OUTSTANDING BOWLING ANALYSES

	O	*M*	*R*	*W*		
J. C. Laker (E)	51.2	23	53	10	v Australia at Manchester	1956
A. Kumble (I)	26.3	9	74	10	v Pakistan at Delhi	1998-99
G. A. Lohmann (E)	14.2	6	28	9	v South Africa at Johannesburg	1895-96
J. C. Laker (E)	16.4	4	37	9	v Australia at Manchester	1956
G. A. Lohmann (E)	9.4	5	7	8	v South Africa at Port Elizabeth	1895-96
J. Briggs (E)	14.2	5	11	8	v South Africa at Cape Town	1888-89
S. C. J. Broad (E)	9.3	5	15	8	v Australia at Nottingham	2015
S. J. Harmison (E)	12.3	8	12	7	v West Indies at Kingston	2003-04
J. Briggs (E)	19.1	11	17	7	v South Africa at Cape Town	1888-89
M. A. Noble (A)	7.4	2	17	7	v England at Melbourne	1901-02
W. Rhodes (E)	11	3	17	7	v Australia at Birmingham	1902

WICKET WITH FIRST BALL IN TEST CRICKET

	Batsman dismissed			
T. P. Horan	W. W. Read	A v E	Sydney	1882-83
A. Coningham	A. C. MacLaren	A v E	Melbourne	1894-95
W. M. Bradley	F. Laver	E v A	Manchester	1899
E. G. Arnold	V. T. Trumper	E v A	Sydney	1903-04
A. E. E. Vogler	E. G. Hayes	SA v E	Johannesburg	1905-06
J. N. Crawford	A. E. E. Vogler	E v SA	Johannesburg	1905-06
G. G. Macaulay	G. A. L. Hearne	E v SA	Cape Town	1922-23
M. W. Tate	M. J. Susskind	E v SA	Birmingham	1924
M. Henderson	E. W. Dawson	NZ v E	Christchurch	1929-30
H. D. Smith	E. Paynter	NZ v E	Christchurch	1932-33
T. F. Johnson	W. W. Keeton	WI v E	The Oval	1939
R. Howorth	D. V. Dyer	E v SA	The Oval	1947
Intikhab Alam	C. C. McDonald	P v A	Karachi	1959-60
R. K. Illingworth	P. V. Simmons	E v WI	Nottingham	1991
N. M. Kulkarni	M. S. Atapattu	I v SL	Colombo (RPS)	1997-98
M. K. G. C. P. Lakshitha	Mohammad Ashraful	SL v B	Colombo (SSC)	2002
N. M. Lyon	K. C. Sangakkara	A v SL	Galle	2011-12
R. M. S. Eranga	S. R. Watson	SL v A	Colombo (SSC)	2011-12
D. L. Piedt	M. A. Vermeulen	SA v Z	Harare	2014-15
G. C. Viljoen	**A. N. Cook**	**SA v E**	**Johannesburg**	**2015-16**

HAT-TRICKS

Most Hat-Tricks

S. C. J. Broad	**2**	H. Trumble	2
T. J. Matthews†	2	Wasim Akram‡	2

† *T. J. Matthews did the hat-trick in each innings of the same match.*
‡ *Wasim Akram did the hat-trick in successive matches.*

Hat-Tricks

There have been **42** hat-tricks in Tests, including the above. Occurrences since 2007:

R. J. Sidebottom	England v New Zealand at Hamilton	2007-08
P. M. Siddle	Australia v England at Brisbane	2010-11
S. C. J. Broad	England v India at Nottingham	2011
Sohag Gazi†	Bangladesh v New Zealand at Chittagong	2013-14
S. C. J. Broad	England v Sri Lanka at Leeds	2014
H. M. R. K. B. Herath	**Sri Lanka v Australia at Galle**	**2016**

† *Sohag Gazi also scored 101 not out.*

M. J. C. Allom, P. J. Petherick and D. W. Fleming did the hat-trick on Test debut. D. N. T. Zoysa took one in the second over of a Test (his first three balls); I. K. Pathan in the first over of a Test.

FOUR WICKETS IN FIVE BALLS

M. J. C. Allom	England v New Zealand at Christchurch *On debut, in his eighth over: W-WWW*	1929-30
C. M. Old	England v Pakistan at Birmingham *Sequence interrupted by a no-ball: WW-WW*	1978
Wasim Akram	Pakistan v West Indies at Lahore (*WW-WW*)	1990-91

MOST WICKETS IN A TEST

19-90	J. C. Laker	England v Australia at Manchester	1956
17-159	S. F. Barnes	England v South Africa at Johannesburg	1913-14
16-136†	N. D. Hirwani	India v West Indies at Madras	1987-88
16-137†	R. A. L. Massie	Australia v England at Lord's	1972
16-220	M. Muralitharan	Sri Lanka v England at The Oval	1998

† *On Test debut.*

There have been 18 further instances of 14 or more wickets in a Test match.

The best bowling figures for the countries not mentioned above are:

15-123	R. J. Hadlee	New Zealand v Australia at Brisbane	1985-86
14-116	Imran Khan	Pakistan v Sri Lanka at Lahore	1981-82
14-149	M. A. Holding	West Indies v England at The Oval	1976
13-132	M. Ntini	South Africa v West Indies at Port-of-Spain	2004-05
12-159	**Mehedi Hasan**	**Bangladesh v England at Mirpur**	**2016-17**
11-255	A. G. Huckle	Zimbabwe v New Zealand at Bulawayo	1997-98

MOST BALLS BOWLED IN A TEST

S. Ramadhin (West Indies) sent down 774 balls in 129 overs against England at Birmingham, 1957, the most delivered by any bowler in a Test, beating H. Verity's 766 for England against South Africa at Durban, 1938-39. In this match Ramadhin also bowled the most balls (588) in any first-class innings, since equalled by Arshad Ayub, Hyderabad v Madhya Pradesh at Secunderabad, 1991-92.

MOST WICKETS IN A SERIES

	T	*R*	*W*	*Avge*		
S. F. Barnes	4	536	49	10.93	England v South Africa	1913-14
J. C. Laker	5	442	46	9.60	England v Australia	1956
C. V. Grimmett	5	642	44	14.59	Australia v South Africa	1935-36
T. M. Alderman	6	893	42	21.26	Australia v England	1981
R. M. Hogg	6	527	41	12.85	Australia v England	1978-79
T. M. Alderman	6	712	41	17.36	Australia v England	1989
Imran Khan	6	558	40	13.95	Pakistan v India	1982-83
S. K. Warne	5	797	40	19.92	Australia v England	2005

The most for South Africa is 37 by H. J. Tayfield against England in 1956-57, for West Indies 35 by M. D. Marshall against England in 1988, for India 35 by B. S. Chandrasekhar against England in 1972-73 (all in five Tests), for New Zealand 33 by R. J. Hadlee against Australia in 1985-86, for Sri Lanka 30 by M. Muralitharan against Zimbabwe in 2001-02, for Zimbabwe 22 by H. H. Streak against Pakistan in 1994-95 (all in three Tests), and for Bangladesh ***19*** *by* ***Mehedi Hasan against England in 2016-17*** *(two Tests).*

MOST WICKETS IN A CALENDAR YEAR

	T	*R*	*W*	*Avge*	*5I*	*10M*	*Year*
S. K. Warne (Australia)	15	2,114	96	22.02	6	2	2005
M. Muralitharan (Sri Lanka)	11	1,521	90	16.89	9	5	2006
D. K. Lillee (Australia)	13	1,781	85	20.95	5	2	1981
A. A. Donald (South Africa)	14	1,571	80	19.63	7	–	1998
M. Muralitharan (Sri Lanka)	12	1,699	80	21.23	7	4	2001
J. Garner (West Indies)	15	1,604	77	20.83	4	–	1984
Kapil Dev (India)	18	1,739	75	23.18	5	1	1983
M. Muralitharan (Sri Lanka)	10	1,463	75	19.50	7	3	2000

MOST WICKETS

		T	*Balls*	*R*	*W*	*Avge*	*5I*	*10M*	*SR*
1	M. Muralitharan (SL/World)	133	44,039	18,180	800	22.72	67	22	55.04
2	S. K. Warne (Australia)	145	40,704	17,995	708	25.41	37	10	57.49
3	A. Kumble (India)	132	40,850	18,355	619	29.65	35	8	65.99
4	G. D. McGrath (Australia)	124	29,248	12,186	563	21.64	29	3	51.95
5	C. A. Walsh (West Indies)	132	30,019	12,688	519	24.44	22	3	57.84
6	**J. M. Anderson (England)**	**122**	**26,840**	**11,310**	**467**	**28.50**	**21**	**3**	**57.47**
7	Kapil Dev (India)	131	27,740	12,867	434	29.64	23	2	63.91
8	R. J. Hadlee (New Zealand)	86	21,918	9,611	431	22.29	36	9	50.85
9	S. M. Pollock (South Africa)	108	24,353	9,733	421	23.11	16	1	57.84
10	**D. W. Steyn (South Africa)**	**85**	**17,286**	**9,303**	**417**	**22.30**	**26**	**5**	**41.45**
	Harbhajan Singh (India)	103	28,580	13,537	417	32.46	25	5	68.53
12	Wasim Akram (Pakistan)	104	22,627	9,779	414	23.62	25	5	54.65
13	C. E. L. Ambrose (WI)	98	22,103	8,501	405	20.99	22	3	54.57
14	M. Ntini (South Africa)	101	20,834	11,242	390	28.82	18	4	53.42
15	I. T. Botham (England)	102	21,815	10,878	383	28.40	27	4	56.95
16	M. D. Marshall (West Indies)	81	17,584	7,876	376	20.94	22	4	46.76
17	Waqar Younis (Pakistan)	87	16,224	8,788	373	23.56	22	5	43.49
18	**S. C. J. Broad (England)**	**102**	**21,000**	**10,503**	**368**	**28.54**	**15**	**2**	**57.06**
19	Imran Khan (Pakistan)	88	19,458	8,258	362	22.81	23	6	53.75
	D. L. Vettori (NZ/World)	113	28,814	12,441	362	34.36	20	3	79.59
21	**H. M. R. K. B. Herath (SL)**	**78**	**21,858**	**10,108**	**357**	**28.31**	**28**	**7**	**61.22**
22	D. K. Lillee (Australia)	70	18,467	8,493	355	23.92	23	7	52.01
	W. P. U. J. C. Vaas (SL)	111	23,438	10,501	355	29.58	12	2	66.02
24	A. A. Donald (South Africa)	72	15,519	7,344	330	22.25	20	3	47.02
25	R. G. D. Willis (England)	90	17,357	8,190	325	25.20	16	–	53.40

		T	*Balls*	*R*	*W*	*Avge*	*5I*	*10M*	*SR*
26	M. G. Johnson (Australia) . . .	73	16,001	8,891	313	28.40	12	3	51.12
27	Zaheer Khan (India)	92	18,785	10,247	311	32.94	11	1	60.40
28	B. Lee (Australia)	76	16,531	9,554	310	30.81	10	–	53.32
29	L. R. Gibbs (West Indies) . . .	79	27,115	8,989	309	29.09	18	2	87.75
30	F. S. Trueman (England). . . .	67	15,178	6,625	307	21.57	17	3	49.43

MOST WICKETS FOR EACH COUNTRY

ENGLAND

J. M. Anderson	**467**	**S. C. J. Broad**	**368**	F. S. Trueman.	307
I. T. Botham.	383	R. G. D. Willis	325	D. L. Underwood	297

AUSTRALIA

S. K. Warne	708	D. K. Lillee	355	B. Lee.	310
G. D. McGrath	563	M. G. Johnson	313	C. J. McDermott.	291

SOUTH AFRICA

S. M. Pollock	421	M. Ntini	390	J. H. Kallis†	291
D. W. Steyn.	**417**	A. A. Donald	330	**M. Morkel**.	**242**

† *J. H. Kallis also took 0-35 and 1-3 for the World XI v Australia (2005-06 Super Series Test).*

WEST INDIES

C. A. Walsh	519	M. D. Marshall.	376	J. Garner.	259
C. E. L. Ambrose	405	L. R. Gibbs.	309	M. A. Holding	249

NEW ZEALAND

R. J. Hadlee	431	C. S. Martin	233	**T. G. Southee**	**201**
D. L. Vettori†	361	C. L. Cairns	218	**T. A. Boult**.	**185**

† *D. L. Vettori also took 1-73 and 0-38 for the World XI v Australia (2005-06 Super Series Test).*

INDIA

A. Kumble	619	Harbhajan Singh.	417	B. S. Bedi	266
Kapil Dev.	434	Zaheer Khan.	311	**R. Ashwin**	**248**

PAKISTAN

Wasim Akram	414	Imran Khan	362	Abdul Qadir	236
Waqar Younis	373	Danish Kaneria.	261	Saqlain Mushtaq.	208

SRI LANKA

M. Muralitharan†	795	W. P. U. J. C. Vaas . . .	355	C. R. D. Fernando	100
H. M. R. K. B. Herath	**357**	S. L. Malinga	101	S. T. Jayasuriya	98

† *M. Muralitharan also took 2-102 and 3-55 for the World XI v Australia (2005-06 Super Series Test).*

ZIMBABWE

p Streak	216
R. W. Price	80
P. A. Strang	70
H. K. Olonga	68
B. C. Strang	56
A. M. Blignaut	53

BANGLADESH

Shakib Al Hasan	**165**
Mohammad Rafique	100
Mashrafe bin Mortaza	78
Shahadat Hossain	72
Enamul Haque jnr	44
Sohag Gazi	38

BEST CAREER AVERAGES

(Qualification: 75 wickets)

Avge		*T*	*W*
10.75	G. A. Lohmann (E)	18	112
16.43	S. F. Barnes (E)	27	189
16.53	C. T. B. Turner (A)	17	101
16.98	R. Peel (E)	20	101
17.75	J. Briggs (E)	33	118
18.41	F. R. Spofforth (A)	18	94
18.56	F. H. Tyson (E)	17	76
18.63	C. Blythe (E)	19	100
20.39	J. H. Wardle (E)	28	102
20.53	A. K. Davidson (A)	44	186
20.94	M. D. Marshall (WI)	81	376
20.97	J. Garner (WI)	58	259
20.99	C. E. L. Ambrose (WI)	98	405

BEST CAREER STRIKE-RATES

(Balls per wicket. Qualification: 75 wickets)

SR		*T*	*W*
34.19	G. A. Lohmann (E)	18	112
38.75	S. E. Bond (NZ)	18	87
41.45	**D. W. Steyn (SA)**	**85**	**417**
41.65	S. F. Barnes (E)	27	189
43.49	Waqar Younis (P)	87	373
44.52	F. R. Spofforth (A)	18	94
45.12	J. V. Saunders (A)	14	79
45.18	J. Briggs (E)	33	118
45.42	F. H. Tyson (E)	17	76
45.46	C. Blythe (E)	19	100
45.74	Shoaib Akhtar (P)	46	178
46.76	M. D. Marshall (WI)	81	376
46.84	**V. D. Philander (SA)**	**40**	**159**
47.02	A. A. Donald (SA)	72	330
48.78	Mohammad Asif (P)	23	106
49.32	C. E. H. Croft (WI)	27	125
49.43	F. S. Trueman (E)	67	307
49.67	**M. A. Starc (A)**	**34**	**143**

BEST CAREER ECONOMY-RATES

(Runs per six balls. Qualification: 75 wickets)

ER		*T*	*W*
1.64	T. L. Goddard (SA)	41	123
1.67	R. G. Nadkarni (I)	41	88
1.88	H. Verity (E)	40	144
1.88	G. A. Lohmann (E)	18	112
1.89	J. H. Wardle (E)	28	102
1.91	R. Illingworth (E)	61	122
1.93	C. T. B. Turner (A)	17	101
1.94	M. W. Tate (E)	39	155
1.94	W. J. O'Reilly (A)	27	144
1.94	H. J. Tayfield (SA)	37	170
1.95	A. L. Valentine (WI)	36	139
1.95	F. J. Titmus (E)	53	153
1.97	S. Ramadhin (WI)	43	158
1.97	R. Peel (E)	20	101
1.97	A. K. Davidson (A)	44	186
1.98	L. R. Gibbs (WI)	79	309

HIGHEST PERCENTAGE OF TEAM'S WICKETS OVER TEST CAREER

(Qualification: 20 Tests)

	Tests	*Wkts*	*Team Wkts*	*% of Team Wkts*
M. Muralitharan (Sri Lanka/World)	133	800	2,070	38.64
S. F. Barnes (England)	27	189	494	38.25
R. J. Hadlee (New Zealand)	86	431	1,255	34.34
C. V. Grimmett (Australia)	37	216	636	33.96
Fazal Mahmood (Pakistan)	34	139	410	33.90
R. Ashwin (India)	**44**	**248**	**747**	**33.19**
Yasir Shah (Pakistan)	**23**	**124**	**381**	**32.54**
W. J. O'Reilly (Australia)	27	144	446	32.28
S. P. Gupte (India)	36	149	470	31.70
Saeed Ajmal (Pakistan)	35	178	575	30.95
Mohammad Rafique (Bangladesh)	33	100	328	30.48
A. V. Bedser (England)	51	236	777	30.37

Excluding the Super Series Test, Muralitharan took 795 out of 2,050 wickets in his 132 Tests for Sri Lanka, a percentage of 38.78.

The percentage shows the proportion of a team's wickets taken by that player in all Tests in which he played, including team wickets in innings in which he did not bowl.

ALL-ROUND RECORDS

HUNDRED AND FIVE WICKETS IN AN INNINGS

England					
A. W. Greig	148	6-164	v West Indies	Bridgetown	1973-74
I. T. Botham	103	5-73	v New Zealand	Christchurch	1977-78
I. T. Botham	108	8-34	v Pakistan	Lord's	1978
I. T. Botham	114	6-58, 7-48	v India	Bombay	1979-80
I. T. Botham	149*	6-95	v Australia	Leeds	1981
I. T. Botham	138	5-59	v New Zealand	Wellington	1983-84
Australia					
C. Kelleway	114	5-33	v South Africa	Manchester	1912
J. M. Gregory	100	7-69	v England	Melbourne	1920-21
K. R. Miller	109	6-107	v West Indies	Kingston	1954-55
R. Benaud	100	5-84	v South Africa	Johannesburg	1957-58
South Africa					
J. H. Sinclair	106	6-26	v England	Cape Town	1898-99
G. A. Faulkner	123	5-120	v England	Johannesburg	1909-10
J. H. Kallis	110	5-90	v West Indies	Cape Town	1998-99
J. H. Kallis	139*	5-21	v Bangladesh	Potchefstroom	2002-03
West Indies					
D. St E. Atkinson	219	5-56	v Australia	Bridgetown	1954-55
O. G. Smith	100	5-90	v India	Delhi	1958-59
G. S. Sobers	104	5-63	v India	Kingston	1961-62
G. S. Sobers	174	5-41	v England	Leeds	1966
R. L. Chase	**137***	**5-121**	**v India**	**Kingston**	**2016**
New Zealand					
B. R. Taylor†	105	5-86	v India	Calcutta	1964-65

India					
V. Mankad	184	5-196	v England	Lord's	1952
P. R. Umrigar	172*	5-107	v West Indies	Port-of-Spain	1961-62
R. Ashwin	103	5-156	v West Indies	Mumbai	2011-12
R. Ashwin	**113**	**7-83**	**v West Indies**	**North Sound**	**2016**
Pakistan					
Mushtaq Mohammad	201	5-49	v New Zealand	Dunedin	1972-73
Mushtaq Mohammad	121	5-28	v West Indies	Port-of-Spain	1976-77
Imran Khan	117	6-98, 5-82	v India	Faisalabad	1982-83
Wasim Akram	123	5-100	v Australia	Adelaide	1989-90
Zimbabwe					
P. A. Strang	106*	5-212	v Pakistan	Sheikhupura	1996-97
Bangladesh					
Shakib Al Hasan	144	6-82	v Pakistan	Mirpur	2011-12
Sohag Gazi	101*	6-77‡	v New Zealand	Chittagong	2013-14
Shakib Al Hasan	137	5-80, 5-44	v Zimbabwe	Khulna	2014-15

† *On debut.* ‡ *Including a hat-trick; Sohag Gazi is the only player to score a hundred and take a hat-trick in the same Test.*

HUNDRED AND FIVE DISMISSALS IN AN INNINGS

D. T. Lindsay	182	6ct	SA v A	Johannesburg	1966-67
I. D. S. Smith	113*	4ct, 1st	NZ v E	Auckland	1983-84
S. A. R. Silva	111	5ct	SL v I	Colombo (PSS)	1985-86
A. C. Gilchrist	133	4ct, 1st	A v E	Sydney	2002-03
M. J. Prior	118	5ct	E v A	Sydney	2010-11
A. B. de Villiers	103*	6ct and 5ct	SA v P	Johannesburg	2012-13
M. J. Prior	110*	5ct	E v NZ	Auckland	2012-13
B-J. Watling	124	5ct	NZ v I	Wellington	2013-14
B-J. Watling	142*	4ct, 1st	NZ v SL	Wellington	2014-15
J. M. Bairstow	**140**	**5ct**	**E v SL**	**Leeds**	**2016**

100 RUNS AND TEN WICKETS IN A TEST

A. K. Davidson	44 80	5-135 6-87	A v WI	Brisbane	1960-61
I. T. Botham	114	6-58 7-48	E v I	Bombay	1979-80
Imran Khan	117	6-98 5-82	P v I	Faisalabad	1982-83
Shakib Al Hasan	137 6	5-80 5-44	B v Z	Khulna	2014-15

Wicketkeeper A. B. de Villiers scored 103 and held 11 catches for South Africa against Pakistan at Johannesburg in 2012-13.*

2,000 RUNS AND 200 WICKETS

	Tests	*Runs*	*Wkts*	*Tests for 1,000/100 Double*
R. Benaud (Australia)	63	2,201	248	32
†I. T. Botham (England)	102	5,200	383	21
S. C. J. Broad (England)	**102**	**2,691**	**368**	**35**
C. L. Cairns (New Zealand)	62	3,320	218	33
A. Flintoff (England/World)	79	3,845	226	43

	Tests	Runs	Wkts	Tests for 1,000/100 Double
R. J. Hadlee (New Zealand)	86	3,124	431	28
Harbhajan Singh (India)	103	2,224	417	62
Imran Khan (Pakistan)	88	3,807	362	30
M. J. Johnson (Australia)	73	2,065	313	37
†J. H. Kallis (South Africa/World)	166	13,289	292	53
Kapil Dev (India)	131	5,248	434	25
A. Kumble (India)	132	2,506	619	56
S. M. Pollock (South Africa)	108	3,781	421	26
†G. S. Sobers (West Indies)	93	8,032	235	48
W. P. U. J. C. Vaas (Sri Lanka)	111	3,089	355	47
D. L. Vettori (New Zealand/World)	113	4,531	362	47
†S. K. Warne (Australia)	145	3,154	708	58
Wasim Akram (Pakistan)	104	2,898	414	45

H. H. Streak scored 1,990 runs and took 216 wickets in 65 Tests for Zimbabwe.

† *J. H. Kallis also took 200 catches, S. K. Warne 125, I. T. Botham 120 and G. S. Sobers 109. These four and C. L. Hooper (5,762 runs, 114 wickets and 115 catches for West Indies) are the only players to have achieved the treble of 1,000 runs, 100 wickets and 100 catches in Test cricket.*

WICKETKEEPING RECORDS

MOST DISMISSALS IN AN INNINGS

7 (all ct)	Wasim Bari	Pakistan v New Zealand at Auckland	1978-79
7 (all ct)	R. W. Taylor	England v India at Bombay	1979-80
7 (all ct)	I. D. S. Smith	New Zealand v Sri Lanka at Hamilton	1990-91
7 (all ct)	R. D. Jacobs	West Indies v Australia at Melbourne	2000-01

The first instance of seven wicketkeeping dismissals in a Test innings was a joint effort for Pakistan v West Indies at Kingston in 1976-77. Majid Khan made four catches, deputising for the injured wicketkeeper Wasim Bari, who made three more catches on his return.

There have been ***30*** *instances of players making six dismissals in a Test innings, the most recent being* ***W. P. Saha (5ct, 1st) for India v West Indies at North Sound in 2016****.*

MOST STUMPINGS IN AN INNINGS

5	K. S. More	India v West Indies at Madras	1987-88

MOST DISMISSALS IN A TEST

11 (all ct)	R. C. Russell	England v South Africa at Johannesburg	1995-96
11 (all ct)	A. B. de Villiers	South Africa v Pakistan at Johannesburg	2012-13
10 (all ct)	R. W. Taylor	England v India at Bombay	1979-80
10 (all ct)	A. C. Gilchrist	Australia v New Zealand at Hamilton	1999-2000

There have been ***26*** *instances of players making nine dismissals in a Test, the most recent being* ***J. M. Bairstow (all ct) for England v Sri Lanka at Leeds in 2016****. S. A. R. Silva made 18 in two successive Tests for Sri Lanka against India in 1985-86.*

The most stumpings in a match is 6 by K. S. More for India v West Indies at Madras in 1987-88.

J. J. Kelly (8ct) for Australia v England in 1901-02 and L. E. G. Ames (6ct, 2st) for England v West Indies in 1933 were the only keepers to make eight dismissals in a Test before World War II.

MOST DISMISSALS IN A SERIES

(Played in 5 Tests unless otherwise stated)

29 (all ct)	B. J. Haddin	Australia v England	2013
28 (all ct)	R. W. Marsh	Australia v England	1982-83
27 (25ct, 2st)	R. C. Russell	England v South Africa	1995-96
27 (25ct, 2st)	I. A. Healy	Australia v England (6 Tests)	1997

S. A. R. Silva made 22 dismissals (21ct, 1st) in three Tests for Sri Lanka v India in 1985-86.

H. Strudwick, with 21 (15ct, 6st) for England v South Africa in 1913-14, was the only wicketkeeper to make as many as 20 dismissals in a series before World War II.

MOST DISMISSALS

			T	*Ct*	*St*
1	M. V. Boucher (South Africa/World)	555	147	532	23
2	A. C. Gilchrist (Australia)	416	96	379	37
3	I. A. Healy (Australia)	395	119	366	29
4	R. W. Marsh (Australia)	355	96	343	12
5	M. S. Dhoni (India)	294	90	256	38
6	B. J. Haddin (Australia)	270	66	262	8
6	P. J. L. Dujon (West Indies)	270	79	265	5
8	A. P. E. Knott (England)	269	95	250	19
9	M. J. Prior (England)	256	79	243	13
10	A. J. Stewart (England)	241	82	227	14
11	Wasim Bari (Pakistan)	228	81	201	27
12	R. D. Jacobs (West Indies)	219	65	207	12
12	T. G. Evans (England)	219	91	173	46
14	**D. Ramdin (West Indies)**	**217**	**74**	**205**	**12**
15	Kamran Akmal (Pakistan)	206	53	184	22
16	A. C. Parore (New Zealand)	201	67	194	7

The record for P. J. L. Dujon excludes two catches taken in two Tests when not keeping wicket; A. J. Stewart's record likewise excludes 36 catches taken in 51 Tests and A. C. Parore's three in 11 Tests.

Excluding the Super Series Test, M. V. Boucher made 553 dismissals (530ct, 23st in 146 Tests) for South Africa, a national record.

W. A. Oldfield made 52 stumpings, a Test record, in 54 Tests for Australia; he also took 78 catches.

The most dismissals by a wicketkeeper playing for the countries not mentioned above are:

		T	*Ct*	*St*
K. C. Sangakkara (Sri Lanka)	151	48	131	20
A. Flower (Zimbabwe)	151	55	142	9
Mushfiqur Rahim (Bangladesh)	**92**	**46**	**81**	**11**

K. C. Sangakkara's record excludes 51 catches taken in 86 matches when not keeping wicket but includes two catches taken as wicketkeeper in a match where he took over when the designated keeper was injured; A. Flower's record excludes nine catches in eight Tests when not keeping wicket, and Mushfiqur Rahim's one catch in five Tests when not keeping wicket.

FIELDING RECORDS

(Excluding wicketkeepers)

MOST CATCHES IN AN INNINGS

5	V. Y. Richardson	Australia v South Africa at Durban	1935-36
5	Yajurvindra Singh	India v England at Bangalore	1976-77
5	M. Azharuddin	India v Pakistan at Karachi	1989-90
5	K. Srikkanth	India v Australia at Perth	1991-92
5	S. P. Fleming	New Zealand v Zimbabwe at Harare	1997-98
5	G. C. Smith	South Africa v Australia at Perth	2012-13

5	D. J. G. Sammy	West Indies v India at Mumbai	2013-14
5	D. M. Bravo	West Indies v Bangladesh at Arnos Vale	2014-15
5	A. M. Rahane	India v Sri Lanka at Galle	2015-16
5	J. Blackwood	West Indies v Sri Lanka at Colombo (PSO)	2015-16

MOST CATCHES IN A TEST

8	A. M. Rahane	India v Sri Lanka at Galle	2015-16
7	G. S. Chappell	Australia v England at Perth	1974-75
7	Yajurvindra Singh	India v England at Bangalore	1976-77
7	H. P. Tillekeratne	Sri Lanka v New Zealand at Colombo (SSC)	1992-93
7	S. P. Fleming	New Zealand v Zimbabwe at Harare	1997-98
7	M. L. Hayden	Australia v Sri Lanka at Galle	2003-04

*There have been **29** instances of players taking six catches in a Test, the most recent being **S. P. D. Smith for Australia v Sri Lanka at Colombo (SSC) in 2016**.*

MOST CATCHES IN A SERIES

(Played in 5 Tests unless otherwise stated)

15	J. M. Gregory	Australia v England	1920-21
14	G. S. Chappell	Australia v England (6 Tests)	1974-75
13	R. B. Simpson	Australia v South Africa	1957-58
13	R. B. Simpson	Australia v West Indies	1960-61
13	B. C. Lara	West Indies v England (6 Tests)	1997-98
13	R. Dravid	India v Australia (4 Tests)	2004-05
13	B. C. Lara	West Indies v India (4 Tests)	2005-06

MOST CATCHES

Ct	*T*		*Ct*	*T*	
210	164†	R. Dravid (India/World)	157	104	M. A. Taylor (Australia)
205	149	D. P. M. D. Jayawardene (SL)	156	156	A. R. Border (Australia)
200	166†	J. H. Kallis (SA/World)	**141**	**140**	**A. N. Cook (England)**
196	168	R. T. Ponting (Australia)	135	134	V. V. S. Laxman (India)
181	128	M. E. Waugh (Australia)	134	115	M. J. Clarke (Australia)
171	111	S. P. Fleming (New Zealand)	**129**	**115**	**Younis Khan (Pakistan)**
169	117†	G. C. Smith (SA/World)	128	103	M. L. Hayden (Australia)
164	131†	B. C. Lara (West Indies/World)	125	145	S. K. Warne (Australia)

er; *Excluding the Super Series Test, Dravid made 209 catches in 163 Tests for India, Kallis 196 in 165 Tests for South Africa, and Lara 164 in 130 Tests for West Indies, all national records. G. C. Smith made 166 catches in 116 Tests for South Africa.*

*The most catches in the field for other countries are Zimbabwe 60 in 60 Tests (A. D. R. Campbell); Bangladesh **30** in 31 Tests (**Mahmudullah**).*

RECORDS

HIGHEST INNINGS TOTALS

952-6 dec	Sri Lanka v India at Colombo (RPS)	1997-98
903-7 dec	England v Australia at The Oval	1938
849	England v West Indies at Kingston	1929-30
790-3 dec	West Indies v Pakistan at Kingston	1957-58
765-6 dec	Pakistan v Sri Lanka at Karachi	2008-09
760-7 dec	Sri Lanka v India at Ahmedabad	2009-10
759-7 dec	**India v England at Chennai**	**2016-17**
758-8 dec	Australia v West Indies at Kingston	1954-55
756-5 dec	Sri Lanka v South Africa at Colombo (SSC)	2006
751-5 dec	West Indies v England at St John's	2003-04

The highest innings totals for the countries not mentioned above are:

690	New Zealand v Pakistan at Sharjah	2014-15
682-6 dec	South Africa v England at Lord's	2003
638	Bangladesh v Sri Lanka at Galle	2012-13
563-9 dec	Zimbabwe v West Indies at Harare	2001

HIGHEST FOURTH-INNINGS TOTALS

To win

418-7	West Indies (needing 418) v Australia at St John's	2002-03
414-4	South Africa (needing 414) v Australia at Perth	2008-09
406-4	India (needing 403) v West Indies at Port-of-Spain	1975-76
404-3	Australia (needing 404) v England at Leeds	1948

To tie

347	India v Australia at Madras	1986-87

To draw

654-5	England (needing 696 to win) v South Africa at Durban	1938-39
450-7	South Africa (needing 458 to win) v India at Johannesburg	2013-14
429-8	India (needing 438 to win) v England at The Oval	1979
423-7	South Africa (needing 451 to win) v England at The Oval	1947

To lose

451	New Zealand (lost by 98 runs) v England at Christchurch	2001-02
450	**Pakistan (lost by 39 runs) v Australia at Brisbane**	**2016-17**
445	India (lost by 47 runs) v Australia at Adelaide	1977-78
440	New Zealand (lost by 38 runs) v England at Nottingham	1973
431	New Zealand (lost by 121 runs) v England at Napier	2007-08

MOST RUNS IN A DAY (BOTH SIDES)

588	England (398-6), India (190-0) at Manchester (2nd day)	1936
522	England (503-2), South Africa (19-0) at Lord's (2nd day)	1924
509	Sri Lanka (509-9) v Bangladesh at Colombo (PSS) (2nd day)	2002
508	England (221-2), South Africa (287-6) at The Oval (3rd day)	1935

MOST RUNS IN A DAY (ONE SIDE)

509	Sri Lanka (509-9) v Bangladesh at Colombo (PSS) (2nd day)	2002
503	England (503-2) v South Africa at Lord's (2nd day)	1924
494	Australia (494-6) v South Africa at Sydney (1st day)	1910-11
482	Australia (482-5) v South Africa at Adelaide (1st day)	2012-13
475	Australia (475-2) v England at The Oval (1st day)	1934

MOST WICKETS IN A DAY

27	England (18-3 to 53 all out and 62) v Australia (60) at Lord's (2nd day)	1888
25	Australia (112 and 48-5) v England (61) at Melbourne (1st day)	1901-02

HIGHEST AGGREGATES IN A TEST

Runs	Wkts			Days played
1,981	35	South Africa v England at Durban	1938-39	10†
1,815	34	West Indies v England at Kingston	1929-30	9‡
1,764	39	Australia v West Indies at Adelaide	1968-69	5
1,753	40	Australia v England at Adelaide	1920-21	6
1,747	25	Australia v India at Sydney	2003-04	5
1,723	31	England v Australia at Leeds	1948	5
1,702	28	Pakistan v India at Faisalabad	2005-06	5

† *No play on one day.* ‡ *No play on two days.*

LOWEST INNINGS TOTALS

26	New Zealand v England at Auckland	1954-55
30	South Africa v England at Port Elizabeth	1895-96
30	South Africa v England at Birmingham	1924
35	South Africa v England at Cape Town	1898-99
36	Australia v England at Birmingham	1902
36	South Africa v Australia at Melbourne	1931-32
42	Australia v England at Sydney	1887-88
42	New Zealand v Australia at Wellington	1945-46
42†	India v England at Lord's	1974
43	South Africa v England at Cape Town	1888-89
44	Australia v England at The Oval	1896
45	England v Australia at Sydney	1886-87
45	South Africa v Australia at Melbourne	1931-32
45	New Zealand v South Africa at Cape Town	2012-13

The lowest innings totals for the countries not mentioned above are:

47	West Indies v England at Kingston	2003-04
49	Pakistan v South Africa at Johannesburg	2012-13
51	Zimbabwe v New Zealand at Napier	2011-12
62	Bangladesh v Sri Lanka at Colombo (PSS)	2007
71	Sri Lanka v Pakistan at Kandy	1994-95

FEWEST RUNS IN A FULL DAY'S PLAY

95	Australia (80), Pakistan (15-2) at Karachi (1st day, 5½ hrs)	1956-57
104	Pakistan (0-0 to 104-5) v Australia at Karachi (4th day, 5½ hrs)	1959-60
106	England (92-2 to 198) v Australia at Brisbane (4th day, 5 hrs). *England were dismissed five minutes before the close of play, leaving no time for Australia to start their second innings.*	1958-59
111	S. Africa (48-2 to 130-6 dec), India (29-1) at Cape Town (5th day, 5½ hrs)	1992-93
112	Australia (138-6 to 187), Pakistan (63-1) at Karachi (4th day, 5½ hrs)	1956-57
115	Australia (116-7 to 165 and 66-5 after following on) v Pakistan at Karachi (4th day, 5½ hrs)	1988-89
117	India (117-5) v Australia at Madras (1st day, 5½ hrs)	1956-57
117	New Zealand (6-0 to 123-4) v Sri Lanka at Colombo (SSC) (5th day, 5¾ hrs)	1983-84

In England

151	England (175-2 to 289), New Zealand (37-7) at Lord's (3rd day, 6 hrs)	1978
158	England (211-2 to 369-9) v South Africa at Manchester (5th day, 6 hrs)	1998
159	Pakistan (208-4 to 350), England (17-1) at Leeds (3rd day, 6 hrs)	1971

LOWEST AGGREGATES IN A COMPLETED TEST

Runs	*Wkts*			*Days played*
234	29	Australia v South Africa at Melbourne	1931-32	3†
291	40	England v Australia at Lord's	1888	2
295	28	New Zealand v Australia at Wellington	1945-46	2
309	29	West Indies v England at Bridgetown	1934-35	3
323	30	England v Australia at Manchester	1888	2

† *No play on one day.*

LARGEST VICTORIES

Largest Innings Victories

Inns & 579 runs	England (903-7 dec) v Australia (201 & 123†) at The Oval	1938
Inns & 360 runs	Australia (652-7 dec) v South Africa (159 & 133) at Johannesburg	2001-02
Inns & 336 runs	West Indies (614-5 dec) v India (124 & 154) at Calcutta	1958-59
Inns & 332 runs	Australia (645) v England (141 & 172) at Brisbane	1946-47
Inns & 324 runs	Pakistan (643) v New Zealand (73 & 246) at Lahore	2002
Inns & 322 runs	West Indies (660-5 dec) v New Zealand (216 & 122) at Wellington	1994-95
Inns & 310 runs	West Indies (536) v Bangladesh (139 & 87) at Dhaka	2002-03
Inns & 301 runs	New Zealand (495-7 dec) v Zimbabwe (51 & 143) at Napier	2011-12

† *Two men absent in both Australian innings.*

Largest Victories by Runs Margin

675 runs	England (521 & 342-8 dec) v Australia (122 & 66†) at Brisbane	1928-29
562 runs	Australia (701 & 327) v England (321 & 145‡) at The Oval	1934
530 runs	Australia (328 & 578) v South Africa (205 & 171§) at Melbourne	1910-11
491 runs	Australia (381 & 361-5 dec) v Pakistan (179 & 72) at Perth	2004-05
465 runs	Sri Lanka (384 and 447-6 dec) v Bangladesh (208 and 158) at Chittagong	2008-09
425 runs	West Indies (211 & 411-5 dec) v England (71 & 126) at Manchester	1976
409 runs	Australia (350 & 460-7 dec) v England (215 & 186) at Lord's	1948
408 runs	West Indies (328 & 448) v Australia (203 & 165) at Adelaide	1979-80
405 runs	Australia (566-8 dec & 254-2 dec) v England (312 & 103) at Lord's	2015

† *One man absent in Australia's first innings; two men absent in their second.*
‡ *Two men absent in England's first innings; one man absent in their second.*
§ *One man absent in South Africa's second innings.*

TIED TESTS

West Indies (453 & 284) v Australia (505 & 232) at Brisbane	1960-61
Australia (574-7 dec & 170-5 dec) v India (397 & 347) at Madras	1986-87

MOST CONSECUTIVE TEST VICTORIES

16	Australia	1999-2000–2000-01
16	Australia	2005-06–2007-08
11	West Indies	1983-84–1984-85
9	Sri Lanka	2001–2001-02
9	South Africa	2001-02–2003
8	Australia	1920-21–1921
8	England	2004–2004-05

MOST CONSECUTIVE TESTS WITHOUT VICTORY

44	New Zealand	1929-30–1955-56
34	Bangladesh	2000-01–2004-05
31	India	1981-82–1984-85
28	South Africa	1935–1949-50
24	India	1932–1951-52
24	Bangladesh	2004-05–2008-09
23	New Zealand	1962-63–1967-68
22	Pakistan	1958-59–1964-65
21	Sri Lanka	1985-86–1992-93
20	West Indies	1968-69–1972-73
20	West Indies	2004-05–2007

WHITEWASHES

Teams winning every game in a series of four Tests or more:

Five-Test Series

Australia beat England	1920-21
Australia beat South Africa	1931-32
England beat India	1959
West Indies beat India	1961-62
West Indies beat England	1984
West Indies beat England	1985-86
South Africa beat West Indies	1998-99
Australia beat West Indies	2000-01
Australia beat England	2006-07
Australia beat England	2013-14

Four-Test Series

Australia beat India	1967-68
South Africa beat Australia	1969-70
England beat West Indies	2004
England beat India	2011
Australia beat India	2011-12
India beat Australia	2012-13

The winning team in each instance was at home, except for West Indies in England, 1984.

PLAYERS

YOUNGEST TEST PLAYERS

Years	*Days*			
15	124	Mushtaq Mohammad	Pakistan v West Indies at Lahore	1958-59
16	189	Aqib Javed	Pakistan v New Zealand at Wellington	1988-89
16	205	S. R. Tendulkar	India v Pakistan at Karachi	1989-90

The above table should be treated with caution. All birthdates for Bangladesh and Pakistan (after Partition) must be regarded as questionable because of deficiencies in record-keeping. Hasan Raza was claimed to be 14 years 227 days old when he played for Pakistan against Zimbabwe at Faisalabad in 1996-97; this age was rejected by the Pakistan Cricket Board, although no alternative has been offered. Suggestions that Enamul Haque jnr was 16 years 230 days old when he played for Bangladesh against England in Dhaka in 2003-04 have been discounted by well-informed local observers, who believe he was 18.

The youngest Test players for countries not mentioned above are:

17	122	J. E. D. Sealy	West Indies v England at Bridgetown	1929-30
17	128	Mohammad Sharif	Bangladesh v Zimbabwe at Bulawayo	2000-01
17	189	C. D. U. S. Weerasinghe	Sri Lanka v India at Colombo (PSS)	1985-86
17	239	I. D. Craig	Australia v South Africa at Melbourne	1952-53
17	352	H. Masakadza	Zimbabwe v West Indies at Harare	2001
18	10	D. L. Vettori	New Zealand v England at Wellington	1996-97
18	149	D. B. Close	England v New Zealand at Manchester	1949
18	340	P. R. Adams	South Africa v England at Port Elizabeth	1995-96

OLDEST PLAYERS ON TEST DEBUT

Years	*Days*			
49	119	J. Southerton	England v Australia at Melbourne	1876-77
47	284	Miran Bux	Pakistan v India at Lahore	1954-55
46	253	D. D. Blackie	Australia v England at Sydney	1928-29
46	237	H. Ironmonger	Australia v England at Brisbane	1928-29
42	242	N. Betancourt	West Indies v England at Port-of-Spain	1929-30
41	337	E. R. Wilson	England v Australia at Sydney	1920-21
41	27	R. J. D. Jamshedji	India v England at Bombay	1933-34
40	345	C. A. Wiles	West Indies v England at Manchester	1933
40	295	O. Henry	South Africa v India at Durban	1992-93

Years	*Days*			
40	216	S. P. Kinneir	England v Australia at Sydney	1911-12
40	110	H. W. Lee	England v South Africa at Johannesburg	1930-31
40	56	G. W. A. Chubb	South Africa v England at Nottingham	1951
40	37	C. Ramaswami	India v England at Manchester	1936

The oldest Test player on debut for New Zealand was H. M. McGirr, 38 years 101 days, v England at Auckland, 1929-30; for Sri Lanka, D. S. de Silva, 39 years 251 days, v England at Colombo (PSS), 1981-82; for Zimbabwe, A. C. Waller, 37 years 84 days, v England at Bulawayo, 1996-97; for Bangladesh, Enamul Haque snr, 35 years 58 days, v Zimbabwe at Harare, 2000-01. A. J. Traicos was 45 years 154 days old when he made his debut for Zimbabwe (v India at Harare, 1992-93) having played three Tests for South Africa in 1969-70.

OLDEST TEST PLAYERS

(Age on final day of their last Test match)

Years	*Days*			
52	165	W. Rhodes	England v West Indies at Kingston	1929-30
50	327	H. Ironmonger	Australia v England at Sydney	1932-33
50	320	W. G. Grace	England v Australia at Nottingham	1899
50	303	G. Gunn	England v West Indies at Kingston	1929-30
49	139	J. Southerton	England v Australia at Melbourne	1876-77
47	302	Miran Bux	Pakistan v India at Peshawar	1954-55
47	249	J. B. Hobbs	England v Australia at The Oval	1930
47	87	F. E. Woolley	England v Australia at The Oval	1934
46	309	D. D. Blackie	Australia v England at Adelaide	1928-29
46	206	A. W. Nourse	South Africa v England at The Oval	1924
46	202	H. Strudwick	England v Australia at The Oval	1926
46	41	E. H. Hendren	England v West Indies at Kingston	1934-35
45	304	A. J. Traicos	Zimbabwe v India at Delhi	1992-93
45	245	G. O. B. Allen	England v West Indies at Kingston	1947-48
45	215	P. Holmes	England v India at Lord's	1932
45	140	D. B. Close	England v West Indies at Manchester	1976

MOST TEST APPEARANCES

200	S. R. Tendulkar (India)	133	M. Muralitharan (Sri Lanka/World)
168	R. T. Ponting (Australia)	133	A. J. Stewart (England)
168	S. R. Waugh (Australia)	132	A. Kumble (India)
166	J. H. Kallis (South Africa/World)	132	C. A. Walsh (West Indies)
164	S. Chanderpaul (West Indies)	131	Kapil Dev (India)
164	R. Dravid (India/World)	131	B. C. Lara (West Indies/World)
156	A. R. Border (Australia)	128	M. E. Waugh (Australia)
149	D. P. M. D. Jayawardene (Sri Lanka)	125	S. M. Gavaskar (India)
147	M. V. Boucher (South Africa/World)	124	Javed Miandad (Pakistan)
145	S. K. Warne (Australia)	124	G. D. McGrath (Australia)
140	**A. N. Cook (England)**	**122**	**J. M. Anderson (England)**
134	V. V. S. Laxman (India)	121	I. V. A. Richards (West Indies)
134	K. C. Sangakkara (Sri Lanka)	120	Inzamam-ul-Haq (Pakistan/World)

Excluding the Super Series Test, J. H. Kallis has made 165 appearances for South Africa, a national record. The most appearances for New Zealand is 112 by D. L. Vettori; for Zimbabwe, 67 by G. W. Flower; and for Bangladesh 61 by Mohammad Ashraful.

MOST CONSECUTIVE TEST APPEARANCES FOR A COUNTRY

153	A. R. Border (Australia)	March 1979 to March 1994
138	**A. N. Cook (England)**	**May 2006 to December 2016**
107	M. E. Waugh (Australia)	June 1993 to October 2002
106	S. M. Gavaskar (India)	January 1975 to February 1987

101†	**B. B. McCullum (New Zealand)**	**March 2004 to February 2016**
98	A. B. de Villiers (South Africa)	December 2004 to January 2015
96†	A. C. Gilchrist (Australia)	November 1999 to January 2008
93	R. Dravid (India)	June 1996 to December 2005
93	D. P. M. D. Jayawardene (Sri Lanka)	November 2002 to January 2013

The most consecutive Test appearances for the countries not mentioned above are:

85	G. S. Sobers (West Indies)	April 1955 to April 1972
56	A. D. R. Campbell (Zimbabwe)	October 1992 to September 2001
53	Javed Miandad (Pakistan)	December 1977 to January 1984
49	**Mushfiqur Rahim (Bangladesh)**	**July 2007 to January 2017**

† *Complete Test career.*

Bold type denotes sequence which was still in progress after January 1, 2017 (or in McCullum's case a career completed during the previous year).

MOST TESTS AS CAPTAIN

	P	*W*	*L*	*D*
G. C. Smith (SA/World)	109	53	29*	27
A. R. Border (A)	93	32	22	38†
S. P. Fleming (NZ)	80	28	27	25
R. T. Ponting (A)	77	48	16	13
C. H. Lloyd (WI)	74	36	12	26
M. S. Dhoni (I)	60	27	18	15
A. N. Cook (E)	**59**	**24**	**22**	**13**
S. R. Waugh (A)	57	41	9	7
A. Ranatunga (SL)	56	12	19	25
M. A. Atherton (E)	54	13	21	20
W. J. Cronje (SA)	53	27	11	15
Misbah-ul-Haq (P)	**53**	**24**	**18**	**11**
M. P. Vaughan (E)	51	26	11	14
I. V. A. Richards (WI)	50	27	8	15
M. A. Taylor (A)	50	26	13	11
A. J. Strauss (E)	50	24	11	15

* *Includes defeat as World XI captain in Super Series Test against Australia.* † *One tie.*

Most Tests as captain of other countries:

	P	*W*	*L*	*D*
Mushfiqur Rahim (B)	**27**	**5**	**13**	**9**
A. D. R. Campbell (Z)	21	2	12	7

A. R. Border captained Australia in 93 consecutive Tests.

W. W. Armstrong (Australia) captained his country in the most Tests without being defeated: ten matches with eight wins and two draws.

Mohammad Ashraful (Bangladesh) captained his country in the most Tests without ever winning: 12 defeats and one draw.

UMPIRES

MOST TESTS

		First Test	*Last Test*
128	S. A. Bucknor (West Indies)	1988-89	2008-09
109	**Aleem Dar (Pakistan)**	**2003-04**	**2016-17**
108	R. E. Koertzen (South Africa)	1992-93	2010
95	D. J. Harper (Australia)	1998-99	2011
92	D. R. Shepherd (England)	1985	2004-05
84	B. F. Bowden (New Zealand)	1999-2000	2014-15
78	D. B. Hair (Australia)	1991-92	2008
74	S. J. A. Taufel (Australia)	2000-01	2012
73	S. Venkataraghavan (India)	1992-93	2003-04
66	H. D. Bird (England)	1973	1996
58	**I. J. Gould (England)**	**2008-09**	**2016-17**
57	S. J. Davis (Australia)	1997-98	2014-15
51	**R. J. Tucker (Australia)**	**2009-10**	**2016-17**

SUMMARY OF TESTS

To January 23, 2017

	Opponents	*Tests*	*Won by* *E*	*A*	*SA*	*WI*	*NZ*	*I*	*P*	*SL*	*Z*	*B*	*Wld*	*Tied*	*Drawn*
England	Australia	**341**	108	140	–	–	–	–	–	–	–	–	–	–	93
	South Africa	**145**	58	–	32	–	–	–	–	–	–	–	–	–	55
	West Indies	**151**	46	–	–	54	–	–	–	–	–	–	–	–	51
	New Zealand	**101**	48	–	–	–	9	–	–	–	–	–	–	–	44
	India	**117**	43	–	–	–	–	25	–	–	–	–	–	–	49
	Pakistan	**81**	24	–	–	–	–	–	20	–	–	–	–	–	37
	Sri Lanka	**31**	12	–	–	–	–	–	–	8	–	–	–	–	11
	Zimbabwe	**6**	3	–	–	–	–	–	–	–	0	–	–	–	3
	Bangladesh	**10**	9	–	–	–	–	–	–	–	–	1	–	–	0
Australia	South Africa	**94**	–	51	23	–	–	–	–	–	–	–	–	–	20
	West Indies	**116**	–	58	–	32	–	–	–	–	–	–	–	1	25
	New Zealand	**57**	–	31	–	–	8	–	–	–	–	–	–	–	18
	India	**90**	–	40	–	–	–	24	–	–	–	–	–	1	25
	Pakistan	**62**	–	31	–	–	–	–	14	–	–	–	–	–	17
	Sri Lanka	**29**	–	17	–	–	–	–	–	4	–	–	–	–	8
	Zimbabwe	**3**	–	3	–	–	–	–	–	–	0	–	–	–	0
	Bangladesh	**4**	–	4	–	–	–	–	–	–	–	0	–	–	0
	ICC World XI	**1**	–	1	–	–	–	–	–	–	–	–	0	–	0
South Africa	West Indies	**28**	–	–	18	3	–	–	–	–	–	–	–	–	7
	New Zealand	**42**	–	–	24	–	4	–	–	–	–	–	–	–	14
	India	**33**	–	–	13	–	–	10	–	–	–	–	–	–	10
	Pakistan	**23**	–	–	12	–	–	–	4	–	–	–	–	–	7
	Sri Lanka	**25**	–	–	14	–	–	–	–	5	–	–	–	–	6
	Zimbabwe	**8**	–	–	7	–	–	–	–	–	0	–	–	–	1
	Bangladesh	**10**	–	–	8	–	–	–	–	–	–	0	–	–	2
West Indies	New Zealand	**45**	–	–	–	13	13	–	–	–	–	–	–	–	19
	India	**94**	–	–	–	30	–	18	–	–	–	–	–	–	46
	Pakistan	**49**	–	–	–	16	–	–	18	–	–	–	–	–	15
	Sri Lanka	**17**	–	–	–	3	–	–	–	8	–	–	–	–	6
	Zimbabwe	**8**	–	–	–	6	–	–	–	–	0	–	–	–	2
	Bangladesh	**12**	–	–	–	8	–	–	–	–	–	2	–	–	2
New Zealand	India	**57**	–	–	–	–	10	21	–	–	–	–	–	–	26
	Pakistan	**55**	–	–	–	–	10	–	24	–	–	–	–	–	21
	Sri Lanka	**32**	–	–	–	–	14	–	–	8	–	–	–	–	10
	Zimbabwe	**17**	–	–	–	–	11	–	–	–	0	–	–	–	6
	Bangladesh	**13**	–	–	–	–	10	–	–	–	–	0	–	–	3
India	Pakistan	**59**	–	–	–	–	–	9	12	–	–	–	–	–	38
	Sri Lanka	**38**	–	–	–	–	–	16	–	7	–	–	–	–	15
	Zimbabwe	**11**	–	–	–	–	–	7	–	–	2	–	–	–	2
	Bangladesh	**8**	–	–	–	–	–	6	–	–	–	0	–	–	2
Pakistan	Sri Lanka	**51**	–	–	–	–	–	–	19	14	–	–	–	–	18
	Zimbabwe	**17**	–	–	–	–	–	–	10	–	3	–	–	–	4
	Bangladesh	**10**	–	–	–	–	–	–	9	–	–	0	–	–	1
Sri Lanka	Zimbabwe	**17**	–	–	–	–	–	–	–	12	0	–	–	–	5
	Bangladesh	**16**	–	–	–	–	–	–	–	14	–	0	–	–	2
Zimbabwe	Bangladesh	**14**	–	–	–	–	–	–	–	–	6	5	–	–	3
		2,248	351	376	151	165	89	136	130	80	11	8	0	2	749

	Tests	*Won*	*Lost*	*Drawn*	*Tied*	*% Won*	*Toss Won*
England	983	351	289	343	–	35.70	475
Australia	797†	376†	213	206	2	47.17	402
South Africa	408	151	135	122	–	37.00	198
West Indies	520	165	181	173	1	31.73	267
New Zealand	419	89	169	161	–	21.24	209
India	507	136	157	213	1	26.82	255
Pakistan	407	130	119	158	–	31.94	195
Sri Lanka	256	80	95	81	–	31.25	140
Zimbabwe	101	11	64	26	–	10.89	58
Bangladesh	97	8	74	15	–	8.24	49
ICC World XI	1	0	1	0	–	0.00	0

† *Includes Super Series Test between Australia and ICC World XI.*

ENGLAND v AUSTRALIA

Season	*Captains* England	Australia	*T*	*E*	*A*	*D*
1876-77	James Lillywhite	D. W. Gregory	2	1	1	0
1878-79	Lord Harris	D. W. Gregory	1	0	1	0
1880	Lord Harris	W. L. Murdoch	1	1	0	0
1881-82	A. Shaw	W. L. Murdoch	4	0	2	2
1882	A. N. Hornby	W. L. Murdoch	1	0	1	0

THE ASHES

Season	*Captains* England	Australia	*T*	*E*	*A*	*D*	*Held by*
1882-83	Hon. Ivo Bligh	W. L. Murdoch	4*	2	2	0	E
1884	Lord Harris[1]	W. L. Murdoch	3	1	0	2	E
1884-85	A. Shrewsbury	T. P. Horan[2]	5	3	2	0	E
1886	A. G. Steel	H. J. H. Scott	3	3	0	0	E
1886-87	A. Shrewsbury	P. S. McDonnell	2	2	0	0	E
1887-88	W. W. Read	P. S. McDonnell	1	1	0	0	E
1888	W. G. Grace[3]	P. S. McDonnell	3	2	1	0	E
1890†	W. G. Grace	W. L. Murdoch	2	2	0	0	E
1891-92	W. G. Grace	J. McC. Blackham	3	1	2	0	A
1893	W. G. Grace[4]	J. McC. Blackham	3	1	0	2	E
1894-95	A. E. Stoddart	G. Giffen[5]	5	3	2	0	E
1896	W. G. Grace	G. H. S. Trott	3	2	1	0	E
1897-98	A. E. Stoddart[6]	G. H. S. Trott	5	1	4	0	A
1899	A. C. MacLaren[7]	J. Darling	5	0	1	4	A
1901-02	A. C. MacLaren	J. Darling[8]	5	1	4	0	A
1902	A. C. MacLaren	J. Darling	5	1	2	2	A
1903-04	P. F. Warner	M. A. Noble	5	3	2	0	E
1905	Hon. F. S. Jackson	J. Darling	5	2	0	3	E
1907-08	A. O. Jones[9]	M. A. Noble	5	1	4	0	A
1909	A. C. MacLaren	M. A. Noble	5	1	2	2	A
1911-12	J. W. H. T. Douglas	C. Hill	5	4	1	0	E
1912	C. B. Fry	S. E. Gregory	3	1	0	2	E
1920-21	J. W. H. T. Douglas	W. W. Armstrong	5	0	5	0	A
1921	Hon. L. H. Tennyson[10]	W. W. Armstrong	5	0	3	2	A
1924-25	A. E. R. Gilligan	H. L. Collins	5	1	4	0	A
1926	A. W. Carr[11]	H. L. Collins[12]	5	1	0	4	E
1928-29	A. P. F. Chapman[13]	J. Ryder	5	4	1	0	E
1930	A. P. F. Chapman[14]	W. M. Woodfull	5	1	2	2	A
1932-33	D. R. Jardine	W. M. Woodfull	5	4	1	0	E
1934	R. E. S. Wyatt[15]	W. M. Woodfull	5	1	2	2	A
1936-37	G. O. B. Allen	D. G. Bradman	5	2	3	0	A
1938†	W. R. Hammond	D. G. Bradman	4	1	1	2	A
1946-47	W. R. Hammond[16]	D. G. Bradman	5	0	3	2	A
1948	N. W. D. Yardley	D. G. Bradman	5	0	4	1	A
1950-51	F. R. Brown	A. L. Hassett	5	1	4	0	A
1953	L. Hutton	A. L. Hassett	5	1	0	4	E
1954-55	L. Hutton	I. W. Johnson[17]	5	3	1	1	E
1956	P. B. H. May	I. W. Johnson	5	2	1	2	E
1958-59	P. B. H. May	R. Benaud	5	0	4	1	A
1961	P. B. H. May[18]	R. Benaud[19]	5	1	2	2	A
1962-63	E. R. Dexter	R. Benaud	5	1	1	3	A
1964	E. R. Dexter	R. B. Simpson	5	0	1	4	A
1965-66	M. J. K. Smith	R. B. Simpson[20]	5	1	1	3	A
1968	M. C. Cowdrey[21]	W. M. Lawry[22]	5	1	1	3	A
1970-71†	R. Illingworth	W. M. Lawry[23]	6	2	0	4	E
1972	R. Illingworth	I. M. Chappell	5	2	2	1	E

	Captains						
Season	*England*	*Australia*	*T*	*E*	*A*	*D*	*Held by*
1974-75	M. H. Denness[24]	I. M. Chappell	6	1	4	1	A
1975	A. W. Greig[25]	I. M. Chappell	4	0	1	3	A
1976-77‡	A. W. Greig	G. S. Chappell	1	0	1	0	—
1977	J. M. Brearley	G. S. Chappell	5	3	0	2	E
1978-79	J. M. Brearley	G. N. Yallop	6	5	1	0	E
1979-80‡	J. M. Brearley	G. S. Chappell	3	0	3	0	—
1980‡	I. T. Botham	G. S. Chappell	1	0	0	1	—
1981	J. M. Brearley[26]	K. J. Hughes	6	3	1	2	E
1982-83	R. G. D. Willis	G. S. Chappell	5	1	2	2	A
1985	D. I. Gower	A. R. Border	6	3	1	2	E
1986-87	M. W. Gatting	A. R. Border	5	2	1	2	E
1987-88‡	M. W. Gatting	A. R. Border	1	0	0	1	—
1989	D. I. Gower	A. R. Border	6	0	4	2	A
1990-91	G. A. Gooch[27]	A. R. Border	5	0	3	2	A
1993	G. A. Gooch[28]	A. R. Border	6	1	4	1	A
1994-95	M. A. Atherton	M. A. Taylor	5	1	3	1	A
1997	M. A. Atherton	M. A. Taylor	6	2	3	1	A
1998-99	A. J. Stewart	M. A. Taylor	5	1	3	1	A
2001	N. Hussain[29]	S. R. Waugh[30]	5	1	4	0	A
2002-03	N. Hussain	S. R. Waugh	5	1	4	0	A
2005	M. P. Vaughan	R. T. Ponting	5	2	1	2	E
2006-07	A. Flintoff	R. T. Ponting	5	0	5	0	A
2009	A. J. Strauss	R. T. Ponting	5	2	1	2	E
2010-11	A. J. Strauss	R. T. Ponting[31]	5	3	1	1	E
2013	A. N. Cook	M. J. Clarke	5	3	0	2	E
2013-14	A. N. Cook	M. J. Clarke	5	0	5	0	A
2015	A. N. Cook	M. J. Clarke	5	3	2	0	E
	In Australia		175	57	91	27	
	In England.		166	51	49	66	
	Totals		341	108	140	93	

* *The Ashes were awarded in 1882-83 after a series of three matches which England won 2–1. A fourth match was played and this was won by Australia.*

† *The matches at Manchester in 1890 and 1938 and at Melbourne (Third Test) in 1970-71 were abandoned without a ball being bowled and are excluded.*

‡ *The Ashes were not at stake in these series.*

The following deputised for the official touring captain or were appointed by the home authority for only a minor proportion of the series:

[1]A. N. Hornby (First). [2]W. L. Murdoch (First), H. H. Massie (Third), J. McC. Blackham (Fourth). [3]A. G. Steel (First). [4]A. E. Stoddart (First). [5]J. McC. Blackham (First). [6]A. C. MacLaren (First, Second and Fifth). [7]W. G. Grace (First). [8]H. Trumble (Fourth and Fifth). [9]F. L. Fane (First, Second and Third). [10]J. W. H. T. Douglas (First and Second). [11]A. P. F. Chapman (Fifth). [12]W. Bardsley (Third and Fourth). [13]J. C. White (Fifth). [14]R. E. S. Wyatt (Fifth). [15]C. F. Walters (First). [16]N. W. D. Yardley (Fifth). [17]A. R. Morris (Second). [18]M. C. Cowdrey (First and Second). [19]R. N. Harvey (Second). [20]B. C. Booth (First and Third). [21]T. W. Graveney (Fourth). [22]B. N. Jarman (Fourth) [23]I. M. Chappell (Seventh). [24]J. H. Edrich (Fourth). [25]M. H. Denness (First). [26]I. T. Botham (First and Second). [27]A. J. Lamb (First). [28]M. A. Atherton (Fifth and Sixth). [29]M. A. Atherton (Second and Third). [30]A. C. Gilchrist (Fourth). [31]M. J. Clarke (Fifth).

HIGHEST INNINGS TOTALS

For England in England: 903-7 dec at The Oval 1938
in Australia: 644 at Sydney 2010-11

For Australia in England: 729-6 dec at Lord's. 1930
in Australia: 659-8 dec at Sydney 1946-47

LOWEST INNINGS TOTALS

For England in England: 52 at The Oval 1948
in Australia: 45 at Sydney 1886-87

For Australia in England: 36 at Birmingham 1902
in Australia: 42 at Sydney 1887-88

DOUBLE-HUNDREDS

For England (13)

364	L. Hutton at The Oval	1938	227	K. P. Pietersen at Adelaide	2010-11
287	R. E. Foster at Sydney	1903-04	216*	E. Paynter at Nottingham	1938
256	K. F. Barrington at Manchester	1964	215	D. I. Gower at Birmingham	1985
251	W. R. Hammond at Sydney	1928-29	207	N. Hussain at Birmingham	1997
240	W. R. Hammond at Lord's	1938	206	P. D. Collingwood at Adelaide	2006-07
235*	A. N. Cook at Brisbane	2010-11	200	W. R. Hammond at Melbourne	1928-29
231*	W. R. Hammond at Sydney	1936-37			

For Australia (24)

334	D. G. Bradman at Leeds	1930	232	S. J. McCabe at Nottingham	1938
311	R. B. Simpson at Manchester	1964	225	R. B. Simpson at Adelaide	1965-66
307	R. M. Cowper at Melbourne	1965-66	219	M. A. Taylor at Nottingham	1989
304	D. G. Bradman at Leeds	1934	215	S. P. D. Smith at Lord's	2015
270	D. G. Bradman at Melbourne	1936-37	212	D. G. Bradman at Adelaide	1936-37
266	W. H. Ponsford at The Oval	1934	211	W. L. Murdoch at The Oval	1884
254	D. G. Bradman at Lord's	1930	207	K. R. Stackpole at Brisbane	1970-71
250	J. L. Langer at Melbourne	2002-03	206*	W. A. Brown at Lord's	1938
244	D. G. Bradman at The Oval	1934	206	A. R. Morris at Adelaide	1950-51
234	S. G. Barnes at Sydney	1946-47	201*	J. Ryder at Adelaide	1924-25
234	D. G. Bradman at Sydney	1946-47	201	S. E. Gregory at Sydney	1894-95
232	D. G. Bradman at The Oval	1930	200*	A. R. Border at Leeds	1993

INDIVIDUAL HUNDREDS

In total, England have scored **239** hundreds against Australia, and Australia have scored **304** against England. The players with at least five hundreds are as follows:

For England

12: J. B. Hobbs.
9: D. I. Gower, W. R. Hammond.
8: H. Sutcliffe.
7: G. Boycott, J. H. Edrich, M. Leyland.
5: K. F. Barrington, D. C. S. Compton, M. C. Cowdrey, L. Hutton, F. S. Jackson, A. C. MacLaren.

For Australia

19: D. G. Bradman.
10: S. R. Waugh.
9: G. S. Chappell.
8: A. R. Border, A. R. Morris, R. T. Ponting.
7: D. C. Boon, M. J. Clarke, W. M. Lawry, M. J. Slater.
6: R. N. Harvey, M. A. Taylor, V. T. Trumper, M. E. Waugh, W. M. Woodfull.
5: M. L. Hayden, J. L. Langer, C. G. Macartney, W. H. Ponsford, S. P. D. Smith.

RECORD PARTNERSHIPS FOR EACH WICKET

For England

323 for 1st	J. B. Hobbs and W. Rhodes at Melbourne	1911-12
382 for 2nd†	L. Hutton and M. Leyland at The Oval	1938
262 for 3rd	W. R. Hammond and D. R. Jardine at Adelaide	1928-29
310 for 4th	P. D. Collingwood and K. P. Pietersen at Adelaide	2006-07
206 for 5th	E. Paynter and D. C. S. Compton at Nottingham	1938
215 for 6th	L. Hutton and J. Hardstaff jnr at The Oval	1938
	G. Boycott and A. P. E. Knott at Nottingham	1977
143 for 7th	F. E. Woolley and J. Vine at Sydney	1911-12
124 for 8th	E. H. Hendren and H. Larwood at Brisbane	1928-29
151 for 9th	W. H. Scotton and W. W. Read at The Oval	1884
130 for 10th	R. E. Foster and W. Rhodes at Sydney	1903-04

For Australia

329 for 1st	G. R. Marsh and M. A. Taylor at Nottingham	1989
451 for 2nd†	W. H. Ponsford and D. G. Bradman at The Oval	1934
276 for 3rd	D. G. Bradman and A. L. Hassett at Brisbane	1946-47
388 for 4th	W. H. Ponsford and D. G. Bradman at Leeds	1934
405 for 5th‡	S. G. Barnes and D. G. Bradman at Sydney	1946-47
346 for 6th†	J. H. Fingleton and D. G. Bradman at Melbourne	1936-37
165 for 7th	C. Hill and H. Trumble at Melbourne	1897-98
243 for 8th†	R. J. Hartigan and C. Hill at Adelaide	1907-08
154 for 9th†	S. E. Gregory and J. McC. Blackham at Sydney	1894-95
163 for 10th†	P. J. Hughes and A. C. Agar at Nottingham	2013

† *Record partnership against all countries.* ‡ *World record.*

MOST RUNS IN A SERIES

England in England	732 (average 81.33)	D. I. Gower	1985
England in Australia	905 (average 113.12)	W. R. Hammond	1928-29
Australia in England	974 (average 139.14)	D. G. Bradman	1930
Australia in Australia	810 (average 90.00)	D. G. Bradman	1936-37

MOST WICKETS IN A MATCH

In total, England bowlers have taken ten or more wickets in a match **40** times against Australia, and Australian bowlers have done it **43** times against England. The players with at least 12 in a match are as follows:

For England

19-90 (9-37, 10-53)	J. C. Laker at Manchester	1956
15-104 (7-61, 8-43)	H. Verity at Lord's	1934
15-124 (7-56, 8-68)	W. Rhodes at Melbourne	1903-04
14-99 (7-55, 7-44)	A. V. Bedser at Nottingham	1953
14-102 (7-28, 7-74)	W. Bates at Melbourne	1882-83
13-163 (6-42, 7-121)	S. F. Barnes at Melbourne	1901-02
13-244 (7-168, 6-76)	T. Richardson at Manchester	1896
13-256 (5-130, 8-126)	J. C. White at Adelaide	1928-29
12-102 (6-50, 6-52)†	F. Martin at The Oval	1890
12-104 (7-36, 5-68)	G. A. Lohmann at The Oval	1886
12-136 (6-49, 6-87)	J. Briggs at Adelaide	1891-92

There are a further 12 instances of 11 wickets in a match, and 17 instances of ten.

For Australia

16-137 (8-84, 8-53)†	R. A. L. Massie at Lord's	1972
14-90 (7-46, 7-44)	F. R. Spofforth at The Oval	1882
13-77 (7-17, 6-60)	M. A. Noble at Melbourne	1901-02
13-110 (6-48, 7-62)	F. R. Spofforth at Melbourne	1878-79
13-148 (6-97, 7-51)	B. A. Reid at Melbourne	1990-91
13-236 (4-115, 9-121)	A. A. Mailey at Melbourne	1920-21
12-87 (5-44, 7-43)	C. T. B. Turner at Sydney	1887-88
12-89 (6-59, 6-30)	H. Trumble at The Oval	1896
12-107 (5-57, 7-50)	S. C. G. MacGill at Sydney	1998-99
12-173 (8-65, 4-108)	H. Trumble at The Oval	1902
12-175 (5-85, 7-90)†	H. V. Hordern at Sydney	1911-12
12-246 (6-122, 6-124)	S. K. Warne at The Oval	2005

There are a further 13 instances of 11 wickets in a match, and 18 instances of ten.

† *On first appearance in England–Australia Tests.*

A. V. Bedser, J. Briggs, J. C. Laker, T. Richardson, R. M. Hogg, A. A. Mailey, H. Trumble and C. T. B. Turner took ten wickets or more in successive Tests.

MOST WICKETS IN A SERIES

England in England	46 (average 9.60)	J. C. Laker	1956
England in Australia	38 (average 23.18)	M. W. Tate	1924-25
Australia in England	42 (average 21.26)	T. M. Alderman (6 Tests)	1981
Australia in Australia	41 (average 12.85)	R. M. Hogg (6 Tests)	1978-79

WICKETKEEPING – MOST DISMISSALS

	M	*Ct*	*St*	*Total*
†R. W. Marsh (Australia)	42	141	7	148
I. A. Healy (Australia)	33	123	12	135
A. P. E. Knott (England)	34	97	8	105
A. C. Gilchrist (Australia)	20	89	7	96
†W. A. Oldfield (Australia)	38	59	31	90
A. A. Lilley (England)	32	65	19	84
B. J. Haddin (Australia)	20	79	1	80
A. J. Stewart (England)	26	76	2	78
A. T. W. Grout (Australia)	22	69	7	76
T. G. Evans (England)	31	64	12	76

† *The number of catches by R. W. Marsh (141) and stumpings by W. A. Oldfield (31) are respective records in England–Australia Tests.*

Stewart held a further six catches in seven matches when not keeping wicket.

SCORERS OF OVER 2,500 RUNS

	T	*I*	*NO*	*R*	*HS*	*100*	*Avge*
D. G. Bradman (Australia)	37	63	7	5,028	334	19	89.78
J. B. Hobbs (England)	41	71	4	3,636	187	12	54.26
A. R. Border (Australia)	47	82	19	3,548	200*	8	56.31
D. I. Gower (England)	42	77	4	3,269	215	9	44.78
S. R. Waugh (Australia)	46	73	18	3,200	177*	10	58.18
G. Boycott (England)	38	71	9	2,945	191	7	47.50
W. R. Hammond (England)	33	58	3	2,852	251	9	51.85
H. Sutcliffe (England)	27	46	5	2,741	194	8	66.85
C. Hill (Australia)	41	76	1	2,660	188	4	35.46
J. H. Edrich (England)	32	57	3	2,644	175	7	48.96
G. A. Gooch (England)	42	79	0	2,632	196	4	33.31
G. S. Chappell (Australia)	35	65	8	2,619	144	9	45.94

BOWLERS WITH 100 WICKETS

	T	*Balls*	*R*	*W*	*5I*	*10M*	*Avge*
S. K. Warne (Australia)	36	10,757	4,535	195	11	4	23.25
D. K. Lillee (Australia)	29	8,516	3,507	167	11	4	21.00
G. D. McGrath (Australia)	30	7,280	3,286	157	10	0	20.92
I. T. Botham (England)	36	8,479	4,093	148	9	2	27.65
H. Trumble (Australia)	31	7,895	2,945	141	9	3	20.88
R. G. D. Willis (England)	35	7,294	3,346	128	7	0	26.14
M. A. Noble (Australia)	39	6,895	2,860	115	9	2	24.86
R. R. Lindwall (Australia)	29	6,728	2,559	114	6	0	22.44
W. Rhodes (England)	41	5,790	2,616	109	6	1	24.00
S. F. Barnes (England)	20	5,749	2,288	106	12	1	21.58
C. V. Grimmett (Australia)	22	9,224	3,439	106	11	2	32.44
D. L. Underwood (England)	29	8,000	2,770	105	4	2	26.38
A. V. Bedser (England)	21	7,065	2,859	104	7	2	27.49
G. Giffen (Australia)	31	6,391	2,791	103	7	1	27.09
W. J. O'Reilly (Australia)	19	7,864	2,587	102	8	3	25.36
C. T. B. Turner (Australia)	17	5,179	1,670	101	11	2	16.53
R. Peel (England)	20	5,216	1,715	101	5	1	16.98
T. M. Alderman (Australia)	17	4,717	2,117	100	11	1	21.17
J. R. Thomson (Australia)	21	4,951	2,418	100	5	0	24.18

RESULTS ON EACH GROUND

In England

	Matches	*England wins*	*Australia wins*	*Drawn*
The Oval	37	16	7	14
Manchester	29	7	7	15†
Lord's	36	7	15	14
Nottingham	22	6	7	9
Leeds	24	7	9	8
Birmingham	14	6	3	5
Sheffield	1	0	1	0
Cardiff	2	1	0	1
Chester-le-Street	1	1	0	0

† *Excludes two matches abandoned without a ball bowled.*

In Australia

	Matches	*England wins*	*Australia wins*	*Drawn*
Melbourne	55	20	28	7†
Sydney	55	22	26	7
Adelaide	31	9	17	5
Brisbane				
Exhibition Ground	1	1	0	0
Woolloongabba	20	4	11	5
Perth	13	1	9	3

† *Excludes one match abandoned without a ball bowled.*

ENGLAND v SOUTH AFRICA

	Captains					
Season	*England*	*South Africa*	*T*	*E*	*SA*	*D*
1888-89	C. A. Smith[1]	O. R. Dunell[2]	2	2	0	0
1891-92	W. W. Read	W. H. Milton	1	1	0	0
1895-96	Lord Hawke[3]	E. A. Halliwell[4]	3	3	0	0

Captains

Season	*England*	*South Africa*	*T*	*E*	*SA*	*D*
1898-99	Lord Hawke	M. Bisset	2	2	0	0
1905-06	P. F. Warner	P. W. Sherwell	5	1	4	0
1907	R. E. Foster	P. W. Sherwell	3	1	0	2
1909-10	H. D. G. Leveson Gower[5]	S. J. Snooke	5	2	3	0
1912	C. B. Fry	F. Mitchell[6]	3	3	0	0
1913-14	J. W. H. T. Douglas	H. W. Taylor	5	4	0	1
1922-23	F. T. Mann	H. W. Taylor	5	2	1	2
1924	A. E. R. Gilligan[7]	H. W. Taylor	5	3	0	2
1927-28	R. T. Stanyforth[8]	H. G. Deane	5	2	2	1
1929	J. C. White[9]	H. G. Deane	5	2	0	3
1930-31	A. P. F. Chapman	H. G. Deane[10]	5	0	1	4
1935	R. E. S. Wyatt	H. F. Wade	5	0	1	4
1938-39	W. R. Hammond	A. Melville	5	1	0	4
1947	N. W. D. Yardley	A. Melville	5	3	0	2
1948-49	F. G. Mann	A. D. Nourse	5	2	0	3
1951	F. R. Brown	A. D. Nourse	5	3	1	1
1955	P. B. H. May	J. E. Cheetham[11]	5	3	2	0
1956-57	P. B. H. May	C. B. van Ryneveld[12]	5	2	2	1
1960	M. C. Cowdrey	D. J. McGlew	5	3	0	2
1964-65	M. J. K. Smith	T. L. Goddard	5	1	0	4
1965	M. J. K. Smith	P. L. van der Merwe	3	0	1	2
1994	M. A. Atherton	K. C. Wessels	3	1	1	1
1995-96	M. A. Atherton	W. J. Cronje	5	0	1	4
1998	A. J. Stewart	W. J. Cronje	5	2	1	2
1999-2000	N. Hussain	W. J. Cronje	5	1	2	2
2003	M. P. Vaughan[13]	G. C. Smith	5	2	2	1

THE BASIL D'OLIVEIRA TROPHY

Captains

Season	*England*	*South Africa*	*T*	*E*	*SA*	*D*	*Held by*
2004-05	M. P. Vaughan	G. C. Smith	5	2	1	2	E
2008	M. P. Vaughan[14]	G. C. Smith	4	1	2	1	SA
2009-10	A. J. Strauss	G. C. Smith	4	1	1	2	SA
2012	A. J. Strauss	G. C. Smith	3	0	2	1	SA
2015-16	**A. N. Cook**	**H. M. Amla[15]**	**4**	**2**	**1**	**1**	**E**
	In South Africa		**81**	**31**	**19**	**31**	
	In England		64	27	13	24	
	Totals		**145**	**58**	**32**	**55**	

The following deputised for the official touring captain or were appointed by the home authority for only a minor proportion of the series:

[1]M. P. Bowden (Second). [2]W. H. Milton (Second). [3]Sir T. C. O'Brien (First). [4]A. R. Richards (Third). [5]F. L. Fane (Fourth and Fifth). [6]L. J. Tancred (Second and Third). [7]J. W. H. T. Douglas (Fourth). [8]G. T. S. Stevens (Fifth). [9]A. W. Carr (Fourth and Fifth). [10]E. P. Nupen (First), H. B. Cameron (Fourth and Fifth). [11]D. J. McGlew (Third and Fourth). [12]D. J. McGlew (Second). [13]N. Hussain (First). [14]K. P. Pietersen (Fourth). [15]A. B. de Villiers (Third and Fourth).

SERIES RECORDS

Highest score	*E*	**258**	**B. A. Stokes at Cape Town**	**2015-16**
	SA	311*	H. M. Amla at The Oval	2012
Best bowling	*E*	9-28	G. A. Lohmann at Johannesburg	1895-96
	SA	9-113	H. J. Tayfield at Johannesburg	1956-57
Highest total	*E*	654-5	at Durban	1938-39
	SA	682-6 dec	at Lord's	2003
Lowest total	*E*	76	at Leeds	1907
	SA	30	at Port Elizabeth	1895-96
	SA	30	at Birmingham	1924

ENGLAND v WEST INDIES

	Captains					
Season	*England*	*West Indies*	*T*	*E*	*WI*	*D*
1928	A. P. F. Chapman	R. K. Nunes	3	3	0	0
1929-30	Hon. F. S. G. Calthorpe	E. L. G. Hoad[1]	4	1	1	2
1933	D. R. Jardine[2]	G. C. Grant	3	2	0	1
1934-35	R. E. S. Wyatt	G. C. Grant	4	1	2	1
1939	W. R. Hammond	R. S. Grant	3	1	0	2
1947-48	G. O. B. Allen[3]	J. D. C. Goddard[4]	4	0	2	2
1950	N. W. D. Yardley[5]	J. D. C. Goddard	4	1	3	0
1953-54	L. Hutton	J. B. Stollmeyer	5	2	2	1
1957	P. B. H. May	J. D. C. Goddard	5	3	0	2
1959-60	P. B. H. May[6]	F. C. M. Alexander	5	1	0	4

THE WISDEN TROPHY

	Captains						
Season	*England*	*West Indies*	*T*	*E*	*WI*	*D*	*Held by*
1963	E. R. Dexter	F. M. M. Worrell	5	1	3	1	WI
1966	M. C. Cowdrey[7]	G. S. Sobers	5	1	3	1	WI
1967-68	M. C. Cowdrey	G. S. Sobers	5	1	0	4	E
1969	R. Illingworth	G. S. Sobers	3	2	0	1	E
1973	R. Illingworth	R. B. Kanhai	3	0	2	1	WI
1973-74	M. H. Denness	R. B. Kanhai	5	1	1	3	WI
1976	A. W. Greig	C. H. Lloyd	5	0	3	2	WI
1980	I. T. Botham	C. H. Lloyd[8]	5	0	1	4	WI
1980-81†	I. T. Botham	C. H. Lloyd	4	0	2	2	WI
1984	D. I. Gower	C. H. Lloyd	5	0	5	0	WI
1985-86	D. I. Gower	I. V. A. Richards	5	0	5	0	WI
1988	J. E. Emburey[9]	I. V. A. Richards	5	0	4	1	WI
1989-90‡	G. A. Gooch[10]	I. V. A. Richards[11]	4	1	2	1	WI
1991	G. A. Gooch	I. V. A. Richards	5	2	2	1	WI
1993-94	M. A. Atherton	R. B. Richardson[12]	5	1	3	1	WI
1995	M. A. Atherton	R. B. Richardson	6	2	2	2	WI
1997-98§	M. A. Atherton	B. C. Lara	6	1	3	2	WI
2000	N. Hussain[13]	J. C. Adams	5	3	1	1	E
2003-04	M. P. Vaughan	B. C. Lara	4	3	0	1	E
2004	M. P. Vaughan	B. C. Lara	4	4	0	0	E
2007	M. P. Vaughan[14]	R. R. Sarwan[15]	4	3	0	1	E
2008-09§	A. J. Strauss	C. H. Gayle	5	0	1	4	WI
2009	A. J. Strauss	C. H. Gayle	2	2	0	0	E
2012	A. J. Strauss	D. J. G. Sammy	3	2	0	1	E
2014-15	A. N. Cook	D. Ramdin	3	1	1	1	E
	In England		83	32	29	22	
	In West Indies		68	14	25	29	
	Totals		151	46	54	51	

† *The Second Test, at Georgetown, was cancelled owing to political pressure and is excluded.*
‡ *The Second Test, at Georgetown, was abandoned without a ball being bowled and is excluded.*
§ *The First Test at Kingston in 1997-98 and the Second Test at North Sound in 2008-09 were called off on their opening days because of unfit pitches and are shown as draws.*

The following deputised for the official touring captain or were appointed by the home authority for only a minor proportion of the series:

[1]N. Betancourt (Second), M. P. Fernandes (Third), R. K. Nunes (Fourth). [2]R. E. S. Wyatt (Third). [3]K. Cranston (First). [4]G. A. Headley (First), G. E. Gomez (Second). [5]F. R. Brown (Fourth). [6]M. C. Cowdrey (Fourth and Fifth). [7]M. J. K. Smith (First), D. B. Close (Fifth). [8]I. V. A. Richards (Fifth). [9]M. W. Gatting (First), C. S. Cowdrey (Fourth), G. A. Gooch (Fifth). [10]A. J. Lamb (Fourth and Fifth). [11]D. L. Haynes (Third). [12]C. A. Walsh (Fifth). [13]A. J. Stewart (Second). [14]A. J. Strauss (First). [15]D. Ganga (Third and Fourth).

SERIES RECORDS

Highest score	*E*	325	A. Sandham at Kingston	1929-30
	WI	400*	B. C. Lara at St John's	2003-04
Best bowling	*E*	8-53	A. R. C. Fraser at Port-of-Spain	1997-98
	WI	8-45	C. E. L. Ambrose at Bridgetown	1989-90
Highest total	*E*	849	at Kingston	1929-30
	WI	751-5 dec	at St John's	2003-04
Lowest total	*E*	46	at Port-of-Spain	1993-94
	WI	47	at Kingston	2003-04

ENGLAND v NEW ZEALAND

	Captains					
Season	*England*	*New Zealand*	*T*	*E*	*NZ*	*D*
1929-30	A. H. H. Gilligan	T. C. Lowry	4	1	0	3
1931	D. R. Jardine	T. C. Lowry	3	1	0	2
1932-33	D. R. Jardine[1]	M. L. Page	2	0	0	2
1937	R. W. V. Robins	M. L. Page	3	1	0	2
1946-47	W. R. Hammond	W. A. Hadlee	1	0	0	1
1949	F. G. Mann[2]	W. A. Hadlee	4	0	0	4
1950-51	F. R. Brown	W. A. Hadlee	2	1	0	1
1954-55	L. Hutton	G. O. Rabone	2	2	0	0
1958	P. B. H. May	J. R. Reid	5	4	0	1
1958-59	P. B. H. May	J. R. Reid	2	1	0	1
1962-63	E. R. Dexter	J. R. Reid	3	3	0	0
1965	M. J. K. Smith	J. R. Reid	3	3	0	0
1965-66	M. J. K. Smith	B. W. Sinclair[3]	3	0	0	3
1969	R. Illingworth	G. T. Dowling	3	2	0	1
1970-71	R. Illingworth	G. T. Dowling	2	1	0	1
1973	R. Illingworth	B. E. Congdon	3	2	0	1
1974-75	M. H. Denness	B. E. Congdon	2	1	0	1
1977-78	G. Boycott	M. G. Burgess	3	1	1	1
1978	J. M. Brearley	M. G. Burgess	3	3	0	0
1983	R. G. D. Willis	G. P. Howarth	4	3	1	0
1983-84	R. G. D. Willis	G. P. Howarth	3	0	1	2
1986	M. W. Gatting	J. V. Coney	3	0	1	2
1987-88	M. W. Gatting	J. J. Crowe[4]	3	0	0	3
1990	G. A. Gooch	J. G. Wright	3	1	0	2
1991-92	G. A. Gooch	M. D. Crowe	3	2	0	1
1994	M. A. Atherton	K. R. Rutherford	3	1	0	2
1996-97	M. A. Atherton	L. K. Germon[5]	3	2	0	1
1999	N. Hussain[6]	S. P. Fleming	4	1	2	1
2001-02	N. Hussain	S. P. Fleming	3	1	1	1
2004	M. P. Vaughan[7]	S. P. Fleming	3	3	0	0
2007-08	M. P. Vaughan	D. L. Vettori	3	2	1	0
2008	M. P. Vaughan	D. L. Vettori	3	2	0	1
2012-13	A. N. Cook	B. B. McCullum	3	0	0	3
2013	A. N. Cook	B. B. McCullum	2	2	0	0
2015	A. N. Cook	B. B. McCullum	2	1	1	0
	In New Zealand		47	18	4	25
	In England		54	30	5	19
	Totals		101	48	9	44

The following deputised for the official touring captain or were appointed by the home authority for only a minor proportion of the series:

[1]R. E. S. Wyatt (Second). [2]F. R. Brown (Third and Fourth). [3]M. E. Chapple (First). [4]J. G. Wright (Third). [5]S. P. Fleming (Third). [6]M. A. Butcher (Third). [7]M. E. Trescothick (First).

SERIES RECORDS

Highest score	*E*	336*	W. R. Hammond at Auckland	1932-33
	NZ	222	N. J. Astle at Christchurch	2001-02
Best bowling	*E*	7-32	D. L. Underwood at Lord's	1969
	NZ	7-74	B. L. Cairns at Leeds	1983
Highest total	*E*	593-6 dec	at Auckland	1974-75
	NZ	551-9 dec	at Lord's	1973
Lowest total	*E*	64	at Wellington	1977-78
	NZ	26	at Auckland	1954-55

ENGLAND v INDIA

Captains

Season	*England*	*India*	*T*	*E*	*I*	*D*
1932	D. R. Jardine	C. K. Nayudu	1	1	0	0
1933-34	D. R. Jardine	C. K. Nayudu	3	2	0	1
1936	G. O. B. Allen	Maharaj of Vizianagram	3	2	0	1
1946	W. R. Hammond	Nawab of Pataudi snr	3	1	0	2
1951-52	N. D. Howard[1]	V. S. Hazare	5	1	1	3
1952	L. Hutton	V. S. Hazare	4	3	0	1
1959	P. B. H. May[2]	D. K. Gaekwad[3]	5	5	0	0
1961-62	E. R. Dexter	N. J. Contractor	5	0	2	3
1963-64	M. J. K. Smith	Nawab of Pataudi jnr	5	0	0	5
1967	D. B. Close	Nawab of Pataudi jnr	3	3	0	0
1971	R. Illingworth	A. L. Wadekar	3	0	1	2
1972-73	A. R. Lewis	A. L. Wadekar	5	1	2	2
1974	M. H. Denness	A. L. Wadekar	3	3	0	0
1976-77	A. W. Greig	B. S. Bedi	5	3	1	1
1979	J. M. Brearley	S. Venkataraghavan	4	1	0	3
1979-80	J. M. Brearley	G. R. Viswanath	1	1	0	0
1981-82	K. W. R. Fletcher	S. M. Gavaskar	6	0	1	5
1982	R. G. D. Willis	S. M. Gavaskar	3	1	0	2
1984-85	D. I. Gower	S. M. Gavaskar	5	2	1	2
1986	M. W. Gatting[4]	Kapil Dev	3	0	2	1
1990	G. A. Gooch	M. Azharuddin	3	1	0	2
1992-93	G. A. Gooch[5]	M. Azharuddin	3	0	3	0
1996	M. A. Atherton	M. Azharuddin	3	1	0	2
2001-02	N. Hussain	S. C. Ganguly	3	0	1	2
2002	N. Hussain	S. C. Ganguly	4	1	1	2
2005-06	A. Flintoff	R. Dravid	3	1	1	1
2007	M. P. Vaughan	R. Dravid	3	0	1	2
2008-09	K. P. Pietersen	M. S. Dhoni	2	0	1	1
2011	A. J. Strauss	M. S. Dhoni	4	4	0	0
2012-13	A. N. Cook	M. S. Dhoni	4	2	1	1
2014	A. N. Cook	M. S. Dhoni	5	3	1	1
2016-17	**A. N. Cook**	**V. Kohli**	**5**	**0**	**4**	**1**
	In England		57	30	6	21
	In India		**60**	**13**	**19**	**28**
	Totals		**117**	**43**	**25**	**49**

* *Since 1951-52, series in India have been for the De Mello Trophy. Since 2007, series in England have been for the Pataudi Trophy.*

The following deputised for the official touring captain or were appointed by the home authority for only a minor proportion of the series:

[1]D. B. Carr (Fifth). [2]M. C. Cowdrey (Fourth and Fifth). [3]Pankaj Roy (Second). [4]D. I. Gower (First). [5]A. J. Stewart (Second).

The 1932 Indian touring team was captained by the Maharaj of Porbandar but he did not play in the Test match.

SERIES RECORDS

Highest score	*E*	333	G. A. Gooch at Lord's	1990
	I	**303***	**K. K. Nair at Chennai**	**2016-17**
Best bowling	*E*	8-31	F. S. Trueman at Manchester	1952
	I	8-55	V. Mankad at Madras	1951-52
Highest total	*E*	710-7 dec	at Birmingham	2011
	I	**759-7 dec**	**at Chennai**	**2016-17**
Lowest total	*E*	101	at The Oval	1971
	I	42	at Lord's	1974

ENGLAND v PAKISTAN

	Captains					
Season	*England*	*Pakistan*	*T*	*E*	*P*	*D*
1954	L. Hutton[1]	A. H. Kardar	4	1	1	2
1961-62	E. R. Dexter	Imtiaz Ahmed	3	1	0	2
1962	E. R. Dexter[2]	Javed Burki	5	4	0	1
1967	D. B. Close	Hanif Mohammad	3	2	0	1
1968-69	M. C. Cowdrey	Saeed Ahmed	3	0	0	3
1971	R. Illingworth	Intikhab Alam	3	1	0	2
1972-73	A. R. Lewis	Majid Khan	3	0	0	3
1974	M. H. Denness	Intikhab Alam	3	0	0	3
1977-78	J. M. Brearley[3]	Wasim Bari	3	0	0	3
1978	J. M. Brearley	Wasim Bari	3	2	0	1
1982	R. G. D. Willis[4]	Imran Khan	3	2	1	0
1983-84	R. G. D. Willis[5]	Zaheer Abbas	3	0	1	2
1987	M. W. Gatting	Imran Khan	5	0	1	4
1987-88	M. W. Gatting	Javed Miandad	3	0	1	2
1992	G. A. Gooch	Javed Miandad	5	1	2	2
1996	M. A. Atherton	Wasim Akram	3	0	2	1
2000-01	N. Hussain	Moin Khan	3	1	0	2
2001	N. Hussain[6]	Waqar Younis	2	1	1	0
2005-06	M. P. Vaughan[7]	Inzamam-ul-Haq	3	0	2	1
2006†	A. J. Strauss	Inzamam-ul-Haq	4	3	0	1
2010	A. J. Strauss	Salman Butt	4	3	1	0
2011-12*U*	A. J. Strauss	Misbah-ul-Haq	3	0	3	0
2015-16*U*	A. N. Cook	Misbah-ul-Haq	3	0	2	1
2016	**A. N. Cook**	**Misbah-ul-Haq**	**4**	**2**	**2**	**0**
	In England		**51**	**22**	**11**	**18**
	In Pakistan		24	2	4	18
	In United Arab Emirates		6	0	5	1
	Totals		**81**	**24**	**20**	**37**

† *In 2008, the ICC changed the result of the forfeited Oval Test of 2006 from an England win to a draw, in contravention of the Laws of Cricket, only to rescind their decision in January 2009.*

U Played in United Arab Emirates.

The following deputised for the official touring captain or were appointed by the home authority for only a minor proportion of the series:

[1]D. S. Sheppard (Second and Third). [2]M. C. Cowdrey (Third). [3]G. Boycott (Third). [4]D. I. Gower (Second). [5]D. I. Gower (Second and Third). [6]A. J. Stewart (Second). [7]M. E. Trescothick (First).

SERIES RECORDS

Highest score	*E*	278	D. C. S. Compton at Nottingham	1954
	P	274	Zaheer Abbas at Birmingham	1971
Best bowling	*E*	8-34	I. T. Botham at Lord's	1978
	P	9-56	Abdul Qadir at Lahore	1987-88
Highest total	*E*	598-9 dec	at Abu Dhabi	2015-16
	P	708	at The Oval	1987
Lowest total	*E*	72	at Abu Dhabi	2011-12
	P	72	at Birmingham	2010

ENGLAND v SRI LANKA

	Captains					
Season	*England*	*Sri Lanka*	*T*	*E*	*SL*	*D*
1981-82	K. W. R. Fletcher	B. Warnapura	1	1	0	0
1984	D. I. Gower	L. R. D. Mendis	1	0	0	1
1988	G. A. Gooch	R. S. Madugalle	1	1	0	0
1991	G. A. Gooch	P. A. de Silva	1	1	0	0
1992-93	A. J. Stewart	A. Ranatunga	1	0	1	0
1998	A. J. Stewart	A. Ranatunga	1	0	1	0
2000-01	N. Hussain	S. T. Jayasuriya	3	2	1	0
2002	N. Hussain	S. T. Jayasuriya	3	2	0	1
2003-04	M. P. Vaughan	H. P. Tillekeratne	3	0	1	2
2006	A. Flintoff	D. P. M. D. Jayawardene	3	1	1	1
2007-08	M. P. Vaughan	D. P. M. D. Jayawardene	3	0	1	2
2011	A. J. Strauss	T. M. Dilshan[1]	3	1	0	2
2011-12	A. J. Strauss	D. P. M. D. Jayawardene	2	1	1	0
2014	A. N. Cook	A. D. Mathews	2	0	1	1
2016	**A. N. Cook**	**A. D. Mathews**	**3**	**2**	**0**	**1**
	In England		**18**	**8**	**3**	**7**
	In Sri Lanka		13	4	5	4
	Totals		**31**	**12**	**8**	**11**

The following deputised for the official touring captain for only a minor proportion of the series:
[1]K. C. Sangakkara (Third).

SERIES RECORDS

Highest score	*E*	203	I. J. L. Trott at Cardiff	2011
	SL	213*	D. P. M. D. Jayawardene at Galle	2007-08
Best bowling	*E*	7-70	P. A. J. DeFreitas at Lord's	1991
	SL	9-65	M. Muralitharan at The Oval	1998
Highest total	*E*	575-9 dec	at Lord's	2014
	SL	628-8 dec	at Colombo (SSC)	2003-04
Lowest total	*E*	81	at Galle	2007-08
	SL	81	at Colombo (SSC)	2000-01

ENGLAND v ZIMBABWE

	Captains					
Season	*England*	*Zimbabwe*	*T*	*E*	*Z*	*D*
1996-97	M. A. Atherton	A. D. R. Campbell	2	0	0	2
2000	N. Hussain	A. Flower	2	1	0	1
2003	N. Hussain	H. H. Streak	2	2	0	0
	In England		4	3	0	1
	In Zimbabwe		2	0	0	2
	Totals		6	3	0	3

SERIES RECORDS

Highest score	*E*	137	M. A. Butcher at Lord's	2003
	Z	148*	M. W. Goodwin at Nottingham	2000
Best bowling	*E*	6-33	R. L. Johnson at Chester-le-Street	2003
	Z	6-87	H. H. Streak at Lord's	2000
Highest total	*E*	472	at Lord's	2003
	Z	376	at Bulawayo	1996-97
Lowest total	*E*	147	at Nottingham	2000
	Z	83	at Lord's	2000

ENGLAND v BANGLADESH

	Captains					
Season	*England*	*Bangladesh*	*T*	*E*	*B*	*D*
2003-04	M. P. Vaughan	Khaled Mahmud	2	2	0	0
2005	M. P. Vaughan	Habibul Bashar	2	2	0	0
2009-10	A. N. Cook	Shakib Al Hasan	2	2	0	0
2010	A. J. Strauss	Shakib Al Hasan	2	2	0	0
2016-17	**A. N. Cook**	**Mushfiqur Rahim**	**2**	**1**	**1**	**0**
	In England		4	4	0	0
	In Bangladesh		**6**	**5**	**1**	**0**
	Totals		**10**	**9**	**1**	**0**

SERIES RECORDS

Highest score	*E*	226	I. J. L. Trott at Lord's	2010
	B	108	Tamim Iqbal at Manchester	2010
Best bowling	*E*	5-35	S. J. Harmison at Dhaka	2003-04
	B	**6-77**	**Mehedi Hasan at Mirpur**	**2016-17**
Highest total	*E*	599-6 dec	at Chittagong	2009-10
	B	419	at Mirpur	2009-10
Lowest total	*E*	**164**	**at Mirpur**	**2016-17**
	B	104	at Chester-le-Street	2005

AUSTRALIA v SOUTH AFRICA

	Captains					
Season	*Australia*	*South Africa*	*T*	*A*	*SA*	*D*
1902-03*S*	J. Darling	H. M. Taberer[1]	3	2	0	1
1910-11*A*	C. Hill	P. W. Sherwell	5	4	1	0
1912*E*	S. E. Gregory	F. Mitchell[2]	3	2	0	1
1921-22*S*	H. L. Collins	H. W. Taylor	3	1	0	2
1931-32*A*	W. M. Woodfull	H. B. Cameron	5	5	0	0
1935-36*S*	V. Y. Richardson	H. F. Wade	5	4	0	1
1949-50*S*	A. L. Hassett	A. D. Nourse	5	4	0	1
1952-53*A*	A. L. Hassett	J. E. Cheetham	5	2	2	1
1957-58*S*	I. D. Craig	C. B. van Ryneveld[3]	5	3	0	2
1963-64*A*	R. B. Simpson[4]	T. L. Goddard	5	1	1	3
1966-67*S*	R. B. Simpson	P. L. van der Merwe	5	1	3	1
1969-70*S*	W. M. Lawry	A. Bacher	4	0	4	0
1993-94*A*	A. R. Border	K. C. Wessels[5]	3	1	1	1
1993-94*S*	A. R. Border	K. C. Wessels	3	1	1	1
1996-97*S*	M. A. Taylor	W. J. Cronje	3	2	1	0
1997-98*A*	M. A. Taylor	W. J. Cronje	3	1	0	2
2001-02*A*	S. R. Waugh	S. M. Pollock	3	3	0	0
2001-02*S*	S. R. Waugh	M. V. Boucher	3	2	1	0
2005-06*A*	R. T. Ponting	G. C. Smith	3	2	0	1
2005-06*S*	R. T. Ponting	G. C. Smith[6]	3	3	0	0
2008-09*A*	R. T. Ponting	G. C. Smith	3	1	2	0
2008-09*S*	R. T. Ponting	G. C. Smith[7]	3	2	1	0
2011-12*S*	M. J. Clarke	G. C. Smith	2	1	1	0
2012-13*A*	M. J. Clarke	G. C. Smith	3	0	1	2
2013-14*S*	M. J. Clarke	G. C. Smith	3	2	1	0
2016-17*A*	**S. P. D. Smith**	**F. du Plessis**	**3**	**1**	**2**	**0**
	In South Africa		50	28	13	9
	In Australia		**41**	**21**	**10**	**10**
	In England		3	2	0	1
	Totals		**94**	**51**	**23**	**20**

S *Played in South Africa.* *A* *Played in Australia.* *E* *Played in England.*

The following deputised for the official touring captain or were appointed by the home authority for only a minor proportion of the series:

[1]J. H. Anderson (Second), E. A. Halliwell (Third). [2]L. J. Tancred (Third). [3]D. J. McGlew (First). [4]R. Benaud (First). [5]W. J. Cronje (Third). [6]J. H. Kallis (Third). [7]J. H. Kallis (Third).

SERIES RECORDS

Highest score	*A*	299*	D. G. Bradman at Adelaide	1931-32
	SA	274	R. G. Pollock at Durban	1969-70
Best bowling	*A*	8-61	M. G. Johnson at Perth	2008-09
	SA	7-23	H. J. Tayfield at Durban	1949-50
Highest total	*A*	652-7 dec	at Johannesburg	2001-02
	SA	651	at Cape Town	2008-09
Lowest total	*A*	47	at Cape Town	2011-12
	SA	36	at Melbourne	1931-32

AUSTRALIA v WEST INDIES

	Captains						
Season	*Australia*	*West Indies*	*T*	*A*	*WI*	*T*	*D*
1930-31*A*	W. M. Woodfull	G. C. Grant	5	4	1	0	0
1951-52*A*	A. L. Hassett[1]	J. D. C. Goddard[2]	5	4	1	0	0
1954-55*W*	I. W. Johnson	D. St E. Atkinson[3]	5	3	0	0	2

THE FRANK WORRELL TROPHY

	Captains							
Season	*Australia*	*West Indies*	*T*	*A*	*WI*	*T*	*D*	*Held by*
1960-61*A*	R. Benaud	F. M. M. Worrell	5	2	1	1	1	A
1964-65*W*	R. B. Simpson	G. S. Sobers	5	1	2	0	2	WI
1968-69*A*	W. M. Lawry	G. S. Sobers	5	3	1	0	1	A
1972-73*W*	I. M. Chappell	R. B. Kanhai	5	2	0	0	3	A
1975-76*A*	G. S. Chappell	C. H. Lloyd	6	5	1	0	0	A
1977-78*W*	R. B. Simpson	A. I. Kallicharran[4]	5	1	3	0	1	WI
1979-80*A*	G. S. Chappell	C. H. Lloyd[5]	3	0	2	0	1	WI
1981-82*A*	G. S. Chappell	C. H. Lloyd	3	1	1	0	1	WI
1983-84*W*	K. J. Hughes	C. H. Lloyd[6]	5	0	3	0	2	WI
1984-85*A*	A. R. Border[7]	C. H. Lloyd	5	1	3	0	1	WI
1988-89*A*	A. R. Border	I. V. A. Richards	5	1	3	0	1	WI
1990-91*W*	A. R. Border	I. V. A. Richards	5	1	2	0	2	WI
1992-93*A*	A. R. Border	R. B. Richardson	5	1	2	0	2	WI
1994-95*W*	M. A. Taylor	R. B. Richardson	4	2	1	0	1	A
1996-97*A*	M. A. Taylor	C. A. Walsh	5	3	2	0	0	A
1998-99*W*	S. R. Waugh	B. C. Lara	4	2	2	0	0	A
2000-01*A*	S. R. Waugh[8]	J. C. Adams	5	5	0	0	0	A
2002-03*W*	S. R. Waugh	B. C. Lara	4	3	1	0	0	A
2005-06*A*	R. T. Ponting	S. Chanderpaul	3	3	0	0	0	A
2007-08*W*	R. T. Ponting	R. R. Sarwan[9]	3	2	0	0	1	A
2009-10*A*	R. T. Ponting	C. H. Gayle	3	2	0	0	1	A
2011-12*W*	M. J. Clarke	D. J. G. Sammy	3	2	0	0	1	A
2015*W*	M. J. Clarke	D. Ramdin	2	2	0	0	0	A
2015-16*A*	**S. P. D. Smith**	**J. O. Holder**	**3**	**2**	**0**	**0**	**1**	**A**
	In Australia		**66**	**37**	**18**	**1**	**10**	
	In West Indies		50	21	14	0	15	
	Totals		**116**	**58**	**32**	**1**	**25**	

A Played in Australia. *W Played in West Indies.*

The following deputised for the official touring captain or were appointed by the home authority for only a minor proportion of the series:

[1]A. R. Morris (Third). [2]J. B. Stollmeyer (Fifth). [3]J. B. Stollmeyer (Second and Third). [4]C. H. Lloyd (First and Second). [5]D. L. Murray (First). [6]I. V. A. Richards (Second). [7]K. J. Hughes (First and Second). [8]A. C. Gilchrist (Third). [9]C. H. Gayle (Third).

SERIES RECORDS

Highest score	*A*	**269***	**A. C. Voges at Hobart**	**2015-16**
	WI	277	B. C. Lara at Sydney	1992-93
Best bowling	*A*	8-71	G. D. McKenzie at Melbourne	1968-69
	WI	7-25	C. E. L. Ambrose at Perth	1992-93
Highest total	*A*	758-8 dec	at Kingston	1954-55
	WI	616	at Adelaide	1968-69
Lowest total	*A*	76	at Perth	1984-85
	WI	51	at Port-of-Spain	1998-99

AUSTRALIA v NEW ZEALAND

	Captains					
Season	*Australia*	*New Zealand*	*T*	*A*	*NZ*	*D*
1945-46*N*	W. A. Brown	W. A. Hadlee	1	1	0	0
1973-74*A*	I. M. Chappell	B. E. Congdon	3	2	0	1
1973-74*N*	I. M. Chappell	B. E. Congdon	3	1	1	1
1976-77*N*	G. S. Chappell	G. M. Turner	2	1	0	1
1980-81*A*	G. S. Chappell	G. P. Howarth[1]	3	2	0	1
1981-82*N*	G. S. Chappell	G. P. Howarth	3	1	1	1

TRANS-TASMAN TROPHY

	Captains						
Season	*Australia*	*New Zealand*	*T*	*A*	*NZ*	*D*	*Held by*
1985-86*A*	A. R. Border	J. V. Coney	3	1	2	0	NZ
1985-86*N*	A. R. Border	J. V. Coney	3	0	1	2	NZ
1987-88*A*	A. R. Border	J. J. Crowe	3	1	0	2	A
1989-90*A*	A. R. Border	J. G. Wright	1	0	0	1	A
1989-90*N*	A. R. Border	J. G. Wright	1	0	1	0	NZ
1992-93*N*	A. R. Border	M. D. Crowe	3	1	1	1	NZ
1993-94*A*	A. R. Border	M. D. Crowe[2]	3	2	0	1	A
1997-98*A*	M. A. Taylor	S. P. Fleming	3	2	0	1	A
1999-2000*N*	S. R. Waugh	S. P. Fleming	3	3	0	0	A
2001-02*A*	S. R. Waugh	S. P. Fleming	3	0	0	3	A
2004-05*A*	R. T. Ponting	S. P. Fleming	2	2	0	0	A
2004-05*N*	R. T. Ponting	S. P. Fleming	3	2	0	1	A
2008-09*A*	R. T. Ponting	D. L. Vettori	2	2	0	0	A
2009-10*N*	R. T. Ponting	D. L. Vettori	2	2	0	0	A
2011-12*A*	M. J. Clarke	L. R. P. L. Taylor	2	1	1	0	A
2015-16*A*	S. P. D. Smith	B. B. McCullum	3	2	0	1	A
2015-16*N*	**S. P. D. Smith**	**B. B. McCullum**	**2**	**2**	**0**	**0**	**A**
	In Australia		31	17	3	11	
	In New Zealand		**26**	**14**	**5**	**7**	
	Totals		**57**	**31**	**8**	**18**	

A Played in Australia. N Played in New Zealand.

The following deputised for the official touring captain: [1]M. G. Burgess (Second). [2]K. R. Rutherford (Second and Third).

SERIES RECORDS

Highest score	*A*	253	D. A. Warner at Perth	2015-16
	NZ	290	L. R. P. L. Taylor at Perth	2015-16
Best bowling	*A*	6-31	S. K. Warne at Hobart	1993-94
	NZ	9-52	R. J. Hadlee at Brisbane	1985-86
Highest total	*A*	607-6 dec	at Brisbane	1993-94
	NZ	624	at Perth	2015-16
Lowest total	*A*	103	at Auckland	1985-86
	NZ	42	at Wellington	1945-46

AUSTRALIA v INDIA

	Captains						
Season	*Australia*	*India*	*T*	*A*	*I*	*T*	*D*
1947-48*A*	D. G. Bradman	L. Amarnath	5	4	0	0	1
1956-57*I*	I. W. Johnson[1]	P. R. Umrigar	3	2	0	0	1
1959-60*I*	R. Benaud	G. S. Ramchand	5	2	1	0	2
1964-65*I*	R. B. Simpson	Nawab of Pataudi jnr	3	1	1	0	1
1967-68*A*	R. B. Simpson[2]	Nawab of Pataudi jnr[3]	4	4	0	0	0
1969-70*I*	W. M. Lawry	Nawab of Pataudi jnr	5	3	1	0	1
1977-78*A*	R. B. Simpson	B. S. Bedi	5	3	2	0	0
1979-80*I*	K. J. Hughes	S. M. Gavaskar	6	0	2	0	4
1980-81*A*	G. S. Chappell	S. M. Gavaskar	3	1	1	0	1
1985-86*A*	A. R. Border	Kapil Dev	3	0	0	0	3
1986-87*I*	A. R. Border	Kapil Dev	3	0	0	1	2
1991-92*A*	A. R. Border	M. Azharuddin	5	4	0	0	1

THE BORDER–GAVASKAR TROPHY

	Captains							
Season	*Australia*	*India*	*T*	*A*	*I*	*T*	*D*	*Held by*
1996-97*I*	M. A. Taylor	S. R. Tendulkar	1	0	1	0	0	I
1997-98*I*	M. A. Taylor	M. Azharuddin	3	1	2	0	0	I
1999-2000*A*	S. R. Waugh	S. R. Tendulkar	3	3	0	0	0	A
2000-01*I*	S. R. Waugh	S. C. Ganguly	3	1	2	0	0	I
2003-04*A*	S. R. Waugh	S. C. Ganguly	4	1	1	0	2	I
2004-05*I*	R. T. Ponting[4]	S. C. Ganguly[5]	4	2	1	0	1	A
2007-08*A*	R. T. Ponting	A. Kumble	4	2	1	0	1	A
2008-09*I*	R. T. Ponting	A. Kumble[6]	4	0	2	0	2	I
2010-11*I*	R. T. Ponting	M. S. Dhoni	2	0	2	0	0	I
2011-12*A*	M. J. Clarke	M. S. Dhoni[7]	4	4	0	0	0	A
2012-13*I*	M. J. Clarke[8]	M. S. Dhoni	4	0	4	0	0	I
2014-15*A*	M. J. Clarke[9]	M. S. Dhoni[10]	4	2	0	0	2	A
	In Australia		44	28	5	0	11	
	In India		46	12	19	1	14	
	Totals		90	40	24	1	25	

A Played in Australia. *I Played in India.*

The following deputised for the official touring captain or were appointed by the home authority for only a minor proportion of the series:

[1]R. R. Lindwall (Second). [2]W. M. Lawry (Third and Fourth). [3]C. G. Borde (First). [4]A. C. Gilchrist (First, Second and Third). [5]R. Dravid (Third and Fourth). [6]M. S. Dhoni (Second and Fourth). [7]V. Sehwag (Fourth). [8]S. R. Watson (Fourth). [9]S. P. D. Smith (Second, Third and Fourth). [10]V. Kohli (First and Fourth).

SERIES RECORDS

Highest score	*A*	329*	M. J. Clarke at Sydney	2011-12
	I	281	V. V. S. Laxman at Kolkata	2000-01
Best bowling	*A*	8-215	J. J. Krejza at Nagpur	2008-09
	I	9-69	J. M. Patel at Kanpur	1959-60
Highest total	*A*	674	at Adelaide	1947-48
	I	705-7 dec	at Sydney	2003-04
Lowest total	*A*	83	at Melbourne	1980-81
	I	58	at Brisbane	1947-48

AUSTRALIA v PAKISTAN

	Captains					
Season	*Australia*	*Pakistan*	*T*	*A*	*P*	*D*
1956-57*P*	I. W. Johnson	A. H. Kardar	1	0	1	0
1959-60*P*	R. Benaud	Fazal Mahmood[1]	3	2	0	1
1964-65*P*	R. B. Simpson	Hanif Mohammad	1	0	0	1
1964-65*A*	R. B. Simpson	Hanif Mohammad	1	0	0	1
1972-73*A*	I. M. Chappell	Intikhab Alam	3	3	0	0
1976-77*A*	G. S. Chappell	Mushtaq Mohammad	3	1	1	1
1978-79*A*	G. N. Yallop[2]	Mushtaq Mohammad	2	1	1	0
1979-80*P*	G. S. Chappell	Javed Miandad	3	0	1	2
1981-82*A*	G. S. Chappell	Javed Miandad	3	2	1	0
1982-83*P*	K. J. Hughes	Imran Khan	3	0	3	0
1983-84*A*	K. J. Hughes	Imran Khan[3]	5	2	0	3
1988-89*P*	A. R. Border	Javed Miandad	3	0	1	2
1989-90*A*	A. R. Border	Imran Khan	3	1	0	2
1994-95*P*	M. A. Taylor	Salim Malik	3	0	1	2
1995-96*A*	M. A. Taylor	Wasim Akram	3	2	1	0
1998-99*P*	M. A. Taylor	Aamir Sohail	3	1	0	2
1999-2000*A*	S. R. Waugh	Wasim Akram	3	3	0	0
2002-03*S/U*	S. R. Waugh	Waqar Younis	3	3	0	0
2004-05*A*	R. T. Ponting	Inzamam-ul-Haq[4]	3	3	0	0
2009-10*A*	R. T. Ponting	Mohammad Yousuf	3	3	0	0
2010*E*	R. T. Ponting	Shahid Afridi[5]	2	1	1	0
2014-15*U*	M. J. Clarke	Misbah-ul-Haq	2	0	2	0
2016-17*A*	**S. P. D. Smith**	**Misbah-ul-Haq**	**3**	**3**	**0**	**0**
	In Pakistan		20	3	7	10
	In Australia		**35**	**24**	**4**	**7**
	In Sri Lanka		1	1	0	0
	In United Arab Emirates		4	2	2	0
	In England		2	1	1	0
	Totals		**62**	**31**	**14**	**17**

P *Played in Pakistan.* *A* *Played in Australia.*
S/U *First Test played in Sri Lanka, Second and Third Tests in United Arab Emirates.*
E *Played in England.*

The following deputised for the official touring captain or were appointed by the home authority for only a minor proportion of the series:

[1]Imtiaz Ahmed (Second). [2]K. J. Hughes (Second). [3]Zaheer Abbas (First, Second and Third). [4]Yousuf Youhana *later known as Mohammad Yousuf* (Second and Third). [5]Salman Butt (Second).

An expanded and regularly updated online version of the Records can be found at www.wisdenrecords.com

SERIES RECORDS

Highest score	*A*	334*	M. A. Taylor at Peshawar	1998-99
	P	237	Salim Malik at Rawalpindi	1994-95
Best bowling	*A*	8-24	G. D. McGrath at Perth	2004-05
	P	9-86	Sarfraz Nawaz at Melbourne	1978-79
Highest total	*A*	**624-8 dec**	**at Melbourne**	**2016-17**
	P	624	at Adelaide	1983-84
Lowest total	*A*	80	at Karachi	1956-57
	P	53	at Sharjah	2002-03

AUSTRALIA v SRI LANKA

Captains

Season	*Australia*	*Sri Lanka*	*T*	*A*	*SL*	*D*
1982-83*S*	G. S. Chappell	L. R. D. Mendis	1	1	0	0
1987-88*A*	A. R. Border	R. S. Madugalle	1	1	0	0
1989-90*A*	A. R. Border	A. Ranatunga	2	1	0	1
1992-93*S*	A. R. Border	A. Ranatunga	3	1	0	2
1995-96*A*	M. A. Taylor	A. Ranatunga[1]	3	3	0	0
1999-2000*S*	S. R. Waugh	S. T. Jayasuriya	3	0	1	2
2003-04*S*	R. T. Ponting	H. P. Tillekeratne	3	3	0	0
2004*A*	R. T. Ponting[2]	M. S. Atapattu	2	1	0	1

THE WARNE–MURALITHARAN TROPHY

Captains

Season	*Australia*	*Sri Lanka*	*T*	*A*	*SL*	*D*	*Held by*
2007-08*A*	R. T. Ponting	D. P. M. D. Jayawardene	2	2	0	0	A
2011-12*S*	M. J. Clarke	T. M. Dilshan	3	1	0	2	A
2012-13*A*	M. J. Clarke	D. P. M. D. Jayawardene	3	3	0	0	A
2016*S*	**S. P. D. Smith**	**A. D. Mathews**	**3**	**0**	**3**	**0**	**SL**
	In Australia		13	11	0	2	
	In Sri Lanka		**16**	**6**	**4**	**6**	
	Totals		**29**	**17**	**4**	**8**	

A Played in Australia. S Played in Sri Lanka.

The following deputised for the official touring captain or was appointed by the home authority for only a minor proportion of the series:

[1]P. A. de Silva (Third). [2]A. C. Gilchrist (First).

SERIES RECORDS

Highest score	*A*	219	M. J. Slater at Perth	1995-96
	SL	192	K. C. Sangakkara at Hobart	2007-08
Best bowling	*A*	7-39	M. S. Kasprowicz at Darwin	2004
	SL	**7-64**	**H. M. R. K. B. Herath at Colombo (SSC)**	**2016**
Highest total	*A*	617-5 dec	at Perth	1995-96
	SL	547-8 dec	at Colombo (SSC)	1992-93
Lowest total	*A*	**106**	**at Galle**	**2016**
	SL	97	at Darwin	2004

AUSTRALIA v ZIMBABWE

Season	*Captains* Australia	Zimbabwe	T	A	Z	D
1999-2000*Z*	S. R. Waugh	A. D. R. Campbell	1	1	0	0
2003-04*A*	S. R. Waugh	H. H. Streak	2	2	0	0
	In Australia		2	2	0	0
	In Zimbabwe		1	1	0	0
	Totals		3	3	0	0

A *Played in Australia.* *Z* *Played in Zimbabwe.*

SERIES RECORDS

Highest score	*A*	380	M. L. Hayden at Perth	2003-04
	Z	118	S. V. Carlisle at Sydney	2003-04
Best bowling	*A*	6-65	S. M. Katich at Sydney	2003-04
	Z	6-121	R. W. Price at Sydney	2003-04
Highest total	*A*	735-6 dec	at Perth	2003-04
	Z	321	at Perth	2003-04
Lowest total	*A*	403	at Sydney	2003-04
	Z	194	at Harare	1999-2000

AUSTRALIA v BANGLADESH

Season	*Captains* *Australia*	*Bangladesh*	*T*	*A*	*B*	*D*
2003*A*	S. R. Waugh	Khaled Mahmud	2	2	0	0
2005-06*B*	R. T. Ponting	Habibul Bashar	2	2	0	0
	In Australia		2	2	0	0
	In Bangladesh		2	2	0	0
	Totals		4	4	0	0

A *Played in Australia.* *B* *Played in Bangladesh.*

SERIES RECORDS

Highest score	*A*	201*	J. N. Gillespie at Chittagong	2005-06
	B	138	Shahriar Nafees at Fatullah	2005-06
Best bowling	*A*	8-108	S. C. G. MacGill at Fatullah	2005-06
	B	5-62	Mohammad Rafique at Fatullah	2005-06
Highest total	*A*	581-4 dec	at Chittagong	2005-06
	B	427	at Fatullah	2005-06
Lowest total	*A*	269	at Fatullah	2005-06
	B	97	at Darwin	2003

AUSTRALIA v ICC WORLD XI

Season	*Australia*	*ICC World XI*	*T*	*A*	*ICC*	*D*
2005-06*A*	R. T. Ponting	G. C. Smith	1	1	0	0

A *Played in Australia.*

SERIES RECORDS

Highest score	*A*	111	M. L. Hayden at Sydney	2005-06
	Wld	76	V. Sehwag at Sydney	2005-06
Best bowling	*A*	5-43	S. C. G. MacGill at Sydney	2005-06
	Wld	4-59	A. Flintoff at Sydney	2005-06
Highest total	*A*	345	at Sydney	2005-06
	Wld	190	at Sydney	2005-06
Lowest total	*A*	199	at Sydney	2005-06
	Wld	144	at Sydney	2005-06

SOUTH AFRICA v WEST INDIES

	Captains					
Season	*South Africa*	*West Indies*	*T*	*SA*	*WI*	*D*
1991-92*W*	K. C. Wessels	R. B. Richardson	1	0	1	0
1998-99*S*	W. J. Cronje	B. C. Lara	5	5	0	0

SIR VIVIAN RICHARDS TROPHY

	Captains						
Season	*South Africa*	*West Indies*	*T*	*SA*	*WI*	*D*	*Held by*
2000-01*W*	S. M. Pollock	C. L. Hooper	5	2	1	2	SA
2003-04*S*	G. C. Smith	B. C. Lara	4	3	0	1	SA
2004-05*W*	G. C. Smith	S. Chanderpaul	4	2	0	2	SA
2007-08 *S*	G. C. Smith	C. H. Gayle[1]	3	2	1	0	SA
2010*W*	G. C. Smith	C. H. Gayle	3	2	0	1	SA
2014-15*S*	H. M. Amla	D. Ramdin	3	2	0	1	SA
	In South Africa		15	12	1	2	
	In West Indies		13	6	2	5	
	Totals		28	18	3	7	

S Played in South Africa. *W Played in West Indies.*

The following deputised for the official touring captain:
[1]D. J. Bravo (Third).

SERIES RECORDS

Highest score	*SA*	208	H. M. Amla at Centurion	2014-15
	WI	317	C. H. Gayle at St John's	2004-05
Best bowling	*SA*	7-37	M. Ntini at Port-of-Spain	2004-05
	WI	7-84	F. A. Rose at Durban	1998-99
Highest total	*SA*	658-9 dec	at Durban	2003-04
	WI	747	at St John's	2004-05
Lowest total	*SA*	141	at Kingston	2000-01
	WI	102	at Port-of-Spain	2010

SOUTH AFRICA v NEW ZEALAND

	Captains					
Season	*South Africa*	*New Zealand*	*T*	*SA*	*NZ*	*D*
1931-32*N*	H. B. Cameron	M. L. Page	2	2	0	0
1952-53*N*	J. E. Cheetham	W. M. Wallace	2	1	0	1
1953-54*S*	J. E. Cheetham	G. O. Rabone[1]	5	4	0	1
1961-62*S*	D. J. McGlew	J. R. Reid	5	2	2	1
1963-64*N*	T. L. Goddard	J. R. Reid	3	0	0	3
1994-95*S*	W. J. Cronje	K. R. Rutherford	3	2	1	0
1994-95*N*	W. J. Cronje	K. R. Rutherford	1	1	0	0
1998-99*N*	W. J. Cronje	D. J. Nash	3	1	0	2

	Captains					
Season	*South Africa*	*New Zealand*	*T*	*SA*	*NZ*	*D*
2000-01*S*	S. M. Pollock	S. P. Fleming	3	2	0	1
2003-04*N*	G. C. Smith	S. P. Fleming	3	1	1	1
2005-06*S*	G. C. Smith	S. P. Fleming	3	2	0	1
2007-08*S*	G. C. Smith	D. L. Vettori	2	2	0	0
2011-12*N*	G. C. Smith	L. R. P. L. Taylor	3	1	0	2
2012-13*S*	G. C. Smith	B. B. McCullum	2	2	0	0
2016*S*	**F. du Plessis**	**K. S. Williamson**	**2**	**1**	**0**	**1**
	In New Zealand		17	7	1	9
	In South Africa		**25**	**17**	**3**	**5**
	Totals		**42**	**24**	**4**	**14**

N Played in New Zealand. S Played in South Africa.

The following deputised for the official touring captain:
[1]B. Sutcliffe (Fourth and Fifth).

SERIES RECORDS

Highest score	*SA*	275*	D. J. Cullinan at Auckland	1998-99
	NZ	262	S. P. Fleming at Cape Town	2005-06
Best bowling	*SA*	8-53	G. B. Lawrence at Johannesburg	1961-62
	NZ	6-60	J. R. Reid at Dunedin	1963-64
Highest total	*SA*	621-5 dec	at Auckland	1998-99
	NZ	595	at Auckland	2003-04
Lowest total	*SA*	148	at Johannesburg	1953-54
	NZ	45	at Cape Town	2012-13

SOUTH AFRICA v INDIA

	Captains					
Season	*South Africa*	*India*	*T*	*SA*	*I*	*D*
1992-93*S*	K. C. Wessels	M. Azharuddin	4	1	0	3
1996-97*I*	W. J. Cronje	S. R. Tendulkar	3	1	2	0
1996-97*S*	W. J. Cronje	S. R. Tendulkar	3	2	0	1
1999-2000*I*	W. J. Cronje	S. R. Tendulkar	2	2	0	0
2001-02*S*†	S. M. Pollock	S. C. Ganguly	2	1	0	1
2004-05*I*	G. C. Smith	S. C. Ganguly	2	0	1	1
2006-07*S*	G. C. Smith	R. Dravid	3	2	1	0
2007-08*I*	G. C. Smith	A. Kumble[1]	3	1	1	1
2009-10*I*	G. C. Smith	M. S. Dhoni	2	1	1	0
2010-11*S*	G. C. Smith	M. S. Dhoni	3	1	1	1
2013-14*S*	G. C. Smith	M. S. Dhoni	2	1	0	1

THE FREEDOM TROPHY

	Captains						
Season	*South Africa*	*India*	*T*	*SA*	*I*	*D*	*Held by*
2015-16*I*	H. M. Amla	V. Kohli	4	0	3	1	I
	In South Africa		17	8	2	7	
	In India		16	5	8	3	
	Totals		33	13	10	10	

S Played in South Africa. I Played in India.

† *The Third Test at Centurion was stripped of its official status by the ICC after a disciplinary dispute and is excluded.*

The following was appointed by the home authority for only a minor proportion of the series:
[1]M. S. Dhoni (Third).

SERIES RECORDS

Highest score	*SA*	253*	H. M. Amla at Nagpur	2009-10
	I	319	V. Sehwag at Chennai	2007-08
Best bowling	*SA*	8-64	L. Klusener at Calcutta	1996-97
	I	7-66	R. Ashwin at Nagpur	2015-16
Highest total	*SA*	620-4 dec	at Centurion	2010-11
	I	643-6 dec	at Kolkata	2009-10
Lowest total	*SA*	79	at Nagpur	2015-16
	I	66	at Durban	1996-97

SOUTH AFRICA v PAKISTAN

	Captains					
Season	*South Africa*	*Pakistan*	*T*	*SA*	*P*	*D*
1994-95*S*	W. J. Cronje	Salim Malik	1	1	0	0
1997-98*P*	W. J. Cronje	Saeed Anwar	3	1	0	2
1997-98*S*	W. J. Cronje[1]	Rashid Latif[2]	3	1	1	1
2002-03*S*	S. M. Pollock	Waqar Younis	2	2	0	0
2003-04*P*	G. C. Smith	Inzamam-ul-Haq[3]	2	0	1	1
2006-07*S*	G. C. Smith	Inzamam-ul-Haq	3	2	1	0
2007-08*P*	G. C. Smith	Shoaib Malik	2	1	0	1
2010-11*U*	G. C. Smith	Misbah-ul-Haq	2	0	0	2
2012-13*S*	G. C. Smith	Misbah-ul-Haq	3	3	0	0
2013-14*U*	G. C. Smith	Misbah-ul-Haq	2	1	1	0
	In South Africa		12	9	2	1
	In Pakistan		7	2	1	4
	In United Arab Emirates		4	1	1	2
	Totals		23	12	4	7

S Played in South Africa. P Played in Pakistan. U Played in United Arab Emirates.

The following deputised for the official touring captain or were appointed by the home authority for only a minor proportion of the series:

[1]G. Kirsten (First). [2]Aamir Sohail (First and Second). [3]Yousuf Youhana *later known as Mohammad Yousuf* (First).

SERIES RECORDS

Highest score	*SA*	278*	A. B. de Villiers at Abu Dhabi	2010-11
	P	146	Khurram Manzoor at Abu Dhabi	2013-14
Best bowling	*SA*	7-29	K. J. Abbott at Centurion	2012-13
	P	6-78	Mushtaq Ahmed at Durban	1997-98
		6-78	Waqar Younis at Port Elizabeth	1997-98
Highest total	*SA*	620-7 dec	at Cape Town	2002-03
	P	456	at Rawalpindi	1997-98
Lowest total	*SA*	124	at Port Elizabeth	2006-07
	P	49	at Johannesburg	2012-13

SOUTH AFRICA v SRI LANKA

	Captains					
Season	*South Africa*	*Sri Lanka*	*T*	*SA*	*SL*	*D*
1993-94*SL*	K. C. Wessels	A. Ranatunga	3	1	0	2
1997-98*SA*	W. J. Cronje	A. Ranatunga	2	2	0	0
2000*SL*	S. M. Pollock	S. T. Jayasuriya	3	1	1	1
2000-01*SA*	S. M. Pollock	S. T. Jayasuriya	3	2	0	1
2002-03*SA*	S. M. Pollock	S. T. Jayasuriya[1]	2	2	0	0

	Captains					
Season	*South Africa*	*Sri Lanka*	*T*	*SA*	*SL*	*D*
2004*SL*	G. C. Smith	M. S. Atapattu	2	0	1	1
2006*SL*	A. G. Prince	D. P. M. D. Jayawardene	2	0	2	0
2011-12*SA*	G. C. Smith	T. M. Dilshan	3	2	1	0
2014*SL*	H. M. Amla	A. D. Mathews	2	1	0	1
2016-17*SA*	**F. du Plessis**	**A. D. Mathews**	**3**	**3**	**0**	**0**
	In South Africa		**13**	**11**	**1**	**1**
	In Sri Lanka		12	3	4	5
	Totals		**25**	**14**	**5**	**6**

SA Played in South Africa. SL Played in Sri Lanka.

The following deputised for the official captain:
[1]M. S. Atapattu (Second).

SERIES RECORDS

Highest score	*SA*	224	J. H. Kallis at Cape Town	2011-12
	SL	374	D. P. M. D. Jayawardene at Colombo (SSC)	2006
Best bowling	*SA*	7-81	M. de Lange at Durban	2011-12
	SL	7-84	M. Muralitharan at Galle	2000
Highest total	*SA*	580-4 dec	at Cape Town	2011-12
	SL	756-5 dec	at Colombo (SSC)	2006
Lowest total	*SA*	168	at Durban	2011-12
	SL	95	at Cape Town	2000-01

SOUTH AFRICA v ZIMBABWE

	Captains					
Season	*South Africa*	*Zimbabwe*	*T*	*SA*	*Z*	*D*
1995-96*Z*	W. J. Cronje	A. Flower	1	1	0	0
1999-2000*S*	W. J. Cronje	A. D. R. Campbell	1	1	0	0
1999-2000*Z*	W. J. Cronje	A. Flower	1	1	0	0
2001-02*Z*	S. M. Pollock	H. H. Streak	2	1	0	1
2004-05*S*	G. C. Smith	T. Taibu	2	2	0	0
2014-15*Z*	H. M. Amla	B. R. M. Taylor	1	1	0	0
	In Zimbabwe		5	4	0	1
	In South Africa		3	3	0	0
	Totals		8	7	0	1

S Played in South Africa. Z Played in Zimbabwe.

SERIES RECORDS

Highest score	*SA*	220	G. Kirsten at Harare	2001-02
	Z	199*	A. Flower at Harare	2001-02
Best bowling	*SA*	8-71	A. A. Donald at Harare	1995-96
	Z	5-101	B. C. Strang at Harare	1995-96
Highest total	*SA*	600-3 dec	at Harare	2001-02
	Z	419-9 dec	at Bulawayo	2001-02
Lowest total	*SA*	346	at Harare	1995-96
	Z	54	at Cape Town	2004-05

SOUTH AFRICA v BANGLADESH

Season	*Captains* *South Africa*	*Bangladesh*	*T*	*SA*	*B*	*D*
2002-03*S*	S. M. Pollock[1]	Khaled Mashud	2	2	0	0
2003*B*	G. C. Smith	Khaled Mahmud	2	2	0	0
2007-08*B*	G. C. Smith	Mohammad Ashraful	2	2	0	0
2008-09*S*	G. C. Smith	Mohammad Ashraful	2	2	0	0
2015*B*	H. M. Amla	Mushfiqur Rahim	2	0	0	2
	In South Africa		4	4	0	0
	In Bangladesh		6	4	0	2
	Totals		10	8	0	2

S Played in South Africa. *B Played in Bangladesh.*

The following deputised for the official captain:
[1]M. V. Boucher (First).

SERIES RECORDS

Highest score	*SA*	232	G. C. Smith at Chittagong	2007-08
	B	75	Habibul Bashar at Chittagong	2003
Best bowling	*SA*	5-19	M. Ntini at East London	2002-03
	B	6-27	Shahadat Hossain at Mirpur	2007-08
Highest total	*SA*	583-7 dec	at Chittagong	2007-08
	B	326	at Chittagong	2015
Lowest total	*SA*	170	at Mirpur	2007-08
	B	102	at Dhaka	2003

WEST INDIES v NEW ZEALAND

Season	*Captains* *West Indies*	*New Zealand*	*T*	*WI*	*NZ*	*D*
1951-52*N*	J. D. C. Goddard	B. Sutcliffe	2	1	0	1
1955-56*N*	D. St E. Atkinson	J. R. Reid[1]	4	3	1	0
1968-69*N*	G. S. Sobers	G. T. Dowling	3	1	1	1
1971-72*W*	G. S. Sobers	G. T. Dowling[2]	5	0	0	5
1979-80*N*	C. H. Lloyd	G. P. Howarth	3	0	1	2
1984-85*W*	I. V. A. Richards	G. P. Howarth	4	2	0	2
1986-87*N*	I. V. A. Richards	J. V. Coney	3	1	1	1
1994-95*N*	C. A. Walsh	K. R. Rutherford	2	1	0	1
1995-96*W*	C. A. Walsh	L. K. Germon	2	1	0	1
1999-2000*N*	B. C. Lara	S. P. Fleming	2	0	2	0
2002*W*	C. L. Hooper	S. P. Fleming	2	0	1	1
2005-06*N*	S. Chanderpaul	S. P. Fleming	3	0	2	1
2008-09*N*	C. H. Gayle	D. L. Vettori	2	0	0	2
2012*W*	D. J. G. Sammy	L. R. P. L. Taylor	2	2	0	0
2013-14*N*	D. J. G. Sammy	B. B. McCullum	3	0	2	1
2014*W*	D. Ramdin	B. B. McCullum	3	1	2	0
	In New Zealand		27	7	10	10
	In West Indies		18	6	3	9
	Totals		45	13	13	19

N Played in New Zealand. *W Played in West Indies.*

The following deputised for the official touring captain or were appointed by the home authority for only a minor proportion of the series:
[1]H. B. Cave (First). [2]B. E. Congdon (Third, Fourth and Fifth).

SERIES RECORDS

Highest score	*WI*	258	S. M. Nurse at Christchurch	1968-69
	NZ	259	G. M. Turner at Georgetown	1971-72
Best bowling	*WI*	7-37	C. A. Walsh at Wellington	1994-95
	NZ	7-27	C. L. Cairns at Hamilton	1999-2000
Highest total	*WI*	660-5 dec	at Wellington	1994-95
	NZ	609-9 dec	at Dunedin (University)	2013-14
Lowest total	*WI*	77	at Auckland	1955-56
	NZ	74	at Dunedin	1955-56

WEST INDIES v INDIA

	Captains					
Season	*West Indies*	*India*	*T*	*WI*	*I*	*D*
1948-49*I*	J. D. C. Goddard	L. Amarnath	5	1	0	4
1952-53*W*	J. B. Stollmeyer	V. S. Hazare	5	1	0	4
1958-59*I*	F. C. M. Alexander	Ghulam Ahmed[1]	5	3	0	2
1961-62*W*	F. M. M. Worrell	N. J. Contractor[2]	5	5	0	0
1966-67*I*	G. S. Sobers	Nawab of Pataudi jnr	3	2	0	1
1970-71*W*	G. S. Sobers	A. L. Wadekar	5	0	1	4
1974-75*I*	C. H. Lloyd	Nawab of Pataudi jnr[3]	5	3	2	0
1975-76*W*	C. H. Lloyd	B. S. Bedi	4	2	1	1
1978-79*I*	A. I. Kallicharran	S. M. Gavaskar	6	0	1	5
1982-83*W*	C. H. Lloyd	Kapil Dev	5	2	0	3
1983-84*I*	C. H. Lloyd	Kapil Dev	6	3	0	3
1987-88*I*	I. V. A. Richards	D. B. Vengsarkar[4]	4	1	1	2
1988-89*W*	I. V. A. Richards	D. B. Vengsarkar	4	3	0	1
1994-95*I*	C. A. Walsh	M. Azharuddin	3	1	1	1
1996-97*W*	C. A. Walsh[5]	S. R. Tendulkar	5	1	0	4
2001-02*W*	C. L. Hooper	S. C. Ganguly	5	2	1	2
2002-03*I*	C. L. Hooper	S. C. Ganguly	3	0	2	1
2005-06*W*	B. C. Lara	R. Dravid	4	0	1	3
2011*W*	D. J. G. Sammy	M. S. Dhoni	3	0	1	2
2011-12*I*	D. J. G. Sammy	M. S. Dhoni	3	0	2	1
2013-14*I*	D. J. G. Sammy	M. S. Dhoni	2	0	2	0
2016*W*	**J. O. Holder**	**V. Kohli**	**4**	**0**	**2**	**2**
	In India		45	14	11	20
	In West Indies		**49**	**16**	**7**	**26**
	Totals		**94**	**30**	**18**	**46**

I Played in India. W Played in West Indies.

The following deputised for the official touring captain or were appointed by the home authority for only a minor proportion of the series:

[1]P. R. Umrigar (First), V. Mankad (Fourth), H. R. Adhikari (Fifth). [2]Nawab of Pataudi jnr (Third, Fourth and Fifth). [3]S. Venkataraghavan (Second). [4]R. J. Shastri (Fourth). [5]B. C. Lara (Third).

SERIES RECORDS

Highest score	*WI*	256	R. B. Kanhai at Calcutta	1958-59
	I	236*	S. M. Gavaskar at Madras	1983-84
Best bowling	*WI*	9-95	J. M. Noreiga at Port-of-Spain	1970-71
	I	9-83	Kapil Dev at Ahmedabad	1983-84
Highest total	*WI*	644-8 dec	at Delhi	1958-59
	I	644-7 dec	at Kanpur	1978-79
Lowest total	*WI*	103	at Kingston	2005-06
	I	75	at Delhi	1987-88

WEST INDIES v PAKISTAN

	Captains					
Season	*West Indies*	*Pakistan*	*T*	*WI*	*P*	*D*
1957-58*W*	F. C. M. Alexander	A. H. Kardar	5	3	1	1
1958-59*P*	F. C. M. Alexander	Fazal Mahmood	3	1	2	0
1974-75*P*	C. H. Lloyd	Intikhab Alam	2	0	0	2
1976-77*W*	C. H. Lloyd	Mushtaq Mohammad	5	2	1	2
1980-81*P*	C. H. Lloyd	Javed Miandad	4	1	0	3
1986-87*P*	I. V. A. Richards	Imran Khan	3	1	1	1
1987-88*W*	I. V. A. Richards[1]	Imran Khan	3	1	1	1
1990-91*P*	D. L. Haynes	Imran Khan	3	1	1	1
1992-93*W*	R. B. Richardson	Wasim Akram	3	2	0	1
1997-98*P*	C. A. Walsh	Wasim Akram	3	0	3	0
1999-2000*W*	J. C. Adams	Moin Khan	3	1	0	2
2001-02*U*	C. L. Hooper	Waqar Younis	2	0	2	0
2004-05*W*	S. Chanderpaul	Inzamam-ul-Haq[2]	2	1	1	0
2006-07*P*	B. C. Lara	Inzamam-ul-Haq	3	0	2	1
2010-11*W*	D. J. G. Sammy	Misbah-ul-Haq	2	1	1	0
2016-17*U*	**J. O. Holder**	**Misbah-ul-Haq**	**3**	**1**	**2**	**0**
	In West Indies		23	11	5	7
	In Pakistan		21	4	9	8
	In United Arab Emirates		**5**	**1**	**4**	**0**
	Totals		**49**	**16**	**18**	**15**

P Played in Pakistan. W Played in West Indies. U Played in United Arab Emirates.

The following were appointed by the home authority or deputised for the official touring captain for a minor proportion of the series:

[1]C. G. Greenidge (First). [2]Younis Khan (First).

SERIES RECORDS

Highest score	*WI*	365*	G. S. Sobers at Kingston	1957-58
	P	337	Hanif Mohammad at Bridgetown	1957-58
Best bowling	*WI*	8-29	C. E. H. Croft at Port-of-Spain	1976-77
	P	7-80	Imran Khan at Georgetown	1987-88
Highest total	*WI*	790-3 dec	at Kingston	1957-58
	P	657-8 dec	at Bridgetown	1957-58
Lowest total	*WI*	53	at Faisalabad	1986-87
	P	77	at Lahore	1986-87

WEST INDIES v SRI LANKA

	Captains					
Season	*West Indies*	*Sri Lanka*	*T*	*WI*	*SL*	*D*
1993-94*S*	R. B. Richardson	A. Ranatunga	1	0	0	1
1996-97*W*	C. A. Walsh	A. Ranatunga	2	1	0	1
2001-02*S*	C. L. Hooper	S. T. Jayasuriya	3	0	3	0
2003*W*	B. C. Lara	H. P. Tillekeratne	2	1	0	1
2005*S*	S. Chanderpaul	M. S. Atapattu	2	0	2	0
2007-08*W*	C. H. Gayle	D. P. M. D. Jayawardene	2	1	1	0
2010-11*S*	D. J. G. Sammy	K. C. Sangakkara	3	0	0	3

THE SOBERS–TISSERA TROPHY

	Captains						
Season	*West Indies*	*Sri Lanka*	*T*	*WI*	*SL*	*D*	*Held by*
2015-16*S*	J. O. Holder	A. D. Mathews	2	0	2	0	SL
	In West Indies		6	3	1	2	
	In Sri Lanka		11	0	7	4	
	Totals		17	3	8	6	

W Played in West Indies. SL Played in Sri Lanka.

SERIES RECORDS

Highest score	*WI*	333	C. H. Gayle at Galle	2010-11
	SL	204*	H. P. Tillekeratne at Colombo (SSC)	2001-02
Best bowling	*WI*	7-57	C. D. Collymore at Kingston	2003
	SL	8-46	M. Muralitharan at Kandy	2005
Highest total	*WI*	580-9 dec	at Galle	2010-11
	SL	627-9 dec	at Colombo (SSC)	2001-02
Lowest total	*WI*	113	at Colombo (SSC)	2005
	SL	150	at Kandy	2005

WEST INDIES v ZIMBABWE

	Captains					
Season	*West Indies*	*Zimbabwe*	*T*	*WI*	*Z*	*D*
1999-2000*W*	J. C. Adams	A. Flower	2	2	0	0

THE CLIVE LLOYD TROPHY

	Captains						
Season	*West Indies*	*Zimbabwe*	*T*	*WI*	*Z*	*D*	*Held by*
2001*Z*	C. L. Hooper	H. H. Streak	2	1	0	1	WI
2003-04*Z*	B. C. Lara	H. H. Streak	2	1	0	1	WI
2012-13*W*	D. J. G. Sammy	B. R. M. Taylor	2	2	0	0	WI
	In West Indies		4	4	0	0	
	In Zimbabwe		4	2	0	2	
	Totals		8	6	0	2	

W Played in West Indies. Z Played in Zimbabwe.

SERIES RECORDS

Highest score	*WI*	191	B. C. Lara at Bulawayo	2003-04
	Z	127*	H. H. Streak at Harare	2003-04
Best bowling	*WI*	6-49	S. Shillingford at Bridgetown	2012-13
	Z	6-73	R. W. Price at Harare	2003-04
Highest total	*WI*	559-6 dec	at Bulawayo	2001
	Z	563-9 dec	at Harare	2001
Lowest total	*WI*	128	at Bulawayo	2003-04
	Z	63	at Port-of-Spain	1999-2000

WEST INDIES v BANGLADESH

	Captains					
Season	*West Indies*	*Bangladesh*	*T*	*WI*	*B*	*D*
2002-03*B*	R. D. Jacobs	Khaled Mashud	2	2	0	0
2003-04*W*	B. C. Lara	Habibul Bashar	2	1	0	1
2009*W*	F. L. Reifer	Mashrafe bin Mortaza[1]	2	0	2	0
2011-12*B*	D. J. G. Sammy	Mushfiqur Rahim	2	1	0	1
2012-13*B*	D. J. G. Sammy	Mushfiqur Rahim	2	2	0	0
2014-15*W*	D. Ramdin	Mushfiqur Rahim	2	2	0	0
	In West Indies		6	3	2	1
	In Bangladesh		6	5	0	1
	Totals		12	8	2	2

B Played in Bangladesh. W Played in West Indies.

The following deputised for the official touring captain for a minor proportion of the series:
[1]Shakib Al Hasan (Second).

SERIES RECORDS

Highest score	*WI*	261*	R. R. Sarwan at Kingston	2003-04
	B	128	Tamim Iqbal at St Vincent	2009
Best bowling	*WI*	6-3	J. J. C. Lawson at Dhaka	2002-03
	B	6-74	Sohag Gazi at Mirpur	2012-13
Highest total	*WI*	648-9 dec	at Khulna	2012-13
	B	556	at Mirpur	2012-13
Lowest total	*WI*	181	at St Vincent	2009
	B	87	at Dhaka	2002-03

NEW ZEALAND v INDIA

	Captains					
Season	*New Zealand*	*India*	*T*	*NZ*	*I*	*D*
1955-56*I*	H. B. Cave	P. R. Umrigar[1]	5	0	2	3
1964-65*I*	J. R. Reid	Nawab of Pataudi jnr	4	0	1	3
1967-68*N*	G. T. Dowling[2]	Nawab of Pataudi jnr	4	1	3	0
1969-70*I*	G. T. Dowling	Nawab of Pataudi jnr	3	1	1	1
1975-76*N*	G. M. Turner	B. S. Bedi[3]	3	1	1	1
1976-77*I*	G. M. Turner	B. S. Bedi	3	0	2	1
1980-81*N*	G. P. Howarth	S. M. Gavaskar	3	1	0	2
1988-89*I*	J. G. Wright	D. B. Vengsarkar	3	1	2	0
1989-90*N*	J. G. Wright	M. Azharuddin	3	1	0	2
1993-94*N*	K. R. Rutherford	M. Azharuddin	1	0	0	1
1995-96*I*	L. K. Germon	M. Azharuddin	3	0	1	2
1998-99*N*†	S. P. Fleming	M. Azharuddin	2	1	0	1
1999-2000*I*	S. P. Fleming	S. R. Tendulkar	3	0	1	2
2002-03*N*	S. P. Fleming	S. C. Ganguly	2	2	0	0
2003-04*I*	S. P. Fleming	S. C. Ganguly[4]	2	0	0	2
2008-09*N*	D. L. Vettori	M. S. Dhoni[5]	3	0	1	2
2010-11*I*	D. L. Vettori	M. S. Dhoni	3	0	1	2
2012-13*I*	L. R. P. L. Taylor	M. S. Dhoni	2	0	2	0

	Captains					
Season	*New Zealand*	*India*	*T*	*NZ*	*I*	*D*
2013-14*N*	B. B. McCullum	M. S. Dhoni	2	1	0	1
2016-17*I*	**K. S. Williamson**[6]	**V. Kohli**	**3**	**0**	**3**	**0**
	In India		**34**	**2**	**16**	**16**
	In New Zealand		23	8	5	10
	Totals		**57**	**10**	**21**	**26**

I Played in India. N Played in New Zealand.

† *The First Test at Dunedin was abandoned without a ball being bowled and is excluded.*

The following deputised for the official touring captain or were appointed by the home authority for a minor proportion of the series:

[1]Ghulam Ahmed (First). [2]B. W. Sinclair (First). [3]S. M. Gavaskar (First). [4]R. Dravid (Second). [5]V. Sehwag (Second). [6]L. R. P. L. Taylor (Second).

SERIES RECORDS

Highest score	*NZ*	302	B. B. McCullum at Wellington	2013-14
	I	231	V. Mankad at Madras	1955-56
Best bowling	*NZ*	7-23	R. J. Hadlee at Wellington	1975-76
	I	8-72	S. Venkataraghavan at Delhi	1964-65
Highest total	*NZ*	680-8 dec	at Wellington	2013-14
	I	583-7 dec	at Ahmedabad	1999-2000
Lowest total	*NZ*	94	at Hamilton	2002-03
	I	81	at Wellington	1975-76

NEW ZEALAND v PAKISTAN

	Captains					
Season	*New Zealand*	*Pakistan*	*T*	*NZ*	*P*	*D*
1955-56*P*	H. B. Cave	A. H. Kardar	3	0	2	1
1964-65*N*	J. R. Reid	Hanif Mohammad	3	0	0	3
1964-65*P*	J. R. Reid	Hanif Mohammad	3	0	2	1
1969-70*P*	G. T. Dowling	Intikhab Alam	3	1	0	2
1972-73*N*	B. E. Congdon	Intikhab Alam	3	0	1	2
1976-77*P*	G. M. Turner[1]	Mushtaq Mohammad	3	0	2	1
1978-79*N*	M. G. Burgess	Mushtaq Mohammad	3	0	1	2
1984-85*P*	J. V. Coney	Zaheer Abbas	3	0	2	1
1984-85*N*	G. P. Howarth	Javed Miandad	3	2	0	1
1988-89*N*†	J. G. Wright	Imran Khan	2	0	0	2
1990-91*P*	M. D. Crowe	Javed Miandad	3	0	3	0
1992-93*N*	K. R. Rutherford	Javed Miandad	1	0	1	0
1993-94*N*	K. R. Rutherford	Salim Malik	3	1	2	0
1995-96*N*	L. K. Germon	Wasim Akram	1	0	1	0
1996-97*P*	L. K. Germon	Saeed Anwar	2	1	1	0
2000-01*N*	S. P. Fleming	Moin Khan[2]	3	1	1	1
2002*P*‡	S. P. Fleming	Waqar Younis	1	0	1	0
2003-04*N*	S. P. Fleming	Inzamam-ul-Haq	2	0	1	1
2009-10*N*	D. L. Vettori	Mohammad Yousuf	3	1	1	1
2010-11*N*	D. L. Vettori	Misbah-ul-Haq	2	0	1	1

Season	Captains: New Zealand	Captains: Pakistan	T	NZ	P	D
2014-15*U*	B. B. McCullum	Misbah-ul-Haq	3	1	1	1
2016-17*N*	**K. S. Williamson**	**Misbah-ul-Haq[3]**	**2**	**2**	**0**	**0**
	In Pakistan		21	2	13	6
	In New Zealand		**31**	**7**	**10**	**14**
	In United Arab Emirates		3	1	1	1
	Totals		**55**	**10**	**24**	**21**

N *Played in New Zealand.* *P* *Played in Pakistan.* *U* *Played in United Arab Emirates.*

† *The First Test at Dunedin was abandoned without a ball being bowled and is excluded.*
‡ *The Second Test at Karachi was cancelled owing to civil disturbances.*

The following were appointed by the home authority for only a minor proportion of the series or deputised for the official touring captain:
[1]J. M. Parker (Third). [2]Inzamam-ul-Haq (Third). [3]Azhar Ali (Second).

SERIES RECORDS

Highest score	*NZ*	204*	M. S. Sinclair at Christchurch	2000-01
	P	329	Inzamam-ul-Haq at Lahore	2002
Best bowling	*NZ*	7-52	C. Pringle at Faisalabad	1990-91
	P	7-52	Intikhab Alam at Dunedin	1972-73
Highest total	*NZ*	690	at Sharjah	2014-15
	P	643	at Lahore	2002
Lowest total	*NZ*	70	at Dacca	1955-56
	P	102	at Faisalabad	1990-91

NEW ZEALAND v SRI LANKA

Season	Captains: New Zealand	Captains: Sri Lanka	T	NZ	SL	D
1982-83*N*	G. P. Howarth	D. S. de Silva	2	2	0	0
1983-84*S*	G. P. Howarth	L. R. D. Mendis	3	2	0	1
1986-87*S*†	J. J. Crowe	L. R. D. Mendis	1	0	0	1
1990-91*N*	M. D. Crowe[1]	A. Ranatunga	3	0	0	3
1992-93*S*	M. D. Crowe	A. Ranatunga	2	0	1	1
1994-95*N*	K. R. Rutherford	A. Ranatunga	2	0	1	1
1996-97*N*	S. P. Fleming	A. Ranatunga	2	2	0	0
1997-98*S*	S. P. Fleming	A. Ranatunga	3	1	2	0
2003*S*	S. P. Fleming	H. P. Tillekeratne	2	0	0	2
2004-05*N*	S. P. Fleming	M. S. Atapattu	2	1	0	1
2006-07*N*	S. P. Fleming	D. P. M. D. Jayawardene	2	1	1	0
2009*S*	D. L. Vettori	K. C. Sangakkara	2	0	2	0
2012-13*S*	L. R. P. L. Taylor	D. P. M. D. Jayawardene	2	1	1	0
2014-15*N*	B. B. McCullum	A. D. Mathews	2	2	0	0
2015-16*N*	B. B. McCullum	A. D. Mathews	2	2	0	0
	In New Zealand		17	10	2	5
	In Sri Lanka		15	4	6	5
	Totals		32	14	8	10

N *Played in New Zealand.* *S* *Played in Sri Lanka.*

† *The Second and Third Tests were cancelled owing to civil disturbances.*

The following was appointed by the home authority for only a minor proportion of the series:
[1]I. D. S. Smith (Third).

SERIES RECORDS

Highest score	*NZ*	299	M. D. Crowe at Wellington	1990-91
	SL	267	P. A. de Silva at Wellington	1990-91
Best bowling	*NZ*	7-130	D. L. Vettori at Wellington	2006-07
	SL	6-43	H. M. R. K. B. Herath at Galle	2012-13
Highest total	*NZ*	671-4	at Wellington	1990-91
	SL	498	at Napier	2004-05
Lowest total	*NZ*	102	at Colombo (SSC)	1992-93
	SL	93	at Wellington	1982-83

NEW ZEALAND v ZIMBABWE

	Captains					
Season	*New Zealand*	*Zimbabwe*	*T*	*NZ*	*Z*	*D*
1992-93*Z*	M. D. Crowe	D. L. Houghton	2	1	0	1
1995-96*N*	L. K. Germon	A. Flower	2	0	0	2
1997-98*Z*	S. P. Fleming	A. D. R. Campbell	2	0	0	2
1997-98*N*	S. P. Fleming	A. D. R. Campbell	2	2	0	0
2000-01*Z*	S. P. Fleming	H. H. Streak	2	2	0	0
2000-01*N*	S. P. Fleming	H. H. Streak	1	0	0	1
2005-06*Z*	S. P. Fleming	T. Taibu	2	2	0	0
2011-12*Z*	L. R. P. L. Taylor	B. R. M. Taylor	1	1	0	0
2011-12*N*	L. R. P. L. Taylor	B. R. M. Taylor	1	1	0	0
2016*Z*	**K. S. Williamson**	**A. G. Cremer**	**2**	**2**	**0**	**0**
	In New Zealand		6	3	0	3
	In Zimbabwe		**11**	**8**	**0**	**3**
	Totals		**17**	**11**	**0**	**6**

N Played in New Zealand. Z Played in Zimbabwe.

SERIES RECORDS

Highest score	*NZ*	**173***	**L. R. P. L. Taylor at Bulawayo**	**2016**
	Z	203*	G. J. Whittall at Bulawayo	1997-98
Best bowling	*NZ*	6-26	C. S. Martin at Napier	2011-12
	Z	8-109	P. A. Strang at Bulawayo	2000-01
Highest total	*NZ*	**582-4 dec**	**at Bulawayo**	**2016**
	Z	461	at Bulawayo	1997-98
Lowest total	*NZ*	207	at Harare	1997-98
	Z	51	at Napier	2011-12

NEW ZEALAND v BANGLADESH

	Captains					
Season	*New Zealand*	*Bangladesh*	*T*	*NZ*	*B*	*D*
2001-02*N*	S. P. Fleming	Khaled Mashud	2	2	0	0
2004-05*B*	S. P. Fleming	Khaled Mashud	2	2	0	0
2007-08*N*	D. L. Vettori	Mohammad Ashraful	2	2	0	0
2008-09*B*	D. L. Vettori	Mohammad Ashraful	2	1	0	1
2009-10*N*	D. L. Vettori	Shakib Al Hasan	1	1	0	0
2013-14*B*	B. B. McCullum	Mushfiqur Rahim	2	0	0	2
2016-17*N*	**K. S. Williamson**	**Mushfiqur Rahim**[1]	**2**	**2**	**0**	**0**
	In New Zealand		**7**	**7**	**0**	**0**
	In Bangladesh		6	3	0	3
	Totals		**13**	**10**	**0**	**3**

B Played in Bangladesh. N Played in New Zealand.

The following deputised for the official touring captain for only a minor proportion of the series:
[1]Tamim Iqbal (Second).

SERIES RECORDS

Highest score	*NZ*	202	S. P. Fleming at Chittagong	2004-05
	B	**217**	**Shakib Al Hasan at Wellington**	**2016-17**
Best bowling	*NZ*	7-53	C. L. Cairns at Hamilton	2001-02
	B	7-36	Shakib Al Hasan at Chittagong	2008-09
Highest total	*NZ*	553-7 dec	at Hamilton	2009-10
	B	**595-8 dec**	**at Wellington**	**2016-17**
Lowest total	*NZ*	171	at Chittagong	2008-09
	B	108	at Hamilton	2001-02

INDIA v PAKISTAN

	Captains					
Season	*India*	*Pakistan*	*T*	*I*	*P*	*D*
1952-53*I*	L. Amarnath	A. H. Kardar	5	2	1	2
1954-55*P*	V. Mankad	A. H. Kardar	5	0	0	5
1960-61*I*	N. J. Contractor	Fazal Mahmood	5	0	0	5
1978-79*P*	B. S. Bedi	Mushtaq Mohammad	3	0	2	1
1979-80*I*	S. M. Gavaskar[1]	Asif Iqbal	6	2	0	4
1982-83*P*	S. M. Gavaskar	Imran Khan	6	0	3	3
1983-84*I*	Kapil Dev	Zaheer Abbas	3	0	0	3
1984-85*P*	S. M. Gavaskar	Zaheer Abbas	2	0	0	2
1986-87*I*	Kapil Dev	Imran Khan	5	0	1	4
1989-90*P*	K. Srikkanth	Imran Khan	4	0	0	4
1998-99*I*	M. Azharuddin	Wasim Akram	2	1	1	0
1998-99*I*†	M. Azharuddin	Wasim Akram	1	0	1	0
2003-04*P*	S. C. Ganguly[2]	Inzamam-ul-Haq	3	2	1	0
2004-05*I*	S. C. Ganguly	Inzamam-ul-Haq	3	1	1	1
2005-06*P*	R. Dravid	Inzamam-ul-Haq[3]	3	0	1	2
2007-08*I*	A. Kumble	Shoaib Malik[4]	3	1	0	2
	In India		33	7	5	21
	In Pakistan		26	2	7	17
	Totals		59	9	12	38

I Played in India. P Played in Pakistan.

† *This Test was part of the Asian Test Championship and was not counted as part of the preceding bilateral series.*

The following were appointed by the home authority for only a minor proportion of the series or deputised for the official touring captain:

[1]G. R. Viswanath (Sixth). [2]R. Dravid (First and Second). [3]Younis Khan (Third). [4]Younis Khan (Second and Third).

SERIES RECORDS

Highest score	*I*	309	V. Sehwag at Multan	2003-04
	P	280*	Javed Miandad at Hyderabad	1982-83
Best bowling	*I*	10-74	A. Kumble at Delhi	1998-99
	P	8-60	Imran Khan at Karachi	1982-83
Highest total	*I*	675-5 dec	at Multan	2003-04
	P	699-5	at Lahore	1989-90
Lowest total	*I*	106	at Lucknow	1952-53
	P	116	at Bangalore	1986-87

INDIA v SRI LANKA

	Captains					
Season	*India*	*Sri Lanka*	*T*	*I*	*SL*	*D*
1982-83*I*	S. M. Gavaskar	B. Warnapura	1	0	0	1
1985-86*S*	Kapil Dev	L. R. D. Mendis	3	0	1	2
1986-87*I*	Kapil Dev	L. R. D. Mendis	3	2	0	1
1990-91*I*	M. Azharuddin	A. Ranatunga	1	1	0	0
1993-94*S*	M. Azharuddin	A. Ranatunga	3	1	0	2
1993-94*I*	M. Azharuddin	A. Ranatunga	3	3	0	0
1997-98*S*	S. R. Tendulkar	A. Ranatunga	2	0	0	2
1997-98*I*	S. R. Tendulkar	A. Ranatunga	3	0	0	3
1998-99*S*†	M. Azharuddin	A. Ranatunga	1	0	0	1
2001*S*	S. C. Ganguly	S. T. Jayasuriya	3	1	2	0
2005-06*I*	R. Dravid[1]	M. S. Atapattu	3	2	0	1
2008*S*	A. Kumble	D. P. M. D. Jayawardene	3	1	2	0
2009-10*I*	M. S. Dhoni	K. C. Sangakkara	3	2	0	1
2010*S*	M. S. Dhoni	K. C. Sangakkara	3	1	1	1
2015-16*S*	V. Kohli	A. D. Mathews	3	2	1	0
	In India		17	10	0	7
	In Sri Lanka		21	6	7	8
	Totals		38	16	7	15

I Played in India. S Played in Sri Lanka.

† *This Test was part of the Asian Test Championship.*

The following was appointed by the home authority for only a minor proportion of the series:
[1]V. Sehwag (Third).

SERIES RECORDS

Highest score	*I*	293	V. Sehwag at Mumbai (BS)	2009-10
	SL	340	S. T. Jayasuriya at Colombo (RPS)	1997-98
Best bowling	*I*	7-51	Maninder Singh at Nagpur	1986-87
	SL	8-87	M. Muralitharan at Colombo (SSC)	2001
Highest total	*I*	726-9 dec	at Mumbai (BS)	2009-10
	SL	952-6 dec	at Colombo (RPS)	1997-98
Lowest total	*I*	112	at Galle	2015-16
	SL	82	at Chandigarh	1990-91

INDIA v ZIMBABWE

	Captains					
Season	*India*	*Zimbabwe*	*T*	*I*	*Z*	*D*
1992-93*Z*	M. Azharuddin	D. L. Houghton	1	0	0	1
1992-93*I*	M. Azharuddin	D. L. Houghton	1	1	0	0
1998-99*Z*	M. Azharuddin	A. D. R. Campbell	1	0	1	0
2000-01*I*	S. C. Ganguly	H. H. Streak	2	1	0	1
2001*Z*	S. C. Ganguly	H. H. Streak	2	1	1	0
2001-02*I*	S. C. Ganguly	S. V. Carlisle	2	2	0	0
2005-06*Z*	S. C. Ganguly	T. Taibu	2	2	0	0
	In India		5	4	0	1
	In Zimbabwe		6	3	2	1
	Totals		11	7	2	2

I Played in India. Z Played in Zimbabwe.

SERIES RECORDS

Highest score	*I*	227	V. G. Kambli at Delhi	1992-93
	Z	232*	A. Flower at Nagpur	2000-01
Best bowling	*I*	7-59	I. K. Pathan at Harare	2005-06
	Z	6-73	H. H. Streak at Harare	2005-06
Highest total	*I*	609-6 dec	at Nagpur	2000-01
	Z	503-6	at Nagpur	2000-01
Lowest total	*I*	173	at Harare	1998-99
	Z	146	at Delhi	2001-02

INDIA v BANGLADESH

	Captains					
Season	*India*	*Bangladesh*	*T*	*I*	*B*	*D*
2000-01*B*	S. C. Ganguly	Naimur Rahman	1	1	0	0
2004-05*B*	S. C. Ganguly	Habibul Bashar	2	2	0	0
2007*B*	R. Dravid	Habibul Bashar	2	1	0	1
2009-10*B*	M. S. Dhoni[1]	Shakib Al Hasan	2	2	0	0
2015*B*	V. Kohli	Mushfiqur Rahim	1	0	0	1
	In Bangladesh		8	6	0	2

B Played in Bangladesh.

The following deputised for the official touring captain for a minor proportion of the series:
[1]V. Sehwag (First).

SERIES RECORDS

Highest score	*I*	248*	S. R. Tendulkar at Dhaka	2004-05
	B	158*	Mohammad Ashraful at Chittagong	2004-05
Best bowling	*I*	7-87	Zaheer Khan at Mirpur	2009-10
	B	6-132	Naimur Rahman at Dhaka	2000-01
Highest total	*I*	610-3 dec	at Mirpur	2007
	B	400	at Dhaka	2000-01
Lowest total	*I*	243	at Chittagong	2009-10
	B	91	at Dhaka	2000-01

PAKISTAN v SRI LANKA

	Captains					
Season	*Pakistan*	*Sri Lanka*	*T*	*P*	*SL*	*D*
1981-82*P*	Javed Miandad	B. Warnapura[1]	3	2	0	1
1985-86*P*	Javed Miandad	L. R. D. Mendis	3	2	0	1
1985-86*S*	Imran Khan	L. R. D. Mendis	3	1	1	1
1991-92*P*	Imran Khan	P. A. de Silva	3	1	0	2
1994-95*S*†	Salim Malik	A. Ranatunga	2	2	0	0
1995-96*P*	Ramiz Raja	A. Ranatunga	3	1	2	0
1996-97*S*	Ramiz Raja	A. Ranatunga	2	0	0	2
1998-99*P*‡	Wasim Akram	H. P. Tillekeratne	1	0	0	1
1998-99*B*‡	Wasim Akram	P. A. de Silva	1	1	0	0
1999-2000*P*	Saeed Anwar[2]	S. T. Jayasuriya	3	1	2	0
2000*S*	Moin Khan	S. T. Jayasuriya	3	2	0	1
2001-02*P*‡	Waqar Younis	S. T. Jayasuriya	1	0	1	0
2004-05*P*	Inzamam-ul-Haq	M. S. Atapattu	2	1	1	0
2005-06*S*	Inzamam-ul-Haq	D. P. M. D. Jayawardene	2	1	0	1
2008-09*P*§	Younis Khan	D. P. M. D. Jayawardene	2	0	0	2
2009*S*	Younis Khan	K. C. Sangakkara	3	0	2	1
2011-12*U*	Misbah-ul-Haq	T. M. Dilshan	3	1	0	2

	Captains					
Season	*Pakistan*	*Sri Lanka*	*T*	*P*	*SL*	*D*
2012*S*	Misbah-ul-Haq[3]	D. P. M. D. Jayawardene	3	0	1	2
2013-14*U*	Misbah-ul-Haq	A. D. Mathews	3	1	1	1
2014*S*	Misbah-ul-Haq	A. D. Mathews	2	0	2	0
2015*S*	Misbah-ul-Haq	A. D. Mathews	3	2	1	0
	In Pakistan		21	8	6	7
	In Sri Lanka		23	8	7	8
	In Bangladesh		1	1	0	0
	In United Arab Emirates		6	2	1	3
	Totals		51	19	14	18

P Played in Pakistan. S Played in Sri Lanka. B Played in Bangladesh.
U Played in United Arab Emirates.

† *One Test was cancelled owing to the threat of civil disturbances following a general election.*
‡ *These Tests were part of the Asian Test Championship.*
§ *The Second Test ended after a terrorist attack on the Sri Lankan team bus on the third day.*

The following deputised for the official touring captain or were appointed by the home authority for only a minor proportion of the series:
[1]L. R. D. Mendis (Second). [2]Moin Khan (Third). [3]Mohammad Hafeez (First).

SERIES RECORDS

Highest score	*P*	313	Younis Khan at Karachi	2008-09
	SL	253	S. T. Jayasuriya at Faisalabad	2004-05
Best bowling	*P*	8-58	Imran Khan at Lahore	1981-82
	SL	9-127	H. M. R. K. B. Herath at Colombo (SSC)	2014
Highest total	*P*	765-6 dec	at Karachi	2008-09
	SL	644-7 dec	at Karachi	2008-09
Lowest total	*P*	90	at Colombo (PSS)	2009
	SL	71	at Kandy	1994-95

PAKISTAN v ZIMBABWE

	Captains					
Season	*Pakistan*	*Zimbabwe*	*T*	*P*	*Z*	*D*
1993-94*P*	Wasim Akram[1]	A. Flower	3	2	0	1
1994-95*Z*	Salim Malik	A. Flower	3	2	1	0
1996-97*P*	Wasim Akram	A. D. R. Campbell	2	1	0	1
1997-98*Z*	Rashid Latif	A. D. R. Campbell	2	1	0	1
1998-99*P*†	Aamir Sohail[2]	A. D. R. Campbell	2	0	1	1
2002-03*Z*	Waqar Younis	A. D. R. Campbell	2	2	0	0
2011-12*Z*	Misbah-ul-Haq	B. R. M. Taylor	1	1	0	0
2013-14*Z*	Misbah-ul-Haq	B. R. M. Taylor[3]	2	1	1	0
	In Pakistan		7	3	1	3
	In Zimbabwe		10	7	2	1
	Totals		17	10	3	4

P Played in Pakistan. Z Played in Zimbabwe.

† *The Third Test at Faisalabad was abandoned without a ball being bowled and is excluded.*

The following were appointed by the home authority for only a minor proportion of the series:
[1]Waqar Younis (First). [2]Moin Khan (Second). [3]H. Masakadza (First).

SERIES RECORDS

Highest score	*P*	257*	Wasim Akram at Sheikhupura	1996-97
	Z	201*	G. W. Flower at Harare	1994-95
Best bowling	*P*	7-66	Saqlain Mushtaq at Bulawayo	2002-03
	Z	6-90	H. H. Streak at Harare	1994-95
Highest total	*P*	553	at Sheikhupura	1996-97
	Z	544-4 dec	at Harare	1994-95
Lowest total	*P*	103	at Peshawar	1998-99
	Z	120	at Harare	2013-14

PAKISTAN v BANGLADESH

	Captains					
Season	*Pakistan*	*Bangladesh*	*T*	*P*	*B*	*D*
2001-02*P*†	Waqar Younis	Naimur Rahman	1	1	0	0
2001-02*B*	Waqar Younis	Khaled Mashud	2	2	0	0
2003-04*P*	Rashid Latif	Khaled Mahmud	3	3	0	0
2011-12*B*	Misbah-ul-Haq	Mushfiqur Rahim	2	2	0	0
2014-15*B*	Misbah-ul-Haq	Mushfiqur Rahim	2	1	0	1
	In Pakistan		4	4	0	0
	In Bangladesh		6	5	0	1
	Totals		10	9	0	1

P Played in Pakistan. B Played in Bangladesh.

† *This Test was part of the Asian Test Championship.*

SERIES RECORDS

Highest score	*P*	226	Azhar Ali at Mirpur	2014-15
	B	206	Tamim Iqbal at Khulna	2014-15
Best bowling	*P*	7-77	Danish Kaneria at Dhaka	2001-02
	B	6-82	Shakib Al Hasan at Mirpur	2011-12
Highest total	*P*	628	at Khulna	2014-15
	B	555-6	at Khulna	2014-15
Lowest total	*P*	175	at Multan	2003-04
	B	96	at Peshawar	2003-04

SRI LANKA v ZIMBABWE

	Captains					
Season	*Sri Lanka*	*Zimbabwe*	*T*	*SL*	*Z*	*D*
1994-95*Z*	A. Ranatunga	A. Flower	3	0	0	3
1996-97*S*	A. Ranatunga	A. D. R. Campbell	2	2	0	0
1997-98*S*	A. Ranatunga	A. D. R. Campbell	2	2	0	0
1999-2000*Z*	S. T. Jayasuriya	A. Flower	3	1	0	2
2001-02*S*	S. T. Jayasuriya	S. V. Carlisle	3	3	0	0
2003-04*Z*	M. S. Atapattu	T. Taibu	2	2	0	0
2016-17Z	**H. M. R. K. B. Herath**	**A. G. Cremer**	**2**	**2**	**0**	**0**
	In Sri Lanka		7	7	0	0
	In Zimbabwe		**10**	**5**	**0**	**5**
	Totals		**17**	**12**	**0**	**5**

S Played in Sri Lanka. Z Played in Zimbabwe.

SERIES RECORDS

Highest score	*SL*	270	K. C. Sangakkara at Bulawayo	2003-04
	Z	266	D. L. Houghton at Bulawayo	1994-95
Best bowling	*SL*	9-51	M. Muralitharan at Kandy	2001-02
	Z	5-106	P. A. Strang at Colombo (RPS)	1996-97
Highest total	*SL*	713-3 dec	at Bulawayo	2003-04
	Z	462-9 dec	at Bulawayo	1994-95
Lowest total	*SL*	218	at Bulawayo	1994-95
	Z	79	at Galle	2001-02

SRI LANKA v BANGLADESH

Season	*Sri Lanka* (Captains)	*Bangladesh* (Captains)	*T*	*SL*	*B*	*D*
2001-02*S*†	S. T. Jayasuriya	Naimur Rahman	1	1	0	0
2002*S*	S. T. Jayasuriya	Khaled Mashud	2	2	0	0
2005-06*S*	M. S. Atapattu	Habibul Bashar	2	2	0	0
2005-06*B*	D. P. M. D. Jayawardene	Habibul Bashar	2	2	0	0
2007*S*	D. P. M. D. Jayawardene	Mohammad Ashraful	3	3	0	0
2008-09*B*	D. P. M. D. Jayawardene	Mohammad Ashraful	2	2	0	0
2012-13*S*	A. D. Mathews	Mushfiqur Rahim	2	1	0	1
2013-14*B*	A. D. Mathews	Mushfiqur Rahim	2	1	0	1
	In Sri Lanka		10	9	0	1
	In Bangladesh		6	5	0	1
	Totals		16	14	0	2

S *Played in Sri Lanka.* *B* *Played in Bangladesh.*

† *This Test was part of the Asian Test Championship.*

SERIES RECORDS

Highest score	*SL*	319	K. C. Sangakkara at Chittagong	2013-14
	B	200	Mushfiqur Rahim at Galle	2012-13
Best bowling	*SL*	7-89	H. M. R. K. B. Herath at Colombo (RPS)	2012-13
	B	5-70	Shakib Al Hasan at Mirpur	2008-09
Highest total	*SL*	730-6 dec	at Mirpur	2013-14
	B	638	at Galle	2012-13
Lowest total	*SL*	293	at Mirpur	2008-09
	B	62	at Colombo (PSS)	2007

An expanded and regularly updated online version of the Records can be found at www.wisdenrecords.com

ZIMBABWE v BANGLADESH

	Captains					
Season	*Zimbabwe*	*Bangladesh*	*T*	*Z*	*B*	*D*
2000-01*Z*	H. H. Streak	Naimur Rahman	2	2	0	0
2001-02*B*	B. A. Murphy[1]	Naimur Rahman	2	1	0	1
2003-04*Z*	H. H. Streak	Habibul Bashar	2	1	0	1
2004-05*B*	T. Taibu	Habibul Bashar	2	0	1	1
2011-12*Z*	B. R. M. Taylor	Shakib Al Hasan	1	1	0	0
2012-13*Z*	B. R. M. Taylor	Mushfiqur Rahim	2	1	1	0
2014-15*B*	B. R. M. Taylor	Mushfiqur Rahim	3	0	3	0
	In Zimbabwe		7	5	1	1
	In Bangladesh		7	1	4	2
	Totals		14	6	5	3

Z Played in Zimbabwe. *B Played in Bangladesh.*

The following deputised for the official touring captain:

[1]S. V. Carlisle (Second).

SERIES RECORDS

Highest score	*Z*	171	B. R. M. Taylor at Harare	2012-13
	B	137	Shakib Al Hasan at Khulna	2014-15
Best bowling	*Z*	6-59	D. T. Hondo at Dhaka	2004-05
	B	8-39	Taijul Islam at Mirpur	2014-15
Highest total	*Z*	542-7 dec	at Chittagong	2001-02
	B	503	at Chittagong	2014-15
Lowest total	*Z*	114	at Mirpur	2014-15
	B	107	at Dhaka	2001-02

TEST GROUNDS

in chronological order

	City and Ground	*First Test Match*		*Tests*
1	**Melbourne, Melbourne Cricket Ground**	**March 15, 1877**	**A v E**	**109**
2	**London, Kennington Oval**	**September 6, 1880**	**E v A**	**99**
3	**Sydney, Sydney Cricket Ground (No. 1)**	**February 17, 1882**	**A v E**	**105**
4	**Manchester, Old Trafford**	**July 11, 1884**	**E v A**	**77**
5	**London, Lord's**	**July 21, 1884**	**E v A**	**133**
6	**Adelaide, Adelaide Oval**	**December 12, 1884**	**A v E**	**75**
7	**Port Elizabeth, St George's Park**	**March 12, 1889**	**SA v E**	**27**
8	**Cape Town, Newlands**	**March 25, 1889**	**SA v E**	**54**
9	Johannesburg, Old Wanderers	March 2, 1896	SA v E	22
	Now the site of Johannesburg Railway Station.			
10	Nottingham, Trent Bridge	June 1, 1899	E v A	61
11	**Leeds, Headingley**	**June 29, 1899**	**E v A**	**75**
12	**Birmingham, Edgbaston**	**May 29, 1902**	**E v A**	**49**
13	Sheffield, Bramall Lane	July 3, 1902	E v A	1
	Sheffield United Football Club have built a stand over the cricket pitch.			
14	Durban, Lord's	January 21, 1910	SA v E	4
	Ground destroyed and built on.			
15	**Durban, Kingsmead**	**January 18, 1923**	**SA v E**	**42**
16	Brisbane, Exhibition Ground	November 30, 1928	A v E	2
	No longer used for cricket.			
17	Christchurch, Lancaster Park	January 10, 1930	NZ v E	40
	Also known under sponsors' names.			
18	Bridgetown, Kensington Oval	January 11, 1930	WI v E	51

	City and Ground	*First Test Match*		*Tests*
19	**Wellington, Basin Reserve**	**January 24, 1930**	**NZ v E**	**59**
20	**Port-of-Spain, Queen's Park Oval**	**February 1, 1930**	**WI v E**	**60**
21	Auckland, Eden Park	February 14, 1930	NZ v E	49
22	Georgetown, Bourda	February 21, 1930	WI v E	30
23	**Kingston, Sabina Park**	**April 3, 1930**	**WI v E**	**49**
24	**Brisbane, Woolloongabba**	**November 27, 1931**	**A v SA**	**59**
25	Bombay, Gymkhana Ground	December 15, 1933	I v E	1
	No longer used for first-class cricket.			
26	**Calcutta (*now Kolkata*), Eden Gardens**	**January 5, 1934**	**I v E**	**40**
27	**Madras (*now Chennai*), Chepauk (Chidambaram Stadium)**	**February 10, 1934**	**I v E**	**32**
28	Delhi, Feroz Shah Kotla	November 10, 1948	I v WI	33
29	Bombay (*now Mumbai*), Brabourne Stadium	December 9, 1948	I v WI	18
	Rarely used for first-class cricket.			
30	Johannesburg, Ellis Park	December 27, 1948	SA v E	6
	Mainly a football and rugby stadium, no longer used for cricket.			
31	**Kanpur, Green Park (Modi Stadium)**	**January 12, 1952**	**I v E**	**22**
32	Lucknow, University Ground	October 25, 1952	I v P	1
	Ground destroyed, now partly under a river bed.			
33	Dacca (*now Dhaka*), Dacca (*now Bangabandhu*) Stadium	January 1, 1955	P v I	17
	Originally in East Pakistan, now Bangladesh, no longer used for cricket.			
34	Bahawalpur, Dring (*now Bahawal*) Stadium	January 15, 1955	P v I	1
	Still used for first-class cricket.			
35	Lahore, Lawrence Gardens (Bagh-e-Jinnah)	January 29, 1955	P v I	3
	Still used for club and occasional first-class matches.			
36	Peshawar, Services Ground	February 13, 1955	P v I	1
	Superseded by new stadium.			
37	Karachi, National Stadium	February 26, 1955	P v I	41
38	Dunedin, Carisbrook	March 11, 1955	NZ v E	10
39	Hyderabad, Fateh Maidan (Lal Bahadur Stadium)	November 19, 1955	I v NZ	3
40	Madras, Corporation Stadium	January 6, 1956	I v NZ	9
	Superseded by rebuilt Chepauk Stadium.			
41	**Johannesburg, Wanderers**	**December 24, 1956**	**SA v E**	**37**
42	Lahore, Gaddafi Stadium	November 21, 1959	P v A	40
43	Rawalpindi, Pindi Club Ground	March 27, 1965	P v NZ	1
	Superseded by new stadium.			
44	Nagpur, Vidarbha CA Ground	October 3, 1969	I v NZ	9
	Superseded by new stadium.			
45	**Perth, Western Australian CA Ground**	**December 11, 1970**	**A v E**	**43**
46	Hyderabad, Niaz Stadium	March 16, 1973	P v E	5
47	Bangalore, Karnataka State CA Ground (Chinnaswamy Stadium)	November 22, 1974	I v WI	21
48	**Bombay (*now Mumbai*), Wankhede Stadium**	**January 23, 1975**	**I v WI**	**25**
49	Faisalabad, Iqbal Stadium	October 16, 1978	P v I	24
50	Napier, McLean Park	February 16, 1979	NZ v P	10
51	Multan, Ibn-e-Qasim Bagh Stadium	December 30, 1980	P v WI	1
	Superseded by new stadium.			
52	St John's (Antigua), Recreation Ground	March 27, 1981	WI v E	22
53	Colombo, P. Saravanamuttu Stadium/ P. Sara Oval	February 17, 1982	SL v E	20
54	Kandy, Asgiriya Stadium	April 22, 1983	SL v A	21
	Superseded by new stadium at Pallekele.			
55	Jullundur, Burlton Park	September 24, 1983	I v P	1
56	Ahmedabad, Sardar Patel (Gujarat) Stadium	November 12, 1983	I v WI	12
57	**Colombo, Sinhalese Sports Club Ground**	**March 16, 1984**	**SL v NZ**	**40**
58	Colombo, Colombo Cricket Club Ground	March 24, 1984	SL v NZ	3
59	Sialkot, Jinnah Stadium	October 27, 1985	P v SL	4
60	Cuttack, Barabati Stadium	January 4, 1987	I v SL	2
61	Jaipur, Sawai Mansingh Stadium	February 21, 1987	I v P	1
62	**Hobart, Bellerive Oval**	**December 16, 1989**	**A v SL**	**13**
63	Chandigarh, Sector 16 Stadium	November 23, 1990	I v SL	1
	Superseded by Mohali ground.			

	City and Ground	*First Test Match*		*Tests*
64	**Hamilton, Seddon Park**	**February 22, 1991**	**NZ v SL**	**22**
	Also known under various sponsors' names.			
65	Gujranwala, Municipal Stadium	December 20, 1991	P v SL	[illegible]
66	Colombo, R. Premadasa (Khettarama) Stadium	August 28, 1992	SL v A	8
67	Moratuwa, Tyronne Fernando Stadium	September 8, 1992	SL v A	4
68	**Harare, Harare Sports Club**	**October 18, 1992**	**Z v I**	**34**
69	Bulawayo, Bulawayo Athletic Club	November 1, 1992	Z v NZ	[illegible]
	Superseded by Queens Sports Club ground.			
70	Karachi, Defence Stadium	December 1, 1993	P v Z	[illegible]
71	Rawalpindi, Rawalpindi Cricket Stadium	December 9, 1993	P v Z	8
72	Lucknow, K. D. "Babu" Singh Stadium	January 18, 1994	I v SL	[illegible]
73	**Bulawayo, Queens Sports Club**	**October 20, 1994**	**Z v SL**	**21**
74	**Mohali, Punjab Cricket Association Stadium**	**December 10, 1994**	**I v WI**	**13**
75	Peshawar, Arbab Niaz Stadium	September 8, 1995	P v SL	6
76	**Centurion (*ex Verwoerdburg*), Centurion Park**	**November 16, 1995**	**SA v E**	**22**
77	Sheikhupura, Municipal Stadium	October 17, 1996	P v Z	2
78	St Vincent, Arnos Vale	June 20, 1997	WI v SL	3
79	**Galle, International Stadium**	**June 3, 1998**	**SL v NZ**	**28**
80	Bloemfontein, Springbok Park	October 29, 1999	SA v Z	4
	Also known under various sponsors' names.			
81	Multan, Multan Cricket Stadium	August 29, 2001	P v B	5
82	Chittagong, Chittagong Stadium	November 15, 2001	B v Z	8
	Also known as M. A. Aziz Stadium.			
83	**Sharjah, Sharjah Cricket Association Stadium**	**January 31, 2002**	**P v WI**	**9**
84	St George's, Grenada, Queen's Park New Stadium	June 28, 2002	WI v NZ	3
85	East London, Buffalo Park	October 18, 2002	SA v B	1
86	Potchefstroom, North West Cricket Stadium	October 25, 2002	SA v B	[illegible]
	Now known under sponsor's name.			
87	**Chester-le-Street, Riverside Ground**	**June 5, 2003**	**E v Z**	**6**
	Also known under sponsor's name.			
88	**Gros Islet, St Lucia, Beausejour Stadium**	**June 20, 2003**	**WI v SL**	**5**
	Now known as Darren Sammy Stadium.			
89	Darwin, Marrara Cricket Ground	July 18, 2003	A v B	2
90	Cairns, Cazaly's Football Park	July 25, 2003	A v B	2
	Also known under sponsor's name.			
91	**Chittagong, Chittagong Divisional Stadium**	**February 28, 2006**	**B v SL**	**15**
	Also known as Bir Shrestha Shahid Ruhul Amin Stadium/Zohur Ahmed Chowdhury Stadium.			
92	Bogra, Shaheed Chandu Stadium	March 8, 2006	B v SL	1
93	Fatullah, Narayanganj Osmani Stadium	April 9, 2006	B v A	2
94	Basseterre, St Kitts, Warner Park	June 22, 2006	WI v I	3
95	**Mirpur (Dhaka), Shere Bangla Natl Stadium**	**May 25, 2007**	**B v I**	**15**
96	Dunedin, University Oval	January 4, 2008	NZ v B	7
97	Providence Stadium, Guyana	March 22, 2008	WI v SL	2
98	**North Sound, Antigua, Sir Vivian Richards Stadium**	**May 30, 2008**	**WI v A**	**5**
99	Nagpur, Vidarbha CA Stadium, Jamtha	November 6, 2008	I v A	5
100	Cardiff, Sophia Gardens	July 8, 2009	E v A	3
	Now known under sponsor's name.			
101	Hyderabad, Rajiv Gandhi Intl Stadium	November 12, 2010	I v NZ	3
102	**Dubai, Dubai Sports City Stadium**	**November 12, 2010**	**P v SA**	**10**
103	**Abu Dhabi, Sheikh Zayed Stadium**	**November 20, 2010**	**P v SA**	**9**
104	**Pallekele, Muttiah Muralitharan Stadium**	**December 1, 2010**	**SL v WI**	**5**
105	Southampton, Rose Bowl	June 16, 2011	E v SL	2
106	Roseau, Dominica, Windsor Park	July 6, 2011	WI v I	4
107	Khulna, Khulna Division Stadium	November 21, 2012	B v WI	3
	Also known as Bir Shrestha Shahid Flight Lt Motiur Rahman/Shaikh Abu Naser Stadium.			
108	**Christchurch, Hagley Oval**	**December 26, 2014**	**NZ v SL**	**4**
109	**Indore, Maharani Usharaje Trust Ground**	**October 8, 2016**	**I v NZ**	**1**
110	**Rajkot, Saurashtra CA Stadium**	**November 9, 2016**	**I v E**	**1**
111	**Visakhapatnam, Andhra CA-Visakhapatnam DCA Stadium**	**November 17, 2016**	**I v E**	**1**

Bold type denotes grounds used for Test cricket since January 1, 2016.

ONE-DAY INTERNATIONAL RECORDS

Matches in this section do not have first-class status.

This section covers one-day international cricket to December 31, 2016. Bold type denotes performances since January 1, 2016, or, in career figures, players who have appeared in one-day internationals since that date.

SUMMARY OF ONE-DAY INTERNATIONALS

1970-71 to December 31, 2016

			Won by															
	Opponents	*Matches*	*E*	*A*	*SA*	*WI*	*NZ*	*I*	*P*	*SL*	*Z*	*B*	*Ass*	*Asia*	*Wld*	*Afr*	*Tied*	*NR*
England	Australia	**136**	51	80	–	–	–	–	–	–	–	–	–	–	–	–	2	3
	South Africa	**56**	24	–	28	–	–	–	–	–	–	–	–	–	–	–	1	3
	West Indies	**88**	42	–	–	42	–	–	–	–	–	–	–	–	–	–	–	4
	New Zealand	**83**	36	–	–	–	41	–	–	–	–	–	–	–	–	–	2	4
	India	**93**	38	–	–	–	–	50	–	–	–	–	–	–	–	–	2	3
	Pakistan	**81**	49	–	–	–	–	–	30	–	–	–	–	–	–	–	–	2
	Sri Lanka	**69**	33	–	–	–	–	–	–	34	–	–	–	–	–	–	1	1
	Zimbabwe	**30**	21	–	–	–	–	–	–	–	8	–	–	–	–	–	–	1
	Bangladesh	**19**	15	–	–	–	–	–	–	–	–	4	–	–	–	–	–	–
	Associates	**22**	19	–	–	–	–	–	–	–	–	–	1	–	–	–	–	2
Australia	South Africa	**96**	–	47	45	–	–	–	–	–	–	–	–	–	–	–	3	1
	West Indies	**139**	–	73	–	60	–	–	–	–	–	–	–	–	–	–	3	3
	New Zealand	**133**	–	90	–	–	37	–	–	–	–	–	–	–	–	–	–	6
	India	**123**	–	72	–	–	–	41	–	–	–	–	–	–	–	–	–	10
	Pakistan	**93**	–	58	–	–	–	–	31	–	–	–	–	–	–	–	1	3
	Sri Lanka	**96**	–	60	–	–	–	–	–	32	–	–	–	–	–	–	–	4
	Zimbabwe	**30**	–	27	–	–	–	–	–	–	2	–	–	–	–	–	–	1
	Bangladesh	**19**	–	18	–	–	–	–	–	–	–	1	–	–	–	–	–	–
	Associates	**23**	–	22	–	–	–	–	–	–	–	–	0	–	–	–	–	1
	ICC World XI	**3**	–	3	–	–	–	–	–	–	–	–	–	–	0	–	–	–
South Africa	West Indies	**61**	–	–	44	15	–	–	–	–	–	–	–	–	–	–	1	1
	New Zealand	**65**	–	–	38	–	22	–	–	–	–	–	–	–	–	–	–	5
	India	**76**	–	–	45	–	–	28	–	–	–	–	–	–	–	–	–	3
	Pakistan	**72**	–	–	47	–	–	–	24	–	–	–	–	–	–	–	–	1
	Sri Lanka	**60**	–	–	29	–	–	–	–	29	–	–	–	–	–	–	1	1
	Zimbabwe	**38**	–	–	35	–	–	–	–	–	2	–	–	–	–	–	–	1
	Bangladesh	**17**	–	–	14	–	–	–	–	–	–	3	–	–	–	–	–	–
	Associates	**23**	–	–	23	–	–	–	–	–	–	–	0	–	–	–	–	–
West Indies	New Zealand	**61**	–	–	–	30	24	–	–	–	–	–	–	–	–	–	–	7
	India	**116**	–	–	–	60	–	53	–	–	–	–	–	–	–	–	1	2
	Pakistan	**130**	–	–	–	69	–	–	58	–	–	–	–	–	–	–	3	–
	Sri Lanka	**56**	–	–	–	28	–	–	–	25	–	–	–	–	–	–	–	3
	Zimbabwe	**47**	–	–	–	35	–	–	–	–	10	–	–	–	–	–	1	1
	Bangladesh	**28**	–	–	–	19	–	–	–	–	–	7	–	–	–	–	–	2
	Associates	**22**	–	–	–	19	–	–	–	–	–	–	2	–	–	–	–	1
New Zealand	India	**98**	–	–	–	–	43	49	–	–	–	–	–	–	–	–	1	5
	Pakistan	**98**	–	–	–	–	42	–	53	–	–	–	–	–	–	–	1	2
	Sri Lanka	**95**	–	–	–	–	45	–	–	41	–	–	–	–	–	–	1	8
	Zimbabwe	**38**	–	–	–	–	27	–	–	–	9	–	–	–	–	–	1	1
	Bangladesh	**28**	–	–	–	–	20	–	–	–	–	8	–	–	–	–	–	–
	Associates	**15**	–	–	–	–	15	–	–	–	–	–	0	–	–	–	–	–
India	Pakistan	**127**	–	–	–	–	–	51	72	–	–	–	–	–	–	–	–	4
	Sri Lanka	**149**	–	–	–	–	–	83	–	54	–	–	–	–	–	–	1	11
	Zimbabwe	**63**	–	–	–	–	–	51	–	–	10	–	–	–	–	–	2	–
	Bangladesh	**32**	–	–	–	–	–	26	–	–	–	5	–	–	–	–	–	1
	Associates	**27**	–	–	–	–	–	25	–	–	–	–	2	–	–	–	–	–
Pakistan	Sri Lanka	**147**	–	–	–	–	–	–	84	58	–	–	–	–	–	–	1	4
	Zimbabwe	**54**	–	–	–	–	–	–	47	–	4	–	–	–	–	–	1	2
	Bangladesh	**35**	–	–	–	–	–	–	31	–	–	4	–	–	–	–	–	–
	Associates	**29**	–	–	–	–	–	–	27	–	–	–	1	–	–	–	1	–
Sri Lanka	Zimbabwe	**50**	–	–	–	–	–	–	–	41	7	–	–	–	–	–	–	2
	Bangladesh	**38**	–	–	–	–	–	–	–	33	–	4	–	–	–	–	–	1
	Associates	**22**	–	–	–	–	–	–	–	21	–	–	1	–	–	–	–	–

	Opponents	Matches	E	A	SA	WI	NZ	I	P	SL	Z	B	Ass	Asia	Wld	Afr	Tied	NR
										Won by								
Zimbabwe	Bangladesh	**67**	–	–	–	–	–	–	–	–	28	39	–	–	–	–	–	[illegible]
	Associates	**62**	–	–	–	–	–	–	–	–	43	–	16	–	–	–	1	[illegible]
Bangladesh	Associates	**38**	–	–	–	–	–	–	–	–	–	26	12	–	–	–	–	[illegible]
Associates	Associates	**193**	–	–	–	–	–	–	–	–	–	–	183	–	–	–	1	[illegible]
Asian CC XI	ICC World XI	**1**	–	–	–	–	–	–	–	–	–	–	–	0	1	–	–	[illegible]
	African XI	**6**	–	–	–	–	–	–	–	–	–	–	–	4	–	1	–	[illegible]
		3,816	328	550	348	377	316	457	457	368	123	101	218	4	1	1	34	[illegible]

Associate and Affiliate Members of ICC who have played one-day internationals are Afghanistan, Bermuda, Canada, East Africa, Hong Kong, Ireland, Kenya, Namibia, Netherlands, Papua New Guinea, Scotland, United Arab Emirates and USA. Sri Lanka, Zimbabwe and Bangladesh played one-day internationals before gaining Test status; these are not counted as Associate results.

RESULTS SUMMARY OF ONE-DAY INTERNATIONALS

1970-71 to December 31, 2016 (3,816 matches)

	Matches	Won	Lost	Tied	No Result	% Won (excl. NR
Australia	891	550	300	9	32	64.55
South Africa	564	348	194	6	16	64.05
Pakistan	866	457	383	8	18	54.36
India	904	457	401	7	39	53.23
West Indies	748	377	338	9	24	52.69
England	677	328	318	8	23	50.76
Sri Lanka	782	368	374	5	35	49.59
New Zealand	714	316	354	6	38	47.18
Bangladesh	321	101	216	–	4	31.86
Zimbabwe	479	123	339	6	11	26.92
Asian Cricket Council XI	7	4	2	–	1	66.66
Papua New Guinea	5	3	2	–	–	60.00
Afghanistan	70	35	34	–	1	50.72
Ireland	110	47	54	3	6	46.63
Netherlands	76	28	44	1	3	39.04
Scotland	87	29	52	–	6	35.80
Hong Kong	16	5	10	–	1	33.33
Kenya	154	42	107	–	5	28.18
ICC World XI	4	1	3	–	–	25.00
Canada	77	17	58	–	2	22.66
Bermuda	35	7	28	–	–	20.00
African XI	6	1	4	–	1	20.00
United Arab Emirates	28	5	23	–	–	17.85
USA	2	–	2	–	–	0.00
East Africa	3	–	3	–	–	0.00
Namibia	6	–	6	–	–	0.00

Matches abandoned without a ball bowled are not included except (from 2004) where the toss took place, in accordance with an ICC ruling. Such matches, like those called off after play began, are now counted as official internationals in their own right, even when replayed on another day. In the percentages of matches won, ties are counted as half a win.

BATTING RECORDS

HIGHEST INDIVIDUAL INNINGS

264	R. G. Sharma	India v Sri Lanka at Kolkata	2014-15
237*	M. J. Guptill	New Zealand v West Indies at Wellington	2014-15
219	V. Sehwag	India v West Indies at Indore	2011-12
215	C. H. Gayle	West Indies v Zimbabwe at Canberra	2014-15

09	R. G. Sharma	India v Australia at Bangalore	2013-14
00*	S. R. Tendulkar	India v South Africa at Gwalior	2009-10
94*	C. K. Coventry	Zimbabwe v Bangladesh at Bulawayo	2009
94	Saeed Anwar	Pakistan v India at Chennai	1997-97
39*	I. V. A. Richards	West Indies v England at Manchester	1984
39*	M. J. Guptill	New Zealand v England at Southampton	2013
89	S. T. Jayasuriya	Sri Lanka v India at Sharjah	2000-01
88*	G. Kirsten	South Africa v UAE at Rawalpindi	1995-96
36*	S. R. Tendulkar	India v New Zealand at Hyderabad	1999-2000
35*	S. R. Watson	Australia v Bangladesh at Mirpur	2010-11
83*	M. S. Dhoni	India v Sri Lanka at Jaipur	2005-06
83	S. C. Ganguly	India v Sri Lanka at Taunton	1999
83	V. Kohli	India v Pakistan at Mirpur	2011-12
81*	M. L. Hayden	Australia v New Zealand at Hamilton	2006-07
81	I. V. A. Richards	West Indies v Sri Lanka at Karachi	1987-88
78*	H. Masakadza	Zimbabwe v Kenya at Harare	2009-10
78	D. A. Warner	Australia v Afghanistan at Perth	2014-15
78	**Q. de Kock**	**South Africa v Australia at Centurion**	**2016-17**
77	P. R. Stirling	Ireland v Canada at Toronto	2010
75*	Kapil Dev	India v Zimbabwe at Tunbridge Wells	1983
75	H. H. Gibbs	South Africa v Australia at Johannesburg	2005-06
75	S. R. Tendulkar	India v Australia at Hyderabad	2009-10
75	V. Sehwag	India v Bangladesh at Mirpur	2010-11
75	C. S. MacLeod	Scotland v Canada at Christchurch	2013-14

he highest individual scores for other Test countries are:

71	**A. D. Hales**	**England v Pakistan at Nottingham**	**2016**
54	Tamim Iqbal	Bangladesh v Zimbabwe at Bulawayo	2009

MOST HUNDREDS

. R. Tendulkar (I)	49	H. H. Gibbs (SA)	21	Mohammad Yousuf (P/As)	15
. T. Ponting (A/World)	30	Saeed Anwar (P)	20	V. Sehwag (I/Wld/Asia)	15
. T. Jayasuriya (SL/Asia)	28	D. P. M. D. Jayawardene (SL/Asia)	19	**L. R. P. L. Taylor (NZ)**	**15**
. Kohli (I)	**26**	B. C. Lara (WI/World)	19		
. C. Sangakkara (SL)	25	M. E. Waugh (A)	18	*Most hundreds for other Test countries:*	
. B. de Villiers (SA)	**24**	D. L. Haynes (WI)	17	M. E. Trescothick (E)	12
. M. Amla (SA)	**23**	J. H. Kallis (SA/Wld/Af)	17	**B. R. M. Taylor (Z)**	**8**
. M. Dilshan (SL)	**22**	N. J. Astle (NZ)	16	**Tamim Iqbal (B)**	**7**
. C. Ganguly (I/Asia)	22	A. C. Gilchrist (A/World)	16		
. H. Gayle (WI/World)	22				

onting's total includes one for the World XI, the only hundred for a combined team.

MOST RUNS

		M	*I*	*NO*	*R*	*HS*	*100*	*Avge*
1	S. R. Tendulkar (India)	463	452	41	18,426	200*	49	44.83
2	K. C. Sangakkara (SL/Asia/World)	404	380	41	14,234	169	25	41.98
3	R. T. Ponting (Australia/World)	375	365	39	13,704	164	30	42.03
4	S. T. Jayasuriya (Sri Lanka/Asia)	445	433	18	13,430	189	28	32.36
5	D. P. M. D. Jayawardene (SL/Asia)	448	418	39	12,650	144	19	33.37
6	Inzamam-ul-Haq (Pakistan/Asia)	378	350	53	11,739	137*	10	39.52
7	J. H. Kallis (S. Africa/World/Africa)	328	314	53	11,579	139	17	44.36
8	S. C. Ganguly (India/Asia)	311	300	23	11,363	183	22	41.02
9	R. Dravid (India/World/Asia)	344	318	40	10,889	153	12	39.16
10	B. C. Lara (West Indies/World)	299	289	32	10,405	169	19	40.48
11	**T. M. Dilshan (Sri Lanka)**	**330**	**303**	**41**	**10,290**	**161***	**22**	**39.27**

The leading aggregates for players who have appeared for other Test countries are:

	M	*I*	*NO*	*R*	*HS*	*100*	*Avg*
S. P. Fleming (New Zealand/World)	280	269	21	8,037	134*	8	32.4
A. Flower (Zimbabwe).	213	208	16	6,786	145	4	35.3
I. R. Bell (England)	161	157	14	5,416	141	4	37.8
Tamim Iqbal (Bangladesh)	**162**	**161**	**3**	**5,120**	**154**	**7**	**32.4**

Excluding runs for combined teams, the record aggregate for Sri Lanka is 13,975 in 397 matches by K. C. Sangakkara; for Australia, 13,589 in 374 matches by R. T. Ponting; for Pakistan, 11,701 in 375 matches by Inzamam-ul-Haq; for South Africa, 11,550 in 323 matches by J. H. Kallis; for West Indies, 10,348 in 295 matches by B. C. Lara; and for New Zealand, 8,007 in 279 matches by S. P. Fleming.

BEST CAREER STRIKE-RATES BY BATSMEN

(Runs per 100 balls. Qualification: 1,000 runs)

SR		*Position*	*M*	*I*	*R*	*Avg*
125.74	**G. J. Maxwell (A)**	**5/6**	**67**	**61**	**1,763**	**33.2**
120.29	**J. C. Buttler (E)**.	**6/7**	**81**	**69**	**2,217**	**38.8**
117.00	Shahid Afridi (P/World/Asia).	2/7	398	369	8,064	23.5
115.07	**L. Ronchi (NZ)**.	**7**	**76**	**59**	**1,206**	**23.6**
111.02	**C. J. Anderson (NZ)**	**6**	**44**	**39**	**1,047**	**29.9**
108.25	**N. L. T. C. Perera (SL)**	**7/8**	**114**	**85**	**1,233**	**17.1**
104.33	V. Sehwag (I/World/Asia)	1/2	251	245	8,273	35.0
103.74	**J. J. Roy (E)**	**1**	**32**	**31**	**1,109**	**38.2**
102.84	**D. A. Miller (SA)**	**5/6**	**87**	**78**	**2,026**	**36.8**
100.05	D. J. G. Sammy (WI)	7/8	126	105	1,871	24.9

Position means a batsman's most usual position(s) in the batting order.

FASTEST ONE-DAY INTERNATIONAL FIFTIES

Balls			
16	A. B. de Villiers.	South Africa v West Indies at Johannesburg	2014-15
17	S. T. Jayasuriya	Sri Lanka v Pakistan at Singapore	1995-96
17	M. D. K. J. Perera	Sri Lanka v Pakistan at Pallekele	2015
17	M. J. Guptill	New Zealand v Sri Lanka at Christchurch	2015-16
18	S. P. O'Donnell	Australia v Sri Lanka at Sharjah.	1989-90
18	Shahid Afridi	Pakistan v Sri Lanka at Nairobi	1996-97
18	Shahid Afridi	Pakistan v Netherlands at Colombo (SSC).	2002
18	G. J. Maxwell	Australia v India at Bangalore	2013-14
18	Shahid Afridi	Pakistan v Bangladesh at Mirpur	2013-14
18	B. B. McCullum	New Zealand v England at Wellington.	2014-15
18	**A. J. Finch**	**Australia v Sri Lanka at Dambulla**	**2016**

FASTEST ONE-DAY INTERNATIONAL HUNDREDS

Balls			
31	A. B. de Villiers	South Africa v West Indies at Johannesburg	2014-15
36	C. J. Anderson.	New Zealand v West Indies at Queenstown.	2013-14
37	Shahid Afridi.	Pakistan v Sri Lanka at Nairobi	1996-97
44	M. V. Boucher.	South Africa v Zimbabwe at Potchefstroom	2006-07
45	B. C. Lara	West Indies v Bangladesh at Dhaka.	1999-2000
45	Shahid Afridi.	Pakistan v India at Kanpur.	2004-05
46	J. D. Ryder	New Zealand v West Indies at Queenstown.	2013-14
46	J. C. Buttler	England v Pakistan at Dubai	2015-16
48	S. T. Jayasuriya	Sri Lanka v Pakistan at Singapore	1995-96

HIGHEST PARTNERSHIP FOR EACH WICKET

86	for 1st	W. U. Tharanga/S. T. Jayasuriya	SL v E	Leeds	2006
72	for 2nd	C. H. Gayle/M. N. Samuels	WI v Z	Canberra	2014-15
58	for 3rd	D. M. Bravo/D. Ramdin	WI v B	Basseterre	2014-15
75*	for 4th	M. Azharuddin/A. Jadeja	I v Z	Cuttack	1997-98
56*	for 5th	D. A. Miller/J-P. Duminy	SA v Z	Hamilton	2014-15
67*	for 6th	G. D. Elliott/L. Ronchi	NZ v SL	Dunedin	2014-15
77	for 7th	J. C. Buttler/A. U. Rashid	E v NZ	Birmingham	2015
38*	for 8th	J. M. Kemp/A. J. Hall	SA v I	Cape Town	2006-07
32	for 9th	A. D. Mathews/S. L. Malinga	SL v A	Melbourne	2010-11
06*	for 10th	I. V. A. Richards/M. A. Holding	WI v E	Manchester	1984

BOWLING RECORDS

BEST BOWLING ANALYSES

8-19	W. P. U. J. C. Vaas	Sri Lanka v Zimbabwe at Colombo (SSC)	2001-02
7-12	Shahid Afridi	Pakistan v West Indies at Providence	2013
7-15	G. D. McGrath	Australia v Namibia at Potchefstroom	2002-03
7-20	A. J. Bichel	Australia v England at Port Elizabeth	2002-03
7-30	M. Muralitharan	Sri Lanka v India at Sharjah	2000-01
7-33	T. G. Southee	New Zealand v England at Wellington	2014-15
7-36	Waqar Younis	Pakistan v England at Leeds	2001
7-37	Aqib Javed	Pakistan v India at Sharjah	1991-92
7-45	**Imran Tahir**	**South Africa v West Indies at Basseterre**	**2016**
7-51	W. W. Davis	West Indies v Australia at Leeds	1983

The best analyses for other Test countries are:

6-4	S. T. R. Binny	India v Bangladesh at Mirpur	2014
6-19	H. K. Olonga	Zimbabwe v England at Cape Town	1999-2000
6-26	Mashrafe bin Mortaza	Bangladesh v Kenya at Nairobi	2006
6-26	Rubel Hossain	Bangladesh v New Zealand at Mirpur	2013-14
6-31	P. D. Collingwood	England v Bangladesh at Nottingham	2005

HAT-TRICKS

Four Wickets in Four Balls

S. L. Malinga — Sri Lanka v South Africa at Providence — 2006-07

Four Wickets in Five Balls

Saqlain Mushtaq — Pakistan v Zimbabwe at Peshawar — 1996-97

Most Hat-Tricks

S. L. Malinga	3	W. P. U. J. C. Vaas†	2
Saqlain Mushtaq	2	Wasim Akram	2

† *W. P. U. J. C. Vaas took the second of his two hat-tricks, for Sri Lanka v Bangladesh at Pietermaritzburg in 2002-03, with the first three balls of the match.*

Hat-Tricks

There have been **40** hat-tricks in one-day internationals, including the above. Those since 2014-15:

P. Utseya	Zimbabwe v South Africa at Harare	2014-15
Taijul Islam†	Bangladesh v Zimbabwe at Mirpur	2014-15
J-P. Duminy	South Africa v Sri Lanka at Sydney	2014-15

S. T. Finn	England v Australia at Melbourne	2014-15
K. Rabada†	South Africa v Bangladesh at Mirpur	2015
J. P. Faulkner	**Australia v Sri Lanka at Colombo (RPS)**	**2016**

† *On debut.*

MOST WICKETS

		M	*Balls*	*R*	*W*	*BB*	*4I*	*Avge*
1	M. Muralitharan (SL/World/Asia)	350	18,811	12,326	534	7-30	25	23.08
2	Wasim Akram (Pakistan)	356	18,186	11,812	502	5-15	23	23.52
3	Waqar Younis (Pakistan)	262	12,698	9,919	416	7-36	27	23.84
4	W. P. U. J. C. Vaas (SL/Asia)	322	15,775	11,014	400	8-19	13	27.53
5	Shahid Afridi (Pakistan/World/Asia)	398	17,670	13,635	395	7-12	13	34.51
6	S. M. Pollock (SA/World/Africa)	303	15,712	9,631	393	6-35	17	24.50
7	G. D. McGrath (Australia/World)	250	12,970	8,391	381	7-15	16	22.02
8	B. Lee (Australia)	221	11,185	8,877	380	5-22	23	23.36
9	A. Kumble (India/Asia)	271	14,496	10,412	337	6-12	10	30.89
10	S. T. Jayasuriya (Sri Lanka/Asia)	445	14,874	11,871	323	6-29	12	36.75
11	J. Srinath (India)	229	11,935	8,847	315	5-23	10	28.08
12	D. L. Vettori (New Zealand/World)	295	14,060	9,674	305	5-7	10	31.71
13	S. K. Warne (Australia/World)	194	10,642	7,541	293	5-33	13	25.73
14	S. L. Malinga (Sri Lanka)	191	9,207	8,082	291	6-38	16	27.77
15	Saqlain Mushtaq (Pakistan)	169	8,770	6,275	288	5-20	17	21.78
	A. B. Agarkar (India)	191	9,484	8,021	288	6-42	12	27.85
17	Zaheer Khan (India/Asia)	200	10,097	8,301	282	5-42	8	29.43
18	J. H. Kallis (S. Africa/World/Africa)	328	10,750	8,680	273	5-30	4	31.79
19	A. A. Donald (South Africa)	164	8,561	5,926	272	6-23	13	21.78
20	J. M. Anderson (England)	194	9,584	7,861	269	5-23	13	29.22
	Abdul Razzaq (Pakistan/Asia)	265	10,941	8,564	269	6-35	11	31.83
	Harbhajan Singh (India/Asia)	236	12,479	8,973	269	5-31	5	33.35
23	M. Ntini (South Africa/World)	173	8,687	6,559	266	6-22	12	24.65
24	Kapil Dev (India)	225	11,202	6,945	253	5-43	4	27.45

The leading aggregates for players who have appeared for other Test countries are:

H. H. Streak (Zimbabwe)	189	9,468	7,129	239	5-32	8	29.82
C. A. Walsh (West Indies)	205	10,882	6,918	227	5-1	7	30.47
Shakib Al Hasan (Bangladesh)	**166**	**8,497**	**6,176**	**220**	**5-47**	**8**	**28.07**

Excluding wickets taken for combined teams, the record for Sri Lanka is 523 in 343 matches by M. Muralitharan; for South Africa, 387 in 294 matches by S. M. Pollock; for Australia, 380 in 249 matches by G. D. McGrath; for India, 334 in 269 matches by A. Kumble; for New Zealand, 297 in 291 matches by D. L. Vettori; and for Zimbabwe, 237 in 187 matches by H. H. Streak.

BEST CAREER STRIKE-RATES BY BOWLERS

(Balls per wicket. Qualification: 1,500 balls)

SR		*M*	*W*
24.73	**M. A. Starc (A)**	**59**	**116**
26.46	**M. J. Henry (NZ)**	**30**	**58**
26.95	Mohammed Shami (I)	47	87
27.10	**Hamid Hassan (Afg)**	**32**	**56**
27.22	S. W. Tait (A)	35	62
27.32	B. A. W. Mendis (SL)	87	152
28.48	**M. J. McClenaghan (NZ)**	**48**	**82**
28.72	R. N. ten Doeschate (Netherlands)	33	55
29.21	S. E. Bond (NZ)	82	147
29.38	G. I. Allott (NZ)	31	52
29.43	B. Lee (A)	221	380
29.58	L. S. Pascoe (A)	29	53
29.76	**M. Morkel (SA/Africa)**	**108**	**181**
29.95	**A. Mishra (I)**	**36**	**64**

BEST CAREER ECONOMY-RATES

(Runs conceded per six balls. Qualification: 50 wickets)

ER		*M*	*W*
3.09	J. Garner (WI)	98	146
3.28	R. G. D. Willis (E)	64	80
3.30	R. J. Hadlee (NZ)	115	158
3.32	M. A. Holding (WI)	102	142
3.40	A. M. E. Roberts (WI)	56	87
3.48	C. E. L. Ambrose (WI)	176	225

WICKETKEEPING AND FIELDING RECORDS

MOST DISMISSALS IN AN INNINGS

(all ct)	A. C. Gilchrist	Australia v South Africa at Cape Town	1999-2000
(all ct)	A. J. Stewart	England v Zimbabwe at Manchester	2000
(5ct, 1st)	R. D. Jacobs	West Indies v Sri Lanka at Colombo (RPS)	2001-02
(5ct, 1st)	A. C. Gilchrist	Australia v England at Sydney	2002-03
(all ct)	A. C. Gilchrist	Australia v Namibia at Potchefstroom	2002-03
(all ct)	A. C. Gilchrist	Australia v Sri Lanka at Colombo (RPS)	2003-04
(all ct)	M. V. Boucher	South Africa v Pakistan at Cape Town	2006-07
(5ct, 1st)	M. S. Dhoni	India v England at Leeds	2007
(all ct)	A. C. Gilchrist	Australia v India at Vadodara	2007-08
(5ct, 1st)	A. C. Gilchrist	Australia v India at Sydney	2007-08
(all ct)	M. J. Prior	England v South Africa at Nottingham	2008
(all ct)	J. C. Buttler	England v South Africa at The Oval	2013
(all ct)	M. H. Cross	Scotland v Canada at Christchurch	2013-14
(5ct, 1st)	Q. de Kock	S. Africa v N. Zealand at Mount Maunganui	2014-15
(all ct)	Sarfraz Ahmed	Pakistan v South Africa at Auckland	2014-15

MOST DISMISSALS

			M	*Ct*	*St*
1	482	K. C. Sangakkara (Sri Lanka/World/Asia)	360	384	98
2	472	A. C. Gilchrist (Australia/World)	282	417	55
3	424	M. V. Boucher (South Africa/Africa)	294	402	22
4	**359**	**M. S. Dhoni (India/Asia)**	**283**	**267**	**92**
5	287	Moin Khan (Pakistan)	219	214	73
6	242	B. B. McCullum (New Zealand)	185	227	15
7	234	I. A. Healy (Australia)	168	195	39
8	220	Rashid Latif (Pakistan)	166	182	38
9	206	R. S. Kaluwitharana (Sri Lanka)	186	131	75
10	204	P. J. L. Dujon (West Indies)	169	183	21

The leading aggregates for players who have appeared for other Test countries are:

171	**Mushfiqur Rahim (Bangladesh)**	**154**	**132**	**39**
165	A. Flower (Zimbabwe)	186	133	32
163	A. J. Stewart (England)	138	148	15

Excluding dismissals for combined teams, the most for Sri Lanka is 473 (378ct, 95st) in 353 matches by K. C. Sangakkara; for Australia, 470 (416ct, 54st) in 281 matches by A. C. Gilchrist; for South Africa, 415 (394ct, 21st) in 289 matches by M. V. Boucher; and for India, ***353*** *(264ct, 89st) in 280 matches by* ***M. S. Dhoni****.*

K. C. Sangakkara's record excludes 19 catches taken in 44 one-day internationals when not keeping wicket; M. V. Boucher's excludes 1 in 1; B. B. McCullum's 35 in 75; R. S. Kaluwitharana's 1 in 3; A. Flower's 8 in 27; A. J. Stewart's 11 in 32; Mushfiqur Rahim's 2 in 11. A. C. Gilchrist played five one-day internationals without keeping wicket, but made no catches in those games. R. Dravid (India) made 210 dismissals (196ct, 14st) in 344 one-day internationals but only 86 (72ct, 14st) in 74 as wicketkeeper (including one where he took over during the match).

MOST CATCHES IN AN INNINGS IN THE FIELD

5	J. N. Rhodes	South Africa v West Indies at Bombay	1993-9

*There have been **35** instances of four catches in an innings.*

MOST CATCHES

Ct	*M*		*Ct*	*M*	
218	448	D. P. M. D. Jayawardene (SL/Asia)	127	273	A. R. Border (Australia)
160	375	R. T. Ponting (Australia/World)	127	398	Shahid Afridi (Pak/World/Asia)
156	334	M. Azharuddin (India)	*Most catches for other Test countries:*		
140	463	S. R. Tendulkar (India)	*Ct*	*M*	
133	280	S. P. Fleming (New Zealand/World)	120	227	C. L. Hooper (West Indies)
131	328	J. H. Kallis (SA/World/Africa)	108	197	P. D. Collingwood (England)
130	262	Younis Khan (Pakistan)	86	221	G. W. Flower (Zimbabwe)
130	350	M. Muralitharan (SL/World/Asia)	**53**	**169**	**Mashrafe bin Mortaza (Ban/As**

*Excluding catches taken for combined teams, the record aggregate for Sri Lanka is 213 in 44 matches by D. P. M. D. Jayawardene; for Australia, 158 in 374 by R. T. Ponting; for New Zealand 132 in 279 by S. P. Fleming; for South Africa, 131 in 323 by J. H. Kallis; and for Bangladesh, **52** i 167 by **Mashrafe bin Mortaza**.*

Younis Khan's record excludes five catches made in three one-day internationals as wicketkeeper

TEAM RECORDS

HIGHEST INNINGS TOTALS

444-3	**(50 overs)**	**England v Pakistan at Nottingham**	**2016**
443-9	(50 overs)	Sri Lanka v Netherlands at Amstelveen	2006
439-2	(50 overs)	South Africa v West Indies at Johannesburg	2014-15
438-4	(50 overs)	South Africa v India at Mumbai	2015-16
438-9	(49.5 overs)	South Africa v Australia at Johannesburg	2005-06
434-4	(50 overs)	Australia v South Africa at Johannesburg	2005-06
418-5	(50 overs)	South Africa v Zimbabwe at Potchefstroom	2006-07
418-5	(50 overs)	India v West Indies at Indore	2011-12
417-6	(50 overs)	Australia v Afghanistan at Perth	2014-15
414-7	(50 overs)	India v Sri Lanka at Rajkot	2009-10
413-5	(50 overs)	India v Bermuda at Port-of-Spain	2006-07
411-4	(50 overs)	South Africa v Ireland at Canberra	2014-15
411-8	(50 overs)	Sri Lanka v India at Rajkot	2009-10
408-5	(50 overs)	South Africa v West Indies at Sydney	2014-15
408-9	(50 overs)	England v New Zealand at Birmingham	2015
404-5	(50 overs)	India v Sri Lanka at Kolkata	2014-15
402-2	(50 overs)	New Zealand v Ireland at Aberdeen	2008
401-3	(50 overs)	India v South Africa at Gwalior	2009-10

The highest totals by other Test countries are:

385-7	(50 overs)	Pakistan v Bangladesh at Dambulla	2010
372-2	(50 overs)	West Indies v Zimbabwe at Canberra	2014-15
351-7	(50 overs)	Zimbabwe v Kenya at Mombasa	2008-09
329-6	(50 overs)	Bangladesh v Pakistan at Mirpur	2014-15

HIGHEST TOTALS BATTING SECOND

438-9	(49.5 overs)	South Africa v Australia at Johannesburg (*Won by 1 wicket*)	2005-06
411-8	(50 overs)	Sri Lanka v India at Rajkot (*Lost by 3 runs*)	2009-10
372-6	**(49.2 overs)**	**South Africa v Australia at Durban** (*Won by 4 wickets*)	**2016-17**
365-9	(45 overs)	England v New Zealand at The Oval (*Lost by 13 runs DLS*)	2015
362-1	(43.3 overs)	India v Australia at Jaipur (*Won by 9 wickets*)	2013-14
351-4	(49.3 overs)	India v Australia at Nagpur (*Won by 6 wickets*)	2013-14
350-3	(44 overs)	England v New Zealand at Nottingham (*Won by 7 wickets*)	2015
350-9	(49.3 overs)	New Zealand v Australia at Hamilton (*Won by 1 wicket*)	2006-07

HIGHEST MATCH AGGREGATES

72-13	(99.5 overs)	South Africa v Australia at Johannesburg	2005-06
25-15	(100 overs)	India v Sri Lanka at Rajkot	2009-10
63-14	(96 overs)	England v New Zealand at The Oval	2015
43-12	**(99.2 overs)**	**South Australia v Australia at Durban**	**2016-17**
30-9	(100 overs)	South Africa v West Indies at Johannesburg	2014-15
26-14	(95.1 overs)	New Zealand v India at Christchurch	2008-09
21-6	(93.3 overs)	India v Australia at Jaipur	2013-14
19-13	**(92.4 overs)**	**England v Pakistan at Nottingham**	**2016**

LOWEST INNINGS TOTALS

5	(18 overs)	Zimbabwe v Sri Lanka at Harare	2003-04
6	(18.4 overs)	Canada v Sri Lanka at Paarl	2002-03
8	(15.4 overs)	Zimbabwe v Sri Lanka at Colombo (SSC)	2001-02
3	(19.5 overs)	Pakistan v West Indies at Cape Town	1992-93
3	(20.1 overs)	Sri Lanka v South Africa at Paarl	2011-12
4	(24.5 overs)	Zimbabwe v Bangladesh at Chittagong	2009-10
5	(40.3 overs)	Canada v England at Manchester	1979
5	(14 overs)	Namibia v Australia at Potchefstroom	2002-03

he lowest totals by other Test countries are:

4	(26.3 overs)	India v Sri Lanka at Sharjah	2000-01
4	(23.2 overs)	West Indies v South Africa at Cape Town	2003-04
8	(18.5 overs)	Bangladesh v West Indies at Mirpur	2010-11
8	(17.4 overs)	Bangladesh v India at Mirpur	2014
4	(35.5 overs)	New Zealand v Pakistan at Sharjah	1985-86
9	(28 overs)	South Africa v Australia at Sydney	1993-94
0	(25.2 overs)	Australia v England at Birmingham	1977
0	(26.3 overs)	Australia v New Zealand at Adelaide	1985-86
6	(32.4 overs)	England v Australia at Manchester	2001

LARGEST VICTORIES

90 runs	New Zealand (402-2 in 50 overs) v Ireland (112 in 28.4 ov) at Aberdeen	2008
75 runs	Australia (417-6 in 50 overs) v Afghanistan (142 in 37.3 overs) at Perth	2014-15
72 runs	South Africa (399-6 in 50 overs) v Zimbabwe (127 in 29 overs) at Benoni	2010-11
58 runs	South Africa (301-8 in 50 overs) v Sri Lanka (43 in 20.1 overs) at Paarl	2011-12
57 runs	India (413-5 in 50 overs) v Bermuda (156 in 43.1 overs) at Port-of-Spain	2006-07
57 runs	South Africa (408-5 in 50 overs) v West Indies (151 in 33.1 overs) at Sydney	2014-15
56 runs	Australia (301-6 in 50 overs) v Namibia (45 in 14 overs) at Potchefstroom	2002-03
56 runs	India (374-4 in 50 overs) v Hong Kong (118 in 36.5 overs) at Karachi	2008
55 runs	**Pakistan (337-6 in 47 overs) v Ireland (82 in 23.4 overs) at Dublin**	**2016**

*There have been **50** instances of victory by ten wickets.*

TIED MATCHES

There have been **34** tied one-day internationals. Australia have tied nine matches; Bangladesh are he only Test country never to have tied. The most recent ties are:

ndia (338 in 49.5 overs) v England (338-8 in 50 overs) at Bangalore	2010-11
ndia (280-5 in 50 overs) v England (270-8 in 48.5 overs) at Lord's (D/L)	2011
ustralia (220 in 49.5 overs) v West Indies (220 in 49.4 overs) at St Vincent	2011-12
Sri Lanka (236-9 in 50 overs) v India (236-9 in 50 overs) at Adelaide	2011-12
South Africa (230-6 in 31 overs) v West Indies (190-6 in 26.1 overs) at Cardiff (D/L)	2013
reland (268-5 in 50 overs) v Netherlands (268-9 in 50 overs) at Amstelveen	2013
Pakistan (229-6 in 50 overs) v West Indies (229-9 in 50 overs) at Gros Islet	2013
Pakistan (266-5 in 47 overs) v Ireland (275-5 in 47 overs) at Dublin (D/L)	2013
New Zealand (314 in 50 overs) v India (314-9 in 50 overs) at Auckland	2013-14
Sri Lanka (286-9 in 50 overs) v England (286-8 in 50 overs) at Nottingham	**2016**
Zimbabwe (257 in 50 overs) v West Indies (257-8 in 50 overs) at Bulawayo	**2016-17**

OTHER RECORDS

MOST APPEARANCES

463	S. R. Tendulkar (I)	334	M. Azharuddin (I)
448	D. P. M. D. Jayawardene (SL/Asia)	**330**	**T. M. Dilshan (SL)**
445	S. T. Jayasuriya (SL/Asia)	328	J. H. Kallis (SA/World/Africa)
404	K. C. Sangakkara (SL/World/Asia)	325	S. R. Waugh (A)
398	Shahid Afridi (P/World/Asia)	322	W. P. U. J. C. Vaas (SL/Asia)
378	Inzamam-ul-Haq (P/Asia)	311	S. C. Ganguly (I/Asia)
375	R. T. Ponting (A/World)	308	P. A. de Silva (SL)
356	Wasim Akram (P)	303	S. M. Pollock (SA/World/Africa)
350	M. Muralitharan (SL/World/Asia)	300	T. M. Dilshan (SL)
344	R. Dravid (I/World/Asia)		

Excluding appearances for combined teams, the record for Sri Lanka is 441 by S. T. Jayasuriya; for Pakistan, 393 by Shahid Afridi; for Australia, 374 by R. T. Ponting; for South Africa, 323 by J. H. Kallis; for West Indies, 295 by B. C. Lara; for New Zealand, 291 by D. L. Vettori; for Zimbabwe, 221 by G. W. Flower; for England, 197 by P. D. Collingwood; and for Bangladesh, 177 by Mohammad Ashraful.

MOST MATCHES AS CAPTAIN

	P	*W*	*L*	*T*	*NR*
R. T. Ponting (A/World)	230	165	51	2	12
S. P. Fleming (NZ)	218	98	106	1	13
M. S. Dhoni (I)	**199**	**110**	**74**	**4**	**11**
A. Ranatunga (SL)	193	89	95	1	8
A. R. Border (A)	178	107	67	1	3
M. Azharuddin (I)	174	90	76	2	6
G. C. Smith (SA/Af)	150	92	51	1	6
S. C. Ganguly (I/Asia)	147	76	66	0	5
Imran Khan (P)	139	75	59	1	4
W. J. Cronje (SA)	138	99	35	1	3
D. P. M. D.	138	99	35	1	3
Jayawardene (SL/As)	129	71	49	1	8
B. C. Lara (WI)	125	59	59	1	7

WORLD CUP FINALS

1975	WEST INDIES (291-8) beat Australia (274) by 17 runs	Lord's
1979	WEST INDIES (286-9) beat England (194) by 92 runs	Lord's
1983	INDIA (183) beat West Indies (140) by 43 runs	Lord's
1987	AUSTRALIA (253-5) beat England (246-8) by seven runs	Calcutta
1992	PAKISTAN (249-6) beat England (227) by 22 runs	Melbourne
1996	SRI LANKA (245-3) beat Australia (241-7) by seven wickets	Lahore
1999	AUSTRALIA (133-2) beat Pakistan (132) by eight wickets	Lord's
2003	AUSTRALIA (359-2) beat India (234) by 125 runs	Johannesburg
2007	AUSTRALIA (281-4) beat Sri Lanka (215-8) by 53 runs (D/L method)	Bridgetown
2011	INDIA (277-4) beat Sri Lanka (274-6) by six wickets	Mumbai
2015	AUSTRALIA (186-3) beat New Zealand (183) by seven wickets	Melbourne

An expanded and regularly updated online version of the Records can be found at www.wisdenrecords.com

TWENTY20 INTERNATIONAL RECORDS

Matches in this section do not have first-class status.

his section covers Twenty20 international cricket to December 31, 2016. Bold type denotes rformances since January 1, 2016, or, in career figures, players who have appeared in Twenty20 ternationals since that date.

RESULTS SUMMARY OF TWENTY20 INTERNATIONALS

2004-05 to December 31, 2016 (573 matches)

	Matches	*Won*	*Lost*	*No Result*	*% Won (excl. NR)*
dia	78	47*	29	2	61.84
outh Africa	91	54	36	1	60.00
akistan	110	65*	45†	–	59.09
i Lanka	87	47*	39	1	54.65
ew Zealand	93	48†	43‡	2	52.74
est Indies	82	41†	38*	3	51.89
ngland	89	44*	41	4	51.76
ustralia	90	46	43†	1	51.68
angladesh	62	20	40	2	33.33
imbabwe	54	14*	40	–	25.92
fghanistan	51	32	19	–	62.74
etherlands	42	23	17	2	57.50
eland	54	24	24	6	50.00
apua New Guinea	6	3	3	–	50.00
ong Kong	21	9	12	–	42.85
cotland	40	15	22	3	40.54
enya	29	10	19	–	34.48
man	13	4	8	1	33.33
nited Arab Emirates	21	6	15	–	28.57
epal	11	3	8	–	27.27
anada	19	4	15*	–	21.05
ermuda	3	–	3	–	0.00

Includes one game settled by a tie-break. † *Includes two settled by a tie-break.*
Includes three settled by a tie-break. Ties were decided by bowling contests or one-over liminators.

latches abandoned without a ball bowled are not included except where the toss took place, when ey are shown as no result.

BATTING RECORDS

HUNDREDS

56	A. J. Finch	Australia v England at Southampton	2013
45*	**G. J. Maxwell**	**Australia v Sri Lanka at Pallekele**	**2016**
24*	**S. R. Watson**	**Australia v India at Sydney**	**2015-16**
23	B. B. McCullum	New Zealand v Bangladesh at Pallekele	2012-13
22	**Babar Hayat**	**Hong Kong v Oman at Fatullah**	**2015-16**
19	F. du Plessis	South Africa v West Indies at Johannesburg	2014-15
18*	**Mohammad Shahzad**	**Afghanistan v Zimbabwe at Sharjah**	**2015-16**
17*	R. E. Levi	South Africa v New Zealand at Hamilton	2011-12
17	C. H. Gayle	West Indies v South Africa at Johannesburg	2007-08
16*	B. B. McCullum	New Zealand v Australia at Christchurch	2009-10

116*	A. D. Hales	England v Sri Lanka at Chittagong	2013-1
114*	M. N. van Wyk	South Africa v West Indies at Durban	2014-1
111*	Ahmed Shehzad	Pakistan v Bangladesh at Mirpur	2013-1
110*	**K. L. Rahul**	**India v West Indies at Lauderhill**	**201**

MOST RUNS

		M	*I*	*NO*	*R*	*HS*	*100*	*Avge*	*SR*
1	B. B. McCullum (New Zealand)	71	70	10	2,140	123	2	35.66	136.2
2	**T. M. Dilshan (Sri Lanka)**	**80**	**79**	**12**	**1,889**	**104***	**1**	**28.19**	**120.4**
3	**M. J. Guptill (New Zealand)**	**61**	**59**	**7**	**1,806**	**101***	**1**	**34.73**	**131.4**
4	**Umar Akmal (Pakistan)**	**82**	**77**	**14**	**1,690**	**94**	**0**	**26.82**	**122.9**
5	**D. A. Warner (Australia)**	**63**	**63**	**3**	**1,686**	**90***	**0**	**28.10**	**139.5**
6	**V. Kohli (India)**	**45**	**41**	**12**	**1,657**	**90***	**0**	**57.13**	**135.4**
7	**J-P. Duminy (South Africa)**	**70**	**64**	**21**	**1,654**	**96***	**0**	**38.46**	**123.6**
8	**Mohammad Hafeez (Pakistan)**	**77**	**75**	**4**	**1,614**	**86**	**0**	**22.73**	**115.0**
9	**Shoaib Malik (Pakistan)**	**82**	**76**	**20**	**1,548**	**75**	**0**	**27.64**	**113.5**
10	**C. H. Gayle (West Indies)**	**50**	**47**	**4**	**1,519**	**117**	**2**	**35.32**	**145.4**
11	D. P. M. D. Jayawardene (Sri Lanka)	55	55	8	1,493	100	1	31.76	133.1
12	**Mohammad Shahzad (Afghanistan)**	**51**	**51**	**2**	**1,480**	**118***	**1**	**30.20**	**137.9**
13	**S. R. Watson (Australia)**	**58**	**56**	**6**	**1,462**	**124***	**1**	**29.24**	**145.3**
14	**E. J. G. Morgan (England)**	**64**	**62**	**12**	**1,460**	**85***	**0**	**29.20**	**130.9**
15	**H. Masakadza (Zimbabwe)**	**50**	**50**	**2**	**1,413**	**93***	**0**	**29.43**	**119.7**
16	**Shahid Afridi (Pakistan)**	**98**	**90**	**12**	**1,405**	**54***	**0**	**18.01**	**150.7**
17	K. C. Sangakkara (Sri Lanka)	56	53	9	1,382	78	0	31.40	119.5
18	**A. B. de Villiers (South Africa)**	**71**	**68**	**10**	**1,368**	**79***	**0**	**23.58**	**131.9**
19	**R. G. Sharma (India)**	**62**	**55**	**12**	**1,364**	**106**	**1**	**31.72**	**129.4**
20	**A. D. Hales (England)**	**45**	**45**	**5**	**1,257**	**116***	**1**	**31.42**	**133.8**
21	**L. R. P. L. Taylor (New Zealand)**	**73**	**65**	**13**	**1,256**	**63**	**0**	**24.15**	**120.0**

The leading aggregate for Bangladesh is:

Shakib Al Hasan	**54**	**54**	**8**	**1,103**	**84**	**0**	**23.97**	**122.4**

FASTEST TWENTY20 INTERNATIONAL FIFTIES

Balls			
12	Yuvraj Singh	India v England at Durban	2007-0
14	**C. Munro**	**New Zealand v Sri Lanka at Auckland**	**2015-1**
17	P. R. Stirling	Ireland v Afghanistan at Dubai	2011-1
17	S. J. Myburgh	Netherlands v Ireland at Sylhet	2013-1
17	C. H. Gayle	West Indies v South Africa at Cape Town	2014-1
18	D. A. Warner	Australia v West Indies at Sydney	2009-1
18	G. J. Maxwell	Australia v Pakistan at Mirpur	2013-1
18	**G. J. Maxwell**	**Australia v Sri Lanka at Pallekele**	**201**

FASTEST TWENTY20 INTERNATIONAL HUNDREDS

Balls			
45	R. E. Levi	South Africa v New Zealand at Hamilton	2011-1
46	F. du Plessis	South Africa v West Indies at Johannesburg	2014-1
46	**K. L. Rahul**	**India v West Indies at Lauderhill**	**201**
47	A. J. Finch	Australia v England at Southampton	201
47	**C. H. Gayle**	**West Indies v England at Mumbai**	**2015-1**
48	**E. Lewis**	**West Indies v India at Lauderhill**	**201**
49	**G. J. Maxwell**	**Australia v Sri Lanka at Pallekele**	**201**

HIGHEST PARTNERSHIP FOR EACH WICKET

71*	**for 1st**	**M. J. Guptill/K. S. Williamson**	**NZ v P**	**Hamilton**	**2015-16**
56	for 2nd	D. P. M. D. Jayawardene/ K. C. Sangakkara	SL v WI	Bridgetown	2010
52	for 3rd	A. D. Hales/E. J. G. Morgan	E v SL	Chittagong	2013-14
61	**for 4th**	**D. A. Warner/G. J. Maxwell**	**A v SA**	**Johannesburg**	**2015-16**
9*	for 5th	Shoaib Malik/Misbah-ul-Haq	P v A	Johannesburg	2007-08
)1*	for 6th	M. E. K. Hussey/C. L. White	A v SL	Bridgetown	2010
91	for 7th	P. D. Collingwood/M. H. Yardy	E v WI	The Oval	2007
80	for 8th	P. L. Mommsen/S. M. Sharif	Scot v Neth	Edinburgh	2015
63	for 9th	Sohail Tanvir/Saeed Ajmal	P v SL	Dubai	2013-14
31*	for 10th	Wahab Riaz/Shoaib Akhtar	P v NZ	Auckland	2010-11

BOWLING RECORDS

BEST BOWLING ANALYSES

-8	B. A. W. Mendis	Sri Lanka v Zimbabwe at Hambantota	2012-13
-16	B. A. W. Mendis	Sri Lanka v Australia at Pallekele	2011-12
-3	H. M. R. K. B. Herath	Sri Lanka v New Zealand at Chittagong	2013-14
-6	Umar Gul	Pakistan v New Zealand at The Oval	2009
-6	Umar Gul	Pakistan v South Africa at Centurion	2012-13
-13	Elias Sunny	Bangladesh v Ireland at Belfast	2012
-13	Samiullah Shenwari	Afghanistan v Kenya at Sharjah	2013-14
-14	**Imad Wasim**	**Pakistan v West Indies at Dubai**	**2016-17**
-18	T. G. Southee	New Zealand v Pakistan at Auckland	2010-11
-19	R. McLaren	South Africa v West Indies at North Sound	2010
-19	M. A. A. Jamil	Netherlands v South Africa at Chittagong	2013-14
-20	N. N. Odhiambo	Kenya v Scotland at Nairobi	2009-10
-22	**Mustafizur Rahman**	**Bangladesh v New Zealand at Kolkata**	**2015-16**
-23	D. Wiese	South Africa v West Indies at Durban	2014-15
-24	A. C. Evans	Scotland v Netherlands at Edinburgh	2015

HAT-TRICKS

. Lee	Australia v Bangladesh at Cape Town	2007-08
. D. P. Oram	New Zealand v Sri Lanka at Colombo	2009
. G. Southee	New Zealand v Pakistan at Auckland	2010-11

MOST WICKETS

		M	*B*	*R*	*W*	*BB*	*4I*	*Avge*	*SR*
1	**Shahid Afridi (Pakistan)**	**98**	**2,144**	**2,362**	**97**	**4-11**	**3**	**24.35**	**6.61**
2	**Umar Gul (Pakistan)**	**60**	**1,203**	**1,443**	**85**	**5-6**	**6**	**16.97**	**7.19**
	Saeed Ajmal (Pakistan)	64	1,430	1,516	85	4-19	4	17.83	6.36
4	**S. L. Malinga (Sri Lanka)**	**62**	**1,307**	**1,582**	**78**	**5-31**	**2**	**20.28**	**7.26**
5	B. A. W. Mendis (Sri Lanka)	39	885	952	66	6-8	5	14.42	6.45
6	**Shakib Al Hasan (Bangladesh)**	**54**	**1,175**	**1,322**	**65**	**4-15**	**3**	**20.33**	**6.75**
	S. C. J. Broad (England)	56	1,173	1,491	65	4-24	1	22.93	7.62
8	**D. W. Steyn (South Africa)**	**42**	**901**	**1,009**	**58**	**4-9**	**2**	**17.39**	**6.71**
	N. L. McCullum (New Zealand)	**63**	**1,123**	**1,278**	**58**	**4-16**	**2**	**22.03**	**6.82**
10	**K. M. D. N. Kulasekara (Sri Lanka)**	**50**	**1,057**	**1,280**	**56**	**4-32**	**1**	**22.85**	**7.26**
11	**R. Ashwin (India)**	**45**	**1,002**	**1,154**	**52**	**4-8**	**2**	**22.19**	**6.91**
	Sohail Tanvir (Pakistan)	**54**	**1,148**	**1,364**	**52**	**3-12**	**0**	**26.23**	**7.12**
	D. J. Bravo (West Indies)	**66**	**1,042**	**1,470**	**52**	**4-28**	**2**	**28.26**	**8.46**
14	G. P. Swann (England)	39	810	859	51	3-13	0	16.84	6.36
15	**Mohammad Nabi (Afghanistan)**	**48**	**1,038**	**1,218**	**50**	**4-17**	**2**	**24.36**	**7.04**

The leading aggregates for other Test countries are:

	M	*B*	*R*	*W*	*BB*	*4I*	*Avge*	*SR*
S. R. Watson (Australia)	**58**	**930**	**1,187**	**48**	**4-15**	**1**	**24.72**	**7.65**
A. G. Cremer (Zimbabwe)	**27**	**534**	**622**	**33**	**3-11**	**0**	**18.84**	**6.98**

WICKETKEEPING AND FIELDING RECORDS

MOST DISMISSALS IN AN INNINGS

5 (3ct, 2st)	Mohammad Shahzad	Afghanistan v Oman at Abu Dhabi	2015-1
4 (all ct)	A. C. Gilchrist	Australia v Zimbabwe at Cape Town	2007-0
4 (all ct)	M. J. Prior	England v South Africa at Cape Town	2007-0
4 (all ct)	A. C. Gilchrist	Australia v New Zealand at Perth	2007-0
4 (all st)	Kamran Akmal	Pakistan v Netherlands at Lord's	200
4 (3ct, 1st)	N. J. O'Brien	Ireland v Sri Lanka at Lord's	200
4 (2ct, 2st)	A. B. de Villiers	South Africa v West Indies at North Sound	201
4 (all ct)	M. S. Dhoni	India v Afghanistan at Gros Islet	201
4 (3ct, 1st)	G. C. Wilson	Ireland v Kenya at Dubai	2011-1
4 (all ct)	A. B. de Villiers	South Africa v Zimbabwe at Hambantota	2012-1
4 (all ct)	M. S. Dhoni	India v Pakistan at Colombo (RPS)	2012-1
4 (all ct)	W. Barresi	Netherlands v Kenya at Dubai	2013-1
4 (2ct, 2st)	Q. de Kock	South Africa v Pakistan at Dubai	2013-1
4 (all st)	D. Ramdin	West Indies v Pakistan at Mirpur	2013-1
4 (3ct, 1st)	**Q. de Kock**	**South Africa v Afghanistan at Mumbai**	**2015-1**
4 (1ct, 3st)	**R. Mutumbami**	**Zimbabwe v Scotland at Nagpur**	**2015-1**

MOST DISMISSALS

			M	*Ct*	*St*
1	**63**	**M. S. Dhoni (India)**	**73**	**41**	**22**
2	60	Kamran Akmal (Pakistan)	53	28	32
3	**51**	**D. Ramdin (West Indies)**	**58**	**32**	**19**
4	**45**	**Mushfiqur Rahim (Bangladesh)**	**53**	**22**	**23**
	45	K. C. Sangakkara (Sri Lanka)	56	25	20
6	**42**	**Mohammad Shahzad (Afghanistan)**	**50**	**21**	**21**
7	**36**	**Q. de Kock (South Africa)**	**29**	**27**	**9**
8	32	B. B. McCullum (New Zealand)	42	24	8

B. B. McCullum's record excludes 11 catches taken in 28 matches when not keeping wicket, and Mushfiqur Rahim's excludes one catch in four matches when not keeping wicket. Kamran Akmal and Mohammad Shahzad both played one match in which they did not keep wicket or take a catch.

MOST CATCHES IN AN INNINGS IN THE FIELD

4	D. J. G. Sammy	West Indies v Ireland at Providence	2010
4	**Babar Hayat**	**Hong Kong v Afghanistan at Mirpur**	**2015-16**

MOST CATCHES

Ct	*M*		*Ct*	*M*	
42	**73**	**L. R. P. L. Taylor (New Zealand)**	**34**	**82**	**Shoaib Malik (Pakistan)**
40	**45**	**A. B. de Villiers (South Africa)**	**33**	**63**	**D. A. Warner (Australia)**
38	**62**	**Umar Akmal (Pakistan)**	**33**	**70**	**J-P. Duminy (South Africa)**
35	**61**	**M. J. Guptill (New Zealand)**	**30**	**66**	**D. J. G. Sammy (West Indies)**
35	**66**	**D. J. Bravo (West Indies)**	**30**	**98**	**Shahid Afridi (Pakistan)**

A. B. de Villiers's record excludes 28 dismissals (21ct, 7st) in 26 matches when keeping wicket; Umar Akmal's excludes 13 (11ct, 2st) in 20 matches.

TEAM RECORDS

HIGHEST INNINGS TOTALS

263-3	**(20 overs)**	**Australia v Sri Lanka at Pallekele**	**2016**
260-6	(20 overs)	Sri Lanka v Kenya at Johannesburg	2007-08
248-6	(20 overs)	Australia v England at Southampton	2013
245-6	**(20 overs)**	**West Indies v India at Lauderhill**	**2016**
244-4	**(20 overs)**	**India v West Indies at Lauderhill**	**2016**
241-6	(20 overs)	South Africa v England at Centurion	2009-10
236-6	(19.2 overs)	West Indies v South Africa at Johannesburg	2014-15
231-7	(20 overs)	South Africa v West Indies at Johannesburg	2014-15
230-8	**(19.4 overs)**	**England v South Africa at Mumbai**	**2015-16**

LOWEST INNINGS TOTALS

39	(10.3 overs)	Netherlands v Sri Lanka at Chittagong	2013-14
53	(14.3 overs)	Nepal v Ireland at Belfast	2015
56	(18.4 overs)	Kenya v Afghanistan at Sharjah	2013-14
60†	(15.3 overs)	New Zealand v Sri Lanka at Chittagong	2013-14
67	(17.2 overs)	Kenya v Ireland at Belfast	2008
68	(16.4 overs)	Ireland v West Indies at Providence	2010
69	(17 overs)	Hong Kong v Nepal at Chittagong	2013-14
69	(17.4 overs)	Nepal v Netherlands at Amstelveen	2015
70	(20 overs)	Bermuda v Canada at Belfast	2008
70	**(15.4 overs)**	**Bangladesh v New Zealand at Kolkata**	**2015-16**

† *One man absent.*

OTHER RECORDS

MOST APPEARANCES

98	**Shahid Afridi (Pakistan)**	**73**	**M. S. Dhoni (India)**
82	**Shoaib Malik (Pakistan)**	**73**	**L. R. P. L. Taylor (New Zealand)**
82	**Umar Akmal (Pakistan)**	**71**	**A. B. de Villiers (South Africa)**
80	**T. M. Dilshan (Sri Lanka)**	71	B. B. McCullum (New Zealand)
77	**Mohammad Hafeez (Pakistan)**	**70**	**J-P. Duminy (South Africa)**

WORLD TWENTY20 FINALS

2007-08	INDIA (157-5) beat Pakistan (152) by five runs	Johannesburg
2009	PAKISTAN (139-2) beat Sri Lanka (138-6) by eight wickets	Lord's
2010	ENGLAND (148-3) beat Australia (147-6) by seven wickets	Bridgetown
2012-13	WEST INDIES (137-6) beat Sri Lanka (101) by 36 runs	Colombo (RPS)
2013-14	SRI LANKA (134-4) beat India (130-4) by six wickets	Mirpur
2015-16	**WEST INDIES (161-6) beat England (155-9) by four wickets**	**Kolkata**

An expanded and regularly updated online version of the Records can be found at www.wisdenrecords.com

MISCELLANEOUS RECORDS

LARGE ATTENDANCES

Test Series

943,000	Australia v England (5 Tests)	1936-37
In England		
549,650	England v Australia (5 Tests)	1953

Test Matches

†‡465,000	India v Pakistan, Calcutta	1998-99
350,534	Australia v England, Melbourne (Third Test)	1936-37

Attendance at India v England at Calcutta in 1981-82 may have exceeded 350,000.

In England		
158,000+	England v Australia, Leeds	1948
140,111	England v India, Lord's	2011
137,915	England v Australia, Lord's	1953

Test Match Day

‡100,000	India v Pakistan, Calcutta (first four days)	1998-99
91,112	Australia v England, Melbourne (Fourth Test, first day)	2013-14
90,800	Australia v West Indies, Melbourne (Fifth Test, second day)	1960-61
89,155	Australia v England, Melbourne (Fourth Test, first day)	2006-07

Other First-Class Matches in England

93,000	England v Australia, Lord's (Fourth Victory Match, 3 days)	1945
80,000+	Surrey v Yorkshire, The Oval (3 days)	1906
78,792	Yorkshire v Lancashire, Leeds (3 days)	1904
76,617	Lancashire v Yorkshire, Manchester (3 days)	1926

One-Day Internationals

‡100,000	India v South Africa, Calcutta	1993-94
‡100,000	India v West Indies, Calcutta	1993-94
‡100,000	India v West Indies, Calcutta	1994-95
‡100,000	India v Sri Lanka, Calcutta (World Cup semi-final)	1995-96
‡100,000	India v Australia, Kolkata	2003-04
93,013	Australia v New Zealand, Melbourne (World Cup final)	2014-15
‡90,000	India v Pakistan, Calcutta	1986-87
‡90,000	India v South Africa, Calcutta	1991-92
87,182	England v Pakistan, Melbourne (World Cup final)	1991-92
86,133	Australia v West Indies, Melbourne	1983-84

Twenty20 International

84,041	Australia v India, Melbourne	2007-08

† *Estimated.*
‡ *No official attendance figures were issued for these games, but capacity at Calcutta (now Kolkata) is believed to have reached 100,000 following rebuilding in 1993.*

LORD'S CRICKET GROUND

Lord's and the Marylebone Cricket Club were founded in London in 1787. The Club has enjoyed an uninterrupted career since that date, but there have been three grounds known as Lord's. The first (1787–1810) was situated where Dorset Square now is; the second (1809–13), at North Bank, had to be abandoned owing to the cutting of the Regent's Canal; and the third, opened in 1814, is the present one at St John's Wood. It was not until 1866 that the freehold of Lord's was secured by MCC. The present pavilion was erected in 1890 at a cost of £21,000.

MINOR CRICKET

HIGHEST INDIVIDUAL SCORES

1,009*	**P. P. Dhanawade, K. C. Gandhi English School v Arya Gurukul at Kalyan** *Dhanawade faced 327 balls in 6 hours 36 minutes and hit 129 fours and 59 sixes*	**2015-16**
628*	A. E. J. Collins, Clark's House v North Town at Clifton College. *A junior house match. His innings of 6 hours 50 minutes was spread over four afternoons*	1899
566	C. J. Eady, Break-o'-Day v Wellington at Hobart	1901-02
546	P. P. Shaw, Rizvi Springfield School v St Francis D'Assisi School at Mumbai	2013-14
515	D. R. Havewalla, B. B. and C. I. Railways v St Xavier's at Bombay	1933-34
506*	J. C. Sharp, Melbourne GS v Geelong College at Melbourne	1914-15
502*	Chaman Lal, Mohindra Coll., Patiala v Government Coll., Rupar at Patiala	1956-57
498	Arman Jaffer, Rizvi Springfield School v IES Raja Shivaji School at Mumbai	2010-11
486*	S. Sankruth Sriram, JSS Intl School U16 v Hebron School U16 at Ootacamund	2014-15
485	A. E. Stoddart, Hampstead v Stoics at Hampstead	1886
475*	Mohammad Iqbal, Muslim Model HS v Government HS, Sialkot at Gujranwala	1958-59
473	Arman Jaffer, Rizvi Springfield School v IES VN Sule School at Mumbai	2012-13
466*	G. T. S. Stevens, Beta v Lambda (University College School house match) at Neasden. *Stevens scored his 466 and took 14 wickets on one day*	1919
461*	Ali Zorain Khan, Nagpur Cricket Academy v Reshimbagh Gymkhana at Nagpur	2010-11
459	J. A. Prout, Wesley College v Geelong College at Geelong	1908-09
451*	V. H. Mol, Maharashtra Under-19 v Assam Under-19 at Nasik	2011-12

The highest score in a Minor County match is 323 by F. E. Lacey for Hampshire v Norfolk at Southampton in 1887; the highest in the Minor Counties Championship is 282 by E. Garnett for Berkshire v Wiltshire at Reading in 1908.*

HIGHEST PARTNERSHIPS

721* for 1st	B. Manoj Kumar and M. S. Tumbi, St Peter's High School v St Philip's High School at Secunderabad	2006-07
664* for 3rd	V. G. Kambli and S. R. Tendulkar, Sharadashram Vidyamandir School v St Xavier's High School at Bombay	1987-88

Manoj Kumar and Tumbi reportedly scored 721 in 40 overs in an Under-13 inter-school match; they hit 103 fours between them, but no sixes. Their opponents were all out for 21 in seven overs.

Kambli was 16 years old, Tendulkar 14. Tendulkar made his Test debut 21 months later.

MOST WICKETS WITH CONSECUTIVE BALLS

There are **two** recorded instances of a bowler taking nine wickets with consecutive balls. Both came in school games: Paul Hugo, for Smithfield School v Aliwal North at Smithfield, South Africa, in 1930-31, and Stephen Fleming (not the future Test captain), for Marlborough College A v Bohally School at Blenheim, New Zealand, in 1967-68. There are five further verified instances of eight wickets in eight balls, the most recent by Mike Walters for the Royal Army Educational Corps v Joint Air Transport Establishment at Beaconsfield in 1979.

TEN WICKETS FOR NO RUNS

There are **25** recorded instances of a bowler taking all ten wickets in an innings for no runs, the most recent by David Morton, for Bayside Muddies v Ranatungas in Brisbane in 1998-99. The previous instance was also in Australia, by the schoolgirl Emma Liddell, for Metropolitan East v West at Penrith (Sydney) in 1995-96. When Jennings Tune did it, for the Yorkshire club Cliffe v Eastrington at Cliffe in 1923, all ten of his victims were bowled. The number has increased by one since last year, following evidence that Wynton Edwards achieved the feat for Queen's College against Selborne College in South Africa in March 1950.

NOUGHT ALL OUT

In minor matches, this is more common than might be imagined. The historian Peter Wynne-Thomas says the first recorded example was in Norfolk, where an Eleven of Fakenham, Walsingham and Hempton were dismissed for nought by an Eleven of Licham, Dunham and Brisley in July 1815.

MOST DISMISSALS IN AN INNINGS

The only recorded instance of a wicketkeeper being involved in all ten dismissals in an innings was by Welihinda Badalge Bennett, for Mahinda College against Richmond College in Ceylon (now Sri Lanka) in 1952-53. His feat comprised six catches and four stumpings. There are three other known instances of nine dismissals in the same innings, one of which – by H. W. P. Middleton for Priory v Mitre in a Repton School house match in 1930 – included eight stumpings. Young Rangers' innings against Bohran Gymkhana in Karachi in 1969-70 included nine run-outs.

The widespread nature – and differing levels of supervision – of minor cricket matches mean that record claims have to be treated with caution. Additions and corrections to the above records for minor cricket will only be considered for inclusion in Wisden *if they are corroborated by independent evidence of the achievement.*

Research: Steven Lynch

RECORD HIT

The Rev. W. Fellows, while at practice on the Christ Church ground at Oxford in 1856, drove a ball bowled by Charles Rogers 175 yards from hit to pitch.

BIGGEST HIT AT LORD'S

The only known instance of a batsman hitting a ball over the present pavilion at Lord's occurred when A. E. Trott, appearing for MCC against Australians on July 31, August 1, 2, 1899, drove M. A. Noble so far and high that the ball struck a chimney pot and fell behind the building.

THROWING THE CRICKET BALL

140 yards 2 feet, Robert Percival, on the Durham Sands racecourse, Co. Durham	c1882
140 yards 9 inches, Ross Mackenzie, at Toronto	1872
140 yards, "King Billy" the Aborigine, at Clermont, Queensland	1872

Extensive research by David Rayvern Allen has shown that these traditional records are probably authentic, if not necessarily wholly accurate. Modern competitions have failed to produce similar distances although Ian Pont, the Essex all-rounder who also played baseball, was reported to have thrown 138 yards in Cape Town in 1981. There have been speculative reports attributing throws of 150 yards or more to figures as diverse as the South African Test player Colin Bland, the Latvian javelin thrower Janis Lusis, who won a gold medal for the Soviet Union in the 1968 Olympics, and the British sprinter Charley Ransome. The definitive record is still awaited.

COUNTY CHAMPIONSHIP

MOST APPEARANCES

762	W. Rhodes	Yorkshire	1898–1930
707	F. E. Woolley	Kent	1906–1938
668	C. P. Mead	Hampshire	1906–1936
617	N. Gifford	Worcestershire (484), Warwickshire (133)	1960–1988
611	W. G. Quaife	Warwickshire	1895–1928
601	G. H. Hirst	Yorkshire	1891–1921

MOST CONSECUTIVE APPEARANCES

423	K. G. Suttle	Sussex	1954–1969
412	J. G. Binks	Yorkshire	1955–1969

J. Vine made 417 consecutive appearances for Sussex in all first-class matches (399 of them in the Championship) between July 1900 and September 1914.

J. G. Binks did not miss a Championship match for Yorkshire between making his debut in June 1955 and retiring at the end of the 1969 season.

UMPIRES

MOST COUNTY CHAMPIONSHIP APPEARANCES

570	T. W. Spencer	1950–1980
531	F. Chester	1922–1955
523	D. J. Constant	1969–2006
517	H. G. Baldwin	1932–1962
511	A. G. T. Whitehead	1970–2005

MOST SEASONS ON ENGLISH FIRST-CLASS LIST

38	D. J. Constant	1969–2006
36	A. G. T. Whitehead	1970–2005
31	K. E. Palmer	1972–2002
31	T. W. Spencer	1950–1980
30	R. Julian	1972–2001
30	P. B. Wight	1966–1995
29	H. D. Bird	1970–1998
28	F. Chester	1922–1955
28	B. Leadbeater	1981–2008
28	R. Palmer	1980–2007
27	B. Dudleston	1984–2010
27	J. W. Holder	1983–2009
27	J. Moss	1899–1929
26	W. A. J. West	1896–1925
25	H. G. Baldwin	1932–1962
25	A. Jepson	1960–1984
25	J. G. Langridge	1956–1980
25	B. J. Meyer	1973–1997
25	D. R. Shepherd	1981–2005

Matthew Lewis, Getty Images

Gloves off: Charlotte Edwards left the international game in 2016.

WOMEN'S TEST RECORDS

This section covers all women's Tests to December 31, 2016. No women's Tests were played in the calendar year 2016.

BATTING RECORDS

HIGHEST INDIVIDUAL INNINGS

242	Kiran Baluch	Pakistan v West Indies at Karachi	2003-04
214	M. D. Raj	India v England at Taunton	2002
209*	K. L. Rolton	Australia v England at Leeds	2001
204	K. E. Flavell	New Zealand v England at Scarborough	1996
204	M. A. J. Goszko	Australia v England at Shenley	2001
200	J. Broadbent	Australia v England at Guildford	1998

1,000 RUNS IN A CAREER

R	*T*		*R*	*T*	
1,935	27	J. A. Brittin (England)	1,110	13	S. Agarwal (India)
1,676	23	C. M. Edwards (England)	1,078	12	E. Bakewell (England)
1,594	22	R. Heyhoe-Flint (England)	1,030	15	S. C. Taylor (England)
1,301	19	D. A. Hockley (New Zealand)	1,007	14	M. E. Maclagan (England)
1,164	18	C. A. Hodges (England)	1,002	14	K. L. Rolton (Australia)

BOWLING RECORDS

BEST BOWLING ANALYSES

8-53	N. David	India v England at Jamshedpur	1995-96
7-6	M. B. Duggan	England v Australia at Melbourne	1957-58
7-7	E. R. Wilson	Australia v England at Melbourne	1957-58
7-10	M. E. Maclagan	England v Australia at Brisbane	1934-35
7-18	A. Palmer	Australia v England at Brisbane	1934-35
7-24	L. Johnston	Australia v New Zealand at Melbourne	1971-72
7-34	G. E. McConway	England v India at Worcester	1986
7-41	J. A. Burley	New Zealand v England at The Oval	1966

MOST WICKETS IN A MATCH

13-226	Shaiza Khan	Pakistan v West Indies at Karachi	2003-04

50 WICKETS IN A CAREER

W	*T*		*W*	*T*	
77	17	M. B. Duggan (England)	60	19	S. Kulkarni (India)
68	11	E. R. Wilson (Australia)	57	16	R. H. Thompson (Australia)
63	20	D. F. Edulji (India)	55	15	J. Lord (New Zealand)
60	13	C. L. Fitzpatrick (Australia)	50	12	E. Bakewell (England)
60	14	M. E. Maclagan (England)			

WICKETKEEPING RECORDS

SIX DISMISSALS IN AN INNINGS

8 (6ct, 2st)	L. Nye	England v New Zealand at New Plymouth	1991-92
6 (2ct, 4st)	B. A. Brentnall	New Zealand v South Africa at Johannesburg	1971-72

25 DISMISSALS IN A CAREER

		T	*Ct*	*St*
58	C. Matthews (Australia)	20	46	12
43	J. Smit (England)	21	39	4
36	S. A. Hodges (England)	11	19	17
28	B. A. Brentnall (New Zealand)	10	16	12

TEAM RECORDS

HIGHEST INNINGS TOTALS

569-6 dec	Australia v England at Guildford	1998
525	Australia v India at Ahmedabad	1983-84
517-8	New Zealand v England at Scarborough	1996
503-5 dec	England v New Zealand at Christchurch	1934-35

LOWEST INNINGS TOTALS

35	England v Australia at Melbourne	1957-58
38	Australia v England at Melbourne	1957-58
44	New Zealand v England at Christchurch	1934-35
47	Australia v England at Brisbane	1934-35
50	Netherlands v South Africa at Rotterdam	2007

WOMEN'S ONE-DAY INTERNATIONAL RECORDS

This section covers women's one-day international cricket to December 31, 2016. Bold type denotes performances in the calendar year 2016 or, in career figures, players who appeared in women's one-day internationals in that year.

BATTING RECORDS

HIGHEST INDIVIDUAL INNINGS

229*	B. J. Clark	Australia v Denmark at Mumbai	1997-98
173*	C. M. Edwards	England v Ireland at Pune	1997-98
171	S. R. Taylor	West Indies v Sri Lanka at Mumbai	2012-13
168*	**T. T. Beaumont**	**England v Pakistan at Taunton**	**2016**
168	S. W. Bates	New Zealand v Pakistan at Sydney	2008-09
157	R. H. Priest	New Zealand v Sri Lanka at Lincoln	2015-16
156*	L. M. Keightley	Australia v Pakistan at Melbourne	1996-97
156*	S. C. Taylor	England v India at Lord's	2006
154*	K. L. Rolton	Australia v Sri Lanka at Christchurch	2000-01
153*	J. Logtenberg	South Africa v Netherlands at Deventer	2007
151	K. L. Rolton	Australia v Ireland at Dublin	2005

MOST RUNS IN A CAREER

R	*M*		*R*	*M*	
5,992	**191**	**C. M. Edwards (England)**	4,064	118	D. A. Hockley (New Zealand)
5,407	**167**	**M. D. Raj (India)**	**3,732**	**98**	**S. R. Taylor (West Indies)**
4,844	118	B. J. Clark (Australia)	**3,375**	**95**	**S. W. Bates (New Zealand)**
4,814	141	K. L. Rolton (Australia)	**3,261**	**101**	**S. J. Taylor (England)**
4,101	126	S. C. Taylor (England)	**3,080**	**131**	**A. J. Blackwell (Australia)**

BOWLING RECORDS

BEST BOWLING ANALYSES

7-4	Sajjida Shah	Pakistan v Japan at Amsterdam	2003
7-8	J. M. Chamberlain	England v Denmark at Haarlem	1991
7-14	A. Mohammed	West Indies v Pakistan at Mirpur	2011-12
7-24	S. Nitschke	Australia v England at Kidderminster	2005
6-10	J. Lord	New Zealand v India at Auckland	1981-82
6-10	M. Maben	India v Sri Lanka at Kandy	2003-04
6-10	S. Ismail	South Africa v Netherlands at Savar	2011-12

MOST WICKETS IN A CAREER

W	*M*		*W*	*M*	
180	109	C. L. Fitzpatrick (Australia)	**136**	**101**	**A. Mohammed (W. Indies)**
177	**151**	**J. N. Goswami (India)**	**123**	**132**	**J. L. Gunn (England)**
146	125	L. C. Sthalekar (Australia)	**120**	**94**	**K. H. Brunt (England)**
141	97	N. David (India)	**114**	**98**	**S. R. Taylor (West Indies)**

WICKETKEEPING RECORDS

MOST DISMISSALS IN AN INNINGS

6 (4ct, 2st)	S. L. Illingworth	New Zealand v Australia at Beckenham	1993
6 (1ct, 5st)	V. Kalpana	India v Denmark at Slough	1993
6 (2ct, 4st)	Batool Fatima	Pakistan v West Indies at Karachi	2003-04
6 (4ct, 2st)	Batool Fatima	Pakistan v Sri Lanka at Colombo (PSO)	2010-11

MOST DISMISSALS IN A CAREER

		M	*Ct*	*St*
133	R. J. Rolls (New Zealand)	104	90	43
121	**T. Chetty (South Africa)**	**80**	**85**	**36**
115	**S. J. Taylor (England)**	**101**	**75**	**40**
114	J. Smit (England)	109	69	45
100	Batool Fatima (Pakistan)	83	54	46
100	J. C. Price (Australia)	84	70	30

Chetty's total includes two catches in two matches, Taylor's two in eight matches and Batool Fatima's three in 15 while not keeping wicket; Price's includes one taken in the field after giving up the gloves mid-game. Rolls did not keep wicket in three matches and Smit in one; neither took any catches in these games.

TEAM RECORDS

HIGHEST INNINGS TOTALS

455-5	New Zealand v Pakistan at Christchurch	1996-97
412-3	Australia v Denmark at Mumbai	1997-98
397-4	Australia v Pakistan at Melbourne	1996-97
378-5	**England v Pakistan at Worcester**	**2016**
376-2	England v Pakistan at Vijayawada	1997-98
375-5	Netherlands v Japan at Schiedam	2003
373-7	New Zealand v Pakistan at Sydney	2008-09

LOWEST INNINGS TOTALS

22	Netherlands v West Indies at Deventer	2008
23	Pakistan v Australia at Melbourne	1996-97
24	Scotland v England at Reading	2001
26	India v New Zealand as St Saviour	2002
27	Pakistan v Australia at Hyderabad (India)	1997-98
28	Japan v Pakistan at Amsterdam	2003
29	Netherlands v Australia at Perth	1988-89

WOMEN'S WORLD CUP WINNERS

1973	England	1993	England	2008-09	England
1977-78	Australia	1997-98	Australia	2012-13	Australia
1981-82	Australia	2000-01	New Zealand		
1988-89	Australia	2004-05	Australia		

WOMEN'S TWENTY20 INTERNATIONAL RECORDS

This section covers women's Twenty20 international cricket to December 31, 2016. Bold type denotes performances in the calendar year 2016 or, in career figures, players who appeared in women's Twenty20 internationals in that year.

BATTING RECORDS

HIGHEST INDIVIDUAL INNINGS

126	M. M. Lanning	Australia v Ireland at Sylhet	2013-14
116*	S. A. Fritz	South Africa v Netherlands at Potchefstroom	2010-11
112*	D. J. S. Dottin	West Indies v South Africa at Basseterre	2010
96*	K. L. Rolton	Australia v England at Taunton	2005
94*	S. W. Bates	New Zealand v Pakistan at Sylhet	2013-14
92*	C. M. Edwards	England v Australia at Hobart	2013-14

MOST RUNS IN A CAREER

R	*M*		*R*	*M*	
2,605	**95**	**C. M. Edwards (England)**	**1,805**	**91**	**D. J. S. Dottin (West Indies)**
2,389	**77**	**S. R. Taylor (West Indies)**	**1,708**	**63**	**M. D. Raj (India)**
2,127	**84**	**S. W. Bates (New Zealand)**	**1,328**	**74**	**Bismah Maroof (Pakistan)**
2,054	**81**	**S. J. Taylor (England)**	**1,262**	**92**	**A. J. Blackwell (Australia)**
1,856	**67**	**M. M. Lanning (Australia)**	**1,223**	**68**	**H. Kaur (India)**

BOWLING RECORDS

BEST BOWLING ANALYSES

6-17	A. E. Satterthwaite	New Zealand v England at Taunton	2007
5-8	**S. E. Luus**	**South Africa v Ireland at Chennai**	**2015-16**
5-10	A. Mohammed	West Indies v South Africa at Cape Town	2009-10
5-11	J. N. Goswami	India v Australia at Visakhapatnam	2011-12
5-11	A. Shrubsole	England v New Zealand at Wellington	2011-12
5-12	A. Mohammed	West Indies v New Zealand at Bridgetown	2013-14
5-15	S. F. Daley	West Indies v Sri Lanka at Colombo (RPS)	2012-13

MOST WICKETS IN A CAREER

W	*M*		*W*	*M*	
104	**89**	**A. Mohammed (West Indies)**	**68**	**47**	**A. Shrubsole (England)**
77	**82**	**E. A. Perry (Australia)**	**67**	**77**	**S. R. Taylor (West Indies)**
73	**70**	**D. Hazell (England)**	**66**	**75**	**Sana Mir (Pakistan)**
72	68	S. F. Daley (West Indies)	**66**	**95**	**J. L. Gunn (England)**

WICKETKEEPING RECORDS

MOST DISMISSALS IN AN INNINGS

5 (1ct, 4st)	Kycia A. Knight	West Indies v Sri Lanka at Colombo (RPS)	2012-13
5 (1ct, 4st)	Batool Fatima	Pakistan v Ireland at Dublin	2013
5 (1ct, 4st)	Batool Fatima	Pakistan v Ireland at Dublin (semi-final)	2013

MOST DISMISSALS IN A CAREER

		M	*Ct*	*St*
68	**S. J. Taylor (England)**	**81†**	**22**	**46**
64	**R. H. Priest (New Zealand)**	**65†**	**34**	**30**
57	**T. Chetty (South Africa)**	**68**	**34**	**23**
55*	**J. L. Gunn (England)**	**95**	**55**	
54*	**L. S. Greenway (England)**	**85**	**54**	
53	**M. R. Aguilleira (West Indies)**	**81†**	**28**	**25**

* *Catches made by non-wicketkeeper in the field.*

† *Taylor's total includes two matches and Priest's one in the field where they made no catches; Aguilleira's total includes ten matches in the field where she made two catches.*

TEAM RECORDS

HIGHEST INNINGS TOTALS

205-1	South Africa v Netherlands at Potchefstroom	2010-11
191-4	West Indies v Netherlands at Potchefstroom	2010-11
191-4	Australia v Ireland at Sylhet	2013-14
188-3	New Zealand v Sri Lanka at Christchurch	2015-16
187-5	**England v Pakistan at Bristol**	**2016**
186-1	Australia v Ireland at Dublin	2015
186-7	New Zealand v South Africa at Taunton	2007
185-2	Australia v Pakistan at Sylhet	2013-14

LOWEST INNINGS TOTALS

44	**Bangladesh v Pakistan at Bangkok**	**2016-17**
54	**Bangladesh v India at Bangkok**	**2016-17**
57	Sri Lanka v Bangladesh at Guanggong	2012-13
60	Pakistan v England at Taunton	2009
60	New Zealand v England at Whangarei	2014-15

WOMEN'S WORLD TWENTY20 WINNERS

2009	England	2012-13	Australia	2015-16	West Indies
2010	Australia	2013-14	Australia		

BIRTHS AND DEATHS

TEST CRICKETERS

Full list from 1876-77 to January 23, 2017

In the Test career column, dates in italics indicate seasons embracing two different years (i.e. non-English seasons). In these cases, only the first year is given, e.g. *1876* for 1876-77. Some non-English series taking place outside the host country's normal season are dated by a single year.

The Test career figures are complete up to January 23, 2017; the one-day international totals up to December 31, 2016, and the Twenty20 international totals up to December 31, 2016. Career figures are for one national team only; those players who have appeared for more than one Test team are listed on page 1441, and for more than one one-day international or Twenty20 international team on page 1443.

The forename by which a player is known is underlined if it is not his first name.

Family relationships are indicated by superscript numbers; where the relationship is not immediately apparent from a shared name, see the notes at the end of this section. (*CY 1889*) signifies that the player was a Wisden Cricketer of the Year in the 1889 Almanack. The 5/10 column indicates instances of a player taking five wickets in a Test innings and ten wickets in a match. O/T signifies number of one-day and Twenty20 internationals played.

[1] *Father and son(s).* [2] *Brothers.* [3] *Grandfather, father and son.* [4] *Grandfather and grandson.* [5] *Great-grandfather and great-grandson.*
† *Excludes matches for another Test team.* ‡ *Excludes matches for another ODI or T20I team.*

ENGLAND (676 players)

	Born	*Died*	*Tests*	*Test Career*	*Runs*	*HS*	*100s*	*Avge*	*Wkts*	*BB*	*5/10*	*Avge*	*Ct/St*	*O/T*
Abel Robert (*CY 1890*)	30.11.1857	10.12.1936	13	1888–1902	744	132*	2	37.20	–	–	–/–	–	13	
Absolom Charles Alfred	7.6.1846	30.7.1889	1	*1878*	58	52	0	29.00	–	–	–/–	–	0	
Adams Christopher John (*CY 2004*)	6.5.1970		5	*1999*	104	31	0	13.00	1	1-42	0/0	59.00	6	5
Afzaal Usman	9.6.1977		3	2001	83	54	0	16.60	1	1-49	0/0	49.00	0	
Agnew Jonathan Philip MBE (*CY 1988*)	4.4.1960		3	1984–1985	10	5	0	10.00	4	2-51	0/0	93.25	0	3
Ali Kabir	24.11.1980		1	2003	10	9	0	5.00	5	3-80	0/0	27.20	0	14
Ali Moeen Munir (*CY 2015*)	18.6.1987		37	2014–*2016*	1,927	155*	5	35.03	98	6-67	2/0	42.22	19	46/19
Allen David Arthur	29.10.1935	24.5.2014	39	*1959*–1966	918	88	0	25.50	122	5-30	4/0	30.97	10	
Allen *Sir* George Oswald Browning ("Gubby")	31.7.1902	29.11.1989	25	1930–*1947*	750	122	1	24.19	81	7-80	5/1	29.37	20	
Allom Maurice James Carrick	23.3.1906	8.4.1995	5	*1929*–*1930*	14	8*	0	14.00	14	5-38	1/0	18.92	0	
Allott Paul John Walter	14.9.1956		13	1981–1985	213	52*	0	14.20	26	6-61	1/0	41.69	4	13
Ambrose Timothy Raymond	1.12.1982		11	*2007*–*2008*	447	102	1	29.80	–	–	–/–	–	31	5/1
Ames Leslie Ethelbert George CBE (*CY 1929*)	3.12.1905	27.2.1990	47	1929–*1938*	2,434	149	8	40.56	–	–	–/–	–	74/23	

	Born	Died	Tests	Test Career	Runs	HS	100s	Avge	Wkts	BB	5/10	Avge	Ct/St	O/T
Amiss Dennis Leslie MBE (*CY 1975*)	7.4.1943		50	1966–1977	3,612	262*	11	46.30	–	–	–/–	–	24	18
Anderson James Michael (*CY 2009*)	30.7.1982		122	2003–*2016*	1,093	81	0	10.21	467	7-43	21/3	28.50	77	194/19
Andrew Keith Vincent	15.12.1929	27.12.2010	2	*1954*–1963	29	15	0	9.66	–	–	–/–	–	1	
Ansari Zafar Shahaan	10.12.1991		3	*2016*	49	32	0	9.80	5	2-76	0/0	55.00	1	1
Appleyard Robert MBE (*CY 1952*)	27.6.1924	17.3.2015	9	1954–1956	51	19*	0	17.00	31	5-51	1/0	17.87	4	
Archer Alfred German	6.12.1871	15.7.1935	1	*1898*	31	24*	0	31.00	–	–	–/–	–	0	
Armitage Thomas	25.4.1848	21.9.1922	2	*1876*	33	21	0	11.00	0	0-15	0/0	–	0	
Arnold Edward George	7.11.1876	25.10.1942	10	*1903*–1907	160	40	0	13.33	31	5-37	1/0	25.41	8	
Arnold Geoffrey Graham (*CY 1972*)	3.9.1944		34	1967–1975	421	59	0	12.02	115	6-45	6/0	28.29	9	14
Arnold John	30.11.1907	4.4.1984	1	1931	34	34	0	17.00	–	–	–/–	–	0	
Astill William Ewart (*CY 1933*)	1.3.1888	10.2.1948	9	*1927–1929*	190	40	0	12.66	25	4-58	0/0	34.24	7	
Atherton Michael Andrew OBE (*CY 1991*)	23.3.1968		115	1989–2001	7,728	185*	16	37.69	2	1-20	0/0	151.00	83	54
Athey Charles William Jeffrey	27.9.1957		23	1980–1988	919	123	1	22.97	–	–	–/–	–	13	31
Attewell William (*CY 1892*)	12.6.1861	11.6.1927	10	*1884–1891*	150	43*	0	16.66	28	4-42	0/0	22.35	9	
Bailey Robert John	28.10.1963		4	1988–*1989*	119	43	0	14.87	–	–	–/–	–	0	4
Bailey Trevor Edward CBE (*CY 1950*)	3.12.1923	10.2.2011	61	1949–*1958*	2,290	134*	1	29.74	132	7-34	5/1	29.21	32	
[1] **Bairstow** David Leslie	1.9.1951	5.1.1998	4	1979–*1980*	125	59	0	20.83	–	–	–/–	–	12/1	21
[1] **Bairstow** Jonathan Marc (*CY 2016*)	26.9.1989		38	2012–*2016*	2,435	167*	3	41.27	–	–	–/–	–	93/5	22/20
Bakewell Alfred Harry (*CY 1934*)	2.11.1908	23.1.1983	6	1931–1935	409	107	1	45.44	0	0-8	0/0	–	3	
Balderstone John Christopher	16.11.1940	6.3.2000	2	1976	39	35	0	9.75	1	1-80	0/0	80.00	1	
Ball Jacob Timothy	14.3.1991		3	2016–*2016*	52	31	0	8.66	2	1-47	0/0	114.00	1	3
Ballance Gary Simon (*CY 2015*)	22.11.1989		21	*2013–2016*	1,413	156	4	39.25	0	0-0	0/0	–	20	16
Barber Robert William (*1967*)	26.9.1935		28	1960–1968	1,495	185	1	35.59	42	4-132	0/0	43.00	21	
Barber Wilfred	18.4.1901	10.9.1968	2	1935	83	44	0	20.75	1	1-0	0/0	0.00	1	
Barlow Graham Derek	26.3.1950		3	*1976*–1977	17	7*	0	4.25	–	–	–/–	–	0	6
Barlow Richard Gorton	28.5.1851	31.7.1919	17	*1881–1886*	591	62	0	22.73	34	7-40	3/0	22.55	14	
Barnes Sydney Francis (*CY 1910*)	19.4.1873	26.12.1967	27	*1901–1913*	242	38*	0	8.06	189	9-103	24/7	16.43	12	
Barnes William (*CY 1890*)	27.5.1852	24.3.1899	21	1880–1890	725	134	1	23.38	51	6-28	3/0	15.54	19	
Barnett Charles John (*CY 1937*)	3.7.1910	28.5.1993	20	1933–1948	1,098	129	2	35.41	0	0-1	0/0	–	14	
Barnett Kim John (*CY 1989*)	17.7.1960		4	1988–1989	207	80	0	29.57	0	0-32	0/0	–	1	1
Barratt Fred	12.4.1894	29.1.1947	5	1929–*1929*	28	17	0	9.33	5	1-8	0/0	47.00	2	
Barrington Kenneth Frank (*CY 1960*)	24.11.1930	14.3.1981	82	1955–1968	6,806	256	20	58.67	29	3-4	0/0	44.82	58	
Barton Victor Alexander	6.10.1867	23.3.1906	1	*1891*	23	23	0	23.00	–	–	–/–	–	0	
Bates Willie	19.11.1855	8.1.1900	15	*1881–1886*	656	64	0	27.33	50	7-28	4/1	16.42	9	
Batty Gareth Jon	13.10.1977		9	*2003–2016*	149	38	0	14.90	15	3-55	0/0	60.93	3	10/1
Bean George	7.3.1864	16.3.1923	3	*1891*	92	50	0	18.40	–	–	–/–	–	4	

	Born	Died	Tests	Test Career	Runs	HS	100s	Avge	Wkts	BB	5/10	Avge	Ct/St	O/T
Bedser *Sir* Alec Victor CBE (*CY 1947*)	4.7.1918	4.4.2010	51	1946–1955	714	79	0	12.75	236	7-44	15/5	24.89	26	
Bell Ian Ronald MBE (*CY 2008*)	11.4.1982		118	2004–*2015*	7,727	235	22	42.69	1	1-33	0/0	76.00	100	161/8
Benjamin Joseph Emmanuel	2.2.1961		1	1994	0	0	0	0.00	4	4-42	0/0	20.00	0	2
Benson Mark Richard	6.7.1958		1	1986	51	30	0	25.50	–	–	–/–	–	0	1
Berry Robert	29.1.1926	2.12.2006	2	1950	6	4*	0	3.00	9	5-63	1/0	25.33	2	
Bicknell Martin Paul (*CY 2001*)	14.1.1969		4	1993–2003	45	15	0	6.42	14	4-84	0/0	38.78	2	7
Binks James Graham (*CY 1969*)	5.10.1935		2	*1963*	91	55	0	22.75	–	–	–/–	–	8	
Bird Morice Carlos	25.3.1888	9.12.1933	10	*1909–1913*	280	61	0	18.66	8	3-11	0/0	15.00	5	
Birkenshaw Jack MBE	13.11.1940		5	*1972–1973*	148	64	0	21.14	13	5-57	1/0	36.07	3	
Blackwell Ian David	10.6.1978		1	*2005*	4	4	0	4.00	0	0-28	0/0	–	0	34
Blakey Richard John	15.1.1967		2	*1992*	7	6	0	1.75	–	–	–/–	–	2	3
Bligh *Hon.* Ivo Francis Walter	13.3.1859	10.4.1927	4	*1882*	62	19	0	10.33	–	–	–/–	–	7	
Blythe Colin (*CY 1904*)	30.5.1879	8.11.1917	19	*1901–1909*	183	27	0	9.63	100	8-59	9/4	18.63	6	
Board John Henry	23.2.1867	15.4.1924	6	*1898–1905*	108	29	0	10.80	–	–	–/–	–	8/3	
Bolus John Brian	31.1.1934		7	1963–*1963*	496	88	0	41.33	0	0-16	0/0	–	2	
Booth Major William (*CY 1914*)	10.12.1886	1.7.1916	2	*1913*	46	32	0	23.00	7	4-49	0/0	18.57	0	
Bopara Ravinder Singh	4.5.1985		13	*2007*–2012	575	143	3	31.94	1	1-39	0/0	290.00	6	120/38
Borthwick Scott George	19.4.1990		1	*2013*	5	4	0	2.50	4	3-33	0/0	20.50	2	2/1
Bosanquet Bernard James Tindal (*CY 1905*)	13.10.1877	12.10.1936	7	*1903*–1905	147	27	0	13.36	25	8-107	2/0	24.16	9	
Botham *Sir* Ian Terence OBE (*CY 1978*)	24.11.1955		102	1977–1992	5,200	208	14	33.54	383	8-34	27/4	28.40	120	116
Bowden Montague Parker	1.11.1865	19.2.1892	2	*1888*	25	25	0	12.50	–	–	–/–	–	1	
Bowes William Eric (*CY 1932*)	25.7.1908	4.9.1987	15	1932–1946	28	10*	0	4.66	68	6-33	6/0	22.33	2	
Bowley Edward Henry (*CY 1930*)	6.6.1890	9.7.1974	5	1929–*1929*	252	109	1	36.00	0	0-7	0/0	–	2	
Boycott Geoffrey OBE (*CY 1965*)	21.10.1940		108	1964–*1981*	8,114	246*	22	47.72	7	3-47	0/0	54.57	33	36
Bradley Walter Morris	2.1.1875	19.6.1944	2	1899	23	23*	0	23.00	6	5-67	1/0	38.83	0	
Braund Leonard Charles (*CY 1902*)	18.10.1875	23.12.1955	23	*1901–1907*	987	104	3	25.97	47	8-81	3/0	38.51	39	
Brearley John Michael OBE (*CY 1977*)	28.4.1942		39	1976–1981	1,442	91	0	22.88	–	–	–/–	–	52	25
Brearley Walter (*CY 1909*)	11.3.1876	30.1.1937	4	1905–1912	21	11*	0	7.00	17	5-110	1/0	21.11	0	
Brennan Donald Vincent	10.2.1920	9.1.1985	2	1951	16	16	0	8.00	–	–	–/–	–	0/1	
Bresnan Timothy Thomas (*CY 2012*)	28.2.1985		23	2009–*2013*	575	91	0	26.13	72	5-48	1/0	32.73	8	85/34
Briggs John (*CY 1889*)	3.10.1862	11.1.1902	33	*1884*–1899	815	121	1	18.11	118	8-11	9/4	17.75	12	
[1] **Broad** Brian Christopher	29.9.1957		25	1984–1989	1,661	162	6	39.54	0	0-4	0/0	–	10	34
[1] **Broad** Stuart Christopher John MBE (*CY 2010*)	24.6.1986		102	*2007–2016*	2,691	169	1	21.35	368	8-15	15/2	28.54	32	121/56
Brockwell William (*CY 1895*)	21.1.1865	30.6.1935	7	1893–1899	202	49	0	16.83	5	3-33	0/0	61.80	6	
Bromley-Davenport Hugh Richard	18.8.1870	23.5.1954	4	*1895–1898*	128	84	0	21.33	4	2-46	0/0	24.50	1	
Brookes Dennis (*CY 1957*)	29.10.1915	9.3.2006	1	*1947*	17	10	0	8.50	–	–	–/–	–	1	

	Born	Died	Tests	Test Career	Runs	HS	100s	Avge	Wkts	BB	5/10	Avge	Ct/St	O/T
Brown Alan	17.10.1935		2	*1961*	3	3*	0	–	3	3-27	0/0	50.00	1	
Brown David John	30.1.1942		26	1965–1969	342	44*	0	11.79	79	5-42	2/0	28.31	7	
Brown Frederick Richard MBE (*CY 1933*)	16.12.1910	24.7.1991	22	1931–1953	734	79	0	25.31	45	5-49	1/0	31.06	22	
Brown George	6.10.1887	3.12.1964	7	1921–*1922*	299	84	0	29.90	–	–	–/–	–	9/3	
Brown John Thomas (*CY 1895*)	20.8.1869	4.11.1904	8	*1894*–1899	470	140	1	36.15	0	0-22	0/0	–	7	
Brown Simon John Emmerson	29.6.1969		1	1996	11	10*	0	11.00	2	1-60	0/0	69.00	1	
Buckenham Claude Percival	16.1.1876	23.2.1937	4	*1909*	43	17	0	6.14	21	5-115	1/0	28.23	2	
[1] **Butcher** Alan Raymond (*CY 1991*)	7.1.1954		1	1979	34	20	0	17.00	0	0-9	0/0	–	0	1
[1] **Butcher** Mark Alan	23.8.1972		71	1997–*2004*	4,288	173*	8	34.58	15	4-42	0/0	36.06	61	
Butcher Roland Orlando	14.10.1953		3	*1980*	71	32	0	14.20	–	–	–/–	–	3	3
Butler Harold James	12.3.1913	17.7.1991	2	1947–*1947*	15	15*	0	15.00	12	4-34	0/0	17.91	1	
Butt Henry Rigden	27.12.1865	21.12.1928	3	*1895*	22	13	0	7.33	–	–	–/–	–	1/1	
Buttler Joseph Charles	8.9.1990		18	2014–*2016*	784	85	0	31.36	–	–	–/–	–	54	81/50
Caddick Andrew Richard (*CY 2001*)	21.11.1968		62	1993–*2002*	861	49*	0	10.37	234	7-46	13/1	29.91	21	54
Calthorpe *Hon.* Frederick Somerset Gough-	27.5.1892	19.11.1935	4	*1929*	129	49	0	18.42	1	1-38	0/0	91.00	3	
Capel David John	6.2.1963		15	1987–*1989*	374	98	0	15.58	21	3-88	0/0	50.66	6	23
Carberry Michael Alexander	29.9.1980		6	*2009–2013*	345	60	0	28.75	–	–	–/–	–	7	6/1
Carr Arthur William (*CY 1923*)	21.5.1893	7.2.1963	11	*1922*–1929	237	63	0	19.75	–	–	–/–	–	3	
Carr Donald Bryce OBE (*CY 1960*)	28.12.1926	12.6.2016	2	*1951*	135	76	0	33.75	2	2-84	0/0	70.00	0	
Carr Douglas Ward (*CY 1910*)	17.3.1872	23.3.1950	1	1909	0	0	0	0.00	7	5-146	1/0	40.28	0	
Cartwright Thomas William MBE	22.7.1935	30.4.2007	5	1964–1965	26	9	0	5.20	15	6-94	1/0	36.26	2	
Chapman Arthur Percy Frank (*CY 1919*)	3.9.1900	16.9.1961	26	1924–*1930*	925	121	1	28.90	0	0-10	0/0	–	32	
Charlwood Henry Rupert James	19.12.1846	6.6.1888	2	*1876*	63	36	0	15.75	–	–	–/–	–	0	
Chatterton William	27.12.1861	19.3.1913	1	*1891*	48	48	0	48.00	–	–	–/–	–	0	
Childs John Henry (*CY 1987*)	15.8.1951		2	1988	2	2*	0	–	3	1-13	0/0	61.00	1	
Christopherson Stanley	11.11.1861	6.4.1949	1	1884	17	17	0	17.00	1	1-52	0/0	69.00	0	
Clark Edward Winchester	9.8.1902	28.4.1982	8	1929–1934	36	10	0	9.00	32	5-98	1/0	28.09	0	
Clarke Rikki	29.9.1981		2	*2003*	96	55	0	32.00	4	2-7	0/0	15.00	1	20
Clay John Charles	18.3.1898	11.8.1973	1	1935	–	–	–	–	0	0-30	0/0	–	1	
Close Dennis Brian CBE (*CY 1964*)	24.2.1931	14.9.2015	22	1949–1976	887	70	0	25.34	18	4-35	0/0	29.55	24	3
Coldwell Leonard John	10.1.1933	6.8.1996	7	1962–1964	9	6*	0	4.50	22	6-85	1/0	27.72	1	
Collingwood Paul David MBE (*CY 2007*)	26.5.1976		68	*2003–2010*	4,259	206	10	40.56	17	3-23	0/0	59.88	96	197/35
[4] **Compton** Denis Charles Scott CBE (*CY 1939*)	23.5.1918	23.4.1997	78	1937–*1956*	5,807	278	17	50.06	25	5-70	1/0	56.40	49	
[4] **Compton** Nicholas Richard Denis (*CY 2013*)	26.6.1983		16	*2012*–2016	775	117	2	28.70	–	–	–/–	–	7	
Cook Alastair Nathan CBE (*CY 2012*)	25.12.1984		140	*2005–2016*	11,057	294	30	46.45	1	1-6	0/0	7.00	141	92/4
Cook Cecil ("Sam")	23.8.1921	5.9.1996	1	1947	4	4	0	2.00	0	0-40	0/0	–	0	

	Born	Died	Tests	Test Career	Runs	HS	100s	Avge	Wkts	BB	5/10	Avge	Ct/St	O/T
Cook Geoffrey	9.10.1951		7	*1981–1982*	203	66	0	15.61	0	0-4	0/0	–	9	6
Cook Nicholas Grant Billson	17.6.1956		15	1983–1989	179	31	0	8.52	52	6-65	4/1	32.48	5	3
Cope Geoffrey Alan	23.2.1947		3	*1977*	40	22	0	13.33	8	3-102	0/0	34.62	1	2
Copson William Henry (*CY 1937*)	27.4.1908	13.9.1971	3	1939–1947	6	6	0	6.00	15	5-85	1/0	19.80	1	
Cork Dominic Gerald (*CY 1996*)	7.8.1971		37	1995–2002	864	59	0	18.00	131	7-43	5/0	29.81	18	32
Cornford Walter Latter	25.12.1900	6.2.1964	4	*1929*	36	18	0	9.00	–	–	–/–	–	5/3	
Cottam Robert Michael Henry	16.10.1944		4	*1968–1972*	27	13	0	6.75	14	4-50	0/0	23.35	2	
Coventry *Hon.* Charles John	26.2.1867	2.6.1929	2	*1888*	13	12	0	13.00	–	–	–/–	–	0	
Cowans Norman George	17.4.1961		19	*1982*–1985	175	36	0	7.95	51	6-77	2/0	39.27	9	23
[1] **Cowdrey** Christopher Stuart	20.10.1957		6	*1984*–1988	101	38	0	14.42	4	2-65	0/0	77.25	5	3
[1] **Cowdrey** *Lord* [Michael <u>Colin</u>] CBE (*CY 1956*)	24.12.1932	4.12.2000	114	*1954–1974*	7,624	182	22	44.06	0	0-1	0/0	–	120	1
Coxon Alexander	18.1.1916	22.1.2006	1	1948	19	19	0	9.50	3	2-90	0/0	57.33	0	
Cranston James	9.1.1859	10.12.1904	1	1890	31	16	0	15.50	–	–	–/–	–	1	
Cranston Kenneth	20.10.1917	8.1.2007	8	1947–1948	209	45	0	14.92	18	4-12	0/0	25.61	3	
Crapp John Frederick	14.10.1912	13.2.1981	7	1948–*1948*	319	56	0	29.00	–	–	–/–	–	7	
Crawford John Neville (*CY 1907*)	1.12.1886	2.5.1963	12	*1905–1907*	469	74	0	22.33	39	5-48	3/0	29.48	13	
Crawley John Paul	21.9.1971		37	1994–*2002*	1,800	156*	4	34.61	–	–	–/–	–	29	13
Croft Robert Damien Bale MBE	25.5.1970		21	1996–2001	421	37*	0	16.19	49	5-95	1/0	37.24	10	50
Curtis Timothy Stephen	15.1.1960		5	1988–1989	140	41	0	15.55	0	0-7	0/0	–	3	
Cuttell Willis Robert (*CY 1898*)	13.9.1863	9.12.1929	2	*1898*	65	21	0	16.25	6	3-17	0/0	12.16	2	
Dawson Edward William	13.2.1904	4.6.1979	5	*1927–1929*	175	55	0	19.44	–	–	–/–	–	0	
Dawson Liam Andrew	1.3.1990		1	*2016*	66	66*	0	66.00	2	2-129	0/0	64.50	0	1/1
Dawson Richard Kevin James	4.8.1980		7	*2001–2002*	114	19*	0	11.40	11	4-134	0/0	61.54	3	
Dean Harry	13.8.1884	12.3.1957	3	1912	10	8	0	5.00	11	4-19	0/0	13.90	2	
DeFreitas Phillip Anthony Jason (*CY 1992*)	18.2.1966		44	*1986*–1995	934	88	0	14.82	140	7-70	4/0	33.57	14	103
Denness Michael Henry OBE (*CY 1975*)	1.12.1940	19.4.2013	28	1969–1975	1,667	188	4	39.69	–	–	–/–	–	28	12
Denton David (*CY 1906*)	4.7.1874	16.2.1950	11	1905–*1909*	424	104	1	20.19	–	–	–/–	–	8	
Dewes John Gordon	11.10.1926	12.5.2015	5	1948–*1950*	121	67	0	12.10	–	–	–/–	–	0	
Dexter Edward Ralph CBE (*CY 1961*)	15.5.1935		62	1958–1968	4,502	205	9	47.89	66	4-10	0/0	34.93	29	
Dilley Graham Roy	18.5.1959	5.10.2011	41	*1979*–1989	521	56	0	13.35	138	6-38	6/0	29.76	10	36
Dipper Alfred Ernest	9.11.1885	7.11.1945	1	1921	51	40	0	25.50	–	–	–/–	–	0	
Doggart George <u>Hubert</u> Graham OBE	18.7.1925		2	1950	76	29	0	19.00	–	–	–/–	–	3	
D'Oliveira Basil Lewis CBE (*CY 1967*)	4.10.1931	18.11.2011	44	1966–1972	2,484	158	5	40.06	47	3-46	0/0	39.55	29	4
Dollery Horace Edgar ("Tom") (*CY 1952*)	14.10.1914	20.1.1987	4	1947–1950	72	37	0	10.28	–	–	–/–	–	1	
Dolphin Arthur	24.12.1885	23.10.1942	1	*1920*	1	1	0	0.50	–	–	–/–	–	1	
Douglas John William Henry Tyler (*CY 1915*)	3.9.1882	19.12.1930	23	*1911–1924*	962	119	1	29.15	45	5-46	1/0	33.02	9	

	Born	Died	Tests	Test Career	Runs	HS	100s	Avge	Wkts	BB	5/10	Avge	Ct/St	O/T
Downton Paul Rupert	4.4.1957		30	*1980*–1988	785	74	0	19.62	–	–	–/–	–	70/5	28
Druce Norman Frank (*CY 1898*)	1.1.1875	27.10.1954	5	*1897*	252	64	0	28.00	–	–	–/–	–	5	
Ducat Andrew (*CY 1920*)	16.2.1886	23.7.1942	1	1921	5	3	0	2.50	–	–	–/–	–	1	
Duckett Ben Matthew (*CY 2017*)	17.10.1994		4	*2016*	110	56	0	15.71	–	–	–/–	–	1	3
Duckworth George (*CY 1929*)	9.5.1901	5.1.1966	24	1924–1936	234	39*	0	14.62	–	–	–/–	–	45/15	
Duleepsinhji Kumar Shri (*CY 1930*)	13.6.1905	5.12.1959	12	1929–1931	995	173	3	58.52	0	0-7	0/0	–	10	
Durston Frederick John	11.7.1893	8.4.1965	1	1921	8	6*	0	8.00	5	4-102	0/0	27.20	0	
Ealham Mark Alan	27.8.1969		8	1996–1998	210	53*	0	21.00	17	4-21	0/0	28.70	4	64
Edmonds Philippe-Henri	8.3.1951		51	1975–1987	875	64	0	17.50	125	7-66	2/0	34.18	42	29
Edrich John Hugh MBE (*CY 1966*)	21.6.1937		77	1963–1976	5,138	310*	12	43.54	0	0-6	0/0	–	43	7
Edrich William John (*CY 1940*)	26.3.1916	24.4.1986	39	1938–*1954*	2,440	219	6	40.00	41	4-68	0/0	41.29	39	
Elliott Harry	2.11.1891	2.2.1976	4	*1927–1933*	61	37*	0	15.25	–	–	–/–	–	8/3	
Ellison Richard Mark (*CY 1986*)	21.9.1959		11	1984–1986	202	41	0	13.46	35	6-77	3/1	29.94	2	14
Emburey John Ernest (*CY 1984*)	20.8.1952		64	1978–1995	1,713	75	0	22.53	147	7-78	6/0	38.40	34	61
Emmett George Malcolm	2.12.1912	18.12.1976	1	1948	10	10	0	5.00	–	–	–/–	–	0	
Emmett Thomas	3.9.1841	29.6.1904	7	*1876–1881*	160	48	0	13.33	9	7-68	1/0	31.55	9	
Evans Alfred John	1.5.1889	18.9.1960	1	1921	18	14	0	9.00	–	–	–/–	–	0	
Evans Thomas Godfrey CBE (*CY 1951*)	18.8.1920	3.5.1999	91	1946–1959	2,439	104	2	20.49	–	–	–/–	–	173/46	
Fagg Arthur Edward	18.6.1915	13.9.1977	5	1936–1939	150	39	0	18.75	–	–	–/–	–	5	
Fairbrother Neil Harvey	9.9.1963		10	1987–*1992*	219	83	0	15.64	0	0-9	0/0	–	4	75
Fane Frederick Luther	27.4.1875	27.11.1960	14	*1905–1909*	682	143	1	26.23	–	–	–/–	–	6	
Farnes Kenneth (*CY 1939*)	8.7.1911	20.10.1941	15	1934–*1938*	58	20	0	4.83	60	6-96	3/1	28.65	1	
Farrimond William	23.5.1903	15.11.1979	4	*1930*–1935	116	35	0	16.57	–	–	–/–	–	5/2	
Fender Percy George Herbert (*CY 1915*)	22.8.1892	15.6.1985	13	*1920*–1929	380	60	0	19.00	29	5-90	2/0	40.86	14	
Ferris John James	21.5.1867	17.11.1900	1†	*1891*	16	16	0	16.00	13	7-37	2/1	7.00	0	
Fielder Arthur (*CY 1907*)	19.7.1877	30.8.1949	6	*1903–1907*	78	20	0	11.14	26	6-82	1/0	27.34	4	
Finn Steven Thomas	4.4.1989		36	*2009–2016*	279	56	0	11.16	125	6-79	5/0	30.40	8	65/21
Fishlock Laurence Barnard (*CY 1947*)	2.1.1907	25.6.1986	4	1936–*1946*	47	19*	0	11.75	–	–	–/–	–	1	
Flavell John Alfred (*CY 1965*)	15.5.1929	25.2.2004	4	1961–1964	31	14	0	7.75	7	2-65	0/0	52.42	0	
Fletcher Keith William Robert OBE (*CY 1974*)	20.5.1944		59	1968–*1981*	3,272	216	7	39.90	2	1-6	0/0	96.50	54	24
Flintoff Andrew MBE (*CY 2004*)	6.12.1977		78§	1998–2009	3,795	167	5	31.89	219	5-58	3/0	33.34	52	138‡/7
Flowers Wilfred	7.12.1856	1.11.1926	8	*1884*–1893	254	56	0	18.14	14	5-46	1/0	21.14	2	
Ford Francis Gilbertson Justice	14.12.1866	7.2.1940	5	*1894*	168	48	0	18.66	1	1-47	0/0	129.00	5	
Foster Frank Rowbotham (*CY 1912*)	31.1.1889	3.5.1958	11	*1911*–1912	330	71	0	23.57	45	6-91	4/0	20.57	11	
Foster James Savin	15.4.1980		7	*2001–2002*	226	48	0	25.11	–	–	–/–	–	17/1	11/5

§ *Flintoff's figures exclude 50 runs and seven wickets for the ICC World XI v Australia in the Super Series Test in 2005-06.*

	Born	*Died*	*Tests*	*Test Career*	*Runs*	*HS*	*100s*	*Avge*	*Wkts*	*BB*	*5/10*	*Avge*	*Ct/St*	*O/T*
Foster Neil Alan (*CY 1988*)	6.5.1962		29	1983–1993	446	39	0	11.73	88	8-107	5/1	32.85	7	48
Foster Reginald Erskine ("Tip") (*CY 1900*)	16.4.1878	13.5.1914	8	*1903*–1907	602	287	1	46.30	–	–	–/–	–	13	
Fothergill Arnold James	26.8.1854	1.8.1932	2	*1888*	33	32	0	16.50	8	4-19	0/0	11.25	0	
Fowler Graeme	20.4.1957		21	1982–*1984*	1,307	201	3	35.32	0	0-0	0/0	–	10	26
Fraser Angus Robert Charles MBE (*CY 1996*)	8.8.1965		46	1989–*1998*	388	32	0	7.46	177	8-53	13/2	27.32	9	42
Freeman Alfred Percy ("Tich") (*CY 1923*)	17.5.1888	28.1.1965	12	*1924*–1929	154	50*	0	14.00	66	7-71	5/3	25.86	4	
French Bruce Nicholas	13.8.1959		16	1986–*1987*	308	59	0	18.11	–	–	–/–	–	38/1	13
Fry Charles Burgess (*CY 1895*)	25.4.1872	7.9.1956	26	*1895*–1912	1,223	144	2	32.18	0	0-3	0/0	–	17	
Gallian Jason Edward Riche	25.6.1971		3	1995–*1995*	74	28	0	12.33	0	0-6	0/0	–	1	
Gatting Michael William OBE (*CY 1984*)	6.6.1957		79	*1977–1994*	4,409	207	10	35.55	4	1-14	0/0	79.25	59	92
Gay Leslie Hewitt	24.3.1871	1.11.1949	1	*1894*	37	33	0	18.50	–	–	–/–	–	3/1	
Geary George (*CY 1927*)	9.7.1893	6.3.1981	14	1924–1934	249	66	0	15.56	46	7-70	4/1	29.41	13	
Gibb Paul Antony	11.7.1913	7.12.1977	8	*1938–1946*	581	120	2	44.69	–	–	–/–	–	3/1	
Giddins Edward Simon Hunter	20.7.1971		4	1999–2000	10	7	0	2.50	12	5-15	1/0	20.00	0	
Gifford Norman MBE (*CY 1975*)	30.3.1940		15	1964–1973	179	25*	0	16.27	33	5-55	1/0	31.09	8	2
Giles Ashley Fraser MBE (*CY 2005*)	19.3.1973		54	1998–*2006*	1,421	59	0	20.89	143	5-57	5/0	40.60	33	62
[2] **Gilligan** Alfred Herbert Harold	29.6.1896	5.5.1978	4	*1929*	71	32	0	17.75	–	–	–/–	–	0	
[2] **Gilligan** Arthur Edward Robert (*CY 1924*)	23.12.1894	5.9.1976	11	*1922–1924*	209	39*	0	16.07	36	6-7	2/1	29.05	3	
Gimblett Harold (*CY 1953*)	19.10.1914	30.3.1978	3	1936–1939	129	67*	0	32.25	–	–	–/–	–	1	
Gladwin Clifford	3.4.1916	9.4.1988	8	1947–1949	170	51*	0	28.33	15	3-21	0/0	38.06	2	
Goddard Thomas William John (*CY 1938*)	1.10.1900	22.5.1966	8	1930–1939	13	8	0	6.50	22	6-29	1/0	26.72	3	
Gooch Graham Alan OBE (*CY 1980*)	23.7.1953		118	1975–*1994*	8,900	333	20	42.58	23	3-39	0/0	46.47	103	125
Gough Darren (*CY 1999*)	18.9.1970		58	1994–2003	855	65	0	12.57	229	6-42	9/0	28.39	13	158‡/2
Gover Alfred Richard MBE (*CY 1937*)	29.2.1908	7.10.2001	4	1936–1946	2	2*	0	–	8	3-85	0/0	44.87	1	
Gower David Ivon OBE (*CY 1979*)	1.4.1957		117	1978–1992	8,231	215	18	44.25	1	1-1	0/0	20.00	74	114
[2] **Grace** Edward Mills	28.11.1841	20.5.1911	1	1880	36	36	0	18.00	–	–	–/–	–	1	
[2] **Grace** George Frederick	13.12.1850	22.9.1880	1	1880	0	0	0	0.00	–	–	–/–	–	2	
[2] **Grace** William Gilbert (*CY 1896*)	18.7.1848	23.10.1915	22	1880–1899	1,098	170	2	32.29	9	2-12	0/0	26.22	39	
Graveney Thomas William OBE (*CY 1953*)	16.6.1927	3.11.2015	79	1951–1969	4,882	258	11	44.38	1	1-34	0/0	167.00	80	
Greenhough Thomas	9.11.1931	15.9.2009	4	1959–1960	4	2	0	1.33	16	5-35	1/0	22.31	1	
Greenwood Andrew	20.8.1847	12.2.1889	2	*1876*	77	49	0	19.25	–	–	–/–	–	2	
[2] **Greig** Anthony William (*CY 1975*)	6.10.1946	29.12.2012	58	1972–1977	3,599	148	8	40.43	141	8-86	6/2	32.20	87	22
[2] **Greig** Ian Alexander	8.12.1955		2	1982	26	14	0	6.50	4	4-53	0/0	28.50	0	
Grieve Basil Arthur Firebrace	28.5.1864	19.11.1917	2	*1888*	40	14*	0	40.00	–	–	–/–	–	0	
Griffith Stewart Cathie CBE ("Billy")	16.6.1914	7.4.1993	3	*1947–1948*	157	140	1	31.40	–	–	–/–	–	5	
[2] **Gunn** George (*CY 1914*)	13.6.1879	29.6.1958	15	*1907–1929*	1,120	122*	2	40.00	0	0-8	0/0	–	15	

	Born	*Died*	*Tests*	*Test Career*	*Runs*	*HS*	*100s*	*Avge*	*Wkts*	*BB*	*5/10*	*Avge*	*Ct/St*	*O/T*
[2] **Gunn** John Richmond (*CY 1904*)	19.7.1876	21.8.1963	6	*1901*–1905	85	24	0	10.62	18	5-76	1/0	21.50	3	
Gunn William (*CY 1890*)	4.12.1858	29.1.1921	11	*1886*–1899	392	102*	1	21.77	–	–	–/–	–	5	
Habib Aftab	7.2.1972		2	1999	26	19	0	8.66	–	–	–/–	–	0	
Haig Nigel Esmé	12.12.1887	27.10.1966	5	1921–*1929*	126	47	0	14.00	13	3-73	0/0	34.46	4	
Haigh Schofield (*CY 1901*)	19.3.1871	27.2.1921	11	*1898*–1912	113	25	0	7.53	24	6-11	1/0	25.91	8	
Hales Alexander Daniel	3.1.1989		11	*2015*–2016	573	94	0	27.28	0	0-2	0/0	–	8	38/45
Hallows Charles (*CY 1928*)	4.4.1895	10.11.1972	2	1921–1928	42	26	0	42.00	–	–	–/–	–	0	
Hameed Haseeb	17.1.1997		3	*2016*	219	82	0	43.80	–	–	–/–	–	4	
Hamilton Gavin Mark	16.9.1974		1	*1999*	0	0	0	0.00	0	0-63	0/0	–	0	0‡
Hammond Walter Reginald (*CY 1928*)	19.6.1903	1.7.1965	85	*1927–1946*	7,249	336*	22	58.45	83	5-36	2/0	37.80	110	
Hampshire John Harry	10.2.1941		8	1969–1975	403	107	1	26.86	–	–	–/–	–	9	3
Hardinge Harold Thomas William ("Wally") (*CY 1915*)	25.2.1886	8.5.1965	1	1921	30	25	0	15.00	–	–	–/–	–	0	
[1] **Hardstaff** Joseph snr	9.11.1882	2.4.1947	5	*1907*	311	72	0	31.10	–	–	–/–	–	1	
[1] **Hardstaff** Joseph jnr (*CY 1938*)	3.7.1911	1.1.1990	23	1935–1948	1,636	205*	4	46.74	–	–	–/–	–	9	
Harmison Stephen James MBE (*CY 2005*)	23.10.1978		62§	2002–2009	742	49*	0	12.16	222	7-12	8/1	31.94	7	58/2
Harris *Lord* [George Robert Canning]	3.2.1851	24.3.1932	4	*1878*–1884	145	52	0	29.00	0	0-14	0/0	–	2	
Hartley John Cabourn	15.11.1874	8.3.1963	2	*1905*	15	9	0	3.75	1	1-62	0/0	115.00	2	
Hawke *Lord* [Martin Bladen] (*CY 1909*)	16.8.1860	10.10.1938	5	*1895–1898*	55	30	0	7.85	–	–	–/–	–	3	
Hayes Ernest George (*CY 1907*)	6.11.1876	2.12.1953	5	*1905*–1912	86	35	0	10.75	1	1-28	0/0	52.00	2	
Hayes Frank Charles	6.12.1946		9	1973–1976	244	106*	1	15.25	–	–	–/–	–	7	6
Hayward Thomas Walter (*CY 1895*)	29.3.1871	19.7.1939	35	*1895*–1909	1,999	137	3	34.46	14	4-22	0/0	36.71	19	
[3] **Headley** Dean Warren	27.1.1970		15	1997–1999	186	31	0	8.45	60	6-60	1/0	27.85	7	13
[2] **Hearne** Alec (*CY 1894*)	22.7.1863	16.5.1952	1	*1891*	9	9	0	9.00	–	–	–/–	–	1	
[1,2] **Hearne** Frank	23.11.1858	14.7.1949	2†	*1888*	47	27	0	23.50	–	–	–/–	–	1	
[2] **Hearne** George Gibbons	7.7.1856	13.2.1932	1	*1891*	0	0	0	0.00	–	–	–/–	–	0	
Hearne John Thomas (*CY 1892*)	3.5.1867	17.4.1944	12	*1891*–1899	126	40	0	9.00	49	6-41	4/1	22.08	4	
Hearne John William (*CY 1912*)	11.2.1891	14.9.1965	24	*1911*–1926	806	114	1	26.00	30	5-49	1/0	48.73	13	
Hegg Warren Kevin	23.2.1968		2	*1998*	30	15	0	7.50	–	–	–/–	–	8	
Hemmings Edward Ernest	20.2.1949		16	1982–*1990*	383	95	0	22.52	43	6-58	1/0	42.44	5	33
Hendren Elias Henry ("Patsy") (*CY 1920*)	5.2.1889	4.10.1962	51	*1920–1934*	3,525	205*	7	47.63	1	1-27	0/0	31.00	33	
Hendrick Michael (*CY 1978*)	22.10.1948		30	1974–1981	128	15	0	6.40	87	4-28	0/0	25.83	25	22
Heseltine Christopher	26.11.1869	13.6.1944	2	*1895*	18	18	0	9.00	5	5-38	1/0	16.80	3	
Hick Graeme Ashley MBE (*CY 1987*)	23.5.1966		65	1991–*2000*	3,383	178	6	31.32	23	4-126	0/0	56.78	90	120
Higgs Kenneth (*CY 1968*)	14.1.1937	7.9.2016	15	1965–1968	185	63	0	11.56	71	6-91	2/0	20.74	4	

§ *Harmison's figures exclude one run and four wickets for the ICC World XI v Australia in the Super Series Test in 2005-06.*

	Born	*Died*	*Tests*	*Test Career*	*Runs*	*HS*	*100s*	*Avge*	*Wkts*	*BB*	*5/10*	*Avge*	*Ct/St*	*O/T*
Hill Allen	14.11.1843	28.8.1910	2	*1876*	101	49	0	50.50	7	4-27	0/0	18.57	1	
Hill Arthur James Ledger	26.7.1871	6.9.1950	3	*1895*	251	124	1	62.75	4	4-8	0/0	2.00	1	
Hilton Malcolm Jameson (*CY 1957*)	2.8.1928	8.7.1990	4	1950–*1951*	37	15	0	7.40	14	5-61	1/0	34.07	1	
Hirst George Herbert (*CY 1901*)	7.9.1871	10.5.1954	24	*1897*–1909	790	85	0	22.57	59	5-48	3/0	30.00	18	
Hitch John William (*CY 1914*)	7.5.1886	7.7.1965	7	*1911*–1921	103	51*	0	14.71	7	2-31	0/0	46.42	4	
Hobbs *Sir* John Berry (*CY 1909*)	16.12.1882	21.12.1963	61	*1907*–1930	5,410	211	15	56.94	1	1-19	0/0	165.00	17	
Hobbs Robin Nicholas Stuart	8.5.1942		7	1967–1971	34	15*	0	6.80	12	3-25	0/0	40.08	8	
Hoggard Matthew James MBE (*CY 2006*)	31.12.1976		67	2000–*2007*	473	38	0	7.27	248	7-61	7/1	30.50	24	26
Hollies William Eric (*CY 1955*)	5.6.1912	16.4.1981	13	*1934*–1950	37	18*	0	5.28	44	7-50	5/0	30.27	2	
[2] **Hollioake** Adam John (*CY 2003*)	5.9.1971		4	1997–*1997*	65	45	0	10.83	2	2-31	0/0	33.50	4	35
[2] **Hollioake** Benjamin Caine	11.11.1977	23.3.2002	2	1997–1998	44	28	0	11.00	4	2-105	0/0	49.75	2	20
Holmes Errol Reginald Thorold (*CY 1936*)	21.8.1905	16.8.1960	5	*1934*–1935	114	85*	0	16.28	2	1-10	0/0	38.00	4	
Holmes Percy (*CY 1920*)	25.11.1886	3.9.1971	7	1921–1932	357	88	0	27.46	–	–	–/–	–	3	
Hone Leland	30.1.1853	31.12.1896	1	*1878*	13	7	0	6.50	–	–	–/–	–	2	
Hopwood John Leonard	30.10.1903	15.6.1985	2	1934	12	8	0	6.00	0	0-16	0/0	–	0	
Hornby Albert Neilson ("Monkey")	10.2.1847	17.12.1925	3	*1878*–1884	21	9	0	3.50	1	1-0	0/0	0.00	0	
Horton Martin John	21.4.1934	3.4.2011	2	1959	60	58	0	30.00	2	2-24	0/0	29.50	2	
Howard Nigel David	18.5.1925	31.5.1979	4	*1951*	86	23	0	17.20	–	–	–/–	–	4	
Howell Henry	29.11.1890	9.7.1932	5	*1920*–1924	15	5	0	7.50	7	4-115	0/0	79.85	0	
Howorth Richard	26.4.1909	2.4.1980	5	1947–*1947*	145	45*	0	18.12	19	6-124	1/0	33.42	2	
Humphries Joseph	19.5.1876	7.5.1946	3	*1907*	44	16	0	8.80	–	–	–/–	–	7	
Hunter Joseph	3.8.1855	4.1.1891	5	*1884*	93	39*	0	18.60	–	–	–/–	–	8/3	
Hussain Nasser OBE (*CY 2003*)	28.3.1968		96	*1989*–2004	5,764	207	14	37.18	0	0-15	0/0	–	67	88
Hutchings Kenneth Lotherington (*CY 1907*)	7.12.1882	3.9.1916	7	*1907*–1909	341	126	1	28.41	1	1-5	0/0	81.00	9	
[1] **Hutton** *Sir* Leonard (*CY 1938*)	23.6.1916	6.9.1990	79	1937–*1954*	6,971	364	19	56.67	3	1-2	0/0	77.33	57	
[1] **Hutton** Richard Anthony	6.9.1942		5	1971	219	81	0	36.50	9	3-72	0/0	28.55	9	
Iddon John	8.1.1902	17.4.1946	5	*1934*–1935	170	73	0	28.33	0	0-3	0/0	–	0	
Igglesden Alan Paul	8.10.1964		3	1989–*1993*	6	3*	0	3.00	6	2-91	0/0	54.83	1	4
Ikin John Thomas	7.3.1918	15.9.1984	18	1946–1955	606	60	0	20.89	3	1-38	0/0	118.00	31	
Illingworth Raymond CBE (*CY 1960*)	8.6.1932		61	1958–1973	1,836	113	2	23.24	122	6-29	3/0	31.20	45	3
Illingworth Richard Keith	23.8.1963		9	1991–*1995*	128	28	0	18.28	19	4-96	0/0	32.36	5	25
Ilott Mark Christopher	27.8.1970		5	1993–*1995*	28	15	0	7.00	12	3-48	0/0	45.16	0	
Insole Douglas John CBE (*CY 1956*)	18.4.1926		9	1950–1957	408	110*	1	27.20	–	–	–/–	–	8	
Irani Ronald Charles	26.10.1971		3	1996–1999	86	41	0	17.20	3	1-22	0/0	37.33	2	31
Jackman Robin David (*CY 1981*)	13.8.1945		4	*1980*–1982	42	17	0	7.00	14	4-110	0/0	31.78	0	15
Jackson *Sir* Francis Stanley (*CY 1894*)	21.11.1870	9.3.1947	20	1893–1905	1,415	144*	5	48.79	24	5-52	1/0	33.29	10	

	Born	*Died*	*Tests*	*Test Career*	*Runs*	*HS*	*100s*	*Avge*	*Wkts*	*BB*	*5/10*	*Avge*	*Ct/St*	*O/T*
Jackson Herbert Leslie (*CY 1959*)	5.4.1921	25.4.2007	2	1949–1961	15	8	0	15.00	7	2-26	0/0	22.14	1	
James Stephen Peter	7.9.1967		2	1998	71	36	0	17.75	–	–	–/–	–	0	
Jameson John Alexander	30.6.1941		4	1971–*1973*	214	82	0	26.75	1	1-17	0/0	17.00	0	3
Jardine Douglas Robert (*CY 1928*)	23.10.1900	18.6.1958	22	1928–*1933*	1,296	127	1	48.00	0	0-10	0/0	–	26	
Jarvis Paul William	29.6.1965		9	*1987–1992*	132	29*	0	10.15	21	4-107	0/0	45.95	2	16
Jenkins Roland Oliver (*CY 1950*)	24.11.1918	22.7.1995	9	*1948*–1952	198	39	0	18.00	32	5-116	1/0	34.31	4	
Jennings Keaton Kent	19.6.1992		2	*2016*	167	112	1	41.75	0	0-20	0/0	–	2	
Jessop Gilbert Laird (*CY 1898*)	19.5.1874	11.5.1955	18	1899–1912	569	104	1	21.88	10	4-68	0/0	35.40	11	
Johnson Richard Leonard	29.12.1974		3	2003–*2003*	59	26	0	14.75	16	6-33	2/0	17.18	0	10
Jones Arthur Owen	16.8.1872	21.12.1914	12	1899–1909	291	34	0	13.85	3	3-73	0/0	44.33	15	
Jones Geraint Owen MBE	14.7.1976		34	*2003–2006*	1,172	100	1	23.91	–	–	–/–	–	128/5	49‡/2
[1] **Jones** Ivor Jeffrey	10.12.1941		15	*1963–1967*	38	16	0	4.75	44	6-118	1/0	40.20	4	
[1] **Jones** Simon Philip MBE (*CY 2006*)	25.12.1978		18	2002–2005	205	44	0	15.76	59	6-53	3/0	28.23	4	8
Jordan Christopher James	4.10.1988		8	2014–*2014*	180	35	0	18.00	21	4-18	0/0	35.80	14	31/19
Jupp Henry	19.11.1841	8.4.1889	2	*1876*	68	63	0	17.00	–	–	–/–	–	2	
Jupp Vallance William Crisp (*CY 1928*)	27.3.1891	9.7.1960	8	1921–1928	208	38	0	17.33	28	4-37	0/0	22.00	5	
Keeton William Walter (*CY 1940*)	30.4.1905	10.10.1980	2	1934–1939	57	25	0	14.25	–	–	–/–	–	0	
Kennedy Alexander Stuart (*CY 1933*)	24.1.1891	15.11.1959	5	*1922*	93	41*	0	15.50	31	5-76	2/0	19.32	5	
Kenyon Donald	15.5.1924	12.11.1996	8	*1951*–1955	192	87	0	12.80	–	–	–/–	–	5	
Kerrigan Simon Christopher	10.5.1989		1	2013	1	1*	0	–	0	0-53	0/0	–	0	
Key Robert William Trevor (*CY 2005*)	12.5.1979		15	2002–*2004*	775	221	1	31.00	–	–	–/–	–	11	5/1
Khan Amjad	14.10.1980		1	*2008*	–	–	–	–	1	1-111	0/0	122.00	0	0/1
Killick *Rev.* Edgar Thomas	9.5.1907	18.5.1953	2	1929	81	31	0	20.25	–	–	–/–	–	2	
Kilner Roy (*CY 1924*)	17.10.1890	5.4.1928	9	1924–1926	233	74	0	33.28	24	4-51	0/0	30.58	6	
King John Herbert	16.4.1871	18.11.1946	1	1909	64	60	0	32.00	1	1-99	0/0	99.00	0	
Kinneir Septimus Paul (*CY 1912*)	13.5.1871	16.10.1928	1	*1911*	52	30	0	26.00	–	–	–/–	–	0	
Kirtley Robert James	10.1.1975		4	2003–*2003*	32	12	0	5.33	19	6-34	1/0	29.52	3	11/1
Knight Albert Ernest (*CY 1904*)	8.10.1872	25.4.1946	3	*1903*	81	70*	0	16.20	–	–	–/–	–	1	
Knight Barry Rolfe	18.2.1938		29	*1961*–1969	812	127	2	26.19	70	4-38	0/0	31.75	14	
Knight Donald John (*CY 1915*)	12.5.1894	5.1.1960	2	1921	54	38	0	13.50	–	–	–/–	–	1	
Knight Nicholas Verity	28.11.1969		17	1995–2001	719	113	1	23.96	–	–	–/–	–	26	100
Knott Alan Philip Eric (*CY 1970*)	9.4.1946		95	1967–1981	4,389	135	5	32.75	–	–	–/–	–	250/19	20
Knox Neville Alexander (*CY 1907*)	10.10.1884	3.3.1935	2	1907	24	8*	0	8.00	3	2-39	0/0	35.00	0	
Laker James Charles (*CY 1952*)	9.2.1922	23.4.1986	46	*1947–1958*	676	63	0	14.08	193	10-53	9/3	21.24	12	
Lamb Allan Joseph (*CY 1981*)	20.6.1954		79	1982–1992	4,656	142	14	36.09	1	1-6	0/0	23.00	75	122
Langridge James (*CY 1932*)	10.7.1906	10.9.1966	8	1933–1946	242	70	0	26.88	19	7-56	2/0	21.73	6	

	Born	Died	Tests	Test Career	Runs	HS	100s	Avge	Wkts	BB	5/10	Avge	Ct/St	O/T
Larkins Wayne	22.11.1953		13	*1979–1990*	493	64	0	20.54	–	–	–/–	–	8	25
Larter John David Frederick	24.4.1940		10	1962–1965	16	10	0	3.20	37	5-57	2/0	25.43	5	
Larwood Harold MBE (*CY 1927*)	14.11.1904	22.7.1995	21	1926–*1932*	485	98	0	19.40	78	6-32	4/1	28.35	15	
Lathwell Mark Nicholas	26.12.1971		2	1993	78	33	0	19.50	–	–	–/–	–	0	
Lawrence David Valentine ("Syd")	28.1.1964		5	1988–*1991*	60	34	0	10.00	18	5-106	1/0	37.55	0	1
Leadbeater Edric	15.8.1927	17.4.2011	2	*1951*	40	38	0	20.00	2	1-38	0/0	109.00	3	
Lee Henry William	26.10.1890	21.4.1981	1	*1930*	19	18	0	9.50	–	–	–/–	–	0	
Lees Walter Scott (*CY 1906*)	25.12.1875	10.9.1924	5	*1905*	66	25*	0	11.00	26	6-78	2/0	17.96	2	
Legge Geoffrey Bevington	26.1.1903	21.11.1940	5	*1927–1929*	299	196	1	49.83	0	0-34	0/0	–	1	
Leslie Charles Frederick Henry	8.12.1861	12.2.1921	4	*1882*	106	54	0	15.14	4	3-31	0/0	11.00	1	
Lever John Kenneth MBE (*CY 1979*)	24.2.1949		21	*1976*–1986	306	53	0	11.76	73	7-46	3/1	26.72	11	22
Lever Peter	17.9.1940		17	*1970*–1975	350	88*	0	21.87	41	6-38	2/0	36.80	11	10
Leveson Gower *Sir* Henry Dudley Gresham	8.5.1873	1.2.1954	3	*1909*	95	31	0	23.75	–	–	–/–	–	1	
Levett William Howard Vincent ("Hopper")	25.1.1908	1.12.1995	1	*1933*	7	5	0	7.00	–	–	–/–	–	3	
Lewis Anthony Robert CBE	6.7.1938		9	*1972*–1973	457	125	1	32.64	–	–	–/–	–	0	
Lewis Clairmonte Christopher	14.2.1968		32	1990–1996	1,105	117	1	23.02	93	6-111	3/0	37.52	25	53
Lewis Jonathan	26.8.1975		1	2006	27	20	0	13.50	3	3-68	0/0	40.66	0	13/2
Leyland Maurice (*CY 1929*)	20.7.1900	1.1.1967	41	1928–1938	2,764	187	9	46.06	6	3-91	0/0	97.50	13	
Lilley Arthur Frederick Augustus ("Dick") (*CY 1897*)	28.11.1866	17.11.1929	35	1896–1909	903	84	0	20.52	1	1-23	0/0	23.00	70/22	
Lillywhite James	23.2.1842	25.10.1929	2	*1876*	16	10	0	8.00	8	4-70	0/0	15.75	1	
Lloyd David	18.3.1947		9	1974–*1974*	552	214*	1	42.46	0	0-4	0/0	–	11	8
Lloyd Timothy Andrew	5.11.1956		1	1984	10	10*	0	–	–	–	–/–	–	0	3
Loader Peter James (*CY 1958*)	25.10.1929	15.3.2011	13	1954–*1958*	76	17	0	5.84	39	6-36	1/0	22.51	2	
Lock Graham Anthony Richard (*CY 1954*)	5.7.1929	30.3.1995	49	1952–*1967*	742	89	0	13.74	174	7-35	9/3	25.58	59	
Lockwood William Henry (*CY 1899*)	25.3.1868	26.4.1932	12	1893–1902	231	52*	0	17.76	43	7-71	5/1	20.53	4	
Lohmann George Alfred (*CY 1889*)	2.6.1865	1.12.1901	18	1886–1896	213	62*	0	8.87	112	9-28	9/5	10.75	28	
Lowson Frank Anderson	1.7.1925	8.9.1984	7	1951–1955	245	68	0	18.84	–	–	–/–	–	5	
Lucas Alfred Perry	20.2.1857	12.10.1923	5	*1878*–1884	157	55	0	19.62	0	0-23	0/0	–	1	
Luckhurst Brian William (*CY 1971*)	5.2.1939	1.3.2005	21	*1970–1974*	1,298	131	4	36.05	1	1-9	0/0	32.00	14	3
Lyth Adam (*CY 2015*)	25.9.1987		7	2015	265	107	1	20.38	0	0-0	0/0	–	8	
Lyttelton *Hon.* Alfred	7.2.1857	5.7.1913	4	1880–1884	94	31	0	15.66	4	4-19	0/0	4.75	2	
Macaulay George Gibson (*CY 1924*)	7.12.1897	13.12.1940	8	*1922*–1933	112	76	0	18.66	24	5-64	1/0	27.58	5	
MacBryan John Crawford William (*CY 1925*)	22.7.1892	14.7.1983	1	1924	–	–	–	–	–	–	–/–	–	0	
McCague Martin John	24.5.1969		3	1993–*1994*	21	11	0	4.20	6	4-121	0/0	65.00	1	
McConnon James Edward	21.6.1922	26.1.2003	2	1954	18	11	0	9.00	4	3-19	0/0	18.50	4	

	Born	Died	Tests	Test Career	Runs	HS	100s	Avge	Wkts	BB	5/10	Avge	Ct/St	O/T
McGahey Charles Percy (*CY 1902*)	12.2.1871	10.1.1935	2	*1901*	38	18	0	9.50	–	–	–/–	–	1	
McGrath Anthony	6.10.1975		4	2003	201	81	0	40.20	4	3-16	0/0	14.00	3	14
MacGregor Gregor (*CY 1891*)	31.8.1869	20.8.1919	8	1890–1893	96	31	0	12.00	–	–	–/–	–	14/3	
McIntyre Arthur John William (*CY 1958*)	14.5.1918	26.12.2009	3	1950–1955	19	7	0	3.16	–	–	–/–	–	8	
MacKinnon Francis Alexander	9.4.1848	27.2.1947	1	*1878*	5	5	0	2.50	–	–	–/–	–	0	
MacLaren Archibald Campbell (*CY 1895*)	1.12.1871	17.11.1944	35	*1894*–1909	1,931	140	5	33.87	–	–	–/–	–	29	
McMaster Joseph Emile Patrick	16.3.1861	7.6.1929	1	*1888*	0	0	0	0.00	–	–	–/–	–	0	
Maddy Darren Lee	23.5.1974		3	1999–*1999*	46	24	0	11.50	0	0-40	0/0	–	4	8/4
Mahmood Sajid Iqbal	21.12.1981		8	2006–*2006*	81	34	0	8.10	20	4-22	0/0	38.10	0	26/4
Makepeace Joseph William Henry	22.8.1881	19.12.1952	4	*1920*	279	117	1	34.87	–	–	–/–	–	0	
Malcolm Devon Eugene (*CY 1995*)	22.2.1963		40	1989–1997	236	29	0	6.05	128	9-57	5/2	37.09	7	10
Mallender Neil Alan	13.8.1961		2	1992	8	4	0	2.66	10	5-50	1/0	21.50	0	
[1] **Mann** Francis George CBE	6.9.1917	8.8.2001	7	*1948*–1949	376	136*	1	37.60	–	–	–/–	–	3	
[1] **Mann** Francis Thomas	3.3.1888	6.10.1964	5	*1922*	281	84	0	35.12	–	–	–/–	–	4	
Marks Victor James	25.6.1955		6	1982–*1983*	249	83	0	27.66	11	3-78	0/0	44.00	0	34
Marriott Charles Stowell ("Father")	14.9.1895	13.10.1966	1	1933	0	0	0	0.00	11	6-59	2/1	8.72	1	
Martin Frederick (*CY 1892*)	12.10.1861	13.12.1921	2	1890–*1891*	14	13	0	7.00	14	6-50	2/1	10.07	2	
Martin John William	16.2.1917	4.1.1987	1	1947	26	26	0	13.00	1	1-111	0/0	129.00	0	
Martin Peter James	15.11.1968		8	1995–1997	115	29	0	8.84	17	4-60	0/0	34.11	6	20
Mason John Richard (*CY 1898*)	26.3.1874	15.10.1958	5	*1897*	129	32	0	12.90	2	1-8	0/0	74.50	3	
Matthews Austin David George	3.5.1904	29.7.1977	1	1937	2	2*	0	–	2	1-13	0/0	32.50	1	
May Peter Barker Howard CBE (*CY 1952*)	31.12.1929	27.12.1994	66	1951–1961	4,537	285*	13	46.77	–	–	–/–	–	42	
Maynard Matthew Peter (*CY 1998*)	21.3.1966		4	1988–*1993*	87	35	0	10.87	–	–	–/–	–	3	14
Mead Charles Philip (*CY 1912*)	9.3.1887	26.3.1958	17	*1911–1928*	1,185	182*	4	49.37	–	–	–/–	–	4	
Mead Walter (*CY 1904*)	1.4.1868	18.3.1954	1	1899	7	7	0	3.50	1	1-91	0/0	91.00	1	
Midwinter William Evans	19.6.1851	3.12.1890	4†	*1881*	95	36	0	13.57	10	4-81	0/0	27.20	5	
Milburn Colin ("Ollie") (*CY 1967*)	23.10.1941	28.2.1990	9	1966–*1968*	654	139	2	46.71	–	–	–/–	–	7	
Miller Audley Montague	19.10.1869	26.6.1959	1	*1895*	24	20*	0	–	–	–	–/–	–	0	
Miller Geoffrey OBE	8.9.1952		34	1976–1984	1,213	98*	0	25.80	60	5-44	1/0	30.98	17	25
Milligan Frank William	19.3.1870	31.3.1900	2	*1898*	58	38	0	14.50	0	0-0	0/0	–	1	
Millman Geoffrey	2.10.1934	6.4.2005	6	*1961*–1962	60	32*	0	12.00	–	–	–/–	–	13/2	
Milton Clement Arthur (*CY 1959*)	10.3.1928	25.4.2007	6	1958–1959	204	104*	1	25.50	0	0-12	0/0	–	5	
Mitchell Arthur	13.9.1902	25.12.1976	6	*1933*–1936	298	72	0	29.80	0	0-4	0/0	–	9	
Mitchell Frank (*CY 1902*)	13.8.1872	11.10.1935	2†	*1898*	88	41	0	22.00	–	–	–/–	–	2	
Mitchell Thomas Bignall	4.9.1902	27.1.1996	5	*1932*–1935	20	9	0	5.00	8	2-49	0/0	62.25	1	
Mitchell-Innes Norman Stewart ("Mandy")	7.9.1914	28.12.2006	1	1935	5	5	0	5.00	–	–	–/–	–	0	

	Born	Died	Tests	Test Career	Runs	HS	100s	Avge	Wkts	BB	5/10	Avge	Ct/St	O/T
Mold Arthur Webb (*CY 1892*)	27.5.1863	29.4.1921	3	1893	0	0*	0	0.00	7	3-44	0/0	33.42	1	
Moon Leonard James	9.2.1878	23.11.1916	4	*1905*	182	36	0	22.75	–	–	–/–	–	4	
Morgan Eoin Joseph Gerard (*CY 2011*)	10.9.1986		16	2010–*2011*	700	130	2	30.43	–	–	–/–	–	11	147‡/64
Morley Frederick	16.12.1850	28.9.1884	4	1880–*1882*	6	2*	0	1.50	16	5-56	1/0	18.50	4	
Morris Hugh	5.10.1963		3	1991	115	44	0	19.16	–	–	–/–	–	3	
Morris John Edward	1.4.1964		3	1990	71	32	0	23.66	–	–	–/–	–	3	8
Mortimore John Brian	14.5.1933	13.2.2014	9	*1958*–1964	243	73*	0	24.30	13	3-36	0/0	56.38	3	
Moss Alan Edward	14.11.1930		9	*1953*–1960	61	26	0	10.16	21	4-35	0/0	29.80	1	
Moxon Martyn Douglas (*CY 1993*)	4.5.1960		10	1986–1989	455	99	0	28.43	0	0-3	0/0	–	10	8
Mullally Alan David	12.7.1969		19	1996–2001	127	24	0	5.52	58	5-105	1/0	31.24	6	50
Munton Timothy Alan (*CY 1995*)	30.7.1965		2	1992	25	25*	0	25.00	4	2-22	0/0	50.00	0	
Murdoch William Lloyd	18.10.1854	18.2.1911	1†	*1891*	12	12	0	12.00	–	–	–/–	–	0/1	
Murray John Thomas MBE (*CY 1967*)	1.4.1935		21	1961–1967	506	112	1	22.00	–	–	–/–	–	52/3	
Newham William	12.12.1860	26.6.1944	1	*1887*	26	17	0	13.00	–	–	–/–	–	0	
Newport Philip John	11.10.1962		3	1988–*1990*	110	40*	0	27.50	10	4-87	0/0	41.70	1	
Nichols Morris Stanley (*CY 1934*)	6.10.1900	26.1.1961	14	*1929*–1939	355	78*	0	29.58	41	6-35	2/0	28.09	11	
Oakman Alan Stanley Myles	20.4.1930		2	1956	14	10	0	7.00	0	0-21	0/0	–	7	
O'Brien *Sir* Timothy Carew	5.11.1861	9.12.1948	5	1884–*1895*	59	20	0	7.37	–	–	–/–	–	4	
O'Connor Jack	6.11.1897	22.2.1977	4	1929–*1929*	153	51	0	21.85	1	1-31	0/0	72.00	2	
Old Christopher Middleton (*CY 1979*)	22.12.1948		46	*1972*–1981	845	65	0	14.82	143	7-50	4/0	28.11	22	32
Oldfield Norman	5.5.1911	19.4.1996	1	1939	99	80	0	49.50	–	–	–/–	–	0	
Onions Graham (*CY 2010*)	9.9.1982		9	2009–2012	30	17*	0	10.00	32	5-38	1/0	29.90	0	4
Ormond James	20.8.1977		2	2001–*2001*	38	18	0	12.66	2	1-70	0/0	92.50	0	
Padgett Douglas Ernest Vernon	20.7.1934		2	1960	51	31	0	12.75	0	0-8	0/0	–	0	
Paine George Alfred Edward (*CY 1935*)	11.6.1908	30.3.1978	4	*1934*	97	49	0	16.16	17	5-168	1/0	27.47	5	
Palairet Lionel Charles Hamilton (*CY 1893*)	27.5.1870	27.3.1933	2	1902	49	20	0	12.25	–	–	–/–	–	2	
Palmer Charles Henry CBE	15.5.1919	31.3.2005	1	*1953*	22	22	0	11.00	0	0-15	0/0	–	0	
Palmer Kenneth Ernest MBE	22.4.1937		1	*1964*	10	10	0	10.00	1	1-113	0/0	189.00	0	
Panesar Mudhsuden Singh ("Monty") (*CY 2007*)	25.4.1982		50	*2005–2013*	220	26	0	4.88	167	6-37	12/2	34.71	10	26/1
Parfitt Peter Howard (*CY 1963*)	8.12.1936		37	*1961*–1972	1,882	131*	7	40.91	12	2-5	0/0	47.83	42	
Parker Charles Warrington Leonard (*CY 1923*)	14.10.1882	11.7.1959	1	1921	3	3*	0	–	2	2-32	0/0	16.00	0	
Parker Paul William Giles	15.1.1956		1	1981	13	13	0	6.50	–	–	–/–	–	0	
Parkhouse William Gilbert Anthony	12.10.1925	10.8.2000	7	1950–1959	373	78	0	28.69	–	–	–/–	–	3	
Parkin Cecil Harry (*CY 1924*)	18.2.1886	15.6.1943	10	*1920*–1924	160	36	0	12.30	32	5-38	2/0	35.25	3	
[1] **Parks** James Horace (*CY 1938*)	12.5.1903	21.11.1980	1	1937	29	22	0	14.50	3	2-26	0/0	12.00	0	
[1] **Parks** James Michael (*CY 1968*)	21.10.1931		46	1954–*1967*	1,962	108*	2	32.16	1	1-43	0/0	51.00	103/11	

	Born	Died	Tests	Test Career	Runs	HS	100s	Avge	Wkts	BB	5/10	Avge	Ct/St	O/T
[1] **Pataudi** Iftikhar Ali Khan, Nawab of (*CY 1932*)	16.3.1910	5.1.1952	3†	*1932*–1934	144	102	1	28.80	–	–	–/–	–	0	
Patel Minal Mahesh	7.7.1970		2	1996	45	27	0	22.50	1	1-101	0/0	180.00	2	
Patel Samit Rohit	30.11.1984		6	*2011–2015*	151	42	0	16.77	7	2-27	0/0	60.14	3	36/18
[2] **Pattinson** Darren John	2.8.1979		1	2008	21	13	0	10.50	2	2-95	0/0	48.00	0	
Paynter Edward (*CY 1938*)	5.11.1901	5.2.1979	20	*1931–1939*	1,540	243	4	59.23	–	–	–/–	–	7	
Peate Edmund	2.3.1855	11.3.1900	9	*1881*–1886	70	13	0	11.66	31	6-85	2/0	22.03	2	
Peebles Ian Alexander Ross (*CY 1931*)	20.1.1908	27.2.1980	13	*1927*–1931	98	26	0	10.88	45	6-63	3/0	30.91	5	
Peel Robert (*CY 1889*)	12.2.1857	12.8.1941	20	*1884*–1896	427	83	0	14.72	101	7-31	5/1	16.98	17	
Penn Frank	7.3.1851	26.12.1916	1	1880	50	27*	0	50.00	0	0-2	0/0	–	0	
Perks Reginald Thomas David	4.10.1911	22.11.1977	2	*1938*–1939	3	2*	0	–	11	5-100	2/0	32.27	1	
Philipson Hylton	8.6.1866	4.12.1935	5	*1891–1894*	63	30	0	9.00	–	–	–/–	–	8/3	
Pietersen Kevin Peter MBE (*CY 2006*)	27.6.1980		104	2005–*2013*	8,181	227	23	47.28	10	3-52	0/0	88.60	62	134‡/37
Pigott Anthony Charles Shackleton	4.6.1958		1	*1983*	12	8*	0	12.00	2	2-75	0/0	37.50	0	
Pilling Richard (*CY 1891*)	11.8.1855	28.3.1891	8	*1881*–1888	91	23	0	7.58	–	–	–/–	–	10/4	
Place Winston	7.12.1914	25.1.2002	3	*1947*	144	107	1	28.80	–	–	–/–	–	0	
Plunkett Liam Edward	6.4.1985		13	*2005*–2014	238	55*	0	15.86	41	5-64	1/0	37.46	3	44/9
Pocock Patrick Ian	24.9.1946		25	*1967–1984*	206	33	0	6.24	67	6-79	3/0	44.41	15	1
Pollard Richard	19.6.1912	16.12.1985	4	1946–1948	13	10*	0	13.00	15	5-24	1/0	25.20	3	
Poole Cyril John	13.3.1921	11.2.1996	3	*1951*	161	69*	0	40.25	0	0-9	0/0	–	1	
Pope George Henry	27.1.1911	29.10.1993	1	1947	8	8*	0	–	1	1-49	0/0	85.00	0	
Pougher Arthur Dick	19.4.1865	20.5.1926	1	*1891*	17	17	0	17.00	3	3-26	0/0	8.66	2	
Price John Sidney Ernest	22.7.1937		15	*1963*–1972	66	32	0	7.33	40	5-73	1/0	35.02	7	
Price Wilfred Frederick Frank	25.4.1902	13.1.1969	1	1938	6	6	0	3.00	–	–	–/–	–	2	
Prideaux Roger Malcolm	31.7.1939		3	1968–*1968*	102	64	0	20.40	0	0-0	0/0	–	0	
Pringle Derek Raymond	18.9.1958		30	1982–1992	695	63	0	15.10	70	5-95	3/0	35.97	10	44
Prior Matthew James (*CY 2010*)	26.2.1982		79	2007–2014	4,099	131*	7	40.18	–	–	–/–	–	243/13	68/10
Pullar Geoffrey (*CY 1960*)	1.8.1935	26.12.2014	28	1959–*1962*	1,974	175	4	43.86	1	1-1	0/0	37.00	2	
Quaife William George (*CY 1902*)	17.3.1872	13.10.1951	7	1899–*1901*	228	68	0	19.00	0	0-6	0/0	–	4	
Radford Neal Victor (*CY 1986*)	7.6.1957		3	1986–*1987*	21	12*	0	7.00	4	2-131	0/0	87.75	0	6
Radley Clive Thornton MBE (*CY 1979*)	13.5.1944		8	*1977*–1978	481	158	2	48.10	–	–	–/–	–	4	4
Ramprakash Mark Ravin MBE (*CY 2007*)	5.9.1969		52	1991–*2001*	2,350	154	2	27.32	4	1-2	0/0	119.25	39	18
Randall Derek William (*CY 1980*)	24.2.1951		47	*1976*–1984	2,470	174	7	33.37	0	0-1	0/0	–	31	49
Ranjitsinhji Kumar Shri (*CY 1897*)	10.9.1872	2.4.1933	15	1896–1902	989	175	2	44.95	1	1-23	0/0	39.00	13	
Rankin William Boyd	5.7.1984		1	*2013*	13	13	0	6.50	1	1-47	0/0	81.00	0	7‡/2‡
Rashid Adil Usman	17.2.1988		10	*2015–2016*	295	61	0	18.43	38	5-64	1/0	42.78	3	37/20
Read Christopher Mark Wells (*CY 2011*)	10.8.1978		15	1999–*2006*	360	55	0	18.94	–	–	–/–	–	48/6	36/1

	Born	*Died*	*Tests*	*Test Career*	*Runs*	*HS*	*100s*	*Avge*	*Wkts*	*BB*	*5/10*	*Avge*	*Ct/St*	*O/T*
Read Holcombe Douglas ("Hopper")	28.1.1910	5.1.2000	1	1935	–	–	–	–	6	4-136	0/0	33.33	0	
Read John Maurice (*CY 1890*)	9.2.1859	17.2.1929	17	1882–1893	461	57	0	17.07	–	–	–/–	–	8	
Read Walter William (*CY 1893*)	23.11.1855	6.1.1907	18	*1882*–1893	720	117	1	27.69	0	0-27	0/0	–	16	
Reeve Dermot Alexander OBE (*CY 1996*)	2.4.1963		3	*1991*	124	59	0	24.80	2	1-4	0/0	30.00	1	29
Relf Albert Edward (*CY 1914*)	26.6.1874	26.3.1937	13	*1903–1913*	416	63	0	23.11	25	5-85	1/0	24.96	14	
Rhodes Harold James	22.7.1936		2	1959	0	0*	0	–	9	4-50	0/0	27.11	0	
Rhodes Steven John (*CY 1995*)	17.6.1964		11	1994–*1994*	294	65*	0	24.50	–	–	–/–	–	46/3	9
Rhodes Wilfred (*CY 1899*)	29.10.1877	8.7.1973	58	1899–*1929*	2,325	179	2	30.19	127	8-68	6/1	26.96	60	
Richards Clifton James ("Jack")	10.8.1958		8	*1986*–1988	285	133	1	21.92	–	–	–/–	–	20/1	22
[2] **Richardson** Derek Walter ("Dick")	3.11.1934		1	1957	33	33	0	33.00	–	–	–/–	–	1	
[2] **Richardson** Peter Edward (*CY 1957*)	4.7.1931		34	1956–1963	2,061	126	5	37.47	3	2-10	0/0	16.00	6	
Richardson Thomas (*CY 1897*)	11.8.1870	2.7.1912	14	1893–*1897*	177	25*	0	11.06	88	8-94	11/4	25.22	5	
Richmond Thomas Leonard	23.6.1890	29.12.1957	1	1921	6	4	0	3.00	2	2-69	0/0	43.00	0	
Ridgway Frederick	10.8.1923	26.9.2015	5	*1951*	49	24	0	8.16	7	4-83	0/0	54.14	3	
Robertson John David Benbow (*CY 1948*)	22.2.1917	12.10.1996	11	1947–*1951*	881	133	2	46.36	2	2-17	0/0	29.00	6	
Robins Robert Walter Vivian (*CY 1930*)	3.6.1906	12.12.1968	19	1929–1937	612	108	1	26.60	64	6-32	1/0	27.46	12	
Robinson Robert Timothy (*CY 1986*)	21.11.1958		29	*1984*–1989	1,601	175	4	36.38	0	0-0	0/0	–	8	26
Robson Samuel David	1.7.1989		7	2014	336	127	1	30.54	–	–	–/–	–	5	
Roope Graham Richard James	12.7.1946	26.11.2006	21	*1972*–1978	860	77	0	30.71	0	0-2	0/0	–	35	8
Root Charles Frederick	16.4.1890	20.1.1954	3	1926	–	–	–	–	8	4-84	0/0	24.25	1	
Root Joseph Edward (*CY 2014*)	30.12.1990		53	*2012–2016*	4,594	254	11	52.80	15	2-9	0/0	48.06	65	78/21
Rose Brian Charles (*CY 1980*)	4.6.1950		9	*1977–1980*	358	70	0	25.57	–	–	–/–	–	4	2
Royle Vernon Peter Fanshawe Archer	29.1.1854	21.5.1929	1	*1878*	21	18	0	10.50	0	0-6	0/0	–	2	
Rumsey Frederick Edward	4.12.1935		5	1964–1965	30	21*	0	15.00	17	4-25	0/0	27.11	0	
Russell Albert Charles ("Jack") (*CY 1923*)	7.10.1887	23.3.1961	10	*1920–1922*	910	140	5	56.87	–	–	–/–	–	8	
Russell Robert Charles ("Jack") (*CY 1990*)	15.8.1963		54	1988–*1997*	1,897	128*	2	27.10	–	–	–/–	–	153/12	40
Russell William Eric	3.7.1936		10	*1961*–1967	362	70	0	21.29	0	0-19	0/0	–	4	
Saggers Martin John	23.5.1972		3	*2003*–2004	1	1	0	0.33	7	2-29	0/0	35.28	1	
Salisbury Ian David Kenneth (*CY 1993*)	21.1.1970		15	1992–*2000*	368	50	0	16.72	20	4-163	0/0	76.95	5	4
Sandham Andrew (*CY 1923*)	6.7.1890	20.4.1982	14	1921–*1929*	879	325	2	38.21	–	–	–/–	–	4	
Schofield Christopher Paul	6.10.1978		2	2000	67	57	0	22.33	0	0-73	0/0	–	0	0/4
Schultz Sandford Spence	29.8.1857	18.12.1937	1	*1878*	20	20	0	20.00	1	1-16	0/0	26.00	0	
Scotton William Henry	15.1.1856	9.7.1893	15	*1881–1886*	510	90	0	22.17	0	0-20	0/0	–	4	
Selby John	1.7.1849	11.3.1894	6	*1876–1881*	256	70	0	23.27	–	–	–/–	–	1	
Selvey Michael Walter William	25.4.1948		3	1976–*1976*	15	5*	0	7.50	6	4-41	0/0	57.16	1	
Shackleton Derek (*CY 1959*)	12.8.1924	28.9.2007	7	1950–1963	113	42	0	18.83	18	4-72	0/0	42.66	1	

	Born	Died	Tests	Test Career	Runs	HS	100s	Avge	Wkts	BB	5/10	Avge	Ct/St	O/T
Shah Owais Alam	22.10.1978		6	*2005–2008*	269	88	0	26.90	0	0-12	0/0	–	2	71/17
Shahzad Ajmal	27.7.1985		1	2010	5	5	0	5.00	4	3-45	0/0	15.75	2	11/3
Sharp John	15.2.1878	28.1.1938	3	1909	188	105	1	47.00	3	3-67	0/0	37.00	1	
Sharpe John William (*CY 1892*)	9.12.1866	19.6.1936	3	1890–*1891*	44	26	0	22.00	11	6-84	1/0	27.72	2	
Sharpe Philip John (*CY 1963*)	27.12.1936	19.5.2014	12	1963–1969	786	111	1	46.23	–	–	–/–	–	17	
Shaw Alfred	29.8.1842	16.1.1907	7	*1876–1881*	111	40	0	10.09	12	5-38	1/0	23.75	4	
Sheppard *Rt Rev. Lord* [David Stuart] (*CY 1953*)	6.3.1929	5.3.2005	22	1950–*1962*	1,172	119	3	37.80	–	–	–/–	–	12	
Sherwin Mordecai (*CY 1891*)	26.2.1851	3.7.1910	3	*1886*–1888	30	21*	0	15.00	–	–	–/–	–	5/2	
Shrewsbury Arthur (*CY 1890*)	11.4.1856	19.5.1903	23	*1881*–1893	1,277	164	3	35.47	0	0-2	0/0	–	29	
Shuter John	9.2.1855	5.7.1920	1	1888	28	28	0	28.00	–	–	–/–	–	0	
Shuttleworth Kenneth	13.11.1944		5	*1970*–1971	46	21	0	7.66	12	5-47	1/0	35.58	1	
[1] **Sidebottom** Arnold	1.4.1954		1	1985	2	2	0	2.00	1	1-65	0/0	65.00	0	
[1] **Sidebottom** Ryan Jay (*CY 2008*)	15.1.1978		22	2001–*2009*	313	31	0	15.65	79	7-47	5/1	28.24	5	25/18
Silverwood Christopher Eric Wilfred	5.3.1975		6	*1996–2002*	29	10	0	7.25	11	5-91	1/0	40.36	2	7
Simpson Reginald Thomas (*CY 1950*)	27.2.1920	24.11.2013	27	*1948–1954*	1,401	156*	4	33.35	2	2-4	0/0	11.00	5	
Simpson-Hayward George Hayward Thomas	7.6.1875	2.10.1936	5	*1909*	105	29*	0	15.00	23	6-43	2/0	18.26	1	
Sims James Morton	13.5.1903	27.4.1973	4	1935–*1936*	16	12	0	4.00	11	5-73	1/0	43.63	6	
Sinfield Reginald Albert	24.12.1900	17.3.1988	1	1938	6	6	0	6.00	2	1-51	0/0	61.50	0	
Slack Wilfred Norris	12.12.1954	15.1.1989	3	*1985*–1986	81	52	0	13.50	–	–	–/–	–	3	2
Smailes Thomas Francis	27.3.1910	1.12.1970	1	1946	25	25	0	25.00	3	3-44	0/0	20.66	0	
Small Gladstone Cleophas	18.10.1961		17	1986–*1990*	263	59	0	15.47	55	5-48	2/0	34.01	9	53
Smith Alan Christopher CBE	25.10.1936		6	*1962*	118	69*	0	29.50	–	–	–/–	–	20	
Smith Andrew Michael	1.10.1967		1	1997	4	4*	0	4.00	0	0-89	0/0	–	0	
Smith Cedric Ivan James (*CY 1935*)	25.8.1906	8.2.1979	5	*1934*–1937	102	27	0	10.20	15	5-16	1/0	26.20	1	
Smith *Sir* Charles Aubrey	21.7.1863	20.12.1948	1	*1888*	3	3	0	3.00	7	5-19	1/0	8.71	0	
[2] **Smith** Christopher Lyall (*CY 1984*)	15.10.1958		8	1983–1986	392	91	0	30.15	3	2-31	0/0	13.00	5	4
Smith David Mark	9.1.1956		2	*1985*	80	47	0	20.00	–	–	–/–	–	0	2
Smith David Robert	5.10.1934	17.12.2003	5	*1961*	38	34	0	9.50	6	2-60	0/0	59.83	2	
Smith Denis (*CY 1935*)	24.1.1907	12.9.1979	2	1935	128	57	0	32.00	–	–	–/–	–	1	
Smith Donald Victor	14.6.1923		3	1957	25	16*	0	8.33	1	1-12	0/0	97.00	0	
Smith Edward Thomas	19.7.1977		3	2003	87	64	0	17.40	–	–	–/–	–	5	
Smith Ernest James ("Tiger")	6.2.1886	31.8.1979	11	*1911–1913*	113	22	0	8.69	–	–	–/–	–	17/3	
Smith Harry	21.5.1891	12.11.1937	1	1928	7	7	0	7.00	–	–	–/–	–	1	
Smith Michael John Knight OBE (*CY 1960*)	30.6.1933		50	1958–1972	2,278	121	3	31.63	1	1-10	0/0	128.00	53	
[2] **Smith** Robin Arnold (*CY 1990*)	13.9.1963		62	1988–*1995*	4,236	175	9	43.67	0	0-6	0/0	–	39	71
Smith Thomas Peter Bromley (*CY 1947*)	30.10.1908	4.8.1967	4	1946–*1946*	33	24	0	6.60	3	2-172	0/0	106.33	1	

	Born	*Died*	*Tests*	*Test Career*	*Runs*	*HS*	*100s*	*Avge*	*Wkts*	*BB*	*5/10*	*Avge*	*Ct/St*	*O/T*
Smithson Gerald Arthur	1.11.1926	6.9.1970	2	*1947*	70	35	0	23.33	–	–	–/–	–	0	
Snow John Augustine (*CY 1973*)	13.10.1941		49	1965–1976	772	73	0	13.54	202	7-40	8/1	26.66	16	9
Southerton James	16.11.1827	16.6.1880	2	*1876*	7	6	0	3.50	7	4-46	0/0	15.28	2	
Spooner Reginald Herbert (*CY 1905*)	21.10.1880	2.10.1961	10	1905–1912	481	119	1	32.06	–	–	–/–	–	4	
Spooner Richard Thompson	30.12.1919	20.12.1997	7	*1951*–1955	354	92	0	27.23	–	–	–/–	–	10/2	
Stanyforth Ronald Thomas	30.5.1892	20.2.1964	4	*1927*	13	6*	0	2.60	–	–	–/–	–	7/2	
Staples Samuel James (*CY 1929*)	18.9.1892	4.6.1950	3	*1927*	65	39	0	13.00	15	3-50	0/0	29.00	0	
Statham John Brian CBE (*CY 1955*)	17.6.1930	10.6.2000	70	*1950*–1965	675	38	0	11.44	252	7-39	9/1	24.84	28	
Steel Allan Gibson	24.9.1858	15.6.1914	13	1880–1888	600	148	2	35.29	29	3-27	0/0	20.86	5	
Steele David Stanley OBE (*CY 1976*)	29.9.1941		8	1975–1976	673	106	1	42.06	2	1-1	0/0	19.50	7	1
Stephenson John Patrick	14.3.1965		1	1989	36	25	0	18.00	–	–	–/–	–	0	
Stevens Greville Thomas Scott (*CY 1918*)	7.1.1901	19.9.1970	10	*1922–1929*	263	69	0	15.47	20	5-90	2/1	32.40	9	
Stevenson Graham Barry	16.12.1955	21.1.2014	2	*1979–1980*	28	27*	0	28.00	5	3-111	0/0	36.60	0	4
[1] **Stewart** Alec James OBE (*CY 1993*)	8.4.1963		133	*1989*–2003	8,463	190	15	39.54	0	0-5	0/0	–	263/14	170
[1] **Stewart** Michael James OBE (*CY 1958*)	16.9.1932		8	1962–*1963*	385	87	0	35.00	–	–	–/–	–	6	
Stoddart Andrew Ernest (*CY 1893*)	11.3.1863	3.4.1915	16	*1887–1897*	996	173	2	35.57	2	1-10	0/0	47.00	6	
Stokes Benjamin Andrew (*CY 2016*)	4.6.1991		32	*2013–2016*	1,902	258	4	33.96	79	6-36	3/0	34.46	22	47/18
Storer William (*CY 1899*)	25.1.1867	28.2.1912	6	*1897*–1899	215	51	0	19.54	2	1-24	0/0	54.00	11	
Strauss Andrew John OBE (*CY 2005*)	2.3.1977		100	2004–2012	7,037	177	21	40.91	–	–	–/–	–	121	127/4
Street George Benjamin	6.12.1889	24.4.1924	1	*1922*	11	7*	0	11.00	–	–	–/–	–	0/1	
Strudwick Herbert (*CY 1912*)	28.1.1880	14.2.1970	28	*1909*–1926	230	24	0	7.93	–	–	–/–	–	61/12	
[2] **Studd** Charles Thomas	2.12.1860	16.7.1931	5	1882–*1882*	160	48	0	20.00	3	2-35	0/0	32.66	5	
[2] **Studd** George Brown	20.10.1859	13.2.1945	4	*1882*	31	9	0	4.42	–	–	–/–	–	8	
Subba Row Raman CBE (*CY 1961*)	29.1.1932		13	1958–1961	984	137	3	46.85	0	0-2	0/0	–	5	
Such Peter Mark	12.6.1964		11	1993–1999	67	14*	0	6.09	37	6-67	2/0	33.56	4	
Sugg Frank Howe (*CY 1890*)	11.1.1862	29.5.1933	2	1888	55	31	0	27.50	–	–	–/–	–	0	
Sutcliffe Herbert (*CY 1920*)	24.11.1894	22.1.1978	54	1924–1935	4,555	194	16	60.73	–	–	–/–	–	23	
Swann Graeme Peter (*CY 2010*)	24.3.1979		60	*2008–2013*	1,370	85	0	22.09	255	6-65	17/3	29.96	54	79/39
Swetman Roy	25.10.1933		11	*1958–1959*	254	65	0	16.93	–	–	–/–	–	24/2	
[1] **Tate** Frederick William	24.7.1867	24.2.1943	1	1902	9	5*	0	9.00	2	2-7	0/0	25.50	2	
[1] **Tate** Maurice William (*CY 1924*)	30.5.1895	18.5.1956	39	1924–1935	1,198	100*	1	25.48	155	6-42	7/1	26.16	11	
Tattersall Roy	17.8.1922	9.12.2011	16	*1950*–1954	50	10*	0	5.00	58	7-52	4/1	26.08	8	
Tavaré Christopher James	27.10.1954		31	1980–1989	1,755	149	2	32.50	0	0-0	0/0	–	20	29
Taylor James William Arthur	6.1.1990		7	2012–*2015*	312	76	0	26.00	–	–	–/–	–	7	27
Taylor Jonathan Paul	8.8.1964		2	*1992*–1994	34	17*	0	17.00	3	1-18	0/0	52.00	0	1
Taylor Kenneth	21.8.1935		3	1959–1964	57	24	0	11.40	0	0-6	0/0	–	1	

	Born	Died	Tests	Test Career	Runs	HS	100s	Avge	Wkts	BB	5/10	Avge	Ct/St	O/T
Taylor Leslie Brian	25.10.1953		2	1985	1	1*	0	–	4	2-34	0/0	44.50	1	2
Taylor Robert William MBE (*CY 1977*)	17.7.1941		57	*1970–1983*	1,156	97	0	16.28	0	0-6	0/0	–	167/7	27
Tennyson *Lord* Lionel Hallam (*CY 1914*)	7.11.1889	6.6.1951	9	*1913*–1921	345	74*	0	31.36	0	0-1	0/0	–	6	
Terry Vivian Paul	14.1.1959		2	1984	16	8	0	5.33	–	–	–/–	–	2	
Thomas John Gregory	12.8.1960		5	*1985*–1986	83	31*	0	13.83	10	4-70	0/0	50.40	0	3
Thompson George Joseph (*CY 1906*)	27.10.1877	3.3.1943	6	1909–*1909*	273	63	0	30.33	23	4-50	0/0	27.73	5	
Thomson Norman Ian	23.1.1929		5	*1964*	69	39	0	23.00	9	2-55	0/0	63.11	3	
Thorpe Graham Paul MBE (*CY 1998*)	1.8.1969		100	1993–2005	6,744	200*	16	44.66	0	0-0	0/0	–	105	82
Titmus Frederick John MBE (*CY 1963*)	24.11.1932	23.3.2011	53	1955–*1974*	1,449	84*	0	22.29	153	7-79	7/0	32.22	35	2
Tolchard Roger William	15.6.1946		4	*1976*	129	67	0	25.80	–	–	–/–	–	5	1
[1] **Townsend** Charles Lucas (*CY 1899*)	7.11.1876	17.10.1958	2	1899	51	38	0	17.00	3	3-50	0/0	25.00	0	
[1] **Townsend** David Charles Humphery	20.4.1912	27.1.1997	3	*1934*	77	36	0	12.83	0	0-9	0/0	–	1	
Townsend Leslie Fletcher (*CY 1934*)	8.6.1903	17.2.1993	4	*1929–1933*	97	40	0	16.16	6	2-22	0/0	34.16	2	
Tredwell James Cullum	27.2.1982		2	*2009–2014*	45	37	0	22.50	11	4-47	0/0	29.18	2	45/17
[4] **Tremlett** Christopher Timothy	2.9.1981		12	2007–*2013*	113	25*	0	10.27	53	6-48	2/0	27.00	4	15/1
[4] **Tremlett** Maurice Fletcher	5.7.1923	30.7.1984	3	*1947*	20	18*	0	6.66	4	2-98	0/0	56.50	0	
Trescothick Marcus Edward MBE (*CY 2005*)	25.12.1975		76	2000–2006	5,825	219	14	43.79	1	1-34	0/0	155.00	95	123/3
[2] **Trott** Albert Edwin (*CY 1899*)	6.2.1873	30.7.1914	2†	*1898*	23	16	0	5.75	17	5-49	1/0	11.64	0	
Trott Ian Jonathan Leonard (*CY 2011*)	22.4.1981		52	2009–*2014*	3,835	226	9	44.08	5	1-5	0/0	80.00	29	68/7
Trueman Frederick Sewards OBE (*CY 1953*)	6.2.1931	1.7.2006	67	1952–1965	981	39*	0	13.81	307	8-31	17/3	21.57	64	
Tudor Alex Jeremy	23.10.1977		10	*1998–2002*	229	99*	0	19.08	28	5-44	1/0	34.39	3	3
Tufnell Neville Charsley	13.6.1887	3.8.1951	1	*1909*	14	14	0	14.00	–	–	–/–	–	0/1	
Tufnell Philip Clive Roderick	29.4.1966		42	*1990*–2001	153	22*	0	5.10	121	7-47	5/2	37.68	12	20
Turnbull Maurice Joseph Lawson (*CY 1931*)	16.3.1906	5.8.1944	9	*1929*–1936	224	61	0	20.36	–	–	–/–	–	1	
[2] **Tyldesley** [George] Ernest (*CY 1920*)	5.2.1889	5.5.1962	14	1921–*1928*	990	122	3	55.00	0	0-2	0/0	–	2	
[2] **Tyldesley** John Thomas (*CY 1902*)	22.11.1873	27.11.1930	31	*1898*–1909	1,661	138	4	30.75	–	–	–/–	–	16	
Tyldesley Richard Knowles (*CY 1925*)	11.3.1897	17.9.1943	7	1924–1930	47	29	0	7.83	19	3-50	0/0	32.57	1	
Tylecote Edward Ferdinando Sutton	23.6.1849	15.3.1938	6	*1882*–1886	152	66	0	19.00	–	–	–/–	–	5/5	
Tyler Edwin James	13.10.1864	25.1.1917	1	*1895*	0	0	0	0.00	4	3-49	0/0	16.25	0	
Tyson Frank Holmes (*CY 1956*)	6.6.1930	27.9.2015	17	1954–*1958*	230	37*	0	10.95	76	7-27	4/1	18.56	4	
Udal Shaun David	18.3.1969		4	*2005*	109	33*	0	18.16	8	4-14	0/0	43.00	1	11
Ulyett George	21.10.1851	18.6.1898	25	*1876*–1890	949	149	1	24.33	50	7-36	1/0	20.40	19	
Underwood Derek Leslie MBE (*CY 1969*)	8.6.1945		86	1966–*1981*	937	45*	0	11.56	297	8-51	17/6	25.83	44	26
Valentine Bryan Herbert	17.1.1908	2.2.1983	7	*1933–1938*	454	136	2	64.85	–	–	–/–	–	2	
Vaughan Michael Paul OBE (*CY 2003*)	29.10.1974		82	*1999*–2008	5,719	197	18	41.44	6	2-71	0/0	93.50	44	86/2
Verity Hedley (*CY 1932*)	18.5.1905	31.7.1943	40	1931–1939	669	66*	0	20.90	144	8-43	5/2	24.37	30	

	Born	Died	Tests	Test Career	Runs	HS	100s	Avge	Wkts	BB	5/10	Avge	Ct/St	O/T
Vernon George Frederick	20.6.1856	10.8.1902	1	*1882*	14	11*	0	14.00	–	–	–/–	–	0	
Vince James Michael	14.3.1991		7	2016	212	42	0	19.27	0	0-0	0/0	–	3	5/5
Vine Joseph (*CY 1906*)	15.5.1875	25.4.1946	2	*1911*	46	36	0	46.00	–	–	–/–	–	0	
Voce William (*CY 1933*)	8.8.1909	6.6.1984	27	*1929–1946*	308	66	0	13.39	98	7-70	3/2	27.88	15	
Waddington Abraham	4.2.1893	28.10.1959	2	*1920*	16	7	0	4.00	1	1-35	0/0	119.00	1	
Wainwright Edward (*CY 1894*)	8.4.1865	28.10.1919	5	1893–*1897*	132	49	0	14.66	0	0-11	0/0	–	2	
Walker Peter Michael	17.2.1936		3	1960	128	52	0	32.00	0	0-8	0/0	–	5	
Walters Cyril Frederick (*CY 1934*)	28.8.1905	23.12.1992	11	1933–1934	784	102	1	52.26	–	–	–/–	–	6	
Ward Alan	10.8.1947		5	1969–1976	40	21	0	8.00	14	4-61	0/0	32.35	3	
Ward Albert (*CY 1890*)	21.11.1865	6.1.1939	7	1893–*1894*	487	117	1	37.46	–	–	–/–	–	1	
Ward Ian James	30.9.1972		5	2001	129	39	0	16.12	–	–	–/–	–	1	
Wardle John Henry (*CY 1954*)	8.1.1923	23.7.1985	28	*1947*–1957	653	66	0	19.78	102	7-36	5/1	20.39	12	
Warner *Sir* Pelham Francis (*CY 1904*)	2.10.1873	30.1.1963	15	*1898*–1912	622	132*	1	23.92	–	–	–/–	–	3	
Warr John James	16.7.1927	9.5.2016	2	*1950*	4	4	0	1.00	1	1-76	0/0	281.00	0	
Warren Arnold	2.4.1875	3.9.1951	1	1905	7	7	0	7.00	6	5-57	1/0	18.83	1	
Washbrook Cyril CBE (*CY 1947*)	6.12.1914	27.4.1999	37	1937–1956	2,569	195	6	42.81	1	1-25	0/0	33.00	12	
Watkin Steven Llewellyn (*CY 1994*)	15.9.1964		3	1991–1993	25	13	0	5.00	11	4-65	0/0	27.72	1	4
Watkins Albert John ("Allan")	21.4.1922	3.8.2011	15	1948–1952	810	137*	2	40.50	11	3-20	0/0	50.36	17	
Watkinson Michael	1.8.1961		4	1995–*1995*	167	82*	0	33.40	10	3-64	0/0	34.80	1	1
Watson Willie (*CY 1954*)	7.3.1920	23.4.2004	23	1951–*1958*	879	116	2	25.85	–	–	–/–	–	8	
Webbe Alexander Josiah	16.1.1855	19.2.1941	1	*1878*	4	4	0	2.00	–	–	–/–	–	2	
Wellard Arthur William (*CY 1936*)	8.4.1902	31.12.1980	2	1937–1938	47	38	0	11.75	7	4-81	0/0	33.85	2	
Wells Alan Peter	2.10.1961		1	1995	3	3*	0	3.00	–	–	–/–	–	0	1
Wharton Alan	30.4.1923	26.8.1993	1	1949	20	13	0	10.00	–	–	–/–	–	0	
Whitaker John James (*CY 1987*)	5.5.1962		1	*1986*	11	11	0	11.00	–	–	–/–	–	1	2
White Craig	16.12.1969		30	1994–*2002*	1,052	121	1	24.46	59	5-32	3/0	37.62	14	51
White David William ("Butch")	14.12.1935	1.8.2008	2	*1961*	0	0	0	0.00	4	3-65	0/0	29.75	0	
White John Cornish (*CY 1929*)	19.2.1891	2.5.1961	15	1921–*1930*	239	29	0	18.38	49	8-126	3/1	32.26	6	
Whysall William Wilfrid (*CY 1925*)	31.10.1887	11.11.1930	4	*1924*–1930	209	76	0	29.85	0	0-9	0/0	–	7	
Wilkinson Leonard Litton	5.11.1916	3.9.2002	3	*1938*	3	2	0	3.00	7	2-12	0/0	38.71	0	
Willey Peter	6.12.1949		26	1976–1986	1,184	102*	2	26.90	7	2-73	0/0	65.14	3	26
Williams Neil FitzGerald	2.7.1962	27.3.2006	1	1990	38	38	0	38.00	2	2-148	0/0	74.00	0	
Willis Robert George Dylan MBE (*CY 1978*)	30.5.1949		90	*1970*–1984	840	28*	0	11.50	325	8-43	16/0	25.20	39	64
[2] **Wilson** Clement Eustace Macro	15.5.1875	8.2.1944	2	*1898*	42	18	0	14.00	–	–	–/–	–	0	
Wilson Donald	7.8.1937	21.7.2012	6	*1963–1970*	75	42	0	12.50	11	2-17	0/0	42.36	1	
[2] **Wilson** Evelyn Rockley	25.3.1879	21.7.1957	1	*1920*	10	5	0	5.00	3	2-28	0/0	12.00	0	

	Born	*Died*	*Tests*	*Test Career*	*Runs*	*HS*	*100s*	*Avge*	*Wkts*	*BB*	*5/10*	*Avge*	*Ct/St*	*O/T*
Woakes Christopher Roger (*CY 2017*)	2.3.1989		17	2013–*2016*	591	66	0	29.55	48	6-70	2/1	29.33	9	55/8
Wood Arthur (*CY 1939*).	25.8.1898	1.4.1973	4	1938–1939	80	53	0	20.00	–	–	–/–	–	10/1	
Wood Barry	26.12.1942		12	1972–1978	454	90	0	21.61	0	0-2	0/0	–	6	13
Wood George Edward Charles	22.8.1893	18.3.1971	3	1924	7	6	0	3.50	–	–	–/–	–	5/1	
Wood Henry (*CY 1891*)	14.12.1853	30.4.1919	4	1888–*1891*	204	134*	1	68.00	–	–	–/–	–	2/1	
Wood Mark Andrew	11.1.1990		8	2015–*2015*	185	32*	0	20.55	25	3-39	0/0	34.40	2	11/1
Wood Reginald.	7.3.1860	6.1.1915	1	*1886*	6	6	0	3.00	–	–	–/–	–	0	
Woods Samuel Moses James (*CY 1889*).	13.4.1867	30.4.1931	3†	*1895*	122	53	0	30.50	5	3-28	0/0	25.80	4	
Woolley Frank Edward (*CY 1911*).	27.5.1887	18.10.1978	64	1909–1934	3,283	154	5	36.07	83	7-76	4/1	33.91	64	
Woolmer Robert Andrew (*CY 1976*)	14.5.1948	18.3.2007	19	1975–1981	1,059	149	3	33.09	4	1-8	0/0	74.75	10	6
Worthington Thomas Stanley (*CY 1937*).	21.8.1905	31.8.1973	9	*1929–1936*	321	128	1	29.18	8	2-19	0/0	39.50	8	
Wright Charles William	27.5.1863	10.1.1936	3	*1895*	125	71	0	31.25	–	–	–/–	–	0	
Wright Douglas Vivian Parson (*CY 1940*)	21.8.1914	13.11.1998	34	1938–*1950*	289	45	0	11.11	108	7-105	6/1	39.11	10	
Wyatt Robert Elliott Storey (*CY 1930*).	2.5.1901	20.4.1995	40	*1927–1936*	1,839	149	2	31.70	18	3-4	0/0	35.66	16	
Wynyard Edward George	1.4.1861	30.10.1936	3	1896–*1905*	72	30	0	12.00	0	0-2	0/0	–	0	
Yardley Norman Walter Dransfield (*CY 1948*) .	19.3.1915	3.10.1989	20	*1938*–1950	812	99	0	25.37	21	3-67	0/0	33.66	14	
Young Harding Isaac ("Sailor")	5.2.1876	12.12.1964	2	1899	43	43	0	21.50	12	4-30	0/0	21.83	1	
Young John Albert	14.10.1912	5.2.1993	8	1947–1949	28	10*	0	5.60	17	3-65	0/0	44.52	5	
Young Richard Alfred	16.9.1885	1.7.1968	2	*1907*	27	13	0	6.75	–	–	–/–	–	6	

AUSTRALIA (450 players)

	Born	*Died*	*Tests*	*Test Career*	*Runs*	*HS*	*100s*	*Avge*	*Wkts*	*BB*	*5/10*	*Avge*	*Ct/St*	*O/T*
a'Beckett Edward Lambert.	11.8.1907	2.6.1989	4	*1928–1931*	143	41	0	20.42	3	1-41	0/0	105.66	4	
Agar Ashton Charles.	14.10.1993		2	2013	130	98	0	32.50	2	2-82	0/0	124.00	0	2/2
Alderman Terence Michael (*CY 1982*)	12.6.1956		41	1981–*1990*	203	26*	0	6.54	170	6-47	14/1	27.15	27	65
Alexander George	22.4.1851	6.11.1930	2	*1880–1884*	52	33	0	13.00	2	2-69	0/0	46.50	2	
Alexander Harry Houston	9.6.1905	15.4.1993	1	*1932*	17	17*	0	17.00	1	1-129	0/0	154.00	0	
Allan Francis Erskine	2.12.1849	9.2.1917	1	*1878*	5	5	0	5.00	4	2-30	0/0	20.00	0	
Allan Peter John	31.12.1935		1	*1965*	–	–	–	–	2	2-58	0/0	41.50	0	
Allen Reginald Charles	2.7.1858	2.5.1952	1	*1886*	44	30	0	22.00	–	–	–/–	–	2	
Andrews Thomas James Edwin	26.8.1890	28.1.1970	16	1921–1926	592	94	0	26.90	1	1-23	0/0	116.00	12	
Angel Jo	22.4.1968		4	*1992–1994*	35	11	0	5.83	10	3-54	0/0	46.30	1	3
[2] **Archer** Kenneth Alan	17.1.1928		5	*1950–1951*	234	48	0	26.00	–	–	–/–	–	0	

	Born	Died	Tests	Test Career	Runs	HS	100s	Avge	Wkts	BB	5/10	Avge	Ct/St	O/T
[2] **Archer** Ronald Graham	25.10.1933	27.5.2007	19	1952–1956	713	128	1	24.58	48	5-53	1/0	27.45	20	
Armstrong Warwick Windridge (*CY 1903*)	22.5.1879	13.7.1947	50	1901–1921	2,863	159*	6	38.68	87	6-35	3/0	33.59	44	
Badcock Clayvel Lindsay ("Jack")	10.4.1914	13.12.1982	7	1936–1938	160	118	1	14.54	–	–	–/–	–	3	
Bailey George John	7.9.1982		5	2013	183	53	0	26.14	–	–	–/–	–	10	90/29
[2] **Bannerman** Alexander Chalmers	21.3.1854	19.9.1924	28	1878–1893	1,108	94	0	23.08	4	3-111	0/0	40.75	21	
[2] **Bannerman** Charles	23.7.1851	20.8.1930	3	1876–1878	239	165*	1	59.75	–	–	–/–	–	0	
Bardsley Warren (*CY 1910*)	6.12.1882	20.1.1954	41	1909–1926	2,469	193*	6	40.47	–	–	–/–	–	12	
Barnes Sidney George	5.6.1916	16.12.1973	13	1938–1948	1,072	234	3	63.05	4	2-25	0/0	54.50	14	
Barnett Benjamin Arthur	23.3.1908	29.6.1979	4	1938	195	57	0	27.85	–	–	–/–	–	3/2	
Barrett John Edward	15.10.1866	6.2.1916	2	1890	80	67*	0	26.66	–	–	–/–	–	1	
Beard Graeme Robert	19.8.1950		3	1979	114	49	0	22.80	1	1-26	0/0	109.00	0	2
Beer Michael Anthony	9.6.1984		2	2010–2011	6	2*	0	3.00	3	2-56	0/0	59.33	1	
[2] **Benaud** John	11.5.1944		3	1972	223	142	1	44.60	2	2-12	0/0	6.00	0	
[2] **Benaud** Richard OBE (*CY 1962*)	6.10.1930	10.4.2015	63	1951–1963	2,201	122	3	24.45	248	7-72	16/1	27.03	65	
Bennett Murray John	6.10.1956		3	1984–1985	71	23	0	23.66	6	3-79	0/0	54.16	5	8
Bevan Michael Gwyl	8.5.1970		18	1994–1997	785	91	0	29.07	29	6-82	1/1	24.24	8	232
Bichel Andrew John	27.8.1970		19	1996–2003	355	71	0	16.90	58	5-60	1/0	32.24	16	67
Bird Jackson Munro	11.12.1986		8	2012–2016	39	19*	0	19.50	34	5-59	1/0	27.47	2	
Blackham John McCarthy (*CY 1891*)	11.5.1854	28.12.1932	35	1876–1894	800	74	0	15.68	–	–	–/–	–	37/24	
Blackie Donald Dearness	5.4.1882	18.4.1955	3	1928	24	11*	0	8.00	14	6-94	1/0	31.71	2	
Blewett Gregory Scott	28.10.1971		46	1994–1999	2,552	214	4	34.02	14	2-9	0/0	51.42	45	32
Bollinger Douglas Erwin	24.7.1981		12	2008–2010	54	21	0	7.71	50	5-28	2/0	25.92	2	39/9
Bonnor George John	25.2.1855	27.6.1912	17	1880–1888	512	128	1	17.06	2	1-5	0/0	42.00	16	
Boon David Clarence MBE (*CY 1994*)	29.12.1960		107	1984–1995	7,422	200	21	43.65	0	0-0	0/0	–	99	181
Booth Brian Charles MBE	19.10.1933		29	1961–1965	1,773	169	5	42.21	3	2-33	0/0	48.66	17	
Border Allan Robert (*CY 1982*)	27.7.1955		156	1978–1993	11,174	205	27	50.56	39	7-46	2/1	39.10	156	273
Boyle Henry Frederick	10.12.1847	21.11.1907	12	1878–1884	153	36*	0	12.75	32	6-42	1/0	20.03	10	
Bracken Nathan Wade	12.9.1977		5	2003–2005	70	37	0	17.50	12	4-48	0/0	42.08	2	116/19
Bradman *Sir* Donald George AC (*CY 1931*)	27.8.1908	25.2.2001	52	1928–1948	6,996	334	29	99.94	2	1-8	0/0	36.00	32	
Bright Raymond James	13.7.1954		25	1977–1986	445	33	0	14.35	53	7-87	4/1	41.13	13	11
Bromley Ernest Harvey	2.9.1912	1.2.1967	2	1932–1934	38	26	0	9.50	0	0-19	0/0	–	2	
Brown William Alfred (*CY 1939*)	31.7.1912	16.3.2008	22	1934–1948	1,592	206*	4	46.82	–	–	–/–	–	14	
Bruce William	22.5.1864	3.8.1925	14	1884–1894	702	80	0	29.25	12	3-88	0/0	36.66	12	
Burge Peter John Parnell (*CY 1965*)	17.5.1932	5.10.2001	42	1954–1965	2,290	181	4	38.16	–	–	–/–	–	23	
Burke James Wallace (*CY 1957*)	12.6.1930	2.2.1979	24	1950–1958	1,280	189	3	34.59	8	4-37	0/0	28.75	18	
Burn Edwin James Kenneth (K. E.)	17.9.1862	20.7.1956	2	1890	41	19	0	10.25	–	–	–/–	–	0	

	Born	Died	Tests	Test Career	Runs	HS	100s	Avge	Wkts	BB	5/10	Avge	Ct/St	O/T
Burns Joseph Antony	6.9.1989		13	2014–2016	873	170	3	37.95	–	–	–/–	–	15	6
Burton Frederick John	2.11.1865	25.8.1929	2	1886–1887	4	2*	0	2.00	–	–	–/–	–	1/1	
Callaway Sydney Thomas	6.2.1868	25.11.1923	3	1891–1894	87	41	0	17.40	6	5-37	1/0	23.66	0	
Callen Ian Wayne	2.5.1955		1	1977	26	22*	0	–	6	3-83	0/0	31.83	1	5
Campbell Gregory Dale	10.3.1964		4	1989–1989	10	6	0	2.50	13	3-79	0/0	38.69	1	12
Carkeek William ("Barlow")	17.10.1878	20.2.1937	6	1912	16	6*	0	5.33	–	–	–/–	–	6	
Carlson Phillip Henry	8.8.1951		2	1978	23	21	0	5.75	2	2-41	0/0	49.50	2	4
Carter Hanson	15.3.1878	8.6.1948	28	1907–1921	873	72	0	22.97	–	–	–/–	–	44/21	
Cartwright Hilton William Raymond	14.2.1992		1	2016	37	37	0	37.00	0	0-15	0/0	–	0	
Casson Beau	7.12.1982		1	2007	10	10	0	10.00	3	3-86	0/0	43.00	2	
[2,4] **Chappell** Gregory Stephen MBE (*CY 1973*)	7.8.1948		87	1970–1983	7,110	247*	24	53.86	47	5-61	1/0	40.70	122	74
[2,4] **Chappell** Ian Michael (*CY 1976*)	26.9.1943		75	1964–1979	5,345	196	14	42.42	20	2-21	0/0	65.80	105	16
[2,4] **Chappell** Trevor Martin	21.10.1952		3	1981	79	27	0	15.80	–	–	–/–	–	2	20
Charlton Percie Chater	9.4.1867	30.9.1954	2	1890	29	11	0	7.25	3	3-18	0/0	8.00	0	
Chipperfield Arthur Gordon	17.11.1905	29.7.1987	14	1934–1938	552	109	1	32.47	5	3-91	0/0	87.40	15	
Clark Stuart Rupert	28.9.1975		24	2005–2009	248	39	0	13.05	94	5-32	2/0	23.86	4	39/9
Clark Wayne Maxwell	19.9.1953		10	1977–1978	98	33	0	5.76	44	4-46	0/0	28.75	6	2
Clarke Michael John (*CY 2010*)	2.4.1981		115§	2004–2015	8,643	329*	28	49.10	31	6-9	2/0	38.19	134	245/34
Colley David John	15.3.1947		3	1972	84	54	0	21.00	6	3-83	0/0	52.00	1	1
Collins Herbert Leslie	21.1.1888	28.5.1959	19	1920–1926	1,352	203	4	45.06	4	2-47	0/0	63.00	13	
Coningham Arthur	14.7.1863	13.6.1939	1	1894	13	10	0	6.50	2	2-17	0/0	38.00	0	
Connolly Alan Norman	29.6.1939		29	1963–1970	260	37	0	10.40	102	6-47	4/0	29.22	17	1
Cook Simon Hewitt	29.1.1972		2	1997	3	3*	0	–	7	5-39	1/0	20.28	0	
Cooper Bransby Beauchamp	15.3.1844	7.8.1914	1	1876	18	15	0	9.00	–	–	–/–	–	2	
[5] **Cooper** William Henry	11.9.1849	5.4.1939	2	1881–1884	13	7	0	6.50	9	6-120	1/0	25.11	1	
Copeland Trent Aaron	14.3.1986		3	2011	39	23*	0	13.00	6	2-24	0/0	37.83	2	
Corling Grahame Edward	13.7.1941		5	1964	5	3	0	1.66	12	4-60	0/0	37.25	0	
Cosier Gary John	25.4.1953		18	1975–1978	897	168	2	28.93	5	2-26	0/0	68.20	14	9
Cottam John Thomas	5.9.1867	30.1.1897	1	1886	4	3	0	2.00	–	–	–/–	–	1	
Cotter Albert ("Tibby")	3.12.1883	31.10.1917	21	1903–1911	457	45	0	13.05	89	7-148	7/0	28.64	8	
Coulthard George	1.8.1856	22.10.1883	1	1881	6	6*	0	–	–	–	–/–	–	0	
Cowan Edward James McKenzie	16.6.1982		18	2011–2013	1,001	136	1	31.28	–	–	–/–	–	24	
Cowper Robert Maskew	5.10.1940		27	1964–1968	2,061	307	5	46.84	36	4-48	0/0	31.63	21	
Craig Ian David	12.6.1935	16.11.2014	11	1952–1957	358	53	0	19.88	–	–	–/–	–	2	
Crawford William Patrick Anthony	3.8.1933	21.1.2009	4	1956–1956	53	34	0	17.66	7	3-28	0/0	15.28	1	

§ *Clarke's figures include 44 runs and one catch for Australia v the ICC World XI in the Super Series Test in 2005-06.*

	Born	Died	Tests	Test Career	Runs	HS	100s	Avge	Wkts	BB	5/10	Avge	Ct/St	O/T
Cullen Daniel James	10.4.1984		1	*2005*	–	–	–	–	1	1-25	0/0	54.00	0	5
Cummins Patrick James	8.5.1993		1	*2011*	15	13*	0	15.00	7	6-79	1/0	16.71	1	21/15
Dale Adam Craig	30.12.1968		2	*1997–1998*	6	5	0	2.00	6	3-71	0/0	31.16	0	30
Darling Joseph (*CY 1900*)	21.11.1870	2.1.1946	34	*1894*–1905	1,657	178	3	28.56	–	–	–/–	–	27	
Darling Leonard Stuart	14.8.1909	24.6.1992	12	*1932–1936*	474	85	0	27.88	0	0-3	0/0	–	8	
Darling Warrick Maxwell	1.5.1957		14	*1977–1979*	697	91	0	26.80	–	–	–/–	–	5	18
Davidson Alan Keith MBE (*CY 1962*)	14.6.1929		44	1953–*1962*	1,328	80	0	24.59	186	7-93	14/2	20.53	42	
Davis Ian Charles	25.6.1953		15	*1973*–1977	692	105	1	26.61	–	–	–/–	–	9	3
Davis Simon Peter	8.11.1959		1	*1985*	0	0	0	0.00	0	0-70	0/0	–	0	39
De Courcy James Harry	18.4.1927	20.6.2000	3	1953	81	41	0	16.20	–	–	–/–	–	3	
Dell Anthony Ross	6.8.1947		2	*1970–1973*	6	3*	0	–	6	3-65	0/0	26.66	0	
Dodemaide Anthony Ian Christopher	5.10.1963		10	*1987–1992*	202	50	0	22.44	34	6-58	1/0	28.02	6	24
Doherty Xavier John	22.12.1982		4	2010–2012	51	18*	0	12.75	7	3-131	0/0	78.28	2	60/11
Donnan Henry	12.11.1864	13.8.1956	5	*1891*–1896	75	15	0	8.33	0	0-22	0/0	–	2	
Doolan Alexander James	29.11.1985		4	*2013–2014*	191	89	0	23.87	–	–	–/–	–	4	
Dooland Bruce (*CY 1955*)	1.11.1923	8.9.1980	3	*1946–1947*	76	29	0	19.00	9	4-69	0/0	46.55	3	
Duff Reginald Alexander	17.8.1878	13.12.1911	22	*1901*–1905	1,317	146	2	35.59	4	2-43	0/0	21.25	14	
Duncan John Ross Frederick	25.3.1944		1	*1970*	3	3	0	3.00	0	0-30	0/0	–	0	
Dyer Gregory Charles	16.3.1959		6	*1986–1987*	131	60	0	21.83	–	–	–/–	–	22/2	23
Dymock Geoffrey	21.7.1945		21	*1973–1979*	236	31*	0	9.44	78	7-67	5/1	27.12	1	15
Dyson John	11.6.1954		30	*1977–1984*	1,359	127*	2	26.64	–	–	–/–	–	10	29
Eady Charles John	29.10.1870	20.12.1945	2	1896–*1901*	20	10*	0	6.66	7	3-30	0/0	16.00	2	
Eastwood Kenneth Humphrey	23.11.1935		1	*1970*	5	5	0	2.50	1	1-21	0/0	21.00	0	
Ebeling Hans Irvine	1.1.1905	12.1.1980	1	1934	43	41	0	21.50	3	3-74	0/0	29.66	0	
Edwards John Dunlop	12.6.1860	31.7.1911	3	1888	48	26	0	9.60	–	–	–/–	–	1	
Edwards Ross	1.12.1942		20	1972–1975	1,171	170*	2	40.37	0	0-20	0/0	–	7	9
Edwards Walter John	23.12.1949		3	*1974*	68	30	0	11.33	–	–	–/–	–	0	1
Elliott Matthew Thomas Gray (*CY 1998*)	28.9.1971		21	*1996*–2004	1,172	199	3	33.48	0	0-0	0/0	–	14	1
Emery Philip Allen	25.6.1964		1	*1994*	8	8*	0	–	–	–	–/–	–	5/1	1
Emery Sidney Hand	15.10.1885	7.1.1967	4	1912	6	5	0	3.00	5	2-46	0/0	49.80	2	
Evans Edwin	26.3.1849	2.7.1921	6	*1881*–1886	82	33	0	10.25	7	3-64	0/0	47.42	5	
Fairfax Alan George	16.6.1906	17.5.1955	10	*1928–1930*	410	65	0	51.25	21	4-31	0/0	30.71	15	
Faulkner James Peter	29.4.1990		1	2013	45	23	0	22.50	6	4-51	0/0	16.33	0	61/21
Favell Leslie Ernest MBE	6.10.1929	14.6.1987	19	*1954–1960*	757	101	1	27.03	–	–	–/–	–	9	
Ferguson Callum James	21.11.1984		1	*2016*	4	3	0	2.00	–	–	–/–	–	0	30/3
Ferris John James (*CY 1889*)	21.5.1867	17.11.1900	8†	*1886*–1890	98	20*	0	8.16	48	5-26	4/0	14.25	4	

	Born	Died	Tests	Test Career	Runs	HS	100s	Avge	Wkts	BB	5/10	Avge	Ct/St	O/T
Fingleton John Henry Webb OBE	28.4.1908	22.11.1981	18	1931–1938	1,189	136	5	42.46	–	–	–/–	–	13	
Fleetwood-Smith Leslie O'Brien ("Chuck")	30.3.1908	16.3.1971	10	1935–1938	54	16*	0	9.00	42	6-110	2/1	37.38	0	
Fleming Damien William	24.4.1970		20	1994–2000	305	71*	0	19.06	75	5-30	3/0	25.89	9	88
Francis Bruce Colin	18.2.1948		3	1972	52	27	0	10.40	–	–	–/–	–	1	
Freeman Eric Walter	13.7.1944		11	1967–1969	345	76	0	19.16	34	4-52	0/0	33.17	5	
Freer Frederick Alfred William	4.12.1915	2.11.1998	1	1946	28	28*	0	–	3	2-49	0/0	24.66	0	
Gannon John Bryant ("Sam")	8.2.1947		3	1977	3	3*	0	3.00	11	4-77	0/0	32.81	3	
Garrett Thomas William	26.7.1858	6.8.1943	19	1876–1887	339	51*	0	12.55	36	6-78	2/0	26.94	7	
Gaunt Ronald Arthur	26.2.1934	30.3.2012	3	1957–1963	6	3	0	3.00	7	3-53	0/0	44.28	1	
Gehrs Donald Raeburn Algernon	29.11.1880	25.6.1953	6	1903–1910	221	67	0	20.09	0	0-4	0/0	–	6	
George Peter Robert	16.10.1986		1	2010	2	2	0	1.00	2	2-48	0/0	38.50	0	
[2] **Giffen** George (*CY 1894*)	27.3.1859	29.11.1927	31	1881–1896	1,238	161	1	23.35	103	7-117	7/1	27.09	24	
[2] **Giffen** Walter Frank	20.9.1861	28.6.1949	3	1886–1891	11	3	0	1.83	–	–	–/–	–	1	
Gilbert David Robert	29.12.1960		9	1985–1986	57	15	0	7.12	16	3-48	0/0	52.68	0	14
Gilchrist Adam Craig(*CY 2002*)	14.11.1971		96§	1999–2007	5,570	204*	17	47.60	–	–	–/–	–	379/37	286‡/13
Gillespie Jason Neil (*CY 2002*)	19.4.1975		71	1996–2005	1,218	201*	1	18.73	259	7-37	8/0	26.13	27	97/1
Gilmour Gary John	26.6.1951	10.6.2014	15	1973–1976	483	101	1	23.00	54	6-85	3/0	26.03	8	5
Gleeson John William	14.3.1938	8.10.2016	29	1967–1972	395	45	0	10.39	93	5-61	3/0	36.20	17	
Graham Henry	22.11.1870	7.2.1911	6	1893–1896	301	107	2	30.10	–	–	–/–	–	3	
[2] **Gregory** David William	15.4.1845	4.8.1919	3	1876–1878	60	43	0	20.00	0	0-9	0/0	–	0	
[1, 2] **Gregory** Edward James	29.5.1839	22.4.1899	1	1876	11	11	0	5.50	–	–	–/–	–	1	
Gregory Jack Morrison (*CY 1922*)	14.8.1895	7.8.1973	24	1920–1928	1,146	119	2	36.96	85	7-69	4/0	31.15	37	
Gregory Ross Gerald	28.2.1916	10.6.1942	2	1936	153	80	0	51.00	0	0-14	0/0	–	1	
[1] **Gregory** Sydney Edward (*CY 1897*)	14.4.1870	31.7.1929	58	1890–1912	2,282	201	4	24.53	0	0-4	0/0	–	25	
Grimmett Clarence Victor (*CY 1931*)	25.12.1891	2.5.1980	37	1924–1935	557	50	0	13.92	216	7-40	21/7	24.21	17	
Groube Thomas Underwood	2.9.1857	5.8.1927	1	1880	11	11	0	5.50	–	–	–/–	–	0	
Grout Arthur Theodore Wallace	30.3.1927	9.11.1968	51	1957–1965	890	74	0	15.08	–	–	–/–	–	163/24	
Guest Colin Ernest John	7.10.1937		1	1962	11	11	0	11.00	0	0-8	0/0	–	0	
Haddin Bradley James	23.10.1977		66	2007–2015	3,265	169	4	32.97	–	–	–/–	–	262/8	126/34
Hamence Ronald Arthur	25.11.1915	24.3.2010	3	1946–1947	81	30*	0	27.00	–	–	–/–	–	1	
Hammond Jeffrey Roy	19.4.1950		5	1972	28	19	0	9.33	15	4-38	0/0	32.53	2	1
Handscomb Peter Stephen Patrick	26.4.1991		4	2016	399	110	2	99.75	–	–	–/–	–	3	
Harris Ryan James (*CY 2014*)	11.10.1979		27	2009–2014	603	74	0	21.53	113	7-117	5/0	23.52	13	21/3
Harry John	1.8.1857	27.10.1919	1	1894	8	6	0	4.00	–	–	–/–	–	1	
Hartigan Roger Joseph	12.12.1879	7.6.1958	2	1907	170	116	1	42.50	0	0-7	0/0	–	1	

§ *Gilchrist's figures include 95 runs, five catches and two stumpings for Australia v the ICC World XI in the Super Series Test in 2005-06.*

	Born	Died	Tests	Test Career	Runs	HS	100s	Avge	Wkts	BB	5/10	Avge	Ct/St	O/T
Hartkopf Albert Ernst Victor	28.12.1889	20.5.1968	1	1924	80	80	0	40.00	1	1-120	0/0	134.00	0	
[2] **Harvey** Mervyn Roye	29.4.1918	18.3.1995	1	1946	43	31	0	21.50	–	–	–/–	–	0	
[2] **Harvey** Robert Neil MBE (*CY 1954*)	8.10.1928		79	1947–1962	6,149	205	21	48.41	3	1-8	0/0	40.00	64	
Hassett Arthur Lindsay MBE (*CY 1949*)	28.8.1913	16.6.1993	43	1938–1953	3,073	198*	10	46.56	0	0-1	0/0	–	30	
Hastings John Wayne	4.11.1985		1	2012	52	32	0	26.00	1	1-51	0/0	153.00	1	28/9
Hauritz Nathan Michael	18.10.1981		17	2004–2010	426	75	0	25.05	63	5-53	2/0	34.98	3	58/3
Hawke Neil James Napier	27.6.1939	25.12.2000	27	1962–1968	365	45*	0	16.59	91	7-105	6/1	29.41	9	
Hayden Matthew Lawrence (*CY 2003*)	29.10.1971		103§	1993–2008	8,625	380	30	50.73	0	0-7	0/0	–	128	160‡/9
Hazlewood Josh Reginald	8.1.1991		26	2014–2016	253	39	0	15.81	109	6-70	4/0	24.78	12	29/7
Hazlitt Gervys Rignold	4.9.1888	30.10.1915	9	1907–1912	89	34*	0	11.12	23	7-25	1/0	27.08	4	
Healy Ian Andrew (*CY 1994*)	30.4.1964		119	1988–1999	4,356	161*	4	27.39	–	–	–/–	–	366/29	168
Hendry Hunter Scott Thomas Laurie ("Stork")	24.5.1895	16.12.1988	11	1921–1928	335	112	1	20.93	16	3-36	0/0	40.00	10	
Henriques Moises Constantino	1.2.1987		4	2012–2016	164	81*	0	23.42	2	1-48	0/0	82.00	1	8/6
Hibbert Paul Anthony	23.7.1952	27.11.2008	1	1977	15	13	0	7.50	–	–	–/–	–	1	
Higgs James Donald	11.7.1950		22	1977–1980	111	16	0	5.55	66	7-143	2/0	31.16	3	
Hilditch Andrew Mark Jefferson	20.5.1956		18	1978–1985	1,073	119	2	31.55	–	–	–/–	–	13	8
Hilfenhaus Benjamin William	15.3.1983		27	2008–2012	355	56*	0	13.65	99	5-75	2/0	28.50	7	25/7
Hill Clement (*CY 1900*)	18.3.1877	5.9.1945	49	1896–1911	3,412	191	7	39.21	–	–	–/–	–	33	
Hill John Charles	25.6.1923	11.8.1974	3	1953–1954	21	8*	0	7.00	8	3-35	0/0	34.12	2	
Hoare Desmond Edward	19.10.1934		1	1960	35	35	0	17.50	2	2-68	0/0	78.00	2	
Hodge Bradley John	29.12.1974		6	2005–2007	503	203*	1	55.88	0	0-8	0/0	–	9	25/15
Hodges John Robart	11.8.1855	d unknown	2	1876	10	8	0	3.33	6	2-7	0/0	14.00	0	
Hogan Tom George	23.9.1956		7	1982–1983	205	42*	0	18.63	15	5-66	1/0	47.06	2	16
Hogg George Bradley	6.2.1971		7	1996–2007	186	79	0	26.57	17	2-40	0/0	54.88	1	123/15
Hogg Rodney Malcolm	5.3.1951		38	1978–1984	439	52	0	9.75	123	6-74	6/2	28.47	7	71
Hohns Trevor Victor	23.1.1954		7	1988–1989	136	40	0	22.66	17	3-59	0/0	34.11	3	
Hole Graeme Blake	6.1.1931	14.2.1990	18	1950–1954	789	66	0	25.45	3	1-9	0/0	42.00	21	
Holland Jonathan Mark	29.5.1987		2	2016	1	1	0	1.00	5	2-72	0/0	54.80	0	
Holland Robert George	19.10.1946		11	1984–1985	35	10	0	3.18	34	6-54	3/2	39.76	5	2
Hookes David William	3.5.1955	19.1.2004	23	1976–1985	1,306	143*	1	34.36	1	1-4	0/0	41.00	12	39
Hopkins Albert John Young	3.5.1874	25.4.1931	20	1901–1909	509	43	0	16.41	26	4-81	0/0	26.76	11	
Horan Thomas Patrick	8.3.1854	16.4.1916	15	1876–1884	471	124	1	18.84	11	6-40	1/0	13.00	6	
Hordern Herbert Vivian MBE	10.2.1883	17.6.1938	7	1910–1911	254	50	0	23.09	46	7-90	5/2	23.36	6	
Hornibrook Percival Mitchell	27.7.1899	25.8.1976	6	1928–1930	60	26	0	10.00	17	7-92	1/0	39.05	7	
Howell William Peter	29.12.1869	14.7.1940	18	1897–1903	158	35	0	7.52	49	5-81	1/0	28.71	12	

§ *Hayden's figures include 188 runs and three catches, for Australia v the ICC World XI in the Super Series Test in 2005-06.*

	Born	Died	Tests	Test Career	Runs	HS	100s	Avge	Wkts	BB	5/10	Avge	Ct/St	O/T
Hughes Kimberley John (*CY 1981*)	26.1.1954		70	1977–1984	4,415	213	9	37.41	0	0-0	0/0	–	50	97
Hughes Mervyn Gregory (*CY 1994*)	23.11.1961		53	1985–1993	1,032	72*	0	16.64	212	8-87	7/1	28.38	23	33
Hughes Phillip Joel	30.11.1988	27.11.2014	26	2008–2013	1,535	160	3	32.65	–	–	–/–	–	15	25/1
Hunt William Alfred	26.8.1908	30.12.1983	1	1931	0	0	0	0.00	0	0-14	0/0	–	1	
Hurst Alan George	15.7.1950		12	1973–1979	102	26	0	6.00	43	5-28	2/0	27.90	3	8
Hurwood Alexander	17.6.1902	26.9.1982	2	1930	5	5	0	2.50	11	4-22	0/0	15.45	2	
Hussey Michael Edward Killeen	27.5.1975		79	2005–2012	6,235	195	19	51.52	7	1-0	0/0	43.71	85	185/38
Inverarity Robert John	31.1.1944		6	1968–1972	174	56	0	17.40	4	3-26	0/0	23.25	4	
Iredale Francis Adams	19.6.1867	15.4.1926	14	1894–1899	807	140	2	36.68	0	0-3	0/0	–	16	
Ironmonger Herbert	7.4.1882	31.5.1971	14	1928–1932	42	12	0	2.62	74	7-23	4/2	17.97	3	
Iverson John Brian	27.7.1915	24.10.1973	5	1950	3	1*	0	0.75	21	6-27	1/0	15.23	2	
Jackson Archibald Alexander	5.9.1909	16.2.1933	8	1928–1930	474	164	1	47.40	–	–	–/–	–	7	
Jaques Philip Anthony	3.5.1979		11	2005–2007	902	150	3	47.47	–	–	–/–	–	7	6
Jarman Barrington Noel	17.2.1936		19	1959–1968	400	78	0	14.81	–	–	–/–	–	50/4	
Jarvis Arthur Harwood	19.10.1860	15.11.1933	11	1884–1894	303	82	0	16.83	–	–	–/–	–	9/9	
Jenner Terrence James	8.9.1944	24.5.2011	9	1970–1975	208	74	0	23.11	24	5-90	1/0	31.20	5	1
Jennings Claude Burrows	5.6.1884	20.6.1950	6	1912	107	32	0	17.83	–	–	–/–	–	5	
Johnson Ian William Geddes CBE	8.12.1917	9.10.1998	45	1945–1956	1,000	77	0	18.51	109	7-44	3/0	29.19	30	
Johnson Leonard Joseph	18.3.1919	20.4.1977	1	1947	25	25*	0	–	6	3-8	0/0	12.33	2	
Johnson Mitchell Guy	2.11.1981		73	2007–2015	2,065	123*	1	22.20	313	8-61	12/3	28.40	27	153/30
Johnston William Arras (*CY 1949*)	26.2.1922	25.5.2007	40	1947–1954	273	29	0	11.37	160	6-44	7/0	23.91	16	
Jones Dean Mervyn (*CY 1990*)	24.3.1961		52	1983–1992	3,631	216	11	46.55	1	1-5	0/0	64.00	34	164
Jones Ernest	30.9.1869	23.11.1943	19	1894–1902	126	20	0	5.04	64	7-88	3/1	29.01	21	
Jones Samuel Percy	1.8.1861	14.7.1951	12	1881–1887	428	87	0	21.40	6	4-47	0/0	18.66	12	
Joslin Leslie Ronald	13.12.1947		1	1967	9	7	0	4.50	–	–	–/–	–	0	
Julian Brendon Paul	10.8.1970		7	1993–1995	128	56*	0	16.00	15	4-36	0/0	39.93	4	25
Kasprowicz Michael Scott	10.2.1972		38	1996–2005	445	25	0	10.59	113	7-36	4/0	32.88	16	43/2
Katich Simon Mathew	21.8.1975		56§	2001–2010	4,188	157	10	45.03	21	6-65	1/0	30.23	39	45/3
Kelleway Charles	25.4.1886	16.11.1944	26	1910–1928	1,422	147	3	37.42	52	5-33	1/0	32.36	24	
Kelly James Joseph (*CY 1903*)	10.5.1867	14.8.1938	36	1896–1905	664	46*	0	17.02	–	–	–/–	–	43/20	
Kelly Thomas Joseph Dart	3.5.1844	20.7.1893	2	1876–1878	64	35	0	21.33	–	–	–/–	–	1	
Kendall Thomas Kingston	24.8.1851	17.8.1924	2	1876	39	17*	0	13.00	14	7-55	1/0	15.35	2	
Kent Martin Francis	23.11.1953		3	1981	171	54	0	28.50	–	–	–/–	–	6	5
Kerr Robert Byers	16.6.1961		2	1985	31	17	0	7.75	–	–	–/–	–	1	4
Khawaja Usman Tariq	18.12.1986		23	2010–2016	1,726	174	5	47.94	–	–	–/–	–	18	15/9

§ *Katich's figures include two runs and one catch for Australia v the ICC World XI in the Super Series Test in 2005-06.*

	Born	*Died*	*Tests*	*Test Career*	*Runs*	*HS*	*100s*	*Avge*	*Wkts*	*BB*	*5/10*	*Avge*	*Ct/St*	*O/T*
Kippax Alan Falconer	25.5.1897	5.9.1972	22	*1924–1934*	1,192	146	2	36.12	0	0-2	0/0	–	13	
Kline Lindsay Francis	29.9.1934	2.10.2015	13	*1957–1960*	58	15*	0	8.28	34	7-75	1/0	22.82	9	
Krejza Jason John	14.1.1983		2	*2008*	71	32	0	23.66	13	8-215	1/1	43.23	4	8
Laird Bruce Malcolm	21.11.1950		21	*1979–1982*	1,341	92	0	35.28	0	0-3	0/0	–	16	23
Langer Justin Lee (*CY 2001*)	21.11.1970		105§	*1992–2006*	7,696	250	23	45.27	0	0-3	0/0	–	73	8
Langley Gilbert Roche Andrews (*CY 1957*)	14.9.1919	14.5.2001	26	*1951–1956*	374	53	0	14.96	–	–	–/–	–	83/15	
Laughlin Trevor John	30.1.1951		3	*1977–1978*	87	35	0	17.40	6	5-101	1/0	43.66	3	6
Laver Frank Jonas	7.12.1869	24.9.1919	15	1899–1909	196	45	0	11.52	37	8-31	2/0	26.05	8	
Law Stuart Grant (*CY 1998*)	18.10.1968		1	*1995*	54	54*	0	–	0	0-9	0/0	–	1	54
Lawry William Morris (*CY 1962*)	11.2.1937		67	1961–*1970*	5,234	210	13	47.15	0	0-0	0/0	–	30	1
Lawson Geoffrey Francis	7.12.1957		46	*1980–1989*	894	74	0	15.96	180	8-112	11/2	30.56	10	79
Lee Brett (*CY 2006*)	8.11.1976		76§	*1999–2008*	1,451	64	0	20.15	310	5-30	10/0	30.81	23	221/25
Lee Philip Keith	15.9.1904	9.8.1980	2	*1931–1932*	57	42	0	19.00	5	4-111	0/0	42.40	1	
Lehmann Darren Scott (*CY 2001*)	5.2.1970		27	*1997–2004*	1,798	177	5	44.95	15	3-42	0/0	27.46	11	117
Lillee Dennis Keith MBE (*CY 1973*)	18.7.1949		70	*1970–1983*	905	73*	0	13.71	355	7-83	23/7	23.92	23	63
Lindwall Raymond Russell MBE (*CY 1949*)	3.10.1921	23.6.1996	61	*1945–1959*	1,502	118	2	21.15	228	7-38	12/0	23.03	26	
Love Hampden Stanley Bray	10.8.1895	22.7.1969	1	*1932*	8	5	0	4.00	–	–	–/–	–	3	
Love Martin Lloyd	30.3.1974		5	2002–2003	233	100*	1	46.60	–	–	–/–	–	7	
Loxton Samuel John Everett OBE	29.3.1921	3.12.2011	12	*1947–1950*	554	101	1	36.93	8	3-55	0/0	43.62	7	
Lyon Nathan Michael	20.11.1987		63	*2011–2016*	640	40*	0	13.61	228	7-94	7/1	34.07	31	13/1
Lyons John James	21.5.1863	21.7.1927	14	*1886–1897*	731	134	1	27.07	6	5-30	1/0	24.83	3	
McAlister Peter Alexander	11.7.1869	10.5.1938	8	*1903*–1909	252	41	0	16.80	–	–	–/–	–	10	
Macartney Charles George (*CY 1922*)	27.6.1886	9.9.1958	35	*1907–1926*	2,131	170	7	41.78	45	7-58	2/1	27.55	17	
McCabe Stanley Joseph (*CY 1935*)	16.7.1910	25.8.1968	39	1930–1938	2,748	232	6	48.21	36	4-13	0/0	42.86	41	
McCool Colin Leslie	9.12.1916	5.4.1986	14	*1945–1949*	459	104*	1	35.30	36	5-41	3/0	26.61	14	
McCormick Ernest Leslie	16.5.1906	28.6.1991	12	*1935*–1938	54	17*	0	6.00	36	4-101	0/0	29.97	8	
McCosker Richard Bede (*CY 1976*)	11.12.1946		25	*1974–1979*	1,622	127	4	39.56	–	–	–/–	–	21	14
McDermott Craig John (*CY 1986*)	14.4.1965		71	*1984–1995*	940	42*	0	12.20	291	8-97	14/2	28.63	19	138
McDonald Andrew Barry	15.6.1981		4	*2008*	107	68	0	21.40	9	3-25	0/0	33.33	2	
McDonald Colin Campbell	17.11.1928		47	*1951*–1961	3,107	170	5	39.32	0	0-3	0/0	–	14	
McDonald Edgar Arthur (*CY 1922*)	6.1.1891	22.7.1937	11	*1920–1921*	116	36	0	16.57	43	5-32	2/0	33.27	3	
McDonnell Percy Stanislaus	13.11.1858	24.9.1896	19	1880–1888	955	147	3	28.93	0	0-11	0/0	–	6	
McGain Bryce Edward	25.3.1972		1	*2008*	2	2	0	1.00	0	0-149	0/0	–	0	
MacGill Stuart Charles Glyndwr	25.2.1971		44§	*1997–2007*	349	43	0	9.69	208	8-108	12/2	29.02	16	3

§ *Langer's figures include 22 runs and one catch, Lee's four runs, two wickets and one catch and MacGill's no runs and nine wickets, for Australia v the ICC World XI in the Super Series Test in 2005-06.*

	Born	Died	Tests	Test Career	Runs	HS	100s	Avge	Wkts	BB	5/10	Avge	Ct/St	O/T
McGrath Glenn Donald (*CY 1998*)	9.2.1970		124§	1993–2006	641	61	0	7.36	563	8-24	29/3	21.64	38	249‡/2
McIlwraith John	7.9.1857	5.7.1938	1	1886	9	7	0	4.50	–	–	–/–	–	1	
McIntyre Peter Edward	27.4.1966		2	1994–1996	22	16	0	7.33	5	3-103	0/0	38.80	0	
McKay Clinton James	22.2.1983		1	2009	10	10	0	10.00	1	1-56	0/0	101.00	1	59/6
Mackay Kenneth Donald MBE	24.10.1925	13.6.1982	37	1956–1962	1,507	89	0	33.48	50	6-42	2/0	34.42	16	
McKenzie Graham Douglas (*CY 1965*)	24.6.1941		60	1961–1970	945	76	0	12.27	246	8-71	16/3	29.78	34	1
McKibbin Thomas Robert	10.12.1870	15.12.1939	5	1894–1897	88	28*	0	14.66	17	3-35	0/0	29.17	4	
McLaren John William	22.12.1886	17.11.1921	1	1911	0	0*	0	–	1	1-23	0/0	70.00	0	
Maclean John Alexander	27.4.1946		4	1978	79	33*	0	11.28	–	–	–/–	–	18	2
[2] **McLeod** Charles Edward	24.10.1869	26.11.1918	17	1894–1905	573	112	1	23.87	33	5-65	2/0	40.15	9	
[2] **McLeod** Robert William	19.1.1868	14.6.1907	6	1891–1893	146	31	0	13.27	12	5-53	1/0	31.83	3	
McShane Patrick George	18.4.1858	11.12.1903	3	1884–1887	26	12*	0	5.20	1	1-39	0/0	48.00	2	
Maddinson Nicolas James	21.12.1991		3	2016	27	22	0	6.75	0	0-9	0/0	–	2	0/2
Maddocks Leonard Victor	24.5.1926	27.8.2016	7	1954–1956	177	69	0	17.70	–	–	–/–	–	19/1	
Maguire John Norman	15.9.1956		3	1983	28	15*	0	7.00	10	4-57	0/0	32.30	2	23
Mailey Arthur Alfred	3.1.1886	31.12.1967	21	1920–1926	222	46*	0	11.10	99	9-121	6/2	33.91	14	
Mallett Ashley Alexander	13.7.1945		38	1968–1980	430	43*	0	11.62	132	8-59	6/1	29.84	30	9
Malone Michael Francis	9.10.1950		1	1977	46	46	0	46.00	6	5-63	1/0	12.83	0	10
Mann Anthony Longford	8.11.1945		4	1977	189	105	1	23.62	4	3-12	0/0	79.00	2	
Manou Graham Allan	23.4.1979		1	2009	21	13*	0	21.00	–	–	–/–	–	3	4
Marr Alfred Percy	28.3.1862	15.3.1940	1	1884	5	5	0	2.50	0	0-3	0/0	–	0	
[1] **Marsh** Geoffrey Robert	31.12.1958		50	1985–1991	2,854	138	4	33.18	–	–	–/–	–	38	117
[1,2] **Marsh** Mitchell Ross	20.10.1991		19	2014–2016	626	87	0	23.18	29	4-61	0/0	37.27	9	46/9
Marsh Rodney William MBE (*CY 1982*)	4.11.1947		96	1970–1983	3,633	132	3	26.51	0	0-3	0/0	–	343/12	92
[1,2] **Marsh** Shaun Edward	9.7.1983		19	2011–2016	1,325	182	4	40.15	–	–	–/–	–	16	51/15
Martin John Wesley	28.7.1931	16.7.1992	8	1960–1966	214	55	0	17.83	17	3-56	0/0	48.94	5	
Martyn Damien Richard (*CY 2002*)	21.10.1971		67	1992–2006	4,406	165	13	46.37	2	1-0	0/0	84.00	36	208/4
Massie Hugh Hamon	11.4.1854	12.10.1938	9	1881–1884	249	55	0	15.56	–	–	–/–	–	5	
Massie Robert Arnold Lockyer (*CY 1973*)	14.4.1947		6	1972–1972	78	42	0	11.14	31	8-53	2/1	20.87	1	3
Matthews Christopher Darrell	22.9.1962		3	1986–1988	54	32	0	10.80	6	3-95	0/0	52.16	1	
Matthews Gregory Richard John	15.12.1959		33	1983–1992	1,849	130	4	41.08	61	5-103	2/1	48.22	17	59
Matthews Thomas James	3.4.1884	14.10.1943	8	1911–1912	153	53	0	17.00	16	4-29	0/0	26.18	7	
Maxwell Glenn James	14.10.1988		3	2012–2014	80	37	0	13.33	7	4-127	0/0	38.71	2	67/36
May Timothy Brian Alexander	26.1.1962		24	1987–1994	225	42*	0	14.06	75	5-9	3/0	34.74	6	47
Mayne Edgar Richard	2.7.1882	26.10.1961	4	1912–1921	64	25*	0	21.33	0	0-1	0/0	–	2	

§ *McGrath's figures include two runs and three wickets for Australia v the ICC World XI in the Super Series Test in 2005-06.*

	Born	Died	Tests	Test Career	Runs	HS	100s	Avge	Wkts	BB	5/10	Avge	Ct/St	O/T
Mayne Lawrence Charles	23.1.1942		6	1964–1969	76	13	0	9.50	19	4-43	0/0	33.05	3	
Meckiff Ian	6.1.1935		18	1957–1963	154	45*	0	11.84	45	6-38	2/0	31.62	9	
Mennie Joe Matthew	24.12.1988		1	2016	10	10	0	5.00	1	1-85	0/0	85.00	0	2
Meuleman Kenneth Douglas	5.9.1923	10.9.2004	1	1945	0	0	0	0.00	–	–	–/–	–	1	
Midwinter William Evans	19.6.1851	3.12.1890	8†	1876–1886	174	37	0	13.38	14	5-78	1/0	23.78	5	
Miller Colin Reid	6.2.1964		18	1998–2000	174	43	0	8.28	69	5-32	3/1	26.15	6	
Miller Keith Ross MBE (*CY 1954*)	28.11.1919	11.10.2004	55	1945–1956	2,958	147	7	36.97	170	7-60	7/1	22.97	38	
Minnett Roy Baldwin	13.6.1888	21.10.1955	9	1911–1912	391	90	0	26.06	11	4-34	0/0	26.36	0	
Misson Francis Michael	19.11.1938		5	1960–1961	38	25*	0	19.00	16	4-58	0/0	38.50	6	
Moody Thomas Masson (*CY 2000*)	2.10.1965		8	1989–1992	456	106	2	32.57	2	1-17	0/0	73.50	9	76
Moroney John	24.7.1917	1.7.1999	7	1949–1951	383	118	2	34.81	–	–	–/–	–	0	
Morris Arthur Robert MBE (*CY 1949*)	19.1.1922	22.8.2015	46	1946–1954	3,533	206	12	46.48	2	1-5	0/0	25.00	15	
Morris Samuel	22.6.1855	20.9.1931	1	1884	14	10*	0	14.00	2	2-73	0/0	36.50	0	
Moses Henry	13.2.1858	7.12.1938	6	1886–1894	198	33	0	19.80	–	–	–/–	–	1	
Moss Jeffrey Kenneth	29.6.1947		1	1978	60	38*	0	60.00	–	–	–/–	–	0	1
Moule William Henry	31.1.1858	24.8.1939	1	1880	40	34	0	20.00	3	3-23	0/0	7.66	1	
Muller Scott Andrew	11.7.1971		2	1999	6	6*	0	–	7	3-68	0/0	36.85	2	
Murdoch William Lloyd	18.10.1854	18.2.1911	18†	1876–1890	896	211	2	32.00	–	–	–/–	–	14	
Musgrove Henry Alfred	27.11.1858	2.11.1931	1	1884	13	9	0	6.50	–	–	–/–	–	0	
Nagel Lisle Ernest	6.3.1905	23.11.1971	1	1932	21	21*	0	21.00	2	2-110	0/0	55.00	0	
Nash Laurence John	2.5.1910	24.7.1986	2	1931–1936	30	17	0	15.00	10	4-18	0/0	12.60	6	
Nevill Peter Michael	13.10.1985		17	2015–2016	468	66	0	22.28	–	–	–/–	–	61/2	0/9
Nicholson Matthew James	2.10.1974		1	1998	14	9	0	7.00	4	3-56	0/0	28.75	0	
Nitschke Homesdale Carl ("Jack")	14.4.1905	29.9.1982	2	1931	53	47	0	26.50	–	–	–/–	–	3	
Noble Montague Alfred (*CY 1900*)	28.1.1873	22.6.1940	42	1897–1909	1,997	133	1	30.25	121	7-17	9/2	25.00	26	
Noblet Geffery	14.9.1916	16.8.2006	3	1949–1952	22	13*	0	7.33	7	3-21	0/0	26.14	1	
North Marcus James	28.7.1979		21	2008–2010	1,171	128	5	35.48	14	6-55	1/0	42.21	17	2/1
Nothling Otto Ernest	1.8.1900	26.9.1965	1	1928	52	44	0	26.00	0	0-12	0/0	–	0	
O'Brien Leo Patrick Joseph	2.7.1907	13.3.1997	5	1932–1936	211	61	0	26.37	–	–	–/–	–	3	
O'Connor John Denis Alphonsus	9.9.1875	23.8.1941	4	1907–1909	86	20	0	12.28	13	5-40	1/0	26.15	3	
O'Donnell Simon Patrick	26.1.1963		6	1985–1985	206	48	0	29.42	6	3-37	0/0	84.00	4	87
Ogilvie Alan David	3.6.1951		5	1977	178	47	0	17.80	–	–	–/–	–	5	
O'Keefe Stephen Norman John	9.12.1984		4	2014–2016	33	23	0	11.00	14	3-53	0/0	32.78	0	0/7
O'Keeffe Kerry James	25.11.1949		24	1970–1977	644	85	0	25.76	53	5-101	1/0	38.07	15	2
Oldfield William Albert Stanley MBE (*CY 1927*)	9.9.1894	10.8.1976	54	1920–1936	1,427	65*	0	22.65	–	–	–/–	–	78/52	
O'Neill Norman Clifford Louis (*CY 1962*)	19.2.1937	3.3.2008	42	1958–1964	2,779	181	6	45.55	17	4-41	0/0	39.23	21	

	Born	Died	Tests	Test Career	Runs	HS	100s	Avge	Wkts	BB	5/10	Avge	Ct/St	O/T
O'Reilly William Joseph OBE (*CY 1935*)	20.12.1905	6.10.1992	27	1931–1945	410	56*	0	12.81	144	7-54	11/3	22.59	7	
Oxenham Ronald Keven	28.7.1891	16.8.1939	7	1928–1931	151	48	0	15.10	14	4-39	0/0	37.28	4	
Paine Timothy David	8.12.1984		4	2010–2010	287	92	0	35.87	–	–	–/–	–	16/1	26/5
Palmer George Eugene ("Joey")	22.2.1859	22.8.1910	17	1880–1886	296	48	0	14.09	78	7-65	6/2	21.51	13	
Park Roy Lindsay	30.7.1892	23.1.1947	1	1920	0	0	0	0.00	0	0-9	0/0	–	0	
Pascoe Leonard Stephen	13.2.1950		14	1977–1981	106	30*	0	10.60	64	5-59	1/0	26.06	2	29
[2] **Pattinson** James Lee	3.5.1990		17	2011–2015	332	42	0	27.66	70	5-27	4/0	26.15	4	15/4
Pellew Clarence Everard ("Nip")	21.9.1893	9.5.1981	10	1920–1921	484	116	2	37.23	0	0-3	0/0	–	4	
Phillips Wayne Bentley	1.3.1958		27	1983–1985	1,485	159	2	32.28	–	–	–/–	–	52	48
Phillips Wayne Norman	7.11.1962		1	1991	22	14	0	11.00	–	–	–/–	–	0	
Philpott Peter Ian	21.11.1934		8	1964–1965	93	22	0	10.33	26	5-90	1/0	38.46	5	
Ponsford William Harold MBE (*CY 1935*)	19.10.1900	6.4.1991	29	1924–1934	2,122	266	7	48.22	–	–	–/–	–	21	
Ponting Ricky Thomas (*CY 2006*)	19.12.1974		168§	1995–2012	13,378	257	41	51.85	5	1-0	0/0	55.20	196	374‡/17
Pope Roland James	18.2.1864	27.7.1952	1	1884	3	3	0	1.50	–	–	–/–	–	0	
Quiney Robert John	20.8.1982		2	2012	9	9	0	3.00	0	0-3	0/0	–	5	
Rackemann Carl Gray	3.6.1960		12	1982–1990	53	15*	0	5.30	39	6-86	3/1	29.15	2	52
Ransford Vernon Seymour (*CY 1910*)	20.3.1885	19.3.1958	20	1907–1911	1,211	143*	1	37.84	1	1-9	0/0	28.00	10	
Redpath Ian Ritchie MBE	11.5.1941		66	1963–1975	4,737	171	8	43.45	0	0-0	0/0	–	83	5
Reedman John Cole	9.10.1865	25.3.1924	1	1894	21	17	0	10.50	1	1-12	0/0	24.00	1	
Reid Bruce Anthony	14.3.1963		27	1985–1992	93	13	0	4.65	113	7-51	5/2	24.63	5	61
Reiffel Paul Ronald	19.4.1966		35	1991–1997	955	79*	0	26.52	104	6-71	5/0	26.96	15	92
Renneberg David Alexander	23.9.1942		8	1966–1967	22	9	0	3.66	23	5-39	2/0	36.08	2	
Renshaw Matthew Thomas	28.3.1996		4	2016	315	184	1	63.00	–	–	–/–	–	5	
Richardson Arthur John	24.7.1888	23.12.1973	9	1924–1926	403	100	1	31.00	12	2-20	0/0	43.41	1	
[4] **Richardson** Victor York OBE	7.9.1894	30.10.1969	19	1924–1935	706	138	1	23.53	–	–	–/–	–	24	
Rigg Keith Edward	21.5.1906	28.2.1995	8	1930–1936	401	127	1	33.41	–	–	–/–	–	5	
Ring Douglas Thomas	14.10.1918	23.6.2003	13	1947–1953	426	67	0	22.42	35	6-72	2/0	37.28	5	
Ritchie Gregory Michael	23.1.1960		30	1982–1986	1,690	146	3	35.20	0	0-10	0/0	–	14	44
Rixon Stephen John	25.2.1954		13	1977–1984	394	54	0	18.76	–	–	–/–	–	42/5	6
Robertson Gavin Ron	28.5.1966		4	1997–1998	140	57	0	20.00	13	4-72	0/0	39.61	1	13
Robertson William Roderick	6.10.1861	24.6.1938	1	1884	2	2	0	1.00	0	0-24	0/0	–	0	
Robinson Richard Daryl	8.6.1946		3	1977	100	34	0	16.66	–	–	–/–	–	4	2
Robinson Rayford Harold	26.3.1914	10.8.1965	1	1936	5	3	0	2.50	–	–	–/–	–	1	
Rogers Christopher John Llewellyn (*CY 2014*)	31.8.1977		25	2007–2015	2,015	173	5	42.87	–	–	–/–	–	15	
Rorke Gordon Frederick	27.6.1938		4	1958–1959	9	7	0	4.50	10	3-23	0/0	20.30	1	

§ *Ponting's figures include 100 runs and one catch for Australia v the ICC World XI in the Super Series Test in 2005-06.*

	Born	Died	Tests	Test Career	Runs	HS	100s	Avge	Wkts	BB	5/10	Avge	Ct/St	O/T
Rutherford John Walter	25.9.1929		1	*1956*	30	30	0	30.00	1	1-11	0/0	15.00	0	
Ryder John	8.8.1889	3.4.1977	20	*1920–1928*	1,394	201*	3	51.62	17	2-20	0/0	43.70	17	
Saggers Ronald Arthur	15.5.1917	17.3.1987	6	1948–*1949*	30	14	0	10.00	–	–	–/–	–	16/8	
Saunders John Victor	21.3.1876	21.12.1927	14	*1901–1907*	39	11*	0	2.29	79	7-34	6/0	22.73	5	
Scott Henry James Herbert	26.12.1858	23.9.1910	8	1884–1886	359	102	1	27.61	0	0-9	0/0	–	8	
Sellers Reginald Hugh Durning	20.8.1940		1	*1964*	0	0	0	0.00	0	0-17	0/0	–	1	
Serjeant Craig Stanton	1.11.1951		12	*1977–1977*	522	124	1	23.72	–	–	–/–	–	13	3
[5] **Sheahan** Andrew Paul	30.9.1946		31	*1967–1973*	1,594	127	2	33.91	–	–	–/–	–	17	3
Shepherd Barry Kenneth	23.4.1937	17.9.2001	9	*1962–1964*	502	96	0	41.83	0	0-3	0/0	–	2	
Siddle Peter Matthew	25.11.1984		62	*2008–2016*	1,063	51	0	14.76	211	6-54	8/0	29.92	16	17/2
Sievers Morris William	13.4.1912	10.5.1968	3	*1936*	67	25*	0	13.40	9	5-21	1/0	17.88	4	
Simpson Robert Baddeley (*CY 1965*)	3.2.1936		62	*1957–1977*	4,869	311	10	46.81	71	5-57	2/0	42.26	110	2
Sincock David John	1.2.1942		3	*1964–1965*	80	29	0	26.66	8	3-67	0/0	51.25	2	
Slater Keith Nichol	12.3.1936		1	*1958*	1	1*	0	–	2	2-40	0/0	50.50	0	
Slater Michael Jonathon	21.2.1970		74	1993–2001	5,312	219	14	42.83	1	1-4	0/0	10.00	33	42
Sleep Peter Raymond	4.5.1957		14	*1978–1989*	483	90	0	24.15	31	5-72	1/0	45.06	4	
Slight James	20.10.1855	9.12.1930	1	1880	11	11	0	5.50	–	–	–/–	–	0	
Smith David Bertram Miller	14.9.1884	29.7.1963	2	1912	30	24*	0	15.00	–	–	–/–	–	0	
Smith Steven Barry	18.10.1961		3	*1983*	41	12	0	8.20	–	–	–/–	–	1	28
Smith Steven Peter Devereux (*CY 2016*)	2.6.1989		50	2010–*2016*	4,752	215	17	60.15	17	3-18	0/0	52.41	67	90/30
Spofforth Frederick Robert	9.9.1853	4.6.1926	18	*1876–1886*	217	50	0	9.43	94	7-44	7/4	18.41	11	
Stackpole Keith Raymond MBE (*CY 1973*)	10.7.1940		43	*1965–1973*	2,807	207	7	37.42	15	2-33	0/0	66.73	47	6
Starc Mitchell Aaron	13.1.1990		34	*2011–2016*	949	99	0	24.33	143	6-50	7/1	28.29	15	59/22
Stevens Gavin Byron	29.2.1932		4	*1959*	112	28	0	16.00	–	–	–/–	–	2	
Symonds Andrew	9.6.1975		26	*2003–2008*	1,462	162*	2	40.61	24	3-50	0/0	37.33	22	198/14
Taber Hedley Brian	29.4.1940		16	*1966–1969*	353	48	0	16.04	–	–	–/–	–	56/4	
Tait Shaun William	22.2.1983		3	2005–*2007*	20	8	0	6.66	5	3-97	0/0	60.40	1	35/21
Tallon Donald (*CY 1949*)	17.2.1916	7.9.1984	21	*1945*–1953	394	92	0	17.13	–	–	–/–	–	50/8	
Taylor John Morris	10.10.1895	12.5.1971	20	*1920*–1926	997	108	1	35.60	1	1-25	0/0	45.00	11	
Taylor Mark Anthony (*CY 1990*)	27.10.1964		104	*1988–1998*	7,525	334*	19	43.49	1	1-11	0/0	26.00	157	113
Taylor Peter Laurence	22.8.1956		13	*1986–1991*	431	87	0	26.93	27	6-78	1/0	39.55	10	83
Thomas Grahame	21.3.1938		8	*1964–1965*	325	61	0	29.54	–	–	–/–	–	3	
Thoms George Ronald	22.3.1927	29.8.2003	1	*1951*	44	28	0	22.00	–	–	–/–	–	0	
Thomson Alan Lloyd ("Froggy")	2.12.1945		4	*1970*	22	12*	0	22.00	12	3-79	0/0	54.50	0	1
Thomson Jeffrey Robert	16.8.1950		51	*1972*–1985	679	49	0	12.81	200	6-46	8/0	28.00	20	50
Thomson Nathaniel Frampton Davis	29.5.1839	2.9.1896	2	*1876*	67	41	0	16.75	1	1-14	0/0	31.00	3	

	Born	*Died*	*Tests*	*Test Career*	*Runs*	*HS*	*100s*	*Avge*	*Wkts*	*BB*	*5/10*	*Avge*	*Ct/St*	*O/T*
Thurlow Hugh Motley ("Pud")	10.1.1903	3.12.1975	1	*1931*	0	0	0	0.00	0	0-33	0/0	–	0	
Toohey Peter Michael	20.4.1954		15	*1977–1979*	893	122	1	31.89	0	0-4	0/0	–	9	5
Toshack Ernest Raymond Herbert	8.12.1914	11.5.2003	12	*1945*–1948	73	20*	0	14.60	47	6-29	4/1	21.04	4	
Travers Joseph Patrick Francis	10.1.1871	15.9.1942	1	*1901*	10	9	0	5.00	1	1-14	0/0	14.00	1	
Tribe George Edward (*CY 1955*)	4.10.1920	5.4.2009	3	*1946*	35	25*	0	17.50	2	2-48	0/0	165.00	0	
[2] **Trott** Albert Edwin (*CY 1899*)	6.2.1873	30.7.1914	3†	*1894*	205	85*	0	102.50	9	8-43	1/0	21.33	4	
[2] **Trott** George Henry Stevens (*CY 1894*)	5.8.1866	10.11.1917	24	1888–*1897*	921	143	1	21.92	29	4-71	0/0	35.13	21	
[2] **Trumble** Hugh (*CY 1897*)	12.5.1867	14.8.1938	32	1890–*1903*	851	70	0	19.79	141	8-65	9/3	21.78	45	
[2] **Trumble** John William	16.9.1863	17.8.1944	7	*1884*–1886	243	59	0	20.25	10	3-29	0/0	22.20	3	
Trumper Victor Thomas (*CY 1903*)	2.11.1877	28.6.1915	48	1899–*1911*	3,163	214*	8	39.04	8	3-60	0/0	39.62	31	
Turner Alan	23.7.1950		14	*1975–1976*	768	136	1	29.53	–	–	–/–	–	15	6
Turner Charles Thomas Biass (*CY 1889*)	16.11.1862	1.1.1944	17	*1886–1894*	323	29	0	11.53	101	7-43	11/2	16.53	8	
Veivers Thomas Robert	6.4.1937		21	*1963–1966*	813	88	0	31.26	33	4-68	0/0	41.66	7	
Veletta Michael Robert John	30.10.1963		8	*1987–1989*	207	39	0	18.81	–	–	–/–	–	12	20
Voges Adam Charles	4.10.1979		20	2015–*2016*	1,485	269*	5	61.87	0	0-3	0/0	–	15	31/7
Wade Matthew Scott	26.12.1987		16	*2011–2016*	673	106	2	30.59	0	0-0	0/0	–	47/4	82/26
Waite Mervyn George	7.1.1911	16.12.1985	2	1938	11	8	0	3.66	1	1-150	0/0	190.00	1	
Walker Maxwell Henry Norman	12.9.1948	28.9.2016	34	*1972*–1977	586	78*	0	19.53	138	8-143	6/0	27.47	12	17
Wall Thomas Welbourn ("Tim")	13.5.1904	26.3.1981	18	*1928*–1934	121	20	0	6.36	56	5-14	3/0	35.89	11	
Walters Francis Henry	9.2.1860	1.6.1922	1	*1884*	12	7	0	6.00	–	–	–/–	–	2	
Walters Kevin Douglas MBE	21.12.1945		74	*1965–1980*	5,357	250	15	48.26	49	5-66	1/0	29.08	43	28
Ward Francis Anthony	23.2.1906	25.3.1974	4	*1936*–1938	36	18	0	6.00	11	6-102	1/0	52.18	1	
Warne Shane Keith (*CY 1994*)	13.9.1969		145§	*1991–2006*	3,154	99	0	17.32	708	8-71	37/10	25.41	125	193‡
Warner David Andrew	27.10.1986		60	*2011–2016*	5,261	253	18	49.16	4	2-45	0/0	67.25	43	88/63
Watkins John Russell	16.4.1943		1	*1972*	39	36	0	39.00	0	0-21	0/0	–	1	
Watson Graeme Donald	8.3.1945		5	*1966*–1972	97	50	0	10.77	6	2-67	0/0	42.33	1	2
Watson Shane Robert	17.6.1981		59§	*2004*–2015	3,731	176	4	35.19	75	6-33	3/0	33.68	45	190/58
Watson William James	31.1.1931		4	*1954*	106	30	0	17.66	0	0-5	0/0	–	2	
[2] **Waugh** Mark Edward (*CY 1991*)	2.6.1965		128	*1990–2002*	8,029	153*	20	41.81	59	5-40	1/0	41.16	181	244
[2] **Waugh** Stephen Rodger (*CY 1989*)	2.6.1965		168	*1985–2003*	10,927	200	32	51.06	92	5-28	3/0	37.44	112	325
Wellham Dirk Macdonald	13.3.1959		6	1981–*1986*	257	103	1	23.36	–	–	–/–	–	5	17
Wessels Kepler Christoffel (*CY 1995*)	14.9.1957		24†	*1982–1985*	1,761	179	4	42.95	0	0-2	0/0	–	18	54‡
Whatmore Davenell Frederick	16.3.1954		7	*1978–1979*	293	77	0	22.53	0	0-11	0/0	–	13	1
White Cameron Leon	18.8.1983		4	*2008*	146	46	0	29.20	5	2-71	0/0	68.40	1	88/47
Whitney Michael Roy	24.2.1959		12	1981–*1992*	68	13	0	6.18	39	7-27	2/1	33.97	2	38

§ *Warne's figures include 12 runs and six wickets, and Watson's 34 runs and no wicket, for Australia v the ICC World XI in the Super Series Test in 2005-06.*

	Born	*Died*	*Tests*	*Test Career*	*Runs*	*HS*	*100s*	*Avge*	*Wkts*	*BB*	*5/10*	*Avge*	*Ct/St*	*O/T*
Whitty William James	15.8.1886	30.1.1974	14	1909–1912	161	39*	0	13.41	65	6-17	3/0	21.12	4	
Wiener Julien Mark	1.5.1955		6	*1979*	281	93	0	25.54	0	0-19	0/0	–	4	7
Williams Brad Andrew	20.11.1974		4	*2003*	23	10*	0	7.66	9	4-53	0/0	45.11	4	25
Wilson John William	20.8.1921	13.10.1985	1	*1956*	–	–	–	–	1	1-25	0/0	64.00	0	
Wilson Paul	12.1.1972		1	*1997*	0	0*	0	–	0	0-50	0/0	–	0	11
Wood Graeme Malcolm	6.11.1956		59	*1977–1988*	3,374	172	9	31.83	–	–	–/–	–	41	83
Woodcock Ashley James	27.2.1947		1	*1973*	27	27	0	27.00	–	–	–/–	–	1	1
Woodfull William Maldon OBE (*CY 1927*)	22.8.1897	11.8.1965	35	1926–1934	2,300	161	7	46.00	–	–	–/–	–	7	
Woods Samuel Moses James (*CY 1889*)	13.4.1867	30.4.1931	3†	1888	32	18	0	5.33	5	2-35	0/0	24.20	1	
Woolley Roger Douglas	16.9.1954		2	*1982–1983*	21	13	0	10.50	–	–	–/–	–	7	4
Worrall John	20.6.1860	17.11.1937	11	*1884*–1899	478	76	0	25.15	1	1-97	0/0	127.00	13	
Wright Kevin John	27.12.1953		10	*1978–1979*	219	55*	0	16.84	–	–	–/–	–	31/4	5
Yallop Graham Neil	7.10.1952		39	*1975–1984*	2,756	268	8	41.13	1	1-21	0/0	116.00	23	30
Yardley Bruce	5.9.1947		33	*1977–1982*	978	74	0	19.56	126	7-98	6/1	31.63	31	7
Young Shaun	13.6.1970		1	1997	4	4*	0	4.00	0	0-5	0/0	–	0	
Zoehrer Timothy Joseph	25.9.1961		10	*1985–1986*	246	52*	0	20.50	–	–	–/–	–	18/1	22

SOUTH AFRICA (329 players)

	Born	*Died*	*Tests*	*Test Career*	*Runs*	*HS*	*100s*	*Avge*	*Wkts*	*BB*	*5/10*	*Avge*	*Ct/St*	*O/T*
Abbott Kyle John	18.6.1987		11	*2012–2016*	95	17	0	6.78	39	7-29	3/0	22.71	4	28/21
Ackerman Hylton Deon	14.2.1973		4	*1997*	161	57	0	20.12	–	–	–/–	–	1	
Adams Paul Regan	20.1.1977		45	*1995–2003*	360	35	0	9.00	134	7-128	4/1	32.87	29	24
Adcock Neil Amwin Treharne (*CY 1961*)	8.3.1931	6.1.2013	26	*1953–1961*	146	24	0	5.40	104	6-43	5/0	21.10	4	
Amla Hashim Mahomed (*CY 2013*)	31.3.1983		100	*2004–2016*	7,799	311*	26	49.99	0	0-4	0/0	–	88	140/37
Anderson James Henry	26.4.1874	11.3.1926	1	*1902*	43	32	0	21.50	–	–	–/–	–	1	
Ashley William Hare	10.2.1862	14.7.1930	1	*1888*	1	1	0	0.50	7	7-95	1/0	13.57	0	
Bacher Adam Marc	29.10.1973		19	*1996–1999*	833	96	0	26.03	0	0-4	0/0	–	11	13
Bacher Aron ("Ali")	24.5.1942		12	1965–*1969*	679	73	0	32.33	–	–	–/–	–	10	
Balaskas Xenophon Constantine	15.10.1910	12.5.1994	9	*1930–1938*	174	122*	1	14.50	22	5-49	1/0	36.63	5	
Barlow Edgar John	12.8.1940	30.12.2005	30	*1961–1969*	2,516	201	6	45.74	40	5-85	1/0	34.05	35	
Baumgartner Harold Vane	17.11.1883	8.4.1938	1	*1913*	19	16	0	9.50	2	2-99	0/0	49.50	1	
Bavuma Temba	17.5.1990		17	*2014–2016*	660	102*	1	30.00	1	1-29	0/0	30.00	8	1
Beaumont Rolland	4.2.1884	25.5.1958	5	1912–*1913*	70	31	0	7.77	0	0-0	0/0	–	2	
Begbie Denis Warburton	12.12.1914	10.3.2009	5	*1948–1949*	138	48	0	19.71	1	1-38	0/0	130.00	2	

	Born	*Died*	*Tests*	*Test Career*	*Runs*	*HS*	*100s*	*Avge*	*Wkts*	*BB*	*5/10*	*Avge*	*Ct/St*	*O/T*
Bell Alexander John	15.4.1906	1.8.1985	16	1929–1935	69	26*	0	6.27	48	6-99	4/0	32.64	6	
Bisset *Sir* Murray	14.4.1876	24.10.1931	3	*1898–1909*	103	35	0	25.75	–	–	–/–	–	2/1	
Bissett George Finlay	5.11.1905	14.11.1965	4	*1927*	38	23	0	19.00	25	7-29	2/0	18.76	0	
Blanckenberg James Manuel	31.12.1892	d unknown	18	*1913*–1924	455	59	0	19.78	60	6-76	4/0	30.28	9	
Bland Kenneth Colin (*CY 1966*)	5.4.1938		21	*1961–1966*	1,669	144*	3	49.08	2	2-16	0/0	62.50	10	
Bock Ernest George.	17.9.1908	5.9.1961	1	*1935*	11	9*	0	–	0	0-42	0/0	–	0	
Boje Nico.	20.3.1973		43	*1999*–2006	1,312	85	0	25.23	100	5-62	3/0	42.65	18	113‡/1
Bond Gerald Edward.	5.4.1909	27.8.1965	1	*1938*	0	0	0	0.00	0	0-16	0/0	–	0	
Bosch Tertius	14.3.1966	14.2.2000	1	*1991*	5	5*	0	–	3	2-61	0/0	34.66	0	2
Botha Johan	2.5.1982		5	*2005–2010*	83	25	0	20.75	17	4-56	0/0	33.70	3	76‡/40
Botten James Thomas ("Jackie").	21.6.1938	14.5.2006	3	1965	65	33	0	10.83	8	2-56	0/0	42.12	1	
Boucher Mark Verdon (*CY 2009*)	3.12.1976		146§	*1997–2011*	5,498	125	5	30.54	1	1-6	0/0	6.00	530/23	290‡/25
Brann William Henry	4.4.1899	22.9.1953	3	*1922*	71	50	0	14.20	–	–	–/–	–	2	
Briscoe Arthur Wellesley ("Dooley").	6.2.1911	22.4.1941	2	*1935–1938*	33	16	0	11.00	–	–	–/–	–	1	
Bromfield Harry Dudley	26.6.1932		9	*1961*–1965	59	21	0	11.80	17	5-88	1/0	35.23	13	
Brown Lennox Sidney.	24.11.1910	1.9.1983	2	*1931*	17	8	0	5.66	3	1-30	0/0	63.00	0	
Burger Christopher George de Villiers.	12.7.1935	5.6.2014	2	*1957*	62	37*	0	20.66	–	–	–/–	–	1	
Burke Sydney Frank	11.3.1934		2	*1961–1964*	42	20	0	14.00	11	6-128	2/1	23.36	0	
Buys Isaac Daniel	4.2.1895	d unknown	1	*1922*	4	4*	0	4.00	0	0-20	0/0	–	0	
Cameron Horace Brakenridge ("Jock") (*CY 1936*).	5.7.1905	2.11.1935	26	*1927*–1935	1,239	90	0	30.21	–	–	–/–	–	39/12	
Campbell Thomas.	9.2.1882	5.10.1924	5	*1909*–1912	90	48	0	15.00	–	–	–/–	–	7/1	
Carlstein Peter Rudolph	28.10.1938		8	*1957–1963*	190	42	0	14.61	–	–	–/–	–	3	
Carter Claude Pagdett.	23.4.1881	8.11.1952	10	1912–1924	181	45	0	18.10	28	6-50	2/0	24.78	2	
Catterall Robert Hector (*CY 1925*)	10.7.1900	3.1.1961	24	*1922–1930*	1,555	120	3	37.92	7	3-15	0/0	23.14	12	
Chapman Horace William	30.6.1890	1.12.1941	2	*1913–1921*	39	17	0	13.00	1	1-51	0/0	104.00	1	
Cheetham John Erskine.	26.5.1920	21.8.1980	24	*1948*–1955	883	89	0	23.86	0	0-2	0/0	–	13	
Chevalier Grahame Anton	9.3.1937		1	*1969*	0	0*	0	0.00	5	3-68	0/0	20.00	1	
Christy James Alexander Joseph.	12.12.1904	1.2.1971	10	1929–*1931*	618	103	1	34.33	2	1-15	0/0	46.00	3	
Chubb Geoffrey Walter Ashton	12.4.1911	28.8.1982	5	1951	63	15*	0	10.50	21	6-51	2/0	27.47	0	
Cochran John Alexander Kennedy	15.7.1909	15.6.1987	1	*1930*	4	4	0	4.00	0	0-47	0/0	–	0	
Coen Stanley Keppel ("Shunter")	14.10.1902	29.1.1967	2	*1927*	101	41*	0	50.50	0	0-7	0/0	–	1	
Commaille John McIllwaine Moore ("Mick") .	21.2.1883	28.7.1956	12	*1909–1927*	355	47	0	16.90	–	–	–/–	–	1	
Commins John Brian.	19.2.1965		3	*1994*	125	45	0	25.00	–	–	–/–	–	2	
Conyngham Dalton Parry	10.5.1897	7.7.1979	1	*1922*	6	3*	0	–	2	1-40	0/0	51.50	1	

§ *Boucher's figures exclude 17 runs and two catches for the ICC World XI v Australia in the Super Series Test in 2005-06.*

	Born	*Died*	*Tests*	*Test Career*	*Runs*	*HS*	*100s*	*Avge*	*Wkts*	*BB*	*5/10*	*Avge*	*Ct/St*	*O/T*
Cook Frederick James	1870	30.11.1915	1	1895	7	7	0	3.50	–	–	–/–	–	0	
[1]**Cook** Stephen Craig	29.11.1982		9	2015–2016	615	117	3	41.00	0	0-16	0/0	–	6	
[1]**Cook** Stephen James (*CY 1990*)	31.7.1953		3	1992–1993	107	43	0	17.83	–	–	–/–	–	0	4
Cooper Alfred Henry Cecil	2.9.1893	18.7.1963	1	1913	6	6	0	3.00	–	–	–/–	–	1	
Cox Joseph Lovell	28.6.1886	4.7.1971	3	1913	17	12*	0	3.40	4	2-74	0/0	61.25	1	
Cripps Godfrey	19.10.1865	27.7.1943	1	1891	21	18	0	10.50	0	0-23	0/0	–	0	
Crisp Robert James	28.5.1911	2.3.1994	9	1935–1935	123	35	0	10.25	20	5-99	1/0	37.35	3	
Cronje Wessel Johannes ("Hansie")	25.9.1969	1.6.2002	68	1991–1999	3,714	135	6	36.41	43	3-14	0/0	29.95	33	188
Cullinan Daryll John	4.3.1967		70	1992–2000	4,554	275*	14	44.21	2	1-10	0/0	35.50	67	138
Curnow Sydney Harry	16.12.1907	28.7.1986	7	1930–1931	168	47	0	12.00	–	–	–/–	–	5	
Dalton Eric Londesbrough	2.12.1906	3.6.1981	15	1929–1938	698	117	2	31.72	12	4-59	0/0	40.83	5	
Davies Eric Quail	26.8.1909	11.11.1976	5	1935–1938	9	3	0	1.80	7	4-75	0/0	68.71	0	
Dawson Alan Charles	27.11.1969		2	2003	10	10	0	10.00	5	2-20	0/0	23.40	0	19
Dawson Oswald Charles	1.9.1919	22.12.2008	9	1947–1948	293	55	0	20.92	10	2-57	0/0	57.80	10	
Deane Hubert Gouvaine ("Nummy")	21.7.1895	21.10.1939	17	1924–1930	628	93	0	25.12	–	–	–/–	–	8	
de Bruyn Zander	5.7.1975		3	2004	155	83	0	38.75	3	2-32	0/0	30.66	0	
de Kock Quinton	17.12.1992		16	2013–2016	1,123	129*	3	51.04	–	–	–/–	–	63/3	69/29
de Lange Marchant	13.10.1990		2	2011	9	9	0	4.50	9	7-81	1/0	30.77	1	4/6
de Villiers Abraham Benjamin	17.2.1984		106	2004–2015	8,074	278*	21	50.46	2	2-49	0/0	52.00	197/5	201‡/71
de Villiers Petrus Stephanus ("Fanie")	13.10.1964		18	1993–1997	359	67*	0	18.89	85	6-23	5/2	24.27	11	83
de Wet Friedel	26.6.1980		2	2009	20	20	0	10.00	6	4-55	0/0	31.00	1	
Dippenaar Hendrik Human ("Boeta")	14.6.1977		38	1999–2006	1,718	177*	3	30.14	0	0-1	0/0	–	27	101‡/1
Dixon Cecil Donovan	12.2.1891	9.9.1969	1	1913	0	0	0	0.00	3	2-62	0/0	39.33	1	
Donald Allan Anthony (*CY 1992*)	20.10.1966		72	1991–2001	652	37	0	10.68	330	8-71	20/3	22.25	18	164
Dower Robert Reid	4.6.1876	15.9.1964	1	1898	9	9	0	4.50	–	–	–/–	–	2	
Draper Ronald George	24.12.1926		2	1949	25	15	0	8.33	–	–	–/–	–	0	
Duckworth Christopher Anthony Russell	22.3.1933	16.5.2014	2	1956	28	13	0	7.00	–	–	–/–	–	3	
Dumbrill Richard	19.11.1938		5	1965–1966	153	36	0	15.30	9	4-30	0/0	37.33	3	
Duminy Jacobus Petrus	16.12.1897	31.1.1980	3	1927–1929	30	12	0	5.00	1	1-17	0/0	39.00	2	
Duminy Jean-Paul	14.4.1984		42	2008–2016	1,982	166	6	34.77	38	4-73	0/0	38.76	33	162/70
Dunell Owen Robert	15.7.1856	21.10.1929	2	1888	42	26*	0	14.00	–	–	–/–	–	1	
du Plessis Francois ("Faf")	13.7.1984		37	2012–2016	2,228	137	6	43.68	0	0-1	0/0	–	22	97/35
du Preez John Harcourt	14.11.1942		2	1966	0	0	0	0.00	3	2-22	0/0	17.00	2	
du Toit Jacobus Francois	2.4.1869	10.7.1909	1	1891	2	2*	0	–	1	1-47	0/0	47.00	1	
Dyer Dennis Victor	2.5.1914	16.6.1990	3	1947	96	62	0	16.00	–	–	–/–	–	0	
Eksteen Clive Edward	2.12.1966		7	1993–1999	91	22	0	10.11	8	3-12	0/0	61.75	5	6

	Born	*Died*	*Tests*	*Test Career*	*Runs*	*HS*	*100s*	*Avge*	*Wkts*	*BB*	*5/10*	*Avge*	*Ct/St*	*O/T*
Elgar Dean	11.6.1987		32	*2012–2016*	1,737	129	6	38.60	13	4-22	0/0	41.61	35	6
Elgie Michael Kelsey ("Kim")	6.3.1933		3	*1961*	75	56	0	12.50	0	0-18	0/0	–	4	
Elworthy Steven	23.2.1965		4	1998–*2002*	72	48	0	18.00	13	4-66	0/0	34.15	1	39
Endean William Russell	31.5.1924	28.6.2003	28	1951–*1957*	1,630	162*	3	33.95	–	–	–/–	–	41	
Farrer William Stephen ("Buster")	8.12.1936		6	*1961–1963*	221	40	0	27.62	–	–	–/–	–	2	
Faulkner George Aubrey	17.12.1881	10.9.1930	25	*1905*–1924	1,754	204	4	40.79	82	7-84	4/0	26.58	20	
Fellows-Smith Jonathan Payn	3.2.1932	28.9.2013	4	1960	166	35	0	27.66	0	0-13	0/0	–	2	
Fichardt Charles Gustav	20.3.1870	30.5.1923	2	*1891–1895*	15	10	0	3.75	–	–	–/–	–	2	
Finlason Charles Edward	19.2.1860	31.7.1917	1	*1888*	6	6	0	3.00	0	0-7	0/0	–	0	
Floquet Claude Eugene	3.11.1884	22.11.1963	1	*1909*	12	11*	0	12.00	0	0-24	0/0	–	0	
Francis Howard Henry	26.5.1868	7.1.1936	2	*1898*	39	29	0	9.75	–	–	–/–	–	1	
Francois Cyril Matthew	20.6.1897	26.5.1944	5	*1922*	252	72	0	31.50	6	3-23	0/0	37.50	5	
Frank Charles Newton	27.1.1891	25.12.1961	3	*1921*	236	152	1	39.33	–	–	–/–	–	0	
Frank William Hughes Bowker	23.11.1872	16.2.1945	1	*1895*	7	5	0	3.50	1	1-52	0/0	52.00	0	
Fuller Edward Russell Henry	2.8.1931	19.7.2008	7	*1952–1957*	64	17	0	8.00	22	5-66	1/0	30.36	3	
Fullerton George Murray	8.12.1922	19.11.2002	7	1947–1951	325	88	0	25.00	–	–	–/–	–	10/2	
Funston Kenneth James	3.12.1925	15.4.2005	18	*1952–1957*	824	92	0	25.75	–	–	–/–	–	7	
Gamsy Dennis	17.2.1940		2	*1969*	39	30*	0	19.50	–	–	–/–	–	5	
Gibbs Herschelle Herman	23.2.1974		90	*1996–2007*	6,167	228	14	41.95	0	0-4	0/0	–	94	248/23
Gleeson Robert Anthony	6.12.1873	27.9.1919	1	*1895*	4	3	0	4.00	–	–	–/–	–	2	
Glover George Keyworth	13.5.1870	15.11.1938	1	*1895*	21	18*	0	21.00	1	1-28	0/0	28.00	0	
Goddard Trevor Leslie	1.8.1931	25.11.2016	41	1955–*1969*	2,516	112	1	34.46	123	6-53	5/0	26.22	48	
Gordon Norman	6.8.1911	2.9.2014	5	*1938*	8	7*	0	2.00	20	5-103	2/0	40.35	1	
Graham Robert	16.9.1877	21.4.1946	2	*1898*	6	4	0	1.50	3	2-22	0/0	42.33	2	
Grieveson Ronald Eustace	24.8.1909	24.7.1998	2	*1938*	114	75	0	57.00	–	–	–/–	–	7/3	
Griffin Geoffrey Merton	12.6.1939	16.11.2006	2	1960	25	14	0	6.25	8	4-87	0/0	24.00	0	
Hall Alfred Ewart	23.1.1896	1.1.1964	7	*1922–1930*	11	5	0	1.83	40	7-63	3/1	22.15	4	
Hall Andrew James	31.7.1975		21	*2001–2006*	760	163	1	26.20	45	3-1	0/0	35.93	16	88/2
Hall Glen Gordon	24.5.1938	26.6.1987	1	*1964*	0	0	0	0.00	1	1-94	0/0	94.00	0	
Halliwell Ernest Austin (*CY 1905*)	7.9.1864	2.10.1919	8	*1891–1902*	188	57	0	12.53	–	–	–/–	–	10/2	
Halse Clive Gray	28.2.1935	28.5.2002	3	*1963*	30	19*	0	–	6	3-50	0/0	43.33	1	
[2] **Hands** Philip Albert Myburgh	18.3.1890	27.4.1951	7	*1913*–1924	300	83	0	25.00	0	0-1	0/0	–	3	
[2] **Hands** Reginald Harry Myburgh	26.7.1888	20.4.1918	1	*1913*	7	7	0	3.50	–	–	–/–	–	0	
Hanley Martin Andrew	10.11.1918	2.6.2000	1	*1948*	0	0	0	0.00	1	1-57	0/0	88.00	0	
Harmer Simon Ross	10.2.1989		5	*2014–2015*	58	13	0	11.60	20	4-61	0/0	29.40	1	
Harris Paul Lee	2.11.1978		37	*2006–2010*	460	46	0	10.69	103	6-127	3/0	37.87	16	3

	Born	*Died*	*Tests*	*Test Career*	*Runs*	*HS*	*100s*	*Avge*	*Wkts*	*BB*	*5/10*	*Avge*	*Ct/St*	*O/T*
Harris Terence Anthony	27.8.1916	7.3.1993	3	1947–*1948*	100	60	0	25.00	–	–	–/–	–	1	
Hartigan Gerald Patrick Desmond	30.12.1884	7.1.1955	5	1912–*1913*	114	51	0	11.40	1	1-72	0/0	141.00	0	
Harvey Robert Lyon	14.9.1911	20.7.2000	2	*1935*	51	28	0	12.75	–	–	–/–	–	0	
Hathorn Christopher Maitland Howard	7.4.1878	17.5.1920	12	*1902–1910*	325	102	1	17.10	–	–	–/–	–	5	
Hayward Mornantau ("Nantie")	6.3.1977		16	*1999*–2004	66	14	0	7.33	54	5-56	1/0	29.79	4	21
[1, 2] **Hearne** Frank	23.11.1858	14.7.1949	4†	*1891–1895*	121	30	0	15.12	2	2-40	0/0	20.00	2	
[1] **Hearne** George Alfred Lawrence	27.3.1888	13.11.1978	3	1922–1924	59	28	0	11.80	–	–	–/–	–	3	
Heine Peter Samuel	28.6.1928	4.2.2005	14	1955–*1961*	209	31	0	9.95	58	6-58	4/0	25.08	8	
Henderson Claude William	14.6.1972		7	*2001–2002*	65	30	0	9.28	22	4-116	0/0	42.18	2	4
Henry Omar	23.1.1952		3	*1992*	53	34	0	17.66	3	2-56	0/0	63.00	2	3
Hime Charles Frederick William	24.10.1869	6.12.1940	1	*1895*	8	8	0	4.00	1	1-20	0/0	31.00	0	
Hudson Andrew Charles	17.3.1965		35	*1991–1997*	2,007	163	4	33.45	–	–	–/–	–	36	89
Hutchinson Philip	25.1.1862	30.9.1925	2	*1888*	14	11	0	3.50	–	–	–/–	–	3	
Imran Tahir	27.3.1979		20	*2011–2015*	130	29*	0	9.28	57	5-32	2/0	40.24	8	64/27
Ironside David Ernest James	2.5.1925	21.8.2005	3	*1953*	37	13	0	18.50	15	5-51	1/0	18.33	1	
Irvine Brian Lee	9.3.1944		4	*1969*	353	102	1	50.42	–	–	–/–	–	2	
Jack Steven Douglas	4.8.1970		2	*1994*	7	7	0	3.50	8	4-69	0/0	24.50	1	2
Johnson Clement Lecky	31.3.1871	31.5.1908	1	*1895*	10	7	0	5.00	0	0-57	0/0	–	1	
Kallis Jacques Henry (*CY 2013*)	16.10.1975		165§	*1995–2013*	13,206	224	45	55.25	291	6-54	5/0	32.63	196	323‡/25
Keith Headley James	25.10.1927	17.11.1997	8	*1952–1956*	318	73	0	21.20	0	0-19	0/0	–	9	
Kemp Justin Miles	2.10.1977		4	*2000–2005*	80	55	0	13.33	9	3-33	0/0	24.66	3	79‡/8
Kempis Gustav Adolph	4.8.1865	19.5.1890	1	*1888*	0	0*	0	0.00	4	3-53	0/0	19.00	0	
Khan Imraan	27.4.1984		1	*2008*	20	20	0	20.00	–	–	–/–	–	1	
[2] **Kirsten** Gary (*CY 2004*)	23.11.1967		101	*1993–2003*	7,289	275	21	45.27	2	1-0	0/0	71.00	83	185
[2] **Kirsten** Peter Noel	14.5.1955		12	*1991*–1994	626	104	1	31.30	0	0-5	0/0	–	8	40
Kleinveldt Rory Keith	15.3.1983		4	*2012*	27	17*	0	9.00	10	3-65	0/0	42.20	2	10/6
Klusener Lance (*CY 2000*)	4.9.1971		49	*1996*–2004	1,906	174	4	32.86	80	8-64	1/0	37.91	34	171
Kotze Johannes Jacobus ("Kodgee")	7.8.1879	7.7.1931	3	*1902*–1907	2	2	0	0.40	6	3-64	0/0	40.50	3	
Kuiper Adrian Paul	24.8.1959		1	*1991*	34	34	0	17.00	–	–	–/–	–	1	25
Kuys Frederick	21.3.1870	12.9.1953	1	*1898*	26	26	0	13.00	2	2-31	0/0	15.50	0	
Lance Herbert Roy ("Tiger")	6.6.1940	10.11.2010	13	*1961–1969*	591	70	0	28.14	12	3-30	0/0	39.91	7	
Langeveldt Charl Kenneth	17.12.1974		6	*2004–2005*	16	10	0	8.00	16	5-46	1/0	37.06	2	72/9
Langton Arthur Chudleigh Beaumont ("Chud")	2.3.1912	27.11.1942	15	1935–*1938*	298	73*	0	15.68	40	5-58	1/0	45.67	8	
Lawrence Godfrey Bernard	31.3.1932		5	*1961*	141	43	0	17.62	28	8-53	2/0	18.28	2	
le Roux Frederick Louis	5.2.1882	22.9.1963	1	*1913*	1	1	0	0.50	0	0-5	0/0	–	0	

§ *Kallis's figures exclude 83 runs, one wicket and four catches for the ICC World XI v Australia in the Super Series Test in 2005-06.*

	Born	Died	Tests	Test Career	Runs	HS	100s	Avge	Wkts	BB	5/10	Avge	Ct/St	O/T
Lewis Percy Tyson	2.10.1884	30.1.1976	1	1913	0	0	0	0.00	–	–	–/–	–	0	
Liebenberg Gerhardus Frederick Johannes	7.4.1972		5	1997–1998	104	45	0	13.00	–	–	–/–	–	1	4
[1] **Lindsay** Denis Thomson	4.9.1939	30.11.2005	19	1963–1969	1,130	182	3	37.66	–	–	–/–	–	57/2	
[1] **Lindsay** John Dixon	8.9.1908	31.8.1990	3	1947	21	9*	0	7.00	–	–	–/–	–	4/1	
Lindsay Nevil Vernon	30.7.1886	2.2.1976	1	1921	35	29	0	17.50	–	–	–/–	–	1	
Ling William Victor Stone	3.10.1891	26.9.1960	6	1921–1922	168	38	0	16.80	0	0-20	0/0	–	1	
Llewellyn Charles Bennett (*CY 1911*)	26.9.1876	7.6.1964	15	1895–1912	544	90	0	20.14	48	6-92	4/1	29.60	7	
Lundie Eric Balfour	15.3.1888	12.9.1917	1	1913	1	1	0	1.00	4	4-101	0/0	26.75	0	
Macaulay Michael John	19.4.1939		1	1964	33	21	0	16.50	2	1-10	0/0	36.50	0	
McCarthy Cuan Neil	24.3.1929	14.8.2000	15	1948–1951	28	5	0	3.11	36	6-43	2/0	41.94	6	
McGlew Derrick John ("Jackie") (*CY 1956*)	11.3.1929	9.6.1998	34	1951–1961	2,440	255*	7	42.06	0	0-7	0/0	–	18	
McKenzie Neil Douglas (*CY 2009*)	24.11.1975		58	2000–2008	3,253	226	5	37.39	0	0-1	0/0	–	54	64/2
McKinnon Atholl Henry	20.8.1932	2.12.1983	8	1960–1966	107	27	0	17.83	26	4-128	0/0	35.57	1	
McLaren Ryan	9.2.1983		2	2009–2013	47	33*	0	23.50	3	2-72	0/0	54.00	0	54/12
McLean Roy Alastair (*CY 1961*)	9.7.1930	26.8.2007	40	1951–1964	2,120	142	5	30.28	0	0-1	0/0	–	23	
McMillan Brian Mervin	22.12.1963		38	1992–1998	1,968	113	3	39.36	75	4-65	0/0	33.82	49	78
McMillan Quintin	23.6.1904	3.7.1948	13	1929–1931	306	50*	0	18.00	36	5-66	2/0	34.52	8	
Maharaj Keshav Athmanand	7.2.1990		4	2016	110	41*	0	36.66	11	3-56	0/0	34.00	0	
Mann Norman Bertram Fleetwood ("Tufty")	28.12.1920	31.7.1952	19	1947–1951	400	52	0	13.33	58	6-59	1/0	33.10	3	
Mansell Percy Neville Frank MBE	16.3.1920	9.5.1995	13	1951–1955	355	90	0	17.75	11	3-58	0/0	66.90	15	
Markham Lawrence Anderson	12.9.1924	5.8.2000	1	1948	20	20	0	20.00	1	1-34	0/0	72.00	0	
Marx Waldemar Frederick Eric	4.7.1895	2.6.1974	3	1921	125	36	0	20.83	4	3-85	0/0	36.00	0	
Matthews Craig Russell	15.2.1965		18	1992–1995	348	62*	0	18.31	52	5-42	2/0	28.88	4	56
Meintjes Douglas James	9.6.1890	17.7.1979	2	1922	43	21	0	14.33	6	3-38	0/0	19.16	3	
Melle Michael George	3.6.1930	28.12.2003	7	1949–1952	68	17	0	8.50	26	6-71	2/0	32.73	4	
Melville Alan (*CY 1948*)	19.5.1910	18.4.1983	11	1938–1948	894	189	4	52.58	–	–	–/–	–	8	
Middleton James	30.9.1865	23.12.1913	6	1895–1902	52	22	0	7.42	24	5-51	2/0	18.41	1	
Mills Charles Henry	26.11.1867	26.7.1948	1	1891	25	21	0	12.50	2	2-83	0/0	41.50	1	
Milton *Sir* William Henry	3.12.1854	6.3.1930	3	1888–1891	68	21	0	11.33	2	1-5	0/0	24.00	2	
Mitchell Bruce (*CY 1936*)	8.1.1909	1.7.1995	42	1929–1948	3,471	189*	8	48.88	27	5-87	1/0	51.11	56	
Mitchell Frank (*CY 1902*)	13.8.1872	11.10.1935	3†	1912	28	12	0	4.66	–	–	–/–	–	0	
Morkel Denijs Paul Beck	25.1.1906	6.10.1980	16	1927–1931	663	88	0	24.55	18	4-93	0/0	45.61	13	
[2] **Morkel** Johannes Albertus	10.6.1981		1	2008	58	58	0	58.00	1	1-44	0/0	132.00	0	56‡/50
[2] **Morkel** Morne	6.10.1984		71	2006–2015	775	40	0	11.56	242	6-23	6/0	29.33	19	105‡/39
Morris Christopher Henry	30.4.1987		2	2015	98	69	0	32.66	4	1-8	0/0	63.25	2	15/11
Murray Anton Ronald Andrew	30.4.1922	17.4.1995	10	1952–1953	289	109	1	22.23	18	4-169	0/0	39.44	3	

	Born	*Died*	*Tests*	*Test Career*	*Runs*	*HS*	*100s*	*Avge*	*Wkts*	*BB*	*5/10*	*Avge*	*Ct/St*	*O/T*
Nel Andre	15.7.1977		36	*2001–2008*	337	34	0	9.91	123	6-32	3/1	31.86	16	79/2
Nel John Desmond	10.7.1928		6	*1949–1957*	150	38	0	13.63	–	–	–/–	–	1	
Newberry Claude	1889	1.8.1916	4	*1913*	62	16	0	7.75	11	4-72	0/0	24.36	3	
Newson Edward Serrurier OBE	2.12.1910	24.4.1988	3	*1930–1938*	30	16	0	7.50	4	2-58	0/0	66.25	3	
Ngam Mfuneko	29.1.1979		3	*2000*	0	0*	0	–	11	3-26	0/0	17.18	1	
Nicholson Frank	17.9.1909	30.7.1982	4	*1935*	76	29	0	10.85	–	–	–/–	–	3	
Nicolson John Fairless William	19.7.1899	13.12.1935	3	*1927*	179	78	0	35.80	0	0-5	0/0	–	0	
Norton Norman Ogilvie	11.5.1881	27.6.1968	1	*1909*	9	7	0	4.50	4	4-47	0/0	11.75	0	
[1] **Nourse** Arthur Dudley (*CY 1948*)	12.11.1910	14.8.1981	34	1935–1951	2,960	231	9	53.81	0	0-0	0/0	–	12	
[1] **Nourse** Arthur William ("Dave")	25.1.1879	8.7.1948	45	*1902*–1924	2,234	111	1	29.78	41	4-25	0/0	37.87	43	
Ntini Makhaya	6.7.1977		101	*1997–2009*	699	32*	0	9.84	390	7-37	18/4	28.82	25	172‡/10
Nupen Eiulf Peter ("Buster")	1.1.1902	29.1.1977	17	*1921–1935*	348	69	0	14.50	50	6-46	5/1	35.76	9	
Ochse Arthur Edward	11.3.1870	11.4.1918	2	*1888*	16	8	0	4.00	–	–	–/–	–	0	
Ochse Arthur Lennox	11.10.1899	5.5.1949	3	*1927*–1929	11	4*	0	3.66	10	4-79	0/0	36.20	1	
O'Linn Sidney	5.5.1927	11.12.2016	7	1960–*1961*	297	98	0	27.00	–	–	–/–	–	4	
Olivier Duanne	9.5.1992		1	*2016*	3	3	0	3.00	5	3-38	0/0	11.40	0	
Ontong Justin Lee	4.1.1980		2	*2001–2004*	57	32	0	19.00	1	1-79	0/0	133.00	1	27‡/14
Owen-Smith Harold Geoffrey ("Tuppy") (*CY 1930*)	18.2.1909	28.2.1990	5	1929	252	129	1	42.00	0	0-3	0/0	–	4	
Palm Archibald William	8.6.1901	17.8.1966	1	*1927*	15	13	0	7.50	–	–	–/–	–	1	
Parker George Macdonald	27.5.1899	1.5.1969	2	1924	3	2*	0	1.50	8	6-152	1/0	34.12	0	
Parkin Durant Clifford	20.2.1873	20.3.1936	1	*1891*	6	6	0	3.00	3	3-82	0/0	27.33	1	
Parnell Wayne Dillon	30.7.1989		5	*2009–2016*	67	23	0	16.75	13	4-51	0/0	26.69	2	54/35
Partridge Joseph Titus	9.12.1932	6.6.1988	11	*1963–1964*	73	13*	0	10.42	44	7-91	3/0	31.20	6	
Pearse Charles Ormerod Cato	10.10.1884	7.5.1953	3	*1910*	55	31	0	9.16	3	3-56	0/0	35.33	1	
Pegler Sidney James	28.7.1888	10.9.1972	16	*1909*–1924	356	35*	0	15.47	47	7-65	2/0	33.44	5	
Petersen Alviro Nathan	25.11.1980		36	*2009–2014*	2,093	182	5	34.88	1	1-2	0/0	62.00	31	21/2
Peterson Robin John	4.8.1979		15	2003–*2013*	464	84	0	27.29	38	5-33	1/0	37.26	9	79/21
Philander Vernon Darryl	24.6.1985		40	*2011–2016*	939	74	0	23.47	159	6-44	11/2	21.40	11	30/7
Piedt Dane Lee-Roy	6.3.1990		7	*2014*–2016	48	19	0	6.85	24	5-153	1/0	36.04	4	
[2] **Pithey** Anthony John	17.7.1933	17.11.2006	17	*1956–1964*	819	154	1	31.50	0	0-5	0/0	–	3	
[2] **Pithey** David Bartlett	4.10.1936		8	*1963–1966*	138	55	0	12.54	12	6-58	1/0	48.08	6	
Plimsoll Jack Bruce	27.10.1917	11.11.1999	1	1947	16	8*	0	16.00	3	3-128	0/0	47.66	0	
[1,2] **Pollock** Peter Maclean (*CY 1966*)	30.6.1941		28	*1961–1969*	607	75*	0	21.67	116	6-38	9/1	24.18	9	
[2] **Pollock** Robert Graeme (*CY 1966*)	27.2.1944		23	*1963–1969*	2,256	274	7	60.97	4	2-50	0/0	51.00	17	
[1] **Pollock** Shaun Maclean (*CY 2003*)	16.7.1973		108	*1995–2007*	3,781	111	2	32.31	421	7-87	16/1	23.11	72	294‡/12

	Born	Died	Tests	Test Career	Runs	HS	100s	Avge	Wkts	BB	5/10	Avge	Ct/St	O/T
Poore Robert Montagu (*CY 1900*)	20.3.1866	14.7.1938	3	*1895*	76	20	0	12.66	1	1-4	0/0	4.00	3	
Pothecary James Edward	6.12.1933	11.5.2016	3	1960	26	12	0	6.50	9	4-58	0/0	39.33	2	
Powell Albert William	18.7.1873	11.9.1948	1	*1898*	16	11	0	8.00	1	1-10	0/0	10.00	2	
Pretorius Dewald	6.12.1977		4	*2001*–2003	22	9	0	7.33	6	4-115	0/0	71.66	0	
Prince Ashwell Gavin	28.5.1977		66	*2001–2011*	3,665	162*	11	41.64	1	1-2	0/0	47.00	47	49‡/1
Prince Charles Frederick Henry	11.9.1874	2.2.1949	1	*1898*	6	5	0	3.00	–	–	–/–	–	0	
Pringle Meyrick Wayne	22.6.1966		4	*1991–1995*	67	33	0	16.75	5	2-62	0/0	54.00	0	17
Procter Michael John (*CY 1970*)	15.9.1946		7	*1966–1969*	226	48	0	25.11	41	6-73	1/0	15.02	4	
Promnitz Henry Louis Ernest	23.2.1904	7.9.1983	2	*1927*	14	5	0	3.50	8	5-58	1/0	20.12	2	
Quinn Neville Anthony	21.2.1908	5.8.1934	12	1929–*1931*	90	28	0	6.00	35	6-92	1/0	32.71	1	
Rabada Kagiso	25.5.1995		14	*2015–2016*	127	32*	0	14.11	63	7-112	5/2	21.76	5	25/16
Reid Norman	26.12.1890	6.6.1947	1	*1921*	17	11	0	8.50	2	2-63	0/0	31.50	0	
Rhodes Jonathan Neil (*CY 1999*)	27.7.1969		52	*1992*–2000	2,532	117	3	35.66	0	0-0	0/0	–	34	245
[2] **Richards** Alfred Renfrew	14.12.1867	9.1.1904	1	*1895*	6	6	0	3.00	–	–	–/–	–	0	
Richards Barry Anderson (*CY 1969*)	21.7.1945		4	*1969*	508	140	2	72.57	1	1-12	0/0	26.00	3	
[2] **Richards** William Henry Matthews	26.3.1862	4.1.1903	1	*1888*	4	4	0	2.00	–	–	–/–	–	0	
Richardson David John	16.9.1959		42	*1991–1997*	1,359	109	1	24.26	–	–	–/–	–	150/2	122
Robertson John Benjamin	5.6.1906	5.7.1985	3	*1935*	51	17	0	10.20	6	3-143	0/0	53.50	2	
Rose-Innes Albert	16.2.1868	22.11.1946	2	*1888*	14	13	0	3.50	5	5-43	1/0	17.80	2	
Routledge Thomas William	18.4.1867	9.5.1927	4	*1891–1895*	72	24	0	9.00	–	–	–/–	–	2	
[2] **Rowan** Athol Matthew Burchell	7.2.1921	22.2.1998	15	1947–1951	290	41	0	17.05	54	5-68	4/0	38.59	7	
[2] **Rowan** Eric Alfred Burchell (*CY 1952*)	20.7.1909	30.4.1993	26	1935–1951	1,965	236	3	43.66	0	0-0	0/0	–	14	
Rowe George Alexander	15.6.1874	8.1.1950	5	*1895–1902*	26	13*	0	4.33	15	5-115	1/0	30.40	4	
Rudolph Jacobus Andries	4.5.1981		48	2003–*2012*	2,622	222*	6	35.43	4	1-1	0/0	108.00	29	43‡/1
Rushmere Mark Weir	7.1.1965		1	*1991*	6	3	0	3.00	–	–	–/–	–	0	4
Samuelson Sivert Vause	21.11.1883	18.11.1958	1	*1909*	22	15	0	11.00	0	0-64	0/0	–	1	
Schultz Brett Nolan	26.8.1970		9	*1992–1997*	9	6	0	1.50	37	5-48	2/0	20.24	2	1
Schwarz Reginald Oscar (*CY 1908*)	4.5.1875	18.11.1918	20	*1905*–1912	374	61	0	13.85	55	6-47	2/0	25.76	18	
Seccull Arthur William	14.9.1868	20.7.1945	1	*1895*	23	17*	0	23.00	2	2-37	0/0	18.50	1	
Seymour Michael Arthur ("Kelly")	5.6.1936		7	*1963–1969*	84	36	0	12.00	9	3-80	0/0	65.33	2	
Shalders William Alfred	12.2.1880	18.3.1917	12	*1898*–1907	355	42	0	16.13	1	1-6	0/0	6.00	3	
Shamsi Tabraiz	18.2.1990		1	*2016*	18	18*	0	–	2	1-49	0/0	75.00	0	3
Shepstone George Harold	9.4.1876	3.7.1940	2	*1895–1898*	38	21	0	9.50	0	0-8	0/0	–	2	
Sherwell Percy William	17.8.1880	17.4.1948	13	*1905–1910*	427	115	1	23.72	–	–	–/–	–	20/16	
Siedle Ivan Julian ("Jack")	11.1.1903	24.8.1982	18	*1927–1935*	977	141	1	28.73	1	1-7	0/0	7.00	7	
Sinclair James Hugh	16.10.1876	23.2.1913	25	*1895–1910*	1,069	106	3	23.23	63	6-26	1/0	31.68	9	

	Born	Died	Tests	Test Career	Runs	HS	100s	Avge	Wkts	BB	5/10	Avge	Ct/St	O/T
Smith Charles James Edward	25.12.1872	27.3.1947	3	*1902*	106	45	0	21.20	–	–	–/–	–	2	
Smith Frederick William	31.3.1861	17.4.1914	3	*1888–1895*	45	12	0	9.00	–	–	–/–	–	2	
Smith Graeme Craig (*CY 2004*)	1.2.1981		116§	*2001–2013*	9,253	277	27	48.70	8	2-145	0/0	110.62	166	196‡/33
Smith Vivian Ian	23.2.1925	25.8.2015	9	1947–*1957*	39	11*	0	3.90	12	4-143	0/0	64.08	3	
Snell Richard Peter	12.9.1968		5	*1991–1994*	95	48	0	13.57	19	4-74	0/0	28.31	1	42
[2] **Snooke** Sibley John ("Tip")	1.2.1881	14.8.1966	26	*1905–1922*	1,008	103	1	22.40	35	8-70	1/1	20.05	24	
[2] **Snooke** Stanley de la Courtte	11.11.1878	6.4.1959	1	1907	0	0	0	0.00	–	–	–/–	–	2	
Solomon William Rodger Thomson	23.4.1872	13.7.1964	1	*1898*	4	2	0	2.00	–	–	–/–	–	1	
Stewart Robert Burnard	3.9.1856	12.9.1913	1	*1888*	13	9	0	6.50	–	–	–/–	–	2	
Steyn Dale Willem (*CY 2013*)	27.6.1983		85	*2004–2016*	1,162	76	0	14.00	417	7-51	26/5	22.30	22	114‡/42
Steyn Philippus Jeremia Rudolf	30.6.1967		3	*1994*	127	46	0	21.16	–	–	–/–	–	0	1
Stricker Louis Anthony	26.5.1884	5.2.1960	13	*1909*–1912	344	48	0	14.33	1	1-36	0/0	105.00	3	
Strydom Pieter Coenraad	10.6.1969		2	*1999*	35	30	0	11.66	0	0-27	0/0	–	1	10
Susskind Manfred John	8.6.1891	9.7.1957	5	1924	268	65	0	33.50	–	–	–/–	–	1	
Symcox Patrick Leonard	14.4.1960		20	*1993–1998*	741	108	1	28.50	37	4-69	0/0	43.32	5	80
Taberer Henry Melville	7.10.1870	5.6.1932	1	*1902*	2	2	0	2.00	1	1-25	0/0	48.00	0	
[2] **Tancred** Augustus Bernard	20.8.1865	23.11.1911	2	*1888*	87	29	0	29.00	–	–	–/–	–	2	
[2] **Tancred** Louis Joseph	7.10.1876	28.7.1934	14	*1902–1913*	530	97	0	21.20	–	–	–/–	–	3	
[2] **Tancred** Vincent Maximillian	7.7.1875	3.6.1904	1	*1898*	25	18	0	12.50	–	–	–/–	–	0	
[2] **Tapscott** George Lancelot ("Dusty")	7.11.1889	13.12.1940	1	*1913*	5	4	0	2.50	–	–	–/–	–	1	
[2] **Tapscott** Lionel Eric ("Doodles")	18.3.1894	7.7.1934	2	*1922*	58	50*	0	29.00	0	0-2	0/0	–	0	
Tayfield Hugh Joseph (*CY 1956*)	30.1.1929	24.2.1994	37	*1949*– 1960	862	75	0	16.90	170	9-113	14/2	25.91	26	
Taylor Alistair Innes ("Scotch")	25.7.1925	7.2.2004	1	*1956*	18	12	0	9.00	–	–	–/–	–	0	
[2] **Taylor** Daniel	9.1.1887	24.1.1957	2	*1913*	85	36	0	21.25	–	–	–/–	–	0	
[2] **Taylor** Herbert Wilfred (*CY 1925*)	5.5.1889	8.2.1973	42	1912–*1931*	2,936	176	7	40.77	5	3-15	0/0	31.20	19	
Terbrugge David John	31.1.1977		7	*1998–2003*	16	4*	0	5.33	20	5-46	1/0	25.85	4	4
Theunissen Nicolaas Hendrik Christiaan de Jong	4.5.1867	9.11.1929	1	*1888*	2	2*	0	2.00	0	0-51	0/0	–	0	
Thornton George	24.12.1867	31.1.1939	1	*1902*	1	1*	0	–	1	1-20	0/0	20.00	1	
Tomlinson Denis Stanley	4.9.1910	11.7.1993	1	1935	9	9	0	9.00	0	0-38	0/0	–	0	
Traicos Athanasios John	17.5.1947		3†	*1969*	8	5*	0	4.00	4	2-70	0/0	51.75	4	0‡
Trimborn Patrick Henry Joseph	18.5.1940		4	*1966–1969*	13	11*	0	6.50	11	3-12	0/0	23.36	7	
Tsolekile Thami Lungisa	9.10.1980		3	*2004*	47	22	0	9.40	–	–	–/–	–	6	
Tsotsobe Lonwabo Lennox	7.3.1984		5	2010–*2010*	19	8*	0	6.33	9	3-43	0/0	49.77	1	61/23
[1] **Tuckett** Lindsay Richard ("Len")	19.4.1885	8.4.1963	1	*1913*	0	0*	0	0.00	0	0-24	0/0	–	2	
[1] **Tuckett** Lindsay Thomas Delville	6.2.1919	5.9.2016	9	1947–*1948*	131	40*	0	11.90	19	5-68	2/0	51.57	9	

§ *G. C. Smith's figures exclude 12 runs and three catches for the ICC World XI v Australia in the Super Series Test in 2005-06.*

	Born	*Died*	*Tests*	*Test Career*	*Runs*	*HS*	*100s*	*Avge*	*Wkts*	*BB*	*5/10*	*Avge*	*Ct/St*	*O/T*
Twentyman-Jones Percy Sydney	13.9.1876	8.3.1954	1	*1902*	0	0	0	0.00	–	–	–/–	–	0	
van der Bijl Pieter Gerhard Vintcent	21.10.1907	16.2.1973	5	*1938*	460	125	1	51.11	–	–	–/–	–	1	
van der Merwe Edward Alexander	9.11.1903	26.2.1971	2	1929–*1935*	27	19	0	9.00	–	–	–/–	–	3	
van der Merwe Peter Laurence	14.3.1937	23.1.2013	15	*1963–1966*	533	76	0	25.38	1	1-6	0/0	22.00	11	
van Jaarsveld Martin	18.6.1974		9	*2002–2004*	397	73	0	30.53	0	0-28	0/0	–	11	11
van Ryneveld Clive Berrange	19.3.1928		19	1951–*1957*	724	83	0	26.81	17	4-67	0/0	39.47	14	
van Zyl Stiaan	19.9.1987		12	*2014*–2016	395	101*	1	26.33	6	3-20	0/0	24.66	6	
Varnals George Derek	24.7.1935		3	*1964*	97	23	0	16.16	0	0-2	0/0	–	0	
Vilas Dane James	10.6.1985		6	2015–*2015*	94	26	0	10.44	–	–	–/–	–	13	0/1
Viljoen G. C. ("Hardus")	6.3.1989		1	*2015*	26	20*	0	26.00	1	1-79	0/0	94.00	0	
Viljoen Kenneth George	14.5.1910	21.1.1974	27	*1930–1948*	1,365	124	2	28.43	0	0-10	0/0	–	5	
Vincent Cyril Leverton	16.2.1902	24.8.1968	25	*1927*–1935	526	60	0	20.23	84	6-51	3/0	31.32	27	
Vintcent Charles Henry	2.9.1866	28.9.1943	3	*1888–1891*	26	9	0	4.33	4	3-88	0/0	48.25	1	
Vogler Albert Edward Ernest (*CY 1908*)	28.11.1876	9.8.1946	15	*1905–1910*	340	65	0	17.00	64	7-94	5/1	22.73	20	
[2] **Wade** Herbert Frederick	14.9.1905	23.11.1980	10	1935–*1935*	327	40*	0	20.43	–	–	–/–	–	4	
[2] **Wade** Walter Wareham ("Billy")	18.6.1914	31.5.2003	11	*1938–1949*	511	125	1	28.38	–	–	–/–	–	15/2	
Waite John Henry Bickford	19.1.1930	22.6.2011	50	1951–*1964*	2,405	134	4	30.44	–	–	–/–	–	124/17	
Walter Kenneth Alexander	5.11.1939	13.9.2003	2	*1961*	11	10	0	3.66	6	4-63	0/0	32.83	3	
Ward Thomas Alfred	2.8.1887	16.2.1936	23	1912–1924	459	64	0	13.90	–	–	–/–	–	19/13	
Watkins John Cecil	10.4.1923		15	*1949–1956*	612	92	0	23.53	29	4-22	0/0	28.13	12	
Wesley Colin	5.9.1937		3	1960	49	35	0	9.80	–	–	–/–	–	1	
Wessels Kepler Christoffel (*CY 1995*)	14.9.1957		16†	*1991*–1994	1,027	118	2	38.03	–	–	–/–	–	12	55‡
Westcott Richard John	19.9.1927	16.1.2013	5	*1953–1957*	166	62	0	18.44	0	0-22	0/0	–	0	
White Gordon Charles	5.2.1882	17.10.1918	17	*1905*–1912	872	147	2	30.06	9	4-47	0/0	33.44	10	
Willoughby Charl Myles	3.12.1974		2	2003	–	–	–	–	1	1-47	0/0	125.00	0	3
Willoughby Joseph Thomas	7.11.1874	11.3.1952	2	*1895*	8	5	0	2.00	6	2-37	0/0	26.50	0	
Wimble Clarence Skelton	22.4.1861	28.1.1930	1	*1891*	0	0	0	0.00	–	–	–/–	–	0	
Winslow Paul Lyndhurst	21.5.1929	24.5.2011	5	*1949*–1955	186	108	1	20.66	–	–	–/–	–	1	
Wynne Owen Edgar	1.6.1919	13.7.1975	6	*1948–1949*	219	50	0	18.25	–	–	–/–	–	3	
Zondeki Monde	25.7.1982		6	2003–*2008*	82	59	0	16.40	19	6-39	1/0	25.26	1	11‡/1
Zulch Johan Wilhelm	2.1.1886	19.5.1924	16	*1909–1921*	983	150	2	32.76	0	0-2	0/0	–	4	

WEST INDIES (309 players)

	Born	*Died*	*Tests*	*Test Career*	*Runs*	*HS*	*100s*	*Avge*	*Wkts*	*BB*	*5/10*	*Avge*	*Ct/St*	*O/T*
Achong Ellis Edgar	16.2.1904	30.8.1986	6	*1929–1934*	81	22	0	8.10	8	2-64	0/0	47.25	6	
Adams James Clive	9.1.1968		54	*1991–2000*	3,012	208*	6	41.26	27	5-17	1/0	49.48	48	127
Alexander Franz Copeland Murray ("Gerry")	2.11.1928	16.4.2011	25	1957–*1960*	961	108	1	30.03	–	–	–/–	–	85/5	
Ali Imtiaz	28.7.1954		1	*1975*	1	1*	0	–	2	2-37	0/0	44.50	0	
Ali Inshan	25.9.1949	24.6.1995	12	*1970–1976*	172	25	0	10.75	34	5-59	1/0	47.67	7	
Allan David Walter	5.11.1937		5	*1961*–1966	75	40*	0	12.50	–	–	–/–	–	15/3	
Allen Ian Basil Alston	6.10.1965		2	1991	5	4*	0	–	5	2-69	0/0	36.00	1	
Ambrose *Sir* Curtly Elconn Lynwall (*CY 1992*)	21.9.1963		98	*1987*–2000	1,439	53	0	12.40	405	8-45	22/3	20.99	18	176
Arthurton Keith Lloyd Thomas	21.2.1965		33	1988–1995	1,382	157*	2	30.71	1	1-17	0/0	183.00	22	105
Asgarali Nyron Sultan	28.12.1920	5.11.2006	2	1957	62	29	0	15.50	–	–	–/–	–	0	
[2] **Atkinson** Denis St Eval	9.8.1926	9.11.2001	22	*1948–1957*	922	219	1	31.79	47	7-53	3/0	35.04	11	
[2] **Atkinson** Eric St Eval	6.11.1927	29.5.1998	8	*1957–1958*	126	37	0	15.75	25	5-42	1/0	23.56	2	
Austin Richard Arkwright	5.9.1954	7.2.2015	2	*1977*	22	20	0	11.00	0	0-5	0/0	–	2	1
Austin Ryan Anthony	15.11.1981		2	2009	39	19	0	9.75	3	1-29	0/0	51.66	3	
Bacchus Sheik Faoud Ahamul Fasiel	31.1.1954		19	*1977–1981*	782	250	1	26.06	0	0-3	0/0	–	17	29
Baichan Leonard	12.5.1946		3	*1974–1975*	184	105*	1	46.00	–	–	–/–	–	2	
Baker Lionel Sionne	6.9.1984		4	*2008*–2009	23	17	0	11.50	5	2-39	0/0	79.00	1	10/3
Banks Omari Ahmed Clemente	17.7.1982		10	*2002*–2005	318	50*	0	26.50	28	4-87	0/0	48.82	6	5
Baptiste Eldine Ashworth Elderfield	12.3.1960		10	*1983–1989*	233	87*	0	23.30	16	3-31	0/0	35.18	2	43
Barath Adrian Boris	14.4.1990		15	*2009*–2012	657	104	1	23.46	0	0-3	0/0	–	13	14/2
Barrett Arthur George	4.4.1944		6	*1970–1974*	40	19	0	6.66	13	3-43	0/0	46.38	0	
Barrow Ivanhoe Mordecai	16.1.1911	2.4.1979	11	*1929*–1939	276	105	1	16.23	–	–	–/–	–	17/5	
Bartlett Edward Lawson	10.3.1906	21.12.1976	5	1928–*1930*	131	84	0	18.71	–	–	–/–	–	2	
Baugh Carlton Seymour	23.6.1982		21	*2002–2011*	610	68	0	17.94	–	–	–/–	–	43/5	47/3
Benjamin Kenneth Charlie Griffith	8.4.1967		26	*1991–1997*	222	43*	0	7.92	92	6-66	4/1	30.27	2	26
Benjamin Winston Keithroy Matthew	31.12.1964		21	*1987–1994*	470	85	0	18.80	61	4-46	0/0	27.01	12	85
Benn Sulieman Jamaal	22.7.1981		26	*2007–2014*	486	42	0	14.29	87	6-81	6/0	39.10	14	47/24
Bernard David Eddison	19.7.1981		3	*2002*–2009	202	69	0	40.40	4	2-30	0/0	46.25	0	20/1
Bess Brandon Jeremy	13.12.1987		1	2010	11	11*	0	11.00	1	1-65	0/0	92.00	0	
Best Carlisle Alonza	14.5.1959		8	*1985–1990*	342	164	1	28.50	0	0-2	0/0	–	8	24
Best Tino la Bertram	26.8.1981		25	*2002–2013*	401	95	0	12.53	57	6-40	2/0	40.19	6	26/6
Betancourt Nelson	4.6.1887	12.10.1947	1	*1929*	52	39	0	26.00	–	–	–/–	–	0	
Binns Alfred Phillip	24.7.1929		5	*1952–1955*	64	27	0	9.14	–	–	–/–	–	14/3	

	Born	*Died*	*Tests*	*Test Career*	*Runs*	*HS*	*100s*	*Avge*	*Wkts*	*BB*	*5/10*	*Avge*	*Ct/St*	*O/T*
Birkett Lionel Sydney	14.4.1905	16.1.1998	4	*1930*	136	64	0	17.00	1	1-16	0/0	71.00	4	
Bishoo Devendra	6.11.1985		21	*2010–2016*	406	45	0	16.91	77	8-49	3/1	37.00	12	14/5
Bishop Ian Raphael	24.10.1967		43	*1988–1997*	632	48	0	12.15	161	6-40	6/0	24.27	8	84
Black Marlon Ian	7.6.1975		6	*2000–2001*	21	6	0	2.62	12	4-83	0/0	49.75	0	5
Blackwood Jermaine	20.11.1991		22	2014–*2016*	1,128	112*	1	31.33	2	2-14	0/0	82.50	19	2
Boyce Keith David (*CY 1974*)	11.10.1943	11.10.1996	21	*1970–1975*	657	95*	0	24.33	60	6-77	2/1	30.01	5	8
Bradshaw Ian David Russell	9.7.1974		5	*2005*	96	33	0	13.71	9	3-73	0/0	60.00	3	62/1
Brathwaite Carlos Ricardo	18.7.1988		3	*2015*–2016	181	69	0	45.25	1	1-30	0/0	242.00	0	20/13
Brathwaite Kraigg Clairmonte	1.12.1992		34	*2010–2016*	2,214	212	5	37.52	12	6-29	1/0	50.91	17	7
[2] **Bravo** Dwayne John	7.10.1983		40	2004–*2010*	2,200	113	3	31.42	86	6-55	2/0	39.83	41	164/66
[2] **Bravo** Darren Michael	6.2.1989		49	*2010–2016*	3,400	218	8	40.00	0	0-2	0/0	–	47	94/12
Breese Gareth Rohan	9.1.1976		1	*2002*	5	5	0	2.50	2	2-108	0/0	67.50	1	
Browne Courtney Oswald	7.12.1970		20	*1994–2004*	387	68	0	16.12	–	–	–/–	–	79/2	46
Browne Cyril Rutherford	8.10.1890	12.1.1964	4	1928–*1929*	176	70*	0	25.14	6	2-72	0/0	48.00	1	
Butcher Basil Fitzherbert (*CY 1970*)	3.9.1933		44	*1958*–1969	3,104	209*	7	43.11	5	5-34	1/0	18.00	15	
Butler Lennox Stephen	9.2.1929	1.9.2009	1	*1954*	16	16	0	16.00	2	2-151	0/0	75.50	0	
Butts Clyde Godfrey	8.7.1957		7	*1984–1987*	108	38	0	15.42	10	4-73	0/0	59.50	2	
Bynoe Michael Robin	23.2.1941		4	*1958–1966*	111	48	0	18.50	1	1-5	0/0	5.00	4	
Camacho George Stephen	15.10.1945	2.10.2015	11	*1967–1970*	640	87	0	29.09	0	0-12	0/0	–	4	
[2] **Cameron** Francis James	22.6.1923	10.6.1994	5	*1948*	151	75*	0	25.16	3	2-74	0/0	92.66	0	
[2] **Cameron** John Hemsley	8.4.1914	13.2.2000	2	1939	6	5	0	2.00	3	3-66	0/0	29.33	0	
Campbell Sherwin Legay	1.11.1970		52	*1994–2001*	2,882	208	4	32.38	–	–	–/–	–	47	90
Carew George McDonald	4.6.1910	9.12.1974	4	*1934–1948*	170	107	1	28.33	0	0-2	0/0	–	1	
Carew Michael Conrad ("Joey")	15.9.1937	8.1.2011	19	1963–*1971*	1,127	109	1	34.15	8	1-11	0/0	54.62	13	
Challenor George	28.6.1888	30.7.1947	3	1928	101	46	0	16.83	–	–	–/–	–	0	
Chanderpaul Shivnarine (*CY 2008*)	16.8.1974		164	*1993–2014*	11,867	203*	30	51.37	9	1-2	0/0	98.11	66	268/22
Chandrika Rajindra	8.8.1989		5	2015–2016	140	37	0	14.00	–	–	–/–	–	2	
Chang Herbert Samuel	2.7.1952		1	*1978*	8	6	0	4.00	–	–	–/–	–	0	
Chase Roston Lamar	22.3.1992		7	2016–*2016*	325	137*	1	29.54	11	5-121	1/0	58.45	1	
Chattergoon Sewnarine	3.4.1981		4	*2007–2008*	127	46	0	18.14	–	–	–/–	–	4	18
[2] **Christiani** Cyril Marcel	28.10.1913	4.4.1938	4	*1934*	98	32*	0	19.60	–	–	–/–	–	6/1	
[2] **Christiani** Robert Julian	19.7.1920	4.1.2005	22	*1947–1953*	896	107	1	26.35	3	3-52	0/0	36.00	19/2	
Clarke Carlos Bertram OBE	7.4.1918	14.10.1993	3	1939	3	2	0	1.00	6	3-59	0/0	43.50	0	
Clarke Sylvester Theophilus	11.12.1954	4.12.1999	11	*1977–1981*	172	35*	0	15.63	42	5-126	1/0	27.85	2	10
[2] **Collins** Pedro Tyrone	12.8.1976		32	*1998–2005*	235	24	0	5.87	106	6-53	3/0	34.63	7	30
Collymore Corey Dalanelo	21.12.1977		30	*1998*–2007	197	16*	0	7.88	93	7-57	4/1	32.30	6	84

	Born	Died	Tests	Test Career	Runs	HS	100s	Avge	Wkts	BB	5/10	Avge	Ct/St	O/T
Constantine *Lord* [Learie Nicholas] MBE (*CY 1940*)	21.9.1901	1.7.1971	18	1928–1939	635	90	0	19.24	58	5-75	2/0	30.10	28	
Cottrell Sheldon Shane	19.8.1989		2	2013–2014	11	5	0	2.75	2	1-72	0/0	98.00	0	2/6
Croft Colin Everton Hunte	15.3.1953		27	1976–1981	158	33	0	10.53	125	8-29	3/0	23.30	8	19
Cuffy Cameron Eustace	8.2.1970		15	1994–2002	58	15	0	4.14	43	4-82	0/0	33.83	5	41
Cummins Anderson Cleophas	7.5.1966		5	1992–1994	98	50	0	19.60	8	4-54	0/0	42.75	1	63‡
Cummins Miguel Lamar	5.9.1990		5	2016–2016	30	24*	0	6.00	10	6-48	1/0	40.80	0	2
Da Costa Oscar Constantine	11.9.1907	1.10.1936	5	1929–1934	153	39	0	19.12	3	1-14	0/0	58.33	5	
Daniel Wayne Wendell	16.1.1956		10	1975–1983	46	11	0	6.57	36	5-39	1/0	25.27	4	18
[2] **Davis** Bryan Allan	2.5.1940		4	1964	245	68	0	30.62	–	–	–/–	–	1	
[2] **Davis** Charles Allan	1.1.1944		15	1968–1972	1,301	183	4	54.20	2	1-27	0/0	165.00	4	
Davis Winston Walter	18.9.1958		15	1982–1987	202	77	0	15.53	45	4-19	0/0	32.71	10	35
De Caires Francis Ignatius	12.5.1909	2.2.1959	3	1929	232	80	0	38.66	0	0-9	0/0	–	1	
Deonarine Narsingh	16.8.1983		18	2004–2013	725	82	0	25.89	24	4-37	0/0	29.70	16	31/8
Depeiza Cyril Clairmonte	10.10.1928	10.11.1995	5	1954–1955	187	122	1	31.16	0	0-3	0/0	–	7/4	
Dewdney David Thomas	23.10.1933		9	1954–1957	17	5*	0	2.42	21	5-21	1/0	38.42	0	
Dhanraj Rajindra	6.2.1969		4	1994–1995	17	9	0	4.25	8	2-49	0/0	74.37	1	6
Dillon Mervyn	5.6.1974		38	1996–2003	549	43	0	8.44	131	5-71	2/0	33.57	16	108
Dowe Uton George	29.3.1949		4	1970–1972	8	5*	0	8.00	12	4-69	0/0	44.50	3	
Dowlin Travis Montague	24.2.1977		6	2009–2010	343	95	0	31.18	0	0-3	0/0	–	5	11/2
Dowrich Shane Omari	30.10.1991		8	2015–2016	409	74	0	34.08	–	–	–/–	–	8/3	
Drakes Vasbert Conniel	5.8.1969		12	2002–2003	386	67	0	21.44	33	5-93	1/0	41.27	2	34
Dujon Peter Jeffrey Leroy (*CY 1989*)	28.5.1956		81	1981–1991	3,322	139	5	31.94	–	–	–/–	–	267/5	169
[2] **Edwards** Fidel Henderson	6.2.1982		55	2003–2012	394	30	0	6.56	165	7-87	12/0	37.87	10	50/20
Edwards Kirk Anton	3.11.1984		17	2011–2014	986	121	2	31.80	0	0-19	0/0	–	15	16
Edwards Richard Martin	3.6.1940		5	1968	65	22	0	9.28	18	5-84	1/0	34.77	0	
Ferguson Wilfred	14.12.1917	23.2.1961	8	1947–1953	200	75	0	28.57	34	6-92	3/1	34.26	11	
Fernandes Maurius Pacheco	12.8.1897	8.5.1981	2	1928–1929	49	22	0	12.25	–	–	–/–	–	0	
Findlay Thaddeus Michael MBE	19.10.1943		10	1969–1972	212	44*	0	16.30	–	–	–/–	–	19/2	
Foster Maurice Linton Churchill	9.5.1943		14	1969–1977	580	125	1	30.52	9	2-41	0/0	66.66	3	2
Francis George Nathaniel	11.12.1897	12.1.1942	10	1928–1933	81	19*	0	5.78	23	4-40	0/0	33.17	7	
Frederick Michael Campbell	6.5.1927	18.6.2014	1	1953	30	30	0	15.00	–	–	–/–	–	0	
Fredericks Roy Clifton (*CY 1974*)	11.11.1942	5.9.2000	59	1968–1976	4,334	169	8	42.49	7	1-12	0/0	78.28	62	12
Fudadin Assad Badyr	1.8.1985		3	2012	122	55	0	30.50	0	0-11	0/0	–	4	
Fuller Richard Livingston	30.1.1913	3.5.1987	1	1934	1	1	0	1.00	0	0-2	0/0	–	0	
Furlonge Hammond Allan	19.6.1934		3	1954–1955	99	64	0	19.80	–	–	–/–	–	0	

	Born	Died	Tests	Test Career	Runs	HS	100s	Avge	Wkts	BB	5/10	Avge	Ct/St	O/T
Gabriel Shannon Terry	28.4.1988		23	2012–2016	112	20*	0	5.89	49	5-96	1/0	38.12	10	8/2
Ganga Daren	14.1.1979		48	1998–2007	2,160	135	3	25.71	1	1-20	0/0	106.00	30	35/1
Ganteaume Andrew Gordon	22.1.1921	17.2.2016	1	1947	112	112	1	112.00	–	–	–/–	–	0	
Garner Joel MBE (*CY 1980*)	16.12.1952		58	1976–1986	672	60	0	12.44	259	6-56	7/0	20.97	42	98
Garrick Leon Vivian	11.11.1976		1	2000	27	27	0	13.50	–	–	–/–	–	2	3
Gaskin Berkeley Bertram McGarrell	21.3.1908	2.5.1979	2	1947	17	10	0	5.66	2	1-15	0/0	79.00	1	
Gayle Christopher Henry	21.9.1979		103	1999–2014	7,214	333	15	42.18	73	5-34	2/0	42.73	96	266/50
Gibbs Glendon Lionel	27.12.1925	21.2.1979	1	1954	12	12	0	6.00	0	0-2	0/0	–	1	
Gibbs Lancelot Richard (*CY 1972*)	29.9.1934		79	1957–1975	488	25	0	6.97	309	8-38	18/2	29.09	52	3
Gibson Ottis Delroy (*CY 2008*)	16.3.1969		2	1995–1998	93	37	0	23.25	3	2-81	0/0	91.66	0	15
Gilchrist Roy	28.6.1934	18.7.2001	13	1957–1958	60	12	0	5.45	57	6-55	1/0	26.68	4	
Gladstone Morais George	14.1.1901	19.5.1978	1	1929	12	12*	0	–	1	1-139	0/0	189.00	0	
Goddard John Douglas Claude OBE	21.4.1919	26.8.1987	27	1947–1957	859	83*	0	30.67	33	5-31	1/0	31.81	22	
Gomes Hilary Angelo ("Larry") (*CY 1985*)	13.7.1953		60	1976–1986	3,171	143	9	39.63	15	2-20	0/0	62.00	18	83
Gomez Gerald Ethridge	10.10.1919	6.8.1996	29	1939–1953	1,243	101	1	30.31	58	7-55	1/1	27.41	18	
[2] **Grant** George Copeland ("Jackie")	9.5.1907	26.10.1978	12	1930–1934	413	71*	0	25.81	0	0-1	0/0	–	10	
[2] **Grant** Rolph Stewart	15.12.1909	18.10.1977	7	1934–1939	220	77	0	22.00	11	3-68	0/0	32.09	13	
Gray Anthony Hollis	23.5.1963		5	1986	48	12*	0	8.00	22	4-39	0/0	17.13	6	25
Greenidge Alvin Ethelbert	20.8.1956		6	1977–1978	222	69	0	22.20	–	–	–/–	–	5	1
Greenidge Cuthbert Gordon MBE (*CY 1977*)	1.5.1951		108	1974–1990	7,558	226	19	44.72	0	0-0	0/0	–	96	128
Greenidge Geoffrey Alan	26.5.1948		5	1971–1972	209	50	0	29.85	0	0-2	0/0	–	3	
Grell Mervyn George	18.12.1899	11.1.1976	1	1929	34	21	0	17.00	0	0-7	0/0	–	1	
Griffith Adrian Frank Gordon	19.11.1971		14	1996–2000	638	114	1	24.53	–	–	–/–	–	5	9
Griffith Charles Christopher (*CY 1964*)	14.12.1938		28	1959–1968	530	54	0	16.56	94	6-36	5/0	28.54	16	
Griffith Herman Clarence	1.12.1893	18.3.1980	13	1928–1933	91	18	0	5.05	44	6-103	2/0	28.25	4	
Guillen Simpson Clairmonte ("Sammy")	24.9.1924	2.3.2013	5†	1951	104	54	0	26.00	–	–	–/–	–	9/2	
Hall *Sir* Wesley Winfield	12.9.1937		48	1958–1968	818	50*	0	15.73	192	7-69	9/1	26.38	11	
Harper Roger Andrew	17.3.1963		25	1983–1993	535	74	0	18.44	46	6-57	1/0	28.06	36	105
Haynes Desmond Leo (*CY 1991*)	15.2.1956		116	1977–1993	7,487	184	18	42.29	1	1-2	0/0	8.00	65	238
[3] **Headley** George Alphonso MBE (*CY 1934*)	30.5.1909	30.11.1983	22	1929–1953	2,190	270*	10	60.83	0	0-0	0/0	–	14	
[3] **Headley** Ronald George Alphonso	29.6.1939		2	1973	62	42	0	15.50	–	–	–/–	–	2	1
Hendriks John Leslie	21.12.1933		20	1961–1969	447	64	0	18.62	–	–	–/–	–	42/5	
Hinds Ryan O'Neal	17.2.1981		15	2001–2009	505	84	0	21.04	13	2-45	0/0	66.92	7	14
Hinds Wavell Wayne	7.9.1976		45	1999–2005	2,608	213	5	33.01	16	3-79	0/0	36.87	32	119/5
Hoad Edward Lisle Goldsworthy	29.1.1896	5.3.1986	4	1928–1933	98	36	0	12.25	–	–	–/–	–	1	
Holder Jason Omar	5.11.1991		20	2014–2016	801	103*	1	28.60	31	5-30	1/0	41.00	16	49/4

	Born	Died	Tests	Test Career	Runs	HS	100s	Avge	Wkts	BB	5/10	Avge	Ct/St	O/T
Holder Roland Irwin Christopher	22.12.1967		11	*1996–1998*	380	91	0	25.33	–	–	–/–	–	9	37
Holder Vanburn Alonzo	10.10.1945		40	1969–*1978*	682	42	0	14.20	109	6-28	3/0	33.27	16	12
Holding Michael Anthony (*CY 1977*)	16.2.1954		60	*1975–1986*	910	73	0	13.78	249	8-92	13/2	23.68	22	102
Holford David Anthony Jerome	16.4.1940		24	1966–*1976*	768	105*	1	22.58	51	5-23	1/0	39.39	18	
Holt John Kenneth Constantine	12.8.1923	3.6.1997	17	1953–1958	1,066	166	2	36.75	1	1-20	0/0	20.00	8	
Hooper Carl Llewellyn	15.12.1966		102	1987–2002	5,762	233	13	36.46	114	5-26	4/0	49.42	115	227
Hope Shai Diego	10.11.1993		7	*2014–2016*	223	41	0	17.15	–	–	–/–	–	4	4
Howard Anthony Bourne	27.8.1946		1	*1971*	–	–	–	–	2	2-140	0/0	70.00	0	
Hunte *Sir* Conrad Cleophas (*CY 1964*)	9.5.1932	3.12.1999	44	*1957–1966*	3,245	260	8	45.06	2	1-17	0/0	55.00	16	
Hunte Errol Ashton Clairmore	3.10.1905	26.6.1967	3	*1929*	166	58	0	33.20	–	–	–/–	–	5	
Hylton Leslie George	29.3.1905	17.5.1955	6	*1934*–1939	70	19	0	11.66	16	4-27	0/0	26.12	1	
Jacobs Ridley Detamore	26.11.1967		65	*1998*–2004	2,577	118	3	28.31	–	–	–/–	–	207/12	147
Jaggernauth Amit Sheldon	16.11.1983		1	*2007*	0	0*	0	0.00	1	1-74	0/0	96.00	0	
Johnson Hophnie Hobah <u>Hines</u>	13.7.1910	24.6.1987	3	*1947*–1950	38	22	0	9.50	13	5-41	2/1	18.30	0	
Johnson Leon Rayon	8.8.1987		9	*2014–2016*	403	66	0	25.18	0	0-9	0/0	–	7	6
Johnson Tyrell Fabian	10.1.1917	5.4.1985	1	1939	9	9*	0	–	3	2-53	0/0	43.00	1	
Jones Charles Ernest Llewellyn	3.11.1902	10.12.1959	4	*1929–1934*	63	19	0	9.00	0	0-2	0/0	–	3	
Jones Prior Erskine Waverley	6.6.1917	21.11.1991	9	*1947–1951*	47	10*	0	5.22	25	5-85	1/0	30.04	4	
Joseph Alzarri Shaheim	20.11.1996		2	2016–*2016*	6	6	0	2.00	5	3-69	0/0	38.00	1	2
Joseph David Rolston Emmanuel	15.11.1969		4	*1998*	141	50	0	20.14	–	–	–/–	–	10	
Joseph Sylvester Cleofoster	5.9.1978		5	2004–2007	147	45	0	14.70	0	0-8	0/0	–	3	13
Julien Bernard Denis	13.3.1950		24	1973–*1976*	866	121	2	30.92	50	5-57	1/0	37.36	14	12
Jumadeen Raphick Rasif	12.4.1948		12	*1971–1978*	84	56	0	21.00	29	4-72	0/0	39.34	4	
Kallicharran Alvin Isaac (*CY 1983*)	21.3.1949		66	*1971–1980*	4,399	187	12	44.43	4	2-16	0/0	39.50	51	31
Kanhai Rohan Bholalall (*CY 1964*)	26.12.1935		79	1957–*1973*	6,227	256	15	47.53	0	0-1	0/0	–	50	7
Kentish Esmond Seymour Maurice	21.11.1916	10.6.2011	2	*1947–1953*	1	1*	0	1.00	8	5-49	1/0	22.25	1	
King Collis Llewellyn	11.6.1951		9	1976–1980	418	100*	1	32.15	3	1-30	0/0	94.00	5	18
King Frank McDonald	14.12.1926	23.12.1990	14	*1952–1955*	116	21	0	8.28	29	5-74	1/0	39.96	5	
King Lester Anthony	27.2.1939	9.7.1998	2	*1961–1967*	41	20	0	10.25	9	5-46	1/0	17.11	2	
King Reon Dane	6.10.1975		19	*1998–2004*	66	12*	0	3.47	53	5-51	1/0	32.69	2	50
Lambert Clayton Benjamin	10.2.1962		5	1991–*1998*	284	104	1	31.55	1	1-4	0/0	5.00	8	11‡
Lara Brian Charles (*CY 1995*)	2.5.1969		130§	*1990–2006*	11,912	400*	34	53.17	0	0-0	0/0	–	164	295‡
Lashley Patrick Douglas ("Peter")	11.2.1937		4	*1960*–1966	159	49	0	22.71	1	1-1	0/0	1.00	4	
Lawson Jermaine Jay Charles	13.1.1982		13	*2002–2005*	52	14	0	3.46	51	7-78	2/0	29.64	3	13
Legall Ralph Archibald	1.12.1925	2003	4	*1952*	50	23	0	10.00	–	–	–/–	–	8/1	

§ *Lara's figures exclude 41 runs for the ICC World XI v Australia in the Super Series Test in 2005-06.*

	Born	Died	Tests	Test Career	Runs	HS	100s	Avge	Wkts	BB	5/10	Avge	Ct/St	O/T
Lewis Desmond Michael	21.2.1946		3	*1970*	259	88	0	86.33	–	–	–/–	–	8	
Lewis Rawl Nicholas	5.9.1974		5	*1997–2007*	89	40	0	8.90	4	2-42	0/0	114.00	0	28/1
Lloyd Clive Hubert CBE (*CY 1971*)	31.8.1944		110	*1966–1984*	7,515	242*	19	46.67	10	2-13	0/0	62.20	90	87
Logie Augustine Lawrence	28.9.1960		52	*1982*–1991	2,470	130	2	35.79	0	0-0	0/0	–	57	158
McGarrell Neil Christopher	12.7.1972		4	*2000–2001*	61	33	0	15.25	17	4-23	0/0	26.64	2	17
McLean Nixon Alexei McNamara	20.7.1973		19	*1997–2000*	368	46	0	12.26	44	3-53	0/0	42.56	5	45
McMorris Easton Dudley Ashton St John	4.4.1935		13	*1957*–1966	564	125	1	26.85	–	–	–/–	–	5	
McWatt Clifford Aubrey	1.2.1922	20.7.1997	6	*1953–1954*	202	54	0	28.85	1	1-16	0/0	16.00	9/1	
Madray Ivan Samuel	2.7.1934	23.4.2009	2	*1957*	3	2	0	1.00	0	0-12	0/0	–	2	
Marshall Malcolm Denzil (*CY 1983*)	18.4.1958	4.11.1999	81	*1978*–1991	1,810	92	0	18.85	376	7-22	22/4	20.94	25	136
[2]**Marshall** Norman Edgar	27.2.1924	11.8.2007	1	*1954*	8	8	0	4.00	2	1-22	0/0	31.00	0	
[2]**Marshall** Roy Edwin (*CY 1959*)	25.4.1930	27.10.1992	4	*1951*	143	30	0	20.42	0	0-3	0/0	–	1	
Marshall Xavier Melbourne	27.3.1986		7	2005–*2008*	243	85	0	20.25	0	0-0	0/0	–	7	24/6
Martin Frank Reginald	12.10.1893	23.11.1967	9	1928–*1930*	486	123*	1	28.58	8	3-91	0/0	77.37	2	
Martindale Emmanuel Alfred	25.11.1909	17.3.1972	10	1933–1939	58	22	0	5.27	37	5-22	3/0	21.72	5	
Mattis Everton Hugh	11.4.1957		4	*1980*	145	71	0	29.00	0	0-4	0/0	–	3	2
Mendonca Ivor Leon	13.7.1934	14.6.2014	2	*1961*	81	78	0	40.50	–	–	–/–	–	8/2	
Merry Cyril Arthur	20.1.1911	19.4.1964	2	1933	34	13	0	8.50	–	–	–/–	–	1	
Miller Nikita O'Neil	16.5.1982		1	2009	5	5	0	2.50	0	0-27	0/0	–	0	46/9
Miller Roy	24.12.1924		1	*1952*	23	23	0	23.00	0	0-28	0/0	–	0	
Mohammed Dave	8.10.1979		5	*2003–2006*	225	52	0	32.14	13	3-98	0/0	51.38	1	7
Moodie George Horatio	26.11.1915	8.6.2002	1	*1934*	5	5	0	5.00	3	2-23	0/0	13.33	0	
Morton Runako Shakur	22.7.1978	4.3.2012	15	2005–*2007*	573	70*	0	22.03	0	0-4	0/0	–	20	56/7
Moseley Ezra Alphonsa	5.1.1958		2	*1989*	35	26	0	8.75	6	2-70	0/0	43.50	1	9
[1]**Murray** David Anthony	29.5.1950		19	*1977–1981*	601	84	0	21.46	–	–	–/–	–	57/5	10
Murray Deryck Lance	20.5.1943		62	1963–1980	1,993	91	0	22.90	–	–	–/–	–	181/8	26
Murray Junior Randalph	20.1.1968		33	*1992–2001*	918	101*	1	22.39	–	–	–/–	–	99/3	55
Nagamootoo Mahendra Veeren	9.10.1975		5	2000–*2002*	185	68	0	26.42	12	3-119	0/0	53.08	2	24
Nanan Rangy	29.5.1953	23.3.2016	1	*1980*	16	8	0	8.00	4	2-37	0/0	22.75	2	
Narine Sunil Philip	26.5.1988		6	2012–*2013*	40	22*	0	8.00	21	6-91	2/0	40.52	2	65/39
Nash Brendan Paul	14.12.1977		21	*2008*–2011	1,103	114	2	33.42	2	1-21	0/0	123.50	6	9
Neblett James Montague	13.11.1901	28.3.1959	1	*1934*	16	11*	0	16.00	1	1-44	0/0	75.00	0	
Noreiga Jack Mollinson	15.4.1936	8.8.2003	4	*1970*	11	9	0	3.66	17	9-95	2/0	29.00	2	
Nunes Robert Karl	7.6.1894	23.7.1958	4	1928–*1929*	245	92	0	30.62	–	–	–/–	–	2	
Nurse Seymour MacDonald (*CY 1967*)	10.11.1933		29	*1959–1968*	2,523	258	6	47.60	0	0-0	0/0	–	21	
Padmore Albert Leroy	17.12.1946		2	*1975*–1976	8	8*	0	8.00	1	1-36	0/0	135.00	0	

	Born	*Died*	*Tests*	*Test Career*	*Runs*	*HS*	*100s*	*Avge*	*Wkts*	*BB*	*5/10*	*Avge*	*Ct/St*	*O/T*
Pagon Donovan Jomo	13.9.1982		2	2004	37	35	0	12.33	–	–	–/–	–	0	
Pairaudeau Bruce Hamilton	14.4.1931		13	1952–1957	454	115	1	21.61	0	0-3	0/0	–	6	
Parchment Brenton Anthony	24.6.1982		2	2007	55	20	0	13.75	–	–	–/–	–	1	7/1
Parry Derick Recaldo	22.12.1954		12	1977–1979	381	65	0	22.41	23	5-15	1/0	40.69	4	6
Pascal Nelon Troy	25.4.1987		2	2010–2010	12	10	0	6.00	0	0-27	0/0	–	1	1
Passailaigue Charles Clarence	4.8.1901	7.1.1972	1	1929	46	44	0	46.00	0	0-15	0/0	–	3	
Patterson Balfour Patrick	15.9.1961		28	1985–1992	145	21*	0	6.59	93	5-24	5/0	30.90	5	59
Payne Thelston Rodney O'Neale	13.2.1957		1	1985	5	5	0	5.00	–	–	–/–	–	5	7
Permaul Veerasammy	11.8.1989		6	2012–2015	98	23*	0	12.25	18	3-32	0/0	43.77	2	6
Perry Nehemiah Odolphus	16.6.1968		4	1998–1999	74	26	0	12.33	10	5-70	1/0	44.60	1	21
Peters Keon Kenroy	24.2.1982		1	2014	0	0	0	0.00	2	2-69	0/0	34.50	0	
Phillip Norbert	12.6.1948		9	1977–1978	297	47	0	29.70	28	4-48	0/0	37.17	5	1
Phillips Omar Jamel	12.10.1986		2	2009	160	94	0	40.00	–	–	–/–	–	1	
Pierre Lancelot Richard	5.6.1921	14.4.1989	1	1947	–	–	–	–	0	0-9	0/0	–	0	
Powell Daren Brentlyle	15.4.1978		37	2002–2008	407	36*	0	7.82	85	5-25	1/0	47.85	8	55/5
Powell Kieran Omar Akeem	6.3.1990		21	2011–2014	1,072	134	3	27.48	–	–	–/–	–	19	28/1
Powell Ricardo Lloyd	16.12.1978		2	1999–2003	53	30	0	17.66	0	0-13	0/0	–	1	109
Rae Allan Fitzroy	30.9.1922	27.2.2005	15	1948–1952	1,016	109	4	46.18	–	–	–/–	–	10	
Ragoonath Suruj	22.3.1968		2	1998	13	9	0	4.33	–	–	–/–	–	0	
Ramadhin Sonny (*CY 1951*)	1.5.1929		43	1950–1960	361	44	0	8.20	158	7-49	10/1	28.98	9	
Ramdass Ryan Rakesh	3.7.1983		1	2005	26	23	0	13.00	–	–	–/–	–	2	1
Ramdin Denesh	13.3.1985		74	2005–2015	2,898	166	4	25.87	–	–	–/–	–	205/12	139/58
Ramnarine Dinanath	4.6.1975		12	1997–2001	106	35*	0	6.23	45	5-78	1/0	30.73	8	4
Rampaul Ravindranath	15.10.1984		18	2009–2012	335	40*	0	14.56	49	4-48	0/0	34.79	3	92/23
Reifer Floyd Lamonte	23.7.1972		6	1996–2009	111	29	0	9.25	–	–	–/–	–	6	8/1
Richards Dale Maurice	16.7.1976		3	2009–2010	125	69	0	20.83	–	–	–/–	–	4	8/1
Richards *Sir* Isaac Vivian Alexander (*CY 1977*)	7.3.1952		121	1974–1991	8,540	291	24	50.23	32	2-17	0/0	61.37	122	187
Richardson *Sir* Richard Benjamin (*CY 1992*)	12.1.1962		86	1983–1995	5,949	194	16	44.39	0	0-0	0/0	–	90	224
Rickards Kenneth Roy	22.8.1923	21.8.1995	2	1947–1951	104	67	0	34.66	–	–	–/–	–	0	
Roach Clifford Archibald	13.3.1904	16.4.1988	16	1928–1934	952	209	2	30.70	2	1-18	0/0	51.50	5	
Roach Kemar Andre Jamal	30.6.1988		37	2009–2015	509	41	0	10.38	122	6-48	6/1	30.23	10	67/11
Roberts Alphonso Theodore	18.9.1937	24.7.1996	1	1955	28	28	0	14.00	–	–	–/–	–	0	
Roberts *Sir* Anderson Montgomery Everton CBE (*CY 1975*)	29.1.1951		47	1973–1983	762	68	0	14.94	202	7-54	11/2	25.61	9	56
Roberts Lincoln Abraham	4.9.1974		1	1998	0	0	0	0.00	–	–	–/–	–	0	
Rodriguez William Vicente	25.6.1934		5	1961–1967	96	50	0	13.71	7	3-51	0/0	53.42	3	

	Born	Died	Tests	Test Career	Runs	HS	100s	Avge	Wkts	BB	5/10	Avge	Ct/St	O/T
Rose Franklyn Albert	1.2.1972		19	*1996*–2000	344	69	0	13.23	53	7-84	2/0	30.88	4	27
Rowe Lawrence George	8.1.1949		30	*1971–1979*	2,047	302	7	43.55	0	0-1	0/0	–	17	11
Russell Andre Dwayne	29.4.1988		1	*2010*	2	2	0	2.00	1	1-73	0/0	104.00	1	51/43
[2] **St Hill** Edwin Lloyd	9.3.1904	21.5.1957	2	*1929*	18	12	0	4.50	3	2-110	0/0	73.66	0	
[2] **St Hill** Wilton H	6.7.1893	d unknown	3	1928–*1929*	117	38	0	19.50	0	0-9	0/0	–	1	
Sammy Darren Julius Garvey	20.12.1983		38	2007–*2013*	1,323	106	1	21.68	84	7-66	4/0	35.79	65	126/66
[2] **Samuels** Marlon Nathaniel (*CY 2013*)	5.1.1981		71	*2000–2016*	3,917	260	7	32.64	41	4-13	0/0	59.63	28	187/51
[2] **Samuels** Robert George	13.3.1971		6	*1995–1996*	372	125	1	37.20	–	–	–/–	–	8	8
Sanford Adam	12.7.1975		11	*2001–2003*	72	18*	0	4.80	30	4-132	0/0	43.86	4	
Sarwan Ramnaresh Ronnie	23.6.1980		87	*1999*–2011	5,842	291	15	40.01	23	4-37	0/0	50.56	53	181/18
Scarlett Reginald Osmond	15.8.1934		3	*1959*	54	29*	0	18.00	2	1-46	0/0	104.50	2	
[1] **Scott** Alfred Homer Patrick	29.7.1934		1	*1952*	5	5	0	5.00	0	0-52	0/0	–	0	
[1] **Scott** Oscar Charles ("Tommy")	14.8.1892	15.6.1961	8	1928–*1930*	171	35	0	17.10	22	5-266	1/0	42.04	0	
Sealey Benjamin James	12.8.1899	12.9.1963	1	1933	41	29	0	20.50	1	1-10	0/0	10.00	0	
Sealy James Edward Derrick	11.9.1912	3.1.1982	11	*1929*–1939	478	92	0	28.11	3	2-7	0/0	31.33	6/1	
Shepherd John Neil (*CY 1979*)	9.11.1943		5	1969–*1970*	77	32	0	9.62	19	5-104	1/0	25.21	4	
Shillingford Grayson Cleophas	25.9.1944	23.12.2009	7	1969–*1971*	57	25	0	8.14	15	3-63	0/0	35.80	2	
Shillingford Irvine Theodore	18.4.1944		4	*1976–1977*	218	120	1	31.14	–	–	–/–	–	1	2
Shillingford Shane	22.2.1983		16	2010–2014	266	53*	0	13.30	70	6-49	6/2	34.55	9	
Shivnarine Sewdatt	13.5.1952		8	*1977–1978*	379	63	0	29.15	1	1-13	0/0	167.00	6	1
Simmons Lendl Mark Platter	25.1.1985		8	*2008–2011*	278	49	0	17.37	1	1-60	0/0	147.00	5	68/38
Simmons Philip Verant (*CY 1997*)	18.4.1963		26	*1987–1997*	1,002	110	1	22.26	4	2-34	0/0	64.25	26	143
Singh Charran Kamkaran	27.11.1935	19.11.2015	2	*1959*	11	11	0	3.66	5	2-28	0/0	33.20	2	
Small Joseph A.	3.11.1892	26.4.1958	3	1928–*1929*	79	52	0	13.16	3	2-67	0/0	61.33	3	
Small Milton Aster	12.2.1964		2	*1983*–1984	3	3*	0	–	4	3-40	0/0	38.25	0	2
Smith Cameron Wilberforce	29.7.1933		5	*1960–1961*	222	55	0	24.66	–	–	–/–	–	4/1	
Smith Devon Sheldon	21.10.1981		38	*2002–2014*	1,593	108	1	24.50	0	0-3	0/0	–	30	47/6
Smith Dwayne Romel	12.4.1983		10	*2003–2005*	320	105*	1	24.61	7	3-71	0/0	49.14	9	105/33
Smith O'Neil Gordon ("Collie") (*CY 1958*)	5.5.1933	9.9.1959	26	*1954–1958*	1,331	168	4	31.69	48	5-90	1/0	33.85	9	
Sobers *Sir* Garfield St Aubrun (*CY 1964*)	28.7.1936		93	*1953–1973*	8,032	365*	26	57.78	235	6-73	6/0	34.03	109	1
Solomon Joseph Stanislaus	26.8.1930		27	*1958–1964*	1,326	100*	1	34.00	4	1-20	0/0	67.00	13	
Stayers Sven Conrad ("Charlie")	9.6.1937	6.1.2005	4	*1961*	58	35*	0	19.33	9	3-65	0/0	40.44	0	
[2] **Stollmeyer** Jeffrey Baxter	11.3.1921	10.9.1989	32	1939–*1954*	2,159	160	4	42.33	13	3-32	0/0	39.00	20	
[2] **Stollmeyer** Victor Humphrey	24.1.1916	21.9.1999	1	1939	96	96	0	96.00	–	–	–/–	–	0	
Stuart Colin Ellsworth Laurie	28.9.1973		6	*2000–2001*	24	12*	0	3.42	20	3-33	0/0	31.40	2	5
Taylor Jaswick Ossie	3.1.1932	13.11.1999	3	*1957–1958*	4	4*	0	2.00	10	5-109	1/0	27.30	0	

	Born	Died	Tests	Test Career	Runs	HS	100s	Avge	Wkts	BB	5/10	Avge	Ct/St	O/T
Taylor Jerome Everton	22.6.1984		46	2003–2015	856	106	1	12.96	130	6-47	4/0	34.46	8	85/23
Thompson Patterson Ian Chesterfield	26.9.1971		2	1995–1996	17	10*	0	8.50	5	2-58	0/0	43.00	0	2
Tonge Gavin Courtney	13.2.1983		1	2009	25	23*	0	25.00	1	1-28	0/0	113.00	0	5/1
Trim John	25.1.1915	12.11.1960	4	1947–1951	21	12	0	5.25	18	5-34	1/0	16.16	2	
Valentine Alfred Louis (*CY 1951*)	28.4.1930	11.5.2004	36	1950–1961	141	14	0	4.70	139	8-104	8/2	30.32	13	
Valentine Vincent Adolphus	4.4.1908	6.7.1972	2	1933	35	19*	0	11.66	1	1-55	0/0	104.00	0	
Walcott *Sir* Clyde Leopold (*CY 1958*)	17.1.1926	26.8.2006	44	1947–1959	3,798	220	15	56.68	11	3-50	0/0	37.09	53/11	
Walcott Leslie Arthur	18.1.1894	27.2.1984	1	1929	40	24	0	40.00	1	1-17	0/0	32.00	0	
Wallace Philo Alphonso	2.8.1970		7	1997–1998	279	92	0	21.46	–	–	–/–	–	9	33
Walsh Courtney Andrew (*CY 1987*)	30.10.1962		132	1984–2000	936	30*	0	7.54	519	7-37	22/3	24.44	29	205
Walton Chadwick Antonio Kirkpatrick	3.7.1985		2	2009	13	10	0	3.25	–	–	–/–	–	10	5/3
Warrican Jomel Andrel	20.5.1992		4	2015	65	21*	0	65.00	11	4-67	0/0	46.27	1	
Washington Dwight Marlon	5.3.1983		1	2004	7	7*	0	–	0	0-20	0/0	–	3	
Watson Chester Donald	1.7.1938		7	1959–1961	12	5	0	2.40	19	4-62	0/0	38.10	1	
[1] **Weekes** *Sir* Everton de Courcy (*CY 1951*)	26.2.1925		48	1947–1957	4,455	207	15	58.61	1	1-8	0/0	77.00	49	
Weekes Kenneth Hunnell	24.1.1912	9.2.1998	2	1939	173	137	1	57.66	–	–	–/–	–	0	
White Anthony Wilbur	20.11.1938		2	1964	71	57*	0	23.66	3	2-34	0/0	50.66	1	
Wight Claude Vibart	28.7.1902	4.10.1969	2	1928–1929	67	23	0	22.33	0	0-6	0/0	–	0	
Wight George Leslie	28.5.1929	4.1.2004	1	1952	21	21	0	21.00	–	–	–/–	–	0	
Wiles Charles Archibald	11.8.1892	4.11.1957	1	1933	2	2	0	1.00	–	–	–/–	–	0	
Willett Elquemedo Tonito	1.5.1953		5	1972–1974	74	26	0	14.80	11	3-33	0/0	43.81	0	
Williams Alvadon Basil	21.11.1949	25.10.2015	7	1977–1978	469	111	2	39.08	–	–	–/–	–	5	
Williams David	4.11.1963		11	1991–1997	242	65	0	13.44	–	–	–/–	–	40/2	36
Williams Ernest Albert Vivian ("Foffie")	10.4.1914	13.4.1997	4	1939–1947	113	72	0	18.83	9	3-51	0/0	26.77	2	
Williams Stuart Clayton	12.8.1969		31	1993–2001	1,183	128	1	24.14	0	0-19	0/0	–	27	57
Wishart Kenneth Leslie	28.11.1908	18.10.1972	1	1934	52	52	0	26.00	–	–	–/–	–	0	
Worrell *Sir* Frank Mortimer Maglinne (*CY 1951*)	1.8.1924	13.3.1967	51	1947–1963	3,860	261	9	49.48	69	7-70	2/0	38.72	43	

NEW ZEALAND (271 players)

	Born	Died	Tests	Test Career	Runs	HS	100s	Avge	Wkts	BB	5/10	Avge	Ct/St	O/T
Adams Andre Ryan	17.7.1975		1	2001	18	11	0	9.00	6	3-44	0/0	17.50	1	42/4
Alabaster John Chaloner	11.7.1930		21	1955–1971	272	34	0	9.71	49	4-46	0/0	38.02	7	
Allcott Cyril Francis Walter	7.10.1896	19.11.1973	6	1929–1931	113	33	0	22.60	6	2-102	0/0	90.16	3	
Allott Geoffrey Ian	24.12.1971		10	1995–1999	27	8*	0	3.37	19	4-74	0/0	58.47	2	31
Anderson Corey James	13.12.1990		13	2013–2015	683	116	1	32.52	16	3-47	0/0	41.18	7	44/25

	Born	Died	Tests	Test Career	Runs	HS	100s	Avge	Wkts	BB	5/10	Avge	Ct/St	O/T
[1] **Anderson** Robert Wickham	2.10.1948		9	1976–1978	423	92	0	23.50	–	–	–/–	–	1	2
[1] **Anderson** William McDougall	8.10.1919	21.12.1979	1	1945	5	4	0	2.50	–	–	–/–	–	1	
Andrews Bryan	4.4.1945		2	1973	22	17	0	22.00	2	2-40	0/0	77.00	1	
Arnel Brent John	3.1.1979		6	2009–2011	45	8*	0	5.62	9	4-95	0/0	62.88	3	
Astle Nathan John	15.9.1971		81	1995–2006	4,702	222	11	37.02	51	3-27	0/0	42.01	70	223/4
Astle Todd Duncan	24.9.1986		2	2012–2016	38	35	0	12.66	1	1-56	0/0	109.00	2	0/2
Badcock Frederick Theodore ("Ted")	9.8.1897	19.9.1982	7	1929–1932	137	64	0	19.57	16	4-80	0/0	38.12	1	
Barber Richard Trevor	3.6.1925	7.8.2015	1	1955	17	12	0	8.50	–	–	–/–	–	1	
Bartlett Gary Alex	3.2.1941		10	1961–1967	263	40	0	15.47	24	6-38	1/0	33.00	8	
Barton Paul Thomas	9.10.1935		7	1961–1962	285	109	1	20.35	–	–	–/–	–	4	
Beard Donald Derek	14.1.1920	15.7.1982	4	1951–1955	101	31	0	20.20	9	3-22	0/0	33.55	2	
Beck John Edward Francis	1.8.1934	23.4.2000	8	1953–1955	394	99	0	26.26	–	–	–/–	–	0	
Bell Matthew David	25.2.1977		18	1998–2007	729	107	2	24.30	–	–	–/–	–	19	7
Bell William	5.9.1931	23.7.2002	2	1953	21	21*	0	–	2	1-54	0/0	117.50	1	
Bennett Hamish Kyle	22.2.1987		1	2010	4	4	0	4.00	0	0-47	0/0	–	0	14
Bilby Grahame Paul	7.5.1941		2	1965	55	28	0	13.75	–	–	–/–	–	3	
Blain Tony Elston	17.2.1962		11	1986–1993	456	78	0	26.82	–	–	–/–	–	19/2	38
Blair Robert William	23.6.1932		19	1952–1963	189	64*	0	6.75	43	4-85	0/0	35.23	5	
Blunt Roger Charles (*CY 1928*)	3.11.1900	22.6.1966	9	1929–1931	330	96	0	27.50	12	3-17	0/0	39.33	5	
Bolton Bruce Alfred	31.5.1935		2	1958	59	33	0	19.66	–	–	–/–	–	1	
Bond Shane Edward	7.6.1975		18	2001–2009	168	41*	0	12.92	87	6-51	5/1	22.09	8	82/20
Boock Stephen Lewis	20.9.1951		30	1977–1988	207	37	0	6.27	74	7-87	4/0	34.64	14	14
Boult Trent Alexander	22.7.1989		49	2011–2016	472	52*	0	14.75	185	6-40	5/1	29.00	22	41/11
[1, 2] **Bracewell** Brendon Paul	14.9.1959		6	1978–1984	24	8	0	2.40	14	3-110	0/0	41.78	1	1
[1] **Bracewell** Douglas Alexander John	28.9.1990		27	2011–2016	568	47	0	13.85	72	6-40	2/0	38.83	10	14/14
[2] **Bracewell** John Garry	15.4.1958		41	1980–1990	1,001	110	1	20.42	102	6-32	4/1	35.81	31	53
[1] **Bradburn** Grant Eric	26.5.1966		7	1990–2000	105	30*	0	13.12	6	3-134	0/0	76.66	6	11
[1] **Bradburn** Wynne Pennell	24.11.1938	25.9.2008	2	1963	62	32	0	15.50	–	–	–/–	–	2	
Brown Vaughan Raymond	3.11.1959		2	1985	51	36*	0	25.50	1	1-17	0/0	176.00	3	3
Brownlie Dean Graham	30.7.1984		14	2011–2013	711	109	1	29.62	1	1-13	0/0	52.00	17	10/5
Burgess Mark Gordon	17.7.1944		50	1967–1980	2,684	119*	5	31.20	6	3-23	0/0	35.33	34	26
Burke Cecil	27.3.1914	4.8.1997	1	1945	4	3	0	2.00	2	2-30	0/0	15.00	0	
Burtt Thomas Browning	22.1.1915	24.5.1988	10	1946–1952	252	42	0	21.00	33	6-162	3/0	35.45	2	
Butler Ian Gareth	24.11.1981		8	2001–2004	76	26	0	9.50	24	6-46	1/0	36.83	4	26/19
Butterfield Leonard Arthur	29.8.1913	5.7.1999	1	1945	0	0	0	0.00	0	0-24	0/0	–	0	
[1] **Cairns** Bernard Lance	10.10.1949		43	1973–1985	928	64	0	16.28	130	7-74	6/1	32.91	30	78

	Born	*Died*	*Tests*	*Test Career*	*Runs*	*HS*	*100s*	*Avge*	*Wkts*	*BB*	*5/10*	*Avge*	*Ct/St*	*O/T*
[1] **Cairns** Christopher Lance (*CY 2000*)	13.6.1970		62	*1989–2004*	3,320	158	5	33.53	218	7-27	13/1	29.40	14	214‡/2
Cameron Francis James MBE	1.6.1932		19	*1961*–1965	116	27*	0	11.60	62	5-34	3/0	29.82	1	
Cave Henry Butler	10.10.1922	15.9.1989	19	1949–1958	229	22*	0	8.80	34	4-21	0/0	43.14	8	
Chapple Murray Ernest	25.7.1930	31.7.1985	14	*1952–1965*	497	76	0	19.11	1	1-24	0/0	84.00	10	
Chatfield Ewen John MBE	3.7.1950		43	*1974–1988*	180	21*	0	8.57	123	6-73	3/1	32.17	7	114
Cleverley Donald Charles	23.12.1909	16.2.2004	2	*1931–1945*	19	10*	0	19.00	0	0-51	0/0	–	0	
Collinge Richard Owen	2.4.1946		35	*1964*–1978	533	68*	0	14.40	116	6-63	3/0	29.25	10	15
Colquhoun Ian Alexander	8.6.1924	26.2.2005	2	*1954*	1	1*	0	0.50	–	–	–/–	–	4	
Coney Jeremy Vernon MBE (*CY 1984*)	21.6.1952		52	*1973–1986*	2,668	174*	3	37.57	27	3-28	0/0	35.77	64	88
Congdon Bevan Ernest OBE (*CY 1974*)	11.2.1938		61	*1964*–1978	3,448	176	7	32.22	59	5-65	1/0	36.50	44	11
Cowie John OBE	30.3.1912	3.6.1994	9	1937–1949	90	45	0	10.00	45	6-40	4/1	21.53	3	
Craig Mark Donald	23.3.1987		15	2014–*2016*	589	67	0	36.81	50	7-94	1/1	46.52	14	
Cresswell George Fenwick	22.3.1915	10.1.1966	3	1949–*1950*	14	12*	0	7.00	13	6-168	1/0	22.46	0	
Cromb Ian Burns	25.6.1905	6.3.1984	5	1931–*1931*	123	51*	0	20.50	8	3-113	0/0	55.25	1	
[2] **Crowe** Jeffrey John	14.9.1958		39	*1982–1989*	1,601	128	3	26.24	0	0-0	0/0	–	41	75
[2] **Crowe** Martin David MBE (*CY 1985*)	22.9.1962	3.3.2016	77	*1981–1995*	5,444	299	17	45.36	14	2-25	0/0	48.28	71	143
Cumming Craig Derek	31.8.1975		11	*2004–2007*	441	74	0	25.94	–	–	–/–	–	3	13
Cunis Robert Smith	5.1.1941	9.8.2008	20	*1963–1971*	295	51	0	12.82	51	6-76	1/0	37.00	1	
D'Arcy John William	23.4.1936		5	1958	136	33	0	13.60	–	–	–/–	–	0	
Davis Heath Te-Ihi-O-Te-Rangi	30.11.1971		5	1994–*1997*	20	8*	0	6.66	17	5-63	1/0	29.35	4	11
de Grandhomme Colin	22.7.1986		4	*2016*	145	37	0	29.00	10	6-41	1/0	26.00	5	4/4
de Groen Richard Paul	5.8.1962		5	*1993–1994*	45	26	0	7.50	11	3-40	0/0	45.90	0	12
Dempster Charles Stewart (*CY 1932*)	15.11.1903	14.2.1974	10	*1929–1932*	723	136	2	65.72	0	0-10	0/0	–	2	
Dempster Eric William MBE	25.1.1925	15.8.2011	5	*1952–1953*	106	47	0	17.66	2	1-24	0/0	109.50	1	
Dick Arthur Edward	10.10.1936		17	*1961*–1965	370	50*	0	14.23	–	–	–/–	–	47/4	
Dickinson George Ritchie	11.3.1903	17.3.1978	3	*1929–1931*	31	11	0	6.20	8	3-66	0/0	30.62	3	
Donnelly Martin Paterson (*CY 1948*)	17.10.1917	22.10.1999	7	1937–1949	582	206	1	52.90	0	0-20	0/0	–	7	
Doull Simon Blair	6.8.1969		32	*1992–1999*	570	46	0	14.61	98	7-65	6/0	29.30	16	42
Dowling Graham Thorne OBE	4.3.1937		39	*1961–1971*	2,306	239	3	31.16	1	1-19	0/0	19.00	23	
Drum Christopher James	10.7.1974		5	*2000–2001*	10	4	0	3.33	16	3-36	0/0	30.12	4	5
Dunning John Angus	6.2.1903	24.6.1971	4	*1932–1937*	38	19	0	7.60	5	2-35	0/0	98.60	2	
Edgar Bruce Adrian	23.11.1956		39	1978–1986	1,958	161	3	30.59	0	0-3	0/0	–	14	64
Edwards Graham Neil ("Jock")	27.5.1955		8	*1976–1980*	377	55	0	25.13	–	–	–/–	–	7	6
Elliott Grant David	21.3.1979		5	*2007–2009*	86	25	0	10.75	4	2-8	0/0	35.00	2	83/16
Emery Raymond William George	28.3.1915	18.12.1982	2	*1951*	46	28	0	11.50	2	2-52	0/0	26.00	0	
Fisher Frederick Eric	28.7.1924	19.6.1996	1	*1952*	23	14	0	11.50	1	1-78	0/0	78.00	0	

	Born	*Died*	*Tests*	*Test Career*	*Runs*	*HS*	*100s*	*Avge*	*Wkts*	*BB*	*5/10*	*Avge*	*Ct/St*	*O/T*
Fleming Stephen Paul	1.4.1973		111	*1993–2007*	7,172	274*	9	40.06	–	–	–/–	–	171	279‡/5
Flynn Daniel Raymond	16.4.1985		24	2008–*2012*	1,038	95	0	25.95	0	0-0	0/0	–	10	20/5
Foley Henry	28.1.1906	16.10.1948	1	*1929*	4	2	0	2.00	–	–	–/–	–	0	
Franklin James Edward Charles	7.11.1980		31	*2000–2012*	808	122*	1	20.71	82	6-119	3/0	33.97	12	110/38
Franklin Trevor John	15.3.1962		21	1983–*1990*	828	101	1	23.00	–	–	–/–	–	8	3
Freeman Douglas Linford	8.9.1914	31.5.1994	2	*1932*	2	1	0	1.00	1	1-91	0/0	169.00	0	
Fulton Peter Gordon	1.2.1979		23	*2005*–2014	967	136	2	25.44	–	–	–/–	–	25	49/12
Gallichan Norman	3.6.1906	25.3.1969	1	1937	32	30	0	16.00	3	3-99	0/0	37.66	0	
Gedye Sidney Graham	2.5.1929	10.8.2014	4	*1963–1964*	193	55	0	24.12	–	–	–/–	–	0	
Germon Lee Kenneth	4.11.1968		12	*1995–1996*	382	55	0	21.22	–	–	–/–	–	27/2	37
Gillespie Mark Raymond	17.10.1979		5	*2007–2011*	76	27	0	10.85	22	6-113	3/0	28.68	1	32/11
Gillespie Stuart Ross	2.3.1957		1	*1985*	28	28	0	28.00	1	1-79	0/0	79.00	0	19
Gray Evan John	18.11.1954		10	1983–*1988*	248	50	0	15.50	17	3-73	0/0	52.11	6	10
Greatbatch Mark John	11.12.1963		41	*1987–1996*	2,021	146*	3	30.62	0	0-0	0/0	–	27	84
Guillen Simpson Clairmonte ("Sammy")	24.9.1924	2.3.2013	3†	*1955*	98	41	0	16.33	–	–	–/–	–	4/1	
Guptill Martin James	30.9.1986		47	*2008–2016*	2,586	189	3	29.38	8	3-11	0/0	37.25	50	140/61
Guy John William	29.8.1934		12	*1955–1961*	440	102	1	20.95	–	–	–/–	–	2	
[1,2] **Hadlee** Dayle Robert	6.1.1948		26	1969–*1977*	530	56	0	14.32	71	4-30	0/0	33.64	8	11
[1,2] **Hadlee** *Sir* Richard John (*CY 1982*)	3.7.1951		86	*1972*–1990	3,124	151*	2	27.16	431	9-52	36/9	22.29	39	115
[1] **Hadlee** Walter Arnold CBE	4.6.1915	29.9.2006	11	1937–*1950*	543	116	1	30.16	–	–	–/–	–	6	
Harford Noel Sherwin	30.8.1930	30.3.1981	8	*1955*–1958	229	93	0	15.26	–	–	–/–	–	0	
Harford Roy Ivan	30.5.1936		3	*1967*	7	6	0	2.33	–	–	–/–	–	11	
[1] **Harris** Chris Zinzan	20.11.1969		23	*1992*–2002	777	71	0	20.44	16	2-16	0/0	73.12	14	250
[1] **Harris** Parke Gerald Zinzan	18.7.1927	1.12.1991	9	*1955–1964*	378	101	1	22.23	0	0-14	0/0	–	6	
Harris Roger Meredith	27.7.1933		2	*1958*	31	13	0	10.33	–	–	–/–	–	0	
[2] **Hart** Matthew Norman	16.5.1972		14	*1993–1995*	353	45	0	17.65	29	5-77	1/0	49.58	9	13
[2] **Hart** Robert Garry	2.12.1974		11	2002–*2003*	260	57*	0	16.25	–	–	–/–	–	29/1	2
Hartland Blair Robert	22.10.1966		9	*1991*–1994	303	52	0	16.83	–	–	–/–	–	5	16
Haslam Mark James	26.9.1972		4	*1992–1995*	4	3	0	4.00	2	1-33	0/0	122.50	2	1
Hastings Brian Frederick	23.3.1940		31	*1968–1975*	1,510	117*	4	30.20	0	0-3	0/0	–	23	11
Hayes John Arthur	11.1.1927	25.12.2007	15	*1950*–1958	73	19	0	4.86	30	4-36	0/0	40.56	3	
Henderson Matthew	2.8.1895	17.6.1970	1	*1929*	8	6	0	8.00	2	2-38	0/0	32.00	1	
Henry Matthew James	14.12.1991		7	2015–*2016*	200	66	0	22.22	17	4-93	0/0	56.11	4	30/5
Hopkins Gareth James	24.11.1976		4	2008–*2010*	71	15	0	11.83	–	–	–/–	–	9	25/10
[2] **Horne** Matthew Jeffery	5.12.1970		35	*1996*–2003	1,788	157	4	28.38	0	0-4	0/0	–	17	50
[2] **Horne** Philip Andrew	21.1.1960		4	*1986–1990*	71	27	0	10.14	–	–	–/–	–	3	4

	Born	Died	Tests	Test Career	Runs	HS	100s	Avge	Wkts	BB	5/10	Avge	Ct/St	O/T
Hough Kenneth William	24.10.1928	20.9.2009	2	1958	62	31*	0	62.00	6	3-79	0/0	29.16	1	
How Jamie Michael	19.5.1981		19	2005–2008	772	92	0	22.70	0	0-0	0/0	–	18	41/5
[2] **Howarth** Geoffrey Philip OBE	29.3.1951		47	1974–1984	2,531	147	6	32.44	3	1-13	0/0	90.33	29	70
[2] **Howarth** Hedley John	25.12.1943	7.11.2008	30	1969–1976	291	61	0	12.12	86	5-34	2/0	36.95	33	9
Ingram Peter John	25.10.1978		2	2009	61	42	0	15.25	–	–	–/–	–	0	8/3
James Kenneth Cecil	12.3.1904	21.8.1976	11	1929–1932	52	14	0	4.72	–	–	–/–	–	11/5	
Jarvis Terrence Wayne	29.7.1944		13	1964–1972	625	182	1	29.76	0	0-0	0/0	–	3	
Jones Andrew Howard	9.5.1959		39	1986–1994	2,922	186	7	44.27	1	1-40	0/0	194.00	25	87
Jones Richard Andrew	22.10.1973		1	2003	23	16	0	11.50	–	–	–/–	–	0	5
Kennedy Robert John	3.6.1972		4	1995	28	22	0	7.00	6	3-28	0/0	63.33	2	7
Kerr John Lambert	28.12.1910	27.5.2007	7	1931–1937	212	59	0	19.27	–	–	–/–	–	4	
Kuggeleijn Christopher Mary	10.5.1956		2	1988	7	7	0	1.75	1	1-50	0/0	67.00	1	16
Larsen Gavin Rolf	27.9.1962		8	1994–1995	127	26*	0	14.11	24	3-57	0/0	28.70	5	121
[1] **Latham** Rodney Terry	12.6.1961		4	1991–1992	219	119	1	31.28	0	0-6	0/0	–	5	33
[1] **Latham** Thomas William Maxwell	2.4.1992		29	2013–2016	2,140	177	6	40.37	–	–	–/–	–	30	49/12
Lees Warren Kenneth MBE	19.3.1952		21	1976–1983	778	152	1	23.57	0	0-4	0/0	–	52/7	31
Leggat Ian Bruce	7.6.1930		1	1953	0	0	0	0.00	0	0-6	0/0	–	2	
Leggat John Gordon	27.5.1926	9.3.1973	9	1951–1955	351	61	0	21.93	–	–	–/–	–	0	
Lissette Allen Fisher	6.11.1919	24.1.1973	2	1955	2	1*	0	1.00	3	2-73	0/0	41.33	1	
Loveridge Greg Riaka	15.1.1975		1	1995	4	4*	0	–	–	–	–/–	–	0	
Lowry Thomas Coleman	17.2.1898	20.7.1976	7	1929–1931	223	80	0	27.87	0	0-0	0/0	–	8	
McCullum Brendon Barrie (*CY 2016*)	27.9.1981		101	2003–2015	6,453	302	12	38.64	1	1-1	0/0	88.00	198/11	260/71
McEwan Paul Ernest	19.12.1953		4	1979–1984	96	40*	0	16.00	0	0-6	0/0	–	5	17
MacGibbon Anthony Roy	28.8.1924	6.4.2010	26	1950–1958	814	66	0	19.85	70	5-64	1/0	30.85	13	
McGirr Herbert Mendelson	5.11.1891	14.4.1964	2	1929	51	51	0	51.00	1	1-65	0/0	115.00	0	
McGregor Spencer Noel	18.12.1931	21.11.2007	25	1954–1964	892	111	1	19.82	–	–	–/–	–	9	
McIntosh Timothy Gavin	4.12.1979		17	2008–2010	854	136	2	27.54	–	–	–/–	–	10	
McKay Andrew John	17.4.1980		1	2010	25	20*	0	25.00	1	1-120	0/0	120.00	0	19/2
McLeod Edwin George	14.10.1900	14.9.1989	1	1929	18	16	0	18.00	0	0-5	0/0	–	0	
McMahon Trevor George	8.11.1929		5	1955	7	4*	0	2.33	–	–	–/–	–	7/1	
McMillan Craig Douglas	13.9.1976		55	1997–2004	3,116	142	6	38.46	28	3-48	0/0	44.89	22	197/8
McRae Donald Alexander Noel	25.12.1912	10.8.1986	1	1945	8	8	0	4.00	0	0-44	0/0	–	0	
[2] **Marshall** Hamish John Hamilton	15.2.1979		13	2000–2005	652	160	2	38.35	0	0-4	0/0	–	1	66/3
[2] **Marshall** James Andrew Hamilton	15.2.1979		7	2004–2008	218	52	0	19.81	–	–	–/–	–	5	10/3
Martin Bruce Philip	25.4.1980		5	2012–2013	74	41	0	14.80	12	4-43	0/0	53.83	0	
Martin Christopher Stewart	10.12.1974		71	2000–2012	123	12*	0	2.36	233	6-26	10/1	33.81	14	20/6

	Born	Died	Tests	Test Career	Runs	HS	100s	Avge	Wkts	BB	5/10	Avge	Ct/St	O/T
Mason Michael James	27.8.1974		1	*2003*	3	3	0	1.50	0	0-32	0/0	–	0	26/3
Matheson Alexander Malcolm	27.2.1906	31.12.1985	2	*1929*–1931	7	7	0	7.00	2	2-7	0/0	68.00	2	
Meale Trevor	11.11.1928	21.5.2010	2	1958	21	10	0	5.25	–	–	–/–	–	0	
Merritt William Edward	18.8.1908	9.6.1977	6	*1929*–1931	73	19	0	10.42	12	4-104	0/0	51.41	2	
Meuli Edgar Milton	20.2.1926	15.4.2007	1	*1952*	38	23	0	19.00	–	–	–/–	–	0	
Milburn Barry Douglas	24.11.1943		3	*1968*	8	4*	0	8.00	–	–	–/–	–	6/2	
Miller Lawrence Somerville Martin	31.3.1923	17.12.1996	13	*1952*–1958	346	47	0	13.84	0	0-1	0/0	–	1	
Mills John Ernest	3.9.1905	11.12.1972	7	*1929–1932*	241	117	1	26.77	–	–	–/–	–	1	
Mills Kyle David	15.3.1979		19	2004–*2008*	289	57	0	11.56	44	4-16	0/0	33.02	4	170/42
Moir Alexander McKenzie	17.7.1919	17.6.2000	17	*1950–1958*	327	41*	0	14.86	28	6-155	2/0	50.64	2	
Moloney Denis Andrew Robert ("Sonny")	11.8.1910	15.7.1942	3	1937	156	64	0	26.00	0	0-9	0/0	–	3	
Mooney Francis Leonard Hugh	26.5.1921	8.3.2004	14	1949–*1953*	343	46	0	17.15	0	0-0	0/0	–	22/8	
Morgan Ross Winston	12.2.1941		20	*1964–1971*	734	97	0	22.24	5	1-16	0/0	121.80	12	
Morrison Bruce Donald	17.12.1933		1	*1962*	10	10	0	5.00	2	2-129	0/0	64.50	1	
Morrison Daniel Kyle	3.2.1966		48	*1987–1996*	379	42	0	8.42	160	7-89	10/0	34.68	14	96
Morrison John Francis MacLean	27.8.1947		17	*1973–1981*	656	117	1	22.62	2	2-52	0/0	35.50	9	18
Motz Richard Charles (*CY 1966*)	12.1.1940	29.4.2007	32	*1961*–1969	612	60	0	11.54	100	6-63	5/0	31.48	9	
Munro Colin	11.3.1987		1	*2012*	15	15	0	7.50	2	2-40	0/0	20.00	0	18/28
Murray Bruce Alexander Grenfell	18.9.1940		13	*1967–1970*	598	90	0	23.92	1	1-0	0/0	0.00	21	
Murray Darrin James	4.9.1967		8	*1994*	303	52	0	20.20	–	–	–/–	–	6	1
Nash Dion Joseph	20.11.1971		32	*1992–2001*	729	89*	0	23.51	93	6-27	3/1	28.48	13	81
Neesham James Douglas Sheehan	17.9.1990		10	*2013–2016*	683	137*	2	37.94	12	3-42	0/0	46.00	7	28/13
Newman *Sir* Jack	3.7.1902	23.9.1996	3	*1931–1932*	33	19	0	8.25	2	2-76	0/0	127.00	0	
Nicholls Henry Michael	15.11.1991		11	*2015–2016*	470	98	0	31.33	–	–	–/–	–	6	11/1
Nicol Robert James	28.5.1983		2	*2011*	28	19	0	7.00	0	0-0	0/0	–	2	22/21
O'Brien Iain Edward	10.7.1976		22	*2004–2009*	219	31	0	7.55	73	6-75	1/0	33.27	7	10/4
O'Connor Shayne Barry	15.11.1973		19	*1997–2001*	103	20	0	5.72	53	5-51	1/0	32.52	6	38
Oram Jacob David Philip	28.7.1978		33	*2002*–2009	1,780	133	5	36.32	60	4-41	0/0	33.05	15	160/36
O'Sullivan David Robert	16.11.1944		11	*1972–1976*	158	23*	0	9.29	18	5-148	1/0	67.83	2	3
Overton Guy William Fitzroy	8.6.1919	7.9.1993	3	*1953*	8	3*	0	1.60	9	3-65	0/0	28.66	1	
Owens Michael Barry	11.11.1969		8	*1992*–1994	16	8*	0	2.66	17	4-99	0/0	34.41	3	1
Page Milford Laurenson ("Curly")	8.5.1902	13.2.1987	14	*1929*–1937	492	104	1	24.60	5	2-21	0/0	46.20	6	
Papps Michael Hugh William	2.7.1979		8	*2003–2007*	246	86	0	16.40	–	–	–/–	–	11	6
[2] **Parker** John Morton	21.2.1951		36	*1972–1980*	1,498	121	3	24.55	1	1-24	0/0	24.00	30	24
[2] **Parker** Norman Murray	28.8.1948		3	*1976*	89	40	0	14.83	–	–	–/–	–	2	1
Parore Adam Craig	23.1.1971		78	1990–*2001*	2,865	110	2	26.28	–	–	–/–	–	197/7	179

	Born	Died	Tests	Test Career	Runs	HS	100s	Avge	Wkts	BB	5/10	Avge	Ct/St	O/T
Patel Dipak Narshibhai	25.10.1958		37	*1986–1996*	1,200	99	0	20.68	75	6-50	3/0	42.05	15	75
Patel Jeetan Shashi (*CY 2015*)	7.5.1980		21	*2005–2016*	343	47	0	12.70	58	5-110	1/0	48.48	12	40/11
Petherick Peter James	25.9.1942	7.6.2015	6	*1976*	34	13	0	4.85	16	3-90	0/0	42.81	4	
Petrie Eric Charlton	22.5.1927	14.8.2004	14	*1955–1965*	258	55	0	12.90	–	–	–/–	–	25	
Playle William Rodger	1.12.1938		8	1958–*1962*	151	65	0	10.06	–	–	–/–	–	4	
Pocock Blair Andrew	18.6.1971		15	*1993–1997*	665	85	0	22.93	0	0-10	0/0	–	5	
Pollard Victor	7.9.1945		32	*1964*–1973	1,266	116	2	24.34	40	3-3	0/0	46.32	19	3
Poore Matt Beresford	1.6.1930		14	*1952–1955*	355	45	0	15.43	9	2-28	0/0	40.77	1	
Priest Mark Wellings	12.8.1961		3	1990–*1997*	56	26	0	14.00	3	2-42	0/0	52.66	0	18
Pringle Christopher	26.1.1968		14	*1990–1994*	175	30	0	10.29	30	7-52	1/1	46.30	3	64
Puna Narotam ("Tom")	28.10.1929	7.6.1996	3	*1965*	31	18*	0	15.50	4	2-40	0/0	60.00	1	
Rabone Geoffrey Osborne	6.11.1921	19.1.2006	12	1949–*1954*	562	107	1	31.22	16	6-68	1/0	39.68	5	
Raval Jeet Ashokbhai	22.5.1988		4	*2016*	237	55	0	33.85	–	–	–/–	–	9	
[1] **Redmond** Aaron James	23.9.1979		8	2008–*2013*	325	83	0	21.66	3	2-47	0/0	26.66	5	6/7
[1] **Redmond** Rodney Ernest	29.12.1944		1	*1972*	163	107	1	81.50	–	–	–/–	–	0	2
Reid John Fulton	3.3.1956		19	*1978–1985*	1,296	180	6	46.28	0	0-0	0/0	–	9	25
Reid John Richard OBE (*CY 1959*)	3.6.1928		58	1949–1965	3,428	142	6	33.28	85	6-60	1/0	33.35	43/1	
Richardson Mark Hunter	11.6.1971		38	*2000–2004*	2,776	145	4	44.77	1	1-16	0/0	21.00	26	4
Roberts Albert William	20.8.1909	13.5.1978	5	*1929*–1937	248	66*	0	27.55	7	4-101	0/0	29.85	4	
Roberts Andrew Duncan Glenn	6.5.1947	26.10.1989	7	*1975–1976*	254	84*	0	23.09	4	1-12	0/0	45.50	4	1
Robertson Gary Keith	15.7.1960		1	*1985*	12	12	0	12.00	1	1-91	0/0	91.00	0	10
Ronchi Luke	23.4.1981		4	2015–*2016*	319	88	0	39.87	–	–	–/–	–	5	72‡/26‡
Rowe Charles Gordon	30.6.1915	9.6.1995	1	*1945*	0	0	0	0.00	–	–	–/–	–	1	
[1] **Rutherford** Hamish Duncan	27.4.1989		16	*2012–2014*	755	171	1	26.96	0	0-2	0/0	–	11	4/7
[1] **Rutherford** Kenneth Robert	26.10.1965		56	*1984–1994*	2,465	107*	3	27.08	1	1-38	0/0	161.00	32	121
Ryder Jesse Daniel	6.8.1984		18	*2008–2011*	1,269	201	3	40.93	5	2-7	0/0	56.00	12	48/22
Santner Mitchell Josef	5.2.1992		13	*2015–2016*	423	73	0	26.43	29	3-60	0/0	38.68	6	25/10
Scott Roy Hamilton	6.3.1917	5.8.2005	1	*1946*	18	18	0	18.00	1	1-74	0/0	74.00	0	
Scott Verdun John	31.7.1916	2.8.1980	10	*1945–1951*	458	84	0	28.62	0	0-5	0/0	–	7	
Sewell David Graham	20.10.1977		1	*1997*	1	1*	0	–	0	0-9	0/0	–	0	
Shrimpton Michael John Froud	23.6.1940	13.6.2015	10	*1962–1973*	265	46	0	13.94	5	3-35	0/0	31.60	2	
Sinclair Barry Whitley	23.10.1936		21	*1962–1967*	1,148	138	3	29.43	2	2-32	0/0	16.00	8	
Sinclair Ian McKay	1.6.1933		2	*1955*	25	18*	0	8.33	1	1-79	0/0	120.00	1	
Sinclair Mathew Stuart	9.11.1975		33	*1999–2009*	1,635	214	3	32.05	0	0-1	0/0	–	31	54/2
Smith Frank Brunton	13.3.1922	6.7.1997	4	*1946–1951*	237	96	0	47.40	–	–	–/–	–	1	
Smith Horace Dennis	8.1.1913	25.1.1986	1	*1932*	4	4	0	4.00	1	1-113	0/0	113.00	0	

	Born	Died	Tests	Test Career	Runs	HS	100s	Avge	Wkts	BB	5/10	Avge	Ct/St	O/T
Smith Ian David Stockley MBE	28.2.1957		63	*1980–1991*	1,815	173	2	25.56	0	0-5	0/0	–	168/8	98
Snedden Colin Alexander	7.1.1918	23.4.2011	1	*1946*	–	–	–	–	0	0-46	0/0	–	0	
Snedden Martin Colin	23.11.1958		25	*1980*–1990	327	33*	0	14.86	58	5-68	1/0	37.91	7	93
Sodhi Inderbir Singh ("Ish")	31.10.1992		14	*2013–2016*	365	63	0	22.81	38	4-60	0/0	46.68	8	13/10
Southee Timothy Grant	11.12.1988		56	*2007–2016*	1,300	77*	0	16.66	201	7-64	6/1	31.45	34	109/38
Sparling John Trevor	24.7.1938		11	1958–*1963*	229	50	0	12.72	5	1-9	0/0	65.40	4	
Spearman Craig Murray	4.7.1972		19	*1995–2000*	922	112	1	26.34	–	–	–/–	–	21	51
Stead Gary Raymond	9.1.1972		5	*1998–1999*	278	78	0	34.75	0	0-1	0/0	–	2	
Stirling Derek Alexander	5.10.1961		6	*1984*–1986	108	26	0	15.42	13	4-88	0/0	46.23	1	6
Styris Scott Bernard	10.7.1975		29	2002–*2007*	1,586	170	5	36.04	20	3-28	0/0	50.75	23	188/31
Su'a Murphy Logo	7.11.1966		13	*1991–1994*	165	44	0	12.69	36	5-73	2/0	38.25	8	12
Sutcliffe Bert MBE (*CY 1950*)	17.11.1923	20.4.2001	42	*1946*–1965	2,727	230*	5	40.10	4	2-38	0/0	86.00	20	
Taylor Bruce Richard	12.7.1943		30	*1964*–1973	898	124	2	20.40	111	7-74	4/0	26.60	10	2
Taylor Donald Dougald	2.3.1923	5.12.1980	3	*1946–1955*	159	77	0	31.80	–	–	–/–	–	2	
Taylor Luteru Ross Poutoa Lote	8.3.1984		80	*2007–2016*	6,015	290	16	46.99	2	2-4	0/0	24.00	122	176/73
Thomson Keith	26.2.1941		2	*1967*	94	69	0	31.33	1	1-9	0/0	9.00	0	
Thomson Shane Alexander	27.1.1969		19	*1989–1995*	958	120*	1	30.90	19	3-63	0/0	50.15	7	56
Tindill Eric William Thomas	18.12.1910	1.8.2010	5	1937–*1946*	73	37*	0	9.12	–	–	–/–	–	6/1	
Troup Gary Bertram	3.10.1952		15	*1976–1985*	55	13*	0	4.58	39	6-95	1/1	37.28	2	22
Truscott Peter Bennetts	14.8.1941		1	*1964*	29	26	0	14.50	–	–	–/–	–	1	
Tuffey Daryl Raymond	11.6.1978		26	*1999–2009*	427	80*	0	16.42	77	6-54	2/0	31.75	15	94/3
Turner Glenn Maitland (*CY 1971*)	26.5.1947		41	*1968–1982*	2,991	259	7	44.64	0	0-5	0/0	–	42	41
Twose Roger Graham	17.4.1968		16	*1995*–1999	628	94	0	25.12	3	2-36	0/0	43.33	5	87
Vance Robert Howard	31.3.1955		4	*1987–1989*	207	68	0	29.57	–	–	–/–	–	0	8
van Wyk Cornelius Francois Kruger	7.2.1980		9	*2011–2012*	341	71	0	21.31	–	–	–/–	–	23/1	
Vaughan Justin Thomas Caldwell	30.8.1967		6	*1992–1996*	201	44	0	18.27	11	4-27	0/0	40.90	4	18
Vettori Daniel Luca	27.1.1979		112§	*1996–2014*	4,523	140	6	30.15	361	7-87	20/3	34.15	58	291‡/34
Vincent Lou	11.11.1978		23	*2001–2007*	1,332	224	3	34.15	0	0-2	0/0	–	19	102/9
[1] **Vivian** Graham Ellery	28.2.1946		5	*1964–1971*	110	43	0	18.33	1	1-14	0/0	107.00	3	1
[1] **Vivian** Henry Gifford	4.11.1912	12.8.1983	7	1931–1937	421	100	1	42.10	17	4-58	0/0	37.23	4	
Wadsworth Kenneth John	30.11.1946	19.8.1976	33	1969–*1975*	1,010	80	0	21.48	–	–	–/–	–	92/4	13
Wagner Neil	13.3.1986		29	2012–*2016*	352	37	0	12.57	118	6-41	4/0	28.58	5	
Walker Brooke Graeme Keith	25.3.1977		5	*2000*–2002	118	27*	0	19.66	5	2-92	0/0	79.80	0	11
Wallace Walter Mervyn	19.12.1916	21.3.2008	13	1937–*1952*	439	66	0	20.90	0	0-5	0/0	–	5	
Walmsley Kerry Peter	23.8.1973		3	*1994–2000*	13	5	0	2.60	9	3-70	0/0	43.44	0	2

§ *Vettori's figures exclude eight runs and one wicket for the ICC World XI v Australia in the Super Series Test in 2005-06.*

	Born	Died	Tests	Test Career	Runs	HS	100s	Avge	Wkts	BB	5/10	Avge	Ct/St	O/T
Ward John Thomas	11.3.1937		8	*1963–1967*	75	35*	0	12.50	–	–	–/–	–	16/1	
Watling Bradley-John	9.7.1985		49	*2009–2016*	2,565	142*	6	38.28	–	–	–/–	–	161/6	27/5
Watson William	31.8.1965		15	1986–*1993*	60	11	0	5.00	40	6-78	1/0	34.67	4	61
Watt Leslie	17.9.1924	15.11.1996	1	*1954*	2	2	0	1.00	–	–	–/–	–	0	
Webb Murray George	22.6.1947		3	*1970–1973*	12	12	0	6.00	4	2-114	0/0	117.75	0	
Webb Peter Neil	14.7.1957		2	*1979*	11	5	0	3.66	–	–	–/–	–	2	5
Weir Gordon Lindsay	2.6.1908	31.10.2003	11	*1929*–1937	416	74*	0	29.71	7	3-38	0/0	29.85	3	
White David John	26.6.1961		2	*1990*	31	18	0	7.75	0	0-5	0/0	–	0	3
Whitelaw Paul Erskine	10.2.1910	28.8.1988	2	*1932*	64	30	0	32.00	–	–	–/–	–	0	
Williamson Kane Stuart (*CY 2016*)	8.8.1990		58	*2010–2016*	4,807	242*	15	50.07	29	4-44	0/0	38.93	51	104/35
Wiseman Paul John	4.5.1970		25	*1997–2004*	366	36	0	14.07	61	5-82	2/0	47.59	11	15
Wright John Geoffrey MBE	5.7.1954		82	*1977–1992*	5,334	185	12	37.82	0	0-1	0/0	–	38	149
Young Bryan Andrew	3.11.1964		35	*1993–1998*	2,034	267*	2	31.78	–	–	–/–	–	54	74
Young Reece Alan	15.9.1979		5	*2010–2011*	169	57	0	24.14	–	–	–/–	–	8	
Yuile Bryan William	29.10.1941		17	*1962–1969*	481	64	0	17.81	34	4-43	0/0	35.67	12	

INDIA (287 players)

	Born	Died	Tests	Test Career	Runs	HS	100s	Avge	Wkts	BB	5/10	Avge	Ct/St	O/T
Aaron Varun Raymond	29.10.1989		9	*2011–2015*	35	9	0	3.88	18	3-97	0/0	52.61	1	9
Abid Ali Syed	9.9.1941		29	*1967–1974*	1,018	81	0	20.36	47	6-55	1/0	42.12	32	5
Adhikari Hemchandra Ramachandra	31.7.1919	25.10.2003	21	*1947–1958*	872	114*	1	31.14	3	3-68	0/0	27.33	8	
Agarkar Ajit Bhalchandra	4.12.1977		26	*1998–2005*	571	109*	1	16.79	58	6-41	1/0	47.32	6	191/4
[2] **Amar Singh** Ladha	4.12.1910	21.5.1940	7	1932–1936	292	51	0	22.46	28	7-86	2/0	30.64	3	
[1,2] **Amarnath** Mohinder (*CY 1984*)	24.9.1950		69	*1969–1987*	4,378	138	11	42.50	32	4-63	0/0	55.68	47	85
[1] **Amarnath** Nanik ("Lala")	11.9.1911	5.8.2000	24	*1933–1952*	878	118	1	24.38	45	5-96	2/0	32.91	13	
[1,2] **Amarnath** Surinder	30.12.1948		10	*1975–1978*	550	124	1	30.55	1	1-5	0/0	5.00	4	3
Amir Elahi	1.9.1908	28.12.1980	1†	*1947*	17	13	0	8.50	–	–	–/–	–	0	
Amre Pravin Kalyan	14.8.1968		11	*1992–1993*	425	103	1	42.50	–	–	–/–	–	9	37
Ankola Salil Ashok	1.3.1968		1	*1989*	6	6	0	6.00	2	1-35	0/0	64.00	0	20
[2] **Apte** Arvindrao Laxmanrao	24.10.1934	5.8.2014	1	1959	15	8	0	7.50	–	–	–/–	–	0	
[2] **Apte** Madhavrao Laxmanrao	5.10.1932		7	*1952*	542	163*	1	49.27	0	0-3	0/0	–	2	
Arshad Ayub	2.8.1958		13	*1987–1989*	257	57	0	17.13	41	5-50	3/0	35.07	2	32
Arun Bharathi	14.12.1962		2	*1986*	4	2*	0	4.00	4	3-76	0/0	29.00	2	4
Arun Lal	1.8.1955		16	*1982–1988*	729	93	0	26.03	0	0-0	0/0	–	13	13

	Born	Died	Tests	Test Career	Runs	HS	100s	Avge	Wkts	BB	5/10	Avge	Ct/St	O/T
Ashwin Ravichandran	17.9.1986		44	2011–2016	1,816	124	4	34.92	248	7-59	24/7	24.96	18	102/45
Azad Kirtivardhan	2.1.1959		7	1980–1983	135	24	0	11.25	3	2-84	0/0	124.33	3	25
Azharuddin Mohammad (*CY 1991*)	8.2.1963		99	1984–1999	6,215	199	22	45.03	0	0-4	0/0	–	105	334
Badani Hemang Kamal	14.11.1976		4	2001	94	38	0	15.66	0	0-17	0/0	–	6	40
Badrinath Subramaniam	30.8.1980		2	2009	63	56	0	21.00	–	–	–/–	–	2	7/1
Bahutule Sairaj Vasant	6.1.1973		2	2000–2001	39	21*	0	13.00	3	1-32	0/0	67.66	1	8
Baig Abbas Ali	19.3.1939		10	1959–1966	428	112	1	23.77	0	0-2	0/0	–	6	
Balaji Lakshmipathy	27.9.1981		8	2003–2004	51	31	0	5.66	27	5-76	1/0	37.18	1	30/5
Banerjee Sarobindu Nath ("Shute")	3.10.1911	14.10.1980	1	1948	13	8	0	6.50	5	4-54	0/0	25.40	0	
Banerjee Subroto Tara	13.2.1969		1	1991	3	3	0	3.00	3	3-47	0/0	15.66	0	6
Banerjee Sudangsu Abinash	1.11.1917	14.9.1992	1	1948	0	0	0	0.00	5	4-120	0/0	36.20	3	
Bangar Sanjay Bapusaheb	11.10.1972		12	2001–2002	470	100*	1	29.37	7	2-23	0/0	49.00	4	15
Baqa Jilani Mohammad	20.7.1911	2.7.1941	1	1936	16	12	0	16.00	0	0-55	0/0	–	0	
Bedi Bishan Singh	25.9.1946		67	1966–1979	656	50*	0	8.98	266	7-98	14/1	28.71	26	10
Bhandari Prakash	27.11.1935		3	1954–1956	77	39	0	19.25	0	0-12	0/0	–	1	
Bharadwaj Raghvendrarao Vijay	15.8.1975		3	1999	28	22	0	9.33	1	1-26	0/0	107.00	3	10
Bhat Adwai Raghuram	16.4.1958		2	1983	6	6	0	3.00	4	2-65	0/0	37.75	0	
Bhuvneshwar Kumar	5.2.1990		16	2012–2016	430	63*	0	22.63	42	6-82	4/0	28.80	5	57/16
[1] **Binny** Roger Michael Humphrey	19.7.1955		27	1979–1986	830	83*	0	23.05	47	6-56	2/0	32.63	11	72
[1] **Binny** Stuart Terence Roger	3.6.1984		6	2014–2015	194	78	0	21.55	3	2-24	0/0	86.00	4	14/3
Borde Chandrakant Gulabrao	21.7.1934		55	1958–1969	3,061	177*	5	35.59	52	5-88	1/0	46.48	37	
Chandrasekhar Bhagwat Subramanya (*CY 1972*)	17.5.1945		58	1963–1979	167	22	0	4.07	242	8-79	16/2	29.74	25	1
Chauhan Chetandra Pratap Singh	21.7.1947		40	1969–1980	2,084	97	0	31.57	2	1-4	0/0	53.00	38	7
Chauhan Rajesh Kumar	19.12.1966		21	1992–1997	98	23	0	7.00	47	4-48	0/0	39.51	12	35
Chawla Piyush Pramod	24.12.1988		3	2005–2012	6	4	0	2.00	7	4-69	0/0	38.57	1	25/7
Chopra Aakash	19.9.1977		10	2003–2004	437	60	0	23.00	–	–	–/–	–	15	
Chopra Nikhil	26.12.1973		1	1999	7	4	0	3.50	0	0-78	0/0	–	0	39
Chowdhury Nirode Ranjan	23.5.1923	14.12.1979	2	1948–1951	3	3*	0	3.00	1	1-130	0/0	205.00	0	
Colah Sorabji Hormasji Munchersha	22.9.1902	11.9.1950	2	1932–1933	69	31	0	17.25	–	–	–/–	–	2	
Contractor Nariman Jamshedji	7.3.1934		31	1955–1961	1,611	108	1	31.58	1	1-9	0/0	80.00	18	
Dahiya Vijay	10.5.1973		2	2000	2	2*	0	–	–	–	–/–	–	6	19
Dani Hemchandra Tukaram	24.5.1933	19.12.1999	1	1952	–	–	–	–	1	1-9	0/0	19.00	1	
Das Shiv Sunder	5.11.1977		23	2000–2001	1,326	110	2	34.89	0	0-7	0/0	–	34	4
Dasgupta Deep	7.6.1977		8	2001	344	100	1	28.66	–	–	–/–	–	13	5
Desai Ramakant Bhikaji	20.6.1939	27.4.1998	28	1958–1967	418	85	0	13.48	74	6-56	2/0	37.31	9	

	Born	Died	Tests	Test Career	Runs	HS	100s	Avge	Wkts	BB	5/10	Avge	Ct/St	O/T
Dhawan Shikhar (*CY 2014*)	5.12.1985		23	*2012–2016*	1,464	187	4	38.52	0	0-0	0/0	–	18	74/22
Dhoni Mahendra Singh	7.7.1981		90	*2005–2014*	4,876	224	6	38.09	0	0-1	0/0	–	256/38	280‡/73
Dighe Sameer Sudhakar	8.10.1968		6	*2000*–2001	141	47	0	15.66	–	–	–/–	–	12/2	23
Dilawar Hussain	19.3.1907	26.8.1967	3	*1933–1936*	254	59	0	42.33	–	–	–/–	–	6/1	
Divecha Ramesh Vithaldas	18.10.1927	11.2.2003	5	*1951–1952*	60	26	0	12.00	11	3-102	0/0	32.81	5	
Doshi Dilip Rasiklal	22.12.1947		33	*1979–1983*	129	20	0	4.60	114	6-102	6/0	30.71	10	15
Dravid Rahul (*CY 2000*)	11.1.1973		163§	1996–*2011*	13,265	270	36	52.63	1	1-18	0/0	39.00	209	340‡/1
Durani Salim Aziz	11.12.1934		29	*1959–1972*	1,202	104	1	25.04	75	6-73	3/1	35.42	14	
Engineer Farokh Maneksha	25.2.1938		46	*1961–1974*	2,611	121	2	31.08	–	–	–/–	–	66/16	5
Gadkari Chandrasekhar Vaman	3.2.1928	11.1.1998	6	*1952–1954*	129	50*	0	21.50	0	0-8	0/0	–	6	
[1] **Gaekwad** Anshuman Dattajirao	23.9.1952		40	*1974–1984*	1,985	201	2	30.07	2	1-4	0/0	93.50	15	15
[1] **Gaekwad** Dattajirao Krishnarao	27.10.1928		11	1952–*1960*	350	52	0	18.42	0	0-4	0/0	–	5	
Gaekwad Hiralal Ghasulal	29.8.1923	2.1.2003	1	*1952*	22	14	0	11.00	0	0-47	0/0	–	0	
Gambhir Gautam	14.10.1981		58	*2004–2016*	4,154	206	9	41.95	0	0-4	0/0	–	38	147/37
Gandhi Devang Jayant	6.9.1971		4	*1999*	204	88	0	34.00	–	–	–/–	–	3	3
Gandotra Ashok	24.11.1948		2	*1969*	54	18	0	13.50	0	0-5	0/0	–	1	
Ganesh Doddanarasiah	30.6.1973		4	*1996*	25	8	0	6.25	5	2-28	0/0	57.40	0	1
Ganguly Sourav Chandidas	8.7.1972		113	1996–*2008*	7,212	239	16	42.17	32	3-28	0/0	52.53	71	308‡
Gavaskar Sunil Manohar (*CY 1980*)	10.7.1949		125	*1970–1986*	10,122	236*	34	51.12	1	1-34	0/0	206.00	108	108
Ghavri Karsan Devjibhai	28.2.1951		39	*1974–1980*	913	86	0	21.23	109	5-33	4/0	33.54	16	19
Ghorpade Jayasinghrao Mansinghrao	2.10.1930	29.3.1978	8	*1952*–1959	229	41	0	15.26	0	0-17	0/0	–	4	
Ghulam Ahmed	4.7.1922	28.10.1998	22	*1948–1958*	192	50	0	8.72	68	7-49	4/1	30.17	11	
Gopalan Morappakam Joysam	6.6.1909	21.12.2003	1	*1933*	18	11*	0	18.00	1	1-39	0/0	39.00	3	
Gopinath Coimbatarao Doraikannu	1.3.1930		8	*1951–1959*	242	50*	0	22.00	1	1-11	0/0	11.00	2	
Guard Ghulam Mustafa	12.12.1925	13.3.1978	2	*1958–1959*	11	7	0	5.50	3	2-69	0/0	60.66	2	
Guha Subrata	31.1.1946	5.11.2003	4	1967–*1969*	17	6	0	3.40	3	2-55	0/0	103.66	2	
Gul Mahomed	15.10.1921	8.5.1992	8†	1946–*1952*	166	34	0	11.06	2	2-21	0/0	12.00	3	
[2] **Gupte** Balkrishna Pandharinath	30.8.1934	5.7.2005	3	*1960–1964*	28	17*	0	28.00	3	1-54	0/0	116.33	0	
[2] **Gupte** Subhashchandra Pandharinath ("Fergie")	11.12.1929	31.5.2002	36	*1951–1961*	183	21	0	6.31	149	9-102	12/1	29.55	14	
Gursharan Singh	8.3.1963		1	*1989*	18	18	0	18.00	–	–	–/–	–	2	1
Hafeez Abdul (see Kardar)														
Hanumant Singh	29.3.1939	29.11.2006	14	*1963–1969*	686	105	1	31.18	0	0-5	0/0	–	11	
Harbhajan Singh	3.7.1980		103	*1997–2015*	2,224	115	2	18.22	417	8-84	25/5	32.46	42	234‡/28
Hardikar Manohar Shankar	8.2.1936	4.2.1995	2	*1958*	56	32*	0	18.66	1	1-9	0/0	55.00	3	
Harvinder Singh	23.12.1977		3	*1997*–2001	6	6	0	2.00	4	2-62	0/0	46.25	0	16

§ *Dravid's figures exclude 23 runs and one catch for the ICC World XI v Australia in the Super Series Test in 2005-06.*

	Born	Died	Tests	Test Career	Runs	HS	100s	Avge	Wkts	BB	5/10	Avge	Ct/St	O/T
Hazare Vijay Samuel	11.3.1915	18.12.2004	30	1946–1952	2,192	164*	7	47.65	20	4-29	0/0	61.00	11	
Hindlekar Dattaram Dharmaji	1.1.1909	30.3.1949	4	1936–1946	71	26	0	14.20	–	–	–/–	–	3	
Hirwani Narendra Deepchand	18.10.1968		17	1987–1996	54	17	0	5.40	66	8-61	4/1	30.10	5	18
Ibrahim Khanmohammad Cassumbhoy	26.1.1919	12.11.2007	4	1948	169	85	0	21.12	–	–	–/–	–	0	
Indrajitsinhji Kumar Shri	15.6.1937	12.3.2011	4	1964–1969	51	23	0	8.50	–	–	–/–	–	6/3	
Irani Jamshed Khudadad	18.8.1923	25.2.1982	2	1947	3	2*	0	3.00	–	–	–/–	–	2/1	
Jadeja Ajaysinhji	1.2.1971		15	1992–1999	576	96	0	26.18	–	–	–/–	–	5	196
Jadeja Ravindrasinh Anirudhsinh	6.12.1988		25	2012–2016	848	90	0	26.50	111	7-48	6/1	24.07	23	126/39
[3] **Jahangir Khan** Mohammad	1.2.1910	23.7.1988	4	1932–1936	39	13	0	5.57	4	4-60	0/0	63.75	4	
Jai Laxmidas Purshottamdas	1.4.1902	29.1.1968	1	1933	19	19	0	9.50	–	–	–/–	–	0	
Jaisimha Motganhalli Laxmanarsu	3.3.1939	6.7.1999	39	1959–1970	2,056	129	3	30.68	9	2-54	0/0	92.11	17	
Jamshedji Rustomji Jamshedji Dorabji	18.11.1892	5.4.1976	1	1933	5	4*	0	–	3	3-137	0/0	45.66	2	
Jayantilal Kenia	13.1.1948		1	1970	5	5	0	5.00	–	–	–/–	–	0	
Johnson David Jude	16.10.1971		2	1996	8	5	0	4.00	3	2-52	0/0	47.66	0	
Joshi Padmanabh Govind	27.10.1926	8.1.1987	12	1951–1960	207	52*	0	10.89	–	–	–/–	–	18/9	
Joshi Sunil Bandacharya	6.6.1969		15	1996–2000	352	92	0	20.70	41	5-142	1/0	35.85	7	69
Kaif Mohammad	1.12.1980		13	1999–2005	624	148*	1	32.84	0	0-4	0/0	–	14	125
Kambli Vinod Ganpat	18.1.1972		17	1992–1995	1,084	227	4	54.20	–	–	–/–	–	7	104
[1] **Kanitkar** Hrishikesh Hemant	14.11.1974		2	1999	74	45	0	18.50	0	0-2	0/0	–	0	34
[1] **Kanitkar** Hemant Shamsunder	8.12.1942	9.6.2015	2	1974	111	65	0	27.75	–	–	–/–	–	0	
Kapil Dev (*CY 1983*)	6.1.1959		131	1978–1993	5,248	163	8	31.05	434	9-83	23/2	29.64	64	225
Kapoor Aashish Rakesh	25.3.1971		4	1994–1996	97	42	0	19.40	6	2-19	0/0	42.50	1	17
Kardar Abdul Hafeez	17.1.1925	21.4.1996	3†	1946	80	43	0	16.00	–	–	–/–	–	1	
Karim Syed Saba	14.11.1967		1	2000	15	15	0	15.00	–	–	–/–	–	1	34
Karthik Krishankumar Dinesh	1.6.1985		23	2004–2009	1,000	129	1	27.77	–	–	–/–	–	51/5	71/9
Kartik Murali	11.9.1976		8	1999–2004	88	43	0	9.77	24	4-44	0/0	34.16	2	37/1
Kenny Ramnath Baburao	29.9.1930	21.11.1985	5	1958–1959	245	62	0	27.22	–	–	–/–	–	1	
Kirmani Syed Mujtaba Hussein	29.12.1949		88	1975–1985	2,759	102	2	27.04	1	1-9	0/0	13.00	160/38	49
Kishenchand Gogumal	14.4.1925	16.4.1997	5	1947–1952	89	44	0	8.90	–	–	–/–	–	1	
Kohli Virat	5.11.1988		53	2011–2016	4,209	235	15	50.10	0	0-0	0/0	–	50	176/45
[2] **Kripal Singh** Amritsar Govindsingh	6.8.1933	22.7.1987	14	1955–1964	422	100*	1	28.13	10	3-43	0/0	58.40	4	
Krishnamurthy Pochiah	12.7.1947	28.1.1999	5	1970	33	20	0	5.50	–	–	–/–	–	7/1	1
Kulkarni Nilesh Moreshwar	3.4.1973		3	1997–2000	5	4	0	5.00	2	1-70	0/0	166.00	1	10
Kulkarni Rajiv Ramesh	25.9.1962		3	1986	2	2	0	1.00	5	3-85	0/0	45.40	1	10
Kulkarni Umesh Narayan	7.3.1942		4	1967	13	7	0	4.33	5	2-37	0/0	47.60	0	
Kumar Praveen	2.10.1986		6	2011	149	40	0	14.90	27	5-106	1/0	25.81	2	68/10

	Born	Died	Tests	Test Career	Runs	HS	100s	Avge	Wkts	BB	5/10	Avge	Ct/St	O/T
Kumar Vaman Viswanath	22.6.1935		2	1960–1961	6	6	0	3.00	7	5-64	1/0	28.85	2	
Kumble Anil (*CY 1996*)	17.10.1970		132	1990–2008	2,506	110*	1	17.77	619	10-74	35/8	29.65	60	269‡
Kunderan Budhisagar Krishnappa	2.10.1939	23.6.2006	18	1959–1967	981	192	2	32.70	0	0-13	0/0	–	23/7	
Kuruvilla Abey	8.8.1968		10	1996–1997	66	35*	0	6.60	25	5-68	1/0	35.68	0	25
Lall Singh	16.12.1909	19.11.1985	1	1932	44	29	0	22.00	–	–	–/–	–	1	
Lamba Raman	2.1.1960	22.2.1998	4	1986–1987	102	53	0	20.40	–	–	–/–	–	5	32
Laxman Vangipurappu Venkata Sai (*CY 2002*)	1.11.1974		134	1996–2011	8,781	281	17	45.97	2	1-2	0/0	63.00	135	86
Madan Lal	20.3.1951		39	1974–1986	1,042	74	0	22.65	71	5-23	4/0	40.08	15	67
Maka Ebrahim Suleman	5.3.1922	7.9.1994	2	1952	2	2*	0	–	–	–	–/–	–	2/1	
Malhotra Ashok Omprakash	26.1.1957		7	1981–1984	226	72*	0	25.11	0	0-0	0/0	–	2	20
Maninder Singh	13.6.1965		35	1982–1992	99	15	0	3.80	88	7-27	3/2	37.36	9	59
[1] **Manjrekar** Sanjay Vijay	12.7.1965		37	1987–1996	2,043	218	4	37.14	0	0-4	0/0	–	25/1	74
[1] **Manjrekar** Vijay Laxman	26.9.1931	18.10.1983	55	1951–1964	3,208	189*	7	39.12	1	1-16	0/0	44.00	19/2	
[1] **Mankad** Ashok Vinoo	12.10.1946	1.8.2008	22	1969–1977	991	97	0	25.41	0	0-0	0/0	–	12	1
[1] **Mankad** Mulvantrai Himmatlal ("Vinoo") (*CY 1947*)	12.4.1917	21.8.1978	44	1946–1958	2,109	231	5	31.47	162	8-52	8/2	32.32	33	
Mantri Madhav Krishnaji	1.9.1921	23.5.2014	4	1951–1954	67	39	0	9.57	–	–	–/–	–	8/1	
Meherhomji Khershedji Rustomji	9.8.1911	10.2.1982	1	1936	0	0*	0	–	–	–	–/–	–	1	
Mehra Vijay Laxman	12.3.1938	25.8.2006	8	1955–1963	329	62	0	25.30	0	0-1	0/0	–	1	
Merchant Vijay Madhavji (*CY 1937*)	12.10.1911	27.10.1987	10	1933–1951	859	154	3	47.72	0	0-17	0/0	–	7	
Mhambrey Paras Laxmikant	20.6.1972		2	1996	58	28	0	29.00	2	1-43	0/0	74.00	1	3
[2] **Milkha Singh** Amritsar Govindsingh	31.12.1941		4	1959–1961	92	35	0	15.33	0	0-2	0/0	–	2	
Mishra Amit	24.11.1982		22	2008–2016	648	84	0	21.60	76	5-71	1/0	35.72	8	36/8
Mithun Abhimanyu	25.10.1989		4	2010–2011	120	46	0	24.00	9	4-105	0/0	50.66	0	5
Modi Rustomji Sheryar	11.11.1924	17.5.1996	10	1946–1952	736	112	1	46.00	0	0-14	0/0	–	3	
Mohammed Shami	3.9.1990		22	2013–2016	233	51*	0	12.94	76	5-47	2/0	32.60	4	47/6
Mohanty Debasis Sarbeswar	20.7.1976		2	1997	0	0*	0	–	4	4-78	0/0	59.75	0	45
Mongia Nayan Ramlal	19.12.1969		44	1993–2000	1,442	152	1	24.03	–	–	–/–	–	99/8	140
More Kiran Shankar	4.9.1962		49	1986–1993	1,285	73	0	25.70	0	0-12	0/0	–	110/20	94
Muddiah Venatappa Musandra	8.6.1929	1.10.2009	2	1959–1960	11	11	0	5.50	3	2-40	0/0	44.66	0	
Mukund Abhinav	6.1.1990		5	2011	211	62	0	21.10	0	0-14	0/0	–	5	
Mushtaq Ali Syed	17.12.1914	18.6.2005	11	1933–1951	612	112	2	32.21	3	1-45	0/0	67.33	7	
Nadkarni Rameshchandra Gangaram ("Bapu")	4.4.1933		41	1955–1967	1,414	122*	1	25.70	88	6-43	4/1	29.07	22	
Naik Sudhir Sakharam	21.2.1945		3	1974–1974	141	77	0	23.50	–	–	–/–	–	0	2
Nair Karun Kaladharan	6.12.1991		3	2016	320	303*	1	160.00	0	0-4	0/0	–	3	2
Naoomal Jeoomal	17.4.1904	28.7.1980	3	1932–1933	108	43	0	27.00	2	1-4	0/0	34.00	0	

	Born	Died	Tests	Test Career	Runs	HS	100s	Avge	Wkts	BB	5/10	Avge	Ct/St	O/T
Narasimha Rao Modireddy Venkateshwar	11.8.1954		4	*1978–1979*	46	20*	0	9.20	3	2-46	0/0	75.66	8	
Navle Janaradan Gyanoba	7.12.1902	7.9.1979	2	1932–*1933*	42	13	0	10.50	–	–	–/–	–	1	
Nayak Surendra Vithal	20.10.1954		2	1982	19	11	0	9.50	1	1-16	0/0	132.00	1	4
[2] **Nayudu** Cottari Kanakaiya (*CY 1933*)	31.10.1895	14.11.1967	7	1932–1936	350	81	0	25.00	9	3-40	0/0	42.88	4	
[2] **Nayudu** Cottari Subbanna	18.4.1914	22.11.2002	11	*1933–1951*	147	36	0	9.18	2	1-19	0/0	179.50	3	
[2] **Nazir Ali** Syed	8.6.1906	18.2.1975	2	1932–*1933*	30	13	0	7.50	4	4-83	0/0	20.75	0	
Nehra Ashish	29.4.1979		17	*1998–2003*	77	19	0	5.50	44	4-72	0/0	42.40	5	117‡/23
Nissar Mohammad	1.8.1910	11.3.1963	6	1932–1936	55	14	0	6.87	25	5-90	3/0	28.28	2	
Nyalchand Sukhlal Shah	14.9.1915	3.1.1997	1	*1952*	7	6*	0	7.00	3	3-97	0/0	32.33	0	
Ojha Naman Vijaykumar	20.7.1983		1	*2015*	56	35	0	28.00	–	–	–/–	–	4/1	1/2
Ojha Pragyan Prayish	5.9.1986		24	*2009–2013*	89	18*	0	8.90	113	6-47	7/1	30.26	10	18/6
Pai Ajit Manohar	28.4.1945		1	*1969*	10	9	0	5.00	2	2-29	0/0	15.50	0	
Palia Phiroze Edulji	5.9.1910	9.9.1981	2	1932–1936	29	16	0	9.66	0	0-2	0/0	–	0	
Pandit Chandrakant Sitaram	30.9.1961		5	1986–*1991*	171	39	0	24.42	–	–	–/–	–	14/2	36
Pankaj Singh	6.5.1985		2	2014	10	9	0	3.33	2	2-113	0/0	146.00	2	1
Parkar Ghulam Ahmed	25.10.1955		1	1982	7	6	0	3.50	–	–	–/–	–	1	10
Parkar Ramnath Dhondu	31.10.1946	11.8.1999	2	*1972*	80	35	0	20.00	–	–	–/–	–	0	
Parsana Dhiraj Devshibhai	2.12.1947		2	*1978*	1	1	0	0.50	1	1-32	0/0	50.00	0	
Patankar Chandrakant Trimbak	24.11.1930		1	*1955*	14	13	0	14.00	–	–	–/–	–	3/1	
[1] **Pataudi** Iftikhar Ali Khan, Nawab of (*CY 1932*)	16.3.1910	5.1.1952	3†	1946	55	22	0	11.00	–	–	–/–	–	0	
[1] **Pataudi** Mansur Ali Khan, Nawab of (*CY 1968*)	5.1.1941	22.9.2011	46	*1961–1974*	2,793	203*	6	34.91	1	1-10	0/0	88.00	27	
Patel Brijesh Pursuram	24.11.1952		21	1974–*1977*	972	115*	1	29.45	–	–	–/–	–	17	10
Patel Jasubhai Motibhai	26.11.1924	12.12.1992	7	*1954–1959*	25	12	0	2.77	29	9-69	2/1	21.96	2	
Patel Munaf Musa	12.7.1983		13	*2005*–2011	60	15*	0	7.50	35	4-25	0/0	38.54	6	70/3
Patel Parthiv Ajay	9.3.1985		23	2002–*2016*	878	71	0	33.76	–	–	–/–	–	52/10	38/2
Patel Rashid	1.6.1964		1	*1988*	0	0	0	0.00	0	0-14	0/0	–	1	1
Pathan Irfan Khan	27.10.1984		29	*2003–2007*	1,105	102	1	31.57	100	7-59	7/2	32.26	8	120/24
Patiala Maharajah of (Yadavendra Singh)	17.1.1913	17.6.1974	1	*1933*	84	60	0	42.00	–	–	–/–	–	2	
Patil Sadashiv Raoji	10.10.1933		1	*1955*	14	14*	0	–	2	1-15	0/0	25.50	1	
Patil Sandeep Madhusudan	18.8.1956		29	*1979–1984*	1,588	174	4	36.93	9	2-28	0/0	26.66	12	45
Phadkar Dattatraya Gajanan	12.12.1925	17.3.1985	31	*1947–1958*	1,229	123	2	32.34	62	7-159	3/0	36.85	21	
Powar Ramesh Rajaram	20.5.1978		2	2007	13	7	0	6.50	6	3-33	0/0	19.66	0	31
Prabhakar Manoj	15.4.1963		39	*1984–1995*	1,600	120	1	32.65	96	6-132	3/0	37.30	20	130
Prasad Bapu Krishnarao Venkatesh	5.8.1969		33	1996–2001	203	30*	0	7.51	96	6-33	7/1	35.00	6	161
Prasad Mannava Sri Kanth	24.4.1975		6	*1999*	106	19	0	11.77	–	–	–/–	–	15	17
Prasanna Erapalli Anatharao Srinivas	22.5.1940		49	*1961–1978*	735	37	0	11.48	189	8-76	10/2	30.38	18	

	Born	Died	Tests	Test Career	Runs	HS	100s	Avge	Wkts	BB	5/10	Avge	Ct/St	O/T
Pujara Cheteshwar Arvind	25.1.1988		43	2010–2016	3,256	206*	10	49.33	0	0-2	0/0	–	30	5
Punjabi Pananmal Hotchand	20.9.1921	4.10.2011	5	1954	164	33	0	16.40	–	–	–/–	–	5	
Rahane Ajinkya Madhukar	6.6.1988		32	2012–2016	2,272	188	8	47.33	–	–	–/–	–	37	72/20
Rahul Kannur Lokesh	18.4.1992		12	2014–2016	795	199	4	41.84	–	–	–/–	–	19	3/5
Rai Singh Kanwar	24.2.1922	12.11.1993	1	1947	26	24	0	13.00	–	–	–/–	–	0	
Raina Suresh Kumar	27.11.1986		18	2010–2014	768	120	1	26.48	13	2-1	0/0	46.38	23	223/62
Rajinder Pal	18.11.1937		1	1963	6	3*	0	6.00	0	0-3	0/0	–	0	
Rajindernath Vijay	7.1.1928	22.11.1989	1	1952	–	–	–	–	–	–	–/–	–	0/4	
Rajput Lalchand Sitaram	18.12.1961		2	1985	105	61	0	26.25	–	–	–/–	–	1	4
Raju Sagi Lakshmi Venkatapathy	9.7.1969		28	1989–2000	240	31	0	10.00	93	6-12	5/1	30.72	6	53
Raman Woorkeri Venkat	23.5.1965		11	1987–1996	448	96	0	24.88	2	1-7	0/0	64.50	6	27
Ramaswami Cotar	16.6.1896	1.1990	2	1936	170	60	0	56.66	–	–	–/–	–	0	
Ramchand Gulabrai Sipahimalani	26.7.1927	8.9.2003	33	1952–1959	1,180	109	2	24.58	41	6-49	1/0	46.31	20	
Ramesh Sadagoppan	16.10.1975		19	1998–2001	1,367	143	2	37.97	0	0-5	0/0	–	18	24
[2] **Ramji** Ladha	10.2.1900	20.12.1948	1	1933	1	1	0	0.50	0	0-64	0/0	–	1	
Rangachari Commandur Rajagopalachari	14.4.1916	9.10.1993	4	1947–1948	8	8*	0	2.66	9	5-107	1/0	54.77	0	
Rangnekar Khanderao Moreshwar	27.6.1917	11.10.1984	3	1947	33	18	0	5.50	–	–	–/–	–	1	
Ranjane Vasant Baburao	22.7.1937	22.12.2011	7	1958–1964	40	16	0	6.66	19	4-72	0/0	34.15	1	
Rathore Vikram	26.3.1969		6	1996–1996	131	44	0	13.10	–	–	–/–	–	12	7
Ratra Ajay	13.12.1981		6	2001–2002	163	115*	1	18.11	0	0-1	0/0	–	11/2	12
Razdan Vivek	25.8.1969		2	1989	6	6*	0	6.00	5	5-79	1/0	28.20	0	3
Reddy Bharath	12.11.1954		4	1979	38	21	0	9.50	–	–	–/–	–	9/2	3
Rege Madhusudan Ramachandra	18.3.1924	16.12.2013	1	1948	15	15	0	7.50	–	–	–/–	–	1	
Roy Ambar	5.6.1945	19.9.1997	4	1969	91	48	0	13.00	–	–	–/–	–	0	
[1] **Roy** Pankaj	31.5.1928	4.2.2001	43	1951–1960	2,442	173	5	32.56	1	1-6	0/0	66.00	16	
[1] **Roy** Pranab	10.2.1957		2	1981	71	60*	0	35.50	–	–	–/–	–	1	
Saha Wriddhaman Prasanta	24.10.1984		20	2009–2016	733	104	1	28.19	–	–	–/–	–	31/7	9
Sandhu Balwinder Singh	3.8.1956		8	1982–1983	214	71	0	30.57	10	3-87	0/0	55.70	1	22
Sanghvi Rahul Laxman	3.9.1974		1	2000	2	2	0	1.00	2	2-67	0/0	39.00	0	10
Sarandeep Singh	21.10.1979		3	2000–2001	43	39*	0	43.00	10	4-136	0/0	34.00	1	5
Sardesai Dilip Narayan	8.8.1940	2.7.2007	30	1961–1972	2,001	212	5	39.23	0	0-3	0/0	–	4	
Sarwate Chandrasekhar Trimbak	22.7.1920	23.12.2003	9	1946–1951	208	37	0	13.00	3	1-16	0/0	124.66	0	
Saxena Ramesh Chandra	20.9.1944	16.8.2011	1	1967	25	16	0	12.50	0	0-11	0/0	–	0	
Sehwag Virender	20.10.1978		103§	2001–2012	8,503	319	23	49.43	40	5-104	1/0	47.35	90	241‡/19
Sekhar Thirumalai Ananthanpillai	28.3.1956		2	1982	0	0*	0	–	0	0-43	0/0	–	0	4

§ *Sehwag's figures exclude 83 runs and one catch for the ICC World XI v Australia in the Super Series Test in 2005-06.*

	Born	*Died*	*Tests*	*Test Career*	*Runs*	*HS*	*100s*	*Avge*	*Wkts*	*BB*	*5/10*	*Avge*	*Ct/St*	*O/T*
Sen Probir Kumar ("Khokhan")	31.5.1926	27.1.1970	14	*1947–1952*	165	25	0	11.78	–	–	–/–	–	20/11	
Sen Gupta Apoorva Kumar	3.8.1939	14.9.2013	1	*1958*	9	8	0	4.50	–	–	–/–	–	0	
Sharma Ajay Kumar	3.4.1964		1	*1987*	53	30	0	26.50	0	0-9	0/0	–	1	31
Sharma Chetan	3.1.1966		23	*1984–1988*	396	54	0	22.00	61	6-58	4/1	35.45	7	65
Sharma Gopal	3.8.1960		5	*1984–1990*	11	10*	0	3.66	10	4-88	0/0	41.80	2	11
Sharma Ishant	2.9.1988		73	2007–*2016*	550	31*	0	8.73	212	7-74	7/1	36.47	14	80/14
Sharma Karan Vinod	23.10.1987		1	*2014*	8	4*	0	8.00	4	2-95	0/0	59.50	0	2/1
Sharma Parthasarathy Harishchandra	5.1.1948	20.10.2010	5	*1974–1976*	187	54	0	18.70	0	0-2	0/0	–	1	2
Sharma Rohit Gurunath	30.4.1987		21	*2013–2016*	1,184	177	2	37.00	2	1-26	0/0	101.00	22	153/62
Sharma Sanjeev Kumar	25.8.1965		2	*1988*–1990	56	38	0	28.00	6	3-37	0/0	41.16	1	23
Shastri Ravishankar Jayadritha	27.5.1962		80	*1980–1992*	3,830	206	11	35.79	151	5-75	2/0	40.96	36	150
Shinde Sadashiv Ganpatrao	18.8.1923	22.6.1955	7	1946–1952	85	14	0	14.16	12	6-91	1/0	59.75	0	
Shodhan Roshan Harshadlal ("Deepak")	18.10.1928	16.5.2016	3	*1952*	181	110	1	60.33	0	0-1	0/0	–	1	
Shukla Rakesh Chandra	4.2.1948		1	*1982*	–	–	–	–	2	2-82	0/0	76.00	0	
Siddiqui Iqbal Rashid	26.12.1974		1	*2001*	29	24	0	29.00	1	1-32	0/0	48.00	1	
Sidhu Navjot Singh	20.10.1963		51	*1983–1998*	3,202	201	9	42.13	0	0-9	0/0	–	9	136
Singh Rabindra Ramanarayan ("Robin")	14.9.1963		1	*1998*	27	15	0	13.50	0	0-16	0/0	–	5	136
Singh Robin	1.1.1970		1	*1998*	0	0	0	0.00	3	2-74	0/0	58.66	1	
Singh Rudra Pratap	6.12.1985		14	*2005*–2011	116	30	0	7.25	40	5-59	1/0	42.05	6	58/10
Singh Vikram Rajvir	17.9.1984		5	*2005*–2007	47	29	0	11.75	8	3-48	0/0	53.37	1	2
Sivaramakrishnan Laxman	31.12.1965		9	*1982–1985*	130	25	0	16.25	26	6-64	3/1	44.03	9	16
Sohoni Sriranga Wasudev	5.3.1918	19.5.1993	4	1946–*1951*	83	29*	0	16.60	2	1-16	0/0	101.00	2	
Solkar Eknath Dhondu	18.3.1948	26.6.2005	27	*1969–1976*	1,068	102	1	25.42	18	3-28	0/0	59.44	53	7
Sood Man Mohan	6.7.1939		1	*1959*	3	3	0	1.50	–	–	–/–	–	0	
Sreesanth Shanthakumaran	6.2.1983		27	*2005*–2011	281	35	0	10.40	87	5-40	3/0	37.59	5	53/10
Srikkanth Krishnamachari	21.12.1959		43	*1981–1991*	2,062	123	2	29.88	0	0-1	0/0	–	40	146
Srinath Javagal	31.8.1969		67	*1991–2002*	1,009	76	0	14.21	236	8-86	10/1	30.49	22	229
Srinivasan Thirumalai Echambadi	26.10.1950	6.12.2010	1	*1980*	48	29	0	24.00	–	–	–/–	–	0	2
Subramanya Venkataraman	16.7.1936		9	*1964–1967*	263	75	0	18.78	3	2-32	0/0	67.00	9	
Sunderam Gundibali Rama	29.3.1930	20.6.2010	2	*1955*	3	3*	0	–	3	2-46	0/0	55.33	0	
Surendranath	4.1.1937	5.5.2012	11	*1958–1960*	136	27	0	10.46	26	5-75	2/0	40.50	4	
Surti Rusi Framroze	25.5.1936	13.1.2013	26	*1960–1969*	1,263	99	0	28.70	42	5-74	1/0	46.71	26	
Swamy Venkatraman Narayan	23.5.1924	1.5.1983	1	*1955*	–	–	–	–	0	0-15	0/0	–	0	
Tamhane Narendra Shankar	4.8.1931	19.3.2002	21	*1954–1960*	225	54*	0	10.22	–	–	–/–	–	35/16	
Tarapore Keki Khurshedji	17.12.1910	15.6.1986	1	*1948*	2	2	0	2.00	0	0-72	0/0	–	0	
Tendulkar Sachin Ramesh (*CY 1997*)	24.4.1973		200	*1989–2013*	15,921	248*	51	53.78	46	3-10	0/0	54.17	115	463/1

	Born	*Died*	*Tests*	*Test Career*	*Runs*	*HS*	*100s*	*Avge*	*Wkts*	*BB*	*5/10*	*Avge*	*Ct/St*	*O/T*
Umrigar Pahlanji Ratanji ("Polly")	28.3.1926	7.11.2006	59	*1948–1961*	3,631	223	12	42.22	35	6-74	2/0	42.08	33	
Unadkat Jaydev Dipakbhai	18.10.1991		1	*2010*	2	1*	0	2.00	0	0-101	0/0	–	0	7/1
Vengsarkar Dilip Balwant (*CY 1987*)	6.4.1956		116	*1975–1991*	6,868	166	17	42.13	0	0-3	0/0	–	78	129
Venkataraghavan Srinivasaraghavan	21.4.1945		57	*1964–1983*	748	64	0	11.68	156	8-72	3/1	36.11	44	15
Venkataramana Margashayam	24.4.1966		1	*1988*	0	0*	0	–	1	1-10	0/0	58.00	1	1
Vijay Murali	1.4.1984		47	*2008–2016*	3,180	167	8	40.25	1	1-12	0/0	147.00	37	17/9
Vinay Kumar Ranganath	12.2.1984		1	*2011*	11	6	0	5.50	1	1-73	0/0	73.00	0	31/9
Viswanath Gundappa Rangnath	12.2.1949		91	*1969–1982*	6,080	222	14	41.93	1	1-11	0/0	46.00	63	25
Viswanath Sadanand	29.11.1962		3	*1985*	31	20	0	6.20	–	–	–/–	–	11	22
Vizianagram Maharajkumar of (*Sir* Vijaya Anand)	28.12.1905	2.12.1965	3	1936	33	19*	0	8.25	–	–	–/–	–	1	
Wadekar Ajit Laxman	1.4.1941		37	1966–1974	2,113	143	1	31.07	0	0-0	0/0	–	46	2
Wasim Jaffer	16.2.1978		31	*1999–2007*	1,944	212	5	34.10	2	2-18	0/0	9.00	27	2
Wassan Atul Satish	23.3.1968		4	1989–1990	94	53	0	23.50	10	4-108	0/0	50.40	1	9
[1, 2] **Wazir Ali** Syed	15.9.1903	17.6.1950	7	1932–1936	237	42	0	16.92	0	0-0	0/0	–	1	
Yadav Jayant	22.1.1990		3	*2016*	221	104	1	73.66	9	3-30	0/0	29.55	1	1
Yadav Nandlal Shivlal	26.1.1957		35	*1979–1986*	403	43	0	14.39	102	5-76	3/0	35.09	10	7
Yadav Umeshkumar Tilak	25.10.1987		26	*2011–2016*	175	30	0	8.75	68	5-93	1/0	38.94	10	62/1
Yadav Vijay	14.3.1967		1	*1992*	30	30	0	30.00	–	–	–/–	–	1/2	19
Yajurvindra Singh	1.8.1952		4	*1976–1979*	109	43*	0	18.16	0	0-2	0/0	–	11	
Yashpal Sharma	11.8.1954		37	1979–1983	1,606	140	2	33.45	1	1-6	0/0	17.00	16	42
[1] **Yograj Singh**	25.3.1958		1	*1980*	10	6	0	5.00	1	1-63	0/0	63.00	0	6
Yohannan Tinu	18.2.1979		3	*2001–2002*	13	8*	0	–	5	2-56	0/0	51.20	1	3
[1] **Yuvraj Singh**	12.12.1981		40	*2003–2012*	1,900	169	3	33.92	9	2-9	0/0	60.77	31	290‡/55
Zaheer Khan (*CY 2008*)	7.10.1978		92	*2000–2013*	1,231	75	0	11.95	311	7-87	11/1	32.94	19	194‡/17

PAKISTAN (226 players)

	Born	*Died*	*Tests*	*Test Career*	*Runs*	*HS*	*100s*	*Avge*	*Wkts*	*BB*	*5/10*	*Avge*	*Ct/St*	*O/T*
Aamer Malik	3.1.1963		14	*1987–1994*	565	117	2	35.31	1	1-0	0/0	89.00	15/1	24
Aamir Nazir	2.1.1971		6	*1992–1995*	31	11	0	6.20	20	5-46	1/0	29.85	2	9
Aamir Sohail	14.9.1966		47	1992–1999	2,823	205	5	35.28	25	4-54	0/0	41.96	36	156
Abdul Kadir	10.5.1944	12.3.2002	4	*1964*	272	95	0	34.00	–	–	–/–	–	0/1	
Abdul Qadir	15.9.1955		67	*1977–1990*	1,029	61	0	15.59	236	9-56	15/5	32.80	15	104
Abdul Razzaq	2.12.1979		46	*1999–2006*	1,946	134	3	28.61	100	5-35	1/0	36.94	15	261‡/32

	Born	Died	Tests	Test Career	Runs	HS	100s	Avge	Wkts	BB	5/10	Avge	Ct/St	O/T
Abdur Rauf	9.12.1978		3	2009–*2009*	52	31	0	8.66	6	2-59	0/0	46.33	0	4/1
Abdur Rehman	1.3.1980		22	*2007*–2014	395	60	0	14.10	99	6-25	2/0	29.39	8	31/8
[2]**Adnan Akmal**	13.3.1985		21	*2010–2013*	591	64	0	24.62	–	–	–/–	–	66/11	5
Afaq Hussain	31.12.1939	25.2.2002	2	*1961–1964*	66	35*	0	–	1	1-40	0/0	106.00	2	
Aftab Baloch	1.4.1953		2	*1969–1974*	97	60*	0	48.50	0	0-2	0/0	–	0	
Aftab Gul	31.3.1946		6	*1968*–1971	182	33	0	22.75	0	0-4	0/0	–	3	
Agha Saadat Ali	21.6.1929	25.10.1995	1	*1955*	8	8*	0	–	–	–	–/–	–	3	
Agha Zahid	7.1.1953		1	*1974*	15	14	0	7.50	–	–	–/–	–	0	
Ahmed Shehzad	23.11.1991		11	*2013*–2015	861	176	3	43.05	0	0-8	0/0	–	3	75/44
Aizaz Cheema	5.9.1979		7	*2011*–2012	1	1*	0	–	20	4-24	0/0	31.90	1	14/5
Akram Raza	22.11.1964		9	*1989–1994*	153	32	0	15.30	13	3-46	0/0	56.30	8	49
Ali Hussain Rizvi	6.1.1974		1	*1997*	–	–	–	–	2	2-72	0/0	36.00	0	
Ali Naqvi	19.3.1977		5	*1997*	242	115	1	30.25	0	0-11	0/0	–	1	
Alim-ud-Din	15.12.1930	12.7.2012	25	1954–1962	1,091	109	2	25.37	1	1-17	0/0	75.00	8	
Amir Elahi	1.9.1908	28.12.1980	5†	*1952*	65	47	0	10.83	7	4-134	0/0	35.42	0	
Anil Dalpat	20.9.1963		9	*1983–1984*	167	52	0	15.18	–	–	–/–	–	22/3	15
Anwar Hussain	16.7.1920	9.10.2002	4	*1952*	42	17	0	7.00	1	1-25	0/0	29.00	0	
Anwar Khan	24.12.1955		1	*1978*	15	12	0	15.00	0	0-12	0/0	–	0	
Aqib Javed	5.8.1972		22	*1988–1998*	101	28*	0	5.05	54	5-84	1/0	34.70	2	163
Arif Butt	17.5.1944	10.7.2007	3	*1964*	59	20	0	11.80	14	6-89	1/0	20.57	0	
Arshad Khan	22.3.1971		9	*1997–2004*	31	9*	0	5.16	32	5-38	1/0	30.00	0	58
Asad Shafiq	28.1.1986		53	*2010–2016*	3,364	137	10	41.02	1	1-32	0/0	69.00	47	58/10
Ashfaq Ahmed	6.6.1973		1	*1993*	1	1*	0	1.00	2	2-31	0/0	26.50	0	3
Ashraf Ali	22.4.1958		8	*1981–1987*	229	65	0	45.80	–	–	–/–	–	17/5	16
Asif Iqbal (*CY 1968*)	6.6.1943		58	*1964–1979*	3,575	175	11	38.85	53	5-48	2/0	28.33	36	10
Asif Masood	23.1.1946		16	*1968–1976*	93	30*	0	10.33	38	5-111	1/0	41.26	5	7
Asif Mujtaba	4.11.1967		25	*1986–1996*	928	65*	0	24.42	4	1-0	0/0	75.75	19	66
Asim Kamal	31.5.1976		12	*2003–2005*	717	99	0	37.73	–	–	–/–	–	10	
Ata-ur-Rehman	28.3.1975		13	1992–1996	76	19	0	8.44	31	4-50	0/0	34.54	2	30
Atif Rauf	3.3.1964		1	*1993*	25	16	0	12.50	–	–	–/–	–	0	
Atiq-uz-Zaman	20.7.1975		1	*1999*	26	25	0	13.00	–	–	–/–	–	5	3
Azam Khan	1.3.1969		1	*1996*	14	14	0	14.00	–	–	–/–	–	0	6
Azeem Hafeez	29.7.1963		18	*1983–1984*	134	24	0	8.37	63	6-46	4/0	34.98	1	15
Azhar Ali	19.2.1985		57	2010–*2016*	4,707	302*	12	47.07	7	2-35	0/0	81.00	55	42
Azhar Khan	7.9.1955		1	*1979*	14	14	0	14.00	1	1-1	0/0	2.00	0	
Azhar Mahmood	28.2.1975		21	*1997*–2001	900	136	3	30.00	39	4-50	0/0	35.94	14	143

	Born	Died	Tests	Test Career	Runs	HS	100s	Avge	Wkts	BB	5/10	Avge	Ct/St	O/T
[2] **Azmat Rana**	3.11.1951	30.5.2015	1	1979	49	49	0	49.00	–	–	–/–	–	0	2
Babar Azam	15.10.1994		6	2016	300	90*	0	27.27	–	–	–/–	–	3	18/4
Basit Ali	13.12.1970		19	1992–1995	858	103	1	26.81	0	0-6	0/0	–	6	50
[3] **Bazid Khan**	25.3.1981		1	2004	32	23	0	16.00	–	–	–/–	–	2	5
Bilawal Bhatti	17.9.1991		2	2013	70	32	0	35.00	6	3-65	0/0	48.50	0	10/9
Danish Kaneria	16.12.1980		61	2000–2010	360	29	0	7.05	261	7-77	15/2	34.79	18	18
D'Souza Antao	17.1.1939		6	1958–1962	76	23*	0	38.00	17	5-112	1/0	43.82	3	
Ehsan Adil	15.3.1993		3	2012–2015	21	12	0	5.25	5	2-54	0/0	52.60	0	6
Ehtesham-ud-Din	4.9.1950		5	1979–1982	2	2	0	1.00	16	5-47	1/0	23.43	2	
Faisal Iqbal	30.12.1981		26	2000–2009	1,124	139	1	26.76	0	0-7	0/0	–	22	18
Farhan Adil	25.9.1977		1	2003	33	25	0	16.50	–	–	–/–	–	0	
Farooq Hamid	3.3.1945		1	1964	3	3	0	1.50	1	1-82	0/0	107.00	0	
Farrukh Zaman	2.4.1956		1	1976	–	–	–	–	0	0-7	0/0	–	0	
Fawad Alam	8.10.1985		3	2009–2009	250	168	1	41.66	–	–	–/–	–	3	38/24
Fazal Mahmood (*CY 1955*)	18.2.1927	30.5.2005	34	1952–1962	620	60	0	14.09	139	7-42	13/4	24.70	11	
Fazl-e-Akbar	20.10.1980		5	1997–2003	52	25	0	13.00	11	3-85	0/0	46.45	2	2
Ghazali Mohammad Ebrahim Zainuddin	15.6.1924	26.4.2003	2	1954	32	18	0	8.00	0	0-18	0/0	–	0	
Ghulam Abbas	1.5.1947		1	1967	12	12	0	6.00	–	–	–/–	–	0	
Gul Mahomed	15.10.1921	8.5.1992	1†	1956	39	27*	0	39.00	–	–	–/–	–	0	
[1, 2] **Hanif Mohammad** (*CY 1968*)	21.12.1934	11.8.2016	55	1952–1969	3,915	337	12	43.98	1	1-1	0/0	95.00	40	
Haroon Rashid	25.3.1953		23	1976–1982	1,217	153	3	34.77	0	0-3	0/0	–	16	12
Hasan Raza	11.3.1982		7	1996–2005	235	68	0	26.11	0	0-1	0/0	–	5	16
Haseeb Ahsan	15.7.1939	8.3.2013	12	1957–1961	61	14	0	6.77	27	6-202	2/0	49.25	1	
[2] **Humayun Farhat**	24.1.1981		1	2000	54	28	0	27.00	–	–	–/–	–	0	5
Ibadulla Khalid ("Billy")	20.12.1935		4	1964–1967	253	166	1	31.62	1	1-42	0/0	99.00	3	
Iftikhar Ahmed	3.9.1990		1	2016	4	4	0	4.00	1	1-1	0/0	13.00	1	2/1
Iftikhar Anjum	1.12.1980		1	2005	9	9*	0	–	0	0-8	0/0	–	0	62/2
Ijaz Ahmed snr	20.9.1968		60	1986–2000	3,315	211	12	37.67	2	1-9	0/0	38.50	45	250
Ijaz Ahmed jnr	2.2.1969		2	1995	29	16	0	9.66	0	0-1	0/0	–	3	2
Ijaz Butt	10.3.1938		8	1958–1962	279	58	0	19.92	–	–	–/–	–	5	
Ijaz Faqih	24.3.1956		5	1980–1987	183	105	1	26.14	4	1-38	0/0	74.75	0	27
[2] **Imran Farhat**	20.5.1982		40	2000–2012	2,400	128	3	32.00	3	2-69	0/0	94.66	40	58/7
Imran Khan (*CY 1983*)	25.11.1952		88	1971–1991	3,807	136	6	37.69	362	8-58	23/6	22.81	28	175
Mohammad **Imran Khan**	15.7.1987		9	2014–2016	6	6	0	1.00	28	5-58	1/0	30.14	0	
Imran Nazir	16.12.1981		8	1998–2002	427	131	2	32.84	–	–	–/–	–	4	79/25
Imtiaz Ahmed	5.1.1928	31.12.2016	41	1952–1962	2,079	209	3	29.28	0	0-0	0/0	–	77/16	

	Born	Died	Tests	Test Career	Runs	HS	100s	Avge	Wkts	BB	5/10	Avge	Ct/St	O/T
Intikhab Alam	28.12.1941		47	*1959–1976*	1,493	138	1	22.28	125	7-52	5/2	35.95	20	4
Inzamam-ul-Haq	3.3.1970		119§	1992–*2007*	8,829	329	25	50.16	0	0-8	0/0	–	81	375‡/1
Iqbal Qasim	6.8.1953		50	*1976–1988*	549	56	0	13.07	171	7-49	8/2	28.11	42	15
Irfan Fazil	2.11.1981		1	*1999*	4	3	0	4.00	2	1-30	0/0	32.50	2	1
Israr Ali	1.5.1927	1.2.2016	4	*1952–1959*	33	10	0	4.71	6	2-29	0/0	27.50	1	
Jalal-ud-Din	12.6.1959		6	*1982–1985*	3	2	0	3.00	11	3-77	0/0	48.81	0	8
Javed Akhtar	21.11.1940	8.7.2016	1	1962	4	2*	0	4.00	0	0-52	0/0	–	0	
Javed Burki	8.5.1938		25	*1960–1969*	1,341	140	3	30.47	0	0-2	0/0	–	7	
Javed Miandad (*CY 1982*)	12.6.1957		124	*1976–1993*	8,832	280*	23	52.57	17	3-74	0/0	40.11	93/1	233
Junaid Khan	24.12.1989		22	*2011*–2015	122	17	0	7.17	71	5-38	5/0	31.73	4	52/9
Kabir Khan	12.4.1974		4	*1994*	24	10	0	8.00	9	3-26	0/0	41.11	1	10
[2] **Kamran Akmal**	13.1.1982		53	*2002*–2010	2,648	158*	6	30.79	–	–	–/–	–	184/22	154/54
Kardar Abdul Hafeez	17.1.1925	21.4.1996	23†	*1952–1957*	847	93	0	24.91	21	3-35	0/0	45.42	15	
Khalid Hassan	14.7.1937	3.12.2013	1	1954	17	10	0	17.00	2	2-116	0/0	58.00	0	
[1] **Khalid Wazir**	27.4.1936		2	1954	14	9*	0	7.00	–	–	–/–	–	0	
Khan Mohammad	1.1.1928	4.7.2009	13	*1952–1957*	100	26*	0	10.00	54	6-21	4/0	23.92	4	
Khurram Manzoor	10.6.1986		16	*2008*–2014	817	146	1	28.17	–	–	–/–	–	8	7/3
Liaqat Ali	21.5.1955		5	*1974*–1978	28	12	0	7.00	6	3-80	0/0	59.83	1	3
Mahmood Hussain	2.4.1932	25.12.1991	27	*1952*–1962	336	35	0	10.18	68	6-67	2/0	38.64	5	
[3] **Majid** Jahangir **Khan** (*CY 1970*)	28.9.1946		63	*1964–1982*	3,931	167	8	38.92	27	4-45	0/0	53.92	70	23
Mansoor Akhtar	25.12.1957		19	*1980–1989*	655	111	1	25.19	–	–	–/–	–	9	41
[2] **Manzoor Elahi**	15.4.1963		6	*1984–1994*	123	52	0	15.37	7	2-38	0/0	27.71	7	54
Maqsood Ahmed	26.3.1925	4.1.1999	16	*1952–1955*	507	99	0	19.50	3	2-12	0/0	63.66	13	
Masood Anwar	12.12.1967		1	*1990*	39	37	0	19.50	3	2-59	0/0	34.00	0	
Mathias Wallis	4.2.1935	1.9.1994	21	*1955–1962*	783	77	0	23.72	0	0-20	0/0	–	22	
Miran Bux	20.4.1907	8.2.1991	2	*1954*	1	1*	0	1.00	2	2-82	0/0	57.50	0	
Misbah-ul-Haq (*CY 2017*)	28.5.1974		72	*2000–2016*	4,951	161*	10	45.84	–	–	–/–	–	49	162/39
Mohammad Akram	10.9.1974		9	*1995–2000*	24	10*	0	2.66	17	5-138	1/0	50.52	4	23
Mohammad Amir (formerly Mohammad Aamer)	13.4.1992		25	2009–*2016*	546	48	0	13.65	81	6-84	3/0	33.72	1	24/31
Mohammad Asif	20.12.1982		23	*2004*–2010	141	29	0	5.64	106	6-41	7/1	24.36	3	35‡/11
Mohammad Aslam Khokhar	5.1.1920	22.1.2011	1	1954	34	18	0	17.00	–	–	–/–	–	0	
Mohammad Ayub	13.9.1979		1	2012	47	25	0	23.50	–	–	–/–	–	1	
Mohammad Farooq	8.4.1938		7	*1960–1964*	85	47	0	17.00	21	4-70	0/0	32.47	1	
Mohammad Hafeez	17.10.1980		50	*2003*–2016	3,452	224	9	39.22	52	4-16	0/0	33.90	43	177/77

§ *Inzamam-ul-Haq's figures exclude one run for the ICC World XI v Australia in the Super Series Test in 2005-06.*

	Born	Died	Tests	Test Career	Runs	HS	100s	Avge	Wkts	BB	5/10	Avge	Ct/St	O/T
Mohammad Hussain	8.10.1976		2	1996–1998	18	17	0	6.00	3	2-66	0/0	29.00	1	14
Mohammad Ilyas	19.3.1946		10	1964–1968	441	126	1	23.21	0	0-1	0/0	–	6	
Mohammad Irfan	6.6.1982		4	2012–2013	28	14	0	5.60	10	3-44	0/0	38.90	0	60/20
Mohammad Khalil	11.11.1982		2	2004	9	5	0	3.00	0	0-38	0/0	–	0	3
Mohammad Munaf	2.11.1935		4	1959–1961	63	19	0	12.60	11	4-42	0/0	31.00	0	
Mohammad Nawaz	21.3.1994		3	2016	50	25	0	12.50	5	2-32	0/0	29.40	2	8/5
Mohammad Nazir	8.3.1946		14	1969–1983	144	29*	0	18.00	34	7-99	3/0	33.05	4	4
Mohammad Ramzan	25.12.1970		1	1997	36	29	0	18.00	–	–	–/–	–	1	
Mohammad Rizwan	1.6.1992		1	2016	13	13*	0	13.00	–	–	–/–	–	1	20/10
Mohammad Salman	7.8.1981		2	2010	25	13	0	6.25	–	–	–/–	–	2/1	7/1
Mohammad Sami	24.2.1981		36	2000–2012	487	49	0	11.59	85	5-36	2/0	52.74	7	87/13
Mohammad Talha	15.10.1988		4	2008–2014	34	19	0	8.50	9	3-65	0/0	56.00	1	3
Mohammad Wasim	8.8.1977		18	1996–2000	783	192	2	30.11	–	–	–/–	–	22/2	25
Mohammad Yousuf (*CY 2007*) (formerly Yousuf Youhana)	27.8.1974		90	1997–2010	7,530	223	24	52.29	0	0-3	0/0	–	65	281‡/3
Mohammad Zahid	2.8.1976		5	1996–2002	7	6*	0	1.40	15	7-66	1/1	33.46	0	11
Mohsin Kamal	16.6.1963		9	1983–1994	37	13*	0	9.25	24	4-116	0/0	34.25	4	19
Mohsin Khan	15.3.1955		48	1977–1986	2,709	200	7	37.10	0	0-0	0/0	–	34	75
[2] **Moin Khan**	23.9.1971		69	1990–2004	2,741	137	4	28.55	–	–	–/–	–	128/20	219
[1] **Mudassar Nazar**	6.4.1956		76	1976–1988	4,114	231	10	38.09	66	6-32	1/0	38.36	48	122
Mufasir-ul-Haq	16.8.1944	27.7.1983	1	1964	8	8*	0	–	3	2-50	0/0	28.00	1	
Munir Malik	10.7.1934	30.11.2012	3	1959–1962	7	4	0	2.33	9	5-128	1/0	39.77	1	
Mushtaq Ahmed (*CY 1997*)	28.6.1970		52	1989–2003	656	59	0	11.71	185	7-56	10/3	32.97	23	144
[2] **Mushtaq Mohammad** (*CY 1963*)	22.11.1943		57	1958–1978	3,643	201	10	39.17	79	5-28	3/0	29.22	42	10
Nadeem Abbasi	15.4.1964		3	1989	46	36	0	23.00	–	–	–/–	–	6	
Nadeem Ghauri	12.10.1962		1	1989	0	0	0	0.00	0	0-20	0/0	–	0	6
[2] **Nadeem Khan**	10.12.1969		2	1992–1998	34	25	0	17.00	2	2-147	0/0	115.00	0	2
Nasim-ul-Ghani	14.5.1941		29	1957–1972	747	101	1	16.60	52	6-67	2/0	37.67	11	1
Nasir Jamshed	6.12.1989		2	2012	51	46	0	12.75	–	–	–/–	–	1	48/18
Naushad Ali	1.10.1943		6	1964	156	39	0	14.18	–	–	–/–	–	9	
Naved Anjum	27.7.1963		2	1989–1990	44	22	0	14.66	4	2-57	0/0	40.50	0	13
Naved Ashraf	4.9.1974		2	1998–1999	64	32	0	21.33	–	–	–/–	–	0	
Naved Latif	21.2.1976		1	2001	20	20	0	10.00	–	–	–/–	–	0	11
Naved-ul-Hasan	28.2.1978		9	2004–2006	239	42*	0	19.91	18	3-30	0/0	58.00	3	74/4
[1] **Nazar Mohammad**	5.3.1921	12.7.1996	5	1952	277	124*	1	39.57	0	0-4	0/0	–	7	
Niaz Ahmed	11.11.1945	12.4.2000	2	1967–1968	17	16*	0	–	3	2-72	0/0	31.33	1	

	Born	Died	Tests	Test Career	Runs	HS	100s	Avge	Wkts	BB	5/10	Avge	Ct/St	O/T
2 **Pervez Sajjad**	30.8.1942		19	*1964–1972*	123	24	0	13.66	59	7-74	3/0	23.89	9	
Qaiser Abbas	7.5.1982		1	*2000*	2	2	0	2.00	0	0-35	0/0	–	0	
Qasim Omar	9.2.1957		26	*1983–1986*	1,502	210	3	36.63	0	0-0	0/0	–	15	31
Rahat Ali	12.9.1988		20	*2012–2016*	136	35*	0	7.55	58	6-127	2/0	37.43	9	14
2 **Ramiz Raja**	14.8.1962		57	*1983–1996*	2,833	122	2	31.83	–	–	–/–	–	34	198
Rashid Khan	15.12.1959		4	*1981–1984*	155	59	0	51.66	8	3-129	0/0	45.00	2	29
Rashid Latif	14.10.1968		37	1992–*2003*	1,381	150	1	28.77	0	0-10	0/0	–	119/11	166
Rehman Sheikh Fazalur	11.6.1935		1	*1957*	10	8	0	5.00	1	1-43	0/0	99.00	1	
Riaz Afridi	21.1.1985		1	*2004*	9	9	0	9.00	2	2-42	0/0	43.50	0	
Rizwan-uz-Zaman	4.9.1961		11	*1981–1988*	345	60	0	19.16	4	3-26	0/0	11.50	4	3
2 **Sadiq Mohammad**	3.5.1945		41	*1969–1980*	2,579	166	5	35.81	0	0-0	0/0	–	28	19
2 **Saeed Ahmed**	1.10.1937		41	*1957–1972*	2,991	172	5	40.41	22	4-64	0/0	36.45	13	
Saeed Ajmal	14.10.1977		35	2009–2014	451	50	0	11.00	178	7-55	10/4	28.10	11	113/64
Saeed Anwar (*CY 1997*)	6.9.1968		55	*1990–2001*	4,052	188*	11	45.52	0	0-0	0/0	–	18	247
Salah-ud-Din	14.2.1947		5	*1964–1969*	117	34*	0	19.50	7	2-36	0/0	26.71	3	
Saleem Jaffer	19.11.1962		14	*1986–1991*	42	10*	0	5.25	36	5-40	1/0	31.63	2	39
Salim Altaf	19.4.1944		21	1967–*1978*	276	53*	0	14.52	46	4-11	0/0	37.17	3	6
2 **Salim Elahi**	21.11.1976		13	*1995–2002*	436	72	0	18.95	–	–	–/–	–	10/1	48
Salim Malik (*CY 1988*)	16.4.1963		103	*1981–1998*	5,768	237	15	43.69	5	1-3	0/0	82.80	65	283
Salim Yousuf	7.12.1959		32	*1981–1990*	1,055	91*	0	27.05	–	–	–/–	–	91/13	86
Salman Butt	7.10.1984		33	*2003*–2010	1,889	122	3	30.46	1	1-36	0/0	106.00	12	78/24
Sami Aslam	12.12.1995		11	*2014–2016*	665	91	0	33.25	–	–	–/–	–	7	4
Saqlain Mushtaq (*CY 2000*)	29.12.1976		49	*1995–2003*	927	101*	1	14.48	208	8-164	13/3	29.83	15	169
Sarfraz Ahmed	22.5.1987		33	*2009–2016*	1,948	112	3	42.34	–	–	–/–	–	86/17	67/25
Sarfraz Nawaz	1.12.1948		55	*1968–1983*	1,045	90	0	17.71	177	9-86	4/1	32.75	26	45
Shabbir Ahmed	21.4.1976		10	*2003–2005*	88	24*	0	8.80	51	5-48	2/0	23.03	3	32/1
Shadab Kabir	12.11.1977		5	1996–*2001*	148	55	0	21.14	0	0-9	0/0	–	11	3
Shafiq Ahmed	28.3.1949		6	1974–*1980*	99	27*	0	11.00	0	0-1	0/0	–	0	3
2 **Shafqat Rana**	10.8.1943		5	*1964–1969*	221	95	0	31.57	1	1-2	0/0	9.00	5	
Shahid Afridi	1.3.1980		27	*1998*–2010	1,716	156	5	36.51	48	5-52	1/0	35.60	10	393‡/98
Shahid Israr	1.3.1950	29.4.2013	1	*1976*	7	7*	0	–	–	–	–/–	–	2	
Shahid Mahboob	25.8.1962		1	*1989*	–	–	–	–	2	2-131	0/0	65.50	0	10
Shahid Mahmood	17.3.1939		1	1962	25	16	0	12.50	0	0-23	0/0	–	0	
Shahid Nazir	4.12.1977		15	*1996–2006*	194	40	0	12.12	36	5-53	1/0	35.33	5	17
Shahid Saeed	6.1.1966		1	*1989*	12	12	0	12.00	0	0-7	0/0	–	0	10
Shakeel Ahmed snr	12.2.1966		1	*1998*	1	1	0	1.00	4	4-91	0/0	34.75	1	

	Born	Died	Tests	Test Career	Runs	HS	100s	Avge	Wkts	BB	5/10	Avge	Ct/St	O/T
Shakeel Ahmed jnr.	12.11.1971		3	*1992–1994*	74	33	0	14.80	–	–	–/–	–	4	2
Shan Masood	14.10.1989		9	*2013*–2016	432	125	1	24.00	0	0-19	0/0	–	6	
Sharjeel Khan	14.8.1989		1	*2016*	44	40	0	22.00	–	–	–/–	–	0	20/15
Sharpe Duncan Albert	3.8.1937		3	*1959*	134	56	0	22.33	–	–	–/–	–	2	
Shoaib Akhtar	13.8.1975		46	*1997–2007*	544	47	0	10.07	178	6-11	12/2	25.69	12	158‡/15
Shoaib Malik	1.2.1982		35	*2001–2015*	1,898	245	3	35.14	32	4-33	0/0	47.46	18	240/82
[1] **Shoaib Mohammad**	8.1.1961		45	*1983–1995*	2,705	203*	7	44.34	5	2-8	0/0	34.00	22	63
Shuja-ud-Din Butt	10.4.1930	7.2.2006	19	1954–*1961*	395	47	0	15.19	20	3-18	0/0	40.05	8	
Sikander Bakht	25.8.1957		26	*1976–1982*	146	22*	0	6.34	67	8-69	3/1	36.00	7	27
Sohail Khan	6.3.1984		9	*2008–2016*	252	65	0	25.20	27	5-68	2/0	41.66	2	13/3
Sohail Tanvir	12.12.1984		2	*2007*	17	13	0	5.66	5	3-83	0/0	63.20	2	62/54
Tahir Naqqash	6.6.1959		15	*1981–1984*	300	57	0	21.42	34	5-40	2/0	41.11	3	40
Talat Ali Malik	29.5.1950		10	*1972–1978*	370	61	0	23.12	0	0-1	0/0	–	4	
Tanvir Ahmed	20.12.1978		5	*2010–2012*	170	57	0	34.00	17	6-120	1/0	26.64	1	2/1
Taslim Arif	1.5.1954	13.3.2008	6	*1979–1980*	501	210*	1	62.62	1	1-28	0/0	28.00	6/3	2
Taufeeq Umar	20.6.1981		44	*2001–2014*	2,963	236	7	37.98	0	0-0	0/0	–	48	22
Tauseef Ahmed	10.5.1958		34	*1979–1993*	318	35*	0	17.66	93	6-45	3/0	31.72	9	70
[2] **Umar Akmal**	26.5.1990		16	*2009–2011*	1,003	129	1	35.82	–	–	–/–	–	12	111/82
Umar Amin	16.10.1989		4	2010	99	33	0	12.37	3	1-7	0/0	21.00	1	15/10
Umar Gul	14.4.1984		47	*2003–2012*	577	65*	0	9.94	163	6-135	4/0	34.06	11	130/60
Wahab Riaz	28.6.1985		24	2010–*2016*	273	39	0	8.27	76	5-63	2/0	34.01	4	75/23
Wajahatullah Wasti	11.11.1974		6	*1998–1999*	329	133	2	36.55	0	0-0	0/0	–	7	15
[2] **Waqar Hassan**	12.9.1932		21	*1952–1959*	1,071	189	1	31.50	0	0-10	0/0	–	10	
Waqar Younis (*CY 1992*)	16.11.1971		87	*1989–2002*	1,010	45	0	10.20	373	7-76	22/5	23.56	18	262
Wasim Akram (*CY 1993*)	3.6.1966		104	*1984–2001*	2,898	257*	3	22.64	414	7-119	25/5	23.62	44	356
Wasim Bari	23.3.1948		81	1967–*1983*	1,366	85	0	15.88	0	0-2	0/0	–	201/27	51
[2] **Wasim Raja**	3.7.1952	23.8.2006	57	*1972–1984*	2,821	125	4	36.16	51	4-50	0/0	35.80	20	54
[2] **Wazir Mohammad**	22.12.1929		20	*1952–1959*	801	189	2	27.62	0	0-2	0/0	–	5	
Yasir Ali	15.10.1985		1	*2003*	1	1*	0	–	2	1-12	0/0	27.50	0	
Yasir Arafat	12.3.1982		3	*2007–2008*	94	50*	0	47.00	9	5-161	1/0	48.66	0	11/13
Yasir Hameed	28.2.1978		25	*2003*–2010	1,491	170	2	32.41	0	0-0	0/0	–	20	56
Yasir Shah	2.5.1986		23	*2014–2016*	332	33	0	11.85	124	7-76	8/2	31.51	16	17/2
[2] **Younis Ahmed**	20.10.1947		4	*1969–1986*	177	62	0	29.50	0	0-6	0/0	–	0	2
Younis Khan (*CY 2017*)	29.11.1977		115	*1999–2016*	9,977	313	34	53.06	9	2-23	0/0	54.55	129	265/25
Yousuf Youhana (*see* Mohammad Yousuf)														
Zaheer Abbas (*CY 1972*)	24.7.1947		78	*1969–1985*	5,062	274	12	44.79	3	2-21	0/0	44.00	34	62

	Born	Died	Tests	Test Career	Runs	HS	100s	Avge	Wkts	BB	5/10	Avge	Ct/St	O/T
Zahid Fazal	10.11.1973		9	*1990–1995*	288	78	0	18.00	–	–	–/–	–	5	19
[2] **Zahoor Elahi**	1.3.1971		2	*1996*	30	22	0	10.00	–	–	–/–	–	1	14
Zakir Khan	3.4.1963		2	*1985–1989*	9	9*	0	–	5	3-80	0/0	51.80	1	17
Zulfiqar Ahmed	22.11.1926	3.10.2008	9	*1952–1956*	200	63*	0	33.33	20	6-42	2/1	18.30	5	
Zulfiqar Babar	10.12.1978		15	*2013–2016*	144	56	0	16.00	54	5-74	2/0	39.42	4	5/7
Zulqarnain	25.5.1962		3	*1985*	24	13	0	6.00	–	–	–/–	–	8/2	16
Zulqarnain Haider	23.4.1986		1	2010	88	88	0	44.00	–	–	–/–	–	2	4/3

SRI LANKA (139 players)

	Born	Died	Tests	Test Career	Runs	HS	100s	Avge	Wkts	BB	5/10	Avge	Ct/St	O/T
Ahangama Franklyn Saliya	14.9.1959		3	*1985*	11	11	0	5.50	18	5-52	1/0	19.33	1	1
Amalean Kaushik Naginda	7.4.1965		2	*1985–1987*	9	7*	0	9.00	7	4-97	0/0	22.28	1	8
Amerasinghe Amerasinghe Mudalige Jayantha Gamini	2.2.1954		2	*1983*	54	34	0	18.00	3	2-73	0/0	50.00	3	
Amerasinghe Merenna Koralage Don Ishara	5.3.1978		1	*2007*	0	0*	0	–	1	1-62	0/0	105.00	0	8
Anurasiri Sangarange Don	25.2.1966		18	*1985–1997*	91	24	0	5.35	41	4-71	0/0	37.75	4	45
Arnold Russel Premakumaran	25.10.1973		44	*1996*–2004	1,821	123	3	28.01	11	3-76	0/0	54.36	51	180/1
Atapattu Marvan Samson	22.11.1970		90	*1990–2007*	5,502	249	16	39.02	1	1-9	0/0	24.00	58	268/2
Bandara Herath Mudiyanselage Charitha Malinga	31.12.1979		8	*1997–2005*	124	43	0	15.50	16	3-84	0/0	39.56	4	31/4
Bandaratilleke Mapa Rallage Chandima Niroshan	16.5.1975		7	*1997–2001*	93	25	0	11.62	23	5-36	1/0	30.34	0	3
Chameera Pathira Vasan Dushmantha	11.1.1992		6	2015–*2016*	61	19	0	6.10	22	5-47	1/0	33.00	3	9/13
Chandana Umagiliya Durage Upul	7.5.1972		16	*1998–2004*	616	92	0	26.78	37	6-179	3/1	41.48	7	147
Chandimal Lokuge Dinesh	18.11.1989		34	*2011–2016*	2,342	162*	7	41.08	–	–	–/–	–	67/10	119/45
Dassanayake Pubudu Bathiya	11.7.1970		11	*1993–1994*	196	36	0	13.06	–	–	–/–	–	19/5	16
de Alwis Ronald Guy	15.2.1959	12.1.2013	11	*1982–1987*	152	28	0	8.00	–	–	–/–	–	21/2	31
de Mel Ashantha Lakdasa Francis	9.5.1959		17	*1981–1986*	326	34	0	14.17	59	6-109	3/0	36.94	9	57
de Saram Samantha Indika	2.9.1973		4	*1999*	117	39	0	23.40	–	–	–/–	–	1	15/1
de Silva Ashley Matthew	3.12.1963		3	*1992–1993*	10	9	0	3.33	–	–	–/–	–	4/1	4
de Silva Dandeniyage Somachandra	11.6.1942		12	*1981*–1984	406	61	0	21.36	37	5-59	1/0	36.40	5	41
de Silva Dhananjaya Maduranga	6.9.1991		8	2016–*2016*	675	129	2	45.00	5	2-91	0/0	51.40	6	11/4
de Silva Ellawalakankanamge Asoka Ranjit	28.3.1956		10	*1985–1990*	185	50	0	15.41	8	2-67	0/0	129.00	4	28
de Silva Ginigalgodage Ramba Ajit	12.12.1952		4	*1981–1982*	41	14	0	8.20	7	2-38	0/0	55.00	0	6

	Born	*Died*	*Tests*	*Test Career*	*Runs*	*HS*	*100s*	*Avge*	*Wkts*	*BB*	*5/10*	*Avge*	*Ct/St*	*O/T*
de Silva Karunakalage Sajeewa Chanaka	11.1.1971		8	*1996–1998*	65	27	0	9.28	16	5-85	1/0	55.56	5	38
de Silva Pinnaduwage Aravinda (*CY 1996*)	17.10.1965		93	1984–2002	6,361	267	20	42.97	29	3-30	0/0	41.65	43	308
de Silva Sanjeewa Kumara Lanka	29.7.1975		3	*1997*	36	20*	0	18.00	–	–	–/–	–	1	11
de Silva Weddikkara Ruwan Sujeewa	7.10.1979		3	2002–2007	10	5*	0	10.00	11	4-35	0/0	19.00	1	
Dharmasena Handunnettige Deepthi Priyantha Kumar	24.4.1971		31	*1993–2003*	868	62*	0	19.72	69	6-72	3/0	42.31	14	141
Dias Roy Luke	18.10.1952		20	*1981–1986*	1,285	109	3	36.71	0	0-17	0/0	–	6	58
Dickwella Dickwella Patabandige Dilantha Niroshan	23.6.1993		4	2014–*2014*	144	72	0	20.57	–	–	–/–	–	15/2	6/3
Dilshan Tillekeratne Mudiyanselage	14.10.1976		87	*1999–2012*	5,492	193	16	40.98	39	4-10	0/0	43.87	88	330/80
Dunusinghe Chamara Iroshan	19.10.1970		5	*1994–1995*	160	91	0	16.00	–	–	–/–	–	13/2	1
Eranga Ranaweera Mudiyanselage Shaminda	23.6.1986		19	*2011*–2016	193	45*	0	12.86	57	4-49	0/0	37.50	5	19/3
Fernando Aththachchi Nuwan Pradeep Roshan	19.10.1986		24	*2011–2016*	121	17*	0	4.84	61	4-62	0/0	42.98	4	16/1
Fernando Congenige Randhi Dilhara	19.7.1979		40	2000–2012	249	39*	0	8.30	100	5-42	3/0	37.84	10	146‡/18
Fernando Ellekutige Rufus Nemesion Susil	19.12.1955		5	*1982–1983*	112	46	0	11.20	–	–	–/–	–	0	7
Fernando Kandage Hasantha Ruwan Kumara	14.10.1979		2	*2002*	38	24	0	9.50	4	3-63	0/0	27.00	1	7
Fernando Kandana Arachchige Dinusha Manoj	10.8.1979		2	*2003*	56	51*	0	28.00	1	1-29	0/0	107.00	0	1
Fernando Muthuthanthrige Vishwa Thilina	18.9.1991		1	2016	0	0*	0	0.00	1	1-16	0/0	16.00	0	
Fernando Thudellage Charitha Buddhika	22.8.1980		9	*2001*–2002	132	45	0	26.40	18	4-27	0/0	44.00	4	17
Gallage Indika Sanjeewa	22.11.1975		1	*1999*	3	3	0	3.00	0	0-24	0/0	–	0	3
Goonatillake Hettiarachige Mahes	16.8.1952		5	*1981–1982*	177	56	0	22.12	–	–	–/–	–	10/3	6
Gunaratne Downdegedara Asela Sampath	8.1.1986		2	*2016*	225	116	1	75.00	0	0-5	0/0	–	2	5/1
Gunasekera Yohan	8.11.1957		2	*1982*	48	23	0	12.00	–	–	–/–	–	6	3
Gunawardene Dihan Avishka	26.5.1977		6	*1998–2005*	181	43	0	16.45	–	–	–/–	–	2	61
Guneratne Roshan Punyajith Wijesinghe	26.1.1962	21.7.2005	1	*1982*	0	0*	0	–	0	0-84	0/0	–	0	
Gurusinha Asanka Pradeep	16.9.1966		41	*1985*–1996	2,452	143	7	38.92	20	2-7	0/0	34.05	33	147
Hathurusinghe Upul Chandika	13.9.1968		26	*1990–1998*	1,274	83	0	29.62	17	4-66	0/0	46.41	7	35
Herath Herath Mudiyanselage Rangana Keerthi Bandara	19.3.1978		78	*1999–2016*	1,396	80*	0	14.69	357	9-127	28/7	28.31	22	71/17
Hettiarachchi Dinuka	15.7.1976		1	*2000*	0	0*	0	0.00	2	2-36	0/0	20.50	0	
Jayasekera Rohan Stanley Amarasiriwardene	7.12.1957		1	*1981*	2	2	0	1.00	–	–	–/–	–	0	2
Jayasundera Madurawelage Don Udara Supeksha	3.1.1991		2	*2015*	30	26	0	7.50	0	0-12	0/0	–	2	
Jayasuriya Sanath Teran (*CY 1997*)	30.6.1969		110	*1990–2007*	6,973	340	14	40.07	98	5-34	2/0	34.34	78	441‡/31
Jayawardene Denagamage Proboth Mahela de Silva (*CY 2007*)	27.5.1977		149	*1997*–2014	11,814	374	34	49.84	6	2-32	0/0	51.66	205	443‡/55

	Born	Died	Tests	Test Career	Runs	HS	100s	Avge	Wkts	BB	5/10	Avge	Ct/St	O/T
Jayawardene Hewasandatchige Asiri Prasanna Wishvanath	9.10.1979		58	2000–*2014*	2,124	154*	4	29.50	–	–	–/–	–	124/32	6
Jeganathan Sridharan	11.7.1951	14.5.1996	2	*1982*	19	8	0	4.75	0	0-12	0/0	–	0	5
John Vinothen Bede	27.5.1960		6	*1982*–1984	53	27*	0	10.60	28	5-60	2/0	21.92	2	45
Jurangpathy Baba Roshan	25.6.1967		2	*1985–1986*	1	1	0	0.25	1	1-69	0/0	93.00	2	
Kalavitigoda Shantha	23.12.1977		1	*2004*	8	7	0	4.00	–	–	–/–	–	2	
Kalpage Ruwan Senani	19.2.1970		11	*1993–1998*	294	63	0	18.37	12	2-27	0/0	64.50	10	86
Kaluhalamulla H. K. S. R. (*see* Randiv, Suraj)														
[2] **Kaluperuma** Lalith Wasantha Silva	25.6.1949		2	*1981*	12	11*	0	4.00	0	0-24	0/0	–	2	4
[2] **Kaluperuma** Sanath Mohan Silva	22.10.1961		4	*1983–1987*	88	23	0	11.00	2	2-17	0/0	62.00	6	2
Kaluwitharana Romesh Shantha	24.11.1969		49	*1992–2004*	1,933	132*	3	26.12	–	–	–/–	–	93/26	189
Kapugedera Chamara Kantha	24.2.1987		8	2006–2009	418	96	0	34.83	0	0-9	0/0	–	6	97/38
Karunaratne Frank Dimuth Madushanka	28.4.1988		36	*2012–2016*	2,200	186	4	32.83	0	0-5	0/0	–	28	17
Kaushal Paskuwal Handi Tharindu	5.3.1993		7	*2014–2015*	106	18	0	10.60	25	5-42	2/0	44.20	3	1
Kulasekara Chamith Kosala Bandara	15.7.1985		1	*2011*	22	15	0	11.00	1	1-65	0/0	80.00	0	4
Kulasekara Kulasekara Mudiyanselage Dinesh Nuwan	22.7.1982		21	*2004*–2014	391	64	0	14.48	48	4-21	0/0	37.37	8	178/50
Kumara Chandradasa Brahammana Ralalage Lahiru Sudesh	13.2.1997		4	*2016*	21	9	0	5.25	15	6-122	1/0	35.20	0	
Kuruppu Don Sardha Brendon Priyantha	5.1.1962		4	*1986*–1991	320	201*	1	53.33	–	–	–/–	–	1	54
Kuruppuarachchi Ajith Kosala	1.11.1964		2	*1985–1986*	0	0*	0	–	8	5-44	1/0	18.62	0	
Labrooy Graeme Fredrick	7.6.1964		9	*1986–1990*	158	70*	0	14.36	27	5-133	1/0	44.22	3	44
Lakmal Ranasinghe Arachchige Suranga	10.3.1987		34	*2010–2016*	312	31	0	8.91	79	5-63	1/0	45.10	8	54/8
Lakshitha Materba Kanatha Gamage Chamila Premanath	4.1.1979		2	2002–*2002*	42	40	0	14.00	5	2-33	0/0	31.60	1	7
Liyanage Dulip Kapila	6.6.1972		9	*1992*–2001	69	23	0	7.66	17	4-56	0/0	39.17	0	16
Lokuarachchi Kaushal Samaraweera	20.5.1982		4	2003–*2003*	94	28*	0	23.50	5	2-47	0/0	59.00	1	21/2
Madugalle Ranjan Senerath	22.4.1959		21	*1981*–1988	1,029	103	1	29.40	0	0-0	0/0	–	9	63
Madurasinghe Madurasinghe Arachchige Wijayasiri Ranjith	30.1.1961		3	1988–*1992*	24	11	0	4.80	3	3-60	0/0	57.33	0	12
Mahanama Roshan Siriwardene	31.5.1966		52	*1985–1997*	2,576	225	4	29.27	0	0-3	0/0	–	56	213
Maharoof Mohamed Farveez	7.9.1984		22	*2003*–2011	556	72	0	18.53	25	4-52	0/0	65.24	7	109/8
Malinga Separamadu Lasith	28.8.1983		30	2004–2010	275	64	0	11.45	101	5-50	3/0	33.15	7	191/62
Mathews Angelo Davis (*CY 2015*)	2.6.1987		65	2009–*2016*	4,470	160	7	46.08	33	4-44	0/0	52.66	49	180/66
Mendis Balapuwaduge Ajantha Winslo	11.3.1985		19	2008–2014	213	78	0	16.38	70	6-99	4/1	34.77	2	87/39
Mendis Balapuwaduge Kusal Gimhan	2.2.1995		14	*2015–2016*	852	176	1	31.55	1	1-10	0/0	18.00	21	17/3

	Born	*Died*	*Tests*	*Test Career*	*Runs*	*HS*	*100s*	*Avge*	*Wkts*	*BB*	*5/10*	*Avge*	*Ct/St*	*O/T*
Mendis Louis Rohan Duleep	25.8.1952		24	*1981*–1988	1,329	124	4	31.64	–	–	–/–	–	9	79
Mirando Magina Thilan Thushara	1.3.1981		10	2003–*2010*	94	15*	0	8.54	28	5-83	1/0	37.14	3	38/6
Mubarak Jehan	10.1.1981		13	2002–*2015*	385	49	0	17.50	0	0-1	0/0	–	15	40/16
Muralitharan Muttiah (*CY 1999*)	17.4.1972		132§	*1992*–2010	1,259	67	0	11.87	795	9-51	67/22	22.67	70	343‡/12
Nawaz Mohamed Naveed	20.9.1973		1	2002	99	78*	0	99.00	–	–	–/–	–	0	3
Nissanka Ratnayake Arachchige Prabath	25.10.1980		4	2003	18	12*	0	6.00	10	5-64	1/0	36.60	0	23
Paranavitana Nishad Tharanga	15.4.1982		32	*2008–2012*	1,792	111	2	32.58	1	1-26	0/0	86.00	27	
Perera Anhettige Suresh Asanka	16.2.1978		3	1998–2001	77	43*	0	25.66	1	1-104	0/0	180.00	1	20
Perera Mahawaduge Dilruwan Kamalaneth	22.7.1982		14	*2013–2016*	331	95	0	14.39	67	6-70	4/1	27.85	8	10/3
Perera Mathurage Don Kusal Janith	17.8.1990		10	*2015–2016*	565	110	1	31.38	–	–	–/–	–	16/8	68/25
Perera Narangoda Liyanaarachchilage Tissara Chirantha	3.4.1989		6	2011–2012	203	75	0	20.30	11	4-63	0/0	59.36	1	114/54
Perera Panagodage Don Ruchira Laksiri	6.4.1977		8	*1998–2002*	33	11*	0	11.00	17	3-40	0/0	38.88	2	19/2
Prasad Kariyawasam Tirana Gamage Dammika	30.5.1983		25	2008–*2015*	476	47	0	12.86	75	5-50	1/0	35.97	6	24/1
Prasanna Seekkuge	27.6.1985		1	*2011*	5	5	0	5.00	0	0-80	0/0	–	0	34/8
Pushpakumara Karuppiahyage Ravindra	21.7.1975		23	*1994–2001*	166	44	0	8.73	58	7-116	4/0	38.65	10	31
Ramanayake Champaka Priyadarshana Hewage	8.1.1965		18	*1987–1993*	143	34*	0	9.53	44	5-82	1/0	42.72	6	62
Ramyakumara Wijekoon Mudiyanselage Gayan	21.12.1976		2	2005	38	14	0	12.66	2	2-49	0/0	33.00	0	0/3
Ranasinghe Anura Nandana	13.10.1956	9.11.1998	2	*1981–1982*	88	77	0	22.00	1	1-23	0/0	69.00	0	9
[2] **Ranatunga** Arjuna (*CY 1999*)	1.12.1963		93	*1981*–2000	5,105	135*	4	35.69	16	2-17	0/0	65.00	47	269
[2] **Ranatunga** Dammika	12.10.1962		2	*1989*	87	45	0	29.00	–	–	–/–	–	0	4
[2] **Ranatunga** Sanjeeva	25.4.1969		9	*1994–1996*	531	118	2	33.18	–	–	–/–	–	2	13
Randiv Suraj (Hewa Kaluhalamullage Suraj Randiv Kaluhalamulla; formerly M. M. M. Suraj)	30.1.1985		12	2010–*2012*	147	39	0	9.18	43	5-82	1/0	37.51	1	31/7
Ratnayake Rumesh Joseph	2.1.1964		23	*1982–1991*	433	56	0	14.43	73	6-66	5/0	35.10	9	70
Ratnayeke Joseph Ravindran	2.5.1960		22	*1981–1989*	807	93	0	25.21	56	8-83	4/0	35.21	1	78
Samarasekera Maitipage Athula Rohitha	5.8.1961		4	1988–*1991*	118	57	0	16.85	3	2-38	0/0	34.66	3	39
[2] **Samaraweera** Dulip Prasanna	12.2.1972		7	*1993–1994*	211	42	0	15.07	–	–	–/–	–	5	5
[2] **Samaraweera** Thilan Thusara	22.9.1976		81	2001–*2012*	5,462	231	14	48.76	15	4-49	0/0	45.93	45	53
Sandakan Paththamperuma Arachchige Don Lakshan Rangika	10.6.1991		3	2016	33	19*	0	16.50	9	4-58	0/0	23.00	1	1
Sangakkara Kumar Chokshanada (*CY 2012*)	27.10.1977		134	2000–*2015*	12,400	319	38	57.40	0	0-4	0/0	–	182/20	397‡/56
Senanayake Charith Panduka	19.12.1962		3	*1990*	97	64	0	19.40	–	–	–/–	–	2	7

§ *Muralitharan's figures exclude two runs, five wickets and two catches for the ICC World XI v Australia in the Super Series Test in 2005-06.*

	Born	Died	Tests	Test Career	Runs	HS	100s	Avge	Wkts	BB	5/10	Avge	Ct/St	O/T
Senanayake Senanayake Mudiyanselage Sachithra Madhushanka	9.2.1985		1	2013	5	5	0	5.00	0	0-30	0/0	–	1	49/24
Shanaka Madagamagamage Dasun	9.9.1991		1	2016	4	4	0	2.00	3	3-46	0/0	15.33	0	9/11
Silva Jayan Kaushal	27.5.1986		35	2011–2016	1,991	139	3	30.16	–	–	–/–	–	30/1	
Silva Kelaniyage Jayantha	2.6.1973		7	1995–1997	6	6*	0	2.00	20	4-16	0/0	32.35	1	1
Silva Lindamlilage Prageeth Chamara	14.12.1979		11	2006–2007	537	152*	1	33.56	1	1-57	0/0	65.00	7	75/16
Silva Sampathawaduge Amal Rohitha	12.12.1960		9	1982–1988	353	111	2	25.21	–	–	–/–	–	33/1	20
Siriwardene Tissa Appuhamilage Milinda	4.12.1985		5	2015–2016	298	68	0	33.11	11	3-25	0/0	23.36	3	14/17
Tharanga Warushavithana Upul	2.2.1985		25	2005–2016	1,412	165	2	32.83	–	–	–/–	–	19	192‡/10
Thirimanne Hettige Don Rumesh Lahiru	8.9.1989		26	2011–2016	1,056	155*	1	24.00	0	0-5	0/0	–	11	107/26
Tillekeratne Hashan Prasantha	14.7.1967		83	1989–2003	4,545	204*	11	42.87	0	0-0	0/0	–	122/2	200
Upashantha Kalutarage Eric Amila	10.6.1972		2	1998–2002	10	6	0	3.33	4	2-41	0/0	50.00	0	12
Vaas Warnakulasuriya Patabendige Ushantha Joseph Chaminda	27.1.1974		111	1994–2009	3,089	100*	1	24.32	355	7-71	12/2	29.58	31	321‡/6
Vandort Michael Graydon	19.1.1980		20	2001–2008	1,144	140	4	36.90	–	–	–/–	–	6	1
Vithanage Kasun Disi Kithuruwan	26.2.1991		10	2012–2015	370	103*	1	26.42	1	1-73	0/0	133.00	10	6/3
Warnapura Bandula	1.3.1953		4	1981–1982	96	38	0	12.00	0	0-1	0/0	–	2	12
Warnapura Basnayake Shalith Malinda	26.5.1979		14	2007–2009	821	120	2	35.69	0	0-40	0/0	–	14	3
Warnaweera Kahakatchchi Patabandige Jayananda	23.11.1960		10	1985–1994	39	20	0	4.33	32	4-25	0/0	31.90	0	6
Weerasinghe Colombage Don Udesh Sanjeewa	1.3.1968		1	1985	3	3	0	3.00	0	0-8	0/0	–	0	
Welagedara Uda Walawwe Mahim Bandaralage Chanaka Asanka	20.3.1981		21	2007–2014	218	48	0	9.08	55	5-52	2/0	41.32	5	10/2
[2] **Wettimuny** Mithra de Silva	11.6.1951		2	1982	28	17	0	7.00	–	–	–/–	–	2	1
[2] **Wettimuny** Sidath (*CY 1985*)	12.8.1956		23	1981–1986	1,221	190	2	29.07	0	0-16	0/0	–	10	35
Wickremasinghe Anguppulige Gamini Dayantha	27.12.1965		3	1989–1992	17	13*	0	8.50	–	–	–/–	–	9/1	4
Wickremasinghe Gallage Pramodya	14.8.1971		40	1991–2000	555	51	0	9.40	85	6-60	3/0	41.87	18	134
Wijegunawardene Kapila Indaka Weerakkody	23.11.1964		2	1991–1991	14	6*	0	4.66	7	4-51	0/0	21.00	0	26
Wijesuriya Roger Gerard Christopher Ediriweera	18.2.1960		4	1981–1985	22	8	0	4.40	1	1-68	0/0	294.00	1	8
Wijetunge Piyal Kashyapa	6.8.1971		1	1993	10	10	0	5.00	2	1-58	0/0	59.00	0	
Zoysa Demuni Nuwan Tharanga	13.5.1978		30	1996–2004	288	28*	0	8.47	64	5-20	1/0	33.70	4	9

ZIMBABWE (100 players)

	Born	Died	Tests	Test Career	Runs	HS	100s	Avge	Wkts	BB	5/10	Avge	Ct/St	O/T
Arnott Kevin John	8.3.1961		4	1992	302	101*	1	43.14	–	–	–/–	–	4	13
Blignaut Arnoldus Mauritius ("Andy")	1.8.1978		19	2000–2005	886	92	0	26.84	53	5-73	3/0	37.05	13	54/1
Brain David Hayden	4.10.1964		9	1992–1994	115	28	0	10.45	30	5-42	1/0	30.50	1	23
Brandes Eddo André	5.3.1963		10	1992–1999	121	39	0	10.08	26	3-45	0/0	36.57	4	59
Brent Gary Bazil	13.1.1976		4	1999–2001	35	25	0	5.83	7	3-21	0/0	44.85	1	70/3
Briant Gavin Aubrey	11.4.1969		1	1992	17	16	0	8.50	–	–	–/–	–	0	5
Bruk-Jackson Glen Keith	25.4.1969		2	1993	39	31	0	9.75	–	–	–/–	–	0	1
Burmester Mark Greville	24.1.1968		3	1992	54	30*	0	27.00	3	3-78	0/0	75.66	1	8
Butchart Iain Peter	9.5.1960		1	1994	23	15	0	11.50	0	0-11	0/0	–	1	20
Campbell Alistair Douglas Ross	23.9.1972		60	1992–2002	2,858	103	2	27.21	0	0-1	0/0	–	60	188
Carlisle Stuart Vance	10.5.1972		37	1994–2005	1,615	118	2	26.91	–	–	–/–	–	34	111
Chakabva Regis Wiriranai	20.9.1987		9	2011–2016	506	101	1	29.76	–	–	–/–	–	9	34/5
Chari Brian Bara	14.2.1992		5	2014–2016	141	80	0	14.10	0	0-3	0/0	–	5	8
Chatara Tendai Larry	28.2.1991		7	2012–2014	82	22	0	6.83	20	5-61	1/0	29.25	0	29/11
Chibhabha Chamunorwa Justice	6.9.1986		2	2016	103	60	0	25.75	1	1-44	0/0	111.00	0	100/30
Chigumbura Elton	14.3.1986		14	2003–2014	569	88	0	21.07	21	5-54	1/0	46.00	6	202‡/47
Chinouya Michael Tawanda	9.6.1986		2	2016	1	1	0	0.50	3	1-45	0/0	62.66	0	2
Coventry Charles Kevin	8.3.1983		2	2005	88	37	0	22.00	–	–	–/–	–	3	39/13
Cremer Alexander Graeme	19.9.1986		15	2004–2016	411	102*	1	15.22	37	4-4	0/0	52.00	9	69/27
Crocker Gary John	16.5.1962		3	1992	69	33	0	23.00	3	2-65	0/0	72.33	0	6
Dabengwa Keith Mbusi	17.8.1980		3	2005	90	35	0	15.00	5	3-127	0/0	49.80	1	37/8
Dekker Mark Hamilton	5.12.1969		14	1993–1996	333	68*	0	15.85	0	0-5	0/0	–	12	23
Duffin Terrence	20.3.1982		2	2005	80	56	0	20.00	–	–	–/–	–	1	23
Ebrahim Dion Digby	7.8.1980		29	2000–2005	1,226	94	0	22.70	–	–	–/–	–	16	82
[2] **Ervine** Craig Richard	19.8.1985		11	2011–2016	670	146	1	33.50	–	–	–/–	–	10	53/16
[2] **Ervine** Sean Michael	6.12.1982		5	2003–2003	261	86	0	32.62	9	4-146	0/0	43.11	7	42
Evans Craig Neil	29.11.1969		3	1996–2003	52	22	0	8.66	0	0-8	0/0	–	1	53
Ewing Gavin Mackie	21.1.1981		3	2003–2005	108	71	0	18.00	2	1-27	0/0	130.00	1	7
Ferreira Neil Robert	3.6.1979		1	2005	21	16	0	10.50	–	–	–/–	–	0	
[2] **Flower** Andrew OBE (*CY 2002*)	28.4.1968		63	1992–2002	4,794	232*	12	51.54	0	0-0	0/0	–	151/9	213
[2] **Flower** Grant William	20.12.1970		67	1992–2003	3,457	201*	6	29.54	25	4-41	0/0	61.48	43	221
Friend Travis John	7.1.1981		13	2001–2003	447	81	0	29.80	25	5-31	1/0	43.60	2	51
Goodwin Murray William	11.12.1972		19	1997–2000	1,414	166*	3	42.84	0	0-3	0/0	–	10	71

	Born	Died	Tests	Test Career	Runs	HS	100s	Avge	Wkts	BB	5/10	Avge	Ct/St	O/T
Gripper Trevor Raymond	28.12.1975		20	*1999–2003*	809	112	1	21.86	6	2-91	0/0	84.83	14	8
Hondo Douglas Tafadzwa	7.7.1979		9	*2001–2004*	83	19	0	9.22	21	6-59	1/0	36.85	5	56
Houghton David Laud	23.6.1957		22	*1992–1997*	1,464	266	4	43.05	0	0-0	0/0	–	17	63
Huckle Adam George	21.9.1971		8	*1997–1998*	74	28*	0	6.72	25	6-109	2/1	34.88	3	19
James Wayne Robert	27.8.1965		4	*1993–1994*	61	33	0	15.25	–	–	–/–	–	16	11
[1] **Jarvis** Kyle Malcolm	16.2.1989		8	*2011–2012*	58	25*	0	7.25	30	5-54	2/0	31.73	3	24/9
[1] **Jarvis** Malcolm Peter	6.12.1955		5	*1992–1994*	4	2*	0	2.00	11	3-30	0/0	35.72	2	12
Johnson Neil Clarkson	24.1.1970		13	*1998*–2000	532	107	1	24.18	15	4-77	0/0	39.60	12	48
Kamungozi Tafadzwa Paul	8.6.1987		1	*2014*	5	5	0	2.50	1	1-51	0/0	58.00	0	14/1
Lamb Gregory Arthur	4.3.1980		1	*2011*	46	39	0	23.00	3	3-120	0/0	47.00	2	15/5
Lock Alan Charles Ingram	10.9.1962		1	*1995*	8	8*	0	8.00	5	3-68	0/0	21.00	0	8
Madondo Trevor Nyasha	22.11.1976	11.6.2001	3	*1997–2000*	90	74*	0	30.00	–	–	–/–	–	1	13
Mahwire Ngonidzashe Blessing	31.7.1982		10	*2002–2005*	147	50*	0	13.36	18	4-92	0/0	50.83	1	23
Maregwede Alester	5.8.1981		2	*2003*	74	28	0	18.50	–	–	–/–	–	1	11
Marillier Douglas Anthony	24.4.1978		5	*2000–2001*	185	73	0	30.83	11	4-57	0/0	29.27	2	48
Maruma Timycen	19.4.1988		1	*2012*	20	10	0	10.00	–	–	–/–	–	1	17/10
[2] **Masakadza** Hamilton	9.8.1983		32	2001–*2016*	1,794	158	4	28.93	16	3-24	0/0	29.56	22	170/50
[2] **Masakadza** Shingirai Winston	4.9.1986		5	*2011–2014*	88	24	0	11.00	16	4-32	0/0	32.18	2	16/7
Masvaure Prince Spencer	7.10.1988		2	2016	55	42	0	13.75	0	0-23	0/0	–	0	
Matambanadzo Everton Zvikomborero	13.4.1976		3	*1996–1999*	17	7	0	4.25	4	2-62	0/0	62.50	0	7
Matsikenyeri Stuart	3.5.1983		8	*2003–2004*	351	57	0	23.40	2	1-58	0/0	172.50	7	113/10
Mawoyo Tinotenda Mbiri Kanayi	8.1.1986		11	*2011–2016*	615	163*	1	29.28	–	–	–/–	–	7	7
Mbangwa Mpumelelo ("Pommie")	26.6.1976		15	*1996–2000*	34	8	0	2.00	32	3-23	0/0	31.43	2	29
Meth Keegan Orry	8.2.1988		2	*2012*	72	31*	0	24.00	4	2-41	0/0	24.50	0	11/2
Moor Peter Joseph	2.2.1991		3	2016–*2016*	211	79	0	35.16	–	–	–/–	–	6/1	14/8
Mpofu Christopher Bobby	27.11.1985		11	*2004–2016*	49	20	0	3.50	25	4-92	0/0	46.80	2	71/20
Mumba Carl Tapfuma	6.5.1995		2	*2016*	14	10*	0	4.66	8	4-50	0/0	37.25	1	1
Mupariwa Tawanda	16.4.1985		1	*2003*	15	14	0	15.00	0	0-136	0/0	–	0	40/4
Murphy Brian Andrew	1.12.1976		11	*1999–2001*	123	30	0	10.25	18	3-32	0/0	61.83	11	31
Mushangwe Natsai	9.2.1991		2	*2014*	8	8	0	2.00	7	4-82	0/0	62.14	2	6/5
Mutendera David Travolta	25.1.1979		1	*2000*	10	10	0	5.00	0	0-29	0/0	–	0	9
Mutizwa Forster	24.8.1985		1	*2011*	24	18	0	12.00	–	–	–/–	–	0	17/3
Mutumbami Richmond	11.6.1989		6	*2012–2014*	217	43	0	19.72	–	–	–/–	–	17/2	31/14
Mwayenga Waddington	20.6.1984		1	*2005*	15	14*	0	15.00	1	1-79	0/0	79.00	0	3
Ncube Njabulo	14.10.1989		1	*2011*	17	14	0	8.50	1	1-80	0/0	121.00	1	1
Nkala Mluleki Luke	1.4.1981		10	2000–*2004*	187	47	0	14.38	11	3-82	0/0	66.09	4	50/1

	Born	Died	Tests	Test Career	Runs	HS	100s	Avge	Wkts	BB	5/10	Avge	Ct/St	O/T
Nyumbu John Curtis	1.3.1983		3	2014–2016	38	14	0	7.60	5	5-157	1/0	75.80	2	19
Olonga Henry Khaaba	3.7.1976		30	1994–2002	184	24	0	5.41	68	5-70	2/0	38.52	10	50
Panyangara Tinashe	21.10.1985		9	2003–2014	201	40*	0	16.75	31	5-59	1/0	26.22	3	65/14
Peall Stephen Guy	2.9.1969		4	1993–1994	60	30	0	15.00	4	2-89	0/0	75.75	1	21
Price Raymond William	12.6.1976		22	1999–2012	261	36	0	8.70	80	6-73	5/1	36.06	4	102/16
Pycroft Andrew John	6.6.1956		3	1992	152	60	0	30.40	–	–	–/–	–	2	20
Ranchod Ujesh	17.5.1969		1	1992	8	7	0	4.00	1	1-45	0/0	45.00	0	3
[2] **Rennie** Gavin James	12.1.1976		23	1997–2001	1,023	93	0	22.73	1	1-40	0/0	84.00	13	40
[2] **Rennie** John Alexander	29.7.1970		4	1993–1997	62	22	0	12.40	3	2-22	0/0	97.66	1	44
Rogers Barney Guy	20.8.1982		4	2004	90	29	0	11.25	0	0-17	0/0	–	1	15
Shah Ali Hassimshah	7.8.1959		3	1992–1996	122	62	0	24.40	1	1-46	0/0	125.00	0	28
Sibanda Vusimuzi	10.10.1983		14	2003–2014	591	93	0	21.10	–	–	–/–	–	16	125‡/26
Sikandar Raza	24.4.1986		6	2013–2016	389	82	0	32.41	6	3-123	0/0	71.00	0	62/26
[2] **Strang** Bryan Colin	9.6.1972		26	1994–2001	465	53	0	12.91	56	5-101	1/0	39.33	11	49
[2] **Strang** Paul Andrew	28.7.1970		24	1994–2001	839	106*	1	27.06	70	8-109	4/1	36.02	15	95
Streak Heath Hilton	16.3.1974		65	1993–2005	1,990	127*	1	22.35	216	6-73	7/0	28.14	17	187‡
Taibu Tatenda	14.5.1983		28	2001–2011	1,546	153	1	30.31	1	1-27	0/0	27.00	57/5	149‡/17
Taylor Brendan Ross Murray	6.2.1986		23	2003–2014	1,493	171	4	34.72	0	0-6	0/0	–	23	167/26
Tiripano Donald Tatenda	17.3.1988		5	2014–2016	173	49*	0	24.71	9	3-91	0/0	52.44	2	13/8
Traicos Athanasios John	17.5.1947		4†	1992	11	5	0	2.75	14	5-86	1/0	40.14	4	27
Utseya Prosper	26.3.1985		4	2003–2013	107	45	0	15.28	10	3-60	0/0	41.00	2	164/35
Vermeulen Mark Andrew	2.3.1979		9	2002–2014	449	118	1	24.94	0	0-5	0/0	–	6	43
Viljoen Dirk Peter	11.3.1977		2	1997–2000	57	38	0	14.25	1	1-14	0/0	65.00	1	53
Vitori Brian Vitalis	22.2.1990		4	2011–2013	52	19*	0	10.40	12	5-61	1/0	38.66	2	20/11
[1] **Waller** Andrew Christopher	25.9.1959		2	1996	69	50	0	23.00	–	–	–/–	–	1	39
[1] **Waller** Malcolm Noel	28.9.1984		11	2011–2016	436	72*	0	20.76	8	4-59	0/0	24.62	10	58/28
Watambwa Brighton Tonderai	9.6.1977		6	2000–2001	11	4*	0	3.66	14	4-64	0/0	35.00	0	
Whittall Andrew Richard	28.3.1973		10	1996–1999	114	17	0	7.60	7	3-73	0/0	105.14	8	63
Whittall Guy James	5.9.1972		46	1993–2002	2,207	203*	4	29.42	51	4-18	0/0	40.94	19	147
Williams Sean Colin	26.9.1986		6	2012–2016	364	119	1	30.33	5	2-95	0/0	57.20	6	101/24
Wishart Craig Brian	9.1.1974		27	1995–2005	1,098	114	1	22.40	–	–	–/–	–	15	90

BANGLADESH (85 players)

	Born	Died	Tests	Test Career	Runs	HS	100s	Avge	Wkts	BB	5/10	Avge	Ct/St	O/T
Abdur Razzak	15.6.1982		12	2005–2013	245	43	0	17.50	23	3-93	0/0	67.39	4	153/34
Abul Hasan	5.8.1992		3	2012	165	113	1	82.50	3	2-80	0/0	123.66	3	6/4
Aftab Ahmed	10.11.1985		16	2004–2009	582	82*	0	20.78	5	2-31	0/0	47.40	7	85/11
Akram Khan	1.11.1968		8	2000–2003	259	44	0	16.18	–	–	–/–	–	3	44
Al-Amin Hossain	1.1.1990		6	2013–2014	68	32*	0	22.66	6	3-80	0/0	76.66	0	14/25
Al Sahariar	23.4.1978		15	2000–2003	683	71	0	22.76	–	–	–/–	–	10	29
Alamgir Kabir	10.1.1981		3	2002–2003	8	4	0	2.00	0	0-39	0/0	–	0	
Alok Kapali	1.1.1984		17	2002–2005	584	85	0	17.69	6	3-3	0/0	118.16	5	69/7
Aminul Islam	2.2.1968		13	2000–2002	530	145	1	21.20	1	1-66	0/0	149.00	5	39
Anamul Haque	16.12.1992		4	2012–2014	73	22	0	9.12	–	–	–/–	–	2	30/13
Anwar Hossain Monir	31.12.1981		3	2003–2005	22	13	0	7.33	0	0-95	0/0	–	0	1
Anwar Hossain Piju	10.12.1983		1	2002	14	12	0	7.00	–	–	–/–	–	0	1
Bikash Ranjan Das	14.7.1982		1	2000	2	2	0	1.00	1	1-64	0/0	72.00	1	
Ehsanul Haque	1.12.1979		1	2002	7	5	0	3.50	0	0-18	0/0	–	0	6
Elias Sunny	2.8.1986		4	2011–2012	38	20*	0	7.60	12	6-94	1/0	43.16	1	4/7
Enamul Haque snr.	27.2.1966		10	2000–2003	180	24*	0	12.00	18	4-136	0/0	57.05	1	29
Enamul Haque jnr.	5.12.1986		15	2003–2012	59	13	0	5.90	44	7-95	3/1	40.61	3	10
Fahim Muntasir	1.11.1980		3	2001–2002	52	33	0	8.66	5	3-131	0/0	68.40	1	3
Faisal Hossain	26.10.1978		1	2003	7	5	0	3.50	–	–	–/–	–	0	6
Habibul Bashar	17.8.1972		50	2000–2007	3,026	113	3	30.87	0	0-1	0/0	–	22	111
Hannan Sarkar	1.12.1982		17	2002–2004	662	76	0	20.06	–	–	–/–	–	7	20
Hasibul Hossain	3.6.1977		5	2000–2001	97	31	0	10.77	6	2-125	0/0	95.16	1	32
Imrul Kayes	2.2.1987		27	2008–2016	1,432	150	3	28.64	0	0-1	0/0	–	27	65/8
Jahurul Islam	12.12.1986		7	2009–2012	347	48	0	26.69	–	–	–/–	–	7	14/3
Javed Omar Belim	25.11.1976		40	2000–2007	1,720	119	1	22.05	0	0-12	0/0	–	10	59
Jubair Hossain	12.9.1995		6	2014–2015	13	7*	0	4.33	16	5-96	1/0	30.81	2	3/1
Junaid Siddique	30.10.1987		19	2007–2012	969	106	1	26.18	0	0-2	0/0	–	11	54/7
Kamrul Islam	10.12.1991		4	2016	41	25*	0	6.83	7	3-87	0/0	42.57	0	
Khaled Mahmud	26.7.1971		12	2001–2003	266	45	0	12.09	13	4-37	0/0	64.00	2	77
Khaled Mashud	8.2.1976		44	2000–2007	1,409	103*	1	19.04	–	–	–/–	–	78/9	126
Liton Das	13.10.1994		3	2015	97	50	0	32.33	–	–	–/–	–	3	9/3
Mahbubul Alam	1.12.1983		4	2008	5	2	0	1.25	5	2-62	0/0	62.80	0	5
Mahmudullah	4.2.1986		31	2009–2016	1,709	115	1	30.51	39	5-51	1/0	44.05	30/1	134/53

	Born	Died	Tests	Test Career	Runs	HS	100s	Avge	Wkts	BB	5/10	Avge	Ct/St	O/T
Manjural Islam	7.11.1979		17	*2000–2003*	81	21	0	3.68	28	6-81	1/0	57.32	4	34
Manjural Islam Rana	4.5.1984	16.3.2007	6	*2003–2004*	257	69	0	25.70	5	3-84	0/0	80.20	3	25
Marshall Ayub	5.12.1988		3	*2013*	125	41	0	20.83	0	0-15	0/0	–	2	
Mashrafe bin Mortaza	5.10.1983		36	*2001*–2009	797	79	0	12.85	78	4-60	0/0	41.52	9	167‡/49
Mehedi Hasan	25.10.1997		4	*2016*	20	10	0	2.50	23	6-77	3/1	24.56	4	
Mehrab Hossain snr.	22.9.1978		9	2000–2003	241	71	0	13.38	0	0-5	0/0	–	6	18
Mehrab Hossain jnr.	8.7.1987		7	2007–*2008*	243	83	0	20.25	4	2-29	0/0	70.25	2	18/2
Mohammad Ashraful	9.9.1984		61	*2001–2012*	2,737	190	6	24.00	21	2-42	0/0	60.52	25	175‡/23
Mohammad Rafique	5.9.1970		33	*2000–2007*	1,059	111	1	18.57	100	6-77	7/0	40.76	7	123‡/1
Mohammad Salim	15.10.1981		2	2003	49	26	0	16.33	–	–	–/–	–	3/1	1
Mohammad Shahid	1.11.1988		5	*2014*–2015	57	25	0	11.40	5	2-23	0/0	57.60	0	1
Mohammad Sharif	12.12.1983		10	*2000–2007*	122	24*	0	7.17	14	4-98	0/0	79.00	5	9
Mominul Haque	29.9.1991		20	*2012–2016*	1,637	181	4	51.15	1	1-10	0/0	192.00	17	26/6
Mushfiqur Rahim	1.9.1988		51	2005–*2016*	2,922	200	4	33.58	–	–	–/–	–	82/11	165/57
Mushfiqur Rahman	1.1.1980		10	*2000–2004*	232	46*	0	13.64	13	4-65	0/0	63.30	6	28
Mustafizur Rahman	6.9.1995		2	2015	3	3	0	3.00	4	4-37	0/0	14.50	0	11/13
Naeem Islam	31.12.1986		8	*2008–2012*	416	108	1	32.00	1	1-11	0/0	303.00	2	59/10
[2] **Nafis Iqbal**	31.1.1985		11	*2004–2005*	518	121	1	23.54	–	–	–/–	–	2	16
Naimur Rahman	19.9.1974		8	*2000–2002*	210	48	0	15.00	12	6-132	1/0	59.83	4	29
Nasir Hossain	30.11.1991		17	*2011*–2015	971	100	1	37.34	8	3-52	0/0	51.62	10	58/31
Nazimuddin	1.10.1985		3	*2011–2012*	125	78	0	20.83	–	–	–/–	–	1	11/7
Nazmul Hossain	5.10.1987		2	*2004–2011*	16	8*	0	8.00	5	2-61	0/0	38.80	0	38/4
Nazmul Hossain Shanto	25.5.1998		1	*2016*	30	18	0	15.00	0	0-13	0/0	–	0	
Nurul Hasan	21.11.1993		1	*2016*	47	47	0	23.50	–	–	–/–	–	2	2/6
Rafiqul Islam	7.11.1977		1	*2002*	7	6	0	3.50	–	–	–/–	–	0	1
Rajin Saleh	20.11.1983		24	*2003–2008*	1,141	89	0	25.93	2	1-9	0/0	134.00	15	43
Raqibul Hasan	8.10.1987		9	*2008–2011*	336	65	0	19.76	1	1-0	0/0	17.00	9	55/5
Robiul Islam	20.10.1986		9	2010–*2014*	99	33	0	9.00	25	6-71	2/0	39.68	5	3/1
Rubel Hossain	1.1.1990		24	*2009–2016*	220	45*	0	9.56	32	5-166	1/0	77.93	11	69/11
Sabbir Rahman	20.8.1991		4	*2016*	209	64*	0	34.83	0	0-11	0/0	–	2	32/26
Sajidul Islam	18.1.1988		3	*2007–2012*	18	6	0	3.00	3	2-71	0/0	77.33	0	0/1
Sanwar Hossain	5.8.1973		9	*2001–2003*	345	49	0	19.16	5	2-128	0/0	62.00	1	27
Shafiul Islam	6.10.1989		9	*2009–2016*	185	53	0	11.56	15	3-86	0/0	53.40	2	56/11
Shahadat Hossain	7.8.1986		38	2005–*2014*	521	40	0	10.01	72	6-27	4/0	51.81	9	51/6
Shahriar Hossain	1.6.1976		3	*2000–2003*	99	48	0	19.80	–	–	–/–	–	0/1	20
Shahriar Nafees	1.5.1985		24	*2005–2012*	1,267	138	1	26.39	–	–	–/–	–	19	75/1

	Born	*Died*	*Tests*	*Test Career*	*Runs*	*HS*	*100s*	*Avge*	*Wkts*	*BB*	*5/10*	*Avge*	*Ct/St*	*O/T*
Shakib Al Hasan	24.3.1987		46	2007–*2016*	3,213	217	4	40.67	165	7-36	15/1	32.14	19	166/54
Shamsur Rahman	5.6.1988		6	*2013–2014*	305	106	1	25.41	0	0-5	0/0	–	7	10/9
Shuvagata Hom	11.11.1986		8	*2014–2016*	244	50	0	22.18	8	2-66	0/0	63.25	8	4/5
Sohag Gazi	5.8.1991		10	*2012–2013*	325	101*	1	21.66	38	6-74	2/0	42.07	5	20/10
Soumya Sarkar	25.2.1993		4	*2014–2016*	229	86	0	32.71	1	1-45	0/0	125.00	0	20/19
Subashis Roy	28.11.1988		1	*2016*	0	0	0	0.00	3	2-89	0/0	40.33	0	1
Suhrawadi Shuvo	21.11.1988		1	*2011*	15	15	0	7.50	4	3-73	0/0	36.50	0	17/1
Syed Rasel	3.7.1984		6	*2005*–2007	37	19	0	4.62	12	4-129	0/0	47.75	0	52/8
Taijul Islam	7.2.1992		11	*2014–2016*	166	32	0	11.85	43	8-39	3/0	32.13	6	4
Talha Jubair	10.12.1985		7	2002–*2004*	52	31	0	6.50	14	3-135	0/0	55.07	1	6
[2]**Tamim Iqbal** (*CY 2011*)	20.3.1989		46	*2007–2016*	3,443	206	8	39.57	0	0-1	0/0	–	12	162/52
Tapash Baisya	25.12.1982		21	2002–2005	384	66	0	11.29	36	4-72	0/0	59.36	6	56
Tareq Aziz	4.9.1983		3	*2003–2004*	22	10*	0	11.00	1	1-76	0/0	261.00	1	10
Taskin Ahmed	3.4.1995		2	*2016*	49	33	0	12.25	2	1-86	0/0	143.00	0	23/13
Tushar Imran	10.12.1983		5	2002–2007	89	28	0	8.90	0	0-48	0/0	–	1	41
Ziaur Rahman	2.12.1986		1	*2012*	14	14	0	7.00	4	4-63	0/0	17.75	0	13/14

Notes

Family relationships in the above lists are indicated by superscript numbers; the following list contains only those players whose relationship is not apparent from a shared name.

In one Test, A. and G. G. Hearne played for England; their brother, F. Hearne, for South Africa.
The Waughs and New Zealand's Marshalls are the only instance of Test-playing twins.
Adnan Akmal: brother of Kamran and Umar Akmal.
Amar Singh, L.: brother of L. Ramji.
Azmat Rana: brother of Shafqat Rana.
Bazid Khan (Pakistan): son of Majid Khan (Pakistan) and grandson of M. Jahangir Khan (India).
Bravo, D. J. and D. M.: half-brothers.
Chappell, G. S., I. M. and T. M.: grandsons of V. Y. Richardson.
Collins, P. T.: half-brother of F. H. Edwards.
Cooper, W. H.: great-grandfather of A. P. Sheahan.
Edwards, F. H.: half-brother of P. T. Collins.
Hanif Mohammad: brother of Mushtaq, Sadiq and Wazir Mohammad; father of Shoaib Mohammad.
Headley, D. W. (England): son of R. G. A. and grandson of G. A. Headley (both West Indies).
Hearne, F. (England and South Africa): father of G. A. L. Hearne (South Africa).
Jahangir Khan, M. (India): father of Majid Khan and grandfather of Bazid Khan (both Pakistan).
Kamran Akmal: brother of Adnan and Umar Akmal.
Khalid Wazir (Pakistan): son of S. Wazir Ali (India).
Kirsten, G. and P. N.: half-brothers.
Majid Khan (Pakistan): son of M. Jahangir Khan (India) and father of Bazid Khan (Pakistan).
Manzoor Elahi: brother of Salim and Zahoor Elahi.
Moin Khan: brother of Nadeem Khan.
Mudassar Nazar: son of Nazar Mohammad.
Murray, D. A.: son of E. D. Weekes.
Mushtaq Mohammad: brother of Hanif, Sadiq and Wazir Mohammad.
Nadeem Khan: brother of Moin Khan.
Nafis Iqbal: brother of Tamim Iqbal.
Nazar Mohammad: father of Mudassar Nazar.
Nazir Ali, S.: brother of S. Wazir Ali.
Pattinson, D. J. (England): brother of J. L. Pattinson (Australia).
Pervez Sajjad: brother of Waqar Hassan.
Ramiz Raja: brother of Wasim Raja.
Ramji, L.: brother of L. Amar Singh.
Richardson, V. Y.: grandfather of G. S., I. M. and T. M. Chappell.
Sadiq Mohammad: brother of Hanif, Mushtaq and Wazir Mohammad.
Saeed Ahmed: brother of Younis Ahmed.
Salim Elahi: brother of Manzoor and Zahoor Elahi.
Shafqat Rana: brother of Azmat Rana.
Sheahan, A. P.: great-grandson of W. H. Cooper.
Shoaib Mohammad: son of Hanif Mohammad.
Tamim Iqbal: brother of Nafis Iqbal.
Umar Akmal: brother of Adnan and Kamran Akmal.
Waqar Hassan: brother of Pervez Sajjad.
Wasim Raja: brother of Ramiz Raja.
Wazir Ali, S. (India): brother of S. Nazir Ali (India) and father of Khalid Wazir (Pakistan).
Wazir Mohammad: brother of Hanif, Mushtaq and Sadiq Mohammad.
Weekes, E. D.: father of D. A. Murray.
Yograj Singh: father of Yuvraj Singh.
Younis Ahmed: brother of Saeed Ahmed.
Yuvraj Singh: son of Yograj Singh.
Zahoor Elahi: brother of Manzoor and Salim Elahi.

Teams are listed only where relatives played for different sides.

PLAYERS APPEARING FOR MORE THAN ONE TEST TEAM

Fourteen cricketers have appeared for two countries in Test matches, namely:

Amir Elahi (India 1, Pakistan 5)
J. J. Ferris (Australia 8, England 1)
S. C. Guillen (West Indies 5, New Zealand 3)
Gul Mahomed (India 8, Pakistan 1)
F. Hearne (England 2, South Africa 4)
A. H. Kardar (India 3, Pakistan 23)
W. E. Midwinter (England 4, Australia 8)
F. Mitchell (England 2, South Africa 3)
W. L. Murdoch (Australia 18, England 1)
Nawab of Pataudi snr (England 3, India 3)
A. J. Traicos (South Africa 3, Zimbabwe 4)
A. E. Trott (Australia 3, England 2)
K. C. Wessels (Australia 24, South Africa 16)
S. M. J. Woods (Australia 3, England 3)

Wessels also played 54 one-day internationals for Australia and 55 for South Africa.

The following players appeared for the ICC World XI against Australia in the Super Series Test in 2005-06: M. V. Boucher, R. Dravid, A. Flintoff, S. J. Harmison, Inzamam-ul-Haq, J. H. Kallis, B. C. Lara, M. Muralitharan, V. Sehwag, G. C. Smith, D. L. Vettori.

In 1970, England played five first-class matches against the Rest of the World after the cancellation of South Africa's tour. Players were awarded England caps, but the matches are no longer considered to have Test status. Alan Jones (born 4.11.1938) made his only appearance for England in this series, scoring 5 and 0; he did not bowl and took no catches.

ONE-DAY AND TWENTY20 INTERNATIONAL CRICKETERS

The following players had appeared for Test-playing countries in one-day internationals or Twenty20 internationals by December 31, 2016, but had not represented their countries in Test matches by January 23, 2017. (Numbers in brackets signify number of one-day internationals for each player: where a second number appears, e.g. (5/1), it signifies the number of Twenty20 internationals for that player.)

By January 2017, K. A. Pollard was the most experienced international player never to have appeared in Test cricket, with 101 one-day internationals and 50 Twenty20 internationals. R. G. Sharma held the record for most international appearances before making his Test debut, with 108 one-day internationals and 36 Twenty20 internationals.

England

M. W. Alleyne (10), I. D. Austin (9), S. W. Billings (6/7), D. R. Briggs (1/7), A. D. Brown (16), D. R. Brown (9), G. Chapple (1), J. W. M. Dalrymple (27/3), S. M. Davies (8/5), J. L. Denly (9/5), J. W. Dernbach (24/34), M. V. Fleming (11), P. J. Franks (1), I. J. Gould (18), A. P. Grayson (2), H. F. Gurney (10/2), G. W. Humpage (3), T. E. Jesty (10), E. C. Joyce (17/2), C. Kieswetter (46/25), G. D. Lloyd (6), A. G. R. Loudon (1), J. D. Love (3), M. B. Loye (7), M. J. Lumb (3/27), M. A. Lynch (3), A. D. Mascarenhas (20/14), S. C. Meaker (2/2), T. S. Mills (0/1), P. Mustard (10/2), P. A. Nixon (19/1), S. D. Parry (2/5), J. J. Roy (32/16), M. J. Smith (5), N. M. K. Smith (7), J. N. Snape (10/1), V. S. Solanki (51/3), R. J. W. Topley (10/6), J. O. Troughton (6), C. M. Wells (2), V. J. Wells (9), A. G. Wharf (13), D. J. Willey (22/12), L. J. Wright (50/51), M. H. Yardy (28/14).

D. R. Brown also played 16 ODIs for Scotland, and E. C. Joyce 46 ODIs and 16 T20Is for Ireland.

Australia

S. A. Abbott (1/3), C. T. Bancroft (0/1), T. R. Birt (0/4), G. A. Bishop (2), S. M. Boland (14/3), C. J. Boyce (0/7), R. J. Campbell (2), D. T. Christian (19/15), M. J. Cosgrove (3), N. M. Coulter-Nile (16/17), B. J. Cutting (4/4), M. J. Di Venuto (9), B. R. Dorey (4), B. R. Dunk (0/3), Fawad Ahmed (3/2), A. J. Finch (77/28), P. J. Forrest (15), B. Geeves (2/1), S. F. Graf (11), I. J. Harvey (73), S. M. Harwood (1/3), T. M. Head (15/4), J. R. Hopes (84/12), D. J. Hussey (69/39), B. Laughlin (5/3), S. Lee (45), M. L. Lewis (7/2), C. A. Lynn (0/5), R. J. McCurdy (11), K. H. MacLeay (16), J. P. Maher (26), J. M. Muirhead (0/5), D. P. Nannes (1/15), A. A. Noffke (1/2), J. S. Paris (2), L. A. Pomersbach (0/1), G. D. Porter (2), N. J. Reardon (0/2), K. W. Richardson (12/3), B. J. Rohrer (0/1), G. S. Sandhu (2), J. D. Siddons (1), M. P. Stoinis (1/1), A. M. Stuart (3), C. P. Tremain (4), G. S. Trimble (2), A. J. Tye (0/3), D. J. Worrall (3), B. E. Young (6), A. Zampa (19/8), A. K. Zesers (2).

R. J. Campbell also played three T20Is for Hong Kong, and D. P. Nannes two T20Is for the Netherlands.

South Africa

Y. A. Abdulla (0/2), S. Abrahams (1), F. Behardien (51/25), D. M. Benkenstein (23), G. H. Bodi (2/1), L. E. Bosman (13/14), R. E. Bryson (7), D. J. Callaghan (29), D. N. Crookes (32), H. Davids (2/9), T. Henderson (0/1), B. E. Hendricks (0/5), R. R. Hendricks (0/5), C. A. Ingram (31/9), J. C. Kent (2), L. J. Koen (5), G. J-P. Kruger (3/1), H. G. Kuhn (0/5), E. Leie (0/2), R. E. Levi (0/13), J. Louw (3/2), D. A. Miller (87/46), P. V. Mpitsang (2), S. J. Palframan (7), A. M. Phangiso (21/11), A. L. Phehlukwayo (6), N. Pothas (3), D. Pretorius (3), A. G. Puttick (1), C. E. B. Rice (3), M. J. R. Rindel (22), R. R. Rossouw (36/15), D. B. Rundle (2), T. G. Shaw (9), M. Shezi (1), E. O. Simons (23), E. L. R. Stewart (6), R. Telemachus (37/3), J. Theron (4/9), A. C. Thomas (0/1), T. Tshabalala (4), R. E. van der Merwe (13/13), J. J. van der Wath (10/8), V. B. van Jaarsveld (2/3), M. N. van Wyk (17/8), C. J. P. G. van Zyl (2), D. Wiese (6/20), H. S. Williams (7), M. Yachad (1).

R. E. van der Merwe also played 11 T20Is for the Netherlands.

West Indies

H. A. G. Anthony (3), S. Badree (0/32), C. D. Barnwell (0/6), M. C. Bascombe (0/1), N. E. Bonner (0/2), D. Brown (3), B. St A. Browne (4), P. A. Browne (5), H. R. Bryan (15), D. C. Butler (5/1), J. L. Carter (17), J. Charles (48/34), D. O. Christian (0/2), R. T. Crandon (1), R. Emrit (2), S. E. Findlay (9/2), A. D. S. Fletcher (25/32), R. S. Gabriel (11), R. C. Haynes (8), R. O. Hurley (9), D. P. Hyatt (9/5), K. C. B. Jeremy (6), E. Lewis (5/5), A. Martin (9/1), G. E. Mathurin (0/3), J. N. Mohammed (2), A. R. Nurse (4/4), W. K. D. Perkins (0/1), K. A. Pollard (101/50), N. Pooran (0/3), R. Powell (4), M. R. Pydanna (3), A. C. L. Richards (1/1), K. Santokie (0/12), K. F. Semple (7), D. C. Thomas (21/3), C. M. Tuckett (1), K. O. K. Williams (0/1), L. R. Williams (15).

New Zealand

G. W. Aldridge (2/1), M. D. Bailey (1), M. D. Bates (2/3), B. R. Blair (14), N. T. Broom (25/10), C. E. Bulfin (4), T. K. Canning (4), P. G. Coman (3), C. de Grandhomme (1/4), A. P. Devcich (12/4), B. J. Diamanti (1/1), M. W. Douglas (6), A. M. Ellis (15/5), L. H. Ferguson (4), B. G. Hadlee (2), L. J. Hamilton (2), R. T. Hart (1), R. L. Hayes (1), R. M. Hira (0/15), P. A. Hitchcock (14/1), L. G. Howell (12), M. J. McClenaghan (48/28), N. L. McCullum (84/63), P. D. McGlashan (4/11), B. J. McKechnie (14), E. B. McSweeney (16), A. W. Mathieson (1), J. P. Millmow (5), A. F. Milne (33/18), T. S. Nethula (5), C. J. Nevin (37), A. J. Penn (5), R. G. Petrie (12), R. B. Reid (9), S. J. Roberts (2), S. L. Stewart (4), L. W. Stott (1), G. P. Sulzberger (3), A. R. Tait (5), E. P. Thompson (1/1), M. D. J. Walker (3), R. J. Webb (3), B. M. Wheeler (6), J. W. Wilson (6), W. A. Wisneski (3), L. J. Woodcock (4/3), G. H. Worker (2/2).

India

S. Aravind (0/1), P. Awana (0/2), A. C. Bedade (13), A. Bhandari (2), Bhupinder Singh snr (2), G. Bose (1), J. J. Bumrah (8/21), Y. S. Chahal (3/3), V. B. Chandrasekhar (7), U. Chatterjee (3), N. A. David (4), P. Dharmani (1), R. Dhawan (3/1), A. B. Dinda (13/9), F. Y. Fazal (1), R. S. Gavaskar (11), R. S. Ghai (6), M. S. Gony (2), Gurkeerat Singh (3), K. M. Jadhav (12/5), Joginder Sharma (4/4), A. V. Kale (1), S. C. Khanna (10), G. K. Khoda (2), A. R. Khurasiya (12), D. S. Kulkarni (12/2), T. Kumaran (8), Mandeep Singh (0/3), J. J. Martin (10), D. Mongia (57/1), S. P. Mukherjee (3), A. M. Nayar (3), P. Negi (0/1), G. K. Pandey (2), M. K. Pandey (12/6), H. H. Pandya (4/16), J. V. Paranjpe (4), Parvez Rasool (1), A. K. Patel (8), A. R. Patel (30/7), Y. K. Pathan (57/22), Randhir Singh (2), S. S. Raul (2), A. T. Rayudu (34/6), A. M. Salvi (4), S. V. Samson (0/1), M. Sharma (26/8), R. Sharma (4/2), S. Sharma (0/2), L. R. Shukla (3), R. P. Singh (2), R. S. Sodhi (18), S. Somasunder (2), B. B. Sran (6/2), S. Sriram (8), Sudhakar Rao (1), M. K. Tiwary (12/3), S. S. Tiwary (3), S. Tyagi (4/1), R. V. Uthappa (46/13), P. S. Vaidya (4), Y. Venugopal Rao (16), Jai P. Yadav (12).

Pakistan

Aamer Hameed (2), Aamer Hanif (5), Aamer Yasin (3/1), Akhtar Sarfraz (4), Anwar Ali (22/16), Arshad Pervez (2), Asad Ali (4/2), Asif Mahmood (2), Awais Zia (0/5), Bilal Asif (3), Faisal Athar (1), Ghulam Ali (3), Haafiz Shahid (3), Hammad Azam (11/5), Haris Sohail (22/4), Hasan Ali (8/3), Hasan Jamil (6), Imad Wasim (14/15), Imran Abbas (2), Imran Khan jnr (0/3), Iqbal Sikandar (4), Irfan Bhatti (1), Javed Qadir (1), Junaid Zia (4), Kamran Hussain (2), Kashif Raza (1), Khalid Latif (5/13), Mahmood Hamid (1), Mansoor Amjad (1/1), Mansoor Rana (2), Manzoor Akhtar (7), Maqsood Rana (1), Masood Iqbal (1), Mohammad Wasim (14/8), Moin-ul-Atiq (5), Mujahid Jamshed (4), Mukhtar Ahmed (0/6), Naeem Ahmed (1), Naeem Ashraf (2), Najaf Shah (1), Naseer Malik (3), Nauman Anwar (0/1), Naumanullah (1), Parvez Mir (3), Rafatullah Mohmand (0/3), Rameez Raja (0/2), Raza Hasan (1/10), Rizwan Ahmed (1), Rumman Raees (0/1), Saad Nasim (3/3), Saadat Ali

(8), Saeed Azad (4), Sajid Ali (13), Sajjad Akbar (2), Salim Pervez (1), Samiullah Khan (2), Shahid Anwar (1), Shahzaib Hasan (3/10), Shakeel Ansar (0/2), Shakil Khan (1), Shoaib Khan (0/1), Sohaib Maqsood (26/20), Sohail Fazal (2), Tanvir Mehdi (1), Usman Khan (0/2), Usman Salahuddin (2), Wasim Haider (3), Zafar Gohar (1), Zafar Iqbal (8), Zahid Ahmed (2).

Sri Lanka

M. A. Aponso (5), K. M. C. Bandara (1/1), J. W. H. D. Boteju (2), A. Dananjaya (1/5), D. L. S. de Silva (2), G. N. de Silva (4), P. C. de Silva (6), L. H. D. Dilhara (9/2), B. Fernando (0/2), E. R. Fernando (3), T. L. Fernando (1), U. N. K. Fernando (2), W. I. A. Fernando (1), J. C. Gamage (4), P. L. S. Gamage (5), W. C. A. Ganegama (4), F. R. M. Goonatilleke (1), P. W. Gunaratne (23), M. D. Gunathilleke (16/5), A. A. W. Gunawardene (1), P. D. Heyn (2), W. S. Jayantha (17), P. S. Jayaprakashdaran (1), C. U. Jayasinghe (0/5), S. A. Jayasinghe (2), D. S. N. F. G. Jayasuriya (6/11), S. H. T. Kandamby (39/5), S. H. U. Karnain (19), H. G. J. M. Kulatunga (0/2), B. M. A. J. Mendis (54/16), C. Mendis (1), A. M. N. Munasinghe (5), E. M. D. Y. Munaweera (0/4), H. G. D. Nayanakantha (3), A. R. M. Opatha (5), S. P. Pasqual (2), S. S. Pathirana (10/2), A. K. Perera (4/2), K. G. Perera (1), H. S. M. Pieris (3), S. M. A. Priyanjan (23), M. Pushpakumara (3/1), C. A. K. Rajitha (0/3), R. L. B. Rambukwella (0/2), S. K. Ranasinghe (4), N. Ranatunga (2), N. L. K. Ratnayake (2), R. J. M. G. M. Rupasinghe (0/2), A. P. B. Tennekoon (4), M. H. Tissera (3), I. Udana (2/7), M. L. Udawatte (9/5), J. D. F. Vandersay (5/7), D. M. Vonhagt (1), A. P. Weerakkody (1), S. Weerakoon (2), K. Weeraratne (15/5), S. R. de S. Wettimuny (3), R. P. A. H. Wickremaratne (3).

Zimbabwe

R. D. Brown (7), T. S. Chisoro (12/7), K. M. Curran (11), S. G. Davies (4), K. G. Duers (6), E. A. Essop-Adam (1), D. A. G. Fletcher (6), T. N. Garwe (1), J. G. Heron (6), R. S. Higgins (11), V. R. Hogg (2), A. J. Ireland (26/1), L. M. Jongwe (22/8), R. Kaia (1), F. Kasteni (3), A. J. Mackay (3), N. Madziva (12/9), G. C. Martin (5), W. P. Masakadza (12/7), M. A. Meman (1), S. F. Mire (10), T. V. Mufambisi (6), T. K. Musakanda (1), C. T. Mutombodzi (11/5), T. Muzarabani (8/9), I. A. Nicolson (2), G. A. Paterson (10), G. E. Peckover (3), E. C. Rainsford (39/2), P. W. E. Rawson (10), H. P. Rinke (18), R. W. Sims (3), G. M. Strydom (12), C. Zhuwao (1/5).

Bangladesh

Abu Haider (0/3), Ahmed Kamal (1), Alam Talukdar (2), Aminul Islam jnr (1), Anisur Rahman (2), Arafat Sunny (16/10), Ather Ali Khan (19), Azhar Hussain (7), Dhiman Ghosh (14/1), Dolar Mahmud (7), Farhad Reza (34/13), Faruq Ahmed (7), Gazi Ashraf (7), Ghulam Faruq (5), Ghulam Nausher (9), Hafizur Rahman (2), Harunur Rashid (2), Jahangir Alam (3), Jahangir Badshah (5), Jamaluddin Ahmed (1), Mafizur Rahman (4), Mahbubur Rahman (1), Mazharul Haque (1), Minhazul Abedin (27), Mithun Ali (2/12), Moniruzzaman (2), Morshed Ali Khan (3), Mosharraf Hossain (5), Mossadek Hossain (8/1), Mukhtar Ali (0/1), Nadif Chowdhury (0/3), Nasir Ahmed (7), Nazmus Sadat (0/1), Neeyamur Rashid (2), Nurul Abedin (4), Rafiqul Alam (2), Raqibul Hasan snr (2), Rony Talukdar (0/1), Saiful Islam (7), Sajjad Ahmed (2), Samiur Rahman (2), Saqlain Sajib (0/1), Shafiuddin Ahmed (11), Shahidur Rahman (2), Shariful Haq (1), Sheikh Salahuddin (6), Tanveer Haider (2), Wahidul Gani (1), Zahid Razzak (3), Zakir Hassan (2).

PLAYERS APPEARING FOR MORE THAN ONE ONE-DAY/TWENTY20 INTERNATIONAL TEAM

The following players have played one-day internationals for the **African XI** in addition to their national side:

N. Boje (2), L. E. Bosman (1), J. Botha (2), M. V. Boucher (5), E. Chigumbura (3), A. B. de Villiers (5), H. H. Dippenaar (6), J. H. Kallis (2), J. M. Kemp (6), J. A. Morkel (2), M. Morkel (3), T. M. Odoyo (5), P. J. Ongondo (1), J. L. Ontong (1), S. M. Pollock (6), A. G. Prince (3), J. A. Rudolph (2), V. Sibanda (2), G. C. Smith (1), D. W. Steyn (2), H. H. Streak (2), T. Taibu (1), S. O. Tikolo (4), M. Zondeki (2). (Odoyo, Ongondo and Tikolo played for Kenya, who do not have Test status.)

The following players have played one-day internationals for the **Asian Cricket Council XI** in addition to their national side:

Abdul Razzaq (4), M. S. Dhoni (3), R. Dravid (1), C. R. D. Fernando (1), S. C. Ganguly (3), Harbhajan Singh (2), Inzamam-ul-Haq (3), S. T. Jayasuriya (4), D. P. M. D. Jayawardene (5), A. Kumble (2), Mashrafe bin Mortaza (2), Mohammad Ashraful (2), Mohammad Asif (3), Mohammad Rafique (2), Mohammad Yousuf (7), M. Muralitharan (4), A. Nehra (3), K. C. Sangakkara (4),

V. Sehwag (7), Shahid Afridi (3), Shoaib Akhtar (3), W. U. Tharanga (1), W. P. U. J. C. Vaas (1), Yuvraj Singh (3), Zaheer Khan (6).

The following players have played one-day internationals for the **ICC World XI** in addition to their national side:

C. L. Cairns (1), R. Dravid (3), S. P. Fleming (1), A. Flintoff (3), C. H. Gayle (3), A. C. Gilchrist (1), D. Gough (1), M. L. Hayden (1), J. H. Kallis (3), B. C. Lara (4), G. D. McGrath (1), M. Muralitharan (3), M. Ntini (1), K. P. Pietersen (2), S. M. Pollock (3), R. T. Ponting (1), K. C. Sangakkara (3), V. Sehwag (3), Shahid Afridi (2), Shoaib Akhtar (2), D. L. Vettori (4), S. K. Warne (1).

K. C. Wessels played one-day internationals (as well as Tests) for both Australia and South Africa. D. R. Brown played ODIs for England plus ODIs and T20Is for Scotland. C. B. Lambert played Tests and ODIs for West Indies and one ODI for USA. E. C. Joyce played ODIs and T20Is for both Ireland and England; E. J. G. Morgan ODIs for Ireland and all three formats for England; and W. B. Rankin ODIs and T20Is for Ireland and all three formats for England. A. C. Cummins played Tests and ODIs for West Indies and ODIs for Canada. G. M. Hamilton played Tests for England and ODIs for Scotland. D. P. Nannes played ODIs and T20Is for Australia and T20Is for the Netherlands. L. Ronchi played ODIs and T20Is for Australia and all three formats for New Zealand. G. O. Jones played all three formats for England and ODIs for Papua New Guinea. R. E. van der Merwe played ODIs and T20Is for South Africa and T20Is for the Netherlands. R. J. Campbell played ODIs for Australia and T20Is for Hong Kong.

ELITE TEST UMPIRES

The following umpires were on the ICC's elite panel in February 2017. The figures for Tests, one-day internationals and Twenty20 internationals and the Test Career dates refer to matches in which they have officiated as on-field umpires (excluding abandoned games). The totals of Tests are complete up to January 23, 2017, the totals of one-day internationals and Twenty20 internationals up to December 31, 2016.

	Country	*Born*	*Tests*	*Test Career*	*ODIs*	*T20Is*
Aleem Dar	P	6.6.1968	109	*2003–2016*	182	41
Dharmasena Handunnettige Deepthi Priyantha Kumar	SL	24.4.1971	43	*2010–2016*	74	22
Erasmus Marais	SA	27.2.1964	40*	*2009–2016*	67	26
Gaffaney Christopher Blair	NZ	30.11.1975	12	*2014–2016*	46	20
Gould Ian James	E	19.8.1957	58	*2008–2016*	114	37
Illingworth Richard Keith	E	23.8.1963	26*	*2012–2016*	49	16
Kettleborough Richard Allan	E	15.3.1973	41	*2010–2016*	65	22
Llong Nigel James	E	11.2.1969	40	*2007–2016*	107	32
Oxenford Bruce Nicholas James	A	5.3.1960	37	*2010–2016*	80	20
Ravi Sundaram	I	22.4.1966	19	*2013–2016*	27	18
Reiffel Paul Ronald	A	19.4.1966	30	2012–*2016*	46	16
Tucker Rodney James	A	28.8.1964	51	*2009–2016*	64	35

* *Includes one Test where he took over mid-match.*

BIRTHS AND DEATHS

OTHER CRICKETING NOTABLES

The following list shows the births and deaths of cricketers, and people associated with cricket, who have *not* played in men's Test matches.

Criteria for inclusion All non-Test players who have either (1) scored 20,000 runs in first-class cricket, or (2) taken 1,500 first-class wickets, or (3) achieved 750 dismissals, or (4) reached both 15,000 runs and 750 wickets. Also included are (5) the leading players who flourished before the start of Test cricket, (6) *Wisden* Cricketers of the Year who did not play Test cricket, and (7) others of particular merit or interest.

Names Where players were normally known by a name other than their first, this is underlined.

Teams Where only one team is listed, this is normally the one for which the player made most first-class appearances. Additional teams are listed only if the player appeared for them in more than 20 first-class matches, or if they are especially relevant to their career. School and university teams are not given unless especially relevant (e.g. for the schoolboys chosen as wartime Cricketers of the Year in the 1918 and 1919 *Wisdens*).

	Teams	*Born*	*Died*
Adams Percy Webster	Cheltenham College; *CY 1919*	5.9.1900	28.9.1962
Aird Ronald MC	Hampshire; sec. MCC 1953–62, pres. MCC 1968–69	4.5.1902	16.8.1986
Aislabie Benjamin	Surrey, secretary of MCC 1822–42	14.1.1774	2.6.1842
Alcock Charles William	Secretary of Surrey 1872–1907	2.12.1842	26.2.1907
Editor, Cricket *magazine, 1882–1907. Captain of Wanderers and England football teams.*			
Alley William Edward	NSW, Somerset; Test umpire; *CY 1962*	3.2.1919	26.11.2004
Alleyne Mark Wayne	Gloucestershire; *CY 2001*	23.5.1968	
Altham Harry Surtees CBE	Surrey, Hants; historian; pres. MCC 1959–60	30.11.1888	11.3.1965
Coach at Winchester for 30 years.			
Arlott Leslie Thomas John OBE	Broadcaster and writer	25.2.1914	14.12.1991
Arthur John Michael	Griq. W, OFS; South Africa coach 2005–10, Australia coach 2011–13, Pakistan coach 2016–	17.5.1968	
Ashdown William Henry	Kent	27.12.1898	15.9.1979
The only player to appear in English first-class cricket before and after the two world wars.			
Ashley-Cooper Frederick Samuel	Historian	22.3.1877	31.1.1932
Ashton *Sir* Hubert KBE MC	Cam. U, Essex; pres. MCC 1960–61; *CY 1922*	13.2.1898	17.6.1979
Austin *Sir* Harold Bruce Gardiner	Barbados	15.7.1877	27.7.1943
Austin Ian David	Lancashire; *CY 1999*	30.5.1966	
Bailey Jack Arthur	Essex; secretary of MCC 1974–87	22.6.1930	
Bainbridge Philip	Gloucestershire, Durham; *CY 1986*	16.4.1958	
Bakewell Enid (*née* Turton)	England Women	16.12.1940	
Bannister John David	Warwickshire; writer and broadcaster	23.8.1930	23.1.2016
Barker Gordon	Essex	6.7.1931	10.2.2006
Bartlett Hugh Tryon	Sussex; *CY 1939*	7.10.1914	26.6.1988
Bates Suzannah Wilson	New Zealand Women	16.9.1987	
Bayliss Trevor Harley	NSW; SL coach 2007–11; Eng. coach 2015–	21.12.1962	
Beauclerk *Rev. Lord* Frederick	Middlesex, Surrey, MCC	8.5.1773	22.4.1850
Beldam George William	Middlesex; photographer	1.5.1868	23.11.1937
Beldham William ("Silver Billy")	Hambledon, Surrey	5.2.1766	26.2.1862
Beloff Michael Jacob QC	Head of ICC Code of Conduct Commission	18.4.1942	
Benkenstein Dale Martin	KwaZulu-Natal, Durham; *CY 2009*	9.6.1974	
Berry Anthony Scyld Ivens	Editor of *Wisden* 2008–11	28.4.1954	
Berry Leslie George	Leicestershire	28.4.1906	5.2.1985
Bird Harold Dennis ("Dickie") OBE	Yorkshire, Leics; umpire in 66 Tests	19.4.1933	
Blofeld Henry Calthorpe OBE	Cambridge Univ; broadcaster	23.9.1939	
Bond John David	Lancashire; *CY 1971*	6.5.1932	
Booth Roy	Yorkshire, Worcestershire	1.10.1926	
Bowden Brent Fraser ("Billy")	Umpire in 84 Tests	11.4.1963	
Bowley Frederick Lloyd	Worcestershire	9.11.1873	31.5.1943
Bradshaw Keith	Tasmania; secretary/chief executive MCC 2006–11	2.10.1963	

	Teams	*Born*	*Died*
Brewer Derek Michael	Secretary/chief executive MCC 2012–	2.4.1958	
Briers Nigel Edwin	Leicestershire; *CY 1993*	15.1.1955	
Brookes Wilfrid H.	Editor of *Wisden* 1936–39	5.12.1894	28.5.1955
Bryan John Lindsay	Kent; *CY 1922*	26.5.1896	23.4.1985
Buchanan John Marshall	Queensland; Australia coach 1999–2007	5.4.1953	
Bucknor Stephen Anthony	Umpire in a record 128 Tests	31.5.1946	
Bull Frederick George	Essex; *CY 1898*	2.4.1875	16.9.1910
Buller John Sydney MBE	Worcestershire; Test umpire	23.8.1909	7.8.1970
Burnup Cuthbert James	Kent; *CY 1903*	21.11.1875	5.4.1960
Caine Charles Stewart	Editor of *Wisden* 1926–33	28.10.1861	15.4.1933
Calder Harry Lawton	Cranleigh School; *CY 1918*	24.1.1901	15.9.1995
Cardus *Sir* John Frederick Neville	Writer	3.4.1888	27.2.1975
Chapple Glen	Lancashire; *CY 2012*	23.1.1974	
Chester Frank	Worcestershire; Test umpire	20.1.1895	8.4.1957
Stood in 48 Tests between 1924 and 1955, a record that lasted until 1992.			
Clark Belinda Jane	Australia Women	10.9.1970	
Clark David Graham	Kent; president MCC 1977–78	27.1.1919	8.10.2013
Clarke Charles Giles CBE	Chairman ECB, 2007–15, pres. ECB, 2015–	29.5.1953	
Clarke William	Nottinghamshire	24.12.1798	25.8.1856
Founded the All-England XI, Trent Bridge ground.			
Collier David Gordon OBE	Chief executive of ECB, 2005–14	22.4.1955	
Collins Arthur Edward Jeune	Clifton College	18.8.1885	11.11.1914
Made 628 in a house match in 1899, the highest score in any cricket until 2016.*			
Conan Doyle *Dr Sir* Arthur Ignatius	MCC	22.5.1859	7.7.1930
Creator of Sherlock Holmes; his only victim in first-class cricket was W. G. Grace.			
Connor Clare Joanne OBE	England Women; administrator	1.9.1976	
Constant David John	Kent, Leics; first-class umpire 1969–2006	9.11.1941	
Cook Thomas Edwin Reed	Sussex	5.1.1901	15.1.1950
Cox George, jnr.	Sussex	23.8.1911	30.3.1985
Cox George, snr.	Sussex	29.11.1873	24.3.1949
Cozier Winston Anthony Lloyd	Broadcaster and writer	10.7.1940	11.5.2016
Dalmiya Jagmohan	Pres. BCCI 2001–04, 2015; Pres. ICC 1997–2000	30.5.1940	20.9.2015
Davies Emrys	Glamorgan; Test umpire	27.6.1904	10.11.1975
Davison Brian Fettes	Rhodesia, Leics, Tasmania, Gloucestershire	21.12.1946	
Dawkes George Owen	Leicestershire, Derbyshire	19.7.1920	10.8.2006
Day Arthur Percival	Kent; *CY 1910*	10.4.1885	22.1.1969
de Lisle Timothy John March Phillipps	Editor of *Wisden* 2003	25.6.1962	
Dennett Edward George	Gloucestershire	27.4.1880	14.9.1937
Dhanawade Pranav Prashant	K. C. Gandhi English School	13.5.2000	
Made the highest score in any cricket, 1,009, in a school match in Mumbai in January 2016.*			
Di Venuto Michael James	Tasmania, Derbys, Durham; Surrey coach 2016–	12.12.1973	
Domingo Russell Craig	South Africa coach 2013–	30.8.1974	
Eagar Edward Patrick	Photographer	9.3.1944	
Edwards Charlotte Marie CBE	England Women; *CY 2014*	17.12.1979	
Ehsan Mani	President of ICC 2003–06	23.3.1945	
Engel Matthew Lewis	Editor of *Wisden* 1993–2000, 2004–07	11.6.1951	
Farbrace Paul	Kent, Middx; SL coach 2014; Eng. asst coach 2014–	7.7.1967	
"Felix" (Nicholas Wanostrocht)	Kent, Surrey, All-England	4.10.1804	3.9.1876
Batsman, artist, author (Felix on the Bat) *and inventor of the Catapulta bowling machine.*			
Ferguson William Henry BEM	Scorer	6.6.1880	22.9.1957
Scorer and baggage-master for five Test teams on 43 tours over 52 years and "never lost a bag".			
Findlay William	Oxford U, Lancs; sec. MCC 1926–36	22.6.1880	19.6.1953
Firth John D'Ewes Evelyn	Winchester College; *CY 1918*	21.2.1900	21.9.1957
Fitzpatrick Cathryn Lorraine	Australia Women	4.3.1968	
Fletcher Duncan Andrew Gwynne OBE	Zimbabwe; England coach 1999–2007; India coach 2011–15	27.9.1948	
Ford Graham Xavier	Natal B; South Africa coach 1999–2002; Sri Lanka coach 2012–14, 2016–	16.11.1960	

	Teams	*Born*	*Died*
Foster Henry Knollys	Worcestershire; *CY 1911*	30.10.1873	23.6.1950
Frindall William Howard MBE	Statistician	3.3.1939	30.1.2009
Frith David Edward John	Writer	16.3.1937	
Gibbons Harold Harry Ian Haywood	Worcestershire	8.10.1904	16.2.1973
Gibson Clement Herbert	Eton, Cam. U, Sussex, Argentina; *CY 1918*	23.8.1900	31.12.1976
Gibson Norman Alan Stanley	Writer	28.5.1923	10.4.1997
Gore Adrian Clements	Eton College; *CY 1919*	14.5.1900	7.6.1990
Grace *Mrs* Martha	Mother and cricketing mentor of WG	18.7.1812	25.7.1884
Grace William Gilbert, jnr.	Gloucestershire; son of WG	6.7.1874	2.3.1905
Graveney David Anthony	Gloucestershire, Somerset, Durham	2.1.1953	
Chairman of England selectors 1997–2008.			
Graves Colin James	Chairman of ECB, 2015–	22.1.1948	
Gray James Roy	Hampshire	19.5.1926	
Gray Malcolm Alexander	President of ICC 2000–03	30.5.1940	
Green David Michael	Lancashire, Gloucestershire; *CY 1969*	10.11.1939	
Grieves Kenneth James	New South Wales, Lancashire	27.8.1925	3.1.1992
Griffith Mike Grenville	Sussex, Camb. Univ; president MCC 2012–13	25.11.1943	
Haigh Gideon Clifford Jeffrey Davidson	Writer	29.12.1965	
Hair Darrell Bruce	Umpire in 78 Tests	30.9.1952	
Hall Louis	Yorkshire; *CY 1890*	1.11.1852	19.11.1915
Hallam Albert William	Lancashire, Nottinghamshire; *CY 1908*	12.11.1869	24.7.1940
Hallam Maurice Raymond	Leicestershire	10.9.1931	1.1.2000
Hallows James	Lancashire; *CY 1905*	14.11.1873	20.5.1910
Harper Daryl John	Umpire in 95 Tests	23.10.1951	
Harrison Tom William	Derbyshire; chief executive of ECB 2015–	11.12.1971	
Hartley Alfred	Lancashire; *CY 1911*	11.4.1879	9.10.1918
Harvey Ian Joseph	Victoria, Gloucestershire; *CY 2004*	10.4.1972	
Hedges Lionel Paget	Tonbridge School, Kent, Glos; *CY 1919*	13.7.1900	12.1.1933
Henderson Robert	Surrey; *CY 1890*	30.3.1865	28.1.1931
Hesson Michael James	New Zealand coach 2012–	30.10.1974	
Hewett Herbert Tremenheere	Somerset; *CY 1893*	25.5.1864	4.3.1921
Heyhoe Flint *Baroness* [Rachael] OBE	England Women	11.6.1939	18.1.2017
Hodson Richard Phillip	Cambridge Univ; president MCC 2011–12	26.4.1951	
Horton Henry	Hampshire	18.4.1923	2.11.1998
Howard Cecil Geoffrey	Middlesex; administrator	14.2.1909	8.11.2002
Hughes David Paul	Lancashire; *CY 1988*	13.5.1947	
Huish Frederick Henry	Kent	15.11.1869	16.3.1957
Humpage Geoffrey William	Warwickshire; *CY 1985*	24.4.1954	
Hunter David	Yorkshire	23.2.1860	11.1.1927
Hutchinson James Metcalf	Derbyshire	29.11.1896	7.11.2000
Believed to be the longest-lived first-class cricketer, at 103 years 344 days.			
Ingleby-Mackenzie Alexander Colin David OBE	Hants; pres. MCC 1996–98	15.9.1933	9.3.2006
Iremonger James	Nottinghamshire; *CY 1903*	5.3.1876	25.3.1956
Isaac Alan Raymond	Chair NZC 2008–10; president ICC 2012–	20.1.1952	
Jackson Victor Edward	NSW, Leicestershire	25.10.1916	30.1.1965
James Cyril Lionel Robert ("Nello")	Writer	4.1.1901	31.5.1989
Jesty Trevor Edward	Hants, Griq W., Surrey, Lancs; umpire; *CY 1983*	2.6.1948	
Johnson Paul	Nottinghamshire	24.4.1965	
Johnston Brian Alexander CBE MC	Broadcaster	24.6.1912	5.1.1994
Jones Alan MBE	Glamorgan; *CY 1978*	4.11.1938	
Played once for England v Rest of the World, 1970, regarded at the time as a Test match.			
Kilburn James Maurice	Writer	8.7.1909	28.8.1993
King John Barton	Philadelphia	19.10.1873	17.10.1965
"Beyond question the greatest all-round cricketer produced by America" – Wisden.			
Knight Roger David Verdon OBE	Surrey, Glos, Sussex; sec. MCC 1994–2005, pres. MCC 2015–16	6.9.1946	
Knight W. H.	Editor of *Wisden* 1864–79	29.11.1812	16.8.1879
Koertzen Rudolf Eric	Umpire in 108 Tests	26.3.1949	

	Teams	*Born*	*Died*
Lacey *Sir* Francis Eden	Hants; secretary of MCC 1898–1926	19.10.1859	26.5.1946
Lamb Timothy Michael	Middlesex, Northamptonshire; chief executive of ECB 1997–2004	24.3.1953	
Langridge John George MBE	Sussex; Test umpire; *CY 1950*	10.2.1910	27.6.1999
Lanning Meghann Moira	Australia Women	25.3.1992	
Lee Peter Granville	Northamptonshire, Lancashire; *CY 1976*	27.8.1945	
Lillywhite Frederick William	Sussex	13.6.1792	21.8.1854
Long Arnold	Surrey, Sussex	18.12.1940	
Lord Thomas	Middlesex; founder of Lord's	23.11.1755	13.1.1832
Lorgat Haroon	Chief executive of ICC 2008–12	26.5.1960	
Lyon Beverley Hamilton	Gloucestershire; *CY 1931*	19.1.1902	22.6.1970
McEwan Kenneth Scott	Eastern Province, Essex; *CY 1978*	16.7.1952	
McGilvray Alan David MBE	NSW; broadcaster	6.12.1909	17.7.1996
MacLaurin *Lord* [Ian Charter]	Chairman of ECB 1997–2002	30.3.1937	
Manohar Shashank Vyankatesh	Pres. BCCI 2008–11, 2015–16; ICC chairman 2015–	29.9.1957	
Marlar Robin Geoffrey	Sussex; writer; pres. MCC 2005–06	2.1.1931	
Marshal Alan	Surrey; *CY 1909*	12.6.1883	23.7.1915
Martin-Jenkins Christopher Dennis Alexander MBE	Writer; broadcaster; pres. MCC 2010–11	20.1.1945	1.1.2013
Mendis Gehan Dixon	Sussex, Lancashire	20.4.1955	
Mercer John	Sussex, Glamorgan; coach and scorer; *CY 1927*	22.4.1893	31.8.1987
Meyer Rollo John Oliver OBE	Somerset	15.3.1905	9.3.1991
Modi Lalit Kumar	Chairman, Indian Premier League 2008–10	29.11.1963	
Moles Andrew James	Warwickshire, NZ coach 2008–09	12.2.1961	
Moores Peter	Sussex; England coach 2007–09, 2014–15	18.12.1962	
Moorhouse Geoffrey	Writer	29.11.1931	26.11.2009
Morgan Derek Clifton	Derbyshire	26.2.1929	
Morgan Frederick David OBE	Chair ECB 2003–07, pres. ICC 2008–10, pres. MCC 2014–15	6.10.1937	
Mynn Alfred	Kent, All-England	19.1.1807	1.11.1861
Neale Phillip Anthony	Worcestershire; England manager; *CY 1989*	5.6.1954	
Newman John Alfred	Hampshire	12.11.1884	21.12.1973
Newstead John Thomas	Yorkshire; *CY 1909*	8.9.1877	25.3.1952
Nicholas Mark Charles Jefford	Hampshire; broadcaster	29.9.1957	
Nicholls Ronald Bernard	Gloucestershire	4.12.1933	21.7.1994
Nielsen Timothy John	South Australia; Australia coach 2007–11	5.5.1968	
Nixon Paul Andrew	Leicestershire, Kent	21.10.1970	
Nyren John	Hampshire	15.12.1764	28.6.1837
Author of The Young Cricketer's Tutor, *1833.*			
Nyren Richard	Hampshire	1734	25.4.1797
Proprietor Bat & Ball Inn, Broadhalfpenny Down.			
Ontong Rodney Craig	Border, Glamorgan, N. Transvaal	9.9.1955	
Ormrod Joseph Alan	Worcestershire, Lancashire	22.12.1942	
Pardon Charles Frederick	Editor of *Wisden* 1887–90	28.3.1850	18.4.1890
Pardon Sydney Herbert	Editor of *Wisden* 1891–1925	23.9.1855	20.11.1925
Parks Henry William	Sussex	18.7.1906	7.5.1984
Parr George	Nottinghamshire, All-England	22.5.1826	23.6.1891
Captain and manager of the All-England XI.			
Partridge Norman Ernest	Malvern College, Warwickshire; *CY 1919*	10.8.1900	10.3.1982
Pawar Sharadchandra Govindrao	Pres. BCCI 2005–08, ICC 2010–12	12.12.1940	
Payton Wilfred Richard Daniel	Nottinghamshire	13.2.1882	2.5.1943
Pearce Thomas Neill	Essex; administrator	3.11.1905	10.4.1994
Pearson Frederick	Worcestershire	23.9.1880	10.11.1963
Perrin Percival Albert ("Peter")	Essex; *CY 1905*	26.5.1876	20.11.1945
Perry Ellyse Alexandra	Australia Women	3.11.1990	
Pilch Fuller	Norfolk, Kent	17.3.1804	1.5.1870
"The best batsman that has ever yet appeared" – Arthur Haygarth, 1862.			
Preston Hubert	Editor of *Wisden* 1944–51	16.12.1868	6.8.1960

	Teams	*Born*	*Died*
Preston Norman MBE	Editor of *Wisden* 1952–80	18.3.1903	6.3.1980
Rait Kerr *Col.* Rowan Scrope	Europeans; sec. MCC 1936–52	13.4.1891	2.4.1961
Raj Mithali	India Women	3.12.1982	
Reeves William	Essex; Test umpire	22.1.1875	22.3.1944
Rice Clive Edward Butler	Transvaal, Nottinghamshire; *CY 1981*	23.7.1949	28.7.2015
Richardson Alan	Warwicks, Middx, Worcs; *CY 2012*	6.5.1975	
Robertson-Glasgow Raymond Charles	Somerset; writer	15.7.1901	4.3.1965
Robins Derrick Harold	Warwickshire; tour promoter	27.6.1914	3.5.2004
Robinson Mark Andrew	Northants, Yorkshire, Sussex, coach	23.11.1966	
Robinson Raymond John	Writer	8.7.1905	6.7.1982
Roebuck Peter Michael	Somerset; writer; *CY 1988*	6.3.1956	12.11.2011
Roland-Jones Tobias Skelton	Middlesex; *CY 2017*	29.1.1988	
Rotherham Gerard Alexander	Rugby School, Warwickshire; *CY 1918*	28.5.1899	31.1.1985
Sainsbury Peter James	Hampshire; *CY 1974*	13.6.1934	12.7.2014
Scott Stanley Winckworth	Middlesex; *CY 1893*	24.3.1854	8.12.1933
Sellers Arthur Brian MBE	Yorkshire; *CY 1940*	5.3.1907	20.2.1981
Seymour James	Kent	25.10.1879	30.9.1930
Shepherd David Robert MBE	Gloucestershire; umpire in 92 Tests	27.12.1940	27.10.2009
Shepherd Donald John	Glamorgan; *CY 1970*	12.8.1927	
Siddons James Darren	Vic., S. Aust.; Bangladesh coach 2007–2011	25.4.1964	
Silk Dennis Raoul Whitehall CBE	Somerset; pres. MCC 1992–94	8.10.1931	
Simmons Jack MBE	Lancashire, Tasmania; *CY 1985*	28.3.1941	
Skelding Alexander	Leicestershire; umpire	5.9.1886	17.4.1960
First-class umpire 1931–58, when he was 72.			
Smith Sydney Gordon	Northamptonshire; *CY 1915*	15.1.1881	25.10.1963
Smith William Charles ("Razor")	Surrey; *CY 1911*	4.10.1877	15.7.1946
Southerton Sydney James	Editor of *Wisden* 1934–35	7.7.1874	12.3.1935
Speed Malcolm Walter	Chief executive of ICC 2001–08	14.9.1948	
Spencer Thomas William OBE	Kent; Test umpire	22.3.1914	1.11.1995
Srinivasan Narayanaswami	Pres. BCCI 2011–14; ICC chair 2014–15	3.1.1945	
Stephenson Franklyn Dacosta	Nottinghamshire, Sussex; *CY 1989*	8.4.1959	
Stephenson Harold William	Somerset	18.7.1920	23.4.2008
Stephenson Heathfield Harman	Surrey, All-England	3.5.1832	17.12.1896
Captained first English team to Australia, 1861-62; umpired first Test in England, 1880.			
Stephenson *Lt-Col.* John Robin CBE	Secretary of MCC 1987–93	25.2.1931	2.6.2003
Studd *Sir* John Edward Kynaston	Middlesex	26.7.1858	14.1.1944
Lord Mayor of London 1928–29; president of MCC 1930.			
Surridge Walter Stuart	Surrey; *CY 1953*	3.9.1917	13.4.1992
Sutherland James Alexander	Victoria; CEO Cricket Australia 2001–	14.7.1965	
Suttle Kenneth George	Sussex	25.8.1928	25.3.2005
Swanton Ernest William ("Jim") CBE	Middlesex; writer	11.2.1907	22.1.2000
Tarrant Francis Alfred	Victoria, Middlesex; *CY 1908*	11.12.1880	29.1.1951
Tanfel Simon James Arnold	Umpire in 74 Tests	21.1.1971	
Taylor Brian	Essex; *CY 1972*	19.6.1932	
Taylor Samantha Claire MBE	England Women; *CY 2009*	25.9.1975	
Taylor Tom Launcelot	Yorkshire; *CY 1901*	25.5.1878	16.3.1960
Thornton Charles Inglis ("Buns")	Middlesex	20.3.1850	10.12.1929
Timms John Edward	Northamptonshire	3.11.1906	18.5.1980
Todd Leslie John	Kent	19.6.1907	20.8.1967
Tunnicliffe John	Yorkshire; *CY 1901*	26.8.1866	11.7.1948
Turner Francis Michael MBE	Leicestershire; administrator	8.8.1934	21.7.2015
Turner Robert Julian	Somerset	25.11.1967	
Ufton Derek Gilbert	Kent	31.5.1928	
van der Bijl Vintcent Adriaan Pieter	Natal, Middx, Transvaal; *CY 1981*	19.3.1948	
Virgin Roy Thomas	Somerset, Northamptonshire; *CY 1971*	26.8.1939	
Ward William	Hampshire	24.7.1787	30.6.1849
Scorer of the first recorded double-century: 278 for MCC v Norfolk, 1820.			
Wass Thomas George	Nottinghamshire; *CY 1908*	26.12.1873	27.10.1953
Watson Frank	Lancashire	17.9.1898	1.2.1976

	Teams	*Born*	*Died*
Webber Roy	Statistician	23.7.1914	14.11.1962
Weigall Gerald John Villiers	Kent; coach	19.10.1870	17.5.1944
West George H.	Editor of *Wisden* 1880–86	1851	6.10.1896
Wheatley Oswald Stephen CBE	Warwickshire, Glamorgan; *CY 1969*	28.5.1935	
Whitaker Edgar Haddon OBE	Editor of *Wisden* 1940–43	30.8.1908	5.1.1982
Wight Peter Bernard	Somerset; umpire	25.6.1930	31.12.2015
Wilson Elizabeth Rebecca ("Betty")	Australia Women	21.11.1921	22.1.2010
Wilson John Victor	Yorkshire; *CY 1961*	17.1.1921	5.6.2008
Wisden John	Sussex	5.9.1826	5.4.1884
"The Little Wonder"; founder of Wisden Cricketers' Almanack, *1864.*			
Wood Cecil John Burditt	Leicestershire	21.11.1875	5.6.1960
Woodcock John Charles OBE	Writer; editor of *Wisden* 1981–86	7.8.1926	
Wooller Wilfred	Glamorgan	20.11.1912	10.3.1997
Wright Graeme Alexander	Editor of *Wisden* 1987–92, 2001–02	23.4.1943	
Wright Levi George	Derbyshire; *CY 1906*	15.1.1862	11.1.1953
Young Douglas Martin	Worcestershire, Gloucestershire	15.4.1924	18.6.1993

CRICKETERS OF THE YEAR, 1889–2017

1889 *Six Great Bowlers of the Year:* J. Briggs, J. J. Ferris, G. A. Lohmann, R. Peel, C. T. B. Turner, S. M. J. Woods.

1890 *Nine Great Batsmen of the Year:* R. Abel, W. Barnes, W. Gunn, L. Hall, R. Henderson, J. M. Read, A. Shrewsbury, F. H. Sugg, A. Ward.

1891 *Five Great Wicketkeepers:* J. M. Blackham, G. MacGregor, R. Pilling, M. Sherwin, H. Wood.

1892 *Five Great Bowlers:* W. Attewell, J. T. Hearne, F. Martin, A. W. Mold, J. W. Sharpe.

1893 *Five Batsmen of the Year:* H. T. Hewett, L. C. H. Palairet, W. W. Read, S. W. Scott, A. E. Stoddart.

1894 *Five All-Round Cricketers:* G. Giffen, A. Hearne, F. S. Jackson, G. H. S. Trott, E. Wainwright.

1895 *Five Young Batsmen of the Season:* W. Brockwell, J. T. Brown, C. B. Fry, T. W. Hayward, A. C. MacLaren.

1896 W. G. Grace.

1897 *Five Cricketers of the Season:* S. E. Gregory, A. A. Lilley, K. S. Ranjitsinhji, T. Richardson, H. Trumble.

1898 *Five Cricketers of the Year:* F. G. Bull, W. R. Cuttell, N. F. Druce, G. L. Jessop, J. R. Mason.

1899 *Five Great Players of the Season:* W. H. Lockwood, W. Rhodes, W. Storer, C. L. Townsend, A. E. Trott.

1900 *Five Cricketers of the Season:* J. Darling, C. Hill, A. O. Jones, M. A. Noble, Major R. M. Poore.

1901 *Mr R. E. Foster and Four Yorkshiremen:* R. E. Foster, S. Haigh, G. H. Hirst, T. L. Taylor, J. Tunnicliffe.

1902 L. C. Braund, C. P. McGahey, F. Mitchell, W. G. Quaife, J. T. Tyldesley.

1903 W. W. Armstrong, C. J. Burnup, J. Iremonger, J. J. Kelly, V. T. Trumper.

1904 C. Blythe, J. Gunn, A. E. Knight, W. Mead, P. F. Warner.

1905 B. J. T. Bosanquet, E. A. Halliwell, J. Hallows, P. A. Perrin, R. H. Spooner.

1906 D. Denton, W. S. Lees, G. J. Thompson, J. Vine, L. G. Wright.

1907 J. N. Crawford, A. Fielder, E. G. Hayes, K. L. Hutchings, N. A. Knox.

1908 A. W. Hallam, R. O. Schwarz, F. A. Tarrant, A. E. E. Vogler, T. G. Wass.

1909 *Lord Hawke and Four Cricketers of the Year:* W. Brearley, Lord Hawke, J. B. Hobbs, A. Marshal, J. T. Newstead.

1910 W. Bardsley, S. F. Barnes, D. W. Carr, A. P. Day, V. S. Ransford.

1911 H. K. Foster, A. Hartley, C. B. Llewellyn, W. C. Smith, F. E. Woolley.

1912 *Five Members of MCC's team in Australia:* F. R. Foster, J. W. Hearne, S. P. Kinneir, C. P. Mead, H. Strudwick.

1913 *Special Portrait:* John Wisden.

1914 M. W. Booth, G. Gunn, J. W. Hitch, A. E. Relf, Hon. L. H. Tennyson.

1915 J. W. H. T. Douglas, P. G. H. Fender, H. T. W. Hardinge, D. J. Knight, S. G. Smith.

1916–17 No portraits appeared.

1918 *School Bowlers of the Year:* H. L. Calder, J. D. E. Firth, C. H. Gibson, G. A. Rotherham, G. T. S. Stevens.

1919 *Five Public School Cricketers of the Year:* P. W. Adams, A. P. F. Chapman, A. C. Gore, L. P. Hedges, N. E. Partridge.

1920 *Five Batsmen of the Year:* A. Ducat, E. H. Hendren, P. Holmes, H. Sutcliffe, E. Tyldesley.

1921 *Special Portrait:* P. F. Warner.

1922 H. Ashton, J. L. Bryan, J. M. Gregory, C. G. Macartney, E. A. McDonald.

1923 A. W. Carr, A. P. Freeman, C. W. L. Parker, A. C. Russell, A. Sandham.

1924 *Five Bowlers of the Year:* A. E. R. Gilligan, R. Kilner, G. G. Macaulay, C. H. Parkin, M. W. Tate.

1925 R. H. Catterall, J. C. W. MacBryan, H. W. Taylor, R. K. Tyldesley, W. W. Whysall.

1926 *Special Portrait:* J. B. Hobbs.
1927 G. Geary, H. Larwood, J. Mercer, W. A. Oldfield, W. M. Woodfull.
1928 R. C. Blunt, C. Hallows, W. R. Hammond, D. R. Jardine, V. W. C. Jupp.
1929 L. E. G. Ames, G. Duckworth, M. Leyland, S. J. Staples, J. C. White.
1930 E. H. Bowley, K. S. Duleepsinhji, H. G. Owen-Smith, R. W. V. Robins, R. E. S. Wyatt.
1931 D. G. Bradman, C. V. Grimmett, B. H. Lyon, I. A. R. Peebles, M. J. Turnbull.
1932 W. E. Bowes, C. S. Dempster, James Langridge, Nawab of Pataudi sen, H. Verity.
1933 W. E. Astill, F. R. Brown, A. S. Kennedy, C. K. Nayudu, W. Voce.
1934 A. H. Bakewell, G. A. Headley, M. S. Nichols, L. F. Townsend, C. F. Walters.
1935 S. J. McCabe, W. J. O'Reilly, G. A. E. Paine, W. H. Ponsford, C. I. J. Smith.
1936 H. B. Cameron, E. R. T. Holmes, B. Mitchell, D. Smith, A. W. Wellard.
1937 C. J. Barnett, W. H. Copson, A. R. Gover, V. M. Merchant, T. S. Worthington.
1938 T. W. J. Goddard, J. Hardstaff jun, L. Hutton, J. H. Parks, E. Paynter.
1939 H. T. Bartlett, W. A. Brown, D. C. S. Compton, K. Farnes, A. Wood.
1940 L. N. Constantine, W. J. Edrich, W. W. Keeton, A. B. Sellers, D. V. P. Wright.
1941–46 No portraits appeared.
1947 A. V. Bedser, L. B. Fishlock, V. (M. H.) Mankad, T. P. B. Smith, C. Washbrook.
1948 M. P. Donnelly, A. Melville, A. D. Nourse, J. D. Robertson, N. W. D. Yardley.
1949 A. L. Hassett, W. A. Johnston, R. R. Lindwall, A. R. Morris, D. Tallon.
1950 T. E. Bailey, R. O. Jenkins, John Langridge, R. T. Simpson, B. Sutcliffe.
1951 T. G. Evans, S. Ramadhin, A. L. Valentine, E. D. Weekes, F. M. M. Worrell.
1952 R. Appleyard, H. E. Dollery, J. C. Laker, P. B. H. May, E. A. B. Rowan.
1953 H. Gimblett, T. W. Graveney, D. S. Sheppard, W. S. Surridge, F. S. Trueman.
1954 R. N. Harvey, G. A. R. Lock, K. R. Miller, J. H. Wardle, W. Watson.
1955 B. Dooland, Fazal Mahmood, W. E. Hollies, J. B. Statham, G. E. Tribe.
1956 M. C. Cowdrey, D. J. Insole, D. J. McGlew, H. J. Tayfield, F. H. Tyson.
1957 D. Brookes, J. W. Burke, M. J. Hilton, G. R. A. Langley, P. E. Richardson.
1958 P. J. Loader, A. J. McIntyre, O. G. Smith, M. J. Stewart, C. L. Walcott.
1959 H. L. Jackson, R. E. Marshall, C. A. Milton, J. R. Reid, D. Shackleton.
1960 K. F. Barrington, D. B. Carr, R. Illingworth, G. Pullar, M. J. K. Smith.
1961 N. A. T. Adcock, E. R. Dexter, R. A. McLean, R. Subba Row, J. V. Wilson.
1962 W. E. Alley, R. Benaud, A. K. Davidson, W. M. Lawry, N. C. O'Neill.
1963 D. Kenyon, Mushtaq Mohammad, P. H. Parfitt, P. J. Sharpe, F. J. Titmus.
1964 D. B. Close, C. C. Griffith, C. C. Hunte, R. B. Kanhai, G. S. Sobers.
1965 G. Boycott, P. J. Burge, J. A. Flavell, G. D. McKenzie, R. B. Simpson.
1966 K. C. Bland, J. H. Edrich, R. C. Motz, P. M. Pollock, R. G. Pollock.
1967 R. W. Barber, B. L. D'Oliveira, C. Milburn, J. T. Murray, S. M. Nurse.
1968 Asif Iqbal, Hanif Mohammad, K. Higgs, J. M. Parks, Nawab of Pataudi jun.
1969 J. G. Binks, D. M. Green, B. A. Richards, D. L. Underwood, O. S. Wheatley.
1970 B. F. Butcher, A. P. E. Knott, Majid Khan, M. J. Procter, D. J. Shepherd.
1971 J. D. Bond, C. H. Lloyd, B. W. Luckhurst, G. M. Turner, R. T. Virgin.
1972 G. G. Arnold, B. S. Chandrasekhar, L. R. Gibbs, B. Taylor, Zaheer Abbas.
1973 G. S. Chappell, D. K. Lillee, R. A. L. Massie, J. A. Snow, K. R. Stackpole.
1974 K. D. Boyce, B. E. Congdon, K. W. R. Fletcher, R. C. Fredericks, P. J. Sainsbury.
1975 D. L. Amiss, M. H. Denness, N. Gifford, A. W. Greig, A. M. E. Roberts.
1976 I. M. Chappell, P. G. Lee, R. B. McCosker, D. S. Steele, R. A. Woolmer.
1977 J. M. Brearley, C. G. Greenidge, M. A. Holding, I. V. A. Richards, R. W. Taylor.
1978 I. T. Botham, M. Hendrick, A. Jones, K. S. McEwan, R. G. D. Willis.
1979 D. I. Gower, J. K. Lever, C. M. Old, C. T. Radley, J. N. Shepherd.
1980 J. Garner, S. M. Gavaskar, G. A. Gooch, D. W. Randall, B. C. Rose.
1981 K. J. Hughes, R. D. Jackman, A. J. Lamb, C. E. B. Rice, V. A. P. van der Bijl.
1982 T. M. Alderman, A. R. Border, R. J. Hadlee, Javed Miandad, R. W. Marsh.

1983 Imran Khan, T. E. Jesty, A. I. Kallicharran, Kapil Dev, M. D. Marshall.
1984 M. Amarnath, J. V. Coney, J. E. Emburey, M. W. Gatting, C. L. Smith.
1985 M. D. Crowe, H. A. Gomes, G. W. Humpage, J. Simmons, S. Wettimuny.
1986 P. Bainbridge, R. M. Ellison, C. J. McDermott, N. V. Radford, R. T. Robinson.
1987 J. H. Childs, G. A. Hick, D. B. Vengsarkar, C. A. Walsh, J. J. Whitaker.
1988 J. P. Agnew, N. A. Foster, D. P. Hughes, P. M. Roebuck, Salim Malik.
1989 K. J. Barnett, P. J. L. Dujon, P. A. Neale, F. D. Stephenson, S. R. Waugh.
1990 S. J. Cook, D. M. Jones, R. C. Russell, R. A. Smith, M. A. Taylor.
1991 M. A. Atherton, M. Azharuddin, A. R. Butcher, D. L. Haynes, M. E. Waugh.
1992 C. E. L. Ambrose, P. A. J. DeFreitas, A. A. Donald, R. B. Richardson, Waqar Younis.
1993 N. E. Briers, M. D. Moxon, I. D. K. Salisbury, A. J. Stewart, Wasim Akram.
1994 D. C. Boon, I. A. Healy, M. G. Hughes, S. K. Warne, S. L. Watkin.
1995 B. C. Lara, D. E. Malcolm, T. A. Munton, S. J. Rhodes, K. C. Wessels.
1996 D. G. Cork, P. A. de Silva, A. R. C. Fraser, A. Kumble, D. A. Reeve.
1997 S. T. Jayasuriya, Mushtaq Ahmed, Saeed Anwar, P. V. Simmons, S. R. Tendulkar.
1998 M. T. G. Elliott, S. G. Law, G. D. McGrath, M. P. Maynard, G. P. Thorpe.
1999 I. D. Austin, D. Gough, M. Muralitharan, A. Ranatunga, J. N. Rhodes.
2000 C. L. Cairns, R. Dravid, L. Klusener, T. M. Moody, Saqlain Mushtaq.
Cricketers of the Century D. G. Bradman, G. S. Sobers, J. B. Hobbs, S. K. Warne, I. V. A. Richards.
2001 M. W. Alleyne, M. P. Bicknell, A. R. Caddick, J. L. Langer, D. S. Lehmann.
2002 A. Flower, A. C. Gilchrist, J. N. Gillespie, V. V. S. Laxman, D. R. Martyn.
2003 M. L. Hayden, A. J. Hollioake, N. Hussain, S. M. Pollock, M. P. Vaughan.
2004 C. J. Adams, A. Flintoff, I. J. Harvey, G. Kirsten, G. C. Smith.
2005 A. F. Giles, S. J. Harmison, R. W. T. Key, A. J. Strauss, M. E. Trescothick.
2006 M. J. Hoggard, S. P. Jones, B. Lee, K. P. Pietersen, R. T. Ponting.
2007 P. D. Collingwood, D. P. M. D. Jayawardene, Mohammad Yousuf, M. S. Panesar, M. R. Ramprakash.
2008 I. R. Bell, S. Chanderpaul, O. D. Gibson, R. J. Sidebottom, Zaheer Khan.
2009 J. M. Anderson, D. M. Benkenstein, M. V. Boucher, N. D. McKenzie, S. C. Taylor.
2010 S. C. J. Broad, M. J. Clarke, G. Onions, M. J. Prior, G. P. Swann.
2011 E. J. G. Morgan, C. M. W. Read, Tamim Iqbal, I. J. L. Trott.
2012 T. T. Bresnan, G. Chapple, A. N. Cook, A. Richardson, K. C. Sangakkara.
2013 H. M. Amla, N. R. D. Compton, J. H. Kallis, M. N. Samuels, D. W. Steyn.
2014 S. Dhawan, C. M. Edwards, R. J. Harris, C. J. L. Rogers, J. E. Root.
2015 M. M. Ali, G. S. Ballance, A. Lyth, A. D. Mathews, J. S. Patel.
2016 J. M. Bairstow, B. B. McCullum, S. P. D. Smith, B. A. Stokes, K. S. Williamson.
2017 B. M. Duckett, Misbah-ul-Haq, T. S. Roland-Jones, C. R. Woakes, Younis Khan.

From 2001 to 2003 the award was made on the basis of all cricket round the world, not just the English season. This ended in 2004 with the start of Wisden's *Leading Cricketer in the World award. Sanath Jayasuriya was chosen in 1997 for his influence on the English season, stemming from the 1996 World Cup. In 2011, only four were named after an ICC tribunal investigating the Lord's spot-fixing scandal made the selection of one of the five unsustainable.*

CRICKETERS OF THE YEAR: AN ANALYSIS

The special portrait of John Wisden in 1913 marked the 50th anniversary of his retirement as a player – and the 50th edition of the Almanack. Wisden died in 1884. The special portraits of P. F. Warner in 1921 and J. B. Hobbs in 1926 were in addition to their earlier selection as a Cricketer of the Year in 1904 and 1909 respectively. These three special portraits and the Cricketers of the Century in 2000 are excluded from the following analysis.

The five players selected to be Cricketers of the Year for 2017 bring the number chosen since selection began in 1889 to 590. They have been chosen from 40 different teams as follows:

Derbyshire	13	Northants	15	Australians	73	Staffordshire	1
Durham	8	Nottinghamshire	29	South Africans	28	Cheltenham College	1
Essex	24	Somerset	19	West Indians	26	Cranleigh School	1
Glamorgan	12	Surrey	49	New Zealanders	10	Eton College	2
Gloucestershire	17	Sussex	21	Indians	15	Malvern College	1
Hampshire	16	Warwickshire	25	Pakistanis	14	Rugby School	1
Kent	26	Worcestershire	17	Sri Lankans	7	Tonbridge School	1
Lancashire	34	Yorkshire	47	Zimbabweans	1	Univ Coll School	1
Leicestershire	8	Oxford Univ	7	Bangladeshis	1	Uppingham School	1
Middlesex	30	Cambridge Univ	10	England Women	2	Winchester College	1

Schoolboys were chosen in 1918 and 1919 when first-class cricket was suspended due to war. The total of sides comes to 615 because 25 players played regularly for two teams (England excluded) in the year for which they were chosen.

Types of Player

Of the 590 Cricketers of the Year, 294 are best classified as batsmen, 160 as bowlers, 97 as all-rounders and 39 as wicketkeepers or wicketkeeper-batsmen.

Research: Robert Brooke

PART EIGHT

The Almanack

OFFICIAL BODIES

INTERNATIONAL CRICKET COUNCIL

The ICC are world cricket's governing body. They are responsible for managing the playing conditions and Code of Conduct for international fixtures, expanding the game and organising the major tournaments, including the World Cup and World Twenty20. Their mission statement says the ICC "will lead by providing a world-class environment for international cricket, delivering major events across three formats, providing targeted support to members and promoting the global game".

Ten national governing bodies are currently Full Members of the ICC; full membership qualifies a nation (or geographic area) to play official Test matches. A candidate for full membership must meet a number of playing and administrative criteria, after which elevation is decided by a vote among existing Full Members. There are also currently 39 Associate Members and 56 Affiliate Members.

The ICC were founded in 1909 as the Imperial Cricket Conference by three Foundation Members: England, Australia and South Africa. Other countries (or geographic areas) became Full Members and thus acquired Test status as follows: India, New Zealand and West Indies in 1926, Pakistan in 1952, Sri Lanka in 1981, Zimbabwe in 1992 and Bangladesh in 2000. South Africa ceased to be a member on leaving the Commonwealth in 1961, but were re-elected as a Full Member in 1991.

In 1965, "Imperial" was replaced by "International", and countries from outside the Commonwealth were elected for the first time. The first Associate Members were Ceylon (later Sri Lanka), Fiji and the USA. Foundation Members retained a veto over all resolutions. In 1989, the renamed International Cricket Council (rather than "Conference") adopted revised rules, aimed at producing an organisation which could make a larger number of binding decisions, rather than simply make recommendations to national governing bodies. In 1993, the Council, previously administered by MCC, gained their own secretariat and chief executive. The category of Foundation Member was abolished.

In 1997, the Council became an incorporated body, with an executive board, and a president instead of a chairman. The ICC remained at Lord's, with a commercial base in Monaco, until August 2005, when after 96 years they moved to Dubai in the United Arab Emirates, which offered organisational and tax advantages.

In 2014, the ICC board approved a new structure, under which they were led by a chairman again, while India, Australia and England took permanent places on key committees. But in 2016 the special privileges given these three were dismantled and, in early 2017, the board agreed to revise the constitution on more egalitarian lines, and to absorb Affiliate Members into the Associate category.

Officers

Chairman: S. V. Manohar. *Chief Executive:* D. J. Richardson.

Chairs of Committees – Chief Executives' Committee: D. J. Richardson. *Finance and Commercial Affairs:* C. G. Clarke. *Cricket:* A. Kumble. *Development:* I. Khwaja. *Code of Conduct Commission:* M. J. Beloff QC. *Women's Committee:* C. J. Connor. *Nominations Committee:* S. V. Manohar. *Disputes Resolution Committee:* M. J. Beloff QC. *Anti-Corruption Unit:* Sir Ronnie Flanagan. *ICC Ethics Officer:* P. Nicholson.

ICC Board: The chairman and chief executive sit on the board *ex officio*. They are joined by G. J. Barclay (New Zealand), W. O. Cameron (West Indies), C. G. Clarke (England), F. Erasmus (Namibia), I. Khwaja (Singapore), V. Limaye (India), R. A. McCollum (Ireland), T. Mukuhlani (Zimbabwe), Nazmul Hassan (Bangladesh), C. Nenzani (South Africa), D. A. Peever (Australia), Shaharyar Khan (Pakistan), T. Sumathipala (Sri Lanka).

Chief Executives' Committee: The chief executive, chairman and the chairs of the cricket committee and women's committee sit on this committee *ex officio*. They are joined by the chief executives of the ten Full Member boards and three Associate Member boards: G. D. Campbell (Papua New Guinea), J. A. Cribbin (Hong Kong), A. M. de Silva (Sri Lanka), W. Deutrom (Ireland), J. M. Grave (West Indies), T. W. Harrison (England), R. Johri (India), H. Lorgat (South Africa), W. Mukondiwa (Zimbabwe), Nizam Uddin Chowdhury (Bangladesh), Subhan Ahmad (Pakistan), J. A. Sutherland (Australia), D. J. White (New Zealand).

Cricket Committee: The chief executive and chairman sit on the committee *ex officio*. They are joined by A. Kumble (*chairman*), C. J. Connor, R. Dravid, D. P. M. D. Jayawardene, R. A. Kettleborough, D. S. Lehmann, R. S. Madugalle, T. B. A. May, K. J. O'Brien, R. J. Shastri, J. P. Stephenson, A. J. Strauss, D. J. White.

General Manager – Cricket: G. J. Allardice. *General Manager – Commercial:* D. C. Jamieson. *General Manager – Anti-Corruption Unit:* TBC. *General Manager – Strategic Communications:* C. Furlong. *Chief Financial Officer:* A. Khanna. *Chief Operating Officer/General Counsel:* I. Higgins. *Head of Media/Communications:* Sami Ul Hasan. *Head of Global Development:* T. L. Anderson. *Head of Internal Audit:* Muhammad Ali.

Membership

Full Members (10): Australia, Bangladesh, England, India, New Zealand, Pakistan, South Africa, Sri Lanka, West Indies and Zimbabwe.

Associate Members* (39): Afghanistan (2001), Argentina (1974), Belgium (2005), Bermuda (1966), Botswana (2005), Canada (1968), Cayman Islands (2002), Denmark (1966), Fiji (1965), France (1998), Germany (1999), Gibraltar (1969), Guernsey (2005), Hong Kong (1969), Ireland (1993), Israel (1974), Italy (1995), Japan (2005), Jersey (2007), Kenya (1981), Kuwait (2005), Malaysia (1967), Namibia (1992), Nepal (1996), Netherlands (1966), Nigeria (2002), Oman (2000), Papua New Guinea (1973), Saudi Arabia (2003), Scotland (1994), Singapore (1974), Suriname (2002), Tanzania (2001), Thailand (2005), Uganda (1998), United Arab Emirates (1990), USA (1965), Vanuatu (1995), Zambia (2003).

Affiliate Members* (56): Austria (1992), Bahamas (1987), Bahrain (2001), Belize (1997), Bhutan (2001), Brazil (2002), Bulgaria (2008), Cameroon (2007), Chile (2002), China (2004), Cook Islands (2000), Costa Rica (2002), Croatia (2001), Cyprus (1999), Czech Republic (2000), Estonia (2008), Falkland Islands (2007), Finland (2000), Gambia (2002), Ghana (2002), Greece (1995), Hungary (2012), Indonesia (2001), Iran (2003), Isle of Man (2004), Lesotho (2001), Luxembourg (1998), Malawi (2003), Maldives (2001), Mali (2005), Malta (1998), Mexico (2004), Morocco (1999), Mozambique (2003), Myanmar (2006), Norway (2000), Panama (2002), Peru (2007), Philippines (2000), Portugal (1996), Qatar (1999), Romania (2013), Russia (2012), Rwanda (2003), St Helena (2001), Samoa (2000), Serbia (2015), Seychelles (2010), Sierra Leone (2002), Slovenia (2005), South Korea (2001), Spain (1992), Swaziland (2007), Sweden (1997), Turkey (2008), Turks & Caicos Islands (2002).

* *Year of election shown in parentheses. Switzerland (1985) were removed in 2012 for failing to comply with the ICC's membership criteria; Cuba (2002) and Tonga (2000) in 2013 for failing to demonstrate a suitable administrative structure; and Brunei in 2014. The USA, Morocco and Turkey were suspended in 2015 and Nepal in 2016.*

Full Member The governing body for cricket of a country recognised by the ICC, or nations associated for cricket purposes, or a geographical area, from which representative teams are qualified to play official Test matches.

Associate Member The governing body for cricket of a country recognised by the ICC, or countries associated for cricket purposes, or a geographical area, which does not qualify as a Full Member, but where cricket is firmly established and organised.

Affiliate Member The governing body for cricket of a country recognised by ICC, or countries associated for cricket purposes, or a geographical area (which is not part of one of those already constituted as a Full Member or Associate Member) where the ICC recognises that cricket is played in accordance with the Laws of Cricket.

Addresses

ICC Street 69, Dubai Sports City, Sh Mohammed Bin Zayed Road, PO Box 500 070, Dubai, United Arab Emirates (+971 4382 8800; website www.icc-cricket.com; email enquiry@icc-cricket.com).

Australia Cricket Australia, 60 Jolimont Street, Jolimont, Victoria 3002 (+61 3 9653 9999; website www.cricket.com.au; email public.enquiries@cricket.com.au).

Bangladesh Bangladesh Cricket Board, Sher-e-Bangla National Cricket Stadium, Mirpur, Dhaka 1216 (+880 2 803 1001; website www.tigercricket.com.bd; email info@tigercricket.com.bd).

England England and Wales Cricket Board (see below).

India Board of Control for Cricket in India, Cricket Centre, 4th Floor, Wankhede Stadium, D Road, Churchgate, Mumbai 400 020 (+91 22 2289 8800; website www.bcci.tv; email office@bcci.tv).

New Zealand New Zealand Cricket, PO Box 8353, Level 4, 8 Nugent Street, Grafton, Auckland 1023 (+64 9 972 0605; website www.blackcaps.co.nz; email info@nzcricket.org.nz).

Pakistan Pakistan Cricket Board, Gaddafi Stadium, Ferozpur Road, Lahore 54600 (+92 42 3571 7231; website www.pcb.com.pk; email online@pcb.com.pk).

South Africa Cricket South Africa, Wanderers Club, PO Box 55009, 21 North Street, Illovo, Northlands 2116 (+27 11 880 2810; website www.cricket.co.za; email info@cricket.co.za).

Sri Lanka Sri Lanka Cricket, 35 Maitland Place, Colombo 07000 (+94 112 681 601; website www.srilankacricket.lk; email info@srilankacricket.lk).

West Indies West Indies Cricket Board, PO Box 616 W, Factory Road, St John's, Antigua (+1 268 481 2450; website www.windiescricket.com; email wicb@windiescricket.com).

Zimbabwe Zimbabwe Cricket, PO Box 2739, 28 Maiden Drive, Highlands, Harare (+263 4 788 090; website www.zimcricket.org; email info@zimcricket.org).

Associate and Affiliate Members' addresses may be found on the ICC website www.icc-cricket.com

ENGLAND AND WALES CRICKET BOARD

The England and Wales Cricket Board (ECB) became responsible for the administration of all cricket – professional and recreational – in England and Wales in 1997. They took over the functions of the Cricket Council, the Test and County Cricket Board and the National Cricket Association, which had run the game in England and Wales since 1968. In 2005, a new constitution streamlined and modernised the governance of English cricket. The Management Board of 18 directors were replaced by a Board of Directors numbering 12, with three appointed by the first-class counties and two by the county boards. In 2010, this expanded to 14, with the appointment of the ECB's first two women directors.

Officers

President: C. G. Clarke. *Chairman:* C. J. Graves. *Chief Executive Officer:* T. W. Harrison.

Board of Directors: C. G. Clarke, M. Darlow, M. V. Fleming, C. J. Graves, T. W. Harrison, I. N. Lovett, A. J. Nash, Lord Patel of Bradford, L. C. Pearson, J. Stichbury, R. W. Thompson, J. Wood, P. G. Wright.

Committee Chairs – Executive Committee: T. W. Harrison. *Anti-Corruption Commission for Education, Standards and Security:* J. Stichbury. *Audit, Risk and Governance:* I. N. Lovett. *Commercial and Communications:* C. J. Graves. *Cricket:* P. G. Wright. *Discipline:* T. J. G. O'Gorman. *Recreational Assembly:* J. Wood. *Remuneration:* C. J. Graves.

Director, England Cricket: A. J. Strauss. *Chief Operating Officer:* G. Hollins. *Chief Financial Officer:* S. Smith. *Director, Communications:* C. Haynes. *Director, Events:* S. Elworthy. *Director, England Cricket Operations:* J. D. Carr. *Director, England Women's Cricket:* C. J. Connor. *Director, Participation and Growth:* M. Dwyer. *Director, Strategy and Public Policy:* D. Mahoney. *Commercial Director:* S. Patel. *People Director:* R. Ranganathan. *Head of Information Technology:* D. Smith. *National Selector:* J. J. Whitaker. *Other Selectors:* A. R. C. Fraser and M. Newell.

ECB: Lord's Ground, London NW8 8QZ (020 7432 1200; website www.ecb.co.uk).

THE MARYLEBONE CRICKET CLUB

The Marylebone Cricket Club evolved out of the White Conduit Club in 1787, when Thomas Lord laid out his first ground in Dorset Square. Their members revised the Laws in 1788 and gradually took responsibility for cricket throughout the world. However, they relinquished control of the game in the UK in 1968, and the International Cricket Council finally established their own secretariat in 1993. MCC still own Lord's and remain the guardian of the Laws. They call themselves "a private club with a public function" and aim to support cricket everywhere, especially at grassroots level and in countries where the game is least developed.

Patron: HER MAJESTY THE QUEEN

Officers

President: 2016–17 – M. V. Fleming. *Club Chairman:* G. M. N. Corbett. *Treasurer:* R. S. Leigh. *Trustees:* P. A. B. Beecroft, A. N. W. Beeson, M. G. Griffith. *Hon. Life Vice-Presidents:* Lord Bramall, E. R. Dexter, G. H. G. Doggart, C. A. Fry, D. J. Insole, A. R. Lewis, Sir Oliver Popplewell, D. R. W. Silk, M. O. C. Sturt, J. C. Woodcock.

Chief Executive and Secretary: D. M. Brewer. *Deputy Secretary:* C. Maynard. *Assistant Secretaries – Cricket:* J. P. Stephenson. *Estates:* R. J. Ebdon. *Finance:* A. D. Cameron. *Legal:* H. A-M. Roper-Curzon. *Commercial:* J. D. Robinson.

MCC Committee: A. J. Alt, A. R. C. Fraser, M. W. Gatting, W. R. Griffiths, C. M. Gupte, C. J. Guyver, S. P. Hughes, G. W. Jones, H. J. H. Loudon, G. T. E. Monkhouse, N. M. Peters, G. J. Toogood. The president, club chairman, treasurer and committee chairmen are also on the committee.

Chairmen of Committees – Arts and Library: D. J. C. Faber. *Cricket:* M. V. Fleming. *Estates:* D. C. Brooks Wilson. *Finance:* R. S. Leigh. *Membership and General Purposes:* Sir Ian Magee. *World Cricket:* J. M. Brearley.

MCC: The Chief Executive and Secretary, Lord's Ground, London NW8 8QN (020 7616 8500; email reception@mcc.org.uk; website www.lords.org. Tickets 020 7432 1000; email ticketing@mcc.org.uk).

PROFESSIONAL CRICKETERS' ASSOCIATION

The Professional Cricketers' Association were formed in 1967 (as the Cricketers' Association) to be the collective voice of first-class professional players, and enhance and protect their interests. During the 1970s, they succeeded in establishing pension schemes and a minimum wage. In recent years their strong commercial operations and greater funding from the ECB have increased their services to current and past players, including education, legal, financial and benevolent help. In 2011, these services were extended to England's women cricketers.

President: A. Flintoff. *Chairman:* D. K. H. Mitchell. *President – Benevolent Fund:* D. A. Graveney. *Non-Executive Chairman:* M. B. H. Wheeler. *Non-Executive Director:* P. G. Read. *Chief Executive:* D. A. Leatherdale. *Commercial Director:* TBC. *Financial Director:* P. Garrett. *Business Development Manager:* G. M. Hamilton. *Commercial Partnerships Manager:* A. Phipps. *Head of Events and Fundraising:* E. Lewis. *Head of Commercial Rights:* E. M. Reid. *Player Rights Manager:* E. Caldwell. *Social Media Executive:* L. Reynolds. *Member Services Manager:* A. Prosser. *Head of Development and Welfare:* I. J. Thomas.

PCA: *London Office* – The Laker Stand, The Oval, Kennington, London SE11 5SS (0207 449 4226; email 903club@thepca.co.uk; website www.thepca.co.uk). *Birmingham Office* – Box 108–9, R. E. S. Wyatt Stand, Warwickshire CCC, Edgbaston, Birmingham B5 7QU.

CRIME AND PUNISHMENT

ICC Code of Conduct – Breaches and Penalties in 2015-16 to 2016-17

R. G. Sharma India v Australia, fifth one-day international at Sydney.
Delayed and screamed "No!" when given out caught behind on 99. Reprimand – J. J. Crowe.

H. H. Pandya India v Australia, first Twenty20 international at Adelaide.
After dismissing C. A. Lynn, ran towards him yelling. Reprimand – J. J. Crowe.

J. R. Hazlewood Australia v New Zealand, Second Test at Christchurch.
Obscene language when DRS review turned down. 15% fine – B. C. Broad.

S. P. D. Smith Australia v New Zealand, Second Test at Christchurch.
Questioned umpire over methods used in DRS review. 30% fine – B. C. Broad.

V. Kohli India v Pakistan, Asia Cup Twenty20 international at Mirpur.
Showed umpire his bat and muttered obscenity when given lbw. 30% fine – J. J. Crowe.

Shakib Al Hasan Bangladesh v Pakistan, Asia Cup Twenty20 international at Mirpur.
Swung bat at stumps after being bowled (but quickly apologised). Reprimand – J. J. Crowe.

J. J. Roy England v Sri Lanka, World Twenty20 match at Delhi.
Obscene language when given lbw; threw bat and helmet at dug-out. 30% fine – J. J. Crowe.

D. J. Willey England v Sri Lanka, World Twenty20 match at Delhi.
Obscene language after dismissing T. A. M. Siriwardene. 15% fine – J. J. Crowe.

F. du Plessis South Africa v Sri Lanka, World Twenty20 match at Delhi.
Looked at bat and shook his head when given lbw. 50% fine – J. J. Crowe.

M. N. Samuels West Indies v England, World Twenty20 final at Kolkata.
Abusive and offensive language to B. A. Stokes in final over. 30% fine – R. S. Madugalle.

J. M. Anderson England v Sri Lanka, Third Test at Lord's.
Disrespect to umpire S. Ravi who told him not to engage with batsman. Reprimand – A. J. Pycroft.

D. M. Bravo West Indies v India, Third Test at Gros Islet.
Persistent verbal engagement with R. G. Sharma. 15% fine – R. S. Madugalle.

R. G. Sharma India v West Indies, Third Test at Gros Islet.
Persistent verbal engagement with D. M. Bravo. 15% fine – R. S. Madugalle.

A. D. Hales England v Pakistan, Fourth Test at The Oval.
Visited third umpire's room to question his dismissal. 15% fine – R. B. Richardson.

S. C. J. Broad England v Pakistan, Fourth Test at The Oval.
Criticised umpires on Twitter after Hales's dismissal. 20% fine – R. B. Richardson.

N. L. T. C. Perera Sri Lanka v Australia, second one-day international at Colombo (RPS).
Provocative behaviour on dismissing D. A. Warner. 15% fine – J. Srinath.

M. A. Starc Australia v Sri Lanka, second one-day international at Colombo (RPS).
Threw the ball towards batsman L. D. Chandimal. Reprimand – J. Srinath.

S. M. S. M. Senanayake Sri Lanka v Australia, first Twenty20 international at Pallekele.
Provocative remarks after dismissing D. A. Warner. 30% fine – J. Srinath.

S. Prasanna Sri Lanka v Australia, second Twenty20 international at Colombo (RPS).
Provocative gestures after dismissing G. J. Maxwell. 15% fine – J. Srinath.

Demerit points were introduced in September 2016; a player receiving four demerit points in a 24-month period could be suspended.

Sabbir Rahman Bangladesh v Afghanistan, first one-day international at Mirpur.
Argued with umpire about lbw decision. 30% fine/2 demerit pts – R. B. Richardson.

R. A. Jadeja India v New Zealand, Third Test at Indore.
Repeatedly ran down protected area of the pitch. 50% fine/3 demerit pts – D. C. Boon.

Mashrafe bin Mortaza Bangladesh v England, second one-day international at Mirpur.
Provocative celebration when J. C. Buttler dismissed. 20% fine/2 demerit pts – J. Srinath.

Sabbir Rahman Bangladesh v England, second one-day international at Mirpur.
Provocative celebration when J. C. Buttler dismissed. 20% fine/1 demerit pt – J. Srinath.

J. C. Buttler England v Bangladesh, second one-day international at Mirpur.
Angry reaction to Bangladesh celebrations when he was out. Reprimand/1 demerit pt – J. Srinath

M. S. Wade Australia v South Africa, fourth one-day international at Port Elizabeth.
Verbal and physical confrontation with bowler T. Shamsi. 25% fine/1 demerit pt – B. C. Broad.

T. Shamsi South Africa v Australia, fourth one-day international at Port Elizabeth.
Verbal and physical confrontation with batsman M. S. Wade. 25% fine/1 demerit pt – B. C. Broad.

Imran Tahir South Africa v Australia, fifth one-day international at Cape Town.
Refused to stop verbally provoking batsman D. A. Warner. 30% fine/2 demerit pts – B. C. Broad.

B. A. Stokes England v Bangladesh, Second Test at Mirpur.
Verbally engaged batsman Sabbir Rahman despite warning. 15% fine/1 demerit pt – R. S. Madugalle.

F. du Plessis South Africa v Australia, Second Test at Hobart.
Applied artificial substance to the ball. 100% of match fee/3 demerit pts – A. J. Pycroft.

R. A. S. Lakmal Sri Lanka v Zimbabwe, one-day international at Bulawayo.
Threw the ball dangerously towards opener C. J. Chibhabha. 50% fine/2 demerit pts – J. Srinath.

B. A. Stokes England v India, Third Test at Mohali.
Reacted to Indian celebration of his dismissal. Reprimand/1 demerit pt – R. S. Madugalle.

Tanveer Haider Bangladesh v New Zealand, second one-day international at Nelson.
Obscene language when N. T. Broom hit him for four. Reprimand/1 demerit pt – B. C. Broad.

D. P. D. N. Dickwella Sri Lanka v South Africa, fourth one-day international at Cape Town.
Inappropriate deliberate physical contact with Rabada. 50% fine/3 demerit pts – R. B. Richardson.

K. Rabada South Africa v Sri Lanka, fourth one-day international at Cape Town.
Inappropriate deliberate physical contact with Dickwella. 50% fine/3 demerit pts – R. B. Richardson.

Twenty-five further breaches took place in Associate Member, Under-19 or women's internationals during this period.

Under ICC regulations on minor over-rate offences, players are fined 10% of their match fee for every over their side fails to bowl in the allotted time, with the captain fined double that amount. There were 12 instances in this period in men's internationals, plus one in a women's ODI:

Azhar Ali/Pakistan v New Zealand, 3rd ODI at Auckland, 20%/10% – D. C. Boon.

Mashrafe bin Mortaza/Bangladesh v India, WT20I at Bangalore, 20%/10% – B. C. Broad.

A. G. Cremer/Zimbabwe v India, T20I at Harare, 40%/20% – R. B. Richardson.

Misbah-ul-Haq/Pakistan v England, 4th Test at The Oval, 20%/10% – R. B. Richardson.

F. du Plessis/South Africa v Australia, 5th ODI at Cape Town, 20%/10% – B. C. Broad.

Misbah-ul-Haq/Pakistan v New Zealand, 1st Test at Christchurch, 40%/20% – R. B. Richardson.
Misbah suspended for one Test as it was his second offence within 12 months.

W. U. Tharanga/Sri Lanka v West Indies, ODI at Bulawayo, 40%/20% – J. Srinath.

Azhar Ali/Pakistan v New Zealand, 2nd Test at Hamilton, 100%/50% – R. B. Richardson.

Mashrafe bin Mortaza/Bangladesh v NZ, 1st ODI at Christchurch, 20%/10% – B. C. Broad.

Misbah-ul-Haq/Pakistan v Australia, 2nd Test at Melbourne, 40%/20% – R. S. Madugalle.

E. J. G. Morgan/England v India, 2nd ODI at Cuttack, 20%/10% – A. J. Pycroft.

Azhar Ali/Pakistan v Australia, 5th ODI at Adelaide, 40%/20% – J. J. Crowe.
Azhar Ali suspended for one ODI as it was his second offence within 12 months.

M. M. Lanning/Aus Women v SA Women, 4th ODI at Coffs Harbour, Reprimand – P. L. Marshall.

INTERNATIONAL UMPIRES' PANELS

In 1993, the ICC formed an international umpires' panel, containing at least two officials from each Full Member. A third-country umpire from this panel stood with a home umpire in every Test from 1994 onwards. In 2002, an elite panel was appointed: two elite umpires – both independent – were to stand in all Tests, and at least one in every ODI, where one home umpire was allowed. A supporting panel of international umpires was created to provide cover at peak times in the Test schedule, and to provide a second umpire in one-day internationals. The ICC also appointed specialist third umpires to give rulings from TV replays. The panels are sponsored by Emirates Airlines.

The elite panel at the start of 2017: Aleem Dar (Pakistan), H. D. P. K. Dharmasena (Sri Lanka), M. Erasmus (South Africa), C. B. Gaffaney (New Zealand), I. J. Gould (England), R. K. Illingworth (England), R. A. Kettleborough (England), N. J. Llong (England), B. N. J. Oxenford (Australia), S. Ravi (India), P. R. Reiffel (Australia) and R. J. Tucker (Australia).

The international panel: Ahsan Raza (Pakistan), Anisur Rahman (Bangladesh), R. J. Bailey (England), G. O. Brathwaite (West Indies), C. M. Brown (New Zealand), A. K. Chowdhury (India), S. D. Fry (Australia), S. George (South Africa), M. A. Gough (England), A. T. Holdstock (South Africa), W. R. Knights (New Zealand), M. D. Martell (Australia), R. E. J. Martinesz (Sri Lanka), T. J. Matibiri (Zimbabwe), R. S. A. Palliyaguruge (Sri Lanka), C. Shamshuddin (India), Sharfuddoula (Bangladesh), Shozab Raza (Pakistan), R. B. Tiffin (Zimbabwe), J. S. Wilson (West Indies).

The third umpires: Ahmed Shahab (Pakistan), N. Duguid (West Indies), S. B. Haig (New Zealand), P. B. Jele (South Africa), Masudur Rahman (Bangladesh), N. N. Menon (India), C. K. Nandan (India), S. J. Nogajski (Australia), L. S. Reifer (West Indies), R. T. Robinson (England), L. Rusere (Zimbabwe), P. Wilson (Australia), R. R. Wimalasiri (Sri Lanka).

Associate and Affiliate panel: Ahmed Shah Durrani (Afghanistan), Ahmed Shah Pakteen (Afghanistan), Akbar Ali (UAE), S. N. Bandekar (USA), R. E. Black (Ireland), K. Cross (New Zealand), M. A. Din (Netherlands), R. D'Mello (Kenya), A. J. T. Dowdalls (Scotland), D. A. Haggo (Scotland), M. Hawthorne (Ireland), C. J. Howard (Hong Kong), Iftikhar Ali (UAE), H. K. G. Jansen (Netherlands), V. K. Jha (Nepal), A. Kapa (PNG), A. W. Louw (Namibia), N. G. Morrison (Vanuatu), A. J. Neill (Ireland), L. Oala (PNG), D. Odhiambo (Kenya), I. O. Oyieko (Kenya), C. A. Polosak (Australia), B. B. Pradhan (Nepal), S. S. Prasad (Singapore), Rabiul Hoque (UAE), I. N. Ramage (Scotland), S. Redfern (England), D. N. Subedi (Nepal), Tabarak Dar (Hong Kong), I. A. Thomson (Hong Kong), C. H. Thorburn (Namibia), P. van Liemt (Netherlands), J. M. Williams (West Indies), C. Young (Cayman Islands).

ICC REFEREES' PANEL

In 1991, the ICC formed a panel of referees to enforce their Code of Conduct for Tests and one-day internationals, to impose penalties for slow over-rates, breaches of the Code and other ICC regulations, and to support the umpires in upholding the conduct of the game. In 2002, the ICC launched an elite panel of referees, on full-time contracts, for all international cricket. The panel is sponsored by Emirates Airlines. At the start of 2017, the panel consisted of D. C. Boon (Australia), B. C. Broad (England), J. J. Crowe (New Zealand), R. S. Madugalle (Sri Lanka), A. J. Pycroft (Zimbabwe), R. B. Richardson (West Indies) and J. Srinath (India). A further panel of regional referees consisted of S. R. Bernard (Australia), D. Govindjee (South Africa), D. T. Jukes (England) and G. F. Labrooy (Sri Lanka).

ENGLISH UMPIRES FOR 2017

First-class: R. J. Bailey, N. L. Bainton, P. K. Baldwin, M. Burns, N. G. B. Cook, N. G. C. Cowley, J. H. Evans, R. Evans, S. C. Gale, S. A. Garratt, M. A. Gough, I. J. Gould, P. J. Hartley, R. K. Illingworth, R. A. Kettleborough, N. J. Llong, G. D. Lloyd, J. W. Lloyds, N. A. Mallender, D. J. Millns, S. J. O'Shaughnessy, R. T. Robinson, M. J. Saggers, B. V. Taylor, A. G. Wharf. *Reserves:* I. D. Blackwell, B. J. Debenham, T. Lungley, J. D. Middlebrook, M. Newell, P. R. Pollard, R. J. Warren, C. M. Watts.

Minor Counties: R. G. B. Allen, J. Attridge, J. S. Beckwith, S. F. Bishopp, D. Browne, T. Caldicott, G. I. Callaway, S. Cobb, K. Coburn, R. G. Eagleton, M. T. Ennis, A. H. Forward, D. J. Gower, R. C. Hampshire, A. C. Harris, Hasan Adnan, I. L. Herbert, A. Hicks, C. Johnson, N. Kent, I. P. Laurence, S. E. Lavis, A. Lunn, S. J. Malone, J. Marshall, P. W. Matten, R. P. Medland, J. D. Middlebrook, Naeem Ashraf, R. J. Newham, P. D. Nicholls, R. Parker, D. N. Pedley, N. E. Piddock, J. Pitcher, M. Pointer, N. Pratt, D. Price, M. Qureshi, G. M. Roberts, S. J. Ross, S. Shanmugam, J. R. Tomsett, D. M. Warburton, M. D. Watton, A. J. Wheeler, R. A. White.

THE DUCKWORTH/LEWIS/STERN METHOD

In 1997, the ECB's one-day competitions adopted a new method to revise targets in interrupted games, devised by Frank Duckworth of the Royal Statistical Society and Tony Lewis of the University of the West of England. The method was gradually taken up by other countries and, in 1999, the ICC decided to incorporate it into the standard playing conditions for one-day internationals.

The system aims to preserve any advantage that one team has established before the interruption. It uses the idea that teams have two resources from which they make runs – an allocated number of overs, and ten wickets. It also takes into account when the interruption occurs, because of the different scoring-rates typical of different stages of an innings. Traditional run-rate calculations relied only on the overs available, and ignored wickets lost.

It uses one table with 50 rows, covering matches of up to 50 overs, and ten columns, from nought to nine wickets down. Each figure gives the percentage of the total runs that would, on average, be scored with a certain number of overs left and wickets lost. If a match is shortened before it begins, to, say, 33 overs a side, the figure for 33 overs and ten wickets remaining would be the starting point.

If overs are lost, the table is used to calculate the percentage of runs the team would be expected to score in those missing overs. This is obtained by reading the figure for the number of overs left, and wickets down, when play stops, and subtracting the figure for the number of overs left when it resumes. If the delay occurs between innings, and the second team's allocation of overs is reduced, then their target is obtained by calculating the appropriate percentage for the reduced number of overs with all ten wickets standing. For instance, if the second team's innings halves from 50 overs to 25, the table shows that they still have 66.5% of their resources left, so have to beat two-thirds of the first team's total, rather than half. If the first innings is complete and the second innings interrupted or prematurely terminated, the score to beat is reduced by the percentage of the innings lost.

The version known as the "Professional Edition" was introduced into one-day internationals from 2003, and subsequently into most national one-day competitions. Using a more advanced mathematical formula (it is entirely computerised), it adjusts the tables to allow for the different scoring-rates that emerge in matches with above-average first-innings scores. In 2014, analysis by Steven Stern of the Queensland University of Technology, responsible for the method after Duckworth and Lewis retired, indicated further modification was needed. The Duckworth/Lewis/Stern method is now used in all one-day and Twenty20 internationals, as well as most national competitions. The original "Standard Edition" is used where computers are unavailable, and at lower levels of the game.

The system also covers first-innings interruptions, multiple interruptions and innings ended by rain. The tables are revised slightly every two years, taking account of changing scoring-rates; the average total in a 50-over international is now just under 249 (up from 225 in 1999).

In the World Cup semi-final between South Africa and New Zealand at Auckland in March 2015, South Africa were 216 for three from 38 overs when seven overs were lost to rain; after the innings resumed, they finished on 281. With three wickets down, the lost overs (39 to 45) constituted 14.85% of South Africa's scoring resources, meaning they used only 85.15%. By contrast, New Zealand's 43-over chase constituted 90% of the resources of a full innings. Their revised target was determined by multiplying South Africa's total, 281, by 90% divided by 85.15% and adding one run: 281 x (90/85.15) + 1 = 298. New Zealand scored 299 for six in 42.5 overs to win, with a six off the penultimate delivery. Had South Africa been two down at the interruption, the lost overs would have constituted a higher percentage of their scoring resources; the revised target would have been 301 and New Zealand would have needed two more runs off the final ball.

A similar system, usually known as the VJD method, is used in some domestic matches in India. It was devised by V. Jayadevan, a civil engineer from Kerala.

POWERPLAYS

In one-day and Twenty20 internationals, two semi-circles of 30-yard (27.43 metres) radius are drawn on the field behind each set of stumps, joined by straight lines parallel to the pitch.

At the instant of delivery in the first ten overs of an uninterrupted one-day international innings (the first six overs in a Twenty20 international), only two fielders may be positioned outside this 30-yard area. During the next 30 overs (11–40), no more than four fielders may be stationed outside it; and in the final ten overs, no more than five. (In Twenty20 internationals, no more than five may be positioned outside the area for the last 14 overs.) In matches affected by the weather, the number of overs in each powerplay stage is reduced in proportion to the overall reduction of overs.

In July 2015, the one-day international requirement for two close fielders in the first ten overs, and the five-over batting powerplay, to be claimed between the 11th and 40th overs, was abolished.

MEETINGS AND DECISIONS IN 2016

ICC BOARD

The ICC Board met in Dubai on February 4, 2016, under new chairman Shashank Manohar, and reconsidered the 2014 changes to the ICC constitution. They agreed to re-establish an independent chairman, who should not hold any post with any member board while in office; to remove the right of India, Australia and England to permanent positions on the leading committees; to require annual audited statements from Full Members; and to conduct a complete review of the 2014 changes. Further details of this meeting appeared in *Wisden 2016*, page 1500.

The board discussed cricket's three formats, the amount of cricket played, and the impact of Twenty20 leagues, with a view to a clearer calendar, underpinned by appropriate funding. They heard a report on dialogue with the International Olympic Committee and the Commonwealth Games Federation.

They appointed an anti-corruption oversight group, to include the executive committee chairman, the chairman of the Anti-Corruption Unit, chief executive David Richardson, former Indian captain Rahul Dravid, legal expert Louis Weston and independent anti-corruption advisor John Abbott.

Following board elections in January, Sri Lanka's membership was fully reinstated, along with funding, and attendance and voting rights. The USA Cricket Association remained suspended, but the ICC had set a budget to support cricket development there, and approved activities to take place in 2016.

A qualification pathway for Under-19 World Cups was agreed: the ten Test countries and the highest-placed Associate in the 2016 tournament would qualify directly for 2018, the remaining five through regional tournaments. The board also received updates on anti-doping matters.

ECB SPONSORSHIP AND BROADCAST DEALS

On February 29, the England and Wales Cricket Board announced that optical retail chain Specsavers had signed a four-year deal to sponsor the County Championship from 2017 to 2020.

The ECB had recently agreed a five-year partnership with Greene King as the Official Beer of England Cricket, and renewed for a further three years its agreement with Yorkshire Tea as the Official Brew of England Cricket; in March, Foster's became the Official Lager of England Cricket for two years.

On May 4, the ECB announced a two-year deal with Talksport radio to broadcast live commentary on the NatWest T20 Blast and Royal London One-Day Cup.

ECB DOMESTIC CRICKET

On March 7, the ECB board agreed changes to the shape of the 2017 domestic season. The Specsavers County Championship was to run throughout the summer, but pause during blocks of limited-overs cricket. There would be two divisions – of eight and ten teams – and 14 rounds rather than 16.

The group stage of the 50-over Royal London One-Day Cup was scheduled for April and May, with the final at Lord's in July; the early start aimed to prepare England players for the Champions Trophy in June. The two group winners would advance directly to the semi-finals, while the teams placed second and third met in two quarter-finals. NatWest T20 Blast matches would be contested on a regional basis, in two blocks in July and August, culminating in finals day. This was intended to attract a family audience in the summer holidays.

On May 9, the ECB announced a new North v South tournament to be played in the UAE in March 2017. There would be three 50-over matches, and some of the players would be selected using the PCA's Most Valuable Player Rankings; it would be a chance for them to press claims for places in the 2019 World Cup.

ICC BOARD

The ICC Board met in Dubai on April 24. They congratulated the West Indies Cricket Board on an unprecedented treble – the Under-19 World Cup, the World Twenty20 and the Women's World Twenty20 – and complimented the Bangladeshi and Indian boards on their staging of these tournaments. But they criticised the behaviour of some West Indian players after the men's World T20 final.

Following the decision to re-establish an independent chairman, the board agreed to elect the chairman by secret ballot in May. All present and past ICC directors were eligible; they must be nominated by two fellow directors and, if elected, give up any national or provincial position with any member board.

Nepal were suspended as an Affiliate Member after a breach of the rule against government interference in members' affairs. ICC management would help develop a sustainable administrative structure in Nepal; in the meantime, their teams were allowed to play in ICC tournaments, but the association would not be entitled to ICC funding.

The board approved a short-term fund of $500,000 each for Afghanistan and Ireland, allowing them to schedule more bilateral one-day series and improve their rankings, and thus their chances of qualification for the 2019 World Cup.

The board were impressed to hear there were now 80,000 cricketers in China, including 35,000 women; the Chinese women's team had narrowly missed qualifying for the Women's WT20. There was a satisfactory report from the USA; it was decided that the World Cricket League Division Four would be staged in Los Angeles in late 2016.

Members confirmed their support for day/night Tests; the first such match had been staged in Adelaide in November 2015, and more were planned. There was further discussion of bilateral international cricket, competitions in all three formats and the need for greater context. The board were updated on cricket's potential participation in the Olympics and the Commonwealth Games.

MCC ANNUAL GENERAL MEETING

The 229th AGM of the Marylebone Cricket Club was held at Lord's on May 4, with president Roger Knight in the chair. He announced that his successor, from October, would be the former Kent captain Matthew Fleming, who had chaired the cricket committee since 2013 and was also a former chairman of the PCA. At 52, he would be the youngest MCC president since Peter May in 1980.

Knight warned members that, although Lord's Tests attracted far greater crowds than those outside London, it was not certain that the ground would continue to host two Tests a year from 2020 onwards, when the current TV rights package requiring seven home Tests would expire.

Resolutions were passed increasing members' entrance fees and annual subscriptions, and amending various rules. A further resolution was approved to commission a review which would include an analysis by a major firm of accountants of the Morley Plan to develop land at the Nursery End; the stand development programme and other capital expenditure required for the current MCC masterplan for Lord's; and MCC's financial projections for the next ten years.

Membership on December 31, 2015, totalled 23,327, made up of 17,832 full members, 5,001 associate members, 334 honorary members, 59 senior members and 101 out-match members. There were 11,649 candidates awaiting election to full membership; 502 vacancies arose in 2015.

ICC CHAIRMAN

On May 12, the ICC announced that Shashank Manohar had been elected chairman unanimously, with no other nominations received. He had already held the role for six months, after becoming president of the Board of Control for Cricket in India; under the 2014 reforms, the BCCI had had the right to nominate the chairman for 2015-16. On election by the ICC board, Manohar immediately stood down as BCCI president. To accommodate the new role of an independent chair, the ICC approved amendments to the constitution, including abolition of the post of ICC president from June.

ICC CRICKET COMMITTEE

The ICC Cricket Committee met at Lord's on May 31–June 1, and heard plans to create greater context through dedicated competitions in the three formats; there was unanimous agreement that the structure of international cricket needed to change.

They acknowledged the success of the inaugural day/night Test in Adelaide, but stressed that day/night Test cricket must be delivered to a consistently high standard across all countries, with the right combination of ball, pitch, lighting levels and environmental conditions to allow an even contest between bat and ball. They expressed concern about the quality of Test pitches, and countries overtly preparing surfaces to suit home teams.

Engineers from the Massachusetts Institute of Technology reported on their testing of the technologies used in the DRS, including edge-detection systems (heat-based and sound-based) and ball-tracking with predictive path. The committee believed the ICC should establish tighter processes to approve new technologies and ensure they were applied more consistently.

After receiving an MCC paper on scientific and statistical evidence that bats had become more powerful through larger sweet spots, the committee thought MCC should consider limiting bat dimensions.

Cricket Australia proposed a two-year trial allowing a concussion substitute in domestic first-class cricket. The committee acknowledged the issue's seriousness but argued that the Laws and playing conditions allowed players to receive the best possible medical treatment, and that further changes were not required at present. They also considered helmet safety after a presentation by ICC medical consultant Dr Craig Ranson. Too many international cricketers still wore helmets not meeting the latest British Standard; the committee recommended enforcing BS-compliant helmets in all international cricket.

The committee noted progress in policing suspect bowling actions, and urged all countries to screen bowlers in domestic cricket before they reached international level.

Clare Connor, chair of the Women's Committee, reported on the impact of the recent Women's World Twenty20 in India, which had attracted 24.5m TV viewers in India alone, as well as an average audience of 100,000 in the USA.

ICC ANNUAL MEETINGS

The ICC annual conference and associated meetings took place in Edinburgh on June 27–July 2. ICC chairman Shashank Manohar thanked outgoing president Zaheer Abbas for his work in the role, which was now being abolished.

The Full Council elected Saudi Arabia as the ICC's 39th Associate Member; they had been an Affiliate since 2003. The suspensions of the USA and Nepal were ratified, though delegations were to visit both countries and report back in October.

The ICC board noted the progress made by the working group reviewing the 2014 constitutional changes which had given greater power to India, England and Australia.

The Chief Executives' Committee discussed the structure of international cricket and new competitions; a workshop in early September would work through the detail.

The board decided to apply for a women's cricket event at the 2022 Commonwealth Games in Durban, to showcase the progress of women's cricket and provide the top players with an additional high-profile competition. There would be further discussions on cricket's potential participation in the Olympics.

The ICC approved a change to the DRS on lbws, slightly increasing the size of the zone the ball had to hit to overturn a not-out decision. They agreed to a trial of the third umpire using instant replays to call no-balls (this was later set for the England–Pakistan one-day series in August); the third umpire would judge no-balls within a few seconds of each delivery, and communicate with the on-field umpire.

On helmet safety, the ICC said helmets should not be mandatory in international cricket but, if used, batting helmets must comply with British Standard BS 7928:2013. Members should educate players on the benefits of BS-compliant helmets, which should be prescribed in clothing and equipment regulations.

The chairman of the Anti-Corruption Unit, Sir Ronnie Flanagan, provided his annual update, including progress on the integrity working party recommendations.

The board extended ICC chief executive David Richardson's contract to 2019.

MCC WORLD CRICKET COMMITTEE

The MCC world cricket committee met at Lord's on July 11–12. A minute's silence was observed in memory of former member Martin Crowe.

The committee agreed the balance between bat and ball had tilted too far towards the bat. The overwhelming view was that it had become too easy to clear the boundary, even with mistimed shots, and there was a risk to the safety of close fielders, bowlers and umpires. It was time to add further limitations on bat sizes to the Laws: in addition to width and length, there should be restrictions on the edge, depth and possibly weight. Manufacturers and scientists would be consulted to finalise the measurements and to investigate the viability of a weight limit.

The committee believed the ICC should apply for Twenty20 cricket to be included in the 2024 Olympics, so the best players (men and women) could inspire and reinvigorate the sport at grassroots level and encourage its growth in new markets.

Having regarded the ICC's 2014 governance changes as bad for the game, they were delighted that, under chairman Shashank Manohar and chief executive David Richardson, the ICC had come to the view that many of those decisions should be reversed.

Richardson outlined ideas to create a better context for Test, one-day and Twenty20 cricket without overcrowding the calendar. The committee felt cricket was thriving in the shorter formats, but the future of Test cricket was uncertain. Remedies were discussed, including more day/night matches, better marketing of the five-day format and increased incentives to play Test cricket. There was strong support for a system of promotion and relegation, with a pinnacle event between the top two teams on a two-yearly cycle.

Shaharyar Khan, chairman of the Pakistan Cricket Board, explained the difficulties they currently faced: having to play home matches in a neutral country, with attendant high costs; no bilateral series against India; and developing grassroots cricket under financial pressure. The committee offered to add one or two promising Pakistani cricketers to the MCC Young Cricketers' intake.

On Law 42.15 – bowler attempting to run out non-striker before delivery – the committee unanimously held that the Law should mirror the ICC playing condition, requiring the non-striker to remain inside the crease before the ball was released. A non-striker out of his crease before this point is either taking an advantage or acting carelessly, and runs the risk of being legitimately run out.

ECB SPONSORSHIP DEAL

On July 28, the ECB announced a new partnership with NatWest, who had been sponsoring various cricket competitions in England and Wales since 1980, as well as the CricketForce volunteering initiative. Over four years from May 2017 – after the conclusion of the board's deal with Waitrose – NatWest would be the ECB's lead commercial partner, supporting work with amateur clubs and leagues, and strengthening the connection between fans and the England teams: men, women, age-groups and national disability sides. The NatWest brand would be emblazoned on all England team shirts.

ECB DOMESTIC CRICKET

The ECB and the chairmen and chief executives of the first-class counties, MCC and the PCA met on September 14 and agreed to plan a new eight-team Twenty20 competition, to be staged in addition to the existing NatWest T20 Blast. The counties were to consult on the proposals, while the PCA would talk to the players. The aim was to broaden the game's appeal, provide greater financial stability for the counties and ensure that each continued to compete in all three formats.

CODE OF CONDUCT AND DECISION REVIEW SYSTEM

Modifications to the ICC Code of Conduct and the DRS regulations came into effect on September 22, ahead of the one-day international between South Africa and Ireland in Benoni.

From this date, in addition to warnings, fines and suspensions, players (or player support personnel) breaching the Code of Conduct would accumulate demerit points, which would remain on their record for two years; the accumulation of four or more points would result in suspension.

There were also new DRS playing conditions relating to lbws. For a not-out decision to be overturned, more than half the ball now had to be impacting the pad within a zone bordered by the outside of off and leg stumps (formerly the centre of off and leg stumps), while the ball had to be hitting the stumps within a zone bordered by the outside (formerly the centre) of off and leg stumps and the bottom of the bails.

ENGLAND PLAYER CONTRACTS

On September 29, the ECB announced a restructuring of the central contract system. Previously, they could award up to 16 central contracts, plus further incremental contracts to players making a certain number of appearances for England during the year. Under the new system, the ECB could award up to 11 contracts each for Test and white-ball cricket, reflecting an increased focus on the shorter formats. Players winning Test contracts (or both) would have their salaries paid in full by the ECB, while those on white-ball contracts would receive a supplement on top of their county salary. A ranking system based on performances, off-field contributions and fitness determined pay levels.

The ECB awarded ten Test contracts to run for 12 months from October 1, 2016. They went to Moeen Ali, James Anderson, Jonny Bairstow, Stuart Broad, Alastair Cook, Steven Finn, Joe Root, Ben Stokes, Chris Woakes and Mark Wood. They also awarded 11 white-ball contracts, to Ali, Root, Stokes and Woakes, plus Jos Buttler, Alex Hales, Eoin Morgan, Liam Plunkett, Adil Rashid, Jason Roy and David Willey. In addition, Gary Ballance was given an incremental contract.

Compared with the previous year, Ian Bell had lost his contract, while Bairstow, Hales, Plunkett, Rashid and Woakes had been promoted from incremental contracts, and Roy and Willey added to the list.

DAY/NIGHT TEST AND CHAMPIONSHIP MATCHES

The ECB announced on October 6 that Edgbaston would host the UK's first day/night Test in 2017. The First Test between England and West Indies (August 17–21), was scheduled to be staged between 2pm and 9pm; players would use pink Dukes balls but wear traditional white clothing. The first day/night Test had been staged at Adelaide, in November 2015, and three more were about to take place, at Dubai in October, Adelaide again in November, and Brisbane in December. Edgbaston had also staged the first day/night List A game in England, a 40-over AXA Life League match between Warwickshire and Somerset in July 1997.

On November 24, it was announced that there would be a round of day/night County Championship matches in June 2017; nine games would start on June 26, with the aim of preparing players for the Edgbaston Test and broadening the audience for four-day cricket.

ICC BOARD

The ICC Board met in Cape Town on October 10–14. Work continued on the governance structure of the ICC, including the revenue-sharing model, and the structure of international bilateral cricket. Proposals were to be presented to the board in February.

Cricket Australia, hosts for the men's and women's World Twenty20 competitions in 2020, proposed holding the women's tournament six months ahead of the men's. They argued that separating the two could boost the women's event, creating space to broadcast it on primetime television. The board agreed, believing the success of the Women's Big Bash League in Australia demonstrated an appetite for women's cricket.

The board approved a governance structure for the USA Cricket Association, including a new constitution with representation across the cricket community, independent directors and elite players. USACA were asked to approve its implementation by December.

The Pakistan Cricket Board requested a special assistance fund because of the financial issues caused by not being able to play at home. The board agreed to provide some form of assistance. They also approved repeat payments of $500,000 to Ireland and Afghanistan (following the ones in April) to stage more ODIs and T20Is, and $250,000 to each of the other Associate Members with ODI and T20I status. It was agreed that Uganda should host the World Cricket League Division Three in 2017, subject to security arrangements and operational costs.

The Chief Executives' Committee approved an application to give first-class status to Ireland's domestic competition, the Inter-Provincial Championship, with List A status for the Inter-Provincial one-day and T20 competitions.

CHANCE TO SHINE

The ECB announced on November 2 that they would double their investment in the Chance to Shine children's cricket charity from £1.25m to £2.5m between 2017 and 2021. Chance to Shine aimed to expand their annual reach from approximately 300,000 primary-school children to more than 500,000 from October 2017, by funding professional coaches and support packages for teachers.

ENGLAND WOMEN'S PLAYER CONTRACTS

On December 16, the ECB introduced two-year contracts for England Women players, to give them greater financial security; unlike their male equivalents, they could not fall back on a professional career in county cricket. There was also a new level of "rookie" contracts for players on the fringe of the international side.

The contracts, to run from February 1, 2017, were awarded to 18 players: Tammy Beaumont, Katherine Brunt, Kate Cross, Georgia Elwiss, Natasha Farrant, Jenny Gunn, Alex Hartley, Danielle Hazell, Amy Jones, Heather Knight, Laura Marsh, Natalie Sciver, Anya Shrubsole, Sarah Taylor, Fran Wilson, Lauren Winfield and Danni Wyatt, plus Beth Langston on the first rookie contract.

Compared with the previous year, Hartley and Langston had been added to the list, while Charlotte Edwards and Lydia Greenway had retired from international cricket, and Rebecca Grundy had been dropped.

MCC WORLD CRICKET COMMITTEE

The MCC world cricket committee met in Mumbai on December 6–7. They recommended to the main MCC committee that the Laws should be revised to limit bat edges to 40mm and bat depths to 67mm (60mm plus 7mm for a possible curve). A bat gauge would enforce the limits in the professional game; there would be a moratorium period for amateur players, allowing them to use existing oversized bats.

The committee also recommended giving umpires the power to send off cricketers for serious disciplinary breaches, such as threatening an umpire, assaulting another player, umpire, official or spectator, or any other act of violence on the field of play. They believed the game needed a mechanism to deal with offences during a match, and not afterwards. Poor behaviour in the recreational game was having an adverse effect; in a recent survey by Portsmouth University, 40% of British umpires said they were questioning whether to continue because of abuse. The committee debated sanctions for lesser offences, including run penalties and sin bins, but did not feel these should be included in the Laws; they could be added as an appendix for governing bodies or leagues to implement within their own playing regulations.

If approved, both these changes would be implemented in the new code of the Laws in October 2017.

The committee did not believe Law 42.3(a) on changing the condition of the ball should be revised, despite a recent incident involving South African Test captain Faf du Plessis in Australia. The Law was clear, and trying to make it more prescriptive by listing banned substances would be counterproductive, as something was bound to be left out.

It was agreed to recommend that catches and stumpings should be permitted after the ball has struck a helmet worn by a fielder, in the same way as if taken off a wicketkeeper's pads. This would include a ball lodged or trapped in the helmet grille.

The committee debated a trial of four-day Tests (last played in 1972-73). On the pro side, there could be clear scheduling, with every Test played Thursday to Sunday to attract greater crowds and television audiences over the last two days. Shorter games would encourage attacking play, which might revive crowds. With more overs scheduled per day, over-rates would have to speed up, so spinners might bowl more. Tours could also be shorter, so fewer Tests would have to be played in the wetter parts of the season. The likelihood that most Tests would run a full four days would make it easier for grounds and broadcasters to schedule staffing and operational costs.

On the other hand, there would probably be more draws. The better team would have less chance of winning, the weaker team more chance of escaping. There could be more doctored pitches to achieve results within four days, or more manufactured games with declaration bowling and cheap runs. Many sides struggled to bowl 90 overs in six and a half hours, so it was unrealistic to think they would bowl many more in a longer day, and spectators might not want to watch for more than seven hours. The committee hoped to hear the thoughts of governing bodies, players, fans, sponsors and broadcasters.

ICC chief executive David Richardson reported on a proposal for a conference-style competition in Test cricket. The committee encouraged the ICC to pursue this; they felt that, though the last six months had seen some competitive Tests, the current rankings system meant lower-ranked nations started so far behind that getting to the top seemed unattainable. A conference system, with all teams starting from scratch, would give more hope of toppling the best nations, and stimulate interest in the ultimate form of the game.

MEETINGS AND DECISIONS IN 2017

ICC BOARD

The ICC Board met in Dubai on February 2–4, 2017. They agreed in principle to recommended changes to the constitution and financial model, and committed to consider further representations from members and to sign off the detail by the April board meeting, for submission to the Full Council in June 2017.

The broader principles agreed included a revised financial distribution, ensuring a more equitable distribution of revenues, and a revised constitution reflecting good governance and clarifying the ICC's roles and objectives to provide leadership in international cricket.

Further constitutional changes proposed included adding Ireland and Afghanistan as Full Members, subject to their meeting membership criteria; removing the Affiliate level of membership, so there would be only two categories, Full and Associate; introducing membership criteria and a membership committee to ensure compliance; an independent female director; equal weight of votes for all board members regardless of status; and all members to be entitled to attend the AGM.

The board also identified their preferred model for all three formats. This included a nine-team Test league, to run over two years, with the remaining three Test sides (assuming Ireland and Afghanistan were promoted) guaranteed a consistent schedule of Tests against the others; a 13-team one-day league to run over three years, leading into qualification for the 2023 World Cup; and a regional Twenty20 structure to be developed as a pathway to qualification for the World Twenty20.

The Chief Executives' Committee agreed to the principle of consistent use of DRS technology across all international cricket. If approved at the annual conference in June, this would be fully implemented from October 2017. In the interim, DRS would be used in the 2017 Champions Trophy, all televised games at the Women's World Cup and all future World Twenty20 televised games (with one review per side). Post-2017, any technology used must be checked and approved by MIT.

DATES IN CRICKET HISTORY

c. 1550 Evidence of cricket being played in Guildford, Surrey.

1610 Reference to "cricketing" between Weald & Upland and North Downs near Chevening, Kent.

1611 Randle Cotgrave's French–English dictionary translates the French word "crosse" as a cricket staff.
Two youths fined for playing cricket at Sidlesham, Sussex.

1624 Jasper Vinall becomes first man known to be killed playing cricket: hit by a bat while trying to catch the ball – at Horsted Green, Sussex.

1676 First reference to cricket being played abroad, by British residents in Aleppo, Syria.

1694 Two shillings and sixpence paid for a "wagger" (wager) about a match at Lewes.

1697 First reference to "a great match" with 11 players a side for 50 guineas, in Sussex.

1700 Cricket match announced on Clapham Common.

1709 First recorded inter-county match: Kent v Surrey.

1710 First reference to cricket at Cambridge University.

1727 Articles of Agreement written governing the conduct of matches between the teams of the Duke of Richmond and Mr Brodrick of Peperharow, Surrey.

1729 Date of earliest surviving bat, belonging to John Chitty, now in the Oval pavilion.

1730 First recorded match at the Artillery Ground, off City Road, central London, still the cricketing home of the Honourable Artillery Company.

1744 Kent beat All-England by one wicket at the Artillery Ground.
First known version of the Laws of Cricket, issued by the London Club, formalising the pitch as 22 yards long.

c. 1767 Foundation of the Hambledon Club in Hampshire, the leading club in England for the next 30 years.

1769 First recorded century, by John Minshull for Duke of Dorset's XI v Wrotham.

1771 Width of bat limited to $4^1/_4$ inches, where it has remained ever since.

1774 Lbw law devised.

1776 Earliest known scorecards, at the Vine Club, Sevenoaks, Kent.

1780 The first six-seamed cricket ball, manufactured by Dukes of Penshurst, Kent.

1787 First match at Thomas Lord's first ground, Dorset Square, Marylebone – White Conduit Club v Middlesex.
Formation of Marylebone Cricket Club by members of the White Conduit Club.

1788 First revision of the Laws of Cricket by MCC.

1794 First recorded inter-school match: Charterhouse v Westminster.

1795 First recorded case of a dismissal "leg before wicket".

1806 First Gentlemen v Players match at Lord's.

1807 First mention of "straight-armed" (i.e. roundarm) bowling: by John Willes of Kent.

1809 Thomas Lord's second ground opened, at North Bank, St John's Wood.

1811 First recorded women's county match: Surrey v Hampshire at Ball's Pond, London.

1814 Lord's third ground opened on its present site, also in St John's Wood.

1827 First Oxford v Cambridge match, at Lord's: a draw.

1828 MCC authorise the bowler to raise his hand level with the elbow.

1833 John Nyren publishes *Young Cricketer's Tutor* and *The Cricketers of My Time.*

1836 First North v South match, for years regarded as the principal fixture of the season.

***c.* 1836** Batting pads invented.

1841 General Lord Hill, commander-in-chief of the British Army, orders that a cricket ground be made an adjunct of every military barracks.

1844 First official international match: Canada v United States.

1845 First match played at The Oval.

1846 The All-England XI, organised by William Clarke, begin playing matches, often against odds, throughout the country.

1849 First Yorkshire v Lancashire match.

***c.* 1850** Wicketkeeping gloves first used.

1850 John Wisden bowls all ten batsmen in an innings for North v South.

1853 First mention of a champion county: Nottinghamshire.

1858 First recorded instance of a hat being awarded to a bowler taking wickets with three consecutive balls.

1859 First touring team to leave England, captained by George Parr, draws enthusiastic crowds in the US and Canada.

1864 "Overhand bowling" authorised by MCC.
John Wisden's *The Cricketer's Almanack* first published.

1868 Team of Australian Aborigines tour England.

1873 W. G. Grace becomes the first player to record 1,000 runs and 100 wickets in a season.
First regulations restricting county qualifications, regarded by some as the official start of the County Championship.

1877 First Test match: Australia beat England by 45 runs at Melbourne.

1880 First Test in England: a five-wicket win against Australia at The Oval.

1882 Following England's first defeat by Australia in England, an "obituary notice" to English cricket in the *Sporting Times* leads to the tradition of the Ashes.

1889 Work begins on present Lord's Pavilion.
South Africa's first Test match.
Declarations first authorised, but only on the third day, or in a one-day match.

1890 County Championship officially constituted.

1895 W. G. Grace scores 1,000 runs in May, and reaches his 100th hundred.

1899 A. E. J. Collins scores 628 not out in a junior house match at Clifton College, the highest recorded individual score in any game – until 2016.
Selectors choose England team for home Tests, instead of host club issuing invitations.

1900 In England, six-ball over becomes the norm, instead of five.

1909 Imperial Cricket Conference (ICC – now the International Cricket Council) set up, with England, Australia and South Africa the original members.

1910 Six runs given for any hit over the boundary, instead of only for a hit out of the ground.

1912 First and only triangular Test series played in England, involving England, Australia and South Africa.

1915 W. G. Grace dies, aged 67.

1926 Victoria score 1,107 v New South Wales at Melbourne, still a first-class record.

1928 West Indies' first Test match.
A. P. Freeman of Kent and England becomes the only player to take more than 300 first-class wickets in a season: 304.

1930 New Zealand's first Test match.
Donald Bradman's first tour of England: he scores 974 runs in five Tests, still a record for any series.

1931 Stumps made higher (28 inches not 27) and wider (nine inches not eight – this was optional until 1947).

1932 India's first Test match.
Hedley Verity of Yorkshire takes ten wickets for ten runs v Nottinghamshire, the best innings analysis in first-class cricket.

1932-33 The Bodyline tour of Australia in which England bowl at batsmen's bodies with a packed leg-side field to neutralise Bradman's scoring.

1934 Jack Hobbs retires, with 197 centuries and 61,237 runs, both records.
First women's Test: Australia v England at Brisbane.

1935 MCC condemn and outlaw Bodyline.

1947 Denis Compton (Middlesex and England) hits a record 3,816 runs in an English season.

1948 First five-day Tests in England.
Bradman concludes Test career with a second-ball duck at The Oval and an average of 99.94 – four runs would have made it 100.

1952 Pakistan's first Test match.

1953 England regain the Ashes after a 19-year gap, the longest ever.

1956 Jim Laker of England takes 19 wickets for 90 v Australia at Manchester, the best match analysis in first-class cricket.

1960 First tied Test: Australia v West Indies at Brisbane.

1963 Distinction between amateurs and professionals abolished in English cricket.
The first major one-day tournament begins in England: the Gillette Cup.

1969 Limited-over Sunday league inaugurated for first-class counties.

1970 Proposed South African tour of England cancelled; South Africa excluded from international cricket because of their government's apartheid policies.

1971 First one-day international: Australia beat England at Melbourne by five wickets.

1973 First women's World Cup: England are the winners.

1975 First men's World Cup: West Indies beat Australia in final at Lord's.

1976 First women's match at Lord's: England beat Australia by eight wickets.

1977 Centenary Test at Melbourne, with identical result to the first match: Australia beat England by 45 runs.
Australian media tycoon Kerry Packer signs 51 of the world's leading players in defiance of the cricketing authorities.

1978 Graham Yallop of Australia is the first batsman to wear a protective helmet in a Test.

1979 Packer and official cricket agree peace deal.

1981 England beat Australia in Leeds Test, after following on with bookmakers offering odds of 500-1 against them winning.

1982 Sri Lanka's first Test match.

1991 South Africa return, with a one-day international in India.

1992 Zimbabwe's first Test match.
Durham become first county since Glamorgan in 1921 to attain first-class status.

1993 The ICC cease to be administered by MCC, becoming an independent organisation.

1994 Brian Lara becomes the first player to pass 500 in a first-class innings: 501 not out for Warwickshire v Durham.

2000 South Africa's captain Hansie Cronje banned from cricket for life after admitting receiving bribes from bookmakers in match-fixing scandal.
Bangladesh's first Test match.
County Championship split into two divisions, with promotion and relegation.

2001 Sir Donald Bradman dies, aged 92.

2003 First Twenty20 game played, in England.

2004 Lara is the first to score 400 in a Test innings, for West Indies v England in Antigua.

2005 England regain the Ashes after 16 years.

2006 Pakistan become first team to forfeit a Test, for refusing to resume at The Oval.
England lose the Ashes after 462 days, the shortest tenure in history.
Shane Warne becomes the first man to take 700 Test wickets.

2007 Australia complete 5–0 Ashes whitewash for the first time since 1920-21.
Australia win the World Cup for the third time running.
India beat Pakistan in the final of the inaugural World Twenty20 tournament.

2008 Indian Premier League of 20-over matches launched.
Sachin Tendulkar becomes the leading scorer in Tests, passing Lara.

2009 Terrorists in Lahore attack buses containing Sri Lankan team and match officials.

2010 Tendulkar scores the first double-century in a one-day international, against South Africa; later in the year, he scores his 50th Test century.
Muttiah Muralitharan retires from Test cricket, after taking his 800th wicket.
Pakistan bowl three deliberate no-balls in Lord's Test against England; the ICC ban the three players responsible.

2011 India become the first team to win the World Cup on home soil.
Salman Butt, Mohammad Asif and Mohammad Amir are given custodial sentences of between six and 30 months for their part in the Lord's spot-fix.
Virender Sehwag makes a world-record 219 in a one-day international, for India against West Indies at Indore.

2012 Tendulkar scores his 100th international century, in a one-day game against Bangladesh at Mirpur.
Hashim Amla makes 311 not out at The Oval, South Africa's first Test triple-century.
England win 2–1 in India, their first Test series victory there since 1984-85.

2013 150th edition of *Wisden Cricketers' Almanack.*
Tendulkar retires after his 200th Test match, with a record 15,921 runs.

2014 Australia complete only the third 5–0 Ashes whitewash.
ICC agree far-reaching changes to their governance, pushed through by India, Australia and England.
Brendon McCullum makes 302, New Zealand's first Test triple-century.
India's Rohit Sharma hits 264 in one-day international against Sri Lanka at Kolkata.
Australian batsman Phillip Hughes, 25, dies after being hit on the neck by a bouncer.

2015 Former Australian captain and TV commentator Richie Benaud dies aged 85.
Australia win World Cup for fifth time, beating New Zealand in final at Melbourne.
England win fourth successive home Ashes series.

2016 Pranav Dhanawade, 15, makes 1,009 not out – the highest recorded individual score in any match – in a school game in Mumbai.
McCullum hits Test cricket's fastest hundred, from 54 balls, in his final match, against Australia at Christchurch.

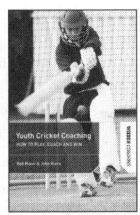

ANNIVERSARIES IN 2017-18

COMPILED BY STEVEN LYNCH

2017

April 28	Mike Brearley (England) born, 1942. *Cerebral Middlesex captain who won the Ashes in 1977, 1978-79 and 1981.*
May 3	J. T. "Jack" Hearne (England) born, 1867. *Middlesex seamer: fourth-highest wicket-taker in all first-class cricket, with 3,061.*
May 12	Hugh Trumble (Australia) born, 1867. *Tall off-spinner who collected 141 Test wickets against England, including two hat-tricks.*
May 24	Ali Bacher (South Africa) born, 1942. *Test batsman and captain, and later a senior administrator.*
June 4	The Bs beat England at Lord's, 1817. *Eleven men whose surname began with B overcame the rest of the alphabet by 114 runs.*
July 2–6	William Lambert (Sussex) scores 107* and 159 v Epsom at Lord's, 1817. *Lambert's last first-class match before he was caught up in a betting scandal.*
August 18	Brian Close (Yorkshire) accused of time-wasting in county match, 1967. *Close was stripped of the England captaincy after slowing down the over-rate against Warwickshire.*
October 17	Martin Donnelly (New Zealand) born, 1917. *Graceful left-hander who scored 206 in the 1949 Lord's Test.*
October 20	Albert "Tibby" Cotter (Australia) killed in action in Palestine, 1917. *The fastest bowler of his time, who featured in five Ashes series.*
October 24	Ian Bishop (West Indies) born, 1967. *Rapid Trinidadian bowler who took 161 Test wickets; later a commentator.*
November 8	Colin Blythe (England) killed in action at Ypres, 1917. *Kent left-arm spinner who took 2,503 wickets at 16.*
November 10	G. H. S. "Harry" Trott (Australia) dies, 1917. *Victoria all-rounder who captained in the 1896 and 1897-98 Ashes.*
November 11	Roy Fredericks (West Indies) born, 1942. *Attacking left-hand opener who scored a rapid century at Perth in 1975-76.*
November 14	C. K. Nayudu (India) dies, 1967. *Legendary figure in Indian cricket, and their first Test captain, in 1932.*
November 23	Gary Kirsten (South Africa) born, 1967. *Adhesive left-hand opener who was the first South African to win 100 Test caps.*
December 8	Ian Johnson (Australia) born, 1917. *Off-spinner who was one of Bradman's Invincibles in 1948, and captain in 1954-55 and 1956 Ashes.*

December 26 Richard Wardill (Victoria) hits the first first-class century in Australia, 1867.
Wardill scored 110 on the first day of the match against New South Wales at Melbourne.

December 31 Arthur Mailey (Australia) dies, 1967.
Whimsical leg-spinner who took 99 Test wickets, including 36 in the 1920-21 Ashes.

2018

January 9 Jimmy Adams (West Indies) born, 1968.
Jamaican left-hander who captained West Indies, and became their director of cricket in 2016.

March 7 Jack Ikin (England) born, 1918.
Lancashire all-rounder who won 18 Test caps.

March 23 Michael Atherton (England) born, 1968.
Lancashire opener who played 115 Tests, 54 as captain; later cricket correspondent of The Times.

March 25 Bill Lockwood (England) born, 1868.
Surrey seamer who could "break back and nip a piece of one's thigh away" (A. E. Knight).

March 28 Nasser Hussain (England) born, 1968.
Essex batsman who played 96 Tests, 45 as captain; later a trenchant TV commentator.

ONE HUNDRED AND FIFTY YEARS AGO

From WISDEN CRICKETERS' ALMANACK 1868

February 15	Cricket match played on the ice at Harewood, Yorkshire, 1838.
May 4	Sawdust introduced on a cricket ground by Lord F. Beauclerk, 1806.
July 15	In the match North v South at Lord's, 1850, John Wisden bowled all the wickets in second innings of South.
July 28	Pavilion at Lord's burnt down, 1825.
August 2	Lord Byron played in Eton and Harrow match at Lord's, 1805.
August 6	Telegraph first used at The Oval, 1849.
August 13	At Gorton, 1859, R. Prestwich was struck by a cricket ball on the temple, from which he died.
September 7	The American Champion Cricketers sailed from Liverpool to Quebec, 1859.

EXTRA MATCHES At Islington, April 22–23, 1867. One Leg (89 and 132) drew with One Arm (143 and 59-9).

ONE HUNDRED YEARS AGO

From WISDEN CRICKETERS' ALMANACK 1918

PREFACE The welcome accorded to *Wisden* a twelvemonth ago made it inevitable that even after three years of war – and as a natural consequence three practically blank cricket seasons – the Almanack should again be brought out. In its general plan the present issue is just the same as the last one. That was unavoidable. The war dominates everything.

NOTES BY THE EDITOR [Sydney Pardon] There can be no question that as regards the propriety of playing cricket in wartime there was a great change of feeling last summer. People realised that with public boxing carried on to an extent never heard of before, and professional billiard matches played in the hottest weather, there was something illogical, not to say absurd, in placing a ban on cricket… All this was diametrically opposite to the state of mind that prevailed during the first summer of the war… [I recall] a conversation I had with Mr Findlay [secretary of Surrey CCC] in the spring of 1915. I asked him whether the nets would be put up for practice at The Oval, and his reply… was something like this: "The nets will be up, but I don't expect our fellows will use them much. They will be afraid of being jeered at by the men on the tram cars." Such fears – perhaps rather imaginary even in 1915 – had quite passed away last summer. We had all come to regard the nightmare of war as a normal condition, and cricket was felt to be as legitimate as any other recreation.

LEICESTERSHIRE IN 1917 The pavilion on the Leicester ground is now the headquarters of the 53rd ASC Remount Depot, and the luncheon pavilion is the official rifle range of the 1st Battalion (Leicester) Leicestershire Volunteer Regiment, which has the cricket ground as an official drill ground.

LANCASHIRE IN 1917 The pavilion at Old Trafford, the members' dining room, and now also the tea room, are in possession of the Red Cross, and there are beds for 90–100 soldiers. The two grounds have been kept regularly mown and rolled.

DERBYSHIRE IN 1917 The pavilion was lent to the Royal Garrison Artillery as a temporary hospital, and during the year the ground was used for military cricket, football, and hockey matches.

NOTTINGHAMSHIRE IN 1917 The ground at Trent Bridge… has been kept in first-class condition, and never looked better than it did during the summer. There are now 100 beds in the pavilion and adjoining buildings, used for the last three years as a hospital. During the season the use of the ground was given free for charity and military matches.

PUBLIC SCHOOL CRICKET IN 1917 by E. B. Noel Public school cricket played an even larger part in the cricket of the year than in the two preceding seasons… There were, of course, a fair number of military teams about, and MCC were able to play a good many schools: Captain P. F. Warner more than once got together a pretty powerful XI, in which some famous cricket heroes took part, notably Lord Harris – the best batsman of his age in England – and Lord Hawke, president of MCC. The Grenadier Guards, too, had quite a useful XI, who were very keen on games against schools when they could be managed.

WINCHESTER COLLEGE v ETON COLLEGE, AT WINCHESTER, JUNE 30, 1917 This was a truly memorable struggle in which Firth accomplished the remarkable performance of taking all ten wickets in the first innings of Eton for 41 runs… Firth's achievement – a record in Winchester cricket – followed within nine days of a striking success in the match at Harrow, where he obtained eight wickets in an innings for 48 runs. Again, this young bowler sent down his leg-breaks with great accuracy of pitch, and varied his pace and flight in puzzling fashion.

There was no first-class cricket in 1917, so Wisden's *Five were School Bowlers of the Year, John D'Ewes Evelyn Firth among them.*

LORD'S SCHOOLS v THE REST, AT LORD'S, AUGUST 6–7, 1917 A most dramatic struggle was this, the Rest who at one point, with only four wickets to fall, wanted 52 runs to escape a single-innings defeat, gaining a memorable victory by 17 runs. Indeed from start to finish the fortunes of the game varied in most sensational fashion… The Lord's Schools had only 78 to make to win… but [Firth] wrought such a transformation, not only getting on a fine leg-break, but keeping a remarkable accuracy of pitch… The great triumph was that of Firth, who not only took seven wickets for 27 runs, but time after time beat the opposing batsman.

DEATHS IN THE WAR, 1917: COLIN BLYTHE The news that Blythe had been killed in France was received everywhere with the keenest regret… the loss is the most serious that cricket has sustained during the war. It is true Blythe had announced his intention of playing no more in first-class matches, but quite possibly this decision was not final. He had certainly no need to think of retiring at the age of 38.

That Blythe was a great bowler is beyond question. He had no warmer admirers than the many famous batsmen who had the satisfaction of making big scores against him. So far as I know they were unanimous in paying tribute to his remarkable powers. He was one of five left-handed slow bowlers of the first rank produced by England in the last 40 years, the other four being Peate, Peel, Briggs, and Rhodes…

Blythe had all the good gifts that pertain to the first-rate slow bowler, and a certain imaginative quality that was peculiarly his own. Very rarely did he get to the end of his resources. To see him bowl to a brilliant hitter was a sheer delight… Blythe's spin was something quite out of the ordinary. On a sticky wicket or on a dry pitch ever so little crumbled, he came off the ground in a way that beat the strongest defence. He had, too, far more pace than most people supposed. The ball that went with his arm often approached the speed of a fast bowler and had of course the advantage of being unsuspected… To sum up his career in a phrase, he will live in cricket history as the greatest Kent bowler of modern days.

DEATHS IN THE WAR, 1917: CAPT. ARTHUR HENDERSON (Argyll and Sutherland Highlanders) In May 1917, was "assumed killed" – at some earlier date. Member of the Ferguslie CC, of Paisley, and one of the best-known players in the Western Cricket Union. Played for Forfarshire. Gained the Military Cross.

In Wisden on the Great War, *Andrew Renshaw, wrote: "He was also awarded the VC posthumously… 'for most conspicuous bravery. During an attack on the enemy trenches this officer, although almost immediately wounded in the left arm, led his company through the front enemy line until he gained his final objective. He then proceeded to consolidate his position, which, owing to heavy gun and machine-gun fire and bombing attacks, was in danger of being isolated. By his cheerful courage and coolness he was enabled to maintain the spirit of his men under most trying conditions. Captain Henderson was killed after he had successfully accomplished his task.' The action took place on April 23 near Fontaine-les-Croisilles, France; he died the next day, aged 23.*

Compiled by Christopher Lane

FIFTY YEARS AGO

From WISDEN CRICKETERS' ALMANACK 1968

OBITUARY: S. F. BARNES by Sir Neville Cardus Most cricketers and students of the game belonging to the period in which S. F. Barnes played were agreed that he was the bowler of the century. Australians as well as English voted him unanimously the greatest. Clem Hill, the famous Australian left-handed batsman, who in successive Test innings scored 99, 98 and 97 v A. C. MacLaren's England team of 1901-2, told me that on a perfect wicket Barnes could swing the new ball in and out "very late", could spin from the ground, pitch on the leg stump and miss the off… Barnes was creative, one of the first bowlers really to use the seam of a new ball and combine swing so subtly with spin that few batsmen could distinguish one from the other…

He was professional in the Lancashire League when A. C. MacLaren, hearing of his skill, invited him to the nets at Old Trafford. "He thumped me on the left thigh. He hit my gloves from a length. He actually said, 'Sorry, sir!' and I said, 'Don't be sorry, Barnes. You're coming to Australia with me.'"…

Throughout his career he remained mysteriously aloof, appearing in the full sky of first-class cricket like a meteor – declaring the death of the most princely of batsmen! He preferred the reward and comparative indolence of Saturday league matches to the daily toil of the county tourney… He was in those days not an easy man to handle on the field of play. There was a Mephistophelian aspect about him. He didn't play cricket out of any green-field starry-eyed idealism. He rightly considered that his talents were worth estimating in cash values. In his old age he mellowed, yet remained humorously cynical.

Sir Donald Bradman argued that W. J. O'Reilly must have been a greater bowler than Barnes because he commanded every ball developed in Barnes's day – plus the googly. I told Barnes of Bradman's remark. "It's quite true," he said, "I never bowled the 'googly.'" Then with a glint in his eye, he added, "I never needed it."… The destruction wreaked by Barnes, and on all his great days, was mostly done by the ball which, bowled from a splendid height, seemed to swing in to the leg stump then spin away from the pitch, threatening the off stump. Barnes assured me that he actually turned the ball by finger twist.

Barnes remained a deadly bowler long after he went out of first-class cricket. So shrewdly did he conserve his energy that in 1928, when he was in his mid-fifties, the West Indies team of that year faced him in a club match and unanimously agreed he was the best they had encountered in the season. For Staffordshire, in his 56th year, he took 76 wickets at 8.21 each…

Barnes had a splendid upright action, right arm straight over. He ran on easy strides, not a penn'orth of energy wasted. He fingered a cricket ball sensitively, like a violinist his fiddle. He always attacked. "Why do these bowlers today send down so many balls the batsman needn't play?" he asked while watching a Test match many years ago. "I didn't. I never gave 'em any rest."

His hatchet face and his suggestion of physical and mental leanness and keenness were part of Barnes's cricket and outlook on the game. He was relentless, a chill wind of antagonism blew from him on the sunniest day.

THE COUNTY CHAMPIONSHIP IN 1967 Yorkshire won the County Championship for the sixth time in nine years, emphasising yet again the vast resources of talent at their command; but this time they emerged with their reputation sullied through the manner in which they wrested two points from Warwickshire at Edgbaston. The [time-wasting] tactics they adopted were condemned by the Advisory County Cricket Committee and led to D. B. Close, the captain, being turned down by MCC for the leadership of the touring team in the West Indies in the early months of [1968]… As it happened, the two ill-gotten points did not come into the final reckoning… The issue was decided on the last day of the season when, with R. Illingworth taking 14 wickets for 64, Yorkshire outplayed Gloucestershire, the bottom club… and finished ten points ahead of Kent and Leicestershire, bracketed second… For the first time in the history of the Championship a county, Nottinghamshire, failed to win any match and *yet did not* finish bottom. They drew 22 of their 28 matches.

SUSSEX v LANCASHIRE, AT HOVE, MAY 3–5, 1967 Play was possible only on the first day, when Sussex established a very favourable position. This had much to do with the form of [Tony] Greig, a 20-year-old South African who hit a sparkling century in his first county match. Six feet seven inches tall, and using his height to produce a lot of power in his strokes, this young man from East London completed 100 in three hours, and then went on for nearly another hour, hitting 22 fours in his 156. Statham and Higgs came in for their share of punishment… Sussex were understandably annoyed at having to sit in the pavilion for the next two days watching the rain.

NOTES BY THE EDITOR [Norman Preston] County cricket has taken its biggest step forward in recent years by opening the door to overseas players through the process of immediate registration. This bold move could be the salvation of the three-day County Championship, and I am only surprised that the plunge was not taken sooner. The numerous provisos safeguard the welfare of English-born players, and the very fact that a heavy responsibility will now rest upon the star cricketer should help the promising youngster to take his place in first-class company without the worry that any temporary failure will weigh heavily against his side… As soon as the way was made clear… the destination of Garry Sobers, the West Indies captain, became the great talking point. Seven counties made inquiries and, after a fortnight of speculation, Nottinghamshire announced on December 14 [1967] their capture of cricket's greatest prize, and that he would captain the side. For the first time in their history Nottinghamshire did not win a match last season, and now they look to Sobers to bring back the crowds to Trent Bridge and revive their fortunes… The financial details of Sobers's contract with Nottinghamshire were not disclosed. It will run for three years and could be worth £7,000 a year, including a flat and a car. One may ask where is the money coming from to pay these expensive stars with county cricket in its present parlous financial state?

THE PUBLIC SCHOOLS IN 1967 by E. M. Wellings Cricket masters at the schools have not succeeded in keeping their over-rates up to acceptable standards and it reflects very badly on the present-day game… At Lord's in 1967 we had a match [MCC Combined Schools v All-India Schools] lasting a full day and producing 116.1 overs. Forty years earlier I played in a Lord's Schools v The Rest match reduced by rain on the first day to a single day. The overs bowled numbered 144.4 – 171 more balls than in 1967. The game has in fact slowed down by four and a half overs an hour, a drop of almost 20%, and it has virtually all happened in the past 15 years… A brisk over-rate is the essential core of a cricket match. Even when we expected 22 overs an hour in Test cricket – England at Lord's in 1930 averaged 23 while Australia were scoring 729 for six, of which Bradman made 254 – cricket was described as a slow game. Now, when we are lucky to get 18 an hour, it has become too slow to maintain sufficient spectator interest to keep the first-class game financially prosperous… The game's rulers have taken steps to boost the county game's tempo. Their players have frustrated them. Before the [1967] season they set 20 overs an hour as the acceptable minimum… Gloucestershire alone met requirements.

OBITUARY: SIR FRANK WORRELL by Sir Learie Constantine Frank Maglinne Worrell was the first hero of the new nation of Barbados, and anyone who doubted that had only to be in the island when his body was brought home in mid-March of 1967. Or in Westminster Abbey when West Indians of all backgrounds and shades of opinion paid their last respects to a man who had done more than any other of their countrymen to bind together the new nations of the Caribbean and establish a reputation for fair play throughout the world. Never before had a cricketer been honoured with a memorial service in Westminster Abbey.

Sir Frank was a man of strong convictions, a brave man and, it goes without saying, a great cricketer. Though he made his name as a player, his greatest contribution was to destroy for ever the myth that a coloured cricketer was not fit to lead a team. Once appointed, he ended the cliques and rivalries between the players of various islands to weld together a team which in the space of five years became the champions of the world. He was a man of true political sense and feeling, a federalist who surely would have made even greater contributions to the history of the West Indies had he not died so tragically in hospital of leukaemia at the early age of 42, a month after returning from India.

People in England can have little idea of the problems of West Indian cricket… Before that wonderful tour of Australia in 1960-61, Barbadians would tend to stick together, and so would the Trinidadians, Jamaicans and Guyanans. Worrell cut across all that. Soon there were no groups. Just one team… So when half a million Australians lined the streets of Melbourne in their ticker-tape farewell to Worrell and his men, they were not only paying a final tribute to the team's great achievements, they were recognising the capacity and potential of equals both on and off the turf…

I have always held that League cricket makes a cricketer, not only as a player but as a man. There is much to learn in the field of human relations from the kind, friendly and warm people of the North of England… Worrell was not just living for the present – as I regret is the case with some of our cricketers – but he was thinking of the future. He took a course at Manchester University and qualified in economics…

I am not one for averages myself. I am more concerned with how a batsman made his runs and not what his average was at the end of the series. Sir Neville Cardus has written of Sir Frank that he never made a crude or an ungrammatical stroke. I agree with that. Worrell was poetry. While Walcott bludgeoned the bowlers and Weekes dominated them, the stylist Worrell waved them away. There was none of the savage aggression of a Sobers in his batting. He was the artist. All three "Ws" were geniuses, but Worrell was my favourite because he had more style and elegance. He had all the strokes and the time and capacity to use them without offence to the eye, without ever being hurried…

[In 1964] Her Majesty the Queen knighted this complete Cricketer, Philosopher and Captain. It was a fitting end to an unforgettable career… Throughout his life, Sir Frank never lost his sense of humour or his sense of dignity… West Indians really laugh their laughs. And Sir Frank laughed louder than most of us. He was a happy man, a good man and a great man. The really tragic thing about his death at the age of 42 was that it cut him off from life when he still had plenty to offer the islands he loved. He was only at the beginning.

ENGLAND v INDIA, FIRST TEST MATCH, AT LEEDS, JUNE 8–13, 1967 England won by six wickets with two and three-quarter hours to spare. India, hit by the weather in May with little chance of accustoming themselves to English conditions, entered the match without a victory to their credit and their reputations so sullied that only small crowds attended… Yet, despite all their misfortunes, the gallant Indians struggled bravely; Pataudi batted magnificently for 64 and 148… Indeed, India, 386 behind on the first innings, accomplished the rare feat of passing 500 in the follow-on… On the first day, after Close won the toss, England for a long time struggled for runs. But they reached 281 for three by the time stumps were drawn… On Friday, England treated the depleted Indian attack mercilessly and in three and a half hours put on 269, before Close declared. Boycott finished with 246 not out… but his lack of enterprise met with much disapproval, and the selectors dropped him for the next Test.

CRICKETER OF THE YEAR, HANIF MOHAMMAD by Ian Wooldridge Few major innings since the war have provoked such contradictory critical appraisal as that played by Pakistan's captain in the Lord's Test of 1967. It began at 4.40 on Friday July 27, and ended only when he ran out of partners at 3.24 the following Monday. His actual entrenchment at the crease, after deductions for rain, meals, sleep and an interminable English sabbath, lasted nine hours two minutes, and his eventual score was 187 not out.

Press comment along the way embraced the full spectrum of colourful opinion: from the outraged puce of those writers who regard themselves as the guardians of sporting entertainment to the purplest prose that could be mustered by others who acclaimed it one of the batting masterpieces of their time. If the reading public were bemused… [Hanif] remained totally unconcerned… As was his habit during times of strain on a tour beset by problems, he returned to his hotel room to listen to sitar music, the beauty of which is a mystery to most Western ears. He brought 12 tapes of it with him from Karachi…

There is not much of Hanif Mohammad to drown. He stands 5ft 6in, and weighs 9¼st at his fittest. In 1967, he was 32, married with children, slightly homesick, distant until you knew him, charming when you did, indifferent to criticism or adulation, physically hampered by recurring styes on the eyes and a leg injury that had threatened his career, in professional life a commercial agent with Pakistan International Airlines and, in confessional moments, a man disturbed by his own capacity for introspection… He has been called the Little Master and, in every sense the description fits him well. Such single-mindedness at the wicket, or in captaincy decisions, has not always endeared him to crowds or critics. The total hours that he has been barracked or slow hand-clapped around the world may well come close to constituting another kind of record. Equally his many refusals to court the slightest risk of defeat on other occasions have earned him many hard words in print. Hanif Mohammad hears the public, reads the Press and proceeds precisely as before. To him there is only one side to the argument: Pakistan first, last and for ever.

NORTHERN ZONE v MCC, AT PESHAWAR, FEBRUARY 1–3, 1967 Brearley annihilated a fair attack which had little support from the field, and achieved the rare distinction of a triple-century. His 312 not out, and MCC's total [514 for 4 dec] have no parallel in a day's play in any match in Pakistan. A new opening partnership of Brearley and Knott realised 208, Knott hitting his maiden first-class century… Hutton finished Northern Zone's first innings with his first hat-trick.

ENGLAND v PAKISTAN, THIRD TEST MATCH, AT THE OVAL, AUGUST 24–28, 1967 Everything else in this match was dwarfed by a wonderful innings of 146 from Asif Iqbal, but it did not save Pakistan from defeat. Still, it provided a rare treat for the Bank Holiday crowd. When Asif arrived at the crease, Pakistan had slumped to 53 for seven, and the match seemed bound to finish before lunch as they still needed 167 to make England bat again. He found a staunch ally in Intikhab, and they indulged in a partnership of 190, a new record for the ninth wicket in Test cricket. Asif's 146 was the highest score by a No. 9 Test batsman… Hitting boldly, Asif excelled with the drive and hook. He raced to 50 out of 56, and Higgs, Arnold and Underwood, so supreme at one stage, all suffered during his drastic punishment. Intikhab's share when the stand reached three figures was 28. A sparkling off-drive from Higgs gave Asif his 14th four and took him to his first Test century in two hours, 19 minutes.

An amazing scene followed. Hundreds of Pakistanis raced to the wicket and hoisted Asif shoulder high. The game was held up for five minutes and, when a squad of police rescued him, the poor fellow was bruised and battered. The team manager revived him with a drink, and he celebrated his great day by striking Higgs for five more boundaries in two overs… [Pakistan] left England only 32 to win and, before the finish, Asif crowned a great personal triumph by disposing of the two England opening batsmen, Close and Cowdrey, so that Barrington was left to make the winning hit.

HAMPSHIRE v MIDDLESEX, AT PORTSMOUTH, AUGUST 23–25, 1967 In an exciting finish, Hampshire tied their match with Middlesex when Cottam was bowled by Herman with the last ball of the game… Fifty runs behind on the first innings, Hampshire took Middlesex wickets cheaply until Murray declared, leaving Hampshire to get 174 in two hours. They reached 100 for three, but with three wickets falling at 154 they were in difficulty… They needed three runs to win with one wicket to fall when Herman began the last over."

Compiled by Christopher Lane

HONOURS AND AWARDS IN 2016-17

In 2016-17, the following were decorated for their services to cricket:

Queen's Birthday Honours, 2016: S. C. J. Broad (Nottinghamshire and England) MBE; A. N. Cook (Essex and England) CBE; S. Heaton (chairman of Lancashire junior league; services to young people and grassroots cricket in Lancashire) BEM; D. Sear (Kent cricket development officer; services to girls' and women's cricket) MBE.

Queen's Birthday Honours (Australia), 2016: M. J. Coward (services to cricket and media as journalist, commentator, author and historian) AM; K. D. Emery (president of Queensland Seniors Cricket; services to cricket and secondary education) OAM.

Queen's Birthday Honours (New Zealand), 2016: B. D. M. Furlong (Central Districts; former chief executive of CD Cricket Association; services to cricket and rugby) QSM; S. B. Heal (former chairman of New Zealand Cricket; services to cricket and the community) MNZM; L. J. Murdoch (formerly on NZC board and convenor of women's selectors; services to sport) ONZM; B. W. Sinclair (Wellington and New Zealand; services to cricket) MNZM; N. G. S. Smith (former president of Otago Cricket Association; services to media and sport) ONZM; G. B. Troup (Auckland and New Zealand; services to sport and the community) ONZM.

New Year's Honours, 2017: J. P. Agnew (Leicestershire and England; services to broadcasting) MBE; S. Nasim (women's coach; services to cricket and young people in London) BEM.

Padma Awards (India), 2017: V. Kohli (Delhi and India) Padma Shri; S. Naik (ex-captain of India Blind team) Padma Shri.

Australia Day Honours, 2017: P. Davis (president of Adelaide and Suburban Cricket Association; services to cricket) OAM; R. G. Holland (New South Wales and Australia) OAM; B. A. H. Palfreyman (Tasmania; former chair of Tasmanian Cricket Assocation; services to cricket) OAM; N. J. Simpson (Warehouse Cricket Umpires' Association; services to cricket) OAM; A. T. Sincock (South Australia; coach and administrator; services to cricket) OAM.

ICC AWARDS

The International Cricket Council's 13th annual awards were announced in December 2016.

Cricketer of the Year (Sir Garfield Sobers Trophy)	**Ravichandran Ashwin (I)**
Test Player of the Year	**Ravichandran Ashwin (I)**
One-Day International Player of the Year	**Quinton de Kock (SA)**
Women's One-Day International Cricketer of the Year	**Suzie Bates (NZ)**
Women's Twenty20 International Cricketer of the Year	**Suzie Bates (NZ)**
Twenty20 International Performance of the Year	**Carlos Brathwaite (WI)**
Emerging Player of the Year	**Mustafizur Rahman (B)**
Associate/Affiliate Player of the Year	**Mohammad Shahzad (Afg)**
Spirit of Cricket Award	**Misbah-ul-Haq (P)**
Umpire of the Year (David Shepherd Trophy)	**Marais Erasmus (SA)**

A panel of five also selected three World XIs from the previous 12 months:

	ICC World Test team		*ICC World one-day team*		*ICC World women's team*
1	David Warner (A)	1	David Warner (A)	1	Suzie Bates (NZ)
2	*Alastair Cook (E)	2	†Quinton de Kock (SA)	2	†Rachel Priest (NZ)
3	Kane Williamson (NZ)	3	Rohit Sharma (I)	3	Smriti Mandhana (I)
4	Joe Root (E)	4	*Virat Kohli (I)	4	*Stafanie Taylor (WI)
5	Adam Voges (A)	5	A. B. de Villiers (SA)	5	Meg Lanning (A)
6	†Jonny Bairstow (E)	6	Jos Buttler (E)	6	Ellyse Perry (A)
7	Ben Stokes (E)	7	Mitchell Marsh (A)	7	Heather Knight (E)
8	Ravichandran Ashwin (I)	8	Ravindra Jadeja (I)	8	Deandra Dottin (WI)
9	Rangana Herath (SL)	9	Mitchell Starc (A)	9	Suné Luus (SA)
10	Mitchell Starc (A)	10	Kagiso Rabada (SA)	10	Anya Shrubsole (E)
11	Dale Steyn (SA)	11	Sunil Narine (WI)	11	Leigh Kasperek (NZ)
12th	Steve Smith (A)	12th	Imran Tahir (SA)	12th	Kim Garth (Ireland)

Previous Cricketers of the Year were Rahul Dravid (2004), Andrew Flintoff and Jacques Kallis (jointly in 2005), Ricky Ponting (2006 and 2007), Shivnarine Chanderpaul (2008), Mitchell Johnson (2009 and 2014), Sachin Tendulkar (2010), Jonathan Trott (2011), Kumar Sangakkara (2012), Michael Clarke (2013) and Steve Smith (2015).

ICC CRICKET HALL OF FAME

The ICC Cricket Hall of Fame was launched in 2009 in association with the Federation of International Cricketers' Associations to recognise legends of the game. In the first year, 60 members were inducted: 55 from the earlier FICA Hall of Fame, plus five new players elected in October 2009 by a voting academy made up of the ICC president, 11 ICC member representatives, a FICA representative, a women's cricket representative, ten journalists, a statistician, and all living members of the Hall of Fame. New members have been elected every year since. Candidates must have retired from international cricket at least five years ago.

The members elected in 2016 were George Lohmann (England), Arthur Morris (Australia), Muttiah Muralitharan (Sri Lanka) and Karen Rolton (Australia), who brought the total to 84.

ICC DEVELOPMENT PROGRAMME AWARDS

The International Cricket Council announced the global winners of their 2015 Development Programme Awards in April 2016.

Best Overall Cricket Development Programme	**Cricket Scotland**
Spirit of Cricket Award	**Vanuatu CA and Malaysia CA**
Photo of the Year	**Rwanda Cricket Association**
Lifetime Service Award	**Jim Bennett (Ireland)**
Volunteer of the Year	**Ivan Thawithemwira (Uganda)**
Women's Cricket Behind the Scenes Award	**Gemma Dunning (Jersey)**

ALLAN BORDER MEDAL

David Warner won the Allan Border Medal, for the best Australian international player of the past 12 months, in January 2016. Previous winners were Glenn McGrath, Steve Waugh, Matthew Hayden, Adam Gilchrist, Ricky Ponting (four times), Michael Clarke (four times), Brett Lee, Shane Watson (twice), Mitchell Johnson and Steve Smith. Warner received 240 votes from team-mates, umpires and journalists, 21 more than Smith, and also took the award for Test Cricketer of the Year. **Glenn Maxwell** was named One-Day International Player of the Year. **Ellyse Perry** won the Belinda Clark Award for the Women's International Cricketer of the Year for the first time. **Adam Voges** of Western Australia won the award for Domestic Cricketer of the Year, and **Alex Ross** of South Australia was Bradman Young Player of the Year.

SHEFFIELD SHIELD PLAYER OF THE YEAR

The Sheffield Shield Player of the Year Award for 2015-16 was won by **Travis Head**, who had led South Australia to their first Shield final for 20 years, and scored 721 runs, including three centuries. The award, instituted in 1975-76, is adjudicated by umpires. The Toyota Futures League Player of the Year award was won by New South Wales batsman **Nick Larkin**. Australia Women's captain **Meg Lanning** was the Player of the Tournament for both the Women's National Cricket League and the Women's Big Bash League. **Brendan Doggett** was the Lord's Taverners Indigenous Cricketer of the Year. **Simon Fry** was Umpire of the Year for the third year running, while the Benaud Spirit of Cricket Awards for fair play went to the men of **Tasmania** and the women of **South Australia**.

CRICKET SOUTH AFRICA AWARDS

In July 2016, **Kagiso Rabada** became the first player to win six CSA awards for the same year. He was named South African Cricketer of the Year, Test Cricketer of the Year, One-Day International Cricketer of the Year, Players' Player of the Year and Fans' Player of the Year, and also won the

Delivery of the Year award for bowling England's Jason Roy in a Twenty20 international at Johannesburg. The Twenty20 International Cricketer of the Year was **Imran Tahir**, and the KFC "So Good!" award went to **Temba Bavuma**, while **Stephen Cook** was International Newcomer of the Year. The Women's Cricketer of the Year was **Dané van Niekerk**. In the domestic categories, first-class champions the Titan collected four awards. **Heino Kuhn** was Sunfoil Series Cricketer of the Year and Domestic Players' Player of the Year, while **Rob Walter** was Coach of the Year and **Albie Morkel** the Ram Slammer of the Season. From the Lions, **Alviro Petersen** was Momentum One-Day Cup Player of the Year, **Nicky van den Bergh** was Domestic Newcomer of the Year and **Dwaine Pretorius** the SACA's Most Valuable Player. **Lungi Ngidi** of Northerns was the first winner of the Africa T20 Cup Player of the Tournament. The **Cape Cobras** won the CSA Fair Play award. **Adrian Holdstock** was Umpire of the Year, and **Bethuel Buthelezi** won the groundsman's award in his first year in charge at the Wanderers.

ENGLAND PLAYERS OF THE YEAR

In May 2016, **Joe Root** was voted Men's Player of the Year, and was also named Test Cricketer and Limited-Overs Cricketer of the Year. In the previous 12 months, he had scored two Ashes centuries plus four one-day international hundreds and he was England's leading scorer in the World Twenty20 tournament. The newly retired England captain **Charlotte Edwards** was voted Women's Player of the Year, while **Anya Shrubsole** was named England Women's Cricketer of the Year for her 32 international wickets across three formats. Essex batsman **Dan Lawrence** was the England Development Programme Cricketer of the Year, after scoring 712 runs for England Under-19 and becoming the third youngest centurion in County Championship history. The England Disability Cricketer of the Year award went to **Callum Flynn**, who was Player of the Series when England won the inaugural Physical Disabilities World Cup, staged in Bangladesh in September 2015. **David Lloyd** was presented with the ECB's Special Achievement Award for the more than 50 years he had spent as a Lancashire and England batsman, coach, umpire and commentator.

PROFESSIONAL CRICKETERS' ASSOCIATION AWARDS

The following awards were announced at the PCA's annual dinner in September 2016.

Reg Hayter Cup (NatWest PCA Player of the Year)	**Ben Duckett** (Northamptonshire)
John Arlott Cup (NatWest PCA Young Player of the Year)	**Ben Duckett** (Northamptonshire)
Investec Test Player of the Summer	**Chris Woakes**
Waitrose Women's Player of the Summer	**Tammy Beaumont**
County MVP of the Summer	**Jeetan Patel** (Warwickshire)
NatWest T20 Blast Player of the Year	**Colin Ingram** (Glamorgan)
Royal London One-Day Cup Player of the Year	**Graeme White** (Northamptonshire)
Sky Sports Sixes Award	**Colin Ingram** (Glamorgan)
Greene King PCA England Masters MVP	**Mal Loye**
Harold Goldblatt Award (PCA Umpire of the Year)	**Michael Gough**
ECB Special Award	**Mike Selvey**
PCA Special Merit Award	**Marcus Trescothick** (Somerset)

PCA Team of the Year **Adam Lyth, Keaton Jennings, Ben Duckett, *Joe Root, †Jonny Bairstow, Liam Dawson, Tim Bresnan, Chris Woakes, Keith Barker, Toby Roland-Jones, Jeetan Patel.**

CHRISTOPHER MARTIN-JENKINS SPIRIT OF CRICKET AWARDS

MCC and the BBC introduced the Spirit of Cricket awards in memory of Christopher Martin-Jenkins, the former MCC president and *Test Match Special* commentator, in 2013. In September 2016, the Elite Award, for the professional cricketer who made the biggest contribution to the Spirit of Cricket in the English season, went to **Tom Fell** of Worcestershire, who had recently returned to the game after treatment for cancer. During a Championship match at Hove, with Sussex chasing 272, Fell made a diving stop on the boundary, but signalled to the umpire that his foot had touched the rope, so Sussex should have four runs. They were eventually bowled out 11 short of victory.

WALTER LAWRENCE TROPHY

The Walter Lawrence Trophy for the fastest century in 2016 went to **Tom Köhler-Cadmore** of Worcestershire, who scored a 43-ball hundred against Durham at Worcester in the season's first match in the NatWest T20 Blast on May 20. He won the trophy plus £3,000. Since 2008, the Trophy has been available for innings in all senior cricket in England; traditionally, it was reserved for the fastest first-class hundred against authentic bowling (in 2016, Samit Patel's 68-ball hundred for Nottinghamshire v Warwickshire at Nottingham on May 18). **Tammy Beaumont** won the Women's Award for her 168 not out from 144 balls for England against Pakistan in the Taunton one-day international. The Universities Award went to **Robbie White** of Loughborough for his 174 off 219 balls against Leeds/Bradford MCCU, which helped Loughborough win the MCCU Championship. Beaumont and White each received a silver medallion and £500. The award for the highest score by a school batsman against MCC went to **Tom Haines**, who scored 187 for Hurstpierpoint College in June, and made his first-class debut for Sussex later in the season; he received a medallion and a Gray-Nicolls bat.

CRICKET WRITERS' CLUB AWARDS

In September 2016, at their 70th anniversary lunch, the Cricket Writers' Club named **Ben Duckett** Young Cricketer of the Year, after he scored 1,338 Championship runs for Northamptonshire at 60, including two double-hundreds. **Keaton Jennings** of Durham, who was the country's leading run-scorer with 1,602 at 64, was County Player of the Year. The first CWC Women's Cricketer of the Year was **Charlotte Edwards**, who led Kent to the County Championship and Twenty20 titles and the Southern Vipers to the first Kia Super League trophy. The Peter Smith Memorial Award "for services to the presentation of cricket to the public" was made to *Guardian* journalist **Mike Selvey**. *The Game of Life* by former *Wisden* editor **Scyld Berry** was the Cricket Book of the Year.

A list of Young Cricketers from 1950 to 2004 appears in Wisden 2005, *page 995. A list of Peter Smith Award winners from 1992 to 2004 appears in* Wisden 2005, *page 745.*

SECOND XI PLAYER OF THE YEAR

The Association of Cricket Statisticians and Historians named **Adam Hose** of Somerset as the Les Hatton Second XI Player of the Year for 2016. Hose scored 644 at 53 in eight matches in the Second XI Championship, culminating in twin unbeaten centuries against Essex – he reached 100 in 76 balls in the second innings. He also scored 370 at 52 in the one-day Second XI Trophy, including two more hundreds, and 184 at 20 in the Twenty20 tournament.

GROUNDSMEN OF THE YEAR

Andy Fogarty retained his title as the ECB's Groundsman of the Year for his four-day pitches at Headingley, with **Stuart Kerrison** of Chelmsford and **Matt Merchant** of Old Trafford sharing the runners-up award. **Steve Birks** of Trent Bridge won the award for the best one-day pitches, ahead of **Lee Fortis** at The Oval. There were commendations for Gary Barwell (Edgbaston) and Andy Mackay (Hove) in the four-day category, and for Kerrison, Vic Demain (Chester-le-Street) and Karl McDermott (the Rose Bowl) in the one-day category. **John Dodds** of Scarborough won the best outground award for the fourth year in five, with Christian Brain of Cheltenham second. The MCC Universities award was shared by **John Moden**, for his final season at Cambridge, and Richard Robinson from Leeds/Bradford's Weetwood ground.

CRICKET SOCIETY AWARDS

Wetherell Award for Leading First-class All-rounder	**Tim Bresnan** (Yorkshire)
Wetherell Award for Leading Schools All-rounder	**Aaran Amin** (Merchant Taylors' School, Northwood)
Most Promising Young Cricketer	**Ben Duckett** (Northamptonshire)
Most Promising Young Woman Cricketer	**Alex Hartley** (Middlesex)
Sir John Hobbs Silver Jubilee Memorial Prize (for Outstanding Under-16 Schoolboy)	**Sam Dorsey** (Swinton High School)
A. A. Thomson Fielding Prize for Best Schoolboy Fielder	**Hamidullah Qadri** (Derby Moor Community Sports College)
Christopher Box-Grainger Memorial Trophy (for schools promoting cricket to the under privileged)	**Swiss Cottage School, Camden**
Don Rowan Memorial Trophy (for schools promoting cricket for disabled children)	**St Philip's School, Kingston**
Ian Jackson Award for Services to Cricket	**Henry Blofeld**
The Perry-Lewis/Kershaw Trophy (for contribution to the Cricket Society XI)	**Jason Fenn**

WOMBWELL CRICKET LOVERS' SOCIETY AWARDS

George Spofforth Cricketer of the Year	**Marcus Trescothick** (Somerset)
Brian Sellers County Captain of the Year	**James Franklin** (Middlesex)
C. B. Fry Young Cricketer of the Year	**Haseeb Hameed** (Lancashire)
Arthur Wood Wicketkeeper of the Year	**Tim Ambrose** (Warwickshire)
Learie Constantine Fielder of the Year	**Marcus Trescothick** (Somerset)
Denis Compton Memorial Award for Flair	**Jos Buttler** (Lancashire/England)
Dr Leslie Taylor Award (best Roses performance)	**Haseeb Hameed** (Lancashire)
Les Bailey Most Promising Young Yorkshire Player	**James Logan**
Ted Umbers Award – Services to Yorkshire Cricket	**Ian Dews***
J. M. Kilburn Cricket Writer of the Year	**John Fuller**

* *For services as Yorkshire CCC's director of cricket development.*

ASIAN CRICKET AWARDS

Professional Player of the Year	**Adil Rashid** (Yorkshire and England)
Professional Young Player of the Year	**Haseeb Hameed** (Lancashire)
Asian Cricket Club of the Year	**Indian Gymkhana CC**
Woman in Cricket Award	**Nalisha Patel** (Lancashire Thunder) and **Shabnim Ismail** (Yorkshire Diamonds)
Professional Coach of the Year	**Cookie Patel** (regional training manager, ECB)
Amateur Coach of the Year	**Shaz Khan** (Oxfordshire CCC/Shrivenham CC)
Posthumous Award	**Hamza Ali** (Hampshire)
Club Cricket Conference Inspiration Award	**Maryam Ali** (community coach, Yorkshire)
Media Award	**Vithushan Ehantharajah**
Grassroots Award	**Shahidul Alam Ratan** (Capital Kids/London Tigers CC)
Behind the Scenes Award	**Amna Rafiq** (Leicestershire)

ECB COUNTY JOURNALISM AWARDS

The ECB announced the winners of the sixth annual County Cricket Journalism Awards for the coverage of domestic cricket on October 25. **Will Macpherson**, a freelance who had worked for ESPNCricinfo and *The Guardian*, was named the Christopher Martin-Jenkins Young Journalist of the Year, and received a £3,000 prize, while runners-up Tim Wigmore (freelance) and Henry Cowen (*All Out Cricket*) received £1,000. **Dave Fletcher** of BBC Radio Derby was the Christopher Martin-Jenkins County Broadcaster of the Year, and was awarded £5,000. The Regional Newspaper of the Year award plus £2,500 went to ***The Sunday Independent*** for its coverage of the South-West, with the *Manchester Evening News* and the *Nottingham Post* commended. ***The Cricket Paper*** was the National Newspaper of the Year, with *The Times* also commended. **ESPNcricinfo** was Online Publication of the Year for the fifth time running.

ECB BUSINESS OF CRICKET AWARDS

The ECB announced the BOCA awards, designed to celebrate Marketing and PR excellence across domestic and international cricket, in November 2016. **Somerset** won the County Recognition Award, the Commercial Partnerships Award and the Marketing and Communications Category B&C Award. The other winners were: Digital Campaign Award – **Glamorgan**; Customer Match Day Experience Award – **Yorkshire**; Marketing and Communications Category A Award – **Nottinghamshire**; Business Change and Innovation Award – **Worcestershire**; Community Engagement Award – **Warwickshire**; ECB Special Award – **Zac Toumazi** (retiring chief executive, Sussex).

ECB OSCAs

The ECB presented the 2016 NatWest Outstanding Service to Cricket Awards to volunteers from recreational cricket in October. The winners were:

NatWest CricketForce Award — **Adam Wilson** (Middlesex)
After the Brondesbury and Primrose Hill clubs merged, he brought together members of both teams, plus parents, juniors and local NatWest staff, for the CricketForce weekend.

Get the Game On — **Mick Bott** (Derbyshire)
Responsible for ensuring an additional 40 games over the past 12 months at Denby CC.

Heartbeat of the Club — **Tim Chambers** (Cambridgeshire)
Served Hemingford Park as chairman, fixture secretary, umpire, groundsman, tea-maker, coach, marketer, school liaison, financial controller, fundraiser and occasional senior player.

Leagues and Boards Award — **Andy Jones** (Leicestershire and Rutland)
Helped to bring three leagues together to form the Leicestershire and Rutland Cricket League.

Officiating – umpires and scorers — **John Bates** (Warwickshire)
Training officer and umpire for the Warwickshire Cricket League and county performance officer for the Warwickshire County Association of Cricket Officials.

Coach of the Year — **Greg Smith** (Lincolnshire)
Coached Legbourne Under-13s, ran Friday evening junior coaching and captained the senior XI.

Young Coach of the Year — **Amara Carr** (Devon)
Mentor to girls at Plympton CC, she also held coaching roles at university, club, county and England Development level (and played for the KSL's Western Storm).

Outstanding Contribution to Coaching — **Rob Arnold** (Buckinghamshire)
Manager of youth cricket at Stony Stratford and coach of Northamptonshire Under-13 girls.

Young Volunteer Award (for under-25s) — **Robert Steadman** (Staffordshire)
Helped coach youngest children at Aldridge CC, in between "picking up boundary flags and coaching cones, putting the covers on, selling raffle tickets and making cups of tea".

Lifetime Achiever — **David Bowden** (Sussex)
President of Sussex and chairman of the Sussex Premier League and Sussex Cricket Foundation.

Outstanding Contribution to Disability Cricket — **David Gavrilovic** (Northamptonshire)
Chairman and captain of Northants Steelbacks Visually Impaired CC; Blind Cricket England & Wales's chairman of competitions and technical director; vice-chairman of British Blind Sport.

Under-19 Twenty20 Club of the Year — **Blagdon Park Young Bulls** (Northumberland)
Players took ownership of their team, completing the U19 T20 Activators course and securing funding and sponsorship; after the official tournament, they continued to arrange friendlies.

ACS STATISTICIAN OF THE YEAR

In March 2017, the Association of Cricket Statisticians and Historians awarded the Brooke-Lambert Statistician of the Year trophy jointly to **Stephen Hill** and **Barry Phillips** for their comprehensive biographical work *Somerset Cricketers 1882–1914*.

2017 FIXTURES

Inv Test	Investec Test match
RL ODI	Royal London one-day international
NW T20I	NatWest Twenty20 international
Champs T	ICC Champions Trophy one-day international
SSCC D1/2	Specsavers County Championship Division 1/Division 2
RLODC	Royal London One-Day Cup
NW T20	NatWest T20 Blast
KSL WT20	Women's Kia Super League
Univs	First-class university match
Univs (nfc)	Non-first-class university match
💡	Day/night or floodlit game

Only the first two of each MCCU's three fixtures carry first-class status.

Sun Mar 26–Wed 29	**Friendly**	MCC	v Middlesex	Abu Dhabi
Tue Mar 28–Thu 30	**Univs**	Cambridge MCCU	v Nottinghamshire	Cambridge
		Glamorgan	v Cardiff MCCU	Cardiff
		Gloucestershire	v Durham MCCU	Bristol
		Kent	v Leeds/Brad MCCU	Canterbury
		Leicestershire	v Loughboro MCCU	Leicester
		Oxford MCCU	v Surrey	Oxford
Sun Apr 2–Tue 4	**Univs**	Cambridge MCCU	v Lancashire	Cambridge
		Yorkshire	v Leeds/Brad MCCU	Leeds
		Oxford MCCU	v Warwickshire	Oxford
		Northamptonshire	v Loughboro MCCU	Northampton
		Essex	v Durham MCCU	Chelmsford
		Hampshire	v Cardiff MCCU	Southampton
Fri Apr 7–Mon 10	**SSCC D1**	Yorkshire	v Hampshire	Leeds
		Surrey	v Warwickshire	The Oval
		Essex	v Lancashire	Chelmsford
	SSCC D2	Northamptonshire	v Glamorgan	Northampton
		Kent	v Gloucestershire	Canterbury
		Leicestershire	v Nottinghamshire	Leicester
Fri Apr 7–Sun 9	**Univs (nfc)**	Durham	v Durham MCCU	Chester-le-Street
		Sussex	v Cardiff MCCU	Hove
		Leeds/Brad MCCU	v Worcestershire	Weetwood
		Derbyshire	v Loughboro MCCU	Derby
		Cambridge MCCU	v Middlesex	Cambridge
		Somerset	v Oxford MCCU	Taunton
Fri Apr 14–Mon 17	**SSCC D1**	Surrey	v Lancashire	The Oval
		Somerset	v Essex	Taunton
		Hampshire	v Middlesex	Southampton
		Warwickshire	v Yorkshire	Birmingham
	SSCC D2	Durham	v Nottinghamshire	Chester-le-Street
		Sussex	v Kent	Hove
		Glamorgan	v Worcestershire	Cardiff
		Derbyshire	v Northamptonshire	Derby
		Gloucestershire	v Leicestershire	Bristol
Fri Apr 21–Mon 24	**SSCC D1**	Lancashire	v Somerset	Old Trafford
		Middlesex	v Essex	Lord's
		Hampshire	v Yorkshire	Southampton
		Warwickshire	v Surrey	Birmingham

Fri Apr21–Mon24	**SSCC D2**	Worcestershire	v Northamptonshire	Worcester
		Nottinghamshire	v Sussex	Nottingham
		Leicestershire	v Glamorgan	Leicester
		Kent	v Derbyshire	Canterbury
		Gloucestershire	v Durham	Bristol
Thu Apr 27	**RLODC**	Northamptonshire	v Warwickshire	Northampton
		Middlesex	v Sussex	Lord's
		Worcestershire	v Nottinghamshire	Worcester
		Gloucestershire	v Glamorgan	Bristol
		Kent	v Hampshire	Canterbury
		Durham	v Derbyshire	Chester-le-Street
Fri Apr 28	**RLODC**	Lancashire	v Leicestershire	Old Trafford
		Somerset	v Surrey	Taunton
Sat Apr 29	**RLODC**	Nottinghamshire	v Yorkshire	Nottingham
Sun Apr 30	**RLODC**	Derbyshire	v Northamptonshire	Derby
		Essex	v Hampshire	Chelmsford
		Glamorgan	v Surrey	Cardiff
		Leicestershire	v Worcestershire	Leicester
		Middlesex	v Gloucestershire	Lord's
		Sussex	v Somerset	Hove
Mon May 1	**RLODC**	Warwickshire	v Durham	Birmingham
		Yorkshire	v Lancashire	Leeds
Tue May 2	**RLODC**	Leicestershire	v Warwickshire	Leicester
		Somerset	v Kent	Taunton
		Surrey	v Essex	The Oval
		Sussex	v Glamorgan	Hove
		Derbyshire	v Nottinghamshire	Derby
Wed May 3	**RLODC**	Hampshire	v Middlesex	Southampton
		Northamptonshire	v Worcestershire	Northampton
		Yorkshire	v Durham	Leeds
Thu May 4	**RLODC**	Essex	v Gloucestershire	Chelmsford
Fri May 5	**RL ODI**	**ENGLAND**	**v IRELAND**	Bristol
	RLODC	Durham	v Leicestershire	Chester-le-Street
		Warwickshire	v Nottinghamshire	Birmingham
		Surrey	v Middlesex	The Oval
		Worcestershire	v Yorkshire	Worcester
		Lancashire	v Northamptonshire	Liverpool
		Kent	v Sussex	Canterbury
		Glamorgan	v Somerset	Cardiff
Sun May 7	**RL ODI**	**ENGLAND**	**v IRELAND**	Lord's
	RLODC	Warwickshire	v Lancashire	Birmingham
		Yorkshire	v Derbyshire	Leeds
		Sussex	v Surrey	Hove
		Nottinghamshire	v Leicestershire	Welbeck
		Kent	v Middlesex	Canterbury
		Glamorgan	v Essex	Cardiff
		Durham	v Northamptonshire	Chester-le-Street
		Hampshire	v Gloucestershire	Southampton
Wed May 10	**RLODC**	Gloucestershire	v Kent	Bristol
		Somerset	v Hampshire	Taunton
		Northamptonshire	v Yorkshire	Northampton
		Derbyshire	v Warwickshire	Derby
		Lancashire	v Worcestershire	Blackpool
		Essex	v Sussex	Chelmsford
		Middlesex	v Glamorgan	Radlett

Matthew Lewis, Getty Images

Branching out: Nottinghamshire revisit Sookholme in May.

Thu May 11	**RLODC**	Nottinghamshire	v Durham	Nottingham	💡
Fri May 12	**ODI**	**IRELAND**	**v BANGLADESH**	**Malahide**	
	RLODC	Lancashire	v Derbyshire	Old Trafford	💡
		Hampshire	v Glamorgan	Southampton	
		Surrey	v Kent	The Oval	
		Worcestershire	v Warwickshire	Worcester	
		Gloucestershire	v Somerset	Bristol	
		Essex	v Middlesex	Chelmsford	
		Leicestershire	v Northamptonshire	Leicester	
Sun May 14	**ODI**	**IRELAND**	**v NEW ZEALAND**	**Malahide**	
	RLODC	Warwickshire	v Yorkshire	Birmingham	
		Worcestershire	v Durham	Worcester	
		Sussex	v Gloucestershire	Eastbourne	
		Surrey	v Hampshire	The Oval	
		Nottinghamshire	v Lancashire	Nottingham	
		Leicestershire	v Derbyshire	Leicester	
		Glamorgan	v Kent	Swansea	
		Somerset	v Essex	Taunton	
Tue May 16	**RLODC**	Northamptonshire	v Nottinghamshire	Northampton	💡
		Derbyshire	v Worcestershire	Derby	💡
		Yorkshire	v Leicestershire	Leeds	💡
		Durham	v Lancashire	Chester-le-Street	💡
Wed May 17	**RLODC**	Hampshire	v Sussex	Southampton	💡
		Kent	v Essex	Canterbury	💡
		Middlesex	v Somerset	Lord's	💡
		Gloucestershire	v Surrey	Bristol	💡
Fri May 19	**ODI**	**IRELAND**	**v BANGLADESH**	**Malahide**	
	Tour match (o-d)	Sussex	v South Africans	Hove	💡
Fri May 19–Mon 22	**SSCC D1**	Middlesex	v Surrey	Lord's	
		Lancashire	v Yorkshire	Old Trafford	
		Essex	v Hampshire	Chelmsford	
		Somerset	v Warwickshire	Taunton	
	SSCC D2	Glamorgan	v Nottinghamshire	Cardiff	
		Leicestershire	v Kent	Leicester	
		Derbyshire	v Worcestershire	Derby	
Sun May 21	**ODI**	**IRELAND**	**v NEW ZEALAND**	**Malahide**	
	Tour match (o-d)	Northamptonshire	v South Africans	Northampton	
Sun May 21–Wed 24	**SSCC D2**	Sussex	v Durham	Hove	
Wed May 24	**RL ODI**	**ENGLAND**	**v SOUTH AFRICA**	**Leeds**	💡
Thu May 25–Sun 28	**SSCC D2**	Derbyshire	v Leicestershire	Derby	
Fri May 26–Mon 29	**SSCC D1**	Somerset	v Hampshire	Taunton	
		Essex	v Surrey	Chelmsford	
	SSCC D2	Nottinghamshire	v Gloucestershire	Nottingham	
		Northamptonshire	v Worcestershire	Northampton	
		Glamorgan	v Durham	Swansea	
		Kent	v Sussex	Tunbridge Wells	
Sat May 27	**RL ODI**	**ENGLAND**	**v SOUTH AFRICA**	**Southampton**	
	Tour match (o-d)	Yorkshire	v South Africa A	Leeds	
Mon May 29	**RL ODI**	**ENGLAND**	**v SOUTH AFRICA**	**Lord's**	
	Tour match (o-d)	Derbyshire	v South Africa A	Derby	
Thur Jun 1	**Champs T**	**ENGLAND**	**v BANGLADESH**	**The Oval**	
	Tour match (o-d)	England Lions	v South Africa A	Nottingham	
Fri Jun 2	**Champs T**	**AUSTRALIA**	**v NEW ZEALAND**	**Birmingham**	

Fri Jun 2–Mon 5	**SSCC D1**	Middlesex	v Somerset	Lord's
		Hampshire	v Warwickshire	Southampton
		Yorkshire	v Lancashire	Leeds
	SSCC D2	Nottinghamshire	v Derbyshire	Nottingham
		Durham	v Northamptonshire	Chester-le-Street
		Sussex	v Worcestershire	Hove
Sat Jun 3	**Champs T**	**SOUTH AFRICA**	**v SRI LANKA**	**The Oval**
	Tour match (o-d)	England Lions	v South Africa A	Northampton
Sun Jun 4	**Champs T**	**INDIA**	**v PAKISTAN**	**Birmingham**
Mon Jun 5	**Champs T**	**AUSTRALIA**	**v BANGLADESH**	**The Oval**
	Tour match (o-d)	England Lions	v South Africa A	Northampton
Tue Jun 6	**Champs T**	**ENGLAND**	**v NEW ZEALAND**	**Cardiff**
Wed Jun 7	**Champs T**	**PAKISTAN**	**v SOUTH AFRICA**	**Birmingham**
Thu Jun 8	**Champs T**	**INDIA**	**v SRI LANKA**	**The Oval**
Thu Jun 8–Sun 11	**Tour match**	Hampshire	v South Africa A	Southampton
	SSCC D2	Kent	v Durham	Canterbury
Fri Jun 9	**Champs T**	**BANGLADESH**	**v NEW ZEALAND**	**Cardiff**
Fri Jun 9–Mon 12	**SSCC D1**	Somerset	v Yorkshire	Taunton
		Lancashire	v Middlesex	Southport
		Surrey	v Essex	Guildford
	SSCC D2	Northamptonshire	v Derbyshire	Northampton
		Worcestershire	v Glamorgan	Worcester
		Leicestershire	v Sussex	Leicester
		Gloucestershire	v Nottinghamshire	Bristol
Sat Jun 10	**Champs T**	**ENGLAND**	**v AUSTRALIA**	**Birmingham**
Sun Jun 11	**Champs T**	**INDIA**	**v SOUTH AFRICA**	**The Oval**
	ODI	**SCOTLAND**	**v NAMIBIA**	**Edinburgh**
Mon Jun 12	**Champs T**	**PAKISTAN**	**v SRI LANKA**	**Cardiff**
Tue Jun 13	**ODI**	**SCOTLAND**	**v NAMIBIA**	**Edinburgh**
	RLODC	**Quarter-final**		
		Quarter-final		
Wed Jun 14	**Champs T**	**Semi-final**		Cardiff
Wed Jun 14–Sat 17	**Tour match**	Sussex	v South Africa A	Arundel
Thu Jun 15	**Champs T**	**Semi-final**		Birmingham
Fri Jun 16	**RLODC**	**Semi-final**		
	Varsity (T20)	Cambridge U	v Oxford U	Cambridge
	W Varsity (T20)	Cambridge U	v Oxford U	Cambridge
Sat Jun 17	**RLODC**	**Semi-final**		
Sun Jun 18	**Champs T**	**Final**		The Oval
	Tour match (o-d)	Leicestershire	v South Africa	Leicester
Mon Jun 19–Thu 22	**SSCC D1**	Lancashire	v Hampshire	Manchester
		Middlesex	v Yorkshire	Lord's
		Essex	v Warwickshire	Chelmsford
	SSCC D2	Durham	v Glamorgan	Chester-le-Street
		Nottinghamshire	v Leicestershire	Nottingham
		Worcestershire	v Kent	Worcester
Wed Jun 21–Sat 24	**NW T20I**	**ENGLAND**	**v SOUTH AFRICA**	**Southampton**
Wed Jun 21–Sat 24	**Tour match**	England Lions	v South Africa A	Canterbury

Fri Jun 23	**NW T20I**	**ENGLAND**	**v SOUTH AFRICA**	**Taunton**	
	Varsity (o-d)	Oxford U	v Cambridge U	Lord's (Nursery)	
	W Varsity (o-d)	Oxford U	v Cambridge U	Lord's (Nursery)	
Sun Jun 25	**NW T20I**	**ENGLAND**	**v SOUTH AFRICA**	**Cardiff**	
Mon Jun 26–Thu 29	**SSCC D1**	Essex	v Middlesex	Chelmsford	💡
		Hampshire	v Somerset	Southampton	💡
		Warwickshire	v Lancashire	Birmingham	💡
		Yorkshire	v Surrey	Leeds	💡
	SSCC D2	Durham	v Worcestershire	Chester-le-Street	💡
		Glamorgan	v Derbyshire	Cardiff	💡
		Northamptonshire	v Leicestershire	Northampton	💡
		Nottinghamshire	v Kent	Nottingham	💡
		Sussex	v Gloucestershire	Hove	💡
Thu Jun 29–Sat Jul 1	**Tour match**	England Lions	v South Africa	Worcester	
Sat Jul 1	**RLODC**	**Final**		Lord's	
Mon Jul 3–Thu 7	**SSCC D1**	Warwickshire	v Middlesex	Birmingham	
		Yorkshire	v Somerset	Scarborough	
		Surrey	v Hampshire	The Oval	
	SSCC D2	Derbyshire	v Durham	Chesterfield	
		Kent	v Northamptonshire	Beckenham	
		Gloucestershire	v Glamorgan	Cheltenham	
Tue Jul 4–Fri 7	**Varsity**	Cambridge U	v Oxford U	Cambridge	
Wed Jul 5–Sat 8	**SSCC D2**	Sussex	v Leicestershire	Arundel	
Thu Jul 6–Mon 10	**1st Inv Test**	**ENGLAND**	**v SOUTH AFRICA**	**Lord's**	
Fri Jul 7	**NW T20**	Yorkshire	v Nottinghamshire	Leeds	💡
		Durham	v Lancashire	Chester-le-Street	💡
		Essex	v Surrey	Chelmsford	💡
		Glamorgan	v Hampshire	Cardiff	💡
		Gloucestershire	v Middlesex	Cheltenham	
		Northamptonshire	v Derbyshire	Northampton	💡
		Worcestershire	v Warwickshire	Worcester	
Sat Jul 8	**NW T20**	Derbyshire	v Yorkshire	Chesterfield	
		Warwickshire	v Nottinghamshire	Birmingham	💡
Sun Jul 9–Wed 12	**SSCC D2**	Gloucestershire	v Worcestershire	Cheltenham	
Sun Jul 9	**NW T20**	Durham	v Northamptonshire	Chester-le-Street	
		Kent	v Essex	Beckenham	
		Lancashire	v Leicestershire	Manchester	
		Surrey	v Somerset	The Oval	
		Sussex	v Glamorgan	Arundel	
Tue Jul 11	**NW T20**	Northamptonshire	v Yorkshire	Northampton	💡
Wed Jul 12	**NW T20**	Sussex	v Hampshire	Hove	💡
Thu Jul 13	**NW T20**	Middlesex	v Surrey	Lord's	💡
		Essex	v Somerset	Chelmsford	💡
		Gloucestershire	v Kent	Cheltenham	
Fri Jul 14–Tue 18	**2nd Inv Test**	**ENGLAND**	**v SOUTH AFRICA**	**Nottingham**	
Fri Jul 14	**NW T20**	Hampshire	v Middlesex	Southampton	💡
		Lancashire	v Yorkshire	Old Trafford	💡
		Surrey	v Kent	The Oval	💡
		Worcestershire	v Leicestershire	Worcester	
		Warwickshire	v Northamptonshire	Birmingham	💡

Sat Jul 15	**NW T20**	Glamorgan	v Somerset	Cardiff
Sun Jul 16	**NW T20**	Middlesex	v Somerset	Uxbridge
		Essex	v Glamorgan	Chelmsford
		Gloucestershire	v Sussex	Cheltenham
		Warwickshire	v Leicestershire	Birmingham
		Lancashire	v Derbyshire	Manchester
Tue Jul 18	**W World Cup**	**Semi-final**		**Bristol**
	NW T20	Kent	v Gloucestershire	Canterbury
Wed Jul 19	**NW T20**	Surrey	v Essex	The Oval
		Worcestershire	v Derbyshire	Worcester
Thu Jul 20	**W World Cup**	**Semi-final**		**Derby**
	NW T20	Middlesex	v Kent	Richmond
		Hampshire	v Sussex	Southampton
		Durham	v Leicestershire	Chester-le-Street
Fri Jul 21	**NW T20**	Worcestershire	v Lancashire	Worcester
		Surrey	v Middlesex	The Oval
		Somerset	v Gloucestershire	Taunton
		Nottinghamshire	v Derbyshire	Nottingham
		Leicestershire	v Northamptonshire	Leicester
		Glamorgan	v Sussex	Cardiff
		Yorkshire	v Warwickshire	Leeds
		Essex	v Hampshire	Chelmsford
Sat Jul 22	**NW T20**	Nottinghamshire	v Northamptonshire	Nottingham
Sun Jul 23	**W World Cup**	**Final**		Lord's
	NW T20	Lancashire	v Durham	Old Trafford
		Warwickshire	v Derbyshire	Birmingham
		Sussex	v Kent	Hove
		Somerset	v Middlesex	Taunton
		Glamorgan	v Essex	Cardiff
		Yorkshire	v Worcestershire	Leeds
		Hampshire	v Surrey	Southampton
Sun Jul 23–Wed 26	**U19 Test**	England U19	v India U19	TBC
Tue Jul 25	**NW T20**	Durham	v Nottinghamshire	Chester-le-Street
		Gloucestershire	v Glamorgan	Bristol
		Leicestershire	v Warwickshire	Leicester
		Derbyshire	v Lancashire	Derby
Wed Jul 26	**NW T20**	Yorkshire	v Durham	Leeds
		Nottinghamshire	v Worcestershire	Nottingham
		Somerset	v Hampshire	Taunton
Thu Jul 27–Mon 31	**3rd Inv Test**	**ENGLAND**	**v SOUTH AFRICA**	**The Oval**
Thu Jul 27	**NW T20**	Northamptonshire	v Worcestershire	Northampton
		Kent	v Somerset	Canterbury
		Middlesex	v Essex	Lord's
Fri Jul 28	**NW T20**	Leicestershire	v Durham	Leicester
		Sussex	v Middlesex	Hove
		Lancashire	v Nottinghamshire	Old Trafford
		Gloucestershire	v Hampshire	Bristol
		Derbyshire	v Northamptonshire	Derby
		Warwickshire	v Yorkshire	Birmingham
		Glamorgan	v Surrey	Cardiff
Sat Jul 29	**NW T20**	Essex	v Gloucestershire	Chelmsford
Sun Jul 30	**NW T20**	Somerset	v Sussex	Taunton
		Warwickshire	v Lancashire	Birmingham

Sun Jul 30	**NW T20**	Kent	v Glamorgan	Canterbury	
		Derbyshire	v Leicestershire	Derby	
		Worcestershire	v Durham	Worcester	
		Nottinghamshire	v Yorkshire	Nottingham	
Mon Jul 31–Thu Aug 3	**U19 Test**	England U19	v India U19	Worcester	
Tue Aug 1–Thu 3	**Tour match**	Essex	v West Indians	Chelmsford	
Tue Aug 1	**NW T20**	Northamptonshire	v Warwickshire	Northampton	💡
		Hampshire	v Kent	Southampton	💡
Wed Aug 2	**NW T20**	Leicestershire	v Nottinghamshire	Leicester	💡
Thu Aug 3	**NW T20**	Glamorgan	v Gloucestershire	Cardiff	💡
		Yorkshire	v Derbyshire	Leeds	💡
		Sussex	v Surrey	Hove	💡
		Middlesex	v Hampshire	Lord's	💡
		Northamptonshire	v Lancashire	Northampton	💡
Fri Aug 4–Tue 8	**4th Inv Test**	**ENGLAND**	**v SOUTH AFRICA**	**Old Trafford**	
Fri Aug 4	**NW T20**	Surrey	v Glamorgan	The Oval	💡
		Warwickshire	v Worcestershire	Birmingham	💡
		Durham	v Yorkshire	Chester-le-Street	💡
		Leicestershire	v Lancashire	Leicester	💡
		Kent	v Sussex	Canterbury	💡
		Gloucestershire	v Somerset	Bristol	💡
		Derbyshire	v Nottinghamshire	Derby	💡
		Hampshire	v Essex	Southampton	💡
Sat Aug 5	**NW T20**	Nottinghamshire	v Durham	Nottingham	
		Worcestershire	v Northamptonshire	Worcester	
Sun Aug 6–Tue 8	**Tour match**	Kent	v West Indians	Canterbury	
Sun Aug 6–Wed 9	**SSCC D1**	Yorkshire	v Essex	Scarborough	
		Middlesex	v Warwickshire	Lord's	
		Hampshire	v Lancashire	Southampton	
	SSCC D2	Leicestershire	v Durham	Leicester	
		Northamptonshire	v Gloucestershire	Northampton	
		Derbyshire	v Nottinghamshire	Derby	
		Worcestershire	v Sussex	Worcester	
Sun Aug 6	**NW T20**	Somerset	v Surrey	Taunton	
Mon Aug 7–Thu 10	**SSCC D1**	Somerset	v Surrey	Taunton	
Mon Aug 7	**U19 ODI**	England U19	v India U19	Cardiff	
Wed Aug 9	**U19 ODI**	England U19	v India U19	Canterbury	💡
Thu Aug 10	**NW T20**	Hampshire	v Glamorgan	Southampton	💡
		Middlesex	v Sussex	Lord's	💡
Fri Aug 11–Sun 13	**Tour match**	Derbyshire	v West Indians	Derby	💡
Fri Aug 11	**NW T20**	Durham	v Worcestershire	Chester-le-Street	💡
		Nottinghamshire	v Warwickshire	Nottingham	💡
		Sussex	v Gloucestershire	Hove	💡
		Northamptonshire	v Leicestershire	Northampton	💡
		Kent	v Hampshire	Canterbury	💡
		Essex	v Middlesex	Chelmsford	💡
		Yorkshire	v Lancashire	Leeds	💡
Sat Aug 12	**NW T20**	Somerset	v Kent	Taunton	
		Leicestershire	v Yorkshire	Leicester	
	U19 ODI	England U19	v India U19	Hove	

Sun Aug 13	**NW T20**	Gloucestershire	v Essex	Bristol
		Somerset	v Glamorgan	Taunton
		Surrey	v Sussex	The Oval
		Worcestershire	v Nottinghamshire	Worcester
		Durham	v Warwickshire	Chester-le-Street
Mon Aug 14	**U19 ODI**	England U19	v India U19	Bristol
Tue Aug 15	**NW T20**	Derbyshire	v Durham	Derby
		Middlesex	v Gloucestershire	TBC
Wed Aug 16	**NW T20**	Lancashire	v Worcestershire	Old Trafford
	U19 ODI	England U19	v India U19	Taunton
Thu Aug 17–Mon 21	**1st Inv Test**	**ENGLAND**	**v WEST INDIES**	**Birmingham**
Thu Aug 17	**NW T20**	Essex	v Kent	Chelmsford
		Leicestershire	v Derbyshire	Leicester
		Surrey	v Gloucestershire	The Oval
		Yorkshire	v Northamptonshire	Leeds
Fri Aug 18	**NW T20**	Lancashire	v Warwickshire	Old Trafford
		Sussex	v Essex	Hove
		Northamptonshire	v Durham	Northampton
		Kent	v Surrey	Canterbury
		Hampshire	v Somerset	Southampton
		Glamorgan	v Middlesex	Cardiff
		Derbyshire	v Worcestershire	Derby
		Nottinghamshire	v Leicestershire	Nottingham
Tue Aug 22	**NW T20**	**Quarter-final**		
Wed Aug 23	**NW T20**	**Quarter-final**		
Thu Aug 24	**NW T20**	**Quarter-final**		
Fri Aug 25–Tue 29	**2nd Inv Test**	**ENGLAND**	**v WEST INDIES**	**Leeds**
Fri Aug 25	**NW T20**	**Quarter-final**		
Mon Aug 28–Thu 31	**SSCC D1**	Surrey	v Middlesex	The Oval
		Lancashire	v Warwickshire	Old Trafford
		Essex	v Somerset	Chelmsford
	SSCC D2	Glamorgan	v Sussex	Colwyn Bay
		Nottinghamshire	v Northamptonshire	Nottingham
		Kent	v Leicestershire	Canterbury
		Worcestershire	v Gloucestershire	Worcester
		Durham	v Derbyshire	Chester-le-Street
Fri Sep 1	**KSL WT20**	**Semi-finals and final**		Hove
Sat Sep 2	**NW T20**	**Semi-finals and final**		Birmingham
Sat Sep 2–Sun 3	**Tour match**	Leicestershire	v West Indians	Leicester
Tue Sep 5–Fri 8	**SSCC D1**	Hampshire	v Surrey	Southampton
		Yorkshire	v Middlesex	Leeds
		Lancashire	v Essex	Old Trafford
		Warwickshire	v Somerset	Birmingham
	SSCC D2	Northamptonshire	v Sussex	Northampton
		Nottinghamshire	v Worcestershire	Nottingham
		Leicestershire	v Gloucestershire	Leicester
		Derbyshire	v Glamorgan	Derby
		Durham	v Kent	Chester-le-Street
Thu Sep 7–Mon 11	**3rd Inv Test**	**ENGLAND**	**v WEST INDIES**	**Lord's**

Tue Sep 12–Fri 15	**SSCC D1**	Warwickshire	v Essex	Birmingham
		Surrey	v Yorkshire	The Oval
		Somerset	v Lancashire	Taunton
		Middlesex	v Hampshire	Uxbridge
	SSCC D2	Worcestershire	v Leicestershire	Worcester
		Sussex	v Derbyshire	Hove
		Glamorgan	v Northamptonshire	Cardiff
		Gloucestershire	v Kent	Bristol
Wed Sep 13	**ODI**	**IRELAND**	**v WEST INDIES**	**Stormont**
Sat Sep 16	**NW T20I**	**ENGLAND**	**v WEST INDIES**	**Chester-le-Street**
Tue Sep 19	**RL ODI**	**ENGLAND**	**v WEST INDIES**	**Old Trafford**
Tue Sep 19-Fri 22	**SSCC D1**	Yorkshire	v Warwickshire	Leeds
		Surrey	v Somerset	The Oval
		Middlesex	v Lancashire	Lord's
		Hampshire	v Essex	Southampton
	SSCC D2	Derbyshire	v Kent	Derby
		Durham	v Sussex	Chester-le-Street
		Glamorgan	v Gloucestershire	Cardiff
		Northamptonshire	v Nottinghamshire	Northampton
Thu Sep 21	**RL ODI**	**ENGLAND**	**v WEST INDIES**	**Nottingham**
Sun Sep 24	**RL ODI**	**ENGLAND**	**v WEST INDIES**	**Bristol**
Mon Sep 25–Thu 29	**SSCC D1**	Lancashire	v Surrey	Old Trafford
		Somerset	v Middlesex	Taunton
		Essex	v Yorkshire	Chelmsford
		Warwickshire	v Hampshire	Birmingham
	SSCC D2	Worcestershire	v Durham	Worcester
		Sussex	v Nottinghamshire	Hove
		Leicestershire	v Northamptonshire	Leicester
		Kent	v Glamorgan	Canterbury
		Gloucestershire	v Derbyshire	Bristol
Wed Sep 27	**RL ODI**	**ENGLAND**	**v WEST INDIES**	**The Oval**
Fri Sep 29	**RL ODI**	**ENGLAND**	**v WEST INDIES**	**Southampton**

ERRATA

Wisden 1913 Page 444		In Cambridgeshire's averages, Mr F. W. Bryan's highest score was 31.
Wisden 2015 Page 780		M. G. Johnson bowled 84 maidens and conceded 1,093 at 23.25 in the calendar year 2015.
	Pages 843 and 847	Further to the *Wisden 2016* Errata, Johnson had 26 maidens, and bowled three maidens in India's second innings at Adelaide.
Wisden 2016 Page 412		The caption should read "…their first victory in the opening Test of an overseas series – other than against Bangladesh – since 2004-05."
	Page 426	Rabada was 20 years 246 days old when he completed his second-innings 6-32.
	Page 460	Yorkshire's pitches had the highest marks for first-class cricket, and Somerset for one-day cricket.
	Page 529	It was Howell and Miles who offered brief resistance.
	Page 583	Shreck was caught by Kerrigan, not Prince.
	Page 635	Craig Overton was suspended for Somerset's final Championship match of 2015 and for their first of 2016 – not for the final two games of 2015. This was an editing error, and – along with an expletive in a quotation – did not appear in the original copy, filed by *Wisden's* Somerset correspondent, Richard Latham.
	Page 804	R. J. Povey's highest score for Rugby was 150*, not 150.
	Pages 1156 and 1158	Imran Khan (in the averages and Trinidad & Tobago's match against Jamaica on February 20–22) is a leg-spinner not a slow left-armer.
	Page 1157	The match between Barbados and Jamaica on November 21–24 was moved from the Bridgetown Oval to Lucas Street.
	Page 1224	Kycia A. Knight scored 34 in the third one-day international between Sri Lanka and West Indies on May 18; her twin sister Kyshona A. Knight was not on this tour.
	Page 1225	In the first Twenty20 international between India and New Zealand, Sophie Devine was out for 70.
	Page 1240	A further 11 instances of three hundreds in successive innings were omitted. They were: **S. C. Cook** (Lions) 147* v Cape Cobras at Potchefstroom, 122 v Titans at Benoni, 122 v Dolphins at Johannesburg; **B. A. Godleman** (Derbyshire) 101 v Leics at Leicester, 108 and 105* v Kent at Derby; **S. P. Jackson** (Saurashtra) 156 v Gujarat at Rajkot, 181* v Punjab at Rajkot, 102 v Maharashtra at Rajkot; **Kamran Akmal** (Nat Bank) 137 v Sui Northern at Karachi, 140 v Lahore Whites at Lahore, 137 v FATA at Sialkot; **R. Paliwal** (Services) 121 and 103 v Saurashtra at Delhi, 107 v Him. Pradesh at

Dharamsala; **Rony Talukder** (Dhaka) 227 v Barisal at Mirpur, 163 v Dhaka Met at Fatullah, 201 v Chittagong at Savar; **B. Sharma** (Him. Pradesh) 119* v Tripura at Agartala, 176 v Hyderabad at Hyderabad, 117* v J&K at Dharamsala; **I. J. L. Trott** (Warwicks) 164 v Northants at Birmingham, 104 v Durham at Birmingham, 211* England Lions v South Africa A at Paarl; **R. V. Uthappa** (Karnataka) 160 v Rajasthan at Jaipur, 148 v Orissa at Mysore, 148 v Delhi at Hubli; **G. L. van Buuren** (Northerns) 150* v Griqualand W at Centurion, 130 v Namibia at Pretoria, 235 v E Province at Centurion; **A. C. Voges** (W Australia) 101 and 139 v Victoria at Perth, 101 v S Australia at Perth.

The first two hundreds by Jackson, Trott and Voges, and the first hundred scored by Kamran, were scored in 2014.

Page 1247 M. H. Yardy also reached 10,000 runs during the calendar year 2016.

An Archive list detailing Errata covering *Wisdens* back to 1920 can be found online at www.bloomsbury.com/uk/special-interest/wisden/errata

CHARITIES IN 2016

ARUNDEL CASTLE CRICKET FOUNDATION – more than 300,000 disadvantaged youngsters, many with special needs, mainly from inner-city areas, have received instruction and encouragement at Arundel since 1986. In 2016, there were 90 days devoted to activities, and 4,500 young people benefited. To donate, please go to www.justgiving.com/arundelcastlecricket. Director of cricket: John Barclay, Arundel Park, Sussex BN18 9LH. Tel: 01903 882602. Website: www.arundelcastlecricketfoundation.co.uk.

THE BRIAN JOHNSTON MEMORIAL TRUST supports cricket for the blind, and aims to ease the financial worries of talented young cricketers through scholarships. The BJMT spin-bowling programme, in support of the ECB, was launched in 2010 to provide expert coaching to all the first-class county Academies and the MCCUs. Registered Charity No. 1045946. Trust administrator: Richard Anstey, 178 Manor Drive North, Worcester Park, Surrey KT4 7RU. Email: contact@lordstaverners.org. Website: www.lordstaverners.org/brian-johnston-memorial-trust.

BRITISH ASSOCIATION FOR CRICKETERS WITH DISABILITIES was formed in 1991 to promote playing opportunities for cricketers with physical and learning difficulties. We work in close partnership with the ECB. President: Bill Higginson, 07455 219526, higgi.b1936@gmail.com. Chairman: David Lloyd, 07739 146762, david53lloyd@googlemail.com.

BUNBURY CRICKET CLUB has raised over £17m for national charities and worthwhile causes. Since 1987, a total of 1,736 boys have played in the Bunbury Festival; 725 have gone on to play first-class cricket, and 78 for England. The 31st Festival, in 2017, will be at Stowe School. The Bunburys also presented the only two Under-15 World Cups ever (in 1996 and 2000). Further information from Dr David English CBE, 1 Highwood Cottages, Nan Clark's Lane, London NW7 4HJ. Email: davidenglishbunbury@gmail.com. Website: www.bunburycricket.co.uk.

CAPITAL KIDS CRICKET, formed in 1989, delivers cricket tuition to boys and girls in state schools in London, establishes and assists emerging clubs, organises residential festivals and competitions in local communities, and runs courses at four London hospitals. Its Indoor Kids Cricket League involves over 140 primary schools and 2,500 children. Chairman: John Challinor, 79 Gore Road, London E9 7HN, johnchallinor@hotmail.com. Director of cricket: Shahidul Alam Ratan, 07748 114811, shahidul.alam@capitalkidscricket.org.uk. Website: www.capitalkidscricket.org.uk.

CHANCE TO SHINE is a national children's charity on a mission to spread the power of cricket throughout schools and communities. Since launching in 2005, Chance to Shine has reached over three million children across 13,000 state schools. Chief executive: Luke Swanson, Kia Oval, Kennington, London SE11 5SW. Tel: 020 7820 9379. Website: www.chancetoshine.org.

THE CHANGE FOUNDATION uses sport to change young lives. In partnership with Investec we use Street20 cricket for the Inner City World Cup in London, and also run the Refugee Cricket Project in partnership with the Refugee Council. Our disability sports programme Hit The Top delivers thriving new clubs and projects. Overseas work has included initiatives in Europe (in partnership with the ICC), as well as Afghanistan, Israel and the West Bank, Brazil, Jamaica, Barbados, Rwanda, Uganda, Sri Lanka, India, Bangladesh, Hong Kong, Ghana, and New York. Chief executive: Andy Sellins, The Cricket Centre, Plough Lane, Wallington, Surrey

SM6 8JQ. Tel: 020 8669 2177. Email: office@thechangefoundation.org.uk. Website: www.thechangefoundation.org.uk.

THE CRICKET SOCIETY TRUST'S principal aim is to support schools and organisations to encourage enjoyment of the game and to develop skills. Particular effort is given to children with special needs, through programmes arranged with the Arundel Castle Cricket Foundation and the Belvoir Castle Cricket Trust. Hon. secretary: Ken Merchant, 16 Louise Road, Rayleigh, Essex SS6 8LW. Tel: 01268 747414. Website: www.cricketsocietytrust.org.uk.

THE DICKIE BIRD FOUNDATION, set up by the former umpire in 2004, helps financially disadvantaged under-18s participate in sport. Grants are made towards the cost of equipment and clothing. Trustee: Ted Cowley, 3 The Tower, Tower Drive, Arthington Lane, Pool-in-Wharfedale, Otley, Yorkshire LS21 1NQ. Tel: 07503 641457. Website: www.thedickiebirdfoundation.co.uk.

ENGLAND AND WALES CRICKET TRUST was established in 2005 to aid community participation in cricket, with a fund for interest-free loans to amateur clubs. In its last financial year (to January 2016) it incurred costs on charitable activities of £9.9m – primarily grants to cricket charities and amateur clubs, and to county boards to support their programmes. Contact: ECB, Lord's Cricket Ground, London NW8 8QZ. Tel: 020 7432 1200. Email: feedback@ecb.co.uk.

THE EVELINA LONDON CHILDREN'S HOSPITAL is the official charity partner of Surrey CCC and The Kia Oval. Evelina is one of the country's leading children's hospitals, treating patients from all over the South-East. Partnership head: Jon Surtees, The Kia Oval, Kennington, London SE11 5SS. Tel: 020 7820 5780. Website: www.kiaoval.com.

FIELDS IN TRUST is the only UK charity protecting and improving green space for future generations to enjoy. We safeguard over 2,600 sites for sport, play and recreation. In the last five years we have added 304 sites where cricket is played. Chief Executive: Helen Griffiths, 36 Woodstock Grove, London W12 8LE. Tel: 020 7427 2110. Website: www.fieldsintrust.org. Facebook: www.facebook.com/fieldsintrust. Twitter @FieldsInTrust.

THE HORNSBY PROFESSIONAL CRICKETERS' FUND supports former professional cricketers and their dependants, through regular financial help or one-off grants towards healthcare or similar essential needs. It was established in 1928 from a bequest from J. H. J. Hornsby (Middlesex, MCC and the Gentlemen), augmented more recently by a bequest from Alec and Eric Bedser, and also by the Walter Hammond Memorial Fund merging with the Trust, which works closely with the PCA and, where appropriate, a player's former county. Secretary: The Rev. Prebendary Mike Vockins OBE, Birchwood Lodge, Birchwood, Storridge, Malvern, Worcestershire WR13 5EZ. Tel: 01886 884366.

THE LEARNING FOR A BETTER WORLD (LBW) TRUST, established in 2006, provides tertiary education to disadvantaged students in the cricket-playing countries of the developing world. In 2016 it was assisting over 2,000 students in India, Pakistan, Nepal, Uganda, Afghanistan, Sri Lanka, South Africa and Jamaica, and in 2017 will include Kenya. Chairman: David Vaux, GPO Box 3029, Sydney, NSW 2000, Australia. Website: www.lbwtrust.com.au.

THE LORD'S TAVERNERS is the UK's leading youth cricket and disability sports charity, dedicated to giving disadvantaged and disabled young people a sporting chance. This year it will donate over £3m to help those of all abilities and backgrounds to play cricket and other sports. Registered Charity No. 306054. The

Lord's Taverners, 90 Chancery Lane, London WC2A 1EU. Tel: 020 7025 0000. Email: contact@lordstaverners.org. Website: www.lordstaverners.org.

THE PCA BENEVOLENT FUND, sponsored by Royal London, is part of the PCA's commitment to supporting players and their dependants in need of a helping hand to readjust to a world beyond cricket, as well as current and past players who have fallen on hard times or are in need of specialist advice or assistance. Head of development and welfare: Ian Thomas, PCA, The Kia Oval, Kennington, London SE11 5SS. Tel: 07768 558050. Website: www.thepca.co.uk.

THE PRIMARY CLUB provides sporting and recreational facilities for the blind and partially sighted. Membership is nominally restricted to those dismissed first ball in any form of cricket; almost 10,000 belong. In total, the club has raised £3m, helped by sales of its tie, popularised by *Test Match Special.* Andrew Strauss is president of the Primary Club Juniors. Hon. secretary: Chris Larlham, PO Box 12121, Saffron Walden, Essex CB10 2ZF. Tel: 01799 586507. Website: www.primaryclub.org.

THE PRINCE'S TRUST helps disadvantaged young people get their lives on track. Founded by HRH The Prince of Wales in 1976, the charity supports 13–30-year-olds who are unemployed, and those struggling at school. The Trust's programmes use a variety of activities, including cricket and other sports, to engage young people and help them gain skills, confidence and qualifications. Prince's Trust House, 9 Eldon Street, London EC2M 7LS. Tel: 0800 842842. Website: www.princes-trust.org.uk.

THE TOM MAYNARD TRUST – formed in 2012 after Tom's tragic death – covers three main areas: helping aspiring young professionals with education projects, currently across six sports; running an academy in Spain for young county cricketers on the first rung of the career ladder; and providing grants for sportspeople to help with travel, kit, coaching, training and education. Contact: Mike Fatkin, 67a Radnor Road, Canton, Cardiff CF5 1RA. Website: www.tommaynardtrust.com.

CRICKET TRADE DIRECTORY

BOOKSELLERS

AARDVARK BOOKS, 10 Briardene Avenue, Scarborough, North Yorkshire YO12 6PL. Tel: 01723 374072; email: pete@aardvarkcricketbooks.co.uk or **pandlaardvark@btinternet.com**. Peter Taylor specialises in *Wisdens*, including rare hardbacks and early editions. *Wisdens* purchased. Restoration of hardbacks and softbacks, cleaning and gilding undertaken.

BOUNDARY BOOKS, The Haven, West Street, Childrey OX12 9UL. Tel: 01235 751021; email: mike@boundarybooks.com; website: boundarybooks.com. Rare and second-hand books, autographs and memorabilia bought and sold. Catalogues issued. Large Oxfordshire showroom open by appointment. Unusual and scarce items always available.

CHRISTOPHER SAUNDERS, Kingston House, High Street, Newnham-on-Severn, Gloucestershire GL14 1BB. Tel: 01594 516030; email: chris@cricket-books.com; website: cricket-books.com. Office/bookroom open by appointment. Second-hand/antiquarian cricket books and memorabilia bought and sold. Regular catalogues issued containing selections from over 12,000 items in stock.

GRACE BOOKS AND CARDS (TED KIRWAN), Donkey Cart Cottage, Main Street, Bruntingthorpe, Lutterworth, Leics LE17 5QE. Tel: 0116 247 8417; email: ted@gracecricketana.co.uk. Second-hand and antiquarian cricket books, *Wisdens*, autographed material and cricket ephemera of all kinds. Now also modern postcards of current international cricketers.

JOHN JEFFERS, The Old Mill, Aylesbury Road, Wing, Leighton Buzzard LU7 0PG. Tel: 01296 688543; mobile: 07846 537692; e-mail: edgwarerover@live.co.uk. *Wisden* specialist. Immediate decision and top settlement for purchase of *Wisden* collections. Why wait for the next auction? Why pay the auctioneer's commission anyway?

J. W. McKENZIE, 12 Stoneleigh Park Road, Ewell, Epsom, Surrey KT19 0QT. Tel: 020 8393 7700; email: mckenziecricket@btconnect.com; website: mckenzie-cricket.co.uk. Specialist since 1971. Antiquarian and second-hand cricket books and memorabilia bought and sold. Catalogues issued regularly. Large shop premises open 9am–5pm Monday–Friday and Saturday by appointment. Thirty minutes from London Waterloo. Please phone before visiting.

KEN FAULKNER, 65 Brookside, Wokingham, Berkshire RG41 2ST. Tel: 0118 978 5255; email: kfaulkner@bowmore.demon.co.uk; website: bowmore.demon.co.uk. Bookroom open by appointment. My stall, with a strong *Wisden* content, will be operating at the Cheltenham Cricket Festival in July 2017. We purchase *Wisden* collections which include pre-1946 editions.

ROGER PAGE, 10 Ekari Court, Yallambie, Victoria 3085, Australia. Tel: (+61) 3 9435 6332; email: rpcricketbooks@unite.com.au; website: rpcricketbooks.com. Australia's only full-time dealer in new and second-hand cricket books. Distributor of overseas cricket annuals and magazines. Agent for Association of Cricket Statisticians and Cricket Memorabilia Society.

ST MARY'S BOOKS & PRINTS, 9 St Mary's Hill, Stamford, Lincolnshire PE9 2DP. Tel: 01780 763033; email: info@stmarysbooks.com; website: stmarysbooks.com. Dealers in *Wisdens* 1864–2016, second-hand, rare cricket books and *Vanity Fair* prints. Book-search service offered.

SPORTSPAGES, 7 Finns Business Park, Mill Lane, Farnham, Surrey GU10 5RX. Tel: 01252 851040; email: info@sportspages.com; website: sportspages.com. Large stock of *Wisdens*, fine sports books and memorabilia, including cricket, rugby, football and golf. Books and memorabilia also purchased, please offer. Visitors welcome to browse by appointment.

TIM BEDDOW, 66 Oak Road, Oldbury, West Midlands B68 0BD. Tel: 0121 421 7117; mobile: 07956 456112; email: wisden1864@hotmail.com. Wanted: cash paid for football, cricket, speedway, motorsport and rugby union memorabilia, badges, books, programmes (amateur and professional), autographed items, match tickets, yearbooks and photographs – anything considered.

WILLIAM H. ROBERTS, Long Low, 27 Gernhill Avenue, Fixby, Huddersfield, West Yorkshire HD2 2HR. Tel: 01484 654463; email: william@roberts-cricket.co.uk; website: williamroberts-cricket.com. Second-hand/antiquarian cricket books, *Wisdens*, autographs and memorabilia bought and sold. Many thanks for your continued support.

WILLOWS PUBLISHING, 17 The Willows, Stone, Staffordshire ST15 0DE. Tel: 01785 814700; email: jenkins.willows@ntlworld.com; website: willowsreprints.com. *Wisden* reprints 1864–1946.

WISDEN DIRECT, website: wisden.com. Various editions of *Wisden Cricketers' Almanack* since 2001 and other Wisden publications, all at discounted prices.

WISDENS.ORG, Tel: 07793 060706; email: wisdens@cridler.com; website: wisdens.org; Twitter: @Wisdens. The unofficial *Wisden* collectors' website. Valuations, guide, discussion forum, all free to use. *Wisden* prices updated constantly. We also buy and sell *Wisdens* for our members. Email us for free advice about absolutely anything to do with collecting *Wisdens*.

WISDENWORLD.COM, Tel: 01480 819272; email: furmedgefamily@btinternet.com; website: wisdenworld.com. A unique and friendly service; quality *Wisdens* bought and sold at fair prices, along with free advice on the value of your collection. The UK's largest *Wisden*-only seller; licensed by Wisden.

AUCTIONEERS

CHRISTIE'S, 8 King Street, St. James's, London SW1Y 6QT. Tel: 0207 389 2674; email: rneelands@christies.com; website: christies.com. Christie's were MCC's auctioneer of choice in 1987 and again in 2010. Rare and valuable cricket books are the firm's speciality. For valuations of complete collections or single items, contact Rupert Neelands, a senior book specialist.

DOMINIC WINTER, Specialist Auctioneers & Valuers, Mallard House, Broadway Lane, South Cerney, Gloucestershire GL7 5UQ. Tel: 01285 860006; website: dominicwinter.co.uk. Check our website for forthcoming specialist sales.

GRAHAM BUDD AUCTIONS in association with Sotheby's, PO Box 47519, London N14 6XD. Tel: 020 8366 2525; website: grahambuddauctions.co.uk. Specialist auctioneer of sporting memorabilia.

KNIGHTS WISDEN, Norfolk. Tel: 01263 768488; email: tim@knights.co.uk; website: knightswisden.co.uk. Established and respected auctioneers. World-record *Wisden* prices achieved in 2007. Four major cricket/sporting memorabilia auctions per year including specialist *Wisden* sale in May. Entries invited.

WISDENAUCTION.COM. Tel: 0800 7 999 501; email:wisdenauction@cridler.com; website: wisdenauction.com. A specially designed auction website for buying and selling *Wisdens*. List your spares today and bid live for that missing year. Every original edition for sale including all hardbacks. Built by collectors for collectors, with the best descriptions on the internet. See advert on page 160.

CRICKET DATABASES

CRICKETARCHIVE: cricketarchive.com. The most comprehensive searchable database on the internet with scorecards of all first-class, List A, pro T20 and major women's matches, as well as a wealth of league and friendly matches. The database currently has more than 1.2m players and over 673,000 full and partial scorecards.

CSW DATABASE FOR PCs. Contact Ric Finlay, email: ricf@netspace.net.au; website: tastats.com.au. Men's and women's international, T20, Australian, NZ and English domestic. Full scorecards and 2,500 searches. Suitable for professionals and hobbyists alike.

WISDEN RECORDS: wisdenrecords.com. Up-to-date and in-depth cricket records from *Wisden*.

CRICKET COLLECTING, MEMORABILIA AND MUSEUMS

CRICKET MEMORABILIA SOCIETY. *See entry in Cricket Speakers and Societies section.*

LORD'S TOURS & MUSEUM, Lord's Cricket Ground, St John's Wood, London NW8 8QN. Tel: 020 7616 8595; email: tours@mcc.org.uk; website: lords.org/tours. A tour of Lord's provides a fascinating behind-the-scenes insight into the world's most famous cricket ground. See the original Ashes urn, plus an outstanding collection of art, cricketing memorabilia and much more.

SIR DONALD BRADMAN'S CHILDHOOD HOME, 52 Shepherd Street, Bowral, NSW 2576, Australia. Tel: (+61) 478 779 642; email: andrewleeming@mac.com; website: 52shepherdstreet.com.au. The house where Don Bradman developed his phenomenal cricketing skills by throwing a golf ball against the base of a tank stand. Open for visits, accommodation, and special events.

WILLOW STAMPS, 10 Mentmore Close, Harrow, Middlesex HA3 0EA. Tel: 020 8907 4200; email: willowstamps@tinyonline.co.uk. Standing order service for new cricket stamp issues, comprehensive back stocks of most earlier issues.

WISDEN COLLECTORS' CLUB: Tel: 01480 819272; email: furmedgefamily@btinternet.com; website: wisdencollectorsclub.co.uk. Free and completely impartial advice on *Wisdens*. We also offer *Wisdens* and other cricket books to our members, usually at no charge except postage. Quarterly newsletter, discounts on publications and a great website. Licensed by Wisden.

CRICKET EQUIPMENT

ACUMEN BOOKS, Pennyfields, New Road, Bignall End, Stoke-on-Trent ST7 8QF. Tel: 01782 720753; email: wca@acumenbooks.co.uk; website: acumenbooks.co.uk. Everything for umpires, scorers, officials, etc. MCC Lawbooks, open-learning manuals, Tom Smith and other textbooks, Duckworth/Lewis, scorebooks, equipment, over & run counters, gauges, heavy and Hi-Vis bails, etc; import/export.

ALL ROUNDER CRICKET, 39 St Michaels Lane, Headingley, Leeds LS6 3BR. Tel: 0113 203 3679; email: info@allroundercricket.com; website: allroundercricket.com. One of the UK's leading cricket retailers, stocking all the top brands, hand-picked by ex-professionals. Open every day, including our new megastore at the Penistone Road Trading Estate in Hillsborough, Sheffield. Also online with next day delivery available.

BOLA MANUFACTURING LTD, 6 Brookfield Road, Cotham, Bristol BS6 5PQ. Tel: 0117 924 3569; email: info@bola.co.uk; website: bola.co.uk. Manufacturer of bowling machines and ball-throwing machines for all sports. Machines for professional and all recreational levels for sale to the UK and overseas.

CHASE CRICKET, Dummer Down Farm, Basingstoke, Hampshire RG25 2AR. Tel: 01256 397499; email: info@chasecricket.co.uk; website: chasecricket.co.uk. Chase Cricket specialises in handmade bats and hi-tech soft goods. Established 1996. "Support British Manufacturing."

FORDHAM SPORTS, 81/85 Robin Hood Way, Kingston Vale, London SW15 3PW. Tel: 020 8974 5654; email: fordham@fordhamsports.co.uk; website: fordhamsports.co.uk. Cricket, hockey and rugby equipment specialist with largest range of branded stock in London at discounted prices. Mail order available.

CRICKET SPEAKERS AND SOCIETIES

COUNCIL OF CRICKET SOCIETIES, Secretary: Dave Taylor, 16 Leech Brook Close, Audenshaw, Manchester M34 5PL. Tel: 0161 336 8536; email: taylor_d2@sky.com; website: councilcricketsocieties.com. For cricket lovers in the winter – join a local society and enjoy speaker evenings with fellow enthusiasts for the summer game.

CRICKET MEMORABILIA SOCIETY, Honorary Secretary: Steve Cashmore, 4 Stoke Park Court, Stoke Road, Bishops Cleeve, Cheltenham, Gloucestershire GL52 8US. Email: cms87@btinternet.com; website: cricketmemorabilia.org. To promote and support the collection and appreciation of all cricket memorabilia. Four meetings annually at first-class grounds with two auctions. Meetings attended by former Test players. Regular members' magazine. Research and valuations undertaken.

LOOK WHO'S TALKING (Ian Holroyd), 20 Mill Street, Warwick, CV34 4HB. Tel: 01926 494323; mobile: 07831 602131; email: ian@look-whos-talking.co.uk; website: look-whos-talking.co.uk. A company specialising in providing first-class public speakers for cricket and other sporting events. Contact us to discuss the event and type of speaker. All budgets catered for.

THE CRICKET SOCIETY, c/o David Wood, Membership Secretary, PO Box 6024, Leighton Buzzard, LU7 2ZS. Email: david.wood@cricketsociety.com; website: cricketsociety.com. A worldwide society which promotes cricket through its awards, acclaimed publications, regular meetings, dinners and special events.

CRICKET TOUR OPERATORS

CRICTOURS – The Cricket Tour Company Ltd, Holmbury House, Skittle Green, Bledlow, Bucks HP27 9PJ. Tel: 01844 343 800; email: tours@crictours.com; website: crictours.com. CricTours is a family-owned company specialising in friendly, luxury, escorted cricket supporters' tours to follow the England team abroad.

GULLIVERS SPORTS TRAVEL, Fiddington Manor, Tewkesbury, Gloucestershire GL20 7BJ. Tel: 01684 879221; email: gullivers@gulliverstravel.co.uk; website: gulliverstravel.co.uk. The UK's longest-established cricket tour operator offers a great choice of supporter packages for the most exciting events around the world – including the Ashes – and playing tours for schools, clubs, military teams and universities.

SMILE GROUP TRAVEL LTD, Gateway House, Stonehouse Lane, Purfleet, Essex RM19 1NS. Tel: 01708 893250; email: info@smilegrouptravel.com; website: smilegrouptravel.com. Smile are experts in tours for both playing and supporters. We work with many professional clubs, including Hampshire, Northamptonshire, Nottinghamshire, etc. Our tours are defined by their excellence and value for money.

PITCHES AND GROUND EQUIPMENT

CRICKET CARPETS DIRECT, Standards House, Meridian East, Meridian Business Park, Leicester LE19 1WZ. Tel: 08702 400 700; email: sales@cricketcarpetsdirect.co.uk; website: cricketcarpetsdirect.co.uk. Installation and refurbishment of artificial cricket pitches. Save money. Top-quality carpets supplied and installed direct from the manufacturer. Over 20 years' experience. Nationwide service.

HUCK NETS (UK) LTD, Gore Cross Business Park, Corbin Way, Bradpole, Bridport, Dorset DT6 3UX. Tel: 01308 425100; email: sales@huckcricket.co.uk; website: huckcricket.co.uk. Alongside manufacturing our unique knotless high-quality polypropylene cricket netting, we offer the complete portfolio of ground and club equipment necessary for cricket clubs of all levels.

NOTTS SPORT, Innovation House, Magna Park, Lutterworth LE17 4XH. Tel: 01455 883730; email: info@nottssport.com; website: nottssport.com. Celebrating over 30 years as a leading supplier of ECB-approved, non-turf cricket pitch systems for coaching, practice and matchplay. Also awarded the ECB NTP Code of Practice Accreditation in 2013.

PLUVIUS, Willow Cottage, Canada Lane, Norton Lindsey, Warwick CV35 8JH. Tel: 07966 597203; email: pluviusltd@aol.com; website: pluvius.uk.com. Manufacturers of value-for-money pitch covers and sightscreens, currently used on Test, county, school and club grounds throughout the UK.

VERDE SPORTS (CRICKET) LTD, Gabbotts Farm Barn, Bury Lane, Withnell, PR6 8SW. Tel: 01254 831666; email: verdesports.cricket@ntlworld.com; website: verdesportscricket.com. With over 40 years' experience, including involvement in the development of all available cricket pitch systems, the company offers two ECB-approved base systems and a range of surfaces.

CHRONICLE OF 2016

JANUARY

3 Ben Stokes hits 258 from 198 balls, with 11 sixes, for England against South Africa at Cape Town. **5** Mumbai schoolboy Pranav Dhanawade scores 1,009 not out, the highest in any organised match. **6** Hashim Amla steps down as South Africa's captain, despite making 201 in drawn Second Test. **7** West Indies draw rain-affected Third Test at Sydney, but Australia win series 2–0. **14 Former South African one-day batsman Gulam Bodi is charged with contriving to fix domestic matches; later banned for 20 years.** **15** Pakistan fast bowler Mohammad Amir returns to international cricket after five-year ban, in Twenty20 match in New Zealand. **16** Stuart Broad takes six for 17 as South Africa are bowled out for 83 at Johannesburg; England win by seven wickets to clinch the series; and India go top of Test rankings. **18** Chris Gayle hits record-equalling 12-ball fifty, with seven sixes, in a Big Bash match in Melbourne. **20** Galle groundsman (and former Sri Lankan Test bowler) Jayananda Warnaweera is suspended for three years for failing to co-operate with ICC match-fixing enquiry. **23** West Indies' most-capped Test player Shivnarine Chanderpaul, 41, confirms international retirement. Former player and commentator Jack Bannister dies, aged 85. **24** Sydney Thunder win the Big Bash. **26** South Africa win Fourth Test at Centurion by 280 runs, Stephen Cook scoring a century on debut, and Kagiso Rabada claiming 13 wickets – but England take series 2–1. **29** Graham Ford appointed Sri Lanka's coach, for a second time.

FEBRUARY

1 Pakistan's oldest Test cricketer Israr Ali dies, aged 88. **4** ICC announce review of 2014 Big Three restructuring. **10** MCC reveal plans to trial red and yellow cards for player misbehaviour. **14** West Indies win Under-19 World Cup. Adam Voges lifts his average above 100 after making 239 in First Test against New Zealand at Wellington; Australia win by an innings. South Africa take one-day series against England 3–2, after being 2–0 down. **17** Andy Ganteaume, who scored 112 in his only Test innings for West Indies, dies, aged 95. **20 In his final match, Brendon McCullum hits the fastest Test century, in 54 balls, at Christchurch; but Australia claim series 2–0, and go top of rankings.** **26** Mumbai win India's Ranji Trophy for 41st time.

MARCH

3 Former New Zealand batsman Martin Crowe dies of cancer, aged 53. **9** Oman beat Ireland in World Twenty20 in India. **16** Gayle hits 47-ball hundred as West Indies overpower England. **18** England stay alive after overhauling South Africa's 229. **21** Guyana clinch West Indies' domestic title. **23** India complete one-run victory over Bangladesh, who lose wickets from the final three balls. **30** England beat New Zealand to reach World T20 final. Victoria win Sheffield Shield final in Adelaide. **31** West Indies beat India to reach World T20 final.

APRIL

3 Carlos Brathwaite smashes four sixes in Ben Stokes's last over as West Indies win the World Twenty20; their women win too. **4** Waqar Younis resigns as Pakistan's coach. **12 Nottinghamshire and England batsman James Taylor forced to retire by serious heart condition.** **18** Inzamam-ul-Haq appointed Pakistan's chairman of selectors. **20** Hong Kong batsman Irfan Ahmed suspended for 30 months for breach of ICC's Anti-Corruption Code. **28** Kane Williamson confirmed as New Zealand captain, succeeding McCullum.

MAY

6 Mickey Arthur appointed coach of Pakistan. **11 England's long-serving captain Charlotte Edwards announces international retirement.** West Indian broadcaster Tony Cozier dies, aged 75. **21** England win First Test against Sri Lanka at Headingley inside three days. **29** Sunrisers Hyderabad win IPL for the first time. **30** Alastair Cook reaches 10,000 runs as England win Second Test at Chester-le-Street. **31** Jimmy Anderson goes top of Test bowling rankings for first time.

JUNE

3 Heather Knight appointed England women's captain. **6** Nottinghamshire hit 445 for eight, the second-highest List A total, against Northamptonshire. **8** Notts make 415 for eight v Worcestershire. **11** Donald Carr, former England captain and administrator, dies, aged 89. **13** England beat Sri Lanka 2–0 after rain-affected Lord's Test is drawn. **21 Liam Plunkett's last-ball six ties first ODI against Sri Lanka, at Nottingham.** **23** Anil Kumble appointed India's coach. **26** Australia beat West Indies in final at Bridgetown to win one-day tri-series also involving South Africa.

JULY

12 MCC's world cricket committee call for restriction on thickness of bats. **14** Hampshire and England opener Michael Carberry diagnosed with cancer. **17 Glamorgan's teenager Aneurin Donald, equals world record with 123-ball double-century against Derbyshire at Colwyn Bay.** Pakistan, for whom Misbah-ul-Haq scores a century and Yasir Shah takes ten wickets, win First Test at Lord's by 75 runs. **18** Marcus Trescothick scores 49th first-class century for Somerset, equalling Harold Gimblett's county record. **19** In their first match at Lord's, Nepal beat MCC. **21** Middlesex's T20 Blast match against Surrey at Lord's draws record crowd of 27,119. **24** India win First Test in Antigua, after Virat Kohli scores 200. **25** England level series against Pakistan with 330-run victory at Manchester, Joe Root making 254. **30** Australia fail to save First Test against Sri Lanka at Pallekele, despite batting through 25 successive maidens on final day.

AUGUST

3 Second Test in Jamaica is drawn. **5** Rangana Herath takes hat-trick as Australia are bowled out for 106 in Second Test at Galle; Sri Lanka win by 229 runs next day. **7** England take 2–1 lead after winning Third Test against Pakistan at Birmingham. **9** Carlos Brathwaite named West Indies' T20 captain. **10** New Zealand win Second Test in Zimbabwe to complete 2–0 sweep. **11 Pakistan batsman Hanif Mohammad dies, aged 81.** **14** Pakistan win Fourth Test at The Oval as series is drawn 2–2. **17** Sri Lanka complete 3–0 whitewash of Australia in Colombo, Herath taking 13 wickets. **20** Northamptonshire beat Durham in T20 Blast final. **21** Southern Vipers, led by Charlotte Edwards, win inaugural women's English T20 Super League. **22** Inadequate covering condemns Fourth Test in Trinidad to a draw: India beat West Indies 2–0, but Pakistan go top of the rankings. **25** ECB confirm England will tour Bangladesh in October, despite security concerns. **27** In Florida, West Indies beat India by the odd run in 489 – a T20 international record. **30** England make an ODI-record 444 for three – Alex Hales 171 – against Pakistan at Nottingham. South Africa beat New Zealand by 204 runs in Second Test at Centurion (the First was a soggy draw).

SEPTEMBER

5 The world's oldest Test cricketer, 97-year-old Lindsay Tuckett, dies in South Africa. **6** Peter Moores appointed Nottinghamshire coach. **12** England's limited-overs captain Eoin Morgan declines to tour Bangladesh; Hales follows suit. **13** Phil Simmons sacked as West Indies coach. **15** Essex clinch Championship second division, and promotion. **17** Warwickshire win Royal London Cup final. **23 Toby Roland-Jones's hat-trick against Yorkshire at Lord's clinches Middlesex's first Championship since 1993.** **26** India win First Test against New Zealand by 197 runs at Kanpur. **28** Australian seamer Max Walker dies, aged 68.

OCTOBER

3 Durham are relegated from Championship first division for running up huge debts; Hampshire stay up. India win Second Test at Kolkata by 178 runs. **5** Pakistan beat West Indies 3–0 in ODI series, Babar Azam scoring a century in each game. **8** Australian mystery spinner John Gleeson dies, aged 78. **11** India complete 3–0 Test sweep over New Zealand at Indore. England win ODI series in Bangladesh 2–1. **12** South Africa round off 5–0 whitewash of Australia (their first such defeat in any format) in home ODI series. **14** Azhar Ali reaches 302 not out in the first day/night Test in Dubai; Pakistan go on to beat West Indies by 56 runs. **20** Australia clinch ICC women's championship. **21** India agree to use DRS in series against England. **24** England complete narrow victory over Bangladesh in First Test, at Chittagong. **25** Pakistan take series against West Indies by winning Second Test in Abu Dhabi. **30 Bangladesh square series with their first Test win over England, by 108 runs inside three days at Mirpur.**

NOVEMBER

2 Sri Lanka win First Test at Harare, Zimbabwe's 100th. **3** Ian Botham becomes Durham's chairman. West Indies win Third Test against Pakistan in Sharjah. **4** Sydney coroner clears players and umpires of blame in death of Phillip Hughes in 2014. **7** South Africa win First Test in Australia by 177 runs at Perth. Former England all-rounder Craig White appointed Hampshire coach. **8** Mohammad Amir signs for Essex in 2017. **10** Herath takes 13 wickets as Sri Lanka win Second Test in Zimbabwe for 2–0 victory. **12 Darren Bravo sent home from West Indies' tour of Zimbabwe after calling WI board president a "big idiot".** Australia bowled out for 85 on first day of Second Test at Hobart; South Africa go on to win series. **13** England finish four wickets short of victory over India in First Test at Rajkot. **14** Andrew Gale succeeds Jason Gillespie as Yorkshire's coach, and steps down as captain. **16** Rod Marsh resigns as Australia's chairman of selectors after Hobart defeat. Former national captain Debbie Hockley is elected New Zealand Cricket's first female president. **19** Zimbabwe and West Indies tie ODI in Bulawayo. **20** New Zealand win First Test against Pakistan at Christchurch by eight wickets. **21** India beat England by 246 runs in Second Test at Visakhapatnam. **22** South African captain Faf du Plessis fined, after TV cameras showed him sucking a mint and applying saliva to the ball. Ex-England rugby international Rob Andrew appointed chief executive of Sussex. **25** Former South African captain Trevor Goddard dies, aged 85. **27** Australia win day/night Test at Adelaide, but South Africa take series 2–1. **29** India go 2–0 up on England with eight-wicket victory at Mohali. New Zealand take nine Pakistan wickets in final session to win Second Test at Hamilton.

DECEMBER

8 Keaton Jennings makes century on debut – but England lose Fourth Test at Mumbai after Virat Kohli replies with 235. **12** A. B. de Villiers resigns as South Africa's Test captain. **15** Gary Ballance named Yorkshire captain. **19** Australia win day/night First Test at Brisbane, after Pakistan fall 40 short of target of 490. With Karun Nair making 303 not out, India reach 759 for seven – their highest total – against England at Chennai; next day they complete 4–0 series victory. **21 South Africa's Alviro Petersen banned for two years for failing to report match-fixing approaches.** **27** Ashley Giles returns to Warwickshire as director of cricket. **30** Pakistan collapse in Second Test at Melbourne to hand victory – and 2–0 series lead – to Australia. South Africa beat Sri Lanka by 206 runs in First Test at Port Elizabeth. **31** Imtiaz Ahmed, who played in all Pakistan's first 39 Test matches, dies, aged 88.

The following items were also reported during 2016:

PRESS TRUST OF INDIA January 3

Two boys aged 16 and 11 were electrocuted, and six others injured, inside a tent being used as a commentary box at a match near Jamnagar in Gujarat. Police said it appeared organisers had illegally tapped into the main power line, and the current had passed through the metal in the tent.

THE GUARDIAN January 4/5

West Indian batsman Chris Gayle asked an Australian TV news reporter for a date while being interviewed live on air. After scoring 41 off 15 balls for Melbourne Renegades in the Big Bash League, he told Network Ten journalist Mel McLaughlin he had played well just so she would interview him. "Your eyes are beautiful. Hopefully we can win this game and then we can have a drink after as well," Gayle told her. "Don't blush, baby." A chorus of anger was led by McLaughlin, who said female sports journalists should be treated as professionals: "We want equality, we always want equality." Gayle, who was later fined, said: "It was just a joke."

SYDNEY MORNING HERALD January 11

Shane Warne agreed to close his charity, the Shane Warne Foundation, to avoid the possibility of its being deregistered after an 11-month investigation by Victoria state officials. Since 2011, the foundation had recorded that 11–32% of funds raised was being sent to sick and underprivileged children, contravening guidelines that suggested 35% as a minimum.

TIMES OF INDIA January 16

Thirty-three aspiring cricketers, some travelling long distances across India, were conned into turning up for nets in the hope of getting a place in Rajkot's new IPL team. They had responded to messages on Facebook instructing them to send sums of up to 3,000 rupees (£36) for the right to attend the trials.

ESPNCRICINFO February 2

Madhya Pradesh dropped all-rounder Rameez Khan from their Ranji Trophy squad after he was arrested for allegedly killing a blackbuck – an antelope protected in India – on a shooting expedition with his father.

OTAGO DAILY TIMES/BBC WORLD SERVICE February 8/20

Eight-year-old Luke Marsh from Dunedin dismissed six batsmen in an over, all bowled, for Kaikorai. He never got the chance for more because the opposition, Taieri, were all out for one in two overs. "It didn't seem real when the ball kept hitting the wickets," Luke's mum Michelle said. It was Luke's first year of hard-ball cricket, having started playing when he was five. Asked by the BBC if he had always been good, he replied: "Hmm… yeah."

BBC February 11

Bapchild in Kent were dismissed for nought in 20 balls in a six-a-side indoor match (no not-out batsman) against Canterbury Christ Church University. "All they needed to do was hit a wall to get one run," said opponent Mike Rose.

THE GUARDIAN February 12

The winner of a $A60,000 Mercedes in a 2015 raffle held by the Shane Warne Foundation, Helen Nolan, was a former general manager of the charity – and Warne's personal assistant between 2005 and 2014. Victorian regulations prohibit only current employees from taking part in charity raffles; a spokesman said the connection was disclosed at the time of the draw. It was also reported that in one financial year the foundation distributed $54,600 to beneficiaries, while paying the chief executive, Warne's brother Jason, a salary of $80,000.

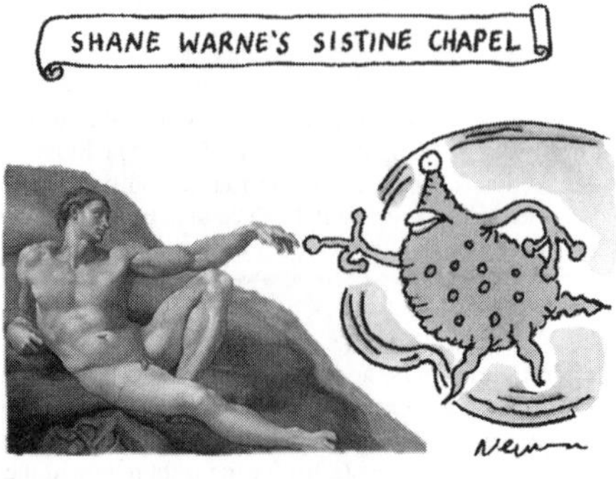

THE GUARDIAN February 15

Shane Warne put forward the theory that humans are descended from extra-terrestrials. He was taking part in the Australian version of *I'm a Celebrity… Get Me Out of Here*, and musing with a fellow contestant, dancer Bonnie Lythgoe, while in the Kruger National Park. Why, he wondered, had the local monkey population not evolved into humans? "Because, I'm saying, aliens. We started from aliens."

MUMBAI MIRROR February 20

Pritam Patil of PYC Hindu Gymkhana hit 306 from 134 balls in a 50-over game in the Maharashtra Cricket Association senior invitation league. PYC scored 594 for six, and beat Nanded by 508 runs. Six of Patil's 36 sixes resulted in lost balls.

CRICKET-ON-ICE.COM February 21

Play was delayed for 20 minutes in the 29th Cricket on Ice tournament in St Moritz because one of the competing teams had forgotten to bring the nails needed to secure the matting.

THE TELEGRAPH, KOLKATA February 23

Nava Nalanda High School beat Gyan Bharati Vidyapith by 812 runs in the Mayor's Cup inter-school tournament. Nava Nalanda made 844 for two in 38 overs, which included 227 penalty runs for a slow over-rate. Second top-scorer was Sreyas Banerjee with 193. Their opponents were all out for 32.

THE AGE, MELBOURNE February 29

Kingsville Baptist CC lost their chance of reaching the semi-finals of the Victorian Turf Cricket Association tournament when the pitch was vandalised. They arrived for the second day of their match against Sunshine, strongly placed to win and finish in the top four, only to find the surface had been dug

DARLING, I'VE BOUGHT US A LOVELY GRADE II LISTED PROPERTY!

March 3

up and covered with oil. No alternative could be found, and Kingsville missed qualification by two points. Sunshine were already out of the running, so suspicion fell on the other contending teams. "It would be hugely disappointing to find out it is someone from the cricket family," said Cricket Victoria chief executive Tony Dodemaide, "but that is the direction it is pointing at the moment."

BBC — March 3

The gasometer outside The Oval, the largest in the world when it was built in 1847, has been given a heritage listing with Grade II status.

BBC — March 11

Shane Warne told critics of his charity he had nothing to hide. "You can all get stuffed if you want to have a go at us for it, but we are very, very proud," he told an interviewer. "It's really disappointing that people want to come after some good people that have raised a lot of money and made a serious difference to seriously underprivileged children."

DAILY NEWS, COLOMBO — March 21

Four students were suspended for five weeks from Rajarata University for playing cricket in front of the main administrative building during college hours. They were said to have interfered with university administration, and damaged vehicles and flowers.

DAILY TELEGRAPH March 24

Scientists have found that batsmen who bat "the wrong way round" have an advantage over players who use traditional methods. Professor Peter Allen of Anglia Ruskin University said that instinctively right-handed or left-handed players who learn to face the bowling the other way, with their dominant hand at the top, have technical and visual advantages. Professor Allen said the same effect may be true in golf and baseball.

THE SUN April 5

Former England fast bowler Steve Harmison has been given a 12-match touchline ban in his role as manager of Northern League football team Ashington. Harmison confronted the referee after one of his players was sent off in a 1–0 defeat by Bishop Auckland.

EXPRESS & STAR, WOLVERHAMPTON April 22

A petition with 1,100 signatures has reached parliament to protest against the National Trust's decision to evict local cricket and football teams from Shugborough Hall, Staffordshire. The Trust has recently taken over the ancestral home of the Earls of Lichfield and its 900-acre estate, and want to return it to grazing land. Milford Hall CC are among the victims.

MAIL ONLINE April 20

Former West Indian Test fast bowler Tino Best said in his autobiography that he had slept with "between 500 and 650" women. "I reckon I'm the best-looking bald guy in the world," he explained.

ESPNcricinfo April 29

Two sons of Test umpire Aleem Dar led to Kilmarnock being demoted from the first division of the Western District Union in Scotland after they were found to have made false claims about their eligibility. They registered under pseudonyms, and said they were born in Glasgow rather than Pakistan.

Press Trust of India May 1

Cricket teams in the Kashmir Valley are causing political concerns because they are being named after militants opposed to India's control of the disputed region. "If this practice is not nipped in the bud, it can create a huge problem in coming months and years," said a security official. "The psyche of the impressionable minds is sought to be influenced."

Peterborough Telegraph May 10

The former Sussex player, Joe Gatting – nephew of Mike – hit six sixes in an over for Swardeston, Norfolk in the National Club Cup. His victim was left-arm seamer Tim Willis, of Huntingdonshire team Ramsey. Gatting scored 160 not out in a 220-run win.

Daily Mirror May 10

Danny Morrison, the former New Zealand cricketer turned commentator, wore a red turban and fake beard when he oversaw the toss in an IPL match in the majority-Sikh city of Mohali. The stunt was widely criticised as insulting, but Morrison insisted he was asked to dress up by the broadcasters, Sony TV. The president of the New Zealand Indian Central Association, Bhikhu Bhana, was supportive: "Cricket can open bridges really, and I think Danny tries to do it sometimes. Look at the crowds there. They're having a good time. From my point of view, I can see nothing culturally offensive from Danny Morrison."

Cricketeurope.com May 11

Off-spinner Rahul Gondhia claimed eight for nought for Campbell College, Belfast, in a 20-over Under-14 match against Dungannon Royal School, who were bowled out for 12. He took them in 18 balls, including a hat-trick, before team-mate Charlie Maskery seized the last two.

The Times May 12

A mining company founded by former England cricketer Phil Edmonds is said to have paid "hundreds of thousands of pounds in alleged bribes" to try to secure a concession in Liberia. The campaign group Global Witness said they had acquired documents implicating Sable Mining, which Edmonds chaired until 2014, in payments to officials. "We have found no evidence to support or justify this attack on the company or its directors, past or present," said Sable's current chairman, Jim Cochrane.

INDEPENDENT.CO.UK May 13

Rwanda's captain Eric Dusingizimana became the latest holder of the world net-batting marathon record by totting up a 51-hour stint in Kigali, the capital. Bowlers included Tony Blair, who happened to be passing. The aim was to raise awareness of Rwandan cricket – and money for a stadium. Dusingizimana was allowed a five-minute break every hour for essential services.

THE NATION, PAKISTAN/THE SPIN May 15/24

National Accountability Bureau sources in Pakistan said officials were investigating a scam involving a fake Belgian team touring the country. However, the Belgian Cricket Federation insisted the visit was genuine. The Federation chairman, Sanjay Vaid, said the allegations were an attempt to smear the Punjab sports and education minister, Rana Mashud, who had helped organise the trip. "We did send a team, a Belgian XI," said Vaid. "I can't call them a national team. But many of them were senior players, and all were eligible to represent Belgium as per the ICC regulations."

BBC May 19

Somerset director of cricket Matthew Maynard has passed his Public Service Vehicle test and is now allowed to drive the team bus. He said he would be able to help out on long journeys and so avoid having to stop and collect another driver.

TIMES OF INDIA May 28

Police in Kanpur are looking for a man alleged to have gambled – and lost – his wife after using her as his stake betting on an IPL match. He was said to have run through all his money in previous bets.

YORKSHIRE POST June 6

Yorkshire coach Jason Gillespie, who became vegan in 2014, said he regretted that Wensleydale Creamery sponsored the club. "Yes, they are a sponsor," he said. "But it doesn't mean I agree with what they do. It's out of my control, just like the fact that cricket balls are made of leather." He added: "Hopefully one day the dairy industry can be shut down. I think it's disgusting and wrong on so many levels."

DEREHAM TIMES/EASTERN DAILY PRESS June 17/30

Will Dewing took hat-tricks in successive weeks for Bradenham in the Norfolk Alliance. In the following game Alex Bates achieved the same feat for the same team. (See also August 16.)

THE TIMES July 1

Several counties are using breathalysers to check whether their players are too drunk to play. Ten counties have been issued with the kits for educational purposes, but some have used them to check up on possible binge-drinking.

MAIL ON SUNDAY/CHRISTIES.COM July 3/13

Commentator Henry Blofeld sold one of Charlie Chaplin's canes at auction to raise money to go travelling with his wife. The cane, previously on display at Blofeld's Chelsea home, is thought to have been used in the 1936 film *Modern Times*, and had been expected to fetch £6,000–9,000. It made £18,750.

HUDDERSFIELD DAILY EXAMINER July 7

A Twenty20 match at Denby Dale against fellow Huddersfield League team Almondbury Wesleyans was abandoned after an Almondbury outfielder allegedly attacked a home spectator. They conceded the match, and the player was suspended, though cricket manager Mark Binns said the police were "not involved to my knowledge," and added: "This is a sporting matter."

ESSEX CHRONICLE July 15

Mike Jones, 45, said he was "living the dream" after being chosen as Essex's latest Eddie the Eagle mascot. Jones, who works for Tesco, was given the job after telling the club that he and his girlfriend Cheryl had dressed up as the Cookie Monster and Elmo from *Sesame Street* for a 1970s weekend at Butlins.

ROTHERHAM ADVERTISER July 29

South African Shawn Dyson hit 40 in an over for Wath against Conisborough in the South Yorkshire Senior League. He struck sixes from the first six balls, one of them a no-ball; the seventh fell inches short. He finished with an unbeaten 151 off 68.

DAILY NEWS, SRI LANKA August 2

A 16-year-old boy in Ambalangoda hanged himself after his parents refused him permission to attend a cricket match, saying he needed to study.

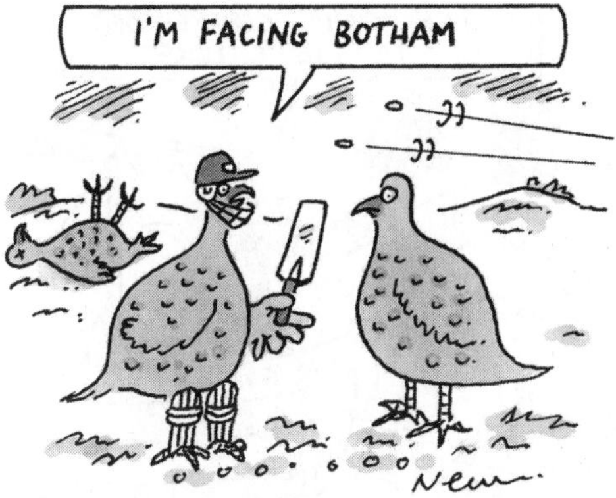

THEGUARDIAN.COM August 12

Sir Ian Botham, in his role as a shooting enthusiast, clashed with BBC wildlife presenter Chris Packham on the Radio 4 *Today* programme on the day the grouse-shooting season began – the "inglorious twelfth" as Packham called it. "It's the gamekeepers who look after the moors," said Botham, who is the figurehead for a campaign group called You Forgot the Birds. "It's only people like Chris that want to sabotage nature by banning success." Packham said grouse moors were ecologically damaged, and endangered birds of prey were being killed by gamekeepers to keep grouse numbers high.

EASTERN DAILY PRESS August 16

Patrick Dewing and Steven Matthews broke the 27-year-old opening partnership record for Bradenham, Norfolk, with 228 against Swardeston B. The previous record, 180, had been set by the same two batsmen in 1989.

MIRROR.CO.UK August 23

A barn owl stopped play when it landed on the stumps in the match between Castle Eden and Seaham Park in County Durham. The owl was a pet called Shadow, and had squeezed through the bars of an aviary. Shadow was reunited with his owner, Steven Franklin, after pictures of him appeared on Facebook. "He's really tame, and he wouldn't know how to catch food for himself in the wild," Franklin said.

DAILY TELEGRAPH August 29

The Keeling family fielded an all-Keeling team for the first time in their annual August Bank Holiday fixture against Sedlescombe in Sussex. They had

August 23

previously come agonisingly close, but were forced to draft in a cousin with a different name. This time four brothers and their seven sons, aged between 59 and 18, achieved their ambition – and won the match. The game is the legacy of Sir John Keeling, who first mustered a family-led team to take on the village before the war, and has been held regularly since its resumption in 1965. "I'm one of eight brothers, so there are quite a lot of first cousins lurking about," said captain Paul Keeling.

DAILY MIRROR, COLOMBO September 25

A 15-year-old bowler, Malinda Nandana Lakshan, died near the Sri Lankan town of Mathugama, after allegedly being clubbed by a 14-year-old batsman, in a dispute over a wide.

RYE & BATTLE OBSERVER September 30

Battle CC marked the 950th anniversary of the Norman Conquest by welcoming a team of French Barbarians, restricted to French-born players, to compete for the Guillaume Trophy. The French lost this time, but creditably.

AUSTRALIAN ASSOCIATED PRESS October 6

Austin Waugh, son of Steve, scored an unbeaten century for Metro New South Wales in the final of the national Under-17 championship against Queensland.

INDIAN EXPRESS October 17

Among the questions in a PE theory exam at a high school in Bhiwandi, Maharashtra, was: "What is Virat Kohli's girlfriend's name?"

FOX SPORTS AUSTRALIA October 18

The pitch for the Premier League match in Melbourne between St Kilda and Footscray Edgewater was eight feet too long, a fact not discovered until after the match, although several players had been puzzled. "Things make sense now," said St Kilda coach Glenn Lalor. "I thought we bowled too short, and I think we bowled 27 wides." The job of preparing the ground at Harry Trott Oval is outsourced to a "curation company", which apologised for what it called "an embarrassing situation".

MID-DAY October 25

After rumours of his death circulated on social media, Farokh Engineer denied them by issuing a message: "Friends, I am alive and kicking. I am very well and let me tell you I don't even need Viagra at 78."

DAILY NEWS, COLOMBO November 1

Mithira Thenwara, captain of the Under-13s at his school, Tissa MMV, took five wickets in five balls against Kalutara Vidyalaya.

BOLTON NEWS November 2

Farnworth CC continued their tradition of burning topical effigies as Bonfire Night guys... by choosing a cricketer. As ever, groundsman Jack Greasley, who has previously chosen crooked MPs, fat-cat bankers and the irritating opera singer from the Go Compare advert, made the decision. "This year, our senior squad were in two major finals and came away with no trophies at all, so there were a lot of disappointed people," explained Greasley. "Because of that, I thought we would burn a cricketer. I do like being a little bit controversial, and it has certainly got people talking."

THE ISLAND, SRI LANKA November 2

Former Sri Lankan captain Mahela Jayawardene walked the length of Sri Lanka – his route took him more than 400 miles – and raised 750m rupees (£4m) for a cancer unit at a hospital in Galle. The walk took a month, in which time he was joined by several leading players. Jayawardene's brother died of cancer 20 years ago.

STUFF.CO.NZ November 8

New Zealand's Broadcasting Standards Authority ordered a radio station to pay $NZ8,000 compensation to Ben Stokes's mother Deborah. She had rung Radio Hauraki to complain about comments made concerning her son's infamous last over in the World Twenty20 final, and found herself talking to presenter Matt Heath, who omitted to mention that they were live on air.

MID-DAY, MUMBAI November 19

Two Mumbai schoolboy openers shared an unbroken partnership of 425 in the Harris Shield. Shrevan Pai had scored 215 and Aryan More 161 when the allotted 45 overs were up. They led Parle Tilak English Medium School to a 302-run win over Cambridge ICSE, Kandivili.

THE GUARDIAN November 22

A councillor in Westbury, Tasmania (population: 1,500), has suggested changing the name of the local cricket ground to the Donald J. Trump Park. "It is in our best interests to extend the hand of friendship to the new president of the United States, who is not a politician and will likely come at things from a different perspective," said councillor John Temple. The response, Temple said later, had been mixed. "The personal conversations I have had have all been positive," he said, but "I have seen things on Facebook calling me an idiot."

ESPNCRICINFO November 22

Three Channel 9 commentators – Shane Warne, Kevin Pietersen and Michael Slater – have each been fined $A300 by Tasmanian police for failing to wear seatbelts. The three were recording a close-of-play update from a car, and were issued with infringement notices after police saw the video on Facebook.

DNA INDIA November 24

In a Tasmanian Under-17 match, Adrian Butterworth of Clarence took five wickets in an over – without managing a hat-trick. He bowled three wides and

a no-ball between the wickets, as well as conceding two from the first ball. Glenorchy still totalled only 23, and Clarence won by 102 runs.

BBC November 24

Coach Gary Kirsten is offering batting tips on the social media platform WhatsApp. Batsmen are invited to send him videos of their technique in exchange for comments by Kirsten. He said 80% of the videos came from India.

ESPNcricinfo December 12

Shania-Lee Swart hit a match-winning 160 while her team-mates contributed no runs between them. Mpumalanga Under-19s made 169 for nine in their Twenty20 match against Easterns at a tournament in Pretoria, but the other nine runs were all extras. Swart hit 18 fours and 12 sixes. In a 50-over game three days earlier, she had scored 289 of her team's 352. "Shania is strong," said her father Baltus. "The bad balls she can hit far; the good balls she can drive down the ground."

Mid-Day, Mumbai December 17

Suryansh Shedge, 13, made a triple-century in a 45-over Giles Shield match in Mumbai. Shedge hit an unbeaten 326 out of a total of 542 for five, as Gundecha Academy won by 487 runs.

Press Trust of India December 18

Pranav Dhanawade, who earlier in the year made the first recorded four-figure individual score at the age of 15, was allegedly involved in a brawl with police after trying to prevent a ground where he was playing cricket being used as a helipad for the visit of a government minister. Dhanawade was taken to the police station and given a warning. After hearing of the incident, the minister, Prakash Javadekar, decided to travel by car. "It is not proper for me to use the playgrounds as helipad," he said.

DAILY NEWS, COLOMBO December 31

Piliyandala Central College won a Singer Trophy Under-19 inter-schools cricket match against Madampa MMV by an innings and 550 runs. Piliyandala scored 648 for three; Madampa were dismissed for 47 and 51.

INDEX OF ADVERTISEMENTS

10 for 10 . . . 927
All Out Cricket . . . 268
Benaud in Wisden . . . 148
Christopher Saunders . . . 122
Cricket Archive . . . 1216
The Cricketer . . . 542
The Cricket Society . . . 139
Cricketing Allsorts . . . 372
Daily Mail . . . 146
DD Designs . . . 258
Edging Towards Darkness . . . 654
Elk Stopped Play . . . 1164
ESPNcricinfo . . . 168
The Essential Wisden . . . 1039
Find *Wisden* online . . . 626
Following On . . . 134
Gilbert . . . 997
The Great Tamasha . . . 792
Half-time . . . 849
Herding Cats . . . 140
J. W. McKenzie . . . endpapers
Leatherbound *Wisdens* . . . 163
The Little Wonder . . . 612
MCC . . . 276
The Nightwatchman . . . 120
The Shorter Wisden . . . 541
Sir Donald Bradman's Childhood Home . . . endpapers
Smile Travel Group . . . 362
Sportspages . . . 126
St Mary's Books . . . 130
The Strangers Who Came Home . . . 1533
Subscribe to *Wisden* . . . endpapers
Tendulkar in Wisden . . . 792
The Times . . . 142
William Hill . . . 288
Willows *Wisden* reprints . . . 158
Wisden at The Oval . . . 584
Wisden Book of Test Cricket . . . 1224
Wisden coaching books . . . 1480
Wisden Collector's Guide . . . 1489
Wisden Cricketers of the Year . . . 1454
Wisden dust jackets . . . endpapers
Wisden India . . . 911
Wisden on Grace . . . 1069
Wisden on the Great War . . . 740
WisdenAuction.com . . . 160
Wisdenworld.com . . . 164

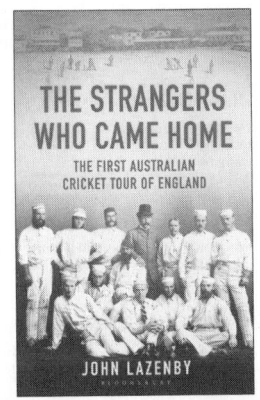

INDEX OF TEST MATCHES

Eight earlier Test series – Sri Lanka v India, Pakistan v England, Sri Lanka v West Indies, Australi v New Zealand, India v South Africa, New Zealand v Sri Lanka, Australia v West Indies, Sout Africa v England – appeared in *Wisden 2016.*

Pag

NEW ZEALAND v AUSTRALIA IN 2015-16

February 12–15	Wellington	Australia won by an innings and 52 runs	95
February 20–24	Christchurch	Australia won by seven wickets	95

ENGLAND v SRI LANKA IN 2016

May 19–21	Leeds	England won by an innings and 88 runs......	26
May 27–30	Chester-le-Street	England won by nine wickets	27
June 9–13	Lord's	Drawn	27

ENGLAND v PAKISTAN IN 2016

July 14–17	Lord's	Pakistan won by 75 runs	29
July 22–25	Manchester	England won by 330 runs	30
August 3–7	Birmingham	England won by 141 runs	30
August 11–14	The Oval	Pakistan won by ten wickets	31

WEST INDIES v INDIA IN 2016

July 21–24	North Sound	India won by an innings and 92 runs	1093
July 30–August 3	Kingston	Drawn..........................	1095
August 9–13	Gros Islet	India won by 237 runs	1096
August 18–22	Port-of-Spain	Drawn..........................	1098

SRI LANKA v AUSTRALIA IN 2016

July 26–30	Pallekele	Sri Lanka won by 106 runs...............	1057
August 4–6	Galle	Sri Lanka won by 229 runs...............	1059
August 13–17	Colombo (SSC)	Sri Lanka won by 163 runs...............	1061

ZIMBABWE v NEW ZEALAND IN 2016

July 28–31	Bulawayo	New Zealand won by an innings and 117 runs	1113
August 6–10	Bulawayo	New Zealand won by 254 runs............	1114

SOUTH AFRICA v NEW ZEALAND IN 2016

August 19–23	Durban	Drawn..........................	1013
August 27–30	Centurion	South Africa won by 204 runs	1014

INDIA v NEW ZEALAND IN 2016-17

September 22–26	Kanpur	India won by 197 runs...................	917
September 30–October 3	Kolkata	India won by 178 runs...................	919
October 8–11	Indore	India won by 321 runs...................	921

Page

PAKISTAN v WEST INDIES IN 2016-17

ber 13–17 (d/n)	Dubai	Pakistan won by 56 runs	991
ber 21–25	Abu Dhabi	Pakistan won by 133 runs	993
ber 30–November 3	Sharjah	West Indies won by five wickets	995

BANGLADESH v ENGLAND IN 2016-17

October 20–24	Chittagong	England won by 22 runs	333
October 28–30	Mirpur	Bangladesh won by 108 runs	337

ZIMBABWE v SRI LANKA IN 2016-17

October 29–November 2	Harare	Sri Lanka won by 225 runs	1118
November 6–10	Harare	Sri Lanka won by 257 runs	1119

AUSTRALIA v SOUTH AFRICA IN 2016-17

November 3–7	Perth	South Africa won by 177 runs	853
November 12–15	Hobart	South Africa won by an innings and 80 runs	856
November 24–27 (d/n)	Adelaide	Australia won by seven wickets	858

INDIA v ENGLAND IN 2016-17

November 9–13	Rajkot	Drawn	350
November 17–21	Visakhapatnam	India won by 246 runs	354
November 26–29	Mohali	India won by eight wickets	357
December 8–12	Mumbai	India won by an innings and 36 runs	363
December 16–20	Chennai	India won by an innings and 75 runs	367

NEW ZEALAND v PAKISTAN IN 2016-17

November 17–20	Christchurch	New Zealand won by eight wickets	962
November 25–29	Hamilton	New Zealand won by 138 runs	964

AUSTRALIA v PAKISTAN IN 2016-17

December 15–19 (d/n)	Brisbane	Australia won by 39 runs	866
December 26–30	Melbourne	Australia won by an innings and 18 runs	869
January 3–7	Sydney	Australia won by 220 runs	870

SOUTH AFRICA v SRI LANKA IN 2016-17

December 26–30	Port Elizabeth	South Africa won by 206 runs	1026
January 2–5	Cape Town	South Africa won by 282 runs	1028
January 12–14	Johannesburg	South Africa won by an innings and 118 runs	1030

NEW ZEALAND v BANGLADESH IN 2016-17

January 12–16	Wellington	New Zealand won by seven wickets	968
January 20–23	Christchurch	New Zealand won by nine wickets	970

INDEX OF UNUSUAL OCCURRENCES

African royalty attend county match .... [illegible]61
Allusion to parents proves costly for Test player .... [illegible]34
Captain declares in one-day game 1204
Celebration is cause for regret 664
County batsman misses game after tussle with fan 494
Dog brings forward Test tea 356
England batsman refunds spectator 310
First-class hat-trick takes three days 468
First-class team declare at 24 for seven on first morning 1103
Illegal bat wins match 674
International team two for one after one ball 1144
Jack Hobbs prospers in Suffolk 762
Kit delays Championship match 444
Maiden first-class hundred reached in dressing-room 975
Match abandoned after umpires simultaneously fall ill 902
Minor County player unexpectedly toothless 723
National Trust bills Surrey 594
Over costs 39 931
PA stops play 509
Run out by a nose 878
Same batsman only wicket to fall in successive first-class games 883
Scorers enforce resumption of game 493
Sightscreen triggers DLS 1154
Sun stops play at both ends of county ground 673
Test captain declares after eavesdropping on umpire 858
Van's inhumanity to van 466

PART TITLES

1 Alastair Cook and Joe Root, July 2016 (page 13) .... Jan Kruger, Getty Images
2 Colin Milburn at Old Trafford, June 1969 (page 121) .... Central Press/Getty Images
3 Bangladesh defeat England, October 2016 (page 241) .... Dibyangshu Sarkar, Getty Images
4 Lord's, Middx v Yorks, September 2016 (page 379) .... Dan Mullan, Getty Images
5 Mitchell Starc at Brisbane, December 2016 (page 791) .... Ryan Pierse, Getty Images
6 Evelyn Jones, August 2016 (page 1165) .... Julian Herbert, Getty Images
7 Karun Nair, India v England, December 2016 (page 1205) .... Danish Siddiqui, Reuters
8 Tibby Cotter, crayon portrait (page 1455) .... Albert Chevallier Tayler, Getty Images

ACT OF SUPREMACY
Joe Root relives his 254 against Pakistan

CAKES, BUSES AND THE SHIPPING FORECAST
Matthew Engel looks back on 60 years of Test Match Special

THE SECRET WORLD OF BALL-TAMPERING
Derek Pringle unpicks the seam

LIFE OF A GENTLEMAN
Vic Marks remembers Tony Cozier

THE GRASS WAS ALWAYS GREENER
Tanya Aldred on cricket and climate change

EVOLUTION OF THE SIX
Gideon Haigh opens his shoulders

THE FIRST ENGLISHMAN TO 10,000
Andy Zaltzman grapples with the curiosities of Alastair Cook

PLUS

CRICKET AND BREXIT

CAST ASIDE BY THE IPL

AND

THE DURHAM DEBACLE

www.wisden.com **£50**

ISBN 978-1-4729-3518-2

9 781472 935182 90100>

Front: Virat Kohli by Danish Siddiqui, Reuters
Back: Jonny Bairstow by Julian Finney, Getty Images